BARRON'S

Finance & Investment Handbook

Third Edition

John Downes
Corporate Financial Consultant
Former Vice President; AVCO Financial Services, Inc.
Office for Economic Development, City of New York

Jordan Elliot Goodman
Senior Finance and Investment Reporter
Money Magazine, Time-Warner Incorporated
Commentator
Cable News Network, Financial News Network,
Mutual Broadcasting System

BARRON'S

New York • London • Sydney • Toronto

All inquiries should be addressed to:
Barron's Educational Series, Inc.
250 Wireless Boulevard
Hauppauge, New York 11788

Library of Congress Catalog Card No.: 89-18307

International Standard Book No.: 0-8120-6188-8

Library of Congress Cataloging-in-Publication Data
Downes, John.
 Barron's finance and investment handbook / John Downes, Jordan Elliot
Goodman. — 3rd ed.
  p. cm.
 Includes bibliographical references (p.
 ISBN 0-8120-6188-8
  1. Finance—Handbooks, manuals, etc. 2. Investments—Handbooks,
manuals, etc. 3. Finance—Dictionaries. 4. Investments—Dictionaries. I.
Goodman, Jordan Elliot. II. Barron's Educational Series, Inc. III. Title. IV.
Finance and investment handbook.
HG173.D66 1990
332.6'78—dc20   89-18307
                                                             CIP

PRINTED IN THE UNITED STATES OF AMERICA

0123   9693   987654321

CONTENTS

	Page
Acknowledgments	vii
Preface to the Third Edition	ix
Introduction	xi

**PART I   HOW TO INVEST YOUR MONEY:
30 KEY PERSONAL INVESTMENT OPPORTUNITIES**

Introduction	3
Personal Investments at a Glance	6
Annuity	9
Bond, Corporate (Interest Bearing)	11
Closed-End Fund	14
Collectibles	17
Common Stock	19
Convertible Security	21
Foreign Stocks and Bonds	24
Futures Contract on a Commodity	27
Futures Contract on an Interest Rate	30
Futures Contract on a Stock Index	32
Government Agency Security	33
Life Insurance (Cash Value)	36
Limited Partnership	38
Money Market Fund	41
Mortgage-Backed (Pass-Through) Security	44
Municipal Security	47
Mutual Funds (Open End)	50
Option Contract (Put or Call)	53
Option Contract on a Futures Contract (Futures Option)	56
Option Contract on an Interest Rate (Debt Option)	58
Option Contract on a Stock Index	60
Option Contract or Futures Contract on a Currency	62
Precious Metals	64
Preferred Stock (Nonconvertible)	67
Real Estate Investment Trust (REIT or FREIT)	70
Real Estate, Physical	73
Savings Alternatives	75
Treasury Securities (Bills, Bonds, and Notes)	79
Unit Investment Trust	81
Zero-Coupon Security	83

Contents

PART II   HOW TO READ AN ANNUAL REPORT

How to Read an Annual Report   89
How to Read a Quarterly Report   118

PART III   HOW TO READ THE FINANCIAL PAGES

How to Read the Financial Pages   121
How to Read Ticker Tapes   159

PART IV   DICTIONARY OF FINANCE AND INVESTMENT

How to Use this Dictionary Effectively   164
Dictionary of Finance and Investment   165

PART V   FINANCE AND INVESTMENT READY REFERENCE

Introduction   568

1. Sources of Information and Assistance   569
      Federal Regulatory Organizations in the United States
        and Canada   569
      U.S. State Attorney Generals' Offices   573
      U.S. State Banking Regulators   577
      U.S. State Insurance Regulators   580
      U.S. State Securities Regulators   584
      Canadian Provincial and Territorial Agencies   588
      Finance and Investment Organizations   589
      Finance and Investment Publications   596
      Computerized Databases for Investors   621
      Personal Computer Software for Investing
        and Financial Planning   627

2. Major Financial Institutions   631
      Federal Reserve System   631
      Primary Government Securities Dealers   634
      Federal Home Loan Banks   637
      Commercial Banks   638
      Canadian Banks   643
      Thrift Institutions   644
      Canadian Trust and Loans   649
      Life Insurance Companies   652
      Brokerage Firms (Full-Service and Discount)   658
      Limited Partnership Sponsors   664
      Accounting Firms   694
      Securities Exchanges Around the World   696

3. Mutual Funds   705
      Open-End Mutual Funds   705
      Closed-End Mutual Funds   757

Contents

4. Futures and Options Contracts   767

5. Historical Data   846
    Amex Market Value Index   847
    Bond Buyer Index (11 bonds)   848
    Bond Buyer Index (20 bonds)   850
    Dow Jones 30 Industrials Stock Average   852
    Dow Jones 20 Transportation Stock Average   856
    Dow Jones 15 Utilities Stock Average   859
    Dow Jones 65 Composite Stock Average   861
    Gold (London morning fix price)   863
    NASDAQ National Market System Composite Index   864
    New York Stock Exchange Composite Index   865
    Standard & Poor's 40 Stock Financial Index   866
    Standard & Poor's 500 Stock Index   867
    Standard & Poor's 400 Industrial Stock Index   869
    Standard & Poor's 20 Transportation Stock Index   871
    Standard & Poor's 40 Utilities Stock Index   873
    Toronto 300 Composite Stock Index   875
    Treasury Bill (3 month) Yields   876
    Treasury Bill (20 year) Yields   877
    Value Line Composite Index   878
    Wilshire 5000 Equity Index   879

    Consumer Price Index   880
    Discount Rate   881
    Federal Funds Rate   884
    Index of Leading Economic Indicators   885
    Money Supply (M-1)   886
    Prime Rate   888
    Producer Price Index   889
    Unemployment Rate (Civilian)   890

6. Publicly Traded Companies   892
    New York Stock Exchange   895
    American Stock Exchange   977
    NASDAQ National Market System   1018
    Toronto Stock Exchange   1137
    American Depositary Receipts   1150
    Free and Discounted Goods and Services for Shareholders   1153

7. Stock Symbols   1155

APPENDIX

Selected Further Reading   1208
Currencies of the World   1214
Abbreviations and Acronyms   1217
Index   1228

ACKNOWLEDGMENTS

A project as massive as this *Handbook* is clearly the work of more than two people, and to thank all adequately would add considerably to its bulk. There are several individuals and organizations, however, without whose help the project in its present form would not have been feasible at all.

A number of leading organizations provided information used in the *Handbook's* reference lists and we are grateful for their generosity and cooperation. These organizations include:

—American Association of Individual Investors
—The American Banker
—American Stock Exchange
—A.M. Best and Company
—Chicago Board of Trade
—Chicago Board Options Exchange
—Chicago Mercantile Exchange
—Chicago Rice and Cotton Exchange
—Coffee, Sugar, and Cocoa Exchange
—Commodity Exchange, Inc.
—Thomas J. Herzfeld and Company
—Interactive Data Corporation
—The Investment Company Institute
—Kansas City Board of Trade
—Longman Financial Services Publishing
—MidAmerica Commodity Exchange
—Minneapolis Grain Exchange
—Montreal Exchange
—The Mutual Fund Education Alliance
—The National Association of Securities Dealers
—New York Cotton Exchange
—New York Futures Exchange
—New York Mercantile Exchange
—New York Stock Exchange
—Pacific Stock Exchange
—Philadelphia Stock Exchange
—Public Accounting Report
—Quotron Systems, Inc.
—The Securities Industry Association
—Robert Stanger & Company
—Toronto Stock Exchange

—Vancouver Stock Exchange
—WEFA Group
—Wilshire Associates
—Winnipeg Commodity Exchange

Scott Robson and Barbara Knight contributed long hours and invaluable assistance to the Ready Reference section. We are grateful to them and also to Seames Clark, who arranged for the stock symbols directory in cooperation with Quotron Systems.

Other people made contributions for which the word acknowledgment is inadequate. Thomas F. Hirsch, Barron's editor for the first two editions, was a full partner in the original project, and we are grateful for his professional guidance and ongoing friendship. John Berseth of Barron's picked up the beat with admirable skill and dedication, and we thank him for his help in bringing this third edition to print.

For help with our original section on How to Read the Financial Pages we called on a veteran New York financial newspaperman, the late Charles Koshetz. The best parts of that chapter remain Charlie's work and a memorial to the insights of a first-rate financial journalist.

Finally, we are indebted for countless reasons to Katie and Annie Downes, Suzanne Koblentz Goodman and, and not least, to Jason Koblentz Goodman, who entered the world just in time to see the finishing touches being put to the Third Edition.

John Downes
Jordan Elliot Goodman

PREFACE TO THE THIRD EDITION

The bankruptcy filing in February 1990 of the Drexel Burnham Lambert Group, the firm whose name was synonymous with high-yield junk bonds and the "merger mania" of the 1980s, marked the end of one of the most colorful if sometimes turbulent periods in American financial history.

A decade that began with a severe recession in 1981–1982 gave way to an unbroken stretch of economic growth and the longest-running bull market in recent history.

But it also saw the federal deficit rise to record levels and America convert from a creditor to a debtor nation in the world economy.

The word "crash," previously reserved for 1929, was reincarnated to describe the unprecedented and terrifying 508-point drop in the Dow Jones Industrial Average on October 19, 1987, a debacle blamed largely on a computer-age phenomenon known as "program trading."

Millions turned out for "Wall Street," a movie inspired by the real-life stories of yuppie millionaires who had sadly learned that insider trading meant trading red suspenders for striped pajamas.

And in the most expensive financial rescue and restructuring project in history, the government was forced to bail out the depositors in hundreds of savings and loan associations that failed because their managers abused the freedoms provided by deregulation.

Many of America's best-known corporations were radically transformed as one major company after another either succumbed to hostile takeovers or leveraged buyouts—or resorted to defensive tactics known by such names as the "poison pill," the "Pac Man strategy," the "scorched-earth policy," or the "white knight."

If the decade would be remembered as the "Roaring Eighties," the 1990s began with events that could only be described as world-shaking.

When McDonald's opened its doors on Red Square, it symbolized the end of the 45-year-old cold war and the failure of communism as an economic system. With perestroika came encouraging early signs that Eastern Bloc countries would eventually become active participants in the world trade and finance community.

The dismantling of the Berlin Wall opened the prospect that a unified Germany would dominate a European community scheduled to be completely free of all trade and economic barriers by 1992.

The emergence of Japan as a leading economic power further reinforced the interdependence of the world's capital markets, symbolized by the addition of Japanese institutions to the list of primary U.S. Government securities dealers. The Tokyo stock market, having kept market-watchers on edge during the 1980s, went into the '90s still selling at stratospheric levels, with the risk that a major sell-off would send reverberations throughout the world.

In the United States massive federal deficits and recession worries created an uncertain investment outlook. Among the most concerned were the holders, including insurance companies and mutual funds, of an estimated $200 billion of junk bonds. Victims of "junk bond phobia" feared that weaker issuers would be unable to meet their obligations in hard economic times, causing massive portfolio losses.

Whatever challenges and opportunities the longer-range future may hold for investors, the basic regulatory and financial framework for investment decisions was established by the revolutionary changes wrought in the 1970s and 1980s.

This third edition takes up-to-date account of those changes and other current developments in investment alternatives; in the way corporations report to investors; in the way financial news is conveyed; in the vocabulary of finance and investment; and in the regulatory establishment and financial marketplace.

Even more than in earlier editions, this revision recognizes the growing global context in which finance and investment decisions will be made as the 1990s lead into the new millennium.

John Downes
Jordan Elliot Goodman

INTRODUCTION

Not since the Great Depression spurred massive reforms in banking and the securities markets has the world of finance and investment seen changes as revolutionary as those of the 1970s and 80s. Deregulation, major tax-law revisions, globalization of markets, and widespread applications of advanced computer and communications technology have altered the world of finance and investment in ways that affect everybody.

As those developments were reshaping the finance and investment landscape in fundamental ways, other historic—sometimes traumatic—events were taking place on the economic and monetary fronts—record high interest rates, world-wide double-digit inflation followed by a major international recession and then disinflation, unprecedented swings in the value of the dollar relative to foreign currencies, and new highs in stock and bond prices.

The far-reaching results include a wider, more complex range of investment choices available to an investment public much more broadly based economically and conscious of such factors as volatility, interest-rate risk, inflation protection, and foreign exchange risk; financial news and corporate reports that are more complex and difficult to understand; an expanded and revised finance and investment vocabulary; a financial marketplace that has increased in size and diversity while spawning a burgeoning information industry using both print and electronic means of communication; and a regulatory establishment that has grown and adapted to a more consumer-oriented investment industry. This *Handbook* is designed as a self-contained reference covering each of these areas — for the individual investor, the student, and the professional.

Deregulation in the brokerage and banking industries, beginning with the "May Day" lifting of fixed commission rates on United States stock exchanges May 1, 1975, and gaining major international thrust with London's "Big Bang" of October 27, 1986, has transformed the financial marketplace. Traditional financial institutions have become diversified organizations mass-marketing a bewildering variety of investment products and services.

The Tax Reform Act of 1986, the most sweeping income tax overhaul in U.S. history, was the last of five major federal tax bills to influence financial and investment decision-making in a single ten-year period. With its enactment, a burdensome marginal tax system fraught with loopholes that had made "tax effects" a key basis of investment judgments has given way to a promising new era of lower tax rates, fewer tax brackets, and investment choices based primarily on economic values.

Internationally, the world has emerged much more interdependent, giving rise to a wide range of investment options denominated in both dollars and foreign currencies, created by firms competing for debt and equity in world-wide markets. Generally, international investment activity has increased as foreign markets have also become deregulated, as communications have improved, and as businesses and financial institutions have expanded beyond national boundaries.

Advances in computer and communications technology, by making possible the linking of markets and the instant processing of tremendous amounts of data, have at once brought greater simplicity and greater complexity to the world of finance and investment, inspiring new investment vehicles, transactions, and methods of limiting risk not previously imaginable.

The *Finance and Investment Handbook* begins with a discussion of 30 key investment alternatives—with their many variations—as they have emerged from this period of historic change. Some are new, others are modernized versions of traditional investment vehicles. Each is presented with an introductory overview followed by questions and answers offering concise information on such crucial matters as costs; minimum purchase amounts; risks; liquidity; tax implications; and suitability for tax-deferred retirement plans. The section's purpose is not to offer specific recommendations, but rather to set forth in an easy-to-read format the vital features distinguishing the various investments so you will be able to make better-informed investment decisions.

Corporate annual reports and other communications of publicly held corporations, as an ironic result of stricter disclosure requirements, have become increasingly elaborate and difficult to understand, leaving many investors more befuddled than enlightened. The second section of the *Handbook* explains what corporate reports contain, what to focus on, and how to analyze and interpret the data provided.

You must know how to read and understand financial information in newspapers in order to make intelligent investment choices and then to follow their progress. Not surprisingly, the proliferation of investment products and the broadening of public participation in the securities markets has fattened the financial sections of daily newspapers with information aimed at individual and institutional investors. Also, with the growth of cable television, many investors are getting their financial news from channels displaying a running ticker tape throughout the business day. The third part of the *Handbook* explains how to read the financial pages and the ticker tape.

Essential to decision-making in any field is understanding the language in which information is communicated. In a technical, dynamic field like finance and investment, keeping up with changing terminology would be a challenge in any event, but developments of the last decade have added a whole new lexicon of finance and investment terms and largely redefined the traditional vocabulary. The argot of the field has also been spiced by a wave of new Wall Street takeover buzzwords, like "greenmail," "poison pill," and "white knight." These and more than 2500 other key terms are defined clearly and comprehensively, with examples and illustrations, in the *Handbook's* fourth major section, the Dictionary of Finance and Investment.

The fifth section of the *Handbook* presents wide-ranging reference material. The information, arranged in an easily accessible manner, is designed to be *used* by investors—beginners and professionals alike—to locate specific data as well as to gain a broader understanding of finance and investment.

The finance and investment marketplace has not only grown in size but has changed character as a result of diversification, mergers, and the introduction of new firms that exist either to market new investment products or to provide information on them. The regulatory establishment, which consists of federal and state government agencies as well as self-regulatory organizations, and relevant trade association and consumer protection groups have expanded and adapted to an industry that has become more consumer-oriented. The most important of these government and nongovernment organizations—including those of Canada—are listed in the opening portions of the *Handbook's* reference listings.

The growing importance of the individual consumer in the investment community has been a catalyst for the burgeoning financial information industry. The *Handbook* lists the major finance and investment publications from national magazines to specialized newsletters, providing addresses and telephone numbers so they can be contacted easily. The industry also has an important electronic dimension in the form of computer databases and software, and the major sources of these products are presented.

"You can't tell the players without a scorecard" goes an old baseball adage, which certainly applies to today's major leagues of financial services. Despite diversification, financial institutions continue to be discussed mainly in terms of their principal and traditional activities—that is, as commercial banks, thrifts, brokerage firms, and life insurance companies. The *Handbook* lists the 100 largest in each of these categories. Also listed are the Federal Reserve and Federal Home Loan banks and branches, the primary government securities dealers, major limited partnership sponsors, the 25 largest accounting firms, and the world's major security and commodity exchanges.

Highly useful information, including name, address, phone number, and investment objective of both open-end and closed-end mutual funds and fund families is provided for those who would rather leave portfolio decisions to a professional manager.

Increasingly, U.S. and Canadian exchanges, in response to growing investor interest, are listing options and futures on financial instruments, stock indexes, and foreign currencies, as well as traditional stock options and futures on agricultural and other commodities. The *Handbook* provides a complete and detailed summary of contracts of all types on all U.S. and Canadian exchanges.

No handbook would be complete if it didn't supply the historical framework of the investment markets and the overall economy. This *Handbook* includes easy to understand but telling historical graphs together with background information and related statistical data on the principal stock and bond market indexes, as well as key economic indicators.

To facilitate ordering through brokers, particularly discount brokers, and to help you take advantage of an increasing willingness on the part of corporations to communicate directly with shareholders or potential shareholders, the *Handbook* provides a list—not readily available elsewhere—of the name, stock symbol, address, phone number, and line of business of approximately 6000 public companies in which you can buy shares or American Depositary Receipts on the New York Stock Exchange, the American Stock Exchange, the Toronto Stock Exchange, and over the counter on the NASDAQ National Market System. In addition, we indicate stocks on which listed options are traded and those offering dividend reinvestment plans. An alphabetical listing of stock symbols with corresponding company names is a feature new to the Third Edition. A limited number of companies offer free merchandise or other items or services of value as part of their shareholder relations efforts. You'll find a list of companies providing such "freebies."

The Appendix is an important part of the *Handbook*. In it you will find an annotated bibliography of selected key works on finance and investment. There is also a listing of the currencies of independent countries, which will be helpful in tracking international developments. At the conclusion of the *Handbook* is one of its most important assets — the index — which will make it easier to find all the information on a particular topic in the book.

HOW TO USE THIS *HANDBOOK* EFFECTIVELY

Each section of this *Handbook* is a self-contained entity. At the same time, however, the relevance of the various sections to each other is clear, since the objective of the *Handbook* is to join in one volume the different elements that together make up today's world of finance and investment. Tempting though it was from an editorial standpoint, cross-referencing has been kept to a minimum in the belief that readers would prefer not to be distracted by such editorial devices. At certain points, however, where reliance on the fuller explanation of a term in the *Handbook's* Dictionary of Finance and Investment seemed preferable to a discussion, cross-references to the dictionary are indicated by small capitals (for instance, ABC AGREEMENT). In any case, the dictionary is a source of comprehensive information on terms and concepts used throughout the *Handbook* and should be consulted whenever an aspect of finance and investment is not clear to you. The Table of Contents and especially the Index will also help you locate related information in different parts of the *Handbook* and should be consulted regularly.

* * *

Although the *Handbook* was a collaborative effort in every sense of the word, primary responsibility was divided as follows: The sections on investment alternatives and reading financial reports were written by John Downes. The section on reading the financial pages was written by Charles Koshetz and edited by John Downes and Jordan Elliot Goodman. The Dictionary of Finance and Investment was authored coequally by John Downes and Jordan Elliot Goodman. The reference lists and the accompanying explanatory material were compiled, edited, and written by Jordan Elliot Goodman.

PART I

How to Invest Your Money: 30 Key Personal Investment Opportunities

INTRODUCTION

Perhaps the most important benefit of deregulation and other recent landmark changes in the securities and banking industries has been the availability to the average individual of investment alternatives that were formerly reserved for the wealthy. But welcome though this development is, it has brought with it choices that are bewildering both in range and complexity. Traditional investment vehicles have been modernized, new ones have been introduced, and, as the marketing departments of financial services conglomerates have sought to give their products mass appeal, the distinctions between different investment alternatives have become blurred.

This section presents 30 basic investment alternatives as they have emerged from the revolutionary events of the 1970s and 80s. It is divided into 30 *basic* alternatives; each discussion, however, includes important variations, which, if counted separately, would more than double the number of alternatives.

The purpose of the section is not to provide advice. Investment decisions must always be made in subjective terms, taking into account one's financial position, risk comfort level, and goals. Rather, the section is designed to set forth in current terms the vital features distinguishing different investments, so you can talk knowledgeably with your investment counselor or, if you are a finance or investment professional, so you can be a better source of advice.

Preceding the discussions of investments is a table showing important characteristics of each investment. The chart is a quick way to learn pertinent facts, but should be used in conjunction with the discussions themselves to make sure you are aware of nuances and exceptions associated with a particular type of investment.

The discussions of investment alternatives begin with short overviews designed to describe the essential features of the investment and, where helpful, provide some historical perspective. These overviews are followed by sections in question-and-answer format designed to present concisely and informatively the basic data needed to evaluate investment alternatives. Let's look at the questions and what they mean. (Remember, if you don't understand a finance or investment term, consult the extensive dictionary in this *Handbook*.)

Buying, Selling, and Holding

How do I buy and sell it? A few years ago, things were simpler: you bought your stocks and bonds from a broker, your life insurance from an insurance agent, and went to a bank with your savings or your loan request. The trend today is toward FULL-SERVICE BROKERS and FINANCIAL SUPERMARKETS that offer all these services and more. We have tried to be as helpful as possible, but there is no universality as to what full-service means from one firm to the next. One thing can be said for certain, though: you won't sound foolish these days if you ask a bank or broker if a given investment—no matter how specialized—can be bought or sold through his or her firm. DISCOUNT BROKERS are a special breed. They handle a variety of securities, but as a rule function strictly as brokers; do not look to them for investment guidance.

Is there a minimum purchase amount, and what is the price range? This question is aimed at giving you an idea of what it costs to get in the game, which is often more than just the minimum DENOMINATION or UNIT in which an investment is issued. The question cannot always be answered in absolute terms, since broker policies vary in terms of minimum orders and there may be SUITABILITY RULES requiring that you prove a certain financial capacity to take the risks associated with a particular investment. Certain securities trade in ROUND LOTS (for instance, 100 shares of common stock), though it is usually possible to buy ODD LOT quantities (for instance, 35 shares) at a higher commission per unit. In any event, call the broker and ask; many large firms have special programs that combine small orders from different investors and thereby make it possible to buy and sell modest amounts at modest commissions.

What fees and charges are involved? Again, we have been specific wherever possible, but with some investments, notably common stocks, commissions are sometimes negotiated, based on the size and nature of the transaction. DISCOUNT BROKERS, which as a rule do not give investment advice but execute trades at rates that are roughly half those of most full-service brokers, also have different rates for different transactions. See the entries for SHARE BROKER and VALUE BROKER in this *Handbook*'s dictionary for discussions of different categories of discount broker. You will also frequently see references to DEALER spreads. This term refers to the MARKDOWNS and markups that are deducted from your selling price or added to your buying price when a broker-dealer is operating as a DEALER rather than simply as a BROKER.

Does it mature, expire, or otherwise terminate? Some investments are issued with a fixed MATURITY DATE, others are not. But even those with a fixed maturity date may be CALLABLE—that is, bought back at the pleasure of the issuer, or as part of a SINKING FUND provision. Others may have PUT OPTIONS, permitting REDEMPTION by the investor before maturity.

Can I sell it quickly? This question has to do with LIQUIDITY, the ability to convert an investment into cash without significant loss of value. Investments normally enjoying high liquidity are those with an active SECONDARY MARKET, in which they are actively traded among other investors subsequent to their original issue. Shares of LISTED SECURITIES have high liquidity. Liquidity can also be provided in other ways: for example, the SPONSOR of a unit investment trust might offer to MAKE A MARKET—to find a buyer to match you as a seller, should the need arise for you to sell.

How is market value determined and how do I keep track of it? MARKET VALUE is the price your investment would fetch in the open market, assuming that it is traded in a SECONDARY MARKET. In these discussions you will often encounter the word, VOLATILE, referring to the extent to which the market price of an investment fluctuates. Professionals use the term SYSTEMATIC RISK or its synonym market risk when discussing an investment's tendency to rise or fall in price as a result of market forces.

Investment Objectives

Should I buy this if my objective is capital appreciation? The purpose here is to identify investments likely to gain in value—to produce CAPITAL GAINS. Although APPRECIATION does not refer to capital growth due to factors such as reinvested dividends or compound interest, such factors are noted as a matter of relevance where they exist to a substantial degree. In the same category is appreciation due to ORIGINAL ISSUE DISCOUNT on fixed-income securities, which is considered interest. Other fixed-income investments bought in the market at a DISCOUNT from PAR because rising rates (or other factors) caused lower prices, create appreciation in the sense of capital gains either at REDEMPTION or when resold in the market at a higher price. Prices can also be at a PREMIUM, meaning higher than par value, when speaking of fixed-income investments.

Should I buy this if my objective is income? Here the purpose is to identify investments whose primary feature is providing regular income, as distinguished from alternatives primarily featuring capital gains or other potential values.

To what extent does it protect against inflation? If the value of an investment usually rises at the same rate or a higher rate than the rate of INFLATION erodes the value of the dollar, the investment is inflation-sensitive. Investments vary in the degree of protection they provide—some provide no protection.

Is it suitable for tax-deferred retirement accounts? Such accounts include INDIVIDUAL RETIREMENT ACCOUNTS (IRAs), KEOGH PLANS, 401(K) PLANS, and other pension plans that are TAX-DEFERRED. The question addresses both the legality and, in some cases, the practicality of using a particular investment in such an account. Investments that might be ruled out for an IRA because of the $2000 annual maximum per person, might be appropriate for an IRA ROLLOVER.

Can I borrow against it? This question considers the general value of an investment as COLLATERAL at a bank or other lending institution, and also the eligibility of an investment for trading in MARGIN ACCOUNTS with brokers under Federal Reserve Board MARGIN REQUIREMENTS. A key consideration is the concept of LEVERAGE, the ability to control a given amount of value with a smaller amount of cash. Borrowing can also be a way of raising cash when an investment is ILLIQUID.

Risk Considerations

How assured can I be of getting my full investment back? Here the discussion concerns safety of PRINCIPAL, which has mainly to do with two types of risk: (1) market or SYSTEMATIC RISK and (2) financial or CREDIT RISK (risk that an issuer will DEFAULT on a contractual obligation or that an EQUITY investment will lose value because of financial difficulty or BANKRUPTCY of an issuer). Insurance considerations and HEDGING, protecting against loss of value through an offsetting position, are also discussed where appropriate.

How assured is my income? Assuming an investment produces income, this question deals with market risk as it may (or may not) affect income, with an issuer's legal obligation to pay income, and with priority of claim in LIQUIDATION.

Are there any other risks unique to this investment? This question intends only to highlight risks peculiar to a particular investment. It is not meant to imply that any risks not included do not exist.

Is it commercially rated? Commercial RATING agencies, such as MOODY'S INVESTORS SERVICE and STANDARD & POOR'S CORPORATION, analyze and rate certain securities and their issuers on a continuous basis. Most ratings are designed to indicate a company's financial strength and thus guide investors as to the degree of CREDIT RISK a security represents, though sometimes other factors are rated. Rating changes usually affect market values.

Tax Considerations

What tax advantages (or disadvantages) does it offer? This discussion is designed to present the tax considerations associated with an investment. Obviously, each individual's tax situation is unique and each investor should obtain professional advice to determine whether an investment with certain tax features represents an advantage or disadvantage in his or her particular case. Many tax advantages formerly enjoyed by investors disappeared with the Tax Reform Act of 1986. Instances where investment values have changed are noted.

Economic Considerations

What economic factors most affect buy, hold, and sell decisions? Here again, only the most general economic considerations are covered and what applies in general might not apply to you.

PERSONAL INVESTMENTS AT A GLANCE

The following chart applies nine key investment criteria to the 30 personal investment alternatives discussed in this section. It is designed simply to answer the question: Is this alternative one I might want to learn more about in view of my own investment objectives? A bullet (●) means that a given characteristic is usually associated, to one degree or another, with a particular alternative. A blank means it is not. A V means that variation within the investment category exists to such an extent that even broad classification would be misleading.

Exceptions abound, and in every case there is a question of degree. In the modern universe of investment alternatives, just about nothing is pure; that fact is indeed what this section of the *Handbook* is all about. So with cognizance of its limitations, use this chart for quick and handy reference and refer to the overviews and questionnaires for more complete understanding.

Investment	Regular Current Income	Capital Appreciation	Tax Benefits	Safety of Principal	Liquidity	Inflation Protection	Leverage*	Future Income or Security	Suitability for IRAs and other Tax-Deferred Accounts
Annuity		●	●	●		V		●	
Bond, Corporate	●	●		●	●				●
Closed-End Fund	●	●		V	●	V			●
Collectible		●				●			
Common Stock	●	●		V	●	●	●		●
Convertible Security	●	●		●	●	●	●		●
Foreign Stocks and Bonds	●	●		V	V	●			●
Futures Contract on a Commodity		●			●		●		
Futures Contract on an Interest Rate		●			●		●		
Futures Contract on a Stock Index		●			●		●		
Government Agency Security	●	●	●	●	●				●
Life Insurance (Cash Value)		●	●	●	●	V		●	

Mortgage-Backed (Pass-Through) Security

Municipal Security

Mutual Fund (Open-End)

Option Contract (Put or Call)

Option Contract on a Futures Contract (Futures Option)

Option Contract on an Interest Rate (Debt Option)

Option Contract on a Stock Index

Option Contract or Futures Contract on a Currency

Precious Metals

Preferred Stock (Nonconvertible)

Real Estate Investment Trust (REIT and FREIT)

Real Estate, Physical

Savings Alternatives

Treasury Securities

Unit Investment Trust

Zero-Coupon Security

* Refers to margin securities and investments wherein large amounts of value can be controlled with small amounts of cash. The general value of investments as loan collateral is covered in the discussions of each of the investment alternatives.

HOW TO INVEST YOUR MONEY: 30 KEY PERSONAL INVESTMENT OPPORTUNITIES

ANNUITY

After a period of modernization, tax rulings, and the shock of a big insurance company bankruptcy, the time-honored annuity is again gaining popularity as an investment alternative. It comes in several varieties, with two basic attractions: (1) tax-deferred capital growth and (2) the option of income for life or a guaranteed period. Among the drawbacks are high penalties (by insurers and the Internal Revenue Service) on premature withdrawal and lower investment returns than could usually be realized directly.

Traditionally, annuities provided fixed income payments for an individual's remaining lifetime in exchange for a lump-sum cash payment. But inflation's negative impact on fixed-income annuities combined with increased life expectancy gave rise, in the late 1950s, to the variable annuity, invested in assets, like stocks, that rise with inflation, thus preserving some purchasing power, although at the price of some market risk.

In the late 1960s and early 70s came the wraparound annuity, which enabled investors to wrap their own mutual funds, savings accounts, or other investments in the annuity vehicle, thus sheltering them from taxes. In the early 1980s, the IRS blew the whistle, ruling that to qualify for tax deferral, annuity investments had to be managed by insurance companies and be available only to annuity contract holders. The annuity has once again become a vehicle largely limited to retirement goals, but it has gained appeal with the modern features acquired along the way.

Annuities are available in two basic types:

Fixed annuities are ''fixed'' in two ways: (1) The amount you invest earns interest (tax-deferred) at a guaranteed rate (1% to 2% under long-term U.S. government bonds, typically) while your principal is guaranteed not to lose value. (2) When you withdraw or opt to ''annuitize'' (begin taking monthly income) you receive a guaranteed amount based on your age, sex, and selection of payment options. Inflation protection is, of course, minimal.

Variable annuities, in contrast, are ''variable'' in two ways: (1) The amount you put in is invested in your choice of a stock, fixed-income bond or money market account, the value and/or earnings of which vary with market conditions. (2) Market value determines the amount available for withdrawals, or (with actuarial factors) the amount the annuitant is paid from one month to the next. Variable annuities thus offer inflation protection in exchange for market risk (minimized somewhat when switching among funds is permitted).

The bankruptcy in the early 1980s of the Baldwin-United Corporation, the biggest name in deferred annuities, shook the confidence of an investor community that had learned to take the financial strength of insurance companies for granted. As it turned out, arrangements were made for investors to regain most of their money, and confidence in the industry, which is heavily regulated and high on any scale of safety, was restored.

In general, annuities, with a variety of optional features for both accumulation and payout, are for long-term investors willing to trade liquidity and some degree of return for safety and tax-deferred capital growth, and whose objective is to defer taxability until later (lower tax-rate) years and/or to guarantee retirement income.

*   *   *

What Is an Annuity?

An annuity is a contract between an insurance company and an annuitant whereby the company, in exchange for a single or flexible premium guarantees a fixed or variable payment to the annuitant at a future time. *Immediate annuities* begin paying out as soon as the premium is paid; *deferred annuities*, which may be paid for in a lump sum or in installments, start paying out at a specified date in the future.

Buying, Selling, and Holding

How do I buy and sell it? Insurance brokers, insurance company sales agents, savings institutions, full-service brokers, commercial banks, and other financial service organizations sell annuities.

Is there a minimum purchase amount, and what is the price range? It varies with the plan, but deferred annuities typically have minimums ranging from $1000 to $5000.

What fees and charges are involved? Fees and charges may include front-end load sales charges ranging from 1% to 10% (although there is a trend toward no initial commissions), premium taxes (imposed on the insurance company by some states and passed on to contract holders), annual fees (typically $15 to $30 per year up to a maximum of 1½% of account value), early withdrawal penalties (typically starting at 7% and decreasing to zero over a seven-year period), and other charges. (See Tax Considerations, below, for tax penalties).

Does it mature, expire, or otherwise terminate? Yes; both the accumulation period and the payout period are specified in the contract.

Can I sell it quickly? Accumulated cash value (principal payments plus investment earnings) can always be withdrawn, but there may be substantial withdrawal penalties as well as tax penalties.

How is market value determined and how do I keep track of it? Annuities do not have secondary market value, but information concerning account balances is supplied by the insurance company.

Investment Objectives

Should I buy an annuity if my objective is capital appreciation? Not in the sense that you would buy an investment at one price and hope to sell it at a higher price. But deferred annuities accumulate value through (tax-deferred) compounding, and variable annuities may be invested in stocks or other securities having capital gains potential.

Should I buy this if my objective is income? Annuities are designed to provide income for future guaranteed periods, so you would not buy a deferred annuity for current income needs.

To what extent does it protect against inflation? Fixed annuities provide no inflation protection. Variable annuities provide protection when their portfolios are invested in inflation-sensitive securities.

Is it suitable for tax-deferred retirement accounts? Yes, but since annuities have tax-deferred status themselves, it may be wiser to use them as supplements to IRAs, Keoghs, and other tax-deferred programs.

Can I borrow against it? Yes.

Risk Considerations

How assured can I be of getting back my full investment in an annuity? Insurance companies are heavily regulated and required to maintain reserves, so with established companies there is low risk of loss due to corporate failure. Most annuities permit early withdrawal of principal, but penalties may apply. Once annuitized (i.e., when payments by the insurance company begin) it becomes a question of how long you live. The insurance company (with the odds in its favor) bets you will die before the annuity is fully paid out.

How assured is my income? While variable annuity income can fluctuate, the risk of default is low. (See previous question.)

Are there any other risks unique to this investment? Although heavily regulated, insurance companies are potentially subject to mismanagement and fraud, and policyholders are not themselves covered by federal protection as bank depositors, for example, are covered by the Federal Deposit Insurance Corporation (FDIC).

Is it commercially rated? Yes. Insurance companies are rated by Best's Rating Service.

Tax Considerations

What tax advantages (or disadvantages) does an annuity offer? Earnings on money invested in deferred annuities, including all interest, dividends, and capital gains, accumulate and compound tax-deferred. Portions of payments to annuitants are returns of investor's principal and thus are not subject to income taxes. Withdrawals of accumulated earnings prior to age 59½ or within 5 years of the purchase date (whichever comes first) are subject to a 10% tax penalty. (An exception is made for life annuities, payable for the lifetimes, or life expectancies, of one or more annuitants.)

Economic Considerations

What economic factors most affect buy, hold, and sell decisions? Although factors such as inflationary expectations and anticipated interest rate movements may guide choices among types of annuities, the decision to buy and hold is based on insurance rather than economic considerations. Annuities are appropriate for people without dependents or heirs, who seek assured income for their remaining lives.

BOND, CORPORATE (INTEREST-BEARING)

The traditional attractions of a corporate bond have been (1) higher yield compared to government bonds and (2) relative safety. Whether secured (usually a mortgage bond) or unsecured (called a debenture), it has a higher claim on earnings than equity investments. If the firm goes out of business, bonds also have a higher claim on the assets of the issuer, whose financial well-being is safeguarded by provisions in bond indentures and is closely monitored by the major bond rating services. Interest on corporates is fully taxable.

Much publicized in the 1980s because of their widespread use in financing corporate takeovers were so-called junk bonds, corporate bonds with lower than investment-grade ratings that pay high yields to compensate for high risk. Although issuers could point to the fact that high-yield bonds in general have had a low default record historically, fears that a prolonged recession would put the more heavily leveraged issuers in trouble caused depressed prices and poor liquidity in the junk bond market as the decade ended.

Bonds are contracts between borrowers and lenders in which the issuer (borrower) promises the bondholder (lender) a specified rate of interest and repayment of principal at maturity.

The face, or par, value of a corporate bond is almost always $1000 (the exceptions being baby bonds with pars of $500 or less), but bonds do not necessarily sell at par value. Particularly in the secondary market, bonds are traded at discounts or premiums relative to par in order to bring their stated (coupon) rates in line with market rates. This inverse relationship between bond prices and interest rate movements causes market risk as the term applies to bonds; when interest rates rise, there is a decline in the price of a bond with a lower fixed interest rate.

Bond prices also vary with the time remaining to maturity. This is because of the time value of money and because time involves risk and risk means higher yield. Bond yields thus normally decrease (and prices increase) as the bond approaches maturity. The concept of yield-to-maturity is basic to bond pricing, and it takes into account the price paid for the bond and all cash inflows and their timing.

The safety and value of corporate bonds are also related to credit risk, quite simply the borrower's ability to pay interest and principal when due. The relative financial strength of the issuer, as reflected in the regularly updated rating assigned to its bonds by the major services, influences yield, which is adjusted by changes in the market price.

Concern that hostile takeovers and recapitalizations would weaken the value of existing holdings has inspired protective provisions in bond indenture agreements. In 1989 Standard & Poor's instituted "Event Risk Covenant Rankings," a system, supplementing its credit ratings, that evaluates such protection. A common provision is the "poison put," which gives bondholders the right to redeem at par if certain designated events occur, such as a hostile takeover, the purchase of a big block of stock, or an excessive dividend payout.

Other considerations influencing corporate bond prices include the existence of call features, which empower the issuer to redeem prior to maturity, often to the disadvantage of the bondholder; call protection periods, which benefit holders; sinking funds, which require the issuer to set aside funds for the retirement of the bonds at maturity; put options giving the investor the right to redeem at specified times prior to maturity; subordinations, which give issues precedence over other issues in liquidation; and guarantees or insurance.

Variable-rate issues, usually called floating-rate notes even though some issues have terms of 30 years, adjust interest rates periodically in line with market rates. These issues generally have lower yields to compensate for the benefit to the holder, but they enjoy greater price stability to the extent the rate adjustments are responsive to market rate movements.

See also the discussions of Convertible Securities and Zero-Coupon Securities.

*   *   *

What Is a Corporate Bond?

A corporate bond is a debt security of a corporation requiring the issuer to pay the holder the par value at a specified maturity and to make agreed scheduled interest payments.

Buying, Selling, and Holding

How do I buy and sell a corporate bond? Through a securities broker-dealer.

Is there a minimum purchase amount, and what is the price range? Bonds are normally issued with $1000 par values, with baby bonds in smaller denominations. Issuers often have 5-bond minimums and broker-dealers trade in round lots of 10 or 100 units. Odd lots may be available at higher brokerage commissions or dealer spreads.

What fees and charges are involved? A per-bond commission of $2.50 to $20, depending on the broker and negotiations with the customer. However, a minimum charge of $30 is common. New issues involve no charges to the investor.

Does it mature, expire, or otherwise terminate? All bonds have maturity dates, but may be callable prior to maturity.

Can I sell it quickly? Usually yes. Most major issues are actively traded, but in large amounts. Small lots can be harder to trade and may involve some price sacrifice and higher transaction costs. Some high-yield junk bonds have been hard to sell because of the fear of default.

How is market value determined and how do I keep track of it? The market value of a fixed-income bond is a function of its yield to maturity and prevailing market interest rates. Prices thus decline when interest rates rise and rise when interest rates decline to result in an appropriate competitive yield. A change in the issuer's rating can also cause a change in price as higher (or lower) risk is reflected in the price/yield relationship. Even without a formal rating change, reduced demand can cause lower bond prices; this has been seen in junk bond prices reflecting fears that a recession will cause defaults. Bond prices are quoted in daily newspapers and electronic databases.

Investment Objectives

Should I buy a corporate bond if my objective is capital appreciation? Usually not, although capital appreciation is possible when bonds can be bought at a discount to their par value, bought prior to a drop in market interest rates, or bought at a favorable price because of a decline in the issuer's credit rating.

Should I buy this if my objective is income? Yes; bonds pay interest, usually semiannually. Yields on top-rated bonds are lower than on bonds of less than investment grade, called junk bonds, which pay more and have higher credit risk.

To what extent does it protect against inflation? Although normal inflationary expectations are built into interest rates, fixed-rate bonds offer no protection against high inflation. Variable-rate issues offer some protection.

Is it suitable for tax-deferred retirement accounts? Yes.

Can I borrow against it? Yes, subject to Federal Reserve margin rules (convertible bonds only) and brokerage-firm and lending-institution policies.

Risk Considerations

How assured can I be of getting my full investment back? If you hold to maturity, it will depend on the issuer's credit, which is evaluated regularly by the major investor's rating services and reflected in ratings from AAA down to D. If you plan to sell in the secondary market before maturity, you are subject also to market risk, the risk that bond prices will be down as a result of higher interest rates. Sophisticated investors sometimes protect against loss of value due to market risk by hedging, using options and futures available on long-term Treasury securities which are similarly affected by interest rate changes.

How assured is my income? Uninterrupted payment of interest depends on the issuer's financial strength and stability of earnings, factors reflected in its bond rating. Inflation can erode the dollar value of fixed-interest payments.

Are there any other risks unique to this investment? A callable bond can be redeemed by the issuer after a certain period has elapsed. Issuers normally force redemption when interest rates have declined and financing can be obtained more cheaply. Under just those circumstances, however, the investor finds the holding most attractive; the market price is up and the coupon interest rate is higher than the prevailing market interest rate. Look for bonds with call protection (typically 10 years). Event risk, the risk of a deterioration in credit quality owing to takeover-related changes in capitalization, is another consideration. Although issuers considering themselves vulnerable may have indenture provisions to protect bondholders (rated by Standard & Poor's Event Risk Covenant Rankings), such measures can result in early redemption and deprive the holder of a long-term investment.

Is it commercially rated? Yes. Fitch Investors Service, Moody's Investors Service, and Standard & Poor's Corporation are the major rating services.

Tax Considerations

What tax advantages (or disadvantages) does a corporate bond offer? None. Bond interest is taxed as ordinary income and appreciation is subject to capital gains tax, except that appreciation resulting from original issue discounts is taxed (as earned) at ordinary income rates.

Economic Considerations

What economic factors most affect buy, hold, or sell decisions? It is best to buy a corporate bond when interest rates are high and the best yields can be obtained. Holding is most attractive when rates are declining, causing an upward move in the market values of fixed-income securities. High inflation erodes the dollar value of fixed interest payments. Poor business conditions over a prolonged period can cause financial weakness and jeopardize a firm's ability to pay.

CLOSED-END FUND

Closed-end funds, so-called because, unlike open-end mutual funds, their sponsoring investment companies do not stand ready to issue and redeem shares on a continuous basis, have a fixed capitalization represented by publicly traded shares that are often listed on the major stock exchanges.

Closed-end funds tend to have specialized portfolios of stocks, bonds, convertibles, or combinations thereof, and may be oriented toward income, capital gains, or a combination of those objectives. Examples are the Korea Fund, which specializes in the stock of Korean firms and is an example of a "single country fund," and ASA Ltd., which invests in South African gold mining stocks. Both are traded on the New York Stock Exchange.

The attraction of a closed-end fund is twofold: (1) Because management is not concerned with continuous buying and selling to accommodate new investors and redemptions, a responsibility of open-end funds that frequently conflicts with ideal market timing, a well-managed closed-end fund can often buy and sell on more favorable terms. (2) Because the popular investor perception is just the opposite— that closed-end funds have less flexibility than open-end funds—shares of closed-end funds can usually be obtained at a discount from net asset value. As a result of these combined factors, annual earnings of closed-end funds sometimes exceed earnings of open-end funds with comparable portfolios.

A special form of closed-end fund is the *dual-purpose fund*. These hybrids have two classes of stock. Preferred shareholders receive all the income from the portfolio—dividends and interest—while common shareholders receive all capital gains realized on the sale of securities in the fund's portfolio. Dual-purpose funds are set up with a specific expiration date, when preferred shares are redeemed at a predetermined price and common shareholders claim the remaining assets, voting either to liquidate or continue the fund on an open-end basis.

Closed-end funds, of which about 80 are publicly and actively traded, are regulated by the Securities and Exchange Commission.

See also the discussion of Mutual Funds.

* * *

What Is a Closed-End Fund?

A closed-end fund is a type of mutual fund that invests in diversified holdings and has a fixed number of shares that are publicly traded.

Buying, Selling, and Holding

How do I buy and sell a closed-end fund? Through a securities broker-dealer.

Is there a minimum purchase amount, and what is the price range? Round-lot 100 share purchases save commissions. Prices vary but many funds sell for $25 or less per share.

What fees and charges are involved? Standard brokerage commissions plus an annual management fee averaging ½% to 1% of the investment.

Does it mature, expire, or otherwise terminate? Funds can be liquidated or converted to open-end funds or operating companies if a majority of shareholders approve. Dual-purpose funds expire, typically in ten years.

Can I sell it quickly? Usually yes. Most funds offer good liquidity.

How is market value determined and how do I keep track of it? By supply and demand factors affecting shares in the market. Whether shares trade at a premium (rare) or at more or less of a discount (the rule) relative to the net asset value of the fund, can depend on the portfolio, yield, the general market, and factors like year-end tax selling. Some funds have stock buyback programs designed to reduce outstanding shares and increase earnings per share. New issues tend initially to sell at premiums, then to slack off when brokers turn their aggressive sales efforts to other products. *The Wall Street Journal* on Monday reports the net asset value, price, and discount or premium for the previous week on actively traded funds.

Investment Objectives

Should I buy a closed-end fund if my objective is capital appreciation? Although fund shares rise and fall in the marketplace, influenced, among other factors, by the value of the fund's portfolio, investors seeking to participate in capital gains would select a fund having appreciation as its primary objective—an aggressive stock fund, for example, as opposed to a bond fund, though gains and losses are possible in both. Dual-purpose funds offer two classes of stock, common shareholders benefiting from all the capital gains, preferred shareholders getting all the interest and dividend income. Funds bought at a discount offer the prospect of additional appreciation through increases in fund share prices.

Should I buy this if my objective is income? Yes, especially funds whose objective is income. (See the preceding question.) Some funds offer guaranteed payouts, but it should be recognized that unless the fund generates income equal to the guaranteed payment, it may come out of funds contributed by investors.

To what extent does it protect against inflation? Some portfolios are more sensitive (less vulnerable) to inflation than others, stocks being better than bonds, for example. Of course, increases in the portfolio benefit investors only when passed on in capital gains distributions or reflected in higher fund share values.

Is it suitable for tax-deferred retirement accounts? Yes.

Can I borrow against it? Yes, subject to Federal Reserve margin requirements and individual lender policies.

Risk Considerations

How assured can I be of getting my full investment back? Fund shares can be just as volatile as common stock. Professionals use various techniques to hedge funds selling at discounts or premiums or converting to open-end funds. These techniques include purchasing options and selling short other funds, treasury securities and futures, and stocks in the same fund's portfolio. Some funds have "open-ending" provisions, whereby they guarantee that investors can choose to collect the full net asset value of fund shares on a specified future debt; it is important to note, however, that although the net asset value may be higher than the market price, it can be lower than your original investment.

How assured is my income? It depends on the quality of the portfolio and the risk characteristics of the investments comprising it. Funds offering guaranteed payouts may have to liquidate capital to make good.

Are there any other risks unique to this investment? The risk unique to closed-end funds is that the value of fund shares can move independently of the value of the securities comprising the fund's portfolio. If this causes shares to trade at a discount to net asset values, it is bad for holders, although it can be viewed as a buying opportunity.

Is it commercially rated? Funds are not usually rated, but information helpful to investors is provided by Standard & Poor's Stock Record Sheets, Moody's Finance Manuals, and other sources.

Tax Considerations

What tax advantages (or disadvantages) does a closed-end fund offer? The tax treatment of closed-end fund shares is the same as for common stock except that until 1988 capital gains distributions enjoy preferential long-term capital gains treatment regardless of how long the fund has been held.

Economic Considerations

What economic factors most affect buy, hold or sell decisions? Most experts say to buy when shares can be obtained at a good discount and the stock market seems poised for a rise. Otherwise, decisions should consider the effects of different economic and market scenarios on various types of portfolios, such as bonds, stocks, or convertibles. It is probably wise to view closed-end funds as long-term investments and to sell when significant appreciation has occurred.

COLLECTIBLE

Collectibles, the name for a diverse range of physical possessions presumed to gain value with time, enjoyed a wave of popularity as a haven for investment money during the inflation-ravaged 1970s. Then the 1981–82 recession revealed how fickle the marketplace can be and how vulnerable collectibles are to adverse economic conditions. When that period was followed by one in which inflation was brought under control and financial investments became attractive again, enthusiasm for collectibles as an investment alternative, exclusive of their utility or personal enjoyment value, waned considerably. Some collectibles did, however, perform very well: One study listing investments that outperformed inflation between 1975 and 1980 included five categories of collectibles along with gold, silver, residential real estate, and money market funds.

There is no universal definition of a collectible. Some experts apply the criteria of rarity, quality, uniqueness, and age, while others put commodities with utilitarian value (like gemstones) or intrinsic value (like coins with gold or silver content) in addition to collector's value in separate categories.

In the broadest definition, however, collectibles are physical assets (not financial or real, in the sense of real estate), that have psychic or utilitarian value for their owners, are unique or in limited supply, and can be expected to increase in value with time and demand. The category thus includes stamps, coins, antiques, gemstones, fine art, photographs, and an almost endless list of other groups and subdivisions ranging from folk art and crafts to baseball cards, comic books, antique automobiles, and miscellaneous collectible junk.

While books have been written on the major categories of collectibles, certain common denominators exist to varying degrees from an investment perspective: often high costs to trade and own; high price volatility; no current income; and undependable or poor liquidity.

These factors plus the opportunity cost of an unproductive investment lead to one conclusion: Collectibles, especially when the relevant group of collectors is solidly in place and in good communication, will probably gain value and outstrip inflation over the long term, but the costs and risks of holding collectibles for investment purposes can be justified only when the assets also provide their owners pleasure or utility.

* * *

What Is a Collectible?

A collectible is a physical asset of a non-real estate and nonfinancial nature that exists in limited supply, usually provides enjoyment or utility to its owner, and is expected to increase in value because of inflation or supply and demand factors such as popularity and rarity.

Buying, Selling, and Holding

How do I buy and sell a collectible? Through dealers, galleries, auctions, private owners, flea markets, and catalogs and other collector publications.

Is there a minimum purchase amount, and what is the price range? Minimums and price ranges vary with the collectible and run a gamut from a few pennies to millions of dollars.

What fees and charges are involved? This depends on the collectible, where it is traded, and many other factors, but fees are an important consideration. Costs may include dealer profits (markups), sales taxes, appraisal fees, storage and safekeeping, maintenance, insurance, as well as opportunity cost—the return you would get if your money were invested more productively.

Does it mature, expire, or otherwise terminate? No.

Can I sell it quickly? A collectible varies in liquidity, from one, like a painting or an antique, bought through established dealers standing ready to repurchase at an agreed-on price, to another salable only through consignment to dealers or auction houses.

How is market value determined and how do I keep track of it? Market value is determined by supply and demand. Some collectibles are more vulnerable to fads than others, and the marketplace can be more efficient in one type of collectible than another because it has more dealers and better communication among dealers and collectors. Some major newspapers, like *The New York Times,* carry advertisements for collectibles of various types; most of the main categories of collectibles are served by specialized periodicals or newsletters; and a number of national magazines contain classified sections and even articles aimed at collectors within their fields of interest. Dealers and appraisers are a source of information about market value, but it is important to satisy oneself as to their objectivity.

Investment Objectives

Should I buy a collectible if my objective is capital appreciation? Yes, but short-term profits depend on a combination of expertise and luck, and long-term appreciation can be affected by fads as well as economic developments.

Should I buy this if my objective is income? No.

To what extent does it protect against inflation? Although there are many risks that can undermine the value of a collectible, if the condition of the collectible remains good and supply and demand factors stay favorable, values will increase with inflation.

Is it suitable for tax-deferred retirement accounts? Collectibles are not legal investments in such accounts unless they are part of portfolios directed by trustees.

Can I borrow against it? Yes; many lenders will accept marketable collectibles as collateral.

Risk Considerations

How assured can I be of getting my full investment back? With most collectibles, this has mainly to do with your level of expertise and the amount of time you hold the asset. In the short term, it is likely that costs and commissions will offset whatever small gain might be realized. In the long run, collectibles become more limited in supply and (assuming good quality and condition) more valuable, but only if the demand has continued strong and economic conditions have not eroded purchasing power. Many collectibles are vulnerable to fads, though some bought from well-established and reputable dealers may be sold back at agreed upon prices.

How assured is my income? Collectibles normally provide no income, and are in fact a drain on cash that might otherwise be invested for income.

Are there any other risks unique to this investment? Collectibles are subject to a wide range of unique risks—forgery and other frauds; physical risk, such as deterioration, fire, and theft; "warehouse finds," where a large supply of a previously limited item is suddenly discovered and becomes a drug on the market; the reverse situation, where a large chunk of a given collectible's supply goes "in collection," leaving so little in circulation that diminished interest reduces demand.

Each category has its own special risks and prospective collectors are advised to research them.

Is it commercially rated? No.

Tax Considerations

What tax advantages (or disadvantages) does it offer? Realized capital gains and capital losses are subject to standard rates for capital assets. Other tax advantages may pertain, depending on whether the collecting is done as a hobby or as a for-profit investment activity. Tax advice should be obtained.

Economic Considerations

What economic factors most affect buy, hold, and sell decisions? Collectibles have traditionally been favored by investors in times of inflation, though the value of this investment category as an inflation hedge is tempered by the many risks. The marketability of collectibles is more dependent on good economic conditions than most other investments.

COMMON STOCK

For total return over the long term, no publicly traded investment alternative offers more potential under normal conditions than common stock.

A share of common stock is the basic unit of equity ownership in a corporation. The shareholder is usually entitled to vote in the election of directors and on other important matters and to share in the wealth created by corporate activities, both through the appreciation of share values and the payment of dividends out of the earnings remaining after debt obligations and holders of preferred stock are satisfied. In the event of liquidation of assets, common shareholders divide the assets remaining after creditors and preferred shareholders have been repaid.

In public corporations, shares have market values primarily based on investor expectations of future earnings and dividends. The relationship of this market price to the actual or expected earnings, called the price-earnings ratio or "multiple," is a measure of these expectations. Stock values are also affected by forecasts of business activity in general and by whatever "investor psychology" is produced by the immediate business and economic environment.

Stocks of young, fast-growing companies, particularly those in industries that are cyclical or high technology-oriented, tend to be volatile, to have high price-earnings ratios, and generally to carry a high degree of risk. Called *growth stocks,* they seldom pay dividends, since earnings are reinvested to finance growth. These stocks are often traded in the over-the-counter market or on the American Stock Exchange.

At the other end of the spectrum, stocks of old, established firms in mature industries and with histories of regular earnings and dividends tend to be characterized by relative price stability and low multiples. These stocks are usually found listed on the New York Stock Exchange (although there are exceptions) and the cream of the crop are known as blue chips. As a general category, these regular dividend payers are called *income stocks.*

Spanning the growth/income continuum is a wide range of common stock investment choices that can be made only in terms of one's personal objectives and risk comfort level. To help in the process is a professional establishment comprised of brokers, investment advisers, and financial planners supported by practitioners of various securities analysis approaches—those trained in fundamental analysis, technical analysis, chartists, and others.

Investors with limited means can gain the advantages of common stock ownership together with the benefits of professional management and portfolio diversification through mutual funds, which are discussed elsewhere in this section.

$$* \quad * \quad *$$

What Is Common Stock?

A common stock represents ownership in a corporation, usually carries voting rights, and often earns dividends (paid out at the discretion of the corporation's board of directors).

Buying, Selling, and Holding

How do I buy and sell common stock? Through a securities broker-dealer.

Is there a minimum purchase amount, and what is the price range? There is no minimum, but buying in round lots (usually 100 shares) saves extra odd-lot (under 100 shares) charges. Some brokers offer programs allowing odd-lot purchases at regular rates. Stock prices range widely, with the majority under $50.

What fees and charges are involved? The brokerage commission, the principal charge, varies by the value and/or size of transaction. Discount brokers charge less than full-service brokers. A nominal transfer tax is imposed on sellers by the federal government and several state governments. Interest and other charges may be incurred in margin accounts, in which qualifying stocks can be traded on credit within requirements of the Federal Reserve Board and individual brokerage firms.

Does it mature, expire, or otherwise terminate? No, although tender offers by issuing companies and outside acquirers often give shareholders the opportunity to sell within a set period at a premium over prevailing stock market prices.

Can I sell it quickly? Usually, yes. Shares of publicly held and actively traded companies are highly liquid.

How is market value determined and how do I keep track of it? Market value is basically determined by investor expectations of future earnings and dividend payments, although the value of assets is also important. Prices may also be affected temporarily by large transactions creating bid-offer imbalances, by rumors of various sorts, and by public tender offers. Newspapers and electronic databases show daily prices on stocks traded on exchanges and over the counter.

Investment Objectives

Should I buy common stock if my objective is capital appreciation? Yes, especially growth stocks of younger firms, which tend to reinvest earnings rather than pay dividends as older, established firms do.

Should I buy this if my objective is income? Yes, especially if your objectives also include some capital appreciation and inflation protection. Established companies are more likely to pay dividends regularly than are fast-growing firms that tend to reinvest earnings.

To what extent does it protect against inflation? Over the long run, stocks rise in value and increase dividends with inflation, though they do not protect against hyperinflation.

Is it suitable for tax-deferred retirement accounts? Yes. Stocks are suitable for IRAs, Keoghs, 401(K) plans, and other tax-deferred plans.

Can I borrow against it? Yes, subject to Federal Reserve margin rules and lender policies concerning marketable securities collateral.

Risk Considerations

How assured can I be of getting my full investment back? There is no concrete assurance. There is always the risk that market prices will decline in value, though some stocks are more volatile than others. When a company goes out of business and liquidates its assets, common shareholders are paid last—after preferred stockholders and creditors.

How assured is my income? Dividends come out of earnings and are declared at the discretion of the board of directors. They can be suspended if profits are off, or if the directors decide reinvestment is preferable. Older, established, blue chip companies are the most dependable dividend payers; young, growth-oriented firms tend to reinvest earnings and thus pay no (or low) dividends.

Are there any other risks unique to this investment? Anything that can affect the fortunes of a company can affect its stock value and dividend payments.

Is it commercially rated? Yes, Moody's, Standard & Poor's, Value Line Investment Survey, and others rate many publicly traded issues.

Tax Considerations

What tax advantages (or disadvantages) does common stock offer? Dividends to individuals, formerly subject to a $100 exclusion ($200 on joint returns), became fully taxable as of December 31, 1986. Gains on the sale of stock held more than six months received preferential long-term capital gains treatment prior to 1987 and were subject to a maximum rate of 28% in 1987. The tax rate differential between ordinary income and capital gains, regardless of the holding period, ended effective with the 1988 tax year. After-tax corporate earnings not paid out as dividends accumulate without being taxed, if not deemed excessive. Corporations can exclude 80% of dividends received from other domestic corporations.

Economic Considerations

What economic factors most affect buy, hold, or sell decisions? Stocks are most attractive as holdings when inflation is moderate, interest rates are low, and business conditions are generally favorable to growth and bigger profits.

CONVERTIBLE SECURITY

Convertible securities—bonds (debentures) or preferred stock convertible into common stock (usually of the issuer but, in rare cases, of the issuer's subsidiary or affiliate)—offer both fixed income and appreciation potential but are not quite the best of both worlds. The yield on the convertible bond or preferred is normally less than that of a "straight" bond or preferred, and the potential for capital gain is less than with a common stock investment.

On the other hand, convertibles (sometimes called CVs and identified that way in the newspaper bond tables, but not the stock tables) do offer less credit risk and market risk than common shares while providing an opportunity to share in the future wealth of the corporation for whose shares the convertible can be exchanged.

In terms of priority of claim on earnings and assets, convertible bonds and convertible preferred stock have the same status as regular bonds and preferred. Bonds, whether convertible or straight, receive payments before preferred stock, whatever its type, and both bonds and preferred have precedence over common stock.

From the investor's standpoint, convertibles must be understood in terms of what is called their *investment value* and their *conversion value*. Investment value is the market value the convertible would have if it were not convertible—its value as a straight bond or straight preferred. Conversion value is the market price of the common stock times the number of shares into which the bond or preferred is convertible (called the conversion rate or ratio).

Since convertible owners hope to capitalize on rises in common shares through conversion and therefore value the conversion privilege, CVs begin trading at a premium over conversion value. As the common rises and the CV is viewed more and more as a common stock investment, the CV tends to sell for its common stock equivalent. Conversion is not advisable until the common dividend has more value than the income on the CV and it is normal for the common price to rise beyond the CV price until that equation is reached.

Of course, common-share prices cannot be guaranteed to rise, and in a down market convertible holders look at their investment in terms of its value as a bond or preferred stock. This investment value represents downside risk protection in the sense that the convertible will never be worth less than this value. Investment value is, however, subject to market risk; it can be pushed down by a general rise in interest rates. But should that happen, investors have downside protection in that the CV will never drop significantly below its conversion value.

Conventional wisdom holds that investors should not buy convertibles unless attracted by the soundness of the underlying common stock. They should be wary also of issues selling at high premiums over the value of the common stock or the prices at which they are callable.

See also the discussion of Zero-coupon Securities.

*   *   *

What Is a Convertible Security?

A convertible security is a preferred stock or debenture (unsecured bond) paying a fixed dividend or rate of interest and convertible into common stock, usually of the issuer, at a specified price or conversion ratio.

Buying, Selling, and Holding

How do I buy and sell a convertible security? Through a securities broker-dealer.

Is there a minimum purchase amount and what is the price range? Convertible preferred stock typically trades in 10-share round lots and has par values ranging from $100 down to $10. Bonds sell in $1000 units but exceptions, called baby bonds, can have lower par values, usually $500 down to $25. Brokers often have minimum orders of 10 bonds or, frequently, 100 bonds. Odd lots involve higher commissions or dealer spreads.

What fees and charges are involved? Standard brokerage commissions or dealer spreads. Bonds usually involve a per-bond commission of $2.50 to $20, depending on the broker and the size of the order. However, a minimum of $30 is common.

Does it mature, expire, or otherwise terminate? Bonds mature; preferred stocks do not. Both may be callable, however, and the regular redemption and retirement of both shares and bonds may be provided for by sinking fund agreements. Of course, once converted to common stock, there are no maturities or calls.

Can I sell it quickly? Most can be readily sold, but trading volume is not ordinarily heavy and prices can fluctuate significantly.

How is market value determined and how do I keep track of it? Market value is influenced both by the market price of the underlying common stock and the investment value of the convertible security—that is, its value as a bond or preferred stock exclusive of the conversion feature. When the conversion premium—the amount by which the price of the convertible security exceeds the price of the underlying common stock—is high, the convertible trades like a bond or preferred stock. When trading like a fixed-income investment, its value fluctuates in inverse relation to interest rates, though it will not decline below its investment value. Once parity has been reached—that is, the price of the convertible and its value assuming conversion are the same—the convertible will rise along with the underlying common stock. Prices of convertibles are reported in the stock or bond tables of daily newspapers and in electronic databases.

Investment Objectives

Should I buy a convertible security if my objective is capital appreciation? Yes; convertibles offer the opportunity to capitalize on growth in common share values while enjoying the greater yield and safety of bonds or preferred.

Should I buy this if my objective is income? Yes; but since growth is a feature, the yield is less than on a straight bond or preferred.

To what extent does it protect against inflation? Convertible prices tend to rise with common share prices, which tend to rise with inflation.

Is it suitable for tax-deferred retirement accounts? Yes, CVs qualify for IRAs, Keoghs, 401(K) plans, and other tax-deferred plans.

Can I borrow against it? Yes, subject to margin rules. CVs are acceptable general collateral, with bonds having more loan value than stock.

Risk Considerations

How assured can I be of getting my full investment back? CVs have downside protection in that their value will not sink below the market value the same investment would have as a straight (nonconvertible) bond or preferred. That "investment value" varies inversely with rates, however, so when rates go up the "floor" goes down. The price of a CV is determined, on the other hand, by the value of its conversion feature, so as long as the common holds up, the CV should not decline to its investment value. Of course, once converted, your investment becomes subject to all the risks of common stock. In liquidation, convertible bonds are paid before convertible preferred stock, and both have precedence over the corporation's common stock.

How assured is my income? The interest on convertible bonds, as a legal obligation of the issuer, has a higher claim on earnings than dividends on convertible preferred stock, which can be omitted if the issuer gets tight for cash. Preferred dividends must be paid before common dividends, however. Assuming the issuer is strong financially and has dependable earnings, there is little to worry about.

Are there any other risks unique to this investment? Dilution—a decrease in the value of common shares into which the CV converts—can happen for many reasons. Provision for such obvious corporate actions as stock splits, new issues, or spinoffs of stock or other properties, is normally made in the bond indenture or preferred stock agreement, but subtle developments, such as small quarterly stock dividends or unplanned events, can be a risk.

Is it commercially rated? Yes, by Moody's, Standard & Poor's, Value Line, and other services.

Tax Considerations

What tax advantages (or disadvantages) does it offer? None, except that gains resulting from conversion to the issuer's common stock are not treated as gains for tax purposes, provided the stock you receive is that of the same corporation that issued the convertible. Corporations can exclude from taxes 80% of preferred dividends.

Economic Considerations

What economic factors most affect buy, hold, or sell decisions? Assuming economic conditions are not threatening the issuer's financial health, convertibles offer holders protection from adverse factors affecting both common stock and fixed-income securities. The CV is thus a security for all seasons, though the price of having it both ways is less appreciation potential than common stock and less yield than straight bonds or preferred stock. It follows that CVs are popular in times of economic and market uncertainty. The ideal time to buy is when rates are high and stocks are low and the best time to hold is in a rising stock market. Stagflation is the worst scenario because stocks are hurt by the stagnation and fixed-income securities are hurt by the inflation; both the conversion and investment values of CVs thus suffer.

FOREIGN STOCKS AND BONDS

Foreign stocks and bonds—those of foreign issuers denominated in foreign currencies—offer opportunities (1) to invest where economies or industry sectors may be faster growing than those at home and (2) to augment total returns through profits on currency movements.

Foreign securities have acquired luster in recent years, as ways to shift money from sluggish United States markets into more vibrant overseas economies (while gaining an edge on domestic inflation) and as "dollar plays," ways of capitalizing on expected declines in the value of the U.S. dollar vis-à-vis foreign currencies. Generally, foreign investment activity has picked up with deregulation of foreign markets, improved communications, and increased internationalization of businesses, banks, and broker-dealers.

Problems that remain, depending on the issue and the market, include inadequate financial information and regulation; high minimum purchase requirements; additional transaction costs and risks; taxes; possible illiquidity; political risk; and the possibility of currency losses. Unless you are wealthy, able to take big risks, and sophisticated in the ways of international interest rates and foreign exchange, you are better advised to achieve international diversification through open-end and closed-end funds or other investment pools specializing in foreign securities.

An exception for some investors might be American Depositary Receipts (ADRs). Many foreign stocks can be owned by way of these negotiable receipts, which are issued by United States banks and represent actual shares held in their foreign branches. ADRs are actively traded on the major stock exchanges and in the over-the-counter market. Although currency risks and foreign withholding taxes remain, the depositary pays dividends and capital gains in U.S. dollars and handles rights offerings, splits, stock dividends, and other corporate actions. ADRs eliminate trading inconveniences and custodial problems that otherwise exist with foreign stocks.

Eurobonds—bonds issued by governments and their agencies, banks, international institutions, and corporations (U.S. and foreign) and sold outside their countries through international syndicates for purchase by international investors—also warrant a special word. They may be denominated in foreign currencies, Eurodollars, or composite currency units, such as Special Drawing Rights (SDRs) or European Units of Account (EUAs) whose certificates representing the combined value of two or more currencies are designed to minimize the effects of currency fluctuations. Most are fixed-income obligations, but some Eurodollar issues have floating rates tied to the London Interbank Offered Rate (LIBOR). Eurobonds, which are issued in bearer form, attract upscale personal investors because they are available in a wide range of maturities, are not subject to a withholding tax, and offer good liquidity.

New issues of Eurobonds may not be sold legally to United States investors until a 90-day seasoning period has expired. Actually, most United States broker-dealers extend this rule to include all new issues in foreign currencies; foreign banks and broker-dealers are generally more solicitous of United States investors in selling new issues. Except for Yankee bonds, obligations of foreign borrowers issued in the United States and denominated in dollars, foreign bonds are not subject to Securities and Exchange Commission regulation.

*   *   *

What Are Foreign Stocks and Bonds?

Foreign stocks and bonds are stock of foreign companies listed on foreign exchanges; stock of foreign companies listed on United States exchanges or represented by listed American Depositary Receipts (ADRs); bonds of foreign government entities and corporations, including Eurobonds and nondollar-denominated bonds issued by local syndicates.

Buying, Selling, and Holding

How do I buy and sell foreign stocks and bonds? Through securities broker-dealers with foreign offices or with expertise in foreign markets, and through foreign banks and their American offices. (ADRs and shares traded on U.S. exchanges can be bought and sold through any broker.)

Is there a minimum purchase amount, and what is the price range? ADRs and U.S. exchange-listed foreign stocks trade just like domestic common stock. Minimums on other stocks and bonds vary widely by issue and dealer, but are often high. With the extra risks, diversification is important, which raises the cost even higher. Unless you are wealthy, you should probably opt for one of the mutual funds or other investment vehicles pooling foreign securities.

What fees and charges are involved? Transaction costs can be a significant consideration. They vary depending on many factors, but may include custodial fees, local turnover or transfer taxes, and currency conversion fees, in addition to broker commissions or dealer spreads. Transaction and custodial costs are minimized with ADRs.

Do foreign stocks and bonds mature, expire, or otherwise terminate? Bonds mature; stocks do not. However remote, the risk exists that a sovereign government will confiscate or devalue assets of foreign investors.

Can I sell them quickly? U.S. exchange-listed foreign stocks and ADRs normally enjoy high liquidity. With other foreign securities, illiquidity is often a problem. Even widely held issues are often kept as permanent investments by governments, banks, and other companies and may not trade actively. Canada, England, and Japan have high average turnover on their stock exchanges.

How is market value determined and how do I keep track of it? Economic, market, and monetary (interest-rate) factors affect foreign stock and bond values the same way they do domestic equity and debt securities, though conditions and growth rates differ among countries. Traditionally, foreign stocks, on average, have been less volatile than domestic issues, because issuers tended to be older firms whose stock was held largely by long-term investors. Today, foreign exchanges list a growing number of young, dynamic companies whose shares are actively traded and often quite volatile. *The Wall Street Journal,* the *Financial Times* (London), and other leading newspapers report on major foreign exchanges, as well as ADRs and foreign stocks and bonds traded in domestic markets.

Investment Objectives

Should I buy foreign stocks and bonds if my objective is capital appreciation? Especially in growing economies, stocks offer potential for both capital and currency appreciation. Unless bought at a discount or in a period of declining interest rates, bonds do not appreciate, although gains due to currency movements are possible.

Should I buy them if my objective is income? Yes, but most foreign stocks have lower dividend yields than domestic stocks, and exchange-rate fluctuations are a factor in the expected returns of both stocks and bonds.

To what extent do they protect against inflation? Foreign stocks can hedge inflation to the extent local economies and industry sectors offer better growth prospects than exist in the United States. But gains from dividends and appreciation can be eroded by foreign-exchange losses.

Are they suitable for tax-deferred retirement accounts? Yes.

Can I borrow against them? Yes; quality securities are acceptable collateral at most banks, and banks headquartered in the country of the issuer will often lend higher percentages of value. Foreign stocks listed on American exchanges are subject to Federal Reserve margin requirements.

Risk Considerations

How assured can I be of getting my full investment back? Although more young, growing firms appear every day on foreign exchanges, most shares represent solid issuers and volatility has traditionally been low, so foreign equities, on average, may actually be safer than many domestic issues, assuming no adverse currency fluctuations. Bondholders, who lack regulatory protection and full credit information, have more credit risk than owners of domestic issues, in addition to having political, interest rate, and currency risks. (Foreign exchange risk can be hedged using currency futures and options.)

How assured is my income? Since issuers tend to be established, reputable firms or governments, there have historically been few defaults on payments of interest or instances of omitted dividends. On the other hand, a lack of full financial disclosure and regulatory supervision makes it difficult to anticipate adverse financial developments. Also, many newer companies, whose securities are riskier than those of traditional foreign issuers, are likewise listed on foreign exchanges. Foreign-exchange risk can also affect income.

Are there any other risks unique to this investment? Political or sovereign risk—the risk, for example, that foreign assets might be expropriated or devalued or that local tax policies might adversely affect debt or equity holders; the risk of transactional losses caused by settlement delays or fraud; with stock not registered with the Securities and Exchange Commission, there are legal difficulties for Americans in subscribing to rights offerings, a fact which can also affect the salability of rights (rights problems do not exist with ADRs or U.S. exchange-listed foreign shares).

Are they commercially rated? Some foreign debt issues are rated. Information can be found in a publication called *Credit Week International,* available at some larger brokerage firms.

Tax Considerations

What tax advantages (or disadvantages) do they offer? Some countries impose a withholding tax, typically from 15% to 20%, on dividends and interest (except Eurobonds). U.S. tax treaties can result in partial reclamation of withholdings in some countries, and the tax can be offset to some extent against federal income taxes. There is usually no capital gains tax imposed by foreign governments, though such gains are taxed by the U.S. government. Special rules apply to 10% or more ownership of a foreign corporation.

Economic Considerations

What economic factors most affect buy, hold, or sell decisions? Foreign securities are best bought when the U.S. dollar is strong against the currency of denomination. To profit from currency movements (or, conversely, to avoid losses) it is best to hold when the dollar is declining against the local currency. Foreign equities are attractive relative to American investments when the foreign economy or industrial sector has a better outlook than its domestic counterpart. Foreign bonds rise and fall in inverse relation to market interest rates.

FUTURES CONTRACT ON A COMMODITY

A futures contract is a commitment to buy or sell a specified quantity of a commodity or financial instrument at a specified price during a particular delivery month. Once restricted largely to agricultural commodities and metals, futures contracts have in recent years been extended to include what are broadly termed financial futures—contracts on debt instruments, such as Treasury bonds and Government National Mortgage Association (''Ginnie Mae'') certificates and on foreign currencies—and, even more recently, contracts on stock indexes. Contract prices are determined through open outcry—a system of verbal communication between sellers and buyers on the floors of regulated commodities exchanges.

The futures markets are broadly divided into two categories of participants: (1) Hedgers have a position in (i.e., own) the underlying commodity or instrument (such as a farmer in the case of an agricultural commodity or an investor in the case of a financial or index future). Hedgers use futures to create countervailing positions, thus protecting against loss due to price (or rate) changes. (2) Speculators do not own the underlying asset for commercial or investment purposes, but instead aim to capitalize on the ups and downs (the volatility) of the contracts themselves. It is the speculators who provide the liquidity essential to the efficient operation of the futures markets.

As with option contracts, which are also discussed in this section, the great majority of futures contracts are closed out before their expiration—or delivery— date. This is done by buying or selling an offsetting contract. It is vital to note that with futures, in contrast to options (which simply expire), the alternative to an offset is a delivery, though this is done with title documentation or, in the case of index futures, cash, not by the legendary dumping of pork bellies on the front steps of absentminded contract holders. When the future is a contract to buy value, delivery of the future is avoided by buying an offsetting future to sell.

The attraction of futures for speculators, again like options, is the enormous leverage they provide. Although brokers normally require investors to meet substantial net worth and income requirements, it is possible to trade contracts with outlays of cash (or sometimes U.S. Treasury securities) equal to 5% to 10% of contract values. Such "margins" (actually good-faith deposits, more in the nature of performance bonds and required of both buyers and sellers) are set by the exchanges, although brokers normally have their own maintenance requirements. Margin calls are normally made when deposits drop to one half the original percentage value.

The commodity exchanges, with oversight by the Commodities Futures Trading Commission (CFTC), each day set limits, based on the previous day's closing price, to the extent a given contract's trading price may vary. While these trading limits help preclude exaggerated short-term volatility and thus make it possible for margin requirements to be kept low, they can also lock a trader into a losing position, where he must meet a margin call but is prevented from trading out of the position because the contract is either up limit or down limit (as high or as low as the daily limit permits it to be traded).

Speculators in futures contracts fall into three groups: (1) the exchange floor traders (scalpers), who make markets in contracts and turn small profits usually within the trading day; (2) spread traders, who hope to profit from offsetting positions in contracts having different maturities but the same underlying commodity or instrument, similar maturities but different (although usually closely related) underlying commodities, or similar contracts in different markets; and (3) position traders, who have the expertise and financial ability to analyze longer-term factors and ride out shorter term fluctuations in the expectation of ultimate gains.

While speculation in futures contracts is not recommended for the average investor, individuals with the money and risk tolerance may participate by choosing among the following alternatives: trading for one's own account, which involves time and expertise; trading through a managed account or a discretionary account with a commodities broker, which utilizes a professional's time and expertise for a fee or sometimes involves a participation in profits; or mutual funds, which offer both professional management and diversification and are regulated by both the CFTC and the Securities and Exchange Commission.

*   *   *

What Is a Commodity Futures Contract?

A commodity futures contract is an agreement to buy or sell a specific amount of a commodity at a particular price in a stipulated future month.

Buying, Selling, and Holding

How do I buy and sell it? Through a full-service broker or firm specializing in commodities transactions.

Is there a minimum purchase amount, and what is the price range? Contract sizes and unit prices vary widely from commodity to commodity, but the exchanges have liberal margin rules making it possible to trade with as little as 5% to 10% down. In some commodities, that can be $100, but brokers often have minimum deposits of $1000 to $2500. (They may also have strict personal income and net worth rules for investors.) One national exchange, the Mid-America Commodity Exchange, offers minicontracts in a number of commodities, currencies, and instruments; they range from one fifth to one half the size of regular contracts.

What fees and charges are involved? Broker commissions, which vary by contract but average $25 to $50 for a round-turn (buy and sell) trade with lower rates for intraday and spread (e.g., buy soybeans, sell soybean oil) transactions. Managed accounts involve management fees and, sometimes, participation in profits.

Does a commodity futures contract mature, expire, or otherwise terminate? Yes. All contracts have a stipulated expiration date.

Can I sell it quickly? Most established contracts are liquid, though daily price limits can create illiquidity when a commodity is down limit or up limit (as high or as low as the daily trading limit permits).

How is market value determined and how do I keep track of it? By supply and demand, which is affected by natural causes as well as general economic developments. Futures prices are quoted daily in the financial pages of newspapers and electronic databases.

Investment Objectives

Should I buy a commodity futures contract if my objective is capital appreciation? Only if you are expert, wealthy, and have a high tolerance for risk. Then, with the high leverage possible, capital gains (and losses) can be huge.

Should I buy this if my objective is income? No. Contracts pay no income.

To what extent does it protect against inflation? Forward commodity prices reflect inflation expectations, but since contracts are short-term oriented, inflation protection is a secondary consideraton.

Is it suitable for tax-deferred retirement accounts? Although not prohibited by the Internal Revenue Service, most brokerage firms rule out futures contracts as too risky for retirement accounts. They may have a limited role in managed accounts, primarily as a hedging tool. Certain pooled investment vehicles trading in futures may be appropriate in selected situations for people with high risk tolerance.

Can I borrow against it? Futures are not acceptable collateral with most lenders. Of course, they provide leverage inherently because of the relatively small deposits required to control contracts.

Risk Considerations

How assured can I be of getting my full investment back? Commodity futures are inherently speculative and it is actually possible to lose more than your investment (though margin calls would usually limit losses to the amount deposited if the account was sold out—that is, liquidated by the broker to meet the margin call).

How assured is my income? Futures provide no income.

Are there any other risks unique to this investment? The possibility of losses in excess of investment and the risk of illiquidity when a contract is down or up limit (thus making it impossible to trade out of a position) are risks unique to commodity futures trading. Of course, there is the risk (nightmare?) of actual delivery of a commodity if you fail to close out a position prior to expiration of a contract.

Is it commercially rated? No.

Tax Considerations

What tax advantages (or disadvantages) does a commodity futures contract offer? Speculators' open positions are marked to market at year end and paper profits and losses taxed as though realized. Prior to the Tax Reform Act of 1986, 60% of profits were taxed as long-term capital gains and 40% at short-term (ordinary income) rates, for a maximum rate of 32%. With the capital gains exclusion ended, net profits are taxable at ordinary rates, although net trading losses can be applied against capital gains on other investments and unused portions carried forward. Other tax treatments apply to nonspeculative and hedging uses and tax advice is recommended.

Economic Considerations

What economic factors most affect buy, hold, and sell decisions? Anything that affects supply and demand for a commodity makes contract values move up and down.

FUTURES CONTRACT ON AN INTEREST RATE

For a general discussion of a futures contract, see Futures Contract on a Commodity.

* * *

What Is a Futures Contract on an Interest Rate?

A futures contract on an interest rate is an agreement to buy or sell a given amount of a fixed-income security, such as a Treasury bill, bond, or note or Government National Mortgage Association security at a particular price in a stipulated future month.

Buying, Selling, and Holding

How do I buy and sell it? Through a full-service broker or firm specializing in commodities transactions.

Is there a minimum purchase amount, and what is the price range? Contract sizes vary with the underlying security and the exchange, but range from $20,000 to $1 million; since exchange margin rules allow trading with as little as 5% deposited, the actual cost of investing can be relatively low.

What fees and charges are involved? Broker commissions averaging $25 to $50 per contract transaction.

Does it mature, expire, or otherwise terminate? Yes; futures contracts have specific expiration dates.

Can I sell it quickly? Yes, except that liquidity may become a problem if the contract reaches the maximum price movement allowable in one day, in effect locking you into a position.

How is market value determined and how do I keep track of it? By market interest rate movements, essentially. When rates go up, the prices of fixed-income securities (and futures related to them) go down, and vice versa. Prices are reported daily in newspapers and electronic databases.

Investment Objectives

Should I buy a futures contract on an interest rate if my objective is capital appreciation? Speculators use the leverage available with futures to capitalize on expected interest rate movements, standing to gain (or lose) substantially more than the amount invested.

Should I buy this if my objective is income? No, though you might use futures to hedge the value of securities bought for income or to lock in the yield on a security to be bought at a later date.

To what extent does it protect against inflation? To the extent inflation expectations are a factor in the volatility of fixed-income investments, futures can offer some protection against loss.

Is it suitable for tax-deferred retirement accounts? Although not prohibited by the Internal Revenue Service, most brokerage firms rule out futures contracts as too risky for retirement accounts. They may have a limited role in managed accounts, primarily as a hedging tool. Certain pooled investment vehicles trading in futures may be appropriate in selected situations for people with high risk tolerance.

Can I borrow against it? No; futures contracts are not acceptable collateral at most lenders. Of course, there is considerable leverage inherent in the small deposit required to control contracts.

Risk Considerations

How assured can I be of getting my full investment back? Just as interest rate movements cannot be predicted with certainty, interest rate futures can result in losses as well as gains; it is in fact possible to lose more than your investment (called open-ended risk) but margin calls would normally limit losses to the amount invested, assuming the account was sold out (liquidated) to meet the call.

How assured is my income? Futures do not provide income.

Are there any other risks unique to this investment? Open-ended risk and the risk of illiquidity when a contract is down limit or up limit, making it impossible to trade out of a position, are risks unique to futures contracts.

Is it commercially rated? No.

Tax Considerations

What tax advantages (or disadvantages) does it offer? Speculators' open positions are marked to market at year end and paper profits and losses taxed as though realized. Prior to the Tax Reform Act of 1986, 60% of profits were taxed as long-term capital gains and 40% at short-term (ordinary income) rates, for a maximum rate of 32%. With the capital gains exclusion ended, net profits are taxable at ordinary rates, although net trading losses can be applied against capital gains on other investments and unused portions carried forward. Other tax treatments apply to nonspeculative and hedging uses and tax advice is recommended.

Economic Considerations

What economic factors most affect buy, hold, and sell decisions? Economic and monetary factors affecting interest rates govern choices having to do with interest rate futures.

FUTURES CONTRACT ON A STOCK INDEX

For a general discussion of a futures contract, see Futures Contract on a Commodity.

* * *

What Is a Futures Contract on a Stock Index?

A futures contract on a stock index is an agreement to buy or sell a stock index at a price based on the index value in a stipulated future month with settlement in cash.

Buying, Selling, and Holding

How do I buy and sell it? Through a full-service broker or firm specializing in commodities transactions.

Is there a minimum purchase amount, and what is the price range? Contracts are priced according to formulas based on index values, and vary in terms both of formulas and index values. For example, the contracts on the New York Stock Exchange Composite Index, the Standard & Poor's 500 Stock Index, and The Value Line Stock Index are priced by multiplying $500 times the index value, which ranges roughly between 100 and 300; if one of those indexes had a value of 200, a contract would cost $100,000, which might require a deposit of 10% or $10,000. To play, though, you would probably have to meet an income and liquid net worth test requiring substantial means.

What fees and charges are involved? Broker commissions.

Does it mature, expire, or otherwise terminate? Yes, all contracts have specific expirations.

Can I sell it quickly? Yes, except that liquidity may become a problem if the contract reaches the maximum price movement allowable in one day (i.e., becomes down limit or up limit).

How is market value determined and how do I keep track of it? By the market performance of the stocks comprising the index as they affect the index value. Index futures are reported with other futures prices in the financial pages of daily newspapers and electronic databases.

Investment Objectives

Should I buy a futures contract on a stock index if my objective is capital appreciation? Speculators use the leverage available with futures to capitalize on expected market movements, standing to gain (or lose) substantially more than the amount invested.

Should I buy this if my objective is income? No, but they are used, mainly by professionals, to hedge the value of income-producing stocks.

To what extent does it protect against inflation? This is not an investment you would hold as an inflation hedge.

Is it suitable for tax-deferred retirement accounts? Although not prohibited by the Internal Revenue Service, most brokerage firms rule out futures contracts as too risky for retirement accounts. They may have a limited role in managed accounts, primarily as a hedging tool. Certain pooled investment vehicles trading in futures may be appropriate in selected situations for people with high risk tolerance.

Can I borrow against it? No; futures are not acceptable collateral at most lenders.

Of course, there is considerable leverage inherent in the relatively small deposit required to control contracts.

Risk Considerations

How assured can I be of getting my full investment back? Just as market movements cannot be predicted with certainty, index futures can result in losses as well as gains; in fact, it is quite possible to lose more than your investment (called openended risk), although margin calls are a safeguard against losses in excess of investment if an account is sold out (liquidated) to meet the call.

How assured is my income? Index futures do not provide income.

Are there any other risks unique to this investment? Index futures and the individual stocks comprising the index may not move exactly together, so it is not a perfect hedging tool.

Is it commercially rated? No.

Tax Considerations

What tax advantages (or disadvantages) does it offer? Speculators' open positions are marked to market at year end and paper profits and losses taxed as though realized. Prior to the Tax Reform Act of 1986, 60% of profits were taxed as longterm capital gains and 40% at short-term (ordinary income) rates, for a maximum rate of 32%. With the capital gains exclusion ended, net profits are taxable at ordinary rates, although net trading losses can be applied against capital gains on other investments and unused portions carried forward. Other tax treatments apply to nonspeculative and hedging uses and tax advice is recommended.

Economic Considerations

What economic factors most affect buy, hold, and sell decisions? The myriad factors affecting the market outlook affect choices having to do with stock index futures, whether they are used to speculate or as a hedging tool.

GOVERNMENT AGENCY SECURITY

Government agency securities, popularly called agencies, are indirect obligations of the United States government, issued by federal agencies and government-sponsored corporations under authority from the United States Congress, but, with a few exceptions, not backed, as U.S. Treasury securities are, by the full faith and credit of the government.

While it is highly unlikely—even unthinkable—that they could ever be allowed to default on principal or interest, these agency securities cannot be considered absolutely risk-free, and therein lies their attraction—because of the slight difference in safety, they generally yield as much as a half percentage point more than direct obligations.

Agencies are also, like Treasuries, exempt from state and local taxes, although there are exceptions—for example, securities guaranteed by the Government National Mortgage Association (GNMA), and issues of the Federal National Mortgage Association (FNMA) and the Federal Home Loan Mortgage Corporation (FHLMC), including both mortgage-backed pass-throughs and bonds and notes issued to finance their operations.

Unlike Treasuries, agencies are not sold by auction but rather are marketed at the best yield possible by the Federal Reserve Bank of New York, as fiscal agent, through its network of primary dealers. Information can be obtained from the Federal Reserve Bank of New York, Treasury and Agency Issues Division, from the issuing agencies, or from dealer commercial banks and securities brokers.

Agencies issuing or guaranteeing securities include:

Asian Development Bank

College Construction Loan Insurance Corporation (Connie Lee)

District of Columbia Armory Board (D.C. Stadium)

Export-Import Bank of the United States

Farmers Home Administration

Federal Agricultural Mortgage Corporation (Farmer Mac)

Federal Farm Credit Consolidated System-Wide Securities

Federal Home Loan Banks

Federal Home Loan Mortgage Corporation

Federal Housing Administration (FHA)

Federal National Mortgage Association (FNMA)

Financing Corp. (FICO)

Government National Mortgage Association (GNMA)

Interamerican Development Bank

International Bank for Reconstruction and Development (World Bank)

Maritime Administration

Resolution Funding Corporation (Refcorp.)

Small Business Administration (SBA)

Student Loan Marketing Association (SLMA)

Tennessee Valley Authority (TVA)

United States Postal Service

Washington Metropolitan Area Transit Authority

* * *

What Is a Government Agency Security?

A government agency security is a negotiable debt obligation of an agency of the United States government, which may be backed by the full faith and credit of the federal government but is more often guaranteed by the sponsoring agency with the implied backing of Congress.

Buying, Selling, and Holding

How do I buy and sell it? Through a securities broker-dealer or at many commercial banks.

Is there a minimum purchase amount, and what is the price range? Denominations and minimums vary widely from $1000 to $25,000 and up, depending on the issue, the issuing agency, and the dealer.

What fees and charges are involved? None in the case of new issues bought from a member of the underwriting group; otherwise a commission or dealer markup.

Does it mature, expire, or otherwise terminate? Yes, maturities range from 30 days to 25 years.

Can I sell it quickly? Yes, but bid and asked spreads tend to be wider than with direct Treasury obligations, which raises the cost of trading in the secondary market.

How is market value determined and how do I keep track of it? Market values vary inversely with market interest rate movements. Daily newspapers, brokers, and large banks provide price information.

Investment Objectives

Should I buy a government agency security if my objective is capital appreciation? No, though appreciation is possible when fixed-rate securities are bought prior to a drop in market interest rates.

Should I buy this if my objective is income? Yes. Yields are a bit higher than those of direct government obligations, but lower than those of corporate obligations.

To what extent does it protect against inflation? As fixed-income securities, agencies offer no protection, though shorter-term issues offer less exposure to inflation risk.

Is it suitable for tax-deferred retirement accounts? Yes.

Can I borrow against it? Yes; lenders will often lend 90% of value.

Risk Considerations

How assured can I be of getting my full investment back? Agencies are second only to Treasury securities as good credit risks. Market prices fall as interest rates rise, however, so you may not get a full return of principal if you sell in the secondary market prior to maturity. Some sophisticated investors hedge market risk using options, futures, and futures options that are available on certain Treasury securities and Government National Mortgage Association securities.

How assured is my income? Very assured. It is highly unlikely the U.S. Treasury, Congress, or a regulatory body like the Federal Reserve Board would allow a government agency to default on interest.

Are there any other risks unique to a government agency security? No, but mortgage-backed pass-through securities issued by government-sponsored entities have different characteristics and are covered separately in this section.

Is it commercially rated? Some issues are rated by major services.

Tax Considerations

What tax advantages (or disadvantages) does it offer? Agencies are fully taxable at the federal level but are exempt from state and local taxes with certain exceptions, such as issues of the Federal National Mortgage Association and the Government National Mortgage Association.

Economic Considerations

What economic factors most affect buy, hold, or sell decisions? It is best to buy when interest rates are high and the best yields can be obtained. Holding is most attractive when rates are declining, causing an upward move in the market values of fixed-income securities, and high inflation is not present to erode the value of fixed returns.

LIFE INSURANCE (CASH VALUE)

For young families as yet without sufficient financial security to provide for expenses in the event of the premature death of the breadwinner or homemaker, life insurance provides essential protection. By far the cheapest and simplest way to obtain that protection is *term life insurance*, a no-frills deal whereby premiums buy insurance but do not create cash value. The alternatives—variously called cash value, straight, whole, permanent, or ordinary life insurance—combine protection with an investment program.

The traditional cash value policy requires a fixed premium for the life of the insured and promises a fixed sum of money on the death of the insured. A portion of the premium covers expenses and actual insurance, the rest earns interest in a tax-deferred savings program, gradually building up a cash value. The latter can be cashed in by canceling the policy (hence the term "cash surrender value"), can be used to buy more protection, or can be borrowed at a below-market or even zero interest rate with the loan balance deducted from the death benefit. On the death of the insured, the beneficiary receives only the death benefit.

Variations called single-premium or limited-payment life policies, have higher up-front premiums so that a policy becomes paid-up—the cash value becomes sufficient to cover the death benefit without further premiums. Later, if the insured is still living, the policy begins paying benefits that can supplement retirement income or be converted to an annuity, thus guaranteeing income for life.

The one serious drawback of cash value policies has been that the interest rate is not competitive with other investments. With soaring interest rates and inflation in the 1970s and in the excitement of new investment products spawned by deregulation in the 1980s, upwardly mobile young investors began questioning the value of insurance policies providing neither competitive investment returns nor the flexibility their dynamic personal financial circumstances required. Faced with cancellations and poor sales, insurers came forth with the following:

> *Universal Life,* which clearly separates the cash value and protection elements of the policy and invests the cash value in a tax-deferred savings program tied to a money market rate. The cost of the insurance is fixed, based on the insured's age and sex, so depending on what the cash value portion earns (it is guaranteed to earn a minimum rate, but can earn more if market rates rise), the premium can vary. The insured may also change the amount of protection at any time. Flexibility is the main feature of this type of policy.
>
> *Variable Life,* which has a fixed premium like straight life, but the cash value goes into a choice of stock, bond, or money market portfolios, which the investor can alternate. The insurer guarantees a minimum death benefit regardless of portfolio performance, although excess gains buy additional coverage. The attraction here is capital growth opportunity.
>
> *Universal Variable Life,* a mid-1980s innovation that combines the flexibility of universal life with the growth potential of variable life.

Even with modern policies, however, the question persists: Why sacrifice a portion of income to an insurance company when pure protection can be more cheaply obtained through term insurance and returns as good or better can be obtained by investing directly? The answer depends on an individual's expertise, self-confidence, and willingness to spend time managing investments.

*   *   *

What Is Cash Value Life Insurance?

Cash value life insurance is a contract combining payment to beneficiaries, in the event of the insured's premature death, with investment programs.

Buying, Selling, and Holding

How do I buy and sell it? Through insurance brokers, insurance company sales agents, savings institutions, full-service brokers, commercial banks, financial planners, and other financial services organizations.

Is there a minimum purchase amount, and what is the price range? Annual premiums vary widely with the type of policy and such factors as the age and sex of the insured.

What fees and charges are involved? Cost of coverage, sales commissions, and insurance company operating costs are built into premiums. Some policies have penalties for cancellation before specified dates.

Does it mature, expire, or otherwise terminate? Policies mature in 10 years to life, depending on the program.

Can I sell it quickly? Yes. Policies can be canceled and cash values claimed anytime (although actual payment may require several weeks of processing time).

How is market value determined and how do I keep track of it? Policies are not traded in a secondary market. Cash values are determined by accumulated premiums plus investment income and performance.

Investment Objectives

Should I buy cash value life insurance if my objective is capital appreciation? Assuming death benefits are your primary objective, you might buy a variable life insurance policy or a universal variable life insurance policy with investments in a stock fund to gain capital appreciation.

Should I buy this if my objective is income? No, although policies combining annuities provide for income payments on annuitization.

To what extent does it protect against inflation? Universal, variable, and universal variable policies can offer some inflation protection through adjustable death benefits and the investment of cash values in inflation-sensitive securities.

Is it suitable for tax-deferred retirement accounts? No; life insurance is not an eligible investment.

Can I borrow against it? Yes. Insurance companies will normally loan cash value at lower-than-market rates and reduce the death benefit by the amount of the loan.

Risk Considerations

How assured can I be of getting my full investment back? Insurance companies are highly regulated and there is little risk they will not meet commitments. However, policies that provide for market returns on cash value investments also carry market risk: e.g., a variable life policy invested in a bond fund would lose cash value if interest rates rose, while one invested in stocks would lose in a down market.

How assured is my income? That depends on how cash values are invested. Policies that invest cash value in money market instruments, for example, are subject to fluctuating income.

Are there any other risks unique to cash value life insurance? Although heavily regulated, insurance companies are potentially subject to mismanagement and fraud and are not themselves covered by federal protection in the sense that banks, for example, are covered by the Federal Deposit Insurance Corporation.

Is it commercially rated? Yes. Insurance companies are rated by Best's Rating Service.

Tax Considerations

What tax advantages (or disadvantages) does it offer? Income earned on cash value accumulates and compounds tax-deferred. Though subject to federal estate taxes (after a $600,000 exclusion) and local inheritance taxes, life insurance proceeds paid to a named beneficiary avoid probate. Proceeds to beneficiaries are normally not subject to federal income taxes. Single-premium life insurance, which offers tax-free cash value accumulation and tax-free access to funds in the form of policy loans, was one of the few tax shelters to survive the Tax Reform Act of 1986. In 1987, however, tax legislation made tax-free borrowings possible only when a test is met requiring substantial insurance coverage relative to premiums over a lengthy time period.

Economic Considerations

What economic factors most affect buy, hold, and sell decisions? Inflation and volatility of interest rates gave rise to life insurance policies whose cash values vary with market conditions. Investors concerned about such factors can choose among such "new breed" alternatives, rather than buying traditional fixed-rate policies, and make their choices based on their expectations. Thus an investor anticipating high inflation and high interest rates would not choose a variable life policy invested in fixed-income bonds but might choose one with a stock fund or one that is money market-oriented. Variable and universal variable life insurance permit switching between bond, stock, and money market funds to afford maximum market flexibility.

LIMITED PARTNERSHIP (LP)

The unique feature of a limited partnership is that financial and tax events flow directly through to individual investors. Until 1987 this meant that limited partners in real estate ventures, oil and gas projects, and other activities (see page   ) could use liberal tax benefits such as depreciation, depletion, intangible drilling costs, and tax credits, as well as operating losses, as deductions against taxable income from wages and investment income. With aggressive marketing by brokers and financial planners, LPs attracted some $100 billion of funds from 12 million investors in the 1980s.

The Tax Reform Act of 1986 severely curtailed the use of LPs as tax shelters by ruling that losses from "passive" sources, like LPs, could be used only against passive income. And while some "economic programs"—those LPs emphasizing income, appreciation, and safety—have continued to provide attractive returns, their ability to shelter cash flow has been lessened by reduced benefits, notably the elimination of accelerated depreciation of real property and the repeal of the investment credit. By the end of the 1980s, hurt by a soft real estate market and previous declines in energy prices, many partnerships, especially those originally touted for their tax advantages, were faltering.

A limited partnership is an organization comprising a general partner with unlimited liability, who is both sponsor and manager, and limited partners, who provide most of the capital, have limited liability, and have no active management role. Most LPs aim to sell or refinance their assets within seven to ten years and distribute proceeds to shareholders.

Limited partnerships may be private, which are restricted to small numbers of wealthy investors and not required to register with the Securities and Exchange Commission, or public, which market shares in typical amounts of $1000 to $5000 to as many limited partners as the sponsor desires. Public LPs must register with the SEC and provide investors with a prospectus and other disclosures.

Limited partnerships are also distinguished in terms of their use of leverage to finance assets. *Leveraged programs,* whose assets are financed 50% or more with borrowed money, offer greater tax benefits because (1) with a larger asset base they generate more deductions, such as depreciation, and because (2) the interest is deductible. *Unleveraged programs* are favored by investors seeking maximum income and less risk.

From the investor's standpoint, one drawback of limited partnerships traditionally has been lack of liquidity. Although a growing number of independent investment firms buy and sell partnership shares, they represent more of a distress market than a formal secondary market for shares. While some sponsors offer market-making services to investors under some circumstances, the selling of shares during the life of the partnership is generally discouraged.

Inspired by investor reservations about the future of tax-advantaged partnerships after tax reform, some sponsors in the mid-1980s began marketing programs featuring depositary receipts, which represent unit interests and can be traded in the open marketplace. Liquidity provided this way is a feature of *master limited partnerships,* a mid-1980s innovation in which corporate assets or private partnerships are reorganized as public limited partnerships combining various objectives. Master limited partnerships, however, will be subject to taxation as corporations starting in 1998.

∗   ∗   ∗

What Is a Limited Partnership?

A limited partnership is a form of business organization, having any of a variety of activities and investment objectives, which is made up of a general partner who organizes and manages the partnership and its operations, and limited partners who contribute capital, have limited liability, and assume no active role in day-to-day business affairs.

Buying, Selling, and Holding

How do I buy and sell it? Unit shares are bought through a securities broker-dealer or financial planner. There is no official secondary market, although some sponsors agree to make markets under certain circumstances and a number of firms trade in partnership shares at distress prices.

Is there a minimum purchase amount, and what is the price range? Public limited partnerships usually have a $1000 to $5000 minimum, with a $2000 minimum for IRAs. Private limited partnerships require at least $20,000. Offerings frequently involve suitability rules, requiring that individuals meet minimum net worth, income, and tax bracket criteria.

What fees and charges are involved? Brokerage commissions and other front-end costs, often totaling 20% or more of the amount invested. There may be additional management fees during the partnership's operating phase.

Does it mature, expire, or otherwise terminate? Most partnerships intend to dispose of their holdings within a specified period (7 to 10 years typically) and distribute the proceeds as capital gains to investors.

Can I sell it quickly? Usually not. There is no secondary market for partnership shares, although some sponsors offer to try to make a market to accommodate investors under certain circumstances. Certain private firms buy LP shares from holders, but the price for this kind of marketability can be high. Some partnerships offer liquidity through depositary receipts, which represent shares and are traded in secondary markets.

How is market value determined and how do I keep track of it? There is no active secondary market for limited partnerships shares and independent firms that buy shares pay widely varying and deeply discounted prices.

The 1986 Tax Act required that sponsors provide annual valuation reports for LPs held in IRAs, and some sponsors provide valuations to all shareholders. Valuation standards are not uniform, however. Industry guidelines recommend that interests be valued at cost for the first three years (even if a high percentage of cost is sales charges unrelated to asset values) and at asset values thereafter; asset appraisals however, may be independent or "direct," meaning estimates are made by the sponsor.

In any event, share values to be ultimately realized as capital gains are affected by various factors, depending on the activities of the partnership and assets it holds.

Investment Objectives

Should I buy a share in a limited partnership if my objective is capital appreciation? Certain types of partnerships emphasize capital gains potential; others do not. Those offering the greatest potential are the riskiest.

Should I buy this if my objective is income? Yes, though not all partnerships have income as a primary objective and some emphasize the tax sheltering of income from other passive sources.

To what extent does it protect against inflation? Some, like all-cash equity programs with investments in inflation-sensitive real estate, offer high protection. Others, such as programs specializing in fixed-rate mortgages, suffer.

Is it suitable for tax-deferred retirement accounts? Yes.

Can I borrow against it? Because of their low liquidity, partnership shares may not be acceptable as marketable securities with many lenders.

Risk Considerations

How assured can I be of getting my full investment back? Safety of principal depends on the type of partnership and the quality of its holdings. Insured mortgage programs held for the life of the partnership offer high safety, but no appreciation, while leveraged programs aimed at high capital gains involve commensurate risk.

How assured is my income? Only insured mortgage programs offer any real assurance of income. Other income partnerships vary with the type and quality of their portfolios.

Are there any other risks unique to this investment? Yes, because limited partners have no active role in management, everything depends on the integrity and management ability of the general partner. In fact, some partnerships (such as those in real estate) are sold as blind pools—that is, the general partner has not even made property selections at the time that investment is made. Programs set up primarily as tax shelters run the risk of being declared abusive, subjecting the investor to heavy penalties and interest as well as back taxes. A sponsor may postpone liquidation to "ride out" a soft market, thus delaying the payout to holders. LPs bought in the secondary market may have hidden tax liabilities stemming from deductions taken by previous shareholders.

Is it commercially rated? Yes. Standard & Poor's Corporation rates limited partnerships, and several firms, such as Robert A. Stanger & Co., analyze limited partnerships and rate such factors as offering terms.

Tax Considerations

What tax advantages (or disadvantages) does it offer? Tax benefits flow through to limited partners. Losses thus generated through 1986 may be used to offset taxable income from any source. Since 1986, however, such "passive" losses have been usable only to offset income from other passive sources and not earned or investment income. The provision phased in over five years, so that 35% of passive losses were disallowed in 1987, 60% in 1988, 80% in 1989, 90% in 1990, and 100% in 1991. Net losses are tax preference items. Unused losses may be carried forward, and after offsetting any gain from the disposition of the passive investment, may be used against any other passive investment. Any excess losses then remaining can be generally applied. At risk rules now include real estate. Master limited partnerships are subject to taxation as corporations after 1998.

Economic Considerations

What economic factors most affect buy, hold, and sell decisions? Because limited partnership investments are generally held for the life of the partnership, hold and sell decisions have limited applicability. Buy decisions should be guided by the outlook for the type of activity in which the partnership specializes and such factors as the expected life of the program and whether it is leveraged or unleveraged.

MONEY MARKET FUND

This special breed of mutual fund gives personal investors the opportunity to own money market instruments that would otherwise be available only to large institutional investors. The attraction is higher yields than individuals could obtain on their own or from most bank money market deposit accounts, plus a high degree of safety and excellent liquidity, complete with checkwriting.

Money market funds are sponsored by mutual fund organizations (investment companies), brokerage firms, and institutions, like insurance companies, which sell and redeem shares without any sales charges or commissions. The company charges only an annual management fee, usually under 1%, although extra services may entail additional charges. Income earned from interest-bearing investments is credited and reinvested (in effect compounded) for shareholders on a daily basis.

The disadvantage of money market funds over other short-term investment alternatives is that income (although normally paid out monthly) fluctuates daily as investments in the fund's portfolio mature and are replaced with new investments bearing current interest rates. In a declining rate market, this can be a disadvantage as compared, say, to a certificate of deposit, which would continue to pay an above-market rate until maturity. As a general rule, fund dividend rates lag behind money market rate changes by a month or so, depending on the average length of their portfolios, which is controlled to an extent by the manager's expectations as to where rates will go. Major sponsors permit switching among different funds in their families.

The market value of a money market fund investment is normally maintained at a constant figure, usually $1 a share. This means capital gains (and the favorable tax treatment they receive) are not a feature of money market funds, though investors may achieve some growth through compounding by opting to reinvest monthly payments.

Funds may differ in terms of the type of securities comprising their portfolios, some specializing only in U.S. Treasury bills or in tax-exempt municipal securities. A general portfolio, however, would typically be comprised of bank and industrial commercial paper, certificates of deposit, acceptances, repurchase agreements, direct and indirect U.S. government obligations, Eurodollar CDs, and other safe and liquid investments. Bonds and foreign debt securities are sometimes included to lift yields.

Money market funds are not covered by federal insurance the way bank deposits are, although funds sponsored by brokerage firms are insured by the Securities Investor Protection Corporation (SIPC) against losses caused by a failure of the firm. Some funds may also be covered by private insurance.

For longer-term investment purposes, alternative investments offer better yield with comparable safety while also providing growth opportunity, tax advantages, and similar inflation protection. The convenience and income of money market funds, although increasingly challenged by bank deposit products, remain attractive for providing for emergencies and for parking temporarily idle cash.

∗ ∗ ∗

What Is a Money Market Fund?

A money market fund is a type of mutual fund in which a pool of money is invested in various money market securities (short-term debt instruments) and which compounds interest daily and pays out (or reinvests) dividends to shareholders monthly.

Buying, Selling, and Holding

How do I buy and sell it? Through sponsoring brokerage firms and mutual fund organizations. Accounts are also offered by insurance companies and other financial institutions as a parking place for temporarily idle funds.

Is there a minimum purchase amount, and what is the price range? The minimum investment usually ranges from $500 to $5000. For funds offered through brokers, $1000 is typical; $2500 is a typical minimum investment for funds offered directly by fund sponsors. Additional investment is usually allowed in increments as small as $100.

What fees and charges are involved? Most are no-load (without sales fee), charging only an annual management fee, which is usually less than 1% of the investment. There may be extra fees for special services, such as money transfers.

Does it mature, expire, or otherwise terminate? No.

Can I sell it quickly? Yes. Shares are redeemable anytime and most funds offer checkwriting privileges, though $500 minimums for checks are common.

How is market value determined and how do I keep track of it? Market values of shares are kept constant. Yields change in response to money market conditions as investments turn over and are calculated on a daily basis. Seven and 30-day average yields are reported weekly in the financial pages of newspapers and current information can be obtained directly by calling the sponsoring organizations.

Investment Objectives

Should I buy this if my objective is capital appreciation? No.

Should I buy this if my objective is income? Yes. The attraction of money market funds is that the individuals can earn the same high yields that would otherwise be available only to institutional investors. Of course, income fluctuates and there is little protection against a decline in market rates.

To what extent does it protect against inflation? Because interest rates on newly offered debt instruments rise with inflation, money market funds, being composed of constantly rotating short-term investments, have performed well in inflation and paid dividends that kept pace with rising price levels.

Is it suitable for tax-deferred retirement accounts? Yes.

Can I borrow against it? Yes, banks and brokers will lend a high percentage (often 90%) of the value of your shares.

Risk Considerations

How assured can I be of getting my full investment back? Your investment in a money market fund is quite safe, since portfolios comprise securities of banks, governments, and top corporations. Investors seeking maximum safety can choose funds investing exclusively in U.S. government direct obligations, though at some sacrifice of yield; while this does not mean the fund is guaranteed by Uncle Sam, the fact that its investments are so guaranteed actually does provide a high degree of security. Some funds are privately insured against default.

How assured is my income? While the risk of default is very small, there is no way of preventing fluctuations in money market interest rates. Dividend rates could therefore decline, although the reaction to market rate changes may be more or less delayed, depending on the average maturity of a portfolio. Most fund sponsors permit shifting into other investment vehicles within their families when adverse developments can be foreseen or when better opportunities exist.

Are there any other risks unique to this investment? A fund that invested relatively long-term just prior to a drastic rise in rates could be forced to sell investments at a loss to meet redemptions. Well-managed and established funds are aware of this obvious risk and take measures to avoid it. Overall, the industry, which is regulated by the Securities and Exchange Commission, has enjoyed an excellent safety record.

Is it commercially rated? A number of organizations record past performance and a few predict future yields, but money market funds are not rated in the sense that bonds and stocks are.

Tax Considerations

What tax advantages (or disadvantages) does it offer? Where portfolios are comprised of tax-exempt securities, investors are exempt from federal taxes and, depending on state laws, possibly state and local taxes. (States may treat tax-exempt funds differently from tax-exempt direct investments.) Otherwise, dividends are fully taxable. Some states that do not tax interest earned on direct investments will tax dividends from funds, even though the fund's income is from interest earned.

Economic Considerations

What economic factors most affect buy, hold, and sell decisions? Money market funds are most attractive when short-term interest rates are high and alternative investments are beset with uncertainty. As a rule, investors use money market funds to park cash temporarily, choosing other investments for longer-term purposes.

MORTGAGE-BACKED (PASS-THROUGH) SECURITY

A mortgage-backed (pass-through) security offers one of the best risk/return deals available to investors, plus excellent liquidity. Two drawbacks, though, are that monthly income payments fluctuate and the term of the investment cannot be predicted with certainty.

Pass-through securities represent shares in pools of home mortgages having approximately the same terms and interest rates. They were introduced in the 1960s to make lenders liquid and stimulate home buying.

The process begins when prospective homeowners apply for mortgages to banks, savings and loan associations and mortgage bankers. The loan paper is sold to intermediaries, such as Freddie Mac or private organizations who repackage it in units represented by certificates, which are marketed to investors. Interest and principal, including prepayments, pass from the homeowner through the intermediary to the investor. When the mortgages mature or are prepaid, the investment expires.

Pass-throughs also enjoy an active secondary market, where securities trade either at discounts or premiums depending on prevailing interest rates. Interestingly, pass-throughs representing pools of low-rate mortgages, when they can be bought favorably to result in attractive yields, are the most desirable holdings because the prepayment risk is low.

The following are principal mortgage-backed securities:

> *Government National Mortgage Association (GNMA):* Ginnie Maes are the most widely-held pass-throughs and are backed by Federal Housing Administration (FHA)-insured and Veterans Administration (VA)-guaranteed mortgages plus the general guarantee of GNMA, which (by virtue of rulings of the Treasury and Justice departments) brings the full faith and credit of the U.S. government behind these securities. They are as safe as Treasury bonds but typically yield 1% to 2% higher.

> *Federal Home Loan Mortgage Corporation (FHLMC):* Freddie Mac PCs (Participation Certificates) are backed by both FHA and VA mortgages and privately insured conventional mortgages plus the general guarantee of FHLMC, a privately managed public institution owned by the Federal Home Loan Bank Board System members. With less safety, PCs yield 15-40 basis points more than GNMAs.

> *Federal National Mortgage Association (FNMA):* Fannie Mae MBSs (Mortgage-Backed Securities) are issued and guaranteed by FNMA, a government-sponsored, publicly held (NYSE-traded) company, and backed by both conventional and FHA and VA mortgages. They are essentially similar to Freddie Macs and tend to have similar yields.

> *Private mortgage participation certificates* issued by lending institutions or conduit firms have varying characteristics and different ratings,

depending on such factors as private mortgage insurance, cash-fund backing, and over-collateralization (the extent to which the market values of underlying properties exceed the mortgages). These include jumbo pools of mortgages from different lenders.

Collateralized mortgage obligations (CMOs), a variation, are instruments, technically mortgage-backed bonds, that break up mortgage pools into separate maturity classes, called tranches. This is accomplished by applying mortgage income first to the bonds with the shortest maturity. Tranches pay different rates of interest and typically mature in 2, 5, 10 and 20 years. Issued by Freddie Mac and private issuers, CMOs are backed by government-guaranteed or other top-grade mortgages and have AAA bond ratings. For a slight sacrifice of yield, CMOs lessen anxiety about the uncertain term of pass-through investments.

Real estate mortgage investment conduits (REMICs), still another variation, created by the Tax Reform Act of 1986. REMICs offer issuers, who may be government or private entities, more flexibility than CMOs and protection from double taxation, which CMOs have avoided with legal technicalities. They are thus able to separate mortgage pools not only into maturity classes but also into classes of risk. The practical effect of this has been that whereas CMOs have financed top-quality mortgages in order to obtain AAA ratings, REMICs have been used to finance mortgages of lesser quality, even some that are financially distressed. More often than not, a REMIC obligation in the late 1980s was a high-yield, junk mortgage bond.

We may be seeing more exceptions, however. In late 1989 Fannie Mae announced a $300 million REMIC issue backed by Ginnie Mae pass-throughs. It was divided into ten parts with average lives from 3.3 to 20.2 years and a range of yields.

Strips: Mortgage-backed securities are also stripped and sold as zero-coupon securities. See the section on zero coupon securities for a discussion of this alternative.

* * *

What Is a Mortgage-Backed (Pass-Through) Security?

A mortgage-backed security is a share in an organized pool of residential mortgages, the principal and interest payments on which are passed through to shareholders, usually monthly. The category includes collateralized mortgage obligations (CMOs), technically mortgage-backed bonds, which provide for different maturities, and real estate mortgage investment conduits (REMICs), which provide for both separate maturity and separate risk classes. It does not include mortgage-backed securities that are corporate bonds or government agency securities and are covered in those sections.

Buying, Selling, and Holding

Where do I buy and sell it? At a securities broker-dealer.

Is there a minimum purchase amount, and what is the price range? Most new pass-throughs are sold in minimum amounts of $25,000, although some older issues can be bought with less and some private issues and CMOs and REMICs can be bought for as little as $1000. Shares of funds, limited partnerships, and unit investment trusts that buy such securities range from $1000-$5000.

What fees and charges are involved? This varies among vehicles and brokers, but can be either a flat fee or a dealer spread. Sponsors deduct modest fees from passed-through income.

Does it mature, expire, or otherwise terminate? Yes, the life of a pool, and its related securities, ends when the mortgages mature or are prepaid. CMOs and REMICs offer investors a choice of earlier or later payouts.

Can I sell it quickly? Yes, liquidity is very good.

How is market value determined and how do I keep track of it? Market value, to the extent mortgage pools have fixed-rate obligations, goes up when market interest rates go down, and vice versa. On the other hand, prepayments rise when rates decline, shrinking the pool and lowering share values. Daily price and yield information is published in the financial pages of newspapers and in electronic databases.

Investment Objectives

Should I buy this if my objective is capital appreciation? Although most investors plan to hold for the life of the issue, capital appreciation is possible as the result of declining market interest rates.

Should I buy this if my objective is income? Yes; mortgage pass-throughs generally offer good yields. The most conservative, Ginnie Maes, normally yield at least 1% more than U.S. Treasury bonds and have the same safety from default. CMOs and REMICs pay slightly lower yields than straight pass-throughs with comparable risk characteristics.

To what extent does it protect against inflation? Because they are based largely on fixed-income mortgages, pass-throughs suffer in high inflation.

Is it suitable for tax-deferred retirement accounts? Yes; except for rollovers, however, the minimum investments exceed IRA limits.

Can I borrow against it? Yes.

Risk Considerations

How assured can I be of getting my full investment back? Although some issues are safer than others (Ginnie Maes are U.S. government-guaranteed against default on underlying mortgages, for example) most pass-throughs are either government-sponsored or otherwise insured in addition to being over-collateralized (i.e., the market value of the real estate behind the mortgages exceeds the face value of the mortgages). They thus offer a high degree of credit safety, although loss of value due to rising interest rates is a risk if sold in the secondary market. REMICs tend to have riskier backing and should be analyzed.

How assured is my income? Income is safe from the credit standpoint (see the previous question) but can vary from month to month as the result of prepayments and other factors.

Are there any other risks unique to this investment? Prepayments may shorten the life of the investment, although the cash they create is of course passed through to investors.

Is it commercially rated? Yes, Standard & Poor's and other services rate mortgage-backed securities.

Tax Considerations

What tax advantages (or disadvantages) does it offer? None. Interest is taxed as ordinary income and profits or losses from the sale of pass-through securities in the secondary market are taxed as capital gains or losses. But the monthly payment received by an investor in a pass-through is only partly interest. Because payments to the investor are simply pass-throughs of payments by homeowners on their mortgages, and those payments are part interest and part principal, the investor pays taxes only on the portion of his payment representing interest; the rest, as principal, is treated as a nontaxable return of capital. Since home mortgage payments have a higher ratio of interest to principal in the earlier years of the mortgage, it follows that income payments on pass-through securities normally have a higher proportion of taxable interest in the earlier years of the life of the pool.

Economic Considerations

What economic factors most affect buy, hold, and sell decisions? Mortgage-backed pass-throughs are most attractive to hold when general interest rates are low relative to the yield on the mortgage pool. However, this scenario can also cause a high rate of prepayments just when the investment is most attractive. The best holding is a pool of low-rate mortgages whose shares are bought at a good discount; that results in an attractive yield for investors, but since the homeowners are also happy with their low-rate mortgages, the risk of prepayment is much less. Of course, inflation erodes the value of fixed payments, which are the basis of income from pass-throughs.

MUNICIPAL SECURITY

A municipal security, or muni, is a debt obligation of a U.S. state or political subdivision, such as a county, city, town, village, or authority.

What has historically made munis special has been their exemption from federal income taxes and, frequently, from state and local income taxes as well. Because of this tax-exempt status, munis have traditionally paid lower rates of interest than taxable securities, making their after-tax return more attractive as an individual's income moved into higher brackets.

The Tax Reform Act of 1986 changed the municipal bond investment environment in fundamental ways primarily by dividing obligations into two basic groups:

Public purpose bonds, also called traditional government purpose bonds or essential purpose bonds, continue to be tax-exempt and to be issued without limit.

Private purpose bonds, vaguely defined as a bond involving more than a 10% benefit to private parties, are taxable unless specifically exempted. Such exempted *permitted private purpose bonds* are subject, with exceptions, to caps.

Whether tax-exempt or not, munis are either (1) *general obligations*, notes or bonds backed by the full faith and credit (including the taxing power) of the issuing entity and used to finance capital expenditures or improvements; or (2) *revenue obligations*, which are used to finance specific projects and are repaid from the revenues of the facilities they finance.

Although munis vary in the degree of credit strength backing them, and although there have been some famous defaults, such as the Washington Public Power Supply System (WHOOPS) in the 1980s, their safety record has generally been excellent, earning them a place between Treasuries and high-grade corporate bonds in terms of investor confidence.

In addition to taxable bonds, recent innovations in the municipal securities field have included *tax-exempt commercial paper*, short-term discounted notes usually backed by bank lines of credit; *bonds with put options* typically exercisable after one to five years, which carry a somewhat lower yield in exchange for the put privilege; *floating (or variable) rate* issues tied to the Treasury bill or another market rate; and *enhanced security* issues, in which the credit of the municipal entity is supplemented by bank lines of credit or other outside resources.

For smaller investors, open and closed-end funds, unit investment trusts, and other pooled vehicles with portfolios of municipal obligations offer diversification and professional management with lower minimums.

Munis are also available as zero-coupon securities and are covered in the section dealing with that investment alternative.

*   *   *

What Is a Municipal Security?

A municipal security is a negotiable bond or note issued by a U.S. state or subdivision. A muni may be a general obligation backed by the full faith and credit (i.e., the borrowing and taxing power) of a government; a revenue obligation paid out of the cash flow from an income-producing project; or a special assessment obligation paid out of taxes specially levied to finance specific public works. Some municipal bonds, such as those to finance low-income housing, may be backed by a federal government agency.

Buying, Selling, and Holding

How do I buy and sell it? Most securities broker-dealers handle municipal securities.

Is there a minimum purchase amount, and what is the price range? Although munis are issued in units of $5000 or $1000 par value as a rule, with exceptions as low as $100, broker-dealers usually require minimum orders of at least $5000 and often want $10,000, $25,000, or up to $100,000. Odd lots are sometimes available from broker-dealers at extra commissions or spreads. Smaller investments can be made through mutual funds, closed-end funds, unit investment trusts and other pooled vehicles with tax-exempt portfolios.

What fees and charges are involved? Sometimes a commission, but usually a spread (rarely exceeding 5%) between the dealer's buying and selling prices.

Does it mature, expire, or otherwise terminate? Yes. Maturities range from one month (notes) to 30 years (bonds). Serial bonds mature in scheduled stages. Munis may also be callable or have put features.

Can I sell it quickly? Some munis have good liquidity, although issues of obscure municipalities and authorities can have inactive markets and be hard to sell.

How is market value determined and how do I keep track of it? Most munis are fixed-income securities and thus rise and fall in opposite relationship to market interest rates. Variable-rate issues, whose rates are periodically adjusted to reflect changes in U.S. Treasury bill yields or other money market rates, tend to sell at or close to their par values. Muni quotes are not normally published in daily newspapers, but prices published in *The Daily Bond Buyer* (mainly new muni issues) and the *Blue List of Current Municipal Offerings* (a Standard and Poor's publication reporting details of secondary market offerings and their size) are available through brokers or directly by subscription.

Investment Objectives

Should I buy a municipal security if my objective is capital appreciation? No, although appreciation is possible when munis sell at discounts because rates have risen or credit questions arise.

Should I buy this if my objective is income? Yes, but only if the after-tax yield in your tax bracket compares favorably to the yield on a taxable investment of comparable safety.

To what extent does it protect against inflation? Fixed-income munis offer no inflation protection. Variable-rate munis would offer some, if interest rates rose.

Is it suitable for tax-deferred accounts? Tax-exempt issues bearing a lower interest rate than a taxable security are not suitable. Taxable munis are suitable.

Can I borrow against it? You can, but the interest you pay is not tax-deductible if the proceeds are used to buy municipals. With the lower rate you earn on most munis, it would hardly pay. While munis are acceptable collateral for other loans, care must be taken to avoid the appearance of a violation of the rule against deducting interest.

Risk Considerations

How assured can I be of getting my full investment back? In most cases, you can be quite sure of getting your investment back at maturity. Munis generally rank between U.S. government securities and corporate bonds in credit safety. But the risk of default varies with the credit of the issuer and the type of obligation (mainly general obligation or revenue obligations). Some munis are covered for default by private insurers. Of course, prices of all fixed-income securities decline when interest rates go up.

How assured is my income? Munis are relatively safe (see the preceding question) but defaults are possible due to such factors as limited ability to impose taxes or disappointing revenues from the use of facilities. Issues may also be callable, enabling the issuer to force redemption after specified times.

Are there any other risks unique to this investment? Munis are not subject to Securities and Exchange Commission regulation, so the legality of the issue must be established. Make sure a legal opinion accompanies the issue.

Is it commercially rated? Moody's Investors Service, Standard & Poor's, and others rate credit. White's Tax-Exempt Bond Rating Service rates market risk.

Tax Considerations

What tax advantages (or disadvantages) does it offer? Interest may be exempt from federal income taxes and frequently from state and local income taxes (36 states tax exempt munis of other states but not their own; 5 states tax their own exempt munis and those of other states; 9 states plus the District of Columbia do not tax any exempt munis). Capital gains are taxable. Permitted private purpose bond interest may be a tax preference item in computing the Alternative Minimum Tax.

Economic Considerations

What economic factors most affect buy, hold, or sell decisions? Personal tax considerations, of course, then interest rate levels and the inflation rate. Buy when rates are high to get good yields; hold as rates decline to see market values rise. Because tax-exempt munis pay a relatively low interest rate, inflation is especially devastating if the rate is fixed. Prolonged economic downturns can increase the risk of municipal defaults. Special supply and demand factors owing to the uncertain status of tax-exempt issues under tax reform legislation then pending, caused abnormally high municipal yields in the mid-1980s.

MUTUAL FUNDS (OPEN END)

An open-end mutual fund is so named because its sponsoring organization, called an investment company or a management company, stands ready at any time to issue new shares or to redeem existing shares at their daily-computed net asset value. An open-end fund offers investors with moderate means the diversification, professional management (for a fee), economy of scale, and, where it might not otherwise exist, the liquidity available only to large investors.

Mutual funds are available with portfolio compositions designed for an almost infinite variety of investment objectives and risk levels. The following is a partial list of types of funds, with their basic portfolio or mode of operation:

Income Fund (stocks paying dividends, preferred stocks, corporate bonds)

Growth Fund (growth stocks)

Aggressive Growth Fund (smaller, riskier growth stocks)

Balanced Fund (growth and income securities)

Performance Fund (high-risk stocks, venture capital investments, etc.)

Conservative Balanced Fund (high-grade income and growth securities)

United States Government Bond Fund (U.S. Treasury or agency bonds)

International Fund (foreign stocks or bonds)

Global Fund (foreign and U.S. stocks or bonds)

Investment Grade Bond Fund (corporates with investment-grade ratings)

Junk Bond Fund (high-yielding corporates below investment grade)

Municipal Bond Fund (tax-exempt municipal securities)

Special Situations Fund (venture capital, debt/equity securities)

Stock Index Fund (replicating or representative of the major stock indexes)

Market Sector Fund or *Specialized Fund* (securities of high-growth industries or specialized industries like gold-mining)

Tax-managed Fund (utility stocks whose dividends are reinvested for long-term capital gains)

Speculative Fund (engages in selling short and leverage)

Commodities Fund (commodity futures contracts)

Option Fund (sells puts and calls for extra income, sometimes speculating by taking positions without owning underlying securities or instruments)

Socially-conscious Fund (excludes investments offensive on moral or ethical grounds)

Fund of Funds (invests in other funds with top performance)

Money Market Fund (short-term, interest-bearing debt instruments)

Tax-exempt Money Market Fund (trades long-term and short-term municipals for best yields and capital gains)

Ginnie-Mae Fund (mortgage-backed pass-through securities guaranteed by Government National Mortgage Association)

Major sponsors allow switching of investments from shares of one fund to another within their fund families. Other services commonly available to investors include term life insurance; automatic reinvestment plans; regular income checks; open account plans allowing fractional share purchases with Social Security or pension checks or other relatively small amounts of cash; loan programs; and toll-free information services.

* * *

What Is an Open-End Mutual Fund?

An open-end mutual fund is an investment company that pools shareholder funds and invests in a diversified securities portfolio having a specified objective. It provides professional management and stands ready to sell new shares and redeem outstanding shares on a continuous (open-end) basis.

Buying, Selling, and Holding

Where do I buy and sell it? Load funds, in which a sales charge is deducted from the amount invested, are bought from securities brokers and financial planners. No-load funds are bought directly from the sponsor. Shares are not sold in the sense that shares of stock are transferred to other owners; rather they are redeemed (by phone, mail, or checkwriting privilege) by the fund at net asset value.

Is there a minimum purchase amount, and what is the price range? Some funds have minimum deposits of $1000–$2500. Others have no minimum. Share prices vary, but a majority are under $20. Many funds offer convenient share accumulation plans for investors of modest means.

What fees and charges are involved? Load funds charge a sales commission, typically 8½% of the amount invested, though with larger purchases the load can go as low as 1½%. No-load funds have no sales commissions. A hybrid, low-load funds, charge commissions of 3% or less. Both load and no-load funds charge annual management fees of from 1/2% to 1% of the value of the investment. There is usually no redemption charge (back-end load, or exit fee), with load funds; no-loads may or may not have a 1% to 2% redemption fee to discourage short-term trading. Various share accumulation plans may involve extra service charges. Some funds discourage frequent switching by imposing extra charges. 12B-1 mutual funds, a type of load fund that builds assets through advertising and publicity, typically charge a promotion fee of 1% less of the fund's value.

Does it mature, expire, or otherwise terminate? No.

Can I sell it quickly? Funds stand ready to redeem shares daily. Some managing companies allow switching among different funds they sponsor at either no charge (no-load fund families) or a small transaction fee.

How is market value determined and how do I keep track of it? Market value, called net asset value, depends on the way various economic and market forces affect the type of investments comprising a particular fund's portfolio; a given economic or interest-rate scenario will have a different effect on bond fund values than stock fund values. Mutual fund quotations are reported daily in newspapers and a fund management company reports, usually quarterly, on the composition of portfolios and transactions during the reporting period.

Investment Objectives

Should I buy an open-end mutual fund if my objective is capital appreciation? Yes, but you would buy a fund with capital gains as a primary objective, such as a growth stock or special situations fund.

Should I buy this if my objective is income? Yes, but you would buy a fund with income as its primary objective, such as a bond or money market fund or a stock fund investing in high-yield stocks.

To what extent does it protect against inflation? That depends on the type of fund. Equity-oriented funds or money market funds offer more protection than fixed-income bond portfolios, which provide little or no protection.

Is it suitable for tax-deferred retirement accounts? Yes, except when the fund is invested in tax-exempt securities, such as municipal bonds.

Can I borrow against it? Yes, subject to Federal Reserve margin rules. Collateral value varies with the type of fund. A lender that might loan 90% of the value of money market fund shares might find a high-risk fund unacceptable as collateral.

Risk Considerations

How assured can I be of getting my full investment back? It depends on the type of fund, the quality of the portfolio, and the adroitness of management in avoiding adverse developments. A money market fund has high safety of principal, whereas a bond fund is vulnerable to interest rate movements and a stock fund is subject to market risk, for example.

How assured is my income? Again, it depends on the type of portfolio, its quality, and the skill of the manager. A fund with AAA bonds will be a safer source of income than one comprised of higher-yielding but riskier junk bonds. Other funds stress capital growth at the expense of income. Money market funds offer assured income at a conservative rate, which goes up and down with market conditions.

Are there any other risks unique to this investment? Except for the fact that funds provide automatic diversification, the same risk considerations apply as affect individual investments.

Is it commercially rated? No, but some funds invest exclusively in securities with given commercial ratings, and a number of organizations rate mutual funds in terms of historical performance.

Tax Considerations

What tax advantages (or disadvantages) does it offer? Income is subject to the same federal income taxes as the investments from which it derives. Thus, a shareholder pays taxes just as if he owned the portfolio directly, except that all capital gains distributions are considered long-term, regardless of the time the fund has been held. Funds invested in tax-exempt municipal securities (some are triple—federal, state, and local—tax-exempt) provide tax-free income, at least at the federal level. States vary in their tax treatment of income from municipal securities (see the discussion of tax considerations in the section on Municipal Securities) and the same rules usually apply to fund income. Some states that would not tax interest will tax dividends from funds, however, even though the fund's income is from interest earned. In such states, dividends from a tax-exempt fund would be taxable.

Economic Considerations

What economic factors most affect buy, hold, or sell decisions? The same economic and market forces that affect individual investments affect funds made up of those investments, so choices should be made in the same terms.

OPTION CONTRACT (PUT or CALL)

Put and call options are contracts that give holders the right, for a price, called a premium, to sell or buy an underlying stock or financial instrument at a specified price, called the exercise or strike price, before a specified expiration date. Option sellers are called writers—covered writers if they own the underlying security or financial instrument, naked writers if they don't—and buyers of options are called option buyers. A put is an option to sell and a call is an option to buy.

Listed options are options traded (since 1973) on national stock and commodity exchanges and thus have both visibility and liquidity, as opposed to conventional over-the-counter options, which are individually negotiated, more expensive, and less liquid. Listed options are available on stocks, stock indexes, debt instruments, foreign currencies, and futures of different types. The issuance and settlement—all the mechanics of options clearing—are handled by the options clearing corporation (OCC), which is owned by the exchanges.

Options make it possible to control a large amount of value with a much smaller amount of money. Because a small percentage change in the value of a financial instrument can result in a much larger percentage change in the value of an option, large gains (and losses) are possible with the leverage that options provide. Although sometimes options are bought with the idea of holding the underlying security as an investment after the exercise of the option, options are usually bought and sold without ever being exercised and settled. They have a life of their own.

The value of options—that is, the amount of their premiums—is mainly determined by the relationship between the exercise price and the market price of the underlying instrument, by the volatility of the underlying instrument, and by the time remaining before expiration.

When the relationship between an option's strike price (exercise price) and the underlying market price is such that the holder would profit (transaction costs aside) by exercising it, an option has intrinsic value and is said to be in the money. In contrast, there is no intrinsic value in an out-of-the-money option—such as a put whose strike price is below the market price or a call whose strike price is above the market price. A premium will normally trade for at least its intrinsic value, if any. An out-of-the-money option, on the other hand, has obviously more risk and a lower premium than an option that is more likely to become profitable. Options on highly volatile securities and instruments command higher premiums because they are more likely to produce profits when and if they move.

Time value influences premiums because the longer the time remaining, the greater the chance of a favorable movement and the higher the present value of the underlying instrument if exercised. This time value, also called net premium, decreases as the option approaches its expiration. (For this reason, options are called wasting assets.) The value of an out-of-the-money option is all time value; that of an in-the-money option is a combination of time value and intrinsic value. In general, the greater the potential for gain, the greater the risk of not achieving it. The farther from expiration and the greater the volatility, the higher the premium an option will have.

Professional traders have multioption strategies, some quite complex, designed to limit risk while capitalizing on premium movements. Called straddles, combinations, and spreads (which have many varieties), they involve close monitoring, expertise, and sometimes onerous commissions. Options trading is not for the average investor.

Options do have a conservative role, however, for personal as well as institutional investors. Options can be used very much like term life insurance policies to protect investors against losses in investments already owned. Option selling (writing) can be a source of added returns.

The use of options as insurance involves the purchase of a put to limit losses or lock in the profit on a position already owned, or the purchase of a call to limit losses or lock in the profit on a short sale. For example, an individual with 100 shares of XYZ at a market value of $60 who expects the price to rise to $70 might buy, at a premium of $125, a put at $55 expiring in three months. If the stock rises, the insurance would have cost $125 and that amount would have to be subtracted from the capital gain. If the stock dropped, however, the put could be exercised and the stock sold for no lower than $55; that would limit the investor's loss to $625—$60 less $55 (times 100 shares) plus the premium of $125. The investor who thought the stock would drop could have sold it short and bought a call to assure the ability to buy the shares to cover at the call price.

Covered option writing—writing calls on stock or other instruments that are owned—is a safe way to increase the income return on an investment, provided the investor is prepared to sell the underlying holding at the exercise price if the price moves that way. Potential gains are limited to the amount of the premium (a significant drawback if the underlying holding rises in value and the option is exercised).

Calls can be written at, in, deep in, out of, or deep out of the money. The farther out of the money it is, the less the chance of exercise and the lower the premium it will command. The main problem with writing covered calls is that to warrant a premium high enough to offset the commissions, the underlying asset has to be volatile, and the option close to the money; the more volatile it is and the closer the option is to the money, the greater the chance it will be exercised. If it's exercised the writer's profit is limited to the premium, when a greater profit could have been made by holding the investment.

Mutual funds that make their income by writing and trading options are an alternative for small investors.

* * *

What Is an Option Contract (Put or Call)?

An option contract is a contract that grants the right, in exchange for a price or premium to buy (call) or sell (put) an underlying security at a specified price within a specified period of time.

Buying, Selling, and Holding

Where do I buy and sell it? At a full-service or discount broker.

Is there a minimum purchase amount, and what is the price range? The minimum is one option contract covering 100 shares. Contracts typically cost a few hundred dollars (usually less than $500).

What fees and charges are involved? In addition to the premium, brokerage commissions are charged for buying, selling, and exercising options. The maximum charge is $25 for a transaction covering one option; the average for multiple-contract transactions is about $14.

Does it mature, expire, or otherwise terminate? Yes; options have a specified expiration date, usually within nine months.

Can I sell it quickly? Yes; most options enjoy good liquidity.

How is market value determined and how do I keep track of it? The market value of an option is its premium value, which is determined by a combination of its intrinsic value (the difference between its exercise price and the market value of the underlying stock) and its time value (the value investors place on the amount of time until the expiration of the option). A small change in a stock price can cause a larger percentage change in an option premium; premium changes are reported daily in the financial sections of newspapers.

Investment Objectives

Should I buy an option contract if my objective is capital appreciation? Because a small change in a stock price causes a higher percentage change in a related option premium, speculators gain leverage using options. Of course, if the underlying stock fails to move in the right direction, the speculator is out the cost of the premium. Options are also used as hedging tools to protect the value of shares held for capital gains.

Should I buy this if my objective is income? Although sellers (writers) of options receive income from premiums and thereby augment the income return on the underlying holding, they may be forced to buy or sell the underlying holding if its price moves adversely. Options are not themselves income-producing investments, although speculators and some mutual funds create income through option writing and various spread strategies.

To what extent does it protect against inflation? Puts and calls, as short-term options, are not designed to capitalize on longer-term movements in common stock prices as might be caused by inflationary factors. Of course, subscription warrants and employee stock options, which are related to put and call options, could be viewed as inflation protection.

Is it suitable for tax-deferred retirement accounts? Although not prohibited by the Internal Revenue Service, most brokerage firms rule out options contracts as too risky for retirement accounts. They may have a limited role in managed accounts, primarily as a hedging tool. Mutual funds or other pooled investments that generate income by writing and speculating in options may be appropriate investments in selected situations for people with high risk tolerance.

Can I borrow against it? No. Although Federal Reserve margin rules allow options transactions in margin accounts, options cannot be used as part of the borrowing base. Of course, options are themselves a source of considerable leverage.

Risk Considerations

How assured can I be of getting my full investment back? Your investment is the premium plus commissions. It is recovered only if the underlying stock or instrument moves favorably to such an extent that the profit gained from selling or exercising the option exceeds the investment; whether it does or not is pure speculation.

How assured is my income? The only income that options provide is from premiums earned in selling them. That is assured income, but it can be more than offset if the underlying stock moves adversely and the option is exercised by its holder.

Are there any other risks unique to this investment? The risk in options ranges from the simple loss of a premium if the option proves valueless to the risk of a magnified loss in the case of uncovered or naked positions—that is, where a put or call is sold without owning the underlying security or instrument. Upon exercise, the security or instrument must be bought or sold at a market price that may be in wide variance from the exercise price.

Is it commercially rated? No.

Tax Considerations

What tax advantages (or disadvantages) does it offer? Options on stocks are subject to the same capital gains taxation as the stocks themselves. Some traditional uses of options to defer income from one year to another have been curtailed by recent tax legislation and advice should be sought. See also the entry for Tax Straddle in Part IV.

Economic Considerations

What economic factors most affect buy, hold, and sell decisions? The same economic factors that affect stock investments in the short term apply essentially to decisions involving put and call options used in speculation and hedging.

OPTION CONTRACT ON A FUTURES CONTRACT (FUTURES OPTION)

For a general discussion of an option, see Option Contract (Put or Call).

* * *

What Is an Option Contract on a Futures Contract?

A futures option is a contract that grants the right, in exchange for a price (premium) to buy (call) or sell (put) a specified futures contract within a specified period of time.

Buying, Selling, and Holding

How do I buy and sell it? At a full-service or discount broker.

Is there a minimum purchase amount, and what is the price range? The minimum purchase is one option on one futures contract. It can cost several hundred to several thousand dollars, depending on the underlying future.

What fees and charges are involved? In addition to the premium, brokerage commissions are charged for buying, selling, and exercising an option. Generally, the maximum charge is $25, and the average charge for multiple option transactions is around $14, with lower rates for high-volume transactions.

Does it mature, expire, or otherwise terminate? Yes; options have a specified expiration date, usually within one year.

Can I sell it quickly? Yes; most futures options have good liquidity and they are not subject to daily trading limits that can affect the liquidity of futures themselves.

How is market value determined and how do I keep track of it? The same factors that affect the market value of futures affect the premium values of futures options. (See the sections Futures Contract on a Commodity and Futures Contract on an Interest Rate.) Prices are reported daily in newspapers and electronic databases.

Investment Objectives

Should I buy a futures option if my objective is capital appreciation? Only if you are a speculator attracted to the high degree of leverage offered by options, although options on futures are used by investors to hedge the value of other investments held for capital gains.

Should I buy this if my objective is income? Although selling options is a source of income, options are not themselves an income-producing investment. Some mutual funds trade in options for the purpose of generating income, however.

To what extent does it protect against inflation? Only to the limited extent that futures offer the opportunity to capitalize on inflation expectations and their effects on interest rates and commodity prices.

Is it suitable for tax-deferred retirement accounts? Although not prohibited by the Internal Revenue Service, most brokerage firms rule out options contracts as too risky for retirement accounts. They may have a limited role in managed accounts, primarily as a hedging tool. Mutual funds or other pooled investments that generate income by writing and speculating in options may be appropriate investments in selected situations for people with high risk tolerance.

Can I borrow against it? No. Although Federal Reserve margin rules allow options transactions in margin accounts, options cannot be used as part of the borrowing base. Of course, options are themselves a source of significant leverage.

Risk Considerations

How assured can I be of getting my full investment back? Your investment is the premium plus commissions. It is recovered only if the underlying futures contract moves favorably to such an extent that the proceeds realized from selling or exercising the option exceed the amount expended; whether it does or not is pure speculation.

How assured is my income? The only income that options provide is from premiums earned in selling them. That is assured income, but it can be more than offset if the underlying future moves adversely and the option is exercised by the holder.

Are there any other risks unique to this investment? Essentially the same risks apply as are involved with regular options and futures on the same underlying assets. A special positive feature, however, is that futures options, particularly on debt instruments, have better liquidity than either straight options or straight futures; that is because of less restrictive trading limits on futures options than on futures, and because the open interest on futures options tends to be much higher than on regular interest-rate (debt) options.

Is it commercially rated? No.

Tax Considerations

What tax advantages (or disadvantges) does it offer? Options on futures are subject to the same tax treatment as futures are. See the section on a Futures Contract on a Commodity.

Economic Considerations

What economic factors most affect buy, hold, and sell decisions? The same economic forces that affect interest rate and commodity futures affect the options available on those contracts.

OPTION CONTRACT ON AN INTEREST RATE (DEBT OPTION)

For a general discussion of an option, see Option Contract (Put or Call).

$$* \quad * \quad *$$

What Is an Option Contract on an Interest Rate?

An interest-rate option is a contract that grants the right, in exchange for a price (premium), to buy (call option) or sell (put option) a certain debt security at a specified price within a specified period of time, thereby producing a particular yield.

Buying, Selling, and Holding

How do I buy and sell it? Through a full-service or discount broker.

Is there a minimum purchase amount, and what is the price range? The minimum purchase is one contract. Premiums, where the underlying security is interest-bearing, are determined as a percentage (in 32nds for Treasury bonds and notes) of par value. Thus a contract on a $100,000 par value U.S. Treasury bond with a premium of 2.50 (2 and 16/32) would cost $2500, while a $20,000 minicontract with a premium of 1.24 (1 and 24/32 or 1¾) would cost $350. Where the underlying security is discounted rather than interest-bearing, as with the 13-week Treasury bill, premiums are quoted with reference to basis point (100ths of one percent) differences between prices, expressed as complements of annualized discount rates. For example, with a 9% yield, a 13-week Treasury bill (par value $1 million) would have a price basis of 91 and might have an option trading at 92.20. With a premium thus quoted at 1.20 (120 basis points), it would cost $3000, calculated: .012 × ¹³⁄₅₂ × $1 million. (A quick way of approximating dollar premiums is to multiply basis points times $25.)

What fees and charges are involved? Brokerage commissions are charged for buying, selling, or exercising options. The maximum charge is $25 for a transaction covering one contract, with reduced rates for larger trades. Margin accounts may entail interest and other added charges. There may also be income and net worth rules to qualify investors.

Does it mature, expire, or otherwise terminate? Yes. All options have expiration dates, usually within nine months.

Can I sell it quickly? Interest rate options have generally good liquidity. Those with the most contracts outstanding (represented by open interest figures in newspapers) are usually easiest to trade.

How is market value determined and how do I keep track of it? Market value, which is premium value, is determined by a combination of intrinsic value (exercise value less market value of the underlying security) and time value (the diminishing value investors place on the time remaining to expiration). Intrinsic value changes with interest rate movements, which are influenced by Federal Reserve Board monetary policy and other economic factors. Option prices are reported daily in newspapers and electronic databases.

Investment Objectives

Should I buy an interest-rate option if my objective is capital appreciation? Speculators use the high leverage possible with options to capitalize on the price volatility resulting from interest rate movements.

Should I buy this if my objective is income? Option writers earn income in addition to the interest they receive on the underlying security, while taking the risk that the option will be exercised if rates move adversely. Investors also use interest rate options to hedge the value of other income-producing investments.

To what extent does it protect against inflation? As short-term instruments, interest-rate options are not designed for dealing with the longer-term effects of inflation on debt securities. However, inflation expectations are a factor in the term structure of interest rates, and it is possible, using options, to capitalize on short-term movements.

Is it suitable for tax-deferred retirement accounts? Although not prohibited by the Internal Revenue Service, most brokerage firms rule out options contracts as too risky for retirement accounts. They may have a limited role in managed accounts, primarily as a hedging tool. Mutual funds or other pooled investments that generate income by writing and speculating in options may be appropriate investments in selected situations for people with high risk tolerance.

Can I borrow against it? No. Although Federal Reserve margin rules allow options transactions in margin accounts, options cannot be used as part of the borrowing base. Of course, options are themselves a source of considerable leverage.

Risk Considerations

How assured can I be of getting my full investment back? Your investment is recovered only if interest rates move favorably to the extent that the proceeds of the sale of the option exceed the premium plus commissions already expended; that is a matter of pure speculation.

How assured is my income? The only income is from premiums earned in selling options and even that can be negated by losses resulting from exercise by the holder.

Are there any other risks unique to this investment? The marketplace of interest-rate options is dominated on one hand by large institutional investors and their portfolio managers and on the other by dealers who handle the large volumes of high-denomination securities that underlie the options. This puts the smaller investor at a disadvantage in terms both of information and transaction cost. Other special risks have to do with the Option Clearing Corporation's power to remedy shortages of underlying securities by permitting substitutions and adjusting strike prices, and with trading hour differences between options and underlying debt instruments. Sellers of options on discount instruments settled in current instruments take a risk to the extent that they cannot hedge perfectly against exercise.

Is it commercially rated? No.

Tax Considerations

What tax advantages (or disadvantages) does it offer? Unlike regular put and call options, traders in interest-rate options are subject to tax rules covering futures trading; this means open positions are marked to market at year-end with paper gains or losses treated as if realized and taxed as net capital gains (see page 31). Tax advice should be sought.

Economic Considerations

What economic factors most affect buy, hold, and sell decisions? Economic and monetary factors affecting interest rates govern choices having to do with interest-rate options.

OPTION CONTRACT ON A STOCK INDEX

For a general discussion of an option, see Option Contract (Put or Call).

* * *

What Is an Option Contract on a Stock Index?

A stock-index option is a contract that grants the right, in exchange for a price (premium), to buy (call option) or sell (put option) the value of an underlying stock index or subindex at a specified price within a specified period of time with settlement in cash.

Buying, Selling, and Holding

How do I buy and sell it? Through a full-service or discount broker.

Is there a minimum purchase amount, and what is the price range? The minimum purchase is one contract. The premium is the difference in index values times $100. A contract based on a 5-point difference between the current (base) value and the exercise value would thus cost $500. Because contracts are settled in cash, margin security in the form of cash or securities is required by brokers, who may also have suitability requirements calling for substantial net worth and income.

What fees and charges are involved? In addition to the premium, brokerage commissions are charged for buying, selling, and exercising options. The maximum charge is $25 for a transaction covering one contract, with reduced rates for large trades. Margin accounts may entail interest and other additional charges.

Does it mature, expire, or otherwise terminate? Yes; options have a specified expiration date.

Can I sell it quickly? Most stock-index options have good liquidity, though newly introduced contracts may have less active markets than contracts that are better established and more popular. Those with many contracts outstanding (represented by large open interest figures in the newspapers) are generally the easiest to trade.

How is market value determined and how do I keep track of it? Premium value is determined by a combination of intrinsic value (exercise price less the index value) and time value (the value investors place on the amount of time remaining to expiration). The intrinsic value is subject to all the forces that make the stock market go up and down; a small movement in the market, as represented by the index, will result in a much larger percentage change in premium value. Indexes are revalued constantly during the trading day and closing prices are published in daily newspapers and electronic databases along with the option values based on them.

Investment Objectives

Should I buy a stock-index option if my objective is capital appreciation? You might if you were a speculator expecting a move in the stock market and were attracted to the high leverage provided by options. You might also use index options to hedge against possible losses in other securities being held for capital gains.

Should I buy this if my objective is income? Although sellers of options receive premium income and thereby increase the income return on their portfolios, options are not themselves income securities.

To what extent does it protect against inflation? Index options are short-term investments and not designed to capitalize on longer-term market movements as might be caused by inflation.

Is it suitable for tax-deferred retirement accounts? Although not prohibited by the Internal Revenue Service, most brokerage firms rule out options contracts as too risky for retirement accounts. They may have a limited role in managed accounts, primarily as a hedging tool. Mutual funds or other pooled investments that generate income by writing and speculating in options may be appropriate investments in selected situations for people with high risk tolerance.

Can I borrow against it? No. Although Federal Reserve margin rules allow options transactions in margin accounts, options cannot be used as part of the borrowing base. Of course, options are themselves a source of significant leverage.

Risk Considerations

How assured can I be of getting my full investment back? Your investment is recovered only if the underlying index value moves favorably to such an extent that the proceeds gained from selling or exercising the option exceed the cost plus commissions; whether it does is pure speculation.

How assured is my income? The only income that options provide is from premiums earned in selling the options. Even that, however, can be negated if the underlying index moves adversely and the option is exercised by the holder.

Are there any other risks unique to this investment? Index options share the same risks as regular puts and calls, but have a few that are unique. These have basically to do with (1) the limitations of index options as a hedging tool (it is impractical to compose a portfolio that duplicates an index exactly and even then there is rarely dollar-for-dollar variation) and with (2) the fact that settlement is made in cash; the settlement figure is the difference between the strike price and the closing value of the index on the day of exercise, and since the seller is not informed of the assignment until the next business day or even later, his hedge position may have lost value. This timing risk must be considered in all multioption strategies using index options. Other risks have to do with trading halts affecting underlying shares (but not the indexes) and causing index values to be based on noncurrent prices, or trading halts in the index options themselves, with the risk that the index value will move adversely before a position can be closed out.

Is it commercially rated? No.

Tax Considerations

What tax advantages (or disadvantages) does it offer? Unlike regular put and call options, index options are subject to tax rules covering futures trading. This means open positions are marked to market at year-end; paper profits or losses are treated as if realized and taxed as net capital gains (see page 31). Tax advice should be sought.

Economic Considerations

What economic factors most affect buy, hold, and sell decisions? Index options are used to make market bets or to protect other holdings against market risk. Any and all economic factors affecting the market become relevant to decisions involving stock options.

OPTION CONTRACT OR FUTURES CONTRACT ON A CURRENCY

For a general discussion of an option, see Option Contract (Put or Call); for a general discussion of a futures contract, see Futures Contract on a Commodity.

* * *

What Is a Futures Contract or an Option Contract on a Currency?

They are contracts to buy or sell (futures) or that represent rights (options) to buy or sell a foreign currency at a particular price within a specified period of time.

Buying, Selling, and Holding

How do I buy and sell them? Through a full-service broker or commodities dealer.

Is there a minimum purchase amount, and what is the price range? Contract sizes vary with different currencies and different markets. The minimum purchase is one contract, which, for an option, typically costs a few hundred dollars. Futures contracts tend to be sizable (standard-size contracts are 12.5 million yen and 125,000 Swiss francs, for example, which on one day in the mid-1980s both equalled about $62,500) but they can be bought with small (1.5% to 4.2%) margins. Also, mini-contracts are traded in several currencies on the Mid-America Commodity Exchange—6.25 million yen and 62,500 Swiss francs, for example.

What fees and charges are involved? Broker's commissions, typically $25 or less per contract for options; $50 to $80 for a round-trip futures contract transaction (purchase and sale). In the event of actual delivery, other fees, charges, or taxes may be required.

Do they mature, expire, or otherwise terminate? Yes; all contracts have specified expiration dates.

Can I sell them quickly? Yes; option and futures contracts enjoy good liquidity, although daily price limits on futures can create illiquidity when contracts are down limit or up limit and it is impossible to trade out of a position, because maximum allowable price movement has occurred during the trading day.

How is market value determined and how do I keep track of it? Premiums and contract values change as the exchange rate between the dollar and the foreign currency changes. The exchange rate is determined by the relative value of two currencies, which can change as events affect either or both of the underlying currencies. Daily prices are published in newspapers and electronic databases.

Investment Objectives

Should I buy them if my objective is capital appreciation? Speculators use the high leverage afforded by options and futures contracts to seek gains on relative currency values.

Should I buy them if my objective is income? Except for premium income earned from selling (writing) options, contracts do not provide income. Contracts are frequently used in hedging strategies to protect other income-producing securities from losses due to currency values.

To what extent do they protect against inflation? Because they are short-term contracts, currency options and futures are not affected directly by inflation.

Are they suitable for tax-deferred retirement accounts? Although not prohibited by the Internal Revenue Service, most brokerage firms rule out options and futures contracts as too risky for retirement accounts. They may have a limited role in managed accounts, primarily as a hedging tool. Mutual funds or other pooled investments that generate income through options and futures may be appropriate investments in selected situations for people with high risk tolerance.

Can I borrow against them? Options can be traded in margin accounts but cannot be used as collateral. Moreover, since foreign currency does not have borrowing value either for margin purposes, purchases as the result of exercise may require extra cash or securities. Futures cannot be used as collateral, but provide leverage because they can be held with small margins, actually good faith deposits.

Risk Considerations

How assured can I be of getting my full investment back? With options, the only investment is the premium plus commissions and it is recovered only when the underlying rate of exchange moves favorably to such an extent that the proceeds gained from sale or exercise exceed the amount expended. Futures are inherently speculative and it is possible to lose more than your investment, although margin calls would normally limit losses to the amount invested, assuming the account was closed out (liquidated) to meet the call.

How assured is my income? Other than premium income from option writing (selling), options and futures provide no income.

Are there any other risks unique to these investments? Since two currencies are involved, developments in either country can affect the values of options and futures. Risks include general economic factors as well as government actions affecting currency valuation and the movements of currencies from one country to another. The quantities of currency underlying option contracts represent odd lots in a market dominated by transactions between banks; this can mean extra transaction costs upon exercise. The fact that options markets may be closed while round-the-clock interbank currency markets are open can create problems due to price and rate discrepancies. With futures, there is always the risk of actual delivery if a position is not closed out prior to expiration of the contract.

Are they commercially rated? No, neither options nor futures are rated.

Tax Considerations

What tax advantages (or disadvantages) do they offer? Options are subject to the same capital gains rules as the underlying assets. Futures are subject to special rules requiring that open positions be marked to market at year-end and be taxed as realized capital gains (see page 31). Net trading losses can be applied against capital gains on other investments and unused portions carried forward. Other tax treatments may apply where contracts are used for hedging purposes. Tax advice should be sought.

Economic Considerations

What economic factors most affect buy, hold, and sell decisions? All factors that affect either currency affect the values of options and futures contracts.

PRECIOUS METALS

Precious metals—gold, silver, platinum, and palladium—are bought by investors primarily to hedge against inflation, economic uncertainty, and foreign exchange risk, in the belief that these metals are repositories of absolute value, whereas paper currencies and securities denominated in such currencies have relative value and are vulnerable to loss.

The economics of precious metals have less to do with the production process, industrial demand, or their greatly diminished monetary role than with the psychology of the financial marketplace. There, precious metals—gold especially—are perceived to be the best store of value available when anxiety causes the value of other assets to go into a tailspin. Historically, in such scenarios gold and other precious metals have risen.

The most famous example was in January 1980 when high international inflation due to rising oil prices, the American-hostage crisis in Iran, and civil disorder in Saudi Arabia combined to cause abnormally heavy buying of precious metals, which drove gold to a record price of $887.50 per ounce and led silver and platinum to peak levels as well. When calmer times returned, however, prices soon fell and stabilized at lower levels. It was a memorable lesson in how volatile this store of value can be.

Physical ownership is one way of owning precious metals, available in bullion form in units ranging from 400-Troy-ounce gold bars to 1-ounce platinum ingots. These are sold by dealers at markups or premiums that fall as weights and dollar values rise. Gold can also be held in coins, such as the South African Krugerrand, the Canadian Maple Leaf, and the U.S. Eagle series, introduced in 1986. Generally, the more popular the coin, the greater its liquidity and the higher its premium. Silver can be bought in bags containing U.S. coins of $1000 total face value, priced at a discount to the silver value to cover melting and refining costs. The drawbacks of physical ownership are mainly the high premiums, safekeeping and insurance costs, and sales taxes.

Certificates—actually warehouse receipts issued by some banks, dealers, and full-service brokers—represent gold, silver, platinum, or palladium held in safekeeping. Typically, for a fee of 3% or higher, the bank or dealer will buy metals in $1000 units and, for a small annual charge, provide insurance and storage. It will also, for 1% or so, sell the bullion or deliver it without a sales tax. The attraction is the convenience and lower transaction costs compared to physical ownership.

Other alternatives include *securities* of companies engaged in mining or processing, including some exchange-traded South African companies (many represented by American Depositary Receipts) as well as highly speculative penny stocks, traded over-the-counter or on regional or Canadian exchanges. There are also *mutual funds* and *closed-end funds* that specialize in both debt and equity issues of precious metals firms.

Finally, *commodity futures, options,* and *options on futures* are traded on precious metals. They provide leverage and hedging opportunities for well-capitalized investors with high expertise and risk tolerance. See separate discussions of these investment vehicles.

* * *

What Are Investments in Precious Metals?

Investments in precious metals involve gold, silver, platinum, and palladium as commodities (i.e., not as money), owned by investors, in physical form or through securities, because of their presumed value as stores of wealth and as hedges against inflation and economic uncertainty. Precious metals are traded by speculators who hope to profit from volatility in the financial marketplace.

Buying, Selling, and Holding

How do I buy and sell them? Through various dealers and brokers, depending on the form of ownership. Coins and certificates are bought and sold through major banks.

Is there a minimum purchase amount, and what is the price range? Precious metals can be bought with almost any amount of money, depending on the form of investment. Certificates generally have $1000 minimums.

What fees and charges are involved? Bullion involves a dealer markup, varying with quantity. Certificates cost 3% and up, with storage and insurance another 1% or more and sales fees of 1% or higher. Domestic and foreign securities and other forms of investment, like mutual funds, are subject to standard fees and commissions. Depending on the form of ownership, other costs may include sales or transfer taxes, shipping and handling, assay fees, insurance, storage, and safekeeping. Physical ownership involves an opportunity cost as well, since the money tied up could otherwise be invested in assets producing income.

Do they mature, expire, or otherwise terminate? Certain investment vehicles, such as options and futures, have specified expirations.

Can I sell them quickly? Usually yes, though platinum and palladium are less liquid than gold and silver. Larger ingots and less popular gold coins can have uncertain liquidity.

How is market value determined and how do I keep track of it? Market value is a complex affair. While investor demand is highest when inflation and economic uncertainty loom largest, industrial demand depends on economic health and certainty. Other factors, such as interest rates and foreign exchange rates, play a key role, and speculators are active. Different forms of investment may be affected in different ways at different times. Dealers are a source of information concerning physical assets; securities and commodities information is reported in the financial pages of daily newspapers.

Investment Objectives

Should I invest in precious metals if my objective is capital appreciation? Yes, but myriad forces affect market value, and a high degree of expertise is required to achieve short-term gains.

Should I buy them if my objective is income? Some forms of ownership, like stocks and mutual funds, may provide income, while others, like physical ownership, provide none and may involve negative returns. In general, precious metals are not purchased for income.

To what extent do they protect against inflation? Although used by investors primarily to hedge political and economic uncertainty, precious metals over the long term have risen in value with inflation. Investors buying precious metals for inflation protection should be mindful, however, that many factors can cause volatility in the shorter term.

Are they suitable for tax-deferred retirement accounts? Except for American gold and silver coins, physical investment is not permitted. Common stocks and mutual fund shares involving precious metals may be suitable for some accounts.

Can I borrow against them? Yes; depending on the form of investment, there are various ways to leverage investments and use them as loan collateral.

Risk Considerations

How assured can I be of getting my full investment back? Precious metals tend to be volatile and offer no assurance that values will be retained.

How assured is my income? Where such investments provide income at all, such as mining stocks paying dividends, the risk is often great.

Are there any other risks unique to these investments? Many investors in precious metals have lost money doing business with unscrupulous dealer-brokers. Political risks in countries where mining is done and related developments, such as the sentiment in the mid-1980s for divestiture of shares of firms doing business in South

Africa, can jeopardize investment values. Inaccurate or misleading estimates of reserves of mining companies is another risk.

Are they commercially rated? Some common stocks are rated by Standard & Poor's and other major services.

Tax Considerations

What tax advantages (or disadvantages) do they offer? Assuming you are not engaged in mining or processing or using gold in a business or profession, dividend income and capital gains and losses are subject to the usual tax treatment. In addition, you may have to pay state sales taxes on physical purchases.

Economic Considerations

What economic factors most affect buy, hold, and sell decisions? Investors favor precious metals to hedge anticipated high inflation; however, many other economic factors can affect the value of precious metals and related investment alternatives, often in different ways.

PREFERRED STOCK (NONCONVERTIBLE)

Preferred stock is a hybrid security that combines features of both common stock and bonds. It is equity, not debt, however, and is thus riskier than bonds. It rarely carries voting rights.

Preferred dividends, like bond interest, are usually a fixed percentage of par value, so share prices, like bond prices, go up when interest rates move down and vice versa. But whereas bond interest is a contractual expense of the issuer, preferred dividends, although payable before common dividends, can be skipped if earnings are low. If the issuer goes out of business, preferred shareholders do not share in assets until bondholders are paid in full, though preferred shareholders rank ahead of common stockholders. Like bonds, preferreds may have sinking funds, be callable, or be redeemable by their holders.

Because preferred issues are designed for insurance companies and other institutional investors which, as corporations, enjoy an 80% tax exclusion on dividends earned, fully taxable yields for individuals are not much better than those on comparable bonds offering more safety. Moreover, trading is often inactive or in big blocks, meaning less liquidity and higher transaction costs for small investors.

Still, personal investors do hold preferred stock. A broker can usually find good buys as investor perceptions of risk in different industrial sectors create yield differences in stocks that are otherwise comparable. Capital appreciation can result from shares bought at a discount from the prices at which a sinking fund will purchase them, or from discounted shares of turnaround firms with dividend arrearages.

Different types of preferred stock include:

Convertible preferred, convertible into common shares and thus offering growth potential plus fixed income; tends to behave differently in the marketplace than straight preferred (see Convertible Security).

Noncumulative preferred is a hangover from the heyday of the railroads and is rare today. Dividends, if unpaid, do not accumulate.

Cumulative preferred is the most common type. Dividends, if skipped, accrue, and common dividends cannot be paid while arrearages exist.

Participating preferred is unusual and typically issued by firms desperate for capital. Holders share in profits with common holders by way of extra dividends declared after regular dividends are paid. This type may have voting rights.

Adjustable (floating or *variable) rate preferred* adjusts the dividend rate quarterly (usually based on the 3-month U.S. Treasury bill) to reflect money market rates. It is aimed at corporate investors seeking after-tax yields combined with secondary market price stability. Individuals, looking at modest, fully taxable dividends that can go down as well as up, might prefer the safety of a money market fund.

Prior preferred stock (or preference shares) has priority of claim on assets and earnings over other preferred shares.

PIK Preferred Stock—PIK is an acronym for payment in kind—refers to an oddity spawned in the wave of leveraged buyouts in the 1980s. PIK preferred pays its dividend in the form of additional preferred stock. It is highly speculative almost by definition, since it implies a dearth of cash and raises a question about the adequacy of the issuer's working capital.

*   *   *

What Is Nonconvertible Preferred Stock?

Nonconvertible preferred is a form of owner's equity, usually nonvoting, paying dividends at a specified rate and having prior claim over common stock on earnings and assets in liquidation.

Buying, Selling, and Holding

How do I buy and sell it? Through a securities broker-dealer.

Is there a minimum purchase amount, and what is the price range? Buying round lots (usually 10 shares) saves commissions. Shares have par (face) values normally ranging from $100 down to $10, and market prices may be higher or lower than par values to bring yields in line with prevailing interest rate levels.

What fees and charges are involved? Standard commissions, with added transaction charges on inactively traded shares.

Does it mature, expire, or otherwise terminate? Preferred stock may be outstanding indefinitely, but many issues have call features or sinking fund provisions, whereby the issuer, usually for a small premium over par value, can require holders to redeem shares. Preferred issues may also have put features, which allow holders to redeem shares.

Can I sell it quickly? In most cases, yes. As a rule, preferreds are less liquid than common stocks and more liquid than bonds. Because large corporate investors dominate, smaller lots can sometimes be difficult for brokers to transact quickly.

How is market value determined and how do I keep track of it? Assuming good financial condition, fixed-income preferreds vary inversely with market interest rates. *Adjustable-rate preferreds* tend to be less volatile because dividends are adjusted quarterly to reflect money market conditions. Preferred prices are reported daily in the stock tables of newspapers and in databases, identified by the abbreviation ''PF'' in newspapers and ''PR'' in most electronic media.

Investment Objectives

Should I buy nonconvertible preferred stock if my objective is capital appreciation? No, although appreciation is possible in shares bought at a discount from par or redemption value or bought prior to a decline in interest rates. Substantial appreciation is possible in turnaround situations where cumulative preferred issues of troubled companies are selling at big discounts and there is a sizable accumulated dividend obligation.

Should I buy this if my objective is income? Yes, but unless you're a corporation or you buy at a discount, your yield won't be much better than that on a comparable corporate bond, and bonds are less risky in terms of both income and principal.

To what extent does it protect against inflation? Fixed-rate preferred offers no protection against inflation. Adjustable-rate preferred offers some.

Is it suitable for tax-deferred retirement accounts? Yes.

Can I borrow against it? Yes, subject to lender policies and Federal Reserve margin requirements.

Risk Considerations

How assured can I be of getting my full investment back? The market value of fixed-rate preferred stock declines as interest rates rise. (Adjustable-rate preferred has greater price stability.) In liquidation, holders of preferred stock are paid after bondholders but before common stockholders.

How assured is my income? Dividends, unlike interest, are not legal obligations and are paid from earnings, so income is as reliable as the issuer's earnings are stable. Established companies, such as utilities, with predictable cash flows are better bets than young firms or firms in cyclical industries, such as housing. Preferred dividends must be paid before common distributions, however; that means common dividends wait until all unpaid preferred dividends of cumulative issues are satisfied.

Are there any other risks unique to this investment? Call features, when present, allow the issuer to force holders to redeem shares, usually at par value plus a small premium. Firms normally call issues when market rates have declined and they can obtain financing more cheaply. But it is exactly under such circumstances that shares are enjoying higher market values and paying higher than market yields to holders who bought before rates declined. So call features represent a risk to investors; indeed the very presence of a call feature can limit upside price potential. Another risk of preferred stock is that should a dividend be omitted, the market may perceive financial weakness and drive down the share values.

Is it commercially rated? Yes. Major issues are rated by Moody's, Standard & Poor's, Value Line Investment Survey, and other services.

Tax Considerations

What tax advantages (or disadvantages) does it offer? None for personal investors. Corporations enjoy an 80% exemption from federal income taxes on dividends from other domestic corporations, effectively raising returns.

Economic Considerations

What economic factors most affect buy, hold, or sell decisions? Since most preferred stock pays a fixed dividend, it is best to buy when market rates are high and the issuer is forced to offer a competitive yield. Prices vary inversely with interest rates, so values increase as interest rates decline. Fixed-rate preferred stock loses value in inflation. Poor business conditions may affect profits and threaten dividends.

REAL ESTATE INVESTMENT TRUST (REIT AND FREIT)

If 1986 Tax Reform spoiled the party for "tax-advantaged" real estate limited partnerships, it made real estate investment trusts, or REITs, which are all about income, more popular than ever. The reasons are two:

First, by extending depreciation from 19 to 27.5 years, tax reform removed one the sweetest tax deductions benefiting limited partners, but REITs had always used a mandatory 35-year schedule, and thus were unaffected. Second, the use of writeoffs against salary and other investment income, a major benefit to limited partners before Tax Reform limited passive loss deductions to passive income, was never a benefit of REITs; REITs generate portfolio income, which is now worth relatively more.

The market environment for REITs has also become more favorable. Overbuilding before Tax Reform, then slow construction when tax benefits dried up, caused both depressed prices and a *projected* dearth of supply in the commercial market. Since this should mean rising rents and values for existing properties, many analysts foresee higher dividends and higher share prices for selected REITs in the 1990s.

REITs were authorized by Congress in the early 1960s to provide small investors with an opportunity to invest in large-scale real estate. After a tumultuous period in the mid-1970s, when rising interest rates and tight money pressured builders, causing loan defaults and forcing many REITs into financial difficulty, the industry, wiser for the experience, enjoyed a resurgence.

Like shares of stock, REITs trade publicly, and like mutual funds their money is invested in a diverse array of assets, from shopping malls and office buildings to health care facilities, apartment complexes and hotels, usually with geographical diversification as well.

Some REITs, called *equity REITs*, take ownership positions in real estate; shareholders receive income from the rents received from the properties and receive capital gains as properties are sold at a profit. Because both rents and property values rise with inflation, inflation protection is an important benefit of equity-oriented real estate investments. Other REITs specialize in lending money to real estate developers. Called *mortgage REITs*, they pass interest income on to shareholders. *Hybrid or balanced* REITs feature a mix of equity and debt investments.

By law, REITs must derive 75% of income from rents, dividends, interest, and gains from the sale of real estate properties, and must pay out 95% to shareholders. Companies meeting those requirements are exempt from federal taxation at the corporate level, although dividends are taxable to shareholders. REITs thus allow investors to share, with limited liability, the financial and tax benefits of real estate while avoiding the double taxation of corporate ownership. REITs also offer liquidity, since you can sell your shares on the market any time you wish.

On the negative side, REIT shares can be just as volatile as shares of stock. When conditions are unfavorable, such as when interest rates are high, materials are short, and the real-estate market is overbuilt, share values suffer.

FREITS: A variation of the REIT is the *finite life real estate investment trust*, or FREIT. FREITs, like limited partnerships, are self-liquidating—that is, they aim to sell or finance their holdings by a given date and distribute the proceeds to investors, thereby enabling them to realize capital gains. Investors thus have the choice of (1) selling their FREIT shares in the market (share values tend to more closely reflect market values of property holding than with REITs) or of (2) waiting to receive the full value of their shares when the portfolio is sold and the cash is distributed. Of course, the disadvantages of REITs apply to FREITs as well—the risk of a soft market at the time of sale or liquidation, and the inability to share in tax-deductible losses.

CMO REITs: A recent and popular innovation has been the CMO REIT, a complex and risky investment created when the issuer of a collateralized mortgage obligation—see section on mortgage-backed (pass-through) securities—sells the CMO's residual cash flows (the spread between the rate paid by mortgage holders and the lower, shorter-term rate paid to CMO investors) to the CMO REIT. REIT shareholders benefit when the spread widens and and get lower returns as the spread narrows.

The main variable affecting the spread is the prepayment rate on the mortgages underlying the CMO. Prepayments fall and spreads widen when market interest rates increase; the reverse happens when rates decrease. Because returns rise and fall with interest rates, CMO REIT investors theoretically enjoy an investment that is countercyclical to other equity investments in real estate, which react adversely to rate increases.

CMO REITs may be vulnerable to more than prepayment risk, however. Depending on how they are structured, an increase in short-term versus long-term interest rates can create a rate squeeze. Moreover, spreads tend to narrow as a function of time as normal prepayments are made and as faster-pay, lower-rate CMO components are paid off, leaving the REIT with more costly longer-term bonds.

CMO REITs, which have been marketed aggressively, can seem appealing because of high initial yields and AAA ratings of the underlying CMOs. But at least one CMO REIT has gone bankrupt, and only investors who understand this sophisticated vehicle and can afford high risk should get involved.

*   *   *

What Is a Real Estate Investment Trust (REIT)?

A REIT is a trust that invests in real estate-related assets, such as properties or mortgages, with funds obtained by selling shares, usually publicly traded, to investors.

Buying, Selling, and Holding

How do I buy and sell it? Through a securities broker-dealer.

Is there a minimum purchase amount, and what is the price range? Like common stocks, shares trade in round lots of 100 shares, with odd-lot transactions involving higher commissions. Prices vary, but most shares trade under $50.

What fees and charges are involved? Standard brokerage commissions.

Does it mature, expire, or otherwise terminate? Not normally. A recent development, called the finite life real estate investment trust or FREIT, is self-liquidating—that is, the management has an expressed intention to sell all its properties and distribute the proceeds within a specified time frame.

Can I sell it quickly? Yes, good liquidity is a major attraction.

How is market value determined and how do I keep track of it? Shares of equity REITs reflect property values, rent trends, and market sentiment about real estate. Mortgage REITs fluctuate as market interest rates affect profits. Balanced REITs—part equity, part mortgage—tend to have greater price stability. CMO REITs tend to rise in value as interest rates increase, and vice versa. FREITs, because shareholders will sooner or later realize capital gains income, tend to have share values somewhat more reflective of underlying property values. Share prices are reported in the stock tables of daily newspapers and in electronic databases.

Investment Objectives

Should I buy this if my objective is capital appreciation? Yes, but the potential for share value increases is greater with equity REITs than mortgage REITs. Also, automatic reinvestment of dividends increases capital gains potential. FREITs aim to pay out realized capital gains within a targeted period.

Should I buy this if my objective is income? Yes, especially since yields are not reduced by taxation at the corporate level. Mortgage REITs and CMO REITs are more income-oriented than equity REITs.

To what extent does it protect against inflation? Since income from rents and capital gains increases with inflation, equity REITs provide excellent inflation protection. Mortgage REITs provide less.

Is it suitable for tax-deferred retirement accounts? Yes.

Can I borrow against it? Yes, subject to Federal Reserve margin rules and individual lender policies.

Risk Considerations

How assured can I be of getting my full investment back? REITs shares have the same market risks as common stocks plus the risk of a decline in property values. Mortgage REIT shares suffer when rising interest rates squeeze profits, and unless insured, can involve the risk of default on mortgages. CMO REITs are subject to special risks (see overview discussion). You should not buy REITs if safety of principal is a paramount concern.

How assured is my income? Assuming REITs are well managed, income, which derives from rents or mortgage interest primarily, should be relatively secure. Still, real estate is sensitive to economic adversity, and there are many safer ways to invest for income. CMO REITs are subject to special risks (see overview discussion).

Are there any other risks unique to this investment? Much depends on expert management in terms of selecting, diversifying, and managing portfolios. Valuation of real estate is anything but an exact science. Certain types of REIT portfolios are riskier than others, those whose portfolios comprise short-term construction loan paper being the riskiest.

Is it commercially rated? Yes, by Standard & Poor's, Moody's, and others.

Tax Considerations

What tax advantages (or disadvantages) does it offer? REITs are not taxed at the corporate level, so dividends are higher. But shareholders personally are taxed. Unlike real estate limited partnerships, REITs cannot offer flow-through tax benefits, but some trustees pass on tax-sheltered cash flow (in excess of income) as a nontaxable return of capital. When shares are sold, however, the cost basis must be adjusted by such returns of capital in calculating capital gains taxes. To meet Internal Revenue Service tax-exemption requirements, 75% of a REIT's income must be real-estate related and 95% of it must be paid out to shareholders.

Economic Considerations

What economic factors most affect buy, hold, or sell decisions? REITs are most attractive to buy and hold when interest rates are low and supply and demand factors in the real estate industry favor growth in property values. Shares tend to be inflation-sensitive as values increase and dividends rise with higher rentals. Real estate is a cyclical industry and the risk-return relationship is maximized when investments are made over the long term. CMO REITs tend to be countercyclical.

REAL ESTATE, PHYSICAL

No investment alternative has been more ballyhooed as a way to get rich quick than real estate. With inflation a fact of life for half a century, this inflation-sensitive investment, with its high potential for leverage through mortgage financing and its abundant tax benefits, has indeed made many millionaires and provided millions of average home owners with nest eggs in the form of home equity.

Although the most liberal tax benefits of investment property were casualties of Tax Reform in 1986 and the baby boom that kept residential property values ascending for 30 years has given way in the 1990s to the baby bust, physical real estate, as long as the country continues to grow, holds the potential for substantial gain for those who know how to locate the best values and have the patience to endure the inevitable cycles, both regional and national.

Real estate has many drawbacks and risks, however, whether owned as an individual; in one of the several forms of joint ownership, which are distinguished mainly in terms of how an interest can be terminated and what happens to it in death or divorce; or through a corporation, which has the advantage of limited liability and the disadvantage of double taxation.

Among the problems of real estate ownership are high carrying costs in the form of property taxes, insurance, maintenance, and repairs; the risk of illiquidity; the risk of loss of value as the result of demographic factors, declining neighborhoods, local economic changes, or government policies (such as a rise in property taxes or the imposition of rent controls); competition from professional and institutional investors affecting local supply and demand factors; changes in federal tax provisions; high costs of selling; and a host of special risks associated with specific types of holdings.

Physical real estate can be categorized as (1) residential, where, because the owner lives there, the utility of shelter or recreational use is an important part of the value but depreciation and maintenance are not allowable tax deductions; (2) rental, where income and tax benefits are primary goals, and appreciation secondary; (3) speculative, where income and utilitarian values are traded off for capital gains potential and losses can result from carrying costs (an example is investment in raw land); and (4) multipurpose, such as a multifamily residence used partly to live in and partly to rent, or a vacation property combining recreational use and rental income (tax implications where the status is not clearly established can be serious).

Properties can also be held in forms of shared ownership, which bring tax advantages and other benefits of home ownership to apartments and town houses. Cooperatives, where owners hold shares in total projects, and condominiums, where apartment units are owned along with a share of commonly shared facilities and amenities, often require a tradeoff of certain lifestyle prerogatives (e.g., a ban on pets) and have eligibility criteria, advertising restrictions, or even prohibitions against renting that can severely limit liquidity. Condominium time-shares, where each of two or more owners has exclusive right of occupancy for a defined period, make condominium units much more affordable. The occupancy rights of some time-shared property even trade in a secondary market, not unlike securities.

The inflation protection, tax breaks, and total returns of real estate are also available through limited partnerships and real estate investment trusts (REITs). Such syndications offer diversification (by type of holding and geography), professional management, economies of scale, and limited liability for small investments, along with some risks and costs of their own.

*   *   *

What Is Physical Real Estate?

Physical real estate includes personal residences and investment properties in the form of developed and undeveloped land, established commercial or residential properties, condominiums, and cooperatives.

Buying, Selling, and Holding

How do I buy and sell it? Through a real estate broker or direct negotiation.

Is there a minimum purchase amount, and what is the price range? There is no minimum purchase amount; the price range is limitless. Properties can generally be financed with a down payment of 5% to 50% of value.

What fees and charges are involved? Real estate involves broker commissions and carrying costs in the form of debt interest, real estate taxes, and maintenance costs. Though there are many tax benefits associated with such costs, they can nonetheless be highly burdensome, especially if a property is not producing income.

Does it mature, expire, or otherwise terminate? Not in a financial sense, although related debt instruments have fixed maturities. Physical real estate is, of course, subject to destructive acts of nature, vandalism, and deterioration from use and time.

Can I sell it quickly? Liquidity varies with the type of property and market conditions; as a general rule, real estate is not a liquid investment.

How is market value determined and how do I keep track of it? Although general economic conditions and such factors as money supply and mortgage interest rates have an important effect, real estate is often characterized by independent markets. One segment of the industry (such as residential homes) can be booming, while another (such as office buildings) is depressed, and market conditions can vary widely from one community or geographical area to another. There is no formalized source of information about real estate prices. Trade associations can be a source of national and regional statistics and real estate brokers keep abreast of local values.

Investment Objectives

Should I buy this if my objective is capital appreciation? Yes.

Should I buy this if my objective is income? Yes, but only rental properties provide regular income.

To what extent does it protect against inflation? Real estate is inflation-sensitive, that is, both property values and rental income increase with inflation.

Is it suitable for tax-deferred retirement accounts? Personal residences are not legal investments. Real estate securities, such as real estate investment trusts (REITs) or income-oriented limited partnerships, can be appropriate investments, however.

Can I borrow against it? Yes; first, second, even third mortgages are common ways of borrowing against real estate. Home equity loans, a popular product of banks and other financial services institutions, are a convenient form of borrowing for home owners. On a professional scale, substantial fortunes have been made and lost using the financial leverage provided by real estate.

Risk Considerations

How assured can I be of getting my full investment back? Real estate offers no guarantees that values will not decline.

How assured is my income? A lease assures income for its term, to the extent the tenant is dependable and creditworthy.

Are there any other risks unique to this investment? Yes, many—including some not invented yet. Common risks include shifting population centers, changing local economies (including tax policies and rent control legislation), zoning changes, acts of nature, crimes like vandalism and arson, and physical deterioration.

Is it commercially rated? No.

Tax Considerations

What tax advantages (or disadvantages) does it offer? The main tax benefits are deductibility from federal income taxes of mortgage interest and property taxes, and on investment property, depreciation (which reduces taxable income without affecting cash flow) and deductible maintenance costs. All rental income is passive, but $25,000 of passive activity losses can be offset against nonpassive income (phased out for high-income taxpayers). Owners of personal residences can defer capital gains taxes by reinvesting the proceeds in another residence of equal or greater value within two years and are entitled to a one-time exemption from capital gains taxes up to certain limits after age 55. Unlike other consumer interest, which becomes nondeductible under the Tax Reform Act of 1986, interest on loans secured by home equity is deductible up to $100,000. The tax code on this has changed several times, however, and you should get up-to-date advice.

Economic Considerations

What economic factors most affect buy, hold, and sell decisions? Real estate values parallel general economic cycles but are also subject to supply and demand conditions in local markets and in segments of the industry (such as commercial, industrial, residential). The most successful real estate investors have diversified portfolios (in terms of geography and type of holding) and stay in an investment until it becomes profitable. These opporitunities, together with professional management and economies of scale, are available to individuals through real estate investment trusts (REITs) and limited partnerships.

SAVINGS ALTERNATIVES

For emergencies and for the sake of prudence, every investor should keep a certain amount of money in cash and in risk-free financial assets. Depending on one's need for liquidity, this often means choosing among the deposit accounts and certificates of deposit offered by banks and thrift institutions and U.S. Savings Bonds.

The following are brief descriptions of major savings alternatives:

> *Deposit accounts* Depositors in subscribing banks, savings and loans, and credit unions are insured up to $100,000, respectively, by the Bank Insurance Fund (BIF), the Savings Association Insurance

Fund (SAIF), and the National Credit Union Administration (NCUA). (BIF and SAIF are units of the Federal Deposit Insurance Corporation (FDIC) that were created in 1989 as part of the regulatory reform accompanying the federal bailout of failing savings and loan associations). Different accounts have different features, however.

Prior to changes in banking laws in the late 1970s and bank deregulation in the early 1980s, choices were relatively simple—a noninterest bearing checking account for day-to-day cash transactions and a passbook savings account paying a modest rate that was limited by law. Then came *Negotiated Order of Withdrawal (NOW) Accounts*, which allowed checkwriting in insured savings accounts but kept the low-interest ceilings. They were followed in 1982 by insured *Money Market Deposit Accounts (MMDAs)* requiring minimum balances but offering liquidity (with limited checkwriting), and paying money market-based rates only slightly lower, on average, than money market mutual funds. In 1983, insured *Super NOW Accounts* were introduced with a minimum balance of $2500, unlimited checking, and market-determined rates that tended to be just under those of MMDAs. A more recent addition, no-minimum checking accounts, require no minimum balance but pay little or no interest on balances and are not really a savings alternative.

With full deregulation in March 1986, institutions became legally free to pay any rate of interest. Because banks and thrift institutions must keep costly reserves, however, and because their federal insurance gives them a marketing advantage, their best rates tend generally to be a hair below money market mutual funds. The exceptions are the more aggressive money center banks and institutions with riskier (thus higher-yielding) loan portfolios or skimpier services.

Certificates of Deposit CDs are issued by banks, savings and loan associations (S&Ls), and credit unions, in various denominations and maturities (some institutions offer designer CDs, with maturities to suit the customer) are also federally insured at member institutions. CDs, which can have similar maturities and vary a couple of points between issuers, are issued both in discount and interest-bearing form and sometimes with variable rates. Other variations include split-rate CDs, where a higher rate is paid early in the CD's term than in its later life; convertible-term CDs, which convert from fixed-rate to variable-rate instruments; and expandable CDs, which allow adding to the investment at the original rate. CDs can also be bought from some brokers, who make bulk purchases of high-yielding CDs from issuing institutions around the country and then resell them; since the brokers make markets in such CDs, buyers have liquidity they would not enjoy as direct investors.

Savings Bonds Savings bonds come with flexible yields (Series EEs, issued on a zero-coupon basis, pay 85% of the average U.S. Treasury note return with a minimum of 6% if held for 5 years), plus deferred federal taxability and exemption from state and local taxes. Previously issued Series E and H bonds can be rolled into EEs or HHs and EEs can be rolled into HHs. HHs are interest-bearing and pay 6% over 10 years. Individuals meeting income qualifications can buy EE bonds to save for a child's higher education and enjoy total or partial federal tax exemption (See Tax Considerations below).

*   *   *

What Are Savings Alternatives?

Savings alternatives include interest-bearing deposit accounts at banks, savings and loans, and credit unions; bank certificates of deposit (CDs); and Series EE and HH U.S. Savings Bonds.

Buying, Selling, and Holding

How do I buy and sell them? Deposit accounts, CDs, and savings bonds may be transacted at banks or other savings and financial services institutions. Series EE bonds may also be available through employer-sponsored payroll savings programs. Series HH bonds can be acquired by exchanging Series E, EE, and freedom share bonds at Federal Reserve banks and branches or the Bureau of Public Debt (Parkersburg, West Virginia 26106). The Federal Reserve or BPD will also redeem HH bonds after six months from issue.

Is there a minimum purchase amount, and what is the price range? Deposit accounts are available with no minimum deposits, but interest may vary with balances and some banks impose charges (negative interest) when low balances become an administrative burden. CDs are usually issued for $500 and up, although some $100 CDs are available. Jumbo CDs are issued for $100,000 and up. Series EE bonds sell for $25 ($50 face value) to $5000 ($10,000 face value). Series HH bonds are issued in $500 to $10,000 denominations.

What fees and charges are involved? Fees and charges on deposit accounts vary with the institution and its product. As a general rule, the higher the balance, the longer the commitment, and the less service, the less the cost to the depositor. Such factors usually are reflected both in rates and in fees and charges. Although CDs involve no fees or charges to buy or to redeem at maturity, the Federal Reserve Board voted in March 1986 to impose a penalty of seven days' interest on amounts withdrawn within the first week from personal CDs. (Institutional CDs were made subject to other penalties for early withdrawal.) Savings bonds involve no fees or charges.

Do they mature, expire, or otherwise terminate? CDs have maturities ranging from 32 days to 10 years. Series EE bonds have adjustable maturities. Series HH bonds mature in 10 years.

Can I sell them quickly? Certain deposit accounts may require notice of withdrawal. CDs may be subject to early withdrawal penalties or the issuer may refuse withdrawal prior to maturity, except in cases of hardship. (Of course, it is usually possible to borrow against such collateral and interest is tax-deductible.) NOW and other savings accounts offer instant liquidity through checkwriting. CDs bought through brokers can be sold in the secondary market. Savings bonds may be redeemed after 6 months, but there may be interest penalties.

How is market value determined and how do I keep track of it? Large CDs traded by dealers and institutional investors and smaller CDs marketed by brokers have secondary market values that rise and fall in inverse relation to prevailing interest rates. There is no secondary market for consumer-size CDs bought directly from banks and other issuing institutions or for savings bonds and deposit accounts.

Investment Objectives

Should I buy these if my objective is capital appreciation? Other than interest compounding, there is no capital gains opportunity except in CDs traded in the secondary market.

Should I buy these if my objective is income? Deposit accounts provide income, although they vary in terms of how rates are determined, how interest is compounded and credited, and how effective annual yields compare competitively. CDs are used for income, but those due in less than one year and zero-coupon CDs are issued on a discount basis—that is, they are sold at less than face value and redeemed at face value. Series EE bonds do not pay interest until maturity and must be held 5 years to receive the full rate on redemption. Series HH bonds pay a fixed rate of 6%.

To what extent do they protect against inflation? To the extent rates move with inflation, deposit accounts offer some protection. Fixed-rate CDs provide none, but short maturities limit risk. Variable-rate CDs provide some protection. Series EE bonds offer some protection because the rate is adjustable. Series HH bonds have a fixed rate and offer none.

Are they suitable for tax-deferred retirement accounts? Deposit accounts are legally eligible, but CDs are a better choice due to their higher yields. Because savings bonds already offer tax deferral, there would be no advantage in putting them in such accounts.

Can I borrow against them? Yes.

Risk Considerations

How assured can I be of getting my full investment back? Most deposits and CDs are insured to $100,000 per depositor by the Bank Insurance Fund (BIF) and the Savings Association Insurance Fund (SAIF)—both are units of the Federal Deposit Insurance Corporation (FDIC)—and by the National Credit Union Administration (NCUA). The FDIC and NCUA are federally sponsored agencies. (Nonmembers are insured by state-backed or private insurers, but check the exact conditions.) Savings bond are direct obligations of the federal government and are risk-free.

How assured is my income? Although rates may in some cases fluctuate, income is very safe because the agencies that insure principal oversee the financial affairs of the institutions.

Are there any other risks unique to these investments? No.

Are they commercially rated? Moody's and other services rate CDs.

Tax Considerations

What tax advantages (or disadvantages) do they offer? Savings bonds are exempt from state and local taxes. Interest on Series EE bonds is tax-deferred until cashed-in or redeemed at maturity; when exchanged for Series HH bonds, interest is tax-deferred until the HH bonds are redeemed. EE bonds used to finance a child's higher education (tuition and fees, but not room and board) are exempt from federal taxes as follows: couples with modified adjusted gross income (income including such items as Social Security and other retirement income) of $60,000 ($40,000 for single taxpayers) *at the time of redemption* may exempt 100% of interest; for higher incomes, the exemption graduates downward and is eliminated entirely at the level of $90,000 for couples ($55,000 for singles). Interest on deposit accounts and CDs is fully taxable.

Economic Considerations

What economic factors most affect buy, hold, and sell decisions? Safety and growth of principal through interest compounding are the main objectives with savings vehicles, although expectations concerning interest rate movements and inflation may guide decisions.

TREASURY SECURITIES (BILLS, BONDS, and NOTES)

United States Treasury securities, called Treasuries for short, are backed by the full faith and credit of the U.S. government and are issued to finance activities ranging from daily cash management to the refinancing of long-term bonded debt.

Investors seeking income thus have a wide choice of maturities, yields, and denominations along with the utmost safety. The government would have to become insolvent before default could occur, and as long as it has the power to create money, that is not a real possibility.

Treasuries also offer excellent liquidity and exemption from taxation at the state and local (but not federal) levels, an advantage that can add significantly to yield in high-tax states and localities.

Being fixed-income securities, however, Treasuries are not immune to the ravages of high inflation, nor are they safe from market risk. When general interest rates move up, the prices of Treasuries, like all fixed-rate investments, move down—unluckily for investors forced to sell prior to maturity in the secondary market. On the other hand, Treasuries, unlike many other fixed-income investments, are not usually callable. With the exception of a recent 20-year issue with a 5-year call provision and some 30-year bonds callable 5 years before maturity, the government cannot force redemption when rates move down.

The major categories of Treasury securities are:

Treasury bills Called T-bills for short, they are issued weekly with 13-week and 26-week maturities and monthly with a 52-week maturity, on a discount basis and in denominations beginning at $10,000 with multiples of $5000 thereafter. They are issued through the Federal Reserve System, and investors may submit tenders either on a competitive basis, specifying terms and risking rejection, or on a noncompetitive basis, in which case the average rate established in the regular auction applies and purchase is assured. T-bills can also be bought for a fee through banks and other dealers.

Treasury bonds and notes These are interest-bearing, paying semi-annually in most cases, and, like T-bills, sold through Federal Reserve banks and branches on a competitive or noncompetitive basis. Maturities of bonds range from 10 to 30 years, those of notes from 2 to 10 years. Bonds and notes can be bought in denominations as low as $1000. Except for 2-year notes, which are usually sold monthly, bonds and notes are offered as the need arises. Of course, outstanding issues with almost any maturity can be bought in the secondary market.

Other Treasury securities, covered elsewhere, include Series EE and HH Savings Bonds and zero-coupon products created by separating the principal and interest coupons from Treasury bonds. A special class, known as flower bonds, is discussed under Tax Considerations below.

Investors may also buy shares of mutual funds or unit investment trusts that invest in portfolios of Treasury securities.

*   *   *

What Is a Treasury Security?

A Treasury security is a negotiable debt obligation of the United States government, backed by its full faith and credit, and issued with various maturities.

Buying, Selling, and Holding

How do I buy and sell it? New issues of bills, bonds, and notes may be purchased through competitive or noncompetitive auction at Federal Reserve banks and branches. They can also be bought and sold at commercial banks, securities broker-dealers, and other financial services companies.

Is there a minimum purchase amount, and what is the price range? Treasury bills are issued in minimum denominations of $10,000 and multiples of $5000 thereafter. Notes and bonds are issued in denominations of $1000, $5000, $10,000, $100,000, and $1 million. Notes due in less than 4 years are usually issued in $5000 denominations.

What fees and charges are involved? Treasury securities bought and redeemed through Federal Reserve banks and branches are without fees. Purchases and sales through banks or broker-dealers involve modest fees (about $25) and/or markups.

Does it mature, expire, or otherwise terminate? Yes. Maturities range from 23 days (cash management bills) to 30 years (bonds).

Can I sell it quickly? Yes; bills, bonds, and notes enjoy an active secondary market and are highly liquid.

How is market value determined and how do I keep track of it? As fixed-income securities, Treasuries rise and fall in price in inverse relation to market interest rates. Because they are risk-free investments, money flows into Treasuries when investors are worried about the credit safety of other debt securities, causing lower yields and higher prices. The financial sections of daily newspapers report new offerings and secondary market yields. The Bureau of Public Debt (Washington, DC 20226) or the Federal Reserve bank or branch in your district will respond to inquiries concerning upcoming offerings.

Investment Objectives

Should I buy this if my objective is capital appreciation? No, but appreciation is possible if market rates decline.

Should I buy this if my objective is income? Yes, particularly Treasuries with longer maturities, but you are sacrificing yield in return for safety. After-tax yields get a boost in high-tax states and localities because interest is not taxed at the state and local levels.

To what extent does it protect against inflation? There is no protection, though short maturities offer less exposure to the risk of inflation.

Is it suitable for tax-deferred retirement accounts? Yes.

Can I borrow against it? Yes, to 90% at most banks and brokers.

Risk Considerations

How assured can I be of getting my full investment back? From the credit standpoint, Treasuries offer the highest degree of safety available. You can be assured of getting your money back at maturity. Should you wish to sell earlier in the secondary market, you may find market prices have declined because of rising market interest rates. (Experts sometimes hedge this risk using interest-rate options, futures, and futures options.) Inflation, of course, erodes dollar values.

How assured is my income? There is virtually no risk the government will default on interest. Some bonds may be callable, terminating interest prematurely. Inflation, of course, can erode the value of fixed-interest payments, and low-yielding securities, like Treasuries, are especially vulnerable in hyperinflation, where the inflation rate can exceed the interest rate.

Are there any other risks unique to this investment? No.

Is it commercially rated? No, since Treasuries are risk-free, there is no need for commercial credit ratings.

Tax Considerations

What tax advantages (or disadvantages) does it offer? Treasuries are fully taxable at the federal level but are exempt from state and local taxes. A special class, called estate tax anticipation bonds or flower bonds, can be used, regardless of cost, at par value in payment of estate taxes, if legally held by the decedent at time of death. Savings bonds, discussed in the section dealing with savings alternatives, are exempt from federal taxes in a specific instance.

Economic Considerations

What economic factors most affect buy, hold, or sell decisions? As with any fixed-income investment, it is best to buy when market rates are high and issues carry a competitive yield. Since prices vary inversely with market interest rates, the holding becomes more attractive as market rates decline. As low-yielding, fixed-income securities, treasuries fare poorly in inflation. Because they are virtually default-proof, they are highly desirable holdings when poor business conditions make other investments vulnerable to default, though yields of Treasuries may decline as a result.

UNIT INVESTMENT TRUST

Like a mutual fund, a unit investment trust (UIT) offers to small investors the advantages of a large, professionally selected and diversified portfolio. Unlike a mutual fund, however, its portfolio is fixed; once structured, it is not actively managed, except for some limited surveillance. It is also self-liquidating, distributing principal as debt securities mature or are redeemed, and paying out the proceeds from equities as they are sold in accordance with predetermined timetables. A one-time sales charge of less than 5% is the only significant cost, and considering this buys you a share in a "millionaire's portfolio," it is one of the attractions.

While sponsors commonly offer instant liquidity as a feature of UITs, liquidity is provided specifically through agreements to make markets in shares or to redeem them; there is not an active secondary market in the public sense, and investors should read the prospectus to determine whether and by what means liquidity provisions exist.

The most common form of UIT is made up of tax-exempt municipal bonds, put together by an investment firm with special expertise in the municipals field. The bonds are deposited with a trustee, usually a bank, which distributes interest and the proceeds from redemptions, calls, and maturities and provides unitholders with audited annual reports. Since unitholders pay taxes as though they were direct investors, portions of income payments representing interest are not taxable, nor are portions representing principal, which are tax-free returns of capital. Capital gains, however, are taxable, technically at the time the trust realizes them, although unitholders commonly recognize them only after their investment in the trust has been recovered from distributions of principal or at the time they sell their shares. It is important to get tax advice on this.

Unit investment trusts are also available with portfolios of money market securities; corporate bonds of different grades; mortgage-backed securities; U.S. government securities; adjustable and fixed-rate preferred stocks; utility common stocks; foreign bonds; replications of stock indexes; and other investments. New varieties of UITs are being created all the time.

Some sponsors offer additional conveniences to investors, including checkwriting, reinvestment options, and exchanging or swapping, for modest fees, among other unit investment trusts under their sponsorship.

*   *   *

What Is a Unit Investment Trust?

A unit investment trust (UIT) is a trust that invests in a fixed portfolio of income-producing securities and sells shares to investors.

Buying, Selling, and Holding

How do I buy and sell it? UITs are bought from sponsoring broker-dealers, who usually stand ready to redeem shares.

Is there a minimum purchase amount, and what is the price range? Shares (units) costing $1000 are typical.

What fees and charges are involved? A sales charge (load) ranging from less than 1% to 5% of your investment (4% is typical, with discounts for volume). An annual fee, usually 0.15%, is factored into the yield. Additional fees (0.30% typically) may apply when the portfolio is insured.

Does it mature, expire, or otherwise terminate? Trusts are self-liquidating. Proceeds are distributed as securities mature or are sold. The life of most UITs is 25 to 30 years, but 10-year trusts are common and some are as short as six months.

Can I sell it quickly? Liquidity is not guaranteed, but it usually exists to some extent because of most sponsors' intentions, once shares are sold, to make markets as an accommodation to holders wishing to sell. Trustees may also redeem shares, but such provisions should be investigated before buying shares. Sponsors may also allow switching into their other investment products at little or no cost.

How is market value determined and how do I keep track of it? Since shares represent units in an investment pool, values are determined by the forces affecting the securities in the pool. Thus trusts composed of fixed-income bonds will increase in value as interest rates decline and vice versa. A trust made up of stocks will be affected by market movements and earnings forecasts for individual stocks, among other factors. Details of a particular trust and its portfolio are set forth in the prospectus that, by law, is provided to investors.

Investment Objectives

Should I buy this if my objective is capital appreciation? UITs usually are set up to provide income (but even with a fixed portfolio, capital gains and losses can result from interest rate movements and other factors). Stock index trusts have capital gains as a primary goal.

Should I buy this if my objective is income? Yes.

To what extent does it protect against inflation? Bond trusts offer no protection; equity trusts and floating-rate trusts offer some.

Is it suitable for tax-deferred retirement accounts? Yes, except those with portfolios of securities that are already tax-exempt.

Can I borrow against it? Yes, subject to Federal Reserve margin rules. The lack of an active secondary market raises a question about ready marketability and the attractiveness of shares as collateral.

Risk Considerations

How assured can I be of getting my full investment back? This varies with the safety of the investments in the trust, government bonds and common equities being at opposite ends of the spectrum. Interest rates may decrease the value of bonds, and therefore of shares, unless held for the life of the trust; market risk is always a question with equities. A growing number of trusts purchase insurance against credit risk.

How assured is my income? Portfolios are well diversified, making income relatively secure.

Are there any other risks unique to this investment? The lack of active management, once the portfolio is established and the shares sold, limits responsive corrective action in the face of adverse portfolio developments. Diversification provides some protection, however.

Is it commercially rated? Yes.

Tax Considerations

What tax advantages (or disadvantages) does it offer? None. UITs are subject to the same taxes (or exemptions) as the investments comprising them. But trusts composed of municipal bonds, some specializing in triple-tax-exempt portfolios for qualified residents, are common, and many taxable UITs are designed for tax-deferred retirement programs.

Economic Considerations

What economic factors most affect buy, hold, or sell decisions? Unit investment trusts are bought with the intention of holding until they self-liquidate. The same considerations that would guide an investor in choosing debt, equity, or money market securities would guide the choice of a particular UIT.

ZERO-COUPON SECURITY

Zero-coupon securities don't pay out their fixed rate of interest like other debt securities; they are issued at deep discounts and accumulate and compound the interest, then pay the full face value at maturity. The attractions for the investor are mainly twofold: (1) They can be bought at very low prices because of the deep discount and (2) Their yield to maturity is locked in, which takes the guesswork out of interest reinvestment.

The mathematical effects of a zero-coupon security, unless one is used to thinking in terms of compound interest over long periods, can seem astonishing: $30.31 invested today in a 12%, 30-year zero-coupon bond will bring $1000 at maturity!

The disadvantages of zeros are that income taxes (unless they are tax-exempt) are payable as interest accrues (and out of cash raised from another source); they are highly volatile; and their value at maturity can erode with inflation. Credit risk, especially with corporate zeros, can be greater than with a regular bond; if the issuer defaults after a certain amount of time has passed, the investor has more to lose, since nothing has been received along the way.

Not surprisingly, a popular use of taxable zeros, with their low purchase prices and automatic compounding, is tax-deferred retirement accounts, where they are sheltered from taxability on imputed interest.

The following are principal types of zeros:

Corporate zero-coupon securities   These are not usually recommended for individual investors because of credit risk and because the yield tends not to be competitive in relation to the risk. One explanation is that these issues are marketed to investors who do not have to pay taxes on imputed interest, such as foreign investors.

Strips and STRIPS   Strips are U.S. Treasury or municipal securities that brokerage firms have separated into principal and interest which, represented by certificates (the actual securities are held in escrow), are marketed as zero-coupon securities under proprietary acronyms like Salomon Brothers' CATS (Certificates of Accrual on Treasury Securities) and M-CATS (Certificates of Accrual on Tax-exempt Securities). Although the obligor is actually the broker, the escrow arrangement assures a high degree of security. Free of risk altogether are STRIPS, Separate Trading of Registered Interest and Principal of Securities, the Treasury's acronym for its own zero-coupon securities. STRIPS are Treasury bonds issued in the traditional way but separated into interest and principal components at the discretion of bondholders using book entry accounts at Federal Reserve banks.

Strips of mortgage-backed securities placed privately or by government agencies are also available. To enter the Federal Reserve's book-entry system, however, federal agency strips must satisfy a technical-ity requiring a minimum of 1% of the principal of the underlying loans; in other words, they can't be 100% interest.

Municipal zero-coupon securities   These securities are issued by state and local governments and are usually exempt from federal taxes and from state taxes in the state of issue. They provide a convenient way of providing for the future goals of high-bracket investors who get an after-tax benefit from their lower interest rates. One caveat, however: some are issued with call features, which can defeat the purpose of a zero from the investor's standpoint, so avoid those.

Zero-coupon convertibles   Introduced in the mid-1980s, these convertibles come in two varieties: one, issued with a put option, converts into common stock, thus providing growth potential; the other, usually a municipal bond, converts into an interest-paying bond, thus enabling the investor to lock in a rate, then, 15 years later, to begin collecting interest.

*   *   *

What Is a Zero-Coupon Security?

A zero-coupon security is a debt security or instrument that does not pay periodic interest but is issued at a deep discount and redeemed at face value.

Buying, Selling, and Holding

How do I buy and sell it? Through a securities broker-dealer and many banks. Some products are proprietary, available only at the dealers marketing them.

Is there a minimum purchase amount, and what is the price range? Because of their deep discount, zero-coupon securities can be bought quite cheaply; a $1000 20-year bond yielding 12% would cost about $97, for example. Broker-dealer minimums of 10 bonds or more are common.

What fees and charges are involved? A broker commission or a dealer spread.

Does it mature, expire or otherwise terminate? Yes; zero-coupon securities have a specified maturity, although some may have put options or be convertible into common stock or interest-bearing bonds. Some zeros have been issued with call features.

Can I sell it quickly? Investors generally buy zeros intending to hold them until maturity. Should you need to sell, the broker-dealer you bought it from can probably make a market, although you would certainly pay a higher transaction cost. Zeros based on treasury securities are somewhat more liquid than corporate or municipal zeros.

How is market value determined and how do I keep track of it? Zeros, being essentially fixed-rate investments, rise and fall in inverse relation to interest rates and are especially volatile. Zeros are listed along with regular bonds in daily newspapers.

Investment Objectives

Should I buy zeros if my objective is capital appreciation? Investing one sum of money and getting back a larger sum is what zeros are all about, so the answer is really yes. Strictly speaking, however, the appreciation is not a capital gain, but is rather compounded interest. Capital gains are possible from secondary market sales after interest rates have declined, but zeros are not usually traded for capital gain.

Should I buy this if my objective is income? No. Zeros pay no periodic income.

To what extent does it protect against inflation? As fixed-rate investments, zeros generally offer no inflation protection. Zeros convertible into common stock offer some.

Is it suitable for tax-deferred retirement accounts? Because zeros are taxed as though annual interest were being paid, they are considered ideal candidates for tax-deferred plans. An exception, of course, would be municipal zeros, which are tax-exempt anyway.

Can I borrow against it? Yes, subject to Federal Reserve margin rules and lender policies.

Risk Considerations

How assured can I be of getting my full investment back? Corporate and municipal issues, unless insured, vary with the credit of the issuer, so credit ratings are important. Treasury issues that are stripped (split into two parts—principal and interest) by brokerage houses and marketed separately as zero-coupon securities represented by receipts or certificates, are highly safe as long as the broker holds the underlying Treasury security in escrow, as is the practice. Some municipal strips issued by brokers (e.g., M-CATS) have indirect U.S. government backing, since they represent prefundings invested in Treasury securities. Direct Treasury zeros (STRIPS) are risk-free. Zeros sold in the secondary market are susceptible to interest rate risk and a wide dealer spread. Of course, full investment, when talking zeros, means face value, not the small amount originally invested, since money is assumed to have a time value.

How assured is my income? Zeros do not pay income; the income return is built into the redemption value.

Are there any other risks unique to this investment? Other than the small risk of an issuing firm going bankrupt in the case of receipts and certificates issued by brokerages, the unique risk of zeros has to do with the degree of exposure; should a zero default, there is more to lose compared with an interest-bearing security, where some portion of interest would have been paid out and presumably been reinvested. Some municipal issues may be callable, which largely defeats the purpose for which most investors hold zeros. Mortgage-backed strips respond to the prepayment experience of the underlying loans. If rates fall, prepayments increase. This shortens the life of strips and decreases the amount of interest earned.

Is it commercially rated? Municipal and corporate issues are rated.

Tax Considerations

What tax advantages (or disadvantages) does it offer? Interest is taxable as it accrues each year, just as if it were paid out. An exception, of course, are tax-exempt municipal zeros, which may also be exempt from taxes in the state of issue. U.S. government zeros are taxable at the federal level but exempt from state and local taxes.

Economic Considerations

What economic factors most affect buy, hold, and sell decisions? Zeros are purchased based on competitive yield considerations and are normally held until maturity, their appeal being a locked-in interest rate as opposed to a yield that varies with the reinvestment value of periodic interest payments in changing markets. Should it be necessary to sell in the secondary market, lower rates mean higher prices. Considerations governing convertible zeros are complex and vary with the provisions of the issue.

PART II

How to Read an
Annual Report

How to Read a Quarterly Report

HOW TO READ AN ANNUAL REPORT

Weekend sailors know an axiom that if you can understand a dinghy you can sail a yacht. It's all in grasping the fundamentals. Annual reports are the yachts of corporate communications, and in full regalia they can be as formidable as they are majestic. Fashioned by accountants and lawyers as well as marketers and executives, and costing major companies as much as $250,000 to $750,000 to publish, the reports are aimed at a variety of audiences—stockholders, potential stockholders, securities analysts, lenders, customers, and even employees. Essentially, however, they are financial statements, and if you can understand the basics, you will find that the rest is elaboration, much of which is legally required and very helpful. Of course, there are other parts that are simply embellishment, and those you take with a grain of salt. First, let's look at a "dinghy."

Basically, a financial statement comprises a *balance sheet* and an *income statement*. Exhibit 1 illustrates a statement reduced to "bare timbers."

EXHIBIT 1
BALANCE SHEET
December 31, 19XX

Cash/near cash	**5**	Accounts and notes payable	15
Accounts receivable	**20**	Accrued liabilities	5
Inventory	35	Current portion, long-term debt	5
CURRENT ASSETS	**60**	**CURRENT LIABILITIES**	**25**
		Long-term liabilities	25
		TOTAL LIABILITIES	**50**
Net fixed assets	35		
Other assets	5	Capital stock	10
		Retained earnings	40
		NET WORTH	**50**
TOTAL ASSETS	**$100**	**TOTAL LIABILITIES AND NET WORTH**	**$100**

THE BASIC BALANCE SHEET

A balance sheet (also called a statement of financial position or a statement of condition) is simply the status of a company's accounts at one moment in time, usually the last business day of a quarter or year. It is often compared to a snapshot, in contrast to a motion picture. On one side, it lists what the company owns—its assets. On the other side it lists what the company owes—its liabilities—and its net worth, or owners' equity, which is what investors have put into the firm plus earnings that have been retained in the business rather than paid out in dividends. The two sides are always equal. Even if a firm were insolvent—that is, owed more than it had in assets—the sides would be equalized by showing a negative (or deficit) net worth. (A minor technical point: Balance sheets can be presented with opposing sides, as just described, which is known as the account form, or with the assets above the liabilities and owners' equity, which is called the report form.)

EXHIBIT 1

INCOME STATEMENT
for the year ended December 31, 19XX

SALES		**$110**
Cost of goods sold	80	
Depreciation	5	
Selling, general, and administrative expenses	15	
	100	
NET OPERATING PROFIT		**10**
Other income or expense	1	
Interest expense	2	
Income taxes	2	
NET INCOME	5	**5**

THE BASIC INCOME STATEMENT

The income statement, which goes by such other names as statement of profit and loss, operating statement, and earnings statement, reports the results of operations over a specified period of time—12 months in the case of an annual report. As customers are billed, and as the costs and expenses of producing goods, running the business, and creating sales are incurred and recorded, the information summarized in the income statement is accumulated.

The income statement will be discussed below in more detail; it is enough for now to understand that its highlights are sales (or revenues), net operating profit (or operating income), and net income. It is this last amount—popularly called the bottom line because it comes after interest expense, unusual income and charges, and income taxes—that is available to pay dividends to shareholders or to be kept in the business as retained earnings.

A word about one expense item, called depreciation, which is important to understand because it is a major factor in cash flow, the net amount of cash taken into the business during a given period and the cash paid out during that period. Depreciation, which is sometimes combined in the figure for cost of goods sold, is merely a bookkeeping entry that reduces income without reducing cash. In other words, depreciation is a noncash expense, and it is added back to net income to determine a company's cash earnings. Net income plus depreciation equals cash flow from operations. More about depreciation and cash flow later.

BASIC RATIO TESTS

With the foregoing information on balance sheets and income statements, it is possible to look at a firm's year-to-year financial statements and make some tentative judgments about the firm's basic financial health and operating trends, particularly if you can compare the figures with those of other firms in a comparable industry. An in-depth look at important financial ratios is at the end of the discussion of the annual report, but much can be learned at a glance by applying the following basic ratio tests.

Current Ratio The current ratio is current assets divided by current liabilities. Current assets are assets expected to be converted to cash within a normal business cycle (usually one year), and current liabilities are obligations that must be paid during the same short-term period. For a manufacturing company (standards vary from industry to industry), a ratio of between 1.5 to 1 and 2 to 1—$1.50 to $2.00 of current assets for each $1.00 of current liabilities—is generally considered an indication that the firm is sufficiently liquid. In other words, there is enough net working capital (the difference between the two figures) to ensure that the firm can meet its current obligations and operate comfortably.

It is important that a company have this cushion because the liquidity of current assets, with the exception of cash and its equivalents, cannot be taken for granted; receivables can become slow or uncollectible (although a reserve for expected write-offs is normally provided) and inventory can lose value or become unsalable. Such things happen in recessions, and can result from poor credit, purchasing, or marketing decisions. Liabilities, unfortunately, remain constant. Of course, a company can have too much liquidity, suggesting inefficient use of cash resources, shrinking operations, or even vulnerability to a takeover attempt by an outside party. Well-run companies are lean, not fat.

Quick Ratio The quick ratio, which is also known as the acid-test ratio, is the current ratio, with inventory, its least liquid and riskiest component, excluded. It is calculated by adding cash, near-cash (for instance, marketable securities), and accounts receivable (sometimes collectively termed monetary assets), and dividing by current liabilities. Assuming no negative trends are revealed in year-to-year comparisons, a ratio of between .50 to 1 and 1 to 1 generally signifies good health, depending on the quality of the accounts receivable.

Average Collection Period A quick way of testing accounts receivable quality is to divide annual sales by 360 and divide the result into the accounts receivable. That tells you the average number of days it takes to collect an account. Since terms of sale in most industries are 30 days, a figure of 30 to 60 would indicate normal collections and basically sound receivables—at least up to the date of the statement. It may be helpful to compare a company's figure with that of other firms in the same industry.

Inventory Turnover Inventory turnover ratio tells the approximate number of times inventory is sold and replaced over a 12 month period and can be a tipoff, when compared with prior years' figures or comparative industry data, to unhealthy accumulations. Inventory should be kept adequate but trim, because it ties up costly working capital and carries market risks. To calculate turnover, divide the balance sheet inventory into sales. (*Note:* Industry comparative data published by Dun & Bradstreet and other firms providing financial data on companies compute this ratio using sales, not cost of goods sold. While cost of goods sold, because it does not include profit, produces a purer result, it is necessary to use sales for the sake of comparability.) As a general rule, high inventory turnover reflects efficient inventory management, but there are exceptions. A firm may be stockpiling raw materials in anticipation of shortages, for instance, or preparing to meet firm orders not yet reflected as sales. If inventory turnover is falling compared to prior years or is out of line with industry data, you should investigate the reasons. Year-to-year comparisons of inventory turnover are of particular significance in high volume–low profit margin industries such as garment manufacturing and retailing.

Debt-to-Equity Ratio The debt-to-equity ratio can be figured in several ways, but for our purposes it is total liabilities divided by net worth. It measures reliance on creditors to finance operations and is one of several capitalization ratios summarized below. Although financial leverage—using other people's money to increase earnings per share—is desirable to a point, too much debt can be a danger sign. Debt involves contractual payments that must be made regardless of earnings levels; it must usually be refinanced when it matures at prevailing (perhaps much higher) money costs; and it has a prior claim on assets in the event of liquidation. Moreover, debt can limit a company's ability to finance additional growth and can adversely affect a firm's credit rating, with implications for the market value of shares. What is considered a proper debt-to-equity ratio varies with the type of company. Those with highly stable earnings, such as many utilities, are able to afford higher ratios than companies with volatile or cyclical earnings. For a typical industrial company, a debt-to-equity ratio significantly higher than 1 to 1 should be looked at carefully.

Operating Profit Margin This figure, obtained by dividing a firm's net operating profit by sales, is a measure of operating efficiency. (Analysts sometimes add depreciation back into net operating profit since it is not a cash expense.) Year-to-year comparisons can be a reflection on cost control or on purchasing and pricing policies. Comparisons with other firms in the same industry provide insight into a company's ability to compete.

Return on Equity This is the bottom line as a percentage of net worth (net worth is divided into net income), and it tells how much the company is earning on shareholder investment. Compared with the figures of prior years and similar companies, it is a measure of overall efficiency—a reflection on financial as well as operational management. But it can also be affected by factors beyond the control of management, such as general economic conditions or higher tax rates. And be suspicious of a firm with abnormally high returns; it could be in for competition from firms willing to sacrifice returns to gain a larger market share. As a rule of thumb, return on equity should be between 10% and 20%.

By applying the foregoing ratio tests to a company's basic balance sheet and income statement, particularly with the help of data on the company's prior years and on other companies in the same industry, you get a sense of whether the company's financial structure and operational trends are essentially sound. There is, however, a great deal you still don't know, such as:

- How reliable are the numbers?
- Are results affected by changes in accounting methods?
- Have there been changes in the company's top management?
- From what product lines did sales and profits largely derive?
- Did any special events affect last year's results?

- What new products are on the horizon?
- Are there any lawsuits or other contingent liabilities that could affect future results or asset values?
- To what extent are the company's operations multinational, and what is its exposure to foreign exchange fluctuations and/or political risk?
- If the company is labor-intensive, what is the status of its union contracts?
- What is the status of the company's debt? Is any financing or refinancing planned that could affect share values?
- How sensitive is the company to changes in interest rates?
- What were the sources and applications of cash?
- Are any major capital expenditures (for instance, real estate, machinery, equipment) being planned? How are existing fixed assets depreciated?
- How much is allocated to research and development?
- What other operational or financial changes has management planned?
- Does the company have a broad base of customers, or a few major customers?
- To what extent is the company dependent on government contracts?
- What is the company's pension liability, and what are its pension assets? Has it adequately provided for other postretirement employee obligations?

WHAT THE ANNUAL REPORT INCLUDES

The majority of annual reports of major public companies include a table of contents on the inside front cover. The following is typical:

Contents
Highlights
Letter to Shareholders
Review of Operations
Financial Statements
  Report of Independent Accountants
  Consolidated Financial Statements
  Statement of Consolidated Cash Flows
  Notes to Financial Statements
  Supplementary Tables
  Management's Discussion and Analysis
Investor's Information
Directors and Officers

Highlights

The highlights greet you at the start of an annual report. Often including charts and other graphics, they present basic information in a clear, comparative way that requires little explanation. At the very least, you should expect to find the company's total sales for the past two years and its net income, expressed both as a total and on a per-share basis. Needless to say, upward trends (usually, but with exceptions) are positive and downward trends negative. But what is most important to understand is that the company and its public relations advisors can include here whatever other information they feel will create the desired impression on the shareholder. That usually means you can expect to find highlights that add up to a positive impression, although it has become lately a matter both of fashion and good business to include a downward trend or two for the sake of credibility. Basically, though, what you can expect to find highlighted, aside from the unavoidable, are the statistics of which the company is most proud. If dividends were up, they will probably be highlighted; if they were down, the same space might be devoted to an increase in research and development (R&D) expenditures, with the implicit promise of a future payoff for shareholders.

Occasionally, you will see information about common shares presented on a primary basis and on a basis assuming full dilution. Dilution occurs when an increased number of shares compete for the same amount of earnings, and it is a potential development when a company has convertible bonds, convertible preferred stock, warrants, or other securities outstanding that, if converted or exercised, would result in the issuance of additional shares. When dilution would significantly affect shareholders, companies are required to report earnings per share on both bases: before dilution (primary) and assuming conversion or exercise of all dilutive securities.

Should you encounter any other unfamiliar figures in the highlights, consult the Ratio Analysis Summary at the end of this discussion of an annual report.

Letter to Shareholders

In the many spoofs that have been written about corporate annual reports and their reputation for obfuscation, the least mercy has been reserved for the letter to shareholders. This review of the year just passed and look at the year ahead leads off the textual part of the report. It is usually signed by the chairperson and president and is often accompanied by a picture of the two together, suggesting amity not always characteristic of their day-to-day relationship.

While it is certainly true that the letter to shareholders is worded to put the best face on the past year's results and to soothe any anxieties that might be aroused by the financial figures to follow, it is nonetheless a statement of management's intentions and, when compared to prior years' messages, a test of management's credibility. Although it is not an audited, formal part of the report, it purports to be a serious comment on the year's results and their financial impact, a report that puts into perspective the major developments affecting shareholders, a statement of management's position on relevant social issues, and an expression of management's plans for the company's future. An impressive letter is one that compares past predictions with actual results and explains in a candid way the disappointments as well as the successes. Be wary of euphemisms (a "challenging" year was probably a bad one) and wording that is vague or qualified; a product area "positioned for growth" may sound promising, but it's not growing yet. If it were, the letter would say so. Much of the meaning of the letter to shareholders is between the lines.

Review of Operations

This review section consists of pictures and prose and often occupies the bulk of the pages of an annual report. Frequently slick, public relations-oriented, and designed to impress a corporation's various publics, the review can nonetheless be a valuable source of information about the company's products, services, facilities, and future direction. Unfortunately, it is also sometimes designed to divert the reader's attention from unpleasant realities. Be suspicious of reviews that stress the future and give the present short shrift or that are built around themes, such as the loyalty of employees or the company's role in building a stronger America. Also, what is not discussed can be more significant that what is discussed. Lack of reference to an aspect of operations described in the preceding year's annual report as an area of rapid growth and expansion may indicate that the company's expectations were not fulfilled and a write-off may be on the horizon. By and large, though, companies are responding to pressures for greater straightforwardness in the way they present themselves. In addition, companies these days are required to provide detailed financial information about the various segments contributing to their sales and profits. Although that information appears later in the supplementary financial data, it allows you to relate the activities being "promoted" to actual results and thus to evaluate the financial significance of different product areas. The Securities and Exchange Commission (SEC) has imposed stricter disclosure requirements in recent years, and these requirements have had a generally positive effect in terms of making annual reports more credible documents.

Financial Statements

Financial statements are, of course, the basic purpose of annual reports, and as the result both of expanded SEC disclosure regulation and companies' own interest in satisfying the information requirements of securities and credit analysts, financial statements have evolved over the years into presentations that elaborate substantially on the basic balance sheet and income statements. Reporting has also become more complex due to the complexity of the companies themselves, which have become diversified in terms both of product lines and geography, with a trend toward multinational operations involving political and currency risks.

Report of Independent Accountants: This report, also known as the auditor's opinion, is sometimes found at the beginning of the financial statement section and sometimes at the end, but it should be the first thing you read. Numbers are only numbers, and the opinion of an independent accounting firm, which is legally required of public companies, certifies that the financial statements were examined and validated. A "clean" or unqualified opinion—we'll get to what a qualified opinion means in a minute—typically reads as shown in Exhibit 2.

EXHIBIT 2

Report of Independent Accountants

To the Shareholders of XYZ Corporation:

We have audited the accompanying consolidated balance sheets of XYZ Corporation and subsidiaries as of December 31, 19X9 and 19X8 and the related consolidated statements of earnings, shareholders' equity, and cash flows for each of the three years in the period ended December 31, 19X9. These financial statements are the responsibility of the Company's management. Our responsibility is to express an opinion on these financial statements based on our audits.

We conducted our audits in accordance with generally accepted auditing standards. Those standards require that we plan and perform the audit to obtain reasonable assurance about whether the financial statements are free of material misstatement. An audit includes examining, on a test basis, evidence supporting the amounts and disclosures in the financial statements. An audit also includes assessing the accounting principles used and significant estimates made by management, as well as evaluating the overall financial statement presentation. We believe that our audits provide a reasonable basis for our opinion.

In our opinion, the financial statements referred to above present fairly, in all material respects, the consolidated financial position of XYZ Corporation and subsidiaries as of 19X9 and 19X8, and the consolidated results of their operations and their cash flows for each of the three years in the period ended December 31, 19X9, in conformity with generally accepted accounting principles.

The above format was adopted by the American Institute of Certified Public Accountants (AIPCA) in 1988 and departs significantly from traditional form.

Until 1988, the words "subject to" in the opinion paragraph were a widely recognized red flag. Such a "qualified opinion" meant the auditors had a reservation about the fairness of the presentation. Typical reasons for qualifying might be a pending lawsuit that, if lost, would materially affect the firm's finances; an indeterminable tax liability relating to an unusual transaction; or an inability to confirm a portion of inventory because of an inaccessible location. Although a qualified opinion was not necessarily negative, it was clear warning that warranted investigation and often led to negative comments by securities analysts with implications for the stock price.

The new format uses explanation rather than qualification where exceptions to "present fairly" are not clear-cut. It is thus possible to have an opinion that is clean but followed by explanations of potential problems.

Advocates of the new form say such disclosure is preferable to a qualified opinion, which implies trouble when it may not materialize. Proponents of the traditional form feel that the reader has inherited the burden of evaluating the seriousness of a potential development and been deprived of the auditor's more competent judgment. In any event, "modified opinions" challenge the reader to understand the issues raised. Explanations are usually found in footnotes to the financial statements and/or the management's discussion and analysis section.

Qualified opinions since 1988 include a statement that "except for" specified problems or departures from generally accepted accounting principles, the report would present fairly the company's financial position. In contrast to traditional qualified opinions, which were fairly common, such language is rare, since it means the Securities and Exchange Commission will require the company to resolve the problem or make the accounting treatment acceptable.

Even rarer are two other types of auditor's opinion, the disclaimer of opinion and the adverse opinion. A disclaimer of opinion states that an opinion is not possible because of a material restriction on the scope of the audit (for example, an inability to verify inventory quantities) or a material uncertainty about the accounts (for example, doubt about the company's continued existence as a going concern). An adverse opinion states that the company's financial statements do not present fairly the financial position or results of operations in accordance with generally accepted accounting principles. Either type of opinion is cause for concern, but you are unlikely to run into these types of opinions since the company will normally take the auditor's advice and make the necessary corrections.

You should be wary of a company's figures if the company regularly replaces the independent auditors. Such conduct could indicate that the company is opinion shopping—looking for auditors whose approach would produce the most favorable sales and earnings figures for the company and thereby perhaps hide problem areas or potential problem areas.

Report by Management: Usually accompanying the Report of Independent Accountants is a similar Report by Management certifying responsibility for the information examined by the accounting firm. This section attests to the objectivity and integrity of the data, estimates, and judgments on which the financial statements were based. It alludes to the company's internal controls and oversight responsibility of the board of directors for the financial statements as carried out through an audit committee composed of directors who are not employees. It is sometimes signed by the chief financial officer of the company and/or the chief executive officer.

Consolidated Financial Statements—Part 1: The Balance Sheet: In the following pages, we will discuss the financial statement of our hypothetical company, XYZ Corporation. As required, the statement presents comparative balance sheets as of the company's two most recent fiscal year ends and income statements for the past three years. Many variations exist on the accounts discussed below, and there are as many unique items as there are companies. But if you grasp the following, you will understand the basis of the vast majority of balance sheets and income statements.

First, an item-by-item explanation of XYZ's balance sheet (see Exhibit 3).

Current Assets

Cash and Cash Equivalents

Cash requires little explanation; it is cash in the bank, on its way to the bank, or in the till. Cash equivalents, sometimes listed separately under cash and called marketable securities, represent idle funds invested in highly safe, highly liquid securities with a maturity, when acquired, of less than 3 months. Examples would be U.S. Treasury bills, certificates of deposit, and commercial paper. They are carried at the lower of their cost or market value. If they are shown at cost, their market value is indicated parenthetically or in a footnote.

Accounts and Notes Receivable

These are customer balances owing. When a company makes a sale, a customer is required either to pay in cash (cash sales) or, as in the majority of cases, within credit terms (credit sales), which tend to be standardized within industries but are typically 30 days and rarely more than 90 days.

Accounts receivable—sometimes called just receivables—are credit accounts that are not yet received. Often there is a reference to a footnote containing an aging schedule, a breakdown of accounts in terms of where they stand in relation to their due dates. This reveals delinquency and trends and is a valuable tool for analysts. Of course, a company expects a certain percentage of uncollectible accounts and, based on its historical experience and current policies (it might, for example decide to liberalize credit policy to boost sales), it sets up a reserve (or allowance) for bad debts, which is deducted from gross receivables to arrive at the balance sheet value. This is either noted on the balance sheet or explained in a footnote. Special attention should be paid to accounts receivable if a company does a significant percentage of its business with a few key customers. If any of these key customers were to have financial problems, the worth of the receivables carried on the company's books would quickly be in jeopardy.

Notes receivable normally account for a small portion of the total and usually represent cases in which special terms were granted and obligations were documented with promissory notes. If a short-term note receivable arose out of a loan or the sale of property or some other nontrade transaction, it would, if material, normally be shown separately or footnoted.

Inventories

This figure, when a company is engaged in manufacturing, is a combination of finished goods, work in process, and raw materials. Conservative accounting practice requires that inventories be carried at the lower of cost or market value, but there are different methods of inventory valuation, principally First In, First Out (FIFO) and Last In, First Out (LIFO).

Under the FIFO method, inventory is assumed to be sold in the chronological order in which it was purchased. Under the LIFO method, the reverse is true: The goods sold in a period are assumed to be those most recently bought. When prices are rising or falling, the difference is reflected in the balance sheet value of inventory. A company using the LIFO method during a period of inflation, because its cost of goods sold reflects the most recent—and higher—prices, will show lower profits on its income statement and a lower balance sheet inventory, since its ending inventory remains valued at older (lower) prices. Because LIFO produces lower taxable income in times of inflation, it is the method adopted by a majority of companies in recent years. Thus, the balance sheet inventories of these companies are undervalued—in other words, they have a "LIFO cushion." It is important to remember that *de*flation would produce the opposite result. An explanation of inventory valuation methods (or, significantly, any change in methods) is provided in the footnotes to the statements, which will also explain adjustments required by the tax law changes.

A company's inventory figure cannot be analyzed in a vacuum. To determine if a company is maintaining adequate inventory control, relate the inventory figure to the growth in sales. Inventory growth should keep pace with sales growth, not exceed it. A buildup of inventory relative to sales should be viewed with skepticism.

Prepaid Expenses

This account represents expenses paid in advance, such as rent, insurance, subscriptions, or utilities, that are capitalized—that is, recognized as asset values, and gradually written off as expenses, as their benefit is realized during the current accounting period. If the amount is important, this account is usually deducted from current assets in computing the current ratio. However, it usually represents an insignificant percentage of current assets and is thus ignored for analytical purposes.

Net Fixed Assets

Property, Plant and Equipment

This section of the balance sheet lists the company's fixed assets, sometimes called capital assets or long-term assets. These assets include land, buildings, machinery and equipment, furniture and fixtures, and leasehold improvements—relatively permanent assets that are used in the production of income. The word tangible is sometimes used in describing these assets, to distinguish them from intangible assets (described below), which similarly produce economic benefits for more than a year but which lack physical substance.

Fixed assets are carried—that is, recorded on the books of the company and therefore reported on its balance sheet—at original cost (the cost the company incurred to acquire them) less accumulated depreciation—the cumulative amount of that original cost that the company has written off through annual depreciation expenses charged to income. Land, however, because it is assumed to have unlimited useful life, is not depreciated. (Companies engaged in mining and other extractive industries, whose capital assets represent natural resources, enjoy depletion allowances, a concept similar to depreciation write-offs.) As a result of depreciation write-downs and inflation, it is not unusual for the book value of a company's fixed assets to be considerably lower than their market value. On the other hand, market value is an indication of what it will cost to keep fixed assets up to date and maintain sufficient capacity to support sales growth. The relationship between sales levels and capital expenditures is therefore an important factor in evaluating a firm's viability. However, businesses vary in terms of how capital-intensive they are; manufacturers rely more on fixed assets to produce sales than wholesalers, for example.

The existence of fully depreciated assets on a company's balance sheet may signal that the company is a likely candidate for a takeover attempt or a leveraged buyout. The company's plant, for instance, has most likely appreciated in market value over the years and the depreciated basis on which it is carried on the balance sheet may have no relationship to reality. Thus, new owners could in part finance the purchase of the company by selling some assets at their higher market value.

EXHIBIT 3

XYZ CORPORATION
Balance Sheet
As of December 31
(Dollars in Millions)

	19X9	19X8
ASSETS		
Cash and cash equivalents	7.6	7.0
Accounts and notes receivable	10.2	9.5
Inventories	23.0	20.9
Prepaid expenses	.3	.2
Total Current Assets	**41.1**	37.6
Property, plant and equipment	83.3	79.4
Less: Accumulated Depreciation	23.5	21.3
Net Fixed Assets	**59.8**	58.1
Other assets	3.8	3.0
Intangible assets	.9	.9
TOTAL ASSETS	**105.6**	99.6
LIABILITIES AND SHAREHOLDERS' EQUITY		
Accounts payable	4.2	4.3
Notes payable	.8	—
Accrued liabilities	3.2	2.7
Federal income taxes payable	8.2	7.1
Current portion (maturity) of long-term debt	.7	.8
Dividends payable	1.4	.9
Total Current Liabilities	**18.5**	15.8
Other liabilities	2.0	1.4
Long-term debt	16.2	17.0
Deferred federal income taxes	.9	.7
TOTAL LIABILITIES	**37.6**	34.9
6% cumulative preferred stock ($100 par value; authorized and outstanding: 50,000 shares)	5.0	5.0
Common stock ($10 par value; authorized 2,500,000 shares; outstanding 1,555,000 shares)	15.6	15.6
Capital surplus	8.2	8.2
Retained earnings	39.2	35.9
TOTAL STOCKHOLDERS' EQUITY	**68.0**	64.7
TOTAL LIABILITIES AND STOCKHOLDERS' EQUITY	**105.6**	99.6

Other Assets

This category can include any number of items such as cash surrender value of life insurance policies taken out to insure the lives of key executives; notes receivable after one year; long-term advance payments; small properties not used in daily business operations; and minority stock ownership in other companies or in subsidiaries that for some reason are not consolidated. Additional types of assets, if significant, would be discussed in the footnotes.

Another category of other assets, which is sometimes broken out separately (as in our example), is generally called intangible assets. These are nonphysical rights or resources presumed to represent an advantage to the firm in the marketplace. The most common intangibles are (1) goodwill and (2) a grouping typically labeled patents, trademarks, and copyrights.

Goodwill refers to a company's worth as an operating entity, or going concern— the prestige and visibility of its name, the morale of its employees, the loyalty of its customers, and other going-concern values. These are values beyond the book value of the firm's assets. Thus, when a company is purchased at a price exceeding its book value, the difference—the value of its goodwill—represents a real cost to the acquiring company. Goodwill, though intangible and abstract, *can* be valued. Because it has no liquidation value, however, it is classified as an intangible asset and must be amortized (written off) over time, in accordance with generally accepted accounting principles. As with fixed assets and depreciation, this is done by annual noncash charges to income. Unlike the case of depreciation deductions, however, there is no tax benefit to the company when intangibles are written off.

Patents, trademarks and copyrights, the other most common intangible assets, have economic value in the sense that they translate into profits, but their carrying value is based on their cost. Being intangibles, they are written off over what accounting practice deems to be their useful lives.

Other intangible assets might include capitalized advertising costs, organization costs, licenses, permits of various sorts, brand names, and franchises.

Because intangible assets are assumed not to have value in liquidation, they are excluded from most ratios used in analyzing values. The term tangible net worth is used to mean shareholder equity less intangible assets.

Current Liabilities

Accounts Payable

This account represents amounts owed to suppliers for raw materials and other goods, supplies, and services purchased on credit for use in the normal operating cycle of the business. In other words, one company's account payable is another company's account receivable. As with receivables, conventional credit terms vary from industry to industry, but 30 days is standard and anything over 90 days is the exception (except in highly seasonal industries, such as garment manufacturing, where longer-term dating is commonplace and liquidity is provided by cashing accounts receivable with finance companies known as factors). The level of accounts payable should vary with sales levels, or, more specifically, with the amount of annual purchases—a part of the cost of goods sold. Any bulging of accounts payable in relation to purchases could mean a firm is relying to an unhealthy extent on trade suppliers as a source of working capital.

Notes Payable

These are usually amounts due banks or financial institutions on short-term loans, often under lines of credit. A line of credit is an arrangement by which a company may borrow working capital up to a limit, and details are usually covered in the footnotes. Notes payable may also be due suppliers under special credit arrangements.

Accrued Liabilities

Accrued liabilities arise when an expense is recognized as an obligation but the cash has not yet actually been paid out. Expenses commonly reflected in this account include payroll, commissions, rent, interest, taxes, and other routine expenses.

Federal Income Taxes Payable

This account is similar to accrued liabilities, but is usually broken out in recognition of its importance. (It is to be distinguished from the account called deferred federal income taxes, a noncurrent liability discussed below.)

Current Portion (Maturity) of Long-Term Debt

When a company has a long-term debt obligation that requires regular payments, the amount due in the next 12 months is recorded here as a current liability.

Dividends Payable

These represent dividends that have been declared by the board of directors but have not been paid. Dividends become an obligation when they are declared, and are normally paid quarterly. They include both preferred and common dividends.

Long-term Liabilities

These are debt obligations due after one year. Included are term loans from financial institutions, mortgages, and debentures (unsecured bonds), as well as capital lease obligations, pension liabilities, and estimated liabilities under long-term warranties. Details are provided in footnotes.

Depending on a company's accounting practices, long-term liabilities may also include an item called deferred federal income taxes. This is often due to the fact that companies may use different rules for tax purposes and reporting purposes, and this creates timing differences. For example, a company using accelerated depreciation for tax purposes would get large depreciation write-offs in the early years of an asset's life, thus saving taxes, but would have higher taxable income in the later years. For reporting purposes, however, the company might wish to use the straight line method of depreciation, which each year produces equal (and lower) charges, thus resulting in higher reported earnings. The amount of taxes deferred are shown on the statement used for reporting purposes (the annual report) as deferred federal income taxes.

Shareholders' Equity

This section of the balance sheet represents the owner's interest—the value of assets after creditors, who have a prior legal claim, have all been paid. It includes accounts for preferred stock, common stock, capital surplus, and retained earnings.

Preferred Stock

Not all companies issue preferred stock, and it exists in several varieties. Several general characteristics are particularly notable: It usually pays a fixed dividend that must be paid before common dividends can be paid; it has precedence over common stock in the distribution of assets in liquidation; and if it is cumulative, unpaid dividends accumulate and must be paid in full before common dividends can be declared.

In recent years companies have used preferred stock as part of antitakeover programs. Referred to as poison-pill preferreds, these shares are created when a hostile takeover attempt is imminent. The new class of preferred stock is designed to raise the cost of the acquisition to a point where it may be abandoned by the company attempting the takeover. You should check whether a company has issued preferred specifically to fend off a takeover attempt and, if so, try to determine the implications such preferred may have for common shareholders.

Common Stock

Shares of common stock are the basic units of ownership in a corporation. Common shareholders follow behind creditors and preferred shareholders in claims on assets and therefore take all the risks inherent in the business. But, with rare exceptions, they vote in elections of directors and on all important matters, and while they may or may not receive dividends, depending on earnings and whether the directors vote to declare dividends, the book value of their shares stands to grow as net worth (shareholders' equity) expands through earnings retained in the business. Common shareholders in publicly traded companies also stand to profit from increases in market prices of shares, which normally reflect expectations of future earnings. But on the balance sheet, common shares are listed either at a par or stated value, an accounting/legal value signifying nothing other than the lowest price at which shares can be initially sold. Sometimes different classes of stock exist and are listed separately, with the privileges or limitations of each indicated parenthetically or in referenced notes.

Capital Surplus

Sometimes seen as additional paid-in capital (as preferred stock and common stock are sometimes called paid-in capital), this account reflects proceeds from issuances of stock that were in excess of the par or stated value of shares. For example, XYZ common has a par value of $10 per share; when 100,000 shares were issued at $12 a share, $1,000,000 was added to common stock and $200,000 was added to capital surplus.

Retained Earnings

This account is made up of corporate earnings not paid out in dividends and instead retained in the business. Retained earnings are not put in a special bank account or stuffed into a figurative mattress—they are simply absorbed as working capital or to finance fixed assets in order to generate more earnings.

Consolidated Financial Statements—Part 2: The Income Statement: The income statement shows the results of operations over a period of 12 months. Results of the two years prior to the year reported on are included for comparative purposes (see Exhibit 4).

Net Sales

Most income statements (or, more formally, Statements of Income), lead off with Net Sales—the total of cash sales (negligible for most industrial companies) and credit sales for the accounting period (12 months for annual reports). Net simply means after returns of merchandise shipped; freight-out; and allowances for shortages, breakage, and other adjustments having to do with day-to-day commerce. (Note that some service companies, including utilities, and financial organizations use the term revenues instead of sales.) Needless to say, the trend of sales as revealed in the three years' worth of figures is a key indicator of how a company is faring in the marketplace. The figures should of course be adjusted for inflation to give an accurate reading of year-to-year changes.

Changes in the components of a company's sales can be more significant than changes in sales figures. If, for example, a chemical company can shift from marketing bulk chemicals (which have a relatively small profit margin) to marketing specialty chemicals (which have a relatively large profit margin) it will ultimately earn more even without an increase in sales. Changes in sales components can be determined by reviewing the business segment information in the annual report (discussed below.)

Cost of Goods Sold

This is the cost of producing inventory and includes raw materials, direct labor, and other overhead that can be directly related to production. It is directly affected by the company's choice of the FIFO or LIFO inventory valuation methods (see Inventories, above). The reason becomes clear when you look at the formula by which cost of goods sold is determined:

Beginning inventory + Purchases during the period − Ending inventory
= Cost of goods sold

When the ending inventory (the balance sheet inventory) is the oldest stock, which is the case when the LIFO method is used, the cost of goods sold, assuming prices are rising with inflation, becomes a higher number than would be the case using FIFO. Of course, the higher the cost of goods sold, the lower will be taxable income, as we will see.

Depreciation

This noncash expense was alluded to at the start of the discussion of an annual report and again under Deferred Federal Income Taxes Payable in the discussion of balance sheet liabilities. To encourage firms to keep facilities modern and thus spur the economy, the U.S. government provides businesses a way to pay less tax and thereby conserve cash. This is accomplished by allowing firms to take an annual percentage (called a depreciation write-off) of what they spent for certain types of fixed assets, such as buildings, machinery, and equipment, and to treat the amount as though it were an actual expense, thus reducing taxable income without requiring an outlay of cash.

Depreciation is a highly complex tax accounting concept, and for purposes of reading annual reports it is not necessary to understand it completely. It is enough to know that tax rules make it possible for companies to recover the cost of certain fixed asset investments on an accelerated basis and thus to get the benefit of tax savings sooner than they would using the straight-line method (now required for newly purchased real property). At the same time, companies are allowed, for purposes of annual reports, to reflect depreciation charges based on the straight line method, whereby the estimated useful life of the asset is divided into its cost to get a uniform annual depreciation charge, which is generally much lower than the figure used for tax purposes. Annual reports thus show higher earnings, while the stockholder has the satisfaction of knowing that the company's tax liability has been minimized. It is all spelled out in the footnotes.

What is more important to know is that depreciation charges have a relationship to the age of the assets and vary with the amount of investment in fixed assets. An increase in depreciation usually reflects increases in depreciable assets—fixed assets like plant and equipment. Decreases usually mean fixed assets have been disposed of or have become fully depreciated. Particularly since straight line depreciation is used by most companies for reporting purposes, lower depreciation charges can signal a need for fixed asset expenditures, meaning long-term financing, which has implications for shareholders in the form either of dilution of share values or higher interest costs. Of course, increased or modernized plant capacity should also translate eventually into higher sales, greater operating efficiency and higher earnings per share.

EXHIBIT 4

XYZ CORPORATION
Income Statement
Fiscal Year Ended December 31
(Dollars in Millions)

	19X9	19X8	19X7
Net Sales	98.4	93.5	88.8
Cost of goods sold	64.9	62.2	59.7
Depreciation and amortization	2.2	3.0	2.0
Selling, general, and administrative expenses	12.1	11.1	10.3
	79.2	76.3	72.0
Net Operating Profit	19.2	17.2	16.8
Other Income or (Expenses)			
Income from dividends and interest	.2		
Interest expense	(1.0)	(.9)	(1.0)
Earnings before income taxes	18.4	16.3	15.8
Provision for income taxes	8.3	7.5	7.3
Net Income	10.1	8.8	8.5

Common shares outstanding: 1,555,000
Net earnings per share (after preferred dividend
requirements in 19X9 and 19X8: 19X9: $6.30; 19X8: $5.47;
19X7: $5.47.

Statement of Retained Earnings

	19X9	19X8	19X7
Retained Earnings Beginning of Year	35.9	33.6	31.3
Net Income for Year	10.1	8.8	8.5
Less: Dividends Paid on:			
Preferred stock ($6 per share)	.3	.3	
Common stock (per share): 19X9: $4.20; 19X8: $4.00;	6.5	6.2	6.2
19X7: $4.00).			
Retained Earnings End of Year	39.2	35.9	33.6

Selling, General, and Administrative (SG&A) Expenses

These are all the expenses associated with the normal operations of the business that were not included in cost of goods sold, which represented direct costs of production. Salaries, rent, utilities, advertising, travel and entertainment, commissions, office payroll, office expenses, and other such items are representative of this category, which varies from industry to industry in terms of its composition and the relative importance of selling expenses versus administrative expenses.

A good test of the quality of a company's management is its ability to control selling, general, and administrative expenses. Many companies have fallen into bankruptcy simply because management was unable or unwilling to control expenses and keep them in line with the growth of sales.

Net Operating Profit

The net operating profit is what is left over after costs of goods sold, depreciation, and SG&A expenses are deducted from sales, and it tells you the company's profit on a normal operating basis—that is, without taking into account unusual items of income or expense or nonoperating expenses such as interest and taxes. As stated above, it is a measure of operating efficiency, and significant variations from year to year or from industry standards should be investigated by looking more closely at the figures behind the totals, many of which are supplied in footnotes or published in the company's form 10-K (see Investor's Information, below). Lower than expected profit due to a rise in SG&A expenses as a percentage of sales might be traceable to a single factor, such as a rise in officers' salaries, for example.

Other Income or Expenses

This category picks up any unusual or nonoperating income or expense items. Examples might include income, gains, or losses from other investments; gains or losses on the sale of fixed assets; or special payments to employees. Nonrecurring items are usually explained in detail in footnotes. In this category is *interest expense,* which, unlike dividends, is a pretax expense. For companies with bonds or other debt outstanding, however, interest expense is a recurring item. Because interest on funded debt is a contractual, fixed expense that, if unpaid, becomes an event of default, analysts follow closely a company's fixed-charge coverage—how many times such fixed charges are covered by pretax annual earnings.

Earnings Before Income Taxes

This figure nets out all pretax income and expense items, but it would not be accurate to say it is the figure on which federal income taxes are based. That is because tax returns of corporations, as we have seen, use difficult methods of depreciation for tax purposes than they use for reporting to shareholders and because other factors, such as tax-loss carrybacks and carryforwards, which are not visible on the current year's statement, may affect the company's tax liability.

Provision for Income Taxes

After taking advantage of all available benefits, this is the company's tax liability for the year in question. Note that it is termed a *provision.* Payments based on estimated taxes have been made during the year, and net payments on this liability are payable according to a timetable determined by the Internal Revenue Service. A portion of the liability will be reflected as a accrued liability, as described above.

A company's effective tax rate should be compared with other companies in the same or similar industries. Although many tax loopholes have been ended by recent tax legislation, it may be a mark of smart and aggressive management if a company has a lower effective rate than other companies similarly engaged.

Net Income

This is the bottom line, the "after everything except dividends" figure. Dividends, by law, must be paid out of earnings, though not necessarily out of current earnings. Below the bottom line, figures for common shares outstanding and earnings per common share are given. Securities analysts usually focus on earnings per share in assessing a company's status. As a rule, earnings per share are expected to grow from year to year, and it may be a sign of trouble if they do not grow according to predictions or if they do not grow at all.

Consolidated Financial Statements — Part 3: The Statement of Retained Earnings (Shareholders' Equity: What typically follows the Income Statement is an analysis showing retained earnings at the beginning of the period; how net income increased retained earnings; dividends paid on preferred stock and common stock during the period; and the retained earnings account at the end of the fiscal year being reported (see Exhibit 4). The last figure will, of course, be the same as the retained earnings figure in the stockholders' equity section of the balance sheet.

A Statement of Retained Earnings may reflect stock dividends—new shares issued to existing shareholders. Stock dividends are accounted for by decreasing retained earnings and increasing common stock in equal amounts (using par or stated value if the stock dividend represents more than 20 to 25 percent of outstanding shares, and market value if it represents less). Many investors are attracted to companies that regularly declare stock dividends. It should be borne in mind, however, that stock dividends in no way enhance the actual assets of a company.

Statement of Consolidated Cash Flows: The Statement of Consolidated Cash Flows (Exhibit 5) replaced the traditional Sources and Uses (or Application) of Funds statement in financial statements issued from 1988 on. "Funds" had previously meant either cash or net working capital (the difference between current assets and current liabilities), and the vast majority of companies used a format focusing on working capital.

By requiring an analysis of changes affecting cash, the Financial Accounting Standards Board (FASB) was recognizing that the viability of a company hinges ultimately on liquidity and that increases in working capital do not necessarily translate into increased cash. For example, a company that relaxed its credit standards to generate increased sales might show higher profits and working capital from one year to another, but it would not be able to meet its obligations unless and until its accounts receivable were collected in cash. Cash means cash and equivalents, defined by FASB as all highly liquid securities with a known market value and a maturity, when acquired, of less than 3 months.

The statement of cash flows puts operating results on a cash basis while showing balance sheet changes as they affect the cash account. (In order to provide a complete "bridge" between two balance sheets, the statement of cash flows will also show major balance sheet changes not affecting cash, such as an exchange of bonds for stock or the purchase of a fixed asset that is 100% financed by long-term debt.)

The FASB requires that cash flows be analyzed in three separate categories: cash flows from operating activities, cash flows from investing activities, and cash flows from financing activities. The most commonly used format is XYZ Corporation's, illustrated in Exhibit 5.

The operating analysis begins with the net income figure (from the income statement) and follows with the adjustments necessary to convert that figure to a cash basis.

Depreciation and amortization, as earlier discussed, are bookkeeping transactions that reduced the net income figure without any expenditure of cash; this item (found on the income statement) is thus added back to net income. The increase in the (balance sheet liability) account called deferred federal income taxes represents the portion of income tax expense not actually paid in cash and is similarly added back to net income.

Next are adjustments to assets and liabilities that changed because of operating activities and provided or used cash. The increase in the accounts and notes receivable is subtracted because it represents sales revenue included in net income but not collected in cash. The increase in inventories is also subtracted because it represents cash spent for inventory purchases in excess of the expense recognized through cost of goods sold. The increase in prepaid expenses is deducted because it represents cash spent but not charged against income. The decrease in XYZ's accounts payable between 19X9 and 19X8 is subtracted because the cash paid to vendors in 19X9 was greater than the amount of expense recorded. (Cash was paid for some 19X8 accounts.) Increases in accrued liabilities and federal income taxes payable were charged to income but not (yet) paid in cash and are thus added back. Other assets and liabilities were either net users (19X9) or providers of cash.

(Note: Adjustments to particular asset and liability accounts will not always equal changes in balance sheet figures as they do in the case of XYZ Corporation. In the case of companies with foreign operations, operating assets and liabilities translated from other currencies have been purified of the effects of currency exchange and a separate line is provided to show the effect of exchange rate changes on cash and cash equivalents. Also, the effects of acquisitions, when accounted for by the PURCHASE ACQUISITION method, and divestitures have been excluded from the operating cash flow adjustments although they are reflected in the balance sheet accounts.)

Cash flows from investing activities include changes in the company's investments in property, plant, and equipment; investments in other companies; and loans made and collected. An increase in investment reduces cash and a decrease (sale) increases cash. It is notable that dividends and interest received are typically treated as operating cash flow, although changes in the same investments are analyzed here. In the case of XYZ, the only changes were those affecting fixed assets. XYZ's only other investments are in the securities comprising cash equivalents; since the whole cash flow statement focuses on cash and cash equivalents, it would be redundant to show those changes here. The small amount of income XYZ received on its cash equivalents is reflected in the net income figure above.

Cash flows from financing activities include all changes in cash resulting from financing, such as short- and long-term borrowings, the issuance or repurchase of common and preferred stock, dividends paid, and changes in dividends payable.

To interpret the cash flow statement it is helpful to remember a basic rule of thumb: In a conservatively operated company, *permanent* capital requirements—fixed assets and the portion of working capital that is not seasonal—should be financed through a combination of retained earnings and either long-term debt or equity. *Short-term* requirements should be financed with short-term liabilities in a cycle that begins when accounts payable are created to purchase inventory, which in turn is sold to create accounts receivable, which are collected to produce cash, and so on.

Once that is understood, the statement can be a valuable analytical tool that reveals healthy or unhealthy trends; a company's capacity for future investment; its future cash requirements; its cash position compared to similar companies; and its actual cash flows versus those anticipated.

A look at Exhibit 5 tells us XYZ Corporation has been generating operating cash flows that generally support its steadily increasing sales. Cash flow from operations has been sufficient to finance annual additions and improvements to its plant and equipment and still pay dividends without impairing its working capital. The statement reveals that in 19X8 the company, despite profitable operations, would have had a negative cash flow (more cash flowing out than in), after meeting $6.5 million of long-term debt repayments, had management not properly planned for the requirement by issuing $5 million of preferred stock.

One final observation: Discontinued operations, although not a factor in XYZ's case, show up frequently as a separate section of the income statements of large companies. Readers are thus able to distinguish between operating results that can be expected to continue in the future and those that have only historical significance. In their statement of cash flows, however, companies are permitted but not required to separately disclose the flows from discontinued operations and extraordinary items.

When companies voluntarily make the separation, they indicate clearly that the analysis of net income and adjustments relates to continuing operations and includes a separate line for net cash provided (or used) by discontinued operations. But when discontinued operations that show up in the income statement are not broken out in the statement of cash flows, it is up to the reader to ascertain if a significant portion of the flows relate to operations that are not ongoing.

Notes to Financial Statements: Footnotes to financial statements, sometimes just called notes, are unfortunately named if there's any implication that they represent superfluous detail. Indeed, the balance sheet, the income statement, and the statement of cash flows contain the sentence: "The Notes to Financial Statements are an integral part of this statement." Footnotes set forth the accounting policies of the business—and provide additional disclosure. They contain information having profound significance for the financial values presented elsewhere in the financial statements.

It would be impossible to list here all the types of information one might find in the notes to financial statements. Here is a sampling, though, and if it succeeds in impressing you with the importance of reading this section of a financial report, it will have accomplished its purpose.

Accounting procedure changes A change in the method of valuing inventory or a change in the company's method of depreciating fixed assets can have significant effects on reported earnings and asset values. You should investigate further if a company frequently changes accounting procedures. The company may, for instance, be trying to hide weak aspects of its operations.

Pension and postretirement benefits A number of companies recently have used overfunded pension plans to generate cash windfalls, but the reverse also occurs: Some are underfunded, so that the company may be faced with the prospect of cash burdens later on. Pension funding is, at best, an inexact science. Estimates based on a variety of actuarial, personnel, and financial assumptions determine the amount of annual expense required to cover future benefits earned by each year's additional service. Not only are these estimates subject to error, but

XYZ CORPORATION
Statement of Consolidated Cash Flow
Fiscal Year Ended December 31
(Dollars in Millions)

	19X9	19X8	19X7
CASH FLOWS FROM OPERATING ACTIVITIES			
Net Income	10.1	8.8	8.5
Adjustments to reconcile net income to net cash provided by operating activities:			
Depreciation and amortization	2.2	3.0	2.0
Deferred income taxes	.2	.3	.2
Accounts receivable	(.7)	(.6)	(.8)
Inventories	(2.1)	(1.9)	(1.2)
Prepaid expenses	(.1)	–	(.1)
Accounts payable	(.1)	1.2	.7
Accrued liabilities	.5	.3	.3
Federal income taxes payable	1.1	.8	.6
Other assets and liabilities, net	(.2)	.5	.5
Net cash from operating activities	**10.9**	**12.4**	**10.7**
CASH FLOWS FROM INVESTING ACTIVITIES			
Additions: property, plant, equipment	(3.9)	(4.2)	(2.8)
Net cash used for investing activities	**(3.9)**	**(4.2)**	**(2.8)**
CASH FLOWS FROM FINANCING ACTIVITIES			
Net change in short-term debt	.7	–	–
Repayments of long-term debt	(.8)	(6.5)	(1.0)
Proceeds from sale of preferred stock		5.0	
Payments of dividends	(6.8)	(6.5)	(6.2)
Increase in dividends payable	.5	.3	–
Net cash used for financing activities	**(6.4)**	**(7.7)**	**(7.2)**
NET INCREASE IN CASH AND EQUIVALENTS	.6	.5	.7
Cash and equivalents, beginning of year	7.0	6.5	5.8
Cash and equivalents at end of year	7.6	7.0	6.5

management has used its discretion over the rate at which pension liabilities are funded to smooth out reported earnings by underfunding in poor years and overfunding in good years. Patterns of underfunding or overfunding can portend future deficiency or surplus, even when estimates are accurate. A liability account termed Unfunded Projected Benefit Obligation is another red flag, in this case meaning that the current return on pension fund investments is inadequate to cover projected future benefit payments.

Closely related are Postemployment Benefits Other than Pensions, consisting mainly of health care benefits payable to employees after retirement and before their eligibility for government benefits such as Medicare and Medicaid. The Financial Accounting Standards Board (FASB) would require companies to fund the present value of estimated future benefits earned by employees. The practice throughout the 1980s, however, was to expense the costs of such benefits as incurred. The appropriate question here is whether benefits actually paid are indicative of future liability. For example, a young company with a young work force would have small current expense, but unless some provision for future liability was made, it would be in for a clobbering when the work force reached retirement age.

Long-term debt Detail on debt maturities makes it possible to anticipate refinancing needs, which have implications for investors in terms of the effect of interest costs on profits or potential dilution of common share values. A company's ability to manage its debt structure so as to obtain money at the lowest rate for the longest maturity is viewed by analysts as demonstrating that the company has a capable management team.

Look here (and also in footnotes concerning preferred stock) for information about antitakeover provisions, or "poison pills." The recent wave of hostile takeovers, usually taking the form of leveraged buyouts, has caused many companies to adopt provisions in their indentures or preferred stock agreements designed to make takeovers prohibitively expensive for acquirers or to protect existing holders from the adverse effects of additional debt or liquidation of assets. A common variety is the "poison put," a provision giving bondholders the right to redeem their bonds at par value in the event of a hostile takeover, thus creating an onerous cash requirement for the acquirer. Although generally designed to protect existing investors from unfavorable events, poison pill provisions can have major implications for a company's finances, and it is important to understand them.

Treasury stock By buying their own shares in the market, companies decrease shares outstanding and thus increase earnings per share for existing stockholders. The existence of an active stock purchase program can be viewed as a two-edged sword. On the one hand, such a program provides in effect a support price for the company's shares as well as a buyer with deep pockets—the company itself. On the other hand, a stock purchase program is frequently used as a defense against a hostile takeover attempt and raises the question whether repurchase of stock is the best way to use assets of the company.

Taxes The prospect of an assessment for a prior year's taxes may be disclosed in the footnotes. Of particular significance is any footnote disclosing that a company's tax returns are being audited or that any of the assumptions utilized by the company in determining the taxable basis of its assets are being questioned by the Internal Revenue Service.

Leases   One of the most significant of the off balance sheet liabilities is the long-term noncapital lease. A footnote dealing with a long-term lease should be reviewed carefully.

Supplementary Tables: The principal supplementary tables are the following.

Segment Reporting

The Financial Accounting Standards Board (FASB) requires companies meeting certain criteria having to do with product and geographical diversification to present certain information in segment form—that is, by product or industry category or markets serviced and by geographical territory. The information required, which covers the same three-year period as the income statement, includes sales or revenues; operating profit or loss; the book value of identifiable assets; aggregate depreciation, depletion, or amortization; and capital expenditures.

These breakdowns enable shareholders to evaluate a company's exposure to the vagaries of various geographical markets, including political and other risks to a company that has foreign operations. For industry or product-line segments, a stockholder is able to evaluate the company's activities in particular areas in terms of the amount of its investment and the return it is realizing on the investment, as well as the year-to-year trends.

Financial Reporting and Changing Prices

Another ruling of the FASB is aimed at accounting for the effect of inflation on the inventory, fixed assets, and the income statement values for cost of goods sold and depreciation as they are related to those assets. Thus, companies are required to present the last five years' figures showing the effects of declines in the purchasing power of the dollar in contrast to the primary values as shown in the financial statements, based on historical cost.

Five-Year Summary of Operations

This required schedule essentially extends the three-year income statement to five years, including preferred and common stock dividend history. It is a useful supplement in terms of permitting analysis of operating trends, and a number of corporations have taken it upon themselves to provide summaries of the last ten years of operations.

Two-Year Quarterly Data

This schedule provides a quarterly breakdown of sales, net income, the high and low stock price, and the common dividend. The operating data is most valuable when a company's operations are subject to seasonal factors, as, for example, a retailer is subject to heavy demand during the Christmas season. The market price and dividend data reveal stock price volatility and the regularity with which the company has made dividend payments.

Management's Discussion and Analysis: The general credibility and informational value of annual reports was significantly advanced in the mid-1980s when the Securities and Exchange Commission began requiring and monitoring the section Management's Discussion and Analysis of the Financial Condition and Results of Operations. This is a narrative presentation designed to present management's candid comments on three key areas of a company's business: results of operations, capital resources, and liquidity. Companies are required to address all material developments affecting these three key areas, favorable or unfavorable, including the effects of inflation. In discussing results of operations, companies are required not only to detail operating and unusual events that affected results for the period under discussion, but also any trends or uncertainties that might affect results in the future. The capital resources part involves questions of fixed asset expenditures and considerations of whether it benefits shareholders more to finance such outlays with stock, bonds, or through lease arrangements. Addressing liquidity means discussing anything that affects net working capital, such as the convertibility into cash of accounts receivable or inventory and the availability of bank lines of credit.

When it made this section a requirement, the SEC sought to elicit, in a company's own words, an interpretation of the significance of past and future financial developments. Its intentions were clearly revealed following enactment of the Tax Reform Act of 1986, when it voted to direct companies to use this section of their 1986 reports to shareholders to quantify certain effects of the new law, such as a reduction in current liabilities for future taxes. Whether it will prove to be a satisfactory substitute for one's own analysis remains to be seen.

Investor's Information

This section of the annual report lists the name of the transfer agent, registrar, and trustees; the exchanges on which the company's securities are traded; the date, time, and place of the annual meeting; and a notice as to when proxy materials will be made available to shareholders of record. If the company has an automatic dividend reinvestment plan, the terms and procedures for participating are stated here.

The number of common shareholders (and preferred, if any) as of the fiscal year-end is also usually indicated in this section.

This section may also invite requests for Form 10-K, the annual Securities and Exchange Commission filing corporations are required to make available to shareholders. The 10-K is filed within 90 days of a company's fiscal year-end. It is a thick, drab report containing a mass of detail. Much of what it contains is in the annual report to shareholders or is incorporated by reference to the public annual report, but other information is unique to the 10-K. Such unique information includes historical background; names of principal security holders; security holdings of management; more detailed financial schedules; information about products or services, properties, markets, distribution systems, backlogs, and competitive factors; detail about patents, licenses, or franchises; number of employees; environmental and other regulatory compliances; information concerning amounts paid directors and their share holdings; and background, including employment history, of executives and their relationships to the firm.

Form 10-Q is a shorter, unaudited, update of the 10-K. It must be filed within 45 days of the end of a company's first, second, and third fiscal quarters. It is mainly useful as a source of information about changes in the status of securities outstanding, compliance with debt agreements, and information on matters to be voted on by shareholders, such as the election of directors.

Directors and Officers

The names of members of the board of directors and their affiliations are listed here as are the names and titles of senior executives. Also usually indicated is the membership of board members on various committees, such as the executive committee, the finance committee, the compensation committee, the committee on corporate responsibility, the research and development committee, and the audit committee. Corporations vary in terms of the use to which they put the backgrounds of their directors—in some cases the role of directors is ceremonial, in others directors are used to advantage—and this section can sometimes provide meaningful insight. The absence of directors unaffiliated with management may indicate a company dominated by senior officers and not responsive to the concerns of outside shareholders. Senior management can also become more entrenched in companies that stagger the terms of directors to help prevent a hostile takeover.

* * *

RATIO ANALYSIS SUMMARY

Ratios are the principal tools of financial statement analysis. By definition, however, ratios indicate relationships, and by excluding considerations such as dollar amounts and the overall size of a company, their meaning in and of themselves can be limited if not misleading. Ratios have their greatest significance when used to make year-to-year comparisons for the purpose of determining trends or when used in comparison with industry data. Composite ratios for different industries are published by Standard & Poor's Corporation, Dun & Bradstreet, Robert Morris Associates, and the Federal Trade Commission. The following is a summary of key ratios and what they signify. Each ratio is computed for XYZ Corporation, whose hypothetical financial statements are shown in the discussion above of the annual report.

Ratios That Measure Liquidity

Ratio	Calculation	XYZ Computation
Current ratio	$\dfrac{\text{Current assets}}{\text{Current liabilities}}$	$\dfrac{41.1}{18.5} = 2.22$

The current ratio measures the extent to which the claims of a firm's short-term creditors are covered by assets expected to be converted to cash within the same short-term period. In XYZ's industry, the standard is 1.9, so its 2.2 ratio indicates comfortable liquidity, although down slightly from last year's ratio of 2.4. In a recession, extra liquidity protection could make a vital difference; slack consumer demand would mean that XYZ's wholesale customers would have lower sales. That would mean less sales and lower inventory turnover for XYZ. As XYZ's customers became tighter for cash and slower ₁paying, or went out of business, XYZ's accounts receivable would become less collectible. Ultimately that could mean insolvency. Hence the importance of this key measure of short-term solvency. Of course, in other types of companies, the current ratio would have less significance. A company whose sales were largely under United States government contracts would have less receivables and inventory risk, for example, and could thus afford a lower current ratio.

Quick ratio	$\dfrac{\text{Current assets-inventory}}{\text{Current liabilities}}$	$\dfrac{41.1 - 23.0}{18.5} = .97$

A refinement of the current ratio, the quick or acid-test ratio answers the question: If sales stopped, could the company meet its current obligations with the readily convertible assets on hand? XYZ has a quick ratio of .97, almost a dollar of quick assets for each dollar of current liabilities, and virtually in line with the industry standard of 1.0. Last year it was slightly better, 1.04 times, but that small a year-to-year difference is probably not enough to signify a negative trend.

Ratios That Measure Activity

Ratio	Calculation	XYZ Computation
Inventory turnover	$\dfrac{\text{Net Sales}}{\text{Inventory}}$	$\dfrac{98.4}{23.0} = 2.8$ times

This tells us the number of times inventory is sold in the course of the year. As a general rule, high turnover means efficient inventory management and more marketable inventory with a lower risk of illiquidity. But it could also be a reflection on pricing policies or could reflect shortages and an inability to meet new orders. XYZ's turnover ratio is 4.3 times, down slightly from the prior year's 4.5 times, and the industry standard is 6.7 times. This should be looked into.

Average collection period	$\dfrac{\text{Accounts receivable}}{\text{Annual credit sales/360 days}}$	$\dfrac{10.2}{.270} = 37$ days

Assuming a company's terms of sale are standard for its industry, the average collection period—which tells if customers are paying bills on time—can be a reflection on credit policy (a liberal policy, involving relaxed credit standards to generate higher sales volume, will usually result in a longer average collection period); on the diligence of a firm's collection effort; on the attractiveness of discounts offered for prompt payment; or on general economic conditions as they affect the finances of the firm's customers. XYZ's collection period was 38 days this year and 37 days last year compared with an industry average of 37 days. It thus enjoys typical collections, apparently reflecting a sound and competitive credit policy. Of course, there could be potential problems not revealed by this test; for example, a concentration of accounts receivable in one industry or with a few customers, which, if affected by adversity, would have a disproportionate effect on the total receivables portfolio. Footnotes to the financial statements will often contain information concerning the composition of accounts receivable and their age relative to the invoice date.

Fixed assets turnover	$\dfrac{\text{Net sales}}{\text{Net fixed assets}}$	$\dfrac{98.4}{59.8} = 1.6$ times

Measured over time and against competitors, this ratio indicates how efficiently a firm is using its property, plant and equipment—its "plant capacity." Increases in fixed assets should produce increases in sales, although the investment will normally lag the sales effect. If, given time, sales fail to increase in relation to plant capacity, it usually reflects poor marketing strategy. XYZ's ratio is low by industry standards. It has recently added to its capacity and has plans to pursue a more aggressive policy aimed at higher sales and increased market share.

Total assets turnover	$\dfrac{\text{Net sales}}{\text{Total assets}}$	$\dfrac{98.4}{105.8} = .93$ times

This ratio measures the amount of sales volume the company is generating on its investment in assets and is thus an indication of the efficiency with which assets are utilized. The relationship between sales and assets is sometimes called operating leverage, since any sales increases that can be generated from the same amount of assets increase profits and return on equity and vice versa. XYZ's turnover of .93, virtually unchanged from the prior year, is considerably under the industry standard of 2.1 meaning XYZ had better increase sales or dispose of some assets. As we observed above, however, it has plans to increase sales and recently added fixed assets in preparation.

Ratios That Measure Profitability

Ratio	Calculation	XYZ Computation
Operating profit margin	$\dfrac{\text{Net operating profit}}{\text{Net sales}}$	$\dfrac{19.2}{98.4} = 19.5\%$

This ratio is the key to measuring a firm's operating efficiency. It is a reflection on management's purchasing and pricing policies and its success in controlling costs and expenses directly associated with the running of the business and the creation of sales, excluding other income and expenses, interest, and taxes. (Some analysts exclude depreciation from this ratio, but we include it here for the sake of comparability.) XYZ's operating profit margin has been quite consistent over the past three years and is somewhat higher than industry averages. That could mean it is in for some competition or that it is exceptionally good at controlling costs. To zero in on the reasons for XYZ's better-than-average performance, relate cost of goods sold to sales and selling, general, and administrative expenses to sales. The explanation may lie in pricing policy or somewhere in the area of selling, general, and administrative expenses.

Net profit margin	$\dfrac{\text{Net income}}{\text{Net sales}}$	$\dfrac{10.1}{98.4} = 10.3\%$

This measures management's overall efficiency—its success not only in managing operations but in terms of borrowing money at a favorable rate, investing idle cash to produce extra income, and taking advantage of tax benefits. XYZ's ratio of 10.3% compares favorably with industry standards. A company in a field where the emphasis was on high volume—a supermarket, for instance—might show a net profit margin of much less—2% for example.

Return on equity	$\dfrac{\text{Net income}}{\text{Total stockholders' equity}}$	$\dfrac{10.1}{68.0} = 15\%$

This ratio measures the overall return on stockholders' equity. It is the bottom line measured against the money shareholders have invested. XYZ's 15% return is above average for the industry, which is good for shareholders as long as it doesn't invite competition.

Ratios That Measure Capitalization (Leverage)

Ratio	Calculation	XYZ Computation
Debt to total assets	$\dfrac{\text{Total liabilities}}{\text{Total assets}}$	$\dfrac{37.6}{105.6} = 36\%$

This measures the proportion of assets financed with debt as opposed to equity. Creditors, such as bankers, prefer that this ratio be low, since it means a greater cushion in the event of liquidation. Owners, on the other hand, may seek higher leverage in order to magnify earnings or may prefer to finance the company's activities through debt rather than yield control. XYZ's ratio is about average for its industry.

Ratio	Calculation	XYZ Computation
Long-term debt to total capitalization	$\dfrac{\text{Long-term debt}}{\text{Long-term debt} + \text{stockholders' equity}}$	$\dfrac{16.2}{68.0} = 24\%$

This ratio tells us the proportion of permanent financing that is represented by long-term debt versus equity. XYZ's ratio of 24% (24% of its permanent capital is debt) is low by industry standards, suggesting it might consider increasing its leverage—that is, financing its future growth through bonds rather than stock.

Debt to equity (debt ratio)	$\dfrac{\text{Total liabilities}}{\text{Total stockholders' equity}}$	$\dfrac{37.6}{68.0} = 55\%$

This is the basic ratio. It measures the reliance on creditors—short and long term—to finance total assets and becomes critical in the event of liquidation, when the proceeds from the sale of assets go to creditors before owners. Since assets tend to shrink in liquidation, the lower this ratio the more secure owners can feel. Also, a high debt ratio makes it more difficult to borrow should the need arise. XYZ's debt ratio of 55% is very conservative, and is another indication that its shareholders could safely benefit from greater leverage.

Times interest earned	$\dfrac{\text{Earnings before taxes and interest charges}}{\text{Interest charges}}$	$\dfrac{19.4}{1.0} = 19 \text{ times}$

This ratio measures the number of times fixed interest charges are covered by earnings. Since failure to meet interest payments would be an event of default under the terms of most debenture agreements, this coverage ratio indicates a margin of safety. Put another way, it indicates the extent to which earnings could shrink—in a recession, for example—before the firm became unable to meet its contractual interest charges. XYZ earns 19 times its annual interest payments, which is substantially more than is normally considered conservative. It is another indication that XYZ should consider increasing its leverage.

Fixed charge coverage	$\dfrac{\text{Earnings before taxes and interest charges}}{\text{Interest charges} + \text{lease payments}}$	$\dfrac{19.4}{1.0} = 19 \text{ times}$

This is the times interest earned ratio expanded to include other fixed charges, notably annual lease payments. XYZ has no lease obligations, so the ratio is the same. It is important to note, however, that the extent of this coverage should be sufficient to ensure that a company can meet its fixed contractual obligations in bad times as well as good times.

Ratios That Measure Stock Values

Ratio	Calculation	XYZ Computation
Price-earnings ratio	$\dfrac{\text{Market price of common share}}{\text{Earnings per common share}}$	$\dfrac{63.00}{6.30} = 10 \text{ times}$

This ratio reflects the value the marketplace puts on a company's earnings and the prospect of future earnings. It is important to shareholders because it represents the value of their holdings, and it is also important from the corporate standpoint in that it is an indication of the firm's cost of capital—the price it could expect to receive if it were to issue new shares. XYZs multiple of ten times earnings is about average for an established company.

Ratio	Calculation	XYZ Computation
Market-to-book ratio	$\dfrac{\text{Market price of common share}}{\text{Book value per share (total assets } - \text{ intangible assets } - \text{ total liabilities and preferred stock/common shares outstanding)}}$	$\dfrac{63.00}{40.00} = 1.58$ times

This indicates the value the market places on a firm's expected earnings—its value as a going concern—in relation to the value of its shares if the company were to be liquidated and the proceeds from the sale of assets, after creditor claims were satisfied, were paid to shareholders. XYZ's common shares have a market value that is half again as much as their value in liquidation, assuming its assets could be liquidated at book value.

Dividend payout ratio	$\dfrac{\text{Dividends per common share}}{\text{Earnings per common share}}$	$\dfrac{4.20}{6.30} = 67\%$

This ratio indicates the percentage of common share earnings that are paid out in dividends. As a general rule, young, growing companies tend to reinvest their earnings to finance expansion and thus have low dividend payout ratios or ratios of zero. XYZ's ratio of 67% is higher than most established companies show.

HOW TO READ A QUARTERLY REPORT

In addition to annual reports, publicly held companies issue interim reports usually on a quarterly basis, which update shareholders about sales and earnings and report any material changes in the company's affairs. Companies are also required to file quarterly information with the Securities and Exchange Commission on Form 10-Q within 45 days of the end of the first, second, and third fiscal quarters. These reports, which contain unaudited financial information and news of changes in securities outstanding, compliance with debt agreements, and matters to be voted on by shareholders, may be available from companies directly; at SEC libraries in Atlanta, Boston, Chicago, Denver, Fort Worth, Los Angeles, New York, Seattle, and the District of Columbia; or through firms that provide all SEC filings (and which advertise in the financial sections of newspapers).

Quarterly shareholder reports vary in comprehensiveness. Some reports provide complete, though usually unaudited, financial statements, but most simply contain summarized updates of the operating highlights of the annual report. Accounting regulations require that companies give at least the following information.

- Sales (or revenues)
- Net income (before and after potential dilution, if pertinent)
- Provision for federal income taxes
- Nonrecurring items of income or expense, with tax implications
- Significant acquisitions or disposals of business segments
- Material contingencies, such as pending lawsuits
- Accounting changes
- Significant changes in financial position, including working capital and capital structure

Accounting regulations require that figures be presented either for the quarter in question or cumulatively for the year-to-date, but prior year data must be included on a comparative basis. That requirement is designed to deal with seasonal factors. For example, the quarterly results of a department store, to cite an industry with marked seasonality (sales bulge at Christmastime), would be meaningless unless compared with the same quarter of the prior year.

The main thing to remember about quarterly reports is that they are designed to update existing shareholders, not to provide prospective shareholders with an overall perspective on the company. They should be read in conjunction with the annual report.

PART III

How to Read the Financial Pages

How to Read Ticker Tapes

HOW TO READ THE
FINANCIAL PAGES

Financial news is a swift-running stream that can be harnessed to power your investment decision-making—or drown you in a flood of statistics. Its volume expanded greatly in the 1970s and 1980s, following deregulation of the financial markets and other developments that increased public participation in a growing investment marketplace, prompting many of us to become our own money managers.

As a result, the financial press has staffed up and daily financial sections have been expanded and redesigned, often along the lines of *The New York Times* free-standing section. *The Wall Street Journal* added a second section and then a third. A relative newcomer, *Investor's Daily*, creates graphs from its computerized data base to show price movements of individual securities. *USA Today* uses innovative graphics to include as much financial information as possible in its pages.

The Financial Times of London responded to the growing appetite for foreign financial news by increasing its international distribution, as did *The Japan Economic Journal* with its weekly English-language edition. *Barron's National Business and Financial Weekly*, long an important weekly source of information for professionals, became more consumer-oriented and added many useful tables and features not found elsewhere.

These and other financial publications have three major goals: (1) To pack as much news as possible into a given space; (2) to attract as many readers as possible; and (3) to allow busy readers to obtain a quick overview and/or easily find whatever specific information they are seeking. These aims are accomplished through packaging the news, and as readers, we must understand how this is done so we can unpackage it to suit ourselves.

THE FIRST PAGE

The outside of the news package—the first page of the financial section of a major daily general-interest newspaper or daily financial newspaper—is aimed at the broadest audience: the consumer, the investor, the civic minded, the curious—all of us, in one way or another. As you move to the inside pages, the information becomes more specific: reports on individual people, companies, markets. The tabular material is the most specific of all, and is included for readers who seek detail—a stock price, currency exchange rates, bond yield, corporate earnings report, or information on a new securities offering, for example. The outside of the package may contain, depending on news developments, one or more of the following elements.

The Digest

The digest presents major stories of the preceding day in summary form, along with summaries of the more important analytical feature stories from that day's newspaper. A good digest also gives you an idea of why an event was important, and what it could lead to. It will also tell you what page to turn to for the full story.

The Economics Story

The fact that a general economics story often appears on the front page of the package is a tribute to the sophistication and interest of the readership. It also reflects the fact that government economic data is scheduled for release well in advance, giving editors and reporters time to reserve space, pull out charts for updating, and line up experts to offer commentary. A monthly cycle of major statistics often starts with the release of data on construction spending and the employment situation (the latter generally is released on the first Friday of the month) and continues with statistics on chain-store sales, crop production, consumer installment credit, industrial production, capacity utilization, housing starts and building permits, producer (wholesale) prices, personal income and outlays, consumer prices, average hourly wages, savings flows, and other matters. The month often ends with a report on the indexes of leading, coincident, and lagging economic indicators. Most of the statistics refer to the previous month, some to two months before. Motor-vehicle manufacturers report on sales every ten days.

Important statistics are also released on a quarterly basis. These statistics include information on U.S. import and export prices, corporate profits, and—of particular significance—the gross national product (GNP). The GNP (especially its inflation-adjusted version, constant dollar or real GNP) is a measure of the total value of goods and services produced by the United States economy. Of key interest is how the seasonally adjusted annual growth rate of the GNP in a particular quarter compares to the previous quarter and to the same quarter in the previous year. Trends in the GNP are our primary measures of whether the U.S. economy is strong or weak, growing or in recession.

For investment purposes, watch for basic themes in overall stories on the economy. Favorable economic signals bode well for corporate profits, and therefore usually for stock prices, and unfavorable signals can have the opposite effect. A weakening economy can lift bond prices, however, because economic slackness means weaker demand for credit and thus lower rates for new loans, which translates into higher prices for existing bonds and notes. But one monthly figure doesn't make a trend, and other factors, including speculation about Federal Reserve Board monetary policy, also affect securities prices. In any event, between the time economic data is released and its appearance in newspapers, there has been ample opportunity for financial markets to react—to "discount the news," as they say on Wall Street. Most stock markets remained open until 4 P.M. EST the day before (the Pacific Stock Exchange closes 30 minutes later) while the bond market, which is mainly located in brokerage house trading rooms, has no official closing. Thus, the opportunity to react effectively to an economic event may have passed by the time you read of it in the newspaper.

The Interest Rate/Bond Market Story

As market interest rates move up or down, the prices of fixed income securities move in the opposite direction to adjust yields to market levels. Yield determines price, and vice versa. Thus, the daily bond market story is essentially an interest rate story. Major daily newspapers always reserve inside space for this story and move it to the outside of the financial package when warranted by major developments. The event could be a big move in bond values, a new prediction by a widely followed interest-rate forecaster, Congressional testimony or other action by the Federal Reserve Board (especially its chairman), or policy changes by foreign central banks. The bigger the development, the more attention will be focused on its significance to consumers—the prospect of higher or lower mortgage and personal borrowing costs, for instance. A complete story will also explain the significance of such news to investors and include comments by analysts and economists. The Federal Reserve's weekly report on the money supply (usually released on Thursday) provides much of the grist for late-week interest rate stories. If the money supply grows faster than the Federal Reserve had planned, the Fed may be tempted to adopt a restrictive monetary policy. That is, the Federal Reserve may reduce the amount of money in the economy to prevent a rise in inflation. Tighter money means higher interest rates, at least on short-term loans and securities, which usually exerts downward pressure on stock and bond prices. If the Fed thinks the money supply is growing too slowly, especially during an economic slowdown, the Fed could be expected to try to ease monetary policy and stimulate money growth. This often leads to lower interest rates and higher prices for fixed income securities, as well as to optimism and higher prices in the stock markets.

The Commodities Story

The roller coaster action in the prices of oil, gold, and silver in recent years helped make activity in the commodities markets a more frequent front-of-the-package story. When the commodities story gets front-page treatment, the consumer implications—for example, the effects on retail prices of gasoline or orange juice—will usually receive most attention. But there will also be economic and market forecasts and comments by professional analysts and traders, designed to inform investors about commodities futures or futures options contracts. Typical questions answered include: How fast has the price of the commodity futures contract reversed direction in the past? Are there new sources of supply that could affect prices—for example, soybeans from Brazil to replace those from Kansas, or beef from Argentina to replace meat from Texas? Is anything happening that could limit supply? What is the outlook for a political development causing activity in precious metals contracts?

The Takeover or Merger Story

Major takeover bids (called public tender offers) or merger announcements make big news partly because they have important implications for the securities prices of the companies involved. In a takeover or merger story look for (1) the price, total and per share, that's being offered for the target company. Also look at the form of payment—cash, securities, or a combination—and how it's being raised. A leveraged buyout, for instance, can sometimes leave the acquired company laden with debt. (2) The reasons for the merger—to combine businesses for greater financial or marketing strength; to avoid an unfriendly takeover; to bail out a troubled corporation, for example. An unfriendly or hostile tender offer could trigger a bidding war which would drive up the price of the target company's stock or prompt legal action. Also, a large-scale takeover or merger runs the risk of antitrust action by the federal government in addition to other impediments. When takeover plans are set back or collapse, the price of the target's stock will most likely drop. (3) Comments by analysts on the acquirer's motives and management skills. A bid substantially above market could mean shares are undervalued or that the acquirer has exciting plans; particularly with reduced float, it might be wiser to hold than tender.

A complete takeover or merger story will also uncover what the risk arbitragers — professional traders who speculate in merger situations — are doing. Heavy buying of the stock of the takeover target combined with short selling of the shares of the acquirer, usually means the professionals think the takeover will succeed.

The Stock Market Story

This daily feature shifts to the front of the financial package when stock indexes undergo an especially big move. Although broader-based and more scientifically weighted indexes exist, the Dow Jones Industrial Average, which tracks 30 blue chip stocks, continues to be the most widely watched barometer and almost invariably is featured in the stock market story. A good roundup should give you the widest possible exploration of factors—the effect of other markets (bonds, commodities, currencies, and to an increased extent, stock options and financial futures), corporate earnings, takeover bids and merger rumors, economic developments, and changing market forecasts. The article should differentiate between different groups of stocks and different markets. The New York Stock Exchange activity often reflects buying and selling by institutional investors while the American Stock Exchange and over the counter (NASDAQ) markets reflect a higher proportion of activity by individual investors interested in less well-known growth stocks. In recent years, market volatility has been intensified by program trading, the computer-driven buying and selling by institutional traders and arbitrage specialists of all stocks in a "basket" or index. Some forms of program trading, particularly index arbitrage, also involve index options, index futures, and stock options, all of which expire together on the third Fridays of March, June, September and December. Although measures have been instituted to process this extra activity with minimum disruption, expiration dates still cause a surge of trading, and the market closing on those Fridays is known on Wall Street as "the triple witching hour." A complete stock market story will usually include predictions by analysts who engage either in fundamental analysis, which focuses on business conditions and the financial strength of companies, or technical analysis, which concentrates on the conditions of the stock market, such as the supply and demand for shares and the emotional cycles of investors. Technical analysts, including those called chartists, who analyze historical market patterns, are usually more willing than fundamentalists to predict near-term market movements for newspaper stories.

The Company Story

Sometimes company stories are the result of breaking news—a profit report, a takeover attempt, a new product—and sometimes they are features that have been planned, and even written, well in advance of publication. Newspapers often carry a company stock story as part of their regular stock market coverage or because it is an important company to the newpaper's readership (it has a plant in town, for instance). Because stories on publicly owned companies can influence market values, there are laws to prevent capitalizing on advance knowledge of their content.

Among the things that you, as an investor or potential investor in a company, want to learn are: (1) The nature of the company's business, and whether or not it's diversified or a one-product operation; the size of its customer base; whether it does business mainly with the government or with private firms; whether it relies heavily on exports and is therefore sensitive to fluctuations in the dollar's value; whether its sources of supply are secure; and whether it can easily pass costs on to consumers. (2) The amount of debt of the company relative to its overall capital and whether it plans to borrow funds, issue more shares, or pay back loans. Among other things, this financial information will tell you whether the value of shares you may already own will undergo dilution, which could reduce earnings per share and thus reduce the market value of shares. (3) The nature of the company's ownership. Is a substantial proportion of stock held by the company's founders or by its current management? Closely held companies cannot be taken over by unwelcome acquirers as easily as widely held companies, but that can also deprive shareholders of profits they might otherwise gain through public tender offers at premiums to market value. You should also be told if financial institutions own large blocks of shares; big institutional positions are an indication of how professional investors regard the company. In the case of companies with relatively few shares, however, that can also cause substantial price swings should institutions gobble up or dump large amounts of shares. Trends in insider or institutional ownership can be solid signals as to the prospects of a company—if top management is accumulating shares, they may know before the public about events that might cause the stock to rise. (4) Trends in the company's earnings history. How steady have profits been? Have they been increasing on a per-share basis? Is the company emerging from a period of weakness? Are earnings mainly the result of ongoing operations or of one-time extraordinary items, such as the sale of company property? (5) Trends in dividend payments.

The Industry Story

You'll find many of the same elements of a company story in an industry story, and you will in addition have the opportunity to look at one company in relation to others. These stories are often accompanied by charts comparing companies in an industrial sector (computer chip makers, retailers, or utilities, for instance) according to sales, per-share earnings, stock price range, recent stock price, price-earnings ratio, and other important data.

Advertisements

Throughout the financial pages of most newspapers—even on the front page—you will find advertisements for bank deposit instruments, mutual funds, and other investments. Early in the year many advertisements for individual retirement accounts appear. Some ads include order forms and encourage you to send a check—sometimes for a hefty amount—right away. Mutual funds and sponsors of other publicly offered securities, however, can't accept an investment from you without first sending you a prospectus. A mutual fund sometimes will print the prospectus as part of the advertisement. Never react impulsively to an attractive rate or yield or special deal. It is difficult to compare rates, yields, and terms because each situation is unique and different institutions use various methods to compute yields. Some have withdrawal penalties and other restrictions that might not be obvious in the ad.

You will also find advertisements for financial publications, advisory newsletters, and computer databases and software, among other products. Often these products can be very helpful, but it is usually best to request a sample or a demonstration to make sure the product suits your needs.

SCANNING THE INSIDE FINANCIAL PAGES

You can get a quick picture of current financial events and trends by scanning the financial pages. The news digest, already discussed, is a good starting point. The inside pages are peppered with daily, weekly, or monthly charts and graphs to give you a snapshot of aspects of business and economics. *The Wall Street Journal,* in addition to its news digest, brings such highlights together in its Markets Diary on the front page (C1) of the Money and Investing section. The Markets Diary, which is illustrated below, shows the prior day's change in key prices and rates in the context of the past week and the past 18 months, giving a quick reading of the status quo and trends. The *Journal's* compact summary provides an excellent overview of the financial markets and is an appropriate introduction to the inside financial pages of any newspaper. Let's look at each of its sections in turn:

Stocks

Stock prices are measured by six major U.S. and foreign indexes and are represented graphically by the Dow Jones Industrial Average. Although by far the most widely watched stock average in the world, the blue-chip DJIA has its limitations: Being "price-weighted," it can be unduly influenced by major moves in higher-priced components, and since it comprises only the stocks of 30 large corporations, primarily

126

MARKETS DIARY 12/5/89

STOCKS Dow Jones Industrial Average

2741.68 −11.95

INDEX	CLOSE	NET CHNG	PCT CHNG	12-MO HIGH	12-MO LOW	12-MO CHNG	PCT	FROM 12/31	PCT
DJIA	2741.68 −	11.95 −	0.43	2791.41	2133.00 +	592.32 +27.56	+	573.11 +26.43	
DJ Equity	327.31 −	1.45 −	0.44	337.63	257.29 +	67.02 +25.75	+	66.57 +25.53	
S&P 500	349.58 −	1.83 −	0.52	359.80	274.24 +	71.99 +25.93	+	71.86 +25.87	
Nasdaq Comp.	458.55 +	0.27 +	0.06	485.73	372.77 +	81.55 +21.63	+	77.17 +20.23	
London (FT 100)	2327.5 +	24.1 +	1.05	2426.0	1747.9 +	560.1 +31.69	+	534.4 +29.80	
Tokyo (Nikkei)	37494.17 +	190.30 +	0.51	37494.17	29470.08 +	7824.79 +26.37	+	7335.17 +24.32	

BONDS Shearson Lehman Hutton T-Bond Index

3464.63 −1.01

INDEX	TUES	TUES YIELD	MON	MON YIELD	YR AGO	12-MO HIGH	12-MO LOW
Shearson Lehman Hutton treas.	3464.63	8.06%	3465.64	8.05%	2907.45	3465.64	2863.49
DJ 20 Bond (Price Return)	93.57	9.22	93.59	9.22	89.30	94.15	87.35
Salomon mortgage-backed	516.15	9.34	516.13	9.34	455.70	516.15	444.82
Bond Buyer municipal	93-29	7.25	93-28	7.25	89-18	95-6	89-4
Merrill Lynch corporate	447.10	9.30	446.93	9.30	392.13	447.10	387.11

INTEREST Federal Funds (N.Y. Fed, Fulton Prebon)

8.53% −0.01

ISSUE	CLOSE	MON	YEAR AGO	12-MO HIGH	12-MO LOW
3-month T-bill	7.56%	7.55%	7.94%	9.10%	7.20%
3-month CD (new)	7.67	7.67	8.44	9.52	7.66
Dealer Comm. Paper (90 days)	8.22	8.25	9.05	10.15	8.13
3-month Eurodollar deposit	8.44	8.44	9.38	10.63	8.25

U.S. DOLLAR J. P. Morgan Index vs. 15 Currencies

90.3 −0.3

CURRENCY	LATE NY	LATE MON	DAY'S HIGH	DAY'S LOW	12-MO HIGH	12-MO LOW — LATE NY —
British pound (in U.S. dollars)	1.5700	1.5625	1.5751	1.5615	1.8605	1.5120
Canadian dollar (in U.S. dollars)	0.8595	0.8595	0.8606	0.8594	0.8595	0.8276
Swiss franc (per U.S. dollar)	1.5920	1.6065	1.5875	1.6095	1.4468	1.7945
Japanese yen (per U.S. dollar)	143.80	143.68	143.55	143.90	121.92	149.46
W. German mark (per U.S. dollar)	1.7780	1.7835	1.7755	1.7910	1.7371	2.0340

COMMODITIES CRB Futures Index (1967=100)

226.30 +0.67

COMMODITY	CLOSE	CHANGE	MON	YR AGO	12-MO HIGH AT CLOSE	12-MO LOW AT CLOSE
Gold (Comex spot), troy oz.	$403.50	$+ 2.40	$401.10	$427.50	$427.50	$358.10
Oil (W. Tex. int. crude), bbl.	20.35	+ 0.10	20.25	15.45	24.65	15.45
Wheat (#2 hard KC), bu.	4.34	+ 0.01	4.33	4.19	4.72	4.07
Steers (Tex.-Okla. choice), 100 lb.	76.50	unch	76.50	73.25	79.75	69.00

NOTE: Monthly charts based on Friday close, except for Federal Funds, which are weekly average rates.

industrial issues, it is not as representative of the overall market as a broader-based index. Nonetheless, the question "How is the market doing?" is almost universally answered by quoting the Dow, which gives it unique status not only as a measure of market performance but as an influential force in market psychology.

Other indexes in the summary include the Dow Jones Equity Index, a relative newcomer made up of 700 stocks, which measures broader market performance; the Standard & Poor's Index of 500 Stocks, also a broad-based index and the most widely followed index after the DJIA; and the NASDAQ (National Association of Securities Dealers Automated Quotations) Composite Index, which measures a large group of mostly smaller companies traded over-the-counter.

The other two indexes track the two most important foreign exchanges: the London Stock Exchange, which is the dominant European market, and the Tokyo Stock Exchange, which is the world's second largest exchange after the New York Stock Exchange. Both the London FT 100 index of 100 stocks (or "Footsie," as it is popularly called) and the Nikkei Stock Average of 225 stocks are, like the Dow Jones Industrial Average, made up of blue-chip companies (called alpha stocks in London and first-section stocks in Tokyo). These indexes are widely watched not only because many people own stocks measured by them, but because of the growing interdependence of financial markets internationally. In reading the tables, keep in mind that Tokyo's trading day precedes London's, which precedes New York's, and that each market is affected by the others.

In the columns from left to right, the table shows the closing value of each index; the net change over the preceding close expressed in points and then as a percentage; the highest and lowest levels reached in the preceding 12-month period; the change both in points and as a percentage within the preceding 12-month period and for the calendar year to date.

What we can learn from the December 5, 1989, Markets Diary illustrated is that while the DJIA and the broad-based indexes were down the previous day, the NASDAQ index was up, indicating a swing, that day at least, from larger-capitalization stocks into smaller companies. The year-to-date comparisons would indicate that for most of the year the reverse was true—that larger stocks, represented exclusively in the DJIA but influencing the DJ Equity and S&P indexes, outperformed the smaller stocks dominating the NASDAQ.

The significance of this is that larger stocks tend to outshine smaller stocks in strong economies and vice versa. In slow economies the greater growth potential of small firms overshadows lower profit margins; thus, their stock prices rise (helped also by the fact that lower-priced stocks tend to register greater percentage changes than higher-priced shares in any market). In contrast, mature companies fare worse in weak economies because their sales and earnings per share tend to go down, taking share prices down with them.

Normally, the 12-month columns would help us detect the trend of stock prices. If, for example, the DJIA outperformed the NASDAQ by a greater amount over a 12-month period than over the shorter period represented by the year-to-date comparisons, one could conclude that smaller stocks were gaining on larger stocks. Of course, we are looking here at the month of December, when the annual figures and the year-to-date figures are within days of being identical.

Bonds

As was observed earlier, bond prices move in the opposite direction of interest rate so this is the market's way of bringing yields in line with prevailing rates. Of course, bond prices and yields are strongly influenced also by risk factors, by inflation expectations, and by supply and demand. Different types of bonds reflect these characteristics to different degrees.

The bond section is highlighted by graphs showing prices of a composite of Treasury bonds. Because T-bonds have the "full faith and credit" of the U.S. Government behind them and, with limited exceptions, are not callable, they are free of risks other than those associated with fluctuating interest rates and inflation. And because they are long-term (10 to 30 years) and not, like short-term Treasury bills, a direct instrument of Federal Reserve monetary policy, T-bond prices and yields reflect more purely than other investments the market's expectations with respect to interest rates and inflation. The T-bond rate is thus the benchmark for all other rates.

The DJ (Dow Jones) 20 Bond index is an arithmetic average of New York Exchange closing prices of 10 industrial and 10 utility bonds with investment-grade ratings from best to intermediate. (The words "price return" in parentheses tell us that changes in the index are the result purely of market activity as it affects prices and yields; in contrast, the other indexes in the group are based on "total return," meaning they reflect, in addition, changes in value resulting from the assumption that interest is reinvested. Under normal conditions this distinction does not materially affect the value of the indexes as indicators of the fixed-income market's direction.)

The Salomon mortgage-backed index tracks prices and yields of pass-through securities backed by home mortgages and issued or guaranteed by U.S. Government agencies such as Ginnie Mae, Freddie Mac, and Fannie Mae. Government-backed mortgage securities yield somewhat more than other government-backed bonds because they are subject to the risk that homeowners will prepay their mortgages, thus shortening the life of the investment. The prepayment risk is greatest when market interest rates decline, affording homeowners an opportunity to refinance at lower rates. Rising rates have the reverse effect and increase the demand for mortgage-backed securities.

The Bond Buyer municipal index, compiled by the *Bond Buyer* daily newspaper, tracks the prices and yields of newly issued AA- and A-rated tax-exempt bonds of states and localities. The Tax Reform Act of 1986 imposed certain restrictions on issuers of municipal securities, thus affecting both demand and supply in the tax-exempt market. The result has been that, on an equivalent taxable yield basis, municipals often yield more than taxable bonds of comparable quality and maturity.

The Merrill Lynch corporate index measures prices and yields of nearly 4,000 investment-grade (AAA to BBB) corporate issues. This index provides essentially the same information as the Dow Jones bond index, but differs in its broader base and its total-return method of computation.

Bond information is presented in six columns. The first four (from left to right) compare the previous day's index value (based on price) and yield with the corresponding figures of day before. The fifth column shows the index value a year ago, and the last two columns indicate the range of prices over the past 12 months.

It is important to understand that all the bonds covered in the foregoing tables are "straight" (not convertible), interest-bearing (not zero-coupon), and fixed-rate (not floating-rate). Such variations would behave differently in the marketplace and not be indicative of fixed-income securities. Also excluded were so-called "junk bonds," whose lower ratings and higher yields reflect their perceived greater risk of default. Indeed, in the latter part of 1989 junk bond prices tumbled when it appeared that some formerly well-regarded junk bond issuers, such as the Campeau Corporation and its U.S. retailing subsidiaries, were close to filing for bankruptcy.

The table illustrates that December 5 was a dull day in the bond market, little changed from the previous day. We do see that prices are substantially higher than a year ago and close to a 12-month high. This, of course, is a reflection of lower rates, and a glimpse at the 18-month graph indicates that higher prices and lower yields were clearly a trend as 1989 was ending.

Interest

Bond prices and yields give an indication of how the market views the future, what existing fixed-income investments might be worth, and what rate of return we could expect from long-term fixed-income investments. Short-term rates, which are highlighted in this section, give an indication as to what the Federal Reserve is doing to regulate the money supply and therby stimulate or slow down the economy. The Fed's actions, in turn, affect other rates and even the prices of stocks, which generally benefit from low rates. Short-term rate levels also have meaning to us directly, since many of the rates we pay—on credit cards, auto loans, adjustable-rate mortgages, and home-equity loans, for example—are "pegged" to the yields on these key money market instruments. And while high minimum purchase requirements exclude most individuals from participating in the short-term money market directly, these instruments are bought and sold by money market funds and affect the yields we get on those widely popular investments.

The charts here plot the federal funds rate, which is the rate banks with excess reserves charge other banks that need reserves for overnight money. Borrowings are heaviest, and the rate highest, when the Federal Reserve, through its monetary policy, is draining reserves from banks so they will have less money to lend and thus provide less stimulus to the economy. The fed funds rate is the most sensitive of rates—so sensitive, in fact, that daily fluctuations could be misleading. For that reason the graph does not plot daily changes but rather a weekly average. A trend in this rate often signals a change in the Fed's discount rate, and that, in turn, is usually followed by a change in the bank prime rate, the maximum rate banks charge their most creditworthy corporate customers. Other rates generally follow the prime.

Other short-term rates shown in the table increase with different degrees of risk and liquidity. The 3 month Treasury bill yield is established weekly at auction, and the bills are traded actively in the secondary market. Buying (and selling) T-bills, thus putting cash into (or taking cash out of) the economy and increasing (or decreasing) bank reserves, is the Fed's primary instrument of monetary policy, so T-bill yields are widely watched as an indicator of rate trends generally. The 90-day bill is also the benchmark for most floating-rate credit.

New 3-month bank certificates of deposit (CDs) tell us what banks are willing to pay for 3-month money. The rate they offer reflects their consensus that, for 3 months, rates are probably not going to drop significantly lower.

Dealer commercial paper (90 days) represents the IOUs of corporate borrowers. (Dealer means this "paper" is bought and sold through brokerage firms rather than issued and redeemed directly.) Commercial paper is unsecured and marketable only by the most creditworthy organizations, which use this method of borrowing as an alternative to more expensive prime rate bank loans. Commercial paper, which lacks secondary market liquidity, competes with risk-free T-bills for investors' cash and naturally commands a higher rate of interest.

The 3-month Eurodollar deposit rate is the rate paid by borrowers of U.S. dollar deposits held in banks, including U.S. bank subsidiaries, outside the United States, primarily, but not exclusively, in Europe. Whereas domestic short-term rates are directly or indirectly controlled by the monetary policies of central banks (such as the Federal Reserve in the United States and the Bank of England in the United Kingdom), the Eurodollar rate is a pure market rate, free to find its own level through supply and demand. This situation has attracted speculators, who are able to buy futures contracts on Eurodollar time deposit rates. Since overseas banks are relatively free of regulation and can operate on narrower spreads, they are able to compete easily with U.S. instruments for investor's money, although arbitrage keeps Eurodollar rates appropriately in line with rates paid by U.S. banks for deposits of similar maturity.

Eurodollar deposit rates and rates on other Eurodollar transactions and securities are based on the London Interbank Offer Rate (LIBOR), the offer side of quotes among major banks in London that trade deposits with each other in the same fashion that U.S. banks trade federal funds. The rate on 3-month Eurodollar deposits is also watched as a harbinger of changes in the U.S. prime rate, which is listed elsewhere in the financial pages. American banks like to maintain a spread of at least 1.5 percentage points between the prime rate and the Eurodollar rate; thus, whenever the spread is wider than that, conditions may be ripe for a drop in the prime.

The rate tables are straightforward and need little explanation. The previous day's closing rates are compared with those of the prior day, followed by columns showing the year-ago closings and the 12-month highs and lows. In the illustrated example, the tables bear out trends evident in the federal funds graph. Interest rates in general had been declining from their spring 1989 highs, and many observers believed a lowering of the Federal Reserve discount rate was overdue.

U.S. Dollar

The globalization of consumer, commercial, and financial markets in recent years has made us appreciate more keenly the effect of varying currency exchange rates. When the dollar becomes stronger—that is, when it buys more pounds, marks, yen, or other units of currency—it becomes cheaper in dollar terms for Americans to travel and shop abroad, to import foreign goods, and to buy foreign stocks and bonds. On the other hand, U.S. companies (and their shares) may suffer under such conditions because cheaper imported goods can hurt the sale of those produced domestically. When the dollar becomes weaker—that is, when it buys fewer units of foreign currencies—the cost of foreign travel and imports rise while U.S. exports become more competitive in world markets. Since the prices of foreign securities and the value of their interest and dividends increase as the dollar weakens, investing in foreign stock markets often means tracking the dollar.

The rates at which one currency can be converted to another are established by bid and offer, not unlike stocks, in a world-wide "over-the-counter" market that uses telephones and computers to link the major financial institutions, exchange brokers, and government agencies that dominate the foreign exchange marketplace. The demand for foreign exchange derives from trade, investment, travel and tourism, government needs of various sorts, and from speculators.

Since the exchange market operates 24 hours a day—when it's midnight in New York it's 2:00 P.M. in Tokyo—there are no closing quotes, although rates are reported at regular times late in the business day, making day-to-day comparisons meaningful. Currency rates are, however, highly sensitive to economic, financial, and political news and subject to rapid and pronounced shifts, which governments, except in extreme instances, are reluctant to counteract through market intervention. The exchange rates reported in newspapers can thus vary considerably from the rates prevailing at the time you read them.

The charts in this section show the J. P. Morgan Index of the dollar's value, one of two major U.S. dollar indexes (the other being the Federal Reserve Index, reported in *The New York Times*), compared with an average, weighted by volume of trade, of 15 foreign currencies. It shows the dollar strengthening between November 1988 and June 1989, then peaking again in September before dropping and leveling off through the first week of December.

The tables compare the dollar to five selected major currencies. The British pound and Canadian dollar rates are expressed in U.S. dollars. For example, late on the trading day in New York on Tuesday, December 5, it would have cost $1.57 to purchase one British pound and about 86 cents to purchase a Canadian dollar. The other currencies are expressed in units "per U.S. dollar." In other words, on that Tuesday the dollar was worth 1.5920 Swiss francs, 143.80 yen, and 1.7780 West German marks. (The difference in the methods has to do simply with custom and practicality, and all rates apply to transactions of at least $1 million.)

The data illustrated show very little change between Tuesday's exchange rates and the prior Monday's. The dollar weakened slightly against the pound, was unchanged against the Canadian dollar, weaker against the Swiss franc, stronger against the yen, and weaker against the mark.

Given the volatility of exchange rates, the two columns showing the high-low range for the trading day can often be more meaningful than the late New York rate by itself. In reading the intraday highs and lows and the 12-month highs and lows, remember that the higher the U.S. dollar figures for the British pound and Canadian dollar, the weaker the dollar, whereas the higher the figure shown for the other currencies, the stronger the dollar.

Thus, consistent with trends revealed by the chart, the dollar on December 5, 1989, was weaker against all the currencies listed in comparison with their 12-month highs but stronger compared to their 12-month lows, with one exception: The Canadian dollar was at a 12-month high and had been even stronger (the U.S. dollar therefore weaker) during the Tuesday trading day. The news story on foreign exchange that day was headlined: "Dollar is mostly lower in slow session; Canadian currency reaches 9-year high." The latter development was attributed to official announcements of Canadian intentions to follow anti-inflation policies and to hold interest rates steady.

Commodities

The commodities section of the Markets Diary highlights key prices and trends in the raw materials and provisions used by commerce and industry to meet our daily wants and needs.

In these Chicago-dominated markets, commodities are bought and sold on either (1) a "spot" basis, meaning the "actuals"—the physical commodities (or warehouse receipts)—are ready for immediate delivery and traded at a "cash price" (for grains) or "spot price" (for other commodities), or (2) a futures basis, meaning a "futures contract" is entered into that provides for delivery and payment in a specified future month at a specified price.

Participants in the market fall into two categories: On one side are businesses buying the commodities for commercial use or using futures contracts to hedge against the risk of loss due to a change in prices. On the other side are traders and speculators who aim to profit from short-term and longer-term price movements.

The average investor may participate in the commodities market through professionally managed pooled investments, or may just be interested in watching commodity price trends for what they reveal about inflationary expectations and the prices of things we eat, drink, wear, or otherwise use in our daily lives.

The Commodity Research Bureau's (CRB) Futures Index tracks futures prices on 21 commodities, including a diverse range of agricultural contracts, oil, lumber, copper, and precious metals. (This index does not include financial futures traded at commodities exchanges, such as those on interest rates and foreign currencies.) Because commodity prices are direct factors in the cost of living, the CRB Index is a highly sensitive barometer of inflation expectations. Increased inflation, of course, usually means higher interest rates and yields and lower bond prices. The diversity of the CRB Index is important to its value as an indicator of the direction of prices in general, since individual commodity prices are subject not only to supply and demand, but also to all manner of other influences including weather conditions, crop failures, trading cycles, political developments, and government actions.

The tables show spot activity in four of the most economically significant and actively traded commodities. Gold, which receives more daily attention in the press than any other single commodity, is shown in U.S. dollars per troy ounce at the closing price on the Commodity Exchange (Comex) in New York. (The Comex close is actually a settlement price determined shortly after trading ends, and represents the futures contract set to expire soonest, the so-called nearest-month contract. Other reports use the morning and afternoon London gold fixings.) The reasons gold is so widely followed, in addition to its industrial and commercial uses, are primarily three: (1) Gold has historically tended to rise in value when the inflation rate increases, so it is viewed as a measure of inflation expectations. (2) Gold is considered a safe haven when political turmoil threatens the value of financial investments, so the price of gold bullion and bullion futures contracts is a measure of international tensions. (3) Gold is used internationally as an alternative to the U.S. dollar, rising as the dollar weakens and vice versa, thus it is seen as a measure of confidence in the dollar.

The other commodities listed reflect changes in the cash or spot prices of the units in which they are traded. Thus, crude oil is quoted in dollars and cents per barrel, wheat in dollars and cents per bushel, and steers in dollars and cents per hundred pounds.

The data illustrated reflect a generally uneventful day in the commodities markets. The *Journal*'s commodities story led with the comment that by holding above $400 an ounce, considered an important psychological level at the time, the outlook for the price of gold was positive, since it had responded to profit-taking the day before by dropping below that level. Elsewhere in the article it was noted that crude oil was responding to increased demand for heating fuel in a " [cold] weather driven market." The only comment on agricultural commodities had to do with corn, which is not included in the Markets Diary but was up in response to reports of a big purchase by the Soviet Union.

Earnings Reports

Quarterly profit reports for corporations are carried in major newspapers like *The New York Times* or *Wall Street Journal* as well as in many other newspapers. In most cases, the abbreviated reports appear in one place, and include the latest sales, net income, net income per share, and shares outstanding, compared with the year-earlier figures. Using year-earlier comparisons rather than comparisons with the previous quarter excludes purely seasonal fluctuations. Department stores, for example, as a rule report the most sales in the fourth quarter, owing to the Christmas season. Comparing the fourth and third quarters, therefore, might give an inaccurate impression of the health of a department-store chain. It is very important also to look at earnings on a per-share basis. Per-share earnings, more than total earnings, are a major determinant of stock prices.

By the time you read the brief earnings reports, the stock market usually has had time to react, since the reports are usually released during trading hours. Occasionally, a company releases earnings after the close of trading, and you may see the price of the stock market react to the news when trading resumes. (Some companies release disappointing earnings late Friday in the hope they will be overlooked or their impact lessened because of the two-day break in trading.)

XYZ PRODUCTS (N)

Qtr to March 31	1986	1985
Revenue	$5,600,000	$4,980,000
Net income	463,000	452,000
Share earns	.22	.22
Shares outstanding	2,100,000	2,050,000

Dividend Reports

Lists of quarterly dividends, organized alphabetically by corporation, appear in greater number during the third through fifth weeks of each calendar quarter when earnings reports are most numerous. The dividend reports are generally divided into categories: Irregular, Increased, Reduced, and Regular. The organization of columns looks like this:

DIVIDEND REPORTS

	Period	Regular Rate	Stk of Record	Pay able
XYZ Corp.	Q	.30	4-10	4-30

The table tells you that the regular dividend for the hypothetical XYZ Corporation is paid quarterly, that the dividend is 30 cents per share (which would result in $1.20 per share annually if the rate held steady), that the dividend will be paid to shareowners of record April 10, and that the actual payment will be made on April 30. It's important to remember that stocks go ex-dividend during the interval between the dividend announcement and the actual payment. This means that the dividend isn't payable to investors who buy the stock during that interval. (On the other hand, if you sell the stock during the ex-dividend period, you still collect the dividend.) Shares listed on the NYSE generally go ex-dividend four days before the stockholder of record date. Stocks normally decline by the amount of the dividend when they enter an ex-dividend trading period.

Securities Offerings

Announcements of newly issued or about-to-be issued stocks and bonds come in two forms. Large newspapers include calendars and digests of expected and newly announced securities issues to be distributed by underwriting groups or syndicates. These groups of investment banking houses also place paid advertisements, known as tombstones in the language of Wall Street, which give a very basic summary of the offerings. (Tombstone ads are also used for other purposes, such as announcing major personnel changes or a firm's important role in an acquisition or merger.)

The newspaper listings come under such headings as Finance Briefs (*The New York Times*) or Financing Business (*The Wall Street Journal*). Because a high proportion of the offerings are bonds, these listings can usually be found near the bond tables and the interest rate/bond market news story.

One advantage of buying new issues (which are often reserved for favored customers) over buying existing securities, is that the buyer pays no commission. The broker-dealer is paid out of the underwriting spread, the difference between the price at which the securities are sold to the public and the lower price paid to the issuer by the underwriters. Even if you're not interested in purchasing securities, these notices give you an idea of the prevailing interest rates (in the case of bonds) and the types of companies that are able to attract capital by issuing shares.

In the accompanying illustration of a typical tombstone ad, the boilerplate (standard legal language) advises you to read the the prospectus before you buy. Many investors, of course, simply rely on the word of their brokers anyway, but the prospectus is a legally required summary of the facts and risks concerning the issue, and

---

New Issue   October 2, 19--

750,000 Shares

ABXY Corporation

Common Stock
($.10 par value)

Price $30 per Share

Copies of the Prospectus may be obtained in any State in which this annoucement is circulated only
from such of the undersigned as may legally offer these securities in such State.

First XYZ Inc.

MNO Inc.

TUV Securities

ABC Inc.   CDE & Co.   Monopoly Inc.

Ajax Inc.   Dustby Inc.   ZXZ Inc.

HIJ Securities

---

investors are well-advised to read it. The tombstone lists the names of the firms comprising the underwriting group and, by alphabetically organized groups, the relative importance of their participation. The par value of the stock, if any, is usually listed, but has no meaning in terms of market value. The offering price, of course, is included; however, this announcement doesn't tell you anything more, for example, how the proceeds of the sale are to be used.

Tender Offer Announcements

In both friendly and unfriendly takeover situations, the advertisements placed by corporations soliciting your shares may offer the greatest source of practical information regarding what you should or could do with your shares. Among other things, these comprehensive tombstone type notices identify the company seeking to acquire another company; state the price being offered for your shares and whether payment will be in cash or securities or a combination of the two; inform you of various deadlines to send in your shares or to withdraw your offer; and announce various other conditions, such as the minimum number of shares the acquiring company requires for the deal to be completed. These notices also include the names of companies that act as soliciting and information agents, such as D.F. King & Co., Georgeson & Co., or the Carter Organization, along with their addresses and phone numbers. Such companies have been paid to provide you with information and prospectuses. Of course, these ads can also be biased and are often followed in a few days with ads placed by the target company, citing reasons to reject the bid.

Redemption Notices

Callable bonds and preferred stock can be redeemed by the issuer prior to maturity, and the likelihood of this happening is greatest when the issuer can replace them with new securities providing lower interest rate or dividends. When redemption takes place, issuers often place paid notices in a local newspaper and/or a major publication, such as *The Wall Street Journal*. These notices provide the serial numbers and demoninations of the securities being redeemed and the call price of the securities.

Short Interest

Around the twentieth of each month, the New York and American stock exchanges and NASDAQ release data on short interest—shares sold when they are not actually owned by the seller (usually they are borrowed). The exchanges break down the statistics by individual stocks and also give a total number of shorted shares of their listed companies compared to the total the month before.

Short interest figures generally signify that professional investors anticipate a decline in share prices. However, the figures are somewhat inflated by the inclusion of the short positions of exchange floor specialists; they sell short as part of their stabilizing function as well as for investment purposes. Market analysts also view large short interest positions as potential buying pressure since short positions must ultimately be covered by purchasing shares.

Other Economic and Financial Indicators

Among the more common weekly graphic features relating to business activity, securities prices, and returns on your savings are the following:

Treasury Bill Bar Chart: This appears in many newspapers, usually on Tuesday, following the Treasury bill auction of the preceding day. This table of 3-month Treasury bill yields shows how discount rates have changed on a weekly basis over the past three months, and gives the year-earlier yield as well. This chart gives you an idea of the direction in which rates on adjustable rate mortgages are heading, and whether you'll earn more or less income from a money market fund or an adjustable rate CD.

Money Supply Chart: This type of chart appears on Friday, following the weekly report on the nation's money supply released by the Federal Reserve Board at 4:30 P.M. EST on Thursday. The chart contains a "cone," made up of diverging lines that indicate the upper and lower targets of money supply growth laid down by the Federal Reserve Board. If the line representing M–1 money supply growth moves above the cone, watch out for jittery speculation about tighter monetary policy—speculation that could hurt bond prices. If the M–1 line is below the cone, be prepared for speculation that the Federal Reserve Board intends to loosen monetary policy and push rates lower—speculation that often supports bond prices. M–1, however, fluctuates week to week because it's narrowly based. Broader measures of the money supply, M–2 and M–3, are reported monthly, and articles often include similar charts for these figures.

New York Stock Exchange Issues

The Dow: Minute by Minute

Position of the Dow Jones industrial average at 30-second intervals yesterday

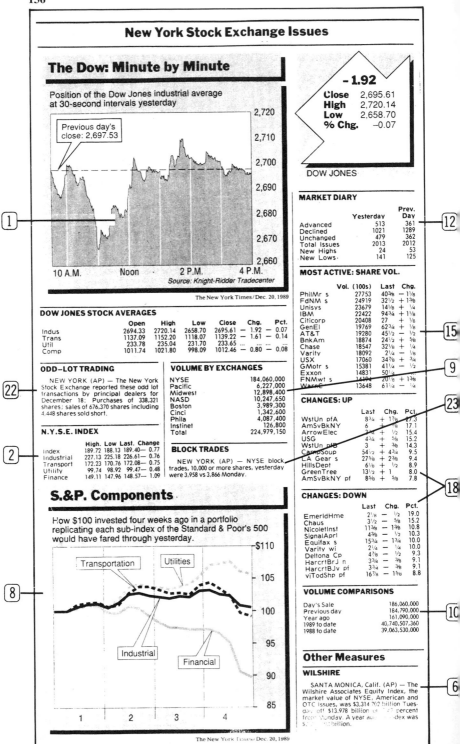

Previous day's close: 2,697.53

2,720
2,710
2,700
2,690
2,680
2,670
2,660

10 A.M.   Noon   2 P.M.   4 P.M.

Source: Knight-Ridder Tradecenter

The New York Times/Dec. 20, 1989

DOW JONES STOCK AVERAGES

	Open	High	Low	Close	Chg.	Pct.
Indus	2694.33	2720.14	2658.70	2695.61	− 1.92	− 0.07
Trans	1137.09	1152.20	1118.07	1139.22	− 1.61	− 0.14
Util	233.78	235.04	231.70	233.65	...	...
Comp	1011.74	1021.80	998.09	1012.46	− 0.80	− 0.08

ODD-LOT TRADING

NEW YORK (AP) — The New York Stock Exchange reported these odd lot transactions by principal dealers for December 18: Purchases of 338,321 shares; sales of 676,370 shares including 4,448 shares sold short.

N.Y.S.E. INDEX

	High.	Low	Last.	Change
Index	189.72	188.13	189.40	− 0.77
Industrial	227.13	225.18	226.61	− 0.76
Transport	172.23	170.76	172.08	− 0.75
Utility	99.74	98.92	99.47	− 0.48
Finance	149.11	147.96	148.57	− 1.09

VOLUME BY EXCHANGES

NYSE	184,060,000
Pacific	6,227,000
Midwest	12,898,400
NASD	10,247,650
Boston	3,989,300
Cinci	1,342,600
Phila	4,087,400
Instinet	126,800
Total	224,979,150

BLOCK TRADES

NEW YORK (AP) — NYSE block trades, 10,000 or more shares, yesterday were 3,958 vs 3,866 Monday.

S.&P. Components

How $100 invested four weeks ago in a portfolio replicating each sub-index of the Standard & Poor's 500 would have fared through yesterday.

Transportation   Utilities

Industrial   Financial

$110
105
100
95
90
85

1   2   3   4

The New York Times/Dec. 20, 1989

−1.92

Close	2,695.61
High	2,720.14
Low	2,658.70
% Chg.	−0.07

DOW JONES

MARKET DIARY

	Yesterday	Prev. Day
Advanced	513	361
Declined	1021	1289
Unchanged	479	362
Total Issues	2013	2012
New Highs	24	53
New Lows	141	125

MOST ACTIVE: SHARE VOL.

	Vol. (100s)	Last	Chg.
PhilMr s	27753	40⅜	− 1⅛
FdNM s	24919	32½	+ 1⅜
Unisys	23679	14⅛	+ ¼
IBM	22422	94¾	+ 1⅛
Citicorp	20408	27	+ ⅛
GenEl	19769	62¾	+ ⅛
AT&T	19280	45½	− ½
BnkAm	18874	24½	+ ⅝
Chase	18547	32⅛	+ ¼
Varity	18092	2¼	− ⅛
USX	17060	34⅞	+ ¾
GMotr s	15381	41¼	− ½
Exxon	14831	50¼	
FNMwl s	14494	20⅛	+ 1⅜
Warne	13648	61¼	− ¼

CHANGES: UP

	Last	Chg.	Pct.
WstUn pfA	8¾	+ 1⅞	27.3
AmSvBkNY	6	+ 1	17.1
ArrowElec	3¾	+ ½	15.4
USG	4¾	+ ⅝	15.2
WstUn pfB	3	+ ⅜	14.3
CampSoup	54½	+ 4¾	9.5
LA Gear s	27⅝	+ 2⅜	9.4
HillsDept	6⅛	+ ½	8.9
GreenTree	13½	+ 1	8.0
AmSvBkNY pf	8⅝	+ ⅝	7.8

CHANGES: DOWN

	Last	Chg.	Pct.
EmerldHme	2⅛	− ½	19.0
Chaus	3½	− ⅝	15.2
NicoletInst	11⅜	− 1⅜	10.8
SignalAprl	4⅜	− ½	10.3
Equifax s	15¾	− 1¾	10.0
Varity wi	2¼	− ¼	10.0
Deltona Cp	4⅞	− ½	9.3
HarcrtBrJ n	3¾	− ⅜	9.1
HarcrtBJv pf	3¾	− ⅜	9.1
viTodShp pf	16⅞	− 1⅝	8.8

VOLUME COMPARISONS

Day's Sale	186,060,000
Previous day	184,790,000
Year ago	161,090,000
1989 to date	40,740,507,360
1988 to date	39,063,530,000

Other Measures

WILSHIRE

SANTA MONICA, Calif. (AP) — The Wilshire Associates Equity Index, the market value of NYSE, American and OTC issues, was $3,314,702 billion Tuesday, off $13.978 billion or ... percent from Monday. A year ago ... dex was $... billion.

The New York Times/Dec. 20, 1989

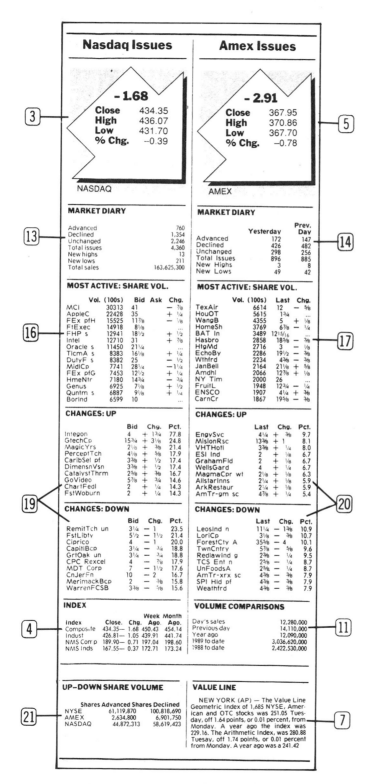

Nasdaq Issues

-1.68

Close	434.35
High	436.07
Low	431.70
% Chg.	−0.39

NASDAQ

Amex Issues

-2.91

Close	367.95
High	370.86
Low	367.70
% Chg.	−0.78

AMEX

MARKET DIARY (Nasdaq)

Advanced	760
Declined	1,354
Unchanged	2,246
Total issues	4,360
New highs	13
New lows	211
Total sales	163,625,300

MARKET DIARY (Amex)

	Yesterday	Prev. Day
Advanced	172	147
Declined	426	482
Unchanged	298	256
Total Issues	896	885
New Highs	3	8
New Lows	49	42

MOST ACTIVE: SHARE VOL. (Nasdaq)

	Vol. (100s)	Bid	Ask	Chg.
MCI	30313	41		− 7/8
AppleC	22428	35		+ 1/4
FEx pfH	15525	117/8		− 1/8
FtExec	14918	81/8		...
FHP s	12941	181/2		+ 1/2
Intel	12710	31		+ 7/8
Oracle s	11450	211/4		...
TlcmA s	8383	161/8		+ 1/4
DutyF s	8382	25		− 1/2
MidlCp	7741	281/4		−11/4
FEx pfG	7453	121/2		+ 1/4
HmeNtr	7180	143/4		− 3/4
Genus	6925	71/8		+ 1/2
Quntm s	6887	91/8		+ 1/4
Borlnd	6599	10		...

MOST ACTIVE: SHARE VOL. (Amex)

	Vol. (100s)	Last	Chg.
TexAir	6614	12	− 5/8
HouOT	5615	13/4	...
WangB	4355	5	+ 1/8
HomeSh	3769	67/8	− 1/4
BAT In	3489	1215/16	...
Hasbro	2858	185/8	− 3/8
HtgMd	2716	3	− 1/8
EchoBy	2286	191/2	− 3/8
Wthfrd	2234	43/8	− 3/8
JanBell	2164	211/8	+ 5/8
Amdhl	2066	127/8	+ 1/8
NY Tim	2000	26	...
FruitL	1948	123/4	− 1/4
ENSCO	1907	41/4	+ 3/8
CarnCr	1867	195/8	− 3/8

CHANGES: UP (Nasdaq)

	Bid	Chg.	Pct.
Integon	4	+ 13/4	77.8
GtechCp	153/4	+ 31/8	24.8
MagicYrs	21/8	+ 3/8	21.4
PerceptTch	41/8	+ 5/8	17.9
CaribSel pf	33/8	+ 1/2	17.4
DimensnVsn	33/8	+ 1/2	17.4
CatalystThrm	25/8	+ 3/8	16.7
GoVideo	57/8	+ 3/4	14.6
ChartFedl	2	+ 1/4	14.3
FstWoburn	2	+ 1/4	14.3

CHANGES: UP (Amex)

	Last	Chg.	Pct.
EngySvc	41/4	+ 3/8	9.7
MislonRsc	133/8	+ 1	8.1
VHTHotl	33/8	+ 1/4	8.0
ESI Ind	2	+ 1/8	6.7
GrahamFld	2	+ 1/8	6.7
WellsGard	4	+ 1/4	6.7
MagmaCpr wt	21/8	+ 1/8	6.3
AllstarInns	21/4	+ 1/8	5.9
ArkRestaur	21/4	+ 1/8	5.9
AmTr-gm sc	47/8	+ 1/4	5.4

CHANGES: DOWN (Nasdaq)

	Bid	Chg.	Pct.
RemitTch un	31/4	− 1	23.5
FstLibty	51/2	− 11/2	21.4
Ciprico	4	− 1	20.0
CapitlBcp	31/4	− 3/4	18.8
GrtOak un	31/4	− 3/4	18.8
CPC Rexcel	4	− 7/8	17.9
MDT Corp	7	− 11/2	17.6
CnJerFn	10	− 2	16.7
MerimackBcp	2	− 3/8	15.8
WarrenFCSB	33/8	− 5/8	15.6

CHANGES: DOWN (Amex)

	Last	Chg.	Pct.
Leosind n	111/4	− 13/8	10.9
LorlCp	31/8	− 3/8	10.7
ForestCty A	355/8	− 4	10.1
TwnCntry	57/8	− 5/8	9.6
Redlawlnd g	23/8	− 1/4	9.5
TCS Ent n	25/8	− 1/4	8.7
UnFoodsA	25/8	− 1/4	8.7
AmTr-xrx sc	43/8	− 3/8	7.9
SPI Hld pf	43/8	− 3/8	7.9
Weathfrd	43/8	− 3/8	7.9

INDEX

Index	Close.	Chg.	Week Ago	Month Ago
Composite	434.35	− 1.68	450.43	454.14
Indust	426.81	− 1.05	439.91	441.74
NMS Comp	189.90	− 0.71	197.04	198.60
NMS Inds	167.55	− 0.37	172.71	173.24

VOLUME COMPARISONS

Day's sales	12,280,000
Previous day	14,110,000
Year ago	12,090,000
1989 to date	3,036,620,000
1988 to date	2,422,530,000

UP–DOWN SHARE VOLUME

	Shares Advanced	Shares Declined
NYSE	61,119,870	100,818,690
AMEX	2,634,800	6,901,750
NASDAQ	44,872,313	58,619,423

VALUE LINE

NEW YORK (AP) — The Value Line Geometric Index of 1,685 NYSE, American and OTC stocks was 251.05 Tuesday, off 1.64 points, or 0.01 percent, from Monday. A year ago the index was 229.16. The Arithmetic Index, was 280.88 Tuesay, off 1.74 points, or 0.01 percent from Monday. A year ago was a 241.42

THE STOCK MARKETS: DAILY SUMMARIES
Key Stock Market Indexes and Charts

It's possible for all but the busiest person to get a quick overview of stock market activity—and even some sense of future market movement—by reviewing the key market indexes and charts clustered at the beginning of the daily stock tables. At first, the mass of figures may overwhelm you. But you can train your eyes and brain to march through such displays, dividing them into mentally digestible components. The principal display of *The Wall Street Journal* appears on the inside front page of the *Money and Investing* (C) section and is headed Stock Market Data Bank. The Market Indicators package of *The New York Times,* shown here, appears at the beginning of its New York Stock Exchange listings. It can be broken down as follows:

Charts 1 to 7   These sets of graphs and tables represent price averages and indexes showing changes in issues listed on the NYSE (1 and 2), NASDAQ (3 and 4), and Amex (5) and, in the case of the Wilshire index (6) and the Value Line index (7), the three markets combined. They simply tell you in which direction the overall group of stocks each covers moved during the most recent trading session. The NYSE receives the most attention, with its list tracked by two families of indexes: the Dow Jones, and the exchange's own NYSE composite. Another important set of indexes, those of Standard & Poor's, are reported separately in *The New York Times* and will be discussed shortly. A composite index includes all the stocks traded on a particular market. A narrower index, such as those that appear here for utilities or transportation shares, tracks relatively few stocks. Utility and financial stocks are sensitive to interest rate changes—and by extension—to the bond market because these industries depend on huge amounts of credit. Therefore, pluses for these indexes immediately indicate the likelihood that the rate situation is stable or improving. Scanning the pluses and minuses in the various markets tells you if the previous day's movements were broadly based or varied from one market to another. The *Times* makes this easy by showing the highlights of the three major indexes in arrow-shaped boxes pointing in the direction the index moved the previous day. Declines for the Amex and NASDAQ next to rising indexes for the NYSE may indicate that institutional investors are more optimistic than individual investors. In the example illustrated, the three indexes all moved in the same direction—down.

Chart 8   This graph varies from day to day and illuminates a relevant aspect of market activity. (*The Wall Street Journal's* counterpart, called *Investment Insight,* appears regularly just below its Markets Diary.) The illustrated example shows how the four subindexes comprising the Standard & Poor's 500 stock index performed relative to each other over a 4-week period. (Current quarterly activity in the S&P 500 is depicted every day in a point-and-figure chart that appears at the beginning of the stock price tables just above another chart showing NYSE volume over the same period.) The S&P 500 is composed mostly of NYSE-listed stocks with some Amex and over-the-counter issues. Although numbers and proportions vary somewhat, its breaks down approximately into 400 industrials, 60 transportation and utility companies, and 40 financial issues. Although broader indexes exist (the Wilshire covers 5,000 stocks and the Value Line about 1,700), the S&P 500 is the most widely followed index of broader market activity and often behaves quite differently than the DJIA index of blue chip stocks. The S&P 100 stock index, which is reported in the table accompanying the graph, has a composition similar to the 500, but it is made up exclusively of stocks for which options are traded.

Charts 9, 10, and 11   Volume can help you determine in which direction the stock market will continue to move. If stock prices rise amid heavy volume, the indication is that many investors chose to invest heavily in stocks, and they intend to hold out for further price rises. Similarly, a market drop on heavy volume is considered a more serious setback than a drop on light volume. A market rise on light volume will cause the market rise to be questioned. The trick, of course, is to have an idea of what normal volume is for any given exchange during any particular season. Bar charts in *The New York Times* and *The Wall Street Journal* indicate daily volume for the NYSE for the past three months and six months, respectively.

Chart 9   This chart shows how the previous day's volume was distributed among the NYSE and the various regional and electronic exchanges on which NYSE-listed stocks are traded.

Charts 10 and 11   These tables compare NYSE and Amex volume figures to the prior day, a year ago, and on a year-to-date basis.

Charts 12, 13, and 14   Called Market Diary here, these figures, like the volume numbers, help you confirm or doubt the validity of changes in the price index. If, for example, the indexes have risen sharply in one of the markets, but the number of issues that advanced are fairly evenly matched with the number of issues that declined, it's possible that the movement of a few stocks was responsible for the rising indexes. Thus, the market isn't as strong as it first appeared. Similarly, the number of stocks that hit 52-week highs during the session indicates how strong the market really was. Major financial sections and publications carry lists of stocks that hit 52-week highs and lows. Obviously, you want to know if any of your stocks are included on these lists.

Charts 15, 16, and 17   The most active issues—stocks with the heaviest trading volume—are given in the descending order of shares traded for each issue—15 for each market. Sometimes stocks appear on the most active list because of a news items or a rumor regarding profits, mergers, or new products. Some stocks, however, constantly appear because they are actively traded by financial institutions, which often are restricted to buying stocks with large market capitalizations (the number of outstanding shares times the market price).

Charts 18, 19, and 20   Because up and down price changes are expressed in percentage terms, you can get a quick idea of the importance of your gain or loss if one of your stocks appears on this list. Cheaper stocks are more apt to be included on this list, since small point changes translate into bigger percentage changes for cheaper stocks than for expensive ones. The list may also help you find (or avoid) volatile stocks.

Chart 21   The up and down share volume helps you gauge the daily strength and weakness of the three major markets. The Advanced column presents the number of shares in each market that were rising when they changed hands, while the Declined column indicates the number of shares sold below the price of the previous sale. Shares sold at the same price are not included. These figures can signal an underlying weakness or strength often masked by the indexes. If stocks rose according to the indexes, but were sold on "weakness" (that is, when the shares were dropping) rather than on "strength" (that is, on rising prices), this could mean that investors were using an overall price rise to take their profits and get out.

Chart 22   Odd-lots, usually stock transactions of fewer than 100 shares, indicate what small investors are doing. Although unflattering to small investors, odd-lot buying or selling is used by contrarian analysts as an example of what *not* to do. In other words, odd-lotters are widely believed to be wrong more often than right. When the proportion of odd-lot short sales rises above normal levels, many analysts predict an imminent market rally. Note that this data, which encompasses NYSE trading, appears two days after the session to which the statistics refer, rather than on the day following the session.

Chart 23   This listing indicates the number of large blocks (10,000 shares or more) of stock handled on the NYSE the previous day. Block activity provides an indication of the portion of total volume transacted by institutional investors. These figures are particularly significant when we know what percentage of block trades was executed above the previous trade (uptick) and below (downtick). When upticks exceed downticks, it is considered a bullish sign and vice versa. This information is provided on Saturdays in *The New York Times* in a section called "Tracking the Markets."

New York Stock Exchange and American Stock Exchange Consolidated Tables

You have to reach into stock tables to find specific information. Stock tables remain the heart of daily financial publications and sections, although the commodity, options, and bond tables are becoming increasingly more important as readers become more familiar with other types of investments. The tables for the two major U.S. stock exchanges, the New York and American stock exchanges, and the NASDAQ national market follow the same format. The information encompasses consolidated trading, which also includes trading on regional exchanges and on the over-the-counter market. Starting with the name of each stock, which we'll call Column 1, the tables offer:

1. Name   It's not always easy to locate a particular stock, because the names are usually radically abbreviated. The abbreviation systems used by the Associated Press and United Press International, which supply most of the tables you see, are different (and not to be confused with stock ticker symbols used on the exchanges); thus, the alphabetical order will differ from one system to the other. Stocks like IBM and AT&T are easy to find; few investors, however, would know immediately that WTPTP is West Point Pepperell. Unless otherwise identified, these are names of common stock. A ''pf'' identifies preferred stock. Preferred

NEW YORK STOCK EXCHANGE

⑨		①	②	③	④	⑤	⑥		⑦	⑧
52-Week				**Yid**	**PE**	**Sales**				
High	**Low**	**Stock**	**Div**	**%**	**Ratio**	**100s**	**High**	**Low**	**Last**	**Chg.**
25	18	XYZ Corp.	.92	2.0	7	623	17⅜	17⅛	17⅜	+⅛

stocks that are convertible to common shares are identified as preferred stock, but the convertability feature is not indicated in the stock tables as it is in the corporate bond tables. A "v" indicates that trading was suspended in the primary market. Stock tables are usually accompanied by explanatory notes defining any letters that may appear. An "A," "B," or other capital letter differentiates between one class of stock and another. A "wt" identifies the security as a warrant. A "vj" indicates that the company is in bankruptcy proceedings, and "wi" means when issued, signifying that the shares have not yet been issued. If the issuance is canceled, the trades will also be canceled. Also included but not identified are exchange-listed American Depositary Receipts (ADRs), which are negotiable receipts representing shares of foreign issuers.

2. Annual dividend   Dividends are listed by dollars and cents per share.   Don't confuse this figure with the amount you'll receive in the mail each quarter. The annual dividend is an estimate, based on the most recent quarterly dividend multiplied by four. If a company has a history of steadily rising dividends, consider this a conservative estimate. An "e" in this column indicates that dividends have been irregular, and that the figure represents the amount paid over the past year, rather than an estimate of future dividends. A "g" means dividends are paid in Canadian currency, although the other stock market data is given in terms of U.S. dollars.

3. Yield   This is the current dividend divided by the lastest closing price, rounded off to the nearest tenth of a percent. A low- or no-yield stock may be a growth stock, which means that profits are reinvested rather than paid out in dividends. Investors purchase growth stocks for capital gains, not for dividends; they hope that stock prices will increase as profits do. Some investors, however, purchase stocks for dividends, or income. This yield figure allows you to compare the dividend income with the income from other types of investments. Remember, however, that while the yield on a stock represents the potential income, the yield on bonds is a combination of both the annual interest income and the lump-sum capital gain or loss that occurs when the bond is redeemed. In a way, therefore, comparing stock and bond yields is similar to comparing apples and oranges.

4. PE ratio   The price earnings ratio is the latest price divided by the last 12 months' earnings per share, rounded to the nearest whole number. Be sure not to confuse PEs with dividends. PEs are used to compare the perceived value of stocks in the marketplace. PEs indicate how investors view the value of a company's profits. Stocks representing solid, uninflated profits that are expected to grow usually have higher PEs than stocks with questionable profits and profit-growth potential. Growth companies may have PEs of 20 or more. On the other hand, a high PE could be the result of a recent drop in earnings, and the prelude to a drop in the stock's price that will drop the PE to its former, lower level. A start-up or turnaround company could be attractive, but could have no earnings—and therefore no PE. PEs give you a way to calculate per share earnings roughly: divide the stock price by the PE.

5. *Sales*   This column gives you the trading volume, in hundreds of shares. A "5," in most cases, means 500 shares changed hands; a "1067" means 106,700 shares were traded. A "z," however, indicates that the full figure is being given. Volume measures how liquid a stock is. Stocks that consistently show large volume and small price changes are liquid; it takes a large imbalance between buy and sell orders to move the price much. Stocks with consistently low trading volume may be subject to wide price swings when large orders are finally placed. Sudden surges in volume, accompanied by rising prices, may indicate that an individual or an organization is building up a stake. (If five percent or more of a company's stock is acquired, however, SEC rule 13(d) requires that information, including a statement of intentions, be filed with its offices, with the company, and with the relevant stock exchange.) Volume surges often trigger takeover rumors, which in turn result in even greater volume and price movements. Financial analysts and journalists often ask company executives about the reasons for unusually heavy volume. A response of "no known reason" may cool speculation, while a "no comment" may fuel the guessing game.

An "x" in the volume column means the stock is ex-dividend. During this time buyers do not receive the most recently declared dividend. Stock prices decline by the amount of the dividend when the shares go ex-dividend, and then usually recover gradually.

6. *High/Low*   These twin columns give the highest and lowest prices during the trading session. A "u" indicates a 52-week high; a "d" indicates a 52-week low.

7. *Last sale*   The last sale is the closing price. Prices are usually expressed in "eighths"; an eighth equals 12.5 cents. Increments of sixteenths (6.25 cents) and thirty-seconds (3.125 cents) are used for cheaper stocks. You'll see these increments most often with over-the-counter stocks. Tables provided by Associated Press don't indicate the location of the last sale. United Press International does include the location, using "p" for Pacific Stock Exchange, "x" for Philadelphia Stock Exchange, "u" for Midwest Stock Exchange, and "g" for over-the-counter.

8. *Change*   This figure represents the change in closing price from the previous day.

9. *52-week High-Low*   The high-low column gives you the annual trading range, the highest and lowest prices of the previous 52 weeks plus the current trading week, up to, but not through, the last session. A broad range indicates that a stock has demonstrated the potential to

make—and lose—money for shareholders. Sometimes, a stock that has traded up and down within a range will meet resistance when it approaches its previous high point, because some investors will use this high point as a benchmark to sell. Similarly, the low point could serve as a buffer against further price drops. At the low point, buyers, hoping history will repeat itself and the stock rise, may purchase shares and thus provide support for the stock's price.

Other Over-the-Counter Stock Tables

The quantity of information available for over-the-counter stocks has grown dramatically over the years. It's still often necessary, however, to call your broker for a price because many of the lesser-known, less expensive stocks aren't included in the daily tables. Your broker will use the pink sheets published by the National Quotations Bureau, which list bid and asked prices, to give you a price. *Barron's* provides extensive over-the-counter tables on a weekly basis. The *National OTC Stock Journal,* another weekly, carries information about penny stocks, which usually sell for less than $1.00. The daily tables included in large newspapers have expanded, in part because of the efforts of the National Association of Securities Dealers, the umbrella group for over-the-counter dealers. Since the early 1970s, the NASD Automated Quotations, or NASDAQ system, has allowed dealers using desktop terminals to view each other's bid quotations (the highest prices they're willing to pay), and asked quotations (the lowest prices they'd accept). NASDAQ also passes this and other information on to wire services for use in daily stock tables. Since the early 1980s, the system has been upgraded to allow dealers to enter transaction prices and sizes of trades. As a result, the tables for the more expensive or more heavily traded NASDAQ stocks are identical to the NYSE and Amex tables. Stocks that are subject to this full-line reporting system are included in tables carrying such headings as NASDAQ National Market or NASDAQ National Market Issues.

However, not all the companies meeting NASD criteria to have their shares listed as part of the National Market System are included there. Instead, more limited market information for the shares of these and other NASDAQ-listed companies is included under the headings of NASDAQ National List or NASDAQ Bid and Asked Quotations. In these tables, you'll mainly find volume figures and closing bid and asked quotations along with the daily change in the bid price from the previous day's closing bid.

The NASDAQ Bid and Asked Quotations table presents the following elements:

1. Name of the stock and its annual dividend, if any.

2. Sales, in hundreds of shares.

3. Last bid of the session, that is, the most a dealer will pay you for

NASDAQ NATIONAL LIST

①	②	③	④	⑤
Stock & Div	**Sales 100s**	**Bid**	**Asked**	**Net Chg.**
ABZ Sys	90	3/8	7/8	− 1/4
Quiljax	2	6	6 3/4	. . .
Zextap Inc .08	14	15 1/2	16	− 1/2

a share. You'll note that the spread between bid and asked prices often is considerable.

4. Last asked quotation of the day, that is, the lowest a dealer will accept for a share.

5. Change in the bid from the end of the previous trading day.

Many over-the-counter stocks appear on neither the National Market nor the National List. Some of the larger financial publications and sections include as many of these stocks as they see fit, usually in an abbreviated form that includes only the name, bid, and asked, but no volume or daily change. These stocks are listed under various headings, including Additional OTC Quotes and NASDAQ Supplemental OTC.

Regional and Foreign Stock Market Tables

A relatively small number of stocks are listed only on regional exchanges, such as the Midwest, Pacific, Philadelphia, and Boston stock exchanges. These shares usually aren't very actively traded and attract mainly a regional following. Regional stock trading information in newspapers usually provides daily data on volume; high, low, and closing prices; and change in price. Readers must calculate dividends, yield, the PE ratio, and seek out 52-week high and low prices.

Of increasing importance are stocks traded on foreign markets. Information about the more important stocks are carried in such major newspapers as *The New York Times* and *The Wall Street Journal*. The stocks are organized by the exchange on which they're traded. The information carried for the Toronto and Montréal markets in Canada is the same as the information carried for the U.S. regional exchange-listed stocks. The data carried for other foreign stocks is more limited: often only the name and the closing price, given in local currency, such as Japanese yen, British pence, French francs, Swiss francs, West German marks, and so on. It's up to the reader to track the daily change, and, if necessary, make use of the foreign exchange tables to translate the price into U.S. dollars and cents. Other tables show foreign securities traded over the counter. The majority of these issues are American Depositary Receipts, representing ownership of securities physically deposited abroad. Where they are not ADRs, the indication ''n'' is used. Quotes are in U.S. dollars and these tables typically have four columns: sales, bid price, asked price, and net change.

STOCK OPTIONS TABLES

Stock options give you both a conservative way to increase the income on your holdings or insure your portfolio against losses, as well as relatively inexpensive and highly speculative ways to invest in stocks. In any case, don't assume you understand these investment vehicles until you at least understand the stock option tables. Although unheard of a generation ago, these tables now comprise a major portion of the inside of financial news packages. The longest tables are generated by the principal options exchanges, the Chicago Board Options Exchange, the American Stock Exchange, and the Philadelphia Stock Exchange. Shorter tables are included for small options trading operations found on other exchanges.

Daily Stock Options Tables

Options tables give you the prices of wasting assets. These contracts, which as a rule last no longer than nine months, give the holder the right, but not the obligation, to buy (call) or sell (put) shares of stock at a specified strike price by a specified expiration date. The daily table format, and what it includes, by columns, is as follows.

STOCK OPTIONS

	①	②	③			④		
	Option &	Strike	Calls—Last			Puts—Last		
	NY Close	Price	May	Aug	Nov	May	Aug	Nov
Ⓐ	XYZ	35	7	6½	6¾	¾	¼	r
Ⓑ	40	40	2	1½	r	1	1½	r
Ⓒ	40	45	¾	¼	r	7	6½	r

1. Name of the underlying stock and under it, the closing price of the underlying stock, repeated for each row of strike prices. (Since New York Stock Exchange tables now generally include sales of NYSE stocks on other exchanges, the NY Close may differ from the NYSE table, which reports later sales on the Pacific Stock Exchange and elsewhere.) In this example, XYZ Corporation stock closed at 40 on the principal stock exchange on which it's traded, most likely the New York Stock Exchange. Because the stock is worth $40 per share, each 100-share options contract has an exercise value of $4000.

2. The strike price is given in this column. This is the price per share at which the option holder is entitled to buy or sell the stock. The accompanying table includes options series for three strike prices— $35, $40, and $45 per share. Therefore, the values of the 100-share contracts are $3500, $4000, and $4500, respectively.

3. and 4. These figures represent the closing prices, or premiums, that were paid for the various puts and calls. The prices are expressed on a per share basis, meaning that you must multiply by 100 shares to determine the cost of the contract. These prices are given for the different months of expiration, usually spaced three months apart. Each contract has a specific month of expiration, with expiration set at 11:59 A.M. EST on the third Saturday of that month. Whether you gain or lose in options trading usually depends on movements in the premium price. That is because options positions are generally closed out with an offsetting purchase or sale or are allowed to expire. Having to exercise the option, that is, actually buying the stock in the case of calls or coming up with the shares to sell in the case of puts, involves more cash than many options holders want to commit.

Notice how the strike prices of the options series straddle the current market value of the stock. This gives investors a choice of intrinsically worthless—but cheap—options as well as options that have considerable value, but which are expensive to buy. Options exchanges constantly create series with new strike prices to maintain this situation as the price of the underlying stock changes. For stocks selling at $25 to $50 per share, the strike prices are usually set in increments of $5; the increments are $10 on contracts for stocks priced $50 to $200 per share. For options on stocks worth $200 or more per share, strike prices are set $20 apart, and for options on stocks worth less than $25 per share, the increments are $2.50.

Using the Associated Press system of symbols, "r" in the premium column means options for that particular strike price and month of expiration did not trade. An "s" indicates that the Options Clearing Corporation, which guarantees your cash or shares when options are exercised or traded, isn't offering that particular contract. United Press International uses "nt" if an option did not trade, and "no" if the OCC isn't offering an option. Associated Press expresses sixteenths as "$1/16$" while United Press uses "1s" to represent that fraction.

The cheapest options are those on which you would lose money (even before considering commission costs) if you exercised them. These are referred to as out-of-the-money options. For example, an XYZ May45 call, giving you the right to pay $45 per share or $4500 per contract for 100 shares of XYZ, costs only 3/4—75 cents per share or $75 per contract. (See Line C, Column 3.) In other words, someone is willing to pay these prices for the right to later pay out $4500 for a stock currently worth $4000. Of course, the hope is that XYZ stock will rise. For example, if the stock rises to $43 per share (which would still mean that the option is intrinsically worthless and out of the money) another investor may be willing to pay more for that option—perhaps 1 1/2 or $1.50 a share. The second investor hopes that the stock will rise to the point at which the option would produce a profit if exercised. In any case, the first buyer, who paid $75 for the contract, could get $150 for the contract—doubling his or her money before subtracting commission costs.

Options with intrinsic value, such as the XYZ May35 calls (which give you the right to pay $3500 for something already worth $4000) are naturally more expensive than those with no intrinsic value. In this table, these options finished the previous section at $7 per share (Line C, Column 4), or $700 per contract. The percentage gains or losses on such options are less than the volatile out-of-the-money options, but there is also less chance that these options will have to be allowed to expire worthless.

These tables also indicate how much money you can make by selling options and thus increase the income from your stock portfolio. For example, if you own 100 shares of XYZ, you may decide to sell calls; that is, you may give another person the right to buy your shares. In return, you receive the premium. Assuming the price of options held steady from the previous day's closing levels, you could expect to receive $150 for selling an XYZ Aug40 call (Line B, Column 3). Of course, if the stock price should rise, the call holder could exercise the option, and you would lose the capital gain. Ideally, you would hope that XYZ stock would hold at around 40 until the option you sold expired. In that case, after brokerage commissions were factored into the equation, it would not be worthwhile for another investor to exercise the option you sold.

If you are worried that your XYZ stock might drop, you can lock in a value of $35 a share through most of August by buying an Aug 35 put (which gives you the right to get $35 a share) for $25 a contract (Line A, Column 4).

In addition to options on individual stocks, options are traded on debt instruments (interest rate options), foreign currencies, stock indexes, and certain futures contracts. What applies to puts and calls on stocks also applies to options on other instruments, with one major exception—index options. Because they are settled in cash and have other distinct features, they deserve special attention.

Daily Index Options Tables

Index options, which give you the right to buy and sell the dollar value of an index (rather than 100 shares of stock, as with stock options) are relatively few; sometimes, however, they are extremely popular. They often dominate the most-active lists that appear at the head of daily option tables. Index options tables run under their exchange headings: Chicago Board Options Exchange (often referred to in the tables as Chicago Board or just Chicago), the American, Philadelphia, Pacific, and New York stock exchanges, and NASD.

Index options are popular because they allow investors to play the whole market, in the case of broad-based indexes, or segments of the market, in the case of indexes that track technology stocks or gold stocks, among others. An index is assigned a value of a certain number of dollars per point—$100, for example. Standard & Poor's has allowed its indexes to be used for such purposes, as have the New York Stock Exchange and Value Line. Sometimes indexes are created specifically for trading options on them. Using the usual format, a hypothetical XYZ index option, which for example, tracks hundreds of stocks, would appear like the accompanying example.

INDEX OPTIONS

①   ②   ③

XYZ Index

	Strike Price	Calls—Last			Puts—Last		
		Feb	Mar	Apr	Feb	Mar	Apr
Ⓐ	290	12⅞	14¼	14⅛	³⁄₁₆	2	4¼
Ⓑ	295	7⅝	10¼	11⅜	¹¹⁄₁₆	3¼	6¾
Ⓒ	300	3¾	7¾	8⅛	1⅞	5⅜	9⅛
Ⓓ	305	1³⁄₁₆	4⅞	6½	4⅜	10½	12
Ⓔ	310	⅜	2⅞	4½	...	14	...

Ⓕ Total call volume 27,435 Total call open int. 78,121
Ⓖ Total put volume 17,477 Total call open int. 75, 940
Ⓗ The index: High 302.55; Low 296.90;
    Close 302.51. + 4.32

Index option tables have the following components:

1. The strike price is the price you would pay (if you owned a call) or would receive (if you owned a put) if the option were exercised. To compute the dollar value, multiple by $100 per point, because the XYZ Index has an assigned value of $100 per point. The 290 strike price, for example, would require the payment of $29,000.

2. Calls-last are the closing prices, or premiums, for calls. Unlike the much longer time periods available for stock options, index options expire in about three months at most. As you can see, investors were paying 12⅞, or $1287.50 per contract, for the expensive, deep-in-the-money Feb290 calls (Line A, Column 2). That's because the index closed at 302.51—the index's closing level is given on Line H—making its monetary value $30,251. The holder of a call with a strike price of 290, or $29,000, has an option with an intrinsic value of $1251 and hopes the value will rise even higher so the option can be sold or exercised at a profit after commissions.

Meanwhile, the 310 strike price call options have no intrinsic value; they are out of the money and thus, cheap. A Feb310 cost only ⅜, or

$37.50 per contract (Line E, Column 2), because it gives the buyer the right to pay $31,000 for an investment that's currently worth only $30,251.

3. Premiums on puts move in the opposite direction of calls. The March puts with a 310 strike price (Line E, Column 3) are expensive, ($1400 per contract) because they are deep in the money; they give the holder the right to demand $31,000 for an index that's worth only $30,152.

F. This line indicates the number of call contracts that were traded during the session and the number of contracts still open (open interest). To some extent, these figures measure investor optimism, because calls are bets that the market index will rise.

G. This line presents the same type of information given in line F, except that line G deals with puts. These figures reflect investor pessimism, because puts are bets that the market will drop, at least insofar as the group of stocks being tracked by the index is concerned.

H. This line indicates how the index performed during the session, in terms of its highest, lowest, and closing values, and change from its previous close. The gain shown in this example, 4.32 points, signifies that the value of the XYZ index rose $432.

Weekly Options Tables

Weekly options tables, such as those found in *Barron's* or the Sunday *New York Times,* follow a format different from the daily tables. Calls and puts are stacked rather than placed next to each other. More information is included in these tables. Index options are still run separately.

In the accompanying example of a typical stock-option table, the columns include the following information:

WEEKLY OPTIONS TABLE

①	②	③	④	⑤		⑥	⑦
Option	Sales	Open Int.	High	Low	Last	Net Chg.	Stock close
ABZ Mar35	1437	10921	6⅛	3¾	4	−1⅛	39
ABZ Mar35 p	99	5089	¹⁄₁₆	¹⁄₁₆	¹⁄₁₆	−¹⁄₁₆	39
ABZ Mar40	5981	7332	1¹⁵⁄₁₆	½	⁹⁄₁₆	−¹⁄₁₆	39
ABZ Mar40 p	237	402	2	1	1¾	+⅜	39

1. Name of the option, as identified by the underlying stock, the expiration month, and the strike price. The closest expiration months and lowest strike prices appear first. A "p" identifies puts; the other options are calls.

2. Sales for the week, in terms of the number of contracts that changed hands.

3. Open interest—the number of contracts in investor and dealer hands that haven't been exercised or closed out yet. Comparing the number of outstanding calls to puts helps you assess the direction speculators expect the price of the stock to take.

4. The highest and lowest premiums, per share, paid for a particular contract during the past week.

5. The closing premium, or price, per share, at the end of the week.

6. Net Change—how much premiums per share rose or fell from the previous weekly close. The 1⅛ ($1.125 per share) loss for ABZ Mar35 calls indicates that the contracts lost $112.50 each.

7. The closing price of the underlying shares, which, when multiplied by 100, equals the exercise value of the contracts, $3900.

FUTURES TABLES

Futures tables are grouped by broad categories—agricultural (grains, edible oils, livestock, coffee, sugar, cocoa, orange juice), metals (gold, silver, platinum, palladium, copper), industrials (lumber, cotton, crude oil, heating oil, gasoline), and financial (U.S. Treasury bonds, notes, and bills, foreign currencies, certificates of deposit, stock index futures). About 50 contracts are listed in various futures markets and included in newspaper tables. Commodity contracts are agreements to deliver or take delivery of a commodity in the future. Hence, the ''Futures Prices'' label for these tables. Most investors in commodities futures contracts are speculators who hope to make big profits by predicting correctly the change in commodity prices. The contracts are identified by their delivery months. A typical table, in this case for cattle, is presented here. The type of contract and the exchange (CME, or Chicago Mercantile Exchange) as well as the size (44,000 pounds) and the units of trade (pennies per pound) are shown in lines B and C.

CATTLE FUTURES

	①	②	③	④	⑤	⑥
	... Season ...					Open
Ⓐ	**High**	**Low**	**High**	**Low**	**Close**	**Chg.**	**Int.**
Ⓑ	CATTLE, LIVE BEEF (CME)						
Ⓒ	44,000 lb.; ¢ per lb.						
Ⓓ	67.07	55.30 Apr	61.75	60.32	60.40	−.30	29,042
Ⓔ	66.60	56.25 Jun	60.52	59.35	59.47	−.28	17.547
Ⓕ	61.75	55.20 Aug	58.40	57.45	57.47	−.25	5,939
Ⓖ	60.60	55.70 Oct	57.20	56.37	56.50	−.15	2,705
Ⓗ	61.75	57.55 Dec	58.80	58.10	58.35	−.02	612
Ⓘ	60.20	58.00 Feb	58.90	58.77	58.77	+.07	56
Ⓙ	Est. sales 21,859. Wed's sales 21.607.						
Ⓚ	Wed.'s open Int 55,901, up 63.						

Other information is presented as follows:

1. The highest and lowest prices paid for a particular delivery month contract since the contract was listed. This indicates the price swings of the contract. The April futures (*Line D*) ranged between 67.07 cents and 55.30 cents per pound, or $29,510 and $24,332 per 44,000-pound contract—a difference of $5178. An investor smart enough or lucky enough to invest $2433 (10% margin when the contract reached its $24,332 low point) and sell when prices peaked would have more than doubled his or her money. On the other hand, someone who invested at the high point could easily have lost all of his or her money. When the loss of a contract's value equals the amount of money that's been invested, brokers will usually demand more margin. If they don't get it, they will sell the contract.

2. The delivery months differentiate one contract from another. The spacing between delivery months and the length of the longest contract varies from one commodity to the next. Most contracts last no longer than one year.

3. The daily high and low prices.

4. The closing price. At 60.40 cents, the close in the April future made that contract worth $26,576.

5. The change in price—the difference from one close to the next. The .3 cent loss for April cattle signifies a $132 loss for the contract.

6. The open interest—the number of contracts that have not been closed through delivery or offsetting transactions. This indicates which contracts will experience the heaviest trading in the future, as most contracts will be closed out through either a sale or a purchase of an offsetting contract, rather than by the delivery of the commodity.

J. This line estimates the number of contracts that changed hands during the last session, as well as the volume of the previous session.

K. This line presents the total open interest of the two previous days, and the change in the number of open contracts.

A great deal of information is omitted from these tables, including delivery days, delivery specifications (the locations to which the commodities would be sent and how they would arrive), and the daily limits in price changes that exchanges impose on most futures contracts. The contract specifications are available from the exchange on which the commodity is traded. Commodities don't possess the uniform qualities of options contracts; the sequence of delivery months and the maximum length of contracts varies from one commodity to another.

Comprehensive commodities tables also include a listing of cash prices, gathered from various sources each day—exchanges, warehouses, fabricators—which give you the immediate value of many of the commodities for which futures contracts are traded as well as other materials, such as wool and cloth and mercury, which have no formal futures market. In the case of futures-related commodities, remember that the current cash price, while often determining the direction of futures contract prices, is usually different. A glut in grain during the harvest could cause an immediate plunge in prices, while prices in the futures market, which anticipate conditions further down the road, could rise.

CORPORATE BOND TABLES

Although corporate bond tables give you valuable insight into a key financial market, they present only part of the picture. While several thousand corporate bonds are traded on the New York and American stock exchanges, many more that are traded through broker/dealers do not appear in the tables of exchange-listed bonds. In addition, exchange-listed bonds traded in lots of 10 or more are also handled off the exchange. According to the Nine Bond Rule, only lots of nine or fewer must be sent to the exchange floor.

Nevertheless, these tables are important because they (1) give you specific information about bonds you may own or are considering buying and (2) indicate the prevailing yields, which can help you estimate the value of similar bonds that you may have in your portfolio or are considering buying.

The table listings look like this:

CORPORATE BONDS

①	②	③	④	⑤
Bonds	**Current Yield**	**Sales in $1,000**	**Last**	**Net Chg.**
ABZ 9⅜s01	11.6	42	81¼	+¼
MXY 8.15x00	9.5	285	85½	−1
KLO 10s09f	18	113	55½	+⅛
STU zr98	...	17	69	+½
WVX 9½ 05	cv	101	141	−1

The accompanying typical bond table presents information as follows:

1. The company abbreviations may vary from the abbreviations used in the stock tables. Also included in this column is the annual interest each bond pays, expressed as a percentage of the par or face value. Most corporate bonds are available in $1000 denominations (though prices are quoted in $100 units), which would mean that ABZ's 9⅜ payout would total $93.75 annually. Where a rate cannot be expressed as a fraction, decimals are used, for example, 8.15 for MXY. The annual interest rate is also referred to as the coupon. Noninterest-paying zero coupon securities are identified by a "zr," as with STU here. The last two numbers in the name cluster represent the year in which the bonds will mature—01 for 2001, 98 for 1998. Among the qualifiers that may also appear after the name is "f," meaning that the bond is trading flat or without accrued interest, and that an interest payment has been missed. The "s" often seen after the bond name is a stylistic embellishment that reflects the verbal description of bonds; for example. "ABZ nine and three eights of 2001."

2. The current yield represents the annual interest payment as a percentage of the last closing price. It provides a comparison with yields for other types of investments. In the case of convertible bonds, or convertibles, where prices, and therefore yields, are governed by movements in the underlying shares, no yield is given. Instead, "cv" is inserted in the yield column to indicate that this is a convertible issue. Of course, no yield is given with zero coupon bonds either.

3. This is volume on the exchange, expressed in sales of $1000 bonds, which is the normal corporate bond denomination. Events—mergers, earnings news, and so on—can cause volume surges, especially in the case of the convertibles. The amount of volume will tell you how liquid the bonds are.

4. The last sale, in terms of $100 units. Multiply by 10 to get the price per $1000 bond. Prices are quoted as a percentage of par value, as though the face value was $100, not $1000. For example, a $1000 face value bond sold at 81¼ actually sold at $812.50.

5. The net change indicates the gain or loss since the previous close, expressed as a percentage of par. Therefore, the + ¼ gain for ABZ translates into 25 cents per $100 face value, or $2.50 per $1000 bond. The − 1 for WVX indicates a $10 loss for $1000 bond. Price changes reflect changes in interest rates. If bond prices have dropped it means interest rates probably rose, and vice versa.

You should also be familiar with the following information, which is not included in the corporate bond tables:

Ratings   These indicate the risk of default by the issuer on payments of interest or principal. The major bond rating agencies are Fitch Investor's Service, Moody's Investors Service and Standard and Poor's Corporation.

Denominations   Not all bonds are available in denominations of $1000. Some, called baby bonds, are denominated in amounts of $500 or less.

Yield to maturity   This represents the return, including both the annual interest payments and the gain or loss realized when the bonds are redeemed, taking into account the timing of payments and the time value of money. Yield to maturity will vary depending on whether you bought the bonds at a discount or a premium in relation to their face value, and with the time remaining to maturity. This type of yield calculation allows you to more easily compare bonds with other types of fixed income investments.

Payment dates   Interest payments on corporate bonds are usually, but not always, made semiannually. In any case, the payment cycles vary.

Callability   If a bond can be redeemed prior to maturity by the issuer, it will most likely be called when rates decline and conditions are favorable to the issuer. For this reason, another yield calculation, yield to call, can have more significance than yield to maturity.

GOVERNMENT SECURITIES TABLES

There's no uniform method of quoting the prices of government securities. In addition, the methods of presenting the values of these bills, notes, and bonds are sometimes as obscure as these markets once were to general investors. Because of the numbers of investors who are now familiar with these markets, however, it's worthwhile for you to know how to extract information from these tables.

Treasury Bills

These obligations—or IOUs—of the U.S. Treasury, are backed by the full faith and credit of the U.S. government. They always mature within one year (3 months, 6 months, 9 months and one year), and are included in many major daily newspapers in the form used in the accompanying table. Information is provided as follows.

TREASURY BILLS

①	②	③	④	⑤
Date	Bid	Asked	Chg	Yield
Mar 13	5.61	5.55	+0.09	5.63

1. This is the date on which the bills mature. The maturity date distinguishes one bill from another.

2. The bid is the price dealers were willing to pay late (there is never an official end) in the last trading session. A bid is presented in a way you may find confusing. It's the discount from the face value demanded by dealers, expressed as an annual percentage. The reason for this is that Treasury bills do not pay interest in the usual sense. Instead, you pay less than the face value of the bills, but you receive the full value when the bills mature. The difference equals the interest you would receive. Thus, if you pay $9000 for a one-year $10,000 bill ($10,000 is the minimum size for a Treasury bill), you're paying 10% less than par, or buying the bill at a 10% discount. A bid of 10 would appear in the table. The higher the discount, the lower the price.

3. The asked price is the price the dealer is willing to accept, again expressed as an annualized percentage discount rate. In these tables, the percentages are carried out to the nearest hundredth, or basis point. Note that the dealer demands a smaller discount—a higher price—when he resells the bonds.

4. The change indicates how much the bid discount rate rose or fell during the session. A plus change actually represents a drop in prices, because it indicates an increased discount from par. Just as a larger discount on merchandise in a store window signifies lower prices, so the .09%, or 9 basis point, indicates an increase in the discount. A minus change means that Treasury bill prices have risen and that the discount rate—and often other types of yields and rates—has dropped.

5. The yield represents a yield to maturity, based on the price you would actually pay for the Treasury bill, rather than its face value. The 10% discount rate tells you that you would pay 10% less than $10,000— or $9000—for a one year Treasury bill, for a difference—representing interest—of $1000. The actual yield, however, is better expressed in terms of the amount you would really pay for this investment—$9000. In addition, a return of $1000 on a $9000 investment is greater than the 10% discount rate; it's an 11.11% yield. Note that the yield shown in the sample table, 5.63, is higher than the 5.61 discount rate bid shown in column 2.

Treasury Notes and Bonds

Treasury note and bond prices are included in the same tables. The only difference is that the notes, designated by an "n" or a "p," mature in from one to ten years after they are issued, while bonds mature in ten years or longer. These tables present the securities in the order of their maturity dates, with the closest maturity date at the top and the furthest (always the much-quoted government long bond) at the bottom. Notice the increase in yields as the period of maturity increases; this reflects the fact that lenders demand a greater return for locking up their money for longer time periods. As with other government bonds, prices are given as dealer bid and asked quotes, not in terms of last sales. The reason for this is that there is no way for the extensive network of government bond dealers to report transaction prices and amounts in order to register them onto a last-sale "tape." Extra care must be taken in reading the bid and asked quotes because the two digits following the decimal points are 32nds rather than hundredths, reflecting the traditional language of the government bond market.

The information on a typical daily table is as follows:

TREASURY BONDS

① Date	② Rate	③ Bid	④ Asked	⑤ Chg.	⑥ Yield
Apr 86 n	11¾	100.19	100.23	+ .4	6.13
Feb 93	6¾	95.18	96.18	+ 1.2	7.39
Nov 02-07	7⅞	97.19	98.3	+ 1.2	8.06
Nov 15 k	9⅜	118.1	118.5	+ 2.2	8.23

1. The date identifies the note or bond by its month and year of maturity; thus an "89" means 1989, a "16" means 2016. In addition, an "n" signifies a note (a "p" signifies notes not subject to withholding tax for foreign owners) while no notation (or a "k" if no withholding tax for foreigner owners is required) appears for bonds. When the maturity figure consists of two years, such as the 02–07 in this table, the second year (2007 here) represents the maturity, while the first year (2002 here) indicates that the bonds could be repaid early, beginning in 2002. Such callability is rare with Treasury securities; it is found only in the final five years of certain 30-year bond issues.

2. The rate is the coupon rate, or the annual interest rate, expressed as a percentage of the face value ($1000 minimum denominations for bonds and $1000 or $5000 for notes).

3. The bid is the price dealers were offering to pay late in the session. It's presented as a percentage of face value. Note, however, that the two digits following the decimal point are 32nds, not tenths or hundredths. The 113.13 bid for the Oct 89 notes equals 113 13/32%. Because 1/32% of $1000 is 31¼ cents, 13/32 equals $4.06¼; the total bid, per $1000 of notes, equals $1134.06¼.

4. The asked, the price at which dealers are offering to sell the securities, is calculated similarly to the bid.

5. The daily change from two previous sessions to yesterday's session is based on the rise or fall of the bid price.

6. This figure represents yield to maturity, which combines your current yield (the percentage return in interest based on the price you actually pay) and the difference between the price you paid and the face value at redemption.

Government Agency Bonds

Securities of U.S. agencies such as the Federal Home Loan Bank and Government National Mortgage Association that appear in *The Wall Street Journal* and *The New York Times* use the same type of bid and asked quotes, expressed in 32nds of a percent, as appear in the Treasury note and bond tables.

Municipal Bonds

You probably won't find municipal bond prices in the financial pages. Even major financial publications include only a sampling of revenue bonds—those repaid from the income of a particular project rather than from general tax dollars. Such tables, typically headed Tax-exempt Authority Bonds, include the issuer's name, maturity date, the bid, the asked, and the daily change in the bid. Information on general obligation bonds is even harder to find. One way of approximating the value of your holdings, though, is to look at yields on newly issued bonds as revealed in tombstone ads placed by underwriters or in the short lists of new issues some papers provide. If the yields on new issues are lower than those your municipals are earning, your bonds are probably selling above face value and vice-versa, assuming the bonds are comparable in terms of quality and type of issuer.

The Tax Reform Act of 1986 profoundly altered the municipal bond landscape, and there are now taxable as well as tax-exempt general obligation and revenue issues. There will undoubtedly be a period of sorting out before reporting practices become conventionally adopted.

MUTUAL FUNDS TABLES

Mutual fund prices are listed several ways in newspapers. Prices of a fund offered by an open-end management company that invests in long-term securities—either stocks or bonds—change with changes in market segments or the market as a whole. These funds sell and redeem their own shares. Large newspapers generally list these prices under the heading Mutual Funds.

MUTUAL FUNDS

①	② NAV	③ Buy	④ Chg.
ABZ Grp:			
Genrl Fd	14.38	NL	+.03
AB Growth	10.50	11.03	+.01
ABZ Incm	5.22	NL	+.02
Tax Ex	8.21	NL	−.01

These tables contain the following information, by column:

1. The names of mutual funds are clustered by family of funds—funds sponsored by a particular management company. The names often reflect the type of investments that comprise each fund; for example, a general stock fund, growth stock fund, income fund, or tax-exempt bond fund.

Some fund names are followed by lowercase letters such as a (meaning a stock dividend was paid in the past 12 months), d (new 52-week low), f (quotation refers to previous day), r (redemption charge may apply), u (new 52-week high), and x (fund is trading ex-dividend).

2. NAV stands for net asset value, the per-share value of the fund's assets, minus management costs. This is the amount you would receive, per share, if you redeemed your shares. The numbers indicate dollars and cents per share. Sometimes the column carries the heading Sell, meaning that you would receive this amount per share if you were the seller.

3. The Buy column may also be headed Offer Price. It tells you, in dollars and cents per share, the price per share, the price you would pay to buy the shares. Funds that carry a sales charge, or front end load, cost more per share than their net asset value. Funds with back end loads discourage withdrawals by charging a fee to redeem your shares. Many funds, however, carry no sales charge; these are no-load funds whose buy-in costs are the same as their net asset values. These funds carry an "NL" or just "n" in the Buy column.

4. Change refers to the daily change in net asset value, determined at the close of each trading day.

Share prices of a fund offered by a closed-end management company, which issues a fixed number of shares that are then traded among investors, are often included in the daily stock tables. Some newspapers also provide weekly tables listing the prices and values of the shares as of the previous day's close-of-the-market.

CLOSED-END FUNDS

①	② N.A. Value	③ Stk Price	④ % Diff
Diversified funds			
ABZ Fund	17.55	21½	+3.1
WXY Fund	10.81	11⅜	−1.8
ZBF Fund	24.74	20½	−5.0
Specialized Equity and Convertible Funds			
ABZ Gold	33.10	33½	+2.2
XYZ Conv	15.77	16	+1.6
XYZ Tech	9.97	10⅛	−4.4

1. Fund names are grouped alphabetically by fund type.

2. Net Asset Values, as of the last close (unless otherwise indicated) are listed in terms of dollars and cents per share.

3. Stock prices are the last close.

4. Percent difference represents the weekly rise or fall of the net asset value of the shares.

Listings of shares of dual purpose funds can be found in stock exchange tables. These closed-end funds have two classes of shares. One class entitles shareholders to capital gains based on the market value of the assets. The other class entitles holders to dividend and interest income from the fund. Some major newspapers also carry weekly tables of the per-share prices of the capital shares, the net asset value of the capital shares, and the weekly percentage or loss of price of those shares. These tables are useful because the daily stock tables don't include net asset values.

Tables for money market funds appear weekly, usually Thursday, after the release of data by Donoghue's money fund average or the National Association of Securities Dealers. Some newspapers print the tables again on Sunday. If you need information on a money market fund before Thursday, you can call the fund organizations. Many fund groups have toll-free 800 phone numbers for shareholders. Most investors need no more than weekly updates because per share values should remain constant at $1.00. These funds, which invest in short-term debt instruments, often are bought because they are liquid (most allow checkwriting) and the yield fluctuates with short-term interest rates. Market movements and the accompanying capital gains and losses don't play a major role in the decision to buy or sell shares. The yield is the main information included in such tables.

MONEY MARKET FUNDS

①	②	③	④	⑤
Fund	Assets ($ million)	Average maturity (days)	7-day average yield (%)	Effective 7-day average yield (%)
ABzz Safety Fst	344.7	20	7.61	7.90
Blxx Liquid Secs	1,343.9	26	7.57	7.73
Xymo Govt. Fund	299.0	22	6.11	6.46

The accompanying table includes the following information, by column:

1. Name of the money-market fund.

2. Assets are stated in millions of dollars, to the nearest $100,000. These figures indicate the size of the fund. Investors constantly debate the advantages and disadvantages of size.

3. The average maturity figure represents how long, on average, it takes for the securities in a money fund's portfolio to mature. Shorter average maturities mean that the fund's yield will react more quickly to general interest-rate changes in the fixed-income securities market. This is beneficial when rates are rising, but disadvantageous when rates are dropping. In the latter case, you would want your fund to hold onto higher-yielding securities as long as possible. The move in the average maturity figure is considered by some to be a good predictor of short-term interest rate direction. If a fund's average maturity increases by several days for several weeks, this is an indication that portfolio managers expect short-term rates to drop. If the average maturity decreases, the managers probably expect short-term rates to rise.

4. The 7-day average yield indicates the average daily total return for that period, and is determined largely by subtracting the fund's costs from the investment income. The result is expressed as a percentage of the average share price:

5. The effective 7-day average yield is the 7-day average yield computed after assuming that the rate continues for a year and that dividends are reinvested. This permits comparison with other instruments whose yields are expressed on the same basis, such as bank certificates of deposit.

OTHER TABLES

Interest and currency rates

The key rates highlighted in the Markets Diary discussed earlier are followed up with more detailed summaries throughout the inside pages.

A complete rate and yield table, for example, would additionally list, with comparisons to the previous day and year ago, the (Federal Reserve) discount rate and the prime rate, whose significance we have already discussed. It might also list yields on 7-year Treasury notes, an important benchmark for intermediate-term corporate and other non-Treasury fixed-income obligations; yields on 30-year Treasury bonds, the ultimate indicator of the entire bond market and often of the stock market, where prices normally move inversely to "long bond" yields; and "telephone" bonds, top-rated obligations of phone companies or other public utilities whose yield is a direct benchmark for other corporate bonds that are riskier to varying degrees. Major newspapers also carry additional lists of rates that are mainly of interest to professional traders. Some, like Eurodollar time deposits, the London Interbank Offer Rate (LIBOR), and commercial paper, were discussed above. Others include banker's acceptances, which are time drafts created in commerce, accepted (guaranteed, in effect) by major banks, and traded as money market instruments; and the broker loan rate (or call loan rate), which is the rate banks charge brokers for overnight loans to cover securities positions of customers. This rate, which usually hovers just above the rate on (also overnight) federal funds, has meaning to individual investors because it determines what brokers charge on margin loans.

Many financial newspapers and other media now carry weekly listings of the banks currently offering the highest interest rates on deposit accounts and certificates of deposit.

The meaning and importance of currency exchange rates was discussed earlier. In addition to highlighting major currency changes, most major financial papers carry full exchange tables, listed alphabetically by country, which provide the exchange rates from the previous two days in four columns—two in terms of dollars per unit of foreign currency, two in terms of units of foreign currency per dollar. Major currencies also list 30-, 90-, and 180-day forward rates. These represent guaranteed future delivery rates offered by banks for customers who must plan ahead and are willing to pay a premium to eliminate the risk of exchange rates moving adversely in the interim.

Some papers, including *The Wall Street Journal,* contain a table showing key currency cross rates. This table lists currencies in terms of each other's value. Complete currency sections also cover futures, options, and futures options on leading currencies.

HOW TO READ TICKER TAPES

With the growth of cable television, an increasing number of investors pick up financial news from cablecasters that cover the securities and commodities markets continuously throughout the business day. Like daily newspapers, the purveyors of electronic financial news aim for a broad audience. Through the creative use of graphics and commentary, they manage generally to communicate complex information in a way nonprofessionals can understand.

But unless you work for an investment firm or spend your leisure time sitting around a board room of a brokerage, the figures and symbols that pass constantly—sometimes with maddening rapidity—across the lower portion of the TV screen may require explanation. What you see there is the stock ticker tape, the same report of trading activity displayed on the floors of the major stock exchanges. The only difference is that to give stock exchange members an advantage, it is transmitted with a 15-minute delay.

The most frequently seen display is the consolidated tape, a combination of two networks (not to be confused with television networks): Network A reports all New York Stock Exchange issues traded on the NYSE or other identified markets, which include five regional exchanges, the over-the-counter market, and other markets, such as Instinet, a computerized market in which large institutional blocks are traded. Network B reports all American Stock Exchange issues traded on the Amex or other identified markets. National Association of Securities Dealers (NASDAQ) over-the-counter quotes are presented separately in the lower band.

Elements of the consolidated tape; which reports actual transactions (the term quotes is loosely used to mean trades in ticker tape jargon, although its proper financial meaning refers to bid and asked quotations) are explained as follows:

Stock Symbol   The first letters are the stock ticker symbol—XON for Exxon, CCI for Citicorp. IBM for IBM, for example. (There is one exception to this, which is that the prefix Q is used when a company is in receivership or bankruptcy.) The ticker symbol may be followed by an abbreviation designating a type of issue, such as Pr to signify preferred stock, which may, in turn, be followed by a letter indicating a class of preferred. Thus XYZPrE means XYZ Corporation's preferred stock series E. If XYZ's preferred stock series E was convertible, the abbreviation .CV would be added to read XYZPrE.CV. Common stock classes, if any, are indicated by a period plus a letter following the ticker symbol. Thus XYZ's class B common would be designated XYZ.B. (A list of ticker symbols is included at the end of Part V of this book.)

Other abbreviations placed after the ticker symbol as necessary are rt for rights; wi for when issued; .WD for when distributed; .WS for warrants (the abbreviation may be preceded by another period and letter to identify the particular issue of warrant); and .XD for ex-dividend.

Market Identifiers   When the information about the stock is followed by an ampersand (&) and a letter, the transaction took place in a market other than the New York Stock Exchange, if you are looking at Network A, or the American Stock Exchange, if you are looking at Network B. The letter identifies the market as follows:

A	American Stock Exchange
B	Boston Stock Exchange
C	Cincinnati Stock Exchange
M	Midwest Stock Exchange
N	New York Stock Exchange
O	Other Markets (mainly Instinet)
P	Pacific Stock Exchange
T	Third market (mainly NASDAQ)
X	Philadelphia Stock Exchange

Volume   The next portion of the transaction information provided on a ticker tape may appear below or to the right of the above stock symbol and market designation. It reports the number of shares traded. However, if the trade is in a round lot of 100 shares, which it usually is, no volume is indicated and the tape simply shows the issue and the price. Thus XYZ 26½ simply means that 100 shares of XYZ were traded at 26.50 a share. Where larger round lot transactions take place, the number of round lots is indicated followed by the letter "s" followed by the price. Thus, XYZ 4 s 26½ means 400 shares were traded at $26.50 a share. Similarly, 1700 shares would be XYZ 17 s 26½ and so on, except that when the volume is 10,000 shares or more the full number is given—XYZ 16,400 s 26½, for example.

Odd lots—quantities other than multiples of 100 or whatever other unit represents the round lot—are not printed on the ticker tape unless approved by an exchange official. If approval is given, odd lots of 50 shares and 150 shares of XYZ would be displayed respectively: XYZ 50 SHRS 26½ and XYZ 150 SHRS 26½.

A limited number of issues—mainly inactive stocks or higher priced preferred issues—trade in round lots of less than 100 shares. On the New York Stock Exchange such round lots are always 10 shares, but on the Amex these round lots can be 10, 25, or 50 shares. Transactions in these special round lots are designated by a number indicating how many lots were traded followed by the symbols. Thus, on the New York Stock Exchange, XYZ Pr 3 ⁚ 55 means 3 10-share lots (30 shares) of XYZ preferred stock were traded at $55 a share. If XYZ were listed on the Amex, you would not know by looking at the tape whether the lot involved was 10, 25, or 50 shares. For that information, you would have to consult a stock guide.

Active Market Procedures   When trading becomes sufficiently heavy to cause the tape to run more than a minute behind, shortcuts are implemented. The most frequently taken measure to keep up with heavy trading is signified by the tape printout DIGITS AND VOLUME DELETED. This means only the unit price digit and fraction will be printed (for example, 9½ instead of 19½) except when the price ends in zero or is an opening transaction. In addition, volume information will be deleted except when trades are 5000 shares or more (the threshold can be raised if required). Another common procedure is to announce REPEAT PRICES OMITTED, meaning that successive transactions at the same price will not be repeated. A third measure is MINIMUM PRICE CHANGES OMITTED, meaning trades will not be displayed unless the price difference exceeds ⅛ of a point. The second and third measures do not apply to opening transactions or to trades of 5000 shares or more. When activity slackens to a more normal level, the tape will read DIGITS AND VOLUME RESUMED with similar indications for the other measures.

Other Abbreviations   When a transaction is being reported out of its proper order, the letters .SLD will follow the symbol as in XYZ .SLD 3s 26½. SLR followed by a number signifies seller's option and number of days until settlement. This indication is found after the price. CORR indicates that a correction of information follows. ERR or CXL indicates a print is to be ignored. OPD signifies an opening transaction that was delayed or one whose price is significantly changed from the previous day's close.

PART IV
Dictionary of Finance and Investment

HOW TO USE THIS DICTIONARY EFFECTIVELY

Alphabetization: All entries are alphabetized by letter rather than by word so that multiple-word terms are treated as single words. For example, **NET ASSET VALUE** follows **NET ASSETS** as though it were spelled **NETASSETVALUE,** without spacing. Similarly, **ACCOUNT EXECUTIVE** follows **ACCOUNTANT'S OPIN-ION.** In unusual cases, abbreviations or acronyms appear as entries in the main text, in addition to appearing in the back of the book in the separate listing of Abbreviations and Acronyms. This is when the short form, rather than the formal name, predominates in common business usage. For example, NASDAQ is more commonly used in speaking of the National Association of Securities Dealers Automated Quotations system than the name itself, so the entry is at **NASDAQ.** Numbers in entry titles are alphabetized as if they were spelled out.

Where a term has several meanings, alphabetical sequence is used for subheads, except in special instances where clarity dictates a different order (for example, under **LEVERAGE** the subhead **Operating leverage** precedes **Financial leverage**). In some entries, the various meanings of the term are presented with simple numerical headings. Securities and Exchange Commission rules are presented in the official numerical order.

Cross references: In order to gain a fuller understanding of a term, it will sometimes help to refer to the definition of another term. In these cases the additional term is printed in SMALL CAPITALS. Such cross references appear in the body of the definition or at the end of the entry (or subentry). Cross references at the end of an entry (or subentry) may refer to related or contrasting concepts rather than give more information about the concept under discussion. As a rule, a term is printed in small capitals only the first time it appears in an entry. Where an entry is fully defined at another entry, a reference rather than a definition is provided; for example, **EITHER-OR ORDER** *see* ALTERNATIVE ORDER.

Italics: Italic type is generally used to indicate that another term has a meaning identical or very closely related to that of the entry. Occasionally, italic type is also used to highlight the fact that a word used is a business term and not just a descriptive phrase. Italics are also used for the titles of publications.

Parentheses: Parentheses are used in entry titles for two reasons. The first is to indicate that an entry's opposite is such an integral part of the concept that only one discussion is necessary; for example, **REALIZED PROFIT (OR LOSS).** The second and more common reason is to indicate that an abbreviation is used with about the same frequency as the term itself; for example, **OVER THE COUNTER (OTC).**

Examples, Illustrations, and Tables: The numerous examples in this Dictionary are designed to help readers gain understanding and to help them relate abstract concepts to the real world of finance and investment. Line drawings are provided in addition to text to clarify concepts best understood visually; for example, technical chart patterns used by securities analysts and graphic concepts used in financial analysis. Tables supplement definitions where essential detail is more effectively condensed and expressed in tabular form; for example, components of the U.S. money supply.

Special Definitions: Some entries are given expanded treatment to enhance their reference value. Examples are **ECONOMIC RECOVERY TAX ACT OF 1981, SECURITIES AND COMMODITIES EXCHANGES, SECURITIES AND EX-CHANGE COMMISSION RULES, STOCK INDEXES AND AVERAGES,** and **TAX REFORM ACT OF 1986.**

DICTIONARY OF FINANCE AND INVESTMENT

a

ABC AGREEMENT agreement between a brokerage firm and one of its employees spelling out the firm's rights when it purchases a New York Stock Exchange membership for the employee. Only individuals can be members of the NYSE, and it is common practice for a firm to finance the purchase of a membership, or SEAT, by one of its employees. The NYSE-approved ABC Agreement contains the following provisions regarding the future disposition of the seat: (1) The employee may retain the membership and buy another seat for an individual designated by the firm. (2) The employee may sell the seat and give the proceeds to the firm. (3) The employee may transfer the seat to another employee of the firm.

ABILITY TO PAY

Finance: borrower's ability to meet principal and interest payments on long-term obligations out of earnings. Also called *ability to service.* See also FIXED CHARGE COVERAGE.

Industrial relations: ability of an employer, especially a financial organization, to meet a union's financial demands from operating income.

Municipal bonds: issuer's present and future ability to generate enough tax revenue to meet its contractual obligations, taking into account all factors concerned with municipal income and property values.

Taxation: the concept that tax rates should vary with levels of wealth or income; for example, the progressive income tax.

ABOVE PAR *see* PAR VALUE.

ABSOLUTE PRIORITY RULE *see* BANKRUPTCY.

ABSORBED

Business: a cost that is treated as an expense rather than passed on to a customer. Also, a firm merged into an acquiring company.

Cost accounting: indirect manufacturing costs (such as property taxes and insurance) are called *absorbed costs.* They are differentiated from variable costs (such as direct labor and materials). See also DIRECT OVERHEAD.

Finance: an account that has been combined with related accounts in preparing a financial statement and has lost its separate identity. Also called *absorption account* or *adjunct account.*

Securities: issue that an underwriter has completely sold to the public.

Also, in market trading, securities are absorbed as long as there are corresponding orders to buy and sell. The market has reached the *absorption point* when further assimilation is impossible without an adjustment in price. See also UNDIGESTED SECURITIES.

ABUSIVE TAX SHELTER LIMITED PARTNERSHIP the Internal Revenue Service deems to be claiming illegal tax deductions—typically, one that inflates the value of acquired property beyond its fair market value. If these writeoffs are denied by the IRS, investors must pay severe penalties and interest charges, on top of back taxes.

ACCELERATED COST RECOVERY SYSTEM (ACRS) provision instituted by the ECONOMIC RECOVERY TAX ACT OF 1981 (ERTA) and modified by the TAX REFORM ACT OF 1986, which establishes rules for the DEPRECIATION (the recovery of cost through tax deductions) of qualifying assets within a shorter period than the asset's expected useful (economic) life. With certain exceptions, the 1986 Act modifications, which generally provide for greater acceleration over longer periods of time than ERTA rules, are effective for property placed in service after 1986. (There are special transition rules applicable to property under contract or construction prior to March 1, 1986, and to specific kinds of property).

The modified rules specify seven ACRS classes determined with reference to their ASSET DEPRECIATION RANGE (ADR). The ADR system, in effect prior to 1981 and now revived, provides upper and lower limits for the designated lifetimes of different types of assets. Thus, the ACRS *three-year* class includes property with an ADR midpoint of four years or less, the *five-year* class includes assets with an ADR midpoint of more than four but less than 10 years, and so on.

ACRS three-year, five-year, seven-year, and ten-year classes are subject to the DOUBLE DECLINING BALANCE DEPRECIATION METHOD (DDB); the fifteen and twenty-year classes use a variation, *the 150% declining balance method*. The real property class, which comprises residential and nonresidential subclasses depreciable over 27½ and 31½ years, respectively (real property was unfavorably affected by the 1986 tax act), uses STRAIGHT-LINE DEPRECIATION.

ACCELERATED DEPRECIATION Internal Revenue Service-approved methods used in the DEPRECIATION of fixed assets placed in service prior to 1980 when the ACCELERATED COST RECOVERY SYSTEM (ACRS) became mandatory. Such methods provided for faster recovery of cost and earlier tax advantages than traditional STRAIGHT LINE DEPRECIATION and included such methods as DOUBLE-DECLINING BALANCE METHOD (now used in some ACRS classes) and SUM-OF-THE-YEARS' DIGITS METHOD.

ACCELERATION CLAUSE provision, normally present in an INDENTURE agreement, mortgage, or other contract, that the unpaid balance is to become due and payable if specified events of default should occur. Such events include failure to meet interest, principal, or sinking fund payments; insolvency; and nonpayment of taxes on mortgaged property.

ACCEPTANCE
In general: agreement created when the drawee of a TIME DRAFT (bill of exchange) writes the word ''accepted'' above the signature and designates a date of payment. The drawee becomes the acceptor, responsible for payment at maturity.

Also, paper issued and sold by sales finance companies, such as General Motors Acceptance Corporation.

Banker's acceptance: time draft drawn on and accepted by a bank, the customary means of effecting payment for merchandise sold in import-export transactions and a source of financing used extensively in international trade. With the credit strength of a bank behind it, the banker's acceptance usually qualifies as a MONEY MARKET instrument. The liability assumed by the bank is called its acceptance liability. *See also* LETTER OF CREDIT.

Trade acceptance: time draft drawn by the seller of goods on the buyer, who becomes the acceptor, and which is therefore only as good as the buyer's credit.

ACCOUNT

In general: contractual relationship between a buyer and seller under which payment is made at a later time. The term *open account* or *charge account* is used, depending on whether the relationship is commercial or personal.

Also, the historical record of transactions under the contract, as periodically shown on the *statement of account.*

Banking: relationship under a particular name, usually evidenced by a deposit against which withdrawals can be made. Among them are demand, time, custodial, joint, trustee, corporate, special, and regular accounts. Administrative responsibility is handled by an *account officer.*

Bookkeeping: assets, liabilities, income, and expenses as represented by individual ledger pages to which debit and credit entries are chronologically posted to record changes in value. Examples are cash, accounts receivable, accrued interest, sales, and officers' salaries. The system of recording, verifying, and reporting such information is called accounting. Practitioners of accounting are called *accountants.*

Investment banking: financial and contractual relationship between parties to an underwriting syndicate, or the status of securities owned and sold.

Securities: relationship between a broker-dealer firm and its client wherein the firm, through its registered representatives, acts as agent in buying and selling securities and sees to related administrative matters. *See also* ACCOUNT EXECUTIVE; ACCOUNT STATEMENT.

ACCOUNTANT'S OPINION statement signed by an independent public accountant describing the scope of the examination of an organization's books and records. Because financial reporting involves considerable discretion, the accountant's opinion is an important assurance to a lender or investor. Depending on the scope of an audit and the auditor's confidence in the veracity of the information, the opinion can be unqualified or, to some degree, qualified. Qualified opinions, though not necessarily negative, warrant investigation. Also called *auditor's certificate.*

ACCOUNT EXECUTIVE brokerage firm employee who advises and handles orders for clients and has the legal powers of an AGENT. Every account executive must pass certain tests and be registered with the NATIONAL ASSOCIATION OF SECURITIES DEALERS (NASD) before soliciting orders from customers. Also called *registered representative. See also* BROKER.

ACCOUNTING PRINCIPLES BOARD (APB) board of the American Institute of Certified Public Accountants (AICPA) that issued (1959–73) a series of ACCOUNTANT'S OPINIONS constituting much of what is known as GENERALLY ACCEPTED ACCOUNTING PRINCIPLES. *See also* FINANCIAL ACCOUNTING STANDARDS BOARD (FASB).

ACCOUNTS PAYABLE amounts owing on open account to creditors for goods and services. Analysts look at the relationship of accounts payable to purchases for indications of sound day-to-day financial management. *See also* TRADE CREDIT.

ACCOUNTS RECEIVABLE money owed to a business for merchandise or services sold on open account, a key factor in analyzing a company's LIQUIDITY—its ability to meet current obligations without additional revenues. *See also* ACCOUNTS RECEIVABLE TURNOVER; AGING SCHEDULE; COLLECTION RATIO.

ACCOUNTS RECEIVABLE FINANCING short-term financing whereby accounts receivable serve as collateral for working capital advances. *See also* FACTORING.

ACCOUNTS RECEIVABLE TURNOVER ratio obtained by dividing total credit sales by accounts receivable. The ratio indicates how many times the receivables portfolio has been collected during the accounting period. *See also* ACCOUNTS RECEIVABLE; AGING SCHEDULE; COLLECTION RATIO.

ACCOUNT STATEMENT

In general: any record of transactions and their effect on charge or open-account balances during a specified period.

Banking: summary of all checks paid, deposits recorded, and resulting balances during a defined period. Also called a *bank statement.*

Securities: statement summarizing all transactions and showing the status of an account with a broker-dealer firm, including long and short positions. Such statements must be issued quarterly, but are generally provided monthly when accounts are active. Also, the OPTION AGREEMENT required when an option account is opened.

ACCREDITED INVESTOR under Securities and Exchange Commission Regulation D, a wealthy investor who does not count as one of the maximum of 35 people allowed to put money into a PRIVATE LIMITED PARTNERSHIP. To be accredited, such an investor must have a net worth of at least $1 million or an annual income of at least $200,000, or must put at least $150,000 into the deal, and the investment must not account for more than 20% of the investor's worth. Private limited partnerships use accredited investors to raise a larger amount of capital than would be possible if only 35 less-wealthy people could contribute.

ACCRETION

1. asset growth through internal expansion, acquisition, or such causes as aging of whisky or growth of timber.
2. adjustment of the difference between the price of a bond bought at an original discount and the par value of the bond.

ACCRUAL BASIS accounting method whereby income and expense items are recognized as they are earned or incurred, even though they may not have been received or actually paid in cash. The alternative is CASH BASIS accounting.

ACCRUED INTEREST interest that has accumulated between the most recent payment and the sale of a bond or other fixed-income security. At the time of sale, the buyer pays the seller the bond's price plus accrued interest, calculated by multiplying the coupon rate by the number of days that have elapsed since the last payment.

Accrued interest is also used in a real estate LIMITED PARTNERSHIP when the seller of a building takes a lump sum in cash at the time of sale and gives a second mortgage for the remainder. If the rental income from the building does not cover the mortgage payments, the seller agrees to let the interest accrue until the building is sold to someone else. Accrued interest deals were curtailed by the 1984 tax act.

ACCRUED MARKET DISCOUNT increase in market value of a DISCOUNT BOND that occurs because of its approaching MATURITY DATE (when it is redeemable at PAR) and not because of declining market interest rates.

ACCUMULATED DIVIDEND dividend due, usually to holders of cumulative preferred stock, but not paid. It is carried on the books as a liability until paid. *See also* CUMULATIVE PREFERRED.

ACCUMULATED PROFITS TAX surtax on earnings retained in a business to avoid the higher personal income taxes they would be subject to if paid out as dividends to the owners.

Accumulations above the specified limit, which is set fairly high to benefit small firms, must be justified by the reasonable needs of the business or be subject to the surtax. Because determining the reasonable needs of a business involves considerable judgment, companies have been known to pay excessive dividends or even to make merger decisions out of fear of the accumulated profits tax. Also called *accumulated earnings tax.*

ACCUMULATION

Corporate finance: profits that are not paid out as dividends but are instead added to the company's capital base. *See also* ACCUMULATED PROFITS TAX.

Investments: purchase of a large number of shares in a controlled way so as to avoid driving the price up. An institution's accumulation program, for instance, may take weeks or months to complete.

Mutual funds: investment of a fixed dollar amount regularly and reinvestment of dividends and capital gains.

ACCUMULATION AREA price range within which buyers accumulate shares of a stock. Technical analysts spot accumulation areas when a stock does not drop below a particular price. Technicians who use the ON-BALANCE VOLUME method of analysis advise buying stocks that have hit their accumulation area, because the stocks can be expected to attract more buying interest. *See also* DISTRIBUTION AREA.

ACCUMULATION AREA

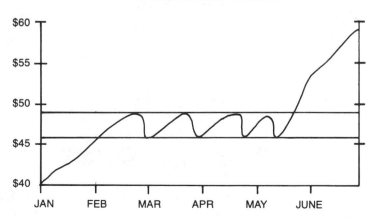

ACID-TEST RATIO *see* QUICK RATIO.

ACKNOWLEDGMENT verification that a signature on a banking or brokerage document is legitimate and has been certified by an authorized person. Acknowledgment is needed when transferring an account from one broker to another, for instance. In banking, an acknowledgment verifies that an item has been received by the paying bank and is or is not available for immediate payment.

ACQUIRED SURPLUS uncapitalized portion of the net worth of a successor company in a POOLING OF INTERESTS combination. In other words, the part of the combined net worth not classified as CAPITAL STOCK.

In a more general sense, the surplus acquired when a company is purchased.

ACQUISITION one company taking over controlling interest in another company. Investors are always looking out for companies that are likely to be acquired, because those who want to acquire such companies are often willing to pay more than the market price for the shares they need to complete the acquisition. *See also* MERGER; POOLING OF INTERESTS; TAKEOVER.

ACROSS THE BOARD movement in the stock market that affects almost all stocks in the same direction. When the market moves up across the board, almost every stock gains in price.

An across-the-board pay increase in a company is a raise of a fixed percent or amount for all employees.

ACTING IN CONCERT two or more investors working together to achieve the same investment goal—for example, all buying stock in a company they want to take over. Such investors must inform the Securities and Exchange Commission if they intend to oust the company's top management or acquire control. It is illegal for those acting in concert to manipulate a stock's price for their own gain.

ACTIVE BOND CROWD members of the bond department of the New York Stock Exchange responsible for the heaviest volume of bond trading. The opposite of the active crowd is the CABINET CROWD, which deals in bonds that are infrequently traded. Investors who buy and sell bonds in the active crowd will tend to get better prices for their securities than in the inactive market, where spreads between bid and asked prices are wider.

ACTIVE BOX collateral available for securing brokers' loans or customers' margin positions in the place—or *box*—where securities are held in safekeeping for clients of a broker-dealer or for the broker-dealer itself. Securities used as collateral must be owned by the firm or hypothecated—that is, pledged or assigned—by the customer to the firm, then by the broker to the lending bank. For margin loans, securities must be hypothecated by the customer to the broker.

ACTIVE MARKET heavy volume of trading in a particular stock, bond, or commodity. The spread between bid and asked prices is usually narrower in an active market than when trading is quiet.

Also, a heavy volume of trading on the exchange as a whole. Institutional money managers prefer such a market because their trades of large blocks of stock tend to have less impact on the movement of prices when trading is generally active.

ACTUALS any physical commodity, such as gold, soybeans, or pork bellies. Trading in actuals ultimately results in delivery of the commodity to the buyer when the contract expires. This contrasts with trading in commodities of, for example, index options, where the contract is settled in cash, and no physical commodity is delivered upon expiration. However, even when trading is in actuals most futures and options contracts are closed out before the contract expires, and so these transactions do not end in delivery.

ACTUARY mathematician employed by an insurance company to calculate premiums, reserves, dividends, and insurance, pension, and annuity rates, using risk factors obtained from experience tables. These tables are based on both the company's history of insurance claims and other industry and general statistical data.

ADDITIONAL PAID-IN CAPITAL see PAID-IN CAPITAL.

ADJUSTABLE RATE MORTGAGE (ARM) mortgage agreement between a financial institution and a real estate buyer stipulating predetermined adjustments of the interest rate at specified intervals. Mortgage payments are tied to some index outside the control of the bank or savings and loan institution, such as the interest rates on U.S. Treasury bills or the average national mortgage rate. Adjustments are made regularly, usually at intervals of one, three, or five years. In return for taking some of the risk of a rise in interest rates, borrowers get lower rates at the beginning of the ARM than they would if they took out a fixed rate mortgage covering the same term. A homeowner who is worried about sharply rising interest rates should probably choose a fixed rate mortgage, whereas one who thinks rates will rise modestly, stay stable, or fall should choose an adjustable rate mortgage. Critics of ARMs charge that these mortgages entice young homeowners to undertake potentially onerous commitments.

ADJUSTED BASIS base price from which to judge capital gains or losses upon sale of an asset like a stock or bond. The cost of commissions in effect is deducted at the time of sale when net proceeds are used for tax purposes. The price must be adjusted to account for any stock splits that have occurred since the initial purchase before arriving at the adjusted basis.

ADJUSTED DEBIT BALANCE (ADB) formula for determining the position of a margin account, as required under Regulation T of the Federal Reserve Board. The ADB is calculated by netting the balance owing the broker with any balance in the SPECIAL MISCELLANEOUS ACCOUNT (SMA), and any paper profits on short accounts. Although changes made in Regulation T in 1982 diminished the significance of ADBs, the formula is still useful in determining whether withdrawals of cash or securities are permissible based on SMA entries.

ADJUSTED EXERCISE PRICE term used in put and call options on Government National Mortgage Association (Ginnie Mae) contracts. To make sure that all contracts trade fairly, the final exercise price of the option is adjusted to take into account the coupon rates carried on all GNMA mortgages. If the standard GNMA mortgage carries an 8% yield, for instance, the price of GNMA pools with 12% mortgages in them are adjusted so that both instruments have the same yield to the investor.

ADJUSTED GROSS INCOME income on which an individual computes federal income tax. Adjusted gross income is determined by subtracting from gross income any unreimbursed business expenses and other deductions—for example Individual Retirement Account (with exceptions outlined in the TAX REFORM ACT OF 1986) and Keogh payments, alimony payments, and disability income. Adjusted gross income is the individual's or couple's income before itemized deductions for such items as medical expenses, state and local income taxes, and real estate taxes.

ADJUSTMENT BOND bond issued in exchange for outstanding bonds when recapitalizing a corporation that faces bankruptcy. Authorization for the exchange comes from the bondholders, who consider adjustment bonds a lesser evil. These bonds promise to pay interest only to the extent earned by the corporation. This gives them one of the characteristics of income bonds, which trade flat—that is, without accrued interest.

ADMINISTRATOR court-appointed individual or bank charged with carrying out the court's decisions with respect to a decedent's estate until it is fully distributed to all claimants. Administrators are appointed when a person dies without having made a will or without having named an executor, or when the named executor cannot or will not serve. The term *administratrix* is sometimes used if the individual appointed is a woman.

In a general sense, an administrator is a person who carries out an organization's policies.

AD VALOREM Latin term meaning "according to value" and referring to a way of assessing duties or taxes on goods or property. As one example, ad valorem DUTY assessment is based on value of the imported item rather than on its weight or quantity. As another example, the city of Englewood, New Jersey, levies an ad valorem tax based on the assessed value of property rather than its size.

ADVANCE-DECLINE (A-D) measurement of the number of stocks that have advanced and the number that have declined over a particular period. It is the ratio of one to the other and shows the general direction of the market. It is considered bullish if more stocks advance than decline on any trading day. It is bearish if declines outnumber advances. The steepness of the A-D line graphically shows whether a strong bull or bear market is underway.

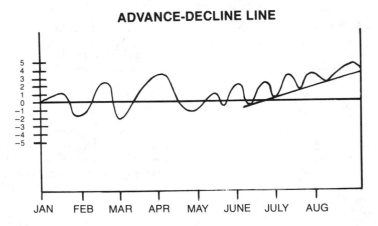

ADVANCE-DECLINE LINE

ADVANCE REFUNDING

Government securities: exchange of maturing government securities prior to their due date for issues with a later maturity. It is through advance refunding that the national debt is extended as an alternative to the economic disruptions that would result from eliminating the debt all at once.

Municipal bonds: sale of new bonds (a *refunding issue*) in advance, usually by some years, of the first call date of the old bonds (*issue to be refunded*). The refunding issue would normally have a lower rate than the issue to be refunded, and the proceeds would be invested, usually in government securities, until the higher-rate bonds become callable. This practice, also called PREREFUNDING, was curtailed by the 1984 and 1986 federal tax acts. *See also* REFUNDING ESCROW DEPOSITS (REDS).

AFFILIATE

In general: two companies are affiliated when one owns less than a majority of the voting stock of the other, or when both are subsidiaries of a third company. A SUBSIDIARY is a company of which more than 50% of the voting shares are owned by another corporation, termed the PARENT COMPANY. A subsidiary is always, by definition, an affiliate, but subsidiary is the preferred term when majority control exists. In everyday use, affiliate is the correct word for inter-company relationships, however indirect, where the parent-subsidiary relationship does not apply.

Banking Act of 1933: any organization that a bank owns or controls by stock holdings, or which the bank's shareholders own, or whose officers are also directors of the bank.

Internal Revenue Service: for purposes of consolidated tax returns an affiliated group is composed of companies whose parent or other inclusive corporation owns at least 80% of voting stock.

Interstate Commerce Commission, Account 706: 1. Controlled by the accounting company alone or with others under a joint agreement. **2.** Controlling the accounting company alone or with others under a joint agreement.

Investment Company Act: company in which there is any direct or indirect ownership of 5% or more of the outstanding voting securities.

AFFILIATED PERSON individual in a position to exert direct influence on the actions of a corporation. Among such persons are owners of 10% or more of the voting shares, directors, and senior elected officers and any persons in a position to exert influence through them—such as members of their immediate family and other close associates. Sometimes called a *control person.*

AFTER ACQUIRED CLAUSE clause in a mortgage agreement providing that any additional mortgageable property acquired by the borrower after the mortgage is signed will be additional security for the obligation.

While such provisions can help give mortgage bonds a good rating and enable issuing corporations to borrow at favorable rates, by precluding additional first mortgages, they make it difficult to finance growth through new borrowings. This gives rise to various maneuvers to remove after acquired clauses, such as redemption or exchange of bonds or changes in indenture agreements.

AFTERMARKET *see* SECONDARY MARKET.

AFTERTAX BASIS basis for comparing the returns on a corporate taxable bond and a municipal tax-free bond. For example, a corporate bond paying 10% would have an aftertax return of 7.2% for someone in the 28% tax bracket. So any municipal bond paying higher than 7.2% would yield a higher aftertax return.

AFTERTAX REAL RATE OF RETURN amount of money, adjusted for inflation, that an investor can keep, out of the income and capital gains earned from investments. Every dollar loses value to inflation, so investors have to keep an eye on the aftertax real rate of return whenever they commit their capital. By and large, investors seek a rate of return that will match if not exceed the rate of inflation.

AGAINST THE BOX SHORT SALE by the holder of a LONG POSITION in the same stock. *Box* refers to the physical location of securities held in safekeeping. When a stock is sold against the box, it is sold short, but only in effect. A short sale is usually defined as one where the seller does not own the shares. Here the seller *does* own the shares (holds a long position) but does not wish to disclose ownership; or perhaps the long shares are too inaccessible to deliver in the time required; or he may be holding his existing position to get the benefit of long-term capital gains tax treatment. In any event, when the sale is made against the box, the shares needed to cover are borrowed, probably from a broker.

AGED FAIL contract between two broker-dealers that is still not settled 30 days after the settlement date. At that point the open balance no longer counts as an asset, and the receiving firm must adjust its capital accordingly.

AGENCY

In general: relationship between two parties, one a principal and the other an AGENT who represents the principal in transactions with a third party.

Finance: certain types of accounts in trust institutions where individuals, usually trust officers, act on behalf of customers. Agency services to corporations are related to stock purchases and sales. Banks also act as agents for individuals.

Government: securities issued by government-sponsored corporations such as Federal Home Loan Banks or Federal Land Banks. Agency securities are exempt from Securities and Exchange Commission (SEC) registration requirements.

Investment: act of buying or selling for the account and risk of a client. Generally, an agent, or broker, acts as intermediary between buyer and seller, taking no financial risk personally or as a firm, and charging a commission for the service.

AGENT individual authorized by another person, called the principal, to act in the latter's behalf in transactions involving a third party. Banks are frequently appointed by individuals to be their agents, and so authorize their employees to act on behalf of principals. Agents have three basic characteristics:
1. They act on behalf of and are subject to the control of the principal.
2. They do not have title to the principal's property.
3. They owe the duty of obedience to the principal's orders.
See also ACCOUNT EXECUTIVE; BROKER; TRANSFER AGENT.

AGGREGATE EXERCISE PRICE in stock options trading, the number of shares in a put or call CONTRACT (normally 100) multiplied by the EXERCISE PRICE. The price of the option, called the PREMIUM, is a separate figure not included in the aggregate exercise price. A July call option on 100 XYZ at 70 would, for example, have an aggregate exercise price of 100 (number of shares) times $70 (price per share), or $7,000, if exercised on or before the July expiration date.

In options traded on debt instruments, which include GOVERNMENT NATIONAL MORTGAGE ASSOCIATION (GNMA) pass-throughs, Treasury bills, Treasury notes, Treasury bonds, and certain municipal bonds, the aggregate exercise price is determined by multiplying the FACE VALUE of the underlying security by the exercise price. For example, the aggregate exercise price of put option Treasury bond December 90 would be $90,000 if exercised on or before its December expiration date, the calculation being 90% times the $100,000 face value of the underlying bond.

AGGREGATE SUPPLY in MACROECONOMICS, the total amount of goods and services supplied to the market at alternative price levels in a given period of time; also called *total output*. The central concept in SUPPLY-SIDE ECONOMICS, it corresponds with aggregate demand, defined as the total amount of goods and services demanded in the economy at alternative income levels in a given period, including both consumer and producers' goods; aggregate demand is also called *total spending*. The aggregate supply curve describes the relationship between price levels and the quantity of output that firms are willing to provide.

AGING SCHEDULE classification of trade ACCOUNTS RECEIVABLE by date of sale. Usually prepared by a company's auditor, the *aging*, as the schedule is called, is a vital tool in analyzing the quality of a company's receivables investment. It is frequently required by grantors of credit.

The schedule is most often seen as: (1) a list of the amount of receivables by the month in which they were created; (2) a list of receivables by maturity, classified as current or as being in various stages of delinquency. The following is a typical aging schedule:

	dollars (in thousands)	
Current (under 30 days)	$14,065	61%
1–30 days past due	3,725	16
31–60 days past due	2,900	12
61–90 days past due	1,800	8
Over 90 days past due	750	3
	$23,240	100%

The aging schedule reveals patterns of delinquency and shows where collection efforts should be concentrated. It helps in evaluating the adequacy of the reserve for BAD DEBTS, because the longer accounts stretch out the more likely they are to become uncollectible. Using the schedule can help prevent the loss of future sales, since old customers who fall too far behind tend to seek out new sources of supply.

AGREEMENT AMONG UNDERWRITERS contract between participating members of an investment banking SYNDICATE; sometimes called *syndicate contract* or *purchase group agreement*. It is distinguished from the *underwriting agreement*, which is signed by the company issuing the securities and the SYNDICATE MANAGER, acting as agent for the underwriting group.

The agreement among underwriters: (1) appoints the originating investment banker as syndicate manager and agent; (2) appoints additional managers, if considered advisable; (3) defines the members' proportionate liability (usually limited to the amount of their participation) and agrees to pay each member's share on settlement date; (4) authorizes the manager to form and allocate units to a SELLING GROUP, and agrees to abide by the rules of the selling group agreement; (5) states the life of the syndicate, usually running until 30 days after termination of the selling group, or ending earlier by mutual consent.

AIR POCKET STOCK stock that falls sharply, usually in the wake of such negative news as unexpected poor earnings. As shareholders rush to sell, and few buyers can be found, the price plunges dramatically, like an airplane hitting an air pocket.

ALIEN CORPORATION company incorporated under the laws of a foreign country regardless of where it operates. "Alien corporation" can be used as a synonym for the term *foreign corporation*. However, "foreign corporation" also is used in U.S. state law to mean a corporation formed in a state other than that in which it does business.

ALLIED MEMBER general partner or voting stockholder of a member firm of the New York Stock Exchange who is not personally a member. Allied members cannot do business on the trading floor. A member firm need have no more than one partner or voting stockholder who owns a membership. So even the chairman of the board of a member firm may be no more than an allied member.

ALLIGATOR SPREAD spread in the options market that "eats the investor alive" with high commission costs. The term is used when a broker arranges a combination of puts and calls that generates so much commission the client is unlikely to turn a profit even if the markets move as anticipated.

ALL OR NONE (AON)

Investment banking: an offering giving the issuer the right to cancel the whole issue if the underwriting is not fully subscribed.

Securities: buy or sell order marked to signify that no partial transaction is to be executed. The order will not automatically be canceled, however, if a complete transaction is not executed; to accomplish that, the order entry must be marked FOK, meaning FILL (for the full number of units) OR KILL.

ALLOTMENT amount of securities assigned to each of the participants in an investment banking SYNDICATE formed to underwrite and distribute a new issue, called *subscribers* or *allottees*. The financial responsibilities of the subscribers are set forth in an allotment notice, which is prepared by the SYNDICATE MANAGER.

ALLOWANCE deduction from the value of an invoice, permitted by a seller of goods to cover damages or shortages. *See also* RESERVE.

ALL-SAVERS CERTIFICATE *see* ECONOMIC RECOVERY TAX ACT OF 1981 (ERTA).

ALPHA
1. coefficient measuring the portion of an investment's RETURN arising from specific (nonmarket) risk. In other words, alpha is a mathematical estimate of the amount of return expected from an investment's inherent values, such as the rate of growth in earnings per share. It is distinct from the amount of return caused by VOLATILITY, which is measured by the BETA coefficient. For example, an alpha of 1.25 indicates that a stock is projected to rise 25% in price in a year when the return on the market and the stock's beta are both expected to be zero. An investment whose price is low relative to its alpha is undervalued and considered a good selection.
2. in the case of a MUTUAL FUND, alpha measures the relationship between the fund's performance and its beta over a three-year period.
3. on the London Stock Exchange, the designation *alpha stocks* applies to the largest and most actively traded companies, comparable to U.S. BLUE CHIPS. As the result of reforms arising from BIG BANG in 1986, alpha shares, which represent some 80% of turnover, are subject to stricter trading regulation than BETA or GAMMA stocks. *See also* DELTA STOCKS.

ALTERNATIVE MINIMUM TAX (AMT) federal tax, revamped by the TAX REFORM ACT OF 1986, aimed at ensuring that wealthy individuals and corporations pay at least some income tax. For individuals, the AMT is computed by adding TAX PREFERENCE ITEMS such as PASSIVE losses from tax shelters, tax-exempt interest on PRIVATE-PURPOSE BONDS issued after August 8, 1986, and deductions claimed for charitable contributions of stock, real estate, art work, and other appreciated property to adjusted gross income, then subtracting $40,000 for a married couple filing jointly or $30,000 if filing singly; 21% of the remainder is the payable tax. The exemption amounts are phased out by 25 cents for each $1 that AMT income exceeds $150,000 for joint filers ($112,500 for individuals). The corporate AMT has the same exemptions but a rate of 20%. Preferences include 50% of the excess of "book" (financial statement) income over total taxable income plus other preferences such as untaxed appreciation of charitable contributions, certain "excess" accelerated depreciation on assets put in service after 1986, tax-exempt interest on private-purpose bonds issued after August 8, 1986, and other industry-specific preferences. After 1989, the corporate AMT is set to be based on the tax definition of earnings and profits, not book income.

ALTERNATIVE ORDER order giving a broker a choice between two courses of action; also called an *either-or order* or a *one cancels the other order*. Such orders are either to buy or to sell, never both. Execution of one course automatically makes the other course inoperative. An example is a combination buy limit/buy stop order, wherein the buy limit is below the current market and the buy stop is above.

AMBAC Indemnity Corporation *see* MUNICIPAL BOND INSURANCE.

AMENDMENT addition to, or change in, a legal document. When properly signed, it has the full legal effect of the original document.

AMERICAN DEPOSITARY RECEIPT (ADR) receipt for the shares of a foreign-based corporation held in the vault of a U.S. bank and entitling the shareholder to all dividends and capital gains. Instead of buying shares of foreign-based companies in overseas markets, Americans can buy shares in the U.S. in the form of an ADR. ADR's are available for hundreds of stocks from numerous countries. Also called *American Depositary Share.*

AMERICAN STOCK EXCHANGE (AMEX) stock exchange located at 86 Trinity Place in downtown Manhattan. The Amex was known until 1921 as the *Curb Exchange,* and it is still referred to as the *Curb* today. For the most part, the stocks and bonds traded on the Amex are those of small to medium-size companies, as contrasted with the huge companies whose shares are traded on the New York Stock Exchange. A large number of oil and gas companies, in particular, are traded on the Amex. The Amex also houses the trading of options on many New York Stock Exchange stocks and some OVER THE COUNTER stocks. More foreign shares are traded on the Amex than on any other U.S. exchange.

AMORTIZATION accounting procedure that gradually reduces the cost value of a limited life or intangible asset through periodic charges to income. For fixed assets the term used is DEPRECIATION, and for wasting assets (natural resources) it is depletion, both terms meaning essentially the same thing as amortization. Most companies follow the conservative practice of writing off, through amortization, INTANGIBLE ASSETS such as goodwill. It is also common practice to amortize any premium over par value paid in the purchase of preferred stock or bond investments. The purpose of amortization is to reflect resale or redemption value.

Amortization also refers to the reduction of debt by regular payments of interest and principal sufficient to pay off a loan by maturity.

Discount and expense on funded debt are amortized by making applicable charges to income in accordance with a predetermined schedule. While this is normally done systematically, charges to profit and loss are permissible at any time in any amount of the remaining discount and expense. Such accounting is detailed in a company's annual report.

ANALYST person in a brokerage house, bank trust department, or mutual fund group who studies a number of companies and makes buy or sell recommendations on the securities of particular companies and industry groups. Most analysts specialize in a particular industry, but some investigate any company that interests them, regardless of its line of business. Some analysts have considerable influence, and can therefore affect the price of a company's stock when they issue a buy or sell recommendation. *See also* CREDIT ANALYST.

AND INTEREST phrase used in quoting bond prices to indicate that, in addition to the price quoted, the buyer will receive ACCRUED INTEREST.

ANKLE BITER stock issue having a MARKET CAPITALIZATION of less than $500 million. Generally speaking, such small-capitalization stocks are more speculative than "high-cap" issues, but their greater growth potential gives them more RELATIVE STRENGTH in recessions. *See also* SMALL FIRM EFFECT.

ANNUAL BASIS statistical technique whereby figures covering a period of less than a year are extended to cover a 12-month period. The procedure, called *annualizing,* must take seasonal variations (if any) into account to be accurate.

ANNUAL MEETING once-a-year meeting when the managers of a company report to stockholders on the year's results, and the board of directors stands for election for the next year. The chief executive officer usually comments on the outlook for the coming year and, with other senior officers, answers questions from shareholders. Stockholders can also request that resolutions on corporate policy be voted on by all those owning stock in the company. Stockholders unable to attend the annual meeting may vote for directors and pass on resolutions through the use of PROXY material, which must legally be mailed to all shareholders of record.

ANNUAL PERCENTAGE RATE (APR) cost of credit that consumers pay, expressed as a simple annual percentage. According to the federal Truth in Lending Act, every consumer loan agreement must disclose the APR in large bold type. *See also* CONSUMER CREDIT PROTECTION ACT OF 1968.

ANNUAL RENEWABLE TERM INSURANCE *see* TERM INSURANCE.

ANNUAL REPORT yearly record of a corporation's financial condition that must be distributed to shareholders under SECURITIES AND EXCHANGE COMMISSION regulations. Included in the report is a description of the company's operations as well as its balance sheet and income statement. The long version of the annual report with more detailed financial information—called the 10-K—is available upon request from the corporate secretary.

ANNUITIZE to begin a series of payments from the capital that has built up in an ANNUITY. The payments may be a fixed amount, or for a fixed period of time, or for the lifetimes of one or two *annuitants,* thus guaranteeing income payments that cannot be outlived. *See also* DEFERRED PAYMENT ANNUITY; FIXED ANNUITY; IMMEDIATE PAYMENT ANNUITY; VARIABLE ANNUITY.

ANNUITY form of contract sold by life insurance companies that guarantees a fixed or variable payment to the annuitant at some future time, usually retirement. In a FIXED ANNUITY the amount will ultimately be paid out in regular installments varying only with the payout method elected. In a VARIABLE ANNUITY, the amount of the payout will vary with the value of the account. All capital and investment proceeds that remain inside the annuity accumulate tax-deferred. Key considerations when buying an annuity are the financial soundness of the insurance company (*see* BEST'S RATING), the returns it has paid on annuities in the past, and the level of fees and commissions paid to annuity salesmen.

ANTICIPATED HOLDING PERIOD time during which a limited partnership expects to hold onto an asset. In the prospectus for a real estate limited partnership, for instance, a sponsor will typically say that the anticipated holding period for a particular property is five to seven years. At the end of that time the property is sold, and, usually, the capital received is returned to the limited partners in one distribution.

ANTICIPATION

In general: paying an obligation before it falls due.

Finance: repayment of debt obligations before maturity, usually to save interest. If a formalized discount or rebate is involved, the term used is *anticipation rate*.

Mortgage instrument: when a provision allows prepayment without penalty, the mortgagee is said to have the *right of anticipation*.

Trade payments: bill that is paid before it is due, not discounted.

ANTITRUST LAWS federal legislation designed to prevent monopolies and restraint of trade. Landmark statutes include:
1. the Sherman Anti-Trust Act of 1890, which prohibited acts or contracts tending to create monopoly and initiated an era of trustbusting.
2. the Clayton Anti-Trust Act of 1914, which was passed as an amendment to the Sherman Act and dealt with local price discrimination as well as with the INTERLOCKING DIRECTORATES. It went further in the areas of the HOLDING COMPANY and restraint of trade.
3. the Federal Trade Commission Act of 1914, which created the Federal Trade Commission or FTC, with power to conduct investigations and issue orders preventing unfair practices in interstate commerce.

ANY-AND-ALL-BID offer to pay an equal price for all shares tendered by a deadline; contrasts with TWO-TIER BID. *See also* TAKEOVER.

APPRECIATION increase in the value of an asset such as a stock, bond, commodity, or real estate.

APPROVED LIST *see* LEGAL LIST.

ARBITRAGE profiting from differences in price when the same security, currency, or commodity is traded on two or more markets. For example, an *arbitrageur* simultaneously buys one contract of gold in the New York market and sells one contract of gold in the Chicago market, locking in a profit because at that moment the price on the two markets is different. (The arbitrageur's selling price is higher than the buying price.) *Index arbitrage* exploits price differences between STOCK INDEX FUTURES and underlying stocks. By taking advantage of momentary disparities in prices between markets, arbitrageurs perform the economic function of making those markets trade more efficiently. *See also* RISK ARBITRAGE.

ARBITRAGE BONDS bonds issued by a municipality in order to gain an interest rate advantage by refunding higher-rate bonds in advance of their call date. Proceeds from the lower-rate refunding issue are invested in Treasuries until the first call date of the higher-rate issue being refunded. Arbitrage bonds, which always raised a question of tax exemption, were further curtailed by the TAX REFORM ACT OF 1986.

ARBITRATION alternative to suing in court to settle disputes between brokers and their clients and between brokerage firms. Traditionally, predispute arbitration clauses in account agreements with brokers automatically assured that disputes would be arbitrated by objective third parties and precluded court cases. In 1989, the Securities and Exchange Commission (SEC) approved sweeping changes that (1) required brokers to disclose clearly when such clauses exist, (2) prohibited any restrictions on customers' rights to file arbitration claims, and (3) imposed stricter qualifying standards for arbitrators. *See also* ARBITRATION BOARD.

ARITHMETIC MEAN simple average obtained by dividing the sum of two or more items by the number of items.

ARM'S LENGTH TRANSACTION transaction that is conducted as though the parties were unrelated, thus avoiding any semblance of conflict of interest. For example, under current law parents may rent real estate to their children and still claim business deductions such as depreciation as long as the parents charge their children what they would charge if someone who is not a relative were to rent the same property.

ARREARAGE

In general: amount of any past-due obligation.

Investments: amount by which interest on bonds or dividends on CUMULATIVE PREFERRED stock is due and unpaid. In the case of cumulative preferred stock, common dividends cannot be paid by a company as long as preferred dividends are in arrears.

ARTICLES OF INCORPORATION document filed with a U.S. state by the founders of a corporation. After approving the articles, the state issues a certificate of incorporation; the two documents together become the CHARTER that gives the corporation its legal existence. The charter embodies such information as the corporation's name, purpose, amount of authorized shares, and number and identity of directors. The corporation's powers thus derive from the laws of the state and from the provisions of the charter. Rules governing its internal management are set forth in the corporation's BYLAWS, which are drawn up by the founders.

ASCENDING TOPS chart pattern tracing a security's price over a period of time and showing that each peak in a security's price is higher than the preceding peak. This upward movement is considered bullish, meaning that the upward trend is likely to continue. *See also* DESCENDING TOPS.

ASE INDEX *see* STOCK INDEXES AND AVERAGES.

ASKED PRICE

1. price at which a security or commodity is offered for sale on an exchange or in the over-the-counter market. Generally, it is the lowest round lot price at which a dealer will sell. Also called the *ask price, asking price, ask,* or OFFERING PRICE.
2. per-share price at which mutual fund shares are offered to the public, usually the NET ASSET VALUE per share plus a sales charge, if any.

ASCENDING TOPS

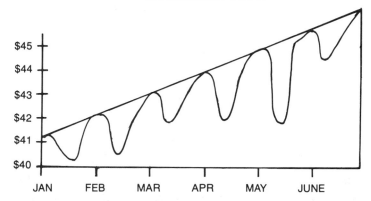

ASSAY test of a metal's purity to verify that it meets the standards for trading on a commodities exchange. For instance, a 100 troy-ounce bar of refined gold must be assayed at a fineness of not less than 995 before the Comex will allow it to be used in settlement of a gold contract.

ASSESSED VALUATION dollar value assigned to property by a municipality for purposes of assessing taxes, which are based on the number of mills per dollar of assessed valuation. If a house is assessed at $100,000 and the tax rate is 50 mills, the tax is $5000. Assessed valuation is important not only to homeowners but also to investors in municipal bonds that are backed by property taxes.

ASSET anything having commercial or exchange value that is owned by a business, institution, or individual. *See also* CAPITAL ASSET; CURRENT ASSETS; DEFERRED CHARGE; FIXED ASSET; INTANGIBLE ASSET; NONCURRENT ASSET.

ASSET ALLOCATION apportioning of investment funds among categories of assets, such as CASH EQUIVALENTS, STOCK, FIXED-INCOME INVESTMENTS, and such tangible assets as real estate, precious metals, and collectibles. Also applies to subcategories such as government, municipal, and corporate bonds, and industry groupings of common stocks. Asset allocation affects both risk and return and is a central concept in personal financial planning and investment management.

ASSET-BACKED SECURITIES bonds or notes backed by loan paper or accounts receivable originated by banks, credit card companies, or other providers of credit and often "enhanced" by a bank LETTER OF CREDIT or by insurance coverage provided by an institution other than the issuer. Typically, the originator of the loan or accounts receivable paper sells it to a specially created trust, which repackages it as securities with a minimum denomination of $1000 and a term of five years or less. The securities are then underwritten by brokerage firms, which reoffer them to the public. Examples are CERTIFICATES FOR AUTOMOBILE RECEIVABLES (CARS) and so-called *plastic bonds*, backed by credit card receivables. Because the institution that originated the underlying loans or receivables is neither the obligor nor the guarantor, investors should evaluate the quality of the original paper, the worth of the guarantor or insurer, and the extent of the protection. *See also* PASS-THROUGH SECURITY.

ASSET COVERAGE extent to which a company's net assets cover a particular debt obligation, class of preferred stock, or equity position.

Asset coverage is calculated as follows: from assets at their total book value or liquidation value, subtract intangible assets, current liabilities, and all obligations prior in claim to the issue in question. Divide the result by the dollar amount of the subject issue (or loan) to arrive at the asset coverage ratio. The same information can be expressed as a percentage or, by using units as the divisor, as a dollar figure of coverage per unit. The variation to determine preferred stock coverage treats all liabilities as paid; the variation to arrive at common stock coverage considers both preferred stock and liabilities paid. The term most often used for the common stock calculation is *net book value per share of common stock.*

These calculations reveal *direct* asset coverage. *Overall* asset coverage is obtained by including the subject issue with the total of prior obligations and dividing the aggregate into total tangible assets at liquidating value.

Asset coverage is important as a cushion against losses in the event of liquidation.

ASSET DEPRECIATION RANGE SYSTEM (ADR) range of depreciable lives allowed by the Internal Revenue Service for particular classes of depreciable assets. The ADR system was replaced when the ECONOMIC RECOVERY TAX ACT OF 1981 (ERTA) introduced the ACCELERATED COST RECOVERY SYSTEM (ACRS) but was revived with modifications of ACRS under the TAX REFORM ACT OF 1986. The ADR system assigns an upper and lower limit to the estimated useful lives of asset classes. ACRS classes are based on the mid-points of these ranges. Under the alternative depreciation system, taxpayers may elect STRAIGHT LINE DEPRECIATION over the applicable ADR-class life.

ASSET FINANCING financing that seeks to convert particular assets into working cash in exchange for a security interest in those assets. The term is replacing *commercial financing* as major banks join commercial finance companies in addressing the financing needs of companies that do not fit the traditional seasonal borrower profile. Although the prevalent form of asset financing continues to be loans against accounts receivable, *inventory loans* are common and *second mortgage loans,* predicated as they usually are on market values containing a high inflation factor, seem to gain popularity by the day. *See also* ACCOUNTS RECEIVABLE FINANCING.

ASSET-LIABILITY MANAGEMENT matching an individual's level of debt and amount of assets. Someone who is planning to buy a new car, for instance, would have to decide whether to pay cash, thus lowering assets, or to take out a loan, thereby increasing debts (or liabilities). Such decisions should be based on interest rates, on earning power, and on the comfort level with debt. Financial institutions carry out asset-liability management when they match the maturity of their deposits with the length of their loan commitments to keep from being adversely affected by rapid changes in interest rates.

ASSET MANAGEMENT ACCOUNT account at a brokerage house, bank, or savings institution that combines banking services like checkwriting, credit cards, and debit cards; brokerage features like buying securities and making loans on margin; and the convenience of having all financial transactions listed on one monthly statement. Such accounts are also termed *central asset accounts* and are known by such proprietary names as the *Cash Management Account* (Merrill Lynch), *Financial Management Account* (Shearson Lehman), and *Active Assets Account* (Dean Witter).

ASSET PLAY stock market term for a stock that is attractive because the current price does not reflect the value of the company's assets. For example, an analyst could recommend a hotel chain, not because its hotels are run well but because its real estate is worth far more than is recognized in the stock's current price. Asset play stocks are tempting targets for takeovers because they provide an inexpensive way to buy assets.

ASSIGN sign a document transferring ownership from one party to another. Ownership can be in a number of forms, including tangible property, rights (usually arising out of contracts), or the right to transfer ownership at some later time. The party who assigns is called the *assignor* and the party who receives the transfer of title—the assignment—is the *assignee*.

Stocks and registered bonds can be assigned by completing and signing a form printed on the back of the certificate—or, as is sometimes preferred for safety reasons, by executing a separate form, called an *assignment separate from certificate* or *stock/bond power.*

When the OPTIONS CLEARING CORPORATION learns of the exercise of an option, it prepares an assignment form notifying a broker-dealer that an option written by one of its clients has been exercised. The firm in turn assigns the exercise in accordance with its internal procedures.

An assignment for the benefit of creditors, sometimes called simply an *assignment,* is an alternative to bankruptcy, whereby the assets of a company are assigned to the creditors and liquidated for their benefit by a trustee.

ASSIMILATION absorption of a new issue of stock by the investing public after all shares have been sold by the issue's underwriters. *See also* ABSORBED.

ASSUMPTION act of taking on responsibility for the liabilities of another party, usually documented by an *assumption agreement.* In the case of a MORTGAGE assumption, the seller remains secondarily liable unless released from the obligation by the lender.

AT PAR at a price equal to the face, or nominal, value of a security. *See also* PAR VALUE.

AT RISK exposed to the danger of loss. Investors in a limited partnership can claim tax deductions only if they can prove that there's a chance of never realizing any profit and of losing their investment as well. Deductions will be disallowed if the limited partners are not exposed to economic risk—if, for example, the general partner guarantees to return all capital to limited partners even if the business venture should lose money.

AT THE CLOSE order to buy or sell a security within the final 30 seconds of trading. Brokers never guarantee that such orders will be executed.

AT THE MARKET *see* MARKET ORDER.

AT THE MONEY at the current price, as an option with an exercise price equal to or near the current price of the stock or underlying futures contract. *See also* DEEP IN/OUT OF THE MONEY; IN THE MONEY; OUT OF THE MONEY.

AT THE OPENING customer's order to a broker to buy or sell a security at the price that applies when an exchange opens. If the order is not executed at that time, it is automatically canceled.

AUCTION MARKET system by which securities are bought and sold through brokers on the securities exchanges, as distinguished from the over-the-counter market, where trades are negotiated. Best exemplified by the NEW YORK STOCK EXCHANGE, it is a double auction system or TWO-SIDED MARKET. That is because, unlike the conventional auction with one auctioneer and many buyers, here we have many sellers and many buyers. As in any auction, a price is established by competitive bidding between brokers acting as agents for buyers and sellers. That the system functions in an orderly way is the result of several trading rules: (1) The first bid or offer at a given price has priority over any other bid or offer at the same price. (2) The high bid and low offer ''have the floor.'' (3) A new auction begins whenever all the offers or bids at a given price are exhausted. (4) Secret transactions are prohibited. (5) Bids and offers must be made in an audible voice.

Also, the competitive bidding by which Treasury bills are sold. *See also* BILL; DUTCH AUCTION.

AUCTION-RATE PREFERRED STOCK *see* DUTCH AUCTION; PREFERRED STOCK.

AUDIT professional examination and verification of a company's accounting documents and supporting data for the purpose of rendering an opinion as to their fairness, consistency, and conformity with GENERALLY ACCEPTED ACCOUNTING PRINCIPLES. *See also* ACCOUNTANT'S OPINION.

AUDITOR'S CERTIFICATE *see* ACCOUNTANT'S OPINION.

AUDIT TRAIL step-by-step record by which accounting data can be traced to their source. Questions as to the validity or accuracy of an accounting figure can be resolved by reviewing the sequence of events from which the figure resulted.

AUTEX SYSTEM electronic system for alerting brokers that other brokers want to buy or sell large blocks of stock. Once a match is made, the actual transaction takes place over the counter or on the floor of an exchange.

AUTHENTICATION identification of a bond certificate as having been issued under a specific indenture, thus validating the bond. Also, legal verification of the genuineness of a document, as by the certification and seal of an authorized public official.

AUTHORITY BOND bond issued by and payable from the revenue of a government agency or a corporation formed to administer a revenue-producing public enterprise. One such corporation is the Port Authority of New York and New Jersey, which operates bridges and tunnels in the New York City area. Because an authority usually has no source of revenue other than charges for the facilities it operates, its bonds have the characteristics of revenue bonds. The difference is that bondholder protections may be incorporated in the authority bond contract as well as in the legislation that created the authority.

AUTHORIZED SHARES maximum number of shares of any class a company may legally create under the terms of its ARTICLES OF INCORPORATION. Normally, a corporation provides for future increases in authorized stock by vote of the stockholders. The corporation is not required to issue all the shares authorized and may initially keep issued shares at a minimum to hold down taxes and expenses. Also called *authorized stock*.

AUTOMATIC REINVESTMENT *see* CONSTANT DOLLAR PLAN; DIVIDEND REINVESTMENT PLAN.

AUTOMATIC WITHDRAWAL mutual fund program that entitles shareholders to a fixed payment each month or each quarter. The payment comes from dividends, including realized capital gains and income on securities held by the fund.

AVERAGE appropriately weighted and adjusted ARITHMETIC MEAN of selected securities designed to represent market behavior generally or important segments of the market. Among the most familiar averages are the Dow Jones industrial and transportation averages.

Because the evaluation of individual securities involves measuring price trends of securities in general or within an industry group, the various averages are important analytical tools.

AVERAGE DOWN strategy to lower the average price paid for a company's shares. An investor who wants to buy 1000 shares, for example, could buy 400 at the current market price and three blocks of 200 each as the price fell. The average cost would then be lower than it would have been if all 1000 shares had been bought at once. Investors also average down in order to realize tax losses. Say someone buys shares at $20, then watches them fall to $10. Instead of doing nothing, the investor can buy at $10, then sell the $20 shares at a capital loss, which can be used at tax time to offset other gains. However, the WASH SALE rule says that in order to claim the capital loss, the investor must not sell the $20 stock until at least 30 days after buying the stock at $10. *See also* CONSTANT DOLLAR PLAN.

AVERAGE EQUITY average daily balance in a trading account. Brokerage firms calculate customer equity daily as part of their procedure for keeping track of gains and losses on uncompleted transactions, called MARK TO THE MARKET. When transactions are completed, profits and losses are booked to each customer's account together with brokerage commissions. Even though daily fluctuations in equity are routine, average equity is a useful guide in making trading decisions and ensuring sufficient equity to meet MARGIN REQUIREMENTS.

AVERAGE UP buy on a rising market so as to lower the overall cost. Buying an equal number of shares at $50, $52, $54, and $58, for instance, will make the average cost $53.50. This is a mathematical reality, but it does not determine whether the stock is worth buying at any or all of these prices.

AVERAGING *see* CONSTANT DOLLAR PLAN.

AWAY FROM THE MARKET expression used when the bid on a LIMIT ORDER is lower or the offer price is higher than the current market price for the security. Away from the market limit orders are held by the specialist for later execution unless FILL OR KILL (FOK) is stipulated on the order entry.

b_____

BABY BOND convertible or straight debt bond having a par value of less than $1000, usually $500 to $25. Baby bonds bring the bond market within reach of small investors and, by the same token, open a source of funds to corporations that lack entree to the large institutional market. On the negative side, they entail higher administrative costs (relative to the total money raised) for distribution and processing and lack the large and active market that ensures the liquidity of conventional bonds.

BACKDATING

In general: dating any statement, document, check or other instrument earlier than the date drawn.

Mutual funds: feature permitting fundholders to use an earlier date on a promise to invest a specified sum over a specified period in exchange for a reduced sales charge. Backdating, which usually accompanies a large transaction, gives retroactive value to purchases from the earlier date in order to meet the requirements of the promise, or LETTER OF INTENT.

BACK-END LOAD redemption charge an investor pays when withdrawing money from an investment. Most common in mutual funds and annuities, the back-end load is designed to discourage withdrawals. Also called *deferred sales charge; exit fee; redemption charge.*

BACKING AWAY broker-dealer's failure, as market maker in a given security, to make good on a bid for the minimum quantity. This practice is considered unethical under the RULES OF FAIR PRACTICE of the NATIONAL ASSOCIATION OF SECURITIES DEALERS.

BACKLOG value of unfilled orders placed with a manufacturing company. Whether the firm's backlog is rising or falling is a clue to its future sales and earnings.

BACK OFFICE bank or brokerage house departments not directly involved in selling or trading. The back office sees to accounting records, compliance with government regulations, and communication between branches. When stock-market trading is particularly heavy, order processing can be slowed by massive volume; this is called a back office crunch.

BACK UP turn around; reverse a stock market trend. When prices are moving in one direction, traders would say of a sudden reversal that the market backed up.

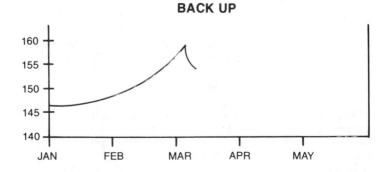

BACK UP

BACKUP LINE BANK LINE of credit in the name of an issuer of commercial paper, covering maturing notes in the event that new notes cannot be marketed to replace them. Ideally, the unused line should always equal the commercial paper outstanding. In practice, something less than total coverage is commonplace, particularly because the compensating balances normally required in support of the line are also available to meet maturing paper.

BACKWARDATION
1. pricing structure in commodities or foreign-exchange trading in which deliveries in the near future have a higher price than those made later on. Backwardation occurs when demand is greater in the near future. *See also* CONTANGO.
2. London Stock Exchange term for the fees and interest due on short sales of stock with delayed delivery.

BAD DEBT open account balance or loan receivable that has proven uncollectible and is written off. Traditionally, companies and financial institutions have maintained a RESERVE for uncollectible accounts, charging the reserve for actual bad debts and making annual tax deductible charges to income to replenish or increase the reserve. The TAX REFORM ACT OF 1986 required companies and large banks ($500 million or more in assets) to convert from the reserve method to a direct charge-off method for tax purposes beginning in 1987, although bad debt reserves will continue to appear on balance sheets for reporting purposes. Small banks and thrift institutions were allowed to continue using the reserve method for tax purposes, although with stricter limitations. The relationship of bad debt write-offs and recoveries to accounts receivable can reveal how liberal or conservative a firm's credit and charge-off policies are.

BAD DELIVERY opposite of GOOD DELIVERY.

BAILOUT BOND BOND issued by RESOLUTION FUNDING CORPORATION (REFCORP) to finance the rescue or disposition of SAVINGS AND LOAN ASSOCIATIONS that were failing in the 1980s. The principal of Refcorp securities is backed by zero-coupon Treasury bonds, and the U.S. Treasury guarantees interest payments. Because this is stronger backing than that enjoyed by other GOVERNMENT SECURITIES issued by agencies, bailout bonds yield only slightly more than TREASURIES of comparable maturity. See also OFFICE OF THRIFT SUPERVISION (OTS).

BALANCED BUDGET *see* BUDGET.

BALANCED MUTUAL FUND fund that buys common stock, preferred stock, and bonds in an effort to obtain the highest return consistent with a low-risk strategy. A balanced fund typically offers a higher yield than a pure stock fund and performs better than such a fund when stocks are falling. In a rising market, however, a balanced mutual fund usually will not keep pace with all-equity funds.

BALANCE OF PAYMENTS system of recording all of a country's economic transactions with the rest of the world during a particular time period. Double-entry bookkeeping is used, and there can be no surplus or deficit on the overall balance of payments. The balance of payments is typically divided into three accounts—current, capital, and gold—and these can show a surplus or deficit. The current account covers imports and exports of goods and services; the capital account covers movements of investments; and the gold account covers gold movements. The balance of payments helps a country evaluate its competitive strengths and weaknesses and forecast the strength of its currency. From the standpoint of a national economy, a surplus on a part of the balance of payments is not necessarily good, nor is a deficit necessarily bad; the state of the national economy and the manner of financing the deficit are important considerations. *See also* BALANCE OF TRADE.

BALANCE OF TRADE net difference over a period of time between the value of a country's imports and exports of merchandise. Movable goods such as automobiles, foodstuffs, and apparel are included in the balance of trade; payments abroad for services and for tourism are not. When a country exports more than it imports, it is said to have a favorable balance of trade; when imports predominate the balance is called unfavorable. The balance of trade should be viewed in the context of the country's entire international economic position, however. For example, a country may consistently have an unfavorable balance of trade that is offset by considerable exports of services; this country would be judged to have a good international economic position. *See also* BALANCE OF PAYMENTS.

BALANCE SHEET financial report, also called *statement of condition* or *statement of financial position*, showing the status of a company's assets, liabilities, and owners' equity on a given date, usually the close of a month. One way of looking at a business enterprise is as a mass of capital (ASSETS) arrayed against the sources of that capital (LIABILITIES and EQUITY). Assets are equal to liabilities and equity, and the balance sheet is a listing of the items making up the two sides of the equation. Unlike a PROFIT AND LOSS STATEMENT, which shows the results of operations over a period of time, a balance sheet shows the state of affairs at one point in time. It is a snapshot, not a motion picture, and must be analyzed with reference to comparative prior balance sheets and other operating statements.

BALLOON final payment on a debt that is substantially larger than the preceding payments. Loans or mortgages are structured with balloon payments when some projected event is expected to provide extra cash flow or when refinancing is anticipated. Balloon loans are sometimes called *partially amortized loans*.

BALLOON INTEREST in serial bond issues, the higher COUPON rate on bonds with later maturities.

BALLOON MATURITY bond issue or long-term loan with larger dollar amounts of bonds or payments falling due in the later years of the obligation.

BANK DISCOUNT BASIS *see* DISCOUNT YIELD.

BANKER'S ACCEPTANCE *see* ACCEPTANCE.

BANK HOLDING COMPANY company that owns or controls two or more banks or other bank holding companies. As defined in the Bank Holding Company Act of 1956, such companies must register with the BOARD OF GOVERNORS of the FEDERAL RESERVE SYSTEM and hence are called registered bank holding companies. Amendments to the 1956 act set standards for acquisitions (1966) and ended the exemption enjoyed by one-bank holding companies (1970), thus restricting bank holding companies to activities related to banking.

BANK INSURANCE FUND (BIF) FEDERAL DEPOSIT INSURANCE CORPORATION (FDIC) unit providing deposit insurance for banks other than thrifts. BIF was formed as part of the 1989 savings and loan association bailout bill to keep separate the administration of the bank and thrift insurance programs. There are thus two distinct insurance entities under FDIC: BIF and SAVINGS ASSOCIATION INSURANCE FUND (SAIF). Deposit insurance coverage remains unaffected. *See also* OFFICE OF THRIFT SUPERVISION (OTS).

BANK LINE bank's moral commitment, as opposed to its contractual commitment, to make loans to a particular borrower up to a specified maximum during a specified period, usually one year. Because a bank line—also called a *line of credit*—is not a legal commitment, it is not customary to charge a commitment fee. It *is* common, however, to require that compensating balances be kept on deposit—typically 10% of the line, with an additional 10% of any borrowings under the line. A line about which a customer is officially notified is called an *advised line* or *confirmed line*. A line that is an internal policy guide about which the customer is not informed is termed a *guidance line*.

BANKMAIL bank's agreement with a company involved in a TAKEOVER not to finance another acquirer's bid.

BANK QUALITY *see* INVESTMENT GRADE.

BANKRUPTCY state of insolvency of an individual or an organization—in other words, an inability to pay debts. There are two kinds of legal bankruptcy under U.S. law: involuntary, when one or more creditors petition to have a debtor judged insolvent by a court; and voluntary, when the debtor brings the petition. In both cases, the objective is an orderly and equitable settlement of obligations.

The 1978 Bankruptcy Reform Act removed some of the rigidities of the old law and permitted more flexibility in procedures. The Bankruptcy Reform Act of 1984 curtailed some of the more liberal provisions (mainly affecting consumer bankruptcy) of the 1978 act.

Chapter 7 of the 1978 act, dealing with LIQUIDATION, provides for a court-appointed interim trustee with broad powers and discretion to make management changes, arrange unsecured financing, and generally operate the debtor business in such a way as to prevent loss. Only by filing an appropriate bond is the debtor able to regain possession from the trustee.

Chapter 11, which deals with REORGANIZATION, provides that, unless the court rules otherwise, the debtor remains in possession of the business and in control of its operation. Debtor and creditors are allowed considerable flexibility in working together. The 1978 law relaxes the old *absolute priority rule,* which gave creditor claims categorical precedence over ownership claims. It also makes possible the negotiation of payment schedules, the restructuring of debt, and even the granting of loans by the creditors to the debtor.

BANK TRUST DEPARTMENT part of a bank engaged in settling estates, administering trusts and guardianships, and performing AGENCY services. As part of its personal trust and ESTATE PLANNING services, it manages investments for large accounts—typically those with at least $50,000 in assets. People who cannot or do not want to make investment decisions are commonly bank trust department clients. Known for their conservative investment philosophy, such departments have custody over billions of dollars, making them a major factor in the movement of stock and bond prices.

Among other things, the departments also act as trustee for corporate bonds, administer pension and profit-sharing plans, and function as TRANSFER AGENTS.

BANK WIRE computerized message system owned and administered by about 250 participating banks in about 75 U.S. cities. Like the FED WIRE, the bank wire transmits large dollar credit transfer information. It also provides information about loan participations, securities transactions, Federal Reserve System funds borrowings, credit history, the payment or nonpayment of "wire fate" items, and other essential matters requiring prompt communication.

BAROMETER selective compilation of economic and market data designed to represent larger trends. Consumer spending, housing starts, and interest rates are barometers used in economic forecasting. The Dow Jones Industrial Average and the Standard & Poor's 500 Stock Index are prominent stock market barometers. The Dow Jones Utility Average is a barometer of market trends in the utility industry.

A *barometer stock* has a price movement pattern that reflects the market as a whole, thus serving as a market indicator. General Motors, for example, is considered a barometer stock.

BARRON'S CONFIDENCE INDEX weekly index of corporate bond yields published by *Barron's*, a Dow Jones financial newspaper. The index shows the ratio of Barron's average yield on 10 top-grade bonds to the Dow Jones average yield on 40 bonds. People who are worried about the economic outlook tend to seek high quality, whereas investors who feel secure about the economy are more likely to buy lower-rated bonds. The spread between high- and low-grade bonds thus reflects investor opinion about the economy.

BARTER trade of goods or services without use of money. When money is involved, whether in such forms as wampum, checks, or bills or coins, a transaction is called a SALE. Although barter is usually associated with undeveloped economies, it occurs in modern complex societies. In conditions of extreme inflation, it can be a preferred mode of commerce. Where a population lacks confidence in its currency or banking system, barter becomes commonplace. In international trade, barter can provide a way of doing business with countries whose soft currencies would otherwise make them unattractive trading partners.

BASE MARKET VALUE average market price of a group of securities at a given time. It is used as a basis of comparison in plotting dollar or percentage changes for purposes of market INDEXING.

BASE PERIOD particular time in the past used as the yardstick when measuring economic data. A base period is usually a year or an average of years; it can also be a month or other time period. The U.S. rate of inflation is determined by measuring current prices against those of a base year; for instance, the consumer price index for May 1983 was determined by comparing prices in that month with prices in the base year of 1967.

BASIS

In general: original cost plus out-of-pocket expenses that must be reported to the Internal Revenue Service when an investment is sold and must be used in calculating capital gains or losses. If a stock was bought for $1000 two years ago and is sold today for $2000, the basis is $1000 and the profit is a capital gain.

Bonds: an investor's YIELD TO MATURITY at a given bond price. A 10% bond selling at 100 has a 10% basis.

Commodities: the difference between the cash price of a hedged money market instrument and a FUTURES CONTRACT.

BASIS POINT smallest measure used in quoting yields on bonds and notes. One basis point is 0.01% of yield. Thus a bond's yield that changed from 10.67% to 11.57% would be said to have moved 90 basis points.

BASIS PRICE

In general: price an investor uses to calculate capital gains when selling a stock or bond. *See also* BASIS.

Odd-lot trading: the price arbitrarily established by an exchange floor official at the end of a trading session for a buyer or seller of an odd lot when the market bid and asked prices are more than $2 apart, or if no round-lot transactions have occurred that day. The customer gets the basis price plus or minus the odd-lot differential, if any. This procedure for determining prices is rare, since most odd lots are transacted at the market bid (if a sale) or asked (if a buy) or at prices based on the next round-lot trade.

BD FORM document that every brokerage house must file with the Securities and Exchange Commission, detailing the firm's financial position and naming its officers. The form must constantly be brought up to date.

BEAR person who thinks a market will fall. Bears may sell a stock short or buy a PUT OPTION to take advantage of the anticipated drop.

BEARER BOND *see* COUPON BOND.

BEARER FORM security not registered on the books of the issuing corporation and thus payable to the one possessing it. A bearer bond has coupons attached, which the bondholder sends in or presents on the interest date for payment, hence the alternative name COUPON BONDS. Bearer stock certificates are negotiable without endorsement and are transferred by delivery. Dividends are payable by presentation of dividend coupons, which are dated or numbered. Most securities issued today are in registered form, including municipal bonds issued since 1983. Many foreign equity securities continue to be issued in bearer form.

In effect, REGISTERED SECURITIES become bearer certificates when properly endorsed, since they can theoretically be negotiated by their holder.

BEAR HUG TAKEOVER bid so attractive in terms of price and other features that directors of the TARGET COMPANY, who might be opposed for other reasons, must approve it or risk shareholder protest.

BEAR MARKET prolonged period of falling prices. A bear market in stocks is usually brought on by the anticipation of declining economic activity, and a bear market in bonds is caused by rising interest rates.

BEAR RAID attempt by investors to manipulate the price of a stock by selling large numbers of shares short. The manipulators pocket the difference between the initial price and the new, lower price after this maneuver. Bear raids are illegal under Securities and Exchange Commission rules, which stipulate that every SHORT SALE be executed on an UPTICK (the last price was higher than the price before it) or a ZERO PLUS TICK (the last price was unchanged but higher than the last preceding different price).

BEAR SPREAD strategy in the options market designed to take advantage of a fall in the price of a security or commodity. Someone executing a bear spread could buy a combination of calls and puts on the same security at different *strike prices* in order to profit as the security's price fell. Or the investor could buy a put of short maturity and a put of long maturity in order to profit from the difference between the two puts as prices fell. *See also* BULL SPREAD.

BELL signal that opens and closes trading on major exchanges—sometimes actually a bell but sometimes a buzzer sound.

BELLWETHER security seen as an indicator of a market's direction. In stocks, International Business Machines (IBM) has long been considered a bellwether because so much of its stock is owned by institutional investors who have much control over supply and demand on the stock market. Institutional trading actions tend to influence smaller investors and therefore the market generally. In bonds, the 20-year U.S. Treasury bond is considered the bellwether, denoting the direction in which all other bonds are likely to move.

BELOW PAR see PAR VALUE.

BENEFICIAL OWNER person who enjoys the benefits of ownership even though title is in another name. When shares of a mutual fund are held by a custodian bank or when securities are held by a broker in STREET NAME, the real owner is the beneficial owner, even though, for safety or convenience, the bank or broker holds title.

BENEFICIARY
1. person to whom an inheritance passes as the result of being named in a will.
2. recipient of the proceeds of a life insurance policy.
3. party in whose favor a LETTER OF CREDIT is issued.
4. one to whom the amount of an ANNUITY is payable.
5. party for whose benefit a TRUST exists.

BEST EFFORT arrangement whereby investment bankers, acting as agents, agree to do their best to sell an issue to the public. Instead of buying the securities outright, these agents have an option to buy and an authority to sell the securities. Depending on the contract, the agents exercise their option and buy enough shares to cover their sales to clients, or they cancel the incompletely sold issue altogether and forgo the fee. Best efforts deals, which were common prior to 1900, entailed risks and delays from the issuer's standpoint. What is more, the broadening of the securities markets has made marketing new issues easier, and the practice of outright purchase by investment bankers, called FIRM COMMITMENT underwriting, has become commonplace. For the most part, the best efforts deals we occasionally see today are handled by firms specializing in the more speculative securities of new and unseasoned companies. *See also* BOUGHT DEAL.

BEST'S RATING rating of financial soundness given to insurance companies by Best's Rating Service. The top rating is A+. A Best's rating is important to buyers of insurance or annuities because it informs them whether a company is financially sound. Best's Ratings are also important to investors in insurance stocks.

BETA
1. coefficient measuring a stock's relative VOLATILITY. The beta is the covariance of a stock in relation to the rest of the stock market. The Standard & Poor's 500 Stock Index has a beta coefficient of 1. Any stock with a higher beta is more volatile than the market, and any with a lower beta can be expected to

rise and fall more slowly than the market. A conservative investor whose main concern is preservation of capital should focus on stocks with low betas, whereas one willing to take high risks in an effort to earn high rewards should look for high-beta stocks. *See also* ALPHA.

2. on the London Stock Exchange, the designation *beta stocks* applies to the second tier in a four-level hierarchy introduced with BIG BANG in October 1986. With ALPHA stocks representing the equivalent of American BLUE CHIP issues, beta stocks represent smaller issues that are less actively traded. *See also* DELTA STOCKS; GAMMA STOCKS.

BID AND ASKED bid is the highest price a prospective buyer is prepared to pay at a particular time for a trading unit of a given security; asked is the lowest price acceptable to a prospective seller of the same security. Together, the two prices constitute a QUOTATION; the difference between the two prices is the SPREAD. Although the bid and asked dynamic is common to all securities trading, "bid and asked" usually refers to UNLISTED SECURITIES traded OVER THE COUNTER.

BIDDING UP practice whereby the price bid for a security is successively moved higher lest an upswing in prices leaves orders unexecuted. An example would be an investor wanting to purchase a sizable quantity of shares in a rising market, using buy limit orders (orders to buy at a specified price or lower) to ensure the most favorable price. Since offer prices are moving up with the market, the investor must move his limit buy price upward to continue accumulating shares. To some extent the buyer is contributing to the upward price pressure on the stock, but most of the price rise is out of his control.

BID WANTED (BW) announcement that a holder of securities wants to sell and will entertain bids. Because the final price is subject to negotiation, the bid submitted in response to a BW need not be specific. A BW is frequently seen on published market quotation sheets.

BIG BANG deregulation on October 27, 1986, of London-based securities markets, an event comparable to MAY DAY in the United States and marking a major step toward a single world financial market.

BIG BLUE popular name for International Business Machines Corporation (IBM), taken from the color of its logotype.

BIG BOARD popular term for the NEW YORK STOCK EXCHANGE.

BIG EIGHT largest U.S. accounting firms as measured by revenue. They do the accounting and auditing for most major corporations, signing the auditor's certificate that appears in every annual report. They also offer various consulting services. Although mergers in the late 1980s reduced the number of top firms to six, there is a significant difference in revenues between them and next echelon and they continue to be referred to as members of the Big Eight. In alphabetical order they are: Arthur Andersen & Co.; Coopers and Lybrand; Deloitte & Touche; Ernst & Young; KPMG Peat Marwick; and Price Waterhouse & Co.

BILL

In general: (1) short for *bill of exchange,* an order by one person directing a second to pay a third. (2) document evidencing a debtor's obligation to a creditor, the kind of bill we are all familiar with. (3) paper currency, like the $5 bill. (4) *bill of sale,* a document used to transfer the title to certain goods from seller to buyer in the same way a deed to real property passes.

Investments: short for *due bill,* a statement of money owed. Commonly used to adjust a securities transaction when dividends, interest, and other distributions are reflected in a price but have not yet been disbursed. For example, when a stock is sold ex-dividend, but the dividend has not yet been paid, the buyer would sign a due bill stating that the amount of the dividend is payable to the seller.

A due bill may accompany delivered securities to give title to the buyer's broker in exchange for shares or money.

U.S. Treasury bill: commonly called bill or T-bill by money market people, a Treasury bill is a short-term (maturities up to a year), discounted government security sold through competitive bidding at weekly and monthly auctions in denominations from $10,000 to $1 million.

The auction at which bills are sold differs from the two-sided auction used by exchanges. Here, in what is sometimes termed a DUTCH AUCTION, the Treasury invites anyone interested to submit a bid, called a TENDER, then awards units to the highest bidders going down a list. Three- and six-month bills are auctioned weekly, nine-month and one-year bills monthly. Although the yield on bills may barely top the inflation rate, the high degree of safety together with the liquidity provided by an active SECONDARY MARKET make bills popular with corporate money managers as well as with banks and other government entities.

Individuals may also purchase bills directly, in amounts under $500,000, at no transaction charge, from a Federal Reserve bank, the Bureau of Federal Debt, or certain commercial banks. Bills bought on this basis are priced by noncompetitive bidding, with subscribers paying an average of the accepted bids.

Treasury bills are the most widely used of all government debt securities and are a primary instrument of Federal Reserve monetary policy.

See also TAX ANTICIPATION BILL; TREASURY DIRECT.

BILLING CYCLE interval between periodic billings for goods sold or services rendered, normally one month, or a system whereby bills or statements are mailed at periodic intervals in order to distribute the clerical workload.

BILL OF EXCHANGE *see* DRAFT.

BLACK FRIDAY sharp drop in a financial market. The original Black Friday was September 24, 1869, when a group of financiers tried to corner the gold market and precipitated a business panic followed by a depression. The panic of 1873 also began on Friday.

BLACK MONDAY October 19, 1987, when the Dow Jones Industrial Average plunged a record 508 points following sharp drops the previous week, reflecting investor anxiety about inflated stock price levels, federal budget and trade deficits, and foreign market activity. Many blamed PROGRAM TRADING for the extreme VOLATILITY.

BLACK-SCHOLES OPTIONS PRICING MODEL model developed by Fischer Black and Myron Scholes to gauge whether options contracts are fairly valued. The model incorporates such factors as the volatility of a security's return, the level of interest rates, the relationship of the underlying stock's price to the *strike* *price* of the option, and the time remaining until the option expires. Current valuations using this model are developed by the Options Monitor Service and are available from Standard & Poor's Trading Systems, 11 Broadway, New York, N.Y. 10004.

BLANKET CERTIFICATION FORM *see* NASD FORM FR-1.

BLANKET FIDELITY BOND insurance coverage against losses due to employee dishonesty. Brokerage firms are required to carry such protection in proportion to their net capital as defined by the Securities and Exchange Commission. Contingencies covered include securities loss, forgery, and fraudulent trading. Also called *blanket bond.*

BLANKET RECOMMENDATION communication sent to all customers of a brokerage firm recommending that they buy or sell a particular stock or stocks in a particular industry regardless of investment objectives or portfolio size.

BLIND POOL limited partnership that does not specify the properties the general partner plans to acquire. If, for example, a real estate partnership is offered in the form of a blind pool, investors can evaluate the project only by looking at the general partner's track record. In a *specified pool*, on the other hand, investors can look at the prices paid for property and the amount of rental income the buildings generate, then evaluate the partnership's potential. In general, blind pool partnerships do not perform better or worse than specified pool partnerships.

BLOCK large quantity of stock or large dollar amount of bonds held or traded. As a general guide, 10,000 shares or more of stock and $200,000 or more worth of bonds would be described as a block.

BLOCK POSITIONER dealer who, to accommodate the seller of a block of securities, will take a position in the securities, hoping to gain from a rise in the market price. Block positioners must register with the Securities and Exchange Commission and the New York Stock Exchange (if member firms). Typically they engage in ARBITRAGE, HEDGING, and SELLING SHORT in order to protect their risk and liquidate their position.

BLOWOUT quick sale of all shares in a new offering of securities. Corporations like to sell securities in such environments, because they get a high price for their stock. Investors are likely to have a hard time getting the number of shares they want during a blowout. Also called *going away* or *hot issue.*

BLUE CHIP common stock of a nationally known company that has a long record of profit growth and dividend payment and a reputation for quality management, products, and services. Some examples of blue chip stocks: International Business Machines, General Electric, and Du Pont. Blue chip stocks typically are relatively high priced and low yielding.

BLUE LIST daily financial publication listing bonds offered for sale by some 700 dealers and banks and representing more than $3 billion in par value. The Blue List mainly contains data on municipal bonds. With its pertinent price, yield, and other data, the Blue List is the most comprehensive source of information on activity and volume in the SECONDARY MARKET for TAX-EXEMPT SECURITIES. Some corporate bonds offered by the same dealers are also included. Full name, Blue List of Current Municipal Offerings.

BLUE-SKY LAW law of a kind passed by various states to protect investors against securities fraud. These laws require sellers of new stock issues or mutual funds to register their offerings and provide financial details on each issue so that investors can base their judgments on relevant data. The term is said to have originated with a judge who asserted that a particular stock offering had as much value as a patch of blue sky.

BOARD BROKER employee of the CHICAGO BOARD OPTIONS EXCHANGE who handles AWAY FROM THE MARKET orders, which cannot immediately be executed. If board brokers act as agents in executing such orders, they notify the exchange members who entered the orders.

BOARD OF ARBITRATION group of three or less individuals selected to adjudicate cases between securities firms and claims brought by customers. Arbitration is the method approved by the NATIONAL ASSOCIATION OF SECURITIES DEALERS, the MUNICIPAL SECURITIES RULE-MAKING BOARD, and the exchanges for resolving disputes, and it applies to both member and nonmember firms. Once the parties to a dispute agree to bring the matter before an arbitration board, the board's ruling is final and binding. Under rule changes approved by the Securities and Exchange Commission (SEC) in 1989, the qualifying standards for arbitrators were made stricter while the number of arbitrators was lowered from five to three in cases involving claims of $500,000 or more. The ceiling for small claims, conducted with one arbitrator, was raised from $5,000 to $10,000. *See also* ARBITRATION.

BOARD OF DIRECTORS group of individuals elected, usually at an annual meeting, by the shareholders of a corporation and empowered to carry out certain tasks as spelled out in the corporation's charter. Among such powers are appointing senior management, naming members of executive and finance committees (if any), issuing additional shares, and declaring dividends. Boards normally include the top corporate executives, termed *inside directors,* as well as OUTSIDE DIRECTORS chosen from business and from the community at large to advise on matters of broad policy. Directors meet several times a year and are paid for their services. They are considered control persons under the securities laws, meaning that their shares are restricted. As insiders, they cannot (1) buy and sell the company's stock within a 6-month period; (2) sell short in the company's stock, and if they sell owned shares must deliver in 20 days and/or place certificates in mail within 5 days; (3) effect any foreign or arbitrage transaction in the company's stock; (4) trade on material information not available to the public.

BOARD OF GOVERNORS OF THE FEDERAL RESERVE SYSTEM seven-member managing body of the FEDERAL RESERVE SYSTEM, commonly called the Federal Reserve Board. The board sets policy on issues relating to banking regulations as well as to the MONEY SUPPLY.

BOARD ROOM

Brokerage house: room where customers can watch an electronic board that displays stock prices and transactions.

Corporation: room where the board of directors holds its meetings.

BOILERPLATE standard legal language, often in fine print, used in most contracts, wills, indentures, prospectuses, and other legal documents. Although what the boilerplate says is important, it rarely is subject to change by the parties to the agreement, since it is the product of years of legal experience.

BOILER ROOM place where high-pressure salespeople use banks of telephones to call lists of potential investors (known in the trade as sucker lists) in order to peddle speculative, even fraudulent, securities. They are called boiler rooms because of the high-pressure selling. Boiler room methods, if not illegal, clearly violate the National Association of Securities Dealers' RULES OF FAIR PRACTICE, particularly those requiring that recommendations be suitable to a customer's account. *See also* BUCKET SHOP.

BOND any interest-bearing or discounted government or corporate security that obligates the issuer to pay the bondholder a specified sum of money, usually at specific intervals, and to repay the principal amount of the loan at maturity. Bondholders have an IOU from the issuer, but no corporate ownership privileges, as stockholders do.

An owner of *bearer bonds* presents the bond coupons and is paid interest, whereas the owner of *registered bonds* appears on the records of the bond issuer.

A SECURED BOND is backed by collateral which may be sold by the bondholder to satisfy a claim if the bond's issuer fails to pay interest and principal when they are due. An *unsecured bond* or DEBENTURE is backed by the full faith and credit of the issuer, but not by any specific collateral.

A CONVERTIBLE bond gives its owner the privilege of exchange for other securities of the issuing company at some future date and under prescribed conditions.

Also, a bond, in finance, is the obligation of one person to repay a debt taken on by someone else, should that other person default. A bond can also be money or securities deposited as a pledge of good faith.

A surety or PERFORMANCE BOND is an agreement whereby an insurance company becomes liable for the performance of work or services provided by a contractor by an agreed-upon date. If the contractor does not do what was promised, the surety company is financially responsible. *See also* INDENTURE; ZERO COUPON SECURITY.

BOND ANTICIPATION NOTE (BAN) short-term debt instrument issued by a state or municipality that will be paid off with the proceeds of an upcoming bond issue. To the investor, BANs offer a safe, tax-free yield that may be higher than other tax-exempt debt instruments of the same maturity.

BOND BROKER broker who executes bond trades on the floor of an exchange. Also, one who trades corporate, U.S. government, or municipal debt issues over the counter, mostly for large institutional accounts.

BOND BUYER, **THE** daily publication containing most of the key statistics and indexes used in the fixed-income markets. *See also* BOND BUYER'S INDEX; THIRTY-DAY VISIBLE SUPPLY.

BOND BUYER'S INDEX index published daily by the *BOND BUYER,* a newspaper covering the municipal bond market. The index provides the yardsticks against which municipal bond yields are measured. One index is composed of 20 long-term bonds rated A or better, and another is made up of 11 AA-rated bonds. Both use newly issued municipals selling at par. The *Bond Buyer* also lists long-term government bonds and compares their aftertax yield with the yield from tax-free municipals. Investors use the publication's Bond Buyer Indexes to plot interest rate patterns.

BOND CROWD exchange members who transact bond orders on the floor of the exchange. The work area in which they congregate is separate from the stock traders, hence the term bond crowd.

BOND POWER form used in the transfer of registered bonds from one owner to another. Sometimes called *assignment separate from certificate,* it accomplishes the same thing as the assignment form on the back of the bond certificate, but has a safety advantage in being separate. Technically, the bond power appoints an attorney-in-fact with the power to make a transfer of ownership on the corporation's books.

BOND RATING method of evaluating the possibility of default by a bond issuer. Standard & Poor's, Moody's Investors Service, and Fitch's Investors Service analyze the financial strength of each bond's issuer, whether a corporation or a government body. Their ratings range from AAA (highly unlikely to default) to D (in default). Bonds rated B or below are not INVESTMENT GRADE—in other words, institutions that invest other people's money may not under most state laws buy them. *See also* RATING.

BOND RATIO *leverage* ratio measuring the percentage of a company's capitalization represented by bonds. It is calculated by dividing the total bonds due after one year by the same figure plus all equity. A bond ratio over 33% indicates high leverage—except in utilities, where higher bond ratios are normal. *See also* DEBT-TO-EQUITY RATIO.

BOND SWAP simultaneous sale of one bond issue and purchase of another. The motives for bond swaps vary: *maturity swaps* aim to stretch out maturities but can also produce a profit because of the lower prices on longer bonds; *yield swaps* seek to improve return and *quality swaps* seek to upgrade safety; *tax swaps* create tax-deductible losses through the sale, while the purchase of a substitute bond effectively preserves the investment. *See also* SWAP, SWAP ORDER.

BOOK
1. in an underwriting of securities, (1) preliminary indications of interest rate on the part of prospective buyers of the issue ("What is the book on XYZ Company?") or (2) record of activity in the syndicate account ("Who is managing the book on XYZ?").
2. record maintained by a specialist of buy and sell orders in a given security. The term derives from the notebook that specialists traditionally used for this purpose. Also, the aggregate of sell orders left with the specialist, as in BUY THE BOOK.
3. as a verb, to book is to give accounting recognition to something. ("They booked a profit on the transaction.")
4. collectively, books are the journals, ledgers, and other accounting records of a business.
   See also BOOK VALUE.

BOOK-ENTRY SECURITIES securities that are not represented by a certificate. Purchases and sales of some municipal bonds, for instance, are merely recorded on customers' accounts; no certificates change hands. This is increasingly popular because it cuts down on paperwork for brokers and leaves investors free from worry about their certificates. *See also* CERTIFICATELESS MUNICIPALS.

BOOK PROFIT OR LOSS *see* UNREALIZED PROFIT OR LOSS.

BOOK VALUE

1. value at which an asset is carried on a balance sheet. For example, a piece of manufacturing equipment is put on the books at its cost when purchased. Its value is then reduced each year as depreciation is charged to income. Thus, its book value at any time is its cost minus accumulated depreciation. However, the primary purpose of accounting for depreciation is to enable a company to recover its cost, not replace the asset or reflect its declining usefulness. Book value may therefore vary significantly from other objectively determined values, most notably MARKET VALUE.

2. net asset value of a company's securities, calculated by using the following formula:

   Total assets *minus* intangible assets (goodwill, patents, etc.) *minus* current liabilities *minus* any long-term liabilities and equity issues that have a prior claim (subtracting them here has the effect of treating them as paid) *equals* total net assets available for payment of the issue under consideration.

   The total net asset figure, divided by the number of bonds, shares of preferred stock, or shares of common stock, gives the *net asset value*—or book value—per bond or per share of preferred or common stock.

   Book value can be a guide in selecting underpriced stocks and is an indication of the ultimate value of securities in liquidation. *See also* ASSET COVERAGE.

BORROWED RESERVES funds borrowed by member banks from a FEDERAL RESERVE BANK for the purpose of maintaining the required reserve ratios. Actually, the proper term is *net borrowed reserves,* since it refers to the difference between borrowed reserves and excess or free reserves. Such borrowings, usually in the form of advances secured by government securities or eligible paper, are kept on deposit at the Federal Reserve bank in the borrower's region. Net borrowed reserves are an indicator of heavy loan demand and potentially TIGHT MONEY.

BORROWING POWER OF SECURITIES amount of money that customers can invest in securities on MARGIN, as listed every month on their brokerage account statements. This margin limit usually equals 50% of the value of their stocks, 30% of the value of their bonds, and the full value of their CASH EQUIVALENT assets, such as MONEY MARKET account funds. The term also refers to securities pledged (hypothecated) to a bank or other lender as loan COLLATERAL. The loan value in this case depends on lender policy and type of security.

BOSTON STOCK EXCHANGE *see* REGIONAL STOCK EXCHANGES.

BOT

1. stockbroker shorthand for bought, the opposite of SL for sold.
2. in finance, abbreviation for balance of trade.
3. in the mutual savings bank industry, abbreviation for board of trustees.

BOTTOM

In general: support level for market prices of any type. When prices fall below that level and appear to be continuing downward without check, we say that the *bottom dropped out.* When prices begin to trend upward again, we say they have *bottomed out.*

Economics: lowest point in an economic cycle.

Securities: lowest market price of a security or commodity during a day, a season, a year, a cycle. Also, lowest level of prices for the market as a whole, as measured by any of the several indexes.

BOTTOM FISHER investor who is on the lookout for stocks that have fallen to their bottom prices before turning up. In extreme cases, bottom fishers buy stocks and bonds of bankrupt or near-bankrupt firms.

BOTTOM-UP APPROACH TO INVESTING search for outstanding performance of individual stocks before considering the impact of economic trends. The companies may be identified from research reports, stock screens, or personal knowledge of the products and services. This approach assumes that individual companies can do well, even in an industry that is not performing well. *See also* TOP-DOWN APPROACH TO INVESTING.

BOUGHT DEAL in securities underwriting, a FIRM COMMITMENT to purchase an entire issue outright from the issuing company. Differs from a STAND-BY COMMITMENT, wherein, with conditions, a SYNDICATE of investment bankers agrees to purchase part of an issue if it is not fully subscribed. Also differs from a BEST EFFORTS commitment, wherein the syndicate agrees to use its best efforts to sell the issue. Most issues in recent years have been bought deals. Typically, the syndicate puts up a portion of its own capital and borrows the rest from commercial banks. Then, perhaps through a selling group, the syndicate resells the issue to the public at slightly more than the purchase price.

BOUTIQUE small, specialized brokerage firm that deals with a limited clientele and offers a limited product line. A highly regarded securities analyst may form a research boutique, which clients use as a resource for buying and selling certain stocks. A boutique is the opposite of a FINANCIAL SUPERMARKET, which offers a wide variety of services to a wide variety of clients.

BOX physical location of securities or other documents held in safekeeping. The term derives from the large metal tin, or tray, in which brokerage firms and banks actually place such valuables. Depending on rules and regulations concerned with the safety and segregation of clients' securities, certificates held in safekeeping may qualify for stock loans or as bank loan collateral.

BRACKET CREEP edging into higher tax brackets as income rises to compensate for inflation. The TAX REFORM ACT OF 1986 collapsed the marginal rate system into two broad brackets, effective in 1988, virtually eliminating bracket creep as a potential problem.

BRANCH OFFICE MANAGER person in charge of a branch of a securities brokerage firm or bank. Branch office managers who oversee the activities of three or more brokers must pass tests administered by various stock exchanges. A customer who is not able to resolve a conflict with a REGISTERED REPRESENTATIVE should bring it to the attention of the branch office manager, who is responsible for resolving such differences.

BREADTH OF THE MARKET percentage of stocks participating in a particular market move. Analysts say there was good breadth if two thirds of the stocks listed on an exchange rose during a trading session. A market trend with good breadth is more significant and probably more long-lasting than one with limited breadth, since more investors are participating. Breadth-of-the-market indexes are alternatively called ADVANCE/DECLINE indexes.

BREAK
Finance: in a pricing structure providing purchasing discounts at different levels of volume, a point at which the price changes—for example, a 10% discount for ten cases.

Investments: (1) sudden, marked drop in the price of a security or in market prices generally; (2) discrepancy in the accounts of brokerage firms; (3) stroke of good luck.

BREAKEVEN POINT
Finance: the point at which sales equal costs. The point is located by breakeven analysis, which determines the volume of sales at which fixed and variable costs will be covered. All sales over the breakeven point produce profits; any drop in sales below that point will produce losses.

Because costs and sales are so complex, breakeven analysis has limitations as a planning tool and is being supplanted by computer-based financial planning systems. *See also* LEVERAGE (operating).

Securities: dollar price at which a transaction produces neither a gain nor a loss.
In options strategy the term has the following definitions:
1. long calls and short uncovered calls: strike price plus premium.
2. long puts and short uncovered puts: strike price minus premium.
3. short covered call: purchase price minus premium.
4. short put covered by short stock: short sale price of underlying stock plus premium.

BREAKING THE SYNDICATE terminating the investment banking group formed to underwrite a securities issue. More specifically, terminating the AGREEMENT AMONG UNDERWRITERS, thus leaving the members free to sell remaining holdings without price restrictions. The agreement among underwriters usually terminates the syndicate 30 days after the selling group, but the syndicate can be broken earlier by agreement of the participants.

BREAKOUT rise in a security's price above a resistance level (commonly its previous high price) or drop below a level of support (commonly the former lowest price). A breakout is taken to signify a continuing move in the same direction.

BREAKOUT

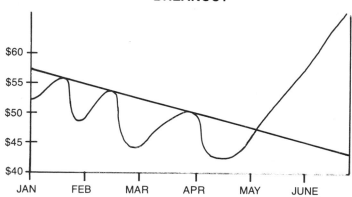

BREAKPOINT SALE in mutual funds, the dollar investment required to make the fundholder eligible for a lower sales charge. *See also* LETTER OF INTENT; RIGHT OF ACCUMULATION.

BREAKUP VALUE *see* PRIVATE MARKET VALUE.

BRETTON WOODS AGREEMENT OF 1944 *see* FIXED EXCHANGE RATE.

BRIDGE LOAN short-term loan, also called a *swing loan,* made in anticipation of intermediate-term or long-term financing.

BROAD TAPE enlargement of the Dow Jones news ticker tape, projected on a screen in the board room of a brokerage firm. It continually reports major news developments and financial information. The term can also refer to similar information provided by Associated Press, United Press International, Reuters, or Munifacts. The broad tape is not allowed on the exchange floor because it would give floor traders an unfair edge.

BROKER

Insurance: person who finds the best insurance deal for a client and then sells the policy to the client.

Real estate: person who represents the seller and gets a commission when the property is sold.

Securities: person who acts as an intermediary between a buyer and seller, usually charging a commission. A broker who specializes in stocks, bonds, commodities, or options acts as AGENT and must be registered with the exchange where the securities are traded. Hence the term *registered representative. See also* ACCOUNT EXECUTIVE; DEALER; DISCOUNT BROKER.

BROKER-DEALER *see* DEALER.

BROKERED CD CERTIFICATE OF DEPOSIT (CD) issued by a bank or thrift institution but bought in bulk by a brokerage firm and resold to brokerage customers. Brokered CDs pay as much as 1% more than those issued directly by major banks, carry federal deposit insurance up to $100,000, enjoy a liquid secondary market made by the broker, and do not require an investor to pay a commission.

BROKER LOAN RATE interest rate at which brokers borrow from banks to cover the securities positions of their clients. The broker loan rate usually hovers a percentage point or so above such short-term interest rates as the federal funds rate and the Treasury bill rate. Since brokers' loans and their customers' margin accounts are usually covered by the same collateral, the term REHYPOTHECATION is used synonymously with *broker loan borrowing.* Because broker loans are callable on 24-hour notice, the term *call loan rate* is also used, particularly in money rate tables published in newspapers.

BUCKET SHOP illegal brokerage firm, of a kind now almost extinct, which accepts customer orders but does not execute them right away as Securities and Exchange Commission regulations require. Bucket-shop brokers confirm the price the customer asked for, but in fact make the trade at a time advantageous to the broker, whose profit is the difference between the two prices. Sometimes bucket shops neglect to fill the customer's order and just pocket the money. *See also* BOILER ROOM.

BUDGET estimate of revenue and expenditure for a specified period. Of the many kinds of budgets, a CASH BUDGET shows cash flow, an expense budget shows projected expenditures, and a CAPITAL BUDGET shows anticipated capital outlays. The term refers to a preliminary financial plan. In a *balanced budget* revenues cover expenditures.

BULGE quick, temporary price rise that applies to an entire commodities or stock market, or to an individual commodity or stock.

BULL person who thinks prices will rise. One can be bullish on the prospects for an individual stock, bond, or commodity, an industry segment, or the market as a whole. In a more general sense, bullish means optimistic, so a person can be bullish on the economy as a whole.

BULL MARKET prolonged rise in the prices of stocks, bonds, or commodities. Bull markets usually last at least a few months and are characterized by high trading volume.

BULL SPREAD option strategy, executed with puts or calls, that will be profitable if the underlying stock rises in value. The following are three varieties of bull spread:

Vertical spread: simultaneous purchase and sale of options of the same class at different strike prices, but with the same expiration date.

Calendar spread: simultaneous purchase and sale of options of the same class and the same price but at different expiration dates.

Diagonal spread: combination of vertical and calendar spreads wherein the investor buys and sells options of the same class at different strike prices and different expiration dates.

An investor who believes, for example, that XYZ stock will rise, perhaps only moderately, buys an XYZ 30 call for 1½ and sells an XYZ 35 call for ½; both options are OUT OF THE MONEY. The 30 and 35 are strike prices and the 1½ and ½ are premiums. The net cost of this spread, or the difference between the premiums, is $1. If the stock rises to 35 just prior to expiration, the 35 call becomes worthless and the 30 call is worth $5. Thus the spread provides a profit of $4 on an investment of $1. If on the other hand the price of the stock goes down, both options expire worthless and the investor loses the entire premium.

BUNCHING
1. combining many round-lot orders for execution at the same time on the floor of an exchange. This technique can also be used with odd-lot orders, when combining many small orders can save the odd-lot differential for each customer.
2. pattern on the ticker tape when a series of trades in the same security appear consecutively.

BURNOUT exhaustion of a tax shelter's benefits, when an investor starts to receive income from the investment. This income must be reported to the Internal Revenue Service, and taxes must be paid on it.

BUSINESS CYCLE recurrence of periods of expansion (RECOVERY) and contraction (RECESSION) in economic activity with effects on inflation, growth, and employment. One cycle extends from a GNP base line through one rise and one decline and back to the base line, a period averaging about 2½ years. A business cycle affects profitability and CASH FLOW, making it a key consideration in corporate dividend policy, and is a factor in the rise and fall of the inflation rate, which in turn affects return on investments.

BUSINESS DAY

In general: hours when most businesses are in operation. Although individual working hours may differ, and particular firms may choose staggered schedules, the conventional business day is 9 A.M. to 5 P.M.

Finance and investments: day when financial marketplaces are open for trading. In figuring the settlement date on a *regular way* securities transaction—which is the fifth business day after the trade date—Saturday, Sunday, and a legal holiday would not be counted, for example.

BUSINESS SEGMENT REPORTING reporting the results of the divisions, subsidiaries, or other segments of a business separately so that income, sales, and assets can be compared. Allocation of central corporate expenses is not required by the Financial Accounting Standards Board. Also called line of business reporting.

BUSTED CONVERTIBLES CONVERTIBLES that trade like fixed-income investments because the market price of the common stock they convert to has fallen so low as to render the conversion feature valueless.

BUST-UP TAKEOVER LEVERAGED BUYOUT in which TARGET COMPANY assets or activities are sold off to repay the debt that financed the TAKEOVER.

BUTTERFLY SPREAD complex option strategy that involves selling two calls and buying two calls on the same or different markets, with several maturity dates. One of the options has a higher exercise price and the other has a lower exercise price than the other two options. An investor in a butterfly spread will profit if the underlying security makes no dramatic movements because the premium income will be collected when the options are sold.

BUY acquire property in return for money. Buy can be used as a synonym for bargain.

BUY AND HOLD STRATEGY strategy that calls for accumulating shares in a company over the years. This allows the investor to pay favorable long-term capital gains tax on profits and requires far less attention than a more active trading strategy.

BUY AND WRITE STRATEGY conservative options strategy that entails buying stocks and then writing covered call options on them. Investors receive both the dividends from the stock and the premium income from the call options. However, the investor may have to sell the stock below the current market price if the call is exercised.

BUYBACK purchase of a long contract to cover a short position, usually arising out of the short sale of a commodity. Also, purchase of identical securities to cover a short sale. Synonym: *short covering. See also* STOCK BUYBACK.

Bond buyback: corporation's purchase of its own bonds at a discount in the open market. This is done in markets characterized by rapidly rising interest rates and commensurately declining bond prices.

BUYER'S MARKET market situation that is the opposite of a SELLER'S MARKET.

BUY HEDGE *see* LONG HEDGE.

BUY IN

Options trading: procedure whereby the responsibility to deliver or accept stock can be terminated. In a transaction called *buying-in* or CLOSING PURCHASE, the writer buys an identical option (only the premium or price is different). The second of these options offsets the first, and the profit or loss is the difference in premiums.

Securities: transaction between brokers wherein securities are not delivered on time by the broker on the sell side, forcing the buy side broker to obtain shares from other sources.

BUYING CLIMAX rapid rise in the price of a stock or commodity, setting the stage for a quick fall. Such a surge attracts most of the potential buyers of the stock, leaving them with no one to sell their stock to at higher prices. This is what causes the ensuing fall. Technical chartists see a buying climax as a dramatic runup, accompanied by increased trading volume in the stock.

BUYING ON MARGIN buying securities with credit available through a relationship with a broker, called a MARGIN ACCOUNT. Arrangements of this kind are closely regulated by the Federal Reserve Board. *See also* MARGIN.

BUYING POWER amount of money available to buy securities, determined by tabulating the cash held in brokerage accounts, and adding the amount that could be spent if securities were margined to the limit. The market cannot rise beyond the available buying power. *See also* PURCHASING POWER.

BUY MINUS order to buy a stock at a price lower than the current market price. Traders try to execute a buy minus order on a temporary dip in the stock's price.

BUY ON THE BAD NEWS strategy based on the belief that, soon after a company announces bad news, the price of its stock will plummet. Those who buy at this stage assume that the price is about as low as it can go, leaving plenty of room for a rise when the news improves. If the adverse development is indeed temporary, this technique can be quite profitable. *See also* BOTTOM FISHER.

BUY ORDER in securities trading, an order to a broker to purchase a specified quantity of a security at the MARKET PRICE or at another stipulated price.

BUYOUT purchase of at least a controlling percentage of a company's stock to take over its assets and operations. A buyout can be accomplished through negotiation or through a tender offer. A LEVERAGED BUYOUT occurs when a small group borrows the money to finance the purchase of the shares. The loan is ultimately repaid out of cash generated from the acquired company's operations or from the sale of its assets. *See also* GOLDEN PARACHUTE.

BUY STOP ORDER BUY ORDER marked to be held until the market price rises to the STOP PRICE, then to be entered as a MARKET ORDER to buy at the best available price. Sometimes called a *suspended market order,* because it remains suspended until a market transaction elects, activates, or triggers the stop. Such an order is not permitted in the over-the-counter market. *See also* STOP ORDER.

BUY THE BOOK order to a broker to buy all the shares available from the specialist in a security and from other brokers and dealers at the current offer price. The book is the notebook in which specialists kept track of buy and sell orders before computers. The most likely source of such an order is a professional trader or a large institutional buyer.

BYLAWS rules governing the internal management of an organization which, in the case of business corporations, are drawn up at the time of incorporation. The charter is concerned with such broad matters as the number of directors and the number of authorized shares; the bylaws, which can usually be amended by the directors themselves, cover such points as the election of directors, the appointment of executive and finance committees, the duties of officers, and how share transfers may be made. Bylaws, which are also prevalent in not-for-profit organizations, cannot countermand laws of the government.

BYPASS TRUST agreement allowing parents to pass assets on to their children to reduce estate taxes. The trust must be made irrevocable, meaning that the terms can never be changed. Assets put in such a trust usually exceed the amount that children and other heirs can receive tax-free at a parent's death. Under the 1981 Tax Act, this amount reaches $600,000 in 1987. Parents can arrange to receive income from the assets during their lifetimes and may even be able to touch the principal in case of dire need. One variation of a bypass trust is the qualified terminable interest property trust, or Q-TIP TRUST.

C

CABINET CROWD members of the New York Stock Exchange who trade in infrequently traded bonds. Also called *inactive bond crowd* or *book crowd*. Buy and sell LIMIT ORDERS for these bonds are kept in steel racks, called cabinets, at the side of the bond trading floor; hence the name cabinet crowd.

CABINET SECURITY stock or bond listed on a major exchange but not actively traded. There are a considerable number of such bonds and a limited number of such stocks, mainly those trading in ten-share units. Cabinets are the metal storage racks that LIMIT ORDERS for such securities are filed in pending execution or cancellation. *See also* CABINET CROWD.

CAGE section of a brokerage firm's back office where funds are received and disbursed.
Also, the installation where a bank teller works.

CALENDAR list of securities about to be offered for sale. Separate calendars are kept for municipal bonds, corporate bonds, government bonds, and new stock offerings.

CALENDAR SPREAD options strategy that entails buying two options on the same security with different maturities. If the EXERCISE PRICE is the same (a June 50 call and a September 50 call) it is a HORIZONTAL SPREAD. If the exercise prices are different (a June 50 call and a September 45 call), it is a DIAGONAL SPREAD. Investors gain or lose as the difference in price narrows or widens.

CALL
Banking: demand to repay a secured loan usually made when the borrower has failed to meet such contractual obligations as timely payment of interest. When

a banker calls a loan, the entire principal amount is due immediately. *See also* BROKER LOAN RATE.

Securities: issuer's right to redeem bonds or preferred stock before maturity (if any). The first dates when an issuer may call securities is specified in the prospectus and in the INDENTURE or preferred stock agreement. *See also* CALLABLE; CALL PRICE.

CALLABLE redeemable by the issuer before the scheduled maturity. The issuer must pay the holders a premium price if such a security is retired early. Bonds are usually called when interest rates fall so significantly that the issuer can save money by floating new bonds at lower rates. *See also* CALL PRICE; DEMAND LOAN.

CALLED AWAY term for a bond redeemed before maturity, or a call or put option exercised against the stockholder, or a delivery required on a short sale.

CALL FEATURE part of the agreement a bond issuer makes with a buyer, called the indenture, describing the schedule and price of redemptions before maturity. Most corporate and municipal bonds have 10-year call features (termed CALL PROTECTION by holders); government securities usually have none. *See also* CALL PRICE.

CALL LOAN RATE *see* BROKER LOAN RATE.

CALL OPTION right to buy 100 shares of a particular stock or stock index at a predetermined price before a preset deadline, in exchange for a premium. For buyers who think a stock will go up dramatically, call options permit a profit from a smaller investment than it would take to buy the stock. These options can also produce extra income for the seller, who gives up ownership of the stock if the option is exercised.

CALL PREMIUM amount that the buyer of a call option has to pay to the seller for the right to purchase a stock or stock index at a specified price by a specified date.

In bonds, preferreds, and convertibles, the amount over par that an issuer has to pay to an investor for redeeming the security early.

CALL PRICE price at which a bond or preferred stock with a *call provision* or CALL FEATURE can be redeemed by the issuer; also known as *redemption price*. To compensate the holder for loss of income and ownership, the call price is usually higher than the par value of the security, the difference being the CALL PREMIUM. *See also* CALL PROTECTION.

CALL PROTECTION length of time during which a security cannot be redeemed by the issuer. U.S. government securities are generally not callable, although there is an exception in certain 30-year Treasury bonds, which become callable after 25 years. Corporate and municipal issuers generally provide 10 years of call protection. Investors who plan to live off the income from a bond should be sure they have call protection, because without it the bond could be CALLED AWAY at any time specified in the indenture.

CANCEL

In general: void a negotiable instrument by annulling or paying it; also, prematurely terminate a bond or other contract.

Securities trading: void an order to buy or sell. *See also* GOOD TILL CANCELED ORDER.

CAPITAL ASSET long-term asset that is not bought or sold in the normal course of business. Generally speaking, the term includes FIXED ASSETS—land, buildings, equipment, furniture and fixtures, and so on. The Internal Revenue Service definition of capital assets includes security investments.

CAPITAL ASSET PRICING MODEL (CAPM) sophisticated model of the relationship between *expected risk* and *expected return*. The model is grounded in the theory that investors demand higher returns for higher risks. It says that the return on an asset or a security is equal to the risk-free return—such as the return on a short-term Treasury security—plus a risk premium.

CAPITAL BUDGET program for financing long-term outlays such as plant expansion, research and development, and advertising. Among the methods used in arriving at a capital budget are NET PRESENT VALUE (NPV), INTERNAL RATE OF RETURN (IRR), and PAYBACK PERIOD.

CAPITAL CONSUMPTION ALLOWANCE amount of depreciation included in the GROSS NATIONAL PRODUCT (GNP), normally around 11%. This amount is subtracted from GNP, on the theory that it is needed to maintain the productive capacity of the economy, to get *net national product (NNP)*. Adjusted further for indirect taxes, NNP equals *national income*. Economists use GNP rather than NNP in the analyses we read every day largely because capital consumption allowance figures are not always available or reliable. *See also* DEPRECIATION.

CAPITAL EXPENDITURE outlay of money to acquire or improve CAPITAL ASSETS such as buildings and machinery.

CAPITAL FLIGHT movement of large sums of money from one country to another to escape political or economic turmoil or to seek higher rates of return. For example, periods of high inflation or political revolution have brought about an exodus of capital from many Latin American countries to the United States, which is perceived as a safe haven for capital.

CAPITAL FORMATION creation or expansion, through savings, of capital or of *producer's goods*—buildings, machinery, equipment—that produce other goods and services, the result being economic expansion.

CAPITAL GAIN difference between an asset's purchase price and selling price, when the difference is positive. When the TAX REFORM ACT OF 1986 was passed, the profit on a CAPITAL ASSET held six months was considered a long-term gain taxable at a lower rate. The 1986 law provided that the differential between long-term capital gain and ordinary income rates be phased out.

CAPITAL GAINS DISTRIBUTION mutual fund's distribution to shareholders of the profits derived from the sale of stocks or bonds. Traditionally, mutual fund shareholders benefited from a lower long-term capital gains tax rate regardless of how long they held fund shares. The TAX REFORM ACT OF 1986 eliminated the rate differential favoring long-term capital gains effective in 1988.

CAPITAL GAINS TAX tax on profits from the sale of CAPITAL ASSETS. The tax law has traditionally specified a minimum HOLDING PERIOD after which a CAPITAL GAIN was taxed at a more favorable rate (recently a maximum of 20% for individuals) than ordinary income. The TAX REFORM ACT OF 1986 provided that all capital gains be taxed at a maximum of 28% in 1987 and at ordinary income rates starting in 1988.

CAPITAL GOODS goods used in the production of other goods—industrial buildings, machinery, equipment—as well as highways, office buildings, government installations. In the aggregate such goods form a country's productive capacity.

CAPITAL-INTENSIVE requiring large investments in CAPITAL ASSETS. Motor-vehicle and steel production are capital-intensive industries. To provide an acceptable return on investment, such industries must have a high margin of profit or a low cost of borrowing. The term capital-intensive is sometimes used to mean a high proportion of fixed assets to labor.

CAPITALISM economic system in which (1) private ownership of property exists; (2) aggregates of property or capital provide income for the individuals or firms that accumulated it and own it; (3) individuals and firms are relatively free to compete with others for their own economic gain; (4) the profit motive is basic to economic life.

Among the synonyms for capitalism are LAISSEZ-FAIRE economy, private enterprise system, and free-price system. In this context *economy* is interchangeable with *system*.

CAPITALIZATION see CAPITALIZE; CAPITAL STRUCTURE; MARKET CAPITALIZATION.

CAPITALIZATION RATE rate of interest used to convert a series of future payments into a single PRESENT VALUE.

CAPITALIZATION RATIO analysis of a company's capital structure showing what percentage of the total is debt, preferred stock, common stock, and other equity. The ratio is useful in evaluating the relative RISK and leverage that holders of the respective levels of security have. *See also* BOND RATIO.

CAPITALIZE
1. convert a schedule of income into a principal amount, called *capitalized value*, by dividing by a rate of interest.
2. issue securities to finance *capital outlays* (rare).
3. record capital outlays as additions to asset accounts, not as expenses. *See also* CAPITAL EXPENDITURE.
4. convert a lease obligation to an asset/liability form of expression called a *capital lease*, that is, to record a leased asset as an owned asset and the lease obligation as borrowed funds.
5. turn something to one's advantage economically—for example, sell umbrellas on a rainy day.

CAPITAL LEASE lease that under Statement 13 of the Financial Accounting Standards Board must be reflected on a company's balance sheet as an asset and corresponding liability. Generally, this applies to leases where the lessee acquires essentially all of the economic benefits and risks of the leased property.

CAPITAL LOSS amount by which the proceeds from the sale of a CAPITAL ASSET are less than the cost of acquiring it. Until the TAX REFORM ACT OF of 1986, $2 of LONG-TERM LOSS could be used to offset $1 of LONG-TERM GAIN and (for non-corporate taxpayers) up to $3000 of ORDINARY INCOME, while short-term losses could be applied dollar-for-dollar against short-term gains and $3000 of ordinary income. Starting in 1987, capital losses were offsetable dollar-for-dollar against capital gains and $3000 of ordinary income. The short-term/long-term distinction ended starting 1988. *See also* TAX LOSS CARRYBACK, CARRYFORWARD.

CAPITAL MARKETS markets where capital funds—debt and equity—are traded. Included are private placement sources of debt and equity as well as organized markets and exchanges.

CAPITAL OUTLAY *see* CAPITAL EXPENDITURE.

CAPITAL REQUIREMENTS
1. permanent financing needed for the normal operation of a business; that is, the long-term and working capital.
2. appraised investment in fixed assets and normal working capital. Whether patents, rights, and contracts should be included is moot.

CAPITAL STOCK stock authorized by a company's charter and having PAR VALUE, STATED VALUE, or NO PAR VALUE. The number and value of issued shares are normally shown, together with the number of shares authorized, in the capital accounts section of the balance sheet.
    Informally, a synonym for COMMON STOCK, though capital stock technically also encompasses PREFERRED STOCK.

CAPITAL STRUCTURE corporation's financial framework, including LONG-TERM DEBT, PREFERRED STOCK, and NET WORTH. It is distinguished from FINANCIAL STRUCTURE, which includes additional sources of capital such as short-term debt, accounts payable, and other liabilities. It is synonymous with *capitalization*, although there is some disagreement as to whether capitalization should include long-term loans and mortgages. Analysts look at capital structure in terms of its overall adequacy and its composition as well as in terms of the DEBT-TO-EQUITY RATIO, called *leverage*. *See also* CAPITALIZATION RATIO; PAR VALUE.

CAPITAL SURPLUS
1. EQUITY—or NET WORTH—not otherwise classifiable as CAPITAL STOCK or RETAINED EARNINGS. Here are five ways of creating surplus:
    a. from stock issued at a premium over par or stated value.
    b. from the proceeds of stock bought back and then sold again.
    c. from a reduction of par or stated value or a reclassification of capital stock.
    d. from donated stock.
    e. from the acquisition of companies that have capital surplus.
2. common umbrella term for more specific classifications such as ACQUIRED SURPLUS, ADDITIONAL PAID-IN CAPITAL, DONATED SURPLUS, and REEVALUATION SURPLUS (arising from appraisals). Most common synonyms: *paid-in surplus; surplus*.

CAPITAL TURNOVER annual sales divided by average stockholder equity (net worth). When compared over a period, it reveals the extent to which a company is able to grow without additional capital investment. Generally, companies with high profit margins have a low capital turnover and vice versa. Also called *equity turnover*.

CAPTIVE FINANCE COMPANY company, usually a wholly owned subsidiary, that exists primarily to finance consumer purchases from the parent company.

Prominent examples are General Motors Acceptance Corporation and Ford Motor Credit Corporation. Although these subsidiaries stand on their own financially, parent companies frequently make SUBORDINATED LOANS to add to their equity positions. This supports the high leverage on which the subsidiaries operate and assures their active participation in the COMMERCIAL PAPER and bond markets.

CARRYBACK, CARRYFORWARD *see* TAX LOSS CARRYBACK, CARRYFORWARD.

CARS *see* CERTIFICATE FOR AUTOMOBILE RECEIVABLES.

CARRYING CHARGE

Commodities: charge for carrying the actual commodity, including interest, storage, and insurance costs.

Margin accounts: fee that a broker charges for carrying securities on credit.

Real estate: carrying cost, primarily interest and taxes, of owning land prior to its development and resale.

Retailing: seller's charge for installment credit, which is either added to the purchase price or to unpaid installments.

CARRYOVER *see* TAX LOSS CARRYBACK, CARRYFORWARD.

CARTEL group of businesses or nations that agree to influence prices by regulating production and marketing of a product. The most famous contemporary cartel is the Organization of Petroleum Exporting Countries (OPEC), which, notably in the 1970s, restricted oil production and sales and raised prices. A cartel has less control over an industry than a MONOPOLY. A number of nations, including the United States, have laws prohibiting cartels. TRUST is sometimes used as a synonym for cartel.

CASH asset account on a balance sheet representing paper currency and coins, negotiable money orders and checks, and bank balances. Also, transactions handled in cash. In the financial statements of annual reports, cash is usually grouped with CASH EQUIVALENTS, defined as all highly liquid securities with a known market value and a maturity, when acquired, of less than 3 months.

To cash is to convert a negotiable instrument, usually into paper currency and coins.

See also CASH EQUIVALENT.

CASH ACCOUNT brokerage firm account whose transactions are settled on a cash basis. It is distinguished from a MARGIN ACCOUNT, for which the broker extends credit. Some brokerage customers have both cash and margin accounts. By law, a CUSTODIAL ACCOUNT for a minor must be a cash account.

CASH BASIS

Accounting: method that recognizes revenues when cash is received and recognizes expenses when cash is paid out. In contrast, the *accrual method* recognizes revenues when goods or services are sold and recognizes expenses when obligations are incurred. A third method, called *modified cash basis*, uses accrual accounting for long-term assets and is the basis usually referred to when the term cash basis is used.

Series EE Savings Bonds: paying the entire tax on these bonds when they mature. The alternative is to prorate the tax each year until the bonds mature.

CASHBOOK accounting book that combines cash receipts and disbursements. Its balance ties to the cash account in the general ledger on which the balance sheet is based.

CASH BUDGET estimated cash receipts and disbursements for a future period. A comprehensive cash budget schedules daily, weekly, or monthly expenditures together with the anticipated CASH FLOW from collections and other operating sources. Cash flow budgets are essential in establishing credit and purchasing policies, as well as in planning credit line usage and short-term investments in COMMERCIAL PAPER and other securities.

CASH COMMODITY commodity that is owned as the result of a completed contract and must be accepted upon delivery. Contrasts with futures contracts, which are not completed until a specified future date. The cash commodity contract specifications are set by the commodity exchanges.

CASH CONVERSION CYCLE elapsed time, usually expressed in days, from the outlay of cash for raw materials to the receipt of cash after the finished goods have been sold. Because a profit is built into the sales, the term *earnings cycle* is also used. The shorter the cycle, the more WORKING CAPITAL a business generates and the less it has to borrow. This cycle is directly affected by production efficiency, credit policy, and other controllable factors.

CASH COW business that generates a continuing flow of cash. Such a business usually has well-established brand names whose familiarity stimulates repeated buying of the products. For example, a magazine company that has a high rate of subscription renewals would be considered a cash cow. Stocks that are cash cows have dependable dividends.

CASH DIVIDEND cash payment to a corporation's shareholders, distributed from current earnings or accumulated profits and taxable as income. Cash dividends are distinguished from STOCK DIVIDENDS, which are payments in the form of stock. *See also* YIELD.

INVESTMENT COMPANY cash dividends are usually made up of dividends, interest income, and capital gains received on its investment portfolio.

CASH EARNINGS cash revenues less cash expenses—specifically excluding noncash expenses such as DEPRECIATION.

CASH EQUIVALENTS instruments or investments of such high liquidity and safety that they are virtually as good as cash. Examples are a MONEY MARKET FUND and a TREASURY BILL.

CASH FLOW
1. in a larger financial sense, an analysis of all the changes that affect the cash account during an accounting period. The STATEMENT OF CASH FLOWS included in annual reports analyzes all changes affecting cash in the categories of operations, investments, and financing. For example, net operating income is an increase, the purchase of a new building is a decrease, and the issuance of stock or bonds is an increase. When more cash comes in than goes out, we speak of a *positive cash flow;* the opposite is a *negative cash flow.* Companies with assets well in excess of liabilities may nevertheless go bankrupt because they cannot generate enough cash to meet current obligations.
2. in investments, NET INCOME plus DEPRECIATION and other noncash charges. In this sense, it is synonymous with CASH EARNINGS. Investors focus on cash

flow from operations because of their concern with a firm's ability to pay dividends. *See also* CASH BUDGET.

CASHIERING DEPARTMENT *see* CAGE.

CASH MARKET transactions in the cash or spot markets that are completed; that is, ownership of the commodity is transferred from seller to buyer and payment is given on delivery of the commodity. The cash market contrasts with the futures market, in which contracts are completed at a specified time in the future.

CASH ON DELIVERY (COD)

Commerce: transaction requiring that goods be paid for in full by cash or certified check or the equivalent at the point of delivery. The term *collect on delivery* has the same abbreviation and same meaning. If the customer refuses delivery, the seller has round-trip shipping costs to absorb or other, perhaps riskier, arrangements to make.

Securities: a requirement that delivery of securities to institutional investors be in exchange for assets of equal value—which, as a practical matter, means cash. Alternatively called *delivery against cost* (DAC) or *delivery versus payment* (DVP). On the other side of the trade, the term is *receive versus payment*.

CASH OR DEFERRED ARRANGEMENT (CODA) *see* 401(K) PLAN.

CASH RATIO ratio of cash and marketable securities to current liabilities; a refinement of the QUICK RATIO. The cash ratio tells the extent to which liabilities could be liquidated immediately. Sometimes called *liquidity ratio*.

CASH SURRENDER VALUE in insurance, the amount the insurer will return to a policyholder on cancellation of the policy. Sometimes abbreviated *CSVLI* (cash surrender value of life insurance), it shows up as an asset on the balance sheet of a company that has life insurance on its principals, called *key man insurance*. Insurance companies make loans against the cash value of policies, often at a better-than-market rate.

CASUALTY LOSS financial loss caused by damage, destruction, or loss of property as the result of an identifiable event that is sudden, unexpected, or unusual. Casualty and theft losses are considered together for tax purposes; are covered by most *casualty insurance* policies; and are tax deductible provided the loss is (1) not covered by insurance or (2) if covered, a claim has been made and denied.

CATS *see* CERTIFICATE OF ACCRUAL ON TREASURY SECURITIES.

CATS AND DOGS speculative stocks that have short histories of sales, earnings, and dividend payments. In bull markets, analysts say disparagingly that even the cats and dogs are going up.

CAVEAT EMPTOR, CAVEAT SUBSCRIPTOR *buyer beware, seller beware*. A variation on the latter is *caveat venditor*. Good advice when markets are not adequately protected, which was true of the stock market before the watchdog SECURITIES AND EXCHANGE COMMISSION was established in the 1930s.

CENTRAL BANK country's bank that (1) issues currency; (2) administers monetary policy, including OPEN MARKET OPERATIONS; (3) holds deposits representing the reserves of other banks; and (4) engages in transactions designed to facilitate the conduct of business and protect the public interest. In the United States, central banking is a function of the FEDERAL RESERVE SYSTEM.

CERTIFICATE formal declaration that can be used to document a fact, such as a birth certificate.

The following are certificates with particular relevance to finance and investments.

1. auditor's certificate, sometimes called certificate of accounts, or ACCOUNTANT'S OPINION.
2. bond certificate, certificate of indebtedness issued by a corporation containing the terms of the issuer's promise to repay principal and pay interest, and describing collateral, if any. Traditionally, bond certificates had coupons attached, which were exchanged for payment of interest. Now that most bonds are issued in registered form, coupons are less common. The amount of a certificate is the par value of the bond.
3. CERTIFICATE OF DEPOSIT.
4. certificate of INCORPORATION.
5. certificate of indebtedness, government debt obligation having a maturity shorter than a bond and longer than a treasury bill (such as a Treasury Note).
6. PARTNERSHIP certificate, showing the interest of all participants in a business partnership.
7. PROPRIETORSHIP certificate, showing who is legally responsible in an individually owned business.
8. STOCK CERTIFICATE, evidence of ownership of a corporation showing number of shares, name of issuer, amount of par or stated value represented or a declaration of no-par value, and rights of the shareholder. Preferred stock certificates also list the issuer's responsibilities with respect to dividends and voting rights, if any.

CERTIFICATE FOR AUTOMOBILE RECEIVABLES (CARS) PASS-THROUGH SECURITY backed by automobile loan paper of banks and other lenders. *See also* ASSET-BACKED SECURITIES.

CERTIFICATELESS MUNICIPALS MUNICIPAL BONDS that have no certificate of ownership for each bondholder. Instead, one certificate is valid for the entire issue. Certificateless municipals save paperwork for brokers and municipalities and allow investors to trade their bonds without having to transfer certificates. *See also* BOOK ENTRY SECURITIES.

CERTIFICATE OF ACCRUAL ON TREASURY SECURITIES (CATS) U.S. Treasury issues, sold at a deep discount from face value. A ZERO-COUPON security, they pay no interest during their lifetime, but return the full face value at maturity. They are appropriate for retirement or education planning. As TREASURY SECURITIES, CATS cannot be CALLED AWAY.

CERTIFICATE OF DEPOSIT (CD) debt instrument issued by a bank that usually pays interest. Institutional CDs are issued in denominations of $100,000 or more, and individual CDs start as low a $100. Maturities range from a few weeks to several years. Interest rates are set by competitive forces in the marketplace. *See also* BROKERED CD.

CERTIFICATE OF DEPOSIT ROLLOVER sophisticated investment strategy that defers taxes from one year to the next. An investor buys a certificate of deposit on margin that will mature in the following year, deducts the interest cost on the loan this year, and moves the income from the certificate into the next year. Internal Revenue Service rules say the interest deduction can be applied against any net investment income, which includes dividends, interest, royalties, and capital gains. Prior to the TAX REFORM ACT OF 1986, $10,000 of investment related interest over and above investment income was deductible. Under the 1986 law, the excess over income will be brought to zero by 1991.

CERTIFIED CHECK check for which a bank guarantees payment. When the check is certified, it legally becomes an obligation of the bank, and the funds to cover it are immediately withdrawn from the depositor's account.

CERTIFIED FINANCIAL PLANNER (CFP) person who has passed examinations accredited by the Denver-based College for Financial Planning, testing the ability to coordinate a client's banking, estate, insurance, investment, and tax affairs. Financial planners usually specialize in one or more of these areas and consult outside experts as needed. Some planners charge only fees and make no money on the implementation of their plans. Others charge a commission on each product or service they sell. *See also* FINANCIAL PLANNER.

CERTIFIED PUBLIC ACCOUNTANT (CPA) accountant who has passed certain exams, achieved a certain amount of experience, reached a certain age, and met all other statutory and licensing requirements of the U.S. state where he or she works. In addition to accounting and auditing, CPAs prepare tax returns for corporations and individuals.

CHAIRMAN OF THE BOARD member of a corporation's board of directors who presides over its meetings and who is the highest ranking officer in the corporation. The chairman of the board may or may not have the most actual executive authority in a firm. The additional title of CHIEF EXECUTIVE OFFICER (CEO) is reserved for the principal executive, and depending on the particular firm, that title may be held by the chairman, the president, or even an executive vice president. In some corporations, the position of chairman is either a prestigious reward for a past president or an honorary position for a prominent person, a large stockholder, or a family member; it may carry little or no real power in terms of policy or operating decision making.

CHAPTER 7 *see* BANKRUPTCY.

CHAPTER 11 *see* BANKRUPTCY.

CHARGE OFF *see* BAD DEBT.

CHARITABLE LEAD TRUST *see* CHARITABLE REMAINDER TRUST.

CHARITABLE REMAINDER TRUST an IRREVOCABLE TRUST that pays income to one or more individuals until the GRANTOR'S death, at which time the balance, which is tax-free, passes to a designated charity. It is a popular tax-saving alternative for individuals without children or who want to benefit children and charity.
The charitable remainder trust is the reverse of a *charitable lead trust*, whereby a charity receives income during the grantor's life and the remainder passes to designated family members upon the grantor's death. The latter trust reduces estate taxes while enabling the family to retain control of the assets.

CHARTER *see* ARTICLES OF INCORPORATION.

CHARTERED FINANCIAL ANALYST (CFA) designation awarded by the Institute of Chartered Financial Analysts (ICFA) Charlottesville, Virginia, to experienced financial analysts who pass examinations in economics, financial accounting, portfolio management, security analysis, and standards of conduct.

CHARTERED FINANCIAL CONSULTANT (ChFC) designation awarded by American College of Bryn Mawr, Pennsylvania, to a professional FINANCIAL PLANNER who completes a four-year program covering economics, insurance, taxation, real estate, and other areas related to finance and investing.

CHARTIST technical analyst who charts the patterns of stocks, bonds, and commodities to make buy and sell recommendations to clients. Chartists believe recurring patterns of trading can help them forecast future price movements. *See also* TECHNICAL ANALYSIS.

CHECK bill of exchange, or draft on a bank drawn against deposited funds to pay a specified sum of money to a specified person on demand. A check is considered as cash and is NEGOTIABLE when endorsed.

CHECKING THE MARKET canvassing securities market-makers by telephone or other means in search of the best bid or offer price.

CHICAGO BOARD OF TRADE *see* SECURITIES AND COMMODITIES EXCHANGES.

CHICAGO BOARD OPTIONS EXCHANGE *see* SECURITIES AND COMMODITIES EXCHANGES.

CHICAGO MERCANTILE EXCHANGE *see* SECURITIES AND COMMODITIES EXCHANGES.

CHIEF EXECUTIVE OFFICER (CEO) officer of a firm principally responsible for the activities of a company. CEO is usually an additional title held by the CHAIRMAN OF THE BOARD, the president, or another senior officer such as a vice chairman or an executive vice president.

CHIEF FINANCIAL OFFICER (CFO) executive officer who is responsible for handling funds, signing checks, keeping financial records, and financial planning for a corporation. He or she typically has the title of vice president-finance or financial vice president in large corporations, that of treasurer or controller (also spelled comptroller) in smaller companies. Since many state laws require that a corporation have a treasurer, that title is often combined with one or more of the other financial titles.

The controllership function requires an experienced accountant to direct internal accounting programs, including cost accounting, systems and procedures, data processing, acquisitions analysis, and financial planning. The controller may also have internal audit responsibilities.

The treasury function is concerned with the receipt, custody, investment, and disbursement of corporate funds and for borrowings and the maintenance of a market for the company's securities.

CHIEF OPERATING OFFICER officer of a firm, usually the president or an executive vice president, responsible for day-to-day management. The chief operating officer reports to the CHIEF EXECUTIVE OFFICER and may or may not be on the board of directors (presidents typically serve as board members). *See also* CHAIRMAN OF THE BOARD.

CHURNING excessive trading of a client's account. Churning increases the broker's commissions, but usually leaves the client worse off or no better off than before. Churning is illegal under SEC and exchange rules, but is difficult to prove.

CINCINNATI STOCK EXCHANGE (CSE) stock exchange established in 1887. The CSE became the first completely automated stock exchange, handling members' transactions without the benefit of a physical trading floor by using computers. The CSE has nominal jurisdiction over the National Securities Trading System (NSTS), known popularly as the "Cincinnati experiment." Participating brokerage firms enter orders into the NSTS computer, which then matches orders and clears the orders back to the brokers. The NSTS contains some of the features envisioned for a national exchange market system.

CIRCLE underwriter's way of designating potential purchasers and amounts of a securities issue during the REGISTRATION period, before selling is permitted. Registered representatives canvass prospective buyers and report any interest to the underwriters, who then circle the names on their list.

CIRCUIT BREAKERS measures instituted by the major stock and commodities exchanges to halt trading temporarily in stocks and stock index futures when the market has fallen by a specified amount in a specified period. Circuit breakers were instituted after BLACK MONDAY in 1987 and modified following another sharp market drop in October, 1989. Their purpose is to prevent a market free fall by permitting a rebalancing of buy and sell orders. See also PROGRAM TRADING.

CITIZEN BONDS form of CERTIFICATELESS MUNICIPALS. Citizen bonds may be registered on stock exchanges, in which case their prices are listed in daily newspapers, unlike other municipal bonds. *See also* BOOK-ENTRY SECURITIES.

CLASS
1. securities having similar features. Stocks and bonds are the two main classes; they are subdivided into various classes—for example, mortgage bonds and debentures, issues with different rates of interest, common and preferred stock, or Class A and Class B common. The different classes in a company's capitalization are itemized on its balance sheet.
2. options of the same type—put or call—with the same underlying security. A class of option having the same expiration date and EXERCISE PRICE is termed a SERIES.

CLASS A/CLASS B SHARES *see* CLASSIFIED STOCK.

CLASSIFIED STOCK separation of equity into more than one CLASS of common, usually designated Class A and Class B. The distinguishing features, set forth in the corporation charter and bylaws, usually give an advantage to the Class A shares in terms of voting power, though dividend and liquidation privileges can also be involved. Classified stock is less prevalent today than in the 1920s, when it was used as a means of preserving minority control.

CLAYTON ANTI-TRUST ACT *see* ANTITRUST LAWS.

CLEAN
Finance: free of debt, as in a clean balance sheet. In banking, corporate borrowers have traditionally been required to *clean up* for at least 30 days each year to prove their borrowings were seasonal and not required as permanent working capital.

International trade: without documents, as in clean vs. documentary drafts.

Securities: block trade that matches corresponding buy or sell orders, thus sparing the block positioner any inventory risk. If the transaction appears on the exchange tape, it is said to be *clean on the tape.* Sometimes such a trade is called a *natural:* "We did a natural for 80,000 XYZ common."

CLEAR

Banking: COLLECTION of funds on which a check is drawn, and payment of those funds to the holder of the check. *See also* CLEARING HOUSE FUNDS.

Finance: asset not securing a loan and not otherwise encumbered. As a verb, to clear means to make a profit: "After all expenses, we *cleared* $1 million."

Securities: COMPARISON of the details of a transaction between brokers prior to settlement; final exchange of securities for cash on delivery.

CLEARING HOUSE FUNDS funds represented by checks or drafts that are transferred between banks through the FEDERAL RESERVE SYSTEM. Unlike FEDERAL FUNDS, which are drawn on reserve balances and are good the same day, clearing house funds require three days to clear. Also, funds used to settle transactions on which there is one day's FLOAT.

CLIFFORD TRUST trust set up for at least ten years and a day which makes it possible to turn over title to income-producing assets, then to reclaim the assets when the trust expires. Prior to the TAX REFORM ACT OF 1986, such trusts were popular ways of shifting income-producing assets from parents to children, whose income was taxed at lower rates. The 1986 Tax Act makes monies put in Clifford Trusts after March 1, 1986, subject to taxation at the grantor's tax rate, thus defeating their purpose. For trusts established before that date, taxes on earnings over $1000 will be paid at the grantor's rate, but only if the child is under the age of 14. *See also* INTER VIVOS TRUST.

CLONE FUND in a FAMILY OF FUNDS, new fund set up to emulate a successful existing fund.

CLOSE

1. the price of the final trade of a security at the end of a trading day.
2. the last half hour of a trading session on the exchanges.
3. in commodities trading, the period just before the end of the session when trades marked for execution AT THE CLOSE are completed.
4. to consummate a sale or agreement. In a REAL ESTATE closing, for example, rights of ownership are transferred in exchange for monetary and other considerations. At a *loan* closing, notes are signed and checks are exchanged. At the close of an *underwriting* deal, checks and securities are exchanged.
5. in accounting, the transfer of revenue and expense accounts at the end of the period—called *closing the books.*

CLOSE A POSITION to eliminate an investment from one's portfolio. The simplest example is the outright sale of a security and its delivery to the purchaser in exchange for payment. In commodities futures and options trading, traders commonly close out positions through offsetting transactions. Closing a position terminates involvement with the investment; hedging, though similar, requires further actions at some point in the future.

CLOSED CORPORATION corporation whose shares are owned by a few people, usually members of management or a family. Shares are not for sale and there is no public market. Also known as *close corporation* or *private corporation*.

CLOSED-END FUND type of fund that has a fixed number of shares, usually listed on a major stock exchange. Unlike open-end mutual funds, closed-end funds do not stand ready to issue and redeem shares on a continuous basis. They tend to have specialized portfolios of stocks, bonds, CONVERTIBLES, or combinations thereof, and may be oriented toward income, capital gains, or a combination of these objectives. Examples are the Korea Fund, which specializes in the stocks of Korean firms, and ASA Ltd., which specializes in South African gold mining stocks. Both are listed on the New York Stock Exchange. Because the managers of closed-end funds are perceived to be less responsive to profit opportunities than open-end fund managers, who must attract and retain shareholders, closed-end fund shares often sell at a discount from net asset value.

A variation of the closed-end fund is the DUAL-PURPOSE FUND, which has two classes of shares representing income and capital gains, respectively.

CLOSED-END MANAGEMENT COMPANY INVESTMENT COMPANY that operates a mutual fund with a limited number of shares outstanding. Unlike an OPEN-END MANAGEMENT COMPANY, which creates new shares to meet investor demand, a closed-end fund starts with a set number of shares. These are often listed on an exchange. *See also* CLOSED-END FUND.

CLOSED-END MORTGAGE mortgage-bond issue with an indenture that prohibits repayment before maturity and the repledging of the same collateral without the permission of the bondholders; also called closed mortgage. It is distinguished from an OPEN-END MORTGAGE.

CLOSED OUT liquidated the position of a client unable to meet a margin call or cover a short sale. *See also* CLOSE A POSITION.

CLOSELY HELD corporation most of whose voting stock is held by a few shareholders; differs from a CLOSED CORPORATION because enough stock is publicly held to provide a basis for trading. Also, the shares held by the controlling group and not considered likely to be available for purchase.

CLOSING COSTS expenses involved in transferring real estate from a seller to a buyer, among them lawyer's fees, survey charges, title searches and insurance, and fees to file deeds and mortgages.

CLOSING PRICE price of the last transaction completed during a day's trading session on an organized securities exchange. *See also* CLOSING RANGE.

CLOSING PURCHASE option seller's purchase of another option having the same features as an earlier one. The two options cancel each other out and thus liquidate the seller's position.

CLOSING QUOTE last bid and offer prices recorded by a specialist or market maker at the close of a trading day.

CLOSING RANGE range of prices (in commodities trading) within which an order to buy or sell a commodity can be executed during one trading day.

CLOSING SALE sale of an option having the same features (i.e., of the same series) as an option previously purchased. The two have the effect of canceling each other out. Such a transaction demonstrates the intention to liquidate the holder's position in the underlying securities upon exercise of the buy.

CODE OF ARBITRATION *see* BOARD OF ARBITRATION.

CODE OF PROCEDURE NATIONAL ASSOCIATION OF SECURITIES DEALERS (NASD) guide for its District Business Conduct Committees in hearing and adjudicating complaints filed between or against NASD members under its Rules of Fair Practice.

COINSURANCE sharing of an insurance risk, common when claims could be of such size that it would not be prudent for one company to underwrite the whole risk. Typically, the underwriter is liable up to a stated limit, and the coinsurer's liability is for amounts above that limit.

Policies on hazards such as fire or water damage often require coverage of at least a specified coinsurance percentage of the replacement cost. Such clauses induce the owners of property to carry full coverage or close to it.

COLLATERAL ASSET pledged to a lender until a loan is repaid. If the borrower defaults, the lender has the legal right to seize the collateral and sell it to pay off the loan.

COLLATERALIZE *see* ASSIGN; COLLATERAL; HYPOTHECATION.

COLLATERALIZED MORTGAGE OBLIGATION (CMO) mortgage-backed bond that separates mortgage pools into different maturity classes, called *tranches*. This is accomplished by applying income (payments and prepayments of principal and interest) from mortgages in the pool in the order that the CMOs pay out. Tranches pay different rates of interest and typically mature in two, five, 10 and 20 years. Issued by Federal Home Loan Mortgage Corporation (Freddie Mac) and private issuers, CMOs are usually backed by government-guaranteed or other top-grade mortgages and have AAA bond ratings. For a slight sacrifice of yield, CMOs lessen the anxiety pass-through holders would have about the uncertain life of their investments. See also CMO REIT, REMIC.

COLLATERAL TRUST BOND corporate debt security backed by other securities, usually held by a bank or other trustee. Such bonds are backed by collateral trust certificates and are usually issued by parent corporations that are borrowing against the securities of wholly owned subsidiaries.

COLLECTIBLE rare object collected by investors. Examples: stamps, coins, oriental rugs, antiques, baseball cards, photographs. Collectibles typically rise sharply in value during inflationary periods, when people are trying to move their assets from paper currency as an inflation hedge, then drop in value during low inflation. Collectible trading for profit can be quite difficult, because of the limited number of buyers and sellers.

COLLECTION
1. presentation of a negotiable instrument such as a draft or check to the place at which it is payable. The term refers not only to check clearing and payment, but to such special banking services as foreign collections, coupon collection, and collection of returned items (bad checks).
2. referral of a past due account to specialists in collecting loans or accounts receivable, either an internal department or a private collection agency.
3. in a general financial sense, conversion of accounts receivable into cash.

COLLECTION PERIOD *see* COLLECTION RATIO.

COLLECTION RATIO ratio of a company's accounts receivable to its average daily sales. Average daily sales are obtained by dividing sales for an accounting period by the number of days in the accounting period—annual sales divided by 365, if the accounting period is a year. That result, divided into accounts receivable (an average of beginning and ending accounts receivable is more accurate), is the collection ratio—the average number of days it takes the company to convert receivables into cash. It is also called *average collection period.* See ACCOUNTS RECEIVABLE TURNOVER for a discussion of its significance.

COLLECTIVE BARGAINING process by which members of the labor force, operating through authorized union representatives, negotiate with their employers concerning wages, hours, working conditions, and benefits.

COLLEGE CONSTRUCTION LOAN INSURANCE ASSOCIATION agency of the U.S. government established in 1987 to guarantee loans for college building programs. Informally called *Connie Lee.*

COMBINATION
1. arrangement of options involving two long or two short positions with different expiration dates or strike (exercise) prices. A trader could order a combination with a long call and a long put or a short call and a short put.
2. joining of competing companies in an industry to alter the competitive balance in their favor is called a combination in restraint of trade.
3. joining two or more separate businesses into a single accounting entity; also called *business combination.* See also MERGER.

COMBINATION ANNUITY *see* HYBRID ANNUITY.

COMBINATION BOND bond backed by the full faith and credit of the governmental unit issuing it as well as by revenue from the toll road, bridge, or other project financed by the bond.

COMBINATION ORDER *see* ALTERNATIVE ORDER.

COMBINED FINANCIAL STATEMENT financial statement that brings together the assets, liabilities, net worth, and operating figures of two or more affiliated companies. In its most comprehensive form, called a combining statement, it includes columns showing each affiliate on an "alone" basis; a column "eliminating" offsetting intercompany transactions; and the resultant combined financial statement. A combined statement is distinguished from a CONSOLIDATED FINANCIAL STATEMENT of a company and subsidiaries, which must reconcile investment and capital accounts. Combined financial statements do not necessarily represent combined credit responsibility or investment strength.

COMEX *see* SECURITIES AND COMMODITIES EXCHANGES.

COMFORT LETTER
1. independent auditor's letter, required in securities underwriting agreements, to assure that information in the registration statement and prospectus is correctly prepared and that no material changes have occurred since its preparation. It is sometimes called *cold comfort letter*—cold because the accountants do not state positively that the information is correct, only that nothing has come to their attention to indicate it is not correct.
2. letter from one to another of the parties to a legal agreement stating that certain actions not clearly covered in the agreement will—or will not—be taken. Such

declarations of intent usually deal with matters that are of importance only to the two parties and do not concern other signers of the agreement.

COMMERCIAL HEDGERS companies that take positions in commodities markets in order to lock in prices at which they buy raw materials or sell their products. For instance, Alcoa might hedge its holdings of aluminum with contracts in aluminum futures, or Eastman Kodak, which must buy great quantities of silver for making film, might hedge its holdings in the silver futures market.

COMMERCIAL LOAN short-term (typically 90-day) renewable loan to finance the seasonal WORKING CAPITAL needs of a business, such as purchase of inventory or production and distribution of goods. Commercial loans—shown on the balance sheet as notes payable—rank second only to TRADE CREDIT in importance as a source of short-term financing. Interest is based on the prime rate. *See also* CLEAN.

COMMERCIAL PAPER short-term obligations with maturities ranging from 2 to 270 days issued by banks, corporations, and other borrowers to investors with temporarily idle cash. Such instruments are unsecured and usually discounted, although some are interest-bearing. They can be issued directly—*direct issuers* do it that way—or through brokers equipped to handle the enormous clerical volume involved. Issuers like commercial paper because the maturities are flexible and because the rates are usually marginally lower than bank rates. Investors— actually lenders, since commercial paper is a form of debt—like the flexibility and safety of an instrument that is issued only by top-rated concerns and is nearly always backed by bank lines of credit. Both Moody's and Standard & Poor's assign ratings to commercial paper.

COMMERCIAL WELLS oil and gas drilling sites that are productive enough to be commercially viable. A limited partnership usually syndicates a share in a commercial well.

COMMINGLING

Securities: mixing customer-owned securities with those owned by a firm in its proprietary accounts. REHYPOTHECATION—the use of customers' collateral to secure brokers' loans—is permissible with customer consent, but certain securities and collateral must by law be kept separate.

Trust banking: pooling the investment funds of individual accounts, with each customer owning a share of the total fund. Similar to a MUTUAL FUND.

COMMISSION

Real estate: percentage of the selling price of the property, paid by the seller.

Securities: fee paid to a broker for executing a trade based on the number of shares traded or the dollar amount of the trade. Since 1975, when regulation ended, brokers have been free to charge whatever they like.

COMMISSION BROKER broker, usually a floor broker, who executes trades of stocks, bonds, or commodities for a commission.

COMMITMENT FEE lender's charge for contracting to hold credit available. Fee may be replaced by interest when money is borrowed or both fees and interest may be charged, as with a REVOLVING CREDIT.

COMMITTEE ON UNIFORM SECURITIES IDENTIFICATION PROCEDURES (CUSIP) committee that assigns identifying numbers and codes for all securities. These CUSIP numbers and symbols are used when recording all buy or sell orders. For International Business Machines the CUSIP symbol is IBM and the CUSIP number is 45920010.

COMMODITIES bulk goods such as grains, metals, and foods traded on a commodities exchange or on the SPOT MARKET. *See also* SECURITIES AND COMMODITIES EXCHANGES.

COMMODITIES EXCHANGE CENTER *see* SECURITIES AND COMMODITIES EXCHANGES.

COMMODITIES FUTURES TRADING COMMISSION *see* REGULATED COMMODITIES.

COMMODITY-BACKED BOND bond tied to the price of an underlying commodity. An investor whose bond is tied to the price of silver or gold receives interest pegged to the metal's current price, rather than a fixed dollar amount. Such a bond is meant to be a hedge against inflation, which drives up the prices of most commodities.

COMMODITY PAPER inventory loans or advances secured by commodities. If the commodities are in transit, a bill of lading is executed by a common carrier. If they are in storage, a trust receipt acknowledges that they are held and that proceeds from their sale will be transmitted to the lender; a warehouse receipt lists the goods.

COMMON MARKET *see* EUROPEAN ECONOMIC COMMUNITY.

COMMON STOCK units of ownership of a public corporation. Owners typically are entitled to vote on the selection of directors and other important matters as well as to receive dividends on their holdings. In the event that a corporation is liquidated, the claims of secured and unsecured creditors and owners of bonds and preferred stock take precedence over the claims of those who own common stock. For the most part, however, common stock has more potential for appreciation. *See also* CAPITAL STOCK.

COMMON STOCK EQUIVALENT preferred stock or bond convertible into common stock, or warrant to purchase common stock at a specified price or discount from market price. Common stock equivalents represent potential dilution of existing common shareholder's equity, and their conversion or exercise is assumed in calculating fully diluted earnings per share. *See also* FULLY DILUTED EARNINGS PER SHARE.

COMMON STOCK FUND MUTUAL FUND that invests only in common stocks.

COMMON STOCK RATIO percentage of total capitalization represented by common stock. From a creditor's standpoint a high ratio represents a margin of safety in the event of LIQUIDATION. From an investor's standpoint, however, a high ratio can mean a lack of *leverage*. What the ratio should be depends largely on the stability of earnings. Electric utilities can operate with low ratios because their earnings are stable. As a general rule, when an industrial company's stock ratio is below 30%, analysts check on earnings stability and fixed charge coverage in bad times as well as good.

COMMUNITY PROPERTY property and income accumulated by a married couple and belonging to them jointly. The two have equal rights to the income from stocks, bonds, and real estate, as well as to the appreciated value of those assets.

COMPANY organization engaged in business as a proprietorship, partnership, corporation, or other form of enterprise. Originally, a firm made up of a group of people as distinguished from a sole proprietorship. However, since few proprietorships owe their existence exclusively to one person, the term now applies to proprietorships as well.

COMPARATIVE STATEMENTS financial statements covering different dates but prepared consistently and therefore lending themselves to comparative analysis, as accounting convention requires. Comparative figures reveal trends in a company's financial development and permit insight into the dynamics behind static balance sheet figures.

COMPARISON
1. short for *comparison ticket,* a memorandum exchanged prior to settlement by two brokers in order to confirm the details of a transaction to which they were parties. Also called comparison sheet.
2. verification of collateral held against a loan, by exchange of information between two brokers or between a broker and a bank.

COMPENSATING BALANCE *or* **COMPENSATORY BALANCE** average balance required by a bank for holding credit available. The more or less standard requirement for a bank line of credit, for example, is 10% of the line plus an additional 10% of the borrowings. Compensating balances increase the effective rate of interest on borrowings.

COMPETITIVE BID sealed bid, containing price and terms, submitted by a prospective underwriter to an issuer, who awards the contract to the bidder with the best price and terms. Many municipalities and virtually all railroads and public utilities use this bid system. Industrial corporations generally prefer to negotiate with their investment bankers on stock issues but sometimes use competitive bidding to select underwriters for bond issues. *See also* NEGOTIATED UNDERWRITING.

COMPLETE AUDIT usually the same as an unqualified audit, because it is so thoroughly executed that the auditor's only reservations have to do with unobtainable facts. A complete audit examines the system of internal control and the details of the books of account, including subsidiary records and supporting documents. This is done with an eye to legality, mathematical accuracy, accountability, and the application of accepted accounting principles.

COMPLETED CONTRACT METHOD accounting method whereby revenues and expenses (and therefore taxes) on long-term contracts, such as government defense contracts, are recognized in the year the contract is concluded, except that losses are recognized in the year they are forecast. This method differs from the *percentage-of-completion method,* where sales and costs are recognized each year based on the value of the work performed. Under the TAX REFORM ACT OF 1986, manufacturers with long-term contracts must elect either the latter method or the *percentage-of-completion capitalized cost method,* requiring that 40% of the contract be included under the percentage-of-completion method and 60% under the taxpayer's normal accounting method.

COMPLETION PROGRAM oil and gas limited partnership that takes over drilling when oil is known to exist in commercial quantities. A completion program is a conservative way to profit from oil and gas drilling, but without the capital gains potential of exploratory wildcat drilling programs.

COMPLIANCE DEPARTMENT department set up in all organized stock exchanges to oversee market activity and make sure that trading complies with Securities and Exchange Commission and exchange regulations. A company that does not adhere to the rules can be delisted, and a trader or brokerage firm that violates the rules can be barred from trading.

COMPOSITE TAPE *see* TAPE.

COMPOUND GROWTH RATE rate of growth of a number, compounded over several years. Securities analysts check a company's compound growth rate of profits for five years to see the long-term trend in profitability.

COMPOUND INTEREST interest earned on principal plus interest that was earned earlier. If $100 is deposited in a bank account at 10%, the depositor will be credited with $110 at the end of the first year and $121 at the end of the second year. That extra $1, which was earned on the $10 interest from the first year, is the compound interest. This example involves interest compounded annually; interest can also be compounded on a daily, quarterly, half-yearly, or other basis.

COMPTROLLER OF THE CURRENCY federal official, appointed by the President and confirmed by the Senate, who is responsible for chartering, examining, supervising, and liquidating all national banks. In response to the *comptroller's call*, national banks are required to submit *call reports* of their financial activities at least four times a year and to publish them in local newspapers. National banks can be declared insolvent only by the Comptroller of the Currency.

COMPUTERIZED MARKET TIMING SYSTEM system of picking buy and sell signals that puts together voluminous trading data in search of patterns and trends. Often, changes in the direction of moving average lines form the basis for buy and sell recommendations. These systems, commonly used by commodity funds and by services that switch between mutual funds, tend to work well when markets are moving steadily up or down, but not in trendless markets.

CONCESSION
1. selling group's per-share or per-bond compensation in a corporate underwriting.
2. right, usually granted by a government entity, to use property for a specified purpose, such as a service station on a highway.

CONDOMINIUM form of real estate ownership in which individual residents hold a deed and title to their houses or apartments and pay a maintenance fee to a management company for the upkeep of common property such as grounds, lobbies, and elevators as well as for other amenities. Condominium owners pay real estate taxes on their units and can sublet or sell as they wish. Some real estate limited partnerships specialize in converting rental property into condominiums. *See also* COOPERATIVE.

CONFIRMATION
1. formal memorandum from a broker to a client giving details of a securities

transaction. When a broker acts as a dealer, the confirmation must disclose that fact to the customer.

2. document sent by a company's auditor to its customers and suppliers requesting verification of the book amounts of receivables and payables. *Positive confirmations* request that every balance be confirmed, whereas *negative confirmations* request a reply only if an error exists.

CONFORMED COPY copy of an original document with the essential legal features, such as the signature and seal, being typed or indicated in writing.

CONGLOMERATE corporation composed of companies in a variety of businesses. Conglomerates were popular in the 1960s, when they were thought to provide better management and sounder financial backing, and therefore generate more profit, than small independent companies. Some conglomerates became so complex that they were difficult to manage. In the 1980s, some conglomerates sold off divisions and concentrated on a few core businesses. Analysts generally consider stocks of conglomerates difficult to evaluate.

CONNIE LEE Nickname for COLLEGE CONSTRUCTION LOAN INSURANCE ASSOCIATION.

CONSIDERATION something of value that one party gives to another in exchange for a promise or act. In law, a requirement of valid contracts. A consideratior can be in the form of money, commodities, or personal services; in many industries the forms have become standardized.

CONSOLIDATED FINANCIAL STATEMENT financial statement that brings together all assets, liabilities, and operating accounts of a parent company and its subsidiaries. *See also* COMBINED FINANCIAL STATEMENT.

CONSOLIDATED MORTGAGE BOND bond issue that covers several units of property and may refinance separate mortgages on these properties. The consolidated mortgage with a single coupon rate is a traditional form of financing for railroads because it is economical to combine many properties in one agreement.

CONSOLIDATED TAPE combined tapes of the New York Stock Exchange and the American Stock Exchange. It became operative in June 1975. Network A covers NYSE-listed securities and identifies the originating market. Network B does the same for Amex-listed securities and securities listed on regional exchanges. *See also* TICKER TAPE.

CONSOLIDATED TAX RETURN return combining reports of companies in what the tax law defines as an affiliated group. A firm is part of an affiliated group if at least 80% owned by another corporation. "Owned" refers to voting stock. (Before the TAX REFORM ACT OF 1986 it also included nonvoting stock.)

CONSOLIDATION LOAN loan that combines and refinances other loans or debt. It is normally an installment loan designed to reduce the dollar amount of an individual's monthly payments.

CONSORTIUM group of companies formed to promote a common objective or engage in a project of benefit to all the members. The relationship normally entails cooperation and a sharing of resources, sometimes even common ownership.

CONSTANT DOLLAR PLAN method of accumulating assets by investing a fixed amount of dollars in securities at set intervals. The investor buys more shares when the price is low and fewer shares when the price is high; the overall cost is lower than it would be if a constant number of shares were bought at set intervals. Also called DOLLAR AVERAGING.

CONSTANT DOLLARS dollars of a base year, used as a gauge in adjusting the dollars of other years in order to ascertain actual purchasing power. Denoted as C$ by the FINANCIAL ACCOUNTING STANDARDS BOARD (FASB), which defines constant dollars as hypothetical units of general purchasing power.

CONSTANT RATIO PLAN a type of FORMULA INVESTING whereby a predetermined ratio is maintained between stock and FIXED-INCOME INVESTMENTS through periodic adjustments. For example, an investor with $200,000 and a 50-50 formula might start out with $100,000 in stock and $100,000 in bonds. If the stock increased in value of $150,000 and the bonds remained unchanged over a given adjustment period, the investor would restore the ratio of $125,000–$125,000 by selling $25,000 of stock and buying $25,000 of bonds.

CONSTRUCTION LOAN short-term real estate loan to finance building costs. The funds are disbursed as needed or in accordance with a prearranged plan, and the money is repaid on completion of the project, usually from the proceeds of a mortgage loan. The rate is normally higher than prime, and there is usually an origination fee. The effective yield on these loans tends to be high, and the lender has a security interest in the real property.

CONSTRUCTIVE RECEIPT term used by Internal Revenue Service for the date when a taxpayer received dividends or other income. IRS rules say that constructive receipt of income is established if the taxpayer has the right to claim it, whether or not the choice is exercised. For instance, if a bond pays interest on December 29, the taxpayer must report the income in that tax year and not in the following year.

CONSUMER CREDIT PROTECTION ACT OF 1968 landmark federal legislation establishing rules of disclosure that lenders must observe in dealings with borrowers. The act stipulates that consumers be told annual percentage rates, potential total cost, and any special loan terms. The act, enforced by the Federal Reserve Bank, is also known as the *Truth in Lending Act.*

CONSUMER DEBENTURE investment note issued by a financial institution and marketed directly to the public. Consumer debentures were a popular means of raising lendable funds for banks during tight money periods prior to deregulation, since these instruments, unlike certificates of deposit, could compete freely with other money-market investments in a high-rate market.

CONSUMER FINANCE COMPANY *see* FINANCE COMPANY.

CONSUMER GOODS goods bought for personal or household use, as distinguished from CAPITAL GOODS or *producer's goods,* which are used to produce other goods. The general economic meaning of consumer goods encompasses consumer services. Thus the *market basket* on which the CONSUMER PRICE INDEX is based includes clothing, food, and other goods as well as utilities, entertainment, and other services.

CONSUMER PRICE INDEX (CPI) measure of change in consumer prices, as determined by a monthly survey of the U.S. Bureau of Labor Statistics. Many pension and employment contracts are tied to changes in consumer prices, as protection against inflation and reduced purchasing power. Among the CPI components are the costs of housing, food, transportation, and electricity. Also known as the *cost-of-living index*.

CONSUMPTION TAX *see* VALUE-ADDED TAX (VAT).

CONTANGO
1. pricing situation in which futures prices get progressively higher as maturities get progressively longer, creating negative spreads as contracts go farther out. The increases reflect carrying costs, including storage, financing, and insurance. The reverse condition, an inverted market, is termed BACKWARDATION.
2. in finance, the costs that must be taken into account in analyses involving forecasts.

CONTINGENT LIABILITY

Banking: potential obligation of a guarantor or accommodation endorser; or the position of a customer who opens a letter of credit and whose account will be charged if a draft is presented. The bank's own responsibility for letters of credit and other commitments, individually and collectively, is its contingent liability.

Corporate reports: pending lawsuits, judgments under appeal, disputed claims, and the like, representing financial liability in the event of an adverse outcome.

CONTINGENT ORDER securities order whose execution depends on the execution of another order; for example, a sell order and a buy order with prices stipulated. Where the purpose is to effect a swap, a price difference might be stipulated as a condition of the order's execution. Generally, brokers discourage these orders, preferring to deal with firm instructions.

CONTINUOUS NET SETTLEMENT (CNS) method of securities clearing and settlement that eliminates multiple fails in the same securities. This is accomplished by using a clearing house, such as the National Securities Clearing Corporation, and a depository, such as DEPOSITORY TRUST COMPANY, to match transactions to securities available in the firm's position, resulting in one net receive or deliver position at the end of the day. By including the previous day's fail position in the next day's selling trades, the firm's position is always up to date and money settlement or withdrawals can be made at any time with the clearing house. The alternative to CNS is window settlement, where the seller delivers securities to the buyer's cashier and receives payment.

CONTRA BROKER broker on the opposite side—the buy side of a sell order or the sell side of a buy order.

CONTRACT in general, agreement by which rights or acts are exchanged for lawful consideration. To be valid, it must be entered into by competent parties, must cover a legal and moral transaction, must possess mutuality, and must represent a meeting of minds.

CONTRACTUAL PLAN plan by which fixed dollar amounts of mutual fund shares are accumulated through periodic investments for 10 or 15 years. The legal vehicle for such investments is the *plan company* or *participating unit investment trust*, a selling organization operating on behalf of the fund's underwriter. The plan company must be registered with the Securities and Exchange Commission, as the underlying fund must be, so the investor receives two prospectuses. Investors in these plans commonly receive other benefits in exchange for their fixed periodic payments, such as decreasing term life insurance. *See also* FRONT END LOAD.

CONTRARIAN investor who does the opposite of what most investors are doing at any particular time. According to contrarian opinion, if everyone is certain that something is about to happen, it won't. This is because most people who say the market is going up are fully invested and have no additional purchasing power, which means the market is at its peak. When people predict decline they have already sold out, so the market can only go up. Some mutual funds follow a contrarian investment strategy, and some investment advisers suggest only out-of-favor securities, whose price/earnings ratio is lower than the rest of the market or industry.

CONTROLLED COMMODITIES commodities regulated by the Commodities Exchange Act of 1936, which set up trading rules for futures in commodities markets in order to prevent fraud and manipulation.

CONTROLLED WILDCAT DRILLING drilling for oil and gas in an area adjacent to but outside the limits of a proven field. Also known as a *field extension*. Limited partnerships drilling in this area take greater risks than those drilling in areas of proven energy reserves, but the rewards can be considerable if oil is found.

CONTROLLER *or* **COMPTROLLER** chief accountant of a company. In small companies the controller may also serve as treasurer. In a brokerage firm, the controller prepares financial reports, supervises internal audits, and is responsible for compliance with Securities and Exchange Commission regulations.

CONTROLLING INTEREST ownership of more than 50% of a corporation's voting shares. A much smaller interest, owned individually or by a group in combination, can be controlling if the other shares are widely dispersed and not actively voted.

CONTROL PERSON *see* AFFILIATED PERSON.

CONTROL STOCK shares owned by holders who have a CONTROLLING INTEREST.

CONVENTIONAL MORTGAGE residential mortgage loan, usually from a bank or savings and loan association, with a fixed rate and term. It is repayable in fixed monthly payments over a period usually 30 years or less, secured by real property, and not insured by the FEDERAL HOUSING ADMINISTRATION or guaranteed by the Veterans Administration.

CONVENTIONAL OPTION put or call contract arranged off the trading floor of a listed exchange and not traded regularly. It was commonplace when options were banned on certain exchanges, but is now rare.

CONVERGENCE movement of the price of a futures contract toward the price of the underlying CASH COMMODITY. At the start of the contract price is higher because of the time value. But as the contract nears expiration the futures price and the cash price converge.

CONVERSION
1. exchange of a convertible security such as a bond into a fixed number of shares

of the issuing corporation's common stock.

2. transfer of mutual-fund shares without charge from one fund to another fund in a single family; also known as fund switching.

3. in insurance, switch from short-term to permanent life insurance.

CONVERSION PARITY common-stock price at which a convertible security can become exchangeable for common shares of equal value.

CONVERSION PREMIUM amount by which the price of a convertible tops the market price of the underlying stock. If a stock is trading at $50 and the bond convertible at $45 is trading at $50, the premium is $5. If the premium is high the bond trades like any fixed income bond. If the premium is low the bond trades like a stock.

CONVERSION PRICE the dollar value at which convertible bonds, debentures, or preferred stock can be converted into common stock, as announced when the convertible is issued.

CONVERSION RATIO relationship that determines how many shares of common stock will be received in exchange for each convertible bond or preferred share when the conversion takes place. It is determined at the time of issue and is expressed either as a ratio or as a conversion price from which the ratio can be figured by dividing the par value of the convertible by the conversion price. The indentures of most convertible securities contain an antidilution clause whereby the conversion ratio may be raised (or the conversion price lowered) by the percentage amount of any stock dividend or split, to protect the convertible holder against dilution.

CONVERSION VALUE

In general: value created by changing from one form to another. For example, converting rental property to condominiums adds to the value of the property.

Convertibles: the price at which the exchange can be made for common stock.

CONVERTIBLES corporate securities (usually preferred shares or bonds) that are exchangeable for a set number of another form (usually common shares) at a prestated price. Convertibles are appropriate for investors who want higher income than is available from common stock, together with greater appreciation potential than regular bonds offer. From the issuer's standpoint, the convertible feature is usually designed as a sweetener, to enhance the marketability of the stock or preferred.

COOLING-OFF PERIOD

1. interval (usually 20 days) between the filing of a preliminary prospectus with the Securities and Exchange Commission and the offer of the securities to the public. *See also* REGISTRATION.

2. period during which a union is prohibited from striking, or an employer from locking out employees. The period, typically 30 to 90 days, may be required by law or provided for in a labor agreement.

COOPERATIVE organization owned by its members.

In real estate, a property whose residents own shares in a cooperative giving them exclusive use of their apartments. Decisions about common areas—hallways, elevators, grounds—are made by a vote of members' shares. Members also approve sales of apartments.

Agriculture cooperatives help farmers sell their products more efficiently. Food cooperatives buy food for their members at wholesale prices, but usually require members to help run the organization.

CORNERING THE MARKET purchasing a security or commodity in such volume that control over its price is achieved. A cornered market in a security would be unhappy news for a short seller, who would have to pay an inflated price to cover. Cornering has been illegal for some years.

CORPORATE BOND debt instrument issued by a private corporation, as distinct from one issued by a government agency or a municipality. Corporates typically have four distinguishing features: (1) they are taxable; (2) they have a par value of $1000; (3) they have a term maturity—which means they come due all at once—and are paid for out of a sinking fund accumulated for that purpose; (4) they are traded on major exchanges, with prices published in newspapers. *See also* BOND; MUNICIPAL BOND.

CORPORATE EQUIVALENT YIELD comparison that dealers in government bonds include in their offering sheets to show the after-tax yield of government bonds selling at a discount and corporate bonds selling at par.

CORPORATE FINANCING COMMITTEE NATIONAL ASSOCIATION OF SECURITIES DEALERS standing committee that reviews documentation submitted by underwriters in compliance with Securities and Exchange Commission requirements to ensure that proposed markups are fair and in the public interest.

CORPORATE INCOME FUND (CIF) UNIT INVESTMENT TRUST with a fixed portfolio made up of high-grade securities and instruments, similar to a MONEY MARKET FUND. Most CIFs pay out investment income monthly.

CORPORATE INSIDER *see* INSIDER.

CORPORATION legal entity, chartered by a U.S. state or by the federal government, and separate and distinct from the persons who own it, giving rise to a jurist's remark that it has "neither a soul to damn nor a body to kick." Nonetheless, it is regarded by the courts as an artificial person; it may own property, incur debts, sue, or be sued. It has three chief distinguishing features:
1. limited liability; owners can lose only what they invest.
2. easy transfer of ownership through the sale of shares of stock.
3. continuity of existence.
   Other factors helping to explain the popularity of the corporate form of organization are its ability to obtain capital through expanded ownership, and the shareholders' ability to profit from the growth of the business.

CORPUS Latin for *body*.
1. in trust banking, the property in a trust—real estate, securities and other personal property, cash in bank accounts, and any other items included by the donor.
2. body of an investment or note, representing the principal or capital as distinct from the interest or income.

CORRECTION reverse movement, usually downward, in the price of an individual stock, bond, commodity, or index. If prices have been rising on the market as a whole, then fall dramatically, this is known as a *correction within an upward trend*. Technical analysts note that markets do not move straight up or down and that corrections are to be expected during any long-term move.

CORRECTION

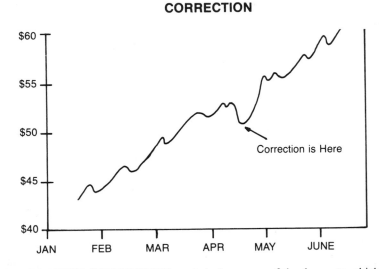

CORRELATION COEFFICIENT statistical measure of the degree to which the movements of two variables are related.

CORRESPONDENT financial organization that regularly performs services for another in a market inaccessible to the other. In banking there is usually a depository relationship that compensates for expenses and facilitates transactions.

COST ACCOUNTING branch of accounting concerned with providing the information that enables the management of a firm to evaluate production costs.

COST BASIS original price of an asset, used in determining capital gains. It usually is the purchase price, but in the case of an inheritance it is the appraised value of the asset at the time of the donor's death.

COST-BENEFIT ANALYSIS method of measuring the benefits expected from a decision, calculating the cost of the decision, then determining whether the benefits outweigh the costs. Corporations use this method in deciding whether to buy a piece of equipment, and the government uses it in determining whether federal programs are achieving their goals.

COST OF CAPITAL rate of return that a business could earn if it chose another investment with equivalent risk—in other words, the OPPORTUNITY COST of the funds employed as the result of an investment decision. Cost of capital is also calculated using a weighted average of a firm's costs of debt and classes of equity. This is also called the *composite cost of capital.*

COST OF CARRY out-of-pocket costs incurred while an investor has an investment position, among them interest on long positions in margin accounts, dividends lost on short margin positions, and incidental expenses.

COST OF GOODS SOLD figure representing the cost of buying raw materials and producing finished goods. Depreciation is considered a part of this cost but is usually listed separately. Included in the direct costs are clear-cut factors such as direct factory labor as well as others that are less clear-cut, such as overhead. *Cost of sales* may be used as a synonym or may mean selling expenses. See also DIRECT OVERHEAD; FIRST IN, FIRST OUT; LAST IN, FIRST OUT.

COST-OF-LIVING ADJUSTMENT (COLA) adjustment of wages designed to offset changes in the cost of living, usually as measured by the CONSUMER PRICE INDEX. COLAs are key bargaining issues in labor contracts and are politically sensitive elements of social security payments and federal pensions because they affect millions of people.

COST-OF-LIVING INDEX *see* CONSUMER PRICE INDEX.

COST OF SALES *see* COST OF GOODS SOLD.

COST-PLUS CONTRACT contract basing the selling price of a product on the total cost incurred in making it plus a stated percentage or a fixed fee—called a *cost-plus-fixed-fee contract.* Cost-plus contracts are common when there is no historical basis for estimating costs and the producer would run a risk of loss— defense contracts involving sophisticated technology, for example. The alternative is a FIXED PRICE contract.

COST-PUSH INFLATION inflation caused by rising prices, which follow on the heels of rising costs. This is the sequence: When the demand for raw materials exceeds the suply, prices go up. As manufacturers pay more for these raw materials they raise the prices they charge merchants for the finished products, and the merchants in turn raise the prices they charge consumers. *See also* DEMAND-PULL INFLATION: INFLATION.

COST RECORDS
1. investor records of the prices at which securities were purchased, which provide the basis for computing capital gains.
2. in finance, anything that can substantiate the costs incurred in producing goods, providing services, or supporting an activity designed to be productive. Ledgers, schedules, vouchers, and invoices are cost records.

COUNCIL OF ECONOMIC ADVISERS group of economists appointed by the President of the United States to provide counsel on economic policy. The council helps to prepare the President's budget message to Congress, and its chairman frequently speaks for the administration's economic policy.

COUPON interest rate on a debt security the issuer promises to pay to the holder until maturity, expressed as an annual percentage of face value. For example, a bond with a 10% coupon will pay $10 per $100 of the face amount per year, usually in installments paid every six months. The term derives from the small detachable segment of a bond certificate which, when presented to the bond's issuer, entitles the holder to the interest due on that date. As the REGISTERED BOND becomes more widespread, coupons are gradually disappearing.

COUPON BOND bond issued with detachable coupons that must be presented to a paying agent or the issuer for semiannual interest payment. These are bearer bonds, so whoever presents the coupon is entitled to the interest. Once universal, the coupon bond has been gradually giving way to the REGISTERED BOND, some of which pay interest through electronic transfers. *See also* BOOK-ENTRY SECURITIES; CERTIFICATELESS MUNICIPALS; COUPON.

COUPON COLLECTION see COLLECTION.

COUPON-EQUIVALENT RATE Same as EQUIVALENT BOND YIELD.

COVARIANCE statistical term for the correlation between two variables multiplied by the standard deviation for each of the variables.

COVENANT promise in a trust indenture or other formal debt agreement that certain acts will be performed and others refrained from. Designed to protect the lender's interest, covenants cover such matters as working capital, debt-equity ratios, and dividend payments. Also called *restrictive covenant* or *protective covenant*.

COVER
1. to buy back contracts previously sold; said of an investor who has sold stock or commodities short.
2. in corporate finance, to meet fixed annual charges on bonds, leases, and other obligations, out of earnings.
3. amount of net-asset value underlying a bond or equity security. Coverage is an important aspect of a bond's safety rating.

COVERED OPTION option contract backed by the shares underlying the option. For instance, someone who owns 300 shares of XYZ and sells three XYZ call options is in a covered option position. If the XYZ stock price goes up and the option is exercised, the investor has the stock to deliver to the buyer. Selling a call brings a premium from the buyer. See also NAKED OPTION.

COVERED WRITER seller of covered options—in other words, an owner of stock who sells options against it to collect premium income. For example, when writing a CALL OPTION, if a stock price stays stable or drops, the seller will be able to hold onto the stock. If the price rises sharply enough, it will have to be given up to the option buyer.

COVERING SHORT see COVER.

CRASH precipitate drop in stock prices and economic activity, as in the crash of 1929, which initiated the Great Depression. Crashes are usually brought on by a loss in investor confidence following periods of high inflation.

CREDIT
In general: loans, bonds, charge-account obligations, and openaccount balances with commercial firms. Also, available but unused bank letters of credit and other standby commitments as well as a variety of consumer credit facilities.
   On another level, discipline in which lending officers and industrial credit people are professionals. At its loftiest it is defined in Dun & Bradstreet's motto: "Credit—Man's Confidence in Man."
Accounting: entry—or the act of making an entry—that increases liabilities, owners' equity, revenue, and gains, and decreases assets and expenses. See also CREDIT BALANCE.
Customer's statement of account: adjustment in the customer's favor, or increase in equity.

CREDIT ANALYST person who (1) analyzes the record and financial affairs of an individual or a corporation to ascertain creditworthiness or (2) determines the credit ratings of corporate and municipal bonds by studying the financial condition and trends of the issuers.

CREDIT BALANCE
In general: account balance in the customer's favor. *See also* CREDIT.

Securities: in cash accounts with brokers, money deposited and remaining after purchases have been paid for, plus the uninvested proceeds from securities sold. In margin accounts, (1) proceeds from short sales, held in escrow for the securities borrowed for these sales; (2) free credit balances, or net balances, which can be withdrawn at will. SPECIAL MISCELLANEOUS ACCOUNT balances are not counted as free credit balances.

CREDIT INSURANCE protection against *abnormal* losses from unpaid accounts receivable, often a requirement of banks lending against accounts receivable.

In consumer credit, life or accident coverage protecting the creditor against loss in the event of death or disability, usually stated as a percentage of the loan balance.

CREDITOR'S COMMITTEE group representing firms that have claims on a company in financial difficulty or bankruptcy; sometimes used as an alternative to legal bankruptcy, especially by smaller firms.

CREDIT RATING formal evaluation of an individual's or company's credit history and capability of repaying obligations. Any number of firms investigate, analyze, and maintain records on the credit responsibility of individuals and businesses— TRW (individuals) and Dun & Bradstreet (commercial firms), for example. The bond ratings assigned by Standard & Poor's and Moody's are also a form of credit RATING. Most large companies and lending institutions assign credit ratings to existing and potential customers.

CREDIT RISK financial and moral risk that an obligation will not be paid and a loss will result.

CREDIT SPREAD difference in the value of two options, when the value of the one sold exceeds the value of the one bought. The opposite of a DEBIT SPREAD.

CREDIT UNION not-for-profit financial institution typically formed by employees of a company, a labor union, or a religious group and operated as a cooperative. Credit unions may offer a full range of financial services and pay higher rates on deposits and charge lower rates on loans than commercial banks. Federally chartered credit unions are regulated and insured by the National Credit Union Administration.

CREEPING TENDER OFFER strategy whereby individuals ACTING IN CONCERT circumvent WILLIAMS ACT provisions by gradually acquiring TARGET COMPANY shares from arbitrageurs and other sellers in the open market. *See also* TENDER OFFER.

CROSS securities transaction in which the same broker acts as agent in both sides of the trade. The practice—called crossing—is legal only if the broker first offers the securities publicly at a price higher than the bid.

CROSSED TRADE manipulative practice prohibited on major exchanges whereby buy and sell orders are offset without recording the trade on the exchange, thus perhaps depriving the investor of the chance to trade at a more favorable price. Also called *crossed sale*.

CROWD group of exchange members with a defined area of function tending to congregate around a trading post pending execution of orders. These are specialists, floor traders, odd-lot dealers, and other brokers as well as smaller groups with specialized functions—the INACTIVE BOND CROWD, for example.

CROWDING OUT heavy federal borrowing at a time when businesses and consumers also want to borrow money. Because the government can pay any interest rate it has to and individuals and businesses can't, the latter are crowded out of credit markets by high interest rates. Crowding out can thus cause economic activity to slow.

CROWN JEWELS the most desirable entities within a diversified corporation as measured by asset value, earning power and business prospects. The crown jewels usually figure prominently in takeover attempts; they typically are the main objective of the acquirer and may be sold by a takeover target to make the rest of the company less attractive to the acquirer.

CROWN LOAN demand loan by a high-income individual to a low-income relative, usually a child or elderly parent. This device was named for Chicago industrialist Harry Crown, who first used it. The money would be invested and the income would be taxable at the borrower's lower rates. For years, the crown loan provided a substantial tax benefit for all parties involved, since such loans could be made interest-free. In 1984 the U.S. Supreme Court ruled that such loans had to be made at the market rate of interest or be subject to gift taxes.

CUM DIVIDEND with dividend; said of a stock whose buyer is eligible to receive a declared dividend. Stocks are usually cum dividend for trades made on or before the fifth day preceding the RECORD DATE, when the register of eligible holders is closed for that dividend period. Trades after the fifth day go EX-DIVIDEND.

CUM RIGHTS with rights; said of stocks that entitle the purchaser to buy a specified amount of stock that is yet to be issued. The cut-off date when the stocks go from cum rights to EX-RIGHTS (without rights) is stipulated in the prospectus accompanying the rights distribution.

CUMULATIVE PREFERRED preferred stock whose dividends if omitted because of insufficient earnings or any other reason accumulate until paid out. They have precedence over common dividends, which cannot be paid if a cumulative preferred obligation exists. Most preferred stock issued today is cumulative.

CUMULATIVE VOTING voting method that improves minority shareholders' chances of naming representatives on the board of directors. In regular or statutory voting, stockholders must apportion their votes equally among candidates for director. Cumulative voting allows shareholders to cast all their votes for one candidate. Assuming one vote per share, 100 shares owned, and six directors to be elected, the regular method lets the shareholder cast 100 votes for each of six candidates for director, a total of 600 votes. The cumulative method lets the same 600 votes be cast for one candidate or split as the shareholder wishes. Cumulative voting is a popular cause among advocates of corporate democracy, but it remains the exception rather than the rule.

CURB *see* AMERICAN STOCK EXCHANGE.

CURRENCY FUTURES contracts in the futures markets that are for delivery in a major currency such as U.S. dollars, British pounds, French francs, German marks, Swiss francs, or Japanese yen. Corporations that sell products around the world can hedge their currency risk with these futures.

CURRENCY IN CIRCULATION paper money and coins circulating in the economy, counted as part of the total money in circulation, which includes DEMAND DEPOSITS in banks.

CURRENT ASSETS cash, accounts receivable, inventory, and other assets such as inventory that are likely to be converted into cash, sold, exchanged, or expensed in the normal course of business, usually within a year.

CURRENT COUPON BOND corporate, federal, or municipal bond with a coupon within half a percentage point of current market rates. These bonds are less volatile than similarly rated bonds with lower coupons because the interest they pay is competitive with current market instruments.

CURRENT LIABILITY debt or other obligation coming due within a year.

CURRENT MARKET VALUE present worth of a client's portfolio at today's market price, as listed in a brokerage statement every month—or more often if stocks are bought on margin or sold short. For listed stocks and bonds the current market value is determined by closing prices; for over-the-counter securities the bid price is used.

CURRENT MATURITY interval between the present time and the maturity date of a bond issue, as distinguished from original maturity, which is the time difference between the issue date and the maturity date. For example, in 1987 a bond issued in 1985 to mature in 2005 would have an original maturity of 20 years and a current maturity of 18 years.

CURRENT PRODUCTION RATE top interest rate allowed on current GOVERNMENT NATIONAL MORTGAGE ASSOCIATION mortgage-backed securities, usually half a percentage point below the current mortgage rate to defray administrative costs of the mortgage servicing company. For instance, when homeowners are paying 13½% on mortgages, an investor in a GNMA pool including those mortgages will get a current production rate of 13%.

CURRENT RATIO current assets divided by current liabilities. The ratio shows a company's ability to pay its current obligations from current assets. For the most part, a company that has a small inventory and readily collectible accounts receivable can operate safely with a lower current ratio than a company whose cash flow is less dependable. *See also* QUICK RATIO.

CURRENT YIELD annual interest on a bond divided by the market price. It is the actual income rate of return as opposed to the coupon rate (the two would be equal if the bond were bought at par) or the yield to maturity. For example, a 10% (coupon rate) bond with a face (or par) value of $1000 is bought at a market price of $800. The annual income from the bond is $100. But since only $800 was paid for the bond, the current yield is $100 divided by $800, or 12½%.

CUSHION
1. interval between the time a bond is issued and the time it can be called. Also termed CALL PROTECTION.

2. margin of safety for a corporation's financial ratios. For instance, if its DEBT-TO-EQUITY RATIO has a cushion of up to 40% debt, anything over that level might be cause for concern.

3. *see* LAST IN, FIRST OUT.

CUSHION BOND callable bond with a coupon above current market interest rates that is selling for a premium. Cushion bonds lose less of their value as rates rise and gain less in value as rates fall, making them suitable for conservative investors interested in high income.

CUSHION THEORY theory that a stock's price must rise if many investors are taking short positions in it, because those positions must be covered by purchases of the stock. Technical analysts consider it particularly bullish if the short positions in a stock are twice as high as the number of shares traded daily. This is because price rises force short sellers to cover their positions, making the stock rise even more.

CUSTODIAL ACCOUNT account that parents create for a minor, usually at a bank or brokerage firm. Minors cannot make securities transactions without the approval of the account trustee. The TAX REFORM ACT OF 1986 taxes earnings over $1000 in a custodial account at the parent's tax rate, but only if the child is younger than 14 years old. For a child 14 years or older, earnings are taxed at the child's rate. *See also* CLIFFORD TRUST; CROWN LOAN; UNIFORM GIFTS TO MINORS ACT.

CUSTODIAN bank or other financial institution that keeps custody of stock certificates and other assets of a mutual fund, individual, or corporate client. *See also* CUSTODIAL ACCOUNT.

CUSTOMER'S LOAN CONSENT agreement signed by a margin customer permitting a broker to borrow margined securities to the limit of the customer's debit balance for the purpose of covering other customers' short positions and certain failures to complete delivery.

CUSTOMER'S MAN traditionally a synonym for *registered representative, account executive,* or *account representative.* Now used rarely, as more women work in brokerages.

CUSTOMERS' NET DEBIT BALANCE total credit extended by New York Stock Exchange member firms to finance customer purchases of securities.

CUTOFF POINT in capital budgeting, the minimum rate of return acceptable on investments.

CYCLE *see* BUSINESS CYCLE.

CYCLICAL STOCK stock that tends to rise quickly when the economy turns up and to fall quickly when the economy turns down. Examples are housing, automobiles, and paper. Stocks of noncyclical industries—such as foods, insurance, drugs—are not as directly affected by economic changes.

d

DAILY TRADING LIMIT maximum that many commodities and options markets are allowed to rise or fall in one day. When a market reaches its limit early and stays there all day, it is said to be having an up-limit or down-limit day. Exchanges usually impose a daily trading limit on each contract. For example, the Chicago Board of Trade limit is two points ($2000 per contract) up or down on its treasury bond futures options contract.

DAISY CHAIN trading between market manipulators to create the appearance of active volume as a lure for legitimate investors. When these traders drive the price up, the manipulators unload their holdings, leaving the unwary investors without buyers to trade with in turn.

DATED DATE date from which accrued interest is calculated on new bonds and other debt instruments. The buyer pays the issuer an amount equal to the interest accrued from the dated date to the issue's settlement date. With the first interest payment on the bond, the buyer is reimbursed.

DATE OF RECORD date on which a shareholder must officially own shares in order to be entitled to a dividend. For example, the board of directors of a corporation might declare a dividend on November 1 payable on December 1 to stockholders of record on November 15. After the date of record the stock is said to be EX-DIVIDEND. Also called *record date*.

DATING in commercial transactions, extension of credit beyond the supplier's customary terms—for example, 90 days instead of 30 days. In industries marked by high seasonality and long lead time, dating, combined with ACCOUNTS RE-CEIVABLE FINANCING, makes it possible for manufacturers with lean capital to continue producing goods. Also called *seasonal dating, special dating*.

DAY LOAN loan from a bank to a broker for the purchase of securities pending delivery through the afternoon clearing. Once delivered the securities are pledged as collateral and the loan becomes a regular broker's call loan. Also called *morning loan*.

DAY ORDER order to buy or sell securities that expires unless executed or canceled the day it is placed. All orders are day orders unless otherwise specified. The main exception is a GOOD-TILL-CANCELED ORDER, though even it can be executed the same day if conditions are right.

DAY TRADE purchase and sale of a position during the same day.

DEALER
1. individual or firm acting as a PRINCIPAL in a securities transaction. Principals trade for their own account and risk. When buying from a broker acting as a dealer, a customer receives securities from the firm's inventory; the confirmation must disclose this. When specialists trade for their own account, as they must as part of their responsibility for maintaining an orderly market, they act as dealers. Since most brokerage firms operate both as brokers and as principals, the term *broker-dealer* is commonly used.
2. one who purchases goods or services for resale to consumers. The element of inventory risk is what distinguishes a dealer from an agent or sales representative.

DEAL STOCK stock affected by TAKEOVER rumors or activities. See also GARBA-TRAGE; IN PLAY; RUMORTRAGE.

DEBENTURE general debt obligation backed only by the integrity of the borrower and documented by an agreement called an INDENTURE. An *unsecured bond* is a debenture.

DEBENTURE STOCK stock issued under a contract providing for fixed payments at scheduled intervals and more like preferred stock than a DEBENTURE, since their status in liquidation is equity and not debt.

Also, a type of bond issued by Canadian and British corporations, which refer to debt issues as stock.

DEBIT BALANCE
1. account balance representing money owed to the lender or seller.
2. money a margin customer owes a broker for loans to purchase securities.

DEBIT SPREAD difference in the value of two options, when the value of the one bought exceeds the value of the one sold. The opposite of a CREDIT SPREAD.

DEBT
1. money, goods, or services that one party is obligated to pay to another in accordance with an expressed or implied agreement. Debt may or may not be secured.
2. general name for bonds, notes, mortgages, and other forms of paper evidencing amounts owed and payable on specified dates or ondemand.

DEBT INSTRUMENT written promise to repay a debt; for instance, a BILL, NOTE, BOND, banker's ACCEPTANCE, CERTIFICATE OF DEPOSIT, or COMMERCIAL PAPER.

DEBTOR person or business that owes money. The person or business on the other side of the transaction is the *creditor*.

DEBT RETIREMENT repayment of debt. The most common method of retiring corporate debt is to set aside money each year in a SINKING FUND.

Most municipal bonds and some corporates are issued in serial form, meaning different portions of an issue—called series—are retired at different times, usually on an annual or semiannual schedule.

Sinking fund bonds and serial bonds are not classes of bonds, just methods of retiring them that are adaptable to debentures, convertibles, and so on. *See also* REFUNDING.

DEBT SECURITY security representing money borrowed that must be repaid and having a fixed amount, a specific maturity or maturities, and usually a specific rate of interest or an original purchase discount. For instance, a BILL, BOND, COMMERCIAL PAPER, or a NOTE.

DEBT SERVICE cash required in a given period, usually one year, for payments of interest and current maturities of principal on outstanding debt. In corporate bond issues, the annual interest plus annual sinking fund payments; in government bonds, the annual payments into the debt service fund. *See also* ABILITY TO PAY.

DEBT-TO-EQUITY RATIO
1. total liabilities divided by total shareholders' equity. This shows to what extent owner's equity can cushion creditors' claims in the event of liquidation.
2. total long-term debt divided by total shareholders' equity. This is a measure of LEVERAGE—the use of borrowed money to enhance the return on owners' equity.

3. long-term debt and preferred stock divided by common stock equity. This relates securities with fixed charges to those without fixed charges.

DECLARE authorize the payment of a dividend on a specified date, an act of the board of directors of a corporation. Once declared, a dividend becomes an obligation of the issuing corporation.

DEDUCTION
1. expense allowed by the Internal Revenue Service as a subtraction from adjusted gross income in arriving at a person's taxable income. Such deductions include interest paid, state and local taxes, charitable contributions.
2. adjustment to an invoice allowed by a seller for a discrepancy, shortage, and so on.

DEED written instrument containing some transfer, bargain, or contract relating to property—most commonly, conveying the legal title to real estate from one party to another.

DEEP DISCOUNT BOND bond selling for a discount of more than about 20% from its face value. Unlike a CURRENT COUPON BOND, which has a higher interest rate, a deep discount bond will appreciate faster as interest rates fall and drop faster as rates rise. Unlike ORIGINAL ISSUE DISCOUNT bonds, deep discounts were issued at a par value of $1000.

DEEP IN/OUT OF THE MONEY CALL OPTION whose exercise price is well below the market price of the underlying stock (deep *in* the money) or well above the market price (deep *out of* the money). The situation would be exactly the opposite for a PUT OPTION. The premium for buying a deep-in-the-money option is high, since the holder has the right to purchase the stock at a striking price considerably below the current price of the stock. The premium for buying a deep-out-of-the-money option is very small, on the other hand, since the option may never be profitable.

DEFAULT failure of a debtor to make timely payments of interest and principal as they come due or to meet some other provision of a bond indenture. In the event of default, bondholders may make claims against the assets of the issuer in order to recoup their principal.

DEFEASANCE

In general: provision found in some debt agreements whereby the contract is nullified if specified acts are performed.

Corporate finance: short for in-substance defeasance, a technique whereby a corporation discharges old, low-rate debt without repaying it prior to maturity. The corporation uses newly purchased securities with a lower face value but paying higher interest or having a higher market value. The objective is a cleaner (more debt free) balance sheet and increased earnings in the amount by which the face amount of the old debt exceeds the cost of the new securities. The use of defeasance in modern corporate finance began in 1982 when Exxon bought and put in an irrevocable trust $312 million of U.S. government securities yielding 14% to provide for the repayment of principal and interest on $515 million of old debt paying 5.8% to 6.7% and maturing in 2009. Exxon removed the defeased debt from its balance sheet and added $132 million—the after-tax difference between $515 million and $312 million—to its earnings that quarter.

In another type of defeasance, a company instructs a broker to buy, for a fee, the outstanding portion of an old bond issue of the company. The broker then exchanges the bond issue for a new issue of the company's stock with an equal market value. The broker subsequently sells the stock at a profit.

DEFENSIVE SECURITIES stocks and bonds that are more stable than average and provide a safe return on an investor's money. When the stock market is weak, defensive securities tend to decline less than the overall market.

DEFERRAL OF TAXES postponement of tax payments from this year to a later year. For instance, an INDIVIDUAL RETIREMENT ACCOUNT (IRA) defers taxes until the money is withdrawn.

DEFERRED ACCOUNT account that postpones taxes until a later date. Some examples: INDIVIDUAL RETIREMENT ACCOUNT, KEOGH PLAN accounts, ANNUITY, PROFIT-SHARING PLAN, SALARY REDUCTION PLAN.

DEFERRED CHARGE expenditure carried forward as an asset until it becomes relevant, such as an advance rent payment or insurance premium. The opposite is *deferred income,* such as advance rent received.

DEFERRED INTEREST BOND bond that pays interest at a later date. A ZERO COUPON BOND, which pays interest and repays principal in one lump sum at maturity, is in this category. In effect, such bonds automatically reinvest the interest at a fixed rate. Prices are more volatile for a deferred interest bond than for a CURRENT COUPON BOND.

DEFERRED PAYMENT ANNUITY annuity whose contract provides that payments to the annuitant be postponed until a number of periods have elapsed—for example, when the annuitant attains a certain age. Also called a *deferred annuity.*

DEFERRED SALES CHARGE *see* BACK-END LOAD.

DEFICIENCY LETTER written notice from the Securities and Exchange Commission to a prospective issuer of securities that the preliminary prospectus needs revision or expansion. Deficiency letters require prompt action; otherwise, the registration period may be prolonged.

DEFICIT
1. excess of liabilities and debts over income and assets. Deficits usually are corrected by borrowing or by selling assets.
2. in finance, an excess of expenditures over budget.

DEFICIT FINANCING borrowing by a government agency to make up for a revenue shortfall. Deficit financing stimulates the economy for a time but eventually can become a drag on the economy by pushing up interest rates. *See also* CROWDING OUT; KEYNESIAN ECONOMICS.

DEFICIT NET WORTH excess of liabilities over assets and capital stock, perhaps as a result of operating losses. Also called *negative net worth.*

DEFICIT SPENDING excess of government expenditures over government revenue, creating a shortfall that must be financed through borrowing. *See also* DEFICIT FINANCING.

DEFINED BENEFIT PENSION PLAN plan that promises to pay a specified amount to each person who retires after a set number of years of service. Such plans pay no taxes on their investments. Employees contribute to them in some cases; in others, all contributions are made by the employer.

DEFLATION decline in the prices of goods and services. Deflation is the reverse of INFLATION; it should not be confused with DISINFLATION, which is a slowing down in the rate of price increases. Generally, the economic effects of deflation are the opposite of those produced by inflation, with two notable exceptions: (1) prices that increase with inflation do not necessarily decrease with deflation—union wage rates, for example; (2) while inflation may or may not stimulate output and employment, marked deflation has always affected both negatively.

DEFLATOR statistical factor or device designed to adjust the difference between real or constant value and value affected by inflation—the *GNP deflator,* for example. *See also* CONSTANT DOLLARS.

DEFLECTION OF TAX LIABILITY legal shift of one person's tax burden to someone else through such methods as the CLIFFORD TRUST, CUSTODIAL ACCOUNTS, and SPOUSAL REMAINDER TRUSTS. Such devices were curtailed but not eliminated by the TAX REFORM ACT OF 1986.

DELAYED DELIVERY delivery of securities later than the scheduled date, which is ordinarily five business days after the trade date. A contract calling for delayed delivery, known as a SELLER'S OPTION, is usually agreed to by both parties to a trade. *See also* DELIVERY DATE.

DELAYED OPENING postponement of the start of trading in a stock until a gross imbalance in buy and sell orders is overcome. Such an imbalance is likely to follow on the heels of a significant event such as a takeover offer.

DELINQUENCY failure to make a payment on an obligation when due. In finance company parlance, the amount of past due balances, determined either on a contractual or recency-of-payment basis.

DELISTING removal of a company's security from an exchange because the firm did not abide by some regulation or the stock does not meet certain financial ratios or sales levels.

DELIVERABLE BILLS financial futures and options trading term meaning Treasury bills that meet all the criteria of the exchange on which they are traded. One such criterion is that the deliverable T-bill is the current bill for the week in which settlement takes place.

DELIVERY DATE
1. first day of the month in which delivery is to be made under a futures contract. Since sales are on a SELLER'S OPTION basis, delivery can be on any day of the month, as long as proper notice is given.
2. fifth business day following a REGULAR WAY transaction on the New York Stock Exchange. Seller's option delivery can be anywhere from 5 to 60 days, though there may be a purchase-price adjustment to compensate for DELAYED DELIVERY. In the case of bonds, regular way delivery means the next business day following a bond sale.

DELIVERY NOTICE
1. notification from the seller to the buyer of a futures contract indicating the date when the actual commodity is to be delivered.
2. in general business transactions, a formal notice documenting that goods have been delivered or will be delivered on a certain date.

DELIVERY VERSUS PAYMENT securities industry procedure, common with institutional accounts, whereby delivery of securities sold is made to the buying customer's bank in exchange for payment, usually in the form of cash. (Institutions are required by law to require "assets of equal value" in exchange for delivery.) Also called CASH ON DELIVERY, delivery against payment, delivery against cash, or, from the sell side, RECEIVE VERSUS PAYMENT.

DELTA
1. measure of the relationship between an option price and the underlying futures contract or stock price. For a call option, a delta of 0.50 means a half-point rise in premium for every dollar that the stock goes up. For a put option contract, the premium rises as stock prices fall. As options near expiration, IN-THE-MONEY contracts approach a delta of 1.
2. on the London Stock Exchange, *delta stocks* are the smallest capitalization issues, and are not shown on the electronic dealing system screens.

DEMAND DEPOSIT account balance which, without prior notice to the bank, can be drawn on by check, cash withdrawal from an automatic teller machine, or by transfer to other accounts using the telephone or home computers. Demand deposits are the largest component of the U.S. MONEY SUPPLY, and the principal medium through which the Federal Reserve implements monetary policy. *See also* COMPENSATING BALANCE.

DEMAND LOAN loan with no set maturity date that can be called for repayment when the lender chooses. Banks usually bill interest on these loans at fixed intervals.

DEMAND-PULL INFLATION price increases occurring when supply is not adequate to meet demand. *See also* COST-PUSH INFLATION.

DEMONETIZATION withdrawal from circulation of a specified form of currency. For example, the Jamaica Agreement between major INTERNATIONAL MONETARY FUND countries officially demonetized gold starting in 1978, ending its role as the major medium of international settlement.

DENOMINATION face value of currency units, coins, and securities. *See also* PAR VALUE.

DEPLETION accounting treatment available to companies that extract oil and gas, coal, or other minerals, usually in the form of an allowance that reduces taxable income. Oil and gas limited partnerships pass the allowance on to their limited partners, who can use it to reduce other tax liabilities.

DEPOSIT
1. cash, checks, or drafts placed with a financial institution for credit to a customer's account. Banks broadly differentiate between demand deposits (check-

ing accounts on which the customer may draw at any time) and time deposits, which usually pay interest and have a specified maturity or require 30 days' notice before withdrawal.
2. securities placed with a bank or other institution or with a person for a particular purpose.
3. sums lodged with utilities, landlords, and service companies as security.
4. money put down as evidence of an intention to complete a contract and to protect the other party in the event that the contract is not completed.

DEPOSITARY RECEIPT *see* AMERICAN DEPOSITARY RECEIPT.

DEPOSITORY INSTITUTIONS DEREGULATION AND MONETARY CONTROL ACT federal legislation of 1980 providing for deregulation of the banking system. The act established the Depository Institutions Deregulation Committee, composed of five voting members, the Secretary of the Treasury and the chair of the Federal Reserve Board, the Federal Home Loan Bank Board, the Federal Deposit Insurance Corporation, and the National Credit Union Administration, and one nonvoting member, the Comptroller of the Currency. The committee is charged with phasing out regulation of interest rates of banks and savings institutions over a six-year period (passbook accounts were deregulated effective April, 1986, under a different federal law). The act authorized interest-bearing NEGOTIABLE ORDER OF WITHDRAWAL (NOW) accounts to be offered anywhere in the country. The act also overruled state usury laws on home mortgages over $25,000 and otherwise modernized mortgages by eliminating dollar limits, permitting second mortgages, and ending territorial restrictions in mortgage lending. Another part of the law permitted stock brokerages to offer checking accounts. *See also* DEREGULATION.

DEPOSITORY TRUST COMPANY central securities repository where stock and bond certificates are exchanged. Most of these exchanges now take place electronically, and few paper certificates actually change hands. The DTC is a member of the Federal Reserve System and is owned by most of the brokerage houses on Wall Street and the New York Stock Exchange.

DEPRECIATED COST original cost of a fixed asset less accumulated DEPRECIATION; this is the *net book value* of the asset.

DEPRECIATION
   Economics: consumption of capital during production—in other words, wearing out of plant and capital goods, such as machines and equipment.
   Finance: amortization of fixed assets, such as plant and equipment, so as to allocate the cost over their depreciable life. Depreciation reduces taxable income but does not reduce cash.
   Among the most commonly used methods are STRAIGHT-LINE DEPRECIATION; ACCELERATED DEPRECIATION; and the ACCELERATED COST RECOVERY SYSTEM. Others include the annuity, appraisal, compound interest, production, replacement, retirement, and sinking fund methods.
   Foreign Exchange: decline in the price of one currency relative to another.

DEPRESSION economic condition characterized by falling prices, reduced purchasing power, an excess of supply over demand, rising unemployment, accumulating inventories, deflation, plant contraction, public fear and caution, and a general decrease in business activity. The Great Depression of the 1930s, centered in the United States and Europe, had worldwide repercussions.

DEREGULATION greatly reducing government regulation in order to allow freer markets to create a more efficient marketplace. After the stock-brokerage industry was deregulated in the mid-1970s, commissions were no longer fixed. After the banking industry was deregulated in the early 1980s, banks were given greater freedom in setting interest rates on deposits and loans. Industries such as communications and transportation have also been deregulated, with similar results: increased competition, heightened innovation, and mergers among weaker competitors. Some government oversight usually remains after deregulation.

DESCENDING TOPS chart pattern wherein each new high price for a security is lower than the preceding high. The trend is considered bearish.

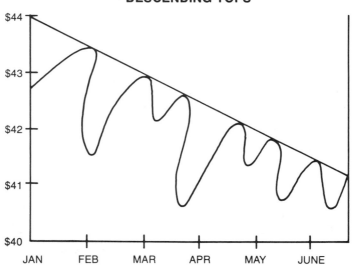

DESCENDING TOPS

DESIGNATED ORDER TURNAROUND (DOT) electronic system used by the New York Stock Exchange to expedite execution of small MARKET ORDERS by routing them directly from the member firm to the SPECIALIST, thus bypassing the FLOOR BROKER. A related system called *Super DOT* routes LIMIT ORDERS.

DESK trading desk, or Securities Department, at the New York FEDERAL RESERVE BANK, which is the operating arm of the FEDERAL OPEN MARKET COMMITTEE. The Desk executes all transactions undertaken by the FEDERAL RESERVE SYSTEM in the money market or the government securities market, serves as the Treasury Department's eyes and ears in these and related markets, and encompasses a foreign desk which conducts transactions in the FOREIGN EXCHANGE market.

DEVALUATION lowering of the value of a country's currency relative to gold and/or the currencies of other nations. Devaluation can also result from a rise in value of other currencies relative to the currency of a particular country.

DEVELOPMENTAL DRILLING PROGRAM drilling for oil and gas in an area with proven reserves to a depth known to have been productive in the past. Limited partners in such a program, which is considerably less risky than an EXPLORATORY DRILLING PROGRAM or WILDCAT DRILLING, have a good chance of steady income, but little chance of enormous profits.

DIAGONAL SPREAD strategy based on a long and short position in the same class of option (two puts or two calls in the same stock) at different striking prices and different expiration dates. Example: a six-month call sold with a striking price of 40 and a three-month call sold with a striking price of 35. *See also* CALENDAR SPREAD; VERTICAL SPREAD.

DIAMOND INVESTMENT TRUST unit trust that invests in high-quality diamonds. Begun in the early 1980s by Thomson McKinnon, these trusts let shareholders invest in diamonds without buying and holding a particular stone. Shares in these trusts do not trade actively and are therefore difficult to sell if diamond prices fall, as they did soon after the first trust was set up.

DIFFERENTIAL small extra charge sometimes called the *odd-lot-differential*—usually ⅛ of a point—that dealers add to purchases and subtract from sales in quantities less than the standard trading unit or ROUND LOT.
  Also, the extent to which a dealer widens his quote to compensate for lack of volume, even though the transaction involves normal trading units.

DIGITS DELETED designation on securities exchange tape meaning that because the tape has been delayed, some digits have been dropped. For example, 26½ . . . 26⅝ . . . 26⅛ becomes 6½ . . . 6⅝ . . . 6⅛.

DILUTION effect on earnings per share and book value per share if all convertible securities were converted or all warrants or stock options were exercised. *See* FULLY DILUTED EARNINGS PER (COMMON) SHARE.

DIP slight drop in securities prices after a sustained uptrend. Analysts often advise investors to buy on dips, meaning buy when a price is momentarily weak.

DIP

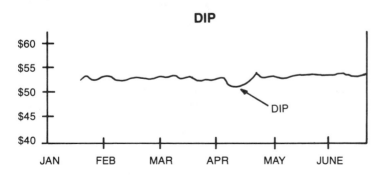

DIRECTOR *see* BOARD OF DIRECTORS.

DIRECT OVERHEAD portion of overhead costs—rent, lights, insurance—allocated to manufacturing, by the application of a standard factor termed a *burden rate*. This amount is absorbed as an INVENTORY cost and ultimately reflected as a COST OF GOODS SOLD.

DIRECT PARTICIPATION PROGRAM program letting investors participate directly in the cash flow and tax benefits of the underlying investments. Such programs are usually organized as LIMITED PARTNERSHIPS, although their uses as tax shelters have been severely curtailed by tax legislation affecting PASSIVE investments.

DIRECT PLACEMENT direct sale of securities to one or more professional investors, typically life-insurance companies. About one third of the new securities offerings in the early 1980s were direct placements, almost all of them bond issues. Also called PRIVATE PLACEMENT.

DISBURSEMENT paying out of money in the discharge of a debt or an expense, as distinguished from a distribution.

DISCHARGE OF BANKRUPTCY order terminating bankruptcy proceedings, ordinarily freeing the debtor of all legal responsibility for specified obligations.

DISCHARGE OF LIEN order removing a lien on property after the originating legal claim has been paid or otherwise satisfied.

DISCLOSURE release by companies of all information, positive or negative, that might bear on an investment decision, as required by the Securities and Exchange Commission and the stock exchanges. *See also* FINANCIAL PUBLIC RELATIONS; INSIDE INFORMATION; INSIDER.

DISCOUNT
1. difference between a bond's current market price and its face or redemption value.
2. manner of selling securities such as treasury bills, which are issued at less than face value and are redeemed at face value.
3. relationship between two currencies. The French franc may sell at a discount to the English pound, for example.
4. to apply all available news about a company in evaluating its current stock price. For instance, taking into account the introduction of an exciting new product.
5. method whereby interest on a bank loan or note is deducted in advance.
6. reduction in the selling price of merchandise or a percentage off the invoice price in exchange for quick payment.

DISCOUNT BOND bond selling below its redemption value. *See also* DEEP DISCOUNT BOND.

DISCOUNT BROKER brokerage house that executes orders to buy and sell securities at commission rates lower than those charged by a FULL SERVICE BROKER.

DISCOUNT DIVIDEND REINVESTMENT PLAN *see* DIVIDEND REINVESTMENT PLAN.

DISCOUNTED CASH FLOW value of future expected cash receipts and expenditures at a common date, which is calculated using NET PRESENT VALUE or INTERNAL RATE OF RETURN and is a factor in analyses of both capital investments and securities investments. The net present value (NPV) method applies a rate of discount (interest rate) based on the marginal cost of capital to future cash flows to bring them back to the present. The internal rate of return (IRR) method finds the average return on investment earned through the life of the investment. It determines the discount rate that equates the present value of future cash flows to the cost of the investment.

DISCOUNTING THE NEWS bidding a firm's stock price up or down in anticipation of good or bad news about the company's prospects.

DISCOUNT RATE
1. interest rate that the Federal Reserve charges member banks for loans, using government securities or ELIGIBLE PAPER as collateral. This provides a floor on interest rates, since banks set their loan rates a notch above the discount rate.
2. interest rate used in determining the PRESENT VALUE of future CASH FLOWS. *See also* CAPITALIZATION RATE.

DISCOUNT WINDOW place in the Federal Reserve where banks go to borrow money at the DISCOUNT RATE. Borrowing from the Fed is a privilege, not a right, and banks are discouraged from using the privilege except when they are short of reserves.

DISCOUNT YIELD yield on a security sold at a discount—U.S. Treasury bills sold at $9750 and maturing at $10,000 in 90 days, for instance. Also called *bank discount basis*. To figure the annual yield, divide the discount ($250) by the face amount ($10,000) and multiply that number by the approximate number of days in the year (360) divided by the number of days to maturity (90). The calculation looks like this:

$$\frac{\$250}{\$10,000} \times \frac{360}{90} = .025 \times 4 = .10 = 10\%.$$

DISCRETIONARY ACCOUNT account giving a broker the power to buy and sell securities, without the client's prior knowledge or consent. Some clients set broad guidelines, such as limiting investments to blue chip stocks.

DISCRETIONARY INCOME amount of a consumer's income spent after essentials like food, housing, and utilities and prior commitments have been covered. The total amount of discretionary income can be a key economic indicator because spending this money can spur the economy.

DISCRETIONARY ORDER order to buy a particular stock, bond, or commodity that lets the broker decide when to execute the trade and at what price.

DISCRETIONARY TRUST
1. mutual fund or unit trust whose investments are not limited to a certain kind of security. The management decides on the best way to use the assets.
2. personal trust that lets the trustee decide how much income or principal to provide to the beneficiary. This can be used to prevent the beneficiary from dissipating funds.

DISINFLATION slowing down of the rate at which prices increase—usually during a recession, when sales drop and retailers are not always able to pass on higher prices to consumers. Not to be confused with DEFLATION, when prices actually drop.

DISINTERMEDIATION movement of funds from low-yielding accounts at traditional banking institutions to higher-yielding investments in the general market—for example, withdrawal of funds from a passbook savings account paying

5½% to buy a Treasury bill paying 10%. As a counter move, banks may pay higher rates to depositors, then charge higher rates to borrowers, which leads to tight money and reduced economic activity. Since banking DEREGULATION, disintermediation is not the economic problem it once was.

DISINVESTMENT reduction in capital investment either by disposing of capital goods (such as plant and equipment) or by failing to maintain or replace capital assets that are being used up.

DISPOSABLE INCOME personal income remaining after personal taxes and noncommercial government fees have been paid. This money can be spent on essentials or nonessentials or it can be saved. *See also* DISCRETIONARY INCOME.

DISTRIBUTING SYNDICATE group of brokerage firms or investment bankers that join forces in order to facilitate the DISTRIBUTION of a large block of securities. A distribution is usually handled over a period of time to avoid upsetting the market price. The term distributing syndicate can refer to a primary distribution or a secondary distribution, but the former is more commonly called simply a syndicate or an underwriting syndicate.

DISTRIBUTION

Corporate finance: allocation of income and expenses to the appropriate subsidiary accounts.

Economics: (1) movement of goods from manufacturers; (2) way in which wealth is shared in any particular economic system.

Estate law: parceling out of assets to the beneficiaries named in a will, as carried out by the executor under the guidance of a court.

Mutual funds and closed-end investment companies: payout of realized capital gains on securities in the portfolio of the fund or closed-end investment company.

Securities: sale of a large block of stock in such manner that the price is not adversely affected. Technical analysts look on a pattern of distribution as a tipoff that the stock will soon fall in price. The opposite of distribution, known as ACCUMULATION, may signal a rise in price.

DISTRIBUTION AREA price range in which a stock trades for a long time. Sellers who want to avoid pushing the price down will be careful not to sell below this range. ACCUMULATION of shares in the same range helps to account for the stock's price stability. Technical analysts consider distribution areas in predicting when stocks may break up or down from that price range. *See also* ACCUMULATION AREA.

DISTRIBUTION STOCK stock part of a block sold over a period of time in order to avoid upsetting the market price. May be part of a primary (underwriting) distribution or a secondary distribution following SHELF REGISTRATION.

DISTRIBUTOR wholesaler of goods to dealers that sell to the consumer market.

DIVERSIFICATION
1. spreading of risk by putting assets in several categories of investments—stocks, bonds, money market instruments, and precious metals, for instance, or several industries, or a mutual fund, with its broad range of stocks in one portfolio.

2. at the corporate level, entering different business areas, as a CONGLOMERATE does.

DIVERSIFIED INVESTMENT COMPANY mutual fund or unit trust that invests in a wide range of securities. Under the Investment Company Act of 1940, such a company may not have more than 5% of its assets in any one stock, bond, or commodity and may not own more than 10% of the voting shares of any one company.

DIVESTITURE disposition of an asset or investment by outright sale, employee purchase, liquidation, and so on.

Also, one corporation's orderly distribution of large blocks of another corporation's stock, which were held as an investment. Du Pont was ordered by the courts to divest itself of General Motors stock, for example.

DIVIDEND distribution of earnings to shareholders, prorated by class of security and paid in the form of money, stock, scrip, or, rarely, company products or property. The amount is decided by the board of directors and is usually paid quarterly. Dividends must be declared as income in the year they are received.

Mutual fund dividends are paid out of income, usually on a quarterly basis from the fund's investments. The tax on such dividends depends on whether the distributions resulted from capital gains, interest income, or dividends received by the fund, although these distinctions largely disappeared in 1988 under the 1986 Tax Act. *See also* EQUALIZING DIVIDEND; EXTRA DIVIDEND.

DIVIDEND CAPTURE *see* DIVIDEND ROLLOVER PLAN.

DIVIDEND DISCOUNT MODEL mathematical model used to determine the price at which a stock should be selling based on the discounted value of projected future dividend payments. It is used to identify undervalued stocks representing capital gains potential.

DIVIDEND EXCLUSION pre-TAX REFORM ACT OF 1986 provision allowing for subtraction from dividends qualifying as taxable income under Internal Revenue Service rules—$100 for individuals and $200 for married couples filing jointly. The 1986 Tax Act eliminated this exclusion effective for the 1987 tax year.

Domestic corporations may exclude from taxable income 80% of dividends received from other domestic corporations. The exclusion was 85% prior to the 1986 Act.

DIVIDEND IN ARREARS the ACCUMULATED DIVIDEND on CUMULATIVE PREFERRED stock, which is payable to the current holder. Preferred stock in a TURNAROUND situation can be an attractive buy when it is selling at a discount and has dividends in arrears.

DIVIDEND PAYOUT RATIO percentage of earnings paid to shareholders in cash. In general, the higher the payout ratio, the more mature the company. Electric and telephone utilities tend to have the highest payout ratios, whereas fast-growing companies usually reinvest all earnings and pay no dividends.

DIVIDEND RECORD publication of Standard & Poor's Corporation that provides information on corporate dividend policies and payment histories.

DIVIDEND REINVESTMENT PLAN automatic reinvestment of shareholder dividends in more shares of the company's stock. Some companies absorb most or all of the applicable brokerage fees, and some also discount the stock price. Dividend reinvestment plans allow shareholders to accumulate capital over the long term using DOLLAR COST AVERAGING. For corporations, dividend reinvestment plans are a means of raising capital funds without the FLOTATION COSTS of a NEW ISSUE.

DIVIDEND REQUIREMENT amount of annual earnings necessary to pay contracted dividends on preferred stock.

DIVIDEND ROLLOVER PLAN method of buying and selling stocks around their EX-DIVIDEND dates so as to collect the dividend and make a small profit on the trade. This entails buying shares about two weeks before a stock goes ex-dividend. After the ex-dividend date the price will drop by the amount of the dividend, then work its way back up to the earlier price. By selling slightly above the purchase price, the investor can cover brokerage costs, collect the dividend, and realize a small capital gain in three or four weeks. This is a short-term gain and is taxed at regular rates. Also called *dividend capture*. *See also* TRADING DIVIDENDS.

DIVIDENDS PAYABLE dollar amount of dividends that are to be paid, as reported in financial statements. These dividends become an obligation once declared by the board of directors and are listed as liabilities in annual and quarterly reports.

DOCUMENTARY DRAFT *see* DRAFT.

DOLLAR BOND
1. municipal revenue bond quoted and traded on a dollar price basis instead of yield to maturity.
2. bond denominated in U.S. dollars but issued outside the United States, principally in Europe.
3. bond denominated in U.S. dollars and issued in the United States by foreign companies.
See also EUROBOND; EURODOLLAR BOND.

DOLLAR COST AVERAGING *see* CONSTANT DOLLAR PLAN.

DOLLAR DRAIN amount by which a foreign country's imports from the United States exceed its exports to the United States. As the country spends more dollars to finance the imports than it receives in payment for the exports, its dollar reserves drain away.

DOLLAR SHORTAGE situation in which a country that imports from the United States can no longer pay for its purchases without U.S. gifts or loans to provide the necessary dollars. After World War II a worldwide dollar shortage was alleviated by massive infusions of American money through the European Recovery Program (Marshall Plan) and other grant and loan programs.

DOLLAR-WEIGHTED RETURN portfolio accounting method that measures changes in total dollar value, treating additions and withdrawals of capital as a part of the RETURN along with income and capital gains and losses. For example, a portfolio (or group of portfolios) worth $100 million at the beginning of a reporting period and $120 million at the end would show a return of 20%; this would be true even if the investments lost money, provided enough new money was infused. While dollar weighting enables investors to compare absolute dollars with financial goals, manager-to-manager comparisons are not possible unless performance is isolated from external cash flows; this is accomplished with the TIME-WEIGHTED RETURN method.

DOMESTIC ACCEPTANCE see ACCEPTANCE.

DOMESTIC CORPORATION corporation doing business in the U.S. state in which it was incorporated. In all other U.S. states its legal status is that of a FOREIGN CORPORATION.

DONATED STOCK fully paid capital stock of a corporation contributed without CONSIDERATION to the same issuing corporation. The gift is credited to the DONATED SURPLUS account at PAR VALUE.

DONATED SURPLUS shareholder's equity account that is credited when contributions of cash, property, or the firm's own stock are freely given to the company. Also termed *donated capital*. Not to be confused with contributed surplus or contributed capital, which is the balances in CAPITAL STOCK accounts plus capital contributed in excess of par or STATED VALUE accounts.

DONOGHUE'S MONEY FUND AVERAGE average of all major money-market fund yields, published weekly for 7- and 30-day yields. Donoghue also tracks the maturity of securities in money-fund portfolios—a short maturity reflecting the conviction of fund managers that interest rates are going to rise. The Donoghue Average is published in many newspapers.

DO NOT REDUCE (DNR) instruction on a LIMIT ORDER to buy, or on a STOP ORDER to sell, or on a STOP-LIMIT ORDER to sell, not to reduce the order when the stock goes EX-DIVIDEND and its price is reduced by the amount of the dividend as usually happens. DNRs do not apply to rights or stock dividends.

DON'T FIGHT THE TAPE don't trade against the market trend. If stocks are falling, as reported on the BROAD TAPE, some analysts say it would be foolish to buy aggressively. Similarly, it would be fighting the tape to sell short during a market rally.

DON'T KNOW Wall Street slang for a *questioned trade*. Brokers exchange comparison sheets to verify the details of transactions between them. Any discrepancy that turns up is called a don't know or a *QT*.

DOUBLE AUCTION SYSTEM see AUCTION MARKET.

DOUBLE-BARRELED municipal revenue bond whose principal and interest are guaranteed by a larger municipal entity. For example, a bridge authority might issue revenue bonds payable out of revenue from bridge tolls. If the city or state were to guarantee the bonds, they would be double-barreled, and the investor would be protected against default in the event that bridge usage is disappointing and revenue proves inadequate.

DOUBLE BOTTOM technical chart pattern showing a drop in price, then a rebound, then another drop to the same level. The pattern is usually interpreted to mean the security has much support at that price and should not drop further. However, if the price does fall through that level, it is considered likely to reach a new low. *See also* DOUBLE TOP.

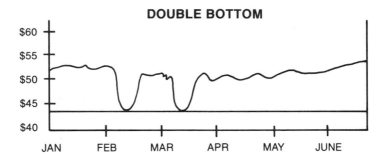

DOUBLE BOTTOM

DOUBLE-DECLINING-BALANCE DEPRECIATION METHOD (DDB) method of accelerated depreciation, approved by the Internal Revenue Service, permitting twice the rate of annual depreciation as the straight-line method. The two methods are compared below, assuming an asset with a total cost of $1000, a useful life of four years, and no SALVAGE VALUE.

YEAR	STRAIGHT LINE		DOUBLE DECLINING BALANCE	
	Expense	Cumulative	Expense	Cumulative
1	$250	$250	$500	$500
2	250	500	250	750
3	250	750	125	875
4	250	1000	63	938
	$1000		$938	

With STRAIGHT-LINE DEPRECIATION the useful life of the asset is divided into the total cost to arrive at the uniform annual charge of $250, or 25% a year. DDB permits twice the straight-line annual percentage rate—50% in this case—to be applied each year to the undepreciated value of the asset. Hence: 50% × $1000 = $500 the first year, 50% × $500 = $250 the second year, and so on.

A variation of DDB, called *150 percent declining balance method,* uses 150% of the straight-line annual percentage rate.

A switch to straight-line from declining balance depreciation is permitted once in the asset's life—logically, at the third year in our example. When the switch is made, however, salvage value must be considered. *See also* ACCELERATED COST RECOVERY SYSTEM; DEPRECIATION.

DOUBLE TAXATION taxation of earnings at the corporate level, then again as stockholder dividends.

DOUBLE TOP technical chart pattern showing a rise to a high price, then a drop, then another rise to the same high price. This means the security is encountering resistance to a move higher. However, if the price does move through that level, the security is expected to go on to a new high. *See also* DOUBLE BOTTOM.

DOW JONES AVERAGES *see* STOCK INDEXES AND AVERAGES.

DOW JONES INDUSTRIAL AVERAGE *see* STOCK INDEXES AND AVERAGES.

DOWNSIDE RISK estimate that a security will decline in value and the extent of the decline, taking into account the total range of factors affecting market price.

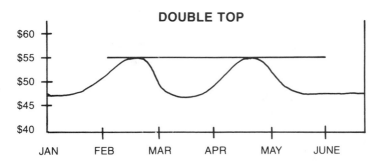

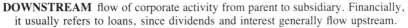

DOWNSTREAM flow of corporate activity from parent to subsidiary. Financially, it usually refers to loans, since dividends and interest generally flow upstream.

DOWNTICK sale of a security at a price below that of the preceding sale. If a stock has been trading at $15 a share, for instance, the next trade is a downtick if it is at 14⅞. Also known as MINUS TICK.

DOWNTURN shift of an economic or stock market cycle from rising to falling. The economy is in a downturn when it moves from expansion to recession, and the stock market is in a downturn when it changes from a bull to a bear market.

DOW THEORY theory that a major trend in the stock market must be confirmed by a similar movement in the Dow Jones Industrial Average and the Dow Jones Transportation Average. According to Dow Theory, a significant trend is not confirmed until both Dow Jones indexes reach the new highs or lows; if they don't, the market will fall back to its former trading range. Dow Theory proponents often disagree on when a true breakout has occurred and, in any case, miss a major portion of the up or down move while waiting for their signals.

DRAFT signed, written order by which one party (drawer) instructs another party (drawee) to pay a specified sum to a third party (payee). Payee and drawer are usually the same person. In foreign transactions, a draft is usually called a *bill of exchange*. When prepared without supporting papers, it is a *clean draft*. With papers or documents attached, it is a *documentary draft*. A *sight draft* is payable on demand. A *time draft* is payable either on a definite date or at a fixed time after sight or demand.

DRAINING RESERVES actions by the Federal Reserve System to decrease the money supply by curtailing the funds banks have available to lend. The Fed does this in three ways: (1) by raising reserve requirements, forcing banks to keep more funds on deposit with Federal Reserve banks; (2) by increasing the rate at which banks borrow to maintain reserves, thereby making it unattractive to deplete reserves by making loans; and (3) by selling bonds in the open market at such attractive rates that dealers reduce their bank balances to buy them. *See also* MULTIPLIER.

DRAWBACK rebate of taxes or duties paid on imported goods that have been reexported. It is in effect a government subsidy designed to encourage domestic manufacturers to compete overseas.

DRAWER *see* DRAFT.

DRILLING PROGRAM *see* BALANCED DRILLING PROGRAM; COMPLETION PRO-

GRAM; DEVELOPMENTAL DRILLING PROGRAM; EXPLORATORY DRILLING PROGRAM; OIL AND GAS LIMITED PARTNERSHIP.

DROPLOCK SECURITY FLOATING RATE NOTE or bond that becomes a FIXED INCOME INVESTMENT when the rate to which it is pegged drops to a specified level.

DUAL BANKING U.S. system whereby banks are chartered by the state or federal government. This makes for differences in banking regulations, in lending limits, and in services available to customers.

DUAL CURRENCY SECURITY stock or bond denominated in more than one currency.

DUAL LISTING listing of a security on more than one exchange to increase liquidity and extend the number of hours when the stock can be traded. Securities may not be listed on both the New York and American stock exchanges.

DUAL PURPOSE FUND exchange-listed CLOSED-END FUND that has two classes of shares. Preferred shareholders receive all the income (dividends and interest) from the portfolio, while common shareholders receive all capital gains. Such funds are set up with a specific expiration date, at which preferred shares are redeemed at a predetermined price and common shareholders claim the remaining assets, voting either to liquidate or to continue the fund on an open-end basis. Dual purpose funds are not closely followed on Wall Street, and there is little trading in them.

DUAL TRADING commodities traders' practice of dealing for their own and their client's accounts at the same time. Reformers favor restricting dual trading to prevent FRONT RUNNING; advocates claim the practice is harmless in itself and economically vital to the industry.

DUE BILL *see* BILL.

DUE DILIGENCE MEETING meeting conducted by the underwriter of a new offering at which brokers can ask representatives of the issuer questions about the issuer's background and financial reliability and the intended use of the proceeds. Brokers who recommend investment in new offerings without very careful due diligence work may face lawsuits if the investment should go sour later. Although, in itself, the legally required due diligence meeting typically is a perfunctory affair, most companies, recognizing the importance of due diligence, hold informational meetings, often in different regions of the country, at which top management representatives are available to answer questions of securities analysts and institutional investors.

DUMPING
   International finance: selling goods abroad below cost in order to eliminate a surplus or to gain an edge on foreign competition. The U.S. Antidumping Act of 1974 was designed to prevent the sale of imported goods below cost in the United States.
   Securities: offering large amounts of stock with little or no concern for price or market effect.

DUN & BRADSTREET (D & B) company that combines credit information obtained directly from commercial firms with data solicited from their creditors, then makes this available to subscribers in reports and a ratings directory. D & B also offers an accounts receivable collection service and publishes financial composite ratios and other financial information. A subsidiary, MOODY'S INVESTORS SERVICE, rates bonds and commercial paper.

DUN'S NUMBER short for Dun's Market Identifier. It is published as part of a list of firms giving information such as an identification number, address code, number of employees, corporate affiliations, and trade styles. Full name: Data Universal Numbering System.

DUTCH AUCTION auction system in which the price of an item is gradually lowered until it meets a responsive bid and is sold. U.S. Treasury bills are sold under this system. Contrasting is the two-sided or DOUBLE AUCTION SYSTEM exemplified by the major stock exchanges. *See also* BILL.

DUTCH AUCTION PREFERRED STOCK type of adjustable-rate PREFERRED STOCK whose dividend is determined every seven weeks in a DUTCH AUCTION process by corporate bidders. Shares are bought and sold at FACE VALUES ranging from $100,000 to $500,000 per share. Also known as *auction rate preferred stock. Money Market Preferred Stock* (Shearson Lehman Brothers Inc.), and by such proprietary acronyms as DARTS (Salomon Brothers Inc.).

DUTY tax imposed on the importation, exportation, or consumption of goods. *See also* TARIFF.

e

EACH WAY commission made by a broker involved on both the purchase and the sale side of a trade. *See also* CROSSED TRADE.

EARLY WITHDRAWAL PENALTY charge assessed against holders of fixed-term investments if they withdraw their money before maturity. Such a penalty would be assessed, for instance, if someone who has a six-month certificate of deposit were to withdraw the money after four months.

EARNED INCOME income (especially wages and salaries) generated by providing goods or services. Also, pension or annuity income.

EARNED SURPLUS *see* RETAINED EARNINGS.

EARNINGS BEFORE TAXES corporate profits after interest has been paid to bondholders, but before taxes have been paid.

EARNINGS MOMENTUM pattern of increasing rate of growth in EARNINGS PER SHARE from one period to another, which usually causes a stock price to go up. For example, a company whose earnings per share are up 15% one year and 35% the next has earnings momentum and should see a gain in its stock price.

EARNINGS PER SHARE portion of a company's profit allocated to each outstanding share of common stock. For instance, a corporation that earned $10 million last year and has 10 million shares outstanding would report earnings of $1 per share. The figure is calculated after paying taxes and after paying preferred shareholders and bondholders. Earnings per share are a key statistic in evaluating a stock's outlook.

EARNINGS-PRICE RATIO relationship of earnings per share to current stock price. Also known as *earnings yield*, it is used in comparing the relative attractiveness of stocks, bonds, and money market instruments. Inverse of PRICE-EARNINGS RATIO.

EASY MONEY *see* TIGHT MONEY.

ECONOMETRICS use of computer analysis and modeling techniques to describe in mathematical terms the relationship between key economic forces such as labor, capital, interest rates, and government policies, then test the effects of changes in economic scenarios. For instance, an econometric model might show the relationship of housing starts and interest rates.

ECONOMIC GROWTH RATE rate of change in the GROSS NATIONAL PRODUCT, as expressed in an annual percentage. If adjusted for inflation, it is called the *real economic growth rate*. Two consecutive quarterly drops in the growth rate mean recession, and two consecutive advances in the growth rate reflect an expanding economy.

ECONOMIC INDICATORS key statistics showing the direction of the economy. Among them are the unemployment rate, inflation rate, factory utilization rate, and balance of trade. *See also* LEADING INDICATORS.

ECONOMIC RECOVERY TAX ACT OF 1981 (ERTA) tax-cutting legislation. Among the key provisions:
1. across-the-board tax cut, which took effect in three stages ending in 1983.
2. indexing of tax brackets to the inflation rate.
3. lowering of top tax rates on long-term capital gains from 28% to 20%. The top rate on dividends, interest, rents, and royalties income dropped from 70% to 50%.
4. lowering of MARRIAGE PENALTY tax, as families with two working spouses could deduct 10% from the salary of the lower-paid spouse, up to $3000.
5. expansion of INDIVIDUAL RETIREMENT ACCOUNTS to all working people, who can contribute up to $2000 a year, and $250 annually for nonworking spouses. Also, expansion of the amount self-employed people can contribute to KEOGH PLAN account contributions.
6. creation of the *all-savers certificate*, which allowed investors to exempt up to $1000 a year in earned interest. The authority to issue these certificates expired at the end of 1982.
7. deductions for reinvesting public utility dividends.
8. reductions in estate and gift taxes, phased in so that the first $600,000 of property can be given free of estate tax starting in 1987. Annual gifts that can be given free of gift tax were raised from $3000 to $10,000. Unlimited deduction for transfer of property to a spouse at death.
9. lowering of rates on the exercise of stock options.
10. change in rules on DEPRECIATION and INVESTMENT CREDIT.
    See also TAX REFORM ACT OF 1986.

EDGE ACT banking legislation, passed in 1919, which allows national banks to conduct foreign lending operations through federal or state chartered subsidiaries, called Edge Act corporations. Such corporations can be chartered by other states and are allowed, unlike domestic banks, to own banks in foreign countries and to invest in foreign commercial and industrial firms. The act also permitted the FEDERAL RESERVE SYSTEM to set reserve requirements on foreign banks that do business in America. Edge Act corporations benefited further from the 1978 International Banking Act, which instructs the Fed to strike any regulations putting

American banks at a disadvantage compared with U.S. operations of foreign banks.

EEC *see* EUROPEAN ECONOMIC COMMUNITY.

EFFECTIVE DATE
In general: date on which an agreement takes effect.
Securities: date when an offering registered with the Securities and Exchange Commission may commence, usually 20 days after filing the registration statement. *See also* SHELF REGISTRATION.
Banking and insurance: time when an insurance policy goes into effect. From that day forward, the insured party is covered by the contract.

EFFECTIVE DEBT total debt owed by a firm, including the capitalized value of lease payments.

EFFECTIVE NET WORTH net worth plus subordinated debt, as viewed by senior creditors. In small business banking, loans payable to principals are commonly subordinated to bank loans. The loans for principals thus can be regarded as effective net worth as long as a bank loan is outstanding and the subordination agreement is in effect.

EFFECTIVE RATE yield on a debt instrument as calculated from the purchase price. The effective rate on a bond is determined by the price, the coupon rate, the time between interest payments, and the time until maturity. Every bond's effective rate thus depends on when it was bought. The effective rate is a more meaningful yield figure than the coupon rate. *See also* RATE OF RETURN.

EFFECTIVE SALE price of a ROUND LOT that determines the price at which the next ODD LOT will be sold. If the last round-lot price was 15, for instance, the odd-lot price might be 15⅛. The added fraction is the *odd-lot differential*.

EFFICIENT MARKET theory that market prices reflect the knowledge and expectations of all investors. Those who adhere to this theory consider it futile to seek undervalued stocks or to forecast market movements. Any new development is reflected in a firm's stock price, they say, making it impossible to beat the market. This vociferously disputed hypothesis also holds that an investor who throws darts at a newspaper's stock listings has as good a chance to outperform the market as any professional investor.

EFFICIENT PORTFOLIO portfolio that has a maximum expected return for any level of risk or a minimum level of risk for any expected return. It is arrived at mathematically, taking into account the expected return and standard deviation of returns for each security, as well as the covariance of returns between different securities in the portfolio.

EITHER-OR ORDER *see* ALTERNATIVE ORDER.

ELASTICITY OF DEMAND AND SUPPLY
Elasticity of demand: responsiveness of buyers to changes in price. Demand for luxury items may slow dramatically if prices are raised, because these purchases are not essential, and can be postponed. On the other hand, demand for necessities such as food, telephone service, and emergency surgery is said to be inelastic. It

remains about the same despite price changes because buyers cannot postpone their purchases without severe adverse consequences.

Elasticity of supply: responsiveness of output to changes in price. As prices move up, the supply normally increases. If it does not, it is said to be inelastic. Supply is said to be elastic if the rise in price means a rise in production.

ELECT

In general: choose a course of action. Someone who decides to incorporate a certain provision in a will elects to do so.

Securities trading: make a conditional order into a market order. If a customer has received a guaranteed buy or sell price from a specialist on the floor of an exchange, the transaction is considered elected when that price is reached. If the guarantee is that a stock will be sold when it reaches 20, and a stop order is put at that price, the sale will be elected at 20.

ELIGIBLE PAPER commercial and agricultural paper, drafts, bills of exchange, banker's acceptances, and other negotiable instruments that were acquired by a bank at a discount and that the Federal Reserve Bank will accept for rediscount.

EMANCIPATION freedom to assume certain legal responsibilities normally associated only with adults, said of a minor who is granted this freedom by a court. If both parents die in an accident, for instance, the 16-year-old eldest son may be emancipated by a judge to act as guardian for his younger brothers and sisters.

EMBARGO government prohibition against the shipment of certain goods to another country. An embargo is most common during wartime, but is sometimes applied for economic reasons as well. For instance, the Organization of Petroleum Exporting Countries placed an embargo on the shipment of oil to the West in the early 1970s to protest Israeli policies and to raise the price of petroleum.

EMERGENCY HOME FINANCE ACT OF 1970 act creating the quasigovernmental Federal Home Loan Mortgage Corporation, also known as Freddie Mac, to stimulate the development of a secondary mortgage market. The act authorized Freddie Mac to package and sell Federal Housing Administration and Veterans Administration-guaranteed mortgage loans. More than half the home mortgages were subsequently packaged and sold to investors in the secondary market in the form of pass-through securities.

EMPLOYEE RETIREMENT INCOME SECURITY ACT (ERISA) 1974 law governing the operation of most private pension and benefit plans. The law eased pension eligibility rules, set up the PENSION BENEFIT GUARANTY CORPORATION, and established guidelines for the management of pension funds.

EMPLOYEE STOCK OWNERSHIP PLAN (ESOP) program encouraging employees to purchase stock in their company. Employees may participate in the management of the company and even take control to rescue the company or a particular plant that would otherwise go out of business. Employees may offer wage and work-rule concessions in return for ownership privileges in an attempt to keep a marginal facility operating.

ENCUMBERED owned by one party but subject to another party's valid claim. A homeowner owns his mortgaged property, for example, but the bank has a security interest in it as long as the mortgage loan is outstanding.

ENDORSE transfer ownership of an asset by signing the back of a negotiable instrument. One can endorse a check to receive payment or endorse a stock or bond certificate to transfer ownership.
See also QUALIFIED ENDORSEMENT.

ENERGY MUTUAL FUND mutual fund that invests solely in energy stocks such as oil, oil service, gas, solar energy, and coal companies and makers of energy-saving devices.

ENTERPRISE a business firm. The term often is applied to a newly formed venture.

ENTREPRENEUR person who takes on the risks of starting a new business. Many entrepreneurs have technical knowledge with which to produce a saleable product or to design a needed new service. Often, VENTURE CAPITAL is used to finance the startup in return for a piece of the equity. Once an entrepreneur's business is established, shares may be sold to the public as an INITIAL PUBLIC OFFERING, assuming favorable market conditions.

EOM DATING arrangement—common in the wholesale drug industry, for example—whereby all purchases made through the 25th of one month are payable within 30 days of the end of the following month; EOM means *end of month.* Assuming no prompt payment discount, purchases through the 25th of April, for example, will be payable by the end of June. If a discount exists for payment in ten days, payment would have to be made by June 10th to take advantage of it. End of month dating with a 2% discount for prompt payment (10 days) would be expressed in the trade either as: *2%-10 days, EOM, 30,* or *2/10 prox. net 30,* where prox., or proximo, means "the next."

EQUAL CREDIT OPPORTUNITY ACT federal legislation passed in the mid-1970s prohibiting discrimination in granting credit, based on race, religion, sex, ethnic background, or whether a person is receiving public assistance or alimony. The Federal Trade Commission enforces the act.

EQUALIZING DIVIDEND special dividend paid to compensate investors for income lost because a change was made in the quarterly dividend payment schedule.

EQUILIBRIUM PRICE
1. price when the supply of goods in a particular market matches demand.
2. for a manufacturer, the price that maximizes a product's profitability.
See illustration, page 256.

EQUIPMENT LEASING PARTNERSHIP limited partnership that buys equipment such as computers, railroad cars, and airplanes, then leases it to businesses. Limited partners receive income from the lease payments as well as tax benefits such as depreciation. Whether a partnership of this kind works out well depends on the GENERAL PARTNER's expertise. Failure to lease the equipment can be disastrous, as happened with railroad hopper cars in the mid-1970s.

EQUIPMENT TRUST CERTIFICATE bond, usually issued by a transportation company such as a railroad or shipping line, used to pay for new equipment. The certificate gives the bondholder the first right to the equipment in the event that interest and principal are not paid when due. Title to the equipment is held in the name of the trustee, usually a bank, until the bond is paid off.

EQUILIBRIUM PRICE

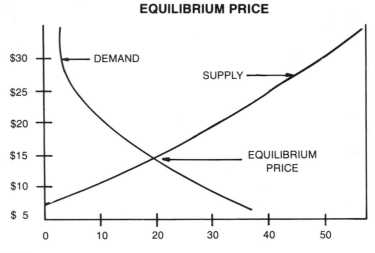

EQUITY

In general: fairness. Law courts, for example, try to be equitable in their judgments when splitting up estates or settling divorce cases.

Banking: difference between the amount a property could be sold for and the claims held against it.

Brokerage account: excess of securities over debit balance in a margin account. For instance, equity would be $28,000 in a margin account with stocks and bonds worth $50,000 and a debit balance of $22,000.

Investments: ownership interest possessed by shareholders in a corporation—stock as opposed to bonds.

EQUITY FINANCING raising money by issuing shares of common or preferred stock. Usually done when prices are high and the most capital can be raised for the smallest number of shares.

EQUITY FUNDING type of investment combining a life insurance policy and a mutual fund. The fund shares are used as collateral for a loan to pay the insurance premiums, giving the investor the advantages of insurance protection and investment appreciation potential.

EQUITY KICKER offer of an ownership position in a deal that involves loans. For instance, a mortgage real estate limited partnership that lends to real estate developers might receive as an equity kicker a small ownership position in a building that can appreciate over time. When the building is sold, limited partners receive the appreciation payout. In return for that equity kicker, the lender is likely to charge a lower interest rate on the loan. Convertible features and warrants are offered as equity kickers to make securities attractive to investors.

EQUITY REIT REAL ESTATE INVESTMENT TRUST that takes an ownership position in the real estate it invests in. Stockholders in equity REITs earn dividends on rental income from the buildings and earn appreciation if properties are sold for a profit. The opposite is a MORTGAGE REIT.

EQUIVALENT BOND YIELD comparison of discount yields and yields on bonds with coupons. Also called *coupon-equivalent rate*. For instance, if a 10%, 90-day Treasury bill with a face value of $10,000 cost $9,750, the equivalent bond yield would be:

$$\frac{\$250}{\$9,750} \times \frac{365}{90} = 10.40\%$$

EQUIVALENT TAXABLE YIELD comparison of the taxable yield on a corporate bond and the tax-free yield on a municipal bond. Depending on the tax bracket, an investor's aftertax return may be greater with a municipal bond than with a corporate bond offering a higher interest rate. For someone in a 28% tax bracket, for instance, a 10% municipal bond would have an equivalent taxable yield of 13.9%. *See* YIELD EQUIVALENCE for method of calculation.

ERISA *see* EMPLOYEE RETIREMENT INCOME SECURITY ACT.

ERTA *see* ECONOMIC RECOVERY TAX ACT OF 1981.

ESCALATOR CLAUSE provision in a contract allowing cost increases to be passed on. In an employment contract, an escalator clause might call for wage increases to keep employee earnings in line with inflation. In a lease, an escalator clause could obligate the tenant to pay for increases in fuel or other costs.

ESCHEAT return of property (for example, land, bank balances, insurance policies) to the state if abandoned or left by a person who died without making a will. If rightful owners or heirs later appear, they can claim the property.

ESCROW money, securities, or other property or instruments held by a third party until the conditions of a contract are met.

ESSENTIAL PURPOSE (or FUNCTION) BOND *see* PUBLIC PURPOSE BOND.

ESTATE all the assets a person possesses at the time of death—such as securities, real estate, interests in business, physical possessions, and cash. The estate is distributed to heirs according to the dictates of the person's will or, if there is no will, a court ruling.

ESTATE PLANNING planning for the orderly handling, disposition, and administration of an estate when the owner dies. Estate planning includes drawing up a will, setting up trusts, and minimizing estate taxes, perhaps by passing property to heirs before death or by setting up a BYPASS TRUST or a TESTAMENTARY TRUST.

ESTATE TAX tax imposed by a state or the federal government on assets left to heirs in a will. Under the Economic Recovery Tax Act of 1981, there is no estate tax on transfers of property between spouses. An exclusion that began at $250,000 in 1982 rose to $600,000 in 1987.

ESTIMATED TAX amount of aniticipated tax for the coming tax year, minus tax credits, based on the higher regular or ALTERNATIVE MINIMUM TAX (AMT). Corporations, estates and trusts, self-employed persons, and persons for whom less than a fixed percentage of income is withheld be employers compute estimated tax and make quarterly payments. The total of withholdings and estimated taxes paid must equal 100% of the prior year's actual tax or 90% of the estimated year's tax.

ETHICAL FUND *see* SOCIAL CONSCIOUSNESS MUTUAL FUND.

EUROBOND bond denominated in U.S. dollars or other currencies and sold to investors outside the country whose currency is used. The bonds are usually issued by large underwriting groups composed of banks and issuing houses from many countries. An example of a Eurobond transaction might be a dollar-denominated debenture issued by a Belgian corporation through an underwriting group comprised of the overseas affiliate of a New York investment banking house, a bank in Holland, and a consortium of British merchant banks; a portion of the issue is sold to French investors through Swiss investment accounts. The Eurobond market is an important source of capital for multinational companies and foreign governments, including Third World governments.

EUROCURRENCY Money deposited by corporations and national governments in banks away from their home countries, called *Eurobanks*. The terms Eurocurrency and Eurobanks do not necessarily mean the currencies or the banks are European, though more often than not, that is the case. For instance, dollars deposited in a British bank or Italian lire deposited in a Japanese bank are considered to be Eurocurrency. The Eurodollar is only one of the Eurocurrencies, though it is the most prevalent. Also known as *Euromoney*.

EURODOLLAR U.S. currency held in banks outside the United States, mainly in Europe, and commonly used for settling international transactions. Some securities are issued in Eurodollars—that is, with a promise to pay interest in dollars deposited in foreign bank accounts.

EURODOLLAR BOND bond that pays interest and principal in Eurodollars, U.S. dollars held in banks outside the United States, primarily in Europe. Such a bond is not registered with the Securities and Exchange Commission, and because there are fewer regulatory delays and costs in the Euromarket, Eurodollar bonds generally can be sold at lower than U.S. interest rates. *See also* EUROBOND.

EURODOLLAR CERTIFICATE OF DEPOSIT CDs issued by banks outside the United States, primarily in Europe, with interest and principal paid in dollars. Such CDs usually have minimum denominations of $100,000 and short-term maturities of less than two years. The interest rate on these CDs is usually pegged to the LONDON INTERBANK OFFERED RATE (LIBOR).

EUROPEAN ECONOMIC COMMUNITY (EEC) economic alliance formed in 1957 by Belgium, France, Italy, Luxembourg, The Netherlands, and West Germany to foster trade and cooperation among its members. Membership was subsequently extended to Great Britain, Ireland, and Denmark (1973); Greece (1984); and Spain and Portugal (1986). Trade barriers were gradually abolished and import duties were standardized with non-EEC countries. Many former European dependencies in Africa and the Caribbean, now independent countries, have preferential trade agreements with the EEC. Central staff headquarters are in Brussels, Belgium, where the Commission of the European Communities set December 31, 1992, as the target date for elimination of all trade barriers between EEC countries and for the adoption of common regulations covering matters as diverse as banking rules and auto-emission standards. Also known as the *European Community*, the *Common Market* and, informally, the United States of Europe.

EUROPEAN OPTION PUT OPTION or CALL OPTION exercisable for a limited time just before expiration. In contrast, an *American option* is exercisable at any time before expiration.

EVALUATOR independent expert who appraises the value of property for which there is limited trading—antiques in an estate, perhaps, or rarely traded stocks or bonds. The fee for this service is sometimes a flat amount, sometimes a percentage of the appraised value.

EVENT RISK the risk that a bond will suddenly decline in credit quality and warrant a lower RATING because of a TAKEOVER-related development, such as additional debt or a RECAPITALIZATION. Corporations whose INDENTURES include protective COVENANTS, such as POISON PUT provisions, are assigned *Event Risk Covenant Rankings* by Standard & Poor's Corporation. Ratings range from E-1, the highest, to E-5 and supplement basic bond ratings.

EXACT INTEREST *see* ORDINARY INTEREST.

EX-ALL sale of a security without dividends, rights, warrants, or any other privileges associated with that security.

EXCESS MARGIN equity in a brokerage firm's customer account, expressed in dollars, above the legal minimum for a margin account or the maintenance requirement. For instance, with a margin requirement of $25,000, as set by REGULATION T and a maintenance requirement of $12,500 set by the stock exchange, the client whose equity is $100,000 would have excess margin of $75,000 and $87,500 in terms of the initial and maintenance requirements, respectively.

EXCESS PROFITS TAX extra federal taxes placed on the earnings of a business. Such taxes may be levied during a time of national emergency, such as in wartime, and are designed to increase national revenue. The excess profits tax is to be distinguished from the WINDFALL PROFITS TAX, designed to prevent excessive corporate profits in special circumstances.

EXCESS RESERVES money a bank holds over and above the RESERVE REQUIREMENT. The money may be on deposit with the Federal Reserve System or with an approved depository bank, or it may be in the bank's possession. Excess reserves are available for loans to other banks or customers or for other corporate uses.

EXCHANGE DISTRIBUTION block trade carried out on the floor of an exchange between customers of a member firm. Someone who wants to sell a large block of stock in a single transaction can get a broker to solicit and bunch a large number of orders. The seller transmits the securities to the buyers all at once, and the trade is announced on the BROAD TAPE as an exchange distribution. The seller, not the buyers, pays a special commission to the broker who executes the trade.

EXCHANGE PRIVILEGE right of a shareholder to switch from one mutual fund to another within one fund family—often, at no additional charge. This enables investors to put their money in an aggressive growth-stock fund when they expect the market to turn up strongly, then switch to a money-market fund when they anticipate a downturn. Some discount brokers allow shareholders to switch between fund families in pursuit of the best performance.

EXCHANGE RATE price at which one country's currency can be converted into another's. The exchange rate between the U.S. dollar and the British pound is different from the rate between the dollar and the West German mark, for example. A wide range of factors influences exchange rates, which generally change slightly each trading day. Some rates are fixed by agreement; *see* FIXED EXCHANGE RATE.

EXCISE TAX federal or state tax on the sale or manufacture of a commodity, usually a luxury item. Examples: federal and state taxes on alcohol and tobacco.

EXCLUSION
1. item not covered by a contract. For instance, an insurance policy may list certain hazards that are excluded from coverage.
2. on a tax return, items that must be reported, but are not taxed. For example, corporations are allowed to exclude 80% of dividends received from other domestic corporations.

EX-DIVIDEND interval between the announcement and the payment of the next dividend. An investor who buys shares during that interval is not entitled to the dividend. Typically, a stock's price moves up by the dollar amount of the dividend as the ex-dividend date approaches, then falls by the amount of the dividend after that date. A stock that has gone ex-dividend is marked with an *x* in newspaper listings.

EX-DIVIDEND DATE date on which a stock goes EX-DIVIDEND, typically about three weeks before the dividend is paid to shareholders of record. Shares listed on the New York Stock Exchange go ex-dividend four business days before the RECORD DATE. This NYSE rule is generally followed by the other exchanges.

EXECUTION
Securities: carrying out a trade. A broker who buys or sells shares is said to have executed an order.
Law: the signing, sealing, and delivering of a contract or agreement making it valid.

EXECUTOR person designated to carry out the wishes expressed in a will as to the administration of the estate and the distribution of the assets in it. An executor may be a bank trust officer or a family member or trusted friend.

EXEMPT SECURITIES stocks and bonds exempt from certain Securities and Exchange Commission and Federal Reserve Board rules. For instance, government and municipal bonds are exempt from SEC registration requirements and from Federal Reserve Board margin rules.

EXERCISE make use of a right available in a contract. In options trading a buyer of a call contract may exercise the right to buy underlying shares at a particular price by informing the option seller. A put buyer's right is exercised when the underlying shares are sold at the agreed-upon price.

EXERCISE LIMIT limit on the number of option contracts of any one class that can be exercised in a span of five business days. For options on stocks, the exercise limit is usually 2000 contracts.

EXERCISE NOTICE notification by a broker that a client wants to exercise a right to buy the underlying stock in an option contract. Such notice is transmitted to the option seller through the Options Clearing Corporation, which ensures that stock is delivered as agreed upon.

EXERCISE PRICE price at which the stock or commodity underlying a call or put option can be purchased (call) or sold (put) over the specified period. For instance, a call contract may allow the buyer to purchase 100 shares of XYZ at any time in the next three months at an exercise or STRIKE PRICE of $63.

EXHAUST PRICE price at which broker must liquidate a client's holding in a stock that was bought on margin and has declined, but has not had additional funds put up to meet the MARGIN CALL.

EXIMBANK *see* EXPORT-IMPORT BANK.

EXIT FEE *see* BACK-END LOAD.

EX-LEGAL municipal bond that does not have the legal opinion of a bond law firm printed on it, as most municipal bonds do. When such bonds are traded, buyers must be warned that legal opinion is lacking.

EXPECTED RETURN *see* MEAN RETURN.

EXPENSE RATIO amount, expressed as a percentage of total investment, that shareholders pay for mutual fund operating expenses and management fees. This money, which may be as high as 1% of shareholder assets, is taken out of the fund's current income and is disclosed in the annual report to shareholders.

EXPIRATION

Banking: date on which a contract or agreement ceases to be effective.

Options trading: last day on which an option can be exercised. If it is not, traders say that the option *expired worthless.*

EXPIRATION CYCLE cycle of expiration dates used in options trading. For example, contracts may be written for one of three cycles: January, April, July, October; February, May, August, November; March, June, September, December. Since options are traded in three-, six-, and nine-month contracts, only three of the four months in the set are traded at once. In our example, when the January contract expires, trading begins on the October contract. Commodities futures expiration cycles follow other schedules.

EX-PIT TRANSACTION purchase of commodities off the floor of the exchange where they are regularly traded and at specified terms.

EXPLORATORY DRILLING PROGRAM search for an undiscovered reservoir of oil or gas—a very risky undertaking. Exploratory wells are called *wildcat* (in an unproven area); *controlled wildcat* (in an area outside the proven limits of an existing field); or *deep test* (within a proven field but to unproven depths). Exploratory drilling programs are usually syndicated, and units are sold to limited partners.

EXPORT-IMPORT BANK (EXIMBANK) bank set up by Congress in 1934 to encourage U.S. trade with foreign countries. Eximbank is an independent entity that borrows from the U.S. Treasury to (1) finance exports and imports; (2) grant direct credit to non-U.S. borrowers;(3) provide export guarantees, insurance against commercial and political risk, and discount loans.

EX-RIGHTS without the RIGHT to buy a company's stock at a discount from the prevailing market price, which was distributed until a particular date. Typically, after that date the rights trade separately from the stock itself. *See also* EX-WARRANTS.

EX-STOCK DIVIDENDS interval between the announcement and payment of a stock dividend. An investor who buys shares during that interval is not entitled to the announced stock dividend; instead, it goes to the seller of the shares, who was the owner on the last recorded date before the books were closed and the stock went EX-DIVIDEND. Stocks cease to be ex-dividend after the payment date.

EXTERNAL FUNDS funds brought in from outside the corporation, perhaps in the form of a bank loan, or the proceeds from a bond offering, or an infusion of cash from venture capitalists. External funds supplement internally generated CASH FLOW and are used for expansion, as well as for seasonal WORKING CAPITAL needs.

EXTRA DIVIDEND dividend paid to shareholders in addition to the regular dividend. Such a payment is made after a particularly profitable year in order to reward shareholders and engender loyalty.

EXTRAORDINARY ITEM nonrecurring occurrence that must be explained to shareholders in an annual or quarterly report. Some examples: writeoff of a division, acquisition of another company, sale of a large amount of real estate, or uncovering of employee fraud that negatively affects the company's financial condition. Earnings are usually reported before and after taking into account the effects of extraordinary items.

EX-WARRANTS stock sold with the buyer no longer entitled to the WARRANT attached to the stock. Warrants allow the holder to buy stock at some future date at a specified price. Someone buying a stock on June 3 that had gone ex-warrants on June 1 would not receive those warrants. They would be the property of the stockholder of record on June 1.

f

FACE-AMOUNT CERTIFICATE debt security issued by face-amount certificate companies, one of three categories of mutual funds defined by the INVESTMENT COMPANY ACT OF 1940. The holder makes periodic payments to the issuer, and the issuer promises to pay the purchaser the face value at maturity or a surrender value if the certificate is presented prior to maturity.

FACE VALUE value of a bond, note, mortgage, or other security as given on the certificate or instrument. Corporate bonds are usually issued with $1000 face values, municipal bonds with $5000 face values, and federal government bonds with $10,000 face values. Although the bonds fluctuate in price from the time they are issued until redemption, they are redeemed at maturity at their face value, unless the issuer defaults. If the bonds are retired before maturity, bondholders normally receive a slight premium over face value. The face value is the amount on which interest payments are calculated. Thus, a 10% bond with a face value of $1000 pays bondholders $100 per year. Face value is also referred to as PAR VALUE or *nominal value*.

FACTORING type of financial service whereby a firm sells or transfers title to its accounts receivable to a factoring company, which then acts as principal, not as agent. The receivables are sold without recourse, meaning that the factor cannot turn to the seller in the event accounts prove uncollectible. Factoring can be done either on a *notification basis,* where the seller's customers remit directly to the factor, or on a *nonnotification basis,* where the seller handles the collections and remits to the factor. There are two basic types of factoring:

1. **Discount factoring** arrangement whereby seller receives funds from the factor prior to the average maturity date, based on the invoice amount of the receivable, less cash discounts, less an allowance for estimated claims, returns, etc. Here the factor is compensated by an interest rate based on daily balances and typically 2% to 3% above the bank prime rate.

2. **Maturity factoring** arrangement whereby the factor, who performs the entire credit and collection function, remits to the seller for the receivables sold each month on the average due date of the factored receivables. The factor's commission on this kind of arrangement ranges from 0.75% to 2%, depending on the bad debt risk and the handling costs.

Factors also accommodate clients with "overadvances," loans in anticipation of sales, which permit inventory building prior to peak selling periods. Factoring has traditionally been most closely associated with the garment industry, but is used by companies in other industries as well.

FAIL POSITION securities undelivered due to the failure of selling clients to deliver the securities to their brokers so the latter can deliver them to the buying brokers. Since brokers are constantly buying and selling, receiving and delivering, the term usually refers to a net delivery position—that is, a given broker owes more securities to other brokers on sell transactions than other brokers owe to it on buy transactions. *See also* FAIL TO DELIVER; FAIL TO RECEIVE.

FAIL TO DELIVER situation where the broker-dealer on the sell side of a contract has not delivered securities to the broker-dealer on the buy side. A fail to deliver is usually the result of a broker not receiving delivery from its selling customer. As long as a fail to deliver exists, the seller will not receive payment. *See also* FAIL TO RECEIVE.

FAIL TO RECEIVE situation where the broker-dealer on the buy side of a contract has not received delivery of securities from the broker-dealer on the sell side. As long as a fail to receive exists, the buyer will not make payment for the securities. *See also* FAIL TO DELIVER.

FAIR CREDIT REPORTING ACT federal law enacted in 1971 giving the right to see and challenge credit records at credit bureaus. *See also* CREDIT RATING.

FAIR MARKET VALUE price at which an asset or service passes from a willing seller to a willing buyer. It is assumed that both buyer and seller are rational and have a reasonable knowledge of relevant facts. *See also* MARKET.

FAIR-PRICE AMENDMENT AMENDMENT, aimed at hostile TWO-TIER BIDS, providing that a SUPERMAJORITY AMENDMENT will be waived if a fair price is offered for all shares of a TAKEOVER target.

FAIR RATE OF RETURN level of profit that a utility is allowed to earn as determined by federal and/or state regulators. Public utility commissions set the fair rate of return based on the utility's needs to maintain service to its customers, pay adequate dividends to shareholders and interest to bondholders, and maintain and expand plant and equipment.

FAIR TRADE ACTS state laws protecting manufacturers from price-cutting by permitting them to establish minimum retail prices for their goods. Fair trade pricing was effectively eliminated in 1975 when Congress repealed the federal laws upholding resale price maintenance.

FAMILY OF FUNDS group of mutual funds managed by the same investment management company. Each fund typically has a different objective; one may be a growth-oriented stock fund, whereas another may be a bond fund or a money market fund. Shareholders in one of the funds can usually switch their money into any of the family's other funds, sometimes at no charge. This system makes it convenient for shareholders to move their assets as different investments become more or less appropriate at different points in the economic cycle, or as their investment needs change. There may be tax consequences when money is transferred from one fund to another. Families of funds with no sales charges are called *no-load families* and are sold directly to investors. Those with sales fees are called *load families* and are typically sold by a broker. *See also* INVESTMENT COMPANY.

FANNIE MAE nickname for the FEDERAL NATIONAL MORTGAGE ASSOCIATION.

FARMER MAC *see* FEDERAL AGRICULTURAL MORTGAGE CORPORATION.

FARTHER OUT; FARTHER IN relative length of option-contract maturities with reference to the present. For example, an options investor in January would call an option expiring in October farther out than an option expiring in July. The July option is farther in than the October option. *See also* DIAGONAL SPREAD.

FAVORABLE TRADE BALANCE situation that exists when the value of a nation's exports is in excess of the value of its imports. *See also* BALANCE OF PAYMENTS; BALANCE OF TRADE.

FAVORITE FIFTY *see* NIFTY FIFTY.

FEDERAL AGENCY SECURITY debt instrument issued by an agency of the federal government such as the Federal National Mortgage Association, Federal Farm Credit Bank, and the Tennessee Valley Authority (TVA). Though not general obligations of the U.S. Treasury, such securities are sponsored by the government and therefore have high safety ratings.

FEDERAL AGRICULTURAL MORTGAGE CORPORATION agency of the U.S. government established in 1988 to provide a secondary market for farm mortgage loans. Informally called *Farmer Mac*.

FEDERAL DEFICIT federal shortfall that results when the government spends more in a fiscal year than it receives in revenue. To cover the shortfall, the government usually borrows from the public by floating long- and short-term debt. Federal deficits, which started to rise in the 1970s and exploded to enormous proportions in the early 1980s, are said by economists to be a cause of high interest rates and inflation, since they compete with private borrowing by businesses and consumers for funds, and add to monetary demand. *See also* CROWDING OUT NATIONAL DEBT.

FEDERAL DEPOSIT INSURANCE CORPORATION (FDIC) federal agency established in 1933 that guarantees (within limits) funds on deposit in member banks and thrift institutions and performs other functions such as making loans to or buying assets from member institutions to facilitate mergers or prevent failures. In 1989, Congress passed savings and loan association bailout legislation that reorganized FDIC into two insurance units: the BANK INSURANCE FUND (BIF) continues the traditional FDIC functions with respect to banking institutions; the SAVINGS ASSOCIATION INSURANCE FUND (SAIF) insures thrift institution deposits, replacing the FEDERAL SAVINGS AND LOAN INSURANCE CORPORATION (FSLIC), which ceased to exist. *See also* OFFICE OF THRIFT SUPERVISION (OTS).

FEDERAL FARM CREDIT BANK government-sponsored institution that consolidates the financing activities of the Federal Land Banks, the Federal Intermediate Credit Banks, and the Banks for Cooperatives. *See* FEDERAL FARM CREDIT SYSTEM.

FEDERAL FARM CREDIT SYSTEM system established by the Farm Credit Act of 1971 to provide credit services to farmers and farm-related enterprises through a network of 12 Farm Credit districts. Each district has a Federal Land Bank, a Federal Intermediate Credit Bank, and a Bank for Cooperatives to carry cut policies of the system. The system sells short-term (5- to 270-day) notes in increments of $50,000 on a discounted basis through a national syndicate of securities dealers. Rates are set by the FEDERAL FARM CREDIT BANK, a unit established to consolidate the financing activities of the various banks. An active secondary market is maintained by several dealers. The system also issues Federal Farm Credit System Consolidated Systemwide Bonds on a monthly basis with 6- and 9-month maturities. The bonds are sold in increments of $5000 with rates set by the system. The bonds enjoy a secondary market even more active than that for the discounted notes. *See also* SECONDARY MARKET.

FEDERAL FUNDS
1. funds deposited by commercial banks at Federal Reserve Banks, including funds in excess of bank reserve requirements. Banks may lend federal funds to each other on an overnight basis at the federal funds rate. Member banks may also transfer funds among themselves or on behalf of customers on a same-day basis by debiting and crediting balances in the various reserve banks. *See* FED WIRE.
2. money used by the Federal Reserve to pay for its purchases of government securities.
3. funds used to settle transactions where there is no FLOAT.

FEDERAL FUNDS RATE interest rate charged by banks with excess reserves at a Federal Reserve district bank to banks needing overnight loans to meet reserve requirements. The federal funds rate is the most sensitive indicator of the direction of interest rates, since it is set daily by the market, unlike the PRIME RATE and the DISCOUNT RATE, which are periodically changed by banks and by the Federal Reserve Board, respectively.

FEDERAL HOME LOAN BANK SYSTEM system supplying credit reserves for SAVINGS AND LOANS, cooperative banks, and other mortgage lenders in a manner similar to the Federal Reserve's role with commercial banks. The Federal Home Loan Bank System is made up of 12 regional Federal Home Loan Banks. It raises money by issuing notes and bonds and lends money to savings and loans and other mortgage lenders based on the amount of collateral the institution can provide. The system was established in 1932 after a massive wave of bank failures. In 1989, Congress passed savings and loan bailout legislation revamping the regulatory structure of the industry. The FEDERAL HOME LOAN BANK BOARD was dismantled and replaced with the FEDERAL HOUSING FINANCE BOARD, which now oversees the home loan bank system. *See also* OFFICE OF THRIFT SUPERVISION (OTS).

FEDERAL HOME LOAN MORTGAGE CORPORATION (FHLMC) publicly chartered agency that buys qualifying residential mortgages from lenders, packages them into new securities backed by those pooled mortgages, provides certain guarantees, and then resells the securities on the open market. The corporation's stock is owned by savings institutions across the U.S. and is held in trust by the Federal Home Loan Bank System. The corporation, nicknamed Freddie Mac, has created an enormous secondary market, which provides more funds for mortgage lending and allows investors to buy high-yielding securities backed by federal guarantees. Freddie Mac formerly packaged only mortgages backed by the Veteran's Administration or the Federal Housing Administration, but now it also resells nongovernmentally backed mortgages. The corporation was established in 1970. *See also* MORTGAGE BACKED CERTIFICATES.

FEDERAL HOUSING ADMINISTRATION (FHA) federally sponsored agency that insures lenders against loss on residential mortgages. It was founded in 1934 in response to the Great Depression to execute the provisions of the National Housing Act. The FHA was the forerunner of a group of government agencies responsible for the growing secondary market for mortgages, such as the Government National Mortgage Association (Ginnie Mae) and the Federal National Mortgage Association (Fannie Mae).

FEDERAL HOUSING FINANCE BOARD U.S. government agency created by Congress in 1989 to assume oversight of the FEDERAL HOME LOAN BANK SYSTEM from the dismantled FEDERAL HOME LOAN BANK BOARD. *See also* OFFICE OF THRIFT SUPERVISION (OTS).

FEDERAL INTERMEDIATE CREDIT BANK one of 12 banks that make funds available to production credit associations, commercial banks, agricultural credit corporations, livestock loan companies, and other institutions extending credit to crop farmers and cattle raisers. Their stock is owned by farmers and ranchers, and the banks raise funds largely from the public sale of short-term debentures. *See also* FEDERAL FARM CREDIT BANK; FEDERAL FARM CREDIT SYSTEM.

FEDERAL LAND BANK one of 12 banks under the U.S. Farm Credit Administration that extend long-term mortgage credit to crop farmers and cattle raisers for buying land, refinancing debts, or other agricultural purposes. To obtain a loan, a farmer or rancher must purchase stock equal to 5% of the loan in any one of approximately 500 local land bank associations; these, in turn, purchase an equal amount of stock in the Federal Land bank. The stock is retired when the loan is repaid. The banks raise funds by issuing Consolidated Systemwide Bonds to the public. *See also* FEDERAL FARM CREDIT BANK; FEDERAL FARM CREDIT SYSTEM.

FEDERAL NATIONAL MORTGAGE ASSOCIATION (FNMA) publicly owned, government-sponsored corporation chartered in 1938 to purchase mortgages from lenders and resell them to investors. The agency, known by the nickname Fannie Mae, mostly packages mortgages backed by the Federal Housing Administration, but also sells some nongovernmentally backed mortgages. Shares of FNMA itself, known as Fannie Maes, are traded on the New York Stock Exchange. The price usually soars when interest rates fall and plummets when interest rates rise, since the mortgage business is so dependent on the direction of interest rates.

FEDERAL OPEN MARKET COMMITTEE (FOMC) key committee in the FEDERAL RESERVE SYSTEM, which sets short-term monetary policy for the Federal Reserve (the Fed). The committee comprises the seven Federal Reserve governors and the presidents of six Federal Reserve Banks. To tighten the money supply, which decreases the amount of money available in the banking system, the Fed sells government securities. The meetings of the committee, which are secret, are the subject of much speculation on Wall Street, as analysts try to guess whether the Fed will tighten or loosen the money supply, thereby causing interest rates to rise or fall. *See also* DESK.

FEDERAL RESERVE BANK one of the 12 banks that, with their branches, make up the FEDERAL RESERVE SYSTEM. These banks are located in Boston, New York, Philadelphia, Cleveland, Richmond, Atlanta, Chicago, St. Louis, Minneapolis, Kansas City, Dallas, and San Francisco. The role of each Federal Reserve Bank is to monitor the commercial and savings banks in its region to ensure that they follow Federal Reserve Board regulations and to provide those banks with access to emergency funds from the DISCOUNT WINDOW. The reserve banks act as depositories for member banks in their regions, providing money transfer and other services. Each of the banks is owned by the member banks in its district.

FEDERAL RESERVE BOARD (FRB) governing board of the FEDERAL RESERVE SYSTEM. Its seven members are appointed by the President of the United States, subject to Senate confirmation, and serve 14-year terms. The Board establishes Federal Reserve System policies on such key matters as reserve requirements and other bank regulations, sets the discount rate, tightens or loosens the availability of credit in the economy, and regulates the purchase of securities on margin.

FEDERAL RESERVE OPEN MARKET COMMITTEE *see* FEDERAL OPEN MARKET COMMITTEE.

FEDERAL RESERVE SYSTEM system established by the Federal Reserve Act of 1913 to regulate the U.S. monetary and banking system. The Federal Reserve System (the Fed) is comprised of 12 regional Federal Reserve Banks, their 25 branches, and all national and state banks that are part of the system. National banks are stockholders of the FEDERAL RESERVE BANK in their region.
　　The Federal Reserve System's main functions are to regulate the national money supply, set reserve requirements for member banks, supervise the printing of currency at the mint, act as clearinghouse for the transfer of funds throughout the banking system, and examine member banks to make sure they meet various Federal Reserve regulations. Although the members of the system's governing board are appointed by the President of the United States and confirmed by the Senate, the Federal Reserve System is considered an independent entity, which is supposed to make its decisions free of political influence. Governors are appointed for terms of 14 years, which further assures their independence. *See also* FEDERAL OPEN MARKET COMMITTEE; FEDERAL RESERVE BOARD; OPEN MARKET OPERATIONS.

FEDERAL SAVINGS AND LOAN ASSOCIATION federally chartered institution with a primary responsibility to collect people's savings deposits and to provide mortgage loans for residential housing. Federal Savings and Loans may be owned either by stockholders, who can trade their shares on stock exchanges, or by depositors, in which case the associations are considered mutual organizations. Federal Savings and Loans are members of the Federal Home Loan Bank System. In the 1970s and early 80s S&Ls expanded into nonhousing-related financial services such as discount stock brokerage, financial planning, credit cards, and consumer loans. *See also* FINANCIAL SUPERMARKET; MUTUAL ASSOCIATION; OFFICE OF THRIFT SUPERVISION (OTS); SAVINGS AND LOAN ASSOCIATION.

FEDERAL SAVINGS AND LOAN INSURANCE CORPORATION (FSLIC) federal agency established in 1934 to insure deposits in member savings institutions. In 1989, Congress passed savings and loan bailout legislation revamping the regulatory structure of the industry. FSLIC was disbanded and its insurance activities assumed by a new agency, SAVINGS ASSOCIATION INSURANCE FUND (SAIF), a unit of the FEDERAL DEPOSIT INSURANCE CORPORATION (FDIC). Responsibility for insolvent institutions previously under FSLIC's jurisdiction was assumed by another newly created agency, RESOLUTION FUNDING CORPORATION (REFCO). *See also* OFFICE OF THRIFT SUPERVISION (OTS).

FEDERAL TRADE COMMISSION (FTC) federal agency established in 1914 to foster free and fair business competition and prevent monopolies and activities in restraint of trade. It administers both antitrust and consumer protection legislation.

FED WIRE high-speed, computerized communications network that connects all 12 Federal Reserve Banks, their 24 branches, the Federal Reserve Board office in Washington, D.C., U.S. Treasury offices in Washington, D.C., and Chicago, and the Washington, D.C. office of the Commodity Credit Corporation; also spelled FedWire and Fedwire. The Fed wire has been called the central nervous system of money transfer in the United States. It enables banks to transfer reserve balances from one to another for immediate available credit and to transfer balances for business customers. Using the Fed wire, Federal Reserve Banks can settle interdistrict transfers resulting from check collections, and the Treasury can shift balances from its accounts in different reserve banks quickly and without cost. It is also possible to transfer bearer short-term Government securities within an hour at no cost. This is done through a procedure called CPD (Commissioner of Public Debt of the Treasury) transfers, whereby one Federal Reserve Bank "retires" a seller's security, while another reserve bank makes delivery of a like amount of the same security from its unissued stock to the buyer.

FICTITIOUS CREDIT the credit balance in a securities MARGIN ACCOUNT representing the proceeds from a short sale and the margin requirement under Federal Reserve Board REGULATION T (which regulates margin credit). Because the proceeds, which are held as security for the loan of securities made by the broker to effect the short sale, and the margin requirement are both there to protect the broker's position, the money is not available for withdrawal by the customer; hence the term "fictitious" credit. It is in contrast to a free credit balance, which can be withdrawn anytime.

FIDELITY BOND *see* BLANKET FIDELITY BOND.

FIDUCIARY person, company, or association holding assets in trust for a beneficiary. The fiduciary is charged with the responsibility of investing the money wisely for the beneficiary's benefit. Some examples of fiduciaries are executors of wills and estates, receivers in bankruptcy, trustees, and those who administer the assets of underage or incompetent beneficiaries. Most U.S. states have laws about what a fiduciary may or may not do with a beneficiary's assets. For instance, it is illegal for fiduciaries to invest or misappropriate the money for their personal gain. *See also* LEGAL LIST; PRUDENT MAN RULE.

FIFO *see* FIRST IN, FIRST OUT.

FILL execute a customer's order to buy or sell a stock, bond, or commodity. An order is filled when the amount of the security requested is supplied. When less than the full amount of the order is supplied, it is known as a *partial fill*.

FILL OR KILL (FOK) order to buy or sell a particular security which, if not executed immediately, is canceled. Often, fill or kill orders are placed when a client wants to buy a large quantity of shares of a particular stock at a particular price. If the order is not executed because it will significantly upset the market price for that stock, the order is withdrawn.

FINANCE CHARGE cost of credit, including interest, paid by a customer for a consumer loan. Under the Truth in Lending Act, the finance charge must be disclosed to the customer in advance. *See also* CONSUMER CREDIT PROTECTION ACT OF 1968; REGULATION Z.

FINANCE COMPANY company engaged in making loans to individuals or businesses. Unlike a bank, it does not receive deposits but rather obtains its financing from banks, institutions, and other money market sources. Generally, finance companies fall into three categories:(1) consumer finance companies, also known as *small loan* or *direct loan companies,* lend money to individuals under the small loan laws of the individual U.S. states; (2) sales finance companies, also called *acceptance companies,* purchase retail and wholesale paper from automobile and other consumer and capital goods dealers; (3) commercial finance companies, also called *commercial credit companies,* make loans to manufacturers and wholesalers; these loans are secured by accounts receivable, inventories, and equipment. Finance companies typically enjoy high credit ratings and are thus able to borrow at the lowest market rates, enabling them to make loans at rates not much higher than banks. Even though their customers usually do not qualify for bank credit, these companies have experienced a low rate of default. Finance companies in general tend to be interest rate-sensitive—increases and decreases in market interest rates affect their profits directly. For this reason, publicly held finance companies are sometimes referred to as "money stocks." *See also* CAPTIVE FINANCE COMPANY.

FINANCIAL ACCOUNTING STANDARDS BOARD (FASB) independent board responsible for establishing and interpreting generally accepted accounting principles. It was formed in 1973 to succeed and continue the activities of the Accounting Principles Board (APB). *See* GENERALLY ACCEPTED ACCOUNTING PRINCIPLES.

FINANCIAL FUTURE FUTURES CONTRACT based on a financial instrument. Such contracts usually move under the influence of interest rates. As rates rise, contracts fall in value; as rates fall, contracts gain in value. Examples of instruments underlying financial futures contracts: Treasury bills, Treasury notes, Government National Mortgage Association (Ginnie Mae) pass-throughs, foreign currencies, and certificates of deposit. Trading in these contracts is governed by the federal Commodities Futures Trading Commission. Traders use these futures to speculate on the direction of interest rates. Financial institutions (banks, insurance companies, brokerage firms) use them to hedge financial portfolios against adverse fluctuations in interest rates.

FINANCIAL INSTITUTION institution that collects funds from the public to place in financial assets such as stocks, bonds, money market instruments, bank deposits, or loans. Depository institutions (banks, savings and loans, savings banks, credit unions) pay interest on deposits and invest the deposit money mostly in loans. Nondepository institutions (insurance companies, pension plans) collect money by selling insurance policies or receiving employer contributions and pay it out for legitimate claims or for retirement benefits. Increasingly, many institutions are performing both depository and nondepository functions. For instance, brokerage firms now place customers' money in certificates of deposit and money market funds and sell insurance. *See* FINANCIAL SUPERMARKET.

FINANCIAL INTERMEDIARY commercial bank, savings and loan, mutual savings bank, credit union, or other "middleman" that smooths the flow of funds between "savings surplus units" and "savings deficit units." In an economy viewed as three sectors—households, businesses, and government—a *savings surplus unit* is one where income exceeds consumption; a *savings deficit unit* is one where current expenditures exceed current income and external sources must be called upon to make up the difference. As a whole, households are savings surplus units, whereas businesses and governments are savings deficit units. Financial intermediaries redistribute savings into productive uses and, in the process, serve two other important functions: By making savers infinitesimally small "shareholders" in huge pools of capital, which in turn are loaned out to a wide number and variety of borrowers, the intermediaries provide both diversification of risk and liquidity to the individual saver. *See also* DISINTERMEDIATION; FINDER'S FEE.

FINANCIAL LEASE lease in which the service provided by the lessor to the lessee is limited to financing equipment. All other responsibilities related to the possession of equipment, such as maintenance, insurance, and taxes, are borne by the lessee. A financial lease is usually noncancellable and is fully paid out *(amortized)* over its term.

FINANCIAL LEVERAGE *see* LEVERAGE.

FINANCIAL MARKET market for the exchange of capital and credit in the economy. Money markets concentrate on short-term debt instruments; capital markets trade in long-term debt and equity instruments. Examples of financial markets: stock market, bond market, commodities market, and foreign exchange market.

FINANCIAL PLANNER professional who analyzes personal financial circumstances and prepares a program to meet financial needs and objectives. Financial planners, who may be accountants, bankers, lawyers, insurance agents, real estate or securities brokers, or independent practitioners, should have knowledge in the areas of wills and estate planning, retirement planning, taxes, insurance, family budgeting, debt management, and investments.

Fee-only planners charge on the basis of service and time and have nothing to sell. *Commission-only* planners offer their services free of charge but sell commission-producing products such as MUTUAL FUNDS, LIMITED PARTNERSHIPS, insurance products, stocks and bonds, and even real estate. *Fee-plus-commission* planners charge an up-front fee for consultation and their written plan, then charge commissions on the financial products they sell. *Fee-offset* planners charge fees against which they apply credits when they sell commission products.

Institute of Certified Financial Planners (ICFP), Denver, Colorado, accredits CERTIFIED FINANCIAL PLANNERS (CFPs) and maintains a referral list; *International Association for Financial Planning (IAFP)*, Atlanta, Georgia, publishes *The Registry of Financial Planning Practitioners,* which listing qualified planners with a CFP, ChFC (CHARTERED FINANCIAL CONSULTANT), CPA, or a law or business degree, who have submitted five client references; *International Association of Registered Financial Planners (IARFP),* Tampa, Florida, designates and lists securities and insurance brokers qualifying as *Registered Financial Planners (RFPs); National Association of Personal Financial Advisors (NAPFA),* Arlington Heights, Illinois, lists fee-only planners.

FINANCIAL POSITION status of a firm's assets, liabilities, and equity accounts as of a certain time, as shown on its FINANCIAL STATEMENT. Also called *financial condition.*

FINANCIAL PUBLIC RELATIONS branch of public relations specializing in corporate disclosure responsibilities, stockholder relations, and relations with the professional investor community. Financial public relations is concerned not only with matters of corporate image and the cultivation of a favorable financial and investment environment but also with legal interpretation and adherence to Securities and Exchange Commission and other government regulations, as well as with the DISCLOSURE requirements of the securities exchanges. Its practitioners, therefore, include lawyers with expertise in such areas as tender offers and take-overs, public offers, proxy solicitation, and insider trading. *See also* INVESTOR RELATIONS DEPARTMENT.

FINANCIAL PYRAMID
1. risk structure many investors aim for in spreading their investments between low-, medium-, and high-risk vehicles. In a financial pyramid, the largest part of the investor's assets is in safe, liquid investments that provide a decent return. Next, some money is invested in stocks and bonds that provide good income and the possibility for long-term growth of capital. Third, a smaller portion of one's capital is committed to speculative investments which may offer higher returns if they work out well. At the top of the financial pyramid, where only a small amount of money is committed, are high-risk ventures that have a slight chance of success, but which will provide substantial rewards if they succeed.
2. acquisition of holding company assets through financial leverage. *See* PYRAMIDING.
   Financial pyramid is not to be confused with fraudulent selling schemes, also sometimes called *pyramiding.*

FINANCIAL PYRAMID

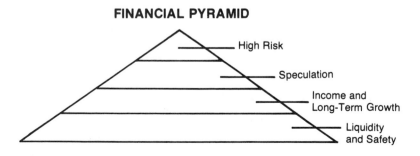

FINANCIAL STATEMENT written record of the financial status of an individual, association, or business organization. The financial statement includes a BAL-

ANCE SHEET and an INCOME STATEMENT (or operating statement or profit and loss statement) and may also include a statement of cash flows, a statement of changes in retained earnings, and other analyses.

FINANCIAL STRUCTURE makeup of the right-hand side of a company's BALANCE SHEET, which includes all the ways its assets are financed, such as trade accounts payable and short-term borrowings as well as long-term debt and ownership equity. Financial structure is distinguished from CAPITAL STRUCTURE, which includes only long-term debt and equity. A company's financial structure is influenced by a number of factors, including the growth rate and stability of its sales, its competitive situation (i.e., the stability of its profits), its asset structure, and the attitudes of its management and its lenders. It is the basic frame of reference for analyses concerned with financial leveraging decisions.

FINANCIAL SUPERMARKET company that offers a wide range of financial services under one roof. For example, some large retail organizations offer stock, insurance, and real estate brokerage, as well as banking services. For customers, having all their assets with one institution can make financial transactions and planning more convenient and efficient, since money does not constantly have to be shifted from one institution to another. For institutions, such all-inclusive relationships are more profitable than dealing with just one aspect of a customer's financial needs. Institutions often become financial supermarkets in order to capture all the business of their customers.

FINANCING CORP. (FICO) agency set up by Congress in 1987 to issue bonds and bail out the Federal Savings and Loan Insurance Corporation (FSLIC). *See also* BAILOUT BONDS.

FINDER'S FEE fee charged by a person or company acting as a finder (intermediary) in a transaction.

FINITE LIFE REAL ESTATE INVESTMENT TRUST (FREIT) REAL ESTATE INVESTMENT TRUST (REIT) that promises to try to sell its holdings within a specified period to realize CAPITAL GAINS.

FIRM
1. general term for a business, corporation, partnership, or proprietorship. Legally, a firm is not considered a corporation since it may not be incorporated and since the firm's principals are not recognized as separate from the identity of the firm itself. This might be true of a law or accounting firm, for instance.
2. solidity with which an agreement is made. For example, a firm order with a manufacturer or a firm bid for a stock at a particular price means that the order or bid is assured.

FIRM COMMITMENT
Securities Underwriting: arrangement whereby investment bankers make outright purchases from the issuer of securities to be offered to the public; also called *firm commitment underwriting*. The underwriters, as the investment bankers are called in such an arrangement, make their profit on the difference between the purchase price—determined through either competitive bidding or negotiation—and the public offering price. Firm commitment underwriting is to be distinguished from conditional arrangements for distributing new securities, such as standby commitments and best efforts commitments. The word

underwriting is frequently misused with respect to such conditional arrangements. It is used correctly only with respect to firm commitment underwritings or, as they are sometimes called, BOUGHT DEALS. *See also* BEST EFFORT; STANDBY COMMITMENT.

Lending: term used by lenders to refer to an agreement to make a loan to a specific borrower within a specific period of time and, if applicable, on a specific property. *See also* COMMITMENT FEE.

FIRM ORDER

Commercial transaction: written or verbal order that has been confirmed and is not subject to cancellation.

Securities: (1) order to buy or sell for the proprietary account of the broker-dealer firm; (2) buy or sell order not conditional upon the customer's confirmation.

FIRM QUOTE securities industry term referring to any round lot bid or offer price of a security stated by a market maker and not identified as a nominal (or subject) quote. Under National Association of Securities Dealers' (NASD) rules and practice, quotes requiring further negotiation or review must be identified as nominal quotes. *See also* NOMINAL QUOTATION.

FIRST BOARD delivery dates for futures as established by the Chicago Board of Trade and other exchanges trading in futures.

FIRST CALL DATE first date specified in the indenture of a corporate or municipal bond contract on which part or all of the bond may be redeemed at a set price. An XYZ bond due in 2010, for instance, may have a first call date of May 1, 1993. This means that, if XYZ wishes, bondholders may be paid off starting on that date in 1993. Bond brokers typically quote yields on such bonds with both yield to maturity (in this case, 2010) and yield to call (in this case, 1993). *See also* YIELD TO CALL; YIELD TO MATURITY.

FIRST IN, FIRST OUT (FIFO) method of accounting for inventory whereby, quite literally, the inventory is assumed to be sold in the chronological order in which it was purchased. For example, the following formula is used in computing the cost of goods sold:

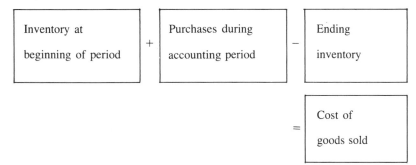

Under the FIFO method, inventory costs flow from the oldest purchases forward, with beginning inventory as the starting point and ending inventory representing the most recent purchases. The FIFO method contrasts with the LIFO or LAST IN, FIRST OUT method, which is FIFO in reverse. The significance of the difference becomes apparent when inflation or deflation affects inventory prices. In an inflationary period, the FIFO method produces a higher ending inventory, a lower cost of goods sold figure, and a higher gross profit. LIFO, on the other hand, produces a lower ending inventory, a higher cost of goods sold figure, and a lower reported profit.

In accounting for the purchase and sale of securities for tax purposes, FIFO is assumed by the IRS unless it is advised of the use of an alternative method.

FIRST MORTGAGE   real estate loan that gives the mortgagee (lender) a primary lien against a specified piece of property. A primary lien has precedence over all other mortgages in case of default. *See also* JUNIOR MORTGAGE; SECOND MORTGAGE.

FIRST PREFERRED STOCK   preferred stock that has preferential claim on dividends and assets over other preferred issues and common stock.

FISCAL AGENT
1. usually a bank or a trust company acting for a corporation under a corporate trust agreement. The fiscal agent handles such matters as disbursing funds for dividend payments, redeeming bonds and coupons, handling taxes related to the issue of bonds, and paying rents.
2. agent of the national government or its agencies or of a state or municipal government that performs functions relating to the issue and payment of bonds. For example, the Federal Reserve is the U.S. government's fiscal agent.

FISCAL POLICY   federal taxation and spending policies designed to level out the business cycle and achieve full employment, price stability, and sustained growth in the economy. Fiscal policy basically follows the economic theory of the 20th-century English economist John Maynard Keynes that insufficient demand causes unemployment and excessive demand leads to inflation. It aims to stimulate demand and output in periods of business decline by increasing government purchases and cutting taxes, thereby releasing more disposable income into the spending stream, and to correct overexpansion by reversing the process. Working to balance these deliberate fiscal measures are the so-called built-in stabilizers, such as the progressive income tax and unemployment benefits, which automatically respond countercyclically. Fiscal policy is administered independently of MONETARY POLICY, by which the Federal Reserve Board attempts to regulate economic activity by controlling the money supply. The goals of fiscal and monetary policy are the same, but Keynesians and Monetarists disagree as to which of the two approaches works best. At the basis of their differences are questions dealing with the velocity (turnover) of money and the effect of changes in the money supply on the equilibrium rate of interest (the rate at which money demand equals money supply). *See also* KEYNESIAN ECONOMICS.

FISCAL YEAR (FY)   accounting period covering 12 consecutive months, 52 consecutive weeks, 13 four-week periods, or 365 consecutive days, at the end of which the books are closed and profit or loss is determined. A company's fiscal year is often, but not necessarily, the same as the calendar year. A seasonal business will frequently select a fiscal rather than a calendar year, so that its year-end figures will show it in its most liquid condition, a choice which also has the advantage of having less inventory to verify physically. The fiscal year of the U.S. government runs from October 1 to September 30.

FIT securities industry jargon describing a situation where the features of a particular investment perfectly match the portfolio requirements of an investor.

FITCH INVESTORS SERVICE, INC. New York and Denver-based RATING firm, which rates corporate and municipal bonds, preferred stock, commercial paper, and obligations of health-care and not-for-profit institutions.

FITCH SHEETS sheets indicating the successive trade prices of securities listed on the major exchanges. They are published by Francis Emory Fitch, Inc. in New York City.

FIVE HUNDRED DOLLAR RULE REGULATION T provision of the Federal Reserve that exempts deficiencies in MARGIN requirements amounting to $500 or less from mandatory remedial action. Brokers are thus not forced to resort to the liquidation of an account to correct a trivial deficiency in a situation where, for example, a customer is temporarily out of town and cannot be reached.

FIVE PERCENT RULE one of the Rules of Fair Practice of the National Association of Securities Dealers (NASD). It proposes an ethical guideline for spreads in dealer transactions and commissions in brokerage transactions, including PROCEEDS SALES and RISKLESS TRANSACTIONS.

FIXATION setting of a present or future price of a commodity, such as the twice-daily London GOLD FIXING. In other commodities, prices are fixed further into the future for the benefit of both buyers and sellers of that commodity.

FIXED ANNUITY investment contract sold by an insurance company that guarantees fixed payments, either for life or for a specified period, to an annuitant. In fixed annuities, the insurer takes both the investment and the mortality risks. A fixed annuity contrasts with a VARIABLE ANNUITY, where payments depend on an uncertain outcome, such as prices in the securities markets. *See also* ANNUITY.

FIXED ASSET tangible property used in the operations of a business, but not expected to be consumed or converted into cash in the ordinary course of events. Plant, machinery and equipment, furniture and fixtures, and leasehold improvements comprise the fixed assets of most companies. They are normally represented on the balance sheet at their net depreciated value.

FIXED-CHARGE COVERAGE ratio of profits before payment of interest and income taxes to interest on bonds and other contractual long-term debt. It indicates how many times interest charges have been earned by the corporation on a pretax basis. Since failure to meet interest payments would be a default under the terms of indenture agreements, the coverage ratio measures a margin of safety. The amount of safety desirable depends on the stability of a company's earnings. (Too much safety can be an indication of an undesirable lack of leverage.) In cyclical companies, the fixed-charge coverage in periods of recession is a telling ratio. Analysts also find it useful to calculate the number of times that a company's *cash flow*—i.e., *after*-tax earnings plus noncash expenses (for example, depreciation)—covers fixed charges. Also known as *times fixed charges*.

FIXED COST cost that remains constant regardless of sales volume. Fixed costs include salaries of executives, interest expense, rent, depreciation, and insurance expenses. They contrast with *variable costs* (direct labor, materials costs), which are distinguished from *semivariable costs*. Semivariable costs vary, but not necessarily in direct relation to sales. They may also remain fixed up to a level of sales, then increase when sales enter a higher range. For example, expenses associated with a delivery truck would be fixed up to the level of sales where a second truck was required. Obviously, no costs are purely fixed; the assumption, however, serves the purposes of cost accounting for limited planning periods. Cost accounting is also concerned with the allocation of portions of fixed costs to inventory costs, also called indirect costs, overhead, factory overhead, and supplemental overhead. *See also* DIRECT OVERHEAD; VARIABLE COST.

FIXED EXCHANGE RATE set rate of exchange between the currencies of countries. At the Bretton Woods international monetary conference in 1944, a system of fixed exchange rates was set up, which existed until the early 1970s, when a FLOATING EXCHANGE RATE system was adopted.

FIXED INCOME INVESTMENT security that pays a fixed rate of return. This usually refers to government, corporate, or municipal bonds, which pay a fixed rate of interest until the bonds mature, and to preferred stock, which pays a fixed dividend. Such investments are advantageous in a time of low inflation, but do not protect holders against erosion of buying power in a time of rising inflation, since the bondholder or preferred shareholder gets the same amount of interest or dividends, even though consumer goods cost more.

FIXED PRICE

Investment: in a public offering of new securities, price at which investment bankers in the underwriting SYNDICATE agree to sell the issue to the public. The price remains fixed as long as the syndicate remains in effect. The proper term for this kind of system is *fixed price offering system*. In contrast, Eurobonds, which are also sold through underwriting syndicates, are offered on a basis that permits discrimination among customers; i.e., the underwriting spread may be adjusted to suit the particular buyer. *See also* EUROBOND.

Contracts: type of contract where the price is preset and invariable, regardless of the actual costs of production. *See also* COST-PLUS CONTRACT.

FIXED RATE (LOAN) type of loan in which the interest rate does not fluctuate with general market conditions. There are fixed rate mortgage (also known as conventional mortgage) and consumer installment loans, as well as fixed rate business loans. Fixed rate loans tend to have higher original interest rates than flexible rate loans such as an ADJUSTABLE RATE MORTGAGE (ARM), because lenders are not protected against a rise in the cost of money when they make a fixed rate loan.

The term fixed rate may also refer to fixed currency exchange rates. *See* FIXED EXCHANGE RATE.

FIXED TRUST UNIT INVESTMENT TRUST that has a fixed portfolio of previously agreed upon securities; also called *fixed investment trust*. The securities are usually of one type, such as corporate, government, or municipal bonds, in order to afford a regular income to holders of units. A fixed trust is distinguished from a PARTICIPATING TRUST.

FIXTURE attachment to real property that is not intended to be moved and would create damage to the property if it were moved—for example, a plumbing fixture. Fixtures are classified as part of real estate when they share the same useful life. Otherwise, they are considered equipment.

FLAG technical chart pattern resembling a flag shaped like a parallelogram with masts on either side, showing a consolidation within a trend. It results from price fluctuations within a narrow range, both preceded and followed by sharp rises or declines. If the flag—the consolidation period—is preceded by a rise, it will usually be followed by a rise; a fall will follow a fall.

FLAG

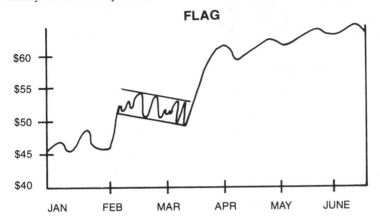

FLASH tape display designation used when volume on an exchange is so heavy that the tape runs more than five minutes behind. The flash interrupts the display to report the current price—called the *flash price*—of a heavily traded security. Current prices of two groups of 50 stocks are flashed at five-minute intervals as long as the tape is seriously behind.

FLAT
  1. in bond trading, without accrued interest. This means that accrued interest will be received by the buyer if and when paid but that no accrued interest is payable to the seller. Issues in default and INCOME BONDS are normally quoted and traded flat. The opposite of a flat bond is an AND INTEREST bond. *See also* LOANED FLAT.
  2. inventory of a market maker with a net zero position—i.e., neither long nor short.
  3. position of an underwriter whose account is completely sold.

FLAT MARKET market characterized by HORIZONTAL PRICE MOVEMENT. It is usually the result of low activity. However, STABILIZATION, consolidation, and DISTRIBUTION are situations marked by both horizontal price movement and active trading.

FLAT SCALE
  Industry: labor term denoting a uniform rate of pay that makes no allowance for volume, frequency, or other factors.
  Municipal bonds: bond trader's term describing a situation where shorter and longer term yields show little difference over the maturity range of a new serial bond issue.

FLAT TAX tax applied at the same rate to all levels of income. It is often discussed as an alternative to the PROGRESSIVE TAX. Proponents of a flat tax argue that people able to retain larger portions of higher income would have added incentive to earn, thus stimulating the economy. Advocates also note its simplicity. Opponents argue it is a REGRESSIVE TAX in effect, comparing it to the sales tax, a uniform tax that puts a greater burden on households with lower incomes. The TAX REFORM ACT OF 1986 instituted a *modified flat tax system*—a progressive tax with fewer tax brackets and lower rates.

FLEXIBLE BUDGET statement of projected revenue and expenditure based on various levels of production. It shows how costs vary with different rates of output or at different levels of sales volume.

FLEXIBLE EXCHANGE RATE *see* FLOATING EXCHANGE RATE.

FLIGHT OF CAPITAL *see* CAPITAL FLIGHT.

FLIGHT TO QUALITY moving capital to the safest possible investment to protect oneself from loss during an unsettling period in the market. For example, when a major bank fails, cautious money market investors may buy only government-backed money market securities instead of those issued by major banks. A flight to quality can be measured by the differing yields resulting from such a movement of capital. In the example just given, the yields on bank-issued money market paper will rise since there will be less demand for it, and the rates on government securities will fall, because there will be more demand for them.

FLIP-IN POISON PILL *see* POISON PILL.

FLIP-OVER POISON PILL *see* POISON PILL.

FLOAT
Banking: time between the deposit of a check in a bank and payment. Long floats are to the advantage of checkwriters, whose money may earn interest until a check clears. They are to the disadvantage of depositors, who must wait for a check to clear before they have access to the funds. As a rule, the further away the paying bank is from the deposit bank, the longer it will take for a check to clear. Some U.S. states limit the amount of float a bank can impose on the checks of its depositors. *See also* UNCOLLECTED FUNDS.
Investments: number of shares of a corporation that are outstanding and available for trading by the public. A small float means the stock will be more volatile, since a large order to buy or sell shares can influence the stock's price dramatically. A larger float means the stock will be less volatile.

FLOATER debt instrument with a variable interest rate tied to another interest rate—for example, the rate paid by Treasury bills. A FLOATING RATE NOTE, for instance, provides a holder with additional interest if the applicable interest rate rises and less interest if the rate falls. It is generally best to buy floaters if it appears that interest rates will rise. If the outlook is for falling rates, investors typically concentrate on fixed-rate instruments. Floaters spread risk between issuers and debtholders.

FLOATING AN ISSUE *see* NEW ISSUE; UNDERWRITE.

FLOATING DEBT continuously renewed or refinanced short-term debt of companies or governments used to finance ongoing operating needs.

FLOATING EXCHANGE RATE movement of a foreign currency exchange rate in response to changes in the market forces of supply and demand; also known as *flexible exchange rate*. Currencies strengthen or weaken based on a nation's reserves of hard currency and gold, its international trade balance, its rate of inflation and interest rates, and the general strength of its economy. Nations generally do not want their currency to be too strong, because this makes the country's goods too expensive for foreigners to buy. A weak currency, on the other hand, may signify economic instability if it has been caused by high inflation or a weak economy. The opposite of the floating exchange rate is the FIXED EXCHANGE RATE system. *See also* PAR VALUE OF CURRENCY.

FLOATING RATE NOTE debt instrument with a variable interest rate. Interest adjustments are made periodically, often every six months, and are tied to a money-market index such as Treasury bill rates. Floating rate notes usually have a maturity of about five years. They provide holders with protection against rises in interest rates, but pay lower yields than fixed rate notes of the same maturity. Also known as a FLOATER.

FLOATING SECURITIES
1. securities bought for the purpose of making a quick profit on resale and held in a broker's name.
2. outstanding stock of a corporation that is traded on an exchange.
3. unsold units of a newly issued security.

FLOATING SUPPLY
Bonds: total dollar amount of municipal bonds in the hands of speculators and dealers that is for sale at any particular time as offered in the BLUE LIST. Someone might say, for instance, "There is $10 billion in floating supply available now in the municipal bond market."
Stocks: number of shares of a stock available for purchase. A dealer might say, "The floating supply in this stock is about 200,000 shares." Sometimes called simply the *float*.

FLOOR BROKER member of an exchange who is an employee of a member firm and executes orders, as agent, on the floor of the exchange for clients. The floor broker receives an order via teletype machine from his firm's trading department, then proceeds to the appropriate trading post on the exchange floor. There he joins other brokers and the specialist in the security being bought or sold, and executes the trade at the best competitive price available. On completion of the transaction, the customer is notified through his registered representative back at the firm, and the trade is printed on the consolidated ticker tape, which is displayed electronically around the country. A floor broker should not be confused with a FLOOR TRADER, who trades as a principal for his or her own account, rather than as a broker.

FLOOR OFFICIAL securities exchange employee, who is present on the floor of the exchange to settle disputes in the auction procedure, such as questions about priority or precedence in the settling of an auction. The floor official makes rulings on the spot and his or her judgment is usually accepted.

FLOOR TICKET summary of the information entered on the ORDER TICKET by the registered representative on receipt of a buy or sell order from a client. The floor ticket gives the floor broker the information needed to execute a securities transaction. The information required on floor tickets is specified by securities industry rules.

FLOOR TRADER member of a stock or commodities exchange who trades on the floor of that exchange for his or her own account. The floor trader must abide by trading rules similar to those of the exchange specialists who trade on behalf of others. The term should not be confused with FLOOR BROKER. *See also* REGISTERED COMPETITIVE TRADER.

FLOTATION (FLOATATION) COST cost of issuing new stocks or bonds. It varies with the amount of underwriting risk and the job of physical distribution. It comprises two elements: (1) the compensation earned by the investment bankers (the underwriters) in the form of the spread between the price paid to the issuer (the corporation or government agency) and the offering price to the public, and (2) the expenses of the issuer (legal, accounting, printing, and other out-of-pocket expenses). Securities and Exchange Commission studies reveal that flotation costs are higher for stocks than for bonds, reflecting the generally wider distribution and greater volatility of common stock as opposed to bonds, which are usually sold in large blocks to relatively few investors. The SEC also found that flotation costs as a percentage of gross proceeds are greater for smaller issues than for larger ones. This occurs because the issuer's legal and other expenses tend to be relatively large and fixed; also, smaller issues tend to originate with less established issuers, requiring more information development and marketing expense. An issue involving a RIGHTS OFFERING can involve negligible underwriting risk and selling effort and therefore minimal flotation cost, especially if the underpricing is substantial.

The UNDERWRITING SPREAD is the key variable in flotation cost, historically ranging from 23.7% of the size of a small issue of common stock to as low as 1.25% of the par value of high-grade bonds. Spreads are determined by both negotiation and competitive bidding.

FLOWER BOND type of U.S. government bond that, regardless of its cost price, is acceptable at par value in payment of estate taxes if the decedent was the legal holder at the time of death; also called *estate tax anticipation bond.* Flower bonds were issued as recently as 1971, and the last of them, with a 3½% coupon, will mature in 1998.

FLOW OF FUNDS

Economics: in referring to the national economy, the way funds are transferred from savings surplus units to savings deficit units through financial intermediaries. *See also* FINANCIAL INTERMEDIARY.

Municipal bonds: statement found in the bond resolutions of municipal revenue issues showing the priorities by which municipal revenue will be applied. Typically, the flow of funds in decreasing order of priority is operation and maintenance, bond debt service, expansion of the facility, and sinking fund for retirement of debt prior to maturity. The flow of funds statement varies in detail from issue to issue.

FLUCTUATION
1. change in prices or interest rates, either up or down. Fluctuation may refer to either slight or dramatic changes in the prices of stocks, bonds, or commodities. *See also* FLUCTUATION LIMIT.
2. the ups and downs in the economy.

FLUCTUATION LIMIT limits placed on the daily ups and downs of futures prices by the commodity exchanges. The limit protects traders from losing too much on a particular contract in one day. If a commodity reaches its limit, it may not trade any further that day. *See also* LIMIT UP, LIMIT DOWN.

FNMA *see* FEDERAL NATIONAL MORTGAGE ASSOCIATION.

FOB *see* FREE ON BOARD.

FOCUS REPORT FOCUS is an acronym for the Financial and Operational Combined Uniform Single report, which broker-dealers are required to file monthly and quarterly with self-regulatory organizations (SROs). The SROs include exchanges, securities associations, and clearing organizations registered with the Securities and Exchange Commission and required by federal securities laws to be self-policing. The FOCUS report contains figures on capital, earnings, trade flow, and other required details.

FOOTSIE popular name for the Financial Times's FT-SE 100 Index (Financial Times-Stock Exchange 100 stock index), a market-value-(capitalization)-weighted index of 100 ALPHA stocks traded on the London Stock Exchange.

FORBES 500 annual listing by *Forbes* magazine of the largest U.S. publicly owned corporations ranked four ways: by sales, assets, profits, and market value. *See also* FORTUNE 500.

FORCED CONVERSION when a CONVERTIBLE security is called in by its issuer. Convertible owners may find it to their financial advantage either to sell or to convert their holdings into common shares of the underlying company or to accept the call price. Such a conversion usually takes place when the convertible is selling above its CALL PRICE because the market value of the shares of the underlying stock has risen sharply. *See also* CONVERTIBLE.

FORECASTING projecting current trends using existing data.
   Stock market forecasters predict the direction of the stock market by relying on technical data of trading activity and fundamental statistics on the direction of the economy.
   Economic forecasters foretell the strength of the economy, often by utilizing complex econometric models as a tool to make specific predictions of future levels of inflation, interest rates, and employment. *See also* ECONOMETRICS.
   Forecasting can also refer to various PROJECTIONS used in business and financial planning.

FORECLOSURE process by which a homeowner who has not made timely payments of principal and interest on a mortgage loses title to the home. The holder of the mortgage, whether it be a bank, a savings and loan, or an individual, must go to court to seize the property, which may then be sold to satisfy the claims of the mortgage.

FOREIGN CORPORATION
   1. corporation chartered under the laws of a state other than the one in which it conducts business. Because of inevitable confusion with the term ALIEN CORPORATION, *out-of-state corporation* is preferred.
   2. corporation organized under the laws of a foreign country; the term ALIEN CORPORATION is usually preferred.

FOREIGN CROWD New York Stock Exchange members who trade on the floor in foreign bonds.

FOREIGN DIRECT INVESTMENT
   1. investment in U.S. businesses by foreign citizens; usually involves majority stock ownership of the enterprise.

2. joint ventures between foreign and U.S. companies.

FOREIGN EXCHANGE instruments employed in making payments between countries—paper currency, notes, checks, bills of exchange, and electronic notifications of international debits and credits.

FORM 3 form filed with the Securities and Exchange Commission and the pertinent stock exchange by all holders of 10% or more of the stock of a company registered with the SEC and by all directors and officers, even if no shares are owned. Form 3 details the number of shares owned as well as the number of warrants, rights, convertible bonds, and options to purchase common stock. Individuals required to file Form 3 are considered insiders, and they are required to update their information whenever changes occur. Such changes are reported on FORM 4.

FORM 4 document, filed with the Securities and Exchange Commission and the pertinent stock exchange, which is used to report changes in the holdings of (1) those who own at least 10% of a corporation's outstanding stock and (2) directors and officers, even if they own no stock. When there has been a major change in ownership, Form 4 must be filed within ten days of the end of the month in which the change took place. Form 4 filings must be constantly updated during a takeover attempt of a company when the acquirer buys more than 10% of the outstanding shares.

FORM 8-K Securities and Exchange Commission required form that a publicly held company must file, reporting on any material event that might affect its financial situation or the value of its shares, ranging from merger activity to amendment of the corporate charter or bylaws. The SEC considers as material all matters about which an average, prudent investor ought reasonably to be informed before deciding whether to buy, sell, or hold a registered security. Form 8-K must be filed within a month of the occurrence of the material event. Timely disclosure rules may require a corporation to issue a press release immediately concerning an event subsequently reported on Form 8-K.

FORM 10-K annual report required by the Securities and Exchange Commission of every issuer of a registered security, every exchange-listed company, and any company with 500 or more shareholders or $1 million or more in gross assets. The form provides for disclosure of total sales, revenue, and pretax operating income, as well as sales by separate classes of products for each of a company's separate lines of business for each of the past five years. A source and application of funds statement presented on a comparative basis for the last two fiscal years is also required. Form 10-K becomes public information when filed with the SEC.

FORM 10-Q quarterly report required by the Securities and Exchange Commission of companies with listed securities. Form 10-Q is less comprehensive than the FORM 10-K annual report and does not require that figures be audited. It may cover the specific quarter or it may be cumulative. It should include comparative figures for the same period of the previous year.

FORMULA INVESTING investment technique based on a predetermined timing or asset allocation model that eliminates emotional decisions. One type of formula investing, called dollar cost averaging, involves putting the same amount of money into a stock or mutual fund at regular intervals, so that more shares will be bought when the price is low and less when the price is high. Another formula investing method calls for shifting funds from stocks to bonds or vice versa as the stock market reaches particular price levels. If stocks rise to a particular point, a certain amount of the stock portfolio is sold and put in bonds. On the other hand, if stocks fall to a particular low price, money is brought out of bonds into stocks. *See also* CONSTANT DOLLAR PLAN; CONSTANT RATIO PLAN.

FORTUNE 500 annual listing by *Fortune* magazine of the 500 largest U.S. industrial (manufacturing) corporations, ranked by sales. The magazine also ranks the assets, net income, stockholders' equity, number of employees, net income as a percent of sales or of stockholders' equity, earnings per share, and total return to investors.

   Fortune publishes another annual directory—the Fortune Service 500—which ranks the 500 largest nonmanufacturing U.S. companies by sales or revenue and by the other criteria used in the Fortune 500 directory. These nonindustrial companies are divided into seven categories: diversified service (housing, health care, etc.), commercial banking, diversified financial (S&Ls, Student Loan Marketing Association, etc.), life insurance, retailing, transportation, and utilities. *See also* FORBES 500.

FORWARD CONTRACT purchase or sale of a specific quantity of a commodity, government security, foreign currency, or other financial instrument at the current or SPOT PRICE, with delivery and settlement at a specified future date. Because it is a completed contract—as opposed to an options contract, where the owner has the choice of completing or not completing—a forward contract can be a COVER for the sale of a FUTURES CONTRACT. *See* HEDGE.

FORWARD EXCHANGE TRANSACTION purchase or sale of foreign currency at an exchange rate established now but with payment and delivery at a specified future time. Most forward exchange contracts have one-, three-, or six-month maturities, though contracts in major currencies can normally be arranged for delivery at any specified date up to a year, and sometimes up to three years.

FORWARD PRICING Securities and Exchange Commission requirement that open-end investment companies, whose share price is always determined by the NET ASSET VALUE of the outstanding shares, base all incoming buy and sell orders on the next net asset valuation of fund shares. *See also* INVESTMENT COMPANY.

FOR YOUR INFORMATION (FYI) prefix to a security price quote by a market maker that indicates the quote is "for your information" and is not a firm offer to trade at that price. FYI quotes are given as a courtesy for purposes of valuation. FVO (for valuation only) is sometimes used instead.

401(K) PLAN also called *cash or deferred arrangement* (CODA) or SALARY REDUCTION PLAN, plan whereby an employee may elect, as an alternative to receiving taxable cash in the form of compensation or a bonus, to contribute pretax dollars to a qualified tax-deferred retirement plan. Effective in 1987, elective deferrals are limited to $7000 (previously $30,000), although employers may continue to contribute the smaller of 25% of compensation or $30,000, less the amount of salary deferral. Withdrawals from 401(K) plans prior to age 59½ are subject to a 10% penalty tax except for death, disability, termination of employment, or qualifying hardship. "Highly compensated" employees are subject to special limitations.

FOURTH MARKET direct trading of large blocks of securities between institutional investors to save brokerage commissions. The fourth market is aided by computers, notably by a computerized subscriber service called *INSTINET*, an acronym for Institutional Networks Corporation. INSTINET is registered with the Securities and Exchange Commission as a stock exchange and numbers among its subscribers a large number of mutual funds and other institutional investors linked to each other by computer terminals. The system permits subscribers to display tentative volume interest and bid-ask quotes to others in the system.

FRACTIONAL DISCRETION ORDER buy or sell order for securities that allows the broker discretion within a specified fraction of a point. For example, "Buy 1000 XYZ at 28, discretion ½ point" means that the broker may execute the trade at a maximum price of 28½.

FRACTIONAL SHARE unit of stock less than one full share. For instance, if a shareholder is in a dividend reinvestment program, and the dividends being reinvested are not adequate to buy a full share at the stock's current price, the shareholder will be credited with a fractional share until enough dividends have been accumulated to purchase a full share.

FRANCHISE

In general: (1) privilege given a dealer by a manufacturer or franchise service organization to sell the franchisor's products or services in a given area, with or without exclusivity. Such arrangements are sometimes formalized in a *franchise agreement,* which is a contract between the franchisor and franchisee wherein the former may offer consultation, promotional assistance, financing, and other benefits in exchange for a percentage of sales or profits. (2) The business owned by the franchisee, who usually must meet an initial cash investment requirement.

Government: legal right given to a company or individual by a government authority permitting the performance of some economic function. For example, an electrical utility might have the right, under the terms of a franchise, to use city property to provide electrical service to city residents.

FRANCHISE TAX state tax, usually regressive (that is, the rate decreases as the tax base increases), imposed on a state-chartered corporation for the right to do business under its corporate name. Franchise taxes are usually levied on a number of value bases, such as capital stock, capital stock plus surplus, or profits.

FRAUD intentional misrepresentation, concealment, or omission of the truth for the purpose of deception or manipulation to the detriment of a person or an organization. Fraud is a legal concept and the application of the term in a specific instance should be determined by a legal expert.

FREDDIE MAC
1. nickname for FEDERAL HOME LOAN MORTGAGE CORPORATION (FHLMC).
2. mortgage-backed securities, issued in minimum denominations of $25,000, that are packaged, guaranteed, and sold by the FHLMC. Mortgage-backed securities are issues in which residential mortgages are packaged and sold to investors.

FREE AND OPEN MARKET market in which price is determined by the free, unregulated interchange of supply and demand. The opposite is a *controlled market,* where supply, demand, and price are artificially set, resulting in an *inefficient market.*

FREE BOX securities industry jargon for a secure storage place ("box") for fully paid (''free'') customers' securities, such as a bank vault or the DEPOSITORY TRUST COMPANY.

FREED UP securities industry jargon meaning that the members of an underwriting syndicate are no longer bound by the price agreed upon and fixed in the AGREEMENT AMONG UNDERWRITERS. They are thus free to trade in the security on a market basis.

FREE ON BOARD (FOB) transportation term meaning that the invoice price includes delivery at the seller's expense to a specified point and no further. For example, ''FOB our Newark warehouse'' means that the buyer must pay all shipping and other charges associated with transporting the merchandise from the seller's warehouse in Newark to the buyer's receiving point. Title normally passes from seller to buyer at the FOB point by way of a bill of lading.

FREERIDING
1. practice, prohibited by the Securities and Exchange Commission and the National Association of Securities Dealers, whereby an underwriting SYNDICATE member withholds a portion of a new securities issue and later resells it at a price higher than the initial offering price.
2. practice whereby a brokerage client buys and sells a security in rapid order without putting up money for the purchase. The practice violates REGULATION T of the Federal Reserve Board concerning broker-dealer credit to customers. The penalty requires that the customer's account be frozen for 90 days. *See also* FROZEN ACCOUNT.

FREE RIGHT OF EXCHANGE ability to transfer securities from one name to another without paying the charge associated with a sales transaction. The free right applies, for example, where stock in STREET NAME (that is, registered in the name of a broker-dealer) is transferred to the customer's name in order to be eligible for a dividend reinvestment plan. *See also* REGISTERED SECURITY.

FRONT-END LOAD sales charge applied to an investment at the time of initial purchase. There may be a front-end load on a mutual fund, for instance, which is sold by a broker. Annuities, life insurance policies, and limited partnerships can also have front-end loads. From the investor's point of view, the earnings from the investment should make up for this up-front fee within a relatively short period of time. *See also* INVESTMENT COMPANY.

FRONT RUNNING practice whereby a securities or commodities trader takes a POSITION to capitalize on advance knowledge of a large upcoming transaction expected to influence the market price. In the stock market, this might be done by buying an OPTION on stock expected to benefit from a large BLOCK transaction. In commodities, DUAL TRADING is common practice and provides opportunities to profit from front running.

FROZEN ACCOUNT
Banking: bank account from which funds may not be withdrawn until a lien is satisfied and a court order is received freeing the balance.
   A bank account may also be frozen by court order in a dispute over the ownership of property.
Investments: brokerage account under disciplinary action by the Federal Reserve Board for violation of REGULATION T. During the period an account is frozen

(90 days), the customer may not sell securities until their purchase price has been fully paid and the certificates have been delivered. The penalty is invoked commonly in cases of FREERIDING.

FULL COUPON BOND bond with a coupon rate that is near or above current market interest rates. If interest rates are generally about 10%, for instance, a 9½% or 11% bond is considered a full coupon bond.

FULL DISCLOSURE

In general: requirement to disclose all material facts relevant to a transaction.

Securities industry: public information requirements established by the Securities Act of 1933, the Securities Exchange Act of 1934, and the major stock exchanges.

See also DISCLOSURE.

FULL FAITH AND CREDIT phrase meaning that the full taxing and borrowing power, *plus* revenue other than taxes, is pledged in payment of interest and repayment of principal of a bond issued by a government entity. U.S. government securities and general obligation bonds of states and local governments are backed by this pledge.

FULL-SERVICE BROKER broker who provides a wide range of services to clients. Unlike a DISCOUNT BROKER, who just executes trades, a full-service broker offers advice on which stocks, bonds, commodities, and mutual funds to buy or sell. A full-service broker may also offer an ASSET MANAGEMENT ACCOUNT; advice on financial planning, tax shelters, and INCOME LIMITED PARTNERSHIPS; and new issues of stock. A full-service broker's commissions will be higher than those of a discount broker. The term *brokerage* is gradually being replaced by variations of the term *financial services* as the range of services offered by brokers expands.

FULLY DILUTED EARNINGS PER (COMMON) SHARE figure showing earnings per common share after assuming the exercise of warrants and stock options, and the conversion of convertible bonds and preferred stock (all potentially *dilutive* securities). Actually, it is more analytically correct to define the term as the smallest earnings per common share figure that can be obtained by computing earnings per share (EPS) for all possible combinations of assumed exercise or conversion (because antidilutive securities—securities whose conversion would add to EPS—may not be assumed to be exercised or converted). Fully diluted EPS must be reported on the profit and loss statement when the figure is 97% or less of earnings available to common shareholders divided by the average number of common shares outstanding during the period. See also DILUTION; PRIMARY EARNINGS PER (COMMON) SHARE.

FULLY DISTRIBUTED term describing a new securities issue that has been completely resold to the investing public (that is, to institutions and individuals and other investors rather than to dealers).

FULLY INVESTED said of an investor or a portfolio when funds in cash or CASH EQUIVALENTS are minimal and assets are totally committed to other investments, usually stock. To be fully invested is to have an optimistic view of the market.

FULLY VALUED said of a stock that has reached a price at which analysts think the underlying company's fundamental earnings power has been recognized by the market. If the stock goes up from that price, it is called OVERVALUED. If the stock goes down, it is termed UNDERVALUED.

FUNDAMENTAL ANALYSIS

Economics: research of such factors as interest rates, gross national product, inflation, unemployment, and inventories as tools to predict the direction of the economy.

Investment: analysis of the balance sheet and income statements of companies in order to forecast their future stock price movements. Fundamental analysts consider past records of assets, earnings, sales, products, management, and markets in predicting future trends in these indicators of a company's success or failure. By appraising a firm's prospects, these analysts assess whether a particular stock or group of stocks is UNDERVALUED or OVERVALUED at the current market price. The other major school of stock market analysis is TECHNICAL ANALYSIS, which relies on price and volume movements of stocks and does not concern itself with financial statistics.

FUNDED DEBT

1. debt that is due after one year and is formalized by the issuing of bonds or long-term notes.
2. bond issue whose retirement is provided for by a SINKING FUND.
   See also FLOATING DEBT.

FUNDING

1. refinancing a debt on or before its maturity; also called REFUNDING and, in certain instances, PREREFUNDING.
2. putting money into investments or another type of reserve fund, to provide for future pension or welfare plans.
3. in corporate finance, the word *funding* is preferred to *financing* when referring to bonds in contrast to stock. A company is said to be funding its operations if it floats bonds.
4. to provide funds to finance a project, such as a research study.
   See also SINKING FUND.

FUNGIBLES bearer instruments, securities, or goods that are equivalent, substitutable, and interchangeable. Commodities such as soybeans or wheat, common shares of the same company, and dollar bills are all familiar examples of fungibles.

Fungibility (interchangeability) of listed options, by virtue of their common expiration dates and strike prices, makes it possible for buyers and sellers to close out their positions by putting offsetting transactions through the OPTIONS CLEARING CORPORATION. *See also* OFFSET; STRIKE PRICE.

FURTHEST MONTH in commodities or options trading, the month that is furthest away from settlement of the contract. For example, Treasury bill futures may have outstanding contracts for three, six, or nine months. The six- and nine-month contracts would be the furthest months, and the three-month contract would be the NEAREST MONTH.

FUTURES CONTRACT agreement to buy or sell a specific amount of a commodity or financial instrument at a particular price in a stipulated future month. The price is established between buyer and seller on the floor of a commodity exchange, using the OPEN OUTCRY system. A futures contract obligates the buyer to purchase the underlying commodity and the seller to sell it, unless the contract is sold to another before settlement date, which may happen if a trader waits to take a profit or cut a loss. This contrasts with options trading, in which the option buyer may choose whether or not to exercise the option by the exercise date. *See also* FORWARD CONTRACT; FUTURES MARKET.

FUTURES MARKET commodity exchange where FUTURES CONTRACTS are traded. Different exchanges specialize in particular kinds of contracts. The major exchanges are Amex Commodity Exchange, the Commodity Exchange Inc. (Comex), the New York Coffee, Sugar and Cocoa Exchange, the New York Cotton Exchange, the New York Mercantile Exchange, and the New York Futures Exchange, all in New York; the Chicago Board of Trade, the International Monetary Market, the Chicago Mercantile Exchange, the Chicago Rice and Cotton Exchange, and the MidAmerica Commodity Exchange, all in Chicago; the Kansas City Board of Trade, in Kansas City, MO; and the Minneapolis Grain Exchange, in Minneapolis. *See also* SPOT MARKET.

FUTURES OPTION OPTION on a FUTURES CONTRACT.

FVO (FOR VALUATION ONLY) *see* FOR YOUR INFORMATION.

g

GAMMA STOCKS classification of stocks traded on the London Stock Exchange. Ranking third behind ALPHA and BETA stocks in terms of capitalization and activity, gamma stocks are less regulated, requiring just two market makers quoting *indicative* (as opposed to *firm*) share prices.

GAP

Finance: amount of a financing need for which provision has yet to be made. For example, ABC company might need $1.5 million to purchase and equip a new plant facility. It arranges a mortgage loan of $700,000, secures equipment financing of $400,000, and obtains new equity of $150,000. That leaves a gap of $250,000 for which it seeks gap financing. Such financing may be available from state and local governments concerned with promoting economic development.

Securities: securities industry term used to describe the price movement of a stock or commodity when one day's trading range for the stock or commodity does not overlap the next day's, causing a range, or gap, in which no trade has occurred. This usually takes place because of some extraordinary positive or negative news about the company or commodity. *See also* PRICE GAP.

GARAGE annex floor on the north side of the main trading floor of the New York Stock Exchange.

GARBATRAGE stock traders' term, combining garbage and ARBITRAGE, for activity in stocks swept upward by the psychology surrounding a major takeover. For example, when two leading entertainment stocks, Time, Inc. and Warner Communications, Inc., were IN PLAY in 1989, stocks with insignificant involvement in the entertainment sector became active. Garbatrage would not apply to activity in bona fide entertainment stocks moving on speculation that other mergers would follow in the wake of Time-Warner. See also RUMORTRAGE.

GAP

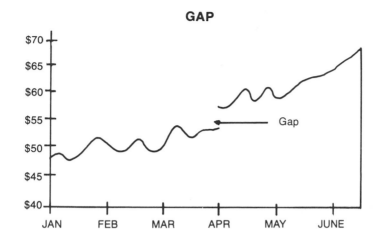

GARNISHMENT court order to an employer to withhold all or part of an employee's wages and send the money to the court or to a person who has won a lawsuit against the employee. An employee's wages will be *garnished* until the court-ordered debt is paid. Garnishing may be used in a divorce settlement or for repayment of creditors.

GATHER IN THE STOPS stock-trading tactic that involves selling a sufficient amount of stock to drive down the price to a point where stop orders (orders to buy or sell at a given price) are known to exist. The stop orders are then activated to become market orders (orders to buy or sell at the best available price), in turn creating movement which touches off other stop orders in a process called SNOWBALLING. Because this can cause sharp trading swings, floor officials on the exchanges have the authority to suspend stop orders in individual securities if that seems advisable. *See also* STOP ORDER.

GENERAL ACCOUNT Federal Reserve Board term for brokerage customer margin accounts subject to REGULATION T, which covers extensions of credit by brokers for the purchase and short sale of securities. The Fed requires that all transactions in which the broker advances credit to the customer be made in this account. *See also* MARGIN ACCOUNT.

GENERAL LEDGER formal ledger containing all the financial statement accounts of a business. It contains offsetting debit and credit accounts, the totals of which are proved by a trial balance. Certain accounts in the general ledger, termed *control accounts*, summarize the detail booked on separate subsidiary ledgers.

GENERAL LIEN LIEN against an individual that excludes real property. The lien carries the right to seize personal property to satisfy a debt. The property seized need not be the property that gave rise to the debt.

GENERAL LOAN AND COLLATERAL AGREEMENT continuous agreement under which a securities broker-dealer borrows from a bank against listed securities to buy or carry inventory, finance the underwriting of new issues, or carry the margin accounts of clients. Synonymous with *broker's loan. See also* BROKER LOAN RATE; MARGIN ACCOUNT; UNDERWRITE.

GENERALLY ACCEPTED ACCOUNTING PRINCIPLES (GAAP) conventions, rules, and procedures that define accepted accounting practice, including broad guidelines as well as detailed procedures. The basic doctrine was set forth by the Accounting Principles Board of the American Institute of Certified Public Accountants, which was superseded in 1973 by the FINANCIAL ACCOUNTING STANDARDS BOARD (FASB), an independent self-regulatory organization.

GENERAL MORTGAGE mortgage covering all the mortgageable properties of a borrower and not restricted to any particular piece of property. Such a blanket mortgage can be lower in priority of claim in liquidation than one or more other mortgages on specific parcels.

GENERAL OBLIGATION BOND municipal bond backed by the FULL FAITH AND CREDIT (which includes the taxing and further borrowing power) of a municipality. A *GO bond,* as it is known, is repaid with general revenue and borrowings, in contrast to the revenue from a specific facility built with the borrowed funds, such as a tunnel or a sewer system. *See also* REVENUE BOND.

GENERAL PARTNER
1. one of two or more partners who are jointly and severally responsible for the debts of a partnership.
2. managing partner of a LIMITED PARTNERSHIP, who is responsible for the operations of the partnership and, ultimately, any debts taken on by the partnership. The general partner's liability is unlimited. In a real estate partnership, the general partner will pick the properties to be bought and will manage them. In an oil and gas partnership, the general partner will select drilling sites and oversee drilling activity. In return for these services, the general partner collects certain fees and often retains a percentage of ownership in the partnership.

GENERAL REVENUE when used in reference to state and local governments taken separately, the term refers to total revenue less revenue from utilities, sales of alcoholic beverages, and insurance trusts. When speaking of combined state and local total revenue, the term refers only to taxes, charges, and miscellaneous revenue, which avoids the distortion of overlapping intergovernmental revenue.

GENERAL REVENUE SHARING unrestricted funds (usable for any purpose) provided by the federal government until 1987 to the 50 states and to more than 38,000 cities, towns, counties, townships, Indian tribes, and Alaskan native villages under the State and Local Fiscal Assistance Act of 1972.

GIFT TAX graduated tax, levied on the donor of a gift by the federal government and most state governments when assets are passed from one person to another. The more money that is given as a gift, the higher the tax rate. The Economic Recovery Tax Act of 1981 allowed a $10,000 federal gift tax exemption per recipient. This means that $10,000 a year can be given free of gift tax to one person ($20,000 to a married couple). The gift tax is computed on the dollar value of the asset being transferred above the $10,000 exemption level. Gifts between spouses are not subject to gift tax. Many states match the $10,000 gift tax exemption, but some allow a smaller amount to be gifted free of tax.

GILT-EDGED SECURITY stock or bond of a company that has demonstrated over a number of years that it is capable of earning sufficient profits to cover dividends on stocks and interest on bonds with great dependability. The term is used with corporate bonds more often than with stocks, where the term BLUE CHIP is more common.

GINNIE MAE nickname for the GOVERNMENT NATIONAL MORTGAGE ASSOCIATION and the certificate issued by that agency. *See also* GINNIE MAE PASS-THROUGH.

GINNIE MAE PASS-THROUGH security backed by a pool of mortgages and guaranteed by the GOVERNMENT NATIONAL MORTGAGE ASSOCIATION (Ginnie Mae), which passes through to investors the interest and principal payments of homeowners. Homeowners make their mortgage payments to the bank or savings and loan that originated their mortgage. After a service charge, usually ½%, the bank forwards the mortgage payments to the pass-through buyers, who may be institutional investors or individuals. Ginnie Mae guarantees that investors will receive timely principal and interest payments even if homeowners do not make mortgage payments on time.

The introduction of Ginnie Mae pass-throughs has benefited the home mortgage market, since more capital has become available for lending. Investors, who are able to receive high, government-guaranteed interest payments, have also benefited. For investors, however, the rate of principal repayment on a Ginnie Mae pass-through is uncertain. If interest rates fall, principal will be repaid faster, since homeowners will refinance their mortgages. If rates rise, principal will be repaid more slowly, since homeowners will hold onto the underlying mortgages. *See also* HALF-LIFE.

GIVE UP
1. term used in a securities transaction involving three brokers, as illustrated by the following scenario: Broker A, a FLOOR BROKER, executes a buy order for Broker B, another member firm broker who has too much business at the time to execute the order. The broker with whom Broker A completes the transaction (the sell side broker) is Broker C. Broker A "gives up" the name of Broker B, so that the record shows a transaction between Broker B and Broker C even though the trade was actually executed between Broker A and Broker C.
2. another application of the term: A customer of brokerage firm ABC Co. travels out of town and, finding no branch office of ABC, places an order with DEF Co., saying he is an account of ABC. After confirming the account relationship, DEF completes a trade with GHI Co., advising GHI that DEF is acting for ABC ("giving up" ABC's name). ABC will then handle the clearing details of the transaction with GHI. Alternatively, DEF may simply send the customer's order directly to ABC for execution. Whichever method is used, the customer pays only one commission.

GLAMOR STOCK stock with a wide public and institutional following. Glamor stocks achieve this following by producing steadily rising sales and earnings over a long period of time. In bull (rising) markets, glamor stocks tend to rise faster than market averages. Although a glamor stock is often in the category of a BLUE CHIP stock, the glamor is characterized by a higher earnings growth rate.

GLASS-STEAGALL ACT OF 1933 legislation passed by Congress authorizing deposit insurance and prohibiting commercial banks from owning brokerage firms. Under Glass-Steagall, these banks may not engage in investment banking activities, such as underwriting corporate securities or municipal revenue bonds. The law was designed to insulate bank depositors from the risk involved when a bank dealt in securities and to prevent a banking collapse like the one that occurred in the Great Depression. In the mid-1980s banks challenged the Glass-Steagall Act by offering money market funds, discount brokerage services, commercial paper, and other investment services.

GNOMES OF ZÜRICH term coined by Labour ministers of Great Britain, during the sterling crisis of 1964, to describe the financiers and bankers in Zürich, Switzerland, who were engaged in foreign exchange speculation.

GNP *see* GROSS NATIONAL PRODUCT.

GO AROUND term used to describe the process whereby the trading desk at the New York Federal Reserve Bank ("the DESK"), acting on behalf of the FEDERAL OPEN MARKET COMMITTEE, contacts primary dealers for bid and offer prices. Primary dealers are those banks and investment houses approved for direct purchase and sale transactions with the Federal Reserve System in its OPEN MARKET OPERATIONS.

GO-GO FUND MUTUAL FUND that invests in highly risky but potentially rewarding stocks. During the 1960s many go-go funds shot up in value, only to fall dramatically later and, in some cases, to go out of business as their speculative investments fizzled.

GOING AHEAD unethical securities brokerage act whereby the broker trades first for his own account before filling his customers' orders. Brokers who go ahead violate the RULES OF FAIR PRACTICE of the National Association of Securities Dealers.

GOING AWAY bonds purchased by dealers for immediate resale to investors, as opposed to bonds purchased *for stock*—that is, to be held in inventory for resale at some future time. The significance of the difference is that bonds bought going away will not overhang the market and cause adverse pressure on prices.

    The term is also used in new offerings of serial bonds to describe large purchases, usually by institutional investors, of the bonds in a particular maturity grouping (or series).

GOING-CONCERN VALUE value of a company as an operating business to another company or individual. The excess of going-concern value over asset value, or LIQUIDATING VALUE, is the value of the operating organization as distinct from the value of assets. In acquisition accounting, going-concern value in excess of asset value is treated as an intangible asset, termed *goodwill*. Goodwill is generally understood to represent the value of a well-respected business name, good customer relations, high employee morale, and other such factors expected to translate into greater than normal earning power. However, because this intangible asset has no independent market or liquidation value, accepted accounting principles require that goodwill be written off over a period of time.

GOING LONG purchasing a stock, bond, or commodity for investment or speculation. Such a security purchase is known as a LONG POSITION. The opposite of going long is GOING SHORT, when an investor sells a security he does not own and thereby creates a SHORT POSITION.

GOING PRIVATE movement from public ownership to private ownership of a company's shares either by the company's repurchase of shares or through purchases by an outside investor. A company usually goes private when the market price of its shares is substantially below their BOOK VALUE and the opportunity thus exists to buy the assets cheaply. Another motive for going private is to ensure the tenure of existing management by removing the company as a takeover prospect.

GOING PUBLIC securities industry phrase used when a private company first offers its shares to the public. The firm's ownership thus shifts from the hands of a few private stockowners to a base that includes public shareholders. At the moment of going public, the stock is called an INITIAL PUBLIC OFFERING. From that point on, or until the company goes private again, its shares have a MARKET VALUE. *See also* NEW ISSUE; GOING PRIVATE.

GOING SHORT selling a stock or commodity that the seller does not have. An investor who goes short borrows stock from his or her broker, hoping to purchase other shares of it at a lower price. The investor will then replace the borrowed stock with the lower priced stock and keep the difference as profit. *See also* SELLING SHORT; GOING LONG.

GOLD BOND bond backed by gold. Such debt obligations are issued by gold-mining companies, who peg interest payments to the level of gold prices. Investors who buy these bonds therefore anticipate a rising gold price. Silver mining companies also issue silver-backed bonds that tie interest payments to silver prices.

GOLDBUG analyst enamored of gold as an investment. Goldbugs usually are worried about possible disasters in the world economy, such as a depression or hyperinflation, and therefore recommend gold as a HEDGE.

GOLDEN HANDCUFFS contract that ties a broker to a brokerage firm. If the broker stays at the firm, he or she will earn lucrative commissions, bonuses, and other compensation. But if the broker leaves and tries to lure clients to another firm, the broker must promise to give back to the firm much of the compensation received while working there. Golden handcuffs are a response by the brokerage industry to the frequent movement of brokers from one firm to another.

GOLDEN PARACHUTE lucrative contract given to a top executive to provide lavish benefits in case the company is taken over by another firm, resulting in the loss of the job. A golden parachute might include generous severance pay, stock options, or a bonus. The TAX REFORM ACT OF 1984 eliminated the deductability of "excess compensation" and imposed an excise tax. The TAX REFORM ACT OF 1986 covered matters of clarification.

GOLD FIXING daily determination of the price of gold by selected gold specialists and bank officials in London, Paris, and Zürich. The price is fixed at 10:30 A.M. and 3:30 P.M. London time every business day, according to the prevailing market forces of supply and demand.

GOLD MUTUAL FUND mutual fund that invests in the shares of gold mining concerns. Some gold mutual funds invest in only U.S. and Canadian stocks; others invest in North American and South African shares. These funds offer investors diversification among many gold mining shares and, frequently, high dividend income, since South African mines typically pay out almost all their earnings as dividends. Such funds have usually performed best during periods of rising inflation. They offer a way of participating in gold as an inflation HEDGE, without the risks incurred by an unsophisticated investor dealing in gold commodities futures trading, bullion, or individual gold stocks.

GOLD STANDARD monetary system under which units of currency are convertible into fixed amounts of gold. Such a system is said to be anti-inflationary. The United States has been on the gold standard in the past. *See also* HARD MONEY.

GOOD DELIVERY securities industry designation meaning that a certificate has the necessary endorsements and meets all other requirements (signature guarantee, proper denomination, and other qualifications), so that title can be transferred by delivery to the buying broker, who is then obligated to accept it. Exceptions constitute *bad delivery*.

GOOD FAITH DEPOSIT

In general: token amount of money advanced to indicate intent to pursue a contract to completion.

Commodities: initial margin deposit required when buying or selling a futures contract. Such deposits generally range from 2% to 10% of the contract value.

Securities:
1. deposit, usually 25% of a transaction, required by securities firms of individuals who are not known to them but wish to enter orders with them.
2. deposit left with a municipal bond issuer by a firm competing for the underwriting business. The deposit typically equals 1% to 5% of the principal amount of the issue and is refundable to the unsuccessful bidders.

GOOD MONEY

Banking: federal funds, which are good the same day, in contrast to CLEARING HOUSE FUNDS. Clearing house funds are understood in two ways: (1) funds requiring three days to clear and (2) funds used to settle transactions on which there is a one-day FLOAT.

Gresham's Law: theory that money of superior intrinsic value, "good money," will eventually be driven out of circulation by money of lesser intrinsic value. *See also* GRESHAM'S LAW.

GOOD-THIS-MONTH ORDER (GTM) order to buy or sell securities (usually at a LIMIT PRICE or STOP PRICE set by the customer) that remains in effect until the end of the month. In the case of a limit price, the customer instructs the broker either to buy at the stipulated limit price or anything lower, or to sell at the limit price or anything higher. In the case of a stop price, the customer instructs the broker to enter a market order once a transaction in the security occurs at the stop price specified.

A variation on the GTM order is the *good-this-week-order* (GTW), which expires at the end of the week if it is not executed.

See also DAY ORDER; GOOD-TILL-CANCELED ORDER; LIMIT ORDER; OPEN ORDER; STOP ORDER.

GOOD THROUGH order to buy or sell securities or commodities at a stated price for a stated period of time, unless canceled, executed, or changed. It is a type of LIMIT ORDER and may be specified GTW (good this week), GTM (GOOD this MONTH ORDER), or for shorter or longer periods.

GOOD-TILL-CANCELED ORDER (GTC) brokerage customer's order to buy or sell a security, usually at a particular price, that remains in effect until executed or canceled. If the GTC order remains unfilled after a long period of time, a broker will usually periodically confirm that the customer still wants the transaction to occur if the stock reaches the target price. *See also* DAY ORDER; GOOD-THIS-MONTH ORDER; OPEN ORDER; TARGET PRICE.

GOODWILL *see* GOING-CONCERN VALUE.

GOVERNMENT NATIONAL MORTGAGE ASSOCIATION (GNMA) government-owned corporation, nicknamed Ginnie Mae, which is an agency of the U.S. Department of Housing and Urban Development. GNMA guarantees, with the full faith and credit of the United States Government, full and timely payment of all monthly principal and interest payments on the mortgage-backed PASS-THROUGH SECURITIES of registered holders. The securities, which are issued by private firms, such as MORTGAGE BANKERS and savings institutions, and typically marketed through security broker-dealers, represent pools of residential mortgages insured or guaranteed by the Federal Housing Administration (FHA), the Farmer's Home Administration (FmHA), or the Veterans Administration (VA). *See also* FEDERAL HOME LOAN MORTGAGE CORPORATION; FEDERAL NATIONAL MORTGAGE ASSOCIATION; GINNIE MAE PASS-THROUGH.

GOVERNMENT OBLIGATIONS U.S. government debt instruments (Treasury bonds, bills, notes, savings bonds) the government has pledged to repay. *See* GOVERNMENTS.

GOVERNMENTS
1. securities issued by the U.S. government, such as Treasury bills, bonds, notes, and savings bonds. Governments are the most creditworthy of all debt instruments since they are backed by the FULL FAITH AND CREDIT of the U.S. government, which if necessary can print money to make payments. Also called TREASURIES.
2. debt issues of federal agencies, which are not directly backed by the U.S. government. *See also* GOVERNMENT SECURITIES.

GOVERNMENT SECURITIES securities issued by U.S. government agencies, such as the RESOLUTION FUNDING CORPORATION (REFCO) or the Federal Land Bank; also called *agency securities*. Although these securities have high credit ratings, they are not considered to be GOVERNMENT OBLIGATIONS and therefore are not directly backed by the FULL FAITH AND CREDIT of the government as TREASURIES are.

GRACE PERIOD
In general: period of time provided in most loan contracts and insurance policies during which default or cancellation will not occur even though payment is past due.
Banking: a provision in some long-term loans, notably EUROCURRENCY syndication loans to foreign governments and multinational firms by groups of banks, whereby repayment of principal does not begin until some point well into the life of the loan. The grace period, which can be as long as five years, is an important point of negotiation between a borrower and a lender; borrowers will sometimes accept a higher interest rate to obtain a longer grace period.

GRADUATED-PAYMENT MORTGAGE (GPM) mortgage featuring lower monthly payments at first, which steadily rise until they level off after a few years. GPMs, also known as "jeeps," are designed for young couples whose income is expected to grow as their careers advance. A graduated-payment mortgage allows such a family to buy a house that would be unaffordable if mortgage payments started out at a high level. Persons planning to take on such a mortgage must be confident that their income will be able to keep pace with the rising payments. *See also* ADJUSTABLE-RATE MORTGAGE; CONVENTIONAL MORTGAGE; REVERSE-ANNUITY MORTGAGE; VARIABLE-RATE MORTGAGE.

GRADUATED SECURITY security whose listing has been upgraded by moving from one exchange to another—for example, from the American Stock Exchange to the more prestigious New York Stock Exchange, or from a regional exchange to a national exchange. An advantage of such a transfer is to widen trading in the security.

GRAHAM AND DODD METHOD OF INVESTING investment approach outlined in Benjamin Graham and David Dodd's landmark book *Security Analysis,* published in the 1930s. Graham and Dodd founded the modern discipline of security analysis with their work. They believed that investors should buy stocks with undervalued assets and that eventually those assets would appreciate to their true value in the marketplace. Graham and Dodd advocated buying stocks in companies where current assets exceed current liabilities and all long-term debt, and where the stock is selling at a low PRICE/EARNINGS RATIO. They suggested that the stocks be sold after a profit objective of between 50% and 100% was reached, which they assumed would be three years or less from the time of purchase. Analysts today who call themselves Graham and Dodd investors hunt for stocks selling below their LIQUIDATING VALUE and do not necessarily concern themselves with the potential for earnings growth.

GRANDFATHER CLAUSE provision included in a new rule that exempts from the rule a person or business already engaged in the activity coming under regulation. For example, an opinion of the Accounting Principles Board (now the Financial Accounting Standards Board) adopted in 1970 requires that businesses amortize (write off) goodwill. The opinion contains a grandfather clause, however, which exempts goodwill acquired before 1970 from the required amortization.

GRANTOR
Investments: options trader who sells a CALL OPTION or a PUT OPTION and collects PREMIUM INCOME for doing so. The grantor sells the right to buy a security at a certain price in the case of a call, and the right to sell at a certain price in the case of a put.
Law: one who executes a deed conveying title to property or who creates a trust. Also called a *settlor.*

GRAVEYARD MARKET bear market wherein investors who sell are faced with substantial losses, while potential investors prefer to stay liquid, that is, to keep their money in cash or cash equivalents until market conditions improve. Like a graveyard, those who are in can't get out and those who are out have no desire to get in.

GREATER FOOL THEORY theory that even though a stock or the market as a whole is FULLY VALUED, speculation is justified because there are enough fools to push it further upward.

GREENMAIL payment by a TAKEOVER target to a potential acquirer, usually to buy back shares at a premium. In exchange, the acquirer agrees not to pursue the takeover bid further. *See also* STANDSTILL AGREEMENT.

GREEN SHOE clause in an underwriting agreement saying that, in the event of exceptional public demand, the issuer will authorize additional shares for distribution by the syndicate.

GRESHAM'S LAW theory in economics that bad money drives out good money. Specifically, people faced with a choice of two currencies of the same nominal value, one of which is preferable to the other because of metal content or because it resists mutilation, will hoard the good money and spend the bad money, thereby driving the good money out of circulation. The observation is named for Sir Thomas Gresham, master of the mint in the reign of Queen Elizabeth I.

GROSS ESTATE total value of a person's assets before liabilities such as debts and taxes are deducted. After someone dies, the executor of the will makes an assessment of the stocks, bonds, real estate, and personal possessions that comprise the gross estate. Debts and taxes are paid, as are funeral expenses and estate administration costs. Beneficiaries of the will then receive their portion of the remainder, which is called the *net estate*.

GROSS LEASE property lease under which the lessor (landlord) agrees to pay all the expenses normally associated with ownership (insurance, taxes, utilities, repairs). An exception might be that the lessee (tenant) would be required to pay real estate taxes above a stipulated amount or to pay for certain special operating expenses (snow removal, grounds care in the case of a shopping center, or institutional advertising, for example). Gross leases are the most common type of lease contract and are typical arrangements for short-term tenancy. They normally contain no provision for periodic rent adjustments, nor are there preestablished renewal arrangements. *See also* NET LEASE.

GROSS NATIONAL PRODUCT (GNP) total value of goods and services produced in the U.S. economy over a particular period of time, usually one year. The GNP growth rate is the primary indicator of the status of the economy. GNP is made up of consumer and government purchases, private domestic and foreign investments in the U.S., and the total value of exports. Figures for GNP on an annual basis are released every quarter, as is an inflation-adjusted version, called *real GNP*.

GROSS PER BROKER gross amount of commission revenues attributable to a particular REGISTERED REPRESENTATIVE during a given period. Brokers, who typically keep one third of the commissions they generate, are often expected by their firms to meet productivity quotas based on their gross.

GROSS PROFIT net sales less the COST OF GOODS SOLD. Also called *gross margin*. *See also* NET PROFIT.

GROSS SALES total sales at invoice values, not reduced by customer discounts, returns or allowances, or other adjustments. *See also* NET SALES.

GROSS SPREAD difference (spread) between the public offering price of a security and the price paid by an underwriter to the issuer. The spread breaks down into the manager's fee, the dealer's (or underwriter's) discount, and the selling concession (i.e., the discount offered to a selling group). *See also* CONCESSION; FLOTATION (FLOATATION) COST.

GROUP OF TEN ten major industrialized countries that try to coordinate monetary and fiscal policies to create a more stable world economic system. The ten are Belgium, Canada, France, Italy, Japan, The Netherlands, Sweden, the United Kingdom, the United States, and West Germany. Also known as the *Paris Club*.

GROUP SALES term used in securities underwriting that refers to block sales made to institutional investors. The securities come out of a syndicate "pot" with credit for the sale prorated among the syndicate members in proportion to their original allotments.

GROWTH FUND mutual fund that invests in growth stocks. The goal is to provide capital appreciation for the fund's shareholders over the long term. Growth funds are more volatile than more conservative income or money market funds. They tend to rise faster than conservative funds in bull (advancing) markets and to drop more sharply in bear (falling) markets. *See also* GROWTH STOCK.

GROWTH STOCK stock of a corporation that has exhibited faster-than-average gains in earnings over the last few years and is expected to continue to show high levels of profit growth. Over the long run, growth stocks tend to outperform slower-growing or stagnant stocks. Growth stocks are riskier investments than average stocks, however, since they usually sport higher price/earnings ratios and make little or no dividend payments to shareholders. *See also* PRICE/EARNINGS RATIO.

GUARANTEE to take responsibility for payment of a debt or performance of some obligation if the person primarily liable fails to perform. A guarantee is a CONTINGENT LIABILITY of the guarantor—that is, it is a potential liability not recognized in accounts until the outcome becomes probable in the opinion of the company's accountant.

GUARANTEED BOND bond on which the principal and interest are guaranteed by a firm other than the issuer. Such bonds are nearly always railroad bonds, arising out of situations where one road has leased the road of another and the security holders of the leased road require assurance of income in exchange for giving up control of the property. Guaranteed securities involved in such situations may also include preferred or common stocks when dividends are guaranteed. Both guaranteed stock and guaranteed bonds become, in effect, DEBENTURE (unsecured) bonds of the guarantor, although the status of the stock may be questionable in the event of LIQUIDATION. In any event, if the guarantor enjoys stronger credit than the railroad whose securities are being guaranteed, the securities have greater value.

Guaranteed bonds may also arise out of parent-subsidiary relationships where bonds are issued by the subsidiary with the parent's guarantee.

GUARANTEED INCOME CONTRACT contract between an insurance company and a corporate profit-sharing or pension plan that guarantees a specific rate of return on the invested capital over the life of the contract. Although the insurance company takes all market, credit, and interest rate risks on the investment portfolio, it can profit if its returns exceed the guaranteed amount. For pension and profit-sharing plans, guaranteed income contracts are a conservative way of assuring beneficiaries that their money will achieve a certain rate of return.

GUARANTEED STOCK *see* GUARANTEED BOND.

GUARANTEE LETTER letter by a commercial bank that guarantees payment of the EXERCISE PRICE of a client's PUT OPTION (the right to sell a given security at a particular price within a specified period) if or when a notice indicating its exercise, called an assignment notice, is presented to the option seller (writer).

GUARANTEE OF SIGNATURE certificate issued by a bank or brokerage firm vouching for the authenticity of a person's signature. Such a document may be necessary when stocks, bonds, or other registered securities are transferred from a seller to a buyer. Banks also require guarantees of signature before they will process certain transactions.

GUN JUMPING
1. trading securities on information before it becomes publicly disclosed.
2. illegally soliciting buy orders in an underwriting, before a Securities and Exchange Commission REGISTRATION is complete.

h

HAIRCUT securities industry term referring to the formulas used in the valuation of securities for the purpose of calculating a broker-dealer's net capital. The haircut varies according to the class of a security, its market risk, and the time to maturity. For example, cash equivalent GOVERNMENTS could have a 0% haircut, equities could have an average 30% haircut, and fail positions (securities with past due delivery) with little prospect of settlement could have a 100% haircut. *See also* CASH EQUIVALENTS; FAIL POSITION.

HALF-LIFE point in time in which half the principal has been repaid in a mortgage-backed security guaranteed or issued by the GOVERNMENT NATIONAL MORTGAGE ASSOCIATION, the FEDERAL NATIONAL MORTGAGE ASSOCIATION, or the FEDERAL HOME LOAN MORTGAGE CORPORATION. Such a security normally has a half-life of 12 years. But specific mortgage pools can have vastly longer or shorter half-lives, depending on interest rate trends. If interest rates fall, more homeowners will refinance their mortgages, meaning that principal will be paid off more quickly, and half-lives will drop. If interest rates rise, homeowners will hold onto their mortgages longer than anticipated, and half-lives will rise.

HALF-STOCK common or preferred stock with a $50 par value instead of the more conventional $100 par value.

HAMMERING THE MARKET intense selling of stocks by those who think prices are inflated. Speculators who think the market is about to drop, and therefore sell short, are said to be hammering the market. *See also* SELLING SHORT.

HARD DOLLARS actual payments made by a customer for services, including research, provided by a brokerage firm. For instance, if a broker puts together a financial plan for a client, the fee might be $1000 in hard dollars. This contrasts with SOFT DOLLARS, which refers to compensation by way of the commissions a broker would receive if he were to carry out any trades called for in that financial plan. Brokerage house research is sold for either hard or soft dollars.

HARD MONEY (HARD CURRENCY)
1. currency in which there is widespread confidence. It is the currency of an economically and politically stable country, such as the U.S. or Switzerland. Countries that have taken out loans in hard money generally must repay them in hard money.
2. gold or coins, as contrasted with paper currency, which is considered *soft money*. Some hard-money enthusiasts advocate a return to the GOLD STANDARD as a method of reducing inflation and promoting economic growth.

HEAD AND SHOULDERS patterns resembling the head and shoulders outline of a person, which is used to chart stock price trends. The pattern signals the reversal of a trend. As prices move down to the right shoulder, a head and shoulders top is formed, meaning that prices should be falling. A reverse head and shoulders pattern has the head at the bottom of the chart, meaning that prices should be rising.

HEAD AND SHOULDERS

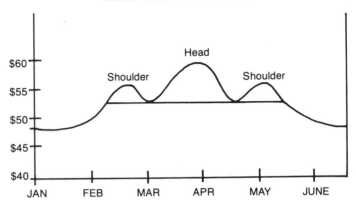

HEAVY MARKET stock, bond, or commodity market with falling prices resulting from a larger supply of offers to sell than bids to buy.

HEDGE/HEDGING strategy used to offset investment risk. A perfect hedge is one eliminating the possibility of future gain or loss.

A stockholder worried about declining stock prices, for instance, can hedge his or her holdings by buying a PUT OPTION on the stock or selling a CALL OPTION. Someone owning 100 shares of XYZ stock, selling at $70 per share, can hedge his position by buying a put option giving him the right to sell 100 shares at $70 at any time over the next few months. This investor must pay a certain amount of money, called a PREMIUM, for these rights. If XYZ stock falls during that time, the investor can exercise his option—that is, sell the stock at $70—thereby preserving the $70 value of the XYZ holdings. The same XYZ stockholder can also hedge his position by selling a call option. In such a transaction, he sells the right to buy XYZ at $70 per share for the next few months. In return, he receives a premium. If XYZ stock falls in price, that premium income will offset to some extent the drop in value of the stock.

SELLING SHORT is another widely used hedging technique.

Investors often try to hedge against inflation by purchasing assets that will rise in value faster than inflation.

Large commercial firms that want to be assured of the price they will receive or pay for a commodity will hedge their position by buying and selling simultaneously in the FUTURES MARKET. For example, Hershey's, the chocolate company, will hedge its supplies of cocoa in the futures market to limit the risk of a rise in cocoa prices.

HEDGE CLAUSE disclaimer seen in market letters, security research reports, or other printed matter having to do with evaluating investments, which purports to absolve the writer from responsibility for the accuracy of information obtained from usually reliable sources. Despite such clauses, which may mitigate liability, writers may still be charged with negligence in their use of information. Typical language of a hedge clause: "The information furnished herein has been obtained from sources believed to be reliable, but its accuracy is not guaranteed."

HEDGED TENDER SELLING SHORT a portion of the shares being tendered to protect against a price drop in the event all shares tendered are not accepted. For example, ABC Company or another company wishing to acquire ABC Company announces a TENDER OFFER at $52 a share when ABC shares are selling at a market price of $40. The market price of ABC will now rise to near the tender price of $52. An investor wishing to sell all his or her 2000 shares at $52 will tender 2000 shares, but cannot be assured all shares will be accepted. To lock in the $52 price on the tendered shares the investor thinks might not be accepted— say half of them or 1000 shares—he or she will sell short that many shares. Assuming the investor has guessed correctly and only 1000 shares are accepted, when the tender offer expires and the market price of ABC begins to drop, the investor will still have sold all 2000 shares for $52 or close to it—half to the tenderer and the other half when the short sale is consummated.

HEDGE FUND securities industry term used to describe certain mutual funds that use hedging techniques. For example, the Prudential-Bache Option Growth Fund has used futures contracts on stock market indexes and short sales with stock options to limit risks (i.e., "to make money in any market environment"). *See* HEDGE/HEDGING.

HEMLINE THEORY whimsical idea that stock prices move in the same general direction as the hemlines of women's dresses. Short skirts in the 1920s and 1960s were considered bullish signs that stock prices would rise, whereas longer dresses in the 1930s and 1940s were considered bearish (falling) indicators. Despite its sometimes uncanny way of being prophetic, the hemline theory has remained more in the area of wishful thinking than serious market analysis.

HIGH CREDIT
Banking: maximum amount of loans outstanding recorded for a particular customer.
Finance: the highest amount of TRADE CREDIT a particular company has received from a supplier at one time.

HIGH FLYER high-priced and highly speculative stock that moves up and down sharply over a short period. The stock of unproven high-technology companies might be high flyers, for instance.

HIGH-GRADE BOND bond rated triple-A or double-A by Standard & Poor's or Moody's rating services. *See also* RATING.

HIGH-PREMIUM CONVERTIBLE DEBENTURE bond with a long-term, high-premium, common stock conversion feature and also offering a fairly competitive interest rate. Premium refers in this case to the difference between the market value of the CONVERTIBLE security and the value at which it is convertible into common stock. Such bonds are designed for bond-oriented portfolios, with the "KICKER," the added feature of convertibility to stock, intended as an inflation hedge.

HIGHS stocks that have hit new high prices in daily trading for the current 52-week period. (They are listed as "highs" in daily newspapers.) Technical analysts consider the ratio between new highs and new LOWS in the stock market to be significant for pointing out stock market trends.

HIGH-TECH STOCK stock of companies involved in high-technology fields (computers, semiconductors, biotechnology, robotics, electronics). Successful high-tech stocks have above-average earnings growth and therefore typically very volatile stock prices.

HISTORICAL COST accounting principle requiring that all financial statement items be based on original cost or acquisition cost. The dollar is assumed to be stable for the period involved.

HISTORICAL TRADING RANGE price range within which a stock, bond, or commodity has traded since going public. A VOLATILE stock will have a wider trading range than a more conservative stock. Technical analysts see the top of a historical range as the RESISTANCE LEVEL and the bottom as the SUPPORT LEVEL. They consider it highly significant if a security breaks above the resistance level or below the support level. Usually such a move is interpreted to mean that the security will go onto new highs or new lows, thus expanding its historical trading range.

HISTORICAL YIELD yield provided by a mutual fund, typically a money market fund, over a particular period of time. For instance, a money market fund may advertise that its historical yield averaged 10% over the last year.

HIT THE BID to accept the highest price offered for a stock. For instance, if a stock's ask price is $50¼ and the current bid price is $50, a seller will hit the bid if he or she accepts $50 a share.

HOLDER OF RECORD owner of a company's securities as recorded on the books of the issuing company or its TRANSFER AGENT as of a particular date. Dividend declarations always specify payability to holders of record as of a specific date.

HOLDING COMPANY corporation that owns enough voting stock in another corporation to influence its board of directors and therefore to control its policies and management. A holding company need not own a majority of the shares of its subsidiaries or be engaged in similar activities. However, to gain the benefits of tax consolidation, which include tax-free dividends to the parent and the ability to share operating losses, the holding company must own 80% or more of the subsidiary's voting stock.

Among the advantages of a holding company over a MERGER as an approach to expansion are the ability to control sizeable operations with fractional ownership and commensurately small investment; the somewhat theoretical ability to take risks through subsidiaries with liability limited to the subsidiary corporation; and the ability to expand through unobtrusive purchases of stock, in contrast to having to obtain the approval of another company's shareholders.

Among the disadvantages of a holding company are partial multiple taxation when less than 80% of a subsidiary is owned, plus other special state and local taxes; the risk of forced DIVESTITURE (it is easier to force dissolution of a holding company than to separate merged operations); and the risks of negative leverage effects in excessive PYRAMIDING.

The following types of holding companies are defined in special ways and are subject to particular legislation: public utility holding company (*see* PUBLIC UTILITY HOLDING COMPANY ACT), BANK HOLDING COMPANY, railroad holding company, and air transport holding company.

HOLDING PERIOD length of time an asset is held by its owner. Through 1987, capital assets held for six months or more qualify for special CAPITAL GAINS TAX treatment. *See also* ANTICIPATED HOLDING PERIOD; INVESTMENT LETTER.

HOLDING THE MARKET entering the market with sufficient buy orders to create price support for a security or commodity, for the purpose of stabilizing a downward trend. The Securities and Exchange Commission views "holding" as a form of illegal manipulation except in the case of stabilization of a new issue cleared with the SEC beforehand.

HOMEOWNER'S EQUITY ACCOUNT credit line offered by banks and brokerage firms allowing a homeowner to tap the built-up equity in his or her home. Such an account is, in effect, a REVOLVING-CREDIT second mortgage, which can be accessed with the convenience of a check. When a homeowner writes a check (takes a loan), a LIEN is automatically placed against the house; the lein is removed after the loan is repaid. A homeowner's equity account often carries a lower interest rate than a second mortgage; typically, the rate is tied to the PRIME RATE. Most such programs require an initial signup fee and payment of additional fees called *points* when the credit line is tapped. Interest on such loans is tax deductible up to $100,000. Rules on deductibility have changed more than once since 1986, however, and a tax specialist should be consulted for the latest information.

HOME RUN large gain by an investor in a short period of time. Someone who aims to hit an investment home run may be looking for a potential TAKEOVER target, for example, since takeover bids result in sudden price spurts. Such investing is inherently more risky than the strategy of holding for the long term.

HORIZON ANALYSIS method of measuring the discounted cash flow (time-adjusted return) from an investment, using time periods or series *(horizons)* that differ from the investment's contractual maturity. The horizon date might be the end of a BUSINESS CYCLE or some other date determined in the perspective of the investor's overall portfolio requirements. Horizon analysis calculations, which include reinvestment assumptions, permit comparison with alternative investments that is more realistic in terms of individual portfolio requirements than traditional YIELD-TO-MATURITY calculations.

HORIZONTAL PRICE MOVEMENT movement within a narrow price range over an extended period of time. A stock would have a horizontal price movement if it traded between $35 and $37 for over six months, for instance. Also known as *sideways price movement*. *See also* FLAT MARKET.

HORIZONTAL SPREAD options strategy that involves buying and selling the same number of options contracts with the same exercise price, but with different maturity dates; also called a CALENDAR SPREAD. For instance, an investor might buy ten XYZ call options with a striking price of $70 and a maturity date of October. At the same time, he would sell ten XYZ call options with the same striking price of $70 but a maturity date of July. The investor hopes to profit by moves in XYZ stock by this means.

HOSPITAL REVENUE BOND bond issued by a municipal or state agency to finance construction of a hospital or nursing home. The latter is then operated under lease by a not-for-profit organization or a for-profit corporation such as Hospital Corporation of America. A hospital revenue bond, which is a variation

HORIZONTAL PRICE MOVEMENT

on the INDUSTRIAL DEVELOPMENT BOND, is tax exempt, but there may be limits to the exemption. *See also* REVENUE BOND.

HOT ISSUE newly issued stock that is in great public demand. Hot issue stocks usually shoot up in price at their initial offering, since there is more demand than there are shares available. Special National Association of Securities Dealers rules apply to the distribution of hot issues by the selling investment banking syndicate. *See also* UNDERWRITE.

HOT MONEY investment funds capriciously seeking high, short-term yields. Borrowers attracting hot money, such as banks issuing high-yielding CERTIFICATES OF DEPOSIT, should be prepared to lose it as soon as another borrower offers a higher rate.

HOT STOCK
1. stock that has been stolen.
2. newly issued stock that rises quickly in price. *See* HOT ISSUE.

HOUSE
1. firm or individual engaged in business as a broker-dealer in securities and/or investment banking and related services.
2. nickname for the London Stock Exchange.

HOUSE ACCOUNT account handled at the main office of a brokerage firm or managed by an executive of the firm; in other words, an account distinguished from one that is normally handled by a salesperson in the territory. Ordinarily, a salesperson does not receive a commission on a house account, even though the account may actually be in his or her territory.

HOUSE CALL brokerage house notification that the customer's EQUITY in a MARGIN ACCOUNT is below the maintenance level. If the equity declines below that point, a broker must call the client, asking for more cash or securities. If the client fails to deliver the required margin, his or her position will be liquidated. House call limits are usually higher than limits mandated by the National Association of Securities Dealers (NASD), a self-regulatory group, and the major exchanges with jurisdiction over these rules. Such a margin MAINTENANCE REQUIREMENT is in addition to the initial margin requirements set by REGULATION T of the Federal Reserve Board. *See also* HOUSE MAINTENANCE REQUIREMENT; MARGIN CALL.

HOUSE MAINTENANCE REQUIREMENT internally set and enforced rules of individual broker-dealers in securities with respect to a customer's MARGIN ACCOUNT. House maintenance requirements set levels of EQUITY that must be maintained to avoid putting up additional equity or having collateral sold out. These levels are normally higher than maintenance levels required by the NATIONAL ASSOCIATION OF SECURITIES DEALERS (NASD) and the stock exchange. *See also* HOUSE CALL; MINIMUM MAINTENANCE.

HOUSE OF ISSUE investment banking firm that underwrites a stock or bond issue and offers the securities to the public. *See also* UNDERWRITE.

HOUSE RULES securities industry term for internal rules and policies of individual broker-dealer firms concerning the opening and handling of customers' accounts and the activities of the customers in such accounts. House rules are designed to assure that firms are in comfortable compliance with the requirements of outside regulatory authorities and in most cases are more stringent than the outside regulations. *See also* HOUSE CALL; HOUSE MAINTENANCE REQUIREMENT.

HOUSING AND URBAN DEVELOPMENT, DEPARTMENT OF (HUD) cabinet-level federal agency, founded in 1965, which is responsible for stimulating housing development in the United States. HUD has several programs to subsidize low- and moderate-income housing and urban renewal projects, often through loan guarantees. The GOVERNMENT NATIONAL MORTGAGE ASSOCIATION (Ginnie Mae), which fosters the growth of the secondary mortgage market, is within HUD.

HOUSING BOND short- or long-term bond issued by a local housing authority to finance short-term construction of (typically) low- or middle-income housing or long-term commitments for housing, plants, pollution control facilities, or similar projects. Such bonds are free from federal income taxes and from state and local taxes where applicable.

Shorter-term bonds sell in $5000 denominations and have maturities from 18 months to 4 years. They cannot be called (redeemed prior to maturity) and are paid at maturity with the proceeds from Federal Housing Administration-insured loans. Longer-term bonds are typically issued by local authorities under federal agency contracts, thus providing complete safety. Yields are competitive.

HULBERT RATING rating by *Hulbert Financial Digest* of how well the recommendations of various investment advisory newsletters have performed over the past few years. The *Digest* ranks several dozen investment advisory newsletters by tabulating the profits and losses of newsletter readers had they followed the advice.

HUNG UP term used to describe the position of an investor whose stocks or bonds have dropped in value below their purchase price, presenting the problem of a substantial loss if the securities were sold.

HURDLE RATE term used in the budgeting of capital expenditures, meaning the REQUIRED RATE OF RETURN in a DISCOUNTED CASH FLOW analysis. If the *expected rate of return* on an investment is below the hurdle rate, the project is not undertaken. The hurdle rate should be equal to the INCREMENTAL COST OF CAPITAL.

HYBRID ANNUITY contract offered by an insurance company that allows an investor to mix the benefits of both fixed and variable annuities; also called *combination annuity*. For instance, an annuity buyer may put a portion of his assets in a FIXED ANNUITY, which promises a certain rate of return, and the remainder in a stock or bond fund VARIABLE ANNUITY, which offers a chance for higher return but takes more risk.

HYPOTHECATION

Banking: pledging property to secure a loan. Hypothecation does not transfer title, but it does transfer the right to sell the hypothecated property in the event of default.

Securities: pledging of securities to brokers as collateral for loans made to purchase securities or to cover short sales, called margin loans. When the same collateral is pledged by the broker to a bank to collateralize a broker's loan, the process is called *rehypothecation*.

i

ILLEGAL DIVIDEND dividend declared by a corporation's board of directors in violation of its charter or of state laws. Most states, for example, stipulate that dividends be paid out of current income or RETAINED EARNINGS; they prohibit dividend payments that come out of CAPITAL SURPLUS or that would make the corporation insolvent. Directors who authorize illegal dividends may be sued by stockholders and creditors and may also face civil and criminal penalties. Stockholders who receive such dividends may be required to return them in order to meet the claims of creditors.

ILLIQUID

Finance: firm that lacks sufficient CASH FLOW to meet current and maturing obligations.

Investments: not readily convertible into cash, such as a stock, bond, or commodity that is not traded actively and would be difficult to sell at once without taking a large loss. Other assets for which there is not a ready market, and which therefore may take some time to sell, include real estate and collectibles such as rare stamps, coins, or antique furniture.

IMBALANCE OF ORDERS too many orders of one kind—to buy or to sell—without matching orders of the opposite kind. An imbalance usually follows a dramatic event such as a takeover, the death of a key executive, or a government ruling that will significantly affect the company's business. If it occurs before the stock exchange opens, trading in the stock is delayed. If it occurs during the trading day, the specialist suspends trading until enough matching orders can be found to make for an orderly market.

IMF *see* INTERNATIONAL MONETARY FUND.

IMMEDIATE FAMILY parents, brothers, sisters, children, relatives supported financially, father-in-law, mother-in-law, sister-in-law, and brother-in-law. This definition is incorporated in the NATIONAL ASSOCIATION OF SECURITIES DEALERS RULES OF FAIR PRACTICE on abuses of *hot issues* through such practices as FREE-RIDING and WITHHOLDING. The ruling prohibits the sale of such securities to members of a broker-dealer's own family or to persons buying and selling for institutional accounts and their families.

IMMEDIATE OR CANCEL ORDER buy or sell order requiring that all or part of the order be executed as soon as the broker enters a bid or offer; the portion not executed is automatically canceled. Such stipulations usually accompany large orders.

IMMEDIATE PAYMENT ANNUITY annuity contract bought with a single payment and with a specified payout plan that starts right away. Payments may be for a specified period or for the life of the annuitant and are usually on a monthly basis. *See also* ANNUITIZE.

IMPAIRED CAPITAL total capital that is less than the stated or par value of the company's CAPITAL STOCK. *See also* DEFICIT NET WORTH.

IMPORT DUTY *see* TARIFF.

IMPUTED INTEREST interest considered to have been paid in effect even though no interest was actually paid. For example, the Internal Revenue Service requires that annual interest be recognized on a ZERO-COUPON SECURITY.

IMPUTED VALUE logical or implicit value that is not recorded in any accounts. Examples: in projecting annual figures, values are imputed for months about which actual figures are not yet available; cash invested unproductively has an imputed value consisting of what it would have earned in a productive investment (OPPORTUNITY COST); in calculating national income, the U.S. Department of Commerce imputes a dollar value for wages and salaries paid in kind, such as food and lodging provided on ships at sea.

INACTIVE ASSET asset not continually used in a productive way, such as an auxiliary generator.

INACTIVE BOND CROWD *see* CABINET CROWD.

INACTIVE POST trading post on the New York Stock Exchange at which inactive stocks are traded in 10-share units rather than the regular 100-share lots. Known to traders as *Post 30*. *See also* ROUND LOT.

INACTIVE STOCK/BOND security traded relatively infrequently, either on an exchange or over the counter. The low volume makes the security ILLIQUID, and small investors tend to shy away from it.

IN-AND-OUT TRADER someone who buys and sells the same security in one day, endeavoring to profit from sharp price moves. *See also* DAY TRADE.

INCENTIVE FEE compensation for producing above-average results. Incentive fees are common for commodities trading advisers who achieve or top a preset return, as well as for a GENERAL PARTNER in a real estate or oil and gas LIMITED PARTNERSHIP.

INCENTIVE STOCK OPTION plan created by the ECONOMIC RECOVERY TAX ACT OF 1981 (ERTA) under which qualifying options are free of tax at the date of grant and the date of exercise. Profits on shares sold after being held one year after exercise were subject to favorable CAPITAL GAINS TAX rates until 1987, when such capital gains became taxable at ordinary rates. *See also* QUALIFYING STOCK OPTION.

INCESTUOUS SHARE DEALING buying and selling of shares in each other's companies to create a tax or other financial advantage.

INCOME AVAILABLE FOR FIXED CHARGES see FIXED-CHARGE COVERAGE.

INCOME AVERAGING method of computing personal income tax whereby tax is figured on the average of the total of current year's income and that of the three preceding years. According to 1984 U.S. tax legislation, income averaging was used when a person's income for the current year exceeded 140% of the average taxable income in the preceding three years. The TAX REFORM ACT OF 1986 repealed income averaging.

INCOME BOND obligation on which the payment of interest is contingent on sufficient earnings from year to year. Such bonds are traded FLAT—that is, with no accrued interest—and are often an alternative to bankruptcy. See ADJUSTMENT BOND.

INCOME INVESTMENT COMPANY management company that operates an income-oriented MUTUAL FUND for investors who value income over growth. These funds may invest in bonds or high-dividend stocks or may write covered call options on stocks. See also INVESTMENT COMPANY.

INCOME LIMITED PARTNERSHIP real estate, oil and gas, or equipment leasing LIMITED PARTNERSHIP whose aim is high income, much of which may be taxable. Such a partnership may be designed for tax-sheltered accounts like Individual Retirement Accounts, Keogh plan accounts, or pension plans.

INCOME PROPERTY real estate bought for the income it produces. The property may be placed in an INCOME LIMITED PARTNERSHIP, or it may be owned by one individual or company. Buyers also hope to achieve capital gains when they sell the property.

INCOME SHARES one of two kinds or classes of capital stock issued by a DUAL—PURPOSE FUND or split investment company, the other kind being *capital shares*. Holders of income shares receive dividends from both classes of shares, generated from income (dividends and interest) produced by the portfolio, whereas holders of capital shares receive capital gains payouts on both calsses. Income shares normally have a minimum income guarantee, which is cumulative.

INCOME STATEMENT see PROFIT AND LOSS STATEMENT.

INCOME TAX annual tax on income levied by the federal government and by certain state and local governments. There are two basic types: the personal income tax, levied on incomes of households and unincorporated businesses, and the corporate (or corporation) income tax, levied on net earnings of corporations.

The U.S. income tax was instituted in 1913 by the Sixteenth Amendment to the Constitution. It has typically accounted for more than half the federal government's total annual revenue. Nearly all states tax individual and corporate incomes, as do many cities, though sales and property taxes are the main sources of state and local revenue. The personal income tax, and to a lesser extent the corporate income tax, were designed to be progressive—that is, to take a larger percentage of higher incomes than lower incomes. The ranges of incomes to which progressively higher rates apply are called TAX BRACKETS, which also determine the value of DEDUCTIONS, such as business costs and expenses, state and local income taxes, or charitable contributions.

In 1986, the individual income tax comprised 15 marginal tax brackets (including the ZERO BRACKET AMOUNT) ranging to a high of 50%. Corporations paid a base rate on the first $25,000 of income, a higher rate on the second $25,000, and a still higher rate on anything over $50,000. LONG-TERM CAPITAL GAINS received preferential tax treatment both for individuals and corporations. Because capital gains rates rewarded taxpayers in a position to take risks, and because LOOPHOLES and TAX SHELTERS enabled the wealthiest corporations and individuals to escape the higher tax brackets, the progressiveness of the tax system was often more theoretical than real.

Spurred by SUPPLY SIDE ECONOMICS, the TAX REFORM ACT OF 1986 introduced a modified FLAT TAX system and contained the most sweeping changes in tax laws since 1913. Signed into law in the Fall of 1986, it drastically reduced tax rates for both individuals and corporations, collapsed the marginal rate structure for individuals into two basic brackets, ended preferential capital gains tax treatment, curtailed loopholes and shelters, and imposed a much stricter ALTERNATIVE MINIMUM TAX applicable to corporations as well as individuals.

INCORPORATION process by which a company receives a state charter allowing it to operate as a corporation. The fact of incorporation must be acknowledged in the company's legal name, using the word *incorporated,* the abbreviation *inc.,* or other acceptable variations. *See also* ARTICLES OF INCORPORATION.

INCREMENTAL CASH FLOW net of cash outflows and inflows attributable to a corporate investment project.

INCREMENTAL COST OF CAPITAL weighted cost of the additional capital raised in a given period. Weighted cost of capital, also called *composite cost of capital,* is the weighted average of costs applicable to the issues of debt and classes of equity that compose the firm's capital structure. Also called *marginal cost of capital.*

INDEMNIFY agree to compensate for damage or loss. The word is used in insurance policies promising that, in the event of a loss, the insured will be restored to the financial position that existed prior to the loss.

INDENTURE formal agreement, also called a deed of trust, between an issuer of bonds and the bondholder covering such considerations as:(1) form of the bond; (2) amount of the issue; (3) property pledged (if not a debenture issue); (4) protective COVENANTS including any provision for a sinking fund; (5) WORKING CAPITAL and CURRENT RATIO; and(6) redemption rights or call privileges. The indenture also provides for the appointment of a trustee to act on behalf of the bondholders, in accordance with the TRUST INDENTURE ACT OF 1939.

INDEPENDENT BROKER New York Stock Exchange member who executes orders for other floor brokers who have more volume than they can handle, or for firms whose exchange members are not on the floor. Formerly called $2 brokers because of their commission for a round lot trade, independent brokers are compensated by commission brokers with fees that once were fixed but are now negotiable. *See also* GIVE UP.

INDEX statistical composite that measures changes in the economy or in financial markets, often expressed in percentage changes from a base year or from the previous month. For instance, the CONSUMER PRICE INDEX uses 1967 as the base year. That index, made up of key consumer goods and services, moves up and down as the rate of inflation changes. By the early 1980s the index had climbed from 100 in 1967 into the low 300s, meaning that the basket of goods the index is based on had risen in price by more than 200%.

Indexes also measure the ups and downs of stock, bond, and commodities markets, reflecting market prices and the number of shares outstanding for the companies in the index. Some well-known indexes are the New York Stock Exchange Index, the American Stock Exchange Index, Standard & Poor's Index, and the Value Line Index. Subindexes for industry groups such as beverages, railroads or computers are also tracked. Stock market indexes form the basis for trading in INDEX OPTIONS. See also STOCK INDEXES AND AVERAGES.

INDEX ARBITRAGE see ARBITRAGE.

INDEX FUND MUTUAL FUND whose portfolio matches that of a broad-based index such as Standard & Poor's Index and whose performance therefore mirrors the market as a whole. Many institutional investors, especially believers in the EFFICIENT MARKET theory, put money in index funds on the assumption that trying to beat the market averages over the long run is futile, and their investments in these funds will at least keep up with the market.

INDEXING
1. weighting one's portfolio to match a broad-based index such as Standard & Poor's so as to match its performance—or buying shares in an INDEX FUND.
2. tying wages, taxes, or other rates to an index. For example, a labor contract may call for indexing wages to the consumer price index to protect against loss of purchasing power in a time of rising inflation.

INDEX OF LEADING INDICATORS see LEADING INDICATORS.

INDEX OPTIONS calls and puts on indexes of stocks. These options are traded on the New York, American, and Chicago Board Options Exchanges, among others. Broad-based indexes cover a wide range of companies and industries, whereas narrow-based indexes consist of stocks in one industry or sector of the economy. Index options allow investors to trade in a particular market or industry group without having to buy all the stocks individually. For instance, someone who thought oil stocks were about to fall could buy a put on the oil index instead of selling short shares in half a dozen oil companies.

INDICATED YIELD coupon or dividend rate as a percentage of the current market price. For fixed rate bonds it is the same as CURRENT YIELD. For common stocks, it is the market price divided into the annual dividend. For preferred stocks, it is the market price divided into the contractual dividend.

INDICATION approximation of what a security's TRADING RANGE (bid and offer prices) will be when trading resumes after a delayed opening or after being halted because of an IMBALANCE OF ORDERS or another reason. Also called *indicated market.*

INDICATION OF INTEREST securities underwriting term meaning a dealer's or investor's interest in purchasing securities that are still *in registration* (awaiting clearance by) the Securities and Exchange Commission. A broker who receives an indication of interest should send the client a preliminary prospectus on the securities. An indication of interest is not a commitment to buy, an important point because selling a security while it is in registration is illegal. *See* CIRCLE.

INDICATOR technical measurement securities market analysts use to forecast the market's direction, such as investment advisory sentiment, volume of stock trading, direction of interest rates, and buying or selling by corporate insiders.

INDIRECT COST AND EXPENSE *see* DIRECT OVERHEAD; FIXED COST.

INDIRECT LABOR COSTS wages and related costs of factory employees, such as inspectors and maintenance crews, whose time is not charged to specific finished products.

INDIVIDUAL RETIREMENT ACCOUNT (IRA) personal, TAX DEFERRED, retirement account that an employed person can set up with a deposit limited to $2000 per year ($4000 for a couple when both work, or $2250 for a couple when one works and the other's income is $250 or less). Under the TAX REFORM ACT OF 1986, rules effective in the tax year 1987 include: deductibility of IRA contributions regardless of income if neither the taxpayer nor the taxpayer's spouse is covered by a QUALIFIED PLAN OR TRUST; even if covered by a qualified plan, taxpayers may deduct IRA contributions if ADJUSTED GROSS INCOME is below $40,000 on a joint return or $25,000 on a single return; couples with incomes of $40,000 to $50,000 and single taxpayers with incomes of $25,000 to $35,000 are allowed partial deductions in amounts reduced proportionately over the $10,000 range with a minimum deduction of $200; taxpayers with incomes over $50,000 (joint) and $35,000 (single) are not allowed deductions, but may make the same contributions (treated as a nontaxable RETURN OF CAPITAL upon withdrawal) and thus gain the benefit of tax-deferral; taxpayers who cannot make deductible contributions because of participation in qualified retirement plans may make nondeductible contributions. Withdrawals from IRAs prior to age 59½ are generally subject to a 10% (of principal) penalty tax.

INDIVIDUAL RETIREMENT ACCOUNT (IRA) ROLLOVER provision of the IRA law that enables persons receiving lump-sum payments from their company's pension or profit-sharing plan because of retirement or other termination of employment to ROLL OVER the amount into an IRA investment plan within 60 days. Also, current IRAs may themselves be transferred to other investment options within the 60-day period. Through an IRA rollover, the capital continues to accumulate tax-deferred until time of withdrawal.

INDUSTRIAL in stock market vernacular, general, catch-all category including firms producing or distributing goods and services that are not classified as utility, transportation, or financial companies.

INDUSTRIAL DEVELOPMENT BOND (IDB) type of MUNICIPAL REVENUE BOND issued to finance FIXED ASSETS that are then leased to private firms, whose payments AMORTIZE the debt. IDBs were traditionally tax-exempt to buyers, but under the TAX REFORM ACT OF 1986, large IDB issues ($1 million plus) are taxable effective August 15, 1986 while tax-exempt small issues for commercial and manufacturing purposes are prohibited after 1986 and 1989 respectively. Also, effective August 8, 1986, banks lost their 80% interest deductibility on borrowings to buy IDBs.

INDUSTRIAL PRODUCTION monthly statistic released by the FEDERAL RESERVE BOARD on the total output of all U.S. factories and mines. These numbers are a key ECONOMIC INDICATOR.

INDUSTRIAL REVENUE BOND *see* INDUSTRIAL DEVELOPMENT BOND.

INEFFICIENCY IN THE MARKET failure of investors to recognize that a particular stock or bond has good prospects or may be headed for trouble. According to the EFFICIENT MARKET theory, current prices reflect all knowledge about securities. But some say that those who find out about securities first can profit by exploiting that information; stocks of small, little-known firms with a large growth potential most clearly reflect the market's inefficiency, they say.

INELASTIC DEMAND OR SUPPLY *see* ELASTICITY OF DEMAND OR SUPPLY.

INFANT INDUSTRY ARGUMENT case made by developing sectors of the economy that their industries need protection against international competition while they establish themselves. In response to such pleas, the government may enact a TARIFF or import duty to stifle foreign competition. The infant industry argument is frequently made in developing nations that are trying to lessen their dependence on the industrialized world. In Brazil, for example, such infant industries as automobile production argue that they need protection until their technological capability and marketing prowess are sufficient to enable competition with well-established foreigners.

INFLATION rise in the prices of goods and services, as happens when spending increases relative to the supply of goods on the market—in other words, too much money chasing too few goods. Moderate inflation is a common result of economic growth. Hyperinflation, with prices rising at 100% a year or more, causes people to lose confidence in the currency and put their assets in hard assets like real estate or gold, which usually retain their value in inflationary times. *See also* COST-PUSH INFLATION; DEMAND-PULL INFLATION.

INFLATION ACCOUNTING showing the effects of inflation in financial statements. The Financial Accounting Standards Board (FASB) requires major companies to supplement their traditional financial reporting with information showing the effects of inflation. The ruling applies to public companies having inventories and fixed assets of more than $125 million or total assets of more than $1 billion.

INFLATION RATE rate of change in prices. Two primary U.S. indicators of the inflation rate are the CONSUMER PRICE INDEX and the PRODUCER PRICE INDEX, which track changes in prices paid by consumers and by producers. The rate can be calculated on an annual, monthly, or other basis.

INFRASTRUCTURE a nation's basic system of transportation, communication, and other aspects of its physical plant. Building and maintaining road, bridge, sewage, and electrical systems provides millions of jobs nationwide. For developing countries, building an infrastructure is a first step in economic development.

INGOT bar of metal. The Federal Reserve System's gold reserves are stored in ingot form. Individual investors may take delivery of an ingot of a precious metal such as gold or silver or may buy a certificate entitling them to a share in an ingot.

INHERITANCE TAX RETURN state counterpart to the federal ESTATE TAX return, required of the executor or administrator to determine the amount of state tax due on the inheritance.

INITIAL MARGIN amount of cash or eligible securities required to be deposited with a broker before engaging in MARGIN transactions. A margin transaction is one in which the broker extends credit to the customer in a MARGIN ACCOUNT.

Under REGULATION T of the Federal Reserve Board, the initial margin is 50% of the purchase price when buying eligible stock or convertible bonds or 50% of the proceeds of a short sale. *See also* MINIMUM MAINTENANCE.

INITIAL PUBLIC OFFERING (IPO) corporation's first offering of stock to the public. IPO's are almost invariably an opportunity for the existing investors and participating venture capitalists to make big profits, since for the first time their shares will be given a market value reflecting expectations for future growth. *See also* HOT ISSUE.

INJUNCTION court order instructing a defendant to refrain from doing something that would be injurious to the plaintiff, or face a penalty. The usual procedure is to issue a temporary restraining order, then hold hearings to determine whether a permanent injunction is warranted.

IN PLAY stock affected by TAKEOVER rumors or activities.

INSIDE INFORMATION corporate affairs that have not yet been made public. The officers of a firm would know in advance, for instance, if the company was about to be taken over, or if the latest earnings report was going to differ significantly from information released earlier. Under Securities and Exchange Commission rules, an INSIDER is not allowed to trade on the basis of such information.

INSIDE MARKET bid or asked quotes between dealers trading for their own inventories. Distinguished from the retail market, where quotes reflect the prices that customers pay to dealers. Also known as *interdealer market; wholesale market.*

INSIDER person with access to key information before it is announced to the public. Usually the term refers to directors, officers, and key employees, but the definition has been extended legally to include relatives and others in a position to capitalize on INSIDE INFORMATION. Insiders are prohibited from trading on their knowledge.

INSOLVENCY inability to pay debts when due. *See also* BANKRUPTCY; CASH FLOW; SOLVENCY.

INSTALLMENT SALE

In general: sale made with the agreement that the purchased goods or services will be paid for in fractional amounts over a specified period of time.

Securities: transaction with a set contract price, paid in installments over a period of time. Gains or losses are generally taxable on a prorated basis.

INSTINET *see* FOURTH MARKET.

INSTITUTIONAL BROKER broker who buys and sells securities for banks, mutual funds, insurance companies, pension funds, or other institutional clients. Institutional brokers deal in large volumes of securities and generally charge their customers lower per-unit commission rates than individuals pay.

INSTITUTIONAL BROKER'S ESTIMATE SYSTEM (IBES) service run by the New York City brokerage firm of Lynch Jones and Ryan, which assembles analysts' estimates of future earnings for thousands of publicly traded companies. These estimates are tabulated, and companies are pinpointed whose estimates have shifted significantly. Reports also detail how many estimates are available on each company and the high, low, and average estimates for each.

INSTITUTIONAL INVESTOR organization that trades large volumes of securities. Some examples are mutual funds, banks, insurance companies, pension funds, labor union funds, corporate profit-sharing plans, and college endowment funds. Typically, more than 50% and sometimes upwards of 70% of the daily trading on the New York Stock Exchange is on behalf of institutional investors.

INSTRUMENT legal document in which some contractual relationship is given formal expression or by which some right is granted—for example, notes, contracts, agreements. *See also* NEGOTIABLE INSTRUMENT.

INSTRUMENTALITY federal agency whose obligations, while not direct obligations of the U.S. Government, are sponsored or guaranteed by the government and backed by the FULL FAITH AND CREDIT of the government. Well over 100 series of notes, certificates, and bonds have been issued by such instrumentalities as Federal Intermediate Credit Banks, Federal Land Banks, Federal Home Loan Bank Board, and Student Loan Marketing Association.

INSURANCE system whereby individuals and companies that are concerned about potential hazards pay premiums to an insurance company, which reimburses them in the event of loss. The insurer profits by investing the premiums it receives. Some common forms of insurance cover business risks, automobiles, homes, boats, worker's compensation, and health. Life insurance guarantees payment to the beneficiaries when the insured person dies. In a broad economic sense, insurance transfers risk from individuals to a larger group, which is better able to pay for losses.

INSURED ACCOUNT account at a bank, savings and loan association, credit union, or brokerage firm that belongs to a federal or private insurance organization. Bank accounts are insured by the BANK INSURANCE FUND (BIF), and savings and loan deposits are insured by the SAVINGS ASSOCIATION INSURANCE FUND (SAIF); both programs are administered by the FEDERAL DEPOSIT INSURANCE CORPORATION (FDIC). Credit union accounts are insured by the *National Credit Union Administration*. Brokerage accounts are insured by the SECURITIES INVESTOR PROTECTION CORPORATION. Such insurance protects depositors against loss in the event that the institution becomes insolvent. Federal insurance systems were set up in the 1930s, after bank failures threatened the banking system with collapse. Some money market funds are covered by private insurance companies.

INTANGIBLE ASSET right or nonphysical resource that is presumed to represent an advantage to the firm's position in the marketplace. Such assets include copyrights, patents, TRADEMARKS, goodwill, computer programs, capitalized advertising costs, organization costs, licenses, LEASES, FRANCHISES, exploration permits, and import and export permits.

INTANGIBLE COST tax-deductible cost. Such costs are incurred in drilling, testing, completing, and reworking oil and gas wells—labor, core analysis, fracturing, drill stem testing, engineering, fuel, geologists' expenses; also abandonment losses, management fees, delay rentals, and similar expenses.

INTERBANK RATE *see* LONDON INTERBANK OFFERED RATE (LIBOR).

INTERCOMMODITY SPREAD spread consisting of a long position and a short position in different but related commodities—for example, a long position in gold futures and a short position in silver futures. The investor hopes to profit from the changing price relationship between the commodities.

INTERDELIVERY SPREAD futures or options trading technique that entails buying one month of a contract and selling another month in the same contract—for instance, buying a June wheat contract and simultaneously selling a September wheat contract. The investor hopes to profit as the price difference between the two contracts widens or narrows.

INTEREST
1. cost of using money, expressed as a rate per period of time, usually one year, in which case it is called an annual rate of interest.
2. share, right, or title in property.

INTEREST COVERAGE *see* FIXED-CHARGE COVERAGE.

INTEREST EQUALIZATION TAX (IET) tax of 15% on interest received by foreign borrowers in U.S. capital markets, imposed in 1963 and removed in 1974.

INTEREST-SENSITIVE STOCK stock of a firm whose earnings change when interest rates change, such as a bank or utility, and which therefore tends to go up or down on news of rate movements.

INTERIM DIVIDEND DIVIDEND declared and paid before annual earnings have been determined, generally quarterly. Most companies strive for consistency and plan quarterly dividends they are sure they can afford, reserving changes until fiscal year results are known.

INTERIM LOAN *see* CONSTRUCTION LOAN.

INTERIM STATEMENT financial report covering only a portion of a fiscal year. Public corporations supplement the annual report with quarterly statements informing shareholders of changes in the balance sheet and income statement, as well as other newsworthy developments.

INTERLOCKING DIRECTORATE membership on more than one company's board of directors. This is legal so long as the companies are not competitors. Consumer activists often point to interlocking directorates as an element in corporate conspiracies. The most flagrant abuses were outlawed by the Clayton Anti-Trust Act of 1914.

INTERMARKET SPREAD *see* INTERDELIVERY SPREAD.

INTERMARKET TRADING SYSTEM (ITS) video-computer display system that links the posts of specialists at the New York, American, Boston, Midwest, Philadelphia, and Pacific Stock Exchanges who are trading the same securities. The quotes are displayed and are firm (good) for at least 100 shares. A broker at one exchange may direct an order to another exchange where the quote is better by marking a card and sending the order electronically. A transaction that is accepted by the broker at the other exchange is termed an electronic handshake; the actual contract is made by telex or telephone.

INTERMEDIARY person or institution empowered to make investment decisions for others. Some examples are banks, savings and loan institutions, insurance companies, brokerage firms, mutual funds, and credit unions. These specialists are knowledgeable about investment alternatives and can achieve a higher return than the average investor can. Furthermore, they deal in large dollar volumes, have lower transaction costs, and can diversify their assets easily. Also called *financial intermediary*.

INTERMEDIATE TERM period between the short and long term, the length of time depending on the context. Stock analysts, for instance, mean 6 to 12 months, whereas bond analysts most often mean 3 to 10 years.

INTERMEDIATION placement of money with a financial INTERMEDIARY like a broker or bank, which invests it in bonds, stocks, mortgages, or other loans, money-market securities, or government obligations so as to achieve a targeted return. More formally called *financial intermediation*. The opposite is DISINTERMEDIATION, the withdrawal of money from an intermediary.

INTERNAL CONTROL method, procedure, or system designed to promote efficiency, assure the implementation of policy, and safeguard assets.

INTERNAL EXPANSION asset growth financed out of internally generated cash— usually termed INTERNAL FINANCING—or through ACCRETION or APPRECIATION. *See also* CASH EARNINGS.

INTERNAL FINANCING funds produced by the normal operations of a firm, as distinguished from external financing, which includes borrowings and new equity. *See also* INTERNAL EXPANSION.

INTERNAL RATE OF RETURN (IRR) discount rate at which the present values of the future cash flows of an investment equal the cost of the investment. It is found by a process of trial and error; when the net present values of cash outflows (the cost of the investment) and cash inflows (returns on the investment) equal zero, the rate of discount being used is the IRR. When IRR is greater than the required return—called the hurdle rate in capital budgeting—the investment is acceptable.

INTERNAL REVENUE SERVICE (IRS) U.S. agency charged with collecting nearly all federal taxes, including personal and corporate income taxes, social security taxes, and excise and gift taxes. Major exceptions include taxes having to do with alcohol, tobacco, firearms, and explosives, and customs duties and tariffs. The IRS administers the rules and regulations that are the responsibility of the U.S. Department of the Treasury and investigates and prosecutes (through the U.S. Tax Court) tax illegalities.

INTERNATIONAL BANK FOR RECONSTRUCTION AND DEVELOPMENT (IBRD) organization set up by the Bretton Woods Agreement of 1944 to help finance the reconstruction of Europe and Asia after World War II. That task accomplished, the *World Bank,* as IBRD is known, turned to financing commercial and infrastructure projects, mostly in developing nations. It does not compete with commercial banks, but it may participate in a loan set up by a commercial bank. World Bank loans must be backed by the government in the borrowing country.

INTERNATIONAL MONETARY FUND (IMF) organization set up by the Bretton Woods Agreement in 1944. Unlike the World Bank, whose focus is on foreign exchange reserves and the balance of trade, the IMF focus is on lowering trade barriers and stabilizing currencies. While helping developing nations pay their debts, the IMF usually imposes tough guidelines aimed at lowering inflation, cutting imports, and raising exports. IMF funds come mostly from the treasuries of industrialized nations. *See also* INTERNATIONAL BANK FOR RECONSTRUCTION AND DEVELOPMENT.

INTERNATIONAL MONETARY MARKET (IMM) division of the Chicago Mercantile Exchange that trades futures in U.S. Treasury bills, foreign currency, certificates of deposit, and Eurodollar deposits.

INTERNATIONAL MUTUAL FUND MUTUAL FUND that invests in securities markets throughout the world so that if one market is in a slump, money can still be made in others. Fund managers must be alert to trends in foreign currencies as well as in world markets. Otherwise, seemingly profitable investments in a rising market could lose money if the national currency is rising against the dollar.

INTERPOLATION estimation of an unknown number intermediate between known numbers. Interpolation is a way of approximating price or yield using bond tables that do not give the net yield on every amount invested at every rate of interest and for every maturity. Interpolation is based on the assumption that a certain percentage change in yield will result in the same percentage change in price. The assumption is not altogether correct, but the variance is small enough to ignore.

INTERPOSITIONING placement of a second broker in a securities transaction between two principals or between a customer and a marketmaker. The practice is regulated by the Securities and Exchange Commission, and abuses such as interpositioning to create additional commission income are illegal.

INTERSTATE COMMERCE COMMISSION (ICC) federal agency created by the Interstate Commerce Act of 1887 to insure that the public receives fair and reasonable rates and services from carriers and transportation service firms involved in interstate commerce. Legislation enacted in the 1970s and 80s substantially curtailed the regulatory activities of the ICC, particularly in the rail, truck, and bus industries.

INTER VIVOS TRUST trust established between living persons—for instance, between father and child. In contrast, a TESTAMENTARY TRUST goes into effect when the person who establishes the trust dies. Also called *living trust.*

IN THE MONEY option contract on a stock whose current market price is above the striking price of a call option or below the striking price of a put option. A call option on XYZ at a striking price of 100 would be in the money if XYZ were selling for 102, for instance, and a put option with the same striking price would be in the money if XYZ were selling for 98. *See also* AT THE MONEY; OUT OF THE MONEY.

IN THE TANK slang expression meaning market prices are dropping rapidly. Stock market observers may say, ''The market is in the tank'' after a day in which stock prices fell.

INTRACOMMODITY SPREAD futures position in which a trader buys and sells contracts in the same commodity on the same exchange, but for different months. For instance, a trader would place an intracommodity spread if he bought a pork bellies contract expiring in December and at the same time sold a pork bellies contract expiring in April. His profit or loss would be determined by the price difference between the December and April contracts.

INTRADAY within the day; often used in connection with high and low prices of a stock, bond, or commodity. For instance, "The stock hit a new intraday high today" means that the stock reached an all-time high price during the day but fell back to a lower price by the end of the day. The listing of the high and low prices at which a stock is traded during a day is called the *intraday price range*.

INTRINSIC VALUE

Financial analysis: valuation determined by applying data inputs to a valuation theory or model. The resulting value is comparable to the prevailing market price.

Options trading: difference between the EXERCISE PRICE or strike price of an option and the market value of the underlying security. For example, if the strike price is $53 on a call option to purchase a stock with a market price of $55, the option has an intrinsic value of $2. Or, in the case of a put option, if the strike price was $55 and the market price of the underlying stock was $53, the intrinsic value of the option would also be $2. Options AT THE MONEY or OUT OF THE MONEY have no intrinsic value.

INVENTORY

Corporate finance: value of a firm's raw materials, work in process, supplies used in operations, and finished goods. Since inventory value changes with price fluctuations, it is important to know the method of valuation. There are a number of inventory valuation methods; the most widely used are FIRST IN, FIRST OUT (FIFO) and LAST IN, FIRST OUT (LIFO). Financial statements normally indicate the basis of inventory valuation, generally the lower figure of either cost price or current market price, which precludes potentially overstated earnings and assets as the result of sharp increases in the price of raw materials.

Personal finance: list of all assets owned by an individual and the value of each, based on cost, market value, or both. Such inventories are usually required for property insurance purposes and are sometimes required with applications for credit.

Securities: net long or short position of a dealer or specialist. Also, securities bought and held by a dealer for later resale.

INVENTORY FINANCING

Factoring: sometimes used as a synonym for overadvances in FACTORING, where loans in excess of accounts receivable are made against inventory in anticipation of future sales.

Finance companies: financing by a bank or sales finance company of the inventory of a dealer in consumer or capital goods. Such loans, also called wholesale financing or *floorplanning*, are secured by the inventory and are usually made as part of a relationship in which retail installment paper generated by sales to the public is also financed by the lender. *See also* FINANCE COMPANY.

INVENTORY TURNOVER ratio of annual sales to inventory, which shows how many times the inventory of a firm is sold and replaced during an accounting period; sometimes called *inventory utilization ratio*. Compared with industry averages, a low turnover might indicate a company is carrying excess stocks of inventory, an unhealthy sign because excess inventory represents an investment with a low or zero rate of return and because it makes the company more vulnerable to falling prices. A steady drop in inventory turnover, in comparison with prior periods, can reveal lack of a sufficiently aggressive sales policy or ineffective buying.

Two points about the way inventory turnover may be calculated: (1) Because sales are recorded at market value and inventories are normally carried at cost, it is more realistic to obtain the turnover ratio by dividing inventory into cost of goods sold rather than into sales. However, it is conventional to use sales as the numerator because that is the practice of Dun & Bradstreet and other compilers of published financial ratios, and comparability is of overriding importance. (2) To minimize the seasonal factor affecting inventory levels, it is better to use an average inventory figure, obtained by adding yearly beginning and ending inventory figures and dividing by 2.

INVERTED SCALE serial bond offering where earlier maturities have higher yields than later maturities. *See also* SERIAL BOND.

INVERTED YIELD CURVE unusual situation where short-term interest rates are higher than long-term rates. Normally, lenders receive a higher yield when committing their money for a longer period of time; this situation is called a POSITIVE YIELD CURVE. An inverted YIELD CURVE occurs when a surge in demand for short-term credit drives up short-term rates on instruments like Treasury bills and money-market funds, while long-term rates move up more slowly, since borrowers are not willing to commit themselves to paying high interest rates for many years. This situation happened in the early 1980s, when short-term interest rates were around 20%, while long-term rates went up to only 16% or 17%. The existence of an inverted yield curve can be a sign of an unhealthy economy, marked by high inflation and low levels of confidence. Also called *negative yield curve*.

INVERTED YIELD CURVE

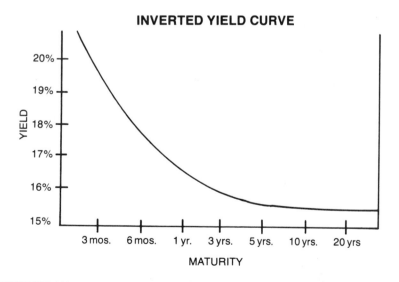

INVESTMENT use of capital to create more money, either through income-producing vehicles or through more risk-oriented ventures designed to result in capital gains. *Investment* can refer to a financial investment (where an investor puts money into a vehicle) or to an investment of effort and time on the part of an individual who wants to reap profits from the success of his labor. Investment connotes the idea that safety of principal is important. SPECULATION, on the other hand, is far riskier.

INVESTMENT ADVISERS ACT legislation passed by Congress in 1940 that requires all investment advisers to register with the Securities and Exchange Commission. The Act is designed to protect the public from fraud or misrepresentation by investment advisers. One requirement, for example, is that advisers must disclose all potential *conflicts of interest* with any recommendations they make to those they advise. A potential conflict of interest might exist where the adviser had a position in a security he was recommending. *See also* INVESTMENT ADVISORY SERVICE.

INVESTMENT ADVISORY SERVICE service providing investment advice for a fee. Investment advisers must register with the Securities and Exchange Commission and abide by the rules of the INVESTMENT ADVISERS ACT. Investment advisory services usually specialize in a particular kind of investment—for example, emerging growth stocks, international stocks, mutual funds, or commodities. Some services only offer advice through a newsletter; others will manage a client's money. The performance of many investment advisory services is ranked by the *Hulbert Financial Digest*. *See* HULBERT RATING.

INVESTMENT BANKER firm, acting as underwriter or agent, that serves as intermediary between an issuer of securities and the investing public. In what is termed FIRM COMMITMENT underwriting, the investment banker, either as manager or participating member of an investment banking syndicate, makes outright purchases of new securities from the issuer and distributes them to dealers and investors, profiting on the spread between the purchase price and the selling (public offering) price. Under a conditional arrangement called BEST EFFORT, the investment banker markets a new issue without underwriting it, acting as agent rather than principal and taking a commission for whatever amount of securities the banker succeeds in marketing. Under another conditional arrangement, called STANDBY COMMITMENT, the investment banker serves clients issuing new securities by agreeing to purchase for resale any securities not taken by existing holders of RIGHTS.

Where a client relationship exists, the investment banker's role begins with preunderwriting counseling and continues after the distribution of securities is completed, in the form of ongoing expert advice and guidance, often including a seat on the board of directors. The direct underwriting responsibilities include preparing the Securities and Exchange Commission registration statement; consulting on pricing of the securities; forming and managing the syndicate; establishing a selling group if desired; and PEGGING (stabilizing) the price of the issue during the offering and distribution period.

In addition to new securities offerings, investment bankers handle the distribution of blocks of previously issued securities, either through secondary offerings or through negotiations; maintain markets for securities already distributed; and act as finders in the private placement of securities.

Along with their investment banking functions, the majority of investment bankers also maintain broker-dealer operations, serving both wholesale and retail clients in brokerage and advisory capacities and offering a growing number of related financial services. *See also* FLOTATION COST; SECONDARY DISTRIBUTION; UNDERWRITE.

INVESTMENT CERTIFICATE certificate evidencing investment in a savings and loan association and showing the amount of money invested. Investment certificates do not have voting rights and do not involve stockholder responsibility. Also called *mutual capital certificate*. *See also* MUTUAL ASSOCIATION.

INVESTMENT CLUB group of people who pool their assets in order to make joint investment decisions. Each member of the club contributes a certain amount of capital, with additional money to be invested every month or quarter. Decisions on which stocks or bonds to buy are made by a vote of members. Besides helping each member become more knowledgeable about investing, these clubs allow people with small amounts of money to participate in larger investments and therefore pay lower commissions. There is a National Association of Investment Clubs, based in Royal Oak, Michigan.

INVESTMENT COMPANY firm that, for a management fee, invests the pooled funds of small investors in securities appropriate for its stated investment objectives. It offers participants more diversification, liquidity, and professional management service than would normally be available to them as individuals.

There are two basic types of investment companies: (1) *open-end*, better known as a MUTUAL FUND, which has a floating number of outstanding shares (hence the name *open-end*) and stands prepared to sell or redeem shares at their current NET ASSET VALUE; and (2) *closed-end*, also known as an *investment trust*, which, like a corporation, has a fixed number of outstanding shares that are traded like stock, often on the major exchanges.

Open-end management companies are divided into two categories, based on their acquisition cost policies: (1) *load funds*, which are sold in the over-the-counter market by broker-dealers, who do not receive a sales commission; instead, a "loading charge" is added to the net asset value at time of purchase. The charge typically runs 8½%, with a reduction for quantity that ranges as low as 4%. There is no redemption charge when load fund shares are sold. (2) *no-load funds*, which are bought directly from sponsoring companies. Such companies do not charge a loading fee, although small redemption charges are not uncommon.

Dealers in closed-end investment companies obtain their sales revenue from regular brokerage commissions.

Both open-end and closed-end investment companies charge annual management fees, typically ranging from ½% to 1% of the value of the investment.

Under the INVESTMENT COMPANY ACT OF 1940, the registration statement and prospectus of every investment company must state its specific investment objectives. Basically, the companies fall into the following categories: diversified common stock funds; balanced funds (mixing bonds and preferred and common stocks); bond and preferred stock funds (featuring fixed income); specialized funds (by industry, groups of industries, geography, size of company); income funds (high-yield securities); performance funds (growth stocks); dual-purpose funds (a form of closed-end investment company offering a choice of dividend shares or capital gain shares); and money market funds (money market instruments).

INVESTMENT COMPANY ACT OF 1940 legislation passed by Congress requiring registration and regulation of investment companies by the Securities and Exchange Commission. The Act sets the standards by which mutual funds and other investment vehicles of investment companies operate, in such areas as promotion, reporting requirements, pricing of securities for sale to the public, and allocation of investments within a fund portfolio. *See also* INVESTMENT COMPANY.

INVESTMENT COUNSEL person with the responsibility for providing investment advice to clients and executing investment decisions. *See also* PORTFOLIO MANAGER.

INVESTMENT CREDIT reduction in income tax liability granted by the federal government over the years to firms making new investments in certain asset categories, primarily equipment; also called *investment tax credit*. The investment credit, designed to stimulate the economy by encouraging capital expenditure, has been a feature of tax legislation on and off, and in varying percentage amounts, since 1962; in 1985 it was 6% or 10% of the purchase price, depending on the life of the asset. As a credit, it has been deducted from the tax bill, not from pretax income, and it has been independent of DEPRECIATION. The TAX REFORM ACT OF 1986 generally repealed the investment credit retroactively for any property placed in service after January 1, 1986. The 1986 Act also provided for a 35% reduction of the value of credits carried over from previous years.

INVESTMENT GRADE term used to describe bonds suitable for purchase by prudent investors. Standard & Poor's rating service designates the bonds in its four top categories (AAA down to BBB) as investment grade. In their FIDUCIARY roles, institutional investors, such as pension funds, insurance companies, and banks, must maintain a certain level of credit quality in the bond portfolios they purchase, so they tend to buy mostly investment grade bonds. Any debt issue below investment grade is considered speculative and is often referred to as a JUNK BOND.

INVESTMENT HISTORY body of prior experience establishing "normal investment practice" with respect to the account relationship between a member firm and its customer. For example, the Rules of Fair Practice of the National Association of Securities Dealers (NASD) prohibit the sale of a new issue to members of a distributing dealer's immediate family unless it can be demonstrated that the number of securities ordered conformed to normal investment practice. In other words, if there was sufficient precedent in the investment history of this particular dealer-customer relationship, the sale would not be a violation of NASD rules.

INVESTMENT LETTER in the private placement of new securities, a letter of intent between the issuer of securities and the buyer establishing that the securities are being bought as an investment and are not for resale. This is necessary to avoid having to register the securities with the Securities and Exchange Commission. (Under provisions of SEC Rule 144, a purchaser of such securities may eventually resell them to the public if certain specific conditions are met, including a mimimum holding period of at least two years.) Use of the investment letter gave rise to the terms *letter stock* and *letter bond* in referring to unregistered issues. *See also* LETTER SECURITY.

INVESTMENT STRATEGY plan to allocate assets among such choices as stocks, bonds, CASH EQUIVALENTS, commodities, and real estate. An investment strategy should be formulated based on an investor's outlook on interest rates, inflation, and economic growth, among other factors, and also taking into account the investor's age, tolerance for risk, amount of capital available to invest, and future needs for capital, such as for financing childrens' college educations or buying a house. An investment adviser will help to devise such a strategy. *See also* INVESTMENT ADVISORY SERVICE.

INVESTMENT STRATEGY COMMITTEE committee in the research department of a brokerage firm that sets the overall investment strategy the firm recommends to clients. The director of research, the chief economist, and several top analysts typically sit on this committee. The group advises clients on the amount of money that should be placed into stocks, bonds, or CASH EQUIVALENTS, as well as the industry groups or individual stocks or bonds that look particularly attractive.

INVESTMENT TAX CREDIT *see* INVESTMENT CREDIT.

INVESTMENT TRUST *see* INVESTMENT COMPANY.

INVESTMENT VALUE OF A CONVERTIBLE SECURITY estimated price at which a CONVERTIBLE security (CV) would be valued by the marketplace if it had no stock conversion feature. The investment value for CVs of major companies is determined by investment advisory services and, theoretically, should never fall lower than the price of the related stock. It is arrived at by estimating the price at which a nonconvertible ("straight") bond or preferred share of the same issuing company would sell. The investment value reflects the interest rate; therefore, the market price of the security will go up when rates are down and vice versa. *See also* PREMIUM OVER BOND VALUE.

INVESTOR RELATIONS DEPARTMENT in major listed companies, a staff position responsible for investor relations, reporting either to the chief financial officer or to the director of public relations. The actual duties will vary, depending on whether the company retains an outside financial public relations firm, but the general responsibilities are as follows:

* to see that the company is understood, in terms of its activities and objectives, and is favorably regarded in the financial and capital markets and the investment community; this means having input into the annual report and other published materials, coordinating senior management speeches and public statements with the FINANCIAL PUBLIC RELATIONS effort, and generally fostering a consistent and positive corporate image.
* to ensure full and timely public DISCLOSURE of material information, and to work with the legal staff in complying with the rules of the SEC, the securities exchanges, and other regulatory authorities.
* to respond to requests for reports and information from shareholders, professional investors, brokers, and the financial media.
* to maintain productive relations with the firm's investment bankers, the specialists in its stock, major broker-dealers, and institutional investors who follow the company or hold sizeable positions in its securities.
* to take direct measures, where necessary, to see that the company's shares are properly valued. This involves identifying the firm's particular investment audience and the professionals controlling its stock float, arranging analysts' meetings and other presentations, and generating appropriate publicity.

The most successful investor relations professionals have been those who follow a policy of full and open dissemination of relevant information, favorable and unfavorable, on a consistent basis. The least successful, over the long run, have been the "touts"—those who emphasize promotion at the expense of credibility.

INVESTORS SERVICE BUREAU New York Stock Exchange public service that responds to written inquiries of all types concerning securities investments.

INVOICE bill prepared by a seller of goods or services and submitted to the purchaser. The invoice lists all the items bought, together with amounts.

INVOLUNTARY BANKRUPTCY *see* BANKRUPTCY.

IRA *see* INDIVIDUAL RETIREMENT ACCOUNT.

IRA ROLLOVER *see* INDIVIDUAL RETIREMENT ACCOUNT ROLLOVER.

IRREDEEMABLE BOND
1. bond without a CALL FEATURE (issuer's right to redeem the bond before maturity) or a REDEMPTION privilege (holder's right to sell the bond back to the issuer before maturity).
2. PERPETUAL BOND.

IRREVOCABLE TRUST trust that cannot be changed or terminated by the one who created it without the agreement of the BENEFICIARY.

IRS *see* INTERNAL REVENUE SERVICE.

ISSUE
1. stock or bonds sold by a corporation or a government entity at a particular time.
2. selling new securities by a corporation or government entity, either through an underwriter or by a private placement.
3. descendants, such as children and grandchildren. For instance, "This man's estate will be passed, at his death, to his issue."

ISSUED AND OUTSTANDING shares of a corporation, authorized in the corporate charter, which have been issued and are outstanding. These shares represent capital invested by the firm's shareholders and owners, and may be all or only a portion of the number of shares authorized. Shares that have been issued and subsequently repurchased by the company are called *treasury stock,* because they are held in the corporate treasury pending reissue or retirement. Treasury shares are legally issued but are not considered outstanding for purposes of voting, dividends, or earnings per share calculations. Shares authorized but not yet issued are called *unissued shares.* Most companies show the amount of authorized, issued and outstanding, and treasury shares in the capital section of their annual reports. *See also* TREASURY STOCK.

ISSUER legal entity that has the power to issue and distribute a security. Issuers include corporations, municipalities, foreign and domestic governments and their agencies, and investment trusts. Issuers of stock are responsible for reporting on corporate developments to shareholders and paying dividends once declared. Issuers of bonds are committed to making timely payments of interest and principal to bondholders.

J

JANUARY BAROMETER market forecasting tool popularized by *The Stock Traders Almanac,* whose statistics show that with over 80% consistency since 1934, the market has risen in years when the STANDARD & POOR'S INDEX of 500 stocks was up in January and dropped when the index for that month was down.

JANUARY EFFECT the phenomenon that stocks (especially small-capitalization stocks) have historically tended to rise markedly during the period starting on the last day of December and ending on the fourth trading day of January. The January Effect is attributed to year-end selling to create tax losses, recognize capital gains, effect portfolio WINDOW DRESSING, or raise holiday cash; since such selling depresses the stocks but has nothing to do with their fundamental worth, bargain hunters quickly buy in, causing the January rally.

JEEP *see* GRADUATED PAYMENT MORTGAGE.

JOBBER
1. wholesaler, especially one who buys in small lots from manufacturers, importers, and/or other wholesalers and sells to retailers.
2. London Stock Exchange term for MARKET MAKER.

JOINT ACCOUNT bank or brokerage account owned jointly by two or more people. Joint accounts may be set up in two ways: (1) either all parties to the account must sign checks and approve all withdrawals or brokerage transactions or (2) any one party can take such actions on his or her own. *See also* JOINT TENANTS WITH RIGHT OF SURVIVORSHIP.

JOINT ACCOUNT AGREEMENT form needed to open a JOINT ACCOUNT at a bank or brokerage. It must be signed by all parties to the account regardless of the provisions it may contain concerning signatures required to authorize transactions.

JOINT AND SURVIVOR ANNUITY annuity that makes payments for the lifetime of two or more beneficiaries, often a husband and wife. When one of the annuitants dies, payments continue to the survivor annuitant in the same amount or in a reduced amount as specified in the contract.

JOINT BOND bond that has more than one obligator or that is guaranteed by a party other than the issuer; also called *joint and several bond*. Joint bonds are common where a parent corporation wishes to guarantee the bonds of a subsidiary. *See* GUARANTEED BOND.

JOINTLY AND SEVERALLY

In general: legal phrase used in definitions of liability meaning that an obligation may be enforced against all obligators jointly or against any one of them separately.

Securities: term used to refer to municipal bond underwritings where the account is undivided and syndicate members are responsible for unsold bonds in proportion to their participations. In other words, a participant with 5% of the account would still be responsible for 5% of the unsold bonds, even though that member might already have sold 10%. *See also* SEVERALLY BUT NOT JOINTLY.

JOINT STOCK COMPANY form of business organization that combines features of a corporation and a partnership. Under U.S. law, joint stock companies are recognized as corporations with unlimited liability for their stockholders. As in a conventional corporation, investors in joint stock companies receive shares of stock they are free to sell at will without ending the corporation; they also elect directors. Unlike in a limited liability corporation, however, each shareholder in a joint stock company is legally liable for all debts of the company.

There are some advantages to this form of organization compared with limited-liability corporations: fewer taxes, greater ease of formation under the common law, more security for creditors, mobility, and freedom from regulation, for example. However, the disadvantages—such as the fact that the joint stock company usually cannot hold title to real estate and, particularly, the company's unlimited liability—tend to outweigh the advantages, with the result that it is not a popular form of organization.

JOINT TENANTS WITH RIGHT OF SURVIVORSHIP when two or more people maintain a JOINT ACCOUNT with a brokerage firm or a bank, it is normally agreed that, upon the death of one account holder, ownership of the account assets passes to the remaining account holders. This transfer of assets escapes probate, but estate taxes may be due, depending on the amount of assets transferred.

JOINT VENTURE agreement by two or more parties to work on a project together. Frequently, a joint venture will be formed when companies with complementary technology wish to create a product or service that takes advantage of the strengths of the participants. A joint venture, which is usually limited to one project, differs from a partnership, which forms the basis for cooperation on many projects.

JUDGMENT decision by a court of law ordering someone to pay a certain amount of money. For instance, a court may order someone who illegally profited by trading on INSIDE INFORMATION to pay a judgment amounting to all the profits from the trade, plus damages. The term also refers to condemnation awards by government entities in payment for private property taken for public use.

JUMBO CERTIFICATE OF DEPOSIT certificate with a minimum denomination of $100,000. Jumbo CDs are usually bought and sold by large institutions such as banks, pension funds, money market funds, and insurance companies.

JUNIOR ISSUE issue of debt or equity that is subordinate in claim to another issue in terms of dividends, interest, principal, or security in the event of liquidation. *See also* JUNIOR SECURITY; PREFERRED STOCK; PRIORITY; PRIOR LIEN BOND; PRIOR PREFERRED STOCK.

JUNIOR MORTGAGE mortgage that is subordinate to other mortgages—for example, a second or a third mortgage. If a debtor defaults, the first mortgage will have to be satisfied before the junior mortgage.

JUNIOR REFUNDING refinancing government debt that matures in one to five years by issuing new securities that mature in five years or more.

JUNIOR SECURITY security with lower priority claim on assets and income than a SENIOR SECURITY. For example, a PREFERRED STOCK is junior to a DEBENTURE, but a debenture, being an unsecured bond, is junior to a MORTGAGE BOND. COMMON STOCK is junior to all corporate securities. Some companies—finance companies, for example—have senior SUBORDINATED and junior subordinated issues, the former having priority over the latter, but both ranking lower than senior (unsubordinated) debt.

JUNK BOND bond with a credit rating of BB or lower by RATING agencies. Junk bonds are issued by companies without long track records of sales and earnings, or by those with questionable credit strength. They are a popular means of financing TAKEOVERS. Since they are more volatile and pay higher yields than INVESTMENT GRADE bonds, many risk-oriented investors specialize in trading them. Institutions with FIDUCIARY responsibilities are regulated. *See* LEGAL LIST.

JURISDICTION defined by the American Bankers Association as "the legal right, power or authority to hear and determine a cause; as in the jurisdiction of a court." The term frequently comes up in finance and investment discussions in connection with the jurisdictions of the various regulatory authorities bearing on the field. For example, the Federal Reserve Board, not the Securities and Exchange Commission (as might be supposed), has jurisdiction in a case involving a brokerage MARGIN ACCOUNT (*see also* REGULATION T).

The term also is important with respect to EUROCURRENCY loan agreements, where it is possible for a loan to be funded in one country but made in another by a group of international banks each from different countries, to a borrower in still another country. The determination of jurisdiction, not to mention the willingness of courts in different countries to accept that jurisdiction, is a matter of obvious urgency in such cases.

JURY OF EXECUTIVE OPINION forecasting method whereby a panel of experts—perhaps senior corporate financial executives—prepare individual forecasts based on information made available to all of them. Each expert then reviews the others' work and modifies his or her own forecasts accordingly. The resulting composite forecast is supposed to be more realistic than any individual effort could be. Also known as *Delphi forecast.*

JUSTIFIED PRICE fair market price an informed buyer will pay for an asset, whether it be a stock, a bond, a commodity, or real estate. *See also* FAIR MARKET VALUE.

JUST TITLE title to property that is supportable against all legal claims. Also called *clear title, good title, proper title.*

k

KAFFIRS term used in Great Britain that refers to South African gold mining shares. These shares are traded over the counter in the U.S. in the form of American Depositary Receipts, which are claims to share certificates deposited in a foreign bank. Under South African law, Kaffirs must pay out almost all their earnings to shareholders as dividends. These shares thus not only provide stockholders with a gold investment to hedge against inflation, but also afford substantial income in the form of high dividend payments. However, investors in Kaffirs must also consider the political risks of investing in South Africa, as well as the risk of fluctuations in the price of gold. *See also* AMERICAN DEPOSITARY RECEIPT.

KANSAS CITY BOARD OF TRADE (KCBT) futures exchange on which contracts for wheat and the Value Line Stock Index are traded.

KEOGH PLAN tax-deferred pension account designated for employees of unincorporated businesses or for persons who are self-employed (either full-time or part-time). As of 1984, eligible people could contribute up to 25% of earned income, up to a maximum of $30,000. Like the INDIVIDUAL RETIREMENT ACCOUNT (IRA), the Keogh plan allows all investment earnings to grow tax deferred until capital is withdrawn, as early as age 59½ and starting no later than age 70½. Almost any investment except precious metals or collectibles can be used for a Keogh account. Typically, people place Keogh assets in stocks, bonds, money-market funds, certificates of deposit, mutual funds, or limited partnerships. The Keogh plan was established by Congress in 1962 and was expanded in 1976 and again in 1981 as part of the Economic Recovery Tax Act.

KEY INDUSTRY industry of primary importance to a nation's economy. For instance, the defense industry is called a key industry since it is crucial to maintaining a country's safety. The automobile industry is also considered key since so many jobs are directly or indirectly dependent on it.

KEYNESIAN ECONOMICS body of economic thought originated by the British economist and government adviser, John Maynard Keynes (1883–1946), whose landmark work, *The General Theory of Employment, Interest and Money,* was published in 1935. Writing during the Great Depression, Keynes took issue with the classical economists, like Adam Smith, who believed that the economy worked best when left alone. Keynes believed that active government intervention in the marketplace was the only method of ensuring economic growth and stability. He held essentially that insufficient demand causes unemployment and that excessive demand results in inflation; government should therefore manipulate the level of aggregate demand by adjusting levels of government expenditure and taxation. For example, to avoid depression Keynes advocated increased government spending and EASY MONEY, resulting in more investment, higher employment, and increased consumer spending.

Keynesian economics has had great influence on the public economic policies of industrial nations, including the United States. In the 1980s, however, after repeated recessions, slow growth, and high rates of inflation in the U.S., a contrasting outlook, uniting monetarists and "supply siders," blamed excessive government intervention for troubles in the economy.

See also AGGREGATE SUPPLY; LAISSEZ-FAIRE; MACROECONOMICS; MONETARIST; SUPPLY-SIDE ECONOMICS.

KICKBACK

Finance: practice whereby sales finance companies reward dealers who discount installment purchase paper through them with cash payments.

Government and private contracts: payment made secretly by a seller to someone instrumental in awarding a contract or making a sale—an illegal payoff.

Labor relations: illegal practice whereby employers require the return of a portion of wages established by law or union contract, in exchange for employment.

KICKER added feature of a debt obligation, usually designed to enhance marketability by offering the prospect of equity participation. For instance, a bond may be convertible to stock if the shares reach a certain price. This makes the bond more attractive to investors, since the bondholder potentially gets the benefit of an equity security in addition to interest payments. Other examples of equity kickers are RIGHTS and WARRANTS. Some mortgage loans also include kickers in the form of ownership participation or in the form of a percentage of gross rental receipts. Kickers are also called *sweeteners.*

KILLER BEES those who aid a company in fending off a takeover bid. "Killer bees" are usually investment bankers who devise strategies to make the target less attractive or more difficult to acquire.

KITING

Commercial banking: (1) depositing and drawing checks between accounts at two or more banks and thereby taking advantage of the FLOAT—that is, the time it takes the bank of deposit to collect from the paying bank. (2) fraudently altering the figures on a check to increase its face value.

Securities: driving stock prices to high levels through manipulative trading methods, such as the creation of artificial trading activity by the buyer and the seller working together and using the same funds.

KNOW YOUR CUSTOMER ethical concept in the securities industry either stated or implied by the rules of the exchanges and the other authorities regulating broker-dealer practices. Its meaning is expressed in the following paragraph from Article 3 of the NASD Rules of Fair Practice: "In recommending to a customer the purchase, sale or exchange of any security, a member shall have reasonable grounds for believing that the recommendation is suitable for such customer upon the basis of the facts, if any, disclosed by such customer as to his other security holdings and as to his financial situation and needs." Customers opening accounts at brokerage firms must supply financial information that satisfies the know your customer requirement for routine purposes.

KONDRATIEFF WAVE theory of the Soviet economist Nikolai Kondratieff in the 1920s that the economies of the Western capitalist world were prone to major up-and-down "supercycles" lasting 50 to 60 years. He claimed to have predicted the economic crash of 1929–30 based on the crash of 1870, 60 years earlier. The Kondratieff wave theory has adherents, but is controversial among economists. Also called *Kondratieff cycle*.

KRUGERRAND gold bullion coin minted by the Republic of South Africa and containing one troy ounce of gold. Krugerrands usually sell for slightly more than the current value of their gold content. Krugerrands were banned for further import into the United States in 1985, although existing coins could still be traded. Other gold coins traded include the Mexican 50-peso, Austrian 100-corona, and Canadian Maple Leaf pieces and the United States Eagle series.

L

LABOR-INTENSIVE requiring large pools of workers. Said of an industry in which labor costs are more important than capital costs. Deep-shaft coal mining, for instance, is labor-intensive.

LAFFER CURVE curve named for U.S. economics professor Arthur Laffer, postulating that economic output will grow if marginal tax rates are cut. The curve is used in explaining SUPPLY-SIDE ECONOMICS, a theory that noninflationary growth is spurred when tax policies encourage productivity and investment.

LAISSEZ-FAIRE doctrine that interference of government in business and economic affairs should be minimal. Adam Smith's *The Wealth Of Nations* (1776) described laissez-faire economics in terms of an "invisible hand" that would provide for the maximum good for all, if businessmen were free to pursue profitable opportunities as they saw them. The growth of industry in England in the early 19th century and American industrial growth in the late 19th century both occurred in a laissez-faire capitalist environment. The laissez-faire period ended by the beginning of the 20th century, when large monopolies were broken up and government regulation of business became the norm. The Great Depression of the 1930s saw the birth of KEYNESIAN ECONOMICS, an influential approach advocating government intervention in economic affairs. The movement toward deregulation of business in the U.S. in the 1970s and 80s is to some extent a return to the laissez-faire philosphy. Laissez-faire is French for "allow to do."

LAPSED OPTION OPTION that reached its expiration date without being exercised and is thus without value.

LAST IN FIRST OUT (LIFO) method of accounting for INVENTORY that ties the cost of goods sold to the cost of the most recent purchases. The formula for cost of goods sold is:

beginning inventory + purchases − ending inventory = cost of goods sold

In contrast to the FIRST IN, FIRST OUT (FIFO) method, in a period of rising prices LIFO produces a higher cost of goods sold and a lower gross profit and taxable income. The artificially low balance sheet inventories resulting from the use of LIFO in periods of inflation give rise to the term *LIFO cushion.*

LAST SALE most recent trade in a particular security. Not to be confused with the final transaction in a trading session, called the CLOSING SALE. The last sale is the point of reference for two Securites and Exchange Commission rules: (1) On a national exchange, no SHORT SALE may be made below the price of the last regular sale. (2) No short sale may be made at the same price as the last sale unless the last sale was at a price higher than the preceding different price. PLUS TICK, MINUS TICK, ZERO MINUS TICK, and ZERO PLUS TICK, used in this connection, refer to the last sale.

LAST TRADING DAY final day during which a futures contract may be settled. If the contract is not OFFSET, either an agreement between the buying and selling parties must be arranged or the physical commodity must be delivered from the seller to the buyer.

LATE TAPE delay in displaying price changes because trading on a stock exchange is particularly heavy. If the tape is more than five minutes late, the first digit of a price is deleted. For instance, a trade at 62¾ is reported as 2¾. *See also* DIGITS DELETED.

LAY OFF

Investment banking: reduce the risk in a standby commitment, under which the bankers agree to purchase and resell to the public any portion of a stock issue not subscribed to by shareowners who hold rights. The risk is that the market value will fall during the two to four weeks when shareholders are deciding whether to exercise or sell their rights. To minimize the risk, investment bankers (1) buy up the rights as they are offered and, at the same time, sell the shares represented by these rights; and (2) sell short an amount of shares proportionate to the rights that can be expected to go unexercised—to ½% of the issue, typically. Also called *laying off.*

Labor: temporarily or permanently remove an employee from a payroll because of an economic slowdown or a production cutback, not because of poor performance or an infraction of company rules.

LEADER
1. stock or group of stocks at the forefront of an upsurge or a downturn in a market. Typically, leaders are heavily bought and sold by institutions that want to demonstrate their own market leadership.
2. product that has a large market share.

LEADING INDICATORS components of an index released monthly by the U.S. Commerce Department's Bureau of Economic Analysis. The components in 1985 were average workweek of production workers; average weekly claims for state unemployment insurance; new orders for consumer goods and materials; vendor performance (companies receiving slower deliveries from suppliers); net business formation; contracts for plant and equipment; new building permits; inventory changes; sensitive materials prices; stock prices; MONEY SUPPLY (M-2); and business and consumer borrowing. The index of leading indicators, the components of which are adjusted for inflation, has accurately forecast ups and downs in the business cycle. Official full name: *Composite Index of 12 Leading Indicators.*

LEASE contract granting use of real estate, equipment, or other fixed assets for a specified time in exchange for payment, usually in the form of rent. The owner of the leased property is called the lessor, the user the lessee. *See also* CAPITAL LEASE; FINANCIAL LEASE; OPERATING LEASE; SALE AND LEASEBACK.

LEASE ACQUISITION COST price paid by a real estate LIMITED PARTNERSHIP, when acquiring a lease, including legal fees and related expenses. The charges are prorated to the limited partners.

LEASEHOLD asset representing the right to use property under a LEASE.

LEASEHOLD IMPROVEMENT modification of leased property. The cost is added to fixed assets and then amortized.

LEASE-PURCHASE AGREEMENT agreement providing that portions of LEASE payments may be applied toward the purchase of the property under lease.

LEG
1. sustained trend in stock market prices. A prolonged bull or bear market may have first, second, and third legs.
2. one side of a spread transaction. For instance, a trader might buy a CALL OPTION that has a particular STRIKE PRICE and expiration date, then combine it with a PUT OPTION that has the same striking price and a different expiration date. The two options are called legs of the spread.
Selling one of the options is termed LIFTING A LEG.

LEGAL computerized data base maintained by the New York Stock Exchange to track enforcement actions against member firms, audits of member firms, and customer complaints. LEGAL is not an acronym, but is written in all capitals.

LEGAL ENTITY person or organization that has the legal standing to enter into a contract and may be sued for failure to perform as agreed in the contract. A child under legal age is not a legal entity; a corporation is a legal entity since it is a person in the eyes of the law.

LEGAL INVESTMENT investment permissible for investors with FIDUCIARY responsibilities. INVESTMENT GRADE bonds, as rated by Standard & Poor's or Moody's, usually qualify as legal investments. Guidelines designed to protect investors are set by the state in which the fiduciary operates. *See also* LEGAL LIST.

LEGAL LIST securities selected by a state agency, usually a banking department, as permissible holdings of mutual savings banks, pension funds, insurance companies, and other FIDUCIARY institutions. To protect the money that individuals place in such institutions, only high quality debt and equity securities are generally included. As an alternative to the list, some states apply the PRUDENT MAN RULE.

LEGAL MONOPOLY exclusive right to offer a particular service within a particular territory. In exchange, the company agrees to have its policies and rates regulated. Electric and water utilities are legal monopolies.

LEGAL OPINION
1. statement as to legality, written by an authorized official such as a city attorney or an attorney general.
2. statement as to the legality of a MUNICIPAL BOND issue, usually written by a law firm specializing in public borrowings. It is part of the *official statement*, the municipal equivalent of a PROSPECTUS. Unless the legality of an issue is established, an investor's contract is invalid at the time of issue and he cannot sue under it. The legal opinion is therefore required by a SYNDICATE MANAGER and customarily accompanies the transfer of municipal securities as long as they are outstanding.

LEGAL TRANSFER transaction that requires documentation other than the standard stock or bond power to validate the transfer of a stock certificate from a seller to a buyer—for example, securities registered to a corporation or to a deceased person. It is the selling broker's responsibility to supply proper documentation to the buying broker in a legal transfer.

LENDER individual or firm that extends money to a borrower with the expectation of being repaid, usually with interest. Lenders create debt in the form of loans, and in the event of LIQUIDATION they are paid off before stockholders receive distributions. But the investor deals in both debt (bonds) and equity (stocks). It is useful to remember that investors in commercial paper, bonds, and other debt instruments are in fact lenders with the same rights and powers enjoyed by banks.

LENDER OF LAST RESORT
1. characterization of a central bank's role in bolstering a bank that faces large withdrawals of funds. The U.S. lender of last resort is the FEDERAL RESERVE BANK. Member banks may borrow from the DISCOUNT WINDOW to maintain reserve requirements or to meet large withdrawals. The Fed thereby maintains the stability of the banking system, which would be threatened if major banks were to fail.
2. government small business financing programs and municipal economic development organizations whose precondition to making loans to private enterprises is an inability to obtain financing from other lending sources.

LENDING AT A PREMIUM term used when one broker lends securities to another broker to cover customer's short position and imposes a charge for the loan. Such charges, which are passed on to the customer, are the exception rather than the rule, since securities are normally LOANED FLAT between brokers, that is, without interest. Lending at a premium might occur when the securities needed are in very heavy demand and are therefore difficult to borrow. The premium is in addition to any payments the customer might have to make to the lending broker to MARK TO THE MARKET or to cover dividends or interest payable on the borrowed securities.

LENDING AT A RATE paying interest to a customer on the credit balance created from the proceeds of a SHORT SALE. Such proceeds are held in ESCROW to secure the loan of securities, usually made by another broker, to cover the customer's short position. Lending at a rate is the exception rather than the rule.

LENDING SECURITIES securities borrowed from a broker's inventory, other MARGIN ACCOUNTS, or from other brokers, when a customer makes a SHORT SALE and the securities must be delivered to the buying customer's broker. As collateral, the borrowing broker deposits with the lending broker an amount of money equal to the market value of the securities. No interest or premium is ordinarily involved in the transaction. The Securities and Exchange Commission requires that brokerage customers give permission to have their securities used in loan transactions, and the point is routinely covered in the standard agreement signed by customers when they open general accounts.

LETTER BOND *see* LETTER SECURITY.

LETTER OF CREDIT (L/C) instrument or document issued by a bank guaranteeing the payment of a customer's drafts up to a stated amount for a specified period. It substitutes the bank's credit for the buyer's and eliminates the seller's risk. It is used extensively in international trade. A *commercial letter of credit* is normally drawn in favor of a third party, called the beneficiary. A *confirmed letter of credit* is provided by a correspondent bank and guaranteed by the issuing bank. A *revolving letter of credit* is issued for a specified amount and automatically renewed for the same amount for a specified period, permitting any number of drafts to be drawn so long as they do not exceed its overall limit. A *traveler's letter of credit* is issued for the convenience of a traveling customer and typically lists correspondent banks at which drafts will be honored. A *performance letter of credit* is issued to guarantee performance under a contract.

LETTER OF INTENT
1. any letter expressing an intention to take (or not take) an action, sometimes subject to other action being taken. For example, a bank might issue a letter of intent stating it will make a loan to a customer, subject to another lender's agreement to participate. The letter of intent, in this case, makes it possible for the customer to negotiate the participation loan.
2. preliminary agreement between two companies that intend to merge. Such a letter is issued after negotiations have been satisfactorily completed.
3. promise by a MUTUAL FUND shareholder to invest a specified sum of money monthly for about a year. In return, the shareholder is entitled to lower sales charges.
4. INVESTMENT LETTER for a LETTER SECURITY.

LETTER SECURITY stock or bond that is not registered with the Securities and Exchange Commission and therefore cannot be sold in the public market. When an issue is sold directly by the issuer to the investor, registration with the SEC can be avoided if a LETTER OF INTENT, called an INVESTMENT LETTER, is signed by the purchaser establishing that the securities are being bought for investment and not for resale. The letter's integral association with the security gives rise to the terms *letter security, letter stock,* and *letter bond.*

LETTER STOCK *see* LETTER SECURITY.

LEVEL DEBT SERVICE provision in a municipal charter stipulating that payments on municipal debt be approximately equal every year. This makes it easier to project the amount of tax revenue needed to meet obligations.

LEVERAGE
Operating leverage: extent to which a company's costs of operating are fixed (rent, insurance, executive salaries) as opposed to variable (materials, direct labor). In a totally automated company, whose costs are virtually all fixed, every dollar of increase in sales is a dollar of increase in operating income once the

BREAKEVEN POINT has been reached, because costs remain the same at every level of production. In contrast, a company whose costs are largely variable would show relatively little increase in operating income when production and sales increased because costs and production would rise together. The leverage comes in because a small change in sales has a magnified percentage effect on operating income and losses. The *degree of operating leverage*—the ratio of the percentage change in operating income to the percentage change in sales or units sold— measures the sensitivity of a firm's profits to changes in sales volume. A firm using a high degree of operating leverage has a breakeven point at a relatively high sales level.

Financial leverage: debt in relation to equity in a firm's capital structure—its LONG-TERM DEBT (usually bonds), PREFERRED STOCK, and SHAREHOLDERS' EQUITY— measured by the DEBT-TO-EQUITY RATIO. The more long-term debt there is, the greater the financial leverage. Shareholders benefit from financial leverage to the extent that return on the borrowed money exceeds the interest costs and the market value of their shares rises. For this reason, financial leverage is popularly called *trading on the equity*. Because leverage also means required interest and principal payments and thus ultimately the risk of default, how much leverage is desirable is largely a question of stability of earnings. As a rule of thumb, an industrial company with a debt to equity ratio of more than 30% is highly leveraged, exceptions being firms with dependable earnings and cash flow, such as electric utilities.

Since long-term debt interest is a fixed cost, financial leverage tends to take over where operating leverage leaves off, further magnifying the effects on earnings per share of changes in sales levels. In general, high operating leverage should accompany low financial leverage, and vice versa.

Investments: means of enhancing return or value without increasing investment. Buying securities on margin is an example of leverage with borrowed money, and extra leverage may be possible if the leveraged security is convertible into common stock. RIGHTS, WARRANTS, and OPTION contracts provide leverage, not involving borrowings but offering the prospect of high return for little or no investment.

LEVERAGED BUYOUT TAKEOVER of a company, using borrowed funds. Most often, the target company's assets serve as security for the loans taken out by the acquiring firm, which repays the loans out of cash flow of the acquired company. Management may use this technique to retain control by converting a company from public to private. A group of investors may also borrow from banks, using their own assets as collateral, to take over another firm. In almost all leveraged buyouts, public shareholders receive a premium over the current market value for their shares.

LEVERAGED COMPANY company with debt in addition to equity in its capital structure. In its popular connotation, the term is applied to companies that are highly leveraged. Although the judgment is relative, industrial companies with more than one third of their capitalization in the form of debt are considered highly leveraged. *See also* LEVERAGE.

LEVERAGED INVESTMENT COMPANY
  1. open-end INVESTMENT COMPANY, or MUTUAL FUND, that is permitted by its charter to borrow capital from a bank or other lender.
  2. dual-purpose INVESTMENT COMPANY, which issues both income and capital shares. Holders of income shares receive dividends and interest on invest-

ments, whereas holders of capital shares receive all capital gains on investments. In effect each class of shareholder leverages the other.

LEVERAGED LEASE LEASE that involves a lender in addition to the lessor and lessee. The lender, usually a bank or insurance company, puts up a percentage of the cash required to purchase the asset, usually more than half. The balance is put up by the lessor, who is both the equity participant and the borrower. With the cash the lessor acquires the asset, giving the lender (1) a mortgage on the asset and (2) an assignment of the lease and lease payments. The lessee then makes periodic payments to the lessor, who in turn pays the lender. As owner of the asset, the lessor is entitled to tax deductions for DEPRECIATION on the asset and INTEREST on the loan.

LEVERAGED STOCK stock financed with credit, as in a MARGIN ACCOUNT. Although not, strictly speaking, leveraged stock, securities that are convertible into common stock provide an extra degree of leverage when bought on margin. Assuming the purchase price is reasonably close to the INVESTMENT VALUE and CONVERSION VALUE, the downside risk is no greater than it would be with the same company's common stock, whereas the appreciation value is much greater.

LIABILITY claim on the assets of a company or individual—excluding ownership EQUITY. Characteristics: (1) It represents a transfer of assets or services at a specified or determinable date. (2) The firm or individual has little or no discretion to avoid the transfer. (3) The event causing the obligation has already occurred. *See also* BALANCE SHEET.

LIBOR *see* LONDON INTERBANK OFFERED RATE.

LIEN creditor's claim against property. For example, a mortgage is a lien against a house; if the mortgage is not paid on time, the house can be seized to satisfy the lien. Similarly, a bond is a lien against a company's assets; if interest and principal are not paid when due, the assets may be seized to pay the bondholders. As soon as a debt is paid, the lien is removed. Liens may be granted by courts to satisfy judgments. *See also* MECHANIC'S LIEN.

LIFE EXPECTANCY age to which an average person can be expected to live, as calculated by an ACTUARY. Insurance companies base their projections of benefit payouts on actuarial studies of such factors as sex, heredity, and health habits and base their rates on actuarial analysis. Life expectancy can be calculated at birth or at some other age and generally varies according to age. Thus, all persons at birth might have an average life expectancy of 70 years and all persons aged 40 years might have an average life expectancy of 75 years.

Life expectancy projections determine such matters as the ages when an INDIVIDUAL RETIREMENT ACCOUNT may start and finish paying out funds. Annuities payable for lifetimes are usually based on separate male or female tables, except that a QUALIFIED PLAN OR TRUST must use unisex tables.

LIFE INSURANCE IN FORCE amount of life insurance that a company has issued, including the face amount of all outstanding policies together with all dividends that have been paid to policyholders. Thus a life insurance policy for $500,000 on which dividends of $10,000 have been paid would count as life insurance in force of $510,000.

LIFO *see* LAST IN, FIRST OUT.

LIFT rise in securities prices as measured by the Dow Jones Industrial Average or other market averages, usually caused by good business or economic news.

LIFTING A LEG closing one side of a HEDGE, leaving the other side as a long or short position. A leg, in Wall Street parlance, is one side of a hedged transaction. A trader might have a STRADDLE—that is, a call and a put on the same stock, at the same price, with the same expiration date. Making a closing sale of the put, thereby lifting a leg—or *taking off a leg*, as it is sometimes called—would leave the trader with the call, or the LONG LEG.

LIMITED COMPANY form of business most common in Britain, where registration under the Companies Act is comparable to incorporation under state law in the United States. It is abbreviated Ltd. or PLC.

LIMITED DISCRETION agreement between broker and client allowing the broker to make certain trades without consulting the client—for instance, sell an option position that is near expiration or sell a stock on which there has just been adverse news.

LIMITED PARTNERSHIP organization made up of a GENERAL PARTNER, who manages a project, and limited partners, who invest money but have limited liability, are not involved in day-to-day management, and usually cannot lose more than their capital contribution. Usually limited partners receive income, capital gains, and tax benefits; the general partner collects fees and a percentage of capital gains and income. Typical limited partnerships are in real estate, oil and gas, and equipment leasing, but they also finance movies, research and development, and other projects. Typically, public limited partnerships are sold through brokerage firms, for minimum investments of $5000, whereas private limited partnerships are put together with fewer than 35 limited partners who invest more than $20,000 each. *See also* INCOME LIMITED PARTNERSHIP; MASTER LIMITED PARTNERSHIP; OIL AND GAS LIMITED PARTNERSHIP; PASSIVE; RESEARCH AND DEVELOPMENT LIMITED PARTNERSHIP; UNLEVERAGED PROGRAM.

LIMITED RISK risk in buying an options contract. For example, someone who pays a PREMIUM to buy a CALL OPTION on a stock will lose nothing more than the premium if the underlying stock does not rise during the life of the option. In contrast, a FUTURES CONTRACT entails *unlimited risk,* since the buyer may have to put up more money in the event of an adverse move. Thus options trading offers limited risk unavailable in futures trading.

Also, stock analysts may say of a stock that has recently fallen in price, that it now has limited risk, reasoning that the stock is unlikely to fall much further.

LIMITED TAX BOND MUNICIPAL BOND backed by the full faith of the issuing government but not by its full taxing power; rather it is secured by the pledge of a special tax or group of taxes, or a limited portion of the real estate tax.

LIMITED TRADING AUTHORIZATION *see* LIMITED DISCRETION.

LIMIT ORDER order to buy or sell a security at a specific price or better. The broker will execute the trade only within the price restriction. For example, a customer puts in a limit order to buy XYZ Corp. at 30 when the stock is selling for 32. Even if the stock reached 30⅛ the broker will not execute the trade. Similarly, if the client put in a limit order to sell XYZ Corp. at 33 when the price is 31, the trade will not be executed until the stock price hits 33.

LIMIT ORDER INFORMATION SYSTEM electronic system that informs subscribers about securities traded on participating exchanges, showing the specialist, the exchange, the order quantities, and the bid and offer prices. This allows subscribers to shop for the most favorable prices.

LIMIT PRICE price set in a LIMIT ORDER. For example, a customer might put in a limit order to sell shares at 45 or to buy at 40. The broker executes the order at the limit price or better.

LIMIT UP, LIMIT DOWN maximum price movement allowed for a commodity FUTURES CONTRACT during one trading day. In the face of a particularly dramatic development, a future's price may move limit up or limit down for several consecutive days.

LINE OF CREDIT see BANK LINE.

LIPPER MUTUAL FUND INDUSTRY AVERAGE average performance level of all mutual funds, as reported by Lipper Analytical Services of New York. The performance of all mutual funds is ranked quarterly and annually, by type of fund—such as aggressive growth fund or income fund. Mutual fund managers try to beat the industry average as well as the other funds in their category. *See also* MUTUAL FUND.

LIQUID ASSET cash or easily convertible into cash. Some examples: money-market fund shares, U.S. Treasury bills, bank deposits. An investor in an ILLIQUID investment such as a real estate or oil and gas LIMITED PARTNERSHIP is required to have substantial liquid assets, which would serve as a cushion if the illiquid deal did not work out favorably.

In a corporation's financial statements, liquid assets are cash, marketable securities, and accounts receivable.

LIQUIDATING DIVIDEND distribution of assets in the form of a DIVIDEND from a corporation that is going out of business. Such a payment may come when a firm goes bankrupt or when management decides to sell off a company's assets and pass the proceeds on to shareholders.

LIQUIDATING VALUE projected price for an asset of a company that is going out of business—for instance, a real estate holding or office equipment. Liquidating value, also called *auction value,* assumes that assets are sold separately from the rest of the organization; it is distinguished from GOING CONCERN VALUE, which may be higher because of what accountants term *organization value* or *goodwill.*

LIQUIDATION
1. dismantling of a business, paying off debts in order of priority, and distributing the remaining assets in cash to the owners. Involuntary liquidation is covered under Chapter 7 of the federal BANKRUPTCY law. *See also* JUNIOR SECURITY; PREFERRED STOCK.
2. forced sale of a brokerage client's securities or commodities after failure to meet a MARGIN CALL. *See also* SELL OUT.

LIQUIDITY
1. characteristic of a security or commodity with enough units outstanding to allow large transactions without a substantial drop in price. A stock, bond, or commodity that has a great many shares outstanding therefore has liquidity.

Institutional investors are inclined to seek out liquid investments so that their trading activity will not influence the market price.

2. ability of an individual or company to convert assets into cash or cash equivalents without significant loss. Investments in money-market funds and listed stocks are much more liquid than investments in real estate, for instance. Having a good amount of liquidity means being able to meet maturing obligations promptly, earn trade discounts, benefit from a good credit rating, and take advantage of market opportunities.

LIQUIDITY DIVERSIFICATION purchase of bonds whose maturities range from short to medium to long term, thus helping to protect against sharp fluctuations in interest rates.

LIQUIDITY FUND Emeryville, California, company that will buy a limited partner's interest in a real estate LIMITED PARTNERSHIP for cash at 25% to 30% below the appraised value.

LIQUIDITY RATIO measure of a firm's ability to meet maturing short-term obligations. *See also* CURRENT RATIO; NET QUICK ASSETS; QUICK RATIO.

LISTED OPTION put or call OPTION that an exchange has authorized for trading, properly called an *exchange-traded option*.

LISTED SECURITY stock or bond that has been accepted for trading by one of the organized and registered securities exchanges in the United States, which list more than 6000 issues of securities of some 3500 corporations. Generally, the advantages of being listed are that the exchanges provide (1) an orderly marketplace; (2) liquidity; (3) fair price determination; (4) accurate and continuous reporting on sales and quotations; (5) information on listed companies; and (6) strict regulations for the protection of security holders. Each exchange has its own listing requirements, those of the New York Stock Exchange being most stringent. Listed securities include stocks, bonds, convertible bonds, preferred stocks, warrants, rights, and options, although not all forms of securities are accepted on all exchanges. Unlisted securites are traded in the OVER-THE-COUNTER market. *See also* LISTING REQUIREMENTS; STOCK EXCHANGE.

LISTING REQUIREMENTS rules that must be met before a stock is listed for trading on an exchange. Among the requirements of the New York Stock Exchange: a corporation must have a minimum of one million publicly held shares with a minimum aggregate market value of $16 million as well as an annual net income topping $2.5 million before federal income tax.

LIVING TRUST *see* INTER VIVOS TRUST.

LOAD sales charge paid by an investor who buys shares in a load MUTUAL FUND or ANNUITY. Loads are usually charged when shares or units are purchased; a charge for withdrawing is called a BACK-END LOAD (or *rear-end load*). A fund that does not charge this fee is called a NO-LOAD FUND. *See also* INVESTMENT COMPANY.

LOAD FUND MUTUAL FUND that is sold for a sales charge by a brokerage firm or other sales representative. Such funds may be stock, bond, or commodity funds, with conservative or aggressive objectives. The stated advantage of a loan fund is that the salesperson will explain the fund to the customer, and advise him or her when it is appropriate to sell the fund, as well as when to buy more shares. A NO-LOAD FUND, which is sold without a sales charge directly to investors by a fund company, does not give advice on when to buy or sell. Increasingly, traditional no-load funds are becoming *low-load funds,* imposing up-front charges of 3% or less with no change in services. *See also* INVESTMENT COMPANY.

LOAD SPREAD OPTION method of allocating the annual sales charge on some contractual mutual funds. In a CONTRACTUAL PLAN, the investor accumulates shares in the fund through periodic fixed payments. During the first four years of the contract, up to 20% of any single year's contributions to the fund may be credited against the sales charge, provided that the total charges for these four years do not exceed 64% of one year's contributions. The sales charge is limited to 9% of the entire contract.

LOAN transaction wherein an owner of property, called the LENDER, allows another party, the *borrower,* to use the property. The borrower customarily promises to return the property after a specified period with payment for its use, called INTEREST. The documentation of the promise is called a PROMISSORY NOTE when the property is cash.

LOAN CROWD stock exchange members who lend or borrow securities required to cover the positions of brokerage customers who sell short—called a crowd because they congregate at a designated place on the floor of the exchange. *See also* LENDING SECURITIES.

LOANED FLAT loaned without interest, said of the arrangement whereby brokers lend securities to one another to cover customer SHORT SALE positions. *See also* LENDING AT A PREMIUM; LENDING AT A RATE; LENDING SECURITIES.

LOAN STOCK *see* LENDING SECURITIES.

LOAN VALUE
1. amount a lender is willing to loan against collateral. For example, at 50% of appraised value, a piece of property worth $800,000 has a loan value of $400,000.
2. with respect to REGULATION T of the FEDERAL RESERVE BOARD, the maximum percentage of the current market value of eligible securities that a broker can lend a margin account customer. Regulation T applies only to securities formally registered or having an unlisted trading privilege on a national securities exchange. For securities exempt from Regulation T, which comprise U.S. government securities, municipal bonds, and bonds of the International Bank for Reconstruction and Development, loan value is a matter of the individual firm's policy.

LOCK BOX
1. cash management system whereby a company's customers mail payments to a post office box near the company's bank. The bank collects checks from the lock box—sometimes several times a day—deposits them to the account of the firm, and informs the company's cash manager by telephone of the deposit. This reduces processing FLOAT and puts cash to work more quickly. The bank's fee for its services must be weighed against the savings from reduced float to determine whether this arrangement is cost-effective.
2. bank service that entails holding a customer's securities and, as agent, receiving and depositing income such as dividends on stock and interest on bonds.
3. box rented in a post office where mail is stored until collected.

LOCKED IN
1. unable to take advantage of preferential tax treatment on the sale of an asset because the required HOLDING PERIOD has not elapsed. *See also* CAPITAL GAIN.
2. commodities position in which the market has an up or down limit day, and investors cannot get in or out of the market.
3. said of a rate of return that has been assured for a length of time through an investment such as a certificate of deposit or a fixed rate bond; also said of profits or yields on securities or commodities that have been protected through HEDGING techniques.

LOCKED MARKET highly competitive market environment with identical bid and ask prices for a stock. The appearance of more buyers and sellers unlocks the market.

LOCK-UP OPTION privilege offered a WHITE KNIGHT (friendly acquirer) by a TARGET COMPANY of buying CROWN JEWELS or additional equity. The aim is to discourage a hostile TAKEOVER.

LONDON INTERBANK OFFERED RATE (LIBOR) rate that the most creditworthy international banks dealing in EURODOLLARS charge each other for large loans. The LIBOR rate is usually the base for other large Eurodollar loans to less creditworthy corporate and government borrowers. For instance, a Third World country may have to pay one point over LIBOR when it borrows money.

LONG BOND 30-year TREASURIES or any bond that matures in more than 10 years. Since these bonds commit investors' money for a long time, they are riskier than shorter-term bonds of the same quality and thus normally pay a higher yield.

LONG COUPON
1. bond issue's first interest payment covering a longer period than the remaining payments, or the bond issue itself. Conventional schedules call for interest payments at six-month intervals. A long COUPON results when a bond is issued more than six months before the date of the first scheduled payment. *See also* SHORT COUPON.
2. interest-bearing bond maturing in more than 10 years.

LONG HEDGE
1. FUTURES CONTRACT bought to protect against a rise in the cost of honoring a future commitment. Also called a *buy hedge*. The hedger benefits from a narrowing of the BASIS (difference between cash price and future price) if the future is bought below the cash price, and from a widening of the basis if the future is bought above the cash price.
2. FUTURES CONTRACT or CALL OPTION bought in anticipation of a drop in interest rates, so as to lock in the present yield on a fixed-income security.

LONG LEG part of an OPTION SPREAD representing a commitment to buy the underlying security. For instance, if a spread consists of a long CALL OPTION and a short PUT OPTION, the long call is the long LEG.

LONG POSITION
1. ownership of a security, giving the investor the right to transfer ownership to someone else by sale or by gift; the right to receive any income paid by the security; and the right to any profits or losses as the security's value changes.
2. investor's ownership of securities held by a brokerage firm.

LONG TERM
1. HOLDING PERIOD of six months or longer, according to the TAX REFORM ACT OF 1984 and applicable in calculating the CAPITAL GAINS TAX until 1988.
2. investment approach to the stock market in which an investor seeks appreciation by holding a stock for a year or more.
3. bond with a maturity of ten years or longer.
    See also LONG BOND; LONG-TERM DEBT; LONG-TERM FINANCING; LONG-TERM GAIN; LONG-TERM LOSS.

LONG-TERM DEBT liability due in a year or more. Normally, interest is paid periodically over the term of the loan, and the principal amount is payable as notes or bonds mature. Also, a LONG BOND with a maturity of 10 years or more.

LONG-TERM FINANCING liabilities not repayable in one year and all equity. *See also* LONG-TERM DEBT.

LONG-TERM GAIN subsequent to the TAX REFORM ACT OF 1984 and prior to provisions of the TAX REFORM ACT OF 1986 effective in 1988, a gain on the sale of a CAPITAL ASSET where the HOLDING PERIOD was six months or more and the profit was subject to the long-term CAPITAL GAINS TAX.

LONG-TERM LOSS negative counterpart to LONG-TERM GAIN as defined by the same legislation. A CAPITAL LOSS can be used to offset a CAPITAL GAIN plus $3000 of ORDINARY INCOME (but the gain and loss must both be either long-term or short-term until the distinction ends in 1988).

LOOPHOLE technicality making it possible to circumvent a law's intent without violating its letter. For instance, a TAX SHELTER may exploit a loophole in the tax law, or a bank may take advantage of a loophole in the GLASS STEAGALL ACT to acquire a DISCOUNT BROKER.

LOSS RATIO ratio of losses paid or accrued by an insurer to premiums earned, usually for a one-year period. *See also* BAD DEBT.

LOSS RESERVE *see* BAD DEBT.

LOT in a general business sense, a lot is any group of goods or services making up a transaction. *See also* ODD LOT; ROUND LOT.

LOW bottom price paid for a security over the past year or since trading in the security began; in the latter sense also called *historic low*.

LOW-LOAD FUND *see* LOAD FUND.

LUMP-SUM DISTRIBUTION single payment to a beneficiary covering the entire amount of an agreement. Participants in Individual Retirement Accounts, pension plans, profit-sharing, and executive stock option plans generally can opt for a lump-sum distribution if the taxes are not too burdensome when they become eligible.

LUXURY TAX tax on goods considered nonessential.

m

MACROECONOMICS analysis of a nation's economy as a whole, using such aggregate data as price levels, unemployment, inflation, and industrial production. *See also* MICROECONOMICS.

MAINTENANCE BOND bond that guarantees against defects in workmanship or materials for a specified period following completion of a contract.

MAINTENANCE CALL call for additional money or securities when a brokerage customer's margin account equity falls below the requirements of the National Association of Securities Dealers (NASD), of the exchanges, or of the brokerage firm. Unless the account is brought up to the levels complying with equity maintenance rules, some of the client's securities may be sold to remedy the deficiency. *See also* MAINTENANCE REQUIREMENT; MINIMUM MAINTENANCE; SELL OUT.

MAINTENANCE FEE annual charge to maintain certain types of brokerage accounts. Such a fee may be attached to an ASSET MANAGEMENT ACCOUNT, which combines securities and money market accounts. Banks and brokers may also charge a maintenance fee for an INDIVIDUAL RETIREMENT ACCOUNT (IRA).

MAINTENANCE REQUIREMENT *see* MINIMUM MAINTENANCE.

MAJORITY SHAREHOLDER one of the shareholders who together control more than half the outstanding shares of a corporation. If the ownership is widely scattered and there are no majority shareholders, effective control may be gained with far less than 51% of the outstanding shares. *See also* WORKING CONTROL.

MAKE A MARKET maintain firm bid and offer prices in a given security by standing ready to buy or sell ROUND LOTS at publicly quoted prices. The dealer is called a *market maker* in the over-the-counter market and a SPECIALIST on the exchanges. A dealer who makes a market over a long period is said to *maintain* a market. *See also* REGISTERED COMPETITIVE MARKET MAKER.

MAKE A PRICE *see* MAKE A MARKET.

MALONEY ACT legislation, also called the Maloney Amendment, enacted in 1938 to amend the SECURITIES EXCHANGE ACT OF 1934 by adding Section 15A, which provides for the regulation of the OVER-THE-COUNTER market (OTC) through national securities associations registered with the Securities and Exchange Commission. *See also* NATIONAL ASSOCIATION OF SECURITIES DEALERS (NASD).

MANAGED ACCOUNT investment account consisting of money that one or more clients entrust to a manager, who decides when and where to invest it. Such an account may be handled by a bank trust department or by an investment advisory firm. Clients are charged a MANAGEMENT FEE and share in proportion to their participation in any losses and gains.

MANAGEMENT combined fields of policy and administration and the people who provide the decisions and supervision necessary to implement the owners' business objectives and achieve stability and growth. The formulation of policy requires analysis of all factors having an effect on short- and long-term profits. The administration of policies is carried out by the CHIEF EXECUTIVE OFFICER, his or her immediate staff, and everybody else who possesses authority delegated by people with supervisory responsibility. Thus the size of management can range from one person in a small organization to multilayered management hierarchies in large, complex organizations. The top members of management, called senior management, report to the owners of a firm; in large corporations, the CHAIRMAN OF THE BOARD, the PRESIDENT, and sometimes other key senior officers report to the BOARD OF DIRECTORS, comprising elected representatives of the owning stockholders. The application of scientific principles to decision-making is called management science. *See also* ORGANIZATION CHART.

MANAGEMENT COMPANY same as INVESTMENT COMPANY.

MANAGEMENT FEE charge against investor assets for managing the portfolio of an open- or closed-end MUTUAL FUND as well as for such services as shareholder relations or administration. The fee, as disclosed in the PROSPECTUS, is a fixed percentage of the fund's asset value, typically 1% or less per year. The fee also applies to a MANAGED ACCOUNT.

MANAGING UNDERWRITER leading—and originating—investment banking firm of an UNDERWRITING GROUP organized for the purchase and distribution of a new issue of securities. The AGREEMENT AMONG UNDERWRITERS authorizes the managing underwriter, or syndicate manager, to act as agent for the group in purchasing, carrying, and distributing the issue as well as complying with all federal and state requirements; to form the selling group; to determine the allocation of securities to each member; to make sales to the selling group at a specified discount—or CONCESSION—from the public offering price; to engage in open market transactions during the underwriting period to stabilize the market price of the security; and to borrow for the syndicate account to cover costs. *See also* FLOTATION COST; INVESTMENT BANKER; UNDERWRITE.

MANIPULATION buying or selling a security to create a false appearance of active trading and thus influence other investors to buy or sell shares. This may be done by one person or by a group acting in concert. Those found guilty of manipulation are subject to criminal and civil penalties. *See also* MINI-MANIPULATION.

MARGIN

In general: amount a customer deposits with a broker when borrowing from the broker to buy securities. Under Federal Reserve Board regulation, the initial margin required since 1945 has ranged from 50 to 100 percent of the security's purchase price. In the mid-1980s the minimum was 50% of the purchase or short sale price, in cash or eligible securities, with a minimum of $2000. Thereafter, MINIMUM MAINTENANCE requirements are imposed by the National Association of Securities Dealers (NASD) and the New York Stock Exchange, in the mid-1980s 25% of the market value of margined securities, and by the individual brokerage firm, whose requirement is typically higher.

Banking: difference between the current market value of collateral backing a loan and the face value of the loan. For instance, if a $100,000 loan is backed by $50,000 in collateral, the margin is $50,000.

Corporate finance: difference between the price received by a company for its products and services and the cost of producing them. Also known as *gross profit margin*.

Futures trading: good-faith deposit an investor must put up when buying or selling a contract. If the futures price moves adversely, the investor must put up more money to meet margin requirements.

MARGIN ACCOUNT brokerage account allowing customers to buy securities with money borrowed from the broker. Margin accounts are governed by REGULATION T, by the National Association of Securities Dealers (NASD), by the New York Stock Exchange, and by individual brokerage house rules. Margin requirements can be met with cash or with eligible securities. In the case of securities sold short, an equal amount of the same securities is normally borrowed without interest from another broker to cover the sale, while the proceeds are keptin escrow as collateral for the lending broker. *See also* MINIMUMMAINTENANCE.

MARGIN AGREEMENT document that spells out the rules governing a MARGIN ACCOUNT, including the HYPOTHECATION of securities, how much equity the customer must keep in the account, and the interest rate on margin loans. Also known as a *hypothecation agreement*.

MARGINAL COST increase or decrease in the total costs of a business firm as the result of one more or one less unit of output. Also called *incremental cost* or *differential cost*. Determining marginal cost is important in deciding whether or not to vary a rate of production. In most manufacturing firms, marginal costs decrease as the volume of output increases due to economies of scale, which include factors such as bulk discounts on raw materials, specialization of labor, and more efficient use of machinery. At some point, however, diseconomies of scale enter in and marginal costs begin to rise; diseconomies include factors like more intense managerial supervision to control a larger work force, higher raw materials costs because local supplies have been exhausted, and generally less efficient input. The marginal cost curve is typically U-shaped on a graph.

A firm is operating at optimum output when marginal cost coincides with average total unit cost. Thus, at less than optimum output, an increase in the rate of production will result in a marginal unit cost lower than average total unit cost; production in excess of the optimum point will result in marginal cost higher than average total unit cost. In other words, a sale at a price higher than marginal unit cost will increase the net profit of the manufacturer even though the sales price does not cover average total unit cost; marginal cost is thus the lowest amount at which a sale can be made without adding to the producer's loss or subtracting from his profits.

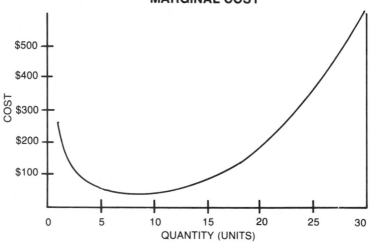

MARGINAL COST

MARGINAL EFFICIENCY OF CAPITAL annual percentage yield earned by the last additional unit of capital. It is also known as *marginal productivity of capital, natural interest rate, net capital productivity,* and *rate of return over cost.* The significance of the concept to a business firm is that it represents the market rate of interest at which it begins to pay to undertake a capital investment. If the market rate is 10%, for example, it would not pay to undertake a project that has a return of 9½%, but any return over 10% would be acceptable. In a larger economic sense, marginal efficiency of capital influences long-term interest rates. This occurs because of the law of diminishing returns as it applies to the yield on capital. As the highest yielding projects are exhausted, available capital moves into lower yielding projects and interest rates decline. As market rates fall, investors are able to justify projects that were previously uneconomical. This process is called *diminishing marginal productivity* or *declining marginal efficiency of capital.*

MARGINAL REVENUE change in total revenue caused by one additional unit of output. It is calculated by determining the difference between the total revenues produced before and after a one-unit increase in the rate of production. As long as the price of a product is constant, price and marginal revenue are the same; for example, if baseball bats are being sold at a constant price of $10 apiece, a one-unit increase in sales (one baseball bat) translates into an increase in total revenue of $10. But it is often the case that additional output can be sold only if the price is reduced, and that leads to a consideration of MARGINAL COST—the added cost of producing one more unit. Further production is not advisable when marginal cost exceeds marginal revenue since to do so would result in a loss. Conversely, whenever marginal revenue exceeds marginal cost, it is advisable to produce an additional unit. Profits are maximized at the rate of output where marginal revenue equals marginal cost.

MARGINAL TAX RATE amount of tax imposed on an additional dollar of income. In the U.S. progressive income tax system, the marginal tax rate increases as income rises. Economists believing in SUPPLY-SIDE ECONOMICS hold that this reduces the incentive to be productive and discourages business investment. In urging that marginal tax rates be cut for individuals and businesses, they argue that the resulting increased work effort and business investment would reduce STAGFLATION. *See also* FLAT TAX.

MARGIN CALL demand that a customer deposit enough money or securities to bring a margin account up to the INITIAL MARGIN or MINIMUM MAINTENANCE requirements. If a customer fails to respond, securities in the account may be liquidated. *See also* FIVE HUNDRED DOLLAR RULE; SELL OUT.

MARGIN DEPARTMENT section within a brokerage firm that monitors customer compliance with margin regulations, keeping track of debits and credits, short sales, and purchases of stock on margin, and all other extensions of credit by the broker. Also known as the *credit department. See also* MARK TO THE MARKET.

MARGIN OF PROFIT relationship of gross profits to net sales. Returns and allowances are subtracted from gross sales to arrive at net sales. Cost of goods sold (sometimes including depreciation) is subtracted from net sales to arrive at gross profit. Gross profit is divided by net sales to get the profit margin, which is sometimes called the *gross margin.* The result is a ratio, and the term is also written as *margin of profit ratio.*

The term profit margin is less frequently used to mean the *net margin,* obtained by deducting operating expenses in addition to cost of goods sold and dividing the result by net sales. Operating expenses are usually shown on profit and loss statements as "selling, general and administrative (SG&A) expenses."

Both gross and net profit margins, when compared with prior periods and with industry statistics, can be revealing in terms of a firm's operating efficiency and pricing policies and its ability to compete successfully with other companies in its field.

MARGIN REQUIREMENT minimum amount that a client must deposit in the form of cash or eligible securities in a margin account as spelled out in REGULA-TION T of the Federal Reserve Board. Reg T requires a minimum 50% of the purchase price of eligible securities bought on margin or 50% of the proceeds of short sales. Also called INITIAL MARGIN. *See also* MARGIN; MARGIN SECURITY; MINIMUM MAINTENANCE; SELLING SHORT.

MARGIN SECURITY security that may be bought or sold in a margin account. Regulation T defines margin securities as: (1) any *registered security* (a LISTED SECURITY or a security having UNLISTED TRADING PRIVILEGES); (2) any *OTC Margin Stock* or *OTC margin bond,* which are defined as any UNLISTED SECURITY that the Federal Reserve Board (FRB) periodically identifies as having the investor interest, marketability, disclosure, and solid financial position of a listed security; (3) any OTC security designated as qualified for trading in the NATIONAL MARKET SYSTEM under a plan approved by the Securities and Exchange Commission; (4) any mutual fund or unit investment trust registered under the Investment Company Act of 1940. Other securities that are not EXEMPT SECURITIES must be transacted in cash.

MARITAL DEDUCTION provision in the Economic Recovery Tax Act of 1981 allowing all the assets of a marriage partner to pass to the surviving spouse free of estate taxes. Previously, a portion of the estate was taxed. The change eliminated double taxation of the surviving spouse's estate.

MARKDOWN
1. amount subtracted from the selling price, when a customer sells securities to a dealer in the OVER THE COUNTER market. Had the securities been purchased from the dealer, the customer would have paid a *markup,* or an amount added to the purchase price. The National Association of Securities Dealers (NASD) RULES OF FAIR PRACTICE established 5% as a reasonable guideline in markups and markdowns, though many factors enter into the question of fairness, and exceptions are common.
2. reduction in the price at which the underwriters offer municipal bonds after the market has shown a lack of interest at the original price.
3. downward adjustment of the value of securities by banks and investment firms, based on a decline in market quotations.
4. reduction in the original retail selling price, which was determined by adding a percentage factor, called a markon, to the cost of the merchandise. Anything added to the markon is called a markup, and the term markdown does not apply unless the price is dropped below the original selling price.

MARKET
1. public place where products or services are bought and sold, directly or through intermediaries. Also called *marketplace.*

2. aggregate of people with the present or potential ability and desire to purchase a product or service; equivalent to demand.
3. securities markets in the aggregate, or the New York Stock Exchange in particular.
4. short for *market value,* the value of an asset based on the price it would command on the open market, usually as determined by the MARKET PRICE at which similar assets have recently been bought and sold.
5. as a verb, to sell. *See also* MARKETING.

MARKETABILITY speed and ease with which a particular security may be bought and sold. A stock that has a large amount of shares outstanding and is actively traded is highly marketable and also liquid. In common use, marketability is interchangeable with LIQUIDITY, but liquidity implies the preservation of value when a security is bought or sold.

MARKETABLE SECURITIES securities that are easily sold. On a corporation's balance sheet, they are assets that can be readily converted into cash—for example, government securities, banker's acceptances, and commercial paper. In keeping with conservative accounting practice, these are carried at cost or market value, whichever is lower.

MARKET ANALYSIS
1. research aimed at predicting or anticipating the direction of stock, bond, or commodity markets, based on technical data about the movement of market prices or on fundamental data such as corporate earnings prospects or supply and demand.
2. study designed to define a company's markets, forecast their directions, and decide how to expand the company's share and exploit any new trends.

MARKET CAPITALIZATION value of a corporation as determined by the market price of its issued and outstanding common stock. It is calculated by multiplying the number of outstanding shares by the current market price of a share. Institutional investors often use market capitalization as one investment criterion, requiring, for example, that a company have a market capitalization of $100 million or more to qualify as an investment. Analysts look at market capitalization in relation to book, or accounting, value for an indication of how investors value a company's future prospects.

MARKET IF TOUCHED ORDER (MIT) order to buy or sell a security or commodity as soon as a preset market price is reached, at which point it becomes a MARKET ORDER. When corn is selling for $4.75 a bushel, someone might enter a market if touched order to buy at $4.50. As soon as the price is dropped to $4.50, the contract would be bought on the customer's behalf at whatever market price prevails when the order is executed.

MARKET INDEX numbers representing weighted values of the components that make up the index. A stock market index, for example, is weighted according to the prices and number of outstanding shares of the various stocks. The Standard and Poor's 500 Stock Index is one of the most widely followed, but myriad other indexes track stocks in various industry groups.

MARKETING moving goods and services from the provider to consumer. This involves product origination and design, development, distribution, advertising, promotion, and publicity as well as market analysis to define the appropriate market.

MARKET LETTER newsletter provided to brokerage firm customers or written by an independent market analyst, registered as an investment adviser with the Securities and Exchange Commission, who sells the letter to subscribers. These letters assess the trends in interest rates, the economy, and the market in general. Brokerage letters typically reiterate the recommendations of their own research departments. Independent letters take on the personality of their writers—concentrating on growth stocks, for example, or basing their recommendations on technical analysis. A HULBERT RATING is an evaluation of such a letter's performance.

MARKET MAKER *see* MAKE A MARKET.

MARKET ORDER order to buy or sell a security at the best available price. Most orders executed on the exchanges are market orders.

MARKET OUT CLAUSE escape clause sometimes written into FIRM COMMITMENT underwriting agreements which essentially allows the underwriters to be released from their purchase commitment if material adverse developments affect the securities markets generally. It is not common practice for the larger investment banking houses to write "outs" into their agreements, since the value of their commitment is a matter of paramount concern. *See also* UNDERWRITE.

MARKETPLACE *see* MARKET.

MARKET PRICE last reported price at which a security was sold on an exchange. For stocks or bonds sold OVER THE COUNTER, the combined bid and offer prices available at any particular time from those making a market in the stock. For an inactively traded security, evaluators or other analysts may determine a market price if needed—to settle an estate, for example.

In the general business world, market price refers to the price agreed upon by buyers and sellers of a product or service, as determined by supply and demand.

MARKET RESEARCH exploration of the size, characteristics, and potential of a market to find out, before developing any new product or service, what people want and need. Market research is an early step in marketing—which stretches from the original conception of a product to its ultimate delivery to the consumer.

In the stock market, market research refers to TECHNICAL ANALYSIS of factors such as volume, price advances and declines, and market breadth, which analysts use to predict the direction of prices.

MARKET RISK *see* SYSTEMATIC RISK.

MARKET SHARE percentage of industry sales of a particular company or product.

MARKET TIMING decisions on when to buy or sell securities, in light of economic factors such as the strength of the economy and the direction of interest rates, or technical indications such as the direction of stock prices and the volume of trading. Investors in mutual funds may implement their market timing decisions by switching from a stock fund to a bond fund to a money market fund and back again, as the market outlook changes.

MARKET TONE general health and vigor of a securities market. The market tone is good when dealers and market makers are trading actively on narrow bid and offer spreads; it is bad when trading is inactive and bid and offer spreads are wide.

MARKET VALUE

In general: market price—the price at which buyers and sellers trade similar items in an open marketplace. In the absence of a market price, it is the estimated highest price a buyer would be warranted in paying and a seller justified in accepting, provided both parties were fully informed and acted intelligently and voluntarily.

Investments: current market price of a security—as indicated by the latest trade recorded.

Accounting: technical definition used in valuing inventory or marketable securities in accordance with the conservative accounting principle of "lower of cost or market." While cost is simply acquisition cost, market value is estimated net selling price less estimated costs of carrying, selling, and delivery, and, in the case of an unfinished product, the costs to complete production. The market value arrived at this way cannot, however, be lower than the cost at which a normal profit can be made.

MARKET VALUE-WEIGHTED INDEX index whose components are weighted according to the total market value of their outstanding shares. Also called *capitalization-weighted index.* The impact of a component's price change is proportional to the issue's overall market value, which is the share price times the number of shares outstanding. For example, the Computer Technology Index, traded on the American Stock Exchange has 30 component stocks. The weighting of each stock constantly shifts with changes in the stock's price and the number of shares outstanding. The index fluctuates in line with the price moves of the stocks.

MARK TO THE MARKET

1. adjust the valuation of a security or portfolio to reflect current market values. For example, MARGIN ACCOUNTS are marked to the market to ensure compliance with maintenance requirements. OPTION and FUTURES CONTRACTS are marked to the market at year end with PAPER PROFIT OR LOSS recognized for tax purposes.
2. in a MUTUAL FUND, the daily net asset value reported to shareholders is the result of marking the fund's current portfolio to current market prices.

MARKUP *see* MARKDOWN.

MARRIAGE PENALTY effect of a tax code that makes a married couple pay more than the same two people would pay if unmarried and filing singly. The $3000 (maximum) two-earner deduction instituted by the ECONOMIC RECOVERY TAX ACT OF 1981 (ERTA) to counter the marriage penalty was repealed, effective for the tax year 1987, by the TAX REFORM ACT OF 1986, which substituted lower tax rates, wider TAX BRACKETS, and an increased STANDARD DEDUCTION.

MARRIED PUT option to sell a certain number of securities at a particular price by a specified time, bought simultaneously with securities of the underlying company so as to hedge the price paid for the securities. *See also* OPTION; PUT OPTION.

MASTER LIMITED PARTNERSHIP (MLP) public LIMITED PARTNERSHIP composed of corporate assets spun off (*roll out*) or private limited partnerships (*roll up*) with income, capital gains, and/or TAX SHELTER orientations. Interests are represented by depositary receipts traded in the SECONDARY MARKET. Investors thus enjoy LIQUIDITY. Flow-through tax benefits, previously possible within PAS-

SIVE income restrictions, were limited by tax legislation passed in 1987 that will treat most MLPs as corporations after a GRANDFATHER CLAUSE expires in 1998.

MATCHED AND LOST report of the results of flipping a coin by two securities brokers locked in competition to execute equal trades.

MATCHED BOOK term used for the accounts of securities dealers when their borrowing costs are equal to the interest earned on loans to customers and other brokers.

MATCHED MATURITIES coordination of the maturities of a financial institution's loans and certificates of deposit. For instance, a savings and loan might make 10-year mortgages at 14%, using the money received for 10-year certificates of deposit with 11% yields. The bank is thus positioned to make a three-point profit for 10 years. If a bank granted 20-year mortgages at a fixed 12%, on the other hand, using short-term funds from money market accounts paying 9%, the bank would lose dramatically if the money market accounts began paying 14%. Such a situation, called a *maturity mismatch,* can cause tremendous problems for the financial institution if it persists.

MATCHED ORDERS
1. illegal manipulative technique of offsetting buy and sell orders to create the impression of activity in a security, thereby causing upward price movement that benefits the participants in the scheme.
2. action by a SPECIALIST to create an opening price reasonably close to the previous close. When an accumulation of one kind of order—either buy or sell—causes a delay in the opening of trading on an exchange, the specialist tries to find counterbalancing orders or trades long or short from his own inventory in order to narrow the spread.

MATCHED SALE PURCHASE TRANSACTION FEDERAL OPEN MARKET COMMITTEE procedure whereby the Federal Reserve Bank of New York sells government securities to a nonbank dealer against payment in FEDERAL FUNDS. The agreement requires the dealer to sell the securities back by a specified date, which ranges from one to 15 days. The Fed pays the dealer a rate of interest equal to the discount rate. These transactions, also called reverse repurchase agreements, decrease the money supply for temporary periods by reducing dealer's bank balances and thus excess reserves. The Fed is thus able to adjust an abnormal monetary expansion due to seasonal or other factors. *See also* REPURCHASE AGREEMENT.

MATRIX TRADING bond swapping whereby traders seek to take advantage of temporary aberrations in YIELD SPREAD differentials between bonds of the same class but with different ratings or between bonds of different classes.

MATURE ECONOMY economy of a nation whose population has stabilized or is declining, and whose economic growth is no longer robust. Such an economy is characterized by a decrease in spending on roads or factories and a relative increase in consumer spending. Many of Western Europe's economies are considerably more mature than that of the United States and in marked contrast to the faster-growing economies of the Far East.

MATURITY DATE
1. date on which the principal amount of a note, draft, acceptance, bond, or

other debt instrument becomes due and payable. Also, termination or due date on which an installment loan must be paid in full.

2. in FACTORING, average due date of factored receivables, when the factor remits to the seller for receivables sold each month.

MAXIMUM CAPITAL GAINS MUTUAL FUND fund whose objective is to produce large capital gains for its shareholders. During a bull market it is likely to rise much faster than the general market or conservative mutual funds. But in a falling market, it is likely to drop much farther than the market averages. This increased volatility results from a policy of investing in small, fast-growing companies whose stocks characteristically are more volatile than those of large, well-established companies.

MAY DAY May 1, 1975, when fixed minimum brokerage commissions ended in the United States. Instead of a mandated rate to execute exchange trades, brokers were allowed to charge whatever they chose. The May Day changes ushered in the era of discount brokerage firms that execute buy and sell orders for low commissions, but give no investment advice. The end of fixed commissions also marked the beginning of diversification by the brokerage industry into a wide range of financial services utilizing computer technology and advanced communications systems.

MEAN RETURN in security analysis, expected value, or mean, of all the likely returns of investments comprising a portfolio; in capital budgeting, mean value of the probability distribution of possible returns. The portfolio approach to the analysis of investments aims at quantifying the relationship between risk and return. It assumes that while investors have different risk-value preferences, rational investors will always seek the maximum rate of return for every level of acceptable risk. It is the mean, or expected, return that an investor attempts to maximize at each level of risk. Also called *expected return. See also* CAPITAL ASSET PRICING MODEL, EFFICIENT PORTFOLIO, PORTFOLIO THEORY.

MECHANIC'S LIEN LIEN against buildings or other structures, allowed by some states to contractors, laborers, and suppliers of materials used in their construction or repair. The lien remains in effect until these people have been paid in full and may, in the event of a liquidation before they have been paid, give them priority over other creditors.

MEDIUM-TERM BOND bond with a maturity of 2 to 10 years. *See also* INTERMEDIATE TERM; LONG TERM; SHORT TERM.

MEMBER BANK bank that is a member of the FEDERAL RESERVE SYSTEM, including all nationally chartered banks and any state-chartered banks that apply for membership and are accepted. Member banks are required to purchase stock in the FEDERAL RESERVE BANK in their districts equal to 6% of their own PAID-IN CAPITAL and paid-in surplus. Half of that investment is carried as an asset of the member bank. The other half is callable by the Fed at any time. Member banks are also required to maintain a percentage of their deposits as reserves in the form of currency in their vaults and balances on deposit at their Fed district banks. These reserve balances make possible a range of money transfer and other services using the FED WIRE system to connect banks in different parts of the country.

MEMBER FIRM brokerage firm that has at least one membership on a major stock exchange, even though, by exchange rules, the membership is in the name of an employee and not of the firm itself. Such a firm enjoys the rights and privileges of membership, such as voting on exchange policy, together with the obligations of membership, such as the commitment to settle disputes with customers through exchange arbitration procedures.

MEMBER SHORT SALE RATIO ratio of the total shares sold short for the accounts of New York Stock Exchange members in one week divided by the total short sales for the same week. Because the specialists, floor traders, and off-the-floor traders who trade for members' accounts are generally considered the best minds in the business, the ratio is a valuable indicator of market trends. A ratio of 82% or higher is considered bearish; a ratio of 68% or lower is positive and bullish. The member short sale ratio appears with other NYSE round lot statistics in the Monday edition of *The Wall Street Journal* and in *Barron's,* a weekly financial newspaper.

MERCANTILE AGENCY organization that supplies businesses with credit ratings and reports on other firms that are or might become customers. Such agencies may also collect past due accounts or trade collection statistics, and they tend to industry and geographical specialization. The largest of the agencies, DUN & BRADSTREET, was founded in 1841 under the name Mercantile Agency. It provides credit information on companies of all descriptions along with a wide range of other credit and financial reporting services.

MERCHANT BANK
1. European financial institution that engages in investment banking, counseling, and negotiating in mergers and acquisitions, and a variety of other services including securities portfolio management for customers, insurance, the acceptance of foreign bills of exchange, dealing in bullion, and participating in commercial ventures. Deposits in merchant banks are negligible, and the prominence of such names as Rothschild, Baring, Lazard, and Hambro attests to their role as counselors and negotiators in large-scale acquisitions, mergers, and the like.
2. The part of an American bank that engages in investment banking functions, such as: advising clients in mergers and acquisitions; underwriting securities; and taking debt or equity positions. The Federal Reserve permits commercial banks to underwrite corporate debt securities but as of December, 1989, has not granted permission to underwrite corporate common stock deals.
3. American bank that has entered into an agreement with a merchant to accept deposits generated by bank credit/charge card transactions.

MERGER combination of two or more companies, either through a POOLING OF INTERESTS, where the accounts are combined; a purchase, where the amount paid over and above the acquired company's book value is carried on the books of the purchaser as goodwill; or a consolidation, where a new company is formed to acquire the net assets of the combining companies. Strictly speaking, only combinations in which one of the companies survives as a legal entity are called mergers or, more formally, statutory mergers; thus consolidations, or statutory consolidations, are technically not mergers, though the term merger is commonly applied to them. Mergers meeting the legal criteria for pooling of interests, where common stock is exchanged for common stock, are nontaxable and are called tax-free mergers. Where an acquisition takes place by the purchase of assets or stock using cash or a debt instrument for payment, the merger is a taxable capital gain to the selling company or its stockholders. There is a potential benefit to such taxable purchase acquisitions, however, in that the acquiring company can write up the acquired company's assets by the amount by which the market value exceeds the book value; that difference can then be charged off to depreciation with resultant tax savings.

Mergers can also be classified in terms of their economic function. Thus a *horizontal merger* is one combining direct competitors in the same product lines and markets; a *vertical merger* combines customer and company or supplier and company; a *market extension merger* combines companies selling the same products in different markets; a *product extension merger* combines companies selling different but related products in the same market; a *conglomerate merger* combines companies with none of the above relationships or similarities. *See also* ACQUISITION.

MEZZANINE BRACKET members of a securities underwriting group whose participations are of such a size as to place them in the tier second to the largest participants. In the newspaper TOMBSTONE advertisements that announce new securities offerings, the underwriters are listed in alphabetical groups, first the lead underwriters, then the mezzanine bracket, then the remaining participants.

MEZZANINE LEVEL stage of a company's development just prior to its going public, in VENTURE CAPITAL language. Venture capitalists entering at that point have a lower risk of loss than at previous stages and can look forward to early capital appreciation as a result of the MARKET VALUE gained by an INITIAL PUBLIC OFFERING.

MICROECONOMICS study of the behavior of basic economic units such as companies, industries, or households. Research on the companies in the airline industry would be a microeconomic concern, for instance. *See also* MACROECONOMICS.

MIDWEST STOCK EXCHANGE *see* REGIONAL STOCK EXCHANGES.

MIG-1 *see* MOODY'S INVESTMENT GRADE.

MILL one-tenth of a cent, the unit most often used in expressing property tax rates. For example, if a town's tax rate is 5 mills per dollar of assessed valuation, and the assessed valuation of a piece of property is $100,000, the tax is $500, or 0.005 times $100,000.

MINI-MANIPULATION trading in a security underlying an option contract so as to manipulate the stock's price, thus causing an increase in the value of the options. In this way the manipulator's profit can be multiplied many times, since a large position in options can be purchased with a relatively small amount of money.

MINIMUM MAINTENANCE equity level that must be maintained in brokerage customers' margin accounts, as required by the New York Stock Exchange (NYSE), the National Association of Securities Dealers (NASD), and individual brokerage firms. Under REGULATION T, $2000 in cash or securities must be deposited with a broker before *any* credit can be extended; then an INITIAL MARGIN requirement must be met, currently 50% of the market value of eligible securities long or short in customers' accounts. The NYSE and NASD, going a step further, both require that a margin be *maintained* equal to 25% of the market value of securities in margin accounts. Brokerage firm requirements are typically a more conservative 30%. When the market value of margined securities falls below these minimums a MARGIN CALL goes out requesting additional equity. If the customer fails to comply, the broker may sell the margined stock and close the customer out. *See also* MARGIN REQUIREMENT; MARGIN SECURITY; MARK TO THE MARKET; SELL OUT.

MINI-WAREHOUSE LIMITED PARTNERSHIP partnership that invests in small warehouses where people can rent space to store belongings. Such partnerships offer tax benefits such as depreciation allowances, but mostly they provide income derived from rents. When the partnership is liquidated, the general partner may sell the warehouse for a profit, providing capital gains to limited partners.

MINORITY INTEREST interest of shareholders who, in the aggregate, own less than half the shares in a corporation. On the consolidated balance sheets of companies whose subsidiaries are not wholly owned, the minority interest is shown as a separate equity account or as a liability of indefinite term. On the income statement, the minority's share of income is subtracted to arrive at consolidated net income.

MINUS symbol (−) preceding a fraction or number in the change column at the far right of newspaper stock tables designating a closing sale lower than that of the previous day.

MINUS TICK *see* DOWNTICK.

MISSING THE MARKET failing to execute a transaction on terms favorable to a customer and thus being negligent as a broker. If the order is subsequently executed at a price demonstrably less favorable, the broker, as the customer's agent, may be required to make good on the amount lost.

MIXED ACCOUNT brokerage account in which some securities are owned (in long positions) and some borrowed (in short positions).

MOBILE HOME CERTIFICATE mortgage-backed security guaranteed by the GOVERNMENT NATIONAL MORTGAGE ASSOCIATION consisting of mortgages on mobile homes. Although the maturity tends to be shorter on these securities than on single-family homes, they have all the other characteristics of regular Ginnie Maes, and the timely payment of interest and the repayment of principal are backed by the FULL FAITH AND CREDIT of the U.S. government.

MODELING designing and manipulating a mathematical representation of an economic system or corporate financial application so that the effect of changes can be studied and forecast. For example, in ECONOMETRICS, a complex economic model can be drawn up, entered into a computer, and used to predict the effect of a rise in inflation or a cut in taxes on economic output.

MODERN PORTFOLIO THEORY *see* PORTFOLIO THEORY.

MOMENTUM rate of acceleration of an economic, price, or volume movement. An economy with strong growth that is likely to continue is said to have a lot of momentum. In the stock market, technical analysts study stock momentum by charting price and volume trends. *See also* EARNINGS MOMENTUM.

MONETARIST economist who believes that the MONEY SUPPLY is the key to the ups and downs in the economy. Monetarists such as Milton Friedman think that the money supply has far more impact on the economy's future course than, say, the level of federal spending—a factor on which KEYNESIAN ECONOMICS puts great stress. Monetarists advocate slow but steady growth in the money supply.

MONETARY POLICY FEDERAL RESERVE BOARD decisions on the MONEY SUPPLY. To make the economy grow faster, the Fed can supply more credit to the banking system through its OPEN MARKET OPERATIONS, or it can lower the member bank reserve requirement or lower the DISCOUNT RATE—which is what banks pay to borrow additional reserves from the Fed. If, on the other hand, the economy is growing too fast and inflation is an increasing problem, the Fed might withdraw money from the banking system, raise the reserve requirement, or raise the discount rate, thereby putting a brake on economic growth. Other instruments of monetary policy range from selective credit controls to simple but often highly effective MORAL SUASION. Monetary policy differs from FISCAL POLICY, which is carried out through government spending and taxation. Both seek to control the level of economic activity as measured by such factors as industrial production, employment, and prices.

MONEY CENTER BANK bank in one of the major financial centers of the world, among them New York, Chicago, San Francisco, Los Angeles, London, Paris, and Tokyo. These banks play a major national and international economic role because they are large lenders, depositories, and buyers of money market instruments and securities as well as large lenders to governments and international corporations. In the stock market, bank analysts usually categorize the money center banks as separate from regional banks—those that focus on one area of the country. Also known as *money market bank.*

MONEY MANAGER *see* PORTFOLIO MANAGER.

MONEY MARKET market for SHORT-TERM DEBT INSTRUMENTS—negotiable certificates of deposit, Eurodollar certificates of deposit, commercial paper, banker's acceptances, Treasury bills, and discount notes of the Federal Home Loan Bank, Federal National Mortgage Association, and Federal Farm Credit System, among others. Federal funds borrowings between banks, bank borrowings from the Federal Reserve Bank WINDOW, and various forms of repurchase agreements are also elements of the money market. What these instruments have in common are safety and LIQUIDITY. The money market operates through dealers, MONEY CENTER BANKS, and the Open Market Trading DESK at the New York Federal Reserve Bank. New York City is the leading money market, followed by London and Tokyo. The dealers in the important money markets are in constant communication with each other and with major borrowers and investors to take advantage of ARBITRAGE opportunities, a practice which helps keep prices uniform worldwide. *See also* MONEY MARKET FUND.

MONEY MARKET DEPOSIT ACCOUNT market-sensitive bank account that has been offered since December 1982. Under Depository Institutions Deregulatory Committee rules, such accounts had a minimum of $1000 (eliminated in 1986) and only three checks may be drawn per month, although unlimited transfers may be carried out at an automatic teller machine. The funds are therefore liquid—that is, they are available to depositors at any time without penalty. The interest rate is generally comparable to rates on money market mutual funds, though any individual bank's rate may be higher or lower. These accounts are insured by the FEDERAL DEPOSIT INSURANCE CORPORATION or the FEDERAL SAVINGS AND LOAN INSURANCE CORPORATION.

MONEY MARKET FUND open-ended MUTUAL FUND that invests in commercial paper, banker's acceptances, repurchase agreements, government securities, certificates of deposit, and other highly liquid and safe securities, and pays money market rates of interest. Launched in the middle 1970s, these funds were especially popular in the early 1980s when interest rates and inflation soared. Management's fee is less than 1% of an investor's assets; interest over and above that amount is credited to shareholders monthly. The fund's net asset value remains a constant $1 a share—only the interest rate goes up or down. Such funds usually offer the convenience of checkwriting privileges.

Most funds are not federally insured, but some are covered by private insurance. Some funds invest only in government-backed securities, which give shareholders an extra degree of safety.

Many money market funds are part of fund families. This means that investors can switch their money from one fund to another and back again without charge. Money in an ASSET MANAGEMENT ACCOUNT usually is automatically swept into a money market fund until the accountholder decides where to invest it next. See also DONOGHUE'S MONEY FUND AVERAGE; FAMILY OF FUNDS; MONEY MARKET DEPOSIT ACCOUNT; TAX-EXEMPT MONEY MARKET FUND.

MONEY SPREAD see VERTICAL SPREAD.

MONEY SUPPLY total stock of money in the economy, consisting primarily of (1) currency in circulation and (2) deposits in savings and checking accounts. Too much money in relation to the output of goods tends to push interest rates down and push prices and inflation up; too little money tends to push interest rates up, lower prices and output, and cause unemployment and idle plant capacity. The bulk of money is in demand deposits with commercial banks, which are regulated by the Federal Reserve Board. It manages the money supply by raising or lowering the reserves that banks are required to maintain and the DISCOUNT RATE at which they can borrow from the Fed, as well as by its OPEN MARKET OPERATIONS— trading government securities to take money out of the system or put it in.

Changes in the financial system, particularly since banking deregulation in the 1980s, have caused controversy among economists as to what really constitutes the money supply at a given time. In response to this, a more comprehensive analysis and breakdown of money was developed. Essentially, the various forms of money are now grouped into two broad divisions: M-1, M-2, and M-3, representing money and NEAR MONEY; and L, representing longer-term liquid funds. The accompanying table shows a detailed breakdown of all four categories. See also MONETARY POLICY.

MONOPOLY control of the production and distribution of a product or service by one firm or a group of firms acting in concert. In its pure form, monopoly, which is characterized by an absence of competition, leads to high prices and a general lack of responsiveness to the needs and desires of consumers. Although the most flagrant monopolistic practices in the United States were outlawed by ANTITRUST LAWS enacted in the late 19th century and early 20th century, monopolies persist in some degree as the result of such factors as patents, scarce essential materials, and high startup and production costs that discourage competition in certain industries. *Public monopolies*—those operated by the government, such as the post office, or closely regulated by the government, such as utilities—ensure the delivery of essential products and services at acceptable prices and generally avoid the disadvantages produced by private monopolies. *Monopsony*, the dominance of a market by one buyer or group of buyers acting together, is less prevalent than monopoly. See also CARTEL; OLIGOPOLY; PERFECT COMPETITION.

MONTHLY COMPOUNDING OF INTEREST see COMPOUND INTEREST.

MONEY SUPPLY

Classification	Components
M-1	currency in circulation commercial bank demand deposits NOW and ATS (automatic transfer from savings) accounts credit union share drafts mutual savings bank demand deposits nonbank travelers checks
M-2	M-1 overnight repurchase agreements issued by commercial banks overnight Eurodollars savings accounts time deposits under $100,000 money market mutual fund shares
M-3	M-2 time deposits over $100,000. term repurchase agreements
L	M-3 and other liquid assets such as: Treasury bills savings bonds commercial paper bankers' acceptances Eurodollar holdings of United States residents (nonbank)

MONTHLY INVESTMENT PLAN plan whereby an investor puts a fixed dollar amount into a particular investment every month, thus building a position at advantageous prices by means of *dollar cost averaging* (*see* CONSTANT DOLLAR PLAN).

MOODY'S INVESTMENT GRADE rating assigned by MOODY'S INVESTORS SERVICE to certain municipal short-term debt securities, classified as MIG-1, 2, 3, and 4 to signify best, high, favorable, and adequate quality, respectively. All four are investment grade or bank quality.

MOODY'S INVESTORS SERVICE headquartered with its parent company, Dun & Bradstreet, in downtown Manhattan, Moody's is one of the two best known bond rating agencies in the country, the other being Standard & Poor's. Moody's also rates commercial paper, preferred and common stocks, and municipal short-term issues. The six bound manuals it publishes annually, supplemented weekly or semiweekly, provide great detail on issuers and securities. The company also publishes the quarterly *Moody's Handbook of Common Stocks,* which charts more than 500 companies, showing industry group trends and company stock price performance. Also included are essential statistics for the past decade, an analysis of the company's financial background, recentfinancial developments, and the outlook. Moody's rates most of the publicly held corporate and municipal bonds and many Treasury and government agency issues, but does not usually rate privately placed bonds.

MORAL OBLIGATION BOND tax-exempt bond issued by a municipality or a state financial intermediary and backed by the moral obligation pledge of a state government. (State financial intermediaries are organized by states to pool local debt issues into single bond issues, which can be used to tap larger investment markets.) Under a moral obligation pledge, a state government indicates its intent to appropriate funds in the future if the primary OBLIGOR, the municipality or intermediary, defaults. The state's obligation to honor the pledge is moral rather than legal because future legislatures cannot be legally obligated to appropriate the funds required.

MORAL SUASION persuasion through influence rather than coercion, said of the efforts of the FEDERAL RESERVE BOARD to achieve member bank compliance with its general policy. From time to time, the Fed uses moral suasion to restrain credit or to expand it.

MORTGAGE debt instrument by which the borrower (mortgagor) gives the lender (mortgagee) a lien on property as security for the repayment of a loan. The borrower has use of the property, and the lien is removed when the obligation is fully paid. A mortgage normally involves real estate. For personal property, such as machines, equipment, or tools, the lien is called a *chattel mortgage. See also* ADJUSTABLE RATE MORTGAGE; CLOSED-END MORTGAGE; CONSOLIDATED MORTGAGE BOND; MORTGAGE BOND; OPEN-END MORTGAGE; VARIABLE RATE MORTGAGE.

MORTGAGE-BACKED CERTIFICATE security backed by mortgages. Such certificates are issued by the FEDERAL HOME LOAN MORTGAGE CORPORATION and the FEDERAL NATIONAL MORTGAGE ASSOCIATION. Others are guaranteed by the GOVERNMENT NATIONAL MORTGAGE ASSOCIATION. Investors receive payments out of the interest and principal on the underlying mortgages. Sometimes banks issue certificates backed by CONVENTIONAL MORTGAGES, selling them to large institutional investors. The growth of mortgage-backed certificates and the secondary mortgage market in which they are traded has helped keep mortgage money available for home financing. *See also* PASS-THROUGH SECURITY.

MORTGAGE-BACKED SECURITY *see* MORTGAGE-BACKED CERTIFICATE.

MORTGAGE BANKER company, or individual, that originates mortgage loans, sells them to other investors, services the monthly payments, keeps related records, and acts as escrow agent to disperse funds for taxes and insurance. A mortgage banker's income derives from origination and servicing fees, profits on the resale of loans, and the spread between mortgage yields and the interest paid on borrowings while a particular mortgage is held before resale. To protect against negative spreads or mortgages that can't be resold, such companies seek commitments from institutional lenders or buy them from the FEDERAL NATIONAL MORTGAGE ASSOCIATION or the GOVERNMENT NATIONAL MORTGAGE ASSOCIATION. Mortgage bankers thus play an important role in the flow of mortgage funds even though they are not significant mortgage holders.

MORTGAGE BOND bond issue secured by a mortgage on the issuer's property, the lien on which is conveyed to the bondholders by a deed of trust. A mortgage bond may be designated senior, underlying, first, prior, overlying, junior, second, third, and so forth, depending on the priority of the lien. Most of those issued by corporations are first mortgage bonds secured by specific real property and also representing unsecured claims on the general assets of the firm. As such, these bonds enjoy a preferred position relative to unsecured bonds of the issuing corporation. *See also* CONSOLIDATED MORTGAGE BOND; MORTGAGE.

MORTGAGE POOL group of mortgages sharing similar characteristics in terms of class of property, interest rate, and maturity. Investors buy participations and receive income derived from payments on the underlying mortgages. The principal attractions to the investor are DIVERSIFICATION and LIQUIDITY, along with a relatively attractive yield. Those backed by government-sponsored agencies such as the FEDERAL HOME LOAN MORTGAGE CORPORATION, FEDERAL NATIONAL MORTGAGE ASSOCIATION, and GOVERNMENT NATIONAL MORTGAGE ASSOCIATION have become popular not only with individual investors but with life insurance companies, pension funds, and even foreign investors.

MORTGAGE REIT REAL ESTATE INVESTMENT TRUST that lends stockholder capital to real estate builders and buyers. Mortgage REITs also borrow from banks and relend that money at higher interest rates. This kind of REIT is highly sensitive to interest rates; as rates rise, its profits are squeezed, because the cost of funds rises faster than income. Profits expand when rates fall, however, as loan income stays the same but the cost of funds drops. The other kind of real estate investment trust—called an EQUITY REIT—takes an ownership position in real estate, as opposed to acting as a lender. Some REITs do both.

MORTGAGE SERVICING administration of a mortgage loan, including collecting monthly payments and penalties on late payments, keeping track of the amount of principal and interest that has been paid at any particular time, acting as escrow agent for funds to cover taxes and insurance, and, if necessary, curing defaults and foreclosing when a homeowner is seriously delinquent. For mortgage loans that are sold in the secondary market and packaged into a MORTGAGE-BACKED CERTIFICATE the local bank or savings and loan that originated the mortgage typically continues servicing the mortgages and collects a fee for doing so.

MOST ACTIVE LIST stocks with the most shares traded on a given day. Unusual VOLUME can be caused by TAKEOVER activity, earnings releases, institutional trading in a widely-held issue, and other factors.

MOVING AVERAGE average of security or commodity prices constructed on a period as short as a few days or as long as several years and showing trends for the latest interval. For example, a thirty-day moving average includes yesterday's figures; tomorrow the same average will include today's figures and will no longer show those for the earliest date included in yesterday's average. Thus every day it picks up figures for the latest day and drops those for the earliest day.

MOVING AVERAGE

MULTINATIONAL CORPORATION corporation that has production facilities or other fixed assets in at least one foreign country and makes its major management decisions in a global context. In marketing, production, research and development, and labor relations, its decisions must be made in terms of host-country customs and traditions. In finance, many of its problems have no domestic counterpart—the payment of dividends in another currency, for example, or the need to shelter working capital from the risk of devaluation, or the choices between owning and licensing. Economic and legal questions must be dealt with in drastically different ways. In addition to foreign exchange risks and the special business risks of operating in unfamiliar environments, there is the specter of political risk—the risk that sovereign governments may interfere with operations or terminate them altogether.

MULTIPLE see PRICE-EARNINGS RATIO.

MULTIPLIER the multiplier—also called the *multiplier effect* or the *multiplier principal*—has two major applications in finance and investments.
1. *investment multiplier* or *Keynesian multiplier:* multiplies the effects of investment spending in terms of total income. An investment in a small plant facility, for example, increases the incomes of the workers who built it, the merchants who provide supplies, the distributors who supply the merchants, the manufacturers who supply the distributors, and so on. Each recipient spends a portion of the income and saves the rest. By making an assumption as to the percentage each recipient saves, it is possible to calculate the total income produced by the investment.
2. *deposit multiplier* or *credit multiplier:* magnifies small changes in bank deposits into changes in the amount of outstanding credit and the money supply. For example, a bank receives a deposit of $100,000, and the RESERVE REQUIREMENT is 20%. The bank is thus required to keep $20,000 in the form of reserves. The remaining $80,000 becomes a loan, which is deposited in the $100,000 could expand into a total of $500,000 in deposits and $400,000 in credit.

MUNICIPAL BOND debt obligation of a state or local government entity. The funds may support general governmental needs or special projects. Issuance must be approved by referendum or by an electoral body. Prior to the TAX REFORM ACT OF 1986, the terms municipal and tax-exempt were synonymous, since virtually all municipal obligations were exempt from federal income taxes and most from state and local income taxes, at least in the state of issue. The 1986 Act, however, divided municipals into two broad groups: (1) PUBLIC PURPOSE BONDS, which remain tax-exempt and can be issued without limitation, and (2) PRIVATE PURPOSE BONDS, which are taxable unless specifically exempted. The tax distinction between public and private purpose is based on the percentage extent to which the bonds benefit private parties: if a tax-exempt public purpose bond involves more than a 10% benefit to private parties, it is taxable. *Permitted private purpose bonds* (those specified as tax-exempt) are generally TAX PREFERENCE ITEMS in computing the ALTERNATIVE MINIMUM TAX and, effective August 15, 1986, are subject to volume caps. *See also* ADVANCE REFUNDING; GENERAL OBLIGATION BOND; HOSPITAL REVENUE BOND; INDUSTRIAL DEVELOPMENT BOND; LIMITED TAX BOND; MUNICIPAL INVESTMENT TRUST; MUNICIPAL REVENUE BOND; SINGLE STATE MUNICIPAL BOND FUND; SPECIAL ASSESSMENT BOND; TAXABLE MUNICIPAL BOND; TAX EXEMPT SECURITY; UNDERLYING DEBT.

MUNICIPAL BOND INSURANCE policies underwritten by private insurers guaranteeing municipal bonds in the event of default. The insurance can be purchased either by the issuing government entity or the investor; it provides that bonds will be purchased from investors at par should default occur. Such insurance is available from a number of large insurance companies, but a major portion is written by two organizations: AMBAC Indemnity Corporation (formerly called American Municipal Bond Assurance Corporation), a unit of Citicorp., and Municipal Bond Insurance Association (MBIA), a pool of private insurers. Insured municipal bonds generally enjoy the highest rating resulting in greater marketability and lower cost to their issuers. From the investor's standpoint, however, their yield is typically lower than similarly rated uninsured bonds because the cost of the insurance is passed on by the issuer to the investor. Some unit investment trusts and mutual funds feature insured municipal bonds for investors willing to trade marginally lower yield for the extra degree of safety.

MUNICIPAL BOND INSURANCE ASSOCIATION *see* MUNICIPAL BOND INSURANCE.

MUNICIPAL IMPROVEMENT CERTIFICATE Certificate issued by a local government in lieu of bonds to finance improvements or services, such as widening a sidewalk, or installing a sewer, or repairing a street. Such an obligation is payable from a special tax assessment against those who benefit from the improvement, and the payments may be collected by the contractor performing the work. Interest on the certificate is usually free of federal, state, and local taxes. *See also* GENERAL OBLIGATION BOND.

MUNICIPAL INVESTMENT TRUST (MIT) UNIT INVESTMENT TRUST that buys municipal bonds and passes the tax-free income on to shareholders. Bonds in the trust's portfolio are normally held until maturity, unlike the constant trading of bonds in an open-ended municipal bond fund's portfolio. MITs are sold through brokers, typically for a sales charge of about 3% of the principal paid, with a minimum investment of $1000. The trust offers diversification, professional management of the portfolio, and monthly interest, compared with the semiannual payments made by individual municipal bonds.

Many MITs invest in the securities of just one state. For California residents who buy a California-only MIT, for example, all the interest is free of federal, state, and local taxes. In contrast, a Californian who buys a national MIT might have to pay state and local taxes on interest derived from out-of-state bonds in the trust's portfolio.

MUNICIPAL NOTE in common usage, a municipal debt obligation with an original maturity of two years or less.

MUNICIPAL REVENUE BOND bond issued to finance public works such as bridges or tunnels or sewer systems and supported directly by the revenues of the project. For instance, if a municipal revenue bond is issued to build a bridge, the tolls collected from motorists using the bridge are committed for paying off the bond. Unless otherwise specified in the indenture, holders of these bonds have no claims on the issuer's other resources.

MUNICIPAL SECURITIES RULEMAKING BOARD *see* SELF-REGULATORY ORGANIZATION.

MUTILATED SECURITY certificate that cannot be read for the name of the issue or the issuer, or for the detail necessary for identification and transfer, or for the exercise of the holder's rights. It is then the seller's obligation to take corrective action, which usually means having the transfer agent guarantee the rights of ownership to the buyer.

MUTUAL ASSOCIATION SAVINGS AND LOAN ASSOCIATION organized as a cooperative owned by its members. Members' deposits represent shares; shareholders vote on association affairs and receive income in the form of dividends. Unlike state-chartered corporate S&Ls, which account for a minority of the industry, mutual associations are not permitted to issue stock, and they are usually chartered by the OFFICE OF THRIFT SUPERVISION (OTS) and belong to the SAVINGS ASSOCIATION INSURANCE FUND (SAIF). Deposits are technically subject to a waiting period before withdrawal, although in practice withdrawals are usually allowed on demand, the association's liquidity being assured by its ability to borrow from the Federal Home Loan Bank using home mortgages as collateral.

MUTUAL COMPANY corporation whose ownership and profits are distributed among members in proportion to the amount of business they do with the company. The most familiar examples are (1) mutual insurance companies, whose members are policy holders entitled to name the directors or trustees and to receive dividends or rebates on future premiums; (2) state-chartered MUTUAL SAVINGS BANKS, whose members are depositors sharing in net earnings but having nothing to do with management; and (3) federal savings and loan associations, MUTUAL ASSOCIATIONS whose members are depositors entitled to vote and receive dividends.

MUTUAL FUND fund operated by an INVESTMENT COMPANY that raises money from shareholders and invests it in stocks, bonds, options, commodities, or money market securities. These funds offer investors the advantages of diversification and professional management. For these services they charge a management fee, typically 1% or less of assets per year.
    Mutual funds may invest aggressively or conservatively. Investors should assess their own tolerance for risk before they decide which fund would be appropriate for them. In addition, the timing of buying or selling depends on the outlook for the economy, the state of the stock and bond markets, interest rates, and other factors.

MUTUAL FUND CUSTODIAN commercial bank or trust company that provides safekeeping for the securities owned by a mutual fund and may also act as TRANSFER AGENT, making payments to and collecting investments from shareholders. Mutual fund custodians must comply with the rules set forth in the INVESTMENT COMPANY ACT OF 1940.

MUTUAL IMPROVEMENT CERTIFICATE certificate issued by a local government in lieu of bonds to finance improvements or services, such as widening a sidewalk, or installing a sewer, or repairing a street. Such an obligation is payable from a special tax assessment against those who benefit from the improvement, and the payments may be collected by the contractor performing the work. Interest on the certificate is free of federal, state, and local taxes. *See also* GENERAL OBLIGATION BOND.

MUTUAL SAVINGS BANK SAVINGS BANK organized under state charter for the ownership and benefit of its depositors. A local board of trustees makes major decisions as fiduciaries, independently of the legal owners. Traditionally, income is distributed to depositors after expenses are deducted and reserve funds are set aside as required. In recent times, many mutual savings banks have begun to issue stock and offer consumer services such as credit cards and checking accounts, as well as commercial services such as corporate checking accounts and commercial real estate loans.

n

NAKED OPTION OPTION for which the buyer or seller has no underlying security position. A writer of a naked CALL OPTION, therefore, does not own a LONG POSITION in the stock on which the call has been written. Similarly, the writer of a naked PUT OPTION does not have a SHORT POSITION in the stock on which the put has been written. Naked options are very risky—although potentially very rewarding. If the underlying stock or stock index moves in the direction sought by the investor, profits can be enormous, because the investor would only have had to put down a small amount of money to reap a large return. On the other hand, if the stock moved in the opposite direction, the writer of the naked option could be subject to huge losses.

For instance, if someone wrote a naked call option at $60 a share on XYZ stock without owning the shares, and if the stock rose to $70 a share, the writer of the option would have to deliver XYZ shares to the call buyer at $60 a share. In order to acquire those shares, he or she would have to go into the market and buy them for $70 a share, sustaining a $10-a-share loss on his or her position. If, on the other hand, the option writer already owned XYZ shares when writing the option, he or she could just turn those shares over to the option buyer. This latter strategy is known as writing a COVERED CALL.

NAKED POSITION securities position that is not hedged from market risk—for example, the position of someone who writes a CALL or PUT option without having the corresponding LONG POSITION or SHORT POSITION on the underlying security. The potential risk or reward of naked positions is greater than that of covered positions. *See* COVERED CALL; HEDGE; NAKED OPTION.

NARROWING THE SPREAD closing the SPREAD between the bid and asked prices of a security as a result of bidding and offering by market makers and specialists in a security. For example, a stock's bid price—the most anyone is willing to pay—may be $10 a share, and the asked price—the lowest price at which anyone will sell—may be $10¾. If a broker or market maker offers to buy shares at $10¼, while the asked price remains at $10¾, the spread has effectively been narrowed.

NARROW MARKET securities or commodities market characterized by light trading and greater fluctuations in prices relative to volume than would be the case if trading were active. The market in a particular stock is said to be narrow if the price falls more than a point between ROUND LOT trades without any apparent explanation, suggesting lack of interest and too few orders. The terms THIN MARKET and *inactive market* are used as synonyms for narrow market.

NASDAQ National Association of Securities Dealers Automated Quotations system, which is owned and operated by the NATIONAL ASSOCIATION OF SECURITIES DEALERS. NASDAQ is a computerized system that provides brokers and dealers with price quotations for securities traded OVER THE COUNTER as well as for many New York Stock Exchange listed securities. NASDAQ quotes are published in the financial pages of most newspapers.

NASD FORM FR-1 form required of foreign dealers in securities subscribing to new securities issues in the process of distribution, whereby they agree to abide by NATIONAL ASSOCIATION OF SECURITIES DEALERS rules concerning a HOT ISSUE. Under NASD Rules of Fair Practice, firms participating in the distribution must make a bona fide public offering at the public offering price. Any sale designed to capitalize on a hot issue—one that on the first day of trading sells at a substantial premium over the public offering price—would be in violation of NASD rules. Violations include a sale to a member of the dealer's family or to an employee, assuming such sales could not be defended as "normal investment practice." Also called *blanket certification form*.

NATIONAL ASSOCIATION OF INVESTMENT CLUBS association that helps investment clubs get established. Investment clubs are formed by people who pool their money and make common decisions about how to invest those assets. *See also* INVESTMENT CLUB.

NATIONAL ASSOCIATION OF SECURITIES DEALERS (NASD) nonprofit organization formed under the joint sponsorship of the Investment Bankers' Conference and the Securities and Exchange Commission to comply with the MALONEY ACT. NASD members include virtually all investment banking houses and firms dealing in the OVER THE COUNTER market. Operating under the supervision of the SEC,the NASD's basic purposes are to (1) standardize practices in the field, (2) establish high moral and ethical standards in securities trading,(3) provide a representative body to consult with the government and investors on matters of common interest, (4) establish and enforce fair and equitable rules of securities trading, and (5) establish a disciplinary body capable of enforcing the above provisions. The NASD also requires members to maintain quick assets in excess of current liabilities at all times. Periodic examinations and audits are conducted to ensure a high level of solvency and financial integrity among members. A special Investment Companies Department is concerned with the problems of investment companies and has the responsibility of reviewing companies' sales literature in that segment of the securities industry.

NATIONAL BANK commercial bank whose charter is approved by the U.S. Comptroller of the Currency rather than by a state banking department. National banks are required to be members of the FEDERAL RESERVE SYSTEM and to purchase stock in the FEDERAL RESERVE BANK in their district (*see* MEMBER BANK). They must also belong to the FEDERAL DEPOSIT INSURANCE CORPORATION.

NATIONAL DEBT debt owed by the Federal government. The national debt is made up of such debt obligations as Treasury bills, Treasury notes, and Treasury bonds. Congress imposes a ceiling on the national debt, which has been increased on occasions when federal spending has risen to the level of the ceiling. In the mid-1980s, the national debt stood at about $1.5 trillion. The interest due on the national debt is one of the major annual expenses of the federal government.

NATIONALIZATION takeover of a private company's assets or operations by a government. The company may or may not be compensated for the loss of assets. In developing nations, an operation is typically nationalized if the government feels the company is exploiting the host country and exporting too high a proportion of the profits. By nationalizing the firm, the government hopes to keep profits at home. In developed countries, industries are often nationalized when they need government subsidies to survive. For instance, the French government nationalized steel and chemical companies in the mid-1980s in order to preserve jobs that would have disappeared if free market forces had prevailed. In some developed countries, however, nationalization is carried out as a form of national policy, often by Socialist governments, and is not designed to rescue ailing industries.

NATIONAL MARKET ADVISORY BOARD board appointed by the Securities and Exchange Commission under provisions of the 1975 Securities Act to study and advise the commission on a national exchange market system (NEMS). NEMS is envisioned as a highly automated, national exchange with continuous auction markets and competing specialists or market makers, but one that would preserve the existing regional exchanges.

NATIONAL MARKET SYSTEM
1. system of trading OVER THE COUNTER stocks under the sponsorship of the NATIONAL ASSOCIATION OF SECURITIES DEALERS (NASD) and NASDAQ. Stocks trading in the National Market System must meet certain criteria for size, profitability, and trading activity. More comprehensive information is available for National Market System stocks than for other stocks traded over the counter. For most over-the-counter stocks, newspapers list the stock name, dividend, trading volume, bid and ask prices, and the change in those prices during a trading day. For National Market System stocks, the listing includes the stock name, dividend, high and low price for the past 52 weeks, trading volume, high and low price during the trading day, closing price on that day, and price change for that day.
2. national system of trading whereby the prices for stocks and bonds are listed simultaneously on the New York Stock Exchange and all regional exchanges. Buyers and sellers therefore are able to get the best prices by executing their trades on the exchange with the most favorable price at the time. This system is not to be confused with the national exchange market system (NEMS) being studied by the Securities and Exchange Commission and other planning groups. *See also* NATIONAL MARKET ADVISORY BOARD.

NATIONAL QUOTATION BUREAU daily service to subscribers that collects bid and offer quotes from MARKET MAKERS in stocks and bonds traded OVER THE COUNTER. Quotes are distributed on PINK SHEETS (for stocks) and YELLOW SHEETS (for corporate bonds). The Bureau is a subsidiary of the Commerce Clearing House, a company engaged in financial publishing.

NATIONAL SECURITIES CLEARING CORPORATION (NSCC) securities clearing organization formed in 1977 by merging subsidiaries of the New York and American Stock Exchanges with the National Clearing Corporation. It functions essentially as a medium through which brokerage firms, exchanges, and other clearing corporations reconcile accounts with each other. *See also* CONTINUOUS NET SETTLEMENT.

NEAREST MONTH in commodity futures or OPTION trading, the expiration dates, expressed as months, closest to the present. For a commodity or an option that had delivery or expiration dates available in September, December, March, and June, for instance, the nearest month would be September if a trade were being made in August. Nearest month contracts are always more heavily traded than FURTHEST MONTH contracts.

NEAR MONEY CASH EQUIVALENTS and other assets that are easily convertible into cash. Some examples are government securities, bank TIME DEPOSITS, and MONEY MARKET FUND shares. Bonds close to REDEMPTION date are also called near money.

NEGATIVE CARRY situation when the cost of money borrowed to finance securities is higher than the yield on the securities. If an investor borrowed at 12% to finance, or "carry," a bond yielding 10%, the bond would have a negative carry, for example. Negative carry does not necessarily mean a loss to the investor, however, and a positive yield can result on an after-tax basis. In this case, the income from the 10% bond may be tax exempt, whereas the interest on the 12% loan is tax deductible.

NEGATIVE CASH FLOW situation in which a business spends more cash than it receives through earnings or other transactions in an accounting period. *See also* CASH FLOW.

NEGATIVE INCOME TAX proposed system of providing financial aid to poverty-level individuals and families, using the mechanisms already in place to collect income taxes. After filing a tax return showing income below subsistence levels, instead of paying an income tax, low-income people would receive a direct subsidy, called a negative income tax, sufficient to bring them up to the subsistence level.

NEGATIVE PLEDGE CLAUSE negative covenant or promise in an INDENTURE agreement that states the corporation will not pledge any of its assets if doing so would result in less security to the debtholders covered under the indenture agreement. Also called *covenant of equal coverage*.

NEGATIVE WORKING CAPITAL situation in which the current liabilities of a firm exceed its current assets. For example, if the total of cash, MARKETABLE SECURITIES, ACCOUNTS RECEIVABLE and notes receivable, inventory, and other current assets is less than the total of ACCOUNTS PAYABLE, short-term notes payable, long-term debt due in one year, and other current liabilities, the firm has a negative working capital. Unless the condition is corrected, the firm will not be able to pay debts when due, threatening its ability to keep operating and possibly resulting in bankruptcy.

To remedy a negative working capital position, a firm has these alternatives: (1) it can convert a long-term asset into a current asset—for example, by selling a piece of equipment or a building, by liquidating a long-term investment, or by renegotiating a long-term loan receivable; (2) it can convert short-term liabilities into long-term liabilities—for example, by negotiating the substitution of a current account payable with a long-term note payable; (3) it can borrow long term; (4) it can obtain additional equity through a stock issue or other sources of paid-in capital; (5) it can retain or "plow back" profits. *See also* WORKING CAPITAL.

NEGATIVE YIELD CURVE situation in which yields on short-term securities are higher than those on long-term securities of the same quality. Normally, short-term rates are lower than long-term rates because those who commit their money for longer periods are taking more risk. But if interest rates climb high enough, borrowers become unwilling to lock themselves into high rates for long periods and borrow short-term instead. Therefore, yields rise on short-term funds and fall or remain stable on long-term funds. Also called an INVERTED YIELD CURVE. *See also* YIELD CURVE.

NEGOTIABLE

In general:
1. something that can be sold or transferred to another party in exchange for money or as settlement of an obligation.
2. matter of mutual concern to one or more parties that involves conditions to be worked out to the satisfaction of the parties. As examples: In a lender-borrower arrangement, the interest rate may be negotiable; in securities sales, brokerage commissions are now negotiable, having historically been fixed; and in divorce cases involving children, the terms of visiting rights are usually negotiable.

Finance: instrument meeting the qualifications of the Uniform Commercial Code dealing with negotiable instruments. *See* NEGOTIABLE INSTRUMENT.

Investments: type of security the title to which is transferable by delivery. A stock certificate with the stock power properly signed is negotiable, for example.

NEGOTIABLE CERTIFICATE OF DEPOSIT large-dollar-amount, short-term certificate of deposit. Such certificates are issued by large banks and bought mainly by corporations and institutional investors. They are payable either to the bearer or to the order of the depositor, and, being negotiable, they enjoy an active SECONDARY MARKET, where they trade in round lots of $5 million. Although they can be issued in any denomination from $100,000 up, the typical amount is $1 million. They have a minimum original maturity of 14 days; most original maturities are under six months. Also called a JUMBO CERTIFICATE OF DEPOSIT.

NEGOTIABLE INSTRUMENT unconditional order or promise to pay an amount of money, easily transferable from one person to another. Examples: check, promissory note, draft (bill of exchange). The Uniform Commercial Code requires that for an instrument to be negotiable it must be signed by the maker or drawer, must contain an unconditional promise or order to pay a specific amount of money, must be payable on demand or at a specified future time, and must be payable to order or to the bearer.

NEGOTIABLE ORDER OF WITHDRAWAL a bank or savings and loan with-drawal ticket that is a NEGOTIABLE INSTRUMENT. The accounts from which such withdrawals can be made, called NOW accounts, are thus, in effect, interest-bearing checking accounts. They were first introduced in the late 1970s and became available nationally in January 1980. In the early and mid-1980s the interest rate on NOW accounts was capped at 5½%; the cap was phased out in the late 1980s. *See also* SUPER NEGOTIABLE ORDER OF WITHDRAWAL (NOW) ACCOUNT.

NEGOTIATED UNDERWRITING underwriting of new securities issue in which the SPREAD between the purchase price paid to the issuer and the public offering price is determined through negotiation rather than multiple competitive bidding. The spread, which represents the compensation to the investment bankers participating in the underwriting (collectively called the *syndicate*), is negotiated between the issuing company and the MANAGING UNDERWRITER, with the consent of the group. Most corporate stock and bond issues and municipal revenue bond issues are priced through negotiation, whereas municipal general obligation bonds and new issues of public utilities are generally priced through competitive bidding. Competitive bidding is mandatory for new issues of public utilities holding companies. *See also* COMPETITIVE BID.

NEST EGG assets put aside for a person's retirement. Such assets are usually invested conservatively to provide the retiree with a secure standard of living for the rest of his or her life. Investment in an INDIVIDUAL RETIREMENT ACCOUNT would be considered part of a nest egg.

NET

In general: figure remaining after all relevant deductions have been made from the gross amount. For example: net sales are equal to gross sales minus discounts, returns, and allowances; net profit is gross profit less operating (sales, general, and administrative) expenses; net worth is assets (worth) less liabilities.

Investments: dollar difference between the proceeds from the sale of a security and the seller's adjusted cost of acquisition—that is, the gain or loss.

As a verb:
1. to arrive at the difference between additions and subtractions or plus amounts and minus amounts. For example, in filing tax returns, capital losses are netted against capital gains.
2. to realize a net profit, as in "last year we netted a million dollars after taxes."

NET ASSETS difference between a company's total assets and liabilities; another way of saying *owner's equity* or NET WORTH. *See* ASSET COVERAGE for a discussion of net asset value per unit of bonds, preferred stock, or common stock.

NET ASSET VALUE (NAV)
1. in mutual funds, the market value of a fund share, synonymous with *bid price*. In the case of no-load funds, the NAV, market price, and offering price are all the same figure, which the public pays to buy shares; load fund market or offer prices are quoted after adding the sales charge to the net asset value. NAV is calculated by most funds after the close of the exchanges each day by taking the closing market value of all securities owned plus all other assets such as cash, subtracting all liabilities, then dividing the result (total net assets) by the total number of shares outstanding. The number of shares outstanding can vary each day depending on the number of purchases and redemptions.
2. book value of a company's different classes of securities, usually stated as net asset value per bond, net asset value per share of preferred stock, and net book value per common share of common stock. The formula for computing net asset value is total assets less any INTANGIBLE ASSET less all liabilities and securities having a prior claim, divided by the number of units outstanding (i.e., bonds, preferred shares, or common shares). *See* BOOK VALUE for a discussion of how these values are calculated and what they mean.

NET CAPITAL REQUIREMENT Securities and Exchange Commission requirement that member firms as well as nonmember broker-dealers in securities maintain a maximum ratio of indebtedness to liquid capital of 15 to 1; also called *net capital rule* and *net capital ratio*. Indebtedness covers all money owed to a firm, including MARGIN loans and commitments to purchase securities, one reason new public issues are spread among members of underwriting syndicates. Liquid capital includes cash and assets easily converted into cash.

NET CHANGE difference between the last trading price on a stock, bond, commodity, or mutual fund from one day to the next. The net change in individual stock prices is listed in newspaper financial pages. The designation + 2½, for example, means that a stock's final price on that day was $2.50 higher than the final price on the previous trading day. The net change in prices of OVER THE COUNTER stocks is usually the difference between bid prices from one day to the next.

NET CURRENT ASSETS difference between current assets and current liabilities; another name for WORKING CAPITAL. Some security analysts divide this figure (after subtracting preferred stock, if any) by the number of common shares outstanding to arrive at working capital per share. Believing working capital per share to be a conservative measure of LIQUIDATING VALUE (on the theory that fixed and other noncurrent assets would more than compensate for any shrinkage in current assets if assets were to be sold), they compare it with the MARKET VALUE of the company's shares. If the net current assets per share figure, or ''minimum liquidating value,'' is higher than the market price, these analysts view the common shares as a bargain (assuming, of course, that the company is not losing money and that its assets are conservatively valued). Other analysts believe this theory ignores the efficiency of capital markets generally and, specifically, obligations such as pension plans, which are not reported as balance sheet liabilities under present accounting rules.

NET EARNINGS *see* NET INCOME.

NET ESTATE *see* GROSS ESTATE.

NET INCOME

In general: sum remaining after all expenses have been met or deducted; synonymous with *net earnings* and with *net profit* or *net loss* (depending on whether the figure is positive or negative).

For a business: difference between total sales and total costs and expenses. Total costs comprise cost of goods sold including depreciation; total expenses comprise selling, general, and administrative expenses, plus INCOME DEDUCTIONS. Net income is usually specified as to whether it is before income taxes or after income taxes. Net income after taxes is the *bottom line* referred to in popular vernacular. It is out of this figure that dividends are normally paid. *See also* OPERATING PROFIT (OR LOSS).

For an individual: gross income less expenses incurred to produce gross income. Those expenses are mostly deductible for tax purposes.

NET INCOME PER SHARE OF COMMON STOCK amount of profit or earnings allocated to each share of common stock after all costs, taxes, allowances for depreciation, and possible losses have been deducted. Net income per share is stated in dollars and cents and is usually compared with the corresponding period a year earlier. For example, XYZ might report that second-quarter net income per share was $1.20, up from 90 cents in the previous year's second quarter. Also known as *earnings per common share* (EPS).

NET INCOME TO NET WORTH RATIO *see* RETURN ON EQUITY.

NET INVESTMENT INCOME PER SHARE income received by an investment company from dividends and interest on securities investments during an accounting period, less management fees and administrative expenses and divided by the number of outstanding shares. Short-term trading profits (net profits from securities held for less than six months) are considered dividend income. The dividend and interest income is received by the investment company, which in turn pays shareholders the net investment income in the form of dividends prorated according to each holder's share in the total PORTFOLIO.

NET LEASE financial lease stipulating that the user (rather than the owner) of the leased property shall pay all maintenance costs, taxes, insurance, and other expenses. Many real estate and oil and gas limited partnerships are structured as net leases with ESCALATOR CLAUSES, to provide limited partners with both depreciation tax benefits and appreciation of investment, minus cash expenses. *See also* GROSS LEASE.

NET OPERATING LOSS (NOL) tax term for the excess of business expenses over income in a tax year. Under TAX LOSS CARRYBACK, CARRYFORWARD provisions, NOLs can (if desired) be carried back three years and forward 15 years. The TAX REFORM ACT OF 1986 limits the use of NOLs, in cases where an acquired loss corporation has had a 50% or more change in ownership, to the loss corporation's FAIR MARKET VALUE multiplied by the long-term tax-exempt bond rate.

NET PRESENT VALUE (NPV) method used in evaluating investments whereby the net present value of all cash outflows (such as the cost of the investment) and cash inflows (returns) is calculated using a given discount rate, usually a REQUIRED RATE OF RETURN. An investment is acceptable if the NPV is positive. In capital budgeting, the discount rate used is called the HURDLE RATE and is usually equal to the INCREMENTAL COST OF CAPITAL.

NET PROCEEDS amount (usually cash) received from the sale or disposition of property, from a loan, or from the sale or issuance of securities after deduction of all costs incurred in the transaction. In computing the gain or loss on a securities transaction for tax purposes, the amount of the sale is the amount of the net proceeds.

NET PROFIT *see* NET INCOME.

NET QUICK ASSETS cash, MARKETABLE SECURITIES, and ACCOUNTS RECEIVABLE, minus current liabilities. *See also* QUICK RATIO.

NET REALIZED CAPITAL GAINS PER SHARE amount of CAPITAL GAINS that an investment company realized on the sale of securities, NET of CAPITAL LOSSES and divided by the number of outstanding shares. Such net gains are distributed at least annually to shareholders in proportion to their shares in the total portfolio. Such distributions have traditionally been treated as tax-favored long-term capital gains to the shareholders, regardless of the length of time they have held shares in the investment company. Capital gains have been taxed at ORDINARY INCOME rates since 1988. *See also* REGULATED INVESTMENT COMPANY.

NET SALES gross sales less returns and allowances, freight out, and cash discounts allowed. Cash discounts allowed is seen less frequently than in past years, since it has become conventional to report as net sales the amount finally received from the customer. Returns are merchandise returned for credit; allowances are deductions allowed by the seller for merchandise not received or received in damaged condition; freight out is shipping expense passed on to the customer.

NET TANGIBLE ASSETS PER SHARE total assets of a company, less any INTANGIBLE ASSET such as goodwill, patents, and trademarks, less all liabilities and the par value of preferred stock, divided by the number of common shares outstanding. *See* BOOK VALUE for a discussion of what this calculation means and how it can be varied to apply to bonds or preferred stock shares. *See also* NET ASSET VALUE.

NET TRANSACTION securities transaction in which the buyer and seller do not pay fees or commissions. For instance, when an investor buys a new issue, no commission is due. If the stock is initially offered at $15 a share, the buyer's total cost is $15 per share.

NET WORTH amount by which assets exceed liabilities. For a corporation, net worth is also known as *stockholders' equity* or NET ASSETS. For an individual, net worth is the total value of all possessions, such as a house, stocks, bonds, and other securities, minus all outstanding debts, such as mortgage and revolving-credit loans. In order to qualify for certain high-risk investments, brokerage houses require that an individual's net worth must be at or above a certain dollar level.

NET YIELD RATE OF RETURN on a security net of out-of-pocket costs associated with its purchase, such as commissions or markups. *See also* MARKDOWN.

NEW ACCOUNT REPORT document filled out by a broker that details vital facts about a new client's financial circumstances and investment objectives. The report may be updated if there are material changes in a client's financial position. Based on the report, a client may or may not be deemed eligible for certain types of risky investments, such as commodity trading or highly leveraged LIMITED PARTNERSHIP deals. *See also* KNOW YOUR CUSTOMER.

NEW ISSUE stock or bond being offered to the public for the first time, the distribution of which is covered by Securities and Exchange Commission (SEC) rules. New issues may be initial public offerings by previously private companies or additional stock or bond issues by companies already public and often listed on the exchanges. New PUBLIC OFFERINGS must be registered with the SEC. PRIVATE PLACEMENTS can avoid SEC registration if a LETTER OF INTENT establishes that the securities are purchased for investment and not for resale to the public. *See also* HOT ISSUE; LETTER SECURITY; PUBLIC OFFERING; UNDERWRITE.

NEW MONEY amount of additional long-term financing provided by a new issue or issues in excess of the amount of a maturing issue or by issues that are being refunded.

NEW MONEY PREFERRED PREFERRED STOCK issued after October 1, 1942, when the tax exclusion for corporate investors receiving preferred stock dividends was raised from 60% to 85%, to equal the exclusion on common stock dividends. The change benefited financial institutions, such as insurance companies, which are limited in the amount of common stocks they can hold, typically 5% of assets.

New money preferreds offer an opportunity to gain tax advantages over bond investments, which have fully taxable interest. The corporate tax exclusion on dividends was lowered to 80% starting in 1987.

NEW YORK COFFEE, SUGAR AND COCOA EXCHANGE *see* SECURITIES AND COMMODITIES EXCHANGES.

NEW YORK COTTON EXCHANGE *see* SECURITIES AND COMMODITIES EXCHANGES.

NEW YORK CURB EXCHANGE *see* AMERICAN STOCK EXCHANGE.

NEW YORK FUTURES EXCHANGE *see* SECURITIES AND COMMODITIES EXCHANGES.

NEW YORK MERCANTILE EXCHANGE *see* SECURITIES AND COMMODITIES EXCHANGES.

NEW YORK STOCK EXCHANGE (NYSE) oldest (1792) and largest stock exchange in the United States, located at 11 Wall Street in New York City; also known as the *Big Board* and *The Exchange*. The NYSE is an unincorporated association governed by a board of directors headed by a full-time paid chairman and comprised of individuals representing the public and the exchange membership in about equal proportion. Operating divisions of the NYSE are market operations, member firm regulation and surveillance, finance and office services, product development and planning, and market services and customer relations. Staff groups handle other specialized functions, such as legal problems, government relations, and economic research; certain operational functions are handled by affiliated corporations, such as DEPOSITORY TRUST COMPANY, NATIONAL SECURITIES CLEARING CORPORATION (NSCC), and SECURITIES INDUSTRY AUTOMATION CORPORATION (SIAC). Total voting membership is currently fixed at 1366 "seats," which are owned by individuals, usually partners or officers of securities firms. The number of firms represented is about 550, some of which are specialists responsible for the maintenance of an orderly market in the securities they handle. Most members execute orders for the public, although a small number—about 30, who are called FLOOR TRADERS—deal exclusively for their own accounts. More than 1500 companies are listed on the NYSE, representing large firms meeting the exchange's uniquely stringent LISTING REQUIREMENTS. STOCKS, BONDS, WARRANTS, OPTIONS, and RIGHTS are traded at 14 electronically equipped installations, called TRADING POSTS, on the FLOOR of the exchange. In the mid-1980s NYSE-listed shares made up approximately 60% of the total shares traded on organized national exchanges in the United States.

NEW YORK STOCK EXCHANGE INDEX *see* STOCK INDEXES AND AVERAGES.

NICHE particular specialty in which a firm has garnered a large market share. Often, the market will be small enough so that the firm will not attract very much competition. For example, a company that makes a line of specialty chemicals for use by only the petroleum industry is said to have a niche in the chemical industry. Stock analysts frequently favor such companies, since their profit margins can often be wider than those of firms facing more competition.

NIFTY FIFTY 50 stocks most favored by institutions. The membership of this group is constantly changing, although companies that continue to produce consistent earnings growth over a long time tend to remain institutional favorites.

Nifty Fifty stocks also tend to have higher than market average price/earnings ratios, since their growth prospects are well recognized by institutional investors. The Nifty Fifty stocks were particularly famous in the bull markets of the 1960s and early 1970s, when many of the price/earnings ratios soared to 50 or more. *See also* PRICE/EARNINGS RATIO.

NINE-BOND RULE New York Stock Exchange (NYSE) requirement that orders for nine bonds or less be sent to the floor for one hour to seek a market. Since bond trading tends to be inactive on the NYSE (because of large institutional holdings and because many of the listed bond trades are handled OVER THE COUNTER), Rule 396 is designed to obtain the most favorable price for small investors. Customers may request that the rule be waived, but the broker-dealer in such cases must then act only as a BROKER and not as a PRINCIPAL (dealer for his own account).

NIKKEI INDEX index of 225 leading stocks traded on the Tokyo Stock Exchange. Called the Nikkei Dow Jones Stock Average until it was renamed in May, 1985, it is similar to the Dow Jones Industrial Average because it is composed of representative BLUE CHIP companies (termed *first-section* companies in Japan) and is a PRICE-WEIGHTED INDEX. That means the movement of each stock, in yen or dollars respectively, is weighed equally regardless of its market capitalization. The Nikkei Stock Average, informally called the Nikkei Index and often still referred to as the Nikkei Dow, is published by The *Nihon Keizai Shimbun* (*Japan Economic Journal*) and is the most widely quoted Japanese stock index.

19c3 STOCK stock listed on a national securities exchange, such as the New York Stock Exchange or the American Stock Exchange, after April 26, 1979, and thus exempt from Securities and Exchange Commission rule 19c3 prohibiting exchange members to engage in OFF-BOARD trading.

NO-ACTION LETTER letter requested from the Securities and Exchange Commission wherein the Commission agrees to take neither civil nor criminal action with respect to a specific activity and circumstances. LIMITED PARTNERSHIPS designed as TAX SHELTERS, which are frequently venturing in uncharted legal territory, often seek no-action letters to clear novel marketing or financing techniques.

NO-BRAINER term used to describe a market the direction of which has become obvious, and therefore requires little or no analysis. This means that most of the stocks will go up in a strong bull market and fall in a bear market, so that it does not matter very much which stock investors buy or sell.

NO-LOAD FUND MUTUAL FUND offered by an open-end investment company that imposes no sales charge (load) on its shareholders. Investors buy shares in no-load funds directly from the fund companies, rather than through a BROKER, as is done in load funds. Many no-load fund families (*see* FAMILY OF FUNDS) allow switching of assets between stock, bond, and money market funds. The listing of the price of a no-load fund in a newspaper is accompanied with the designation NL. The net asset value, market price, and offer prices of this type of fund are exactly the same, since there is no sales charge. *See also* LOAD FUND.

NOMINAL EXERCISE PRICE EXERCISE PRICE (strike price) of a GOVERNMENT NATIONAL MORTGAGE ASSOCIATION (GNMA or Ginnie Mae) option contract, obtained by multiplying the unpaid principal balance on a Ginnie Mae certificate by the ADJUSTED EXERCISE PRICE. For example, if the unpaid principal balance is $96,000 and the adjusted exercise price is 58, the nominal exercise price is $55,680.

NOMINAL INTEREST RATE *see* NOMINAL YIELD.

NOMINAL QUOTATION bid and offer prices given by a market maker for the purpose of valuation, not as an invitation to trade. Securities industry rules require that nominal quotations be specifically identified as such; usually this is done by prefixing the quote with the letters FYI (FOR YOUR INFORMATION) or FVO (for valuation only).

NOMINAL YIELD annual dollar amount of income received from a fixed-income security divided by the PAR VALUE of the security and stated as a percentage. Thus a bond that pays $90 a year and has a par value of $1000 has a nominal yield of 9%, called its *coupon rate*. Similarly, a preferred stock that pays a $9 annual dividend and has a par value of $100 has a nominal yield of 9%. Only when a stock or bond is bought exactly at par value is the nominal yield equal to the actual yield. Since market prices of fixed-income securities go down when market interest rates go up and vice versa, the actual yield, which is determined by the market price and coupon rate (nominal yield), will be higher when the purchase price is below par value and lower when the purchase price is above par value. *See also* RATE OF RETURN.

NOMINEE person or firm, such as a bank official or brokerage house, into whose name securities or other properties are transferred by agreement. Securities held in STREET NAME, for example, are registered in the name of a BROKER (nominee) to facilitate transactions, although the customer remains the true owner.

NONCALLABLE preferred stock or bond that cannot be redeemed at the option of the issuer. A bond may offer CALL PROTECTION for a particular length of time, such as ten years. After that, the issuer may redeem the bond if it chooses and can justify doing so. U.S. government bond obligations are not callable until close to maturity. Provisions for noncallability are spelled out in detail in a bond's INDENTURE agreement or in the prospectus issued at the time a new preferred stock is floated. Bond yields are often quoted to the first date at which the bonds could be called. *See also* YIELD TO CALL.

NONCLEARING MEMBER member firm of the New York Stock Exchange or another organized exchange that does not have the operational facilities for clearing transactions and thus pays a fee to have the services performed by another member firm, called a *clearing member*. The clearing process involves comparison and verification of information between the buying and selling brokers and then the physical delivery of certificates in exchange for payment, called the *settlement*.

NONCOMPETITIVE BID method of buying Treasury bills without having to meet the high minimum purchase requirements of the regular DUTCH AUCTION; also called *noncompetitive tender*. The process of bidding for Treasury bills is split into two parts: competitive and noncompetitive bids.

　　COMPETITIVE BIDS are entered by large government securities dealers and brokers, who buy millions of dollars worth of bills. They offer the best price they can for the securities, and the highest bids are accepted by the Treasury in what is called the Dutch auction.

Noncompetitive bids are submitted by smaller investors through a Federal Reserve Bank, the Bureau of Federal Debt, or certain commercial banks. These bids will be executed at the average of the prices paid in all the competitive bids accepted by the Treasury. The minimum noncompetitive bid for a Treasury bill is $10,000. *See also* TREASURY DIRECT.

NONCUMULATIVE term describing a preferred stock issue in which unpaid dividends do not accrue. Such issues contrast with CUMULATIVE PREFERRED issues, where unpaid dividends accumulate and must be paid before dividends on common shares. Most preferred issues are cumulative. On a noncumulative preferred, omitted dividends will, as a rule, never be paid. Some older railroad preferred stocks are of this type.

NONCURRENT ASSET asset not expected to be converted into cash, sold, or exchanged within the normal operating cycle of the firm, usually one year. Examples of noncurrent assets include FIXED ASSETS, such as real estate, machinery, and other equipment; LEASEHOLD IMPROVEMENTS; INTANGIBLE ASSETS, such as goodwill, patents, and trademarks; notes receivable after one year; other investments; miscellaneous assets not meeting the definition of a CURRENT ASSET. Prepaid expenses (also called DEFERRED CHARGES or *deferred expenses*), which include such items as rent paid in advance, prepaid insurance premiums, and subscriptions, are usually considered current assets by accountants. Credit analysts, however, prefer to classify these expenses as noncurrent assets, since prepayments do not represent asset strength and protection in the way that other current assets do, with their convertibility into cash during the normal operating cycle and their liquidation value should operations be terminated.

NONMEMBER FIRM brokerage firm that is not a member of an organized exchange. Such firms execute their trades either through member firms, on regional exchanges, or in the THIRD MARKET. *See* MEMBER FIRM; REGIONAL STOCK EXCHANGES.

NONPARTICIPATING PREFERRED STOCK *see* PARTICIPATING PREFERRED STOCK.

NONPRODUCTIVE LOAN type of commercial bank loan that increases the amount of spending power in the economy but does not lead directly to increased output; for example, a loan to finance a LEVERAGED BUYOUT. The Federal Reserve has on occasion acted to curtail such lending as one of its early steps in implementing monetary restraint.

NONPUBLIC INFORMATION information about a company, either positive or negative, that will have a material effect on the stock price when it is released to the public. Insiders, such as corporate officers and members of the board of directors, are not allowed to trade on material nonpublic information until it has been released to the public, since they would have an unfair advantage over unsuspecting investors. Some examples of important nonpublic information are an imminent takeover announcement, a soon-to-be-released earnings report that is more favorable than most analysts expect, or the sudden resignation of a key corporate official. *See also* DISCLOSURE; INSIDER.

NONPURPOSE LOAN loan for which securities are pledged as collateral but which is not used to purchase or carry securities. Under Federal Reserve Board REGULATION U, a borrower using securities as collateral must sign an affidavit called a PURPOSE STATEMENT, indicating the use to which the loan is to be put. Regulation U limits the amount of credit a bank may extend for purchasing and carrying margin securities, where the credit is secured directly or indirectly by stock.

NONQUALIFYING ANNUITY annuity purchased outside of an IRS-approved pension plan. The contributions to such an annuity are made with after-tax dollars. Just as with a QUALIFYING ANNUITY, however, the earnings from the nonqualifying annuity can accumulate tax deferred until withdrawn. Assets may be placed in either a FIXED ANNUITY, a VARIABLE ANNUITY, or a HYBRID ANNUITY.

NONQUALIFYING STOCK OPTION employee stock option not meeting the Internal Revenue Service criteria for QUALIFYING STOCK OPTIONS (INCENTIVE STOCK OPTIONS) and therefore triggering a tax upon EXERCISE. (The issuing employer, however, can deduct the nonqualifying option during the period when it is exercised, whereas it would not have a deduction when a qualifying option is exercised.) A STOCK OPTION is a right issued by a corporation to an individual, normally an executive employee, to buy a given amount of shares at a stated price within a specified period of time. Gains realized on the exercise of nonqualifying options are treated as ordinary income in the tax year in which the options are exercised. Qualifying stock options, in contrast, are taxed neither at the time of granting nor the time of exercise; only when the underlying stock is sold and a CAPITAL GAIN realized, does a tax event occur.

NONRECOURSE LOAN type of financial arrangement used by limited partners in a DIRECT PARTICIPATION PROGRAM, whereby the limited partners finance a portion of their participation with a loan secured by their ownership in the underlying venture. They benefit from the LEVERAGE provided by the loan. In case of default, the lender has no recourse to the assets of the partnership beyond those held by the limited partners who borrowed the money.

NONRECURRING CHARGE one-time expense or WRITE-OFF appearing in a company's financial statement; also called *extraordinary charge*. Nonrecurring charges would include, for example, a major fire or theft, the write-off of a division, and the effect of a change in accounting procedure.

NONREFUNDABLE provision in a bond INDENTURE that either prohibits or sets limits on the issuer's retiring the bonds with the proceeds of a subsequent issue, called REFUNDING. Such a provision often does not rule out refunding altogether but protects bondholders from REDEMPTION until a specified date. Other such provisions may preclude refunding unless new bonds can be issued at a specified lower rate. *See also* CALL PROTECTION.

NONVOTING STOCK corporate securities that do not empower a holder to vote on corporate resolutions or the election of directors. Such stock is sometimes issued in connection with a takeover attempt, when management creates nonvoting shares to dilute the target firm's equity and thereby discourage the merger attempt. Except in very special circumstances, the New York Stock Exchange does not list nonvoting stock. Preferred stock is normally nonvoting stock. *See also* VOTING STOCK; VOTING TRUST CERTIFICATE.

NO-PAR-VALUE STOCK stock with no set (par) value specified in the corporate charter or on the stock certificate; also called *no-par stock*. Companies issuing no-par value shares may carry whatever they receive for them either as part of the CAPITAL STOCK account or as part of the CAPITAL SURPLUS (paid-in capital) account, or both. Whatever amount is carried as capital stock has an implicit value, represented by the number of outstanding shares divided into the dollar amount of capital stock.

The main attraction of no-par stock to issuing corporations, historically, had to do with the fact that many states imposed taxes based on PAR VALUE, while other states, like Delaware, encouraged incorporations with no-par-value stock.

For the investor, there are two reservations: (1) that unwise or inept directors may reduce the value of outstanding shares by accepting bargain basement prices on new issues (shareholders are protected, to some extent, from this by PRE-EMPTIVE RIGHT—the right to purchase enough of a new issue to protect their power and equity) and (2) that too great an amount of net worth may be channeled into the capital surplus account, which is restricted by the law of many states from being a source of dividend payments. *See* ILLEGAL DIVIDEND.

Still, no-par stock, along with low-par stock, remains an appealing alternative, from the issuer's standpoint, to par-value shares because of investor confusion of par value and real value.

Most stock issued today is either no-par or low-par value.

NORMAL INVESTMENT PRACTICE history of investment in a customer account with a member of the National Association of Securities Dealers as defined in their rules of fair practice. It is used to test the bona fide PUBLIC OFFERINGS requirement that applies to the allocation of a HOT ISSUE. If the buying customer has a history of purchasing similar amounts in normal circumstances, the sale qualifies as a bona fide public offering and is not in violation of the Rules of Fair Practice. A record of buying only hot issues is not acceptable as normal investment practice. *See also* NASD FORM FR-1.

NORMAL TRADING UNIT standard minimum size of a trading unit for a particular security; also called a ROUND LOT. For instance, stocks have a normal trading unit of 100 shares, although inactive stocks trade in 10-share round lots. Any securities trade for less than a round lot is called an ODD LOT trade.

NOTE written promise to pay a specified amount to a certain entity on demand or on a specified date. *See also* MUNICIPAL NOTE; PROMISSORY NOTE; TREASURIES.

NOT-FOR-PROFIT type of incorporated organization in which no stockholder or trustee shares in profits or losses and which usually exists to accomplish some charitable, humanitarian, or educational purpose; also called *nonprofit*. Such groups are exempt from corporate income taxes but are subject to other taxes on income-producing property or enterprises. Donations to these groups are usually tax deductible for the donor. Some examples are hospitals, colleges and universities, foundations, and such familiar groups as the Red Cross and Girl Scouts.

NOT HELD instruction (abbreviated NH) on a market order to buy or sell securities, indicating that the customer has given the FLOOR BROKER time and price discretion in executing the best possible trade but will not hold the broker responsible if the best deal is not obtained. Such orders, which are usually for large blocks of securities, were originally designed for placement with specialists, who could hold an order back if they felt prices were going to rise. The Securities and Exchange Commission no longer allows specialists to handle NH orders, leaving floor brokers without any clear alternative except to persuade the customer to change the order to a LIMIT ORDER. The broker can then turn the order over to a SPECIALIST, who could sell pieces of the block to floor traders or buy it for his own account. *See* SPECIALIST BLOCK PURCHASE AND SALE. An older variation of NH is DRT, meaning disregard tape.

NOT RATED indication used by securities rating services (such as Standard & Poor's or Moody's) and mercantile agencies (such as Dun & Bradstreet) to show that a security or a company has not been rated. It has neither negative nor positive implications. The abbreviation NR is used.

NOVATION
1. agreement to replace one party to a contract with a new party. The novation transfers both rights and duties and requires the consent of both the original and the new party.
2. replacement of an older debt or obligation with a newer one.

NOW ACCOUNT *see* NEGOTIABLE ORDER OF WITHDRAWAL.

O

OBLIGATION BOND type of mortgage bond in which the face value is greater than the value of the underlying property. The difference compensates the lender for costs exceeding the mortgage value.

OBLIGOR one who has an obligation, such as an issuer of bonds, a borrower of money from a bank or another source, or a credit customer of a business supplier or retailer. The obligor (*obligator, debtor*) is legally bound to pay a debt, including interest, when due.

ODD LOT securities trade made for less than the NORMAL TRADING UNIT (termed a ROUND LOT). In stock trading, any purchase or sale of less than 100 shares is considered an odd lot, although inactive stocks generally trade in round lots of 10 shares. An investor buying or selling an odd lot pays a higher commission rate than someone making a round-lot trade. This odd-lot differential varies among brokers but for stocks is often ⅛ of a point (12½¢) per share. For instance, someone buying 100 shares of XYZ at $70 would pay $70 a share plus commission. At the same time, someone buying only 50 shares of XYZ would pay $70⅛ a share plus commission. *See also* ODD-LOT DEALER; ODD-LOT SHORT-SALE RATIO; ODD-LOT THEORY.

ODD-LOT DEALER originally a dealer who bought round lots of stock and resold it in odd lots to retail brokers who, in turn, accommodated their smaller customers at the regular commission rate plus an extra charge, called the odd-lot differential. The assembling of round lots from odd lots is now a service provided free by New York Stock Exchange specialists to member brokers, and odd-lot transactions can be executed through most brokers serving the retail public. Brokers handling odd lots do, however, receive extra compensation; it varies with the broker, but ⅛ of a point (12½¢) per share in addition to a regular commission is typical. *See also* ODD-LOT.

ODD-LOT SHORT-SALE RATIO ratio obtained by dividing ODD LOT short sales by total odd-lot sales, using New York Stock Exchange (NYSE) statistics; also called the *odd-lot selling indicator*. Historically, odd-lot investors—those who buy and sell in less than 100-share round lots—react to market highs and lows;

when the market reaches a low point, odd-lot short sales reach a high point, and vice versa. The odd-lot ratio has followed the opposite pattern of the NYSE MEMBER SHORT SALE RATIO. *See also* ODD-LOT THEORY.

ODD-LOT THEORY historical theory that the ODD LOT investor—the small personal investor who trades in less than 100-share quantities—is usually guilty of bad timing and that profits can be made by acting contrary to odd-lot trading patterns. Heavy odd-lot buying in a rising market is interpreted by proponents of this theory as a sign of technical weakness and the signal of a market reversal. Conversely, an increase of odd-lot selling in a declining market is seen as a sign of technical strength and a signal to buy. In fact, analyses of odd-lot trading over the years fail to bear out the theory with any real degree of consistency, and it has fallen into disfavor in recent years. It is also a fact that odd-lot customers generally, who tend to buy market leaders, have fared rather well in the upward market that has prevailed over the last fifty years or so. *See also* ODD-LOT SHORT-SALE RATIO.

OFF-BOARD off the exchange (the New York Stock Exchange is known as the Big Board, hence the term). The term is used either for a trade that is executed OVER THE COUNTER or for a transaction entailing listed securities that is not completed on a national exchange. Over-the-counter trading is handled by telephone, with competitive bidding carried on constantly by market makers in a particular stock. The other kind of off-board trade occurs when a block of stock is exchanged between customers of a brokerage firm, or between a customer and the firm itself if the brokerage house wants to buy or sell securities from its own inventory. *See also* THIRD MARKET.

OFFER price at which someone who owns a security offers to sell it; also known as the ASKED PRICE. This price is listed in newspapers for stocks traded OVER THE COUNTER. The bid price—the price at which someone is prepared to buy—is also shown. The bid price is always lower than the offer price. *See also* OFFERING PRICE.

OFFERING *see* PUBLIC OFFERING.

OFFERING CIRCULAR *see* PROSPECTUS.

OFFERING DATE date on which a distribution of stocks or bonds will first be available for sale to the public. *See also* DATED DATE; PUBLIC OFFERING.

OFFERING PRICE price per share at which a new or secondary distribution of securities is offered for sale to the public; also called PUBLIC OFFERING PRICE. For instance, if a new issue of XYZ stock is priced at $40 a share, the offering price is $40.

When mutual fund shares are made available to the public, they are sold at NET ASSET VALUE, also called the *offering price* or the ASKED PRICE, plus a sales charge, if any. In a NO-LOAD FUND, the offering price is the same as the net asset value. In a LOAD FUND, the sales charge is added to the net asset value, to arrive at the offering price. *See also* OFFER.

OFFERING SCALE prices at which different maturities of a SERIAL BOND issue are offered to the public by an underwriter. The offering scale may also be expressed as yields to maturity. *See also* YIELD TO MATURITY.

OFFER WANTED (OW) notice by a potential buyer of a security that he or she is looking for an offer by a potential seller of the security. The abbreviation OW is frequently seen in the PINK SHEETS (listing of stocks) and YELLOW SHEETS (listing of corporate bonds) published by the NATIONAL QUOTATION BUREAU for securities traded by OVER THE COUNTER dealers. *See also* BID WANTED.

OFF-FLOOR ORDER order to buy or sell a security that originates off the floor of an exchange. These are customer orders originating with brokers, as distinguished from orders of floor members trading for their own accounts (ON-FLOOR ORDERS). Exchange rules require that off-floor orders be executed before orders initiated on the floor.

OFFICE OF MANAGEMENT AND BUDGET (OMB) at the federal level, an agency within the Office of the President responsible for (1) preparing and presenting to Congress the president's budget; (2) working with the Council of Economic Advisers and the Treasury Department in developing a fiscal program; (3) reviewing the administrative policies and performance of government agencies; and (4) advising the president on legislative matters.

OFFICE OF THRIFT SUPERVISION (OTS) agency of the U.S. Treasury Department created by Congress's "bailout bill" of August 4, 1989, to replace the disbanded FEDERAL HOME LOAN BANK BOARD and assume responsibility for the nation's ailing savings and loan industry. The legislation empowered OTS to institute new regulations, charter new federal savings and loan associations, and supervise state-chartered banks and savings and loan holding companies.

The bailout bill also created: (1) RESOLUTION TRUST CORPORATION (RTC), which, operating under the management of the FEDERAL DEPOSIT INSURANCE CORPORATION (FDIC), was charged with closing or merging institutions that become insolvent between 1989 and 1992; (2) RESOLUTION FUNDING CORPORATION (REFCORP), charged with borrowing from private capital markets to fund RTC activities and to manage the remaining assets and liabilities taken over by the FEDERAL SAVINGS AND LOAN INSURANCE CORPORATION FSLIC) prior to 1989; (3) SAVINGS ASSOCIATION INSURANCE FUND (SAIF, pronounced "safe"), to replace FSLIC as insurer of thrift deposits and to be administered by FDIC separately from its bank deposit insurance program, which became the BANK INSURANCE FUND (BIF); and (4) FEDERAL HOUSING FINANCE BOARD (FHFB), charged with overseeing the FEDERAL HOME LOAN BANK SYSTEM.

Resolution Trust Corporation (RTC) was scheduled to terminate after 1996, when its responsibilities would shift to SAIF.

See also BAILOUT BOND.

OFFICIAL NOTICE OF SALE notice published by a municipality inviting investment bankers to submit competitive bids for an upcoming bond issue. The notice provides the name of a municipal official from whom further detail can be obtained and states certain basic information about the issue, such as its par value and important conditions. The *Bond Buyer* regularly carries such notices.

OFFICIAL STATEMENT *see* LEGAL OPINION.

OFFSET

Accounting: (1) amount equaling or counterbalancing another amount on the opposite side of the same ledger or the ledger of another account. *See also* ABSORBED. (2) amount that cancels or reduces a claim of any sort.

Banking: (1) bank's legal right to seize deposit funds to cover a loan in default—called *right of offset*. (2) number stored on a bank card that, when related to the code number remembered by the cardholder, represents the depositor's identification number, called *PAN-PIN pair*.

Securities, commodities, options: (1) closing transaction involving the purchase or sale of an OPTION having the same features as one already held. (2) HEDGE, such as the SHORT SALE of a stock to protect a capital gain or the purchase of a future to protect a commodity price, or a STRADDLE representing the purchase of offsetting put and call options on a security.

OFFSHORE term used in the United States for any financial organization with a headquarters outside the country. A MUTUAL FUND with a legal domicile in the Bahamas or the Cayman Islands, for instance, is called an *offshore fund*. To be sold in the United States, such funds must adhere to all pertinent federal and state regulations. Many banks have offshore subsidiaries that engage in activities that are either heavily regulated or taxed or not allowed under U.S. law.

OIL AND GAS LIMITED PARTNERSHIP partnership consisting of one or more limited partners and one or more general partners that is structured to find, extract, and market commercial quantities of oil and natural gas. The limited partners, who assume no liability beyond the funds they contribute, buy units in the partnership, typically for at least $5000 a unit, from a broker registered to sell that partnership. All the limited partners' money then goes to the GENERAL PARTNER, the partner with unlimited liability, who either searches for oil and gas (an exploratory or wildcat well), drills for oil and gas in a proven oil field (a DEVELOPMENTAL DRILLING PROGRAM), or pumps petroleum and gas from an existing well (a COMPLETION PROGRAM). The riskier the chance of finding oil and gas, the higher the potential reward or loss to the limited partner. Conservative investors who mainly want to collect income from the sale of proven oil and gas reserves are safest with a developmental or completion program.

Subject to PASSIVE income rules, limited partners also receive tax breaks, such as depreciation deductions for equipment used for drilling and oil depletion allowances for the value of oil extracted from the fields. If the partnership borrows money for increased drilling, limited partners also can get deductions for the interest cost of the loans. *See also* EXPLORATORY DRILLING PROGRAM; INCOME LIMITED PARTNERSHIP; INTANGIBLE COSTS; LIMITED PARTNERSHIP.

OIL AND GAS LOTTERY program run by the Bureau of Land Management at the U.S. Department of the Interior that permits anyone filing an application to be selected for the right to drill for oil and gas on selected parcels of federal land. Both large oil companies and small speculators enter this lottery. An individual winning the drawing for a particularly desirable plot of land may sublet the property to an oil company, which will pay him or her royalties if the land yields commercial quantities of oil and gas.

OLIGOPOLY market situation in which a small number of selling firms control the market supply of a particular good or service and are therefore able to control the market price. An oligopoly can be *perfect*—where all firms produce an identical good or service (cement)—or *imperfect*—where each firm's product has a different identity but is essentially similar to the others (cigarettes). Because each firm in an oligopoly knows its share of the total market for the product or service it produces, and because any change in price or change in market share by one firm is reflected in the sales of the others, there tends to be a high degree of interdependence among firms; each firm must make its price and output decisions with regard to the responses of the other firms in the oligopoly, so that oligopoly prices, once established, are rigid. This encourages nonprice competition, through advertising, packaging, and service—a generally nonproductive form of resource allocation. Two examples of oligopoly in the United States are airlines serving the same routes and tobacco companies. *See also* OLIGOPSONY.

OLIGOPSONY market situation in which a few large buyers control the purchasing power and therefore the output and market price of a good or service; the buy-side counterpart of OLIGOPOLY. Oligopsony prices tend to be lower than the prices in a freely competitive market, just as oligopoly prices tend to be higher. For example, the large tobacco companies purchase all the output of a large number of small tobacco growers and therefore are able to control tobacco prices.

OMITTED DIVIDEND dividend that was scheduled to be declared by a corporation, but instead was not voted for the time being by the board of directors. Dividends are sometimes omitted when a company has run into financial difficulty and its board decides it is more important to conserve cash than to pay a dividend to shareholders. The announcement of an omitted dividend will typically cause the company's stock price to drop, particularly if the announcement is a surprise.

ON ACCOUNT
In general: in partial payment of an obligation.
Finance: on credit terms. The term applies to a relationship between a seller and a buyer wherein payment is expected sometime after delivery and the obligation is not documented by a NOTE. Synonymous with *open account.*

ON A SCALE *see* SCALE ORDER.

ON-BALANCE VOLUME TECHNICAL ANALYSIS method that attempts to pinpoint when a stock, bond, or commodity is being accumulated by many buyers or is being distributed by many sellers. The on-balance volume line is superimposed on the stock price line on a chart, and it is considered significant when the two lines cross. The chart indicates a buy signal when accumulation is detected and a sell signal when distribution is spotted. The on-balance method can be used to diagnose an entire market or an individual stock, bond, or commodity.

ONE-CANCELS-THE-OTHER ORDER *see* ALTERNATIVE ORDER.

ONE-DECISION STOCK stock with sufficient quality and growth potential to be suitable for a BUY AND HOLD STRATEGY.

ON-FLOOR ORDER security order originating with a member on the floor of an exchange when dealing for his or her own account. The designation separates such orders from those for customers' accounts (OFF-FLOOR ORDERS), which are generally given precedence by exchange rules.

ON MARGIN *see* MARGIN.

OPD ticker tape symbol designating (1) the first transaction of the day in a security after a DELAYED OPENING or (2) the opening transaction in a security whose price has changed significantly from the previous day's close—usually 2 or more points on stocks selling at $20 or higher, 1 or more points on stocks selling at less than $20.

OPEN
Securities:
1. status of an order to buy or sell securities that has still not been executed. A

GOOD-TILL-CANCELED ORDER that remains pending is an example of an open order.

2. to establish an account with a broker.

Banking: to establish an account or a LETTER OF CREDIT.

Finance: unpaid balance.

See also OPEN-END LEASE; OPEN-END MANAGEMENT COMPANY; OPEN-END MORTGAGE; OPEN INTEREST; OPEN ORDER; OPEN REPO.

OPEN-END LEASE lease agreement providing for an additional payment after the property is returned to the lessor, to adjust for any change in the value of the property.

OPEN-END MANAGEMENT COMPANY INVESTMENT COMPANY that sells MUTUAL FUNDS to the public. The terms arises from the fact that the firm continually creates new shares on demand. Mutual fund shareholders buy the shares at NET ASSET VALUE and can redeem them at any time at the prevailing market price, which may be higher or lower than the price at which the investor bought. The shareholder's funds are invested in stocks, bonds, or money market instruments, depending on the type of mutual fund company. The opposite of an open-end management company is a CLOSED-END MANAGEMENT COMPANY, which issues a limited number of shares, which are then traded on a stock exchange.

OPEN-END MORTGAGE

Real estate finance: MORTGAGE that allows the issuance of additional bonds having equal status with the original issue, but that protects the original bondholders with specific restrictions governing subsequent borrowing under the original mortgage. For example, the terms of the original INDENTURE might permit additional mortgage-bond financing up to 75% of the value of the property acquired, but only if total fixed charges on all debt, including the proposed new bonds, have been earned a stated number of times over the previous 5 years. The open-end mortgage is a more practical and acceptable (to the mortgage holder) version of the *open mortgage,* which allows a corporation to issue unlimited amounts of bonds under the original first mortgage, with no protection to the original bondholders. An even more conservative version is the *limited open-end mortgage,* which usually contains the same restrictions as the open-end, but places a limit on the amount of first mortgage bonds that can be issued, and typically provides that proceeds from new bond issues be used to retire outstanding bonds with the same or prior security.

Trust banking: corporate trust indenture that permits the trustee to authenticate and deliver bonds from time to time in addition to the original issue. See also AUTHENTICATION.

OPENING

1. price at which a security or commodity starts a trading day. Investors who want to buy or sell as soon as the market opens will put in an order at the opening price.

2. short time frame of market opportunity. For instance, if interest rates have been rising for months, and for a few days or weeks they fall, a corporation that has wanted to FLOAT bonds at lower interest rates might seize the moment to issue the bonds. This short time frame would be called an *opening in the market* or a *window of opportunity.* See also WINDOW.

OPEN INTEREST total number of contracts in a commodity or options market that are still open; that is, they have not been exercised, closed out, or allowed to expire. The term also applies to a particular commodity or, in the case of options, to the number of contracts outstanding on a particular underlying security. The level of open interest is reported daily in newspaper commodity and options pages.

OPEN-MARKET OPERATIONS activities by which the Securities Department of the Federal Reserve Bank of New York—popularly called the DESK—carries out instructions of the FEDERAL OPEN MARKET COMMITTEE designed to regulate the money supply. Such operations involve the purchase and sale of government securities, which effectively expands or contracts funds in the banking system. This, in turn, alters bank reserves, causing a MULTIPLIER effect on the supply of credit and, therefore, on economic activity generally. Open-market operations represent one of three basic ways the Federal Reserve implements MONETARY POLICY, the others being changes in the member bank RESERVE REQUIREMENTS and raising or lowering the DISCOUNT RATE charged to banks borrowing from the Fed to maintain reserves.

OPEN-MARKET RATES interest rates on various debt instruments bought and sold in the open market that are directly responsive to supply and demand. Such open-market rates are distinguished from the DISCOUNT RATE, set by the FEDERAL RESERVE BOARD as a deliberate measure to influence other rates, and from bank commercial loan rates, which are directly influenced by Federal Reserve policy. The rates on short-term instruments like COMMERCIAL PAPER and banker's AC-CEPTANCES are examples of open-market rates, as are yields on interest-bearing securities of all types traded in the SECONDARY MARKET.

OPEN ON THE PRINT BLOCK POSITIONER's term for a BLOCK trade that has been completed with an institutional client and "printed" on the consolidated tape, but that leaves the block positioner open—that is, with a risk position to be covered. This usually happens when the block positioner is on the sell side of the transaction and sells SHORT what he lacks in inventory to complete the order.

OPEN ORDER buy or sell order for securities that has not yet been executed or canceled; a GOOD-TILL-CANCELED ORDER.

OPEN OUTCRY method of trading on a commodity exchange. The term derives from the fact that traders must shout out their buy or sell offers. When a trader shouts he wants to sell at a particular price and someone else shouts he wants to buy at that price, the two traders have made a contract that will be recorded.

OPEN REPO REPURCHASE AGREEMENT in which the repurchase date is unspecified and the agreement can be terminated by either party at any time. The agreement continues on a day-to-day basis with interest rate adjustments as the market changes.

OPERATING LEASE type of LEASE, normally involving equipment, whereby the contract is written for considerably less than the life of the equipment and the lessor handles all maintenance and servicing; also called *service lease*. Operating leases are the opposite of capital leases, where the lessee acquires essentially all the economic benefits and risks of ownership. Common examples of equipment financed with operating leases are office copiers, computers, automobiles, and trucks. Most operating leases are cancellable, meaning the lessee can return the equipment if it becomes obsolete or is no longer needed.

OPERATING LEVERAGE *see* LEVERAGE.

OPERATING PROFIT (OR LOSS) the difference between the revenues of a business and the related costs and expenses, excluding income derived from sources other than its regular activities and before income deductions; synonymous with *net operating profit (or loss), operating income (or loss),* and *net operating income (or loss).* Income deductions are a class of items comprising the final section of a company's income statement, which, although necessarily incurred in the course of business and customarily charged before arriving at net income, are more in the nature of costs imposed from without than costs subject to the control of everyday operations. They include interest; amortized discount and expense on bonds; income taxes; losses from sales of plants, divisions, major items of property; prior-year adjustments; charges to contingency reserves; bonuses and other periodic profit distributions to officers and employees; write-offs of intangibles; adjustments arising from major changes in accounting methods, such as inventory valuation base; fire, flood, and other extraordinary losses; losses on foreign exchange; and other material and nonrecurrent items.

OPERATING RATIO any of a group of ratios that measure a firm's operating efficiency and effectiveness by relating various income and expense figures from the profit and loss statement to each other and to balance sheet figures. Among the ratios used are sales to cost of goods sold, operating expenses to operating income, net profits to gross income, net income to net worth. Such ratios are most revealing when compared with those of prior periods and with industry averages.

OPERATIONS DEPARTMENT BACK OFFICE of a brokerage firm where all clerical functions having to do with clearance, settlement, and execution of trades are handled. This department keeps customer records and handles the day-to-day monitoring of margin positions.

OPM
1. other people's money; Wall Street slang for the use of borrowed funds by individuals or companies to increase the return on invested capital. *See also* FINANCIAL LEVERAGE.
2. options pricing model. *See* BLACK-SCHOLES OPTION PRICING MODEL.

OPPORTUNITY COST

In general: highest price or rate of return an alternative course of action would provide.

Corporate finance: concept widely used in business planning; for example, in evaluating a CAPITAL INVESTMENT project, a company must measure the projected return against the return it would earn on the highest yielding alternative investment involving similar risk. *See also* COST OF CAPITAL.

Securities investments: cost of forgoing a safe return on an investment in hopes of making a larger profit. For instance, an investor might buy a stock that shows great promise but yields only 4%, even though a higher safe return is available in a money market fund yielding 10%. The 6% yield difference is called the opportunity cost.

OPTIMUM CAPACITY level of output of manufacturing operations that produces the lowest cost per unit. For example, a tire factory may produce tires at $30 apiece if it turns out 10,000 tires a month, but the tires can be made for $20 apiece if the plant operates at its optimum capacity of 100,000 tires a month. *See also* MARGINAL COST.

OPTION

In general: right to buy or sell property that is granted in exchange for an agreed-upon sum. If the right is not exercised after a specified period, the option expires and the option buyer forfeits the money. *See also* EXERCISE.

Securities: securities transaction agreement tied to stocks, commodities, or stock indexes. Options are traded on many exchanges.

1. a CALL OPTION gives its buyer the right to buy 100 shares of the underlying security at a fixed price before a specified date in the future—usually three, six, or nine months. For this right, the call option buyer pays the call option seller, called the writer, a fee called a PREMIUM, which is forfeited if the buyer does not exercise the option before the agreed-upon date. A call buyer therefore speculates that the price of the underlying shares will rise within the specified time period. For example, a call option on 100 shares of XYZ stock may grant its buyer the right to buy those shares at $100 apiece anytime in the next three months. To buy that option, the buyer may have to pay a premium of $2 a share, or $200. If at the time of the option contract XYZ is selling for $95 a share, the option buyer will profit if XYZ's stock price rises. If XYZ shoots up to $120 a share in two months, for example, the option buyer can EXERCISE his or her option to buy 100 shares of the stock at $100 and then sell the shares for $120 each, keeping the difference as profit (minus the $2 premium per share). On the other hand, if XYZ drops below $95 and stays there for three months, at the end of that time the call option will expire and the call buyer will receive no return on the $2 a share investment premium of $200.

2. the opposite of a call option is a PUT OPTION, which gives its buyer the right to sell a specified number of shares of a stock at a particular price within a specified time period. Put buyers expect the price of the underlying stock to fall. Someone who thinks XYZ's stock price will fall might buy a three-month XYZ put for 100 shares at $100 apiece and pay a premium of $2. If XYZ falls to $80 a share, the put buyer can then exercise his or her right to sell 100 XYZ shares at $100. The buyer will first purchase 100 shares at $80 each and then sell them to the put option seller (writer) at $100 each, thereby making a profit of $18 a share (the $20 a share profit minus the $2 a share cost of the option premium).

In practice, most call and put options are rarely exercised. Instead, investors buy and sell options before expiration, trading on the rise and fall of premium prices. Because an option buyer must put up only a small amount of money (the premium) to control a large amount of stock, options trading provides a great deal of LEVERAGE and can prove immensely profitable. Options traders can write either covered options, in which they own the underlying security, or far riskier naked options, for which they do not own the underlying security. Often, options traders lose many premiums on unsuccessful trades before they make a very profitable trade. More sophisticated traders combine various call and put options in SPREAD and STRADDLE positions. Their profits or losses result from the narrowing or widening of spreads between option prices.

An *incentive stock option* is granted to corporate executives if the company achieves certain financial goals, such as a level of sales or profits. The executive is granted the option of buying company stock at a below-market price and selling the stock in the market for a profit.

See also CALL; COVERED OPTION; DEEP IN (OUT OF) THE MONEY; IN THE MONEY; NAKED OPTION; OPTION WRITER; OUT OF THE MONEY.

OPTION AGREEMENT form filled out by a brokerage firm's customer when opening an option account. It details financial information about the customer, who agrees to follow the rules and regulations of options trading. This agreement, also called the *option information form,* assures the broker that the customer's financial resources are adequate to withstand any losses that may occur from options trading. The customer must receive a prospectus from the OPTIONS CLEARING CORPORATION before he or she can begin trading.

OPTIONAL DIVIDEND dividend that can be paid either in cash or in stock. The shareholder entitled to the dividend makes the choice.

OPTIONAL PAYMENT BOND bond whose principal and/or interest are payable, at the option of the holder, in one or more foreign currencies as well as in domestic currency.

OPTION HOLDER someone who has bought a call or put OPTION but has not yet exercised or sold it. A call option holder wants the price of the underlying security to rise; a put option holder wants the price of the underlying security to fall.

OPTION MUTUAL FUND MUTUAL FUND that either buys or sells options in order to increase the value of fund shares. OPTION mutual funds may be either conservative or aggressive. For instance, a conservative fund may buy stocks and increase shareholders' income through the PREMIUM earned by selling put and call options on the stocks in the fund's portfolio. This kind of fund would be called an *option income fund.* At the opposite extreme, an aggressive *option growth fund* may buy puts and calls in stocks that the fund manager thinks are about to fall or rise sharply; if the fund manager is right, large profits can be earned through EXERCISE of the options. The LEVERAGE that options provide makes it possible to multiply the return on invested funds many times over.

OPTION PREMIUM amount per share paid by an OPTION buyer to an option seller for the right to buy (call) or sell (put) the underlying security at a particular price within a specified period. Option premium prices are quoted in increments of eighths or sixteenths of 1% and are printed in the options tables of daily newspapers. A PREMIUM of $5 per share means an option buyer would pay $500 for an option on 100 shares. *See also* CALL OPTION; PUT OPTION.

OPTIONS CLEARING CORPORATION (OCC) corporation that handles options transactions on the stock exchanges and is owned by the exchanges. It issues all options contracts and guarantees that the obligations of both parties to a trade are fulfilled. The OCC also processes the exchange of money on all options trades and maintains records of those trades. Its prospectus is given to all investors to read before they can trade in options. This prospectus outlines the rules and risks of trading and sets the standards for ethical conduct on the part of options traders. *See also* OPTION.

OPTION SERIES options of the same class (puts or calls with the same underlying security) that also have the same EXERCISE PRICE and maturity month. For instance, all XYZ October 80 calls are a series, as are all ABC July 100 puts. *See also* OPTION.

OPTION SPREAD buying and selling of options within the same CLASS at the same time. The investor who uses the OPTION spread strategy hopes to profit from the widening or narrowing of the SPREAD between the various options. Option spreads can be designed to be profitable in either up or down markets.
    Some examples:
    (1) entering into two options at the same EXERCISE PRICE, but with different

maturity dates. For instance, an investor could buy an XYZ April 60 call and sell an XYZ July 60 call.

(2) entering into two options at different STRIKE PRICES with the same expiration month. For example, an investor could buy an XYZ April 60 call and sell an XYZ April 70 call.

(3) entering into two options at different strike prices with different expiration months. For instance, an investor could buy an XYZ April 60 call and sell an XYZ July 70 call.

OPTION WRITER person or financial institution that sells put and call options. A writer of a PUT OPTION contracts to buy 100 shares of stock from the put option buyer by a certain date for a fixed price. For example, an option writer who sells XYZ April 50 put agrees to buy XYZ stock from the put buyer at $50 a share any time until the contract expires in April.

A writer of a CALL OPTION, on the other hand, guarantees to sell the call option buyer the underlying stock at a particular price before a certain date. For instance, a writer of an XYZ April 50 call agrees to sell stock at $50 a share to the call buyer any time before April.

In exchange for granting this right, the option writer receives a payment called an OPTION PREMIUM. For holders of large portfolios of the premiums from stocks, option writing therefore is a source of additional income.

OR BETTER Indication, abbreviated OB on the ORDER TICKET of a LIMIT ORDER to buy or sell securities, that the broker should transact the order at a price better than the specified LIMIT PRICE if a better price can be obtained.

ORDER

Investments: instruction to a broker or dealer to buy or sell securities or commodities. Securities orders fall into four basic categories: MARKET ORDER, LIMIT ORDER, time order, and STOP ORDER.

Law: direction from a court of jurisdiction, or a regulation.

Negotiable instruments: payee's request to the maker, as on a check stating, "Pay to the order of (when presented by) John Doe."

Trade: request to buy, sell, deliver, or receive goods or services which commits the issuer of the order to the terms specified.

ORDER TICKET form completed by a registered representative (ACCOUNT EXECUTIVE) of a brokerage firm, upon receiving order instructions from a customer. It shows whether the order is to buy or to sell, the number of units, the name of the security, the kind of order (ORDER MARKET, LIMIT ORDER or STOP ORDER) and the customer's name or code number. After execution of the order on the exchange floor or in the firm's trading department (if over the counter), the price is written and circled on the order ticket, and the completing broker is indicated by number. The order ticket must be retained for a certain period in compliance with federal law.

ORDINARY INCOME income from the normal activities of an individual or business, as distinguished from CAPITAL GAINS from the sale of assets. Prior to the TAX REFORM ACT OF 1986, the long-term CAPITAL GAINS TAX was lower than that on ordinary income. The 1986 Act eliminated the preferential capital gains rate, but it kept the separate statutory language to allow for future increases in ordinary income rates.

ORDINARY INTEREST simple interest based on a 360-day year rather than on a 365-day year (the latter is called *exact interest*). The difference between the two bases when calculating daily interest on large sums of money can be substantial. The ratio of ordinary interest to exact interest is 1.0139.

ORGANIZATION CHART chart showing the interrelationships of positions within an organization in terms of authority and responsibility. There are basically three patterns of organization: *line organization,* in which a single manager has final authority over a group of foremen or middle management supervisors; *functional organization,* in which a general manager supervises a number of managers identified by function; and *line and staff organization,* which is a combination of line and functional organization, with specialists in particular functions holding staff positions where they advise line officers concerned with actual production.

ORIGINAL COST
1. in accounting, all costs associated with the acquisition of an asset.
2. in public utilities accounting, the acquisition cost incurred by the entity that first devotes a property to public use; normally, the utility company's cost for the property. It is used to establish the rate to be charged customers in order to provide the utility company with a FAIR RATE OF RETURN on capital.

ORIGINAL ISSUE DISCOUNT discount from PAR VALUE at the time a bond is issued. (Although the par value of bonds is normally $1000, $100 is used when traders quote prices.) A bond may be issued at $50 ($500) per bond instead of $100 ($1000), for example. The bond will mature at $100 ($1000), however, so that an investor has a built-in gain if the bond is held until maturity. The most extreme version of an original issue discount is a ZERO-COUPON BOND, which is originally sold at far below par value and pays no interest until it matures.
   The tax treatment of original issue discount bonds is complex. The Internal Revenue Service assumes a certain rate of appreciation of the bond every year until maturity. No capital gain or loss will be incurred if the bond is sold for that estimated amount. But if the bond is sold for more than the assumed amount, a CAPITAL GAINS TAX or a tax at the ORDINARY INCOME rate is due.

ORIGINAL MATURITY interval between the issue date and the maturity date of a bond, as distinguished from current maturity, which is the time difference between the present time and the maturity date. For example, in 1987 a bond issued in 1985 to mature in 2005 would have an original maturity of 20 years and a current maturity of 18 years.

ORIGINATOR
1. bank, savings and loan, or mortgage banker that initially made the mortgage loan comprising part of a pool of mortgages.
2. investment banking firm that worked with the issuer of a new securities offering from the early planning stages and that usually is appointed manager of the underwriting SYNDICATE; more formally called the *originating investment banker.*
3. in banking terminology, the initiator of money transfer instructions.

OTC *see* OVER THE COUNTER.

OTC MARGIN STOCK shares of certain large firms traded OVER THE COUNTER that qualify as margin securities under REGULATION T of the Federal Reserve

Board. Such stock must meet rigid criteria, and the list of eligible OTC shares is under constant review by the Fed. *See also* MARGIN SECURITY.

OTHER INCOME heading on a profit and loss statement for income from activities not in the normal course of business; sometimes called *other revenue*. Examples: interest on customers' notes, dividends and interest from investments, profit from the disposal of assets other than inventory, gain on foreign exchange, miscellaneous rent income. *See also* EXTRAORDINARY ITEM.

OTHER PEOPLE'S MONEY *see* OPM.

OUT-OF-FAVOR INDUSTRY OR STOCK industry or stock that is currently unpopular with investors. For example, the investing public may be disenchanted with an industry's poor earnings outlook. If interest rates were rising, interest-sensitive stocks such as banks and savings and loans would be out of favor because rising rates might harm these firms' profits. CONTRARIAN investors—those who consciously do the opposite of most other investors—tend to buy out-of-favor stocks because they can be bought cheaply. When the earnings of these stocks pick up, contrarians typically sell the stocks. Out-of-favor stocks tend to have a low PRICE/EARNINGS RATIO.

OUT OF LINE term describing a stock that is too high or too low in price in comparison with similar-quality stocks. A comparison of this sort is usually based on the PRICE/EARNINGS RATIO (PE), which measures how much investors are willing to pay for a firm's earnings prospects. If most computer industry stocks had PEs of 15, for instance, and XYZ Computers had a PE of only 10, analysts would say that XYZ's price is out of line with the rest of the industry.

OUT OF THE MONEY term used to describe an OPTION whose STRIKE PRICE for a stock is either higher than the current market value, in the case of a CALL, or lower, in the case of a PUT. For example, an XYZ December 60 CALL option would be out of the money when XYZ stock was selling for $55 a share. Similarly, an XYZ December 60 PUT OPTION would be out of the money when XYZ stock was selling for $65 a share.

Someone buying an out-of-the-money option hopes that the option will move IN THE MONEY, or at least in that direction. The buyer of the above XYZ call would want the stock to climb above $60 a share, whereas the put buyer would like the stock to drop below $60 a share.

OUTSIDE DIRECTOR member of a company's BOARD OF DIRECTORS who is not an employee of the company. Such directors are considered important because they are presumed to bring unbiased opinions to major corporate decisions and also can contribute diverse experience to the decision-making process. A retailing company may have outside directors with experience in finance and manufacturing, for instance. To avoid conflict of interest, outside directors never serve on the boards of two directly competing corporations. Directors receive fees from the company in return for their service, usually a set amount for each board meeting they attend.

OUTSTANDING
1. unpaid; used of ACCOUNTS RECEIVABLE and debt obligations of all types.
2. not yet presented for payment, as a check or draft.
3. stock held by shareholders, shown on corporate balance sheets under the heading of CAPITAL STOCK issued and outstanding.

OUT THE WINDOW term describing the rapid way a very successful NEW ISSUE of securities is marketed to investors. An issue that goes out the window is also called a BLOWOUT. *See also* HOT ISSUE.

OVERALL MARKET PRICE COVERAGE total assets less intangibles divided by the total of (1) the MARKET VALUE of the security issue in question and (2) the BOOK VALUE of liabilities and issues having a prior claim. The answer indicates the extent to which the market value of a particular CLASS of securities is covered in the event of a company's liquidation.

OVERBOOKED *see* OVERSUBSCRIBED.

OVERBOUGHT description of a security or a market that has recently experienced an unexpectedly sharp price rise and is therefore vulnerable to a price drop (called a CORRECTION by technical analysts). When a stock has been overbought, there are fewer buyers left to drive the price up further. *See also* OVERSOLD.

OVERHANG sizable block of securities or commodities contracts that, if released on the market, would put downward pressure on prices. Examples of overhang include shares held in a dealer's inventory, a large institutional holding, a secondary distribution still in registration, and a large commodity position about to be liquidated. Overhang inhibits buying activity that would otherwise translate into upward price movement.

OVERHEAD
1. costs of a business that are not directly associated with the production or sale of goods or services. Also called INDIRECT COSTS AND EXPENSES, *burden* and, in Great Britain, *oncosts*.
2. sometimes used in a more limited sense, as in manufacturing or factory overhead.
   See also DIRECT OVERHEAD.

OVERHEATING term describing an economy that is expanding so rapidly that economists fear a rise in INFLATION. In an overheated economy, too much money is chasing too few goods, leading to price rises, and the productive capacity of a nation is usually nearing its limit. The remedies in the United States are usually a tightening of the money supply by the Federal Reserve and curbs in federal government spending. *See also* MONETARY POLICY; OPTIMUM CAPACITY.

OVERISSUE shares of CAPITAL STOCK issued in excess of those authorized. Preventing overissue is the function of a corporation's REGISTRAR (usually a bank acting as agent), which works closely with the TRANSFER AGENT in canceling and reissuing certificates presented for transfer and in issuing new shares.

OVERLAPPING DEBT municipal accounting term referring to a municipality's share of the debt of its political subdivisions or the special districts sharing its geographical area. It is usually determined by the ratio of ASSESSED VALUATION of taxable property lying within the corporate limits of the municipality to the assessed valuation of each overlapping district. Overlapping debt is often greater than the direct debt of a municipality, and both must be taken into account in determining the debt burden carried by taxable real estate within a municipality when evaluating MUNICIPAL BOND investments.

OVERNIGHT POSITION broker-dealer's LONG POSITION or SHORT POSITION in a security at the end of a trading day.

OVERNIGHT REPO overnight REPURCHASE AGREEMENT; an arrangement whereby securities dealers and banks finance their inventories of Treasury bills, notes, and bonds. The dealer or bank sells securities to an investor with a temporary surplus of cash, agreeing to buy them back the next day. Such transactions are settled in immediately available FEDERAL FUNDS, usually at a rate below the federal funds rate (the rate charged by banks lending funds to each other).

OVERSOLD description of a stock or market that has experienced an unexpectedly sharp price decline and is therefore due, according to some proponents of TECHNICAL ANALYSIS, for an imminent price rise. If all those who wanted to sell a stock have done so, there are no sellers left, and so the price will rise. *See also* OVERBOUGHT.

OVERSUBSCRIBED underwriting term describing a new stock issue for which there are more buyers than available shares. An oversubscribed, or *overbooked,* issue often will jump in price as soon as its shares go on the market, since the buyers who could not get shares will want to buy once the stock starts trading. In some cases, an issuer will increase the number of shares available if the issue is oversubscribed. *See also* GREEN SHOE; HOT ISSUE.

OVER THE COUNTER (OTC)
1. security that is not listed and traded on an organized exchange.
2. market in which securities transactions are conducted through a telephone and computer network connecting dealers in stocks and bonds, rather than on the floor of an exchange.

    Over-the-counter stocks are traditionally those of smaller companies that do not meet the LISTING REQUIREMENTS of the New York Stock Exchange or the American Stock Exchange. In recent years, however, many companies that qualify for listing have chosen to remain with over-the-counter trading, because they feel that the system of multiple trading by many dealers is preferable to the centralized trading approach of the New York Stock Exchange, where all trading in a stock has to go through the exchange SPECIALIST in that stock. The rules of over-the-counter stock trading are written and enforced largely by the NATIONAL ASSOCIATION OF SECURITIES DEALERS (NASD), a self-regulatory group. Prices of over-the-counter stocks are published in daily newspapers, with the NATIONAL MARKET SYSTEM stocks listed separately from the rest of the over-the-counter market. Other over-the-counter markets include those for government and municipal bonds. *See also* NASDAQ.

OVERTRADING

Finance: practice of a firm that expands sales beyond levels that can be financed with normal WORKING CAPITAL. Continued overtrading leads to delinquent ACCOUNTS PAYABLE and ultimately to default on borrowings.

New issue underwriting: practice whereby a member of an underwriting group induces a brokerage client to buy a portion of a new issue by purchasing other securities from the client at a premium. The underwriter breaks even on the deal because the premium is offset by the UNDERWRITING SPREAD.

Securities: excessive buying and selling by a broker in a DISCRETIONARY ACCOUNT. *See also* CHURNING.

OVERVALUED description of a stock whose current price is not justified by the earnings outlook or the PRICE/EARNINGS RATIO. It is therefore expected that the stock will drop in price. Overvaluation may result from an emotional buying spurt, which inflates the market price of the stock, or from a deterioration of the company's financial strength. The opposite of overvalued is UNDERVALUED. *See also* FULLY VALUED.

OVERWRITING speculative practice by an OPTION WRITER who believes a security to be overpriced or underpriced and sells CALL OPTIONS or PUT OPTIONS on the security in quantity, assuming they will not be exercised. *See also* OPTION.

P

PACIFIC SOCK EXCHANGE *see* REGIONAL STOCK EXCHANGES.

PAC-MAN STRATEGY technique used by a corporation that is the target of a takeover bid to defeat the acquirer's wishes. The TARGET COMPANY defends itself by threatening to take over the acquirer and begins buying its common shares. For instance, if company A moves to take over company B against the wishes of the management of company B, company B will begin buying shares in company A in order to thwart A's takeover attempt. The Pac-Man strategy is named after a popular video game of the early 1980s, in which each character that does not swallow its opponents is itself consumed. *See also* TAKEOVER; TENDER OFFER.

PAID-IN CAPITAL capital received from investors in exchange for stock, as distinguished from capital generated from earnings or donated. The paid-in capital account includes CAPITAL STOCK and contributions of stockholders credited to accounts other than capital stock, such as an excess over PAR value received from the sale or exchange of capital stock. It would also include surplus resulting from RECAPITALIZATION. Paid-in capital is sometimes classified more specifically as *additional paid-in capital, paid-in surplus,* or *capital surplus.* Such accounts are distinguished from RETAINED EARNINGS or its older variation, EARNED SURPLUS. *See also* DONATED STOCK.

PAID-IN SURPLUS *see* PAID-IN CAPITAL.

PAINTING THE TAPE
1. illegal practice by manipulators who buy and sell a particular security among themselves to create artificial trading activity, causing a succession of trades to be reported on the CONSOLIDATED TAPE and luring unwary investors to the "action." After causing movement in the market price of the security, the manipulators hope to sell at a profit.
2. consecutive or frequent trading in a particular security, resulting in its repeated appearances on the ticker tape. Such activity is usually attributable to special investor interest in the security.

PAIRED SHARES common stocks of two companies under the same management that are sold as a unit, usually appearing as a single certificate printed front and back. Also called *Siamese shares* or *stapled stock.*

P & L *see* PROFIT AND LOSS STATEMENT.

PAPER PROFIT OR LOSS unrealized CAPITAL GAIN or CAPITAL LOSS in an investment or PORTFOLIO. Paper profits and losses are calculated by comparing the current market prices of all stocks, bonds, mutual funds, and commodities in a portfolio to the prices at which those assets were originally bought. These profits or losses become realized only when the securities are sold.

PAR equal to the nominal or FACE VALUE of a security. A bond selling at par, for instance, is worth the same dollar amount it was issued for or at which it will be redeemed at maturity—typically, $1000 per bond.

With COMMON STOCK, par value is set by the company issuing the stock. At one time, par value represented the original investment behind each share of stock in goods, cash, and services, but today this is rarely the case. Instead, it is an assigned amount (such as $1 a share) used to compute the dollar accounting value of the common shares on a company's balance sheet. Par value has no relation to MARKET VALUE, which is determined by such considerations as NET ASSET VALUE, YIELD, and investors' expectations of future earnings. Some companies issueNO-PAR VALUE STOCK. *See also* STATED VALUE.

Par value has more importance for bonds and PREFERRED STOCK. The interest paid on bonds is based on a percentage of a bond's par value—a 10% bond pays 10% of the bond's par value annually. Preferred dividends are normally stated as a percentage of the par value of the preferred stock issue.

PAR BOND bond that is selling at PAR, the amount equal to its nominal value or FACE VALUE. A corporate bond redeemable at maturity for $1000 is a par bond when it trades on the market for $1000.

PARENT COMPANY company that owns or controls subsidiaries through the ownership of voting stock. A parent company is usually an operating company in its own right; where it has no business of its own, the term HOLDING COMPANY is often preferred.

PARETO'S LAW theory that the pattern of income distribution is constant, historically and geographically, regardless of taxation or welfare policies; also called *law of the trivial many and the critical few* or *80-20 law*. Thus, if 80% of a nation's income will benefit only 20% of the population, the only way to improve the economic lot of the poor is to increase overall output and income levels.

Other applications of the law include the idea that in most business activities a small percentage of the work force produces the major portion of output or that 20% of the customers account for 80% of the dollar volume of sales. The law is attributed to Vilfredo Pareto, an Italian-Swiss engineer and economist (1848–1923).

Pareto is also credited with the concept called *Paretian optimum* (or *optimality*) that resources are optimally distributed when an individual cannot move into a better position without putting someone else into a worse position.

PARITY PRICE price for a commodity or service that is pegged to another price or to a composite average of prices based on a selected prior period. As the two sets of prices vary, they are reflected in an index number on a scale of 100. For example, U.S. farm prices are pegged to prices based on the purchasing power of farmers in the period from 1910 to 1914. If the parity ratio is below 100, reflecting a reduction in purchasing power to the extent indicated, the government compensates the farmer by paying a certain percentage of parity, either in the form of a direct cash payment, in the purchase of surplus crops, or in a NONRE-COURSE LOAN.

The concept of parity is also widely applied in industrial wage contracts as a means of preserving the real value of wages.

PARKING placing assets in a safe investment while other investment alternatives are under consideration. For instance, an investor will park the proceeds of a stock or bond sale in an interest-bearing money market fund while considering what other stocks or bonds to purchase.

PARTIAL DELIVERY term used when a broker does not deliver the full amount of a security or commodity called for by a contract. If 10,000 shares were to be delivered, for example, and only 7000 shares are transferred, it is called a partial delivery.

PARTICIPATING PREFERRED STOCK PREFERRED STOCK that, in addition to paying a stipulated dividend, gives the holder the right to participate with the common stockholder in additional distributions of earnings under specified conditions. One example would be an arrangement whereby preferred shareholders are paid $5 per share, then common shareholders are paid $5 per share, and then preferred and common shareholders share equally in further dividends up to $1 per share in any one year.

Participating preferred issues are rare. They are used when special measures are necessary to attract investors. Most preferred stock is *nonparticipating preferred stock,* paying only the stipulated dividends.

PARTICIPATION CERTIFICATE certificate representing an interest in a POOL of funds or in other instruments, such as a MORTGAGE POOL. The following quasi-governmental agencies issue and/or guarantee such certificates (also called PASS-THROUGH SECURITIES): FEDERAL HOME LOAN MORTGAGE CORPORATION, FEDERAL NATIONAL MORTGAGE ASSOCIATION, GOVERNMENT NATIONAL MORTGAGE ASSOCIATION.

PARTICIPATION LOAN

Commercial lending: loan made by more than one lender and serviced (administered) by one of the participants, called the *lead bank* or *lead lender.* Participation loans make it possible for large borrowers to obtain bank financing when the amount involved exceeds the legal lending limit of an individual bank (approximately 10% of a bank's capital).

Real estate: mortgage loan, made by a lead lender, in which other lenders own an interest.

PARTNERSHIP contract between two or more people in a joint business who agree to pool their funds and talent and share in the profits and losses of the enterprise. Those who are responsible for the day-to-day management of the partnership's activities, whose individual acts are binding on the other partners, and who are personally liable for the partnership's total liabilities are called *general partners.* Those who contribute only money and are not involved in management decisions are called *limited partners;* their liability is limited to their investment.

Partnerships are a common form of organization for service professions such as accounting and law. Each accountant or lawyer made a partner earns a percentage of the firm's profits.

Limited partnerships are also sold to investors by brokerage firms, financial planners, and other registered representatives. These partnerships may be either public (meaning that a large number of investors will participate and the partnership's plans must be filed with the Securities and Exchange Commission) or private (meaning that only a limited number of investors may participate and the plan need not be filed with the SEC). Both public and private limited partnerships invest in real estate, oil and gas, research and development, and equipment leasing. Some of these partnerships are oriented towards offering tax advantages and capital gains to limited partners, while others are designed to provide mostly income and some capital gains.

See also GENERAL PARTNER; LIMITED PARTNERSHIP; OIL AND GAS LIMITED PARTNERSHIP; PRIVATE LIMITED PARTNERSHIP; PUBLIC LIMITED PARTNERSHIP.

PAR VALUE *see* PAR.

PAR VALUE OF CURRENCY ratio of one nation's currency unit to that of another country, as defined by the official exchange rates between the two countries; also called *par of exchange* or *par exchange rate*. Since 1971, exchange rates have been allowed to float; that is, instead of official rates of exchange, currency values are being determined by the forces of supply and demand in combination with the buying and selling by countries of their own currencies in order to stabilize the market value, a form of PEGGING.

PASSED DIVIDEND *see* OMITTED DIVIDEND; CUMULATIVE PREFERRED.

PASSIVE income or loss from activities in which a taxpayer does not materially participate, such as LIMITED PARTNERSHIPS, as distinguished from (1) income from wages and active trade or business or (2) *investment (or portfolio) income*, such as dividends and interest. Under the TAX REFORM ACT OF 1986, losses and credits from passive activities are deductible only against income and tax from passive activities, although one passive activity can offset another and unused passive losses can be carried forward. For preenactment passive interests, 65% of net passive losses can be applied against nonpassive income in 1987, 40% in 1988, 20% in 1989, and 10% in 1990. Real estate rental activities are considered passive regardless of material participation, but $25,000 can be deducted against nonpassive activities (phasing out for incomes over $100,000 with special provisions for low-income and rehabilitation housing).

PASSIVE BOND BOND that yields no interest. Such bonds sometimes arise out of reorganizations or are used in NOT-FOR-PROFIT fund raising.

PASSIVE INVESTING
1. putting money in an investment deemed *passive* by the Internal Revenue Service, such as a LIMITED PARTNERSHIP.
2. investing in a MUTUAL FUND that replicates a market index, such as the STANDARD & POOR'S INDEX, thus assuring investment performance no worse (or better) than the market as a whole. An INDEX FUND charges a much lower MANAGEMENT FEE than an ordinary mutual fund.

PASS-THROUGH SECURITY security, representing pooled debt obligations repackaged as shares, that passes income from debtors through the intermediary to investors. The most common type of pass-through is a MORTGAGE-BACKED CERTIFICATE, usually government-guaranteed, where homeowners' principal and interest payments pass from the originating bank or savings and loan through a governmental agency or investment bank to investors, net of service charges. Pass-throughs representing other types of assets, such as auto loan paper or student loans, are also widely marketed. *See also* CERTIFICATE OF AUTOMOBILE RECEIVABLES (CARS); COLLATERALIZED MORTGAGE OBLIGATION; REMIC.

PAYBACK PERIOD in capital budgeting; the length of time needed to recoup the cost of a CAPITAL INVESTMENT. The payback period is the ratio of the initial investment (cash outlay) to the annual cash inflows for the recovery period. The major shortcoming of the payback period method is that it does not take into account cash flows after the payback period and is therefore not a measure of the profitability of an investment project. For this reason, analysts generally prefer the DISCOUNTED CASH FLOW methods of capital budgeting—namely, the INTERNAL RATE OF RETURN and the NET PRESENT VALUE methods.

PAYDOWN

Bonds: refunding by a company of an outstanding bond issue through a smaller new bond issue, usually to cut interest costs. For instance, a company that issued $100 million of 12% bonds a few years ago will pay down (refund) that debt with a new $80 million issue with an 8% yield. The amount of the net deduction is called the paydown.

Lending: repayment of principal short of full payment. *See also* ON ACCOUNT.

PAYING AGENT agent, usually a bank, that receives funds from an issuer of bonds or stock and in turn pays principal and interest to bondholders and dividends to stockholders, usually charging a fee for the service. Sometimes called *disbursing agent.*

PAYMENT DATE date on which a declared stock dividend or a bond interest payment is scheduled to be paid.

PAYOUT RATIO percentage of a firm's profits that is paid out to shareholders in the form of dividends. Young, fast-growing companies reinvest most of their earnings in their business and usually do not pay dividends. Regulated electric, gas, and telephone utility companies have historically paid out larger proportions of their highly dependable earnings in dividends than have other industrial corporations. Since these utilities are limited to a specified return on assets and are thus not able to generate from internal operations the cash flow needed for expansion, they pay large dividends to keep their stock attractive to investors desiring yield and are able to finance growth through new securities offerings. *See also* RETENTION RATE.

PAY UP
1. situation when an investor who wants to buy a stock at a particular price hesitates and the stock begins to rise. Instead of letting the stock go, he "pays up" to buy the shares at the higher prevailing price.
2. when an investor buys shares in a high quality company at what is felt to be a high price. Such an investor will say "I realize that I am paying up for this stock, but it is worth it because it is such a fine company."

PEGGING stabilizing the price of a security, commodity, or currency by intervening in a market. For example, until 1971 governments pegged the price of gold at certain levels to stabilize their currencies and would therefore buy it when the price dropped and sell when the price rose. Since 1971, a FLOATING EXCHANGE RATE system has prevailed, in which countries use pegging—the buying or selling of their own currencies—simply to offset fluctuations in the exchange rate. The U.S. government uses pegging in another way to support the prices of agricultural commodities; *see* PARITY PRICE.

In floating new stock issues, the managing underwriter is authorized to try to peg the market price and stabilize the market in the issuer's stock by buying shares in the open market. With this one exception, securities price pegging is illegal and is regulated by the Securities and Exchange Commission. *See also* STABILIZATION.

PENALTY CLAUSE clause found in contracts, borrowing agreements, and savings instruments providing for penalties in the event a contract is not kept, a loan payment is late, or a withdrawal is made prematurely. *See also* PREPAYMENT PENALTY.

PENNANT technical chart pattern resembling a pointed flag, with the point facing to the right. Unlike a FLAG pattern, in which rallies and peaks occur in a uniform range, it is formed as the rallies and peaks that give it its shape become less pronounced. A pennant is also characterized by diminishing trade volume. With these differences, this pattern has essentially the same significance as a flag; that is, prices will rise or fall sharply once the pattern is complete.

PENNANT

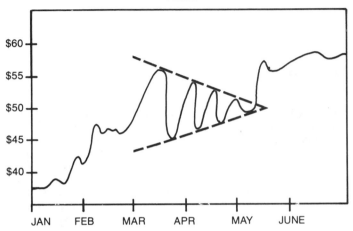

PENNY STOCK stock that typically sells for less than $1 a share, although it may rise to as much as $10 a share after the initial PUBLIC OFFERING, usually because of heavy promotion. Penny stocks are issued by companies with a short or erratic history of revenues and earnings, and therefore such stocks are more VOLATILE than those of large, well-established firms traded on the New York or American stock exchanges. Many brokerage houses therefore have special precautionary rules about trading in these stocks.

All penny stocks are traded OVER-THE-COUNTER, many of them in the local markets of Denver, Vancouver, or Salt Lake City. These markets have had a history of boom and bust, with a speculative fervor for oil, gas, and gold-mining stocks in the Denver penny stock market in the late 1970s turning to bust by the early 1980s.

PENSION BENEFIT GUARANTY CORPORATION (PBGC) federal corporation established under the EMPLOYEE RETIREMENT INCOME SECURITY ACT of 1974 (ERISA) to guarantee basic pension benefits in covered plans by administering terminated plans and placing liens on corporate assets for certain pension liabilities that were not funded. To be covered, a plan must promise clearly defined benefits to more than 25 employees. *See also* PENSION FUND.

PENSION FUND fund set up by a corporation, labor union, governmental entity, or other organization to pay the pension benefits of retired workers. Pension funds invest billions of dollars annually in the stock and bond markets, and are therefore a major factor in the supply-demand balance of the markets. Earnings on the investment portfolios of pension funds are TAX DEFERRED. Fund managers make actuarial assumptions about how much they will be required to pay out to pensioners and then try to ensure that the RATE OF RETURN on their portfolios equals or exceeds that anticipated payout need. *See also* APPROVED LIST; EMPLOYEE RETIREMENT INCOME SECURITY ACT; PRUDENT-MAN RULE; VESTING.

PER CAPITA DEBT total bonded debt of a municipality, divided by its population. A more refined version, called *net per capita debt*, divides the total bonded debt less applicable sinking funds by the total population. The result of either ratio, compared with ratios of prior periods, reveals trends in a municipality's debt burden, which bond analysts evaluate, bearing in mind that, historically, defaults in times of recession have generally followed overexpansion of debts in previous boom periods.

PERCENTAGE-OF-COMPLETION CAPITALIZED COST METHOD *see* COMPLETED CONTRACT METHOD.

PERCENTAGE ORDER order to a securities broker to buy or sell a specified number of shares of a stock after a fixed number of these shares have been traded. It can be a LIMIT ORDER or a MARKET ORDER and usually applies to one day.

PERFECT COMPETITION market condition wherein no buyer or seller has the power to alter the market price of a good or service. Characteristics of a perfectly competitive market are a large number of buyers and sellers, a homogeneous (similar) good or service, an equal awareness of prices and volume, an absence of discrimination in buying and selling, total mobility of productive resources, and complete freedom of entry. Perfect competition exists only as a theoretical ideal. Also called *pure competition*.

PERFECT HEDGE *see* HEDGE/HEDGING.

PERFORMANCE BOND surety bond given by one party to another, protecting the second party against loss in the event the terms of a contract are not fulfilled. The surety company is primarily liable with the principal (the contractor) for nonperformance. For example, a homeowner having a new kitchen put in may request a performance bond from the home improvement contractor so that the homeowner would receive cash compensation if the kitchen was not done satisfactorily within the agreed upon time.

PERFORMANCE FEE *see* INCENTIVE FEE.

PERFORMANCE FUND MUTUAL FUND designed for growth of capital. A performance fund invests in high-growth companies that do not pay dividends or that pay small dividends. Investors in such funds are willing to take higher-than-average risks in order to earn higher-than-average returns on their invested capital. *See also* GROWTH STOCK; PERFORMANCE STOCK.

PERFORMANCE STOCK high-growth stock that an investor feels will significantly rise in value. Also known as GROWTH STOCK, such a security tends to pay either a small dividend or no dividend at all. Companies whose stocks are in this category tend to retain earnings rather than pay dividends in order to finance their rapid growth. *See also* PERFORMANCE FUND.

PERIODIC PAYMENT PLAN plan to accumulate capital in a mutual fund by making regular investments on a monthly or quarterly basis. The plan has a set pay-in period, which may be 10 or 20 years, and a mechanism to withdraw funds from the plan after that time. Participants in periodic payment plans enjoy the advantages of DOLLAR COST AVERAGING and the diversification among stocks or bonds that is available through a mutual fund. Some plans also include completion insurance, which assures that all scheduled contributions to the plan will continue so that full benefits can be passed on to beneficiaries in the event the participant dies or is incapacitated.

PERIODIC PURCHASE DEFERRED CONTRACT ANNUITY contract for which fixed-amount payments, called *premiums,* are paid either monthly or quarterly and that does not begin paying out until a time elected by the holder (the *annuitant*). In some cases, premium payments may continue after payments from the annuity have begun. A periodic purchase deferred contract can be either fixed or variable. *See also* FIXED ANNUITY; VARIABLE ANNUITY.

PERIOD OF DIGESTION time period after the release of a NEW ISSUE of stocks or bonds during which the trading price of the security is established in the marketplace. Particularly when an INITIAL PUBLIC OFFERING is released, the period of digestion may entail considerable VOLATILITY, as investors try to ascertain an appropriate price level for it.

PERMANENT FINANCING

Corporate finance: long-term financing by means of either debt (bonds or long-term notes) or equity (common or preferred stock).

Real estate: long-term mortgage loan or bond issue, usually with a 15-, 20-, or 30-year term, the proceeds of which are used to repay a CONSTRUCTION LOAN.

PERPENDICULAR SPREAD option strategy using options with similar expiration dates and different strike prices (the prices at which the options can be exercised). A perpendicular spread can be designed for either a bullish or a bearish outlook.

PERPETUAL BOND bond that has no maturity date, is not redeemable, and pays a steady stream of interest indefinitely; also called *annuity bond.* The only notable perpetual bonds in existence are the consols first issued by the British Treasury to pay off smaller issues used to finance the Napoleonic Wars (1814). Some persons in the United States believe it would be more realistic to issue perpetual government bonds than constantly to refund portions of the national debt, as is the practice.

PERPETUAL INVENTORY inventory accounting system whereby book inventory is kept in continuous agreement with stock on hand; also called *continuous inventory.* A daily record is maintained of both the dollar amount and the physical quantity of inventory, and this is reconciled to actual physical counts at short intervals. Perpetual inventory contrasts with *periodic inventory.*

PERPETUAL WARRANT investment certificate giving the holder the right to buy a specified number of common shares of stock at a stipulated price with no expiration date. *See also* SUBSCRIPTION WARRANT.

PETRODOLLARS dollars paid to oil-producing countries and deposited in Western banks. In the 1970s, Middle Eastern oil producers built up huge surpluses of petrodollars, which the banks lent to oil-importing countries around the world. By the mid-1980s, these surpluses had shrunk, and many of the borrowing countries were having trouble repaying their huge debts. The flow of petrodollars, therefore, is very important in understanding the current world economic situation. Also called *petrocurrency* or *oil money*.

PHANTOM STOCK PLAN executive incentive concept whereby an executive receives a bonus based on the market appreciation of the company's stock over a fixed period of time. The hypothetical (hence phantom) amount of shares involved in the case of a particular executive is proportionate to his or her salary level. The plan works on the same principle as a CALL OPTION (a right to purchase a fixed amount of stock at a set price by a particular date). Unlike a call option, however, the executive pays nothing for the option and therefore has nothing to lose.

PHILADELPHIA STOCK EXCHANGE *see* REGIONAL STOCK EXCHANGES.

PHYSICAL COMMODITY actual commodity that is delivered to the contract buyer at the completion of a commodity contract in either the SPOT MARKET or the FUTURES MARKET. Some examples of physical commodities are corn, cotton, gold, oil, soybeans, and wheat. The quality specifications and quantity of the commodity to be delivered are specified by the exchange on which it is traded.

PHYSICAL VERIFICATION procedure by which an auditor actually inspects the assets of a firm, particularly inventory, to confirm their existence and value, rather than relying on written records. The auditor may use statistical sampling in the verification process.

PICKUP value gained in a bond swap. For example, bonds with identical coupon rates and maturities may have different market values, mainly because of a difference in quality, and thus in yields. The higher yield of the lower-quality bond received in such a swap compared with the yield of the higher-quality bond that was exchanged for it results in a net gain for the trader, called his or her pickup on the transaction.

PICKUP BOND bond that has a relatively high coupon (interest) rate and is close to the date at which it is callable—that is, can be paid off prior to maturity—by the issuer. If interest rates fall, the investor can look forward to picking up a redemption PREMIUM, since the bond will in all likelihood be called.

PICTURE Wall Street jargon used to request bid and asked prices and quantity information from a specialist or from a dealer regarding a particular security. For example, the question "What's the picture on XYZ?" might be answered, "58⅜ [best bid] to ¾ [best offer is 58¾], 1000 either way [there are both a buyer and a seller for 1000 shares]."

PIGGYBACK REGISTRATION situation when a securities UNDERWRITER allows existing holdings of shares in a corporation to be sold in combination with an offering of new public shares. The PROSPECTUS in a piggyback registration will reveal the nature of such a public/private share offering and name the sellers of the private shares. *See also* PUBLIC OFFERING.

PIK (PAYMENT-IN-KIND) SECURITIES bonds or PREFERRED STOCK that pay interest/dividends in the form of additional bonds or preferred stock. PIK securities have been used in TAKEOVER financing in lieu of cash and are highly speculative.

PINK SHEETS daily publication of the NATIONAL QUOTATION BUREAU that details the BID AND ASKED prices of thousands of OVER THE COUNTER (OTC) stocks. Many of these stocks are not carried in daily OTC newspaper listings. Brokerage firms subscribe to the pink sheets—named for their color—because the sheets not only give current prices but list market makers who trade each stock. Debt securities are listed separately on YELLOW SHEETS.

PIPELINE term referring to the underwriting process that involves securities being proposed for public distribution. The phrase used is "in the pipeline." The entire underwriting process, including registration with the Securities and Exchange Commission, must be completed before a security can be offered for public sale. Underwriters attempt to have several securities issues waiting in the pipeline so that the issues can be sold as soon as market conditions become favorable. In the municipal bond market, the pipeline is called the "Thirty Day Visible Supply" in the *Daily Bond Buyer* newspaper.

PLACE to market new securities. The term applies to both public and private sales but is more often used with reference to direct sales to institutional investors, as in PRIVATE PLACEMENT. The terms FLOAT and *distribute* are preferred in the case of a PUBLIC OFFERING.

PLACEMENT RATIO ratio, compiled by the *Bond Buyer* as of the close of business every Thursday, indicating the percentage of the past week's new MUNICIPAL BOND offerings that have been bought from the underwriters. Only issues of $1 million or more are included.

PLANT assets comprising land, buildings, machinery, natural resources, furniture and fixtures, and all other equipment permanently employed. Synonymous with FIXED ASSET.

   In a limited sense, the term is used to mean only buildings or only land and buildings: "property, plant, and equipment" and "plant and equipment."

PLASTIC BONDS *see* ASSET-BACKED SECURITIES.

PLEDGING transferring property, such as securities or the CASH SURRENDER VALUE of life insurance, to a lender or creditor as COLLATERAL for an obligation. *Pledge* and *hypothecate* are synonymous, as they do not involve transfer of title. ASSIGN, although commonly used interchangeably with *pledge* and *hypothecate,* implies transfer of ownership or of the right to transfer ownership at a later date. *See also* HYPOTHECATION.

PLOW BACK to reinvest a company's earnings in the business rather than pay out those profits as dividends. Smaller, fast-growing companies usually plow back most or all earnings in their businesses, whereas more established firms pay out more of their profits as dividends.

PLUS
   1. plus sign (+) that follows a price quotation on a Treasury note or bond, indicating that the price (normally quoted as a percentage of PAR value refined to 32ds) is refined to 64ths. Thus 95.16 + (95^{16}/$_{32}$ + or 95^{32}/$_{64}$ +) means 95^{33}/$_{64}$.
   2. plus sign after a transaction price in a listed security (for example, 39½ +), indicating that the trade was at a higher price than the previous REGULAR WAY transaction. *See also* PLUS TICK.
   3. plus sign before the figure in the column labeled "Change" in the newspaper stock tables, meaning that the closing price of the stock was higher than the previous day's close by the amount stated in the "Change" column.

PLUS TICK expression used when a security has been traded at a higher price than the previous transaction in that security. A stock price listed as 28 + on the CONSOLIDATED TAPE has had a plus tick from 27⅞ or below on previous trades. It is a Securities and Exchange Commission rule that short sales can be executed only on plus ticks or ZERO PLUS TICKS. Also called *uptick*. *See also* MINUS TICK; TICK; ZERO-MINUS TICK.

POINT

Bonds: percentage change of the face value of a bond expressed as a point. For example, a change of 1% is a move of one point. For a bond with a $1000 face value, each point is worth $10, and for a bond with a $5000 face value, each point is $50.

Bond yields are quoted in basis points: 100 basis points make up 1% of yield. *See* BASIS POINT.

Real estate and other commercial lending: upfront fee charged by the lender, separate from interest but designed to increase the overall yield to the lender. A point is 1% of the total principal amount of the loan. For example, on a $100,000 mortgage loan, a charge of 3 points would equal $3000.

Stocks: change of $1 in the market price of a stock. If a stock has risen 5 points, it has risen by $5 a share.

The movements of stock market averages, such as the Dow Jones Industrial Average, are also quoted in points. However, those points refer not to dollar amounts but to units of movement in the average, which is a composite of weighted dollar values. For example, a 10-point move in the Dow Jones Average from 1200 to 1210 does *not* mean the Dow now stands at $1210.

POINT AND FIGURE CHART graphic technique used in TECHNICAL ANALYSIS to follow the up or down momentum in the price moves of a security. Point and figure charting disregards the element of time and is solely used to record changes in price. Every time a price move is upward, an X is put on the graph above the previous point. Every time the price moves down, an O is placed one square down. When direction changes, the next column is used. The resulting lines of Xs and Os will indicate whether the security being charted has been maintaining an up or a down momentum over a particular time period.

POISON PILL strategic move by a takeover-target company to make its stock less attractive to an acquirer. For instance, a firm may issue a new series of PREFERRED STOCK that gives shareholders the right to redeem it at a premium price after a TAKEOVER. Two variations: a *flip-in poison pill* allows all existing holders of target company's shares except the acquirer to buy additional shares at a bargain price; a *flip-over poison pill* allows holders of common stock to buy (or holders of preferred stock to convert into) the acquirer's shares at a bargain price in the event of an unwelcome merger. Such measures raise the cost of an ACQUISITION and cause DILUTION, hopefully deterring a takeover bid.

POISON PUT provision in an INDENTURE giving bondholders the privilege of redemption at PAR if certain designated events occur, such as a hostile TAKEOVER, the purchase of a big block of shares, or an excessively large dividend payout. Poison puts, or *superpoison puts* as the more stringent variations are called, are popular antitakeover devices because they create an onerous cash obligation for the acquirer. They also protect the bondholder from the deterioration of credit quality and RATING that might result from a LEVERAGED BUYOUT that added to the issuer's debt. *See also* EVENT RISK.

POINT AND FIGURE CHART

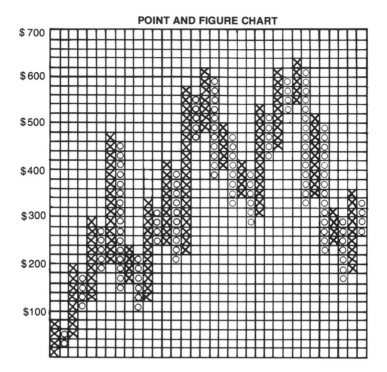

POLICY LOAN loan from an insurance company secured by the CASH SURRENDER VALUE of a life insurance policy. The amount available for such a loan depends on the number of years the policy has been in effect, the insured's age when the policy was issued, and the size of the death benefit. Such loans are often made at below-market interest rates to policyholders, although more recent policies usually only allow borrowing at rates that fluctuate in line with money market rates. If the loan is not repaid by the insured, the death benefit of the life insurance policy will be reduced by the amount of the loan plus accrued interest.

POOL

Capital Budgeting: as used in the phrase "pool of financing," the concept that investment projects are financed out of a pool of funds rather than out of bonds, preferred stock, and common stock individually. A weighted average cost of capital is thus used in analyses evaluating the return on investment projects. *See also* COST OF CAPITAL.

Industry: joining of companies to improve profits by reducing competition. Such poolings are generally outlawed in the United States by various ANTITRUST LAWS.

Insurance: association of insurers who share premiums and losses in order to spread risk and give small insurers an opportunity to compete with larger ones.

Investments:

1. combination of resources for a common purpose or benefit. For example, an INVESTMENT CLUB pools the funds of its members, giving them the opportunity to share in a PORTFOLIO offering greater diversification and the hope of a better return on their money than they could get individually. A *commodities pool*

entrusts the funds of many investors to a trading professional and distributes profits and losses among participants in proportion to their interests.

2. group of investors joined together to use their combined power to manipulate security or commodity prices or to obtain control of a corporation. Such pools are outlawed by regulations governing securities and commodities trading. *See also* MORTGAGE POOL.

POOLING OF INTERESTS accounting method used in the combining or merging of companies following an acquisition, whereby the balance sheets (assets and liabilities) of the two companies are simply added together, item by item. This tax-free method contrasts with the PURCHASE ACQUISITION method, in which the buying company treats the acquired company as an investment and any PREMIUM paid over the FAIR MARKET VALUE of the assets is reflected on the buyer's balance sheet as GOODWILL. Because reported earnings are higher under the pooling of interests method, most companies prefer it to the purchase acquisition method, particularly when the amount of goodwill is sizable.

The pooling of interests method can be elected only when the following conditions are met:

1. The two companies must have been autonomous for at least two years prior to the pooling and one must not have owned more than 10% of the stock of the other.

2. The combination must be consummated either in a single transaction or in accordance with a specific plan within one year after the plan is initiated; no contingent payments are permitted.

3. The acquiring company must issue its regular common stock in exchange for 90% or more of the common stock of the other company.

4. The surviving corporation must not later retire or reacquire common stock issued in the combination, must not enter into an arrangement for the benefit of former stockholders, and must not dispose of a significant portion of the assets of the combining companies for at least two years.

See also MERGER.

PORTFOLIO combined holding of more than one stock, bond, commodity, real estate investment, CASH EQUIVALENT, or other asset by an individual or institutional investor. The purpose of a portfolio is to reduce risk by diversification. *See also* PORTFOLIO BETA SCORE; PORTFOLIO THEORY.

PORTFOLIO BETA SCORE relative VOLATILITY of an individual securities portfolio, taken as a whole, as measured by the BETA coefficients of the securities making it up.

PORTFOLIO INSURANCE the use, by a PORTFOLIO MANAGER, of STOCK INDEX FUTURES to protect stock portfolios against market declines. Instead of selling actual stocks as they lose value, managers sell the index futures; if the drop continues, they repurchase the futures at a lower price, using the profit to offset losses in the stock portfolio. The inability of the markets on BLACK MONDAY to process such massive quantities of stock efficiently and the subsequent instituting of CIRCUIT BREAKERS all but eliminated portfolio insurance. *See also* PROGRAM TRADING.

PORTFOLIO MANAGER professional responsible for the securities PORTFOLIO of an individual or INSTITUTIONAL INVESTOR. Also called a *money manager* or, especially where personalized service is involved, in INVESTMENT COUNSEL. A portfolio manager may work for a mutual fund, pension fund, profit-sharing plan, bank trust department, or insurance company, as well as private investors. In return for a fee, the manager has the fiduciary responsibility to manage the assets prudently and make them grow as much as possible. In making such decisions, a portfolio manager must choose whether stocks, bonds, CASH EQUIVALENTS, real estate, or some other assets present the best opportunities for profit at any particular time. *See also* PORTFOLIO THEORY; PRUDENT-MAN RULE.

PORTFOLIO THEORY sophisticated investment decision approach that permits an investor to classify, estimate, and control both the kind and the amount of expected risk and return; also called *portfolio management theory* or *modern portfolio theory*. Essential to portfolio theory are its quantification of the relationship between risk and return and the assumption that investors must be compensated for assuming risk. Portfolio theory departs from traditional security analysis in shifting emphasis from analyzing the characteristics of individual investments to determining the statistical relationships among the individual securities that comprise the overall portfolio. The portfolio theory approach has four basic steps: *security valuation*—describing a universe of assets in terms of expected return and expected risk; *asset allocation decision*—determining how assets are to be distributed among classes of investment, such as stocks or bonds; *portfolio optimization*—reconciling risk and return in selecting the securities to be included, such as determining which portfolio of stocks offers the best return for a given level of expected risk; and *performance measurement*—dividing each stock's performance (risk) into market-related (systematic) and industry/security-related (residual) classifications.

POSITION

Banking: bank's net balance in a foreign currency.

Finance: firm's financial condition.

Investments:

1. investor's stake in a particular security or market. A LONG POSITION equals the number of shares *owned;* a SHORT POSITION equals the number of shares *owed* by a dealer or an individual. The dealer's long positions are called his *inventory of securities*.

2. Used as a verb, to take on a long or a short position in a stock.

POSITION BUILDING process of buying shares to accumulate a LONG POSITION or of selling shares to accumulate a SHORT POSITION. Large institutional investors who want to build a large position in a particular security do so over time to avoid pushing up the price of the security.

POSITION LIMIT

Commodities trading: number of contracts that can be acquired in a specific commodity before a speculator is classified as a "large trader." Large traders are subject to special oversight by the COMMODITIES FUTURES TRADING COMMISSION (CFTC) and the exchanges and are limited as to the number of contracts they can add to their positions. The position limit varies with the type of commodity.

Options trading: maximum number of exchange-listed OPTION contracts that can be owned or controlled by an individual holder, or by a group of holders acting jointly, in the same underlying security. The current limit is 2000 contracts on the same side of the market (for example, long calls and short puts are one side of the market); the limit applies to all expiration dates.

POSITION TRADER commodities trader who takes a long-term approach—six months to a year or more—to the market. Usually possessing more than average experience, information, and capital, these traders ride through the ups and downs of price fluctuations until close to the delivery date, unless drastic adverse developments threaten. More like insurance underwriters than gamblers, they hope to achievelong-term profits from calculated risks as distinguished from pure speculation.

POSITIVE CARRY situation in which the cost of money borrowed to finance securities is lower than the yield on the securities. For example, if a fixed-income bond yielding 13% is purchased with a loan bearing 11% interest, the bond has positive carry. The opposite situation is called NEGATIVE CARRY.

POSITIVE YIELD CURVE situation in which interest rates are higher on long-term debt securities than on short-term debt securities of the same quality. For example, a positive yield curve exists when 20-year Treasury bonds yield 14% and 3-month Treasury bills yield 10%. Such a situation is common, since an investor who ties up his money for a longer time is taking more risk and is usually compensated by a higher yield. When short-term interest rates rise above long-term rates, there is a NEGATIVE YIELD CURVE. *See* illustration, page 407.

POSITIVE YIELD CURVE

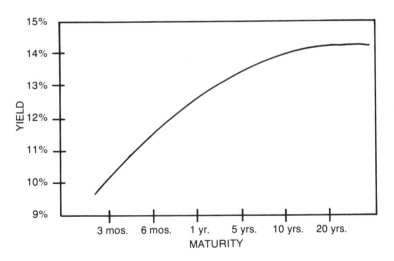

POST

Accounting: to transfer from a journal of original entry detailed financial data, in the chronological order in which it was generated, into a ledger book. Banks post checking account deposits and withdrawalsin a ledger, then summarize these transactions on the monthly bankstatement.

Investments: horseshoe-shaped structure on the floor of the New York Stock Exchange where specialists trade specific securities. Video screens surround the post, displaying the bid and offer prices available for stocks traded at that location. Also called *trading post*.

POT securities underwriting term meaning the portion of a stock or bond issue returned to the MANAGING UNDERWRITER by the participating investment bankers to facilitate sales to INSTITUTIONAL INVESTORS. Institutions buying from the pot designate the firms to be credited with pot sales. *See also* RETENTION.

POT IS CLEAN MANAGING UNDERWRITER'S announcement to members of the underwriting group that the POT—the portion of the stock or bond issue withheld to facilitate institutional sales—has been sold.

POWER OF ATTORNEY

In general: written document that authorizes a particular person to perform certain acts on behalf of the one signing the document. The document, which must be witnessed by a notary public or some other public officer, may bestow either *full power of attorney* or *limited power of attorney*. It becomes void upon the death of the signer.

Investments: *full power of attorney* might, for instance, allow assets to be moved from one brokerage or bank account to another. A *limited power of attorney,* on the other hand, would only permit transactions within an existing account. A broker given a limited power of attorney, for instance, may buy and sell securities in an account but may not remove them. Such an account is called a DISCRETIONARY ACCOUNT. *See also* DISCRETIONARY ORDER; PROXY; STOCK POWER.

PRECEDENCE priority of one order over another on the floor of the exchanges, according to rules designed to protect the DOUBLE-AUCTION SYSTEM. The rules basically are that the highest bid and lowest offer have precedence over other bids and offers, that the first bid or first offer at a price has priority over other bids or offers at that price, and that the size of the order determines precedence thereafter, large orders having priority over smaller orders. Where two orders of equal size must compete for the same limited quantity after the first bid is filled, the impasse is resolved by a flip of the coin. *See also* MATCHED AND LOST. Exchange rules also require that public orders have precedence over trades for floor members' own accounts. *See also* OFF-FLOOR ORDER; ON-FLOOR ORDER.

PRECOMPUTE in installment lending, methods of charging interest whereby the total amount of annual interest either is deducted from the face amount of the loan at the time the loan proceeds are disbursed or is added to the total amount to be repaid in equal installments. In both cases, the EFFECTIVE RATE to the borrower is higher than the stated annual rate used in the computation. "Truth in lending" laws require that the effective annual rate be expressed in SIMPLE INTEREST terms.

PREEMPTIVE RIGHT right giving existing stockholders the opportunity to purchase shares of a NEW ISSUE before it is offered to others. Its purpose is to protect shareholders from dilution of value and control when new shares are issued. Although 48 U.S. states have preemptive right statutes, most states also either permit corporations to pay stockholders to waive their preemptive rights or state in their statutes that the preemptive right is valid only if set forth in the corporate charter. As a result, preemptive rights are the exception rather than the rule. Where they do exist, the usual procedure is for each existing stockholder to receive, prior to a new issue, a SUBSCRIPTION WARRANT indicating how many new shares the holder is entitled to buy—normally, a proportion of the shares he or she already holds. Since the new shares would typically be priced below the market, a financial incentive exists to exercise the preemptive right. *See also* SUBSCRIPTION RIGHT.

PREFERENCE ITEM *see* TAX PREFERENCE ITEM.

PREFERENCE SHARES *see* PRIOR-PREFERRED STOCK.

PREFERRED DIVIDEND COVERAGE net income after interest and taxes (but before common stock dividends) divided by the dollar amount of preferred stock dividends. The result tells how many times over the preferred dividend requirement is covered by current earnings.

PREFERRED STOCK class of CAPITAL STOCK that pays dividends at a specified rate and that has preference over common stock in the payment of dividends and the liquidation of assets. Preferred stock does not ordinarily carry voting rights.

   Most preferred stock is *cumulative;* if dividends are passed (not paid for any reason), they accumulate and must be paid before common dividends. A PASSED DIVIDEND on *noncumulative preferred* stock is generally gone forever. *Participating preferred* stock entitles its holders to share in profits above and beyond the declared dividend, along with common shareholders, as distinguished from *nonparticipating preferred,* which is limited to the stipulated dividend. *Adjustable-rate preferred* stock pays a dividend that is adjustable, usually quarterly, based on changes in the Treasury bill rate or other money market rates. *Convertible preferred stock* is exchangeable for a given number of common shares and thus tends to be more VOLATILE than *nonconvertible preferred,* which behaves more like a fixed-income bond. *See also* CONVERTIBLE; CUMULATIVE PREFERRED; PARTICIPATING PREFERRED; PIK (PAYMENT-IN-KIND) SECURITIES; PRIOR-PREFERRED STOCK.

PREFERRED STOCK RATIO PREFERRED STOCK at PAR value divided by total CAPITALIZATION; the result is the percentage of capitalization—bonds and net worth—represented by preferred stock.

PRELIMINARY PROSPECTUS first document released by an underwriter of a NEW ISSUE to prospective investors. The document offers financial details about the issue but does not contain all the information that will appear in the final or statutory prospectus, and parts of the document may be changed before the final prospectus is issued. Because portions of the cover page of the preliminary prospectus are printed in red ink, it is popularly called the *red herring*.

PREMIUM

In general: extra payment usually made as an incentive.

Bonds:
1. amount by which a bond sells above its face (PAR) value. For instance, a bond with a face value of $1000 would sell for a $100 premium when it cost $1100. The same meaning also applies to preferred stock. *See also* PREMIUM BOND; PREMIUM OVER BOND VALUE; PREMIUM OVER CONVERSION VALUE.
2. amount by which the REDEMPTION PRICE to the issuer exceeds the face value when a bond is called. *See also* CALL PREMIUM.

Insurance: fee paid to an insurance company for insurance protection. Also, the single or multiple payments made to build an ANNUITY fund.

Options: price a put or call buyer must pay to a put or call seller (writer) for an option contract. The premium is determined by market supply and demand forces. *See also* OPTION; PREMIUM INCOME.

Stocks:
1. charge occasionally paid by a short seller when stock is borrowed to make delivery on a SHORT SALE.

2. amount by which a stock's price exceeds that of other stocks to which it is comparable. For instance, securities analysts might say that XYZ Foods is selling at a 15% premium to other food company stocks—an indication that the stock is more highly valued by investors than its industry peers. It does not necessarily mean that the stock is overpriced, however. Indeed, it may indicate that the investment public has only begun to recognize the stock's market potential and that the price will continue to rise. Similarly, analysts might say that the food industry is selling for a 20% premium to Standard & Poor's 500 index, indicating the relative price strength of the industry group to the stock market as a whole.

3. in new issues, amount by which the trading price of the shares exceeds the OFFERING PRICE.

4. amount over market value paid in a *tender offer*. See also PREMIUM RAID.

PREMIUM BOND bond with a selling price above face or redemption value. A bond with a face value of $1000, for instance, would be called a premium bond if it sold for $1050. This price does not include any ACCRUED INTEREST due when the bond is bought. When a premium bond is called before scheduled maturity, bondholders are usually paid more than face value, though the amount may be less than the bond is selling for at the time of the CALL.

PREMIUM INCOME income received by an investor who sells a PUT OPTION or a CALL OPTION. An investor collects premium income by writing a COVERED OPTION, if he or she owns the underlying stock, or a NAKED OPTION, if he or she does not own the stock. An investor who sells options to collect premium income hopes that the underlying stock will not rise very much (in the case of a call) or fall very much (in the case of a put).

PREMIUM OVER BOND VALUE upward difference between the market value of a CONVERTIBLE bond and the price at which a straight bond of the same company would sell in the same open market. A convertible bond, eventually convertible to common stock, will normally sell at a PREMIUM over its bond value because investors place a value on the conversion feature. The higher the market price of the issuer's stock is relative to the price at which the bond is convertible, the greater the premium will be, reflecting the investor's tendency to view it more as a stock than as a bond. When the stock price falls near or below the conversion price, investors then tend to view the convertible as a bond and the premium narrows or even disappears. Other factors affecting the prices of convertible bonds generally include lower transaction costs on the convertibles than would be incurred in buying the stock outright, an attraction that exerts some upward pressure on the premium; the demand from life insurance companies and other institutional investors that are limited by law as to the common stock investments they can have and that gain their equity participation through convertibles; the duration period of the option to convert—the longer it is, the more valuable the future and the higher the premium; high dividends on the issuer's common stock, a factor increasing demand for the common versus the convertible, and therefore a downward pressure. See also PREMIUM OVER CONVERSION VALUE.

PREMIUM OVER CONVERSION VALUE amount by which the MARKET PRICE of a CONVERTIBLE preferred stock or convertible bond exceeds the price at which it is convertible. Convertibles (CVs) usually sell at a PREMIUM for two basic reasons: (1) if the convertible is a bond, the bond value—defined as the price at which a straight bond of the same company would sell in the same open market— is the lowest value the CV will reach; it thus represents DOWNSIDE RISK protection, which is given a value in the marketplace, generally varying with the VOLATILITY of the common stock; (2) the conversion privilege is given a value by investors because they might find it profitable eventually to convert the securities.

At relatively high common-stock price levels, a convertible tends to sell for its common stock equivalent and the conversion value becomes negligible. This occurs because investors are viewing the security as a common stock, not as a bond, and because conversion would be preferable to redemption if the bond were called. On the other hand, when the market value of the convertible is close to its bond value, the conversion feature has little value and the security is valued more as a bond. It is here that the CONVERSION PREMIUM is highest. The conversion premium is also influenced to some extent by transaction costs, insurance company investment restrictions, the duration of the conversion OPTION, and the size of common dividends. *See also* PREMIUM OVER BOND VALUE.

PREMIUM RAID surprise attempt to acquire a position in a company's stock by offering holders an amount—or premium—over the market value of their shares. The term *raid* assumes that the motive is control and not simply investment. Attempts to acquire control are regulated by federal laws that require disclosure of the intentions of those seeking shares. *See also* TENDER OFFER; WILLIAMS ACT.

PRENUPTIAL CONTRACT agreement between a future husband and wife that details how the couple's financial affairs are to be handled both during the marriage and in the event of divorce. The agreement may cover insurance protection, ownership of housing and securities, and inheritance rights. Such contracts may not be accepted in a court of law.

PREPAYMENT

In general: paying a debt obligation before it comes due.

Accounting: expenditure for a future benefit, which is recorded in a BALANCE SHEET asset account called a DEFERRED CHARGE, then written off in the period when the benefit is enjoyed. For example, prepaid rent is first recorded as an asset, then charged to expense as the rent becomes due on a monthly basis.

Banking: paying a loan before maturity. Some loans (particularly mortgages) have a prepayment clause that allows prepayment at any time without penalty, while others charge a fee if a loan is paid off before due.

Installment credit: making payments before they are due. *See also* RULE OF THE 78s.

Securities: paying a seller for a security before the settlement date.

Taxes: prepaying taxes, for example, to have the benefit of deducting state and local taxes from one's federal income tax return in the current calendar year rather than in the next year.

PREPAYMENT PENALTY fee paid by a borrower to a bank when a loan or mortgage that does not have a prepayment clause is repaid before its scheduled maturity.

PREREFUNDING procedure in which a bond issuer floats a second bond in order to pay off the first bond at the first CALL date. The proceeds from the sale of the second bond are safely invested, usually in Treasury securities, that will mature at the first call date of the first bond issue. Those first bonds are said to be prerefunded after this operation has taken place. Bond issuers prerefund bonds during periods of lower interest rates in order to lower their interest costs. *See also* ADVANCE REFUNDING; REFUNDING.

PRESALE ORDER order to purchase part of a new MUNICIPAL BOND issue that is accepted by an underwriting SYNDICATE MANAGER before an announcement of the price or COUPON rate and before the official PUBLIC OFFERING. Municipals are exempt from registration requirements and other rules of the Securities and Exchange Commission, which forbids preoffering sales of corporate bond issues. *See also* PRESOLD ISSUE.

PRESENT VALUE value today of a future payment, or stream of payments, discounted at some appropriate compound interest—or discount—rate. For example, the present value of $100 to be received 10 years from now is about $38.55, using a discount rate equal to 10% interest compounded annually.

The present value method, also called the DISCOUNTED CASH FLOW method, is widely used in corporate finance to measure the return on a CAPITAL INVESTMENT project. In security investments, the method is used to determine how much money should be invested today to result in a certain sum at a future time. Present value calculations are facilitated by present value tables, which are compound interest tables in reverse. Also called *time value of money*.

PRESIDENT highest-ranking officer in a corporation after the CHAIRMAN OF THE BOARD, unless the title CHIEF EXECUTIVE OFFICER (CEO) is used, in which case the president can outrank the chairman. The president is appointed by the BOARD OF DIRECTORS and usually reports directly to the board. In smaller companies the president is usually the CEO, having authority over all other officers in matters of day-to-day management and policy decision-making. In large corporations the CEO title is frequently held by the chairman of the board, leaving the president as CHIEF OPERATING OFFICER, responsible for personnel and administration on a daily basis.

PRESIDENTIAL ELECTION CYCLE THEORY hypothesis of investment advisers that major stock market moves can be predicted based on the four-year presidential election cycle. According to this theory, stocks decline soon after a president is elected, as the chief executive takes the harsh and unpopular steps necessary to bring inflation, government spending, and deficits under control. During the next two years or so, taxes may be raised and the economy will slip into a recession. About midway into the four-year cycle, stocks should start to rise in anticipation of the economic recovery that the incumbent president wants to be roaring at full steam by election day. The cycle then repeats itself with the election of a new president or the reelection of an incumbent. This theory worked remarkably well from the late 1960s to the mid-1980s.

PRESOLD ISSUE issue of MUNICIPAL BONDS or government bonds that is completely sold out before the price or yield is publicly announced. Corporate bond issues, which must be offered to the public with a Securities and Exchange Commission registration statement, cannot legally be presold. *See also* PRESALE ORDER.

PRETAX EARNINGS OR PROFITS NET INCOME (earnings or profits) before federal income taxes.

PRETAX RATE OF RETURN yield or capital gain on a particular security before taking into account an individual's tax situation. *See also* RATE OF RETURN.

PRICE CHANGE net rise or fall of the price of a security at the close of a trading session, compared to the previous session's CLOSING PRICE. A stock that rose $2 in a day would have a +2 after its final price in the newspaper stock listings. A stock that fell $2 would have a − 2. The average of the price changes for groups of securities, in indicators such as the Dow Jones Industrial Average and Standard & Poor's 500 Stock Index, is calculated by taking into account all the price changes in the components of the average or index.

PRICE/EARNINGS RATIO (P/E) price of a stock divided by its earnings per share. The P/E ratio may either use the reported earnings from the latest year (called a *trailing P/E*) or employ an analyst's forecast of next year's earnings (called a *forward P/E*). The trailing P/E is listed along with a stock's price and trading activity in the daily newspapers. For instance, a stock selling for $20 a share that earned $1 last year has a trailing P/E of 20. If the same stock has projected earnings of $2 next year, it will have a forward P/E of 10.

The price/earnings ratio, also known as the *multiple,* gives investors an idea of how much they are paying for a company's earning power. The higher the P/E, the more investors are paying, and therefore the more earnings growth they are expecting. High P/E stocks—those with multiples over 20—are typically young, fast-growing companies. They are far riskier to trade than low P/E stocks, since it is easier to miss high-growth expectations than low-growth predictions. Low P/E stocks tend to be in low-growth or mature industries, in stock groups that have fallen out of favor, or in old, established, BLUE-CHIP companies with long records of earnings stability and regular dividends. In general, low P/E stocks have higher yields than high P/E stocks, which often pay no dividends at all.

PRICE GAP term used when a stock's price either jumps or plummets from its last trading range without overlapping that trading range. For instance, a stock might shoot up from a closing price of $20 a share, marking the high point of an $18–$20 trading range for that day, and begin trading in a $22–$24 range the next day on the news of a takeover bid. Or a company that reports lower than expected earnings might drop from the $18–$20 range to the $13–$15 range without ever trading at intervening prices. Price gaps are considered significant movements by technical analysts, who note them on charts, because such gaps are often indications of an OVERBOUGHT or OVERSOLD position.

PRICE LIMIT *see* LIMIT PRICE.

PRICE RANGE high/low range in which a stock has traded over a particular period of time. In the daily newspaper, a stock's 52-week price range is given. In most companies' annual reports, a stock's price range is shown for the FISCAL YEAR.

PRICE SPREAD OPTIONS strategy in which an investor simultaneously buys and sells two options covering the same security, with the same expiration months, but with different exercise prices. For example, an investor might buy an XYZ May 100 call and sell an XYZ May 90 call.

PRICE SUPPORT government-set price floor designed to aid farmers or other producers of goods. For instance, the government sets a minimum price for sugar that it guarantees to sugar growers. If the market price drops below that level, the government makes up the difference. *See also* PARITY PRICE.

PRICE-WEIGHTED INDEX index in which component stocks are weighted by their price. Higher-priced stocks therefore have a greater percentage impact on the index than lower-priced stocks. In recent years, the trend of using price-weighted indexes has given way to the use of MARKET-VALUE WEIGHTED INDEXES.

PRICEY term used of an unrealistically low bid price or unrealistically high offer price. If a stock is trading at $15, a pricey bid might be $10 a share, and a pricey offer $20 a share.

PRIMARY DEALER one of the three dozen or so banks and investment dealers authorized to buy and sell government securities in direct dealings with the FEDERAL RESERVE BANK of New York in its execution of Fed OPEN MARKET OPERATIONS. Such dealers must be qualified in terms of reputation, capacity, and adequacy of staff and facilities.

PRIMARY DISTRIBUTION sale of a new issue of stocks or bonds, as distinguished from a SECONDARY DISTRIBUTION, which involves previously issued stock. All issuances of bonds are primary distributions. Also called *primary offering*, but not to be confused with *initial public offering*, which refers to a corporation's *first* distribution of stock to the public.

PRIMARY EARNINGS PER (COMMON) SHARE earnings available to common stock (which is usually net earnings after taxes and preferred dividends) divided by the number of common shares outstanding. This figure contrasts with earnings per share after DILUTION, which assumes warrants, rights, and options have been exercised and convertibles have been converted. *See also* CONVERTIBLE; FULLY DILUTED EARNINGS PER (COMMON) SHARE; SUBSCRIPTION WARRANT.

PRIMARY MARKET market for new issues of securities, as distinguished from the SECONDARY MARKET, where previously issued securities are bought and sold. A market is primary if the proceeds of sales go to the issuer of the securities sold. The term also applies to government securities auctions and to opening option and futures contract sales.

PRIME
Banking: PRIME RATE.
Investments: acronym for Prescribed Right to Income and Maximum Equity. PRIME is a UNIT INVESTMENT TRUST, sponsored by the Americus Shareowner Service Corporation, which separates the income portion of a stock from its appreciation potential. The income-producing portion is called PRIME, and the appreciation potential is called SCORE (an acronym for Special Claim on Residual Equity). PRIME and SCORE together make up a unit share investment trust, known by the acronym USIT. Both PRIME and SCORE trade on the American Stock Exchange.

The first version of this unit came into existence with American Telephone and Telegraph stock in late 1983, as AT&T was undergoing divestiture. PRIME units entitled their holders to the dividend income that a holder of one common share of the old AT&T would have gotten plus a proportionate share of the dividends of the seven regional operating companies split off from AT&T. PRIME holders also received all price APPRECIATION in the stock up to the equivalent of $75 a share. SCORE holders received all appreciation over $75, but no dividend income.

This form of unit trust allows investors who want income from a stock to maximize that income, and investors who want capital gains to have increased leverage in achieving those gains. *See also* CAPITAL GAIN.

PRIME PAPER highest quality COMMERCIAL PAPER, as rated by Moody's Investor's Service and other rating agencies. Prime paper is considered INVESTMENT GRADE, and therefore institutions with FIDUCIARY responsibility can invest in it.

Moody's has three ratings of prime paper:
P-1: Highest quality
P-2: Higher quality
P-3: High quality
Commercial paper below P-3 is not considered prime paper.

PRIME RATE interest rate banks charge to their most creditworthy customers. The rate is determined by the market forces affecting a bank's cost of funds and the rates that borrowers will accept. The prime rate tends to become standard across the banking industry when a major bank moves its prime rate up or down. The rate is a key interest rate, since loans to less-creditworthy customers are often tied to the prime rate. For example, a BLUE CHIP company may borrow at a prime rate of 10%, but a less-well-established small business may borrow from the same bank at prime plus 2, or 12%. Although the major bank prime rate is the definitive "best rate" reference point, many banks, particularly those in outlying regions, have a two-tier system, whereby smaller companies of top credit standing may borrow at an even lower rate.

PRIME RATE FUND *mutual fund* that buys portions of corporate loans from banks and passes interest, which is designed to approximate the PRIME RATE, along to shareholders net of load charges and management fees. Although the bank loans are senior obligations and fully collateralized, they are subject to DEFAULT, particularly in recessions. Prime rate funds thus pay 2-3% more than the yield on one-year CERTIFICATES OF DEPOSIT (CDs); but management fees tend to be higher than those of other mutual funds. Another possible disadvantage is limited liquidity; the only way investors can get out is to sell their shares back to the funds once each quarter.

PRINCIPAL

In General:
1. major party to a transaction, acting as either a buyer or a seller. A principal buys and sells for his or her own account and at his or her own risk.
2. owner of a privately held business.

Banking and Finance:
1. face amount of a debt instrument or deposit on which interest is either owed or earned.
2. balance of an obligation, separate from interest. *See also* PRINCIPAL AMOUNT.

Investments: basic amount invested, exclusive of earnings.

PRINCIPAL AMOUNT FACE VALUE of an obligation (such as a bond or a loan) that must be repaid at maturity, as separate from the INTEREST.

PRINCIPAL STOCKHOLDER stockholder who owns a significant number of shares in a corporation. Under Securities and Exchange Commission (SEC) rules, a principal stockholder owns 10% or more of the voting stock of a REGISTERED COMPANY. These stockholders are often on the board of directors and are considered insiders by SEC rules, so that they must report buying and selling in the company's stock. *See also* AFFILIATED PERSON; CONTROL STOCK; INSIDER.

PRINCIPAL SUM

Finance: also used as a synonym for PRINCIPAL, in the sense of the obligation due under a debt instrument exclusive of interest. Synonymous with CORPUS. *See also* TRUST.

Insurance: amount specified as payable to the beneficiary under a policy, such as the death benefit.

PRIORITY system used in an AUCTION MARKET, in which the first bid or offer price is executed before other bid and offer prices, even if subsequent orders are larger. Orders originating off the floor (*see* OFF-FLOOR ORDER) of an exchange also have priority over ON-FLOOR ORDERS. *See also* MATCHED AND LOST; PRECEDENCE.

PRIOR-LIEN BOND bond that has precedence over another bond of the same issuing company even though both classes of bonds are equally secured. Such bonds usually arise from REORGANIZATION. *See also* JUNIOR ISSUE.

PRIOR-PREFERRED STOCK PREFERRED STOCK that has a higher claim than other issues of preferred stock on dividends and assets in the event of LIQUIDATION; also known as *preference shares*.

PRIVATE LIMITED PARTNERSHIP LIMITED PARTNERSHIP not registered with the Securities and Exchange Commission (SEC) and having a maximum of 35 limited partners. *See also* ACCREDITED INVESTOR.

PRIVATE MARKET VALUE (PMV) the aggregate market value of a company if each of its parts operated independently and had its own stock price. Also called *breakup value* or *takeover value*. Analysts look for high PMV in relation to market value to identify bargains and potential TARGET COMPANIES. PMV differs from LIQUIDATION VALUE, which excludes GOING CONCERN VALUE and BOOK VALUE; the latter is an accounting concept.

PRIVATE PLACEMENT sale of stocks, bonds, or other investments directly to an institutional investor like an insurance company. A PRIVATE LIMITED PARTNERSHIP is also considered a private placement. A private placement does not have to be registered with the Securities and Exchange Commission, as a PUBLIC OFFERING does, if the securities are purchased for investment as opposed to resale. *See also* LETTER SECURITY.

PRIVATE PURPOSE BOND category of MUNICIPAL BOND distinguished from PUBLIC PURPOSE BOND in the TAX REFORM ACT OF 1986 because 10% or more of the bond's benefit goes to private activities. Private purpose obligations, which are also called *private activity bonds* or *nonessential function bonds*, are taxable unless their use is specifically exempted. Even tax-exempt *permitted private activity bonds*, if issued after August 8, 1986, are TAX PREFERENCE ITEMS, except those issued for 501(c)(3) organizations (hospitals, colleges, universities). Private purpose bonds specifically *prohibited* from tax-exemption effective August 15, 1986, include those for sports, trade, and convention facilities and large-issue (over $1 million) INDUSTRIAL DEVELOPMENT BONDS. Permitted issues, except those for 501(c)(3) organizations, airports, docks, wharves, and government-owned solid-waste disposal facilities, are subject to volume caps, effective August 15, 1986, of $75 per capita or $250 million per state (whichever is larger), dropping to $50 per capita or $150 million per state in 1988. *See also* TAXABLE MUNICIPAL BOND.

PROBATE judicial process whereby the will of a deceased person is presented to a court and an EXECUTOR or ADMINISTRATOR is appointed to carry out the will.

PROCEEDS
1. funds given to a borrower after all interest costs and fees are deducted.
2. money received by the seller of an asset after commissions are deducted—for example, the amount a stockholder receives from the sale of shares, less broker's commission. *See also* PROCEEDS SALE.

PROCEEDS SALE OVER THE COUNTER securities sale where the PROCEEDS are used to purchase another security. Under the FIVE PERCENT RULE of the NATIONAL ASSOCIATION OF SECURITIES DEALERS (NASD), such a trade is considered one transaction and the NASD member's total markup or commission is subject to the 5% guideline.

PRODUCER PRICE INDEX measure of change in wholesale prices (formerly called the *wholesale price index*), as released monthly by the U.S. Bureau of Labor Statistics. The index is broken down into components by commodity, industry sector, and stage of processing. *See also* CONSUMER PRICE INDEX.

PRODUCTION RATE coupon (interest) rate at which a PASS-THROUGH SECURITY guaranteed by the GOVERNMENT NATIONAL MORTGAGE ASSOCIATION (GNMA) is issued. The rate is set a half percentage point under the prevailing Federal Housing Administration (FHA) rate, the maximum rate allowed on residential mortgages insured and guaranteed by the FHA and the Veterans Administration.

PROFIT
Finance: positive difference that results from selling products and services for more than the cost of producing these goods. *See also* NET PROFIT.
Investments: difference between the selling price and the purchase price of commodities or securities when the selling price is higher.

PROFIT AND LOSS STATEMENT (P & L) summary of the revenues, costs, and expenses of a company during an accounting period; also called INCOME STATEMENT, *operating statement, statement of profit and loss, income and expense statement.* Together with the BALANCE SHEET as of the end of the accounting period, it constitutes a company's financial statement. *See also* COST OF GOODS SOLD; NET INCOME; NET SALES.

PROFIT CENTER segment of a business organization that is responsible for producing profits on its own.

PROFIT MARGIN *see* MARGIN OF PROFIT.

PROFIT-SHARING PLAN agreement between a corporation and its employees that allows the employees to share in company profits. Annual contributions are made by the company, when it has profits, to a profit-sharing account for each employee, either in cash or in a deferred plan, which may be invested in stocks, bonds, or cash equivalents. The funds in a profit-sharing account generally accumulate tax deferred until the employee retires or leaves the company. Many plans allow employees to borrow against profit-sharing accounts for major expenditures such as purchasing a home or financing children's education. Because corporate profit-sharing plans have custody over billions of dollars, they are major institutional investors in the stock and bond markets.

PROFIT TAKING action by short-term securities or commodities traders to cash in on gains earned on a sharp market rise. Profit taking pushes down prices, but only temporarily; the term implies an upward market trend.

PRO FORMA Latin for "as a matter of form"; refers to a presentation of data, such as a BALANCE SHEET or INCOME STATEMENT, where certain amounts are hypothetical. For example, a pro forma balance sheet might show a debt issue that has been proposed but has not yet been consummated.

PROGRAM TRADING computer-driven buying *(buy program)* or selling *(sell program)* of baskets of 15 or more stocks by *index* ARBITRAGE specialists or institutional traders. Program refers to computer programs that constantly monitor stock, futures, and options markets, giving buy and sell signals when opportunities for arbitrage profits occur or when market conditions warrant portfolio accumulation or liquidation transactions. Program trading has been blamed for excessive volatility in the markets, especially on Black Monday in 1987, when PORTFOLIO INSURANCE—the since discredited use of index options and futures to hedge stock portfolios—was an important contributing factor to the sharp decline in prices.

PROGRESSIVE TAX INCOME TAX system in which those with higher incomes pay taxes at higher rates than those with lower incomes; also called *graduated tax. See also* FLAT TAX; REGRESSIVE TAX.

PROGRESS PAYMENTS
1. periodic payments to a supplier, contractor, or subcontractor for work satisfactorily performed to date. Such schedules are provided in contracts and can significantly reduce the amount of WORKING CAPITAL required by the performing party.
2. disbursements by lenders to contractors under construction loan arrangements. As construction progresses, bills and LIEN waivers are presented to the bank or savings and loan, which advances additional funds.

PROJECTION estimate of future performance made by economists, corporate planners, and credit and securities analysts. Economists use econometric models to project GROSS NATIONAL PRODUCT (GNP), inflation, unemployment, and many other economic factors. Corporate financial planners project a company's operating results and CASH FLOW, using historical trends and making assumptions where necessary, in order to make budget decisions and to plan financing. Credit analysts use projections to forecast DEBT SERVICE ability. Securities analysts tend to focus their projections on earnings trends and cash flow per share in order to predict market values and dividend coverage. *See also* ECONOMETRICS.

PROJECT LINK econometric model linking all the economies in the world and forcasting the effects of changes in different economies on other economies. The project is identified with 1980 Nobel Memorial Prize in Economics winner Lawrence R. Klein. *See also* ECONOMETRICS.

PROJECT NOTE short-term debt issue of a municipal agency, usually a housing authority, to finance the construction of public housing. When the housing is finished, the notes are redeemed and the project is financed with long-term bonds. Both project notes and bonds usually pay tax-exempt interest to note- and bondholders, and both are also guaranteed by the U.S. Department of Housing and Urban Development.

PROMISSORY NOTE written promise committing the maker to pay the payee a specified sum of money either on demand or at a fixed or determinable future date, with or without interest. Instruments meeting these criteria are NEGOTIABLE. Often called, simply, a NOTE.

PROPORTIONAL REPRESENTATION method of stockholder voting, giving individual shareholders more power over the election of directors than they have under STATUTORY VOTING, which, by allowing one vote per share per director, makes it possible for a majority shareholder to elect all the directors. The most familiar example of proportional representation is CUMULATIVE VOTING, under which a shareholder has as many votes as he has shares of stock, multiplied by the number of vacancies on the board, all of which can be cast for one director. This makes it possible for a minority shareholder or a group of small shareholders to gain at least some representation on the board. Another variety provides for the holders of specified classes of stock to elect a number of directors in certain circumstances. For example, if the corporation failed to pay preferred dividends, the preferred holders might then be given the power to elect a certain proportion of the board. Despite the advocacy of stockholders' rights activists, proportional representation has made little headway in American corporations.

PROPRIETORSHIP unincorporated business owned by a single person. The individual proprietor has the right to all the profits from the business and also has responsibility for all the firm's liabilities. Since proprietors are considered self-employed, they are eligible for Keogh accounts for their retirement funds. *See also* KEOGH PLAN.

PRO RATA Latin for "according to the rate"; a method of proportionate allocation. For example, a pro rata property tax rebate might be divided proportionately (prorated) among taxpayers based on their original assessments, so that each gets the same percentage.

PROSPECTUS formal written offer to sell securities that sets forth the plan for a proposed business enterprise or the facts concerning an existing one that an investor needs to make an informed decision. Prospectuses are also issued by MUTUAL FUNDS, describing the history, background of managers, fund objectives, a financial statement, and other essential data. A prospectus for a PUBLIC OFFERING must be filed with the Securities and Exchange Commission and given to prospective buyers of the offering. The prospectus contains financial information and a description of a company's business history, officers, operations, pending litigation (if any), and plans (including the use of the proceeds from the issue).

Before investors receive the final copy of the prospectus, called the *statutory prospectus,* they may receive a PRELIMINARY PROSPECTUS, commonly called a *red herring.* This document is not complete in all details, though most of the major facts of the offering are usually included. The final prospectus is also called the *offering circular.*

Offerings of limited partnerships are also accompanied by prospectuses. Real estate, oil and gas, equipment leasing, and other types of limited partnerships are described in detail, and pertinent financial information, the background of the general partners, and supporting legal opinions are also given.

PROTECTIVE COVENANT *see* COVENANT.

PROVISION *see* ALLOWANCE.

PROXY

In general: person authorized to act or speak for another.

Business:

1. written POWER OF ATTORNEY given by shareholders of a corporation, authorizing a specific vote on their behalf at corporate meetings. Such proxies nor-

mally pertain to election of the BOARD OF DIRECTORS or to various resolutions submitted for shareholders' approval.
2. person authorized to vote on behalf of a stockholder of a corporation.

PROXY FIGHT technique used by an acquiring company to attempt to gain control of a TAKEOVER target. The acquirer tries to persuade the shareholders of the TARGET COMPANY that the present management of the firm should be ousted in favor of a slate of directors favorable to the acquirer. If the shareholders, through their PROXY votes, agree, the acquiring company can gain control of the company without paying a PREMIUM price for the firm.

PROXY STATEMENT information that the Securities and Exchange Commission requires must be provided to shareholders before they vote by proxy on company matters. The statement contains proposed members of the BOARD OF DIRECTORS, inside directors' salaries, and pertinent information regarding their bonus and option plans, as well as any resolutions of minority stockholders and of management.

PRUDENT-MAN RULE standard adopted by some U.S. states to guide those with responsibility for investing the money of others. Such fiduciaries (executors of wills, trustees, bank trust departments, and administrators of estates) must act as a prudent man or woman would be expected to act, with discretion and intelligence, to seek reasonable income, preserve capital, and, in general, avoid speculative investments. States not using the prudent-man system use the LEGAL LIST system, allowing fiduciaries to invest only in a restricted list of securities, called the *legal list*.

PUBLIC HOUSING AUTHORITY BOND obligation of local public housing agencies, which is centrally marketed through competitive sealed-bid auctions conducted by the U.S. Department of Housing and Urban Development (HUD). These obligations are secured by an agreement between HUD and the local housing agency that provides that the federal government will loan the local authority a sufficient amount of money to pay PRINCIPAL and INTEREST to maturity.
    The proceeds of such bonds provide low-rent housing through new construction, rehabilitation of existing buildings, purchases from private builders or developers, and leasing from private owners. Under special provisions, low-income families may also purchase such housing.
    The interest on such bonds is exempt from federal income taxes and may also be exempt from state and local income taxes.

PUBLIC LIMITED PARTNERSHIP real estate, oil and gas, equipment leasing, or other LIMITED PARTNERSHIP that is registered with the Securities and Exchange Commission and offered to the public through registered broker/dealers. Such partnerships may be oriented to producing income or capital gains, or within PASSIVE income rules, to generating tax advantages for limited partners. The number of investors in such a partnership is limited only by the sponsor's desire to cap the funds raised. A public limited partnership, which does not have an active secondary market, is distinguished from a PRIVATE-LIMITED PARTNERSHIP, which is limited to 35 limited partners plus ACCREDITED INVESTORS, and a MASTER LIMITED PARTNERSHIP (MLP) which is publicly traded, often on the major stock exchanges.

PUBLICLY HELD corporation that has shares available to the public at large. Such companies are regulated by the Securities and Exchange Commission.

PUBLIC OFFERING

1. offering to the investment public, after registration requirements of the Securities and Exchange Commission (SEC) have been complied with, of new securities, usually by an investment banker or a syndicate made up of several investment bankers, at a public offering price agreed upon between the issuer and the investment bankers. Public offering is distinguished from PRIVATE PLACEMENT of new securities, which is subject to different SEC regulations. *See also* REGISTERED NEW ISSUE; UNDERWRITE.
2. SECONDARY DISTRIBUTION of previously issued stock. *See also* REGISTERED SECONDARY OFFERING.

PUBLIC OFFERING PRICE price at which a NEW ISSUE of securities is offered to the public by underwriters. *See also* OFFERING PRICE; UNDERWRITE.

PUBLIC OWNERSHIP

Government: government ownership and operation of a productive facility for the purpose of providing some good or service to citizens. The government supplies the capital, controls management, sets prices, and generally absorbs all risks and reaps all profits—similar to a private enterprise. When public ownership displaces private ownership in a particular instance, it is called NATIONALIZATION.

Investments: portion of a corporation's stock that is publicly traded.

PUBLIC PURPOSE BOND category of MUNICIPAL BOND, as defined in the TAX REFORM ACT OF 1986, which is exempt from federal income taxes provided it provides no more than 10% benefit to private parties; also called *public activity, traditional government purpose,* and *essential purpose* bond. Although not defined in specific terms, public purpose bonds are presumed to include purposes such as roads, libraries, and government buildings.

PUBLIC SECURITIES ASSOCIATION association representing dealers, banks, and brokers underwriting municipal, U.S. government, and federal agency debt securities, as well as dealers in mortgage-backed securities.

PUBLIC UTILITY HOLDING COMPANY ACT OF 1935 major landmark in legislation regulating the securities industry, which reorganized the financial structures of HOLDING COMPANIES in the gas and electric utility industries and regulated their debt and dividend policies. Prior to the Act, abuses by holding companies were rampant, including WATERED STOCK, top-heavy capital structures with excessive fixed-debt burdens, and manipulation of the securities markets.
   To summarize the four basic provisions of the Act:
1. It requires holding companies operating interstate and persons exercising a controlling influence on utilities and holding companies to register with the Securities and Exchange Commission (SEC) and to provide information on the organizational structure, finances, and means of control.
2. It provides for SEC control of the operation and performance of registered holding companies and SEC approval of all new securities offerings, resulting in such reforms as the elimination of NONVOTING STOCK, the prevention of the milking of subsidiaries, and the outlawing of the upstreaming of dividends (payment of dividends by operating companies to holding companies).
3. It provides for uniform accounting standards, periodic administrative and financial reports, and reports on holdings by officers and directors, and for the end of interlocking directorates with banks or investment bankers.
4. It began the elimination of complex organizational structures by allowing only

one intermediate company between the top holding company and its operating companies (the GRANDFATHER CLAUSE).

PURCHASE ACQUISITION accounting method used in a business MERGER whereby the purchasing company treats the acquired company as an investment and adds the acquired company's assets to its own at their fair market value. Any premium paid over and above the FAIR MARKET VALUE of the acquired assets is reflected as GOODWILL on the buyer's BALANCE SHEET and must be written off against future earnings. Goodwill amortization is not deductible for tax purposes, so the reduction of reported future earnings can be a disadvantage of this method of merger accounting as compared with the alternative POOLING OF INTERESTS method. The purchase acquisition method is mandatory unless all the criteria for a pooling of interests combination are met.

PURCHASE FUND provision in some PREFERRED STOCK contracts and BOND indentures requiring the issuer to use its best efforts to purchase a specified number of shares or bonds annually at a price not to exceed par value. Unlike SINKING FUND provisions, which require that a certain number of bonds be retired annually, purchase funds require only that a tender offer be made; if no securities are tendered, none are retired. Purchase fund issues benefit the investor in a period of rising rates when the redemption price is higher than the market price and the proceeds can be put to work at a higher return.

PURCHASE GROUP group of investment bankers that, operating under the AGREEMENT AMONG UNDERWRITERS, agrees to purchase a NEW ISSUE of securities from the issuer for resale to the investment public; also called the UNDERWRITING GROUP or *syndicate*. The purchase group is distinguished from the SELLING GROUP, which is organized by the purchase group and includes the members of the purchase group along with other investment bankers. The selling group's function is DISTRIBUTION.

The agreement among underwriters, also called the *purchase group agreement,* is distinguished from the underwriting or purchase agreement, which is between the underwriting group and the issuer. *See also* UNDERWRITE.

PURCHASE GROUP AGREEMENT *see* PURCHASE GROUP.

PURCHASE-MONEY MORTGAGE MORTGAGE given by a buyer in lieu of cash for the purchase of property. Such mortgages make it possible to sell property when mortgage money is unavailable or when the only buyers are unqualified to borrow from commercial sources.

PURCHASE ORDER written authorization to a vendor to deliver specified goods or services at a stipulated price. Once accepted by the supplier, the purchase order becomes a legally binding purchase CONTRACT.

PURCHASING POWER

Economics: value of money as measured by the goods and services it can buy. For example, the PURCHASING POWER OF THE DOLLAR can be determined by comparing an index of consumer prices for a given base year to the present.

Investment: amount of credit available to a client in a brokerage account for the purchase of additional securities. Purchasing power is determined by the dollar amount of securities that can be margined. For instance, a client with purchasing power of $20,000 in his or her account could buy securities worth $40,000 under the Federal Reserve's currently effective 50% MARGIN REQUIREMENT. *See also* MARGIN SECURITY.

PURCHASING POWER OF THE DOLLAR measure of the amount of goods and services that a dollar can buy in a particular market, as compared with prior periods, assuming always an INFLATION or a DEFLATION factor and using an index of consumer prices. It might be reported, for instance, that one dollar in 1970 has 59 cents of purchasing power in 1990 because of the erosion caused by inflation. Deflation would increase the dollar's purchasing power.

PURE PLAY stock market jargon for a company that is virtually all devoted to one line of business. An investor who wants to invest in that line of business looks for such a pure play. For instance, General Dynamics may be considered a pure play in the defense business. The opposite of a pure play is a widely diversified company, such as a CONGLOMERATE.

PURPOSE LOAN loan backed by securities and used to buy other securities under Federal Reserve Board MARGIN and credit regulations.

PURPOSE STATEMENT form filed by a borrower that details the purpose of a loan backed by securities. The borrower agrees not to use the loan proceeds to buy securities in violation of any Federal Reserve regulations. *See also* NONPURPOSE LOAN; REGULATION U.

PUT BOND bond that allows its holder to redeem the issue on specified dates before maturity and receive full FACE VALUE. In return for this privilege, a bond buyer sacrifices some yield when choosing a put bond over a fixed-rate bond, that cannot be redeemed before maturity.

PUT-CALL RATIO total puts divided by total calls outstanding on a security or index. The ratio is one of the SENTIMENT INDICATORS.

PUT OPTION

Bonds: bondholder's right to redeem a bond before maturity. *See also* PUT BOND.

Options: contract that grants the right to sell at a specified price a specific number of shares by a certain date. The put option buyer gains this right in return for payment of an OPTION PREMIUM. The put option seller grants this right in return for receiving this premium. For instance, a buyer of an XYZ May 70 put has the right to sell 100 shares of XYZ at $70 to the put seller at any time until the contract expires in May. A put option buyer hopes the stock will drop in price, while the put option seller (called a *writer*) hopes the stock will remain stable, rise, or drop by an amount less than his or her profit on the premium.

PUT TO SELLER phrase used when a PUT OPTION is exercised. The OPTION WRITER is obligated to buy the underlying shares at the agreed-upon price. If an XYZ June 40 put were "put to seller," for instance, the writer would have to buy 100 shares of XYZ at $40 a share from the put holder even though the current market price of XYZ may be far less than $40 a share.

PYRAMIDING

In general: form of business expansion that makes extensive use of financial LEVERAGE to build complex corporate structures.

Fraud: scheme that builds on nonexistent values, often in geometric progression, such as a chain letter, now outlawed by mail fraud legislation. A famous example was the Ponzi scheme, perpetrated by Charles Ponzi in the late 1920s. Investors were paid ''earnings'' out of money received from new investors until the scheme collapsed.

Investments: using unrealized profits from one securities or commodities POSITION as COLLATERAL to buy further positions with funds borrowed from a broker. This use of leverage creates increased profits in a BULL MARKET, and causes MARGIN CALLS and large losses in a BEAR MARKET.

Marketing: legal marketing strategy whereby additional distributorships are sold side-by-side with consumer products in order to multiply market reach and maximize profits to the sales organization.

q———————————————————————————

Q-TIP TRUST *q*ualified *t*erminable *i*nterest *p*roperty *trust*, which allows assets to be transferred between spouses. The grantor of a Q-tip trust directs income from the assets to his or her spouse for life but has the power to distribute the assets upon the death of the spouse. Such trusts qualify the grantor for the unlimited marital deduction if the spouse should die first.

A Q-tip trust is often used to provide for the welfare of a spouse while keeping the assets out of the estate of another (such as a future marriage partner) if the grantor dies first.

QUALIFIED ENDORSEMENT endorsement (signature on the back of a check or other NEGOTIABLE INSTRUMENT transferring the amount to someone other than the one to whom it is payable) that contains wording designed to limit the endorser's liability. ''Without recourse,'' the most frequently seen example, means that if the instrument is not honored, the endorser is not responsible. Where qualified endorsements are restrictive (such as ''for deposit only'') the term *restricted endorsement* is preferable.

QUALIFIED OPINION language in the auditor's opinion accompanying financial statements that calls attention to limitations of the audit or exceptions the auditor takes to items in the statements. Typical reasons for qualified opinions: a pending lawsuit that, if lost, would materially affect the financial condition of the company; an indeterminable tax liability relating to an unusual transaction; inability to confirm a portion of the inventory because of inaccessible location. *See also* ACCOUNTANT'S OPINION.

QUALIFIED PLAN OR TRUST plan set up by an employer for the benefit of employees that adheres to the rules set forth by the Internal Revenue Service (IRS) in 1954. Such a plan—for example, a profit-sharing or a pension plan—allows employees to build up savings, which are paid out at retirement or upon termination of employment. The employees pay taxes on this money only when they draw it out, usually at retirement; until such time, the funds accumulate tax deferred. The employer makes the payments to the plan, and is therefore entitled to certain deductions and other tax benefits as stated in the IRS Code.

QUALIFYING ANNUITY ANNUITY approved by the Internal Revenue Service (IRS) for inclusion as an investment in Keogh plans, IRAs, and other IRS-approved pension and profit-sharing plans. *see also* KEOGH PLAN; INDIVIDUAL RETIREMENT ACCOUNT (IRA).

QUALIFYING SHARE share of COMMON STOCK owned in order to qualify as a director of the issuing corporation.

QUALIFYING STOCK OPTION privilege granted to an employee of a corporation that permits the purchase, for a special price, of shares of its CAPITAL STOCK, under conditions sustained in the Internal Revenue Service Code. The law states (1) that the OPTION plan must be approved by the stockholders, (2) that the option is not transferable, (3) that the EXERCISE PRICE must not be less than the MARKET PRICE of the shares at the time the option is issued, and (4) that the grantee may not own more than 5% of the company's voting power or 5% of the value of all classes of its outstanding stock (10% if equity capital is under $1 million). No income tax is payable by the employee either at the time of the grant or at the time the option is exercised. If the market price falls below the option price, another option with a lower exercise price can be issued. There is a $100,000 per employee limit on the value of stock covered by options that are exercisable in any one calendar year. Also called INCENTIVE STOCK OPTION.

QUALIFYING UTILITY utility in which shareholders were able (until the end of 1985) to defer taxes by reinvesting up to $750 in dividends ($1500 for a couple filing jointly) in the company's stock. Taxes were due when the stock was sold. This plan was enacted by the Economic Recovery Tax Act of 1981 as a means of helping utilities raise investment capital cheaply. Most of the utilities qualifying for the plan were electric utilities.

QUALITATIVE ANALYSIS

In general: analysis that evaluates factors that cannot be precisely measured.

Securities and credit analysis: analysis that is concerned with such questions as the experience, character, and general caliber of management; employee morale; and the status of labor relations rather than with the actual financial data about a company. *See also* QUANTITATIVE ANALYSIS.

QUALITY CONTROL process of assuring that products are made to consistently high standards of quality. Inspection of goods at various points in their manufacture is usually an important part of the quality control process.

QUALITY OF EARNINGS phrase describing a corporation's earnings that are attributable to increased sales and cost controls, as distinguished from artificial profits created by inflationary values in inventories or other assets. In a period of high inflation, the quality of earnings tends to suffer, since a large portion of a firm's profits is generated by the rising value of inventories. In a lower inflation period, a company that achieves higher sales and maintains lower costs produces a higher quality of earnings—a factor often appreciated by investors, who are frequently willing to pay more for a higher quality of earnings.

QUANT person with mathematical and computer skills who provides numerical and analytical support services in the securities industry.

QUANTITATIVE ANALYSIS analysis dealing with measurable factors as distinguished from such qualitative considerations as the character of management or the state of employee morale. In credit and securities analysis, examples of quantitative considerations are the value of assets; the cost of capital; the historical and projected patterns of sales, costs, and profitability and a wide range of considerations in the areas of economics; the money market; and the securities markets. Although quantitative and qualitative factors are distinguishable, they must be combined to arrive at sound business and financial judgments. *See also* QUAL-ITATIVE ANALYSIS.

QUARTERLY

In general: every three months (one quarter of a year).

Securities: basis on which earnings reports to shareholders are made; also, usual time frame of dividend payments.

QUARTER STOCK stock with a par value of $25 per share.

QUASI-PUBLIC CORPORATION corporation that is operated privately and often has its stock traded publicly, but that also has some sort of public mandate and often has the government's backing behind its direct debt obligations; for instance, the FEDERAL NATIONAL MORTGAGE ASSOCIATION (Fannie Mae), and the STUDENT LOAN MARKETING ASSOCIATION (Sallie Mae).

QUICK RATIO cash, MARKETABLE SECURITIES, and ACCOUNTS RECEIVABLE divided by current liabilities. By excluding inventory, this key LIQUIDITY ratio focuses on the firm's more LIQUID ASSETS, and helps answer the question "If sales stopped, could this firm meet its current obligations with the readily convertible assets on hand?" Assuming there is nothing happening to slow or prevent collections, a quick ratio of 1 to 1 or better is usually satisfactory. Also called *acid-test ratio, quick asset ratio.*

QUID PRO QUO

In general: from the Latin, meaning "something for something." By mutual agreement, one party provides a good or service for which he or she gets another good or service in return.

Securities industry: arrangement by a firm using institutional research that it will execute all trades based on that research with the firm providing it, instead of directly paying for the research. This is known as paying in SOFT DOLLARS.

QUIET PERIOD period an ISSUER is "in registration" and subject to an SEC embargo on promotional publicity. It dates from the preunderwriting decision to 40 or 90 days after the EFFECTIVE DATE.

QUOTATION

Business: price estimate on a commercial project or transaction.

Investments: highest bid and lowest offer (asked) price currently available on a security or a commodity. An investor who asks for a quotation ("quote") on XYZ might be told "60 to 60½," meaning that the best bid price (the highest price any buyer wants to pay) is currently $60 a share and that the best offer (the lowest price any seller is willing to accept) is $60½ at that time. Such quotes assume ROUND-LOT transactions—for example, 100 shares for stocks.

QUOTATION BOARD electronically controlled board at a brokerage firm that displays current price quotations and other financial data such as dividends, price ranges of stocks, and current volume of trading.

QUOTED PRICE price at which the last sale and purchase of a particular security or commodity took place.

r

RACKETEER INFLUENCED AND CORRUPT ORGANIZATION ACT *see* RICO.

RADAR ALERT close monitoring of trading patterns in a company's stock by senior managers to uncover unusual buying activity that might signal a TAKEOVER attempt. *See also* SHARK WATCHER.

RAIDER individual or corporate investor who intends to take control of a company by buying a controlling interest in its stock and installing new management. Raiders who accumulate 5% or more of the outstanding shares in the TARGET COMPANY must report their purchases to the Securities and Exchange Commission, the exchange of listing, and the target itself. *See also* BEAR RAID; WILLIAMS ACT.

RALLY marked rise in the price of a security, commodity future, or market after a period of decline or sideways movement.

R & D *see* RESEARCH AND DEVELOPMENT.

RANDOM WALK theory about the movement of stock and commodity futures prices hypothesizing that past prices are of no use in forecasting future price movements. According to the theory, stock prices reflect reactions to information coming to the market in random fashion, so they are no more predictable than the walking pattern of a drunken person. The random walk theory was first espoused in 1900 by the French mathematician Louis Bachelier and revived in the 1960s. It is hotly disputed by advocates of TECHNICAL ANALYSIS, who say that charts of past price movements enable them to predict future price movements.

RANGE high and low end of a security, commodity future, or market's price fluctuations over a period of time. Daily newspapers publish the 52-week high and low price range of stocks traded on the New York Stock Exchange, American Stock Exchange, and over-the-counter markets. Advocates of TECHNICAL ANALYSIS attach great importance to trading ranges because they consider it of great significance if a security breaks out of its trading range by going higher or lower. *See also* BREAKOUT.

RATE BASE value established for a utility by a regulatory body such as a Public Utility Commission on which the company is allowed to earn a particular rate of return. Generally the rate base includes the utility's operating costs but not the cost of constructing new facilities. Whether modernization costs should be included in the rate base, and thus passed on to customers, is a subject of continuing controversy. *See also* FAIR RATE OF RETURN.

RATE COVENANT provision in MUNICIPAL REVENUE BOND agreements or resolutions covering the rates, or methods of establishing rates, to be charged users of the facility being financed. The rate covenant usually promises that rates will be adjusted when necessary to cover the cost of repairs and maintenance while continuing to provide for the payment of bond interest and principal.

RATE OF EXCHANGE *see* EXCHANGE RATE; PAR VALUE OF CURRENCY.

RATE OF INFLATION *see* CONSUMER PRICE INDEX; INFLATION RATE; PRODUCER PRICE INDEX.

RATE OF RETURN

Fixed-income securities (bonds and preferred stock): CURRENT YIELD, that is, the coupon or contractual dividend rate divided by the purchase price. *See also* YIELD TO AVERAGE LIFE; YIELD TO CALL; YIELD TO MATURITY.

Common stock: (1) dividend yield, which is the annual dividend divided by the purchase price. (2) TOTAL RETURN rate, which is the dividend plus capital appreciation.

Corporate finance: RETURN ON EQUITY or RETURN ON INVESTED CAPITAL.

Capital budgeting: INTERNAL RATE OF RETURN.

See also FAIR RATE OF RETURN; HORIZON ANALYSIS; MEAN RETURN; REAL INTEREST RATE; REQUIRED RATE OF RETURN; TOTAL RETURN; YIELD.

RATING

Credit and investments: evaluation of securities investment and credit risk by rating services such as Fitch Investors Service, Inc., MOODY'S INVESTORS SERVICE, STANDARD & POOR'S CORPORATION, and VALUE LINE INVESTMENT SURVEY. *See also* CREDIT RATING; EVENT RISK; NOT RATED.

Insurance: using statistics, mortality tables, probability theory, experience, judgment, and mathematical analysis to establish the rates on which insurance premiums are based. There are three basic rating systems: *class rate,* applying to a homogeneous grouping of clients; *schedule system,* relating positive and negative factors in the case of a particular insured (for example, a smoker or nonsmoker in the case of a life policy) to a base figure; and *experience rating,* reflecting the historical loss experience of the particular insured. Also called *rate-making.*

Insurance companies are also rated; *see* BEST'S RATING.

LEADING BOND RATING SERVICES Explanation of corporate/municipal bond ratings	RATING SERVICE		
	Fitch	*Moody's*	*Standard & Poor's*
Highest quality, "gilt edged"	AAA	Aaa	AAA
High quality	AA	Aa	AA
Upper medium grade	A	A	A
Medium grade	BBB	Baa	BBB
Predominantly speculative	BB	Ba	BB
Speculative, low grade	B	B	B
Poor to default	CCC	Caa	CCC
Highest speculation	CC	Ca	CC
Lowest quality, no interest	C	C	C
In default, in arrears, questionable value	{ DDD DD D		DDD DD D

Fitch and Standard & Poor's may use + or − to modify some ratings. Moody's uses the numerical modifiers 1 (highest), 2, and 3 in the range from Aa1 through Ca3.

RATIO ANALYSIS method of analysis, used in making credit and investment judgments, which utilizes the relationship of figures found in financial statements to determine values and evaluate risks and compares such ratios to those of prior periods and other companies to reveal trends and identify eccentricities. Ratio analysis is only one tool among many used by analysts. *See also* ACCOUNTS RECEIVABLE TURNOVER; ACID TEST RATIO; BOND RATIO; CAPITALIZATION RATIO; CAPITAL TURNOVER; CASH RATIO; COLLECTION PERIOD; COMMON STOCK RATIO; CURRENT RATIO; DEBT-TO-EQUITY RATIO; DIVIDEND PAYOUT RATIO; EARNINGS-PRICE

RATIO; FIXED CHARGE COVERAGE; LEVERAGE; NET TANGIBLE ASSETS PER SHARE; OPERATING RATIO; PREFERRED STOCK RATIO; PRICE-EARNINGS RATIO; PROFIT MARGIN; QUICK RATIO; RETURN ON EQUITY; RETURN ON INVESTED CAPITAL; RETURN ON SALES.

RATIO WRITER OPTIONS writer who sells more CALL contracts than he has underlying shares. For example, an investor who writes (sells) 10 calls, 5 of them covered by the 500 owned shares of the underlying stock and the other 5 of them uncovered (or "naked"), has a 2 for 1 ratio write.

REACHBACK ability of a LIMITED PARTNERSHIP or other tax shelter to offer deductions at the end of the year that reach back for the entire year. For instance, the investor who buys an OIL AND GAS LIMITED PARTNERSHIP in late December might be able to claim deductions for the entire year's drilling costs, depletion allowance, and interest expenses. Reachback on tax shelters was considered to be abusive by the Internal Revenue Service, and it was substantially eliminated in 1983 and 1984.

REACTION drop in securities prices after a sustained period of advancing prices, perhaps as the result of PROFIT TAKING or adverse developments. *See also* CORRECTION.

READING THE TAPE judging the performance of stocks by monitoring changes in price as they are displayed on the TICKER tape. An analyst reads the tape to determine whether a stock is acting strongly or weakly, and therefore is likely to go up or down. An investor reads the tape to determine whether a stock trade is going with or against the flow of market action. *See also* DON'T FIGHT THE TAPE.

REAGANOMICS economic program followed by the administration of President Ronald Reagan beginning in 1981. Reaganomics stressed lower taxes, higher defense spending, and curtailed spending for social services. After a reduction of growth in the money supply by the Federal Reserve Board combined with Reaganomics to produce a severe recession in 1981–82, the Reagan years were characterized by huge budget deficits, low interest and inflation rates, and continuous economic growth.

REAL ESTATE piece of land and all physical property related to it, including houses, fences, landscaping, and all rights to the air above and earth below the property. Assets not directly associated with the land are considered *personal property*.

REAL ESTATE INVESTMENT TRUST (REIT) company, usually traded publicly, that manages a portfolio of real estate in order to earn profits for shareholders. Patterned after INVESTMENT COMPANIES, REITs make investments in a diverse array of real estate from shopping centers and office buildings to apartment complexes and hotels. Some REITs, called EQUITY REITS, take equity positions in real estate; shareholders receive income from the rents received from the properties and receive capital gains as buildings are sold at a profit. Other REITs specialize in lending money to building developers; such MORTGAGE REITS pass interest income on to shareholders. Some REITs have a mix of equity and debt investments. To avoid taxation at the corporate level, 75% or more of the REIT's income must be from real property and 95% of its taxable income must be distributed to shareholders. The TAX REFORM ACT OF 1986 generally gave REITs more flexibility.

REAL INCOME income of an individual, group, or country adjusted for changes in PURCHASING POWER caused by inflation. A price index is used to determine the difference between the purchasing power of a dollar in a base year and the purchasing power now. The resulting percentage factor, applied to total income, yields the value of that income in constant dollars, termed real income. For instance, if the cost of a market basket increases from $100 to $120 in ten years, reflecting a 20% decline in purchasing power, salaries must rise by 20% if real income is to be maintained.

REAL INTEREST RATE current interest rate minus inflation rate. The real interest rate may be calculated by comparing interest rates with present or, more frequently, with predicted inflation rates. The real interest rate gives investors in bonds and other fixed-rate instruments a way to see whether their interest will allow them to keep up with or beat the erosion in dollar values caused by inflation. With a bond yielding 10% and inflation of 3%, for instance, the real interest rate of 7% would bring a return high enough to beat inflation. If inflation were at 15%, however, the investor would fall behind as prices rise.

REALIZED PROFIT (OR LOSS) profit or loss resulting from the sale or other disposal of a security. Capital gains taxes may be due when profits are realized; realized losses can be used to offset realized gains for tax purposes. Such profits and losses differ from a PAPER PROFIT OR LOSS, which (except for OPTION and FUTURES CONTRACTS) has no tax consequences.

REAL RATE OF RETURN RETURN on an investment adjusted for inflation.

REBATE
1. in lending, unearned interest refunded to a borrower if the loan is paid off before maturity.
2. in consumer marketing, payment made to a consumer after a purchase is completed, to induce purchase of a product. For instance, a customer who buys a television set for $500 may be entitled to a rebate of $50, which is received after sending a proof of purchase and a rebate form to the television manufacturer. *See also* RULE OF THE 78S.

RECAPITALIZATION alteration of a corporation's CAPITAL STRUCTURE, such as an exchange of bonds for stock. BANKRUPTCY is a common reason for recapitalization; debentures might be exchanged for REORGANIZATION BONDS that pay interest only when earned A healthy company might seek to improve its tax situation by replacing preferred stock with bonds to take advantage of the tax deductibility of interest. *See also* DEFEASANCE.

RECAPTURE
1. contract clause allowing one party to recover some degree of possession of an asset. In leases calling for a percentage of revenues, such as those for shopping centers, the recapture clause provides that the developer get a percentage of profits in addition to a fixed rent.
2. in the tax code, the reclamation by the government of tax benefits previously taken. For example, where a portion of the profit on the sale of a depreciable asset represented ACCELERATED DEPRECIATION or the INVESTMENT CREDIT, all or part of that gain would be "recaptured" and taxed as ORDINARY INCOME, with the balance subject to the favorable CAPITAL GAINS TAX. Effective with the TAX REFORM ACT OF 1986, dispositions of property are taxed at ordinary rates uniformly. Recapture also has specialized applications in oil and other industries. Recapture assumed a new meaning under the 1986 Act whereby banks with assets of $500 million or more were required to take into income

the balance of their RESERVE for BAD DEBTS. The Act called for recapture of income at the rate of 10%, 20%, 30%, and 40% for the years 1987 through 1990, respectively.

RECEIVER court-appointed person who takes possession of, but not title to, the assets and affairs of a business or estate that is in a form of BANKRUPTCY called *receivership* or is enmeshed in a legal dispute. The receiver collects rents and other income and generally manages the affairs of the entity for the benefit of its owners and creditors until a disposition is made by the court.

RECEIVER'S CERTIFICATE debt instrument issued by a RECEIVER, who uses the proceeds to finance continued operations or otherwise to protect assets in receivership. The certificates constitute a LIEN on the property, ranking ahead of all other secured or unsecured liabilities in LIQUIDATION.

RECEIVE VERSUS PAYMENT instruction accompanying sell orders by institutions that only cash will be accepted in exchange for delivery of the securities at the time of settlement. Institutions are generally required by law to accept only cash. Also called *receive against payment*.

RECESSION downturn in economic activity, defined by many economists as at least two consecutive quarters of decline in a country's GROSS NATIONAL PRODUCT.

RECLAMATION
Banking: restoration or correction of a NEGOTIABLE INSTRUMENT—or the amount thereof—that has been incorrectly recorded by the *clearing house*.

Finance: restoration of an unproductive asset to productivity, such as by using landfill to make a swamp developable.

Securities: right of either party to a securities transaction to recover losses caused by *bad delivery* or other irregularities in the settlement process.

RECORD DATE *see* DATE OF RECORD; EX-DIVIDEND DATE; PAYMENT DATE.

RECOURSE LOAN
1. loan for which an endorser or guarantor is liable for payment in the event the borrower defaults.
2. loan made to a DIRECT PARTICIPATION PROGRAM or LIMITED PARTNERSHIP whereby the lender, in addition to being secured by specific assets, has recourse against the general assets of the partnership. *See also* NONRECOURSE LOAN.

RECOVERY
Economics: period in a business cycle when economic activity picks up and the GROSS NATIONAL PRODUCT grows, leading into the expansion phase of the cycle.

Finance: (1) absorption of cost through the allocation of DEPRECIATION; (2) collection of an ACCOUNT RECEIVABLE that had been written off as a bad debt; (3) residual cost, or salvage value, of a fixed asset after all allowable depreciation.

Investment: period of rising prices in a securities or commodities market after a period of falling prices.

REDEEMABLE BOND *see* CALLABLE.

REDEMPTION repayment of a debt security or preferred stock issue, at or before maturity, at PAR or at a premium price.
    Mutual fund shares are redeemed at NET ASSET VALUE when a shareholder's holdings are liquidated.

REDEMPTION PRICE *see* CALL PRICE.

RED HERRING *see* PRELIMINARY PROSPECTUS.

REDISCOUNT DISCOUNT short-term negotiable debt instruments, such as banker's ACCEPTANCES and COMMERCIAL PAPER, that have been *discounted* with a bank—in other words, exchanged for an amount of cash adjusted to reflect the current interest rate. The bank then discounts the paper a second time for its own benefit with another bank or with a Federal Reserve bank. Rediscounting was once the primary means by which banks borrowed additional reserves from the Fed. Today most banks do this by discounting their own notes secured by GOVERNMENT SECURITIES or other ELIGIBLE PAPER. But *rediscount rate* is still used as a synonym for DISCOUNT RATE, the rate charged by the Fed for all bank borrowings.

REDS *see* REFUNDING ESCROW DEPOSITS.

REFCORP *see* RESOLUTION FUNDING CORPORATION.

REFINANCING

Banking: extending the maturity date, or increasing the amount of existing debt, or both.

Bonds: REFUNDING; retiring existing bonded debt by issuing new securities to reduce the interest rate, or to extend the maturity date, or both.

Personal finance: revising a payment schedule, usually to reduce the monthly payments and often to modify interest charges.

REFUNDING
1. replacing an old debt with a new one, often in order to lower the interest costs of the issuer. For instance, a corporation or municipality that has issued 14% bonds may want to refund them by issuing 10% bonds if interest rates have dropped. *See also* PREREFUNDING; REFINANCING.
2. in merchandising, returning money to the purchaser—for example, a consumer who has paid for an appliance and is not happy with it.

REFUNDING ESCROW DEPOSITS (REDS) financial instruments used to circumvent 1984 and 1986 tax law restrictions on tax-exempt PREREFUNDINGS for certain kinds of state or local projects, such as airports, solid-waste disposal facilities, wharves, and convention centers. The object of prerefundings was to lock in a lower current rate in anticipation of maturing higher-rate issues. REDs accomplish this by way of a forward purchase contract that obligates the investor to buy bonds at a predetermined rate when they are issued at a future date. The future date coincides with the first optional call date on existing high-rate bonds. In the interim, the investor's money is invested in Treasury bonds bought in the secondary market. The Treasuries are held in escrow, in effect securing the investor's deposit and paying taxable annual income. The Treasuries mature around the call date on the existing bonds, providing the money to buy the new issue and redeem the old one. Also called *municipal forwards*.

REGIONAL BANK bank that specializes in collecting deposits and making loans in one region of the country, as distinguished from a MONEY CENTER BANK, which operates nationally and internationally.

REGIONAL STOCK EXCHANGES organized national securities exchanges located outside of New York City and registered with the Securities and Exchange Commission. They include: the Boston, Cincinnati, Intermountain (Salt Lake

City), Midwest (Chicago), Pacific (Los Angeles and San Francisco), Philadelphia (Philadelphia and Miami), and Spokane stock exchanges. These exchanges list not only regional issues, but many of the securities that are listed on the New York exchanges. Companies listed on the NEW YORK STOCK EXCHANGE and the AMERICAN STOCK EXCHANGE will often be listed on regional exchanges as well to broaden the market for their securities. Using the INTERMARKET TRADING SYSTEM (ITS), a SPECIALIST on the floor of one of the New York or regional exchanges can see competing prices for the securities he trades on video screens. Regional exchanges handle only a small percentage of the total volume of the New York exchanges, though more than 50% of companies listed in New York are also listed regionally. *See also* DUAL LISTING; GRADUATED SECURITY; SECURITIES AND COMMODITIES EXCHANGES.

REGISTERED BOND bond that is recorded in the name of the holder on the books of the issuer or the issuer's REGISTRAR and can be transferred to another owner only when ENDORSED by the registered owner. A bond registered for principal only, and not for interest, is called a *registered coupon bond*. One that is not registered is called a *bearer bond;* one issued with detachable coupons for presentation to the issuer or a paying agent when interest or principal payments are due is termed a COUPON BOND. Bearer bonds are NEGOTIABLE INSTRUMENTS payable to the holder and therefore do not legally require endorsement. Bearer bonds that may be changed to registered bonds are called *interchangeable bonds*.

REGISTERED CHECK check issued by a bank for a customer who places funds aside in a special register. The customer writes in his name and the name of the payee and the amount of money to be transferred. The bank, which collects a fee for the service, then puts on the bank's name and the amount of the check and gives the check a special number. The check has two stubs, one for the customer and one for the bank. The registered check is similar to a money order for someone who does not have a checking account at the bank.

REGISTERED COMPANY company that has filed a REGISTRATION STATEMENT with the Securities and Exchange Commission in connection with a PUBLIC OFFERING of securities and must therefore comply with SEC DISCLOSURE requirements.

REGISTERED COMPETITIVE MARKET MAKER
1. securities dealer registered with the NATIONAL ASSOCIATION OF SECURITIES DEALERS (NASD) as a market maker in a particular OVER-THE-COUNTER stock— that is, one who maintains firm bid and offer prices in the stock by standing ready to buy or sell round lots. Such dealers must announce their quotes through NASDAQ, which requires that there be at least two market makers in each stock listed in the system; the bid and asked quotes are compared to ensure that the quote is a *representative spread*. See also MAKE A MARKET.
2. REGISTERED COMPETITIVE TRADER on the New York Stock Exchange. Such traders are sometimes called market makers because, in addition to trading for their own accounts, they are expected to help correct an IMBALANCE OF ORDERS. *See also* REGISTERED EQUITY MARKET MAKER.

REGISTERED COMPETITIVE TRADER one of a group of New York Stock Exchange members who buy and sell for their own accounts. Because these members pay no commissions, they are able to profit on small changes in market prices and thus tend to trade actively in stocks doing a high volume. Like SPECIALISTS, registered competitive traders must abide by exchange rules, including a requirement that 75% of their trades be *stabilizing*. This means they cannot sell unless the last trading price on a stock was up, or buy unless the last trading price was down. Orders from the general public take precedence over those of registered competitive traders, which account for less than 1% of volume. Also called *floor trader* or *competitive trader*.

REGISTERED COUPON BOND *see* REGISTERED BOND.

REGISTERED EQUITY MARKET MAKER AMERICAN STOCK EXCHANGE member firm registered as a trader for its own account. Such firms are expected to make stabilizing purchases and sales when necessary to correct imbalances in particular securities. *See also* REGISTERED COMPETITIVE MARKET MAKER.

REGISTERED FINANCIAL PLANNER (RFP) *see* FINANCIAL PLANNER.

REGISTERED INVESTMENT COMPANY investment company, such as an open-end or closed-end MUTUAL FUND, which files a registration statement with the Securities and Exchange Commission and meets all the other requirements of the INVESTMENT COMPANY ACT OF 1940.

REGISTERED OPTIONS TRADER specialist on the floor of the AMERICAN STOCK EXCHANGE who is responsible for maintaining a fair and orderly market in an assigned group of options.

REGISTERED REPRESENTATIVE employee of a stock exchange member broker/dealer who acts as an ACCOUNT EXECUTIVE for clients. As such, the registered representative gives advice on which securities to buy and sell, and he collects a percentage of the commission income he generates as compensation. To qualify as a registered representative, a person must acquire a background in the securities business and pass a series of tests, including the General Securities Examination and state securities tests. "Registered" means licensed by the Securities and Exchange Commission and by the New York Stock Exchange.

REGISTERED RETIREMENT SAVINGS PLAN (RRSP) tax-deductible and tax-sheltered retirement plan for individuals in Canada, similar in concept to the INDIVIDUAL RETIREMENT PLAN (IRA) in the United States.

REGISTERED SECONDARY OFFERING offering, usually through investment bankers, of a large block of securities that were previously issued to the public, using the abbreviated Form S-16 of the Securities and Exchange Commission. Such offerings are usually made by major stockholders of mature companies who may be *control persons* or institutions who originally acquired the securities in a private placement. Form S-16 relies heavily on previously filed SEC documents such as the S-1, the 10-K, and quarterly filings. Where listed securities are concerned, permission to sell large blocks off the exchange must be obtained from the appropriate exchange. *See also* LETTER SECURITY; SECONDARY DISTRIBUTION; SECONDARY OFFERING; SHELF REGISTRATION.

REGISTERED SECURITY
1. security whose owner's name is recorded on the books of the issuer or the issuer's agent, called a *registrar*—for example, a REGISTERED BOND as opposed to a *bearer bond,* the former being transferable only by endorsement, the latter payable to the holder.
2. securities issue registered with the Securities and Exchange Commission as a new issue or as a SECONDARY OFFERING. *See also* REGISTERED SECONDARY OFFERING; REGISTRATION.

REGISTRAR agency responsible for keeping track of the owners of bonds and the issuance of stock. The registrar, working with the TRANSFER AGENT, keeps current files of the owners of a bond issue and the stockholders in a corporation. The registrar also makes sure that no more than the authorized amount of stock is in circulation. For bonds, the registrar certifies that a bond is a corporation's genuine debt obligation.

REGISTRATION process set up by the Securities Exchange Acts of 1933 and 1934 whereby securities that are to be sold to the public are reviewed by the Securities and Exchange Commission. The REGISTRATION STATEMENT details pertinent financial and operational information about the company, its management, and the purpose of the offering. Incorrect or incomplete information will delay the offering.

REGISTRATION FEE charge made by the Securities and Exchange Commission and paid by the issuer of a security when a public offering is recorded with the SEC.

REGISTRATION STATEMENT document detailing the purpose of a proposed public offering of securities. The statement outlines financial details, a history of the company's operations and management, and other facts of importance to potential buyers. *See also* REGISTRATION.

REGRESSION ANALYSIS statistical technique used to establish the relationship of a dependent variable, such as the sales of a company, and one or more independent variables, such as family formations, GROSS NATIONAL PRODUCT, per capita income, and other ECONOMIC INDICATORS. By measuring exactly how large and significant each independent variable has historically been in its relation to the dependent variable, the future value of the dependent variable can be predicted. Essentially, regression analysis attempts to measure the degree of correlation between the dependent and independent variables, thereby establishing the latter's predictive value. For example, a manufacturer of baby food might want to determine the relationship between sales and housing starts as part of a sales forecast. Using a technique called a scatter graph, it might plot on the X and Y axes the historical sales for ten years and the historical annual housing starts for the same period. A line connecting the average dots, called the regression line, would reveal the degree of correlation between the two factors by showing the amount of unexplained variation—represented by the dots falling outside the line. Thus, if the regression line connected all the dots, it would demonstrate a direct relationship between baby food sales and housing starts, meaning that one could be predicted on the basis of the other. The proportion of dots scattered outside the regression line would indicate, on the other hand, the degree to which the relationship was less direct, a high enough degree of unexplained variation meaning there was no meaningful relationship and that housing starts have no predictive value in terms of baby food sales. This proportion of unexplained variations is termed the *coefficient of determination,* and its square root the CORRELATION COEFFICIENT. The correlation coefficient is the ultimate yardstick of regression analysis: a correlation coefficient of 1 means the relationship is direct—baby food and housing starts move together; -1 means there is a negative relationship— the more housing starts there are, the less baby food is sold; a coefficient of zero means there is no relationship between the two factors.

Regression analysis is also used in securities' markets analysis and in the risk-return analyses basic to PORTFOLIO THEORY.

REGRESSION ANALYSIS
SCATTER GRAPH

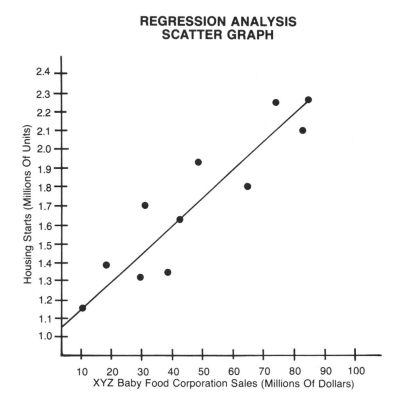

XYZ Baby Food Corporation Sales (Millions Of Dollars)

Housing Starts (Millions Of Units)

REGRESSIVE TAX

1. system of taxation in which tax rates decline as the tax base rises. For example, a system that taxed values of $1000 to $5000 at 5%, $5000 to $10,000 at 4% and so on would be regressive. A regressive tax is the opposite of a PRO-GRESSIVE TAX.

2. tax system that results in a higher tax for the poor than for the rich, in terms of percentage of income. In this sense, a sales tax is regressive even though the same rate is applied to all sales, because people with lower incomes tend to spend most of their incomes on goods and services. Similarly, payroll taxes are regressive because they are borne largely by wage earners and not by higher income groups. Local property taxes also tend to be regressive because poorer people spend more of their incomes on housing costs, which are directly affected by property taxes. *See also* FLAT TAX.

REGULAR WAY DELIVERY (AND SETTLEMENT) completion of securities transaction at the office of the purchasing broker on (but not before) the fifth full business day following the date of the transaction, as required by the NEW YORK STOCK EXCHANGE. Government transactions are an exception; for them, regular way means delivery and settlement the next business day following a transaction.

REGULATED COMMODITIES commodities under the jurisdiction of the COMMODITIES FUTURES TRADING COMMISSION, which include all commodities traded in organized contract markets. The CFTC was established in 1974 by the U.S. Congress, succeeding the Commodities Exchange Act of 1936. It polices matters of information and disclosure, fair trading practices, registration of firms and individuals, and the protection of customer funds, record keeping, and the maintenance of orderly futures and options markets.

REGULATED INVESTMENT COMPANY MUTUAL FUND or UNIT INVESTMENT TRUST eligible under *Regulation M* of the Internal Revenue Service to pass capital gains, dividends, and interest earned on fund investments directly to its shareholders to be taxed at the personal level. The process, designed to avoid double taxation, is called the *conduit theory.* To qualify as a regulated investment company, the fund must meet such requirements as 97% minimum distribution of interest and dividends received on investments and 90% distribution of capital gain net income. Shareholders must pay taxes even if they reinvest their distributions.

REGULATION A
1. Securities and Exchange Commission provision for simplified REGISTRATION of small issues of securities. A Regulation A issue requires a shorter form of PROSPECTUS and carries lesser liability for officers and directors for false or misleading statements.
2. Federal Reserve Board statement of the means and conditions under which Federal Reserve banks make loans to member and other banks at what is called the DISCOUNT WINDOW. *See also* REDISCOUNT.

REGULATION G Federal Reserve Board rule regulating lenders other than commercial banks, brokers or dealers who, in the ordinary course of business, extend credit to individuals to purchase or carry securities. Special provision is made for loans by corporations and credit unions to finance purchases under employee stock option and stock purchase plans.

REGULATION Q Federal Reserve Board ceiling on the rates that banks and other savings institutions can pay on savings and other time deposits. THE DEPOSITORY INSTITUTIONS DEREGULATION AND MONETARY CONTROL ACT OF 1980 provided for phasing out Regulation Q by 1986.

REGULATION T Federal Reserve Board regulation covering the extension of credit to customers by securities brokers, dealers, and members of the national securities exchanges. It establishes INITIAL MARGIN requirements and defines registered (eligible), unregistered (ineligible), and exempt securities. *See also* MARGIN REQUIREMENT; MARGIN SECURITIES.

REGULATION U Federal Reserve Board limit on the amount of credit a bank may extend a customer for purchasing and carrying MARGIN SECURITIES. *See also* NONPURPOSE LOAN.

REGULATION Z Federal Reserve Board regulation covering provisions of the CONSUMER CREDIT PROTECTION ACT OF 1968, known as the Truth in Lending Act.

REHYPOTHECATION pledging by brokers of securities in customers' MARGIN ACCOUNTS to banks as collateral for broker loans under a GENERAL LOAN AND COLLATERAL AGREEMENT. Broker loans cover the positions of brokers who have made margin loans to customers for margin purchases and SELLING SHORT. Margin loans are collateralized by the HYPOTHECATION of customers' securities to the broker. Their rehypothecation is authorized when the customer originally signs a GENERAL ACCOUNT agreement.

REINSURANCE sharing of RISK among insurance companies. Part of the insurer's risk is assumed by other companies in return for a part of the premium fee paid by the insured. By spreading the risk, reinsurance allows an individual company to take on clients whose coverage would be too great a burden for one insurer to carry alone.

REINVESTMENT PRIVILEGE right of a shareholder to reinvest dividends in order to buy more shares in the company or MUTUAL FUND, usually at no additional sales charge.

REINVESTMENT RATE rate of return resulting from the reinvestment of the interest from a bond or other fixed-income security. The reinvestment rate on a ZERO-COUPON BOND is predictable and locked in, since no interest payments are ever made, and therefore all imputed interest is reinvested at the same rate. The reinvestment rate on coupon bonds is less predictable because it rises and falls with market interest rates.

REIT *see* REAL ESTATE INVESTMENT TRUST.

REJECTION

Banking: refusal to grant credit to an applicant because of inadequate financial strength, a poor credit history, or some other reason.

Insurance: refusal to underwrite a risk, that is, to issue a policy.

Securities: refusal of a broker or a broker's customer to accept the security presented to complete a trade. This usually occurs because the security lacks the necessary endorsements, or because of other exceptions to the rules for GOOD DELIVERY.

RELATIVE STRENGTH rate at which a stock falls relative to other stocks in a falling market or rises relative to other stocks in a rising market. Analysts reason that a stock that holds value on the downside will be a strong performer on the upside and vice versa.

RELEASE CLAUSE provision in a MORTGAGE agreement allowing the freeing of pledged property after a proportionate amount of payment has been made.

REMARGINING putting up additional cash or eligible securities to correct a deficiency in EQUITY deposited in a brokerage MARGIN ACCOUNT to meet MINIMUM MAINTENANCE REQUIREMENTS. Remargining usually is prompted by a MARGIN CALL.

REMIC acronym for *real estate mortgage investment conduit*, a pass-through vehicle created under the TAX REFORM ACT OF 1986 to issue multiclass mortgage-backed securities. REMICs may be organized as corporations, partnerships, or trusts, and those meeting qualifications are not subject to DOUBLE TAXATION. Interests in REMICs may be *regular* (debt instruments) or *residual* (equity interests).

REMIT pay for purchased goods or services by cash, check, or electronic payment.

REORGANIZATION financial restructuring of a firm in BANKRUPTCY. *See also* TRUSTEE IN BANKRUPTCY; VOTING TRUST CERTIFICATE.

REORGANIZATION BOND debt security issued by a company in REORGANIZATION proceedings. The bonds are generally issued to the company's creditors on a basis whereby interest is paid only if and when it is earned. *See also* ADJUSTMENT BOND; INCOME BOND.

REPATRIATION return of the financial assets of an organization or individual from a foreign country to the home country.

REPLACEMENT COST ACCOUNTING accounting method allowing additional DEPRECIATION on part of the difference between the original cost and current replacement cost of a depreciable asset.

REPURCHASE AGREEMENT (REPO; RP) agreement between a seller and a buyer, usually of U.S. Government securities, whereby the seller agrees to repurchase the securities at an agreed upon price and, usually, at a stated time. Repos, also called RPs or buybacks, are widely used both as a money market investment vehicle and as an instrument of Federal Reserve MONETARY POLICY. Where a repurchase agreement is used as a short-term investment, a government securities dealer, usually a bank, borrows from an investor, typically a corporation with excess cash, to finance its inventory, using the securities as collateral. Such RPs may have a fixed maturity date or be OPEN REPOS, callable at any time. Rates are negotiated directly by the parties involved, but are generally lower than rates on collateralized loans made by New York banks. The attraction of repos to corporations, which also have the alternatives of COMMERCIAL PAPER, CERTIFICATES OF DEPOSIT, TREASURY BILLS and other short-term instruments, is the flexibility of maturities that makes them an ideal place to "park" funds on a very temporary basis. Dealers also arrange *reverse repurchase agreements*, whereby they agree to buy the securities and the investor agrees to repurchase them at a later date.

The FEDERAL RESERVE BANK also makes extensive use of repurchase agreements in its OPEN MARKET OPERATIONS as a method of fine tuning the MONEY SUPPLY. To temporarily expand the supply, the Fed arranges to buy securities from nonbank dealers who in turn deposit the proceeds in their commercial bank accounts thereby adding to reserves. Timed to coincide with whatever length of time the Fed needs to make the desired adjustment, usually 1 to 15 days, the dealer repurchases the securities. Such transactions are made at the Federal Reserve DISCOUNT RATE and accounts are credited in FEDERAL FUNDS. When it wishes to reduce the money supply temporarily, the Fed reverses the process. Using a procedure called the MATCHED SALE PURCHASE TRANSACTION, it sells securities to a nonbank dealer who either draws down bank balances directly or takes out a bank loan to make payment, thereby draining reserves.

In a third variation of the repurchase agreement, banks and thrift institutions can raise temporary capital funds with a device called the *retail repurchase agreement*. Using pooled government securities to secure loans from individuals, they agree to repurchase the securities at a specified time at a price including interest. Despite its appearance of being a deposit secured by government securities, the investor has neither a special claim on the securities nor protection by the FEDERAL DEPOSIT INSURANCE CORPORATION in the event the bank liquidates.

See also OVERNIGHT REPO.

REQUIRED RATE OF RETURN return required by investors before they will commit money to an investment at a given level of risk. Unless the expected return exceeds the required return, an investment is unacceptable. *See also* HURDLE RATE; INTERNAL RATE OF RETURN; MEAN RETURN.

RESCIND cancel a contract agreement. The Truth in Lending Act confers the RIGHT OF RESCISSION, which allows the signer of a contract to nullify it within three business days without penalty and have any deposits refunded. Contracts may also be rescinded in cases of fraud, failure to comply with legal procedures, or misrepresentation. For example, a contract signed by a child under legal age may be rescinded, since children do not have the right to take on contractual obligations.

RESEARCH AND DEVELOPMENT (R&D) scientific and marketing evolution of a new product or service. Once such a product has been created in a laboratory or other research setting, marketing specialists attempt to define the market for the product. Then, steps are taken to manufacture the product to meet the needs of the market. Research and development spending is often listed as a separate item in a company's financial statements. In industries such as high-technology and pharmaceuticals, R&D spending is quite high, since products are outdated or attract competition quickly. Investors looking for companies in such fast-changing fields check on R&D spending as a percentage of sales because they consider this an important indicator of the company's prospects. *See also* RESEARCH AND DEVELOPMENT LIMITED PARTNERSHIP.

RESEARCH AND DEVELOPMENT LIMITED PARTNERSHIP plan whose investors put up money to finance new product RESEARCH AND DEVELOPMENT. In return, the investors get a percentage of the product's profits, if any, together with such benefits as DEPRECIATION of equipment. R&D partnerships may be offered publicly or privately, usually through brokerage firms. Those that are offered to the public must be registered with the Securities and Exchange Commission. *See also* LIMITED PARTNERSHIP.

RESEARCH DEPARTMENT division within a brokerage firm, investment company, bank trust department, insurance company, or other institutional investing organization that analyzes markets and securities. Research departments include analysts who focus on particular securities, commodities, and whole industries as well as generalists who forecast movements of the markets as a whole, using both FUNDAMENTAL ANALYSIS and TECHNICAL ANALYSIS. An analyst whose advice is followed by many investors can have a major impact on the prices of individual securities.

RESERVE
1. segregation of RETAINED EARNINGS to provide for such payouts as dividends, contingencies, improvements, or retirement of preferred stock.
2. VALUATION RESERVE, also called ALLOWANCE, for DEPRECIATION, BAD DEBT losses, shrinkage of receivables because of discounts taken, and other provisions created by charges to the PROFIT AND LOSS STATEMENT.
3. hidden reserves, represented by understatements of BALANCE SHEET values.
4. deposit maintained by a commercial bank in a FEDERAL RESERVE BANK to meet the Fed's RESERVE REQUIREMENT.

RESERVE REQUIREMENT FEDERAL RESERVE SYSTEM rule mandating the financial assets that member banks must keep in the form of cash and other liquid assets as a percentage of DEMAND DEPOSITS and TIME DEPOSITS. This money must be in the bank's own vaults or on deposit with the nearest regional FEDERAL RESERVE BANK. Reserve requirements, set by the Fed's Board of Governors, are one of the key tools in deciding how much money banks can lend, thus setting the pace at which the nation's money supply and economy grow. The higher the reserve requirement, the tighter the money—and therefore the slower the economic growth. *See also* MONETARY POLICY; MONEY SUPPLY; MULTIPLIER.

RESIDENTIAL ENERGY CREDIT tax credit granted to homeowners prior to 1986 by the federal government for improving the energy efficiency of their homes. Installation of storm windows and doors, insulation, or new fuel-saving heating systems before the end of 1985 meant a maximum federal credit on expenditures of $300. Equipping a home with renewable energy devices such as solar panels or windmills meant a maximum federal credit of $4000. Many states offer incentives for installing such devices.

RESIDUAL SECURITY SECURITY that has a potentially dilutive effect on earnings per common share. Warrants, rights, convertible bonds, and preferred stock are potentially dilutive because exercising or converting them into common stock would increase the number of common shares competing for the same earnings, and earnings per share would be reduced. *See also* DILUTION: FULLY DILUTED EARNINGS PER (COMMON) SHARE.

RESIDUAL VALUE
1. realizable value of a FIXED ASSET after costs associated with the sale.
2. amount remaining after all allowable DEPRECIATION charges have been subtracted from the original cost of a depreciable asset.
3. scrap value, which is the value to a junk dealer.
    Also called *salvage value*.

RESISTANCE LEVEL

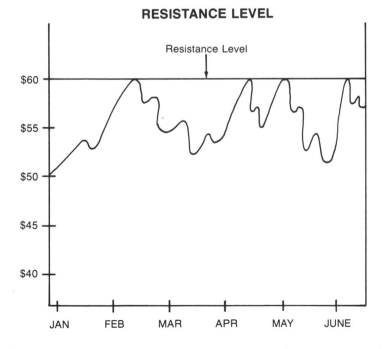

RESISTANCE LEVEL price ceiling at which technical analysts note persistent selling of a commodity or security. If XYZ's stock generally trades between a low of $50 and a high of $60 a share, $50 is called the SUPPORT LEVEL and $60

is called the resistance level. Technical analysts think it significant when the stock breaks through the resistance level because that means it usually will go on to new high prices. *See also* BREAKOUT; TECHNICAL ANALYSIS.

RESOLUTION
1. in general, expression of desire or intent.
2. formal document representing an action of a corporation's BOARD OF DI-RECTORS—perhaps a directive to management, such as in the declaration of a dividend, or a corporate expression of sentiment, such as acknowledging the services of a retiring officer. A *corporate resolution*, which defines the authority and powers of individual officers, is a document given to a bank.
3. legal order or contract by a government entity—called a *bond resolution*—authorizing a bond issue and spelling out the rights of bondholders and the obligations of the issuer.

RESTRICTED ACCOUNT MARGIN ACCOUNT with a securities broker in which the EQUITY is less than the INITIAL MARGIN requirement set by the Federal Reserve Board's REGULATION T. A customer whose account is restricted may not make further purchases and must, in accordance with Regulation T's *retention requirement*, retain in the account a percentage of the proceeds of any sales so as to reduce the deficiency (debit balance). This retention requirement is currently set at 50%. *See also* MARGIN CALL.

RESTRICTED SURPLUS portion of RETAINED EARNINGS not legally available for the payment of dividends. Among the circumstances giving rise to such restriction: dividend arrearages in CUMULATIVE PREFERRED stock, a shortfall in the minimum WORKING CAPITAL ratio specified in an INDENTURE, or simply a vote by the BOARD OF DIRECTORS. Also called *restricted retained earnings*.

RESOLUTION FUNDING CORPORATION (REFCORP) U.S. government agency created by Congress in 1989 to (1) issue BAILOUT BONDS and raise industry funds to finance activities of the RESOLUTION TRUST CORPORATION (RTC) and (2) merge or close sick institutions inherited from the disbanded FEDERAL SAVINGS AND LOAN INSURANCE CORPORATION (FSLIC). *See also* OFFICE OF THRIFT SUPERVISION (OTS).

RESOLUTION TRUST CORPORATION (RTC) U.S. government agency created by the 1989 "bailout bill" to merge or close savings and loan institutions becoming insolvent between 1989 and August 1992. RTC was scheduled to terminate after 1996 and shift its responsibilities to the SAVINGS ASSOCIATION INSURANCE FUND (SAIF), a unit of the FEDERAL DEPOSIT INSURANCE CORPORATION. The *Resolution Trust Corporation Oversight Board*, an arm of the executive branch, oversees broad policy and the dispensing of funds to sick S&Ls by RTC. *See also* OFFICE OF THRIFT SUPERVISION (OTS).

RESTRICTIVE COVENANT *see* COVENANT.

RESYNDICATION LIMITED PARTNERSHIP partnership in which existing properties are sold to new limited partners, who can gain tax advantages that had been exhausted by the old partnership. For instance, a partnership with government-subsidized housing may have given partners substantial tax benefits five years ago. Now the same housing development may be sold to a resyndication partnership, which will start the process of DEPRECIATION over again and claim additional tax benefits for its new limited partners. Resyndication partnerships are usually offered as PRIVATE PLACEMENTS through brokerage houses, although a few have been offered to the public.

RETAIL HOUSE brokerage firm that caters to retail investors instead of institutions. Such a firm may be a large national broker called a WIRE HOUSE, with a large RESEARCH DEPARTMENT and a wide variety of products and services for individuals, or it may be a small BOUTIQUE serving an exclusive clientele with specialized research or investment services.

RETAIL INVESTOR investor who buys securities and commodities futures on his own behalf, not for an organization. Retail investors typically buy shares of stock or commodity positions in much smaller quantities than institutions such as mutual funds, bank trust departments, and pension funds and therefore are usually charged commissions higher than those paid by the institutions. In recent years, market activity has increasingly been dominated by INSTITUTIONAL INVESTORS.

RETAINED EARNINGS net profits kept to accumulate in a business after dividends are paid. Also called *undistributed profits* or *earned surplus*. Retained earnings are distinguished from *contributed capital*—capital received in exchange for stock, which is reflected in CAPITAL STOCK or CAPITAL SURPLUS and DONATED STOCK or DONATED SURPLUS. STOCK DIVIDENDS—the distribution of additional shares of capital stock with no cash payment—reduce retained earnings and increase capital stock. Retained earnings plus the total of all the capital accounts represent the NET WORTH of a firm. *See also* ACCUMULATED PROFITS TAX; PAID-IN CAPITAL.

RETAINED EARNINGS STATEMENT reconciliation of the beginning and ending balances in the RETAINED EARNINGS account on a company's BALANCE SHEET. It breaks down changes affecting the account, such as profits or losses from operations, dividends declared, and any other items charged or credited to retained earnings. A retained earnings statement is required by GENERALLY ACCEPTED ACCOUNTING PRINCIPLES whenever comparative balance sheets and income statements are presented. It may appear in the balance sheet, in a combined PROFIT AND LOSS STATEMENT and retained earnings statement, or as a separate schedule. It may also be called *statement of changes in earned surplus* (or *retained income*).

RETENTION in securities underwriting, the number of units allocated to a participating investment banker (SYNDICATE member) minus the units held back by the syndicate manager for facilitating institutional sales and for allocation to firms in the selling group that are not also members of the syndicate. *See also* UNDERWRITE.

RETENTION RATE percentage of aftertax profits credited to RETAINED EARNINGS. It is the opposite of the DIVIDEND PAYOUT RATIO.

RETENTION REQUIREMENT *see* RESTRICTED ACCOUNT.

RETIREMENT
1. cancellation of stock or bonds that have been reacquired or redeemed. *See also* CALLABLE; REDEMPTION.
2. removal from service after a fixed asset has reached the end of its useful life or has been sold and appropriate adjustments have been made to the asset and depreciation accounts.
3. repayment of a debt obligation.

4. permanent withdrawal of an employee from gainful employment in accordance with an employer's policies concerning length of service, age, or disability. A retired employee may have rights to a pension or other retirement provisions offered by the employer. Employer retirement benefits may supplement payments from an INDIVIDUAL RETIREMENT ACCOUNT (IRA) or KEOGH PLAN.

RETURN

Finance and investment: profit on a securities or capital investment, usually expressed as an annual percentage rate. *See also* RATE OF RETURN; RETURN ON EQUITY; RETURN ON INVESTED CAPITAL; RETURN ON SALES; TOTAL RETURN.

Retailing: exchange of previously sold merchandise for REFUND or CREDIT against future sales.

Taxes: form on which taxpayers submit information required by the government when they file with the INTERNAL REVENUE SERVICE. For example, form 1040 is the tax return used by individual tax payers.

Trade: physical return of merchandise for credit against an invoice.

RETURN OF CAPITAL distribution of cash resulting from DEPRECIATION tax savings, the sale of a CAPITAL ASSET or of securities in a portfolio, or any other transaction unrelated to RETAINED EARNINGS. Returns of capital are not directly taxable but may result in higher CAPITAL GAINS taxes later on if they reduce the acquisition cost base of the property involved. Also called *return of basis*.

RETURN ON EQUITY amount, expressed as a percentage, earned on a company's common stock investment for a given period. It is calculated by dividing common stock equity (NET WORTH) at the beginning of the accounting period into NET INCOME for the period after preferred stock dividends but before common stock dividends. Return on equity tells common shareholders how effectually their money is being employed. Comparing percentages for current and prior periods reveals trends, and comparison with industry composites reveals how well a company is holding its own against its competitors.

RETURN ON INVESTED CAPITAL amount, expressed as a percentage, earned on a company's total capital—its common and preferred stock EQUITY plus its long-term FUNDED DEBT—calculated by dividing total capital into earnings before interest, taxes, and dividends. Return on invested capital, usually termed *return on investment*, or *ROI*, is a useful means of comparing companies, or corporate divisions, in terms of efficiency of management and viability of product lines.

RETURN ON SALES net pretax profits as a percentage of NET SALES—a useful measure of overall operational efficiency when compared with prior periods or with other companies in the same line of business. It is important to recognize, however, that return on sales varies widely from industry to industry. A supermarket chain with a 2% return on sales might be operating efficiently, for example, because it depends on high volume to generate an acceptable RETURN ON INVESTED CAPITAL. In contrast, a manufacturing enterprise is expected to average 4% to 5%, so a return on sales of 2% is likely to be considered highly inefficient.

REVALUATION change in the value of a country's currency relative to others that is based on the decision of authorities rather than on fluctuations in the market. Revaluation generally refers to an increase in the currency's value; DEVALUATION refers to a decrease. *See also* FLOATING EXCHANGE RATE; PAR VALUE OF CURRENCY.

REVENUE ANTICIPATION NOTE (RAN) short-term debt issue of a municipal entity that is to be repaid out of anticipated revenues such as sales taxes. When the taxes are collected, the RAN is paid off. Interest from the note is usually tax-free to RAN holders.

REVENUE BOND *see* MUNICIPAL REVENUE BOND.

REVENUE NEUTRAL guiding criterion in drafting the TAX REFORM ACT OF 1986 whereby provisions estimated to add revenue were offset by others estimated to reduce revenue, so that on paper the new bill would generate the same amount of revenue as the old tax laws. The concept was theoretical rather than real, since estimates are subject to variation.

REVENUE SHARING

Limited partnerships: percentage split between the general partner and limited partners of profits, losses, cash distributions, and other income or losses which result from the operation of a real estate, oil and gas, equipment leasing, or other partnership. *See also* LIMITED PARTNERSHIP.

Taxes: return of tax revenue to a unit of government by a larger unit, such as from a state to one of its municipalities. GENERAL REVENUE SHARING between the federal government and states, localities, and other subunits existed between 1972 and 1987.

REVERSAL change in direction in the stock or commodity futures markets, as charted by technical analysts. If the Dow Jones Industrial Average has been climbing steadily from 1100 to 1200, for instance, chartists would speak of a reversal if the average started a sustained fall back toward 1100.

REVERSAL

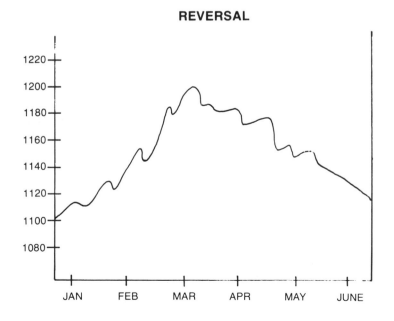

REVERSE ANNUITY MORTGAGE (RAM) MORTGAGE instrument that allows an elderly person to live off the equity in a fully paid-for house. Such a homeowner would enter into a reverse annuity mortgage agreement with a financial institution such as a bank, which would guarantee a lifelong fixed monthly income in return for gradually giving up ownership of the house. The longer the payments continue, the less equity the elderly owner would retain. At the owner's death the bank gains title to the real estate, which it can sell at a profit. The law also permits such arrangements between relatives, so that, for instance, a son or daughter might enter into a reverse annuity mortgage transaction with his or her retiring parents, thus providing the parents with cash to invest in income-yielding securities and the son or daughter with the depreciation and other tax benefits of real estate ownership. *See also* ARM'S LENGTH TRANSACTION.

REVERSE A SWAP restore a bond portfolio to its former position following a swap of one bond for another to gain the advantage of a YIELD SPREAD or a tax loss. The reversal may mean that the yield differential has disappeared or that the investor, content with a short-term profit, wishes to stay with the original bond for the advantages that may be gained in the future. *See also* BOND SWAP.

REVERSE CONVERSION technique whereby brokerage firms earn interest on their customers' stock holdings. A typical reverse conversion would work like this: A brokerage firm sells short the stocks it holds in customers' margin accounts, then invests this money in short-term money market instruments. To protect against a sharp rise in the markets, the firm hedges its short position by buying CALL options and selling PUT options. To unwind the reverse conversion, the firm buys back the stocks, sells the call, and buys the put. *See also* MARGIN ACCOUNT; OPTION.

REVERSE MORTGAGE arrangement whereby a homeowner borrows against home equity and receives regular payments (tax-free) from the lender until the accumulated principal and interest reach the credit limit of equity; at that time, either the lender gets repayment in a lump sum or takes the house. Reverse mortgages are available privately and through the Federal Housing Administration (FHA). They are appropriate for cash-poor but house-rich older borrowers who want to stay in their homes and expect to live long enough to amortize high up-front fees but not so long that the lender winds up with the house. Lower income but greater security is provided by a variation, the REVERSE ANNUITY MORTGAGE (RAM).

REVERSE REPURCHASE AGREEMENT *see* REPURCHASE AGREEMENT.

REVERSE SPLIT procedure whereby a corporation reduces the number of shares outstanding. The total number of shares will have the same market value immediately after the reverse split as before it, but each share will be worth more. For example, if a firm with 10 million outstanding shares selling at $10 a share executes a reverse 1 for 10 split, the firm will end up with 1 million shares selling for $100 each. Such splits are usually initiated by companies wanting to raise the price of their outstanding shares because they think the price is too low to attract investors. Also called *split down*. *See also* SPLIT.

REVISIONARY TRUST IRREVOCABLE TRUST that becomes a REVOCABLE TRUST after a specified period, usually over 10 years or upon the death of the GRANTOR.

REVOCABLE TRUST agreement whereby income-producing property is deeded to heirs. The provisions of such a TRUST may be altered as many times as the GRANTOR pleases, or the entire trust agreement can be canceled, unlike irrevocable trusts. The grantor receives income from the assets, but the property passes directly to the beneficiaries at the grantor's death, without having to go through PROBATE court proceedings. Since the assets are still part of the grantor's estate, however, estate taxes must be paid on this transfer. This kind of trust differs from an IRREVOCABLE TRUST, which permanently transfers assets from the estate during the grantor's lifetime and therefore escapes estate taxes.

REVOLVING CREDIT

Commercial banking: contractual agreement between a bank and its customer, usually a company, whereby the bank agrees to make loans up to a specified maximum for a specified period, usually a year or more. As the borrower repays a portion of the loan, an amount equal to the repayment can be borrowed again under the terms of the agreement. In addition to interest borne by notes, the bank charges a fee for the commitment to hold the funds available. A COMPENSATING BALANCE may be required in addition.

Consumer banking: loan account requiring monthly payments of less than the full amount due, and the balance carried forward is subject to a financial charge. Also, an arrangement whereby borrowings are permitted up to a specified limit and for a specified period, usually a year, with a fee charged for the commitment. Also called *open-end credit* or *revolving line of credit*.

REVOLVING LINE OF CREDIT *see* REVOLVING CREDIT.

RICH
1. term for a security whose price seems too high in light of its price history. For bonds, the term may also imply that the yield is too low.
2. term for rate of interest that seems too high in relation to the borrower's risk.
3. synonym for *wealthy*.

RICO acronym for RACKETEER INFLUENCED AND CORRUPT ORGANIZATION ACT, a federal law that was aimed originally at organized crime but was used to convict firms and individuals of INSIDER TRADING in the late 1980s. Many critics charged that the law was excessively enforced, and several indictments were dismissed for lack of evidence.

RIGGED MARKET situation in which the prices for a security are manipulated so as to lure unsuspecting buyers or sellers. *See also* MANIPULATION.

RIGHT *see* SUBSCRIPTION RIGHT.

RIGHT OF REDEMPTION right to recover property transferred by a MORTGAGE or other LIEN by paying off the debt either before or after foreclosure. Also called *equity of redemption*.

RIGHT OF RESCISSION right granted by the federal CONSUMER CREDIT PROTECTION ACT OF 1968 to void a contract within three business days with full refund of any down payment and without penalty. The right is designed to protect consumers from high-pressure door-to-door sales tactics and hastily made credit commitments which involve their homes as COLLATERAL, such as loans secured by second mortgages.

RIGHT OF SURVIVORSHIP right entitling one owner of property held jointly to take title to it when the other owner dies. *See also* JOINT TENANTS WITH RIGHT OF SURVIVORSHIP; TENANTS IN COMMON.

RIGHTS OFFERING offering of COMMON STOCK to existing shareholders who hold rights that entitle them to buy newly issued shares at a discount from the price at which shares will later be offered to the public. Rights offerings are usually handled by INVESTMENT BANKERS under what is called a STANDBY COMMITMENT, whereby the investment bankers agree to purchase any shares not subscribed to by the holders of rights. *See also* PREEMPTIVE RIGHT; SUBSCRIPTION RIGHT.

RING location on the floor of an exchange where trades are executed. The circular arrangement where traders can make bid and offer prices is also called a *pit*, particularly when commodities are traded.

RISING BOTTOMS technical chart pattern showing a rising trend in the low prices of a security or commodity. As the range of prices is charted daily, the lows reveal an upward trend. Rising bottoms signify higher and higher basic SUPPORT LEVELS for a security or commodity. When combined with a series of ASCENDING TOPS, the pattern is one a follower of TECHNICAL ANALYSIS would call bullish.

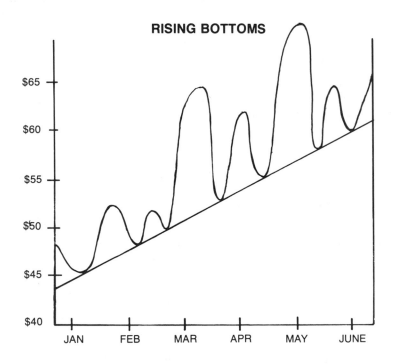

RISING BOTTOMS

RISK measurable possibility of losing or not gaining value. Risk is differentiated from uncertainty, which is not measurable. Among the commonly encountered types of risk are these:

Actuarial risk: risk an insurance underwriter covers in exchange for premiums, such as the risk of premature death.

Exchange risk: chance of loss on foreign currency exchange.

Inflation risk: chance that the value of assets or of income will be eroded as inflation shrinks the value of a country's currency.

Interest rate risk: possibility that a fixed-rate debt instrument will decline in value as a result of a rise in interest rates.

Inventory risk: possibility that price changes, obsolescence, or other factors will shrink the value of INVENTORY.

Liquidity risk: possibility that an investor will not be able to buy or sell a commodity or security quickly enough or in sufficient quantities because buying or selling opportunities are limited.

Political risk: possibility of NATIONALIZATION or other unfavorable government action.

Repayment (credit) risk: chance that a borrower or trade debtor will not repay an obligation as promised.

Risk of principal: chance that invested capital will drop in value.

Underwriting risk: risk taken by an INVESTMENT BANKER that a new issue of securities purchased outright will not be bought by the public and/or that the market price will drop during the offering period.

RISK-ADJUSTED DISCOUNT RATE in PORTFOLIO THEORY and CAPITAL BUDGET analysis, the rate necessary to determine the PRESENT VALUE of an uncertain or risky stream of income; it is the risk-free rate (generally the return on short-term U.S. Treasury securities) plus a risk premium that is based on an analysis of the risk characteristics of the particular investment or project.

RISK ARBITRAGE ARBITRAGE involving risk, as in the simultaneous purchase of stock in a company being acquired and sale of stock in its proposed acquirer. Also called *takeover arbitrage*. Traders called *arbitrageurs* attempt to profit from TAKEOVERS by cashing in on the expected rise in the price of the target company's shares and drop in the price of the acquirer's shares. If the takeover plans fall through, the traders may be left with enormous losses. Risk arbitrage differs from riskless arbitrage, which entails locking in or profiting from the differences in the prices of two securities or commodities trading on different exchanges. *See also* RISKLESS TRANSACTION.

RISK AVERSE term referring to the assumption that, given the same return and different risk alternatives, a rational investor will seek the security offering the least risk—or, put another way, the higher the degree of risk, the greater the return that a rational investor will demand. *See also* CAPITAL ASSET PRICING MODEL; EFFICIENT PORTFOLIO; MEAN RETURN; PORTFOLIO THEORY.

RISK CAPITAL *see* VENTURE CAPITAL.

RISK CATEGORY classification of risk elements used in analyzing MORTGAGES.

RISK-FREE RETURN the YIELD on a risk-free investment. The three-month Treasury bill is considered a riskless investment because it is a direct obligation of the U.S. government and its term is short enough to minimize the risks of inflation and market interest rate changes. The CAPITAL ASSET PRICING MODEL used in modern PORTFOLIO THEORY has the premise that the return on a security is equal to the risk-free return plus a RISK PREMIUM.

RISKLESS TRANSACTION
1. trade guaranteeing a profit to the trader that initiates it. An *arbitrageur* may lock in a profit by trading on the difference in prices for the same security or commodity in different markets. For instance, if gold were selling for $400 an ounce in New York and $398 in London, a trader who acts quickly could

buy a contract in London and sell it in New York for a riskless profit.

2. concept used in evaluating whether dealer MARKUPS and MARKDOWNS in OVER THE COUNTER transactions with customers are reasonable or excessive. In what is known as the FIVE PERCENT RULE, the NATIONAL ASSOCIATION OF SECURITIES DEALERS (NASD) takes the position that markups (when the customer buys) and markdowns (when the customer sells) should not exceed 5%, the proper charge depending on the effort and risk of the dealer in completing a trade. The maximum would be considered excessive for a riskless transaction, in which a security has high marketability and the dealer does not simply act as a broker and take a commission but trades from or for inventory and charges a markup or markdown. Where a dealer satisfies a buy order by making a purchase in the open market for inventory, then sells the security to the customer, the trade is called a *simultaneous transaction*. To avoid NASD criticism, broker-dealers commonly disclose the markups and markdowns to customers in transactions where they act as dealers.

RISK PREMIUM in PORTFOLIO THEORY, the difference between the RISK-FREE RETURN and the TOTAL RETURN from a risky investment. In the CAPITAL ASSET PRICING MODEL, the risk premium reflects market-related risk (SYSTEMATIC RISK) as measured by BETA. Other models also reflect specific risk as measured by ALPHA.

ROCKET SCIENTIST investment firm creator of innovative securities.

ROLL DOWN move from one OPTION position to another one having a lower EXERCISE PRICE. The term assumes that the position with the higher exercise price is closed out.

ROLL FORWARD move from one OPTION position to another with a later expiration date. The term assumes that the earlier position is closed out before the later one is established. If the new position involves a higher EXERCISE PRICE, it is called a *roll-up and forward*; if a lower exercise price, it is called a *roll-down and forward*. Also called *rolling over*.

ROLLING STOCK equipment that moves on wheels, used in the transportation industry. Examples include railroad cars and locomotives, tractor-trailers, and trucks.

ROLLOVER

1. movement of funds from one investment to another. For instance, an INDIVIDUAL RETIREMENT ACCOUNT may be rolled over when a person retires into an ANNUITY or other form of pension plan payout system. When a BOND or CERTIFICATE OF DEPOSIT matures, the funds may be rolled over into another bond or certificate of deposit. The proceeds from the sale of a house may be rolled over into the purchase of another house within two years without tax penalty. A stock may be sold and the proceeds rolled over into the same stock, establishing a different cost basis for the shareholder. *See also* THIRTY DAY WASH RULE.

2. term often used by banks when they allow a borrower to delay making a PRINCIPAL payment on a loan. Also, a country that has difficulty in meeting its debt payments may be granted a rollover by its creditors. With governments themselves, rollovers in the form of REFUNDINGS or REFINANCINGS are routine. *See also* CERTIFICATE OF DEPOSIT ROLLOVER.

ROLL UP move from one OPTION position to another one having a higher EXERCISE PRICE. The term assumes that the earlier position is closed out before the new position is established. *See also* MASTER LIMITED PARTNERSHIP.

ROUND LOT generally accepted unit of trading on a securities exchange. On the New York Stock Exchange, for example, a round lot is 100 shares for stock and $1000 or $5000 par value for bonds. In inactive stocks, the round lot is 10 shares. Increasingly, there seems to be recognition of a 500-share round lot for trading by institutions. Large-denomination CERTIFICATES OF DEPOSIT trade on the OVER THE COUNTER market in units of $1 million. Investors who trade in round lots do not have to pay the DIFFERENTIAL charged on ODD LOT trades.

ROUND TRIP TRADE purchase and sale of a security or commodity within a short time. For example, a trader who continually is making short-term trades in a particular commodity is making round trip or *round turn* trades. Commissions for such a trader are likely to be quoted in terms of the total for a purchase and sale—$100 for the round trip, for instance. Excessive round trip trading is called CHURNING.

ROYALTY payment to the holder for the right to use property such as a patent, copyrighted material, or natural resources. For instance, inventors may be paid royalties when their inventions are produced and marketed. Authors may get royalties when books they have written are sold. Land owners leasing their property to an oil or mining company may receive royalties based on the amount of oil or minerals extracted from their land. Royalties are set in advance as a percentage of income arising from the commercialization of the owner's rights or property.

ROYALTY TRUST oil or gas company *spin-off* of oil reserves to a trust, which avoids DOUBLE TAXATION, eliminates the expense and risk of new drilling, and provides DEPLETION tax benefits to shareholders. In the mid-1980s Mesa Royalty Trust, which pioneered the idea, led other trusts in converting to a MASTER LIMITED PARTNERSHIP form of organization, offering tax advantages along with greater flexibility and liquidity.

RULE 405 New York Stock Exchange codification of an ethical concept recognized industrywide by those dealing with the investment public. These so-called KNOW YOUR CUSTOMER rules recognize that what is suitable for one investor may be less appropriate for another and require investment people to obtain pertinent facts about a customer's other security holdings, financial condition, and objectives. *See also* SUITABILITY RULES.

RULE OF 72 formula for approximating the time it will take for a given amount of money to double at a given COMPOUND INTEREST rate. The formula is simply 72 divided by the interest rate. In six years $100 will double at a compound annual rate of 12%, thus; 72 divided by 12 equals 6.

RULE OF THE 78s method of computing REBATES of interest on installment loans. It uses the SUM-OF-THE-YEAR'S-DIGITS basis in determining the interest earned by the FINANCE COMPANY for each month of a year, assuming equal monthly payments, and gets its name from the fact that the sum of the digits 1 through 12 is 78. Thus interest is equal to12/78ths of the total annual interest in the first month, 11/78ths in the second month, and so on.

RULES OF FAIR PRACTICE set of rules established by the Board of Governors of the NATIONAL ASSOCIATION OF SECURITIES DEALERS (NASD), a self-regulatory organization comprising investment banking houses and firms dealing in the OVER

THE COUNTER securities market. As summarized in the NASD bylaws, the rules are designed to foster just and equitable principles of trade and business; high standards of commercial honor and integrity among members; the prevention of fraud and manipulative practices; safeguards against unreasonable profits, commissions, and other charges; and collaboration with governmental and other agencies to protect investors and the public interest in accordance with Section 15A of the MALONEY ACT. *See also* FIVE PERCENT RULE; IMMEDIATE FAMILY; KNOW YOUR CUSTOMER; MARKDOWN; RISKLESS TRANSACTION.

RUMORTRAGE stock traders' term, combining rumor and *arbitrage,* for buying and selling based on rumor of a TAKEOVER. *See also* DEAL STOCKS; GARBATRAGE.

RUN

Banking: demand for their money by many depositors all at once. If large enough, a run on a bank can cause it to fail, as hundreds of banks did in the Great Depression of the 1930s. Such a run is caused by a breach of confidence in the bank, perhaps as a result of large loan losses or fraud.

Securities:

1. list of available securities, along with current bid and asked prices, which a market maker is currently trading. For bonds the run may include the par value as well as current quotes.
2. when a security's price rises quickly, analysts say it had a quick run up, possibly because of a positive earnings report.

RUNDOWN

In general: status report or summary.

Municipal bonds: summary of the amounts available and the prices on units in a SERIAL BOND that has not yet been completely sold to the public.

RUNNING AHEAD illegal practice of buying or selling a security for a broker's personal account before placing a similar order for a customer. For example, when a firm's analyst issues a positive report on a company, the firm's brokers may not buy the stock for their own accounts before they have told their clients the news. Some firms prohibit brokers from making such trades for a specific period, such as two full days from the time of the recommendation.

RUNOFF printing of an exchange's closing prices on a TICKER tape after the market has closed. The runoff may take a long time when trading has been very heavy and the tape has fallen far behind the action.

S——————————————————————————

SAFE HARBOR

1. financial or accounting step that avoids legal or tax consequences. Commonly used in reference to *safe harbor leasing,* as permitted by the ECONOMIC RECOVERY TAX ACT OF 1981 (ERTA). An unprofitable company unable to use the INVESTMENT CREDIT and ACCELERATED COST RECOVERY SYSTEM (ACRS) liberalized depreciation rules, could transfer those benefits to a profitable firm seeking to reduce its tax burden. Under such an arrangement, the profitable company would own an asset the unprofitable company would otherwise have purchased itself; the profitable company would then lease the asset to the

unprofitable company, presumably passing on a portion of the tax benefits in the form of lower lease rental charges. Safe harbor leases were curtailed by provisions in the TAX EQUITY AND FISCAL RESPONSIBILITY ACT OF 1982 (TEFRA).
2. provision in a law that excuses liability if the attempt to comply in good faith can be demonstrated. For example, safe harbor provisions would protect management from liability under Securities and Exchange Commission rules for financial PROJECTIONS made in good faith.
3. form of SHARK REPELLENT whereby a TARGET COMPANY acquires a business so onerously regulated it makes the target less attractive, giving it, in effect, a safe harbor.

SAFEKEEPING storage and protection of a customer's financial assets, valuables, or documents, provided as a service by an institution serving as AGENT and, where control is delegated by the customer, also as custodian. An individual, corporate, or institutional investor might rely on a bank or a brokerage firm to hold stock certificates or bonds, keep track of trades, and provide periodic statements of changes in position. Investors who provide for their own safekeeping usually use a *safe deposit box*, provided by financial institutions for a fee. *See also* STREET NAME.

SAIF *see* SAVINGS ASSOCIATION INSURANCE FUND (SAIF).

SALARY REDUCTION PLAN plan allowing employees to contribute pretax compensation to a qualified TAX-DEFERRED retirement plan. Until the TAX REFORM ACT OF 1986, the term was synonymous with 401(K) PLAN, but the 1986 Act prohibited employees of state and local governments and tax-exempt organizations from establishing new 401(K) plans and added restrictions to existing government and tax-exempt unfunded deferred compensation arrangements and tax-sheltered annuity arrangements creating, in effect, a broadened definition of salary reduction plan. The 1986 law limits annual maximum deferral amounts for unfunded deferred compensation arrangements to the lesser of $7500 or ⅓ of an individual's compensation and imposes a $9500 annual limit on elective deferrals under 403(B) Plans (annuity programs for municipalities and not-for-profits).

SALE

In general: any exchange of goods or services for money. *Contrast with* BARTER.

Finance: income received in exchange for goods and services recorded for a given accounting period, either on a cash basis (as received) or on an accrual basis (as earned). *See also* GROSS SALES.

Securities: in securities trading, a sale is executed when a buyer and a seller have agreed on a price for the security.

SALE AND LEASEBACK form of LEASE arrangement in which a company sells an asset to another party—usually an insurance or finance company, a leasing company, a limited partnership, or an institutional investor—in exchange for cash, then contracts to lease the asset for a specified term. Typically, the asset is sold for its MARKET VALUE, so the lessee has really acquired capital that would otherwise have been tied up in a long-term asset. Such arrangements frequently have tax benefits for the lessee, although there is normally little difference in the effect on income between the lease payments and the interest payments that would have existed had the asset been purchased with borrowed money. A company generally opts for the sale and leaseback arrangement as an alternative to straight financing when the rate it would have to pay a lender is higher than the cost of rental or when it wishes to show less debt on its BALANCE SHEET (called *off-balance-sheet financing*). *See also* CAPITAL LEASE.

SALES CHARGE fee paid to a brokerage house by a buyer of shares in a load MUTUAL FUND or a LIMITED PARTNERSHIP. Normally, the sales charge for a mutual fund starts at 8½% of the capital invested and decreases as the size of the investment increases. The sales charge for a limited partnership is often even higher— typically 10%. In return for the sales charge, investors are entitled to investment advice from the broker on which fund or partnership is best for them. A fund that carries no sales charge is called a NO-LOAD FUND. *See also* FRONT-END LOAD; LETTER OF INTENT; LOAD FUND.

SALES LITERATURE

In general: written material designed to help sell a product or a service.

Investments: written material issued by a securities brokerage firm, mutual fund, underwriter, or other institution selling a product that explains the advantages of the investment product. Such literature must be truthful and must comply with disclosure regulations issued by the Securities and Exchange Commission and state securities agencies.

SALES LOAD *see* SALES CHARGE.

SALLIE MAE *see* STUDENT LOAN MARKETING ASSOCIATION.

SALVAGE VALUE *see* RESIDUAL VALUE.

SAME-DAY SUBSTITUTION offsetting changes in a MARGIN ACCOUNT in the course of one day, resulting in neither a MARGIN CALL nor a credit to the SPECIAL MISCELLANEOUS ACCOUNT. Examples: a purchase and a sale of equal value; a decline in the MARKET VALUE of some margin securities offset by an equal rise in the market value of others.

S & P PHENOMENON tendency of stocks newly added to the STANDARD & POOR'S INDEX to rise temporarily in price as S&P-related INDEX FUNDS adjust their portfolios, creating heavy buying activity.

SATURDAY NIGHT SPECIAL sudden attempt by one company to take over another by making a public TENDER OFFER. The term was coined in the 1960s after a rash of such surprise maneuvers, which were often announced over weekends. The WILLIAMS ACT of 1968 placed severe restrictions on tender offers and required disclosure of direct or indirect ownership of 5% or more of any class of EQUITY. It thus marked the end of what, in its traditional form, was known as the "creeping tender."

SAUCER technical chart pattern signaling that the price of a security or a commodity has formed a bottom and is moving up. An inverse saucer shows a top in the security's price and signals a downturn. *See also* TECHNICAL ANALYSIS.

SAVINGS AND LOAN ASSOCIATION depository financial institution, federally or state chartered, that obtains the bulk of its deposits from consumers and holds the majority of its assets as home mortgage loans. A few such specialized institutions were organized in the 19th century under state charters but with minimal regulation. Reacting to the crisis in the banking and home building industries precipitated by the Great Depression, Congress in 1932 passed the

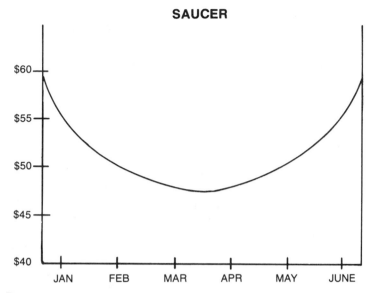

Federal Home Loan Bank Act, establishing the FEDERAL HOME LOAN BANK SYSTEM to supplement the lending resources of state-chartered savings and loans (S&Ls). The Home Owners' Loan Act of 1933 created a system for the federal chartering of S&Ls under the supervision of the Federal Home Loan Bank Board. Deposits in federal S&Ls were insured with the formation of the Federal Savings and Loan Insurance Corporation in 1934.

A second wave of restructuring occurred in the 1980s. The DEPOSITORY INSTITUTIONS DEREGULATION AND MONETARY CONTROL ACT of 1980 set a six-year timetable for the removal of interest rate ceilings, including the S&Ls' quarter-point rate advantage over the commercial bank limit on personal savings accounts. The act also allowed S&Ls limited entry into some markets previously open only to commercial banks (commercial lending, nonmortgage consumer lending, trust services) and, in addition, permitted MUTUAL ASSOCIATIONS to issue INVESTMENT CERTIFICATES. In actual effect, interest rate parity was achieved by the end of 1982.

The Garn-St Germain Depository Institutions Act of 1982 accelerated the pace of deregulation and gave the Federal Home Loan Bank Board wide latitude in shoring up the capital positions of S&Ls weakened by the impact of record-high interest rates on portfolios of old, fixed-rate mortgage loans. The 1982 act also encouraged the formation of stock savings and loans or the conversion of existing mutual (depositor-owned) associations to the stock form, which gave the associations another way to tap the capital markets and thereby to bolster their net work.

In 1989, responding to a massive wave of insolvencies caused by misma- nagement, corruption, and economic factors, Congress passed a savings and loan "bailout bill" that revamped the regulatory structure of the industry under a newly created agency, the OFFICE OF THRIFT SUPERVISION (OTS). Disbanding the Federal Savings and Loan Insurance Corporation (FSLIC), the bill created the SAVINGS ASSOCIATION INSURANCE FUND (SAIF) to provide deposit insurance under the administration of the FEDERAL DEPOSIT INSURANCE CORPORATION (FDIC). It also created the RESOLUTION TRUST CORPORATION (RTC) and RESOLUTION FUND- ING CORPORATION (REFCO) to deal with insolvent institutions. The Federal

Home Loan Bank Board was replaced by the FEDERAL HOUSING FINANCE BOARD, which now oversees the Federal Home Loan Bank System. *See also* SAVINGS BANK.

SAVINGS ASSOCIATION INSURANCE FUND (SAIF) U.S. government entity created by Congress in 1989 as part of its SAVINGS AND LOAN ASSOCIATION "bailout bill" to replace the FEDERAL SAVINGS AND LOAN INSURANCE CORPORATION (FSLIC) as the provider of deposit insurance for thrift institutions. SAIF, pronounced to rhyme with "safe," is administered by the FEDERAL DEPOSIT INSURANCE CORPORATION (FDIC) separately from its bank insurance program, which was renamed *Bank Insurance Fund (BIF)*. The new organization provides the same protection ($100,00 per depositor) as FSLIC. After 1996, SAIF will assume responsibility for insolvent institutions from RESOLUTION TRUST CORPORATION (RTC). *See also* OFFICE OF THRIFT SUPERVISION (OTS).

SAVINGS BANK depository financial institution that primarily accepts consumer deposits and makes home mortgage loans. Historically, savings banks were of the mutual (depositor-owned) form and chartered in only 16 states; the majority of savings banks were located in the New England states, New York, and New Jersey. Prior to the passage of the Garn-St Germain Depository Institutions Act of 1982, state-chartered savings bank deposits were insured along with commercial bank deposits by the FEDERAL DEPOSIT INSURANCE CORPORATION (FDIC). The Garn-St Germain Act gave savings banks the options of a federal charter, mutual-to-stock conversion, supervision by the Federal Home Loan Bank Board, and insurance from the FEDERAL SAVINGS AND LOAN INSURANCE CORPORATION (FSLIC). In 1989, the Federal Home Loan Bank Board was replaced by the FEDERAL HOUSING FINANCE BOARD (FHFB) and FSLIC by the newly created SAVINGS ASSOCIATION INSURANCE FUND (SAIF), a unit of the FDIC. *See also* MUTUAL SAVINGS BANK; SAVINGS AND LOAN ASSOCIATION.

SAVINGS BOND U.S. government bond issued in FACE VALUE denominations ranging from $50 to $10,000. Issued at a discount, these bonds are redeemed at face value at maturity. From 1941 to 1979, the government issued SERIES E BONDS. Starting in 1980, Series EE and HH bonds were issued. Series EE bonds range from $50 to $10,000; Series HH bonds, from $500 to $10,000. Both earn interest for ten years, though the U.S. Congress often extends that date. As of November 1, 1986, Series EE bonds, if held for five years, pay 85% of the average yields on five-year Treasury securities or 6%, whichever is more. Series HH bonds, available only through an exchange of at least $500 in Series E or EE bonds, pay a fixed annual 6% rate in two semiannual payments.

The interest from savings bonds is exempt from state and local taxes, and no federal tax is due until the bonds are redeemed. Bondholders wanting to defer the tax liability on their maturing Series EE bonds can exchange them for Series HH.

SCALE

Labor: wage rate for specific types of employees. For example: "Union scale for carpenters is $15.60 per hour."

Production economics: amount of production, as in "economy or diseconomy of scale." *See also* MARGINAL COST.

Serial bonds: vital data for each of the scheduled maturities in a new SERIAL BOND issue, including the number of bonds, the date they mature, the COUPON rate, and the offering price.

See also SCALE ORDER.

SCALE ORDER order for a specified number of shares that is to be executed in stages in order to average the price. Such an order might provide for the purchase of a total of 5000 shares to be executed in lots of 500 shares at each quarter-point interval as the market declines. Since scale orders are clerically cumbersome, not all brokers will accept them.

SCALPER

In general: speculator who enters into quasi-legal or illegal transactions to turn a quick and sometimes unreasonable profit. For example, a scalper buys tickets at regular prices for a major event and when the event becomes a sellout, resells the tickets at the highest price possible.

Securities:

1. investment adviser who takes a position in a security before recommending it, then sells out after the price has risen as a result of the recommendation. *See also* INVESTMENT ADVISERS ACT.
2. market maker who, in violation of the RULES OF FAIR PRACTICE of the NATIONAL ASSOCIATION OF SECURITIES DEALERS, adds an excessive markup or takes an excessive MARKDOWN on a transaction. *See also* FIVE PERCENT RULE.
3. commodity trader who trades for small gains, usually establishing and liquidating a position within one day.

SCHEDULE 13D form required under Section 13d of the SECURITIES ACT OF 1934 within ten business days of acquiring direct or BENEFICIAL OWNERSHIP of 5% or more of any class of equity securities in a PUBLICLY HELD corporation. In addition to filing with the Securities and Exchange Commission, the purchaser of such stock must also file the 13d with the stock exchange on which the shares are listed (if any) and with the company itself. Required information includes the way the shares were acquired, the purchaser's background, and future plans regarding the target company. The law is designed to protect against insidious TAKEOVER attempts and to keep the investing public aware of information that could affect the price of their stock. *See also* WILLIAMS ACT.

SCORCHED-EARTH POLICY technique used by a company that has become the target of a TAKEOVER attempt to make itself unattractive to the acquirer. For example, it may agree to sell off the most attractive parts of its business, called the CROWN JEWELS, or it may schedule all debt to become due immediately after a MERGER. *See also* POISON PILL; SHARK REPELLENT.

SCORE acronym for "Special Claim on Residual Equity," a certificate issued by the Americus Shareowner Service Corporation, a privately held company formed to market the product. A SCORE gives its holder the right to all the appreciation on an underlying security above a specified price, but none of the dividend income from the security. Its counterpart, called PRIME, passes all dividend income to its holders, who get the benefit of price appreciation up to the limit where SCORE begins. PRIME and SCORE together form a unit share investment trust (USIT), and both are listed on the American Stock Exchange. A buyer of a SCORE unit is hoping that the underlying stock will rise steeply in value.

The first USIT was formed with the shares of American Telephone and Telegraph. PRIME holders got all dividends and price appreciation in AT&T up to $75 a share; SCORE holders received all appreciation above $75.

SCREEN (STOCKS) to look for stocks that meet certain predetermined investment and financial criteria. Often, stocks are screened using a computer and a data base containing financial statistics on thousands of companies. For instance, an investor may want to screen for all those companies that have a PRICE/EARNINGS RATIO of less than 10, an earnings growth rate of more than 15%, and a dividend yield of more than 4%.

SCRIP

In general: receipt, certificate, or other representation of value recognized by both payer and payee. Scrip is not currency, but may be convertible into currency.

Securities: temporary document that is issued by a corporation and that represents a fractional share of stock resulting from a SPLIT, exchange of stock, or SPIN-OFF. Scrip certificates may be aggregated or applied toward the purchase of full shares. Scrip dividends have historically been paid in lieu of cash dividends by companies short of cash.

SCRIPOPHILY practice of collecting stock and bond certificates for their scarcity value, rather than for their worth as securities. The certificate's price rises with the beauty of the illustration on it and the importance of the issuer in world finance and economic development. Many old certificates, such as those issued by railroads in the 19th century or by Standard Oil before it was broken up in the early 20th century, have risen greatly in value since their issue, even though the issuing companies no longer exist.

SDR *see* SPECIAL DRAWING RIGHTS.

SEASONALITY variations in business or economic activity that recur with regularity as the result of changes in climate, holidays, and vacations. The retail toy business, with its steep sales buildup between Thanksgiving and Christmas and pronounced dropoff thereafter, is an example of seasonality in a dramatic form, though nearly all businesses have some degree of seasonal variation. It is often necessary to make allowances for seasonality when interpreting or projecting financial or economic data, a process economists call *seasonal adjustment*.

SEASONED ISSUE securities (usually from established companies) that have gained a reputation for quality with the investing public and enjoy LIQUIDITY in the SECONDARY MARKET.

SEAT figurative term for a membership on a securities or commodities exchange. Seats are bought and sold at prices set by supply and demand. A seat on the New York Stock Exchange, for example, traded for over $1 million prior to BLACK MONDAY in 1987 and just over $400,000 in late 1989. *See also* ABC AGREEMENT; MEMBER FIRM.

SEC *see* SECURITIES AND EXCHANGE COMMISSION.

SEC FEE small (one cent per several hundred dollars) fee charged by the Securities and Exchange Commission (SEC) to sellers of EQUITY securities that are exchange traded.

SECONDARY DISTRIBUTION public sale of previously issued securities held by large investors, usually corporations, institutions, or other AFFILIATED PERSONS, as distinguished from a NEW ISSUE or PRIMARY DISTRIBUTION, where the seller is the issuing corporation. As with a primary offering, secondaries are usually handled by INVESTMENT BANKERS, acting alone or as a syndicate, who purchase the shares from the seller at an agreed price, then resell them, sometimes with the help of a SELLING GROUP, at a higher PUBLIC OFFERING PRICE, making their profit on the difference, called the SPREAD. Since the offering is registered with the Securities and Exchange Commission, the syndicate manager can legally stabilize—or peg—the market price by bidding for shares in the open market. Buyers of securities offered this way pay no commissions, since all costs are borne by the selling investor. If the securities involved are listed, the CONSOLIDATED TAPE will announce the offering during the trading day, although the offering is not made until after the market's close. Among the historically large secondary distributions were the Ford Foundation's offering of Ford Motor Company stock in 1956 (approximately $658 million) handled by 7 firms under a joint management agreement and the sale of Howard Hughes' TWA shares ($566 million) through Merrill Lynch, Pierce, Fenner & Smith in 1966.

A similar form of secondary distribution, called the SPECIAL OFFERING, is limited to members of the New York Stock Exchange and is completed in the course of the trading day.

See also EXCHANGE DISTRIBUTION; REGISTERED SECONDARY OFFERING; SECURITIES AND EXCHANGE COMMISSION RULES 144 and 237.

SECONDARY MARKET

1. exchanges and over-the-counter markets where securities are bought and sold subsequent to original issuance, which took place in the PRIMARY MARKET. Proceeds of secondary market sales accrue to the selling dealers and investors, not to the companies that originally issued the securities.
2. market in which money-market instruments are traded among investors.

SECONDARY MORTGAGE MARKET buying, selling, and trading of existing mortgage loans and mortgage-backed securities. Original lenders are thus able to sell loans in their portfolios in order to build LIQUIDITY to support additional lending. Mortgages originated by lenders are purchased by government agencies (such as the FEDERAL HOME LOAN MORTGAGE CORPORATION, and the FEDERAL NATIONAL MORTGAGE ASSOCIATION) and by investment bankers. These agencies and bankers, in turn, create pools of mortgages, which they repackage as mortgage-backed securities, called PASS-THROUGH SECURITIES or PARTICIPATION CERTIFICATES, which are then sold to investors. The secondary mortgage market thus encompasses all activity beyond the PRIMARY MARKET, which is between the homebuyers and the originating mortgage lender.

SECONDARY OFFERING *see* SECONDARY DISTRIBUTION.

SECONDARY STOCKS used in a general way to mean stocks having smaller MARKET CAPITALIZATION, less quality, and more risk than BLUE CHIP issues represented by the Dow Jones Industrial Average. Secondary stocks, which often behave differently than blue chips, are tracked by the Amex Market Value Index, the NASDAQ Composite Index, and broad indexes, such as the STANDARD & POOR'S INDEX. Also called *second-tier stocks*.

SECOND MORTGAGE LENDING advancing funds to a borrower that are secured by real estate previously pledged in a FIRST MORTGAGE loan. In the case of DEFAULT, the first mortgage has priority of claim over the second.

A variation on the second mortgage is the *home equity loan*, in which the loan is secured by independent appraisal of the property value. A home equity loan may also be in the form of a line of credit, which may be drawn down on by using a check or even a credit card. *See also* HOMEOWNER'S EQUITY ACCOUNT; RIGHT OF RESCISSION.

SECOND-PREFERRED STOCK preferred stock issue that ranks below another preferred issue in terms of priority of claim on dividends and on assets in liquidation. Second-preferred shares are often issued with a CONVERTIBLE feature or with a warrant to make them more attractive to investors. *See also* JUNIOR SECURITY; PREFERRED STOCK; PRIOR-PREFERRED STOCK; SUBSCRIPTION WARRANT.

SECOND ROUND intermediate stage of VENTURE CAPITAL financing, coming after the SEED MONEY (for START-UP) and *first round* stages and before the MEZZANINE LEVEL, when the company has matured to the point where it might consider a LEVERAGED BUYOUT by management or an INITIAL PUBLIC OFFERING (IPO).

SECTOR particular group of stocks, usually found in one industry. SECURITIES ANALYSTS often follow a particular sector of the stock market, such as airline or chemical stocks.

SECTOR FUND SPECIALIZED MUTUAL FUND that invests in one industry.

SECULAR long-term (10–50 years or more) as distinguished from seasonal or cyclical time frames.

SECURED BOND bond backed by the pledge of COLLATERAL, a MORTGAGE, or other LIEN. The exact nature of the security is spelled out in the INDENTURE. Secured bonds are distinguished from unsecured bonds, called DEBENTURES.

SECURED DEBT debt guaranteed by the pledge of assets or other COLLATERAL. *See also* ASSIGN; HYPOTHECATION.

SECURITIES ACT OF 1933 first law enacted by Congress to regulate the securities markets, approved May 26, 1933, as the Truth in Securities Act. It requires REGISTRATION of securities prior to public sale and adequate DISCLOSURE of pertinent financial and other data in a PROSPECTUS to permit informed analysis by potential investors. It also contains antifraud provisions prohibiting false representations and disclosures. Enforcement responsibilities were assigned to the SECURITIES AND EXCHANGE COMMISSION by the SECURITIES EXCHANGE ACT OF 1934. The 1933 act did not supplant BLUE SKY LAWS of the various states.

SECURITIES ACTS AMENDMENTS OF 1975 federal legislation enacted on June 4, 1975, to amend the SECURITIES EXCHANGE ACT OF 1934. The 1975 amendments directed the SECURITIES AND EXCHANGE COMMISSION to work with the industry toward establishing a NATIONAL MARKET SYSTEM together with a system for the nationwide clearance and settlement of securities transactions. Because of these provisions, the 1975 laws are sometimes called the *National Exchange Market System Act*. New regulations were also introduced to promote prompt and accurate securities handling, and clearing agencies were required to register with and report to the SEC. The 1975 amendments required TRANSFER AGENTS other than banks to register with the SEC and provided that authority with respect to bank transfer agents would be shared by the SEC and bank regulatory agencies. The Municipal Securities Rulemaking Board was created to regulate brokers, dealers, and banks dealing in municipal securities, with rules subject to SEC approval and enforcement shared by the NATIONAL ASSOCIATION OF SECURITIES DEALERS and bank regulatory agencies. The law also required the registration of broker-dealers in municipals, but preserved the exemption of issuers from REGISTRATION requirements. The amendments contained the prohibition of fixed commission rates, adopted earlier by the SEC in its Rule 19b-3.

SECURITIES ANALYST individual, usually employed by a stock brokerage house, bank, or investment institution, who performs investment research and examines the financial condition of a company or group of companies in an industry and in the context of the securities markets. Many analysts specialize in a single industry or SECTOR and make investment recommendations to buy, sell, or hold in that area. Among a corporation's financial indicators most closely followed by ANALYSTS are sales and earnings growth, CAPITAL STRUCTURE, stock price trend and PRICE/EARNINGS RATIO, DIVIDEND PAYOUTS, and RETURN ON INVESTED CAPITAL. Securities analysts promote corporate financial disclosure by sponsoring forums through local associations, the largest of which is the New York Society of Security Analysts; and through its national body, the Financial Analysts Federation. *See also* FORECASTING; FUNDAMENTAL ANALYSIS; QUALITATIVE ANALYSIS; QUANTITATIVE ANALYSIS; TECHNICAL ANALYSIS.

SECURITIES AND COMMODITIES EXCHANGES organized, national exchanges where securities, options, and futures contracts are traded by members for their own accounts and for the accounts of customers. The stock exchanges are registered with and regulated by the SECURITIES AND EXCHANGE COMMISSION (SEC); the commodities exchanges are registered with and regulated by the Commodity Futures Trading Commission (*see* REGULATED COMMODITIES); where options are also traded on an exchange, such activity is regulated by the SEC.

STOCKS, BONDS, SUBSCRIPTION RIGHTS, SUBSCRIPTION WARRANTS and in some cases OPTIONS are traded on nine STOCK EXCHANGES in the United States. The FUTURES MARKET is represented by 13 leading commodities exchanges.

Exchanges listing basic securities—stocks, bonds, rights, warrants and options on individual stocks—are described under the entries for New York Stock Exchange, American Stock Exchange, and regional stock exchanges. The exchanges listing commodity and other futures contracts and options in addition to those on individual stocks are:

American Stock Exchange (New York) *index options:* Computer Technology Index, Institutional Index, International Market Index, Major Market Index, Oil Index. *interest rate options:* U.S. Treasury bills, U.S. Treasury notes.

Chicago Board of Trade (Chicago) *futures:* CBOE 250, corn, gold, Government National Mortgage Association CDR, Major Market Index, Major Market Index "MAXI", Municipal Bond Index, NASDAQ-100 Index, oats, silver, soybeans, soybean meal, soybean oil, Treasury bonds, Treasury notes, wheat. *futures options:* corn, silver, soybeans, soybean meal, soybean oil, Treasury bonds, Treasury notes.

Chicago Board Options Exchange (Chicago) *index options:* Standard & Poor's 100 Index, Standard & Poor's 500 Index, Standard & Poor's Over The Counter 250 Index. *interest rate options:* U.S. Treasury bonds, U.S. Treasury notes.

Chicago Mercantile Exchange (Chicago) *futures:* feeder cattle, live cattle, live hogs, lumber, Over The Counter 250 Industrial Stock Price Index, pork bellies, Standard & Poor's 500 Index, Treasury bills. *futures options:* Australian dollar, British pound, Canadian dollar, Deutsche mark, Eurodollar, feeder cattle, Japanese yen, live cattle, live hogs, lumber, pork bellies, Standard & Poor's 500 stock index, Swiss franc, Treasury bills.

Chicago Rice and Cotton Exchange (Chicago) *futures:* rough rice.

Commodity Exchange, Inc. (COMEX)* (New York) *futures:* aluminum, copper, gold, Moody's Corporate Bond Index, silver. *futures options:* copper, gold, silver.

Kansas City Board of Trade (Kansas City) *futures:* sorghum, Value Line Maxi Index, Value Line Mini Index, wheat. *futures options:* wheat.

MidAmerica Commodity Exchange (Chicago) *futures:* British pound, Canadian dollar, corn, Deutsche Mark, gold, Japanese yen, live cattle, live hogs, oats, platinum, silver, soybeans, soybean meal, Swiss franc, U.S. Treasury bills, U.S. Treasury bonds, wheat. *futures options:* soybeans, wheat.
New York Cotton Exchange* (New York) *futures:* cotton, orange juice, propane. *futures options:* cotton, orange juice. **Finex** (a division of the Cotton Exchange), *futures:* European Currency Unit, U.S. dollar, Treasury index.
New York Futures Exchange (division of the New York Stock Exchange) (New York) *futures:* Commodity Research Bureau Futures Price Index, NYSE Composite Index, Russell 2000 Index, Russell 3000 Index, Treasury bonds. *futures options:* NYSE Composite Index.
New York Mercantile Exchange* (New York) *futures:* crude oil, gasoline, no. 2 heating oil, palladium, platinum, propane. *futures options:* crude oil, heating oil.
New York Stock Exchange (New York) *basket trading:* New York Stock Exchange Portfolio. *index options:* New York Stock Exchange Options Index.
Pacific Stock Exchange (San Francisco) *index options:* Financial News Composite Index.
Philadelphia Stock Exchange (Philadelphia) *foreign currency futures:* Australian dollar, British pound, Canadian dollar, Deutsche Mark, European Currency Unit, French franc, Japanese yen, Swiss franc. *futures:* National Over-The-Counter Index Futures. *index options:* Gold/Silver Index, National OTC Index, Value Line Composite Index.

SECURITIES AND EXCHANGE COMMISSION (SEC) federal agency created by the SECURITIES EXCHANGE ACT OF 1934 to administer that act and the SECURITIES ACT OF 1933, formerly carried out by the FEDERAL TRADE COMMISSION. The SEC is made up of five commissioners, appointed by the President of the United States on a rotating basis for five-year terms. The chairman is designated by the President and, to insure its independence, no more than three members of the commission may be of the same political party. The statutes administered by the SEC are designed to promote full public DISCLOSURE and protect the investing public against malpractice in the securities markets. All issues of securities offered in interstate commerce or through the mails must be registered with the SEC; all national securities exchanges and associations are under its supervision, as are INVESTMENT COMPANIES, investment counselors and advisers, OVER THE COUNTER brokers and dealers, and virtually all other individuals and firms operating in the investment field. In addition to the 1933 and 1934 securities acts, responsibilities of the SEC include the PUBLIC UTILITY HOLDING COMPANY ACT of 1935, the TRUST INDENTURE ACT of 1939, the INVESTMENT COMPANY ACT of 1940 and the INVESTMENT ADVISERS ACT of 1940. It also administers the SECURITIES ACTS AMENDMENTS OF 1975, which directed the SEC to facilitate the establishment of a NATIONAL MARKET SYSTEM and a nationwide system for clearance and settlement of transactions

---

*These exchanges, though independent, share space and other facilities at 4 World Trade Center, in New York City, and are collectively called the Commodity Exchange Center.

and established the Municipal Securities Rulemaking Board, a self-regulatory organization whose rules are subject to SEC approval. *See also* SECURITIES AND EXCHANGE COMMISSION RULES.

SECURITIES AND EXCHANGE COMMISSION RULES The following are some of the more commonly encountered rules of the SEC. The list highlights the most prominent features of the rules and is not intended as a legal interpretation. The rules are listed in numerical order.

Rule 3b-3: Definition of Short Sale defines short sale as one in which the seller does not own the SECURITY sold or which is consummated by delivery of a borrowed security; ownership is defined in terms of securities, CONVERTIBLES, OPTIONS, and SUBSCRIPTION WARRANTS.

Rule 10a-1: Short sales known as the SHORT SALE RULE, prohibits a short sale of securities below the price of the last regular trade and at that price unless it was higher than the last different price preceding it. In determining the price at which a short sale can be made after a security goes EX-DIVIDEND, EX-RIGHTS, or ex- any other distribution, all sales prices prior to the ex- date may be reduced by the amount of the distribution.

Rule 10b-2: Solicitation of purchases on an exchange to facilitate distribution of securities prohibits parties concerned with a PRIMARY DISTRIBUTION or a SECONDARY DISTRIBUTION of a security from soliciting orders for the issue other than through the offering circular or formal PROSPECTUS.

Rule 10b-4: Short tendering of securities prohibits a SHORT TENDER—the sale of borrowed securities (as in SELLING SHORT) to a person making a TENDER OFFER.

Rule 10b-6: Prohibitions against trading by persons interested in a distribution rule that prohibits issuers, underwriters, broker-dealers, or others involved in a DISTRIBUTION of securities from buying the issue, or rights to it, during the distribution. The section permits transactions between the issuer and the underwriters and among the participating underwriters as required to carry out a distribution. The law extends to a repurchase by the issuer or to a purchase by participants in a new issue of CONVERTIBLE securities already on the market and convertible into the securities being offered.

Rule 10b-7: Stabilizing to effect a distribution provisions governing market STABILIZATION activities by issuers or underwriters in securities offerings.

Rule 10b-8: Distributions through rights prohibits market price MANIPULATION by interested parties in a RIGHTS OFFERING.

Rule 10b-10: Confirmation of transactions sets minimum information and disclosure requirements for the written confirmations of sales or purchases that broker-dealers send to clients, including disclosure of whether a firm is acting as AGENT (broker) or as PRINCIPAL (dealer).

Rule 10b-13: Other purchases during tender offer or exchange offer prohibits a person making a cash TENDER OFFER or an offer to exchange one EQUITY security for another from taking a position in the security being tendered or in a security CONVERTIBLE into the security being tendered until the tender offer or exchange offer expires.

Rule 10b-16: Credit terms in margin transactions terms and conditions concerning the interest charges on MARGIN loans to brokerage customers and the broker's disclosure responsibilities to borrowers.

Rule 11A: Floor trading regulations rules governing floor trading by exchange members, including those concerning PRIORITY and PRECEDENCE of transactions, transactions for the accounts of persons associated with members, HEDGE transactions, exchange bond trading, transactions by REGISTERED COMPETITIVE MARKET MAKERS and REGISTERED EQUITY MARKET MAKERS, and member transactions.
Rule 12b–1: *See* 12b–1 MUTUAL FUND.

Rule 13d: Acquisition of beneficial interest disclosures required by any person who directly or indirectly acquires a beneficial interest of 5% or more of any class of a registered equity security. *See also* WILLIAMS ACT.

Rule 13e: Repurchase of shares by issuers prohibits purchase by an issuer of its own shares during a TENDER OFFER for its shares and regulates GOING PRIVATE transactions by issuers or their affiliates.

Rule 14a: Solicitation of proxies sets forth the information and documentation required with PROXY materials distributed to shareholders of a public corporation.

Rule 14d: Tender offers regulations and restrictions covering public TENDER OFFERS and related disclosure requirements. *See also* WILLIAMS ACT.

Rule 15c2-1: Hypothecation of customers' securities regulates a broker-dealer's SAFEKEEPING of customers' securities in a MARGIN ACCOUNT, prohibiting the COMMINGLING of customers' accounts without the consent of the respective customers and the commingling of customers' accounts with the securities of noncustomers, and limiting broker borrowings secured by customers' collateral to the aggregate amount of customers' indebtedness. *See also* HYPOTHECATION.

Rule 15c3-1: Net capital requirements for brokers or dealers covers NET CAPITAL REQUIREMENTS relative to the aggregate indebtedness of brokers and dealers of different types.

Rule 15c3-2: Customers' free credit balances requires a broker-dealer to notify customers with credit balances in their accounts that such balances may be withdrawn on demand.

Rule 15c3-3: Customer-protection reserves and custody of securities regulates the handling of customers' fully paid securities and excess MARGIN securities (security value in excess of MARGIN REQUIREMENTS) with broker-dealers. Fully paid securities must be segregated, and the broker must make weekly deposits to a Special Reserve Bank Account for the Exclusive Benefit of Customers.

Rule 17f-1: Missing, lost, counterfeit, or stolen securities requires exchanges, broker-dealers, clearing agencies, banks and transfer agents to report promptly to both the SEC and the appropriate law enforcement agency any knowledge of missing, lost, counterfeit, or stolen securities and to check with the SEC whenever a security comes into their possession to make sure it has not been reported at large.

Rule 19b-3: Prohibiting fixing of rates of commission by exchanges prohibits fixed commissions on stock exchange transactions pursuant to the SECURITIES ACT AMENDMENTS OF 1975.

Rule 19c-3: Off-board trading by exchange members permits securities listed on an exchange after April 26, 1979, to be traded off the exchange by member firms, a step toward an experimental NATIONAL MARKET SYSTEM in compliance with the SECURITIES ACT AMENDMENTS OF 1975.

Rule 144: Public sale of unregistered securities sets forth the conditions under which a holder of unregistered securities may make a public sale without filing a formal REGISTRATION STATEMENT. No LETTER SECURITY purchased through a PRIVATE PLACEMENT may be sold for at least two years after the date of purchase. Thereafter, during any three-month period, the following amounts may be sold: if listed securities, the greater of 1 % of the amount outstanding or the average trading volume within the preceding weeks; if unlisted, 1% of outstandings. Securities may be sold only in broker's transactions.

Rule 145: Securities acquired in recapitalization persons who acquire securities as a result of reclassification, MERGER, consolidation, or transfer of corporate assets may sell such securities without REGISTRATION under stipulated conditions.

Rule 156: Mutual fund sales literature forbids false and misleading sales materials promoting INVESTMENT COMPANY securities.

Rule 237: Public sale of unregistered securities expanding on Rule 144, provides that five years after full payment for the purchase of privately placed securities, the lesser of $50,000 of such securities or 1% of the securities outstanding in a particular CLASS may be sold within a one year period.

Rule 254: Registration of small issues provides for simplified registration of small issues ($1.5 million or less in the mid-1980s) including a short-form REGISTRATION STATEMENT and PROSPECTUS. *See also* REGULATION A.

Rule 415: Shelf registration permits corporations to file a REGISTRATION for securities they intend to issue in the future when market conditions are favorable. *See also* SHELF REGISTRATION.

SECURITIES EXCHANGE ACT OF 1934 law governing the securities markets, enacted June 6, 1934. The act outlaws misrepresentation, MANIPULATION, and other abusive practices in the issuance of securities. It created the SECURITIES AND EXCHANGE COMMISSION (SEC) to enforce both the SECUEITIES ACT OF 1933 and the Securities Exchange Act of 1934.

Principal requirements of the 1934 act are as follows:

1. REGISTRATION of all securities listed on stock exchanges, and periodic DISCLOSURES by issuers of financial status and changes in condition.
2. regular disclosures of holdings and transactions of "INSIDERS"—the officers and directors of a corporation and those who control at least 10% of equity securities.
3. solicitation of PROXIES enabling shareholders to vote for or against policy proposals.
4. registration with the SEC of stock exchanges and brokers and dealers to ensure their adherence to SEC rules through self-regulation.
5. surveillance by the SEC of trading practices on stock exchanges and over-the-counter markets to minimize the possibility of insolvency among brokers and dealers.
6. regulation of MARGIN REQUIREMENTS for securities purchased on credit; the FEDERAL RESERVE BOARD sets those requirements.
7. SEC subpoena power in investigations of possible violations and in enforcement actions.

The SECURITIES ACT AMENDMENTS OF 1975 ratified the system of free-market determination of brokers' commissions and gave the SEC authority to oversee development of a NATIONAL MARKET SYSTEM.

SECURITIES INDUSTRY ASSOCIATION (SIA) trade group that represents broker-dealers. The SIA lobbies for legislation affecting the brokerage industry. It also educates its members and the public about industry trends and keeps statistics on revenues and profits of brokers. The SIA represents only the segment of broker-dealers that sells taxable securities. Tax-exempt bond, government bond, and mortgage-backed security dealers are represented by the PUBLIC SECURITIES ASSOCIATION.

SECURITIES INDUSTRY AUTOMATION CORPORATION (SIAC) organization established in 1972 to provide communications and computer systems and services for the New York Stock Exchange (NYSE) and the American Stock Exchange (AMEX). It is two-thirds owned by NYSE and one-third owned by AMEX.

SECURITIES INVESTOR PROTECTION CORPORATION (SIPC) nonprofit corporation, established by Congress under the Securities Investors Protection Act of 1970, that insures the securities and cash in the customer accounts of member brokerage firms against the failure of those firms. All brokers and dealers registered with the Securities and Exchange Commission and with national stock exchanges are required to be members of SIPC. The Corporation acts similarly to the FEDERAL DEPOSIT INSURANCE CORPORATION (FDIC), which insures banks, and the FEDERAL SAVINGS AND LOAN INSURANCE CORPORATION (FSLIC), which insures savings and loans. When a brokerage firm fails, SIPC will first try to merge it into another brokerage firm. If this fails, SIPC will liquidate the firm's assets and pay off account holders up to an overall maximum of $500,000 per customer, with a limit of $100,000 on cash or cash equivalents. SIPC does not protect investors against market risk. *See also* SEPARATE CUSTOMER.

SECURITIES LOAN
1. loan of securities by one broker to another, usually to cover a customer's short sale. The lending broker is secured by the cash proceeds of the sale.
2. in a more general sense, loan collateralized by MARKETABLE SECURITIES. These would include all customer loans made to purchase or carry securities by broker-dealers under Federal Reserve Board REGULATION T margin rules, as well as by banks under REGULATION U and other lenders under REGULATION G. Loans made by banks to brokers to cover customers' positions are also collateralized by securities, but such loans are called *broker's loans* or *call loans*. *See also* HYPOTHECATION; LENDING AT A PREMIUM; LENDING AT A RATE; LENDING SECURITIES; REHYPOTHECATION; SELLING SHORT.

SECURITY
Finance: collateral offered by a debtor to a lender to secure a loan called *collateral security*. For instance, the security behind a mortgage loan is the real estate being purchased with the proceeds of the loan. If the debt is not repaid, the lender may seize the security and resell it.
    Personal security refers to one person or firm's GUARANTEE of another's primary obligation.
Investment: instrument that signifies an ownership position in a corporation (a stock), a creditor relationship with a corporation or governmental body (a bond), or rights to ownership such as those represented by an OPTION, SUBSCRIPTION RIGHT, and SUBSCRIPTION WARRANT.

SECURITY MARKET LINE relationship between the REQUIRED RATE OF RETURN on an investment and its SYSTEMATIC RISK.

SECURITY RATINGS evaluations of the credit and investment risk of securities issues by commercial RATING agencies.

SEED MONEY venture capitalist's first contribution toward the financing or capital requirements of a START-UP business. It frequently takes the form of a loan, often SUBORDINATED, or an investment in convertible bonds or preferred stock. Seed money provides the basis for additional capitalization to accommodate growth. *See also* MEZZANINE LEVEL; SECOND ROUND; VENTURE CAPITAL.

SEEK A MARKET to look for a buyer (if a seller) or a seller (if a buyer) of securities.

SEGREGATION OF SECURITIES Securities and Exchange Commission rules (8c and 15c2-1) designed to protect customers' securities used by broker-dealers to secure broker loans. Specifically, broker-dealers may not (1) commingle the securities of different customers without the written consent of each customer, (2) commingle a customer's securities with those of any person other than a bonafide customer, or (3) borrow more against customers' securities than the customers, in the aggregate, owe the broker-dealer against the same securities. *See also* COMMINGLING; HYPOTHECATION; REHYPOTHECATION; SECURITIES AND EXCHANGE COMMISSION RULE 15c2-1.

SELECTED DEALER AGREEMENT agreement governing the SELLING GROUP in a securities underwriting and distribution. *See also* UNDERWRITE.

SELF-DIRECTED IRA INDIVIDUAL RETIREMENT ACCOUNT (IRA) that can be actively managed by the account holder, who designates a CUSTODIAN to carry out investment instructions. The account is subject to the same conditions and early withdrawal limitations as a regular IRA. Investors who withdraw money from a qualified IRA plan have 60 days in which to roll over the funds to another plan before they become liable for tax penalties. Most corporate and U.S. government securities are eligible to be held by a self-directed IRA, as are limited partnerships, but collectibles and precious metals (art, gems, gold coins) are not.

SELF-REGULATORY ORGANIZATION (SRO) principal means contemplated by the federal securities laws for the enforcement of fair, ethical, and efficient practices in the securities and commodities futures industries. It is these organizations that are being referred to when "industry rules" are mentioned, as distinguished from the regulatory agencies such as the Securities and Exchange Commission or the Federal Reserve Board. The SROs include all the national SECURITIES AND COMMODITIES EXCHANGES as well as the NATIONAL ASSOCIATION OF SECURITIES DEALERS (NASD), which represents all the firms operating in the over-the-counter market, and the *Municipal Securities Rulemaking Board,* created under the Securities Acts Amendments of 1975 to regulate brokers, dealers and banks dealing in municipal securities. Rules made by the MSRB are subject to approval by the SEC and are enforced by the NASD and bank regulatory agencies.

SELF-SUPPORTING DEBT bonds sold for a project that will produce sufficient revenues to retire the debt. Such debt is usually issued by municipalities building a public structure (for example, a bridge or tunnel) that will be producing revenue through tolls or other charges. The bonds are not supported by the taxing power of the municipality issuing them. *See also* REVENUE BOND.

SELF-TENDER *see* SHARE REPURCHASE PLAN.

SELLER'S MARKET situation in which there is more demand for a security or product than there is available supply. As a result, the prices tend to be rising, and the sellers can set both the prices and the terms of sale. It contrasts with a buyer's market, characterized by excess supply, low prices, and terms suited to the buyer's desires.

SELLER'S OPTION securities transaction in which the seller, instead of making REGULAR WAY DELIVERY, is given the right to deliver the security to the purchaser on the date the seller's option expires or before, provided written notification of the seller's intention to deliver is given to the buyer one full business day prior to delivery. Seller's option deliveries are normally not made before 6 business days following the transaction or after 60 days.

SELLING CLIMAX sudden plunge in security prices as those who hold stocks or bonds panic and decide to dump their holdings all at once. Technical analysts see a climax as both a dramatic increase in volume and a sharp drop in prices on a chart. To these analysts, such a pattern usually means that a short-term rally will soon follow, since there are few sellers left after the climax. Sometimes, a selling climax can signal the bottom of a BEAR MARKET, meaning that after the climax the market will start to rise.

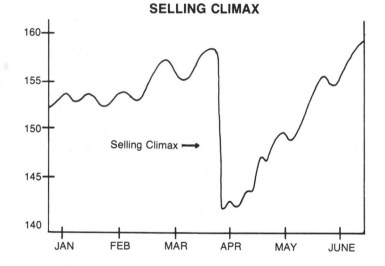

SELLING CLIMAX

SELLING CONCESSION discount at which securities in a NEW ISSUE offering (or a SECONDARY DISTRIBUTION) are allocated to the members of a SELLING GROUP by the underwriters. Since the selling group cannot sell to the public at a price higher than the PUBLIC OFFERING PRICE, its compensation comes out of the difference between the price paid to the issuer by the underwriters and the public offering price, called the SPREAD. The selling group's portion, called the CONCESSION, is normally one half or more of the gross spread, expressed as a discount off the public offering price. *See also* FLOTATION COST; UNDERWRITE; UNDERWRITING SPREAD.

SELLING DIVIDENDS questionable practice by sales personnel dealing in MUTUAL FUNDS whereby a customer is induced to buy shares in a fund in order to get the benefit of a dividend scheduled in the near future. Since the dividend is already part of the NET ASSET VALUE of the fund and therefore part of the share price, the customer derives no real benefit.

SELLING, GENERAL, AND ADMINISTRATIVE (SG&A) EXPENSES grouping of expenses reported on a company's PROFIT AND LOSS STATEMENT between COST OF GOODS SOLD and INCOME DEDUCTIONS. Included are such items as salespersons' salaries and commissions, advertising and promotion, travel and entertainment, office payroll and expenses, and executives' salaries. SG&A expenses do not include such items as interest or amortization of INTANGIBLE ASSETS, which would be listed as income deductions. *See also* OPERATING PROFIT (OR LOSS).

SELLING GROUP group of dealers appointed by the syndicate manager of an UNDERWRITING GROUP, as AGENT for the other underwriters, to market a new or secondary issue to the public; also called *selling syndicate*. The selling group typically includes members of the underwriting group but varies in size with the size of the issue, sometimes running into several hundred dealers. The selling group is governed by the selling group agreement, also called the SELECTED DEALER AGREEMENT. It sets forth the terms of the relationship, establishes the commission (or SELLING CONCESSION, as it is called), and provides for the termination of the group, usually in 30 days. The selling group may or may not be obligated to purchase unsold shares. *See also* UNDERWRITE.

SELLING OFF selling securities or commodities under pressure to avoid further declines in prices. Technical analysts call such action a *sell-off*. *See also* DUMPING.

SELLING ON THE GOOD NEWS practice of selling a stock soon after a positive news development is announced. Most investors, cheered by the news of a successful new product or higher earnings, buy a stock because they think it will go higher; this pushes up the price. Someone selling on this good news believes that the stock will have reached its top price once all those encouraged by the development have bought the stock. Therefore, it is better to sell at this point than to wait for more good news or to be holding the stock if the next announcement is disappointing. *Compare with* BUYING ON THE BAD NEWS.

SELLING SHORT sale of a security or commodity futures contract not owned by the seller; a technique used (1) to take advantage of an anticipated decline in the price or (2) to protect a profit in a LONG POSITION (*see* SELLING SHORT AGAINST THE BOX).

An investor borrows stock certificates for delivery at the time of short sale. If the seller can buy that stock later at a lower price, a profit results; if the price rises, however, a loss results.

A commodity sold short represents a promise to deliver the commodity at a set price on a future date. Most commodity short sales are COVERED before the DELIVERY DATE.

Example of a short sale involving stock: An investor, anticipating a decline in the price of XYZ shares, instructs his or her broker to sell short 100 XYZ when XYZ is trading at $50. The broker then loans the investor 100 shares of XYZ, using either its own inventory, shares in the MARGIN ACCOUNT of another customer, or shares borrowed from another broker. These shares are used to make settlement with the buying broker within five days of the short sale transaction, and the proceeds are used to secure the loan. The investor now has what is known as a SHORT POSITION—that is, he or she still does not own the 100 XYZ and, at some point, must buy the shares to repay the lending broker. If the market price of XYZ drops to $40, the investor can buy the shares for $4000, repay the lending broker, thus covering the short sale, and claim a profit of $1000, or $10 a share.

Short selling is regulated by REGULATION T of the Federal Reserve Board. *See also* LENDING AT A RATE; LENDING AT A PREMIUM; LOANED FLAT; MARGIN REQUIREMENT; SHORT SALE RULE.

SELLING SHORT AGAINST THE BOX SELLING SHORT stock actually owned by the seller but held in SAFEKEEPING, called the BOX in Wall Street jargon. The motive for the practice, which assumes that the securities needed to COVER are borrowed as with any short sale, may be simply inaccessibility of the box or that the seller does not wish to disclose ownership. The main motive traditionally, however, has been to protect a CAPITAL GAIN in the shares that are owned, while deferring a LONG-TERM GAIN into another tax year. This practice had particular benefit when the tax rate on long-term gains was significantly lower than that on ORDINARY INCOME and a six-month HOLDING PERIOD was required to qualify. Under the TAX REFORM ACT OF 1986, long-term capital gains rates for individuals rose to 28% in 1987 compared with a maximum ordinary income rate of 38.5% in that year. Beginning in 1988, capital gains and ordinary income become taxable at the same rates, eliminating the tax deferral motive for selling short against the box, except in extreme cases where taxpayers are moving from the 28% to the 15% bracket.

SELL OUT
1. liquidation of a MARGIN ACCOUNT by a broker after a MARGIN CALL has failed to produce additional equity to bring the margin to the required level. *See also* CLOSE A POSITION; MARGIN REQUIREMENT; MINIMUM MAINTENANCE.
2. action by a broker when a customer fails to pay for securities purchased and the securities received from the selling broker are sold to cover the transaction. Term also applies to commodities futures transactions.
3. expression used when all the securities in a NEW ISSUE underwriting have been distributed.

SELL PLUS sell order with instructions to execute only if the trading price in a security is higher than the last different preceding price. *See also* SHORT-SALE RULE.

SELL-STOP ORDER *see* STOP ORDER.

SELL THE BOOK order to a broker by the holder of a large quantity of shares of a security to sell all that can be ABSORBED at the current bid price. The term derives from the SPECIALIST'S BOOK—the record of all the buy and sell orders members have placed in the stock he or she handles. In this scenario, the buyers potentially include those in the specialist's book, the specialist for his or her own account, and the broker-dealer CROWD.

SENIOR DEBT loans or DEBT SECURITIES that have claim prior to junior obligations and EQUITY on a corporation's assets in the event of LIQUIDATION. Senior debt commonly includes funds borrowed from banks, insurance companies, or other financial institutions, as well as notes, bonds, or debentures not expressly defined as junior or subordinated.

SENIOR REFUNDING replacement of securities maturing in 5 to 12 years with issues having original maturities of 15 years or longer. The objectives may be to reduce the bond issuer's interest costs, to consolidate several issues into one, or to extend the maturity date.

SENIOR SECURITY security that has claim prior to a junior obligation and EQUITY on a corporation's assets and earnings. Senior securities are repaid before JUNIOR SECURITIES in the event of LIQUIDATION. Debt, including notes, bonds, and debentures, is senior to stock; first mortgage bonds are senior to second mortgage bonds; and all mortgage bonds are senior to debentures, which are unsecured.

SENSITIVE MARKET market easily swayed by good or bad news.

SENSITIVITY ANALYSIS study measuring the effect of a change in a variable (such as sales) on the risk or profitability of an investment.

SENTIMENT INDICATORS measures of the bullish or bearish mood of investors. Many technical analysts look at these indicators as contrary indicators—that is, when most investors are bullish, the market is about to drop, and when most are bearish, the market is about to rise. Some financial newsletters measure swings in investor sentiment by tabulating the number of INVESTMENT ADVISORY SERVICES that are bullish or bearish.

SEPARATE CUSTOMER concept used by the SECURITIES INVESTOR PROTECTION CORPORATION (SIPC) in allocating insurance coverage. If there is a difference in the way investment accounts are owned, each account is viewed as a separate customer entitled to the maximum protection; thus two accounts, one in the name of John Jones and the other in the name of John Jones and his wife Mary Jones, would be treated as separate accounts and separate persons. On the other hand, a CASH ACCOUNT, a MARGIN ACCOUNT, and a special convertible bond account all owned by John Jones are not treated as separate customer accounts but as one.

SERIAL BOND bond issue, usually of a municipality, with various MATURITY DATES scheduled at regular intervals until the entire issue is retired. Each bond certificate in the series has an indicated REDEMPTION DATE.

SERIES E BOND savings bond issued by the U.S. government from 1941 to 1979. The bonds were then replaced by Series EE and Series HH bonds. Outstanding Series E bonds, which may be exchanged for the newer varieties, will continue to pay interest for between 25 and 40 years from their issue date. Those issued from 1941 to 1952 accrue interest for 40 years; those issued in 1979, for 25 years. There is a sliding scale for Series E bonds issued between 1952 and 1979. Their interest is exempt from state and local taxes. *See also* SAVINGS BOND.

SERIES EE BOND *see* SAVINGS BOND.

SERIES HH BOND *see* SAVINGS BOND.

SERIES OF OPTION class of OPTION, either all CALL OPTIONS or all PUT OPTIONS, on the same underlying security, all of which have the same EXERCISE PRICE (strike price) and maturity date. For example, all XYZ May 50 calls would form a series of options.

SETTLE

In general: to pay an obligation.

Estates: distribution of an estate's assets by an executor to beneficiaries after all legal procedures have been completed.

Law: (1) to resolve a legal dispute short of adjudication; (2) to arrange for disposition of property, such as between spouses or between parents and children, if there has been a dispute such as a divorce.

Securities: to complete a securities trade between brokers acting as AGENTS or between a broker and his customer. A trade is settled when the customer has paid the broker for securities bought or when the customer delivers securities that have been sold and the customer receives the proceeds from the sale. *See also* CONTINUOUS NET SETTLEMENT.

SETTLEMENT DATE date by which an executed order must be settled, either by a buyer paying for the securities with cash or by a seller delivering the securities and receiving the proceeds of the sale for them. In a REGULAR-WAY DELIVERY of stocks and bonds, the settlement date is five business days after the trade was executed. For listed options and government securities, settlement is required by the next business day. *See also* SELLER'S OPTION.

SETTLOR person who creates an INTER VIVOS TRUST as distinguished from a TESTAMENTARY TRUST. Also called *donor, grantor,* or *trustor.*

SEVERALLY BUT NOT JOINTLY form of agreement used to establish the responsibility for selling a portion of the securities in an underwriting. UNDERWRITING GROUP members agree to buy a certain portion of an issue (severally) but do not agree to joint liability for shares not sold by other members of the syndicate. In a less common form of underwriting arrangement, called a *several and joint agreement*, syndicate members agree to sell not only the shares allocated to them, but also any shares not sold by the rest of the group. *See also* UNDERWRITE.

SG&A EXPENSES *see* SELLING, GENERAL, AND ADMINISTRATIVE EXPENSES.

SHADOW CALENDAR backlog of securities issues in REGISTRATION with the Securities and Exchange Commission for which no OFFERING DATE has been set pending clearance.

SHAKEOUT change in market conditions that results in the elimination of marginally financed participants in an industry. For example, if the market for microcomputers suddenly becomes glutted because there is more supply than demand, a shakeout will result, meaning that companies will fall by the wayside. In the securities markets, a shakeout occurs when speculators are forced by market events to sell their positions, usually at a loss.

SHARE
1. unit of equity ownership in a corporation. This ownership is represented by a stock certificate, which names the company and the shareowner. The number of shares a corporation is authorized to issue is detailed in its corporate charter. Corporations usually do not issue the full number of AUTHORIZED SHARES.
2. unit of ownership in a mutual fund. *See also* INVESTMENT COMPANY.
3. interest, normally represented by a certificate, in a general or LIMITED PARTNERSHIP.

SHARE BROKER DISCOUNT BROKER whose charges are based on the number of shares traded. The more shares in a trade, the lower the per-share cost will be. Trading with a share broker is usually advantageous for those trading at least 500 shares, or for those trading in high-priced shares, who would otherwise pay a percentage of the dollar amount. Those trading in small numbers of shares, or lower-priced ones, may pay lower commissions with a VALUE BROKER, the other kind of discount brokerage firm.

SHAREHOLDER
1. owner of one or more shares of STOCK in a corporation. A common shareholder

is normally entitled to four basic rights of ownership: (1) claim on a share of the company's undivided assets in proportion to number of shares held; (2) proportionate voting power in the election of DIRECTORS and other business conducted at shareholder meetings or by PROXY; (3) DIVIDENDS when earned and declared by the BOARD OF DIRECTORS; and (4) PREEMPTIVE RIGHT to subscribe to additional stock offerings before they are available to the general public except when overruled by the ARTICLES OF INCORPORATION or in special circumstances, such as where stock is issued to effect a merger.

2. owner of one or more shares or units in a MUTUAL FUND. Mutual fund investors have voting rights similar to those of stock owners.

Shareholders' rights can vary according to the articles of incorporation or BYLAWS of the particular company.

See also PREFERRED STOCK.

SHAREHOLDER'S EQUITY total ASSETS minus total LIABILITIES of a corporation. Also called *stockholder's equity*, EQUITY, and NET WORTH.

SHARE REPURCHASE PLAN program by which a corporation buys back its own shares in the open market. It is usually done when shares are UNDERVALUED. Since it reduces the number of shares outstanding and thus increases EARNINGS PER SHARE, it tends to elevate the market value of the remaining shares held by stockholders. *See also* GOING PRIVATE; TREASURY STOCK.

SHARES AUTHORIZED number of shares of stock provided for in the ARTICLES OF INCORPORATION of a company. This figure is ordinarily indicated in the capital accounts section of a company's BALANCE SHEET and is usually well in excess of the shares ISSUED AND OUTSTANDING. A corporation cannot legally issue more shares than authorized. The number of authorized shares can be changed only by amendment to the corporate charter, with the approval of the shareholders. The most common reason for increasing authorized shares in a public company is to accommodate a stock SPLIT.

SHARES OUTSTANDING *see* ISSUED AND OUTSTANDING.

SHARK REPELLENT measure undertaken by a corporation to discourage unwanted TAKEOVER attempts. Also called *porcupine provision*. For example:

(1) fair price provision requiring a bidder to pay the same price to all shareholders. This raises the stakes and discourages TENDER OFFERS designed to attract only those shareholders most eager to replace management.

(2) GOLDEN PARACHUTE contract with top executives that makes it prohibitively expensive to get rid of existing management.

(3) defensive merger, in which a TARGET COMPANY combines with another organization that would create antitrust or other regulatory problems if the original, unwanted takeover proposal was consummated. *See also* SAFE HARBOR.

(4) STAGGERED BOARD OF DIRECTORS, a way to make it more difficult for a corporate RAIDER to install a majority of directors sympathetic to his or her views.

(5) supermajority provision, which might increase from a simple majority to two-thirds or three-fourths the shareholder vote required to ratify a takeover by an outsider.

See also POISON PILL; SCORCHED-EARTH POLICY.

SHARK WATCHER firm specializing in the early detection of TAKEOVER activity. Such a firm, whose primary business is usually the solicitation of proxies for client corporations, monitors trading patterns in a client's stock and attempts to determine the identity of parties accumulating shares.

SHELF REGISTRATION term used for SECURITIES AND EXCHANGE COMMISSION RULE 415 adopted in the 1980s, which allows a corporation to comply with REGISTRATION requirements up to two years prior to a PUBLIC OFFERING of securities. With the registration "on the shelf," the corporation, by simply updating regularly filed annual, quarterly, and related reports to the SEC, can go to the market as conditions become favorable with a minimum of administrative preparation. The flexibility corporate issuers enjoy as the result of shelf registration translates into substantial savings of time and expense.

SHELL CORPORATION company that is incorporated but has no significant assets or operations. Such corporations may be formed to obtain financing prior to starting operations, in which case an investment in them is highly risky. The term is also used of corporations set up by fraudulent operators as fronts to conceal tax evasion schemes.

SHERMAN ANTI-TRUST ACT OF 1890 *see* ANTITRUST LAWS.

SHOGUN SECURITY security issued and distributed exclusively in Japan by a non-Japanese company and denominated in a currency other than the yen.

SHOP
1. area of a business location where production takes place, as distinguished from the office or warehouse areas.
2. factory work force of an employer, as in a "union shop."
3. office of a broker-dealer in securities.
4. the act of canvassing dealers for the most favorable price, as in shopping securities dealers for the best bid or offer.
5. a small retail establishment.

SHORT AGAINST THE BOX *see* SELLING SHORT AGAINST THE BOX.

SHORT BOND
1. bond with a short maturity; a somewhat subjective concept, but generally meaning two years or less. *See also* SHORT TERM.
2. bond repayable in one year or less and thus classified as a CURRENT LIABILITY in accordance with the accounting definition of SHORT-TERM DEBT.
3. SHORT COUPON bond.

SHORT COUPON
1. bond interest payment covering less than the conventional six-month period. A short coupon payment occurs when the original issue date is less than a half year from the first scheduled interest payment date. Depending on how short the coupon is, the ACCRUED INTEREST makes a difference in the value of the bond at the time of issue, which is reflected in the offering price.
2. bond with a relatively short maturity, usually two years or less.
See also LONG COUPON.

SHORT COVERING actual purchase of securities by a short seller to replace those borrowed at the time of a short sale. *See also* LENDING SECURITIES; SELLING SHORT.

SHORT HEDGE transaction that limits or eliminates the risk of declining value in a security or commodity without entailing ownership. Examples:
(1) SELLING SHORT AGAINST THE BOX leaves the owned securities untouched, possibly to gain in value, while protecting against a decline in value, since that would be offset by a profit on the short sale.
(2) purchasing a PUT OPTION to protect the value of a security that is owned limits loss to the cost of the option.
(3) buying a futures contract on raw materials at a specific price protects a manufacturer committed to sell a product at a certain price at a specified future time but who cannot buy the raw materials at the time of the commitment. Thus, if the price of the materials goes up, the manufacturer makes a profit on the contract; if the price goes down, he or she makes a profit on the product.
Compare with LONG HEDGE.

SHORT INTEREST total amount of shares of stock that have been sold short and have not yet been repurchased to close out SHORT POSITIONS. The short interest figure for the New York Stock Exchange, which is published monthly in newspapers, indicates how many investors think stock prices are about to fall. The Exchange reports all issues in which there are at least 5000 shares sold short, and in which the short interest position had changed by at least 2000 shares in the preceding month. The higher the short interest, the more people are expecting a downturn. Such short interest also represents potential buying pressure, however, since all short sales must eventually be covered by the purchase of shares. For this reason, a high short interest position is viewed as a bullish sign by many sophisticated market watchers. *See also* SELLING SHORT; SHORT INTEREST THEORY.

SHORT INTEREST THEORY theory that a large SHORT INTEREST in a stock presages a rise in the market price. It is based on the reasoning that even though short selling reflects a belief that prices will decline, the fact that short positions must eventually be covered is a source of upward price pressure. It is also called the CUSHION THEORY, since short sales can be viewed as a cushion of imminent buy orders. *See also* MEMBERS' SHORT-SALE RATIO; ODD-LOT SHORT-SALE RATIO; SELLING SHORT; SPECIALIST'S SHORT-SALE RATIO.

SHORT POSITION
Commodities: contract in which a trader has agreed to sell a commodity at a future date for a specific price.
Stocks: stock shares that an individual has sold short (by delivery of borrowed certificates) and has not covered as of a particular date.
See also COVER; SELLING SHORT.

SHORT SALE *see* SELLING SHORT.

SHORT-SALE RULE Securities and Exchange Commission rule requiring that short sales be made only in a rising market; also called PLUS TICK rule. A short sale can be transacted only under these conditions: (1) if the last sale was at a higher price than the sale preceding it (called an UPTICK or PLUS TICK); (2) if the last sale price is unchanged but higher than the last preceding different sale (called a ZERO-PLUS TICK). The short sale rule was designed to prevent abuses perpetuated by so-called pool operators, who would drive down the price of a stock by heavy short selling, then pick up the shares for a large profit.

SHORT SQUEEZE situation when prices of a stock or commodity futures contract start to move up sharply and many traders with short positions are forced to buy stocks or commodities in order to COVER their positions and prevent losses. This sudden surge of buying leads to even higher prices, further aggravating the losses of short sellers who have not covered their positions. *See also* SELLING SHORT.

SHORT TENDER using borrowed stock to respond to a TENDER OFFER. The practice is prohibited by SECURITIES AND EXCHANGE COMMISSION RULE 10b-4.

SHORT TERM

Accounting: assets expected to be converted into cash within the normal operating cycle (usually one year), or liabilities coming due in one year or less. *See also* CURRENT ASSETS; CURRENT LIABILITY.

Investment: investment with a maturity of one year or less. This includes bonds, although in differentiating between short-, medium-, and long-term bonds short term often is stretched to mean two years or less. *See also* SHORT BOND; SHORT-TERM DEBT; SHORT-TERM GAIN OR LOSS.

Taxes: HOLDING PERIOD of six months or less, used to differentiate SHORT-TERM GAIN OR LOSS from LONG TERM GAIN and LONG TERM LOSS until the TAX REFORM ACT OF 1986 eliminated the short/long distinction in 1988.

SHORT-TERM DEBT all debt obligations coming due within one year; shown on a balance sheet as current liabilities. *See also* CURRENT LIABILITY.

SHORT-TERM GAIN OR LOSS for tax purposes, the profit or loss realized from the sale of securities or other capital assets held six months or less. Short term gains are taxable at ordinary income rates to the extent they are not reduced by offsetting short term losses. *See also* CAPITAL GAIN; CAPITAL LOSS.

SIDE-BY-SIDE TRADING trading of a security and an OPTION on that security on the same exchange.

SIDEWAYS MARKET period in which prices trade within a narrow range, showing only small changes up or down. Also called HORIZONTAL PRICE MOVEMENT. *See also* FLAT MARKET.

SILENT PARTNER
1. limited partner in a DIRECT PARTICIPATION PROGRAM, such as real estate and oil and gas limited partnerships, in which CASH FLOW and tax benefits are passed directly through to shareholders. Such partners are called silent because, unlike general partners, they have no direct role in management and no liability beyond their individual investment.
2. general partner in a business who has no role in management but represents a sharing of the investment and liability. Silent partners of this type are often found in family businesses, where the intent is to distribute tax liability. *See also* LIMITED PARTNERSHIP.

SILVER THURSDAY the day—March 27, 1980—when the extremely wealthy Hunt brothers of Texas failed to meet a MARGIN CALL by the brokerage firm of Bache Halsey Stuart Shields (which later became Prudential-Bache Securities) for $100 million in silver futures contracts. Their position was later covered and Bache survived, but the effects on the commodities markets and the financial markets in general were traumatic.

SIMPLE INTEREST interest calculation based only on the original principal amount. Simple interest contrasts with COMPOUND INTEREST, which is applied to principal plus accumulated interest. For example, $100 on deposit at 12% simple interest would yield $12 per year (12% of $100). For computing interest on loans, simple interest is distinguished from various methods of calculating interest on a precomputed basis. *See also* PRECOMPUTE; CONSUMER CREDIT PROTECTION ACT OF 1968.

SIMPLIFIED EMPLOYEE PENSION (SEP) PLAN pension plan in which both the employee and the employer contribute to an INDIVIDUAL RETIREMENT ACCOUNT (IRA). Under the TAX REFORM ACT OF 1986, employees (except those participating in SEPs of state or local governments) may elect to have employer contributions made to the SEP or paid to the employee in cash as with cash or deferred arrangements [401(K) PLANS]. Elective contributions, which are excludable from earnings for income tax purposes but includable for employment tax (FICA and FUTA) purposes, are limited to $7000, while employer contributions may not exceed $30,000. SEPs are limited to small employers (25 or fewer employees) and at least 50% of employees must participate. Special provisions concern the integration of SEP contributions and Social Security benefits and limit tax deferrals for highly compensated individuals.

SINGLE OPTION term used to distinguish a PUT OPTION or a CALL OPTION from a SPREAD or a STRADDLE, each of which involves two or more put or call options. *See also* OPTION.

SINGLE-PREMIUM DEFERRED ANNUITY (SPDA) tax-deferred investment similar to an INDIVIDUAL RETIREMENT ACCOUNT, without many of the IRA restrictions. An investor makes a lump-sum payment to an insurance company selling the annuity. That lump sum can be invested in either a fixed-return instrument like a CD or a variable-return portfolio that can be switched among stocks, bonds, and money-market accounts. Proceeds are taxed only when distributions are taken. In contrast to an IRA, there is no limit to the amount that may be invested in an SPDA. Like the IRA, the tax penalty for withdrawals before age 59½ is 10%.

SINGLE-PREMIUM LIFE INSURANCE WHOLE LIFE INSURANCE policy requiring one premium payment. Since this large, up-front payment begins accumulating cash value immediately, the policy holder will earn more than holders of policies paid up in installments. With its tax-free appreciation (assuming it remains in force); low or no net-cost; tax-free access to funds through POLICY LOANS; and tax-free proceeds to beneficiaries, this type of policy emerged as a popular TAX SHELTER under the TAX REFORM ACT OF 1986.

SINGLE-STATE MUNICIPAL BOND FUND MUTUAL FUND that invests entirely in tax-exempt obligations of governments and government agencies within a single state. Therefore, dividends paid on fund shares are not taxable to residents of that state when they file state tax returns, although capital gains, if any, are taxable (at ORDINARY INCOME rates starting in 1988).

SINKER industry term for a bond with a SINKING FUND.

SINKING FUND money accumulated on a regular basis in a separate custodial account that is used to redeem debt securities or preferred stock issues. A bond indenture or preferred stock charter may specify that payments be made to a sinking fund, thus assuring investors that the issues are safer than bonds (or preferred stocks) for which the issuer must make payment all at once, without the benefit of a sinking fund. *See also* PURCHASE FUND.

SIZE
1. number of shares or bonds available for sale. A market maker will say, when asked for a quote, that a particular number of shares (the size) is available at a particular price.
2. term used when a large number of shares are for sale—a trader will say that "shares are available in size," for instance.

SKIP-PAYMENT PRIVILEGE
1. clause in some MORTGAGE contracts and installment loan agreements that allows the borrower to miss a payment if payments are ahead of schedule.
2. option offered to bank credit-card holders meeting certain requirements whereby they may defer the December payment on balances due.

SLD LAST SALE indication, meaning "sold last sale," that appears on the CONSOLIDATED TAPE when a greater than normal change occurs between transactions in a security. The designation, which appears after the STOCK SYMBOL, is normally used when the change is a point or more on lower-priced issues (below $20) or two points or more on higher-priced issues.

SLEEPER stock in which there is little investor interest but which has significant potential to gain in price once its attractions are recognized. Sleepers are most easily recognized in retrospect, after they have already moved up in price.

SLEEPING BEAUTY potential TAKEOVER target that has not yet been approached by an acquirer. Such a company usually has particularly attractive features, such as a large amount of cash, or undervalued real estate or other assets.

SMALL BUSINESS ADMINISTRATION (SBA) federal agency created in 1953 to provide financial assistance (through direct loans and loan guarantees) as well as management assistance to businesses that lack the access to CAPITAL MARKETS enjoyed by larger more creditworthy corporations. Further legislation authorized the SBA to contribute to the VENTURE CAPITAL requirements of START-UP companies by licensing and funding small business investment companies (SBICs), to maintain a loan fund for rehabilitation of property damaged by natural disasters, and to provide loans, counseling and training for small businesses owned by minorities, the economically disadvantaged, and the disabled. The SBA finances its activities through direct grants approved by Congress.

SMALL FIRM EFFECT tendency of stocks of smaller firms, defined by MARKET CAPITALIZATION, to outperform larger firms. Theories to explain this phenomenon vary, but include the following: (1) smaller companies tend to have more growth potential; (2) small capitalization groupings include more companies in financial difficulty; when fortunes recover, price gains are dramatic and lift the return of the group as a whole; (3) small firms are generally neglected by analysts and hence by institutions, but once discovered, they become appropriately valued, registering dramatic gains in the process. *See also* ANKLE BITER.

SMALL INVESTOR individual investor who buys small amounts of stock or bonds, often in ODD LOT quantities; also called the RETAIL INVESTOR. Although there are millions of small investors, their total holdings are dwarfed by the share ownership of large institutions such as mutual funds and insurance companies.

Together with the proliferation of mutual funds, recent developments in the brokerage industry and its diversification along full-service lines have brought new programs specifically designed to make investing more convenient for small investors. Thus, much cash traditionally kept in savings banks has found its way into the stock and bond markets. *See also* ODD-LOT SHORT-SALE RATIO; ODD-LOT THEORY.

SNOWBALLING process by which the activation of STOP ORDERS in a declining or advancing market causes further downward or upward pressure on prices, thus triggering more stop orders and more price pressure, and so on.

SOCIAL CONSCIOUSNESS MUTUAL FUND mutual fund that is managed for capital appreciation while at the same time investing in securities of companies that do not conflict with certain social priorities. As a product of the social consciousness movements of the 1960s and 1970s, this type of mutual fund might not invest in companies that derive significant profits from defense contracts or whose activities cause environmental pollution, nor in companies with significant interests in countries with repressive or racist governments.

SOFT CURRENCY funds of a country that are not acceptable in exchange for the hard currencies of other countries. Soft currencies, such as the Soviet Union's ruble, are fixed at unrealistic exchange rates and are not backed by gold, so that countries with hard currencies, like U.S. dollars or British pounds, are reluctant to convert assets into them. *See also* HARD MONEY (HARD CURRENCY).

SOFT DOLLARS means of paying brokerage firms for their services through commission revenue, rather than through direct payments, known as *hard-dollar fees*. For example, a mutual fund may offer to pay for the research of a brokerage firm by executing trades generated by that research through that brokerage firm. The broker might agree to this arrangement if the fund manager promises to spend at least $100,000 in commissions with the broker that year. Otherwise, the fund would have to pay a hard-dollar fee of $50,000 for the research. *Compare with* HARD DOLLARS.

SOFT LANDING term used by optimists amid growing recession fears in the late 1980s to connote a rate of economic growth sufficient to avoid recession but slow enough to prevent high inflation and interest rates.

SOFT MARKET market characterized by an excess of supply over demand. A soft market in securities is marked by inactive trading, wide bid-offer spreads, and pronounced price drops in response to minimal selling pressure. Also called *buyer's market*.

SOFT SPOT weakness in selected stocks or stock groups in the face of a generally strong and advancing market.

SOLD-OUT MARKET commodities market term meaning that futures contracts in a particular commodity or maturity range are largely unavailable because of contract liquidations and limited offerings.

SOLVENCY state of being able to meet maturing obligations as they come due. *See also* INSOLVENCY.

SOURCE AND APPLICATIONS OF FUNDS STATEMENT analysis of changes in the FINANCIAL POSITION of a firm from one accounting period to another; also called *sources and uses of funds statement*. It is usually presented as part of a complete FINANCIAL STATEMENT and appears in the ANNUAL REPORTS of publicly held companies. It consists of two parts: (1) *sources of funds* summarizes the transactions that increased WORKING CAPITAL, such as NET INCOME, DEPRECIA-TION, the issue of bonds, the sale of stock, or an increase in deferred taxes; (2) *applications of funds* summarizes the way funds were used, such as the purchase or improvement of plant and equipment, the payment of dividends, the repayment of long-term debt, or the redemption or repurchase of shares.

SOVEREIGN RISK risk that a foreign government will default on its loan or fail to honor other business commitments because of a change in national policy. A country asserting its prerogatives as an independent nation might prevent the REPATRIATION of a company or country's funds through limits on the flow of capital, tax impediments, or the nationalization of property. Sovereign risk became a factor in the growth of international debt that followed the oil price increases of the 1970s. Several developing countries that borrowed heavily from Western banks to finance trade deficits had difficulty later keeping to repayment schedules. Banks had to reschedule loans to such countries as Mexico and Argentina to keep them from defaulting. These loans ran the further risk of renunciation by political leaders, which also would have affected loans to private companies that had been guaranteed by previous governments. Beginning in the 1970s, banks and other multinational corporations developed sophisticated analytical tools to measure sovereign risk before committing to lend, invest, or begin operations in a given foreign country. Throughout periods of worldwide economic volatility, the United States has been able to attract foreign investment because of its perceived lack of sovereign risk. Also called *country risk* or *political risk.*

SPECIAL ARBITRAGE ACCOUNT special MARGIN ACCOUNT with a broker reserved for transactions in which the customer's risk is hedged by an offsetting security transaction or position. The MARGIN REQUIREMENT on such a transaction is substantially less than in the case of stocks bought on credit and subject to price declines. *See also* HEDGE/HEDGING.

SPECIAL ASSESSMENT BOND municipal bond that is repaid from taxes imposed on those who benefit directly from the neighborhood-oriented public works project funded by the bond; also called *special assessment limited liability bond, special district bond, special purpose bond,* SPECIAL TAX BOND. For example, if a bond finances the construction of a sewer system, the homeowners and businesses hooked up to the sewer system pay a special levy that goes to repay the bonds. The interest from special assessment bonds is tax free to resident bondholders. These are not normally GENERAL OBLIGATION BONDS, and the FULL FAITH AND CREDIT of the municipality is not usually behind them. Where the full faith and credit does back such bonds, they are called general obligation special assessment bonds.

SPECIAL BID infrequently used method of purchasing a large block of stock on the New York Stock Exchange whereby a MEMBER FIRM, acting as a broker, matches the buy order of one client, usually an institution, with sell orders solicited from a number of other customers. It is the reverse of an EXCHANGE DISTRIBUTION. The member broker makes a fixed price offer, which is announced in advance on the CONSOLIDATED TAPE. The bid cannot be lower than the last sale or the current regular market bid. Sellers of the stock pay no commissions; the buying customer pays both the selling and buying commissions. The transaction is completed during regular trading hours.

SPECIAL BOND ACCOUNT special MARGIN ACCOUNT with a broker that is reserved for transactions in U.S. government bonds, municipals, and eligible listed and unlisted nonconvertible corporate bonds. The restrictions under which brokers may extend credit with margin securities of these types are generally more liberal than in the case of stocks.

SPECIAL CASH ACCOUNT same as CASH ACCOUNT.

SPECIAL DISTRICT BOND *see* SPECIAL ASSESSMENT BOND.

SPECIAL DRAWING RIGHTS (SDR) measure of a nation's reserve assets in the international monetary system; known informally as "paper gold." First issued by the INTERNATIONAL MONETARY FUND (IMF) in 1970, SDRs are designed to supplement the reserves of gold and convertible currencies (or hard currencies) used to maintain stability in the foreign exchange market. For example, if the U.S. Treasury sees that the British pound's value has fallen precipitously in relation to the dollar, it can use its store of SDRs to buy excess pounds on the foreign exchange market, thereby raising the value of the remaining supply of pounds.

This neutral unit of account was made necessary by the rapid growth in world trade during the 1960s. International monetary officials feared that the supply of the two principal reserve assets—gold and U.S. dollars—would fall short of demand, causing the value of the U.S. currency to rise disproportionately in relation to other reserve assets. (At the time SDRs were introduced, the price of gold was fixed at about $35 per ounce.)

The IMF allocates to each of its more than 140 member countries an amount of SDRs proportional to its predetermined quota in the fund, which in turn is based on its GROSS NATIONAL PRODUCT (GNP). Each member agrees to back its SDRs with the full faith and credit of its government, and to accept them in exchange for gold or convertible currencies.

Originally, the value of one SDR was fixed at one dollar and at the dollar equivalent of other key currencies on January 1, 1970. As world governments adopted the current system of FLOATING EXCHANGE RATES, the SDR's value fluctuated relative to the "basket" of major currencies. Increasing reliance on SDRs in settling international accounts coincided with a decline in the importance of gold as a reserve asset.

Because of its inherent equilibrium relative to any one currency, the SDR has been used to denominate or calculate the value of private contracts, international treaties, and securities on the EUROBOND market.

SPECIALIST member of a stock exchange who maintains a fair and orderly market in one or more securities. A specialist or SPECIALIST UNIT performs two main functions: executing LIMIT ORDERS on behalf of other exchange members for a portion of the FLOOR BROKER's commission, and buying or selling—sometimes SELLING SHORT—for the specialist's own account to counteract temporary imbalances in supply and demand and thus prevent wide swings in stock prices. The specialist is prohibited by exchange rules from buying for his own account when there is an unexecuted order for the same security at the same price in the SPECIALIST'S BOOK, the record kept of limit orders in each price category in the sequence in which they are received. Specialists must meet strict minimum capital requirements before receiving formal approval by the New York Stock Exchange. *See also* SPECIALIST BLOCK PURCHASE AND SALE; SPECIALIST'S SHORT SALE RATIO.

SPECIALIST BLOCK PURCHASE AND SALE transaction whereby a SPE-

CIALIST on a stock exchange buys a large block of securities either to sell for his own account or to try and place with another block buyer and seller, such as a FLOOR TRADER. Exchange rules require that such transactions be executed only when the securities cannot be ABSORBED in the regular market. *See also* NOT HELD.

SPECIALIST'S BOOK record maintained by a SPECIALIST that includes the specialist's own inventory of securities, market orders to sell short, and LIMIT ORDERS and STOP ORDERS that other stock exchange members have placed with the specialist. The orders are listed in chronological sequence. For example, for a stock trading at 57 a broker might ask for 500 shares when the price falls to 55. If successful at placing this limit order, the specialist notifies the member broker who entered the request, and collects a commission. The specialist is prohibited from buying the stock for his own account at a price for which he has previously agreed to execute a limit order.

SPECIALIST'S SHORT-SALE RATIO ratio of the amount of stock sold short by specialists on the floor of the New York Stock Exchange to total short sales. The ratio signals whether specialists are more or less bearish (expecting prices to decline) on the outlook for stock prices than other NYSE members and the public. Since specialists must constantly be selling stock short in order to provide for an orderly market in the stocks they trade, their short sales cannot be entirely regarded as an indication of how they perceive trends. Still, their overall short sales activity reflects knowledge, and technical analysts watch the specialist's short-sale ratio carefully for a clue to imminent upturns or downturns in stock prices. Traditionally, when the ratio rises above 60%, it is considered a bearish signal. A drop below 45% is seen as bullish and below 35% is considered extremely bullish. *See also* ODD-LOT SHORT-SALE RATIO; SELLING SHORT; SPECIALIST.

SPECIALIST UNIT stock exchange SPECIALIST (individual, partnership, corporation, or group of two or three firms) authorized by an exchange to deal as PRINCIPAL and AGENT for other brokers in maintaining a stable market in one or more particular stocks. A specialist unit on the New York Stock Exchange is required to have enough capital to buy at least 5000 shares of the common stock of a company it handles and 1000 shares of the company's CONVERTIBLE preferred stock.

SPECIALIZED MUTUAL FUND fund that limits its investments to a particular sector of the marketplace—for example, the energy industry or the health care-related field. In some mutual fund groups, there is a PORTFOLIO of specialized funds for shareholders to choose from, so that when one area no longer looks promising, they can shift assets into another area. For example, investors may want to sell their shares in an interest-sensitive financial services fund and reinvest the proceeds in a defense-stock fund if they think interest rates are about to rise and defense spending is about to increase dramatically.

SPECIAL MISCELLANEOUS ACCOUNT (SMA) memorandum account of the funds in excess of the MARGIN REQUIREMENT. Such excess funds may arise from the proceeds of sales, appreciation of market values, dividends, or cash or securities put up in response to a MARGIN CALL. An SMA is not under the jurisdiction of REGULATION T of the Federal Reserve Board, as is the INITIAL MARGIN requirement, but this does not mean the customer is free to withdraw balances from it. The account is maintained essentially so that the broker can gauge how far the customer might be from a margin call. Any withdrawals require the broker's permission.

SPECIAL OFFERING method of selling a large block of stock that is similar to a SECONDARY DISTRIBUTION but is limited to New York Stock Exchange members and takes place during normal trading hours. The selling member announces the impending sale on the CONSOLIDATED TAPE, indicating a fixed price, which is usually based on the last transaction price in the regular market. All costs and commissions are borne by the seller. The buyers are member firms that may be buying for customer accounts or for their own inventory. Such offerings must have approval from the Securities and Exchange Commission.

SPECIAL SITUATION
1. undervalued stock that should soon rise in value because of an imminent favorable turn of events. A special situation stock may be about to introduce a revolutionary new product or be undergoing a needed management change. Many securities analysts concentrate on looking for and analyzing special situation stocks.
2. stock that fluctuates widely in daily trading, often influencing market averages, because of a particular news development, such as the announcement of a TAKEOVER bid.

SPECIAL TAX BOND
1. MUNICIPAL REVENUE BOND that will be repaid through excise taxes on such purchases as gasoline, tobacco, and liquor. The bond is not backed by the ordinary taxing power of the municipality issuing it. The interest from these bonds is tax free to resident bondholders.
2. SPECIAL ASSESSMENT BOND.

SPECTAIL term for broker-dealer who is part retail broker but preponderantly dealer/speculator.

SPECULATION assumption of risk in anticipation of gain but recognizing a higher than average possibility of loss. Speculation is a necessary and productive activity. It can be profitable over the long term when engaged in by professionals, who often limit their losses through the use of various HEDGING techniques and devices, including OPTIONS trading, SELLING SHORT, STOP LOSS ORDERS, and transactions in FUTURES CONTRACTS. The term speculation implies that a business or investment risk can be analyzed and measured, and its distinction from the term INVESTMENT is one of degree of risk. It differs from gambling, which is based on random outcomes.
See also VENTURE CAPITAL.

SPIN-OFF form of corporate DIVESTITURE that results in a subsidiary or division becoming an independent company. In a traditional spin-off, shares in the new entity are distributed to the parent corporation's shareholders of record on a PRO RATA basis. Spin-offs can also be accomplished through a LEVERAGED BUYOUT by the subsidiary or division's management, or through an EMPLOYEE STOCK OWNERSHIP PLAN (ESOP).

SPLIT increase in a corporation's number of outstanding shares of stock without any change in the shareholders' EQUITY or the aggregate MARKET VALUE at the time of the split. In a split, also called a *split up*, the share price declines. If a stock at $100 par value splits 2-for-1, the number of authorized shares doubles (for example, from 10 million to 20 million) and the price per share drops by half, to $50. A holder of 50 shares before the split now has 100 shares at the lower price. If the same stock splits 4-for-1, the number of shares quadruples to 40 million and the share price falls to $25. Dividends per share also fall proportionately. Directors of a corporation will authorize a split to make ownership more affordable to a broader base of investors. Where stock splits require an increase in AUTHORIZED SHARES and/or a change in PAR VALUE of the stock, shareholders must approve an amendment of the corporate charter.

See also REVERSE SPLIT.

SPLIT COMMISSION commission divided between the securities broker who executes a trade and another person who brought the trade to the broker, such as an investment counselor or financial planner. Split commissions between brokers are also common in real estate transactions.

SPLIT DOWN see REVERSE SPLIT.

SPLIT OFFERING new municipal bond issue, part of which is represented by SERIAL BONDS and part by term maturity bonds.

SPLIT ORDER large transaction in securities that, to avoid unsettling the market and causing fluctuations in the market price, is broken down into smaller portions to be executed over a period of time.

SPLIT RATING situation in which two major rating agencies, such as Standard & Poor's and Moody's Investors Service, assign a different rating to the same security.

SPLIT UP see SPLIT.

SPONSOR

Limited partnerships: GENERAL PARTNER who organizes and sells a LIMITED PARTNERSHIP. Sponsors (also called *promoters*) rely on their reputation in past real estate, oil and gas, or other deals to attract limited partners to their new deals.

Mutual funds: investment company that offers shares in its funds. Also called the *underwriter*.

Stocks: important investor—typically, an institution, mutual fund, or other big trader—whose favorable opinion of a particular security influences other investors and creates additional demand for the security. Institutional investors often want to make sure a stock has wide sponsorship before they invest in it, since this should ensure that the stock will not fall dramatically.

SPOT COMMODITY COMMODITY traded with the expectation that it will actually be delivered to the buyer, as contrasted to a FUTURES CONTRACT that will usually expire without any physical delivery taking place. Spot commodities are traded in the SPOT MARKET.

SPOT DELIVERY MONTH nearest month of those currently being traded in which a commodity could be delivered. In late January, therefore, the spot delivery month would be February for commodities with a February contract trade.

SPOT MARKET commodities market in which goods are sold for cash and delivered immediately. Trades that take place in FUTURES CONTRACTS expiring in the current month are also called *spot market trades*. The spot market tends to be conducted OVER-THE-COUNTER—that is, through telephone trading—rather than on the floor of an organized commodity exchange. Also called *actual market, cash market* or *physical market*. See also FUTURES MARKET.

SPOT PRICE current delivery price of a commodity traded in the SPOT MARKET. Also called *cash price*.

SPOUSAL IRA INDIVIDUAL RETIREMENT ACCOUNT that may be opened in the name of a nonworking spouse. In the mid-1980s, the maximum annual IRA contribution for a married couple, only one of whom was employed, was $2250. The couple could allocate the $2250 any way they wished between two accounts, as long as either account did not exceed the $2000 limit imposed on all IRAs. If both spouses worked, they could each contribute up to $2000 to their respective IRAs, or a combined maximum of $4000.

SPOUSAL REMAINDER TRUST means used prior to the TAX REFORM ACT OF 1986 to shift income to a person taxable at a lower rate. Income-producing property, such as securities, is transferred by the grantor to the trust for a specific time, typically five years. Trust income is distributed to the beneficiary (or to a minor's CUSTODIAL ACCOUNT) to be used for expenses such as a child's college education. The income is therefore taxed at the beneficiary's lower tax rate. When the trust term expires, the property passes irrevocably to the grantor's spouse. The TAX REFORM ACT OF 1986 provided that effective for trusts established or contributions to trusts made after March 1, 1986, income must be taxed at the grantor's tax rate if the beneficiary is under age 14 and the property can revert to the grantor or the grantor's spouse.

SPREAD

Commodities: in futures trading, the difference between delivery months in the same or different markets.

Fixed-income securities:
1. difference between yields on securities of the same quality but different maturities. For example, the spread between 10% short-term Treasury bills and 14% long-term Treasury bonds is 4 percentage points.
2. difference between yields on securities of the same maturity but different quality. For instance, the spread between a 14% long-term Treasury bond and a 17% long-term bond of a B-rated corporation is 3 percentage points, since an investor's risk is so much less with the Treasury bond. See also YIELD SPREAD.

Foreign exchange: in ARBITRAGE terminology, a larger-than-normal difference in currency exchange rates between two markets.

Options: difference in premiums (prices) resulting from a combination of put and call OPTIONS within the same CLASS on the same underlying security. STRIKE PRICE and expiration month may be the same or different. For example, an investor could create a spread by buying an XYZ November 40 call and selling an XYZ November 30 call. See also BEAR SPREAD; BULL SPREAD; BUTTERFLY SPREAD; CALENDAR SPREAD; CREDIT SPREAD; DEBIT SPREAD; DIAGONAL SPREAD; OPTION; PRICE SPREAD; VERTICAL SPREAD.

Stocks and bonds:
1. difference between the bid and offer price. If a stock is bid at $45 and offered at $46, the spread is one dollar. This spread narrows or widens according to the supply and demand for the security being traded.

2. difference between the high and low price of a particular security over a given period.

Underwriting: difference between the proceeds an issuer of a new security receives and the price paid by the public for the issue. This spread is taken by the underwriting syndicate as payment for its services. A security issued at $100 may entail a spread of $2 for the underwriter, so the issuer receives $98 from the offering. *See also* UNDERWRITING SPREAD.

SPREADING practice of buying and selling OPTION contracts of the same CLASS on the same underlying security in order to profit from moves in the price of that security. *See also* SPREAD.

SPREAD OPTION SPREAD position involving the purchase of an OPTION at one EXERCISE PRICE and the simultaneous sale of another option on the same underlying security at a different exercise price and/or expiration date. *See also* DIAGONAL SPREAD; HORIZONTAL SPREAD; VERTICAL SPREAD.

SPREAD ORDER OPTIONS market term for an order designating the SERIES of LISTED OPTIONS the customer wishes to buy and sell, together with the desired SPREAD—or difference in option premiums (prices)—shown as a net debit or net credit. The transaction is completed if the FLOOR BROKER can execute the order at the requested spread.

SPREAD POSITION status of an account in which a SPREAD has been executed.

SPREADSHEET ledger sheet on which a company's financial statements, such as BALANCE SHEETS, INCOME STATEMENTS, and sales reports, are laid out in columns and rows. Spreadsheets are used by securities and credit analysts in researching companies and industries. Since the advent of personal computers, spreadsheets have come into wide use, because software makes them easy to use. In an electronic spreadsheet on a computer, any time one number is changed, all the other numbers are automatically adjusted according to the relationships the computer operator sets up. For instance, in a spreadsheet of a sales report of a company's many divisions, the updating of a single division's sales figure will automatically change the total sales for the company, as well as the percentage of total sales that division produced.

SQUEEZE

Finance: (1) tight money period, when loan money is scarce and interest rates are high, making borrowing difficult and expensive—also called a *credit crunch*; (2) any situation where increased costs cannot be passed on to customers in the form of higher prices.

Investments: situation when stocks or commodities futures start to move up in price, and investors who have sold short are forced to COVER their short positions in order to avoid large losses. When done by many short sellers, this action is called a SHORT SQUEEZE. *See also* SELLING SHORT; SHORT POSITION.

SRO *see* SELF-REGULATORY ORGANIZATION.

STABILIZATION

Currency: buying and selling of a country's own currency to protect its exchange value, also called PEGGING.

Economics: leveling out of the business cycle, unemployment, and prices through fiscal and monetary policies.

Market trading: action taken by REGISTERED COMPETITIVE TRADERS on the New York Stock Exchange in accordance with an exchange requirement that 75% of their trades be stabilizing—in other words, that their sell orders follow a PLUS TICK and their buy orders a MINUS TICK.

New issues underwriting: intervention in the market by a managing underwriter in order to keep the market price from falling below the PUBLIC OFFERING PRICE during the offering period. The underwriter places orders to buy at a specific price, an action called PEGGING that, in any other circumstance, is a violation of laws prohibiting MANIPULATION in the securities and commodities markets.

STAG speculator who makes it a practice to get in and out of stocks for a fast profit, rather than to hold securities for investment.

STAGFLATION term coined by economists in the 1970s to describe the previously unprecedented combination of slow economic growth and high unemployment (stagnation) with rising prices (inflation). The principal factor was the fourfold increase in oil prices imposed by the Organization of Petroleum Exporting Countries (OPEC) cartel in 1973-74, which raised price levels throughout the economy while further slowing economic growth. As is characteristic of stagflation, fiscal and monetary policies aimed at stimulating the economy and reducing unemployment only exacerbated the inflationary effects.

STAGGERED BOARD OF DIRECTORS board of directors of a company in which a portion of the directors are elected each year, instead of all at once. A board is often staggered in order to thwart unfriendly TAKEOVER attempts, since potential acquirers would have to wait longer than one ANNUAL MEETING before they could take control of a company's board through the normal voting procedure.

STAGGERING MATURITIES technique used to lower risk by a bond investor. Since long-term bonds are more volatile than short-term ones, an investor can HEDGE against interest rate movements by buying short-, medium- and long-term bonds. If interest rates decline, the long-term bonds will rise faster in value than the shorter-term bonds. If rates rise, however, the shorter-term bonds will hold their value better than long-term debt obligations, which could fall precipitously.

STAGNATION

Economics: period of no or slow (3% or less) economic growth or of economic decline, in real (inflation-adjusted) terms.

Securities: period of low volume and inactive trading.

STAGS acronym for *S*terling *T*ransferable *A*ccruing *G*overnment *S*ecurities, ZERO-COUPON SECURITIES denominated in pounds sterling and created by separating interest payments from the principal of British Treasury bonds (gilts). *See also* STRIP.

STANDARD & POOR'S CORPORATION subsidiary of McGraw-Hill, Inc. that provides a broad range of investment services, including RATING corporate and municipal bonds, common stocks, preferred stocks, and COMMERCIAL PAPER; compiling the Standard & Poor's Composite Index of 500 Stocks, the Standard & Poor's 400 Industrial Index, and the Standard & Poor's 100 Index among other indexes; publishing a wide variety of statistical materials, investment advisory reports, and other financial information, including: *Bond Guide*, a summary of data on corporate and municipal bonds; *Earnings Forecaster*, earnings-per-share estimates on more than 1600 companies; *New Issue Investor*, information and analysis on the new issue market; *Stock Guide*, investment data on listed and unlisted common and preferred stocks and mutual funds; *Analyst's Handbook*, per-share data on the stocks and industry groups making up the 400 index, plus 15 transportation, financial and utility groups; *Corporation Records*, six volumes of information on more than 10,000 publicly held companies; *Stock Reports*, 2-page analytical reports on listed and unlisted companies. A subsidiary publishes the daily BLUE LIST of municipal and corporate bonds. Standard & Poor's also publishes *Poor's Register*, a national directory of companies and their officers; *Securities Dealers of North America*, a directory of investment banking and brokerage firms in North America; and provides a range of back office and electronic services. See also BOND RATING; STANDARD & POOR'S RATING; STOCK INDEXES AND AVERAGES.

STANDARD & POOR'S INDEX broad-based measurement of changes in stock-market conditions based on the average performance of 500 widely held common stocks; commonly known as the *Standard & Poor's 500* (or *S&P 500*). The selection of stocks, their relative weightings to reflect differences in the number of outstanding shares, and publication of the index itself are services of STANDARD & POOR'S CORPORATION, a financial advisory, securities rating, and publishing firm. The index tracks industrial, transportation, financial, and utility stocks; since mid-1989, the composition of the 500 stocks has been more flexible and the number of issues in each sector has varied. See also S&P PHENOMENON; STOCK INDEXES AND AVERAGES.

STANDARD & POOR'S RATING classification of stocks and bonds according to risk issued by STANDARD AND POOR'S CORPORATION. S&P's top four debt grades—called INVESTMENT GRADE AAA, AA, A, and BBB—indicate a minimal risk that a corporate or municipal bond issue will default in its timely payment of interest and principal. Common stocks are ranked A+ through C on the basis of growth and stability, with a ranking of D signifying reorganization. See also EVENT RISK; LEGAL LIST.

STANDARD COST estimate, based on engineering and accounting studies, of what the costs of production should be, assuming normal operating conditions. Standard costs differ from budgeted costs, which are forecasts based on expectations. Variances between standard costs and actual costs measure productive efficiency and are a basis of cost control.

STANDARD DEDUCTION individual taxpayer alternative to itemizing deductions. Under TAX REFORM ACT OF 1986, which indexes them to inflation starting in 1989, they were:

	1987	1988
Single Taxpayer	$2540	$3000
Head of Household	$2540	$4400
Married Filing Jointly	$3760	$5000
Married Filing Separately	$1880	$2500

STANDARD DEVIATION statistical measure of the degree to which an individual value in a probability distribution tends to vary from the mean of the distribution. It is widely applied in modern PORTFOLIO THEORY, for example, where the past performance of securities is used to determine the range of possible future performances and a probability is attached to each performance. The standard deviation of performance can then be calculated for each security and for the portfolio as a whole. The greater the degree of dispersion, the greater the risk. *See also* PORTFOLIO THEORY; REGRESSION ANALYSIS.

STANDARD INDUSTRIAL CLASSIFICATION (SIC) SYSTEM federally designed standard numbering system identifying companies by industry and providing other information. It is widely used by market researchers, securities analysts, and others. Computerized data bases frequently make use of the system.

STANDBY COMMITMENT

Securities: agreement between a corporation and an investment banking firm or group (the *standby underwriter*) whereby the latter contracts to purchase for resale, for a fee, any portion of a stock issue offered to current shareholders in a RIGHTS OFFERING that is not subscribed to during the two- to four-week standby period. A right, often issued to comply with laws guaranteeing the shareholder's PREEMPTIVE RIGHT, entitles its holder, either an existing shareholder or a person who has bought the right from a shareholder, to purchase a specified amount of shares before a PUBLIC OFFERING and usually at a price lower than the PUBLIC OFFERING PRICE.

The risk to the investment banker in a standby commitment is that the market price of shares will fall during the standby period. *See also* LAY OFF for a discussion of how standby underwriters protect themselves. *See also* FLOTATION COST; SUBSCRIPTION RIGHT; UNDERWRITE.

Lending: a bank commitment to loan money up to a specified amount for a specific period, to be used only in a certain contingency. The most common example would be a commitment to repay a construction lender in the event a permanent mortgage lender cannot be found. A COMMITMENT FEE is normally charged.

STANDBY UNDERWRITER *see* STANDBY COMMITMENT.

STANDSTILL AGREEMENT accord by a RAIDER to abstain from buying shares of a company for a specified period. *See also* GREENMAIL.

START-UP new business venture. In VENTURE CAPITAL parlance, start-up is the earliest stage at which a venture capital investor or investment pool will provide funds to an enterprise, usually on the basis of a business plan detailing the background of the management group along with market and financial PROJECTIONS. Investments or loans made at this stage are also called SEED MONEY.

STATE BANK bank organized under a charter granted by a regulatory authority in one of the 50 U.S. states, as distinguished from a NATIONAL BANK, which is federally chartered. The powers of a state-chartered commercial bank are generally consistent with those of national banks, since state laws tend to conform to federal initiatives and vice versa. State banks' deposits are insured by the FEDERAL DEPOSIT INSURANCE CORPORATION. State banks have the option of joining the FEDERAL RESERVE SYSTEM, and even if they reject membership, they may purchase support services from the Fed, including check-processing and coin and currency services.

STATED VALUE assigned value given to a corporation's stock for accounting purposes in lieu of par value. For example, the stated value may be set at $1 a share, so that if a company issued 10 million shares, the stated value of its stock would be $10 million. The stated value of the stock has no relation to its market price. It is, however, the amount per share that is credited to the CAPITAL STOCK account for each share outstanding and is therefore the legal capital of the corporation. Since state law generally prohibits a corporation from paying dividends or repurchasing shares when doing so would impair its legal capital, stated value does offer stockholders a measure of protection against loss of value.

STATEMENT
1. summary for customers of the transactions that occurred over the preceding month. A bank statement lists all deposits and withdrawals, as well as the running account balances. A brokerage statement shows all stock, bond, commodity futures, or options trades, interest and dividends received, margin debt outstanding, and other transactions, as well as a summary of the worth of the accounts at month end. A trade supplier provides a summary of open account transactions. See also ASSET MANAGEMENT ACCOUNT.
2. statement drawn up by businesses to show the status of their ASSETS and LIABILITIES and the results of their operations as of a certain date. See also FINANCIAL STATEMENT.

STATEMENT OF CONDITION
Banking: sworn accounting of a bank's resources, liabilities, and capital accounts as of a certain date, submitted in response to periodic "calls" by bank regulatory authorities.
Finance: summary of the status of assets, liabilities, and equity of a person or a business organization as of a certain date. See also BALANCE SHEET.

STATEMENT OF INCOME see PROFIT AND LOSS STATEMENT.

STATEMENT OF OPERATIONS see PROFIT AND LOSS STATEMENT.

STATUTORY INVESTMENT investment specifically authorized by state law for use by a trustee administering a trust under that state's jurisdiction.

STATUTORY MERGER legal combination of two or more corporations in which only one survives as a LEGAL ENTITY. It differs from *statutory consolidation*, in which all the companies in a combination cease to exist as legal entities and a new corporate entity is created. See also MERGER.

STATUTORY PROSPECTUS see PROSPECTUS.

STATUTORY VOTING one-share, one-vote rule that governs voting procedures in most corporations. Shareholders may cast one vote per share either for or against each nominee for the board of directors, but may not give more than one vote to one nominee. The result of statutory voting is that, in effect, those who control over 50% of the shares control the company by ensuring that the majority of the board will represent their interests. *Compare with* CUMULATIVE VOTING. *See also* PROPORTIONAL REPRESENTATION.

STAYING POWER ability of an investor to stay with (not sell) an investment that has fallen in value. For example, a commodity trader with staying power is able to meet margin calls as the commodities FUTURES CONTRACTS he has bought fall in price. He can afford to wait until the trade ultimately becomes profitable. In real estate, an investor with staying power is able to meet mortgage and maintenance payments on his or her properties and is therefore not harmed as interest rates rise or fall, or as the properties become temporarily difficult to sell.

STICKY DEAL new securities issue that the underwriter fears will be difficult to sell. Adverse market conditions, bad news about the issuing entity, or other factors may lead underwriters to say, "This will be a sticky deal at the price we have set." As a result, the price may be lowered or the offering withdrawn from the market.

STOCK

1. ownership of a CORPORATION represented by shares that are a claim on the corporation's earnings and assets. COMMON STOCK usually entitles the shareholder to vote in the election of directors and other matters taken up at shareholder meetings or by proxy. PREFERRED STOCK generally does not confer voting rights but it has a prior claim on assets and earnings—dividends must be paid on preferred stock before any can be paid on common stock. A corporation can authorize additional classes of stock, each with its own set of contractual rights. *See also* ARTICLES OF INCORPORATION; AUTHORIZED SHARES; BLUE CHIP; BOOK VALUE; CAPITAL STOCK; CERTIFICATE; CLASS; CLASSIFIED STOCK; CLOSELY HELD; COMMON STOCK; COMMON STOCK EQUIVALENT; CONVERTIBLES; CONTROL STOCK; CORPORATION; CUMULATIVE PREFERRED; DIVIDEND; EARNINGS PER SHARE; EQUITY; FLOAT; FRACTIONAL SHARES; GOING PUBLIC; GROWTH STOCK; INACTIVE STOCK; INITIAL PUBLIC OFFERING; ISSUED AND OUTSTANDING; JOINT STOCK COMPANY; LETTER SECURITY; LISTED SECURITY; MARKET VALUE; NONVOTING STOCK; NO-PAR VALUE STOCK; OVER THE COUNTER; PAR VALUE; PARTICIPATING PREFERRED; PENNY STOCK; PREEMPTIVE RIGHT; PREFERENCE SHARES; PREFERRED STOCK; PRIOR PREFERRED STOCK; QUARTER STOCK; REGISTERED SECURITY; REGISTRAR; REVERSE SPLIT; SCRIP; SECURITY; SHARE; SHAREHOLDER; SPLIT; STATED VALUE; STOCK CERTIFICATE; STOCK DIVIDEND; STOCK EXCHANGE; STOCKHOLDER; STOCKHOLDER OF RECORD; STOCK MARKET; STOCK POWER; STOCK PURCHASE PLAN; STOCK SYMBOL; STOCK WATCHER; TRANSFER AGENT; TREASURY STOCK; VOTING STOCK; VOTING TRUST CERTIFICATE; WATERED STOCK.
2. inventories of accumulated goods in manufacturing and retailing businesses.
3. *see* ROLLING STOCK.

STOCK AHEAD situation in which two or more orders for a stock at a certain price arrive about the same time, and the exchange's PRIORITY rules take effect. New York Stock Exchange rules stipulate that the bid made first should be executed first or, if two bids came in at once, the bid for the larger number of shares receives priority. The bid that was not executed is then reported back to the broker, who informs the customer that the trade was not completed because there was stock ahead. *See also* MATCHED AND LOST.

STOCK BUYBACK corporation's purchase of its own outstanding stock. A buyback may be financed by borrowings, sale of assets, or operating CASH FLOW. Its purpose is commonly to increase EARNINGS PER SHARE and thus the market price, often to discourage a TAKEOVER. When a buyback involves a PREMIUM paid to an acquirer in exchange for a promise to desist from takeover activity, the payment is called GREENMAIL. A buyback having a formula and schedule may also be called a SHARE REPURCHASE PLAN or SELF-TENDER. *See also* TREASURY STOCK.

STOCK CERTIFICATE documentation of a shareholder's ownership in a corporation. Stock certificates are engraved intricately on heavy paper to deter forgery. They indicate the number of shares owned by an individual, their PAR VALUE (if any), the CLASS of stock (for example, common or preferred), and attendant voting rights. To prevent theft, shareholders often store certificates in safe deposit boxes or take advantage of a broker's SAFEKEEPING service. Stock certificates become negotiable when endorsed.

STOCK DIVIDEND payment of a corporate dividend in the form of stock rather than cash. The stock dividend may be additional shares in the company, or it may be shares in a SUBSIDIARY being spun off to shareholders. The dividend is usually expressed as a percentage of the shares held by a shareholder. For instance, a shareholder with 100 shares would receive 5 shares as the result of a 5% stock dividend. From the corporate point of view, stock dividends conserve cash needed to operate the business. From the stockholder point of view, the advantage is that additional stock is not taxed until sold, unlike a cash dividend, which is declarable as income in the year it is received.

STOCK EXCHANGE organized marketplace in which stocks, COMMON STOCK EQUIVALENTS, and bonds are traded by members of the exchange, acting both as agents (brokers) and as principals (dealers or traders). Such exchanges have a physical location where brokers and dealers meet to execute orders from institutional and individual investors to buy and sell securities. Each exchange sets its own requirements for membership; the New York Stock Exchange has the most stringent requirements. *See also* AMERICAN STOCK EXCHANGE; LISTING REQUIREMENTS; NEW YORK STOCK EXCHANGE; REGIONAL STOCK EXCHANGES; SECURITIES AND COMMODITIES EXCHANGES.

STOCKHOLDER individual or organization with an ownership position in a corporation; also called a SHAREHOLDER or *shareowner*. Stockholders must own at least one share, and their ownership is confirmed by either a stock certificate or a record by their broker, if shares are in the broker's custody.

STOCKHOLDER OF RECORD common or preferred stockholder whose name is registered on the books of a corporation as owning shares as of a particular date. Dividends and other distributions are made only to shareholders of record. Common stockholders are usually the only ones entitled to vote for candidates for the board of directors or on other matters requiring shareholder approval.

STOCK INDEXES AND AVERAGES indicators used to measure and report value changes in representative stock groupings. Strictly speaking, an AVERAGE is simply the ARITHMETIC MEAN of a group of prices whereas an INDEX is an average expressed in relation to an earlier established BASE MARKET VALUE. (In practice, the distinction between indexes and averages is not always clear; the AMEX Major Market Index is an average, for example.) Indexes and averages may be broad based—that is, comprised of many stocks and designed to be representative of the overall market—or narrow based—meaning made up of a smaller number of stocks and designed to reflect a particular industry or market SECTOR. Selected indexes and averages are also used as the underlying value of STOCK INDEX FUTURES, INDEX OPTIONS, or options on index futures, which enable investors to make a "market bet" or to HEDGE a POSITION against general market movement at relatively little cost. An extensive number and variety of indexes and averages exist. Among the best known and most widely used are:
AMEX Major Market Index price-weighted (high-priced issues have more influence than low-priced issues) average of 20 BLUE CHIP industrial stocks. It is designed to replicate the Dow Jones Industrial Average (DJIA) in measuring representative performance in the stocks of major industrial corporations. It is produced by the American Stock Exchange (AMEX) but is composed of stocks listed on the New York Stock Exchange (NYSE), 15 of which are also components

of the DJIA. Futures on the Major Market Index are traded on the Chicago Board of Trade.

AMEX Market Value Index (AMVI) formerly known as the ASE Index and prepared on a different basis, AMVI is a capitalization or MARKET VALUE-WEIGHTED INDEX (i.e., the impact of a component's price change is proportionate to the overall market value of the issue) introduced at a base level of 100.00 in September 1973 and adjusted to half that level in July 1983. It measures the collective performance of more than 800 issues, representing all major industry groups, traded on the AMEX, including AMERICAN DEPOSITARY RECEIPTS and warrants as well as common stocks. Uniquely, cash dividends paid by component stocks are assumed to be reinvested and are thus reflected in the index. Options on the AMVI are listed on the American Stock Exchange.

Dow Jones Industrial Average (DJIA) price-weighted average of 30 actively traded blue chip stocks, primarily industrials but including American Express Company and American Telephone and Telegraph Company. Prepared and published by Dow Jones & Company, it is the oldest and most widely quoted of all the market indicators. The components, which change from time to time, represent between 15% and 20% of the market value of NYSE stocks. The DJIA is calculated by adding the closing prices of the component stocks and using a divisor that is adjusted for SPLITS and STOCK DIVIDENDS equal to 10% or more of the market value of an issue as well as for substitutions and mergers. The average is quoted in points, not in dollars. Dow Jones & Company has refused to allow the DJIA to be used as a basis for speculation with futures or options. Subindexes similarly prepared are the *Dow Jones Transportation Average (DJTA)*—20 railroad, airline and trucking stocks (*see also* DOW THEORY); and the *Dow Jones Utility Average (DJUA)*—15 geographically representative gas and electric utility companies.

The Dow Jones Composite, also called the *65 Stock Average*, combines the DJIA, DJTA, and DJUA. Dow Jones also puts out two prominent bond averages—the *Dow Jones 40 Bond Average*, representative of six different bond groups, and the *Dow Jones Municipal Bond Yield Average*, a weekly average of leading state and major city tax-exempt yields.

New York Stock Exchange Composite Index market value-weighted index which relates all NYSE stocks to an aggregate market value as of December 31, 1965, adjusted for capitalization changes. The base value of the index is $50 and point changes are expressed in dollars and cents. Futures and futures options are traded on the New York Futures Exchange (NYFE), a division of the NYSE. Index options are traded on the NYSE itself. The *New York Stock Exchange Telephone Index*, similarly prepared, is comprised of the eight common stocks of companies that made up predivestiture AT&T. Index options in the Telephone Index are listed on the NYSE, but no futures are traded. NYSE subindexes include the *NYSE Industrial, NYSE Transportation, NYSE Utility,* and *NYSE Financial* Indexes.

Standard & Poor's Composite Index of 500 Stocks market value-weighted index showing the change in the aggregate market value of 500 stocks relative to the base period 1941-43. It is composed mostly of NYSE-listed companies with some AMEX and over-the-counter stocks, in the following proportions: 400 industrials, 60 transportation and utility companies, and 40 financial issues. The index represents about 80% of the market value of all issues traded on the NYSE. Index options are traded on the Chicago Board Options Exchange and futures and futures options are traded on the Chicago Mercantile Exchange. *The Standard & Poor's 100 Stock Index*, calculated on the same basis as the 500 stock index, is made up of stocks for which options are listed on the Chicago Board Options Exchange.

Its components are mainly NYSE industrials, but some transportation, utility and financial stocks are also included. Options on the 100 Index are listed on the Chicago Board Options Exchange and futures are traded on the Chicago Mercantile Exchange. Futures options are not traded.

NASDAQ-OTC Price Index this index is based on the National Association of Securities Dealers Automated Quotations (NASDAQ) and represents all domestic OVER-THE-COUNTER stocks except those traded on exchanges and those having only one MARKET MAKER, a total of some 3500 stocks. It is market value-weighted and was introduced with a base value of 100.00 on February 5, 1971. Options and futures are not traded on this index.

Value Line Composite Index equally-weighted geometric average of approximately 1700 NYSE, AMEX, and over the counter stocks tracked by the VALUE LINE INVESTMENT SURVEY. The index uses a base value of 100.00 established June 30, 1961, and changes are expressed in index numbers rather than dollars and cents. This index is designed to reflect price changes of typical industrial stocks and being neither price nor market value-weighted, it largely succeeds. Options are traded on the Philadelphia Exchange, and futures are available on the Kansas City Board of Trade.

Wilshire 5000 Equity Index broadest of all the averages and indexes, the Wilshire Index is market value-weighted and represents the value, in billions of dollars, of all NYSE, AMEX, and over the counter issues for which quotes are available, some 5000 stocks in all. Changes are measured against a base value established December 31, 1980. Options and futures are not traded on the Wilshire Index, which is prepared by the Wilshire Associates of Santa Monica, California.

Barron's Group Stock Averages simple, arithmetic averages of stocks in more than 30 different industrial groupings, adjusted for splits and large stock dividends since 1937. Options and futures are not traded.

See also BARRON'S CONFIDENCE INDEX; BOND BUYER'S INDEX; LIPPER MUTUAL FUND INDUSTRY AVERAGE; SECURITIES AND COMMODITIES EXCHANGES.

STOCK INDEX FUTURE security that combines features of traditional commodity futures trading with securities trading using composite stock indexes. Investors can speculate on general market performance or can buy an index future contract to hedge a LONG POSITION or SHORT POSITION against a decline in value. Settlement is in cash, since it is obviously impossible to deliver an index of stocks to a futures buyer. Among the most popular stock index futures traded are the New York Stock Exchange Composite Index on the New York Futures Exchange (NYFE), the Standard & Poor's 500 Index on the Chicago Mercantile Exchange (CME), and the Value Line Composite Index on the Kansas City Board of Trade (KCBT).

It is also possible to buy options on stock index futures; the Standard & Poor's 500 Stock Index futures options are traded on the Chicago Mercantile Exchange and the New York Stock Exchange Composite Index futures options are traded on the New York Futures Exchange, for example. Unlike stock index futures or INDEX OPTIONS, however, futures options are not settled in cash; they are settled by delivery of the underlying stock index futures contracts.

See also FUTURES CONTRACT; HEDGE/HEDGING; SECURITIES AND COMMODITIES EXCHANGES.

STOCK LIST function of the organized stock exchanges that is concerned with LISTING REQUIREMENTS and related investigations, the eligibility of unlisted companies for trading privileges, and the delisting of companies that have not complied with exchange regulations and listing requirements. The New York Stock Exchange department dealing with listing of securities is called the Department of Stock List.

STOCK MARKET general term referring to the organized trading of securities through the various exchanges and the OVER THE COUNTER market. The securities involved include COMMON STOCK, PREFERRED STOCK, BONDS, CONVERTIBLES, OPTIONS, rights, and warrants. The term may also encompass commodities when used in its most general sense, but more often than not the stock market and the commodities (or futures) market are distinguished. The query "How did the market do today?" is usually answered by a reference to the Dow Jones Industrial Average, comprised of stocks listed on the New York Stock Exchange. *See also* SECURITIES AND COMMODITIES EXCHANGES.

STOCK OPTION
1. right to purchase or sell a stock at a specified price within a stated period. OPTIONS are a popular investment medium, offering an opportunity to hedge positions in other securities, to speculate in stocks with relatively little investment, and to capitalize on changes in the MARKET VALUE of options contracts themselves through a variety of options strategies.
   See also CALL OPTION; PUT OPTION.
2. widely used form of employee incentive and compensation, usually for the executives of a corporation. The employee is given an OPTION to purchase its shares at a certain price (at or below the market price at the time the option is granted) for a specified period of years.
   See also INCENTIVE STOCK OPTION; QUALIFYING STOCK OPTION.

STOCK POWER power of attorney form transferring ownership of a REGISTERED SECURITY from the owner to another party. A separate piece of paper from the CERTIFICATE, it is attached to the latter when the security is sold or pledged to a brokerage firm, bank, or other lender as loan COLLATERAL. Technically, the stock power gives the owner's permission to another party (the TRANSFER AGENT) to transfer ownership of the certificate to a third party. Also called *stock/bond power*.

STOCK PURCHASE PLAN organized program for employees of a company to buy shares of its stock. The plan could take the form of compensation if the employer matches employee stock purchases. Also, a corporation can offer to reinvest dividends in additional shares as a service to shareholders, or it can set up a program of regular additional share purchases for participating shareholders who authorize periodic, automatic payments from their wages for this purpose.

    Another form of stock purchase plan is the EMPLOYEE STOCK OWNERSHIP PLAN (ESOP), whereby employees regularly accumulate shares and may ultimately assume control of the company.

STOCK RECORD control, usually in the form of a ledger card or computer report, used by brokerage firms to keep track of securities held in inventory and their precise location within the firm. Securities are recorded by name and owner.

STOCK SPLIT *see* SPLIT.

STOCK SYMBOL letters used to identify listed companies on the securities exchanges on which they trade. These symbols, also called *trading symbols,* identify trades on the CONSOLIDATED TAPE and are used in other reports and documents whenever such shorthand is convenient. Some examples: ABT (Abbott Laboratories), AA (Aluminum Company of America), XON (Exxon), KO (Coca Cola). Stock symbols are not necessarily the same as abbreviations used to identify the same companies in the stock tables of newspapers. *See also* COMMITTEE ON UNIFORM SECURITIES IDENTIFICATION PROCEDURES (CUSIP).

STOCK-TRANSFER AGENT *see* TRANSFER AGENT.

STOCK WATCHER (NYSE) computerized service that monitors all trading activity and movement in stocks listed on the New York Stock Exchange. The system is set up to identify any unusual activity due to rumors or MANIPULATION or other illegal practices. The stock watch department of the NYSE is prepared to conduct investigations and to take appropriate action, such as issuing clarifying information or turning questions of legality over to the Securities and Exchange Commission. *See also* SURVEILLANCE DEPARTMENT OF EXCHANGES.

STOP-LIMIT ORDER order to a securities broker with instructions to buy or sell at a specified price or better (called the *stop-limit price*) but only after a given *stop price* has been reached or passed. It is a combination of a STOP ORDER and a LIMIT ORDER. For example, the instruction to the broker might be "buy 100 XYZ 55 STOP 56 LIMIT" meaning that if the MARKET PRICE reaches $55, the broker enters a limit order to be executed at $56 or a better (lower) price. A stop-limit order avoids some of the risks of a stop order, which becomes a MARKET ORDER when the stop price is reached; like all price-limit orders, however, it carries the risk of missing the market altogether, since the specified limit price or better may never occur. The American Stock Exchange prohibits stop-limit orders unless the stop and limit prices are equal.

STOP LOSS

Insurance: promise by a reinsurance company that it will cover losses incurred by the company it reinsures over and above an agreed-upon amount.

Stocks: customer order to a broker that sets the sell price of a stock below the current MARKET PRICE. A stop-loss order therefore will protect profits that have already been made or prevent further losses if the stock drops.

STOP ORDER order to a securities broker to buy or sell at the MARKET PRICE once the security has traded at a specified price called the *stop price*. A stop order may be a DAY ORDER, a GOOD-TILL-CANCELED ORDER, or any other form of time-limit order. A stop order to buy, always at a stop price above the current market price, is usually designed to protect a profit or to limit a loss on a short sale (*see* SELLING SHORT). A stop order to sell, always at a price below the current market price, is usually designed to protect a profit or to limit a loss on a security already purchased at a higher price. The risk of stop orders is that they may be triggered by temporary market movements or that they may be executed at prices several points higher or lower than the stop price because of market orders placed ahead of them. Also called *stop-loss order*. *See also* GATHER IN THE STOPS; STOP LIMIT ORDER; STOP LOSS (stocks).

STOP-OUT PRICE lowest dollar price at which Treasury bills are sold at a particular auction. This price and the beginning auction price are averaged to establish the price at which smaller purchasers may purchase bills under the NONCOMPETITIVE BID system. *See also* BILL; DUTCH AUCTION.

STOP PAYMENT revocation of payment on a check after the check has been sent or delivered to the payee. So long as the check has not been cashed, the writer has up to six months in which to request a stop payment. The stop payment right does not carry over to electronic funds transfers.

STOPPED OUT term used when a customer's order is executed under a STOP ORDER at the price predetermined by the customer, called the *stop price*. For instance, if a customer has entered a stop-loss order to sell XYZ at $30 when the stock is selling at $33, and the stock then falls to $30, his or her position will Be stopped out. A customer may also be stopped out if the order is executed at a guaranteed price offered by a SPECIALIST. *See also* GATHER IN THE STOPS; STOPPED STOCK.

STOPPED STOCK guarantee by a SPECIALIST that an order placed by a FLOOR BROKER will be executed at the best bid or offer price then in the SPECIALIST'S BOOK unless it can be executed at a better price within a specified period of time.

STOP PRICE *see* STOP ORDER.

STORY STOCK/BOND security with values or features so complex that a "story" is required to persuade investors of its merits. Story stocks are frequently from companies with some unique product or service that is difficult for competitors to copy.

STRADDLE strategy consisting of an equal number of PUT OPTIONS and CALL OPTIONS on the same underlying stock, stock index, or commodity future at the same STRIKE PRICE and maturity date. Each OPTION may be exercised separately, although the combination of options is usually bought and sold as a unit.

STRAIGHT-LINE DEPRECIATION method of depreciating a fixed asset whereby the asset's useful life is divided into the total cost less the estimated salvage value. The procedure is used to arrive at a uniform annual DEPRECIATION expense to be charged against income before figuring income taxes. Thus, if a new machine purchased for $1200 was estimated to have a useful life of ten years and a salvage value of $200, annual depreciation under the straight-line method would be $100, charged at $100 a year. This is the oldest and simplest method of depreciation and is used by many companies for financial reporting purposes, although faster depreciation of some assets with greater tax benefits in the early years is allowed under the ACCELERATED COST RECOVERY SYSTEM (ACRS).

STRAP OPTION contract combining one PUT OPTION and two CALL OPTIONS of the same SERIES, which can be bought at a lower total premium than that of the three options bought individually. The put has the same features as the calls—same underlying security, exercise price, and maturity. Also called *triple option*. *Compare with* STRIP.

STRATEGIC BUYOUT *acquisition* based on analysis of the operational benefits of consolidation. Implicitly contrasts with the type of TAKEOVER based on "paper values" that characterized the "merger mania" of the 1980s—undervalued stock bought using JUNK BONDS ultimately repayable from the liquidation of acquired assets and activities. A strategic buyout focuses on how companies fit together and anticipates enhanced long-term earning power. *See also* SYNERGY.

STREET short for Wall Street, referring to the financial community in New York City and elsewhere. It is common to hear "The Street likes XYZ." This means there is a national consensus among securities analysts following XYZ that its prospects are favorable. *See also* STREET NAME.

STREET NAME phrase describing securities held in the name of a broker or another nominee instead of a customer. Since the securities are in the broker's custody, transfer of the shares at the time of sale is easier than if the stock were registered in the customer's name and physical certificates had to be transferred.

STRIKE PRICE *see* EXERCISE PRICE.

STRIP

Bonds: brokerage-house practice of separating a bond into its CORPUS and COUPONS, which are then sold separately as ZERO-COUPON SECURITIES. The 1986 Tax Act permitted MUNICIPAL BOND strips. Some, such as Salomon Brothers' tax-exempt M-CATS, represent PREREFUNDINGS backed by U.S. Treasury securities held in escrow. Other strips include Treasuries stripped by brokers, such as TIGERS, and stripped mortgage-backed securities of government-sponsored issuers like Fannie Mae. A variation known by the acronym STRIPS (Separate Trading of Registered Interest and Principal of Securities) is a prestripped zero-coupon bond that is a direct obligation of the U. S. Treasury.

Options: OPTION contract consisting of two PUT OPTIONS and one CALL OPTION on the same underlying stock or stock index with the same strike and expiration date. *Compare with* STRAP.

Stocks: to buy stocks with the intention of collecting their dividends. Also called *dividend stripping. See also* DIVIDEND ROLLOVER PLAN.

STUB STOCK common stocks or instruments convertible to equity in a company that is overleveraged as the result of a BUYOUT or RECAPITALIZATION and may have DEFICIT NET WORTH. Stub stock is highly speculative and highly volatile but, unlike JUNK BONDS, has unlimited potential for gain if the company succeeds in restoring financial balance.

STUDENT LOAN MARKETING ASSOCIATION (SLMA) publicly traded stock corporation that guarantees student loans traded on the SECONDARY MARKET. It was established by federal decree in 1972 to increase the availability of education loans to college and university students made under the federally sponsored Guaranteed Student Loan Program and the Health, Education Assistance Loan Program. Known as *Sallie Mae*, it purchases student loans from originating financial institutions and provides financing to state student loan agencies. It also sells short- and medium-term notes, some FLOATING RATE NOTES.

SUBCHAPTER M Internal Revenue Service regulation dealing with what is commonly called the *conduit theory,* in which qualifying investment companies and real estate investment trusts avoid double taxation by passing interest and dividend income and capital gains directly through, without taxation, to shareholders, who are taxed as individuals. *See also* REAL ESTATE INVESTMENT TRUST; REGULATED INVESTMENT COMPANY.

SUBCHAPTER S section of the Internal Revenue Code giving a corporation that has 35 or fewer shareholders and meets certain other requirements the option of being taxed as if it were a PARTNERSHIP. Thus a small corporation can distribute its income directly to shareholders and avoid the corporate income tax while enjoying the other advantages of the corporate form. These companies are known as *S corporations, tax-option corporations,* or *small business corporations.*

SUBJECT Wall Street term referring to a bid and/or offer that is negotiable—that is, a QUOTATION that is not firm. For example, a broker looking to place a sizable order might call several dealers with the question, "Can you give me a *subject quote* on 20,000 shares of XYZ?"

SUBJECT QUOTE *see* SUBJECT.

SUBORDINATED junior in claim on assets to other debt, that is, repayable only after other debts with a higher claim have been satisfied. Some subordinated debt may have less claim on assets than other subordinated debt; a *junior subordinated debenture* ranks below a subordinated DEBENTURE, for example.

It is also possible for unsubordinated (senior) debt to become subordinated at the request of a lender by means of a subordination agreement. For example, if an officer of a small company has made loans to the company instead of making a permanent investment in it, a bank might request the officer's loan be subordinated to its own loan as long as the latter is outstanding. This is accomplished by the company officer's signing a subordination agreement. *See also* EFFECTIVE NET WORTH; JUNIOR SECURITY.

SUBSCRIPTION agreement of intent to buy newly issued securities. *See also* NEW ISSUE; SUBSCRIPTION RIGHT; SUBSCRIPTION WARRANT.

SUBSCRIPTION PRICE price at which existing shareholders of a corporation are entitled to purchase common shares in a RIGHTS OFFERING or at which subscription warrants are exercisable. *See also* SUBSCRIPTION RIGHT; SUBSCRIPTION WARRANT.

SUBSCRIPTION PRIVILEGE right of existing shareholders of a corporation, or their transferees, to buy shares of a new issue of common stock before it is offered to the public. *See also* PREEMPTIVE RIGHT; SUBSCRIPTION RIGHT.

SUBSCRIPTION RATIO *see* SUBSCRIPTION RIGHT.

SUBSCRIPTION RIGHT privilege granted to existing shareholders of a corporation to subscribe to shares of a new issue of common stock before it is offered to the public; better known simply as a *right*. Such a right, which normally has a life of two to four weeks, is freely transferable and entitles the holder to buy the new common stock below the PUBLIC OFFERING PRICE. While in most cases one existing share entitles the stockholder to one right, the number of rights needed to buy a share of a new issue (called the *subscription ratio*) varies and is determined by a company in advance of an offering. To subscribe, the holder sends or delivers to the company or its agent the required number of rights plus the dollar price of the new shares.

Rights are sometimes granted to comply with state laws that guarantee the shareholders' PREEMPTIVE RIGHT—their right to maintain a proportionate share of ownership. It is common practice, however, for corporations to grant rights even when not required by law; protecting shareholders from the effects of DILUTION is seen simply as good business.

The actual certificate representing the subscription is technically called a SUBSCRIPTION WARRANT, giving rise to some confusion. The term *subscription warrant*, or simply *warrant*, is commonly understood in a related but different sense—as a separate entity with a longer life than a right—maybe 5, 10, or 20 years or even perpetual—and with a SUBSCRIPTION PRICE higher at the time of issue than the MARKET VALUE of the common stock.

Subscription rights are offered to shareholders in what is called a RIGHTS OFFERING, usually handled by underwriters under a STANDBY COMMITMENT.

SUBSCRIPTION WARRANT type of security, usually issued together with a BOND or PREFERRED STOCK, that entitles the holder to buy a proportionate amount of common stock at a specified price, usually higher than the market price at the time of issuance, for a period of years or to perpetuity; better known simply as a *warrant*. In contrast, rights, which also represent the right to buy common shares, normally have a subscription price lower than the current market value of the common stock and a life of two to four weeks. A warrant is usually issued as a SWEETENER, to enhance the marketability of the accompanying fixed income securities. Warrants are freely transferable and are traded on the major exchanges. They are also called *stock-purchase warrants*. *See also* PERPETUAL WARRANT; SUBSCRIPTION RIGHT.

SUBSIDIARY company of which more than 50% of the voting shares are owned by another corporation, called the PARENT COMPANY. *See also* AFFILIATE.

SUBSTITUTION

Banking: replacement of COLLATERAL by other collateral.

Contracts: replacement of one party to a contract by another. *See also* NOVATION.

Economics: concept that, if one product or service can be replaced by another, their prices should be similar.

Law: replacement of one attorney by another in the exercise of stock powers relating to the purchase and sale of securities. *See also* STOCK POWER.

Securities:
1. exchange or SWAP of one security for another in a client's PORTFOLIO. Securities analysts often advise substituting a stock they currently favor for a stock in the same industry that they believe has less favorable prospects.
2. substitution of another security of equal value for a security acting as COLLATERAL for a MARGIN ACCOUNT. *See also* SAME-DAY-SUBSTITUTION.

SUICIDE PILL POISON PILL with potentially catastrophic implications for the company it is designed to protect. An example might be a poison pill providing for an exchange of stock for debt in the event of a HOSTILE TAKEOVER; that would discourage an acquirer by making the TAKEOVER prohibitively expensive, but its implementation could put the TARGET COMPANY in danger of bankruptcy.

SUITABILITY RULES guidelines that those selling sophisticated and potentially risky financial products, such as limited partnerships or commodities futures contracts, must follow to ensure that investors have the financial means to assume the risks involved. Such rules are enforced through self-regulation administered by such organizations as the NATIONAL ASSOCIATION OF SECURITIES DEALERS, the SECURITIES AND COMMODITIES EXCHANGES, and other groups operating in the securities industry. Individual brokerage firms selling the products have their own guidelines and policies. They typically require the investor to have a certain level of NET WORTH and LIQUID ASSETS, so that he or she will not be irreparably harmed if the investment sours. A brokerage firm may be sued if it has allowed an unsuitable investor to buy an investment that goes sour. *See also* KNOW YOUR CUSTOMER.

SUM-OF-THE-YEARS'-DIGITS METHOD (SOYD) method of ACCELERATED DEPRECIATION that results in higher DEPRECIATION charges and greater tax savings in the earlier years of a FIXED ASSET'S useful life than the STRAIGHT-LINE DEPRE-

CIATION method, where charges are uniform throughout. Sometimes called just *sum-of-digits method*, it allows depreciation based on an inverted scale of the total of digits for the years of useful life. Thus, for four years of life, the digits 4, 3, 2, and 1 are added to produce 10. The first year's rate becomes 4/10ths of the depreciable cost of the asset (cost less salvage value), the second year's rate 3/10ths, and so on. The effects of this method of accelerated depreciation are compared with the straight-line method in the following illustration, which assumes an asset with a total cost of $1000, a useful life of four years, and no salvage value:

YEAR	STRAIGHT LINE		SUM-OF-YEARS' DIGITS	
	Expense	Cumulative	Expense	Cumulative
1	$250	$250	$400	$400
2	$250	$500	$300	$700
3	$250	$750	$200	$900
4	$250	$1000	$100	$1000
	$1000		$1000	

See also ACCELERATED COST RECOVERY SYSTEM (ACRS).

SUNRISE INDUSTRIES figurative term for the emerging growth sectors that some believe will be the mainstays of the future economy, taking the place of declining *sunset industries*. Although the latter, including such mature industries as the automobile, steel, and other heavy manufacturing industries, will continue to be important, their lead role as employers of massive numbers of workers is expected to be superseded by the electronics and other computer-related high-technology, biotechnology, and genetic engineering sectors and by service industries.

SUNSET PROVISION condition in a law or regulation that specifies an expiration date unless reinstated by legislation. For example, a sunset provision in the TAX REFORM ACT OF 1986 prohibits tax-exempt single-family mortgage bonds after 1988.

SUNSHINE LAWS state or federal laws (also called *government in the sunshine laws*) that require most meetings of regulatory bodies to be held in public and most of their decisions and records to be disclosed. Many of these statutes were enacted in the 1970s because of concern about government abuses during the Watergate period. Most prominent is the federal Freedom of Information (FOI) Act, which makes it possible to obtain federal documents.

SUPERMAJORITY AMENDMENT corporate AMENDMENT requiring that a substantial majority (usually 67% to 90%) of stockholders approve important transactions, such as mergers.

SUPER DOT *see* DESIGNATED ORDER TURNAROUND (DOT).

SUPER NOW ACCOUNT deregulated transaction account authorized for depository institutions in 1982. It paid interest higher than on a conventional NOW (NEGOTIABLE ORDER OF WITHDRAWAL) account but slightly lower than that on the MONEY MARKET DEPOSIT ACCOUNT (MMDA). With the deregulation of banking deposit accounts in 1986, however, banks are free to pay whatever rates they feel cost considerations and competitive conditions warrant. Although some banks continue to offer MMDA accounts which pay a slightly higher rate to compensate for the fact that checkwriting is limited to three checks a month, most banks now offer one transaction account with unlimited checkwriting.

SUPER SINKER BOND bond with long-term COUPONS (which might equal a 20-year-bond's yield) but with short maturity. Typically, super sinkers are HOUSING BONDS, which provide home financing. If homeowners move from their homes and prepay their mortgages, bondholders receive their principal back right away. Super sinkers may therefore have an actual life of as little as three to five years, even though their yield is about the same as bonds of much longer maturities.

SUPERVISORY ANALYST member firm research analyst who has passed a special New York Stock Exchange examination and is deemed qualified to approve publicly distributed research reports.

SUPPLEMENTAL AGREEMENT agreement that amends a previous agreement and contains additional conditions.

SUPPLY-SIDE ECONOMICS theory of economics contending that drastic reductions in tax rates will stimulate productive investment by corporations and wealthy individuals to the benefit of the entire society. Championed in the late 1970s by Professor Arthur Laffer (*see* LAFFER CURVE) and others, the theory held that MARGINAL TAX RATES had become so high (primarily as a result of big government) that major new private spending on plant, equipment, and other "engines of growth" was discouraged. Therefore, reducing the size of government, and hence its claim on earned income, would fuel economic expansion.

Supporters of the supply-side theory claimed they were vindicated in the first years of the administration of President Ronald W. Reagan, when marginal tax rates were cut just prior to a sustained economic recovery. However, members of the opposing KEYNESIAN ECONOMICS school maintained that the recovery was a classic example of "demand-side" economics—growth was stimulated not by increasing the supply of goods, but by increasing consumer demand as disposable incomes rose. Also clashing with the supply-side theory were MONETARIST economists, who contended that the most effective way of regulating aggregate demand is for the Federal Reserve to control growth in the money supply. *See also* AGGREGATE SUPPLY.

SUPPORT LEVEL price level at which a security tends to stop falling because there is more demand than supply. Technical analysts identify support levels as prices at which a particular security or market has bottomed in the past. When a stock is falling towards its support level, these analysts say it is "testing its support," meaning that the stock should rebound as soon as it hits the support price. If the stock continues to drop through the support level, its outlook is considered very bearish. The opposite of a support level is a RESISTANCE LEVEL. *See* illustration.

SURCHARGE charge added to a charge, cost added to a cost, or tax added to a tax. *See also* SURTAX.

SURPLUS connotes either CAPITAL SURPLUS or EARNED SURPLUS. *See also* PAID-IN CAPITAL; RETAINED EARNINGS.

SURTAX tax applied to corporations or individuals who have earned a certain level of income. For instance, a government might impose a surtax of 10% on all those with an ADJUSTED GROSS INCOME of $50,000 or more.

SUPPORT LEVEL

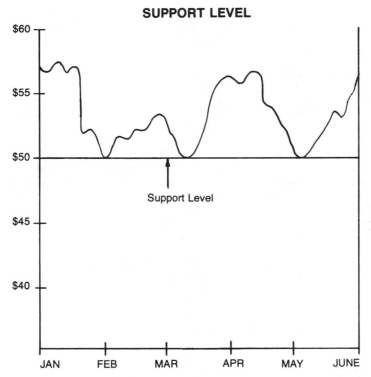

SURVEILLANCE DEPARTMENT OF EXCHANGES division of a stock exchange that is constantly watching to detect unusual trading activity in stocks, which may be a tipoff to an illegal practice. These departments cooperate with the Securities and Exchange Commission in investigating misconduct. *See also* STOCK WATCHER.

SUSPENDED TRADING temporary halt in trading in a particular security, in advance of a major news announcement or to correct an imbalance of orders to buy and sell. Using telephone alert procedures, listed companies with material developments to announce can give advance notice to the New York Stock Exchange Department of Stock List or the American Stock Exchange Securities Division. The exchanges can then determine if trading in the securities affected should be suspended temporarily to allow for orderly dissemination of the news to the public. Where advance notice is not possible, a *floor governor* may halt trading to stabilize the price of a security affected by a rumor or news development. Destabilizing developments might include a MERGER announcement, an unfavorable earnings report, or a major resource discovery. *See also* CIRCUIT BREAKER; DISCLOSURE; FORM 8-K; INVESTOR RELATIONS DEPARTMENT.

SUSPENSE ACCOUNT in accounting, an account used temporarily to carry receipts, disbursements, or discrepancies, pending their analysis and permanent classification.

SWAP exchange one security for another. A swap may be executed to change the maturities of a bond PORTFOLIO or the quality of the issues in a stock or bond portfolio, or because investment objectives have shifted. Investors with bond portfolio losses often swap for other higher-yielding bonds to be able to increase the return on their portfolio and realize tax losses. *See also* BOND SWAP; SUBSTITUTION.

SWAP ORDER *see* CONTINGENT ORDER.

SWEETENER feature added to a securities offering to make it more attractive to purchasers. A bond may have the sweetener of convertibility into common stock added, for instance. *See also* KICKER.

SWITCHING

Mutual Funds: moving assets from one mutual fund to another, either within a FAMILY OF FUNDS or between different fund families. There is no charge for switching within a no-load family of mutual funds, which offers a variety of stock, bond, and money market funds. A sales charge would have to be paid when switching from one LOAD FUND to another. Switching usually occurs at the shareholder's initiative, as a resultof changes in market conditions or investment objectives. *See also* NO-LOAD FUND.

Securities: selling stocks or bonds to replace them with other stocks and bonds with better prospects for gain. *See also* SWAP.

SWITCH ORDER *see* CONTINGENT ORDER.

SYNDICATE *see* PURCHASE GROUP; UNDERWRITING GROUP.

SYNDICATE MANAGER *see* MANAGING UNDERWRITER.

SYNERGY ideal sought in corporate mergers and acquisitions that the performance of a combined enterprise will exceed that of its previously separate parts. For example, a MERGER of two oil companies, one with a superior distribution network and the other with more reserves, would have synergy and would be expected to result in higher earnings per share than if the companies remained separate. *See also* STRATEGIC BUYOUT.

SYNTHETIC ASSET value that is artificially created by using other assets, such as securities, in combination. For example, the simultaneous purchase of a CALL OPTION and sale of a PUT OPTION on the same stock creates *synthetic stock* having the same value, in terms of CAPITAL GAIN potential, as the underlying stock itself.

SYSTEMATIC RISK that part of a security's risk that is common to all securities of the same general class (stocks and bonds) and thus cannot be eliminated by DIVERSIFICATION; also known as *market risk*. The measure of systematic risk in stocks is the BETA COEFFICIENT. *See also* PORTFOLIO BETA SCORE, PORTFOLIO THEORY.

t

TAFT-HARTLEY ACT federal law (in full, Labor Management Relations Act) enacted in 1947, which restored to management in unionized industries some of the bargaining power it had lost in prounion legislation prior to World War II. Taft-Hartley prohibited a union from

- refusing to bargain in good faith
- coercing employees to join a union
- imposing excessive or discriminatory dues and initiation fees
- forcing employers to hire union workers to perform unneeded or nonexistent tasks (a practice known as *featherbedding*)
- striking to influence a bargaining unit's choice between two contesting unions (called a *jurisdictional strike*)
- engaging in secondary boycotts against businesses selling or handling nonunion goods
- engaging in sympathy strikes in support of other unions

Taft-Hartley also

- imposed disclosure requirements to regulate union business dealings and uncover fraud and racketeering
- prohibited unions from directly making contributions to candidates running for federal offices
- authorized the President of the United States to postpone strikes in industries deemed essential to national economic health or national security by declaring an 80-day "cooling-off period"
- permitted states to enact right-to-work laws, which outlaw compulsory unionization.

TAIL

Insurance: interval between receipt of premium income and payment of claims. For example, REINSURANCE companies have a long tail as compared to CASUALTY INSURANCE companies.

Treasury auctions: spread in price between the lowest COMPETITIVE BID accepted by the U.S. Treasury for bills, bonds, and notes and the average bid by all those offering to buy such Treasury securities. *See also* TREASURIES.

Underwriting: decimal places following the round-dollar amount of a bid by a potential UNDERWRITER in a COMPETITIVE BID underwriting. For instance, in a bid of $97.3347 for a particular bond issue, the tail is .3347.

TAILGATING unethical practice of a broker who, after a customer has placed an order to buy or sell a certain security, places an order for the same security for his or her own account. The broker hopes to profit either because of information the customer is known or presumed to have or because of the customer's purchase is of sufficient size to put pressure on the security price.

TAKE

In general:
1. profit realized from a transaction.
2. gross receipts of a lottery or gambling enterprise.
3. open to bribery, as in *being on the take*.

Law: to seize possession of property. When a debtor defaults on a debt backed by COLLATERAL, that property is taken back by the creditor.

Securities: act of accepting an OFFER price in a transaction between brokers or dealers.

TAKE A BATH to suffer a large loss on a SPECULATION or investment, as in "I took a bath on my XYZ stock when the market dropped last week."

TAKE A FLIER to speculate, that is, to buy securities with the knowledge that the investment is highly risky.

TAKE A POSITION

1. to buy stock in a company with the intent of holding for the long term or, possibly, of taking control of the company. An acquirer who takes a position of 5% or more of a company's outstanding stock must file information with the Securities and Exchange Commission, the exchange the TARGET COMPANY is listed on, and the target company itself.

2. phrase used when a broker/dealer holds stocks or bonds in inventory. A position may be either long or short. *See also* LONG POSITION; SHORT POSITION.

TAKEDOWN

1. each participating INVESTMENT BANKER'S proportionate share of the securities to be distributed in a new or a secondary offering.

2. price at which the securities are allocated to members of the UNDERWRITING GROUP, particularly in municipal offerings.
See also UNDERWRITE.

TAKE-OR-PAY CONTRACT agreement between a buyer and a seller that obligates the buyer to pay a minimum amount of money for a product or a service, even if the product or service is not delivered. These contracts are most often used in the utility industry to back bonds to finance new power plants. A take-or-pay contract stipulates that the prospective purchaser of the power will take the power from the bond issuer or, if construction is not completed, will repay bondholders the amount of their investment. Take-or-pay contracts are a common way to protect bondholders. In a precedent-setting case in 1983, however, the Washington State Supreme Court voided take-or-pay contracts that many utilities had signed to support the building of the Washington Public Power Supply System (known as WHOOPS) nuclear plants. This action caused WHOOPS to default on some of its bonds, putting a cloud over the validity of the take-or-pay concept.

TAKEOUT

Real estate finance: long-term mortgage loan made to refinance a short-term construction loan (INTERIM LOAN). *See also* STANDBY COMMITMENT.

Securities: withdrawal of cash from a brokerage account, usually after a sale and purchase has resulted in a net CREDIT BALANCE.

TAKEOVER change in the controlling interest of a corporation. A takeover may be a friendly acquisition or an unfriendly bid the TARGET COMPANY might fight with SHARK REPELLENT techniques. A hostile takeover (aiming to replace existing management) is usually attempted through a public TENDER OFFER. Other approaches might be unsolicited merger proposals to directors, accumulations of shares in the open market, or PROXY FIGHTS that seek to install new directors. *See also* ANY-AND-ALL BID; BEAR HUG; BUST-UP TAKEOVER; CROWN JEWELS; FAIR-PRICE AMENDMENT; GARBATRAGE; GOLDEN PARACHUTE; GREENMAIL; IN PLAY; KILLER BEES; LEVERAGED BUYOUT; LOCK-UP OPTION; MERGER; PAC-MAN STRATEGY; POISON PILL; POISON PUT; RADAR ALERT; RAIDER; RISK ARBITRAGE; RUMORTRAGE; SAFE HARBOR; SATURDAY NIGHT SPECIAL; SCHEDULE 13D; SCORCHED EARTH POLICY; SHARK WATCHER; SLEEPING BEAUTY; STAGGERED BOARD OF DIRECTORS; STANDSTILL AGREEMENT; SUICIDE PILL; STOCK BUYBACK; STRATEGIC BUYOUT; SUPERMAJORITY AMENDMENT; TWO-TIER BID; WHITE KNIGHT; WHITE SQUIRE; WILLIAMS ACT.

TAKEOVER ARBITRAGE *see* RISK ARBITRAGE.

TAKING DELIVERY

In general: accepting receipt of goods from a common carrier or other shipper, usually documented by signing a bill of lading or other form of receipt.

Commodities: accepting physical delivery of a commodity under a FUTURES CONTRACT or SPOT MARKET contract. Delivery requirements, such as the size of the contract and the necessary quality of the commodity, are established by the exchange on which the commodity is traded.

Securities: accepting receipt of stock or bond certificates that have recently been purchased or transferred from another account.

TANGIBLE ASSET any asset not meeting the definition of an INTANGIBLE ASSET, which is a nonphysical right to something presumed to represent an advantage in the marketplace, such as a trademark or patent. Thus tangible assets are clearly those having physical existence, like cash, real estate, or machinery. Yet in accounting, assets such as ACCOUNTS RECEIVABLE are considered tangible, even though they are no more physical than a license or a lease, both of which are considered intangible. In summary: if an asset has physical form it is tangible; if it doesn't, consult a list of what accountants have decided are intangible assets.

TANGIBLE COST oil and gas drilling term meaning the cost of items that can be used over a period of time, such as casings, well fittings, land, and tankage, as distinguished from intangible costs such as drilling, testing, and geologist's expenses. In the most widely used LIMITED PARTNERSHIP sharing arrangements, tangible costs are borne by the GENERAL PARTNER (manager) while intangible costs are borne by the limited partners (investors), usually to be taken as tax deductions. In the event of a dry hole, however, all costs become intangibles. *See also* INTANGIBLE COST.

TANGIBLE NET WORTH total ASSETS less INTANGIBLE ASSETS and total LIABILITIES; also called *net tangible assets*. Intangible assets include nonmaterial benefits such as goodwill, patents, copyrights, and trademarks.

TAPE

1. service that reports prices and size of transactions on major exchanges. Also called *composite type* and *ticker tape* (because of the sound made by the machine that printed the tape before the process was computerized).
2. tape of Dow Jones and other news wires, usually called the BROAD TAPE. *See also* CONSOLIDATED TAPE.

TARGET COMPANY firm that has been chosen as attractive for TAKEOVER by a potential acquirer. The acquirer may buy up to 5% of the target's stock without public disclosure, but it must report all transactions and supply other information to the Securities and Exchange Commission, the exchange the target company is listed on, and the target company itself once 5% or more of the stock is acquired. *See also* TOEHOLD PURCHASE; SCHEDULE 13D; SLEEPING BEAUTY; TENDER OFFER; WILLIAMS ACT.

TARGET PRICE

Finance: price at which an acquirer aims to buy a company in a TAKEOVER.

Options: price of the underlying security after which a certain OPTION will become profitable to its buyer. For example, someone buying an XYZ 50 call for a PREMIUM of $200 could have a target price of 52, after which point the premium will be recouped and the CALL OPTION will result in a profit when exercised.

Stocks: price that an investor is hoping a stock he or she has just bought will rise to within a specified period of time. An investor may buy XYZ at $20, with a target price of $40 in one year's time, for instance.

TARIFF
1. federal tax on imports or exports usually imposed either to raise revenue (called a *revenue tariff*) or to protect domestic firms from import competition (called a *protective tariff*). A tariff may also be designed to correct an imbalance of payments. The money collected under tariffs is called DUTY or *customs duty*.
2. schedule of rates or charges, usually for freight.

TAXABLE INCOME amount of income (after all allowable deductions and adjustments to income) subject to tax. On an individual's federal income tax return, taxable income is ADJUSTED GROSS INCOME (the sum of wages, salaries, dividends, interest, capital gains, business income, etc., less adjustments for INDIVIDUAL RETIREMENT ACCOUNT contributions, moving expenses, unreimbursed business expenses) less itemized or standard deductions and the total of personal exemptions. Once taxable income is known, the individual taxpayer finds the total income tax obligation by checking the Internal Revenue Service tax tables or by calculating the tax according to a rate schedule. TAX CREDITS reduce the tax liability dollar-for-dollar.

NET INCOME of a self-employed person (self-proprietorship) and distributions to members of a partnership are included in adjusted gross income, and hence taxable income, on an individual tax return.

Taxable income of an incorporated business, also called *net income before taxes,* consists of total revenues less cost of goods sold, selling and administrative expenses, interest, and extraordinary items.

TAXABLE MUNICIPAL BOND taxable debt obligation of a state or local government entity, an outgrowth of the TAX REFORM ACT OF 1986 (which restricted the issuance of traditional TAX-EXEMPT SECURITIES). Taxable MUNICIPAL BONDS are issued as PRIVATE PURPOSE BONDS to finance such prohibited projects as a sports stadium; as MUNICIPAL REVENUE BONDS where caps apply; or as PUBLIC PURPOSE BONDS where the 10% private use limitation has been exceeded.

TAX AND LOAN ACCOUNT account in a private-sector depository institution, held in the name of the district Federal Reserve Bank as fiscal agent of the United States, that serves as a repository for operating cash available to the U.S. Treasury. Withheld income taxes, employers' contributions to the Social Security fund, and payments for U.S. government securities routinely go into a tax and loan account.

TAX ANTICIPATION BILL (TAB) short-term obligation issued by the U.S. Treasury in competitive bidding at maturities ranging from 23 to 273 days. TABs typically come due within 5 to 7 days after the quarterly due dates for corporate tax payments, but corporations can tender them at PAR value on those tax deadlines in payment of taxes without forfeiting interest income. Since 1975, TABs have been supplemented by cash management bills, due in 30 days or less, and issued in minimum $10 million blocks. These instruments, which are timed to coincide with the maturity of existing issues, provide the Treasury with additional cash management flexibility while giving large investors a safe place to park temporary funds.

TAX ANTICIPATION NOTE (TAN) short-term obligation of a state or municipal government to finance current expenditures pending receipt of expected tax payments. TAN debt evens out the cash flow and is retired once corporate and individual tax revenues are received.

TAX BASIS

Finance: original cost of an ASSET, less accumulated DEPRECIATION, that goes into the calculation of a gain or loss for tax purposes. Thus, a property acquired for $100,000 that has been depreciated by $40,000 has a tax basis of $60,000 assuming no other adjustments; sale of that property for $120,000 results in a taxable CAPITAL GAIN of $60,000.

Investments: price at which a stock or bond was purchased, plus brokerage commission. The law requires that a PREMIUM paid on the purchase of an investment be amortized.

TAX BRACKET point on the income-tax rate schedules where TAXABLE INCOME falls; also called *marginal tax bracket*. It is expressed as a percentage to be applied to each additional dollar earned over the base amount for that bracket. Under a PROGRESSIVE TAX system, increases in taxable income lead to higher marginal rates in the form of higher brackets. The TAX REFORM ACT OF 1986, introducing a modified flat tax system, reduced the number of tax brackets for individuals from 15 to 2, starting with the 1988 tax year. (A five-bracket structure, with rates ranging from 11% to 38.5%, was provided for the 1987 transition year.) The two brackets set by the law were 15% and 28%, but a 5% surtax effectively put high-income taxpayers in a marginal tax bracket of 33%. For example, a single taxpayer in the 15% bracket paid $15 on each taxable $100 up to $17,850, and 28%, or $28, of each taxable dollar over that level. The 5% surtax applied to single incomes between $43,150 and $89,560; different income figures were involved for heads of household and married couples filing jointly. A DEDUCTION came off the last marginal dollar earned; thus the 28% taxpayer in the above example would save $28 in taxes with each additional $100 of deductions until he worked his way back into the 15% bracket where each $100 deduction would save $15. (A deduction should not be confused with a TAX CREDIT.)

For corporations the 1986 law reduced the number of brackets from five to three. Effective July 1, 1987 (with blended rates applicable to any fiscal year that included that date), firms with taxable income of $50,000 or less were subject to a 15% rate; incomes from $50,000 to $75,000 were taxed at 25%; and incomes from $75,000 and up were taxed at 34%. An additional 5% tax was imposed on income between $100,000 and $335,000, which in effect created a flat tax rate of 34% for corporations with taxable income of $335,000 or more and a 39% effective rate on taxable income in the $100,000 to $335,000 phaseout range.

TAX CREDIT direct, dollar-for-dollar reduction in tax liability, as distinguished from a tax deduction, which reduces taxes only by the percentage of a taxpayer's TAX BRACKET. (A taxpayer in the 28% tax bracket would get a 28 cent benefit from each $1.00 deduction, for example.) In the case of a tax credit, a taxpayer owing $10,000 in tax would owe $9000 if he took advantage of a $1000 tax credit. Under certain conditions, tax credits are allowed for a pensioner above age 65, income tax paid to a foreign country, child care expenses, rehabilitation of historic properties, conducting research and development, building low-income housing, and providing jobs for economically disadvantaged people. The TAX REFORM ACT OF 1986 repealed many tax credits, such as the INVESTMENT CREDIT.

TAX DEFERRED term describing an investment whose accumulated earnings are free from taxation until the investor takes possession of them. For example, the holder of an INDIVIDUAL RETIREMENT ACCOUNT postpones paying taxes on interest, dividends, or capital appreciation if he or she waits until after age 59½ to cash in those gains. Other examples of tax-deferred investment vehicles include KEOGH PLANS; ANNUITIES; VARIABLE LIFE INSURANCE, WHOLE LIFE INSURANCE, and UNIVERSAL LIFE INSURANCE policies; STOCK PURCHASE or DIVIDEND REINVESTMENT PLANS; and Series EE and Series HH U.S. SAVINGS BONDS.

TAX EQUITY AND FISCAL RESPONSIBILITY ACT OF 1982 (TEFRA) federal legislation to raise tax revenue, mainly through closing various loopholes and instituting tougher enforcement procedures. Among its major components:

1. penalties for noncompliance with tax laws were increased, and various steps were taken to facilitate tax collection by the Internal Revenue Service (IRS).
2. ten percent of interest and dividends earned was required to be withheld from all bank and brokerage accounts and forwarded directly to the IRS. (This provision was later canceled by Congress after a major lobbying campaign to overturn it.)
3. TAX PREFERENCE ITEMS were added to the old add-on minimum tax to strengthen the ALTERNATIVE MINIMUM TAX.
4. the floor for medical expense deductions was raised from 3% to 5% of ADJUSTED GROSS INCOME.
5. casualty and theft losses were made deductible only if each loss exceeds $100 and the total excess losses exceed 10% of adjusted gross income.
6. deductions for original issue discount bonds were limited to the amount the issuer would deduct as interest if it issued bonds with a face amount equivalent to the actual proceeds and paying the market rate of interest. This amount must be reduced by the amount of deductions for actual interest.
7. more rapid rates for recovering costs under the ACCELERATED COST RECOVERY SYSTEM (ACRS), which had been scheduled to go into effect in 1985 and 1986, were repealed.
8. most of the rules providing for SAFE HARBOR leasing transactions authorized under the ECONOMIC RECOVERY TAX ACT OF 1981 were repealed. Formerly, companies were allowed to trade unusable tax benefits for cash, but Congress considered the practice abusive.
9. excise taxes were raised to 3% on telephone use, to 16 cents a pack on cigarettes, and to 8% on airline tickets.
10. the Federal Unemployment Tax Act wage base and tax rate were increased.
11. numerous tax incentives for corporate mergers and takeovers were reduced.
12. net extraction losses in foreign oil and gas operations in one country were allowed to offset net extraction income from such operations in other countries in the computation of oil and gas extraction taxes.
13. most bonds were required to be registered so that the government could ensure that bondholders are reporting interest.
14. As long as they are not prohibited by a Foreign Corrupt Practices Act, payments to foreign officials were authorized to be deducted as legitimate business expenses.
15. the basis of assets that generate tax INVESTMENT CREDITS was reduced by one-half the amount of the credit.
16. pension and profit-sharing qualified plans were curtailed with a series of new rules that restricted plan loans, required withholding on plan distributions, limited estate-tax exclusions on certain plan distributions, and restricted "top-heavy" plans, those tilted to benefit mostly the top-earning employees of a company.
17. changes were made in the way life insurance companies were taxed.

TAX-EXEMPT MONEY MARKET FUND MONEY MARKET FUND invested in short-term municipal securities that are tax-exempt, thus the fund generates and distributes income tax-free to shareholders. Such funds have a lower yield than taxable funds and should be evaluated on an AFTERTAX BASIS.

TAX-EXEMPT SECURITY obligation whose interest is exempt from taxation by federal, state, and/or local authorities. It is frequently called a MUNICIPAL BOND (or simply a *municipal*), even though it may have been issued by a state government or agency or by a county, town, or other political district or subdivision. The security is backed by the FULL FAITH AND CREDIT or by anticipated revenues of the issuing authority. Interest income from tax-exempt municipals is free from federal income taxation as well as from taxation in the jurisdiction where the securities have been issued. Thus, New York City obligations are TRIPLE TAX-EXEMPT to city residents whose income is taxed on the federal, state, and local levels. (A very few municipalities tax residents for their own otherwise tax-exempt issues.)

MUTUAL FUNDS that invest exclusively in tax-exempt securities confer the same tax advantages on their shareholders. However, while a fund's dividends would be entirely tax-exempt on a shareholder's federal tax return, they would be free from state income tax only in proportion to the amount of interest income derived from the taxpayer's home state, assuming no interstate reciprocity arrangements pertain.

The return to investors from a tax-exempt bond is less than that from a corporate bond, because the tax exemption provides extra compensation; the higher the TAX BRACKET of the investor, the more attractive the tax-free alternative becomes. Municipal bond yields vary according to local economic factors, the issuer's perceived ability to repay, and the security's quality RATING assigned by one of the bond-rating agencies. *See also* MORAL OBLIGATION BOND.

TAX LOSS CARRYBACK, CARRYFORWARD tax benefit that allows a company or individual to apply losses to reduce tax liability. A company may OFFSET the current year's capital or net operating losses against profits in the three immediately preceding years, with the earliest year first. After the carryback, it may carry forward (also called a *carryover*) capital losses five years and net operating losses up to 15 years. By then it will presumably have regained financial health.

Individuals may carry over capital losses until they are used up for an unlimited number of years to offset capital gains. Unlike corporations, however, individuals generally cannot carry back losses to apply to prior years' tax returns. The 1986 tax act curbed tax-motivated BUYOUTS by limiting the use of NOLs where a loss corporation has had a 50% or more ownership change in a three-year period. A special set of complex rules pertains to carryback of losses for trading in commodity futures contracts.

TAX PREFERENCE ITEM item specified by the tax law that a taxpayer must include when calculating ALTERNATIVE MINIMUM TAX (AMT). Under the TAX REFORM ACT OF 1986, preference items include: net PASSIVE losses at 100% of value (that is, without the transition benefits the regular tax allows for interests purchased before enactment); benefits from ACCELERATED DEPRECIATION (calculated in different ways for personal property and real property); certain INTANGIBLE COSTS; the excess of fair market value at exercise date over option cost for INCENTIVE STOCK OPTIONS; tax-exempt interest on PRIVATE PURPOSE BONDS of municipalities issued after August 8, 1986; and the untaxed appreciation of property contributed to charity. Corporate preferences are generally the same as for individuals, but in addition include: charges to increase BAD DEBT reserves when they exceed levels reflecting actual experience (applicable to small banks and other financial institutions); earnings based on percentage-of-completion accounting for longterm contracts entered into after February 1, 1986; gains on dispositions of dealer property in the year of disposition (as opposed to the installment method of accounting) effective March 1, 1986; and an amount equal to 50% of the difference between a corporation's book income and its AMT liability. The last-mentioned preference, which is aimed at profits reported to shareholders but not regularly taxed, expired in 1989. *See also* TAX REFORM ACT OF 1976; TAX EQUITY AND FISCAL RESPONSIBILITY ACT OF 1982.

TAX REFORM ACT OF 1976 federal legislation that tightened several provisions and benefits relating to taxation, beginning in the 1976 tax year. Among its major provisions:

1. extended the long-term CAPITAL GAINS holding period from six months to nine months in 1977 and to 12 months beginning in 1978.
2. instituted new rules on determining the TAX BASIS of inherited property.
3. set a new minimum capital gains tax on the sale of a house.
4. established, for homeowners over age 65, a once-in-a-lifetime exclusion of up to $35,000 in capital gains tax on the sale of a principal residence. (This amount was later raised by other tax bills, until it stood at $125,000 in the mid-1980s.)
5. increased the maximum net CAPITAL LOSS deduction from ordinary income on a personal income tax return to $3000 beginning in 1978.
6. extended the period of tax loss carryforward from five years to seven; gave companies the option of carrying losses forward without having first to carry them back; and prohibited acquiring corporations from taking advantage of an acquired firm's loss carryovers unless it gave the acquired firm's stockholders continuing ownership in the combined company.
7. limited deductions for home-office expenses to cases where homes are used as principal business locations, or for meeting with clients.
8. disallowed owners who rent their vacation homes from reporting losses, deducting maintenance costs or taking depreciation on those rentals unless the owners themselves used the homes less than two weeks per year, or less than 10% of total rental time.
9. instituted a deduction up to $3000 for "indirect" moving costs if a new job is more than 35 miles from a previous job.
10. established a child-care tax credit of up to $400 for one child and up to $800 for more than one child.
11. allowed a divorced parent, if contributing at least $1200 in child support, to claim a child as a dependent deduction.
12. instituted a spousal INDIVIDUAL RETIREMENT ACCOUNT, which allowed nonworking spouses to contribute up to $250.
13. disallowed losses on tax shelters financed through loans made without any obligation to pay, or where taxpayer's risk is limited by a form of guarantee or REPURCHASE AGREEMENT, except for real estate investments.
14. treated the exercise of a STOCK OPTION as ordinary income rather than as a CAPITAL GAIN.

TAX REFORM ACT OF 1984 legislation enacted by Congress as part of the Deficit Reduction Act of 1984 to reduce the federal budget deficit. The following are highlights from the more than 100 provisions in the Act:

1. shortened the minimum holding period for assets to qualify for long-term capital gains treatment from one year to six months.
2. allowed contributions to be made to an INDIVIDUAL RETIREMENT ACCOUNT

no later than April 15 after the tax year for which an IRA benefit is sought; previously the cut-off was the following October 15.
3. allowed the Internal Revenue Service to tax the benefits of loans made on below-market, interest-free, or "gift" terms.
4. tightened INCOME AVERAGING requirements.
5. set a $150 per capita limit on the amount of INDUSTRIAL DEVELOPMENT BONDS that a state could issue in a year, and permitted interest to be tax-exempt only for certain "small issues."
6. retained the 15% minimum tax on corporate TAX PREFERENCE ITEMS as in the TAX REFORM ACT OF 1976, but increased from 15% to 20% the deduction allowed for a tax preference item.
7. restricted GOLDEN PARACHUTE payments to executives by eliminating the corporate tax deductibility of these payments and subjecting them to a non-deductible 20% excise tax.
8. required registration of TAX SHELTERS with the Internal Revenue Service and set penalties for failure to comply. Also set penalties for overvaluing assets used for depreciation in a tax shelter.
9. expanded rules in ERTA to cover additional types of stock and options transactions that make up TAX STRADDLES.
10. repealed the 30% withholding tax on interest, dividends, rents, and royalties paid to foreign investors by U.S. corporations and government agencies.
11. raised the liquor tax, reduced the cigarette tax, and extended the 3% telephone excise tax.
12. delayed to 1987 the scheduled decline in estate and gift taxes.
13. granted a specific tax exemption for many fringe benefits.
14. extended mortgage subsidy bonds through 1988.
15. required ALTERNATIVE MINIMUM TAX quarterly estimated payments.
16. changed the rules affecting taxation of life insurance companies.
17. disqualified from eligibility for long-term capital gains tax the appreciation of market discounts on newly issued ORIGINAL ISSUE DISCOUNT bonds.
18. real estate depreciation was lengthened from 15 to 18 years.
19. delayed implementation of new finance leasing rules until 1988.
20. restricted the sale of unused depreciation tax deductions by tax-exempt entities to companies that can use the deductions.
21. phased out the graduated corporate income tax on the first $100,000 of income for corporations with income over $1 million.
22. created Foreign Sales Corporations (FSCs) to provide American companies with tax deferral advantages to encourage exports.
23. limited tax breaks for luxury automobiles to a maximum writeoff of $16,000 in the first three years of ownership.
24. increased the earned income tax credit for lower-income taxpayers from 10% to a maximum of 11% of the first $5000 of income.
25. eliminated the tax on property transfers in a divorce.
26. increased the standard automobile mileage rate from 9 cents a mile to 12 cents a mile for expenses incurred in volunteer charity work.
27. tightened rules and increased penalties for those who try to inflate deductions by overvaluing property donated to charity.

TAX REFORM ACT OF 1986 landmark federal legislation that made comprehensive changes in the system of U.S. taxation. Among the law's major provisions:

Provisions Affecting Individuals
1. lowered maximum marginal tax rates from 50% to 28%, beginning in 1988

and reduced the number of basic TAX BRACKETS from 14 to 2—28% and 15%. Also instituted a 5% rate surcharge for high-income taxpayers.

2. eliminated the preferential tax treatment of CAPITAL GAINS. Starting in 1988, all gains realized on asset sales are taxed at ordinary income rates, no matter how long the asset was held.
3. increased the personal exemption to $1900 in 1987, $1950 in 1988, and $2000 in 1989. Phased out exemption for high-income taxpayers.
4. increased the STANDARD DEDUCTION, and indexed it to inflation starting in 1989.
5. repealed the deduction for two-earner married couples.
6. repealed income averaging for all taxpayers.
7. repealed the $100 ($200 for couples) dividend exclusion.
8. restricted the deductibility of IRA contributions.
9. mandated the phaseout of consumer interest deductibility by 1991.
10. allowed investment interest expense to be offset against investment income, dollar-for-dollar, without limitation.
11. limited unreimbursed medical expenses that can be deducted to amounts in excess of 7.5% of adjusted gross income.
12. limited the tax deductibility of interest on a first or second home mortgage to the purchase price of the house plus the cost of improvements and amounts used for medical or educational purposes.
13. repealed the deductibility of state and local sales taxes.
14. limited miscellaneous deductions to expenses exceeding 2% of adjusted gross income.
15. limited the deductibility of itemized charitable contributions.
16. strengthened the ALTERNATIVE MINIMUM TAX, and raised the rate to 21%.
17. tightened home office deductions.
18. lowered the deductibility of business entertainment and meal expenses from 100% to 80%.
19. eliminated the benefits of CLIFFORD TRUSTS and other income-shifting devices by taxing unearned income over $1000 on gifts to children under 14 years old at the grantor's tax rate.
20. repealed the tax credit for political contributions.
21. limited the use of losses from PASSIVE activity to offsetting income from passive activity.
22. lowered the top rehabilitation tax credit from 25% to 20%.
23. made all unemployment compensation benefits taxable.
24. repealed the deduction for attending investment seminars.
25. eased the rules for exercise of INCENTIVE STOCK OPTIONS.
26. imposed new limitations on SALARY REDUCTION PLANS and SIMPLIFIED EMPLOYEE PENSION (SEP) PLANS.

Provisions Affecting Business
27. lowered the top corporate tax rate to 34% from 46%, and lowered the number of corporate tax brackets from five to three.
28. applied the ALTERNATIVE MINIMUM TAX (AMT) to corporations, and set a 20% rate.
29. repealed the investment tax credit for property placed in service after 1985.
30. altered the method of calculating DEPRECIATION.
31. limited the deductibility of charges to BAD DEBT reserves to financial institutions with less than $500 million in assets.
32. extended the research and development tax credit, but lowered the rate from 25% to 20%.

33. eliminated the deductibility of interest that banks pay to finance tax-exempt securities holdings.
34. eliminated the deductibility of GREENMAIL payments by companies warding off hostile takeover attempts.
35. restricted COMPLETED CONTRACT METHOD accounting for tax purposes.
36. limited the ability of a company that acquires more than 50% of another firm to use NET OPERATING LOSSES to offset taxes.
37. reduced the corporate DIVIDEND EXCLUSION from 85% to 80%.
38. limited cash and installment method accounting for tax purposes.
39. restricted tax-exemption on MUNICIPAL BONDS to PUBLIC PURPOSE BONDS and specified PRIVATE PURPOSE BONDS. Imposed caps on the dollar amount of permitted private purpose bonds. Limited PREREFUNDING. Made interest on certain private purpose bonds subject to the AMT.
40. amended the rules for qualifying as a REAL ESTATE INVESTMENT TRUST and the taxation of REITs.
41. set up tax rules for real estate mortgage investment conduits (REMICs).
42. changed many rules relating to taxation of foreign operations of U.S. multinational companies.
43. liberalized the requirements for employee VESTING rules in a company's qualified pension plan, and changed other rules affecting employee benefit plans.
44. enhanced benefit of SUBCHAPTER S corporation status.

TAX SELLING selling of securities, usually at year end, to realize losses in a PORTFOLIO, which can be used to OFFSET capital gains and thereby lower an investor's tax liability. *See also* LONG TERM GAIN; LONG TERM LOSS; SELLING SHORT AGAINST THE BOX; SHORT TERM GAIN OR LOSS; SWAP; THIRTY-DAY WASH RULE.

TAX SHELTER method used by investors to legally avoid or reduce tax liabilities. Legal shelters include those using DEPRECIATION of assets like real estate or equipment or DEPLETION allowances for oil and gas exploration. LIMITED PARTNERSHIPS have traditionally offered investors limited liability and tax benefits including "flow through" operating losses usable to offset income from other sources. The TAX REFORM ACT OF 1986 dealt a severe blow to such tax shelters by ruling that PASSIVE losses could be used only to offset passive income, by lengthening depreciation schedules, and by extending AT RISK rules to include real estate investments. Vehicles that allow tax-deferred capital growth, such as INDIVIDUAL RETIREMENT ACCOUNTS (IRAs) and KEOGH PLANS (which also provide current tax deductions for qualified taxpayers), SALARY REDUCTION PLANS, and SINGLE PREMIUM LIFE INSURANCE, are also popular tax shelters as are tax-exempt MUNICIPAL BONDS.

TAX STRADDLE technique whereby OPTION or FUTURES CONTRACTS are used to eliminate economic risk while creating an advantageous tax position. In its most common use, an investor with a CAPITAL GAIN would take a position creating an offsetting "artificial" loss in the current tax year and postponing the gain until the next tax year. The ECONOMIC RECOVERY TAX ACT OF 1981 curtailed this practice by requiring traders to MARK TO THE MARKET at year-end and include unrealized gains in taxable income. The TAX REFORM ACT OF 1986 introduced a change whereby an exception for COVERED WRITERS of calls is denied if the taxpayer fails to hold the covered CALL OPTION for 30 days after the related stock is disposed of at a loss, if gain on the termination or disposition of the option is included in the next year.

TAX UMBRELLA tax loss carryforwards stemming from losses of a company in past years, which act to shield profits earned in the current and future tax years from taxes. *See also* TAX LOSS CARRYBACK, CARRYFORWARD.

TEAR SHEET sheet from one of a dozen loose-leaf books comprising Standard & Poor's Stock Reports, which provide essential background and financial data on more than 4000 companies. Brokers often tear and mail these sheets to satisfy customer inquiries on specific companies (hence the name).

TECHNICAL ANALYSIS research into the demand and supply for securities and commodities based on trading volume and price studies. Technical analysts use charts or computer programs to identify price trends in a market, security, or commodity future, which they think will foretell price movements. Most analysis is done for the short- or intermediate-term outlook for the security or commodity in question, but some technicians also predict long-term cycles based on charts and other data. Unlike fundamental analysts, technical analysts generally do not concern themselves with the financial position of a company, such as its earnings, or the strength of its balance sheet. *See also* ADVANCE/DECLINE (A-D); ASCENDING TOPS; BREAKOUT; CORRECTION; DESCENDING TOPS; DIP; DOUBLE BOTTOM; DOUBLE TOP; FLAG; FUNDAMENTAL ANALYSIS; GAP; HEAD AND SHOULDERS; HORIZONTAL PRICE MOVEMENT; MOVING AVERAGE; PENNANT; POINT AND FIGURE CHART; RESISTANCE LEVEL; REVERSAL; RISING BOTTOMS; SAUCER; SELLING CLIMAX; SUPPORT LEVEL; TRIANGLE; V FORMATION; VERTICAL LINE CHARTING; W FORMATION.

TECHNICAL RALLY short rise in securities or commodities futures prices within a general declining trend. Such a rally may result because investors are bargain-hunting or because analysts have noticed a particular SUPPORT LEVEL at which securities usually bounce up.

TECHNICAL SIGN short-term trend that TECHNICAL ANALYSIS can identify as significant in the price movement of a security or a commodity.

TEFRA *see* TAX EQUITY AND FISCAL RESPONSIBILITY ACT OF 1982.

TELEPHONE SWITCHING process of shifting assets from one MUTUAL FUND or VARIABLE ANNUITY portfolio to another by telephone. Such a switch may be among the stock, bond, or money-market funds of a single FAMILY OF FUNDS, or it may be from a fund in one family to a fund in another. Transfers involving portfolios in annuity contracts do not trigger taxation of gains as do mutual fund switches.

TENANCY IN COMMON ownership of property by two or more persons in such a way that when one of them dies, the deceased's undivided interest passes to his or her heirs and not to the surviving tenant(s). This arrangement is distinguished from joint tenancy (*see* JOINT TENANTS WITH THE RIGHT OF SURVIVORSHIP) and tenancy by the entirety (a similar arrangement pertaining to a married couple where the husband or wife automatically acquires the other's share upon death).

TENANT
   Real Estate: (1) holder or possessor of real property; (2) lessee.
   Securities: part owner of a security.
   See also JOINT TENANTS WITH RIGHT OF SURVIVORSHIP; TENANCY IN COMMON.

TENDER

1. act of surrendering one's shares in a corporation in response to an offer to buy them at a set price. *See also* TENDER OFFER.
2. to submit a formal bid to buy a security, as in a U.S. Treasury bill auction. *See also* DUTCH AUCTION.
3. offer of money or goods in settlement of a prior debt or claim, as in the delivery of goods on the due date of a FUTURES CONTRACT.
4. agreed-upon medium for the settlement of financial transactions, such as U.S. currency, which is labeled "legal tender for all debts, public and private."

TENDER OFFER offer to buy shares of a corporation, usually at a PREMIUM above the shares' market price, for cash, securities, or both, often with the objective of taking control of the TARGET COMPANY. A tender offer may arise from friendly negotiations between the company and a corporate suitor or may be unsolicited and possibly unfriendly, resulting in countermeasures being taken by the target firm. The Securities and Exchange Commission requires any corporate suitor accumulating 5% or more of a target company to make disclosures to the SEC, the target company, and the relevant exchange. *See also* SCHEDULE 13D; TAKE-OVER; TREASURY STOCK.

10-K REPORT *see* FORM 10-K.

1099 annual statement sent to the Internal Revenue Service and to taxpayers by the payers of dividends (1099-DIV) and interest (1099-INT) and by issuers of taxable ORIGINAL ISSUE DISCOUNT securities (1099-OID).

TEN PERCENT GUIDELINE MUNICIPAL BOND analysts' guideline that funded debt over 10% of the ASSESSED VALUATION of taxable property in a municipality is excessive.

TERM

1. period of time during which the conditions of a contract will be carried out. This may refer to the time in which loan payments must be made, or the time when interest payments will be made on a certificate of deposit or a bond. It also may refer to the length of time a life insurance policy is in force. *See also* TERM LIFE INSURANCE.
2. provision specifying the nature of an agreement or contract, as in *terms and conditions*.
3. period of time an official or board member is elected or appointed to serve. For example, Federal Reserve governors are appointed for 14-year terms.

TERM CERTIFICATE CERTIFICATE OF DEPOSIT with a longer-term maturity date. Such CDs can range in length from one year to ten years, though the most popular term certificates are those for one or two years. Certificate holders usually receive a fixed rate of interest, payable semiannually during the term, and are subject to costly EARLY WITHDRAWAL PENALTIES if the certificate is cashed in before the scheduled maturity.

TERM LIFE INSURANCE form of life insurance, written for a specified period, that requires the policyholder to pay only for the cost of protection against death; that is, no cash value is built up as in WHOLE LIFE INSURANCE. Every time the policy is renewed, the premium is higher, since the insured is older and therefore statistically more likely to die. Term insurance is far cheaper than whole life, giving policyholders the alternative of using the savings to invest on their own.

TERM LOAN intermediate- to long-term (typically, two to ten years) secured credit granted to a company by a commercial bank, insurance company, or commercial finance company usually to finance capital equipment or provide working capital. The loan is amortized over a fixed period, sometimes ending with a BALLOON payment. Borrowers under term loan agreements are normally required to meet minimum WORKING CAPITAL and debt to net worth tests, to limit dividends, and to maintain continuity of management.

TEST

In general: examination to determine knowledge, competence, or qualifications.

Finance: criterion used to measure compliance with financial ratio requirements of indentures and other loan agreements (for example, a current asset to current liability test, or a debt to net worth test).

Securities: term used in reference to a price movement that approaches a SUPPORT LEVEL or a RESISTANCE LEVEL established earlier by a commodity future, security, or market. A test is passed if the levels are not penetrated and is failed if prices go on to new lows or highs. Technical analysts say, for instance, that if the Dow Jones Industrials last formed a solid base at 1000, and prices have been falling from 1100, a period of testing is approaching. If prices rebound once the Dow hits 1000 and go up further, the test is passed. If prices continue to drop below 1000, however, the test is failed. *See also* TECHNICAL ANALYSIS.

TESTAMENTARY TRUST trust created by a will, as distinguished from an INTER VIVOS TRUST created during the lifetime of the GRANTOR.

THEORETICAL VALUE (OF A RIGHT) mathematically determined MARKET VALUE of a SUBSCRIPTION RIGHT after the offering is announced but before the stock goes EX-RIGHTS. The formula includes the current market value of the common stock, the subscription price, and the number of rights required to purchase a share of stock:

theoretical value of a right

$$= \frac{\text{market value of common stock} - \text{subscription price per share}}{\text{number of rights needed to buy 1 share} + 1}$$

Thus, if the common stock market price is $50 per share, the subscription price is $45 per share, and the subscription ratio is 4 to 1, the value of one right would be $1:

$$\frac{50 - 45}{4 + 1} = \frac{5}{5} = 1$$

THIN MARKET market in which there are few bids to buy and few offers to sell. A thin market may apply to an entire class of securities or commodities futures—such as small OVER THE COUNTER stocks or the platinum market—or it may refer to a particular stock, whether exchange-listed or over-the-counter. Prices in thin markets are more volatile than in markets with great LIQUIDITY, since the few trades that take place can affect prices significantly. Institutional investors who buy and sell large blocks of stock tend to avoid thin markets, because it is difficult for them to get in or out of a POSITION without materially affecting the stock's price.

THIRD MARKET nonexchange-member broker/dealers and institutional investors trading OVER THE COUNTER in exchange-listed securities. The third market rose to importance in the 1950s when institutional investors began buying common stocks as an inflation hedge and fixed commission rates still prevailed on the exchanges. By trading large blocks with nonmember firms, they both saved commissions and avoided the unsettling effects on prices that large trades on the exchanges produced. After commission rates were deregulated in May 1975, a number of the firms active in the third market became member firms so they could deal with members as well as nonmembers. At the same time, member firms began increasingly to move large blocks of stock off the floor of the exchanges, in effect becoming participants in the third market. Before selling securities off the exchange to a nonmember, however, a member firm must satisfy all LIMIT ORDERS on the SPECIALIST'S BOOK at the same price or higher. *See also* OFF-FLOOR ORDER.

THIRD-PARTY CHECK
1. check negotiated through a bank, except one payable to the writer of the check (that is, a check written for cash). The *primary party* to a transaction is the bank on which a check is drawn. The *secondary party* is the drawer of the check against funds on deposit in the bank. The *third party* is the payee who endorses the check.
2. double-endorsed check. In this instance, the payee endorses the check by signing the back, then passes the check to a subsequent holder, who endorses it prior to cashing it. Recipients of checks with multiple endorsers are reluctant to accept them unless they can verify each endorser's signature.
3. payable-through drafts and other negotiable orders not directly serviced by the providing company. For example, a check written against a money market mutual fund is processed not by the mutual fund company but typically by a commercial bank that provides a "third-party" or "payable-through" service. Money orders, credit union share drafts, and checks drawn against a brokerage account are other examples of payable-through or third-party items.

THIRTY-DAY VISIBLE SUPPLY total dollar volume of new MUNICIPAL BONDS carrying maturities of 13 months or more that are scheduled to reach the market within 30 days. The figure is supplied on Thursdays in the BOND BUYER.

THIRTY-DAY WASH RULE Internal Revenue Service rule stating that losses on a sale of stock may not be used as losses for tax purposes (that is, used to OFFSET gains) if equivalent stock is purchased within 30 days before or 30 after the date of sale.

THRIFT INSTITUTION organization formed primarily as a depository for consumer savings, the most common varieties of which are the SAVINGS AND LOAN ASSOCIATION and the SAVINGS BANK. Traditionally, savings institutions have loaned most of their deposit funds in the residential mortgage market and continued to do so after legislation in the early 1980s expanded their range of depository services and allowed them to make commercial and consumer loans. CREDIT UNIONS are sometimes included in the thrift institution category, since their principal source of deposits is also personal savings, though they have traditionally made small consumer loans, not mortgage loans. *See also* DEPOSITORY INSTITUTIONS DEREGULATION AND MONETARY CONTROL ACT; MUTUAL ASSOCIATION; MUTUAL SAVINGS BANK.

TICK upward or downward price movement in a security's trades. Technical analysts watch the tick of a stock's successive up or down moves to get a feel of the stock's trend. *See also* DOWNTICK; MINUS TICK; PLUS TICK; SHORT SALE RULE; TECHNICAL ANALYSIS; UPTICK; ZERO-MINUS TICK; ZERO-PLUS TICK.

TICKER system that produces a running report of trading activity on the stock exchanges, called the TICKER TAPE. The name derives from machines that, in times past, printed information by punching holes in a paper tape, making an audible ticking sound as the tape was fed forth. Today's ticker tape is a computer screen and the term is used to refer both to the CONSOLIDATED TAPE, which shows the STOCK SYMBOL, latest price, and volume of trades on the exchanges, and to news ticker services. *See also* QUOTATION BOARD.

TICKER SYMBOL letters that identify a security for trading purposes on the CONSOLIDATED TAPE, such as XON for Exxon Corporation. *See also* STOCK SYMBOL; TICKER TAPE.

TICKER TAPE device that relays the STOCK SYMBOL and the latest price and volume on securities as they are traded to investors around the world. Prior to the advent of computers, this machine had a loud printing device that made a ticking sound. Since 1975, the New York Stock Exchange and the American Stock Exchange have used a CONSOLIDATED TAPE that indicates the New York or REGIONAL STOCK EXCHANGE on which a trade originated. Other systems, known as news tickers, pass along the latest economic, financial and market news developments. See also TAPE.

GM	MMM&P	IBM&T		XON&M	
3S41⅝		83½	4S124¼		2S41

Sample section of the consolidated tape.
Trades in General Motors, Minnesota Mining and Manufacturing, IBM, and Exxon are shown. Letters following the ampersands in the upper line indicate the marketplace in which the trade took place: P signifies the Pacific Stock Exchange, T the THIRD MARKET, M the Midwest Exchange; no indication means the New York Stock Exchange. Other codes not illustrated are X for Philadelphia Stock Exchange, B for Boston Stock Exchange, O for other markets, including INSTINET. In the lower line, where a number precedes the letter S, a multiple of 100 shares is indicated. Thus, 300 shares of General Motors were transacted at a price of 41⅝ on the New York Stock Exchange; 100 shares of Minnesota Mining were traded on the Pacific Exchange at 83½, and so on.

TIGER acronym for Treasury Investors Growth Receipt, a form of ZERO-COUPON SECURITY first created by the brokerage firm of Merrill Lynch, Pierce, Fenner & Smith. TIGERS are U.S. government-backed bonds that have been stripped of their COUPONS. Both the CORPUS (principal) of the bonds and the individual coupons are sold separately at a deep discount from their face value. Investors receive FACE VALUE for the TIGERS when the bonds mature but do not receive periodic interest payments. Under Internal Revenue Service rules, however, TIGER holders owe income taxes on the imputed interest they would have earned had the bond been a FULL COUPON BOND. To avoid having to pay taxes without having the benefit of the income to pay them from, most investors put TIGERS in Individual Retirement or Keogh accounts or in other TAX DEFERRED plans. Also called *TIGR*.

TIGHT MARKET market in general or market for a particular security marked by active trading and narrow bid-offer price spreads. In contrast, inactive trading and wide spreads characterize a *slack market. See also* SPREAD.

TIGHT MONEY economic condition in which credit is difficult to secure, usually as the result of Federal Reserve action to restrict the MONEY SUPPLY. The opposite is *easy money*. *See also* MONETARY POLICY.

TIME DEPOSIT savings account or CERTIFICATE OF DEPOSIT held in a financial institution for a fixed term or with the understanding that the depositor can withdraw only by giving notice. While a bank is authorized to require 30 days' notice of withdrawal from savings accounts, passbook accounts are generally regarded as readily available funds. Certificates of deposit, on the other hand, are issued for a specified term of 30 days or more, and provide penalties for early withdrawal. Financial institutions are free to negotiate any maturity term a customer might desire on a time deposit or certificate, as long as the term is at least 30 days, and to pay interest rates as high or low as the market will bear. *See also* DEPOSITORY INSTITUTIONS DEREGULATION AND MONETARY CONTROL ACT; REGULATION Q.

TIME DRAFT DRAFT payable at a specified or determinable time in the future, as distinguished from a *sight draft,* which is payable on presentation and delivery.

TIMES FIXED CHARGES *see* FIXED-CHARGE COVERAGE.

TIME SPREAD OPTION strategy in which an investor buys and sells PUT OPTION and CALL OPTION contracts with the same EXERCISE PRICE but with different expiration dates. The purpose of this and other option strategies is to profit from the difference in OPTION PREMIUMS—the prices paid to buy the options. *See also* CALENDAR SPREAD; HORIZONTAL SPREAD; SPREAD.

TIME VALUE

In general: price put on the time an investor has to wait until an investment matures, as determined by calculating the PRESENT VALUE of the investment at maturity. *See also* YIELD TO MATURITY.

Options: that part of a stock option PREMIUM that reflects the time remaining on an option contract before expiration. The premium is composed of this time value and the INTRINSIC VALUE of the option.

Stocks: difference between the price at which a company is taken over and the price before the TAKEOVER occurs. For example, if XYZ Company is to be taken over at $30 a share in two months, XYZ shares might presently sell for $28.50. The $1.50 per share difference is the cost of the time value those owning XYZ must bear if they want to wait two months to get $30 a share. As the two months pass, the time value will shrink, until it disappears on the day of the takeover. The time that investors hold XYZ has a price because it could be used to invest in something else providing a higher return. *See also* OPPORTUNITY COST.

TIME-WEIGHTED RETURN portfolio accounting method that measures investment performance (income and price changes) as a percentage of capital "at work," effectively eliminating the effects of additions and withdrawals of capital and their timing that distort DOLLAR-WEIGHTED RETURN accounting. Since exact time-weighting is impractical, the industry accepts an approximation that assumes all additions and withdrawals occur simultaneously at the midpoint of a reporting period. Performance thus equals the return on the value of assets at the beginning of the measuring period plus the return on the net amount of additions and withdrawals during the period divided in half. The periods, usually quarters, are then linked to produce a compound average TOTAL RETURN.

TIP

In general: payment over and above a formal cost or charge, ostensibly given in appreciation for extra service, to a waiter, bellhop, cabdriver, or other person engaged in service. Also called a *gratuity*.

Investments: information passed by one person to another as a basis for buy or sell action in a security. Such information is presumed to be of material value and not available to the general public. The Securities and Exchange Commission regulates the use of such information by so-called insiders, and court cases have established the liability of persons receiving and using or passing on such information (called tippees) in certain circumstances. *See also* INSIDER; INSIDE INFORMATION.

TOEHOLD PURCHASE accumulation by an acquirer of less than 5% of the shares of a TARGET COMPANY. Once 5% is acquired, the acquirer is required to file with the Securities and Exchange Commission, the appropriate stock exchange, and the target company, explaining what is happening and what can be expected. *See also* SCHEDULE 13D; WILLIAMS ACT.

TOLL REVENUE BOND MUNICIPAL BOND supported by revenues from tolls paid by users of the public project built with the bond proceeds. Toll revenue bonds frequently are floated to build bridges, tunnels, and roads. *See also* REVENUE BOND.

TOMBSTONE advertisement placed in newspapers by investment bankers in a PUBLIC OFFERING of securities. It gives basic details about the issue and lists the UNDERWRITING GROUP members involved in the offering in alphabetically organized groupings according to the size of their participations. It is not "an offer to sell or a solicitation of an offer to buy," but rather it calls attention to the PROSPECTUS, sometimes called the *offering circular*. A tombstone may also be placed by an investment banking firm to announce its role in a PRIVATE PLACEMENT, corporate MERGER, or ACQUISITION; by a corporation to announce a major business or real estate deal; or by a firm in the financial community to announce a personnel development or a principal's death. *See also* MEZZANINE BRACKET.

TON bond traders' jargon for $100 million.

TOP-DOWN APPROACH TO INVESTING method in which an investor first looks at trends in the general economy, and next selects industries and then companies that should benefit from those trends. For example, an investor who thinks inflation will stay low might be attracted to the retailing industry, since consumers' spending power will be enhanced by low inflation. The investor then might look at Macy's, Federated Department Stores, and other major retailers to see which company has the best earnings prospects in the near term. The opposite method is called the BOTTOM-UP APPROACH TO INVESTING.

TOPPING OUT term denoting a market or a security that is at the end of a period of rising prices and can now be expected to stay on a plateau or even to decline.

TOTAL CAPITALIZATION CAPITAL STRUCTURE of a company, including LONG-TERM DEBT and all forms of EQUITY.

TOTAL COST

Accounting: (usually pl.) sum of FIXED COSTS, semivariable costs, and VARIABLE COSTS.

Investments: contract price paid for a security plus the brokerage commission plus any ACCRUED INTEREST due the seller (if the security is a bond). The figure is not to be confused with the COST BASIS for the purpose of figuring the CAPITAL GAINS TAX, which may involve other factors such as amortization of bond premiums.

TOTAL RETURN annual return on an investment including appreciation and dividends or interest. For bonds, total return is YIELD TO MATURITY. For stocks, future appreciation is projected using the current PRICE/EARNINGS RATIO. In options trading, total return means dividends plus capital gains plus premium income.

TOTAL VOLUME total number of shares or contracts traded in a stock, bond, commodity future, or option on a particular day. For stocks and bonds, this is the aggregate of trades on national exchanges like the New York and American stock exchanges and on regional exchanges. For commodities futures and options, it represents the volume of trades executed around the world in one day. For over-the-counter securities, total volume is measured by the NASDAQ index.

TOUT to promote a particular security aggressively, usually done by a corporate spokesman, public relations firm, broker, or analyst with a vested interest in promoting the stock. Touting a stock is unethical if it misleads investors. *See also* INVESTMENT ADVISERS ACT; INVESTOR RELATIONS DEPARTMENT.

TRADE

In general:
1. buying or selling of goods and services among companies, states, or countries, called *commerce*. The amount of goods and services imported minus the amount exported makes up a country's BALANCE OF TRADE. *See also* TARIFF; TRADE DEFICIT.
2. those in the business of selling products are called *members of the trade*. As such, they receive DISCOUNTS from the price the public has to pay.
3. group of manufacturers who compete in the same market. These companies form trade associations and publish trade journals.
4. commercial companies that do business with each other. For example, ACCOUNTS PAYABLE to suppliers are called *trade accounts payable*; the term TRADE CREDIT is used to describe accounts payable as a source of WORKING CAPITAL financing. Companies paying their bills promptly receive *trade discounts* when available.
5. synonymous with BARTER, the exchange of goods and services without the use of money.

Securities: to carry out a transaction of buying or selling a stock, a bond, or a commodity future contract. A trade is consummated when a buyer and seller agree on a price at which the trade will be executed. A TRADER frequently buys and sells for his or her own account securities for short-term profits, as contrasted with an investor who holds his positions in hopes of long-term gains.

TRADE BALANCE *see* BALANCE OF TRADE.

TRADE CREDIT open account arrangements with suppliers of goods and services, and a firm's record of payment with the suppliers. Trade liabilities comprise a company's ACCOUNTS PAYABLE. DUN & BRADSTREET is the largest compiler of trade credit information, rating commercial firms and supplying published reports. Trade credit data is also processed by MERCANTILE AGENCIES specializing in different industries.

Trade credit is an important external source of WORKING CAPITAL for a company, although such credit can be highly expensive. Terms of 2% 10 days, net 30 days (2% discount if paid in 10 days, the net [full] amount due in 30 days) translate into a 36% annual interest rate if not taken advantage of. On the other hand, the same terms translate into a borrowing rate of slightly over 15% if payment is made in 60 days instead of 30.

TRADE DATE day on which a security or a commodity future trade actually takes place. The SETTLEMENT DATE usually follows the trade date by five business days, but varies depending on the transaction and method of delivery used. *See also* DELAYED DELIVERY; DELIVERY DATE; REGULAR-WAY DELIVERY (AND SETTLEMENT); SELLER'S OPTION.

TRADE DEFICIT OR SURPLUS excess of imports over exports (*trade deficit*) or of exports over imports (*trade surplus*), resulting in a negative or positive BALANCE OF TRADE. The balance of trade is made up of transactions in merchandise and other movable goods and is only one factor comprising the larger *current account* (which includes services and tourism, transportation, and other *invisible items*, such as interest and profits earned abroad) in the overall BALANCE OF PAYMENTS. Factors influencing a country's balance of trade include the strength or weakness of its currency in relation to those of the countries with which it trades (a strong U.S. dollar, for example, makes goods produced in other countries relatively cheap for Americans), production advantages in key manufacturing areas (Japanese automobiles, for instance), or the domestic economy of a trading country where production may or may not be meeting demand.

TRADEMARK distinctive name, symbol, motto, or emblem that identifies a product, service, or firm. In the United States, trademark rights—the right to prevent competitors from using similar marks in selling or advertising—arise out of use; that is, registration is not essential to establish the legal existence of a mark. A trademark registered with the U.S. Patent and Trademark Office is good for 20 years, renewable as long as used. Products may be both patented and protected by trademark, the advantage being that when the patent runs out, exclusivity can be continued indefinitely with the trademark. A trademark is classified on a BALANCE SHEET as an INTANGIBLE ASSET.

Although, like land, trademarks have an indefinite life and cannot technically be amortized, in practice accountants do amortize trademarks over their estimated life, not to exceed 40 years.

TRADER

In general: anyone who buys and sells goods or services for profit; a DEALER or *merchant*. *See also* BARTER; TRADE.

Investments:

1. individual who buys and sells securities, such as STOCKS, BONDS, OPTIONS, or commodities, such as wheat, gold, or FOREIGN EXCHANGE, for his or her own account—that is, as a dealer or PRINCIPAL—rather than as a BROKER or AGENT.

2. individual who buys and sells securities or commodities for his or her own account on a short-term basis in anticipation of quick profits; a *speculator*. *See also* DAY TRADE; COMPETITIVE TRADER; FLOOR TRADER; REGISTERED COMPETITIVE MARKET MAKER; REGISTERED COMPETITIVE TRADER; SPECULATION.

TRADING AUTHORIZATION document giving a brokerage firm employee acting as AGENT (BROKER) the POWER OF ATTORNEY in buy-sell transactions for a customer.

TRADING DIVIDENDS technique of buying and selling stocks in other firms by a corporation in order to maximize the number of DIVIDENDS it can collect. This action is advantageous, because 80% of the dividend income it receives from the stocks of other companies is not taxed, according to Internal Revenue Service regulations. *See also* DIVIDEND EXCLUSION.

TRADING HALT *see* SUSPENDED TRADING.

TRADING LIMIT *see* DAILY TRADING LIMIT; LIMIT UP, LIMIT DOWN.

TRADING PATTERN long-range direction of a security or commodity future price. This pattern is charted by drawing a line connecting the highest prices the security has reached and another line connecting the lowest prices the security has traded at over the same time frame. These two lines will be pointing either up or down, indicating the security's long-term trading pattern.

    See also TRENDLINE.

TRADING PATTERN

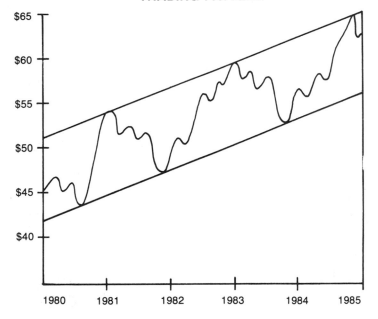

TRADING POST physical location on a stock exchange floor where particular securities are bought and sold. It is here that the SPECIALIST in a particular security performs his market-making functions and that the CROWD (floor brokers with orders in that security) congregates. The New York Stock Exchange, for example, has 22 trading posts, most handling around 100 stocks. *See also* FLOOR BROKER; FLOOR TRADER; MAKE A MARKET.

TRADING RANGE

Commodities: trading limit set by a COMMODITIES futures exchange for a particular commodity. The price of a commodity future contract may not go higher or lower than that limit during one day's trading. *See also* LIMIT UP, LIMIT DOWN.

Securities: range between the highest and lowest prices at which a security or a market has traded. The trading range for XYZ Corporation might be $40 to $60 over the last two years, for example. If a security or a market seems to be stuck in a narrow price range, analysts say that it is a trading range market, which will eventually be followed by a significant up or down move. *See also* FLAG; PENNANT; TRIANGLE; WEDGE.

TRADING UNIT number of SHARES, BONDS, or other securities that is generally accepted for ordinary trading purposes on the exchanges. *See also* ODD LOT; ROUND LOT; UNIT OF TRADING.

TRADING VARIATION fractions to which securities transaction prices are rounded. For example, stocks are rounded up or down to the nearest eighth of a point. Options over $3 are also rounded to an eighth, but options under $3 are rounded to $1/16$. Corporate and municipal bonds are rounded to $1/8$, medium- and long-term government notes and bonds to $1/32$, and shorter-term government bonds to $1/64$. *See also* PLUS.

TRANCH *see* COLLATERALIZED MORTGAGE OBLIGATION (CMO).

TRANSACTION

Accounting: event or condition recognized by an entry in the books of account.

Securities: execution of an order to buy or sell a security or commodity futures contract. After the buyer and seller have agreed on a price, the seller is obligated to deliver the security or commodity involved, and the buyer is obligated to accept it. *See also* TRADE.

TRANSACTION COSTS cost of buying or selling a security, which consists mainly of the BROKERAGE COMMISSION, the dealer MARKDOWN or markup, or fee (as would be charged by a bank or broker-dealer to buy or sell Treasuries, for example) but also includes direct taxes, such as the SEC TAX and any state-imposed TRANSFER TAXES.

TRANSFER AGENT agent, usually a commercial bank, appointed by a corporation, to maintain records of stock and bond owners, to cancel and issue certificates, and to resolve problems arising from lost, destroyed, or stolen certificates. (Preventing OVERISSUE of shares is the function of the REGISTRAR.) A corporation may also serve as its own transfer agent.

TRANSFER PRICE price charged by individual entities in a multi-entity corporation on transactions among themselves; also termed *transfer cost*. This concept is used where each entity is managed as a PROFIT CENTER—that is, held responsible for its own RETURN ON INVESTED CAPITAL—and must therefore deal with the other internal parts of the corporation on an arm's-length (or market) basis. *See also* ARM'S LENGTH TRANSACTION.

TRANSFER TAX

1. combined federal tax on gifts and estates. *See* ESTATE TAX; GIFT TAX.
2. federal tax on the sale of all bonds (except obligations of the United States, foreign governments, states, and municipalities) and all stocks. The tax is paid

by the seller at the time ownership is transferred and involves a few pennies per $100 of value.

3. tax levied by some state and local governments on the transfer of such documents as deeds to property, securities, or licenses. Such taxes are paid, usually with stamps, by the seller or donor and are determined by the location of the transfer agent. States with transfer taxes on stock transactions are New York, Florida, South Carolina, and Texas. New York bases its tax on selling price; the other states apply the tax to PAR value (giving NO-PAR-VALUE STOCK a value of $100). Bonds are not taxed at the state level.

TRANSMITTAL LETTER letter sent with a document, security, or shipment describing the contents and the purpose of the transaction.

TREASURER company officer responsible for the receipt, custody, investment, and disbursement of funds, for borrowings, and, if it is a public company, for the maintenance of a market for its securities. Depending on the size of the organization, the treasurer may also function as the CONTROLLER, with accounting and audit responsibilities. The laws of many states require that a corporation have a treasurer. *See also* CHIEF FINANCIAL OFFICER (CFO).

TREASURIES NEGOTIABLE debt obligations of the U.S. government, secured by its FULL FAITH AND CREDIT and issued at various schedules and maturities. The income from Treasury securities is exempt from state and local, but not federal, taxes.

1. *Treasury bills*—short-term securities with maturities of one year or less issued at a discount from FACE VALUE. Auctions of 91-day and 182-day BILLS take place weekly, and the yields are watched closely in the money markets for signs of interest rate trends. Many floating-rate loans and variable-rate mortgages have interest rates tied to these bills. The Treasury also auctions 52-week bills once every four weeks. At times it also issues very short-term cash management bills, TAX ANTICIPATION BILLS, and treasury certificates of indebtedness. Treasury bills are issued in minimum denominations of $10,000, with $5000 increments above $10,000 (except for cash management bills, which are sold in minimum $10 million blocks). Individual investors who do not submit a COMPETITIVE BID are sold bills at the average price of the winning competitive bids. Treasury bills are the primary instrument used by the Federal Reserve in its regulation of MONEY SUPPLY through OPEN MARKET OPERATIONS. *See also* DUTCH AUCTION; REPURCHASE AGREEMENT.

2. *Treasury bonds*—long-term debt instruments with maturities of 10 years or longer issued in minimum denominations of $1000.

3. *Treasury notes*—intermediate securities with maturities of 1 to 10 years. Denominations range from $1000 to $1 million or more. The notes are sold by cash subscription, in exchange for outstanding or maturing government issues, or at auction.

TREASURY BILL *see* BILL; TREASURIES.

TREASURY BOND *see* TREASURIES.

TREASURY DIRECT system through which an individual investor can make a NONCOMPETITIVE BID on U.S. Treasury securities (TREASURIES), thus bypassing middlemen like banks or broker-dealers and avoiding their fees. The system works through FEDERAL RESERVE BANKS and branches; the minimum purchase is $10,000.

TREASURY STOCK stock reacquired by the issuing company and available for RETIREMENT or resale. It is issued but not outstanding. It cannot be voted and it pays or accrues no dividends. It is not included in any of the ratios measuring values per common share. Among the reasons treasury stock is created are (1) to provide an alternative to paying taxable dividends, since the decreased amount of outstanding shares increases the per share value and often the market price; (2) to provide for the exercise of stock options and warrants and the conversion of convertible securities; (3) in countering a TENDER OFFER by a potential acquirer; (4) to alter the DEBT-TO-EQUITY RATIO by issuing bonds to finance the reacquisition of shares; (5) as a result of the STABILIZATION of the market price during a NEW ISSUE. Also called *reacquired stock* and *treasury shares. See also* ISSUED AND OUTSTANDING; UNISSUED STOCK.

TREND

In general: any general direction of movement. For example: "There is an upward (downward, level) trend in XYZ sales," or "There is a trend toward increased computerization of trading on Wall Street."

Securities: long-term price or trading volume movements either up, down, or sideways, which characterize a particular market, commodity or security. Also applies to interest rates and yields.

TRENDLINE line used by technical analysts to chart the past direction of a security or commodity future in order to help predict future price movements. The trend-line is made by connecting the highest or lowest prices to which a security or commodity has risen or fallen within a particular time period. The angle of the resulting line will indicate if the security or commodity is in a downtrend or uptrend. If the price rises above a downward sloping trendline or drops below a rising uptrend line, technical analysts say that a new direction may be emerging. *See also* TECHNICAL ANALYSIS; TRADING PATTERN.

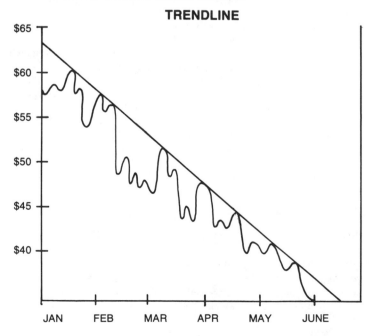

TRENDLINE

TRIANGLE technical chart pattern that has two base points and a top point, formed by connecting a stock's price movements with a line. In a typical triangle pattern, the apex points to the right, although in reverse triangles the apex points to the left. In a typical triangle, there are a series of two or more rallies and price drops where each succeeding peak is lower than the preceding peak, and each bottom is higher than the preceding bottom. In a right-angled triangle, the sloping part of the formation often points in the direction of the breakout. Technical analysts find it significant when a security's price breaks out of the triangle formation, either up or down, because that usually means the security's price will continue in that direction. *See also* PENNANT; TECHNICAL ANALYSIS; WEDGE.

TRIANGLE

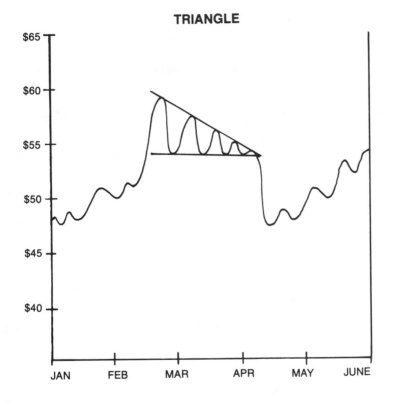

TRICKLE DOWN theory that economic growth can best be achieved by letting businesses flourish, since their prosperity will ultimately trickle down to middle- and lower-income people, who will benefit by increased economic activity. Economists who argue for this method say that it produces more long-term growth than if government made direct welfare grants to the middle- and lower-income sectors. *See also* SUPPLY-SIDE ECONOMICS.

TRIPLE TAX EXEMPT feature of MUNICIPAL BONDS in which interest is exempt from federal, state, and local taxation for residents of the states and localities that issue them. Such bonds are particularly attractive in states with high income tax rates. Many municipal bond funds buy only triple tax exempt bonds and market them to residents of the state and city of the issuer. *See also* SINGLE-STATE MUNICIPAL BOND FUND.

TRIPLE WITCHING HOUR last trading hour on the third Friday of March, June, September, and December, when OPTIONS and futures on stock indexes expire concurrently. Massive trades in index futures, options, and underlying stocks by hedge strategists and arbitrageurs cause abnormal activity (NOISE) and VOLATILITY. Smaller-scale *witching hours* occur in the other eight months, usually on the third Friday, when index futures or options expire.

TRUNCATION shortening of processing steps, in an effort to reduce paperwork and operating costs. For example, check truncation, or check SAFEKEEPING, where the bank holds the checks or microfilm records of them in a central file.

TRUST

Business: type of corporate combination that engaged in monopolies and restraint of trade and that operated freely until the ANTITRUST LAWS of the late 19th century and early 20th century. The name derived from the use of the voting trust, in which a small number of trustees vote a majority of the shares of a corporation. The voting trust survives as a means of facilitating the reorganization of firms in difficulty. *See also* INVESTMENT COMPANY; VOTING TRUST CERTIFICATE.

Law: FIDUCIARY relationship in which a person, called a *trustee,* holds title to property for the benefit of another person, called a BENEFICIARY. The person creating the trust is the *creator, settlor,* GRANTOR, or *donor;* the property itself is called the CORPUS, *trust res, trust fund,* or *trust estate,* which is distinguished from any income earned by it. If the trust is created while the donor is living, it is called a *living trust* or INTER VIVOS TRUST. A trust created by a will is called a TESTAMENTARY TRUST. The trustee is usually charged with investing trust property productively and, unless specifically limited, can sell, mortgage, or lease the property as he or she deems warranted. *See also* CHARITABLE REMAINDER TRUST; CLIFFORD TRUST; INVESTMENT TRUST; REVISIONARY TRUST; TRUST COMPANY; TRUSTEE IN BANKRUPTCY; TRUST INDENTURE ACT OF 1939.

TRUST COMPANY organization, usually combined with a commercial bank, which is engaged as a trustee, FIDUCIARY, or AGENT for individuals or businesses in the administration of TRUST funds, estates, custodial arrangements, stock transfer and registration, and other related services. Trust companies also engage in fiduciary investment management functions and estate planning. They are regulated by state law.

TRUSTEE *see* TRUST.

TRUSTEE IN BANKRUPTCY trustee appointed by a U.S. district court or by creditors to administer the affairs of a bankrupt company or individual. Under Chapter 7 of the U.S. BANKRUPTCY Code, the trustee has the responsibility for liquidating the property of the company and making distributions of liquidating dividends to creditors. Under the Chapter 11 provision, which provides for REORGANIZATION, a trustee may or may not be appointed. If one is, the trustee is responsible for seeing that a reorganization plan is filed and often assumes responsibility for the company.

TRUST INDENTURE ACT OF 1939 federal law requiring all corporate bonds and other debt securities to be issued under an INDENTURE agreement approved by the SECURITIES AND EXCHANGE COMMISSION (SEC) and providing for the appointment of a qualified trustee free of conflict of interest with the issuer. The Act provides that indentures contain protective clauses for bondholders, that bondholders receive semiannual financial reports, that periodic filings be made with the SEC showing compliance with indenture provisions, and that the issuer be liable for misleading statements. Securities exempted from regulation under the SECURITIES ACT OF 1933 are also exempted from the Trust Indenture Act, but some securities not requiring registration under the 1933 Act do fall under the provisions of the Trust Indenture Act, such as bonds issued in REORGANIZATION or RECAPITALIZATION.

TRUTH IN LENDING LAW legislation stipulating that lenders must disclose to borrowers the true cost of loans and make the interest rate and terms of the loan simple to understand. *See also* CONSUMER CREDIT PROTECTION ACT OF 1968; RIGHT OF RESCISSION.

TURKEY disappointing investment. The term may be used with reference to a business deal that went awry, or to the purchase of a stock or bond that dropped in value sharply, or to a new securities issue that did not sell well or had to be sold at a loss.

TURNAROUND favorable reversal in the fortunes of a company, a market, or the economy at large. Stock market investors speculating that a poorly performing company is about to show a marked improvement in earnings might profit handsomely from its turnaround.

TURNKEY any project constructed or manufactured by a company that ultimately turns it over in finished form to the company that will use it, so that all the user has to do is turn the key, so to speak, and the project is underway. The term is used of housing projects that, after construction, are turned over to property managers. There are also turnkey computer systems, for which the user needs no special computer knowledge and which can therefore be put right to work once they are installed.

TURNOVER
Finance:
1. number of times a given asset is replaced during an accounting period, usually a year. *See also* ACCOUNTS RECEIVABLE TURNOVER; INVENTORY TAKEOVER.
2. ratio of annual sales of a company to its NET WORTH, measuring the extent to which a company can grow without additional capital investment when compared over a period. *See also* CAPITAL TURNOVER.

Great Britain: annual sales volume.

Industrial relations: total employment divided by the number of employees replaced during a given period.

Securities: volume of shares traded as a percentage of total shares listed on an exchange during a period, usually either a day or a year. The same ratio is applied to individual securities and the portfolios of individual or institutional investors.

12b-1 MUTUAL FUND MUTUAL FUND that assesses shareholders for some of its promotion expenses. These funds are usually no-load, so no brokers are involved in the sale to the public. Instead, the funds normally rely on advertising and public relations to build their assets. The charge usually amounts to about 1% or less of a fund's assets. A 12b-1 fund must be specifically registered as such with the Securities and Exchange Commission, and the fact that such charges are levied must be disclosed. *See also* NO-LOAD FUND.

TWENTY-DAY PERIOD period required by the Securities and Exchange Commission (SEC) after filing of the REGISTRATION STATEMENT and PRELIMINARY PROSPECTUS in a NEW ISSUE or SECONDARY DISTRIBUTION during which they are reviewed and, if necessary, modified. The end of the twenty-day period—also called the COOLING-OFF PERIOD—marks the EFFECTIVE DATE when the issue may be offered to the public. The period may be extended by the SEC if more time is needed to respond to a DEFICIENCY LETTER.

TWENTY-FIVE PERCENT RULE MUNICIPAL BOND analyst's guideline that bonded debt over 25% of a municipality's annual budget is excessive.

TWENTY-PERCENT CUSHION RULE guideline used by analysts of MUNICIPAL REVENUE BONDS that estimated revenues from the financed facility should exceed the operating budget plus maintenance costs and DEBT SERVICE by a 20% margin or "cushion" to allow for unanticipated expenses or error in estimating revenues.

TWISTING unethical practice of convincing a customer to trade unnecessarily, thereby generating a commission for the broker or salesperson. For example, a broker may induce a customer to sell one mutual fund with a sales charge in order to buy another fund, also with a sales charge, thereby generating a commission. Also called CHURNING.

TWO-DOLLAR BROKER *see* INDEPENDENT BROKER.

200 PERCENT DECLINING BALANCE METHOD *see* DOUBLE DECLINING-BALANCE DEPRECIATION METHOD (DDB).

TWO-SIDED MARKET market in which both the BID AND ASKED sides are firm, such as that which a SPECIALIST and others who MAKE A MARKET are required to maintain. In a two-sided market, both buyers and sellers are assured of their ability to complete transactions. Also called *two-way market.*

TWO-TIER BID TAKEOVER bid where the acquirer offers to pay more for the shares needed to gain control than for the remaining shares; contrasts with ANY-AND-ALL BID.

U

ULTRA VIRES ACTIVITIES actions of a corporation that are not authorized by its charter and that may therefore lead to shareholder or third-party suits. *See also* ARTICLES OF INCORPORATION.

UNAMORTIZED BOND DISCOUNT difference between the FACE VALUE (par value) of a bond and the proceeds received from the sale of the bond by the issuing company, less whatever portion has been amortized, that is, written off to expense as recorded periodically on the PROFIT AND LOSS STATEMENT. At the time of issue, a company has two alternatives: (1) it can immediately absorb as an expense the amount of discount plus costs related to the issue, such as legal, printing, REGISTRATION, and other similar expenses, or (2) it can decide to treat the total discount and expenses as a DEFERRED CHARGE, recorded as an ASSET to be written off over the life of the bonds or by any other schedule the company finds desirable. The amount still to be expensed at any point is the unamortized bond discount.

UNAMORTIZED PREMIUMS ON INVESTMENTS unexpensed portion of the amount by which the price paid for a security exceeded its PAR value (if a BOND or PREFERRED STOCK) or MARKET VALUE (if common stock). A PREMIUM paid in acquiring an investment is in the nature of an INTANGIBLE ASSET, and conservative accounting practice dictates it be written off to expense over an appropriate period. *See also* GOING-CONCERN VALUE.

UNCOLLECTED FUNDS portion of bank deposit made up of checks that have not yet been collected by the depository bank—that is, payment has not yet been acknowledged by the bank on which a check was drawn. A bank will usually not let a depositor draw on uncollected funds. *See also* FLOAT.

UNCOVERED OPTION OPTION contract for which the owner does not hold the underlying investment (should delivery on the option be required). *See also* NAKED OPTION; UNDERLYING FUTURES CONTRACT; UNDERLYING SECURITY; WRITING NAKED.

UNDERBANKED said of a NEW ISSUE underwriting when the originating INVESTMENT BANKER is having difficulty getting other firms to become members of the UNDER-WRITING GROUP, or syndicate. *See also* UNDERWRITE.

UNDERBOOKED said of a NEW ISSUE of securities during the preoffering REGISTRATION period when brokers canvassing lists of prospective buyers report limited INDICATIONS OF INTEREST. The opposite of underbooked would be *fully circled*. *See also* CIRCLE.

UNDERCAPITALIZATION situation in which a business does not have enough capital to carry out its normal business functions. *See also* CAPITALIZATION; WORKING CAPITAL.

UNDERLYING DEBT MUNICIPAL BOND term referring to the debt of government entities within the jurisdiction of larger government entities and for which the larger entity has partial credit responsibility. For example, a township might share responsibility for the general obligations of a village within the township, the debt of the village being underlying debt from the township's standpoint. The term OVERLAPPING DEBT is also used to describe underlying debt, but overlapping debt can also exist with entities of equal rank where, for example, a school district crosses boundaries of two or more townships.

UNDERLYING FUTURES CONTRACT FUTURES CONTRACT that underlies an OPTION on that future. For example, the Chicago Board of Trade offers a U.S. Treasury bond futures option. The underlying future is the Treasury bond futures contract traded on the Board of Trade. If the option contract were exercised, delivery would be made in the underlying futures contract.

UNDERLYING SECURITY
   Options: security that must be delivered if a PUT OPTION or CALL OPTION contract is exercised. Stock INDEX OPTIONS and STOCK INDEX FUTURES, however, are settled in cash, since it is not possible to deliver an index of stocks.
   Securities: common stock that underlies certain types of securities issued by corporations. This stock must be delivered if a SUBSCRIPTION WARRANT or SUBSCRIPTION RIGHT is exercised, if a CONVERTIBLE bond or PREFERRED STOCK is converted into common shares, or if an INCENTIVE STOCK OPTION is exercised.

UNDERMARGINED ACCOUNT MARGIN ACCOUNT that has fallen below MARGIN REQUIREMENTS or MINIMUM MAINTENANCE requirements. As a result, the broker must make a MARGIN CALL to the customer.

UNDERVALUED security selling below its LIQUIDATION value or the MARKET VALUE analysts believe it deserves. A company's stock may be undervalued because the industry is out of favor, because the company is not well known or has an erratic history of earnings, or for many other reasons. Fundamental analysts try to spot companies that are undervalued so their clients can buy before the stocks become FULLY VALUED. Undervalued companies are also frequently targets of TAKEOVER attempts, since acquirers can buy assets cheaply this way. *See also* FUNDAMENTAL ANALYSIS.

UNDERWRITE

Insurance: to assume risk in exchange for a PREMIUM.

Investments: to assume the risk of buying a NEW ISSUE of securities from the issuing corporation or government entity and reselling them to the public, either directly or through dealers. The UNDERWRITER makes a profit on the difference between the price paid to the issuer and the PUBLIC OFFERING PRICE, called the UNDERWRITING SPREAD.

Underwriting is the business of investment bankers, who usually form an UNDERWRITING GROUP (also called a PURCHASE GROUP or syndicate) to pool the risk and assure successful distribution of the issue. The syndicate operates under an AGREEMENT AMONG UNDERWRITERS, also termed a *syndicate contract* or PURCHASE GROUP contract.

The underwriting group appoints a MANAGING UNDERWRITER, also known as *lead underwriter, syndicate manager,* or simply *manager,* that is usually the *originating investment banker*—the firm that began working with the issuer months before to plan details of the issue and prepare the REGISTRATION materials to be filed with the SECURITIES AND EXCHANGE COMMISSION. The manager, acting as agent for the group, signs the UNDERWRITING AGREEMENT (or *purchase contract*) with the issuer. This agreement sets forth the terms and conditions of the arrangement and the responsibilities of both issuer and underwriter. During the offering period, it is the manager's responsibility to stabilize the MARKET PRICE of the issuer's shares by bidding in the open market, a process called PEGGING. The manager may also appoint a SELLING GROUP, comprised of dealers and the underwriters themselves, to assist in DISTRIBUTION of the issue.

Strictly speaking, *underwrite* is properly used only in a FIRM COMMITMENT underwriting, also known as a BOUGHT DEAL, where the securities are purchased outright from the issuer.

Other investment banking arrangements to which the term is sometimes loosely applied are BEST EFFORT, ALL OR NONE, and STANDBY COMMITMENTS; in each of these, the risk is shared between the issuer and the INVESTMENT BANKER.

The term is also sometimes used in connection with a REGISTERED SECONDARY OFFERING, which involves essentially the same process as a new issue, except that the proceeds go to the selling investor, not to the issuer. For these arrangements, the term *secondary offering* or SECONDARY DISTRIBUTION is preferable to *underwriting,* which is usually reserved for new, or primary, distributions.

There are two basic methods by which underwriters are chosen by issuers and underwriting spreads are determined: NEGOTIATED UNDERWRITINGS and COMPETITIVE BID underwritings. Generally, the negotiated method is used in corporate equity (stock) issues and most corporate debt (bond) issues, whereas the competitive bidding method is used by municipalities and public utilities.

See also ALLOTMENT; BLOWOUT; FLOATING AN ISSUE; FLOTATION COST; HOT ISSUE; INITIAL PUBLIC OFFERING; PRESOLD ISSUE; PRIMARY MARKET; PUBLIC OFFERING; STANDBY UNDERWRITER.

UNDERWRITER

Insurance: company that assumes the cost risk of death, fire, theft, illness, etc., in exchange for payments, called *premiums*.

Securities: INVESTMENT BANKER who, singly or as a member of an UNDERWRITING GROUP or syndicate, agrees to purchase a NEW ISSUE of securities from an issuer and distribute it to investors, making a profit on the UNDERWRITING SPREAD. *See also* UNDERWRITE.

UNDERWRITING AGREEMENT agreement between a corporation issuing new securities to be offered to the public and the MANAGING UNDERWRITER as agent for the UNDERWRITING GROUP. Also termed the *purchase agreement* or *purchase contract*, it represents the underwriters' commitment to purchase the securities, and it details the PUBLIC OFFERING PRICE, the UNDERWRITING SPREAD (including all discounts and commissions), the net proceeds to the issuer, and the SETTLEMENT DATE.

The issuer agrees to pay all expenses incurred in preparing the issue for resale, including the costs of REGISTRATION with the SECURITIES AND EXCHANGE COMMISSION (SEC) and of the PROSPECTUS, and agrees to supply the managing underwriter with sufficient copies of both the PRELIMINARY PROSPECTUS (red herring) and the final, statutory prospectus. The issuer guarantees (1) to make all required SEC filings and to comply fully with the provisions of the SECURITIES ACT OF 1933; (2) to assume responsibility for the completeness, accuracy, and proper certification of all information in the registration statement and prospectus; (3) to disclose all pending litigation; (4) to use the proceeds for the purposes stated; (5) to comply with state securities laws; (6) to work to get listed on the exchange agreed upon; and (7) to indemnify the underwriters for liability arising out of omissions or misrepresentations for which the issuer had responsibility.

The underwriters agree to proceed with the offering as soon as the registration is cleared by the SEC or at a specified date thereafter. The underwriters are authorized to make sales to members of a SELLING GROUP.

The underwriting agreement is not to be confused with the AGREEMENT AMONG UNDERWRITERS. *See also* BEST EFFORT; FIRM COMMITMENT; STANDBY COMMITMENT; UNDERWRITE.

UNDERWRITING GROUP temporary association of investment bankers, organized by the originating INVESTMENT BANKER in a NEW ISSUE of securities. Operating under an AGREEMENT AMONG UNDERWRITERS, it agrees to purchase securities from the issuing corporation at an agreed-upon price and to resell them at a PUBLIC OFFERING PRICE, the difference representing the UNDERWRITING SPREAD. The purpose of the underwriting group is to spread the risk and assure successful distribution of the offering. Most underwriting groups operate under a *divided syndicate contract*, meaning that the liability of members is limited to their individual participations. Also called DISTRIBUTING SYNDICATE, PURCHASE GROUP, *investment banking group*, or *syndicate*. *See also* FIRM COMMITMENT; UNDERWRITE; UNDERWRITING AGREEMENT.

UNDERWRITING SPREAD difference between the amount paid to an issuer of securities in a PRIMARY DISTRIBUTION and the PUBLIC OFFERING PRICE. The amount of SPREAD varies widely, depending on the size of the issue, the financial strength of the issuer, the type of security involved (stock, bonds, rights), the status of the security (senior, junior, secured, unsecured), and the type of commitment made by the investment bankers. The range may be from a fraction of 1% for a bond issue of a big utility company to 25% for the INITIAL PUBLIC OFFERING of a small company. The division of the spread between the MANAGING UNDERWRITER, the SELLING GROUP, and the participating underwriters also varies, but in a two-point spread the manager might typically get 0.25%, the selling group 1%, and the underwriters 0.75%. It is usual, though, for the underwriters also to be members of the selling group, thus picking up 1.75% of the spread, and for the manager to be in all three categories, thus picking up the full 2%. See also COMPETITIVE BID; FLOTATION COST; GROSS SPREAD; NEGOTIATED UNDERWRITING; SELLING CONCESSION; UNDERWRITE.

UNDIGESTED SECURITIES newly issued stocks and bonds that remain undistributed because there is insufficient public demand at the OFFERING PRICE. See also UNDERWRITE.

UNDISTRIBUTED PROFITS (EARNINGS, NET INCOME) see RETAINED EARNINGS.

UNDIVIDED PROFITS account shown on a bank's BALANCE SHEET representing profits that have neither been paid out as DIVIDENDS nor transferred to the bank's SURPLUS account. Current earnings are credited to the undivided profits account and are then either paid out in dividends or retained to build up total EQUITY. As the account grows, round amounts may be periodically transferred to the surplus account.

UNEARNED DISCOUNT account on the books of a lending institution recognizing interest deducted in advance and which will be taken into income as earned over the life of the loan. In accordance with accounting principles, such interest is initially recorded as a LIABILITY. Then, as months pass and it is gradually "earned," it is recognized as income, thus increasing the lender's profit and decreasing the corresponding liability. See also UNEARNED INCOME.

UNEARNED INCOME (REVENUE)

Accounting: income received but not yet earned, such as rent received in advance or other advances from customers. Unearned income is usually classified as a CURRENT LIABILITY on a company's BALANCE SHEET, assuming that it will be credited to income within the normal accounting cycle. See also DEFERRED CHARGE.

Income taxes: income from sources other than wages, salaries, tips, and other employee compensation—for example, DIVIDENDS, INTEREST, rent.

UNEARNED INTEREST interest that has already been collected on a loan by a financial institution, but that cannot yet be counted as part of earnings because the principal of the loan has not been outstanding long enough. Also called DISCOUNT and UNEARNED DISCOUNT.

UNENCUMBERED property free and clear of all liens (creditors' claims). When a homeowner pays off his mortgage, for example, the house becomes unencumbered property. Securities bought with cash instead of on MARGIN are unencumbered.

UNIFIED CREDIT federal TAX CREDIT that may be applied against the gift tax, the estate tax, and, under specified conditions, the generation-skipping transfer tax.

UNIFORM GIFTS TO MINORS ACT (UGMA) law adopted by most U.S. states that sets up rules for the distribution and administration of assets in the name of a child. The Act provides for a CUSTODIAN of the assets, often the parents, but sometimes an independent TRUSTEE. When minors reach majority, custodial accounts become the child's property unless other arrangements have been specified. The practice of shifting income to a minor's account to gain lower income-tax rates was curtailed by the TAX REFORM ACT OF 1986, which made unearned income over $1000 to a child under 14 years old subject to taxation at the grantor's rate.

UNIFORM PRACTICE CODE rules of the NATIONAL ASSOCIATION OF SECURITIES DEALERS (NASD) concerned with standards and procedures for the operational handling of OVER THE COUNTER securities transactions, such as delivery, SETTLEMENT DATE, EX-DIVIDEND DATE, and other ex-dates (such as EX-RIGHTS and EX-WARRANTS), and providing for the arbitration of disputes through Uniform Practice committees.

UNIFORM SECURITIES AGENT STATE LAW EXAMINATION test required of prospective REGISTERED REPRESENTATIVES in many U.S. states. In addition to the examination requirements of states, all registered representatives, whether employees of member firms or OVER THE COUNTER brokers, must pass the General Securities Representative Examination (also known as the Series 7 Examination), administered by the National Association of Securities Dealers (NASD).

UNISSUED STOCK shares of a corporation's stock authorized in its charter but not issued. They are shown on the BALANCE SHEET along with shares ISSUED AND OUTSTANDING. Unissued stock may be issued by action of the board of directors, although shares needed for unexercised employee STOCK OPTIONS, rights, warrants, or convertible securities must not be issued while such obligations are outstanding. Unissued shares cannot pay dividends and cannot be voted. They are not to be confused with TREASURY STOCK, which is issued but not outstanding.

UNIT

In general: any division of quantity accepted as a standard of measurement or of exchange. For example, in the commodities markets, a unit of wheat is a bushel, a unit of coffee a pound, and a unit of shell eggs a dozen. The unit of U.S. currency is the dollar.

Banking: bank operating out of only one office, and with no branches, as required by states having unit banking laws.

Finance:
1. segment or subdivision (division or subsidiary, product line, or plant) of a company.
2. in sales or production, quantity rather than dollars. One might say, for example, "Unit volume declined but dollar volume increased after prices were raised."

Securities:
1. minimum amount of stocks, bonds, commodities, or other securities accepted for trading on an exchange. *See also* ODD LOT; ROUND LOT; UNIT OF TRADING.
2. group of specialists on a stock exchange, who maintain fair and orderly mar-

kets in particular securities. *See also* SPECIALIST; SPECIALIST UNIT.
3. more than one class of securities traded together; one common share and one SUBSCRIPTION WARRANT might sell as a unit, for example.
4. in primary and secondary distributions of securities, one share of stock or one bond.

UNITED STATES GOVERNMENT SECURITIES direct GOVERNMENT OBLI-GATIONS—that is, debt issues of the U.S. government, such as Treasury bills, notes, and bonds and Series EE and Series HH SAVINGS BONDS as distinguished from government-sponsored AGENCY issues. *See also* GOVERNMENT SECURITIES; TREASURIES.

UNIT INVESTMENT TRUST investment vehicle, registered with the SECURITIES AND EXCHANGE COMMISSION under the INVESTMENT COMPANY ACT OF 1940, that purchases a fixed PORTFOLIO of income-producing securities, such as corporate, municipal, or government bonds, mortgage-backed securities, or PREFERRED STOCK. Units in the trust, which usually cost at least $1000, are sold to investors by brokers, for a LOAD charge of about 4%. Unit holders receive an undivided interest in both the principal and the income portion of the portfolio in proportion to the amount of capital they invest. The portfolio of securities remains fixed until all the securities mature and unit holders have recovered their principal. Most brokerage firms maintain a SECONDARY MARKET in the trusts they sell, so that units can be resold if necessary.
    In Britain, open-end mutual funds are called *unit trusts*.
    See also INVESTMENT COMPANY; MORTGAGE-BACKED CERTIFICATE; UNIT SHARE INVESTMENT TRUST.

UNIT OF TRADING normal number of shares, bonds, or commodities comprising the minimum unit of trading on an exchange. For stocks, this is usually 100 shares, although inactive shares trade in 10-share units. For corporate bonds on the NYSE, the unit for exchange trading is $1000 or $5000 par value. Commodities futures units vary widely, according to the COMMODITY involved. *See also* FUTURES CONTRACT; ODD LOT; ROUND LOT.

UNIT SHARE INVESTMENT TRUST (USIT) specialized form of UNIT INVESTMENT TRUST comprising one unit of PRIME and one unit of SCORE.

UNIVERSAL LIFE INSURANCE form of life insurance, first marketed in the early 1980s, that combines the low-cost protection of TERM LIFE INSURANCE with a savings portion, which is invested in a tax-deferred account earning money-market rates of interest. The policy is flexible; that is, as age and income change, a policyholder can increase or decrease premium payments and coverage, or shift a certain portion of premiums into the savings account, without additional sales charges or complications. A new form of the policy; called *universal variable life insurance*, combines the flexibility of universal life with the growth potential of variable life. *See also* VARIABLE LIFE INSURANCE; WHOLE LIFE INSURANCE.

UNLEVERAGED PROGRAM LIMITED PARTNERSHIP whose use of borrowed funds to finance the acquisition of properties is 50% or less of the purchase price. In contrast, a *leveraged program* borrows 50% or more. Investors seeking to maximize income tend to favor unleveraged partnerships, where interest expense and other deductions from income are at a minimum. Investors looking for TAX SHEL-TERS favor leveraged programs despite the higher risk because of the larger DE-

PRECIATION writeoffs on the greater amount of property acquired with the borrowed money and the greater amount of tax deductible interest.

UNLIMITED TAX BOND MUNICIPAL BOND secured by the pledge to levy taxes at an unlimited rate until the bond is repaid.

UNLISTED SECURITY security that is not listed on an organized exchange, such as the NEW YORK STOCK EXCHANGE, the AMERICAN STOCK EXCHANGE, or the REGIONAL STOCK EXCHANGES, and is traded in the OVER THE COUNTER market.

UNLISTED TRADING trading of securities not listed on an organized exchange but traded on that exchange as an accommodation to its members. An exchange wishing to trade unlisted securities must file an application with the SECURITIES AND EXCHANGE COMMISSION and make the necessary information available to the investing public. The New York Stock Exchange does not allow unlisted trading privileges, and the practice has declined at the American Stock Exchange and other organized exchanges.

UNLOADING

Finance: selling off large quantities of merchandise inventory at below-market prices either to raise cash quickly or to depress the market in a particular product.

Investments: selling securities or commodities when prices are declining to preclude further loss.

See also DUMP; PROFIT TAKING; SELLING OFF.

UNPAID DIVIDEND dividend that has been declared by the board of directors of a corporation but has not reached its PAYMENT DATE. Once a board acts to DECLARE a dividend, it is then recognized as a corporate LIABILITY until paid.

UNREALIZED PROFIT (OR LOSS) profit or loss that has not become actual. It becomes a REALIZED PROFIT (OR LOSS) when the security or commodity future contract in which there is a gain or loss is actually sold. Also called a *paper profit or loss.*

UNREGISTERED STOCK *see* LETTER SECURITY.

UNSECURED DEBT obligation not backed by the pledge of specific COLLATERAL.

UNWIND A TRADE to reverse a securities transaction through an offsetting transaction. *See also* OFFSET.

UPSET PRICE term used in auctions that represents the minimum price at which a seller of property will entertain bids.

UPSIDE POTENTIAL amount of upward price movement an investor or an analyst expects of a particular stock, bond, or commodity. This opinion may result from either FUNDAMENTAL ANALYSIS or TECHNICAL ANALYSIS.

UPSTAIRS MARKET transaction completed within the broker-dealer's firm and without using the stock exchange. Securities and Exchange Commission and stock exchange rules exist to ensure that such trades do not occur at prices less favorable to the customer than those prevailing in the general market. *See also* OFF BOARD.

UPTICK transaction executed at a price higher than the preceding transaction in that security; also called PLUS TICK. A plus sign is displayed throughout the day next to the last price of each stock that showed a higher price than the preceding transaction in that stock at the TRADING POST of the SPECIALIST on the floor of the New York Stock Exchange. Short sales may only be executed on upticks or ZERO-PLUS TICKS. *See also* MINUS TICK; SELLING SHORT; TICK.

UPTREND upward direction in the price of a stock, bond, or commodity future contract or overall market. *See also* TRENDLINE.

UTILITY REVENUE BOND MUNICIPAL BOND issued to finance the construction of electric generating plants, gas, water and sewer systems, among other types of public utility services. These bonds are repaid from the revenues the project produces once it is operating. Such bonds usually have a reserve fund that contains an amount equal to one year's DEBT SERVICE, which protects bondholders in case there is a temporary cash shortage or revenues are less than anticipated. *See also* REVENUE BOND.

V

VALUATION RESERVE reserve or allowance, created by a charge to expenses (and therefore, in effect, taken out of profits) in order to provide for changes in the value of a company's assets. Accumulated DEPRECIATION, allowance for BAD DEBTS, and UNAMORTIZED BOND DISCOUNT are three familiar examples of valuation reserves. Also called *valuation account.*

VALUE-ADDED TAX (VAT) consumption tax levied on the value added to a product at each stage of its manufacturing cycle as well as at the time of purchase by the ultimate consumer. The value-added tax is a fixture in European countries and a major source of revenue for the European Common Market. Advocates of a value-added tax for the U.S. contend that it would be the most efficient method of raising revenue and that the size of its receipts would permit a reduction in income tax rates. Opponents argue that in its pure form it would be the equivalent of a national sales tax and therefore unfair and regressive, putting the greatest burden on those who can least afford it. As an example, for each part that goes into the assembling of an automobile, the auto manufacturer would pay a value-added tax to the supplier, probably a percentage of the purchase price, as is the case with a sales tax. When the finished car is sold, the consumer pays a value-added tax on the cost of the finished product less the material and supply costs that were taxed at earlier stages. This avoids double taxation and thus differs from a flat sales tax based on the total cost of purchase.

VALUE BROKER DISCOUNT BROKER whose rates are based on a percentage of the dollar value of each transaction. It is usually advantageous to place orders through a value broker for trades of low-priced shares or small numbers of shares, since commissions will be relatively smaller than if a shareholder used a SHARE BROKER, another type of discount broker, who charges according to the number and the price of the shares traded.

VALUE CHANGE change in a stock price adjusted for the number of outstanding shares of that stock, so that a group of stocks adjusted this way are equally weighted. A unit of movement of the group—called an INDEX—is thus representative of the average performance.

VALUE DATE
Banking: official date when money is transferred, that is, becomes good funds to the depositor. The value date differs from the *entry date* when items are received from the depositor, since the items must then be forwarded to the paying bank or otherwise collected. The term is used mainly with reference to foreign accounts, either maintained in a domestic bank or maintained by a domestic bank in foreign banks. *See also* FLOAT.

Eurodollar and foreign currency transactions: synonymous with SETTLEMENT DATE or DELIVERY DATE, which on spot transactions involving North American currencies (U.S. dollar, Canadian dollar, and Mexican peso) is one business day and on spot transactions involving other currencies, two business days. In the forward exchange market, value date is the maturity date of the contract plus one business day for North American currencies, two business days for other currencies. *See also* FORWARD EXCHANGE TRANSACTION; SPOT MARKET.

VALUE LINE INVESTMENT SURVEY investment advisory service that ranks hundreds of stocks for "timeliness" and safety. Using a computerized model based on a company's earnings momentum, Value Line projects which stocks will have the best or worst relative price performance over the next 12 months. In addition, each stock is assigned a risk rating, which identifies the VOLATILITY of a stock's price behavior relative to the market average. The service also ranks all major industry groups for timeliness. Value Line's ranking system for both timeliness and safety of individual stock is as follows:
1—highest rank
2—above average rank
3—average rank
4—below average rank
5—lowest rank
The weekly writeups of companies that Value Line subscribers receive include detailed financial information about a company, as well as such data as corporate INSIDER buying and selling decisions and the percentage of a company's shares held by institutions.

VA MORTGAGE *see* VETERANS ADMINISTRATION (VA) MORTGAGE.

VARIABLE ANNUITY life insurance ANNUITY contract whose value fluctuates with that of an underlying securities PORTFOLIO or other INDEX of performance. The variable annuity contrasts with a conventional or FIXED ANNUITY, whose rate of return is constant and therefore vulnerable to the effects of inflation. Income on a variable annuity may be taken periodically, beginning immediately or at any future time. The annuity may be a single-premium or multiple-premium contract. The return to investors may be in the form of a periodic payment that varies with the MARKET VALUE of the portfolio or a fixed minimum payment with add-ons based on the rate of portfolio appreciation. *See also* SINGLE PREMIUM DEFERRED ANNUITY.

VARIABLE COST cost that changes directly with the amount of production—for example, direct material or direct labor needed to complete a product. *See also* FIXED COST.

VARIABLE LIFE INSURANCE innovation in WHOLE LIFE INSURANCE that gives policyholders the opportunity to earn substantial CAPITAL GAINS on their insurance investment. As the inflation and high interest rates of the 1970s and early 80s made the rates of return on whole life policies uncompetitive, insurance companies began to underwrite a variable life policy that allows the cash value of the policy to be invested in stock, bond, or money market portfolios. Investors can elect to move from one portfolio to another or can rely on the company's professional money managers to make such decisions for them. As in whole life insurance, the annual premium is fixed, but part of it is earmarked for the investment PORTFOLIO. The policyholder bears the risk of securities investments, while the insurance company guarantees a minimum death benefit unaffected by any portfolio losses. When portfolio investments rise substantially, a portion of the increased cash value is put into additional insurance coverage. As in usual whole life policies, borrowings can be made against the accumulated cash value, or the policy can be cashed in. As in an INDIVIDUAL RETIREMENT ACCOUNT, earnings from variable life policies are tax deferred until distributed. Income is then taxed only to the extent that it exceeds the total premiums paid into the policy. Death benefits are taxed not as individual income but as taxable estate income, which has an exclusion rising to $600,000 in 1987.

Variable life insurance is different from UNIVERSAL LIFE INSURANCE. Universal life allows policyholders to increase or decrease premiums and change the death benefit. It also accrues interest at market-related rates on premiums over and above insurance charges and expenses.

VARIABLE-RATE DEMAND NOTE note representing borrowings (usually from a commercial bank) that is payable on demand and that bears interest tied to a money market rate, usually the bank PRIME RATE. The rate on the note is adjusted upward or downward each time the base rate changes.

VARIABLE RATE MORTGAGE (VRM) home mortgage loan with an interest rate that varies with money market rates or the lending institution's cost of funds. The VRM—also called ADJUSTABLE RATE MORTGAGE—grew out of a depressed mortgage market caused by record high interest rates in the late 1970s and reached a peak of popularity from 1980 to 1984 with lenders offering initial below-market rates. As rates began to fall in 1984, the popularity of the VRM began to wane and the fixed-rate mortgage, now affordable, again became attractive to home-buyers who placed a value on its predictability.

The VRM is not to be confused with a GRADUATED PAYMENT MORTGAGE, which is issued at a fixed rate with monthly payments designed to increase as the borrower's income grows.

VARIANCE

Accounting: difference between actual cost and STANDARD COST in the categories of direct material, direct labor, and DIRECT OVERHEAD. A positive variation (when the actual cost is lower than the standard or anticipated cost) would translate into a higher profit unless offset by negative variances elsewhere.

Finance:
1. difference between corresponding items on a comparative BALANCE SHEET and PROFIT AND LOSS STATEMENT.
2. difference between actual experience and budgeted or projected experience in any financial category. For example, if sales were projected to be $2 million for a period and were actually $2.5 million, there would be a positive variance of $500,000, or 25%.

Statistics: measure of the dispersion of a distribution. It is the sum of the squares of the deviations from the mean. *See also* STANDARD DEVIATION.

VELOCITY rate of spending, or turnover of money—in other words, how many times a dollar is spent in a given period of time. The concept of ''income velocity of money'' was first explained by the economist Irving Fisher in the 1920s as bearing a direct relationship to GROSS NATIONAL PRODUCT (GNP). GNP is the product of total MONEY SUPPLY and its velocity measure. Velocity affects the amount of economic activity generated by a given money supply, which includes bank deposits and cash in circulation. Velocity is a factor in the Federal Reserve Board's management of MONETARY POLICY, because an increase in velocity may obviate the need for a stimulative increase in the money supply. Conversely, a decline in velocity might dampen economic growth, even if the money supply holds steady. An increase in income velocity since World War II has been partly attributed to active cash management by corporations using electronic technology to move funds rapidly in and out of various bank accounts and investment vehicles. *See also* FISCAL POLICY.

VENDOR
1. supplier of goods or services of a commercial nature; may be a manufacturer, importer, or wholesale distributor. For example, one component of the Index of LEADING INDICATORS is vendor performance, meaning the rate at which suppliers of goods are making delivery to their commercial customers.
2. retailer of merchandise, especially one without an established place of business, as in *sidewalk vendor*.

VENTURE CAPITAL important source of financing for START-UP companies or others embarking on new or TURNAROUND ventures that entail some investment risk but offer the potential for above average future profits; also called *risk capital*. Prominent among firms seeking venture capital in the 1980s are those classified as emerging-growth or high-technology companies. Sources of venture capital include wealthy individual investors; subsidiaries of banks and other corporations organized as small business investment companies (SBICs); groups of investment banks and other financing sources who pool investments in venture capital funds or VENTURE CAPITAL LIMITED PARTNERSHIPS. The SMALL BUSINESS ADMINISTRATION (SBA) promotes venture capital programs through the licensing and financing of SBICs. Venture capital financing supplements other personal or external funds that an ENTREPRENEUR is able to tap, or takes the place of loans of other funds that conventional financial institutions are unable or unwilling to risk. Some venture capital sources invest only at a certain stage of entrepreneurship, such as the start-up or SEED MONEY stage, the *first round* or SECOND ROUND phases that follow, or at the MEZZANINE LEVEL immediately preceding an INITIAL PUBLIC OFFERING. In return for taking an investment risk, venture capitalists are usually rewarded with some combination of PROFITS, PREFERRED STOCK, ROYALTIES on sales, and capital appreciation of common shares.

VENTURE CAPITAL LIMITED PARTNERSHIP investment vehicle organized by a brokerage firm or entrepreneurial company to raise capital for START-UP companies or those in the early processes of developing products and services. The partnership will usually take shares of stock in the company in return for capital supplied. Limited partners receive income from profits the company may earn. If the company is successful and goes public, limited partners' profits could be realized from the sale of formerly private stock to the public. This type of partnership differs from a RESEARCH AND DEVELOPMENT LIMITED PARTNERSHIP in that R&D deals receive revenue only from the particular products they UNDERWRITE, whereas a venture capital partnership participates in the profits of the company, no matter what product or service is sold. *See also* ENTREPRENEUR; LIMITED PARTNERSHIP.

VERTICAL LINE CHARTING form of technical charting on which the high, low, and closing prices of a stock or a market are shown on one vertical line with the closing price indicated by a short horizontal mark. Each vertical line represents another day, and the chart shows the trend of a stock or a market over a period of days, weeks, months, or years. Technical analysts discern from these charts whether a stock or a market is continually closing at the high or low end of its trading range during a day. This is useful in understanding whether the market's action is strong or weak, and therefore whether prices will advance or decline in the near future. *See also* TECHNICAL ANALYSIS.

VERTICAL LINE CHARTING

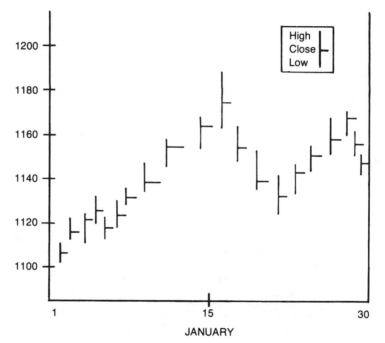

JANUARY

VERTICAL SPREAD OPTION strategy that involves purchasing an option at one STRIKE PRICE while simultaneously selling another option of the same class at the next higher or lower strike price. Both options have the same expiration date. For example, a vertical spread is created by buying an XYZ May 30 call and selling an XYZ May 40 call. The investor who buys a vertical spread hopes to profit as the difference between the option premium on the two option positions widens or narrows. Also called a PRICE SPREAD. *See also* OPTION PREMIUM.

VESTING right an employee gradually acquires by length of service at a company to receive employer-contributed benefits, such as payments from a PENSION FUND, PROFIT-SHARING PLAN, or other QUALIFIED PLAN OR TRUST. Under the TAX REFORM ACT OF 1986, employees must be vested 100% after five years of service or at 20% a year starting in the third year and becoming 100% vested after seven years.

VETERANS ADMINISTRATION (VA) MORTGAGE home mortgage loan granted by a lending institution to qualified veterans of the U.S. armed forces or to their surviving spouses and guaranteed by the VA. The guarantee reduces risk to the lender for all or part of the purchase price on conventional homes, mobile homes, and condominiums. Because of this federal guarantee, banks and thrift institutions can afford to provide 30-year VA mortgages on favorable terms with a relatively low down payment even during periods of TIGHT MONEY. Interest rates on VA mortgages, formerly fixed by the Department of Housing and Urban Development together with those on Federal Housing Administration (FHA) mortgages, are now set by the VA.

VA mortgages comprise an important part of the mortgage pools packaged and sold as securities by such quasi-governmental organizations as the FEDERAL HOME MORTGAGE CORPORATION (Freddie Mac) and the GOVERNMENT NATIONAL MORTGAGE ASSOCIATION (Ginnie Mae).

V FORMATION technical chart pattern that forms a V. The V pattern indicates that the stock, bond, or commodity being charted has bottomed out and is now in a bullish (rising) trend. An upside-down (inverse) V is considered bearish (indicative of a falling market). *See also* BOTTOM; TECHNICAL ANALYSIS.

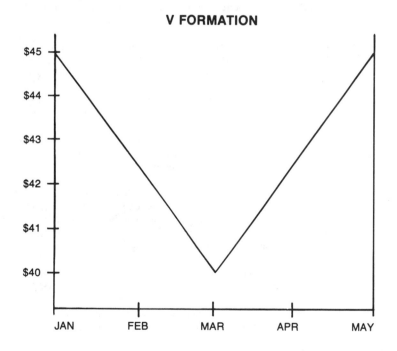

V FORMATION

VOIDABLE contract that can be annulled by either party after it is signed because fraud, incompetence, or another illegality exists or because a RIGHT OF RESCISSION applies.

VOLATILE tending to rapid and extreme fluctuations. The term is used to describe the size and frequency of the fluctuations in the price of a particular stock, bond, or commodity. A stock may be volatile because the outlook for the company is particularly uncertain, because there are only a few shares outstanding (*see also* THIN MARKET), or because of various other reasons. Where the reasons for the variation have to do with the particular security as distinguished from market conditions, return is measured by a concept called ALPHA. A stock with an alpha factor of 1.25 is projected to rise in price by 25% in a year on the strength of its inherent values such as growth in earnings per share and regardless of the performance of the market as a whole. Market-related volatility, also called SYSTEMATIC RISK, is measured by BETA.

VOLATILITY characteristic of a security, commodity, or market to rise or fall sharply in price within a short-term period. A measure of the relative volatility of a stock to the overall market is its BETA. *See also* VOLATILE.

VOLUME total number of stock shares, bonds, or commodities futures contracts traded in a particular period. Volume figures are reported daily by exchanges, both for individual issues trading and for the total amount of trading executed on the exchange. Technical analysts place great emphasis on the amount of volume that occurs in the trading of a security or a commodity futures contract. A sharp rise in volume is believed to signify future sharp rises or falls in price, because it reflects increased investor interest in a security, commodity, or market. *See also* TECHNICAL ANALYSIS; TURNOVER.

VOLUME DELETED note appearing on the CONSOLIDATED TAPE, usually when the tape is running behind by two minutes or more because of heavy trading, that only the STOCK SYMBOL and the trading price will be displayed for transactions of less than 5000 shares.

VOLUNTARY ACCUMULATION PLAN plan subscribed to by a MUTUAL FUND shareholder to accumulate shares in that fund on a regular basis over time. The amount of money to be put into the fund and the intervals at which it is to be invested are at the discretion of the shareholder. A plan that invests a set amount on a regular schedule is a dollar cost averaging plan or CONSTANT DOLLAR PLAN.

VOLUNTARY BANKRUPTCY legal proceeding that follows a petition of BANKRUPTCY filed by a debtor in the appropriate U.S. district court under the Bankruptcy Act. Petitions for voluntary bankruptcy can be filed by any insolvent business or individual except a building and loan association or a municipal, railroad, insurance, or banking corporation.

VOTING STOCK shares in a corporation that entitle the shareholder to voting and PROXY rights. When a shareholder deposits such stock with a CUSTODIAN that acts as a voting TRUST, the shareholder retains rights to earnings and dividends but delegates voting rights to the trustee. *See also* COMMON STOCK; PROPORTIONAL REPRESENTATION; VOTING TRUST CERTIFICATE.

VOTING TRUST CERTIFICATE transferable certificate of beneficial interest in a *voting trust,* a limited-life trust set up to center control of a corporation in the hands of a few individuals, called *voting trustees.* The certificates, which are issued by the voting trust to stockholders in exchange for their common stock, represent all the rights of common stock except voting rights. The common stock is then registered on the books of the corporation in the names of the trustees. The usual purpose for such an arrangement is to facilitate REORGANIZATION of a corporation in financial difficulty by preventing interference with management.

Voting trust certificates are limited to the five-year life of a TRUST but can be extended with the mutual consent of the holders and trustees.

VULTURE FUND type of LIMITED PARTNERSHIP that invests in depressed property, usually real estate, aiming to profit when prices rebound.

W

WAITING PERIOD TWENTY-DAY period required by the SECURITIES AND EXCHANGE COMMISSION between the filing of a REGISTRATION in a securities offering and the time the securities can legally be offered to the investing public. This COOLING-OFF PERIOD may be extended if more time is needed to make corrections or add information to the REGISTRATION STATEMENT and PROSPECTUS.

WALLFLOWER stock that has fallen out of favor with investors. Such stocks tend to have a low PRICE/EARNINGS RATIO.

WALL STREET
1. common name for the financial district at the lower end of Manhattan in New York City, where the New York and American Stock Exchanges and numerous brokerage firms are headquartered. The New York Stock Exchange is actually located at the corner of Wall and Broad Streets.
2. investment community, such as in "Wall Street really likes the prospects for that company" or "Wall Street law firm," meaning a firm specializing in securities law and mergers. Also referred to as "the Street."

WANTED FOR CASH TICKER tape announcement that a bidder will pay cash the same day for a specified block of securities. Cash trades are executed for delivery and settlement at the time the transaction is made.

WAR BABIES jargon for the stocks and bonds of corporations engaged primarily as defense contractors. Also called *war brides*.

WAREHOUSE RECEIPT document listing goods or commodities kept for SAFEKEEPING in a warehouse. The receipt can be used to transfer ownership of that commodity, instead of having to deliver the physical commodity. Warehouse receipts are used with many commodities, particularly precious metals like gold, silver, and platinum, which must be safeguarded against theft.

WARRANT *see* SUBSCRIPTION WARRANT.

WASH SALE purchase and sale of a security either simultaneously or within a short period of time. It may be done by a single investor or (where MANIPULATION is involved) by two or more parties conspiring to create artificial market activity in order to profit from a rise in the security's price. Wash sales taking place within 30 days of the underlying purchase do not qualify as tax losses under Internal Revenue Service rules.

Under the TAX REFORM ACT OF 1984, wash sale rules were extended to all taxpayers except those trading in securities in the normal course of business, such as securities dealers. Prior to the 1984 Act, noncorporate taxpayers engaged in a trade or business were exempt from wash sale rules. The Act also extended the wash sale prohibition to closing short sales of substantially identical securities, or to instances where short sales are made within 30 days of closing.

See also THIRTY-DAY WASH RULE.

WASTING ASSET
1. fixed asset, other than land, that has a limited useful life and is therefore subject to DEPRECIATION.
2. natural resource that diminishes in value because of extractions of oil, ores, or gas, or the removal of timber, or similar depletion and that is therefore subject to AMORTIZATION.
3. security with a value that expires at a particular time in the future. An OPTION contract, for instance, is a wasting asset, because the chances of a favorable move in the underlying stock diminish as the contract approaches expiration, thus reducing the value of the option.

WATCH LIST list of securities singled out for special surveillance by a brokerage firm or an exchange or other self-regulatory organization to spot irregularities. Firms on the watch list may be TAKEOVER candidates, companies about to issue new securities, or others that seem to have attracted an unusually heavy volume of trading activity. *See also* STOCK WATCHER; SURVEILLANCE DEPARTMENT OF EXCHANGES.

WATERED STOCK stock representing ownership of OVERVALUED assets, a condition of overcapitalized corporations, whose total worth is less than their invested capital. The condition may result from inflated accounting values, gifts of stock, operating losses, or excessive stock dividends. Among the negative features of watered stock from the shareholder's standpoint are inability to recoup full investment in LIQUIDATION, inadequate return on investment, possible liability exceeding the PAR value of shares, low MARKET VALUE because of poor dividends and possible adverse publicity, reduced ability of the firm to issue new stock or debt securities to capitalize on growth opportunity, and loss of competitive position because of the need to raise prices to provide a return acceptable to investors. To remedy the situation, a company must either increase its assets without increasing its OUTSTANDING shares or reduce outstanding shares without reducing assets. The alternatives are to increase RETAINED EARNINGS or to adjust the accounting values of assets or of stock.

WEAK MARKET market characterized by a preponderance of sellers over buyers and a general declining trend in prices.

WEDGE technical chart pattern similar to but varying slightly from a TRIANGLE. Two converging lines connect a series of peaks and troughs to form a wedge. These converging lines move in the same direction, unlike a triangle, in which one rises while the other falls or one rises or falls while the other line stays horizontal. Falling wedges usually occur as temporary interruptions of upward price rallies, rising wedges as interruptions of a falling price trend. *See also* TECHNICAL ANALYSIS.

W FORMATION technical chart pattern of the price of a stock, bond, or commodity that shows the price has hit a SUPPORT LEVEL two times and is moving up; also called a *double bottom*.
   A reverse W is just the opposite; the price has hit a resistance level and is headed down. This is called a DOUBLE TOP.

WHEN DISTRIBUTED transactions conditional on the SECONDARY DISTRIBUTION of shares ISSUED AND OUTSTANDING but CLOSELY HELD, as those of a wholly owned subsidiary, for example. *See also* WHEN ISSUED.

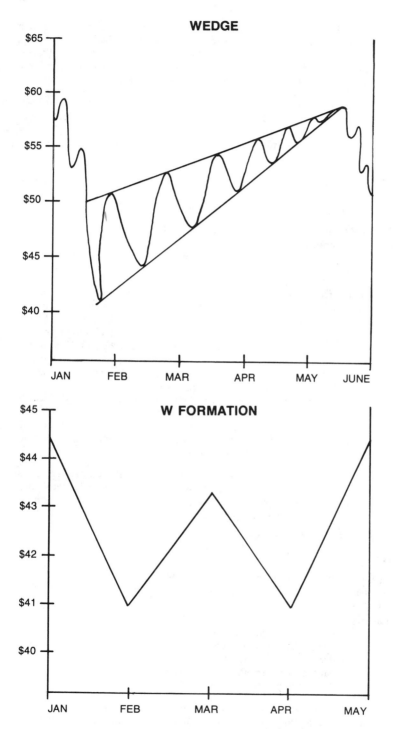

WHEN ISSUED short form of "when, as, and if issued." Term refers to a transaction made conditionally because a security, although authorized, has not yet been issued. NEW ISSUES of stocks and bonds, stocks that have SPLIT, and Treasury securities are all traded on a when issued basis. In a newspaper listing, a "WI" is placed next to the price of such a security. *See also* WHEN DISTRIBUTED.

WHIPSAWED to be caught in VOLATILE price movements and make losing trades as prices rise and fall. A trader is whipsawed if he or she buys just before prices fall and sells just before prices rise.

Term is also used in TECHNICAL ANALYSIS referring to misleading signals in the chart trends of markets or particular securities.

WHITE KNIGHT friendly acquirer sought by the target of an unfriendly TAKEOVER.

WHITE SQUIRE WHITE KNIGHT who buys less than a majority interest.

WHITE'S RATING White's Tax-Exempt Bond Rating Service's classification of municipal securities, which is based on market factors rather than credit considerations and which attempts to determine appropriate yields. *See also* MUNICIPAL BOND.

WHOLE LIFE INSURANCE form of life insurance policy that offers protection in case the insured dies and also builds up cash value. The policy stays in force for the lifetime of the insured, unless the policy is canceled or lapses. The policyholder usually pays a set annual PREMIUM for whole life, which does not rise as the person grows older (as in the case with TERM INSURANCE). The earnings on the cash value in the policy accumulate tax-deferred, and can be borrowed against in the form of a POLICY LOAN. The death benefit is reduced by the amount of the loan, if the loan is not repaid. Because whole life insurance traditionally offered a low return on the policyholder's investment, many policyholders beginning in the 1970s switched to new, higher-earning forms of whole life, such as UNIVERSAL LIFE INSURANCE and VARIABLE LIFE INSURANCE. Whole life insurance is also known as *ordinary* life, *permanent* life, or *straight* life insurance. *See also* SINGLE-PREMIUM LIFE INSURANCE.

WHOLE LOAN SECONDARY MORTGAGE MARKET term that distinguishes an investment representing an original residential mortgage loan (whole loan) from a loan representing a participation with one or more lenders or a PASS-THROUGH SECURITY representing a pool of mortgages.

WHOLESALE PRICE INDEX *see* PRODUCER PRICE INDEX.

WHOLESALER

In general: middleman or DISTRIBUTOR who sells mainly to retailers, JOBBERS, other merchants, and industrial, commercial, and institutional users as distinguished from consumers. *See also* VENDOR.

Securities:

1. INVESTMENT BANKER acting as an UNDERWRITER in a NEW ISSUE or as a distributor in a secondary offering of securities. *See also* SECONDARY DISTRIBUTION.

2. broker-dealer who trades with other broker-dealers, rather than with the retail investor, and receives discounts and selling commissions.

3. SPONSOR of a MUTUAL FUND.

WHOOPS nickname for the Washington Public Power Supply System. In the late 1970s and early 80s, WHOOPS raised billions of dollars through MUNICIPAL BOND offerings to finance construction of five nuclear plants in the state of Washington. Because of cost overruns, bad management, and numerous delays, two of the plants were canceled, and it was doubtful that two others would ever be completed. WHOOPS defaulted on the payments to bondholders on the two canceled plants after the Washington Supreme Court ruled that the TAKE-OR-PAY CONTRACTS with the many utilities in the Northwest that had backed the bonds were invalid. This was the largest municipal bond default in history.

WIDE OPENING abnormally large SPREAD between the BID AND ASKED prices of a security at the OPENING of a trading session.

WIDGET symbolic American gadget, used wherever a hypothetical product is needed to illustrate a manufacturing or selling concept.

WIDOW-AND-ORPHAN STOCK stock that pays high dividends and is very safe. It usually has a low BETA COEFFICIENT and is involved in a noncyclical business. For years American Telephone and Telegraph was considered the premier widow-and-orphan stock, but its status was reevaluated following the court ordered-divestiture of local operating companies in the mid-1980s.

WILDCAT DRILLING exploring for oil or gas in an unproven area. A wildcat OIL AND GAS LIMITED PARTNERSHIP is structured so that investors take high risks but can reap substantial rewards if oil or gas is found in commercial quantities.

WILLIAMS ACT federal legislation enacted in 1968 that imposes requirements with respect to public TENDER OFFERS. It was inspired by a wave of unannounced TAKEOVERS in the 1960s, which caught managers unawares and confronted stockholders with decisions they were ill prepared to make. The Williams Act and amendments now comprise Sections 13(d) and 14(d) of the SECURITIES EXCHANGE ACT OF 1934. The law requires the bidder opening a tender to file with both the SECURITIES AND EXCHANGE COMMISSION and the TARGET COMPANY a statement detailing the terms of the offer, the bidder's background, the cash source, and his or her plans for the company if there is a takeover. The same information is required within 10 days from any person or company acquiring 5% or more of another company. The law mandates a minimum offering period of 20 days and gives tendering shareholders 15 days to change their minds. If only a limited number of shares are accepted, they must be prorated among the tendering stockholders. *See also* SATURDAY NIGHT SPECIAL.

WINDFALL PROFIT profit that occurs suddenly as a result of an event not controlled by the person or company profiting from the event. For example, oil companies profited in the 1970s from an explosion in the price of oil brought about by the Arab oil embargo and the price increases demanded by the Organization of Petroleum Exporting Countries. *See also* WINDFALL PROFITS TAX.

WINDFALL PROFITS TAX tax on profits that result from a sudden windfall to a particular company or industry. In 1980, federal legislation was passed that levied such a tax on oil companies because of the profits they earned as a result of the sharp increase in oil prices in the 1970s.

WINDOW
1. limited time during which an opportunity should be seized, or it will be lost. For example, a period when new stock issues are welcomed by the public only lasts for a few months, or maybe as long as a year—that time is called the *window of opportunity.*

2. DISCOUNT WINDOW of a Federal Reserve bank.
3. cashier department of a brokerage firm, where delivery and settlement of securities transactions takes place.

WINDOW DRESSING

1. trading activity near the end of a quarter or fiscal year that is designed to dress up a PORTFOLIO to be presented to clients or shareholders. For example, a fund manager may sell losing positions in his portfolio so he can display only positions that have gained in value.
2. accounting gimmickry designed to make a FINANCIAL STATEMENT show a more favorable condition than actually exists—for example by omitting certain expenses, by concealing liabilities, by delaying WRITE-OFFS, by anticipating sales, or by other such actions, which may or may not be fraudulent.

WIRE HOUSE national or international brokerage firm whose branch offices are linked by a communications system that permits the rapid dissemination of prices, information, and research relating to financial markets and individual securities. Although smaller retail and regional brokers currently have access to similar data, the designation of a firm as a wire house dates back to the time when only the largest organizations had access to high-speed communications. Therefore, *wire house* still is used to refer to the biggest brokerage houses.

WIRE ROOM operating department of a brokerage firm that receives customers' orders from the REGISTERED REPRESENTATIVE and transmits the vital data to the exchange floor, where a FLOOR TICKET is prepared, or to the firm's trading department for execution. The wire room also receives notices of executed trades and relays them to the appropriate registered representatives. Also called *order department, order room,* or *wire and order.*

WITCHING HOUR see TRIPLE WITCHING HOUR.

WITHDRAWAL PLAN program available through most open-end MUTUAL FUND companies in which shareholders can receive fixed payments of income or CAPITAL GAINS (or both) on a regular basis, usually monthly or quarterly.

WITHHOLDING

Securities: violation of the RULES OF FAIR PRACTICE of the NATIONAL ASSOCIATION OF SECURITIES DEALERS whereby a participant in a PUBLIC OFFERING fails to make a bona fide public offering at the PUBLIC OFFERING PRICE—for example, by withholding shares for his or her own account or selling shares to a family member, an employee of the dealer firm, or another broker-dealer—in order to profit from the higher market price of a HOT ISSUE. *See also* IMMEDIATE FAMILY; INVESTMENT HISTORY.

Taxes:
1. deduction from salary payments and other compensation to provide for an individual's tax liability. Federal income taxes and Social Security contributions are withheld from paychecks and are deposited in a Treasury TAX AND LOAN ACCOUNT with a bank. The yearly amount of withholding is reported on an income statement (form W-2), which must be submitted with the federal, state, and local tax returns. Liability not provided for by withholding must be paid in for ESTIMATED TAX payments.
2. withholding by corporations and financial institutions of a flat 10% of interest and dividend payments due securities holders, as required under the TAX EQUITY AND FISCAL RESPONSIBILITY ACT OF 1982. The purpose was to levy a tax on

people whose earnings escaped tracking by the Internal Revenue Service. The 10% withholding requirement was repealed in 1983. As a compromise, "backup withholding" was instituted, whereby, using Social Security numbers, payments can be reported to the IRS and matched against the actual income reported.

3. withholdings from pension and annuity distributions, sick pay, tips, and sizeable gambling winnings, as stipulated by law.

4. 30% withholding requirement on income from U.S. securities owned by foreigners—repealed by the TAX REFORM ACT OF 1984.

WORKING CAPITAL funds invested in a company's cash, ACCOUNTS RECEIVABLE, INVENTORY, and other CURRENT ASSETS (*gross working capital*); usually refers to *net working capital*—that is, current assets minus current liabilities (*see* CURRENT LIABILITY). Working capital finances the CASH CONVERSION CYCLE of a business—the length of time required to convert raw materials into finished goods, finished goods into sales, and accounts receivable into cash. These factors vary with the type of industry and the scale of production, which varies in turn with seasonality and with sales expansion and contraction.

Internal sources of working capital include RETAINED EARNINGS, operating efficiencies and the allocation of CASH FLOW from sources like DEPRECIATION or deferred taxes to working capital. External sources include bank and other short-term borrowings, TRADE CREDIT, and term debt and EQUITY FINANCING not channeled into long-term assets. *See also* CURRENT RATIO; NET CURRENT ASSETS.

WORKING CONTROL effective control of a corporation by a shareholder or shareholders with less than 51% voting interest. Working control by a minority holder, or by two or more minority holders working in concert, is possible when share ownership of a firm is otherwise widely dispersed.

WORKING INTEREST direct participation with unlimited liability, as distinguished from passive LIMITED PARTNERSHIP shares. The TAX REFORM ACT OF 1986 let investors with working interests in drilling ventures, such as GENERAL PARTNERS, offset losses against all types of income.

WORKOUT situation, such as a bad loan or troubled firm, where remedial measures are being taken.

WORLD BANK *see* INTERNATIONAL BANK FOR RECONSTRUCTION AND DEVELOPMENT.

WRAPAROUND ANNUITY ANNUITY contract allowing an annuitant discretion in the choice of underlying investments. Wraparound refers to the protection the annuity vehicle provides through its TAX-DEFERRED status, which becomes precarious when the annuity vehicle is being used as a technical way to avoid tax payment. The tax courts have ruled against tax deferment where money can be allocated by an annuity owner to a portfolio managed by an annuitant and where the annuitant can switch among funds of the sponsoring insurance company that are also marketed independently of annuities. On the other hand, the IRS has upheld tax deferral where an individual could not buy such funds without also buying the annuity. In any event, the insurer must legally own the annuity money.

WRAPAROUND MORTGAGE second mortgage that increases a borrower's indebtedness while leaving the original mortgage contract in force. The wraparound mortgage becomes the JUNIOR MORTGAGE and is held by the lending institution as security for the total mortgage debt. The borrower makes payments on both loans to the wraparound lender, who in turn makes scheduled installment payments on the original *senior mortgage*. It is a convenient way for a property owner to obtain additional credit without having to pay off an existing mortgage.

WRINKLE novel feature that may attract a buyer for a new product or a security. For example, ZERO COUPON SECURITIES were a new wrinkle when they were introduced in the early 1980s, but soon thereafter became quite commonplace.

WRITE-OFF charging an ASSET amount to expense or loss. The effect of a write-off is to reduce or eliminate the value of the asset and reduce profits. Write-offs are systematically taken in accordance with allowable tax DEPRECIATION of a FIXED ASSET, and with the AMORTIZATION of certain other assets, such as an INTANGIBLE ASSET and a capitalized cost (like premiums paid on investments). Write-offs are also taken when assets are, for whatever reason, deemed worthless, the most common example being uncollectible ACCOUNTS RECEIVABLE. Where such write-offs can be anticipated and therefore estimated, the usual practice has been to charge income regularly in amounts needed to maintain a RESERVE, the actual losses then being charged to the reserve. The TAX REFORM ACT OF 1986 required that BAD DEBT write-offs be charged directly to income by taxpayers other than small banks and thrift institutions. *See also* EXTRAORDINARY ITEM; NONRECURRING CHARGE.

WRITE OUT procedure followed when a SPECIALIST on an exchange makes a trade involving his own inventory, on one hand, and an order he is holding for a FLOOR BROKER, on the other. Exchange rules require a two-part transaction: the broker first completes a trade with the specialist, who then completes the transaction by a separate trade with the customer. The write out involves no charge other than the normal broker's commission.

WRITER
  1. person who sells PUT OPTION and CALL OPTION contracts, and therefore collects PREMIUM INCOME. The writer of a put option is obligated to buy (and the writer of a call option is obligated to sell) the UNDERLYING SECURITY at a predetermined price by a particular date if the OPTION is exercised. *See also* COVERED CALL; NAKED OPTION; WRITING NAKED.
  2. insurance UNDERWRITER.

WRITING CASH-SECURED PUTS OPTION strategy that a trader who wants to sell PUT OPTIONS uses to avoid having to use a MARGIN ACCOUNT. Rather than depositing MARGIN with a broker, a put WRITER can deposit cash equal to the option EXERCISE PRICE. With this strategy, the put option writer is not subject to additional margin requirements in the event of changes in the underlying stock's price. The put writer can also be earning money by investing the PREMIUM he or she receives in MONEY MARKET instruments.

WRITING NAKED strategy used by an OPTION seller in which the trader does not own the UNDERLYING SECURITY. This strategy can lead to large profits if the stock moves in the hoped-for direction, but it can lead to large losses if the stock moves in the other direction, since the trader will have to go into the marketplace to buy the stock in order to deliver it to the option buyer. *See also* NAKED OPTION.

WRITING PUTS TO ACQUIRE STOCK strategy used by an OPTION writer (seller) who believes a stock is going to decline and that its purchase at a given price would represent a good investment. By writing a PUT OPTION exercisable at that price, the writer cannot lose. If the stock, contrary to his expectation, goes up, the option will not be exercised and he is at least ahead the amount of the PREMIUM he received. If, as expected, the stock goes down and the option is exercised, he has bought the stock at what he had earlier decided was a good buy, and he has the premium income in addition.

WRITTEN-DOWN VALUE BOOK VALUE of an asset after DEPRECIATION or other AMORTIZATION; also called *net book value.* For example, if the original cost of a piece of equipment was $1000 and accumulated depreciation charges totaled $400, the written-down value would be $600. *See also* INTANGIBLE ASSET.

WT abbreviation for *warrant. See also* SUBSCRIPTION WARRANT.

X

X or XD symbol used in newspapers to signify that a stock is trading EX-DIVIDEND, that is, without dividend. The symbol X is also used in bond tables to signify without interest.

XR symbol used in newspapers to signify that a stock is trading EX-RIGHTS, that is, without rights attached. *See also* SUBSCRIPTION RIGHT.

XW symbol used in newspapers to signify that a stock is trading EX-WARRANTS, that is, without warrants attached. *See also* SUBSCRIPTION WARRANT.

Y

YANKEE BOND MARKET dollar-denominated bonds issued in the U.S. by foreign banks and corporations. The bonds are issued in the U.S. when market conditions there are more favorable than on the EUROBOND market or in domestic markets overseas. Similarly, Yankee CERTIFICATES OF DEPOSIT are negotiable CDs issued in the U.S. by branches and agencies of foreign banks.

YELLOW SHEETS daily publication of the NATIONAL QUOTATION BUREAU that details the BID AND ASKED prices and firms that MAKE A MARKET in CORPORATE BONDS traded in the OVER THE COUNTER (OTC) market. Much of this information is not available in the daily OTC newspaper listings. The sheets are named for their color. OTC equity issues are covered separately on PINK SHEETS and regional OTC issues of both classes are listed on white sheets.

YEN BOND in general terms, any bond issue denominated in Japanese yen. International bankers using the term are usually referring to yen-denominated bonds issued or held outside Japan. Yen bonds have historically been an unimportant factor in international credit because of strict exchange controls and financial industry regulation by the Japanese government. An accord announced in May 1984 by the U.S. Treasury Department and Japanese Ministry of Finance was designed to open Japan to international money, capital, and securities markets and increase the importance of the yen in world trade and government reserve holdings. As a result, yen bonds are expected to increase their share of international debt offerings currently dominated by U.S. dollars. *See also* EUROBOND.

YIELD

In general: RETURN on an investor's CAPITAL INVESTMENT. A piece of real estate may yield a certain return, or a business deal may offer a particular yield. *See also* RETURN ON INVESTED CAPITAL.

Agriculture: agricultural output in terms of quantity of a crop.

Bonds:

1. COUPON rate of interest divided by the purchase price, called CURRENT YIELD. For example, a bond selling for $1000 with a 10% coupon offers a 10% current yield. If that same bond were selling for $500, however, it would offer a 20% yield to an investor who bought it for $500. (As a bond's price falls, its yield rises and vice versa.)

2. rate of return on a bond, taking into account the total of annual interest payments, the purchase price, the redemption value, and the amount of time remaining until maturity; called *maturity yield* or YIELD TO MATURITY. *See also* YIELD TO AVERAGE LIFE; YIELD TO CALL.

Lending: total money earned on a loan—that is, the ANNUAL PERCENTAGE RATE of interest multiplied by the term of the loan.

Stocks: percentage rate of return paid on a common or preferred stock in dividends. For example, a stock that sells for $20 and pays an annual dividend of $2 per share has a yield, also called a *dividend yield*, of 10%.

Taxes: amount of revenue received by a governmental entity as a result of a tax.

YIELD ADVANTAGE extra amount of return an investor will earn if he or she purchases a CONVERTIBLE security instead of the common stock of the same issuing corporation. If an XYZ Corporation convertible yields 10% and an XYZ common share yields 5%, the yield advantage is 5%. *See also* YIELD SPREAD.

YIELD CURVE graph showing the term structure of interest rates by plotting the yields of all bonds of the same quality with maturities ranging from the shortest to the longest available. The resulting curve shows if short-term interest rates are higher or lower than long-term rates. If short-term rates are lower, it is called a POSITIVE YIELD CURVE. If short-term rates are higher, it is called a NEGATIVE (or INVERTED) YIELD CURVE. If there is little difference between short-term and long-term rates, it is called a *flat yield curve*. For the most part, the yield curve is positive, since investors who are willing to tie up their money for a longer period of time usually are compensated for the extra risk they are taking by receiving a higher yield. The most common version of the yield curve graph plots Treasury securities, showing the range of yields from a three-month TREASURY BILL to a 20- or 30-year TREASURY BOND.

Fixed-income analysts study the yield curve carefully in order to make judgments about the direction of interest rates.

YIELD EQUIVALENCE the rate of interest at which a tax-exempt bond and a taxable security of similar quality provide the same return. In the day of the 50% TAX BRACKET, for example, a tax-exempt bond paying 10% was the equivalent of a taxable corporate bond of 20%. To calculate the yield that must be provided by a taxable security to equal that of a tax-exempt bond for investors in different tax brackets, the tax exempt yield is divided by the reciprocal of the tax bracket (100 less 28%, for example) to arrive at the taxable yield.

Thus, a person in the 28% tax bracket, for example, who wished to figure the taxable equivalent of a 10% tax free municipal bond would divide 10% by 72% (100 minus 28%) to get 13.9%—the yield a corporate taxable bond would have to provide to be equivalent, after taxes, to the 10% municipal bond. To convert a taxable yield to a tax-exempt yield, the formula is reversed—that is, the tax exempt yield is equal to the taxable yield multiplied by the reciprocal of the tax bracket.

YIELD SPREAD difference in YIELD between various issues of securities. In comparing bonds, it usually refers to issues of different credit quality since issues of the same maturity and quality would normally have the same yields, as with Treasury securities, for example. Yield spread also refers to the differential between dividend yield on stocks and the CURRENT YIELD on bonds. The comparison might be made, for example, between the STANDARD & POOR'S INDEX (of 500 stocks) dividend yield and the current yield of an index of corporate bonds. A significant difference in bond and stock yields, assuming similar quality, is known as a *yield gap*.

YIELD TO AVERAGE LIFE yield calculation used, in lieu of YIELD TO MATURITY or YIELD TO CALL, where bonds are retired systematically during the life of the issue, as in the case of a SINKING FUND with contractual requirements. Because the issuer will buy its own bonds on the open market to satisfy its sinking fund requirements if the bonds are trading below PAR, there is to that extent automatic price support for such bonds; they therefore tend to trade on a yield-to-average-life basis.

YIELD TO CALL yield on a bond assuming the bond will be redeemed by the issuer at the first CALL date specified in the INDENTURE agreement. The same calculations are used to calculate yield to call as YIELD TO MATURITY except that the principal value at maturity is replaced by the first CALL PRICE and the maturity date is replaced by the first call date. Assuming the issuer will put the interest of the company before the interest of the investor and will call the bonds if it is favorable to do so, the lower of the yield to call and the yield to maturity can be viewed as the more realistic rate of return to the investor.

YIELD TO MATURITY (YTM) concept used to determine the rate of return an investor will receive if a long-term, interest-bearing investment, such as a bond, is held to its MATURITY DATE. It takes into account purchase price, REDEMPTION value, time to maturity, COUPON yield, and the time between interest payments. Recognizing time value of money, it is the DISCOUNT RATE at which the PRESENT VALUE of all future payments would equal the present price of the bond, also known as INTERNAL RATE OF RETURN. It is implicitly assumed that coupons are reinvested at the YTM rate. YTM can be approximated using a bond value table (also called a bond yield table) or can be determined using a programmable calculator equipped for bond mathematics calculations. *See also* HORIZON ANALYSIS; YIELD TO AVERAGE LIFE; YIELD TO CALL.

YO-YO STOCK stock that fluctuates in a VOLATILE manner, rising and falling quickly like a yo-yo.

Z

ZERO-BASE BUDGETING (ZBB) method of setting budgets for corporations and government agencies that requires a justification of all expenditures, not only those that exceed the prior year's allocations. Thus all budget lines are said to begin at a zero base and are funded according to merit rather than according to the level approved for the preceding year, when circumstances probably differed.

ZERO-BRACKET AMOUNT until the TAX REFORM ACT OF 1986, the STANDARD DEDUCTION, that is, the income automatically not subject to federal income tax for taxpayers choosing not to itemize deductions. The zero-bracket amount was built into the tax tables and schedules used to compute tax. The 1986 Act replaced the zero-bracket amount with an increased standard deduction, which was subtracted from income before computing taxes rather than being part of the rate tables. The new standard deduction, indexed to inflation and containing special provisions for the blind and elderly, was set to become fully effective in 1988.

ZERO-COUPON CONVERTIBLE SECURITY
1. Zero-coupon BOND convertible into the common stock of the issuing company when the stock reaches a predetermined price. Introduced as Liquid Yield Option Notes (LYONS), these securities have a PUT OPTION that permits holders to redeem the bonds within three years after the initial offering. They tend to trade at a small PREMIUM OVER CONVERSION VALUE and provide a lower YIELD TO MATURITY than their nonconvertible counterparts.
2. Zero-coupon bond, usually a MUNICIPAL BOND, convertible into an interest bearing bond at some time before maturity. For example, a zero-coupon (tax-free) municipal bond would automatically accumulate and compound interest for its first 15 years at which time it would convert to a regular income-paying bond. Thus, an investor is able to lock in a current interest rate with a small initial investment. Varieties are marketed under the acronyms GAINS (Growth And Income Securities) and FIGS (Future Income and Growth Securities).

ZERO-COUPON SECURITY security that makes no periodic interest payments but instead is sold at a deep discount from its face value. The buyer of such a bond receives the rate of return by the gradual APPRECIATION of the security, which is redeemed at FACE VALUE on a specified maturity date. For tax purposes, the Internal Revenue Service maintains that the holder of a zero-coupon bond owes income tax on the interest that has accrued each year, even though the bondholder does not actually receive the cash until maturity. Because of this interpretation, many financial advisors recommend that zero-coupon securities be used for INDIVIDUAL RETIREMENT ACCOUNTS or KEOGH ACCOUNTS, where they remain tax-sheltered.
    There are many kinds of zero-coupon securities. The most commonly known is the zero-coupon bond, which either may be issued at a deep discount by a corporation or may be created by a brokerage firm when it strips the coupons off a bond and sells the CORPUS and the coupons separately. This technique is used frequently with Treasury bonds, and the zero-coupon issue is marketed under such names as Cat or Tiger. Zero-coupon bonds are also issued by municipalities. Buying a municipal zero frees its purchaser of the worry about paying taxes on imputed interest, since the interest is tax-exempt. Zero-coupon certificates of deposit and zero mortgages also exist; they work on the same principal as zero-coupon bonds—the CD or mortgage holder receives face value at maturity, and no payments until then.

Zero-coupon securities are frequently used to plan for a specific investment goal. For example, a parent knowing his child will enter college in 10 years can buy a zero that will mature in 10 years, and thus be assured of having money available for tuition. Similarly, a worker wanting to provide for retirement in 25 years can buy a 25-year zero.

Because zero-coupon securities bear no interest, they are the most VOLATILE of all fixed-income securities. Since zero-coupon bondholders do not receive interest payments, zeros fall more dramatically than bonds paying out interest on a current basis when interest rates rise. However, when interest rates fall, zero-coupon securities rise more rapidly in value, because the bonds have locked in a particular rate of reinvestment that becomes more attractive the further rates fall. The greater the number of years that a zero-coupon security has until maturity, the less an investor has to pay for it, and the more LEVERAGE is at work for him. For instance, a bond that will mature in 5 years may double, but one that matures in 25 years may increase in value 10 times, depending on the interest rate of the bond.

See also CERTIFICATE OF ACCRUAL ON TREASURY SECURITIES (CATS); COUPON BOND; DEEP DISCOUNT BOND; TIGER.

ZERO-MINUS TICK sale that takes place at the same price as the previous sale, but at a lower price than the last different price; also called a *zero downtick*. For instance, stock trades may be executed consecutively at prices of $52, $51, and $51. The final trade at $51 was made at a zero-minus tick, because it was made at the same price as the previous trade, but at a lower price than the last different price.

ZERO-PLUS TICK securities trade that takes place at the same price as the previous transaction but at a higher price than the last different price; also called *zero uptick*. For instance, with trades executed consecutively at $51, $52, and $52, the last trade at $52 was made at a zero-plus tick—the same price as the previous trade but a higher price than the last different price. Short sales must be executed only on zero-plus ticks or on PLUS TICKS. *See also* SHORT SALE RULE.

PART V

Finance and Investment
Ready Reference

INTRODUCTION

In today's complex world of finance and investment, it's crucial not only to know *how* different investments work, but also *where* to find the information essential to making wise decisions about those investments.

In the following pages you will find an enormous wealth of information concerning finance and investment. In some cases, the data presented is designed mainly to help you tap the many sophisticated sources available to investors. In other cases, we present well-organized data that can offer important insight into the workings of finance and investment. *In all cases, you are given information you can use.* The address and telephone number is given for just about every institution, organization, and firm listed, and you are encouraged to make direct contact in order to obtain the data required to make a well-informed investment decision.

The section is divided into the following principal parts:

Sources of Information and Assistance Public and private agencies and associations that help investors are listed as are major financial publications and databases.

Major Financial Institutions In this part are listed the names, addresses, and phone numbers of commercial banks, thrift institutions, life insurance companies, brokerage firms, sponsors of publicly available limited partnerships, accounting firms, and major stock and commodity exchanges around the world.

Mutual Funds Both open-end and closed-end funds are presented.

Futures and Options Contracts Detailed specifications of each contract are presented in tabular form, along with a list of where each contract is traded.

Historical Data This section provides graphs and tabular matter showing important longer-term financial and economic trends. Dow Jones and other indexes are included.

Publicly Traded Companies About 6000 corporations are listed, according to the place where the shares trade: NYSE, AMEX, NASDAQ, and Toronto Stock Exchange. Listings include name, stock symbol, address, phone number, line of business, option availability, and whether the firm offers a dividend reinvestment plan. These listings are followed by a compilation of important American Depositary Receipts (ADRs) and a listing of benefits some companies offer shareholders such as free merchandise or services.

1. SOURCES OF INFORMATION AND ASSISTANCE

When trying to make decisions and keep up-to-date in the increasingly complex world of finance and investment, it is often necessary to turn to others. This section of the *Handbook* is designed to guide you to the organizations that can help you.

Since the financial markets are so heavily regulated by the government today, it is important to know which federal and state regulators can be of assistance. The first part of this section gives a brief description of major federal, state and provincial regulatory agencies in the United States and Canada, and how to contact them.

A government agency sometimes is not the best place to turn. Private associations, trade groups and self-regulatory organizations are often well equipped to deal with problems or questions related to finance and investment. The second part of this section lists many of these private groups.

For advice on where to invest and how to manage your financial affairs, there is an enormous pool of advice available in finance and investment publications. The third part of this section gives you the information you need to contact a great number of worthy publications that contain such advice.

To tap information about financial markets in an even speedier fashion, you can use computer databases, which are listed in the fourth part of this section. In addition, we have selected some of the best software that can make sense of the massive amounts of information these databases contain.

FEDERAL REGULATORY ORGANIZATIONS IN THE UNITED STATES AND CANADA

This is a list of the major governmental agencies that regulate the finance and investment markets in the United States and Canada. Each agency's address and telephone number is accompanied by a brief description of its major responsibilities. These agencies primarily oversee the fairness and efficiency of finance and investment markets. In that role, consumers and investors can complain to them about perceived abuses or illegality in the marketplace. Many of the agencies are discussed in more detail in the Dictionary section of the Handbook, along with the legislation that created the agency. The regulatory aspect of some of the agencies is less important than other functions.

Agencies of the United States Government

Bureau of Economic Analysis
1401 K Street, N.W.
Washington, D.C. 20230
(202) 523-0777

Compiles, analyzes and publishes data on economic activity, including gross national product, personal income, corporate profits and leading economic indicators.

Bureau of Labor Statistics
441 G Street, N.W.
Washington, D.C. 20212
(202) 523-1221

Compiles, analyzes and publishes data on labor activity such as unemployment, consumer price index, producer price index and wages.

Commerce Department
14th Street and E Street, S.W.
Washington, D.C. 20230
(202) 377-3263

Regulates international trade and helps American businesses expand in a variety of ways. Publishes a large amount of data about the U.S. economy.

Commodity Futures Trading Commission
2033 K Street, N.W.
Washington, D.C. 20581
(202) 254-8630

Regulates the trading of commodity futures and options contracts. Investigates charges of fraud against commodity dealers. The CFTC also approves all new contracts that Exchanges want to trade.

Comptroller of the Currency
490 L'Enfant Plaza, S.W.
Washington, D.C. 20219
(202) 447-1800

Regulates all national banks in the United States and handles consumer complaints against those banks.

Consumer Product Safety Commission
1111 18th Street, N.W.
Washington, D.C. 20207
(301) 492-6800

Regulates and monitors the safety of con-

sumer products. Provides information to the public on, and develops manufacturing standards for, consumer goods.

Council of Economic Advisers
17th Street and Pennsylvania Avenue, N.W.
Washington, D.C. 20500
(202) 395-5084

Monitors and analyzes the economy and advises the president on economic developments, trends and policies. Also prepares the economic reports of the president to Congress.

Farm Credit Administration
1501 Farm Credit Drive
McLean, Virginia 22102
(703) 883-4056

Supervises and regulates lending activities of the Farm Credit System, which provides funding for agricultural, aquatic and rural electric enterprises.

Federal Deposit Insurance Corporation
550 17th Street, N.W.
Washington, D.C. 20429
(202) 898-6947

Insures deposits in member institutions up to $100,000 per depositor. Also regularly examines banks and replies to consumer complaints about federally insured state banks. Helps arrange the merger of weak banks into stronger ones.

Federal Home Loan Mortgage Corporation
1776 G Street, N.W.
Washington, D.C. 20552
(202) 789-4448

Freddie Mac, as it is known, encourages the growth of the secondary mortgage market by buying mortgages from lenders, packaging and guaranteeing them, and reselling them as mortgage-backed securities.

Federal Housing Finance Board
1700 G Street, N.W.
Washington, D.C. 20552
(202) 906-6590

Supervises the 12 regional Federal Home Loan Banks.

Federal Reserve System
20th Street and C Street, N.W.
Washington, D.C. 20551
(202) 452-3215

Regulates national money supply, oversees activities of, and supplies credit to, member banks, and supervises the printing of money at the mint. Investors can also buy Treasury securities directly from the Fed or any of its district banks or branches.

Federal Trade Commission
Sixth Street and Pennsylvania Avenue, N.W.
Washington, D.C. 20580
(202) 523-3598

Enforces antitrust laws and consumer protection legislation. For instance, the FTC oversees the Truth-in-Lending laws, and seeks to curtail unfair sales practices and deceptive advertising.

Internal Revenue Service
1111 Constitution Avenue, N.W.
Washington, D.C. 20224
(202) 566-4115

Collects personal and corporate taxes for the Federal Government and administers rules and regulations of the Treasury Department.

International Monetary Fund
700 19th Street, N.W.
Washington, D.C. 20431
(202) 623-7100

An intergovernmental organization that maintains funds contributed by, and available to, member nations. Payments are designed to promote world trade and aid members with temporary problems.

International Trade Administration
14th Street and Constitution Avenue, N.W.
Washington, D.C. 20230
(202) 377-3022

Regulates and promotes non-agricultural trade between the U.S. and its trading partners. Also develops global policies to expand U.S. exports.

Interstate Commerce Commission
12th Street and Constitution Avenue, N.W.
Washington, D.C. 20423
(202) 275-7572

Monitors the flow of products carried between states by surface transportation, such as rail, truck, water and pipeline.

National Credit Union Administration
1776 G Street, N.W.
Washington, D.C. 20456
(202) 357-1050

Regulates federally chartered credit unions and offers assistance in establishing credit unions.

Office of Thrift Supervision
1700 G Street, N.W.
Washington, D.C. 20552
(202) 906-6000

Charters federal savings and loan associations, supervises and examines federally and state chartered thrifts.

Pension Benefit Guaranty Corporation
2020 K Street, N.W.
Washington, D.C. 20006
(202) 956-5000

Ensures that participants in private pension plans will receive at least basic retirement benefits should a program run short of funds.

Resolution Trust Corporation
550 17th Street, N.W.
Washington, D.C. 20429
(202) 898-8750

Responsible for merging ailing thrifts with healthy savings and loans or selling off the assets of failed thrifts to pay creditors.

Securities and Exchange Commission
450 Fifth Street, N.W.
Washington, D.C. 20549
(202) 272-2800

Regulates the securities industry. Registers issues of securities, investigates fraud and insider trading, supervises investment companies, investment advisers, accounting firms and self-regulatory organizations like the stock exchanges and the National Association of Securities Dealers.

Securities Investor Protection Corporation
805 15th Street, N.W.
Washington, D.C. 20005
(202) 371-8300

Insures brokerage customers' holdings up to $500,000 per customer, with a limit of $100,000 in cash or cash equivalents against losses due to financial failure of a firm. SIPC does not cover losses due to market fluctuations or default by the issuers of securities. Helps arrange mergers of failing brokerage firms into stronger firms.

Small Business Administration
1441 L Street, N.W.
Washington, D.C. 20416
(202) 653-6365

Offers advice and below-market rate loans and loan guarantees to qualifying small businesses, with special programs for veterans and women, among other groups. Also licenses and funds Small Business Investment Companies (SBICs).

Social Security Administration
6401 Security Boulevard
Baltimore, Maryland 21235
(301) 594-7700

Regulates eligibility and payments of social security benefits to workers after they retire or become disabled. Also administers supplemental income programs for the aged, blind and dependents.

Treasury Department
Main Treasury Building
Washington, D.C. 20220
(202) 566-5252

Regulates the issuance of government debt (Treasury bills, bonds and notes) in coordination with the Federal Reserve and issues savings bonds. Plays a large role in coordinating economic and financial issues with foreign governments.

United State International Trade Commission
500 E Street, S.W.
Washington, D.C. 20436
(202) 252-1822

Studies factors relating to U.S. foreign trade and its relation to domestic production, employment and competitiveness. Also provides technical advice for government and private policy-makers.

United States Tax Court
400 Second Street, N.W.
Washington, D.C. 20217
(202) 376-2754

Hears cases involving disputes between the IRS and taxpayers.

Federal Government Agencies of Canada

Bank of Canada
Ottawa, Ontario K1A 0G9
(613) 782-8111

Regulates the money supply of Canada. It also acts as fiscal agent for the Government of Canada in managing the public debt. The Bank of Canada also has the sole right to issue Canadian paper money.

Business Centre
Department of Regional Industrial Expansion
235 Queen Street
Ottawa, Ontario K1A OH5
(613) 995-5771

The center helps business people get useful information about federal programs and services, industrial and trade topics, and in general improves the relationship of government with the business community.

Canada Deposit Insurance Corporation
P.O. Box 2340, Station D
Ottawa, Ontario K1P 5W5
(613) 996-2081

Insures deposits up to $60,000 per depositor in member institutions. Membership in the Corporation is restricted to banks, trust companies and mortgage loan companies.

Canada Mortgage and Housing Corporation
Montreal Road
Ottawa, Ontario K1A OP7
(613) 748-2000

The Corporation administers the National Housing Act and is responsible for delivering housing assistance to increase the supply of housing. The Corporation also insures mortgage loans made by approved lenders on the open market, and makes direct loans to areas not served by approved lenders.

Consumer and Corporate Affairs Canada
Place du Portage
Tower 1
Ottawa/Hull, Ontario K1A OC9
(819) 997-1670

Regulates many business activities and oversees consumer protection. Among its many responsibilities, the agency regulates product safety, consumer complaints, misleading advertising, federal corporation law, patents, copyrights and trademark law, and inspection of meat, fish and other foods.

Export Development Corporation
151 O'Connor Street
Ottawa, Ontario K1P 5T9
(613) 598-2500

Assists Canadian companies to export their products and services.

External Affairs Department, International
  Trade Development
125 Sussex Drive
Ottawa, Ontario K1A OG2
(800) 267-8376

Coordinates international trade policy, and helps Canadian companies export their products and services.

Federal Business Development Bank
CP 335,Tour de la Bourse
Montreal, Quebec H4Z 1L4
(514) 283-5904

Provides capital and equity financing and management services to Canadian businesses.

Finance Department
Ottawa, Ontario K1A OG5
(613) 992-5225

Conducts the financial affairs and economic planning for the Canadian government.

Inspector-General of Banks
Department of Finance
Ottawa, Ontario K1A OG5
(613) 992-0377

Division of the Finance Department that inspects banks for soundness of their financial condition.

Insurance Department Canada
140 O'Connor Street
Ottawa, Ontario K1A OH2
(613) 996-8587

Regulates all insurance companies in Canada, including life insurance, health insurance and property and casualty insurance.

Revenue Canada, Taxation
Communications Directorate
875 Heron Road
Ottawa, Ontario K1A OI8
(613) 957-3503

Collects corporate and individual taxes from Canadians.

Statistics Canada
Ottawa, Ontario K1A OT6
(613) 951-2422

Compiles many of the economic and financial statistics for the government of Canada.

Treasury Board
140 O'Connor Street
Ottawa, Ontario K1A OR5
(613) 957-2400

A Cabinet committee, brought into existence by the Financial Administration Act, which advises the rest of the Cabinet on the optimum allocation of public funds among government programs to permit the most efficient use of the government's manpower, financial and material resources.

U.S. STATE ATTORNEY GENERAL'S OFFICES

The attorney general's office is the place to go for a wide variety of consumer complaints. The attorney general is particularly concerned with stopping fraud, and frequently several attorneys general will coordinate their efforts to stop a multistate fraudulent business. Those who suspect a solicitation to be fraudulent should contact their state's attorney general on this list before handing over any money.

Besides taking consumer complaints, the attorney general's office promulgates rules and regulations which promote fair business practices. Areas in their jurisdiction include deceptive advertising and contract law, for example. When appropriate, attorneys general also appeal to legislative bodies to pass new consumer protection laws. To enforce these laws, attorneys general pursue both civil and criminal prosecution of violators.

   Your state attorney general's offices may also be a source of help when considering a purchase decision. These offices usually publish helpful publications giving tips on what to avoid in entering certain kinds of sales contracts, for instance. Even if one is not sure where to turn for help for a particular consumer problem, the attorney general is often a good place to start.

ALABAMA
Attorney General
Alabama State House
Montgomery, Alabama 36130
(205) 261-7300, (800) 392-5658

ALASKA
Attorney General
Capital Building
P.O. Box K
Juneau, Alaska 99811
(907) 465-3600

ARIZONA
Attorney General
1275 W. Washington Street
Phoenix, Arizona 85007
(602) 542-4266, (800) 8431

ARKANSAS
Attorney General
200 Tower Building
4th & Center Street
Little Rock, Arkansas 72201
(501) 682-2007, (800) 482-8982

CALIFORNIA
Attorney General
1515 K Street, Suite 511
Sacramento, California 94244-2550
(916) 324-5437, (800) 952-5548

COLORADO
Attorney General
1525 Sherman Street
Denver, Colorado 80203
(303) 866-3611

CONNECTICUT
Attorney General
55 Elm Street
Hartford, Connecticut 06106
(203) 566-2026, (800) 842-2649

DELAWARE
Attorney General
820 North French Street
Wilmington, Delaware 19801
(302) 571-3838

DISTRICT OF COLUMBIA
Department of Consumer and Regulatory
   Affairs
614 H Street, N.W.
Washington, D.C. 20001
(202) 727-7000

FLORIDA
Attorney General
State Capitol
Tallahassee, Florida 32399-1050
(904) 487-1963, (800) 342-2176

GEORGIA
Attorney General
40 Capitol Square
Atlanta, Georgia 30334
(404) 656-3300, (800) 282-5808

HAWAII
Attorney General
State Capital
415 Beretania Street, Room 405
Honolulu, Hawaii 96813
(808) 548-4740

IDAHO
Attorney General
Statehouse, Room 210
Boise, Idaho 83720
(208) 334-2400

ILLINOIS
Attorney General
500 South Second Street
Springfield, Illinois 62706
(217) 782-1090

INDIANA
Attorney General
219 State House
Indianapolis, Indiana 46204
(317) 232-6201, (800) 382-5516

IOWA
Attorney General
Hoover Building, 2nd Floor
Des Moines, Iowa 50319
(515) 281-5164

KANSAS
Attorney General
Judicial Center, 2nd Floor
Topeka, Kansas 66612
(913) 296-2215, (800) 432-2310

KENTUCKY
Attorney General
116 Capitol Building
Frankfort, Kentucky 40601
(502) 564-7600, (800) 432-9257

LOUISIANA
Attorney General
P.O. Box 94005
Baton Rouge, Louisiana 70804-9005
(504) 342-7013

MAINE
Attorney General
State House, Station 6
Augusta, Maine 04333
(207) 289-3661

MARYLAND
Attorney General
200 St. Paul Place
Baltimore, Maryland 21202
(301) 576-6300

MASSACHUSETTS
Attorney General
One Ashburton Place
Boston, Massachusetts 02108
(617) 727-8400

MICHIGAN
Attorney General
525 W. Ottawa Street, 7th Floor
Lansing, Michigan 48913
(517) 373-1110

MINNESOTA
Attorney General
State Capitol
St. Paul, Minnesota 55155
(612) 297-6196

MISSISSIPPI
Attorney General
P.O. Box 220
Jackson, Mississippi 39205
(601) 359-3680, (800) 222-7622

MISSOURI
Attorney General
P.O. Box 899
Jefferson City, Missouri 65102
(314) 751-3321, (800) 392-8222

MONTANA
Attorney General
Justice Building
215 N. Sanders
Helena, Montana 59620
(406) 444-2026

NEBRASKA
Attorney General
2115 State Capitol Building
P.O. Box 98920
Lincoln, Nebraska 68509
(402) 471-2682

NEVADA
Attorney General
Heroes Memorial Bldg.
Carson City, Nevada 89710
(702) 687-4170, (800) 992-0900

NEW HAMPSHIRE
Attorney General
208 State House Annex
Concord, New Hampshire 03301-6397
(603) 271-3658

NEW JERSEY
Attorney General
Justice Complex, CN 080
Trenton, New Jersey 08625
(609) 292-8740

NEW MEXICO
Attorney General
P.O. Drawer 1508
Santa Fe, New Mexico 87504-1508
(505) 827-6000

NEW YORK
Attorney General
State Capitol
Albany, New York 12224
(518) 474-7124

NORTH CAROLINA
Attorney General
Department of Justice Building
P.O. Box 629
Raleigh, North Carolina 27602
(919) 733-3377

NORTH DAKOTA
Attorney General
State Capitol Building, 1st Floor
Bismarck, North Dakota 58505
(701) 224-2210, (800) 472-2600

OHIO
Attorney General
30 E. Broad Street
Columbus, Ohio 43266-0410
(614) 466-4320, (800) 282-0515

OKLAHOMA
Attorney General
112 State Capitol Building
Oklahoma City, Oklahoma 73105
(405) 521-3921

OREGON
Attorney General
100 Justice Building
Salem, Oregon 97310
(503) 378-4400

PENNSYLVANIA
Attorney General
Strawberry Square, 16th Floor
Harrisburg, Pennsylvania 17120
(717) 787-3391

PUERTO RICO
Department of Justice
P.O. Box 192
Old San Juan, Puerto Rico 00902
(809) 721-2900

RHODE ISLAND
Attorney General
72 Pine Street
Providence, Rhode Island 02903-2856
(401) 274-4400

SOUTH CAROLINA
Attorney General
P.O. Box 11549
Columbia, South Carolina 29211
(803) 734-3970, (800) 922-1594

SOUTH DAKOTA
Attorney General
State Capitol
Pierre, South Dakota 57501-5090
(605) 773-3215, (800) 592-1865

TENNESSEE
Attorney General
450 James Robertson Parkway
Nashville, Tennessee 37219
(615) 741-2368, (800) 342-8385

TEXAS
Attorney General
Supreme Court Building
P.O. Box 12548
Austin, Texas 78711-2548
(512) 463-2100

UTAH
Attorney General
236 State Capitol
Salt Lake City, Utah 84114
(801) 538-1015

VERMONT
Attorney General
Pavilion Office Building
Montpelier, Vermont 05602
(802) 828-3171, (800) 642-5149

VIRGINIA
Attorney General
101 N. 8th Street
Richmond, Viginia 23219
(804) 786-2071, (800)552-9963

VIRGIN ISLANDS OF THE UNITED STATES
Consumer Services Administration
P.O. Box 5468
Charlotte Amalie, St. Thomas
U.S. Virgin Islands 00801
(809) 774-3130

WASHINGTON
Attorney General
Highways Licenses Building
7th Floor, MS PB-71
Olympia, Washington 98504
(206) 753-6200, (800) 551-4636

WEST VIRGINIA
Attorney General
State Capitol Building
Room E-26
Charleston, West Virginia 25305
(304) 348-2021

WISCONSIN
Attorney General
P.O. Box 7857
Madison, Wisconsin 53707-7857
(608) 266-1221, (800) 362-8189

WYOMING
Attorney General
123 State Capitol
Cheyenne, Wyoming 82002
(307) 777-7841

U.S. STATE BANKING REGULATORS

The regulators listed here are charged with supervising the activities of state-chartered banks. These are banks not regulated at the national level, where the Comptroller of the Currency and Federal Reserve Board do the supervision. Depending on the state, state chartered banks may have more or fewer powers than federally regulated banks. For example, the amount of money state banks can lend to customers as a percent of deposits varies widely from state to state. State banking regulators also oversee the financial soundness of the banks in their jurisdictions, and help to merge failing banks into healthy ones. These regulators do not insure state bank deposits, however; that is usually done by the Federal Deposit Insurance Corporation.

State bank regulators also pursue consumer complaints against banks in their state. For example, it would be appropriate to contact a regulator if a state bank was preventing checks from clearing within a reasonable time or if fees were excessive. Complaints about deceptive advertising or promotional materials by banks can also be addressed to these agencies. Questions about credit, and the denial of credit privileges, are also handled by the agencies in this list.

State banking agencies are also helpful when shopping for a bank. They will usually publish helpful literature about banks and bank services. Do not expect these agencies to do comparisons of yields paid on bank accounts or interest rates charged on loans—these numbers change too frequently for the agencies to track them.

ALABAMA
Banking Department
166 Commerce Street
Montgomery, Alabama 36130
(205) 261-3452

ALASKA
Director of Banking and Securities
State Office Building
P.O. Box D
Juneau, Alaska 99811
(907) 465-2521

ARIZONA
Superintendent of Banks Office
Suite 815, Century Plaza
3225 North Central
Phoenix, Arizona 85012
(602) 255-4421

ARKANSAS
State Bank Commissioner's Office
323 Center Street, Suite 500
Little Rock, Arkansas 72201
(501) 371-1117

CALIFORNIA
Superintendent of Banks Office
Suite 1100, 111 Pine Street
San Francisco, California 94111-5613
(415) 557-3232

COLORADO
State Bank Commissioner's Office
Room 700, State Office Building
303 West Colfax
Denver, Colorado 80204
(303) 620-4358

CONNECTICUT
Banking Commissioner's Office
44 Capitol Avenue
Hartford, Connecticut 06106
(203) 566-4560

DELAWARE
State Bank Commissioner's Office
P.O. Box 1401
Dover, Delaware 19903
(302) 736-4235

DISTRICT OF COLUMBIA
Comptroller of the Currency
490 L'Enfant Plaza, S.W.
Washington, D.C. 20219
(202) 447-1750

FLORIDA
State Comptroller's Office
State Capitol Building
Tallahassee, Florida 32399-0350
(904) 488-0370

GEORGIA
Commissioner of Banking and Finance
Suite 200, 2990 Brandywine Road
Atlanta, Georgia 30341-5565
(404) 986-1633

HAWAII
Division of Financial Institutions
P.O. Box 2054
Honolulu, Hawaii 96805
(808) 548-5855

IDAHO
Department of Finance Office
Statehouse Mall
Boise, Idaho 83720
(208) 334-3313

ILLINOIS
Commissioner of Banks and Trust
 Companies
Room 400, Reisch Building
119 South 5th Street
Springfield, Illinois 62701-1291
(217) 782-7966

INDIANA
Department of Financial Institutions Office
Room 1024, Indiana State Office Building
Indianapolis, Indiana 46204
(317) 232-3955

IOWA
Superintendent of Banking Office
200 E. Grand Avenue
Des Moines, Iowa 50319
(515) 281-4014

KANSAS
State Bank Commissioner's Office
Suite 300, 700 Jackson Street, S.W.
Topeka, Kansas 66603
(913) 296-2266

KENTUCKY
Commissioner of the Department of
 Financial Institutions
911 Leawood Drive
Frankfort, Kentucky 40601
(502) 564-3390

LOUISIANA
Commissioner of Financial Institutions
P.O. Box 94095, Capitol Station
Baton Rouge, Louisiana 70804
(504) 925-4661

MAINE
Superintendent of Banking
State House Station—36
Augusta, Maine 04333
(207) 289-3231

MARYLAND
Bank Commissioner
Suite 800, The Brokerage
34 Market Place
Baltimore, Maryland 21202
(301) 659-6262

MASSACHUSETTS
Commissioner of Banks
100 Cambridge Street, Room 2004
Boston, Massachusetts 02202
(617) 727-3145

MICHIGAN
Financial Institutions Bureau
P.O. Box 30224
Lansing, Michigan 48909
(517) 373-3460

MINNESOTA
Deputy Commissioner of Commerce
5th Floor, 500 Metro Square Building
St. Paul, Minnesota 55101
(612) 296-2715

MISSISSIPPI
Department of Banking and
 Consumer Finance
P.O. Box 731
Jackson, Mississippi 39205
(601) 359-1031

MISSOURI
Director Savings and Loan Division
P.O. Box 836
Jefferson City, Missouri 65102
(314) 751-4243

MONTANA
Commissioner of Financial
 Institutions
1424 9th Avenue
Helena, Montana 59620
(406) 444-2091

NEBRASKA
Director of Banking and Finance Office
P.O. Box 95006
Lincoln, Nebraska 68509
(402) 471-2171

NEVADA
Administrator of Financial Institutions
 Office
406 East Second Street
Carson City, Nevada 89710
(702) 885-4260

NEW HAMPSHIRE
Bank Commissioner
45 S. Main Street
Concord, New Hampshire 03301
(603) 271-3561

NEW JERSEY
Commissioner of Banking
20 West State Street, CN040
Trenton, New Jersey 08625
(609) 292-3420

NEW MEXICO
Financial Institutions Division
Regulations and Licensing Department
Bataan Memorial Building
Santa Fe, New Mexico 87503
(505) 827-7740

NEW YORK
Superintendent of Banks
2 Rector Street
New York, New York 10006-1894
(212) 618-6557

NORTH CAROLINA
Commissioner of Banks
430 Salisbury Street
Raleigh, North Carolina 27611
(919) 733-3016

NORTH DAKOTA
Commissioner of Banking and
 Financial Institutions
State Capitol, 600 E. Boulevard Avenue
Bismarck, North Dakota 58505
(701) 224-2253

OHIO
Superintendent of Banks
77 South High Street
Columbus, Ohio 43266-0544
(614) 466-2932

OKLAHOMA
Bank Commissioner
Malco Building
4100 North Lincoln Boulevard
Oklahoma City, Oklahoma 73105
(405) 521-2782

OREGON
Administrator of the Financial
 Institutions Division
280 Court Street, N.E.
Salem, Oregon 97310
(503) 378-4140

PENNSYLVANIA
Secretary of Banking
16th Floor, 333 Market Street
Harrisburg, Pennsylvania 17101-2290
(717) 787-6991

PUERTO RICO
Bureau of Banks and Financial
 Institutions
P.O. Box 5-4515
San Juan, Puerto Rico 00905
(809) 721-5242

RHODE ISLAND
Superintendent Banking Division
233 Richmond Street
Providence, Rhode Island 02903
(401) 277-2246

SOUTH CAROLINA
Commissioner of Banking
Room 309, 1015 Sumter Street
Columbia, South Carolina 29201
(803) 734-2001

SOUTH DAKOTA
Director of Banking and Finance
State Capitol, 910 Sioux
Pierre, South Dakota 57501
(605) 773-3421

TENNESSEE
Commissioner of Financial
 Institutions
4th Floor, John Sevier Building,
Nashville, Tennessee 37219-5384
(615) 741-2236

TEXAS
Banking Commissioner
2601 North Lamar
Austin, Texas 78705-4294
(512) 479-1200

UTAH
Commissioner of Financial
 Institutions
P.O. Box 89
Salt Lake City, Utah 84110
(801) 530-6500

VERMONT
Commissioner of Banking and
  Insurance
120 State Street
Montpelier, Vermont 05602
(802) 828-3301

VIRGINIA
Commissioner of Financial
  Institutions
Suite 1600,701 East Byrd Street
Richmond, Virginia 23205
(804) 786-3657

VIRGIN ISLANDS OF THE UNITED STATES
Chairman of the the Banking Board
P.O. Box 450
St. Thomas, Virgin Islands 00801
(809) 774-2991

WASHINGTON
Supervisor of Banking
Room 218, General Administration
Building, MS AX-22
Olympia, Washington 98504
(206) 753-6520

WEST VIRGINIA
Commissioner of Banking
Room 311, State Office Building 3
1800 Washington Street, E.
Charleston, West Virginia 25305
(304) 348-2294

WISCONSIN
Commissioner of Banking
P.O. Box 7876
Madison, Wisconsin 53707-7876
(608) 266-1621

WYOMING
State Examiner
4th Floor West,Herschler Building
122 W. 25th Street
Cheyenne, Wyoming 82002
(307) 777-6600

U.S. STATE INSURANCE REGULATORS

Every state has its own laws and regulations which govern all types of insurance. Unlike most other areas in the financial services field, there is very little regulation of the insurance industry at the federal level. The state agencies listed here enforce all state insurance laws. Insurance commissioners must approve of the sale of all life, health, automobile and homeowners insurance products in their states. Some states, such as New York and California, are particularly rigorous in approving any new product for sale to state residents. If a product has been approved for sale in one of those states, it is often approved elsewhere as well.

When there are problems with an insurance company, these regulators step in. For example, they oversee the process of merging failing insurance companies into strong ones. They also protect policyholders by assuring that insurance companies keep adequate reserves. In the case of an insurance company failure, they see to it that policyholders' interests are protected as much as possible. State insurance offices also respond to consumer complaints against insurance companies on such issues as unfair pricing, denial of insurance claims, and deceptive advertising practices. Before bringing a complaint to one of these agencies, however, it is important to complain to the insurance company first. If the problem has not been resolved at that level, then these agencies should be consulted.

These insurance regulators also offer assistance to those looking to purchase insurance coverage. They may provide helpful literature about the kinds of insurance policies being offered, and also be able to inform buyers about patterns of complaints against particular companies.

ALABAMA
Commissioner of Insurance
135 South Union Street
Montgomery, Alabama 36130
(205) 269-3550

ALASKA
Director of Insurance
State Office Building, P.O. Box D.
Juneau, Alaska 99811
(907) 465-2515

ARIZONA
Director of Insurance
3030 North 3rd Street, Suite 1100
Phoenix, Arizona 85012
(602) 542-5400

ARKANSAS
Insurance Commissioner
400 University Tower Building
Little Rock, Arkansas 72204
(501) 371-1325

CALIFORNIA
Insurance Commissioner
17th Floor, 100 Van Ness Avenue
San Francisco, California 94102
(415) 557-9624

COLORADO
Commissioner of Insurance Office
5th Floor, 303 West Colfax
Denver, Colorado 80204
(303) 573-3410

CONNECTICUT
Insurance Commissioner
165 Capitol Avenue
State Office Building
Hartford, Connecticut 06106
(203) 297-3800

DELAWARE
Insurance Commissioner
841 Silver Lake Plaza
Dover, Delaware 19901
(302) 736-4251

DISTRICT OF COLUMBIA
Administrator of Insurance
Suite 1120, 614 H Street, N.W.
Washington, D.C. 20001
(202) 727-8001

FLORIDA
Insurance Commissioner
Plaza Level 11, State Capitol Building
Tallahassee, Florida 32399
(904) 488-3440

GEORGIA
Insurance Commissioner's Office
Suite 716, West Tower Floyd Building
#2 Martin Luther King Jr. Drive
Atlanta, Georgia 30334
(404) 656-2056

HAWAII
Insurance Commissioner
P.O. Box 3614
Honolulu, Hawaii 96811
(808) 548-6522

IDAHO
Director of Insurance
700 West State Street
Boise, Idaho 83720
(208) 334-2250

ILLINOIS
Director of Insurance
4th Floor, 320 W. Washington Street
Springfield, Illinois 62767
(217) 782-4515

INDIANA
Commissioner of Insurance
311 W. Washington Street, Suite 300
Indianapolis, Indiana 46204
(317) 232-2386

IOWA
Commissioner of Insurance
Ground Floor, State Office Building, G23
Des Moines, Iowa 50319
(515) 281-5705

KANSAS
Commissioner of Insurance
420 Southwest 9th Street
Topeka, Kansas 66612
(913) 296-3071

KENTUCKY
Insurance Commissioner
229 West Main Street
Frankfort, Kentucky 40602
(502) 564-3630

LOUISIANA
Commissioner of Insurance
P.O. Box 94214
Baton Rouge, Louisiana 70804
(504) 342-5328

MAINE
Superintendent of Insurance
Hollowell Annex
State House, Station #34
Augusta, Maine 04333
(207) 289-3101

MARYLAND
Insurance Commissioner Office
7th Floor South
501 St. Paul Place
Baltimore, Maryland 21202
(301) 659-6300

MASSACHUSETTS
Commissioner of Insurance
100 Cambridge Street
Boston, Massachusetts 02202
(617) 727-3333

MICHIGAN
Commissioner of Insurance
P.O. Box 30018
Lansing, Michigan 48909
(517) 335-2049

MINNESOTA
Deputy Commissioner of Commerce
5th Floor, 500 Metro Square Building
St. Paul, Minnesota 55101
(612) 296-6907

MISSISSIPPI
Commissioner of Insurance
P.O. Box 79
Jackson, Mississippi 39205
(601) 359-3569

MISSOURI
Director of Insurance
P.O. Box 690
Jefferson City, Missouri 65102
(314) 751-2451

MONTANA
Deputy Commissioner of Insurance
Mitchell Building, Room 270
Helena, Montana 59604
(406) 444-2040

NEBRASKA
Director of Insurance
941 O Street, Suite 400
Lincoln, Nebraska 68509
(402) 471-2201

NEVADA
Commissioner of Insurance
Nye Building
201 South Falls Street
Carson City, Nevada 89710
(702) 885-4270

NEW HAMPSHIRE
Insurance Commissioner
169 Manchester Street
Concord, New Hampshire 03301
(603) 271-2261

NEW JERSEY
Commissioner of Insurance
20 West State Street, CN 325
Trenton, New Jersey 08625
(609) 292-5360

NEW MEXICO
Superintendent of Insurance
PERA Building, P.O. Drawer 1269
Santa Fe, New Mexico 87504
(505) 827-4535

NEW YORK
Superintendent of Insurance
Empire State Plaza, Building 1
Albany, New York 10013
(518) 474-6600

NORTH CAROLINA
Commissioner of Insurance
430 North Salisbury Street
P.O. Box 26387
Raleigh, North Carolina 27611
(919) 733-7343, (800) 662-7777

NORTH DAKOTA
Commissioner of Insurance
5th Floor, Capitol Building
Bismarck, North Dakota 58505
(701) 224-2440

OHIO
Director of Insurance
2100 Stella Court
Columbus, Ohio 43266
(614) 644-2658

OKLAHOMA
Insurance Commissioner
1901 North Walnut
Oklahoma City, Oklahoma 73105
(405) 521-2828

OREGON
Insurance Commissioner
21 Labor and Industries Building
Salem, Oregon 97310
(503) 378-4120

PENNSYLVANIA
Commissioner of Insurance
1326 Strawberry Square
Harrisburg, Pennsylvania 17120
(717) 787-5173

PUERTO RICO
Commissioner of Insurance
P.O. Box 8330
Fernandez Juntos Station
Santurce, Puerto Rico 00910
(809) 724-6565

RHODE ISLAND
Insurance Director
233 Richmond Street
Providence, Rhode Island 02903
(401) 277-2223

SOUTH CAROLINA
Insurance Commissioner
P.O. Box 10015
Columbia, South Carolina 29202
(803) 758-3266

SOUTH DAKOTA
Director of Insurance
910 Sioux
State Capitol Building
Pierre, South Dakota 57501
(605) 773-4104

TENNESSEE
Assistant Commissioner of Insurance
Volunteer Plaza Building
500 James Robertson Parkway
Nashville, Tennessee 37219
(615) 741-2176

TEXAS
State Board of Insurance
1110 San Jacinto Boulevard
Austin, Texas 78701
(512) 463-6169

UTAH
Commissioner of Insurance
P.O. Box 45803
Salt Lake City, Utah 84145
(801) 530-6400

VERMONT
Commissioner of Banking and Insurance
120 State Street
Montpelier, Vermont 05602
(802) 828-3301

VIRGINIA
Commissioner of Insurance
Jefferson Building
1220 Bank Street, P.O. Box 1157
Richmond, Virginia 23209
(804) 786-3396

VIRGIN ISLANDS
Commissioner of Insurance
Office of Lieutenant Governor
P.O. Box 450, Charlotte Amalie
St. Thomas, Virgin Islands 00801
(809) 774-2991

WASHINGTON
Insurance Commissioner
Insurance Building AQ21
Olympia, Washington 98504
(206) 753-7301

WEST VIRGINIA
Insurance Commissioner
2019 Washington Street East
Charleston, West Virginia 25305
(304) 348-3354

WISCONSIN
Commissioner of Insurance
P.O. Box 7873
Madison, Wisconsin 53707
(608) 266-3585

WYOMING
Insurance Commissioner
122 West 25th Street, Herschler Building
Cheyenne, Wyoming 82002
(307) 777-7401

U.S. STATE SECURITIES REGULATORS

Anyone dealing with the potential purchase or sale of securities might want to consult with the state regulators listed here. Brokerage firms and financial planners selling securities must pass tests adminstered by state securities departments. In the event of any malfeasance on the part of those with a license to sell securities, the state securities department will look into the complaint, and possibly revoke the license, if such action is called for.

These regulators protect buyers of securities sold in their states in another way: They screen all securities offering documents such as prospectuses to ensure that adequate information has been disclosed and that the deal is not fraudulent. The securities office will not judge each deal on its investment potential, but it will reject offerings which it deems abusive. This prescreening process is commonly called the blue-sky process, because a judge once asserted that a particular offering had as much value as a patch of blue sky. It is important to ask these state securities regulators, therefore, if a particular security, such as a mutual fund or limited partnership, has passed the blue sky process in one's state. If it has not, state residents are not allowed to buy it.

Besides watching over the securities industry in their states and screening new securities offerings, state securities offices can be helpful in explaining the pros and cons of various kinds of securities. They often have helpful literature describing what investors should watch for in making good investments and avoiding bad ones. In general, these offices will be one of the best places to contact about any question that might come up regarding a security sold in one's state.

ALABAMA
Securities Commissioner
2nd Floor, 166 Commerce Street
Montgomery, Alabama 36130
(205) 261-2984

ALASKA
Banking, Securities & Corporations
Division & Economic
  Development Department
Post Office Box D
Juneau, Alaska 99811
(907) 465-2521

ARIZONA
Securities Division
Corporation Commission
1200 West Washington
Phoenix, Arizona 85007
(602) 255-4242

ARKANSAS
Securities Commissioner
201 East Markham
Little Rock, Arkansas 72201
(501) 371-1011

CALIFORNIA
Securities Commissioner
Department of Corporations
Suite 205, 1025 P Street
Sacramento, California 95814
(916) 445-8200

COLORADO
Division of Securities
Department of Regulatory Agencies
1560 Broadway, Suite 1450
Denver, Colorado 80202
(303) 866-2607

CONNECTICUT
Securities & Business Investments
Department of Banking
44 Capitol Avenue
Hartford, Connecticut 06106
(203) 566-4560

DELAWARE
Secretary of State
Townsend Building
Dover, Delaware 19901
(302) 736-4111

DISTRICT OF COLUMBIA
Deputy Mayor for Financial Management
Suite 423, 1350 Pennsylvania Avenue, N.W.
Washington, D.C. 20004
(202) 727-2476

FLORIDA
Securities Division
Department of Banking & Finance
The Capitol
Tallahassee, Florida 32301
(904) 488-9805

GEORGIA
Securities Director
Room 214, 270 Washington Street
Atlanta, Georgia 30334
(404) 656-2174

HAWAII
Business Registration Division
Commerce & Consumer Affairs Department
1010 Richards Street
Honolulu, Hawaii 96810
(808) 548-6521

IDAHO
Department of Finance
700 West State Street
Boise, Idaho 83720
(208) 334-3684

ILLINOIS
Secretary of State
213 State House
Springfield, Illinois 62756
(217) 782-2201

INDIANA
Securities Commissioner
Suite 560, 1 North Capitol Street
Indianapolis, Indiana 46204
(317) 232-6681

IOWA
Securities Division
Insurance Department
Lucas Stone Office Building
Des Moines, Iowa 50319
(515) 281-4441

KANSAS
Securities Commissioner
Suite 212, 503 Kansas Avenue
Topeka, Kansas 66603
(913) 296-3307

KENTUCKY
Financial Institutions Department
Public Protection & Regulation Cabinet
911 Leawood Drive
Frankfort, Kentucky 40601
(502) 564-3390

LOUISIANA
Securities Commission
Suite 315, 325 Loyola Avenue
Baton Rouge, Louisiana 70112
(514) 568-5515

MAINE
Bureau of Banking; Business, Occupational
& Professional Regulations Department
Suite 36, State House Station
Augusta, Maine 04333
(207) 289-3231

MARYLAND
Division of Securities, Office of
the Attorney General
4th Floor, 7 North Calvert Street
Baltimore, Maryland 21202
(301) 576-6360

MASSACHUSETTS
Securities Division, the Office
of Secretary of Commonwealth
Suite 337, State House
Boston, Massachusetts 02133
(617) 727-3548

MICHIGAN
Securities Division, Department of
Commerce
6546 Mercantile Way
Lansing, Michigan 48909
(517) 334-6200

MINNESOTA
Registration & Licensing Division
of the Department of Commerce
5th Floor, Metro Square Building
St. Paul, Minnesota 55101
(612) 296-2594

MISSISSIPPI
Securities Division
Office of Secretary of State
401 Mississippi Street
Jackson, Mississippi 39201
(601) 359-1350

MISSOURI
Division of Securities
Office of Secretary of State
Truman Building, Box 778
Jefferson City, Missouri 65102
(314) 751-4136

MONTANA
Securities Division
Office of State Auditor
Capitol Station
Helena, Montana 59620
(406) 444-2040

NEBRASKA
Department of Banking & Finance
P.O. Box 95006
301 Centennial Mall South
Lincoln, Nebraska 68509
(402) 471-2171

NEVADA
Securities and Fraud Division
Office of Secretary of State
State Capitol
Carson City, Nevada 89710
(702) 885-5203

NEW HAMPSHIRE
Division of Securities
Department of Insurance
169 Manchester Street
Concord, New Hampshire 03301
(603) 271-2261

NEW JERSEY
Bureau of Securities
Suite 308, 80 Mulberry Street
Newark, New Jersey 07102
(201) 648-2040

NEW MEXICO
Securities Division
Regulation & Licensing Department
Bataan Memorial Building
Santa Fe, New Mexico 87503
(505) 827-7750

NEW YORK
Bureau of Investor Protection & Securities
120 Broadway
New York, New York 10271
(212) 341-2222

NORTH CAROLINA
Division of Securities
Office of Secretary of State
Suite 302, 300 North Salisbury Street
Raleigh, North Carolina 27611
(919) 733-3924

NORTH DAKOTA
Securities Commissioner
P.O. Box 95006
00th floor, State Capitol
Bismarck, North Dakota 58505
(701) 224-2910

OHIO
Division of Securities of the
  Department of Commerce
77 South High Street
Columbus, Ohio 43266
(614) 466-3723

OKLAHOMA
Securities Commissioner
Post Office Box 53595
Oklahoma City, Oklahoma 73152
(405) 521-2451

OREGON
Division of Securities
Department of Insurance and Finance
21 Labor and Industries Building
Salem, Oregon 97310
(503) 378-4100

PENNSYLVANIA
Securities Commissioner
2nd Floor, 1010 North 7th Street
Harrisburg, Pennsylvania 17102
(717) 787-8061

PUERTO RICO
Securities Commissioner's Office
Department of the Treasury
P.O. Box 3508
San Juan, Puerto Rico 00904
(809) 723-1122

RHODE ISLAND
Banking Division
Department of Business Regulation
100 North Main Street
Providence, Rhode Island 02903
(401) 277-2405

SOUTH CAROLINA
Securities Division
P.O. Box 11350
Columbia, South Carolina 29211
(803) 758-21584

SOUTH DAKOTA
Division of Securities
Commerce & Regulations Department
910 Sioux, State Capitol
Pierre, South Dakota 57501
(605) 773-3177

TENNESSEE
Securities Division
Department of Commerce & Insurance
500 James Robertson Parkway
Nashville, Tennessee 37219
(615) 741-2241

TEXAS
Securities Board
1800 San Jacinto
Austin, Texas 78711
(512) 474-2233

UTAH
Securities Commissioner
Department of Commerce
Post Office Box 45802
Salt Lake City, Utah 84145
(801) 530-6607

VERMONT
Securities Commissioner
Department of Banking & Insurance
120 State Street
Montpelier, Vermont 05602
(802) 828-3301

VIRGINIA
Securities and Retail
  Franchising Bureau
Post Office Box 1197
1220 Bank Street
Richmond, Virginia 23219
(804) 786-7751

VIRGIN ISLANDS
Corporations & Trade Names Division
Office of Lieutenant Governor
P.O. Box 450
St. Thomas, Virgin Islands 00801
(809) 774-2991

WASHINGTON
Securities Division
Department of Licensing
Highways-Licensing Building
Olympia, Washington 98504
(206) 753-6928

WEST VIRGINIA
Securities Division
Office of State Auditor
100 State Capitol Building
Charleston, West Virginia 25305
(304) 348-2257

WISCONSIN
Commissioner of Securities
P.O. Box 1768
111 West Wilson Street
Madison, Wisconsin 53703
(608) 266-3431

WYOMING
Secretary of State
State Capitol
Cheyenne, Wyoming 82002
(307) 777-7378

CANADIAN PROVINCIAL AGENCIES

The provincial and territorial agencies listed here have many of the same powers as state regulators in the United States. We have listed the two major finance and investment agencies in each province. The Consumer and Corporate Affairs Agencies regulate such areas as consumer protection, mortgages, insurance, credit, and securities, among other areas. The Finance Departments of each province run the financial affairs of government and collect taxes.

ALBERTA
Consumer & Corporate Affairs Department
22nd Floor, 10025 Jasper Avenue,
Edmonton, Alberta T5J 3Z5
(403) 422-3935

Treasury Department
434 Terrace Building
9515 107th Street
Edmonton, Alberta T5K 2C3
(403) 427-9957

BRITISH COLUMBIA
Ministry of Consumer & Corporate Affairs
940 Blanshard Street
Victoria, British Columbia V8W 3E6
(604) 387-3126

Ministry of Finance
Parliament Buildings
Victoria, British Columbia V8V 1X4
(604) 387-9278

MANITOBA
Consumer & Corporate Affairs Department
114 Garry Street
Winnipeg, Manitoba R3C 1G1
(204) 956-2040

Department of Finance
109 Legislative Building
Winnipeg, Manitoba R3C OV8
(204) 945-3754

NEW BRUNSWICK
Consumer Affairs Division
Justice Department
P.O. Box 6000
Fredericton, New Brunswick E3B 5H1
(506) 453-2682

Department of Finance
Centennial Building
P.O. Box 6000
New Brunswick E3B 5H1
(506) 453-2511

NEWFOUNDLAND
Department of Consumers Affairs and
 Communications
Elizabeth Towers, P.O. Box 4750
St. John's, Newfoundland A1C 5T7
(709) 576-2600

Department of Finance
Confederation Building, P.O. Box 4750
St. John's, Newfoundland A1C 5T7
(709) 576-2924

NORTHWEST TERRITORIES
Department of Finance
P.O. Box 2703
Whitehorse, Yukon Territory Y1A 2C6
(403) 667-5343

NOVA SCOTIA
Department of Consumer Affairs
P.O. Box 998
Halifax, Nova Scotia B3J 2X3
(902) 424-4690

Department of Finance
P.O. Box 187
Halifax, Nova Scotia B3J 2N3
(902) 424-5720

ONTARIO
Ministry of Consumer & Commercial
 Relations
555 Yonge Street
Toronto, Ontario M7A 2H6
(416) 963-1111

Ministry of Treasury and Economics
4th Floor, Frost Building South
Queen's Park, Toronto M7A 1Z2
(416) 965-4746

PRINCE EDWARD ISLAND
Consumer Services Division,
 Justice Department
P.O. Box 2000
Charlottetown,
Prince Edward Island C1A 7N8
(902) 368-4588

Department of Finance
P.O. Box 2000
Charlottetown, Prince Edward I. C1A 7N8
(902) 368-4050

QUEBEC
Ministère des Finances
12 rue St. Louis
Quebec, P.Q. G1R 5L3
(418) 691-2233

Ministère de la Protection du Consommateur
6 rue de L'Université
Quebec, P.Q. G1R 5G8
(418) 643-1557

SASKATCHEWAN
Department of Consumer and Commercial
Affairs
1871 Smith Street
Regina, Saskatchewan S4P 3V7
(306) 787-1928

Department of Finance
10th Floor, Treasury Board Division,
2350 Albert Street
Regina, Saskatchewan S4P 4A6
(306) 787-6532

FINANCE AND INVESTMENT ORGANIZATIONS

This is a list of the most important organizations in the finance and investment field. Included are trade associations, which educate the public about their industry and lobby for their political positions in Congress; self-regulatory organizations, which regulate the conduct of the marketplace under the supervision of a federal regulatory agency; and consumer and investor organizations, which educate consumers and investors and help them resolve problems.

American Association of Commodity Traders
9 South William Street
New York, New York

Represents traders of commodity futures and options and educates the public about the commodity markets.

American Association of Individual Investors
625 North Michigan Avenue
Chicago, Illinois 60611
(312) 280-0170

Educates individual investors about opportunities in stocks, bonds and mutual funds and investment computer software. Conducts seminars, workshops and offers home study courses.

American Bankers Association
1120 Connecticut Avenue, N.W.
Washington, D.C. 20036
(202) 663-5000

Represents commercial banks in legislative and regulatory activities and legal action. Also educates the public about banking.

American Council of Life Insurance
1001 Pennsylvania Avenue, N.W.
Washington, D.C. 20004
(202) 624-2000

Represents life insurance companies in lobby-

ing on life insurance-related issues and educates the public about insurance.

American Financial Services Association
1101 14th Street, N.W.
Washington, D.C. 20005
(202) 289-0400

Represents companies that lend to consumers, mostly finance companies. Lobbies on issues related to consumer lending, and also educates the public about use of credit and budgeting.

American Institute of Certified Public Accountants
1211 Avenue of the Americas
New York, New York 10036
(212) 575-6200

Professional society of certified public accountants which establishes auditing and reporting standards and prepares the Uniform CPA Examination for state licensing bodies.

American Insurance Association
Suite 1000, 1130 Connecticut Avenue, N.W.
Washington, D.C. 20036
(202) 828-7100

Represents property and liability insurance companies in lobbying on insurance-related issues. Educates the public about safety issues and suggests codes to governments on such areas as industrial safety and fire prevention.

American League of Financial Institutions
Suite 201, 1709 New York Avenue
Washington, D.C. 20006
(202) 628-5624

Represents minority savings and loan associations. Provides counseling, consulting and technical assistance to member associations.

American Management Association
135 West 50th Street
New York, New York 10020
(212) 586-8100

Non-profit educational organization working to improve management skills in government and industry.

American Society of Chartered Life
    Underwriters and Chartered Financial
    Consultants
270 Bryn Mawr Avenue
Bryn Mawr, Pennsylvania 19010
(215) 526-2500

Professional society of insurance agents and executives, accountants, attorneys and trust officers who hold the CLU (Chartered Life Underwriter) or the ChFC (Chartered Financial Consultant) designation. These designations are earned by attending certain seminars and passing certain examinations.

Appraisers Association of America
60 East 42nd Street
New York, New York 10165
(212) 867-9775

Represents those who give professional appraisals of the value of property, usually for tax or insurance purposes.

Associated Credit Bureaus
16211 Park Ten Place
Houston, Texas 77218
(713) 492-8155

Represents consumer credit bureaus, which maintain files on credit histories of individuals. Consumers can take complaints about a local credit bureau to the Associated Credit Bureaus for resolution.

Association of Financial Guaranty Insurors
122 South Swan Street
Albany, New York 12210
(518) 449-4698

Represents municipal bond, corporate and other bond insurers and financial guarantee

reinsurers. Serves as a forum to discuss issues of mutual concern, to seek acceptable legislation and regulation of the financial guarantee industry, and to promote public understanding of the benefits of financial guarantees.

Association of Publicly Traded Investment
    Funds
201 North Charles Street
Baltimore, Maryland 21201
(301) 752-5900

Represents companies that offer closed-end mutual funds to the public, both in public education about the funds and lobbying on issues relating to the funds.

Bank Administration Institute
60 Gould Center
Rolling Meadows, Illinois 60008
(312) 228-6200, (800) 323-8552,
(800) 942-8861 inside Illinois

Conducts research, sponsors developmental programs and serves as the banking industry's major resource in management, administrative and technical specialties.

Bond Investors Association
Suite 240, 5979 N.W. 151st Street
Miami Lakes, Florida 33014
(305) 557-1832

A non-profit organization that educates and informs members and the general public about legislation and developments affecting bondholders.

Bond & Share Society
26 Broadway
New York, New York 10004
(212) 943-1880

Society for promoting the hobby of scripophily, that is, the collection and study of antique stock and bond certificates.

Canadian Securities Institute
Suite 360, 33 Yonge Street
Toronto, Ontario M5E 1G4 Canada
(416) 364-9130

Provides education on investments to Canadian brokerage firms and the general public.

Consumer Bankers Association
Suite 1200, 1300 North 17th Street
Arlington, Virginia 22209
(703) 276-1750

Represents commercial banks, savings and

loans and credit unions and educates the public about banking.

College For Financial Planning
4695 South Monaco Street
Denver, Colorado 80237
(303) 220-1200

Provides mail-order educational material and administers tests for financial planners. A person who has passed the College's multi-part test, is a certified financial planner, and is entitled to use the CFP designation.

Council of Better Business Bureaus
1515 Wilson Boulevard
Arlington, Virginia 22209
(703) 276-0100

Mediates disputes between consumers and businesses and promotes ethical business standards.

Credit Union National Association
P.O. Box 431
Madison, Wisconsin 53701
(608) 231-4000

Represents credit unions in lobbying on issues related to credit unions. Promotes credit union membership and the formation of new credit unions, and educates the public about credit unions.

Coalition of Publicly Traded Partnerships
Suite 200, 1625 K Street, N.W.
Washington, D.C. 20006
(202) 857-0670

Represents master limited partnerships and their corporate sponsors in legislative and lobbying matters.

Commercial-Investment Real Estate Council
430 North Michigan Avenue
Chicago, Illinois 60601
(312) 329-8624, (800) 621-7035

Represents real estate brokers, developers and mortgage bankers involved in commercial investment.

Council of Institutional Investors
Suite 405, 1420 16th Street, N.W.
Washington, D.C. 20036
(202) 745-0800

Represents trustees from public and union pension funds, non-profit foundations and endowment funds. Educates members about corporate actions and ways to boost returns on investments.

Electronic Funds Transfer Association
Suite 310, 1421 Prince Street
Alexandria, Virginia 22314
(703) 549-9800

Provides a forum for financial institutions, retailers, telecommunications companies and other businesses involved in the transfer of funds by computer.

Employee Benefit Research Institute
Suite 600, 2121 K Street
Washington, D.C. 20037
(202) 659-0670

Made up of corporations, banks, insurance companies, unions and other organizations concerned with the future of employee benefit programs.

Financial Accounting Foundation
Suite 7, 401 Merritt
Norwalk, Connecticut 06856
(203) 847-0700

Maintains the Financial Accounting Standards Board, which sets financial reporting standards for private-sector organizations, and the Governmental Accounting Standards Board, which sets standards for state and local governments.

Financial Analysts Federation
5 Boar's Head Lane
Charlottesville, Virginia 22903
(804) 977-8977, (800) 247-8132

International organization of investment professionals, designed to further the education and enhance the standards of its members and the general investment community.

Financial Executives Institute
10 Madison Avenue
Morristown, New Jersey 07962
(201) 898-4600

Organization of executives (such as controllers, treasurers, vice presidents of finance and chief financial officers) who perform finance functions in corporations.

Financial Products Standards Board
Suite 320, 10065 East Harvard Avenue
Denver, Colorado 80231
(303) 751-7600

Sets standards for financial products to aid financial planners and the public in evaluating investment strategies.

Futures Industry Association
1825 Eye Street, N.W.
Washington, D.C. 20006
(202) 466-5460

Represents brokerage firms that deal in stock index and commodity futures, both in lobbying on futures-related issues and educating the public about the futures industry.

Gold Institute, The
1026 16th Street, N.W.
Washington, D.C. 20036
(202) 783-0500

Represents gold mining, manufacturing and retailing firms, conducts research on technology and industrial uses. Also compiles statistics on gold production, distribution and sales.

Health Insurance Association of America
Suite 1200, 1025 Connecticut Avenue, N.W.
Washington, D.C. 20036
(202) 223-7780

Represents accident and health insurance companies.

Independent Bankers Association of America
Suite 950, 1 Thomas Circle, N.W.
Washington, D.C. 20005
(202) 659-8111

Represents small- and medium-sized commercial banks in lobbying on banking issues. Provides its members with income-producing and cost-saving programs in areas such as credit cards, equipment purchasing, advertising, loan participations and insurance.

Industry Council For Tangible Assets
25 E Street, N.W.
Washington, D.C. 20001
(202) 783-3500

Monitors regulations and legislation concerning the manufacture, sale and distribution of precious metals, stamps, coins and gems.

Institute of Certified Financial Planners
Suite 320, 10065 East Harvard Avenue
Denver, Colorado 80231
(303) 751-7600, (800) 282-7526

Represents financial planners who have earned the CFP (Certified Financial Planner) designation. Provides continuing education for planners, and refers consumers who inquire about CFP's in their area.

Institute of Chartered Financial Analysts
P.O. Box 3668
Charlottesville, Virginia 22903
(804) 977-6600

Represents financial analysts who have passed the CFA (Chartered Financial Analyst) examination. Conducts continuing education seminars of financial and investment analysis.

Insurance Information Institute
110 William Street
New York, New York 10038
(212) 669-9200,
(800) 221-4954

Represents property and liability insurance companies to educate the public about insurance issues. Maintains a consumer insurance hotline.

Insurance Institute of America
720 Providence Road
Malvern, Pennsylvania 19355
(215) 644-2100

Sponsors educational programs for property and liability insurance personnel.

Insurance Services Office
160 Water Street
New York, New York 10038
(212) 487-5000

Establishes rate guidelines for property and liability insurance companies.

International Association for Financial Planning
2 Concourse Parkway, Suite 800
Atlanta, Georgia 30328
(404) 395-1605

Represents those in the financial services industry who are involved with financial planning. Promotes education of financial planners and offers assistance to the public in finding planners in their area.

International Credit Association
243 North Lindbergh Boulevard
St. Louis, Missouri 63141
(314) 991-3030

Represents members of the credit industry. Conducts continuing education programs on credit issues.

International Franchise Association
1025 Connecticut Avenue, N.W.
Washington, D.C. 20036
(202) 659-0790

Represents franchisors and franchisees of many different kinds of businesses by lobbying Congress on issues of concern to the industry. Gives advice to those wanting to evaluate franchise opportunities.

Investment Company Institute
Suite 600, 1600 M Street, N.W.
Washington, D.C. 20036
(202) 293-7700

Represents load and no-load mutual fund companies, open-end and closed-end funds and unit investment trusts. Lobbies on mutual fund issues in Congress and educates the public about the uses of mutual funds.

Investment Counsel Association of America
20 Exchange Place
New York, New York 10005
(212) 344-0999

Represents firms that invest clients' money in stocks and bonds for a fee. Provides a list of money managers for those looking for one.

Investment Management Consultants
  Association
Suite 340C, 10200 East Girard Avenue
Denver, Colorado 80231
(303) 337-2424

Represents brokers, consultants and money managers. Works to increase public awareness and knowledge of investment management consultants. Also certifies consultants.

Investment Partnership Association
Suite 500, 1100 Connecticut Avenue, N.W.
Washington, D.C. 20036
(202) 775-9750

Works to promote and preserve the investment partnership among investors in energy, leasing, real estate, research and development and telecommunications.

Investor Responsibility Research Center
Suite 600, 1755 Massachusetts Avenue, N.W.
Washington, D.C. 20036
(202) 939-6500

Publishes impartial reports and analyses on contemporary business and public policy issues for corporations and institutional investors that vote proxies independently.

Life Insurance Marketing and Research
  Association
P.O. Box 208
Hartford, Connecticut 06141
(203) 677-0033

Conducts research, seminars and schools for the life insurance industry.

Managed Futures Trade Association
P.O. Box 22184
Pittsburgh, Pennsylvania 15222
(203) 221-1260

Represents and educates trading advisors, brokers and individuals in the area of managed futures.

Microcomputer Investors Association
902 Anderson Drive
Fredricksburg, Virginia 22405
(703) 371-5474

Represents and educates professional investors using microcomputers. Also operates hardware and software library and compiles investing statistics.

Mortgage Bankers Association of America
1125 15th Street, N.W.
Washington, D.C. 20005
(202) 861-6500

Represents mortgage lenders such as mortgage bankers, commercial banks, savings and loans and insurance companies. The MBAA lobbies on housing finance issues before Congress and conducts continuing education seminars for members of the industry.

Municipal Securities Rulemaking Board
1818 N Street, N.W.
Washington, D.C. 20036
(202) 223-9347

A self-regulatory agency for brokers and dealers in the municipal securities industry.

Mutual Fund Education Alliance
Suite 1632, 520 North Michigan Avenue
Chicago Illinois 60611
(312) 527-1454

Represents no-load mutual funds and provides information to consumers on the name, telephone number and kinds of funds available.

National Association of Business Economists
Suite 300, 28790 Chagrin Boulevard
Cleveland, Ohio 44122
(216) 464-7986

Society comprised of corporate and governmental economists and those with an active
interest in applied, practical economics.

National Association of Futures Trading
  Advisors
111 East Wacker Drive
Chicago, Illinois 60601
(312) 644-6610

Represents commodity trading advisors in
industry matters and to government agencies.

National Association of Investment
  Companies
915 15th Street, N.W.
Washington, D.C. 20005
(202) 347-8600

Provides technical assistance and monitors
legislation for investment companies supplying capital to minority-owned small businesses.

National Association of Investors Corporation
1515 East 11 Mile Road
Royal Oak, Michigan 48067
(313) 543-0612

Represents investment clubs. Helps people
set up such clubs, and monitors performance
of the clubs.

National Association of Manufacturers
1331 Pennsylvania Avenue, N.W.
Washington, D.C. 20004
(202) 637-3000

Represents industry views to government on
national and international issues. Also reviews
legislation, administrative rulings and judicial
decisions affecting industry.

National Association of OTC Companies
Suite 950, 1707 L Street, N.W.
Washington, D.C. 20036
(202) 785-9200

Represents companies with stocks traded over
the counter.

National Association of Personal Financial
  Advisors
Suite 105, 1130 Lake Cook Road
Buffalo Grove, Illinois 60089
(312) 537-7722

Represents financial planners who work only

for a consulting fee, and do not take commissions for selling products.

National Association of Real Estate
  Investment Trusts
Suite 705, 1129 20th Street, N.W.
Washington, D.C. 20036
(202) 785-8717

Represents real estate investment trusts before Congress in lobbying on REIT-related
issues, and educates the public about REITs.

National Association of Realtors
430 North Michigan Avenue
Chicago, Illinois 60611
(312) 329-8200

Represents Realtors by lobbying Congress on
real estate-related issues and educates the
public about the realty business.

National Association of Securities Dealers
1735 K Street, N.W.
Washington, D.C. 20006
(202) 728-8000

Organization formed under the supervision of
the Securities and Exchange Commission to
self-regulate the securities markets, particularly the NASDAQ (National Association of
Securities Dealers Automated Quotations)
system, which it owns and operates. Also
responsible for the over-the-counter municipal securities and government securities
markets.

National Association of Small Business
  Investment Companies
Suite 1101, 1156 15th Street, N.W.
Washington, D.C. 20005
(202) 833-8230

Represents small business investment companies (SBICs) that are publicly traded or private companies that invest in private small
businesses. The Association lobbies Congress
on issues related to the industry and educates
the public about SBICs.

National Association of Women Business
  Owners
918 6th Street, N.W.
Washington, D.C. 20006
(202) 955-5790

Provides technical assistance, management
training and business and economic information to women business owners and represents members in legislative and lobbying
efforts.

National Council of Savings Institutions
1101 15th Street, N.W.
Washington, D.C. 20005
(202) 857-3100

Represents savings and loans and savings banks in educating its members and the public about issues relating to banking and housing finance.

National Foundation For Consumer Credit
8701 Georgia Avenue
Silver Spring, Maryland 20910
(301) 589-5600

Represents grantors of credit to consumers such as finance companies, retailers and banks. Sponsors Consumer Credit Counseling Service centers around the country to give low- or no-cost aid to consumers in credit difficulty.

National Futures Association
Suite 1600, 200 West Madison Street
Chicago, Illinois 60606
(800) 621-3570,
(800) 572-9400 in Illinois

Represents and sets standards for the firms and individuals that sell commodity futures and options on commodities. Resolves disputes between its members and customers with complaints against those members.

National Insurance Consumer Organziation
121 North Payne Street
Alexandria, Virginia 22314
(703) 548-8050

Represents and educates consumers about insurance issues.

National Investor Relations Institute
1730 M Street, N.W.
Washington, D.C. 20036
(202) 861-0630

Represents executives in the investor relations and financial communications fields. Conducts continuing education programs for members.

National Venture Capital Association
1655 North Fort Meyer Drive
Arlington, Virginia 22209
(703) 528-4370

Represents venture capitalists seeking to invest money in growing enterprises. Lobbies in Congress for programs to improve the environment for venture capital investing.

New York Society of Security Analysts
2nd Floor, 71 Broadway
New York, New York 10006
(212) 344-8450

Affiliate of the Financial Analysts Federation which conducts regular meetings between securities analysts and managements of companies followed by those analysts. This is the largest society in the country, though there are similar societies in most major American cities as well.

North American Securities Adminstrators
Association
Suite 750, 555 New Jersey Avenue
Washington, D.C. 20001
(202) 737-0900

Represents state and local officials enforcing "blue sky" laws in the sale of securities.

Overseas Private Investment Corporation
1615 M Street, N.W.
Washington, D.C. 20527
(202) 457-7000

Supports and assists qualified U.S. investors in private ventures in less developed countries.

Public Securities Association
40 Broad Street
New York, New York 10004
(212) 809-7000

International trade association of banks and broker/dealers in U.S. government and federal agency securities, municipal securities, mortgage-backed securities and money-market securities.

Real Estate Securities and Syndication
Institute
Suite 650, 430 North Michigan Avenue
Chicago, Illinois 60611
(312) 670-6760

Represents realtors and broker/dealers engaged in real estate syndication, limited partnerships and other real estate securities. Works to improve the skills and raise the standards of members.

Securities Industry Association
120 Broadway
New York, New York 10271
(212) 608-1500

Represents securities broker/dealers, underwriters and investment bankers in lobbying Congress on issues of concern to the securities industry. Educates the public about the securities industry.

Stockholders of America
1625 Eye Street, N.W.
Washington, D.C. 20006
(202) 783-3430

Monitors legislation and regulations affecting stockholders.

United Shareholders Association
Suite 770, 1667 K Street, N.W.
Washington, D.C. 20006
(202) 393-4600

Works to increase shareholders' rights and battle abuses by corporate management. Represents members in lobbying efforts.

United States Chamber of Commerce
1615 H Street, N.W.
Washington, D.C. 20062
(202) 463-5000

Represents the business community's views on business, the economy and other issues at the federal, state and local level. Sponsors educational programs and maintains a business forecast and survey center.

United States League of Savings Institutions
Suite 801, 1709 New York Avenue, N.W.
Washington, D.C. 20006
(202) 637-8900

Represents savings and loans in lobbying before Congress on issues affecting the thrift industry. Educates the public about the savings and loan and housing industries.

FINANCE AND INVESTMENT PUBLICATIONS

The following is a list of just about all of the major publications that can help keep you informed about the fast-changing world of finance and investment. The list encompasses the full spectrum of publications, from mass circulation business magazines to investment newsletters that reach only a handful of subscribers. The publications also cover a wide variety of topics, from investment advice about stocks, bonds, money market instruments, and commodities to mutual funds, taxation, entrepreneurship, and corporate finance. Other subjects covered include international investing, banking, precious metals, collectibles, management trends, economic forecasting, socially conscious investing, estate planning, venture capital, insider trading, real estate, and options. The title of each newsletter will often give you a clue to its subject matter.

Almost all the publications are available for a subscription charge; some also require that you join the organization that puts out the publication. Many will send you a sample either free or for a nominal charge.

Before subscribing to a newsletter, you must assess your needs and level of sophistication. Some letters listed here are designed for the novice investor with a relatively small amount of money to put into stocks or mutual funds. Other publications are aimed at a highly sophisticated audience that is knowledgeable about technical analysis, commodities trading, or some other specialty. In general, the more complex the publication, the higher the subscription fee.

Whichever publications you read, employ an appropriate amount of caution before following specific investment recommendations. Despite many advisors' claims, no one calls every move in the complex financial markets right every time. You should be satisfied if you find a few letters that offer a style you are comfortable with and have a good long-term track record at spotting unfolding investment trends.

AAII Journal
Suite 1900, 625 North Michigan Avenue
Chicago, Illinois 60611 (312) 280-0170

Acquisition Mart, The
Business Publications, Inc.
Suite D, 10055 Barnes Canyon Road
San Diego, California 92121
(619) 457-7577, (800) 523-7543,
(800) 453-2646 inside California

Addison Report, The
P.O. Box 402
Franklin, Massachusetts 02038
(617) 528-8678

Advisor, The
P.O. Box 13645
Houston, Texas 77019

ACCU Comm Futures Forecast
Suite 187, 3645 28th Street, Southeast
Grand Rapids, Michigan 49508
(616) 676-9765

AgBiotech Stock Letter
AgBiotech Investors
P.O. Box 40460
Berkeley, California 94704 (415) 843-1842

Agriculture (newspaper)
AgriData Resources, Inc.
330 East Kilbourn Avenue
Milwaukee, Wisconsin 53202
(414) 278-7676, (800) 558-9044

Aflak Market Report
P.O. Box 4808
Foster City, California 94404

Alan Shawn Feinstein Insiders Report
37-41 Alhambra Circle
Cranston, Rhode Island 02905
(401) 467-5155

Alexander Letter
Brexmarl, P.O. Box 231
Hamilton 5, Bermuda (809) 295-2686

All-Weather Fund Investor
P.O. Box 6600
Rapid City, South Dakota 57709
(605) 341-1971

America's Fastest Growing Companies
John S. Herold, Inc.
5 Edgewood Avenue
Greenwich, Connecticut 06830 (203) 869-2585

American Banker (newspaper)
One State Street Plaza
New York, New York 10004 (212) 943-8200

American Stock Exchange Weekly Bulletin
86 Trinity Place
New York, New York 10006 (212) 306-1445

ASC Mutual Fund Advisor
American Strategic Capital
Suite 105, 4281 Katella Avenue
Los Alamitos, California 90720
(714) 527-1223

ASTRO Stock Market Advisory
5816 Webster Street
Omaha, Nebraska 68132 (402) 551-3203

Astute Investor, The
Investor's Analysis
P.O. Box 988
Paoli, Pennsylvania 19301
(215) 296-2411, (800) 227-8883

Astute Investor, The
Route 3, Box 310-D
Kingston, Tennessee 37763 (615) 376-2732

Bankers Monthly Magazine
200 West 57th Street
New York, New York 10019 (212) 399-1084

Banking Week (newspaper)
International Thomson Publishing Corp.
One State Street Plaza
New York, New York 10004 (212) 943-6700

Banking Quotation Records
William B. Dana, Co.
213 Silver Beach Avenue
Daytona Beach, Florida 32118
(800) 962-3262

Bankruptcy Data Source, The
Krause & Co.
190 Lombard Street
San Francisco, California 94111
(415) 397-5444

Bankruptcy Opportunities Service
Southeast Executive Park, 100 Executive Drive
Brewster, New York 10509
(914) 278-6500, (800) 772-0024

Barron's National Business and Financial Weekly
200 Liberty Street
New York, New York 10281 (212) 416-2700

Bartlett Letters
P.O. Box 465
Aurora, Illinois 60507 (312) 896-3143

Bauer Financial Reports
Bauer Communications, Inc.
P.O. Drawer 145510
Coral Gables, Florida 33114
(305) 441-2062,
outside Florida (800) 447-0011

Baxter Letter
1030 East Putnam Avenue
Greenwich, Connecticut 06836
(203) 637-4559

Bench Investment Letter
222 Bridge Plaza South
Fort Lee, New Jersey 07024 (201) 585-2333

Best's Insurance Management Reports
A.M. Best Company
Oldwick, New Jersey 08858 (201)-439-2200

Better Investing
National Association of Investors Corp.
1515 East Eleven Mile Road
Royal Oak, Michigan 48067 (313) 543-0612

BioCycle
JG Press
P.O. Box 323
Emmaus, Pennsylvania 10849
(215) 967-4135

BI Research
P.O. Box 133
Redding, CT 06875 (914) 763-5816

Blanchard's American Rarities
Blanchard & Co.
2400 Jefferson Highway
Jefferson, Louisiana 70121 (800) 877-7633

Blue Book of Canadian Business Service Stock
  Reports
Marpep Publishing Ltd.
133 Richmond Street West
Toronto, Ontario M5H 3M8 Canada
(416) 869-1177

Blue Chip Economic Indicators
Blue Chip Financial Forecasts
Capitol Publications, Inc.
Suite 444, 1101 King Street
Alexandria, Virginia 22313
(703) 684-4100, (800) 327-7206

Boardroom Reports
330 West 42nd Street
New York, New York 10036 (212) 239-9000

Board Watch
P.O. Box 2141
Spokane, Washington 99210

Bob Brinker's Marketimer
P.O. Box 7005
Princeton, New Jersey 08543 (201) 359-8838

Bonanza Report
BFG Publishers
Suite 1, 3855 South Valley View Boulevard
Las Vegas, Nevada 89103 (702) 364-1844

Bond Buyer
One State Street Plaza
New York, New York 10004 (212) 943-8200

Bond Fund Survey
Survey Publications
P.O. Box 4180, Grand Central Station
New York, New York 10163 (212) 988-2498

Bond Market Advisor
Suite 290, 900 Ashwood Parkway
Atlanta, Georgia 30338 (404) 668-0508

Bond Profit Report
KCI Communications
Suite 400, 1101 King Street
Alexandria, Virginia 22314 (203) 548-2400

Bondweek
Institutional Investor, Inc.
488 Madison Avenue
New York, New York 10022 (212) 303-3300

Boot Cove Economic Forecast
Voight Industries, Inc.
P.O. Box 220
Lubec, Maine 04652 (207) 733-5593

Bottom Line
330 West 42nd Street
New York, New York 10036 (212) 239-9000

Bowser Report
P.O. Box 6278
Newport News, Virginia 23606
(804) 877-5979

Braun's Stock Index
317 Wyntfield Drive
Lewisville, North Carolina 27023
(919) 945-9110

Breakthrough Investing
American Media Group
Suite 300, 951 Broken Sound Parkway N.W.
Boca Raton, Florida 33431 (407) 241-1800

Bretz's Juncture Recognition
P.O. Box 1209
Pompano Beach, Florida 33061
(305) 564-0643

Broadcast Banking
Broadcast Investor
Broadcast Investor Charts
Broadcast Stats
Paul Kagan Associates
126 Clock Tower Place
Carmel, California 93923 (408) 624-1536

Browning Newsletter
Fraser Management Associates, Inc.
P.O. Box 494
Burlington, Vermont 05402 (802) 658-0322

Bruce Gould on Commodities
P.O. Box 16
Seattle, Washington 98111

Bullish Review Of Commodity Futures
  Markets
14600 Blaine Avenue East
Rosemount, Minnesota 55068
(612) 423-4949

Business Month
488 Madison Avenue
New York, New York 10022 (212) 326-2600

Business Week Magazine
1221 Avenue of the Americas
New York, New York 10020 (212) 512-2511

Cable TV Investor
Cable TV Investor Charts
Paul Kagan Associates
126 Clock Tower Place
Carmel, California 93923 (408) 624-1536

Cabot Market Letter, The
P.O. Box 3044
Salem, Massachusetts 01970
(617) 745-5532

Cadence Universe Performance Report by CDA:
Mutual Fund Performance Review
Investment Advisors Equity Performance
Bank Commingled Funds
Insurance Company Commingled Funds
CDA Overview of Market Indices

CDA Investment Technologies, Inc.
Suite 220, 1355 Piccard Drive
Rockville, Maryland 20850 (301) 975-9600

Cafritz Report, The
Box 8565
Silver Spring, Maryland 20907
(301) 588-1957

California Technology Stock Letter
Murenove, Inc.
Suite 200, 1620 Montgomery Street
San Francisco, California 94111
(415) 982-0125

Cambridge Financial Manager
Cambridge Financial Management
Riverfront 2, 55 Cambridge Parkway
Cambridge, Massachusetts 02142
(617) 621-8500

Canadian Business Service
Marpep Publishing, Ltd.
Suite 700, 133 Richmond Street West
Toronto, Ontario M5H 3M8 Canada
(416) 869-1177

Canadian Guide To International Investing
CCH Canadian Limited
6 Garamond Court
Don Mills, Ontario M3C 1Z5 Canada
(416) 441-2992

Canadian Market Confidential
Phoenix Communications Group, Ltd.
Colorado Springs, Colorado 80901
(719) 576-9200

Catalyst
64 Main Street
Montpelier, Vermont 05602 (802) 223-7943

Certified Coin Dealer
P.O. Box 11099
Torrance, California 90510 (213) 515-7534

Chartcraft Publications:
Investor's Intelligence
Long Term Point and Figure Chartbook
Monthly Point and Figure Chartbook of NYSE/
  ASE
Quarterly Mutual Funds Point and Figure
  Chartbook
Quarterly Options Relative Strength Chartbook
Quarterly Options Point and Figure Chartbook
Quarterly Over the Counter Point and Figure
Chartbook

Point and Figure Method Book
Weekly Breakout Service NYSE
Weekly Breakout Service ASE/OTC
Weekly Mutual Funds Breakout Service
Weekly Commodity Service
Weekly Options Service
Weekly Service on NYSE/ASE
Technical Indicator Review
Chartcraft, Inc.
30 Church Street
New Rochelle, New York 10801
(914) 632-0422

Charting The Economy
P.O. Box 829
New Haven, Connecticut 06504
(203) 666-8664

Chartist, The
P.O. Box 758
Seal Beach, California 90740 (213) 596-2385

CHEAP Investor
Mathews and Associates, Inc.
Suite 10, 36 King Arthur Court
Northlake, Illinois 60164 (708) 562-0021

Clean Yield
P.O. Box 1880
Greensboro Bend, Vermont 05842
(802) 533-7178

CMI Stock and Index Options Trader
P.O. Box 3289
Newport Beach, California 92659
(714) 851-9079

Coinage Magazine
James Miller Publications
2660 East Main Street
Ventura, California 93003 (805) 643-3664

Coin Dealer Newsletter
P.O. Box 11099
Torrance, California 90510 (213) 515-7369

Comex Daily Market Report
Comex Weekly Market Report
Comex Diary
Commodity Exchange, Inc.
4 World Trade Center, 7th Floor
New York, New York 10048 (212) 938-2900

Commercial & Financial Chronicle
William B. Dana, Co.
213 Silver Beach Avenue
Daytona Beach, Florida 32118
(800) 962-3262

Commodity Closeup
Oster Communications
P.O. Box 6, Cedar Falls, Iowa 50613
(319) 277-1271

Commodity Futures Forecast
Commodex
The Mall at the Galaxy
7000 Boulevard East
Guttenberg, New Jersey 07093
(201) 868-2600

Commodity Traders Consumer Report
Suite 149, 1731 Howe Avenue
Sacramento, California 9582 (916) 677-7562

Computerized Investing
American Association of Individual Investors
Suite 1900, 625 North Michigan Avenue
Chicago, Illinois 60611 (312) 280-0170

Computer Trading Tutor
Bruce Babcock Jr.
Suite 149, 1731 Howe Avenue
Sacramento, California 95825
(916) 677-7562

Consensus
Suite 401, 1737 McGee Street
Kansas City, Missouri 64108 (816) 471-3862

Consultant's Certified Coin Report
P.O. Box 8277
Fountain Valley, California 92728
(714) 662-0237

Contrary Investor
Contrary Investor Follow-Up
Fraser Management Associates, Inc.
P.O. Box 494
Burlington, Vermont 05402 (802) 658-0322

Corporate Buyback Opportunities Report
Southeast Executive Park, 100 Executive Drive
Brewster, New York 10509
(914) 278-6500, (800) 772-0024

Corporate Cashflow Magazine
6255 Barfield Road
Atlanta, Georgia 30328 (404) 256-9800

Corporate Financing Week
Institutional Investor, Inc.
488 Madison Avenue
New York, New York 10022 (212) 303-3300

Crain Communications Publications:
Advertising Age

Business Insurance
Business Marketing
City & State
Crain's Chicago Business
Crain's Cleveland Business
Crain's Detroit Business
Crain's New York Business
Pensions & Investment Age
Crain Communications Inc.
740 Rush Street
Chicago, Illinois 60611 (312) 649-5200

Crawford Perspectives
205 East 78th Street
New York, New York 10021 (212) 628-1156

CRB Futures Chart Service
Commodity Research Bureau
100 Church Street
New York, New York 10007 (212) 406-4545

Credit Union News
150 Nassau Street
New York, New York 10038 (212) 267-7707

Creditweek
Standard and Poor's Corp.
25 Broadway
New York, New York 10004 (212) 208-8000

CSCRPM Journal of Commodity Research
A View From Naples
P.O. Box 2302,
Naples, Florida 33939 (813) 263-3114

CTCR (Commodity Traders Consumer Report)
Suite 149, 1731 Howe Avenue
Sacramento, California 95825 (916) 677-7562

Cumulative Average, The
Sibbet Publications
1091 East Woodbury Road
Pasadena, California 91104 (818) 791-5157

Currency Dealer Newsletter
P.O. Box 11099
Torrance, California 90510 (213) 515-7534

Cylinder Theory Reports
P.O. Box 4526
Albuquerque, New Mexico 87196
(505) 843-7749

Daily Graphs
William O'Neil & Co.
P.O. Box 24933
Los Angeles, California 90024
(213) 820-2583

Daily Trader, The
P.O. Box 46709
Cincinnati, Ohio 45246 (800) 922-4869

Danbell Energy Alert
Danbell Energy Letter
Daniels & Bell
99 Wall Street
New York, New York 10005 (212) 422-1710

Dave Remark Market Letter
Suite 2200, 1001 4th Avenue
Seattle, Washington 90154 (800) 426-9490

Davis-Zweig Futures Hotline
Davis-Zweig Bond Fund Timer
Davis-Zweig Futures, Inc.
P.O. Box 360
Bellmore, New York 11710 (516) 785-1300

Deal Base
Business Publications, Inc.
Suite D, 10055 Barnes Canyon Road
San Diego, California 92121
(619) 457-7577, (800) 523-7543,
(800) 453-2646 inside California

Defaulted Bonds Newsletter
Bond Investors Association, Inc.
P.O. Box 4427
Miami Lakes, Florida 33014
(305) 557-1454, (800) 557-1454

Deliberations: The Ian McAvity Market Letter
P.O. Box 182, Adelaide Street Station
Toronto, Ontario M5C 2J1, Canada
(416) 867-1100

Dessauer's Journal of Financial Markets
Limmat Publications, Inc.
P.O. Box 1718
Orleans, Massachusetts 02653
(508) 255-1651

Dick Davis Digest
P.O. Box 2828, Ocean View Station
Miami Beach, Florida 33140
(305) 531-7777

Digest, The
College For Financial Planning
9725 East Hampden Avenue
Denver, Colorado 80231 (303) 755-7101

Dines Letter, The
James Dines & Co.
P.O. Box 22
Belvedere, California 94920

Donoghue's Moneyletter
Donoghue's Mutual Funds Almanac
P.O. Box 6640
Holliston, Massachusetts 01746
(508) 429-5930

Dowbeaters
P.O. Box 284
Ironia, New Jersey 07845 (201) 543-4860

Dow Theory Comment
10 Upland Road
Colorado Springs, Colorado 90806

Dow Theory Forecast
7412 Calumet Avenue
Hammond, Indiana 46324 (219) 931-6480

Dow Theory Letters
P.O. Box 1759
La Jolla, California 92038 (619) 454-0481

Dunn & Hargitt Commodity Service
P.O. Box 1100, 22 North Second Street
Lafayette, Indiana 47902 (317) 423-2624

Economist, The
10 Rockefeller Plaza
New York, New York 10020
(212) 541-5730, (800) 456-6086

Educated Investor
Wall Street Research
P.O. Box 354
Scarsdale, New York 10583

Ehrenkrantz Report, The
50 Broadway
New York, New York 10004
(212) 425-5328, (800) 854-0085

Elder Viewpoint On Futures
Elder Viewpoint Futures
P.O. Box 20555, Columbus Circle
New York, New York 10583

Eliot Sharp's Financing News
Dealers' Digest, Inc.
2 World Trade Center, 18th Floor
New York, New York 10048 (212) 227-1200

Elliott Wave Theorist
Elliott Wave Commodity Forecast
New Classics Library
P.O. Box 1618
Gainesville, Georgia 30503 (404) 536-0309

Emerging and Special Situations
Standard and Poor's Corp.
25 Broadway
New York, New York 10004 (212) 208-8000

Equity Research Associates
540 Madison Avenue
New York, New York 10022 (212) 940-0236

Estate Planning
Prentice Hall
Route 9-W
Englewood Cliffs, New Jersey 07632
(201) 592-2000

Estate Planning Magazine
Warren Gorham and Lamont
210 South Street
Boston, Massachusetts 02111
(617) 423-2020

Estate Planning and Taxation Coordinator
Research Institute of America, Inc.
111 Radio Circle
Mt. Kisco, New York 10549 (800) 431-9025

Estate Planning Review
Financial and Estate Planning
Financial and Estate Planning Ideas & Trends
Commerce Clearing House, Inc.
4025 West Peterson Avenue
Chicago, Illinois 60646 (312) 583-8500

Estates, Gifts and Trusts Journal
Tax Management, Inc.
Bureau of National Affairs
1227 25th Street, N.W.
Washington, D.C. 20037 (202) 452-7566

Factor Report
1539 County Road 13
Nisswa, Minnesota 56468 (218) 963-3554

Farm Futures Magazine
AgriData Resources, Inc.
330 East Kilbourn Avenue
Milwaukee, Wisconsin 53202
(414) 278-7676, (800) 558-9044

Fastest Growing Stocks
Worden & Worden
P.O. Box 3458
Chapel Hill, North Carolina 27515
(919) 933-6956

FEDWATCH
Money Market Services
275 Shoreline Drive
Redwood City, California 94065
(415) 595-0610

FIA Review
Futures Industry Association
Suite 1040, 1825 Eye Street N.W.
Washington, D.C. 20006 (202) 466-5460

Fidelity Monitor
P.O. Box 1294
Rocklin, California 95677 (916) 624-0191

Financial Analysts Journal
Financial Analysts Federation
Suite 1602, 1633 Broadway
New York, New York 10102 (212) 957-2860

Financial Executive Magazine
Financial Executives Institute
P.O. Box 1938, 10 Madison Avenue
Morristown, New Jersey 07962
(201) 898-4600

Financial Freedom Report Magazine
1831 Fort Union Boulevard
Salt Lake City, Utah 84121 (801) 943-1280

Financial Services Week
Fairchild Publications
7 East 12th Street
New York, New York 10003 (212) 337-3130

Financial Times of London
14 East 60th Street
New York, New York 10022 (212) 752-4500

Financial World Magazine
1450 Broadway
New York, New York 10018
(212) 869-1616, (800) 666-6639

Five Point Investment Strategy
Suite 3850, 200 West Madison Street
Chicago, Illinois 60606 (312) 853-2820

Forbes Magazine
60 Fifth Avenue
New York, New York 10011 (212) 620-2200

Ford Data Base Report
Ford Investment Management Report
Ford Value Report
Ford Investor Services, Inc.
Suite 1, 11722 Sorrento Valley Road
San Diego, California 92121 (619) 755-1327

Forecaster
Forecaster Publishing Company
19623 Ventura Boulevard
Tarzana, California 91356 (818) 345-4421

Forecasts & Strategies
Phillips Publishing, Inc.
7811 Montrose Road
Potomac, Maryland 20854 (301) 340-2100

Fortune Magazine
Time-Warner Inc.
1271 Avenue of the Americas
New York, New York 10020 (212) 522-1212

Fraser Opinion Letter
Fraser Management Associates, Inc.
P.O. Box 494
Burlington, Vermont 05402 (802) 658-0322

Free Market Analyst
P.O. Box 16312
Baltimore, Maryland 21210

Fund Exchange
Paul A. Merriman & Associates, Inc.
Suite 507, 1200 Westlake Avenue N
Seattle, Washington 98109
(206) 285-8877

Fundline
David H. Menhashe & Co.
P.O. Box 663
Woodland Hills, California 91365
(818) 346-5637

Futures Magazine
219 Parkade
Cedar Falls, Iowa 50613 (319) 277-6341

FXC Investors
62-19 Cooper Avenue
Glendale, New York 11385 (718) 417-1330

Gann Angles
Gannworld, Inc.
3315 Martin Road
Carmel, California 93923

Garside Forecast
P.O. Box 1812
Santa Ana, California 92702 (714) 259-1670

Generic Stock News, The
Generic Stock Investment Service, Inc.
Suite 612, Norstar Bank Building
Ithaca, New York 14850 (607) 272-2583

Georgeson Report
Georgeson & Co.
Wall Street Plaza
New York, New York 10005 (212) 440-9800

Global Markets
Lenape Investment Corporation
P.O. Box 724
Morrisville, Pennsylvania 19067

Going Public, The IPO Reporter
2 World Trade Center, 18th Floor
New York, New York 10048 (212) 227-1200

Gold Investment Review
P.O. Drawer A
Sandy Hook, Connecticut 06482
(203) 426-7790
Gold Newsletter
Blanchard & Co.
2400 Jefferson Highway
Jefferson, Louisiana 70121 (800) 877-7633

Goldsmith-Nagan Bond and Money Market Letter
1545 New York Avenue, N.E.
Washington, D.C. 20002 (202) 628-1600

Gold Standard News
1805 Grand Avenue
Kansas City, Missouri 64108 (816) 842-4653

Gold Stocks Advisory
P.O. Box 20345
Columbus, Ohio 43220 (614) 459-4590

Good Money
Good Money Publications
P.O. Box 363
Worcester, Vermont 05682 (802) 223-3911

Gordon Market Timer
P.O. Box 1424
Englewood Cliffs, New Jersey 07632

Graham-Rea Investment Analysis
10966 Chalon Road
Los Angeles, California 90077 (213) 471-1917

Grandich Letter
Suite 2B, 4255 Route 9
Freehold, New Jersey 07728

Granville Market Letter
P.O. Box 413006
Kansas City, Missouri 64141
(816) 474-5353

Ground Floor
The Hirsch Organization
6 Deer Trail
Old Tappan, New Jersey 07675
(201) 664-3400

Growth Fund Guide
Growth Fund Research Building
P.O. Box 6600
Rapid City, South Dakota 57709
(605) 341-1971

Growth Stock Outlook
P.O. Box 15381
Chevy Chase, Maryland 20815
(301) 654-5205

Growth Stock Report
American Media Group
Suite 300, 951 Broken Sound Parkway, N.W.
Boca Raton, Florida 33431 (407) 241-1800

Guide To Corporate Buybacks
Southeast Executive Park, 100 Executive Drive
Brewster, New York 10509
(914) 278-6500, (800) 772-0024

Hampton Market Letter
P.O. Box 1507
Beaverton, Oregon 97075

Hard Money Digest
P.O. Box 37
Corte Madera, California 94925
(415) 924-1612

Harmonic Research
650 Fifth Avenue
New York, New York 10019
(212) 484-2065

Harry Browne's Special Reports
P.O. Box 5586
Austin, Texas 78763 (512) 453-7313

Heim Investment Letter
P.O. Box 19435
Portland, Oregon 97219

High Technology and Other Growth Stocks
402 Border Road
Concord, Massachussetts 01742
(508) 371-0096

High Yield Advisor
P.O. Box 46709
Cincinnati, Ohio (800) 922-4869

Holt Advisory
Weiss Research Publications
P.O. Box 2923
West Palm Beach, Florida 33402
(407) 684-8100

Howard Prenzel Technical Alert Letter
P.O. Box 893
Floral City, Florida 32636 (904) 726-1339

Hulbert Financial Digest
316 Commerce Street
Alexandria, Virginia 22314 (703) 683-5905

Hume Publications:
MoneyLetter
Super Investor Files
Super Investor Hot Sheet
Tax Letter
Hume Publishing Company
Suite 502, 4100 Yonge Street
Toronto, Ontario M2P 2B9 (416) 221-4596

Hutchinson National's Investment Newsletter
20 West Second Street, P.O. Box 1488
Hutchinson, Kansas 67501 (316) 662-0561

In Business
JG Press
P.O. Box 323
Emmaus, Pennsylvania 18049
(215) 967-4135

Inc. Magazine
38 Commercial Wharf
Boston, Massachusetts 02110
(617) 227-4700

Income & Safety
Institute For Econometric Research
3471 North Federal Highway
Ft. Lauderdale, Florida 33306
(800) 327-6720

Independent Investor Newsletter, The
82 Devonshire Street, Department L8A
Boston, Massachusetts 02109
(617) 570-2987

Independent Thinker
P.O. Box 107
Clementon, New Jersey 08021

Index Option Advisor
P.O. Box 46709
Cincinnati, Ohio 45246 (800) 922-4869

Indicator Digest
Money Growth Institute, Inc.
451 Grand Avenue
Palisades Park, New Jersey 07650
(201) 947-8056

Industries in Transition
Business Communication Co.
Suite 13, 25 Van Zant Street
Norwalk, Connecticut 06855
(203) 853-4266

Industry Forecast
Levy Economic Forecasts
P.O. Box 26
Chappaqua, New York 10514 (914) 238-3665

Insider Indicator
2920 NE 24th
Portland, Oregon 97212

Insider Opportunities Report
Southeast Executive Park, 100 Executive Drive
Brewster, New York 10509
(914) 278-6500, (800) 772-0024

Insider Outlook
S.R.S. Advisors
120 Broadway
New York, New York 10271 (212) 349-2372

Insiders, The
Institute for Econometric Research
3471 North Federal Highway
Fort Lauderdale, Florida 33306
(800) 327-6720

Insider's Chronicle
Suite 206, 398 West Camino Gardens
Boulevard
Boca Raton, Florida 33427 (407) 394-3404

Insider's Report, The
Boardroom Reports, Inc.
330 West 42nd Street
New York, New York 10036 (212) 239-9000

Insights
Suite 1502
200 Park Avenue
New York, New York 10166 (212) 599-1630

Insights
TFS, Inc.
238 Littleton Road
Westford, Massachusetts 01886
(508) 692-2290

Insight: The Advisory Letter for Concerned
Investors
Insight: Investing for a Better World
Franklin Research and Development Corp.
711 Atlantic Avenue
Boston, Massachusetts 02111
(617) 423-6655

Insurance Investing Newsletter
P.O. Box 2090
Huntington Beach, California 92646
(714) 893-7332

Institute of Certified Financial Planners
Journal
Institute Today
Suite 320, 10065 East Harvard Avenue
Denver, Colorado 80231 (303) 751-7600

Institutional Investor Magazine
Institutional Investor, Inc.
488 Madison Avenue
New York, New York 10022 (212) 303-3300

Interest Rate Review
International Institute for Economic Research,
Inc.
P.O. Box 338
Washington Depot, Connecticut 06794
(203) 868-7772, (800) 221-7514

Intermarket Magazine
Suite 3100, 11 South La Salle Street
Chicago, Illinois 60603 (312) 726-0050

International Fund Monitor
P.O. Box 5754
Washington, D.C. 20016

International Gold Digest
Money Growth Institute, Inc.
451 Grand Avenue
Palisades Park, New Jersey 07650
(201) 947-8800

International Harry Schultz Letter
FERC Ltd.
P.O. Box 622
CH-1001 Lausanne, Switzerland
(32) 16-544-684

Intervest Daily Energy Report
Intervest Research Services, Inc.
Suite 555, 18321 Ventura Boulevard
Tarzana, California 91356 (818) 342-0710

InvesTech Market Analyst
InvestTech Mutual Fund Advisor
2472 Birch Glen
Whitefish, Montana 59937 (406) 862-7777

Investment and Tax Shelter Blue Book
Securities Investigations, Inc.
P.O. Box 888
Woodstock, New York 12498 (914) 679-2300

Investment Dealers' Digest
2 World Trade Center, 18th Floor
New York, New York 10048 (212) 227-1200

Investment Educators Commodity Letter
719 South Fourth Street
Watseka, Illinois 60970 (815) 432-4334

Investment Horizons
Investment Information Services, Inc.
205 West Wacker Drive
Chicago, Illinois 60606 (312) 750-9300

Investment Letter
P.O. Box 36358
Grosse Pointe, Michigan 48236

Investment Quality Trends
Suite 4, 7440 Girard Avenue
La Jolla, California 92037
(619) 459-3818

Investment Reporter, The
Marpep Publishing Limited
133 Richmond Street
Toronto, Ontario M5H 3M8 Canada
(416) 869-1177

Investment Strategist
Money Growth Institute
37 Van Reipen Avenue
Jersey City, New Jersey 07306
(201) 792-0801

*Investment Strategy and Market Timing
Update*
Institute of Wall Street Studies
P.O. Box 3039
Boca Raton, Florida 33432
(800) 453-8837

Investor News
Prescott, Ball and Turben
1331 Euclid Avenue
Cleveland, Ohio 44115 (216) 574-7300

Investor Relations Newsletter
Enterprise Publications
20 North Wacker Drive
Chicago, Illinois 60606 (312) 332-3571

Investor Relations Update
National Investor Relations Institute
Suite 701, 2000 L Street, N.W.
Washington, D.C. 20036 (202) 861-0630

Investor, U.S.A.
Seahorse Financial Advisers
18 Seatuck Lane, P.O. Box 370
Remsenburg, New York 11960
(516) 325-0507

Investor's Daily (newspaper)
1941 Armacost Avenue
Los Angeles, California 90025
(213) 207-1832

Investor's Digest of Canada
Financial Post Co.
777 Bay Street
Toronto, Ontario M5G 2E4 Canada
(416) 596-5612

Investor's Hotline
Suite S-6, 10616 Beaver Dam Road
Hunt Valley, Maryland 21030 (301) 771-0064

Investors Intelligence
Chartcraft, Inc.
30 Church Street
New Rochelle, New York 10801
(914) 632-0422

It's Your Money/The Jorgensen Report
Jorgensen & Associates, Inc.
P.O. Box 37
Corte Madera, California 94925
(415) 924-1612

Jerome Wenger's Special Situation Report
PSN Communications
9145 Guilford Road
Columbia, Maryland 21045 (301) 792-2848

Journal of Futures Markets
John Wiley & Sons, Inc.
605 Third Avenue
New York, New York 10158 (212) 850-6000

Journal of Portfolio Management
Institutional Investor, Inc.
488 Madison Avenue
New York, New York 10022 (212) 303-3300

JS & A Advisory
P.O. Box 1271
Wichita, Kansas 67201

Jumbo Rate News
Bauer Communications, Inc.
P.O. Drawer 145510
Coral Gables, Florida 33114
(305) 441-2062,
(800) 447-0011 outside Florida

Juncture Recognition
P.O. Box 1209
Pompano Beach, Florida 33061

Kalenda Market Letter
Suite 50, 42751 East Florida
Hemet, California 92344

Kenneth Gerbino Investment Letter
Suite 200, 9595 Wilshire Boulevard
Beverly Hills, California 90212
(800) 821-8897,
(800) 922-3434 in California

Key-Volume Strategies
P.O. Box 407
White Plains, New York 10602
(914) 997-1276

Kimball Letter
Kimball Associates
4640 Rummell Road
St. Cloud, Florida 32769 (407) 892-8555

Kinsman's Low-Risk Growth Letter
Suite 150, 4340 Redwood Highway
San Rafael, California 94903 (415) 479-3200

Kiplinger Washington Letter
1729 H Street, N.W.
Washington, D.C. 20006 (202) 887-6400

Kirkpatrick's Market Strategist
P.O. Box 4376
Portsmouth, New Hampshire 03801
(603) 431-1411

Klein-Wolman Investment Letter
P.O. Box 727
Princeton Junction, New Jersey 08550
(609) 799-3885

Kondratieff Wave Analyst
Donald J. Hoppe Analysis
P.O. Box 977
Crystal Lake, Illinois 60014

Kon-Lin Letter, The
Kon-Lin Research and Analysis Corp.
5 Water Road
Rocky Point, New York 11778 (516) 744-8536

LaLoggia's Special Situation Report
P.O. Box 167
Rochester, New York 14601 (716) 232-1240

Laser Report
1 Technology Park Drive, P.O. Box 989
Westford, Massachusetts 01886
(508) 392-2132

Long Term Investing
Concept Publishing
P.O. Box 500
York, New York 14592 (716) 243-3148

Long Term Values
William O'Neil & Co.
P.O. Box 24933
Los Angeles, California 90024 (213) 820-2583

Lowe Financial Letter
Suite 500, 44 Montgomery Street
San Francisco, California 94104

Low Priced Stock Survey, The
Dow Theory Forecasts
7412 Calumet Avenue
Hammond, Indiana 46324 (219) 931-6480

Magic T Theory Forecast
P.O. Box 539
Nantucket, Massachusetts 02554

Main Street Journal
Claremont Economics Institute
Suite E, 143 North Harvard
Claremont, California 91711 (714) 625-1441

Major Trends
250 West Coventry Court
Milwaukee, Wisconsin 53217 (414) 352-8460

Managed Account Reports
Suite 213, 5513 Twin Knolls Road
Columbia, Maryland 21045 (301) 730-5365

Margo's Market Monitor
P.O. Box 642
Lexington, Massachusetts 02173
(617) 861-0302

Marketarian
Research Publications
P.O. Box 84902
Phoenix, Arizona 85071
(602) 252-4477, (800) 528-0559

Market Beat, Inc.
1436 Granada
Ann Arbor, Michigan 48103 (313) 426-2146

Market Charts, a Point & Figure Technical
Library
20 Exchange Place
New York, New York 10005 (212) 509-0944

Market Chronicle (newspaper)
William B. Dana Co.
213 Silver Beach Avenue
Daytona Beach, Florida 32118
(800) 962-3262

Market/Cycle Investing
995 Oak Park Drive
Morgan Hill, California 95037

Market Fax
P.O. Box 1234
Pacifica, California 94044 (415) 355-9666

Market Guide
Market Guide, Inc.
49 Glen Head Road
Glen Head, New York 11545 (516) 759-1253

Market Insider Bulletin
Evasona Co.
P.O. Box 541
Thornhill, Ontario L3T 2C0 Canada
(416) 883-4843

*Market Insights, Special Situations in the
Futures Markets*
Bruce Babcock, Jr.
Suite 149, 1731 Howe Avenue
Sacramento, California 95825 (916) 677-7562

Market Logic
Institute for Econometric Research
3471 North Federal Highway
Fort Lauderdale, Florida 33306
(800) 327-6720

Market Mania
P.O. Box 1234
Pacifica, California 94044 (415) 355-9666

Market Master
Suite 101, 23185 La Cadena
Laguna Hills, California 92653 (714) 951-8466

Market Monthly
Lenape Investment Corp.
P.O. Box 724
Morrisville, Pennsylvania 19067

Marketrend-Technical
1615 Northern Boulevard
Manhasset, New York 11030 (516) 627-1600

Market Sentiment
P.O. Box 25430
Rochester, New York 14625

Market Timing Report
P.O. Box 225
Tucson, Arizona 85702 (602) 624-6364

Market Vantage
Orion Publishing
P.O. Box 517
Mt. Kisco, New York 10549 (914) 277-5801

Marpep Publications:
*Blue Book Of Canadian Business Service Stock
  Reports*
Canadian News Facts
Canadian PennyMines Analyst
Developers & Chains
Investment Reporter
Low-Priced Stock Analyst
Money Reporter
Personal Wealth Reporter
Marpep Publishing Limited
133 Richmond Street West
Toronto, Ontario, M5H 3M8 Canada
(416) 869-1177

Marples Business Newsletter
Pacific Northwest Investor
Suite 509, 911 Western Avenue
Seattle, Washington 98104 (206) 622-0155

Master Indicator of the Stock Market
P.O. Box 3024
West Palm Beach, Florida 33402
(305) 793-8316

MBH Weekly Commodity Letter
P.O. Box 353
Winnetka, Illinois 60093
(708) 291-1870, (800) 678-5253

McAlvany Intelligence Advisor
Research Publications
P.O. Box 84904
Phoenix, Arizona 85071 (602) 252-4477
(800) 528-0559

McKeever Strategy Letter, The
Omega Financial Services
P.O. Box 4130
Medford, Oregon 97501 (503) 826-9279

McShane Letter
155 East 55th Street
New York, New York 10022 (212) 688-2387

Media General Financial Weekly (newspaper)
301 East Grace Street
Richmond, Virginia 23219 (804) 649-6587

Medical Technology Stock Letter
Piedmont Venture Group
P.O. Box 40460
Berkeley, California 94704 (415) 843-1857

Memo To Clients
Sherwood Moran Investment Timing
7550 Panthera Court
Orlando, Florida 32822 (409) 275-3901

Merrill Lynch Market Letter
Merrill Lynch Stockfinder Research Service
World Financial Center, North Tower,
  20th Floor
New York, New York 10281 (212) 449-8076

Merriman Market Analyst
MMA Gold and Silver Report
P.O. Box 1074
Birmingham, Michigan 48012 (313) 626-3034

Middle/Fixed Income Letter
MASTCA Publishing Corp.
P.O. Box 55
Loch Sheldrake, New York 12759
(914) 794-5792

Money and Markets Newsletter
Weiss Research, Inc.
P.O. Box 2923
West Palm Beach, Florida 33402
(407) 684-8100

Money Dynamics Letter
Raymond James & Associates
5051 Westheimer, 1440 Post Oak Tower
Houston, Texas 77056

Money Fund Safety Ratings
Institute for Econometric Research
3471 North Federal Highway
Fort Lauderdale, Florida 33306
(800) 327-6720

Money Magazine
Time-Warner Inc.
1271 Avenue of the Americas
New York, New York 10020 (212) 522-1212

Money Maker Magazine
5705 North Lincoln Avenue
Chicago, Illinois 60659 (312) 275-3590

Money Manager Portfolios
H F Pearson & Co.
33 Queen Street
Syosset, New York 11791 (516) 427-3107

Money Market Fund Survey
Survey Publications
P.O. Box 4180, Grand Central Station
New York, New York 10163 (212) 988-2498

Money Master
American Media Group
Suite 300, 951 Broken Sound Parkway N.W.
Boca Raton, Florida 33431 (407) 241-1800

Moneypaper, The
930 Mamaroneck Avenue
Mamaroneck, New York 10538
(914) 381-5400

Money Reporter
Marpep Publishing
133 Richmond Street West
Toronto, Ontario M5H 3M8, Canada
(416) 869-1177

Money Trends
Sammut Capital Management
P.O. Box 569
Skaneateles, New York 13152 (315) 685-8889

Monthly Summary, The
P.O. Box 11099
Torrance, California 90510 (213) 515-7534

Moody's Investors Service Publications:
Bank and Finance Manual and News Reports
Bond Record
Bond Survey
Dividend Record
Handbook of Common Stocks

Handbook of OTC Stocks
Industrial Manual and News Reports
Industry Review
International Manual and News Reports
Municipal and Government Manual and News
Reports
OTC Industrial Manual and News Reports
OTC Unlisted Manual and News Reports
Public Utility Manual and News Reports
Transportation Manual and News Reports
Moody's Investors Service
99 Church Street
New York, New York 10007
(212) 553-0300

Mortgage Commentary Publications:
Bank Accountant
Bank Attorney
Bank Board Watch
Bond Counsel
Credit Union Accountant
FDIC Watch
Mortgage Accountant
Mortgage Commentary
Mortgage Marketplace
Mortgage Securities Watch
NCUA Watch
Public Finance Accountant
Savings and Loan Reporter
TDC Financial Services Retailer
Thrift Accountant
Thrift Attorney
Thrift D&O Watch
Mortgage Commentary Publications
P.O. Box 30240
Bethesda, Maryland 20814
(301) 654-5580

MPT Fund Review
MPT Review
Navellier & Associates, Inc.
P.O. Box 6349
Incline Village, Nevada 89450
(702) 831-7800

Muni Week
One State Street
New York, New York (212) 943-8200

Mutual Funds Guide
Commerce Clearing House, Inc.
4025 West Peterson Avenue
Chicago, Illinois 60646 (312) 583-8500

Mutual Fund Fact Book
Guide To Mutual Funds
Investment Company Institute
1600 M Street
Washington, D.C. 20036 (202) 293-7700

Mutual Fund Forecaster
Institute for Econometric Research
3471 North Federal Highway
Fort Lauderdale, Florida 33306
(800) 327-6720

Mutual Fund Investing
Phillips Publishing
7811 Montrose Road
Potomac, Maryland 20854 (301) 340-2100

Mutual Fund Letter, The
Investment Information Services
205 West Wacker Drive
Chicago, Illinois 60606 (312) 750-9300

Mutual Fund Specialist
P.O. Box 1025
Eau Claire, Wisconsin 54702 (715) 834-7425

Mutual Fund Strategist
P.O. Box 446
Burlington, Vermont 05402 (802) 658-3513

Mutual Fund Switch Service
235 Greenbriar Street
Elk Grove Village, Illinois 60007
(312) 437-1123

Mutual Fund Trends
P.O. Box 6600
Rapid City, South Dakota 57709
(605) 563-9000

National Association of Investors Corp
Investor Advisory Service
1515 East Eleven Mile Road
Royal Oak, Michigan 48067 (313) 543-0612

National Association of Small Business
Investment Company News
1156 15th Street, N.W.
Washington, D.C. 20005 (202) 833-8230

National Farm Finance News
Suite 1300, 212 West 35th Street
New York, New York 10001 (212) 563-4273

National OTC Stock Journal (newspaper)
Suite 400, 1780 South Bellaire
Denver, Colorado 80222 (303) 758-9131

National Thrift & Mortgage News
212 West 35th Street
New York, New York 10001 (212) 563-4008

National Underwriter (newspaper)
Suite A2110, 175 West Jackson Boulevard
Chicago, Illinois 60604 (312) 922-2704

Nation's Business
1615 H Street, N.W.
Washington, D.C. 20062 (202) 463-5650

Nelson Publications:
Directory of Investment Managers
Directory of Investment Research
Financial Mailing Lists
Guide To "Neglected" Stocks
Research Monthly
Nelson Publications
1 Gateway Plaza, P.O. Box 591
Port Chester, New York 10573
(914) 937-8400

New Issues
Institute for Econometric Research
3471 North Federal Highway
Fort Lauderdale, Florida 33306
(800) 327-6720

Newsletter Digest
2335 Pansy Street
Huntsville, Alabama 35801 (205) 536-0901

Newsworthy
The Institute of Certified Financial Planners
3443 South Galena
Denver, Colorado 80231 (303) 751-7600

Ney Mutual Fund Report
Ney Report
Richard Ney & Associates Asset Management
P.O. Box 91109
Pasadena, California 91109 (818) 441-2222

Nicholson Report
P.O Box 56-1065
Miami, Florida 33256 (305) 252-4090

Nielsen's International Investment Letter
P.O. Box 7532
Olympia, Washington 98507

No-Load Fund Investor
P.O. Box 283
Hastings-on-Hastings, New York 10706
(914) 693-7420

*NoLoad Fund*X*
Dal Investment Co.
235 Montgomery Street
San Francisco, California 94104
(415) 986-7979

North American Gold Mining Stocks
P.O. Box 1065
Jackson Heights, New York 11372
(718) 457-1426

Norwood Index
Norwood Securities
6134 North Milwaukee Avenue
Chicago, Illinois 60646 (312) 763-1540

NYFEline
New York Futures Exchange
20 Broad Street, 10th Floor
New York, New York 10005 (212) 656-4949

Ober Income Letter
Securities Investigations, Inc.
Mill Hill Road, P.O. Box 888
Woodstock, New York 12498
(914) 679-2300

Oberweis Securities
Oberweis Securities Inc.
1771 Drehl Road
Naperville, Illinois (312) 416-8300

Off Shore Banking News
301 Plymouth Drive, N.E.
Dalton, Georgia 30721 (404) 259-6035

Oil and Gas Investor
Hart Publications
Suite 400, 1900 Grant
Denver, Colorado 80203 (303) 832-1917

Oil/Energy Statistics Bulletin
One Map Hill Drive
Box 127
Babson Park, Massachusetts 02157
(617) 237-6620

Opportunities in Options
P.O. Box 2126
Malibu, California 90265 (213) 457-3199

Option Advisor
Investment Research Institute Inc.
P.O. Box 46709
Cincinnati, Ohio 45246 (800) 922-4869

Ostaro's Market Newsletter
Cardinal Star Corp.
P.O. Box A76
New York, New York 10163 (212) 686-4121

OTC Growth Stock Watch
P.O. Box 305
Brookline, Massachusetts 02146
(617) 327-8420

OTC Insight
Insight Capital Management, Inc.
P.O. Box 127
Moraga, California 94556 (415) 376-1362

OTC Handbook
Standard & Poor's Corp.
25 Broadway
New York, New York 10004
(212) 208-8000

OTC Review
OTC Special Situations
OTC Review, Inc.
110 Pennsylvania Avenue
Oreland, Pennsylvania 19075
(215) 887-9000

Ottawa Letter
CCH Canadian Limited
6 Garamond Court
Don Mills, Ontario M3C 1Z5, Canada
(416) 441-2992
Outlook, The
Standard & Poor's Corp.
25 Broadway
New York, New York 10004
(212) 208-8000

Outstanding Investor Digest
Suite 501, 14 East 4th Street
New York, New York 10012
(212) 777-3330

Outten Quarterly Stock Evaluation
435 Winslow Avenue
Long Beach, California 90814
(213) 498-1965

Paul Kagan Associates Publications:
Broadcast Banker/Broker
Broadcast Investor
Broadcast Investor Charts
Broadcast Stats
Cable TV Advertising
Cable TV Investor
Cable TV Investor Charts
Cable TV Law Reporter
Cable TV Programming
Cable TV Tax Letter
Cable TV Technology
Cellular Investor
Euromedia Investor
Euro TV Investor
Home Shopping Investor
Kagan Media Index
Media Mergers & Acquisitions
Media Sports & Business
Motion Picture Investor
Movie Stats
Multicast
Newspaper Investor
Pay TV Movie Log
Pay TV Newsletter
SMATV News

TV Program Investor
TV Program Stats
Video Investor
Paul Kagan Associates, Inc.
126 Clock Tower Place
Carmel, California 93923 (408) 624-1536

Patient Investor
Ariel Capital Management
307 North Michigan Avenue
Chicago, Illinois 60601 (312) 726-0140

Pattern Proportion Number
P.O. Box 5601
Denver, Colorado 80217

Pearson Investment Letter
3801 Sydney Road
Dover, Florida 33527 (813) 659-2560

Penny Fortune Newsletter
Phoenix Communications Group, Ltd.
P.O. Box 670
Colorado Springs, Colorado 80901
(719) 576-9200

Penny Stocks Newsletter
31731 Outer Highway 10
Redlands, California 92373 (714) 794-3716

Penny Stock Ventures
451 Garand Avenue
Palisades Park, New Jersey 07650

Pensions & Investment Age
Pensions and Investments Performance Evalu-
  ation Reports (PIPER)
Crain Communications
740 North Rush Street
Chicago, Illinois 60611 (312) 649-5200

Pension World
6255 Barfield Road
Atlanta, Georgia 30328 (404) 256-9800

Performance Guide Publications, Mutual Funds
  and Timing and Managed Accounts
P.O. Box 2604
Palos Verdes, California 90274
(213) 547-5036

Perlow Letter
319 Lovell Avenue
Mill Valley, California 94941 (415) 383-7464

Personal Advantage/Finance
Boardroom Reports, Inc.
330 West 42nd Street
New York, New York 10036
(212) 239-9000

Personal Finance
KCI Communications
Suite 400, 1101 King Street
Alexandria, Virginia 22314 (800) 772-9200

Personal Investor Magazine
Plaza Communications, Inc.
Suite 280, 18818 Teller Avenue
Irvine, California 92715 (714) 851-2220

Personal Portfolio Manager
Infocomm Systems, Inc.
P.O. Box 439
Purdys, New York 10578 (800) 523-2407

Personal Wealth Reporter
Marpep Publishing Ltd.
133 Richmond Street West
Toronto, M5H 3M8 Canada (416) 869-1177

Peter Dag Investment Letter
65 Lake Front Drive
Akron, Ohio 44319 (216) 644-2782

Peterson Report — Stocks Under Ten Dollars
7322 Pinewood Street
Falls Church, Virginia 22046
(202) 785-0037

Petzold On The Market
Petzold On Stocks
4455 Torrance Boulevard
Torrance, California 90503 (213) 431-0180

Phelps Investment Service
George E. Phelps Co.
18351 Beach Boulevard, Suite H
Huntington Beach, California 92648
(714) 841-3387

Phillips Publications:
Jay Schabaker's Mutual Fund Investing
Mark Skousen's Forecasts & Strategies
Retirement Letter, The
Richard C. Young's Intelligence Report
Richard C. Young's International Gold Report
Phillips Publishing, Inc.
7811 Montrose Road
Potomac, Maryland 20854
(301) 424-3700, (800) 722-9000

Plain Talk Investor
Suite 203, 1500 Skokie Boulevard
Northbrook, Illinois 60062 (312) 564-1955

Portfolio Letter
Institutional Investor
488 Madison Avenue
New York, New York 10022
(212) 303-3300

Portfolios Investment Advisory
P.O. Box 997
Lynchburg, Virginia 24505 (804) 845-1335

Potential Profits
Financial Guidance, Inc.
P.O. Box 3831
Albany, Georgia 31706 (912) 883-7774

Powell Monetary Analyst
Reserve Research Ltd.
P.O. Box 4135, Station A
Portland, Maine 04101 (207) 878-3144

PQ Wall Forecast
P.O. Box 5601, Terminal Annex
Denver, Colorado 80217 (303) 455-1523

Precision Timing
P.O. Box 11722
Atlanta, Georgia 30355 (404) 355-0447

Predictions
Euler Enterprises, Inc.
Suite 1200, 7910 Woodmont Avenue
Bethesda, Maryland 20814 (301) 951-3800

Predictor & Tillman Survey
P.O. Drawer 3010
Lompoc, California 93438 (805) 688-9905

Prentice Hall Publications:
Estate Planning
Estate Planning Ideas Newsletter
Financial Planning
Financial Planning Ideas Newsletter
Life Insurance Planning
Life Insurance Ideas Newsletter
Real Estate Investment Planning
Real Estate Investment Ideas Newsletter
Successful Estate Planning Ideas & Methods
Prentice Hall Law & Business
855 Valley Road
Clifton, New Jersey 07013 (201) 592-2000

Primary Trend
Arnold Investment Counsel
700 North Water Street
Milwaukee, Wisconsin 53202 (414) 271-2726

Prime Investment Alert
P.O. Box 701
Bangor, Maine 04401 (207) 945-0241

Pring Market Review
International Institute for Economic Research,
Inc.
P.O. Box 329
Washington Depot, Connecticut 06794
(203) 868-7772, (800) 221-7514

Princeton Portfolios, The
Suite 229, 301 North Harrison
Princeton, New Jersey 08540 (609) 497-0362

Privileged Information
Boardroom Reports, Inc.
330 West 42nd Street
New York, New York 10036 (212) 239-9000

Professional Investor
Lynatrace, Inc.
P.O. Box 2144
Pompano Beach, Florida 33061
(305) 946-6353

Professional Tape Reader, The
RADCAP Inc.
P.O. Box 2407
Hollywood, Florida 33022 (305) 923-3733

Professional Timing Service
P.O. Box 7483
Missoula, Montana 59807 (406) 543-4131

Prudent Speculator, The
P.O. Box 1767
Santa Monica, California 90406
(213) 395-5275

Puryear Money Report
45 John Street
New York, New York 10038 (212) 513-1271

PSR Prophet
1001 Bridgeway, P.O. Box 244
Sausalito, California 94965 (415) 381-3PSR

Psychic Forecaster, The
3443 Parkway Center Court
Orlando, Florida 32808 (800) 333-5697

Public Investor
Government Finance Officers Association
Suite 800, 180 North Michigan Avenue
Chicago, Illinois 60601 (312) 977-9700

Puetz Investment Report
Division & 100 East
Fowler, Indiana 47944 (317) 884-0600

Quarterly Performance Report
LJR Communications
5513 Twin Knolls Road
Columbia, Maryland 21045 (301) 730-5365

Quote American
Quote New York
Quote OTC
Harry Lankford Co.
P.O. Box 213
Wichita, Kansas 67201 (316) 262-2111

Ragland Market Letter
Investors Research Corp.
P.O. Box 33103 Decatur, Georgia 30033
(404) 938-9674

Rate Watch
Bauer Communications, Inc.
P.O. Drawer 145510
Coral Gables, Florida 33114 (305) 441-2062,
outside Florida (800) 447-0011

Realty Stock Review
Audit Investments
136 Summit Avenue
Montvale, New Jersey 07645 (201) 358-2735

Reaper, The
Research Publications
P.O. Box 84902
Phoenix, Arizona 85071
(602) 252-4477, (800) 528-0559

REIT Line
National Association of Real Estate Invest-
   ment Trusts, Inc.
Suite 705, 1129 20th Street, N.W.
Washington, D.C. 20036 (202) 785-8717

Research Institute of America:
Complete Internal Revenue Code
Corporate Capital Transactions Coordinator
Corporation and Partnership Tax Return Guide
Employee Benefits Alert
Employee Benefits Compliance Coordinator
Employment Coordinator
Employment Discrimination Coordinator
Employment Alert
Estate Planners Alert
Estate Planning & Taxation Coordinator
Executive Compensation & Taxation
   Coordinator
Farmers Federal Tax Alert
Federal Income Tax Regulations
Federal Tax Coordinator 2d
Fiduciary Tax Return Guide
Guide To Travel and Entertainment
   Deductions
Individual Tax Return Guide
Labor Relations Forms & Agreements
Master Federal Tax Manual
Oil and Gas Tax Alert
Partnership & S Corporation Coordinator
Pension Coordinator
Real Estate Coordinator
Small Business Tax Planner
State Tax Action Coordinator
Tax Action Coordinator
Tax-Favored Benefits for Small Business
   Owners
Tax Guide
Tax Preparers Liability Service

Tax Return Organizer
Weekly Alert
Year-End Tax Saving Tactics
Research Institute of America
111 Radio Circle
Mt. Kisco, New York 10549 (800) 431-9025

Retirement Letter
Phillips Publishing
7811 Montrose Road
Potomac, Maryland 20854 (301) 340-2100

RHM Survey of Warrants, Options &
  Low-Priced Stocks
RHM Convertible Survey
RHM Associates
172 Forest Avenue
Glen Cove, New York 11542
(516) 759-2904

Richland Report
P.O. Box 222
La Jolla, California 92038 (619) 459-2611

Rickenbacker Report
P.O. Box 1000
Atkinson, New Hampshire 03811

Robbins Report
William Spencer Educational Foundation
3118 Hillcrest Drive
San Antonio, Texas 78201 (512) 733-0051

Roesch Market Memo, The
P.O. Box 4242
Shawnee Mission, Kansas 66204
(913) 381-0857

Ronald Sadoff's Major Trends
250 West Coventry Court
Milwaukee, Wisconsin 53217
(414) 352-8460

ROG/Bond and Money Market Letter
1545 New York Avenue, N.E.
Washington, D.C. 20002 (202) 628-1600

Rosner Market Letter
P.O. Box 5279
West Bloomfield, Michigan 48033

Ruff Times, The
Target, Inc.
4457 Willow Road
Pleasanton, California 94566
(415) 463-2200

Ryals Investment Report
Suite 202, 2930 Honolulu Avenue
La Crescenta, California 91214
(818) 248-1486

S.A. Advisory
2274 Arbor Lane
Salt Lake City, Utah 84117
(801) 272-4761

Sales and Marketing Digest
Suite 300, 951 Broken Sound Parkway N.W.
Boca Raton, Florida 33431 (407) 241-1800

Scientific Market Analysis
P.O. Box 28261, Rancho Bernardo
San Diego, California 92128

SEC Docket
Commerce Clearing House, Inc.
4025 West Peterson Avenue
Chicago, Illinois 60646 (312) 583-8500

SEC News Digest
Washington Service Bureau
Suite 270, 655 15th Street, N.W.
Washington, D.C. 20005 (202) 833-9200

Sector Fund Connection
8949 La Riviera Drive
Sacramento, California 95826
(916) 363-2055

Sector Funds Newsletter
P.O. Box 1210
Escondido, California 92025 (619) 748-0805

Securities and Federal Corporate Law Report
Clark Boardman Co.
375 Hudson Street
New York, New York 10014 (212) 929-7500

Securities Traders' Monthly
Dealers' Digest. Inc.
2 World Trade Center, 18th Floor
New York, New York 10048 (212) 227-1200

Securities Week
McGraw-Hill Publications
1221 Avenue of the Americas
New York, New York 10020 (212) 512-3144

Sentinel Investment Letter
Hanover Investment Management Corp.
P.O. Box 189, 52 South Main Street
New Hope, Pennsylvania 18938
(215) 862-5454

Shelburne Securities Forecast
P.O. Box 5566
Arlington, Virginia 22205 (703) 532-4416

Silver and Gold Report
Precious Metals Report, Inc.
P.O. Box 510
Bethel, Connecticut 06801 (203) 748-2036

Silver Baron
Suite 909, 101 Convention Center Drive
Las Vegas, Nevada 89109 (702) 786-0307

Silver Magazine
P.O. Box 1243
Whittier, California 90609 (213) 696-6738

Sindlinger Fax Service
405 Osborne Lane
Wallingford, PA 19086 (215) 565-0247

Small Cap Opportunities Report
100 Executive Drive, Southeast Executive Park
Brewster, New York 10509 (914) 278-6500
(800) 772-0024

Smart Money
The Hirsch Organization
6 Deer Trail
Old Tappan, New Jersey 07675
(201) 664-3400

Sound Advice
Suite 6, 191 North Hartz Avenue
Danville, California 94526
(415) 838-8100, (800) 423-8423

Southeast Business Alert
Word Merchants Inc.
Suite 990, 2000 Riveredge Parkway
Atlanta, Georgia 30328 (404) 984-0151

Special Growth Stocks
P.O. Box 1768
Champaign, Illinois 61820

Special Investment Situations
P.O. Box 4254, 6305 Forest Park Drive
Signal Mountain, Tennessee 37405
(615) 886-1628

Special Option Situations
Phoenix Communications Group, Ltd.
P.O. Box 670
Colorado Springs, Colorado 80901
(719) 576-9200

Special Situations Newsletter
C.H. Kaplan Research Associates
150 Nassau Street
New York, New York 10038 (212) 233-0660

Special Situation Report
P.O. Box 167
Rochester, New York 14601 (716) 232-1240

Spectrum by CDA:
Convertibles

*Five Percent Ownership based on 13D, 13G
  and 14D-1 Filings
Insider Ownership
Institutional Portfolios
Institutional Stock Holdings Survey
U.S. and European Investment Company
  Portfolios
U.S. and European Investment Company
  Stock Holdings Survey*
CDA Investment Technologies, Inc.
Suite 220, 1355 Piccard Drive
Rockville, Maryland 20850 (301) 975-9600

Speculative Ventures
Orion Publishing
P.O. Box 517
Mt. Kisco, New York 10549 (914) 277-5801

Speculator, The
Growth In Funds, Inc.
77 South Palm Avenue
Sarasota, Florida 34236 (813) 954-0330

*Spread Scope Commodity Spread Charts
Spread Scope Spread Letter
Spread Scope Long-Term Weekly Charts*
Spread Scope, Inc.
P.O. Box 5841
Mission Hills, California 91345
(818) 365-4579, (800) 232-7285

Standard and Poor's Publications:
*Amex Handbook
Analyst's Handbook
Blue List
Bond Guide
Called Bond Record
CD Ratings Service
Commercial Paper Ratings Guide
Corporate Registered Bond Interest Record
Corporation Records
CreditWeek
CreditWeek International
Current Market Perspectives
CUSIP Directories
Daily Action Stock Charts
Daily Stock Price Record (NYSE, AMEX and
  OTC)
Directors and Executives
Directory of Bond Agents
Dividend Record
Earnings Forecaster
Emerging and Special Situations
Growth Stocks Handbook
High Tech Stocks Handbook
High Yield Quarterly
Income Stocks Handbook
Index Services
Industry Surveys*

Insurance Rating Services
Municipal Bond Book
Municipal Registered Bond Interest Record
Mutual Fund Profiles
Oil and Gas Stocks Handbook
OTC Handbook
OTC Chart Manual
Outlook, The
P.C. Investor
Register of Corporations
Review of Securities Regulation
Security Dealers of North America
Statistical Service
Stock Guide
Stock Market Encyclopedia
Stock Reports
Stock Summary
Trendline Stock Chart Services
Unit Investment Trusts
Standard & Poor's Corp.
25 Broadway
New York, New York 10004
(212) 208-8000

Stanger Register
Stanger Report
Stanger Review
Stanger & Co.
1129 Broad Street
Shrewsbury, New Jersey 07701
(201) 389-3600, (800) 631-2291

Staton's Stock Market Advisory
Suite B-4, 300 East Boulevard
Charlotte, North Carolina 28203
(704) 335-0276

Stein Synopsis
Stein Investment Company
P.O. Box 148028
Chicago, Illinois 60614 (312) 880-5090

Stock Market Brief
P.O. Box 490128
Atlanta, Georgia 30349 (404) 991-2384

Stock Market Cycles
Suite 305, 2260 Cahuenga Boulevard
Los Angeles, California 90068
(213) 465-5543

Stock Market Magazine
Gazette Press
16 School Street
Yonkers, New York 10701 (914) 423-4566

Stock Market Monitor
P.O. Box 403
Naperville, Illinois 60566 (312) 852-6276

Stock and Option Trading Form
Demand Supply Index
P.O. Box 24242
Fort Lauderdale, Florida 33307
(407) 566-4500

Stock Transfer Guide
Commerce Clearing House, Inc.
4025 West Peterson Avenue
Chicago, Illinois 60646 (312) 583-8500

Strategic Investment
Agora Publishing, Inc.
824 East Baltimore Street
Baltimore, Maryland 21202 (800) 433-1528

Street Smart Investing
100 Executive Drive, Southeast Executive Park
Brewster, New York 10509
(914) 278-6500, (800) 772-0024

Strongest Stocks
P.O. Box 565
Sausalito, California 94966

Supergrowth Technology USA
21st Century Research
8200 Boulevard East
North Bergen, New Jersey 07047
(201) 868-0881

Switch Fund Advisory
Phillips Publishing
7811 Montrose Road
Potomac, Maryland 20854 (301) 340-2100

Switch Fund Timing
P.O. Box 25430
Rochester, New York 14625 (716) 385-3122

Systems and Forecasts
Signalert Corp.
150 Great Neck Road
Great Neck, New York 11021 (516) 829-6444

Tactics and Technics
Gruntal & Co.
14 Wall Street, 14th Floor
New York, New York 10004 (212) 858-6000

Taking Stock
1400 Temple Building
Rochester, New York 14604
(716) 232-4548

Target Publications:
Finance Over 50
Jack Anderson Confidential
Ruff Times

Woman Sense
Target Publications
4557 Willow Road
Pleasanton, California 94566 (415) 463-2200

Taurus Publications:
Mega-Dollar
Mega-Yen Record
Taurus Corp.
P.O. Box 767
Winchester, Virginia 22601 (703) 667-4827

Tax Avoidance Digest
Euler Enterprises, Inc.
Suite 1200, 7910 Woodmont Avenue
Bethesda, Maryland 20814 (301) 951-3800

Tax Hotline
Boardroom Reports, Inc.
330 West 42nd Street
New York, New York 10036 (212) 239-9000

Taxletter
Hume Publishing Company
Suite 502, 4100 Yonge Street
Willowdale, Ontario M2P 2B9 Canada
(416) 221-4596

Tax Planning Review
Commerce Clearing House, Inc.
4025 West Peterson Avenue
Chicago, Illinois 60646 (312) 583-8500

Tax Shelter Blue Book
Securities Investigations, Inc.
P.O. Box 888
Woodstock, New York 12498 (914) 679-2300

*Technical Analysis of Stocks & Commodities
Magazine*
9131 California Avenue, S.W.
Seattle, Washington 98136 (206) 938-0570
(800) 832-4642

Technical Comments
Charting Techniques, Inc.
802 South Westmoreland Road
Dallas, Texas 75211

Technical Indicator Review
Chartcraft, Inc.
30 Church Street
New Rochelle, New York 10801
(914) 632-0422

Technical Trends
P.O. Box 792
Wilton, Connecticut 06897 203-762-0229

Tech Street Journal
TFS, Inc.
238 Littleton Road
Westford, Massachusetts 01886
(508) 692-2290

Telephone Switch Newsletter
P.O. Box 2538
Huntington Beach, California 92647
(714) 898-2588

Texas Trader's Relative Strength Trendex
Trendex Research Management
P.O. Box 1978
San Antonio, Texas 78297 (512) 225-6581

13D Opportunities Report
13F Opportunities Report
100 Executive Drive, Southeast Executive Park
Brewster, New York 10509
(914) 278-6500, (800) 772-0024

Timer Digest
P.O. Box 1688
Greenwich, Connecticut 06836
(203) 629-3503

Time Your Switch
P.O. Box 673
Andover, Massachusetts 01810
(508) 470-3511

Timing
Suite 135, 3320 East Shea Boulevard
Phoenix, Arizona 85028 (602) 996-1800

Timing & Tactics
Wilson Foster & Co.
Suite 100, 4987 Olivas Park Drive
Ventura, California 93003 (805) 644-8207

Today's Investor
PSN Communications
9145 Guilford Road
Columbia, Maryland 21045
(301) 792-2848

Todd Market Timer
Suite 3-182, 26861 Trabuco Road
Mission Viejo, California 92691

Tomorrow's Commodities
Tomorrow's Commodity Options
Tomorrow's Options
Tomorrow's Stocks
Techno-Fundamental Investments
P.O. Box 6216
Scottsdale, Arizona 85261 (602) 996-2908

Tony Henfrey's Gold Letter
P.O. Box 9137
Allentown, Pennsylvania 18105

Toronto Stock Exchange Daily Record
Toronto Stock Exchange
2 First Canadian Place, Exchange Tower
Toronto, Ontario M5X 1J2, Canada
(416) 947-4200

Tradecenter Market Letter
Knight-Ridder Financial Information
55 Broadway
New York, New York 10006 (212) 269-1110

Trends in Mutual Fund Activity
Investment Company Institute
1600 M Street, N.W.
Washington, D.C. 20036 (202) 293-7700

Trendway Advisory Service
P.O. Box 7184
Louisville, Kentucky 40207 (502) 893-7765

Trusts and Estates Magazine
Communication Channels
6255 Barfield Road
Atlanta, Georgia 30328 (404) 256-9800

Turnaround Letter, The
New Generations, Inc.
Suite 801, 225 Friend Street
Boston, Massachusetts 02114
(617) 573-9550

Turning Point
P.O. Box 12176
Scottsdale, Arizona 85267 (602) 991-3410

United and Babson Investment Report
United Mutual Fund Selector
210 Newbury Street
Boston, Massachusetts 02116
(617) 267-8855

United States Banker
Kalo Communications
10 Valley Drive
Greenwich, Connecticut 06831 (203) 869-8200

U.S.A. Investment
P.O. Box 47128
Wichita, Kansas 67201

Utility Forecaster
KCI Communications
Suite 400, 1101 King Street
Alexandria, Virginia 22314 (703) 548-2400

Value Line Convertibles
Value Line Investment Survey
Value Line New Issues Service
Value Line Options
Value Line Special Situations Service
711 Third Avenue
New York, New York 10017 (212) 687-3965

Venture Capital Journal
Suite 700, 75 Second Avenue
Needham, Massachusetts 02194
(617) 449-2100

Vickers Weekly Insider Report
Vickers Stock Research
P.O. Box 59
Brookside, New Jersey 07926
(201) 539-1336

Volume Reversal Survey
P.O. Box 1546
Chicago, Illinois 60690
(312) 432-1120, (800) 554-5551

Wall Street Computer Review
2 World Trade Center, 18th Floor
New York, New York 10048 (212) 227-1200

Wall Street Digest
214 Carnegie Center
Princeton, New Jersey 08540 (609) 452-8111

Wall Street Edge
American Media Group
Suite 300, 951 Broken Sound Parkway N.W.
Boca Raton, Florida 33431 (407) 241-1000

Wall Street Generalist
MarketMetrics, Inc.
Suite 6, 1266 First Street
Sarasota, Florida 33577 (813) 366-5645

Wall Street Inquirer
263 Orange Avenue
Goleta, California 93117 (805) 964-8275

Wall Street Journal
200 Liberty Street
New York, New York 10281 (212) 416-2000

Wall Street Letter
Institutional Investor
488 Madison Avenue
New York, New York 10022 (212) 303-3300

Wall Street Micro Investor
P.O. Box 6
Riverdale, New York 10471 (212) 884-5408

Wall Street Money Letter
Institute of Wall Street Studies
P.O. Box 3039
Boca Raton, Florida 33432 (800) 453-8837

Wall Street Reports
Wall Street Transcript
99 Wall Street, 22nd Floor
New York, New York 10005
(212) 747-9500

Washington International Business Report
818 Connecticut Avenue, N.W., 12th Floor
Washington, D.C. 20006 (202) 872-8181

Weber's Fund Advisor
P.O. Box 3490
New Hyde Park, New York 11040
(516) 466-1252

Weiss Research Publications:
Business Forecast
Holt Advisory
Money and Markets Newsletter
WOW Indexes (Who Owns What in the Futures
  Markets)
P.O. Box 2923
West Palm Beach, Florida 33402
(407) 684-8100

Wellington Letter
Wellington Special Bulletin
Wellington Tradeline
733 Bishop Street
Honolulu, Hawaii 96813 (808) 524-8063

Western Monetary Report
Western Monetary Consultants
P.O. Box 430
Fort Collins, Colorado 80522
(303) 224-5555, (800) 525-4956

Whisper on Wall Street
221 West Avenue
Darien, Connecticut 06820 (203) 655-7011

Who Is Financing What
Euler Enterprises, Inc.
Suite 1200, 7910 Woodmont Avenue
Bethesda, Maryland 20814 (301) 951-3800

Wiesenberger Investment Companies Service
Current Performance and Dividend Report
Management Results
Mutual Fund Investment Analyzer
Mutual Funds Investment Report
Panorama
Warren Gorham and Lamont
210 South Street
Boston, Massachusetts 02111
(617) 423-2020, (800) 950-1217

Wilsearch Investment Letter
620 South 42nd Street
Boulder, Colorado 80303
(303) 494-0404, (800) 777-0057

WMP Publications:
INVESTigate
Market Express
Short Alert
World Market Perspective
WMP Enterprises, Inc.
3443 Parkway Center Court
Orlando, Florida 42808 (407) 290-9600

Wolfe's Version
P.O. Box 99
Blue Springs, Missouri 64015
(816) 229-1666

Women's Investment Newsletter
Phoenix Communications Group, Ltd.
P.O. Box 670
Colorado Springs, Colorado 80901
(719) 576-9200

Worden Report
Worden & Worden
P.O. Box 3458
Chapel Hill, North Carolina 27515

Approved Wright Investment List
Comparative Investment Analysis
Wright Bankers' Service
Wright Newsletter
Wright's Monthly Report
Wright Investors Service
10 Middle Street, Park City Plaza
Bridgeport, Connecticut 06604
(203) 333-6666

Young's World Money Forecast
Young Research & Publishing, Inc.
Federal Building, Thames Street
Newport, Rhode Island 02840
(401) 849-2131

Your Window Into The Future
Moneypower
P.O. Box 22586
Minneapolis, Minnesota 55422
(612) 537-8096

Z-900 Report
Intervest Research Services Inc.
Suite 555, 18321 Ventura Boulevard
Tarzana, California 91356 (818) 342-0710

Zweig Forecast
Zweig Performance Ratings Report
P.O. Box 360
Bellmore, New York 11710 (516) 785-1300

COMPUTERIZED DATABASES FOR INVESTORS

The following firms offer investors with computers and modems the opportunity to follow price movements in investment markets with up-to-the-second accuracy. Investors can tap into these data banks to download both current and historical price and volume information as well as news about investment markets. Some of these databases also allow investors to execute trades through their computers.

Almont Analytical Corp.:
MBS Database System
80 West Avon Road
Avon, Connecticut 06001 (203) 673-0634

Analex Inc.:
Branch Deposit Data
1901 Chapel Hill Road
Durham, North Carolina 27707
(919) 493-5448

Argus Research Corp.:
Argus On-Line
17 Battery Place
New York, New York 10004 (212) 425-7500

Bechtel Information Services:
Orderline
SEC/Express
15740 Shady Grove Road
Gaithersburg, Maryland 20877
(800) 231-3282

Black River Systems Corp.:
Macro World Forecaster
Macro World Investor
4680 Brownsboro Road, Building C
Winston-Salem, North Carolina 27106
(919) 721-0928

Bloomberg L.P.:
Financial Markets
499 Park Avenue
New York, New York 10022 (212) 980-5800

Bridge Information Systems:
Market Data Systems
717 Office Parkway
St. Louis, Missouri 63141 (800) 325-3282

Bond Buyer, The:
Bond Buyer Full Text
One State Street Plaza
New York, New York 10004 (212) 943-6303

Burlington Hall Asset Management, Inc.:
LaPorte Portfolio Allocation System
126 Petersburg Road
Hackettstown, New Jersey 07840
(201) 852-1694

BusinessWeek:
Mutual Fund Scoreboard
Top 100 and Top 1000 Elite
S-2, Princeton Road
Hightstown, New Jersey 08520
(800) 553-3575

Cablesoft, Inc.:
LiveWire
307 West Burlington Avenue
Fairfield, Iowa 52556 (800) 467-7916

CDA Investment Technologies, Inc.:
Cadence
Mutual Fund Hypotheticals
Spectrum
1355 Piccard Drive
Rockville, Maryland 20850
(301) 590-1330

CISCO:
Daily Data
Daily News
Data Bank
Express
Market Profile
Suite 1133, 327 South LaSalle Street
Chicago, Illinois 60604 (800) 666-1223

Codeworks, Inc.:
Dial-Up Historic Tick Data Service
P.O. Box 9581
Pensacola, Florida 32513
(904) 476-7231

Commodity Quotations, Inc.:
ComStock
ComStock Real-Time Market Quotations
ComStock Terminal Interface Device
Dow Jones Corporate Report
Liquidity Data Bank
670 White Plains Road
Scarsdale, New York 10583
(914) 725-3477

Compuserve, Inc.:
Securities Market Data
10K Plus
5000 Arlington Centre Boulevard
Columbus, Ohio 43220 (614) 457-8600

Comtex Scientific Corp.:
NewsGrid
OTC NewsAlert
911 Hope Street
Stamford, Connecticut 06907
(203) 358-0007

CQG, Inc.:
CQG System One
TQ 20-20
P.O. Box 758
Glenwood Springs, Colorado 81602
(800) 525-7082

CQI, McGraw-Hill Financial Services Co.:
ComStock
670 White Plains Road
Scarsdale, New York 10583
(914) 725-3477, (800) 431-5019

CSI:
Quicktrieve
200 West Palmetto Park Road
Boca Raton, Florida 33432 (407) 392-8663

Dataline Inc.:
Canquote
Insider Trading Monitor
Money Center
Quotron
Teledat
Suite 700, 67 Richmond Street West
Toronto, Ontario M5H 1Z5 (416) 365-1616

Datastream International:
Equity and Fixed Income Services
Worldview
Suite 6069, One World Trade Center
New York, New York 10048 (212) 524-8400

Detroyat Associates:
Euro Equities
535 Madison Avenue, 37th Floor
New York, New York 10022 (212) 759-0160

Disclosure, Inc.:
Compact Disclosure
Disclosure/Spectrum Ownership
5161 River Road
Bethesda, Maryland 20816 (301) 951-1300

Dow Jones & Company:
Capital Markets Report
International Newswire
News Services Broadtape
Professional Investor Report
200 Liberty Street
New York, New York 10281 (212) 416-2420

Dow Jones News/Retrieval:
Dow Jones News/Retrieval
P.O. Box 300
Princeton, New Jersey 08540
(609) 520-4000

DRI/McGraw-Hill:
AIBD Eurobonds
Commodities
Current Economic Indicators
Financial and Credit Statistics
Financial Market Indices
International Economic Monitoring Service
McCleod Young Weir Canadian Fixed
   Income
McGraw-Hill News
Morgan Stanley Capital International Indices
NIKKEI Corporate
Securities Industry
Standard & Poor's Industry Financial
U.S. Bonds
U.S. and Canadian Equities
U.S. Central
U.S. Economic Monitoring Service
Suite 1111, 625 North Michigan Avenue
Chicago, Illinois 60611 (312) 440-2400

Equis International:
Technician
P.O. Box 26743
Salt Lake City, Utah 84126 (800) 882-3040

EuroAmerican Group Inc.:
Hermes II
Suite 516, 50 Broad Street
New York, New York 10275 (212) 269-6686

Evans Economics, Inc.:
Electronic News Service
Equity Market Service
Suite 310, 1725 Eye Street
Washington, D.C. 20006 (202) 467-4900

Expert Object Company:
Plus Tick
Suite 210, 7250 Cicero Avenue
Lincolnwood, Illinois 60646 (312) 676-5555

Extel Financial Ltd.:
Exshare
Two World Trade Center, 18th Floor
New York, New York 10048
(212) 513-1570

Fast Track Systems:
Options Group Services
Suite 2301, 61 Broadway
New York, New York 10006 (800) 633-3282

Filequest Corp.:
System Software
Suite 1102, 19 Rector Street
New York, New York 10006 (212) 747-9140

Finsoft, Inc.:
System Workstations
P.O. Box 270359
Houston, Texas 77277 (713) 667-2876

Ford Investor Services, Inc.:
Epic Diskette
Epic On-Line
Hiper On-Line
Suite 1, 11722 Sorrento Valley Road
San Diego, California 92121
(619) 755-1327

FP Online, The Financial Post Information
  Service:
Annual Record of New Issues
Corporate Database
Dividend Database
Financial Post Electronic Edition
Five Year Corporate Database
Historical Earnings Database
Key Items Corporate Database
Portfolio Pricing Service
Securities Database
777 Bay Street
Toronto, Ontario M5G 2E4 Canada
(416) 593-3118

Futures Update:
Futures Update
219 Parkade
Cedar Falls, Iowa 50613 (800) 553-2910

Hale Systems, Inc.:
Dial/Data
Merlin
2 Seaview Boulevard
Port Washington, New York 11050
(516) 484-4545

Houston Computer Services, Inc.:
Octacomm
Suite 200, 11001 South Wilcrest Drive
Houston, Texas 77099 (713) 568-9900

IDD Information Services:
Corporate New Issues
Mergers and Acquisitions
Public Finance New Issues
Tradeline Securities
Two World Trade Center
New York, New York 10048
(212) 432-0045

Info Globe:
Canadian Financial Database
Marketscan
Reportline
Report On Business Corporate Database
444 Front Street West
Toronto, Ontario M5V 259 (416) 585-5250

Information Sources, Inc.:
Business Software Data Base
Software CD
1173 Colusa Avenue
Berkeley, California 94707 (415) 525-6220

Information Technologies:
Telescan
Suite 400, 2900 Wilcrest Drive
Houston, Texas 77042 (713) 952-1060,
(800) 727-4636

Intelcom Data Services:
Storm
20 Exchange Place
New York, New York 10005
(212) 269-8100

Interactive Data Corp.:
Call/Sinking Fund Database
Commodities Database
Compustat Database
Exshare (International Securities Database)
Exstat (International Fundamental Database)
Foreign Exchange Database
Fund Pricing
I/B/E/S (Institutional Brokers Estimate
  System)
Institutional Bond Quotes Database
International German Bonds Database
Masterpiece
Money-Market Database
Monthly/Quarterly Database
Mortgage-Backed Securities Database
Municipal Bond Database
Prices Database
Real-Time
Security Master Database
Split & Dividend Database
Value Line Database
Zacks Earnings Estimates Database
95 Hayden Avenue
Lexington, Massachusetts 02173
(617) 860-8206

Investment Company Data, Inc.:
Mutual Fund Database Online
406 Merle Hay Tower
Des Moines, Iowa 50310
(800) 255-2255, ext. 5222

Sources of Information and Assistance

Invest/Net:
Insider Trading Monitor
Suite 237, 99 NW 183rd Street
North Miami, Florida (305) 652-1721

I.P. Sharp Associates:
Infomagic
Suite 1900, 2 First Canadian Place
Toronto, Ontario M5X 1E3 Canada
(416) 364-2910

Key Data:
Bankers Dial-Up Data Access
Dial-Up Data Access
44342 Soft Avenue
Lancaster, California 93536 (805) 949-8022

Knight-Ridder Financial Information
  Services:
American Quotation Systems
Commodity New Services
Commodity Perspective
Commodity Research Bureau
CNS Analyst II
Financial News
Journal Of Commerce
MoneyCenter
TradeCenter
Unicom
VU/Text Information Services
One Exchange Plaza, 55 Broadway
New York, New York 10006 (800) 433-8430

KR Trade Center:
KR TradeCenter
25 Hudson Street, 12th Floor
New York, New York 10013
(212) 966-6473

Lotus Information Network Corp.:
Signal
1900 South Norfolk Street
San Mateo, California 94403
(800) 367-4670

Lotus One Source:
CD/Banking
CD/Corporate
CD/International
CD/Investment
CD/Private
55 Cambridge Parkway
Cambridge, Massachussetts 02142
(617) 577-8500 ext. 5747, (800) 554-5501
outside Massachussetts

Lynch, Jones & Ryan:
Institutional Brokers Estimate System
345 Hudson Street
New York, New York 10014 (212) 243-3137

Market Guide Inc.:
Market Guide Database
49 Glen Head Road
Glen Head, New York 11545 (516) 759-1253

Mead Data Central, Inc.:
Lexis Financial Information Service
Nexis Service
P.O. Box 933
Dayton, Ohio 45401 (800) 227-4908

MJK Associates:
Data Bases
Databases
122 Saratoga Avenue
Santa Clara, California 95051
(408) 247-5102

MMS International:
Asia/Pacific Market Analysis
Canadian Market Analysis
Currency Market Analysis
Debt Market Analysis
Equity Market Analysis
Gilt Market Analysis
Yen Market Report
275 Shorline Drive
Redwood City, California 94065
(800) 227-7304

MP Software:
Market Base
P.O. Box 37
Needham Heights, Massachusetts 02194
(617) 449-8460

Myriad Data Corp.:
Fixed Income Descriptive Databases
1415 Linden Avenue
Allentown, Pennsylvania 18105
(215) 437-2659

National CD Network, Inc.:
Qwick-Rate CD Software
Suite 304, 1800 Sandy Plains Parkway
Marietta, Georgia 30066 (800) 331-7805

National Computer Network:
CD Infoline
Nite-Line
Optdat
Suite A1038, 175 West Jackson
Chicago, Illinois 60604 (312) 427-5125

Newport Associates Ltd.:
BancBase 1
Energy Data Base
Suite 320, 7400 East Orchard Road
Englewood, Colorado 80111
(303) 779-5515

Newsnet, Inc.:
Newsnet
945 Haverford Road
Bryn Mawr, Pennsylvania 19010
(215) 527-8030

New York Futures Exchange:
NYFE Market Data
20 Broad Street
New York, New York 10005 (212) 656-5384

Nikkei Telecom:
NEEDS-Net
Suite 1802, 1221 Avenue of the Americas
New York, New York 10020
(212) 512-3600

Optima Futures Analysis:
T-Bond & Euro$/T-Bill Futures Update
Suite 612, 327 South LaSalle Street
Chicago, Illinois 60604 (312) 427-3616

Options Group, The:
TOG Services
Suite 2000, 50 Broadway
New York, New York 10004 (212) 785-5555

Oster Communications, Inc.:
FutureLink
219 Parkside
Cedar Falls, Iowa 50613 (319) 277-1271

Paradyne Corp.:
3455 Multiple Virtual Modem
8550 Ulmerton Road
Largo, Florida 34641 (800) 482-3333

PC Quote, Inc.:
PC Quote
Suite 1600, 401 South LaSalle Street
Chicago, Illinois 60605 (312) 786-5400,
(800) 225-5657

Quotron Systems, Inc.:
Australian Sharewatch
Bid/Ask Montage
Bridgewater
Commodity Class Display
Commodity Trading Monitor
Comtex OTC News Alert
Disclosure
Dow Jones News Service
Dynamic Option Class Display
Enhanced Monitor Service
Equity Transaction Service
Financial Data Base Services
FX Quote
Intraday Graphs
List Quote
MarketWire

Moneywatch
Monitor Service
Munifacts
Nomura Research Institute
Option Class Display
Option Trading Information Service
Optract Plus
Price and Market Data Base
Quote
Quoteline
Real Time Ticker Service
Research Distribution Service
Standard Ticker Service
Stewart Data
Vickers Holdings
Vickers Insider Trading
5454 Beethoven Street
Los Angeles, California 90066
(213) 827-4600

QV Trading Systems, Inc.:
Market Data Interface
11 Broadway
New York, New York 10004
(212) 344-8470

Real Decisions Corp.:
Dart
22 Thorndal Circle
Darien, Connecticut 06820 (203) 656-1500

Reuters America Inc.:
Aviation Link
Blend
Chartist
Company Newsyear
Country Reports
Instant-Link
Market View
Pricelink
Spotline
Supplyline
Textline
1700 Broadway
New York, New York 10019 (212) 603-3300

Shaw Data Services, Inc.:
Quotes
Research
122 East 42nd Street
New York, New York 10168 (212) 682-8877

Source Telecomputing Corp.:
Associated Press
Bizdate
Business Update
CDA Mutual Fund Analyses
Commodity World News
Donoghue's Money Letter
High Tech Europe

Investext
Historical Quotes
Media General Stock Analysis
OTC Newswire
Risk/Reward Analysis
Standard & Poor's Invest I
United Press International
1616 Anderson Road
McLean, Virginia 22102 (800) 336-3366

Standard & Poor's Compustat Services, Inc.:
Aggregate
Bank
Business Information
Canadian
Industrial
Prices-Dividends-Earnings
Telecommunication
Utility
7400 South Alton Court
Englewood, Colorado 80112
(800) 525-8640

Standard & Poor's Corp:
MarketScope
Unistock
Vestor
25 Broadway
New York, New York 10004 (212) 208-8731

Stratus Computer, Inc.:
SQL2000 Relational Database Management
System
55 Fairbanks Boulevard
Marlboro, Massachusetts 01752
(508) 460-2192

Street Software Technology, Inc.:
Daily Pricing Service
40 Wall Street
New York, New York 10005 (212) 425-9450

Telekurs (North America) Inc.:
INDES
International Securities Cross Reference
  Service
InvestData System
North American New Issue Newswire
Teledata System
Titelbulletin
ValorData System
Valor Register
P.O. Box 4999
Stamford, Connecticut 06907
(203) 353-8100

Telemet America, Inc.:
Pocket Quote Pro
Radio Exchange
325 First Street
Alexandria, Virginia 22314 (703) 548-2042

Telerate Systems, Inc.:
AutoQuote
Database Services
MarketFeed
Quick Quote
One World Trade Center
New York, New York 10048 (212) 938-5400

Thomson Financial Networks:
Investext
11 Farnsworth Street, 4th Floor
Boston, Massachusetts 02210
(617) 345-2000, (800) 662-7878

Tick Data, Inc.:
Historical Tick Data for Futures and Options
Suite 115, 720 Kipling Street
Lakewood, Colorado 80215 (303) 232-3701

Toronto Stock Exchange:
Consolidated Canadian Data Feed
Two First Canadian Place
Toronto, Ontario M5X 1J2 Canada
(416) 947-4456

Trade Plus, Inc.:
Trade Plus
Suite 301, 480 California Avenue
Palo Alto, California 94306 (415) 324-4554

Track Data Corp.:
MarkeTrack
MX-386
Optrack
Suite 2801, 61 Broadway
New York, New York 10048 (212) 938-5400

Trapp Information Services, Inc.:
COM Information Service
Suite 2001, 275 Madison Avenue
New York, New York 10566 (212) 682-1010

Max Ule & Co.:
Ticker Screen
Suite 200, 26 Broadway
New York, New York 10004 (212) 809-1160

Value Line Inc.:
Convertible Database
DataBase II
Estimates & Projections
Valuemaster
711 Third Avenue
New York, New York 10017 (212) 687-3965

Vickers Stock Research:
Vickers On-Line
226 New York Avenue
Huntington, New York 11743
(800) 645-5043,
(800) 832-5280 inside New York

VuText Information Services, Inc.:
VuText Information Services
Suite 1300, 325 Chestnut Street
Philadelphia, Pennsylvania 19106
(215) 574-4400

Wang Financial Information Services:
Shark
120 Wall Street
New York, New York 10005
(800) 423-2002

Warner Computer Systems:
Estinet
Finpak
17-01 Pollitt Drive
Fair Lawn, New Jersey 07432 (201)
(201) 794-4800

Wright Investor's Service:
Worldscope Database
Worldscope Financial and Service Company
Profiles

Worldscope Industrial Profiles
10 Middle Street
Bridgeport, Connecticut 06604
(203) 333-6666

World'Vest-Base Partnership:
5867 Walnut Ridge Road
Three Oaks, Michigan 49128
(616) 756-9711

XPress Information Services, Ltd.:
XPress Executive
XPress/XChange
P.O. Box 4153
Englewood, Colorado 80155
(800) 772-6397

Zacks Investment Research:
Estimate Service
Indicator
Two North Riverside Plaza
Chicago, Illinois 60606
(312) 559-9405

PERSONAL COMPUTER SOFTWARE FOR INVESTING AND FINANCIAL PLANNING

The following lists contain a sampling of software packages that can help investors to make better investment decisions and to improve record-keeping, as well as to perform personal financial planning. There are, of course, hundreds of software packages on the market to perform these tasks. Those listed here have proven themselves by being on the market for some time. They are all marketed by established companies in the software business.

The software programs in group one perform asset allocation functions. These programs evaluate the potential risks and returns on different classes of assets, such as stocks, bonds and cash. This allows investors to allocate their money among assets for maximum returns at acceptable levels of risk.

The group two programs are designed for fixed income analysis. These programs analyze the quality and maturity structures of bond portfolios. They also allow investors to maximize returns on the bond portion of their portfolios based on different interest rate assumptions.

The programs in group three are designed to help an individual do financial planning. This means that investments can be tracked, tax strategy formulated, real estate decisions examined, and retirement and estate planning options explored. One particular advantage of these programs is that once data has been entered into the computer for one part of a program, it is stored for use in other parts of the program. For instance, when a stock sale that generates a taxable capital gain is entered in the investment records section, it is also recorded in the income tax preparation part of the program.

The programs in group four allow users to screen lists of stocks to isolate the companies that meet certain fundamental investment criteria. The information on companies comes either from a disk that is updated monthly or from a continuously updated online database, which is accessed by telephone line. Usually these disks or on-line databases are available for an annual fee. There are many kinds of screens investors can perform with this software, depending on what kinds of stocks they want to find. For example, an investor looking for high income could find the highest-yielding stocks in the database. Someone looking for growth stocks could find the companies with fast earnings growth records.

Programs in the fifth group enable users to keep track of their investment portfolios. Once stocks, bonds and other instruments are entered into the computer, the value of the portfolio can be easily updated by tapping into a database. These programs also reveal the tax implications of potential investment moves.

Programs in the sixth group are designed to pick stocks based on technical considerations, such as price movements and volume. These programs usually display data in chart form, allowing investors to isolate stocks with technical indicators thought to point to a good buying or selling opportunity.

1. Asset Allocation Software

AAT (Asset Allocation Tools)
Scientific Press
507 Seaport Court
Redwood City, California 94063
(415) 366-2577

Asset Mix Optimizer
CDA Investment Technologies, Inc.
1355 Piccard Drive
Rockville, Maryland 20850 (301) 590-1330

Fixed Asset System
Best Programs, Inc.
2700 South Quincy Street
Arlington, Virginia 22206 (703) 820-9300

Portfolio Investment Selection Optimizer
Suite 400, 2995 Woodside Road
Woodside, California 94062
(415) 368-7655

2. Fixed Income Analysis Software

BondEdge, The
Capital Management Sciences
Suite 1203, 10920 Wilshire Boulevard
Los Angeles, California 90024
(213) 824-9715

Bondseye
Ergo, Inc.
1419 Wyant Road
Santa Barbara, California 93108
(805) 969-9366

Bondspec
Interactive Data Corp.
95 Hayden Avenue
Lexington, Massachusetts 02173
(617) 863-8295

Fixed Income Security Trading System
(FISTS)
Bond-Tech Inc.
P.O. Box 192
Englewood, Ohio 45322 (513) 836-3991

Street Wise Bond Machine
Street Wise, Inc.
Box 1150 M
Bayshore, New York 11706 (516) 665-5963

3. Financial Planning Software

Managing Your Money
MECA Ventures
Riverside Avenue
327 Westport, Connecticut 06880
(203) 222-9087

Wealth Builder By Money Magazine
Reality Technologies, Inc.
3624 Market Street
Philadelphia, Pennsylvania 19104
(215) 387-6055, (800) 346-2024

4. Fundamental Analysis Software

DataWindow
Interactive Data Corp.
95 Hayden Avenue
Lexington, Massachusetts 02173
(617) 860-8314

FAME Software
FAME (Citicorp)
641 Lexington Avenue
New York, New York 10043 (212) 344-5020

Fundamental Investor, The
Savant Corp.
P.O. Box 440278
Houston, Texas 77244 (713) 556-8363

Market Microscope
Dow Jones & Co.
P.O. Box 300
Princeton, New Jersey 08543
(609) 520-4641

N-Squared Analyzer-XL Program
N-Squared Computing
5318 Forest Ridge Road
Silverton, Oregon 97381 (503) 873-4420

Stock and Commodity Selection
Fortunet, Inc.
Suite 400, 2995 Woodside Road
Woodside, California 94062 (415) 368-7655

StockPak II
Standard & Poor's Corp.
26 Broadway
New York, New York 10004 (212) 208-8408

Stockpro
Techserve, Inc.
P.O. Box 70056
Bellevue, Washington 98007
(206) 747-5598

Value/Screen Plus
Value Line, Inc.
711 Third Avenue
New York, New York 10017 (212) 687-3965

Zacks' EASY Software
Zacks Investment Research
Two North Riverside Plaza
Chicago, Illinois 60606 (312) 559-9405

5. Portfolio Management Software

Dow Jones Market Manager PLUS
Dow Jones & Co.
P.O. Box 300
Princeton, New Jersey 08543
(609) 520-4641

Investment Manager I
Investment Manager II
Integrated Decision Systems, Inc.
Suite 225, 1950 Sawtelle Boulevard
Los Angeles, California 90025
(213) 478-4015

Investor's Portfolio
Savant Corp.
P.O. Box 440278
Houston, Texas 77244 (800) 231-9900

Personal Investor
Best Programs, Inc.
2700 South Quincy Street
Arlington, Virginia 22206 (703) 820-9300

Portfolio Evaluator
Financial Applications, Inc.
P.O. Box 75124
Houston, Texas 77275 (713) 947-2899

Portfolio Management Information System
ITS Associates, Inc.
36 Washington Street
Wellesley, Massachussetts 02181
(617) 237-7750

Value Line Portfolio Manager
Value Line, Inc.
711 Third Avenue
New York, New York 10017 (212) 687-3965

6. Technical Analysis Software

CNS Analyst II
Knight-Ridder Commodity News Services
2100 West 89th Street
Leawood, Kansas 66206 (800) 255-6490

CompuTrac
CompuTrac, Inc.
P.O. Box 15951
New Orleans, Louisiana 70115
(800) 535-7990

CSL Stock Analyses
MetaStock Professional
Info Globe
444 Front Street West
Toronto, Ontario M5V 2S9 (416) 585-5250

Dow Jones Market Analyzer
Dow Jones & Co.
P.O. Box 300
Princeton, New Jersey 08543
(609) 520-4642

Equalizer, The
Charles Schwab & Co.
Schwab Building, 101 Montgomery Street
San Francisco, California 94104
(415) 627-7000

Insight
Bristol Financial Services, Inc.
23 Bristol Place
Wilton, Connecticut 06897 (203) 834-0040

INVESTigator
Investment Technology
5104 Utah
Greenville, Texas 75401 (214) 455-3255

MetaStock
Equis International
P.O. Box 26743
Salt Lake City, Utah 84126
(801) 974-5115, (800) 882-3040

N-Squared Analyzer-XL Program
N-Squared Computing
5318 Forest Ridge Road
Silverton, Oregon 97381 (503) 873-4420

PC Quote
PC Quote, Inc.
401 South LaSalle Street
Chicago, Illinois 60605 (800) 225-5657

Technical Analysis Charts
Technical Analysis, Inc.
P.O. Box 46518
9131 California Avenue, S.W.
Seattle, Washington 98136 (800) 432-4642

Technical Investor, The
Savant Corp.
P.O. Box 440278
Houston, Texas 77244 (713) 556-8363

Telescan
Informaton Technologies
Suite 400, 2900 Wilcrest Drive
Houston, Texas 77042
(713) 952-1060, (800 727-4636

Trendline
Standard & Poor's Corp.
26 Broadway
New York, New York 10004 (212) 208-8792

Volume Reversal
Volume Reversal Survey
P.O. Box 1451
Sedona, Arizona 86336 (602) 282-1275

2. MAJOR FINANCIAL INSTITUTIONS

This section of the *Finance and Investment Handbook* provides listings of major financial institutions, such as banks, life insurance companies, brokerages, limited partnership sponsors, and securities and commodities exchanges. All provide vital financial services. Personal investors deal directly with most of the institutions, and at least indirectly with all. Introductions to the lists provide background information on the types of institutions covered; for additional information it is best to contact an institution directly.

The first part of this section provides lists of the major institutions of the banking system. The 12 banks and the 25 branches that make up the Federal Reserve System and the 12 banks that comprise the Federal Home Loan Bank System are listed. Then follows a list of the primary dealers in government securities, which interact with the Federal Reserve banks. Next is a compilation of the 100 largest commercial banks in the United States and the commercial banks of Canada, followed by a listing of the 100 largest thrift institutions (savings and loans and savings banks) in the United States and the trust and loans of Canada.

The second part of this section provides a listing of the top 100 life-insurance companies in the U.S. and Canada. Insurance companies are important not only because of the protection they provide to policyholders, but also because they are major institutional investors.

A listing of the top 100 full-service brokerage firms and a listing of major discount brokers follow. Full-service brokers play a key role in raising capital for corporations and government bodies, and distributing securities and a wide array of financial services to individual and institutional investors. Investors can save on commissions by dealing with discount brokers.

This section continues with a compilation of major sponsors of limited partnerships, broken down by category of investment, such as real estate, oil and gas, and equipment leasing. By allowing individual investors to participate in markets previously accessible mainly to large institutions and the wealthy, these sponsors have greatly broadened the markets in which they compete.

Next is a listing of the 25 leading accounting firms. These firms, which in the past generally restricted their activities to auditing and accounting, have diversified recently into a variety of financial services. The final part of this section presents stock and commodity exchanges around the world. As financial markets have grown and become more interdependent, foreign exchanges have become more important to North Americans looking for investment opportunities.

FEDERAL RESERVE BANKS

The following is list of the names, addresses and telephone numbers of the 12 banks and 25 branch banks that make up the Federal Reserve System. These banks supervise the activities of commercial banks and savings banks in their regions. Each branch is associated with one of the 12 Federal Reserve banks—on the list of branches, the parent bank is shown in parentheses. Nationally chartered banks must join the Federal Reserve system; state-chartered banks join on a voluntary basis. The Fed banks ensure that the banks they supervise follow Federal Reserve rules and provide member banks with access to emergency funds through the discount window. Each regional bank is owned by the member banks in its region.

The Federal Reserve System was set up by Congress in 1913 to regulate the U.S. monetary and banking system. The System regulates the nation's money supply by buying and selling government securities on the open market, setting reserve requirements for member banks, setting the discount rate at which it lends funds to members banks, supervising printing of the currency at the mint, acting as a clearinghouse for the transfer of funds throughout the banking system, and examining member banks to ensure that they meet Federal Reserve regulations.

Members of the top policy-making body of the Federal Reserve—the Board of Governors—are appointed by the President of the United States with the consent of the Senate. However, in conducting monetary policy, the Fed is designed to operate independently, so that the rate of growth of the money supply is not directly controlled by Congress or the President. To assure independence, members of the Board of Governors of the Federal Reserve are appointed to 14-year terms. Statements by members of the Board of Governors—especially the Chairman—often have much influence in the finance and investment community.

Depositors and borrowers can complain to the Federal Reserve about practices of member banks considered unfair or abusive. The Fed has jurisdiction over consumer credit, for instance, so consumers can bring complaints about problems with bank lending policies, credit cards, or advertising. In addition, consumers wanting to buy U.S. Treasury and government agency securities without the fees that banks and brokers usually charge can buy them directly through any of the Federal Reserve banks or branches on this list. Also, Federal Reserve banks publish a variety of economic reports and studies that can be helpful to an investor.

Board of Governors

Board of Governors of the
Federal Reserve System
21st and Constitution Avenue, N.W.
Washington, D.C. 20551
(202) 452-3000

Federal Reserve Banks

ATLANTA
Federal Reserve Bank of Atlanta
104 Marietta Street, N.W.
Atlanta, Georgia 30303
(404) 521-8500

BOSTON
Federal Reserve Bank of Boston
600 Atlantic Avenue
Boston, Massachusetts 02106
(617) 973-3000

CHICAGO
Federal Reserve Bank of Chicago
230 South LaSalle Street
Chicago, Illinois 60604
(312) 322-5322

CLEVELAND
Federal Reserve Bank of Cleveland
1455 East Sixth Street, P.O. Box 6387
Cleveland, Ohio 44101
(216) 579-2000

DALLAS
Federal Reserve Bank of Dallas
400 South Akard Street
Dallas, Texas 75222
(214) 651-6111

KANSAS CITY
Federal Reserve Bank of Kansas City
925 Grand Avenue
Kansas City, Missouri 64198
(806) 881-2000

MINNEAPOLIS
Federal Reserve Bank of Minneapolis
250 Marquette Avenue
Minneapolis, Minnesota 55480
(612) 340-2345

NEW YORK
Federal Reserve Bank of New York
Federal Reserve Postal Station
New York, New York 10045
(212) 720-5000

PHILADELPHIA
Federal Reserve Bank of Philadelphia
Ten Independence Mall
Philadelphia, Pennsylvania 19106
(215) 574-6000

RICHMOND
Federal Reserve Bank of Richmond
701 East Byrd Street, P.O. Box 27622
Richmond, Virginia 23261
(804) 697-8000

ST. LOUIS
Federal Reserve Bank of St. Louis
411 Locust Street
St. Louis, Missouri 63166
(314) 444-8444

SAN FRANCISCO
Federal Reserve Bank of San Francisco
101 Market Street
San Francisco, California 94120
(415) 974-2000

Federal Reserve Branch Banks

BALTIMORE (Richmond)
502 South Sharp Street
Baltimore, Maryland 21203
(301) 576-3300

BIRMINGHAM (Atlanta)
1801 Fifth Avenue North
Birmingham, Alabama 35202
(205) 252-3141

BUFFALO (New York)
160 Delaware Avenue
Buffalo, New York 14240
(716) 849-5000

CHARLOTTE (Richmond)
401 South Tryon Street
Charlotte, North Carolina 28230
(704) 373-0200

CINCINNATI (Cleveland)
150 East Fourth Street
Cincinnati, Ohio 45201
(513) 721-4787

DENVER (Kansas City)
1020 16th Street
Denver, Colorado 80217
(303) 292-4020

DETROIT (Chicago)
160 Fort Street West
Detroit, Michigan 48231
(313) 961-6880

EL PASO (Dallas)
301 East Main Street
El Paso, Texas 79999
(915) 544-4730

HELENA (Minneapolis)
400 North Park Avenue
Helena, Montana 59601
(406) 442-3860

HOUSTON (Dallas)
1701 San Jacinto Street
Houston, Texas 77001
(713) 659-4433

JACKSONVILLE (Atlanta)
515 Julia Street
Jacksonville, Florida 32231
(904) 632-4400

LITTLE ROCK (St. Louis)
325 West Capitol Avenue
Little Rock, Arkansas 72203
(501) 372-5451

LOS ANGELES (San Francisco)
409 West Olympic Boulevard
Los Angeles, California 90051
(213) 683-8563

LOUISVILLE (St. Louis)
410 South Fifth Street
Louisville, Kentucky 40232
(502) 587-7351

MEMPHIS (St. Louis)
200 North Main Street
Memphis, Tennessee 38101
(800) 238-5293

MIAMI (Atlanta)
9100 N.W. Thirty-Sixth Street Extension
Miami, Florida 33178
(305) 591-2065

NASHVILLE (Atlanta)
301 Eighth Avenue North
Nashville, Tennessee 37203
(615) 259-4006

NEW ORLEANS (Atlanta)
525 St. Charles Avenue
New Orleans, Louisiana 70161
(504) 586-1505

OKLAHOMA CITY (Kansas City)
226 Northwest Third Street
Oklahoma City, Oklahoma 73125
(405) 235-1721

OMAHA (Kansas City)
102 South Seventeenth Street
Omaha, Nebraska 68102
(402) 341-3610

PITTSBURGH (Cleveland)
717 Grant Street
Pittsburgh, Pennsylvania 15230
(412) 261-7800

PORTLAND (San Francisco)
915 S.W. Stark Street
Portland, Oregon 97208
(503) 221-5900

SALT LAKE CITY (San Francisco)
120 South State Street
Salt Lake City, Utah 84130
(801) 322-7900

SAN ANTONIO (Dallas)
126 East Nueva Street
San Antonio, Texas 78295
(512) 224-2141

SEATTLE (San Francisco)
1015 Second Avenue
Seattle, Washington 98124
(206) 442-1650

PRIMARY GOVERNMENT SECURITIES DEALERS

The following is a list of banks and brokerage firms that act as primary government securities dealers, reporting to the Federal Reserve Bank of New York. In this role, they facilitate the Fed's open market operations by buying and selling Treasury securities directly through the New York Fed's Securities Department, commonly called The Desk. These dealers are therefore key players in the execution of Federal Reserve policy, as set down by the Federal Open Market Committee, which decides to tighten or loosen the money supply to combat inflation or to ease the money supply to stimulate economic growth. When the Fed wants to tighten money supply, it sells government securities to the primary dealers—the dollars the dealers pay for the securities are thus taken out of circulation, and the money supply contracts. When the Fed, on the other hand, wants to expand the money supply, it buys government securities from the dealers—the proceeds from these sales then go into the economy, and the money supply increases.

When the government issues new Treasury securities, these primary dealers also play a key role, because they are among other large dealers and investors making competitive bids for the securities. Under the competitive bid system, also known as a Dutch auction, bidders offer higher prices for the securities, and the highest prices are accepted. Most individual investors do not participate in this auction. Rather than risk losing out to a higher bidder, they buy Treasury securities with noncompetitive bids, for which the investor accepts whatever price is determined by the competitive auction.

In order to become a primary dealer, a firm must show the Federal Reserve that the company has an excellent reputation, large capacity for trading in government securities, and adequate staff and facilities. It is considered to be very presitigous to be accepted into the inner circle of primary government securities dealers.

Aubrey G. Lanston & Co., Inc.
20 Broad Street
New York, New York 10005
(212) 612-1605

Bankers Trust Co.
130 Liberty Street
New York, New York 10015
(212) 775-1270

Barclays De Zoete Wedd Government
Securities Inc.
46th floor, 55 Water Street
New York, New York 10004
(212) 412-4000

Bear, Stearns & Co.
245 Park Avenue
New York, New York 10167
(212) 272-5502

Carroll McEntee & McGinley Inc.
40 Wall Street
New York, New York 10005
(212) 825-5885

Chase Securities, Inc.
One Chase Manhattan Plaza
New York, New York 10081
(212) 552-3141

Chemical Bank
277 Park Avenue, 9th Floor
New York, New York 10172
(212) 310-4215

Citicorp
55 Water Street, 47th Floor
New York, New York 10043
(212) 310-4215

Continental Bank
231 South LaSalle Street
Chicago, Illinois 60697
(312) 828-4535

CRT Government Securities Ltd.
7 Hanover Square
New York, New York 10004
(212) 858-5661

Daiwa Securities America, Inc.
1 World Financial Center, Tower A
200 Liberty Street, 25th Floor
New York, New York 10281
(212) 341-5828

Dean Witter Reynolds, Inc.
2 World Trade Center, 60th Floor
New York, New York 10048
(212) 392-3990

Dillon Read & Co., Inc.
535 Madison Avenue
New York, New York 10022
(212) 906-7442

Discount Corporation of New York
58 Pine Street
New York, New York 10005
(212) 906-7442

Donaldson, Lufkin & Jenrette Securities
Corp.
140 Broadway
New York, New York 10005
(212) 504-3240

Drexel Burnham Lambert Government
Securities, Inc.
60 Broad Street
New York, New York 10004
(212) 361-8100

The First Boston Corp.
Park Avenue Plaza
New York, New York 10055
(212) 909-3265

First National Bank of Chicago
Suite 0401, 1 First National Plaza
Chicago, Illinois 60670
(312) 732-8075

Goldman, Sachs & Co.
85 Broad Street, 27th Floor
New York, New York 10004
(212) 902-8340

Greenwich Capital Markets, Inc.
600 Steamboat Road
Greenwich, Connecticut 06830
(203) 625-2818

Harris Government Securities, Inc.
111 West Monroe Street
Chicago, Illinois 60690
(312) 461-3180

Irving Securities, Inc.
1 Wall Street
New York, New York 10015
(212) 635-1400

Kidder, Peabody & Co., Inc.
10 Hanover Square, 18th Floor
New York, New York 10005
(212) 510-4990

Kleinwort Benson Government Securities,
Inc.
140 South Dearborn Street
Chicago, Illinois 60603
(312) 899-4766

Lloyds Government Securities Corp.
1 Seaport Plaza
199 Water Street
New York, New York 10038
(212) 607-5140

Manufacturers Hanover Securities Corp.
270 Park Avenue
New York, New York 10017
(212) 286-2400

Merrill Lynch Government Securities, Inc.
Merrill Lynch World Headquarters
North Tower, World Financial Center
New York, New York 10281
(212) 449-5633

Midland Montagu Securities, Inc.
444 Market Street, 17th Floor
San Francisco, California 94111
(415) 274-5604

J.P. Morgan Securities Inc.
23 Wall Street
New York, New York 10015
(212) 483-4224

Morgan Stanley & Co., Inc.
1251 Avenue of the Americas
New York, New York 10020
(212) 296-5000

Nikko Securities Co., International Inc.
1 World Financial Center, Tower A
200 Liberty Street
New York, New York 10281

Nomura Securities International, Inc.
180 Maiden Lane
New York, New York 10038
(212) 208-9614

PaineWebber Inc.
1285 Avenue of the Americas, 11th Floor
New York, New York 10019
(212) 713-2973

Prudential-Bache Securities Inc.
1 Seaport Plaza
New York, New York 10292
(212) 214-3346

Salomon Brothers Inc.
1 New York Plaza
New York, New York 10004
(212) 747-7265

Sanwa-BGK Securities Co., L.P.
599 Lexington Avenue
New York, New York 10022
(212) 527-2500

Security Pacific National Bank
300 South Grand Avenue, 19th Floor
Los Angeles, California 90071
(213) 229-1044

S.G. Warburg & Co. Inc.
787 Seventh Avenue, 26th Floor
New York, New York 10019
(212) 459-7001

Shearson Lehman Government Securities,
Inc.
World Financial Center, Tower C
New York, New York 10285
(212) 640-8135

Smith Barney, Harris Upham & Co., Inc.
1345 Avenue of the Americas, 46th Floor
New York, New York 10105
(212) 698-6521

UBS Securities Inc.
299 Park Avenue
New York, New York 10171
(212) 230-4000

Wertheim Schroder & Co. Inc.
787 Seventh Avenue
New York, New York 10019
(212) 492-6600

Westpac Pollock Government Securities Inc.
160 Water Street
New York, New York 10038
(212) 797-5820

Yamaichi International (America), Inc.
2 World Trade Center
New York, New York 10048
(212) 432-8525

FEDERAL HOME LOAN BANKS

The following are the names, addresses and telephone numbers of the 12 banks of the Federal Home Loan Bank System. The Federal Home Loan Bank System, established by Congress in 1932 after the collapse of the banking system during the Great Depression, raises money by issuing notes and bonds and lends money to savings and loans and other mortgage lenders based on the amount of collateral the borrowing institution can provide. The Federal Home Loan Banks supply credit reserves to federally and state chartered savings and loans, cooperative banks and other mortgage lenders in their regions. Each Home Loan Bank is owned by the member financial institutions in its region.

Prior to the Thrift Bailout Bill of 1989, the Federal Home Loan Banks were supervised by the Federal Home Loan Bank Board. With the bailout, however, the FHLBB was eliminated and was replaced by two organizations: the Office of Thrift Supervision and the Federal Housing Finance Board. The Office of Thrift Supervision regulates federal- and state-chartered thrifts. The Federal Housing Finance Board supervises the 12 Federal Home Loan Banks.

National Headquarters

Federal Housing Finance Board
1700 G Street, N.W.
Washington, D.C. 20552
(202) 785-5400

Office of Thrift Supervision
1700 G Street, N.W.
Washington, D.C. 20552
(202) 906-6000

Federal Home Loan Banks

ATLANTA
Federal Home Loan Bank of Atlanta
Coastal States Building
260 Peachtree Street, N.W.
Atlanta, Georgia 30343
(404) 522-2450

BOSTON
Federal Home Loan Bank of Boston
One Financial Center
Boston, Massachusetts 02110
(617) 542-0150

CHICAGO
Federal Home Loan Bank of Chicago
111 East Wacker Drive, Suite 800
Chicago, Illinois 60601
(312) 565-5700

CINCINNATI
Federal Home Loan Bank of Cincinnati
2000 Atrium II
221 East 4th Street
Cincinnati, Ohio 45202
(513) 852-7500

DALLAS
Federal Home Loan Bank of Dallas
600 East John Carpenter Freeway
Dallas/Ft. Worth, Texas 75261
(214) 659-8500

DES MOINES
Federal Home Loan Bank of Des Moines
907 Walnut Street
Des Moines, Iowa 50309
(515) 243-4211

INDIANAPOLIS
Federal Home Loan Bank of Indianapolis
1350 Merchants Plaza, South Tower
115 West Washington Street
Indianapolis, Indiana 46204
(317) 631-0130

NEW YORK
Federal Home Loan Bank of New York
One World Trade Center, Floor 103
New York, New York 10048
(212) 432-2000

PITTSBURGH
Federal Home Loan Bank of Pittsburgh
20 Stanwix Street
One Riverfront Center
Pittsburgh, Pennsylvania 15222
(412) 288-3400

SAN FRANCISCO
Federal Home Loan Bank of San Francisco
600 California Street
San Francisco, California 94120
(415) 393-1000

SEATTLE
Federal Home Loan Bank of Seattle
600 Stewart Street
Seattle, Washington 98101
(206) 624-3980

TOPEKA
Federal Home Loan Bank of Topeka
3 Townsite Plaza
120 East 6th Street
Topeka, Kansas 66603
(913) 233-0508

COMMERCIAL BANKS

The following is an alphabetical list of the names, addresses and telephone numbers of the headquarters of the 100 largest commercial banks in the United States. The institutions listed here are the largest based on their total deposits, the criterion generally used for comparing the size of banks. These deposits are made up of deposits by corporations, individuals, correspondent banks, government agencies, not-for-profit organizations and many other groups. They are in such forms as checking accounts and certificates of deposit and other time deposits. Another way of ranking banks is by the amount of permanent capital. This capital has been built over the years by offerings of stock to the public and retained earnings. The top 100 institutions would basically be the same using either method of ranking.

Most banks listed here are national banks, because they are chartered by the federal government. Any bank with the initial N (meaning National) or with national in its name is a national bank. Although there are about 14,000 banks in the United States, there is a high amount of concentration of deposits and capital in the largest banks. The two largest banks, Citibank N.A. and Bank of America N.T. & S.A., have $104 billion and $70 billion in deposits respectively. The top 29 banks have deposits in excess of $10 billion. The banks that rank near number 100, in contrast, have about $3 billion in deposits.

In the 1980s there were many bank mergers, as banks sought to compete better in the new, less regulated environment brought about largely by the Depository Institutions Deregulation and Monetary Control Act in 1980. Some large banks operate newly acquired banks as separate subsidiaries. Chase Manhattan's Chase Lincoln First, for example, is larger than many small banks. Since they are run independently, though still under the corporate umbrella, they are listed here separately.

This list of the largest commercial banks (current as of the end of 1988) is courtesy of the American Banker newspaper [1 State Street Plaza, New York, New York 10004 (212) 943-6700].

American Security Bank, N.A.
1501 Pennsylvania Avenue N.W.
Washington, D.C. 20013
(202) 624-4000

AmeriTrust Company, N.A.
900 Euclid Avenue
Cleveland, Ohio 44101
(216) 737-5000

AmSouth Bank, N.A.
Post Office Box 11007
Birmingham, Alabama 35288
(205) 326-5120

BancOhio National Bank
155 East Broad Street
Columbus, Ohio 43215
(614) 463-7100

Banco Popular de Puerto Rico
Banco Popular Center
Hato Rey
San Juan, Puerto Rico 00919
(809) 765-9800

Bankers Trust Company
280 Park Avenue
New York, New York 10017
(212) 250-2500

Bank of America National Trust &
Savings Association
555 California Street
San Francisco, California 94137
(415) 622-3456

Bank of California
400 California Street
San Francisco, California 94104
(415) 765-0400

Bank of Hawaii
Financial Plaza of the Pacific
111 South King Street
Honolulu, Hawaii 96846
(808) 537-8111

Bank of New England
28 State Street
Boston, Massachusetts 02109
(617) 742-4000

The Bank of New York
48 Wall Street
New York, New York 10286
(212) 495-1784

Bank of Tokyo Trust Company
100 Broadway
New York, New York 10005
(212) 766-3400

Barnett Bank of South Florida, N.A.
15400 N.W. 77
Court, Florida 33016
(305) 821-9010

Boston Safe Deposit & Trust Company
1 Boston Place
Boston, Massachusetts 02106
(617) 722-7000

Central Fidelity Bank, N.A.
111 Franklin Road S.W.
Roanoke, Virginia 24032
(703) 983-8045

Chase Lincoln First Bank, N.A.
One Lincoln First Square
Rochester, New York 14643
(716) 258-5000

The Chase Manhattan Bank
One Chase Manhattan Plaza
New York, New York 10081
(212) 552-2222

Chemical Bank
277 Park Avenue
New York, New York 10172
(212) 310-3849

Citibank N.A.
399 Park Avenue
New York, New York 10043
(212) 559-1000

Citibank (New York State)
99 Garnsey Road
Fairport, New York 14450
(716) 546-0506

Citizens and Southern National Bank
35 Broad Street
Atlanta, Georgia 30302
(404) 581-2121

Citizens and Southern National Bank
of Florida
One Financial Plaza
Fort Lauderdale, Florida 33340
(305) 765-2000

Comerica Bank
211 West Fort Street
Detroit , Michigan 48275
(313) 222-3300

Connecticut Bank & Trust Company N.A.
One Constitution Plaza
Hartford, Connecticut 06115
(203) 244-5000

Connecticut National Bank
777 Main Street
Hartford, Connecticut 06115
(203) 728-2000

Continental Bank N.A.
231 South La Salle Street
Chicago, Illinois 60697
(312) 828-2345

Crestar Bank
919 East Main Street
Richmond, Virginia 23261
(804) 782-5000

European American Bank
156 West 56th Street
New York, New York 10019
(212) 708-8000

Fidelity Bank, N.A.
135 South Broad Street
Philadelphia, Pennsylvania 19109
(215) 985-6000

First Alabama Bank
8 Commerce Street
Montgomery, Alabama 35134
(205) 832-8011

First Bank N.A.
P.O. Box A512, First Bank Place
Minneapolis, Minnesota 55480
(612) 370-4141

First City, Texas
1001 Main Street
Houston, Texas 77002
(713) 658-6011

First Fidelity Bank, N.A.
550 Broad Street
Newark, New Jersey 07102
(201) 565-3200

First Florida Bank, N.A.
111 Madison Avenue
Tampa, Florida 33601
(813) 224-1111

First Hawaiian Bank
P.O. Box 3200
Honolulu, Hawaii 96847
(808) 525-7000

First Interstate Bank of Arizona, N.A.
First Interstate Bank Plaza
Phoenix, Arizona 85072
(602) 271-6000

First Interstate Bank of California
707 Wilshire Boulevard
Los Angeles, California 90017
(213) 614-4111

First Interstate Bank of Oregon, N.A.
1300 Southwest Fifth Avenue
Portland, Oregon 97201
(503) 225-2111

First Interstate Bank of Texas
1000 Louisiana Street
Houston, Texas 77002
(713) 224-6611

The First National Bank of Atlanta
Two Peachtree Street N.W.
Atlanta, Georgia 30383
(404) 332-5000

First National Bank of Chicago
One First National Plaza
Chicago, Illinois 60670
(312) 732-4000

First National Bank of Maryland
25 South Charles Street
Baltimore, Maryland 21203
(301) 244-4000

First Pennsylvania Bank, N.A.
Centre Square
16th and Market Streets
Philadelphia, Pennsylvania 19101
(215) 786-5000

First Tennessee Bank, N.A.
165 Madison Avenue
Memphis, Tennessee 38101
(901) 523-4444

First Union National Bank of Florida
200 W. Forsyth Street
Jacksonville, Florida 32202
(904) 361-2265

First Union National Bank of North Carolina
First Union Plaza, 301 South Tryon Street
Charlotte, North Carolina 28288
(704) 374-6161

Fleet National Bank
111 Westminster Street
Providence, Rhode Island 02903
(401) 278-6000

Florida National Bank
225 Water Street
General Mail Center
Jacksonville, Florida 32202
(904) 359-5111

Greenwood Trust Company
12 Read's Way
New Castle, Delaware 19720
(302) 323-7184

Harris Trust & Savings Bank
111 West Monroe Street
Chicago, Illinois 60603
(312) 461-2121

Hibernia National Bank
P.O. Box 61540
New Orleans, Louisiana 70161
(504) 586-5552

Huntington National Bank
The Huntington National Bank Building
17 South High Street
Columbus, Ohio 43287
(614) 476-8300

Irving Trust Company
One Wall Street
New York, New York 10005
(212) 487-2121

Israel Discount Bank
511 Fifth Avenue
New York, New York 10017
(212) 551-8500

Manufacturers Hanover Trust Company
270 Park Avenue
New York, New York 10017
(212) 286-6000

Manufacturers National Bank
Manufacturers Bank Tower
100 Renaissance Center
Detroit, Michigan 48243
(313) 222-4000

Marine Midland Bank, N.A.
140 Broadway
New York, New York 10015
(212) 440-1000

Maryland National Bank
Baltimore and Light Streets
Baltimore, Maryland 21202
(301) 244-5000

MBank Dallas, N.A.
1717 Main Street
Dallas, Texas 75265
(214) 290-2000

Mellon Bank, N.A.
One Mellon Square
Pittsburgh, Pennsylvania 15258
(412) 234-5000

Meridian Bank
35 North 6th Street
Reading, Pennsylvania 19603
(215) 320-2000

Michigan National Bank
24040 Orchard Lake Road
Farmington Hills, Michigan 48024
(313) 477-3330

Midlantic National Bank
80 Park Plaza
Newark, New Jersey 07101
(201) 266-6000

Morgan Guaranty Trust Company
23 Wall Street
New York, New York 10015
(212) 483-2323

National Bank of Detroit
611 Woodward Avenue
Detroit, Michigan 48226
(313) 225-1000

National City Bank
1900 East 9th Street
Cleveland, Ohio 44114
(216) 575-2000

National Westminster Bank N.J.
Exchange Place Centre
Jersey City, New Jersey 07302
(201) 547-7000

National Westminster Bank U.S.A.
175 Water Street
New York, New York 10038
(212) 602-1000

NCNB National Bank
One NCNB Plaza
Charlotte, North Carolina 28255
(704) 374-5000

NCNB National Bank of Florida
400 North Lashley St.
Tampa, Florida 33631
(813) 224-5270

NCNB Texas National Bank
Pacific at Ervay St.
Dallas, Texas 75283
(214) 922-5000

Norstar Bank
69 State Street
Albany, New York 12201
(518) 447-4000

Northern Trust Bank
50 South La Salle Street
Chicago, Illinois 60675
(312) 630-6000

Norwest Bank Minnesota, N.A.
Sixth Street and Marquette Avenue
Minneapolis, Minnesota 55479
(612) 667-8123

Philadelphia National Bank
Broad and Chestnut Streets
Philadelphia, Pennsylvania 19101
(215) 585-5000

Pittsburgh National Bank
Fifth Avenue & Wood Street
Pittsburgh, Pennsylvania 15222
(412) 762-2000

Premier Bank
451 Florida Boulevard
Baton Rouge, Louisiana 70821
(504) 389-4011

Provident National Bank
Broad and Chestnut Streets
Philadelphia, Pennsylvania 19101
(215) 585-5000

Republic National Bank of New York
452 Fifth Avenue
New York, New York 10018
(212) 525-5000

Riggs National Bank
1503 Pennsylvania Avenue, N.W.
Washington, D.C. 20074
(202) 835-6000

Sanwa Bank California
444 Market Street
San Francisco, California 94111
(415) 765-9500

Seattle-First National Bank
701 Fifth Avenue
Seattle, Washington 98124
(206) 358-3000

Security Pacific Bank
101 North First Avenue
Phoenix, Arizona 85002
(602) 262-2000

Security Pacific Bank Washington
Security Pacific Bank Tower
Seattle, Washington 98124
(206) 621-4111

Security Pacific National Bank
333 South Hope Street
Los Angeles, California 90071
(213) 345-5871

Shawmut Bank of Boston, N.A.
One Federal Street
Boston, Massachusetts 02211
(617) 292-2000

Signet Bank/Virginia
7 North Eighth Street
Richmond, Virginia 23260
(804) 747-2000

Society National Bank
800 Superior Avenue
Cleveland, Ohio 44114
(216) 689-3000

South Carolina National Bank
1426 Main Street
Columbia, South Carolina 29226
(803) 765-3000

Southeast Bank, N.A.
One Southeast Financial Center
Miami, Florida 33131
(305) 375-7500

Sovran Bank, N.A.
12th and Main Streets
Richmond, Virginia 23261
(804) 788-2000

State Street Bank & Trust Company
225 Franklin Street
Boston, Massachusetts 02101
(617) 786-3000

Texas Commerce Bank,N.A.
712 Main Street
Houston, Texas 77252
(713) 236-4865

Trust Company Bank
25 Park Place N.E.
Atlanta, Georgia 30302
(404) 588-7711

Union Bank
350 California Street
San Francisco, California 94120
(415) 445-0200

United States National Bank of Oregon
U.S. Bancorp Tower
111 Southwest Fifth Avenue
Portland, Oregon 97208
(503) 275-6111

Valley National Bank
Valley Bank Center
241 North Central Avenue
Phoenix, Arizona 85004
(602) 261-2900

Wachovia Bank and Trust Company, N.A.
301 North Main Street
Winston-Salem, North Carolina 27101
(919) 770-5000

CANADIAN BANKS

The following is a list of the 10 major banks of Canada. Unlike the United States, where there are 14,000 banks, Canadian banking is highly concentrated into a few large institutions that provide the full range of banking services to consumers and institutions. These banks are regulated at the federal and provincial levels in a similar way to American banks. Deposits are insured to $60,000.

Bank of Montreal
First Bank Tower
1 First Canadian Place
Toronto, Ontario M5X 1A1
(416) 867-5000

Bank of Nova Scotia
44 King Street West
Toronto, Ontario M5H 1H1
(416) 866-6161

BC Bancorp
Suite 1235, Two Bentall Centre
555 Burrard Street
Vancouver, British Columbia V7X 1K1
(604) 681-3911

Canadian Imperial Bank of Commerce
Commerce Court
Toronto, Ontario M5L 1A2
(416) 980-2211

Canadian Western Bank
Suite 1200, 10040 104 Street
Edmonton, Alberta T5J 3X6
(403) 423-8888

Continental Bank of Canada
130 Adelaide Street West
Toronto, Ontario M5H 3RZ
(416) 864-1019

Laurentian Bank of Canada
1981 McGill College Avenue
Montreal, Quebec H3A 3K3
(514) 284-3931

National Bank of Canada
600 de La Gauchetiere ouest
Montreal, Quebec H3B 4L2
(514) 394-4000

Royal Bank of Canada
1 Place Ville Marie
Montreal, Quebec H3C 3A9
(514) 874-2110

Toronto-Dominion Bank
1 Toronto-Dominion Centre
Toronto, Ontario M5K 1A2
(416) 982-8222

THRIFT INSTITUTIONS

The following is an alphabetical list of the names, addresses and telephone numbers of the headquarters of the 100 largest savings and loans and savings banks in the United States, ranked by total deposits as of the end of 1988, as tabulated by the American Banker newspaper (1 State Street Plaza, New York, New York 10004 (212) 943-6700). Total deposits, made up mostly of certificates of deposit and money-market accounts from individual and institutional investors, are the best measure of thrift institution size, and they are therefore commonly used in ranking savings and loans and savings banks. Some tabulations compare thrifts by the amount of their total assets—mostly mortgage loans. In either case, the list of the top 100 institutions would be similar.

Savings and loans were initially founded predominantly in the western states, particularly California, as a mechanism for pioneer settlers in the 19th century to finance the construction of homes. They were largely regulated by state authorities until 1932, when the Federal Home Loan Bank Board was set up in reaction to the crisis of the banking and home building industries during the Great Depression. Savings and loans are now regulated at both the federal and state levels and most deposits are insured by the Savings Association Insurance Fund.

Savings banks were initially found mainly on the East Coast, where, like savings and loans, they catered to consumers and made home loans. They are chartered and regulated by both state authorities and the Federal Reserve Board, as well as the Office of Thrift Supervision in some cases. Most deposits are insured by the Federal Deposit Insurance Corporation (FDIC). Over the years, the few distinctions between savings banks and savings and loans have largely faded away.

Historically, both types of thrifts have been distinguished from commercial banks in that they obtained most of their deposits from consumers, and lent that money out in the form of fixed-rate mortgages to homebuyers. To give them an edge in attracting deposits, they were allowed (under Regulation Q) to pay 1/4% more interest on passbook savings accounts than commercial banks. Starting in the late 1970s, when the general level of interest rates started to rise dramatically, many thrifts ran into financial trouble, because their income from mortgages was fixed at low rates, while they had to pay out higher rates on unregulated certificates of deposit to retain depositors. The pressure from this predicament ultimately led to the Depository Institutions Deregulation and Monetary Control Act of 1980 and the Garn-St Germain Act of 1982, which mandated the gradual phase-out of control on interest rates on all deposits, and permitted thrifts to offer adjustable-rate mortgages. They were also allowed to enter businesses from which they had previously been banned, such as commercial lending, issuing credit cards and providing trust services.

By the mid 1980s, thrifts played a prominent and highly competitive role in providing financial services. Many institutions went after consumer dollars by paying among the highest interest rates in the country on money-market deposits and certificates of deposit. These savings and loans and savings banks often arranged to take deposits over the phone. They sometimes brought in millions of dollars by allying with a securities brokerage firm that sells certificates of deposit. With the ability to bring in large amounts of money quickly, many thrifts became aggressive lenders as well.

By the late 1980s and early 1990s, many thrifts had gotten into severe financial trouble becauase they had taken excessive risks or because of fraud. A federal bailout had to be arranged to merge failed institutions into healthy ones. The bailout bill created a new regulatory structure for the industry by replacing the Federal Savings and Loan Insurance Corporation with the Savings Association Insurance Fund. The Federal Home Loan Bank Board became the Office of Thrift Supervision, and a new agency, the Resolution Trust Corporation, was formed to dispose of thrift assets.

American Savings & Loan Association
222 N. El Dorado Street
Stockton, California 95201
(209) 948-1116

American Savings & Loan
Association of Florida
17801 N.W. Second Avenue
Miami, Florida 33169
(305) 653-5353

American Savings Bank, FSB
1133 Avenue of the Americas
New York, New York 10036
(212) 880-7600

AmeriFirst Federal Savings &
Loan Association
One Southeast Third Avenue
Miami, Florida 33131
(305) 577-6100

Anchor Savings Bank, FSB
225 Main Street
Northport, New York 11768
(516) 596-3900

Apple Bank for Savings
Maiden Lane and Water Street
New York, New York 10017
(800) 525-1525

Astoria Federal Savings & Loan Association
37-16 30th Avenue
Long Island City, New York 11103
(718) 545-4400

Atlantic Financial Federal
50 Monument Road
Bala Cynwyd, Pennsylvania 19004
(215) 668-9440

Bank Western Federal Savings Bank
700 17th Street
Denver, Colorado 80202
(303) 370-1212

Benjamin Franklin Federal Savings & Loan
Association
501 Southeast Hawthorne Boulevard
Portland, Oregon 97228
(503) 275-1234

Bright Banc Savings Association
2355 Stemmons, Suite 400
Dallas, Texas 75204
(214) 638-9500

California Federal Savings & Loan
Association
5670 Wilshire Boulevard
Los Angeles, California 90036
(213) 932-4321

Capitol Federal Savings & Loan Association
700 Kansas Avenue
Topeka, Kansas 66603
(913) 235-1341

Carteret Savings Bank, F.A.
200 South Street
Morristown, New Jersey 07960
(201) 326-1000

CenTrust Savings Bank
101 East Flagler Street
Miami, Florida 33131
(305) 376-5000

Chevy Chase Savings & Loan Inc.
8401 Connecticut Avenue
Chevy Chase, Maryland 20815
(301) 986-7000

Citicorp Savings, F.S. & L.A.
260 California Street
San Francisco, California 94111
(415) 981-3180

Citicorp Savings of Illinois, F.S.A.
One South Dearborn Street
Chicago, Illinois 60603
(312) 977-5000

Citizens Federal Bank, A FSB
999 Brickell Avenue
Miami, Florida 33131
(305) 577-0400

City Federal Savings & Loan Association
Route 202-206
Bedminster, New Jersey 07921
(201) 658-4100

Coast Savings & Loan Association
855 South Hill Street
Los Angeles, California 90014
(213) 624-2110

Columbia Savings & Loan Association
8800 Wilshire Boulevard
Beverly Hills, California 90212
(213) 657-6303

Columbia Savings Federal Savings & Loan
Association
5850 South Ulster Circle East
Englewood, Colorado 80111
(303) 773-3444

Commercial Federal Savings & Loan
Association
2120 South 72nd Street
Omaha, Nebraska 68124
(402) 554-9200

Community Federal Savings & Loan
Association
1 Community Federal Center
St. Louis, Missouri 63131
(314) 822-5000

Consolidated Federal Bank, FSB
3100 Monticello Road
Dallas, Texas 75205
(214) 443-9000

Crossland Savings, FSB
211 Montague Street
Brooklyn, New York 11201
(718) 780-0400

Dime Savings Bank of New York, FSB
9 DeKalb Avenue
Brooklyn, New York 11201
(718) 403-7500

Dollar Dry Dock Savings Bank
2530 Grand Concourse
Bronx, New York 10458
(212) 584-6000

Downey Savings & Loan Association
3501 Jamboree Road
Newport Beach, California 92660
(714) 854-3100

Emigrant Savings Bank
5 East 42nd Street
New York, New York 10017
(212) 883-5800

Empire of America, FSB
One Main Place
Buffalo, New York 14202
(716) 845-7000

Farm & Home Savings Association
221 West Cherry
Nevada, Missouri 64772
(417) 667-3333

Far West Savings & Loan Association
4001 MacArthur Boulevard
Newport Beach, California 92660
(714) 833-8383

Fidelity Federal Savings & Loan Association
600 North Brand Boulevard
Glendale, California 91209
(213) 244-4181

First Federal of Michigan
1001 Woodward Avenue
Detroit, Michigan 48226
(313) 965-1400

First Federal Savings & Loan Association of
Pittsburgh
300 Sixth Avenue
Pittsburgh, Pennsylvania 15222
(412) 392-5500

First Federal Savings & Loan Association of
Rochester
One First Federal Place
Rochester, New York 14614
(716) 454-4010

First Minnesota Savings Bank, FSB
77 South 7th Street
St. Paul, Minnesota 55402
(612) 371-3700

First Nationwide Savings, FSB
700 Market Street
San Francisco, California 94102
(415) 991-5200

First Texas Savings Association
14951 Dallas Parkway
Dallas, Texas 75240
(214) 960-4500

Florida Federal Savings & Loan Association
360 Central Avenue
St. Petersburg, Florida 33731
(813) 893-1131

Fortune Savings Bank
2120 U.S. 19 South
Clearwater, Florida 33546
(813) 538-1000

Franklin Savings Association
One Franklin Plaza
Ottawa, Kansas 66067
(913) 242-1400

Georgia Federal Bank, FSB
20 Marietta Street N.W.
Atlanta, Georgia 30348
(404) 588-2600

Gibraltar Savings
9111 Wilshire Boulevard
Beverly Hills,California 90210
(213) 278-8720

Glendale Federal Savings and Loan
Association
800 North Brand Boulevard
Glendale, California 91209
(818) 500-2000

Goldome, FSB
One Fountain Plaza
Buffalo, New York 14203
(716) 847-5800

Great American First Savings Bank
600 B Street
San Diego, California 92112
(619) 231-1885

Great Western Bank, FSB
8484 Wilshire Boulevard
Beverly Hills, California 90211
(213) 852-3411

Green Point Savings Bank
807 Manhattan Avenue
Brooklyn, New York 11222
(718) 670-7500

Guarantee Federal Savings & Loan
Association
6116 N. Central Expressway
Dallas, Texas 75231
(214) 696-0097

Hill Financial Savings Association
400 Main Street
Red Hill, Pennsylvania 18076
(215) 679-9506

Home Federal Savings & Loan Association
of San Diego
707 Broadway
San Diego, California 92101
(619) 450-7000

Home Owners Federal Savings and Loan
Association
3 Burlington Woods
Burlington, Massachusetts 01803
(617) 965-2026

Home Savings Association of Kansas City
1006 Grand Avenue
Kansas City, Missouri 64106
(816) 221-7100

Home Savings of America, F.A.
1001 Commerce Drive
Irwindale, California 91706
(818) 960-6311

Homestead Savings, F.S. & L.A.
979 Broadway
Millbrae, California 94030
(415) 692-1432

Household Bank, FSB
4301 MacArthur Boulevard
Newport Beach, California
(714) 955-4600

Howard Savings Bank
150 S. White Horse Pike
Berlin, New Jersey 08009
(609) 767-5857

Hudson City Savings Bank
West 80 Century Road
Paramus, New Jersey 07652
(201) 967-0950

Imperial Savings Association
8787 Complex Drive
San Diego, California 92123
(619) 292-6500

Lincoln Savings & Loan Association
18200 Von Karman Street
Irvine, California 92714
(714) 553-0200

Lincoln Savings Bank, FSB
200 Park Avenue
New York, New York 10166
(212) 972-9500

Long Island Savings Bank, FSB
50 Jackson Avenue
Syosset, New York 11791
(516) 677-5000

Manhattan Savings Bank
385 Madison Avenue
New York, New York 10017
(212) 688-3000

MeraBank, FSB
3003 North Central Avenue
Phoenix, Arizona 85012
(602) 968-5600

Meritor Savings Bank
1212 Market Street
Philadelphia, Pennsylvania 19107
(215) 636-6000

Metropolitan Federal Bank, FSB
215 North Fifth Street
Fargo, North Dakota 58108
(701) 293-2600

Midwest Federal Savings & Loan
Association
801 Nicollet Mall
Minneapolis, Minnesota 55402
(612) 372-6123

Northeast Savings, F.A.
50 State Street
Hartford, Connecticut 06103
(203) 280-1000

Old Stone Bank, FSB
150 South Main Street
Providence, Rhode Island 02903
(401) 278-2000

Olney Savings Association
300 East Main
Olney, Texas 76374
(817) 564-5502

Pacific First Federal Savings Bank
1145 Broadway
Tacoma, Washington 98401
(206) 383-7605

People's Bank
899 Main Street
Bridgeport, Connecticut 06602
(203) 579-7171

Perpetual Savings Bank, FSB
8200 Greensboro Drive
McLean, Virginia 22102
(703) 356-1802

Pima Savings and Loan Association
4801 East Broadway
Tucson, Arizona 85732
(602) 747-8484

Rochester Community Savings Bank
40 Franklin Street
Rochester, New York 14604
(716) 263-4400

San Antonio Savings Association
11221 Katy Freeway, Suite 101
Houston, Texas 77079
(713) 467-8900

San Francisco Federal Savings & Loan
Association
99 Post Street
San Francisco, California 94104
(415) 955-5800

Santa Barbara Savings & Loan Association
1035 State Street
Santa Barbara, California 93102
(805) 963-0561

San Jacinto Savings Association
P.O. Box 35700
Houston, Texas 77235
(713) 661-7000

Seamen's Bank for Savings, FSB
30 Wall Street
New York, New York 10005
(212) 428-4500

Sears Savings Bank
701 North Brand Street
Glendale, California 91203
(818) 956-1800

Society for Savings
31 Pratt Street
Hartford, Connecticut 06145-2200
(203) 727-5000

Southwest Savings Association
200 Crescent Court, Suite 1660
Dallas, Texas 75201
(214) 871-5600

Standard Federal Bank
2401 West Big Beaver Road
Troy, Michigan 48084
(313) 643-9600

St. Paul Federal Bank for Savings
6700 West North Avenue
Chicago, Illinois 60635
(312) 622-5000

Sunbelt Savings Association of Texas
4901 LBJ Freeway
Dallas, Texas 75234
(214) 386-0444

Talman Home Federal Savings & Loan
Association
5501 South Kedzie Avenue
Chicago, Illinois 60633
(312) 434-3322

TCF Banking and Savings, F.A.
801 Marquette Avenue
Minneapolis, Minnesota 55402
(612) 370-7000

Third Federal Savings and Loan Association
of Cleveland
7007 Broadway Avenue
Cleveland, Ohio 44105
(216) 441-6000

Transohio Savings Bank, FSB
1 Penton Plaza, 1111 Chester Avenue
Cleveland, Ohio 44114
(216) 579-7700

United Savings Association of Texas
3200 Southwest Freeway, Suite 2000
Dallas, Texas 77027
(713) 981-2300

University Savings Association
1160 Dairy Ashford
Houston, Texas 77079
(713) 596-1000

Valley Federal Savings & Loan Association
6842 Van Nuys Boulevard
Van Nuys, California 91405
(818) 904-3000

Washington Mutual Savings Bank
1101 Second Avenue
Seattle, Washington 98111
(206) 464-4400

Western Federal Savings and Loan
Association
13160 Mindanao Way
Marina del Rey, California 90295
(213) 306-6500

Western Savings & Loan Association
3443 North Central Avenue
Phoenix, Arizona 85011
(602) 248-4600

Williamsburgh Savings Bank
One Hanson Place
Brooklyn, New York 11243
(718) 270-4242

World Savings Federal Savings & Loan
Association
1901 Harrison Street
Oakland, California 94612
(415) 645-9200

CANADIAN TRUST AND LOANS

The equivalent of the U. S. savings and loan in Canada is called a trust and loan. These trust and loans act as executors, trustees and administrators of wills and trust agreements; serve as transfer agents, registrars and bond trustees for corporations; take deposits that are invested in fixed term instruments; offer unit investment trusts; manage profit-sharing and pension plans for companies; and offer mortgage loans, mostly to residential home buyers. The following is an alphabetical list of Canadian Trust and Loans.

Acadia Trust Company
798 Prince Street
Truro, Nova Scotia B2N 1H1
(902) 895-5484

Atlantic Trust Company of Canada
1741 Barrington Street
Halifax, Nova Scotia B3J 3C4
(902) 422-1701

Bayshore Trust Company
825 Eglington Avenue West, 5th Floor
Toronto,Ontario M5N 1E7
(416) 787-1787

Cabot Trust Company
Suite 402, 1055 Wilson Avenue
Downsview, Ontario M3K 1Y9
(416) 633-4400

Canada Trustco Mortgage Company
Canada Trust Tower, 275 Dundas Street
London, Ontario N6A 4S4
(519) 663-1940

Canadian Trust Company
1 Place Ville Marie
Montreal, Quebec H3B 4A8
(514) 397-7119

CanWest Trust Company
1195 West Broadway, Suite 200
Vancouver, British Columbia V6H 3Z1
(604) 734-6515

Central Trust Company
1801 Hollis Street
Halifax, Nova Scotia B3J 3C8
(902) 420-2000

Chancellor Trust Company
360 Bay Street, 5th floor
Toronto, Ontario M5H 2V6
(416) 869-7980

CIBC Mortgage Corporation
Commerce Court Postal Station
Toronto, Ontario M5L 1A2
(416) 784-7391

Citizens Trust Company
815 West Hastings Street
Vancouver, British Columbia V6C 1B4
(604) 682-7171

Community Trust Company
2271 Bloor Street West
Toronto, Ontario M6S 1P1
(416) 763-2291

Co-operative Trust Company of Canada
333 3rd Avenue North
Saskatoon, Saskatchewan S7K 2M2
(306) 244-1900

Coronet Trust Company
160 bloor Street East, Suite 160
Toronto, Ontario M4W 1B9
(416) 928-3965

Counsel Trust Company
36 Toronto Street, Suite 300
Toronto, Ontario M5C 2C5
(416) 365-3100

Dominion Trust Company
121 King Street West
Toronto, Ontario M5H 3T9
(416) 362-8282

Effort Trust Company
240 Main Street East
Hamilton, Ontario L8N 1H5
(416) 528-8956

Evangeline Savings and Mortgage Company
494 King Street
Windsor, Nova Scotia B0N 2T0
(902) 798-8326

Family Trust Corporation
5954 Highway 7
Markham, Ontario L3P 1A2
(416) 294-1310

Fiducie Canadienne Italienne
6999 Boulevard St. Laurent
Montreal, Quebec H2S 3E1
(514) 270-4124

Fiducie du Quebec
1 Complexe Desjardins, Tour Sud, C.P. 34
Montreal, Quebec H5B 1E4
(514) 286-9441

Financial Trust Company
55 Yonge Street, Suite 700
Toronto, Ontario M5E 1S4
(416) 366-8999

First City Trust Company
14th Floor, 777 Hornby Street
Vancouver, British Columbia V6Z 1S4
(604) 685-2489

Guaranty Trust Company of Canada
625 Church Street
Toronto, Ontario M4Y 2G1
(416) 975-4500

Guardian Trust Company
618 Rue St. Jacques
Montreal, Quebec H3C 1E3
(514) 842-7161

Household Trust Company
85 Bloor Street East
Toronto, Ontario M4W 1B4
(416) 960-0665

Huronia Trust Company
2 Mississauga Street East
Orillia, Ontario L3V 6H9
(705) 325-2328

Income Trust Company
181 Main Street West
Hamilton, Ontario L8N 3N9
(416) 528-9811

Inland Trust and Savings Corporation
1054 Portage Avenue
Winnipeg, Manitoba R3G 3M2
(204) 786-7801

International Trust Company
Royal Bank Plaza, North Tower
Toronto, Ontario M5J 2J2
(416) 865-0515

Investors Group Trust Company
One Canada Centre, 447 Portage Avenue
Winnipeg, Manitoba R3C 3B6
(204) 956-8441

Merchant Trust Company
1809 Barrington Street, Suite 804
Halifax, Nova Scotia B3J 3K8
(902) 421-1966

Metropolitan Trust Company
6 Crescent Road
Toronto, Ontario M4W 3K9
(416) 967-1813

Monarch Trust Company
21 St. Clair Avenue East, Suite 1005
Toronto, Ontario M4T 1L9
(416) 922-4545

Montreal Trust Company
1 Place Ville Marie
Montreal, Quebec H3B 3L6
(514) 397-7119

Morgan Trust Company of Canada
630 Rene Levesque Boulevard West, Suite
  900
Montreal, Quebec H3B 1S6
(514) 878-3861

Municipal Trust Company
70 Collier Street
Barrie, Ontario L4M 4S9
(705) 726-7200

Mutual Trust Company
70 University Avenue
Toronto, Ontario M5J 2M4
(416) 598-2665

National Trust Company
21 King Street East
Toronto, Ontario M5C 1B3
(416) 361-4222

North West Trust Company
10205 101 Street, Toronto Dominion Tower
Edmonton, Alberta T5J 4G1
(403) 429-9300

Pacific & Western Trust Comapny
242 22nd Street East
Saskatoon, Saskatchewan S7K OE8
(306) 244-1868

Peace Hills Trust Company
P.O. Box 60
Hobberna, Alberta T0C 1N0
(403) 421-1606

Peoples Trust Company
1050 West Pender Street, Suite 610
Vancouver, British Columbia V6E 3S7
(604) 683-2881

Premier Trust Company
1155 Yonge Street
Toronto, Ontario M4T 1W2
(416) 964-1124

Regent Trust Company
877 Portage Avenue
Winnipeg, Manitoba R3G ON8
(204) 783-8995

Royal Trust
Royal Trust Tower
P.O. Box 7500, Station A
Toronto, Ontario M5W 1P9
(416) 864-7000

Saskatchewan Trust Company
171 2nd Avenue South
Saskatoon, Saskatchewan S7K 1K6
(306) 244-8744

Sherbrooke Trust
455 King Street West
Sherbrooke, Quebec J1H 6E8
(819) 822-9550

Societe Nationale de Fiducie
425 de Mainsonneuve West
Montreal, Quebec H3A 3G5
(514) 844-2050

Standard Trust Company
69 Yonge Street
Toronto, Ontario M5E 1K3
(416) 868-6900

Sterling Trust Corporation
220 Bay Street, Suite 500
Toronto, Ontario M5J 2K8
(416) 364-7495

Trust General du Canada
1100 rue University
Montreal, Quebec H3B 2G7
(514) 871-7100

Trust La Laurentienne du Canada
1981 McGill College Avenue
Montreal, Quebec H3A 2Y2
(514) 284- 7000

Trust Pret et Revenu (Savings and
Investment Trust)
850 place d'Youville
Quebec City, Quebec G1K 7P3
(418) 692- 1221

Vanguard Trust of Canada Limited
70 University Avenue, Suite 1200
Toronto, Ontario M5J 2M4
(416) 591-1133

LIFE INSURANCE COMPANIES

The following is an alphabetical list of the headquarters addresses and telephone numbers of the 100 largest life insurance companies in the United States and Canada. The list is provided courtesy of A.M. Best Company of Oldwick, New Jersey 08858 (tel. 201 439-2200), which tracks the life insurance industry.

Life insurance companies are normally ranked in one of three ways: by admitted assets, by life insurance in force, or by total premium income. Although any of these rankings would include most of the same companies, this particular list is based on admitted assets. Such assets include all the assets a life insurance company has accumulated over the years, including investments in real estate, stocks, and bonds, based on the current market value of these assets. Because of the enormous size of these assets, insurance companies have become extremely important institutional investors. The other two methods of ranking these companies, by life insurance in force and by total premium income, show the amount of coverage insurance companies are providing and the dollar amount of their sales. These are also important figures to judge a company by, but they do not provide as direct an indication of a company's importance in the finance and investment markets.

The life insurance industry is characterized by a few giant firms with a high percentage of the industry's total assets and a large number of smaller companies. The top two firms, Prudential Insurance Company of America and Metropolitan Life Insurance Company, had assets at the end of 1988 of $116 billion and $94 billion, respectively. Only the top 22 companies had assets of around $10 billion or more. The 100th largest company had a a little more than $2 billion in assets.

The companies on this list represent two distinct types of insurance company. One is owned by stockholders, and its or its parent company's shares are traded on the New York or American stock exchange or over the counter. This type of company is in business to write life insurance policies, invest premiums, and the difference between investment income and insurance claims ultimately reaches shareholders as dividends or increases in shareholder's equity. The other type of company, called a mutual life insurance company (the word mutual is usually in the name), is owned by policyholders, who receive any profits the company may earn. Mutual companies have no outstanding stock traded on an exchange, since the company is owned solely by its policyholders.

As in other areas of the financial services industry, competition has been increasing among life insurers. The advent in the early 1980s of universal life insurance, which ties cash value buildup to money-market rates, put additional pressure on all insurers to make policies more competitive. By the 1990s, the life insurance industry had produced a panoply of products which allow policyholders a wide range of flexibility in paying premiums, building cash value and buying insurance protection. In addition to traditional whole life and term policies, companies now offer universal life, variable life (where the policyholder chooses between stock, bond, and money-market investments), universal variable life, and a wide range of annuity and Individual Retirement Account products. Many insurers also offer financial planning services.

In addition to their role as insurers of lives, life insurance companies have become an important source of capital for world capital markets. Insurance companies are a major force in the stock market; the municipal, corporate, and government bond markets; in real estate (both as owners and lenders); and as providers of venture capital. Some insurance companies have expanded their offerings by acquiring brokerage and money management firms.

Aetna Life Insurance and Annuity Company
151 Farmington Avenue
Hartford, Connecticut 06156
(203) 273-0123

Aetna Life Insurance Company
151 Farmington Avenue
Hartford, Connecticut 06156
(203) 273-0123

Aid Association for Lutherans
4321 North Ballard Road
Appleton, Wisconsin 54919
(414) 734-5721

Alexander Hamilton Life Insurance Company
of America
33045 Hamilton Boulevard
Farmington Hills, Michigan 48018
(313) 553-2000

Allstate Life Insurance Company
Allstate Plaza West
Northbrook, Illinois 60062
(312) 402-5000

American Family Life Assurance Company
of Columbus
1932 Wynnton Road
Columbus, Georgia 31999
(404) 323-3431

American General Life and Accident
Insurance Company
American General Center
Nashville, Tennessee 37250
(615) 749-1000

American Life Insurance Company
One Alico Plaza
Wilmington, Delaware 19801
(302) 594-2000

American National Insurance Company
One Moody Plaza
Galveston, Texas 77550-7999
(409) 763-4661

American United Life Insurance Company
One American Square
Indianapolis, Indiana 46204
(317) 263-1877

The Canada Life Assurance Company
330 University Avenue
Toronto, Ontario, Canada M5G 1R8
(416) 597-1456

Commonwealth Life Insurance Company
Commonwealth Building, Broadway at
Fourth Avenue
Louisville, Kentucky 40202
(502) 587-7371

Confederation Life Insurance Company
321 Bloor Street, East
Toronto, Ontario, Canada M4W 1H1
(416) 323-8111

Connecticut General Life Insurance
Company
900 Cottage Grove Road
Bloomfield, Connecticut 06002
(203) 726-6000

Connecticut Mutual Life Insurance
Company
140 Garden Street
Hartford, Connecticut 06154
(203) 727-6500

Continental Assurance Company
CNA Plaza
Chicago, Illinois 60685
(312) 822-5000

Crown Life Insurance Company
120 Bloor Street East
Toronto, Ontario, Canada M4W 1B8
(416) 928-4500

The Equitable Life Assurance Society of the
United States
787 Seventh Avenue
New York, New York 10019
(212) 554-1234

Equitable Variable Life Insurance Company
787 Seventh Avenue
New York, New York 10019
(212) 714-5107

Executive Life Insurance Company
Executive Life Center,
11444 West Olympic Boulevard
Los Angeles, California 90064
(213) 312-1000

Executive Life Insurance Company of
New York
390 North Broadway
Jericho, New York 11753
(516) 931-6400

Family Life Insurance Company
Park Place, 1200 Sixth Avenue
Seattle, Washington 98101
(206) 292-1000

Fidelity Bankers Life Insurance Company
1011 Boulder Springs Drive
Richmond, Virginia 23225
(804) 323-1011

Fidelity and Guaranty Life Insurance
Company
100 Light Street
Baltimore, Maryland 21202
(301) 547-3000

First Capital Life Insurance Company
10241 Wateridge Circle
San Diego, California 92121-2733
(619) 452-9060

First Colony Life Insurance Company
700 Main Street
Lynchburg, Virginia 24504
(804) 845-0911

The Franklin Life Insurance Company
Franklin Square
Springfield, Illinois 62713
(217) 528-2011

General American Life Insurance Company
700 Market Street
St. Louis, Missouri 63101
(314) 231-1700

Great American Life Insurance Company
6330 San Vicente Boulevard
Los Angeles, California 90048
(213) 937-8000

The Great-West Life Assurance Company
100 Osborne Street North
Winnipeg, Manitoba, Canada R3C 3A5
(204) 946-1190

The Guardian Life Insurance Company
of America
201 Park Avenue South
New York, New York 10003
(212) 598-8000

Hartford Life Insurance Company
Hartford Plaza
Hartford, Connecticut 06115
(203) 547-5000

Home Life Insurance Company
75 Wall Street
New York, New York 10005
(212) 428-2000

IDS Life Insurance Company
IDS Tower 10
Minneapolis, Minnesota 55440
(612) 327-3131

The Imperial Life Assurance Company
of Canada
96 St. Clair Avenue, West
Toronto, Canada M4V 1N7
(416) 926-2600

The Independent Order of Foresters
789 Don Mills Road
Don Mills, Ontario, Canada M3C 1T9
(416) 429-3000

Integrated Resources Life Insurance
Company
3737 Westown Parkway
West Des Moines, Iowa 50265
(515) 223-3000

Jackson National Life Insurance Company
5901 Executive Drive
Lansing, Michigan 48911
(517) 394-3400

Jefferson-Pilot Life Insurance Company
101 North Elm Street
Greensboro, North Carolina 27401
(919) 378-2011

John Alden Life Insurance Company
5100 Gamble Drive
St. Louis Park, Minnesota 55416
(305) 470-3100

John Hancock Mutual Life Insurance
Company
John Hancock Place
Boston, Massachusetts 02117
(617) 572-6000

Kemper Investors Life Insurance Company
120 South LaSalle Street
Chicago, Illinois 60603
(312) 781-1121

Keystone Provident Life Insurance Company
15 Westminster Street
Providence, Rhode Island 02903
(617) 338-3500

Knights of Columbus
1 Columbus Plaza
New Haven, Connecticut 06507-0901
(203) 772-2130

Liberty National Life Insurance Company
2001 Third Avenue South
Birmingham, Alabama 35233
(205) 325-2722

The Life Insurance Company of Virginia
6610 West Broad Street
Richmond, Virginia 23230
(804) 281-6000

The Lincoln National Life Insurance
Company
1300 South Clinton Street
Fort Wayne, Indiana 46801
(219) 427-2000

Lincoln National Pension Insurance
Company
1300 South Clinton Street
Fort Wayne, Indiana 46801
(219) 427-2000

Lutheran Brotherhood
625 Fourth Avenue South
Minneapolis, Minnesota 55415
(612) 340-7000

The Manufacturers Life Insurance
Company
200 Bloor Street East
Toronto, Ontario, Canada M4W 1E5
(416) 926-0100

Massachusetts Mutual Life Insurance
Company
1295 State Street
Springfield, Massachusetts 01111
(413) 788-8411

Metropolitan Insurance and Annuity
Company
One Madison Avenue
New York, New York 10010
(212) 578-2211

Metropolitan Life Insurance Company
One Madison Avenue
New York, New York 10010-3690
(212) 578-2211

The Minnesota Mutual Life Insurance
Company
Minnesota Mutual Life Center,
400 North Robert Street
St. Paul, Minnesota 55101
(612) 298-3500

Monarch Life Insurance Company
One Monarch Place
Springfield, Massachusetts 01133
(413) 784-2000

The Mutual Benefit Life Insurance
Company
520 Broad Street
Newark, New Jersey 07102-3184
(201) 481-8000

The Mutual Life Assurance Company of
Canada
227 King Street South
Waterloo, Ontario, Canada N2J 4C5
(519) 888-2290

The Mutual Life Insurance Company of
New York
1740 Broadway at 55th Street
New York, New York 10019
(212) 708-2000

Mutual of America Life Insurance Company
666 Fifth Avenue
New York, New York 10103
(212) 399-1600

National Home Life Assurance Company
222 Monroe Street
Jefferson City, Missouri 65101
(215) 648-5000

National Life Insurance Company
510 Munoz Rivera Avenue
Hato Rey, Puerto Rico 00919
(809) 758-8080

Nationwide Life Insurance Company
One Nationwide Plaza
Columbus, Ohio 43216
(614) 249-7111

New England Mutual Life Insurance
  Company
501 Boylston Street
Boston, Massachusetts 02117
(617) 578-2000

New York Life Insurance and Annuity
  Corporation
300 Delaware Avenue
Wilmington, Delaware 19801
(212) 576-7000

New York Life Insurance Company
51 Madison Avenue, Room 250
New York, New York 10010
(212) 576-7000

North American Life Assurance Company
5650 Yonge Street
North York, Ontario, Canada M2M 4G4
(416) 229-4515

The Northwestern Mutual Life Insurance
  Company
720 East Wisconsin Avenue
Milwaukee, Wisconsin 53202
(414) 271-1444

Pacific Mutual Life Insurance Company
700 Newport Center Drive
Newport Beach, California 92660
(714) 640-3011

The Penn Mutual Life Insurance Company
530 Walnut Street
Philadelphia, Pennsylvania 19172
(215) 625-5000

Peoples Security Life Insurance Company
300 West Morgan Street
Durham, North Carolina 27701
(919) 687-8200

Phoenix Mutual Life Insurance Company
One American Row
Hartford, Connecticut 06115
(203) 275-5000

Principal Mutual Life Insurance Company
711 High Street
Des Moines, Iowa 50309
(515) 247-5111

Provident Life and Accident Insurance
  Company
One Fountain Square
Chattanooga, Tennessee 37402
(615) 755-1011

Provident Mutual Life Insurance Company
  of Philadelphia
1600 Market Street
Philadelphia, Pennsylvania 19103
(215) 636-5000

Provident National Assurance Company
One Fountain Square
Chattanooga, Tennessee 37402
(615) 755-1011

Pruco Life Insurance Company
213 Washington Street
Newark, New Jersey 07102
(201) 802-2000

The Prudential Insurance Company
  of America
Prudential Plaza
Newark, New Jersey 07101
(201) 802-6000

Safeco Life Insurance Company
Safeco Plaza
Seattle, Washington 98185
(206) 545-5000

Southwestern Life Insurance Company
500 North Akard
Dallas, Texas 75201
(214) 954-7111

State Farm Life Insurance Company
One State Farm Plaza
Bloomington, Illinois 61710
(309) 766-2311

State Mutual Life Assurance Company
  of America
440 Lincoln Street
Worcester, Massachusetts 01605
(508) 852-1000

Sun Life Assurance Company of Canada
150 King Street West
Toronto, Ontario, Canada M5H 1J9
(416) 979-9966

Sun Life Assurance Company of Canada
(U.S.)
One Sun Life Executive Park
Wellesley Hills, Massachusetts 02181
(617) 237-6030

Sun Life Insurance Company of America
260 Peachtree Street, N.W.
Atlanta, Georgia 30303
(404) 223-2500

Tandem Insurance Group, Inc.
1700 Broadway, 10th Floor
New York, New York 10019
(212) 713-8340

Teachers Insurance and Annuity Association
of America
750 Third Avenue
New York, New York 10017
(212) 490-9000

Transamerica Life Insurance and Annuity
Company
1150 South Olive Street
Los Angeles, California 90015
(213) 742-3111

Transamerica Occidental Life Insurance
Company
Transamerica Center,
1150 South Olive Street
Los Angeles, California 90015
(213) 742-2111

The Travelers Insurance Company
One Tower Square, 4PB
Hartford, Connecticut 06183-1071
(203) 277-0111

The Travelers Life and Annuity Company
One Tower Square, 4PB
Hartford, Connecticut 06183-1071
(203) 277-0111

Unum Life Insurance Company
2211 Congress Street
Portland, Maine 04122
(207) 770-2211

Unum Life Insurance Company of America
2211 Congress Street
Portland, Maine 04122
(207) 770-2211

The Union Central Life Insurance Company
1876 Waycross Road
Cincinnati, Ohio 45240
(513) 595-2200

United Insurance Company of America
One East Wacker Drive
Chicago, Illinois 60601
(312) 661-4500

United of Omaha Life Insurance Company
Mutual of Omaha Plaza
Omaha, Nebraska 68175
(402) 342-7600

United Pacific Life Insurance Company
33301 9th Avenue South
Federal Way, Washington 98003
(215) 864-5900

The Variable Annuity Life Insurance
Company
2929 Allen Parkway
Houston, Texas 77019
(713) 526-5251

Western National Life Insurance Company
205 East 10th Street
Amarillo, Texas 79101
(806) 378-3400

The Western and Southern Life Insurance
Company
400 Broadway
Cincinnati, Ohio 45202
(513) 629-1800

BROKERAGE FIRMS

The following is a list of the top 100 full-service and the top discount brokerage firms in the United States and Canada. Traditionally, brokers sold mostly stocks and bonds to their customers, who were primarily persons of substanial means. Today, these firms allow customers to buy and sell stocks, bonds, commodities, options, mutual funds, bank certificates of deposit, limited partnerships and many other financial products. Brokers also offer asset management accounts, which combine holdings of assets like stocks and bonds with a money-market fund which provides checkwriting and credit card features. Most brokers in addition offer individualized financial planning services. As a result of this wide range of products, brokers today have a much more diverse clientele, ranging from young persons just starting to invest to wealthy retired people who are experienced investors.

On May 1, 1975, known as May Day in the brokerage industry, the era of fixed commissions ended. This move brought much more competition within the industry and ushered in a new breed of broker—the discounter. These brokers specialize in executing buy and sell orders for stocks, bonds and options. As a rule, they charge commissions far lower than full-service brokers. Discounters do not give advice about which securities to buy or sell, however, so investors who use them generally are more experienced and knowledgable. Some discount brokers were acquired in the 1980s by commercial banks, who under the Glass-Steagall Act of 1933 are not allowed to act as full-service brokers. Banks were allowed to make such acquisitions because discount brokers do not give advice or underwrite securities. Full-service firms offer far more guidance on what investments are appropriate for each client. For this guidance, however, clients must pay significantly higher charges.

Within the full-service brokerage firm category, two varieties exist. The largest firms are known as wire houses, because they have a large network of offices nationally linked by advanced communications equipment. National wire house firms also tend to have an important presence overseas. In contrast, regional brokerage firms concentrate on serving customers in a particular area of the country. Such firms typically do not offer as wide an array of financial products, although they usually provide all the basics. Regional firms tend to concentrate on finding investment opportunities not yet discovered by large national firms.

In addition to providing services to individuals, brokers who also engage in investment banking play an important role in raising capital for federal, state and local governments and for corporations. Such firms underwrite new issues of debt securities for governments and equity and debt issues for corporations and distribute them to both institutional and individual investors. In addition, brokers act as advisers to corporations involved in merger and acquisition activity and other areas of corporate finance. Increasingly, brokerage firms are expanding their operations internationally, to facilitate trading of foreign currencies, and foreign debt and equity securities.

This alphabetical list contains the top 100 brokerage firms as measured by amount of capital. Capital is crucial to a brokerage firm because it must constantly be put at risk in underwriting and trading securities. The two largest firms on the list, Shearson Lehman Hutton Inc. and Salomon Brothers Inc., had about $6.6 billion and $3.1 billion in capital, respectively, in 1988. The two next largest firms, Merrill Lynch, Pierce, Fenner & Smith Incorporated, and Goldman Sachs & Co., had capital of over $2 billion. All other brokerage firms listed here had less than $2 billion of capital. The smallest of the 100 firms on the list had $32 million in capital.

Most of these brokerage firms were originally formed as partnerships, but in recent years, many incorporated and a number offered shares of stock in their companies to the public. Such public offerings are often the best way for a brokerage firm to raise the additional capital it needs to be competitive.

Following the list of 100 full-service firms is an alpabetical list of the top discount brokers, also ranked by capital. These lists are provided courtesy of the brokerage industry's trade association, the Securities Industry Association, [120 Broadway, New York, New York 10005 (212) 608-1500].

Full-Service Brokerage Firms

ABD Securities Corporation
One Battery Park Plaza
New York, New York 10004
(212) 363-5100

Advest, Inc.
280 Trumbull Street
Hartford, Connecticut 06103
(203) 525-1421

Alliance Capital Management L.P.
1345 Avenue of the Americas
New York, New York 10105
(212) 969-1000

Arnhold and S. Bleichroeder, Inc.
45 Broadway
New York, New York 10006
(212) 943-9200

Robert W. Baird & Co., Incorporated
777 East Wisconsin Avenue
Milwaukee, Wisconsin 53202
(414) 765-3500

The Bank of Tokyo Trust Company
100 Broadway
New York, New York 10005
(212) 766-3400

The Bear Stearns Companies Inc.
245 Park Avenue
New York, New York 10167
(212) 272-2000

William Blair & Company
135 South LaSalle Street
Chicago, Illinois 60603
(312) 236-1600

Blunt Ellis & Loewi Incorporated
111 E. Kilbourn Avenue
Milwaukee, Wisconsin 53202
(414) 347-3400

Boettcher & Company, Inc.
828 Seventeenth Street
Denver, Colorado 80202
(303) 628-8000

J.C. Bradford & Co.
330 Commerce Street
Nashville, Tennessee 37201-1809
(615) 748-9000

Alex. Brown & Sons Incorporated
135 East Baltimore Street
Baltimore, Maryland 21202
(301) 727-1700

Chase Securities, Inc.
One Chase Manhattan Plaza
New York, New York 10081
(212) 552-2301

The Chicago Corporation
208 South LaSalle Street
Chicago, Illinois 60604
(312) 855-7600

CL Global Partners Securities Corporation
95 Wall Street, 17th Floor
New York, New York 10005
(212) 428-6100

Commerzbank Capital Markets Corporation
One World Trade Center, Suite 4047
New York, New York 10048
(212) 432-8200

Crowell,Weeden and Co.,
One Wilshire Building, Suite 2800
Los Angeles, California 90017
(213) 620-1850

Daiwa Securities America,Inc.
One World Financial Center,
200 Liberty Street, Tower A
New York, New York 10281
(212) 945-0100

Dean Witter Reynolds Inc.
2 World Trade Center
New York, New York 10048
(212) 392-2222

Deutsche Bank Capital Corporation
31 West 52nd Street, 3rd Floor
New York, New York 10019
(212) 474-7000

Dillon Read & Co. Inc.
535 Madison Avenue
New York, New York 10022
(212) 906-7000

Dominick & Dominick Incorporated
90 Broad Street
New York, New York 10004
(212) 558-8800

Donaldson, Lufkin and Jenrette Securities
Corporation
140 Broadway
New York, New York 10005
(212) 504-3000

Eaton Vance Distributors, Inc.
24 Federal Street
Boston, Massachusetts 02110
(617) 482-8260

A.G. Edwards & Sons, Inc.
One North Jefferson
St. Louis, Missouri 63103
(314) 289-3000

Eppler, Guerin & Turner, Inc.
144 Ross Avenue, Ste. 2300
Dallas, Texas 75202
(214) 880-9000

Federated Securities Corp.
Federated Investors Tower
Pittsburgh, Pennsylvania 15222-3779
(412) 288-1900

First Boston Inc.
Park Avenue Plaza
New York, New York 10055
(212) 909-2000

Furman Selz Mager Dietz & Birney
Incorporated
230 Park Avenue
New York, New York 10169
(212) 309-8200

Glickenhaus & Co.
6 East 43rd Street
New York, New York 10017
(212) 953-7800

Goldman Sachs & Co.
85 Broad Street
New York, New York 10004
(212) 902-1000

Greenwich Capital Markets, Inc.
600 Steamboat Road
Greenwich, Connecticut 06830
(203) 625-2700

Gruntal & Co. Incorporated
14 Wall Street
New York, New York 10005
(212) 267-8800

Hambrecht & Quist Incorporated
One Bush Street
San Francisco, California 94104
(415) 576-3300

Herzog, Heine, Geduld, Inc.
26 Broadway
New York, New York 10004
(212) 908-4000

J.J.B. Hilliard, W.L. Lyons Inc.
Hilliard Lyons Center
Louisville, Kentucky 40232-2760
(502) 588-8400

Integrated Resources Equity Corporation
10 Union Square East
New York, New York 10003
(212) 353-7000

Inter-Regional Financial Group, Inc.
100 Dain Tower
Minneapolis, Minnesota 55402
(612) 371-7750

Interstate/Johnson Lane Corporation
2700 NCNB Plaza
101 South Tryon Street
Charlotte, North Carolina 28280
(704) 379-9000

Janney Montgomery Scott Inc.
5 Penn Center Plaza
Philadelphia, Pennsylvania 19103
(215) 665-6000

Jefferies & Company, Inc.
445 South Figueroa Street, Suite 3300
Los Angeles, California 90071
(213) 624-3333

Edward D. Jones & Co.
201 Progress Parkway
St. Louis, Missouri 63043
(314) 851-2000

Keefe,Bruyette & Woods ,Inc.
Suite 8566, Two World Trade Center
New York, New York 10048
(212) 323-8300

Kemper Clearing Corp.
411 East Mason Street
Milwaukee, Wisconsin 53202
(414) 225-4100

Kemper Financial Services, Inc.
120 South LaSalle Street
Chicago, Illinois 60603
(312) 781-1121

Kidder Peabody & Co., Incorporated
10 Hanover Square
New York, New York 10005
(212) 510-3000

C. J. Lawrence, Morgan Grenfell Inc.
1290 Avenue of the Americas
New York, New York 10104-0101
(212) 468-5000

Lazard Freres & Co.
One Rockefeller Plaza
New York, New York 10020
(212) 489-6600

Legg Mason, Inc.
Legg Mason Tower
111 South Calvert Street
Baltimore, Maryland 21202
(301) 539-3400

Levesque, Beaubien Inc.
1155 Metcalfe Street, 5th Floor
Montreal, Quebec H3B 4S9 Canada
(514) 879-2222

Mabon, Nugent & Co.
One Liberty Plaza, 165 Broadway
New York, New York 10006
(212) 732-2820

Bernard L. Madoff Investment Securities
885 Third Avenue
New York, New York 10022
(212) 230-2424

McDonald & Company Securities, Inc.
2100 The Society Building
Cleveland, Ohio 44114
(216) 443-2300

Merrill Lynch, Pierce, Fenner & Smith Inc.
North Tower, World Financial Center
New York, New York 10281-1332
(212) 449-1000

Mesirow Financial Holdings, Inc.
350 North Clark Street, Suite 300
Chicago, Illinois 60610
(312) 670-6000

Miller Tabak Hirsch & Company
331 Madison Avenue
New York, New York 10017
(212) 370-0040

Montgomery Securities
600 Montgomery Street
San Francisco, California 94111
(415) 627-2000

Morgan Keegan & Company, Inc.
50 Front Street
Memphis, Tennessee 38103
(901) 524-4100

J. P. Morgan Securities Inc.
23 Wall Street
New York, New York 10015
(212) 483-2323

Morgan Stanley & Co. Inc.
1251 Avenue of the Americas
New York, New York 10020
(212) 703-4000

Nesbitt Thomson Bonguard Inc.
Sun Life Tower, Sun Life Center,
150 King Street West, Suite 2200
Toronto, Ontario M5H 3W2 Canada
(416) 586-3600

Neuberger & Berman
522 Fifth Avenue
New York, New York 10036
(212) 730-7370

New Japan Securities International, Inc.
One World Trade Center, Suite 9133
New York, New York 10048
(212) 839-0001

The Nikko Securities Co. International, Inc.
200 Liberty Street
New York, New York 10281
(212) 416-5400

Nomura Securities International
180 Maiden Lane
New York, New York 10038
(212) 208-9300

John Nuveen and Co. Inc.
333 West Wacker Drive
Chicago, Illinois 60606
(312) 917-7700

The Ohio Company
155 East Broad Street
Columbus, Ohio 43215
(614) 464-6811

Oppenheimer & Company, Inc.
Oppenheimer Tower, World Financial Center
New York, New York 10281
(212) 667-7000

PaineWebber Group Inc.
1285 Avenue of the Americas
New York, New York 10019
(212) 713-2000

Pemburton Securities Inc.
666 Burrard Street
Vancouver, British Columbia V6C 3C7 Canada
(604) 688-8411

Piper, Jaffray & Hopwood Incorporated
Piper Jaffray Tower
222 South 9th Street
Minneapolis, Minnesota 55440
(612) 342-6000

Prescott, Ball and Turben, Inc.
1331 Euclid Avenue
Cleveland, Ohio 44115
(216) 574-7300

Prudential-Bache Securities Inc.
One Seaport Plaza
199 Water Street
New York, New York 10292
(212) 791-1000

Raymond James & Associates, Inc.
880 Carillon Parkway
St. Petersburg, Florida 33733-2749
(813) 573-3800

The Robinson-Humphrey Company, Inc.
Atlanta Financial Center
3333 Peachtree Road, N.E.
Atlanta, Georgia 30326
(404) 266-6000

Rodman & Renshaw, Inc.
120 South LaSalle Street
Chicago, Illinois 60603
(312) 977-7800

Salomon Brothers Inc.
One New York Plaza
New York, New York 10004
(212) 747-7000

SBCI Swiss Bank Corporation Investment
Banking, Inc.
222 Broadway, 4th Floor
New York, New York 10038
(212) 335-1000

M.A. Schapiro & Co., Inc.
One Chase Manhattan Plaza
New York, New York 10005
(212) 425-6600

ScotiaMcCleod (U.S.A.) Inc.
59 Maiden Lane
New York, New York 10038
(212) 804-5400

Securities Settlement Corporation
One Whitehall Street
New York, New York 10004
(212) 709-8000

Shearson Lehman Hutton Inc.
American Express Tower
World Financial Center
New York, New York 10285
(212) 298-2000

Smith Barney, Harris Upham & Company, Inc.
1345 Avenue of the Americas
New York, New York 10105
(212) 399-6000

Smith New Court, Carl Marks Inc.
77 Water Street
New York, New York 10005
(212) 437-7000

Spear, Leeds & Kellogg
115 Broadway
New York, New York 10006
(212) 587-8800

Stephens Inc.
114 East Capitol Avenue
Little Rock, Arkansas 72203
(501) 374-4361

Tucker, Anthony Incorporated
1 Beacon Street
Boston, Massachusetts 02108
(617) 725-2000

UBS Securities,Inc.
299 Park Avenue
New York, New York 10171
(212) 230-4000

Van Kampen Merritt Inc.
1001 Warrenville Road
Lisle, Illinois 60532
(312) 719-6000

Walwyn Stodgell Cochran Murray Limited
70 University Avenue
Toronto, Ontario M5J 2M5 Canada
(416) 591-6000

S. G. Warburg & Co. Inc.
787 Seventh Avenue
New York, New York 10019
(212) 459-7000

Weiss, Peck & Greer
One New York Plaza
New York, New York 10004
(212) 908-9570

Wertheim Schroder & Co. Incorporated
Equitable Center
787 Seventh Avenue
New York, New York 10019-6016
(212) 492-6000

Westpac Pollock Government Securities Inc.
160 Water Street
New York, New York 10038
(212) 797-5800

Yamaichi International (America), Inc.
Two World Trade Center
New York, New York 10048
(212) 912-6400

The Ziegler Company, Inc.
215 North Main Street
West Bend, Wisconsin 53095
(414) 334-5521

Discount Brokerage Firms

Bidwell
209 S.W. Oak Street
Portland, Oregon 97204
(503) 790-9000, (800) 547-6337
(800) 452-6774

Burke Christensen & Lewis
303 West Madison Street
Chicago, Illinois 60606
(312) 346-8283, (800) 621-0392

Fidelity Brokerage Services Inc.
161 Devonshire Street
Boston, Massachusetts 02110
(800) 225-1799, (617) 570-7000

Heartland Securities
208 South LaSalle Street
Chicago, Illinois 60604
(312) 372-0075, (800) 621-0662
(800) 972-0580

Pacific Brokerage Services
5757 Wilshire Boulevard
Beverly Hills, California 90211
(800) 421-8395, (213) 939-1100

Quick & Reilly, Inc.
120 Wall Street
New York, New York 10005
(800) 221-5220, (212) 943-8686

Charles Schwab and Co.
101 Montgomery Street
San Francisco, California
(800) 342-5472, (415) 398-1000

Muriel Siebert and Co.
444 Madison Avenue
New York, New York 10022
(800) 872-0711, (212) 644-2400

York Securities
11 Wall Street
New York, New York 10005
(212) 349-9700

LIMITED PARTNERSHIP SPONSORS

The following is a list of major sponsors of publicly available limited partnerships. All the sponsors act as general partner in managing the assets of the partnership for the benefit of the limited partners. In return for management services, general partners receive management fees and often a percentage of profits generated by partnership investments.

In recent years, there has been a proliferation of different types of limited partnerships. These programs, which formerly were marketed only to wealthy investors, are now sold to investors of more modest means, mostly through brokerage firms and financial planners.

Some partnerships are designed to provide current income—often at least partially sheltered from taxation. Such income is derived from interest on loans the partnership has made, from rents that tenants pay to occupy real estate owned by the partnership, from sales of oil and gas that have been extracted by the partnership, or from other sources.

Other partnerships are designed to produce long-term capital gains for limited partners. These plans pay out little, if any, current income to participants. Capital gains can be achieved through purchases and resale at a higher price of real estate, oil and gas properties, equipment like computers or airplanes, cable television systems, or other investments. The skill of the general partner in buying undervalued properties and increasing their worth over time is key in realizing such capital gains.

Some partnerships strive not only for income or capital gains, but also for tax savings for the limited partners. Tax benefits from depreciation, tax credits, depletion allowances, intangible drilling costs, operating losses or other tax savings under current law, pass directly through to limited partners in direct proportion to their holdings in the partnership. Before 1987, these benefits could be applied without limit to taxable earnings from salaries, investments, or any other source of income. The Tax Reform Act of 1986 severely curtailed the use of limited partnerships as tax shelters by ruling that the applicability of such passive source deductions would, after a five-year transaction period, be limited to income from other passive sources. For purposes of the alternative minimum tax, the new law was even tougher on limited partnerships: Net passive losses were made a tax preference item at 100% of value effective in 1987.

All units of limited partnerships must be purchased through qualified broker/dealers. These dealers have the responsibility of doing a due diligence investigation of the partnership's management, objectives, and track record. Once the deal has cleared this process, brokers are allowed to sell units to customers who meet certain suitability requirements. Usually, a certain level of yearly income and net worth is called for, in addition to the assurance that the investor is sophisticated enough to understand the potential risks of the investment. Investors must be given the partnership's prospectus before they invest. Each unit of a partnership typically costs $1000, and the minimum purchase is from 1 to 5 units. For Individual Retirement Accounts, the minimum is usually 2 units, or $2000. Out of this amount, broker/dealers usually charge a sales commission of at least 5%, and sometimes as much as 10%, of the principal invested. In general, partnership shares are not actively traded, though general partners usually will attempt to buy back partnership interests or place the units with another person if an existing partner wants to liquidate a position. In a few cases, partnership units are listed on the New York or American stock exchanges or traded over the counter.

The listing that follows is divided into the nine main types of limited partnerships. These are Agricultural/Livestock; Cable Television; Commodities and Financial Futures; Equipment Leasing; Film, Theater and Video Production; Medical Equipment and Services; Miscellaneous; Oil and Gas; Real Estate, and Research and Development. The general partners in each category are the ones with the largest sales to the public in their specialty. They are listed alphabetically, along with their addresses and telephone numbers.

This list is courtesy of Robert Stanger & Company, a firm which tracks the limited partnership industry. Stanger is located at 1129 Broad Street, Shrewsbury, New Jersey 07701 [(201) 389-3600 or (800) 631-2291].

Agriculture/Livestock

Agriculture/Livestock partnerships invest in a wide variety of agricultural properties that pass income and tax benefits through to limited partners. These programs may involve growing grain or fruits and vegetables or producing lumber. Other partnerships involve raising livestock and selling the cattle for slaughter. The success or failure of the partnership depends on the management of the farm as well as the price the partnership gets for its products. Higher returns in general result when prices are high and rising than when prices are low and falling.

Agrifuture, Inc.
3651 Pegasus Drive, Suite 101
Bakersfield, California 93308
(805) 393-2550

First Winthrop Corp.
225 Franklin Street
Boston, Massachusetts 02110
(617) 439-4200, (800) 343-9533

FPI Agribusiness, Inc.
737 Bishop Street
Honolulu, Hawaii 96813
(800) 367-5214

Granada Management Corp.
10900 Richmond Avenue, P.O. Box 42298
Houston, Texas 77242
(713) 977-7000, (800) 231-2183

Marley Orchards Corp.
Cowiche City Street
Cowiche, Washington 98923
(212) 668-4620, (509) 678-4123

Mauna Loa Resources, Inc.
827 Fort Street
Honolulu, Hawaii 96813
(808) 536-4461

Met Farm and Ranch Properties, Inc.
8717 West 110th Street, Suite 700
Overland Park, Kansas 66210
(913) 451-8282

Millenium Genetics, Inc.
West Highway 26
Broadwater, Nebraska 69125
(308) 489-5411, (303) 297-1030

Scott Davenport Farms
816 Park Lane, Suite D
Lee's Summit, Missouri 64063
(816) 932-7244

Two Rivers Cattle Company, Inc.
116 South Capitol Street
Mount Sterling, Illinois 62353
(217) 773-3622

Viking Ranches, Inc.
19968 Bear Valley Road
Apple Valley, California 92308
(619) 247-5896

Vintech Almond Advisers, Inc.
2455 Bennett Valley Road, Suite 314B
Santa Rosa, California 95404
(800) 233-3080

Cable Television

These partnerships build or buy cable television systems, upgrade their services in an attempt to increase subscriptions, and sell the systems in five to ten years. Limited partners receive capital gains resulting from the sale of the systems as well as any tax benefits that may flow from the partnership's investment in the business. These partnerships typically provide little, if any income to partners, since the revenue from operations is generally reinvested in the business.

Cencom Cable Associates, Inc.
14522 South Outer 40 Road, Suite 300
Chesterfield, Massachusetts 01012
(314) 576-4446

Enstar Communications Corp.
6100 Lake Forest Drive, Suite 300
Atlanta, Georgia 30328
(404) 252-0061, (800) 241-1005

Falcon Cable Investors Group
199 South Los Robles Avenue, Suite 640
Pasadena, California 91101
(818) 792-7132

First Ameri-Cable Corp.
801 Kingsmill Parkway
Columbus, Ohio 43229
(614) 888-8080, (800) 641-2505

Galaxy Cablevision Management
1100 North Main
Sikeston, Missouri
(314) 471-3080, (800) 851-4193

Integrated Resources
10 Union Square East
New York, New York 10003
(212) 353-7000, (800) 821-5100

Integrated Resources
2930 East Third Avenue
Denver, Colorado 80206
(800) 821-5100

International Capital Monitoring Corp.
12835 East Arapahoe Road
Tower Two, Penthouse
Englewood, Colorado 80112
(303) 790-0330

Jones Intercable, Inc.
9697 East Mineral Avenue
Englewood, Colorado 80111
(303) 792-3131, (800) 572-6520

Northland Communications Corp.
3500 One Union Square Building
Seattle, Washington 98101
(206) 621-1351

Phoenix Cable, Inc.
1891 Francisco Boulevard
San Rafael, California 94901
(415) 485-4600, (800) 227-2626

Prime Cable Corp.
600 Congress Avenue
3000 One American Center
Austin, Texas 78704
(512) 476-7888

Rifkin Cable Management Partners
360 South Monroe Street
Denver, Colorado 80209
(303) 333-1215

Signet Cablevision Co.
15124 Kercheval
Grosse Pointe Park, Michigan 48230
(313) 824-5454

U.S.A.T.V. Co.
1016 Northwest 82nd Street
Oklahoma City, Oklahoma 73114
(405) 848-0733

Commodities and Financial Futures

The following partnerships hire money managers who invest in the commodities and financial futures markets for capital gains. These markets are very volatile and are difficult for individuals to play on their own. By pooling resources with many other investors, partnerships allow the small investor to hire professional advisors who follow the markets closely and make timely investment decisions. Each partnership will usually invest in many commodities and financial futures markets simultaneously so that losses in one market can be offset by profits in another. These partnerships are designed to achieve capital gains, not income. With a few profitable trades, the returns to partners can be substantial—average annual returns of 20% or more are not uncommon. Limited partners are allowed to take money out of the partnership at specified intervals—usually once or twice a year. The investment advisor will not normally put all the partnership's assets at risk in the markets, so that a cushion remains if the futures positions result in losses. If losses are severe, a partnership may be dissolved, and the remaining capital returned to limited partners.

Advisors Futures Fund, Inc.
141 West Jackson Boulevard, Suite 1633
Chicago, Illinois 60604
(312) 341-5962

Agrifuture, Inc.
3651 Pegasus Drive, Suite 101
Bakersfield, California 93308
(805) 393-2550

ATA Research Inc.
6500 Greenville Avenue, Suite 300
Dallas, Texas 75206
(214) 373-7606, (214) 750-1300,
(800) 348-3601

Ceres Investment Co.
1 North Jefferson Avenue
St. Louis, Missouri 63103
(314) 289-3049

CIS Investments Inc.
141 West Jackson Boulevard
Chicago, Illinois 60604
(312) 435-8000

Demeter Management Corp.
Two World Trade Center, 22nd Floor
New York, New York 10048
(212) 392-2642

Dunn & Hargitt Investment Management, Inc.
22 North Second Street, P. 1100
Lafayette, Indiana 47901
(317) 423-2624

Everest Futures Management, Inc.
508 North Second Street, Suite 302
Fairfield, Iowa 52556
(515) 472-5500

Geldermann Futures Management Corp.
One Financial Place, 20th Floor
Chicago, Illinois 60605
(312) 663-7500

Hayden Commodities Corp.
17 Battery Place, 4th Floor
New York, New York 10004
(212) 668-5464, (212) 623-9647

Heinold Asset Management, Inc.
250 South Wacker Drive, 4th Floor
Chicago, Illinois 60606
(312) 648-8000, (800) 527-1010,
(800) 621-0266

Index Asset Management Partners
222 West Adams Street, Suite 1249
Chicago, Illinois 60606
(312) 207-5700, (312) 419-5800

Index Management Services, Inc.
90 West Street, Suite 1801
New York, New York 10006
(212) 227-5208, (800) 221-2917

International Futures Fund Partners
208 South LaSalle Street, Suite 200
Chicago, Illinois 60604
(312) 855-7720

IR Futures Corp.
372 Danbury Road
Wilton, Connecticut 06897
(203) 762-8511, (800) 833-3369

Lind-Waldock Financial Partners, Inc.
30 South Wacker Drive, Suite 1712
Chicago, Illinois 60606
(312) 648-1400

McCormick Futures Management, Inc.
135 South LaSalle Street, Suite 2006
Chicago, Illinois 60603
(312) 263-3300, (312) 443-7362

Merchant Funds Management, Inc.
141 West Jackson Boulevard, Suite 2700
Chicago, Illinois 60604
(312) 939-7000

North American Investment Futures, Inc.
8100 Connecticut Boulevard
East Hartford, Connecticut 06108
(800) 243-4322

Paul Tudor Jones
160 Broadway, Suite 905
New York, New York 10006
(212) 608-0901

Randell Commodity Corp.
889 Ridge Lake Boulevard
Memphis, Tennessee 38119
(901) 763-0370, (901) 761-5100

RJO Commodities Management, Inc.
550 West Jackson Boulevard, Suite 400
Chicago, Illinois 60606
(312) 648-7300, (800) 825-5595

Rockwell Future Management, Inc.
Bergen Park Business Plaza
1202 Highway 74, Suite 212
Evergreen, Colorado 80439
(303) 674-1328, (303) 572-1000

Rudolf Wolff Equity Management
295 Madison Avenue
New York, New York 10002
(212) 573-0400, (212) 490-5900

Seaport Futures Management, Inc.
100 Gold Street, 7th Floor
New York, New York 10038
(212) 791-4429, (212) 776-4429

Stotler Funds, Inc.
141 West Jackson Boulevard, Suite 1600-A
Chicago, Illinois 60604
(312) 987-2937, (312) 704-9000,
(800) 423-8320

U.S. Futures Corp.
102 South Tejon Street, Suite 1100
Colorado Springs, Colorado 80903
(303) 578-3328

Virginia Futures Management Corp.
141 West Jackson Boulevard
Chicago, Illinois 60604
(312) 922-1717

Equipment Leasing

Equipment Leasing partnerships specialize in buying a wide range of equipment and leasing it to users. For example, one of these partnerships might buy computers and lease them to a company preferring to rent rather than buy. The rental income from the computers is passed through to the limited partners as are all tax benefits, such as depreciation on the equipment. When the lease expires, the partnership either re-leases the computers or sells them and distributes the proceeds to limited partners. In addition to leasing computer equipment, such partnerships may also lease transportation equipment such as airplanes and railroad cars.

AFG Aircraft Management Corp.
Exchange Place
Boston, Massachusetts 02109
(617) 542-1200

Airlease Management Services, Inc.
2988 Campus Drive
San Mateo, California 94403
(415) 627-9300

Atel Financial Corp.
160 Sansome Street, 7th Floor
San Francisco, California 94104
(415) 989-8800, (800) 543-ATEL

CAI Equipment Leasing I Corp.
31 East Platte Avenue
Colorado Springs, Colorado 80903
(303) 442-0100

Capital Partners Management Co.
2995 Baseline Road
Boulder, Colorado 80303
(303) 442-0100

CIS Equipment Management Corp.
909 Montgomery Street
San Francisco, California 94133
(415) 788-7900, (800) 222-2372

CSA Financial Corp.
2 Oliver Street
Boston, Massachusetts 02189
(617) 482-4671, (800) 336-0005

Dean Witter Reynolds, Inc.
Two World Trade Center
New York, New York 10006
(212) 524-2906, (800) 462-6631

Equitec Financial Group, Inc.
7677 Oakport Street, P.O. Box 2470
Oakland, California 94614
(415) 430-9900, (800) 445-9020

Fidelity Leasing Associates
259 Radnor-Chester Road
Radnor, Pennsylvania 19087
(215) 971-6605, (800) 223-3543

Finalco Group, Inc.
8200 Greensboro Drive, Suite 1500
McLean, Virginia 22102
(703) 790-0970, (800) 346-2526

First of Michigan Leasing
100 Renaissance Center
Detroit, Michigan 48243
(313) 259-2600

Greenbrier Partners, Inc.
633 Battery Street
San Francisco, California 94111
(813) 345-3199, (800) 237-4240

ICON Properties, Inc.
One Summit Avenue
White Plains, New York 10606
(914) 428-9000, (800) 222-4266

Integrated Resources
One Union Square East
New York, New York 10003
(212) 353-7000, (800) 821-5100,
(800) 223-1424

Intermodal Equipment Associates
540 Howard Street
San Francisco, California 94105
(415) 543-7363

Leastec Corp.
1440 Maria Lane, Suite 200
Walnut Creek, California 94596
(415) 938-3443, (800) 821-2456

McDonnell Douglas Capital Corp.
5455 Corporate Drive, Suite 210
Troy, Michigan 48098
(313) 641-9797, (800) 444-4911

Meridian-Columbia Management Corp.
570 Lake Cook Road, Suite 300
Deerfield, Illinois 60015
(212) 804-6819, (312) 940-1200

Pegasus Aircraft Management Corp.
One Montgomery Street
San Francisco, California 94104
(415) 434-3900

Phoenix Leasing Inc.
1891 Francisco Boulevard
San Rafael, California 94901
(415) 485-4600, (800) 227-2626

PLM Financial Services, Inc.
655 Montgomery Street
San Francisco, California 94111
(800) 227-0830

Polaris Aircraft Leasing Corp.
600 Montgomery Street, 3rd Floor
San Francisco, California 94111
(415) 362-0333, (800) 227-3530

R&D Funding Corp./Prudential-Bache
3945 Freedom Circle, Suite 800
Santa Clara, California 95054
(408) 980-0990

RJ Leasing, Inc.
1400 66th Street North
St. Petersburg, Florida 33710
(813) 345-3199, (800) 237-4240

Republic Management, Inc.
P.O. Box 919
Olympia, Washington 98507
(206) 754-6227

Super Fund Capital L.P.
90 West Street, Suite 2115
New York, New York 10006
(212) 962-0100, (800) 221-2917

Textainer Capital Corp.
Spear Street Tower, Suite 347
1 Market Plaza
San Francisco, California 94105
(415) 434-0551, (800) 356-1739

Torchmark Leasing Programs, Inc.
600 Atlantic Avenue
Boston, Massachusetts 02210
(617) 482-8000

Troy Capital Services, Inc.
5455 Corporate Drive, Suite 210
Troy, Michigan 48098
(313) 641-9797

U.S. Investment Management Services, Inc.
733 Front Street ·
San Francisco, California 94111
(415) 627-9200

Van Arnem Financial Services, Inc.
870 Bowers Street
Birmingham, Michigan 48009
(303) 694-5106

Waddell & Reed Leasing, Inc.
2400 Pershing Road, P.O. Box 418343
Kansas City, Missouri 64108
(816) 283-4000, (816) 283-4231

Wellesley Leasing Partnership
711 Atlantic Avenue
Boston, Massachusetts 02210
(617) 482-8000

Western Cogen Management
5613 DTC Parkway
Englewood, Colorado 80111
(303) 771-7550

Film, Theater and Video Productions, Media Properties

Film, Theater and Video Production partnerships invest in the production and distribution of motion pictures, plays and the acquisition of media properties such as television and radio stations. Partners help to finance the production costs of a portfolio of films, plays or video productions, or the acquisition of several media properties. Partners then receive royalties when the film is released to the public in theaters, on cable television or in videocassette form. The success of the partnership depends on the commercial success of the film, play or video production, or the growth in the value of the radio and television station. Limited partners usually receive no income in the start-up or acquisition phase of the partnership, but receive distributions once a film, play or media property generates revenues. A certain amount of this income is sheltered by the tax benefits generated by film, play or video production.

Bagdasian & Bloom Productions
532 West 50th Street, Suite 4-AR
New York, New York 10019
(212) 581-3320

Bejan, Nelson Entertainment Ltd.
433 West 46th Street 4RE
New York, New York 10036
(212) 245-0001

BFI Partners
4849 Golf Road
Skokie, Illinois 60777
(312) 677-2900

Broadcast Ventures, Inc.
9800 Richmond Avenue, Suite 300
Houston, Texas 77042
(713) 781-0781

Cates Films, Inc.
57 East 74th Street
New York, New York 10021
(212) 517-7100

CineGroup, Inc. & John P. Finegan
1503 Walnut Street
Philadelphia, Pennsylvania 19102
(215) 568-6010

Communications Investment Corp.
5401 West Kennedy Boulevard
Tampa, Florida 33609
(813) 381-3800

DEG Management Corp.
8670 Wilshire Boulevard
Beverly Hills, California 90211
(213) 854-7000

Delphi Co.
711 Third Avenue, 17th Floor
New York, New York 10017
(212) 986-1921

Denim Productions, Inc. & Lee Guber
41 East 57th Street, Room 901
New York, New York 10022
(212) 759-2810

Dynasty Production Management,
   Inc.
500 South 500 West
Sandy, Utah 84070
(801) 566-9455

Entertainment America, Inc.
6244 Clark Center Avenue, Unit 4
Sarasota, Florida 34238
(813) 924-7848

Entertainment Development Co. II
636 Northland Boulevard
Cincinnati, Ohio 45240
(513) 851-5700

Entertainment, Inc.
204 Brazilian Avenue, Suite 200
Palm Beach, Florida 33480
(407) 659-1660

First Artists Media Entertainment
1221 Brickell Avenue
Miami, Florida 33131
(800) 885-FAME

Flamingo Bay Films, Inc.
19377 North East 10th Avenue, Suite 311
North Miami Beach, Florida 33179
(305) 653-1766

FMC Communications, Inc.
12832 Harbor Boulevard, Suite 260
Garden Grove, California 92640
(800) 533-7480

HBO Film Management, Inc.
1100 Avenue of the Americas
New York, New York 10036
(212) 986-1921, (212) 512-1172

Jones 21st Century Management, Inc.
9697 East Mineral Avenue
Englewood, Colorado 80112
(303) 792-3131, (800) 572-6520

Kagan Media Capital, Inc.
126 Clock Tower Place
Carmel, California 93923
(201) 902-3113, (408) 624-1536

Kings Road Entertainment, Inc.
1901 Avenue of the Stars, Suite 605
Los Angeles, California 90067
(213) 552-0057, (714) 253-4687

Lake Land Fire Films, Inc.
111 Barrow Street
New York, New York 10014
(212) 620-7393

Lorimar Film Partners
3970 Overland Avenue
Culver City, California 90230
(213) 202-2000, (213) 202-2128

Malrite Broadcast Partners, Inc.
1200 Statler Office Tower
1128 Euclid Avenue
Cleveland, Ohio 44115
(516) 222-6954

Media Opportunity Management Partners
World Financial Center, North Tower
New York, New York 10281
(212) 449-2011

Media Partners
130 Franklin Center
29100 Northwestern Highway
Southfield, Michigan 48034
(313) 353-3333

New South Pictures, Inc.
5600 Roswell Road, Suite 290
Atlanta, Georgia 30350
(404) 252-9102

NMV Hollywood, Inc.
2701 Rocky Point Drive, Suite 700
Tampa, Florida 33607
(813) 884-4433

Omnibus Productions
1576 Broadway, Suite 308
New York, New York 10036
(212) 265-2238

Orbit Entertainment, Inc.
Paramount Studios, 5555 Melrose Avenue
Hollywood, California 90038
(213) 468-5960

Producers Circle Company
1350 Sixth Avenue, Penthouse
New York, New York 10019
(212) 765-6760

Shearson Premiere Corp.
14 Wall Street
New York, New York 10005
(212) 577-5250, (212) 635-4424

Silver Screen Management Services, Inc.
595 Madison Avenue
New York, New York 10002
(212) 995-7600, (212) 310-1500

Star Partners
180 Park Avenue North
Winter Park, Florida 32789
(800) 421-7827

TGP Communications, Inc.
860 Via de la Paz Street
Pacific Palisades, California 90272
(213) 459-8181

The Gamble, Inc.
13 Ashland Street
Medford, Massachusetts 02155
(617) 391-6864

Theater Management Associates, Inc.
240 West 44th Street
New York, New York 10036
(303) 279-1596

Video Investors, Ltd.
10350 Santa Monica Boulevard, Suite 200
Los Angeles, California 90025
(213) 277-0711

Medical Equipment and Services

These limited partnerships invest in the research and development of new medical equipment and drugs, and the operation of medical service operations such as outpatient clinics and specialized healthcare facilities. Limited partners usually receive a low level of income from operations in the early years of the partnership, but can receive large capital gains if the medical equipment or health care facility gains acceptance in the marketplace and becomes profitable.

Cetus Development Corp.
1400 53rd Street
Emeryville, California 94608
(415) 420-3300

H.H.S.V. MRI Corp.
1111 Goffle Road
Hawthorne, New Jersey 07506
(201) 423-0300

Hospital Development & Service Corp.
401 North West 42nd Avenue
Plantation, Florida 33317
(615) 383-4444
(305) 587-5010

MedInc
Two Vantage Way, Suite 500
Nashville, Tennessee 37228
(615) 244-1008

Med Venture, Inc.
Business & Technology Center
511 11th Avenue South, Room 406
Minneapolis, Minnesota 55415
(612) 332-7211

Nuclear Medicine, Inc.
400 Arthur Godfrey Road
Miami Beach, Florida 33140
(305) 921-5500

Omega Health Services of Birmingham, Inc.
7770 Poplar Avenue, Suite 105
Germantown, Tennessee 38138
(901) 757-0435

Rocky Mountain Stone Management, Inc.
601 East Hampden, Suite 580
Englewood, Colorado 80110
(303) 788-6866

PAMCO Medical Management, Inc.
101 Madison Avenue
Morristown, New Jersey 07961
(201) 993-0866

Wendt-Bristol Diagnostics Co.
1550 Kenny Road
Columbus, Ohio 43212
(614) 486-9411

Physicians Clinical Services, Ltd.
10 Penn Center Plaza, Suite 1000
Philadelphia, Pennsylvania 19103
(215) 569-3884

Miscellaneous

These partnerships invest in a variety of activities that do not fit into any of the other categories presented here. Coin partnerships buy a portfolio of selected rare coins, which will be held for several years before being sold, with any profits distributed to limited partners. Master limited partnerships are traded on exchanges, and tend to hold assets such as real estate and oil and gas properties, from which they receive income which they pass on to limited partners. Partnerships that invest in leveraged buyouts and financings gain equity stakes in established companies by helping those companies finance leveraged buyouts. Partners receive income from loans made to these companies and have the potential to receive capital gains when the private companies go public again sometime in the future. Telecommunications partnerships invest in the construction and operation of cellular or coin-operated pay telephone systems. Partners receive income from the operations, and hope to receive capital gains if the systems are later sold for a profit. Some partnerships participate in many activities in different fields, thus diversifying limited partners' risk.

Alpha Pay Phones (telecommunications)
8113 Ridgepoint Drive, Suite 209
Irving, Texas 75063
(817) 267-5621

Avalon Cellular, Inc. (telecommunications)
13360 Firestone Boulevard, Suite A
Santa Fe Springs, California 90670
(213) 457-1642

Cedar Fair L.P. (master limited partnership
on NYSE)
P.O. Box CN 5006
Sandusky, Ohio 44871
(419) 626-0830

Emkay Rare Coin Associates, Ltd. (coins)
517 Route 111
Hauppauge, New York 11788
(516) 724-1855, (800) 824-0023

Equus Capital Corp. (leveraged buyouts, mezzanine financing)
P.O. Box 13197
Houston, Texas 77219
(713) 529-0900, (800) 654-3423

Far West Capital, Inc. (oil and gas, real estate,
agriculture, hydroelectric, geothermal)
921 Executive Park Drive, Suite B
Salt Lake City, Utah 84117
(801) 268-4444

Food-N-Fuel Partners (convenience stores,
retail gas)
2801 Glenda Avenue
Fort Worth, Texas 76111
(817) 831-0761

Freeport-McMoran Resource Partners, Inc.
(master limited partnerships)
1615 Poydras Street
New Orleans, Louisiana 70112
(504) 582-4000

Maritrans GP, Inc. (master limited
partnership)
1400 Three Parkway
Philadelphia, Pennsylvania
(215) 864-1200

Gene Morgan Management Co. (real estate,
futures, venture capital)
Bunker Hill Tower
800 West First Street
Los Angeles, California 90012
(213) 622-1234

Numismatic Ventures, Inc. (coins)
2117 Hollywood Boulevard
Hollywood, Florida 33020
(305) 921-2646

Reich & Tang, Inc. (master limited
partnerships)
100 Park Avenue
New York, New York 10017
(212) 370-1110

SDI Partners (master limited partnership)
One Logan Square
Philadelphia, Pennsylvania 19103
(215) 665-3650

SSI Partners (common stock, warrants)
9 West 57th Street
New York, New York 10019
(212) 750-8300

Thomas H. Lee Advisors II (LBOs and
recapitalizations)
75 State Street
Boston, Massachusetts 02109
(617) 227-1050

Oil and Gas

   Oil and Gas limited partnerships are involved in the exploration, drilling and
production of oil and gas. The riskiest and potentially most rewarding partnerships do
exploratory drilling to find oil and gas reserves. If the driller is successful, revenues
from the sale of oil and gas flow through to limited partners, along with tax benefits
such as the oil depletion allowance and depreciation on drilling equipment.

   More conservative programs either drill where oil and gas reserves are proven or
just pump out oil and gas from wells that have already been successfully drilled. The
success or failure of any oil and gas limited partnership depends not only on the finding
and pumping of petroleum and/or natural gas, however. The price of oil and gas is also
a crucial determinant of success. In general, the programs offer higher returns to
limited partners when oil and gas prices are high and rising than when prices are low
and falling.

Apache Corp.
730 Second Avenue South
Minneapolis, Minnesota 55402
(612) 347-8884, (800) 328-7187

APCO Group, Inc.
15919 Stuebner Airline
Spring, Texas 77379
(713) 376-0100

Bataa Energy, Inc.
5401 West 10th Street
Greeley, Colorado 80634
(303) 356-5699

Baytide Petroleum, Inc.
1000 One Boston Plaza
20 East 5th Street
Tulsa, Oklahoma 74103
(918) 585-8150, (800) 622-6301

Benton Petroleum Co.
2021 Sperry Avenue
Ventura, California 93003
(805) 644-7741

Bogert Oil Co.
The Oil Center, Suite 1000-W
2601 N.W. Expressway
Oklahoma City, Oklahoma 73111
(800) 824-7591

Cannon Resources, Inc.
1800 S. Washington, Suite 300
Amarillo, Texas 79102
(800) 327-2733

Chesterfield Energy Corp.
203 West Main St.
Clarksburg, West Virginia 26301
(304) 623-5467

Chimayo Energy Corp.
619 South Taylor Street
Amarillo, Texas 79101
(806) 373-7672

Clinton Oil Co.
4770 Indianaola Avenue
Columbus, Ohio 43214
(614) 888-9558

Coastal Corp.
4990 Speak Lane, Suite 280
San Jose, California 95118
(408) 723-7411
    and
Coastal Tower
9 Greenway Plaza
Houston, Texas 77046
(713) 877-6821

Columbia Petroleum Partners
One Townsite Plaza, N. Concourse
Topeka, Kansas 66603
(913) 232-7283, (800) 255-3569,
(913) 234-0581

Conquest Oil Co.
3400 West 16th Street
Greeley, Colorado 80631
(602) 993-7844

Continental Reserves Management, Inc.
308 Keisling Building
102 Broadway Avenue
Carnegie, Pennsylvania 15106
(412) 276-7100

Continental Resources, Inc.
4 Smithfield Street, Suite 200
Pittsburgh, Pennsylvania 15222
(412) 566-1751

Culton Petroleum & Exploration, Inc.
Route 6, Box 39F
London, Kentucky 40741
(606) 864-4215

Cuyahoga Petroleum Group
100 Jericho Quadrangle
Jericho, New York 11753
(516) 433-8000

Deep Wilcox Corp.
1301 Dove Street, Suite 700
Newport Beach, California 92660
(714) 752-4902, (714) 497-1999,
(714) 499-1969

Dyco Petroleum Corp.
1100 Interchange Tower
Wayzata Blvd. at Hwy. 18
Minneapolis, Minnesota 55426
(612) 591-4100, (612) 545-2828

ECC Resources Corp.
1535 E. Olive, Suite A
Fresno, California 93728
(209) 485-8060

Egolf Co.
50 Penn Place, Suite 1410
Oklahoma City, Oklahoma 73118
(405) 840-3293

Energy Sciences Corp.
1221 Lamar Street, Suite 1500
Houston, Texas 77010
(206) 572-3901, (800) 223-1445

Energysearch Inc.
211 South Broad Street
Philadelphia, Pennsylvania 19107
(215) 985-5085, (215) 985-5255

Enex Resources Corp.
800 Rockmead Drive
3 Kingwood Place, Suite 200
Kingwood, Texas 77339
(713) 358-8401, (713) 358-4454,
(800) 231-0444

Everflow Eastern Inc.
132 South Broad Street
P.O. Box 354
Canfield, Ohio 44406
(216) 533-2692

Graham Resources
P.O. Box 3134
Covington, Louisiana 70434
(800) 821-5724

Hawkins Oil & Gas, Inc.
400 South Boston, Suite 800
Tulsa, Oklahoma 74103
(918) 585-3121

Hayden Oil Co.
200 East 7th Street, Suite 300
Loveland, Colorado 80537
(303) 663-0766

Hite Operating Co.
1112 South Villa Drive
Evansville, Indiana 47714
(812) 479-8946, (800) 247-7774

Hold Oil Corp. & Keyston Production Co.
7136 South Yale Avenue, Suite 208
Tulsa, Oklahoma 74136
(215) 688-6051

IRI Fund Asset Management
50 Briar Hollow, Suite 490
Houston, Texas 77027
(304) 623-6671

Integrated Resources
1331 17th Street, Suite 900
Denver, Colorado 80202
(303) 298-1807, (800) 525-4004

JR Operating Co.
104 Sixth Street, S.W.
Canton, Ohio 44702
(216) 443-2730

Kelly Oil Corp.
601 Jefferson Street, Suite 1100
Dresser Tower
Houston, Texas 77002
(212) 838-6070, (713) 652-5211

Kidder, Peabody
10 Hanover Square
New York, New York 10005
(800) 772-9417

Levengood Oil & Gas, Inc.
2301 Progress Street
Dover, Ohio 44622
(216) 364-4550

Lincam Oil & Gas, Inc.
25231 Grogan's Mill Road, Suite 340
The Woodlands, Texas 77380
(713) 367-9995

Mack & Mullen Management Services
Inc.
15301 Ventura Boulevard, Suite 300
Sherman Oaks, California 91403
(818) 995-3007

Merrico Resources, Inc.
1000 Energy Center
1505 North Commerce
P.O. Box 849
Ardmore, Oklahoma 73402
(405) 226-6700, (800) 654-4597

Morgan Energy Corp.
309 West First Avenue
Denver, Colorado 80223
(303) 777-4143

North Coast Energy, Inc.
5311 Northfield Road, Suite 320
Bedford Heights, Ohio 44146
(216) 663-1668, (800) 645-6427

Northstar Exploration Co.
2904 Parklawn Drive
Midwest City, Oklahoma 73110
(405) 733-0041

NYLIFE Equity Inc. & American
Exploration Co.
885 Third Avenue, Suite 2500
New York, New York 10022
(212) 576-6486, (212) 576-7309,
(800) 824-4636

Olympia Energy, Inc.
2030 Las Vegas Trail, Suite 1D
Fort Worth, Texas 76116
(214) 922-9245

Oxford Oil and Gas Inc.
1901 Avenue of the Stars, Suite 1450
Los Angeles, California 90067
(213) 284-6600

Paine Webber
Avanti Building, 5th Floor
810 South Cincinnati Avenue
Tulsa, Oklahoma 74119
(918) 583-5525

Pan Exploration and Development Inc.
5501 Foxridge Drive
Shawnee Mission, Kansas 66202
(913) 722-5958

Parker & Parsley Petroleum Co.
800 Empire Plaza
Midland, Texas 79702
(915) 683-4768, (800) 831-3332

Petrolane Partners
1600 East Hill Street
Long Beach, California 90806
(713) 759-4520, (213) 427-5471

Petroleum Development Corp.
103 East Main Street
Bridgeport, West Virginia 26330
(800) 624-3821

Petroleum Research Corp.
1900 East Flamingo, Suite 262
Las Vegas, Nevada 89121
(702) 796-2901

Pioneer Western Energy Corp.
600 Cleveland Street, Suite 800
P.O. Box 5068
Clearwater, Florida 33518
(813) 446-3333, (800) 237-9783

PRC Drilling Corp.
2900 East Flamingo Road, Suite 262
Las Vegas, Nevada 89121
(702) 796-2901

Prudential-Bache
One Seaport Plaza
199 Water Street
New York, New York 10292
(212) 214-1768, (212) 214-1761

Quinoco Energy, Inc.
645 Fifth Avenue, East Wing
New York, New York 10022
(800) 421-4374

Ramco Oil & Gas Corp.
P.O. Box 2347
Hollywood, Florida 33022
(305) 920-2441

Red Eagle Exploration Co.
1601 Northwest Expressway, 17th Floor
P.O. Box 54320
Oklahoma City, Oklahoma 73156
(405) 843-8066, (203) 658-1760,
(800) 654-9274

Resource Exploration, Inc.
2876 S. Arlington Road
Akron, Ohio 44312
(202) 244-1200

Seville Energy Development Corp.
10 Esquire Road
New City, New York 10956
(914) 638-2200

Snyder Exploration Co.
1360 Post Oak Blvd., Suite 1500
Houston, Texas 77056
(713) 963-9188

Southwest Royalties Inc.
530 Western United Life Building
P.O. Drawer 11390
Midland, Texas 79702
(915) 686-9927

Sterling Drilling and Production Co.
150 Grand Street
White Plains, New York 10601
(914) 684-5830

Stone Petroleum Corp.
710 Hugh Wallis Road
Lafayette, Louisiana 70505
(318) 237-0410

Stratigraphic Petroleum, Inc.
5956 Sherry Lane, Suite 505
Dallas, Texas 75225
(214) 739-0300

Swift Energy Co.
16825 Northchase Drive, Suite 400
Houston, Texas 77060
(713) 874-2700, (800) 777-2750

Valero Natural Gas Co.
530 McCullough Avenue
San Antonio, Texas 78215
(512) 246-2444

Vineyard Oil & Gas Co.
10299 West Main Road
P.O. Box 391
North East, Pennsylvania 16428
(814) 725-8742

Wells Development Co.
8325 Ohio River Boulevard
Pittsburgh, Pennsylvania 15202
(412) 734-7494

Real Estate

Real Estate limited partnerships buy equity interests in, and make loans to owners of, a wide variety of real estate properties, such as office buildings, apartment complexes, shopping centers and miniwarehouse storage centers. Partnerships that mainly buy such properties plan to sell them in five to ten years, and pass through any capital gains to limited partners. In the meantime, they collect rents and improve the properties, if necessary, passing along income and tax benefits, such as depreciation, to limited partners.

The other type of real estate partnership makes mortgage loans to real estate owners or those constructing buildings. In some cases, these programs also have some equity participation in the real estate for which they are making loans. In general, mortgage loan partnerships are more conservative investments than equity programs, and loan offerings pay higher current income to limited partners.

Action Capital, Inc.
4003 East Speedway Boulevard, Suite 122
Tucson, Arizona 85712
(800) 877-3569

AEI Real Estate Funds
101 West Burnsville Parkway, Suite 200
Minneapolis, Minnesota 55337
(612) 894-8800, (800) 328-3519

Aetna/AREA Corporation
26 Broadway, Suite 532
New York, New York 10007
(212) 969-2214, (800) 421-8866

AFC Capital Corp.
881 Alma Real Drive, Suite 205
Pacific Palisades, California 90272
(213) 829-1700, (800) 624-3770

AFPC Equity
222 Third Avenue North, Suite 240
Nashville, Tennessee 37201
(615) 371-0001

AGS Leasing Inc.
177 Bovet Road, Suite 575
San Mateo, California 94402
(415) 570-7100, (800) 551-1006

AI Housing, Inc.
129 South Street
Boston, Massachusetts 02111
(617) 350-0250

Aldrich, Eastman & Waltch, Inc.
P.O. Box 709
Valley Forge, Pennsylvania 19482
(800) 522-5555

Allstar Inns G.P. Inc.
2020 De La Vina Street
Santa Barbara, California 93105
(805) 687-3383

America First Capital Associates
1004 Farnam Street, Suite 400
Omaha, Nebraska 68102
(402) 444-1630, (800) 228-4681

American Finance Group
American Pacific Advisors
401 North La Cadena Drive
Colton, California 92324
(714) 824-3303

Amrecorp Realty, Inc.
Two Bent Tree Tower
16479 Dallas Parkway
Dallas, Texas 75248
(214) 380-8000

Anchorage Realty Fund, Inc.
500 Post Road East, Suite 300
Westport, Connecticut 06880
(203) 454-2300

Angeles Securities Corporation
10301 West Pico Boulevard
Los Angeles, California 90064
(213) 277-4900, (800) 421-4374

Angell Care, Inc.
Salem Center
Yadkin Valley Road
Advance, North Carolina 27006
(919) 998-8445, (919) 723-7580

APSC Realty Corp.
1901 Avenue of the Stars, Suite 938
Los Angeles, California 90057
(213) 553-6740

APT Advisors, Inc.
18200 Von Karman, Suite 800
Irvine, California 92715
(714) 553-8511

Armored Storage, Inc.
2702 North Third Street
Phoenix, Arizona 85004
(714) 752-0522, (800) 272-1055

ARP Zero Coupon Mortgage Investors, Inc.
2909 Cole Avenue, Suite 300
Dallas, Texas 75204
(303) 449-7780

Asa W. Candler Properties, Inc.
1215 Hightower Trail, Suite C-240
Atlanta, Georgia 30350
(404) 998-1171

ASB Enterprises, Inc.
6634 Valjean Avenue
Van Nuys, California 91406
(619) 431-9100

Aspen Enterprise Ltd.
2757 44th Street, S.W., Suite 306
Grand Rapids, Michigan 49509
(616) 531-9100

Associated Planners Realty Corp.
1901 Avenue of the Stars, Suite 938
Los Angeles, California 90067
(213) 553-6740

ATA Research, Inc.
6500 Greenville Avenue, Suite 300
Dallas, Texas 75206
(214) 373-7606, (214) 750-1300,
(800) 348-3601

August Financial Partners
3545 Long Beach Boulevard, 5th Floor
P.O. Box 22630
Long Beach, California 90807
(800) 821-3332, (800) 352-3718 in California

Automotive Service Centers, Inc.
10936 North 56th Street, Suite 201
Tampa, Florida 33617
(813) 254-3133, (800) 237-4120 ext. 22

Avron B. Fogelman
5400 Poplar Avenue
Memphis, Tennessee 38119
(901) 767-6500, (800) 952-9952

Balcor Co.
Balcor Plaza, 4849 Golf Road
Skokie, Illinois 60077
(312) 677-2900, (800) 422-5267

Bass, Marion Real Estate Group, Inc.
4000 Park Road
Charlotte, North Carolina
(704) 523-9407

Bell Land Investments, Inc.
4420 North Saddlebag Trail, Suite 202
Scottsdale, Arizona 85251
(602) 945-4573

Bellevue Capital Corp.
1240 Bayshore Highway, Suite 300
Burlingame, California 94010
(415) 697-3760

Benton Investment Co. & ISC Realty
Corp.
441 North Cherry Street
P.O. Box 21
Winston-Salem, North Carolina 27101
(919) 722-8182

Berg Harmon Associates
One Harmon Meadow Boulevard
Secaucus, New Jersey 07094
(201) 865-2200, (800) 342-5242

Berry & Boyle Realty Advisors
River Place, 57 River Street
Wellesley Hills, Massachusetts
(617) 237-0544, (800) 223-6026

BH Group
2757 44th Street, S.W.
Grand Rapids, Michigan 49509
(616) 531-9100

Big Tree Mortgage Advisors Inc.
11947 North Freeway, Suite 610
Houston, Texas 77060
(713) 820-0570

Birtcher Real Estate Partners
915 Broadway
New York, New York 10010
(212) 505-4400, (800) 223-1460

Bizanz, Robert S. & Terrance E. Troy
1018 Pioneer Building
St. Paul, Minnesota 55101
(612) 223-2500, (612) 227-6925

BMF Management, Inc.
1507 West Yale Avenue
Orange, California 92667
(714) 998-7797, (800) 258-6691

Boettcher & Co.
828 17th Street
Denver, Colorado 80202
(303) 628-8000

Boston Capital Associates
c/o Boston Capital Partners
313 Congress Street
Boston, Massachusetts 02210
(617) 439-0077, (800) 632-3642

Boston Financial Group, Inc.
225 Franklin Street, 29th Floor
Boston, Massachusetts 02110
(617) 542-4475

Boston Historic Partners
50 Rowes Wharf, Suite 400
Boston, Massachusetts 02110
(617) 330-7700, (800) 825-7700

Brauvin Realty Inc.
333 West Wacker Drive, 10th Floor
Chicago, Illinois 60606
(312) 443-0922, (800) 272-8846

Brichard Properties, Inc.
650 California Street, 12th Floor
San Francisco, California 94104
(415) 989-2000, (800) 228-5727

Brown Equity Income Properties, Inc.
3810 Buena Vista Road
Columbus, Georgia 31906
(301) 727-4083

Brunner Management Limited Partnership
104 East Third Street
Dayton, Ohio 45402
(513) 228-2741

BT Venture Partners
3710 One First Union Center
301 South College Street
Charlotte, North Carolina 28202
(704) 333-1367

Budget Storage Equities, Inc.
Board of Trade Center
120 South Market Street, Suite 400
Wichita, Kansas 67202
(316) 263-5848

Cal Fed Investment Management Co.
5670 Wilshire Boulevard, Suite 2200
Los Angeles, California 90036
(213) 932-4196

California Retirement Villas, Inc.
245 Fischer Avenue, Suite D-1
Costa Mesa, California 92626
(714) 751-7400

Capital Builders, Inc.
2010 North First Street, Suite 200
San Jose, California 95131
(408) 436-8402

Capitol Corp.
American First Tower, Suite 1330
101 North Robinson Avenue
Oklahoma City, Oklahoma 73102
(800) 421-1296

Cardinal Industries, Inc.
2040 Hamilton Road
Columbus, Ohio 43232
(614) 861-3211, (614) 755-6556

Carlsberg Resources Corp.
2800 28th, Suite 222
Santa Monica, California 90405
(213) 450-9696

Casino Development, Inc.
Dunes Casino Hotel
Albany Avenue and The Boardwalk
Atlantic City, New Jersey 08401
(609) 345-6000

Centennial Beneficial Corp.
282 South Anita Drive
Orange, California 92668
(714) 634-9200, (800) 854-8442

Century Capital Group, Ltd.
240 Algoma Boulevard
Oshkosh, Wisconsin 54901
(800) 426-1405, (800) 426-1404 WI

Certified Financial Services
1180 Spring Centre South Boulevard
Altamonte Springs, Florida 37214
(305) 869-9800, (800) 327-1092

CG Historic, Inc.
1800 Eight Penn Center Plaza
Philadelphia, Pennsylvania 19103
(215) 751-9411

Charter Pacific Corp.
2702 North Third Street, Suite 2006
Phoenix, Arizona 85004
(602) 266-0699

Chesapeake Associates
21 West Colony Road, Suite 250
Durham, North Carolina 27705
(919) 682-2154

Chrisken Income Properties, Inc.
345 North Canal Street, Suite 700
Chicago, Illinois 60606
(312) 454-1626, (800) 433-8395

CIGNA Realty Resources, Inc.
900 Cottage Grove Road, South Building
Bloomfield, Connecticut 06002
(203) 726-5120, (203) 726-3595

C.I.P. Management Corp.
23 West Park Avenue
Merchantville, New Jersey 08109
(609) 662-1116, (800) 999-2323

Clark Financial Corp.
2144 South Highland Drive, Suite 200
Salt Lake City, Utah 84106
(801) 485-2321

Clifton Investment Properties
6400 El Dorado Circle
Tucson, Arizona 85715
(800) 527-6946

Clover Financial Corp.
23 West Park Avenue
Merchantville, New Jersey 08109
(609) 662-1116, (800) 999-2323

CM Plus Corp.
5200 Town Center Circle, 4th Floor
Boca Raton, Florida 33486
(407) 394-9260

CNL Realty Corp.
400 East South Street, Suite 500
Orlando, Florida 32801
(407) 422-1574, (800) 522-3863

Coachman Inns of America, Inc.
301 N.W. 63rd Street, Suite 500
Oklahoma City, Oklahoma 73116
(405) 840-4667, (800) 421-1296

CoastFed Realty, Inc.
9171 Wilshire Boulevard
Beverly Hills, California 90210
(213) 274-5553

Commodore Realty Investments, Inc.
1140 Atlanta Center
250 Piedmont Avenue, N.E.
Atlanta, Georgia 30309
(404) 524-4415

Common Goal Capital Group, Inc.
5900 York Road, Suite 200
Baltimore, Maryland 21212
(301) 435-6700, (800) 822-3863

Concord Assets Group, Inc.
5200 Town Center Circle, 4th Floor
Boca Raton, Florida 33486
(407) 394-9260, (800) 624-2565

Concord Associates
745 Fifth Avenue
New York, New York 10151
(212) 688-1776

Condey Associates
2551 Lucien Way, Suite 300
Maitland, Florida 32751
(407) 660-1984, (800) 848-1984

Connecticut General
950 Cottage Grove Road
Bloomfield, Connecticut 06002
(203) 726-2820

Consolidated Capital Corp.
1900 Powell Street
Emeryville, California 94608
(415) 652-7171, (800) 227-1870

Consolidated Resources Corp. of America
2245 Perimeter Park, Suite 3
Atlanta, Georgia 30341
(800) 241-3395

Continental Capital Realty
3773 Ellsworth Road East
Ann Arbor, Michigan 48108
(313) 971-1866

Continental Wingate Properties, Inc.
Old Central Wharf
75 Central Street
Boston, Massachusetts 02109
(617) 574-9000

Copley Real Estate Advisors
399 Boylston Street
Boston, Massachusetts 02159
(617) 578-1188, (800) 225-7670

Corporate Realty Income Fund
1700 Broadway, 34th Floor
New York, New York 10019
(212) 603-8916

Covington Technologies
2451 East Orangethorpe Avenue
Fullerton, Calfornia 92631
(714) 879-0111

C.R.I. Management Corp.
The C.R.I. Building
11200 Rockville Pike
Rockville, Maryland 20852
(301) 468-9200, (800) 669-6591

Crown Management Corp.
23 West Park Avenue
Merchantville, New Jersey 08109
(609) 662-1116, (800) 999-2323

Dain Properties, Inc.
1820 Dain Tower
Minneapolis, Minnesota 55402
(612) 371-7810, (612) 371-2827

Daniel Priority Fund, Inc.
One Meadow Brook
Corporate Park
P.O. Box 43250
Birmingham, Alabama 35242
(205) 991-4500, (800) 9-DANIEL

Datek Securities Corp.
4522 Fort Hamilton Parkway
Brooklyn, New York 11219
(212) 687-7000, (718) 435-7100

DBSI Housing, Inc.
1070 North Curtis Road, Suite 270
Boise, Idaho 83706
(208) 322-5858

DeAnza Corp.
9171 Wilshire Boulevard, Suite 627
Beverly Hills, California 90210
(213) 550-1111

Dean Witter Reynolds
130 Liberty Street
New York, New York 10006
(212) 524-4578, (800) 732-5891

Decade Co.
1800 West Sarah Lane
Brookfield Lakes Corporation Center
Brookfield, Wisconsin 53005
(414) 792-9201

Deines, John, T. Kegley, G. White & C. Tadema
1370 Stewart Street
Seattle, Washington 98109
(206) 623-3784

Del Taco
345 Baker Street
Costa Mesa, California 92626
(800) 854-8393

Dexter R. Yager & Faison S. Kuester
730 East Trade Street, Suite 1010
Charlotte, North Carolina 28202
(704) 372-1300

DiVall Real Estate Corp.
100 North Hamilton
Madison, Wisconsin 53703
(608) 251-5559

Dover Historic Properties, Inc.
1700 Market Street
Philadelphia, Pennsylvania 19103
(215) 561-0264, (800) 468-4017

Drew R. Prell
10717 Camino Ruiz, Suite 267
San Diego, California 92126
(619) 695-0830

Drexel Burnham Lambert, Inc.
55 Broad Street, 11th Floor
New York, New York 10006
(212) 480-5077

DSI Properties, Inc.
3701 Long Beach Boulevard
Long Beach, California 90801
(213) 595-7711

Duke Realty Advisors
8900 Keystone Crossing
Indianapolis, Indiana 46240
(317) 848-7400

Emerald Homes, Inc.
5333 North 7th Street, Suite 30
Phoenix, Arizona 85014
(602) 995-9100

Equimax Time Shares, Inc.
4209 Hillcrest Drive
Los Angeles, California 90008
(213) 296-1181

Equitable Life Assurance Society of the U.S.
3414 Peachtree Road N.E.
Atlanta, Georgia 30326
(404) 239-5001, (212) 980-8532

Equitec Financial Group, Inc.
7677 Oakport Street
P.O. Box 2470
Oakland, California 94614
(800) 445-0920

Equity Capital Corp.
631 Second Avenue South
Nashville, Tennessee 37201
(615) 371-1969

Equity Management Syndications, Inc.
1685 Mcfarland Road
Pittsburgh, Pennsylvania 15216
(412) 787-8066

Equity Realty, Inc.
3840 Lindell Boulevard
St. Louis, Missouri 63108
(314) 843-1972

EQK Green Acres Corp.
3 Bala Plaza East
Bala Cynwyd, Pennsylvania 19034
(215) 667-2300

Ernst, Diessner Management
4501 North 22nd Street, Suite 190
Phoenix, Arizona 85016
(602) 956-2489

Essex Property Corp.
777 California
Palo Alto, California 94303
(415) 494-3700

Excellex Corp.
410 Ware Boulevard, Suite 1111
Tampa, Florida 33619
(813) 623-5469, (813) 684-6670

FCA Corp.
3000 Post Oak Boulevard, Suite 1790
Houston, Texas 77056
(713) 965-0077

FDIP, Inc.
179 West Washington Street, Suite 325
Chicago, Illinois 60602
(312) 346-2070, (800) 225-9498

FFCA Management Co.
Financial Center
3443 North Central Avenue, Suite 500
Phoenix, Arizona 85012
(602) 264-9636, (800) 528-1179

First Capital Properties Corp.
Two North Riverside Plaza
Chicago, Illinois 60606
(312) 207-0020

First Security Equity Mortgage, Inc.
1050 17th Street, Suite 900
Denver, Colorado 80265
(303) 298-9300, (800) 874-3863

First Washington Development Group, Inc.
727 15th Street, N.W.
Washington, D.C. 20005
(301) 539-3400

Florida Sun International, Inc.
2828 Edgewater Drive
Orlando, Florida 32804
(305) 422-5423

FMA Realty, Inc.
210 Gateway Mall North, Suite 102
Lincoln, Nebraska 68505
(402) 467-6964

FMG Western Region Aquisitions, Inc.
15303 Ventura Boulevard, Suite 1400
Sherman Oaks, California 91403
(215) 964-7000

Fogelman Properties, Inc.
5400 Poplar Avenue
Memphis, Tennessee 38119
(901) 767-6500, (800) 952-9952

Forum Retirement, Inc.
8900 Keystone Crossing, Suite 1200
Indianapolis, Indiana 46240
(317) 846-0700

Founders Income Properties
477 Madison Avenue
New York, New York 10022
(212) 688-2747

Fox Group of Companies
950 Tower Lane
Foster City, California 94404
(415) 378-7000, (800) 227-6707

FPI Real Estate
25 Cadillac Drive
Sacramento, California 95825
(916) 929-3636

Franchise Finance Corp. of America
3443 North Central Avenue, Suite 500
Phoenix, Arizona 85012
(602) 264-9639, (800) 528-1179

Franklin Resources Inc.
777 Mariners Island Boulevard
P.O. Box 7777
San Mateo, California 94404
(800) 872-5612, (800) 448-3153

Frederick Investment Corp.
3900 Barrett Drive, Suite 301
Raleigh, North Carolina 27609
(919) 781-6009

Freeman Diversified Properties, Inc.
2517 Lebanon Road
Nashville, Tennessee 37215
(615) 889-8250, (800) 221-3947

Freeman, William T. & John L. Thompson
619 Greene Street
Augusta, Georgia 30901
(404) 724-0010

Giant Investments, Inc. & Gerald I.
   Schulman
11300 Weddington Street
North Hollywood, California 91601
(818) 509-0900

Givens, Dicks & Smith
520 Crown Oak Centre Drive
Longwood, Florida 32750
(305) 331-8004

Glencurt Corp.
141 Stevens Avenue, Suite 14
P.O. Box 188
Oldsmar, Florida 34677
(813) 855-2428

Goodstore Associates, Inc.
5638 Desert View Drive
La Jolla, California 92037
(619) 459-4874

Gradvantage, Inc.
580 Building, 580 Walnut Street
Cincinnati, Ohio 45216
(513) 579-5000

Gran-Mark Properties, Inc.
6845 Elm Street, Suite 711
McLean, Virginia 22101
(703) 790-3190

Griffin Investment Corp.
8300 Humboldt Avenue, South
Minneapolis, Minnesota 55431
(800) 328-3788, (800) 762-3793

Group Five Financial Corp.
12140 Woodcrest Executive Drive, Suite 230
St. Louis, Missouri 63141
(314) 434-7955, (800) 447-6875

Guy E. Hatfield
6153 Fairmount Avenue, Suite 201
San Diego, California 92120
(619) 563-8800

Harbor American Capital Group
3567 East Sunrise Drive
Tucson, Arizona 85718
(602) 577-1108, (800) 332-4244

HC Mortgage Company, Inc.
227 South Main Street, Suite 202
South Bend, Indiana 46601
(219) 234-2535

HCW Inc.
101 Summer Street
Boston, Massachusetts 02110
(617) 542-2880, (800) 343-9132

Healthvest Properties, Inc.
One Urban Centre, Suite 595-A
4830 West Kennedy Boulevard
Tampa, Florida 33609
(813) 873-7244, (813) 964-2817

Heritage Group Associates
429 Santa Monica Boulevard, Suite 300
Santa Monica, California 90401
(213) 458-1911

Hilliard Lyons Real Estate Finance, Inc.
545 South Third Street, Suite 306
Louisville, Kentucky 40202
(502) 588-8457

Historic Landmark Corp.
100 Marietta Station Walk, Suite 350
Marietta, Georgia 30060
(404) 428-0055

HLFL Management, Inc.
30 South Front Street
Philadelphia, Pennsylvania 19106
(215) 922-0900

Holden Group
11365 West Olympic Boulevard
Los Angeles, California 90064
(800) 654-8076

Horizon Health Systems, Inc.
615 Commerce Street, Suite 250
Tacoma, Washington 98402
(206) 627-7264

Hoyt Partners III
5453 West 61st Place
Mission, Kansas 66205
(913) 384-5700, (800) 255-0037

Huntington Warehouse, Inc.
5847 San Felipe, Suite 3800
Houston, Texas 77057
(713) 953-0888

IML Properties Development Corp.
1110 Brickell Avenue, Suite 800
Miami, Florida 33131
(305) 371-8333

Income Growth Management, Inc.
215 South Highway 101, Suite 100
Solana Beach, California 92075
(800) 624-8115

Independent American Real Estate, Inc.
1341 West Mockingbird Lane, Suite 1200 East
Dallas, Texas 75062
(214) 570-8700

Inland Real Estate Investment Corp.
2901 Butterfield Road
Oakbrook, Illinois 60521
(312) 218-8000, (800) 826-8228

Integrated Resources
10 Union Square East
New York, New York 10003
(212) 353-7000, (800) 821-5100

Interstate General Management Corp.
222 Smallwood Village Center
St. Charles, Maryland 20602
(301) 843-8600

Intrust, Inc.
1270 Springbrook Road
Walnut Creek, California 94596
(415) 947-6868

I.R.E. Income Advisors Corp.
1320 South Dixie Highway
Coral Gables, Florida 33146
(800) 858-6750

ISC Realty Corp.
2650 NCNB Plaza
Charlotte, North Carolina 28280
(704) 379-9164

Jacques-Miller, Inc.
211 Seventh Avenue North
Nashville, Tennessee 37219
(615) 248-7400
(800) 251-2003

Jason-Northco Properties, Inc.
6860 Washington Avenue South
Eden Prairie, Minnesota 55344
(612) 332-2212

JLI Properties, Inc.
7008 Security Boulevard
Baltimore, Maryland 21207
(301) 764-3555

JMB Realty Corp.
875 North Michigan Avenue
Chicago, Illinois 60611
(312) 440-5080, (800) 521-1870

John Hancock Realty Equities, Inc.
One Exeter Plaza
699 Boylston Street
Boston, Massachusetts 02161
(617) 424-8148

JRD Partners, Ltd.
1624 Market Street, Suite 204
Denver, Colorado 80202
(303) 623-2300

K-A Southeastern Income Partners
707 East Main Street
Richmond, Virginia 23219
(804) 649-2311

Kemper Real Estate, Inc.
630 Hansen Way
Palo Alto, California 94304
(800) 468-4881, (800) 421-0226

Keyes Property Advisors, Inc.
100 North Biscayne Boulevard
Miami, Florida 33132
(305) 371-3592, (800) 225-7059

Keystone Properties
99 High Street
Boston, Massachusetts 02110
(617) 338-3430, (800) 633-4900

Keystone Mortgage Company
11340 West Olympic Boulevard, Suite 300
Los Angeles, California 90064
(213) 473-4993, (800) 344-4055

Kimmins Realty Investment, Inc.
1501 Second Avenue
P.O. Box 75321
Tampa, Florida 33605
(813) 248-3678, (800) 533-3447

KP Realty Advisors, Inc.
10 Hanover Square, 19th Floor
New York, New York 10005
(212) 510-4337, (212) 510-4345

Krupp Corp.
470 Atlantic Avenue
Boston, Massachusetts 02210
(617) 574-8300, (800) 255-7877

La Quinta Realty Corp.
10010 San Pedro Avenue
San Antonio, Texas 78216
(512) 366-6106

Land Financial Group
165 North Meramec
Clayton, Missouri 63105
(314) 862-1834

Landmark Capital Corp.
222 Third Avenue North, Suite 420
Nashville, Tennessee 37207
(615) 256-4714, (615) 371-0001

Lansing Corp.
800 El Camino Real, Suite 400
Menlo Park, California 94025
(415) 321-7100, (800) 227-8228

Legg Mason Realty Partners, Inc.
100 Light Street
Baltimore, Maryland 21202
(301) 539-3400, (800) 852-1991

L.C.L. Equities
322 Route 46 West
Parsippany, New Jersey 07054
(201) 882-5050

Leperq Capital Partners
345 Park Avenue
New York, New York 10154
(212) 702-0260, (800) 525-8904

Liberty Real Estate Corp.
Federal Reserve Plaza
Boston, Massachusetts 02110
(617) 722-6060, (800) 526-2606

Life Assurance Co. of Pennsylvania
222 North Michigan Avenue
Chicago, Illinois 60601
(312) 263-2282, (800) 437-9202

Linpro Enterprises, Ltd.
900 East Eighth Avenue
King of Prussia, Pennsylvania 19406
(215) 251-9100

Love Development and Investment Co.
515 Olive Street, Suite 1400
St. Louis, Missouri 63101
(314) 621-1200, (314) 982-0744

Lutheran Brotherhood Real Estate
Products Co.
625 Fourth Avenue South
Minneapolis, Minnesota 55415
(612) 340-7215

Madison Pizza Associates, Inc.
1015 Grandview Avenue
P.O. Box 25066
Glendale, California 91201
(818) 246-3060, (800) 762-6267

Michael C. Mahler
4720 Lincoln Boulevard, Suite 200
Marina Del Rey, California 90292
(213) 312-1191, (800) TRAWEEK

Mariner Capital Management, Inc.
13987 McGregor Boulevard, S.W.
Fort Meyers, Florida 33919
(813) 481-2011

Marion Bass Real Estate Group, Inc.
4000 Park Road
Charlotte, North Carolina 28209
(704) 523-9407

Marriot RIBM Two Corp.
10400 Fernwood Road
Bethesda, Maryland 20817
(301) 380-1390

MB Investment Propeties, Inc.
290 Westminster Street
Providence, Rhode Island 02906
(401) 751-8600, (800) 333-4726

McCombs Corp.
2392 Morse Avenue
Irvine, California 92714
(714) 863-1901, (800) 622-6227

McCracken Intervest
2550 South Oneida Street, Suite 203
Denver, Colorado 80224
(303) 759-2677, (800) 835-7851

McGuinness and Associates
1101 Bayside Drive, Suite 100
Corona Del Mar, California 92625
(714) 760-0505

McNeil Realty Investors Corp.
2855 Campus Drive
San Mateo, California 94403
(415) 572-0660, (800) 227-6537

Mendik Corp.
330 Madison Avenue
New York, New York 10017
(212) 969-2254

Meridian Healthcare Investments, Inc.
225 East Redwood Street
Baltimore, Maryland 21202
(301) 727-4083

Merit I Corp.
1110 Financial Center
Des Moines, Iowa 50309
(515) 288-0830, (800) 451-1141

Merrill Lynch Hubbard, Inc.
Two Broadway
New York, New York 10004
(212) 908-8532

Metro Self-Storage Capital Corp.
13000 West Route 176
Lake Bluff, Illinois 60044
(312) 295-8414, (800) 423-5344

Meyer Investment Properties, Inc.
222 South Harbor Boulevard, Suite 7
Anaheim, California 92805
(714) 778-8425

Mortgage BancFund Corp.
100 West Main Street, Suite 10
Tustin, California 92680
(714) 669-0611, (800) 343-0611

Motel 6, Inc.
51 Hitchcock Way
Santa Barbara, California 93105
(805) 682-6666

Motels of America Investment Corp.
10992 San Diego Mission Road, Suite 300
San Diego, California 92108
(619) 563-8800

MSS Management Co.
13000 West Route 176
Lake Bluff, Illinois 60044
(800) 423-5344

Murphy Favre Properties, Inc.
1109 Second Avenue
Seattle, Washington 98101
(206) 464-5985

Murray Realty Investors, Inc.
5520 LBJ Freeway
Dallas, Texas 75240
(214) 851-6600, (800) 527-5909

Mutual Benefit Life Insurance Co.
290 Westminster Street
Providence, Rhode Island 02906
(401) 751-8600, (800) 333-4726

N.A. Properties, Inc.
1600 Plaza 600 Building
Seattle, Washington 98101
(206) 441-2900

National Corp. for Housing Partnerships
1133 15th Street, N.W.
Washington, D.C. 20005
(202) 347-6247

National Development & Investment, Inc.
13555 Bishops Court
Brookfield, Wisconsin 53008
(414) 784-7000, (800) 558-1312

National Marinas
7601 North Federal Highway, Suite 250
Boca Raton, Florida 33487
(407) 997-0616, (800) 622-DOCK

National Partnership Investments Corp.
9090 Wilshire Boulevard, 2nd Floor
Beverly Hills, California 90211
(213) 278-2191

National Realty Partners, Inc.
8320 Old Courthouse Road, Suite 200
Vienna, Virginia 22180
(703) 790-8484

National Western Capital Corp.
7201 East Camelback, Suite 206
Scottsdale, Arizona 85251
(602) 998-1155

New England Life Properties, Inc.
535 Boylston Street, 12th Floor
Boston, Massachusetts 02116
(617) 578-1139, (800) 225-7670

NHT, Inc.
40 Grove Street
Wellesley, Massachusetts
(302) 571-8100

Nooney Investors, Inc.
7701 Forsyth Boulevard
St. Louis, Missouri 63105
(314) 863-7700, (800) 325-0893

NPI Management Corp.
666 Third Avenue
New York, New York 10017
(212) 551-6000, (800) 223-1424

NTS Corp.
10172 Linn Station Road
Louisville, Kentucky 40223
(502) 426-4800, (800) 421-1492

NYLIFE Realty, Inc.
51 Madison Avenue, Room 1700
New York, New York 10010
(212) 576-7309, (800) 332-5774

Occidental Land Research
22632 East Golden Springs Drive, Suite 300
Diamond Bar, California 91765
(714) 861-6211, (800) 831-2078

Oliver Realty, Inc.
900 Roosevelt Parkway, Suite 540
Chesterfield, Missouri 63017
(314) 532-7751, (800) 628-3581

Oppenheimer Industries, Inc.
The Oppenheimer Building, 16th Floor
21 West 10th Street
Kansas City, Missouri 64105
(816) 471-1750, (800) 432-4020

Oxford Development Corp.
7316 Wisconsin Avenue, Suite 300
Bethesda, Maryland 20814
(301) 654-3100

Pacific Partners Joint Venture
1723 8th Avenue North
Seattle, Washington 98109
(206) 285-8118, (800) 523-2758

Pacific Peninsula Equities Corp.
23133 Hawthorne Boulevard
Torrance, California 90505
(213) 373-7795, (800) 824-8194

Pacifica Breakers Associates, Inc.
1901 Newport Boulevard
Costa Mesa, California 92627
(714) 631-8600

Paine Webber
100 Federal Street
Boston, Massachusetts 02188
(212) 780-8876, (800) 342-5797

Paradigm Capital
7001 South 900 East, Suite 250
Midvale, Utah 84047
(801) 566-7737

Paul V. Fitch
1925 Banks Mill Road
P.O. Box 2184
Aiken, South Carolina 29801
(803) 649-0576

Performance Investments, Inc.
1740 Independence Boulevard
Charlotte, North Carolina 28205
(704) 372-2565

Perkins Management Co.
6401 Poplar Avenue
Memphis, Tennessee 38119
(901) 766-6400

P.I. Associates
484 Pierce Street
Birmingham, Michigan 48009
(313) 645-1260

Pioneer Western Properties Corp.
600 Cleveland Street
Clearwater, Florida 34615
(813) 585-6565, (800) 237-9783

PLA Associates
3939 Vincennes Road
Indianapolis, Indiana 46268
(800) 346-3789

PlanVest Capital Corp.
1332 Park View Avenue, Suite 200
Manhattan Beach, California 90266
(800) 752-6778, (800) 752-6878 in California

Portfolio Advisory Services, Inc.
One Post Office Square
Boston, Massachusetts 02109
(617) 330-7700

Preferred Capital Investments, Inc.
1699 Wall Street
Mount Prospect, Illinois 60056
(312) 956-4800

Presidential Management Co.
21031 Ventura Boulevard
Woodland Hills, California 91364
(818) 992-8999

Prime Plus Corp.
1601 LBJ Freeway, Suite 200
Dallas, Texas 75234
(214) 406-6400, (800) 888-2311

Prime-American Realty Corp.
710 Route 46 East
P.O. Box 2746
Fairfield, New Jersey 07007
(201) 882-1880

Principal Growth Realty Management, Inc.
31 West 52nd Street, 16th Floor
New York, New York 10019
(212) 767-2717

Professional Capital VII, Inc.
800 Plaza 600 Building
Seattle, Washington 98101
(206) 448-4800

Prometheus Development Co.
20300 Stevenson Creek Boulevard, Suite 100
Cupertino, California 95014
(408) 446-0157

Property Resources, Inc.
15951 Los Gatos Boulevard
Los Gatos, California 95032
(408) 358-4211, (800) 872-5612

Prudential-Bache Securities
One Seaport Plaza, 33rd Floor
199 Water Street
New York, New York 100
(212) 214-1000

PSI Associates II
1015 Grandview Avenue
P.O. Box 25050
Glendale, California 91201
(818) 244-8080, (800) 421-2856,
(800) 331-3388

Public Storage, Inc.
1015 Grandview Avenue
Glendale, California 91201
(818) 244-8080, (800) 421-2856

QSV Properties, Inc.
Pillsbury Center, MS 4046
200 South Sixth Street
Minneapolis, Minnesota 55402
(612) 330-4966, (612) 330-8345

Qualicorp Management, Inc.
One Davis Boulevard
Tampa, Florida 33606
(813) 254-6330, (800) 237-8520

Quinn-L Equities, Inc.
3003 Knight Street
Shreveport, Louisiana 71105
(318) 865-8493, (800) 551-8244

Radnor Financial Group, Inc.
250 King of Prussia Road
Radnor, Pennsylvania 19406
(215) 964-7303

RAL Asset Management Group
20875 Crossroads Circle
Suite 800
Brookfield, Wisconsin 53186
(414) 798-8470, (800) 888-8470

Rancon Financial Corp.
27720 Jefferson Avenue
Temecula, California 92390
(714) 676-6664, (800) 877-3660

Real America Investors, Inc.
4333 Edgewood Road, N.E.
Cedar Rapids, Iowa 52402
(319) 398-8789, (800) 553-4287

Realmark Properties, Inc.
680 Statler Towers
Buffalo, New York 14202
(716) 854-6767, (800) 348-0016

Realty Advisors, Inc.
15010 Avenue of Science, Suite 100
San Diego, California 92128
(619) 485-9400, (800) 333-9235

Realty Income Corp.
220 West Crest Street
Escondido, California 92025
(800) 854-1967, (800) 542-6030 in California

Realty Parking Corp.
225 East Redwood Street
Baltimore, Maryland 21202
(301) 727-4140

Recorp Partners, Inc.
7000 East Shea Boulevard, Suite 250
Scottsdale, Arizona 85254
(602) 991-2288

Red Lion Properties, Inc.
4001 Main Street
Vancouver, Washington 98663
(206) 696-0001

REIF Partners
1711 West County Road B, Suite 300 South
Roseville, Minnesota 55113
(612) 636-5779

Related Companies, Inc.
645 Fifth Avenue
New York, New York 10022
(212) 421-5333, (800) 831-4826

Resources Pension Advisory Corp.
666 Third Avenue
New York, New York 10017
(212) 551-6398, (800) 223-1424

Restaurant Management IV
1479 West Gene Street
Winter Park, Florida 32789
(407) 645-4811

Retirement Living Communities
6900 South Gray Road
Indianapolis, Indiana 46237
(317) 783-5461

Richard Roberts Co., Inc.
35 Tower Lane
Avon, Connecticut 06001
(800) 431-7011

Ridgely Development Co.
15 North 21st Street
P.O. Box 11633
Birmingham, Alabama 35203
(205) 252-3681

RJ Properties, Inc.
880 Carillon Parkway
St. Petersburg, Florida
(813) 578-3800, (800) 233-1687]

Robin Lynn, Inc. & Linsan Corp.
21031 Ventura Boulevard
Woodland Hills, California 91364
(818) 992-8999

Royalty Management Corp.
2610 West Shaw Avenue, #103
Fresno, California 93711
(209) 435-6112, (800) 533-0109

RWB Realty Corp.
938 Lafayette Street
New Orleans, Louisiana 70113
(504) 525-7000, (800) 525-0789

SBF Partners
2665 South Moorland Road, Suite 206
New Berlin, Wisconsin 53151
(414) 789-1800

SCA Realty Holding, Inc.
218 North Charles Street, Suite 500
Baltimore, Maryland 21201
(301) 962-0595

Scarsdale Enterprises, Inc.
1606 Hinman Avenue
Evanston, Illinois 60201
(312) 782-8888

Scott D. Christopher
10330 North Dale Mabry, Suite 205
Tampa, Florida 33607
(813) 968-2434

S.D.I., Inc.
6910 East 5th Avene
Scottsdale, Arizona 85251
(602) 949-7144

Secured Investment Resources
5453 West 61st Place
Mission, Kansas 66205
(913) 384-9056, (800) 255-0037

Securities Properties, Inc.
2201 Sixth Avenue, Suite 1500
Seattle, Washington 98121
(206) 623-8313

Security Capital Real Estate Corp.
1290 Avenue of the Americas
New York, New York 10104
(212) 408-2918

SGS Associates
1600 Plaza 600 Building
Seattle, Washington 98101
(206) 441-2900

Shearson Lehman Hutton
American Express Tower, 12th Floor
World Financial Center
New York, New York 10281
(212) 298-4500, (212) 767-2935

Shelter Development Corp.
One East Lexington Street, Suite 204
Baltimore, Maryland 21202
(301) 962-0595

Shelter Realty Corp.
One Shelter Place
P.O. Box 2347
Greenville, South Carolina 29602
(803) 239-1000

Shelter Resource Corp.
3880 Michelson Drive, Suite 200
Irvine, California 92715
(714) 786-0506

Shurguard, Inc.
999 Third Avenue, Suite 1001
Seattle, Washington 98104
(206) 628-3200, (800) 231-3955

Sierra Capital Realty Advisors, Inc.
One Maritime Plaza, Suite 500
San Francisco, California 94104
(415) 543-4141, (800) 982-4141

Signature Inns, Inc.
8335 Allison Pointe Trail, Suite 300
Indianapolis, Indiana 46250
(317) 577-1111

Signet Cablevision Co.
15124 Kercheval
Gross Pointe Park, Michigan 48230
(313) 824-5454, (214) 458-2555

Silent Management, Inc.
1407 West Lancaster
Fort Worth, Texas 76102
(817) 336-9211

Southeast Acquisitions, Inc
King of Prussia Road
Radnor, Pennsylvania 19406
(215) 964-7254

Southmark Capital Corp.
401 East Ocean Boulevard
Long Beach, California 90802
(213) 491-5501, (800) 421-3757

Southwest Capital Financial Corp.
1201 South Alma School Road, Suite 7550
Mesa, Arizona 85210
(602) 461-1600

Spring and Roe Partners, Inc.
16655 West Bluemond Road
Brookfield, Wisconsin 53005
(414) 786-8200

Standard Pacific L.P.
1565 West MacArthur Boulevard
Costa Mesa, California 92656
(714) 546-1161

Sterling Historic Properties, Inc.
1615 Northern Boulevard
Manhasset, New York 11030
(516) 627-5223, (800) 492-4902

Sungrowth Equities Corp.
The Sungrowth Building
1120 Pacific Coast Highway
Huntington Beach, California 92648
(714) 960-4357

Super 8 Motels, Inc.
1700 South El Camino Real, Suite 503
San Mateo, California 94402
(415) 572-1868

TCC Center Development, Inc.
330 Second Avenue South, Suite 850
Minneapolis, Minnesota 55401
(612) 342-6000, (612) 342-6313

Teachers Management & Investment Corp.
#6 Upper Newport Plaza
Newport Beach, California 92660
(714) 955-9100

Tempo GP, Inc.
3414 Peachtree Road, N.E., Suite 600
Atlanta, Georgia 30326
(404) 239-0927, (800) 843-3164

Tessier Properties
5110 North 44th Street, Suite 120L
Phoenix, Arizona 85018
(602) 840-6850, (800) 228-4426

Titan Realty Corp.
17862 17th Street, Suite 102
Tustin, California 92680
(714) 669-1451

222 Partners, Inc.
222 Third Avenue, Suite 420
Nashville, Tennessee 37201
(615) 256-4714

Trammell Crow Ventures Co.
Suite 3500 Trammell Crow Center
2001 Ross Avenue
Dallas, Texas 75201
(214) 979-5100

Traweek Real Estate Corp.
4720 Lincoln Boulevard, Suite 200
Marina Del Rey, California 90292
(213) 822-9157, (800) TRAWEEK

Trion, Ltd.
888 Prospect Street
La Jolla, California 92037
(619) 456-1954

Triple Check Partners II
727 South Main Street
Burbank, California 91506
(818) 885-7415

T. Rowe Price Associates, Inc.
100 East Pratt Street
Baltimore, Maryland 21202
(301) 625-7752, (800) 638-7890

Uniprop, Inc.
280 Daines Street
Birmingham, Michigan 48009
(313) 645-1260

United Investors Real Estate, Inc.
2400 Pershing Road
P.O. Box 418343
Kansas City, Missouri 64108
(816) 283-4431, (800) 832-3541

United Stor-All Corp.
1009 Grant Street, Suite 203
Denver, Colorado 80203
(303) 832-3541, (800) 832-3541

USAA Financial Services Co.
9800 Fredricksburg Road
San Antonio, Texas 78288
(512) 690-2211, (800) 531-8000

USAllied Development Corp.
44 Page Street, 5th Floor
San Francisco, California 94102
(415) 392-7600

USAssets General Partner, Inc.
10 Second Street, N.E., Suite 301
Minneapolis, Minnesota 55413
(612) 623-4220, (800) 328-4827

USC, Inc.
1711 West County Road B, Suite 300S
Roseville, Minnesota 55113
(612) 636-8050

Vanderbilt Realty Joint Venture
3100 West End Avenue
Nashville, Tennessee 37203
(615) 298-5700

VMS Realty Investors
8700 West Bryn Mawr Avenue
Chicago, Illinois 60631
(312) 399-8700, (800) 992-9281

Volador Associates, Ltd.
8125 North 23rd Avenue, Suite 151
Phoenix, Arizona 85021
(602) 995-1151, (800) 826-1672

Walsmith Associates Two
7320 Six Forks Road, Suite 210
Raleigh, North Carolina 27615
(919) 848-2038

WDH Services, Inc.
16700 Valley View Avenue
La Mirada, California 90638
(714) 739-8100

Welch-Wagner Associates
22005 West Outer Drive
Dearborn, Michigan 48124
(313) 562-5005

Wells Capital, Inc.
3885 Holcomb Bridge Road
Norcross, Georgia 30092
(404) 449-7800, (800) 448-1010

Wendy's of West Michigan, Inc.
50 Louis Street, N.W.
Grand Rapids, Michigan 49503
(616) 242-0876, (616) 459-1588

Wespac Financial Corp.
4701 Von Karman
Newport Beach, California 92660
(714) 851-4032, (800) 854-4050

Western Development Corp.
1204 Wisconsin Avenue, N.W.
Washington, D.C. 20007
(202) 965-3600

Westfield Properties Corp.
4750 Von Karman, Suite 101
Newport Beach, California 92660
(800) 451-1643, (800) 255-7490 in California

Westin Financial Group
2614 Telegraph Avenue
Berkeley, California 94704
(415) 548-6600

Westin Realty Corp.
Westin Building
2001 Sixth Avenue
Seattle, Washington 98121
(206) 443-5154

Westminster Financial Corp.
9720 Wilshire Boulevard
Beverly Hills, California 90212
(213) 858-8117

Westmoreland Capital Corp.
680 Statler Towers
Buffalo, New York 14202
(800) 348-0016, (800) 854-4554 in New York

Whitehall Income Co.
1200-B North El Dorado Place
Tucson, Arizona 85715
(602) 721-0200, (800) 528-7180

Wildwood of America, Inc.
5401 West Kennedy Boulevard, Suite 300
Tampa, Florida 33609
(813) 287-2449

Windsor Corp.
120 West Grand Avenue, Suite 206
Escondido, California 92025
(800) 821-4715, (800) 821-3736 in California

Wingate Development Corp.
Old Central Wharf
75 Center Street
Boston, Massachusetts 02189
(617) 574-9000

Wooley Capital Corp.
5215 North O'Connor Road
Irving, Texas 75039
(214) 869-8282

W.P. Carey & Co.
689 Fifth Avenue
New York, New York 10022
(212) 888-7700

Major Financial Institutions

Research and Development

The following partnerships help finance research into new products or services that small but promising companies cannot finance on their own. In addition, such partnerships use funds to develop and market a product or service so that it will gain acceptance in the marketplace. Most commonly, Research and Development partnerships finance a number of unrelated ventures in the high-technology field. If one of the projects becomes commercially successful, the payoff to limited partners can be great. The risk of loss is also large, however, since many ideas which may be technically feasible do not become ultimately commercially viable. In addition to receiving distributions from the partnership if projects are profitable, limited partners can also receive tax benefits in the form of tax credits and depreciation on equipment. It often takes at least five, and sometimes ten, years before a significant discovery is made, tested, and marketed successfully.

Daleco Research & Development, Inc.
3388 Via Lido 4th Floor
Newport Beach, California 92663
(800) 432-5326

R&D Funding Corporation
1290 Ridder Park Drive #1
San Jose, California 95131
(408) 980-0990

Lamtech Electronics Corporation
5615 Corporate Boulevard, Suite 8F
Baton Rouge, Louisiana 70808
(504) 924-4830, (504) 925-0491

Technology Funding Inc.
2000 Alameda de la Pulgas, Suite 250
San Mateo, California 94402
(415) 345-2200, (800) 821-5323

ACCOUNTING FIRMS

The following is a list of the names, addresses and telephone numbers of the headquarters of the 25 largest U.S. certified public accounting firms, based on revenue generated in 1988. These firms are organized as partnerships of the certified public accountants who work in them. CPAs, who must pass examinations to earn their licenses, mainly do corporate accounting and auditing and prepare tax returns.

Recent mergers have brought changes among the industry leaders, formerly known as the Big Eight. Deloitte Haskins & Sells joined with Touche Ross & Co. to create Deloitte & Touche, while Ernst & Whinney combined with Arthur Young & Co. to form Ernst & Young. These actions have reduced the Big Eight to the Big Six. The other firms at the top are: Arthur Andersen & Co.; Coopers & Lybrand; KPMG Peat, Marwick & Co.; and Price Waterhouse & Co. Most major corporations deal with one of these six companies, and their revenues are far larger than other accounting firms. For instance, in 1988, Ernst & Young, the largest firm, had annual revenues of a little over $4 billion and Price Waterhouse, the sixth member of the Big Six, had $2 billion in revenue. Beyond the Big Six, revenue per firm dropped dramatically. The seventh-largest firm, Laventhol & Horwath, had revenues of $328 million and the 25th-ranked firm, Richard A. Eisner & Co., had revenues of just $27 million.

Accounting firms have also been branching out beyond their traditional functions of auditing and accounting and into other business services, particularly management consulting. A number of these firms now offer specialized advice for clients in such industries as financial services, health care and telecommunications.

This list is provided courtesy of *Public Accounting Report* (50 South Ninth Street, Minneapolis, Minnesota 55403, 612-332-1022), a newsletter that tracks the accounting industry.

Altschuler, Melvoin and Glasser
30 South Wacker Drive
Chicago, Illinois 60606
(312) 207-2800

Arthur Andersen & Co.
69 West Washington Street
Chicago, Illinois 60602
(312) 580-0069

Baird Kurtz & Dobson
318 Park Central East
Springfield, Missouri 65806
(417) 865-8701

BDO Seidman
1430 Broadway
New York, New York 10018
(212) 302-0100

Cherry, Bekaert & Holland
One NCNB Plaza
Charlotte, North Carolina 28280
(704) 377-1678

Clifton, Gunderson & Co.
900 Commercial National Bank Building
Peoria, Illinois 61602
(309) 671-4500

Coopers & Lybrand
1251 Avenue of the Americas
New York, New York 10020
(212) 536-2000

Crowe, Chizek
330 East Jefferson Boulevard
South Bend, Indiana 46624
(219) 232-3992

Deloitte & Touche
1114 Avenue of the Americas
New York, New York 10036
(212) 790-0500

Ernst & Young
2000 National City Center
Cleveland, Ohio 10020
(216) 861-5000

Grant Thornton
Prudential Plaza
Chicago, Illinois 60601
(312) 856-0001

KMG Main Hurdman
55 East 52nd Street
New York, New York 10055
(212) 909-5000

Laventhol and Horwath
1845 Walnut Street
Philadelphia, Pennsylvania 10103
(215) 299-1600

Kenneth Leventhal & Co.
2049 Century Park East
Los Angeles, California 90067
(213) 277-0880

McGladrey Hendrickson & Pullen
640 Capital Square
Des Moines, Iowa 50309
(515) 284-8680

Moss Adams
2830 Bank of California Center
Seattle, Washington 98164
(206) 223-1820

George S. Olive & Co.
320 North Meridian Street
Indianapolis, Indiana 46204
(317) 267-8400

Pannell Kerr Forster
262 North Belt East
Houston, Texas 77060
(713) 999-5134

KPMG Peat, Marwick, Main & Co.
345 Park Avenue
New York, New York 10022
(212) 758-9700

Plante & Moran
26211 Central Park Boulevard
Southfield, Michigan 48037
(313) 352-2500

Price Waterhouse & Co.
1251 Avenue of the Americas
New York, New York 10020
(212) 489-8900

Reznick Fedder & Silverman
Suite 300, 4520 East-West Highway
Bethesda, Maryland 20814
(301) 652-9100

Richard A. Eisner   Wipfli, Ullrich & Bertelsen
575 Madison Avenue   P.O. Box 8010
New York, New York 10022   Wausau, Wisconsin 54402
(212) 355-1700   (715) 845-3111

Spicer & Oppenheim
7 World Trade Center
New York, New York 10048
(212) 422-1000

SECURITIES AND FUTURES EXCHANGES AROUND THE WORLD

The following is a list of the name and address of major securities and futures exchanges around the world. Telephone numbers are provided for American, Canadian and several other major exchanges. The list is arranged alphabetically by country.

The most active financial markets are those in the industrialized countries of North America, Western Europe and Japan. In these countries, there is more regulation of securities markets, and companies have to disclose more about their financial status; the regulation and disclosure requirements of U.S. exchanges are by far the strictest. The more active markets are more competitive and therefore are characterized by narrower spreads between bid and asked prices.

The stock markets of the less industrialized countries offer both greater rewards and greater risks to investors. Regulation of these markets tends to be looser and financial disclosure rules less stringent. With less trading activity, the spreads between bid and asked prices tend to be wide. In some cases, investment by nonnationals of the country is banned or strictly limited. Many of these markets provide rich opportunities to participate in some of the world's fastest growing economies, such as South Korea, Taiwan, and Singapore.

The shares of some prominent companies listed on these and other exchanges are also traded in the United States as American Depositary Receipts (ADRs). For investors who are interested in participating in these foreign markets, but do not have the time or expertise to do so directly, there are a number of mutual funds, both closed-end and open-end, specializing in buying securities in markets around the world.

Argentina

Bolsa de Comercio de Buenos Aires
Sarmiento 299
Buenos Aires 1353

Australia

Stock Exchange of Adelaide
55 Exchange Place
Adelaide, 5001 S.A.

Brisbane Stock Exchange
Network House
344 Queen Street
Brisbane, 4001 Queensland

Stock Exchange of Melbourne
351 Collins Street
Melbourne, 3001 Victoria

Stock Exchange of Perth
68 St. George's Terrace
Perth, 6001 W.A.

Sydney Futures Exchange
13-15 O'Connell Street
Sydney, N.S.W. 2000
61 (02) 233-7633

Sydney Stock Exchange
20 Bond Street
Australia Square
Syndey, N.S.W. 2000
61 (02) 225-6600, (02) 221-0000

Austria

Wiener Boersekammer
Wipplingerstrasse 34
A-1011 Wien, 1
(01) 534-990

Belgium

Fondsen-En Wisselbeurs Van Antwerpen
Korte Klarenstraat 1
2000 Antwerpen

Bourse de Bruxelles
Palais de la Bourse
1000 Bruxelles
(02) 512-5110

Fondsen-Ed Wisselbeurs Van Gent
Kouter, 29
9000 Gent

Bourse de Fonds Public de Liege
Boulevard D'Avroy, 3/022
4000 Liege

Brazil

Bolsa Brasileira de Futuros
Avenue Rio Branco 110, 14th Floor
20040 Rio de Janiero
(5521) 224-6062

Bolsa de Mercadorias de Sao Paulo
Rua Libero Badaro 471, 4th Floor
Sao Paulo 01009
(5511) 32-3101

Bolsa de Valores do Rio de Janiero
Praca XV de Novembro 20
Rio de Janiero RJ

Bolsa de Valores de Sao Paulo
Rua Alvares Penteado No. 151-60 Andar
01012 Sao Paulo, SP

Bolsa Mercantil and de Futuros
Praca Antonio Prado, 48
Sao Paulo/SP 01010
(5511) 239-5511

Canada

Alberta Stock Exchange
300 5th Avenue, S.W.
Calgary, Alberta T2P 3C4
(403) 262-7791

Montreal Exchange
Tour de la Bourse
800 Victoria Square
Montreal, Quebec HAZ 1A9
(514) 871-2424

Toronto Futures Exchange
Toronto Stock Exchange
The Exchange Tower
2 First Canadian Place
Toronto, Ontario M5X 1J2
(416) 947-4700, (416) 947-4487

Vancouver Stock Exchange
Stock Exchange Tower
P.O. Box 10333
609 Granville Street
Vancouver, British Columbia V7Y 1H1
(604) 689-3334

Winnipeg Commodity Exchange
500 Commodity Exchange Tower
360 Main Street
Winnipeg, Manitoba R3C 3Z4
(204) 949-0495

Winnipeg Stock Exchange
167 Lombard Avenue
Winnipeg, Manitoba R3B OV3
(204) 942-8431

Chile

Bolsa de Comercio de Santiago
Casilla 123-D
Santiago

China, Republic of (Taiwan)

Taiwan Stock Exchange
8-10th Floor, City Building
85 Yen-Ping South Road
Taipei

Colombia

Bolsa de Bogota
Carrera 8, 13-82 Piso 8
Bogota

Denmark

Kobenhavns Fondsbors
2 Nikolaj Plads
1067 Kobenhavn K
(01) 93-3366

Equador

Bolsa de Valores de Quito
Avenue Rio Amazonas 540 y Jeronimo
Carrion, Piso 8
Apartado Postal 3772
Quito

Egypt

Cairo Stock Exchange
4-A Cherifein Street
Cairo

Finland

Helsingin Arvopapereriporssi
Fabianinkatu 14
00100 Helsinki 10

France

Bourse de Bordeaux
Palais de la Bourse
13-Bordeaux

Bourse de Lille
68 Palais Bourse
Place du Theatre
59-Lille

Bourse de Lyon
Palais du Commerce
Place de la Bourse
69289 Lyon

Bourse de Marseille
Palais de la Bourse
Marseille

Bourse de Nancy
40 Rue Henri Poincare
54000 Nancy

Bourse de Nantes
Palais de la Bourse
Place du Commerce
44-Nantes

Bourse de Paris
4 Place de la Bourse
75080 Paris
(14) 261-8590

Compagnie Des Commissionaires Agrees
(CCA)
Bourse de Commerce
2 Rue de Viarmes
Paris 75001
33 4508-8250

Lille Potato Futures Market
Centre Mercure
445 Boulevard Gambetta
59200 Tourcoing
33 2026-2213

Marche a Terme Des Instruments Financiers
(MATIF)
Conseil du Marche a Terme
108 Rue de Richileu
Paris 75002
331 4015-2001

Paris Commodity Exchange
Bourse de Commerce
2 Rue de Viarmes B.P. 53/01
75040 Paris

Great Britain

Baltic Futures Exchange
24-28 St. Mary Avenue
London EC3A 8EP
44 (1) 283-5146

Belfast Stock Exchange
Northern Bank House
10 High Street
Belfast BT1 1BP

International Petroleum Exchange of London
1 Commodity Quay
St. Katherine Docks
London E1 9AX
44 (1) 481-2080

International Stock Exchange
Old Broad Street
London EC2N 1HP
44 (01) 588-2355

London Commodity Exchange
Cereal House, 58 Mark Lane
London EC3R 7NE

London Futures and Options Exchange
(FOX)
1 Commodity Quay
St. Katherine Docks
London E1 9AX
44 (1) 481-2080

London International Financial
Futures Exchange (LIFFE)
Royal Exchange
London EC3V 3PJ
44 (1) 623-0444

London Metal Exchange (LME)
Plantation House
Fenchurch Street
London EC3M 3AP
44 (1) 623-0444

London Stock Exchange
Old Broad and Threadneedle Streets
London EC2N 1HP
44 (1) 588-2355

Midlands & Western Stock Exchange
Margaret Street
Birmingham B3 3J1

Northern Stock Exchange
2/6 Norfolk Street
Manchester M2 1DS

Provincial Stock Exchange
Room 402, 4th Floor
London EC2N 1HP

Scottish Stock Exchange
Stock Exchange House
69 St. George's Place
Glasgow G2 1BU
   and
12 Dublin Street
Edinburgh EH1 3PP

Greece

Athens Stock Exchange
10 Sophocleous Street
Athens 121

Hong Kong

Hong Kong Futures Exchange
Hong Kong Stock Exchange
New World Trade Tower, 12th Floor
16-18 Queen's Road Central
Hong Kong
852 (2) 868-0338, (05) 262-967

India

Bombay Stock Exchange
Dalal Street
Fort, Bombay 40001

Calcutta Stock Exchange Association
7 Lyons Range
Calcutta 700001

Delhi Stock Exchange Association
3 & 4/4B Asaf Ali Road
New Delhi 110002

Madras Stock Exchange
Stock Exchange Building
11 Second Line Beach
Madras 60001

Indonesia

Stock Exchange of Indonesia
Perserikatan Perdagangan
Uang dan Efek-Efek
P.O. Bo. 1224/Dak,
Jakarta-Kota

Ireland

Irish Stock Exchange
28 Anglesea Street
Dublin 2

Israel

Tel-Aviv Stock Exchange
113 Allenby Road
Tel-Aviv 65127

Italy

Borsa Valori di Bologna
Piazza della Costituzione, 8
Palazzo degli Affari
40100 Bologna

Borsa Valori de Firenze
Piazza Mentana, 2
50122 Firenze

Borsa Valori di Genova
Via G. Boccardo, 1
16121 Genova

Borsa Valori di Milano
Piazza degli Afferi, 6
20123 Milano
(02) 8534-4662

Borsa Valori di Napoli
Via S. Aspreno, 2
80133 Napoli

Borsa Valori di Palermo
Via E. Amari, 11
90139 Palermo

Borsa Valori di Roma
Via de' Burro, 147
00186 Roma

Borsa Valori di Torino
Via S. Francesco da Paola, 28
10123 Torino

Borsa Valori de Trieste
Via Cassa di Risparmio, 2
34100 Trieste

Borsa Valori di Venezia
Via XXII Marzo, 2034
30124 Venezia

Jamaica

Jamaica Stock Exchange
Bank of Jamaica Tower
P.O. Box 621
Nethersole Place, Kingston

Japan

Fukuoka Stock Exchange
2-14-2 Tenjin, Chuohku
Fukuokashi

Hiroshima Stock Exchange
14-18 Ginzancho
Hiroshimashi

Hokkaido Grain Exchange
3 Odori Nishi 5-chome
Chuo-ku
Sapporo, Hokkaido 060

Kanmon Commodity Exchange
1-5, Nabecho
Shimonoseki-shi
Yamaguchi 750

Kobe Grain Exchange
2-4-16 Honmachi
Hyogo-ku, Kobe-shi
Hyogo 652

Kobe Raw Silk Exchange
126 Higashicho
Kobe Silk Center Building, 8th Floor
Chuo-ku, Kobe-shi
Hyogo, 650

Kobe Rubber Exchange
49, Harimacho
Chuo-ku, Kobe-shi
Hyogo 650

Kyoto Stock Exchange
66 Tateuri Nishimachi
Tohdohin Higashihairu
Shijohdohri, Shimokyoku
Kyoto

Maebashi Dried Cocoon Exchange
1-49-1 Furuichi-Machi
Maebashi City
Gunma prefecture 371

Nagoya Grain and Sugar Exchange
2-3-2 Meiekiminami
Nakamura-ku, Nagoya-shi
Aichi 450

Nagoya Stock Exchange
3-3-17 Sakae, Naka-ku
Nagoyashi

Nagoya Textile Exchange
3-2-15 Nishiki
Naka-ku, Nagoya-shi
Aichi 460

Nilgata Securities Exchange
1245 Hachibancho
Kamiohkawamaedohri
Niigatashi

Osaka Grain Exchange
1-10-14 Awaza
Nish-ku, Osaka-shi
Osaka 550

Osaka Securities Exchange
Kitahama 2-chome
Higashi-Ku
Osaka 541
81 (6) 203-1151

Osaka Sugar Exchange
3-32-1 Kitakyutaro-Machi
Higashi-ku, Osaka-shi
Osaka 541

Osaka Textile Exchange
3-32-1 Kitakyutaro-Machi
Higanshiku
Osaka 541

Sapporo Stock Exchange
5-14-1 Nishi
Minami Ichijoh, Chuoku
Sappororshi

Tokyo Commodity Exchange (TCE)
Tosen Building
10-8 Nihonbashi
Horidomecho 1-chome
Chuo-ku, Tokyo
81 (3) 661-9191

Tokyo Grain Exchange (TGE)
12-5 Kakigara-cho
1-chome Nihonbashi
Chuo-ku, Tokyo 103
81 (3) 668-9311

Tokyo Stock Exchange (TSE)
2-1-1 Nihombashi-Kayaba-cho
2-chome, Chuo-ku
Tokyo, 103
81 (03) 666-0141

Tokyo Sugar Exchange (TSUE)
9-4 Koamicho
Nihonbashi, Chuo-ku
Tokyo 103

Toyohashi Cocoon Exchange
52-2 Ekimae-odori
Toyohashi City
Aichi Prefecture 440
81 (0) 532-526231

Yokohama Raw Silk Exchange
Silk Center, 4th Floor
1 Yamashita-cho
Naka-ku, Yokohama-shi
Knagawa 231

Kenya

Nairobi Stock Exchange
Stanbank House
Moi Avenue
P.O. Box 43633
Nairobi

Luxembourg

Societe de la Bourse de Luxembourg
11 avenue de la Porte-Neuve BP 165
2011 Luxembourg
352-477-9361

Malaysia

Kuala Lumpur Commodity Exchange (KLCE)
Podium Block, 4th Floor
Dayabumi Complex
P.O. Box 11260
50740 Kuala Lumpur
60 (3) 293-6822

Kuala Lumpur Stock Exchange
4th Floor Block C, Damansara Centre
Damansara Heights
Kuala Lumpur 23-04

Mexico

Bolsa Mexicana de Valores
Uruguay 68 Colonia Centro
CP 06000, Mexico City DF
Mexico 1. D.F.
(05) 510-4620

Bolsa de Valores de Monterey
Escobedo Sur #733
Monterey, N.L.

Morocco

Bourse Des Valeurs De Casablanca
Chamber of Commerce Building
98 Boulevard Mohamed V
Casablanca

Netherlands

Amsterdam Pork and Potato Exchange
(APPE)
Koopmansbeurs
Damrak 62a
Amsterdam
31 (20) 22 8654

Amsterdam Stock Exchange
Beursplein 5, P.O. Box 19163
1012 JW Amsterdam
(20) 237911

European Options Exchange (EOE)
Rokin 65
1012 KK Amsterdam
31 (20) 550-4550

Financiele Termijnmarkt Amsterdam NV
(FTA)
Nes 49
Amsterdam 1012 KD
P.O. Box 10220
1001 EE Amsterdam
31 (20) 550-4550

New Zealand

Auckland Stock Exchange
C.M.L. Centre
Queen Street
Auckland 1

Christchurch Invercargill Stock Exchange
128 Oxford Terrace
P.O. Box 639

Dunedin Stock Exchange
Queens Building
109 Princes Street
P.O. Box 483
Dunedin C.1

New Zealand Futures Exchange (NZFE)
P.O. Box 6734 Wellesley Street
Auckland
64 (9) 398-308

Wellington Stock Exchange
Government Life Insurance Building
Brandon Street
P.O. Box 767
Wellington C.1

Nigeria

Nigerian Stock Exchange
NIDB House, 15th Floor
63/71, Broad Street
P.O. Box 2457
Lagos

Norway

Aalesunds Bors
Roysegate 14
6001 Aalesund

Bergen Bors
Olav Kyrresgate 11
Postboks 832
5000 Bergen

Fredrikstad Bors
Nygaardsgaten 5
Fredrikstad

Oslo Bors
P.O. Box 460 Sentrum
0152 Oslo 1
(02) 42-3880

Trondheim Bors
Dronningensgt
Trondheim

Pakistan

Karachi Stock Exchange
Stock Exchange Road
Karachi 2

Lahore Stock Exchange
17 Bank Square
Lahore

Peru

Bolsa De Valores De Lima
Jiron Antonio Miro Quesada 265
Apartado 1538
Lima 100

Philippines

Makati Stock Exchange
Makati Stock Exchange Building
Ayala Avenue
Makati, Metro Manila

Manila International Futures Exchange
(MIFE)
Producers Bank Centre, 7th Floor
Paseo de Roxas
Makati, Metro Manila
63 818-5496

Manila Stock Exchange
Manila Stock Exchange Building
Prensa Street, Cor. Muelle de la Industria
Binondo, Manila

Metropolitan Stock Exchange
Padilla Arcade, 2nd Floor
Greenhills Commercial Center
San Juan, Metro Manila

Portugal

Bolsa De Valores De Lisboa
Praca do Comercio
Torreao Oriental
Lisboa

Singapore

Stock Exchange of Singapore
702/1403, Hong Leong Building
Raffles Quay OUB Centre
Singapore 0104
(65) 535-3788

Singapore International Monetary Exchange
(SIMEX)
1 Maritime Square
09-39 World Trade Center
Singapore 0409
(65) 278-6363

South Africa

Johannesburg Stock Exchange
P.O. Box 1174
Diagonal Street
Johannesburg, 2000
(01) 833-6580

South Korea

Korean Stock Exchange
1-116, Yoido-Dong
Youngdeungpo-Ku
Seoul

Spain

Bolsa de Barcelona
Paseo Isabel 11, Consulado 2
Barcelona 3

Bolsa de Bilbao
Jose Maria Olabarri 1
Bilbao 1

Bolsa de Comercio de Madrid
Plaza de la Lealtad 1
Madrid 28014
(01) 231-2290

Bolsa Oficial de Comercio de Valencia
Calle Pascual y Genis 19
Valencia

Sri Lanka

Colombo Brokers' Association
P.O. Box 101
59 Janadipathi Mawatha
Colombo 1

Sweden

Stockholms Fondbors
Box 1256, Kallargrand 2
S-111 82 Stockholm
(08) 14-3160

Stockholm Options Market (SOM)
Birger Jarlsgatan 18
Box 5015
S-102 41, Stockholm
46 (8) 114-070

Sweden Options and Futures Exchange
(SOFE)
Regeringsgatan 38
P.O. Box 7267
Stockholm
46 (8) 791-4080

Switzerland

Borsenkammer Des Kantons Basel-Stadt
Freie Strasse 3
CH-4001 Basel

Berner Borseenverein
Aabergergasse 30
CH-3011 Bern

Chambre De La Bourse De Geneve
10, rue Peitot
Case Postale 228
1211 Geneve

Bourse De Lausanne
Societe de Banque Suisse
16, Place St. Francois
CH-1003 Lausanne

Bourse De Neuchatel
Coq d-Inde 24
2000 Neuchatel

Effektenboersenverein Zurich
Bleicherweg 5
Postfach
8021 Zurich
(01) 229-2111

Swiss Options and Financial Futures
Exchange (SOFFEX)
Talstrasse 11
Zurich 8021
41 (1) 21135

Thailand

Securities Exchange of Thailand
Siam Center, 4th Floor
965 Rama 1 Road
Bangkok, Metropolis 5

United States

American Stock Exchange (AMEX)
86 Trinity Place
New York, New York 10006
(212) 306-1000

Boston Stock Exchange (BSE)
One Boston Place
Boston, Massachusetts 02108
(617) 723-9500

Chicago Board of Trade (CBOT)
141 West Jackson Boulevard
Chicago, Illinois 60604
(312) 435-3500

Chicago Board Options Exchange (CBOE)
400 South LaSalle Street
Chicago, Illinois 60605
(312) 786-5600

Chicago Mercantile Exchange (CME),
Index and Options Market (IOM) and
International Monetary Market (IMM)
30 South Wacker Drive
Chicago, Illinois 60606
(312) 930-1000

Chicago Rice & Cotton Exchange (CRCE)
141 West Jackson Street
Chicago, Illinois 60604
(312) 341-3078

Cincinnati Stock Exchange (CSE)
205 Dixie Terminal Building
Cincinnati, Ohio 45202
(513) 621-1410

Coffee, Sugar & Cocoa Exchange (CSCE)
4 World Trade Center
New York, New York 10048
(212) 938-2800

Commodity Exchange, Inc. (COMEX)
4 World Trade Center
New York, New York 10048
(212) 938-2900

Intermountain Stock Exchange (ISE)
373 South Main Street
Salt Lake City, Utah 84111
(801) 363-2531

Kansas City Board of Trade (KCBT)
4800 Main Street
Kansas City, Missouri 64112
(816) 753-7500

MidAmerica Commodity Exchange (MIDAM)
141 West Jackson Boulevard
Chicago, Illinois 60604
(312) 341-3000, (312) 341-3078

Midwest Stock Exchange (MSE)
440 South LaSalle Street
Chicago, Illinois 60605
(312) 663-2222

Minneapolis Grain Exchange (MGE)
400 South Fourth Street
Minneapolis, Minnesota 55415
(612) 338-6212

New York Cotton Exchange (NYCE)
4 World Trade Center
New York, New York 10048
(212) 938-2650, 938-2652

New York Futures Exchange (NYFE)
20 Broad Street
New York, New York 10005
(212) 656-4949, (800) 221-7722

New York Mercantile Exchange (NYMEX)
4 World Trade Center
New York, New York 10048
(212) 938-2222

New York Stock Exchange (NYSE)
11 Wall Street
New York, New York 10005
(212) 656-3000

Pacific Stock Exchange (PSE)
301 Pine Street
San Francisco, California 94104
(415) 393-4000

Philadelphia Stock Exchange (PHLX)
Philadelphia Board of Trade (PBOT)
1900 Market Street
Philadelphia, Pennsylvania 19103
(215) 496-5000, 496-5165

Spokane Stock Exchange (SSE)
225 Peyton Building
Spokane, Washington 99201
(509) 624-4632

West Germany

Berliner Wertpapierborse
Hardenbergstrasse 16-18
1000 Berlin 12

Rheinisch-Westfalische Borse zu Dusseldorf
Ernst-Schneider-Platz 1
4000 Dusseldorf

Frankfurter Wertpapierborse
Borsenplatz 6, Postfach 100811
6000 Frankfurt am Main 1
(69) 21-970

Hanseatische Wertpapierborse Hamburg
Adolphsplatz, Borse, Zimmer 151
2000 Hamburg 11

Bayerische Borse in Munchen
Lenbachplatz 2 a
8000 Munchen 2

3. MUTUAL FUNDS

OPEN-END MUTUAL FUNDS

The following is a list of the names, addresses and telephone numbers of American open-end mutual funds. Most organizations offer more than one fund, and the funds in this list are grouped under the name of the firm to which they belong. In order to obtain information about a fund you may be interested in, look first for the name of its management group. Newspaper listings also usually group mutual funds by family.

The funds on this list are both load and no-load. Load funds are sold through brokers and financial planners for commissions that generally range from about 3% (this is called a low-load fund) to as much as 8$^1/_2$%. In return for this sales charge, customers should expect expert advice on which fund is most appropriate for their investment needs and goals. A broker should also tell the customer when to get out of the fund, as well as when to get in. No-load funds, on the other hand, charge no commissions. Investors buy shares directly from the management companies over the phone, by mail or in person. The management company representative will offer information on the funds the firm offers, but they may not advise investors on which fund to buy. No one will call when the time comes to switch from one fund to another—that is left totally up to the individual shareholder.

The funds on this list are each categorized by the investment objective of the fund manager. The following is a brief characterization of each objective, the abbreviation of which is given in parentheses after each fund's name in the list of funds.

Aggressive Growth (AG) Aggressive-growth funds seek maximum capital gains; current income is not a consideration. Fund managers may use several strategies, such as buying high-technology stocks, emerging growth stocks, or companies that have fallen on hard times or are out of favor. Some aggressive funds make use of options and futures, and/or borrow against funds shares to buy stock. Aggressive-growth funds typically provide dramatic gains and losses for shareholders, and should therefore be monitored closely.

Balanced (B) Balanced mutual funds generally invest in both stocks and bonds, with the intent of providing capital gains and income. Preservation of principal is a primary objective of balanced fund managers. These funds are for conservative investors who are looking for some growth of capital.

Corporate Bond (CB) Corporate-bond funds seek to pay a high level of income to shareholders by buying corporate bonds. Some conservative bond funds buy only the debt of highly rated corporations. The yield on this kind of fund would be lower than on that of a fund buying bonds from lower-rated corporations—frequently called junk bonds or high-yield bonds. Although income, not capital gains, is the primary objective of most corporate bond shareholders, gains can be significant if the country's general level of interest rates falls. On the other hand, losses can also be substantial if interest rates rise.

Flexible Portfolio (FP) Flexible portfolio funds give the fund manager great flexibility in deciding which asset offers the best risk-return tradeoff at any particular time. Therefore, such funds may invest in stocks, bonds, money-market instruments, options, futures or foreign securities at various times. Such funds are sometimes called asset-allocation funds. Shareholders of flexible funds desire some current income, but also are expecting superior long-term capital gains.

Growth (G) Growth funds invest in the common stock of growth companies. The primary aim is to achieve capital gains, and income is of little concern. Growth funds vary widely in the amount of risk they are willing to take, but in general they take less risk than aggressive-growth funds because the stocks they buy are those of more seasoned companies.

Global Bond (GB) Global Bond funds invest in fixed-income securities that are for the most part not denominated in U. S. dollars. Such funds may purchase bonds issued by foreign corporations or by U.S. corporations in non-dollar currencies. Global bond funds also invest in bonds issued by foreign governments or their agencies. Investors in global bond funds expect a high level of current income, and capital gains, if the direction of interest rates and currency rates is favorable.

Growth and Income (G + I) Growth and income funds seek to provide both capital gains and a steady stream of income by buying the shares of high-yielding, conservative stocks. Growth and income fund managers look for companies with solid records of increasing their dividend payments, as well as showing earnings gains. These funds are more conservative than pure growth funds.

Global (GLB) Global funds invest in securities anywhere in the world. They buy stocks, bonds and money-market instruments in both the United States and in foreign countries, depending on where the fund manager sees the best opportunity for growth. Global funds' main objective is long-term capital appreciation, though they may provide some current income.

GNMA Fund (GNMA) These funds buy Government National Mortgage Association (GNMA or Ginnie Mae) certificates, which are securities backed by home mortgages. GNMA funds are designed to provide a high level of current income to shareholders and to minimize risk to capital. These funds are subject to fluctuation because of the ups and downs of interest rates, however. They are also affected by the rate at which homeowners refinance their mortgages. When interest rates fall, more mortgages are refinanced, and therefore shareholders in GNMA funds see their yields fall. When rates rise, on the other hand, fewer mortgages are refinanced, and so the fund maintains its yield, but it does not grow very quickly. GNMA funds are designed for conservative, income-oriented investors.

High Yield Bond (HYB) High yield bond funds buy the debt securities issued by non-investment grade corporations and municipalities. Because these securities offer higher risks than investment-grade bonds, high-yield bonds pay higher yields. Since the companies and municipalities that issue high-yield bonds are more highly leveraged than top-quality issuers, their bonds are more subject to default, particularly if there is an economic downturn in the issuer's industry or region. Such defaults would not only cut the yield on high-yield bond funds, but also erode the capital value of the shares. Investors in high-yield bond funds, therefore, should be well aware that they are taking an extra degree of default risk in exchange for a higher level of current income than is available from more conservative bond funds.

Income (I) Income funds seek to provide a high level of current income by buying government and corporate bonds as well as high-yielding common and preferred stocks. Income funds are not designed to provide major capital gains, but their shares do rise when interest rates fall. (Conversely, the shares fall in value when interest rates rise.) Income funds are designed for conservative, income-oriented investors.

Income Bond (IB) Income bond funds invest in a variety of bonds to produce high taxable current income for shareholders. Such funds usually invest in corporate or government bonds, but may also buy foreign bonds. They are usually managed more conservatively than bond funds that buy high-yield bonds, and therefore offer lower current yields.

Income Equity (IE) Income equity funds invest in bonds and high-yielding stocks with the objective of providing shareholders with a moderate level of current income and a moderate level of long-term capital appreciation. Income-equity funds are slightly more conservatively managed, and usually have a higher percentage of their assets in bonds than growth and income funds.

International (INT) International funds invest in stocks of companies around the world as well as in bonds issued by foreign companies and governments. Some funds (also called global funds) buy American and Canadian shares in addition to those of companies in other countries, while others are restricted to buying non-North American shares. International funds provide investors with diversification among countries as well as industries. Such funds are strongly influenced by the rise and fall of foreign exchange rates —a factor important to consider before buying shares. For Americans, it would generally be beneficial to buy an international fund when the outlook is for the dollar to fall against other currencies. Conversely, international-fund performance usually suffers when the dollar strengthens. International funds are for those willing to take some risk; understanding of the effect of currency changes on holdings is essential.

Long Term Municipal Bond (LTMB) These funds aim to provide a high level of tax-exempt income to shareholders by buying the debt obligations of cities, states and other municipal government agencies. Depending on the state in which a shareholder resides, interest earned is either totally or partially free of federal, state, and local income taxes. While such funds are designed to provide current income, their value also rises and falls inversely with the country's general level of interest rates. The municipal bonds these funds usually buy tend to mature anywhere from 10 to 20 years in the future.

Money Market (MM) Money-market mutual funds buy short-term securities sold in the money markets to provide current income to shareholders. Because of the short-term nature of their holdings, these funds reflect changes in short-term interest rates rather quickly. The principal in money-market funds is extremely safe. Some money funds buy commercial instruments like commercial paper, banker's acceptances and repurchase agreements, while others restrict themselves to buying U.S. Treasury obligations like Treasury bills. The portfolios of some money-market funds are insured by private insurance companies. Most money funds allow checkwriting, often with a minimum check size of $250 or $500. Money market funds are frequently included in asset management accounts offered by brokerage firms, and are used as parking places for funds while shareholders decide where the best place to invest long-term might be. Otherwise, money-market funds are for extremely conservative investors, who want virtually no risk of capital loss.

Option Income (OI) Option-income funds provide high current returns by writing call options on a portfolio of dividend-paying stocks. The current return derives from dividends on stock as well as premium income earned by writing options. If the value of the stock in the portfolio declines, the net asset value of the fund will also decline, though the income earned will somewhat offset that decline. Option-income funds are designed for investors wanting high current return while being willing to risk declines in the value of their shares.

Precious Metals-Gold (PMG) Such funds invest in the shares of gold and silver mining companies. These shares often pay high dividends, and therefore the funds often can pay high yields. As with all precious-metal investments, these funds reflect the ups and downs of investor psychology as it relates to the outlook for inflation as well as political upheaval. These funds tend to perform better when inflation is high and rising and there is considerable political turmoil in the world. Some funds invest largely in South African mines, while others restrict themselves to shares in North American mining companies.

Short-Term Municipal Bond (STMB) These funds buy short-term obligations of cities, states and municipal government agencies, and pass along tax-exempt income to shareholders. Since the bonds are short-term, they are less risky and usually have a lower yield than longer-term obligations. Some short-term municipal bond funds operate like tax-free money-market funds and allow check writing, usually with a $250 or $500 per check minimum. These funds are generally for conservative investors in income-tax brackets high enough to take advantage of tax-free income.

State Municipal Bond-Long Term (STMB-LT) These funds buy debt obligations of cities and municipal authorities in one state only. The interest from these bonds is usually tax exempt to residents of the particular state. Thus, shareholders can have a higher after-tax yield than if they bought shares in an out-of-state fund on which they had to pay taxes. These funds typically buy longer-term bonds maturing in 10 to 20 years. As a result, they fluctuate considerably with the ups and downs of the general level of interest rates.

State Municipal Bond-Short Term (STMB-ST) These funds buy the debt obligations of cities and municipal authorities in one state only. The interest from these bonds is usually tax exempt to residents of the particular state. Thus, shareholders can obtain a higher after-tax yield than if they bought the shares in an out-of-state fund on which they had to pay taxes. These funds typically buy short-term debt obligations with maturities from a few days or months to as much as five years. Therefore, they are not as subject to interest rate fluctuations as long-term funds. The funds generally allow shareholders to write checks, typically with a minimum withdrawal of $250 to $500 per check.

U.S. Government Income (USGI) These funds invest only in direct obligations of the U.S. Treasury. The funds therefore buy U.S. Treasury bills, bonds and notes and federally backed mortgage securities. Shareholders of such funds want a high level of current income as well as maximum safety against default. Some funds have short maturities, while others buy bonds with maturities as long as 20 or 30 years. The longer the portfolio's overall maturity, the more the fund will fluctuate with general interest-rate movements.

This listing of mutual funds was made possible through the generous cooperation of two mutual fund trade associations, the Investment Company Institute and the Mutual Fund Educational Alliance. The Investment Company Institute (1600 M Street, N.W., Washington, D.C. 20036 (202) 293-7700) has both load and no-load members, and regularly keeps track of new fund groups and funds. It publishes an annual directory of members.

The Mutual Fund Educational Alliance (Suite 1632, 520 North Michigan Avenue, Chicago, Illinois 60611 (312) 527-1454) also has a large membership of no-load and low-load funds.

Abbreviations of Fund Objectives

AG	Aggressive Growth
B	Balanced
CB	Corporate Bond
FP	Flexible Portfolio
G	Growth
GB	Global Bond
G + I	Growth and Income
GLB	Global
GNMA	Government National Mortgage Association Fund
HYB	High Yield Bond
I	Income
IB	Income Bond
IE	Income Equity
INT	International
LTMB	Long-Term Municipal Bond
MM	Money Market
OI	Option Income
PMG	Precious Metals-Gold
STMB	Short-Term Municipal Bond
SMB-LT	State Municipal Bond-Long Term
SMB-ST	State Municipal Bond-Short Term
USGI	U.S. Government Income

AAL Funds
222 West College Avenue
Appleton, Wisconsin 54919
(414) 734-5721, (800) 553-6319

AAL Capital Growth Fund (G), AAL Income Fund (I), AAL Municipal Bond Fund (LTMB)

AARP Investments
160 Federal Street
Boston, Massachusetts 02110-1706
(800) 253-2277

AARP Capital Growth (G), AARP General Bond, AARP Ginnie Mae (GNMA), AARP Growth and Income (G + I), AARP Tax Free Bond (LTMB), AARP Tax Free Shares (STMB)

ABD Securities Corp.
One Battery Park Plaza
New York, New York 10004
(212) 363-5100

ABD American Capital Markets Funds: ABD Common Stock Fund (G), ABD Investment Grade Bond Fund (I), ABD Money Market Fund (MM)

ABT Family of Funds
205 Royal Palm Way
Palm Beach, Florida 33480
(407) 655-7255, (800) 441-6580

ABT Growth and Income Trust (G+I), ABT Investment Series: ABT Emerging Growth Fund (AG), ABT Security Income Fund (OI), ABT Money Market Series: ABT Prime Portfolio (MM), ABT Tax-Free Portfolio (STMB), ABT Utility Income Fund (IE)

Accrued Equities
295 Northern Boulevard
Great Neck, New York 11021
(516) 466-0808

New Alternatives Fund (G)

Acorn
Two North LaSalle Street, Suite 500
Chicago, Illinois 60602-379
(312) 621-0630

Acorn Fund (G)

ADTEK Fund
4920 West Vliet Street
Milwaukee, Wisconsin 53208
(414) 257-1842

ADTEK Fund (FP)

Advantage Trust
16030 Ventura Boulevard, Suite 500
Encino, California 91436
(818) 501-5215

Advantage Trust: Advantage Tax-Free Bond Fund (LTMB), Advantage U.S. Government Securities Fund (USGI)

Advest Advantage Funds
60 State Street
Boston, Massachusetts 02109
(617) 742-5900, (800) 243-8115

Advantage Government Securities Fund (USGI), Advantage Growth Fund (G), Advantage Income Fund (I), Advantage Special Fund (G)

Aetna
151 Farmington Avenue
Hartford, Connecticut 06156
(203) 273-4808

Aetna Guaranteed Equity Trust (G + I), Aetna Income Shares (IB), Aetna Investment Adviser Fund (B), Aetna Variable Fund (G)

Afuture Fund. *see* Carlisle-Asher Management Company.

AIM Group
11 Greenway Plaza, Suite 1919
Houston, Texas 77046
(713) 626-1919, (800) 231-0803
and
Three University Plaza
Hackensack, New Jersey 07601
(201) 342-6066, (800) 433-1918

AIM Convertible Securities (CB), Aim Equity Funds: AIM Charter Fund (G + I), AIM Constellation Fund (AG), AIM Weingarten Fund (G), AIM Government Funds: AIM U.S. Government Securities Fund (USGI), AIM Tax-Exempt Funds, Inc.: AIM California Tax-Free Intermediate Fund (SMB-LT) Cortland Trust: AIM General Money Market Fund (MM), General Money Market Fund (MM), Tax-Free Money Market Fund (STMB), U.S. Government Fund (MM), High Yield Securities (HYB), Short-Term Investments Co.: AIM Limited Maturity Treasury Shares (USGI), Limited Maturity Treasury Portfolio A (USGI), Limited Maturity Treasury Portfolio B (USGI), Prime Portfolio (MM), Treasury Portfolio (MM), Silver Star Fund: Government Portfolio (MM), Prime Portfolio (MM), Summit Investors Fund (G), Tax-Free Investments Trust: AIM Tax-Free Intermediate Shares (LTMB), Flag Investors Tax-Free Cash Reserve Shares (STMB), Institutional Cash Reserve Shares (STMB), Institutional Intermediate Shares (LTMB)

Alex. Brown
135 East Baltimore Street, P.O. Box 515
Baltimore, Maryland 21203
(301) 727-1700
Flag Investors Fund Telephone Income Shares Series (I)

Alger Funds
75 Maiden Lane
New York, New York 10038
(212) 806-8800, (800) 992-FUND
Alger American Fund: Alger American Growth Portfolio (G), Alger American Income and Growth Portfolio (IE), Alger American Money Market Portfolio (MM), Alger American Small Capitalization Portfolio (AG), Alger Fund: Alger Fixed Income Portfolio (IB), Alger Growth Portfolio (G), Alger High Yield Portfolio (HYB), Alger Income and Growth Portfolio (IE), Alger Money Market Portfolio (MM), Alger Small Capitilization Portfolio (AG)

Alliance Capital Management
1345 Avenue of the Americas
New York, New York 10105
(212) 969-1000, (800) 221-5672
and
40 Rector Street
New York, New York 10006
(212) 513-4200, (800) 443-4430
Alliance Balanced Shares (B), Alliance Bond Fund: High-Yield Portfolio (HYB), Monthly Income Portfolio (CB), U.S. Government Portfolio (USGI), Alliance Capital Reserves (MM), Alliance Convertible Fund (G + I), Alliance Counterpoint Fund (G), Alliance Dividend Shares (G + I), Alliance Fund (G), Alliance Global Fund: Canadian Fund (INT), World Equities Fund (INT), Alliance Government Reserves (MM), Alliance International Fund (INT), Alliance Mortgage Securities Income Fund (GNMA), Alliance Short-Term Multi-Market Fund (MM), Alliance Tax Exempt Reserves: California Portfolio (STMB), New York Portfolio (STMB), Tax-Exempt Reserves (General) (STMB), Alliance Tax-Free Income Fund: California Portfolio (SMB-LT), High Bracket Tax-Free Portfolio (LTMB), High Income Tax-Free Portfolio (LTMB), Insured California Portfolio (SMB-LT), New York Portfolio (SMB-LT), Alliance Technology Fund (AG), Fiduciary Management Associates (AG), Quasar Associates (AG), Surveyor Fund (G), Austria Fund

Allied Advisory Inc.
1666 K Street, N.W., Suite 901
Washington, D.C. 20006
(202) 331-1112
Allied Capital Fund I (B), Allied Capital Fund II

Allstate Investment Management Co.
One World Trade Center
New York, New York 10048
(212) 392-1600
Allstate Municipal Income Opportunities Trust II (SMB-LT), Allstate Municipal Income Trust Opportunities III (SMB-LT)

Altamira Investment Services
250 Bloor Street East, Suite 301
Toronto, Ontario, Canada M4W 1E6
(416) 925-1623
Altamira Canadian Balanced (G + I), Altamira Diversified Fund (G + I)

AMA Advisers
5 Sentry Parkway West, Suite 120
P.O. Box 1111
Blue Bell, Pennsylvania 19422
(215) 825-0400, (800) AMA-FUND,
(800) 262-3863
AMA Growth Fund: Classic Growth (G), Classic Income (B), Global Growth (GLB), Growth Plus Income (G + I), AMA Income Fund: Global Income (GB), Global Short Term (GB), U.S. Government Income Plus (IB), AMA Money Fund: Prime Portfolio (MM), Treasury Portfolio (MM), Medical Technology Fund (AG)

American Asset Trust
Suite 100, 107 South Main Street
Salt Lake City, Utah 84111
(801) 328-3333
American Asset Management Corporation: American Asset Dividend Fund (IE), American Asset Yield Fund (IE)

American Capital
2800 Post Oak Boulevard
Houston, Texas 77056
(713) 993-0500, (800) 421-5666
American Capital California Tax-Exempt Trust (SMB-LT), American Capital Comstock Fund (G), American Capital Corporate Bond Fund (CB), American Capital Enterprise Fund (AG), American Captial Exchange Fund (G), American Capital Federal Mortgage Trust (GNMA), American Capital Government Money Market Trust (MM), American Captial Government Securities (USGI), American Capital Growth

Fund (G), American Capital Harbor Fund (G + I), American Capital High Yield Investments (HYB), American Capital Life Investment Trust: American Captial Common Stock Portfolio (G + I), American Capital Corporate Bond Portfolio (CB), American Capital Government Portfolio (USGI), American Capital Money Market Portfolio (MM), American Capital Multiple Strategy Portfolio (FP), American Capital Municipal Bond Fund (LTMB), American Capital Over-The-Counter Securities (AG), American Capital Pace Fund (G), American Capital Reserve Fund (MM), American Capital Tax-Exempt Trust: High Yield Municipal Portfolio (LTMB), Insured Municipal Portfolio (LTMB), Money Market Municipal Portfolio (STMB), New York Municipal Portfolio (SMB-LT), American Capital Venture Fund (AG), American General Equity Accumulaltion Fund (AG), American General High Yield Accumulation Fund (HYB), American General Money Market Accumulation Fund (MM), Common Sense Trust: Common Sense Government Fund (USGI), Common Sense Growth and Income Fund (G + I), Common Sense Growth Fund (G), Common Sense Money Market Fund (MM), Common Sense Municipal Bond Fund (LTMB), Fund of America (G), Provident Fund for Income (I)

American Eagle
100 Light Street
Baltimore, Maryland 21202
(301) 547-3894, (800) 622-3363

American Eagle Fund: American Eagle Balanced Series (G + I), American Eagle Growth Series (G), American Eagle Income Series (IE), American Eagle Money Market Series

American Express Funds. *see* Shearson Lehman Hutton.

American Fund Advisors
50 Broad Street
New York, New York 10004
(212) 482-8100, (800) 654-0001

National Aviation & Technology Corporation (G), National Telecommunications & Technology Fund (G), National Value Fund (G)

American General Funds. *see* VALIC.

American Growth
410 17th Street, Suite 800
Denver, Colorado 80202
(303) 623-6137, (800) 525-2406

American Growth Fund (G)

American Investors
777 West Putnam Avenue
P.O. Box 2500
Greenwich, Connecticut 06836
(203) 531-5000, (800) 243-5353

American Investors Growth Fund (AG), American Investors Income Fund (HYB), American Investors Money Fund (MM), American Investors Option Fund (G)

American National
Two Moody Plaza
Galveston, Texas 77550
(409) 763-2767, (800) 231-4639

American National Growth Fund (G), American National Income Fund (IE), American National Money Market Fund (MM), Triflex Fund, (B)

American Pension Investors
2316 Atherholt Road
P.O. Box 2529
Lynchburg, Virginia 24501
(804) 846-1361, (800) 533-4115, (800) 544-6060

American Pension Investors Trust: Balanced Fund (B), Growth Fund (AG), Investment Grade Securities Fund (CB), Precious Resources Fund (PMG), U.S. Government Intermediate Fund (USGI)

American Shares Funds. *see* Templeton Funds.

American United Life
One American Square
Indianapolis, Indiana 46204
(317) 263-1877

AUL American Series Funds: Equity Portfolio (G), Bond Portfolio (I), Money Market Portfolio (MM), Managed Portfolio (FP)

Ameritas Investment Advisors
5900 "O" Street
Lincoln, Nebraska 68510
(402) 467-1122

Sower Series Fund: Bond Portfolio (IB), Discretionary Portfolio (FP), Growth Portfolio (G), Money Market Portfolio (MM)

AMEV Funds
P.O. Box 64284
St. Paul, Minnesota 55164
(612) 738-4000, (800) 872-2638

AMEV Advantage Portfolios: Asset Allocation Portfolio (G + I), Capital Appreciation Portfolio (G), High Yield Portfolio (HYB), AMEV

Capital Fund (G + I), AMEV Fiduciary Fund (AG), AMEV Growth Fund (G), AMEV Money Fund (MM), AMEV Tax-Free Fund: Minnesota Portfolio (SMB-LT), National Portfolio (LTMB). AMEV U.S. Government Securities Fund (USGI)

Amherst Investment Management
Company, Inc.
One Monarch Place, 12th Floor
Springfield, Massachusetts 01144
(413) 784-6857, (413) 781-3000

Variable Investors Series: Cash Management Series (MM), Common Stock Series (G), High Yield Series (HYB), Multiple Strategy Series (FP), Natural Resources Series (G), Real Estate Series (G + I), U.S. Government High Quality Series (IB)

Amway
7575 East Fulton Road
Ada, Michigan 49355
(616) 676-6288, (800) 346-2670

Amway Mutual Fund (G)

Analytic Investment Management
2222 Martin Street, Suite 230
Irvine, California 92715
(714) 833-0294

Analytic Optioned Equity Fund (G + I)

Anchor Pathway Funds
2201 East Camelback
Phoenix, Arizona 85016
(602) 955-0300, (800) 528-9679

Anchor Pathway Fund: Cash Management Series (MM), Growth Series (G), Growth-Income Series (G + I), High-Yield Bond Series (HYB), U.S. Government Guaranteed/AAA-Rated Securities Series (USGI)

Aquila Group
200 Park Avenue, Suite 4515
New York, New York 10017
(212) 697-6666

Capital Cash Management Trust (MM), Cash Assets Trust: Cash Assets Trust (MM), Tax-Free Cash Assets Trust (STMB), U.S. Treasuries Cash Assets Trust (MM), Cash Reserves Trust (MM), Churchill Tax-Free Trust: Churchill Tax-Free Cash Fund (STMB), Churchill Tax-Free Fund of Kentucky (SMB-LT), Hawaiian Tax-Free Trust (SMB-LT), Prime Cash Fund (MM), Short Term Asset Reserves (MM), Tax-Free Fund of Colorado (SMB-LT), Tax-Free Trust of Arizona (SMB-LT), Tax-Free Trust of Oregon (SMB-LT)

Armstrong
1445 Ross, Suite 1490
Dallas, Texas 75202
(214) 720-9101

Armstrong Associates (G)

Arnold Investment Counsel
First Financial Centre
700 North Water Street
Milwaukee, Wisconsin 53202
(414) 271-7870, (800) 443-6544

Primary Trend Fund (FP), Primary Income Funds: Primary Money Market Fund (MM), Primary U.S. Government Fund (USGI)

Associated Planners Group, Inc.
1925 Century Park East, 19th Floor
Los Angeles, California 90067
(213) 553-6740

Associated Planners Investment Trust: Associated Planners California Tax-Free Fund (SMB-LT), Associated Planners Government Securities Fund (USGI), Associated Planners Stock Fund (G)

Aster Capital Management
60 East Sir Francis Drake Boulevard, Suite 306
Larkspur, California 94939
(415) 461-8770, (800) 446-6662

Meridian Fund (G)

Avondale
1105 Holliday
Wichita Falls, Texas 76301
(817) 761-3777

Avondale Investment Trust: Avondale Government Securities Fund (USGI), Avondale Total Return Fund (G + I)

Axe-Houghton Management Inc.
400 Benedict Avenue
Tarrytown, New York 10591
(914) 333-5200, (914) 631-8131,
(800) 366-0444, (800) 431-1030

Axe-Houghton Fund B (G + I), Axe-Houghton Income Fund (IB), Axe-Houghton Money Market Fund (MM), Axe-Houghton Stock Fund (G)

Babson Funds. *see* Jones & Babson

Bailard, Biehl & Kaiser
2755 Campus Drive
San Mateo, California 94403
(415) 571-5800

Bailard, Biehl & Kaiser International Fund (AG), BB&K Fund Group: BB&K Diversa Fund (G + I)

Baird
777 East Wisconsin Avenue
Milwaukee, Wisconsin 53202
(414) 765-3500, (800) 792-2473

Baird Blue Chip Fund (G + I), Baird Capital
Development Fund (G)

Baker Fentress & Co.
200 West Madison Street
Chicago, Illinois 60606
(312) 236-9190

Baker Fentress Fund (G + I)

Baker Funds. *see* James Baker & Co.

Bank Investment Fund
265 Franklin Street
Boston, Massachusetts 02110
(617) 439-4416

Bank Investment Fund: Fund One (USGI),
Liquidity Fund (MM)

Bankers National
101 Gibraltar Drive
Morris Plains, New Jersey 07950
(201) 644-5200, (800) 445-8539

Bankers National Series Trust: BNL Common
Stock Portfolio (G), BNL Convertible Portfolio
(G + I), BNL Government Securities Portfolio
(USGI), BNL High Yield Portfolio (HYB), BNL
Money Market Portfolio (MM), BNL Mort-
gaged-Backed Securities Portfolio (GNMA),
BNL Multiple Strategies Portfolio (FP)

Bankers Systems
6815 Saukview Drive
P.O. Box 517
St. Cloud, Minnesota 56302
(612) 251-3060, (800) 328-1375

Bankers Systems GRANIT Fixed Income Fund
(IB), Bankers Systems GRANIT Government
Securities Fund (USGI), Bankers Systems
GRANIT Growth Stock Fund (G), Bankers
Systems GRANIT Money Market Fund (MM),
Bankers Systems GRANIT Stock Fund (G + I),
Bankers Systems GRANIT Tax Exempt Fund
(LTMB)

Baron Capital
450 Park Avenue
New York, New York 10022
(212) 759-7700, (800) 99-BARON

Baron Asset Fund (AG)

Bartlett & Company
36 East Fourth Street
Cincinnati, Ohio 45202
(513) 621-4612, (800) 543-0863

Bartlett Capital Trust: Basic Value Fund (G + I),
Fixed Income Fund (IB), Bartlett Management
Trust: Bartlett Enhanced Cash Reserves (I),
Bartlett Strategic Income Fund (I)

Bass Capital
4000 Park Road
Charlotte, North Carolina 28209
(704) 523-9407, (800) 366-2277

Harvest Funds: Growth Portfolio (G), Income
Portfolio (I)

B.C. Ziegler
215 North Main Street
West Bend, Wisconsin 53095
(414) 334-5521, (800) 826-4600

Principal Preservation Portfolios: Dividend
Achievers Portfolio (IE), Government Plus
Portfolio (USGI), Insured Tax-Exempt Plus
Portfolio (LTMB), Retirement Portfolio (B),
S&P 100 Plus Portfolio (G + I), Tax-Exempt
Plus Portfolio (LTMB)

Beacon Hill Management, Inc.
75 Federal Street
Boston, Massachusetts 02110-1904
(617) 482-0795

Beacon Hill Mutual (G)

Bench Group
222 Bridge Plaza South
Fort Lee, New Jersey 07024
(201) 585-2333, (800) 422-3624

Bench Portfolios Fund: Blue Chip Portfolio (G)

Benham Capital Management Group
755 Page Mill Road
Palo Alto, California 94304
(415) 858-2400, (800) 227-8380,
(800) 4-SAFETY

Benham California Tax Free Insured Trust
(SMB-LT), Benham California Tax-Free Trust:
High Yield Portfolio (SMB-LT), Intermediate-
Term Portfolio (SMB-LT), Long-Term Portfo-
lio (SMB-LT), Money Market Portfolio (SMB-
ST), Benham Equity Fund: Benham Gold Equi-
ties Index Fund (PMG), Benham Government
Income Trust: Benham GNMA Income Fund
(GNMA), Benham National Tax-Free Trust:
Intermediate-Term Portfolio (LTMB), Long-

Term Portfolio (LTMB), Money Market Portfolio (STMB), Benham Target Maturities Trust: Series 1990 (USGI), Series 1995 (USGI), Series 2000 (USGI), Series 2005 (USGI), Series 2010 (USGI), Series 2015 (USGI), Benham Variable Insurance Trust: Asset Allocation Portfolio (FP), Equity Index Portfolio (G), Natural Resources Portfolio (G), U.S. Government and High Quality Income Portfolio (I), U.S. Government and High Quality Money Market Portfolio (MM), U.S. Government Zero-Coupon Portfolio-1995 (USGI), U.S. Government Zero-Coupon Portfolio-2000 (USGI), U.S. Government Zero-Coupon Portfolio-2005 (USGI), Capital Preservation Fund (MM), Capital Preservation Fund II (MM), Capital Preservation Treasury Note Trust (USGI)

Berger & Associates
899 Logan Street, Suite 211
Denver, Colorado 80203
(303) 837-1020, (800) 333-1001
One Hundred and One Fund (G + I), One Hundred Fund (G)

Bernstein
767 Fifth Avenue
New York, New York 10153
(212) 486-5800
Sanford C. Bernstein Fund: Bernstein Diversified Municipal Portfolio (LTMB), Bernstein Government Short Duration Portfolio (USGI), Bernstein Intermediate Duration Portfolio (I), Bernstein New York Municipal Portfolio (SMB-LT), Bernstein Short Duration Plus Portfolio (I)

Better Investing Fund
National Association of Investors Corp.
1515 East Eleven Mile Road
Royal Oak, Michigan 48067
(313) 543-0612
Better Investing Fund (G)

Blackstone Star Trust, Inc.
One Seaport Plaza
New York, New York 10292
(212) 214-3334
Blackstone Star Fund (G)

William Blair & Company
135 South LaSalle Street
Chicago, Illinois 60603
(312) 346-4830
Growth Industry Shares Fund (G)

BMI Equity
67 Wall Street
New York, New York 10005
(212) 422-1619
BMI Equity Fund (G)

The Boston Company Advisors, Inc.
P.O. Box 2537
Boston, Massachusetts 02208-9983
(800) 225-5267, (800) 343-6324
Boston Company Funds: Asset Allocation (G + I), Blue Chip Fund (G + I), Bond Index (G + I), California Tax-Free Bond (SMB-LT), California Tax-Free Money (SMB-LT), Capital Appreciation (G), Cash Management Fund (MM), Cash Management Plus (I), Contrarian Fund (G), Equity Index (G + I), GNMA Fund (I), Government Money (MM), International (INT), Massachusetts Tax-Free Bond (SMB-LT), Massachusetts Tax-Free Money (SMB-LT), Managed Income (I), New York Tax-Free Bond (SMB-LT), New York Tax-Free Money (SMB-ST), Small Capital Equity Index (G + I), Special Growth Fund (G), Tax-Free Bond (STMB), Tax-Free Money (MM)

Brandywine Fund
Freiss Associates, Inc.
3908 Kennett Pike
Greenville, Delaware 19807
(302) 656-6200
Brandywine Fund (G)

Bridges
8401 West Dodge Road
256 Durham Plaza
Omaha, Nebraska 68114
(402) 397-4700
Bridges Investment Fund (G + I)

Bruce & Co.
20 North Wacker Drive, Suite 1425
Chicago, Illinois 60606
(312) 236-9161
Bruce Fund (AG)

Bull & Bear Group
11 Hanover Square, 11th Floor
New York, New York 10005
(212) 785-0900, (212) 363-1100, (800) 847-4200
Bull & Bear Capital Growth Fund (G), Bull & Bear Equity Income Fund (G), Bull & Bear Financial News Composite Fund (G), Bull & Bear Inc.: Bull & Bear Dollar Reserves (MM), Bull & Bear High Yield Fund (HYB), Bull & Bear

U.S. Government Guaranteed Securities Fund (USGI), Bull & Bear Municipal Securities: Bull & Bear Tax-Free Income Fund (LTMB), Bull & Bear Overseas Fund Ltd. (INT), Bull & Bear Special Equities Fund (AG), Golconda Investors (PMG)

Calamos Group
2001 Spring Road, Suite 750
Oak Brook, Illinois 60521
(312) 571-7115 (800) 323-9943

Calamos Convertible Income Fund (I), CFS Investment Trust: Kalliston Convertible Total Return Fund (G + I), Kalliston Preferred Plus Fund (IE)

California Investment Trust
44 Montgomery Street, Suite 2200
San Francisco, California 94104
(415) 398-2727, (800) 225-8778,
(800) 826-8166

California Investment I: California Tax-Free Income Fund (SMB-LT), California Tax-Free Money Market Fund (SMB-LT), California Investment Trust II: U.S. Government Securities Fund (USGI)

Calvert Group
1700 Pennsylvania Avenue, N.W.
Washington, D.C. 20006
(202) 951-4820, (800) 368-2748

Ariel Growth Fund (G), Calvert Fund: Equity Portfolio (G), Income Portfolio (IB), Limited Term Government Portfolio (USGI), U.S. Government Income Portfolio (USGI), Calvert Social Investment Fund: Bond Portfolio (CB), Equity Portfolio (G), Managed Growth Portfolio (FP), Money Market Portfolio (MM), Calvert Tax-Free Reserves: Limited-Term Portfolio (STMB), Long-Term Portfolio (LTMB), Money Market Portfolio (STMB), First Variable Rate Fund for Government Income (MM), Money Management Plus: Government Portfolio (MM), Prime Portfolio (MM), Tax Free Portfolio (STMB), Washington Area Growth Fund (G)

CAM Fund
P.O. Box 1987
Valley Forge, Pennsylvania 19481
(215) 783-6789, (800) 423-2345

Consolidated Asset Management Fund (MM)

Capiello/Colleague Multi-Asset Fund
Metropark
510 Thornall Street
Edison, New Jersey 08837-2212
(201) 494-1223

Capiello/Colleague Multi-Asset Fund (G + I)

Capital Research & Management
333 South Hope Street
Los Angeles, California 90071
(213) 486-9200, (800) 421-0180
and
Four Embarcadero Center
P.O. Box 7650
San Francisco, California 94120-7650
(415) 421-9360, (800) 421-0180
and
1101 Vermont Avenue, N.W.
Washington, D.C. 20005
(202) 842-5665

AMCAP Fund (G), American Balanced Fund (B), American Funds Income Series: U.S. Government Guaranteed Securities Fund (USGI), American High-Income Trust (HYB), American Life/Annuity Series: Cash Management Fund (MM), Growth Fund (G), Growth-Income Fund (G + I), High Yield Bond Fund (HYB), U.S. Government Guaranteed/AAA-Rated Securities Fund (USGI), American Mutual Fund (G + I), American Variable Insurance Series: Cash Management Series (MM), Growth Series (G), Growth Income Series (G + I), High Yield Bond Series (HYB), U.S. Government Guaranteed/AAA-Rated Securities Series (USGI), Bond Fund of America (IB), Bond Portfolio of Endowments (IB), Capital Income Builder (G + I), Capital World Bond Fund (GB), Cash Management Trust of America (MM), Endowments (G + I), EuroPacific Growth Fund (INT), Fundamental Investors (G + I), Growth Fund of America (G), Income Fund of America (I), Intermediate Bond Fund of America (CB), Investment Company of America (G + I), New Economy Fund (G), New Perspective Fund (GLB), New World Investment Fund (INT), Tax-Exempt Bond Fund of America (LTMB), Tax-Exempt Fund of California (SMB-LT), Tax-Exempt Fund of Maryland (SMB-LT), Tax-Exempt Fund of Virginia (SMB-LT), Washington Mutual Investors Fund (G + I)

Capital Supervisors, Inc.
20 North Clark Street, Suite 700
Chicago, Illinois 60602
(312) 236-8271

Capital Supervisors Helios Fund (G)

Capstone Group
1100 Milan Street, Suite 3500
P.O. Box 3167
Houston, Texas 77253-3167
(713) 750-8000, (800) 262-6631

Capstone Equity Series: Capstone EquityGuard Stock Fund (G), Cashman Farrell Value Fund (G + I), Fund of the Southwest (AG), Investors

Cash Reserve Fund (MM), Investors Income Fund (IB), Investors International Series Trust European Fund (INT), Medical Research Investment Fund (G), PBHG Growth Fund (AG), U.S. Trend Fund (AG)

Cardinal
155 East Broad Street
Columbus, Ohio 43215
(614) 464-7041, (614) 464-5511,
(800) 848-7734
Cardinal Fund (G), Cardinal Government Guaranteed Fund (USGI), Cardinal Government Securities Trust (MM), Cardinal Tax Exempt Money Trust (STMB)

Carillon Investments
1876 Waycross Road
P.O. Box 5304
Cincinnati, Ohio 45201
(513) 595-2600
Carillon Cash Reserves (MM), Carillon Fund: Bond Portfolio (CB), Equity Portfolio (G + I), Money Market Portfolio (MM), Carillon Capital Fund (FP)

Carlisle-Asher Management Co.
122 Willowbrook Lane
West Chester, Pennsylvania 19382
(215) 344-7910, Z (800) 523-7594
Afuture Fund (G)

Carnegie Capital Management, Inc.
1100 Halle Building
1288 Euclid Avenue
Cleveland, Ohio 44115-1831
(216) 781-4440, (800) 321-2322
Carnegie Government Securities Trust: Carnegie High Yield Government Series (USGI), Carnegie Intermediate Government Series (USGI), Carnegie Long Government Series (USGI), Carnegie Short Government Series (USGI), Carnegie Tax Exempt Income Trust: Georgia Insured Fund (SMB-LT), Minnesota Insured Fund (SMB-LT), National High-Yield Fund (LTMB), National Insured Fund (LTMB), Ohio Insured Fund (SMB-LT), Short-Term Fund (STMB), Short-Term Fund (STMB), Carnegie Tax Free Income Trust (STMB), Carnegie-Cappiello Trust: Growth Series (G), Total Return Series (G + I), Liquid Capital Income Trust (MM)

Century Shares Trust
One Liberty Square
Boston, Massachusetts 02109
(617) 482-3060, (800) 321-1928
Century Shares Trust (G + I)

Chartwell Capital Corp.
5299 DTC Boulevard, Suite 260
Englewood, Colorado 80111
(303) 694-1700
Chartwell Capital Fund (G)

Chase Manhattan Bank
P.O. Box 419261
Kansas City, Missouri 64179
800-64-VISTA
Vista Capital Growth (G), Vista Growth & Income (G + I), Vista NY Tax Free Income (SMB-LT), Vista New York Tax Free Money Market (SMB-ST), Vista Tax Free Income (STMB), Vista Tax Free Money Market (MM), Vista U.S. Government Income (USGI), Vista U.S. Government Money Market (MM)

Chile Fund
One Citicorp Center, 58th Floor
153 East 53rd Street
New York, New York 10022
(212) 832-2626
Chile Fund (INT)

Christos Fund
975 Oak Street, Suite 625
Eugene, Oregon 97401
(503) 686-2744, (800) 999-3303
Christos Trust: Christos Fund (FP)

Chubb Securities
One Granite Place
Concord, New Hampshire 03301
(603) 224-7741
Chubb Investment Funds: Chubb Government Securities Fund (GNMA), Chubb Growth Fund (G), Chubb Money Market Fund (MM), Chubb Tax-Exempt Fund (LTMB), Chubb Total Return Fund (G + I)

CIGNA
1350 Main Street
Springfield, Massachusetts 01103
(413) 781-7776, (800) 56CIGNA
and
Hartford, Connecticut 06152
(203) 726-6000, (800) 562-4462
CIGNA Aggressive Growth Fund (AG), CIGNA Annuity Fund: Aggressive Equity Fund (AG), Equity Fund (G), Growth and Income Fund (G + I), Income Fund (I), Money Market Fund (MM), CIGNA Cash Funds: CIGNA Cash Fund (MM), CIGNA Tax-Exempt Cash Fund (STMB), CIGNA Government Securities Fund (USGI), CIGNA Growth Fund (G), CIGNA High Yield Fund (HYB), CIGNA Income Fund (IB), CIGNA

Money Market Fund (MM), CIGNA Municipal Bond Fund (LTMB), CIGNA Utilities Fund (IE), CIGNA Value Fund (G + I), CIGNA Variable Products Group: Companion Fund (G)

Citibank
153 East 53rd Street
New York, New York 10043
(212) 559-9416, (800) CITI-IRA

Collective Investment Trust for Citibank IRAs: Balanced Portfolio (G + I), Equity Portfolio (G), Income Portfolio (G), Short Term Portfolio (MM)

Clemenson Capital Management Group
West 421 Riverside
Spokane, Washington 99201
(509) 747-7520, (800) 331-4603 (I.D.)

Northwest Investors Tax-Exempt Business Trust: Idaho Extended Maturity Tax-Exempt Fund (SMB-LT), Idaho Limited Maturity Tax-Exempt Fund (SMB-LT)

Clipper Fund
9601 Wilshire Boulevard, Suite 828
Beverly Hills, California 90201
(213) 278-4461

Clipper Fund (G)

CMC
1300 S.W. Sixth Street
P.O. Box 1350
Portland, Oregon 97207-1350
(503) 222-3600

CMC Small Cap Fund (AG)

College Prepayment Fund, Inc.
4807 Bethesda Avenue, Suite 193
Bethesda, Maryland 20814
(800) 288-6866

College Prepayment Fund (B)

Colonial Management Associates
One Financial Center
Boston, Massachusetts 02111
(617) 426-3750, (800) 225-2365

Colonial Advanced Strategies Gold Trust (PMG), Colonial California Tax-Exempt Trust (SMB-LT), Colonial Corporate Cash Trust I (I), Colonial Corporate Cash Trust II (I), Colonial Fund (G), Colonial Equity Index Portfolios: Colonial International Equity Index Trust (INT), Colonial Small Stock Index Trust (G + I), Colonial United States Equity Index Trust (G + I), Colonial Fund (G + I), Colonial Government Money Market Trust (MM), Colonial Govern-

ment Securities Plus Trust (USGI), Colonial Growth Shares Trust (G), Colonial High Yield Securities Trust (HYB), Colonial Income Trust (I), Colonial Massachusetts Tax-Exempt Trust (SMB-LT), Colonial Michigan Tax-Exempt Trust (SMB-LT), Colonial Minnesota Tax-Exempt Trust (SMB-LT), Colonial New York Tax-Exempt Trust (SMB-LT), Colonial Ohio Tax-Exempt Trust (SMB-LT), Colonial Investment Grade Municipal Trust (LTMB), Colonial Strategic Income Trust: Portfolio I (OI), Portfolio II (OI), Colonial Tax-Exempt Money Market Trust (STMB), Colonial Tax-Exempt Trust: Colonial Tax-Exempt High Yield Fund (LTMB), Colonial U.S. Government Trust (USGI), Colonial Value Investing Portfolios-Equity Portfolio: Aggressive Growth Fund (AG), Diversified Return Fund (GLB), Inflation Hedge Fund (G + I), Colonial Value Investing Portfolios - Income Portfolio: Federal Securities Fund (USGI), High Income Fund (HYB), High Yield Municipal Bond Fund (LTMB), Money Market (MM), Colonial/Hancock Liberty Trust: Colonial/Hancock Liberty Agressive Growth Fund (AG), Colonial/Hancock Liberty Aggressive Income Fund (HYB), Colonial/Hancock Liberty Asset Allocation Fund (FP), Colonial Hancock Liberty Growth and Income Fund (G + I), Colonial/Hancock Liberty Inflation Hedge Fund (G + I), Colonial Hancock Liberty Investment Grade Income Fund (USGI), Colonial/Hancock Liberty Money Market Fund (MM), Colonial Intermarket Income Trust I

Colorado Funds
717 17th Street, Suite 2700
Denver, Colorado 80202
(303) 292-0300

Colorado Double Tax-Exempt Fund (SMB-LT)

Columbia
1301 S.W. 5th Avenue
P.O. Box 1350
Portland, Oregon 97207
(503) 222-3600, (800) 547-1037

Columbia Daily Income Company (MM), Columbia Fixed Income Securities Fund (IB), Columbia Growth Fund (G), Columbia Municipal Bond Fund (SMB-LT), Columbia Special Fund (AG), Columbia U.S. Government Guaranteed Securities Fund (USGI)

Commonwealth Group
1500 Forest Avenue, Suite 223
P.O. Box 8687
Richmond, Virginia 23226
(804) 285-8211, (800) 527-9500

Commonwealth Group: Bowser Growth Fund

(G), Newport Far East Fund (INT), Newport Global Growth Fund (GLB)

Community Assets Management, Inc.
50 South Steele Street, Suite 660
Denver, Colorado 80209-2807
(303) 399-9300

Community Bankers Mutual Fund (USGI)

Composite
West 601 Riverside, 9th Floor
Seafirst Financial Center
Spokane, Washington 99201
(509) 624-4118, (800) 544-6093

Composite Bond & Stock Fund (B), Composite Cash Management Company: Money Market Portfolio (MM), Tax-Exempt Money Market Portfolio (STMB), Composite Deferred Series Inc.: Growth Portfolio (G), Income Portfolio (CB), Money Market (MM), Composite Growth Fund (G + I), Composite Income Fund (I), Composite Select Fund: High Yield Portfolio (HYB), Northwest Portfolio (G + I), Value Portfolio (G), Composite Tax-Exempt Bond Fund (LTMB), Composite U.S. Government Securities (GNMA)

Concord Financial
156 West 56th Street, 19th Floor
New York, New York 10019
(212) 492-1600, (212) 422-6644,
(800) 367-6075, (800) 332-3863

Horizon Funds: Horizon Intermediate Government Fund (USGI), Horizon Intermediate Tax-Exempt Fund (LTMB), Horizon Prime Fund (MM), Horizon Tax-Exempt Money Fund (STMB), Horizon Treasury Fund (MM), Pacific Horizon California Tax-Exempt Bond Portfolio (SMB-LT), Pacific Horizon Funds: Aggressive Growth Portfolio (AG), Convertible Securities Fund (G + I), GNMA Extra Fund (GNMA), Government Money Market Portfolio (MM), High Yield Bond Portfolio (HYB), Money Market Portfolio (MM), Pacific Horizon Tax-Exempt Money Market Portfolios (STMB)

Connecticut Mutual
140 Garden Street
Hartford, Connecticut 06154
(203) 727-6500, (800) 243-0018

Connecticut Mutual Financial Services Series Fund I: Growth Portfolio (G), Income Portfolio (IB), Money Market Portfolio (MM), Total Return Portfolio (G), Connecticut Mutual Investment Accounts: Connecticut Mutual Government Securities Account (USGI), Connecticut Mutual Growth Account (G), Connecticut Mutual Income Account (I), Connecticut Mu-

tual Liquid Account (MM), Connecticut Mutual Total Return Account (G + I)

Continental Equities
180 Maiden Lane
New York, New York 10038
(212) 440-3863, (800) 626-3863

Continental Equity Plus Fund (G + I), Continental Money Market (MM), Continental Option Income Plus Fund (OI), Continental Tax-Exempt Fund (STMB), Continental U.S. Government Plus Fund (USGI)

Continental Heritage
535 16th Street, Suite 900
Denver, Colorado 80202
(303) 595-3333, (800) 345-4561

Continental Heritage Mutual Fund Trust: Continental Heritage California Municipal Series (SMB-LT), Continental Heritage Government Income Series (GNMA), Continental Heritage Tax Free Income Series (LTMB)

Copley Financial Services Corporation
315 Pleasant Street, P.O. Box 3287
Fall River, Massachusetts 02722
(508) 674-8459

Copley Fund (G + I)

Counsellors Funds
466 Lexington Avenue
New York, New York 10017-3147
(212) 878-0600, (800) 888-6878

Counsellors Capital Appreciation Fund (G), Counsellors Cash Reserve Fund (MM), Counsellors Emerging Growth Fund (AG), Counsellors Fixed Income Fund (IB), Counsellors Intermediate Maturity Government Fund (USGI), Counsellors International Equity Fund (INT), Counsellors New York Municipal Bond Fund (SMB-LT), Counsellors New York Tax Exempt Fund (SMB-LT)

Country Capital
1701 Towanda Avenue
Bloomington, Illinois 61701
(309) 557-2444

Country Capital Growth Fund (G), Country Capital Income Fund (I), Country Capital Money Market Fund (MM), Country Capital Tax-Exempt Bond Fund (LTMB)

Craig-Hallum, Inc.
701 4th Avenue South, Suite 1000
Minneapolis, Minnesota 55415-1655
(612) 332-1212, (800) 331-4923

General Securities (G)

Criterion Group
1000 Louisiana, Suite 6000
Houston, Texas 77002
(713) 751-2400, (800) 999-3863,
(800) 231-4645
Criterion Bond Fund: Criterion Limited Term Institutional Trust (USGI), Criterion U.S. Government Institutional Trust (USGI), Investment Quality Interest Portfolio (IB), U.S. Government High Yield Trust (USGI), Criterion Income Trust: Commerce Income Shares (I), Criterion Special Equity Portfolios: Lowry Market Timing Fund (AG), Criterion Special Series: Criterion Special Blue Chip Fund (G), Criterion Special Convertible Securities Fund (G + I), Criterion Special Emerging Growth Fund (AG), Criterion Special Global Growth Fund (GLB), Criterion Special Government Income Fund (USGI), Criterion Special High Yield Bond Fund (HYB), Criterion Special High Yield Tax Free Fund (LTMB), Criterion Special Money Market (MM), Criterion Special Natural Resources Fund (G), Criterion Technology Fund (AG), Current Interest: Money Market Portfolio (MM), Premium Cash Reserves (MM), U.S. Government Portfolio (MM), Pilot Fund (AG), Sunbelt Growth Fund (G), Insured Quality Tax Free Bond Portfolio (LTMB)

Crossland Trust
211 Montague Street
Brooklyn, New York 11201
(718) 780-0543
Crossland Equity Income Fund (G), Crossland New York Tax-Free Bond Fund (SMB-ST), Crossland Taxable Bond Fund (IB), Crossland Tax-Free Bond Fund (USGI), Crossland Tax-Free Money Fund (STMB)

Cross-Market
2600 Virginia Avenue, N.W., Suite 701
Washington, D.C. 20037
(202) 333-1864, (800) 346-2521
Cross-Market Opportunity Fund (GLB)

Cumberland Advisors
614 Landis Avenue
Vineland, New Jersey 08360
(800) 257-7013, (800) 232-6692 (NJ),
(609) 692-6690
Cumberland Growth Fund (G)

Currency Funds, Inc.
61 Broadway
New York, New York 10006
(212) 363-3300
Currency Funds: British Pound Sterling Portfolio (INT), Japanese Yen Portfolio (INT), U.S. Dollar Portfolio (MM)

Dayton Kahn Heppe Hancock
Architect's Building, Suite 1905
Philadelphia, Pennsylvania 19103
(215) 988-0277
Gibraltar Fund (G)

Dean Witter
One World Trade Center, 59th Floor
New York, New York 10048
(212) 938-4554, (800) 221-2685
Active Assets Government Securities Trust (MM), Active Assets Money Trust (MM), Active Assets Tax-Free Trust (STMB), Dean Witter American Value Fund (G), Dean Witter California Tax-Free Income Fund (SMB-LT), Dean Witter Convertible Securities Trust (G + I), Dean Witter Developing Growth Securities Trust (AG), Dean Witter Dividend Growth Securities (G + I), Dean Witter Government Securities Plus (USGI), Dean Witter High Yield Securities (HYB), Dean Witter Managed Assets Trust (FP), Dean Witter Natural Resource Development Securities (G), Dean Witter New York Tax-Free Income Fund (SMB-LT), Dean Witter Option Income Trust (OI), Dean Witter Strategist Fund (G + I), Dean Witter Tax-Advantaged Corporate Trust (I), Dean Witter Tax-Exempt Securities Trust (LTMB), Dean Witter U.S. Government Securities Trust (USGI), Dean Witter Utilities Fund (G + I), Dean Witter Value-Added Market Series: Equity Portfolio (G + I), Dean Witter Variable Investment Series: Equity Portfolio (G), High Yield Portfolio (HYB), Managed Assets Portfolio (FP), Money Market Portfolio (MM), Quality Income Plus Portfolio (IB), Dean Witter World Wide Investment Trust (GLB), Dean Witter/Sears California Tax-Free Daily Income Trust (SMB-ST), Dean Witter/Sears Liquid Asset Fund (MM), Dean Witter/Sears Tax-Free Daily Income Trust (STMB), Dean Witter/Sears U.S. Government Money Market Trust (MM), Sears Tax-Exempt Reinvestment Fund (LTMB)

Delaware Group
One Commerce Square, 10 Penn Center Plaza
Philadelphia, Pennsylvania 19103
(215) 988-1200, (215) 988-1333,
(800) 523-4640
Delaware Group Cash Reserve (MM), Delaware Group Decatur Fund: Decatur I Series (IE), Decatur II Series (IE), Delaware Group Delaware Fund (B), Delaware Group DelCap

Fund: Concept I Series (G), Delaware Group Delchester High-Yield Bond Fund: Delchester I (HYB), Delchester II (HYB), Delaware Group Government Fund: Government Income Series (GNMA), Delaware Group Tax-Free Fund: USA Insured Series (LTMB), USA Series (LTMB), Delaware Group Tax-Free Money Fund (STMB), Delaware Group Treasury Reserves: Cashiers Series (MM), Investors Series (USGI), Delaware Group Trend Fund (AG), Delaware Group Value Fund (AG), DMC Tax-Free Income Trust - PA (SMB-LT)

Dillon, Read Capital, Inc.
535 Madison Avenue, 36th Floor
New York, New York 10022
(212) 906-7658, (800) 522-8895,
(800) 227-1597, (800) 356-6454
DR Balanced Fund (B), DR Equity Fund (G + I)

Dividend/Growth Fund
107 North Adams Street
Rockville, Maryland 20850
(301) 251-1002, (800) 638-2042

Dividend/Growth Fund: Dividend Shares (G + I), Laser & Advanced Technology Series (G)

Dodge & Cox
One Post Street, 35th Floor
San Francisco, California 94104
(415) 981-1710

Dodge & Cox Balanced Fund (B), Dodge & Cox Income Fund (I), Dodge & Cox Stock Fund (G + I)

Dollar Dry Dock
50 Main Street
White Plains, New York 10606
(914) 397-2168, (800) 541-0830
Investors Preference Fund for Income (GNMA)

Domini & Co.
6 St. James Avenue
Boston, Massachusetts 02116
(617) 432-1679
Domini Social Index Fund (G)

Dreman Mutual Group
30 Montgomery Street
Jersey City, New Jersey 07302
(201) 332-8228, (800) 533-1608
Dreman Mutual Group: Dreman Bond Portfolio (IB), Dreman Contrarian Portfolio (G), Dreman High Return Portfolio (G + I)

Drexel Burnham Lambert
60 Broad Street
New York, New York 10004
(212) 232-5000, (800) 272-2700
DBL Cash Fund: Government Securities Portfolio (MM), Money Market Portfolio (MM), DBL Tax-Free Fund: Limited Term Portfolio (LTMB), Long Term Series (LTMB), Money Market Portfolio (STMB), Drexel Burnham Fund (G + I), Drexel Series Trust: Bond-Debenture Series (IB), Convertible Securities Series (G + I), Emerging Growth Series (AG), Government Securities Series (USGI), Growth Series (G), Limited Term Government Series (USGI), Money Market Series (MM), Option Income Series (OI), Priority Selection Series (G), Fenimore International Fund; Equity Series (INT), Fixed Income Series (GB)

Dreyfus
One World Financial Centre
200 Liberty Avenue
New York, New York 10281
(212) 945-0100
and
666 Old Country Road
Garden City, New York 11530
(718) 895-1206, (516) 794-5210,
(800) 645-6561, (800) 821-1185,
(800) 346-3621, (800) 242-8671
and
767 Fifth Avenue
New York, New York 10153
(718) 895-1347, (800) 648-9048,
(800) 451-6200
Daiwa Money Fund (MM), Dreyfus A Bonds Plus (CB), Dreyfus California Tax Exempt Bond Fund (SMB-LT), Dreyfus California Tax Exempt Money Market Fund (SMB-ST), Dreyfus Capital Value Fund (G + I), Dreyfus Cash Management (MM), Dreyfus Cash Management Plus (MM), Dreyfus Convertible Securities Fund (I), Dreyfus Dollar International Fund (MM), Dreyfus Foreign Investors GNMA Fund (GNMA), Dreyfus Foreign Investors U.S. Government Bond Fund, L.P. (USGI), Dreyfus Fund Incorporated (G + I), Dreyfus GNMA Fund (GNMA), Dreyfus Government Cash Management (MM), Dreyfus Growth Opportunity Fund (G), Dreyfus Institutional Money Market Fund: Government Series (MM), Money Market Series (MM), Dreyfus Insured Tax Exempt Bond Fund (LTMB), Dreyfus Intermediate Tax Exempt Bond Fund (LTMB), Dreyfus Leverage Fund (AG), Dreyfus Liquid Assets (MM), Dreyfus Massachusetts Tax Exempt Bond Fund (SMB-LT), Dreyfus Money Market Instruments: Government Securities Series (MM), Money

Market Series (MM), Dreyfus New Jersey Tax Exempt Bond Fund (SMB-LT), Dreyfus New Jersey Tax Exempt Money Market Fund (SMB-ST), Dreyfus New Leaders Fund (G), Dreyfus New York Insured Tax Exempt Bond Fund (SMB-LT), Dreyfus New York Tax Exempt Bond Fund (SMB-LT), Dreyfus New York Tax Exempt Intermediate Bond Fund (SMB-LT), Dreyfus New York Tax Exempt Money Market Fund (SMB-ST), Dreyfus Short-Intermediate Government Fund (USGI), Dreyfus Short-Intermediate Tax Exempt Bond Fund (LTMB), Dreyfus Strategic Aggressive Investing, L.P. (AG), Dreyfus Strategic Income (I), Dreyfus Strategic Investing (AG), Dreyfus Strategic World Investing L.P. (GLB), Dreyfus Strategic World Revenues, L.P. (GB), Dreyfus Tax Exempt Bond Fund (LTMB), Dreyfus Tax Exempt Cash Management (STMB), Dreyfus Tax Exempt Money Market Fund (STMB), Dreyfus Third Century Fund (G), Dreyfus Treasury Cash Management (MM), Dreyfus U.S. Government Bond Fund, L.P. (USGI), Dreyfus U.S. Government Intermediate Securities, L.P. (USGI), Dreyfus U.S. Guaranteed Money Market Account, L.P. (MM), Dreyfus Worldwide Dollar Money Market Fund (MM), First Lakeshore Diversified Asset Fund (I), First Lakeshore Money Market Fund: Government Series (MM), Money Market Series (MM), First Lakeshore Tax Exempt Bond Fund: Intermediate Series (LTMB), Long-Term Series (LTMB), First Lakeshore Tax Exempt Money Market Fund (STMB), FN Network Tax Free Money Market Fund (STMB), General Aggressive Growth Fund (AG), General California Tax Exempt Money Market Fund (SMB-ST), General Government Securities Money Market Fund (MM), General Money Market Fund (MM), General New York Tax Exempt Intermediate Bond Fund (SMB-LT), General New York Tax Exempt Money Market Fund (SMB-ST), General Tax Exempt Bond Fund (LTMB), General Tax Exempt Money Market Fund (STMB), McDonald Money Market Fund (MM), McDonald Tax Exempt Money Market Fund (STMB), Premier California Tax Exempt Bond Fund (SMB-LT), Premier GNMA Fund (GNMA), Premier Income Fund (LTMB), Premier New York Tax Exempt Bond Fund (SMB-LT), Premier State Tax Exempt Bond Fund: Connecticut Series (SMB-LT), Florida Series (SMB-LT), Maryland Series (SMB-LT), Massachusetts Series (SMB-LT), Michigan Series (SMB-LT), Minnesota Series (SMB-LT), Ohio Series (SMB-LT), Pennsylvania Series (SMB-LT), Texas Series (SMB-LT), Premier Tax Exempt Bond Fund (LTMB)

Eaton Vance
24 Federal Street
Boston, Massachusetts 02110
(617) 482-8260, (800) 225-6265

Capital Exchange Fund (G + I), Depositors Fund of Boston (G + I), Diversification Fund (G + I), Eaton & Howard Stock Fund (G + I), Eaton Vance Cash Management Fund (MM), Eaton Vance Corporate High Income Dollar Fund, L.P. (HYB), Eaton Vance Government Obligations Trust (USGI), Eaton Vance Growth Fund (G), Eaton Vance High Yield Fund (I), Eaton Vance Income Fund of Boston (I), Eaton Vance Investors Fund (B), Eaton Vance Marathon Group: Eaton Vance California Municipals Trust (SMB-LT), Eaton Vance Equity-Income Trust (G + I), Eaton Vance High Income Trust (HYB), Eaton Vance High Yield Municipals Trust (LTMB), Eaton Vance Liquid Assets Trust (MM), Eaton Vance Natural Resources Trust (G), Eaton Vance Municipal Bond Fund (LTMB), Eaton Vance Prime Rate Reserves (MM), Eaton Vance Special Equities Fund (G), Eaton Vance Tax Free Reserves (STMB), Eaton Vance Total Return Trust (G + I), Eaton Vance U.S. Government Income Dollar Fund, L.P. (USGI), Exchange Fund of Boston (G + I), Fiduciary Exchange Fund (G + I), Leverage Fund of Boston (AG), Nautilus Fund (AG), Second Fiduciary Exchange Fund (G + I), Vance Sanders Exchange Fund (G + I), Vance Sanders Special Fund (G), Wright Managed Bond Trust: Wright Current Income Fund (IB), Wright Government Obligations Fund (USGI), Wright Near Term Bond Fund (IB), Wright Tax Free Bond Fund (LTMB), Wright Total Return Bond Fund (CB), Wright Managed Equity Trust: Wright Junior Blue Chip Equities Fund (G + I), Wright Quality Core Equities Fund (G + I), Wright Selected Blue Chip Equities Fund (G + I), Wright Managed Money Market Trust (MM)

EBI Funds. see INVESCO Capital Management

Eclipse Equity
Towneley Capital Management, Inc.
144 East 30th Street
New York, New York 10016
(800) 872-2710, (212) 696-4130
Eclipse Equity Fund (G + I)

Edgemont Asset Management Corp.
17 Battery Place, Suite 2624
New York, New York 10004
(212) 344-3337
The Kaufmann Fund (AG)

Elite Group
1206 IBM Building
Seattle, Washington 98101
(206) 624-5863, (800) 654-5261

Elite Group: Elite Growth & Income Fund (G + I), Elite Income Fund (IB)

Emerald Advisers, Inc.
312 Plum Street, Suite 900
Cincinnati, Ohio 45202
(513) 721-7227

Emerald Funds: Emerald Aggressive Growth (AG), Emerald Disciplined Asset Allocation (FP), Emerald Growth & Income (G + I), Emerald High Yield (HYB), Emerald International ADR (INT), Emerald Market Plus (G), Emerald Money Market (MM), Emerald Quality Income (I)

Empire of America
320 Empire Tower
Buffalo, New York 14202
(716) 855-7891

Big E Pathfinder Family of Mutual Funds: Big E Pathfinder Government Plus Fund (USGI), Big E Pathfinder New York Tax-Free Income Fund (SMB-LT), Big E Pathfinder Tax-Free Income Fund (LTMB), Big E Pathfinder Total Return Fund (G + I)

Endeavor Series Trust
1101 Bayside Drive, Suite 100
Corona del Mar, California 92625
(714) 760-0505

Endeavor Series Trust Funds: Domestic Managed Asset Allocation Portfolio (FP), Domestic Money Market Portfolio (MM), Finite Time Portfolio (IB), Global Growth Portfolio (GLB), Global Managed Asset Allocation Portfolio (GLB)

Enterprise Group of Funds
250 Piedmont Avenue, N.E., Suite 102
Atlanta, Georgia 30365
(404) 521-6545, (800) 443-3521

Enterprise Equity Portfolios: Enterprise Aggressive Growth Portfolio (AG), Enterprise Growth and Income Portfolio (IE), Enterprise Growth Portfolio (G), Enterprise International Growth Portfolio (INT), Enterprise Income Portfolios: Enterprise Corporate Bond Portfolio (CB), Enterprise GNMA Portfolio (GNMA), Enterprise Government Securities Portfolio (USGI), Enterprise High-Yield Bond Portfolio (HYB), Enterprise Tax-Exempt Income Portfolio (SMB-LT), Enterprise Specialty Portfolios: Enterprise Precious Metals Portfolio (PMG)

Engemann Management Co.
600 North Rosemead Boulevard
Pasadena, California 91107
(818) 351-4276, (800) 882-2855

Pasadena Fortress Fund (G), Pasadena Growth Fund (G)

Equitable Capital Management
1285 Avenue of the Americas
New York, New York 10019
(212) 641-8100

Equitable Funds: Equitable Balanced Fund (G + I), Equitable Capital High Yield Plus Fund (HYB), Equitable Government Securities Fund (USGI), Equitable Growth Fund (G), Equitable Tax Exempt Fund (LTMB)

EquitiLink International Management
One Seaport Plaza
New York, New York 10292
(212) 214-1215

First Australia Prime Income Fund (INT)

Evaluation Associates
200 Connecticut Avenue, 8th Floor
Norwalk, Connecticut 06854
(203) 855-2200

Management of Managers Group of Funds: Capital Appreciation Fund (IE), Core Equity Fund (G), Fixed Income Securities Fund (I), Income Equity Fund (IE), Intermediate Mortgage Securities Fund (GNMA), International Equity Fund (INT), Money Market Fund (MM), Municipal Bond Fund (LTMB), Precious Metals Fund (PMG), Short and Intermediate Fixed Income Securities Fund (IB), Short Term Fixed Income Securities Fund (I), Short Term Municipal Bond Fund (STMB), Special Equity Fund (G)

Evergreen Funds. see Saxton Woods Asset Management Corp.

Fairmont
Morton H. Sachs & Co.
1346 Third Street
Louisville, Kentucky 40208
(502) 636-5633

Fairmont Fund (AG)

Farm Bureau
5400 University Avenue
West Des Moines, Iowa 50265
(515) 225-5400, (800) 247-4170

FBL Institutional Fund: Ginnie Mae Portfolio (GNMA), Growth Common Stock Portfolio (G), High Grade Bond Portfolio (IB), FBL Money

Market Fund (MM), FBL Series Fund: Aggressive Growth Common Stock Portfolio (AG), Blue Chip Portfolio (G), Ginnie Mae Portfolio (GNMA), Growth Common Stock Portfolio (G + I), High Quality Bond Portfolio (IB), High Yield Bond Portfolio (HYB), Managed Portfolio (FP), Money Market Portfolio (MM)

Fasciano Company
135 S. LaSalle Street, Suite 1209
Chicago, Illinois 60603
(312) 782-6232
Fasciano Fund (G)

Federated
Federated Investors Tower
Pittsburgh, Pennsylvania 15222-3779
(412) 288-1900, (412) 288-1948,
(800) 245-4770, (800) 245-3391,
(800) 245-5000, (800) 245-5051,
(800) 245-0242, (800) 245-4770

A.T. Ohio Tax-Free Money Fund (SMB-ST), Aetna Series Trust: Aetna High Income Securities Fund (HYB), Aetna High Quality Stock Fund (G + I), Aetna Municipal Bond Fund (LTMB), Aetna U.S. Government Bond Fund (USGI), American Leaders Fund (G + I), Automated Cash Management Trust (MM), Automated Government Money Trust (MM), Convertible Securities and Income (G + I), Edward D. Jones & Co. Daily Passport Cash Trust (MM), EGT Money Market Trust (MM), Federated Bond Fund (IB), Federated Corporate Cash Trust (I), Federated Floating Rate Trust (CB), Federated GNMA Trust (GNMA), Federated Growth Trust (AG), Federated High Income Securities (HYB), Federated High Quality Stock Fund (G + I), Federated High Yield Trust (HYB), Federated Income Trust (USGI), Federated Intermediate Government Trust (USGI), Federated Intermediate Municipal Trust (LTMB), Federated Master Trust (MM), Federated Short-Intermediate Government Trust (USGI), Federated Short-Intermediate Municipal Trust (LTMB), Federated Short-Term U.S. Government Trust (MM), Federated Stock and Bond Fund (B), Federated Stock Trust (G + I), Federated Tax-Free Income Fund (LTMB), Federated Tax-Free Trust (STMB), Federated U.S. Government Fund (USGI), Federated Utility Trust (IE), Federated Variable Rate Mortgage Securities Trust (GNMA), Fort Washington Money Market Fund (MM), Fortress High Yield Municipal Fund (LTMB), Fortress Total Performance U.S. Treasury Fund (USGI), FT International Trust (INT), Fund for U.S. Government Securities (USGI), Government Income Securities (USGI), High Yield Cash Trust (MM), Liberty U.S. Government Money Mar-

ket Trust (MM), Liquid Cash Trust (MM), Money Market Management (MM), Money Market Trust (MM), New York Municipal Cash Trust (SMB-ST), Progressive Income Equity Fund (IE), Tax Free Instruments Trust (STMB), Trust for Short-Term U.S. Government Securities (MM), Trust for U.S. Treasury Obligations (MM), Value Plus U.S. Treasury Obligations Fund (USGI)

Fenimore
Box 399
Cobleskill, New York 12043
(518) 234-7543
Fenimore Asset Management Trust: FAM Value Fund (G + I)

Fidelity Investments
82 Devonshire St.
Boston, Massachusetts 02109
(617) 570-7000, (617) 523-1919,
(800) 544-666, (800) 343-9184,
(800) 723-6181, (800) 522-7297,
(800) 343-5409

Daily Money Fund: Money Market Portfolio (MM), U.S. Treasury Portfolio (MM), Daily Tax-Exempt Money Fund (STMB), Equity Portfolio-Growth (AG), Equity Portfolio-Income (IE), Fidelity California Tax Free Fund: High Yield Porfolio (SMB-LT), Insured Portfolio (SMB-LT), Money Market Portfolio (SMB-ST), Fidelity Capital Trust: Fidelity Capital Appreciation Fund (AG), Fidelity Value Fund (G), Fidelity Cash Reserves (MM), Fidelity Charles Street Trust: Fidelity U.S. Government Reserves (MM), Fidelity Congress Street Fund (G + I), Fidelity Contrafund (G), Fidelity Corporate Trust: Fidelity Adjustable Rate Preferred Portfolio (I), Fidelity Court Street Trust: Fidelity Connecticut Tax-Free Portfolio (SMB-LT), Fidelity High Yield Municipals (LTMB), Fidelity New Jersey Tax-Free High Yield Portfolio (SMB-LT), Fidelity New Jersey Tax-Free Money Market Portfolio (SMB-ST), Fidelity Daily Income Trust (MM), Fidelity Destiny Portfolios: Destiny I (G), Destiny II (G), Fidelity Devonshire Trust: Fidelity Equity-Income Fund (IE), Fidelity Real Estate Investment Portfolio (G + I), Fidelity Utilities Income Fund (IE), Fidelity Exchange Fund (G + I), Fidelity Financial Trust: Fidelity Convertible Securities Fund (G + I), Fidelity Freedom Fund (AG), Fidelity Fixed-Income Trust: Fidelity Flexible Bond Portfolio (CB), Fidelity Short-Term Bond Portfolio (CB), Fidelity Fund (G + I), Fidelity Government Securities Fund (USGI), Fidelity Growth Company Fund (AG), Fidelity High Income Fund (HYB), Fidelity Income Fund: Fidelity Ginnie Mae Portfolio (GNMA), Fidelity Mortgage Securities Portfolio (GNMA), Fidelity Short-Term Government Portfolio (USGI), Fidelity Institutional Cash Portfolios: Domestic Money Market Portfolio (MM), Money Market Portfolio (MM), U.S. Government Portfolio (MM), U.S. Treasury Portfolio I (MM), U.S. Treasury Portfolio II (MM), Fidelity Institutional Tax-Exempt Cash Portfolios (STMB), Fidelity Institutional Trust: Fidelity U.S. Bond Index Portfolio (IB), Fidelity U.S. Equity Index Portfolio (G + I), Fidelity Intermediate Bond Fund (CB), Fidelity Investment Trust: Fidelity Canada Fund (INT), Fidelity Europe Fund (INT), Fidelity Global Fund (GB), Fidelity International Growth & Income Fund (INT), Fidelity Overseas Fund (INT), Fidelity Pacific Basin Fund (INT), Fidelity Limited Term Municipals (LTMB), Fidelity Magellan Fund (AG), Fidelity Massachusetts Tax-Free Fund: High Yield Portfolio (SMB-LT), Money Market Portfolio (SMB-ST), Fidelity Money Market Trust: Domestic Money Market Portfolio (MM), U.S. Government Portfolio (MM), U.S. Treasury Portfolio (MM), Fidelity Municipal Trust: Fidelity Aggressive Tax-Free Portfolio (LTMB), Fidelity Insured Tax-Free Portfolio (LTMB), Fidelity Michigan Tax-Free Portfolio (SMB-LT), Fidelity Minnesota Tax-Free Portfolio (SMB-LT), Fidelity Municipal Bond Portfolio (LTMB), Fidelity Ohio Tax-Free Portfolio (SMB-LT), Fidelity Pennsylvania Tax-Free High Yield Portfolio (SMB-LT), Fidelity Pennsylvania Tax-Free Money Market Portfolio (SMB-ST), Fidelity Short-Term Tax-Free Portfolio (SMB-LT), Fidelity Texas Tax-Free Portfolio (SMB-LT), Fidelity New York Tax-Free Fund: High Yield Portfolio (SMB-LT), Insured Portfolio (SMB-LT), Fidelity Puritan Trust: Fidelity Balanced Fund (B), Fidelity Puritan Fund (IE), Fidelity Qualified Dividend Fund (I), Fidelity Securities Fund: Fidelity Blue Chip Portfolio (G), Fidelity Growth & Income Portfolio (G + I), Fidelity OTC Portfolio (AG), Fidelity Select Portfolios: Air Transportation Portfolio (AG), American Gold Portfolio (PMG), Automation and Machinery Portfolio (AG), Automotive Portfolio (AG), Biotechnology Portfolio (AG), Broadcast and Media Portfolio (AG), Brokerage and Investment Management Portfolio (AG), Capital Goods Portfolio (AG), Chemicals Portfolio (AG), Computers Portfolio (AG), Defense and Aerospace Portfolio (AG), Electric Utilities Portfolio (AG), Electronics Portfolio (AG), Energy Portfolio (AG), Energy Service Portfolio (AG), Financial Services Portfolio (AG), Food and Agriculture Portfolio (AG), Health Care Portfolio (AG), Housing Portfolio (AG), Industrial Materials Portfolio (AG), Leisure Portfolio (AG), Life Insurance Portfolio (AG), Medical Delivery Portfolio (AG), Money Market Portfolio (MM), Paper and Forest Prod-

ucts Portfolio (AG), Precious Metals and Minerals Portfolio (PMG), Property and Casualty Insurance Portfolio (AG), Regional Banks Portfolio (AG), Restaurant Industry Portfolio (AG), Retailing Portfolio (AG), Savings and Loan Portfolio (AG), Software and Computer Services Portfolio (AG), Technology Portfolio (AG), Telecommunications Portfolio (AG), Transportation Portfolio (AG), Utilities Portfolio (AG), Fidelity Special Situations Fund (AG), Fidelity Tax-Exempt Money Market Trust (STMB), Fidelity Trend Fund (G), Fidelity U.S. Treasury Money Market Fund (MM), Financial Reserves Fund (MM), Income Portfolios: Limited Term Series (IB), Short Fixed-Income Series (I), Short Government Series (USGI), Short-Intermediate Fixed-Income Series (I), State and Local Asset Management California Portfolio (MM), State and Local Asset Management Government Money Market Portfolio (MM), North Carolina Cash Management Trust: Cash Portfolio (MM), Term Portfolio (CB), Plymouth Fund: Plymouth Aggressive Income Portfolio (HYB), Plymouth Government Securities Portfolio (USGI), Plymouth Growth Opportunities Portfolio (G), Plymouth Income & Growth Portfolio (B), Plymouth Short-Term Bond Portfolio (IB), Plymouth Investment Series: Plymouth Global Natural Resources Portfolio (GLB), Plymouth High Income Municipal Portfolio (LTMB), Plymouth Securities Trust: Market Access Plus Bear Value Portfolio (I), Market Access Plus Bull Value Portfolio (I), Tax-Exempt Portfolios: Limited Term Series (LTMB), Short-Intermediate Term Series (STMB), Variable Insurance Products Fund: Equity Income Portfolio (IE), High Income Portfolio (HYB), Money Market Portfolio (MM), Overseas Portfolio (INT), Zero Coupon Bond Fund: 1993 Portfolio (USGI), 1998 Portfolio (USGI), 2003 Portfolio (USGI)

Fiduciary Management, Inc.
222 East Mason Street
Milwaukee, Wisconsin 53202
(414) 271-6666
Fiduciary Capital Growth (AG)

Financial Programs, Inc.
7800 East Union Avenue
Denver, Colorado 80237
(303) 779-1233, (800) 525-8085,
(800) 525-9769 in Colorado
Financial Daily Income Shares (MM), Financial Dynamics Fund (AG), Financial High Yield Portfolio (I), Financial Industrial Income (IE), Financial Industrial Fund (G + I), Financial Select Income Portfolio (I), Financial Strategic Portfolio-Energy (AG), Financial Strategic

Portfolio-European (INT), Financial Strategic Portfolio-Financial Services (G), Financial Strategic Portfolio-Gold (PMG), Financial Strategic Portfolio-Health Sciences (AG), Financial Strategic Portfolio-Leisure (AG), Financial Strategic Portfolio-Pacific Basin (INT), Financial Strategic Portfolio-Technology (AG), Financial Strategic Portfolio-Utilities (G + I), Financial Tax Free Income Shares (LTMB), Financial Tax-Free Money Fund (STMB), Financial U.S. Government Portfolio (USGI)

First Eagle Fund
45 Broadway
New York, New York 10006
(212) 943-9200, (800) 451-3623
First Eagle Fund of America (G)

First Investors Management Co.
120 Wall Street
New York, New York 10005
(212) 208-6000
Executive Investors Trust: Executive Investors High Yield Fund (HYB), First Investors Bond Appreciation Fund (HYB), First Investors Cash Management Fund (MM), First Investors Discovery Fund (AG), First Investors Fund: First Investors Blue Chip Fund (IE), First Investors Fund for Growth (AG), First Investors Fund for Income (HYB), First Investors Government Fund (USGI), First Investors High Yield Fund (HYB), First Investors International Securities Fund (GLB), First Investors Life Series Fund: Bond Appreciation Series (HYB), Cash Management Series (MM), Discovery Series (AG), Growth Series (G), High Yield Series (I), First Investors Multi-State Insured Tax Free Fund: California Series (SMB-LT), Massachusetts Series (SMB-LT), Michigan Series (SMB-LT), Minnesota Series (SMB-LT), New Jersey Series (SMB-LT), Ohio Series (SMB-LT), First Investors New York Tax Free Fund (SMB-LT), First Investors Qualified Dividend Fund (I), First Investors Special Bond Fund (HYB), First Investors Tax Exempt Fund (LTMB), First Investors Tax Exempt Money Market (STMB), First Investors U.S. Government Plus Fund 1st Series (USGI), First Investors U.S. Government Plus Fund 2nd Series (USGI), First Investors U.S. Government Plus Fund 3rd Series (USGI), First Investors Value Fund (G)

First Pacific Advisors
10301 West Pico Blvd
Los Angeles, California 90064
(213) 277-4900, (800) 421-4374
FPA Capital Fund (G), FPA New Income (IB),

FPA Paramount Fund (G + I), FPA Perennial Fund (G +. I)

First Pacific Management
1270 Queen Emma Street, Suite 607
Honolulu, Hawaii 96813
(808) 599-2400
First Pacific Mutual Fund: First Hawaii Municipal Bond Fund (SMB-LT)

First Trust/Clayton Brown
500 West Madison, Suite 3000
Chicago, Illinois 60606
(312) 559-3000, (800) 621-4770
First Trust America Fund (GNMA), First Trust Fund: U.S. Government Series (USGI), First Trust Tax-Free Bond Fund: Income Series (LTMB), Insured Series (LTMB)

Fischer Francis Trees & Watts, Inc.
717 Fifth Avenue
New York, New York 10022
(212) 350-8050
FFTW Institutional Reserves Fund (MM)

Flag Investors
135 East Baltimore Street
P.O. Box 515
Baltimore, Maryland 21203
(301) 727-1700
and
P.O. Box 17250
Baltimore, Maryland 21203
(301) 321-4444
Alex. Brown Cash Reserve Fund: Government Series (MM), Prime Series (MM), Flag Investors Corporate Cash Trust (I), Flag Investors Emerging Growth Fund (AG), Flag Investors International Trust (INT), Flag Investors Telephone Income Trust (I), Total Return U.S. Treasury Fund: C.J. Lawrence Total Return U.S. Treasury Fund (USGI), Flag Investors Total Return U.S. Treasury Fund (USGI)

Flagship
One First National Plaza, Suite 910
Dayton, Ohio 45402
(513) 461-0332, (800) 227-4648
Flagship Basic Value Fund (I), Flagship Tax Exempt Funds: All-American Tax Exempt Fund (LTMB), Arizona Double Tax Exempt Fund (SMB-LT), Colorado Double Tax Exempt Fund (SMB-LT), Connecticut Double Tax Exempt Fund (SMB-LT), Georgia Double Tax Exempt Fund (SMB-LT), Insured Tax Exempt Fund (LTMB), Kentucky Triple Tax Exempt Fund (SMB-LT), Limited Term Tax Exempt Fund

(LTMB), Michigan Triple Tax Exempt Fund (SMB-LT), Missouri Double Tax Exempt Fund (SMB-LT), North Carolina Triple Tax Exempt Fund (SMB-LT), Ohio Double Tax Exempt Fund (SMB-LT), Pennsylvania Triple Tax Exempt Fund (SMB-LT), Tennessee Double Tax Exempt Fund (SMB-LT), Virginia Double Tax Exempt Fund (SMB-LT)

Flex Funds. *see* Meeder & Associates

Frank Russell
P.O. Box 1591
Tacoma, Washington 98401-1591
(206) 627-7001, (800) 972-0700

Frank Russell Investment Company: Diversified Bond (IB), Diversified Equity (G + I), Equity I (G + I), Equity II (G), Equity III (IE), Equity Income (IE), Fixed Income I (IB), Fixed Income II (IB), International (INT), International Securities (INT), Limited Volatility Tax Free (STMB), Money Market (MM), Special Growth (G), U.S. Government Money Market (MM), Volatility Constrained Bond (IB), Frank Russell Quantitative Equity Fund (G + I), Frank Russell Tax Free Money Market Fund (STMB)

Franklin Group of Funds
777 Mariners Island Blvd.
San Mateo, California 94404
(415) 570-3000, (415) 378-2000,
(800) 632-2180, (800) DIAL-BEN

AGE High Income Fund (HYB), Franklin California Tax-Free Income Fund (SMB-LT), Franklin California Tax-Free Trust: Franklin California Insured Tax-Free Income Fund (SMB-LT), Franklin California Tax-Exempt Money Fund (SMB-ST), Franklin Corporate Cash Management Fund (I), Franklin Custodian Funds: DynaTech Series (AG), Growth Series (G), Income Series (I), U.S. Government Securities Series (GNMA), Utilities Series (G + I), Franklin Equity Fund (G), Franklin Federal Money Fund (MM), Franklin Federal Tax-Free Income Fund (LTMB), Franklin Gold Fund (PMG), Franklin Investors Securities Trust: Franklin Adjustable Rate Mortgage Fund (GNMA), Franklin Convertible Securities Fund (G + I), Franklin Global Opportunity Income Fund (GB), Franklin Short-Intermediate U.S. Government Securities Fund (USGI), Franklin Special Equity Income Fund (IE), Franklin Managed Trust: Franklin Corporate Cash Portfolio (I), Franklin Investment Grade Income Portfolio (CB), Franklin Rising Dividends Portfolio (G), Franklin Money Fund (MM), Franklin New York Tax-Exempt Money Fund (SMB-ST), Franklin New York Tax-Free Income Fund (SMB-LT), Franklin Option Fund

(OI), Franklin Partners Funds: Franklin Tax-Advantaged High Yield Securities Fund (HYB), Franklin Tax-Advantaged U.S. Government Securities Fund (GNMA), Franklin Pennsylvania Investors Fund: Equity Portfolio (G), High Income Portfolio (HYB), U.S. Government Securities Portfolio (GNMA), Franklin Tax-Exempt Money Fund (STMB), Franklin Tax-Free Trust: Franklin Alabama Tax-Free Income Fund (SMB-LT), Franklin Arizona Tax-Free Income Fund (SMB-LT), Franklin Colorado Tax-Free Income Fund (SMB-LT), Franklin Connecticut Tax-Free Income Fund (SMB-LT), Franklin Florida Tax-Free Income Fund (SMB-LT), Franklin Georgia Tax-Free Income Fund (SMB-LT), Franklin High Yield Tax-Free Income Fund (LTMB), Franklin Indiana Tax-Free Income Fund (SMB-LT), Franklin Insured Tax-Free Income Fund (LTMB), Franklin Louisiana Tax-Free Income Fund (SMB-LT), Franklin Maryland Tax-Free Income Fund (SMB-LT), Franklin Massachusetts Insured Tax-Free Income Fund (SMB-LT), Franklin Michigan Insured Tax-Free Income Fund (SMB-LT), Franklin Minnesota Insured Tax-Free Income Fund (SMB-LT), Franklin Missouri Tax-Free Income Fund (SMB-LT), Franklin New Jersey Tax-Free Income Fund (SMB-LT), Franklin North Carolina Tax-Free Income Fund (SMB-LT), Franklin Ohio Insured Tax-Free Income Fund (SMB-LT), Franklin Oregon Tax-Free Income Fund (SMB-LT), Franklin Pennsylvania Tax-Free Income Fund (SMB-LT), Franklin Puerto Rico Tax-Free Income Fund (SMB-LT), Franklin Texas Tax-Free Income Fund (SMB-LT), Franklin Virginia Tax-Free Income Fund (SMB-LT), Institutional Fiduciary Trust: Equity Portfolio (G + I), Federal Tax-Exempt Portfolio (LTMB), Franklin Government Investors Money Market Portfolio (MM), Franklin U.S. Government Securities Money Market Portfolio (MM), GNMA Portfolio (GNMA), Money Market Portfolio (MM), Precious Metals Portfolio (PMG)

44 Wall Street
MDB Asset Management Corp.
26 Broadway
New York, New York 10004
(212) 248-8080, (800) 543-2620

44 Wall Street Fund (AG)

Founders Mutual Depositor Corp.
3033 East First Avenue, Suite 810
Denver, Colorado 80206
(303) 394-4404, (800) 525-2440

Founders Blue Chip Fund (G + I), Founders Equity Income (B), Founders Frontier Fund

(AG), Founders Growth Fund (G), Founders Special Fund (AG)

Fountaine Trust
Richard Fountaine Associates, Inc.
111 South Calvert Street, Suite 1500
Baltimore, Maryland 21202
(301) 385-1591

Fountaine Capital Appreciation Fund (G + I)

Freedom Family of Funds
One Beacon Street
Boston, Massachusetts 02108
(617) 523-3170, (800) 225-6258

Freedom Investment Trust: Freedom Equity Value Fund (G), Freedom Gold & Government Trust (USGI), Freedom Government Plus Fund (USGI), Freedom Managed Tax Exempt Fund (LTMB), Freedom Money Market Fund (MM), Freedom Regional Bank Fund (G), Freedom Investment Trust II: Freedom Global Fund (GLB), Freedom Global Income Plus Fund (GB), Freedom Investment Trust III: Freedom Environmental Fund (G), Tucker Anthony Group of Tax Exempt Funds: Tucker Anthony Tax Exempt Money Fund (STMB), Tucker Anthony Mutual Fund: Cash Management Fund (MM), Government Securities Fund (MM)

Froley, Revy Investment Co.
1000 Wilshire Blvd, Suite 800
Los Angeles, California 90017-2465
(213) 625-1611

Dolphin FRIC Convertible Fund (G + I)

Fundamental Portfolio Advisors, Inc.
111 Broadway, Suite 1107
New York, New York 10006
(800) 225-6864, (212) 608-6864

California Muni Fund (SMB-LT), Fundamental Fixed-Income Fund: High Yield Municipal (LTMB), New York Municipal Fund (SMB-LT)

Fund Asset Management Inc.
800 Scudders Mill Road
Plainsboro, New Jersey 08536
(609) 282-2800

Apex Municipal Fund (STMB)

Furman, Anderson & Co.
19 Rector Street
New York, New York 10006
(212) 509-8532

Rainbow Fund (G)

Furman Selz
230 Park Avenue, 13th Floor
New York, New York 10169
(212) 309-8400, (800) 845-8406

Empire Builder Tax Free Bond Fund (SMB-LT), FFB Funds Trust: FFB Cash Management Fund (MM), FFB Equity Fund (G), FFB Tax-Free Money Market Fund (STMB), FFB U.S. Government Fund (MM), FFB U.S. Treasury Fund (MM), Fund Source: BIL International Growth Fund (GLB), Government Trust (MM), International Equity Trust (INT), Money Trust (MM), Olympus Equity Plus Fund (G), Olympus U.S. Government Trust (USGI), Washington Money Trust (MM), FundTrust: FundTrust Aggressive Growth Fund (AG), FundTrust Growth & Income Fund (G + I), FundTrust Growth Fund (G), FundTrust Income Fund (IB), FundTrust Managed Total Return Fund (G + I)

Gabelli Funds
P.O. Box 1634
Grand Central Station
New York, New York 10163
(212) 490-3670, (800) 422-3554

Gabelli Asset Fund (G), Gabelli Growth Fund (G), Gabelli Value Fund (G)

Gabelli-O'Connor
8 Sound Shore Drive
Greenwich, Connecticut 06830
(203) 629-2090, (800) 877-3863

Gabelli-O'Connor Treasurer's Fund: Auction Rate Preferred Portfolio (I), Domestic Prime Money Market Portfolio (MM), Limited Term Portfolio (I), Money Market Plus Portfolio (MM), Tax Exempt Limited Term Portfolio (LTMB), Tax Exempt Money Market Portfolio (STMB)

Gardner Companies
105 Hazel Path
P.O. Box 1256
Hendersonville, Tennessee 37077-1256
(615) 824-8027, (800) 247-2392

Gardner Managed Assets Trust (G + I)

Gateway Investment Advisers, Inc.
400 TechneCenter Drive, Suite 220
Milford, Ohio 45150
(513) 248-2700, (800) 354-6339

Gateway Trust: Gateway Government Bond Fund (USGI), Gateway Growth Plus Fund (G), Gateway Option Index Fund (OI)

GEICO
GEICO Plaza
Washington, D.C. 20076
(301) 986-2200, (800) 832-6232
GEICO Qualified Dividend Fund (I), Government Securities Cash Fund (MM)

General Funds. *see* Dreyfus

General Securities Fund. *see* Craig-Hallum, Inc.

Gintel Equity Management, Inc.
Greenwich Office Park OP-6
Greenwich, Connecticut 06830
(203) 622-6400, (800) 243-5808
Gintel Capital Appreciation (AG), Gintel ERISA (G + I), Gintel Fund (G)

GIT Investment Funds
1655 North Fort Myer Drive
Arlington, Virginia 22209
(703) 528-6500, (800) 336-3063
GIT Equity Trust: GIT Equity Income Portfolio (I), GIT Equity Select Growth Portfolio (G), GIT Equity Special Growth Portfolio (AG), GIT Income Trust: GIT Income Trust A-Rated Income Portfolio (IB), GIT Income Trust Maximum Income Portfolio (HYB), GIT Tax-Free Trust: High Yield Portfolio (LTMB), Money Market Portfolio (STMB), Virginia Portfolio (SMB-LT), Government Investors Trust (MM)

GNA Capital
3300 One Union Square
Seattle, Washington 98101
(206) 625-1755, (800) 433-0684
GNA Investors Trust: U.S. Government Securities Fund (USGI)

Golden Financial Group
P.O. Box 5179, FDR Station
New York, New York 10150
(212) 688-7070
and
909 Third Avenue
New York, New York 10022
and
520 Broad Street
Newark, New Jersey 07102-3184
(201) 481-8000
Golden American Fundtrust Separate Account B: Fundtrust Aggressive Growth Series (AG), Fundtrust Growth Series (G), Fundtrust Growth and Income Series (G + I), Fundtrust Income Series (I), Mutual Benefit Variable Contract Account 11: All-Growth Series (G), Fully

Managed Series (FP), Limited Maturity Bond Series (IB), Liquid Asset Series (I), Multiple Allocation Series (FP), Natural Resources Series (PMG), Real Estate Division (G)

Gradison
The 580 Building
6th & Walnut Streets
Cincinnati, Ohio 45202-3198
(513) 579-5700, (800) 543-1818
Gradison Cash Reserves Trust (MM), Gradison Custodian Trust: Gradison Government Income Fund (USGI), Gradison Growth Trust: Established Growth Fund (G), Opportunity Growth Fund (AG), Gradison U.S. Government Trust (MM)

Greenfield Fund
230 Park Avenue, Suite 910
New York, New York 10169
(212) 986-2600
Greenfield Fund (G + I)

Greenspring Fund
The Quadrangle, Suite 322
Village of Cross Keys
Baltimore, Maryland 21210
(301) 435-9000
Greenspring Fund Inc. (G)

Growth Fund of Washington
1101 Vermont Avenue, N.W.
Washington, D.C. 20005
(202) 842-5665, (800) 972-9274
Growth Fund of Washington (G)

Growth Industry Shares
135 South LaSalle Street
Chicago, Illinois 60603
(312) 346-4830
Growth Industry Shares (G), William Blair Ready Reserves (MM)

G.T. Global Funds
50 California Street, Suite 2700
San Francisco, California 94111
(415) 392-6181, (800) 824-1580
G.T. Global Growth Series: G.T. America Growth Fund (G), G.T. Europe Growth Fund (INT), G.T. International Growth Fund (INT), G.T. Japan Growth Fund (INT), G.T. Pacific Growth Fund (INT), G.T. Worldwide Growth Fund (GLB), G.T. Global Income Series: G.T. Global Bond Fund (GB), G.T. Global Government Income Fund (GB), G.T. Money Market Series: G.T. Government Obligations Fund (MM)

Guardian Life
201 Park Avenue South
New York, New York 10003
(212) 598-8259, (800) 221-3253

Guardian Cash Management Trust (MM), Guardian Park Avenue Fund (G)

Harbor Capital Advisors, Inc.
One SeaGate
Toledo, Ohio 43666
(419) 247-2477, (800) 442-1050

Harbor Fund: Harbor Bond Fund (IB), Harbor Growth Fund (G), Harbor International Fund (INT), Harbor Money Market Fund (MM), Harbor U.S. Equities Fund (G + I), Harbor Value Fund (IE)

Harris Associates
2 North LaSalle Street, Suite 500
Chicago, Illinois 60602
(312) 621-0630

Acorn Fund (G)

Hartford
200 Hopmeadow Street
P.O. Box 2999
Hartford, Connecticut 06104-2999
(203) 683-8245, (203) 683-8255,
(800) 227-1371, (800) 343-1250

Hartford Bond/Debt Securities Fund (IB), Hartford GNMA/Mortgage Security Fund (GNMA), Hartford Index Fund (G + I), Hartford Money Market Fund (MM), Hartford U.S. Government Money Market Fund (MM), Hartford Zero Coupon Treasury Fund (USGI), HVA Advisers Fund (G + I), HVA Aggressive Growth Fund (AG), HVA Money Market Fund (MM), HVA Stock Fund (G)

Hartwell Management Co.
515 Madison Avenue, 31st Floor
New York, New York 10022
(212) 308-3355, (800) 645-6405

Hartwell Emerging Growth (AG), Hartwell Growth Fund (AG)

J.B. Havre Securities, Inc.
1188 Bishop Street, Suite 1202
Honolulu, Hawaii 96813
(808) 521-4831

Hawaii Mutual Fund (G)

Hawaii Trust Co.
200 Park Avenue, Suite 4515
New York, New York 10017
(212) 697-6666

Hawaii Tax Free Trust (SMB-ST)

Heartland Group
790 North Milwaukee Street
Milwaukee, Wisconsin 53202
(414) 347-7000, (800) 558-1015

Heartland Group: Heartland Money Market Fund (MM), Heartland U.S. Government Fund (USGI), Heartland Value Fund (G)

Heine Management Group
253 Post Road West
P.O. Box 830
Westport, Connecticut 06881
(203) 222-1624, (800) 422-2564

LMH Fund Ltd (G + I)

Heine Securities
51 JFK Parkway
Short Hills, New Jersey 07078
(201) 912-2100, (800) 448-3863

Mutual Series Fund: Mutual Beacon Fund (G + I), Mutual Qualified Fund (G + I), Mutual Shares Fund (G + I)

Heitner Corp.
515 Olive Street, 11th Floor
St. Louis, Missouri 63101
(314) 421-4422, (800) 325-7159

THC Fund: Municipal Utilities Tax-Exempt Fund (Midwest) (LTMB), Municipal Utilities Tax-Exempt Fund (Missouri) (SMB-LT)

Heritage Asset Management, Inc.
880 Carillon Parkway
St. Petersburg, Florida 33716
(813) 573-3800

Heritage Capital Appreciation Trust (G), Heritage Cash Trust (MM), Heritage Convertible Income-Growth Trust (G + I), Heritage Income Trust (G + I)

Hidden Strength Funds
One Harmon Meadow Boulevard, 4th Floor
Secaucus, New Jersey 07094
(201) 867-2904, (800) 872-8037

Hidden Strength Funds: Aggressive Asset Allocation Portfolio (G), Conservative Asset Allocation Portfolio (IE), Growth Portfolio (G), Moderate Asset Allocation Portfolio (B), Money Market Portfolio (MM), U.S. Government High Yield Portfolio (USGI)

Hilliard-Lyons
P.O. Box 32760
Louisville, Kentucky 40232-2760
(502) 588-8400, (800) 444-1854

Hilliard-Lyons Government Fund (MM)

Home Group
59 Maiden Lane, 21st Floor
New York, New York 10038
(212) 530-6016
Home Group Trust: Home Cash Reserves (MM), Home Federal Tax-Free Reserves (STMB), Home Government Reserves (MM), Home Government Securities Fund (USGI), Home Growth and Income Fund (G + I), Home High Yield Bond Fund (HYB), Home New York Tax-Free Reserves (SMB-ST)

Home Life
One Centennial Plaza
Piscataway, New Jersey 08854
(212) 428-2000
Home Life Bond Fund (IB), Home Life Equity Fund (G), Home Life Liquid Fund (MM)

Horace Mann
One Horace Mann Plaza
Springfield, Illinois 62715
(217) 789-2500
Horace Mann Balanced Fund (B), Horace Mann Growth Fund (G), Horace Mann Income Fund (I), Horace Mann Short-Term Investment Fund (I)

Huntington Advisers, Inc.
251 South Lake Avenue, Suite 600
Pasadena, California 91101
(213) 681-3700,
(800) 826-0188
Huntington Investment Trust: Huntington CPI+ Fund (G + I), Huntington Short-Term Government Mortgage Fund (GNMA), International Cash Portfolios: Australian Cash Portfolio (MM), Canadian Cash Portfolio (MM), D-Mark Cash Portfolio (MM), Global Cash Portfolio (MM), Sterling Cash Portfolio (MM), Swiss Franc Cash Portfolio (MM), U.S. CASH Portfolio (MM), Yen Cash Portfolio (MM)

Hutchinson Advisers
208 South LaSalle Street, Suite 1816
Chicago, Illinois 60604
(312) 726-2688,
(800) 322-6573
Municipal Lease Securities Fund (LTMB)

Hyperion Capital Management, Inc.
One Seaport Plaza
New York, New York 10292
(212) 214-3334
Hyperion Total Return and Income Fund (B)

IAI Group
1100 Dain Tower
P.O. Box 357
Minneapolis, Minnesota 55440
(612) 371-7780, (612) 371-2884
IAI Apollo Fund (AG), IAI Bond Fund (IB), IAI International Fund (INT), IAI Regional Fund (G), IAI Reserve Fund (I), IAI Stock Fund (G + I)

IDEX Funds
201 Highland Avenue
Largo, Florida 34640
(813) 585-6565, (800) 237-3055
IDEX Fund (G), IDEX Fund 3 (G), IDEX II (G), IDEX Total Income Trust (IB)

IDS Mutual Fund Group
IDS Tower 10
Minneapolis, Minnesota 55440
(612) 372-3131, (800) 328-8300
IDS Bond Fund (CB), IDS California Tax-Exempt Trust: IDS California Tax-Exempt Fund (SMB-LT), IDS Cash Management Fund (MM), IDS Discovery Fund (AG), IDS Equity Plus Fund (G + I), IDS Extra Income Fund (HYB), IDS Federal Income Fund (USGI), IDS Growth Fund (G), IDS High Yield Tax-Exempt Fund (LTMB), IDS International Fund (INT), IDS Life Capital Resource Fund (G), IDS Life Managed Fund (G + I), IDS Life Moneyshare Fund (MM), IDS Life Special Income Fund (IB), IDS Managed Retirement Fund (FP), IDS Mutual (B), IDS New Dimensions Fund (G), IDS Precious Metals Fund (PMG), IDS Progressive Fund (AG), IDS Selective Fund (CB), IDS Special Tax-Exempt Series Trust: IDS Insured Tax-Exempt Fund (LTMB), IDS Massachusetts Tax-Exempt Fund (SMB-LT), IDS Michigan Tax-Exempt Fund (SMB-LT), IDS Minnesota Tax-Exempt Fund (SMB-LT), IDS New York Tax-Exempt Fund (SMB-LT), IDS Ohio Tax-Exempt Fund (SMB-LT), IDS Stock Fund (G + I), IDS Strategy Fund: Aggressive Equity Portfolio (AG), Equity Portfolio (G + I), Income Portfolio (CB), Money Market Portfolio (IB), Pan Pacific Portfolio (GLB), IDS Tax-Exempt Bond Fund (LTMB), IDS Tax-Free Money Fund (STMB), IDS Utilities Income Fund (IE)

Imperial Portfolios
9275 Sky Park Court
P.O. Box 82997
San Diego, California 92138
(619) 292-2379, (800) 347-5588
Imperial Portfolios: California Tax-Free Portfolio (SMB-LT), High Grade Corporate Bond

Portfolio (CB), High Yield Portfolio (HYB), S&P 100 Portfolio (G), U.S. Government Portfolio (USGI)

Industrial Series Trust Funds. *see* Mackenzie Group of Funds

Integra Fund
600 New Hampshire Avenue, N.W., Suite 720
Washington, D.C. 20037
(202) 965-4150
Integra Fund (B)

Integrated Resources
10 Union Square East
New York, New York 10003
(212) 353-7000, (800) 821-5100
and
One Bridge Plaza
Fort Lee, New Jersey 07024
(201) 461-0606

Home Investors Government Guaranteed Income Fund (GNMA), Integrated Capital Appreciation Fund (G), Integrated Cash Fund (MM), Integrated Corporate Investors Fund (I), Integrated Equity Portfolios: Aggressive Growth Portfolio (AG), Growth Portfolio (G), Integrated Income Plus Fund (CB), Integrated Income Portfolios: Convertible Securities Portfolio (I), Government Securities Plus Portfolio (USGI), High Yield Portfolio (HYB), Integrated Money Market Securities (MM), Integrated Resources Series Trust: Aggressive Growth Portfolio (AG), Aggressive Multi-Asset Portfolio (G + I), Convertible Securities Portfolio (I), Fixed Income Portfolio (I), Foreign Securities Portfolio (INT), Government Securities Portfolio (USGI), Growth Portfolio (G), High Yield Portfolio (HYB), Money Market Portfolio (MM), Multi-Asset Portfolio (G + I), Natural Resources Portfolio (G + I), Total Return Portfolio (G + I), Integrated Tax Free Portfolios: STRIPES Portfolio (LTMB), Tax Free California Municipal Bond Portfolio (SMB-LT), Tax Free Money Market Portfolio (STMB), U.S. Tax Free Income Portfolio (LTMB)

Interstate Asset Management, Inc.
2600 NCNB Plaza
Charlotte, North Carolina 28280
(704) 379-9097

Interstate Capital Growth Fund (G), Southeastern Savings Instititutions Fund (G)

INVESCO Capital Management
1315 Peachtree Street, N.E., Suite 500
Atlanta, Georgia 30309
(404) 892-0666, (800) 554-1156

EBI Cash Management (MM), EBI Equity (G + I), EBI Income (IB), EBI Series Trust: EBI Flex Fund (FP), International Fund (INT), INVESCO Institutional Series Trust: INVESCO Institutional Equity Fund (G + I), INVESCO Institutional Flex Fund (FP), INVESCO Institutional Income Fund (IB), INVESCO Institutional International Fund (INT), INVESCO Treasurers Series Trust: Money Reserve Fund (MM), Tax-Exempt Fund (STMB)

Investors Research Corp.
P.O. Box 419200
Kansas City, Missouri 64141-5575
(816) 531-5575, (800) 345-2021

Twentieth Century Balanced (G + I), Twentieth Century Cash Reserves (MM), Twentieth Century Giftrust (AG), Twentieth Century Growth (G), Twentieth Century Heritage (G), Twentieth Century Long-Term (I), Twentieth Century Select (G), Twentieth Century Tax-Exempt: Intermediate (LTMB), Twentieth Century Tax-Exempt: Long (LTMB), Twentieth Century U.S. Government (USGI), Twentieth Century Ultra (AG), Twentieth Century Vista (AG)

IRI Funds
One Appletree Square
Minneapolis, Minnesota 55425
(612) 853-9500, (800) 328-1010

IRI Stock Fund (G), Midas Gold Shares & Bullion (PMG)

Isaak Bond Investments
600 17th Street, Suite 2610
South Tower
Denver, Colorado 80202
(303) 623-7500, (800) 242-0094

North Dakota Double Tax-Exempt Bond Fund (SMB-LT)

Ivy Management, Inc.
40 Industrial Park Road
Hingham, Massachusetts 02043
(617) 749-1416, (800) 235-3322

Ivy Fund: Ivy Growth Fund (G), Ivy Institutional Investors Fund (G), Ivy International Fund (INT), Ivy Money Market Fund (MM), Ivy U.S. Government Income Fund (USGI)

James Baker & Co.
1601 N.W. Expressway, 20th Floor
Oklahoma City, Oklahoma 73118
(405) 842-1400, (800) 654-3248

Baker Fund: Equity Series (G), U.S. Government Series (USGI)

Janus Capital Corp.
100 Fillmore Street, Suite 300
Denver, Colorado 80206-4923
(303) 525-3713, (303) 333-3863,
(800) 525-3713

Janus Flexible Income Fund (FP), Janus Fund (G), Janus Value Fund (G), Janus Venture Fund (AG)

John Hancock
101 Huntington Avenue
Boston, Massachusetts 02199
(617) 375-1760, (800) 225-5291

John Hancock Asset Allocation Trust (FP), John Hancock Bond Trust (CB), John Hancock Cash Management Trust (MM), John Hancock Global Trust (GLB), John Hancock Growth Trust (G), John Hancock High Income Trust: Federal Securities Plus Portfolio (USGI), Fixed Income Portfolio (HYB), John Hancock Special Equities Trust (AG), John Hancock Tax-Exempt Income Trust (LTMB), John Hancock Tax-Exempt Series Trust: California Portfolio (SMB-LT), Massachusetts Portfolio (SMB-LT), New York Portfolio (SMB-LT), John Hancock U.S. Government Guaranteed Mortgages Trust (GNMA), John Hancock U.S. Government Securities Trust (USGI), John Hancock World Trust: Pacific Basin Equities Portfolio (INT), World Fixed Income Portfolio (GB)

Jones & Babson
3 Crown Center, 2440 Pershing Road
Kansas City, Missouri 64108
(816) 471-5200, (800) 4-BABSON

Babson Bond Trust (IB), Babson Enterprise Fund (AG), Babson Growth Fund (G), Babson Money Market: Federal Portfolio (MM), Babson Money Market: Prime Portfolio (MM), Babson Shadow Stock Fund (G), Babson-Stewart Ivory International (G), Babson Tax-Free Income Fund (MM), Babson Value Fund (G + I), UMB Bond Fund (IB), UMB Money Market Fund: Federal Portfolio (MM), UMB Money Market Fund: Prime Portfolio (MM), UMB Qualified Dividend (AG), UMB Stock Fund (G + I), UMB Tax-Free Money Market (MM)

J.W. Grant
1515 North Federal Highway, Suite 310
Boca Raton, Florida 33432
(407) 338-2145
J.W. Grant Fund (AG)

Kaufmann Fund. see Edgemont Asset Management Corp.

Kemper Financial Services
120 South LaSalle Street
Chicago Illinois 60603
(312) 781-1121, (800) 621-1048,
(800) 621-1148

Cash Equivalent Fund: Government Securities Portfolio (MM), Money Market Portfolio (MM), Tax-Exempt Portfolio (STMB), Investment Portfolios: Equity Portfolio (G), Government Plus Portfolio (USGI), High Yield Portfolio (IB), Money Market Portfolio (MM), Option Income Portfolio (OI), Total Return Portfolio (G + I), Kemper Blue Chip Fund (G + I), Kemper California Tax-Free Income Fund (SMB-LT), Kemper Enhanced Government Income Fund (USGI), Kemper Global Income Fund (GB), Kemper Gold Fund (PMG), Kemper Government Money Market Fund (MM), Kemper Growth Fund (G), Kemper Guaranteed Retirement Fund - Series 1999 (B), Kemper High Yield Fund (HYB), Kemper Income & Capital Preservation Fund (IB), Kemper International Fund (INT), Kemper Money Market Fund (MM), Kemper Municipal Bond Fund (LTMB), Kemper Municipal Income Trust (LTMB), Kemper New York Tax-Free Income Fund (SMB-LT), Kemper Option Income Fund (OI), Kemper Summit Fund (AG), Kemper Technology Fund (G), Kemper Total Return Fund (G + I), Kemper U.S. Government Securities Fund (USGI), Money Market Portfolios Trust: Tax-Exempt Portfolio (STMB), Tax-Exempt California Money Market Fund (SMB-ST)

Keystone Group
99 High Street
Boston, Massachusetts 02110
(617) 338-3200, (800) 343-2898

Aggressive Stock Trust (AG), Cash Income Trust (MM), Government Guaranteed Securities Trust (GNMA), Government Securities Zero Coupon Trust: 1991 Series (USGI), 1996 Series (USGI), High Yield Bond Trust (HYB), Keystone America Equity Income Fund (IE), Keystone America Fund of Growth Stock (IE), Keystone America Global Opportunity Fund (GLB), Keystone America Government Securities Fund (USGI), Keystone America High Yield Bond Fund (HYB), Keystone America Investment Grade Bond Fund (CB), Keystone America Money Market Fund (MM), Keystone America Tax Free Income Fund (LTMB), Keystone America Tax Free Money Market Fund (STMB), Keystone Custodian Funds, B-1 Series (IB), Keystone Custodian Funds, B-2 Series (CB), Keystone Custodian Funds, B-4 Series (HYB), Keystone Custodian Funds, K-1 Series

(IE), Keystone Custodian Funds, K-2 Series (G), Keystone Custodian Funds, S-1 Series (G + I), Keystone Custodian Funds, S-3 Series (G), Keystone Custodian Funds, S-4 Series (AG), Keystone International Fund (GLB), Keystone Liquid Trust (MM), Keystone Precious Metals Holdings (PMG), Keystone Tax Exempt Trust (LTMB), Keystone Tax Free Fund (LTMB), Managed Assets Trust (G + I), Managed Growth Stock Trust (G), Money Market/ Options Investments (OI), Mortgage Securities Income Trust (GNMA), Salem Funds: Salem Fixed Income Portfolio (I), Salem Growth Portfolio (G), Salem Money Market Portfolio (MM), Salem Tax Free Money Market Portfolio (STMB), Salem Tax Free Portfolio (LTMB)

Kidder Peabody Funds. *see* Webster

Kleinwort Benson International
200 Park Avenue
New York, New York 10166
(212) 687-2515, (800) 237-4218

Transatlantic Growth Fund (INT), Transatlantic Income Fund (GB)

Knox Funds
6 St. James Avenue
Boston, Massachusetts 02116
(617) 423-0800

Knox Managed Growth Fund (G), Knox Managed Income Fund (I), Knox Managed Total Return Fund (B), Knox Money Market Fund (MM)

Kotrozo
4141 North Scottsdale Road, Suite 100
Scottsdale, Arizona 85251
(602) 949-1369

Kotrozo Mutual Fund Group: Kotrozo Arizona Tax Free Fund (SMB-LT), Kotrozo Option Income Fund (OI)

Landmark Funds
6 St. James Avenue
Boston, Massachusetts 02116
(617) 423-1679

Landmark Institutional Cash Reserves (MM)

Lazard Freres
One Rockefeller Plaza
New York, New York 10020
(212) 957-5403, (212) 489-6600,
(800) 854-8525

HT Insight Funds: HT Insight Cash Management Fund (MM), HT Insight Convertible Fund (G + I), HT Insight Equity Fund (G), HT Insight

Government Fund (MM), HT Insight Tax-Free Money Market Fund (STMB), Lazard Freres Funds: Lazard Freres Cash Management Fund (MM), Lazard Freres Equity Fund (G), Lazard Freres Government Fund (MM), Lazard Freres Tax-Free Money Market Fund (STMB), Lazard Freres Total Return Fund (IB), Lazard Freres Institutional Fund: Lazard Freres Institutional Cash Portfolio (MM), Lazard Freres Institutional Government Portfolio (MM), Lazard Freres Institutional Prime Portfolio (MM), Lazard Freres Institutional Tax-Free Portfolio (STMB), Lazard Freres Institutional Treasury Portfolio (MM), Lazard Special Equity Fund (AG)

Legg Mason Wood Walker, Inc.
111 South Calvert Street
Baltimore, Maryland 21202
(301) 539-3400, (800) 822-5544,
(800) 368-2558

Legg Mason Cash Reserve Trust (MM), Legg Mason Income Trust: Legg Mason Investment Grade Income Portfolio (IB), Legg Mason U.S. Government Intermediate-Term Portfolio (USGI), Legg Mason Special Investment Fund (AG), Legg Mason Tax-Exempt Trust (STMB), Legg Mason Total Return Trust (G + I), Legg Mason Value Trust (G)

Lehman
55 Water Street, 34th Floor
New York, New York 10041
(212) 668-8578, (800) 221-5350

Lehman Capital Fund (AG), Lehman Investors Fund (G + I), Lehman Opportunity Fund (G)

Lepercq de Neuflize & Co.
345 Park Avenue
New York, New York 10154
(212) 702-0174, (212) 702-0175,
(800) 548-7878

Lepercq-Istel Aggressive Growth (AG), Lepercq-Istel International (INT), Lepercq-Istel Trust: Lepercq-Istel Fund (G + I)

Lexington Management Corp.
Park 80 West, Plaza Two
P.O. Box 1515
Saddle Brook, New Jersey 07662
(201) 845-7300, (800) 526-0056,
(800) 526-0057

Lexington Corporate Leaders Trust Fund (G + I), Lexington Global Fund (GLB), Lexington GNMA Income Fund (GNMA), Lexington Goldfund (PMG), Lexington Government Securities Money Market (MM), Lexington

Growth Fund (G), Lexington Money Market Trust (MM), Lexington Research Fund (G), Lexington Tax Exempt Bond (LTMB), Lexington Tax Free Money Fund (STMB), Lexington Technical Strategy Fund (G)

Life of Virginia
6610 West Broad Street
Richmond, Virginia 23230
(804) 281-6000, (800) 822-6000

Life of Virginia Series Fund: Bond Portfolio (CB), Common Stock Portfolio (G), Money Market Portfolio (MM), Total Return Portfolio (G + I)

Lindner Management Corp.
200 South Bemiston
P.O. Box 11208
St. Louis, Missouri 63105
(314) 727-5305

Lindner Growth Fund (G), Lindner Dividend Fund (B)

Loch Ness
7039 Encina Lane
Boca Raton, Florida 33433
(407) 488-3589

Loch Ness Option Fund (OI)

Loomis-Sayles. see New England/Loomis-Sayles

Lord Abbett
General Motors Building
767 Fifth Avenue
New York, New York 10153
(212) 848-1800, (800) 223-4224

Affiliated Fund (G + I), Lord Abbett Bond-Debenture Fund (HYB), Lord Abbett California Tax-Free Income Fund (SMB-LT), Lord Abbett Cash Reserve Fund (MM), Lord Abbett Developing Growth Fund (AG), Lord Abbett Fundamental Value Fund (G + I), Lord Abbett Global Fund: Equity Series (GLB), Income Series (GB), Lord Abbett Tax-Free Income Fund: National Series (LTMB), New York Series (SMB-LT), Texas Series (SMB-LT), Lord Abbett U.S. Government Securities Fund (USGI), Lord Abbett Value Appreciation Fund (G)

Lutheran Brotherhood
625 Fourth Avenue, South
Minneapolis, Minnesota 55415
(612) 339-8091, (800) 328-4552

LBVIP Series Fund: Growth Series (G), High Yield Series (HYB), Income Series (I), Money Market Series (MM). Lutheran Brotherhood

Fund (G + I), Lutheran Brotherhood High Yield Fund (HYB), Lutheran Brotherhood Income Fund (IB), Lutheran Brotherhood Money Market Fund (MM), Lutheran Brotherhood Municipal Bond Fund (LTMB)

MacKay-Shields
51 Madison Avenue
New York, New York 10010
(212) 576-7000, (800) 522-4202

MacKay-Shields MainStay Series Fund: MacKay-Shields Capital Appreciation Fund (AG), MacKay-Shields Convertible Fund (G + I), MacKay-Shields Global Fund (GLB), MacKay-Shields Gold & Precious Metals Fund (PMG), MacKay-Shields Government Plus Fund (USGI), MacKay-Shields High Yield Corporate Bond Fund (HYB), MacKay-Shields Money Market (MM), MacKay-Shields Tax Free Bond Fund (LTMB), MacKay-Shields Total Return Fund (B), MacKay-Shields Value Fund (G)

Mackenzie Group of Funds
1200 North Federal Highway
Boca Raton, Florida 33432
(407) 393-8900, (800) 222-2274

Industrial Series Trust: Mackenzie American Fund (G), Mackenzie California Municipal Fund (SMB-LT), Mackenzie Cash Management Fund (MM), Mckenzie Fixed Income Trust (CB), Mackenzie Government Securities Trust (USGI), Mackenzie National Municipal Fund (LTMB), Mackenzie New York Municipal Fund (SMB-LT), Mackenzie Option Income Fund (OI), Mackenzie Funds: Canada Fund (INT), Growth and Income Fund (G + I)

Manufacturers
200 Bloor Street East
North Tower 5
Toronto, Ontario, Canada M4W 1E5
(416) 926-6700

ManuLife Series Fund: Balanced Assets Fund (B), Capital Growth Bond Fund (I), Common Stock Fund (G + I), Emerging Growth Equity Fund (AG), Money Market Fund (MM), Real Estate Securities Fund (G + I)

Mariner
9003 Greentree Commons, Suite I
Marlton, New Jersey 08053
(609) 596-9300, (800) 634-2536

Mariner Funds Trust: Mariner Bond Market Fund (CB), Mariner Cash Management Fund (MM), Mariner Equity Fund (G), Mariner Government Fund (MM), Mariner Intermediate Government Bond Fund (USGI), Mariner New

York Tax-Free Money Market Fund (SMB-ST), Mariner Tax-Free Money Market Fund (STMB), Mariner U.S. Treasury Fund (MM)

Massachusetts Financial
500 Boylston Street
Boston, Massachusetts 02116
(617) 954-5000, (800) 343-2829
Massachusetts Capital Development Fund (G), Massachusetts Cash Management Trust: Government Series (MM), Prime Series (MM), Massachusetts Financial Bond Fund (CB), Massachusetts Financial Development Fund (G + I), Massachusetts Financial Emerging Growth Trust (AG), Massachusetts Financial High Income Trust - I (HYB), Massachusetts Financial High Income Trust - II (HYB), Massachusetts Financial International Trust-Bond Portfolio (GB), Massachusetts Financial Special Fund (AG), Massachusetts Financial Total Return Trust (I), Massachusetts Investors Growth Stock Fund (G), Massachusetts Investors Trust (G + I), Massachusetts Tax-Exempt Money Market Fund (SMB-ST), MFS Government Guaranteed Securities Trust (USGI), MFS Government Securities High Yield Trust (USGI), MFS Lifetime Investment Program: Lifetime Capital Growth Trust (G), Lifetime Dividends Plus Trust (IE), Lifetime Emerging Growth Trust (AG), Lifetime Global Equity Trust (GLB), Lifetime Gold & Precious Metals Trust (PMG), Lifetime Government Income Plus Trust (USGI), Lifetime High Income Trust (HYB), Lifetime Intermediate Income Trust (GB), Lifetime Managed Municipal Bond Trust (LTMB), Lifetime Managed Sectors Trust (G), Lifetime Money Market Trust (MM), MFS Managed California Tax-Exempt Trust (SMB-LT), MFS Managed Multi-State Tax-Exempt Trust: Georgia Series (SMB-LT), Maryland Series (SMB-LT), Massachusetts Series (SMB-LT), Michigan Series (SMB-LT), Minnesota Series (SMB-LT), New Jersey Series (SMB-LT), New York Series (SMB-LT), North Carolina Series (SMB-LT), Ohio Series (SMB-LT), South Carolina Series (SMB-LT), Tennessee Series (SMB-LT), Virginia Series (SMB-LT), West Virginia Series (SMB-LT), MFS Managed Municipal Bond Trust (LTMB), MFS Managed Sectors Trust (G), MFS Principal Income Trust (USGI), Municipal Working Capital Trust (STMB), Trust for Thrift Institutions (HYB)

MassMutual Life
1295 State Street
Springfield, Massachusetts 01111
(413) 788-8411, (800) 542-6767
MassMutual Integrity Funds: MassMutual

Balanced Fund (B), MassMutual Capital Appreciation Fund (G), MassMutual Corporate Cash Fund (IE), MassMutual Investment Grade Bond Fund (CB), MassMutual Money Market Fund (MM), MassMutual Tax-Exempt Bond Fund (LTMB), MassMutual Tax-Exempt Money Market (STMB), MassMutual U.S. Government Securities Fund (USGI), MassMutual Value Stock Fund (G + I)

Mathers & Co.
100 Corporate North, Suite 201
Bannockburn, Illinois 60015
(312) 295-7400, (800) 962-3863
Mathers Fund (G)

Maxus Investment Group
3550 Lander Road, 2nd Floor
Pepper Pike, Ohio 44124
(216) 292-3434
Maxus Fund (FP)

McDonald & Co.
2100 Society Building
Cleveland, Ohio 44114
(216) 443-2300
McDonald U.S. Government Money Market Fund (MM)

Meeder & Associates, Inc.
6000 Memorial Drive
Dublin, Ohio 43017
(614) 766-7000, (800) 325-FLEX
Flex Bond Fund (IB), Flex Growth Fund (G), Flex Income & Growth Fund (IE), Flex Money Market Fund (MM), Flex Muirfield Fund (G), Flex Retirement Growth Fund (FP)

Meeschaert & Co.
28 Hill Farm Road
RFD #2 Box 151
St. Johnsbury, Vermont 05819
(802) 748-2400
Meeschaert Capital Accumulation Trust (G), Meeschaert Gold and Currency Trust (PMG), Meeschaert International Bond Fund (GB)

Merrill Lynch
P.O. Box 9011
Princeton, New Jersey 08543-9011
(201) 560-5507, (609) 282-2800,
(609) 282-2000, (800) 262-4636,
(800) 221-3150, (800) 637-3863
and
One Financial Center, 15th Floor
Boston, Massachusetts 02111
(617) 357-1460, (800) 225-1576

CBA Money Fund (MM), CMA Government Securities Fund (MM), CMA Money Fund (MM), CMA Multi-State Municipal Series Trust: CMA California Tax-Exempt Fund (SMB-ST), CMA New York Tax-Exempt Fund (SMB-ST), CMA Tax-Exempt Fund (STMB), Corporate Fund Investment Accumulation Program (CB), Developing Capitalism Fund (INT), Merrill Lynch Basic Value Fund (G + I), Merrill Lynch California Municipal Series Trust: Merrill Lynch California Municipal Bond Fund (SMB-LT), Merrill Lynch Capital Fund (G + I), Merrill Lynch High Yield Municipal Fund (SMB-ST), Merrill Lynch Corporate Bond Fund: High Income Portfolio (HYB), High Quality Portfolio (CB), Intermediate Term Portfolio (CB), Merrill Lynch Corporate Dividend Fund (I), Merrill Lynch Equi-Bond I Fund (G + I), Merrill Lynch EuroFund (INT), Merrill Lynch Federal Securities Trust (USGI), Merrill Lynch Fund for Tomorrow (G), Merrill Lynch Global Allocation Fund (FP), Merrill Lynch Global Convertible Fund (GLB), Merrill Lynch Government Fund (MM), Merrill Lynch Institutional Fund (MM), Merrill Lynch Institutional Intermediate Fund (USGI), Merrill Lynch Institutional Tax-Exempt Fund (STMB), Merrill Lynch International Holdings (GLB), Merrill Lynch Multi-State Municipal Series Trust: Merrill Lynch New York Municipal Bond Fund (SMB-LT), Merrill Lynch Municipal Bond Fund: High Yield Portfolio (LTMB), Insured Portfolio (LTMB), Limited Maturity Portfolio (LTMB), Merrill Lynch Municipal Income Fund (STMB), Merrill Lynch Natural Resources Trust (G), Merrill Lynch Pacific Fund (INT), Merrill Lynch Phoenix Fund (AG), Merrill Lynch Ready Assets Trust (MM), Merrill Lynch Retirement Benefit Investment Program: Full Investment Portfolio (B), Merrill Lynch Retirement Equity Fund (G + I), Merrill Lynch Retirement Global Fund (GB), Merrill Lynch Retirement Reserves Money Fund (MM), Merrill Lynch Retirement/Income Fund (GNMA), Merrill Lynch Series Fund: Balanced Portfolio (B), Capital Stock Portfolio (G + I), Global Strategy Portfolio (GLB), Growth Stock Portfolio (G), High Yield Portfolio (HYB), Intermediate Government Bond Portfolio (USGI), Long Term Corporate Bond Portfolio (CB), Money Reserve Portfolio (MM), Multiple Strategy Portfolio (G + I), Natural Resources Portfolio (G), Merrill Lynch Special Value Fund (G), Merrill Lynch Strategic Dividend Fund (G + I), Merrill Lynch U.S.A. Government Reserves (MM), Merrill Lynch Variable Series Funds: American Balanced Fund (B), Equity Growth Fund (G), Flex Strategy Fund (G + I), High Current Income Fund (HYB), Natural Resources Focus Fund (G), Prime Bond Fund (CB), Qual-

ity Equity Fund (G + I), Reserve Assets Fund (MM), Municipal Fund Investment Accumulation Program (LTMB), Sci-Tech Holdings (GLB), Summit Cash Reserve Fund (MM), Merrill Lynch Munihealth Fund (LTMB), Merrill Lynch Prime Fund (I)

Merriman Investment
1200 Westlake Avenue, North, Number 507
Seattle, Washington 98109
(206) 285-8877, (800) 423-4893

Merriman Investment Trust: Merriman Timed Government Fund (USGI)

Mesirow Financial Corporation
350 North Clark Street
Chicago, Illinois 60610
(312) 670-6035, (800) 458-5222

Skyline Fund: Balanced Portfolio (B), Monthly Income Portfolio (HYB), Special Equities Portfolio (AG)

M&I Investment Management Corp.
330 East Kilbourn Avenue
Two Plaza East, Suite 1150
Milwaukee, Wisconsin 53202
(414) 347-1141, (800) 247-7039

Newton Growth Fund (G), Newton Income Fund: Newton Income Fund (IB), Newton Money Fund (MM)

MidAmerica
433 Edgewood Road, N.E.
Cedar Rapids, Iowa 52499
(319) 398-8511, (800) 553-4287

MidAmerica High Growth Fund (AG), MidAmerica High Yield Fund (HYB), MidAmerica Mutual Fund (G), MidAmerica Tax-Exempt Bond Fund (LTMB)

Midwest Group
700 Dixie Terminal Building
Cincinnati, Ohio 45202
(513) 629-2000, (800) 543-8721

Financial Independence Trust: Growth Fund (G), U.S. Government Securities Fund (GNMA), U.S. Treasury Allocation Fund (USGI), Midwest Group State Tax Exempt Trust, Midwest Group Tax Free Trust: Limited Term Portfolio (LTMB), Money Market Portfolio (STMB), Ohio Tax Free Money Fund (SMB-LT), Midwest Income Trust: Institutional Government Fund (MM), Intermediate Term Government Fund (USGI), Short Term Government Fund (MM), Train, Smith New York Tax-Exempt Money Fund (SMB-ST), Train, Smith Tax-Exempt Money Fund (SMB-ST)

Miller, Anderson & Sherrerd
Two Bala Plaza
Bala Cynwyd, Pennsylvania 19004
(800) 332-5577, (215) 668-0850

MAS Pooled Trust Equity Portfolio (G + I),
MAS Pooled Trust Fixed Income Portfolio (I),
MAS Pooled Trust Quantitative Growth (G + I),
MAS Pooled Trust Select Fixed Income (I),
MAS Pooled Trust Small Capitalization (G + I),
MAS Pooled Trust Value Portfolio (IE)

Mills Value
1108 East Main Street, 14th Floor
Richmond, Virginia 23219
(804) 649-2400

Mills Value Fund (IE)

MIM Mutual Funds
4500 Rockside Road, Suite 440
Independence, Ohio 44131-6809
(216) 642-3000, (800) 233-1240

MIM Mutual Funds: Bond Income Fund (IB),
Money Market Fund (MM), Stock Appreciation
Fund (AG), Stock, Convertible & Option Growth
Fund (G), Stock, Convertible & Option Income
Fund (IE)

MIMLIC
400 North Robert Street
St. Paul, Minnesota 55101-2098
(612) 223-4252, (800) 443-3677

MIMLIC Asset Allocation Fund (G + I), MIMLIC
Cash Fund (MM), MIMLIC Fixed Income Secu-
rities Fund (I), MIMLIC Investors Fund I (G + I),
MIMLIC Money Market Fund (MM), MIMLIC
Mortgage Securities Income Fund (GNMA)

Monetta
1776-B South Naperville Road, Suite 101
Wheaton, Illinois 60187-8133
(312) 462-9800

Monetta Fund (G)

Money Management Associates
4922 Fairmont Avenue
Bethesda, Maryland 20814
(301) 657-1500, (800) 343-3355

Rushmore Over-The-Counter Index Plus (G),
Rushmore Stock Market Index Plus (G + I),
Rushmore U.S. Government Intermediate-
Term Securities (LTMB), Rushmore U.S.
Government Long-Term Securities (LTMB)

Monitrend Mutual Fund
272 Closter Dock Road, Suite 1
Closter, New Jersey 07624
(201) 886-2300, (800) 251-1970

Monitrend Mutual Fund: Gold Series (PMG),
Government Series (USGI), S&P 100 Index
Series (G), Value Series (G)

MONY
500 Frank W. Burr Boulevard 71-13
Glenpointe Center West
Teaneck, New Jersey 07666
(212) 907-6669

MONY Series Fund: Diversified Portfolio (B),
Equity Growth Portfolio (G), Equity Income
Portfolio (IE), Intermediate Term Bond Portfo-
lio (IB), Long Term Bond Portfolio (IB), Money
Market Portfolio (MM), MONY Variable Ac-
count-A (G), MONY Variable Account-B (MM)

Moore & Schley
Park 80 West, Plaza Two
Saddle Brook, New Jersey 07662
(201) 845-7300, (800) 526-0056

Concord Income Trust: Convertible Portfolio
(G + I), National Tax Exempt Portfolio (LTMB),
U.S. Government Guaranteed Portfolio (USGI)

Morgan Keegan
50 Front Street, 21st Floor
Memphis, Tennessee 38103
(901) 524-4100, (800) 238-7127

Morgan Keegan Southern Capital Fund (G)

Morison Asset Management
1201 Marquette, Suite 400
P.O. Box 3709
Minneapolis, Minnesota 55403
(612) 332-1588

Morison Asset Allocation Fund (FP)

M.S.B. Fund
Savings Banks Trust Company
330 Madison Avenue
New York, New York 10017
(212) 551-1800

M.S.B. Fund (G)

M.S.D. & T. Funds, Inc.
One Exchange Place, 9th Floor
Boston, Massachusetts 02109
(800) 441-7379

M.S.D. & T. Tax-Exempt Money Market Fund
(STMB)

Municipal Capital Group
16450 Los Gatos Boulevard, Suite 115
Los Gatos, California 95030
(408) 356-2411

California Municipal Income Fund (SMB-LT)

Mutual Benefit
520 Broad Street
Newark, New Jersey 07101
(401) 751-8600, (201) 481-8000,
(800) 333-4726
MAP-Government Fund (MM), Mutual Benefit Fund (G)

Mutual of America
666 Fifth Avenue
New York, New York 10103
(212) 399-1600, (800) 223-0898

Mutual of America Investment Corporation: Bond Fund (IB), Composite Fund (FP), Money Market (MM), Stock Fund (G + I)

Mutual of Omaha
10235 Regency Circle
Omaha, Nebraska 68114
(402) 397-8555, (800) 228-9596

Mutual of Omaha America Fund (USGI), Mutual of Omaha Cash Reserve Fund (MM), Mutual of Omaha Growth Fund (G), Mutual of Omaha Income Fund (I), Mutual of Omaha Money Market Account (MM), Mutual of Omaha Tax-Free Income Fund (LTMB)

Mutual Group of Funds. see Heine Securities

Mutual Selection Management
2610 Park Avenue
P.O. Box 209
Muscatine, Iowa 52761
(319) 264-8000

Mutual Selection Fund (G)

NASL Series
695 National Avenue
P.O. Box 9064 GMF
Boston, Massachusetts 02205
and
North American Security Trust
695 Atlantic Avenue
Boston, Massachusetts 02111
(617) 439-6960, (800) 344-1029

NASL Series Trust: Bond Portfolio (CB), Convertible Securities Portfolio (G + I), Equity Portfolio (G), Global Equities Portfolio (GLB), Global Government Bond Portfolio (GB), Money Market Portfolio (MM), North American Security Trust: Aggressive Asset Allocation Trust (FP), Conservative Asset Allocation Trust (FP), Growth Trust (G), Moderate Asset Allocation Trust (FP), Money Market Trust (MM), U.S. Government High Yield Trust (USGI)

National Aviation & Technology Fund. see American Fund Advisors

National Bank of Washington
619 14th Street, N.W.
Washington, D.C. 20005
(800) 845-8406, (212) 309-8400
Washington Money Trust (MM)

National Securities
605 Third Avenue, 12th Floor
New York, New York 10158
(212) 661-3000, (800) 223-7757

California Tax Exempt Bonds (SMB-LT), Fairfield Fund (AG), National Bond Fund (HYB), National Cash Reserves (MM), National Federal Securities Trust (USGI), National Growth Fund (G), National Precious Metals Fund (PMG), National Preferred Fund (IE), National Premium Income Fund (I), National Real Estate Trust: National Real Estate Income Fund (I), National Real Estate Stock Fund (AG), National Securities Tax Exempt Bonds (STMB), National Stock Fund (G + I), National Strategic Allocation Fund (G + I), National Total Income Fund (I), National Total Return Fund (G + I)

Nationwide Financial Services
One Nationwide Plaza
P.O. Box 182008
Columbus, Ohio 43218
(614) 249-7855, (800) 533-5622,
(800) 848-0920

Financial Horizons Investment Trust: Cash Reserve Fund (MM), Government Bond Fund (USGI), Growth Fund (G), Municipal Bond Fund (LTMB), Nationwide Investing Foundation: Bond Fund (CB), Growth Fund (G), Money Market Fund (MM), Nationwide Fund (G + I). Nationwide Separate Account Trust: Bond Fund (CB), Common Stock Fund (G + I), Money Market Fund (MM). Nationwide Tax-Free Fund (LTMB)

ND Capital
201 South Broadway
Minot, North Dakota 58701
(701) 852-5292

North Dakota Tax-Free Fund (SMB-LT)

Neuberger & Berman Management
342 Madison Avenue
New York, New York 10173
(212) 850-8300, (800) 223-6448
and
522 Fifth Avenue
New York, New York 10036
(212) 850-8300, (800) 223-6448

Advisers Management Trust: Growth Portfolio (G), Limited Maturity Bond Portfolio (IB), Liquid Asset Portfolio (MM). Guardian Mutual

Fund (G + I), Liberty Fund (HYB), Manhattan Fund (G), Neuberger & Berman Cash Reserves (MM), Neuberger & Berman Genesis (G), Neuberger & Berman Government Money Fund (MM), Neuberger & Berman Limited Maturity Bond (I), Neuberger & Berman Money Market Plus (IB), Neuberger & Berman Municipal Securities (LTMB), Neuberger & Berman Municipal Money (STMB), Neuberger & Berman Partner's Fund (G), Neuberger & Berman Selected Sectors Plus Energy (G)

New England/Loomis-Sayles
399 Boylston Street, 9th Floor
Boston, Massachusetts 02116
(617) 267-6600, (617) 267-7055,
(800) 888-4823, (800) 343-7104,
(800) 634-8025
and
Back Bay Annex
P.O. Box 449
Boston, Massachusetts 02117
(617) 578-1333, (800) 345-4048
and
501 Boylston Street
Boston, Massachusetts 02117
(617) 267-7055, (800) 634-8025

Investment Trust of Boston: Growth Opportunity Portfolio (G + I), High Income Portfolio (HYB), Liquid Reserves Portfolio (MM), Massachusetts Tax Free Income Portfolio (SMB-LT), Premium Income Portfolio (G + I), World Income Portfolio (GB), Loomis-Sayles Capital Development Fund (G), Loomis-Sayles Mutual Fund (B), New England Bond Income Fund (IB), New England Cash Management Trust: Money Market Series (MM), U.S. Government Series (MM), New England Equity Income Fund (G + I), New England Global Government Fund (GB), New England Government Securities Fund (USGI), New England Growth Fund (G), New England Retirement Equity Fund (G), New England Tax Exempt Income Fund (LTMB), New England Tax Exempt Money Market Trust (STMB), New England Zenith Fund: Bond Income Series (IB), Capital Growth Series (G), Managed Series (G + I), Money Market Series (MM), Stock Index Series (G + I)

Newport Securities
3151 Airway Avenue, Suite H-1
Costa Mesa, California 92626
(714) 957-1217

Orange County Growth Fund (G)

Newton. see M&I Investment Management Corp.

Nicholas Company, Inc.
700 North Water Street, Suite 1010
Milwaukee, Wisconsin 53202
(414) 272-6133, (800) 227-5987

Nicholas Fund (G), Nicholas II (G), Nicholas Income Fund (I), Nicholas Limited Edition (G), Nicholas Money Market (MM)

Noddings Investment Group
Two MidAmerica Plaza, Suite 920
Oakbrook Terrace, Illinois 60181
(312) 954-1322, (800) 544-7785

Noddings Convertible Strategies Fund (AG)

Nomura Capital Management
180 Maiden Lane
New York, New York 10038
(212) 208-9300, (800) 833-0018

Nomura Pacific Basic Fund (INT)

Northeast Management & Research Co.
50 Congress Street
Boston, Massachusetts 02109
(617) 523-3588, (800) 225-6704

Northeast Investors Growth (G), Northeast Investors Trust (I)

Nuveen
333 West Wacker Drive
Chicago, Illinois 60606
(312) 917-7844, (312) 917-7843,
(312) 917-7824, (800) 621-7210,
(800) 858-4084, (800) 621-2431

Nuveen California Tax-Free Fund: Nuveen California Insured Portfolio (SMB-LT), Nuveen California Money Market Portfolio (SMB-ST), Nuveen California Special Bond Portfolio (SMB-LT), Nuveen Insured Tax-Free Bond Fund: Massachusetts Portfolio (SMB-LT), National Portfolio (LTMB), New York Portfolio (SMB-LT), Nuveen Municipal Bond Fund (LTMB), Nuveen Performance Plus Municipal Fund (STMB), Nuveen Tax-Exempt Money Market Fund (STMB), Nuveen Tax-Free Bond Fund: Massachusetts Portfolio (SMB-LT), New York Portfolio (SMB-LT), Ohio Portfolio (SMB-LT), Nuveen Tax-Free Money Market Fund: Massachusetts Portfolio (SMB-ST), New York Portfolio (SMB-ST), Nuveen Tax-Free Reserves (STMB)

Oberweis Securities
841 North Lake Street
Aurora, Illinois 60506
(312) 897-7100, (800) 722-0834

Oberweis Emerging Growth Fund: Emerging Growth Portfolio (AG)

Ohio National Fund
237 William Howard Taft
Cincinnati, Ohio 45219
(513) 861-3600

Ohio National Fund: Bond Portfolio (CB), Equity Portfolio (G), Money Market Portfolio (MM), Omni Portfolio (B)

OLDE
751 Griswold
Detroit, Michigan 48226
(313) 961-6666

OLDE Custodian Fund: OLDE Intermediate C.U. Investment Series (I), OLDE Special Ventures Equity Series (AG)

Olympic Trust
800 West 6th Street, Suite 540
Los Angeles, California 90017-2708
(213) 623-7833

Olympic Trust: Balanced Income Fund (B), Equity Income Fund (IE), Small Cap Fund (AG)

Oppenheimer/Centennial
3410 South Galena Street
Denver, Colorado 80231
(303) 671-3200, (800) 525-7048,
(800) 327-3069, (800) 548-1225
and
Two World Trade Center
New York, New York 10048-0669
(212) 323-0200, (800) 525-7048

Centennial California Tax-Exempt Trust (STMB), Centennial Government Trust (MM), Centennial Money Market Trust (MM), Centennial Tax Exempt Trust (STMB), Champion High Yield Fund-USA (HYB), Constitution Funds: Equity Income Fund (IE), High Yield Fund (HYB), Tax-Exempt Income Fund (LTMB), U.S. Government Fund (USGI), Daily Cash Accumulation Fund (MM), Main Street Funds: Capital Preservation Fund (G), Government Securities Fund (USGI), Income and Growth Fund (IE), Oppenheimer Asset Allocation Fund (FP), Oppenheimer Blue Chip Fund (G + I), Oppenheimer California Tax Exempt Fund (SMB-LT), Oppenheimer Cash Reserves (MM), Oppenheimer Directors Fund (AG), Oppenheimer Equity Income Fund (IE), Oppenheimer Fund (AG), Oppenheimer Global Bio-Tech Fund (GLB), Oppenheimer Global Fund (GLB), Oppenheimer GNMA Fund (GNMA), Oppenheimer Gold & Special Minerals Fund (PMG), Oppenheimer High Yield Fund (HYB), Oppenheimer Money Market Fund (MM), Oppenheimer New York Exempt Fund (SMB-LT), Oppenheimer New York Tax-Exempt Cash Reserves (SMB-ST), Oppenheimer Ninety-Ten

Fund (I), Oppenheimer OTC Fund (AG), Oppenheimer Pennsylvania Tax Exempt Fund (SMB-LT), Oppenheimer Premier Income Fund (OI), Oppenheimer Regency Fund (AG), Oppenheimer Special Fund (AG), Oppenheimer Target Fund (AG), Oppenheimer Tax-Exempt Cash Reserves (STMB), Oppenheimer Tax-Free Bond Fund (LTMB), Oppenheimer Time Fund (AG), Oppenheimer Total Income Fund (IB), Oppenheimer Total Return Fund (FP), Oppenheimer U.S. Government Trust (USGI), Oppenheimer Variable Account Funds: Oppenheimer Bond Fund (CB), Oppenheimer Capital Appreciation Fund (AG), Oppenheimer Growth Fund (G), Oppenheimer High Income Fund (HYB), Oppenheimer Money Fund (MM), Oppenheimer Multiple Strategies Fund (FP)

Over-The-Counter
275 Commerce Drive, Suite 228
P.O. Box 1537
Fort Washington, Pennsylvania 19034-1537
(215) 643-2510, (800) 523-2578

Over-The-Counter Securities Fund (G)

Pacific American
707 Wilshire Boulevard, W9-1
Los Angeles, California 90017
(213) 614-7697

Pacific American Fund: Money Market Portfolio (MM), Short Term Government Portfolio (MM)

Pacific Investment Management Company
840 Newport Center Drive, Suite 300
Newport Beach, California 92660
(714) 640-3031, (800) 443-6915

Pacific Investment Management Institutional Trust: Growth Stock Portfolio (G), International Bond Portfolio (GB), Long Duration Portfolio (IB), Low Duration Portfolio (IB), Market Mirror Stock Portfolio (G + I), Mortgage Plus Portfolio (GNMA), Short-Term Portfolio (I), Total Return Portfolio (IB)

PaineWebber
1285 Avenue of the Americas
PaineWebber Building
New York, New York 10019
(212) 713-2000, (800) 544-9300,
(800) 647-1568, (800) RMA-1000

PaineWebber California Tax Exempt Income Fund (SMB-LT), PaineWebber Cashfund (MM), PaineWebber Classic Atlas Fund (GLB), PaineWebber Classic Growth and Income Fund (G + I), PaineWebber Classic Growth Fund (G), PaineWebber Fixed Income Portfolios: GNMA Portfolio (GNMA), High Yield Bond Portfolio

(HYB), Investment Grade Bond Portfolio (CB), PaineWebber Investment Series: PaineWebber Master Energy-Utility Fund (G + I), Paine-Webber Master Global Income Fund (GB), PaineWebber Managed Municipal Trust: Paine-Webber Tax-Exempt Income Fund (LTMB), PaineWebber Master Series: PaineWebber Master Asset Allocation Fund (FP), Paine-Webber Master Growth Fund (G), PaineWebber Master Income Fund (IB), PaineWebber Master Money Fund (MM), PaineWebber Municipal Series: PaineWebber Classic New York Tax-Free Fund (SMB-LT), PaineWebber High Yield Municipal Bond Fund (LTMB), Paine-Webber RMA Money Fund: California Tax Free Fund (SMB-ST), Money Market Portfolio (MM), New York Tax Free Fund (SMB-ST), Paine-Webber Retirement Money Fund (MM), U.S. Government Portfolio (MM), PaineWebber RMA Tax-Exempt Fund (STMB), PaineWebber Series Trust: Asset Allocation Portfolio (FP), Corporate Bond Portfolio (CB), Global Growth Portfolio (GLB), Global Income Portfolio (GB), Growth & Income Portfolio (G + I), Growth Portfolio (G), High Yield Bond Portfolio (HYB), Money Market Portfolio (MM)

Paribas
787 Seventh Avenue, 30th Floor
Equitable Building
New York, New York 10019
(212) 841-3200

Paribas Trust for Institutions: Quantas Equity Managed Portfolio (G), Quantas II (G)

Parkway
985 Old Eagle School Road
Wayne, Pennsylvania 19087
(215) 688-8165, (800) 992-2207

Parkway Cash Fund (MM), Parkway Tax-Free Reserve Fund (STMB)

Parnassus Financial
244 California Street
San Francisco, California 94111
(415) 362-3505

Parnassus Fund (G)

Pasadena Investment Trust
600 North Rosemead Boulevard
Pasadena, California 91107-2101
(818) 351-4276, (800) 882-2855

Pasadena Investment Trust: Pasadena Growth Fund (AG), Pasadena Fundamental Value Fund (G)

Patriot Group, Inc.
211 Congress Street
Boston, Massachusetts 02110
(617) 426-3310, (800) 843-0090

Patriot Group Investment Trust: Patriot Corporate Cash Fund (IE)

Pax World
224 State Street
Portsmouth, New Hampshire 03801
(603) 431-8022

Pax World Fund (B)

Pennsylvania Mutual
1414 Avenue of the Americas
New York, New York 10019
(212) 355-7311, (800) 221-4268

Pennsylvania Mutual Fund (G), Royce Fund: Income Series (HYB), Total Return Series (IE), Value Series (AG)

Perritt Investments
205 West Wacker Drive, 5th Floor
Chicago, Illinois 60606
(312) 750-9304, (800) 338-1579

Perritt Capital Growth Fund (AG)

Phoenix
101 Munson Street
Greenfield, Massachusetts 01301
(413) 774-3151, (800) 243-1574

Phoenix Multi-Portfolio Fund: Phoenix Tax-Exempt Bond Portfolio (LTMB). Phoenix Series Fund: Phoenix Balanced Fund Series (B), Phoenix Convertible Fund Series (G + I), Phoenix Growth Fund Series (G), Phoenix High Quality Bond Fund Series (CB), Phoenix High Yield Fund Series (HYB), Phoenix Money Market Fund Series (MM), Phoenix Stock Fund Series (G), Phoenix U.S. Government Securities Fund Series (USGI), Phoenix Total Return Fund (AG)

Pilgrim
101000 Santa Monica Boulevard, 21st Floor
Los Angeles, California 90067
(213) 551-0833, (800) 334-3444

Pilgrim Corporate Investors Fund (I), Pilgrim Foreign Investors: Pilgrim Government Securities Fund (GNMA), Pilgrim High Income Fund (CB), Pilgrim International Bond Fund (GB), Pilgrim GNMA Fund (GNMA), Pilgrim High Yield Trust (I), Pilgrim MagnaCap Fund (G) Pilgrim Money Market Fund: General Portfolio (MM), Pilgrim Preferred Fund (I)

Pioneer
60 State Street
Boston, Massachusetts 02109-1975
(617) 742-7825, (800) 225-6292
Pioneer Bond Fund (CB), Pioneer Cash Reserve (MM), Pioneer Fund (G + I), Pioneer II (G + I), Pioneer Municipal Bond Fund (LTMB), Pioneer Tax-Free Money Market Fund (STMB), Pioneer Three (G + I), Pioneer U.S. Government Money Market Fund (MM), Pioneer U.S. Government Trust (USGI)

Piper Jaffray Investment Trust
222 South 9th Street
Piper Jaffray Tower
Minneapolis, Minnesota 55402
(612) 342-6426
American Opportunity Income Fund (G + I), Piper Jaffray Investment Trust: Balanced Fund (B), Government Income Fund (GNMA), Institutional Government Income Fund (USGI), Minnesota Tax-Exempt Fund (SMB-LT), Money Market Fund (MM), National Tax-Exempt Fund (LTMB), Sector Performance Fund (G), Tax-Exempt Money Market (STMB), U.S. Government Money Market Fund (MM), Value Fund (G)

Planco Financial Services
16 Industrial Boulevard
Paoli, Pennsylvania 19301
(215) 251-0550, (800) 523-7798
RBB Fund: Bedford Government Money Market Portfolio (MM), Bedford Money Market Portfolio (MM), Bedford Tax-Free Money Market Portfolio (STMB), Cash Preservation Money Market Portfolio (MM), Cash Preservation Tax-Free Money Market Portfolio (STMB), SafeGuard Balanced Portfolio (B), SafeGuard Equity Growth and Income Portfolio (IE), Safeguard Money Market Portfolio (MM), Safe-Guard Tax-Free Money Market Portfolio (STMB), SafeGuard Tax-Free Portfolio (LTMB), Sansom Street Government Money Market Portfolio (MM), Sansom Street Money Market Portfolio (MM), Sansom Street Tax-Free Money Market Portfolio (STMB)

Portfolios Inc.
1445 Ross Avenue, LB212
Dallas, Texas 75202
(214) 720-9101
Armstrong Associates (G)

PNC Financial Corp.
Webster Building, Suite 204
Concord Plaza
3411 Silverside Road
Wilmington, Delaware 19810
(302) 478-1630
PNC Equity Portfolio (G), PNC Fixed Income (B), PNC Money Market Portfolio (MM), PNC Government Money Market Portfolio (MM), PNC Tax-Free Money Market Portfolio (USGI)

P.N.C.G. Fund Advisors, Inc.
121 S.W. Morrison, Suite 1415
Portland, Oregon 97205
(503) 295-0919, (800) 541-9732
Oregon Municipal Bond Fund (SMB-LT), P.N.C.G. Growth Fund (G + I)

T. Rowe Price Funds. see T. Rowe Price under "T"

Princor
711 High Street
Des Moines, Iowa 50309
(515) 247-5711, (800) 247-4123
Princor Aggressive Growth Fund (AG), Princor Bond Fund (CB), Princor Capital Accumulation Fund (G + I), Princor Cash Management Fund (MM), Princor Government Securities Income Fund (GNMA), Princor Growth Fund (G), Princor High Yield Fund (HYB), Princor Managed Fund (FP), Princor Tax-Exempt Bond Fund (LTMB), Princor Tax-Exempt Cash Management Fund (STMB), Princor World Fund (GLB)

Providentmutual Investment Management Co.
1600 Market Street
P.O. Box 7378
Phildelphia, Pennsylvania 19101
(215) 636-5000
Market Street Fund: Bond Portfolio (PM Variable Bond Sep. Acct. III) (IB), Growth Portfolio (PM Variable Growth Sep. Acct. I) (G), Managed Portfolio (PM Variable Managed Sep. Acct. IV) (FP), Money Market Portfolio (PM Variable Money Market Sep. Acct. II) (MM)

Prudent Speculator
4023 West 6th Street
Los Angeles, California 90020
(213) 386-0260, (800) 444-4778
Prudent Speculator Fund: Prudent Speculator Leveraged Fund (AG)

Prudential Mutual Funds
One Seaport Plaza
New York, New York 10292
(212) 214-1215, (800) 872-7787

Command Government Fund (MM), Command Money Fund (MM), Command Tax-Free Fund (STMB), Prudential Institutional Liquidity Portfolio: Institutional Domestic Liquid Assets Series (MM), Institutional Government Series (MM), Institutional Money Market Series (MM), Institutional Tax-Exempt Series (STMB), Prudential-Bache California Municipal Fund (SMB-LT), Prudential-Bache Corporate Dividend Fund (G + I), Prudential-Bache Equity Fund (G), Prudential-Bache Equity Income Fund (IE), Prudential-Bache FlexiFund: Aggressively Managed Portfolio (FP), Conservatively Managed Portfolio (FP), Prudential-Bache Global Fund (GLB), Prudential-Bache Global Genesis Fund (GLB), Prudential-Bache Global Natural Resources Fund (GLB), Prudential-Bache GNMA Fund (GNMA), Prudential-Bache Government Securities Trust: Intermediate Term Series (USGI), Money Market Series (MM), Prudential-Bache Government Plus Fund (USGI), Prudential-Bache Government Plus Fund II (USGI), Prudential-Bache Growth Opportunity Fund (AG), Prudential-Bache High Yield Fund (HYB), Prudential-Bache Income-Vertible Plus Fund (I), Prudential-Bache Money-Mart Assets (MM), Prudential-Bache Municipal Bond Fund: High Yield Series (LTMB), Insured Series (LTMB), Modified Term Series (LTMB), Prudential-Bache Municipal Series Fund: Arizona Series (SMB-LT), Georgia Series (SMB-LT), Maryland Series (SMB-LT), Massachusetts Series (SMB-LT), Michigan Series (SMB-LT), Minnesota Series (SMB-LT), New Jersey Series (SMB-LT), New York Money Market Series (SMB-ST), New York Series (SMB-LT), North Carolina Series (SMB-LT), Ohio Series (SMB-LT), Oregon Series (SMB-LT), Pennsylvania Series (SMB-LT), Prudential-Bache National Municipals Fund (LTMB), Prudential-Bache Option Growth Fund (G), Prudential-Bache Research Fund (G), Prudential-Bache Special Situations Fund (AG), Prudential-Bache Tax Free Money Fund (STMB), Prudential-Bache Utility Fund (IE)

Prudent Speculator Group
P.O. Box 75231
Los Angeles, California 90075-0231
(800) 444-4778

Prudent Speculator Leveraged Fund (AG)

Public Service Investment
618 South 19th Street
Arlington, Virginia 22202
(703) 521-0785, (804) 782-7347

Public Employees Retirement Trust (G + I)

Putnam Funds
One Post Office Square
Boston, Massachusetts 02109
(617) 292-1000, (800) 225-2465

George Putnam Fund of Boston (B), Putnam California Tax Exempt Income Fund (SMB-LT), Putnam California Tax Exempt Money Market Fund (SMB-ST), Putnam Capital Manager Trust: PCM Fixed Account (I), PCM Growth and Income Fund (G + I), PCM High Yield Fund (HYB), PCM Money Market Fund (MM), PCM Multi-Strategy Fund (FP), PCM U.S. Government and High Grade Bond Fund (IB), PCM Voyager Fund (AG), Putnam Capital Preservation/Income Trust (USGI), Putnam Convertible Income - Growth Trust (G + I), Putnam Corporate Cash Trust - Adjustable Rate Preferred Portfolio (I), Putnam Corporate Cash Trust - Diversified Strategies Portfolio (I), Putnam Daily Dividend Trust (MM), Putnam Dividend Income (I), Putnam Diversified Income Trust (I), Putnam Energy-Resources Trust (AG), Putnam Fund for Growth and Income (G + I), Putnam Global Governmental Income Trust (GB), Putnam GNMA Plus Trust (GNMA), Putnam Health Sciences Trust (AG), Putnam High Income Government Trust (USGI), Putnam High Yield Trust (HYB), Putnam High Yield Trust II (HYB), Putnam Income Fund (I), Putnam Information Sciences Trust (AG), Putnam International Equities Fund (GLB), Putnam Investors Fund (G), Putnam Massachusetts Tax Exempt Income Fund (SMB-LT), Putnam Michigan Tax Exempt Income Fund (SMB-LT), Putnam Minnesota Tax Exempt Income Fund (SMB-LT), Putnam New York Tax Exempt Income Fund (SMB-LT), Putnam New York Tax Exempt Money Market Fund (SMB-ST), Putnam Ohio Tax Exempt Income Fund (SMB-LT), Putnam Option Income Trust (OI), Putnam Option Income Trust II (OI), Putnam OTC Emerging Growth Fund (AG), Putnam Tax Exempt Income Fund (LTMB), Putnam Tax Exempt Money Market Fund (STMB), Putnam Tax-Free Income Trust: High Yield Fund (LTMB), Insured Fund (LTMB), Putnam U.S. Government Guaranteed Securities Income Trust (GNMA), Putnam Vista Basic Value Fund (AG), Putnam Voyager Fund (AG)

Quantum
605 Madison Avenue
Covington, Kentucky 41011
(606) 491-4271

Quantum Fund (AG)

Quest For Value
Oppenheimer Tower
World Financial Center
New York, New York 10281
(212) 667-7587, (800) 862-7778

Quest For Value Accumulation Trust: Bond Trust (IB), Equity Fund (G), Managed Fund (FP), Money Market Fund (MM), SmallCap Fund (G), Quest For Value Cash Management Trust (MM), Quest for Value Fund (AG), Quest for Value Investment Trust: U.S. Government High Income Fund (USGI)

Rea-Graham
10966 Chalon Road
Los Angeles, California 90077
(213) 471-1917, (800) 433-1998

Rea-Graham Fund (G)

Reich & Tang, Inc.
100 Park Avenue
New York, New York 10017
(212) 370-1252

Reich & Tang Equity (AG)

Republic National Bank of New York
230 Park Avenue
New York, New York 10169
(212) 309-8400, (800) 845-8406

Fund Trust Aggressive Growth (AG), Fund Trust Growth (G), Fund Trust Growth and Income (G + I), Fund Trust Income (I), Money Trust (MM)

Reserve Management Co.
810 Seventh Avenue
New York, New York 10019
(212) 977-9675, (800) 421-0261

Reserve Equity Trust-Contrarian Portfolio (G + I)

Rightime Econometrics
Forst Pavilion, Suite 1000
218 Glenside Avenue
Wyncote, Pennsylvania 19095-1595
(215) 572-7288, (215) 887-8111,
(800) 242-1421

Rightime Fund: Rightime Blue Chip Fund (G), Rightime Fund (FP), Rightime Government Securities Fund (USGI), Rightime Growth Fund (FP)

RNC Mutual Fund Group
11601 Wilshire Boulevard, 24th Floor
Los Angeles, California 90025
(213) 312-3393, (800) 225-9655

RNC Convertible Securities Fund (G + I), RNC Corporate Cash Management Fund (IE), RNC Income Fund (IB), RNC Liquid Assets Fund (MM), RNC Regency Fund (G), RNC Short-Intermediate Government Securities Fund (USGI), RNC Westwind Fund (G + I)

Robertson, Colman & Stephens
One Embarcadero Center, Suite 3100
San Francisco, California 94111
(415) 781-9700, (800) 821-9687

RCS Emerging Growth Fund (AG)

Rochester
379 Park Avenue
Rochester, New York 14607
(716) 442-5500

Rochester Convertible Funds: Growth Fund (CB), Income Fund (HYB), Rochester Fund Municipals (LTMB), Rochester Growth Fund (G), Rochester Tax Managed Fund (G + I)

Rockwood Growth Fund
545 Shoup Avenue, Suite 334
P.O. Box 50313
Idaho Falls, Idaho 83405
(208) 522-5593

Rockwood Growth Fund (G),

Rodney Square
Rodney Square North
Wilmington, Delaware 19890
(302) 651-1923, (800) 225-5084

Rodney Square Benchmark U.S. Treasury Fund (USGI), Rodney Square Fund: Money Market Portfolio (MM), U.S. Government Portfolio (MM), Rodney Square International Securities Fund: Rodney Square International Equity Fund (INT), Rodney Square Multi-Manager Fund: Growth Portfolio (AG), Total Return Portfolio (G + I), Value Portfolio (G), Rodney Square Tax-Exempt Fund (STMB)

T. Rowe Price Funds. see T. Rowe Price under "T"

Ruane, Cunniff & Co.
1370 Avenue of the Americas
New York, New York 10019
(212) 245-4500

Sequoia Fund (G)

Rushmore Funds. see Money Management Associates

RXR Group
30 Buxton Farm Road, Suite 116
Stamford, Connecticut 06905
(203) 323-5015, (800) 654-5311

RXR Dynamic Government Fund (USGI)

Ryland Acceptance Advisors, Inc.
325 Columbia Turnpike
Florham Park, New Jersey 07932
(201) 514-2000

Mortgage Liquidity Fund (GNMA)

SAFECO Asset Management Company
SAFECO Plaza, T-15
Seattle, Washington 98185
(206) 545-5530, (800) 426-6730

SAFECO California Tax-Free Income (SMB-LT), SAFECO Equity Fund (G + I), SAFECO Growth Fund (G), SAFECO High-Yield Bond (HYB), SAFECO Income Fund (IE), SAFECO Intermediate-Term Bond (IB), SAFECO Money Market Mutual Fund (MM), SAFECO Municipal Bond Fund (LTMB), SAFECO Tax-Free Money Market (STMB), SAFECO U.S. Government Securities (USGI)

Salem Funds
99 High Street
Boston, Massachusetts 02110
(704) 331-0710, (800) 343-3424

Salem Growth (G)

Saxton Woods Asset Management
550 Mamaroneck Avenue
Harrison, New York 10528
(914) 698-5711, (800) 235-0064

Evergreen American Retirement (G + I), Evergreen Fund (AG), Evergreen Money Market Trust (MM), Evergreen Total Return (G + I), Evergreen Value Timing Fund (G)

Schafer Capital Management
645 Fifth Avenue, 7th Floor
New York, New York 10022
(212) 644-1800

Schafer Value Fund (G)

Schield Management Co.
390 Union Boulevard, Suite 410
Denver, Colorado 80228
(303) 985-9999, (800) 826-8154

Schield Portfolios Series: Aggressive Growth Portfolio (AG), High Yield Bond Portfolio (HYB), Timed Asset Allocation Multi-Fund (FP), Value Portfolio (G)

Schroder Capital
787 Seventh Avenue, 29th Floor
New York, New York 10019
(212) 422-6550

Schroder Capital Funds: Schroder U.S. Equity Fund (G)

Schroder Capital Management International
230 Park Avenue
New York, New York 10169
(212) 309-8400, (800) 845-8406

International Equity Trust (INT)

Scudder Stevens & Clark, Inc.
175 Federal Street
Boston, Massachusetts 02110
(617) 439-4640, (617) 482-3990,
(800) 253-2277, (800) 225-2471
and
345 Park Avenue
New York, New York 10154
(212) 326-6200, (617) 439-4640,
(800) 225-2470

AARP Cash Investment Funds: AARP Money Fund (MM), AARP Growth Trust: AARP Capital Growth Fund (G), AARP Growth and Income Fund (G + I), AARP Income Trust: AARP General Bond Fund (CB), AARP GNMA and U.S. Treasury Fund (USGI), AARP Insured Tax Free Income Trust: AARP Insured Tax Free General Bond Fund (LTMB), AARP Insured Tax Free Short Term Fund (STMB) Japan Fund (INT), Korea Fund (INT), Scudder California Tax Free Fund (SMB-LT), Scudder California Tax Free Money (SMT-ST), Scudder Capital Growth Fund (G), Scudder Cash Investment Trust (MM), Scudder Development Fund (AG), Scudder Equity Income Fund (G + I), Scudder GNMA Fund (GNMA), Scudder Global Fund (GLB), Scudder Gold Fund (PMG), Scudder Government Money Fund (MM), Scudder Growth & Income Free (G + I), Scudder High Yield Tax-Free (LTMB), Scudder Income Fund (I), Scudder International Bond Fund (I), Scudder International Fund (INT), Scudder Massachusetts Tax Free Fund (SMB-LT), Scudder Managed Municipal (SMB-LT), Scudder New York Tax Free Fund (SMB-LT), Scudder New York Tax Free Money (SMB-ST), Scudder Ohio Tax Free Fund (SMB-LT), Scudder Pennsylvania Tax Free Fund (SMB-LT), Scudder Target Fund: General 90 (IB), General 94 (IB), Government 90 (USGI), U.S. Government 1990 Zero Coupon (USGI), U.S. Government 1995 Zero Coupon (USGI), U.S. Government 2000 Zero Coupon (USGI), Scudder Tax-Free Target Fund: Tax Free 90 (LTMB), Tax Free 93 (LTMB),

Tax Free 96 (LTMB), Scudder Tax-Free Money Fund (MM), Scudder Tax-Free Target Fund (LTMB), Scudder U.S. Government Zero Coupon Bond (I), Scudder Treasurers Trust: Treasurers Money Portfolio (MM), Treasurers Tax Exempt Money Portfolio (STMB)

Sea Investment Management
6991 East Camelback Road, Suite B304
Scottsdale, Arizona 85251
(602) 998-5557
Arizona Tax Free Fund (SMB-LT)

Seafirst
701 Fifth Avenue
P.O. Box 84248
Seattle, Washington 98124
(206) 358-6119, (800) 323-9919

Collective Investment Trust for Seafirst Retirement Accounts: Asset Allocation Fund (FP), Blue Chip Fund (G), Bond Fund (IB), Money Market Fund (MM)

SECURAL Group
2401 South Memorial Drive
Appleton, Wisconsin 54915
(414) 739-3161, (800) 426-5975
SECURAL Mutual Funds: Fixed Income Fund (I), Government Bond Fund (LTMB), Municipal Bond Fund (LTMB), Special Equity Fund (AG), Stock Fund (G + I)

Security Benefit Group
700 Harrison Street, 6th Floor
Topeka, Kansas 66636
(913) 295-3127, (800) 255-2461,
(800) 432-3536
Security Action Fund (G), Security Cash Fund (MM), Security Equity Fund (G) Security Income Fund: Corporate Bond Series (CB), High Yield Series (HYB), U.S. Government Series (GNMA), Security Investment Fund (G + I), Security Omni Fund (AG), Security Tax-Exempt Fund (LTMB), Security Ultra Fund (AG)

SEI Financial Services
680 East Swedesford Road, No. 7
Wayne, Pennsylvania 19087
(215) 254-1000, (800) 345-1151
SEI Cash+Plus Trust: Federal Securities Portfolio (MM), GNMA Portfolio (GNMA), Government Portfolio (MM), Intermediate Term Government Portfolio (USGI), Money Market Portfolio (MM), Prime Obligation Portfolio (MM), Short-Term Government Portfolio (USGI), SEI Index Funds: Bond Index Portfolio (IB), S&P 500 Index Portfolio (G + I), SEI

Institutional Managed Trust: Balanced Portfolio (B), Bond Portfolio (IB), Capital Appreciation Portfolio (G), Equity Income Portfolio (IE), Limited Volatility Bond Portfolio (IB), Value Portfolio (G + I), SEI Liquid Asset Trust: Commercial Portfolio (MM), Government Portfolio (MM), Prime Obligation Portfolio (MM), Treasury II Portfolio (MM), Treasury Portfolio (MM), SEI Tax Exempt Trust: Institutional Tax Free Portfolio (STMB), Tax Free Portfolio (STMB)

Selected
1331 Euclid Avenue
Cleveland, Ohio 44115
(216) 696-3360, (800) 553-5533
Selected American Shares (G + I), Selected Capital Preservation Trust: Selected Daily Government Fund (MM), Selected Daily Income Fund (MM), Selected Daily Tax-Exempt Fund (STMB), Selected Government Total Return Fund (USGI), Selected Special Shares (G)

Seligman
One Bankers Trust Plaza
New York, New York 10006
(212) 488-0200, (800) 221-2450
Seligman California Tax-Exempt Fund Series: High-Yield Series (SMB-LT), Money Market Series (SMB-ST), Quality Series (SMB-LT), Seligman Capital Fund (AG), Seligman Cash Management Fund: Government Portfolio (MM), Prime Portfolio (MM), Seligman Common Stock Fund (G + I), Seligman Communications and Information Fund (AG), Seligman Growth Fund (G), Seligman High Income Fund Series: High-Yield Bond Series (HYB), Secured Mortgage Income Series (GNMA), U.S. Government Guaranteed Securities Series (USGI), Seligman Income Fund (I), Seligman Mutual Benefit Portfolios: Seligman Capital Portfolio (AG), Seligman Cash Management Portfolio (MM), Seligman Common Stock Portfolio (G + I), Seligman Fixed Income Securities Portfolio (IB), Seligman Income Portfolio (I), Seligman New Jersey Tax-Exempt Fund (SMB-LT), Seligman Pennsylvania Tax-Exempt Fund Series: High-Yield Series (SMB-LT), Quality Series (SMB-LT), Seligman Tax-Exempt Fund Series: Colorado Tax-Exempt Series (SMB-LT), Florida Tax-Exempt Series (SMB-LT), Georgia Tax-Exempt Series (SMB-LT), Louisiana Tax-Exempt Series (SMB-LT), Maryland Tax-Exempt Series (SMB-LT), Massachusetts Tax Exempt Series (SMB-LT), Michigan Tax-Exempt Series (SMB-LT), Minnesota Tax-Exempt Series (SMB-LT), Missouri

Tax-Exempt Series (SMB-LT), National Tax-Exempt Series (LTMB), New York Tax-Exempt Series (SMB-LT), Ohio Tax-Exempt Series (SMB-LT), Oregon Tax-Exempt Series (SMB-LT), South Carolina Tax-Exempt Series (SMB-LT)

Sentinel
National Life Drive
Montpelier, Vermont 05604
(802) 229-3900, (800) 282-3863
Sentinel Cash Management Fund (MM), Sentinel Group Funds: Balanced Fund Series (B), Bond Fund Series (IB), Common Stock Fund Series (G + I), Government Securities Fund (USGI), Growth Fund Series (G)

Sentry
1800 North Point Drive
Stevens Point, Wisconsin 54481
(715) 346-6000, (800) 826-0266
Sentry Fund (G)

Sequoia Fund. see Ruane, Cuniff & Co.

Shearson Lehman Hutton
1 Boston Place
Boston, Massachusetts 02019
(617) 956-9740, (617) 451-2010,
(800) 225-5267
and
3512 Silverside Road
The Commons, Number 6
Wilmington, Delaware 19810
(302) 478-6945, (800) 441-7379
and
2 World Trade Center
New York, New York 10048
(212) 321-7155, (212) 321-7160,
(212) 528-2744
and
One Battery Park Plaza
New York, New York 10004
(212) 742-5000
and
31 West 52nd Street, 15th Floor
New York, New York 10019
(212) 969-5300, (800) 334-4636
(212) 528-2744
and
1300 South University Drive, 6th Floor
Fort Worth, Texas 76107
(817) 335-3051, (800) 221-3636
American Telecommunication Trust: SLH AT&T Growth Portfolio (G), SLH AT&T Income Portfolio (G + I), Arch Fund: Discretionary Portfolio (MM), Non-Discretionary Portfolio (MM), Arch Tax-Exempt Trust: Discretionary Portfolio

(STMB), Non-Discretionary Portfolio (STMB), Bison Money Market Fund: Discretionary Portfolio - Class B (MM), Non-Discretionary Portfolio - Class A (MM), Tax-Exempt Discretionary Portfolio (STMB), Tax-Exempt Non-Discretionary Portfolio (STMB), Boston Company Fund: Capital Appreciation Fund (G), Cash Management Fund (MM), GNMA Fund (GNMA), Government Income Fund (CB), Government Money Fund (MM), Special Growth Fund (G), Boston Company Index and Blue Chip Trust: Blue Chip Fund (G + I), Bond Index Fund (IB), Equity Index Fund (G), Small Capitalization Equity Index Fund (G), Boston Company Tax-Free Municipal Funds: California Tax-Free Bond Fund (SMB-LT), California Tax-Free Money Fund (SMB-ST), Massachusetts Tax-Free Bond Fund (SMB-LT), Massachusetts Tax-Free Money Fund (SMB-ST), New York Tax-Free Bond Fund (SMB-LT), New York Tax-Free Money Fund (SMB-ST), Tax Free Bond Fund (LTMB), Tax-Free Money Fund (STMB), Chestnut Street Cash Fund: Portfolio A (MM), Portfolio B (MM), E.F. Hutton Municipal Series: SLH Arizona Municipal Fund (SMB-LT), Galaxy Fund: Government Fund (MM), Money Market Fund (MM), Tax Exempt Money Market Fund (STMB), Hutton Investment Series: Bond & Income Series (IB), SLH European Portfolio (INT), SLH Global Equity Portfolio (GLB), SLH Government Fund (USGI), SLH Growth Portfolio (G), SLH Investment Grade Bond Portfolio (AG), SLH Pacific Portfolio (INT), SLH Precious Metal Portfolio (PMG), SLH Special Equities Portfolio (AG), Hutton Master Series: SLH Convertible Securities Fund (G + I), International Fund for Institutions (INT), Marketmaster Money Market Trust (MM), Marketmaster Trust: Government Fund (MM), Money Market Fund (MM), Tax Exempt Fund (STMB), Municipal Fund for California Investors (SMB-ST), Municipal Fund for New York Investors (SMB-ST), Municipal Fund for Temporary Investment: InterMuni Fund (LTMB), LongMuni Fund (STMB), Muni-Cash (STMB), Muni-Cash (STMB), Muni-Fund (STMB), Portfolios for Diversified Investment: Diversified Equity Appreciation Fund (G), Diversified Fixed Income Fund (IB), Shearson Lehman California Daily Tax Fund (SMB-LT), Shearson Lehman Series Fund: SLH IDS Appreciation Portfolio (G), SLH IDS Government Portfolio (USGI), SLH IDS High Income Portfolio (HYB), SLH IDS Money Market Portfolio (MM), SLH IDS Total Return Portfolio (G + I), Shearson Lehman Special Equity Portfolios: SLH Growth and Opportunity Portfolio (G), SLH Sector Analysis Portfolio (G), SLH Special International Equity Portfolio (INT),

SLH Strategic Investors Portfolio (FP), Shearson Lehman Special Income Portfolios: SLH Convertible Portfolio (G + I), SLH Global Bond Portfolio (GB), SLH High Income Bond Portfolio (HYB), SLH Intermediate Term Government Portfolio (USGI), SLH Long Term Government Portfolio (USGI), SLH Mortgage Securities Portfolio (GNMA), SLH Option/Income Portfolio (OI), SLH Special Income Money Market Portfolios (MM), SLH Tax Exempt Income Portfolio (LTMB), SLH Utility Portfolio (I), SLH Aggressive Growth Fund (AG), SLH Appreciation (G), SLH California Municipal Fund (SMB-LT), SLH Daily Dividend Fund (MM), SLH Daily Tax-Free Dividend Fund (STMB), SLH Fundamental Value Fund (G), SLH Global Opportunities Fund (GLB), SLH Government and Agencies Income Fund (MM), SLH High Yield Fund (HYB), SLH Managed Governments (GNMA), SLH Managed Municipals (LTMB), SLH Massachusetts Municipals (MB-LT), SLH Michigan Municipals (SMB-LT), SLH Multiple Opportunities Portfolio L.P. (FP), SLH New York Daily Tax-Free Fund (SMB-ST), SLH New York Municipals (SMB-LT), SLH Ohio Municipals (SMB-LT), SLH Precious Metals and Minerals (PMG), SLH Principal Return Fund: Zeros and Appreciation Series 1996 (G), SLH Small Capitalization (AG), Temporary Investment Fund: TempCash (MM), TempFund (MM), Trust for Federal Securities: FedFund (MM), ShortFed Fund (USGI), T-Fund (MM)

Sheffield Management
1 Pitcairn Place
Jenkintown, Pennsylvania 19046
(215) 887-6700
and
41 Madison Avenue, 24th Floor
New York, New York 10010
(212) 779-7979, (800) 922-7771

Blanchard Government Money Market Fund (MM), Blanchard Precious Metals Fund (PMG), Blanchard Strategic Growth Fund (FP)

Sherman, Dean
6061 N.W. Expressway, Suite 465, IH 10(W)
San Antonio, Texas 78201
(512) 735-7700, (800) 247-6375

Sherman, Dean Fund (AG)

Siebel Capital
80 East Sir Francis Drake Boulevard
Larkspur, California 94939
(415) 461-3850
and
7677 Oakport Street
P.O. Box 2470
Oakland, California 94614

(415) 430-9900, (800) 445-9020
Adam Investors (G + I), Equitec Siebel Fund Group: Equitec Siebel Aggressive Growth Fund Series (AG), Equitec Siebel Cash Equivalent Fund Series (MM), Equitec Siebel Global Fund Series (GLB), Equitec Siebel High Yield Bond Fund Series (HYB), Equitec Siebel Precious Metals Fund Series (PMG), Equitec Siebel Total Return Fund Series (G + I), Equitec Siebel U.S. Government Securities Fund Series (USGI), Equitec Siebel Fund Group II: Equitec Siebel California Tax-Exempt Municipal Bond Fund Series (SMB-LT), Equitec Siebel Equity Plus Fund Series (IE), Equitec Siebel Series Trust: Agressive Growth Portfolio (AG), High Yield Bond Portfolio (HYB), Money Market Portfolio (MM), Total Return Portfolio (G + I), Gamma Partners (G + I), Siebel Capital Partners (G + I)

Sigma
3801 Kennett Park, Suite C-200
Wilmington, Delaware 19087
(302) 652-3091, (800) 441-9490
and
100 Oliver Street
Boston, Massachusetts 02110
(617) 268-7575, (800) 441-9490

ISI Growth Fund (G), ISI Trust Fund (G + I), Sigma Capital Shares (AG), Sigma Federal Moneyfund (MM), Sigma Income Shares (IB), Sigma Investment Shares (G + I), Sigma MoneyFund (MM), Sigma Pennsylvania Tax-Free Trust (SMB-LT), Sigma Special Fund (G), Sigma Tax-Free Bond Fund (LTMB), Sigma Tax-Free Fund: Money Market Portfolio (STMB), SIGMA Trust Shares (B), Sigma U.S. Government Fund (USGI), Sigma Value Shares (G), Sigma Venture Shares (AG), Sigma World Fund (INT)

SIT Investment Associates
1714 First Bank Place West
Minneapolis, Minnesota 55402
(612) 332-3223, (800) 332-5580

Sit "New Beginning" Growth (AG), Sit "New Beginning" Income & Growth (IE), Sit "New Beginning" Investment Reserve (IB), Sit "New Beginning" Tax-Free Income (LTMB), Sit "New Beginning" U.S. Government Securities (USGI)

SMA Investment Trust
440 Lincoln Street
Worcester, Massachusetts 01605
(508) 852-1000

SMA Investment Trust: Growth Fund (G), Income Appreciation Fund (G + I), Money Market Fund (MM)

Smith Barney
1345 Avenue of the Americas
New York, New York 10105
(212) 399-6000, (800) 544-7835

Muni Bond Funds: California Portfolio (SMB-LT), Limited Term Portfolio (LTMB), National Portfolio (LTMB), New York Portfolio (SMB-LT), National Liquid Reserves: NLR Cash Portfolio (MM), NLR Government Portfolio (MM), NLR Retirement Portfolio (MM), Smith Barney Equity Funds (G), Smith Barney Funds: Income & Growth Portfolio (G + I), Income Return Account Portfolio (I), Monthly Payment Government Portfolio (GNMA), U.S. Government Securities Portfolio (GNMA), Tax Free Money Fund (STMB), Vantage Money Market Funds: Vantage Cash Portfolio (MM), Vantage Government Portfolio (MM)

Smith Hayes Financial Services
NBC Center, Suite 780
Lincoln, Nebraska 68508
(402) 476-3000

Smith Hayes Trust: Asset Allocation Portfolio (FP), Balanced Portfolio (FP), Convertible Portfolio (IE), Convertible Preferred Portfolio (G + I), Covered Option Writing Portfolio (G), Defensive Growth Portfolio (G), Government/Quality Bond Portfolio (USGI), Value Portfolio (G)

SoGen Securities Corp.
767 Fifth Avenue
New York, New York 10153
(212) 832-0022, (800) 334-2143

SoGen International Fund (INT)

Sound Shore Management, Inc.
P.O. Box 1810
8 Sound Shore Drive
Greenwich, Connecticut 06836
(203) 629-1980

Sound Shore Fund (G)

Southeastern Asset
860 Ridgelake Boulevard, Suite 301
Memphis, Tennessee 38119
(901) 761-2474, (800) 445-9469

Southeastern Asset Management Value Trust (G)

Southern Farm Bureau
1401 Livingston Lane, Suite 300
P.O. Box 691
Jackson, Mississippi 39205
(601) 982-7800, (800) 647-8053

Southern Farm Bureau Cash Fund (MM)

Sovereign
985 Old Eagle School Road, Suite 515A
Wayne, Pennsylvania 19087
(215) 254-0703

Sovereign Investors (G + I)

Spears, Benzak, Salomon & Farrell
45 Rockefeller Plaza, 33rd Floor
New York, New York 10111
(212) 903-1200, (800) 422-7273

SBSF Funds: SBSF Convertible Securities Fund (G + I), SBSF Growth Fund (G), SBSF Money Market Fund (MM)

Spencer
908 Town & Country Boulevard, Suite 602
Houston, Texas 77024
(713) 621-7688, (800) 458-1446

Spencer Trust: Spencer Growth Fund (G)

Standish Ayer & Wood, Inc.
One Financial Center
Boston, Massachusetts 02111
(617) 350-6100

Standish Marathon Fund (AG)

State Farm
One State Farm Plaza
Bloomington, Illinois 61710
(309) 766-2029

State Farm Balanced Fund (B), State Farm Growth Fund (G), State Farm Interim Fund (USGI), State Farm Municipal Bond Fund (LTMB)

State Street
One Financial Center, 30th Floor
Boston, Massachusetts 02111
(617) 348-2000, (800) 882-0052
(617) 482-3920

MetLife-State Street Equity Trust: MetLife-State Street Capital Appreciation Fund (AG), MetLife-State Street Equity Income Fund (IE), MetLife-State Street Equity Investment Fund (G + I), MetLife-State Street Fixed Income Trust: MetLife-State Street Government Income Fund (USGI), MetLife-State Street Income Trust: MetLife-State Street Government Securities Fund (USGI), MetLife-State Street High Income Fund (HYB), MetLife-State Street Managed Assets (I), MetLife-State Street Money Market Trust: MetLife-State Street Money Market Fund (MM), MetLife-State Street Tax-Exempt Trust: MetLife-State Street High Income Tax-Exempt Fund (LTMB), State Street

Open-End Mutual Funds   **751**

Capital Fund (AG), State Street Exchange Fund (G&I), State Street Fund for Foundations and Endowments: Equity Growth Portfolio (G), Equity Income Portfolio (IE), Fixed Income Portfolio (I), State Street Growth Fund (G + I), State Street Investment Corporation (G + I)

Steinhardt Advisers, Inc.
605 Third Avenue
New York, New York 10158
(212) 490-2727

Steinhardt Fund (G)

SteinRoe & Farnham/Liberty Mutual
300 West Adams Street
P.O. Box 1143
Chicago, Illinois 60690
(312) 368-7700, (312) 368-7800,
(800) 338-2550
and
Federal Reserve Plaza
Boston, Massachusetts 02210
(617) 722-6000, (800) 433-3399

Liberty Mutual Tax Exempt Income Trust (LTMB), Liberty Mutual U.S. Government Guaranteed Securities Income Trust (GNMA), SteinRoe Equity Trust: SteinRoe Capital Opportunities Fund (AG), SteinRoe Growth & Income (G + I), SteinRoe International Growth (INT), SteinRoe Prime Equities (G), SteinRoe Special Fund (AG), SteinRoe Stock Fund (G), SteinRoe Total Return Fund (G + I), SteinRoe Income Trust: SteinRoe Cash Reserves (MM), SteinRoe Government Reserves (MM), Stein-Roe Government Plus (USGI), SteinRoe High-Yield Bonds (HYB), SteinRoe Managed Bonds (IB), SteinRoe Tax-Exempt Income Trust: SteinRoe High-Yield Municipals (LTMB), Stein-Roe Intermediate Municipals (LTMB), Stein-Roe Managed Municipals (LTMB), SteinRoe Tax-Exempt Money Fund (STMB)

Stephens Inc.
114 East Capitol Avenue
Little Rock, Arkansas 72201
(501) 374-4361, (800) 643-9691

Overland Express Funds: Asset Allocation Fund (FP), California Tax-Free Bond Fund (SMB-LT), Special Income Fund (G + I), Tax-Free Money Market Fund (STMB)

Stratton Management Co.
610 West Germantown Pike, Suite 361
Plymouth Meeting, Pennsylvania 19462
(215) 941-0255, (800) 634-5726

Stratton Growth Fund (G + I), Stratton Monthly Dividend Shares (IE)

Strong/Corneliuson Capital Management, Inc.
100 Heritage Reserve
Menomonee Falls, Wisconsin 53051
(414) 359-1400, (800) 368-3863
and
P.O. Box 2936
Milwaukee, Wisconsin 53201
(414) 359-3400, (800) 368-3863

Strong Advantage Fund (I), Strong Discovery Fund (AG), Strong Government Securities Fund (USGI), Strong Income Fund (G + I), Strong Investment Fund (G + I), Strong Money Market Fund (MM), Strong Municipal Bond (LTMB), Strong Municipal Money Market (MM), Strong Opportunity Fund (AG), Strong Short-Term Bond Fund (IB), Strong Tax-Free Funds: Strong Tax-Free Income Fund (LTMB), Strong Tax-Free Money Market Fund (STMB), Strong Total Return Fund (FP), Strong U.S. Government Reserves Fund (USGI)

Sun Growth
One Sun Life Executive Park
Wellesley Hills, Massachusetts 02181
(617) 237-6030, (800) 225-3950

Sun Growth Variable Annuity Fund (G)

T. Rowe Price
100 East Pratt Street
Baltimore, Maryland 21202
(301) 547-2000, (800) 638-5660

T. Rowe Price California Tax-Free Income Trust: California Tax-Free Bond Fund (SMB-LT), California Tax-Free Money Fund (SMB-ST), T. Rowe Price Capital Appreciation Fund (G), T. Rowe Price Equity Income Fund (IE), T. Rowe Price GNMA Fund (GNMA), T. Rowe Price Growth & Income Fund (G + I), T. Rowe Price Growth Stock Fund (G), T. Rowe Price High Yield Fund (HYB), T. Rowe Price Institutional Trust: Tax-Exempt Reserve Portfolio (STMB), T. Rowe Price International Discovery Fund (INT), T. Rowe Price International Trust: T. Rowe Price International Bond Fund (GB), T. Rowe Price International Stock Fund (INT), T. Rowe Price New America Growth Fund (AG), T. Rowe Price New Era Fund (G), T. Rowe Price New Horizons Fund (AG), T. Rowe Price New Income Fund (IB), T. Rowe Price Prime Reserve Fund (MM), T. Rowe Price Science & Technology Fund (AG), T. Rowe Price Short-Term Bond Fund (IB), T. Rowe Price Small-Cap Value Fund (AG), T. Rowe Price State Tax-Free Income Trust: Maryland Tax-Free Bond Fund (SMB-LT), New York Tax-Free Bond Fund (SMB-LT), New York Tax-Free Money Fund

(SMB-ST), T. Rowe Price Tax-Exempt Money Fund (STMB), T. Rowe Price Tax-Free High Yield Fund (LTMB), T. Rowe Price Tax-Free Income Fund (LTMB), T. Rowe Price Tax-Free Short-Intermediate Fund (LTMB), T. Rowe Price U.S. Treasury Money Fund (MM)

Taft Philanthropic
11150 Sunset Hills Road, Suite 240
Reston, Virginia 22090
(703) 689-2300
Taft Philanthropic Trust (GLB)

Templeton
700 Central Avenue
P.O. Box 33030
St. Petersburg, Florida 33733-8030
(813) 823-8712, (800) 237-0738
Templeton Funds: Foreign Fund (INT), World Fund (GLB), Templeton Global Funds: Templeton Global Fund (GLB), Templeton Growth Fund (GLB), Templeton Income Fund (GB), Templeton Money Fund (MM), Templeton Real Estate Trust (G)

Texas Commerce Bank
16 HCB 98
P.O. Box 2558
Houston, Texas 77252-8098
(713) 546-7775
Retirement Investment Trust: Balanced Fund (G + I), Equity Growth Fund (G), Equity Income Fund (IE), Income Fund (I), Money Market Fund (MM)

Thompson, Unger & Plumb
4610 University Avenue
P.O. Box 55320
Madison, Wisconsin 53705
(608) 231-1676
Thompson, Unger & Plumb Fund (G + I)

Thomson McKinnon
Financial Square
New York, New York 10005
(212) 482-5894, (800) 628-1237
Cash Accumulation Trust: National Government Fund (MM), National Money Market Fund (MM), National Tax-Exempt Fund (STMB), Thomson McKinnon Convertible Securities Fund (G + I), Thomson McKinnon Global Fund (GLB), Thomson McKinnon Growth Fund (G), Thomson McKinnon Income Fund (IB), Thomson McKinnon Opportunity Fund (AG), Thomson McKinnon Precious Metals & Natural Resources Fund (PMG), Thomson McKinnon Short-Term Fund (MM), Thomson McKinnon Tax-Exempt Fund (LTMB), Thomson McKinnon U.S. Government Fund (USGI)

Thornburg Management
119 East Marcy Street, Suite 202
Santa Fe, New Mexico 87501
(505) 984-0200
Thornburg Income Trust (USGI)

Thornton Group
230 California Street, Suite 300
P.O. Box 2749
San Francisco, California 94126-2749
(415) 544-8701
Thornton Group: Thornton Oriental Income and Growth Fund (GB), Thornton Tiger South East Asia Fund (INT)

Towneley Capital
144 East 30th Street
New York, New York 10016
(212) 696-4130, (800) 872-2710
Eclipse Financial Asset Trust: Eclipse Equity Fund (G + I)

Transamerica
P.O. Box 2598
Los Angeles, California 90051-1598
(213) 741-7702
Transamerica Cash Reserve (MM)
Transatlantic Fund: see Kleinwort Benson International

Tremont Select Funds
700 Dixie Terminal Building
Cincinnati, Ohio 45202
(513) 629-2000
Tremont Funds: Global Equity Fund (GLB), Growth and Value Fund (G), High Yield Fund (HYB), Money Market Plus Fund (MM), Real Estate Fund (G), U.S. Treasury Management Fund (USGI), Zero Coupon Treasury Fund (I)

Tri-Magna Corp.
205 East 42nd Street, Suite 2020
New York, New York 10017
(212) 682-3300
Tri-Magna Fund (AG)

Trinity Capital Management
183 East Main Street, Suite 1135
Rochester, New York 14604
(716) 262-4080, (800) 456-7780
Pinnacle Government Fund (MM), Trinity Liquid Assets Trust: Trinity Money Market Fund (MM)

Tudor Management Company, Inc.
One New York Plaza
New York, New York 10004
(212) 908-9500, (800) 223-3332
Tudor Fund (AG), WPG Growth Fund (G)

Twentieth Century Funds. *see* Investors Research Corp.

Tyndall Newport Fund Management
1500 Forest Avenue, Suite 223
Richmond, Virginia 23229
(804) 285-8211

Tyndall-Newport Fund (INT)

Unified Management Corporation
429 North Pennsylvania Street
Indianapolis, Indiana 46204-1897
(317) 634-3300, (800) 862-7283
and
100 Kentucky Tower
Louisville, Kentucky 40202
(502) 581-0741

Amana Mutual Funds Trust: Income Series (IE), Liquid Green Tax-Free Trust (STMB), Liquid Green Trust (MM), Professional Portfolios Trust: Aggressive Growth Fund (AG), Government Securities Fund (USGI), High Yield Fund (HYB), International Fund (INT), Timed Equity Fund (G), Total Return Fund (G + I), Tower Series Funds: Bond Series (CB), Equity Income Series (IE), Unified Growth Fund (A), Unified Income Fund (I), Unified Municipal Fund: General Series (LTMB), Indiana Series (SMB-LT), Unified Mutual Shares (G + I)

United Funds
2400 Pershing Road
P.O. Box 418343
Kansas City, Missouri 64141-9343
(816) 283-4000, (800) 821-5664

United Cash Management Fund (MM), United Continental Income Fund (B), United Funds: United Accumulative Fund (G), United Bond Fund (IB), United Income Fund (IE), United Science and Energy Fund (G), United Gold & Government Fund (PMG), United Government Securities Fund (USGI), United High Income Fund II (HYB), United High Income Fund (HYB), United International Growth Fund (GLB), United Municipal Bond Fund (LTMB), United Municipal High Income Fund (LTMB), United New Concepts Fund (AG), United Retirement Shares (G + I), United Vanguard Fund (AG)

United Services Advisors
P.O. Box 29467
San Antonio, Texas 78229-0467
(512) 696-1234, (800) 873-8637

United Services Funds: Gold Shares Fund (PMG), Good & Bad Times Fund (G), Growth Fund (G), Income Fund (IE), LoCap Fund (AG),

New Prospector Fund (PMG), Real Estate Fund (G), Tax Free Fund (LTMB), U.S. GNMA Fund (GNMA), U.S. Tresury Securities Fund (MM)

USAA Investment Management Company
USAA Building
San Antonio, Texas 78288
(512) 498-8000, (800) 531-8000

USAA Investment Trust: Cornerstone Fund (B), Gold Fund (PMG), International Fund (INT), USAA LIFE Portfolio Series: USAA LIFE Balanced Portfolio (B), USAA LIFE Growth Portfolio (G), USAA LIFE Income Portfolio (I), USAA LIFE Money Market Portfolio (MM), USAA Mutual Fund: Aggressive Growth Fund (AG), Growth Fund (G), Income Fund (I), Income Stock Fund (IE), Money Market Fund (MM), USAA Tax Exempt Fund: High Yield Fund (LTMB), Intermediate-Term Fund (LTMB), Short Term Fund (STMB), Tax Exempt Money Market Fund (STMB)

U.S. Boston Investment
6 New England Executive Park
Burlington, Massachusetts 01803
(617) 272-6420

U.S. Boston Investment Company: Boston Foreign Growth and Income (INT), Boston Growth and Income (G + I)

VALIC
2929 Allen Parkway
P.O. Box 3206
Houston, Texas 77253
(713) 526-5251

American General Series Portfolio Company: Capital Accumulation Fund (AG), Capital Conservation Fund (G&I), Goverment Securities Fund (USGI), Money Market Fund (MM), Quality Growth Fund (G + I), Stock Index Fund (G), Timed Opportunity Fund (G)

Valley Forge Management Corporation
P.O. Box 262
Valley Forge, Pennsylvania 19481
(215) 688-6839

Valley Forge Growth and Income Fund (G + I)

Value Line
711 Third Avenue
New York, New York 10017
(212) 687-3965, (800) 223-0818

Value Line Aggressive Income Trust (HYB), Value Line Cash Fund (MM), Value Line Centurion Fund (G), Value Line Convertible Fund (G + I), Value Line Fund (G), Value Line Income Fund (I), Value Line Leveraged Growth Investors (AG), Value Line New York Tax Exempt

Trust (SMB-LT), Value Line Special Situtation Fund (AG), Value Line Strategic Asset Management Trust (FP), Value Line Tax Exempt Fund: High Yield Portfolio (LTMB), Money Market Portfolio (STMB), Value Line U.S. Government Securities Fund (USGI), Value Line U.S. Government Securities Trust (USGI)

Van Eck
122 East 42nd Street
New York, New York 10168
(212) 687-5200, (800) 221-2220

International Investors Incorporated (PMG), Van Eck Funds: Gold/Resources Fund (PMG), U.S. Government Money Fund (MM), World Income Fund (GB), World Trends Fund (GLB)

Vanguard Group of Investment Companies
Vanguard Financial Center
P.O. Box 2600
Valley Forge, Pennsylvania 19482
(215) 648-6000, (800) 662-7447,
(800) 662-2739

Explorer Fund (AG), Explorer II (AG), Naess & Thomas Special Fund (AG), PRIMECAP Fund (G), Trustees Commingled Fund, Vanguard Adjustable Rate Preferred Stock Fund (IE), Vanguard Asset Allocation Fund (FP), Vanguard Bond Market Fund (IB), Vanguard California Tax-Free: Insured Long-Term Portfolio (SMB-LT), California Money Market Portfolio (SMB-ST), Vanguard Convertible Securities (G + I), Vanguard Equity Income Fund (IE), Vanguard Explorer Fund (AG), Vanguard Explorer II Fund (AG), Vanguard Fixed-Income Securities: GNMA Portfolio (GNMA), High Yield Bond Portfolio (HYB), Investment Grade Bond Portfolio (IB), Short Term Bond Portfolio (IB), Short Term Government Bond Portfolio (USGI), U.S. Treasury Bond Portfolio (USGI), Vanguard High Yield Stock Fund (IE), Vanguard Index Trust: 500 Portfolio (G + I), Extended Market Portfolio (G), Vanguard Money Market Reserves/Federal Portfolio (MM), Vanguard Money Market Reserves/Insured Portfolio (MM), Vanguard Money Market Reserves/Prime Portfolio (MM), Vanguard Municipal Bond Fund/High Yield Portfolio (LTMB), Vanguard Municipal Bond Fund/Insured Long-Term Municipal Bond Portfolio (LTMB), Vanguard Municipal Bond Fund/Intermediate-Term Portfolio (LTMB), Vanguard Municipal Bond Fund/Limited Term Portfolio (LTMB), Vanguard Municipal Bond Fund/Long Term Portfolio (LTMB), Vanguard Municipal Bond Fund/Money Market Portfolio (STMB), Vanguard Municipal Bond Fund/Short-Term Portfolio

(STMB), Vanguard Naess & Thomas Special Fund (AG), Vanguard New Jersey Tax-Free Fund: Insured Tax-Free Portfolio (SMB-LT), Money-Market Portfolio (SMB-ST), Vanguard New York Insured Tax-Free (SMB-LT), Vanguard Pennsylvania Insured Tax-Free (SMB-LT), Vanguard Pennsylvania Money Market Fund (SMB-ST), Vanguard Preferred Stock Fund (IE), Vanguard PRIMECAP Fund (G), Vanguard Quantitative Portfolios (G + I), Vanguard Specialized Portfolios: Energy Portfolio (AG), Vanguard Specialized Portfolios: Gold and Precious Metals Portfolio (PMG), Vanguard Specialized Portfolios: Health Care Portfolio (AG), Vanguard Specialized Portfolios: Service Economy Portfolio (AG), Vanguard Specialized Portfolios: Technology Portfolio (AG), Vanguard STAR Fund (B), Vanguard Trustees Commingled-International Equity Portfolio (INT), Vanguard Trustees Commingled U.S. Equity Portfolio (G + I), Vanguard W.L. Morgan Growth Fund (G), Vanguard Wellesley Income Fund (G + I), Vanguard Wellington Fund (G + I), Vanguard Windsor Fund (G + I), Vanguard Windsor II Fund (G + I), Vanguard World Fund-International Growth Portfolio (G), Vanguard World Fund-U.S. Growth Portfolio (G)

Van Kampen Merritt
1001 Warrenville Road
Lisle, Illinois 60532
(312) 719-6000, (800) 225-2222

Van Kampen Merritt California Insured Tax Free Fund (SMB-LT), Van Kampen Merritt California Municipal Trust (SMB-LT), Van Kampen Merritt Growth and Income Fund (G + I), Van Kampen Merritt High Yield Fund (HYB), Van Kampen Merritt Intermediate Term Trust (I), Van Kampen Merritt Insured Tax Free Income Fund (LTMB), Van Kampen Merritt Limited Term High Income Trust Fund (HYB), Van Kampen Merritt Managed Municipal Income Trust (LTMB), Van Kampen Merritt Money Market Fund (MM), Van Kampen Merritt Pennsylvania Tax Free Income Fund (SMB-LT), Van Kampen Merritt Prime Rate Income Trust (CB), Van Kampen Merritt Tax Free High Income Fund (LTMB), Van Kampen Merritt Tax Free Money Fund (STMB), Van Kampen Merritt U.S. Government Fund (USGI)

Van Liew Capital
One Turks Head Place
Providence, Rhode Island 02903
(401) 421-1411, (800) 331-3186

VLC Trust (SMB-LT)

Venture Advisers
124 East Marcy Street
P.O. Box 1688
Santa Fe, New Mexico 87504-1688
(505) 983-4335, (800) 545-2098,
(800) 458-6557

New York Venture Fund (AG), Retirement Planning Funds of America: Bond Fund (USGI), Equity Fund (AG), Money Market Fund (MM), Venture Income (+) Plus (HYB), Venture Muni (+) Plus (LTMB), Venture Trust Money Market Fund: General Purpose Portfolio (MM), Government Portfolio (MM), Venture Trust Tax-Free Fund: Money Market Portfolio (STMB)

Vintage Advisors
29 West Susquehanna Avenue, Suite 112
Towson, Maryland 21204
(301) 494-8488, (800) 234-4111

Treasury First (USGI)

Wade Fund
5100 Poplar Avenue, Suite 2224
Memphis, Tennessee 38137
(901) 682-4613

Wade Fund (G)

Warburg, Pincus Counsellors, Inc.
466 Lexington Avenue
New York, New York 10017
(800) 888-6878, (212) 878-9272

Counsellors Capital Appreciation (G), Counsellors Cash Reserves (MM), Counsellors Emerging Growth (AG), Counsellors Fixed Income (I), Counsellors Intermediate Maturity Government (USGI), Counsellors New York Muni Bond (SMB-LT), Counsellors New York Tax-Exempt (MM)

Wasatch Advisors
68 South Main Street
Salt Lake City, Utah 84101
(801) 533-0777

Wasatch Advisors Funds: Wasatch Aggressive Equity Fund (AG), Wasatch Growth Fund (G), Wasatch Income Fund (I)

Washington Square
20 Washington Avenue South
Minneapolis, Minnesota 55401
(612) 372-5605

Select Capital Growth Fund (G), Select Cash Management Fund (MM), Select High Yield Fund (HYB), Select Managed Fund (G), Washington Square Cash Fund (MM)

Wayne Hummer Management Co.
175 West Jackson Boulevard
Chicago, Illinois 60604-2884
(312) 431-1700,
(800) 621-4477

Wayne Hummer Growth Fund (G + I), Wayne Hummer Money Fund Trust: Money Market Portfolio (MM)

Wealth Monitors, Inc.
1001 East 101st Terrace, Suite 220
Kansas City, Missouri 64131
(816) 941-7990, (800) 338-1579

Wealth Monitors Fund (G)

Webster
20 Exchange Place
New York, New York 10005
(212) 510-5552

Kidder, Peabody California Tax Exempt Money Market Fund (SMB-ST), Kidder, Peabody Equity Income Fund (IE), Kidder, Peabody Exchange Money Market Fund (MM), Kidder, Peabody Government Income Fund (USGI), Kidder, Peabody Government Money Fund (MM), Kidder, Peabody MarketGuard Appreciation Fund (G), Kidder, Peabody Premium Account Fund (MM), Kidder, Peabody Special Growth Fund (AG), Kidder, Peabody Tax Exempt Money Fund (STMB), Kidder, Peabody Tax Free Income Fund: National Series (LTMB), New York Series (SMB-LT), Webster Cash Reserve Fund (MM)

Weiss Peck & Greer
One New York Plaza, 31st Floor
New York, New York 10004
(212) 908-9582,
(800) 223-3332

Tudor Fund (AG), Weiss Peck & Greer Funds Trust: WPG Dividend Income Fund (IE), WPG Government Securities Fund (USGI), WPG Short Term Income Fund (MM), WPG Tax Free Money Market Fund (STMB), WPG Fund (G + I), WPG Growth Fund (AG), WPG International Fund (INT)

Weitz & Co.
9290 West Dodge Road
The Mark, Suite 405
Omaha, Nebraska 68114-3323
(402) 391-1980

Weitz Series Fund: Fixed Income Series (I), Weitz Value Fund (G)

Western Capital
1925 Century Park East, Suite 2350
Los Angeles, California 90067
(213) 556-5499, (800) 423-4891

Western Capital Specialty Managers Trust:
All-Growth Series (G), Fully Managed Series
(FP), Limited Maturity Bond Series (IB), Liquid
Asset Series (MM), Multiple Allocation Series
(B), Natural Resources Series (IE), Real Estate
Series (G + I)

Weston Financial Group
45 William Street
Wellesley, Massachusetts 02181
(617) 239-0445

Weston Portfolios: New Century Capital Portfolio (G + I), New Century I Portfolio (I)

Westwood Management
885 Third Avenue
New York, New York 10022
(212) 688-2323, (800) 323-7023

Westwood Fund (G + I)

Wheat, First Securities
707 East Main Street
Richmond, Virginia 23219
(804) 649-2311, (800) 321-0038

Southeastern Growth Fund (G)

Woodstock Common Trust Fund
Wood County Trust Co.
181 Second Street South
Wisconsin Rapids, Wisconsin 54494
(715) 423-7600

Woodstock Funds: Woodstock Corporate Fixed
Income Portfolio (CB), Woodstock Equity
Portfolio (G), Woodstock Fixed Income Port-
folio (IB), Woodstock Multiple Opportunities
Portfolio (B), Woodstock Municipal Income
Portfolio (LTMB), Woodstock U.S. Govern-
ment Fixed Income Portfolio (USGI)

Wood Struthers & Winthrop
140 Broadway, 42nd Floor
New York, New York 10005
(212) 504-4000, (800) 225-8011,
(800) 521-3036, (800) 221-5672

Neuwirth Fund (AG), Pine Street Fund (G + I),

Winthrop Focus Fund: Winthrop Fixed Income
Portfolio (CB), Winthrop Growth Portfolio (G)

Working Assets
230 California Street, Suite 500
San Francisco, California 94111
(415) 989-3200, (800) 223-7010,
(800) 543-8800

Working Assets Money Fund (MM)

World Money Managers
7 Fourth Street, Suite 14
Petaluma, California 94952
(512) 453-7558, (800) 531-5142

Permanent Porfolio (G), Permanent Treasury
Bill Portfolio (B)

WPG Advisors
One New York Plaza
New York, New York 10004
(800) 223-3332 (212) 908-9500

WPG Dividend Income Fund (IE), WPG Fund
(G + I), WPG Government Securities Fund (I)

Wright Investors' Service
24 Federal Street
Boston, Massachusetts 02110
(617) 482-8260

Equifund-Wright National Fiduciary Equity
Funds: Australian National Fiduciary Equity
Fund (INT), Austrian National Fiduciary Equity
Fund (INT), Belgian/Luxembourg National
Fiduciary Equity Fund (INT), Canadian Na-
tional Fiduciary Equity Fund (INT), Dutch Na-
tional Fiduciary Equity Fund (INT), French
National Fiduciary Equity Fund (INT), German
National Fiduciary Equity Fund (INT), Italian
National Fiduciary Equity Fund (INT), Japa-
nese National Fiduciary Equity Fund (INT),
Pacific Basin National Fiduciary Equity Fund
(INT), Scandinavian National Fiduciary Equity
Fund (INT), Spanish National Fiduciary Equity
Fund (INT), Swiss National Fiduciary Equity
Fund (INT), United Kingdom National Fiduci-
ary Equity Fund (INT)

Yamaichi Funds
Two World Trade Center, Suite 9840
New York, New York 10048
(212) 466-6830

Yamaichi Funds: Yamaichi Global Fund (GLB)

CLOSED-END MUTUAL FUNDS

The following is a compilation of the names, ticker symbols and addresses of American closed-end mutual funds, with the types of investments made by each. The notation *bond* means the fund buys only bonds, and is therefore likely to pay a high yield. The notation *convertible* means that the fund mainly buys convertible bonds, which pay a higher yield than stocks, but also have more potential to rise in value than bonds. The notation *dual purpose* means that the fund is split into two, with one part of the fund designed for investors who want income, and the other part designed for shareholders intent upon capital gains. The notation *equity* means the fund buys stocks, mostly for capital gains purposes. The notation *gold* means the fund exclusively buys shares of gold-mining companies, which usually have a high yield, but are subject to the ups and downs of gold prices. The notation *specialized equity* means that the fund buys only particular kinds of stocks for the purpose of capital appreciation. Some funds, for instance, only buy stocks of medical companies, while others concentrate on the stocks of a particular foreign country like Japan.

Closed-end mutual funds issue a fixed number of shares, which are then traded either on exchanges or over-the-counter. Funds traded on the New York Stock Exchange are notated with an NYSE, those on the American Stock Exchange, with an ASE, and those traded over the counter, with an OTC. Closed-end funds contrast with open-ended mutual funds, which create new shares whenever additional funds are received from customers. But closed-end fund managers buy and sell stocks, bonds and convertible securities just like open-end mutual fund managers.

Open-end funds sell at the net asset value (NAV) of their holdings on a particular day (plus a charge, or load, in some cases) and always stand ready to redeem shares at the NAV. In contrast, closed-end funds usually sell above or below their net asset value. The price of the shares is determined by the same forces of supply and demand that affect the value of any publicly traded security. Therefore, those buying shares in a closed-end fund when it is selling below net asset value are, in effect, buying a dollar's worth of securities for less than a dollar, and those buying such a fund when it is trading at a premium to its (NAV) receive less than a dollar's worth of securities for each dollar invested.

This list is provided courtesy of Thomas J. Herzfeld, author of *The Investor's Guide To Closed-End Funds* (McGraw-Hill) and *The Thomas J. Herzfeld Encyclopedia of Closed-End Funds*. Mr. Herzfeld, who can be reached at P.O. Box 161465, Miami, Florida 33116 (305) 271-1900, is an investment advisor specializing in closed-end funds.

ACM Government Income Fund, Inc., ACG, NYSE (Bond)
1345 Avenue of the Americas
New York, New York 10105 (800) 221-5672

ACM Government Opportunity Fund, AOF, NYSE (Bond)
1345 Avenue of the Americas
New York, New York 10105 (800) 221-5672

ACM Government Securities Fund, Inc. GSF, NYSE (Bond)
1345 Avenue of the Americas
New York, New York 10105 (800) 221-5672

ACM Government Spectrum Fund, SI, NYSE (Bond)
1345 Avenue of the Americas
New York, New York 10105 (800) 221-5672

Adams Express Company, ADX, NYSE (Equity)
Suite 1140, 7 St. Paul Street
Baltimore, Maryland 21202 (301) 752-5900

Allied Capital Corporation, ALLC, OTC (Equity)
Suite 901, 1666 K Street, N.W.
Washington, D.C. 20006 (202) 331-1112

Allstate Municipal Income Opportunities
Trust, AMO, NYSE (Bond)
2 Montgomery Street
Jersey City, New Jersey 07302
(800) 526-3143

Allstate Municipal Income Trust, ALM, NYSE
(Bond)
One World Trade Center
New York, New York 10048
(212) 938-4500

Allstate Municipal Income Trust II, ALT,
NYSE (Bond)
One World Trade Center
New York, New York 10048
(212) 938-4500

Allstate Municipal Premium Income Fund,
ALT, NYSE (Bond)
2 Montgomery Street
Jersey City, New Jersey 07303
(800) 526-3143

Alterman Investment Fund, Inc., OTC (Bond)
Suite 104, 1218 West Paces Ferry Road
N.W.
Atlanta, Georgia 30327 (404) 237-9891

American Capital Bond Fund, Inc., ACB,
NYSE (Bond)
2800 Post Oak Boulevard
Houston, Texas 77056 (713) 993-0500

American Capital Convertible Securities,Inc.,
AGS, NYSE (Convertible-Bond)
2800 Post Oak Boulevard
Houston, Texas 77056 (713) 993-0500

American Capital Income Trust, ACD, NYSE
(Bond)
2300 Post Oak Boulevard
Houston, Texas 77056 (713) 421-9696

American Government Income Fund, Inc.,
AGF, NYSE (Bond)
Piper Jaffray Tower, 220 South Ninth Street
Minneapolis, Minnesota 55402
(800) 333-6000 ext. 6418

American Government Income Portfolio Inc.,
AAF, NYSE (Bond)
Piper Jaffray Tower, 222 South Ninth Street
Minneapolis, Minnesota 55402
(800) 333-6000

American Government Term Trust, AGT,
NYSE (Bond)
Piper Jaffray Tower, 222 South Ninth Street
Minneapolis, Minnesota 55402
(800) 333-6000

Americas All-Season Fund Inc., FUND, OTC
(Equity)
Suite 300, 422 West Fairbanks Avenue
Winter Park, Florida 32789 (800) 333-4222

AMEV Securities, Inc. AMV, NYSE (Bond)
P.O. Box 6284
St. Paul, Minnesota 55164 (612) 738-4000

ASA Limited, ASA, NYSE (Specialized
Equity)
P.O. Box 269
Florham Park, New Jersey 07932
(201) 377-3535

Asia Pacific Fund, Inc., APB, NYSE (Equity)
One Seaport Plaza
New York, New York 10292
(800) 451-6788, (212) 214-3334

Baker Fentress & Co., BKF, ASE (Equity)
Suite 3510, 200 West Madison Street
Chicago, Illinois 60606 (312) 236-9190

Bancroft Convertible Fund, Inc., BCV, NYSE
(Convertible-Bond)
Suite 1310, 56 Pine Street
New York, New York 10005 (212) 269-9236

Bando-McGlocklin Capital Corp.,BMCC, OTC
(Specialized Bond)
13555 Bishops Court
Brookfield, Wisconsin 53005
(414) 784-9010

Bergstrom Capital, BEM, ASE (Equity)
Suite 220, 505 Madison Street
Seattle, Washington 98104 (206) 623-7302

Blackstone Income Trust, BKT, NYSE (Bond)
One Seaport Plaza
New York, New York 10292
(212) 214-3334

Blackstone Target Term Trust, BTT, NYSE
(Bond)
One Seaport Plaza
New York, New York 10292 (212) 214-3334

Blue Chip Value Fund, BLU, NYSE (Equity)
633 17th Street
Denver, Colorado 80202 (303) 293-5999

Brazil Fund, Inc. BZF, NYSE (Equity)
345 Park Avenue
New York, New York 10154 (212) 326-6200

Bunker Hill Income Securities, Inc., BHL,
NYSE (Bond)
P.O. Box 4602
Pasadena, California 91106 (213) 229-1260

Capital Investments Inc., OTC (Equity)
744 4th Street
Milwaukee, Wisconsin 53203
(414) 273-6560

Capital Southwest Corporation, CSWC, OTC
(Specialized Equity)
Suite 700, 12900 Preston Road
Dallas, Texas 75230 (214) 233-8242

Castle Convertible Fund, Inc., CVF, ASE
(Convertible-Bond)
75 Maiden Lane
New York, New York 10038 (212) 806-8800

Central Fund of Canada Limited, CEF, ASE
(Gold)
P.O. Box 7319
Ancaster, Ontario L9G 3N6, Canada
(416) 648-7878

Central Securities Corporation, CET, ASE
(Equity)
375 Park Avenue
New York, New York 10152 (212) 688-3011

CIGNA High Income Shares, HIS, NYSE
(Bond)
1380 Main Street
Springfield, Massachusetts 01103
(413) 781-7776, (800) 523-2097

CIM High Yield Securities, CIM, ASE (Bond)
One Boston Place
Boston, Massachusetts 02108
(617) 426-3750

Circle Income Shares, Inc., CINS, OTC
(Bond)
P.O. Box 44027
Indianapolis, Indiana 46244 (317) 639-8180

Clarion Capital Corporation, CLRN, OTC
(Miscellaneous)
3555 Curtis Boulevard
Eastlake, Ohio 44094 (216) 953-0555

Clemente Global Growth Fund Inc., CLM,
NYSE (Equity)
767 Third Avenue
New York, New York 10017 (212) 759-3339

CNA Income Shares Inc., CNN, NYSE (Bond)
CNA Plaza
Chicago, Illinois 60685 (312) 822-4181

Colonial Intermediate High Income Fund,
Inc., CIF, NYSE (Bond)
One Financial Center
Boston, Massachusetts 02111
(617) 426-3750

Colonial Municipal Income Trust, CMU,
NYSE (Bond)
One Financial Center
Boston, Massachusetts 02111
(617) 526-3750

Combined Penny Stock Fund, Inc.
(Specialized Equity)
Unit 11, 2616 West Colorado Avenue
Colorado Springs, Colorado 80904
(719) 636-1511

Comstock Partners Strategy Fund Inc., CPF,
NYSE (Bond)
45 Broadway
New York, New York 10006
(212) 943-9100, (800) 543-6217

Convertible Holdings Inc., CNV, NYSE (Dual-
Purpose)
P.O. Box 9011
Princeton, New Jersey 08543
(609) 282-3200

Counsellors Tandem Securities Fund, Inc.
CTF, NYSE (Dual-Purpose)
466 Lexington Avenue
New York, New York 10017
(212) 878-0600, (800) 888-6878

Current Income Shares, Inc., CUR, NYSE
(Bond)
P.O. Box 30151, Terminal Annex
Los Angeles, California 90030
(213) 236-7940

Cypress Fund, Inc., WJR, ASE (Specialized
Equity)
1285 Avenue of the Americas
New York, New York 10019

Dean Witter Government Income Trust, GVT,
NYSE (Bond)
One World Trade Center
New York, New York 10048 (212) 938-4500

DK Investors, Inc., OTC (Bond)
276 Fifth Avenue
New York, New York 10001 (212) 684-7074

Dover Regional Financial Shares, DVRFS,
OTC (Specialized Equity)
Suite 800, 1811 Chestnut Street
Philadelphia, Pennsylvania 19103
(215) 561-0264, (800) 468-4017

Dreyfus California Municipal Income Inc.,
DCM, ASE (Bond)
666 Old Country Road
Garden City, New York 11530
(516) 794-5120

Dreyfus Municipal Income Inc., DMF, ASE
(Bond)
666 Old Country Road
Garden City, New York 11530
(516) 794-5120

Dreyfus New York Municipal Income Inc.,
DNM, ASE (Bond)
666 Old Country Road
Garden City, New York 11530
(516) 794-5120

Dreyfus Strategic Government Income
Trust, DSI, NYSE (Bond)
666 Old Country Road
Garden City, New York 11530
(516) 794-5210

Dreyfus Strategic Municipals Income Inc.,
LEO, NYSE (Bond)
767 Fifth Avenue, 35th Floor
New York, New York 10153 (800) 334-6899

Duff & Phelps Selected Utilities, DNP, NYSE
(Specialized Equity)
55 East Monroe Street
Chicago, Illinois 60604 (312) 368-5510

Duke and Company, Inc., DKE, Philadelphia
Stock Exchange (Specialized Equity)
Suite 608, 302 East Carson Avenue
Las Vegas, Nevada 89101 (702) 384-7021

1838 Bond-Debenture Trading Fund, BDF,
NYSE (Bond)
3 Mellon Bank Center, 32nd Floor
Philadelphia, Pennsylvania 19102
(215) 963-3500, (800) 232-1838

Ellsworth Convertible Growth & Income
Fund, ECF, NYSE (Convertible Bond)
56 Pine Street
New York, New York 10005 (212) 269-9236

Engex, Inc., EGX, ASE (Equity)
44 Wall Street
New York, New York 10005 (212) 459-4000

Excelsior Income Shares, Inc., EIS, NYSE
(Bond)
Suite 2300, 45 Wall Street
New York, New York 10005 (212) 425-7120

Financial News Composite Fund Inc., FIF,
NYSE (Equity)
320 South Boston
Tulsa, Oklahoma 74103 (918) 599-0045

First Australia Fund, IAF, ASE (Equity)
One Seaport Plaza
New York, New York 10292 (212) 214-3334

First Australia Prime Income Fund, FAX, ASE
(Bond)
One Seaport Plaza
New York, New York 10292 (212) 214-3334

First Boston Income Fund, Inc., FBF, NYSE
(Bond)
c/o The Vanguard Group, Vanguard Financial
Center
Valley Forge, Pennsylvania 19482
(215) 648-6069

First Boston Strategic Income Fund, Inc.
FBI, NYSE (Bond)
c/o Vanguard Group, Vanguard Financial
Center
Valley Forge, Pennsylvania 19482
(215) 648-6069

First Financial Fund, Inc., FF, NYSE
(Specialized Equity)
One Seaport Plaza
New York, New York 10292 (212) 214-3334

First Iberian Fund, Inc., IBF, ASE (Equity)
One Seaport Plaza
New York, New York 10292 (212) 214-3334

Flexible Bond Trust, FLX, NYSE (Bond)
1285 Avenue of the Americas
New York, New York 10019
(212) 713-2084

Fort Dearborn Income Securities,Inc., FTD,
NYSE (Bond)
Suite 123, One North State Street
Chicago, Illinois 60602 (312) 346-0676

France Fund, Inc., FRN, NYSE (Equity)
535 Madison Avenue
New York, New York 10022 (212) 701-2875

Franklin Corporation, FKLN, ASE
(Miscellaneous)
777 Mariners Island Boulevard
San Mateo, California 94404
(415) 378-2000

Franklin Principal Maturity Trust, FDT, NYSE
(Bond)
777 Mariners Island Boulevard
San Mateo, California 94404
(415) 378-2000

Franklin Universal Trust, FT, NYSE (Bond)
770 Mariners Island Boulevard
San Mateo, California 94404
(415) 378-2000, (800) 342-5236

Gabelli Equity Trust, Inc. GAB, NYSE
   (Equity)
8 Sound Shore Drive
Greenwich, Connecticut 06830
(203) 625-0028

Gemini II, GMI, NYSE (Dual-Purpose)
c/o The Vanguard Financial Center
Valley Forge, Pennsylvania 19482
(800) 662-2739

General American Investors Company,Inc.,
   GAM, NYSE (Equity)
330 Madison Avenue
New York, New York 10017
(212) 916-8400

Germany Fund, GER, NYSE (Equity)
40 Wall Street
New York, New York 10005 (800) 642-0144

Global Government Plus Fund, Inc., GOV,
   NYSE (Bond)
One Seaport Plaza
New York, New York 10292 (212) 214-3332

Global Growth and Income Fund Inc., GGF,
   NYSE (Dual Purpose)
c/o The Vanguard Group, Vanguard Financial
   Center
Valley Forge, Pennsylvania 19482
(215) 648-6205

Global Income Plus Fund, Inc., GLI, NYSE
   (Bond)
1285 Avenue of the Americas
New York, New York 10019 (212) 713-2710

Global Yield Fund, Inc., PGY, NYSE (Bond)
One Seaport Plaza
New York, New York 10292 (800) 451-6588

Greater Washington Investors, Inc., GWA,
   ASE (Equity)
5454 Wisconsin Avenue
Chevy Chase, Maryland 20815
(301) 656-0626

Growth Stock Outlook Trust, Inc., GSO,
   NYSE (Equity)
4405 East-West Highway
Bethesda, Maryland 20814 (301) 986-5866

Hampton Utilities Trust, NYSE (Specialized
   Equity)
222 Broadway
New York, New York 10038
(212) 238-2000

H&Q Healthcare Investors, HQH, NYSE
   (Specialized Equity)
50 Rowes Wharf, 4th Floor
Boston, Massachusetts 02109
(617) 574-0500

Hatteras Income Securities, Inc., HAT, NYSE
   (Bond)
One NCNB Plaza, 8th Floor
Charlotte, North Carolina 28255
(704) 333-7808

Helvetia Fund, SWZ, NYSE (Equity)
521 Fifth Avenue
New York, New York 10175
(212) 867-7660

High Income Advantage Trust, YLD, NYSE
   (Bond)
One World Trade Center
New York, New York 10048 (800) 221-2685

High Income Advantage Trust II, YLT, NYSE
   (Bond)
One World Trade Center, 59th Floor
New York, New York 10048 (800) 221-2685

High Income Advantage Trust III, YLH, NYSE
   (Bond)
One World Trade Center, 59th Floor
New York, New York 10048 (800) 221-2685

High Yield Income Fund, Inc., HYI, NYSE
   (Bond)
One Seaport Plaza
New York, New York 10292 (212) 214-3334

High Yield Plus Fund, HYP, NYSE (Bond)
One Seaport Plaza
New York, New York 10292 (212) 214-3334

HITK Corporation, HITK, OTC (Equity)
777 Summer Street
Stamford, Connecticut 06901
(203) 323-7773

INA Investment Securities, Inc., IIS, NYSE
   (Bond)
P.O. Box 13856
Philadelphia, Pennsylvania 19101
(203) 726-6271

Independence Square Income Securities,
Inc., ISIS, OTC (Bond)
3 Radnor Corporate Center,
100 Matsonford Road
Radnor, Pennsylvania 19087
(215) 964-8882

India Growth Fund, IGF, NYSE (Equity)
200 Park Avenue
New York, New York 10166
(212) 878-8000

Intercapital Income Securities, Inc., ICB,
NYSE (Bond)
One World Trade Center
New York, New York 10048
(212) 938-4553

Israel Investors Corporation, IICR, OTC
(Equity)
475 Park Avenue South, 8th Floor
New York, New York 10016
(212) 213-2200

Italy Fund, Inc., ITA, NYSE (Equity)
31 West 53rd Street
New York, New York 10018
(212) 767-3034

John Hancock Income Securities Trust, JHS,
NYSE (Bond)
101 Huntington Avenue
Boston, Massachusetts 02199
(617) 375-1500

John Hancock Investors, Inc., JHI, NYSE
(Bond)
John Hancock Place, P.O. Box 111
Boston, Massachusetts 02117
(617) 412-4506

Kemper High Income Trust, KHI, NYSE
(Bond)
120 South LaSalle Street
Chicago, Illinois 60603 (800) 621-1048

Kemper Multi-Market Income Trust, KMM,
NYSE (Bond)
120 South LaSalle Street
Chicago, Illinois 60603 (800) 621-1048

Kemper Intermediate Government Trust,
KGT, NYSE (Bond)
120 South LaSalle Street
Chicago, Illinois 60603 (800) 621-1048

Kemper Municipal Income Trust, KTF, NYSE
(Bond)
120 South LaSalle Street
Chicago, Illinois 60603 (800) 442-2848

Kleinwort Benson Australian Income Fund,
Inc., KBA, NYSE (Bond)
200 Park Avenue
New York, New York 10166 (212) 972-9315

Korea Fund, Inc., KF, NYSE (Equity)
345 Park Avenue
New York, New York 10154 (212) 325-6439

Lehman Corporation, LEM, NYSE (Equity)
55 Water Street
New York, New York 10041 (212) 668-8578

Liberty All-Star Equity Fund, USA, NYSE
(Equity)
600 Atlantic Avenue
Boston, Massachusetts 02210
(800) 542-3863

Lincoln National Convertible Securities
Fund, Inc., LNV, NYSE (Convertible-Bond)
1300 Clinton Street
Fort Wayne, Indiana 46801 (219) 427-2210

Lincoln National Direct Placement Fund,
Inc., LND, NYSE (Bond)
1300 Clinton Street
Fort Wayne, Indiana 46801 (219) 427-2210

Lomas Mortgage Securities, LSF, NYSE
(Bond)
Suite 3600, 2001 Bryan Tower
Dallas, Texas 75201 (214) 746-7111

Malaysia Fund, Inc., MF, NYSE (Equity)
Vanguard Financial Center
Valley Forge, Pennsylvania 19482
(800) 332-5577, (215) 648-6116

MassMutual Corporate Investors,Inc., MCI,
NYSE (Bond)
1295 State Street
Springfield, Massachusetts 01111
(413) 788-8411

MassMutual Participation Investors, MPV,
NYSE (Bond)
1295 State Street
Springfield, Massachusetts 01111
(413) 788-8411

Mexico Fund,Inc., MXF, NYSE (Equity)
Impulsora del Fondo Mexico, S.A.,
77 Aristoleles Street, 3rd Floor
11560 Mexico DF Mexico (212) 492-6485

MFS Government Markets Income Trust,
MGI, NYSE (Bond)
500 Boylston Street
Boston, Massachusetts 02116
(617) 954-5000

MFS Income & Opportunity Trust, MFO,
NYSE (Bond)
500 Boylston Street
Boston, Massachusetts 02116
(617) 954-5000

MFS Intermediate Income Trust, MIN, NYSE
(Bond)
500 Boylston Street
Boston, Massachusetts 02116
(617) 954-5000

MFS Multimarket Income Trust, MMT, NYSE
(Bond)
500 Boylston Street
Boston, Massachusetts 02116
(617) 954-5000

MFS Multimarket Total Return Trust, MFT,
NYSE (Bond)
500 Boylston Street
Boston, Massachusetts 02116
(617) 954-5000

MFS Municipal Income Trust, MFM, NYSE
(Bond)
500 Boylston Street
Boston, Massachusetts 02116
(617) 954-5000

Montgomery Street Income Securities, Inc.,
MTS, NYSE (Bond)
Suite 1608, 315 Montgomery Street
San Francisco, California 94104
(415) 982-8020

Morgan Grenfell SMALLCap Fund, Inc.,
MGC, NYSE (Specialized Equity)
855 Third Avenue
New York, New York 10022 (212) 230-2600

Municipal High Income Fund, MHF, NYSE
(Bond)
Two World Trade Center, 106th Floor
New York, New York 10048 (212) 321-7155

MuniEnhanced Fund, Inc., MIF, ASE (Bond)
800 Scudders Mill Road
Plainsboro, New Jersey 08536
(609) 282-2800

MuniInsured Fund Inc., MIF, ASE (Bond)
800 Scudders Mill Road
Plainsboro, New Jersey 08536
(609) 282-2800

MuniVest Fund, MVF, ASE (Bond)
800 Scudders Mill Road
Plainsboro, New Jersey 08536
(609) 282-2800

Mutual of Omaha Interest Shares,Inc., MUO,
NYSE (Bond)
10235 Regency Circle
Omaha, Nebraska 68114 (402) 397-8555

New America High Income Fund, Inc., HYB,
NYSE (Bond)
99 Bedford Street
Boston, Massachusetts 02111
(617) 426-0182

New York Tax-Exempt Income Fund, Inc.,
XTX, ASE (Bond)
Suite 3000, 500 West Madison Street
Chicago, Illinois 60606 (312) 559-3000

Niagara Share Corporation, NGS, NYSE
(Equity)
70 Niagara Street
Buffalo, New York 14202 (716) 856-2600

Nicholas Applegate Growth Equity Fund,
Inc., GEF, NYSE (Bond)
Suite 2040, 701 B. Street
San Diego, California 92101 (619) 234-4472

Nuveen California Municipal Income Fund,
Inc., NCA, NYSE (Bond)
333 West Wacker Drive
Chicago, Illinois 60606 (312) 917-7812

Nuveen California Municipal Value Fund,
Inc., NCM, NYSE (Bond)
333 West Wacker Drive
Chicago, Illinois 60606 (312) 917-7812

Nuveen Municipal Income Fund, Inc., NMI,
NYSE (Bond)
333 West Wacker Drive
Chicago, Illinois 60606 (312) 917-7812

Nuveen Municipal Value Fund, Inc., NUV,
NYSE (Bond)
333 West Wacker Drive
Chicago, Illinois 60606 (312) 917-8200

Nuveen New York Municipal Income Trust,
NNM, ASE (Bond)
333 West Wacker Drive
Chicago, Illinois 60606 (312) 917-7812

Nuveen New York Municipal Value Fund,
NNY, NYSE (Bond)
333 West Wacker Drive
Chicago, Illinois 60606 (312) 917-7812

Nuveen Premium Income Municipal Fund,
NPI, NYSE (Bond)
333 West Wacker Drive
Chicago, Illinois 60606 (312) 917-7810

Oppenheimer Multi-Government Trust, OGT,
  NYSE (Bond)
Two World Trade Center
New York, New York 10048-0669
(212) 323-0200

Oppenheimer Multi-Sector Income Trust,
  OMS, NYSE (Bond)
Two World Trade Center
New York, New York 10048-0669
(800) 525-7048

Pacific American Income Shares, Inc., PAI,
  NYSE (Bond)
117 East Colorado Boulevard
Pasadena, California 91105 (818) 449-0309

Patriot Premium Dividend Fund, Inc., PDF,
  NYSE (Specialized Equity)
211 Congress Street
Boston, Massachusetts 02110
(617) 426-3310

Penny Stock Fund of North America, Inc.,
  OTC (Specialized Equity)
P.O. Box 3039
Colorado Springs, California 80934
(719) 636-1511

Petroleum & Resources Corporation, PEO,
  NYSE (Specialized Equity)
Suite 1140, Seven St. Paul Street
Baltimore, Maryland 21201 (301) 752-5900

Pilgrim Regional Bank Shares, PBS, NYSE
  (Specialized Equity)
10100 Santa Monica Boulevard
Los Angeles, California 90067
(800) 331-1080

Pro-Med Capital, Inc., PMC, ASE (Equity)
Suite 225, 1380 N.E. Miami Gardens Drive
North Miami Beach, Florida 33179
(305) 949-590

Prospect Street High Income Portfolio, PHY,
  NYSE (Bond)
One Financial Center
Boston, Massachusetts 02111
(617) 350-5718

Providence Investors Company, OTC
  (Equity)
1902 Fleet National Bank Building
Providence, Rhode Island 02903
(401) 421-1141

Prudential Intermediate Income Fund, PIF,
  NYSE (Bond)
One Seaport Plaza
New York, New York 10292 (212) 214-3334

Prudential Strategic Income Fund, PSF,
  NYSE (Bond)
One Seaport Plaza
New York, New York 10292
(212) 214-3334

Putnam High Income Convertible & Bond
  Fund, PCF, NYSE (Convertible Bond)
One Post Office Square
Boston, Massachusetts 02109
(617) 292-1000

Putnam Intermediate Government Income
  Trust, PGT, NYSE (Bond)
One Post Office Square
Boston, Massachusetts 02109
(617) 292-1000

Putnam Master Income Trust, PMT, NYSE
  (Bond)
One Post Office Square
Boston, Massachusetts 02109
(617) 292-1000

Putnam Master Intermediate Income Trust,
  PIM, NYSE (Bond)
One Post Office Square
Boston, Massachusetts 02109
(617) 292-1000

Putnam Premium Income Trust, PPT, NYSE
  (Bond)
One Post Office Square
Boston, Massachusetts 02109
(617) 292-1000

Quest for Value Dual Purpose Fund, Inc.,
  KFV, NYSE (Dual-Purpose)
Oppenheimer Tower, World Financial Center
New York, New York 10281
(212) 667-7561

RAC Income Fund, Inc., RMF, NYSE (Bond)
10221 Wincopin Circle
Columbia, Maryland 21044
(301) 964-8260

Rand Capital Corporation, RAND, OTC
  (Specialized Equity)
1300 Rand Building
Buffalo, New York 14203 (716) 853-0802

Real Estate Securities Income Fund, RIF,
ASE (Specialized Equity)
757 Third Avenue, 16th Floor
New York, New York 10017
(212) 832-10017

Real Silk Hosiery Mills, Inc., OTC (Equity)
757 Third Avenue, 16th Floor
New York, New York 10017 (212) 832-3232

Regional Financial Shares Investment Fund,
Inc. BNC, NYSE (Specialized Equity)
1285 Avenue of the Americas
New York, New York 10019 (212) 713-2000

Renaissance Fund, Inc., OTC (Specialized
Equity)
70 Maple Avenue
Katonah, New York 10536 (914) 232-3800

Revere Fund, Inc., PREV, OTC (Bond)
745 Fifth Avenue
New York, New York 10151 (212) 808-9090

Rockies Fund, Inc., ROCK, OTC (Equity)
Suite 202, 8301 East Prentice Avenue
Englewood, Colorado 80111
(303) 779-4208

Royce Value Trust Inc., RVT, NYSE (Equity)
1414 Avenue of the Americas
New York, New York 10019 (212) 355-7311

Schafer Value Trust Inc., SAT, NYSE
(Equity)
18th Floor, 645 Fifth Avenue
New York, New York 10022 (212) 644-1002

Scudder New Asia Fund, Inc., SAF, NYSE
(Equity)
345 Park Avenue
New York, New York 10154 (212) 326-6200

Source Capital, Inc., SOR, NYSE (Equity)
10301 West Pico Boulevard
Los Angeles, California 90064
(213) 277-4900

Spain Fund, SNF, NYSE (Equity)
1345 Avenue of the Americas
New York, New York 10105 (800) 247-4145

Spectra Fund, Inc., OTC (Equity)
75 Maiden Lane
New York, New York 10038 (212) 547-3600

State Mutual Securities Trust, SMS, NYSE
(Bond)
440 Lincoln Street
Worcester, Massachusetts 01605
(617) 852-1000

Sterling Capital Corporation, SPR, ASE
(Specialized Equity)
635 Madison Avenue
New York, New York 10022 (212) 980-3360

Summit Tax-Exempt Bond Fund, SUA, ASE
(Bond)
P.O. Box 2016, Peck Slip Station
New York, New York 10272
(800) 253-6672

Taiwan Fund Inc. (Equity)
111 Devonshire Street
Boston, Massachusetts 02109
(617) 570-6327

TCW Convertible Securities Fund, Inc., CVT,
NYSE (Convertible Bond)
400 South Hope Street
Los Angeles, California 90071
(213) 683-4000

Templeton Emerging Markets Fund, Inc.,
EMF, ASE (Equity)
700 Central Avenue
St. Petersburg, Florida 33701
(813) 823-8712

Templeton Global Government Income Fund,
TGG, NYSE (Bond)
700 Central Avenue
St. Petersburg, Florida 33701
(813) 823-8712

Templeton Global Income Fund, Inc., GIM,
NYSE (Bond)
700 Central Avenue
St. Petersburg, Florida 33701
(813) 823-8712

Templeton Value Fund, TVF, NYSE (Equity)
700 Central Avenue
St. Petersburg, Florida 33701
(813) 823-8712

Thai Fund, Inc., TTF, NYSE (Equity)
Vanguard Financial Center, P.O. Box 1102
Valley Forge, Pennsylvania 19482
(215) 648-6000

Transamerica Income Shares, Inc., TAI,
NYSE (Bond)
1150 South Olive Street
Los Angeles, California 90051
(213) 742-4141

Tri-Continental Corporation, TY, NYSE
(Equity)
One Bankers Trust Plaza
New York, New York 10006
(800) 221-2450

United Kingdom Fund, Inc., USKM, NYSE
(Equity)
7th Floor, 245 Park Avenue
New York, New York 10041

USF&G Packholder Fund, PHF, ASE (Bond)
The Spectrum Office Tower, Suite 700,
11260 Chester Road
Cincinnati, Ohio 45246
(513) 771-5150

USLIFE Income Fund,Inc., UIF, NYSE (Bond)
125 Maiden Lane
New York, New York 10038
(212) 709-6000

Van Kampen Merritt California Municipal
Trust, VKC, ASE (Bond)
1001 Warrenville Road
Lisle, Illinois 60532 (312) 719-6000

Van Kampen Merritt Intermediate Term High
Income Trust, VIT, NYSE (Bond)
1001 Warrenville Road
Lisle, Illinois 60532 (312) 719-6000

Van Kampen Merritt Municipal Income
Trust, VMT, NYSE (Bond)
1001 Warrenville Road
Lisle, Illinois 60532 (800) 225-2222

Vestaur Securities,Inc., VES, NYSE (Bond)
11th Floor, 16th & Market Streets
Philadelphia, Pennsylvania 19101
(215) 567-3969

World Income Fund, WOI, ASE (Bond)
800 Scudders Mill Road
Plainsboro, New Jersey 08536
(609) 282-2800

Worldwide Value Fund, Inc., VLU, NYSE
(Equity)
7 East Redwood Street
Baltimore, Maryland 21202 (301) 539-3400

Zenith Income Fund, Inc., ZIF, NYSE (Bond)
Two World Trade Center
New York, New York 10048 (212) 321-7155

Z-Seven Fund, Inc., ZSEV, Pacific Stock
Exchange (Specialized Equity)
Suite 21, 90 Broad Street
New York, New York 10004 (212) 809-1880

Zweig Fund, Inc. (Specialized Equity)
900 Third Avenue
New York, New York 10022 (212) 486-7110

Zweig Total Return Fund, ZTR, NYSE
(Equity)
900 Third Avenue
New York, New York 10022 (212) 486-7110

4. FUTURES AND OPTIONS CONTRACTS

On the following pages, you will find a list of commodity and option contracts being traded in the United States and Canada. These contracts are listed by the exchange on which they are traded. Within each exchange, the listings are broken down into the kind of products they are: foreign currency options, futures, futures options, index options, or interest rate options. Each contract is then listed alphabetically within its category.

Contract specifications set by each Exchange and approved by either the Commodities Futures Trading Commission or the Securities and Exchange Commission are listed with each contract.

The basic facts about each futures contract include the following information, although not all of these categories are relevant to each contract.

Trading Unit: What underlying commodity or group of stocks is being traded, and the quantity.

Prices Quoted In: The form in which prices are quoted (such as cents per bushel).

Minimum Price Fluctuation: What is the smallest move, up or down, the contract can make? This is indicated first in increments that the contract can move in, and then as a dollar figure for the amount of money that the move means to the commodity trader.

Dollar Value of a 1 Cent Move: The dollars an investor will make or lose, at least on paper, if a contract moves 1 cent up or down.

Daily Contract Limit: Many exchanges do not allow prices to rise or fall beyond certain limits within a day. Such limits, if any, are shown first in the increment of the contract, and then as a dollar figure.

Settlement: The way contracts are settled when they expire. Some contracts provide for the physical delivery of a commodity. Specific rules must be followed on how and where commodities are delivered from seller to buyer. Other contracts involve no physical delivery. These contracts are settled in cash.

Last Trading Day: The last day trading can occur in a contract.

Contract Months: Although all of these contracts trade constantly, most expire in only certain months of the year. This column presents the months in which contracts expire.

Trading Hours: The hours during which a contract is traded, in local time. EST means Eastern Standard Time, CST means Central Standard Time and PST means Pacific Standard Time.

Ticker Symbol: The symbol by which a contract's current price and trading activity can be checked through an electronic price quote service.

For index, interest rate and futures options contracts, other information is given:

Exercise Limits: Each exchange limits the number of contracts one trader can take a position in, either on the long or short side of a trade.

Strike Prices: These are set both above and below the current market price of the future or index, so puts and calls can be traded in both directions. This column also gives the intervals at which strike prices are set, and when new strike prices are added.

Expiration Day : If options are not exercised, they expire. This column details when options expire.

Index By Contract (U.S.)

Aluminum: futures (COMEX)
Australian Dollar: foreign currency futures (CME); foreign currency options (PHSE); futures options (CME)
Bank Certificates of Deposit: futures (IMM)
Barley: futures (WCE); futures options (CME)
British Pound: foreign currency futures (CME); foreign currency options (PHSE); futures (MIDAM); futures options (CME)
Canadian Dollar: foreign currency options (CME); foreign currency futures (PHSE); futures (MIDAM); futures options (CME)
CBOE 250 Index: futures (CBOT)
Cocoa: futures (CSCE); futures options (CSCE)
Coffee: futures (CSCE); futures options (CSCE)
Commodity Research Bureau Price Index: futures (NYFE)
Computer Technology Index: index options (AMEX)
Consumer Price Index-Wages: futures (CSCE)
Copper: futures (COMEX); futures options (COMEX)
Corn: futures (CBOT, MIDAM); futures options (CBOT)
Corn Syrup: futures (MGE)
Cotton: futures (NYCE); futures options (NYCE)
CRB Futures Price Index: futures (NYFE)
Crude Oil: futures (NYMEX); futures options (NYMEX)
Deutsche Mark: foreign currency futures (CME); foreign currency options (PHSE); futures (MIDAM); futures options (CME)
Eurodollars: foreign currency futures (CME); futures options (CME)
European Currency Units: foreign currency futures (CME); futures (FINEX); foreign currency options (PHSE)
Exchange Stock Portfolio: basket trading (NYSE)
Feeder Cattle: futures options (CME)
Financial News Composite Index: index options (PSE)
French Franc: foreign currency futures (CME); foreign currency options (PHSE)

Gasoline: futures (NYMEX)
Gold: futures (CBOT, COMEX, MIDAM); futures options (COMEX, MIDAM); index options (PHSE)
Government National Mortgage Association CDR: futures (CBOT)
Heating Oil: futures (NYMEX); futures options (NYMEX)
High Fructose Corn Syrup: futures (MGE)
International Market Index: index options (AMEX)
Institutional Index: index options (AMEX)
Japanese Yen: foreign currency futures (CME); foreign currency options (PHSE); futures (MIDAM); futures options (CME)
Live Cattle: futures (CME, MIDAM); futures options (CME)
Live Hogs: futures (CME, MIDAM); futures options (CME)
Lumber: futures (CME); futures options (CME)
Major Market Index: index options (AMEX)
Major Market Index "Maxi": futures (CBOT)
Moody's Corporate Bond Index: futures (COMEX)
Municipal Bond Index: futures (CBOT); futures options (CBOT)
National OTC Index: futures (PHSE); index options (PHSE)
NYSE Composite Index: futures (NYFE); futures options (NYFE); index options (NYSE)
NYSE Options Index: index options (NYSE)
Oats: futures (CBOT, MIDAM)
Oil Index: index options (AMEX)
Orange Juice: futures (NYCE); futures options (NYCE)
Palladium: futures (NYMEX)
Platinum: futures (MIDAM, NYMEX)
Pork Bellies: futures options (CME)
Propane: futures (NYCE, NYMEX)
Rough Rice: futures (CRCE)
Russell Index: futures (NYFE)
Silver: futures (CBOT, COMEX, MIDAM); futures options (CBOT, COMEX)
Sorghum: futures (KCBT)
Soybeans: futures (CBOT, MIDAM); futures options (CBOT, MIDAM)
Soybean Meal: futures (CBOT, MIDAM); futures options (CBOT)
Soybean Oil: futures (CBOT); futures options (CBOT)
Standard and Poor's 100 Index: index options (CBOE)
Standard and Poor's 500 Index: futures (CME); futures options (CME); index options (CBOE)
Sugar: futures (CSCE); futures options (CSCE)
Swiss Franc: foreign currency futures (CME); foreign currency options (PHSE); futures (MIDAM); futures options (CME)
Treasury Bills: futures (CME, MIDAM); futures options (CME); interest rate options (AMEX)
Treasury Bonds: futures (CBOT, MIDAM, NYFE); futures options (CBOT); interest rate options (CBOE)
Treasury Index (Five Year): futures (FINEX)
Treasury Notes: futures (CBOT); futures options (CBOT); interest rate options (AMEX, CBOE)
U.S. Dollar: futures (FINEX)
Value Line Index: futures (KCBT); index options (PHSE)
Wheat: futures (CBOT, KCBT, MGE, MIDAM); futures options (CBOT, KCBT, MGE, MIDAM)

Key To Abbreviations of U.S. Exchanges:

AMEX: American Stock Exchange
CBOE: Chicago Board Options Exchange
CBOT: Chicago Board of Trade
CME: Chicago Mercantile Exchange
COMEX: Commodity Exchange, Inc.
CRCE: Chicago Rice and Cotton Exchange
CSCE: Coffee, Sugar and Cocoa Exchange
KCBT: Kansas City Board of Trade
MGE: Minneapolis Grain Exchange
MIDAM: MidAmerica Commodity Exchange
NYCE: New York Cotton Exchange
  [Also FINEX]
NYFE: New York Futures Exchange
NYMEX: New York Mercantile Exchange
NYSE: New York Stock Exchange
PHSE: Philadelphia Stock Exchange
PSE: Pacific Stock Exchange

Index By Contract (International)

Alberta Feed Barley: futures (WCE)
All Ordinaries Share Price Index: futures (SFE); futures options (SFE)
Aluminum, primary and high grade: futures (LME); futures options (LME)
American Soybeans: futures (TGE)
Australian Dollar: futures (SFE); futures options (SFE)
Australian 90-day Bank Accepted Bills: futures (SFE); futures options (SFE)
Australian 10-year Treasury Bond: futures (SFE); futures options (SFE)
Australian 3-year Treasury Bond: futures (SFE); futures options (SFE)
Baltic Freight Index: futures (BFE)
Barclays Share Price Index: futures (NZFE)
Barley: futures (BFE); futures options (BFE)
Bond Index: futures options (EOE)
Brazilian Coffee: futures (BMF)
Brazilian Domestic 60 and 90 day CD's: futures (BMF)
Brazilian Treasury Bonds: futures (BMF); futures options (BMF)
Brent Blend Crude Oil: futures (IPE)
British Pound: futures (LIFFE), (SIMEX); futures options: (EOE), (LIFFE)
Broilers (Frozen and Chilled): futures (BMF)
Canadian 3-month Bankers Acceptance: futures (ME)
Canadian Bonds: futures (ME); futures options (TFE)
Canadian Dollar: futures (ME); futures options (VSE)
Canadian Treasury Bills: futures (ME, TFE)
Canola/Rapeseed: futures (WCE)
Cattle: futures (BFE, SFE)
Chinese Soybeans: futures (TGE)
Cocoa: futures (FOX), (KLCE); futures options (FOX)
Cocoa Beans: futures (PFE)
Cocoa Butter: futures (PFE)
Coffee: futures (FOX, PFE); futures options (FOX)
Copper (Grade A and Standard): futures (LME); futures options (LME)

Cotton Yarn: futures (TCE)
Crude Oil: futures (IPE)
Crude Palm Oil: futures (KLCE)
Deutsche Mark: futures (LIFFE, SIMEX); futures options (SIMEX)
Domestic Feed Barley: futures (WCE)
Domestic Feed Oats: futures (WCE)
Domestic Feed Wheat: futures (WCE)
Dutch Government Bonds: futures options: (EOE)
Dutch Guilder Bond Future: futures (FTA)
EEC Barley: futures (BFE); futures options (BFE)
EEC Wheat: futures (BFE); futures options (BFE)
EOE Stock Index: futures options (EOE)
Eurodollar 90-day Time Deposit: futures (SIMEX); futures options (SIMEX)
Eurodollar 3-month Time Deposit: futures (LIFFE), (SFE); futures options (LIFFE)
Financial Times Stock Exchange 100 Index (FTSE): futures (LIFFE); futures options
    (ISE)
Flaxseed: futures (WCE)
French Government National Bond: futures (MATIF); futures options (MATIF)
French Treasury 90-day Bill: futures (MATIF)
Gas Oil: futures (IPE); futures options (IPE)
German Government Bond: futures (LIFFE)
Gold: futures (BMF, HKFE, ME, SFE, TCE); futures options (BMF, EOE, VSE)
Hang Seng Index: futures (HKFE)
Japanese Government Bond: futures (LIFFE)
Japanese 10-year and 20-year Government Bond: futures (TSE)
Japanese Soybeans: futures (TGE)
Japanese Yen: futures (LIFFE, SIMEX); futures options (SIMEX)
Lead: futures (LME); futures options (LME)
Live Cattle: futures (BFE, BMF, SFE)
Live Hogs: futures (BMF)
Lumber: futures (ME)
Major Market Index: futures options (EOE)
New Zealand Dollar: futures (NZFE)
New Zealand 5-year Government Stock Number 2: futures (NZFE)
New Zealand 90-day Bank Accepted Bills: futures (NZFE)
Nickel: futures (LME); futures options (LME)
Nikkei Stock Average: futures (OSE, SIMEX)
Oats: futures (WCE)
OMX Index: futures (SOM); futures options (SOM)
Oil and Gas Stock Index: futures (TFE)
Osaka Stock Futures 50: futures (OSE)
Pig: futures (BFE)
Platinum: futures (ME, TCE); futures options (VSE)
Potato Starch: futures (TGE)
Potatoes: futures (BFE, LPFM); futures options (BFE)
Rapeseed: futures (WCE)
Red Beans: futures (TGE)
Robusta Coffee: futures (PFE)
Rubber: futures (KLCE, TCE)
Rye: futures (WCE)
Sao Paulo Stock Exchange Index: futures (BMF)
Silver: futures (LME, TCE); futures options (EOE, TFE, VSE)

Soybeans: futures (HKFE)
Soybean Meal: futures (BFE)
Sugar: futures (FOX, HKFE, TSUE); futures options (FOX)
Swedish 5-year Treasury Note: futures options (SOM)
Swiss Franc: futures (LIFFE)
SX 16 Stock Index: futures (SOFE); futures options (SOFE)
Tin: futures (KLCE)
Tokyo Stock Price Index: futures (TSE)
Toronto 35 Index: futures (TFE); futures options (TSEX)
TSE 300 Spot Contract: futures (TFE)
United Kingdom, Long Gilt: futures (LIFFE); futures options (LIFFE)
United Kingdom LTOM 63 Equity Options: futures options (ISE)
United Kingdom Medium Gilt: futures (LIFFE)
United Kingdom Short Gilt: futures (LIFFE)
United Kingdom 3-month Sterling: futures (LIFFE); futures options (LIFFE)
United States Dollar: futures (BMF, NZFE, TFE); futures options (BMF, EOE)
United States Dollar: futures (BMF, NZFE); futures options (BMF, EOE)
United States Dollar-Deutsche Mark: futures options (ISE)
United States Dollar-Deutsche Mark Currency: futures (SFE); futures options (LIFFE)
United States Dollar-Sterling: futures options (ISE)
United States Treasury Bond: futures (LIFFE, SFE); futures options (LIFFE)
Wheat: futures (BFE, WCE)
White Beans: futures (TGE)
White Sugar: futures (PFE)
Wool: futures (SFE)
Woolen Yarn: futures (TCE)
Zinc (High Grade): futures (LME); futures options (LME)

Key to Abbreviations of International Exchanges

BFE: Baltic Futures Exchange (Britain)
[includes Baltic International Freight Futures Exchange, London Grain Futures Market, London Meat Futures Market, London Potato Futures Market, Soya Bean Meal Futures Association]
BMF: Bolsa Mercantil & De Futuros (Brazil)
EOE: European Options Exchange (The Netherlands)
FOX: London Futures and Options Exchange (Britain)
FTA: Financiale Terminjmarkt Amsterdam (The Netherlands)
HKFE: Hong Kong Futures Exchange (Hong Kong)
KLCE: Kuala Lumpur Commodity Exchange (Malaysia)
IPE: International Petroleum Exchange of London (Britain)
ISE: International Stock Exchange (Britain)
LIFFE: London International Financial Futures Exchange
LME: London Metal Exchange
LPFM: Lille Potato Futures Market (France)
MATIF: Marche A Terme Des Instrument Financiers (France)
ME: Montreal Exchange (Canada)
NZFE: New Zealand Futures Exchange
OSE: Osaka Securities Exchange (Japan)
PFE: Paris Futures Exchange (France)

SFE: Sydney Futures Exchange (Australia)
SIMEX: Singapore International Monetary Exchange (Singapore)
SOFE: Swedish Options and Futures Exchange (Sweden)
SOM: Stockholm Options Market (Sweden)
TCE: Tokyo Commodity Exchange (Japan)
TFE: Toronto Futures Exchange (Canada)
TGE: Tokyo Grain Exchange (Japan)
TSE: Tokyo Stock Exchange (Japan)
TSEX: Toronto Stock Exchange (Canada)
TSUE: Tokyo Sugar Exchange
VSE: Vancouver Stock Exchange (Canada)
WCE: Winnipeg Commodity Exchange (Canada)

UNITED STATES SECURITIES, FUTURES AND OPTIONS EXCHANGES

American Stock Exchange (AMEX)

Index Options

Contract	Underlying Index	Trading Unit	Prices Quoted In	Minimum Price Fluctuation
• Computer Technology Index	major computer stocks	index × $100	index points	$^1/_{16}$ up to 3, $^1/_8$ over 3
• Institutional Index	75 major institutional holdings	index × $100	index points	$^1/_{16}$ up to 3, $^1/_8$ over 3
• International Market Index	50 foreign equities	index × $100	index points	$^1/_{16}$ up to 3, $^1/_8$ over 3
• Major Market Index	20 Blue Chip stocks	index × $100	index points	$^1/_{16}$ up to 3, $^1/_8$ over 3
• Oil Index	major oil stocks	index × $100	index points	$^1/_{16}$ up to 3, $^1/_8$ over 3

Interest Rate Options

Contract	Underlying Security	Trading Unit	Prices Quoted In	Minimum Price Fluctuation
• Treasury Bills	current 13-week T-bill	$1 million T-bills	basis points	1 basis point ($25)
• Treasury Notes	current 10-year T-note	$100,000 T-notes	basis points	$^1/_{32}$ of a point ($31.25)

Strike Prices	Settlement	Contract Months	Trading Hours	Ticker Symbol
5 points apart	in cash	3 nearest months plus Mar, June Sept, Dec	9:30 a.m.- 4:10 p.m. EST	XCI
5 points apart	in cash	3 nearest months plus Mar, June Sept, Dec	9:30 a.m.- 4:15 p.m. EST	XII
5 points apart	in cash	3 nearest months plus Mar, June, Sept, Oct	9:30 a.m.- 4:15 p.m. EST	ADR
5 points apart	in cash	3 nearest months plus Mar, June, Sept, Dec	9:30 a.m.- 4:15 p.m. EST	XMI
5 points apart	in cash	3 nearest months plus Jan, Apr, July, Oct	9:30 a.m.- 4:10 p.m. EST	XOI

Strike Prices	Settlement	Contract Months	Trading Hours
20 basis points apart	in Treasury bills	Mar, June, Sept, Dec	9:30 a.m.- 3:00 p.m. EST
2 basis points apart	in Treasury notes	Feb, May Aug, Nov	9:30 a.m.- 3:00 p.m. EST

Chicago Board of Trade (CBOT)

Futures

Contract	Trading Unit	Prices Quoted In	Minimum Price Fluctuation
• CBOE 250 Index	index of CBOE 250 × $500	full points and $1/20$ of a point	$1/20$ of a point ($25)
• Corn	5000 bushels	cents and $1/4$ cents a bushel	$1/4$ of a cent, ($12.50)
• Gold (Kilo)	1 kilogram (32.15 troy ounces)	dollars and cents a troy ounce	10 cents a troy ounce ($3.22)
• Gold (Ounce)	100 troy ounces	dollars and cents a troy ounce	10 cents a troy ounce ($10.00)
• GNMA-CDR (Collateralized Depositary Receipt)	$100,000 of GNMA 8% coupon	full points and 32nds of a point	$1/32$ of a point ($31.25)
• Major Market Maxi Index	index of 20 Blue Chip stocks × $250	full points and $1/20$ of a point	$1/20$ of a point ($12.50)
• Municipal Bond Index	Bond Buyer Muni Index × $1000	full points and 32nds of a point	$1/32$ of a point ($31.25)
• Oats	5000 bushels	cents and $1/4$ cents a bushel	$1/4$ of a cent a bushel ($12.50)
Silver • (1000 Ounces)	1000 troy ounces	dollars and cents a troy ounce	$1/10$ of a cent a troy ounce ($1)
• Silver (5000 Ounces)	5000 troy ounces	dollars and cents a troy ounce	$1/10$ of a cent a troy ounce ($5)
• Soybeans	5000 bushels	cents and $1/4$ cents a bushel	$1/4$ of a bushel ($12.50)
• Soybean Meal	100 tons (200,000 pounds)	dollars and cents a ton	10 cents a ton ($10)
• Soybean Oil	60,000 pounds	dollars and cents per hundredweight	$1/100$ of a cent per pound ($6)

Daily Contract Limit	Dollar Value of 1 Cent Move	Contract Months	Trading Hours	Ticker Symbol
50 index points ($25,000)	$500	3 nearest months and Mar, June, Sept, Dec	8:30 a.m.-3:15 p.m. CST	JV
10 cents ($500)	$50	Mar, May, July, Sept, Dec	9:30 a.m.-1:15 p.m CST	C
$50 a troy ounce ($1607.50)	—	3 nearest months and Feb, Apr, June, Aug, Oct, Dec	8:00 a.m.-1:40 p.m. CST	KI
$50 a troy ounce ($5,000)	—	3 nearest months and Feb, Apr, June, Aug, Oct, Dec	7:20 a.m.-1:40 p.m. CST	GH
$^{64}/_{32}$ per contract ($2000)	—	Mar, June, Sept, Dec	8:00 a.m.-2:00 p.m. CST	M
None	—	monthly	8:15 a.m.-3:15 p.m. CST	BC
$^{96}/_{32}$ per contract ($3000)	—	Mar, June, Sept, Dec	7:20 a.m.-2:00 p.m. CST	MB
10 cents a bushel ($500)	$50	Mar, May, July, Sept, Dec	9:30 a.m.-1:15 p.m. CST	O
$1 a troy ounce	$10	3 nearest months and Feb, Apr, June, Aug, Oct, Dec	7:25 a.m.-1:25 p.m. CST	AG
$1 a troy ounce	$50	3 nearest months and Feb, Apr, June, Aug, Oct, Dec	7:25 a.m.-1:25 p.m. CST	SV
30 cents a bushel ($1500)	$50	Jan, Mar, May, July, Aug, Sept, Nov	9:30 a.m.-1:15 p.m. CST	S
$10 a ton ($1000)	$1	Jan, Mar, May, July, Aug, Sept, Oct, Dec	9:30 a.m.-1:15 p.m. CST	SM
1 cent per pound ($600)	—	Jan, Mar, May, July, Aug, Sept, Oct, Dec	9:30 a.m.-1:15 p.m. CST	BO

Contract	Trading Unit	Prices Quoted In	Minimum Price Fluctuation
• 30-Day Interest Rate	$5 million	$41.67 per basis point	$1/100$ of a percent ($41.67)
• Treasury Bonds	$100,000 of Treasury bond 8% coupon	full points and 32nds of a point	$1/32$ of a point ($31.25)
• Treasury Notes	$100,000 of Treasury notes	full points and 32nds of a point	$1/32$ of a point ($31.25)
• Treasury Notes (Five-Year)	$100,000 of Treasury notes	32nds of a point	$1/2$ of $1/32$ of a point ($15.63)
• Wheat	5000 bushels	cents and $1/4$ cents a bushel	$1/4$ of a cent a bushel ($12.50)

Futures Options

Contract	Trading Unit	Prices Quoted In	Minimum Price Fluctuation	Strike Prices
• Corn	1 CBT corn futures contract	$1/8$ of a cent ($50)	$1/8$ of a point ($6.25)	10 cents apart
• Municipal Bond Index	1 CB municipal bond index futures contract	full points ($1000) and 64ths of a point	$1/64$ of a point ($15.63)	2 points apart
• Silver	1 CBT silver futures contract	$1/10$ of a cent ($1)	$1 a troy ounce ($1000)	25 cents to $20 apart
• Soybeans	1 CBT soybean futures contract	$1/8$ of a cent ($50)	$1/8$ of a point ($6.25)	25 cents apart
• Soybean Meal	1 CBT soybean meal futures contract	5 cents a ton ($5)	$1/8$ of point ($6.25)	$10 apart
• Soybean Oil	1 CBT soybean oil futures contract	0.005 cent a pound ($3)	$1/8$ of a point ($6.25)	1 cent apart
• Treasury Bonds	1 CBT T-bond futures contract	$1/64$ of 1% of $100,000	$1/64$ of a point ($15.63)	2 points apart
• Treasury Notes	1 CBT T-note futures contract	$1/64$ of 1% $100,000	$1/64$ of a point ($15.63)	1 point apart
• Wheat	1 CBT wheat futures contract	$1/8$ cent ($50)	$1/8$ cent a bushel ($6.25)	10 cents apart

Daily Contract Limit	Dollar Value of 1 Cent Move	Contract Months	Trading Hours	Ticker Symbol
150 basis point	—	first 7 calendar months and 2 from Mar, June, Sept, Dec	7:20 a.m.- 2:00 p.m. CST	FF
$^{96}/_{32}$ of a point ($3000)	—	Mar, June, Sept, Dec	7:20 a.m.- 2:00 p.m. CST	US
$^{96}/_{32}$ of a point ($3000)	—	Mar, June, Sept, Dec	7:20 a.m.- 2:00 p.m. CST	TY
$^{96}/_{32}$ of a point ($3000)	—	Mar, June, Sept, Dec	7:20 a.m.- 2:00 p.m. CST	FV
20 cents a bushel ($1000)	—	Mar, May, July, Sept, Dec	9:30 a.m.- 1:15 p.m. CST	W

Expiration Day	Last Trading Day	Contract Months	Trading Hours	Ticker Symbol
Saturday after last trading day	Friday before first futures notice day	Mar, May, July, Sept, Dec	9:30 a.m.- 1:15 p.m. CST	CY (calls) PY (puts)
8:00 p.m. on last day of trading	2:00 p.m. on last day of trading	Mar, June, Sept, Dec	7:20 a.m.- 2:00 p.m. CST	QC (calls) QP (puts)
Saturday after last trading day	Friday before first futures notice day	Feb, Apr, June, Aug, Oct, Dec	7:25 a.m.- 1:25 p.m. CST	AC (calls) AP (puts)
Saturday after last trading day	Friday before first futures notice day	Jan, Mar, May, July, Aug, Sept, Nov	9:30 a.m.- 1:15 p.m. CST	CZ (calls) PZ (puts)
Saturday after last trading day	Friday before first futures notice day	Jan, Mar, May, July, Aug, Sept, Oct	9:30 a.m.- 1:15 p.m. CST	MY (calls) MZ (puts)
Saturday after last trading day	Friday before first futures notice day	Jan, Mar, May, July, Aug, Sept, Oct, Dec	9:30 a.m.- 1:15 p.m. CST	OY (calls) OZ (puts)
Saturday after last trading day	Friday before first futures notice day	Mar, June, Sept, Dec	7:20 a.m.- 2:00 p.m. CST	CG (calls) PG (puts)
Saturday after last trading day	Friday before first futures notice day	Mar, June, Sept, Dec	7:20 a.m.- 2:00 p.m. CST	TO (calls) TP (puts)
Saturday after last trading day	Friday before first futures notice day	Mar, May, July, Sept, Dec	9:30 a.m.- 1:15 p.m. CST	WY (calls) WZ (puts)

Chicago Board Options Exchange (CBOE)

Index Options

Contract	Underlying Index	Trading Unit	Prices Quoted In	Minimum Price Fluctuation
• S&P 100 Index	S&P 100 Stock Index	index × $100	dollars and cents	$1/16$ up to 3, $1/8$ over 3
• S&P 500 Index	S&P 500 Stock Index	index × $100	dollars and cents	$1/16$ up to 3, $1/8$ over 3
• S&P 500 Index	S&P 500 Stock Index	index × $100	dollars and cents	$1/16$ up to 3, $1/8$ over 3
• S&P 500 Index	S&P 500 Stock Index	index × $100	dollars and cents	$1/16$ up to 3, $1/8$ over 3

Interest Rate Options

Contract	Underlying Security	Trading Unit	Prices Quoted In	Minimum Price Fluctuation
• Long-Term Rates	long-term government bonds		points and $1/16$ of a point	$1/16$ of a point ($6)
• Short-Term Rates	short-term government bonds		points and $1/16$ of a point	$1/16$ of a point ($6)
• U.S. Treasury Bonds	Treasury bonds	$100,000 in bonds	points and $1/32$ of a point	$1/32$ of a point ($31.25)
• U.S. Treasury Notes	Treasury notes	$100,000 in notes	points and $1/32$ of a point	$1/32$ of a point ($31.25)

Chicago Mercantile Exchange (CME)

Foreign Currency Futures

Contract	Trading Unit	Prices Quoted In	Minimum Price Fluctuation
• Australian Dollar	100,000 Australian dollars	cents per Australian dollar	1 point or $.0001 per Australian dollar ($10)
• British Pound	62,500 British pounds	cents per pound	2 points or $.0002 per pound ($12.50)

Strike Prices	Settlement	Last Trading Day	Contract Months	Trading Hours	Ticker Symbol
5 points apart	in cash	3rd Friday of contract month	4 nearest months	8:30 a.m.- 3:15 p.m. CST	OEX
5 points apart	in cash	3rd Friday of contract month	Mar, June, Sept, Oct, Dec	8:30 a.m.- 3:00 p.m. CST	SPX
25 points apart	in cash	3rd Friday of contract month	Mar, June, Sept, Oct, Dec	8:30 a.m.- 3:00 p.m. CST	SPL
5 points apart	in cash	3rd Thursday of contract month	Mar, June Sept, Oct Dec	8:30 a.m.- 3:15 p.m. CST	NSX

Strike Prices	Settlement	Last Trading Day	Contract Months	Trading Hours	Ticker Symbol
2¹/₂ points apart	in principal			7:20 a.m.- 2:00 p.m.	LTX
2¹/₂ points apart	in principal			7:20 a.m.- 2:00 p.m. CST	IRX
1 point apart	in Treasury bonds	3rd Friday of contract month	Mar, June, Sept, Dec	8:00 a.m.- 2:00 p.m. CST	YBQ, YBR
1 point apart	in Treasury notes	3rd Friday of contract month	Mar, June, Sept, Dec	8:00 a.m.- 2:00 p.m. CST	YFD, YFC

Daily Price Limit	Last Trading Day	Contract Months	Trading Hours	Ticker Symbol
150 points	2nd business day before 3rd Wednesday of month	Mar, June, Sept, Dec	7:20 a.m.- 2:00 p.m. CST	AD
400 points	2nd business day before 3rd Wednesday of month	Mar, June, Sept, Dec	7:20 a.m.- 2:00 p.m. CST	BP

Contract	Trading Unit	Prices Quoted In	Minimum Price Fluctuation
• Canadian Dollar	100,000 Canadian dollars	cents per Canadian dollar	1 point or $.0001 per Canadian dollar ($10)
• Deutsche Mark	125,000 German marks	cents per German mark	1 point or $.0001 per German mark ($12.50)
• Eurodollar 90-Day Time Deposit	1 million Eurodollars	index points	1 point ($25)
• European Currency Unit	125,000 European Currency Units	cents per European Currency Unit	1 point or $.0001 per European Currency Unit ($12.50)
• French Franc	250,000 French francs	cents per French franc	5 points or $.0005 per French franc ($12.50)
• Japanese Yen	12.5 million Japanese yen	cents per Japanese yen	1 point or $.000001 per Japanese yen ($12.50)
• Swiss Franc	125,000 Swiss francs	cents per Swiss franc	1 point or $.0001 per Swiss franc ($12.50)

Futures

Contract	Trading Unit	Prices Quoted In	Minimum Price Fluctuation	Daily Price Limit
• Feeder Cattle	44,000 pounds	dollars per hundred pounds	2.5 cents per hundred pounds ($11)	1.5 cents per pound ($660)
• Live Cattle	40,000 pounds	dollars per hundred pounds	2.5 cents per hundred pounds ($10)	1.5 cents per pound ($600)
• Live Hogs	30,000 pounds	dollars per hundred pounds	2.5 cents per hundred pounds ($7.50)	1.5 cents per pound ($450)
• Lumber	150,000 board feet	dollars per thousand board feet	10 cents per thousand board feet ($15)	$5 per thousand board feet ($750)
• Pork Bellies	40,000 pounds	dollars per hundred pounds	2.5 cents per hundred pounds ($10)	2 cents per pound ($800)
• S&P 500 Index	S&P 500 × $500	cents	5 cents (5 points) ($25)	None
• U.S. Treasury Bills	$1 million 3-month Treasury bill	index points	1 index point ($25)	None

Daily Price Limit	Last Trading Day	Contract Months	Trading Hours	Ticker Symbol
100 points	2nd business day before 3rd Wednesday of month	Mar, June, Sept, Dec	7:20 a.m.- 2:00 p.m. CST	CD
150 points	2nd business day before 3rd Wednesday of month	Mar, June, Sept, Dec	7:20 a.m.- 2:00 p.m. CST	DM
none	2nd London business day before 3rd Wednesday of month	Mar, June, Sept, Dec	7:20 a.m.- 2:00 p.m. CST	ED
150 points	2nd business day before 3rd Wednesday of month	Mar, June, Sept, Dec	7:10 a.m.- 2:00 p.m. CST	EC
500 points	2nd business day before 3rd Wednesday of month	Mar, June, Sept, Dec	7:20 a.m.- 2:00 p.m. CST	FR
150 points	2nd business day before 3rd Wednesday of month	Mar, June, Sept, Dec	7:20 a.m.- 2:00 p.m. CST	JY
150 points	2nd business day before 3rd Wednesday of contract	Mar, June, Sept, Dec	7:20 a.m.- 2:00 p.m. CST	SF

Dollar Value Of 1 Cent Move	Last Trading Day	Contract Months	Trading Hours	Ticker Symbol
$440	last Thursday of contract month	Jan, Mar, Apr, May, Aug, Sept, Oct	9:05 a.m.- 1:00 p.m. CST	FC
$400	20th day of contract month	Feb, Apr, June, Aug, Sept, Oct, Dec	9:05 a.m.- 1:00 p.m. CST	LC
$300	20th day of contract month	Feb, Apr, June, July, Aug, Oct, Dec	9:10 a.m.- 1:00 p.m. CST	LH
$1	15th day of contract month	Jan, Mar, May, July, Sept, Nov	9:00 a.m.- 1:05 p.m. CST	LB
$400	6 days before end of contract month	Feb, Mar, May, July, Aug	9:10 a.m.- 1:00 p.m. CST	PB
—	Thursday before 3rd Friday of contract month	Mar, June, Sept, Dec	8:30 a.m.- 3:15 p.m. CST	SP
—	last trading day	Mar, June, Sept, Dec	7:20 a.m.- 2:00 p.m. CST	TB

Futures Options

Contract	Trading Unit	Prices Quoted In	Minimum Price Fluctuation	Strike Prices
● Australian Dollar	1 Australian dollar futures contract	cents per Australian dollar	.0001 cent ($10)	1 cent per Australian dollar apart
● British Pound	1 pound futures contract	cents per pound	2 cents ($12.50)	2.5 cents per pound apart
● Canadian Dollar	1 Canadian dollar futures contract	cents per Canadian dollar	.0001 cent ($10)	.005 cent per Canadian dollar apart
● Deutsche Mark	1 Deutsche mark futures contract	cents per Deutsche mark	.0001 cent ($12.50)	1 cent per Deutsche mark apart
● Eurodollars	1 Eurodollar futures contract	index points (.01 points = $25)	.01 points ($25)	50 index points apart
● Feeder Cattle	1 feeder cattle futures contract	cents per pound	2.5 cents per 100 pounds ($11)	2 cents apart
● Japanese Yen	1 Japanese yen futures contract	cents per Japanese yen	.000001 cent ($12.50)	.0001 cent per yen apart
● Live Cattle	1 cattle futures contract	cents per pound	.025 per pound ($10)	2 cents apart
● Live Hogs	1 hogs futures contract	cents per pound	.025 per pound ($7.50)	2 cents apart
● Lumber	1 lumber futures contract	cents per board foot	10 cents per thousand board feet ($15)	$5 apart
● Pork Bellies	1 pork belly futures contract	cents per pound	.025 cents per pound ($10)	2 cents apart
● S&P 500 Stock Index	1 S&P 500 futures contract	index points (.01 point = $5)	.05 points ($25)	.05 points apart
● Swiss Franc	1 Swiss franc futures contract	cents per Swiss franc	1 cent ($12.50)	1 cent per Swiss franc apart
● Treasury Bills	1 T-bill futures contract	index points (.01 points = $25)	.01 points ($25)	50 index points apart

Expiration Day	Last Trading Day	Contract Months	Trading Hours	Ticker Symbol
on last trading day	2nd Friday before 3rd Wednesday a month	every month	7:20 a.m.- 2:00 p.m. CST	KA (call) JA (put)
on last trading day	2nd Friday before 3rd Wednesday of month	every month	7:20 a.m.- 2:00 p.m. CST	CP (call) PP (put)
on last trading day	2nd Friday before 3rd Wednesday of month	every month	7:20 a.m.- 2:00 p.m. CST	CV (call) PV (put)
on last trading day	2nd Friday before 3rd Wednesday of month	every month	7:20 a.m.- 2:00 p.m. CST	CM (call) PM (put)
on last trading day	2nd London business day before 3rd Wednesday of month	Mar, June, Sept, Dec	7:20 a.m.- 2:00 p.m. CST	CE (call) PE (put)
on last trading day	last Thursday of month	Jan, Mar, Apr, May, Aug, Sept, Oct, Nov	9:05 a.m.- 1:00 p.m. CST	KF (call) JF (put)
on last trading day	2nd Friday before 3rd Wednesday of month	every month	7:20 a.m.- 2:00 p.m. CST	CJ (call) PJ (put)
on last trading day	last Friday before first day of month	Feb, Apr, June, Aug, Sept, Oct, Dec	9:05 a.m.- 1:00 p.m. CST	CK (call) PK (put)
on last trading day	last Friday before first day of month	Feb, Apr, June, July, Aug, Oct, Dec	9:10 a.m.- 1:00 p.m. CST	CH (call) PH (put)
on last trading day	last Friday before first day of month	Jan, Mar, May, July, Sept, Nov	9:00 a.m.- 1:05 p.m. CST	KL (call) JL (put)
on last trading day	last Friday before first day of month	Feb, Mar, May, July, Aug	9:10 a.m.- 1:00 p.m. CST	KP (call) JP (put)
3rd Friday of month	3rd Thursday or Friday of month	every month	8:30 a.m.- 3:15 p.m. CST	CS (call) PS (put)
on last trading day	2nd Friday before 3rd Wednesday of month	every month	7:20 a.m.- 2:00 p.m. CST	CF (call) PF (put)
on last trading day	varies	Mar, June, Sept, Dec	7:20 a.m.- 2:00 p.m. CST	CQ (call) PQ (put)

Chicago Rice and Cotton Exchange (CRCE)

Futures

Contract	Trading Unit	Prices Quoted In	Minimum Fluctuation
● Rough Rice	2000 hundredweight	cents per hundredweight	.005 per hundredweight ($10)

Coffee, Sugar and Cocoa Exchange (CSCE)

Futures

Contract	Trading Unit	Prices Quoted In	Minimum Fluctuation	Daily Price Limit
● Cocoa	10 metric tons	dollars per metric ton	$1 per metric ton ($10)	$88 per metric ton
● Coffee	37,500 pounds	cents per pound	$5/100$ of a cent per pound ($18.75)	6 cents per pound
● International Market Index (IMI)	$250 × index	dollars	0.05 point ($12.50)	30 points below, 50 points above, previous day
● Sugar Number 11	50 long tons	cents per pound	$1/100$ of a cent per pound ($11.20)	$1/2$ cent per pound = $560
● Sugar Number 14	50 long tons	cents per pound	$1/100$ of a cent per pound ($11.20)	$1/2$ cent per pound = $560
● World White Sugar	50 metric tons	cents per ton	20 cents per ton ($10)	$10 per ton = $500

Futures Options

Contract	Trading Unit	Prices Quoted In	Minimum Price Fluctuation	Strike Prices
● Cocoa	1 cocoa futures contract	dollars per metric ton	$1 per ton ($10)	$100 under $3600 $200 above $3600
● Coffee	1 coffee futures contract	cents per pound	$1/100$ of a cent per pound = $3.75	5 cents under 200 cents, 10 cents above 200 cents
● Sugar	1 sugar futures contract	cents per pound	1 cent per pound ($11.20)	varies

Daily Price Limit	Last Trading Day	Contract Months	Trading Hours	Ticker Symbol
30 cents per hundredweight ($600)	8th to last day of month	Jan, Mar, May, Sept, Nov	9:15 a.m.- 1:30 p.m. CST	NR

Last Trading Day	Contract Months	Trading Hours	Ticker Symbol
one business day prior to last notice day	Mar, May, July, Sept, Dec	9:30 a.m.- 2:15 p.m. EST	CC
one business day prior to last notice day	Mar, May, July, Sept, Dec	9:45 a.m.- 2:28 p.m. EST	KC
one business day prior to 3rd Friday	most months	9:30 a.m.- 4:15 p.m. EST	DR
last business day of the month preceding the delivery month	Mar, May, July, Oct	10:00 a.m.- 1:43 p.m. EST	SB
8th calendar day of the month preceding the delivery month	Jan, Mar, May, July, Sept, Nov	9:40 a.m.- 1:43 p.m. EST	SE
15th of month preceding the delivery month	Jan, Mar, May, July Oct	9:45 a.m. - 1:43 p.m. EST	WS

Expiration Day	Last Trading Day	Contract Months	Trading Hours
on last trading day (by 4:00 p.m.)	1st Friday of month before contract month	Mar, May, July, Sept, Dec	9:30 a.m.- 3:00 p.m. EST
on last trading day (by 4:00 p.m.)	1st Friday of month before contract month	Mar, May, July, Sept, Dec	9:45 a.m.- 3:34 p.m. EST
on last trading day (by 3:00 p.m.)	2nd Friday of month before contract month	Mar, May, July, Oct	10:00 a.m.- 1:58 p.m. EST

Commodity Exchange Inc. (COMEX)

Futures

Contract	Trading Unit	Prices Quoted In	Minimum Price Fluctuation	Daily Contract Limit
● Aluminum	44,000 pounds	cents per pound	$5/100$ of a cent ($20)	5 cents a pound
● Copper	25,000 pounds	cents per pound	$5/100$ of a cent ($12.50)	5 cents a pound
● Gold	100 troy ounces	cents per troy ounce	10 cents per troy ounce ($10)	$25 per troy ounce
● Silver	5000 troy ounces	cents per troy ounce	$1/10$ of a cent per troy ounce ($5)	50 cents per troy ounce

Futures Options

Contract	Trading Unit	Prices Quoted In	Minimum Price Fluctuation	Strike Prices
● Copper	1 copper futures contract	cents per pound	$5/100$ of a cent per pound	1 to 5 cents apart, depending on copper price
● Gold	1 gold futures contract	cents per troy ounce	10 cents per troy ounce	$10 to $40 apart, depending on gold price
● Silver	1 silver futures contract	cents per troy ounce	$1/10$ of a cent per troy ounce	25 cents to $1 apart, depending on silver price

Dollar Value of 1 Cent Move	Last Trading Day	Contract Months	Trading Hours	Ticker Symbol
$400	3rd to last day of month	3 nearest months and Feb, Apr, June, Aug, Oct, Dec	8:30 a.m.- 2:30 p.m. EST	AL
$250	3rd to last day of month	Jan, Mar, May, July, Sept, Dec	9:25 a.m.- 2:00 p.m. EST	HG
$1	3rd to last day of month	3 nearest months and Feb, Apr, June, Aug, Oct, Dec	8:20 a.m.- 2:30 p.m. EST	GC
$50	3rd to last day of month	3 nearest months and Jan, Mar, May, July	8:25 a.m.- 2:25 p.m. EST	SI

Expiration Day	Last Trading Day	Contract Months	Trading Hours	Ticker Symbol
on last trading day	2nd Friday of month before futures delivery	Mar, May, July, Sept, Dec	9:25 a.m.- 2:00 p.m. EST	HX
on last trading day	2nd Friday of month before futures delivery	12 months: Jan–Dec	8:25 a.m.- 2:30 p.m. EST	OG
on last trading day	2nd Friday of month before futures delivery	Mar, May, July, Sept, Dec	8:25 a.m.- 2:25 p.m. EST	SO

Kansas City Board of Trade (KCBT)

Futures

Contract	Trading Unit	Prices Quoted In	Minimum Price Fluctuation	Daily Contract Limit
• Sorghum	5000 bushels	cents and $^1/_4$ cents per bushel	$^1/_4$ cent per bushel ($12.50)	15 cents
• Value Line Maxi Index	index × $500	index points	$25 per tick	50 points
• Value Line Mini Index	index × $100	index points	$5 per tick	50 points
• Wheat	5000 bushels	cents and $^1/_4$ cents per bushel	$^1/_4$ cent per bushel ($12.50)	25 cents

• Futures Options

Contract	Trading Unit	Prices Quoted In	Minimum Price Fluctuation	Strike Prices
• Wheat	1 wheat futures contract	cents per bushel	$^1/_8$ of a cent per bushel ($6.25)	10 cents per bushel apart

MidAmerica Commodity Exchange (MIDAM)
[An Affiliate of the Chicago Board of Trade]

Futures

Contract	Trading Unit	Prices Quoted In	Minimum Price Fluctuation
• British Pound	12,500 British pounds	dollars per British pound	$.0005 ($6.25)
• Canadian Dollar	50,000 Canadian dollars	U.S. dollars per Canadian dollar	$.0001 ($6.25)
• Corn	1000 bushels	dollars and cents per bushel	.0125 of a cent per bushel ($6.25)
• Deutsche Mark	62,500 Deutsche marks	U.S. dollars per Deutsche mark	$.0001 ($6.25)
• Gold	33.2 troy ounces	dollars per troy ounce	10 cents per troy ounce ($3.32)

Dollar Value of 1 Cent Move	Last Trading Day	Contract Months	Trading Hours	Ticker Symbol
$50	8th day before end of month	Mar, May, July, Sept, Dec	9:30 a.m.- 1:15 p.m. CST	GS
—	3rd Friday of month	Mar, June, Sept, Dec	9:00 a.m.- 3:15 p.m. CST	KV
—	3rd Friday of month	Mar, June, Sept, Dec	9:30 a.m.- 3:15 p.m. CST	MV
$50	8th day before end of month	Mar, May, June, Sept, Dec	9:30 a.m.- 1:15 p.m. CST	KW

Expiration Day	Last Trading Day	Contract Months	Trading Hours	Ticker Symbol
1st Saturday after last trading day	Friday at least 5 trading days before end of month	Mar, May, July, Sept, Dec	9:30 a.m.- 1:20 p.m. CST	WC (call) WP (put)

Daily Contract Limit	Last Trading Day	Contract Months	Trading Hours
none	2 days before 3rd Wednesday	Mar, June, Sept, Dec	7:20 a.m.- 1:34 p.m. CST
none	2 days before 3rd Wednesday	Mar, June, Sept, Dec	7:20 a.m.- 1:36 p.m. CST
10 cents a bushel ($100)	8 days before end of month	Mar, May, July, Sept, Dec	9:30 a.m.- 1:30 p.m. CST
none	2 days before 3rd Wednesday	Mar, June, Sept, Dec	7:20 a.m.- 1:30 p.m. CST
$25 per troy ounce ($830)	3 days before end of month	every month	8:00 a.m.- 1:40 p.m. CST

Contract	Trading Unit	Prices Quoted In	Minimum Price Fluctuation
• Japanese Yen	6,250,000 yen	U.S. dollars per yen	$.000001 ($6.25)
• Live Cattle	22,000 pounds	cents per pound	$.025 per pound ($5)
• Live Hogs	15,000 pounds	cents per pound	$.025 per pound ($3.75)
• Oats	1000 bushels	cents per bushel	$.025 per bushel ($6.25)
• Platinum	25 troy ounces	cents per troy ounce	10 cents per troy ounce ($2.50)
• Silver	1000 troy ounces	cents per troy ounce	$.001 of a cent per troy ounce ($1)
• Soybeans	1000 bushels	cents per bushel	$.0125 per bushel ($6.25)
• Soybean Meal	20 tons	cents per ton	10 cents per ton ($2)
• Swiss Franc	62,500 Swiss francs	U.S. dollars per Swiss franc	$.0001 ($6.25)
• Treasury Bills	$500,000 in 90-day T-bills	100 minus T-bill yield	1 basis point ($12.50)
• Treasury Bonds	$50,000 in 15 year T-bonds	in 32nds of a % of par	$1/32$ of a percentage point ($15.625)
• Wheat	1000 bushels	cents per bushel	$.0125 per bushel ($1.25)

Futures Options

Contract	Trading Unit	Prices Quoted In	Minimum Price Fluctuation	Strike Prices
• Gold	1 gold futures contract	cents per troy ounce	$.025 per troy ounce ($2.50)	$10-$40 per troy ounce apart
• Soybeans	1 soybean futures contract	cents per bushel	$.0125 per bushel ($1.00)	25 cents per bushel apart
• Wheat	1 wheat futures contract	cents per bushel	$.0125 per bushel ($1.25)	10 cents per bushel apart

Daily Contract Limit	Last Trading Day	Contract Months	Trading Hours
none	2 days before 3rd Wednesday	Mar, June, Sept, Dec	7:20 a.m.- 1:30 p.m. CST
$.015 per pound ($300)	20th day of the month	Feb, Apr, June, Aug, Oct, Dec	9:05 a.m.- 1:15 p.m. CST
$.015 per pound ($225)	20th day of the month	Feb, Apr, June, July, Aug, Sept, Oct, Dec	9:10 a.m.- 1:15 p.m. CST
10 cents per bushel ($100)	8th day before end of month	Mar, May, July, Sept,	9:30 a.m.- 1:30 p.m. CST
$25 per troy ounce ($625)	4th day before end of month	nearest month Jan, Apr, July, Oct	8:00 a.m.- 1:40 p.m. CST
50 cents per troy ounce ($500)	3rd day before end of month	every month	8:05 a.m.- 1:40 p.m. CST
30 cents per bushel ($300)	8th day before end of month	Jan, Mar, May, July, Aug, Sept, Nov	9:30 a.m.- 1:30 p.m. CST
$10 per ton ($200)	8th day before end of month	Jan, Mar, May, July, Aug, Sept, Oct, Dec	9:30 a.m.- 1:30 p.m. CST
none	2 days before 3rd Wednesday	Mar, June, Sept, Dec	7:20 a.m.- 1:36 p.m. CST
none	day before T-bill delivery date on Int'l Monetary Mkt.	Mar, June Sept, Dec	7:20 a.m.- 2:15 p.m. CST
$^{64}/_{32}$ of a percentage point ($1000)	8th day before end of month	Feb, Mar, May, June, Aug, Sept, Nov, Dec	8:00 a.m.- 2:15 p.m. CST
20 cents per bushel ($200)	8th day before end of month	Mar, May, July, Sept, Dec	9:30 a.m.- 1:30 p.m. CST

Expiration Day	Last Trading Day	Contract Months	Trading Hours
Saturday after last trading day	last Friday, at least 5 days before delivery of futures contract	Feb, Apr, June, Aug, Oct, Dec	8:00 a.m.- 1:40 p.m. CST
Saturday after last trading day	last Friday, at least 10 days before delivery of futures contract	Jan, Mar, May, July, Aug, Sept, Nov	9:30 a.m.- 1:30 p.m. CST
Saturday after last trading day	last Friday, at least 10 days before delivery of futures contract	Mar, May, July, Sept, Dec	9:30 a.m.- 1:30 p.m. CST

Minneapolis Grain Exchange (MGE)

Futures

Contract	Trading Unit	Prices Quoted In	Minimum Price Fluctuation
• High Fructose Corn Syrup	37,000 pounds	dollars and cents per hundredweight	2 cents per trading unit ($7.40)
• Oats	5000 bushels	cents and $^{1}/_{4}$ cents per bushel	$^{1}/_{4}$ of a cent per bushel ($12.50)
• Spring Wheat	5000 bushels	cents and $^{1}/_{4}$ cents per bushel	$^{1}/_{8}$ per bushel ($6.25)
• White Wheat	5000 bushels	cents and $^{1}/_{4}$ cents per bushel	$^{1}/_{4}$ of a cent per bushel ($12.50)

Futures Options

Contract	Trading Unit	Prices Quoted In	Minimum Price Fluctuation	Strike Prices
• Spring Wheat, American	1 wheat futures contract	cents and $^{1}/_{8}$ cents per bushel	$.012 cent per bushel ($6.25)	10 cents per bushel apart
• Spring Wheat, European	1 wheat futures contract	cents and $^{1}/_{8}$ cents per bushel	$.012 cent per bushel ($6.25)	10 cents per bushel apart

New York Cotton Exchange (NYCE)

Futures

Contract	Trading Unit	Prices Quoted In	Minimum Price Fluctuation	Daily Contract Limit
• Cotton	50,000 pounds	cents and $^{1}/_{100}$'s of a cent per pound	$^{1}/_{100}$ of a cent per pound ($5)	2 cents per pound ($1000) (No limit on or after 1st notice day of current delivery month)
• Orange Juice	15,000 pounds	cents and $^{1}/_{100}$'s a cent per pound	$^{5}/_{100}$ of a cent per pound ($7.50)	5 cents per pound ($750)

Daily Contract Limit	Last Trading Day	Contract Months	Trading Hours	Ticker Symbol
$1 per hundredweight ($37)	8th day before end of month	Mar, May, July, Sept, Dec	9:00 a.m.-1:25 p.m. CST	HF
10 cents per bushel ($500)	8th day before end of month	Mar, May, July, Sept, Dec	9:30 a.m. 1:15 p.m. CST	OM
20 cents per bushel ($1000)	8th day before end of month	Mar, May, July, Sept, Dec	9:30 a.m.-1:15 p.m. CST	MW
20 cents per bushel ($1000)	8th day before end of month	Mar, May, July, Sept, Dec	9:30 a.m.-1:15 p.m. CST	NW

Expiration Day	Last Trading Day	Contract Months	Trading Hours	Ticker Symbol
1st Saturday after last trading day	1st Friday, at least 10 days before delivery of futures contract	Mar, May, July, Sept, Dec	9:35 a.m.-1:15 p.m. CST	CW (call) PW (put)
1st Saturday after last trading day	1st Friday, at least 10 days before delivery of futures contract	Mar, May, July, Sept, Dec	9:35 a.m.-1:15 p.m. CST	MC (call) ME (put)

Dollar Value of 1 Cent Move	Last Trading Day	Contract Months	Trading Hours	Ticker Symbol
$500	17 days before end of month	Mar, May, July, Oct, Dec	10:30 a.m.-3:00 p.m. EST	CT
$1.50	9 days before last delivery day	Jan, Mar, May, July, Sept, Nov	10:15 a.m.-2:45 p.m. EST	JO

Futures Options

Contract	Trading Unit	Prices Quoted In	Minimum Price Fluctuation	Strike Prices
• Cotton	1 cotton futures contract	cents and $^1/_{100}$ of a cent	$^1/_{100}$ of a cent ($5)	1 cent apart
• Frozen Concentrated Orange Juice	1 orange juice futures contract	cents and $^1/_{100}$ of a cent	$^5/_{100}$ of a cent ($7.50)	2.50 cents increments

FINEX
[A division of the New York Cotton Exchange]

Futures

Contract	Trading Unit	Prices Quoted In	Minimum Price Fluctuation
• European Currency Units	100,000 ECU	cents and $^1/_{100}$ of a cent per ECU ($1000)	.01 of a cent per ECU ($1000)
• U.S. Dollar Index	Dollar index × $500	index points relative to its base (100)	.01 of an index point ($5)
• U.S. Treasury Index (Five Year)	5-year U.S. Treasury note	percentage of par value	$15.625

New York Futures Exchange (NYFE)

Futures

Contract	Trading Unit	Prices Quoted In	Minimum Price Fluctuation
• CRB Futures Price Index	commodity index × $500	index points	5 basis points ($25)
• NYSE Composite Index	index × $500	index points	5 basis points ($25)
• Treasury Bonds	$100,000 Treasury bond	32nds of a point	$^1/_2$ of $^1/_{32}$ of 1%

Expiration Day	Last Trading Day	Contract Months	Trading Hours	Ticker Symbol
on last trading day	1st Friday of month before delivery month	Mar, May, July, Oct, Dec	10:30 a.m.-3:00 p.m. EST	CO
on last trading day	1st Friday of month before delivery month	Jan, Mar, May, July, Sept, Nov	10:15 a.m.-2:45 p.m. EST	OJ

Daily Contract Limit	Last Trading Day	Contract Months	Trading Hours	Ticker Symbol
None	3 days before 3rd Thursday of month	Mar, June, Sept, Dec	8:20 a.m.-2:40 p.m. EST	EU
Varies	3rd Wednesday of month	Mar, June, Sept, Dec	8:20 a.m.-3:00 p.m. EST	DX
None	last Monday of contract month	Mar, June, Sept, Dec	8:25 a.m.-3:10 p.m. EST	FYTR

Daily Contract Limit	Last Trading Day	Contract Months	Trading Hours	Ticker Symbol
none	3rd business day of month	Mar, May, July, Sept, Dec	9:00 a.m.-3:15 p.m. EST	CRB
18 points	Thursday before 3rd Friday of month	Mar, June, Sept, Dec	9:30 a.m.-4:15 p.m. EST	YX
$^{96}/_{32}$ (3 points)	8th day before end of month	Mar, June, Sept, Dec	8:20 a.m.-4:15 p.m. EST	UB

Futures Options

Contract	Underlying Index	Prices Quoted In	Minimum Price Fluctuation	Strike Prices
• CRB Index Contract	CRB index futures	index points 1 point = $5	5 points ($125)	numbers divisible by 5
• NYSE Composite Index Contract	NYSE composite index	index points 1 point = $5	5 points ($25)	numbers divisible by 2

New York Mercantile Exchange (NYMEX)

Futures

Contract	Trading Unit	Prices Quoted In	Minimum Price Fluctuation
• Crude Oil	1000 barrels	dollars and cents per barrel	1 cent per barrel ($10)
• Gasoline	1000 barrels	dollars and cents per gallon	.01 cent per gallon ($4.20)
• Number 2 Heating Oil	1000 barrels	dollars and cents per gallon	.01 cent per gallon ($420)
• Palladium	100 troy ounces	dollars and cents per troy ounce	5 cents per troy ounce ($5)
• Platinum	50 troy ounces	dollars and cents per troy ounce	10 cents per troy ounce ($5)
• Propane	1000 barrels	dollars and cents per troy ounce	.01 cents per gallon ($4.20)

Futures Options

Contract	Trading Unit	Prices Quoted In	Minimum Price Fluctuation	Strike Prices
• Crude Oil	1 crude oil futures contract	dollars and cents per barrel	1 cent ($10)	$1 apart
• Number 2 Heating Oil	1 number 2 heating oil futures contract	dollars and cents per barrel	1 cent ($4.20)	2 cents apart

Expiration Day	Last Trading Day	Contract Months	Trading Hours
on last trading day	last day of futures delivery month	Mar, May, July, Sept, Dec	9:00 a.m.- 3:15 p.m.
on last trading day	last day of futures delivery month	Mar, June, Sept, Dec	9:30 a.m.- 4:15 p.m. EST

Daily Contract Limit	Last Trading Day	Contract Months	Trading Hours	Ticker Symbol
$1 per barrel ($1000)	3rd day before 25th of month	every month	9:45 a.m.- 3:10 p.m. EST	CL
2 cents per gallon ($840)	last day of month before delivery month	every month	9:50 a.m.- 3:05 p.m. EST	HU
2 cents per gallon ($840)	last day of month before delivery month	every month	9:50 a.m.- 3:05 p.m. EST	HO
$6 per troy ounce ($600)	4th day before end of delivery month	Mar, June, Sept, Dec	8:50 a.m.- 2:20 p.m. EST	PA
$25 per troy ounce ($1250)	4th day before end of delivery month	Jan, Apr, July, Oct	9:00 a.m.- 2:30 p.m. EST	PL
2 cents per gallon ($840)	last day of month before delivery month	every month	9:50 a.m.- 3:10 p.m. EST	PN

Expiration Day	Last Trading Day	Contract Months	Trading Hours	Ticker Symbol
on last trading day	2nd Friday of month before delivery month	6 nearest months	9:45 a.m.- 3:10 p.m. EST	LO
on last trading day	2nd Friday of month before delivery month	6 nearest months	9:50 a.m. - 3:10 p.m. EST	OH

New York Stock Exchange (NYSE)

Basket Trading

Contract	Underlying Index	Trading Unit	Prices Quoted In
• Exchange Stock Portfolio	S&P 500 index	index × $100	index points

Index Options

Contract	Underlying Index	Trading Unit	Prices Quoted In	Minimum Price Fluctuation
• NYSE Options Index	NYSE composite index	index × $100	index points	$1/16$ of a point ($6.25)

Pacific Stock Exchange (PSE)

Index Option

Contract	Underlying Index	Trading Unit	Prices Quoted In	Minimum Price Fluctuation
• Financial News Composite Index	Financial News index	index × $100	index points	—

Philadelphia Stock Exchange (PHLX)

Foreign Currency Options

Contract	Trading Unit	Prices Quoted In	Minimum Price Fluctuation	Strike Prices
• Australian Dollar	50,000 Australian dollars	cents per Australian dollar	.0001 cents ($5)	1 cent apart
• British Pound	31,250 British pounds	cents per British pound	($3.125)	$2^1/2$ cents apart
• Canadian Dollar	50,000 Canadian dollars	cents per Canadian dollar	1 cent ($5)	1 cent apart
• Deutsche Mark	62,500 Deutsche marks	cents per Deutsche mark	1 cent ($6.25)	1 cent apart

Minimum Price Fluctuation	Settlement	Trading Hours	Ticker Symbol
.01 index points	in cash	9:30 a.m.- 4:00 p.m. EST	—

Strike Prices	Settlement	Last Trading Day	Contract Months	Trading Hours	Ticker Symbol
5 points apart	in cash	3rd Thursday of month	nearest 3 months	9:30 a.m.- 4:15 p.m. EST	NYA

Strike Prices	Settlement	Last Trading Day	Contract Months	Trading Hours	Ticker Symbol
5 points apart	in cash	Saturday after 3rd Friday of contract month	nearest 4 months	6:30 a.m.- 1:15 p.m. PST	—

Expiration Day	Contract Months	Trading Hours	Ticker Symbol
Saturday before 3rd Wednesday of month	Mar, June, Sept, Dec and 2 nearest months	4:30 a.m.- 2:30 p.m. EST*	XAD
Saturday before 3rd Wednesday of month	Mar, June, Sept, Dec and 2 nearest months	4:30 a.m.- 2:30 p.m. EST*	XBP
Saturday before 3rd Wednesday of month	Mar, June, Sept, Dec and 2 nearest months	4:30 a.m.- 2:30 p.m. EST*	XCD
Saturday before 3rd Wednesday of month	Mar, June, Sept, Dec and 2 nearest months	4:30 a.m.- 2:30 p.m. EST*	XDM

* Also 6:00 p.m.–10:00 p.m. EST

Contract	Trading Unit	Prices Quoted In	Minimum Price Fluctuation	Strike Prices
• European Currency Units	10 European currencies	62,500 cents per ECU	1 cent per ECU ($6.25)	2 cents apart ($6.25)
• French Franc	250,000 French francs	$1/10$ of a cent per French franc	($5.00)	$1/4$ of a cent apart
• Japanese Yen	6,250,000 Japanese yen	$1/100$ of a cent per Japanese yen	5 cents ($6.25)	$1/100$ of a cent apart
• Swiss Franc	62,500 Swiss francs	cents per Swiss franc	1 cent ($6.25)	1 cent apart

Futures

Contract	Trading Unit	Prices Quoted In	Minimum Price Fluctuation
• National OTC Index Futures	index × $500	index points	5 cents per point ($25)

Index Options

Contract	Underlying Index	Trading Unit	Prices Quoted In	Minimum Price Fluctuation
• Gold/Silver Index	7 gold and silver mining stocks	and index × $100	index points (1 point = $100)	.01 points
• National OTC Index	OTC 100 stocks	index × $100	index points (1 point = $100)	.01 points
• Utility Index	20 utility company stocks	index × $100	index points (1 point = $100)	.01 points
• Value Line Composite Index	1700 Value Line stocks	index × $100	index points (1 point = $100)	$1/16$ point ($6.25)

Futures and Options Contracts

Expiration Day	Contract Months	Trading Hours	Ticker Symbol
Friday before 3rd Wednesday of month	Mar, June, Sept, Dec and 2 nearest months	4:30 a.m.- 2:30 p.m. EST*	ECU
Saturday before 3rd Wednesday of month	Mar, June, Sept, Dec and 2 nearest months	4:30 a.m.- 2:30 p.m. EST*	XFF
Saturday before 3rd Wednesday of month	Mar, June, Sept, Dec and 2 nearest months	4:30 a.m.- 2:30 p.m. EST*	XJY
Saturday before 3rd Wednesday of month	Mar, June, Sept, Dec and 2 nearest months	4:30 a.m.- 2:30 p.m. EST*	XSF

* Also 6:00 p.m.–10:00 p.m. EST

Daily Contract Limit	Last Trading Day	Contract Months	Trading Hours	Ticker Symbol
none	3rd Friday of month	Feb, Mar, Apr, June, Sept	10:00 a.m.- 4:15 p.m. EST	OX

Strike Prices	Settlement	Last Trading Day	Contract Months	Trading Hours	Ticker Symbol
5 points apart	in cash	1st day before expiration	Mar, June, Sept, Dec and 2 nearest months	9:30 a.m.- 4:10 p.m. EST	XAU
5 points apart	in cash	1st day before expiration	Mar, June, Sept, Dec and 2 nearest months	10:00 a.m.- 4:10 p.m. EST	XOC
5 points apart	in cash	1st day before expiration	Mar, June, Sept, Dec and 2 nearest months	9:30 a.m. 4:15 p.m. EST	UTY
5 points apart	in cash	1st day before expiration	Mar, June, Sept, Dec and 2 nearest months	9:30 a.m.- 4:15 p.m. EST	XVL

CANADIAN SECURITIES, FUTURES AND OPTIONS EXCHANGES
Montreal Exchange (ME)

Futures

Contract	Trading Unit	Prices Quoted In	Minimum Price Fluctuation
• Canadian Banker's Acceptance — Three Month	1 million Canadian dollars in Banker's Acceptances	index minus yield	one basis point
• Lumber	140,000 feet board measure (FBM)	U.S. dollars per thousand FBM	10 cents per thousand ($14)

Futures Options

Contract	Trading Unit	Prices Quoted In	Minimum Price Fluctuation	Strike Prices
• Canadian Bonds	$25,000 in Canadian bonds	Canadian dollars and cents	.01% of $100 (Canadian)	2.5 points apart
• Canadian Dollar	50,000 Canadian dollars	Canadian dollars and cents	.0001 cent per Canadian dollar	1 cent apart
• Canadian T-Bills	$250,000 in Canadian T-bills	basis points	one basis point	50 basis points apart
• Gold	10 troy ounces	dollars and cents per ounce	10 cents per ounce	$10 apart
• Platinum	10 troy ounces	dollars and cents per ounce	10 cents per ounce	$10 apart

Toronto Futures Exchange (TFE)

Futures

Contract	Trading Unit	Prices Quoted In	Minimum Price Fluctuation
• Oil & Gas Stock Index	Canadian Oil & Gas Stocks	index points	one index point ($10)
• Toronto Stock Exchange 300 Index	300 TSE stocks	index points	one index point ($10)
• Toronto 35 Index	35 TSE stocks	index points	two index points ($10)

Daily Contract Limit	Last Trading Day	Contract Months	Trading Hours
none	2nd London business day before 3rd Wednesday of month	Mar, June, Sept, Dec	9:00 a.m.-3:00 p.m. EST
$5 per thousand FBM	business day before the 16th of a contract month	Jan, Mar, May, July, Sept, Nov	10:00 a.m.-2:30 p.m. EST

Expiration Day	Last Trading Day	Contract Months	Trading Hours
Saturday after 3rd Friday of month	—	Mar, June, Sept, Dec and 3 nearest months	9:00 a.m.-4:00 p.m. EST
Monday after 3rd Friday of month	3rd Friday of month	Mar, June, Sept, Dec and 3 nearest months	8:00 a.m.-2:30 p.m. EST
day after auction	3rd Friday of month	Mar, June, Sept, Dec and 3 nearest months	8:35 a.m.-3:00 p.m. EST
Monday after 3rd Friday of month	3rd Friday of month	Feb, May, Aug, Nov and 3 nearest months	9:00 a.m.-2:30 p.m. EST
Monday after 3rd Friday of month	3rd Friday of month	Mar, June, Sept, Dec and 3 nearest months	9:00 a.m.-2:30 p.m. EST

Daily Contract Limit	Last Trading Day	Contract Months	Trading Hours	Ticker Symbol
250 index points ($2500)	3rd Friday of month	next 3 months	9:20 a.m.-4:10 p.m. EST	TOX
150 index points ($1500)	none	monthly	9:20 a.m.-4:10 p.m. EST	TCX
13.50 points ($6750)	Thursday before 3rd Friday of month	3 nearest months	9:15 a.m.-4:15 p.m. EST	TXF

Contract	Trading Unit	Prices Quoted In	Minimum Price Fluctuation
• Treasury Bills (Canadian)	$1 million of 91-day Canadian T-bills		one basis point ($24)
• Treasury Bonds (Canadian)	$100,000 of 15 year Canadian T-bonds		$1/32$ of a point ($31.25)
• U.S. Dollar	50,000 U.S. dollars	Canadian dollars per $100 U.S.	1 Canadian cent, 1 point = $5

Options

Contract	Trading Unit	Prices Quoted In	Minimum Price Fluctuation	Strike Prices
• Silver	100 troy ounces	U.S. cents per ounce	one cent	25 cents apart
• Treasury Bonds (Canadian)	$25,000 in T-bonds	.05% of $100 face value	.05% of $100 face value	2.5 points apart

Toronto Stock Exchange (TSEX)

Options

Contract	Trading Unit	Prices Quoted In	Minimum Price Fluctuation	Strike Prices
• Toronto 35 Index	TSE 35 index × $100	Canadian cents per index	one cent	5 points apart

Vancouver Stock Exchange (VSE)

Commodity Options

Contract	Trading Unit	Prices Quoted In	Minimum Price Fluctuation	Strike Prices
• Canadian Dollar	$50,000 Canadian dollars	U.S. dollars per Canadian dollars	1 cent per Canadian dollar ($5)	2 cents per Canadian dollar apart

Daily Contract Limit	Last Trading Day	Contract Months	Trading Hours	Ticker Symbol
60 basis points ($1440)	T-bill auction before last Friday of delivery month	current month plus Mar, June, Sept, Dec	9:00 a.m.- 3:15 p.m. EST	TBT
2 points ($2000)	6th to last day of delivery month	Mar, June, Sept, Dec	9:00 a.m.- 3:15 p.m. EST	GCB
250 points ($12.50)	3rd Wednesday of month	3 nearest months and Mar, June, Sept, Dec	8:30 a.m.- 4:00 p.m. EST	USD

Expiration Day	Last Trading Day	Contract Months	Trading Hours	Ticker Symbol
Saturday after 3rd Friday of month	3rd Friday of month	3 nearest months	9:05 a.m.- 4:00 p.m. EST	SVR
Saturday after 3rd Friday of month	3rd Friday of month	Mar, June, Sept, Dec	9:00 a.m.- 4:00 p.m. EST	OBC

Expiration Day	Last Trading Day	Contract Months	Trading Hours	Ticker Symbol
3rd Friday of month	Thursday before 3rd Friday of month	3 nearest months	9:15 a.m.- 3:15 p.m. EST	TXO

Expiration Day	Last Trading Day	Contract Months	Trading Hours	Ticker Symbol
Monday after 3rd Friday of month	3rd Friday of month	5 nearest months and Mar, June, Sept, Dec	11:30 a.m.- 4:00 p.m. PST	CAN

Contract	Trading Unit	Prices Quoted In	Minimum Price Fluctuation	Strike Prices
• Gold	10 troy ounces	U.S. dollars and cents per ounce	10 cents per ounce ($1)	$10 apart apart
• Platinum	10 troy ounces	U.S. dollars and cents per ounce	10 cents per ounce ($1)	$10 apart apart
• Silver	1000 troy ounces	U.S. dollars and cents per ounce	1 cent per ounce ($10)	25 cents apart

Winnipeg Commodity Exchange (WCE)

Futures

Contract	Trading Unit	Prices Quoted In	Minimum Price Fluctuation
• Barley (Alberta)	20 metric tons	dollars and cents per ton	10 cents per ton
• Barley (Domestic)	100 metric tons	dollars and cents per ton	10 cents per ton
• Flaxseed	100 metric tons	dollars and cents per ton	10 cents per ton
• Oats	100 metric tons	dollars and cents per ton	10 cents per ton
• Rapeseed	100 metric tons	dollars and cents per ton	10 cents per ton
• Rye	20 metric tons	dollars and cents per ton	10 cents per ton
• Wheat	20 metric tons	dollars and cents per ton	10 cents per ton

Expiration Day	Last Trading Day	Contract Months	Trading Hours	Ticker Symbol
Monday after 3rd Friday of month	3rd Friday of month	Feb, May, Aug, Nov	11:30 a.m.- 4:00 p.m. PST	OR
Monday after 3rd Friday of month	3rd Friday of month	Mar, June, Sept, Dec and 3 nearest months	11:30 a.m. - 4:00 p.m. PST	PX
Monday after 3rd Friday of month	3rd Friday of month	Mar, June, Sept, Dec	7:30 a.m.- 4:30 p.m. PST	SIT

Daily Contract Limit	Last Trading Day	Contract Months	Trading Hours	Ticker Symbol
$5 per ton	last business day of month	Feb, Apr, June, Sept, Nov	9:30 a.m.- 1:15 p.m. CST	AB
$5 per ton	last business day of contract month	Mar, May, July, Oct, Dec	9:30 a.m.- 1:15 p.m. CST	B
$10 per ton	last business day of contract month	Mar, May, July, Oct, Dec	9:30 a.m.- 1:15 p.m. CST	F
$5 per ton	last business day of contract month	Mar, May, July, Oct, Dec	9:30 a.m.- 1:15 p.m. CST	O
$10 per ton	8th day before end of month	Jan, Mar, June, Sept, Nov	9:30 a.m.- 1:15 p.m. CST	RS
$5 per ton	last business day of contract month	Mar, May, July, Oct, Dec	9:30 a.m.- 1:15 p.m. CST	R
$5 per ton	last business day of contract month	Mar, May, July, Oct, Dec	9:30 a.m.- 1:15 p.m. CST	W

AUSTRALIAN SECURITIES, FUTURES AND OPTIONS EXCHANGE

Sydney Futures Exchange (SFE)

Futures

Contract	Trading Unit	Prices Quoted In	Minimum Price Fluctuation
● All Ordinaries Index	index × $100	index points	1 basis point ($10)
● Australian Dollar	100,000 Australian dollars	U.S. dollars and cents	.0001 cents
● Australian T-Bond (3-year)	$100,000 of Australian bonds	100 minus yield	.01 point ($11.50)
● Australian T-Bond (10-year)	$100,000 of Australian bonds	100 minus annual yield	.005 percentage point ($25)
● Bank Accepted Bills (90-Day)	500,000 Australian dollars	100 minus yield	.01 percentage point ($11.50)
● Cattle	10,000 kilograms	U.S. dollars and cents per kilogram	0.1 cent per kilogram ($10)
● Eurodollar	1 million U.S. dollars	basis points	01 percentage point ($25)
● Gold	10 troy ounces	U.S. dollars and cents per ounce	.0001 cent ($10)
● U.S. T-Bond	$100,000 U.S. bond	basis points	$1/32$ of a point ($31.25)
● Wool	1500 kilograms	cents per kilogram	1 cent per kilogram ($25)

Futures Options

Contract	Trading Unit	Prices Quoted In	Minimum Price Fluctuation	Strike Prices
● All Ordinaries Index	1 All Ordinaries futures contract	index points	0.1 index point	25 points apart
● Australian Dollar	1 Australian dollar futures contract	dollars and cents	.0001 U.S. cent per Australian dollar ($10 U.S.)	1 cent apart apart
● Australian T-Bond (3-Year)	1 3-Year T-bond futures contract	100 minus annual yield	.01 of a percentage point ($25)	.25 of a percentage point apart

Last Trading Day	Contract Months	Trading Hours
2nd to last business day of month	Mar, June, Sept, Dec	9:30 a.m-12:30 p.m. and 2:00 p.m.-3:45 p.m.
next to last day before 3rd Wednesday of month	Mar, June, Sept, Dec	8:30 a.m.-4:30 p.m.
15th business day of month	Mar, June, Sept, Dec	8:30 a.m.-12:30 p.m. and 2:00 p.m.-4:30 p.m.
15th business day of month	Mar, June, Sept, Dec	8:30 a.m.-12:30 p.m., and 2:00 p.m.-3:30 p.m.
Wednesday before 2nd Friday of month	Mar, June, Sept, Dec and 6 nearest months	8:30 a.m.-12:30 p.m. and 2:00 p.m.-4:30 p.m.
3rd Wednesday of month	monthly	10:30 a.m.-12:30 p.m. and 2:00 p.m.-4 p.m.
—	Mar, June, Sept, Dec and 6 nearest months	8:35 a.m.-6:15 p.m.
3rd to last day of month	Feb, Apr, June, Aug, June, Aug, Oct, Dec and 3 nearest months	8:35 a.m.-4:00 p.m.
7th business day before end of month	Mar, June, Sept, Dec	8:35 a.m.-6:15 p.m.
day after final auction	Mar, May, July, Oct, Dec	10:30 a.m.-12:30 p.m and 2:00 p.m. -4 p.m.

Expiration Day	Contract Months	Trading Hours
last day of underlying futures contract	Mar, June, Sept, Dec	9:30 a.m.-12:30 p.m. and 2:00 p.m.-3:45 p.m.
last trading day	Mar, June, Sept, Dec	8:30 a.m.-4:30 p.m.
last trading day	Mar, June, Sept, Dec	8:30 a.m.-12:30 p.m. and 2:00 p.m.-4:30 p.m.

Contract	Trading Unit	Prices Quoted In	Minimum Price Fluctuation	Strike Prices
• Australian T-Bond (10-Year)	1 10-Year T-bond futures contract	100 minus annual yield	.005 of a percentage point ($25)	.25 of a percentage point apart
• Bank Accepted Bills (90-Day)	1 bank accepted futures contract	100 minus annual yield	.01 of a percentage point ($11.50)	.50 of a percentage point apart

BRAZILIAN SECURITIES, FUTURES AND OPTIONS EXCHANGE

Bolsa Mercantil & De Futuros (BMF)

Futures

Contract	Trading Unit	Prices Quoted In	Minimum Price Fluctuation
• Brazil Coffee	100 bags	cruzados per 60 kilogram bag	10 cruzados per bag
• Brazilian T-Bond	1000 Brazilian T-bonds	cruzados per bond	0.01 cruzados per bond
• Broilers	12 metric tons	cruzados per kilogram	0.01 cruzado per kilogram
• Dollar	$5000	cruzados per dollar	0.01 cruzado = $1
• Domestic CD (60 & 90 Day)	1 million cruzados	points	0.1 point = 10 cruzados
• Gold	250 grams	cruzados per gram	0.1 cruzado per gram
• Live Cattle	330 net arrobas	cruzados per net arroba	0.10 cruzado per arroba
• Live Hogs	8000 net kilograms	cruzados per net kilogram	0.01 cruzado per kilogram
• Sao Paulo Stock Index	index × 50 cruzados	index points	0.05 points = 50 cruzados

Expiration Day	Contract Months	Trading Hours
last day of underlying futures contract	Mar, June, Sept, Dec	8:30 a.m.-12:30 p.m. and 2:00 p.m.-4:30 p.m
Friday before settlement of underlying futures contract	Mar, June, Sept, Dec Sept, Dec	8:30 a.m.-12:30 p.m. and 2:00 p.m.-4:30 p.m.

Last Trading Day	Contract Months	Trading Hours
last business day of contract month	Mar, May, July, Sept, Dec	10:45 a.m.-4:00 p.m.
last business day before bond's expiration	every month	10:30 a.m.-4:00 p.m.
last business day of delivery month	even months	2:15 p.m.-2:35 p.m. and 2:40 p.m.-3:00 p.m.
1st business day of delivery month	every month	10:00 a.m.-10:20 a.m. and 10:30 a.m.-3:45 p.m.
3rd Wednesday of contract month	4 nearest months, even months	11:15 a.m.-12:30 p.m. and 3:15 p.m.-4:00 p.m.
last business day of previous month	odd months	10:00 a.m.-4:30 p.m.
last business day of contract month	even months	2:15 p.m.-2:35 p.m. and 2:40 p.m.-3:00 p.m.
last business day of contract month	even months	2:15 p.m.-2:35 p.m. and 2:30 p.m.-3:00 p.m.
Wednesday nearest 15th day of contract month	even months	9:30 a.m.-1:15 p.m.

Futures Options

Contract	Trading Unit	Prices Quoted In	Minimum Price Fluctuation	Strike Prices
• Brazilian T-Bond	1000 Brazilian T-bonds	cruzados per bond	0.01 cruzado per bond	varies
• Dollar	$5000	cruzados $1 per dollar	0.01 cruzado $1	varies
• Gold	250 grams	cruzados per gram	0.10 cruzado per gram	varies

BRITISH SECURITIES, FUTURES AND OPTIONS EXCHANGES

Baltic Futures Exchange (BFE)
(Baltic International Freight Futures Exchange)

Futures

Contract	Trading Unit	Prices Quoted In	Minimum Price Fluctuation
• Baltic Freight Index	index × $10	dollars per index point	5 cents ($5)

(London Grain Futures Market)

Futures

Contract	Trading Unit	Prices Quoted In	Minimum Price Fluctuation
• Barley	100 metric tons	pence per ton	.05 pence (5 pounds)
• Wheat	100 metric tons	pence per ton	.05 pence (5 pounds)

Expiration Day	Contract Months	Trading Hours
last trading day	every month	10:30 a.m.-4:00 p.m.
last trading day	odd months	10:00 a.m.-10:20 a.m. and 10:30 a.m.-3:45 p.m.
last trading day	odd months	10:00 a.m.-4:30 p.m.

Last Trading Day	Contract Months	Trading Hours
last business day of month	Jan, Apr, July, Oct	10:15 a.m.-12:30 p.m. and 2:30 p.m.-4:15 p.m.

Last Trading Day	Contract Months	Trading Hours
23rd day of month	Jan, Mar, May, Sept, Nov	11:00 a.m.-12:30 p.m. and 2:45 p.m.-4:00 p.m.
23rd day of month	Jan, Mar, May, July, Sept, Nov	11:00 a.m.-12:30 p.m. and 2:45 p.m.-4:00 p.m.

Futures Options

Contract	Trading Unit	Prices Quoted In	Minimum Price Fluctuation	Strike Prices
● Barley	1 barley futures contract	pence per ton	5 pence (5 pounds)	1 pound per ton apart
● Wheat	1 wheat futures contract	pence per ton	5 pence (5 pounds)	1 pound per ton apart

(London Meat Futures Market)

Futures

Contract	Trading Unit	Prices Quoted In	Minimum Price Fluctuation
● Cattle	5000 kilograms	pence per kilogram	5 pence (5 pounds)
● Pig	3250 kilograms	pence per kilogram	1 pence (3.25 pounds)

(London Potato Futures Market)

Futures

Contract	Trading Unit	Prices Quoted In	Minimum Price Fluctuation
● Potatoes (Cash Settled)	40 metric tons	pence per ton	10 pence per ton
● Potatoes (Main Crop)	40 metric tons	pence per ton	10 pence per ton

Futures Options

Contract	Trading Unit	Prices Quoted In	Minimum Price Fluctuation	Strike Prices
● Potatoes (Main Crop)	1 potato futures contract	pence per ton	10 pence per ton	5 pence apart

Expiration Day	Contract Months	Trading Hours
day after last trading day	Jan, Mar, May, Nov	11:00 a.m.-12:30 p.m. and 2:45 p.m.-6:00 p.m.
day after last trading day	Jan, Mar, May, July, Sept, Nov	11:00 a.m.-12:30 p.m. and 2:45 p.m.-6:00 p.m.

Last Trading Day	Contract Months	Trading Hours
last Friday of month	Jan, Feb, Mar, Apr, Sept, Oct, Nov	10:00 a.m.-12:00 p.m. and 2:15 p.m.-3:45 p.m.
last Tuesday of month	Feb, Apr, June, Aug, Oct, Nov	10:00 a.m.-12:00 p.m. and 2:15 p.m.-3:45 p.m.

Last Trading Day	Contract Months	Trading Hours
last Tuesday of month	Mar, July, Aug, Sept	11:00 a.m.-12:30 p.m. and 2:45 p.m.-4:00 p.m.
10th day of month	Feb, Apr, May, Nov	11:00 a.m.-12:30 p.m. and 2:45 a.m.-4:00 p.m.

Expiration Day	Contract Months	Trading Hours
last business day	Mar, Apr, May, Nov	11:00 a.m.-12:30 p.m. 2:45 p.m.-4:00 p.m.

(Soya Bean Meal Futures Association)

Futures

Contract	Trading Unit	Prices Quoted In	Minimum Price Fluctuation
• Soybean Meal	20 metric tons	pounds per ton	10 pounds (2 pounds)

International Petroleum Exchange of London (IPE)

Futures

Contract	Trading Unit	Prices Quoted In	Minimum Price Fluctuation
• Crude Oil	1000 barrels Brent crude	dollars and cents per barrel	1 cent per barrel
• Gas Oil	100 tons gas oil	dollars and cents per ton	25 cents per ton

Futures Options

Contract	Trading Unit	Prices Quoted In	Minimum Price Fluctuation	Strike Prices
• Gas Oil	1 gas oil futures contract	dollars and cents per ton	5 cents per ton	$5 apart

International Stock Exchange (ISE)

Futures Options

Contract	Trading Unit	Prices Quoted In	Minimum Price Fluctuation	Strike Prices
• Financial Times Stock Index	10 pounds × index	pence per 10 pounds	.005 pence	25 index points apart
• LTOM (63 UK Equity Options)	1000 shares	pence per underlying share	.0025 pence	10 points apart

Last Trading Day	Contract Months	Trading Hours
22nd day of month	Feb, Apr, June, Aug, Oct, Dec	10:30 a.m.-12:00 p.m. and 2:45 p.m.-4:00 p.m.

Last Trading Day	Contract Months	Trading Hours
10th day of month before contract	6 nearest months	9:15 a.m.-12:15 p.m. and 2:30 p.m.- 5:15 p.m.
3 business days before 13th day of month	9 nearest months	9:15 a.m.-12:15 p.m. and 2:30 p.m.-5:15 p.m.

Expiration Day	Contract Months	Trading Hours
3rd Wednesday of month before contract	9 nearest months	9:15 a.m.-12:24 p.m. and 2:30 p.m.-5:25 p.m.

Expiration Day	Contract Months	Trading Hours
last trading day	4 nearest months	9:05 a.m.-3:40 p.m.
2 days before end of month	Jan, Apr, July, Oct or Feb, May, Aug, Nov or Mar, June, Sept, Dec	9:05 a.m.-4:05 p.m.

Contract	Trading Unit	Prices Quoted In	Minimum Price Fluctuation	Strike Prices
• U.S. Dollar-Deutsche Mark	62,500 Deutsche marks	dollars and cents per mark	1 cent	1 cent apart
• U.S. Dollar-Sterling	12,000 British pounds	dollars and cents per pound	5 cents	5 cents apart

London Futures and Options Exchange (FOX)

Futures

Contract	Trading Unit	Prices Quoted In	Minimum Price Fluctuation
• Cocoa	10 metric tons	pounds per ton	1 pound per ton
• Coffee	5 tons	pounds per ton	1 pound per ton
• Sugar (Raw)	50 tons	dollars and cents per ton	20 cents per ton
• Sugar (White)	50 tons	dollars and cents per ton	10 cents per ton

Futures Options

Contract	Trading Unit	Prices Quoted In	Minimum Price Fluctuation	Strike Prices
• Cocoa	1 cocoa futures contract	pounds per ton	1 pound per ton	50 pounds per ton
• Coffee	1 coffee futures contract	pounds per ton	1 pound per ton	50 pounds per ton
• Sugar (Raw)	1 sugar futures contract	cents per ton	5 cents per ton	$5 apart

Expiration Day	Contract Months	Trading Hours
last trading day	Mar, June, Sept, Dec and and 2 of 3 nearest months	9:00 a.m.-3:40 p.m.
last trading day	Mar, June, Sept, Dec and 2 of 3 nearest months	9:05 a.m.-3:40 p.m.

Last Trading Day	Contract Months	Trading Hours
last market day of month	Mar, May, July, Sept, July, Sept, Dec	10:00 a.m.-12:58 p.m. and 2:30 p.m.-4:45 p.m.
last market day of month	Jan, Mar, May, July, Sept, Nov, Jan	9:45 a.m.-12:32 p.m. and 2:30 p.m.-5:02 p.m.
last market day of month before contract	Mar, May, Aug, Oct, Dec	10:30 a.m.-12:30 p.m. and 2:30 p.m.-7:00 p.m.
last market day before 15th of month	Mar, May, Aug, Oct, Dec	9:45 a.m.-7:10 p.m.

Expiration Day	Contract Months	Trading Hours
3rd Wednesday of month before contract	Mar, May, July, Sept, Dec	10:00 a.m.-1:00 p.m. and 2:30 p.m.-5:00 p.m.
3rd Wednesday of month before contract	Jan, Mar, May, July, Sept, Nov	9:45 a.m.-12:30 p.m. and 2:30 p.m.-5:00 p.m.
3rd Wednesday of month before contract	Mar, May, Aug, Oct, Dec	10:30 a.m.-12:30 p.m. and 2:30 p.m.-7:00 p.m.

London International Financial Futures Exchange (LIFFE)

Futures

Contract	Trading Unit	Prices Quoted In	Minimum Price Fluctuation
• British Pound	25,000 British pounds	dollars and cents per pound	1 cent ($2.50)
• Deutsche Mark	125,000 Deutsche marks	dollars and cents per mark	1 cent ($12.50)
• Eurodollar	$1 million	100 minus interest rate	1 cent ($25)
• Financial Times Stock Index	25 pounds per index point	index divided by 10	.05 pound (12.50 pounds)
• German Government Bond	250,000 mark bond (6% coupon)	per 100 marks	.01 mark (25 marks)
• Gilt (Long)	50,000 British pound bond (12% coupon)	per 100 pounds	$1/32$ pound (15.625 pounds)
• Gilt (Medium)	50,000 British pound bond (9% coupon)	per 100 pounds	$1/32$ pound (15.625 pounds)
• Gilt (Short)	100,000 British pound bond (10% coupon)	per 100 pounds	$1/64$ pound (15.625 pounds)
• Japanese Government Bond	100,000,000 yen bond (6% coupon)	per 100 yen	.01 yen (10,000 yen)
• Japanese Yen	12,500,000 yen	dollars and cents per 100 yen	1 cent ($12.50)
• Sterling (3-Month)	500,000 pounds	100 minus interest rate	.01 pound (12.50 pounds)
• Swiss Franc	125,000 Swiss francs	dollars and cents per franc	1 cent ($12.50)
• U.S. Dollar-Deutsche Mark	$50,000 against marks	dollars and cents per mark	.0001 cent (5 marks)
• U.S. Treasury Bond	$100,000 bond (8% coupon)	per $100	$1/32$ dollar ($31.25)

Last Trading Day	Contract Months	Trading Hours
2 business days before delivery	Mar, June, Sept, Dec	8:32 a.m.-4:02 p.m.
2 business days before delivery	Mar, June, Sept, Dec	8:34 a.m.-4:04 p.m.
2 business days before 3rd Wednesday of month	Mar, June, Sept, Dec	8:10 a.m.-4:00 p.m.
last business day of month	Mar, June, Sept, Dec	9:05 a.m.-4:05 p.m.
3 business days before delivery	Mar, June, Sept, Dec	8:10 a.m.-4:00 p.m.
2 business days before end of month	Mar, June, Sept, Dec	9:00 a.m.-4:15 p.m.
2 business days before end of month	Mar, June, Sept, Dec	8:55 a.m.-4:10 p.m.
2 business days before end of month	Mar, June, Sept, Dec	9:05 a.m.-4:20 p.m.
1 business day before end of month	Mar, June, Sept, Dec	8:10 a.m.-4:05 p.m.
2 business days before delivery	Mar, June, Sept, Dec	8:30 a.m.-4:00 p.m.
3rd Wednesday of month	Mar, June, Sept, Dec	8:20 a.m.-4:02 p.m.
2 business days before delivery	Mar, June, Sept, Dec	8:36 a.m.-4:06 p.m.
2 business days before delivery	Mar, June, Sept, Dec	8:34 a.m.-4:04 p.m.
7 CBOT business days before end of month	Mar, June, Sept, Dec	8:15 a.m.-4:10 p.m.

Futures Options

Contract	Trading Unit	Prices Quoted In	Minimum Price Fluctuation	Strike Prices
• British Pound	25,000 pounds	dollars and cents per pound	1 cent ($2.50)	5 cents apart
• Eurodollar	1 Eurodollar futures contract	.01 cent multiples	1 cent ($25)	25 cents apart
• Long Gilt	1 long gilt futures contract	multiples of $1/64$ pound	$1/64$ of a pound	2 pounds apart
• Sterling (3-Month)	1 sterling futures contract	pence	1 pence (12.50 pounds)	25 pence apart
• U.S. Dollar- Deutsche Mark	$50,000 against marks	dollars and cents per mark	.01 pfennig per dollar (5 marks)	5 pfennigs per dollar apart
• U.S. Treasury Bond	1 $100,000 T-bond futures contract	multiples of $1/64$ of a point	$1/64$ ($15.625)	2 points apart

London Metal Exchange (LME)

Futures

Contract	Trading Unit	Prices Quoted In	Minimum Price Fluctuation
• Aluminum (High Grade)	25 metric tons	dollars and cents per ton	1 cent ($25)
• Aluminum (Primary)	25 metric tons	pounds and pence per ton	50 pence per ton (12.50 pounds)
• Copper (Grade A)	25 metric tons	pounds and pence per ton	50 pence per ton (12.50 pounds)
• Copper (Standard)	25 metric tons	pounds and pence per ton	50 pence per ton (12.50 pounds)

Expiration Day	Contract Months	Trading Hours
last trading day	Mar, June, Sept, Dec	8:34 a.m.-4:02 p.m.
last trading day	Mar, June, Sept, Dec	8:32 a.m.-4:00 p.m.
last trading day	Mar, June, Sept, Dec	9:02 a.m.-4:15 p.m.
last trading day	Mar, June, Sept, Dec	8:22 a.m.-4:02 p.m.
3 business days before 3rd Wednesday of month	Mar, June, Sept, Dec and 3 nearest months	8:36 a.m.-4:04 p.m.
1st Friday at least 6 CBOT working days before delivery	Mar, June, Sept, Dec	8:17 a.m.-4:10 p.m.

Last Trading Day	Contract Months	Trading Hours
—	daily between spot and 3 nearest months	11:55 a.m.-12:00 p.m. and 12:55 p.m.-1:00 p.m.; also 3:40 p.m.-3:45 p.m. and 4:20 p.m.-4:25 p.m.
—	daily between spot and 3 nearest months	11:50 a.m.-11:55 a.m. and 12:50 p.m.-12:55 p.m.; also 3:35 p.m.-3:40 p.m. and 4:15 p.m.-4:20 p.m.
—	daily between spot and 3 nearest months	12:00 p.m.-12:05 p.m. and 12:30 p.m.-12:35 p.m.; also 3:30 p.m.-3:35 p.m. and 4:10 p.m.-4:15 p.m.
—	daily between spot and 3 nearest months	12:00 p.m.-12:05 p.m. and 12:35 p.m.-12:40 p.m.; also 3:30 p.m.-3:35 p.m. and 4:10 p.m.-4:15 p.m.

Contract	Trading Unit	Prices Quoted In	Minimum Price Fluctuation
● Lead	25 metric tons	pounds and pence per ton	25 pence per ton (6.25 pounds)
● Nickel	6 metric tons	pounds and pence per ton	1 pound (6 pounds)
● Silver (10,000 ounces)	10,000 troy ounces	cents per ounce	10 cents ($10)
● Silver (2,000 ounces)	2,000 troy ounces	cents per ounce	10 cents ($2)
● Zinc	25 metric tons	pounds and pence per ton	25 pence per ton (6.25 pounds)

Futures Options

Contract	Trading Unit	Prices Quoted In	Minimum Price Fluctuation	Strike Prices
● Aluminum (High Grade)	1 25 metric ton aluminum futures contract	dollars or pounds per ton	—	$25 or 25 pounds per ton apart
● Aluminum (Primary)	1 25 metric ton aluminum futures contract	dollars or pounds per ton	—	$25 or 25 pounds per ton apart
● Copper (Grade A)	1 25 metric ton copper futures contract	pounds per ton	0.50 pounds per ton	$25 or 25 pounds per ton apart
● Lead	1 25 metric ton lead futures contract	pounds per ton	0.25 pounds per ton	$20 or 20 pounds per ton apart
● Nickel	1 6 metric ton nickel futures contract	pounds per ton	1 pound per ton	$50 or 50 pounds per ton apart
● Zinc	1 25 metric ton zinc futures contract	pounds per ton	0.25 pounds per ton	$20 or 20 pounds per ton apart

Last Trading Day	Contract Months	Trading Hours
—	daily between spot and 3 nearest months	12:05 p.m.-12:10 p.m. and 12:40 p.m.-12:45 p.m.; also 3:20 p.m.-3:25 p.m. and 4:00 p.m.-4:05 p.m.
—	daily between spot and 3 nearest months	12:15 p.m.-12:20 p.m. and 1:00 p.m.-1:05 p.m.; also 3:45 p.m.-3:50 p.m. and 4:25 p.m.-4:30 p.m.
—	daily between spot and 3 nearest months	11:45 a.m.-11:50 a.m. and 1:05 p.m.-1:05 p.m.; also 3:50 p.m.-3:55 p.m. and 4:30 p.m.-4:35 p.m.
—	daily between spot and 3 nearest months	11:45 a.m.-12:15 p.m. and 1:05 p.m.-1:10 p.m.; also 3:50 p.m.-3:55 p.m. and 4:30 p.m.-4:35 p.m.
—	daily between spot and 3 nearest months	12:10 p.m.-12:15 p.m. and 12:45 p.m.-12:50 p.m.; also 3:25 p.m.-3:30 p.m. and 4:05 p.m.-4:10 p.m.

Expiration Day	Contract Months	Trading Hours
—	Jan and every 2nd month after that	all day
—	Jan and every 2nd month after that	all day
—	Jan and every 2nd month after that	all day
—	Feb and every 2nd month after that	all day
—	Feb and every 2nd month after that	all day
—	Feb and every 2nd month after that	all day

FRENCH SECURITIES, FUTURES AND OPTIONS EXCHANGES

Lille Potato Futures Market (LPFM)

Futures

Contract	Trading Unit	Prices Quoted In	Minimum Price Fluctuation
• Potatoes	20 tons	francs per kilogram	25 francs per 100 kilograms

Marche A Terme Instrument Financiers (MATIF)

Futures

Contract	Trading Unit	Prices Quoted In	Minimum Price Fluctuation
• French Gov't National Bond	500,000 franc bond (10% coupon)	percent of par in basis points	.05 points = 250 francs
• French T-Bill (90-Day)	5 million franc bond	100 minus interest rate	.01 points = 125 francs

Futures Options

Contract	Trading Unit	Prices Quoted In	Minimum Price Fluctuation	Strike Prices
• French Gov't National Bond	1 French gov't national bond futures contract	percent of par in basis points	0.01 points = 50 francs	even strike prices

Last Trading Day	Contract Months	Trading Hours
2nd Tuesday of contract month	Feb, Apr, May, Nov	11:00 a.m.-12:45 p.m. and 3:00 p.m.-4:30 p.m.

Last Trading Day	Contract Months	Trading Hours
4 days before last business day of month	Mar, June, Sept, Dec	10:00 a.m.-3:00 p.m.
business day after T-bills 3rd monthly adjudication	Mar, June, Sept, Dec	10:00 a.m.-3:00 p.m.

Expiration Day	Contract Months	Trading Hours
last day of trading	Mar, June, Sept, Dec	10:00 a.m.-3:00 p.m.

Paris Futures Exchange (PFE)

Futures

Contract	Trading Unit	Prices Quoted In	Minimum Price Fluctuation
• Cocoa Beans	10 metric tons	francs per kilogram	50 francs per 100 kilograms
• Cocoa Butter	10 metric tons	francs per kilogram	1 franc per 100 kilograms
• Coffee	5 metric tons	francs per kilogram	1 franc per 100 kilograms
• White Sugar	50 metric tons	francs per ton	1 franc per ton

HONG KONG SECURITIES, FUTURES EXCHANGE

Hong Kong Futures Exchange (HKFE)

Futures

Contract	Trading Unit	Prices Quoted In	Minimum Price Fluctuation
• Gold	100 troy ounces	dollars and cents per ounce	10 cents = $100
• Hang Seng Index	50 Hong Kong dollars × index	index points	1 index point
• Soybeans	30,000 kilograms	Hong Kong dollars and cents	20 cents per 60 kilograms
• Sugar	50 long tons	dollars and cents per pound	$1/_{100}$ cent = $11.20

Last Trading Day	Contract Months	Trading Hours
last day of contract month	Mar, May, July, Sept, Dec	10:30 a.m.-1:00 p.m. and 3:00 p.m.-5:30 p.m.
20th day of month before contract month	Mar, May, July, Sept, Dec	11:15 a.m.-1:00 p.m. and 3:00 p.m.-5:30 p.m.
last day of contract month	Jan, Mar, May, July, Sept, Nov	10:15 a.m.-1:00 p.m. and 3:00 p.m.-5:30 p.m.
last day of contract month	Mar, May, Aug, Oct, Dec	10:45 a.m.-1:00 p.m. and 3:00 p.m.-7:00 p.m.

Last Trading Day	Contract Months	Trading Hours
last business day of contract month	2 nearest months, even months, spot months	9:00 a.m.-12:00 p.m. and 2:00 p.m.-5:30 p.m.
2nd business day of trading month	3 even months	10:00 a.m.-12:30 p.m. and 2:30 p.m.-3:30 p.m.
15th day of contract month	6 nearest months	9:00 a.m.-10:50 a.m. and 12:50 p.m.-2:50 p.m.
business day before first day of contract month	Jan, Mar, May, July, Sept, Oct	10:30 a.m.-12:00 p.m. and 2:25 p.m.-4:00 p.m.

JAPANESE SECURITIES, FUTURES EXCHANGES

Osaka Securities Exchange (OSE)

Futures

Contract	Trading Unit	Prices Quoted In	Minimum Price Fluctuation
• Nikkei Stock Average	average × 1000	yen per average	10 yen per average
• Osaka Stock Futures 50	index of 50 stocks	index average	$^1/_{10}$ yen

Tokyo Commodity Exchange (TCE)

Futures

Contract	Trading Unit	Prices Quoted In	Minimum Price Fluctuation
• Cotton Yarn	4000 pounds	yen per pound	0.1 yen per 1 pound
• Gold	1 kilogram bar	yen per gram	1 yen per gram
• Platinum	500 grams	yen per gram	1 yen per gram
• Rubber	5000 kilograms	yen per kilogram	0.1 yen per 1 kilogram
• Silver	30 kilograms	yen per gram	0.1 yen per 10 grams
• Woolen Yarn	500 kilograms	yen per gram	1 yen per 1 gram

Last Trading Day	Contract Months	Trading Hours
3rd day before settlement	Mar, June, Sept, Dec	9:00 a.m.-11:15 a.m. and 2:00 p.m.-3:15 p.m.
6th day before delivery	Mar, June, Sept, Dec	9:00 a.m.-11:00 a.m. and 1:00 p.m.-3:00 p.m.

Last Trading Day	Contract Months	Trading Hours
4th business day before delivery	6 nearest months	8:50 a.m. and 10:00 a.m.; 1:50 p.m. and 3:10 p.m.
3rd business day before delivery	odd months after an even month; each even month within 1 year of odd month	9:10 a.m., 10:30 a.m., 11:30 a.m.; 1:10 p.m., 2:30 p.m., 3:45 p.m.
3rd business day before delivery	odd months after an even month; each even month within 1 year of odd month	after silver calls
5th business day before delivery	4 nearest months, then each even month	9:45 a.m., 10:45 a.m.; 1:45 p.m., 2:45 p.m., 3:30 p.m.
end of contract month	odd months after an even month; each even month within 1 year of odd month	after gold calls
4th business day before delivery	6 nearest months	after cotton yarn calls

Tokyo Grain Exchange (TGE)

Futures

Contract	Trading Unit	Prices Quoted In	Minimum Price Fluctuation
• American Soybeans	15 tons	yen per kilogram	10 yen per 60 kilograms
• Chinese Soybeans	250 bags	yen per kilogram bag	10 yen per 60 kilogram bag
• Japanese Soybeans	40 bags	yen per kilogram bag	10 yen per 60 kilogram bag
• Potato Starch	100 bags	yen per kilogram bag	1 yen per 25 kilogram bag
• Red Beans	80 bags	yen per kilogram bag	10 yen per 30 kilogram bag
• White Beans	40 bags	yen per kilogram bag	10 yen per kilogram bag

Tokyo Stock Exchange (TSE)

Futures

Contract	Trading Unit	Prices Quoted In	Minimum Price Fluctuation
• Japanese Gov't Bond (10 Year)	10-year yen bond	—	0.01 yen per 100 yen
• Japanese Gov't Bond (20 Year)	20-year yen bond	—	0.01 yen per 100 yen
• Tokyo Stock Price Index	stock index	index points	1 index point

Last Trading Day	Contract Months	Trading Hours
2 days before last business day of contract month	even months	10:00 a.m.-11:00 a.m. and 1:00 p.m.-2:00 p.m.
—	6 nearest months	10:00 a.m.-11:00 a.m. and 1:00 p.m.- 2:00 p.m.
—	3 nearest months	3:00 p.m.
—	3 nearest months	3:00 p.m.
—	6 nearest months	9:00 a.m.-11:00 a.m. and 1:00 p.m.-3:00 p.m.
—	6 nearest months	3:00 p.m.

Last Trading Day	Contract Months	Trading Hours
9th business day before delivery	Mar, June, Sept, Dec	9:00 a.m.-11:00 a.m. and 1:00 p.m.-3:00 p.m.
9th business day before delivery	Mar, June, Sept, Dec	9:00 a.m.-11:15 a.m. and 1:00 p.m.-3:00 p.m.
3rd business day before delivery	Mar, June, Sept, Dec	9:00 a.m.-11:15 a.m. and 1:00 p.m.-3:15 p.m.

Tokyo Sugar Exchange (TSUE)

Futures

Contract	Trading Unit	Prices Quoted In	Minimum Price Fluctuation
• Raw Sugar	10 metric tons	—	—
• Refined White Sugar	9 metric tons	—	—

MALAYSIAN SECURITIES, FUTURES EXCHANGE

Kuala Lumpur Commodity Exchange (KLCE)

Futures

Contract	Trading Unit	Prices Quoted In	Minimum Price Fluctuation
• Cocoa	10 metric tons	dollars per ton	$1 per ton
• Crude Palm Oil	25 metric tons	Malaysian dollars per ton	1 Malaysian dollar per ton
• Rubber	20 metric tons (for contract months), 60 metric tons for distant delivery	Malaysian dollars and cents per kilogram	$^1/_4$ Malaysian cent per kilogram
• Rubber	10 tons (for single contract months), 30 tons for delivery quarter	Malaysian dollars and cents per kilogram	$^1/_4$ Malaysian cent per kilogram
• Tin	5 tons	dollars per ton	$5 per ton

Last Trading Day	Contract Months	Trading Hours
—	odd months	9:30 a.m., 10:30 a.m., 1:30 p.m., 3:30 p.m.
—	6 nearest months	9:30 a.m., 10:30 a.m., 1:30 p.m., 3:30 p.m.

Last Trading Day	Contract Months	Trading Hours
20th day of month	Jan, Mar, May, July, Sept, Nov, Dec	11:15 a.m.-12:00 p.m. and 4:00 p.m.- 6:00 p.m.
15th day of preceding month	6 nearest months	11:00 a.m.-12:30 p.m. and 3:30 p.m.-6:00 p.m.
—	—	10:00 a.m.-1:00 p.m. and 4:00 p.m.-6:00 p.m.
last business day of month before contract	nearest 4 to 6 months	10:00 a.m.-1:00 p.m. and 4:00 p.m.-6:00 p.m.
3rd to last business day of month	4 nearest months	12:15 p.m.-1:00 p.m. and 4:00 p.m.-6:00 p.m.

THE NETHERLANDS SECURITIES, FUTURES AND OPTIONS EXCHANGES

European Options Exchange (EOE)

Futures Options

Contract	Trading Unit	Prices Quoted In	Minimum Price Fluctuation	Strike Prices
● Bond Index	100 Dutch florin × index	index points	0.05 Dutch florin	2.50 Dutch florin apart
● British Pound	10,000 pounds	Dutch florin per 100 pounds	0.05 Dutch florin apart	5 Dutch florin apart
● Dollar	$10,000	Dutch florin per $100	0.05 Dutch florin	5 Dutch florin apart
● Dutch Gov't Bonds	10,000 Dutch florin bond	100 units	0.10 Dutch florin	2.50% of principal apart
● EOE Stock Index	100 Dutch florin × index	index points	0.10 Dutch florin	5 Dutch florin apart
● Gold	10 troy ounces	dollars and cents per troy ounce	10 cents = $1	$10 apart
● Major Market Index	index × $100	index points	$^1/_8$ point	5 points apart
● Silver	250 troy ounces	dollars and cents per ounce	1 cent = $2.50	25 cents apart

Financiale Terminjmarkt Amsterdam (FTA)

Futures

Contract	Trading Unit	Prices Quoted In	Minimum Price Fluctuation
● Guilder Bond	1000 Dutch florin × bond index	index points	0.01 point = 10 Dutch

Expiration Day	Contract Months	Trading Hours
3rd Saturday after last trading day	Feb, May, Aug, Nov	10:30 a.m.-4:30 p.m.
3rd Saturday after last trading day	Mar, June, Sept, Dec	10:00 a.m.-4:30 p.m.
3rd Saturday after last trading day	Mar, June, Sept, Dec	10:00 a.m.-4:30 p.m.
3rd Saturday after last trading day	Feb, May, Aug, Nov	11:30 a.m.-4:30 p.m.
3rd Saturday after last trading day	Jan, Apr, July, Oct	10:30 a.m.-4:30 p.m.
3rd Saturday after last trading day	3 nearest months	10:00 a.m.-4:30 p.m.
3rd Saturday after last trading day	3 nearest months	12:00 p.m.-4:30 p.m.
3rd Saturday after last trading day	Mar, June, Sept, Dec	10:00 a.m.-4:30 p.m.

Last Trading Day	Contract Months	Trading Hours
last business day of month	Feb, May, Aug, Nov	10:45 a.m.-4:30 p.m.

NEW ZEALAND SECURITIES, FUTURES EXCHANGES

New Zealand Futures Exchange (NZFE)

Futures

Contract	Trading Unit	Prices Quoted In	Minimum Price Fluctuation
• Barclays Share Price Index	20 New Zealand dollars × index	index points	—
• Dollar	$50,000 per	dollars per New Zealand dollar	0.00001 cent
• Five-Year Gov't Stock	$100,000 New Zealand gov't stock (10% coupon)	—	0.01%
• New Zealand Dollar	100,000 New Zealand dollars	dollars and cents per New Zealand dollar	0.00001 cent
• 90-Day Bank Accepted Bills	$500,000 New Zealand principal	100 minus price	0.01%

SINGAPORE SECURITIES, FUTURES AND OPTIONS EXCHANGES

Singapore International Monetary Exchange (SIMEX)

Futures

Contract	Trading Unit	Prices Quoted In	Minimum Price Fluctuation
• British Pound	62,500 pounds	dollars and cents per pound	0.0002 cent = $12.50
• Deutsche Mark	125,000 German marks	dollars and cents per mark	0.0001 cent = $12.50

Last Trading Day	Contract Months	Trading Hours
2nd to last business day of contract month	3 nearest months and Mar, June, Sept, Dec	9:15 a.m.-3:45 p.m.
1st Wednesday after 9th day of settlement month	4 nearest months and Mar, June, Sept, Dec	8:15 a.m.-4:45 p.m.
1st Wednesday after 9th day of settlement month	Mar, June, Sept, Dec	8:00 a.m.-5:00 p.m.
2 business days before 1st Wednesday of settlement month	3 nearest months	8:05 a.m.-4:55 p.m.
1st Wednesday after 9th day of settlement month	3 nearest months and Mar, June, Sept, Dec	8:10 a.m. -4:50 p.m.

Last Trading Day	Contract Months	Trading Hours
2nd business day before 3rd Wednesday of contract month	Spot, Mar, June, Sept, Dec	8:25 a.m.-5:15 p.m.
2nd business day before 3rd Wednesday of contract month	Spot, Mar, June, Sept, Dec	8:20 a.m.-5:10 p.m.

Contract	Trading Unit	Prices Quoted In	Minimum Price Fluctuation
• Eurodollar 90-Day Time Deposit	$1 million principal	percent of par in basis points	0.01 point = $25
• Japanese Yen	12,500,000 yen	dollars and cents per yen	0.000001 point = $12.50
• Nikkei Stock Average	average × 500 yen	index points	0.05 points = 2500 yen

Futures Options

Contract	Trading Unit	Prices Quoted In	Minimum Price Fluctuation	Strike Prices
• Deutsche Mark	1 mark futures contract	points of 100%	0.01 point = $12.50	1 cent apart
• Eurodollar 90-Day Time Deposit	1 Eurodollar futures contract	points of 100%	0.01 point = $25	0.50 point apart
• Japanese Yen	1 yen futures contract	points of 1000%	0.001 point = $12.50	0.01 point apart

SWEDISH SECURITIES, FUTURES AND OPTIONS EXCHANGES

Stockholm Options Market (SOM)

Forwards

Contract	Trading Unit	Prices Quoted In	Minimum Price Fluctuation
• OMX Index	index	index points	—

Last Trading Day	Contract Months	Trading Hours
2nd London business day before 3rd Wednesday of contract month	Spot, Mar, June, Sept, Dec	8:30 a.m.-5:20 p.m.
2nd business day before 3rd Wednesday of contract month	Spot, Mar, June, Sept, Dec	8:15 a.m.-5:05 p.m.
3rd Wednesday of contract month	Spot, Mar, June, Sept, Dec	8:00 a.m.-2:15 p.m.

Expiration Day	Contract Months	Trading Hours
last trading day	Mar, June, Sept, Dec, and serial months	8:20 a.m.-5:10 p.m.
last trading day	Mar, June, Sept, Dec	
2 Fridays before 3rd Wednesday of contract months	Mar, June, Sept, Dec and serial months	8:15 a.m.-5:05 p.m.

Last Trading Day	Contract Months	Trading Hours
4th Friday of expiration month	Jan, Mar, May, July, Sept, Nov	10:00 a.m.-4:00 p.m.

Futures Options

Contract	Trading Unit	Prices Quoted In	Minimum Price Fluctuation	Strike Prices
• OMX Index	index	percentage of option	0.01 of option	20 index points apart
• Swedish T-Note (5-Year)	1,000,000 Swedish krona note	percentage of option	0.01 of option	20 index points apart

Swedish Options and Futures Exchange (SOFE)

Forwards

Contract	Trading Unit	Prices Quoted In	Minimum Price Fluctuation
• SX 16 Stock Index	index × 1000	index points points	0.05 Swedish krona

Futures Options

Contract	Trading Unit	Prices Quoted In	Minimum Price Fluctuation	Strike Prices
• SX 16 Stock Index	index × 100	index points	0.05 Swedish krona	10 Swedish krona apart

Expiration Day	Contract Months	Trading Hours
last trading day	Jan, Mar, May, July, Sept, Nov	10:00 a.m.-4:00 p.m.
last trading day	—	9:30 a.m.-3:00 p.m.

Last Trading Day	Contract Months	Trading Hours
last day before expiration	monthly	9:45 a.m.-10:00 p.m.

Expiration Day	Contract Months	Trading Hours
4th Friday of contract month	monthly	9:45 a.m.-10:00 p.m.

5. HISTORICAL DATA

This section of the *Handbook* allows you to follow the major ups and downs of the financial markets and the United States economy during the 20th Century. Although history never repeats itself exactly, it is important to understand historical market cycles if you are to understand where the markets and economy stand today, as well as where they might be going in the future.

The historical section is presented with graphs accompanied by tabular data and explanations of what the information signifies to you as an investor. Graphs are based on end-of-month closing stock index values; municipal bond yields compiled the first week of each month; month-end London morning fix prices of gold; monthly average Treasury bill and bond yields; monthly average discount, prime, and federal funds rates; and monthly or monthly average government economic statistics.

The tabular data show annual highs, lows, and year-end figures on the same monthly bases as the above with these exceptions: stock indexes are based on daily closing figures; the consumer and producer price indexes and money supply (M-1) statistics are annual percentage changes (for instance, November 1989 vs. November 1988); gold prices are daily London morning fixings; and the discount and prime rates are day-end figures.

Note that the month-end data points on which the stock index graphs are based may reflect different highs and lows than the daily closing data. The month-end data plot long-term trends with a minimum of aberrations caused by PROGRAM TRADES and other NOISE, while the daily data are more subject to short-term fluctuations. The graphs showing trends of the discount and prime rates, because they are based on monthly averages, will also differ from the accompanying tables, which are based on day-end rates.

Much of the securities data have been provided courtesy of Interactive Data Corporation, a securities and financial data base service. Interactive, with headquarters at 95 Hayden Avenue, Lexington, Massachusetts 02173 (phone: 617-863-8100) provided numbers for the charts as far back as their data banks went. This usually meant 1968, though in some cases, indexes were not created until later. Much of the economic data have been provided courtesy of the WEFA Group, with headquarters at 150 Monument Road, Bala Cynwyd, Pennsylvania 19004 (phone:215-667-6000). If data were received from another source, such as the Federal Reserve Board, the U.S. Bureau of Labor Statistics, Dow Jones and Company or Standard and Poor's Corporation, either IDC or WEFA and that source have been credited.

AMEX MARKET VALUE INDEX

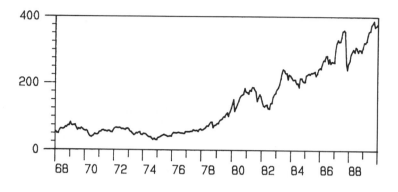

Source: American Stock Exchange, Interactive Data Corporation

This graph shows the movement of the American Stock Exchange Market Value Index. Formerly known as the American Stock Exchange Index, the AMVI is a market value-weighted index (i.e., the impact of a component's price change is proportionate to the overall market value of the issue). The index measures the performance of more than 800 issues, representing all major industry groups, including shares, American Depositary Receipts and warrants. The companies listed on the Amex tend to be medium-sized and smaller growth firms. One unique aspect of this index is that cash dividends paid by the component stocks are assumed to be reinvested and thus are reflected in the index.

Year	High	Low	Close
1968	74.82	48.66	73.69
1969	84.49	57.22	60.01
1970	62.77	36.10	49.21
1971	60.86	49.09	58.49
1972	69.18	58.55	64.52
1973	65.23	42.16	45.16
1974	51.01	29.13	30.16
1975	48.43	31.10	41.74
1976	54.92	42.16	54.92
1977	63.95	54.31	63.95
1978	88.44	59.87	75.28
1979	123.67	76.02	123.54
1980	185.38	107.85	174.49
1981	190.18	138.38	160.31
1982	170.93	118.65	170.30
1983	249.03	169.61	223.01
1984	227.73	189.16	204.26
1985	246.13	202.06	246.13

Year	High	Low	Close
1986	285.19	240.30	263.27
1987	365.01	231.90	260.35
1988	309.59	260.35	306.01
1989	397.03	305.24	378.00

BOND BUYER INDEX (11 BONDS)

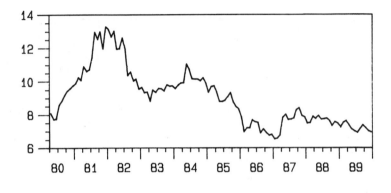

Source: Bond Buyer, Interactive Data Corporation

This graph shows the movement of the *Bond Buyer* Index of 11 bonds. The *Bond Buyer* is a daily newspaper covering the municipal bond market. This index is made up of the yields of 11 newly issued general obligation municipal bonds averaging 20 years to maturity rated Aa and selling at par. The issuers of these bonds, whose average rating is second only to Aaa, are among the most creditworthy of all those issuing bonds in the municipal market. The yield offered by these bonds, therefore, is lower than that of less creditworthy municipalities, but it acts as a benchmark against which market participants compare other municipal bond yields.

Year	High	Low	Close
1917	4.55	3.88	4.60
1918	4.65	4.39	4.42
1919	4.53	4.42	4.53
1920	5.25	4.53	5.03
1921	5.16	4.48	4.35
1922	4.37	4.05	4.14
1923	4.38	4.10	4.35
1924	4.35	4.07	4.15
1925	4.23	3.98	4.19
1926	4.19	4.05	4.10

Year	High	Low	Close
1927	4.10	3.89	3.83
1928	4.15	3.83	4.13
1929	4.47	4.13	4.19
1930	4.25	3.92	4.05
1931	4.23	3.60	4.66
1932	4.66	4.02	3.81
1933	4.90	3.81	4.50
1934	4.50	3.38	3.30
1935	3.30	2.79	2.84
1936	2.84	2.35	2.35
1937	2.90	2.35	2.75
1938	2.75	2.42	2.36
1939	2.94	2.26	2.24
1940	2.66	1.82	1.80
1941	2.13	1.57	1.91
1942	2.79	1.72	1.80
1943	1.80	1.35	1.44
1944	1.44	1.30	1.32
1945	1.43	1.06	1.14
1946	1.66	1.04	1.62
1947	2.13	1.53	2.11
1948	2.25	1.98	1.97
1949	2.00	1.84	1.86
1950	1.87	1.54	1.50
1951	2.04	1.43	1.92
1952	2.20	1.84	2.21
1953	2.88	2.21	2.37
1954	2.37	2.10	2.24
1955	2.50	2.22	2.41
1956	3.10	2.29	3.08
1957	3.43	2.81	2.85
1958	3.51	2.70	3.26
1959	3.70	3.17	3.65
1960	3.65	3.12	3.26
1961	3.44	3.16	3.28
1962	3.28	2.92	2.97
1963	3.24	2.95	3.19
1964	3.25	3.06	3.01
1965	3.47	2.99	3.45
1966	4.14	3.43	3.66
1967	4.37	3.32	4.27
1968	4.72	3.96	4.72
1969	6.74	4.68	6.42
1970	7.00	5.02	5.47
1971	6.04	4.75	4.82
1972	5.35	4.78	4.98

Year	High	Low	Close
1973	5.45	4.87	5.05
1974	6.71	5.04	6.62
1975	7.23	5.94	6.45
1976	6.57	5.36	5.36
1977	5.57	5.18	5.37
1978	6.28	5.32	6.22
1979	7.02	5.77	6.85
1980	10.08	6.63	9.27
1981	12.89	9.04	12.89
1982	13.05	8.90	9.18
1983	9.86	8.54	9.57
1984	10.95	9.34	9.78
1985	9.74	8.25	8.26
1986	8.24	6.64	6.70
1987	9.05	6.40	7.72
1988	7.85	7.22	7.40
1989	7.78	6.75	6.84

BOND BUYER INDEX (20 BONDS)

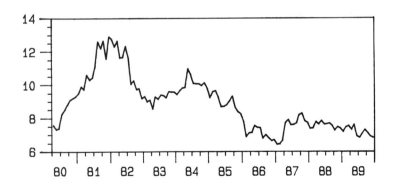

Source: Bond Buyer, Interactive Data Corporation

This graph shows the movement of the *Bond Buyer* Index of 20 bonds. The *Bond Buyer* is a daily newspaper covering the municipal bond market. This index is made up of the yields of 20 newly issued general obligation municipal bonds with an average maturity of 20 years, rated from Baa to AAA, (thus including all those of investment grade) and selling at par. The issuers of these bonds are among the most creditworthy of all those issuing bonds in the municipal market.

Year	High	Low	Close
1917	4.56	3.92	4.62
1918	4.72	4.40	4.44
1919	4.55	4.44	4.56
1920	5.27	4.56	5.06
1921	5.26	4.50	5.06
1922	4.41	4.09	4.16
1923	4.40	4.11	4.37
1924	4.37	4.11	4.16
1925	4.26	3.99	4.23
1926	4.23	4.10	4.13
1927	4.13	3.93	3.87
1928	4.18	3.87	4.17
1929	4.49	4.17	4.23
1930	4.29	3.97	4.12
1931	4.45	3.74	4.87
1932	5.09	4.57	4.61
1933	5.69	4.48	5.48
1934	5.48	3.89	3.81
1935	3.81	3.23	3.25
1936	3.25	2.69	2.62
1937	3.17	2.62	3.16
1938	3.19	2.83	2.78
1939	3.30	2.66	2.59
1940	3.00	2.18	2.14
1941	2.43	1.90	2.24
1942	2.51	2.13	2.17
1943	2.17	1.69	1.77
1944	1.77	1.59	1.62
1945	1.72	1.35	1.42
1946	1.91	1.29	1.85
1947	2.35	1.78	2.36
1948	2.48	2.20	2.19
1949	2.21	2.08	2.07
1950	2.07	1.70	1.06
1951	2.23	1.58	2.11
1952	2.39	2.03	2.40
1953	3.09	2.40	2.54
1954	2.54	2.26	2.38
1955	2.63	2.37	2.56
1956	3.24	2.42	3.23
1957	3.57	2.96	2.97
1958	3.59	2.85	3.40
1959	3.81	3.26	3.78
1960	3.78	3.27	3.39
1961	3.55	3.26	3.37
1962	3.37	2.98	3.05

Year	High	Low	Close
1963	3.31	3.01	3.26
1964	3.32	3.12	3.07
1965	3.56	3.04	3.53
1966	4.24	3.51	3.76
1967	4.45	3.40	4.38
1968	4.85	4.07	4.85
1969	6.90	4.82	6.61
1970	7.12	5.33	5.74
1971	6.23	4.97	5.03
1972	5.54	4.96	5.08
1973	5.59	4.99	5.18
1974	7.15	5.16	7.08
1975	7.67	6.27	7.13
1976	7.13	5.83	5.83
1977	5.93	5.45	5.66
1978	6.67	5.58	6.61
1979	7.38	6.08	7.23
1980	10.56	7.11	9.76
1981	13.30	9.49	13.30
1982	13.44	9.25	9.56
1983	10.04	8.78	9.76
1984	11.07	9.51	9.91
1985	9.87	8.36	8.36
1986	8.33	6.77	6.83
1987	9.17	6.54	7.86
1988	7.97	7.33	7.50
1989	7.72	6.86	6.97

DOW JONES 30 INDUSTRIALS STOCK AVERAGE

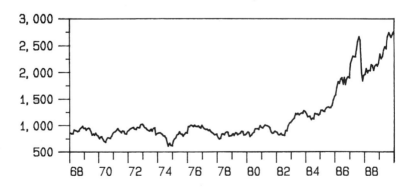

Source: Dow Jones and Company, Interactive Data Corporation

The graph on the opposite page shows the movement of the Dow Jones 30 Industrials Stock Average, the oldest and most widely of all stock market indicators. When people ask "What did the market do today?" they usually expect to hear whether this average was up or down for the day. The price-weighted average is comprised of the stocks of 30 blue-chip stocks, primarily manufacturing companies but also service companies like American Express. The components, which change from time to time, represent between 15 percent and 20 percent of the market value of all NYSE stocks. The Dow, as it is known, is calculated by adding the closing prices of the component stocks and using a divisor that adjusts for splits and stock dividends equal to 10% or more of the market issue as well as for mergers and changes in the components of the list. The Dow Jones 65 Composite Stock Average is composed of the Dow Jones 30 industrials, the Dow Jones 20 transportations and the Dow Jones 15 utilities.

The components of the Dow Jones Industrial Average (DJIA) are:

Allied-Signal Company
Aluminum Company of America
American Can Company
American Express Company
American Telephone & Telegraph
Bethlehem Steel
Chevron
DuPont
Eastman Kodak Company
Exxon Corporation
General Electric Company
General Motors Corporation
Goodyear Tire & Rubber Company
Inco Incorporated
International Business Machines Corporation
International Paper Company
McDonald's Corporation
Merck & Company
Minnesota Mining & Manufacturing Company
Navistar International
Owens-Illinois, Inc.
Philip Morris Company
Procter & Gamble Corporation
Sears, Roebuck and Company
Texaco Incorporated
Union Carbide Corporation
United Technologies Company
USX Corporation
Westinghouse Electric Corporation
F.W. Woolworth & Company

Year	High	Low	Close
1897	55.82	38.49	49.41
1898	60.97	42.00	60.52
1899	77.61	58.27	66.08
1900	71.04	52.96	70.71
1901	78.26	61.52	64.56
1902	68.44	59.57	64.29

Year	High	Low	Close
1903	67.70	42.15	49.11
1904	73.23	46.41	69.61
1905	96.56	68.76	96.20
1906	103.00	85.18	93.63
1907	96.37	53.00	58.75
1908	88.38	58.62	86.15
1909	100.53	79.91	99.05
1910	98.34	73.62	81.36
1911	87.06	72.94	81.68
1912	94.15	80.15	87.87
1913	88.57	72.11	78.78
1914	83.43	53.17	53.17
1915	99.21	54.22	99.15
1916	110.15	84.96	95.00
1917	99.18	65.95	74.38
1918	89.07	73.38	82.20
1919	119.62	79.15	107.23
1920	109.88	66.75	71.95
1921	81.50	63.90	81.10
1922	103.43	78.59	98.73
1923	105.38	85.76	95.52
1924	120.51	88.33	120.51
1925	159.39	115.00	156.66
1926	166.64	135.20	157.20
1927	202.40	152.73	202.40
1928	300.00	191.33	300.00
1929	381.17	198.69	248.48
1930	294.07	157.51	164.58
1931	194.36	73.79	77.90
1932	88.78	41.22	59.93
1933	108.67	50.16	99.90
1934	110.74	85.51	104.04
1935	148.44	96.71	144.13
1936	184.90	143.11	179.90
1937	194.40	113.64	120.85
1938	158.41	98.95	154.76
1939	155.92	121.44	150.24
1940	152.80	111.84	131.13
1941	133.59	106.34	110.96
1942	119.71	92.92	119.40
1943	145.82	119.26	135.89
1944	152.53	134.22	152.32
1945	195.82	151.35	192.91
1946	212.50	163.12	177.20

Year	High	Low	Close
1947	186.85	163.21	181.16
1948	193.16	165.39	177.30
1949	200.52	161.60	200.13
1950	235.47	196.81	235.41
1951	276.37	238.99	269.23
1952	292.00	256.35	291.90
1953	293.79	255.49	280.90
1954	404.39	279.87	404.39
1955	488.40	388.20	488.40
1956	521.05	462.35	499.47
1957	520.77	419.79	435.69
1958	583.65	436.89	583.65
1959	679.36	574.46	679.36
1960	685.47	566.05	615.89
1961	734.91	610.25	731.14
1962	726.01	535.76	652.10
1963	767.21	646.79	762.95
1964	891.71	766.08	874.13
1965	969.26	840.59	969.26
1966	995.15	744.32	785.69
1967	943.08	786.41	905.11
1968	985.21	825.13	943.75
1969	968.85	769.93	800.36
1970	842.00	631.16	838.92
1971	950.82	797.97	890.20
1972	1036.27	889.15	1020.02
1973	1051.70	788.31	850.86
1974	891.66	577.60	616.24
1975	881.81	632.04	852.41
1976	1014.79	858.71	1004.65
1977	999.75	800.85	831.17
1978	907.74	742.12	805.01
1979	897.61	796.67	838.74
1980	1000.17	759.13	963.99
1981	1024.05	824.01	875.00
1982	1070.55	776.92	1046.55
1983	1287.20	1027.04	1258.64
1984	1286.64	1086.57	1211.57
1985	1553.10	1184.96	1546.67
1986	1955.57	1502.29	1895.95
1987	2722.42	1738.74	1938.83
1988	2183.50	1879.14	2168.57
1989	2791.41	2144.64	2753.20

DOW JONES 20 TRANSPORTATION STOCK AVERAGE

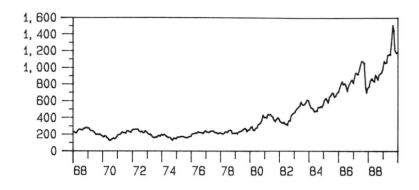

Source: Dow Jones and Company, Interactive Data Corporation

This graph shows the movement of the Dow Jones 20 Transportation Stock Average. This price-weighted average consists of the stocks of the 20 large companies in the transportation business, which includes airlines, railroads and trucking. The Transportation Average is important not only in that it tracks the movement of a major segment of American industry, but also because it is watched by the proponents of the Dow Theory, which maintains that a significant trend is not confirmed until both the Dow Jones Industrial Average and Transportation Average reach new highs or lows; if they don't, the market will fall back to its former trading range, according to this theory. From 1897 to 1969, this average was called the Dow Jones Railroad Average. The Dow Jones 65 Composite Average is composed of the Dow Jones 20 Transportation Stock Average, as well as the Dow Jones 30 Industrials and the Dow Jones 15 Utilities.

The components of the Dow Jones Transportation Average are:
AMR Corporation
American President Lines
Burlington Northern Railroad
Canadian Pacific Railroad
Carolina Freight Corporation
Consolidated Freight Corporation
CSX Corporation
Delta Air Lines
Federal Express Company
Leaseway Transportation Company
Norfolk Southern Railway
NWA Incorporated
Norfolk Southern Corporation
Pan American Corporation
Piedmont Aviation, Inc.
Ryder System Incorporated
Santa Fe Pacific Company
TWA Corporation
UAL Incorporated
Union Pacific Corporation
USAir Group

Year	High	Low	Close
1897	67.23	48.12	62.29
1898	74.99	55.89	74.99
1899	87.04	72.48	77.73
1900	94.99	72.99	94.99
1901	117.86	92.66	114.85
1902	129.36	111.73	118.98
1903	121.28	88.80	98.33
1904	119.46	91.31	117.43
1905	133.51	114.52	133.26
1906	138.36	120.30	129.80
1907	131.95	81.41	88.77
1908	120.05	86.04	120.05
1909	134.46	113.90	130.41
1910	129.90	105.59	114.06
1911	123.86	109.80	116.83
1912	124.35	114.92	116.84
1913	118.10	100.50	103.72
1914	109.43	87.40	88.53
1915	108.28	87.85	108.05
1916	112.28	99.11	105.15
1917	105.76	70.75	79.73
1918	92.91	77.21	84.32
1919	91.13	73.63	75.30
1920	85.37	67.83	75.96
1921	77.56	65.52	74.27
1922	93.99	73.43	86.11
1923	90.63	76.78	80.86
1924	99.50	80.23	98.33
1925	112.93	92.98	112.93
1926	123.33	102.41	120.86
1927	144.82	119.29	140.30
1928	152.70	132.60	151.14
1929	189.11	128.07	144.72
1930	157.94	91.65	96.58
1931	111.58	31.42	33.63
1932	41.30	13.23	25.90
1933	56.53	23.43	40.80
1934	52.97	33.19	36.44
1935	41.84	27.31	40.48
1936	59.89	40.66	53.63
1937	64.46	28.91	29.46
1938	33.98	19.00	33.98
1939	35.90	24.14	31.83
1940	32.67	22.14	28.13
1941	30.88	24.25	25.42
1942	29.28	23.31	27.39
1943	38.30	27.59	33.56

Year	High	Low	Close
1944	48.40	33.45	48.40
1945	64.89	47.03	62.80
1946	68.31	44.69	51.13
1947	53.42	41.16	52.48
1948	64.95	48.13	52.86
1949	54.29	41.03	52.76
1950	77.89	51.24	77.64
1951	90.08	72.39	81.70
1952	112.53	82.03	111.27
1953	112.21	90.56	94.03
1954	146.23	94.84	145.86
1955	167.83	137.84	163.29
1956	181.23	150.44	153.23
1957	157.67	95.67	96.96
1958	157.91	99.89	157.65
1959	173.56	146.65	154.05
1960	160.43	123.37	130.85
1961	152.93	131.06	143.84
1962	149.83	114.86	141.04
1963	179.46	142.03	178.54
1964	224.91	178.81	205.34
1965	249.55	187.29	247.48
1966	271.72	184.34	202.97
1967	274.49	205.16	233.24
1968	279.48	214.58	271.60
1969	279.88	169.03	176.34
1970	183.31	116.69	171.52
1971	248.33	169.70	243.72
1972	275.71	212.24	227.17
1973	228.10	151.97	196.19
1974	202.45	125.93	143.44
1975	174.57	146.47	172.65
1976	237.03	175.69	237.03
1977	246.64	199.60	217.18
1978	261.49	199.31	206.56
1979	271.77	205.78	252.39
1980	425.68	233.69	398.10
1981	447.38	335.48	380.30
1982	464.55	292.12	448.38
1983	612.57	434.24	598.59
1984	612.63	444.03	558.13
1985	723.31	553.03	708.21
1986	866.74	686.97	807.17
1987	1101.16	661.00	748.86
1988	973.61	737.57	969.84
1989	1532.01	959.95	1177.81

DOW JONES 15 UTILITIES STOCK AVERAGE

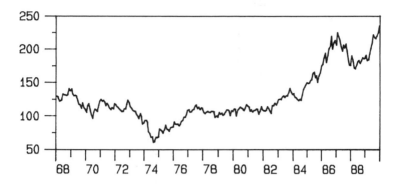

Source: Dow Jones and Company, Interactive Data Corporation

This graph shows the movement of the Dow Jones 15 Utilities Stock Average. This price-weighted average is composed of 15 geographically representative and well-established gas and electric utility companies. Since utilities are heavy borrowers, their stock prices are inversely affected by the ups and downs of interest rates. The Dow Jones 65 Composite Stock Average is composed of the Dow Jones 15 Utilities Stock Average, the Dow Jones 30 industrials and the Dow Jones 20 transportations.

The components of the Dow Jones Utilities Average are:
American Electric Power Company
Centerior Energy
Columbia Gas System
Commonwealth Edison Company
Consolidated Edison Company
Consolidated Natural Gas Company
Detroit Edison Company
Houston Industries
Niagra Mohawk Power Company
Pacific Gas & Electric Company
Panhandle Eastern Company
Peoples Energy Corporation
Philadelphia Electric Company
Public Service Enterprise Group Incorporated
Southern California Edison Company

Year	High	Low	Close
1929	144.61	64.72	88.27
1930	108.62	55.14	60.80
1931	73.40	30.55	31.41
1932	36.11	16.53	27.50
1933	37.73	19.33	23.29
1934	31.03	16.83	17.80

Year	High	Low	Close
1935	29.78	14.46	29.55
1936	36.08	28.63	34.83
1937	37.54	19.65	20.35
1938	25.19	15.14	23.02
1939	27.10	20.71	25.58
1940	26.45	18.03	19.85
1941	20.65	13.51	14.02
1942	14.94	10.58	14.54
1943	22.30	14.69	21.87
1944	26.37	21.74	26.37
1945	39.15	26.15	38.13
1946	43.74	33.20	37.27
1947	37.55	32.28	33.40
1948	36.04	31.65	33.55
1949	41.31	33.36	41.29
1950	44.26	37.40	40.98
1951	47.22	41.47	47.22
1952	52.64	47.53	52.60
1953	53.88	47.87	52.04
1954	62.47	52.22	62.47
1955	66.68	61.39	64.16
1956	71.17	63.03	68.54
1957	74.61	62.10	68.58
1958	91.00	68.94	91.00
1959	94.70	85.05	87.83
1960	100.07	85.02	100.02
1961	135.90	99.75	129.16
1962	130.85	103.11	129.23
1963	144.37	129.19	138.99
1964	155.71	137.30	155.17
1965	163.32	149.84	152.63
1966	152.39	118.96	136.18
1967	140.43	120.97	127.91
1968	141.30	119.79	137.17
1969	139.95	106.31	110.08
1970	121.84	95.86	121.84
1971	128.39	108.03	117.75
1972	124.14	105.06	119.50
1973	120.72	84.42	89.37
1974	95.09	57.93	68.76
1975	87.07	72.02	83.65
1976	108.38	84.52	108.38
1977	118.67	104.97	111.28
1978	110.98	96.35	98.24
1979	109.74	98.24	106.60
1980	117.34	96.04	114.42
1981	117.81	101.28	109.02

Year	High	Low	Close
1982	122.83	103.22	119.46
1983	140.70	119.51	131.84
1984	149.93	122.25	149.52
1985	174.96	146.54	174.81
1986	219.15	169.47	206.01
1987	227.83	160.98	175.08
1988	190.02	167.08	186.28
1989	235.98	181.84	235.04

DOW JONES 65 COMPOSITE STOCK AVERAGE

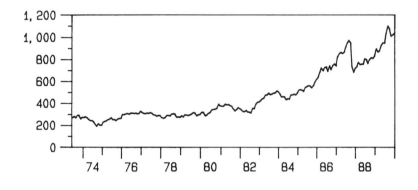

Source: Dow Jones and Company, Interactive Data Corporation

This graph shows the movement of the Dow Jones 65 Composite Stock Average. This average is made up of the 30 stocks in the Dow Jones Industrial Average, the 20 stocks in the Dow Jones Transportation Average and the 15 stocks in the Dow Jones Utility Average. The average therefore is significant because it combines the three blue chip averages and thus gives a good indication of the overall direction of the largest, most established companies.

Year	High	Low	Close
1939	53.0	40.4	50.6
1940	51.7	37.2	44.0
1941	44.9	35.5	39.4
1942	39.6	31.5	39.6
1943	50.9	39.8	47.1
1944	56.6	47.0	56.6
1945	73.5	55.9	73.5
1946	79.4	58.5	65.4
1947	67.1	57.3	65.1

Year	High	Low	Close
1948	71.9	59.9	64.7
1949	71.9	57.8	71.9
1950	87.2	70.3	87.2
1951	100.0	86.9	97.4
1952	113.6	96.1	113.6
1953	114.0	98.2	108.0
1954	150.2	106.0	150.2
1955	174.2	137.8	174.2
1956	184.1	164.3	174.2
1957	179.9	142.8	149.4
1958	202.4	147.4	202.4
1959	233.5	200.1	219.5
1960	222.6	190.4	206.1
1961	251.4	204.8	249.6
1962	245.8	187.4	228.9
1963	269.1	228.7	269.1
1964	314.2	269.1	307.5
1965	340.9	290.4	340.9
1966	352.4	261.3	290.3
1967	337.3	282.7	314.1
1968	353.1	290.1	352.7
1969	346.2	253.0	268.3
1970	273.2	208.7	273.2
1971	318.4	270.2	310.1
1972	338.5	302.1	338.5
1973	334.1	247.7	272.5
1974	282.5	184.2	199.7
1975	268.2	205.3	261.7
1976	325.5	264.5	325.5
1977	324.9	274.3	287.2
1978	315.3	260.7	272.2
1979	315.1	274.3	298.3
1980	388.9	271.7	373.4
1981	394.6	320.6	347.8
1982	416.3	299.4	409.2
1983	515.1	401.0	502.9
1984	514.0	421.4	489.9
1985	619.4	480.9	616.5
1986	767.9	602.8	736.8
1987	992.2	653.7	714.2
1988	830.2	700.7	825.9
1989	1115.1	816.9	1035.1

GOLD (London Morning Fix Price)

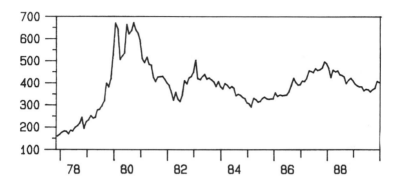

Source: Interactive Data Corporation

This graph shows the movement of the per troy ounce gold price, according to the month-end morning fixings in London. Twice each business day (at 10:30 a.m. and 3:30 p.m.), five major metals dealers meet in London to fix a benchmark price for gold, after assessing supply and demand at that time. Gold has traditionally been considered a store of value against both the erosion through inflation of a currency's purchasing power and political instability or turmoil. From the 1930s until the early 70s, gold was fixed at $35 an ounce in the United States. When trading in the metal resumed, gold at first rose to about $200 an ounce, then fell to about $100, then rose again modestly in the mid-1970's. In the late 1970s and early 80s, with inflation driven by rising oil prices, compounded by Middle East tensions, the gold price soared. It then dropped precipitously and after a period of relative stability in the mid-1980s began falling as a reflection of disinflation.

Year	High	Low	Close
1977	168.15	156.65	165.60
1978	243.65	165.60	224.50
1979	524.00	216.50	524.00
1980	843.00	474.00	589.50
1981	599.25	391.75	400.00
1982	488.50	297.00	448.00
1983	511.50	374.75	381.50
1984	406.85	303.25	309.00
1985	339.30	285.00	327.00
1986	442.75	326.00	390.90
1987	502.75	390.90	486.50
1988	486.50	389.05	410.15
1989	417.15	358.10	401.00

NASDAQ NATIONAL MARKET SYSTEM COMPOSITE INDEX

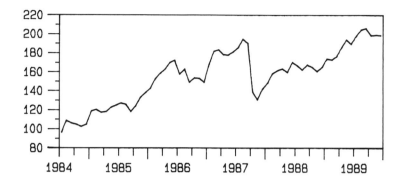

Source: National Association of Securities Dealers, Interactive Data Corporation

This graph shows the movement of the National Association of Securities Dealers Automated Quotations (NASDAQ) National Market System Composite Index. This market-value weighted index is composed of all the stocks traded on the National Market System of the over-the-counter market, which is supervised by the National Association of Securities Dealers. The companies in this index are smaller growth companies, many of them in high technology and financial services. The direction of the index is used by analysts to gauge investor interest in more speculative stocks. In times of enthusiasm for small stocks, this index will rise dramatically, and it will fall just as much when investors opt for safety instead of risk.

Year	High	Low	Close
1973	136.84	88.67	92.19
1974	96.53	54.87	59.82
1975	88.00	60.70	77.62
1976	97.88	78.06	97.88
1977	105.05	93.66	105.05
1978	139.25	99.09	117.98
1979	152.29	117.84	151.14
1980	208.15	124.09	202.34
1981	223.47	175.03	195.84
1982	240.70	159.14	232.41
1983	328.91	230.59	278.60
1984	278.90	225.30	247.35
1985	307.76	245.91	324.93
1986	411.16	323.01	348.83
1987	455.26	291.88	330.47
1988	396.11	331.97	381.38
1989	485.73	378.56	454.82

NEW YORK STOCK EXCHANGE COMPOSITE INDEX

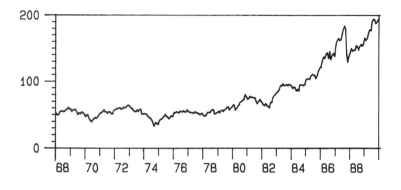

Source: New York Stock Exchange, Interactive Data Corporation

This graph shows the movement of the New York Stock Exchange Composite Index. This market-value weighted index is composed of four subindexes—the NYSE Industrial, Transportation, Utilities, and Finance indexes. As such, the Composite Index provides a broader measure of the performance of the New York Stock Exchange than the more widely quoted Dow Jones Industrial Average. Some newspapers, such as the New York Times, provide a graph of the NYSE Composite on a daily basis. Stock index futures and options are traded on the NYSE Composite on the New York Futures Exchange.

Year	High	Low	Close
1968	61.27	48.70	58.90
1969	59.32	49.31	51.53
1970	52.36	37.69	50.23
1971	57.76	49.60	56.43
1972	65.14	56.23	64.48
1973	65.48	49.05	51.82
1974	53.37	32.89	36.13
1975	51.24	37.06	47.64
1976	57.88	48.04	57.88
1977	57.69	49.78	52.50
1978	60.38	48.37	53.62
1979	63.39	53.88	61.95
1980	81.02	55.30	77.86
1981	79.14	64.96	71.41
1982	82.35	58.80	81.03
1983	99.63	79.79	95.18
1984	98.12	85.13	96.38
1985	121.90	94.60	121.58

Year	High	Low	Close
1986	145.75	117.75	138.58
1987	187.99	125.91	138.23
1988	159.42	136.72	156.26
1989	199.34	154.98	195.04

STANDARD & POOR'S 40 STOCK FINANCIAL INDEX

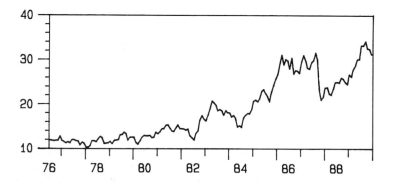

Source: Standard & Poor's Corporation, Interactive Data Corporation

This graph shows the movement of the Standard & Poor's Financial Index. This market-value weighted index is composed of 40 large financial institutions such as banks and insurance companies. As such, the stocks in the index tend to move inversely with interest rates. The S&P Financial Index is combined with the S&P 400 Industrials, 20 Transportations and 40 Utilities to form the Standard and Poor's 500, one of the main benchmarks of performance of the stock market.

Year	High	Low	Close
1976	12.79	11.25	12.79
1977	12.67	10.57	11.15
1978	13.18	10.14	11.22
1979	13.90	11.05	12.57
1980	13.76	10.39	13.70
1981	16.56	13.15	14.47
1982	18.05	11.55	16.58
1983	20.99	15.77	18.13
1984	18.88	14.09	18.80
1985	25.87	18.37	25.72
1986	31.13	25.19	26.92
1987	32.56	20.39	21.63
1988	24.63	24.46	24.49
1989	35.24	24.30	31.30

STANDARD AND POOR'S 500 STOCK INDEX

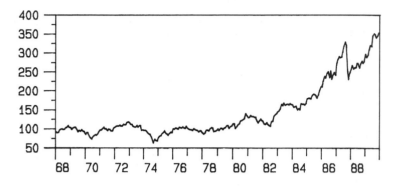

Source: Standard and Poor's Corporation, Interactive Data Corporation

This graph shows the movement of Standard & Poor's 500 Stock Index. This market-value weighted index is composed of the S&P 400 Industrials, the S&P 20 Transportations, the S&P 40 Financials and the S&P 40 Utilities. Most of the stocks in the S&P 500 are found on the New York Stock Exchange, though there are a few from the American Stock Exchange and the over-the-counter market. The index represents about 80 percent of the market value of all the issues traded on the NYSE. The S&P is commonly considered the benchmark against which the performance of individual stocks or stock groups is measured. It is a far broader measure of market activity than the Dow Jones Industrial Average, even though the DJIA is quoted more widely. There are mutual funds, called index funds, which aim to mirror the performance of the S&P 500. Such funds appeal to investors who wish to match the general performance of the stock market. Stock index futures and options are also traded on the S&P 500 and its smaller version, the S&P 100, on the Chicago Mercantile Exchange and the Chicago Board Options Exchange.

Year	High	Low	Close
1930	25.92	14.44	15.34
1931	18.17	7.72	8.12
1932	9.31	4.40	6.89
1933	12.20	5.53	10.10
1934	11.82	8.36	9.50
1935	13.46	8.06	13.43
1936	17.69	13.40	17.18
1937	18.68	10.17	10.55
1938	13.79	8.50	13.21
1939	13.23	10.18	12.49
1940	12.77	8.99	10.58
1941	10.86	8.37	8.69
1942	9.77	7.47	9.77

Year	High	Low	Close
1943	12.64	9.84	11.67
1944	13.29	11.56	13.28
1945	17.68	13.21	17.36
1946	19.25	14.12	15.30
1947	16.20	13.71	15.30
1948	17.06	13.84	15.20
1949	16.79	13.55	16.76
1950	20.43	16.65	20.41
1951	23.85	20.69	23.77
1952	26.59	23.09	26.57
1953	26.66	22.71	24.81
1954	35.98	24.80	35.98
1955	46.41	34.58	45.48
1956	49.74	43.11	46.67
1957	49.13	38.98	39.99
1958	55.21	40.33	55.21
1959	60.71	53.58	59.89
1960	60.39	52.30	58.11
1961	72.64	57.57	71.55
1962	71.13	52.32	63.10
1963	75.02	62.69	75.02
1964	86.28	75.43	84.75
1965	92.63	81.60	92.43
1966	94.06	73.20	80.33
1967	97.59	80.38	96.47
1968	108.37	87.72	103.86
1969	106.16	89.20	92.06
1970	93.46	69.29	92.15
1971	104.77	90.16	102.09
1972	119.12	101.67	118.05
1973	120.24	92.16	97.55
1974	99.80	62.28	68.56
1975	95.61	70.04	90.19
1976	107.83	90.90	107.46
1977	107.97	90.71	95.10
1978	106.99	86.90	96.11
1979	111.27	96.13	107.94
1980	140.52	98.22	135.76
1981	138.12	112.77	122.55
1982	143.02	102.42	140.64
1983	172.65	138.34	164.93
1984	170.41	147.82	167.24
1985	212.02	163.68	211.28
1986	254.00	203.49	242.17
1987	336.77	223.92	247.08
1988	283.66	276.83	277.72
1989	359.80	275.31	353.40

STANDARD & POOR'S 400 INDUSTRIAL STOCK INDEX

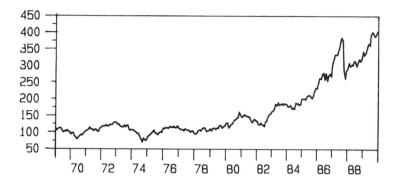

Source: Standard and Poor's Corporation, Interactive Data Corporation

This graph shows the movement of Standard & Poor's 400 Industrial Stock Index, commonly known as the S&P 400. This market-value weighted index is made up of 400 large, established industrial companies, most of which are traded on the New York Stock Exchange. The stocks in the Dow Jones Industrial Average are also included in the S&P 400, but the S&P index provides a much broader picture of the performance of industrial stocks. Standard and Poor's 500 index is comprised of the S&P 400 plus the S&P 40 Utilities, 20 Transportations and 40 Financials Indexes.

Year	High	Low	Close
1930	20.32	11.33	11.90
1931	14.07	6.02	6.32
1932	7.26	3.52	5.18
1933	10.25	4.24	9.26
1934	10.54	7.63	9.12
1935	12.84	7.90	12.77
1936	17.02	12.67	16.50
1937	18.10	9.73	10.26
1938	13.66	8.39	13.07
1939	13.08	9.92	12.17
1940	12.42	8.70	10.37
1941	10.62	8.47	8.78
1942	9.94	7.54	9.93
1943	12.58	10.00	11.61
1944	13.18	11.43	13.05
1945	17.06	12.97	16.79
1946	18.53	13.64	14.75
1947	15.83	13.40	15.18
1948	16.93	13.58	15.12
1949	16.52	13.23	16.49

Year	High	Low	Close
1950	20.60	16.34	20.57
1951	24.33	20.85	24.24
1952	26.92	23.30	26.89
1953	26.99	22.70	24.87
1954	37.24	24.84	37.24
1955	49.54	35.66	48.44
1956	53.28	45.71	50.08
1957	53.25	41.98	42.86
1958	58.97	43.20	58.97
1959	65.32	57.02	64.50
1960	65.02	55.34	61.49
1961	76.69	60.87	75.72
1962	75.22	54.80	66.00
1963	79.25	65.48	79.25
1964	91.29	79.74	89.62
1965	98.55	86.43	98.47
1966	100.60	77.89	85.24
1967	106.15	85.31	105.11
1968	118.03	95.05	113.02
1969	116.24	97.75	101.49
1970	102.87	75.58	100.90
1971	115.84	99.36	112.72
1972	132.95	112.19	131.87
1973	134.54	103.37	109.14
1974	111.65	69.53	76.47
1975	107.40	77.71	100.88
1976	120.89	101.64	119.46
1977	118.92	99.88	104.71
1978	118.71	95.52	107.21
1979	124.99	107.08	121.02
1980	160.96	111.09	154.45
1981	157.02	125.93	137.12
1982	159.66	114.08	157.62
1983	194.84	154.95	186.24
1984	191.48	167.75	186.36
1985	235.75	182.24	234.56
1986	282.77	224.88	269.93
1987	393.17	255.43	285.86
1988	326.84	320.18	321.26
1989	410.49	318.66	403.49

STANDARD AND POOR'S 20 TRANSPORTATION
STOCK INDEX

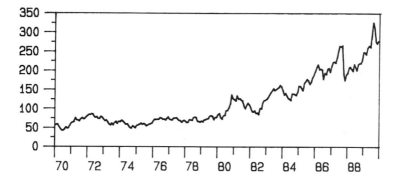

Source: Standard and Poor's Corporation, Interactive Data Corporation

This graph shows the movement of the Standard & Poor's 20 Transportation Stock Index. This market-value weighted index is made up of 20 large transportation companies in the airline, trucking and railroad businesses. It is combined with the S&P 400 Industrials, S&P 40 Utilities and S&P 40 Financials to make up the Standard & Poor's 500 Index.

Year	High	Low	Close
1930	46.34	28.27	30.20
1931	34.75	10.08	10.57
1932	13.02	4.32	8.72
1933	18.97	7.69	13.89
1934	17.77	11.15	12.25
1935	14.81	9.36	14.32
1936	20.95	14.40	18.90
1937	22.07	9.76	9.89
1938	11.23	6.58	11.23
1939	12.04	7.80	10.47
1940	10.78	7.25	9.47
1941	10.22	7.77	8.21
1942	10.12	7.75	9.43
1943	13.34	9.52	11.65
1944	15.85	11.57	15.85
1945	21.33	15.45	20.83
1946	22.74	13.86	15.61
1947	16.46	11.95	14.46
1948	17.26	13.34	13.92
1949	14.49	11.24	13.86

Year	High	Low	Close
1950	19.39	13.34	19.34
1951	21.93	17.59	20.08
1952	25.41	20.16	24.90
1953	25.13	19.79	20.33
1954	30.48	20.42	30.38
1955	35.78	28.54	34.17
1956	37.57	30.45	31.36
1957	32.48	20.82	20.95
1958	34.39	21.57	34.39
1959	38.03	31.98	33.82
1960	34.92	27.17	29.55
1961	35.30	29.64	33.25
1962	34.48	26.81	32.73
1963	40.70	32.88	40.65
1964	49.87	40.54	45.82
1965	51.56	41.06	51.28
1966	56.32	37.91	41.04
1967	51.46	41.35	43.71
1968	56.08	40.82	54.15
1969	56.96	35.26	37.16
1970	38.94	24.65	35.40
1971	48.32	35.03	44.61
1972	48.31	40.40	44.26
1973	45.80	32.50	45.80
1974	47.36	29.38	35.59
1975	40.18	34.02	38.12
1976	78.11	67.57	78.11
1977	78.72	63.29	69.50
1978	82.48	63.14	65.12
1979	84.11	65.33	76.73
1980	136.71	70.72	126.22
1981	135.29	96.13	110.44
1982	126.93	81.77	123.12
1983	164.97	119.45	158.81
1984	161.46	117.21	143.91
1985	192.35	141.56	188.72
1986	217.28	176.16	197.27
1987	274.20	167.59	190.17
1988	229.61	228.10	228.17
1989	331.07	226.42	278.48

STANDARD & POOR'S 40 UTILITIES STOCK INDEX

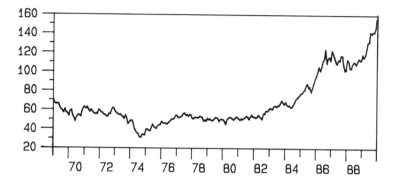

Source: Standard and Poor's Corporation, Interactive Data Corporation

This graph shows the movement of Standard & Poor's 40 Utilities Stock Index. This market-value weighted index is made up of 40 large and geographically representative electric and gas utilities. It is combined with the S&P 400 Industrials, S&P 20 Transportations, and S&P 40 Financials to make up Standard & Poor's 500 Index.

Year	High	Low	Close
1930	67.83	35.33	38.75
1931	49.17	22.38	23.66
1932	26.77	12.49	21.97
1933	27.41	14.73	16.21
1934	21.78	11.35	12.13
1935	20.46	9.52	20.25
1936	24.61	19.36	23.46
1937	25.26	13.47	13.96
1938	17.04	10.90	15.97
1939	17.77	14.23	16.81
1940	17.36	12.65	13.08
1941	13.48	7.77	8.21
1942	8.88	6.65	8.69
1943	12.72	8.79	12.07
1944	13.72	11.98	13.51
1945	20.61	13.63	19.96
1946	23.54	16.95	19.58
1947	19.83	15.89	16.28
1948	18.01	15.56	16.04
1949	19.94	15.90	19.93
1950	21.45	18.35	19.42

Year	High	Low	Close
1951	21.72	19.61	21.72
1952	24.55	21.73	24.55
1953	25.30	22.25	25.10
1954	29.82	25.16	29.82
1955	32.87	29.53	31.70
1956	33.93	31.15	31.76
1957	34.29	28.96	32.14
1958	43.28	32.32	43.28
1959	45.45	41.87	44.74
1960	51.76	43.74	51.76
1961	67.97	51.42	64.83
1962	65.11	50.21	61.09
1963	67.99	61.26	66.42
1964	74.97	66.36	74.52
1965	78.20	72.03	75.51
1966	75.37	59.03	69.35
1967	72.59	62.21	66.08
1968	72.30	61.06	69.69
1969	70.74	54.33	56.09
1970	61.71	47.67	61.71
1971	64.81	54.48	59.83
1972	62.99	52.02	61.05
1973	61.57	43.51	46.91
1974	49.44	29.37	33.54
1975	45.61	35.31	44.45
1976	54.24	44.70	54.24
1977	57.56	51.60	54.73
1978	54.47	48.23	48.47
1979	52.85	47.14	50.24
1980	53.97	43.29	52.45
1981	55.75	48.96	52.98
1982	61.69	50.31	60.45
1983	70.30	60.22	66.17
1984	76.47	62.90	75.89
1985	93.26	74.70	93.17
1986	123.74	90.33	112.29
1987	124.04	91.80	102.12
1988	112.94	112.21	112.64
1989	155.29	111.15	156.04

TORONTO 300 COMPOSITE STOCK INDEX

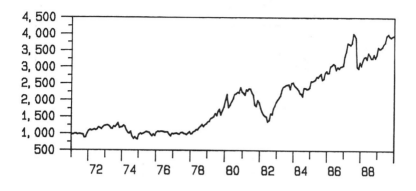

Source: Toronto Stock Exchange, Interactive Data Corporation

This graph shows the movement of the Toronto 300 Composite Stock Index. This is the major index for Canadian stocks, since most of the stock market trading in Canada takes place in Toronto. The index is composed of the Industrial, Transportation, Utilities and Financial Indexes maintained by the Toronto Stock Exchange. Stock index futures are traded on the Composite 300 on the Toronto Futures Exchange.

Year	High	Low	Close
1971	1036.09	879.80	990.54
1972	1226.58	990.54	1226.58
1973	1319.26	1122.34	1187.78
1974	1276.81	821.10	835.42
1975	1081.96	862.74	942.94
1976	1100.55	931.17	1011.52
1977	1067.35	961.04	1059.59
1978	1332.71	998.19	1309.99
1979	1813.17	1315.82	1813.17
1980	2402.23	1702.51	2268.70
1981	2390.50	1812.48	1954.24
1982	1958.08	1346.35	1958.08
1983	2598.26	1949.81	2552.35
1984	2585.73	2079.69	2400.33
1985	2900.60	2348.55	2900.60
1986	3129.20	2754.06	3066.18
1987	4112.89	2837.90	3160.10
1988	3465.40	2978.00	3390.00
1989	3985.11	3350.50	3969.79

TREASURY BILL (3 MONTH) YIELDS

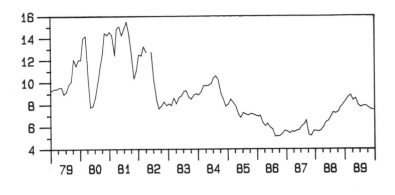

Source: Federal Reserve Bulletin, Interactive Data Corporation

This graph shows the movement of the yields of 3-month U.S. Treasury bills. These yields are considered the most important yardsticks of short-term interest rates, and they are therefore watched closely by credit market analysts for signs that rates might be rising or falling. Many floating-rate loans and variable-rate mortgages are tied to the Treasury bill rate. The minimum purchase amount of a Treasury bill is $10,000. Auctions for Treasury bills are held weekly. Individual investors who do not submit a competitive bid are sold bills at the average price of the winning competitive bids. Treasury bills are the primary instrument used by the Federal Reserve in its regulation of the money supply through open market operations. Futures are traded on Treasury bills on the International Monetary Market and the MidAmerica Commodity Exchange. Futures options on T-bills are traded on the Chicago Mercantile Exchange, and the interest rate options on T-bills are traded on the American Stock Exchange.

Year	Average Rates	Year	Average Rates
1965	4.37%	1978	9.08%
1966	4.96%	1979	12.04%
1967	4.96%	1980	15.49%
1968	5.94%	1981	10.85%
1969	7.81%	1982	7.94%
1970	4.87%	1983	9.00%
1971	4.01%	1984	8.06%
1972	5.07%	1985	7.10%
1973	7.45%	1986	
1974	7.15%	1987	
1975	5.44%	1988	
1976	4.35%	1989	
1977	6.07%		

TREASURY BOND (20 YEAR) YIELDS

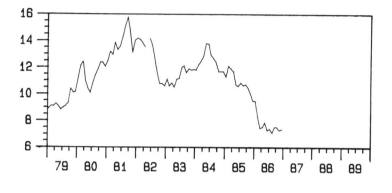

Source: Federal Reserve Bulletin, Interactive Data Corporation

This graph shows the movement of the yields of 20-year Treasury bonds. Treasury-bond yields are considered the most important yardsticks of long-term interest rates, and they are therefore watched closely by credit market analysts for signs that rates might be rising or falling. The minimum denomination of a Treasury bond is $1000 and maturities range from 10 to 30 years, with the 20-year T-bond representing a large percentage of the bonds traded. Futures are traded on Treasury bonds on the Chicago Board of Trade and the MidAmerica Commodity Exchange. Futures options on T-bonds are traded on the Chicago Board of Trade, and interest rate options on T-bonds are traded on the Chicago Board Options Exchange.

Year	Average Rates	Year	Average Rates
1965	4.50%	1978	8.90%
1966	4.76%	1979	10.18%
1967	5.59%	1980	12.49%
1968	5.88%	1981	13.73%
1969	6.97%	1982	10.62%
1970	6.28%	1983	12.02%
1971	6.00%	1984	11.64%
1972	5.96%	1985	9.75%
1973	7.29%	1986	
1974	7.91%	1987	
1975	8.23%	1988	
1976	7.30%	1989	
1977	7.87%		

VALUE LINE COMPOSITE INDEX

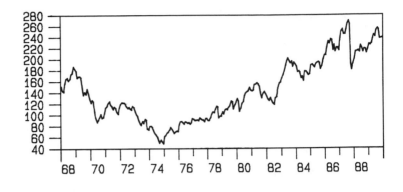

Source: Value Line, Inc., Interactive Data Corporation

This graph shows the movement of the Value Line Composite Index. This equally weighted geometric average is composed of the approximately 1700 stocks traded on the New York Stock Exchange, American Stock Exchange, and over-the-counter that are tracked by the Value Line Investment Survey. This index is particularly broad in scope, since Value Line covers both large industrial companies as well as smaller growth firms. Futures are traded on the Value Line Composite Index on the Kansas City Board of Trade, and index options are traded on the index on the Philadelphia Stock Exchange.

Year	High	Low	Close
1968	188.64	138.92	183.18
1969	183.67	127.40	130.56
1970	135.46	84.23	103.60
1971	125.76	97.36	112.94
1972	125.98	107.11	114.05
1973	116.20	70.50	73.61
1974	83.41	47.03	48.97
1975	80.88	51.12	70.69
1976	93.47	71.62	93.47
1977	96.34	86.53	93.92
1978	119.77	88.67	97.97
1979	125.25	98.88	121.91
1980	149.76	100.60	144.20
1981	159.03	125.66	137.81
1982	161.37	112.32	158.94
1983	208.51	156.70	194.35
1984	200.32	162.46	177.98
1985	214.86	176.61	214.86

Year	High	Low	Close
1986	246.80	210.84	225.62
1987	289.36	180.14	201.62
1988	241.35	200.70	232.68
1989	278.98	231.46	258.78

WILSHIRE 5000 EQUITY INDEX

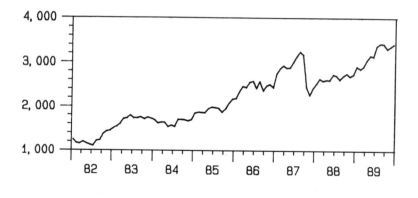

Source: Wilshire Associates, Interactive Data Corporation

This graph shows the movement of the Wilshire 5000 Equity Index. This market-value weighted index of 5000 stocks is the broadest of all the indexes and averages, and represents the value, in billions of dollars, of all New York Stock Exchange, American Stock Exchange and over-the-counter stocks for which quotes are available. The index is used as a measure of how all stocks are doing as a group, as opposed to a particular segment of the market.

Year	High	Low	Close
1971	955.26	871.15	949.26
1972	1090.31	976.73	1090.31
1973	1059.76	854.60	861.73
1974	863.57	550.04	590.34
1975	840.17	675.54	784.15
1976	954.18	879.52	954.18
1977	919.19	851.60	887.59
1978	1004.15	822.27	922.77
1979	1101.82	935.84	1100.71
1980	1466.64	1026.03	1404.60
1981	1415.04	1208.47	1286.24

Year	High	Low	Close
1982	1451.59	1099.70	1451.59
1983	1791.70	1508.98	1723.63
1984	1702.11	1536.91	1702.01
1985	2164.69	1845.24	2164.69
1986	2598.03	2109.61	2434.95
1987	3299.44	2188.11	2434.95
1988	2794.44	2398.01	2738.42
1989	3523.47	2718.59	3419.88

CONSUMER PRICE INDEX

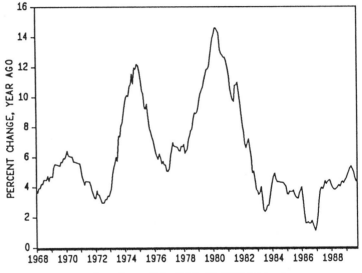

Source: Bureau of Labor Statistics, The WEFA Group

This graph shows the movement of the Consumer Price Index. The line represents the rolling 12-month average of changes in consumer prices—a method which best shows the ups and downs of the inflation rate. Each month, the U.S. Bureau of Labor Statistics shops a fixed market basket of goods and services available to an average urban wage earner. The market basket of goods is updated every few years. The major groups included in the CPI are food, shelter, fuel oil and coal, gas and electricity, apparel, private transportation, public transportation, medical care, entertainment, services and commodities. The CPI is important because many pension and employment contracts are tied to changes in it. The inflationary spike of the 1970s did much damage to the world economy and had profound consequences, including the strongly anti-inflationary monetary policies in the middle 1980s. Futures on the Consumer Price Index are traded on the Coffee, Sugar and Cocoa Exchange.

Year	Annual Change in CPI	Year	Annual Change in CPI
1967	2.9%	1979	11.3%
1968	4.2%	1980	13.5%
1969	5.4%	1981	10.4%
1970	5.9%	1982	6.1%
1971	4.3%	1983	3.2%
1972	3.3%	1984	4.3%
1973	6.2%	1985	3.6%
1974	11%	1986	1.9%
1975	9.1%	1987	3.7%
1976	5.8%	1988	4.1%
1977	6.5%	1989	4.6%
1978	7.7%		

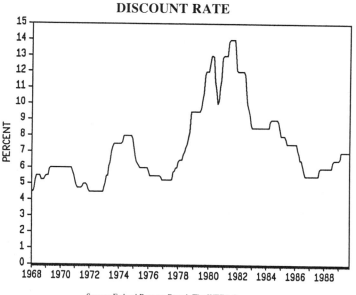

DISCOUNT RATE

Source: Federal Reserve Board, The WEFA Group

This graph shows the movement of the discount rate, which is the rate the Federal Reserve charges its member banks for loans from the discount window. Credit market analysts watch the Fed's discount rate moves very carefully, since changes in the rate are a major indication of whether the Fed wants to ease or tighten the money supply. When the Fed wants to ease the money supply to stimulate the economy, it cuts the discount rate. When the Fed wants to tighten the money supply to slow the economy and thereby to try to lower the inflation rate, it raises the discount rate. The discount rate acts as a floor on interest rates, since banks set their loan rates, such as the prime rate, a notch above the disount rate.

Year	High	Low	Close
1914	6%	5%	6%
1915	5%	4%	4%
1916	4%	3%	3%
1917	3.50%	3%	3%
1918	3.50%	4%	4%
1919	4.75%	4%	4.75%
1920	7%	4.75%	7%
1921	7%	4.50%	4.50%
1922	4.50%	4%	4%
1923	4.50%	4%	4.50%
1924	4.50%	3%	3%
1925	3.50%	3%	3.50%
1926	4%	3.50%	4%
1927	4%	3.50%	4%
1928	5%	3.50%	5%
1929	6%	4.50%	4.50%
1930	4.50%	2%	2%
1931	3.50%	1.50%	3.50%
1932	3.50%	2.50%	2.50%
1933	3.50%	2%	2%
1934	2%	1.50%	1.50%
1935	1.50%	1.50%	1.50%
1936	1.50%	1.50%	1.50%
1937	1.50%	1%	1%
1938	1%	1%	1%
1939	1%	1%	1%
1940	1%	1%	1%
1941	1%	1%	1%
1942	1%	50%	50%
1943	1%	50%	50%
1944	1%	50%	50%
1945	1%	50%	50%
1946	1%	50%	50%
1947	1%	1%	1%
1948	1.50%	1%	1.50%
1949	1.50%	1.50%	1.50%
1950	1.75%	1.50%	1.75%
1951	1.75%	1.75%	1.75%
1952	1.75%	1.75%	1.75%
1953	2%	1.75%	2%
1954	2%	1.50%	2%
1955	2.50%	1.50%	2.50%
1956	3%	2.50%	3%
1957	3.50%	3%	3%
1958	3%	1.75%	3%
1959	4%	2.50%	4%

Year	High	Low	Close
1960	4%	3%	3%
1961	3%	3%	3%
1962	3%	3%	3%
1963	3.50%	3%	3.50%
1964	4%	3.50%	4%
1965	4.50%	4%	4.50%
1966	4.50%	4.50%	4.50%
1967	4.50%	4%	4.50%
1968	5.50%	4.50%	5.50%
1969	6%	5.5%	6%
1970	6%	5.5%	5.5%
1971	5%	4.5%	4.5%
1972	4.5%	4.5%	4.5%
1973	7.5%	4.5%	7.5%
1974	8%	7.75%	7.75%
1975	7.75%	6%	6%
1976	6%	5.25%	5.25%
1977	6%	5.25%	6%
1978	9.5%	6%	9.5%
1979	12%	9.5%	12%
1980	10%	13%	13%
1981	14%	12%	12%
1982	12%	8.5%	8.5%
1983	8.5%	8.5%	8.5%
1984	9%	8%	8%
1985	8%	7.5%	7.5%
1986	7.5%	5.5%	5.5%
1987	7%	5.5%	6%
1988	6.5%	6%	6.5%
1989	7%	6.5%	7%

FEDERAL FUNDS RATE

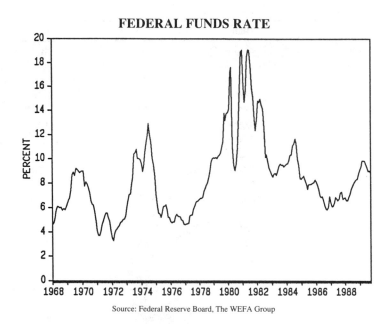

Source: Federal Reserve Board, The WEFA Group

This graph shows the movement of the federal funds rate, which is the rate at which banks with excess reserves lend to banks needing overnight loans to meet reserve requirements. The fed funds rate is the most sensitive of all short-term interest rates, and therefore it is carefully watched by credit market analysts as a precursor of moves in other interest rates. For instance, when the fed funds rate consistently stays below the discount rate, analysts often anticipate that the Federal Reserve will cut the discount rate.

Year	High	Low	Close
1968	6.12%	4.6%	6.02%
1969	9.19%	6.3%	8.97%
1970	8.98%	4.9%	4.9%
1971	5.57%	3.71%	4.14%
1972	5.33%	3.29%	5.33%
1973	10.78%	5.94%	9.95%
1974	12.92%	8.53%	8.53%
1975	7.13%	5.20%	5.20%
1976	5.48%	4.65%	4.65%
1977	6.56%	4.61%	7.75%
1978	10.03%	6.70%	10.03%
1979	13.78%	10.01%	13.78%
1980	18.90%	9.03%	18.90%
1981	19.08%	12.37%	12.37%
1982	14.94%	8.95%	8.95%
1983	9.56%	8.51%	9.47%
1984	11.64%	8.38%	8.38%
1985	8.58%	7.53%	8.27%

Year	High	Low	Close
1986	8.14%	5.85%	6.91%
1987	7.29%	6.10%	6.77%
1988	8.76%	6.58%	8.76%
1989	9.95%	8.46%	8.52%

INDEX OF LEADING ECONOMIC INDICATORS

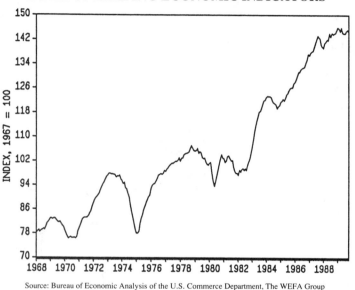

Source: Bureau of Economic Analysis of the U.S. Commerce Department, The WEFA Group

This graph shows the movement of the Index of Leading Economic Indicators. This composite of 12 economic indicators (adjusted for inflation) is designed to forecast whether the economy will gain or lose strength, and is therefore an important tool for economists and others doing business planning. On the whole, it has been an accurate barometer of future economic activity. The 12 components of the Index are: average workweek of production workers; average weekly claims for unemployment insurance; new orders for consumer goods and materials; vendor performance (companies receiving slower deliveries from suppliers); contracts for plant and equipment; new building permits; durable goods order backlog; sensitive materials prices; stock prices; money supply as measured by M-2; and consumer expectations. The index is released monthly.

Year	High	Low	December
1968	111.5	104.4	111.5
1969	112.7	109.1	109.1
1970	107.5	104.4	107.3
1971	118.0	108.6	118.0
1972	131.4	119.2	131.4
1973	134.2	128.7	128.7
1974	128.7	109.2	109.2

Year	High	Low	December
1975	122.8	107.6	122.8
1976	134.5	126.1	134.5
1977	142.4	134.5	142.4
1978	147.9	141.0	147.2
1979	149.3	140.1	140.5
1980	143.4	130.9	143.0
1981	144.6	136.2	136.2
1982	140.9	134.7	140.9
1983	163.4	145.2	163.4
1984	168.2	163.9	164.1
1985	171.5	166.3	171.5
1986	137.2	128.1	137.2
1987	143.3	136.8	139.7
1988	145.1	139.3	145.1
1989	146.0	144.0	144.7

MONEY SUPPLY (M-1)

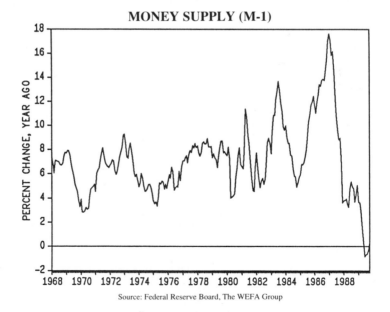

Source: Federal Reserve Board, The WEFA Group

This graph shows the movement of changes in the money supply in the United States, as measured by M-1. The line represents the rolling 12-month change in the money supply. The percentage change is calculated by comparing, for example, the December 1989 figure with the December 1988 figure. This method best shows the ups and downs of the growth of the amount of money circulating in the economy. The rate of change in the money supply is important because it has an important bearing on how quickly or slowly the economy will be growing in the future. Monetarist economists believe changes in the money supply are the key to economic ups and downs. When the Federal Reserve, which strongly influences the money supply through its conduct of open market operations and by setting bank reserve requirements and the discount rate, wants the economy to expand, it eases the money supply. When the Fed is concerned that inflation may be accelerating, it will slow the economy by tightening the money supply. The components of the M-1 measure of the money supply are: currency in circulation; commercial and mutual savings bank demand deposits; NOW and ATS (automatic transfer from savings) accounts; credit union share drafts; and nonbank travelers checks.

Year	High	Low	December
1968	7.93%	3.21%	3.21%
1969	5.25%	2.77%	5.25%
1970	8.19%	4.61%	6.56%
1971	9.19%	5.93%	9.19%
1972	9.42%	5.52%	5.52%
1973	6.05%	4.36%	4.36%
1974	5.57%	3.55%	4.90%
1975	6.60%	4.68%	6.60%
1976	8.33%	6.90%	8.06%
1977	8.89%	7.37%	8.26%
1978	8.54%	7.13%	7.16%
1979	8.37%	4.30%	6.63%
1980	11.08%	4.34%	6.51%
1981	9.04%	4.59%	8.83%
1982	13.79%	7.79%	8.83%
1983	9.70%	4.64%	5.78%
1984	11.57%	5.89%	11.57%
1985	9.55%	7.13%	8.02%
1986	9.55%	5.75%	6.31%
1987	7.62%	5.95%	6.81%
1988	9.22%	6.38%	8.86%
1989	9.95%	8.46%	

PRIME RATE

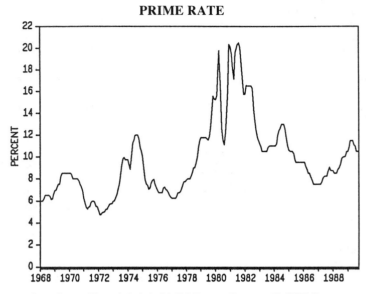

Source: Bureau of Economic Analysis of the U.S. Commerce Department, The WEFA Group

This graph shows the movement of the prime rate, which is the interest rate banks charge their most creditworthy customers. The rate is determined by market forces affecting a bank's cost of funds and the rates borrowers will accept. The prime often moves up or down in concert with the Federal Reserve discount rate. The prime rate tends to become standard across the banking industry when a major bank moves its rate up or down. The rate is a key interest rate, since loans to less creditworthy customers are often tied to the prime.

Year	High	Low	Close
1968	6.75%	6%	6.75%
1969	8.5%	6.75%	8.5%
1970	8.5%	6.75%	6.75%
1971	6.75%	5.25%	5.25%
1972	6%	5%	6%
1973	10%	6%	10%
1974	12%	8.75%	10.5%
1975	10.5%	7%	7%
1976	7.25%	6.25%	6.25%
1977	7.75%	6.5%	7.75%
1978	11.75%	7.75%	11.75%
1979	15.75%	11.5%	15%
1980	21.50%	10.75%	21.50%
1981	20.5%	15.75%	15.75%
1982	17%	11.5%	11.5%
1983	11.5%	10.5%	11%
1984	13%	10.75%	10.75
1985	10.75%	9.5%	9.5%

Year	High	Low	Close
1986	9.5%	7.5%	7.5%
1987	9.25%	7.5%	8.75%
1988	10.5%	8.5%	10.5%
1989	11.5%	10.5%	10.5%

PRODUCER PRICE INDEX

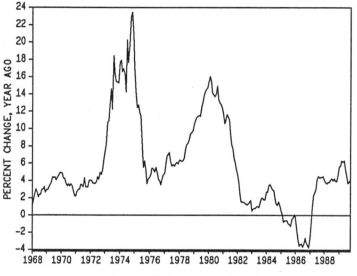

Source: U.S. Bureau of Labor Statistics, The WEFA Group

This graph shows the movement of the Producer Price Index. The line represents the rolling 12-month average of changes in producer prices—a method that best shows the ups and downs of the wholesale inflation rate. Each month, the U.S. Bureau of Labor Statistics measures changes in the prices of all commodities, at all stages of processing, produced for sale in primary markets in the United States. Approximately 3400 commodity prices are collected by the Bureau from sellers. The prices are generally the first significant large-volume commercial transaction for each commodity—either the manufacturer's selling price or the selling price from an organized commodity exchange. The major commodity groups that are represented in the PPI are: farm products; processed food and feed; textiles and apparel; hides, skins and leather; fuels; chemicals; rubber and plastic products; lumber and wood products; pulp and paper products; metals and metal products; machinery and equipment; furniture and household durables; nonmetallic mineral products; and transportation equipment. The PPI is important not only because it is a good gauge of what is happening in the industrial economy but also because it gives an indication of the future trend in consumer prices.

Year	Annual Percent Change	Year	Annual Percent Change
1961	-0.2%	1964	0.4%
1962	0%	1965	3.4%
1963	-0.1%	1966	1.7%

Year	Annual Percent Change	Year	Annual Percent Change
1967	1.0%	1979	12.6%
1968	2.8%	1980	14.1%
1969	4.8%	1981	9.2%
1970	2.2%	1982	2.0%
1971	4.0%	1983	1.3%
1972	6.5%	1984	2.4%
1973	13.1%	1985	-0.6%
1974	18.9%	1986	2.9%
1975	9.2%	1987	2.1%
1976	4.6%	1988	4.0%
1977	6.1%	1989	
1978	7.8%		

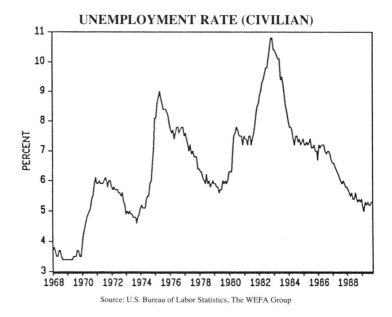

UNEMPLOYMENT RATE (CIVILIAN)

Source: U.S. Bureau of Labor Statistics, The WEFA Group

This graph shows the movement of the unemployment rate. This is the rate of civilians, 16 years of age and older, who were not employed, and who made specific efforts to find a job within the previous four weeks and who were available for work. Persons on layoff from a job or waiting to report to a new job within 30 days are also classified as unemployed. The unemployment rate is a lagging indicator—that is, it rises months after business has already slowed down, and it falls months after business has picked up.

MONTHLY RATE

Year	High	Low	December
1968	3.7%	3.3%	3.3%
1969	3.6%	3.3%	3.4%
1970	5.9%	3.8%	5.9%
1971	5.9%	5.7%	5.9%
1972	5.7%	5.1%	5.1%
1973	4.9%	4.5%	4.8%
1974	7%	5%	7%
1975	8.8%	7.9%	8.1%
1976	7.8%	7.2%	7.6%
1977	7.5%	6.3%	6.3%
1978	6.3%	5.7%	5.9%
1979	5.9%	5.5%	5.9%
1980	7.7%	6.2%	7.1%
1981	8.4%	7.1%	8.4%
1982	10.6%	8.5%	10.6%
1983	10.3%	8.1%	8.1%
1984	7.9%	7.0%	7.1%
1985	7.3%	6.8%	6.8%
1986	7.2%	6.7%	6.7%
1987	6.6%	5.8%	5.8%
1988	5.8%	5.3%	5.3%
1989	5.4%	5.1%	5.4%

6. PUBLICLY TRADED COMPANIES

On the following pages, you will find a comprehensive list of the companies whose common stock is traded on the New York Stock Exchange, the American Stock Exchange, and on the over-the-counter market. The OTC stocks listed here are those in the National Market System of NASDAQ (National Association of Securities Dealers Automated Quotation system). Each of the three markets is listed separately. In addition, there is a listing of the 300 largest capitalization stocks traded on the Toronto Stock Exchange.

Following the overall company lists are two lists of special interest: the first presents companies offering free or reduced-price goods or services to shareholders; the second, foreign companies whose American Depositary Receipts (ADRs) are traded in the United States. Following this, in Section 7, is an alphabetical list of the stock symbols of all the companies on the NYSE, AMEX and OTC markets.

The New York Stock Exchange is the home of almost all the largest, most established public companies, though many smaller growth companies are traded there as well. The NYSE operates with a specialist system of trading, where buyers and sellers are brought together by a specialist on the floor of the Exchange. The specialist steps in to buy or sell shares if there is an imbalance of orders on one side of the market or the other. The requirements the NYSE imposes for being listed on the exchange are the most stringent of all the places where stocks are traded in the United States. Two of the most important requirements are that a corporation must have (1) a minimum aggregate market value of $16 million and (2) annual net income topping $2.5 million before federal income taxes.

The American Stock Exchange is where medium and smaller-sized companies are traded. In addition, many foreign companies are listed on the AMEX. The American Stock Exchange uses the same specialist trading system employed by the New York Stock Exchange. The AMEX's listing requirements are less stringent than of the NYSE, though the exchange requires that a company have a reliably profitable business.

The over-the-counter market is populated for the most part with smaller, emerging growth companies without long histories of earnings and dividends. Of late, many firms that formerly graduated from the OTC market to the AMEX and NYSE as they increased in size have instead been staying on the OTC market. Unlike on the two exchanges, trading on the OTC market is done under a system of competing marketmakers who communicate by telephone and computer terminal. The market is overseen by the National Association of Securities Dealers, an self-regulatory organization. Price quotes that appear in newspapers come from the NASDAQ electronic system. The requirements for being traded over-the-counter are far less stringent than those of the NYSE or AMEX. For the most part, companies whose shares are being publicly traded for the first time, called initial public offerings, begin to trade on the OTC market. The list of companies in this section does not include every company whose stock is traded over the counter. Instead, it features the great majority of the most actively traded companies on NASDAQ. As a group, they are called the

National Market System stocks. There is more price and volume information available on NMS stocks than on other OTC stocks, which tend to be of very small companies.

Each listing includes up to seven elements: the company's name, stock symbol, address, telephone number, line of business, if it has a dividend reinvestment plan and whether options are traded on the stock.

Company Name: We have used each company's full corporate name, though words such as Incorporated, Company and Corporation are abbreviated to become Inc., Co. and Corp. The lists are arranged alphabetically, by company name.

Stock Symbol: The stock symbol—usually three or four capital letters—follows each company's name. When asking a broker to look up the price or other information about a stock, it is usually necessary to provide the stock symbol. The symbol is then entered into a computer terminal, which retrieves data about the company. The stock symbol is not the same abbreviation as one sees in newspaper stock tables, however.

Address: The street address or post office box listed refers to the executive office at the headquarters of the company. In the case of foreign companies, the home address of the company usually is listed, though the address of a contact office in the U.S. may be given.

Telephone Number: The phone number is that of the executive offices at the company's headquarters. If you require further information about the company because you are considering whether to invest in it, you should ask for the investor relations department, which will send annual and quarterly financial reports and other data about the firm.

Line Of Business: This is a brief description of the main business of the company. Some companies specialize in a narrow field—in this case, the description is quite specific to its line of business. Other companies engage in diverse activities, and for them, we have listed the largest segments of their business, or when no business is dominant, we have labeled the company a conglomerate. To find out each company's exact product line, you must call or write the firm's investor relations department.

Dividend Reinvestment Plan: If the letters DRP are in brackets on the final line of an entry for a company, this means that shareholders can use a company plan to reinvest cash dividends into more of the company's stock, instead of receiving a cash payment. Usually, there will be little or no commission cost to the shareholder who participates in a plan. Many companies also allow shareholders to make cash payments in addition to reinvesting dividends to buy more shares, usually at no commission charge.

Some companies offer an extra bonus in their dividend reinvestment plan. Companies on the list with a 5% following the DRP listing offer a 5% discount on the purchase price of newly issued stock for the amount of reinvested dividends. Thus, a shareholder who reinvested $100 of dividends would be credited with purchasing $105 worth of stock. Some companies allow the 5% discount on both dividends reinvested as well as additional cash put up by the shareholder.

Most companies allow shareholders to participate in a dividend reinvestment plan while owning as little as one share. If the dividend is not sufficient to purchase a full share, a shareholder's account is credited with the appropriate fractional share.

The information on dividend reinvestment plans was compiled by Duane Frederic, who publishes a monthly list tracking company plans. A sample copy of this list is available for $10 from Mr. Frederic at 8908 East Pilgrim Drive, Chagrin Falls, Ohio 44022, or by calling (216) 543-9176.

Options: Also on the final line of a company entry is a notation of whether options are traded on the company's stock. This is signified with the letter O. Stock options may be traded on the American Stock Exchange, the Chicago Board Options

Exchange, the Pacific Stock Exchange or the Philadelphia Stock Exchange. Options of larger companies may trade on more than one of these exchanges simultaneously. Stock options can be used by an investor to make a speculative bet on a stock going up or down. Other investors use options to increase their income or hedge the value of their stock holdings.

In today's fast-moving world of finance and investment, a company may merge with another, add or drop a line of business, change its address or telephone number, move from one exchange to another, or even go out of business. Despite such changes, this list will remain an indispensable resource for investors and others in the finance and investment community.

NEW YORK STOCK EXCHANGE

AAR Corporation AIR
1111 Nicholas Boulevard
Elk Grove Village, IL 60007 (312) 439-3939
aerospace components DRP

Abbott Laboratories ABT
Abbott Park
North Chicago, IL 60064 (312) 937-6100
medical supplies DRP O

Abitibi-Price, Inc. ABY
2 First Canadian Place
Toronto, ON Canada M5X 1A9
(416) 369-6700
paper and newsprint

ACM Government Income Fund ACG
1345 Avenue of the Americas
New York, NY 10105 (800) 221-5672
government securities bond fund DRP

ACM Government Opportunity Fund AOF
1345 Avenue of the Americas
New York, NY 10105 (800) 247-4154
government securities bond fund DRP

ACM Government Securities Fund GSF
1345 Avenue of the Americas
New York, NY 10105 (800) 221-5672
government securities bond fund DRP

ACM Government Spectrum Fund SI
1345 Avenue of the Americas
New York, NY 10105 (800) 247-4154
government securities bond fund DRP

ACM Managed Income Fund AMF
1345 Avenue of the Americas
New York, NY 10105 (800) 247-4154
government and junk bond fund DRP

Acme-Cleveland Corp. AMT
30195 Chagrin Boulevard
Cleveland, OH 44124 (216) 292-2100
metalworking and communications equipment
DRP

Acme Electric Corporation ACE
260 North Union Street
Olean, NY 14760 (716) 373-3050
power conversion equipment, transformers

Acuson Corp. ACN
1220 Charleston Road
Mountain View, CA 94039 (415) 969-9112
ultrasound imaging systems O

Adams Express Company ADX
Suite 1140, 7 St. Paul Street
Baltimore, MD 21202 (301) 752-5900
closed-end stock mutual fund DRP

Adobe Resources Corporation ADB
667 Madison Avenue
New York, NY 10021 (212) 758-8110
oil and gas exploration and development

Advanced Micro Devices, Inc. AMD
901 Thompson Place
Sunnyvale, CA 94088 (408) 732-2400
semiconductors O

Advest Group (The), Inc. ADV
One Commercial Plaza
Hartford, CT 06103 (203) 525-1421
brokerage firm DRP

Aetna Life And Casualty Company AET
151 Farmington Avenue
Hartford, CT 06115 (203) 273-0123
insurance DRP 5% O

Affiliated Publications AFP
135 Morrissey Boulevard
Boston, MA 02107 (617) 929-3300
publishing newspapers and magazines O

A.G. Edwards Inc. AGE
1 North Jefferson
St. Louis, MO 63103 (314)289-3000
brokerage firm O

Ahmanson H.F. & Company AHM
660 South Figueroa Street
Los Angeles, CA 90017 (213) 955-4200
savings and loan O

Aileen Inc. AEE
1411 Broadway
New York, NY 10018 (212) 398-9770
apparel, sportswear

Air Products & Chemicals Inc. APD
P. O. Box 538
Allentown, PA 18105 (215) 481-4911
industrial gases/equipment, chemicals DRP O

Airborne Freight Corporation ABF
3101 Western Avenue
Seattle, WA 98111 (206) 285-4600
freight forwarding

Airgas, Inc. ARG
5 Radnor Corporate Center
Radnor, PA 19087 (215) 687-5253
industrial gases, protective equipment

Airlease Ltd., L.P. FLY
2988 Campus Drive
San Mateo, CA 94403 (415) 574-5729
leases commercial aircraft

Alaska Air Group Inc. ALK
19300 Pacific Highway South
Seattle, WA 98168 (206) 433-3200
regional airline O

Albany International Corp. AIN
1373 Broadway
Albany, NY 12204 (518) 445-2200
fabrics for paper industry

Alberto-Culver Company ACV
2525 Armitage Ave
Melrose Park, IL 60160 (312) 450-3000
personal care products

Albertson's Inc. ABS
250 Parkcenter Boulevard
Boise, ID 83726 (208) 385-6200
food stores O

Alcan Aluminum, Ltd AL
1188 Sherbrooke Street West
Montreal Quebec, CDA H3A 2G2
(514) 848-8000
aluminum refining DRP 5% O

Alco Standard Corporation ASN
825 Duportail Road, P.O. Box 834
Valley Forge, PA 19482 (215) 296-8000
paper and office products, foodservices DRP

Alexander & Alexander Services, Inc. AAL
1211 Avenue of the Americas
New York, NY 10036 (212) 840-8500
insurance brokers O

Alexanders Inc. ALX
500 Seventh Avenue
New York, NY 10018 (212) 560-2121
retailing, real estate

Alleghany Corporation Y
Park Avenue Plaza
New York, NY 10055 (212) 752-1356
financial services, insurance, fasteners

Allegheny International, Inc. AG
2 Oliver Plaza
Pittsburgh, PA 15230 (412) 562-4000
household appliances

Allegheny Ludlum Corp. ALS
1000 Six PPG Place
Pittsburgh, PA 15222 (412) 394-2800
specialty steel products

Allegheny Power System Inc. AYP
320 Park Avenue
New York, NY 10022 (212) 752-2121
electric utility DRP

Allen Group Inc. ALN
534 Broad Hollow Road
Melville, NY 11747 (516) 293-5500
auto parts, testing equipment

Alliance Capital Management L.P. AC
1345 Avenue of the Americas
New York, NY 10105 (212) 969-1000
investment advisory services

Allied Products Corporation ADP
10 South Riverside Plaza
Chicago, IL 60606 (312) 454-1020
agricultural and industrial products

Allied-Signal Inc. ALD
Columbia Road & Park Avenue
Morristown, NJ 07962 (201) 455-2000
aerospace, automotive, plastics DRP O

Allstate Municipal Income Opportunities AMO
One World Trade Center
New York, NY 10048 (212) 938-4500
municipal bond closed-end mutual fund DRP

Allstate Municipal Income Trust ALM
One World Trade Center
New York, NY 10048 (212) 938-4500
municipal bond closed-end mutual fund DRP

Allstate Municipal Income Trust II ALT
One World Trade Center
New York, NY 10048 (212) 938-4500
municipal bond closed-end mutual fund DRP

Allstate Municipal Premium Income Trust ALI
One World Trade Center
New York, NY 10048 (212) 938-4500
municipal bond closed-end mutual fund DRP

ALLTEL Corporation AT
100 Executive Parkway
Hudson, OH 44236 (216) 650-7000
telephone equipment and services

Aluminum Company of America AA
1501 Alcoa Building, 425 6th Avenue
Pittsburgh, PA 15219 (412)553-4545
aluminum production DRP O

Amax Gold Inc. AU
1707 Cole Boulevard
Golden, CO 80401 (303) 231-0444
gold and silver production

AMAX Inc. AMX
200 Park Avenue
New York, NY 10166 (212) 856-4200
minerals mining, oil and gas O

AMCA International Ltd. AIL
Dartmouth National Bank Bldg
Hanover, NH 03755 (603) 643-5454
engineering and heavy construction

Amcast Industrial AIZ
3931 South Dixie Avenue
Kettering, OH 45439 (513) 298-5251
metal products, auto parts DRP

Amdura Corp. ADU
1800 Landmark Towers, 345 St. Peter St.
St. Paul, MN 55102 (612) 293-4904
hardware distributor, recycling equipment

Amerada Hess Corporation AHC
1185 Avenue of the Americas
New York, NY 10036 (212) 997-8500
oil and gas refining and marketing DRP O

American Barrick Resources Corp. ABX
24 Hazelton Avenue
Toronto, Ontario, CDA M5R 2E2
(416) 923-9400
gold production O

American Brands Inc. AMB
1700 East Putnam Avenue
Old Greenwich, CT 06870 (203) 698-5000
tobacco, consumer products DRP O

American Building Maintenance Ind. ABM
333 Fell Street
San Francisco, CA 94102 (415) 864-5150
building maintenance

American Business Products Inc. ABP
Suite 1200, 2100 River Edge Parkway
Atlanta, GA 30328 (404) 953-8300
business forms DRP

American Capital Bond Fund, Inc. ACB
2800 Post Oak Boulevard
Houston, TX 77056 (713) 993-0500
closed-end bond fund DRP

American Capital Convertible Sec. Inc ACS
2800 Post Oak Boulevard
Houston, TX 77056 (713) 993-0500
closed end convertible fund DRP

American Capital Income Trust ACD
2800 Post Oak Boulevard
Houston, TX 77056 (800) 421-9696
closed end bond fund DRP

American Capital Management & Research
ACA
2800 Post Oak Boulevard
Houston, TX 77056 (713) 993-0500
investment advisory services

American Century Corporation ACT
600 Commerce Plaza,111 Soledad
San Antonio, TX 78205 (512) 226-2222
savings and loan, real estate

American Cyanamid Company ACY
859 Berdan Ave.,
One Cyanamid Plaza
Wayne, NJ 07470 (201) 831-2000
chemicals, drugs DRP O

American Electric Power Company, Inc. AEP
1 Riverside Plaza
Columbus, OH 43215 (614) 223-1000
electric utility DRP O

American Express Company AXP
American Express Tower,
World Financial Center
New York, NY 10285 (212) 640-2000
financial and travel services DRP O

American Family Corporation AFL
1932 Wynnton Road
Columbus, GA 31999 (404) 323-3431
insurance DRP O

American General Corporation AGC
2929 Allen Parkway
Houston, TX 77019 (713) 522-1111
insurance, financial services DRP O

American Government Income Fund Inc. AGF
Piper Jaffray Tower, 222 South Ninth Street
Minneapolis, MN 55402 (800) 333-6000
government securities closed-end mutual
fund

American Government Income Portfolio Inc.
AAF
Piper Jaffray Tower, 222 South Ninth Street
Minneapolis, MN 55402 (800) 333-6000
government securities closed-end mutual
fund

American Government Term Trust Inc. AGT
Piper Jaffray Tower, 222 South Ninth Street
Minneapolis, MN 55402 (800) 333-6000
government securities closed-end mutual
fund

American Health Properties Inc. AHE
Suite 600, 9665 Wilshire Boulevard
Beverly Hills, CA 90212 (213) 276-6245
health care real estate investment trust DRP

American Heritage Life Investment Corp. AHL
11 East Forsyth Street
Jacksonville, FL 32202 (904) 354-1776
insurance DRP

American Home Products Corp. AHP
685 Third Avenue
New York, NY 10017 (212) 986-1000
drugs, food and medical products DRP O

American Information Technologies Corp. AIT
30 South Wacker Drive
Chicago, IL 60606 (312) 750-5000
telecommunications services DRP O

American International Group Inc. AIG
70 Pine Street
New York, NY 10270 (212) 770-7000
insurance O

American Medical International Inc. AMI
414 North Camden Drive
Beverly Hills, CA 90210 (213) 278-6200
hospitals, health services DRP O

American President Companies Ltd APS
1800 Harrison Street
Oakland, CA 94612 (415) 272-8284
shipping O

American Real Estate Partners L.P. ACP
666 Third Avenue
New York, NY 10017 (212) 551-6000
real estate limited partnership DRP

American Realty Trust ARB
Suite 1100, 15770 Dallas Parkway
Dallas, TX 75248 (214) 233-0100
real estate investment trust

American Savings Bank ASB
99 Church Street
White Plains, NY 10601 (914) 287-2600
savings bank

American Ship Building Company ABG
2502 Rocky Point Road
Tampa, FL 33607 (813) 885-5537
ship building

American Stores Company ASC
Suite 500, 19100 Von Karman Avenue
Irvine, CA 92715 (714) 476-4400
food and drug stores O

American Telephone and Telegraph
Company T
550 Madison Avenue
New York, NY 10022 (212) 605-5500
telecommunications, computers DRP O

American Water Works Company Inc. AWK
1025 Laurel Oak Road
Voorhees, NJ 08043 (609) 346-8200
water utility

Americana Hotels and Realty Corp. AHR
535 Boylston Street
Boston, MA 02116 (617) 247-3358
hotels and real estate

Ameron Inc. AMN
4700 Ramona Boulevard, P.O. Box 3000
Monterey Park, CA 91754 (213) 268-4111
pipe, construction, industrial products

Ames Department Stores ADD
2418 Main Street
Rocky Hill, CT 06067 (203) 563-8234
department stores DRP O

AMETEK Inc. AME
410 Park Avenue
New York, NY 10022 (212) 935-8640
instruments and industrial equipment

AMEV Securities Inc. AMV
500 Bielenberg Drive
St. Paul, MN 55164 (612) 738-4000
closed-end bond mutual fund DRP

AM International AM
Suite 900, 333 West Wacker Drive
Chicago, IL 60606 (312) 558-1966
graphics industry products

Amoco Corporation AN
200 East Randolph Drive
Chicago, IL 60601 (312) 856-6111
oil and gas production and marketing DRP O

AMP Inc. AMP
470 Friendship Road
Harrisburg, PA 17105 (717) 564-0100
electronic connecting devices DRP O

Ampco-Pittsburgh Corporation AP
Suite 4600,600 Grant Street
Pittsburgh, PA 15219 (412) 456-4400
air and liquid handling equipment, metals

AMR Corporation AMR
P.O. Box 61616
DFW Airport, TX 75261 (817) 355-1234
airline flights and services O

AMRE, Inc. AMM
4949 West Royal Lane
Irving, TX 75063 (214) 929-4088
home improvement contractor

AMREP Corporation AXR
10 Columbus Circle
New York, NY 10019 (212) 541-7300
real estate, magazine distributor

Amsouth Bancorporation ASO
1400 First National-Southern Building
Birmingham, AL 35203 (205) 320-7151
banking DRP 5%

Anacomp, Inc. AAC
Suite 600, 11550 N Meridian Street
Indianapolis, IN 46240 (317) 844-9666
computer and micrographic services

Anadarko Petroleum Corp.
16855 Northchase Drive
Houston, TX 77060 (713) 875-1101
oil and gas exploration and production O

Analog Devices, Inc. ADI
Route 1, Industrial Park
Norwood, MA 02062 (617) 329-4700
electronic measuring equipment O

Anchor Glass Container ANC
1 Anchor Place, 1100 Anchor Street
Tampa, FL 33607 (813) 870-6120
glass containers

Angelica Corporation AGL
10176 Corporate Square Drive
St. Louis, MO 63132 (314) 991-4150
health care uniforms

Angell Real Estate Company ACR
915 West Fourth Street
Winston-Salem, NC 27102 (919) 723-7580
real estate investment trust

Anheuser-Busch Companies, Inc. BUD
1 Busch Place
St. Louis, MO 63118 (314) 577-2000
beer and food products DRP O

Anthem Electronics, Inc. ATM
1040 East Brokaw Road
San Jose, CA 95131 (408) 295-4200
semiconductor distributor

Anthony Industries, Inc. ANT
4900 Triggs Street
City of Commerce, CA 90022 (213) 268-4877
fishing tackle, swimming pools

AON Corp. AOC
123 North Wacker Drive
Chicago, IL 60606 (312) 701-3000
insurance DRP

Apache Corp. APA
1700 Lincoln Street
Denver, CO 80203 (303) 837-5000
oil and gas exploration and production DRP O

Apple Bank for Savings APK
205 East 42nd Street
New York, NY 10017 (212) 573-8000
savings bank

Applied Magnetics Corp. APM
75 Robin Hill Road
Goleta, CA 93117 (805) 683-5353
computer magnetic storing heads O

Archer-Daniels-Midland Company ADM
4666 Faries Parkway
Decatur, IL 62525 (217) 424-5200
grain processing, food products O

ARCO Chemical Company RCM
3801 West Chester Pike
Newtown Square, PA 19073 (215) 359-2000
chemicals O

Aristech Chemical Corporation ARS
600 Grant Street
Pittsburgh, PA 15230 (412) 433-2747
chemicals O

Arkla, Inc. ALG
P.O. Box 21734, 525 Milam Street
Shreveport, LA 71151 (318) 429-2700
natural gas production and transmission DRP
O

Armada Corporation ABW
630 Buhl Building
Detroit, MI 48226 (313) 963-3100
specialty alloys

Armco, Inc. AS
300 Interspace Parkway
Parsippany, NJ 07054 (201) 316-5200
steel producer O

Armstrong World Industries, Inc. ACK
P.O. Box 3001, West Liberty Street
Lancaster, PA 17604 (717) 397-0611
flooring products DRP O

Arrow Electronics Inc. ARW
25 Hub Drive
Melville, NY 11747 (516) 391-1300
electronics distributor

ARTRA Group Inc. ATA
500 Central Avenue
Northfield, IL 60093 (312) 628-2554
scientific instruments, jewelry

Arvin Industries Inc. ARV
1531 13th Street
Columbus, IN 47201 (812) 379-3000
auto parts

ARX, Inc. ARX
35 South Service Road
Plainview, NY 11803 (516) 694-6700
military and industrial products

ASA Ltd. Inc. ASA
P.O. Box 269, 140 Columbia Turnpike
Florham Park, NJ 07932 (201) 377-3535
closed-end gold mutual fund DRP O

ASARCO Inc. AR
180 Maiden Lane
New York, NY 10038 (212) 510-2000
metals mining DRP O

Ashland Coal, Inc. ACI
2205 Fifth Street Road
Huntington, WV 25771 (304) 526-3333
mines and markets coal

Ashland Oil Inc. ASH
1000 Ashland Drive
Ashland, KY 41114 (606) 329-3333
oil refining, chemicals DRP 5% O

Asia Pacific Fund, Inc. APB
One Seaport Plaza
New York, NY 10292 (212) 214-3334
Asian stock closed-end mutual fund DRP

Asset Investors Corp. AIC
Suite 1000, 3600 Yosemite Street
Denver, CO 80237 (303) 773-1100
real estate investment trust

Atalanta/Sosnoff Capital Corp. ATL
499 Park Avenue
New York, NY 10022 (212) 755-2800
investment management services

Athlone Industries Inc. ATH
200 Webro Road
Parsippany, NJ 07054 (201) 887-9100
specialty metals, fasteners

Atlanta Gas Light Company ATG
235 Peachtree Street N.E.
Atlanta, GA 30302 (404) 584-4000
natural gas utility DRP

Atlantic Energy, Inc. ATE
1199 Black Horse Pike
Pleasantville, NJ 08232 (609) 645-4500
electric utility DRP

Atlantic Richfield Company ARC
515 South Flower Street
Los Angeles, CA 90071 (213) 486-3511
oil/gas exploration and marketing DRP O

Atlas Corporation AZ
353 Nassau Street
Princeton, NJ 08540 (609) 921-2000
gold mining, building products

Atmos Energy Corp. ATO
Suite 1800, 3 Lincoln Centre
Dallas, TX 75240 (214) 934-9227
natural gas distributor DRP

Audio/Video Affiliates, Inc. AVA
2875 Needmore Road
Dayton, OH 45414 (513) 276-3931
consumer electronics retailer

Augat, Inc. AUG
89 Forbes Blvd., P.O. Box 448
Mansfield, MA 02048 (508) 543-4300
electromechancial components

Ausimont N.V. AUS
128 Technology Drive
Waltham, MA 02254 (617) 899-3000
specialty chemicals

Automatic Data Processing Inc. AUD
One ADP Boulevard
Roseland, NJ 07068 (201) 994-5000
data processing O

Avalon Corporation AVL
101 East 52nd Street
New York, NY 10022 (212) 751-8700
oil and gas exploration

AVEMCO Corporation AVE
411 Aviation Way
Frederick, MD 21701 (301) 694-5700
aviation insurance

Avery International Corporation AVY
150 North Orange Grove Boulevard
Pasadena, CA 91103 (818) 304-2000
self-adhesive labels, paper products DRP

Avnet Inc. AVT
80 Cutter Mill Road
Great Neck, NY 11021 (516) 466-7000
electronics distributor DRP O

Avon Products, Inc. AVP
9 West 57th Street
New York, NY 10019 (212) 546-6015
cosmetics, fragrances, jewelry DRP O

AVX Corporation AVX
60 Cutter Mill Road
Great Neck, NY 11021 (516) 829-8500
ceramic capacitors

Aydin Corporation AYD
700 Dresher Road, P.O. Box 349
Horsham, PA 19044 (215) 657-7510
microwave, data communications equipment

Bairnco Corp. BZ
200 Park Avenue
New York, NY 10166 (212) 490-8722
laminated products, shielding systems

Baker, Fentress & Co. BKF
Suite 3510, 200 West Madison Street
Chicago, IL 60606 (312) 236-9190
closed-end stock mutual fund DRP

Baker Hughes, Inc. BHI
3900 Essex Lane
Houston, TX 77027 (713) 439-8600
oil field services, heavy machinery DRP O

Baldor Electric Company BEZ
5711 South 7th Street
Fort Smith, AR 72902 (501) 646-4711
electric motors

Ball Corporation BLL
345 South High Street
Muncie, IN 47307 (317) 747-6100
metal/glass containers, aerospace DRP 5%

Bally Manufacturing Corporation BLY
8700 West Bryn Mawr Avenue
Chicago, IL 60631 (312) 399-1300
casino, health clubs, lottery equipment O

Baltimore Bancorp BBB
Baltimore and Charles Street
Baltimore, MD 21202 (301) 244-3360
banking DRP

Baltimore Gas & Electric BGE
Gas & Electric Building, Charles Center
Baltimore, MD 21203 (301) 234-5502
electric and gas utility DRP

Banc One Corporation ONE
100 East Broad Street
Columbus, OH 43271 (614) 248-5944
banking DRP O

BancFlorida Financial Corp. BFL
5801 Pelican Bay Boulevard
Naples, FL 33963 (813) 597-1611
banking

Banco Central SA BCM
49 Alcala
Madrid, Spain (341) 232-8810
banking

Banco Santander STD
Paseo de Pereda, 10-12
39004 Santander, Spain (42) 22-12-00
banking

BancTEXAS Group Inc. BTX
1601 Elm Street
Dallas, TX 75201 (214) 969-6400
banking

Bandag Inc. BDG
Bandag Center
Muscatine, IA 52761 (319) 262-1400
tire retreader

Bank of Boston Corporation BKB
100 Federal Street
Boston, MA 02110 (617) 434-2200
banking DRP 5% O

Bank of New England NEB
28 State Street
Boston, MA 02109 (617) 742-4000
banking

Bank of New York Co. BK
48 Wall Street
New York, NY 10286 (212) 495-1784
banking DRP 5% O

BankAmerica Corporation BAC
Bank Of America Center
San Francisco, CA 94104 (415) 622-2091
banking O

Bankers Trust New York Corporation BT
280 Park Avenue
New York, NY 10017 (212) 250-2500
banking and financial services DRP 3% O

Banner Industries Inc. BNR
25700 Science Park Drive
Cleveland, OH 44122 (216) 464-3650
aerospace parts, water treatment equipment

Barclays PLC BCS
54 Lombard Street
London, England EC3P 3AH
(011) 441-626-1567
banking

Bard C R Inc. BCR
730 Central Avenue
Murray Hill, NJ 07974 (201) 277-8000
medical supplies DRP O

Barnes Group Inc. B
123 Main Street
Bristol, CT 06010 (203) 583-7070
spring manufacturing, aerospace

Barnett Banks, Inc. BBI
100 Laura Street
Jacksonville, FL 32202 (904) 791-7720
banking DRP

Baroid Corp. BRC
3000 North Belt East
Houston, TX 77032 (713) 987-4000
oil industry products and services

Barry Wright Corporation BAR
680 Pleasant Street
Watertown, MA 02172 (617) 965-5800
computer shock protection equipment

BASIX Corporation BAS
475 Park Avenue South
New York, NY 10016 (212) 696-7589
printing, computer systems, oil

Battle Mountain Gold Co. BMG
42nd Floor, 333 Clay Street
Houston, TX 77002 (713) 650-6400
gold mining O

Bausch & Lomb Inc. BOL
1 Lincoln First Square
Rochester, NY 14601 (716) 338-6000
contact lenses, optical instruments DRP O

Baxter International Inc. BAX
1 Baxter Parkway
Deerfield, IL 60015 (312) 948-2000
medical supplies DRP O

Bay Financial Corporation BAY
200 State Street
Boston, MA 02109 (617) 439-6046
real estate investment

Bay State Gas Company BGC
120 Royall Street
Canton, MA 02021 (617) 828-8650
gas utility DRP

BCE Inc. BCE
800 Square Victoria
Montreal, Quebec, CDA H4Z IG8
(514) 499-7000
telecommunications services DRP O

Bear Stearns Companies Inc. BSC
245 Park Avenue
New York, NY 10167 (212) 272-2000
brokerage firm O

Bearings Inc. BER
3600 Euclid Avenue
Cleveland, OH 44115 (216) 881-2838
bearings and power transmissions

Beazer PLC BZR
Beazer House, Lower Bristol Road
Bath, Avon BA2 3EY England (0225) 28401
homebuilding, building materials

Beckman Instruments BEC
2500 Harbor Boulevard
Fullerton, CA 92634 (714) 871-4848
laboratory instruments

Becton, Dickinson and Company BDX
One Becton Drive
Franklin Lakes, NJ 07417 (201) 848-6800
medical supplies DRP O

Belding Hemingway Company Inc. BHY
1430 Broadway
New York, NY 10018 (212) 944-6040
fabrics, threads, buttons

Bell Atlantic Corporation BEL
1600 Market Street
Philadelphia, PA 19103 (215) 963-6000
telecommunications DRP O

Bell Industries, Inc. BI
11812 San Vicente Boulevard
Los Angeles, CA 90049 (213) 826-6778
electronics distributor, building products

BellSouth Corporation BLS
675 West Peachtree Street NE
Atlanta, GA 30375 (404) 249-2000
telecommunications DRP 5% O

Belo A H Corporation BLC
Young & Houston Streets
Dallas, TX 75265 (214) 977-8730
publishing, broadcasting

Bemis Company Inc. BMS
800 Northstar Center
Minneapolis, MN 55402 (612) 340-6000
consumer/industrial packaging material

Beneficial Corporation BNL
400 Bellevue Parkway
Wilmington, DE 19809 (302) 798-0800
personal credit, financial services DRP O

Benguet Corporation BE
12 San Miguel Avenue, Mandaluyong
Metro Manila, Philippines (011) 632-721-1239
gold and silver mines

Berkey Inc. BKY
1 Water Street
White Plains, NY 10601 (914) 428-9460
photo equipment and supplies

Berkshire Hathaway Inc. BRK
1440 Kiewit Plaza
Omaha, NE 68131 (402) 846-1400
insurance, media, investments

Best Buy Co., Inc. BBY
4400 West 78th Street
Minneapolis, MN 55435 (612) 896-2300
consumer electronics retailing

Bethlehem Steel Corporation BS
701 East Third Street
Bethlehem, PA 18016 (215) 694-2424
steel mills, steel products O

BET Public Limited Co. BEP
Stratton House
Piccadilly, London W1X 6AS, UK
(01) 629-8886
industrial and commercial services

Beverly Enterprises BEV
873 South Fair Oaks Avenue
Pasadena, CA 91105 (818) 577-6111
nursing homes O

Biocraft Laboratories Inc. BCL
92 Route 46
Elmwood Park, NJ 07407 (201) 796-3434
generic drugs

Birmingham Steel Corp. BIR
Suite 1000, 3000 Riverchase Galleria
Birmingham, AL 35244 (205) 985-9290
steel mini-mills

Black & Decker Corporation BDK
701 East Joppa Road
Towson, MD 21204 (301) 583-3900
power tools and household appliances DRP O

Black Hills Corporation BKH
625 9th Street
Rapid City, SD 57709 (605) 348-1700
electric utility, coal mining DRP 5%

Blackstone Income Trust, Inc. BKT
One Seaport Plaza
New York, NY 10292 (212) 214-3334
closed-end mortgage securities mutual fund

Blackstone Target Term Trust, Inc. BTT
One Seaport Plaza
New York, NY 10292 (212) 214-3334
closed-end mortgage securities mutual fund

Block (H&R) Inc. HRB
4410 Main Street
Kansas City, MO 64111 (816) 753-6900
tax return preparation, databases DRP O

BMC Industries Inc. BMC
2 Appletree Square
Minneapolis, MN 55425 (612) 851-6000
electronic circuits, optics

Blockbuster Entertainment Corp. BV
901 East Las Olas Boulevard
Ft. Lauderdale, FL 33301 (305) 524-8200
videocassette retail stores

Blue Arrow PLC BAW
31 Worship Street
London EC2A 2DX, England (414) 961-1000
employment agency

Blue Chip Value Fund, Inc. BLU
755 New York Avenue
Huntington, NY 11743 (516) 351-1113
closed-end stock mutual fund

Boeing Company BA
7755 East Marginal Way South
Seattle, WA 98108 (206) 655-2121
aircraft manufacturer O

Boise Cascade Corporation BCC
1 Jefferson Square
Boise, ID 83728 (208) 384-6161
paper and wood products DRP O

Bolt Beranek And Newman Inc. BBN
10 Fawcett Street
Cambridge, MA 02238 (617) 873-2000
computer research, consulting services

Bond International Gold, Inc. BIG
Cayman Int. Trust Building
Georgetown, Grand Cayman BWI
(809) 949-2081
gold mining

Borden Chemicals & Plastics L.P. BCP
Highway 73
Geismar, LA 70734 (504) 387-5101
chemicals, plastics, industrial gases O

Borden Inc. BN
277 Park Avenue
New York, NY 10172 (212) 573-4000
dairy and food products, chemicals DRP O

Boston Celtics L.P. BOS
150 Causeway Street
Boston, MA 02114 (617) 523-6050
professional basketball team

Boston Edison Company BSE
800 Boylston Street
Boston, MA 02199 (617) 424-2000
electric utility DRP 5%

Bowater Inc. BOW
1 Parklands Drive
Darien, CT 06820 (203) 656-7200
newsprint, coated paper DRP 5% O

BRE Properties, Inc. BRE
Suite 2500, One Montgomery Street
San Francisco, CA 94104 (415) 445-6530
real estate investment trust

Brazil Fund, Inc. BZF
345 Park Avenue
New York, NY 10154 (212) 326-6200
Brazilian stock closed-end mutual fund

Briggs & Stratton Corporation BGG
12301 West Wirth Street
Wauwatosa, WI 53222 (414) 259-5333
power equipment engines, locks DRP

Bristol-Myers Company BMY
345 Park Avenue
New York, NY 10022 (212) 546-4000
drugs, cosmetics, personal care DRP O

British Airways PLC BAB
Speedbird House, Heathrow Airport
Hounslow, Middlesex TW6 2JA
(441) 759-5511
international airline

British Gas PLC BRG
Rivermill House, 152 Grosvenor Road
London SW1V 3JL, England
(011) 441-821-1444
gas utility

British Petroleum Company PLC BP
Britannic House, Moor Lane
London, EC2Y 9BU, England (212) 887-9385
oil and gas production O

British Telecommunications PLC BTY
81 Newgate Street
London EC1A 7AJ (441) 356-5000
telecommunications services in UK

Broad, Inc. BRO
11601 Wilshire Boulevard
Los Angeles, CA 90025 (213) 312-5000
life insurance, financial services O

Broken Hill Proprietary Company Ltd. BHP
BHP House, 140 William Street
Melbourne, Victoria 3000, Australia 60-0701
(011) 603-609-3333
petroleum, minerals, steel

Brooklyn Union Gas Company BU
195 Montague Street
Brooklyn, NY 11201 (718) 403-2000
gas utility DRP

Brown & Sharpe Manufacturing Company
BNS
Precision Park, Frenchtown Road
North Kingston, RI 02852 (401) 886-2000
machine tools, measuring instruments DRP

Brown Group Inc. BG
8400 Maryland Avenue
St. Louis, MO 63105 (314) 854-4000
footwear, fabric DRP

Browning-Ferris Industries Inc. BFI
757 North Eldridge
Houston, TX 77253 (713) 870-8100
waste management DRP O

BRT Realty Trust BRT
60 Cutter Mill Road
Great Neck, NY 11021 (516) 466-3100
real estate investment trust

Brunswick Corporation BC
1 Brunswick Plaza
Skokie, IL 60076 (312) 470-4700
recreation products DRP O

Brush Wellman Inc. BW
1200 Hanna Building
Cleveland, OH 44115 (216) 443-1000
beryllium products DRP

Buckeye Parnters L.P. BPL
100 Buckeye Road
Emmaus, PA 18049 (215) 820-8300
petroleum pipeline

Bunker Hill Income Securities Inc. BHL
P.O. Box 70220
Pasadena, CA 91107 (213) 229-1290
closed-end bond mutual fund DRP

Burger King Investors L.P. BKP
Suite 610, 200 South Sixth Street
Minneapolis, MN 55402 (612) 330-8345
fast food restaurants

Burlington Coat Factory Warehouse Corp.
BCF
1830 Route 130
Burlington, NJ 08016 (609) 387-7800
apparel stores

Burlington Northern Inc. BNI
3800 Continental Plaza, 777 Main Street
Ft. Worth, TX 76102 (817) 878-2000
railroads O

Burlington Resources Inc. BR
999 Third Avenue
Seattle, WA 98104 (206) 467-3838
pipeline, oil and gas, forest products

Burndy Corporation BDC
Richards Avenue
Norwalk, CT 06856 (203) 838-4444
electrical connectors

Businessland Inc. BLI
1001 Ridder Park Drive
San Jose, CA 95131 (408) 437-0400
computer retailing

C3 Inc. CEE
460 Herndon Parkway
Herndon, VA 22070 (703) 471-6000
computer systems, software

Cabot Corporation CBT
950 Winter Street
Waltham, MA 02254 (617) 890-0200
carbon black, oil, gas DRP

Caesars World Inc. CAW
1801 Century Park East
Los Angeles, CA 90067 (213) 552-2711
entertaining, gaming, resort facilities O

Cal Fed Income Parnters L.P. CFI
5670 Wilshire Boulevard
Los Angeles, CA 90036 (213) 932-4928
real estate partnership

CalFed Inc. CAL
5670 Wilshire Boulevard
Los Angeles, CA 90036 (213) 932-4200
banking and insurance O

California Real Estate Investment Trust CT
Suite 100, 850 Montgomery Street
San Francisco, CA 94133 (415) 433-1855
real estate investment trust

Callahan Mining Corporation CMN
11811 North Tatum Boulevard
Phoenix, AZ 85028 (602) 953-5965
silver mining, flexible hose

CalMat Company CZM
3200 San Fernando Road
Los Angeles, CA 90065 (213) 258-2777
cement, concrete, stone products

Calton, Inc. CN
500 Craig Road
Freehold, NJ 07728 (201) 780-1800
residential housing builder

Cameron Iron Works Inc. CIW
13013 Northwest Freeway
Houston, TX 77040 (713) 939-2211
oil tools, forgings, and valves

Campbell Resources Inc. CCH
111 Richmond Street West
Toronto, ON, CDA M5H 2G4 (416) 366-5201
gold and copper mining

Campbell Soup Company CPB
Campbell Place
Camden, NJ 08103 (609) 342-4800
canned and frozen food DRP O

Canadian Pacific Limited CP
910 Peel Street
Montreal, CDA H3C 3E4 (514) 395-5151
transportation, energy, real estate DRP O

Canal Capital Corp. COW
717 Fifth Avenue
New York, NY 10022 (212) 826-6040
stockyards, real estate, investments

Capital Cities Communications/ABC Inc. CCB
77 West 66th Street
New York, NY 10023 (212) 456-7777
radio/TV broadcasting, publishing O

Capital Holding Corp. CPH
Commonwealth Building
Louisville, KY 40202 (502) 560-2000
life, accident, health insurance DRP

Carter-Wallace Inc. CAR
767 Fifth Ave.
New York, NY 10153 (212) 758-4500
health care/personal care/pet products

CareerCom Corp. PTA
Harrisview Office Center, 108 Lowther Street
Lemoyne, PA 17043 (717) 774-1477
vocational schools

Cascade Natural Gas Corporation CGC
222 Fairview Avenue North
Seattle, WA 98109 (206) 624-3900
gas utility DRP

Carlisle Companies, Inc. CSL
250 East Fifth Street
Cincinnati, OH 45202 (513) 241-2500
rubber, plastics, tires, wire

Castle & Cooke, Inc. CKE
10900 Wilshire Boulevard
Los Angeles, CA 90024 (213) 824-1500
food products, real estate O

Carolco Pictures Inc. CRC
8800 Sunset Boulevard
Los Angeles, CA 90069 (213) 850-8800
motion picture production

Caterpillar, Inc. CAT
100 North East Adams Street
Peoria, IL 61629 (309) 675-1000
farm/construction/mining machinery DRP O

Carolina Freight Corporation CAO
North Carolina Highway 150 East
Cherryville, NC 28021 (704) 435-6811
trucking DRP

CBI Industries Inc. CBH
800 Jorie Boulevard
Oak Brook, IL 60522 (312) 572-7000
contracting services, gases DRP

Carolina Power & Light Company CPL
411 Fayetteville Street
Raleigh, NC 27602 (919) 836-6111
electric utility DRP 3%

CBS Inc. CBS
51 West 52nd Street
New York, NY 10019 (212) 975-4321
broadcasting DRP O

Carpenter Technology Corporation CRS
101 West Bern Street
Reading, PA 19603 (215) 371-2000
steel mills DRP

CCX Inc. CCX
1200 Route 22
Bridgewater, NJ 08807 (201) 231-8888
wire and cable, alloy steels

Carriage Industries, Inc. CGE
South Industrial Boulevard
Calhoun, GA 30701 (404) 629-9234
carpeting

CDI Corp. CDI
10 Penn Center
Philadelphia, PA 19103 (215) 569-2200
engineering services, temporary help

Carson Pirie Scott & Company CRN
36 South Wabash Avenue
Chicago, IL 60603 (312) 641-8000
department stores

Cedar Fair L.P. FUN
One Causeway Drive
Sandusky, OH 44871 (419) 626-0830
amusement parks

Carter Hawley Hale Stores Inc. CHH
550 South Flower Street
Los Angeles, CA 90071 (213) 620-0150
retail/department stores O

Centel Corporation CNT
O'Hare Plaza, 8725 East River Road
Chicago, IL 60631 (312) 399-2500
telephone, communications systems DRP O

Centerior Energy Corp. CX
6200 Oak Tree Boulevard
Independence, OH 44131 (216) 447-3100
electric utility DRP O

Centex Corporation CTX
3333 Lee Parkway
Dallas, TX 75219 (214) 559-6500
residential construction, cement

Central & South West Corporation CSR
Suite 2500, 2121 San Jacinto Street
Dallas, TX 75201 (214) 754-1000
electric utility DRP

Central Hudson Gas & Electric Corp. CNH
284 South Avenue
Poughkeepsie, NY 12601 (914) 452-2000
electric and gas utility DRP

Central Illinois Public Service Co. CIP
607 East Adams Street
Springfield, IL 62701 (217) 523-3600
electric and gas utility DRP

Central Louisiana Electric Co. Inc. CNL
2030 Donahue Ferry Road
Pineville, LA 71360 (318) 484-7400
electric utility DRP 5%

Central Maine Power Company CTP
Edison Drive
Augusta, ME 04336 (207) 623-3521
electric utility DRP 5%

Central Vermont Public Service Corp. CV
77 Grove Street
Rutland, VT 05701 (802) 773-2711
electric utility DRP 5%

Century Telephone Enterprises, Inc. CTL
Suite 700, 1900 North 18th
Monroe, LA 71201 (318) 388-9500
communications service DRP 5%

Cenvill Investors, Inc. CVI
Century Village Adm. Building
West Palm Beach, FL 33417 (407) 686-2577
real estate investment trust

Champion International Corporation CHA
1 Champion Plaza
Stamford, CT 06921 (203) 358-7000
paper and containers, forest products O

Champion Spark Plug Company CHM
900 Upton Avenue, P.O. Box 910
Toledo, OH 43607 (419) 535-2567
auto parts, accessories

Chaparral Steel Co. CSM
300 Ward Road
Midlothian, TX 76065 (214) 775-8241
steel products

Charter Company CHR
1 East Fourth Street
Cincinnati, OH 45202 (513) 579-2482
oil refining/marketing/production, gas

Chase Manhattan Corporation CMB
1 Chase Manhattan Plaza
New York, NY 10081 (212) 552-2222
banking DRP 5% O

Chaus (Bernard) Inc. CHS
1410 Broadway
New York, NY 10018 (212) 354-1280
women's clothing

Chelsea Industries Inc. CHD
1360 Soldiers Field Road
Boston, MA 02135 (617) 787-9010
plastic products, electronic components

Chemed Corporation CHE
1200 Dubois Tower
Cincinnati, OH 45202 (513) 762-6900
specialty chemicals, health products

Chemical Banking Corporation CHL
277 Park Avenue
New York, NY 10172 (212) 310-6161
banking DRP 5% O

Chemical Waste Management Inc. CHW
3001 Butterfield Road
Oak Brook, IL 60521 (312) 218-1500
hazardous waste management services O

Chesapeake Corporation CSK
1021 East Cary Street
Richmond, VA 23218 (804) 697-1000
paper products, containers DRP

Chevron Corporation CHV
225 Bush Street
San Francisco, CA 94104 (415) 894-7700
oil production/refining/marketing DRP O

Chicago Milwaukee Corporation CHG
547 West Jackson Boulevard
Chicago, IL 60606 (312) 822-0400
real estate investments

Chock Full O'Nuts Corporation CHF
370 Lexington Avenue
New York, NY 10017 (212) 532-0300
coffee, real estate

Christiana Companies, The CST
9171 Towne Center Drive
San Diego, CA 92122 (619) 587-0123
real estate development

Chrysler Corporation C
12000 Chrysler Drive
Highland Park, MI 48288 (313) 956-5252
auto manufacturer, finance DRP O

Chubb Corporation CB
15 Mountain View Road
Warren, NJ 07061 (212) 580-2000
fire, marine, casualty insurance O

Church's Fried Chicken Inc. CHU
355A Spencer Lane
San Antonio, TX 78284 (512) 735-9392
chicken restaurants

Chyron Corporation CHY
265 Spagnoli Road
Melville, NY 11747 (516) 845-2000
electronic TV titling, graphics equipment

CIGNA Corporation CI
1 Logan Square
Philadelphia, PA 19103 (215) 523-4000
life, auto, fire, casualty insurance DRP O

CIGNA High Income Shares HIS
1380 Main Street
Springfield, MA 01103 (413) 784-0100
closed-end bond mutual fund

CILCORP Inc. CER
300 Liberty Street
Peoria, IL 61602 (309) 672-5271
electric utility DRP

Cincinnati Bell Inc. CSN
201 East 4th Street
Cincinnati, OH 45201 (513) 397-9900
telephone service DRP

Cincinnati Gas & Electric Company CIN
139 East 4th Street
Cincinnati, OH 45202 (513) 381-2000
electric and gas utility DRP

Cincinnati Milacron Inc. CMZ
4701 Marburg Avenue
Cincinnati, OH 45209 (513) 841-8100
machine tools, plastics machinery DRP O

Cineplex Odeon Corp. CPX
1303 Yonge Street
Toronto, Ontario, CDA M4T 2Y9
(416) 323-6600
movie theater operations O

Circle K Corporation CKP
1601 North 7th Street
Phoenix, AZ 85006 (602) 253-9600
convenience food stores O

Circuit City Stores Inc. CC
2040 Thalbro Street
Richmond, VA 23230 (804) 257-4292
consumer electronics retailer O

Circus Circus Enterprises Inc. CIR
2880 Las Vegas Boulevard South
Las Vegas, NV 89109 (702) 734-0410
casino-hotels O

Citicorp CCI
399 Park Avenue
New York, NY 10043 (212) 559-1000
banking, financial services DRP O

Citizen's & Southern Corp. CTZ
35 Broad Street
Atlanta, GA 30303 (404) 581-2121
banking DRP O

Citytrust Bancorp, Inc. CYT
945 Main Street
Bridgeport, CT 06601 (203) 384-5400
banking

Clabir Corporation CLG
485 West Putnam Avenue
Greenwich, CT 06830 (203) 625-0300
ice cream, chocolate products

Claire's Stores Inc. CLE
6095 N.W. 167th Street
Miami, FL 33015 (305) 558-2577
apparel stores

Clark Equipment Company CKL
100 North Michigan Street
South Bend, IN 46634 (219) 239-0100
fork lifts, axles, transmissions

Clayton Homes Inc. CMH
New Topside Road at Alcoa Highway
Knoxville, TN 37901 (615) 970-7200
manufactured homes producer

Clemente Global Growth Fund, Inc. CLM
767 Third Avenue
New York, NY 10017 (212) 759-3339
closed-end global stock mutual fund DRP

Cleveland-Cliffs Inc. CLF
1100 Superior Avenue
Cleveland, OH 44114 (216) 694-5700
iron ore

Clorox Company CLX
1221 Broadway
Oakland, CA 94612 (415) 271-7000
soaps and cleansers DRP O

Club Med Inc. CMI
309 Grand Cayman Islands
Georgetown, BWI (809) 949-2081
operator of vacation resorts

CML Group Inc. CML
524 Main Street
Acton, MA 01720 (617) 264-4155
specialty retailing, recreation

CMS Energy Corp. CMS
Suite 1100, Fairlane Plaza South
300 Town Center Drive
Dearborn, MI 48126 (313) 436-9261
electric and gas utility

CNA Financial Corporation CNA
CNA Plaza
Chicago, IL 60685 (312) 822-5000
fire, marine, casualty, title insurance O

CNA Income Shares Inc. CNN
CNA Plaza
Chicago, IL 60685 (312) 822-4181
closed end bond mutual fund DRP

CNW Corporation CNW
1 Northwestern Center
Chicago, IL 60606 (312) 559-7000
railroads O

Coachmen Industries Inc. COA
601 East Beardsley Avenue
Elkhart, IN 46514 (219) 262-0123
recreational vehicles

Coast Savings & Loan Association CSA
1000 Wilshire Boulevard
Los Angeles, CA 90017 (213) 688-2000
savings and loan

Coastal Corporation CGP
9 Greenway Plaza
Houston, TX 77046 (713) 877-1400
refining and marketing of oil, gas, coal O

Coca Cola Company KO
310 North Avenue N.W.
Atlanta, GA 30313 (404) 676-2121
soft drinks, juices, foods DRP O

Coca-Cola Enterprises, Inc. CCE
One Coca-Cola Plaza N.W.
Atlanta, GA 30313 (404) 676-2100
coca-cola bottling operations O

Coles Myer Ltd. CM
800 Toorak Road
Tooronga 3146, Victoria, Australia
(03) 829-3688
department and food stores

Colgate-Palmolive Company CL
300 Park Avenue
New York, NY 10022 (212) 310-2000
household/personal/health items DRP O

Collins Foods International Inc. CF
12655 West Jefferson Boulevard
Los Angeles, CA 90066 (213) 827-2300
restaurants

Colonial High Income Municipal Trust CXE
1 Financial Center
Boston, MA 02111 (617) 426-3750
closed-end municipal bond mutual fund DRP

Colonial Intermediate High Income Fund CIF
1 Financial Center
Boston, MA 02111 (617) 426-3750
closed-end junk bond mutual fund DRP

Colonial Municipal Income Trust CMU
1 Financial Center
Boston, MA 02111 (617) 426-3750
closed-end municipal bond mutual fund DRP

Columbia Gas System, Inc. CG
20 Montchanin Road
Wilmington, DE 19807 (302) 429-5000
gas utility DRP

Columbia Pictures Entertainment, Inc. KPE
711 Fifth Avenue
New York, NY 10022 (212) 751-4400
motion picture production O

Columbia Savings and Loan Association CSV
8840 Wilshire Boulevard
Beverly Hills, CA 90211 (213) 657-6134
savings and loan

Combustion Engineering, Inc. CSP
900 Long Ridge Road
Stamford, CT 06904 (203) 329-8771
energy generation, engineering DRP O

Comdisco Inc. CDO
6111 River Road
Rosemont, IL 60018 (312) 698-3000
remarket/lease IBM computer equipment O

Commercial Metals Company CMC
7800 Stemmons Freeway
Dallas, TX 75247 (214) 689-4300
metals fabrication

Commodore International Limited CBU
1200 Wilson Drive
West Chester, PA 19380 (215) 431-9100
computer systems, electronic products O

Commonwealth Edison Company CWE
1 First National Plaza, 37th Floor
Chicago, IL 60690 (312) 294-4321
electric utility DRP 5% O

Commonwealth Energy System CES
One Main Street
Cambridge, MA 02142 (617) 225-4000
electric and gas utility DRP

Commonwealth Mortgage of America L.P.
CMA
2425 West Loop South
Houston, TX 77027 (713) 439-7200
mortgage banking

Communications Satellite Corporation CQ
950 L'Enfant Plaza South S.W.
Washington, DC 20024 (202) 863-6000
satellite telecommunications DRP O

Community Psychiatric Centers CMY
517 Washington Street
San Francisco, CA 94111 (415) 831-1166
acute psychiatric hospitals O

COMPAQ Computer Corp. CPQ
20555 FM 149
Houston, TX 77070 (713) 370-0670
computers

Comprehensive Care Corp. CMP
18551 Von Karman Avenue
Irvine, CA 92715 (714) 851-2273
psychiatric hospitals O

Computer Associates International, Inc. CA
711 Stewart Avenue
Garden City, NY 11530 (516) 227-3300
computer software O

Computer Factory Inc. CFA
399-A Executive Boulevard
Elmsford, NY 10523 (914) 347-5000
computer retailing

Computer Sciences Corporation CSC
2100 East Grand Avenue
El Segundo, CA 90245 (213) 615-0311
computer services O

Computer Task Group, Inc. TSK
800 Delaware Avenue
Buffalo, NY 14209 (716) 882-8000
computer services

Comstock Partners Strategy Fund, Inc. CPF
45 Broadway
New York, NY 10006 (212) 943-9100
closed-end bond mutual fund

ConAgra Inc. CAG
Conagra Center, 1 Central Park Plaza
Omaha, NE 68102 (402) 978-4000
bakery, flour, feeds, poultry DRP O

Connecticut Energy Corporation CNE
880 Broad Street
Bridgeport, CT 06604 (203) 382-8111
gas utility DRP

Connecticut Natural Gas Corporation CTG
100 Columbus Boulevard
Hartford, CT 06144 (203) 727-3000
gas utility DRP

Conseco, Inc. CNC
11825 North Pennsylvania Street
Carmel, IN 46032 (317) 573-6100
life and health insurance

Consolidated Edison Co. of New York, Inc. ED
4 Irving Place
New York, NY 10003 (212) 460-4600
electric and gas utility DRP O

Consolidated Freightways Inc. CNF
3240 Hillview Avenue, P.O. Box 10340
Palo Alto, CA 94303 (415) 494-2900
trucking, air freight O

Consolidated Natural Gas Company CNG
4 Gateway Center, CNG Tower
Pittsburgh, PA 15222 (412) 227-1000
gas utility, oil and gas production DRP O

Consolidated Rail Corporation CRR
6 Penn Plaza
Philadelphia, PA 19103 (215) 977-4000
railroad operations O

Consolidated Stores Corporation CNS
2020 Corvair Avenue
Columbus, OH 43207 (614) 224-1297
retail stores

Constar International Inc. CTR
One Central Plaza, 835 Georgia Avenue
Chattanooga, TN 37402 (615) 267-2973
plastic containers

Contel Corporation CTC
245 Perimeter Center Parkway
Atlanta, GA 30346 (404) 391-8000
telecommunications services DRP O

Continental Corporation CIC
180 Maiden Lane
New York, NY 10038 (212) 440-3980
property-casualty insurance DRP O

Continental Illinois Corporation (NEW) CIL
231 South La Salle Street
Chicago, IL 60697 (312) 828-2345
banking

Continental Illinois Holding Corp. CIH
231 South La Salle Street
Chicago, IL 60697 (312) 828-2345
banking

Continental Information Systems Corp. CNY
1 CIS Parkway
Syracuse, NY 13221 (315) 437-1900
computer leasing

Control Data Corporation CDA
8100 34th Avenue South
Minneapolis, MN 55440 (612) 853-8100
computer hardware and services DRP O

Convertible Holdings Inc. CNV
P.O. Box 9011
Princeton, NJ 08543 (609) 282-2050
closed-end dual purpose mutual fund

Cooper Companies, Inc. COO
3145 Porter Drive
Palo Alto, CA 94304 (415) 856-5000
medical products, contact lenses O

Cooper Industries Inc. CBE
First City Tower
Houston, TX 77002 (713) 739-5400
electrical/electronic products DRP O

Cooper Tire & Rubber Company CTB
Lima & Western Avenues
Findlay, OH 45839 (419) 423-1321
tires

Copperweld Corporation COS
4 Gateway Center
Pittsburgh, PA 15222 (412) 263-3200
alloy steel, specialty tubing DRP

Core Industries, Inc. CRI
500 North Woodward Avenue
Bloomfield Hills, MI 48013 (313) 642-3400
electronics, farm equipment, fluid controls

Corning Glass Works GLW
Houghton Park
Corning, NY 14830 (607) 974-9000
glass products, medical equipment DRP O

Corroon & Black Corporation CBL
Wall Street Plaza
New York, NY 10005 (212) 363-4100
insurance brokers DRP

Counsellors Tandem Securities Fund, Inc. CTF
466 Lexington Avenue
New York, NY 10017 (212) 878-0600
closed-end utility stock mutual fund

Countrywide Credit Industries Inc. CCR
155 North Lake Avenue
Pasadena, CA 91101 (818) 304-8400
mortgage banking

Countrywide Mortgage Investments, Inc.
CWM
155 North Lake Avenue
Pasadena, CA 91109 (818) 304-8400
mortgage real estate investment trust

CPC International Inc. CPC
International Plaza
Englewood Cliffs, NJ 07632 (201) 894-4000
grocery food products DRP O

CPI Corp. CPY
1706 Washington Avenue
St. Louis, MO 63103 (314) 231-1575
photo portrait studios

Craig Corporation CRA
116 North Robertson Boulevard
Los Angeles, CA 90048 (213) 659-6641
supermarkets

Crane Company CR
757 Third Avenue
New York, NY 10017 (212) 415-7300
aerospace, construction products DRP

Cray Research, Inc. CYR
608 2nd Avenue South
Minneapolis, MN 55402 (612) 333-5889
supercomputers O

CRI Insured Mortgage Investments L.P. CRM
1 Central Plaza, 11200 Rockville Pike
Rockville, MA 20852 (301) 468-9200
real estate investment partnership

CRI Insured Mortgage Investments Inc. II CII
1 Central Plaza, 11200 Rockville Pike
Rockville, MA 20852 (301) 468-9200
real estate investment partnership

CRI Insured Mortgage Investments III L.P.
CTH
1 Central Plaza, 11200 Rockville Pike
Rockville, MA 20852 (301) 468-9200
real estate investment partnership

Crompton & Knowles Corporation CNK
1 Station Place
Stamford, CT 06902 (203) 353-5400
industrial chemicals and machinery DRP

CrossLand Savings, F.S.B. CRL
211 Montague Street
Brooklyn, NY 11201 (718) 780-0400
savings bank O

Crown Cork & Seal Company, Inc. CCK
9300 Ashton Road
Philadelphia, PA 19136 (215) 698-5358
metal cans, filling & packaging machinery

CRS Sirrine Inc. CRX
Suite 900, 1177 West Loop South
Houston, TX 77027 (713) 552-2000
architecture and engineering services

Crystal Brands Inc. CBR
Crystal Brands Road
Southport, CT 06490 (203) 254-6200
sportswear, accessories

CSX Corporation CSX
1 James Center
Richmond, VA 23261 (804) 782-1400
railroads, coal O

CTS Corporation CTS
905 North West Boulevard
Elkhart, IN 46514 (219) 293-7511
electronic components

Culbro Corporation CUC
387 Park Avenue
New York, NY 10016 (212) 561-8700
tobacco and industrial products

Cummins Engine Company, Inc. CUM
500 Jackson Street
Columbus, IN 47202 (812) 377-5000
diesel engines DRP

Current Income Shares Inc. CUR
445 South Figeroa Street
Los Angeles, CA 90071 (213) 236-7096
closed end bond mutual fund DRP

Curtiss-Wright Corporation CW
1200 Wall Street West
Lyndhurst, NJ 07071 (201) 896-8400
aerospace, process equipment

CyCare Systems, Inc. CYS
Suite 320, 4343 East Camelback Road
Phoenix, AZ 85018 (602) 952-5300
healthcare computer services

Cyclops Industries CYC
650 Washington Street
Pittsburgh, PA 15228 (412) 343-4000
steel products

Cypress Semiconductor Corporation CY
3901 North First Street
San Jose, CA 95134 (408) 943-2600
custom semiconductors

Cyprus Minerals Company CYM
9100 East Mineral Circle
Englewood, CO 80112 (303) 643-5000
copper, coal, gold mining O

Dallas Corporation DLS
6750 LBJ Freeway
Dallas, TX 75240 (214) 233-6611
transportation and construction doors

Dana Corporation DCN
4500 Dorr Street
Toledo, OH 43615 (419) 535-4500
auto parts, accessories DRP O

Danaher Corporation DHR
3524 Water Street N.W.
Washington, DC 20007 (202) 333-1805
auto parts, instruments

Daniel Industries Inc. DAN
9753 Pine Lake Drive
Houston, TX 77055 (713) 467-6000
measuring and fluid control devices

Data-Design Laboratories DDL
7925 Center Ave.
Cucamonga, CA 91730 (714) 987-2511
circuit boards, engineering services

Data General Corporation DGN
4400 Computer Drive
Westboro, MA 01580 (508) 366-8911
minicomputers O

Datapoint Corporation DPT
9725 Datapoint Drive
San Antonio, TX 78229 (512) 699-7000
data processing systems

Davis Water & Waste Industries, Inc. DWW
1820 Metcalf Avenue
Thomasville, GA 31792 (912) 226-5733
pipe, valves, water equipment

Dayton-Hudson Corporation DH
777 Nicollet Mall
Minneapolis, MN 55402 (612) 370-6948
department/discount/specialty stores DRP O

DCNY Corporation DCY
900 Market Street
Wilmington, DE 19801 (302) 421-7900
securities trading, investment management

Dean Foods Company DF
3600 North River Road
Franklin Park, IL 60131 (312) 625-6200
dairy and other food products DRP

Dean Witter Government Income Trust GVT
1 World Trade Center
New York, NY 10048 (212) 938-4500
closed-end government bond mutual fund

Deere & Company DE
John Deere Road
Moline, IL 61265 (309) 765-8000
farm/construction/mining machinery DRP O

Del-Val Financial Corporation DVL
24 River Road
Bogota, NJ 07603 (201) 487-1300
real estate investment trust

Delmarva Power & Light Company DEW
800 King Street
Wilmington, DE 19899 (302) 429-3011
electric utility DRP

Delta Air Lines, Inc. DAL
Hartsfield Atlanta International Airport
Atlanta, GA 30320 (404) 765-2600
airline DRP O

Delta Woodside Industries, Inc. DLW
Suite 200, 233 North Main Street
Greenville, SC 29601 (803) 232-8301
textile fabrics, apparel

Deltona Corporation DLT
3250 S.W. 3rd Avenue
Miami, FL 33129 (305) 854-1111
real estate development

Deluxe Corporation DLX
1080 West Country Road
St. Paul, MN 55126 (612) 483-7111
imprinted bank checks, forms O

Dennison Manufacturing Company DSN
275 Wyman Street
Waltham, MA 02254 (617) 890-6350
stationery, packaging products DRP

DeSoto Inc. DSO
1700 South Mt. Prospect Road
Des Plaines, IL 60017 (312) 391-9000
paints, coatings, detergents

Detroit Edison Company DTE
2000 2nd Avenue
Detroit, MI 48226 (313) 237-8000
electric utility DRP O

Dexter Corporation, The DEX
1 Elm Street
Windsor Locks, CT 06096 (203) 627-9051
specialty chemicals, biotechnology DRP

Diagnostic Products Corporation DP
5700 West 96th Street
Los Angeles, CA 90045 (213) 776-0180
health products test kits

Di Giorgio Corporation DIG
1 Maritime Plaza
San Francisco, CA 94111 (415) 765-0100
food distributor, building products DRP

Diamond Shamrock Offshore Partners L.P.
DSP
717 North Harwood Street
Dallas, TX 75201 (214) 953-2000
oil investment partnership

Diamond Shamrock R&M, Inc. DRM
9830 Colonnade Boulevard
San Antonio, TX 78230 (512) 641-6800
oil refining and marketing

Diana Corporation DNA
Suite 1900, 111 East Wisconsin Avenue
Milwaukee, WI 53202 (414) 289-9797
food distribution

Diebold Inc. DBD
818 Mulberry Road S.E.
Canton, OH 44711 (216) 489-4000
record storage, bank security, ATM's O

Digital Communications Associates, Inc. DCA
1000 Alderman Drive
Alpharetta, GA 30201 (404) 442-4000
computer communications products O

Digital Equipment Corporation DEC
146 Main Street
Maynard, MA 01754 (508) 493-5111
data processing equipment O

Dime Savings Bank of New York, F.S. B. DME
1225 Franklin Avenue
Garden City, NY 11530 (516) 227-6030
savings bank

Disney, Walt Company DIS
500 South Buena Vista Street
Burbank, CA 91521 (818) 840-1000
amusement parks, films, TV DRP O

Diversified Energies, Inc. DEI
201 South 7th Street
Minneapolis, MN 55402 (612) 372-5101
gas and oil pipelines and exploration DRP

Diversified Industries Inc. DMC
101 South Hanley Road
Clayton, MO 63105 (314) 862-8200
metals trading, exercise equipment

Dixons Group PLC DXN
29 Farm Street
London W1X 7RD, England
(011) 441-499-3494
consumer electronics retailing

Dominion Resources Inc. D
701 East Byrd Street
Richmond, VA 23261 (804) 775-7500
electric utility DRP O

Donaldson Company, Inc. DCI
1400 West 94th Street
Minneapolis, MN 55431 (612) 887-3131
engine air cleaners, mufflers DRP

Donnelley, R H, & Sons Company DNY
2223 Martin Luther King Drive
Chicago, IL 60616 (312) 326-8000
printing DRP O

Dover Corporation DOV
277 Park Avenue
New York, NY 10172 (212) 826-7160
elevators, petroleum equipment O

Dow Chemical Company DOW
2030 Williard H. Dow Center
Midland, MI 48640 (517) 636-1000
chemicals, plastics, pharmaceuticals DRP O

Dow Jones & Company Inc. DJ
200 Liberty Street
New York, NY 10281 (212) 416-2000
business and financial news services DRP O

Downey Savings & Loan Association DSL
3501 Jamboree Road
Newport Beach, CA 92660 (714) 854-3100
savings and loan

DPL Inc. DPL
Courthouse Plaza Southwest
Dayton, OH 45402 (513) 224-6000
gas and electric utility DRP

Dravo Corporation DRV
1 Oliver Plaza
Pittsburgh, PA 15222 (412) 566-3000
construction aggregates

Dresher, Inc. DSR
7200 South Mason Avenue
Bedford Park, IL 60499 (312) 594-8900
brass beds

Dresser Industries Inc. DI
1525 Elm Street
Dallas, TX 75221 (214) 740-6000
oil and gas services DRP O

Dreyfus Corporation, The DRY
767 5th Avenue
New York, NY 10153 (212) 715-6000
mutual fund management and investment O

Dreyfus Strategic Government Income, Inc.
DSI
666 Old Country Road
Garden City, NY 11530 (516) 794-5210
closed-end government bond mutual fund

Dreyfus Strategic Municipals, Inc. LEO
666 Old Country Road
Garden City, NY 11530 (516) 794-5210
closed-end municipal bond mutual fund

Duff & Phelps Selected Utilities, Inc. DNP
55 East Monroe Street
Chicago, IL 60603 (312) 368-5510
closed-end utility stock mutual fund

Duke Power Company DUK
422 South Church Street, P.O. Box 33189
Charlotte, NC 28242 (704) 373-4011
electric utility DRP O

Duke Realty Investments Inc. DRE
8445 Keystone Crossing
Indianapolis, IN 46240 (317) 257-8688
real estate investment trust

Dun & Bradstreet Corporation DNB
299 Park Avenue
New York, NY 10171 (212) 593-6800
business info publishing/marketing/TV O

Du Pont de Nemours, E.I., & Co. DD
1007 Market Street
Wilmington, DE 19898 (302) 774-1000
chemicals, oil and gas production DRP O

Duquesne Light Company DQU
1 Oxford Centre, 301 Grant Street
Pittsburgh, PA 15279 (412) 393-6000
electric utility DRP 3%

Dynamics Corporation of America DYA
475 Steamboat Road
Greenwich, CT 06830 (203) 869-3211
appliances, metal fabrication

E-Systems ESY
6250 LBJ Freeway, P.O. Box 6030
Dallas, TX 75266 (214) 661-1000
electronic and aerospace equipment O

Eagle-Picher Industries Inc. EPI
580 Walnut Street, P.O. Box 779
Cincinnati, OH 45202 (513) 721-7010
auto parts, industrial machinery

Eastern Enterprises EFU
9 Riverside Road
Weston, MA 02193 (617) 647-2300
gas utility, coal, barges DRP O

Eastern Utilities Associates EUA
1 Liberty Square
Boston, MA 02109 (617) 357-9590
electric utility DRP 5%

Eastman Kodak Company EK
343 State Street
Rochester, NY 14650 (716) 724-4000
photographic equipment, chemicals, drugs
DRP O

Eaton Corporation ETN
100 Erieview Plaza
Cleveland, OH 44114 (216) 523-5000
automotive, electrical components DRP 5% O

ECC International Corp. ECC
175 Strafford Avenue
Wayne, PA 19087 (215) 687-2600
military weapons simulators

Echlin Inc. ECH
100 Double Beach Road
Branford, CT 06405 (203) 481-5751
auto parts, accessories O

Ecolab Inc. ECL
Ecolab Center
St. Paul, MN 55102 (612) 293-2233
cleaning and lawn care services DRP

Edison Brothers Stores, Inc. EBS
501 North Broadway
St. Louis, MO 63178 (314) 331-6000
women's shoe and apparel stores

EDO Corporation EDO
14-04 111th Street
College Point, NY 11356 (718) 445-6000
marine and military electronic equipment

Edwards (A.G.), Inc. AGE
1 North Jefferson Street
St. Louis, MO 63103 (314) 289-3000
regional brokerage

1838 Bond-Debenture Trading Fund BDF
32nd Floor, 3 Mellon Bank Center
Philadelphia, PA 19102 (215) 963-3560
closed-end bond mutual fund

EG&G Inc. EGG
45 William Street, Wellesley Office Park
Wellesley, MA 02181 (617) 237-5100
electronic, nucleonic systems DRP 0

Ekco Group, Inc. EKO
Suite 102, 98 Spit Brock Road
Nashua, NH 03062 (603) 888-1212
kitchen tools, houseware products

Elcor Corporation ELK
14643 Dallas Parkway
Dallas, TX 75240 (214) 851-0500
roofing and industrial products

Eldon Industries, Inc. ELD
9920 La Cienega Boulevard
Inglewood, CA 90301 (213) 642-7716
office products, electronic repair

Electronic Associates, Inc. EA
185 Monmount Parkway
West Long Branch, NJ 07764 (201) 229-1100
simulator computer systems

Eljer Industries, Inc. ELJ
901 Tenth Street
Plano, TX 75074 (214) 881-7177
plumbing, heating, air conditioning

Elscint Ltd ELT
Advanced Technology Center, P.O. Box 550
Haifa 31004, Israel (972) 450540
scientific, medical instruments

EMC Corporation EMC
171 South Street
Hopkinton, MA 01748 (508) 435-1000
computer expansion boards

Emerald Homes L.P. EHP
Suite 310, 5333 North 7th Street
Phoenix, AZ 85014 (602) 995-9100
homebuilding

Emerald Mortgage Investments Corporation
EIC
Suite 219, 5333 North 7th Street
Phoenix, AZ 85014 (602) 265-8541
mortgage real estate investment trust

Emerson Electric Company EMR
8000 West Florissant, P.O. Box 4100
St. Louis, MO 63136 (314) 553-2000
electrical and electronic products DRP 0

Emerson Radio Corporation EME
1 Emerson Lane
North Bergen, NJ 07047 (201) 854-6600
consumer electronics

Empire District Electric Company EDE
602 Joplin Street
Joplin, MO 64801 (417) 623-4700
electric utility DRP 5%

Empressa Nacional de Electricidad, S.A. ELE
Principe de Vergara, 187
Madrid 28002, Spain (341) 416-8011
Spanish electric utility

Energen Corporation EGN
2101 6th Avenue North
Birmingham, AL 35203 (205) 326-2700
gas utility DRP

Engelhard Corporation EC
Menlo Park CN-40
Edison, NJ 08818 (201) 632-6000
specialty catalysts, precious metals DRP O

Ennis Business Forms Inc. EBF
107 North Sherman Street
Ennis, TX 75119 (214) 875-6581
business forms, paper products

Enron Corporation ENE
1400 Smith Street
Houston, TX 77002 (713) 853-6161
gas pipeline, oil exploration DRP O

ENSERCH Corporation ENS
300 South St. Paul Street
Dallas, TX 75201 (214) 651-8700
oil and gas, gas utility/pipeline DRP O

Enserch Exploration Partners Ltd EP
1817 Wood Street
Dallas, TX 75201 (214) 748-1110
oil and gas investment partnership

Ensource Inc. EEE
Suite 1900, 1001 Fannin
Houston, TX 77002 (713) 739-0200
oil and gas exploration and production

Entergy Corporation ETR
225 Baronne Street
New Orleans, LA 70112 (504) 529-5262
electric utility

Enterra Corporation EN
P.O. Box 1535
Houston, TX 77251 (713) 672-7600
rents oil drilling equipment

Environmental Systems Company ESC
333 Executive Court
Little Rock, AK 72205 (501) 223-4100
hazardous waste management services

EQK Green Acres, L.P. EGA
3 Bala Plaza East Suite 500
Bala Cynwyd, PA 19004 (215) 667-2300
real estate investment trust

EQK Realty Investors I EKR
3 Bala Plaza East Suite 500
Bala Cynwyd, PA 19004 (215) 667-2300
real estate investment trust

Equifax Inc. EFX
1600 Peachtree Street N.W.
Atlanta, GA 30302 (404) 885-8000
risk management, financial services

Equimark Corporation EQK
Equibank Building, 2 Oliver Plaza
Pittsburgh, PA 15222 (412) 288-5000
banking DRP

Equitable Real Estate Shopping Centers L.P.
EQM
American Express Tower,
World Financial Center
New York, NY 10285 (212) 298-4500
shopping center limited partnership

Equitable Resources Inc. EQT
420 Boulevard of the Allies
Pittsburgh, PA 15219 (412) 261-3000
gas utility DRP

Equitec Financial Group Inc. EFG
7677 Oakport Street P O Box 2470
Oakland, CA 94614 (415) 430-9900
financial services, real estate

Erbamont N V ERB
1266 Main Street
Stamford, CT 06902 (203) 967-4882
drugs

ERC International, Inc. ERC
3211 Germantown Road
Fairfax, VA 22030 (703) 246-0200
government consulting

Esselte Business Systems Inc. ESB
71 Clinton Road
Garden City, NY 11530 (516) 741-1477
office supply/graphics products

Esterline Corporation ESL
Suite 600, 10800 NE 8th Street
Bellevue, WA 98004 (206) 453-6001
circuit board automation, instrumentation

Ethyl Corporation EY
330 South 4th Street, P.O. Box 2189
Richmond, VA 23217 (804) 788-5000
chemicals, plastics, aluminum O

Excelsior Income Shares EIS
45 Wall Street
New York, NY 10005 (212) 425-7120
closed end bond mutual fund DRP

Exxon Corporation XON
1251 Avenue of the Americas
New York, NY 10020 (212) 333-1000
oil/gas production and marketing DRP O

Fabri-Centers of America FCA
23550 Commerce Park Road
Beachwood, OH 44122 (216) 464-2500
retail fabric stores

FAI Insurances Limited FAI
FAI Insurance Building, 185 Macquarie St.
Sydney, NSW 2000, Australia (02) 221-1155
insurance, investment services

Fairchild Industries, Inc. FEN
300 West Service Road, P.O. Box 10803
Chantilly, VA 22021 (703) 478-5800
aerospace DRP

Fairfield Communities, Inc. FCI
2800 Cantrell Road
Little Rock, AR 72202 (501) 664-6000
real estate development, time sharing

Family Dollar Stores FDO
P.O. Box 25800, 10401 Old Monroe Road
Charlotte, NC 28212 (704) 847-6961
discount stores

Fansteel Inc. FNL
1 Tantalum Place
North Chicago, IL 60064 (312) 689-4900
specialty metals refining

Far West Financial Corporation FWF
1800 Avenue of the Americas
Los Angeles, CA 90067 (213) 551-0322
savings and loan

Farah Inc. FRA
8889 Gateway West
El Paso, TX 79925 (915) 593-4444
jeans and slacks for men and boys

Fay's Drug Company, Inc. FAY
7245 Henry Clay Boulevard
Liverpool, NY 13088 (315) 451-8000
discount drug stores

Fedders Corporation FJQ
158 Highway 206, P.O. Box 265
Peapack, NJ 07977 (201) 234-2100
air conditioning equipment

Federal Express Corporation FDX
2005 Corporate Avenue, P.O. Box 727
Memphis, TN 38194 (901) 369-3600
freight and package forwarding O

Federal Home Loan Mortgage Corporation FRE
Pr
1759 Business Center Drive
Reston, VA 22090 (703) 759-8000
packages mortgages for secondary market

Federal National Mortgage Assoc. FNM
3900 Wisconsin Avenue, N.W.
Washington, DC 20016 (202) 537-7000
mortgage-backed securities DRP O

Federal Paper Board Company, Inc. FBO
75 Chestnut Ridge Road
Montvale, NJ 07645 (201) 391-1776
paperboard, pulp, folding cartons DRP O

Federal Realty Investment Trust FRT
Suite 500, 4800 Hampden Lane
Bethesda, MD 20814 (301) 652-3360
real estate investment trust DRP 5%

Federal Signal Corporation FSS
1415 22nd Street Room 1100
Oak Brook, IL 60521 (312) 954-2000
electric outdoor signs and signals DRP

Ferro Corporation FOE
1 Erieview Plaza
Cleveland, OH 44144 (216) 641-8580
specialty coatings and chemicals DRP

Fieldcrest Cannon, Inc. FLD
326 East Stadium Drive
Eden, NC 27288 (919) 627-3000
bed and bath products, carpets, textiles

Filtertek Companies FTK
11411 Price Road
Hebron, IL 60034 (815) 648-2416
auto and health care filters

Financial Corporation of Santa Barbara FSB
3908 State Street, P.O. Box 1109
Santa Barbara, CA 93105 (805) 682-2300
savings and loan

Financial News Composite Fund, Inc. FIF
1285 Avenue of the Americas
New York, NY 10019 (212) 713-2000
closed-end index mutual fund

Fine Homes International L.P. FHI
10 Stamford Forum
Stamford, CT 06901 (203) 356-1400
real estate brokerage, relocation services

Finevest Foods, Inc. FVF
191 Mason Street
Greenwich, CT 06830 (203) 629-8014
frozen food distributor, dairy products

Fireman's Fund Corporation FFC
777 San Marin Drive
Novato, CA 94998 (415) 899-2000
property and casualty insurance

First Bank System Inc. FBS
1200 1st Bank Place East
Minneapolis, MN 55480 (612) 370-5100
banking, financial services DRP 5%

First Boston Income Fund, Inc. FBF
Vanguard Financial Center
Valley Forge, PA 19482 (215) 648-6069
closed-end bond mutual fund

First Boston Strategic Income Fund, Inc. FBI
Vanguard Financial Center
Valley Forge, PA 19482 (215) 648-6116
closed-end bond mutual fund

First Capital Holdings Corporation FCH
1900 Avenue of the Stars
Los Angeles, CA 90067 (213) 551-1000
life insurance

First Chicago Corporation FNB
1 First National Plaza
Chicago, IL 60670 (312) 732-4000
banking DRP 5% O

First City Bancorp of Texas FBT
1001 Main Street
Houston, TX 77002 (713) 658-6011
banking

First Fidelity Bancorporation FFB
550 Broad Street
Newark, NJ 07192 (201) 565-3200
banking DRP 5%

First Financial Fund, Inc. FF
One Seaport Plaza
New York, NY 10292 (212) 214-3334
closed-end stock mutual fund DRP

First Interstate Bancorp I
707 Wilshire Boulevard
Los Angeles, CA 90054 (213) 614-3001
banking DRP O

First Mississippi Corporation FRM
700 North Street, P.O. Box 1249
Jackson, MS 39215 (601) 948-7550
fertilizer, chemicals, oil and gas DRP O

First Pennsylvania Corporation FPA
Centre Square West, 16th and Market Streets
Philadelphia, PA 19101 (215) 786-5000
banking

First Union Corporation FTU
First Union Plaza
Charlotte, NC 28288 (704) 374-6565
banking DRP O

First Union R.E. Eq. Mtge. Investments FUR
Suite 1900, 55 Public Square
Cleveland, OH 44113 (216) 781-4030
real estate investment trust DRP

First Virginia Banks Inc. FVB
6400 Arlington Boulevard
Falls Church, VA 22046 (703) 241-4000
banking DRP 5%

First Wachovia Corporation FW
301 North Main Street
Winston-Salem, NC 27150 (919) 770-5000
banking DRP 5%

Firstar Corporation FSR
777 East Wisconsin Avenue
Milwaukee, WI 53202 (414) 765-4321
banking DRP

FirstFed Financial Corporation FED
401 Wilshire Boulevard
Santa Monica, CA 90401 (213) 458-3011
savings and loan

Fischbach Corporation FIS
485 Lexington Avenue
New York, NY 10017 (212) 986-4100
electrical and mechanical contracting

Fleet/ Norstar Financial Group, Inc. FNG
55 Kennedy Plaza
Providence, RI 02903 (401) 278-5800
banking, financial services DRP

Fleetwood Enterprises, Inc. FLE
P.O. Box 7638, 3125 Myers Street
Riverside, CA 92523 (714) 351-3500
mobile homes, travel trailers O

Fleming Companies Inc. FLM
6301 Waterford Boulevard, Box 26647
Oklahoma City, OK 73126 (405) 840-7200
wholesale food distributor DRP 5%

FlightSafety International, Inc. FSI
Marine Air Terminal, La Guardia Airport
Flushing, NY 11371 (718) 565-4100
pilot and marine training

Floating Point Systems, Inc. FLP
3601 SW Murray Boulevard
Beaverton, OR 97005 (503) 641-3151
hi-speed array processor computers O

Florida East Coast Industries Inc. FLA
1 Malaga Street
St. Augustine, FL 32084 (904) 829-3421
railroads, real estate

Florida Progress Corporation FPC
270 First Avenue South
St. Petersburg, FL 33701 (813) 895-1700
electric utility DRP 5%

Flow General, Inc. FGN
7655 Old Springhouse Road
McLean, VA 22102 (703) 893-5915
biomedical products, research services

Flowers Industries, Inc. FLO
U.S. Highway 19 South
Thomasville, GA 31799 (912) 226-9110
baked goods, snack foods, frozen foods

Fluor Corporation FLR
333 Michelson Drive
Irvine, CA 92730 (714) 975-2000
general contracting, coal, lead O

FMC Corporation FMC
200 East Randolph Drive
Chicago, IL 60601 (312) 861-6000
chemicals and machinery DRP O

FMC Gold Company FGL
5011 Meadowood Way
Reno, NV 89502 (702) 827-3777
gold and silver mining

Foote, Cone & Belding Communications Inc.
FCB
101 East Erie Street
Chicago, IL 60611 (312) 751-7000
advertising agency DRP

Foothill Group, Inc. FGI
30343 Canwood Street
Agoura Hills, CA 91301 (818) 706-0131
commercial finance

Ford Motor Company F
The American Road
Dearborn, MI 48121 (313) 322-3000
auto/truck/farm/defense equipment DRP O

Fort Dearborn Securities Inc. FTD
Suite 0123, 1 North State Street
Chicago, IL 60602 (312) 346-0676
closed end bond mutual fund DRP

Foster Wheeler Corporation FWC
Perryville Corporate Park
Clinton, NJ 08809 (201) 730-4000
energy and process equipment/plants DRP O

Foxboro Company, The FOX
Bristol Park
Foxboro, MA 02035 (617) 543-8750
industrial control instrument systems

FPL Group Inc FPL
11770 U.S. Highway #1
North Palm Beach, FL 33408 (407) 694-6300
electric utility, insurance DRP O

France Fund, Inc. FRN
535 Madison Avenue
New York, NY 10022 (212) 701-2875
closed-end French stock mutual fund

Franklin Principal Maturity Trust FPT
777 Mariners Island Boulevard
San Mateo, CA 94404 (415) 570-3000
closed-end bond mutual fund DRP

Franklin Resources, Inc. BEN
777 Mariners Island Boulevard
San Mateo, CA 94404 (415) 570-3000
mutual funds, investment management

Franklin Universal Trust FT
777 Mariners Island Boulevard
San Mateo, CA 94404 (415) 378-2000
closed-end stock and bond mutual fund

Freeport-McMoran Copper Company, Inc.
FCX
6110 Plumas Street
Reno, NV 89509 (702) 826-3000
copper, gold and silver mining

Freeport McMoran Energy Partners Ltd FMP
1615 Poydras Street
New Orleans, LA 70112 (504) 582-4000
oil investment partnership

Freeport McMoran Gold Company FAU
1615 Poydras Street
New Orleans, LA 70112 (504) 582-4000
gold mining

Freeport McMoran Inc. FTX
1615 Poydras Street
New Orleans, LA 70112 (504) 582-4000
agricultural minerals, oil and gas DRP O

Freeport McMoran O & G Royalty Trust FMR
First City Financial Center, 1301 Fannin
Houston, TX 77002 (713) 658-7639
oil and gas royalty trust

Freeport-McMoran Resource Partners L.P.
FRP
1615 Poydras Street
New Orleans, LA 70112 (504) 582-4000
fertilizer, sulphur

Fuqua Industries Inc. FQA
4900 Georgia-Pacific Center
Atlanta, GA 30303 (404) 658-9000
sporting goods, lawn equipment,
photofinishing O

Furr's/Bishop's Cafeterias, L.P. CAF
6901 Quaker Avenue
Lubbock, TX 79413 (806) 792-7151
cafeteria limited partnership

Gabelli Equity Trust, Inc. GAB
8 Sound Shore Drive
Greenwich, CT 06830 (203) 625-0028
closed-end stock mutual fund DRP

Gallagher, Arthur J. & Co. AJG
10 Gould Center, Golf Road
Rolling Meadows, IL 60008 (312) 640-8500
insurance brokerage

Galoob, Lewis Toys, Inc. GAL
500 Forbes Boulevard
South San Francisco, CA 94080
(415) 952-1678
toys

Galveston-Houston Company GHX
Suite 1200, 4900 Woodway
Houston, TX 77056 (713) 966-2500
mining, construction, energy equipment

Gannett Company Inc. GCI
1000 Wilson Boulevard
Arlington, VA 20044 (703) 284-6000
newspapers, TV and radio stations DRP O

Gap, Inc. (The) GPS
900 Cherry Avenue, P.O. Box 60
San Bruno, CA 94066 (415) 952-4400
apparel and accessory stores O

Gateway Corporation GAT
Silbury Court, 418 Silbury Boulevard
Milton Keynes, MK9 2NB, UK (0908) 607171
food and specialty retailing

GATX Corporation GMT
120 South Riverside Plaza
Chicago, IL 60606 (312) 621-6200
railcar leasing, shipping DRP

GEICO Corporation GEC
GEICO Plaza
Chevy Chase, MD 20076 (301) 986-3000
property and casualty insurance

Gemini II Inc. GMI
Vanguard Financial Center
Valley Forge, PA 19482 (800) 662-7447
closed end dual purpose mutual fund

GenCorp Inc. GY
175 Ghent Road
Fairlawn, OH 44313 (216) 869-4440
aerospace, automotive, polymers DRP O

Genentech, Inc. GNE
460 Point San Bruno Boulevard
South San Francisco, CA 94080
(415) 266-1000
biotechnology

General American Investors Co. Inc. GAM
330 Madison Avenue
New York, NY 10017 (212) 916-8400
closed-end stock mutual fund DRP

General Cinema Corporation GCN
P.O. Box 1000, 27 Boylston Street
Chestnut Hill, MA 02167 (617) 232-8200
movie theatres, retailing, candy DRP O

General Datacomm Industries, Inc. GDC
1 Kennedy Avenue
Middlebury, CT 06762-1299 (203) 574-1118
electronic data transmission systems

General Development Corporation GDV
1111 South Bayshore Drive
Miami, FL 33131 (305) 350-1200
develops planned communities

General Dynamics Corporation GD
Pierre LaClede Center
St. Louis, MO 63105 (314) 889-8200
aerospace industries, submarines O

General Electric Company GE
3135 Easton Turnpike
Fairfield, CT 06431 (203) 373-2211
aerospace, broadcasting, appliances DRP O

General Energy Development, Ltd. GED
Suite 900, 1201 Louisiana
Houston, TX 77002 (713) 654-9110
oil and gas production

General Homes Corporation GHO
7322 Southwest Freeway
Houston, TX 77074 (713) 270-4177
construction of single family homes

General Host Corporation GH
22 Gate House Road
Stamford, CT 06904 (203) 357-9900
nursery and crafts retailing

General Housewares Corporation GHW
6 Suburban Avenue, P.O. Box 10265
Stamford, CT 06904-2265 (203) 325-4141
cookware and giftware

General Instrument Corporation GRL
767 5th Avenue
New York, NY 10153 (212) 207-6200
electronic components and systems O

General Mills, Inc. GIS
1 General Mills Boulevard
Minneapolis, MN 55426 (612) 540-2311
foods, restaurants DRP O

General Motors Corporation GM
3044 West Grand Boulevard
Detroit, MI 48202 (313) 556-5000
autos, trucks, defense, space DRP O

GEO International Corporation GX
1 Landmark Square
Stamford, CT 06901 (203) 964-1955
graphics and oilfield equipment

General Motors Class E Common Stock GME
7171 Forest Lane
Dallas, TX 75230 (214) 604-6000
computer services O

Georgia Gulf Corporation GGC
Suite 595, 400 Perimeter Center Terrace
Atlanta, GA 30346 (404) 395-4500
commodity and specialty chemicals O

General Motors Class H Common Stock GMH
3044 West Grand Boulevard
Detroit, MI 48202 (313) 556-3510
defense and automotive products

Georgia-Pacific Corporation GP
133 Peachtree Street N.W.
Atlanta, GA 30303 (404) 521-4000
building products, packaging, paper DRP O

General Nutrition, Inc. GNC
921 Penn Avenue
Pittsburgh, PA 15222 (412) 288-4600
health food production and retailing DRP

Gerber Products Company GEB
445 State Street
Fremont, MI 49412 (616) 928-2000
baby foods, apparel, toys DRP O

General Public Utilities Corporation GPU
100 Interpace Parkway
Parsippany, NJ 07054 (201) 263-6500
electric utility

Gerber Scientific Inc. GRB
83 Gerber Road West
South Windsor, CT 06074 (203) 644-1551
automatic electronic drafting systems O

General Re Corporation GRN
Financial Centre, 695 East Main Street
Stamford, CT 06904 (203) 328-5000
property-casualty reinsurance O

Germany Fund, Inc. GER
40 Wall Street
New York, NY 10005 (212) 612-0676
closed-end German stock mutual fund

General Signal Corporation GSX
High Ridge Park
Stamford, CT 06904 (203) 357-8800
electrical control equipment DRP

Getty Petroleum Corporation GTY
125 Jericho Turnpike
Jericho, NY 11753 (516) 338-6000
distribution of gasoline, gas stations

Genesco Inc. GCO
111 7th Avenue South
Nashville, TN 37202 (615) 367-7000
produces/sells footwear and men's wear

GF Corporation GFB
4944 Belmont Avenue
Youngstown, OH 44501 (216) 759-8888
metal office furniture

GenRad Inc. GEN
300 Baker Avenue
Concord, MA 01742 (508) 369-4400
electronic test equipment O

GIANT Group Ltd GPO
Highway 453, P.O. Box 218
Harleyville, SC 29448 (803) 496-7880
cement

Genuine Parts Company GPC
2999 Circle 75 Parkway
Atlanta, GA 30339 (404) 953-1700
distribution of auto and industrial parts O

Gibraltar Financial Corporation GFC
9111 Wilshire Boulevard
Beverly Hills, CA 90210 (213) 278-8720
savings and loan

Gillette Company GS
Prudential Plaza
Boston, MA 02199 (617) 421-7000
personal care products, pens DRP O

Gitano Group, Inc. GIT
1411 Broadway
New York, NY 10018 (212) 819-0707
men's, women's and children's apparel

Glaxo Holdings PLC GLX
Clarges House, 6-12 Clarges Street
London W1Y 8DH England (01) 493-4060
pharmaceuticals O

Gleason Corporation GLE
30 Corporate Woods
Rochester, NY 14692 (716) 272-6000
bevel gear machinery, industrial products

GLENFED, Inc. GLN
700 North Brand Boulevard
Glendale, CA 91209 (818) 500-2000
savings and loan O

Global Government Plus Fund, Inc. GOV
One Seaport Plaza
New York, NY 10292 (800) 451-6788
closed-end global bond mutual fund DRP

Global Income Plus Fund, Inc. GLI
1285 Avenue of the Americas
New York, NY 10019 (212) 713-2710
closed-end global bond mutual fund DRP

Global Growth & Income Fund, Inc. GGF
Vanguard Financial Center
Valley Forge, PA 19482 (800) 662-7447
closed-end dual purpose mutual fund

Global Marine Inc. GLM
777 North Eldridge Road
Houston, TX 77079 (713) 596-5100
offshore drilling, oil and gas exploration

Global Yield Fund, Inc. PGY
One Seaport Plaza
New York, NY 10292 (212) 214-1215
closed-end global bond mutual fund DRP

Golden Nugget, Inc. GNG
129 Fremont Street
Las Vegas, NV 89101 (702) 385-7111
hotel-casino complexes O

Golden Valley Microwave Foods, Inc. GVF
7450 Metro Boulevard
Edina, MN 55435 (612) 835-6900
microwave-based foods O

Golden West Financial Corporation GDW
1901 Harrison Street
Oakland, CA 94612 (415) 446-6000
savings and loan O

Goldome GDM
1 Fountain Plaza
Buffalo, NY 14203 (716) 847-5800
savings bank

Goodrich, BF, Company GR
3925 Embassy Parkway
Akron, OH 44313 (216) 374-3985
chemical, plastic, aerospace products DRP O

Goodyear Tire & Rubber Company GT
1144 East Market Street
Akron, OH 44316 (216) 796-2121
rubber/plastic/chemical products DRP 5% O

Gordon Jewelry Corporation GOR
820 Fannin Street
Houston, TX 77002 (713) 222-8080
retail jewelry store chain

Gottschalks Inc. GOT
860 Fulton Mall
Fresno, CA 93721 (209) 485-1111
department stores

Grace, W R Company GRA
Grace Plaza, 1114 Avenue of the Americas
New York, NY 10036 (212) 819-5500
chemicals, energy, consumer products DRP
O

Graco Inc. GGG
4050 Olson Memorial Highway
Golden Valley, MN 55422 (612) 623-6000
fluid-handling equipment

Grainger, W W Inc GWW
5500 West Howard Street
Skokie, IL 60077 (312) 982-9000
electrical, mechanical products

Great American First Savings Bank GTA
600 B Street
San Diego, CA 92183 (619) 231-1885
savings and loan

Great Atlantic & Pacific Tea Co., Inc. GAP
2 Paragon Drive
Montvale, NJ 07645 (201) 573-9700
supermarkets, coffee processing

Great Lakes Chemical Corporation GLK
Highway 52 Northwest
West Lafayette, IN 47906 (317) 497-6100
chemicals

Great Northern Iron Ore Properties GNI
W-2081 1st National Bank Building
St. Paul, MN 55101 (612) 224-2385
leasing iron ore properties to mine firms

Great Northern Nekoosa Corporation GNN
401 Merritt 7, P.O. Box 5120
Norwalk, CT 06856 (203) 845-9000 DRP O
newsprint, paper, packaging

Great Western Financial Corporation GWF
8484 Wilshire Boulevard
Beverly Hills, CA 90211 (213) 852-3411
savings and loan DRP O

Green Mountain Power Corporation GMP
25 Green Mountain Drive
South Burlington, VT 05402 (802) 864-5731
electric utility DRP 5%

Green Tree Acceptance Inc. GNT
1100 Landmark Tower, 345 St. Peter Street
St. Paul, MN 55102 (612) 293-3400
purchases housing contracts

Greyhound Corporation G
Greyhound Tower
Phoenix, AZ 85077 (602) 248-4000
consumer products, bus manufacturing O

Grow Group Inc. GRO
200 Park Avenue
New York, NY 10166 (212) 599-4400
specialty coatings, chemical products O

Growth Stock Outlook Trust GSO
4405 East West Highway
Bethesda, MD 20814 (301) 654-5205
closed-end stock mutual fund DRP

Grubb & Ellis Company GBE
1 Montgomery Street, Telesis Tower
San Francisco, CA 94014 (415) 956-1990
real estate broker

Grumman Corporation GQ
1111 Stewart Avenue
Bethpage, NY 11714 (516) 575-0574
government aircraft, trucks, radar DRP O

GTE Corporation GTE
1 Stamford Forum
Stamford, CT 06904 (203) 965-2000
telecommunication systems, equipment DRP
O

Guardsman Products, Inc. GPI
2960 Lucerne Drive S.E.
Grand Rapids, MI 49501 (616) 957-2600
industrial coatings, consumer polishes

Guilford Mills Inc. GFD
4925 West Market Street
Greensboro, NC 27407 (919) 292-7550
textiles for apparel/upholstery/autos

Gulf Resources & Chemical Corporation GRE
99 High Street
Boston, MA 02110 (617) 482-2555
coal, specialty clays, oil and gas

Gulf States Utilities Company GSU
350 Pine Steeet
Beaumont, TX 77701 (409) 838-6631
electric utility

Hadson Corporation HAD
101 Park Avenue
Oklahoma City, OK 73102 (405) 235-9531
energy products and services

Hall, Frank B & Company, Inc. FBH
549 Pleasantville Road
Briarcliff Manor, NY 10510 (914) 769-9200
insurance brokers O

Halliburton Company HAL
3600 Lincoln Plaza
Dallas, TX 75201 (214) 978-2600
oil field services/engineering O

Hallwood Group Inc. HWG
767 Third Avenue
New York, NY 10017 (212) 319-2360
real estate, financial services

Handleman Company HDL
500 Kirts Boulevard
Troy, MI 48084 (313) 362-4400
sells and distributes music and books DRP

Handy & Harman HNH
850 Third Avenue
New York, NY 10022 (212) 752-3400
metals, auto parts, electronic items DRP

Hanna M.A. Company MAH
Suite 3600, 1301 East 9th Street
Cleveland, OH 44114 (216) 589-4000
formulated polymers, iron ore

Hannaford Bros. Company HRD
145 Pleasant Hill Road
Scarborough, ME 04074 (207) 883-2911
supermarkets, drug stores DRP

Hanson PLC Han
1 Grosvenor Place
London SW1X 7JH, England (441) 245-1245
consumer, industrial, building products O

Harcourt Brace Jovanovich Inc. HBJ
6277 Sea Harbor Drive
Orlando, FL 32887 (305) 345-2000
book, journal, and magazine publishing O

Harland, John H. Company JH
2939 Miller Road
Decatur, GA 30035 (404) 981-9460
check printing

Harley-Davidson, Inc. HDI
3700 West Juneau Avenue
Milwaukee, WI 53208 (414) 342-4680
motorcycles, recreational vehicles

Harman International Industries, Inc. HAR
1155 Connecticut Avenue N.W.
Washington, DC 20036 (202) 955-6130
makes audio and video equipment

Harnischfeger Industries, Inc. HPH
13400 Bishops Lane
Brookfield, WI 53201 (414) 671-4400
papermaking, material handling equipment O

Harris Corporation HRS
1025 West NASA Boulevard
Melbourne, FL 32919 (407) 727-9100
electronic communications equipment DRP O

Harsco Corporation HSC
350 Poplar Church Road
Wormleysburg, PA 17001 (717) 763-7064
metals fabrication DRP

Hartmarx Corporation HMX
101 North Wacker Drive
Chicago, IL 60606 (312) 372-6300
clothing manufacturer/retailer DRP

Hatteras Income Securities Inc. HAT
1 NCNB Plaza, P.O. Box 120
Charlotte, NC 28255 (704) 333-7808
closed-end bond mutual fund DRP

Hawaiian Electric Industries Inc. HE
900 Richards Street
Honolulu, HI 96813 (808) 548-5670
electric utility DRP 5%

Health & Rehabilitation Properties Trust HRP
215 First Street
Cambridge, MA 02142 (617) 661-3112
health care real estate investment trust DRP

Health Care Property Investors Inc. HCP
Suite 1200, 10990 Wilshire Boulevard
Los Angeles, CA 90024 (213) 473-1990
health care real estate investment trust DRP

Hecla Mining Company HL
Hecla Building, 6500 Mineral Drive
Coeur d'Alene, ID 83814 (208) 769-4100
silver, gold mining O

Heilig-Meyers Company HMY
2235 Staples Mill Road
Richmond, VA 23230 (804) 359-9171
retail furniture stores

Heinz, H J Company HNZ
600 Grant Street
Pittsburgh, PA 15219 (412) 237-5757
food products DRP O

Helene Curtis Industries, Inc. HC
325 North Wells Street
Chicago, IL 60610 (312) 661-0222
beauty and hair care products

Helmerich & Payne Inc. HP
Utica at 21st Street
Tulsa, OK 74114 (918) 742-5531
oil field services/exploration O

Helvetia Fund, Inc. SWZ
521 Fifth Avenue
New York, NY 10175 (212) 867-7660
closed-end Swiss stock mutual fund DRP

Hercules Inc. HPC
900 Market Place
Wilmington, DE 19894 (302) 594-5000
chemicals and plastics products DRP O

Hershey Foods Corporation HSY
100 Mansion Road East
Hershey, PA 17033 (717) 534-4000
chocolate candy, pasta DRP O

Hewlett-Packard Company Inc. HWP
3000 Hanover Street
Palo Alto, CA 94304 (415) 857-1501
measurement and computer products O

Hexcel Corporation HXL
11555 Dublin Boulevard
Dublin, CA 94568 (415) 828-4200
honeycomb cores for aerospace DRP 5%

Hi-Shear Industries, Inc. HSI
3333 New Hyde Park Road
North Hills, NY 10042 (516) 627-8600
aerospace fastener devices

High Income Advantage Trust YLD
1 World Trade Center
New York, NY 10048 (212) 938-4553
closed-end bond mutual fund DRP

High Income Advantage Trust II YLT
1 World Trade Center
New York, NY 10048 (212) 938-4500
closed-end bond mutual fund DRP

High Income Advantage Trust III YLH
1 World Trade Center
New York, NY 10048 (212) 938-4500
closed-end bond mutual fund DRP

High Yield Income Fund, Inc. HYI
One Seaport Plaza
New York, NY 10292 (212) 214-3334
closed-end bond mutual fund

High Yield Plus Fund, Inc. HYP
One Seaport Plaza
New York, NY 10292 (212) 214-3334
closed-end bond mutual fund

Hillenbrand Industries Inc. HB
Highway 46
Batesville, IN 47006 (812) 934-7000
burial caskets, medical equipment, luggage

Hills Department Stores, Inc. HDS
15 Dan Road
Canton, MA 02021 (617) 821-1000
discount department stores

Hilton Hotels Corporation HLT
9336 Civic Center Drive
Beverly Hills, CA 90209 (213) 278-4321
hotels and casinos O

HIMONT Inc. HMT
3 Little Falls Centre, 2801 Centerville Road
Wilmington, DE 19850 (302) 996-6000
polypropylene producer

Hitachi, Ltd HIT
6, Kanda-Surugadai 4 Chome
Chiyoda-Ku, Tokyo 101, Japan
(914) 332-5800
electrical and industrial equipment O

Holiday Corporation HIA
1023 Cherry Road
Memphis, TN 38117 (901) 762-8600
hotels, hotel-casinos O

Home Depot Inc. HD
2727 Paces Ferry Road
Atlanta, GA 30339 (404) 433-8211
retail building material stores O

Home Group, Inc. HME
59 Maiden Lane
New York, NY 10038 (212) 530-6800
insurance, brokerage, banking

Home Owners Federal S&L Assoc. HFS
21 Milk Street
Boston, MA 02109 (617) 482-0630
savings and loan

HomeFed Corporation HFD
625 Broadway
San Diego, CA 92101 (619) 699-8000
savings and loan O

Homestake Mining Company HM
650 California Street
San Francisco, CA 94108 (415) 981-8150
gold/uranium/lead/zinc/silver mining DRP O

Homestead Financial Corporation HFL
979 Broadway
Milbrae, CA 94030 (415) 692-9940
savings and loan

Honda Motor Company Ltd HMC
No. 1-1, 2-chome, Minami-Aoyama
Minato-ku, Tokyo 107, Japan (03) 423-1111
motorcycles, autos, light trucks O

Honeywell Inc. HON
Honeywell Plaza
Minneapolis, MN 55408 (612) 870-5200
controls, space and aviation DRP O

Hong Kong Telecommunications, Ltd. HKT
15th Floor, 3 Exchange Square
Hong Kong 852-58488787
telecommunications services

Hopper Soliday Corporation HS
1600 Market Street
Philadelphia, PA 19103 (215) 977-7474
brokerage, investment banking

Horizon Corporation HZN
16838 East Palisades Boulevard
Fountain Hills, AZ 85268 (602) 837-1685
develops and sells planned communities

Horizon Healthcare Corporation HHC
Suite 530, 6001 Indian School Road
Albuquerque, NM 87110 (505) 881-4961
retirement housing centers

Hotel Investors Trust/Corporation HOT
21031 Venture Boulevard
Woodland Hills, CA 91364 (818) 883-9500
hotel real estate investment trust DRP

Houghton Mifflin Company HTN
1 Beacon Street
Boston, MA 02108 (617) 725-5000
text and trade books DRP O

House of Fabrics HF
13400 Riverside Drive
Sherman Oaks, CA 91423 (818) 995-7000
retailer of sewing notions and fabrics

Household International Inc. HI
2700 Sanders Road
Prospect Heights, IL 60070 (312) 564-3663
consumer and commercial finance, insurance
DRP O

Houston Industries Inc. HOU
5 Post Oak Park
Houston, TX 77210 (713) 629-3000
electric utility DRP O

Houston Oil Royalty Trust RTH
1301 Fannin
Houston, TX 77002 (713) 658-7639
royalties of oil and gas properties

Howell Corporation HWL
Suite 1800, 1010 Lamar
Houston, TX 77002 (713) 658-4000
oil and gas exploration and refining

H&Q Healthcare Investors HQH
50 Rowes Wharf
Boston, MA 02110 (617) 574-0500
closed-end health stock mutual fund DRP

HRE Properties HRE
530 5th Avenue - 21st Floor
New York, NY 10036 (212) 642-4800
real estate investment trust DRP 5%

Huffy Corporation HUF
7701 Byers Road
Miamisburg, OH 45342 (513) 866-6251
bicycles, juvenile products DRP

Hughes Supply Inc. HUG
521 West Central Boulevard
Orlando, FL 32802 (407) 841-4755
wholesaler of electrical and plumbing items

Hughes Tool Company HT
5425 Polk Avenue
Houston, TX 77023 (713) 924-2222
oil and gas equipment and services DRP O

Humana Inc. HUM
P.O. Box 1438 500 West Main Street
Louisville, KY 40201-1438 (502) 580-1000
acute care community hospitals DRP O

Hunt Manufacturing Company HUN
230 South Broad Street
Philadelphia, PA 19102 (215) 732-7700
art and office supplies

Huntingdon International Holdings PLC HTD
Wooley Road, Alconbury, Huntingdon
Cambridgeshire PE18 6ES England
0480-890431
life sciences research and enginerring

Huntway Partners L.P. HWY
23822 West Valencia Boulevard
Valencia, CA 91355 (805) 253-1799
refines asphalt and petroleum products

Hydraulic Company THC
835 Main Street
Bridgeport, CT 06601 (203) 367-6621
water utility DRP 5%

IBP, Inc. IBP
Dakota City, NE 68731 (402) 494-2061
beef and pork products

ICM Property Investors Inc. ICM
600 Third Avenue
New York, NY 10016 (212) 986-5640
real estate investment trust DRP

ICN Pharmaceuticals Inc. ICN
3300 Hyland Avenue
Costa Mesa, CA 92626 (714) 545-0113
pharmaceuticals, biomedicals

Idaho Power Company IDA
P.O. Box 70 1220 West Idaho Street
Boise, ID 83707 (208) 383-2200
electric utility DRP

Ideal Basic Industries Inc. IDL
Ideal Plaza, 950 17th Street
Denver, CO 80201 (303) 623-5661
portland cement

IE Industries, Inc. IEL
200 First Street S.E.
Cedar Rapids, IA 52401 (319) 398-4411
electric and gas utility DRP

Illinois Central Transportation Co. IC
2 Illinois Center, 233 North Michigan Avenue
Chicago, IL 60601 (312) 819-7500
railroad

Illinois Power Company IPC
500 South 27th Street
Decatur, IL 62525 (217) 424-6600
electric and gas utility

Illinois Tool Works, Inc. ITW
8501 West Higgins Road
Chicago, IL 60631 (312) 693-3040
fasteners, tools, plastic containers

IMC Fertilizer Group, Inc. IFL
2100 Sanders Road
Northbrook, IL 60062 (312) 272-9200
phosphate chemicals, potash, fertilizer

IMO Industries, Inc. IMD
3450 Princeton Pike
Lawrenceville, NJ 08648 (609) 896-7600
instruments, controls, power systems

Imperial Chemical Industries PLC ICI
Imperial Chemical House, Millbank
London England SW1P 3JF (212) 644-9292
chemicals O

Imperial Corporation of America ICA
9275 Sky Park Court
San Diego, CA 92123 (619) 292-3000
savings and loan

INA Investment Securities Inc. IIS
1600 Arch Street
Philadelphia, PA 19103 (203) 726-6271
closed-end bond mutual fund DRP

INCO Limited N
Royal Trust Tower
Toronto, CDA M5K 1N4 (416) 361-7511
nickel, copper, precious metals O

India Growth Fund, Inc. IGF
Boston Company Advisors, One Boston Place
Boston, MA 02108 (216) 687-5745
closed-end Indian stock mutual fund DRP

Indiana Energy Inc. IEI
1630 North Meridian Street
Indianapolis, IN 46202 (317) 926-3351
gas utility DRP

Ingersoll-Rand Company IR
200 Chestnut Ridge Road
Woodcliff Lake, NJ 07675 (201) 573-0123
non-electrical machinery and equipment DRP
O

Inland Steel Industries IAD
30 West Monroe Street
Chicago, IL 60603 (312) 346-0300
steel, steel service centers O

Inspiration Resources Corp. IRC
250 Park Avenue
New York, NY 10177 (212) 503-3100
metals, agricultural chemicals

Integra Hotel and Restaurant Company ITG
4441 West Airport Freeway
Irving, TX 75015 (214) 258-8500
restaurants, hotels

Integrated Resources Inc. IRE
666 Third Avenue
New York, NY 10017 (212) 551-6000
insurance, investment management

Intelogic Trace, Inc. IT
Turtle Creek Tower I
San Antonio, TX 78229 (512) 558-5700
computer maintenance services

Inter-Regional Financial Group, Inc. IFG
100 Dain Tower
Minneapolis, MN 55402 (612) 371-7750
investment banking, securities brokerage

InterCapital Income Securities Inc. ICB
1 World Trade Center
New York, NY 10048 (212) 938-4500
closed-end bond mutual fund DRP

INTERCO Inc. ISS
101 South Hanley Road
St. Louis, MO 63105 (314) 863-1100
apparel, footwear, home furnishings

Interlake Corporation IK
701 Harger Road
Oak Brook, IL 60521 (312) 572-6600
metals, materials handling DRP 5%

International Aluminum Corporation IAL
767 Monterey Pass Road
Monterey Park, CA 91754 (213) 264-1670
aluminum products

International Business Machines Corporation
IBM
Old Orchard Road
Armonk, NY 10504 (914) 765-1900
computers, information systems DRP O

International Flavors & Fragrances Inc. IFF
521 West 57th Street
New York, NY 10019 (212) 765-5500
industrial flavor and fragrance products O

International Minerals & Chemical Corp IGL
2315 Sanders Road
Northbrook, IL 60062 (312) 564-8600
medical products, chemicals, fragrances DRP
O

International Multifoods Corporation IMC
Multifoods Tower Box 2942
Minneapolis, MN 55402 (612) 340-3300
foodservice distribution, foods DRP

International Paper Company IP
2 Manhattanville Road
Purchase, NY 10577 (914) 397-1500
pulp, paper, lumber, plywood DRP O

International Rectifier Corporation IRF
233 Kansas Street
El Segundo, CA 90245 (213) 772-2000
semiconductor products

International Technology Corporation ITX
23456 Hawthorne Boulevard
Torrance, CA 90505 (213) 378-9933
environmental projects and services

Interpublic Group of Companies Inc. IPG
1271 Avenue of the Americas
New York, NY 10020 (212) 399-8000
advertising agencies DRP O

Interstate/Johnson Lane, Inc. IS
2700 NCNB Plaza
Charlotte, NC 28280 (704) 379-9000
securities brokerage

Interstate Power Company IPW
1000 Main Street
Dubuque, IA 52001 (319) 582-5421
electric utility DRP

InterTAN Inc. ITN
2000 Two Tandy Center
Fort Worth, TX 76102 (817) 332-7181
consumer electronics retailing

Iowa-Illinois Gas & Electric Company IWG
206 East 2nd Street
Davenport, IA 52808 (319) 326-7111
gas and electric utility DRP 5%

Iowa Resources Inc. IOR
P.O. Box 657, 666 Grand Avenue
Des Moines, IA 50303 (515) 281-2900
electric utility DRP 5%

IP Timberlands Ltd IPT
77 West 45th Street
New York, NY 10036 (212) 536-6000
investment partnerships - timber

IPALCO Enterprises Inc. IPL
25 Monument Circle
Indianapolis, IN 46206 (317) 261-8261
electric utility DRP

IPCO Corporation IHS
1025 Westchester Avenue
White Plains, NY 10604 (914) 682-4500
makes/distributes medical/optical supplies

IP Timberlands, Ltd. IPT
2 Manhattanville Road
Purchase, NY 10577 (914) 397-1500
timberland limited partnership

IRT Property Company IRT
Suite 1400, 200 Galleria Parkway
Atlanta, GA 30339 (404) 955-4406
real estate investment trust

Italy Fund Inc. ITA
2 World Trade Center — 106th Floor
New York, NY 10048 (212) 321-7476
closed-end Italian stock mutual fund

ITT Corporation ITT
320 Park Avenue
New York, NY 10022 (212) 752-6000
insurance, automotive, hotels, defense DRP
O

Jackpot Enterprises, Inc. J
2900 South Highland Drive
Las Vegas, NV 89109 (702) 369-3424
gambling machines

James River Corporation of Virginia JR
P.O. Box 2218, Tredegar Street
Richmond, VA 23217 (804) 644-5411
paper products O

Jamesway Corporation JMY
40 Hartz Way
Secaucus, NJ 07094 (201) 330-6000
discount department stores

Jefferson-Pilot Corporation JP
101 North Elm Street
Greensboro, NC 27420 (919) 378-2417
life, accident, health insurance DRP

Jepson Corporation JEP
360 West Butterfield Road
Elmhurst, IL 60126 (312) 834-3710
manages leveraged buyout companies

JHM Mortgage Securities L.P. JHM Pr
9th Floor, 8300 Greensboro Drive
McLean, VA 22102 (703) 883-2900
mortgage securities limited partnership

John Hancock Income Securities Trust JHS
101 Huntington Avenue
Boston, MA 02199 (617)375-1500
closed-end bond mutual fund DRP

John Hancock Investors Trust JHI
101 Huntington Avenue
Boston, MA 02199 (617) 421-4506
closed-end bond mutual fund DRP

Johnson Controls Inc. JCI
5757 North Green Bay Avenue, P.O. Box 591
Milwaukee, WI 53201 (414) 228-1200
building automation systems, batteries DRP
O

Johnson & Johnson Company JNJ
1 Johnson & Johnson Plaza
New Brunswick, NJ 08933 (201) 524-0400
health care products O

Johnston Industries, Inc. JII
30 Rockefeller Plaza
New York, NY 10020 (212) 247-5460
industrial and apparel textiles

Johnstown/Consolidated Realty Trust JCT
2000 Powell Street
Emeryville, CA 94608 (415) 652-7171
real estate investment trust

Jorgensen, Earle M Company JOR
10700 Alameda Street
Lynwood, CA 90262 (213) 567-1122
distribution of metals DRP

Jostens Inc. JOS
5501 Norman Center Drive
Minneapolis, MN 55437 (612) 830-3300
custom mementos for schools, business DRP

J.P. Industries, Inc. JPI
325 East Eisenhower Parkway
Ann Arbor, MI 48104 (313) 663-6749
automotive products

JWP Inc. JWP
2975 Westchester Avenue
Purchase, NY 10577 (914) 935-4000
electrical contractor, water utility

Kaiser Aluminum & Chemical Corporation
KLU
300 Lakeside Drive
Oakland, CA 94643 (415) 271-3300
aluminum products, oil, gas, chemicals

Kaiser Cement Corporation KCC
Kaiser Building 300 Lakeside Drive
Oakland, CA 94612 (415) 271-2000
cement, concrete, aggregates

Kaneb Services Inc. KAB
Suite 600, 2400 Lakeside Boulevard
Richardson, TX 75081 (214) 699-4000
oil/gas exploration/production pipeline

Kansas City Power & Light Company KLT
1330 Baltimore Avenue
Kansas City, MO 64105 (816) 551-2312
electric utility

Kansas City Southern Industries Inc. KSU
114 West 11th Street
Kansas City, MO 64105 (816) 556-0303
railroads, financial services

Kansas Gas and Electric Company KGE
201 North Market Street
Wichita, KS 67201 (316) 261-6611
electric utility DRP 5%

Kansas Power & Light Company KAN
818 Kansas Avenue
Topeka, KS 66612 (913) 296-6300
electric and gas utility DRP

Katy Industries Inc. KT
853 Dundee Avenue
Elgin, IL 60120 (312) 379-1121
jewelry, spas, industrial machinery

Kaufman & Broad Home Corporation KBH
11601 Wilshire Boulevard
Los Angeles, CA 90025 (213) 312-1200
residential construction

Kay Jewelers, Inc. KJI
320 King Street
Alexandria, VA 22314 (703) 683-3800
jewelry retailing

Kellogg Company K
1 Kellogg Square, 235 Porter Street
Battle Creek, MI 49016 (616) 961-2000
convenience foods, cereal DRP O

Kellwood Company KWD
600 Kellwood Parkway
St. Louis, MO 63178 (314) 576-3100
apparel, home fashions, recreational items

Kemper High Income Trust KHI
120 South LaSalle Street
Chicago, IL 60603 (800) 537-6006
closed-end bond mutual fund DRP

Kemper Intermediate Government Trust KGT
120 South LaSalle Street
Chicago, IL 60603 (800) 537-6006
closed-end bond mutual fund DRP

Kemper Multi-Market Income Trust KMM
120 South LaSalle Street
Chicago, IL 60603 (800) 537-6006
closed-end bond mutual fund DRP

Kemper Municipal Income Trust KTF
120 South LaSalle Street
Chicago, IL 60603 (800) 537-6006
closed-end bond mutual fund DRP

Kennametal Inc. KMT
Route 981 at Westmoreland County Airport
Latrobe, PA 15650 (412) 539-5000
tungsten-based carbide tools DRP 5%

Kentucky Utilities Company KU
1 Quality Street
Lexington, KY 40507 (606) 255-1461
electric utility DRP

Kerr Glass Manufacturing Corporation KGM
1840 Century Park East
Los Angeles, CA 90067 (213) 556-2200
glass containers, plastic packaging

Kerr-McGee Corporation KMG
Kerr McGee Center, P.O. Box 25861
Oklahoma City, OK 73125 (405) 270-1313
oil and gas exploration/production DRP O

KeyCorp KEY
1 Keycorp Plaza
Albany, NY 12201 (518) 486-8000
banking DRP

Keystone Consolidated Industries Inc. KES
Suite 1440, 5430 LBJ Freeway
Dallas, TX 75240 (214) 458-0028
steel and wire products, fasteners

Keystone International Inc. KII
9600 West Gulf Bank Drive
Houston, TX 77240 (713) 466-1176
flow control products and systems DRP

Kimberly-Clark Corporation KMB
P.O. Box 619100, DFW Airport Station
Dallas, TX 75261 (214) 830-1200
paper products, lumber, pulp, newsprint DRP
O

KLM Royal Dutch Airlines KLM
Amsterdamseweg 55
Amstelveen, Netherlands (020) 499123
international airline

K Mart Corporation KM
3100 West Big Beaver Road
Troy, MI 48084 (313) 643-1000
discount and variety stores O

KN Energy, Inc. KNE
12055 West Second Place
Lakewood, CO 80215 (303) 989-1740
natural gas pipeline DRP

King World Productions, Inc. KWP
830 Morris Turnpike
Short Hills, NJ 07078 (201) 376-1313
television program syndicator O

Kleinwort Benson
Australian Income
Fund, Inc. KBA
200 Park Avenue
New York, NY 10166 (212) 972-9315
closed-end Australian bond mutual fund DRP

Knight-Ridder, Inc. KRI
1 Herald Plaza, Suite 624
Miami, FL 33101 (305) 376-3800
newspapers, business information O

Knogo Corporation KNO
350 Wireless Boulevard
Hauppauge, NY 11788 (516) 232-2100
electronic anti-shoplifting systems

Koger Properties Inc. KOG
3986 Boulevard Center Drive
Jacksonville, FL 32207 (904) 396-4811
owns and operates office buildings DRP 5%

Korea Fund Inc. KF
c/o Scudder Stevens & Clark, 345 Park Ave
New York, NY 10154 (212) 326-6200
closed-end Korean stock fund DRP

Kroger Company KR
1014 Vine Street
Cincinnati, OH 45202 (513) 762-4000
supermarkets, foods, drug stores DRP O

Kubota Ltd KUB
2-47, Shikitsuhigashi 1-chome
Naniwa-ku, Osaka 556-91, Japan
(06) 648-2111
agricultural machinery, pipe

Kuhlman Corporation KUH
2565 West Maple Road
Troy, MI 48084 (313) 649-9300
transformers, auto parts, springs

Kyocera Corporation KYO
5-22 Kitainoue-cho, Yamashina-Ku
Kyoto 607, Japan (075) 592-3851
ceramics for industrial and electronic use

Kysor Industrial Corporation KZ
1 Madison Avenue
Cadillac, MI 49601 (616) 779-2200
truck parts, refrigeration products

Laclede Gas Company LG
720 Olive Street
St. Louis, MO 63101 (314) 342-0500
gas utility DRP

LAC Minerals Ltd. LAC
21st Floor, North Tower, Royal Bank Plaza
Toronto, Ontario, CDA M5J 2J4
(416) 865-0722
gold mining O

L.A. Gear, Inc. LA
4221 Redwood Avenue
Los Angeles, CA 90066 (213) 822-1995
athletic footwear

Lafarge Corporation LAF
Suite 300, 11130 Sunrise Valley Drive
Reston, VA 22091 (703) 264-3600
cement, concrete DRP

Lamson & Sessions Company LMS
25701 Science Park Drive
Beachwood, OH 44122 (216) 464-3400
industrial, construction products

Landmark Bancshares Corporation LBC
10 South Brentwood Boulevard
Clayton, MO 63105 (314) 889-9500
banking DRP

Lands' End, Inc. LE
Lands' End Lane
Dodgeville, WI 53595 (608) 935-9341
mail order clothing retailing

La Quinta Motor Inns, Inc. LQM
La Quinta Plaza, 10010 San Pedro
San Antonio, TX 78216 (512) 366-6000
operates motor inns

La Quinta Motor Inns, L.P. LQP
La Quinta Plaza, 10010 San Pedro
San Antonio, TX 78216 (512) 366-6030
motor inns partnership

Lawter International Inc. LAW
990 Skokie Boulevard
Northbrook, IL 60062 (312) 498-4700
chemicals for inks and paints

La-Z-Boy Chair Company LZB
1284 North Telegraph Street
Monroe, MI 48161 (313) 242-1444
residential and office furniture DRP

Lea-Ronal Inc. LRI
272 Buffalo Avenue
Freeport, NY 11520 (516) 868-8800
electro-plating and metal finishing

Lee Enterprises Inc. LEE
130 East 2nd Street
Davenport, IA 52801 (319) 383-2202
newspaper publishing, broadcasting

Legg Mason Inc. LM
111 South Calvert Street
Baltimore, MD 21203 (301) 539-3400
brokerage services

Leggett and Platt Inc. LEG
1 Leggett Road
Carthage, MO 64836 (417) 358-8131
furniture springs, bedding products

Lehman Corporation LEM
55 Water Street
New York, NY 10041 (212) 668-8578
closed-end stock mutual fund DRP O

Leisure Technology, Inc. LVX
12223 West Olympic Boulevard
Los Angeles, CA 90064 (213) 826-1000
develops retirement communities

Lennar Corporation LEN
700 Northwest 107th Avenue
Miami, FL 33172 (305) 559-4000
residential construction

Leslie Fay Companies, Inc. LES
1400 Broadway
New York, NY 10018 (212) 221-4000
women's apparel

Leucadia National Corporation LUK
315 Park Avenue South
New York, NY 10010 (212) 460-1900
insurance, manufacturing, investments

Liberty All-Star Equity Fund USA
Federal Reserve Plaza
Boston, MA 02210 (617) 722-6000
closed-end stock mutual fund

Liberty Corporation LC
P.O. Box 789, Wade Hampton Boulevard
Greenville, SC 29602 (803) 268-8283
insurance, broadcasting

Liggett Group, Inc. LIG
300 North Duke Street
Durham, NC 27702 (919) 683-9000
cigarette manufacturer

Lilly, Eli and Company LLY
307 East McCarty Street
Indianapolis, IN 46285 (317) 276-2000
medicines, medical instruments O

Limited Inc., The LTD
2 Limited Parkway
Columbus, OH 43216 (614) 479-7000
women's apparel stores O

Lincoln National Convertible Sec. Fund, Inc.
LNV
1300 South Clinton Street
Fort Wayne, IN 46801 (219) 427-2210
closed-end bond mutual fund DRP

Lincoln National Corporation LNC
1300 South Clinton Street
Fort Wayne, IN 46801 (219) 427-2000
life/health/casualty insurance DRP

Lincoln Nat'l Direct Placement Fund Inc. LND
1300 South Clinton Street
Fort Wayne, IN 46801 (312) 427-3909
closed-end bond mutual fund

Litton Industries Inc. LIT
360 North Crescent Drive
Beverly Hills, CA 90210 (213) 859-5000
electronic, defense, automation systems O

LL&E Royalty Trust LRT
1st City National Bank of Houston
Houston, TX 77002 (713) 658-7639
oil and gas exploration

L & N Housing Corporation LHC
2001 Bryan Tower
Dallas, TX 75201 (214) 746-7111
real estate investment trust

Lockheed Corporation LK
4500 Park Granada Boulevard
Calabasas, CA 91399 (818) 712-2000
aerospace, aeronautic, marine systems O

Loctite Corporation LOC
10 Columbus Boulevard
Hartford, CT 06106 (203) 520-5000
adhesives, sealants, coatings DRP

Loews Corporation Inc. LTR
667 Madison Avenue
New York, NY 10021 (212) 545-2000
insurance, cigarettes, watches, broadcasting
O

Logicon Inc. LGN
3701 Skypark Drive
Torrance, CA 90505 (213) 373-0220
electronic systems, aerospace

Lomas Financial Corporation LFC
2001 Bryan Tower
Dallas, TX 75201 (214) 746-7111
mortgage banking, leasing, insurance

Lomas Mortgage Corporation LMC
2001 Bryan Tower
Dallas, TX 75201 (214) 746-7111
mortgage real estate investment trust

Lomas Mortgage Securities Fund, Inc. LSF
Suite 3600, 2001 Bryan Tower
Dallas, TX 75201 (214) 746-7111
closed-end mortgage securities mutual fund

Lomas & Nettleton Mortgage Investors LOM
2001 Bryan Tower, P.O. Box 655644
Dallas, TX 75265 (214) 746-7111
mortgage real estate investment trust

Lone Star Industries Inc. LCE
1 Greenwich Plaza
Greenwich, CT 06836 (203) 661-3100
cement, concrete, sand, crushed stone O

Long Island Lighting Company LIL
175 East Old Country Road
Hicksville, NY 11801 (516) 933-4590
electric and gas utility

Longs Drug Stores Corporation LDG
141 North Civic Drive
Walnut Creek, CA 94596 (415) 937-1170
drugstore chain

Longview Fibre Company LFB
P.O. Box 639
Longview, WA 98632 (206) 425-1550
tree farms, paper, logs

Loral Corporation LOR
600 Third Avenue
New York, NY 10016 (212) 697-1105
military electronics, aircraft braking O

Louisiana General Services Inc. LGS
1233 West Bank Expressway
Harvey, LA 70058 (504) 367-7000
gas utility, oil exploration DRP

Louisiana Land & Exploration Co. LLX
909 Poydras Street
New Orleans, LA 70112 (504) 566-6500
oil and gas exploration and production O

Louisiana-Pacific Corporation LPX
111 SW 5th Avenue
Portland, OR 97204 (503) 221-0800
lumber, plywood, pulp DRP O

Louisville Gas & Electric Company LOU
311 West Chesnut Street, P.O. Box 32010
Louisville, KY 40232 (502) 566-4011
electric and gas utility DRP

Lowe's Companies, Inc. LOW
Highway 268 East, P.O. Box 1111
North Wilkesboro, NC 28656 (919) 651-4000
retailer of building products DRP O

LTV Corporation LTV
2001 Ross Avenue
Dallas, TX 75201 (214) 979-7711
steel products, aerospace

Lubrizol Corporation, The LZ
29400 Lakeland Boulevard
Wickliffe, OH 44092 (216) 943-4200
chemical additives for petroleum industry O

Luby's Cafeterias, Inc. LUB
2211 NE Loop 410, P.O. Box 33069
San Antonio, TX 78265 (512) 654-9000
cafeterias

Lukens Inc. LUC
50 South First Avenue
Coatesville, PA 19320 (215) 383-2000
steel plate DRP

LVI Group, Inc. LVI
345 Hudson Street
New York, NY 10014 (212) 337-6600
interior construction management

Lyondell Petrochemical Company LYO
1221 McKinney Avenue
Houston, TX 77010 (713) 652-7200
petrochemicals, refined petroleum

M/A-Com Inc MAI
7 New England Executive Park
Burlington, MA 01803 (617) 272-9600
microwave and digital communications O

M A Hanna Company HNM
100 Erieview Plaza
Cleveland, OH 44114 (216) 589-4000
iron mining

MAI Basic Four, Inc., MBF
14101 Myford Road
Tustin, CA 92680 (714) 731-5100
computer systems

Malaysia Fund, Inc. MF
Vanguard Financial Center
Valley Forge, PA 19482 (800) 332-5577
closed-end Malaysian stock mutual fund DRP

Manhattan National Corporation MLC
1876 Waycross Road
Cincinnati, OH 45420 (513) 595-5400
life insurance

Manor Care, Inc. MNR
10750 Columbia Pike
Silver Spring, MD 20901 (301) 681-9400
nursing homes for elderly, inns O

Manufacturers Hanover Corporation MHC
270 Park Avenue
New York, NY 10017 (212) 286-6000
banking DRP O

Manville Corporation MVL
Ken-Caryl Ranch
Denver, CO 80217 (303) 978-2000
forest products, mining, fiber glass

MAPCO Incorporated MDA
1800 South Baltimore Avenue
Tulsa, OK 74119 (918) 581-1800
produces/markets coal/oil/gas liquid DRP O

Marcade Group, Inc. MAR
275 Madison Avenue
New York, NY 10016 (212) 532-6565
women's and men's apparel manufacturer

Marion Laboratories Inc. MKC
9221 Ward Parkway
Kansas City, MO 64114 (816) 966-5000
pharmaceuticals DRP O

Maritrans Partners L.P. TUG
702 Goldsborough Building, 1102 West Street
Wilmington, DE 19801 (302) 656-7242
marine transport of petroleum products

Mark IV Industries, Inc. IV
501 John James Audubon Highway
Amherst, NY 14228 (716) 689-4972
audio, aerospace, automotive products

Marriott Corporation MHS
10400 Fernwood Road
Bethesda, MD 20058 (301) 380-9000
hotels, restaurants, food services O

Marsh & McClennan Corporation MMC
1221 Avenue of the Americas
New York, NY 10020 (212) 997-2000
insurance brokerage and agency services O

Marshall Industries MI
9674 Telstar Avenue
El Monte, CA 91731 (818) 459-5500
electronic and industrial products distributor

Martin Marietta Corporation ML
6801 Rockledge Drive
Bethesda, MD 20817 (301) 897-6000
aerospace, defense, communications O

Masco Corporation MAS
21001 van Born Road
Taylor, MI 48180 (313) 274-7400
plumbing products, furniture, cabinets O

MassMutual Corporate Investors Inc. MCI
1295 State Street
Springfield, MA 01111 (413) 788-8411
closed-end bond mutual fund DRP

MassMutual Participation Investors MPV
1295 State Street
Springfield, MA 01111 (413) 788-8411
closed-end bond mutual fund DRP

Matsushita Electric Industrial Co. Ltd MC
Kadoma, Osaka, Japan
375 Park Avenue, NY, NY 10152
(212) 371-4116
consumer electrical and electronic products

Mattel, Inc. MAT
5150 Rosecrans Avenue
Hawthorne, CA 90250 (213) 978-5150
toys O

Mauna Loa Macadamia Partners L.P. NUT
827 Fort Street
Honolulu, HI 96813 (808) 544-6112
macadamia nut-growing partnership

Maxus Energy Corporation
717 North Harwood Street
Dallas, TX 75201 (214) 953-2000
oil and gas exploration and production O

May Department Stores Company MA
611 Olive Street
St. Louis, MO 63101 (314) 342-6300
department, discount, shoe stores O

Maytag Company MYG
403 West 4th Street North
Newton, IA 50208 (515) 792-8000
major home appliances, repair parts DRP O

MBIA, Inc. MBI
445 Hamilton Avenue
White Plains, NY 10601 (914) 681-1300
municipal bond insurance

MCA Inc. MCA
100 Universal City Plaza
Universal City, CA 91608 (818) 777-1000
film entertainment, records DRP O

McClatchy Newspapers, Inc. MNI
2100 Q Street
Sacramento, CA 95816 (916) 321-1000
newspaper publishing

McDermott International Corporation MDR
1010 Common Street
New Orleans, LA 70112 (504) 587-5400
construction in energy industries O

McDonald & Company Investments, Inc.
MDD
2100 Society Building
Cleveland, OH 44114 (216) 443-2300
securities brokerage

McDonald's Corporation MCD
McDonald's Plaza
Oak Brook, IL 60521 (312) 575-3000
fast-food restaurant chain DRP O

McDonnell Douglas Corporation MD
P.O. Box 516
St. Louis, MO 63166 (314) 232-0232
aerospace industries, information systems O

Medtronic, Inc. MDT
3055 Old Highway Eight P O Box 1453
Minneapolis, MN 55440 (612) 574-4000
implantable medical devices, monitoring O

McGraw-Hill, Inc. MHP
1221 Avenue of the Americas
New York, NY 10020 (212) 512-2000
books, magazines, info services, TV DRP O

MEI Diversified, Inc. MEI
800 Marquette Bank Minneapolis Building
Minneapolis, MN 55402 (612) 339-8853
distributes candy, nuts, snack foods

McKesson Corporation MCK
1 Post Street 37th Floor
San Francisco, CA 94104 (415) 983-8300
distributor of drugs, health products DRP O

Medusa Corporation MSA
3008 Monticello Boulevard
Cleveland Heights, OH 44118 (216) 371-4000
cement, aggregates, construction services

MCN Corporation MCN
500 Griswold Street
Detroit, MI 48226 (313) 256-5500
gas utility DRP

Mellon Bank Corporation MEL
1 Mellon Bank Center
Pittsburgh, PA 15258 (412) 234-5000
banking DRP 5% O

MCorp M
1802 Commerce Street
Dallas, TX 75201 (214) 290-5000
banking

Melville Corporation MES
3000 Westchester Avenue
Harrison, NY 10528 (914) 253-8000
footwear, apparel, health, toy stores O

MDC Holdings, Inc. MDC
Suite 900, 3600 South Yosemite Street
Denver, CO 80237 (303) 773-1100
developer of houses and real estate

Mercantile Stores Company Inc. MST
1100 North Market Street
Wilmington, DE 19801 (302) 575-1816
department stores, beauty salons

MDU Resources Group Inc. MDU
400 North 4th Street
Bismark, ND 58501 (701) 222-7900
electric/gas utility, gas pipeline DRP 5%

Merck & Company, Inc. MRK
126 East Lincoln Avenue
Rahway, NJ 07065 (201) 574-4000
human and animal health products DRP O

Mead Corporation MEA
World Headquarters Courthouse Plaza NE
Dayton, OH 45463 (513) 222-6323
paper, wood products, publishing DRP O

Mercury Finance Company MFN
40 Skokie Boulevard
Northbrook, IL 60062 (312) 564-3720
purchases installment sales contracts

Measurex Corporation MX
1 Results Way
Cupertino, CA 95014 (408) 255-1500
paper industry process control systems

Mercury Savings & Loan Association MSL
7812 Edinger Avenue
Huntington Beach, CA 92647 (714) 842-9333
savings and loan

Meditrust MT
128 Technology Center
Waltham, MA 02154 (617) 736-1500
health care real estate investment trust

Meredith Corporation MDP
1716 Locust Street
Des Moines, IA 50336 (515) 284-3000
magazine and book publishing, broadcasting

Merrill Lynch & Company Inc. MER
World Financial Center
New York, NY 10281 (212) 449-1000
investment services and brokerage DRP O

Mesa Limited Partnership MLP
1 Mesa Square, P.O. Box 2009
Amarillo, TX 79189 (806) 378-1000
oil and gas exploration and production

Mesa Offshore Trust MOS
Texas Commerce Bank, 712 Main Street
Houston, TX 77002 (713) 236-6369
oil and gas production

Mesa Royalty Trust MTR
Texas Commerce Bank, 712 Main Street
Houston, TX 77002 (713) 236-6369
royalty interests in oil and gas

Mesabi Trust MSB
P.O. Box 318, Church Street Station
New York, NY 10015 (212) 250-6696
leasehold mining royalties

Mestek, Inc. MCC
209 North Elm Street
Westfield, MA 01085 (413) 568-9571
heating, air conditioning equipment

Metropolitan Financial Corporation MFC
1600 Radisson Tower
Fargo, ND 58108 (701) 293-2600
savings and loan, real estate broker DRP

Mexico Fund Inc. MXF
477 Madison Avenue
New York, NY 10022 (212) 326-3500
closed-end Mexican stock fund

MFS Government Markets Income Trust MGF
200 Berkeley Street
Boston, MA 02116 (617) 423-3500
closed-end bond mutual fund DRP

MFS Income & Opportunity Trust MFO
200 Berkeley Street
Boston, MA 02116 (617) 423-3500
closed-end bond mutual fund DRP

MFS Intermediate Income Trust MIN
200 Berkeley Street
Boston, MA 02116 (617) 423-3500
closed-end bond mutual fund DRP

MFS Multimarket Income Trust MMT
200 Berkeley Street
Boston, MA 02116 (617) 954-5000
closed-end bond mutual fund DRP

MFS Multimarket Total Return Trust MFT
200 Berkeley Street
Boston, MA 02116 (617) 954-5000
closed-end bond mutual fund DRP

MFS Municipal Income Trust MFM
200 Berkeley Street
Boston, MA 02116 (617) 954-5000
closed-end municipal bond mutual fund DRP

MGI Properties MGI
30 Rowes Wharf
Boston, MA 02110 (617) 330-5335
real estate investment trust

MGM/UA Communications MGM
450 North Roxbury Drive
Beverly Hills, CA 90210 (213) 281-4000
motion pictures and television shows

MHI Group, Inc. MH
2032-D Thomasville Road
Tallahassee, FL 32312 (904) 385-8883
funeral homes, cemeteries

Mickelberry Corporation MBC
405 Park Avenue
New York, NY 10022 (212) 832-0303
printing, advertising agencies

Midway Airlines, Inc. MDW
5959 South Cicero Avenue
Chicago, IL 60638 (312) 838-0001
airline O

Midwest Energy Company MWE
401 Douglas Street, P.O. Box 1348
Sioux City, IA 51102 (712) 277-7400
electric and gas utility DRP

Millipore Corporation MIL
80 Ashby Road
Bedford, MA 01730 (617) 275-9200
fluid filtration systems DRP

Milton Roy Company MRC
Suite 900, 111 Second Avenue
St. Petersburg, FL 33733 (813) 823-4444
pumps, laboratory instruments DRP

Minnesota Mining & Manufacturing Company
MMM
3M Center Building
St. Paul, MN 55144 (612) 733-1110
industrial and consumer tapes, abrasives DRP
O

Minnesota Power & Light Company MPL
30 West Superior Street
Duluth, MN 55802 (218) 722-2641
electric utility DRP

Mitel Corporation MLT
350 Leggett Drive
Kanata, Ontario CDA K2K 1X3
(613) 592-2122
telecommunications equipment O

MNC Financial, Inc. MNC
10 Light Street
Baltimore, MD 21203 (301) 244-6737
banking DRP

Mobil Corporation MOB
150 East 42nd Street
New York, NY 10017 (212) 883-4242
oil refining and marketing DRP O

Monarch Capital Corporation MON
1 Monarch Place
Springfield, MA 01144 (413) 781-3000
life and disability insurance

Monarch Machine Tool Company MMO
615 North Oak Street
Sidney, OH 45365 (513) 492-4111
lathes for metal-working industry

Monsanto Company MTC
800 North Lindbergh Boulevard
St. Louis, MO 63167 (314) 694-1000
chemicals, drugs, sweeteners DRP O

Montana Power Company, The MTP
40 East Broadway
Butte, MT 59701 (406) 723-5421
electric and gas utility DRP 5%

Montedison S.P.A. MNT
Foro Buonaparte n. 31
20121 Milan, Italy (212) 764-0414
chemicals, energy, pharmaceuticals

Montgomery Street Income Securities, Inc.
MTS
Suite 1608, 315 Montgomery Street
San Francisco, CA 94104 (415) 982-8191
closed-end bond mutual fund DRP

MONY Real Estate Investors MYM
1740 Broadway
New York, NY 10019 (212) 586-6716
real estate investment trust DRP

Moore Corporation Ltd MCL
1 First Canadian Place, P.O. Box 78
Toronto, Ontario, CDA M5X 1G5
(416) 364-2600
business forms DRP 5% O

Morgan, J.P. & Company, Inc. JPM
23 Wall Street
New York, NY 10015 (212) 483-2323
banking and financial services DRP 5% O

Morgan Grenfell SMALLCAP Fund, Inc. MGC
885 Third Avenue
New York, NY 10022 (212) 230-2600
closed-end stock mutual fund

Morgan Keegan, Inc. MOR
50 Front Street
Memphis, TN 38103 (901) 524-4100
regional brokerage services

Morgan Products Ltd. MGN
601 Oregon Street
Oshkosh, WI 54903 (414) 235-7170
wooden doors, window systems

Morgan Stanley Group, Inc. MS
1251 Avenue of the Americas
New York, NY 10020 (212) 703-4000
investment banking, brokerage O

Morrison Knudsen Corporation MRN
1 Morrison Knudsen Plaza
Boise, ID 83707 (208) 386-8000
engineering, construction services DRP

Mortgage & Realty Trust MRT
8360 Old York Road
Elkins Park, PA 19117 (215) 881-1525
real estate investment trust DRP 5%

Morton International, Inc. MTI
110 North Wacker Drive
Chicago, IL 60606 (312) 807-2000
chemicals, salt, automotive systems O

Motel 6, L.P. SIX
14651 Dallas Parkway
Dallas, TX 75240 (214) 386-6161
motels

Motorola, Inc. MOT
Motorola Center 1303 East Algonquin Road
Schaumburg, IL 60196 (312) 397-5000
electronic equipment and systems O

Municipal High Income Fund, Inc. MHF
31 West 52nd Street
New York, NY 10019 (212) 767-3700
closed-end municipal bond mutual fund

MuniEnhanced Fund, Inc. MEN
800 Scudders Mill Road
Plainsboro, NJ 08536 (609) 282-2800
closed-end municipal bond mutual fund

Munsingwear, Inc. MUN
724 North First Street
Minneapolis, MN 55401 (612) 340-4713
men's, women's and children's apparel

Murphy Oil Corporation MUR
200 Peach Street
El Dorado, AR 71730 (501) 862-6411
oil and gas services, exploration O

Mutual of Omaha Interest Shares, Inc. MUO
10235 Regency Circle
Omaha, NE 68114 (402) 397-8555
closed-end bond mutual fund DRP

Myers, L E Company Group MYR
1010 Jorie Boulevard
Oak Brook, IL 60521 (312) 990-4666
construction of electric utility plants

Mylan Laboratories, Inc. MYL
1030 Century Building
Pittsburgh, PA 15222 (412) 232-0100
generic drugs O

NACCO Industries, Inc. NC
12800 Shaker Boulevard
Cleveland, OH 44120 (216) 752-1000
coal mining, engines, household appliances

Nalco Chemical Company NLC
1 Nalco Center
Naperville, IL 60566 (312) 961-9500
specialized industrial chemicals DRP O

Nashua Corporation NSH
44 Franklin Street
Nashua, NH 03061 (603) 880-2323
office copy products, labels

National Australia Bank Ltd. NAB
500 Bourke Street
Melbourne, Victoria 3000, Australia
(03) 605-3500
banking

National City Corporation NCC
National City Center, 1900 East 9th Street
Cleveland, OH 44114 (216) 575-2000
banking DRP

National Convenience Stores, Inc. NCS
100 Waugh Drive
Houston, TX 77007 (713) 863-2200
self-service food stores

National Education Corporation NEC
18400 Von Karman Avenue
Irvine, CA 92715 (714) 474-9400
vocational training, educational publishing O

National Enterprises, Inc. NEI
Earl Avenue at Wallace Street
Lafayette, IN 47904 (317) 448-2000
panelized homes, homesites, construction

National Fuel Gas Company NFG
30 Rockefeller Plaza
New York, NY 10112 (212) 541-7533
gas utility DRP

National Heritage, Inc. NHR
Suite 500, 15770 North Dallas Parkway
Dallas, TX 75248 (214) 233-3900
nursing homes

National Intergroup, Inc. NII
20 Stanwix Street
Pittsburgh, PA 15222 (412) 394-4100
drug distribution, aluminum, steel

National Medical Enterprises, Inc. NME
11620 Wilshire Boulevard
Los Angeles, CA 90025 (213) 479-5526
general and specialty hospitals DRP O

National Mine Service Company NMS
795 Old Route 119 North
Indiana, PA 15701 (412) 349-7100
mining equipment and supplies, hydraulics

National Presto Industries, Inc. NPK
3925 North Hastings Way
Eau Claire, WI 54703 (715) 839-2121
electrical appliances

National Semiconductor Corporation NSM
2900 Semiconductor Drive
Santa Clara, CA 95051 (408) 721-5000
semiconductor components O

National Service Industries, Inc. NSI
1180 Peachtree Street N.E.
Atlanta, GA 30309 (404) 892-2400
lighting, textile rental, chemicals

National-Standard Company NSD
1618 Terminal Road
Niles, MI 49102 (616) 683-8100
wire products and machinery

National Westminster Bank PLC NW
41 Lothbury
London EC2P, England (011) 441-726-1000
banking

Nationwide Health Properties, Inc. NHP
99 South Oakland Avenue
Pasadena, CA 91101 (818) 405-0195
health care real estate investment trust

Navistar International Corporation NAV
401 West Michigan Avenue
Chicago, IL 60611 (312) 836-2000
truck manufacturer

NBB Bancorp, Inc. NBB
174 Union Street
New Bedford, MA 02742 (617) 996-5000
banking

NBD Bancorp Inc. NBD
611 Woodward Avenue
Detroit, MI 48226 (313) 225-1000
banking DRP

NBI Inc. NBI
3450 Mitchell Lane, P.O. Box 9001
Boulder, CO 80301 (303) 444-5710
software, word processing systems O

NCH Corporation NCH
2727 Chemsearch Boulevard
Irving, TX 75015 (214) 438-0211
cleaning chemicals and equipment

NCNB Corporation NCB
1 NCNB Plaza
Charlotte, NC 28255 (704) 374-5000
banking DRP 5% O

NCR Corporation NCR
1700 South Patterson Boulevard
Dayton, OH 45479 (513) 445-5000
business info processing systems DRP O

Neiman-Marcus Group, Inc. NMG
27 Boylston Street
Chestnut Hill, MA 02167 (617) 232-0760
specialty retailing

NERCO, Inc. NER
111 Southwest Columbia
Portland, OR 97201 (503) 796-6600
coal and precious metals, gas

Nevada Power Company NVP
6226 West Sahara Avenue
Las Vegas, NV 89102 (702) 367-5000
electric utility DRP

New America High Income Fund, Inc. HYB
99 Bedford Street
Boston, MA 02111 (617) 426-0182
closed-end bond mutual fund DRP

New American Shoe Company, Inc. NSO
19 West 34th Street
New York, NY 10001 (212) 643-0300
athletic footwear, slippers

New England Electric System NES
25 Research Drive
Westborough, MA 01582 (508) 366-9011
electric utility DRP 5%

New Jersey Resources Corporation NJR
1415 Wyckoff Road
Wall, NJ 07719 (201) 938-1480
gas utility DRP

New Plan Realty Trust NPR
1120 Avenue of the Americas
New York, NY 10036 (212) 869-3000
real estate investment trust DRP

New York State Electric & Gas Corporation
NGE
4500 Vestral Parkway East
Binghamton, NY 13903 (607) 729-2551
electric and gas utility DRP

Newell Company NWL
Newell Center, 29 East Stephenson Street
Freeport, IL 61032 (815)235-4171
consumer hardware and housewares

Newhall Land and Farming Company NHL
23823 Valencia Boulevard
Valencia, CA 91355 (805) 255-4000
land development limited partnership

Newmont Gold Company O
1700 Lincoln Street
Denver, CO 80203 (303) 863-7414
gold mining O

Newmont Mining Corporation NEM
1700 Lincoln Street
Denver, CO 80203 (303) 863-7414
gold, coal mining DRP O

News Corporation Limited NWS
2 Holt Street, Sydney
New South Wales 2010, Australia
(011) 612-288-3000
newspaper and magazine publishing,
broadcasting

Niagara Mohawk Power Corporation NMK
300 Erie Boulevard West
Syracuse, NY 13202 (315) 474-1511
electric and gas utility DRP O

Niagara Share Corporation NGS
344 Delaware Avenue
Buffalo, NY 14202 (716) 856-2600
closed-end stock mutual fund DRP

Nicholas-Applegate Growth Equity Fund, Inc.
GEF
One Seaport Plaza
New York, NY 10292 (212) 214-2833
closed-end stock mutual fund DRP

Nicolet Instrument Corporation NIC
5225 Verona Road
Madison, WI 53711 (608) 271-3333
electronic measurement instruments

NICOR, Inc. GAS
1700 West Ferry Road
Naperville, IL 60566 (312) 242-4470
gas utility, oil/gas production DRP 5%

NIPSCO Industries, Inc. NI
5265 Hohman Avenue
Hammond, IN 46320 (219) 853-5200
electric and gas utility DRP

N.L. Industries, Inc. NL
3000 North Sam Houston Parkway East
Houston, TX 77032 (713) 987-5900
pigments, specialty chemicals DRP

Noble Affiliates Inc. NBL
110 West Broadway
Ardmore, OK 73402 (405) 223-4110
oil and gas exploration and production O

Nord Resources Corporation NRD
8150 Washington Village Drive
Dayton, OH 45458 (513) 433-6307
explores and develops minerals and ores

Norfolk Southern Corporation NSC
1 Commercial Place
Norfolk, VA 23510 (804) 629-2600
railroad, motor carrier DRP O

Norsk Hydro A.S. NHY
Bygdoy alle 2, N-0257
Oslo 2, Norway (02) 43 21 00
agriculture, oil and gas, metals

Nortek, Inc. NTK
50 Kennedy Plaza
Providence, RI 02903 (401) 751-1600
building products, aerospace, electrical

North European Oil Royalty Trust NET
Suite 19A, 43 West Front Street
Red Bank, NJ 07701 (201) 741-4008
oil and gas producer

Northeast Savings, F.A. NSB
50 State House Square
Hartford, CT 06103 (203) 280-1000
savings bank

Northeast Utilities NU
Selden Street
Berlin, CT 06037 (203) 665-5000
electric utility DRP

Northern States Power Company NSP
414 Nicollet Mall
Minneapolis, MN 55401 (612) 330-5500
electric and gas utility DRP

Northern Telecom Limited NT
3 Robert Speck Parkway
Mississauga, Ont., CDA L4Z 2G5
(416) 897-9000
telecommunications equipment O

Northgate Exploration Limited NGX
Suite 2701, 1 First Canadian Place
Toronto, Ont., CDA M5X 1C7 (416) 362-6683
gold mining

Northrop Corporation NOC
1840 Century Park East Century City
Los Angeles, CA 90067 (213) 553-6262
aerospace products and services DRP O

Norton Company NRT
120 Front Street
Worcester, MA 01608 (508) 795-5000
abrasives, ceramics, drilling products O

Norwest Corporation NOB
Norwest Center, 6th and Marquette
Minneapolis, MN 55479 (612) 667-1234
diversified financial services DRP 5%

NOVA Corporation of Alberta NVA
801 Seventh Avenue S.W.
Calgary, Alberta T2P 2N6 (403) 290-6000
petrochemicals, pipelines, gas marketing DRP
O

Novo Industri A/S NVO
Novo Alle, DK-2880
Bagsvaerd, Denmark (45) 2-982333
industrial enzymes, insulin O

Nucor Corporation NUE
4425 Randolph Road
Charlotte, NC 28211 (704) 366-7000
steel products DRP

NUI Corporation NUI
550 Route 202-206, P.O. Box 760
Bedminster, NJ 07921 (201) 781-0500
gas utility DRP 5%

Nuveen California Municipal Income Fund, Inc.
NCM
333 West Wacker Drive
Chicago, IL 60606 (312) 917-7812
closed-end municipal bond mutual fund

Nuveen California Municipal Value Fund, Inc.
NCA
333 West Wacker Drive
Chicago, IL 60606 (312) 917-7812
closed-end municipal bond mutual fund DRP

Nuveen Municipal Income Fund, Inc. NMI
333 West Wacker Drive
Chicago, IL 60606 (312) 917-7812
closed-end municipal bond mutual fund DRP

Nuveen Municipal Value Fund, Inc. NUV
333 West Wacker Drive
Chicago, IL 60606 (312) 917-7812
closed-end municipal bond mutual fund DRP

Nuveen New York Municipal Value Fund, Inc.
NNY
333 West Wacker Drive
Chicago, IL 60606 (312) 917-7812
closed-end municipal bond mutual fund DRP

Nuveen Premium Income Municipal Fund, Inc.
NPI
333 West Wacker Drive
Chicago, IL 60606 (312) 917-7812
closed-end municipal bond mutual fund DRP

NWA Inc. NWA
2700 Lone Oak Parkway
Eagan, MN 55121 (612) 726-2111
airline O

NYNEX Corporation NYN
335 Madison Avenue
New York, NY 10017 (212) 370-7400
telecommunications services DRP O

Oak Industries, Inc. OAK
16510 Via Esprillo
Rancho Bernardo, CA 92127 (619) 485-9300
switches, communications equipment

Oakwood Homes Corporation OH
2225 South Holden Road
Greensboro, NC 27417 (919) 855-2400
mobile homes

Occidental Petroleum Corporation OXY
10889 Wilshire Boulevard
Los Angeles, CA 90024 (213) 879-1700
oil/coal/gas exploration/production DRP O

Ocean Drilling and Exploration Company ODR
1600 Canal Street
New Orleans, LA 70161 (504) 561-2811
oil and gas contract drilling O

Ogden Corporation OG
2 Pennsylvania Plaza
New York, NY 10121 (212) 868-6100
operating services, environmental plants O

Ohio Edison Company OEC
76 South Main Street
Akron, OH 44308 (216) 384-5100
electric utility DRP

OHM Corporation OHM
16406 U.S. Route 224 East
Findlay, OH 45840 (419) 423-3529
environmental testing services

Oklahoma Gas & Electric Company OGE
P.O. Box 321, 321 North Harvey Avenue
Oklahoma City, OK 73102 (405) 272-3000
electric utility DRP

Olin Corporation OLN
120 Long Ridge Road
Stamford, CT 06904 (203) 356-2000
chemicals, metals, ammunition DRP O

Omnicare, Inc. OCR
1300 Fountain Square South
Cincinnati, OH 45202 (513) 762-6666
hospital services, equipment, supplies

Oneida Limited OCQ
Oneida, NY 13421 (315) 361-3000
tableware/cookware, industrial wire DRP 5%

ONEOK Inc. OKE
100 West Fifth Street
Tulsa, OK 74102 (918) 588-7000
gas utility, oil and gas production

On-Line Software International, Inc. OSI
Fort Lee Executive Park, 2 Executive Drive
Fort Lee, NJ 07024 (201) 592-0009
software

Oppenheimer Capital L.P. OCC
Oppenheimer Tower, World Financial Center
New York, NY 10281 (212) 667-7588
investment management services partnership

Oppenheimer Multi-Government Trust OGT
2 World Trade Center
New York, NY 10048 (212) 323-0200
closed-end government bond mutual fund
DRP

Oppenheimer Multi-Sector Income Trust OMS
2 World Trade Center
New York, NY 10048 (212) 323-0200
closed-end bond mutual fund DRP

Orange & Rockland Utilities, Inc. ORU
1 Blue Hill Plaza
Pearl River, NY 10965 (914) 352-6000
electric and gas utility DRP

Orange-co, Inc. OJ
300 Alternate Highway 27 South
Lake Hamilton, FL 33851 (813) 439-1585
citrus juices, petroleum distributor

Orient-Express Hotels, Inc. OEH
1155 Avenue of the Americas
New York, NY 10036 (212) 302-5055
European hotels, trains

Orion Capital Corporation OC
30 Rockefeller Plaza
New York, NY 10112 (212) 541-4646
life, accident, health insurance

Orion Pictures Corporation OPC
711 Fifth Avenue
New York, NY 10022 (212) 758-5100
film-making, television production

Oryx Energy Company ORX
5656 Blackwell, 4 NorthPark East
Dallas, TX 75231 (214) 890-6000
oil and gas exploration and production

Outboard Marine Corporation OM
100 Sea-Horse Drive
Waukegan, IL 60085 (312) 689-6200
outboard motors, lawn/turf equipment DRP

Overseas Shipholding Group, Inc. OSG
1114 Avenue of the Americas
New York, NY 10036 (212) 869-1222
bulk ocean transport

Owens-Corning Fiberglas Corporation OCF
Fiberglas Tower
Toledo, OH 43659 (419) 248-8000
glass fiber insulation, industrial materials O

Owens & Minor, Inc. OMI
2727 Enterprise Parkway
Richmond, VA 23229 (804) 747-9794
health products and drug distributor

Oxford Industries, Inc. OXM
222 Piedmont Avenue N.E.
Atlanta, GA 30308 (404) 659-2424
men's and women's apparel

Pacific American Income Shares, Inc. PAI
117 East Colorado Boulevard
Pasadena, CA 91105 (818) 584-4300
closed-end bond mutual fund DRP

Pacific Enterprises PET
801 South Grand Avenue
Los Angeles, CA 90017 (213) 895-5000
gas utility, drug stores DRP O

Pacific Gas & Electric Company PCG
77 Beale Street
San Francisco, CA 94106 (415) 972-7000
electric and gas utility DRP O

Pacific Scientific Company PSX
620 Newport Center Drive
Newport Beach, CA 92660 (714) 720-1714
aerospace products, specialty motors

Pacific Telesis Group PAC
130 Kearny Street
San Francisco, CA 94108 (415) 394-3000
telecommunications services DRP O

PacifiCorp PPW
851 Southwest 6th Avenue
Portland, OR 97204 (503) 464-6000
electric and telephone utility, coal DRP

PaineWebber Group, Inc. PWJ
1285 Avenue of the Americas
New York, NY 10019 (212) 713-2000
investment services, brokerage O

Pan Am Corporation PN
Pan Am Building
New York, NY 10017 (212) 880-1234
airline

Panhandle Eastern Corporation PEL
5400 Westheimer Court
Houston, TX 77056 (713) 627-5400
gas pipelines DRP 5% O

Pansophic Systems, Inc. PNS
709 Enterprise Drive
Oak Brook, IL 60521 (312) 572-6000
standardized systems software products O

Paramount Communications Inc. PCI
1 Gulf & Western Plaza
New York, NY 10023 (212) 373-8000
movie production, publishing DRP O

Park Electrochemical Corporation PKE
5 Dakota Drive
Lake Success, NY 11042 (516) 354-4100
printed circuit materials

Parker Drilling Company PKD
Parker Building, 8 East Third Street
Tulsa, OK 74103 (918) 585-8221
contract oil drilling service

Parker Hannifin Corporation PH
17325 Euclid Avenue
Cleveland, OH 44112 (216) 531-3000
fluid power systems and components O

Par Pharaceutical, Inc. PRX
1 Ram Ridge Road
Spring Valley, NY 10977 (914) 425-7100
generic drug manufacturer

PAR Technology Corporation PTC
220 Seneca Turnpike
New Hartford, NY 13413 (315) 738-0600
point-of-sale terminals, government software

Pathe Communications Corporation PCC
8670 Wilshire Boulevard
Beverly Hills, CA 90211 (213) 658-2100
movie production and theaters

Patrick Petroleum Company PPC
301 West Michigan Avenue
Jackson, MI 49201 (517) 787-6633
oil and gas exploration and production

Patriot Premium Dividend Fund, Inc. PDF
211 Congress Street
Boston, MA 02110 (617) 426-3310
closed-end preferred stock mutual fund

Patten Corporation PAT
Main Road
Stamford, VT 05352 (802) 694-1581
markets rural properties

Penn Central Corporation PC
1 East Fourth Street
Cincinnati, OH 45202 (513) 579-6600
wire and cable, defense systems, real estate
O

Penney, J.C. Company, Inc. JCP
1481 North Dallas Parkway
Dallas, TX 75240 (214) 591-1000
department stores, drug stores DRP O

Pennsylvania Power & Light Company PPL
2 North 9th Street
Allentown, PA 18101 (215) 770-5151
electric utility DRP

Pennzoil Company PZL
P.O. Box 2967, 1 Pennzoil Place
Houston, TX 77252 (713) 546-4000
oil and gas, sulphur, filters DRP O

Peoples Energy Corporation PGL
122 South Michigan Avenue
Chicago, IL 60603 (312) 431-4000
gas utility DRP

Pep Boys - Manny Moe & Jack PBY
3111 West Allegheny Avenue
Philadelphia, PA 19132 (215) 229-9000
auto parts retail chain

PepsiCo, Inc. PEP
World Headquarters
Purchase, NY 10577 (914) 253-2000
beverages, snack foods, restaurants DRP O

Perkin-Elmer Corporation, The PKN
761 Main Avenue
Norwalk, CT 06856 (203) 762-1000
analytic equipment, optics, avionics DRP O

Perkins Family Restaurants, L.P. PFR
6075 Poplar Avenue
Memphis, TN 38119 (901) 766-6400
restaurants

Permian Basin Royalty Trust PBT
P.O. Box 1317
Fort Worth, TX 76101 (817) 390-6905
royalty oil interests

Permian Partners, L.P. PPA Pr
2500 CityWest Boulevard
Houston, TX 77251 (713) 787-2222
crude oil transportation

Perry Drug Stores Inc. PDS
5400 Perry Drive
Pontiac, MI 48056 (313) 334-1300
drug stores

Petrie Stores Corporation PST
70 Enterprise Avenue
Secaucus, NJ 07094 (201) 866-3600
women's specialty store chain O

Petrolane Parnters L.P. LPG
1600 East Hill Street
Long Beach, CA 90806 (213) 427-5471
markets liquefied petroleum gas

Petroleum & Resources Corporation PEO
7 St. Paul Street
Baltimore, MD 21202 (301) 752-5900
closed-end energy stock mutual fund DRP

Petroleum Investments Limited PIL
Suite 1410, 50 Penn Place
Oklahoma City, OK 73118 (405) 840-3293
oil and gas limited partnership

Pfizer, Inc. PFE
235 East 42nd Street
New York, NY 10017 (212) 573-2323
health/agriculture/chemical products DRP O

Phelps Dodge Corporation PD
2600 North Central Avenue
Phoenix, AZ 85004 (602) 234-8100
copper mining, carbon black O

PHH Group, Inc. PHH
11333 McCormick Road
Hunt Valley, MD 21031 (301) 771-1900
personnel/vehicle fleet/leasing services

Philadelphia Electric Company PE
2301 Market Street
Philadelphia, PA 19101 (215) 841-4000
electric and gas utility DRP O

Philadelphia Suburban Corporation PSC
762 Lancaster Avenue
Bryn Mawr, PA 19010 (215) 527-8000
water utility DRP

Philip Morris Companies, Inc. MO
120 Park Avenue
New York, NY 10017 (212) 880-5000
cigarettes, brewing, food DRP O

Philips Industries, Inc. PHL
4801 Springfield Street, P.O. Box 943
Dayton, OH 45401 (513) 253-7171
construction, building products O

Philips N.V. PHG
Groenewoudseweg 1,5621 BA
Eindhoven, Netherlands (314) 073-2312
electrical and electronics products O

Phillips Petroleum Company P
244 Adams Building
Bartlesville, OK 74004 (918) 661-6600
oil production/refining/marketing DRP O

Phillips-Van Heusen Corporation PVH
1290 Avenue of the Americas
New York, NY 10104 (212) 541-5200
men's apparel, footwear

PHLCORP, Inc. PHX
1700 Market Street
Philadelphia, PA 19103 (215) 557-1800
property/casualty insurance, trading stamps

PHM Corporation PHM
Suite 200, 33 Bloomfield Hills Parkway
Bloomfield Hills, MI 48013 (313) 644-7300
residential homebuilder

Piedmont Natural Gas Company, Inc. PNY
1915 Rexford Road
Charlotte, NC 28211 (704) 364-3120
gas utility DRP 5%

Pier 1 Imports, Inc. PIR
Suite 600, 301 Commerce Street
Fort Worth, TX 76102 (817) 878-8000
import specialty furnishings stores

Pilgrim Regional Bank Shares, Inc. PBS
10100 Santa Monica Boulevard
Los Angeles, CA 90067 (213) 551-0833
closed-end bank mutual fund DRP

Pilgrim's Pride Corporation CHX
110 South Texas Street
Pittsburg, TX 75686 (214) 856-7901
chicken and egg producer

Pinnacle West Capital Corporation PNW
2828 North Central Avenue
Phoenix, AZ 85072 (602) 234-1142
electric utility, banking DRP

Pioneer Electronic Corporation PIO
4-1 Meguro 1-Chome Meguro-Ku
Tokyo 153 Japan (03) 494-1111
high-fidelity stereo and video products

Pitney-Bowes Inc. PBI
Walter H. Wheeler Jr Drive
Stamford, CT 06926 (203) 356-5000
business equipment and supplies DRP 0

Pittston Company PCO
1 Pickwick Plaza
Greenwich, CT 06830 (203) 622-0900
coal, freight forwarding, security DRP 0

Placer Dome, Inc. PDG
Suite 3500, IBM Tower,
Toronto-Dominion Centre
Toronto, Ontario, CDA M5K 1N3
(416) 868-6060
gold, silver mining, oil and gas production

Plains Petroleum Company PLP
12596 West Bayaud
Lakewood, CO 80215 (303) 969-9325
oil and gas exploration and production

Playboy Enterprises, Inc. PLA
919 North Michigan Avenue
Chicago, IL 60611 (312) 751-8000
magazines, licensing, video operations

Plessey Company PLC PLY
Millbank Tower, 21-24 Millbank
London SWIP 40P England (212) 698-2102
telecommunications, electronic components

PNC Financial Corporation PNC
Fifth Avenue and Wood Street
Pittsburgh, PA 15222 (412) 762-2666
banking DRP 0

Pogo Producing Company PPP
600 Travis
Houston, TX 77208 (713) 651-4300
oil and gas exploration and development

Polaroid Corporation PRD
549 Technology Square
Cambridge, MA 02139 (617) 577-2000
photographic equipment and film DRP 0

Pope & Talbot, Inc. POP
1500 South West 1st Avenue
Portland, OR 97201 (503) 228-9161
wood, pulp, and paper products

Portec, Inc. POR
300 Windsor Drive
Oak Brook, IL 60521 (312) 573-4600
railway track and construction equipment

Portland General Corporation PGN
121 Southwest Salmon Street
Portland, OR 97204 (503) 464-8000
electric utility DRP

Potlatch Corporation PCH
1 Maritime Plaza
San Francisco, CA 94119 (415) 576-8800
pulp, paperboard, lumber, paper DRP

Potomac Electric Power Company POM
1900 Pennsylvania Avenue N.W.
Washington, DC 20068 (202) 872-2000
electric utility DRP

PPG Industries Inc. PPG
1 PPG Place
Pittsburgh, PA 15272 (412) 434-3131
glass, paint, resins, fiber glas DRP O

Premark International, Inc. PMI
1717 Deerfield Road
Deerfield, IL (312) 405-6000
tupperware, food equipment

Premier Industrial Corporation PRE
4500 Euclid Avenue
Cleveland, OH 44103 (216) 391-8300
electronic and industrial products DRP

Primark Corporation PMK
Suite 700, 8251 Greensboro Drive
McLean, VA 22102 (703) 790-7600
aviation services, financial services

Prime Motor Inns, Inc. PDQ
700 Route 46 East
Fairfield, NJ 07007 (201) 882-1010
motels and motel construction O

Prime Motor Inns, L.P. PMP
700 Route 46 East
Fairfield, NJ 07006 (201) 882-1010
motor inn partnership O

Primerica Corporation PA
65 East 55th Street
New York, NY 10022 (212) 891-8900
financial services, brokerage, insurance O

Procter & Gamble Company PG
1 Procter & Gamble Plaza
Cincinnati, OH 45202 (513) 983-1100
household/food/grooming products DRP O

Products Research & Chemical Corporation
PRC
5430 San Fernando Road
Glendale, CA 91203 (818) 240-2060
sealants, coatings, specialty chemicals

Progressive Corporation (Ohio)
6000 Parkland Boulevard
Mayfield Heights, OH 44124 (216) 464-8000
property-casualty insurance

Proler International Corporation PS
7501 Wallisville Road
Houston, TX 77020 (713) 675-2281
upgrades ferrous scrap metal

Prospect Street High Income Portfolio, Inc.
PHY
1 Financial Center
Boston, MA 02111 (617) 350-5718
closed-end junk bond mutual fund

Prudential Realty Trust PRT
Prudential Plaza
Newark, NJ 07101 (201) 877-4302
real estate investment trust

Prudential Strategic Income Fund, Inc. PSF
1 Seaport Plaza
New York, NY 10292 (212) 214-3334
closed-end bond mutual fund DRP

PS Group, Inc. PSG
4370 LaJolla Village Drive
San Diego, CA 92122 (619) 546-5001
aircraft leasing, fuel distribution, travel

PSI Holdings, Inc. PIN
1000 East Main Street
Plainfield, NJ 46168 (317) 839-9611
electric utility

Public Service Company of New Hampshire
PNH
1000 Elm Street
Manchester, NH 03105 (603) 669-4000
electric utility

Public Service Company of Colorado PSR
550 15th Street
Denver, CO 80202 (303) 571-7511
electric and gas utility DRP

Public Service Company of New Mexico PNM
Alvarado Square
Albuquerque, NM 87158 (505) 848-2700
electric, gas and water utility

Public Service Enterprise Group, Inc. PEG
80 Park Plaza
Newark, NJ 07101 (201) 430-7000
electric and gas utility DRP

Publicker Industries, Inc. PUL
1445 East Putnam Avenue, P.O. Box 1978
Old Greenwich, CT 06870 (203) 637-4500
liquid and solid carbon dioxide

Puerto Rican Cement Company, Inc. PRN
P.O. Box 4487
San Juan, Puerto Rico 00936 (809) 783-3000
cement, paper and packaging

Puget Sound Power & Light Company PSD
Puget Power Building
Bellevue, WA 98004 (206) 454-6363
electric utility DRP

Putnam High Income Convertible and Bond
Fund PCF
1 Post Office Square
Boston, MA 02109 (617) 292-1000
closed-end convertible and bond mutual fund
DRP

Putnam Intermediate Government Income
Trust PGT
1 Post Office Square
Boston, MA 02109 (617) 292-1000
closed-end government bond mutual fund
DRP

Putnam Managed Municipal Income Trust
PMM
1 Post Office Square
Boston, MA 02109 (617) 292-1000
closed-end municipal bond mutual fund DRP

Putnam Master Income Trust PMT
1 Post Office Square
Boston, MA 02109 (617) 292-1000
closed-end bond mutual fund DRP

Putnam Master Intermediate Income Trust
PIM
1 Post Office Square
Boston, MA 02109 (617) 292-1000
closed-end bond mutual fund DRP

Putnam Premier Income Trust PPT
1 Post Office Square
Boston, MA 02109 (617) 292-1000
closed-end bond mutual fund DRP

Pyro Energy Corporation BTU
653 South Hebron Avenue
Evansville, IN 47715 (812) 473-8600
coal mining

Qantel Corporation BQC
129 Littleton Road
Parsippany, NJ 07054 (201) 299-8240
minicomputers

QMS, Inc. AQM
1 Magnum Pass
Mobile, AL 36618 (205) 633-4300
intelligent computer printers

Quaker Oats Company OAT
Quaker Tower, 321 North Clark Street
Chicago, IL 60604 (312) 222-7111
grocery products, toys, pet food DRP O

Quaker State Corporation KSF
255 Elm Street
Oil City, PA 16301 (814) 676-7676
auto products, lubricants, fuels DRP O

Quanex Corporation NX
Suite 1500, 1900 West Loop South
Houston, TX 77027 (713) 961-4600
seamless and welded steel tubing, bars DRP

Quantum Chemical Corporation CUE
99 Park Avenue
New York, NY 10016 (212) 949-5000
chemicals, propane marketing DRP O

Questar Corporation STR
180 East First South Street
Salt Lake City, UT 84147 (801) 534-5000
gas distribution, oil and gas exploration

Quest for Value Dual Purpose Fund, Inc. KFV
Oppenheimer Tower, World Financial Center
New York, NY 10281 (212) 667-7587
closed-end dual purpose mutual fund

Quick & Reilly Group, Inc. BQR
120 Wall Street
New York, NY 10005 (212) 943-8686
discount brokerage firm

RAC Income Fund, Inc. RMF
10221 Wincopin Circle
Columbus, MD 21044 (301) 964-8260
closed-end mortgage securities mutual fund
DRP

RAC Mortgage Investment Corporation RMR
10221 Wincopin Circle
Columbus, MD 21044 (301) 730-7222
mortgage real estate investment trust

Racal Telecom PLC RTG
The Courtyard, 2-4 London Road Newbury
Berkshire RG13 1JL, England
(011) 44-635-33251
English cellular telephone network

Radice Corporation RI
600 Corporate Drive
Fort Lauderdale, FL 33334 (305) 493-5003
develops and sells houses and condominiums

Ralston Purina Company RAL
Checkerboard Square
St. Louis, MO 63164 (314) 982-1000
groceries, pet foods, feed, batteries DRP O

Ramada, Inc. RAM
P.O. Box 52035
Phoenix, AZ 85072 (602) 273-4000
hotels, casino-hotels, restaurants

Ranger Oil Limited RGO
425 First Street S.W.
Calgary, AL, CDA T2P 3L8 (403) 263-1500
oil and gas exploration and production O

Raychem Corporation RYC
300 Constitution Drive
Menlo Park, CA 94025 (415) 361-3333
plastic and elastomeric products O

Raymond James Financial, Inc. RJF
880 Carillon Parkway
St. Petersburg, FL 33176 (813) 573-3800
securities brokerage, investment banking

Rayonier Timberlands, L.P. LOG
1177 Summer Street
Stamford, CT 06904 (203) 348-7000
timber limited partnership

Raytech Corporation RAY
100 Oakview Drive
Trumbull, CT 06611 (203) 372-7544
automotive equipment, fasteners

Raytheon Company RTN
141 Spring Street
Lexington, MA 02173 (617) 862-6600
electronic products, aircraft, appliances DRP
O

Reading & Bates Corporation RB
3200 Mid-Continent Tower, 401 South Boston
Tulsa, OK 74103 (918) 583-8521
oil/gas drilling, water treatment

Real Estate Investment Trust of California
RCT
Suite 700, 12011 San Vicente Boulevard
Los Angeles, CA 90049 (213) 476-7793
real estate investment trust

Realty ReFund Trust RRF
1385 Eaton Center, 1111 Superior Avenue
Cleveland, OH 44114 (216) 771-7660
real estate investment trust

Recognition Equipment, Inc. REC
2701 East Grauwyler Road
Irving, TX 75061 (214) 579-6000
optical character recognition systems

Reebok International Ltd. RBK
150 Royall Street
Canton, MA 02021 (617) 821-2800
footwear and apparel O

Reece Corporation RCE
800 South Street
Waltham, MA 02254 (617) 894-9220
industrial sewing machines

Regal International, Inc. RGL
256 North Belt East
Houston, TX 77060 (713) 445-7700
rubber products for oil and gas industry

Regional Financial Shares Investment Fund, Inc. BNC
1285 Avenue of the Americas
New York, NY 10019 (212) 713-2000
closed-end bank stock mutual fund DRP

Reich & Tang, L.P. RTP
100 Park Avenue
New York, NY 10017 (212) 370-1110
mutual fund and investment management partnership

Reliance Group Holdings, Inc. REL
Park Avenue Plaza
55 East 52nd Street
New York, NY 10055 (212) 909-1100
property-casualty insurance, investments

Republic Gypsum Company RGC
3625 Miller Park Drive
Garland, TX 75042 (214) 272-0441
gypsum, paperboard

Republic New York Corporation RNB
452 5th Avenue
New York, NY 10018 (212) 525-6100
banking

Rexene Corporation RXN
5005 LBJ Freeway
Dallas, TX 75244 (214) 450-9000
petrochemicals, plastic film

Reynolds Metals Company RLM
6601 Broad Street Road
Richmond, VA 23261 (804) 281-2000
aluminum products DRP O

Reynolds & Reynolds Company REY
115 South Ludlow Street
Dayton, OH 45402 (513) 443-2000
business forms, data processing products

Rite Aid Corporation RAD
Trindle Road and Railroad Avenue
Shiremanstown, PA 17011 (717) 761-2633
discount drug store chain DRP O

River Oaks Industries, Inc. ROI
150 East 58th Street
New York, NY 10155 (212) 980-9670
housewares distribution, mobile home financing

RLC Corporation RLC
1 Rollins Plaza P O Box 1791
Wilmington, DE 19899 (302) 479-2700
trucking leasing DRP

RLI Corporation RLI
9025 North Lindbergh Drive
Peoria, IL 61615 (309) 692-1000
property/casualty insurance

Robertson H.H. Company RHH
2 Gateway Center
Pittsburgh, PA 15222 (412) 281-3200
commercial construction and products

Rochester Gas & Electric Corporation RGS
89 East Avenue
Rochester, NY 14649 (716) 546-2700
electric and gas utility DRP

Rochester Telephone Corporation RTC
180 South Clinton Avenue
Rochester, NY 14646 (716) 777-1000
telephone service DRP

Rockefeller Center Properties, Inc. RCP
1166 Avenue of the Americas
New York, NY 10036 (212) 841-7760
real estate investment trust DRP

Rockwell International Corporation ROK
2230 East Imperial Highway
El Segundo, CA 90245 (213) 647-5000
aerospace, electronics, automotive DRP O

Rodman & Renshaw Capital Group, Inc. RR
120 South LaSalle Street
Chicago, IL 60603 (312) 977-7800
securities brokerage, investment banking

Rohm & Haas Company ROH
Independence Mall West
Philadelphia, PA 19105 (215) 592-3000
chemicals, plastics O

Rohr Industries, Inc. RHR
Foot of H Street
Chula Vista, CA 92012 (619) 691-4111
aircraft, aerospace components O

Rollins Environmental Services, Inc. REN
1 Rollins Plaza
Wilmington, DE 19803 (302) 492-2757
industrial waste disposal DRP O

Rollins, Inc. ROL
2170 Piedmont Road N.E.
Atlanta, GA 30324 (404) 888-2000
pest control, security services DRP

Rorer Group, Inc. ROR
500 Virginia Drive
Fort Washington, PA 19034 (215) 628-6000
prescription and over-the-counter drugs DRP
O

Rowan Companies, Inc. RDC
1900 Post Oak Tower Building,
5051 Westheimer
Houston, TX 77056 (713) 621-7800
contract drilling, air charter service

Royal Dutch Petroleum Company RD
30 Carel van Bylandtlaan
2596HR The Hague, Netherlands
(212) 632-4870
oil production and marketing O

Royal International Optical Corporation RIO
2760 Irving Boulevard
Dallas, TX 75207 (214) 638-1397
optical stores

Royce Value Trust, Inc. RVT
1414 Avenue of the Americas
New York, NY 10019 (212) 355-7311
closed-end stock mutual fund DRP

RPC Energy Services, Inc. RES
2170 Piedmont Road NE
Atlanta, GA 30301 (404) 888-2950
oil and gas industry services, boats

RPS Realty Trust RPS
666 Third Avenue
New York, NY 10017 (212) 551-6000
real estate investment trust DRP

Rubbermaid, Inc. RBD
1147 Akron Road
Wooster, OH 44691 (216) 264-6464
plastic and rubber products O

Russ Berrie and Company, Inc. RUS
111 Bauer Drive
Oakland, NJ 07436 (201) 337-9000
impulse gift items

Russ Togs, Inc. RTS
1411 Broadway
New York, NY 10018 (212) 647-8500
apparel for women and girls

Russell Corporation RML
Alexander City, AL 35010
(205) 329-4000
leisure apparel, athletic uniforms DRP

Ryder System, Inc. R
3600 N.W. 82nd Avenue
Miami, FL 33166 (305) 593-3726
truck and airplane leasing/services DRP O

Rykoff-Sexton, Inc. RYK
761 Terminal Street
Los Angeles, CA 90021 (213) 622-4131
food distributor to institutions

Ryland Group, Inc. RYL
10221 Wincopin Circle
Columbia, MD 21044 (301) 730-7222
single-family home construction

Rymer Foods, Inc. RYR
Suite 1106, 300 West Washington Street
Chicago, IL 60606 (312) 419-0060
meat products for restaurants, food stores

Saatchi & Saatchi Company PLC SAA
15 Lower Regent Street
London SW1Y 4LR, England
advertising, public relations

Sabine Royalty Trust SBR
NCNB Texas National Bank, P.O. Box 83650
Dallas, TX 75283 (214) 977-2400
royalties of oil and gas properties

Safeguard Scientifics, Inc. SFE
630 Park Avenue
King of Prussia, PA 19406 (215) 265-4000
power transmission, information processing

Safety-Kleen Corporation SK
777 Big Timber Road
Elgin, IL 60123 (312) 697-8460
parts cleaning services

Sahara Casino Partners, L.P. SAH
2535 Las Vegas Boulevard South
Las Vegas, NV 89109 (702) 737-2111
hotel and casino partnership

Saint Joseph Light & Power Company SAJ
520 Francis Street
St. Joseph, MO 64502 (816) 233-8888
electric utility DRP

Salant Corporation SLT
1155 Avenue of the Americas
New York, NY 10036 (212) 221-7500
slacks, jeans, apparel

Salomon, Inc. SB
1 New York Plaza
New York, NY 10004 (212) 747-7000
investment services, commodity trading DRP
O

San Juan Basin Royalty Trust SJT
Texas American Bank/ Ft Worth,
P.O. Box 2604
Fort Worth, TX 76113 (817) 884-4417
oil & gas royalty interest

San Juan Racing Association, Inc. SJR
65th Infantry Station
Rio Piedras, Puerto Rico 00929
(809) 724-6060
racetrack, transmission towers

Santa Anita Companies SAR
1 Wilshire Building
Los Angeles, CA 90017 (213) 485-9220
racetrack, commercial real estate DRP 5%

Santa Fe Energy Partners, L.P. SFP
Suite 1000, 1616 South Voss Road
Houston, TX 77057 (713) 783-2401
oil and gas partnership

Santa Fe Pacific Corporation SFX
224 South Michigan Avenue
Chicago, IL 60604 (312) 786-6000
railroad, real estate O

Santa Fe Pacific Pipeline Partners, L.P. SFL
888 South Figueroa
Los Angeles, CA 90017 (213) 614-1095
petroleum pipeline partnership

Sara Lee Corporation SLE
3 First National Plaza
Chicago, IL 60602 (312) 726-2600
food processor, consumer products DRP O

Savin Corporation SVB
9 West Broad Street, P.O. Box 10270
Stamford, CT 06904 (203) 967-5000
copying machines

SCANA Corporation SCG
1426 Main Street
Columbus, SC 29201 (803) 748-3000
electric and gas utility DRP

SCEcorp
2244 Walnut Grove Avenue
Rosemead, CA 91770 (818) 302-1212
electric utility DRP O

Schafer Value Trust, Inc. SAT
18th Floor, 645 Fifth Avenue
New York, NY 10022 (212) 644-1800
closed-end stock mutual fund

Schering-Plough Corporation SGP
1 Giralda Farms
Madison, NJ 07940 (201) 822-7000
drugs, personal care products DRP O

Schlumberger Limited SLB
277 Park Avenue
New York, NY 10172 (212) 350-9400
oil drilling services, measurement systems O

Schwab (Charles) Corporation SCH
101 Montgomery Street
San Francisco, CA 94104 (415) 627-7000
discount securities brokerage

Schwitzer, Inc. SCZ
1125 Brookside Avenue
Indianapolis, IN 46206 (317) 269-3100
turbochargers, auto engine components

Scientific-Atlanta, Inc. SFA
1 Technology Parkway, Box 105600
Atlanta, GA 30348 (404) 441-4000
communications equipment, instruments O

SCOR U.S. Corporation SUR
Suite 1400, 110 William Street
New York, NY 10038 (212) 513-1777
property and casualty reinsurance

Scotsman Industries, Inc. SCT
775 Corporate Woods Parkway
Vernon Hills, IL 60061 (312) 215-4500
commercial refrigeration products

Scott Paper Company SPP
1 Scott Plaza
Philadelphia, PA 19113 (215) 522-5000
paper products DRP O

Scotty's, Inc. SHB
Recker Highway
Winter Haven, FL 33882 (813) 299-1111
building materials retailer

Scudder New Asia Fund SAF
345 Park Avenue
New York, NY 10154 (212) 326-6200
closed-end Asian stock mutual fund

Sea Containers Limited SCR
41 Cedar Avenue, P.O. Box 1179
Hamilton 5, Bermuda (809) 295-2244
sea cargo container chassis, ferries O

Seagram Company Limited VO
1430 Peel Street
Montreal, Quebec CDA H3A 1S9
(514) 849-5271
wine and distilled spirits, chemicals O

Seagull Energy Corporation SGO
First City Tower, 1001 Fannin
Houston, TX 77002 (713) 951-4700
natural gas pipeline

Sealed Air Corporation SEE
Park 80 Plaza East
Saddle Brook, NJ 07662 (201) 791-7600
packaging products and systems

Sears Roebuck & Company S
Sears Tower
Chicago, IL 60684 (312) 875-2500
retailing, insurance, brokerage DRP O

Security Pacific Corporation SPC
333 South Hope Street
Los Angeles, CA 90071 (213) 345-6211
banking DRP 5% O

Sequa Corporation SQA.A
200 Park Avenue
New York, NY 10166 (212) 986-5500
aerospace, machinery, chemicals, barges

Service Corporation International SRV
1929 Allen Parkway, P.O. Box 13548
Houston, TX 77219 (713) 522-5141
funeral services, cemetery O

ServiceMaster L.P. SVM
2300 Warrenville Road
Downers Grove, IL 60515 (312) 964-1300
industrial and consumer maintenance services

Service Resources Corporation SRC
11 East 36th Street
New York, NY 10016 (212) 219-0800
facilities management

Shaw Industries, Inc. SHX
616 East Walnut Avenue
Dalton, GA 30720 (404) 278-3812
carpet manufacturer

Shawmut National Corporation SNC
1 Federal Street
Boston, MA 02211 (617) 292-2000
banking DRP O

Shearson Lehman Hutton Holdings, Inc. SLH
American Express Tower,
World Financial Center
New York, NY 10285 (212) 298-2000
brokerage and investment banking O

Shelby Williams Industries, Inc. SY
1348 Merchandise Mart
Chicago, IL 60654 (312) 527-3593
seating products, vinyl wall coverings

Shell Transport & Trading Company SC
Shell Centre
London SE1 7NA England (212) 632-4870
oil and gas exploration and production O

Sherwin-Williams Company SHW
101 Prospect Avenue N.W.
Cleveland, OH 44115 (216) 566-2000
paint and varnish manufacturer O

Shoney's, Inc. SHN
1727 Elm Hill Pike
Nashville, TN 37202 (615) 391-5201
restaurants and motels

Showboat, Inc. SBO
2800 East Fremont Street
Las Vegas, NV 89104 (702) 385-9141
hotel and casino

Sierra Pacific Resources SRP
6100 Neil Road
Reno, NV 89511 (702) 689-3600
electric, gas, water utility DRP

Signal Apparel Company, Inc. SIA
Suite 922, 701 Market Street
Chattanooga, TN 37402 (615) 756-8146
apparel and accessories

Signet Banking Corporation SBK
7 North Eighth Street
Richmond, VA 23260 (804) 747-2000
banking

Sizeler Property Investors, Inc. SIZ
2542 Williams Boulevard
Kenner, LA 70062 (504) 466-5363
real estate investment trust

Skyline Corporation SKY
2520 By-pass Road
Elkhart, IN 46515 (219) 294-6521
mobile homes, recreational vehicles O

SL Industries, Inc. SL
Suite 201, 3 Greentree Center
Marlton, NJ 08053 (609) 596-7800
specialty industrial products

Slattery Group Inc SGI
1044 Northern Boulevard
Roslyn, NY 11576 (516) 484-1360
heavy construction services

Smith International, Inc. SII
17832 Gillette Avenue
Irvine, CA 92714 (714) 752-9000
oil drilling equipment, services

SmithKline Beckman Corporation SKB
1 Franklin Plaza
Philadelphia, PA 19101 (215) 751-4000
drugs, medical instruments DRP O

Smucker, J.M. Company SJM
Strawberry Lane
Orrville, OH 44667 (216) 682-0015
preserves, jams and jellies DRP

Snap-on Tools Corporation SNA
2801 80th Street
Kenosha, WI 53141 (414) 656-5200
hand tools for automotive maintenance

Snyder Oil Partners, L.P. SOI
2500 First Republicbank Tower
Fort Worth, TX 76102 (817) 338-4043
oil and gas exploration and development

Solitron Devices, Inc. SOD
1177 Blue Heron Boulevard
Riviera Beach, FL 33404 (305) 848-4311
aerospace electronic components

Sonat, Inc. SNT
First National-Southern Natural Building
Birmingham, AL 35203 (205) 325-3800
gas pipeline, oil and gas drilling DRP O

Sony Corporation SNE
7-35 Kitashinagawa 6-chome, Shinagawa-ku
Tokyo, 141 Japan (03) 448-2111
(212) 371-5800
consumer/industrial electronics, recorded
music O

Soo Line Corporation SOO
800 Soo Line Building, 5th and Marquette
Minneapolis, MN 55440 (612) 347-8000
railroad, real estate

Source Capital, Inc. SOR
10301 West Pico Boulevard
Los Angeles, CA 90064 (213) 277-4900
closed-end stock mutual fund DRP

South Jersey Industries, Inc. SJI
1 South Jersey Plaza, Route 4
Folsom, NJ 08037 (609) 561-9000
gas utility, sand mining, oil exploration DRP

Southdown, Inc. SDW
Suite 2200, 1200 Smith Street
Houston, TX 77002 (713) 658-8921
cement, concrete, oil and gas production

Southeast Banking Corporation STB
1 Southeast Financial Center
Miami, FL 33131 (305) 375-7500
banking DRP 5%

Southern Company SO
64 Perimeter Center East
Atlanta, GA 30346 (404) 393-0650
electric utility DRP O

Southern Indiana Gas & Electric Company
SIG
20-24 N.W. 4th Street
Evansville, IN 47741 (812) 424-6411
gas and electric utility DRP

Southern New England Telecommunications
Corp. SNG
227 Church Street
New Haven, CT 06506 (203) 771-5200
telephone service DRP

Southern Union Company SUG
1800 Renaissance Tower
Dallas, TX 75270 (214) 748-8511
gas utility, oil exploration DRP

Southmark Corporation SM
Suite 800, 1601 LBJ Freeway
Dallas, TX 75234 (214) 241-8787
real estate, financial services

Southwest Airlines, Inc. LUV
P.O. Box 37611, Love Field
Dallas, TX 75235 (214) 902-1100
regional airline O

Southwest Gas Corporation SWX
5241 Spring Mountain Road, P.O. Box 98510
Las Vegas, NV 89193 (702) 876-7011
natural gas utility, savings and loan DRP

Southwestern Bell Corporation SBC
1 Bell Center
St. Louis, MO 63101 (314) 235-9800
telecommunications service DRP O

Southwestern Energy Company SWN
1083 Sain Street
Fayetteville, AR 72702 (501) 521-1141
gas utility, oil and gas exploration DRP

Southwestern Public Service Company SPS
SPS Tower, 6th and Tyler Streets
Amarillo, TX 79170 (806) 378-2121
electric utility DRP

Sovran Financial Corporation SOV
Sovran Center, One Commercial Place
Norfolk, VA 23510 (804) 441-4000
banking DRP

Spain Fund, Inc. SNF
1345 Avenue of the Americas
New York, NY 10105 (212) 964-0700
closed-end Spanish stock mutual fund

Sparton Corporation SPA
2400 East Ganson Street
Jackson, MI 49202 (517) 787-8600
sonobuoys, industrial electronics, auto parts

Springs Industries, Inc. SMI
205 North White Street
Fort Mill, SC 29715 (803) 547-3650
fabrics, home furnishings

SPS Technologies, Inc. ST
Route 332
Newton, PA 18940 (215) 860-3000
industrial fasteners, metal materials

SPX Corporation SPW
100 Terrace Plaza
Muskegon, MI 49443 (616) 724-5000
auto and industrial parts DRP

Square D Company SQD
Executive Plaza, 1415 South Rosell Street
Palatine, IL 60067 (312) 397-2600
electrical and electronic equipment DRP

Squibb Corporation SQB
P.O. Box 4000
Princeton, NJ 08540 (609) 921-4000
drugs, medical products DRP O

SSMC, Inc. SSM
1077 Bridgeport Avenue
Shelton, CT 06484 (203) 925-4200
consumer and industrial sewing machines

Standard Brands Paint Company SBP
4300 West 190th Street
Torrance, CA 90509 (213) 214-2411
paint and home decorating centers

Standard Commercial Corporation STW
2201 Miller Road
Wilson, NC 27894 (919) 291-5507
tobacco leaf dealer, wool DRP

Standard Federal Bank SFB
2401 West Big Beaver Road
Troy, MI 48084 (313) 643-9600
savings banking

Standard Motor Products, Inc. SMP
37-18 Northern Boulevard
Long Island City, NY 11101 (718) 392-0200
auto parts

Standard Pacific L.P. SPF
1565 West MacArthur Boulevard
Costa Mesa, CA 92626 (714) 546-1161
residential home construction partnership

Standard Products Company SPD
2130 West 110th Street
Cleveland, OH 44102 (216) 281-8300
auto parts

Standex International Corporation SXI
6 Manor Parkway
Salem, NH 03079 (603) 893-9701
diversified manufacturing, graphics DRP

Stanhome, Inc. STH
333 Western Avenue
Westfield, MA 01085 (413) 562-3631
personal care products, giftware

Stanley Works SWK
1000 Stanley Drive
New Britain, CT 06050 (203) 225-5111
hardware products, tools DRP O

Starret, L.S. Company SCX
121 Crescent Street
Athol, MA 01331 (508) 249-3551
mechanics' measuring tools

State Mutual Securities Trust SMS
440 Lincoln Street
Worcester, MA 01605 (508) 852-1000
closed-end bond mutual fund DRP

Steego Corporation STG
319 Clematis Street
West Palm Beach, FL 33402 (305) 655-9700
auto and farm parts, office products

Sterling Bancorp STL
540 Madison Avenue
New York, NY 10022 (212) 826-8000
banking

Sterling Chemicals, Inc. STX
Suite 3700, 333 Clay Street
Houston, TX 77002 (713) 650-3700
petrochemicals

Stifel Financial Corporation SF
500 North Broadway
St. Louis, MO 63102 (314) 342-2000
regional brokerage firm

Stone Container Corporation STO
150 North Michigan Avenue
Chicago, IL 60601 (312) 346-6600
containerboard, paper, pulps, bags O

Stone & Webster, Inc. SW
1 Penn Plaza, 250 West 34th Street
New York, NY 10119 (212) 290-7500
engineering/construction contractors DRP

Stoneridge Resources, Inc. SRE
Suite 300, 2000 North Woodward Avenue
Bloomfield Hills, MI 48013 (313) 540-9040
citrus fruit juices, groves

Storage Equities, Inc. SEQ
1015 Grandview Avenue
Glendale, CA 91201 (818) 244-8080
mini-warehouse real estate investment trust

Storage Technology Company STK
2270 South 88th Street
Louisville, CO 80028 (303) 673-5151
computer data storage equipment, printers

Strategic Mortgage Investments, Inc. STM
700 North Central Avenue
Glendale, CA 91203 (818) 247-6057
mortgage loan real estate investment trust
DRP

Stride Rite Corporation SRR
5 Cambridge Center
Cambridge, MA 02142 (617) 491-8800
children's shoe retailer, manufacturer DRP O

Student Loan Marketing Association SLM
1050 Thomas Jefferson Street N.W.
Washington, DC 20007 (202) 333-8000
student loan financing O

Suave Shoe Corporation SWV
14100 NW 60th Avenue
Miami Lakes, FL 33014 (305) 822-7880
shoe manufacturer and importer

Sun Company, Inc. SUN
100 Matsonford Road
Radnor, PA 19087 (215) 293-6000
oil and gas refining, marketing DRP O

Sun Distributors, L.P. SDP
Suite 2600, 1 Logan Square
Philadelphia, PA 19103 (215) 665-3650
industrial product wholesaling partnership

Sun Electric Corporation SE
1 Sun Parkway
Crystal Lake, IL 60014 (815) 459-7700
automotive test equipment

Sun Energy Partners, L.P. SLP
5656 Blackwell, Four NorthPark East
Dallas, TX 75231 (214) 890-6000
oil and gas exploration, production

Sundstrand Corporation SNS
4949 Harrison Avenue
Rockford, IL 61125 (815) 226-6000
aerospace parts, industrial products DRP

Sunshine Mining Company SSC
300 Crescent Court
Dallas, TX 75201 (214) 855-8700
silver mining oil and gas exploration

SunTrust Banks, Inc. STI
25 Park Place N.E.
Atlanta, GA 30303 (404) 588-7455
banking DRP

Super Valu Stores, Inc. SVU
11840 Valley View Road
Eden Prairie, MN 55344 (612) 828-4000
food wholesaler and retailer O

Symbol Technologies, Inc. SBL
116 Wilbur Place
Bohemia, NY 11716 (516) 563-2400
laser-based bar-code readers O

Syms Corporation SYM
Syms Way
Secaucus, NJ 07094 (201) 902-9600
discount apparel stores

Syntex Corporation SYN
3401 Hillview Avenue
Palo Alto, CA 94304 (415) 855-5050
drugs, diagnostic products O

Sysco Corporation SYY
1390 Enclave Parkway
Houston, TX 77077 (713) 584-1190
food distribution and service O

Systems Center, Inc. SMX
1800 Alexander Bell Drive
Reston, VA 22091 (703) 264-8000
systems software producer, maintenance

Tacoma Boatbuilding Company TBO
1840 Marine View Drive
Tacoma, WA 98422 (206) 572-3600
medium size aluminum and steel vessels

Taiwan Fund, Inc. TWN
111 Devonshire Street
Boston, MA 02109 (617) 570-6327
closed-end Taiwanese stock mutual fund DRP

Talley Industries, Inc. TAL
2800 North 44th Street
Phoenix, AZ 85008 (602) 957-7711
industrial products, propellants, insecticide

Tambrands, Inc. TMB
1 Marcus Avenue
Lake Success, NY 11042 (516) 358-8300
feminine hygiene products DRP O

Tandem Computers, Inc. TDM
19333 Vallco Parkway
Cupertino, CA 95014 (408) 725-6000
fault-tolerant mainframe computers O

Tandy Corporation TAN
1800 One Tandy Center
Fort Worth, TX 76102 (817) 390-3700
consumer electronics, computer retailer O

Tandycrafts, Inc. TAC
1400 Everman Parkway
Fort Worth, TX 76140 (817) 551-9600
leather crafts, picture frames

TCBY Enterprises, Inc. TBY
1100 TCBY Tower, 425 West Capitol Avenue
Little Rock, AK 72212 (501) 688-8229
frozen yogurt stores O

TCW Convertible Securities Fund, Inc. CVT
400 South Hope Street
Los Angeles, CA 90071 (213) 683-4000
closed-end convertibles mutual fund DRP

TDK Corporation TDK
1-13-1, Nihonbashi, Chuo-ku
Tokyo 103, Japan (516) 625-0100
ferrite, ceramics, magnetic tape

Tech-Sym Corporation TSY
10500 Westoffice Drive
Houston, TX 77042 (713) 785-7790
defense electronics

TECO Energy, Inc. TE
702 North Franklin Street
Tampa, FL 33602 (813) 228-4111
electric utility, transport services

Tektronix, Inc. TEK
14150 S.W. Karl Braun Drive
Beavertown, OR 97077 (503) 627-7111
oscilloscopes, information display monitors O

TeleCom Corporation TEL
Suite 7000, 1545 West Mockingbird Lane
Dallas, TX 75235 (214) 638-0638
heating and air conditioning equipment

Telecom*USA, Inc. TTT
61 Perimeter Park N.E.
Atlanta, GA 30341 (404) 458-4927
long distance telephone service

Teledyne Inc. TDY
1901 Avenue of the Stars
Los Angeles, CA 90067 (213) 277-3311
aviation, engines, metals, insurance O

Telefonica de Espana, S.A. TEF
Gran Via 28
Madrid 28013, Spain (011) 341-459-3050
Spanish telephone utility

Telerate, Inc. TLR
1 World Trade Center
New York, NY 10048 (212) 938-5200
computerized financial information network O

Temple-Inland, Inc. TIN
303 South Temple Drive
Diboll, TX 75941 (409) 829-2211
paper, containers, building products DRP

Templeton Global Governments Income Trust
TGG
700 Central Avenue
St. Petersburg, FL 33701 (813) 823-8712
closed-end global bond mutual fund DRP

Templeton Global Income Fund, Inc. GIM
700 Central Avenue
St. Petersburg, FL 33701 (813) 823-8712
closed-end global bond mutual fund DRP

Templeton Value Fund TVF
700 Central Avenue
St. Petersburg, FL 33701 (813) 823-8712
closed-end global stock mutual fund DRP

Tenneco, Inc. TGT
Tenneco Building, P.O. Box 2511
Houston, TX 77252 (713) 757-2131
oil and gas, pipelines, farm equipment DRP O

Teradyne, Inc. TER
321 Harrison Avenue
Boston, MA 02118 (617) 482-2700
electronic test equipment O

Tesoro Petroleum Corporation TSO
8700 Tesoro Drive
San Antonio, TX 78286 (512) 828-8484
oil and gas exploration and production O

Texaco, Inc. TX
2000 Westchester Avenue
White Plains, NY 10650 (914) 253-4000
oil refining and marketing, chemicals O

Texas American Bancshares, Inc. TXA
500 Throckmorton Street
Fort Worth, TX 76102 (817) 884-4040
banking

Texas Eastern Corporation TET
1221 McKinney Street
Houston, TX 77252 (713) 759-3131
gas pipeline DRP O

Texas Industries, Inc. TXI
8100 Carpenter Freeway
Dallas, TX 75247 (214) 637-3100
cement, concrete products, steel

Texas Instruments, Inc. TXN
13500 North Central Expressway
Dallas, TX 75265 (214) 995-3773
electronics, defense, digital products O

Texas Pacific Land Trust TPL
61 Broadway
New York, NY 10006 (212) 269-2266
oil land holdings and royalties

Texas Utilities Company TXU
2001 Bryan Tower
Dallas, TX 75201 (214) 812-4600
electric utility DRP 5% O

Texfi Industries, Inc. TXF
400 English Road
Rocky Mount, NC 27804 (919) 443-5001
fabrics for the apparel industry

Textron, Inc. TXT
40 Westminster Street
Providence, RI 02903 (401) 421-2800
aerospace, finance, auto parts DRP O

TGI Friday's, Inc. TGI
14665 Midway Road
Dallas, TX 75244 (214) 450-5400
restaurant chain

Thackeray Corporation THK
Suite 3509, 1 Penn Plaza
New York, NY 10119 (212) 967-8600
ribbons, wire, hardware, real estate

The Williams Companies WMB
1 Williams Center
Tulsa, OK 74172 (918) 588-2000
gas pipelines, fertilizer, oil, gas O

Thai Fund, Inc. TTF
Vanguard Financial Center, P.O. Box 1102
Valley Forge, PA 19482 (800) 332-5577
closed-end Thai stock mutual fund

Thermo Electron Corporation TMO
101 First Avenue
Waltham, MA 02254 (617) 622-1111
cogeneration, instruments, process
equipment

Thiokol Corporation TKC
2475 Washington Boulevard
Ogden, UT 84401 (801) 629-2000
aerospace

Thomas & Betts Corporation TNB
1001 Frontier Road
Bridgewater, NJ 08807 (201) 685-1600
electrical and electronic connectors DRP

Thomas Industries, Inc. TII
4360 Brownsboro Road
Louisville, KY 40207 (502) 893-4600
electric light fixtures, tools, hardware

Thomson McKinnon Asset Management, L.P.
TMA
1 State Street Plaza
New York, NY 10004 (212) 482-5894
investment management partnership

Thor Industries, Inc. THO
419 West Pike Street
Jackson Center, OH 45334 (513) 596-6849
motor homes, trailers

Thortec International, Inc. THT
2000 Alameda de las Puglas
San Mateo, CA 94403 (415) 574-5000
engineering and architectural services

Tidewater, Inc. TDW
1440 Canal Street
New Orleans, LA 70112 (504) 568-1010
offshore oil service vessels

Tiffany & Company TIF
727 Fifth Avenue
New York, NY 10022 (212) 755-8000
fine jewelry, gifts

Time-Warner, Inc. TL
1271 Avenue of the Americas
New York, NY 10020 (212) 522-1212
magazines, books, TV, movies, records DRP
0

Times Mirror Company TMC
Times Mirror Square
Los Angeles, CA 90053 (213) 237-3700
newspaper, book, magazine publishing, TV

Timken Company TKR
1835 Deuber Ave S.W.
Canton, OH 44706 (216) 438-3000
bearings, alloy steel DRP

TIS Mortgage Investment Company TIS
Suite 700, 550 Kearny Street
San Francisco, CA 94108 (415) 393-8000
mortgage real estate investment trust

Titan Corporation TTN
9191 Towne Centre Drive
San Diego, CA 92122 (619) 453-9592
defense computers and systems

TJX Companies, Inc. TJX
1 Mercer Road
Natick, MA 01760 (508) 651-6000
discount apparel stores

TNP Enterprises, Inc. TNP
4100 International Plaza
Fort Worth, TX 76109 (817) 731-0099
electric utility DRP

Todd Shipyards Corporation TOD
1102 S.W. Massachusetts Street
Seattle, WA 98134 (206) 223-1560
builds and repairs ships

Tokheim Corporation TOK
10501 Corporate Drive
Fort Wayne, IN 46801 (219) 423-2552
equipment for gas stations

Toll Brothers, Inc. TOL
3103 Philmont Avenue
Huntingdon Valley, PA 19006 (215) 938-8000
single family home builder

Tonka Corporation TKA
6000 Clearwater Drive
Minnetonka, MN 55343 (612) 936-3300
toys

Tootsie Roll Industries, Inc. TR
7401 South Cicero Avenue
Chicago, IL 60629 (312) 838-3400
candies

Torchmark Corporation TMK
2001 Third Avenue South
Birmingham, AL 35233 (205) 325-4200
insurance and financial services O

Toro Corporation TTC
8111 Lyndale Avenue South
Bloomington, MN 55420 (612) 888-8801
outdoor maintenance equipment DRP

Tosco Corporation TOS
2401 Colorado Avenue
Santa Monica, CA 90406 (213) 207-6000
petroleum refiner, oil development

Toys "R" Us, Inc. TOY
461 From Road
Paramus, NJ 07652 (201) 262-7800
toy supermarkets O

Trammell Crow Real Estate Investors TCR
3500 Trammel Crow Center,
2001 Ross Avenue
Dallas, TX 75201 (214) 979-5100
real estate investment trust

Transamerica Corporation TA
600 Montgomery Street
San Francisco, CA 94111 (415) 983-4000
insurance, lending, leasing DRP O

Transamerica Income Shares, Inc. TAI
P.O. Box 2438
Los Angeles, CA 90051 (213) 742-4141
closed end bond mutual fund DRP

TransCanada PipeLines Limited TRP
Commerce Court West
Toronto, ON, CDA M5L 1C2 (416) 869-2111
gas pipeline DRP O

TransCapital Financial Corporation TFC
Suite 1300, 1100 Superior Avenue
Cleveland, OH 44114 (216) 579-7700
banking

Transco Energy Company E
2800 South Post Oak Boulevard,
P.O. Box 1396
Houston, TX 77251 (713) 439-2000
gas pipeline and marketing, coal O

Transco Exploration Partners, Ltd. EXP
Transco Tower, 2800 Post Oak Boulevard
Houston, TX 77056 (713) 439-2000
oil and gas partnership

Transcon, Inc. TCL
5700 South Eastern Avenue
Los Angeles, CA 90040 (213) 726-8555
trucking

TransTechnology Corporation TT
15303 Ventura Boulevard
Sherman Oaks, CA 91403 (818) 990- 5920
aerospace, defense, automation equipment

Travelers Corporation TIC
1 Tower Square
Hartford, CT 06183 (203) 277-0111
insurance, financial services DRP O

TRE Corporation TRE
9460 Wilshire Boulevard
Los Angeles, CA 90212 (213) 470-7120
aerospace material, hardware

Tribune Company TRB
435 North Michigan Avenue
Chicago, IL 60611 (312) 222-9100
newspapers, broadcasting, forest products O

Tri-Continental Corporation TY
130 Liberty Street
New York, NY 10006 (212) 432-4100
closed-end stock mutual fund DRP O

Trinity Industries, Inc. TRN
2525 Stemmons Freeway
Dallas, TX 75207 (214) 631-4420
railcars, structural and marine products

Trinova Corporation TNV
1705 Indian Wood Circle
Maumee, OH 43537 (419) 891-2200
fluid power and plastics products DRP O

Triton Energy Corporation OIL
1400 1 Energy Square,
4925 Greenville Avenue
Dallas, TX 75206 (214) 691-5200
oil and gas exploration and development

Triton Group Ltd. TGL
Suite 206, 1020 Prospect Street
La Jolla, CA 92037 (619) 456-1556
engine repair, building products, restaurants

TRW, Inc. TRW
1900 Richmond Road
Cleveland, OH 44124 (216) 291-7000
space, defense, auto parts, information DRP
O

Tucson Electric Power Company TEP
220 West 6th Street, P.O. Box 711
Tucson, AZ 85702 (602) 622-6661
electric utility DRP

Tultex Corporation TTX
22 East Church Street
Martinsville, VA 24115 (703) 632-2961
sportswear and yarn

Twin Disc, Inc. TDI
1328 Racine Street
Racine, WI 53403 (414) 634-1981
power transmission equipment DRP

Tyco Laboratories, Inc. TYC
1 Tyco Park
Exeter, NH 03833 (603) 778-9700
fire protection systems, electrical DRP O

Tyler Corporation TYL
3200 San Jacinto Tower
Dallas, TX 75201 (214) 754-7800
industrial explosives, pipe, coatings

UAL Corporation UAL
1200 Algonquin Road
Elk Grove Township, IL 60666 (312) 952-4000
airline O

UDC-Universal Development L.P. UDC
4812 South Mill Avenue
Tempe, AZ 85282 (602) 820-4488
home building, land development

UGI Corporation UGI
460 North Gulph Road
Valley Forge, PA 19482 (215) 337-1000
electric and gas utility, liquefied gases DRP
5%

UNC, Inc. UNC
175 Admiral Cochrane Drive
Annapolis, MD 21401 (301) 266-7333
aerospace, defense, environmental services

Ultimate Corporation ULT
717 Ridgedale Avenue
East Hanover, NJ 07936 (201) 887-9222
minicomputer systems

UniFirst Corporation UNF
68 Jonspin Road
Wilmington, MA 01887 (508) 658-8888
garment rental services

Unilever N.V. UN
Burgemeester's Jacobplein 1 3015 CA
Rotterdam, The Netherlands (212) 418-8829
food, chemicals, detergents, paper O

Unilever PLC UL
Unilever House
London EC4P 4BQ, England (212) 418- 8829
foods, chemicals, detergents, paper

Union Camp Corporation UCC
1600 Valley Road
Wayne, NJ 07470 (201) 628-9000
paper, packaging, wood products DRP O

Union Carbide Corporation UK
39 Old Ridgebury Road
Danbury, CT 06817 (203) 794-2000
chemicals, plastics, gases, carbon DRP O

Union Corporation UCO
50 Washington Street
South Norwalk, CT 06854 (203) 866-1099
financial services

Union Electric Company UEP
1901 Gratiot Street
St. Louis, MO 63103 (314) 621-3222
electric and gas utility DRP

Union Exploration Partners Limited UXP
900 Executive Plaza West, 4635 SW Freeway
Houston, TX 77207 (713) 623-8000
oil and gas exploration and production

Union Pacific Corporation UNP
Martin Tower, Eighth and Eaton Avenues
Bethlehem, PA 18018 (215) 861-3200
railroads, trucking, oil and gas O

Union Planters Corporation UPC
67 Madison Avenue
Memphis, TN 38103 (901) 523-6656
banking DRP

Union Texas Petroleum Holdings, Inc. UTH
1330 Post Oak Boulevard
Houston, TX 77056 (713) 623-6544
oil and gas production

UnionFed Financial Corporation UFF
523 Sixth Street
Los Angeles, CA 90014 (213) 688-8400
savings and loan

Unisys Corporation UIS
Township and Union Meetings Road
Blue Bell, PA 19424 (215) 542-4011
information systems O

Unit Corporation UNT
1000 Galleria Tower 1, 7130 South Lewis
Tulsa, OK 74136 (918) 493-7700
onshore contract drilling for oil and gas

United Asset Management Corporation UAM
1 International Place
Boston, MA 02110 (617) 330-8900
investment management services

United Brands Company UB
1 East Fourth Street
Cincinnati, OH 45202 (513) 784-8011
bananas, meat processing

United Cable Television Corporation UCT
4700 South Syracuse Parkway
Denver, CO 80237 (303) 779-5999
cable television systems

United Illuminating Company UIL
80 Temple Street
New Haven, CT 06506 (203) 787-7200
electric utility DRP

United Industrial Corporation UIC
18 East 48th Street
New York, NY 10017 (212) 752-8787
defense, combustion products, plastics

United Inns, Inc. UI
2300 Clark Tower
Memphis, TN 38137 (901) 767-2880
hotels, furniture

United Jersey Banks UJB
301 Carneigie Center
Princeton, NJ 08543 (609) 987-3200
banking DRP

United Kingdom Fund, Inc. UKM
245 Park Avenue
New York, NY 10167 (212) 530-8446
closed-end British stock mutual fund

United Merchants and Manufacturers, Inc.
UMM
1407 Broadway
New York, NY 10018 (212) 930-3900
textiles, apparel, home furnishings

United Park City Mines Company UPK
309 Kearns Building, 136 South Main Street
Salt Lake City, UT 84101 (801) 532-4031
mine leasing

USAir Group, Inc. U
1911 Jefferson Davis Highway
Arlington, VA 22202 (703) 892-7224
airline O

U.S. Home Corporation UH
1800 West Loop South, P.O. Box 2863
Houston, TX 77252 (713) 877-2311
residential homebuilding

United States Shoe Corporation USR
1 Eastwood Drive
Cincinnati, OH 45227 (513) 527-7000
footwear manufacturing and retailing DRP O

United States Surgical Corporation USS
150 Glover Avenue
Norwalk, CT 06856 (203) 866-5050
surgical staples

United Technologies Corporation UTX
United Technologies Building
Hartford, CT 06101 (203) 728-7000
aerospace, air conditioning, elevators O

United Telecommunications, Inc. UT
2330 Shawnee Mission Parkway
Westwood, KS 66205 (913) 676-3000
local and long distance telephone service DRP
O

United Water Resources, Inc. UWR
200 Old Hook Road
Harrington Park, NJ 07640 (201) 784-9434
water utility DRP 5%

Unitrode Corporation UTR
5 Forbes Road
Lexington, MA 02173 (617) 861-6540
semiconductor devices

Univar Corporation UVX
1600 Norton Building
Seattle, WA 98104 (206) 447-5911
industrial chemicals

Universal Corporation UVV
Hamilton Street at Broad
Richmond, VA 23230 (804) 359-9311
tobacco, title insurance, commodities DRP

Universal Foods Corporation UFC
433 East Michigan Street
Milwaukee, WI 53202 (414) 271-6755
foods products DRP 5%

Universal Health Realty Income Trust UHT
367 South Gulph Road
King of Prussia, PA 19046 (215) 265-0688
health care real estate investment trust

Universal Medical Buildings, L.P. UMB
839 North Jefferson Street
Milwaukee, WI 53202 (414) 278-0100
medical facilities partnership

Unocal Corporation UCL
1201 West Fifth Street
Los Angeles, CA 90051 (213) 977-7600
oil exploration and production DRP O

UNUM Corporation UNM
2211 Congress Street
Portland, ME 04122 (207) 770-2211
disability, health, life insurance

Upjohn Company UPJ
7000 Portage Road
Kalamazoo, MI 49001 (616) 323-4000
pharmaceuticals, health care, seeds DRP O

USAir Group, Inc. U
1911 Jefferson Davis Highway
Arlington, VA 22202 (703) 892-7224
airline O

USACafes, L.P. USF
Suite 500, 8080 North Central Expressway
Dallas, TX 75206 (214) 891-8400
restaurant franchise partnership

USF&G Corporation FG
100 Light Street
Baltimore, MD 21002 (301) 547-3000
property-casualty, life insurance DRP 5% O

USG Corporation USG
101 South Wacker Drive
Chicago, IL 60606 (312) 606-4000
gypsum-based and other building products
DRP O

US Home Corporation UH
1800 West Loop South
Houston, TX 77027 (713) 877-2300
residential construction

USLICO Corporation USC
4601 Fairfax Drive
Arlington, VA 22203 (703) 875-3600
life, property-casualty insurance DRP

USLIFE Corporation USH
125 Maiden Lane
New York, NY 10038 (212) 709-6000
insurance and financial services DRP

USLIFE Income Fund, Inc. UIF
125 Maiden Lane
New York, NY 10038 (212) 709-6000
closed-end bond mutual fund DRP

UST, Inc. UST
100 West Putnam Avenue
Greenwich, CT 06830 (203) 661-1100
tobacco products, wines DRP O

US West, Inc. USW
7800 East Orchard Road
Englewood, CO 80111 (303) 793-6500
telecommunications service DRP O

USX Corporation X
600 Grant Street
Pittsburgh, PA 15230 (412) 433-1121
steel products, oil and gas DRP O

Utilicorp United, Inc. UCU
2000 Commerce Tower, 911 Main Street
Kansas City, MO 64199 (816) 421-6600
gas and electric utility DRP

Valero Energy Corporation VLO
530 McCullough Avenue, P.O. Box 500
San Antonio, TX 78215 (512) 246-2000
petroleum refining, gas pipelines O

Valero Natural Gas Partners, L.P. VLP
530 McCullough Avenue
San Antonio, TX 78215 (512) 246-2000
gas pipelines, gas liquids

Valhi, Inc. VHI
5430 LBJ Freeway
Dallas, TX 75240 (214) 386-4110
chemicals, petroleum services, sugar

Valley Industries, Inc. VI
900 Walnut Street
St. Louis, MO 63102 (314) 231-2160
steel products

Van Dorn Company VDC
2700 East 79th Street
Cleveland, OH 44104 (216) 361-5234
containers, plastic molding machinery DRP

Van Kampen Merritt Intermediate Term High
Income Trust VIT
1001 Warrenville Road
Lisle, IL 60532 (312) 719-6000
closed-end bond mutual fund

Van Kampen Merritt Municipal Income Trust
VMT
1001 Warrenville Road
Lisle, IL 60532 (312) 719-6000
closed-end municipal bond mutual fund

Varco International, Inc. VRC
743 North Eckhoff Street
Orange, CA 92668 (714) 978-1900
oil and gas drilling tools and equipment

Varian Associates Inc. VAR
611 Hansen Way
Palo Alto, CA 94394 (415) 493-4000
microwave tubes, semiconductor items DRP
O

Varity Corporation VAT
595 Bay Street
Toronto, Ontario CDA M5G 2C3
(416) 593-3811
farm and industrial machinery, engines

Vestaur Securities, Inc. VES
Centre Square West
Philadelphia, PA 19101 (215) 567-3969
closed-end bond mutual fund DRP

Vestron, Inc. VV
1010 Washington Boulevard
Stamford, CT 06901 (203) 978-5400
pre-recorded videocassettes, motion pictures

V.F. Corporation VFC
1047 North Park Road
Wyomissing, PA 19610 (215) 378-1151
leisure and intimate apparel DRP O

Vishay Intertechnology, Inc. VSH
63 Lincoln Highway
Malvern, PA 19355 (215) 644-1300
electronic resistors, measurement
instruments

Vista Chemical Company VC
900 Threadneedle Drive
Houston, TX 77224 (713) 588-3000
commodity and specialty chemicals O

Vons Companies, Inc. VON
10150 Lower Azusa Road
El Monte, CA 91731 (818) 579-1400
supermarkets and drugstores

Vornado, Inc. VNO
174 Passaic Street
Garfield, NJ 07026 (201) 773-4000
real estate leasing, shopping centers

Vulcan Materials Company VMC
1 Metroplex Drive
Birmingham, AL 35209 (205) 877-3000
construction materials, chemicals

Wackenhut Corporation WAK
1500 San Remo Avenue
Coral Gables, FL 33146 (305) 666-5656
security and investigative services

Wainoco Oil Corporation WOL
Suite 1500, 1200 Smith Street
Houston, TX 77002 (713) 658-9900
oil and gas exploration and production

Walgreen Company WAG
200 Wilmot Road
Deerfield, IL 60015 (312) 940-2500
drug stores DRP O

Wallace Computer Services, Inc. WCS
4600 West Roosevelt Road
Hillside, IL 60162 (312) 626-2000
business forms, labels, catalogs

Wal-Mart Stores, Inc. WMT
702 Southwest 8th Street
Bentonville, AR 72712 (501) 273-4000
discount retailing O

Warner Communications Inc. WCI
75 Rockefeller Plaza
New York, NY 10019 (212) 484-8000
film, television, records, magazines O

Warner Computer Systems, Inc. WCP
17-01 Pollitt Drive
Fair Lawn, NJ 07410 (201) 794-4800
computer processing, databases

Warner-Lambert Company WLA
201 Tabor Road
Morris Plains, NJ 07950 (201) 540-2000
medical products, drugs, gums, mints DRP O

Washington Gas Light Company WGL
1100 H Street N.W.
Washington, DC 20080 (202) 750-4440
gas utility DRP

Washington National Corporation WNT
1630 Chicago Avenue
Evanston, IL 60201 (312) 570-5500
life, health insurance, annuities DRP 5%

Washington Water Power Company WWP
East 1411 Mission Avenue
Spokane, WA 99202 (509) 489-0500
electric and gas utility DRP

Waste Management, Inc. WMX
3003 Butterfield Road
Oak Brook, IL 60521 (312) 572-8800
solid/ chemical waste management DRP O

Watkins-Johnson Company WJ
3333 Hillview Avenue
Palo Alto, CA 94304 (415) 493-4141
electronic systems and devices

Wean, Inc. WID
13 South, 3 Gateway Center
Pittsburgh, PA 15222 (412) 456-5300
sheet and strip steel machinery

Webb, Del E Corporation WBB
2231 East Camelback Road
Phoenix, AZ 85038 (602) 468-6800
development of planned real estate
communities

Wedgestone Financial WDG
181 Wells Avenue
Newton, MA 02159 (617) 965-8330
mortgage loan real estate investment trust

Weingarten Realty Investors WRI
2600 Citadel Plaza Drive
Houston, TX 77292 (713) 868-6000
real estate investment trust

Weis Markets, Inc. WMK
1000 South Second Street
Sunbury, PA 17801 (717) 286-4571
supermarkets DRP

Wellman, Inc. WLM
67 Walnut Avenue
Clark, NJ 07066 (201) 388-0120
recycles plastic and fiber wastes

Wells Fargo & Company WFC
420 Montgomery Street
San Francisco, CA 94163 (415) 396-0123
banking DRP O

Wells Fargo Mortgage & Equity Trust WFM
420 Montgomery Street
San Francisco, CA 94163 (415) 396-3381
real estate investment trust DRP

Wendy's International, Inc. WEN
4288 West Dublin-Granville Road
Dublin, OH 43017 (614) 764-3100
fast-food restaurants DRP O

West Company, Inc. WST
West Bridge Street
Phoenixville, PA 19460 (215) 935-4500
pharmaceutical packaging

West Point-Pepperell, Inc. WPM
400 West 10th Street
West Point, GA 31833 (404) 654-4000
household/ apparel/industrial fabrics O

Westcoast Energy, Inc. WE
1333 West Georgia Street
Vancouver BC CDA V6E 3K9 (604) 664-5500
gas pipeline DRP 5% O

Western Company of North America WSN
6000 Western Place, P.O. Box 186
Fort Worth, TX 76107 (817) 731-5100
oil drilling services

Western Gas Processors, Ltd. WGP Pr
10701 Melody Drive
Denver, CO 80234 (303) 452-5603
natural gas pipeline construction and
operation

Western Savings and Loan Association WSL
6001 North 24th Street
Phoenix, AZ 85016 (602) 468-4600
savings and loan

Western Union Corporation WU
1 Lake Street
Upper Saddle River, NJ 07458
(201) 825-5000
electronic messaging services

Westinghouse Electric Corporation WX
Westinghouse Building Gateway Center
Pittsburgh, PA 15222 (412) 244-2000
industrial, electric and electronic equipment O

Westvaco Corporation W
299 Park Avenue
New York, NY 10171 (212) 688-5000
pulp, paper, paper products, lumber DRP O

Weyerhaeuser Company WY
33663 32nd Drive South
Tacoma, WA 98477 (206) 924-2345
pulp, paper, packaging, logs, chips DRP O

Wheeling-Pittsburgh Steel Corporation WHX
1134 Market Street
Wheeling, WV 26003 (304) 234-2400
steel and steel products

Whirlpool Corporation WHR
2000 U.S. 33 North
Benton Harbor, MI 49022 (616) 926-5000
major home appliances DRP O

Whitehall Corporation WHT
2659 Nova Drive
Dallas, TX 75229 (214) 247-8747
seismic survey and defense electronics

Whitman Corporation WH
1 Illinois Center, 111 East Wacker Drive
Chicago, IL 60601 (312) 565-3000
specialty foods, bottling, auto repair DRP O

Whittaker Corporation WKR
10880 Wilshire Boulevard
Los Angeles, CA 90024 (213) 475-9411
aerospace, chemicals

WICOR, Inc. WIC
777 East Wisconsin Avenue
Milwaukee, WI 53201 (414) 291-7026
gas utility DRP

Wilfred American Educational Corporation
WAE
1657 Broadway
New York, NY 10019 (212) 582-6690
career school systems

Willcox & Gibbs, Inc. WG
1440 Broadway
New York, NY 10018 (212) 869-1800
electrical components, apparel industry
supplies

Williams A.L. Corporation ALW
Building 1200, 3100 Breckinridge Boulevard
Duluth, GA 30136 (404) 381-1674
life insurance, securities brokerage

Williams Companies WMB
1 Williams Center
Tulsa, OK 74172 (918) 588-2000
oil and gas pipelines, telecommunications
DRP O

Wilshire Oil Company of Texas WOC
921 Bergen Avenue
Jersey City, NJ 07306 (201) 420-2796
oil and gas exploration and production

Winchell's Donut Houses, L.P. WDH
16424 Valley View Avenue
La Mirada, CA 90637 (714) 670-5300
donut house partnership

Windmere Corporation WND
5980 Miami Lakes Drive
Miami Lakes, FL 33014 (305) 362-2611
electric appliances, personal care products O

Winn-Dixie Stores, Inc. WIN
5050 Edgewood Court
Jacksonville, FL 32203 (904) 783-5000
supermarkets DRP

Winnebago Industries, Inc. WGO
Junction of Highways 9 and 69
Forest City, IA 50436 (515) 582-3535
motor homes and recreational vehicles O

Winners Corporation WNR
101 Winners Circle Maryland Farms
Brentwood, TN 37027 (615) 377-4400
restaurants

Wisconsin Energy Corporation WEC
231 West Michigan Street
Milwaukee, WI 53201 (414) 221-2345
electric utility DRP

Wisconsin Public Service Corporation WPS
700 North Adams Street
Green Bay, WI 54307 (414) 433-1445
electric and gas utility

Witco Corporation WIT
520 Madison Avenue
New York, NY 10022 (212) 605-3800
oil, chemical, and detergent products DRP

WMS Industries, Inc. WMS
767 Fifth Avenue
New York, NY 10153 (212) 751-5300
amusement games, casinos

Wolverine World Wide, Inc. WWW
9341 Courtland Drive N.E.
Rockford, MI 49351 (616) 866-5500
footwear

Woolworth, F.W. Company Z
233 Broadway
New York, NY 10279 (212) 553-2000
variety/apparel/shoe store chains DRP O

WorldCorp, Inc. WOA
Suite 490, 13873 Park Center Road
Herndon, VA 22017 (703) 834-9200
contract flight services

Worldwide Value Fund, Inc. VLU
111 South Calvert Street
Baltimore, MD 21203 (301) 539-3400
closed-end global stock mutual fund

WPL Holdings, Inc. WPH
222 West Washington Avenue
Madison, WI 53703 (608) 252-3311
electric, gas, water utility DRP

Wrigley, Wm. Jr. Company WWY
410 North Michigan Avenue
Chicago, IL 60611 (312) 644-2121
chewing gum DRP O

WurlTech Industries, Inc. WUR
Suite 250, 4265 San Felipe
Houston, TX 77027 (713) 622-7216
manufacturing

Wyle Laboratories WYL
128 Maryland Street
El Segundo, CA 90245 (213) 678-4251
distribution of electronic components DRP

Wynn's International, Inc. WN
2600 East Nutwood Avenue
Fullerton, CA 92631 (714) 992-2000
engine additives and treatment solutions

Wyse Technology WYS
3571 North First Street
San Jose, CA 95134 (408) 433-1000
computers and terminals O

Xerox Corporation XRX
P.O. Box 1600, 800 Long Ridge Road
Stamford, CT 06904 (203) 968-3000
office automation equipment, finance DRP O

XTRA Corporation XTR
60 State Street
Boston, MA 02109 (617) 367-5000
leases intermodal transportation equipment

Zapata Corporation ZOS
Zapata Tower, P.O. Box 4240
Houston, TX 77210 (713) 226-6000
oil/gas production and services, fishing O

Zemex Corporation ZMX
280 Park Avenue
New York, NY 10017 (212) 557-2020
industrial minerals and materials

Zenith Electronics Corporation ZE
1000 Milwaukee Avenue
Glenview, IL 60025 (312) 391-7000
consumer electronics, computer systems O

Zenith Income Fund, Inc. ZIF
2 World Trade Center
New York, NY 10048 (212) 321-7155
closed-end bond mutual fund DRP

Zenith Laboratories, Inc. ZEN
140 LeGrand Avenue
Northvale, NJ 07647 (201) 767-1700
generic drug manufacturer

Zenith National Insurance Corporation ZNT
21255 Cailfa Street
Woodland Hills, CA 91367 (818) 713-1000
workers' compensation and other insurance

Zero Corporation ZRO
444 South Flower Street
Los Angeles, CA 90071 (213) 629-7000
electronic equipment, enclosures DRP

Zurn Industries, Inc. ZRN
1 Zurn Place
Erie, PA 16505 (814) 452-2111
waste-to-energy, water quality systems DRP

Zweig Fund, Inc. ZF
900 Third Avenue
New York, NY 10022 (212) 486-7110
closed-end stock and bond mutual fund DRP

Zweig Total Return Fund, Inc. ZTR
900 Third Avenue
New York, NY 10022 (212) 486-7110
closed-end stock and bond mutual fund DRP

AMERICAN STOCK EXCHANGE

ABIOMED, Inc. ABD
33 Cherry Hill Drive
Danvers, MA 01923 (508) 777-5410
medical devices, cardiac support systems

ABM Gold Corporation AGO
Suite 206, 595 Howe Street
Vancouver, British Columbia V6C 2T5
(604) 669-1814
gold mining

Acme United Corporation ACU
425 Post Road
Fairfield, CT 06430 (203) 255-2744
medical shears and scissors, rulers

Action Industries, Inc. ACX
Allegheny Industrial Park, 460 Nixon Road
Cheswick, PA 15024 (412) 782-4800
merchandising programs for retailers

Acton Corporation ATN
Suite 200, 4600 Marriott Drive
Raleigh, NC 27612 (919) 781-5611
insurance, real estate development

Adams Resources & Energy, Inc. AE
6910 Fannin
Houston, TX 77030 (713) 797-9966
markets and transports petroleum products

Adams-Russell, Inc. AEI
1380 Main Street
Waltham, MA 02154 (617) 894-8540
defense electronics

AIFS, Inc. AIF
3661 Buchanan Street
San Francisco, CA 94123 (415) 563-2500
foreign study for students

Air Express International Corporation AEX
120 Tokeneke Road
Darien, CT 06820 (203) 655-7900
freight forwarding

AIRCOA Hotel Partners, L.P. AHT
Suite 1200, 4600 South Ulster Street
Denver, CO 80237 (303) 220-2000
hotel and resort partnership

A.L. Laboratories, Inc. BMD
1 Executive Drive
Fort Lee, NJ 07024 (201) 947-7774
pharmaceuticals, animal health products

Alamco, Inc. AXO
200 West Main Street P.O. Box 1740
Clarksburg, WV 26301 (304) 623-6671
oil and gas exploration and production

Alba-Waldensian, Inc. AWS
201 St. Germain Avenue, SW, P.O. Box 100
Valdese, NC 28690 (704) 874-2191
hosiery, apparel, health care

Alfin, Inc. AFN
720 Fifth Avenue
New York, NY 10019 (212) 333-7700
fragrances

Alliance Bancorporation ABK
1500 West Benson Boulevard
Anchorage, AL 99503 (907) 258-7890
banking

Allstar Inns, L.P. SAI
2020 De La Vina Street
Santa Barbara, CA 93130 (805) 687-3383
motel partnership

Alpha Industries, Inc. AHA
20 Sylvan Road
Woburn, MA 01801 (617) 935-5150
microwave computer devices

Alpine Group, Inc. AGI
3 University Plaza
Hackensack, NJ 07601 (201) 343-7600
industrial products, information displays

ALZA Corporation AZA
950 Page Mill Road, P.O. Box 10950
Palo Alto, CA 94303 (415) 494-5000
controlled release drug products O

AmBrit, Inc. ABI
10101 9th Street North
St. Petersburg, FL 33716 (813) 577-5007
manufactures/distributes ice cream bars

AMC Entertainment, Inc. AEN
106 West 14th Street Suite 1700
Kansas City, MO 64105 (816) 221-4000
operates movie theaters

Amdahl Corporation AMH
1250 East Arques Avenue, P.O. Box 3470
Sunnyvale, CA 94088 (408) 746-6000
high-performance computer systems O

America First PREP Fund 2 L.P. PF
1004 Farnam Street
Omaha, NE 68102 (402) 444-1630
mortgage limited partnership

American Bank of Connecticut BKC
2 West Main Street
Waterbury, CT 06723 (203) 757-9401
savings banking

American Biltrite Inc. ABL
57 River Street
Wellesley Hills, MA 02181 (617) 237-6655
floor coverings, tape products, footwear

American Capital Corporation ACC
Suite 2650, 1221 Brickell Avenue
Miami, FL 33131 (305) 536-1400
savings and loan

American Exploration Company AX
Suite 2100, 700 Louisiana
Houston, TX 77002 (713) 237-0800
oil and gas properties and royalties

American Fructose Corporation AFC.A
250 Harbor Drive
Stamford, CT 06904 (203) 356-9000
high fructose corn syrup

American Healthcare Management, Inc. AHI
Suite 900, 14160 Dallas Parkway
Dallas, TX 75240 (214) 385-7000
health care facilities

American Israeli Paper Mills Ltd. AIP
P.O.B. 142, Industrial Zone
Hadera, Israel 38101 (06) 333666
paper manufacturing from imported pulp

American List Corporation AMZ
98 Cutter Mill Road
Great Neck, NY 11021 (516) 466-0602
rents lists of students to schools

American Maize-Products Company AZE.A
250 Harbor Drive
Stamford, CT 06904 (203) 356-9000
corn sweeteners and starches, tobacco

American Medical Buildings, Inc. A
735 North Water Street
Milwaukee, WI 53202 (414) 227-0222
construction of medical buildings, clinics

American Oil and Gas Corporation AOG
Suite 2000, 333 Clay Street
Houston, TX 77002 (713) 739-2900
oilfield crews and rigs

American Petrofina, Inc. API.A
Fina Plaza
Dallas, TX 75206 (214) 750-2900
oil refining and marketing

American Precision Industries Inc. APR
2777 Walden Avenue
Buffalo, NY 14225 (716) 684-9700
industrial processing equipment, electronics

American Restaurant Partners, L.P. RMC
Suite 3102, 555 North Woodlawn
Wichita, KS 67208 (316) 684-5119
restaurant partnership

American Science & Engineering, Inc. ASE
Fort Washington
Cambridge, MA 02139 (617) 868-1600
energy, space, medical systems

American Shared Hospital Services AMS
Suite 2420, 444 Market Street
San Francisco, CA 94111 (415) 788-5300
provides medical services to hospitals

American Southwest Mortgage Investments
Corporation ASR
Suite 300, 5210 East Williams Circle
Tucson, AZ 85711 (602) 790-5847
mortgage real estate investment trust

American Technical Ceramics Corp. AMK
1 Norden Lane
Huntington Station, NY 11746 (516) 271-9600
ceramic and porcelain capacitors

Americus Trust for American Express
Shares XP
15 West 39th Street
New York, NY 10018 (212) 575-8670
unit trust for American Express shares

Americus Trust for American Home Products
Shares HPP
15 West 39th Street
New York, NY 10018 (212) 575-8670
unit trust for American Home Products shares

Americus Trust for AT & T Shares,
Series 2 ATU
15 West 39th Street
New York, NY 10018 (212) 575-8670
unit trust for AT & T shares

Americus Trust for Amoco Shares AOU
15 West 39th Street
New York, NY 10018 (212) 575-8670
unit trust for Amoco shares

Americus Trust for Arco Shares RFU
15 West 39th Street
New York, NY 10018 (212) 575-8670
unit trust for Arco shares

Americus Trust for Bristol-Myers Shares BYU
15 West 39th Street
New York, NY 10018 (212) 575-8670
unit trust for Bristol-Myers shares

Americus Trust for Chevron Shares CVU
15 West 39th Street
New York, NY 10018 (212) 575-8670
unit trust for Chevron shares

Americus Trust for Coca Cola Shares KKU
15 West 39th Street
New York, NY 10018 (212) 575-8670
unit trust for Coca Cola shares

Americus Trust for Dow Chemical Shares DOU
15 West 39th Street
New York, NY 10018 (212) 575-8670
unit trust for Dow Chemical shares

Americus Trust for Du Pont Shares DPU
15 West 39th Street
New York, NY 10018 (212) 575-8670
unit trust for Du Pont shares

Americus Trust for Kodak Shares KDU
15 West 39th Street
New York, NY 10018 (212) 575-8670
unit trust for Kodak shares

Americus Trust for Exxon Shares XNU
15 West 39th Street
New York, NY 10018 (212) 575-8670
unit trust for Exxon shares

Americus Trust for Ford Shares FCU
15 West 39th Street
New York, NY 10018 (212) 575-8670
unit trust for Ford shares

Americus Trust for GTE Shares LDU
15 West 39th Street
New York, NY 10018 (212) 575-8670
unit trust for GTE shares

Americus Trust for GE Shares LDU
15 West 39th Street
New York, NY 10018 (212) 575-8670
unit trust for GE shares

Americus Trust for GM Shares GCU
15 West 39th Street
New York, NY 10018 (212) 575-8670
unit trust for GM shares

Americus Trust for Hewlett-Packard Shares
HLU
15 West 39th Street
New York, NY 10018 (212) 575-8670
unit trust for Hewlett-Packard shares

Americus Trust for IBM Shares BZU
15 West 39th Street
New York, NY 10018 (212) 575-8670
unit trust for IBM shares

Americus Trust for Johnson & Johnson
Shares BZU
15 West 39th Street
New York, NY 10018 (212) 575-8670
unit trust for Johnson & Johnson shares

Americus Trust for Merck Shares MKU
15 West 39th Street
New York, NY 10018 (212) 575-8670
unit trust for Merck shares

Americus Trust for Mobil Shares MBU
15 West 39th Street
New York, NY 10018 (212) 575-8670
unit trust for Mobil shares

Americus Trust for Philip Morris Shares HMU
15 West 39th Street
New York, NY 10018 (212) 575-8670
unit trust for Philip Morris shares

Americus Trust for Procter & Gamble
Shares OGU
15 West 39th Street
New York, NY 10018 (212) 575-8670
unit trust for Procter & Gamble shares

Americus Trust for Sears Shares RSU
15 West 39th Street
New York, NY 10018 (212) 575-8670
unit trust for Sears shares

Americus Trust for Union Pacific Shares UPU
15 West 39th Street
New York, NY 10018 (212) 575-8670
unit trust for Union Pacific shares

Americus Trust for Xerox Shares XXU
15 West 39th Street
New York, NY 10018 (212) 575-8670
unit trust for Xerox shares

AmeriHealth, Inc. AHH
Suite 1500, 2859 Paces Ferry Road
Atlanta, GA 30339 (404) 435-1776
hospital management

Ampal-American Israel Corporation AIS.A
10 Rockefeller Plaza
New York, NY 10020 (212) 586-3232
loans/investments in Israel

Amwest Insurance Group, Inc. AMW
Suite 300, 6320 Canoga Avenue
Woodland Hills, CA 91367 (818) 704-1111
property-casualty insurance

Andal Corporation ADL
550 Lexington Avenue
New York, NY 10022 (212) 688-4440
specialty steel, tubing

Andrea Radio Corp. AND
11-40 45th Road
Long Island City, NY 11101 (718) 729-8500
audio-electronic equipment

Angeles Corporation ANG
10301 West Pico Boulevard
Los Angeles, CA 90064 (213) 277-4900
oil/gas/real estate partnerships

Angeles Finance Partners ANF
10301 West Pico Boulevard
Los Angeles, CA 90064 (213) 277-4900
short-term secured loans

Angeles Mortgage Partners, Ltd. ANM
10301 West Pico Boulevard
Los Angeles, CA 90064 (800) 421-4374
mortgage partnership

AOI Coal Company AOI
Suite 500, 300 West Texas
Midland, TX 79701 (915) 684-3773
coal mining/processing/marketing

ARC International Corporation ATV
4000 Chesswood Drive
Downsview, Ontario CDA M3J 2B9
(416) 630-0200
cable TV equipment

Arctic Alaska Fisheries Corporation ICE
Fishermen's Center, Fisherman's Terminal
Seattle, WA 98199 (206) 282-3445
fishing

Arizona Commerce Bank AZB
110 South Church Avenue
Tucson, AZ 85701 (602) 628-9800
banking

Arizona Land Income Corporation AZL
Suite 1800, 3443 North Central Avenue
Phoenix, AZ 85012 (602) 264-8800
mortgage real estate investment trust

Ark Restaurants Corporation RK
158 West 29th Street
New York, NY 10001 (212) 760-0520
restaurants and bars

Armatron International, Inc. ART
Two Main Street
Melrose, MA 02176 (617) 321-2300
lawn and garden products

Arrow Automotive Industries, Inc. AI
5 Speen Streeet, P.O. Box 856
Framingham, MA 01701 (617) 872-3711
rebuilds auto replacement parts

Astrex, Inc. ASI
205 Express Street
Plainview, NY 11803 (516) 433-1700
electronics showrooms/distribution

Astrotech International Corporation AIX
Suite 240, Two Chatham Center
Pittsburgh, PA 15219 (412) 391-1896
oil services

AT&E Corporation ATW
1 Maritime Plaza
San Francisco, CA 94111 (415) 433-0430
communications equipment

ATI Medical, Inc. ATI
640 Paula Avenue
Glendale, CA 91201 (818) 502-9984
rents equipment to hospitals

Atari Corporation ATC
1196 Borregas Avenue
Sunnyvale, CA 94086 (408) 745-2000
personal computers, video games

Atlantis Group, Inc. AGH
Suite 801, 2665 South Bayshore Drive
Miami, FL 33133 (305) 858-2200
plastics and furniture manufacturing

Atlas Consolidated Mining & Dev. Corporation
ACM.B
8776 Paseo de Roxas, Makati
Metro Manila, Philippines (212) 758-2430
copper, gold, silver mining

Audiotronics Corporation ADO
7428 Bellaire Avenue
North Hollywood, CA 91605 (818) 765-2645
audio and visual components/equipment

Audiovox Corporation VOX
150 Marcus Boulevard
Hauppauge, NY 11788 (516) 231-7750
automotive aftermarket products

Badger Meter, Inc. BMI
4545 West Brown Deer Road
Milwaukee, WI 53223 (414) 355-0400
utility water meters, flow measurement

Baker, Michael Corporation BKR
4301 Dutch Ridge Road, Box 280
Beaver, PA 15009 (412) 495-7711
engineering consulting services

Baldwin Securities Corporation BAL
342 Madison Avenue
New York, NY 10173 (212) 972-8170
originates loans

Baldwin Technology Company, Inc. BLD
417 Shippan Avenue
Stamford, CT 06902 (203) 348-4400
printing press equipment

Balfour Maclaine Corporation BML
Wall Street Plaza
New York, NY 10005 (212) 425-2100
commodity trading and brokerage

Bamberger Polymers, Inc. BPI
3003 New Hyde Park Road
New Hyde Park, NY 11042 (516) 328-2772
thermoplastic resins

Baruch-Foster Corporation BFO
4925 Greenville Ave.,1160 One Energy Square
Dallas, TX 75206 (214) 368-5886
oil and gas development

Bancroft Convertible Fund, Inc. BCV
56 Pine Street
New York, NY 10005 (212) 269-9236
closed-end convertible mutual fund   DRP

B. A. T. Industries PLC BTI
Windsor House, 50 Victoria Street
London SW1H ONL England (01) 222-7979
tobacco, retailing, paper, insurance

Banister Continental Ltd. BAN
9910 39th Avenue
Edmonton, Alberta T6E 5H8 (403) 462-9430
utility construction

B.B. Real Estate Investment Corporation BBR
Suite A, 705 University Avenue
Sacramento, CA 95285 (916) 929-5433
real estate investment trust

Bank Building & Equipment Corporation of
America BB
3630 South Geyer Road
St. Louis, MO 63127 (314) 821-2265
designs/builds/remodels/equips banks

Bayou Steel Corporation BYX
River Road
LaPlace, LA 70068 (504) 652-4900
steel minimill

Beard Oil Company BOC
Suite 200, 5600 North May Avenue
Oklahoma City, OK 73112 (405) 824-2333
oil and gas development, iodine, carbon
dioxide

Bank of San Francisco Company BOF
550 Montgomery Street
San Francisco, CA 94111 (415) 391-9000
banking

BankAtlantic Financial Corporation BFC
1320 South Dixie Highway
Coral Gables, FL 33146 (305) 665-8100
banking

Belden & Blake Energy Company BBE
7555 Freedom Avenue, N.W.
North Canton, OH 44720 (216) 499-1660
oil and gas exploration and development

Barnwell Industries, Inc. BRN
Suite 2085, 2828 Paa Street
Honolulu, HI 96819 (808) 836-0136
oil and gas production

Belvedere Corporation BLV
90 William Street
New York, NY 10038 (212) 797-7770
property-casualty insurance

Barr Laboratories, Inc. BRL
2 Quaker Road
Pomona, NY 19070 (914) 362-1100
generic drug manufacturer

Bergen Brunswig Corporation BBC.A
4000 Metropolitan Drive
Orange, CA 92668 (714) 385-4000
drugs, health products, video cassettes

Barrister Information Systems Corporation BIS
1 Technology Center, 45 Oak Street
Buffalo, NY 14203 (716) 845-5010
computer-based information for lawyers

Bergstrom Capital Corporation BEM
Suite 220, 505 Madison Street
Seattle, WA 98104 (206) 623-7302
closed-end stock mutual fund

Barry, R.G. Corporation RGB
13405 Yarmouth Road N.W.
Pickerington, OH 43147 (614) 864-6400
slippers, comfort footwear

Bermuda Star Line, Inc. BSL
1086 Teaneck Road
Teaneck, NJ 07666 (201) 837-0400
cruise vacations

Bethlehem Corporation BET
25th & Lennox Streets, P.O. Box 348
Easton, PA 18044 (215) 258-7111
energy and environmental products

B+H Maritime Carriers, Ltd. BHM
73 Front Street
Hamilton 5, Bermuda (809) 295-8513
dry and liquid bulk cargo vessels

B+H Ocean Carriers, Ltd. BHO
73 Front Street
Hamilton 5, Bermuda (809) 295-8313
dry and liquid bulk cargo vessels

BIC Corporation BIC
Wiley Street
Milford, CT 06460 (203) 783-2000
low-cost disposable pens, lighters, razors

Binks Manufacturing Company BIN
9201 West Belmont Avenue
Franklin Park, IL 60131 (312) 671-3000
coatings application equipment

Bio-Rad Laboratories, Inc. BIO.B
1000 Alfred Nobel Drive
Hercules, CA 94547 (415) 234-4130
medical test kits, analytic instruments

Biopharmaceutics, Inc. BPH
990 Station Road
Bellport, NY 11713 (516) 286-5800
generic drug manufacturer

Biotherapeutics, Inc. BRX
357 Riverside Drive
Franklin, TN 37064 (615) 794-4700
cancer biotherapy laboratory services

Biscayne Holdings, Inc. BHA
Suite 801, 2665 South Bayshore Drive
Miami, FL 33133 (305) 858-2200
women's and children's apparel

Blessings Corporation BCO
645 Martinsville Road
Liberty Corner, NJ 07938 (201) 647-7980
plastic film and geriatric products

Blount, Inc. BLT.A
4520 Executive Park Drive, P.O. Box 949
Montgomery, AL 36116 (205) 244-4000
construction/engineering, chain saw parts

Boddie-Noell Restaurant Properties, Inc. BNP
1021 Noell Lane
Rocky Mount, NC 27802 (919) 937-2000
restaurant real estate investment trust

Bolar Pharmaceutical Company, Inc. BLR
33 Ralph Avenue
Copiague, NY 11726 (516) 842-8383
generic prescription drugs

Bow Valley Industries Ltd. BVI
Suite 1800, 321 Sixth Avenue
Calgary, Alberta CDA T2P 3R2 (403) 261-6100
oil and gas development O

Bowl America, Inc. BWL.A
6446 Edsall Road
Alexandria, VA 22312 (703) 941-6300
bowling centers

Bowmar Instrument Corporation BOM
5050 North 40th Street
Phoenix, AZ 85018 (602) 957-0271
electromechanical components

Bowne & Company, Inc. BNE
345 Hudson Street
New York, NY 10014 (212) 924-5500
financial printer

Brascan Ltd. BRS.A
Suite 4800, Commerce Court West
Toronto, Ontario M5L 1B7 (416) 363-9491
natural resources, consumer products,
finance O

Brown-Forman, Inc. BF.B
850 Dixie Highway P.O. Box 1080
Louisville, KY 40210 (502) 585-1100
wine, spirits, china, luggage DRP

BSD Bancorp, Inc. BSD
Suite 1320, 225 Broadway
San Diego, CA 92101 (619) 237-5367
banking

BSN Corporation BSN
1901 Diplomat
Dallas, TX 75234 (214) 484-9484
sports equipment

Buell Industries, Inc. BUE
130 Huntington Avenue
Waterbury, CT 06708 (203) 574-1800
fasteners for auto industry

Buffton Corporation BFX
501 City Center Tower, 201 Main Street
Fort Worth, TX 76102 (817) 332-4761
avionic, electronic, plastic products

Burnham Pacific Properties, Inc. BPP
610 West Ash Street
San Diego, CA 92101 (619) 236-1555
real estate investment trust

Bush Industries, Inc. BSH
1 Mason Drive
Jamestown, NY 14702 (716) 665-2000
electronics furniture

Cablevision Systems Corporation CVC
One Media Crossways
Woodbury, NY 11797 (516) 364-8450
operates cable systems

Caesars New Jersey, Inc. CJN
Suite 2600, 1801 Century Park East
Los Angeles, CA 90067 (213) 552-2711
casino-hotel

Cagle's, Inc. CGL.A
2000 Hills Avenue, N.W.
Atlanta, GA 30318 (404) 355-2820
poultry producer, food distributor

California Energy Company, Inc. CE
601 California Street
San Francisco, CA 94108 (415) 391-7700
geothermal power producer

California Jockey Club CJ
Suite 506, 2121 South El Camino Real
San Mateo, CA 94403 (415) 349-2562
horse racing real estate investment trust

Calprop Corporation CPP
5456 McConnell Avenue
Los Angeles, CA 90066 (213) 306-4314
single family homebuilder

Canadian Marconi Company CMW
2442 Trenton Avenue
Montreal, Quebec H3P 1Y9 (514) 341-7630
communications equipment   O

Canadian Occidental Petroleum Ltd. CXY
Suite 1500, 635 8th Avenue S.W.
Calgary, Alberta T2P 3Z1 (403) 234-6700
oil and gas, chemicals, alternate fuels   O

Canandaigua Wine Company, Inc. CDG.B
116 Buffalo Street
Canandaigua, NY 14424 (716) 394-7900
domestic wine producer

Carmel Container Systems, Ltd. KML
12 Kehilat Venetzia Street
Tel Aviv, Israel 61240 (03) 490794
designs and manufactures containers

Carnival Cruise Lines, Inc. CCL
3915 Biscayne Boulevard
Miami, FL 33137 (305) 573-6030
cruise line   O

Cash America Investments, Inc. PWN
Suite 1000, 306 West 7th Street
Fort Worth, TX 76102 (817) 335-1100
pawnshops and jewelry stores

Caspen Oil, Inc. CNO
Suite 1100, 300 Crescent Court
Dallas, TX 75201 (214) 855-2990
oil and gas development

Castle, A.M. & Company CAS
3400 North Wolf Road
Franklin Park, IL 60131 (312) 625-6411
metal products distributor

Castle Convertible Fund, Inc. CVF
75 Maiden Lane
New York, NY 10038 (212) 806-8800
closed-end convertible mutual fund

Catalina Lighting, Inc. LTG
6073 N.W. 167th Street
Miami, FL 33015 (305) 558-4777
decorative lighting and ceiling fans

Cavalier Homes, Inc. CXV
600 Bank Building
Wichita Falls, TX 76307 (817) 723-5523
manufactured homes

Centennial Group, Inc. CEG
282 South Anita Drive
Orange, CA 92668 (714) 634-9200
real estate development

Central Fund of Canada Ltd. CEF
55 Broad Leaf Crescent
Ancaster, Ontario, CDA L9G 3N6
(416) 648-7878
gold and silver bullion

Central Pacific Corporation CTA
5016 California Avenue
Bakersfield, CA 93380 (805) 861-5211
banking

Central Securities Corporation CET
375 Park Avenue
New York, NY 10152 (212) 688-3011
closed-end stock mutual fund

CenTrust Savings Bank DLP
101 East Flagler Street
Miami, FL 33131 (305) 376-5000
savings and loan

Century Communications Corporation CTY
50 Locust Avenue
New Canaan, CT 06840 (203) 966-8746
cable television, cellular telephone

Cenvill Development Corporation CVL
1926 Tenth Avenue
Lake Worth, FL 33461 (407) 533-9500
develops retirement communities

Chambers Development Company, Inc. CDV.A
10700 Frankstown Road
Pittsburgh, PA 15235 (412) 242-6237
waste management, security services

Champion Enterprises, Inc. CHB
5573 East North Street
Dryden, MI 48428 (313) 796-2211
manufactured homes

Chariot Group, Inc. CGR
45 Rockefeller Plaza
New York, NY 10020 (212) 489-6380
plastic containers, windows and doors

Charter Power Systems, Inc. CHP
3043 Walton Road
Plymouth Meeting, PA 19462 (215) 828-9000
battery power systems

Chase Medical Group, Inc. CGO
7950 N.W. 53rd Street
Miami, FL 33166 (305) 594-1000
medical centers

Chicago Rivet & Machine Company CVR
901 Frontenac Road
Naperville, IL 60540 (312) 357-8500
rivets and related machinery

CIM High Yield Securities CIM
1 Boston Place
Boston, MA 02108 (617) 687-5745
closed-end bond mutual fund   DRP

Citadel Holding Corporation CDL
600 North Brand Boulevard
Glendale, CA 91203 (818) 956-7100
savings and loan

Citizens First Bancorp, Inc. CFB
208 Harrison Road
Glen Rock, NJ 07452 (201) 445-3400
banking   O

Clear Channel Communications, Inc. CCU
500 2 RepublicBank Plaza,
175 East Houston Street
San Antonio, TX 78205 (512) 225-4231
radio and television stations

CMI Corporation CMX
I-40 and Morgan Road P.O. Box 1985
Oklahoma City, OK 73101 (405) 787-6020
automated road-building equipment

Coast Distribution System CRV
1982 Zanker Road
San Jose, CA 95112 (408) 436-0877
recreational vehicle parts distributor

Coeur d'Alene Mines Corporation CDE
505 Front Street
Coeur d'Alene, ID 83814 (208) 667-3511
silver and gold mining

Cognitronics Corporation CGN
25 Crescent Street
Stamford, CT 06906 (203) 327-5307
optical scan/voice response components

Cohu, Inc. COH
5755 Kearny Villa Road
San Diego, CA 92123 (619) 277-6700
electronic devices, TV equipment

Collins Industries, Inc. GO
421 East 30th Avenue
Hutchinson, KS 67502 (316) 663-5551
ambulances, specialty vehicles

Color Systems Technology, Inc. CLR
Suite 100, 4553 Glencoe Avenue
Marina Del Rey, CA 90292 (213) 822-6567
converts black and white films to color

Colorado Prime Corporation CPE
1 Michael Avenue
Farmingdale, NY 11735 (516) 694-1111
gourmet foods and food appliances

Columbia Real Estate Investments, Inc. CIV
10440 Little Patuxent Parkway
Columbia, MD (301) 964-8875
mortgage real estate investment trust

Com Systems, Inc. CTM
7900 Haskell Avenue
Van Nuys, CA 91409 (818) 988-3010
long-distance telephone service

ComFed Bancorp, Inc. CFK
45 Central Street
Lowell, MA 01853 (617) 454-5663
banking

Cominco Ltd. CLT
Suite 2300, 200 Granville Street
Vancouver, BC V6C 2R2 (604) 682-0611
lead, zinc mining, fertilizers, chemicals O

Commtron Corporation CMR
1501 50th Street
West Des Moines, IA 50265 (515) 226-3000
prerecorded videocassette distributor

Comptek Research, Inc. CTK
110 Broadway
Buffalo, NY 14203 (716) 842-2700
defense electronics

CompuDyne Corporation CDC
90 State House Square
Hartford, CT 06103 (203) 240-2980
defense electronics equipment

CompuTrac, Inc. LLB
222 Municipal Drive
Richardson, TX 75080 (214) 234-4241
computer systems for lawyers

Concord Fabrics Inc. CIS
1359 Broadway
New York, NY 10018 (212) 760-0300
woven and knitted fabrics

Connelly Containers, Inc. CON
Righters Ferry Rd. and Schuylkill River
Bala Cynwyd, PA 19004 (215) 839-6400
containers, food processing

Conquest Exploration Company CQX
Suite 500, 4201 FM 1960 West
Houston, TX 77068 (713) 440-2000
oil and gas exploration and development

Consolidated Energy Partners, L.P. CPS
Suite 1100, 1860 Lincoln Street
Denver, CO 80295 (303) 861-5252
oil and gas partnership

Conston Corporation KCS
3250 South 76th Street
Philadelphia, PA 19153 (215) 492-9700
specialty retailer of women's clothing

Continental Materials Corporation CUO
325 North Wells Street
Chicago, IL 60610 (312) 661-7200
minerals, building materials, furnaces

Continuum Company, Inc. CNV
9500 Arboretum Boulevard
Austin, TX 78759 (512) 345-5700
computer software for insurance industry

ConVest Energy Partners, Ltd. CEP
Suite 700, 2401 Fountain View Drive
Houston, TX 77057 (713) 780-1952
oil and gas exploration and development

Copley Properties, Inc. COP
399 Boylston Street
Boston, MA 02116 (617) 578-1200
real estate investment trust

Corcap, Inc. CCP
Suite 2121, 90 State House Square
Hartford, CT 06103 (203) 240-2900
elastomer products

Corona Corporation ICR.A
Suite 1900, 120 Adelaide Street West
Toronto, Ontario, CDA M5H 1T1
(416) 862-2000
gold mining

Courtaulds PLC COU
18 Hanover Square
London, England W1A 2BB
textiles, paint, plastics, chemicals

Cross, A.T. Co. ATXA
One Albion Road
Lincoln, RI 02865 (401) 333-1200
high-priced writing instruments/accessories

Crowley, Milner & Company COM
2301 West Lafayette Boulevard
Detroit, MI 48216 (313) 962-2400
department stores

Crown Central Petroleum Corporation CNP.A
One North Charles, P.O. Box 1168
Baltimore, MD 21203 (301) 539-7400
petroleum refining and marketing

Crown Crafts, Inc. CRW
Edmond St., P.O. Box 12371
Calhoun, GA 30701 (404) 629-7941
home furnishings products

Cruise America, Inc. RVR
Suite 250, 5959 Blue Lagoon Drive
Miami, FL 33126 (305) 262-9611
rents motorhomes and vans

Crystal Oil Company COR
229 Milam Street, P.O. Box 21101
Shreveport, LA 71101 (318) 222-7791
oil and gas development

CSS Industries, Inc. CSS
1401 Walnut Street
Philadelphia, PA 19102 (215) 569-9900
business forms, specialty metal containers

Cubic Corporation CUB
9333 Balboa Avenue
San Diego, CA 92123 (619) 277-6780
defense electronics, elevators, fare collection

Curtice Burns Foods, Inc. CBI
One Lincoln First Square, P.O. Box 681
Rochester, NY 14603 (716) 325-1020
canned, frozen, snack foods   DRP

Customedix Corporation CUS
Route 513
Califon, NJ 07830 (201) 832-5171
health care piping components

CXR Telcom Corporation CXR
501 Charcot Avenue
San Jose, CA 95131 (408) 425-8520
telecommunications test equipment

Cypress Fund, Inc. WJR
1285 Avenue of the Americas
New York, NY 10019 (212) 713-2000
closed-end stock mutual fund

Damon Creations, Inc. DNI
16 East 34th Street
New York, NY 10016 (212) 683-2465
men's furnishings and sportswear

Damson Energy Company, L.P. DEP.A
366 Madison Avenue
New York, NY 10017 (212) 503-8500
oil and gas development/investments

Datametrics Corporation DC
8966 Comanche Avenue
Chatsworth, CA 91311 (818) 341-2901
defense computer peripherals

Dataproducts Corporation DPC
6200 Canoga Avenue
Woodland Hills, CA 91365 (818) 887-8000
computer printers, aerospace   O

Dataram Corporation DTM
Princeton Road
West Windsor Township, NJ 08512
(609) 799-0071
minicomputer-related memory products

Daxor Corporation DXR
645 Madison Avenue
New York, NY 10022 (212) 935-1430
sperm bank, blood storage

De Laurentiis Film Partners, L.P. DFP
8670 Wilshire Boulevard
Beverly Hills, CA 90211 (213) 854-7000
motion picture partnership

De Rose Industries, Inc. DRI
2621 West Airport Freeway
Irving, TX 75062 (214) 258-0330
mobile homes

Decorator Industries, Inc. DII
2755 W. 8th Avenue
Hialeah, FL 33010 (305) 885-4661
manufactures and distributes draperies

Del Laboratories, Inc. DLI
565 Broad Hollow Road
Farmingdale, NY 11735 (516) 293-7070
drugs and cosmetics

Delmed, Inc. DMD
120 Albany Street
New Brunswick, NJ 08903 (201) 249-9393
dialysis sterile solutions

Designatronics, Inc. DSG
2101 Jericho Turnpike
New Hyde Park, NY 11040 (516) 328-3300
electro-mechanical components

Designcraft Industries, Inc. DJI
23 W. 47th Street
New York, NY 10036 (212) 719-3960
precious metals industry components, jewelry

Devon Energy Corporation DVN
1500 Mid-America Tower
Oklahoma City, OK 73102 (405) 235-3611
oil and gas development and production

Diagnostic/Retrieval Systems, Inc. DRS.A
8 Wright Way
Oakland, NJ 07436 (201) 337-3800
anti-submarine warfare computer systems

Diasonics, Inc. DIA
280 Utah Avenue
South San Francisco, CA 94080
(415) 872-2722
magnetic resonance imaging systems,
ultrasound

Dickenson Mines, Ltd. DML.A
Suite 2600, 130 Adelaide Street West
Toronto, Ontario CDA M5H 3P5
(416) 361-0402
gold, silver, limestone mining   O

DI Industries, Inc. DRL
Suite 625, 450 Gears Road
Houston, TX 77067 (713) 874-0202
contract oil and gas drilling

Dillard Department Stores, Inc. DDS.A
900 West Capitol Avenue, P.O. Box 486
Little Rock, AR 72203 (501) 376-5200
department stores

Diodes, Inc. DIO
9957 Canoga Avenue
Chatsworth, CA 91311 (818) 882-4920
semiconductor devices

Direct Action Marketing, Inc. DMK
200 Madison Avenue
New York, NY 10016 (212) 953-0100
retail marketing by direct mail

Divi Hotels, N.V. DVH
54 Gunderman Road
Ithaca, NY 14850 (607) 277-3484
operates Caribbean resort hotels

Dixon Ticonderoga Company DXT
756 Beachland Boulevard
Vero Beach, FL 32963 (407) 231-3190
writing and office products, graphite

Donnelly Corporation DON
414 East 40th Street
Holland, MI 49423 (616) 394-2200
rearview mirrors, modular windows

Dreyfus California Municipal Income, Inc.
DCM
666 Old Country Road
Garden City, NY 11530 (516) 794-5210
closed-end municipal bond mutual fund

Dreyfus Municipal Income, Inc. DMF
666 Old Country Road
Garden City, NY 11530 (516) 794-5210
closed-end municipal bond mutual fund

Dreyfus New York Municipal Income, Inc.
DNM
666 Old Country Road
Garden City, NY 11530 (516) 794-5210
closed-end municipal bond mutual fund

Driver-Harris Company DRH
308 Middlesex Street
Harrison, NJ 07029 (201) 483-4800
wire and cable non-ferrous alloys

Ducommun Inc. DCO
4710 Southeastern Avenue
Los Angeles, CA 90040 (213) 727-7400
aerospace and electronics components

Duplex Products Inc. DPX
1947 Bethany Road
Sycamore, IL 60178 (815) 895-2101
continuous business forms

DWG Corporation DWG
6917 Collins Avenue
Miami Beach, FL 33141 (305) 866-7771
apparel textiles, LP gas, soft drinks

EAC Industries, Inc. EAC
224 South Michigan Avenue
Chicago, IL 60604 (312) 922-7111
hardware, aircraft and defense products

Eagle Clothes, Inc. EGL
Suite 6501, 350 Fifth Avenue
New York, NY 10118 (212) 736-4831
manufacture and retail of menswear

Eagle Financial Corporation EAG
222 Main Street
Bristol, CT 06010 (203) 589-4600
savings and loan

Earl Scheib, Inc. ESH
8737 Wilshire Boulevard
Beverly Hills, CA 90211 (213) 652-4880
auto painting, body repairs

Eastern Company EML
112 Bridge Street
Naugatuck, CT 06770 (203) 729-2255
security products, metal castings   DRP

EastGroup Properties EGP
300 1 Jackson Place, 188 East Capitol Street
Jackson, MS 39201 (601) 948-4091
real estate investment trust

Echo Bay Mines, Ltd. ECO
3300 Manulife Place, 10180 101st Street
Edmonton, AL, CDA T5J 3S4 (403) 429-5811
gold mining   O

EECO Inc. EEC
1601 East Chestnut Avenue
Santa Ana, CA 92702 (714) 835-6000
computer keyboards, switches

Ecology and Environment, Inc. EEI
368 Pleasantview Drive
Lancaster, NY 14086 (716) 684-8060
environmental consulting amd testing

Ehrlich Bober Financial Corporation EB
101 Park Avenue
New York, NY 10178 (212) 856-4300
municipal securities investment banking

Eldorado Bancorp ELB
17752 East 17th Street
Tustin, CA 92680 (714) 830-8800
banking

ElectroSound Group, Inc. ESG
800 Veterans Memorial Highway
Hauppauge, NY 11788 (516) 724-3700
manufactures records and audio tapes

Ellsworth Convertible Growth &
Income Fund, Inc. ECF
Suite 1310, 56 Pine Street
New York, NY 10005 (212) 269-9236
closed-end convertible mutual fund DRP

Elsinore Corporation ELS
202 East Fremont Street
Las Vegas, NV 89101 (702) 385-4011
resort hotels and casinos

Empire of America, FSB EOA
1 Empire Tower
Buffalo, NY 14202 (716) 845-7000
savings banking

Empire of Carolina, Inc. EMP
441 South Federal Highway
Deerfield Beach, FL 33441 (305) 428-9001
children's plastic toys, decorative items

Endevco, Inc. EI
8080 North Central Expressway
Dallas, TX 75206 (214) 691-5536
natural gas processing and transportation

Energy Development Partners Ltd. EDP
4582 South Ulster Street Parkway
Denver, CO 80237 (303) 850-7373
oil and gas exploration and production

Energy Service Company, Inc. ESV
1201 Dairy Ashford
Houston, TX 77079 (713) 496-6060
contract drilling, oil-field tubular goods

Engex, Inc. EGX
44 Wall Street
New York, NY 10005 (212) 495-4000
closed-end stock mutual fund

ENSR Corporation ENX
3000 Richmond Avenue
Houston, TX 77098 (713) 520-9494
industrial and environmental consulting

ENSTAR Indonesia, Inc. ESR
120 White Plains Road
Tarrytown, NY 10591 (914) 333-2000
oil and gas development in Indonesia

Entertainment Marketing, Inc. EM
10310 Harwin Drive
Houston, TX 77036 (713) 995-4433
consumer electronics retailing

Entertainment Publishing Corporation ENT
1400 North Woodward Avenue
Birmingham, MI 48011 (313) 642-8300
discount coupon books

Enviropact, Inc. ENV
4790 N.W. 157th Street
Miami, FL 33014 (305) 620-1700
environmental consulting services

Enzo Biochem, Inc. ENZ
345 Hudson Street
New York, NY 10014 (212) 337-3355
genetic engineering research

Equity Income Fund (AT&T) ATF
Bank of New York, 21 West Street
New York, NY 10015 (212) 612-7055
unit investment trust for ATT shares DRP

Escagenetics Corporation ESN
830 Bransten Road
San Carlos, CA 94070 (415) 595-5335
plant biotechnology

ESI Industries, Inc. ESI
4925 Greenville Avenue
Dallas, TX 75206 (214) 363-9487
specialized truck bodies, modular homes

Espey Manufacturing & Electronics
Corporation ESP
Ballston & Congress Avenues, P.O. Box 422
Saratoga Springs, NY 12866 (518) 584-4100
electronic power supply systems

Esprit Systems, Inc. ETI
100 Marcus Drive
Melville, NY 11747 (516) 293-5600
markets video display terminals

Esquire Radio & Electronics, Inc. EE
4100 First Avenue
Brooklyn, NY 11232 (718) 499-0020
consumer electronics distributor

Etz Lavaud, Ltd. ETZ
P.O. Box 38
Petah Tikva, Israel 49100 (03) 914931
plastic and wood products, aviation materials

Everest & Jennings International EJ.A
2310 So. Sepulveda Boulevard
Los Angeles, CA 90064 (213) 479-4141
wheelchairs, medical equipment

Excel Industries, Inc. EXC
1120 North Main Street
Elkhart, IN 46514 (219) 264-2131
windows for vehicles

Fab Industries, Inc. FIT
200 Madison Avenue
New York, NY 10016 (212) 279-9000
fabrics and laces

Falcon Cable Systems Company FAL
Suite 500, 10866 Wilshire Boulevard
Los Angeles, CA 90024 (213) 470-4884
cable TV systems operator

FFP Partners, L.P. FFP
2801 Glenda Avenue
Fort Worth, TX 76117 (817) 831-0761
convenience stores

Fibreboard Corporation FBD
1000 Burnett Avenue
Concord, CA 94520 (415) 686-0700
lumber, plywood, insulation

Fidelity National Financial, Inc. FNF
Suite 400, 2100 S.E. Main Street
Irvine, CA 92714 (714) 852-9770
title insurance

First Australia Fund, Inc. IAF
One Seaport Plaza
New York, NY 10292 (212) 214-3334
closed-end Australian stock mutual fund DRP

First Australia Prime Income Fund, Inc. FAX
One Seaport Plaza
New York, NY 10292 (212) 214-3334
closed-end Australian bond mutual fund DRP

First Central Financial Corporation FCC
266 Merrick Road
Lynbrook, NY 11563 (516) 593-7070
property-casualty insurance

First Connecticut Small Business Investment
Company FCO
177 State Street
Bridgeport, CT 06604 (203) 366-4726
loans to small businesses

First Empire State Corporation FES
1 M&T Plaza
Buffalo, NY 14240 (716) 842-5445
banking DRP

First Federal Bancorp, Inc. FFS
761 West Huron Street
Pontiac, MI 48053 (313) 333-7071
savings and loan

First Iberian Fund, Inc. IBF
1 Seaport Plaza
New York, NY 10292 (212) 214-3334
closed-end Spanish stock mutual fund

First National Corporation FN
401 West A Street
San Diego, CA 92101 (619) 233-5588
banking

First Republic Bancorp, Inc. FRC
221 Pine Street
San Francisco, CA 94104 (415) 392-1400
savings and loan

Firstcorp, Inc. FCR
300 South Salisbury Street
Raleigh, NC 27601 (919) 831-4200
savings and loan

FirstFed America, Inc. FFA
851 Fort Street Mall
Honolulu, HI 96813 (808) 531-9411
savings and loan

Fischer & Porter Company FP
125 East County Line Road
Warminster, PA 18974 (215) 674-6000
industrial process control equipment

Fitchburg Gas & Electric Light Company FGE
285 John Fitch Highway
Fitchburg, MA 01420 (508) 343-6931
electric and gas utility

Flanigan's Enterprises, Inc. BDL
2841 Cypress Creek Road
Ft. Lauderdale, FL 33309 (305) 974-9003
liquor stores, cocktail lounges

Flexible Bond Trust, Inc. FLX
1285 Avenue of the Americas
New York, NY 10019 (212) 713-2000
closed-end bond mutual fund DRP

Florida Rock Industries, Inc. FRK
155 East 21st Street
Jacksonville, FL 32206 (904) 355-1781
ready-mixed concrete products, aggregates

Fluke, John Manufacturing Company, Inc.
FKM
6920 Seaway Boulevard
Everett, WA 98203 (206) 347-6100
test and measurement instruments/systems

Foodarama Supermarkets, Inc. FSM
303 West Main Street, P.O. Box 592
Freehold, NJ 07728 (201) 462-4700
supermarkets

Ford Motor of Canada, Ltd. FC
The Canadian Road
Oakville, Ontario, CDA L6J 5E4
(416) 845-2511
automaker

Forest City Enterprises, Inc. FCE.A
10800 Brookpark Road
Cleveland, OH 44130 (216) 267-1200
real estate, building materials

Forest Laboratories, Inc. FRX
150 East 58th Street 20th Floor
New York, NY 10155 (212) 421-7850
ethical and non-prescription drugs

Forum Retirement Partners, L.P. FRL
Suite 1200, 8900 Keystone Crossing
Indianapolis, IN 46240 (317) 846-0700
retirement living centers partnership

FPA Corporation FPO
2507 Philmont Avenue
Huntingdon Valley, PA 19006 (215) 947-8900
community development, leisure services

Franklin Holding Corporation FKL
767 Fifth Avenue
New York, NY 10153 (212) 486-2323
closed-end small business investment
company

Frederick's of Hollywood FHO
6608 Hollywood Boulevard
Los Angeles, CA 90028 (213) 466-5151
apparel stores, mail order

Frequency Electronics, Inc. FEI
55 Charles Lindbergh Boulevard
Mitchel Field, NY 11553 (516) 794-4500
electronic control products

Friedman Industries, Inc. FRD
4001 Homestead Road
Houston, TX 77028 (713) 672-9433
processes steel coils into plates/sheets

Fries Entertainment, Inc. FE
6922 Hollywood Boulevard
Los Angeles, CA 90028 (213) 466-2266
produces made-for-TV-movies

Frisch's Restaurants, Inc. FRS
2800 Gilbert Avenue
Cincinnati, OH 45206 (513) 961-2660
operates coffee shops, motels

Frozen Food Express Industries, Inc. JIT
318 Cadiz Street
Dallas, TX 75207 (214) 428-7661
refrigerated motor carrier

Fruit of the Loom, Inc. FTL
233 South Wacker Drive
Chicago, IL 60606 (312) 876-1724
underwear, screen print shirts

Fur Vault, Inc. FRV
360 West 31st Street
New York, NY 10001 (212) 563-7070
wholesaler/retailer of fur apparel

Gainsco, Inc. GNA
5701 East Loop 820 South
Fort Worth, TX 76119 (817) 483-0007
property-casualty insurance

Galaxy Cablevision, L.P. GTV
1100 North Main Street
Sikeston, MO 63801 (314) 471-3080
cable television partnership

Garan, Inc. GAN
350 Fifth Avenue
New York, NY 10118 (212) 563-2000
knitted/woven apparel

Gaylord Container Corporation GCR
Suite 400, 500 Lake Cook Road
Deerfield, IL 60015 (312) 405-5500
containers, containerboard, paper bags

Gelman Sciences, Inc. GSC
600 South Wagner Road, Box 1448
Ann Arbor, MI 48106 (313) 665-0651
lab health devices, filters

Gemco National, Inc. GNL
216 Willowbrook Lane
West Chester, PA 19382 (215) 430-8124
holding company

General Automation, Inc. GA
1055 South East Street
Anaheim, CA 92805 (714) 778-4800
advanced computing products

General Employment Enterprises, Inc. JOB
Oakbrook Terrace Tower, 1 Tower Lane
Oakbrook Terrace, IL 60181 (312) 954-0400
personnel placement service

General Microwave Corporation GMW
5500 New Horizons Boulevard
Amityville, NY 11701 (516) 226-8900
electron measuring and control equipment

Genisco Technology Corporation GES
14930 East Alondra Boulevard
La Mirada, CA 90638 (714) 523-7001
computer graphics, peripherals

Genovese Drug Stores, Inc. GDX.A
80 Marcus Drive
Melville, NY 11747 (516) 420-1900
drug and general merchandise chain

Geothermal Resources International, Inc. GEO
Suite 900, 1825 South Grant Street
San Mateo, CA 94402 (415) 349-3232
develops geothermal properties

Giant Food, Inc. GFS.A
6300 Sheriff Road
Landover, MD 20785 (301) 341-4100
supermarkets, drug stores, foods   DRP, O

Giant Yellowknife Mines, Ltd. GYK
Suite 1900, 95 Wellington Street West
Toronto, Ontario, CDA M5J 2N7
(416) 363-5470
gold mining

Gibson, C.R. Company GIB
32 Knight Street
Norwalk, CT 06856 (203) 847-4543
gift, stationery and memory items

Glatfelter, P.H. Company GLT
228 South Main Street
Spring Grove, PA 17362 (717) 225-4711
printing/writing/technical papers

Glenmore Distilleries Co. GDS.B
1700 Citizens Plaza
Louisville, KY 40202 (502) 589-0130
domestic, imported liquors

Global Natural Resources, Inc. GNR
Suite 900, 5300 Memorial Drive
Houston, TX 77007 (713) 880-5464
oil and gas exploration and production

Global Ocean Carriers, Ltd. GLO
67 Akti Miaouli
Piraeus, Greece (30) 1452-3601
cargo bulk carriers

Goldfield Corporation GV
Suite 500, 100 Rialto Place
Melbourne, FL 32901 (407) 724-1700
electrical construction, copper, silver mining

Gorman-Rupp Company GRC
305 Bowman Street
Mansfield, OH 44901 (419) 755-1011
pump products manufacturer

Gould Investors, L.P. GLP
60 Cutter Mill Road
Great Neck, NY 11021 (516) 466-3100
real estate partnership

Graham Corporation GHM
20 Florence Avenue
Batavia, NY 14020 (716) 343-2216
vacuum and heat transfer equipment

Graham-Field Health Products, Inc. GFI
400 Rabro Drive
Hauppauge, NY 11788 (516) 582-5900
medical sundries, healthcare products

Granges Exploration, Ltd. GXL
900-625 Howe Street
Vancouver, BC CDA V6C 2T6 (604) 687-2831
gold mining

Graphic Technology, Inc. GRT
14824 West 117th Street
Olathe, KS 66062 (913) 829-8000
bar-coded labels for inventory control

Greater Washington Investors, Inc. GWA
5454 Wisconsin Avenue
Chevy Chase, MD 20815 (301) 656-0626
venture capital investments

Greenman Brothers, Inc. GMN
105 Price Parkway
Farmingdale, NY 11735 (516) 293-5300
wholesale/retail distribution of toys

Greiner Engineering, Inc. GII
Suite 1210, 300 East Carpenter Freeway
Irving, TX 75062 (214) 258-6208
engineering and architectural services

GRI Corporation GRR
65 East Wacker Place
Chicago, IL 60601 (312) 977-3700
consumer products by mail

GTI Corporation GTI
Suite 310, 9191 Towne Centre Drive
San Diego, CA 92131 (619) 578-3111
electronic components

Guardian Bancorp GB
800 South Figueroa Street
Los Angeles, CA 90017 (213) 239-0800
banking

Gulf Canada Resources, Ltd. GOU
401 9th Avenue S.W.
Calgary, Alberta T2P 2H7 (403) 233-4000
oil and gas exploration and production O

Gundle Environmental Systems, Inc. GUN
19103 Gundle Road
Houston, TX 77073 (713) 443-8564
lining systems to prevent water contamination

GW Utilities Ltd. GWT
Suite 2700, 2 First Canadian Place
Toronto, Ontario CDA M5X 1B5
(416) 862-5600
gas utility, pipelines

HAL, Inc. HA
1164 Bishop Street
Honolulu, HI 96820 (808) 836-7365
airline

Halifax Engineering, Inc. HX
5250 Cherokee Avenue
Alexandria, VA 22312 (703) 750-2202
professional/technical support services

Halsey Drug Company, Inc. HDG
1827 Pacific Street
Brooklyn, NY 11233 (718) 467-7500
generic drug manufacturer

Hampton Industries, Inc. HAI
2000 Greenville Highway, P.O. Box 614
Kinston, NC 28502 (919) 527-8011
men's and boys' shirts, women's blouses

Hampton Utilities Trust HU
777 Mariners Island Boulevard
San Mateo, CA 94403 (800) 221-0856
closed-end utility stock mutual fund

Harvey Group, Inc. HRA
245 Great Neck Road
Great Neck, NY 11022 (516) 621-3366
distributes electronics, brokers food

Hasbro, Inc. HAS
1027 Newport Avenue
Pawtucket, RI 02862 (401) 727-5000
toys, board and card games O

Hastings Manufacturing Company HMF
325 North Hanover Street
Hastings, MI 49058 (616) 945-2491
manufactures auto replacement parts

Healthcare International HII
9737 Great Hills Trail
Austin, TX 78759 (512) 346-4300
psychiatric and rehabilitation services

Health Care REIT, Inc. HCN
Suite 1950, 1 Seagate
Toledo, OH 43604 (419) 247-2800
nursing home real estate investment trust

Health-Chem Corporation HCH
1107 Broadway
New York, NY 10010 (212) 691-7550
time-release drug delivery system

Health-Mor, Inc. HMI
151 East 22nd Street
Lombard, IL 60148 (312) 953-9700
vacuum cleaners, metal tubing

HealthVest HVT
9737 Great Hills Trail
Austin, TX 78759 (512) 343-5234
health care real estate investment trust

HEICO Corporation HEI
3000 Taft Street
Hollywood, FL 33021 (305) 987-6101
jet engine and laboratory products

Hein-Werner Corporation HNW
1005 Perkins Avenue
Waukesha, WI 53187 (414) 542-6611
hydraulic jacks and pumps for auto repair

Heldor Industries, Inc. HDR
1 Corey Road
Morristown, NJ 07960 (201) 898-9445
in-ground swimming pools

Helm Resources, Inc. H
66 Field Point Road
Greenwich, CT 06830 (203) 629-1400
thermoplastic resins, industrial products

Heritage Entertainment, Inc. HHH
7920 Sunset Boulevard
Los Angeles, CA 90046 (213) 850-5858
motion picture production for TV

Heritage Media Corporation HTG
Suite 1500, 13355 Noel Road
Dallas, TX 75240 (214) 702-7380
radio and TV broadcasting, in-store
advertising

Hershey Oil Corporation HSO
101 West Walnut Street
Pasadena, CA 91103 (818) 405-8888
oil and gas exploration and development

Hinderliter Industries Inc. HND
Suite 600, 7134 South Yale Avenue
Tulsa, OK 74136 (918) 494-0992
liquid gas transfer equipment, heat treating

Hipotronics, Inc. HIP
Route 22, P.O. Box A
Brewster, NY 10509 (914) 279-8091
high voltage testing/power supply equipment

HMG/Courtland Properties, Inc. HMG
2701 South Bayshore Drive
Coconut Grove, FL 33133 (305) 854-6803
real estate investment trust

Hofmann Industries, Inc. HOF
3145 Shillington Road
Sinking Spring, PA 19608 (215) 678-8051
electric welded steel tubing

Holco Mortgage Acceptance Corporation
HOL.A
Suite 308, 333 North Second Street
Niles, MI 49120 (616) 683-7510
GNMA investments

Holly Corporation HOC
Suite 2600, 717 North Harwood Street
Dallas, TX 75201 (214) 979-0210
petroleum refining and marketing

Home Shopping Network, Inc. HSN
12000 25th Court North
St. Petersburg, FL 33716 (813) 572-8585
retailing over TV, TV station ownership   O

Hooper Holmes, Inc. HH
170 Mount Airy Road
Basking Ridge, NJ 07920 (201) 766-5000
healthcare information for insurance
companies

Hormel, George A. & Company HRL
501 16th Avenue, N.E., P.O. Box 800
Austin, MN 55912 (507) 437-5737
meat processor, especially pork products

Horn & Hardart Company HOR
730 Fifth Avenue
New York, NY 10019 (212) 398-9000
fast food restaurants, mail order items

Houston Oil Trust HO
First City National Bank, P.O. Box 809
Houston, TX 77001 (713) 658-7145
royalties of oil/gas properties

Hovnanian Enterprises, Inc. HOV
10 Route 35, P. O. Box 500
Red Bank, NJ 07701 (201) 747-7800
multifamily home builder

Howell Industries, Inc. HOW
17515 West Nine Mile Road
Southfield, MI 48075 (313) 424-8220
auto steel parts, seat guides

Howe Richardson, Inc. HRI
680 Van Houten Avenue
Clifton, NJ 07015 (201) 471-3400
electronic control and measurement devices

Howtek, Inc. HTK
21 Park Avenue
Hudson, NH 03051 (603) 882-5200
ink jet printers

Hubbell Inc. HUB.B
584 Derby Milford Road
Orange, CT 06477 (203) 789-1100
heavy electrical equipment

HUBCO, Inc. HCO
3100 Bergenline Ave.
Union City, NJ 07087 (201) 348-2300
banking

Hudson Foods, Inc. HFI
Hudson Road and 13th Street
Rogers, AR 72757 (501) 636-1100
produces/markets poultry products

Hudson General Corporation HGC
111 Great Neck Road
Great Neck, NY 11021 (516) 487-8610
aviation services, land development

I.C.H. Corporation ICH
4211 Norbourne Boulevard, P. O. Box 7769
Louisville, KY 40207 (502) 897-1861
insurance

ICN Biomedicals, Inc. BIM
3300 Hyland Avenue
Costa Mesa, CA 92626 (714) 545-0113
medical research chemicals

IGI, Inc. IG
2285 East Landis Avenue
Vineland, NJ 08360 (609) 691-2411
vaccines, pharmaceuticals

Imperial Oil, Ltd. IMO.A
111 St. Clair Avenue West
Toronto, Ontario, CDA M5W 1K3
(416) 968-4111
petroleum refiner and marketer   O

Income Opportunity Realty Trust IOT
Suite 200, 1601 LBJ Freeway
Dallas, TX 75234 (214) 406-6423
real estate investment trust

INCSTAR Corporation ISR
1951 Northwestern Avenue
Stillwater, MN 55082 (612) 439-9710
immunological diagnostic test kits

Insteel Industries, Inc. III
1373 Boggs Drive
Mount Airy, NC 27030 (919) 786-2141
wire manufacturer

Instron Corporation ISN
100 Royall Street
Canton, MA 02021 (617) 828-2500
material testing equipment

Instrument Systems Corporation ISY
100 Jericho Quadrangle
Jericho, NY 11753 (516) 938-5544
home furnishings, textiles, communications

Intelligent Systems Master L.P. INP
4355 Shackleford Road
Norcross, GA 30093 (404) 381-2900
microcomputer related products

Inter-City Gas Corporation ICG
20 Queen Street West
Toronto, Ontario, CDA M5H 3RS
(416) 598-0101
gas utility, heating equipment   DRP, O

Intermark Inc. IMI
1020 Prospect Street, P. O. Box 1149
La Jolla, CA 92037 (619) 459-3841
operating/holding company

International Banknote Company, Inc. IBK
230 Park Avenue
New York, NY 10169 (212) 697-6600
currencies/securities printing, holograms

International Income Property, Inc. IIP
100 Park Avenue
New York, NY 10017 (212) 972-4080
real estate investments

International Power Machines Corporation
PWR
2975 Miller Park North
Garland, TX 75042 (212) 272-8000
uninterruptible power systems for computers

International Proteins Corporation PRO
123 Fairfield Road
Fairfield, NJ 07006 (201) 227-2710
manufacturer/distributor of fishmeal

International Recovery Corporation INT
Suite 800,
700 South Royal Poinciana Boulevard
Miami Springs, FL 33166 (305) 884-2001
waste management services, recycling,
aviation

International Telecharge, Inc. ITI
108 South Akard
Dallas, TX 75202 (214) 744-0240
long-distance telephone service, equipment

International Thoroughbred Breeders Inc. ITB
202 Abbington Drive
East Windsor, NJ 08520 (609) 443-6111
breeding, thoroughbred/harness race tracks

Interstate General Company, L.P. IGC
222 Smallwood Village Center
St. Charles, MD 20601 (301) 843-7333
real estate partnership

Ionics, Inc. ION
65 Grove Street
Watertown, MA 02172 (617) 926-2500
water treatment equipment and services

IPM Technology, Inc. IPM
6851 West Imperial Highway
Los Angeles, CA 90045 (213) 646-2994
airport ancillary services

Iroquois Brands, Ltd. IBL
20405 F.M. 149
Houston, TX 77070 (713) 320-8593
nutritional and gourmet products, industrial

IRT Corporation IX
3030 Callan Road
San Diego, CA 92121 (619) 450-4343
automated inspection systems and services

ISI Systems, Inc. SYS
161 Forbes Road
Braintree, MA 02184 (617) 848-4620
data processing for insurance industry

ISS-International Service System, Inc. ISI
1430 Broadway
New York, NY 10018 (212) 382-9800
building maintenance

IVAX Corporation IVX
8800 N.W. 36th Street
Miami, FL 33166 (305) 590-2200
specialty chemicals, drug research

Iverson Technology Corporation IVT
1356 Beverly Road
McLean, VA 22101 (703) 749-1200
modifies computers to specifications

Jaclyn, Inc. JLN
635 59th Street
West New York, NJ 07093 (201) 868-9400
popular-priced handbags

Jacobs Engineering Group, Inc. JEC
251 South Lake Avenue
Pasadena, CA 91101 (213) 681-3781
full-service engineering organization

James Madison, Ltd. JML
1730 M Street N.W.
Washington, DC 20036 (202) 452-5500
banking

Jan Bell Marketing, Inc. JBM
7501 West Oakland Park Boulevard
Ft. Lauderdale, FL 33319 (305) 741-2383
distributes diamond, gold jewelry

Jetronic Industries, Inc. JET
Main & Cotton Streets
Philadelphia, PA 19127 (215) 482-7660
electronic equipment manufacturer

Jewelmasters, Inc. JEM
777 South Flagler Drive
West Palm Beach, FL 33401 (407) 655-7260
designs and sells fine jewelry

Johnson Products Company, Inc. JPC
8522 South Lafayette Avenue
Chicago, IL 60620 (312) 483-4100
hair products, cosmetics geared to blacks

Jones Intercable Investors, L.P. JTV
9697 East Mineral Avenue
Englewood, CO 80112 (303) 792-3111
cable TV partnership

Joule, Inc. JOL
1245 U.S. Route 1 South
Edison, NJ 08837 (201) 494-6500
temporary help and contract engineering

Jumping-Jacks Shoes, Inc. JJS
100 Fifth Street
Monett, MO 65708 (417) 235-3122
manufacturer/distributor children's shoes

Kappa Networks, Inc. KPA
1443 Pinewood Street
Rahway, NJ 07065 (201) 396-9400
electronic components

Keithley Instruments, Inc. KEI
28775 Aurora Road
Solon, OH 44139 (216) 248-0400
electronic test and measurement instruments

Kelley Oil & Gas Partners, L.P. KLY
1100 Dresser Tower, 601 Jefferson Street
Houston, TX 77002 (301) 652-5200
oil and gas partnership

Kent Electronics Corporation KEC
5600 Bonhomme Road
Houston, TX 77036 (713) 780-7770
electronics products distributor

Kenwin Shops, Inc. KWN
4747 Granite Drive
Tucker, GA 30084 (404) 938-0451
ladies' and children's apparel

Kerkhoff Industries, Inc. KIX
Suite 310, 15225 104th Avenue
Surrey, BC CDA V3R 6Y8 (604) 585-2001
real estate construction and development

Ketchum & Company, Inc. KCH
77 Brant Avenue
Clark, NJ 07066 (201) 815-4700
drug and health products distributor

Ketema, Inc. KTM
2333 State Road
Bensalem, PA 19020 (215) 639-2255
aluminum extrusions, aerospace parts

Keystone Camera Products Corporation KYC
468 Getty Avenue
Clifton, NJ 07015 (201) 546-2800
35 mm cameras and photographic equipment

Killearn Properties, Inc. KPI
7118 Beech Ridge Trail
Tallahassee, FL 32312 (904) 893-2111
developer of communities

Kinark Corporation KIN
7060 South Yale Avenue, P.O. Box 1499
Tulsa, OK 74136 (918) 494-0964
chemical storage and packaging

Kirby Exploration Company, Inc. KEX
1717 St. James Place, P.O. Box 1745
Houston, TX 77251 (713) 629-9370
barge transportation, insurance

Kit Manufacturing Company KIT
530 East Wardlow Road, P.O. Box 848
Long Beach, CA 90801 (213) 595-7451
mobile homes, recreational vehicles

Kleer-Vu Industries, Inc. KVU
2016 Main Street
Houston, TX 77002 (713) 654-7777
plastic transparent items

KMW Systems Corporation KMW
6034 West Courtyard Drive
Austin, TX 78730 (512) 338-3000
computer graphics, communications
equipment

Koala Technologies Corporation KOA
1560 Montague Expressway
San Jose, CA 95131 (408) 432-7500
computer peripherals, plastics, paints

Koger Equity, Inc. KE
3986 Boulevard Center Drive
Jacksonville, FL 32207 (904) 398-3403
real estate investment trust

KV Pharmaceutical Company KV
2503 South Hanley Road
St. Louis, MO 63144 (314) 645-6600
drug products

LaBarge, Inc. LB
707 North Second Street
St. Louis, MO 63102 (314) 231-5960
interconnect assemblies, electronics

La Jolla Bancorp LJC
1075 Wall Street
LaJolla, CA 92037 (619) 450-1000
banking

Lancer Corporation LAN
235 West Turbo
San Antonio, TX 78216 (512) 344-3071
beverage dispensing systems

Landmark Land Company, Inc. LML
Suite 200, 100 Clock Tower Place
Carmel, CA 93923 (408) 625-4060
savings and loan, real estate development

Landmark Savings Association LSA
335 Fifth Avenue
Pittsburgh, PA 15222 (412) 553-7744
savings banking

Landsing Pacific Fund LPF
800 El Camino Real
Menlo Park, CA 94025 (415) 321-7100
real estate investment trust DRP

Larizza Industries LII
Suite 1040, 201 West Big Beaver Road
Troy, MI 48084 (313) 689-5800
plastic and electrical components for cars

Laser Industries, Ltd. LAS
Atidim Science-Based Industrial Park
Neve Sharett, Tel-Aviv, Israel 61131
(9723) 493241
surgical laser systems

Latshaw Enterprises, Inc. LAT
2533 South West Street
Wichita, KS 67217 (316) 942-7266
mechanical controls, molded plastic

Laurentian Capital Corporation LQ
Suite 300, 640 Lee Road
Wayne, PA 19087 (215) 889-7400
life, accident, and health insurance

Lawrence Insurance Group, Inc. LWR
770 Broadway
New York, NY 10003 (212) 674-8753
property-casualty insurance

Lawson Mardon Group, Ltd. LMG
Suite 401, 6711 Mississauga Road
Mississauga, Ontario, CDA L5N ZW3
(416) 821-9711
packaging and printing

Lazare Kaplan International, Inc. LKI
529 Fifth Avenue
New York, NY 10017 (212) 972-9700
cutter and merchant of diamonds

Lee Pharmaceuticals LPH
1444 Santa Anita Avenue, P.O. Box 3836
South El Monte, CA 91733 (213) 442-3141
nail care, orthodontic products

Leiner P. Nutritional Products Corporation PLI
1845 West 205th Street
Torrance, CA 90501 (213) 328-9610
vitamin suppliers

Lifetime Corporation LFT
99 Summer Street
Boston, MA 02110 (617) 330-5080
home health care services

Lillian Vernon Corporation LVC
510 South Fulton Avenue
Mount Vernon, NY 10550 (914) 699-4131
direct mail marketing of specialty items

Lincoln N.C. Realty Fund, Inc. LRF
101 Lincoln Centre Drive
Foster City, CA 94404 (415) 571-2250
real estate investment trust

Linpro Specified Properties LPO
200 Berwyn Park
Berwyn, PA 19312 (215) 251-9111
real estate investment trust

Lionel Corporation LIO
441 Lexington Avenue
New York, NY 10017 (212) 818-0630
self-service toy supermarkets

Littlefield, Adams & Company LFA
1302 Rockland Avenue N.W.
Roanoke, VA 24012 (703) 563-2565
imprinted leisurewear

Lori Corporation LRC
500 Central Avenue, P.O. Box 8902
Northfield, IL 60093 (312) 441-7300
distributor of costume jewelry

LSB Industries, Inc. LSB
16 South Pennsylvania
Oklahoma City, OK 73107 (405) 235-4546
bearings, machine tools, air conditioning

Lumex, Inc. LUM
100 Spence Street
Bay Shore, NY 11706 (516) 273-2200
hospital furniture/equipment

Luria, L., & Son, Inc. LUR
5770 Miami Lakes Drive
Miami Lakes, FL 33014 (305) 557-9000
catalog showroom retailer

Lydall, Inc. LDL
One Colonial Road
Manchester, CT 06040 (203) 646-1233
fiber materials for specialized applications

Lynch Corporation LGL
8 Sound Shore Drive
Greenwich, CT 06830 (203) 629-3333
glass machinery, transports vehicles, quartz

MacGregor Sporting Goods, Inc. MGS
25 East Union Avenue
East Rutherford, NJ 07073 (201) 935-6300
manufactures/imports athletic equipment

MacNeal-Schwendler Corporation MNS
815 Colorado Boulevard
Los Angeles, CA 90041 (213) 258-9111
software for computer-aided engineering

Magma Copper Company MCU
P.O. Box M
San Manuel, AZ 85631 (602) 385-3100
copper mining

Maine Public Service Company MAP
209 State Street, P.O. Box 1209
Presque Isle, ME 04769 (207) 768-5811
electric utility

Malartic Hygrade Gold Mines (Canada) Ltd.
MHG
Suite 2402, 1 Dundas Street West
Toronto, Ontario, CDA M5G 1Z3
(416) 977-4653
gold mining

Manufactured Homes, Inc. MNH
P.O. Box 24549
Winston-Salem, NC 27114 (919) 768-9890
manufactured homes retailer

Marlton Technologies, Inc. MTY
3000 G Lincoln Drive East
Marlton, NJ 08053 (609) 985-1933
audiotext manufacturing and service

Mars Graphic Services, Inc. WMD
1 Deadline Drive
Westville, NJ 08093 (609) 456-8666
printing for direct mail marketing

Matec Corporation MXC
75 South Street
Hopkinton, MA 01748 (508) 435-9039
electronic components/systems, cable

Material Sciences Corporation MSC
2300 East Pratt Boulevard
Elk Grove Village, IL 60007 (312) 439-8270
steel coil protective coatings

Materials Research Corporation MTL
Route 303
Orangeburg, NY 10962 (914) 359-4200
film coating, etching, high purity metals

Matlack Systems, Inc. MLK
1 Rollins Plaza, 2200 Concord Pike
Wilmington, DE 19803 (302) 479-2700
bulk commodities trucking

Matthews & Wright Group, Inc. MW
14 Wall Street
New York, NY 10005 (212) 267-4470
municipal securities

MAXXAM, Inc. MXM
10880 Wilshire Boulevard
Los Angeles, CA 90024 (213) 474-6264
real estate management, forest products

McFaddin Ventures, Inc. MV
Suite 100, 1900 Yorktown
Houston, TX 77056 (713) 871-0212
operates entertainment clubs

McRae Industries, Inc. MRI.B
Wadeville Community, Highway 109 North
Mount Gilead, NC 27306 (919) 439-6147
combat boots, apparel

MedChem Products, Inc. MCH
43 Nagog Park
Acton, MA 01720 (617) 938-9328
biomedical products for surgery

Media General, Inc. MEG.A
333 East Grace Street
Richmond, VA 23219 (804) 649-6000
newspaper publishing, newsprint, TV   DRP

Medical Management of America, Inc. MMA
3101 North Harlem Avenue
Chicago, IL 60634 (312) 889-9900
eye care center management

Medical Properties, Inc. MPP
16633 Ventura Boulevard
Encino, CA 91436 (818) 902-2270
health care real estate investment trust

Medicore, Inc. MDK
2201 West 76th Street
Hialeah, FL 33016 (305) 558-4000
kidney dialysis centers, electromechancial
parts

MEDIQ, Inc. MED
One MEDIQ Plaza
Pennsauken, NJ 08110 (609) 665-9300
medical services/equipment leasing

MEM Company, Inc. MEM
Union Street Extension
Northvale, NJ 07647 (201) 767-0100
men's toiletries, fragrances, cosmetics

Merchants Group, Inc. MGP
250 Main Street
Buffalo, NY 14202 (716) 849-3333
property-casualty insurance

Merrimac Industries, Inc. MRM
41 Fairfield Place
West Caldwell, NJ 07007 (201) 575-1300
signal processing subsystems

Met-Pro Corporation MPR
160 Cassell Road
Harleysville, PA 19438 (215) 723-6751
pollution control, fluid handling, filters

Metrobank MBN
10900 Wilshire Boulevard
Los Angeles, CA 90024 (213) 824-5700
banking

Metropolitan Realty Corporation MET
2550 West Grand Boulevard
Detroit, MI 48208 (313) 896-2600
real estate investment trust

Michaels Stores, Inc. MKE
5931 Campus Circle Drive, Las Colinas Park
Irving, TX 75063 (214) 580-8242
specialty retail stores

Micron Products, Inc. PMR
320 Lexington Avenue
New York, NY 10016 (212) 889-7676
hospital and medical supplies distributor

Middleby Corporation MBY
8300 Austin Avenue
Morton Grove, IL 60053 (312) 966-8300
commercial foodservice equipment

Midland Company MLA
537 East Pete Rose Way
Cincinnati, OH 45202 (513) 721-3777
insurance, mobile homes, barges

Mission Resource Partners, L.P. MRP
1151 Harbor Bay Parkway
Alameda, CA 94501 (415) 748-6100
oil and gas partnership

Mission West Properties MSW
Suite 120, 12555 High Bluff Drive
San Diego, CA 92130 (619) 481-5181
real estate investment trust

Mitchell Energy & Development Corporation
MND
2001 Timberloch Place, P.O. Box 4000
The Woodlands, TX 77387 (713) 363-5500
oil and gas, real estate development O

Moog, Inc. MOG.A
East Aurora, NY 14052 (716) 652-2000
aerospace servovalves, industrial controls

Moore Medical Corporation MMD
389 John Downey Drive
New Britain, CT 06050 (203) 225-2225
drugs, medical/beauty products distributor

Morgan's Foods, Inc. MR
Suite 300, 6690 Beta Drive
Cleveland, OH 44143 (216) 461-6200
restaurants

Mortgage Investments Plus, Inc. MIP
6320 Canoga Avenue
Woodland Hills, CA 91367 (818) 715-0311
real estate investment trust

Mott's Super Markets, Inc. MSM
59-65 Leggett Street
East Hartford, CT 06108 (203) 289-3301
supermarkets

Mountain Medical Equipment, Inc. MTN
10488 West Centennial Road
Littleton, CO 80127 (303) 973-1200
oxygen concentrators

MSA Realty Corporation SSS
115 West Washington Street
Indianapolis, IN 46204 (317) 263-7030
real estate investment trust

MSR Exploration Ltd. MSR
CBM Building, P.O. Box 250
Cut Bank, MT 59427 (406) 873-2235
oil and gas exploration and development

MuniInsured Fund, Inc. MIF
800 Scudders Mill Road
Plainsboro, NJ 08536 (609) 282-2800
closed-end municipal bond mutual fund   DRP

MuniVest Fund, Inc. MVF
P.O. Box 9011
Princeton, NJ 08543 (609) 282-2800
closed-end municipal bond mutual fund   DRP

Myers Industries, Inc. MYE
1293 South Main Street
Akron, OH 44301 (216) 253-5592
tire service equipment and supplies

Nabors Industries, Inc. NBR
900 Third Avenue
New York, NY 10022 (212) 832-4646
contract drilling, oilfield transportation

Nantucket Industries, Inc. NAN
105 Madison Avenue
New York, NY 10016 (212) 889-5656
hosiery and underwear

Nasta International, Inc. NAS
200 Fifth Avenue
New York, NY 10010 (212) 929-8085
design and marketing of toys

National Gas & Oil Company NLG
1500 Granville Road, P.O. Drawer A-F
Newark, OH 43055 (614) 344-2102
natural gas supplier

National HealthCorp, L.P. NHC
814 South Church Street
Murfreesboro, TN 37130 (615) 896-5921
health care centers, home health care

National Patent Development Corp. NPD
9 West 57th Street
New York, NY 10019 (212) 826-8500
emerging technology commercial products   O

National Realty L.P. NLP
Suite 560, 1601 LBJ Freeway
Dallas, TX 75234 (214) 960-9383
real estate partnership

NCF Financial Corporation NFC
230 South Tryon Street
Charlotte, NC 28202 (704) 335-5700
savings and loan

NECO Enterprises, Inc. NPT
12 Turner Road
Middletown, RI 02840 (401) 847-4480
electric utility DRP

Nelson Holdings International, Ltd. NHI
Suite 100, 200 Granville Street
Vancouver, BC V6C 1S4 (604) 689-9356
home videotape publisher

New Line Cinema Corporation NLN
575 Eighth Avenue
New York, NY 10018 (212) 239-8880
motion picture production

New Mexico and Arizona Land Company NZ
2810 North Third Street
Phoenix, AZ 85004 (602) 266-5455
land rental, minerals

New Process Company NOZ
220 Hickory Street
Warren, PA 16366 (814) 723-3600
mail order apparel and home furnishings

New York Tax-Exempt Income Fund, Inc. XTX
500 West Madison Street
Chicago, IL 60606 (312) 559-3000
closed-end municipal bond mutual fund   DRP

New York Times Company NYT.A
229 West 43rd Street
New York, NY 10036 (212) 556-1234
newspapers, magazines, TV stations   DRP, O

Newcor, Inc. NEW
3270 West Big Beaver Rd. Suite 430
Troy, MI 48084 (313) 643-7730
specialized industrial machinery

Newmark & Lewis, Inc. NLI
595 South Broadway
Hicksville, NY 11802 (516) 681-6900
retail electrical/appliance stores

Nichols Institute LAB
26441 Via de Anza
S.J. Capistrano, CA 92675 (714) 661-8000
clinical testing services

Nichols, S.E. Inc. NCL
275 Seventh Avenue
New York, NY 10001 (212) 206-9400
discount department stores

North Canadian Oils, Ltd. NCD
Suite 700, 112 Fourth Avenue S.W.
Calgary, Alberta T2P 4B2 (403) 261-3100
oil and gas exploration and pipeline

NRM Energy Company, L.P. NRM
2121 San Jacinto Street
Dallas, TX 75201 (214) 880-0243
oil and gas exploration and production

NS Group, Inc. NSS
Ninth and Lowell Streets
Newport, KY 41072 (606) 292-6809
steel products

Nu Horizons Electronics Corporation NUH
6000 New Horizons Boulevard
North Amityville, NY 11701 (516) 226-6000
distributor of semiconductor parts

Nuclear Data, Inc. NDI
1330 East Golf Street
Schaumburg, IL 60196 (312) 884-3600
printed circuit boards manufacturing

Numac Oil & Gas, Ltd. NMC
1400, 9915 108th Street
Edmonton, Alberta, CDA T5K 2G8
(403) 423-1718
oil and gas exploration

Nuveen New York Municipal Income Fund,
Inc. NNM
333 West Wacker Drive
Chicago, IL 60606 (312) 917-7812
closed-end muncipal bond mutual fund

NVRyan L.P. NVR
Suite 300, 7601 Lewinsville Road
McLean, VA 22102 (703) 761-2000
homebuilding partnership

O'Brien Energy Systems, Inc. OBS
225 South Eighth Avenue
Philadelphia, PA 19106 (215) 627-5500
cogeneration and alternative fuels

Odetics, Inc. O.A
1515 South Manchester Avenue
Anaheim, CA 92802 (714) 774-5000
intelligent machines, robots

OEA, Inc. OEA
34501 East Quincy Avenue, P. O. Box 10488
Denver, CO 80210 (303) 693-1248
aerospace systems, airbag parts

Ohio Art Company OAR
1 Toy Street, P.O. Box 111
Bryant, OH 43506 (419) 636-3141
manufactures toys

Olsten Corporation OLS
One Merrick Avenue
Westbury, NY 11590 (516) 832-8200
temporary personnel services

OMI Corporation OMM
90 Park Avenue
New York, NY 10016 (212) 986-1960
bulk shipping

One Liberty Properties, Inc. OLP
Suite 3304, 515 Madison Avenue
New York, NY 10022 (212) 935-0931
real estate investment trust

Oneita Industries, Inc. ONA
Highway 41, Conifer Street
Andrews, SC 29510 (803) 264-5225
t-shirts, infantswear, underwear, fabrics

O'okiep Copper Company, Ltd. OKP
75 Fox Street
Johannesburg, 2001, South Africa
(212) 880-5100
copper mining

Oppenheimer Industries, Inc. OPP
21 West 10th Street
Kansas City, MO 64105 (816) 471-1750
cattle agency, ranch broker

Oregon Steel Mills, Inc. OS
14400 North Rivergate Boulevard
Portland, OR 97203 (503) 286-9651
steel plate and pipe manufacturer

Organogenesis, Inc. ORG
83 Rogers Street
Cambridge, MA 02142 (617) 577-1717
makes living organ equivalents

Oriole Homes Corporation OHC.A
1151 N.W. 24th Street
Pompano Beach, FL 33064 (305) 972-7660
homes and condominium apartments

Ormand Industries, Inc. OMD
1055 South Vail Avenue
Montebello, CA 90640 (213) 724-4052
distributes containers

O'Sullivan Corporation OSL
1944 Valley Avenue
Winchester, VA 22601 (703) 667-6666
plastic products for automotive industry

Oxford Energy Company OEN
3510 Unocal Place
Santa Rosa, CA 95403 (707) 575-3929
energy generation from renewable resources

Pall Corporation PLL
30 Sea Cliff Avenue
Glen Cove, NY 11542 (516) 671-4000
fluid filters and equipment

Parker & Parsley Development Partners,
L.P. PDP
Suite 800, 508 West Wall Street
Midland, TX 79701 (915) 683-4768
oil and gas partnership

Pauley Petroleum, Inc. PP
410 East College Boulevard
Roswell, NM 88201 (505) 625-8700
oil and gas exploration and refining

PAXAR Corporation PXR
275 North Middletown Road
Pearl River, NY 10965 (914) 735-9200
product identification materials for apparel

Pay-Fone Systems, Inc. PYF
8100 Balboa Boulevard
Van Nuys, CA 91406 (818) 997-0808
payroll service systems

PEC Israel Economic Corporation IEC
511 Fifth Avenue
New York, NY 10017 (212) 687-2400
finance and organize companies in Israel

Peerless Tube Company PLS
58-76 Locust Avenue
Bloomfield, NJ 07003 (201) 743-5100
metal, plastic aerosol containers

Pegasus Gold, Inc. PGU
Suite 400, North 9 Post
Spokane, WA 99201 (509) 624-4653
gold and silver mining

Penn Engineering & Manufacturing
Corporation PNN
Old Easton Road, P. O. Box 1000
Danboro, PA 18916 (215) 766-8853
self-clinching fasteners, electric motors

Penn Traffic Company PNF
319 Washington Street
Johnstown, PA 15901 (814) 536-9900
supermarkets, dairy processing

Pennsylvania Real Estate Investment Trust PEI
Suite 135, 455 Pennsylvania Avenue
Fort Washington, PA 19034 (215) 542-9250
real estate investment trust

Penobscot Shoe Company PSO
450 North Main Street, P.O. Box 545
Old Town, ME 04468 (207) 827-4431
casual sport footwear

Penril Corporation PNL
7811 Montrose Road
Potomac, MD 20854 (301) 762-4949
data communications equipment, test
instruments

Perini Corporation PCR
73 Mount Wayte Avenue
Framingham, MA 01701 (617) 875-6171
construction, real estate development

Perini Investment Properties, Inc. PNV
490 Union Avenue
Framingham, MA 01701 (617) 875-6975
real estate management

Peters J.M. Company, Inc. JMP
Suite 200, 3501 Jamboree Road
Newport Beach, CA 92660 (714) 854-2500
single-family homebuilder

Petroleum Heat & Power Company, Inc. PHP
Davenport Street
Stamford, CT 06904 (203) 323-2121
home heating oil distributor

Philippine Long Distance Telephone Company
PHI
PLDT Building, Legazpi Street
Makati, Metro Manila, Philippines
local and long distance telephone service

Pico Products, Inc. PPI
103 Commerce Boulevard
Liverpool, NY 13088 (315) 451-7700
telecommunications signals products

Pioneer Systems, Inc. PAE
375 Park Avenue
New York, NY 10152 (212) 889-1800
needlework, paint crafts, hobby crafts

Pitt-DesMoines, Inc. PDM
3400 Grand Avenue, Neville Island
Pittsburgh, PA 15225 (412) 331-3000
steel fabricating, contracting

Pittsburgh & West Virginia Railroad PW
Suite 410, 3 PPG Place
Pittsburgh, PA 15222 (212) 687-4956
leased rail line

Pittway Corporation PRY
333 Skokie Boulevard
Northbrook, IL 60065 (312) 498-1260
aerosol products, burglar and smoke alarms

PLM International, Inc. PLM
Suite 1200, 655 Montgomery Street
San Francisco, CA 94111 (415) 989-1860
transport equipment leasing/managing

Ply Gem Industries, Inc. PGI
919 Third Avenue
New York, NY 10022 (212) 832-1550
specialty wood products, filtration products

Plymouth Rubber Company, Inc. PLR.A
104 Revere Street
Canton, MA 02021 (617) 828-0220
plastic and rubber specialties

Pneumatic Scale Corporation PNU
65 Newport Avenue
Quincy, MA 02171 (617) 328-6100
packaging and bottling machinery

Polaris Industries Partners, L.P. SNO
1225 North County Road 18
Minneapolis, MN 55441 (612) 542-0500
snowmobile and recreational vehicles

Porta Systems Corporation PSI
575 Underhill Blvd.
Syosset, NY 11791 (516) 364-9300
manufactures telecommunications equipment

Portage Industries Corporation PTG
1325 Adams Street
Portage, WI 53901 (608) 742-7123
specialized packaging materials

Prairie Oil Royalties Company, Ltd. POY
715 5th Avenue S.W.
Calgary, Alberta T2P 2X7 (403) 231-0111
oil and gas exploration and development

Pratt & Lambert, Inc. PM
75 Tonowanda Street P.O. Box 22
Buffalo, NY 14207 (716) 873-6000
architectural finishes, special coatings

Pratt Hotel Corporation PHC
Suite 2200, 2 Galleria Tower, 13455 Noel Road
Dallas, TX 75240 (214) 386-9777
hotels and casinos

Precision Aerotech, Inc. PAR
Suite 120, 7777 Fay Avenue
La Jolla, CA 92037 (619) 456-2992
precision aerospace components

Preferred Health Care, Ltd. PY
Suite 300, 15 River Road
Wilton, CT 06897 (203) 762-0993
mental health programs

Pre-Paid Legal Services, Inc. PPD
321 East Main Street
Ada, OK 74820 (405) 436-1234
pre-paid legal service contracts

Presidential Realty Corporation PDL.B
180 South Broadway
White Plains, NY 10605 (914) 948-1300
real estate investment trust

Presidio Oil Co. PRS.B
Suite 750, 5613 DTC Parkway
Englewood, CO 80111 (303) 773-0100
oil and gas exploration and development

Price Communications Corporation PR
Suite 3201, 45 Rockefeller Plaza
New York, NY 10020 (212) 757-5600
TV/radio, newspaper, outdoor advertising

Prime Financial Partners, L.P. PFP
Suite 130, 4141 North Scottsdale Road
Scottsdale, AZ 85251 (602) 941-4141
real estate consulting partnership

Princeton Diagnostic Labs of America, Inc.
PDA
100 Corporate Court
South Plainfield, NJ 07080 (201) 769-8500
clinical testing services

Prism Entertainment Corporation PRZ
Suite 1000, 1888 Century Park East
Los Angeles, CA 90067 (213) 277-3270
home video and TV syndication

Professional Care, Inc. PCE
125 East Bethpage Road
Plainview, NY 11803 (516) 694-8700
supplemental health care personnel

Pro-Med Capital PMC
Suite 225, 1380 N.E. Miami Gardens Drive
North Miami Beach, FL 33179 (305) 949-5900
makes loans to health care professionals

Property Capital Trust PCT
200 Clarendon Street
Boston, MA 02116 (617) 536-8600
real estate investment trust

Providence Energy Corporation PVY
100 Weybosset Street
Providence, RI 02903 (401) 272-5040
gas utility

PSE, Inc. POW
9432 Old Katy Road
Houston, TX 77055 (713) 464-9451
cogeneration, waste heat recovery plants

Punta Gorda Isles, Inc. PGA
1625 West Marion Avenue
Punta Gorda, FL 33950 (813) 637-3881
land development, home builder

Quaker Fabric Corporation CFQ
941 Grinnell Street
Fall River, MA 02721 (617) 678-1951
upholstery fabric for home furnishings

Quebecor, Inc. PQB
612 St. Jacques Street West
Montreal, Quebec, CDA H3C 4M8
(514) 282-9600
publishing, printing, forest products

Ragan Brad, Inc. BRD
1 Center South,
4404-G Stuart Andrew Boulevard
Charlotte, NC 28210 (704) 529-6666
tire retreading, retail tire stores

Raven Industries, Inc. RAV
205 East 6th Street, P.O. Box 1007
Sioux Falls, SD 57117 (605) 336-2750
sportswear, balloons, plastics, electronics

RB & W Corporation RBW
5970 Heisley Road
Mentor, OH 44060 (216) 357-1200
metal parts, industrial fasteners

Real Estate Securities Income Fund, Inc. RIF
757 Third Avenue
New York, NY 10017 (212) 832-3232
closed-end real estate stock mutual fund

Realty South Investors, Inc. RSI
1850 Parkway Place
Marietta, GA 30067 (404) 426-0327
real estate investment trust

Re Capital Corporation RCC
6 Stamford Forum, P.O. Box 10148
Stamford, CT 06904 (203) 977-6100
property-casualty reinsurance

RECO International, Inc. RNT
5680 East Houston
San Antonio, TX 78220 (512) 662-5700
industrial refrigeration equipment

Red Lion Inns, L.P. RED
4001 Main Street
Vancouver, WA 98663 (206) 696-0001
hotel partnership

Redlaw Industries, Inc. RDL
255 West Street South, P.O. Box 1100
Orillia, Ontario, CDA L3V 6L3 (705) 325-6121
automotive and transportation products

Regal-Beloit Corporation RBC
5330 East Rockton Road, P.O. Box 38
South Beloit, IL 61080 (815) 389-1920
cutting tools, power transmissions

Residential Mortgage Investments, Inc. RMI
2624 West Freeway
Fort Worth, TX 76102 (817) 390-2000
mortgage real estate investment trust

Resort Income Investors, Inc. RII
Suite 2790, 190 South LaSalle Street
Chicago, IL 60603 (312) 444-1400
resort real estate investment trust

Resource Recycling Technologies, Inc. RRT
300 Plaza Drive
Binghampton, NY (607) 729-9331
processes glass, metal and plastic containers

Riedel Environmental Technologies, Inc. RIE
4611 North Channel Avenue
Portland, OR 97217 (503) 286-4656
hazardous waste management services

Rio Algom, Ltd. ROM
Suite 2600, 120 Adelaide Street West
Toronto, Ontario, CDA M5H 1W5
(416) 367-4000
copper, uranium mining, stainless steel

Riser Foods, Inc. RSR
5300 Richmond Road
Bedford Heights, OH 44146 (216) 292-7000
supermarkets, wholesale grocery operations

Riverbend International Corporation RIV
15749 East Ventura Boulevard
Sanger, CA 93657 (209) 787-2501
food processing and marketing

RMS International, Inc. RMS
621 Route 46
Hasbrouck Heights, NJ 07604 (201) 288-8833
cable TV communications equipment

Robert-Mark, Inc. RMK.A
Route 52 & Old State Road
Hopewell Junction, NY 12533 (914) 221-3700
real estate brokerage and mortgage banking

Rogers Corporation ROG
One Technology Drive
Rogers, CT 06263 (203) 774-9605
polymer products, electronic interconnectors

Royal Palm Beach Colony, L.P. RPB
540 N.W. 165th Street Road
Miami, FL 33169 (305) 949-2100
real estate

Ruddick Corporation RDK
2000 First Union Plaza
Charlotte, NC 28282 (704) 372-5404
supermarkets, threads, yarns, business forms

RYMAC Mortgage Investment Corporation RM
20251 Century Boulevard
Germantown, MD 20874 (301) 353-9210
mortgage real estate investment trust

Salem Corporation SBS
P.O. Box 2222
Pittsburgh, PA 15230 (412) 923-2200
heavy equipment for coal/metal industries

Samson Energy Company L.P. SAM
2 West Second Street, Samson Plaza
Tulsa, OK 74103 (918) 583-1791
oil and gas exploration and development

San Carlos Milling Company, Inc. SAN
San Carlos, Occidental Negros
Philippines
sugar cane milling

Sandy Corporation SDY
1500 West Big Beaver Road
Troy, MI 48084 (313) 649-0800
markets corporate training programs

Sanmark-Stardust, Inc. SMK
136 Madison Avenue
New York, NY 10016 (212) 679-7260
manufacturer of women's and men's apparel

Saxon Oil Development Partners, L.P. SAX
Suite 1500, 3710 Rawlins
Dallas, TX 75219 (214) 528-5588
oil and gas exploration and development

Sbarro, Inc. SBA
763 Larkfield Road
Commack, NY 11725 (516) 864-0200
Italian fast-food restaurants

Scandinavia Company, Inc. SCF
136 Nassau Road
Huntington, NY 11743 (516) 385-9580
invests in Scandinavian companies

Sceptre Resources, Ltd. SRL
3100 West Tower, 150 6th Avenue S.W.
Calgary, Alberta, CDA T2P 3Y7
(403) 298-9800
oil and gas exploration and production

Science Management Corporation SMG
140 Allen Road
Liberty Corner, NJ 07938 (201) 647-7000
management, engineering consulting services

Scope Industries SCP
233 Wilshire Boulevard
Santa Monica, CA 90401 (213) 458-1574
waste material recycling, oil and gas

Scurry-Rainbow Oil, Ltd. SRB
1700 Home Oil Tower, 324 8th Avenue S.W.
Calgary, Alberta, CDA T2P 2Z5
(403) 232-7101
oil and gas exploration and development

Seaboard Corporation SEB
200 Boylston Street
Newton, MA 02167 (617) 332-8492
flour milling, grain storage

Seamen's Corporation SMN
Suite 1700, 5949 Sherry Lane
Dallas, TX 75225 (214) 739-3900
savings and loan

Seaport Corporation SEO
425 North 7th Street
Sacramento, CA 95814 (916) 443-4602
auto replacement parts

Seitel, Inc. SEI
16010 Barker's Point Lane
Houston, TX 77079 (713) 558-1990
seismic data bank

Selas Corporation of America SLS
2034 Limekiln Pike
Dresher, PA 19025 (215) 646-6600
heat processing equipment

Seligman & Associates, Inc. SLG
1760 South Telegraph Road
Bloomfield Hills, MI 48013 (313) 334-7300
builds homes, manages property

Semtech Corporation SMH
652 Mitchell Road
Newbury Park, CA 91320 (805) 498-2111
manufactures silicon rectifiers

Servotronics, Inc. SVT
3901 Union Road
Buffalo, NY 14225 (716) 633-5990
manufactures cutlery and servocontrols

SFM Corporation SFM
27th Floor, Park Omni Hotel, 870 7th Avenue
New York, NY 10019 (212) 757-1717
machinery and electric motors, toys

Shaer Shoe Corporation SHS
Canal & Dow Streets
Manchester, NH 03101 (603) 625-8566
women's fashion footwear

Shelter Components Corporation SST
27217 C.R. #6, P.O. Box 4026
Elkhart, IN 46514 (219) 262-4541
manufactured housing, RV components

Sherwood Group, Inc. SHD
1 Exchange Plaza
New York, NY 10006 (212) 482-4000
securities, financial services

Shopco Laurel Centre, L.P. LSC
Shearson Lehman Hutton,
World Financial Center
New York, NY 10285 (212) 767-3400
shopping mall partnership

Sierra Capital Realty Trust Company IV SZD
1 Market Plaza, Steuart Street Tower
San Francisco, CA 94105 (415) 543-4141
real estate investment trust   DRP

Sierra Capital Realty Trust Company VI SZF
1 Market Plaza, Steuart Street Tower
San Francisco, CA 94105 (415) 543-4141
real estate investment trust   DRP

Sierra Capital Realty Trust Company VII SZG
1 Market Plaza, Steuart Street Tower
San Francisco, CA 94105 (415) 543-4141
real estate investment trust   DRP

Sierra Health Services, Inc. SIE
333 South Rancho Drive
Las Vegas, NV 89106 (702) 646-8180
owns and operates an HMO

Sierracin Corporation SER
12780 San Fernando Road
Sylmar, CA 91342 (818) 362-6802
aerospace, industrial components

SIFCO Industries, Inc. SIF
970 East 64th Street
Cleveland, OH 44103 (216) 881-8600
precision forgings, machined parts

Sikes Corporation SK.A
One Sikes Boulevard
Lakeland, FL 33801 (813) 687-7171
ceramic tile products

Silvercrest Industries, Inc. SLV
1108 West 17th Street
Santa Ana, CA 92706 (714) 542-2606
manufactures mobile homes

SIPCO, Inc. SFT.Pr
1900 AA Street
Greeley, CO 80631 (303) 351-0083
meat processing

SJW Corporation SJW
374 West Santa Clara Street
San Jose, CA 95196 (408) 279-7810
water utility DRP

Skolniks, Inc. SKN
Suite 308, 10801 Electron Drive
Louisville, KY 40299 (502) 267-7667
bagel restaurants

Smith, A.O. Corporation SMC.B
11270 West Park Place
Milwaukee, WI 53223 (414) 359-4000
auto and truck equipment, water heaters

Sorg, Inc. SRG
111 Eighth Avenue
New York, NY 10011 (212) 741-6600
financial and corporate printing

Sotheby's Holdings, Inc. BID
1334 York Avenue
New York, NY 10021 (212) 606-7000
art auctioneer

Southwest Bancorp SWB
410 South Melrose Drive
Vista, CA 92083 (619) 726-5870
banking

Southwest Realty, Ltd. SWL
7424 Greenville Avenue
Dallas, TX 75231 (214) 369-1995
real estate partnership

Spartech Corporation SEH
Suite 1001, 7777 Bonhomme
Clayton, MO 63105 (314) 721-4242
plastic sheet, plastic alloys, polyethylene

Speed-O-Print Business Machines Corporation
SBM
1801 West Larchmont Avenue
Chicago, IL 60613 (312) 249-8000
office copy-making machines

Spelling Entertainment, Inc. SP
1041 North Formosa Avenue
Los Angeles, CA 90046 (213) 850-2413
produces television series, movies

SPI Holding, Inc. SPH Pr
1501 North Plano Road
Richardson, TX 75081 (214) 234-2721
in-room entertainment services for hotels

SPI Pharmaceuticals, Inc. SPI
ICN Plaza, 3300 Hyland Avenue
Costa Mesa, CA 92626 (714) 545-0100
pharmaceuticals

Stage II Apparel Corporation SA
350 Fifth Avenue
New York, NY 10118 (212) 564-5865
men's and boy's casual apparel

Standard Shares, Inc. SWD
333 Skokie Boulevard
Northbrook, IL 60065 (312) 498-1260
alarms and security products, publishing

Starrett Housing Corporation SHO
909 Third Avenue
New York, NY 10022 (212) 751-3100
develops/constructs multi-unit housing

Stepan Company SCL
Edens & Winnetka
Northfield, IL 60093 (312) 446-7500
basic/intermediate chemicals

Sterling Capital Corporation SPR
635 Madison Avenue
New York, NY 10022 (212) 980-3360
investment company

Sterling Electronics Corporation SEC
4201 Southwest Freeway
Houston, TX 77027 (713) 623-6600
manufactures electronic equipment

Sterling Software, Inc. SSW
8080 North Central Expressway
Dallas, TX 75206 (214) 891-8600
markets computer software products

St. Joe Gold Corporation SJG
7733 Forsyth Boulevard
Clayton, MO 63105 (314) 726-9500
gold/silver mining

Stevens Graphics Corporation SVG.A
5500 Airport Freeway
Fort Worth, TX 76117 (817) 831-3911
printing presses, business forms equipment

Struthers Wells Corporation SUW
1003 Pennsylvania Avenue West
Warren, PA 16365 (814) 726-1000
heat transfer equipment

Summit Tax Exempt Bond Fund, L.P. SUA
625 Madison Avenue
New York, NY 10022 (212) 421-5333
closed-end municipal securities mutual fund
DRP

Sunbelt Nursery Group, Inc. SBN
Suite 600, 6500 West Freeway
Fort Worth, TX 76116 (817) 738-8111
retailer of nursery and garden products

Sun City Industries, Inc. SNI
Suite 304, 8600 Doral Boulevard
Miami, FL 33166 (305) 593-2355
production and marketing of eggs

Sunshine-Jr. Stores, Inc. SJS
17th St. & June Avenue, P.O. Box 2498
Panama City, FL 32402 (904) 769-1661
convenience stores, supermarkets

Super Food Services, Inc. SFS
3185 Elbee Road
Dayton, OH 45439 (513) 294-1731
food wholesaler

Superior Industries International, Inc. SUP
7800 Woodley Avenue
Van Nuys, CA 91406 (818) 781-4973
highly stylized car wheels, accessories

Superior Surgical Manufacturing Company,
Inc. SGC
10099 Seminole Boulevard
Seminole, FL 34642 (813) 397-9611
hospital and industrial uniforms

Swift Energy Company SFY
Suite 400, 16825 Northchase Drive
Houston, TX 77060 (713) 874-2700
oil and gas exploration and development

Synalloy Corporation SYO
Camp Croft, P. O. Box 5627
Spartanburg, SC 29304 (803) 585-3605
metal and chemical processor

Systems Industries, Inc. SYI
560 Cottonwood Drive
Milpitas, CA 95035 (408) 432-1212
computer data storage systems

Tab Products Company TBP
1400 Page Mill Road
Palo Alto, CA 94304 (415) 852-2400
office/computer furniture

Tandy Brands, Inc. TAB
Suite 660, 550 Bailey
Fort Worth, TX 76107 (817) 334-8200
leather goods, specialty retailing

Tasty Baking Company TBC
2801 Hunting Park Avenue
Philadelphia, PA 19129 (215) 221-8500
small cakes, pies, graphic equipment

Team, Inc. TMI
1019 South Hood Street
Alvin, TX 77511 (713) 331-6154
pipe repair services, transportation

TEC, Inc. TCK
3561 East Sunrise
Tucson, AZ 85718 (602) 792-2230
plumbing products

Technitrol, Inc. TNL
Suite 10, 8200 Flourtown Avenue
Wyndmoor, PA 19118 (215) 233-9500
electronic and mechanical products

Technodyne, Inc. TND
3000 Marcus Avenue
Lake Success, NY 11042 (516) 354-5353
health and beauty aids distributor, antennas

Tech/Ops Landauer, Inc. TO
2 Science Road
Glenwood, IL 60425 (312) 755-7000
radon gas detection, radiation monitoring

Tech/Ops Sevcon, Inc. TOC
1 Beacon Street
Boston, MA 02108 (617) 523-2030
electric vehicle controls

Tejon Ranch Company TRC
P. O. Box 1000
Lebec, CA 93243 (805) 248-6774
seed, cattle, oil, land, farming

TeleConcepts Corporation TCC
36 Holly Drive
Newington, CT 06111 (203) 666-5666
decorative telephones

Teleflex, Inc. TFX
155 South Limerick Road
Limerick, PA 19468 (215) 948-5100
car/boat/plane precision equipment

Telephone & Data Systems, Inc. TDS
79 West Monroe Street
Chicago, IL 60603 (312) 630-1900
telephone service

Telesphere International, Inc. TSP
Suite 500, 2 Mid America Plaza
Oakbrook Terrace, IL 60181 (312) 954-7700
long-distance telephone service

Templeton Emerging Markets Fund, Inc. EMF
700 Central Avenue
St. Petersburg, FL 33701 (813) 823-8712
closed-end global stock mutual fund

TENERA, L.P. TLP
1995 University Avenue
Berkeley, CA 94704 (415) 845-5200
utility software and consulting partnership

Tenney Engineering, Inc. TNY
1090 Springfield Road
Union, NJ 07083 (201) 686-7870
environmental test equipment

Texas Air Corporation TEX
Suite 4040, Capital Bank Plaza
Houston, TX 77002 (713) 658-9588
airline

Texas Meridian Resources, Ltd. TMR
Suite 825, 580 Westlake Park Boulevard
Houston, TX 77079 (713) 558-8080
oil and gas production

Thermedics, Inc. TMD
470 Wildwood Street, P.O. Box 2999
Woburn, MA 01888 (617) 938-3786
biomedical products, analytical instruments

Thermo Cardiosystems, Inc. TCA
470 Wildwood Street
Woburn, MA 01888 (617) 932-8668
blood-pumping devices for heart patients

Thermo Environmental, Inc. TEV
101 First Avenue
Waltham, MA 02254 (617) 622-1620
environmental testing services, water
management

Thermo Instrument Systems, Inc. THI
101 First Avenue
Waltham, MA 02254 (617) 622-1605
spectrometers, radiation and air instruments

Thermo Process Systems, Inc. TPI
101 First Avenue
Waltham, MA 02254 (617) 622-1000
thermal processing systems, hazardous waste

Thor Energy Resources, Inc. THR
719 West Front Street
Tyler, TX 75702 (214) 531-6000
oil and gas exploration and production

Three D Departments, Inc. TDD.B
18012 Mitchell South
Irvine, CA 92714 (714) 261-1042
linens and bedding discount stores

TII Industries, Inc. TI
1385 Akron Street
Copiague, NY 11726 (516) 789-5000
overvoltage protectors, power supply systems

Timberland Company TBL
11 Merrill Industrial Drive
Hampton, NH 03842 (603) 926-1600
footwear

Tofutti Brands, Inc. TOF
1098 Randolph Avenue
Rahway, NJ 07065 (201) 499-8500
non-dairy frozen dessert products

Torotel, Inc. TTL
13402 South 71 Highway
Grandview, MO 64030 (816) 761-6314
magnetic components

Total Petroleum North America Ltd. TPN
One Denver Place, 999 18th Street
Denver, CO 80202 (303) 291-2000
oil and gas refining and marketing O

TPA of America, Inc. TPS
Suite 1100, 6701 Center Drive West
Los Angeles, CA 90045 (213) 641-1400
health insurance plan administrator

Town & Country Corporation TNC
25 Union Street
Chelsea, MA 02150 (617) 884-8500
fine jewelry manufacturer and marketer

Transcisco Industries, Inc. TNI.B
655 Montgomery Street
San Francisco, CA 94111 (415) 544-8227
railroad equipment manufacture and
maintenance

Trans-Lux Corporation TLX
110 Richards Avenue
Norwalk, CT 06854 (203) 853-4321
display/print-out equipment, theaters

Tranzonic Companies TNZ
30195 Chagrin Boulevard
Pepper Pike, OH 44124 (216) 831-5757
disposable consumer products, housewares

TRC Companies, Inc. TRR
800 Connecticut Boulevard
East Hartford, CT 06108 (203) 289-8631
environmental engineering and consulting

Triangle Corporation TRG
62 Southfield Avenue
Stamford, CT 06904 (203) 327-9050
mechanics' hand tools

Triangle Home Products, Inc. THP
945 East 93rd Street
Chicago, IL 60619 (312) 374-4400
lighting fixtures, bathroom cabinets

Tridex Corporation TDX
1 Gotham Island
Westport, CT 06880 (203) 226-1144
electronic components, coaxial connectors

Tri-State Motor Transit Company of Delaware
TSM
Post Office Box 113
Joplin, MO 64802 (417) 624-3131
transports explosives, radioactive material

Trust America Service Corporation TRS
Suite 300, 1700 66th Street North
St. Petersburg, FL 33710 (813) 384-0833
mortgage banking

T 2 Medical, Inc. TSQ
610 Colonial Park Drive
Roswell, GA 30075 (404) 594-0475
home care infusion therapy centers

Tubos de Acero de Mexico TAM
Campos Eliseos 400
11000 Mexico, D.F. (905) 202-0003
seamless steel pipe and tubing

Turner Broadcasting System, Inc. TBS.A
1 CNN Center,
100 International Boulevard, N.W.
Atlanta, GA 30348 (404) 827-1700
cable news, TV broadcasting, sports

Turner Corporation TUR
633 Third Avenue
New York, NY 10017 (212) 878-0400
diversified builder, real estate

Two Pesos, Inc. TWP
1 Westchase Center, 10777 Westheimer
Houston, TX 77042 (713) 781-0067
Mexican restaurants

UniCARE Financial Corporation UFN
Suite 600, 2201 DuPont Drive
Irvine, CA 92715 (714) 955-2170
workers' compensation insurance

Unicorp American Corporation UAC
156 East 46th Street
New York, NY 10017 (212) 972-6100
banking, real estate

Unimar Company UMR
120 White Plains Road
Tarrytown, NY 10591 (914) 333-2000
oil and gas exploration in Indonesia

Union Valley Corporation UVC
2209 Route 9, Corporate Office Center
Howell, NJ 07731 (201) 905-9000
develops retirement communities

United Capital Corporation ICU
110 East 59th Street
New York, NY 10022 (212) 371-1781
real estate, engineered products

United Foods, Inc. UFD.B
100 Dawson Avenue
Bells, TN 38006 (901) 663-2341
frozen vegetables marketer

United Medical Corporation UM
56 Haddon Avenue
Haddonfield, NJ 08033 (609) 354-2200
medical services and products

United States Cellular Corporation USM
Suite 700, 8410 West Bryn Mawr
Chicago, IL 60631 (312) 399-8900
cellular telephone systems

Unitel Video, Inc. UNV
515 West 57th Street
New York, NY 10019 (212) 265-3600
videotape recording, post-production

UNITIL Corporation UTL
216 Epping Road
Exeter, NH 03833 (603) 772-0775
electric utility   DRP 5%

University Bank, N.A. UBN
25 Needham Street
Newtown, MA 02161 (617) 965-8800
banking, real estate lending

University Patents, Inc. UPT
1465 Post Road East, P.O. Box 901
Westport, CT 06881 (203) 255-6044
computer-based education, optical products

Uno Restaurant Corporation UNO
100 Charles Park Road
West Roxbury, MA 02132 (617) 323-9200
pizza restaurants

USF&G Pacholder Fund, Inc. PHF
11260 Chester Road
Cincinnati, OH 45246 (513) 771-5150
closed-end bond mutual fund   DRP

USP Real Estate Investment Trust URT
4333 Edgewood Road, N.E.
Cedar Rapids, IA 52499 (319) 398-8975
real estate investment trust

Vader Group, Inc. VDR
10 State Street
Moonachie, NJ 07074 (201) 440-2600
holding company

Valley Forge Corporation VF
Suite 326, 100 Smith Ranch Road
San Rafael, CA 94903 (415) 492-1500
recreational marine products, industrial

Valley Resources, Inc. VR
1595 Mendon Road
Cumberland, RI 02864 (401) 333-1595
gas utility   DRP 5%

Valspar Corporation VAL
1101 Third Street South
Minneapolis, MN 55415 (612) 332-7371
paints and coatings

Van Kampen Merritt California
Municipal Trust VKC
1001 Warrenville Road
Lisle, IL 60532 (312) 719-6000
closed-end municipal bond mutual fund

Verit Industries, Inc. VER
11131 Dora Street
Sun Valley, CA 91352 (213) 875-0508
distributes close-out merchandise

Vermont American Corporation VAC.A
100 East Liberty Street
Louisville, KY 40202 (502) 587-6851
cutting tools, power tool accessories

Vermont Research Corporation VRE
Precision Park
North Springfield, VT 05150 (802) 886-2256
magnetic computer memories

Versar, Inc. VSR
6850 Versar Center, P.O. Box 1549
Springfield, VA 22151 (703) 750-3000
environmental technical services

Viacom, Inc. VIA
200 Elm Street
Dedham, MA 02026 (617) 461-1600
entertainment, TV programs, cable TV

Viatech, Inc. VTK
One Aerial Way
Syosset, NY 11791 (516) 822-4940
engineering services, packaging equipment

Vicon Industries, Inc. VII
525 Broad Hollow Road
Melville, NY 11747 (516) 293-2200
closed-circuit TV security equipment

Washington Post Company WPO.B
1150 15th Street, N.W.
Washington, DC 20071 (202) 334-6600
newspapers, magazines, TV, newsprint

Vintage Enterprises, Inc. VIN
3825 Northeast Expressway
Atlanta, GA 30340 (404) 458-3144
manufacturer/retailer mobile homes

Washington Real Estate Investment Trust WRE
4936 Fairmont Avenue
Bethesda, MD 20814 (301) 652-4300
real estate investment trust   DRP

Virco Manufacturing Corporation VIR
15134 South Vermont Avenue
Los Angeles, CA 90247 (213) 532-3570
chairs, tables, contract seating

Watsco, Inc. WSO.A
2665 South Bayshore Drive
Coconut Grove, FL 33133 (305) 858-1204
climate control devices, temporary personnel

VMS Hotel Investment Fund VHT
8700 West Bryn Mawr Avenue
Chicago, IL 60631 (312) 399-8700
real estate investment trust

Weatherford International, Inc. WII
Suite 1000, 1360 Post Oak Boulevard
Houston, TX 77056 (713) 439-9400
oil field services/equipment/rental

VMS Short Term Income Trust VST
8700 West Bryn Mawr Avenue
Chicago, IL 60631 (312) 399-8700
real estate investment trust

Wedco Technology, Inc. WED
Route 173
West Portal, NJ 08802 (201) 479-4181
grinding services, machinery manufacture

Voplex Corporation VOT
800 Stephenson Highway
Troy, MI 48083 (313) 597-6300
plastic auto and industrial parts

Weiman Company, Inc. WC
4801 West Peterson Avenue
Chicago, IL 60646 (312) 286-1121
photo service, mail order jewelry

VTX Electronics Corporation
61 Executive Boulevard
Farmingdale, NY 11735 (516) 293-9880
electronic wire and cable distributor

Weldotron Corporation WLD
1532 South Washington Avenue
Piscataway, NJ 08855 (201) 752-6700
industrial packaging equipment

Vulcan International VUL
6 East 4th Street
Cincinnati, OH 45202 (513) 621-2850
shoe lasts/heels, bowling pins

Wellco Enterprises, Inc. WLC
Georgia Avenue and Pine Street
Waynesville, NC 28786 (704) 456-3545
manufacturer of footwear, shoe machinery

Vyquest, Inc. VY
2421 South Nappanee Street
Elkhart, IN 46517 (219) 294-2126
manufactured homes, recreational vehicles

Wells American Corporation WAC
3243 Sunset Boulevard
West Columbia, SC 29169 (803) 796-7800
desktop microcomputers

Wang Laboratories, Inc. WAN.B
One Industrial Avenue
Lowell, MA 01851 (508) 459-5000
office automation products, computers   O

Wells-Gardner Electronics Corporation WGA
2701 North Kildare Avenue
Chicago, IL 60639 (312) 252-8220
video monitors, TV receivers

Wesco Financial Corporation WSC
315 East Colorado Boulevard
Pasadena, CA 91101 (818) 449-2345
savings and loan, insurance, steel, electrical

Wespercorp WP
17032 Murphy
Irvine, CA 92715 (714) 261-0606
computer components, voice response
systems

WestAir Holding, Inc. WAH
5570 Air Terminal Drive
Fresno, CA 93727 (209) 294-6915
regional airline

Westamerica Bancorporation WAB
1108 Fifth Avenue
San Rafael, CA 94901 (415) 456-8000
banking

Westbridge Capital Corporation WBC
777 Main Street
Fort Worth, TX 76102 (817) 878-3300
life, accident, and health insurance

Westcorp, Inc. WES
1111 East Katella Avenue
Orange, CA 92667 (714) 532-7200
savings and loan, auto finance

Western Digital Corporation WDC
2445 McCabe Way
Irvine, CA 92714 (714) 863-0102
semiconductor devices, disk drives O

Western Health Plans, Inc. WHP
3702 Ruffin Road
San Diego, CA 92123 (619) 571-3102
health maintenance organizations

Western Investment Real Estate Trust WIR
3450 California Street
San Francisco, CA 94118 (415) 929-0211
real estate investment trust

Wichita River Oil Corporation WRO
3300 Anaconda Tower, 555 17th Street
Denver, CO 80202 (303) 292-3300
oil and gas exploration and production

Wiener Enterprises, Inc. WPB
5725 Powell Street, P.O. Box 23607
Harahan, LA 70183 (504) 733-7055
retail apparel and shoe stores

Winston Resources, Inc. WRS
535 Fifth Avenue
New York, NY 10017 (212) 557-5000
personnel recruitment, temporary help

Winthrop Insured Mortgage Investors II WMI
260 Franklin Street
Boston, MA 02110 (617) 330-8600
investments in insured mortgage loans

Wolf, Howard B., Inc. HBW
3809 Parry Avenue
Dallas, TX 75226 (214) 823-9941
women's fashion apparel

World Income Fund, Inc. WOI
800 Scudders Mill Road
Plainsboro, NJ 08536 (609) 282-2800
closed-end global bond mutual fund DRP

Worthen Banking Corporation WOR
Worthen Bank Building
200 West Capitol Avenue
Little Rock, AR 72201 (501) 378-1521
banking

Wrather Corp. WCO
270 North Canon Drive
Beverly Hills, CA 90210 (213) 278-8521
owns tv syndication rights, hotel

Yankee Companies, Inc. YNK
175 Derby Street
Hingham, MA 02043 (617) 740-4411
environmental and oilfield services

NASDAQ NATIONAL MARKET SYSTEM

Aaron Rents, Inc. ARON
1100 Aaron Building, 3001 North Fulton Drive
Atlanta, GA 30363 (404) 231-0011
furniture and appliance rental

Acme Steel Company ACME
13500 South Perry Avenue
Riverdale, IL 60627 (312) 849-2500
iron and steel products

ABQ Corporation ABQC
6501 Americas Parkway, N.E.
Albuquerque, NM 87110 (505) 889-1153
banking, investments

Action Auto Rental, Inc. AXXN
6830 Cochran Road
Solon, OH 44139 (216) 349-4440
rents autos for insurance replacement

Abrams Industries, Inc. ABRI
5775-A Glenridge Drive, N.E.
Atlanta, GA 30328 (404) 256-9785
contracting and engineering

Action Auto Stores, Inc. AAST
2128 South Dort Highway
Flint, MI 48507 (313) 235-5600
discount auto parts stores

ABS Industries, Inc. ABSI
Interstate Square, Suite 300
Willoughby, OH 44094 (216) 946-2274
finished metal

Action Products International, Inc. APII
344 Cypress Road
Ocala, FL 32672 (904) 687-2202
museum gift shop items, aerospace products

Academy Insurance Group, Inc. ACIG
6600 Peachtree-Dunwoody Road
Atlanta, GA 30328 (404) 698-7000
sells insurance to armed forces

Acxiom Corporation ACXM
301 Industrial Boulevard
Conway, AR 72032 (501) 329-6836
provides marketing information to businesses

ACC Corporation ACCC
39 State Street
Rochester, NY 14614 (716) 987-3000
long distance telephone service

ADAC Laboratories ADAC
540 Alder Drive
Milpitas, CA 95035 (408) 945-2990
medical imaging and information supplies

ACCEL International Corporation ACLE
475 Metro Place North
Dublin, OH 43017 (614) 764-7000
specialty insurance

Adage, Inc. ADGE
One Fortune Drive
Billerica, MA 01821 (617) 667-7070
computer graphics workstations

Accuray Corp. ACRA
650 Ackerman Road
Columbus, OH 43202 (614) 261-2495
electronic instruments DRP

Adaptec, Inc. ADPT
580 Cottonwood Drive
Milpitas, CA 95035 (408) 432-8600
computer controllers

Aceto Corporation ACET
126-02 Northern Boulevard
Flushing, NY 11368 (718) 898-2300
makes and distributes chemicals, drugs

ADC Telecommunications, Inc. ADCT
5501 Green Valley Drive
Bloomington, MN 55437 (612) 835-6800
telecommunications equipment

Addington Resources, Inc. ADDR
9431 Route 60
Ashland, KY 41101 (606) 928-3433
coal mining

Adia Services, Inc. ADIA
64 Willow Place
Menlo Park, CA 94025 (415) 324-0696
temporary personnel services

Adobe Systems, Inc. ADBE
1585 Charleston Road
Mountain View, CA 94039 (415) 961-4400
desktop publishing systems

Advance Circuits, Inc. ADVC
6101 Baker Road
Minnetonka, MN 55345 (612) 933-8812
electronic circuits

Advance Ross Corporation AROS
111 West Monroe Street
Chicago, IL 60603 (312) 346-9126
pollution control devices

Advanced Computer Techniques Corporation
ACTP
16 East 32nd Street
New York, NY 10016 (212) 696-3600
health computer systems, programming

Advanced Marketing Services, Inc. ADMS
4747 Morena Boulevard
San Diego, CA 92117 (619) 581-2232
supplies books to warehouse clubs

Advanced Polymer Systems, Inc. APOS
3696-C Haven Avenue
Redwood City, CA 94063 (415) 366-2626
controlled-release drug systems

Advanced Semiconductor Materials
International ASMIF
Jan Steenlaan 9, 3723 BS
Bilthoven, The Netherlands
(31) (030) 781-836
semiconductor devices and integrated
circuits

Advanced Telecommunications Corporation
ATEL
148 International Boulevard
Atlanta, GA 30303 (404) 688-2475
long-distance telephone service

ADVANTA Corporation ADVN
300 Welsh Road
Horsham, PA 19044 (215) 657-4000
direct-marketing consumer financial services

ADVO-System, Inc. ADVO
1 Univac Lane
Windsor, CT 06095 (203) 285-6100
direct-mail marketing

AEGON N.V. AEGNY
Mariahoeveplein 50, P.O. Box 202
The Hague, The Netherlands (70) 443210
life, accident and health insurance

AEL Industries, Inc. AELNA
306 Richardson Road
Lansdale, PA 19446 (215) 822-2929
electronic defense equipment

AEP Industries, Inc. AEPI
20 Knickerbocker Road
Moonachie, NJ 07074 (201) 935-6500
plastic film products

Aequiton Medical, Inc. AQTN
14800 28th Avenue North
Plymouth, MN 55447 (612) 557-9200
medical electronic products

Aerosonic Corporation ASON
1212 North Hercules Drive
Clearwater, FL 33518 (813) 461-3000
flight instruments for airplanes

Aero Systems, Inc. AESM
5415 N.W. 36th Street
Miami, FL 33152 (305) 871-1300
aircraft electronic equipment

Affiliated Banc Corporation ABCV
143 Chestnut Street
Holyoke, MA 01040 (413) 534-8000
savings banking

Affiliated Bankshares of Colorado, Inc. AFBK
Suite 1500, 1125 17th Street
Denver, CO 80202 (303) 269-7788
banking

AFP Imaging Corporation AFPC
250 Clearbrook Road
Elmsford, NY 10523 (914) 592-6100
medical diagnostic equipment

Agency Rent-A-Car, Inc. AGNC
30000 Aurora Road
Solon, OH 44139 (216) 349-1000
auto rental for insurance replacement

Agnico-Eagle Mines, Ltd. AEAGF
Suite 2302, 401 Bay Street
Toronto, Ontario, CDA M5H 2Y4
(416) 947-1212
gold and silver mining

Agouron Pharmaceuticals AGPH
505 Coast Boulevard South
La Jolla, CA 92037 (619) 456-5320
drugs for health care and food industries

AIRCOA Hospitality Services, Inc. AIRC
Suite 1200, 4600 South Ulster Street
Denver, CO 80237 (303) 220-2000
hotel and resort management

Air Midwest, Inc. AMWI
2203 Air Cargo Road
Wichita, KS 67277 (316) 942-8137
regional airline

Air Wis Services, Inc. ARWS
Outagamie County Airport,
203 Challenger Drive
Appleton, WI 54915 (414) 739-5123
regional airline

AirTran Corporation ATCC
6201 34th Avenue South
Minneapolis, MN 55450 (612) 726-5151
regional airline

Alaska Apollo Gold Mines, Ltd. APLOF
1600-609 Granville Street
Vancouver, BC, CDA V7Y 1C3 (602) 279-2070
gold mining

Alaska Mutual Bancorporation AMAB
1500 West Benson Boulevard
Anchorage, AK 99509 (907) 274-3561
banking

AlaTenn Resources, Inc. ATNG
P.O. Box 918
Florence, AL 35631 (205) 383-3631
natural gas distributor

ALC Communications Corporation ALCC
30300 Telegraph Road
Birmingham, MI 48010 (313) 647-4060
long-distance telephone services

Alco Health Services Corporation AAHS
P.O. Box 959
Valley Forge, PA 19482 (215) 296-4480
distributes drugs, health and beauty aids

Alden Electronics, Inc. ADNEA
Washington Street
Westboro, MA 01581 (617) 366-8851 •
weather data display terminals

Aldus Corporation ALDC
Suite 200, 411 First Avenue South
Seattle, WA 98104 (206) 622-5500
desktop publishing software

Alex. Brown Inc. ABSB
135 East Baltimore Street
Baltimore, MD 21202 (301) 727-1700
brokerage and investment banking

Alexander & Baldwin, Inc. ALEX
822 Bishop Street
Honolulu, HI 96801 (808) 525-6611
shipping, real estate, sugar plantations

Alexander Energy Corporation AEOK
501 N.W. Expressway
Oklahoma City, OK 73118 (405) 840-5020
oil and gas exploration and development

Alfa Corporation ALFA
2108 East South Boulevard
Montgomery, AL 36116 (205) 288-3900
life insurance

Algorex Corporation ALGO
70 Corporate Drive
Hauppauge, NY 11788 (516) 434-9400
electronic systems testing

Alico, Inc. ALCO
P.O. Box 338
LaBelle, FL 33935 (813) 675-2966
citrus fruit, cattle, timber, mining

Allegheny & Western Energy Corporation
ALGH
1600 Kanawha Valley Building
Charleston, WV 25301 (304) 343-4567
gas exploration and development

Allen Organ Company AORGB
Macungie, PA (215) 966-2200
electronic keyboard musical instruments

Alliance Financial Corporation ALFL
Suite 233, 23400 Michigan Avenue
Dearborn, MI 48124 (313) 277-5780
banking

Alliant Computer Systems Corporation ALNT
1 Monarch Drive
Littleton, MA 01460 (508) 486-4950
minisupercomputers

Allied Capital Corporation ALLC
Suite 901, 1666 K Street
Washington, DC 20006 (202) 331-1112
small business investment company

ALLIED Group, Inc. ALGR
701 Fifth Avenue
Des Moines, IA 50309 (515) 280-4211
property-casualty and life insurance

Allied Research Corporation ARAI
P.O. Box 1000
Severna Park, MD 21146 (301) 269-5404
ammunition and weapons systems

Alloy Computer Products, Inc. ALOY
100 Pennsylvania Avenue
Framingham, MA 01701 (508) 875-6100
computer subsystems, tape storage

Allwaste, Inc. ALWS
Suite 1300, 3040 Post Oak Boulevard
Houston, TX 77477 (713) 632-8777
environmental services

Alpha Microsystems, Inc. ALMI
3501 Sunflower Street
Santa Ana, CA 92704 (714) 957-8500
microcomputer systems

Alpha 1 Biomedicals ALBM
777 14th Street N.W.
Washington, D.C. 20005 (202) 628-9898
drugs for immune system problems

Alpharel, Inc. AREL
3601 Calle Tecate
Camarillo, CA 93010 (805) 482-9815
computerized document management
systems

Altera Corporation ALTR
3525 Monroe Street
Santa Clara, CA 95051 (408) 984-2800
integrated circuits

Altos Computer Systems ALTO
2641 Orchard Parkway
San Jose, CA 95134 (408) 946-6700
microcomputer systems

Altron, Inc. ALRN
1 Jewel Drive
Wilmington, MA 01887 (508) 658-5800
electronic circuit boards, panels

Altus Bank ALTS
851 South Beltline Highway
Mobile, AL 36606 (205) 473-0500
savings banking

AMCORE Financial, Inc. AMFI
501 Seventh Street
Rockford, IL 61104 (815) 968-2241
banking

A.M.E., Inc. AMEA
1133 North Hollywood Way
Burbank, CA 91505 (818) 841-7440
videotape post-production services

Ameriana Savings Bank, FSB ASBI
2118 Bundy Avenue
New Castle, IN 47362 (317) 529-2230
savings banking, insurance

Ameribanc Investors Group AINVS
Suite 900, 7630 Little River Turnpike
Annandale, VA 22003 (703) 658-2720
savings banking, real estate lending

American Bankers Insurance Group, Inc.
ABIG
11222 Quail Roost Drive
Miami, FL 33157 (305) 253-2244
insurance

American Carriers, Inc. ACIXQ
9393 West 110th Street
Overland Park, KS 66210 (913) 451-2811
trucking

American City Business Journals AMBJ
3535 Broadway
Kansas City, MO 64111 (816) 753-4300
weekly regional business newspapers

American Colloid Company ACOL
1500 West Shure Drive
Arlington Heights, IL 60004 (312) 392-4600
bentonite mineral blends, transportation,
polymers

American Communications & Television, Inc.
ASTVC
7061 South Tamiami Trail
Sarasota, FL 34231 (813) 923-3700
television stations

American Consumer Products, Inc. ACPI
5777 Grant Avenue
Cleveland, OH 44105 (216) 271-4000
consumer hardware manufacturer and
distributor

American Continental Corporation AMCC
2735 East Camelback Road
Phoenix, AZ 85016 (602) 957-7170
savings and loan, real estate investment

American Cytogenetics ACYT
6440 Coldwater Canyon Avenue
North Hollywood, CA 91606 (818) 766-1286
conducts cancer tests

American Ecology Corporation ECOL
30423 Canwood Street
Agoura Hills, CA 91301 (818) 991-7361
waste disposal, environmental services

American Film Technologies, Inc. AFT
1265 Drummers Lane
Wayne, PA 19087 (215) 688-1322
converts black and white films to color

American First Corporation AFCO
Suite 1340, American First Tower
Oklahoma City, OK 73102 (405) 270-5300
municipal and government bond trading

American Franchise Group, Inc. BUCS
3000 N.E. 30th Place
Fort Lauderdale, FL 33306 (305) 563-1224
prints business cards and stationery

American Greetings Corporation AGREA
10500 American Road
Cleveland, OH 44144 (216) 252-7300
greeting cards

American Health Services AHTS
4440 Von Karman
Newport Beach, CA 92660 (714) 476-0733
provides diagnostic/treatment services

American Home Shield Corporation AHSC
Suite 200, 90 South E Street
Santa Rosa, CA 95404 (707) 578-2800
major appliance and home systems
warranties

American Indemnity Financial Corporation
AIFC
1 American Indemnity Plaza
Galveston, TX 77550 (409) 766-4600
casualty insurance

American Integrity Corporation AIIC
2 Penn Center Plaza
Philadelphia, PA 19102 (215) 561-1400
health insurance

American Magnetics Corporation AMMG
13535 Ventura Boulevard
Sherman Oaks, CA 91423 (818) 783-8900
card reader products, data management
systems

American Management Systems, Inc. AMSY
1777 North Kent Street
Arlington, VA 22209 (703) 841-6000
computer consulting, systems engineering

American Medical Electronics, Inc. AMEI
4125 Keller Springs Road
Dallas, TX 75244 (214) 248-6000
orthopedic medical devices

American Midland Corporation AMCO
270 Sylvan Avenue
Englewood Cliffs, NJ 07632 (201) 871-3800
operates nursing homes, real estate
developer

American National Insurance Company ANAT
1 Moody Plaza
Galveston, TX 77550 (409) 763-4661
life insurance

American Nuclear Corporation ANUC
314 Midwest Avenue
Casper, WY 82602 (307) 265-7912
uranium production

American Pacesetter AEC
4300 Campus Drive
Newport Beach, CA 92660 (714) 975-8530
savings and loan

American Pacific Corporation APFC
4045 South Spencer Street
Henderson, NV 89015 (702) 735-2200
ammonium perchlorate manufacturer

American Physicians Service Group AMPH
1301 Capital of Texas Highway
Austin, TX 78746 (512) 328-0888
business support to medical professionals

American Recreation Centers, Inc. AMRC
9261 Folsom Boulevard
Sacramento, CA 95860 (916) 362-2695
operates bowling centers DRP

American Software, Inc. AMSWA
470 East Paces Ferry Road, N.E.
Atlanta, GA 30305 (404) 261-4381
applications software producer

American Steel & Wire Corporation RODS
4300 East 49th Street
Cuyahoga Heights, OH 44125 (216) 883-3800
steel rod and wire

American Television and Communications
ATCMA
160 Inverness Drive West
Englewood, CO 80112 (303) 799-1200
cable televison systems

American Travellers Corporation ATVC
1800 Street Road
Warrington, PA 18976 (215) 343-1000
health insurance

American Western Corporation AWST
1208 West Elkhorn
Sioux Falls, SD 57117 (605) 334-0334
polyethylene film products

American Woodmark Corporation AMWD
3102 Shawnee Drive
Winchester, VA 22601 (703) 665-9100
kitchen cabinets and vanities

America West Airlines AWAL
4000 East Sky Harbor Boulevard
Phoenix, AZ 85034 (602) 894-0800
regional airline

AmeriFirst Bank, FSB AMRI
1 S.E. Third Avenue
Miami, FL 33131 (305) 557-6100
savings banking

Ameritrust Corporation AMTR
900 Euclid Avenue
Cleveland, OH 44101 (216) 737-6478
banking

Amgen, Inc. AMGN
1900 Oak Terrace Lane
Thousand Oaks, CA 91320 (805) 499-5725
biotechnology

Amistar Corporation AMTA
237 Via Vera Cruz
San Marcos, CA 92069 (619) 471-1700
printed circuit board equipment

Amoskeag Bank Shares, Inc. AMKG
875 Elm Street
Manchester, NH 03105 (603) 647-3200
banking

Amoskeag Company AMOS
Suite 4500, Prudential Center
Boston, MA 02199 (617) 262-4000
textiles, railroad, modular housing

Amplicon, Inc. AMPI
Suite 401, 2020 East First Street
Santa Ana, CA 92705 (714) 834-0525
leases and sells computer equipment

AMSERV, Inc. AMSR
1201 Corporate Boulevard
Reno, NV 89502 (702) 348-1000
supplies temporary nursing personnel

AmVestors Financial Corporation AVFC
415 Southwest 8th Avenue
Topeka, KS 66603 (913) 232-6945
life insurance products

Analysis & Technology, Inc. AATI
Technology Park, Route 2
North Stonington, CT 06359 (203) 599-3910
engineering and analytical services

Anaren Microwave, Inc. ANEN
6635 Kirkville Road
East Syracuse, NY 13057 (315) 432-8909
microwave signal processing devices

Analogic Corporation ALOG
8 Centennial Drive
Peabody, MA 01961 (508) 977-3000
measurement, signal translation equipment

Analysts International Corporation ANLY
7615 Metro Boulevard
Minneapolis, MN 55435 (612) 835-2330
software programming, analysis

Anchor Savings Bank, FSB ABKR
1420 Broadway
Hewlett, NY 11557 (516) 596-3900
savings banking

An-Con Genetics, Inc. ANCN
1 Huntington Quadrangle
Melville, NY 11747 (516) 694-8470
medical products for biotechnology industry

Andersen Group ANDR
1280 Blue Hills Avenue
Bloomfield, CT 06002 (203) 242-0761
communications electronics, medical
equipment

Andover Controls Corporation ANDO
York and Haverhill Streets
Andover, MA 01810 (617) 470-0555
computer automation systems

Andover Togs, Inc. ATOG
1 Penn Plaza
New York, NY 10119 (212) 244-0700
sells children's sportwear

Andrew Corporation ANDW
10500 West 153rd Street
Orland Park, IL 60462 (312) 349-3300
specialized antennas, transmission lines

Andrews Group, Inc. AGRP
2813 West Alameda Avenue
Burbank, CA 91505 (818) 840-7000
comic and children's books

Andros Analyzers, Inc. ANDY
2332 Fourth Street
Berkeley, CA 94710 (415) 849-5700
sophisticated gas analyzers

Anglo American Corporation of South Africa
ANGLY
44 Main Street
Johannesburg 2001, South Africa
gold, diamond, platinum, copper mining

Anglo American Gold Investment Company,
Ltd. AAGIY
44 Main Street
Johannesburg 2001, South Africa
gold mining

Animed, Inc. VETS
25 Lumber Road
Roslyn, NY 11576 (516) 484-2700
veterinary services

Anitec Image Techology Corp. ANTC
40 Charles Street
Binghamton, NY 13902 (201) 573-6908
photo equipment

Apogee Enterprises, Inc. APOG
7900 Xerxes Avenue South
Minneapolis, MN 55431 (612) 835-1874
window and glass products

Apogee Robotics, Inc. APGE
2643 Midpoint Drive
Fort Collins, CO 80525 (303) 221-1122
materials handling sytems

Apple Computer, Inc. AAPL
20525 Mariani Avenue
Cupertino, CA 95014 (408) 996-1010
personal computers, software, peripherals O

Applied Bioscience International, Inc. APBI
Mettlers Road
East Millstone, NJ 08873 (201) 873-2550
toxicological testing services

Applied Biosystems, Inc. ABIO
850 Lincoln Centre Drive
Foster City, CA 94404 (415) 570-6667
instruments, reagents for research labs O

Applied Data Communications, Inc. ADCC
14272 Chambers Road
Tustin, CA 92680 (714) 731-9000
disk drive equipment

Applied Materials, Inc. AMAT
3050 Bowers Avenue
Santa Clara, CA 95054 (408) 727-5555
semiconductor production equipment

Applied Power, Inc. APWRA
13000 West Silver Spring Drive
Butler, WI 53005 (414) 781-6600
hydraulic work tools

Applied Solar Energy Corporation SOLR
15251 East Don Julian Road
City of Industry, CA 91746 (213) 968-6581
photovoltaic products

Aquanautics Corporation AQNT
Suite 101, 980 Atlantic Avenue
Alameda, CA 94501 (415) 521-4331
oxygen control technologies

Arabian Shield Development Company ARSD
10830 North Central Expressway
Dallas, TX 75231 (214) 692-7872
mineral exploration, oil refinery

Arbor Drugs, Inc. ARBR
1818 Maplelawn
Troy, MI 48084 (313) 643-9420
drugstores

Archive Corporation ACHV
1650 Sunflower Avenue
Costa Mesa, CA 92626 (714) 641-0279
computer cartridge tape drives

Arch Petroleum, Inc. ARCH
777 Taylor Street
Fort Worth, TX 76102 (817) 332-9209
oil and gas exploration and development

Arden Group, Inc. ARDNA
2020 South Central Avenue
Compton, CA 90220 (213) 638-2842
supermarkets, communications equipment

Argonaut Group, Inc. AGII
1800 Avenue of the Stars
Los Angeles, CA 90067 (213) 553-0561
property-casualty insurance

Aris Corporation FOAM
2501 East Magnolia
Phoenix, AZ 85036 (602) 275-4711
foam cups, containers, insulation

Arkansas Freightways Corporation AFWY
512 U.S. Highway 62-65 North
Harrison, AR 72601 (501) 741-9000
trucking

Armor All Products Corporation ARMR
22 Corporate Park
Irvine, CA 92714 (714) 553-1003
car care products

Arnold Industries, Inc. AIND
625 South Fifth Avenue
Lebanon, PA 17042 (717) 274-2521
trucking

Arnox Corporation ARNX
20 Dayton Avenue
Greenwich, CT 06830 (203) 661-0556
fire retardant products

Arrow Bank Corporation AROW
250 Glen Street
Glens Falls, NY 12801 (518) 793-4121
banking

Artel Communications AXXX
93 Grand Street
Worcester, MA 01610 (617) 752-5690
fiber optics communications equipment

ASEA AB ASEAY
S-72183
Vasteras, Sweden (46) 21-100000
power plants and transmission

Ashton-Tate TATE
20101 Hamilton Avenue
Torrance, CA 90502 (213) 329-8000
microcomputer software O

ASK Computer Systems, Inc. ASKI
2440 West El Camino Real
Mountain View, CA 94039 (415) 969-4442
turnkey minicomputer systems

Aspen Ribbons, Inc. ARIB
555 Aspen Ridge Drive
Lafayette, CO 80026 (303) 666-5750
computer printer ribbons

Associated Banc Corporation ASBC
222 Cherry Street
Green Bay, WI 54307 (414) 433-3166
banking

Associated Communications Corporation
ACCM
Gateway Towers
Pittsburgh, PA 15222 (412) 281-1907
communication

AST Research, Inc. ASTA
2121 Alton Avenue
Irvine, CA 92714 (714) 863-1333
personal computers and accessories

Astec Industries, Inc. ASTE
4101 Jerome Avenue
Chattanooga, TN 37407 (615) 867-4210
asphalt equipment

Astradyne Computer ACIIQ
600 Old Country Road
Garden City, NY 11530 (516) 742-9500
bank and hospital software

Astrocom Corporation ACOM
120 West Plato Boulevard
St. Paul, MN 55107 (612) 227-8651
data communications equipment

Astro-Med, Inc. ALOT
600 East Greenwich Avenue
West Warwick, RI 02893 (401) 828-4000
specialty high-speed printers

Astronics Corporation ATRO
80 South Davis Street
Orchard Park, NY 14127 (716) 662-6640
paper products, gears, lighting

Astrosystems, Inc. ASTR
Six Nevada Drive
Lake Success, NY 11042 (516) 328-1600
electronic precision measurement products

Atek Metals Center, Inc. ATKM
10052 Commerce Park Drive
Cincinnati, OH 45246 (513) 874-3490
aerospace superalloys

Athey Products Corporation ATPC
Route 1-A North
Raleigh, NC 27602 (919) 556-5171
loading and hauling equipment

Atico Financial Corporation ATFC
150 S.E. Third Avenue
Miami, FL 33131 (305) 577-7781
agricultural products

Atkinson (Guy F.) Company of California ATKN
10 West Orange Avenue
South San Francisco, CA 94080
(415) 876-1000
construction, auto parts, pipe, waste
management

Atlantic American Corporation AAME
4370 Peachtree Road, N.E.
Atlanta, GA 30319 (404) 266-5500
property-casualty, health, life insurance

Atlantic Financial Federal ATLF
50 Monument Road
Bala Cynwyd, PA 19004 (215) 668-6600
savings and loan

Atlantic Southeast Airlines, Inc. ASAI
1688 Phoenix Parkway
College Park, GA 30349 (404) 996-4562
regional airline

Attention Medical Company ATMD
3007 Skyway Circle North
Irving, TX 75038 (214) 258-6300
distributes hospital and surgical supplies

Atwood Oceanics, Inc. ATWD
15835 Park Ten Place Drive
Houston, TX 77218 (713) 492-2929
offshore oil and gas drilling

Ault, Inc. AULT
1600 Freeway Boulevard
Minneapolis, MN 55430 (612) 560-9300
power conversion products for computers

Autoclave Engineers, Inc. ACLV
2930 West 22nd Street
Erie, PA 16512 (814) 838-2071
industrial research equipment

Autodesk, Inc. ACAD
2320 Marinship Way
Sausalito, CA 94965 (415) 332-2344
computer-aided design software

Autodie Corporation ADIE
44 Coldbrook, N.W.
Grand Rapids, MI 49503 (616) 454-9361
stamping dies and molds for automakers

Automated Language Processing AILP
295 Chipeta Way
Salt Lake City, UT 84108 (801) 584-3000
language translation software

Automated Systems, Inc. ASII
1505 Commerce Avenue
Brookfield, WI 53005 (414) 784-6400
sophisticated printed circuit boards

Automatix, Inc. AITX
755 Middlesex Turnpike
Billerica, MA 01821 (508) 667-7900
factory automation software

Automotive Industries, Inc. AUIN
7900 Glades Road
Boca Raton, FL 33433 (407) 483-4444
auto parts distributors

Autotrol Corporation AUTR
5730 North Glen Park Road
Milwaukee, WI 53209 (414) 228-9100
water treatment

Auto-Trol Technology Corporation ATTC
12500 North Washington Street
Denver, CO 80233 (303) 452-4919
computer-aided graphics, publishing

Avant-Garde Computing, Inc. AVGA
8000 Commerce Parkway
Mt. Laurel, NJ 08054 (609) 778-7000
data communications software

Avantek, Inc. AVAK
4401 Great America Parkway
Santa Clara, CA 95054 (408) 727-0700
microwave components, defense electronics

Avatar Holdings, Inc. AVTR
201 Alhambra Circle
Coral Gables, FL 33134 (305) 442-7000
real estate, water utility, cable TV

Avino Mines & Resources, Ltd. AVMRF
Suite 100, 455 Granville Street
Vancouver, BC, CDA V6C 1T1 (604) 682-3701
gold and silver mining

Avondale Industries, Inc. AVDL
5100 River Road
Avondale, LA 70094 (504) 436-2121
construction and repair of ships

A&W Brands, Inc. SODA
709 Westchester Avenue
White Plains, NY 10604 (914) 397-1700
soft drinks

AW Computer Systems, Inc. AWCSA
9000A Commerce Parkway
Mt. Laurel, NJ 08054 (609) 234-3939
retail point-of-sale equipment

Aztec Manufacturing Company AZTC
400 North Tarrant Street
Crowley, TX 76036 (817) 297-4361
oil field tubing processor

Babbage's, Inc. BBGS
10741 King William Drive
Dallas, TX 75220 (214) 401-9000
computer software retail stores

Baker, J., Inc. JBAK
65 Sprague Street
Readville, MA 02137 (617) 364-3000
footwear retailing

Baldwin & Lyons, Inc. BWINA
3100 North Meridian Street
Indianapolis, IN 46208 (317) 636-9800
trucking casualty insurance

Baldwin Piano & Organ Company BPAO
422 Wards Corner Road
Loveland, OH 45140 (513) 576-4500
pianos, electronic keyboards

Baltek Corporation BTEK
10 Fairway Court
Northvale, NJ 07647 (201) 767-1400
balsa wood products, shrimp farming

Banco Popular De Puerto Rico BPOP
Banco Popular Center
Hato Rey, PR 00936 (809) 765-9800
banking

BancOklahoma Corporation BOKCC
Bank of Oklahoma Tower
Tulsa, OK 74192 (918) 588-6000
banking

Bancorp Hawaii, Inc. BNHI
111 South King Street
Honolulu, HI 96813 (808) 537-8111
banking DRP 5%

BancTec, Inc. BTEC
4435 Spring Valley Road
Dallas, TX 75244 (214) 450-7700
financial transaction computer systems

Bangor Hydro-Electric Company BANG
33 State Street
Bangor, ME 04401 (207) 945-5621
electric utility

Banker's Note, Inc. BKNT
4900 Highland Parkway
Smyrna, GA 30080 (404) 432-0636
ladies apparel stores

Bank of Granite GRAN
123 North Main Street
Granite Falls, NC 28630 (704) 396-3141
banking

Bank of Montreal BMO
Place d'Armes, P.O. Box 6002
Montreal, Quebec, CDA H2Y 3S8
(514) 877-7110
banking DRP 0

Bank of New England Corporation BKNE
28 State Street
Boston, MA 02109 (617) 742-4000
banking DRP 3%

Bank of Nova Scotia BNS
44 King Street West
Toronto, Ontario, CDA M5H 1H1
(416) 866-6161
banking DRP 0

Bank South Corporation BKSO
55 Marietta Street N.W.
Atlanta, GA 30303 (404) 529-4111
banking

BankEast Corporation BENH
One Wall Street
Manchester, NH 03105 (603) 624-6000
banking

Bankers First Corporation (Georgia) BNKF
985 Broad Street
Augusta, GA 30901 (404) 823-3200
banking

Banknorth Group, Inc. BKNG
8 North Main Street
St. Albans, VT 05478 (802) 524-5951
banking

Banks of Iowa, Inc. BIOW
520 Walnut Street
Des Moines, IA 50306 (515) 245-6320
banking

Banks of Mid-America, Inc. BOMA
100 Broadway
Oklahoma City, OK 73102 (405) 231-6000
banking

BankVermont Corp. BKVT
148 College Street
Burlington, VT 05402 (802) 658-1810
banking

BankWorcester Corporation BNKW
365 Main Street
Worcester, MA 01608 (508) 831-4000
banking

Banponce Corporation BDEP
268 Munoz Rivera Avenue
San Juan, PR 00936 (809) 754-9400
banking

Banta Corporation BNTA
100 Main Street
Menasha, WI 54952 (414) 722-7777
printing, graphic, video services

Barden Corporation (The) BARD
200 Park Avenue
Danbury, CT 06813 (203) 744-2211
precision ball bearings

Barris Industries, Inc. BRRS
1990 South Bundy Drive
Los Angeles, CA 90025 (213) 280-2100
game shows, television shows, films

Barton Industries, Inc. BART
2401 North Highway 177
Shawnee, OK 74801 (405) 273-7660
valves and oil drilling equipment

Barry's Jewelers, Inc. BARY
1430 Huntington Drive
Duarte, CA 91010 (818) 303-4741
retail jewelry stores

Base Ten Systems, Inc. BASEA
Number One Electronics Drive
Trenton, NJ 08619 (609) 586-7010
aircraft weapons control systems

Basic American Medical, Inc. BAMI
4000 East Southport Road, P.O. Box 27120
Indianapolis, IN 46227 (317) 783-5461
operates acute care hospitals, retirement
homes

Basic Resources International (Bahamas) Ltd.
BBAH
650 Fifth Avenue
New York, NY 10019 (212) 541-8920
oil & gas

Bassett Furniture Industries, Inc. BSET
P.O. Box 626
Bassett, VA 24055 (703) 629-7511
wood furniture

Bay View Federal S&L Association BVFS
2121 South El Camino Real
San Mateo, CA 94403 (415) 573-7300
savings and loan

BayBanks, Inc. BBNK
175 Federal Street
Boston, MA 02110 (617) 482-1040
banking DRP

Bayly Corporation BAYL
5500 South Valencia Way
Englewood, CO 80111 (303) 773-3850
leisure and utility apparel

BB&T Financial Corporation BBTF
223 West Nash Street
Wilson, NC 27893 (919) 399-4291
banking DRP

BCE Development BD
999 West Hastings Street
Vancouver, BC CDA V6C 2W7 (604) 688-2171
real estate development

BeautiControl Cosmetics, Inc. BUTI
3311-400 Boyington
Carrolton, TX 75006 (214) 458-0601
direct sales of women's cosmetics

Beauty Labs, Inc. LABB
3000 Marcus Avenue
Lake Success, NY 11042 (516) 775-7800
specialty beauty products

Beeba's Creations, Inc. BEBA
9220 Activity Road
San Diego, CA 92126 (619) 549-2922
women's sportswear and intimate apparel

Beecham Group, PLC. BECHY
Beecham House, Great West Road
Brentford, Middlesex, UK TW8 9BD
drugs and consumer products

BEI Holdings, Ltd. BEIH
Suite 300, 4751 Best Road
Atlanta, GA 30337 (404) 768-5689
financial institutions consulting

Belcor, Inc. BLCR
18004 Skypark Circle
Irvine, CA 92714 (714) 261-7522
oil and gas exploration and development

Bel Fuse, Inc. BELF
198 Van Vorst Street
Jersey City, NJ 07302 (201) 432-0463
computer delay lines, fuses, circuits

Bell (W) & Company, Inc. BLLW
12401 Twinbrook Parkway
Rockville, MD 20852 (301) 881-2000
catalog showroom retailing

Bell Savings Holdings, Inc. BSBX
9 South 69th Street
Upper Darby, PA 19082 (215) 734-1000
savings banking

Benihana National Corporation BNHN
8685 Northwest 53rd Terrace
Miami, FL 33166 (305) 593-0770
Japanese-style restaurants

Ben & Jerry's Homemade, Inc. BJICA
Route 100, P.O. Box 240
Waterbury, VT 05676 (802) 244-5641
super premium ice cream products

Benjamin Franklin Federal S&L Association
BENJ
501 S.E. Hawthorne Boulevard
Portland, OR 97214 (503) 275-1234
savings and loan

Berkley (W. R.) Corporation BKLY
165 Mason Street
Greenwich, CT 06836 (203) 629-2880
specialty property-casualty insurance

Berkshire Gas Company (The) BGAS
115 Cheshire Road
Pittsfield, MA 01201 (413) 442-1511
gas utility DRP

Berry Petroleum Company BRRYA
1000 Hovey Hills Road
Taft, CA 93268 (805) 769-8811
oil and gas exploration and development

Betz Laboratories, Inc. BETZ
4636 Somerton Road
Trevose, PA 19047 (215) 355-3300
specialty chemicals for water treatment

BGS Systems, Inc. BGSS
128 Technology Center
Waltham, MA 02254 (617) 891-0000
data processing software

Big B, Inc. BIGB
2600 Morgan Road, S.E.
Bessemer, AL 35023 (205) 424-3421
discount drug stores

Bindley Western Industries, Inc. BIND
4212 West 71st Street
Indianapolis, IN 46268 (317) 298-9900
drug distributor

Bingo King Company, Inc. BNGO
400 East Mineral Avenue
Littleton, CO 80122 (303) 795-2625
sells bingo cards and supplies

Biocontrol Technology, Inc. BICO
300 Indian Springs Road
Indiana, PA 15701 (412) 349-1811
implantable medical devices

Biogen, Inc. BGEN
14 Cambridge Center
Cambridge, MA 02142 (617) 864-8900
biotechnology drugs

Bio-logic Systems Corporation BLSC
1 Bio-logic Plaza
Mundelein, IL 60060 (312) 949-5200
medical electrodiagnostic systems

Bio-Medicus, Inc. BMDS
9600 West 76th Street
Eden Prairie, MN 55344 (612) 944-7784
cardiovascular medical devices

Biomerica, Inc. BMRA
1533 Monrovia Avenue
Newport Beach, CA 92663 (714) 645-2111
medical diagnostic test kits

Biomet, Inc. BMET
Airport Industrial Park
Warsaw, IN 46580 (219) 267-6639
surgical implants, prostheses

Bioplasty, Inc. BIOP
1385 Centennial Drive
St. Paul, MN 55113 (612) 636-4112
wound care and plastic surgery products

Biosearch Medical Products Inc. BMPI
35 Industrial Pkwy.
Somerville, NJ 08876 (201) 722-5000
medical supplies

Biospherics, Inc. BINC
12051 Indian Creek Court
Beltsville, MD 20705 (301) 369-3900
environmental and health services

Biotech Research Laboratories, Inc. BTRL
1600 East Gude Drive
Rockville, MD 20850 (301) 251-0800
viral diagnostic kits, antibodies

BioTechnica International, Inc. BIOT
85 Bolton Street
Cambridge, MA 02140 (617) 864-0040
dental diagnostics, agricultural biotechnology

Bird Inc. BIRD
1 Dedham Place
Westwood, MA 02090 (617) 461-1414
building and roofing materials

Birtcher Corporation (The) BIRT
4501 North Arden Drive
El Monte, CA 91731 (818) 575-8144
electronic medical instruments

Bishop, Inc. BISH
5388 Sterling Center Drive
Westlake Village, CA 91359 (818) 991-2600
engineering, architectural design products

Black Industries, Inc. BLAK
2816 North Roxboro Street
Durham, NC 27704 (919) 477-0485
construction

Blinder International BINL
6455 South Yosemite Street
Englewood, CO 80111 (303) 773-8200
securities brokerage

Block Drug Company, Inc. BLOCA
257 Cornelison Avenue
Jersey City, NJ 07302 (201) 434-3000
dental care and drug products

Blue Ridge Real Estate— Big Boulder Corp.
BLRGZ
Route 940 and Mosey Wood Road
Blakeslee, PA 18610 (717) 443-8433
ski resorts

Blyvooruitzicht Gold Mining Company, Ltd.
BLYVY
The Corner House, 63 Fox Street
Johannesburg 2001, South Africa
gold and silver mining

BMA Corporation BMAC
BMA Tower
Kansas City, MO 64141 (816) 753-8000
life and health insurance DRP

BMC Software, Inc. BMCS
1 Sugar Creek Center
Sugar Land, TX 77478 (713) 240-8800
systems software

BMR Financial Group, Inc. BMRG
2302 Parklake Drive, N.E.
Atlanta, GA 30345 (404) 934-9994
finance and management services, banking

BNH Bankshares, Inc. BNHB
209 Church Street
New Haven, CT 06510 (203) 865-4500
banking

Boatmen's Bancshares, Inc. BOAT
800 Market Street
St. Louis, MO 63101 (314) 554-7720
banking DRP

Bobbie Brooks, Inc. BBKS
3830 Kelley Avenue
Cleveland, OH 44114 (216) 881-5300
women's coats and outerwear

Bob Evans Farms, Inc. BOBE
3776 South High Street
Columbus, OH 43207 (614) 491-2225
restaurants, pork sausage DRP

Bogert Oil Company BOGO
Oil Center West, 2601 N.W. Expressway
Oklahoma City, OK 73112 (405) 848-5808
oil and gas exploration and development

Bohemia, Inc. BOHM
2280 Oakmont Way
Eugene, OR 97401 (503) 342-6262
forest products

Bonneville Pacific Corporation BPCO
257 East 200 South
Salt Lake City, UT 84111 (801) 363-2520
alternative energy power producer

Bonray Drilling Corporation BNRY
2644 N.W. 63rd Street
Oklahoma City, OK 73116 (405) 843-5787
onshore oil and gas contract driller

Boole & Babbage, Inc. BOOL
510 Oakmead Parkway
Sunnyvale, CA 94086 (408) 735-9550
computer analysis software

Boonton Electronics Corporation BOON
791 Route 10
Randolph, NJ 07869 (201) 584-1077
electronic testing and measuring instruments

Boston Bancorp. SBOS
460 West Broadway
South Boston, MA 02127 (617) 268-2500
banking

Boston Digital Corporation BOST
Granite Park
Milford, MA 01757 (617) 473-4561
machining systems and software

Boston Five Bancorp, Inc. BFCS
10 School Street
Boston, MA 02108 (617) 742-6000
savings banking

Bouton Corproation BOTN
2960 Post Road
Southport, CT 06490 (203) 259-4967
optical equipment

Bowater Industries PLC BWTRY
Bowater House
Knightsbridge, London UK SW1X 7NN
packaging, industrial products, timber

Bradley Real Estate Trust BRLYS
250 Boylston Street
Boston, MA 02116 (617) 421-0750
real estate investment trust

Brady (W. H.) Company BRCOA
727 West Glendale Avenue
Milwaukee, WI 53201 (414) 332-8100
chemicals, adhesives, coatings

BRAE Corporation BRAE
160 Spear Street
San Francisco, CA 94105 (415) 995-1700
leases railcars

Brajdas Corporation BRJS
21550 Oxnard Street
Woodland Hills, CA 91367 (818) 710-7730
electronic parts distributor

Bralorne Resources, Ltd. BRALF
3100-205 5th Avenue S.W.
Calgary, AB, CDA T2P 2V7 (403) 268-0700
oil and gas products and services

Brand Companies, Inc. BRAN
1420 Renaissance Drive
Park Ridge, IL 60068 (312) 298-1200
insulation, asbestos removal contractor

Brandon Systems Corporation BRDN
1 Harmon Plaza
Secaucus, NJ 07094 (201) 392-0800
temporary computer personnel

Braniff, Inc. BAIRD
7701 Lemmon Avenue
Dallas, TX 75209 (214) 358-6011
regional airline

Breakwater Resources, Ltd. BWRLF
1440 625 Howe Street
Vancouver, BC CDA V6C 2T6 (604) 669-1918
gold mining

Brenco, Inc. BREN
P.O. Box 389
Petersburg, VA 23804 (804) 732-0202
railroad car bearings, industrial equipment

Brendle's, Inc. BRDL
1919 North Bridge Street
Elkin, NC 28621 (919) 526-5600
discount retail stores

Brenton Banks, Inc. BRBK
Capital Square, 400 Locust
Des Moines, IA 50309 (515) 283-2394
banking

Bridgford Foods Corporation BRID
1308 North Patt Street
Anaheim, CA 92801 (714) 526-5533
frozen and snack foods

Brilund, Ltd. BRILF
3280 Howell Mill Road, N.W.
Atlanta, GA 30327 (404) 351-5315
oil, gas, minerals rights

Brinkmann Instruments, Inc. BRIK
Cantiague Road
Westbury, NY 11590 (516) 334-7500
scientific instruments, lab disposables

BRIntec Corporation BRIX
1600 West Main Street
Willimantic, CT 06226 (203) 456-8000
electronic interconnection components

Bristol Holdings, Inc. BRST
2900 South Highland Drive
Las Vegas, NV 89109 (702) 369-3424
operates and installs slot machines

Britton Lee, Inc. BLII
14600 Winchester Boulevard
Los Gatos, CA 95030 (408) 378-7000
relational database software

Brock Exploration Corporation BKE
225 Baronne Street
New Orleans, LA 70112 (504) 586-1815
oil and gas production

Brown, Robert C. & Company RCBI
655 Montgomery Street
San Francisco, CA 94111 (415) 981-4050
investment management, securities
brokerage

Brown Transport Company BTCI
352 University Avenue S.W.
Atlanta, GA 30315 (404) 752-5151
trucking

Bruno's, Inc. BRNO
300 Research Parkway
Birmingham, AL 35211 (205) 940-9400
supermarkets, drug and food stores

BSD Medical Corporation BSDM
420 Chipeta Way
Salt Lake City, UT 84108 (801) 582-5550
hyperthermia systems for cancer treatment

BT Financial Corporation BTFC
532-534 Main Street
Johnstown, PA 15907 (814) 536-7801
non-bank finance

BTR Realty, Inc. BTRI
817 Maiden Choice Lane
Baltimore, MD 21228 (301) 247-4991
real estate

Buckeye Financial Corporation BCKY
36 East Gay Street
Columbus, OH 43215 (614) 225-2100
savings and loan

Buffets, Inc. BOCB
10260 Viking Drive
Eden Prairie, MN 55344 (612) 942-9760
buffet restaurants

Buffelsfontein Gold Mining Company BFELY
General Mining Building, 6 Hollard Street
Johannesburg, South Africa 2001
gold and uranium mining

Buffton Corporation BUFF
1415 Interfirst Tower
Fort Worth, TX 76102 (817) 332-4761
oil and gas

Builders Transport, Inc. TRUK
U.S. Hwy. 1
Camden, SC 29020 (803) 432-1400
trucking

Bull & Bear Group, Inc. BNBGA
11 Hanover Square
New York, NY 10005 (212) 785-0900
investment management, discount brokerage

Bull Run Gold Mines, Ltd. BULL
1600 Stout Street
Denver, CO 80202 (303) 620-9300
gold mining

Burmah Oil Public Limited Company BURMY
Pipers Way
Swindon, UK SN3 1RE (07) 9330151
auto lubricants, transports gas, oil

Burnup & Sims, Inc. BSIM
One North University Drive
Fort Lauderdale, FL 33324 (305) 587-4512
installs cable TV, telephone, theaters

Burr-Brown Corporation BBRC
International Airport Industrial Park
Tucson, AZ 85734 (602) 746-1111
precision microelectronic products

Burritt InterFinancial Bancorporation BANQ
267 Main Street
New Britain, CT 06050 (203) 225-7601
savings and loan

Business Men's Assurance Co. of America
BMAC
BMA Tower
Kansas City, MO 64108 (816) 753-8000
insurance DRP

Butler Manufacturing Company BTLR
BMA Tower, Penn Valley Park
Kansas City, MO 64141 (816) 968-3000
custom-designed buildings, products DRP

Butler National Corporation BUTL
8246 Nieman Road
Lenexa, KS 66214 (913) 888-8585
electronic machinery

Bytex Corporation BYTX
Southborough Office Park, 120 Turnpike Road
Southborough, MA 01772 (508) 480-0840
electronic matrix switching systems

C.A. Blockers, Inc. LUNG
4018 Glenview Avenue
Louisville, KY 40222 (502) 584-2554
products to slow cancer from cigarettes

Cabot Medical Corporation CBOT
2021 Cabot Boulevard West
Langorne, PA 19047 (215) 752-8300
female reproductive healthcare devices

Cache, Inc. CACH
1460 Broadway
New York, NY 10036 (212) 840-4242
high-fashion women's apparel stores

CACI International CACI
1700 North Moore Street
Arlington, VA 22209 (703) 841-7800
computer analysis and services

Cadbury Schweppes P.L.C. CADBY
1-4 Connaught Place
London, England W2 2EX (01) 262-1212
confectionary food and soft drinks

Cade Industries, Inc. CADE
1219 North Cass
Milwaukee, WI 53202 (414) 223-3790
components for aircraft and autos

Cadema Corporation CDMA
569 North Street
Middletown, NY 10940 (914) 343-7474
radiology and nuclear medicine drugs

Cadence Design Systems CDNC
2455 Augustine Drive
Santa Clara, CA 95054 (408) 727-0264
computer-aided design software

Cadmus Communications Corporation CDMS
2901 Byrdhill Road
Richmond, VA 23230 (804) 264-2885
graphics arts printing

Calgene, Inc. CGNE
1920 Fifth Street
Davis, CA 95616 (916) 753-6313
applies DNA technology to plants

Calgon Carbon Corporation CRBN
400 Media Drive
Robinson Township, PA 15230
(412) 787-6700
makes and markets activated carbons

California Amplifier, Inc. CAMP
460 Calle San Pablo
Camarillo, CA 93010 (805) 987-9000
microwave components for defense products

California Biotechnology, Inc. CBIO
2450 Bayshore Parkway
Mountain View, CA 94043 (415) 966-1550
biotechnology healthcare products

California Financial Holding CFHC
212 North San Joaquin Street
Stockton, CA 95202 (209) 948-6870
savings and loan

California Microwave, Inc. CMIC
990 Almanor Avenue
Sunnyvale, CA 94086 (408) 732-4000
electronic communications equipment

California Water Service Company CWTR
1720 North First Street
San Jose, CA 95112 (408) 453-8414
water utility DRP

Callon Petroleum Company CLNP
200 North Canal Street
Natchez, MS 39120 (601) 442-1601
oil and gas

Calumet Industries, Inc. CALI
3 Illinois Center, Suite 424
Chicago, IL 60601 (312) 565-4120
refining and marketing crude oil

Cambrex Corporation CBAM
40 Avenue A
Bayonne, NJ 07002 (201) 858-7900
chemical products manaufacturer

Cambridge Analytical Associates, Inc. CAAN
1105 Commonwealth Avenue
Boston, MA 02215 (617) 232-2207
environmental services

Cambridge BioScience CBCX
365 Plantation Street
Worcester, MA 01605 (617) 272-6626
infectious disease diagnostic tests

Canal-Randolph Ltd. Partnership CANL
717 Fifth Avenue
New York, NY 10022 (212) 826-6040
investment company

Canonie Environmental Services Corporation
CANO
800 Canonie Drive
Porter, IN 46304 (219) 926-8651
hazardous waste disposal services

Cannon Express, Inc. CANX
1901 Robinson
Springdale, AR 72764 (501) 751-9209
trucking

Canon, Inc. CANNY
7-1, Nishi-shinjuku 2-chome
Shinjuku-ku, Tokyo 163, Japan
business machines, cameras

Cape Cod Bank & Trust Company CCBT
307 Main Street
Hyannis, MA 02601 (508) 394-1300
banking

Capital Associates, Inc. CAII
31 East Platte Avenue
Colorado Springs, CO 80903 (303) 633-1177
equipment leasing and remarketing

Capital Southwest Corporation CSWC
12900 Preston Road
Dallas, TX 75230 (214) 233-8242
venture capital investment company

Capitol Bancorporation CAPB
One Bulfinch Place
Boston, MA 02114 (617) 723-5300
banking

Capitol Transamerica Corporation CATA
4610 University Avenue
Madison, WI 53705 (608) 231-4450
property-casualty, health insurance

Captain Crab, Inc. CRAB
Bayshore Executive Plaza
Miami, FL 33161 (305) 895-9505
restaurants

Cardiac Control Systems CCSC
3 Commerce Boulevard
Palm Coast, FL 32037 (904) 445-5450
implantable cardiac pacemakers

Cardinal Distribution, Inc. CDIC
655 Metro Place South
Dublin, OH 43017 (614) 761-8700
distributes drugs and medical supplies

Care Plus, Inc. CPLS
Suite 700, 6700 North Andrews Avenue
Fort Lauderdale, FL 33309 (305) 493-6464
home infusion therapies

Carl Karcher Enterprises, Inc. CARL
1200 North Harbor Boulevard
Anaheim, CA 92801 (714) 778-7109
restaurants

Carlton Communications CCTVY
10 East Road
London N1 6AJ, UK (01) 251-1533
television products and services

Carme, Inc. CAME
84 Galli Drive
Novato, CA 94949 (415) 883-3367
hair and skin products

Carmike Cinemas, Inc. CMIKA
1301 First Avenue
Columbus, GA 31901 (404) 576-3400
motion picture theaters

Carolina Bancorp, Inc. FFCA
620 North Main Street
High Point, NC 27260 (919) 884-5071
savings and loan

Carriage Industries, Inc. CARG
P.O. Box 542
Calhoun, GA 30701 (404) 629-9234
rugs and carpets

Carrington Laboratories, Inc. CARN
9200 Carpenter Freeway
Dallas, TX 75247 (214) 638-7686
wound care drugs, antiviral agents

Carver Corporation CAVR
20121 48th Avenue West
Lynnwood, WA 98036 (206) 775-1202
high-fidelity audio systems

Cascade Corporation CASC
2020 S.W. 4th Avenue
Portland, OR 97201 (503) 227-0024
materials handling equipment

Cascade International, Inc. KOSM
2424 North Federal Highway
Boca Raton, FL 33431 (407) 338-8278
women's apparel and cosmetics stores

Casey's General Stores, Inc. CASY
1299 N.E. Broadway Avenue
Des Moines, IA 50313 (515) 263-3700
convenience stores

Casual Male Corporation CMLE
418 Boston Turnpike
Shrewsbury, MA 01545 (508) 842-2300
larger-size menswear stores

Cato Corporation CACOA
8100 Denmark Road
Charlotte, NC 28217 (704) 554-8510
women's apparel stores

Cavco Industries CVCO
301 East Bethany Home Road
Phoenix, AZ 85012 (602) 265-0580
manufactured housing producers

C B & T Bancshares, Inc. CBTB
1148 Broadway
Columbus, GA 31902 (404) 649-2197
banking DRP

CCB Financial Corporation CCBF
111 Corcoran Street
Durham, NC 27701 (919) 683-7777
banking DRP

C-Cor Electronics, Inc. CCBL
60 Decibel Road
State College, PA 16801 (814) 238-2461
cable TV equipment, data communications

CCNB Corporation CCNC
331 Bridge Street
New Cumberland, PA 17070 (717) 774-7000
banking

Celgene Corporation CELG
7 Powder Horn Drive
Warren, NJ 07060 (201) 271-1001
biotechnology specialty chemicals

Cellular Communications, Inc. COMM
919 Third Avenue
New York, NY 10022 (212) 319-7014
cellular telephone systems

Cellular Products, Inc. CELP
688 Main Street
Buffalo, NY 14202 (716) 842-6270
diagnostic and blood screening tests

Cel-Sci Corporation CELI
Suite 202, 601 Wythe Street
Alexandria, VA 22314 (703) 549-5293
biomedical research

CEM Corporation CEMX
3100 Smith Farm Road
Matthews, NC 28106 (704) 821-7015
testing and analysis instruments

CenCor, Inc. CNCR
12th & Baltimore, City Center Square
Kansas City, MO 64196 (816)474-4750
temporary help services

Centocor, Inc. CNTO
244 Great Valley Parkway
Malvern, PA 19355 (215) 296-4488
diagnostic and therapeutic products

Central Bancshares of the South, Inc. CBSS
701 South 20th Street
Birmingham, AL 35296 (205) 933-3000
banking DRP

Central Fidelity Banks, Inc. CFBS
1021 East Cary Street
Richmond, VA 23219 (804) 782-4000
banking DRP

Central Holding Company CHOL
36800 Gratiot Avenue
Mount Clemens, MI 48043 (313) 792-8055
savings and mortgage banking, real estate

Central Jersey Bancorp CJER
Route Nine, P.O. Box 30
Freehold Township, NJ 07728 (201) 462-0011
banking DRP

Central Pennsylvania Financial CPSA
100 West Independence Street
Shamokin, PA 17872 (717) 644-0861
savings bank

Central Reserve Life Corporation CRLC
343 West Bagley Road
Berea, OH 44017 (216) 826-4100
life, accident, health insurance

Central Sprinkler Corporation CNSP
451 North Cannon Avenue
Lansdale, PA 19446 (215) 362-0700
fire sprinkler systems

Centuri, Inc. CENT
300 Plaza Drive
Binghamton, NY 13903 (607) 729-5313
outdoor sporting equipment

Ceradyne, Inc. CRDN
3169 Redhill Avenue
Costa Mesa, CA 92626 (714) 549-0421
ceramic products for aerospace

CERBCO, Inc. CERB
5600 Columbia Pike
Bailey's Crossroads, VA 22041
(703) 379-4500
defense engineering and analysis

Cermetek Microelectronics Inc. CRMK
1308 Borregas Avenue
Sunnyvale, CA 94088 (408) 752-5000
computer communications equipment

Cerner Corporation CERN
2800 Rockcreek Parkway
Kansas City, MO 64117 (816) 221-1024
healthcare information systems

CerProbe Corporation CRPB
600 South Rockford Drive
Tempe, AZ 85281 (602) 967-7885
electronics probing and interface products

Certron Corporation CRTN
5439 East La Palma Avenue
Anaheim, CA 92807 (714) 634-4280
audio and video tapes, floppy disks

Cetus Corporation CTUS
1400 53rd Street
Emeryville, CA 94608 (415) 420-3300
biotechnology healthcare products O

CF&I Steel Corporation CFIP
P.O. Box 316
Pueblo, CO 81002 (303) 561-6500
steel rails, tubular steel, wire, bar

CFS Financial Corporation, Inc. CFSC
4020 University Drive
Fairfax, VA 22030 (703) 691-4400
savings & loan

Challenger International, Ltd. CSTIF
Sea Venture Building, 10 Parliament Street
Hamilton, Bermuda HM GX (713) 622-1502
crude oil refining and marketing

Champion Parts, Inc. CREB
2525 22nd Street
Oak Brook, IL 60521 (312) 573-6600
rebuilds automotive parts

Chancellor Corporation CHCR
Federal Reserve Plaza
Boston, MA 02210 (617) 723-3500
transportation equipment leasing

Chandler Insurance Company, Ltd. CHANF
P.O. Box 1289, Elizabethan Square
Grand Cayman, BWI (809) 949-7823
casualty insurance

Chantal Pharmaceutical Corporation CHTLE
575 Madison Avenue
New York, NY 10022 (212) 605-0545
acne, baldness drugs

Chaparral Resources, Inc. CHAR
621 17th Street
Denver, CO 80293 (303) 293-2340
oil and gas exploration and production

Chapman Energy, Inc. CHPN
9400 North Central Expressway
Dallas, TX 75231 (214) 692-1800
oil and gas exploration and production

Charlotte Charles, Inc. CAKE
2501 North Elston Avenue
Chicago, IL 60647 (312) 772-8310
gourmet and specialty food products

Charming Shoppes, Inc. CHRS
450 Winks Lane
Bensalem, PA 19020 (215) 245-9100
women's specialty apparel stores O

Charter Federal S&L Association CHFD
110 Piedmont Avenue
Bristol, VA 24201 (703) 669-5101
savings and loan

Charter One Financial, Inc. COFI
1215 Superior Avenue
Cleveland, OH 44114 (216) 586-5300
savings banking

Chartwell Group, Ltd. CTWL
55 Green Farms Road
Westport, CT 06880 (203) 454-4800
accessory furniture products

Chattem, Inc. CHTT
1715 West 38th Street
Chattanooga, TN 37409 (615) 821-4571
health and beauty products, chemicals

Checkpoint Systems, Inc. CHEK
550 Grove Road
Thorofare, NJ 08086 (609) 848-1800
electronic article surveillance systems

Check Technology Corporation CTCQ
1284 Corporate Center Drive
St. Paul, MN 55121 (612) 454-9300
printing equipment

Chefs International, Inc. CHEF
62 Broadway
Point Pleasant Beach, NJ 08742
(201) 295-0350
restaurants

ChemDesign Corporation CDCC
99 Development Road
Fitchburg, MA 01420 (508) 345-9999
makes custom chemicals

Chemex Pharmaceuticals, Inc. CHMX
7400 East Orchard Street
Denver, CO 80237 (303) 770-7744
skin cancer drugs

Chemical Fabrics Corporation CMFB
701 Daniel Webster Hwy.
Merrimack, NH 03054 (603) 424-9000
textiles for extreme environments

Chemfix Technologies, Inc. CFIX
Metairie Centre, Edenborn Avenue
Metairie, LA 70001 (504) 831-3600
waste treatment, environmental services

Cherry Corporation CHER
3600 Sunset Avenue
Waukegan, IL 60087 (312) 662-9200
snap-action switches, electrical products

Chesapeake Utilities Corporation CHPK
350 South Queen Street
Dover, DE 19901 (302) 734-6700
gas utility

Cheyenne Software, Inc. CHEY
55 Bryant Avenue
Roslyn, NY 11576 (516) 484-5110
specialized computer software

Chief Consolidated Mining Company CFCM
866 Second Avenue
New York, NY 10017 (212) 688-8130
minerals mining

Child World, Inc. CWLD
25 Littlefield Street
Avon, MA 02322 (617) 588-7300
toy supermarkets

Chili's, Inc. CHLI
Suite 200, 6820 LBJ Freeway
Dallas, TX 75240 (214) 980-9917
restaurants

Chips and Technologies, Inc. CHPS
3050 Zanker Road
San Jose, CA 95134 (408) 434-0600
semiconductor hardware and software

Chipwich, Inc. CHIPA
358 East 57th Street
New York, NY 10022 (212) 688-8890
ice cream products

Chiron Corporation CHIR
4560 Horton Street
Emeryville, CA 94608 (415) 655-8730
therapeutic and diagnostic biotechnology

Chittenden Corporation CNDN
Two Burlington Square
Burlington, VT 05401 (802) 658-4000
banking

Chronar Corporation CRNR
195 Clarkville Road
Lawrenceville, NJ 08648 (609) 799-8800
photovoltaic panels

Church & Dwight Company, Inc. CRCH
469 North Harrison Street
Princeton, NJ 08543 (609) 683-5900
sodium bicarbonate

CIMCO, Inc. CIMC
265 Briggs Avenue
Costa Mesa, CA 92626 (714) 546-4460
thermoplastic components

Cimflex Teknowledge Corporation CMTK
1850 Embarcadero Road
Palo Alto, CA 94303 (415) 424-0500
computer integrated manufacturing systems

Cincinnati Financial Corporation CINF
6200 South Gilmore Road
Fairfield, OH 45014 (513) 870-2000
property-casualty, life insurance

Cincinnati Microwave, Inc. CNMW
One Microwave Plaza
Cincinnati, OH 45249 (513) 489-5400
radar warning receivers

Cintas Corporation CTAS
11255 Reed Hartman Highway
Cincinnati, OH 45241 (513) 489-4000
uniform sale and rental

Cipher Data Products, Inc. CIFR
9715 Businesspark Avenue
San Diego, CA 92131 (619) 578-9100
data storage hardware and subsystems

Ciprico, Inc. CPCI
2955 Xenium Lane
Plymouth, MN 55441 (612) 559-2034
disk controllers, computer tape adapters

Circadian, Inc. CKDN
3942 North First Street
San Jose, CA 95134 (408) 943-9222
diagnostic medical instruments

Circle Express, Inc. CEXX
3334 Founders Road
Indianapolis, IN 46268 (317) 872-4011
trucking

Circle Fine Art Corporation CFNE
875 North Michigan Avenue
Chicago, IL 60611 (312) 943-0664
art galleries

Circon Corporation CCON
460 Ward Drive
Santa Barbara, CA 93111 (805) 967-0404
medical video systems, endoscopes

C.I.S. Technologies CISIF
6846 South Canton
Tulsa, OK 74136 (918) 496-2451
health care data processing

Citizens Banking Corporation CBCF
One Citizens Banking Center
Flint, MI 48502 (313) 766-7500
banking

CleveTrust Realty Investors CTRI
1020 Ohio Savings Plaza
Cleveland, OH 44114 (216) 621-3366
real estate investment trust

Citizens Growth Properties CITG
200 Peoples Bank Bldg.
Jackson, MS 39201 (601) 948-4091
real estate investment trust

Clinical Data, Inc. CLDA
1172 Commonwealth Avenue
Boston, MA 02134 (617) 734-3700
medical diagnostics products and services

Citizens Savings Financial Corporation CSFCB
999 Brickell Avenue
Miami, FL 33131 (305) 577-0400
savings and loan

Clini-Therm Corporation CLIN
11410 Pagemill Road
Dallas, TX 75243 (214) 343-2180
cancer treatment equipment

Citizens Security Group, Inc. CSGI
406 Main Street
Red Wing, MN 55066 (612) 388-7171
property-casualty insurance

Clinton Gas Systems, Inc. CGAS
4770 Indianola Avenue
Columbus, OH 43214 (614) 888-9588
oil and gas exploration, real estate

Citizens Utilities Company CITUB
High Ridge Park
Stamford, CT 06905 (203) 329-8800
telephone, electric, gas, water utilities DRP

Clothestime, Inc. (The) CTME
5325 East Hunter Avenue
Anaheim, CA 92807 (714) 779-5881
women's apparel stores

City National Corporation CTYN
400 North Roxbury Drive
Beverly Hills, CA 90210 (213) 550-5400
banking

CMS Enhancements, Inc. ACMS
1372 Valencia Avenue
Tustin, CA 92680 (714) 259-9555
personal computer accessories

CityFed Financial Corporation CTYF
293 South County Road
Palm Beach, FL 33480 (305) 655-5919
savings and loan DRP 5%

CNB Bancshares CNBE
20 N.W. Third Street
Evansville, IN 47708 (812) 464-3400
banking

Clairson International Corporation CLIC
720 S.W. 17th Street
Ocala, FL 32674 (904) 368-4000
coated wire products for home storage

Coast Federal S&L Association CFSF
1777 Main Street
Sarasota, FL 33578 (813) 366-7000
savings and loan

CLARCOR, Inc. CLRK
2323 Sixth Street
Rockford, IL 61125 (815) 962-8867
filters, packaging, paper tubes

Cobb Resources Corporation COBB
313 Washington S.E.
Albuquerque, NM 87108 (505) 265-2622
oil and gas exploration and development

Clean Harbors, Inc. CLHB
325 Wood Road
Braintree, MA 02184 (617) 849-1800
environmental services, waste treatment

COBE Laboratories, Inc. COBE
Suite 500C, 12600 West Colfax
Lakewood, CO 80215 (303) 232-6800
kidney and heart medical products

Coca-Cola Bottling Company Consolidated
COKE
1900 Redford Road
Charlotte, NC 28211 (704) 551-4400
soft drinks DRP

CoCa Mines, Inc. COCA
910 Denver Center Building,
1776 Lincoln Street
Denver, CO 80203 (303) 861-5400
gold and silver mining

Code-Alarm, Inc. CODL
950 East Whitcomb
Madison Heights, MI 48071 (313) 583-9620
electronic auto security systems

Codenoll Technology Corporation CODN
1086 North Broadway
Yonkers, NY 10701 (914) 965-6300
data communications fiber optics

Coherent, Inc. COHR
3210 Porter Drive
Palo Alto, CA 94304 (415) 493-2111
medical laser, optics products

Collaborative Research, Inc. CRIC
2 Oak Park
Bedford, MA 01730 (617) 275-0004
genetic engineering, biotechnology

Collagen Corporation CGEN
2500 Faber Place
Palo Alto, CA 94303 (415) 856-0200
plastic surgery, dermatology products

Collective Bancorp COFD
158 Philadelphia Avenue
Egg Harbor City, NJ 08215 (609) 965-1234
savings banking

Colonial BancGroup, Inc. (The) CLBGA
1 Commerce Street
Montgomery, AL 36192 (205) 240-5000
banking

Colonial Gas Company CGES
40 Market Street
Lowell, MA 01852 (508) 458-3171
gas utility DRP

Colonial Group, Inc. (The) COGRA
1 Financial Center
Boston, MA 02111 (617) 426-3750
investment management, mutual funds

Colonial Life & Accident Insurance Company
CACCB
1200 Colonial Life Boulevard
Columbia, SC 29202 (803) 798-7000
life, accident, health insurance

Colorado National Bankshares, Inc. COLC
950 Seventeenth Street
Denver, CO 80217 (303) 629-1968
banking

Colorocs Corporation CLRX
2830 Peterson Place
Norcross, GA 30071 (404) 448-9799
color copiers and printing devices

Comair Holdings, Inc. COMR
P.O. Box 75021, Greater Cincinnati Airport
Cincinnati, OH 45275 (606) 525-2550
regional airline

COMARCO, Inc. CMRO
160 S. Springs Road
Anaheim, CA 92808 (714) 921-0672
engineering and computer services

Comcast Corporation CMCSA
One Belmont Avenue
Bala Cynwyd, PA 19004 (215) 667-4200
cable TV systems operator

Comcoa, Inc. CCOA
Suite 200, 411 North Webb Road
Wichita, KS 67206 (316) 683-4411
rental of household durable goods

Comdial Corporation CMDL
1180 Seminole Trail
Charlottesville, VA 22906 (804) 978-2500
telephone instruments

Comerica, Inc. CMCA
211 West Fort Street
Detroit, MI 48226 (313) 222-3300
banking DRP

Commerce Bancorp, Inc. COBA
336 Route 70
Marlton, NJ 08053 (609) 983-6300
banking

Commerce Bancshares, Inc. CBSH
1000 Walnut
Kansas City, MO 64106 (816) 234-2000
banking

Commerce Clearing House, Inc. CCLR
2700 Lake Crook Road
Riverwoods, IL 60015 (312) 940-4600
tax and business law publishing, services

Commercial Bancorporation of Colorado
CBOC
3300 East First Avenue
Denver, CO 80206 (303) 321-1234
banking

Commercial Decal, Inc. COME
650 South Columbus Avenue
Mount Vernon, NY 10550 (914) 664-1610
ceramic decals, plastic foils

Commercial Federal Corporation CFCN
2120 South 72nd Street
Omaha, NE 68124 (402) 554-9200
savings and loan

Commercial Intertech Corporation CTEK
1775 Logan Avenue
Youngstown, OH 44501 (216) 746-8011
hydraulic components, metal products, filters

Commercial National Corporation CNCL
P.O. Box 21119
Shreveport, LA 71152 (318) 429-1616
banking

Commonwealth Bancshares Corporation
CBKS
101 West Third Street
Williamsport, PA 17703 (717) 327-5011
banking

Communications & Cable, Inc. CCAB
North Haverhill Road
West Palm Beach, FL 33417 (305) 683-4767
cable TV systems, recreation facilities

Communications Systems Inc. CSII
213 South Main Street
Hector, MN 55342 (612) 848-6231
telecommunications equipment, services

Communications Transmission, Inc. CTIA
3307 Northland Drive
Austin, TX 78731 (512) 451-0131
long-distance transmission capacity

Comnet Corporation CNET
6404 Ivy Lane
Greenbelt, MD 20770 (301) 220-5400
computer services and software

Comp-U-Check, Inc. CMUC
16250 Northland Drive
Southfield, MI 48075 (313) 569-1448
check guarantee, collection services

Compression Labs, Inc. CLIX
2860 Junction Avenue
San Jose, CA 95134 (408) 435-3000
videoconferencing systems

CompuChem Corporation CCEM
3308 Chapel Hill/ Nelson Highway
Research Triangle Park, NC 27709
(919) 549-8263
environmental and drug testing

Computer Communications, Inc. CCMM
2610 Columbia Street
Torrance, CA 90503 (213) 320-9101
data communications systems

Computer & Communications Technology
Corporation CCTC
9177 Skypark Court
San Diego, CA 92123 (619) 279-8973
magnetic recording head products

Computer Automation, Inc. CAUT
2181 Dupont Drive
Irvine, CA 92713 (714) 833-8830
electronic automatic test equipment

Computer Data Systems, Inc. CPTD
One Curie Court
Rockville, MD 20850 (301) 921-7000
management consulting, data processing

Computer Entry Systems Corporation CESC
2120 Industrial Parkway
Silver Spring, MD 20904 (301) 622-3500
cash management, payment processing
systems

Computer Horizons Corporation CHRZ
747 Third Avenue
New York, NY 10017 (212) 371-9600
custom software development

Computer Identics Corporation CIDN
5 Shawmut Road
Canton, MA 02021 (617) 821-0830
automatic identification products

Computer Language Research, Inc. CLRI
2395 Midway Road
Carrollton, TX 75006 (214) 250-7000
income tax processing services

Computer Memories, Inc. CMIN
9811 Independence Avenue
Chatsworth, CA 91311 (818) 700-2671
disk drives

Computer Products, Inc. CPRD
2900 S.W. 14th Street
Pompano Beach, FL 33069 (305) 974-5500
power conversion products, measurement

Computer Resources, Inc. CRII
4520 West 160th Street
Cleveland, OH 44135 (216) 362-1020
computer equipment

Comshare, Inc. CSRE
3001 South State Street
Ann Arbor, MI 48108 (313) 994-4800
software and computer services

Comstock Group, Inc. CSTK
38 Old Ridgebury Road
Danbury, CT 06810 (203) 792-9800
design and engineering services

Comtech Telecommunications Corporation
CMTL
63 Oser Avenue
Hauppauge, NY 11788 (516) 435-4646
satellite communications systems

Comtex Scientific Corporation CMTX
911 Hope Street
Stamford, CT 06907 (203) 838-7200
distributes electronic news and information

Comtrex Systems Corporation COMX
109 Gaither Drive
Mt. Laurel, NJ 08054 (609) 778-0090
electronic cash registers

Concept, Inc. CCPT
11311 Concept Boulevard
Largo, FL 34643 (813) 392-6464
medical-surgical products

Concord Computing Corporation CEFT
7 Alfred Circle
Bedford, MA 01730 (617) 275-1730
computers

Concorde Career Colleges, Inc. CNCD
City Center Square, 12th & Baltimore
Kansas City, MO 64196 (816) 474-4750
vocational career training programs

Concurrent Computer Corporation CCUR
106 Apple Street
Tinton Falls, NJ 07724 (201) 758-7000
computers for time-critical applications

Confertech International, Inc. CFER
2801 Youngfield
Golden, CO 80401 (303) 237-5151
audio teleconferencing systems

Conmed Corporation CNMD
310 Broad Street
Utica, NY 13501 (315) 797-8375
electrocardiograph products

Connaught Biosciences, Inc. CSESF
55 University Avenue
Toronto, Ontario, CDA M5J 2H7
(416) 941-8770
biological products

Connecticut Water Service, Inc. CTWS
93 West Main Street
Clinton, CT 06413 (203) 669-8636
water utility DRP 5%

Conner Peripherals, Inc. CNNR
2221 Old Oakland Road
San Jose, CA 95131 (408) 433-3340
produces Winchester disk drives

Consolidated-Bathhurst, Inc. CB.A
800 boul, Dorchester Ouest
Montreal, Quebec, CDA H3B 1Y9
(514) 875-2160
forest products and packaging

Consolidated Capital Income Trust CCITS
2000 Powell Street
Emeryville, CA 94608 (415) 652-7171
real estate investment trust

Consolidated Capital Specialty Trust CCSTS
2000 Powell Street
Emeryville, CA 94608 (415) 652-7171
real estate investment trust

Consolidated Capital Realty Investors CCPLS
2000 Powell Street
Emeryville, CA 94608 (415) 652-7171
real estate investment trust

Consolidated Fibres, Inc. CFIB
50 California Street
San Francisco, CA 94111 (415) 788-5300
textiles

Consolidated Papers, Inc. CPER
P.O. Box 50
Wisconsin Rapids, WI 54494 (715) 422-3111
enamel paper, coated specialty papers

Consolidated Products, Inc. COPI
500 Century Building,
36 South Pennsylvania St.
Indianapolis, IN 46204 (317) 633-4100
restaurants

Consolidated-Tomoka Land Company CTLC
2570 Volusia Avenue
Daytona Beach, FL 32020 (904) 255-7558
citrus operations

Constellation Bancorp CSTL
68 Broad Street
Elizabeth, NJ 07207 (201) 354-4080
banking DRP

Consul Restaurant Corporation CNSL
4815 West 77th Street
Minneapolis, MN 55435 (612) 893-0230
restaurants

Consumers Financial Corporation CFIN
1110 Fernwood Avenue
Camp Hill, PA 17011 (717) 761-4230
life, accident, health insurance

Consumers Water Company CONW
3 Canal Plaza
Portland, ME 04112 (207) 773-6438
water utility DRP

Contel Cellular CCXLA
9000 Central Park West
Atlanta, GA 30328 (404) 391-8217
cellular telephone service

Continental Bancorp, Inc. CBRP
1500 Market Street
Philadelphia, PA 19102 (215) 564-7000
banking DRP

Continental General Company CGIC
8901 Indian Hills Drive
Omaha, NE 68114 (402) 397-3200
life, accident, health insurance

Continental Health Affiliates, Inc. CTHL
900 Sylvan Avenue
Englewood Cliff, NJ 07632 (201) 567-4600
outpatient healthcare services

Continental Healthcare Systems, Inc. CHSI
8900 Indian Creek Pkwy.
Overland Park, KS 66210 (913) 451-6161
health services

Continental Homes Holding CONH
11000 North Scottsdale Road
Scottsdale, AZ 85254 (602) 483-0006
single family homebuilder

Continental Medical Systems CONT
650 Wilson Lane
Mechanicsburg, PA 17055 (717) 691-8047
medical rehabilitation and long-term services

Continuum Company, Inc. (The) CTUC
9500 Arboretum Boulevard
Austin, TX 78759 (512) 345-5700
software for insurance industry

Control Resource Industries, Inc. CRIX
670 Mariner Drive
Michigan City, IN 46360 (219) 872-8686
asbestos abatement services

Convergent Solutions, Inc. CSOL
100 Metro Park South
Laurence Harbor, NJ 08878 (201) 290-0090
software

Conversion Industries, Inc. CVSNF
101 East Green Street
Pasadena, CA 91105 (818) 793-7526
hydroelectric, cogeneration power production

Convex Computer Corporation CNVX
701 North Plano Road
Richardson, TX 75081 (214) 952-0200
supercomputers

Co-operative Bank of Concord (The) COBK
97 Lowell Road
Concord, MA 01742 (617) 369-2400
banking

Cooper Development, Inc. COOL
3145 Porter Drive
Palo Alto, CA 94304 (415) 856-5000
automated medical diagnostic systems

Cooper Life Sciences, Inc. ZAPS
3145 Porter Drive
Palo Alto, CA 94304 (408) 720-1100
medical products

Coors, Adolph Company ACCOB
Golden, CO 80401 (303) 279-6565
beer brewing

Copytele, Inc. COPY
900 Walt Whitman Road
Huntington Station, NY 11746
(516) 549-5900
computer flat panel displays

Coral Gold Corporation CGLDF
Suite 100, 455 Granville Street
Vancouver, BC, CDA V6C 1T1 (604) 682-3701
gold mining

Corcom, Inc. CORC
1600 Winchester Road
Libertyville, IL 60048 (312) 680-7400
noise pollution control devices

Cordis Corporation CORD
10555 West Flagler Street
Miami, FL 33174 (305) 551-2000
cardiovascular disease devices

CoreStates Financial Corporation CSFN
Broad and Chestnut Streets
Philadelphia, PA 19101 (215) 629-3504
banking DRP

Corporate Capital Resources, Inc. CCRS
32123 Lindero Canyon Road
Westlake Village, CA 91361 (818) 991-3111
venture capital investments

Corporate Software, Inc. CSOF
410 University Avenue
Westwood, MA 02090 (617) 329-3500
computer hardware and software

Corrections Corporation of America CCAX
28 White Bridge Road
Nashville, TN 37205 (615) 356-1885
privatization of prisons

Corvus Systems, Inc. CRVS
160 Great Oaks Boulevard
San Jose, CA 95119 (408) 281-4100
local area networks

Cosmetics & Fragrance Concepts COSF
10551 Ewing Road
Beltsville, MD 20705 (301) 937-8840
cosmetics stores

Cosmo Communications Corporation CSMO
16501 N.W. 16th Court
Miami, FL 33169 (305) 621-4227
consumer electronic products

Costar Corporation CSTR
205 Broadway
Cambridge, MA 02139 (617) 868-6200
precision plastic products for labs

Costco Wholesale Corporation COST
10809 120th Avenue, N.E.
Kirkland, WA 98083 (206) 828-8100
cash-and-carry membership warehouses

Cotton States Life and Health Insurance
Company CSLH
244 Perimeter Center Parkway
Atlanta, GA 30346 (404) 391-8600
life, health, accident insurance

Country Lake Foods, Inc. CLFI
1930 Wooddale Drive
St. Paul, MN 55164 (612) 735-6700
milk, ice cream, dairy products

Country Wide Transport CWTS
1110 South Reservoir Street
Pomona, CA 91766 (714) 629-0229
trucking

County Savings Bank CSBA
3760 State Street
Santa Barbara, CA 93105 (805) 682-2400
savings banking

Courier Corporation CRRC
165 Jackson Street
Lowell, MA 01852 (617) 458-6351
specialty printing

Courier Dispatch Group, Inc. CDGI
180 Interstate North
Atlanta, GA 30302 (404) 955-8646
air and ground courier services

Cousins Properties, Inc. COUS
2500 Windy Ridge Parkway
Marietta, GA 30067 (404) 955-2200
real estate investment trust

Covington Development Group, Inc. COVT
2451 East Orangethorpe Avenue
Fullerton, CA 92631 (714) 879-0111
single and multiple family housing developer

CPC Rexcel CPST
500 Washington Avenue
St. Louis, MO 63101 (314) 436-2822
consumer plastic containers

CPT Corporation CPTC
8100 Mitchell Road
Eden Prairie, MN 55344 (612) 937-8000
computers

Cracker Barrel Old Country Store, Inc. CBRL
Hartmann Drive, P.O. Box 787
Lebanon, TN 37088 (615) 444-5533
restaurants

Craftmatic/ Contour Industries, Inc. CRCC
2500 Interplex Drive
Trevose, PA 19047 (215) 639-1310
electric adjustable beds, reclining chairs

Crawford & Company CRAW
5620 Glenridge Drive, N.E.
Atlanta, GA 30342 (404) 256-0830
insurance claims administration

Crazy Eddie, Inc. CRZY
140 Carter Drive
Edison, NJ 08817 (201) 248-1410
consumer electronics stores

Crescott, Inc. CRCT
645 Madison Avenue
New York, NY 10022 (212) 308-6920
operates vending machines

Crestar Financial Corporation CRFC
919 East Main Street
Richmond, VA 23261 (804) 782-5000
banking DRP

Crestmont Federal S & L CRES
2035 Lincoln Highway
Edison, NJ 08817 (201) 287-3838
savings and loan

Critical Industries, Inc. FYBR
5815 Gulf Freeway
Houston, TX 77023 (713) 923-1300
asbestos abatement services

Criticare Systems, Inc. CXIM
Suite 398, 20900 Swenson Drive
Waukesha, WI 53186 (414) 797-8282
patient-monitoring medical devices

Cronus Industries, Inc. CRNS
Suite 1400, 1111 West Mockingbird
Dallas, TX 75247 (214) 905-2590
real estate recording, election services

Crop Genetics International Corporation CROP
7170 Standard Drive
Hanover, MD 21076 (301) 621-2900
agricultural biotechnology

Cross & Trecker Corporation CTCO
505 North Woodward Avenue
Bloomfield Hills, MI 48013 (313) 644-4343
machine tools, materials handling equipment

Crown Auto, Inc. CRNI
7550 Corporate Way
Eden Prairie, MN 55344 (612) 831-5232
auto parts retailing

Crown Books Corporation CRWN
3300 75th Avenue
Landover, MD 20785 (301) 731-1200
book retailing

CrownAmerica CRNA
701 Chattanooga Avenue
Dalton, GA 30720 (404) 278-1422
textiles for carpet industry

CSP, Inc. CSPI
40 Linnell Circle
Billerica, MA 01821 (617) 272-6020
electronic equipment, data processing

C-TEC Corporation CTEX
46 Public Square
Wilkes-Barre, PA 18703 (717) 825-1100
telephone, cable TV services

CT Financial Services CFS
275 Dundas Street
London, Ontario, CDA N6A 3S4
(519) 663-1938
mortgage banking

CUC International, Inc. CUCD
707 Summer Street
Stamford, CT 06904 (203) 324-9261
computerized merchandising and travel
services

Cucos, Inc. CUCO
3009 25th Street
Metairie, LA 70002 (504) 835-0306
Mexican restaurants

Cullen/Frost Bankers, Inc. CFBI
100 West Houston Street
San Antonio, TX 78296 (512) 220-4011
banking

Culp, Inc. CULP
2020 Logan Street
High Point, NC 27263 (919) 889-5161
upholstery fabrics, mattress tickings

CVB Financial Corporation CVBF
701 North Haven Avenue
Ontario, CA 91764 (714) 980-4030
banking

CVN Companies, Inc. CAVN
1405 Xenium Lane North
Minneapolis, MN 55441 (612) 559-8000
direct marketing of consumer products

Cybertek Corporation CKCP
6133 Bristol Parkway
Culver City, CA 90230 (213) 649-2450
insurance software and data processing

Cytogen Corporation CYTO
201 College Road East
Princeton, NJ 08540 (609) 987-8200
biotechnological diagnosis systems

Dahlberg, Inc. DAHL
600 South County Road
Minneapolis, MN 55426 (612) 542-1118
hearing aids and accessories

Dairy Mart Convenience Stores, Inc. DMCVB
240 South Road
Enfield, CT 06082 (203) 741-3611
convenience stores

Daisy Systems Corporation DAZY
700 East Middlefield Road
Mountain View, CA 94043 (415) 960-0123
computer-aided engineering design systems

DAKA International DKAI
3636 Medical Drive
San Antonio, TX 78229 (512) 692-0040
institutional food service, restaurants

Dallas Semiconductor Corporation DSMI
4350 Beltwood Parkway South
Dallas, TX 75244 (214) 450-0400
specialized integrated circuits

Damon Biotech, Inc. DBIO
119 Fourth Avenue
Needham Heights, MA 02194 (617) 449-6002
biotechnology, biomedical products

Dart Drug Stores, Inc. DDRGC
3301 Pennsy Drive
Landover, MD 20785 (301) 772-6000
drug, health and beauty aids stores

Dataflex Corporation DFLX
777 New Durham Road
Edison, NJ 08817 (201) 321-1100
personal computer and peripheral sales

Datamarine International, Inc. DMAR
53 Portside Drive
Pocasset, MA 02559 (508) 563-7151
recreational marine electronic products

Data Measurement Corproation DMCB
15884 Gaither Drive
Gaithersburg, MD 20877 (301) 948-2450
computerized measurement systems

Data I/O Corporation DAIO
10525 Willows Roads N.E.
Redmond, WA 98073 (206) 881-6444
integrated circuit testing systems

Datascope Corporation DSCP
580 Winters Avenue
Paramus, NJ 07653 (201) 265-8800
clinical health care products

Datasouth Computer Corporation DSCC
4216 Stuart Andrew Boulevard
Charlotte, NC 28217 (704) 523-8500
computer printers

Data Switch Corporation DASW
One Enterprise Drive
Shelton, CT 06484 (203) 926-1801
data processing management control

Data Translation, Inc. DATX
100 Locke Drive
Marlborough, MA 01752 (508) 481-3700
image-processing computer boards

Data Transmission Network DTLN
8805 Indian Hills Drive
Omaha, NE 68114 (402) 390-2328
electronic agricultural marketing information

Datavision, Inc. DVIS
160 SW 12th Avenue
Deerfield Beach, FL 33442 (305) 481-2801
computerized security monitoring systems

DataVend, Inc. DATV
Suite 3040, 1502 Joh Avenue
Baltimore, MD 21227 (301) 644-3100
videocassette vending machine retailing

Datron Systems, Inc. DTSI
200 West Los Angeles Avenue
Simi Valley, CA 93065 (805) 584-1717
satellite communication terminals

Datum, Inc. DATM
1363 South State College Boulevard
Anaheim, CA 92806 (714) 533-6333
timing instrumentation products

Dauphin Deposit Corporation DAPN
213 Market Street
Harrisburg, PA 17105 (717) 255-2121
banking

Davis Water & Waste Industries, Inc. DWWS
P. O. Box 1419
Thomasville, GA 31792 (912) 226-5733
pollution control equipment

Davox Corporation DAVX
3 Federal Street
Billerica, MA 01821 (508) 667-4455
data communications and telephone
automation

Dawson Geophysical Company DWSN
208 South Marienfeld Street
Midland, TX 79701 (915) 682-7356
oil and gas seismic services

DBA Systems, Inc. DBAS
1200 South Woody Burke Road
Melbourne, FL 32902 (407) 727-0660
defense electronics systems

DDI Pharmaceuticals, Inc. DDIX
518 Logue Avenue
Mountain View, CA 94043 (415) 964-7676
osteoarthritis treatment drugs

De Beers Consolidated Mines, Ltd. DBRSY
36 Stockdale Street
Kimberley 8300, South Africa
diamond mining and marketing, gold mining

Deb Shops, Inc. DEBS
9401 Blue Grass Road
Philadelphia, PA 19114 (215) 676-6000
sportswear apparel stores

Decision Systems, Inc. DCSN
200 Route 17
Mahwah, NJ 07430 (201) 529-1440
computer systems analysis, hardware sales

Decom Systems, Inc. DSII
340 Rancheros Drive
San Marcos, CA 92009 (619) 431-1945
aerospace telecommunications equipment

Decor Corporation DCOR
1519 Alum Creek Drive South
Columbus, OH 43209 (614) 258-2871
graphic reproductions, art stores

Defiance Precision Products, Inc. DEFI
1125 Precision Way
Defiance, OH 43512 (419) 782-3334
transportation products and services

DEKALB Energy Company ENRGB
110 16th Street
Denver, CO 80202 (303) 595-0707
oil and gas production

DEKALB Genetics Corporation SEEDB
3100 Sycamore Road
DeKalb, IL 60115 (815) 758-3461
agricultural seeds, hybrid swine, hens

Delaware Otsego Corporation DOCP
1 Railroad Avenue
Cooperstown, NY 13326 (607) 547-2555
railroad, real estate

Delchamps, Inc. DLCH
305 Delchamps Drive
Mobile, AL 36602 (205) 433-0431
supermarkets

Delta Natural Gas Company, Inc. DGAS
3617 Lexington Road
Winchester, KY 40391 (606) 744-6171
gas utility

Deltak Corporation DLTK
13330 12th Avenue North
Plymouth, MN 55441 (612) 554-3371
heat recovery generators, energy conversion

Denison Mines, Ltd. DEN.A
Suite 3900, Royal Bank Plaza
Toronto, Ontario, CDA M5J 2K2
(416) 865-1991
uranium, potash, coal mines

Dento-Med Industries, Inc. DTMD
941 Clint Moore Road
Boca Raton, FL 33431 (305) 994-6191
oral hygiene products

DEP Corporation DEPC
2101 East Via Arado Avenue
Rancho Dominguez, CA 90220
(213) 604-0777
hair and skin care products, soaps,
fragrances

Deposit Guaranty Corporation DEPS
210 East Capitol Street
Jackson, MS 39215 (601) 354-8564
banking DRP

Designs, Inc. DESI
1244 Boylston Street
Boston, MA 02167 (617) 739-6722
specialty jeans retail stores

DEST Corporation DEST
1201 Cadillac Court
Milpitas, CA 95035 (408) 946-7100
desktop document scanners

Detection Systems, Inc. DETC
130 Perinton Parkway
Fairport, NY 14450 (716) 223-4060
electronic security instruments

Detrex Corporation DTRX
Suite 1100, 4000 Town Center
Southfield, MI 48075 (313) 358-5800
chemicals for oil, chemical and metal
industries

Devcon International Corporation DEVC
1350 East Newport Center Drive
Deerfield Beach, FL 33442 (305) 429-1500
heavy construction services

Develcon Electronics, Ltd. DLCFF
856 51st East
Saskatoon, SK, CDA S7K 5C7 (306) 933-3300
data communications equipment

Devon Group, Inc. DEVN
1600 Summer Street
Stamford, CT 06905 (203) 964-1444
computer typesetting and printing

Dewey Electronics Corporation (The) DEWYE
27 Muller Road
Oakland, NJ 07436 (201) 337-4700
electronic measuring instruments

DFSoutheastern, Inc. DFSE
250 East Ponce de Leon Avenue
Decatur, GA 30030 (404) 371-4000
savings and loan

DH Technology, Inc. DHTK
15070 Avenue of Science
San Diego, CA 92128 (619) 451-3485
computer printers and accessories

Diagnostic Products Corp. DPCZ
5700 West 96th Street
Los Angeles, CA 90045 (213) 776-0180
medical diagnostic products

Dial REIT, Inc. DEAL
11506 Nicholas Street
Omaha, NE 68154 (402) 496-7184
real estate investment trust

Dibrell Brothers, Inc. DBRL
512 Bridge Street
Danville, VA 24541 (804) 792-7511
redries and packs leaf tobacco

Diceon Electronics, Inc. DICN
18522 Von Karman Avenue
Irvine, CA 92715 (714) 833-0870
electronic circuit boards

Dick Clark Productions, Inc. DCPI
3003 West Olive Avenue
Burbank, CA 91510 (818) 841-3003
television programming and motion pictures

Digilog, Inc. DILO
1370 Welsh Road
Montgomeryville, PA 18936 (215) 628-4530
data communications test products

Digital Microwave DMIC
170 Rose Orchard Way
San Jose, CA 95134 (408) 943-0777
digital microwave communications products

Digital Products Corporation DIPC
4021 N.E. 5th Terrace
Fort Lauderdale, FL 3334 (305) 564-0521
telephone dialing systems

Digitech, Inc. DGTC
15 Progress Parkway
St. Louis, MO 63043 (314) 878-1200
telephone equipment

Digitext, Inc. DIGT
325 Hillcrest Drive
Thousand Oaks, CA 91360 (805) 495-3456
digital electronic keyboard products

Dionex Corporation DNEX
1228 Titan Way
Sunnyvale, CA 94088 (408) 737-0700
chromatography systems

Distributed Logic Corporation DLOG
1555 South Sinclair Street
Anaheim, CA 92806 (714) 937-5700
communications controllers, data storage

Diversco, Inc. DVRS
Road 57
Spartansburg, SC 29304 (803) 579-3420
provides skilled and unskilled personnel

Diversified Human Resources Group, Inc.
HIRE
5001 Spring Valley
Dallas, TX 75244 (214) 458-8500
places permanent and temporary personnel

Diversified Investment Group, Inc. DING
6958 Torresdale Avenue
Philadelphia, PA 19135 (215) 624-9000
savings and loan

Diversified Retail Group, Inc. DRGX
601-20 Dover Road
Rockville, MD 20850 (301) 279-8677
apparel, candy and framing stores

Dixie Yarns, Inc. DXYN
1100 South Watkins Street
Chattanooga, TN 37404 (615) 698-2501
specialty yarns, industrial threads, fabrics

DNA Plant Technology Corporation DNAP
2611 Branch Pike
Cinnaminson, NJ 08077 (609) 829-0110
biotechnology, food production

D&N Financial Corporation DNFC
400 Quincy Street
Hancock, MI 49930 (906) 482-2700
savings banking

D.O.C. Optics Corporation DOCO
19800 West Eight Mile Road
Southfield, MI 48075 (313) 354-7100
optical products retailing

Dollar General Coporation DOLR
427 Beech Street
Scottsville, KY 42164 (502) 237-5444
discount general merchandise stores

Domain Technology DOMN
311 Turquoise Street
Milpitas, CA 95035 (408) 262-4100
computer thin-film disks

Dominion Bankshares Corporation DMBK
213 South Jefferson Street
Roanoke, VA 24040 (703) 563-7000
banking DRP 5%

Dominion Textile, Inc. DTX
1950 rue Sherbrooke
Montreal, Quebec, CDA H3H 1E7
(514) 989-6000
textile products

Dorchester Hugoton, Ltd. DHULZ
9696 Skillman Street
Dallas, TX 75243 (214) 739-2002
oil and gas properties

Doskocil Companies, Inc. DOSK
321 North Main Street
South Hutchinson, Kansas 67505
(316) 663-1005
specialty precooked meats for restaurants

Dotronix, Inc. DOTX
160 First Street S.E.
New Brighton, MN 55112 (612) 633-1742
cathode ray tube displays

Douglas & Lomason Company DOUG
24600 Hallwood Court
Farmington Hills, MI 48331 (313) 478-7800
automotive metal parts

Dress Barn (The), Inc. DBRN
88 Hamilton Avenue
Stamford, CT 06902 (203) 327-4242
women's apparel stores

Drew Industries, Inc. DRWI
200 Mamaroneck Avenue
White Plains, NY 10601 (914) 428-9098
home construction products

Drexler Techology Corporation DRXR
2557 Charleston Road
Mountain View, CA 94043 (415) 969-7277
optical data storage, semiconductors

Dreyer's Grand Ice Cream, Inc. DRYR
5929 College Avenue
Oakland, CA 94618 (415) 652-8187
ice cream, dessert products

Driefontein Consolidated, Ltd. DRFNY
Gold Fields Building, 75 Fox Street
Johannesburg, South Africa 2001
(212) 880-5100
gold mining

Drug Emporium, Inc. DEMP
7760 Oletangy River Road
Columbus, OH 43235 (614) 888-6876
discount drug stores

DSC Communications Corporation DIGI
1000 Coit Road
Plano, TX 75075 (214) 519-3000
telecommunications equipment O

DST Systems, Inc. DSTS
1004 Baltimore Avenue
Kansas City, MO 64105 (816) 221-5545
mutual fund shareholder services, software

Dumagami Mines, Ltd. DMI
401 Bay Street, Suite 1612
Toronto, Ontario CDA M5H 2Y4
(416) 947-1212
gold mining

Dunkin' Donuts, Inc. DUNK
Pacella Park Drive, P.O. Box 317
Randolph, MA 02368 (617) 961-4000
donut and coffee shops DRP

Durakon Industries, Inc. DRKN
3200 Beecher Road
Flint, MI 48532 (313) 230-0633
pickup truckbed liners

Duramed Pharmaceuticals DRMDC
5040 Lester Road
Cincinnati, OH 45213 (513) 731-9900
generic drug manufacturer

Duratek Corporation DRTK
6411 Ivy Lane
Greenbelt, MD 20770 (301) 474-2100
isolates radioactive material from water

Durham Corporation DUCO
2610 Wycliff Road, P.O. Box 27807
Raleigh, NC 27611 (919) 782-6110
life, health, property-casualty insurance

Duriron Company, Inc. (The) DURI
425 North Findlay Street
Dayton, OH 45404 (513) 226-4000
fluid movement and control equipment DRP

Durr-Fillauer Medical, Inc. DUFM
218 Commerce Street
Montgomery, AL 36104 (205) 241-8800
distributes drugs, medical products

Dyansen Corporation DYAN
3 East 54th Street
New York, NY 10022 (212) 644-5100
art and sculpture galleries

DYATRON Corporation DYTR
210 Automation Way
Birmingham, AL 35201 (205) 956-7500
computer services, software

Dycom Industries, Inc. DYCO
450 Australia Avenue South
West Palm Beach, FL 33401 (305) 659-6301
telecommunications services

Dynamics Research Corporation DRCO
60 Concord Street
Wilmington, MA 01887 (508) 658-6100
defense technical services, measuring
devices

Dynascan Corporation DYNA
6460 West Cortland Street
Chicago, IL 60635 (312) 889-8870
telephones, answering machines, CBs

Dynatech Corporation DYTC
3 New England Executive Park
Burlington, MA 01803 (617) 272-6100
electronic measurement instruments

EA Engineering, Sciences & Technology, Inc.
EACO
15 Loveton Circle
Sparks, MD 21152 (301) 771-4950
environmental and health consulting

Eagle Telephonics, Inc. EGLA
375 Oser Avenue
Hauppauge, NY 11788 (516) 273-6700
electronic telephone keyset systems

Earth Technology Corporation ETCO
100 West Broadway
Long Beach, CA 90802 (213) 495-4449
environmental services

Easco Hand Tools, Inc. TOOL
318 Clubhouse Lane
Hunt Valley, MD 21031 (301) 584-9200
mechanics' hand tools

Eastco Industrial Safety Corporation ESTO
130 West 10th Street
Huntington Station, NY 11746
(516) 427-1802
disposable, protective clothing

Eastover Corporation EAST
P.O. Box 22728
Jackson, MS 39225 (601) 948-4091
investment services

Eaton Vance Corporation EAVN
24 Federal Street
Boston, MA 02110 (617) 482-8260
investment management, mutual funds

E&B Marine, Inc. EDMI
201 Meadow Road
Edison, NJ 08818 (201) 819-7400
marine supplies retailing

ECI Telecom, Ltd. ECILF
88, Yigal Allon Street
Tel-Aviv, Israel 67891 (03) 333-3241
telecommunications equipment

Edgcomb Corporation EDGC
30 Rockefeller Plaza
New York, NY 10112 (212) 246-1000
metals service business

Education Systems & Publications ESPC
195 Cortlandt Street
Belleville, NJ 07109 (201) 759-1520
direct mail printing

Egghead, Inc. EGGS
22011 S.E. 51st
Issaquah, WA 98027 (206) 391-0800
personal computer software retailing

E.I.L. Instruments, Inc. EILI
10 Loveton Circle
Sparks, MD 21152 (301) 771-4800
distributes electronic equipment

EIP Microwave, Inc. EIPM
4500 Campus Drive
Newport Beach, CA 92660 (714) 756-8171
microwave test equipment

Elan Corporation, PLC ELANY
1300 Gould Drive
Gainesville, GA 30501 (404) 534-8239
drug absorption and delivery technologies

Elbit Computers, Ltd. ELBTF
Advanced Technology Center
Haifa 31053, Israel (972) 4556677
military computerized systems

El Chico Corporation ELCH
12200 Stemmons Freeway
Dallas, TX 75234 (214) 241-5500
Mexican restaurants

Elco Industries, Inc. ELCN
1111 Samuelson Road
Rockford, IL 61125 (815) 397-5151
specialty fasteners, custom components

Elcotel, Inc. ECTL
6428 Parkland Drive
Sarasota, FL 34243 (813) 758-0389
private pay telephone manufacturer

Eldec Corporation ELDC
16700 13th Avenue West
Lynnwood, WA 98046 (206) 743-1313
electronic aerospace products

Electro-Catheter Corporation ECTH
2100 Felver Court
Rahway, NJ 07065 (201) 382-5600
diagnostic and therapeutic catheters

Electromagnetic Sciences, Inc. ELMG
125 Technology Park/ Atlanta
Norcross, GA 30092 (404) 448-5770
microwave components, data terminals

Electromedics, Inc. ELMD
7337 South Revere Parkway
Englewood, CO 80112 (303) 790-8700
open-heart surgery medical products

Electronic Tele-Communications Inc. ETCI
1915 MacArthur Road
Waukesha, WI 53188 (414) 542-5600
electronic communications equipment

Electro Rent Corporation ELRC
6060 Sepulveda Boulevard
Van Nuys, CA 91411 (818) 786-2525
electronic test equipment rental

Electro Scientific Industries, Inc. ESIO
13900 N.W. Science Park Drive
Portland, OR 97229 (503) 641-4141
computer-controlled laser systems

Electro-Sensors, Inc. ELSE
7251 Washington Avenue South
Minneapolis, MN 55435 (612) 941-8171
medical supplies

Elexis Corporation ELEX
7000 N.W. 46th Street
Miami, FL 33166 (305) 592-6069
sports/fitness products, pet care

El Paso Electric Company ELPA
P.O. Box 982
El Paso, TX 79960 (915) 543-5958
electric utility DRP

Elron Electronic Industries, Ltd. ELRNF
Advanced Technology Center
Haifa, Israel (212) 819-1644
military electronics, medical imaging

ELXSI Corporation EXLXS
2334 Lundy Place
San Jose, CA 95131 (408) 942-0900
minisupercomputers

EMC Insurance Group, Inc. EMCI
717 Mulberry Street
Des Moines, IA 50309 (515) 280-2581
property-casualty insurance

EMCON Associates MCON
1921 Ringwood Avenue
San Jose, CA 95131 (408) 275-1444
environmental engineering and consulting

Employers Casualty Company ECRC
1301 Young Street
Dallas, TX 75202 (214) 760-6100
worker's compensation, casualty insurance

EMS Systems, Ltd. EMSIF
1325 Capital Parkway
Carrolton, TX 75006 (214) 446-2900
electronic components, telecommunications

Emulex Corporation EMLX
3545 Harbor Boulevard
Costa Mesa, CA 92626 (714) 662-5600
computer data storage enhancements

Encore Computer Corporation ENCC
257 Cedar Hill Street
Marlborough, MA 01752 (508) 460-0500
parallel processing computer systems

Energy Assets International Corporation EAIC
1221 Lamar
Houston. TX 77010 (713) 759-0336
oil and gas industry financing

Energy Conversion Devices, Inc. ENERC
1675 West Maple Road
Troy, MI 48084 (313) 280-1900
photovoltaics, imaging systems, materials

EnergyNorth, Inc. ENNI
1260 Elm Street
Manchester, NH 03105 (603) 625-4000
gas utility DRP

ENEX Resources Corporation ENEX
800 Rockmead Drive
Kingwood, TX 77339 (713) 358-8401
oil and gas exploration and development

Engineered Support Systems, Inc. EASI
1270 North Price Road
St. Louis, MO 63132 (314) 993-5880
military ground support equipment

Engineering Measurements Company EMCO
600 Diagonal Highway
Longmont, CO 80501 (303) 651-0550
liquid, air, gas measurement devices

Engraph, Inc. ENGH
2635 Century Parkway NE
Atlanta, GA 30345 (404) 329-0332
printed packaging, identification materials

Enscor, Inc. ENCRF
156 Duncan Mill Road
Don Mills, Ontario, CDA M3B 3N2
(416) 449-3535
homebuilding, land development

Enseco, Inc. NCCO
205 Alewite Brook Parkway
Cambridge, MA 02138 (617) 661-3111
environmental testing laboratories

Envirodyne Industies, Inc. ENVR
142 East Ontario Street
Chicago, IL 60611 (312) 649-0600
plastic food packaging products

Enviromental Control Group, Inc. ECGI
1000 Lenola Road
Maple Shade, NJ 08052 (609) 866-1616
asbestos abatement services

Environmental Power POWR
53 State Street
Boston, MA 02109 (617) 720-5550
alternative power generation

Environmental Tectonics Corporation ENVT
County Line Industrial Park
Southampton, PA 18966 (215) 355-9100
waste measuring equipment

Envirosafe Services, Inc. ENVI
900 East 8th Avenue
King of Prussia, PA (215) 962-0800
hazardous-waste disposal services

Enzon, Inc. ENZN
300-C Corporate Court
South Plainfield, NJ 07080 (201) 668-1800
therapeutic agent enzymes

Epsilon Data Management, Inc. EPSI
50 Cambridge Street
Burlington, MA 01803 (617) 273-0250
marketing databases, direct response

Equitable Bancorporation EBNC
100 South Charles Center
Baltimore, MD 21201 (301) 547-4000
banking

Equitable of Iowa Companies EQICB
699 Walnut Street
Des Moines, IA 50306 (515) 282-1335
life insurance, retail stores

Equitex, Inc. EQTX
7315 East Peakview Avenue
Englewood, CO 80111 (303) 796-8940
venture capital investment company

Equity Oil Company EQTY
10 West Broadway
Salt Lake City, UT 84101 (801) 521-3515
oil and gas exploration and development

Ericsson Telephone Company (L.M.) ERICY
S-126 25
Stockholm, Sweden (468) 719-0000
(212) 685-4030
public and private communications systems

Erie Lackawanna, Inc. ERIE
1302 Midland Bldg.
Cleveland, OH 44115 (216) 621-4617
investment company

ERLY Industries ERLY
10960 Wilshire Boulevard
Los Angeles, CA 90024 (213) 879-1480
rice and wine marketing

ESELCO, Inc. EDSE
725 East Portage Avenue
Sault St. Marie, MI 49783 (906) 632-2221
electric utility

ESSEF Corporation ESSF
7010 Lindsay Drive
Mentor, OH 44060 (216) 942-1200
engineered plastics and polymers

Escalade, Inc. ESCA
817 Maxwell Avenue
Evansville, IN 47717 (812) 426-2281
graphics art equipment and supplies

Essex Corporation ESEX
333 North Fairfax Street
Alexandria, VA 22314 (703) 548-4500
engineering and technical services to govt.

Essex County Gas Company ECGC
7 North Hunt Road
Amesbury, MA 01913 (508) 388-4000
gas utility

E'Town Corporation EWAT
1 Elizabethtown Plaza
Elizabeth, NJ 07202 (201) 354-4444
water utility DRP

Evans, Inc. EVAN
36 South State Street
Chicago, IL 60603 (312) 855-2000
fur apparel retailer

Evans & Sutherland Computer Corporation
ESCC
580 Arapeen Drive
Salt Lake City, UT 84108 (801) 582-5847
pilot training and engineering computers

Everex Systems, Inc. EVRX
4831 Milmont Drive
Fremont, CA 94538 (415) 498-1111
personal computers and peripherals

EVRO Financial Corporation EVRO
Suite 7, 2218 Jackson Boulevard
Rapid City, SD 57709 (605) 348-9187
oil and gas exploration and production

Exar Corporation EXAR
2222 Qume Drive
San Jose, CA 95131 (408) 434-6400
telecommunications integrated circuits

Excelan, Inc. EXLN
2180 Fortune Drive
San Jose, CA 95131 (408) 434-2300
local area network products

Exchange Bancorp Inc. EXCG
120 South LaSalle Street
Chicago, IL 60603 (312) 781-8000
banking

Executone Information Systems XTON
8300 East Raintree Drive
Scottsdale, AZ 85260 (602) 998-2200
markets key telephone systems

Exovir, Inc. XOVR
111 Great Neck Road
Great Neck, NY 11021 (516) 466-2110
biological materials to treat disease

Expeditors International of Washington, Inc.
EXPD
19119 16 Avenue South
Seattle, WA 98121 (206) 246-3711
air and ocean freight forwarding

EZ-E-M, Inc. EZEM
7 Portland Avenue
Westbury, NY 11590 (516) 333-8230
diagnostic imaging products

Fabricland, Inc. FBRC
2035 N.E. 181st Avenue
Portland, OR 97230 (503) 666-4511
fabrics retailing

Fair, Isaac & Company, Inc. FICI
120 North Redwood Drive
San Rafael, CA 94903 (415) 472-2211
scoring systems for credit analysis

Falcon Oil & Gas Company, Inc. FLOG
5030 East University
Odessa, TX 79762 (915) 367-4126
oil and gas exploration and development

Falcon Products, Inc. FLCP
9387 Dielman Industrial Drive
St. Louis, MO 63132 (314) 991-9200
furniture, foodservice, healthcare equipment

Falconbridge, Ltd. FALCF
Commerce Court West
Toronto, Ontario, CDA M5L 1B4
(416) 863-7000
nickel, copper, zinc mining and refining

Falstaff Brewing Corporation FALB
312 West 8 Street
Vancouver, WA 98660 (206) 695-3381
beer and malt beverages

Family Steak Houses of Florida, Inc. RYFL
2113 Florida Boulevard
Neptune Beach, FL 32233 (904) 249-4197
restaurants

Famous Restaurants, Inc. FAMS
4725 North Scottsdale Road
Scottsdale, AZ 85251 (602) 990-1123
Mexican restaurants

Faraday Labatories, Inc. FDLB
100 Hoffman Place
Hillside, NJ 07205 (201) 375-3304
chemical products

Farm & Home Financial Corporation FAHS
221 West Cherry
Nevada, MO 64772 (417) 667-3333
savings and loan

Farmer Brothers Company FARM
20333 South Normandie Avenue
Torrance, CA 90502 (213) 320-1212
produces coffee, spices, food products

Farr Company FARC
2221 Park Place
El Segundo, CA 90245 (213) 772-5221
filters and filtration equipment

Fastenal Company FAST
2001 Theurer Boulevard
Winona, MN 55987 (507) 454-5374
threaded fastener supplies

FDP Corporation FDPC
2140 South Dixie Highway
Miami, FL 33133 (305) 858-8200
life insurance software

Federal Screw Works FSCR
2400 Buhl Building
Detroit, MI 48226 (313) 963-2323
automotive industrial components

Ferrofluidics Corporation FERO
40 Simon Street
Nashua, NH 03061 (603) 883-9800
magnetic fluid technology equipment

FHP International Corporation
9900 Talbert Avenue
Fountain Valley, CA 92728 (714) 963-7233
health maintenance organization

Fibronics International, Inc. FBRX
Communications Way, Independence Park
Hyannis, MA 02601 (508) 778-0700
fiber optic computer connectors

Fidelity Federal S & L of Tennessee FFTN
401 Union Street
Nashville, TN 37219 (615) 244-0571
savings and loan

Fifth Third Bancorp FITB
38 Fountain Square Plaza
Cincinnati, OH 45263 (513) 579-5300
banking DRP

Figgie International, Inc. FIGI
4420 Sherwin Road
Willoughby, OH 44094 (216) 953-2700
fire protection, materials handling, sports

FileNet Corporation FILE
3565 Harbor Boulevard
Costa Mesa, CA 92626 (714) 966-3400
optical disk computer systems

Final Test, Inc. FNLT
10858 Harry Hines Boulevard
Dallas, TX 75220 (214) 352-4500
assembles and tests circuit boards

Financial News Network, Inc. FNNI
6701 Center Drive West
Los Angeles, CA 90405 (213) 670-1100
financial news cable TV network

Financial Trust Corporation FITC
1 West High Street
Carlisle, PA 17013 (717) 243-3212
financial services

Fingermatrix, Inc. FINX
30 Virginia Road
North White Plains, NY 10603
(914) 428-5441
fingerprint identification technology

Finnigan Corporation FNNG
355 River Oaks Parkway
San Jose, CA 95134 (408) 433-4800
mass spectrometers

First Alabama Bancshares, Inc. FABC
P.O. Box 1448
Montgomery, AL 36102 (205) 832-8486
banking DRP

First Albany Companies, Inc. FACT
41 State Street
Albany, NY 12207 (518) 447-8500
securities brokerage, investment
management

First of America Bank Corporation FABK
108 East Michigan Avenue
Kalamazoo, MI 49007 (616) 383-9000
banking DRP 5%

First American Bank and Trust FIAMA
401 Northlake Boulevard
North Palm Beach, FL 33408 (407) 533-1700
banking

First American Corporation FATN
First American Center
Nashville, TN 37237 (615) 748-2000
banking DRP

First American Federal S & L Association
FAMF
1900 Memorial Pkwy.
Huntsville, AL 35801 (205) 539-5761
savings and loan

First American Financial Corporation (The)
FAMR
114 East Fifth Street
Santa Ana, CA 92701 (714) 558-3211
title insurance

First Bancorporation of Ohio FBOH
106 South Main Street
Akron, OH 44308 (216) 384-8000
banking DRP

First Banc Securities, Inc. FBSI
201 High Street
Morgantown, WV 26505 (304) 291-7700
banking

First Capital Corporation FCAP
248 East Capitol Street
Jackson, MS 39205 (601) 354-5111
banking

First Capitol Financial Corporation FCFI
3300 South Parker Road
Aurora, CO 80014 (303) 671-1000
savings and loan

First Charter Corporation FCTR
22 Union Street
Concord, NC 28026 (704) 786-3300
banking DRP

First Colonial Bankshares Corporation FCOLA
30 North Michigan Avenue
Chicago, IL 60602 (312) 419-9891
banking

First Commerce Corporation FCOM
210 Baronne Street
New Orleans, LA 70160 (504) 561-1371
banking DRP

First Commercial Bancorp FCOB
550 J Street
Sacramento, CA 95814 (916) 447-7700
banking

First Commercial Corporation FCLR
Capitol and Broadway Streets
Little Rock, AR 72201 (501) 371-7000
banking

First Community Bancorp FRFD
124 North Water Street
Rockford, IL 61110 (815) 962-3003
banking

First Constitution Financial Corporation FCON
80 Elm Street
New Haven, CT 06510 (203) 782-4570
banking

First Continental REIT FCRE
1360 Post Oak Blvd.
Houston, TX 77056 (713) 622-2084
real estate investment trust

First Eastern Corporation FEBC
11 West Market Street
Wilkes-Barre, PA 18768 (717) 826-4600
banking

First Executive Corporation FEXC
11444 West Olympic Boulevard
Los Angeles, CA 90064 (213) 312-1000
life insurance

First Family Group, Inc. FFAM
3081 Gilcrist Road
Akron, OH 44305 (216) 733-1475
appliance, consumer electronics retailing

First Federal Savings Bank of Montana FFSM
202 Main Street
Kalispell, MT 59901 (406) 752-7101
banking

First Federal S & L Association of Charleston
FFCH
34 Broad Street
Charleston, SC 29401 (803) 724-0800
savings and loan

First Federal S & L Association of Fort Myers
FFMY
2201 Second Street
Fort Myers, FL 33901 (813) 334-4106
savings and loan

First Federal S & L Association of SC FTSC
301 College Street
Greenville, SC 29601 (803) 271-7222
savings and loan

FirstFed Michigan Corporation FFOM
1001 Woodward Avenue
Detroit, MI 48226 (313) 965-1400
savings banking

First Financial Bancorp FFBC
108 South Main Street
Monroe, OH 45050 (513) 867-4700
banking

First Financial Corporation FFHC
1305 Main Street
Stevens Point, WI 54481 (715) 341-0400
savings and loan

First Financial Holdings, Inc. FFCH
34 Broad Street
Charleston, SC 29401 (803) 724-0800
savings and loan DRP

First Financial Management Corporation
FFMC
3 Corporate Square
Atlanta, GA 30329 (404) 321-0120
financial services data processing

First Florida Banks, Inc. FFBK
First Florida Tower, 111 Madison Street
Tampa, FL 33601 (813) 224-1111
banking

First Hawaiian, Inc. FHWN
165 South King Street
Honolulu, HI 96813 (808) 525-7000
banking

FirsTier Financial, Inc. FRST
1700 Farnam Street
Omaha, NE 68102 (402) 348-6000
banking

First Illinois Corporation FTIL
800 Davis Street
Evanston, IL 60204 (312) 866-6000
banking DRP

First Indiana Corporation FISB
135 North Pennsylvania Street
Indianapolis, IN 46204 (317) 269-1200
banking, real estate lending

First Interstate Corporation of Wisconsin FIWI
636 Wisconsin Avenue
Sheboygan, WI 53081 (414) 459-2000
banking

First Interstate of Iowa, Inc. FIIA
900 First Interstate Bank Building
Locust at Sixth Avenue
Des Moines, IA 50309 (515) 245-7230
banking DRP

First Michigan Bank Corporation FMBC
115 Clover Avenue
Holland, MI 49423 (616) 396-9000
banking DRP

First Midwest Bancorp, Inc. FMBI
Suite 302, 1230 East Diehl Road
Naperville, IL 60566 (312) 357-3500
banking DRP

FirstMISS Gold, Inc. FRMG
5250 Neil Road
Reno, NV 89502 (702) 827-0211
gold mining

First National Bancorp (of Gainesville) FBAC
111 Green Street, N.E.
Gainesville, GA 30503 (404) 535-5500
banking

First Northern S & L Association FNGB
201 North Monroe Avenue
Green Bay, WI 54301 (414) 437-7101
savings and loan

First of America Bank Corporation FABK
108 East Michigan Avenue
Kalamazoo, MI 49007 (616) 383-9000
banking DRP

First Ohio Bancshares, Inc. FIRO
606 Madison Avenue
Toledo, OH 43604 (419) 259-6960
banking

First Regional Bancorp FRGB
1801 Century Park East
Los Angeles, CA 90067 (213) 552-1776
banking

First Savings Bank of Florida, FSB FSBF
101 Federal Place
Tarpon Springs, FL 33589 (813) 934-5721
banking

First Security Corporation FSCO
79 South Main
Salt Lake City, UT 84111 (801) 350-5325
banking DRP 5%

First Security Corporation of Kentucky FSKY
One First Security Plaza
Lexington, KY 40507 (606) 231-1000
banking DRP

1st Source Corporation SRCE
100 North Michigan Street
South Bend, IN 46601 (219) 236-2000
banking

First Tennessee National Corporation FTEN
165 Madison Avenue
Memphis, TN 38103 (901) 523-4161
banking DRP

First United Bancshares, Inc. UNTD
Main and Washington Streets
El Dorado, AR 71730 (501) 863-3181
banking

First United Financial Services, Inc. FUFS
111 East Busse Avenue
Mount Prospect, IL 60056 (312) 398-4000
financial services

First Western Financial Corporation FWES
First Western Square,
2700 West Sahara Avenue
Las Vegas, NV 89102 (702) 871-2000
savings and loan

Fiserv, Inc. FISV
2152 South 114th Street
Milwaukee, WI 53227 (414) 546-5000
data processing for financial institutions

Fisher Scientific Group FSHG
11255 North Torrey Pines Road
La Jolla, CA 92037 (619) 457-3565
medical instruments and supplies, software

Fisons PLC FISNY
Fison House, Princes Street, Ipswich
Suffolk 1P1 1QH, UK (0473) 56721
medicines and medical supplies

Flagler Bank Corporation (The) FLGL
Flagler Center
West Palm Beach, FL 33401 (305) 659-2265
banking

Flamemaster Corporation FAME
11120 Sherman Way
Sun Valley, CA 91352 (818) 982-1650
flame retardant coatings and sealants

Flexsteel Industries, Inc. FLXS
P.O. Box 877
Dubuque, IA 52001 (319) 556-7730
upholstered furniture

Flextronics, Inc. FLEX
35325 Fircrest Street
Newark, CA 94560 (415) 794-3539
printed circuit boards, electronics

Flock Industries, Inc. FLOK
251 Grant Avenue
East Newark, NJ 07029 (201) 481-6600
produces flocked materials and fibers

Florida Federal Savings Bank FLFE
360 Central Avenue
St. Petersburg, FL 33171 (813) 893-1131
savings banking

Florida National Banks of Florida, Inc. FNBF
225 Water Street
Jacksonville, FL 32202 (904) 359-5020
banking DRP 5%

Florida Public Utilities Company FPUT
401 South Dixie Highway
West Palm Beach, FL 33402 (305) 832-2461
electric utility

Flow Systems, Inc. FLOW
21440 68th Avenue South
Kent, WA 98032 (206) 872-4900
waterjet and abrasivejet cutting systems

FlowMole Corporation MOLE
21409 72nd Avenue South
Kent, WA 98032 (206) 395-0200
installs underground cables and pipes

Fluorocarbon Company (The) FCBN
27611 La Paz Road
Laguna Niguel, CA 92656 (714) 831-5350
rubber components and sealing devices

F & M National Corporation FMNT
38 Rouss Avenue
Winchester, VA 22601 (703) 665-4200
banking

Fonar Corporation FONR
110 Marcus Drive
Melville, NY 11747 (516) 694-2929
magnetic resonance imaging devices

Food Lion, Inc. FDLNB
P.O. Box 1330
Salisbury, NC 28145 (704) 633-8250
supermarkets

Foremost Corporation of America FCOA
5800 Foremost Drive S.E., P.O. Box 2450
Grand Rapids, MI 49501 (616) 942-3000
mobile home and recreational vehicle
insurance

Forest Oil Corporation FOIL
78 Main Street
Bradford, PA 16701 (814) 368-7171
oil and gas exploration and development

Forschner Group, Inc. (The) FSNR
151 Long Hill Crossroads
Shelton, CT 06484 (203) 929-6391
knives

Fortune Financial Group, Inc. FORF
2120 U.S. Highway 19 South
Clearwater, FL 34624 (813) 538-1000
savings banking

Forum Group, Inc. FOUR
Suite 1200, 8900 Keystone Crossing
Indianapolis, IN 46240 (317) 846-0700
retirement living centers, nursing homes

Forum Re Group FRMBF
Emporium Building, Front Street
Hamilton 1254, HMFX Bermuda
(809) 295-4239
international reinsurance

Foster (L.B.) Company FSTRA
415 Holiday Drive
Pittsburgh, PA 15220 (412) 928-3400
pipe for energy industry, transportation
products

Fourth Financial Corporation FRTH
100 North Broadway, P.O. Box 4
Wichita, KS 67201 (316) 261-4444
banking DRP

Frances Denney Companies, Inc. DNNY
437 Madison Avenue
New York, NY 10022 (212) 230-0340
fragrances, cosmetics, skin-care treatments

Franklin Computer Corporation FDOS
122 Burrs Road
Mt. Holly, NJ 08060 (609) 261-4800
hand-held computer reference products

Franklin Electric Company, Inc. FELE
400 East Spring Street
Bluffton, IN 46714 (219) 824-2900
submersible electric motors, special motors

Franklin Savings Bank, FSB FSVB
26400 West Twelve Mile Road
Southfield, MI 48086 (313) 358-4710
savings banking

Fremont General Corporation FRMT
1633 26th Street
Santa Monica, CA 90404 (213) 315-5500
life insurance, financial services

Fretter, Inc. FTTR
35901 Schoolcraft Road
Livonia, MI 48150 (313) 591-0600
consumer electronics retailing

Freymiller Trucking, Inc. FRML
1400 South Union Avenue
Bakersfield, CA 93307 (805) 397-4151
trucking

Frontier Insurance Group, Inc. FRTR
217 Broadway
Monticello, NY 12701 (914) 794-8000
property-casualty insurance, reinsurance

FSI International, Inc.
322 Lake Hazeltine Drive
Chaska, MN 55138 (612) 448-5440
semiconductor equipment

Fuji Photo Film Company, Ltd. FUJIY
26-30 Nishiazabu 2-chome
Minato-ku, Tokyo 106, Japan
photographic films, floppy disks, tape

Fuller (H. B.) Company FULL
2400 Energy Park Drive
St. Paul, MN 55108 (612) 645-3401
adhesives, sealants, coatings, paint DRP

Fulton Federal S & L Assocaition FFSL
One Georgia Center,
600 West Peachtree Street N.W.
Atlanta, GA 30308 (404) 249-7000
savings and loan

Furnishings 2000, Inc. FURNC
11230 Sorrento Valley Road
San Diego, CA 92121 (619) 452-5560
home furnishings retailing

Galactic Resources, Ltd. GALCF
935-355 Burrard Street
Vancouver, BC V6C 2GB (604) 687-7169
gold mining

Galileo Electro-Optics Corporation GAEO
Galileo Park P.O. Box 550
Sturbridge, MA 01566 (508) 347-9191
fiber and electro-optic components,
multipliers

Gambro AB GAMBY
Magistratsvagen 16
S-220 10 Lund, Sweden (011) 46 169000
hemodialysis and hemofiltration products

Gamma Biologicals, Inc. GAMA
3700 Mangum Road
Houston, TX 77092 (713) 681-8481
in vitro diagnostic testing reagents

Gandalf Technologies Inc. GANDF
130 Colonnade Road South
Nepean, Ontario, CDA K2E 7J5
(613) 723-6500
data communications equipment, network systems

Gander Mountain, Inc. GNDR
Highway W, P.O. Box 128
Wilmot, WI 53192 (414) 862-2331
hunting, fishing, camping products retailing

Gantos, Inc. GTOS
3260 Patterson Avenue S.E.
Grand Rapids, MI 49508 (616) 949-7000
women's apparel specialty stores

Gateway Bank GTWY
50 Main Street
South Norwalk, CT 06856 (203) 853-2265
banking

Gateway Communications, Inc. GWAY
2941 Alton Avenue
Irvine, CA 92714 (714) 553-1555
local area networking communications products

Gencor Industries GCOR
2140 West Washington Street
Orlando, FL 32805 (305) 843-9880
highway construction capital goods

Gen-Probe, Inc. GPRO
9880 Campus Point Drive
San Diego, CA 92121 (619) 546-8000
genetic probe medical diagnostic products

General Binding Corporation GBND
One GBC Plaza
Northbrook, IL 60062 (312) 272-3700
office machines and supplies

General Building Products GBLD
2599 Route 112
Medford, NY 11763 (516) 645-3500
lumber and building products retailing

General Computer Corporation GCCC
2045 Midway Drive
Twinsburg, OH 44087 (216) 425-3241
computers for pharmacy industry

General Devices, Inc. GDIC
207 East Main Street
Norristown, PA 19404 (215) 272-4477
contract technical services

General Magnaplate Corporation GMCC
1331 U.S. Route One
Linden, NJ 07036 (201) 862-6200
corrosion and wear-resistant coatings

General Parametrics Corporation GPAR
1250 Ninth Street
Berkeley, CA 94710 (415) 524-3950
desktop presentation graphics products

Genessee Corporation GENBB
445 St. Paul Street
Rochester, NY 14605 (716) 546-1030
beer brewing

Genetics Institute GENI
87 Cambridge Park Drive
Cambridge, MA 02140 (617) 876-1170
biotechnology drug products

Genex Corporation GNEX
16020 Industrial Drive
Gaithersburg, MD 20877 (301) 258-0552
genetically engineered proteins

Genicom Corporation GECM
Genicom Drive
Waynesboro, VA 22980 (703) 949-1000
computer printers, hermetically sealed relays

Genlyte Group, Inc. GLYT
100 Lighting Way
Secaucus, NJ 07094 (201) 864-3000
indoor and outdoor lighting fixtures

Gentex Corporation GNTX
10985 Chicago Drive
Zeeland, MI 49464 (616) 392-7195
automatic rearview mirrors, fire protection

Geodynamics Corporation GDYN
5520 Ekwill Street
Santa Barbara, CA 93111 (805) 964-9905
engineering and custom applications software

Geodyne Resources, Inc. GEOD
320 South Boston Avenue
Tulsa, OK 74103 (918) 583-5525
oil and gas exploration

Genzyme Corporation GENZ
75 Kneeland Street
Boston, MA 02111 (617) 451-1923
health care biological products

Georgia Bonded Fibers, Inc. GBFH
15 Nuttman Street
Newark, NJ 07103 (201) 642-3547
elstomeric fiber, cushion insole materials

Geotel, Inc. GETE
25 Davids Drive
Hauppauge, NY 11788 (516) 436-7230
instrumentation

Geraghty & Miller, Inc. GMGW
125 East Bethpage Road
Plainview, NY 11803 (516) 249-7600
ground-water development and protection

Geriatric & Medical Centers, Inc. GEMC
5601 Chesnut Street
Philadelphia, PA 19139 (215) 476-2250
nursing care facilities, ambulance services

Germania Bank, FSB GMFD
701 Market, Gateway One on the Mall
St. Louis, IL 63101 (314) 241-8856
savings banking

Gibson Greetings, Inc. GIBG
2100 Section Road
Cincinnati, OH 45237 (513) 841-6600
greeting cards, gift wrap

Giga-tronics Inc. GIGA
2495 Estand Way
Pleasant Hill, CA 94523 (415) 680-8160
defense electronics

Gilbert Associates, Inc. GILBA
P.O. Box 1498
Reading, PA 19603 (215) 775-5900
power station engineering services

Gish Biomedical, Inc. GISH
2350 Pullman Avenue
Santa Ana, CA 92705 (714) 261-1330
disposable cardiovascular medical products

G&K Services, Inc. GKSR
400 South County Road 18
Minneapolis, MN 55426 (612) 546-7440
rents and launders textile products

Glenex Industries, Inc. GLXIF
185 Davenport Road
Toronto, Ontario, CDA M5R 1J1
(416) 962-9292
entertainment, oil and gas, specialty
chemicals

GMI Group, Inc. GMED
373 Route 46 West
Fairfield, NJ 07006 (201) 227-5000
marketing communications, publishing

GNI Group, Inc. GNUC
Suite 4656, 1001 Fannin
Houston, TX 77002 (713) 759-0350
environmental services, waste treatment

Gold Company of America GCAPZ
1 Seaport Plaza
New York, NY 10292 (212) 214-1000
acquires gold for limited partners

Golden Corral Realty Corporation GCRA
5151 Glenwood Avenue
Raleigh, NC 27612 (919) 781-5310
real estate investment trust

Golden Cycle Gold Corporation GCGC
228 North Cascade Avenue
Colorado Springs, CO 80903 (719) 471-9013
gold mining

Golden Enterprises, Inc. GLDC
2101 Magnolia Avenue
Birmingham, AL 35205 (205) 326-6101
snack foods, steel bolts and fasteners

Golden Poultry Company CHIK
244 Perimeter Center Parkway N.E.
Atlanta, GA 30346 (404) 393-5000
processes and distributes poultry products

Golden Triangle Royalty & Oil, Inc. GTRO
Kamon House, 1304 Avenue L
Cisco, TX 76437 (817) 442-2665
oil and gas royalty interests

Goldex Mines, Ltd. GLX
401 Bay Street
Toronto, Ontario, CDA M5H 2Y4
(416) 947-1212
gold mining

Good Guys, Inc. GGUY
601 Van Ness Avenue
San Francisco, CA 94102 (415) 885-2121
consumer electronics stores

GoodMark Foods, Inc. GDMK
6131 Falls of Neuse Road
Raleigh, NC 27609 (919) 790-9940
meat snack products

Goody Products, Inc. GOOD
969 Newark Turnpike
Kearny, NJ 07032 (201) 997-3000
hair care accessory products, cosmetics

Goulds Pumps, Inc. GULD
240 Fall Street
Seneca Falls, NY 13148 (315) 568-2811
centifugal liquid handling pumps DRP

Gradco Systems, Inc. GRCO
7 Morgan
Irvine, CA 92718 (714) 770-1223
paper-handling equipment for copiers

Graphic Industries, Inc. GRPH
2155 Monroe Drive, N.E.
Atlanta, GA 30324 (404) 874-3327
financial, commercial printing

Graphic Scanning Corporation GSCC
25 Rockwood Place
Englewood, NJ 07631 (201) 894-8000
radio paging, data communications

Great American Management & Investment
GAMI
2 North Riverside Plaza
Chicago, IL 60606 (312) 648-5656
financial services, industrial products,
chemicals

Great American Communications GACC
1 East 4th Street
Cincinnati, OH 45202 (513) 579-2177
radio and TV broadcasting and production

Great Eastern Energy & Development GREN
5990 Greenwood Plaza Boulevard
Englewood, CO 80111 (303) 773-6016
oil and gas production

Great Falls Gas Company GFGC
1 River Park Tower
Great Falls, MT 59403 (406) 761-7100
gas utility

Great Lakes Bancorp, FSB GLBC
401 East Liberty Street
Ann Arbor, MI 48107 (313) 769-8300
savings banking

Great Pacific Industries, Inc. GPI
1600-1055 West Hastings Street
Vancouver, BC CDA V6E 2H2 (604) 688-6764
international finance

Greater New York Savings Bank GRTR
1 Penn Plaza
New York, NY 10119 (212) 613-4000
savings banking

Green A.P. Industries, Inc. APGI
Green Boulevard
Mexico, MO 65265 (314) 473-3626
heat-resistant refractory products

Greenery Rehabilitation Group GRGI
215 First Street
Cambridge, MA 02142 (617) 824-7200
rehabilitation and nursing facilities

Greenwich Pharmaceuticals, Inc. GRPI
501 Office Center Drive
Ft. Washington, PA 19034 (215) 540-9500
drugs for inflammatory diseases

Grenada Sunburst System Corporation GSSC
2000 Gateway
Grenada, MS 38901 (601) 226-1100
banking

Grey Advertising, Inc. GREY
777 Third Avenue
New York, NY 10017 (212) 546-2000
advertising

Griffin Technology Inc. GRIF
6132 Victor-Manchester Road
Victor, NY 14564 (716) 924-7121
business data processing

Grist Mill Company GRST
21340 Hayes Avenue
Lakeville, MN 55044 (612) 469-4981
cereal, snack, confectionary products

Grossman's, Inc. GROS
200 Union Street
Braintree, MA 02184 (617) 848-0100
lumber, building products retailing

Grubb & Ellis Realty Income Trust GRIT
One Montgomery Street
San Francisco, CA 94104 (415) 781-4748
real estate investment trust

GTECH Corporation GTCH
101 Dyer Street
Providence, RI 02903 (401) 273-7700
lottery computer systems

GTS Corporation GTSC
Suite 151, 16801 Greenspoint Park Drive
Houston, TX 77060 (713) 874-9300
data processing for oil & gas industry

Guest Supply, Inc. GEST
720 U.S. Highway One
North Brunswick, NJ 08902 (201) 246-3011
personal care items for hotel guests

Gulf Applied Technologies, Inc. GATS
1233 West Loop South
Houston, TX 08902 (201) 246-3011
pipeline engineering, environmental
consulting

GWC Corporation GWCC
3219 Philadelphia Pike
Claymont, DE 19703 (302) 798-3883
water utility

Haber, Inc. HABE
470 Main Road
Towaco, NJ 07082 (201) 263-0990
develops advanced chemical technologies

Hadco Corporation HDCO
10 Manor Parkway
Salem, NH 03079 (603) 898-8000
printed circuits, electronics

Hadron, Inc. HDRN
9990 Lee Highway
Fairfax, VA 22030 (703) 359-6201
engineering and computer consulting

Hako Minuteman, Inc. HAKO
111 South Route 53
Addison, IL 60101 (312) 627-6900
commercial and industrial cleaning products

Hall Financial Group, Inc. HALL
10100 North Central Expressway
Dallas, TX 75231 (214) 750-7646
real estate financial services

Hamilton Oil Corporation HAML
1560 Broadway
Denver, CO 80202 (303) 863-3000
oil and gas exploration and production

Hammond Company (The) THCO
4910 Campus Drive
Newport Beach, CA 92660 (714) 752-6671
mortgage banking, insurance, savings and
loan

Hana Biologics, Inc. HANA
850 Marina Village Parkway
Alameda, CA 94501 (415) 748-3000
transplants cells to replace damaged cells

Hanover Insurance Co. (The) HINS
100 North Parkway
Worcester, MA 01605 (508) 853-7200
property-casulaty insurance

HarCor Energy, Inc. HARC
Suite 570, 9401 Wilshire Boulevard
Beverly Hills, CA 90212 (213) 859-8284
oil and gas exploration and production

Harding Associates, Inc. HRDG
7655 Redwood Boulevard
Novato, CA 94945 (415) 892-0821
environmental engineering services

Harken Oil & Gas, Inc. HOGI
4001 Airport Freeway
Bedford, TX 76021 (817) 267-1777
markets petroleum products

Harleysville Group, Inc. HGIC
355 Maple Avenue
Harleysville, PA 19438 (215) 256-5000
property-casualty insurance

Harlyn Products, Inc. HRLN
1515 South Main Street
Los Angeles, CA 90015 (213) 746-0745
gold and silver jewelry

Harmon Industries, Inc. HRMN
P.O. Box 1570
Blue Springs, MO 64015 (816) 229-3345
railroad signal and communications
equipment

Harper Group (The) HARG
260 Townsend Street
San Francisco, CA 94107 (415) 978-0600
freight forwarding

Harris & Harris Group, Inc. HHGP
620 Fifth Avenue
New York, NY 10020 (212) 307-4380
insurance brokerage and consulting

Hartford National Corporation HNAT
777 Main Street
Hartford, CT 06115 (203) 728-2000
banking DRP 5%

Hartford Steam Boiler Inspection & Insurance
Co. HBOL
One State Street
Hartford, CT 06102 (203) 722-1866
property-casualty insurance for boilers DRP

Hathaway Corporation HATH
Suite 200, 350 Interlocken Parkway
Broomfield, CO 80020 (303) 460-1500
electronic measuring and recording
equipment

Hauserman, Inc. HASR
5711 Grant Avenue
Cleveland, OH 44105 (216) 883-1400
office furniture, walls, storage

Haverty Furniture Companies, Inc. HAVT
866 West Peachtree Street N.W.
Atlanta, GA 30308 (404) 881-1911
furniture stores

Hawkeye Bancorporation HWKB
600 First Building, 319 7th Street
Des Moines, IA 50307 (515) 284-1930
banking

HBO & Company HBOC
301 Perimeter Center North
Atlanta, GA 30346 (404) 393-6000
hospital computer information systems

HCC Industries HCCI
16311 Ventura Boulevard
Encino, CA 91436 (213) 995-4131
hermetic seals, electronic connectors

Healthcare Services Group, Inc. HCSG
2643 Huntingdon Pike
Huntingdon Valley, PA 19006 (215) 938-1661
housekeeping, laundry services for nursing
homes

Healthco International, Inc. HLCO
25 Stuart Street
Boston, MA 02116 (617) 423-6045
dental profession products and services

Healthdyne, Inc. HDYN
1850 Parkway Place
Marietta, GA 30067 (404) 423-4500
home health care products and services

Health Images, Inc. HIMG
8601 Dunwoody Place
Atlanta, GA 30350 (404) 587-5084
magnetic resonance imaging diagnostic
services

HEALTHSOUTH Rehabilitation Corporation
HSRC
Two Perimeter Park South
Birmingham, AL 35243 (205) 967-7116
medical rehabilitation services and equipment

Heart Federal Savings and Loan Association
HFED
649 Lincoln Way
Auburn, CA 95603 (916) 823-7283
savings and loan

Hechinger Company HECHB
3500 Pennsy Drive
Landover, MD 20785 (301) 341-1000
do-it-yourself home centers

Heekin Can, Inc. HEKN
11310 Cornell Park Drive
Cincinnati, OH 45242 (513) 489-3200
steel food cans, aluminum beverage cans

HEI Corporation HEIC
Suite 112, 7676 Woodway
Houston, TX 77063 (713) 780-7802
operates acute-care hospitals

Heist (C.H.) Corporation CHHC
810 North Belcher Road
Clearwater, FL 33575 (813) 461-5656
special construction

Helen of Troy Corporation HELE
6827 Market Street
El Paso, TX 79915 (915) 779-6363
hair care appliances, beauty supply

Helix Technology Corporation HELX
Kelvin Park, 204 Second Avenue
Waltham, MA 02254 (617) 890-9292
cryogenic (low temperature) technology

Hemodynamics, Inc. HMDY
6000 Park of Commerce Boulevard
Boca Raton, FL 33487 (407) 994-4700
devices to detect blood-flow abnormalities

HemoTec, Inc. HEMO
7103 South Revere Parkway
Englewood, CO 80112 (303) 790-7900
blood clotting medical instruments

Henley Group, Inc. HENG
11255 North Torrey Pines Road
La Jolla, CA 92037 (619) 455-9494
lab and medical equipment, real estate

Henry, Jack and Associates, Inc. JKHY
P.O. Box 807
Monett, MO 65708 (417) 235-6652
data processing for banks

Heritage Financial Services, Inc. HERS
12015 South Western Avenue
Blue Island, IL 60406 (312) 385-2900
banking

Herley Microwave Systems, Inc. HRLY
10 Industry Drive
Lancaster, PA 17603 (717) 397-2777
defense electronics

H & H Oil Tool Company, Inc. HHOT
201 South Hallock Drive
Santa Paula, CA 93060 (805) 647-5595
oil and gas drilling equipment

Hibernia Corporation HIBC
313 Carondelet Street
New Orleans, LA 70161 (504) 586-5332
banking DRP 5%

Hibernia Savings Bank HSBK
263 Washington Street
Boston, MA 02108 (617) 227-9031
savings banking

Hickam (Dow B.), Inc. DBHI
10410 Corporate Drive, P.O. Box 2006
Sugar Land, TX 77478 (713) 240-1000
drugs, dietary fibers

High Plains Corporation HIPC
333 North Waco
Wichita, KS 67201 (316) 269-4310
makes ethanol as a gasoline additive

Highland Superstores, Inc. HIGH
21405 Trolley Drive
Taylor, MI 48180 (313) 291-7800
consumer electronics retailing

Hi-Port Industries, Inc. HIPT
Suite 560, 11811-10 East Freeway
Houston, TX 77029 (713) 455-0007
contract packaging service, lubricants

HITK Corporation HITK
3835 Green Leaf Drive
Las Vegas, NV 89120 (702) 435-3307
venture capital investments

HMO America, Inc. HMOA
540 North LaSalle Street
Chicago, IL 60610 (312) 751-7500
health maintenance organization

H.M.S.S., Inc. HMSS
12450 Greenspoint Drive
Houston, TX 77060 (713) 873-4677
home infusion therapies

Hogan Systems, Inc. HOGN
5080 Spectrum Drive
Dallas, TX 75248 (214) 386-0020
banking software

Hollywood Park Realty Enterprises HTRFZ
P.O. Box 50332
Pasadena, CA 91105 (213) 627-8145
horse track real estate investment trust

Home Beneficial Corporation HBENB
3901 West Broad Street
Richmond, VA 23261 (804) 358-8431
life, health, accident insurance

Home Federal Savings Bank of Georgia HFGA
Washington & Green Streets
Gainesville, GA 30503 (404) 535-0950
savings and loan

Home Federal S & L Association of Upper
East Tenn. HFET
2112 North Roan Street
Johnson City, TN 37601 (615) 282-6311
savings and loan

Home Intensive Care, Inc. KDNY
16401 N.W. Second Avenue
North Miami Beach, FL 33169
(305) 944-8887
home hemodialysis services

Home Office Reference Laboratory, Inc.
HORL
10310 West 84th Terrace
Lenexa, KS 66214 (913) 888-1770
laboratory testing services for insurance
industry

Home Savings Bank HMSB
315 Wyckoff Avenue
Brooklyn, NY 11237 (718) 417-2440
savings banking

Home Unity S & L Association HUSB
618 Germantown Pike
Lafayette Hill, PA 19444 (215) 825-8900
savings and loan

HON Industries, Inc. HONI
414 East Third Street
Muscatine, IA 52761 (319) 264-7400
office furniture, fireplaces, stoves

Horizon Industries, Inc. HRZN
South Industrial Boulevard
Calhoun, GA 30701 (404) 629-7721
carpet manufacturer

Howard Bancorp HOBC
111 Main Street
Burlington, VT 05401 (802) 658-1010
banking

Howard Savings Bank (The) HWRD
200 South Orange Avenue
Livingston, NJ 07039 (201) 533-7400
savings banking

HPSC, Inc. HPSC
25 Stuart Street
Boston, MA 02116 (617) 423-6043
dental equipment

Hudson's Bay Company HBC
401 Bay Street
Toronto, Ontario, CDA M5H 2Y4
(416) 861-4894
department stores, merchandising, real estate
DRP

Huffman Koos, Inc. HUFK
Route 4 and Main Street
River Edge, NJ 07661 (201) 343-4300
furniture and accessories retailing

Humphrey, Inc. HUPH
9212 Balboa Avenue
San Diego, CA 92123 (619) 565-6631
control and measuring precision instruments

Hunt (J.B.) Transport Services, Inc. JBHT
Highway 71 North
Lowell, AR 72745 (501) 659-8800
trucking

Huntington Bancshares, Inc. HBAN
41 South High Street
Columbus, OH 43287 (614) 476-8300
banking DRP 5%

Hurco Companies, Inc. HURC
6460 Saguaro Court
Indianapolis, IN 46268 (317) 293-5309
metalworking machines, numerical controls

Hutchinson Technology, Inc. HTCH
40 West Highland Park
Hutchinson, MN 55350 (612) 587-3797
disk drives, computer peripherals

HWC Distribution HWCD
7413 Mesa Drive
Houston, TX 77028 (713) 635-4600
wire and cable distributors

Hycor Biomedical, Inc. HYBD
7272 Chapman Avenue
Garden Grove, CA 92641 (714) 895-9558
medical diagnostic products for urinalysis

Hydro Flame Corporation HFLM
1874 South Pioneer Road
Salt Lake City, UT 84104 (801) 972-4621
wood burning stove, furnace manufacturer

Hytek Microsystems, Inc. HTEK
980 University Avenue
Los Gatos, CA 95030 (408) 395-2300
hybrid electronic circuits

ICOT Corporation ICOT
3801 Zanker Road
San Jose, CA 95150 (408) 433-3300
data communications equipment

IDB Bankholding Corporation, Ltd. IDBBY
511 Fifth Avenue
New York, NY 10017 (212) 551-8500
banking

IDB Communications Group, Inc. IDBX
10525 West Washington Boulevard
Culver City, CA 90232 (213) 870-9000
satellite transmission services

IEH Corporation IEHC
109 Prince Street
New York, NY 10012 (212) 677-1881
aerospace electronics, interconnection
devices

IFR Systems, Inc. IFRS
10200 West York Street
Wichita, KS 67215 (316) 522-4981
electronic test equipment

I.I.S. Intelligent Information Systems Ltd.
IISL
Technion City, P.O. Box 1640
Haifa 31015, Israel (004) 293-0200
computer peripherals

ILC Technology, Inc. ILCT
399 Java Drive
Sunnyvale, CA 94089 (408) 745-7900
light sensing products

Imatron Inc. IMAT
389 Oyster Point Boulevard
South San Francisco, CA 94080
(415) 583-9964
computed tomography scanners
manufacturer

Immunex Corporation IMNX
51 University Street
Seattle, WA 98101 (206) 587-0430
immunological therapeutic products

Immunomedics IMMU
150 Mount Bethel Road
Warren, NJ 07060 (201) 647-5400
cancer detection biotechnology

Impact Systems, Inc. MPAC
1075 East Brodaw Road
San Jose, CA 95131 (408) 293-7000
paper-making control systems

Imperial Bancorp IBAN
9920 South La Cienega Boulevard
Inglewood, CA 90301 (213) 417-5600
banking

Imperial Holly Corporation IHKS
Suite 200, 1 Imperial Square
Sugar Land, TX 77487 (713) 491-9181
sugar refining and marketing

IMRE Corporation IMRE
130 Fifth Avenue North
Seattle, WA 98109 (206) 448-1000
cancer treatment products

Imreg, Inc. IMRGA
Suite 1400, 144 Elk Place
New Orleans, LA 70112 (504) 523-2875
immune systems diagnosis and treatment

Inacomp Computer Centers, Inc. INAC
1824 West Maple Road
Troy, MI 48084 (313) 649-5580
computer retailing

INB Financial Corporation INBF
1 Indiana Square
Indianapolis, IN 46266 (317) 266-6000
banking DRP

Incomnet, Inc. ICNT
31225 LaBaya Drive
Westlake Village, CA 91362 (818) 707-4141
data communications network hardware and
software

Independence Bancorp, Inc. INBC
1 Hillendale Road
Perkasie, PA 18944 (215) 257-2402
banking DRP

Independent Bank Corporation IBCP
230 West Main Street
Ionia, MI 48846 (616) 527-9450
banking

Independent Insurance Group, Inc. INDHK
1 Independent Drive
Jacksonville, FL 32276 (904) 358-5151
life, accident, health, property insurance

Index Technology Corporation INDX
1 Main Street
Cambridge, MA 02142 (617) 494-8200
computer-aided software engineering
products

Indiana Financial Investors, Inc. IFII
151 North Delaware Street
Indianapolis, IN 46204 (317) 637-3000
real estate investment company

Industrial Acoustics Company, Inc. IACI
1160 Commerce Avenue
Bronx, NY 10462 (212) 931-8000
noise control building products

Industrial Resources, Inc. INDR
111 West Monroe Street
Chicago, IL 60603 (312) 346-9126
coal, sodium, limestone holdings

Infodata System, Inc. INFD
5 Tobey Village Office Park
Pittsford, NY 14534 (716) 381-7430
database management software

Information International, Inc. IINT
5933 Slauson Avenue
Culver City, CA 90230 (213) 390-8611
computerized prepress publishing systems

Information Resources, Inc. IRIC
150 North Clinton Street
Chicago, IL 60606 (312) 726-1221
computer-based marketing research services

Information Science Inc. INSI
95 Chestnut Ridge Road
Montvale, NJ 07645 (201) 391-1600
business services

Informix Corporation IFMX
4100 Bohannon Drive
Menlo Park, CA 94025 (415) 322-4100
relational database management software

Infotechnology, Inc. ITCH
320 Park Avenue
New York, NY 10022 (212) 891-7500
venture capital investments, broadcasting

Infotron Systems Corporation INFN
9 North Olney Avenue,
Cherry Hill Industrial Center
Cherry Hill, NJ 08003 (609) 424-9400
data and voice communications systems

Ingles Markets, Inc. IMKTA
Highway 70, P.O. Box 6676
Asheville, NC 28816 (704) 669-2941
supermarkets

Inmac Corporation INMC
2465 Augustine Drive
Santa Clara, CA 95054 (408) 727-1970
direct-response marketing of computer
products

InnoVet, Inc. IVET
Suite 110, 3401 North Federal Highway
Boca Raton, FL 33431 (407) 394-0621
animal healthcare products

Innovex, Inc. INVX
1313 Fifth Street South
Hopkins, MN 55343 (612) 938-4155
professional photo-processing printers

Insituform East, Inc. INEI
3421 Pennsy Drive
Landover, MD 20785 (301) 386-4100
repairs underground sewers and pipes

Insituform Group, Ltd. IGLSF
Borough House, Trinity Square
Guernsey, Channel Isl. (444) 812-3806
repairs underground sewers and pipes

Insituform Mid-America, Inc. INSMA
17988 Edison Avenue, P.O. Box 1026
Chesterfield, MO 63017 (314) 532-6137
repairs underground sewers and pipes

Insituform of North America, Inc. INSUA
3315 Democrat Road
Memphis, TN 38118 (901) 363-2105
repairs underground sewers and pipes

Insituform Southeast Corporation ISEC
11511 Phillips Highway South
Jacksonville, FL 32256 (904) 262-5802
repairs underground sewers and pipes

InSpeech, Inc. INSP
2570 Boulevard of Generals
Norristown, PA 19403 (215) 631-9300
rehabilitative speech therapy services

Instrumentarium Corporation INMRY
P.O. Box 357 SF-00101
Helsinki, Finland (358) 0-735-172
hospital equipment and supplies

Intech, Inc. INTE
282 Brokaw Road
Santa Clara, CA 95050 (408) 727-0500
assembled electronic circuits

Integon Corporation ITGN
500 West 5th Street
Winston-Salem, NC 27152 (919) 770-2000
life and property-casualty insurance

Integra Financial Corporation ITGR
Pennbank Center
Titusville, PA 16354 (814) 827-2751
banking DRP

Integrated Device Technology, Inc. IDTI
3236 Scott Boulevard
Santa Clara, CA 95051 (408) 727-6116
integrated circuit design and manufacture

Integrated Genetics, Inc. INGN
31 New York Avenue
Framingham, MA 01701 (617) 875-1336
diagnostic and therapeutic biotechnology
products

INTEK Diversified Corporation IDCC
5800 West Jefferson Boulevard
Los Angeles, CA 90016 (213) 870-7665
aerospace injected molded products

Intel Corporation INTC
3065 Bowers Avenue
Santa Clara, CA 95051 (408) 987-8080
semiconductor components, computers O

Intellicall, Inc. INCL
Suite 410, 2155 Cheanault
Carrolton, TX 75006 (214) 416-0022
markets pay telephone to independent
vendors

IntelliCorp, Inc. INAI
1975 El Camino Real West
Mountain View, CA 94040 (415) 965-5500
artificial intelligence software

Intelligent Electronics INEL
35 East Uwchlan Avenue
Exton, PA 19341 (215) 524-1800
markets microcomputer systems

Intelligent Systems Corporation INTS
4355 Shackelford Road
Norcross, GA 30093 (404) 441-0611
computers and accessories

Interactive Technologies, Inc. ITXI
2266 North 2nd Street
North St. Paul, MN 55109 (612) 777-2690
wireless security and monitoring systems

InterContinental Life Corporation ILCO
8310 Capital of Texas Highway
Austin, TX 78731 (512) 338-1100
life, accident and health insurance

Interface, Inc. IFSIA
Orchard Hill Road
LaGrange, GA 30241 (404) 882-1891
free-lay carpet tiles

Interface Systems, Inc. INTF
5855 Interface Drive
Ann Arbor, MI 48103 (313) 769-5900
computer printers and interfaces

Interferon Sciences, Inc. IFSC
783 Jersey Avenue
New Brunswick, NJ 08901 (201) 249-3250
interferon biopharmaceuticals

Intergraph Corporation INGR
One Madison Industrial Park
Huntsville, AL 35807 (205) 772-2000
computer-aided design systems O

Interhome Energy, Inc. IHEIF
324 Eighth Avenue S.W.
Calgary, AB, CDA T2P 2Z5 (403) 232-5500
oil pipeline, natural gas processing

Interim Systems Corporation INSY
4 Brighton Road
Clifton, NJ 07015 (201) 777-6500
temporary personnel and healthcare services

Interleaf, Inc. LEAF
10 Canal Park
Cambridge, MA 02141 (617) 577-9800
electronic publishing systems and software

Intermagnetics General Corporation INMA
Charles Industrial Park, New Karner Road
Guilderland, NY 12084 (518) 456-5456
magnetic resonance imaging diagnostic
equipment

INTERMEC Corporation INTR
4405 Russell Road
Lynnwood, WA 98046 (206) 348-2600
bar-code printers and readers

Intermet Corporation INMT
Suite 1600, 2859 Paces Ferry Road
Atlanta, GA 30339 (404) 431-6000
iron foundry, castings

Intermetrics, Inc. IMET
733 Concord Avenue
Cambridge, MA 02138 (617) 661-1840
systems engineering software

International American Homes, Inc. HOME
1620 Route 22
Union, NJ 07083 (201) 851-2320
homebuilder

International Broadcasting Corporation IBCA
5101 IDS Center
Minneapolis, MN 55402 (612) 333-5100
manages Harlem Globetrotters, Ice Capades

International Capital Equipment Ltd. ICEY
1840 Palmer Avenue
Larchmont, NY 10538 (914) 834-5011
equipment leasing

International Container Systems, Inc. ICSI
5401 West Kennedy Boulevard
Tampa, FL 33609 (813) 287-8940
plastic soft-drink bottle cases

International Dairy Queen INDQA
5701 Green Valley Drive
Minneapolis, MN 55437 (612) 830-0200
soft serve dairy products, beverages

International Game Technology IGAM
520 South Rock Boulevard
Reno, NV 89502 (702) 323-5060
gaming products, gaming monitoring
systems

International Genetic Engineering, Inc. IGEI
1545 17th Street
Santa Monica, CA 90404 (213) 829-7681
specialty chemical, drug, food industry
research

International Holding Capital Corporation ISLH
841 Bishop Street
Honolulu, HI 96813 (808) 547-5110
savings and loan

International Lease Finance Corporation ILFC
8484 Wilshire Boulevard
Beverly Hills, CA 90211 (213) 658-7871
aircraft leasing

International Microelectronic Products IMPX
2830 North First Street
San Jose, CA 95134 (408) 432-9100
application-specific integrated circuits

International Mobile Machines Corporation
IMMC
100 North 20th Street
Philadelphia, PA 19103 (215) 665-7800
digital radio telephone system

International Research and Development
Corporation IRDV
500 North Main Street
Mattawan, MI 49071 (616) 668-3336
pre-clinical safety evaluation of drugs,
chemicals

International Shipholding Corporation INSH
650 Poydras Street
New Orleans, LA 70130 (504) 529-5461
shipping services

International Totalizator Systems, Inc. ITSI
2131 Faraday Avenue
Carlsbad, CA 92008 (619) 931-4000
computerized lottery and pari-mutuel wagering
systems

InterPharm Laboratories, Ltd. IPLLF
Science-Based Industrial Park
Kiryat Weizmann, Ness-Ziona 76110 Israel
healthcare biotechnology products, growth
hormone

Interphase Corporation INPH
2925 Merrell Road
Dallas, TX 75229 (214) 350-9000
peripheral controller products

Interpoint Corporation INTP
10301 Willows Road
Redmond, WA 98073 (206) 882-3100
hybrid microcircuit products

Interspec, Inc. ISPC
1100 East Hector Street
Conshohocken, PA 19428 (215) 834-1511
medical ultrasound systems and supplies

Inter-Tel, Inc. INTLA
6505 West Chandler Boulevard
Chandler, AZ 85226 (602) 961-9000
digital key and hybrid electronic telephones

Intertrans Corporation ITRN
8505 Freeport Parkway
Irving, TX 75063 (214) 929-8888
air freight forwarding and shipping

Invacare Corporation IVCR
899 Cleveland Street
Elyria, OH 44036 (216) 329-6000
wheelchairs, hospital beds, health equipment

Invention, Design, Engineering Associates,
Inc. IDEA
500 Alaska Avenue
Torrance, CA 90503 (213) 320-9462
automation equipment to test and assemble
electronics

Investment Technologies, Inc. IVES
Metropark, 510 Thornall Street
Edison, NJ 08837 (201) 494-1200
computerized system for asset allocation
model

Investors Financial Corporation INVF
9201 Forest Hill Avenue
Richmond, VA 23235 (804) 323-4500
banking

Investors S & L Association ISLA
5008 Monument Avenue
Richmond, VA 23230 (804) 254-1300
savings and loan

Invitron Corporation INVN
4649 Le Bourget Drive
St. Louis, MO 63134 (314) 426-5000
mammalian cell culture systems for
biotechnology

Iomega Corporation IOMG
1821 West 4000 South
Roy, UT 84067 (801) 778-1000
computer disk drives

Iowa Southern, Inc. IUTL
300 Sheridan Avenue
Centerville, IA 52544 (515) 437-4400
electric and gas utility

IPL Systems, Inc. IPLS
360 Second Avenue
Waltham, MA 02154 (617) 890-6620
computer mainframes and subsystems

Isco, Inc. ISKO
4700 Superior Street
Lincoln, NE 68504 (402) 464-0231
chemical, scientific research instruments

Isomedix, Inc. ISMX
11 Apollo Drive
Whippany, NJ 07981 (201) 887-4700
irradiation services, sterilize medical devices

Isomet Corporation IOMT
5263 Port Royal Road
Springfield, VA 22151 (703) 321-8301
laser equipment and accessories

Itel Corporation ITEL
Suite 1950, 2 North Riverside Plaza
Chicago, IL 60606 (312) 902-1515
container and railcar leasing, cable distributor
0

Ito-Yokado Company, Ltd. IYCOY
1-4, Shibakoen 4-chome
Minato-ku, Tokyo 105, Japan (03) 459-2111
clothing, food, household goods retailing

IWC Resources Corporation IWCR
1220 Waterway Boulevard
Indianapolis, IN 46202 (317) 639-1501
water utility

Jack Carl/312-Futures FUTR
222 West Adams Street
Chicago, IL 60606 (312) 407-5700
futures brokerage and clearing services

Jacobson Stores, Inc. JCBS
3333 Sargeant Road
Jackson, MI 49201 (517) 764-6400
women's apparel stores, home furnishings

Jaco Electronics, Inc. JACO
145 Oser Avenue
Hauppauge, NY 11788 (516) 273-5500
semiconductor and electronics distributor

Jacor Communications, Inc. JCOR
1300 Central Trust Center
Cincinnati, OH 45202 (513) 621-1300
operates radio stations

Jaguar plc JAGRY
Browns Lane, Allesley,
Coventry CV5 9DR, UK (0203) 402121
luxury automobile manufacturer

Jay Jacobs, Inc. JAYJ
1530 5th Avenue
Seattle, WA 98101 (206) 622-5400
fashion apparel specialty retailing

JB's Restaurants, Inc. JBBB
1010 West 2610 South
Salt Lake City, UT 84119 (801) 974-4300
restaurants

Jefferies Group, Inc. JEFG
445 South Figueroa Street
Los Angeles, CA 90071 (213) 624-3333
equity securities transactions, brokerage

Jefferson Bankshares, Inc. JBNK
123 East Main Street
Charlottesville, VA 22901 (804) 972-1100
banking DRP

Jefferson Smurfit Corporation JJSC
401 Alton Street
Alton, IL 62002 (618) 463-6000
paperboard and packaging, newsprint

Jennifer Convertibles, Inc. JENN
331 Route 4 West
Paramus, NJ 07652 (201) 343-1610
sofabed retailing

Jerrico, Inc. JERR
101 Jerrico Drive
Lexington, KY 40579 (606) 263-6000
fish restaurants, coffee shops O

Jesup Group JGRP
100 First Stamford Place
Stamford, CT 06902 (203) 324-9862
plastic and polymer type products

Jiffy Lube International, Inc. JLUB
6000 Metro Drive
Baltimore, MD 21215 (301) 764-3555
fast automotive lubrication service centers

J&J Snack Foods Corporation JJSF
6000 Central Highway
Pennsauken, NJ 08109 (609) 665-9533
snack foods, baked goods

JLG Industries, Inc. JLGI
JLG Drive
McConnellsburg, PA 17233 (717) 485-5161
work platforms, hydraulic cranes

JMB Realty Trust JMBRS
875 North Michigan Avenue
Chicago, IL 60611 (312) 440-4800
real estate investment trust

John Adams Life Corporation JALC
11845 West Olympic Boulevard
Los Angeles, CA 90064 (213) 444-5252
life insurance

Johnson Electronics, Inc. JHSN
4301 Metric Drive
Winter Park, FL 32792 (305) 677-4030
transmission and reception of broadcast
signals

Johnson Worldwide Associates JWAIA
4041 North Main Street
Racine, WI 53402 (414) 631-2100
fishing, camping, diving products
manufacturer

Jones Intercable, Inc. JOIN
5275 DTC Pkwy.
Englewood, CO 80111 (303) 740-9700
operates cable TV systems

Jones Medical Industries, Inc. JMED
11710 Lackland Industrial Drive
St. Louis, MO 63146 (314) 432-7557
drugs and food supplements

Joslyn Corporation JOSL
30 South Wacker Drive
Chicago, IL 60606 (312) 454-2900
electrical transmission equipment DRP

Judy's Inc. JUDY
7710 Haskell Avenue
Van Nuys, CA 91406 (213) 873-6200
apparel stores

Juno Lighting, Inc. JUNO
2001 South Mount Prospect Road
Des Plaines, IL 60017 (312) 827-9880
recessed and track lighting fixtures

Justin Industries, Inc. JSTN
2821 West 7th Street
Fort Worth, TX 76107 (817) 336-5125
face brick, footwear, cooling towers DRP

Kahler Corporation KHLR
20 S.W. 2nd Avenue
Rochester, MN 55902 (507) 282-2581
hotel and resort operations, formal wear
rental

Kaman Corporation KAMNA
1332 Blue Hills Avenue
Bloomfield, CT 06002 (203) 243-8311
aerospace and industrial products, music
DRP

Kamenstein, (M) Inc. MKCO
190 East Post Road
White Plains, NY 10601 (914) 946-2290
wood household products for food, storage

Kasler Corporation KASL
27400 East Fifth Street
Highland, CA 92346 (714) 884-4811
roadway, bridge, public works construction

Kaydon Corporation KDON
2860 McCracken Street
Muskegon, MI 49443 (616) 755-3741
anti-friction bearings, filters, rings

Kaypro Corporation KPRO
533 Stevens Avenue
Solana Beach, CA 92075 (619) 481-4300
portable microcomputers

Keane, Inc. KEAN
10 City Square
Boston, MA 02129 (617) 241-9200
customizes software for data processing

Kelly Services, Inc. KELYA
999 West Big Beaver Road
Troy, MI 48084 (313) 362-4444
temporary personnel

Kemper Corporation KEMC
Kemper Center
Long Grove, IL 60049 (312) 540-2000
property-casualty, life insurance, investments

KenCope Energy Companies KCOP
12500 San Pedro
San Antonio, TX 78216 (512) 494-1179
oil and gas services and exploration

Kenilworth Systems Corporation KENS
151 Dupont Street
Plainview, NY 11803 (516) 349-0990
manufactures cashless wagering systems

Kentucky Central Life Insurance Company
KENCA
Kincaid Towers
Lexington, KY 40507 (606) 253-5111
life insurance, consumer finance,
broadcasting

Keptel, Inc. KPTL
56 Park Road
Trinton Falls, NJ 07724 (201) 389-8800
testing equipment for local telephone
companies

Kevlin Microwave Corporation KVLM
26 Conn Street
Woburn, MA 01801 (617) 935-4800
microwave equipment, high-frequency
connectors

Kewaunee Scientific Corporation KEQU
1144 Wilmette Avenue
Wilmette, IL 60091 (312) 251-7100
scientific laboratory furniture and equipment

Key Centurion Bancshares KEYC
Virginia and Capitol Streets
Charleston, WV 25324 (304) 526-4303
banking

Key Tronic Corporation KTCC
North 4424 Sullivan Road
Spokane, WA 99216 (509) 928-8000
computer keyboards

Keystone Financial, Inc. KSTN
P.O. Box 708
Altoona, PA 16603 (814) 946-6689
banking

Keystone Heritage Group, Inc. KHGI
P.O. Box 448
Lebanon, PA 17042 (717) 274-6800
investment company

Kimball International, Inc. KBALB
1600 Royal Street
Jasper, IN 47546 (812) 482-1600
wood office furniture, pianos

Kimmins Environmental Service Corporation
KEVN
1501 Second Avenue
Tampa, FL 33675 (813) 248-3878
environmental services, real estate
development

Kinder-Care, Inc. KNDR
2400 Presidents Drive
Montgomery, AL 36116 (205) 277-5090
day care centers, financial services, retailing
0

Kinder-Care Learning Centers, Inc. KIND
2400 Presidents Drive
Montgomery, AL 36116 (205) 277-5090
day care centers

Kinetic Concepts, Inc. KNCI
3440 East Houston Street
San Antonio, TX 78219 (512) 225-4092
rents specialized beds for acutely ill patients

Kings Road Entertainment, Inc. KREN
1901 Avenue of the Stars
Los Angeles, CA 90067 (213) 552-0057
produces theatrical motion pictures

KLA Instruments Corporation KLAC
3530 Bassett Street
Santa Clara, CA 95054 (408) 988-6100
semiconductor equipment

KLLM Transport Services, Inc. KLLM
3475 Lakeland Drive
Jackson, MS 39208 (601) 939-2545
temperature-controlled trucking

Kloof Gold Mining Company, Ltd. KLOFY
Gold Fields Building, 75 Fox Street
Johannesburg, 2001, South Africa
gold mining

KMS Industries, Inc. KMSI
3853 Research Park Drive
Ann Arbor, MI 48106 (313) 769-1100
energy research and development

Knape & Vogt Manufacturing Company KNAP
2700 Oak Industrial Drive,
Grand Rapids, MI 49505 (616) 459-3311
specialty hardware products, shelving
systems

Komag, Inc. KMAG
591 Yosemite Drive
Milpitas, CA 95035 (408) 946-2300
thin film rigid disks for disk drives

K.R.M. Petroleum KRMC
150 Grand Street
White Plains, NY 10601 (914) 684-5830
oil and gas exploration and production

Krueger (W.A.) Company KRUE
7301 East Helm Drive
Scottsdale, AZ 85260 (602) 948-5650
prints magazines, books, catalogs

KRUG International Corporation KRUG
Suite 500, 6 Gem Plaza
Dayton, OH 45402 (513) 224-9066
waste removal systems, aerospace research

K-Tron International, Inc. KTII
Routes 55 and 553
Pitman, NJ 08071 (609) 589-0500
digital measurement products

Kulicke and Soffa Industries, Inc. KLIC
2101 Blair Mill Road
Willow Grove, PA 19090 (215) 784-6000
semiconductor equipment, wire bonders

Kurzweil Music Systems, Inc. KURM
411 Waverly Oaks Road
Waltham, MA 02154 (617) 893-5900
computer-based musical instruments

Kustom Electronics, Inc. KUST
8320 Nieman Road
Shawnee Mission, KS 66214 (913) 492-1400
traffic safety radar systems, communications
products

Kyle Technology Corporation KYLE
3500 N.W. Stewart Parkway
Roseburg, OR 97470 (503) 672-5953
makes terminals for heart pacemakers

La Petite Academy, Inc. LPAI
12th and Baltimore City Center
Kansas City, MO 64196 (816) 474-4750
day care centers

Laclede Steel Company LCLD
Equitable Building, 10 Broadway
St. Louis, MO 63102 (314) 425-1400
carbon and alloy steel

Ladd Furniture, Inc. LADF
One Plaza Center
High Point, NC 27261 (919) 889-0333
furniture manufacturer

Laidlaw Transportation, Ltd. LDMFB
3221 North Service Road
Burlington, Ontario, CDA L7N 3G2
(416) 336-1800
waste management, school bus operations

Lakeland Industries, Inc. LAKE
3601 Hempstead Turnpike
Levittown, NY 11756 (516) 579-6161
industrial safety apparel

Lake Shore Bancorp, Inc. LSNB
605 North Michigan Avenue
Chicago, IL 60611 (312) 787-1900
banking

Lam Research Corporation LRCX
4650 Cushing Parkway
Fremont, CA 94538 (415) 659-0200
semiconductor fabricating systems

Lancaster Colony Corporation LANC
37 West Broad Street
Columbus, OH 43215 (614) 224-7141
housewares, automotive products, foods

Lance, Inc. LNCE
8600 South Boulevard
Charlotte, NC 28232 (704) 554-1421
snack foods, breadbasket items DRP

Langley Corporation LCOR
310 Euclid Avenue
San Diego, CA 92114 (619) 264-3181
aerospace precision metal parts

Laser Photonics, Inc. LAZR
12351 Research Parkway
Orlando, FL 32826 (305) 281-4103
solid-state laser products

Laser Precision Corporation LASR
17819 Gillette Avenue
Irvine, CA 92714 (714) 660-8801
makes test and measurement
instrumentation

Lastertechnics, Inc. LASX
5500 Wilshire Avenue
Albuquerque, NM 87113 (505) 822-1123
laser marking systems, laser printers

Lawson Products, Inc. LAWS
1666 East Touhy Avenue
Des Plaines, IL 60018 (312) 827-9666
distributes fasteners, repair parts

LCS Industries, Inc. LCSI
120 Brighton Road
Clifton, NJ 07012 (201) 778-5588
direct marketing services

LDB Corporation LDBC
444 Sidney Baker South
Kerrville, TX 78028 (512) 257-2000
pizza restaurants

LDI Corporation LDIC
1375 East 9th Street
Cleveland, OH 44114 (216) 687-0100
leases new and used computers

Lee Data Corporation LEDA
7075 Flying Cloud Drive
Eden Prairie, MN 55344 (612) 828-0300
computer terminals

LEGENT Corporation LGNT
2 Allegheny Center
Pittsburgh, PA 15212 (412) 323-2600
computer systems software

LESCO, Inc. LSCO
20005 Lake Road
Rocky River, OH 44116 (216) 333-9250
golf course and lawn care products

Levon Resources LVNVF
455 Granville Street
Vancouver, BC, CDA V6C 1T1 (604) 682-3701
gold and silver mining

Lexicon Corporation LEXI
1541 North West 65th Avenue
Ft. Lauderdale, FL 33313 (305) 792-4400
military and industrial technology

Liberty Homes, Inc. LIBH
1101 Eisenhower Drive North
Goshen, IN 46526 (219) 533-0431
manufactured homes

Liberty National Bancorp, Inc. LNBC
416 West Jefferson, P.O. Box 32500
Louisville, KY 40232 (502) 566-2000
banking DRP

Life Investors Inc. LINV
4333 Edgewood Road, North East
Cedar Rapids, IA 52499 (319) 398-8511
insurance

Lifeline Systems, Inc. LIFE
1 Arsenal Marketplace
Watertown, MA 02172 (617) 923-4141
hospital emergency response system

Life Technologies, Inc. LTEK
8717 Grovemont Circle
Gaithersburg, MD 20877 (301) 840-8000
life sciences research products

Lilly Industrial Coatings Inc. LICIA
733 South West Street, P.O. Box 946
Indianapolis, IN 46225 (317) 634-8512
industrial coatings, furniture finishes

LIN Broadcasting Corporation LINB
1370 Avenue of the Americas
New York, NY 10019 (212) 765-1902
broadcasting, cellular telephone service O

Lincoln Bancorp LCNB
16030 Ventura Boulevard
Encino, CA 91436 (818) 907-9122
banking

Lincoln Logs, Ltd. LLOG
Riverside Drive
Chestertown, NY 12817 (518) 494-4777
complete log home packages for
homebuilders

Lincoln Foodservice Products, Inc. LINN
1111 North Hadley Road
Fort Wayne, IN 46804 (219) 432-9511
conveyor ovens, commercial cooking
equipment

Lincoln Telecommunications Company LTEC
1440 M Street
Lincoln, NE 68508 (402) 474-2211
local telephone service DRP

Lindal Cedar Homes, Inc. LNDL
4300 South 104th Place
Seattle, WA 98178 (206) 725-0900
cedar home manufacturer

Lindberg Corporation LIND
8600 West Bryn Mawr Avenue
Chicago, IL 60631 (312) 693-2021
commercial heat treating services for
metalworking

Lindsay Manufacturing Company LINZ
East Highway 91
Lindsay, NE 68644 (402) 428-2131
agricultural irrigation systems

Linear Technology Corporation LLTC
1630 McCarthy Boulevard
Milpitas, CA 95035 (408) 432-1900
makes linear integrated circuits

Liposome Companies, Inc. LIPO
1 Research Way, Princeton Forrestal Center
Princeton, NJ 08540 (609) 452-7060
researches liposome technology for drugs

Liqui-Box Corporation LIQB
6950 Worthington-Galena Road
Worthington, OH 43085 (614) 888-9280
plastic packaging, containers

Live Entertainment, Inc. LIVE
500 North Ventu Park Road
Newbury Park, CA 91320 (805) 499-5827
distributes video and audio cassettes

Liz Claiborne, Inc. LIZC
1441 Broadway
New York, NY 10018 (212) 354-4900
women's and men's apparel manufacturer O

Loan America Financial Corporation LAFCB
8100 Oak Lane
Miami Lakes, FL 33016 (305) 557-9282
mortgage banking services

Local Federal Savings & Loan Association
LOCL
3601 North West 63rd Street
Oklahoma City, OK 73126 (405) 841-2100
savings and loan

Lodgistix, Inc. LDGX
1938 North Woodlawn
Wichita, KS 67208 (316) 685-2216
computerized property management systems

Lone Star Technologies, Inc. LSST
2200 West Mockingbird Lane
Dallas, TX 75235 (214) 352-3981
tubular steel, incineration units, banking

Lotus Development Corporation LOTS
55 Cambridge Parkway
Cambridge, MA 02142 (617) 577-8500
microcomputer applications software

Lowrance Electronics, Inc. LEIX
12000 East Skelly Drive
Tulsa, OK 74128 (918) 437-6881
sonar for recreational boats

Loyola Capital Corporation LOYC
1300 North Charles Street
Baltimore, MD 21201 (301) 332-7000
savings and loan

LPL Investment Group, Inc. LPLI
358 Hall Avenue
Wallingford, CT 06492 (203) 265-8600
leveraged buyout investments

LSB Bancshares, Inc. LXBK
One LSB Plaza
Lexington, NC 27292 (704) 246-6500
investment company

LSI Lighting Systems Inc. LYTS
4201 Malsbary Road
Cincinnati, OH 45242 (513) 793-3200
outdoor lighting products

LSI Logic Corporation LLSI
1551 McCarthy Boulevard
Milpitas, CA 95035 (408) 433-8000
custom semiconductors O

LTX Corporation LTXX
LTX Park at University Avenue
Westwood, MA 02090 (617) 461-1000
semiconductor test equipment

Luskin's, Inc. LUSK
7125 Columbia Gateway
Columbia, MD 21046 (301) 290-1111
consumer electronics retailing

Lyphomed, Inc. LMED
10401 West Touhy Avenue
Rosemont, IL 60018 (312) 390-6500
nutritional intravenous drug products

MacDermid, Inc. MACD
50 Brookside Road
Waterbury, CT 06708 (203) 575-5700
specialty chemicals for electronics industry
DRP

Machine Technology, Inc. MTEC
25 Eastmans Road
Parsippany, NJ 07054 (201) 386-0600
semiconductor production equipment

Mack Trucks, Inc. MACK
2100 Mack Boulevard
Allentown, PA 18105 (215) 439-3011
heavy-duty truck manufacturer

MacMillan Bloedel, Ltd. MMBLF
1075 West Georgia Street
Vancouver, BC, CDA V6E 3R9 (604) 661-8000
newsprint, specialty papers, containerboard

Madison Gas and Electric Company MDSN
133 South Blair Street
Madison, WI 53701 (608) 252-7963
electric and gas utility DRP

Magma Power Company MGMA
11770 Bernardo Plaza Court
San Diego, CA 92128 (619) 487-9412
geothermal power plants

Magna Group, Inc. MAGI
19 Public Square
Belleville, IL 62220 (618) 234-0020
banking

Magna International Inc. MAGAF
36 Apple Creek Boulevard
Markham, Ontario, CDA L3R 4Y4
(416) 477-7766
automotive components

Mail Boxes, Etc. MAIL
5555 Oberlin Drive
San Diego, CA 92121 (619) 452-1553
postal, business and communications
services

Mallard Coach Company MALC
26535 U.S. Highway 6
Nappanee, IN 46550 (219) 773-2471
recreational vehicle manufacturer

Management Company Entertainment Group,
Inc. MCEG
575 Fifth Avenue
New York, NY 10017 (212) 983-5799
motion picture production and distribution

Management Science America, Inc. MSAI
3445 Peachtree Road, N.E.
Atlanta, GA 30326 (404) 239-2000
applications software

Manatron, Inc. MANA
2970 South 9th Street
Kalamazoo, MI 49009 (616) 375-5300
microcomputer data processing systems

Manitowoc Company, Inc. (The) MANT
500 South Sixteenth Street
Manitowoc, WI 54220 (414) 684-6621
construction machinery, cranes, ice machines

Manufacturers National Corporation MNTL
One Hundred Renaissance Center
Detroit, MI 48243 (313) 222-4000
banking DRP

M/A/R/C Inc. MARC
7850 Beltline Road
Irving, TX 75063 (214) 506-3400
marketing research

Marcus Corporation (The) MRCS
212 West Wisconsin Avenue
Milwaukee, WI 53203 (414) 272-6020
hotels, restaurants, movie theaters

Margaux, Inc. MRGX
5005 Brandin Court
Fremont, CA 94538 (415) 498-1650
commercial refrigeration components

Marine Corporation (The) MCOR
East Old State Capitol Plaza
Springfield, IL 62701 (217) 525-9600
banking

Marine Petroleum Trust MARPS
P.O. Box 2964
Dallas, TX 75221 (214) 922-6148
oil and gas lease royalties

Marine Transport Lines, Inc. MTLI
150 Meadowland Parkway
Secaucus, NJ 07096 (201) 330-0200
shipping of oil and commodities

Mark Controls Corporation MRCC
5202 Old Orchard Road
Skokie, IL 60077 (312) 470-8585
industrial valves, flow control products

Mark Twain Bancshares, Inc. MTWN
8820 Ladue Road
St. Louis, MO 63124 (314) 727-1000
banking DRP

Markel Corproation MAKL
4551 Cox Road
Glen Allen, VA 23060 (804) 747-0136
specialty insurance broker, claims
administration

Market Facts, Inc. MFAC
676 North Saint Clair Street
Chicago, IL 60611 (312) 280-9100
marketing research services

MarkitStar, Inc. MARK
475 Tenth Avenue
New York, NY 10018 (212) 629-5777
retail interactive communications systems

Marquest Medical Products, Inc. MMPI
11039 East Lansing Circle
Englewood, CO 80112 (303) 790-4835
disposable medical products, home
healthcare

Marsam Pharmaceuticals, Inc. MSAM
Building 31, Olney Avenue
Cherry Hill, NJ 08034 (609) 424-5600
injectable generic prescription drugs

Marsh Supermarkets, Inc. MARS
501 Depot Street
Yorktown, IN 47396 (317) 759-8101
supermarkets, convenience stores DRP

Marshall & Isley Corporation MRIS
770 North Water Street
Milwaukee, WI 53202 (414) 765-7801
banking DRP

Marten Transport, Ltd. MRTN
129 Marten Street
Mondovi, WI 54755 (715) 926-4216
trucking

Martin Lawrence Limited Editions, Inc. MLLE
16250 Stagg Street
Van Nuys, CA 91406 (818) 988-0630
retail art galleries, limited-edition graphics

Masco Industries, Inc. MASX
21001 Van Born Road
Taylor, MI 48180 (313) 274-7405
custom industrial engineered components

Masstor Systems Corporation MSCO
5200 Great America Parkway
Santa Clara, CA 95052 (408) 988-1008
computer data storage equipment

Maxco, Inc. MAXC
Suite 1050, 1 Michigan Avenue
Lansing, MI 48933 (517) 484-1414
construction supplies, auto refinishing
products

Maxim Integrated Products, Inc. MXIM
120 Gabriel Drive
Sunnyvale, CA 94086 (408) 737-7600
makes analog circuits

Maxtor Corporation MXTR
211 River Oaks Parkway
San Jose, CA 95134 (408) 432-1700
computer data storage products O

Maxwell Laboratories, Inc. MXWL
8888 Balboa Avenue
San Diego, CA 92123 (619) 279-5100
pulsed power equipment

Mayfair Industries, Inc. MAYF
1407 Broadway
New York, NY 10018 (212) 921-1717
manufactures clothing

Mayfair Super Markets, Inc. MYFRA
681 Newark Avenue
Elizabeth, NJ 07208 (201) 352-6400
supermarkets

Maynard Oil Company MOIL
Suite 660, 8080 North Central Expressway
Dallas, TX 75206 (214) 891-8880
oil and gas exploration and production

Mays, (J. W.) Inc. MAYS
510 Fulton Street
Brooklyn, NY 11201 (212) 624-7400
retailing

MBS Textbook Exchange, Inc. MBSX
1711 Paris Road
Columbia, MD 65201 (314) 442-3171
wholesaler of college textbooks

McCormick & Company, Inc. MCCRK
11350 McCormick Road
Hunt Valley, MD 21031 (301) 771-7301
spices, food products DRP

McFarland Energy, Inc. MCFE
10425 South Painter Avenue
Santa Fe Springs, CA 90670 (213) 944-0181
oil and gas exploration and production

McGill Manufacturing Company Inc. MGLL
909 North Lafayette Street
Valparaiso, IN 46383 (219) 465-2200
anti-friction bearings, electrical products

McGrath RentCorp MGRC
10760 Bigge Street
San Leandro, CA 94577 (415) 568-8866
rents modular offices and instruments

MCI Communications Corporation MCIC
1133 19th Street, N.W.
Washington, DC 20036 (202) 872-1600
long-distance telephone service O

MDT Corporation MDTC
2300 205th Street
Toarrance, CA 90501 (213) 618-9269
sterility assurance systems

Mechanical Technology, Inc. MTIX
968 Albany-Shaker Road
Latham, NY 12110 (518) 785-2211
aerospace systems, manufacturing research

Medalist Industries, Inc. MDIN
10218 North Port Washington
Mequon, WI 53092 (414) 241-8500
industrial fasteners, warmth-related clothing
DRP

Medar, Inc. MDXR
38700 Grand River Avenue
Farmington Hills, MI 48018 (313) 477-3900
computer-controlled automation equipment

Medco Containment Services, Inc. MCCS
1900 Pollitt Drive
Fair Lawn, NJ 07410 (201) 794-9010
prescription drugs by mail O

Medco Research, Inc. MEDR
8733 Beverly Boulevard
Los Angeles, CA 90048 (213) 854-1954
develops drugs for cardiovascular diseases

Medex, Inc. MDEX
3637 Lacon Road
Hilliard, OH 43026 (614) 876-2413
life-support products

MEDIAGENIC MGNC
3885 Bohannon Drive
Menlo Park, CA 94025 (415) 329-0800
interactive electronic media, software, games

Medical Care International, Inc. MEDC
Suite 600, 15110 Dallas Parkway
Dallas, TX 75248 (214) 490-3190
ambulatory surgical centers

Medical Graphics Corporation MGCC
350 Oak Grove Parkway
St. Paul, MN 55127 (612) 484-4874
computerized diagnostic systems

Medical Sterilization, Inc. MSTI
225 Underhill Blvd.
Syosset, NY 11791 (516) 496-8822
health services

Medicine Shoppe International, Inc. MSII
1100 North Lindbergh Boulevard
St. Louis, MO 63132 (314) 993-6000
prescription pharmacies

Medstone International, Inc. MSHK
1607 Monrovia Avenue
Costa Mesa, CA 92627 (714) 646-8211
shock wave system to disintegrate kidney
stones

Megadata Corporation MDTA
35 Orville Drive
Bohemia, NY 11716 (516) 589-6800
intelligent video display computer terminals

Melamine Chemicals, Inc. MTWO
Highway 19W, P.O. Box 748
Donaldsonville, LA 70346 (504) 473-3121
produces melamine

Mellon Participating Mortgage Trust MPMT
551 Madison Avenue
New York, NY 10022 (212) 702-4040
mortgage investments

Mentor Corporation MNTR
600 Pine Avenue
Santa Barbara, CA 93117 (805) 967-3451
surgically implantable medical devices,
condoms

Mentor Graphics Corporation MENT
8500 S.W. Creekside Place
Beaverton, OR 97005 (503) 626-7000
computer-aided engineering software

Mercantile Bancorporation, Inc. MTRC
Mercantile Tower, P.O. Box 524
St. Louis, MO 63166 (314) 425-2525
banking DRP

Mercantile Bankshares Corporation MRBK
2 Hopkins Plaza
Baltimore, MD 21203 (301) 237-5900
banking DRP 5%

Merchant Bank of California (The) MCAL
9100 Wilshire Blvd.
Beverly Hills, CA 90212 (213) 274-9820
banking

Merchants Bancorp, Inc. MRBA
702 Hamilton Mall
Allentown, PA 18101 (215) 821-7215
banking

Merchants Bancshares, Inc. MBVT
123 Church Street
Burlington, VT 05401 (802) 658-3400
banking

Merchants Bank of New York (The) MBNY
434 Broadway
New York, NY 10013 (212) 669-6600
banking

Merchants Capital Corporation MCBKB
125 Tremont Street
Boston, MA 02108 (617) 484-2800
banking, investment management, brokerage

Merchants National Corp. MCHN
One Merchants Plaza
Indianapolis, IN 46255 (317) 267-6100
banking

Mercury General Corporation MRCY
4484 Wilshire Boulevard
Los Angeles, CA 90010 (213) 937-1060
auto and homeowners insurance

Meret, Inc. MRETC
645 South Grant Avenue
Columbus, OH 43206 (614) 469-0444
strategic planning and consulting

Meridian Bancorp, Inc. MRDN
35 North Sixth Street
Reading, PA 19603 (215) 320-2000
banking DRP 5%

Meridian Diagnostics, Inc. KITS
3471 River Hills Drive
Cincinnati, OH 45244 (513) 271-3700
immunodiagnostic test kits and reagents

Meridian Insurance Group, Inc. MIGI
2955 North Meridian Street
Indianapolis, IN 46206 (317) 927-8100
home and auto insurance

Meritor Savings Bank MTOR
1212 Market Street
Philadelphia, PA 19107 (215) 636-6000
savings banking, mortgage banking

Merrill Corporation MRLL
1 Merrill Circle, Energy Park
St. Paul, MN 55108 (612) 646-4501
prints financial and corporate documents

Merrimac Industries, Inc. MMAC
41 Fairfield Place
West Caldwell, NJ 07007 (201) 575-1300
electronic equipment

Merry-Go-Round Enterprises, Inc. MGRE
1220 East Joppa Road
Towson, MD 21204 (301) 828-1000
specialty apparel retailing

Merry Land & Investment Company, Inc.
MERY
624 Ellis Street
Augusta, GA 30903 (404) 722-6756
real estate investments

Mesa Airlines, Inc. MESL
1296 West Navajo Street
Farmington, NM 87401 (505) 327-0271
regional airline

Met-Coil Systems Corporation METS
425 Second Street, S.E.
Cedar Rapids, IA 52401 (319) 363-6566
machinery to process metal coils and sheets

Methode Electronics, Inc. METH
7444 Wilson Avenue
Harwood Heights, IL 60656 (312) 867-9600
printed circuit boards, connectors

Metro Airlines, Inc. MAIR
1 Metro Center, 1700 West 20th Street
DFW Airport, TX 75261 (214) 453-4400
regional airline

MetroBanc, Federal Savings Bank MTBC
201 Monroe Avenue, N.W.
Grand Rapids, MI 49503 (616) 459-3161
savings banking

Metro Mobile CTS, Inc. MCTAC
110 East 59th Street
New York, NY 10022 (212) 319-7444
cellular telephone systems

Metropolitan Federal S & L Association MFTN
230 Fourth Avenue North
Nashville, TN 37202 (615) 259-2800
savings and loan

Metropolitan S & L Association MSLA
5944 Luther Lane
Dallas, TX 75225 (214) 369-2700
savings and loan

Metro-Tel Corporation MTRO
485-13 South Broadway
Hicksville, NY 11801 (516) 937-3420
telephone cable test equipment

Meyer, Fred Inc. MEYR
3800 S.E. 22nd Avenue
Portland, OR 97202 (503) 232-8844
department stores

Michael Anthony Jewelers, Inc. MAJL
70 South MacQuesten Parkway
Mount Vernon, NY 10550 (914) 699-9480
jewelry manufacturer

Michael Foods, Inc. MIKL
5353 Wayzata Boulevard
Minneapolis, MN 55416 (612) 546-1500
egg, potato, dairy, food items

Michigan National Corporation MNCO
27777 Inkster Road
Farmington Hills, MI 48018 (313) 473-8600
banking DRP

MicroAge, Inc. MICA
2308 South 55th Street
Tempe, AZ 85282 (602) 968-3168
microcomputer retail stores

Microbilt Corporation BILT
6190 Powers Ferry Road
Atlanta, GA 30339 (404) 955-0313
data communications systems

Microbiological Sciences, Inc. MBLS
771 Main Street
West Warwick, RI 02893 (401) 828-5250
microbiological culture media products

Microcom, Inc. MNPI
1400 Providence Highway
Norwood, MA 02062 (617) 762-9310
computer communications networks

Microdyne Corporation MCDY
491 Oak Road
Ocala, FL 32672 (904) 687-4633
earth station components for satellites

Micro Mask, Inc. MCRO
695 Vaqueros Avenue
Sunnyvale, CA 94086 (408) 245-7342
photomasks for semiconductor industry

Micron Technology, Inc. MCRN
2805 East Columbia Road
Boise, ID 83706 (208) 383-4000
semiconductor manufacturer

Micropolis Corporation MLIS
21123 Nordhoff Street
Chatsworth, CA 91311 (818) 709-3300
computer disk drives

MicroPro International Corporation MPRO
33 San Pablo Avenue
San Rafael, CA 94903 (415) 499-1200
word processing software

Microsemi Corporation MSCC
2830 South Fairview Street
Santa Ana, CA 92704 (714) 979-8220
semiconductor products and assemblies

Micros Systems, Inc. MCRS
12000 Baltimore Avenue
Beltsville, MD 20705 (301) 490-2000
point-of-sale electronic information systems

Microsoft Corporation MSFT
16011 N.E. 36th Way, P.O. Box 97017
Redmond, WA 98073 (206) 882-8080
operating systems and application software

Microwave Filter Company, Inc. MFCO
6743 Kinne Street
East Syracuse, NY 13057 (315) 437-3953
interference filters, communications
consulting

Mid-America Bancorp MABC
500 West Broadway
Louisville, KY 40202 (502) 562-5439
banking

Mid-American National Bank and Trust
Company MIAM
222 South Main Street
Bowling Green, OH 43402 (419) 352-5271
banking

MidConn Bank MIDC
346 Main Street
Kensington, CT 06037 (203) 828-0301
banking

Middlesex Water Company MSEX
1500 Ronson Road
Iselin, NJ 08830 (201) 634-1500
water utility DRP

Midlantic Corporation MIDL
Metro Park Plaza
Edison, NJ 08818 (201) 321-8000
banking DRP

Mid-Hudson Savings Bank, FSB MHBK
Route 52, P.O. Box M
Fishkill, NY 12524 (914) 896-6215
savings banking

Mid-Maine Savings Bank, FSB MMSB
Great Falls Plaza
Auburn, ME 04210 (207) 784-3581
savings banking

MidSouth Corporation MSRR
111 East Capitol Street
Jackson, MS 39201 (601) 353-7508
regional railroad

Mid-State Federal S & L Association MSSL
3300 S.W. 34th Avenue
Ocala, FL 32674 (904) 854-0177
savings and loan

Midwest Communications Corporation MCOM
1 Sperti Drive
Edgewood, KY 41017 (606) 331-8990
supplies equipment to television industry

Miller Building Systems, Inc. MTIK
Suite 390, 102 Wilmot Road
Deerfield, IL 60015 (312) 945-3222
nonresidential temporary and modular
structures

Miller, Herman MLHR
8500 Byron Road
Zeeland, MI 49464 (616) 772-3300
office and institutional furniture

Millicom, Inc. MILL
153 East 53rd Street
New York, NY 10022 (212) 355-3440
operates cellular telphone systems

Mills-Jennings Company JKPT
4673 AirCenter Circle
Reno, NV 89502 (702) 827-8110
makes electronic slot machines

Miltope Group, Inc. MILT
733 Third Avenue
New York, NY 10017 (212) 661-6343
specialty computers for military applications

Mindscape, Inc. MIND
3444 Dundee Road
Northbrook, IL 60062 (312) 480-7667
entertainment and education computer
software

Mine Safety Appliances Company MNES
121 Gamma Drive, RIDC Industrial Park
Pittsburgh, PA 15238 (412) 967-3000
health and safety products for miners

MiniScribe Corporation MINY
1861 Lefthand Circle
Longmont, CO 80501 (303) 651-6000
microcomputer disk drives

Minnetonka Corporation MINL
8400 Normandale Lake Boulevard
Bloomington, MN 55437 (612) 897-5400
fragrances, health and beauty products

Minnova, Inc. MVA
Commerce Court West, P.O. Box 91
Toronto, Ontario, CDA M51 1C7
(416) 982-7270
gold, copper, silver, zinc mining

Minntech Corporation MNTX
14905 28th Avenue North
Minneapolis, MN 55441 (612) 553-3300
kidney dialysis treatment devices

Minorco SA MNRCY
P.O. Box HM650
Hamilton, Bermuda (352) 497311
gold mining, commodities trading

Mischer Corporation (The) MSHR
2727 North Loop West, #200
Houston, TX 77008 (713) 869-7800
building construction

M/I Schottenstein Homes, Inc. MIHO
41 South High Street
Columbus, OH 43215 (614) 221-5700
single-family home builder

Mitsui & Company, Ltd. MITSY
2-1, Ohtemachi 1-Chome
Chiyoda-ku, Tokyo, Japan (212) 878-4000
international trading company

MLX Corporation MLXX
Suite 804, 100 East Big Beaver Road
Troy, MI 48083 (313) 528-2400
distributes refrigeration and A/C products

MMI Medical, Inc. MMIM
1902 Royalty Drive
Pomona, CA 91767 (714) 620-0391
health services, supplies

MMR Holding Corporation MMRH
15981 Airline Highway
Baton Rouge, LA 70817 (504) 292-3500
electrical and mechanical specialty contractor

MNX, Inc. MNXI
5310 St. Joseph Avenue
St. Joseph, MO 64505 (816) 233-3158
trucking

Mobile Gas Service Corporation MBLE
2828 Dauphin Street
Mobile, AL 36606 (205) 476-2720
gas utility DRP

Modern Controls, Inc. MOCO
6820 Shingle Creek Parkway
Minneapolis, MN 55430 (612) 560-2900
packaging materials test instruments

Modine Manfacturing Company MODI
1500 DeKoven Avenue
Racine, WI 53401 (414) 636-1200
heat-transfer products for automakers

Molecular Biosystems MOBI
10030 Barnes Canyon Road
San Diego, CA 92121 (619) 452-0681
develops biological and biochemical products

Molecular Genetics, Inc. MOGN
10320 Bren Road East
Minnetonka, MN 55343 (612) 935-7335
corn hybrids research, biotechnology

Molex, Inc. MOLX
2222 Wellington Court
Lisle, IL 60532 (312) 969-4550
electronic interconnection equipment O

Monarch Avalon, Inc. MAHI
4517 Harford Road
Baltimore, MD 21214 (301) 254-9200
printing, toys and games

Moniterm Corporation MTRM
5740 Green Circle Drive
Minnetonka, MN 55343 (612) 935-4151
high-resolution computer monitors

Monitor Technologies, Inc. MLAB
10180 Scripps Ranch Boulevard
San Diego, CA 92131 (619) 578-5060
equipment to monitor air pollution

Monoclonal Antibodies, Inc. MABS
2319 Charleston Road
Mountain View, CA 94043 (415) 960-1320
medical diagnostic kits using monoclonal
antibodies

Moore Financial Group, Inc. MFGI
101 South Capitol Boulevard
Boise, ID 83733 (208) 383-7000
banking DRP

Moore-Handley, Inc. MHCO
Highway 31 South
Pelham, AL 35124 (205) 663-8011
hardware distributor

Moore Products Company MORP
Sumneytown
Spring House, PA 19477 (215) 646-7400
industrial instruments and measuring gauges

Morehouse Industries, Inc. MIXS
1600 West Commonwealth Avenue
Fullerton, CA 92634 (714) 738-5000
industrial processing equipment

Moran, J.T. Financial Corporation JTMC
1 Whitehall Street
New York, NY 10004 (212) 363-5959
investment banking and securities brokerage

Mor-Flo Industries, Inc. MORF
18450 South Miles Road
Cleveland, OH 44128 (216) 663-7300
gas, electric and solar water heaters

Morgro Chemical Company MRGR
145 West Central Avenue
Salt Lake City, UT 84115 (801) 266-1132
snow and ice melting products, garden
chemicals

Morino, Inc. MRNO
8615 Westwood Center Drive
Vienna, VA 22180 (703) 734-9494
mainframe systems software

Morris County Savings Bank (The) MCSB
21 South Street
Morristown, NJ 07960 (201) 539-0500
savings banking

Morrison, Inc. MORR
4721 Morrison Drive
Mobile, AL 36625 (205) 344-3000
cafeterias O

MOSCOM Corporation MSCM
300 Main Street
East Rochester, NY 14445 (716) 385-6440
telecommunications management systems

Mosinee Paper Corporation MOSI
1244 Kronenwetter Drive
Mosinee, WI 54455 (715) 693-4470
industrial specialty paper and plastic products

Moto Photo, Inc. MOTO
4444 Lake Center Drive
Dayton, OH 45426 (513) 854-6686
one-hour photoprocessing franchises

Motor Club of America MOTR
484 Central Avenue
Newark, NJ 07107 (201) 733-1234
homeowners and automobile insurance

MPSI Systems, Inc. MPSG
8282 South Memorial Drive
Tulsa, OK 74133 (918) 250-9611
software, data processing

Mr. Gasket Company MRGC
8700 Brookpark Road
Brooklyn, OH 44129 (216) 398-8300
auto parts

M.S. Carriers, Inc. MSCA
3150 Starnes Cove
Memphis, TN 38116 (901) 332-2500
trucking

Mt. Baker Bank, A Savings Bank MBSB
1621 Cornwall Avenue
Bellingham, WA 98227 (206) 676-2300
banking

MTS Systems Corporation MTSC
14000 Technology Drive
Eden Prairie, MN 55344 (612) 937-4000
engineering design and materials test
systems

Mueller, Paul Company MUEL
1600 West Phelps Street
Springfield, MO 65802 (417) 831-3000
stainless steel tanks for dairy and meat
industries

Multibank Financial Corporation MLTF
100 Rustcraft Road
Dedham, MA 02026 (617) 461-1820
banking DRP 3%

Multi-Color Corporation LABL
4575 Eastern Avenue
Cincinnati, OH 45226 (513) 321-5381
supplies printed in-mold labels on plastic
containers

Multimedia, Inc. MMEDC
305 South Main Street, P.O. Box 1688
Greenville, SC 29602 (803) 298-4373
publishing, TV, radio and cable broadcasting

Mutual Home Federal Savings Bank MHFS
171 Monroe Avenue, N.W.
Grand Rapids, MI 49503 (616) 451-4521
savings and loan

Mutual Savings Life Insurance Company
MUTS
P.O. Box 2222
Decatur, AL 35601 (205) 552-7011
life insurance

Mycogen Corporation MYCO
5451 Oberlin Drive
San Diego, CA 92121 (619) 453-8030
biological insecticides and herbicides

Myo-Tech Corporation MYOT
5301 North Federal Highway
Boca Raton, FL 33487 (407) 994-4700
digital myograph to detect soft-tissue
damage

NAC Re Corporation NREC
1 Greenwich Plaza
Greenwich, CT 06836 (203) 622-5200
property-casualty reinsurance

Napa Valley Bancorp NVBC
One Financial Plaza
Napa, CA 94558 (707) 255-8300
banking

Napco Security Systems, Inc. NSSC
333 Bayview Avenue
Amityville, NY 11701 (516) 842-9400
burglar alarm equipment

Nash-Finch Company NAFC
3381 Gorham Avenue
St. Louis Park, MN 55426 (612) 929-0371
food stores, supplies supermarkets DRP

Nashville City Bank & Trust Co. NCBT
315 Union Street
Nashville, TN 37201 (615) 251-9200
banking

National Bancorp of Alaska, Inc. NBAK
301 West Northern Lights Boulevard
Anchorage, AK 99510 (907) 276-1132
banking

National Bankshares Corporation of Texas
NBCTC
430 Soledad Street
San Antonio, TX 78291 (512) 225-2511
banking

National Business Systems, Inc. NBSIF
3220 Orlando Drive
Mississauga, Ontario, CDA L4V 1R5
(416) 671-3334
embossing products for transaction card
issuers

National Capital Management Corporation
NCMC
Suite 3300, 50 California Street
San Francisco, CA 94111 (415) 989-2661
rental real estate, business investments

National City Bancorporation NCBM
75 South Fifth Street
Minneapolis, MN 55402 (612) 340-3183
banking

National City Corporation NCTY
1900 East Ninth Street
Cleveland, OH 44114 (216) 575-2000
banking DRP

National Commerce Bancorporation NCBC
One Commerce Square
Memphis, TN 38150 (901) 523-3242
banking

National Community Banks, Inc. NCBR
113 West Essex
Maywood, NJ 07607 (201) 845-1000
banking DRP

National Computer Systems, Inc. NLCS
11000 Prairie Lakes Drive
Minneapolis, MN 55440 (612) 829-3000
optical mark-scanning systems to score tests

National Data Corporation NDTA
One National Data Plaza
Atlanta, GA 30329 (404) 329-8500
credit card transaction processing

National Environmental Controls, Inc. NECT
2424 Edenborn Avenue
Metairie, LA 70001 (504) 831-3600
solid waste disposal services

National FSI, Inc. NFSI
2777 Stemmons Freeway
Dallas, TX 75207 (214) 689-3200
employee benefits and financial software
systems

National Healthcare, Inc. NHCI
2727 Paces Ferry Road
Atlanta, GA 30339 (404) 431-1500
healthcare services to rural communities

National HMO Corporation NHMO
Suite F, 2800 Aurora Road
Melbourne, FL 32935 (407) 242-8513
outpatient medical and dental offices

National Health Laboratories, Inc. NHLI
7590 Fay Avenue
La Jolla, CA 92037 (619) 454-3314
clinical laboratories

National Lampoon, Inc. NLPI
155 Avenue of the Americas
New York, NY 10013 (212) 645-5040
humor and satire magazine and
videocassettes

National Lumber & Supply, Inc. NTLB
17102 Newhope Street
Fountain Valley, CA 92708 (714) 751-3970
do-it-yourself home improvement centers

National Micronetics, Inc. NMIC
5600 Kearney Mesa Road
San Diego, CA 92111 (619) 279-7500
makes recording heads for disk drives

National Penn Bancshares, Inc. NPBC
Philadelphia and Reading
Boyertown, PA 19512 (215) 367-6001
banking

National Pizza Company PIZA
720 West 20th Street
Pittsburg, KS 66762 (316) 231-3390
pizza restaurants

National Security Insurance Company NSIC
661 East Davis Street
Elba, AL 36323 (205) 897-2273
life, health, accident insurance

National Technical Systems NTSC
24007 Ventura Boulevard
Calabasas, CA 91302 (818) 348-7101
engineering and testing services to
government

National Western Life Insurance Company
NWLIA
850 East Anderson Lane
Austin, TX 78752 (512) 836-1010
life insurance, government securities
brokerage

Nationwide Power Corporation NPWR
1300 S.W. 12th Avenue
Pompano Beach, FL 33069 (305) 782-3110
power equipment

Nature's Bounty, Inc. NBTY
90 Orville Drive
Bohemia, NY 11716 (516) 567-9500
food supplements and vitamins

Nature's Sunshine Products, Inc. NATR
1655 North Main
Spanish Fork, UT 84660 (801) 798-9861
nutritional products, vitamins, water purifier

Navigators Group, Inc. NAVG
84 William Street
New York, NY 10038 (212) 809-3710
marine and aviation property-casualty
insurance

NBSC Corporation NSCB
207 North Main Street
Sumter, SC 29150 (803) 775-1211
banking

ND Resources NUDYE
37 Castle Pines Drive North
Castle Rock, CO 80104 (303) 688-1411
oil, gas, minerals exploration, development

NEC Corporation NIPNY
33-1, Shiba 5-chome
Minato-ku, Tokyo 108 Japan (034) 454-1111
electronic equipment, communications

NEECO, Inc. NEEC
70 Shawmut Road
Canton, MA 02021 (617) 821-4100
personal computer retailing

Nellcor, Inc. NELL
25495 Whitesell Street
Hayward, CA 94545 (415) 887-5858
electronic patient-monitoring instruments

NEOAX, Inc. NOAX
5 High Ridge Park, P.O. Box 10309
Stamford, CT 06904 (203) 322-8333
custom motor vehicles, metal recycling

NESB Corporation NESB
63 Eugene O'Neill Drive
New London, CT 06320 (203) 444-3400
savings banking

Network Equipment Technologies NETX
400 Penobscot Drive
Redwood City, CA 94063 (415) 366-4400
communications network management
products

Network General Corporation NETG
1945A Charleston Road
Mountain View, CA 94043 (415) 965-1800
local area network analysis tools

Networks Electronic Corporation NWRK
9750 DeSoto Avenue
Chatsworth, CA 91311 (818) 341-0440
specialized bearings, electro-pyrotechnic
devices

Network Systems Corporation NSCO
7600 Boone Avenue North
Minneapolis, MN 55428 (612) 424-4888
high-speed computer network equipment O

Neutrogena Corporation NGNA
5755 West 96th Street
Los Angeles, CA 90045 (213) 642-1150
specialty soaps, skin and hair-care products

New Brunswick Scientific Company, Inc.
NBSC
44 Talmadge Road
Edison, NJ 08818 (201) 287-1200
scientific instruments, laboratory equipment

New England Business Service, Inc. NEBS
500 Main Street
Groton, MA 01450 (617) 448-6111
business forms and related products

New England Critical Care, Inc. NECC
165 Forest Street
Marlborough, MA 01752 (508) 480-0503
home infusion therapy services

New Hampshire Savings Bank Corporation
NHSB
27 North State Street
Concord, NH 03301 (603) 224-7711
banking

New Jersey Steel Corporation NJST
North Crossman Road
Sayreville, NJ 08872 (201) 721-6600
operates steel mini-mill

Neworld Bancorp, Inc. NWOR
55 Summer Street
Boston, MA 02110 (617) 482-2600
banking

Newport Corporation NEWP
18235 Mount Baldy Circle
Fountain Valley, CA 92708 (714) 963-9811
laser research and experimentation

Newport Electronics, Inc. NEWE
630 East Young Street
Santa Ana, CA 92705 (714) 540-4914
precision digital electronic instruments

Newport Pharmaceuticals International, Inc.
NWPH
897 West 16th Street
Newport Beach, CA 92663 (714) 642-7511
viral infection drugs

New York Marine and General Insurance
Company NYMG
100 Park Avenue
New York, NY 10017 (212) 953-0580
marine and aircraft insurance

NHD Stores, Inc. NHDI
365 Washington Street
Stoughton, MA 02072 (617) 341-1810
hardware and houseware stores

Niagra Exchange Corporation NIEX
741 Delaware Avenue
Buffalo, NY 14209 (716) 884-8970
property-casualty insurance

Nichols-Homeshield, Inc. NHIC
1470 North Farnsworth Avenue
Aurora, IL 60507 (312) 851-5430
aluminum building products

Nichols Research Corporation NRES
4040 South Memorial Parkway
Huntsville, AL 35802 (205) 883-1140
optics technology research for defense

NIKE, Inc. NIKE
3900 South West Murray Boulevard
Beaverton, OR 97005 (503) 641-6453
athletic footwear and apparel O

Nobel Insurance Ltd. NOBL
3010 LBJ Freeway
Dallas, TX 75234 (214) 484-5626
insurance

Nobility Homes, Inc. NOBH
3741 S.W. 7th Street
Ocala, FL 32678 (904) 732-5157
mobile home manufacturer

Noble Drilling Corporation NDCO
17 East 7th Street
Tulsa, OK 74119 (918) 599-9700
oil and gas drilling

Nodaway Valley Company NVCO
220 North First Street
Clarinda, IA 51632 (712) 542-5125
editorial and pre-press services to book
publishers

Noland Company NOLD
2700 Warwick Boulevard
Newport News, VA 23607 (804) 928-9147
building materials distibutor

Nordson Corporation NDSN
28601 Clemens Road
Westlake, OH 44145 (216) 892-1580
industrial application equipment

Nordstrom, Inc. NOBE
1501 Fifth Avenue
Seattle, WA 98101 (206) 628-2111
specialty apparel retailing O

Norsk Data A.S. NORKZ
Postboks 25, Bogerud N-0621
Oslo-6, Norway (011) 472-626000
markets minicomputers

Norstan, Inc. NRRD
2905 Northwest Boulevard
Minneapolis, MN 55441 (612) 420-1100
private telephone systems distributor

North American Biologicals, Inc. NBIO
16500 N.W. 15th Avenue
Miami, FL 33169 (305) 625-5303
collects and processes human blood plasma

North American National Corporation NAMC
1251 Dublin Road
Columbus, OH 43216 (614) 488-4881
life insurance

North American Ventures, Inc. NAVI
333 East River Drive
East Hartford, CT 06108 (203) 528-0232
venture capital investments

North Atlantic Industries, Inc. NATL
60 Plant Avenue
Hauppauge, NY 11788 (516) 582-6500
computer peripherals, testing instruments

North Carolina Natural Gas Corporation NCNG
150 Rowan Street
Fayetteville, NC 28302 (919) 483-0315
gas utility DRP

Northeast Bancorp, Inc. NBIC
300 Main Street
Stamford, CT 06904 (203) 348-6211
banking DRP

North East Insurance Company NEIC
959 Brighton Avenue
Portland, ME 04102 (207) 772-3733
property-casualty insurance

North Fork Bancorporation, Inc. NFBC
9025 Main Road
Mattituck, NY 11952 (516) 298-5000
banking DRP

North Hills Electronics, Inc. NOHL
Alexander Place
Glen Cove, NY 11542 (516) 671-5700
electronic components, instruments

Northern Trust Corporation NTRS
50 South LaSalle Street
Chicago, IL 60675 (312) 630-6000
banking

Northwestern States Portland Cement NSTS
12 Second Street N.E.
Mason City, IA 50401 (515) 421-3202
produces Portland cement products

Northwest Natural Gas Company NWNG
1 Pacific Square, 220 N.W. Second Avenue
Portland, OR 97209 (503) 226-4211
gas utility DRP

North-West Telecommunications, Inc. NOWT
901 Kilbourn Avenue
Tomah, WI 54660 (608) 372-4151
telephone service, cable TV, directory
publishing

Northwest Teleproductions, Inc. NWTL
4455 West 77th Street
Minneapolis, MN 55435 (612) 835-4455
television commercials, videotape and film
production

Northwestern Public Service Company NWPS
Third Street and Dakota Avenue South
Huron, SD 57350 (605) 352-8411
electric and gas utility DRP 5%

Novametrix Medical Systems Inc. NMTX
3 Sterling Drive
Wallingford, CT 06492 (203) 265-7701
medical electronic oxygen-monitoring
instruments

Nova Pharmaceutical Corporation NOVX
6200 Freeport Centre
Baltimore, MD 21224 (301) 522-7000
drug research and development

Novar Electronics Corporation NOVR
24 Brown Street
Barberton, OH 44203 (216) 745-0074
electronic security and energy-management
systems

Novell, Inc. NOVL
748 North, 1340 West
Orem, UT 84057 (801) 226-8202
local area network computer systems

Novo Corporation NOVO
481 Doremus Avenue
Newark, NJ 07105 (201) 578-2000
home improvement product manufacturer

Nowsco Well Service, Ltd. NWELF
1300, 801 6th Avenue S.W.
Calgary, AB, CDA T2P 4E1 (403) 261-2990
oil and gas well equipment

Noxell Corporation NOXL
P.O. Box 1799
Baltimore, MD 21203 (301) 785-7300
beauty and health aids, cosmetics O

Nu-Med, Inc. NUMS
16633 Ventura Boulevard
Encino, CA 91436 (818) 990-2000
acute-care hospital operator

Nuclear Metals, Inc. NUCM
2229 Main Street
Concord, MA 01742 (617) 369-5410
specialty metal products, uranium, powders

Nuclear Support Services, Inc. NSSI
West Market Street
Campbelltown, PA 17010 (717) 838-8125
provides personnel for nuclear power plants

Numerax, Inc. NMRX
230 Passaic Street
Maywood, NJ 07607 (201) 368-0170
transportation services

Numerex Corporation NUMR
7101 Northland Circle
Minneapolis, MN 55428 (612) 533-4716
machinery

Numerica Financial Corporation NUME
1155 Elm Street
Manchester, NH 03105 (603) 624-2424
savings and loan DRP

Nutmeg Industries, Inc. NUTM
4408 West Linebaugh Avenue
Tampa, FL 33624 (813) 963-6153
sportswear imprinted with logos and insignia

NuVision, Inc. NUVI
2284 South Ballenger Highway
Flint, MI 48503 (313) 767-0900
eyecare products retailing

NWNL Companies, Inc. NWNL
20 Washington Avenue South
Minneapolis, MN 55401 (612) 372-5432
life insurance

NYCOR, Inc. NYCO
158 Highway 206
Peapack, NJ 07977 (201) 781-5400
automotive components

Oak Hill Sportswear Corporation OHSC
1411 Broadway
New York, NY 10018 (212) 354-0444
women's apparel manufacturer

Oceaneering International, Inc. OCER
16001 Park Ten Place
Houston, TX 77084 (713) 578-8868
services for offshore oil and gas industry

OCG Technology OCGT
42 Executive Boulevard
Farmingdale, NY 11735 (516) 454-0981
heart disease detection systems

Ocilla Industries, Inc. OCIL
Highway 129 North, P.O. Box 100
Ocilla, GA 31774 (912) 468-7485
manufactured housing manufacturer

Occupational-Urgent Care OUCH
1215 Howe Avenue
Sacramento, CA 95825 (916) 924-5200
workers' compensation and group health
programs

Octel Communications Corporation OCTL
890 Tasman Drive
Milpitas, CA 95035 (408) 942-6500
makes voice processing systems

Office Depot, Inc. ODEP
851 Broken Sound Parkway, N.W.
Boca Raton, FL 33487 (407) 994-2131
office supply retailing

Offshore Logistics, Inc. OLOG
224 Rue de Jean, P.O. Box 5-C
Lafayette, LA 70505 (318) 233-1221
provides transportation to offshore oil rigs

Oglebay Norton Company OGLE
1100 Superior Avenue
Cleveland, OH 44114 (216) 861-3300
shipping, coal and iron ore mining

Ohio Bancorp OHBC
801 Dollar Bank Building
Youngstown, OH 44503 (216) 744-2093
banking

Ohio Casualty Corporation OCAS
136 North Third Street
Hamilton, OH 45025 (513) 867-3000
property-casualty insurance

O.I. Corporation OICO
P.O. Box 2980
College Station, TX 77841 (409) 690-1711
water quality measurement instruments

Oil-Dri Corporation of America OILC
520 North Michigan Avenue
Chicago, IL 60611 (312) 321-1515
absorbent mineral products

Oilgear Company (The) OLGR
2300 South 51st Street
Milwaukee, WI 53219 (414) 327-1700
oil drilling equipment

OKC Limited Partnership OKC
P.O. Box 102, 4835 LBJ Freeway
Dallas, TX 75244 (214) 233-7100
oil and gas properties

Old Kent Financial Corporation OKEN
One Vandenberg Center
Grand Rapids, MI 49503 (616) 774-5000
banking

Old National Bancorp OLDB
420 Main Street
Evansville, IN 47708 (812) 464-1200
banking

Old Republic International Corporation OLDR
307 North Michigan Avenue
Chicago, IL 60601 (312) 346-8100
property, liability, life, title, mortgage
insurance DRP

Old Spaghetti Warehouse, Inc. OSWI
6120 Aldwick Drive
Garland, TX 75043 (214) 226-6000
Italian food restaurants

Old Stone Corporation OSTN
150 South Main Street
Providence, RI 02903 (401) 278-2000
banking

Olson Industries, Inc. OLSN
13400 Riverside Drive
Sherman Oaks, CA 91423 (818) 995-1238
foam egg cartons, plastic packaging

Omnicom Group, Inc. OMCM
909 Third Avenue
New York, NY 10022 (212) 935-5660
international advertising agency networks

Oncogene Science, Inc. ONCS
350 Community Drive
Manhasset, NY 11030 (516) 365-9300
cancer detection biotechnology products

One Bancorp (The) TONE
One Maine Savings Plaza
Portland, ME 04101 (207) 871-1111
banking

One Price Clothing Stores, Inc. ONPR
290 Commerce Park, Highway 290
Duncan, SC 29334 (803) 439-6666
women's apparel store with uniform price

Optek Technology, Inc. OPTX
1215 West Crosby Road
Carrolton, TX 75006 (214) 323-2200
infrared optoelectronic components,
assemblies

Optelecom, Inc. OPTC
15930 Luanne Drive
Gaithersburg, MD 20877 (301) 840-2121
optical fiber communications, laser systems

Optical Coating Laboratory, Inc. OCLI
2789 Northpoint Parkway
Santa Rosa, CA 95407 (707) 545-6440
optical thin-filmed coated products to control
light

Optical Radiation Corporation ORCO
1300 Optical Drive
Azusa, CA 91702 (818) 969-3344
precision optical components, vision care

Optical Specialties, Inc. OSI
4281 Technology Drive
Fremont, CA 94538 (415) 490-6400
semiconductor wafer inspection stations

Opto Mechanik, Inc. OPTO
425 North Drive
Melbourne, FL 32936 (305) 254-1212
optical devices for weapons fire control

Optrotech, Ltd. OPTKF
Industrial Zone B, P.O. Box 69
Nes-Ziona 70450 Israel (008) 487-111
printed circuit board optical inspection

Oracle Systems Corporation ORCL
20 Davis Drive
Belmont, CA 94002 (415) 598-8000
database and applications software

Orbit Instrument Corporation ORBT
80 Cabot Court
Hauppauge, NY 11788 (516) 435-8300
military electronic components

Oregon Metallurgical Corporation OREM
530 West 34th Avenue
Albany, OR 97321 (503) 926-4281
titanium and alloys for aircraft manufacturers

Oshkosh B'Gosh, Inc. GOSHA
112 Otter Avenue
Oshkosh, WI 54902 (414) 231-8800
children's apparel

Oshkosh Truck Corporation OTRKB
2307 Oregon Street
Oshkosh, WI 54903 (414) 235-9150
truck manufacturer

Oshman's Sporting Goods, Inc. OSHM
2302 Maxwell Lane
Houston, TX 77023 (713) 928-3171
sporting goods retailing

Osicom Technologies, Inc. OSIC
198 Green Pond Road
Rockaway Township, NJ 07866
(201) 586-2550
distributes disk drives, computers, tape
backups

Osmonics, Inc. OSMO
5951 Clearwater Drive
Minnetonka, MN 55343 (612) 933-2277
filters and pumps for water purification

Otter Tail Power Company OTTR
215 South Cascade Street
Fergus Falls, MN 56537 (218) 739-8200
electric utility DRP

Outlet Communications, Inc. OCOAC
111 Dorrance Street
Providence, RI 02903 (401) 276-6200
television and radio stations

PACCAR, Inc. PCAR
777-106th Avenue, N.E.
Bellevue, WA 98004 (206) 455-7400
heavy-duty trucks, auto parts O

PACE Membership Warehouse, Inc. PMWI
3350 Peoria Street
Aurora, CO 80010 (303) 364-0700
wholesale/retail mass merchandiser

Pacer Technology PTCH
1600 Dell Avenue
Campbell, CA 95008 (408) 379-9701
adhesives and sealants

PacifiCare Health Systems, Inc. PHSY
5995 Plaza Drive
Cypress, CA 90630 (714) 952-1121
operates health maintenance organizations

Pacific First Financial Corporation PFFS
Tacoma Financial Center, 1145 Broadway
Tacoma, WA 98401 (206) 383-7605
savings banking

Pacific Gold Corporation PAGO
13315 Washington Boulevard
Los Angeles, CA 90066 (213) 301-8444
gold mining

Pacific International Services PISC
1600 Kapiolani Boulevard
Honolulu, HI 96814 (808) 926-4242
car rental services

Pacific Nuclear Systems PACN
1010 South 336th Street
Federal Way, WA 98003 (206) 874-2235
handles radioactive waste for nuclear plants

Pacific Telecom, Inc. PTCM
805 Broadway
Vancouver, WA 98668 (206) 696-0983
independent telephone holding company

Pacific Western Bancshares PAWB
333 West Santa Clara Street
San Jose, CA 95113 (408) 244-1700
banking

Packaging Systems Corporation PAKS
275 North Middletown Road
Pearl River, NY 10965 (914) 735-9200
packaging products

Paco Pharmaceutical Services, Inc. PPSI
1200 Paco Way
Lakewood, NJ 08701 (201) 367-9000
drug packaging products

Pacwest Bancorp PWST
1211 Southwest Fifth Avenue
Portland, OR 97204 (503) 790-7501
banking

Pancho's Mexican Buffet, Inc. PAMX
3500 Noble Avenue
Ft. Worth, TX 76111 (817) 831-0081
Mexican restaurants

Pantera's Corporation PANT
2930 Stemmons Freeway
Dallas, TX 75247 (214) 638-7250
operates pizza restaurants

Panatech Research and Development
Corporation PNTC
655 Deep Valley Drive
Rolling Hills Estates, CA 90274
(213) 541-0221
medical supplies

Parallel Petroleum Corporation PLLL
1 Marienfield Place
Midland, TX 79701 (915) 684-3727
acquires oil and gas properties

Paris Business Forms, Inc. PBFI
122 Kissel Road
Burlington, NJ 08016 (609) 387-7300
business forms manufacturer

Park Communications, Inc. PARC
Terrace Hill
Ithaca, NY 14850 (607) 272-9020
television, radio stations, newspapers

Park-Ohio Industries, Inc. PKOH
20600 Chagrin Blvd.
Cleveland, OH 44122 (216) 991-9700
machined products, containers, industrial
rubber

Parkway Company (The) PKWY
120 North Congress Street
Jackson, MS 39225 (601) 948-4091
financial services

Parlex Corporation PRLX
145 Milk Street
Methuen, MA 01844 (617) 685-4341
semiconductor equipment

Patlex Corporation PTLX
533 South Avenue West
Westfield, NJ 07090 (201) 654-6620
enforces and exploits patents, lasers

Patrick Industries, Inc. PATK
1800 South 14th Street
Elkhart, IN 46515 (219) 294-7511
makes building materials for mobile homes

Paul Harris Stores, Inc. PHRS
6003 Guion Road
Indianapolis, IN 46268 (317) 293-3900
women's business apparel retailing

Paxton, Frank Company PAXTA
9229 Ward PArkway
Kansas City, MO 64114 (816) 361-7110
supplies hardwood lumber and plywood

Paychex, Inc. PAYX
911 Panorama Trail South
Rochester, NY 14625 (716) 385-6666
payroll services

Payco American Corporation PAYC
180 North Executive Drive
Brookfield, WI 53005 (414) 784-9035
collection agency

PCA International, Inc. PCAI
815 Matthews-Mint Hill Road
Matthews, NC 28105 (704) 847-8011
color portrait photography

PCS, Inc. PCSI
9060 East Via Linda
Scottsdale, AZ 85258 (602) 391-4600
prescription drug claims processing

PDA Engineering PDAS
2975 Redhill Avenue
Costa Mesa, CA 92626 (714) 540-8900
mechanical engineering software

Peerless Manufacturing Company PMFG
2819 Walnut Hill Lane
Dallas, TX 75229 (214) 357-6181
liquid and solid separators and filters

Pelsart Resources NL PELRY
100 Railway Parade
West Perth, W.A. 6005 Australia
(09) 322-5911
gold, silver, copper mining

Penn Virginia Corporation PVIR
2500 Fidelity Bldg.
Philadelphia, PA 19109 (215) 545-6600
coal mining, oil, gas, limestone, timber

Pennsylvania Enterprises, Inc. PENT
39 Public Square
Wilkes-Barre, PA 18711 (717) 829-8600
gas and water utility DRP

Pentair, Inc. PNTA
1700 West Highway 36
St. Paul, MN 55113 (612) 636-7920
paper, industrial products, ammunition DRP

Penta Systems International, Inc. PSLI
309 East Federal Street
Baltimore, MD 21202 (301) 685-7258
composition and pagination computer
systems

Pentech International, Inc. PNTK
999 New Durham Road
Edison, NJ 08817 (201) 287-6640
colorful writing and drawing instruments

PENWEST, LTD. PENW
777 108th Avenue N.E.
Bellevue, WA 98004 (206) 462-6000
supplies specialty starch products, food
ingredients

Peoples Bancorp of Worcester, Inc. PEBW
120 Front Street
Worcester, MA 01608 (617) 791-3861
banking

Peoples Bancorporation PBNC
130 South Franklin Street
Rocky Mount, NC 27802 (919) 977-4811
banking

Peoples Heritage Financial Group, Inc.
1 Portland Square
Portland, ME 04112 (207) 761-8500
savings banking

Peoples Westchester Savings PWSB
3 Skyline Drive
Hawthorne, NY 10532 (914) 347-3800
savings banking

Perception Technology Corporation PCEP
40 Shawmut Road
Canton, MA 02021 (617) 821-0320
interactive telephone information response
systems

Perceptronics, Inc. PERC
21135 Erwin Street
Woodland Hills, CA 91367 (818) 884-7470
computer-based military training systems

PerfectData Corporation PERF
9174 Deering Avenue
Chatsworth, CA 91311 (818) 988-2400
computer maintenance equipment

Perpetual Financial Corporation PFCP
2034 Eisenhower Avenue
Alexandria, VA 22314 (703) 838-6000
savings banking

Personal Computer Products, Inc. PCPI
11590 West Bernardo Court
San Diego, CA 92127 (619) 485-8411
microprocessor products for computers

Personal Diagnostics, Inc. PERS
628 Route 10
Whippany, NJ 07981 (201) 884-2034
medical device development

Petrol Industries, Inc. PTRL
1200 North Market Street
Shreveport, LA 71107 (313) 424-6396
oil and gas

Petroleum Equipment Tools Company PTCO
Suite 600, 11000 Richmond Street
Houston, TX 77042 (713) 953-1141
rents oil and gas drilling equipment

Petroleum Helicopters, Inc. PHELK
5728 Jefferson Highway
New Orleans, LA 70183 (504) 733-6790
provides helicopter transport to oil rigs

Petrolite Corporation PLIT
100 North Broadway
St. Louis, MO 63102 (314) 241-8370
specialty chemicals and polymers

Petrominerals Corporation PTRO
Suite 9, 12362 Beach Boulevard
Stanton, CA 90680 (714) 895-6370
oil and gas exploration and production

P&F Industries, Inc. PFINA
300 Smith Street
Farmingdale, NY 11735 (516) 694-1800
ductwork contracting, pneumatic tools

Pharmacia AB PHAB
S-751 82
Uppsala, Sweden (46) 18163000
instruments and biotechnology chemicals

PharmaControl Corporation PHAR
661 Palisade Avenue
Englewood Cliffs, NJ 07632 (201) 567-9004
drugs and vitamins

Phoenix American, Inc. PHXA
2401 Kerner Boulevard
San Rafael, CA 94901 (415) 485-4500
equipment leasing limited partnerships

Phoenix Medical Technology, Inc. PHNX
P.O. Box 346
Andrews, SC 29510 (803) 221-5100
medical supplies

Phoenix Re Corporation PXRE
80 Maiden Lane
New York, NY 10038 (212) 837-9520
commercial and property reinsurance

Phoenix Technologies, Ltd. PTEC
320 Norwood Park South
Norwood, MA 02062 (617) 769-7020
software compatibility products

PhoneMate, Inc. PHMT
325 Maple Avenue
Torrance, CA 90503 (213) 618-9910
telephone answering machines

Photo Control Corporation PHOC
4800 Quebec Avenue North
Minneapolis, MN 55428 (612) 537-3601
cameras, film, photo accessories

Photographic Sciences Corporation PSCX
770 Basket Road
Webster, NY 14580 (716) 265-1600
bar-code instruments and scanners

Photronic Labs, Inc. PLAB
15 Secor Road
Brookfield, CT 06804 (203) 775-9000
makes photomasks for integrated circuits

Physicians Insurance Company of Ohio PICO
P.O. Box 281
Pickerington, OH 43147 (614) 864-7100
insurance

Pic N' Save Corporation PICN
2430 East Del Amo Boulevard
Dominguez, CA 90220 (213) 537-9220
retailing close-out merchandise

Piccadilly Cafeterias, Inc. PICC
3232 Sherwood Forest Boulevard,
P.O. Box 2467
Baton Rouge, LA 70821 (504) 293-9440
cafeteria restaurants

Piedmont BankGroup Inc. PBGI
P.O. Box 4751
Martinsville, VA 24115 (703) 632-2971
banking

Piedmont Management Company, Inc. PMAN
80 Maiden Lane
New York, NY 10038 (212) 363-4650
reinsurance, investment management

Piedmont Mining Company, Inc. PIED
4215 Stuart Andrew Boulevard
Charlotte, NC 28217 (704) 523-6866
gold mining

Pioneer Financial Corporation PION
5601 Ironbridge Parkway
Chester, VA 23831 (804) 748-9733
savings banking

Pioneer Financial Services, Inc. PFSI
304 North Main Street
Rockford, IL 61101 (815) 987-5000
life, accident, health insurance

Pioneer Group, Inc. (The) PIOG
60 State Street
Boston, MA 02109 (617) 742-7825
investment services, mutual funds

Pioneer Hi-Bred Internmational, Inc. PHYB
6800 Pioneer Parkway
Johnston, IA 50131 (515) 270-3100
hybrid seed corn, plant inoculants DRP

Pioneer Savings Bank PSBF
Pioneer Center, 5770 Roosevelt Boulevard
Clearwater, FL 34620 (813) 530-7600
savings banking

Pioneer-Standard Electronics, Inc. PIOS
4800 East 131st Street
Garfield Heights, OH 44105 (216) 587-3600
industrial electronics components distributor

Piper Jaffray, Inc. PIPR
222 South Ninth Street
Minneapolis, MN 55402 (612) 342-6000
securities brokerage, investment banking

Plains Resources, Inc. PLNS
1601 Northwest Expressway
Oklahoma City, OK 73118 (405) 842-2008
oil and gas exploration and production

Planters Corporation (The) PNBT
131 North Church Street
Rocky Mount, NC 27804 (919) 977-8211
banking DRP

Plasti-Line, Inc. SIGN
623 East Emory Road
Knoxville, TN 37950 (615) 938-1511
indoor and outdoor signs

Plaza Commerce Bancorp PLZA
55 Almaden Boulevard
San Jose, CA 95113 (408) 294-8940
banking

Plenum Publishing Corporation PLEN
233 Spring Street
New York, NY 10013 (212) 620-8000
publishing, books

Plexus Resources Corporation PLUSF
175 South West Temple Street
Salt Lake City, UT 84101 (801) 363-9152
develops oil, gas and natural resources
properties

Polk Audio, Inc. POLK
5601 Metro Drive
Baltimore, MD 21215 (301) 358-3600
loudspeaker systems

Policy Management Systems Corporation
PMSC
One PMS Center
Columbia, SC 29202 (803) 735-4000
software for insurance companies

Ponce Federal Bank, FSB PFBS
Villa and Concordia Streets
Ponce, PR 00731 (809) 844-8100
banking

Ports of Call, Inc. POCI
2121 Valentia Street
Denver, CO 80220 (303) 321-6767
arranges travel packages

Possis Corporation POSS
750 Pennsylvania Avenue South
Minneapolis, MN 55426 (612) 545-1471
engineering, design and manufacturing
services

Poughkeepsie Savings Bank, FSB (The) PKPS
2 Garden Street
Poughkeepsie, NY 12601 (914) 431-6200
savings banking

Powell Industries, Inc. POWL
8550 Mosley Drive
Houston, TX 77075 (713) 944-6900
electrical distribution equipment

Prab Robots, Inc. PRAB
6007 Sprinkle Road
Kalamazoo, MI 49003 (616) 329-0835
industrial robots, automation systems,
conveyors

Praxis Biologics, Inc. PRXS
Suite 300, 30 Corporate Woods
Rochester, NY 14623 (716) 272-7000
purified vaccines for infectious diseases

Precision Castparts Corporation PCST
4600 S.E. Harney Drive
Portland, OR 97206 (503) 652-3550
investment castings of aerospace components
0

Preferred Risk Life Insurance Company PFDR
1111 Ashworth Road
West Des Moines, IA 50265 (515) 225-5000
life, health insurance for non-users of alcohol

Premier Bancorp, Inc. PRBC
P.O. Box 3399
Baton Rouge, LA 70821 (504) 389-4206
banking

Presidential Life Corporation PLFE
69 Lydecker Street
Nyack, NY 10960 (914) 358-2300
life insurance

Preston Corporation PTRK
151 Easton Boulevard
Preston, MD 21655 (301) 673-7151
trucking services

Preway, Inc. PRW
595 Summer Street
Stamford, CT 06901 (203) 357-1006
gas barbecue grills, space heaters

Priam Corporation PRIA
20 West Montague Expressway
San Jose, CA 95134 (408) 434-9300
computer disk drives

Price, T. Rowe Associates, Inc. TROW
100 East Pratt Street
Baltimore, MD 21202 (301) 547-2000
investment management, mutual funds

Price Company (The) PCLB
2657 Ariane Drive
San Diego, CA 92117 (619) 581-4600
wholesale membership merchandise outlets
0

Price Stern Sloan, Inc. PSSP
360 North La Cienega Boulevard
Los Angeles, CA 90048 (213) 657-6100
children's books, educational aids, novelties

Pricor, Inc. PRCO
440 Metroplex Drive
Nashville, TN 37211 (615) 834-3030
detention and correctional services for
government

Pride Petroleum Services, Inc. PRDE
Suite 1500, 3040 Post Oak Boulevard
Houston, TX 77056 (713) 871-8567
oil and gas well servicing

Prime Medical Services PMSI
240 Madison Avenue
New York, NY 10016 (212) 685-3570
cardiac rehabilitation, diagnostic imaging
services

Printronix, Inc. PTNX
17500 Cartwright Road
Irvine, CA 92713 (714) 863-1900
computer printers

Production Operators Corporation PROP
11302 Tanner Road
Houston, TX 77041 (713) 466-0980
oil and gas services

Professional Investors Insurance Group, Inc.
PROF
9933 East 16th Street
Tulsa, OK 74128 (918) 665-8280
life, health, accident, crop insurance

Profit Systems, Inc. PFTS
80 West Sunrise Highway
Valley Stream, NY 11581 (516) 791-1551
air freight services

Profit Technology, Inc. PRTE
17 Battery Place
New York, NY 10004 (212) 809-3500
productivity and training software

Programming and Systems, Inc. PSYS
269 West 40th Street
New York, NY 10018 (212) 944-9200
vocational school training

Progress Federal Savings Bank PBNK
One Montgomery Plaza
Norristown, PA 19401 (215) 272-3500
banking

ProGroup, Inc. PRGR
6201 Mountainview Road
Ooltewah, TN 37363 (615) 238-5890
golf equipment, sporting apparel

ProNet, Inc. PNET
2400 Lakeside Boulevard
Richardson, TX 75081 (214) 235-5111
automated paging systems for doctors

Property Trust of America PTRAS
4487 North Mesa
El Paso, TX 79902 (915) 532-3901
real estate investment trust

Prospect Group, Inc. PROS
645 Madison Avenue
New York, NY 10022 (212) 758-8500
investment company, railroad, knives

Prospect Park Financial Corporation PPSA
989 McBride Avenue
West Paterson, NJ 07424 (201) 890-1234
savings and loan

Protective Life Corporation PROT
2801 Highway 280 South
Birmingham, AL 35223 (205) 879-9230
life, health insurance

Provident Bankshares Corporation PBKS
144 East Lexington Street
Baltimore, MD 21202 (301) 281-7349
savings banking

Provident Life & Accident Insurance Co. of America PACCB
Fountain Square
Chattanooga, TN 37402 (615) 755-1011
life, health, accident insurance

PSICOR, Inc. PCOR
16818 Via del Campo Court
San Diego, CA 92127 (619) 485-5599
supplies technicians and equipment for heart surgery

Pubco Corporation PUBO
3830 Kelley Avenue
Cleveland, OH 44114 (216) 861-5300
commercial printing, outerwear apparel

Public Service Company of North Carolina, Inc. PSNC
400 Cox Road
Gastonia, NC 28053 (704) 864-6731
gas utility DRP

Publishers Equipment PECN
16660 Dallas Parkway
Dallas, TX 75248 (214) 931-2312
newspaper production equipment

Puget Sound Bancorp PSNB
1119 Pacific Avenue
Tacoma, WA 98402 (206) 593-3600
banking

Pulaski Furniture Corporation PLFC
1 Pulaski Square, P.O. Box 1371
Pulaski, VA 24301 (703) 980-7330
furniture

Pulitzer Publishing Company PLTZ
900 North Tucker Boulevard
St. Louis, MO 63101 (314) 622-7000
newspapers, television and radio stations

Puritan-Bennett Corporation PBEN
9401 Indian Creek Parkway, P.O. Box 25905
Overland Park, KS 66225 (913) 661-0444
inhalation therapy, pulmonary diagnostic equipment

PWA Corporation PWA
Suite 2800, 700 2nd Street S.W.
Calgary, AB, CDA T2P 2W2 (403) 294-2000
airline

Pyramid Oil Company PYOL
2008 21st Street
Bakersfield, CA 93301 (805) 325-1000
oil and gas drilling

Pyramid Technology Corporation PYRD
1295 Charleston Road
Mountain View, CA 94039 (415) 965-7200
supermini and minimainframe computers

QED Exploration, Inc. QEDX
Suite 1560, 1616 Glenarm Place
Denver, CO 80202 (303) 572-7832
oil and gas exploration and production

Qintex Entertainment, Inc. QNTX
345 North Maple Drive
Beverly Hills, CA 90210 (213) 281-2600
television production, film distribution

QMax Technology Group, Inc. QMAX
1001 Brown School Road
Vandalia, OH 45377 (513) 890-5231
cosmetics, skin care, fragrances, drugs

Q-Med, Inc. QEKG
67 Walnut Avenue
Clark, NJ 07066 (201) 381-6880
cardiac monitors

Quadrax Corporation QDRX
300 High Point Avenue
Portsmouth, RI 02871 (401) 683-6600
develops composites for aerospace uses

Quadrex Corporation QUAD
1700 Dell Avenue
Campbell, CA 95008 (408) 866-4510
nuclear power engineering services

Quaker Chemical Corporation QCHM
Elm and Lee Streets
Conshohocken, PA 19428 (215) 828-4250
specialty chemicals for industrial applications

Quality Food Centers QFCI
10112 N.E. 10th Street
Bellevue, WA 98004 (206) 454-8107
supermarkets

Quality Systems, Inc. QSII
17822 East 17th Street
Tustin, CA 92680 (714) 731-7171
dental and medical computer systems

Quantronix Corporation QUAN
49 Wireless Boulevard
Smithtown, NY 11787 (516) 273-6900
solid-state lasers for semiconductor
manufacturing

Quantum Corporation QNTM
1804 McCarthy Boulevard
Milpitas, CA 95035 (408) 432-1100
computer disk drives

Quarex Industries, Inc. QRXI
47-05 Metropolitan Avenue
Ridgewood, NY 11385 (718) 821-0011
wholesale meat, poultry, grocery services

Quest Biotechnology, Inc. QBIO
320 Fisher Building
Detroit, MI 48202 (313) 873-0200
produces recombinant monoclocal antibodies

QuesTech, Inc. QTEC
7600 Leesburg Pike
Falls Church, VA 22043 (703) 760-1000
engineering for defense department

Quest Medical, Inc. QMED
4103 Billy Mitchell Drive
Dallas, TX 75244 (214) 387-2740
intravenous, surgical hospital products

Quiksilver, Inc. QUIK
1740 Monrovia Avenue
Costa Mesa, CA 92627 (714) 645-1395
men's and boys beachwear and casual
clothing

Quixote Corporation QUIX
One East Wacker Drive
Chicago, IL 60601 (312) 467-6755
highway crash cushions, transcription
systems

QVC Network, Inc. QVCN
Goshen Corporate Park
West Chester, PA 19380 (215) 430-1000
consumer products marketing over cable TV

Rabbit Software Corporation RABT
7 Great Valley Parkway East
Malvern, PA 19355 (215) 647-0440
communications hardware and software

Radiation Systems, Inc. RADS
1501 Moran Road
Sterling, VA 22170 (703) 450-5680
communication antennas

Radiant Technology Corporation RTCC
5395 East Hunter Avenue
Anaheim, CA 92807 (714) 970-1522
infrared ovens for electronic circuitry makers

Ragen Corporation RAGN
9 Porete Avenue
North Arlington, NJ 07032 (201) 997-1000
mechanical and electronic components for
high-tech

Ramapo Financial Corporation RMPO
64 Mountain View Blvd.
Wayne, NJ 07470 (201) 696-6100
banking

Ramsay Health Care, Inc. RHCI
1 Poydras Plaza, 639 Loyola Avenue
New Orleans, LA 70113 (504) 525-2505
acute-care psychiatric hospitals

Rangaire Corporation RANG
501 South Wilhite Street
Cleburne, TX 76031 (817) 477-2161
lighting fixtures, range hoods, freezers,
limestone

Rank Organization, PLC RANKY
11 Hill Street
London W1X 8AE UK (312) 297-2124
film and TV services, recreation parks,
duplicating

Rauch Industries, Inc. RCHI
6048 South York Road
Gastonia, NC 28053 (704) 867-5333
glass and satin Christmas tree ornaments

Rax Restaurants, Inc. RAXR
1266 Dublin Road
Columbus, OH 43215 (614) 486-3669
restaurants

Raymond Corporation (The) RAYM
Canal Street
Greene, NY 13778 (607) 656-2311
materials handling systems for warehouses

ReadiCare, Inc. REDI
3 Corporate Plaza Drive
Newport Beach, CA 92660 (714) 476-8743
outpatient medical centers

Reading Company RDGC
1101 Market Street, Reading Center
Philadelphia, PA 19107 (215) 922-3303
real estate development, windows, walls

Realist, Inc. RLST
16288 Megal Drive
Menemonee Falls, WI 53051 (414) 251-8100
micrographic products, surveying
instruments

Recoton Corporation RCOT
46-23 Crane Street
Long Island City, NY 11101 (718) 392-6442
consumer electronics accessories

Red Eagle Resources Corporation REDX
1601 Northwest Expressway
Oklahoma City, OK 73118 (405) 843-8066
oil and gas development

Reeds Jewelers, Inc. REED
2525 South 17th Street
Wilmington, NC 28401 (919) 350-3100
retail jewelry stores

Reeves Communications Corporation RVCC
708 Third Avenue
New York, NY 10017 (212) 573-8880
produces television programs

Refac Technology Development Corporation
REFC
122 East 42nd Street
New York, NY 10168 (212) 687-4741
acquires rights to manufacture electronic
products

Reflectone, Inc. RFTN
5125 Tampa West Boulevard
Tampa, FL 33634 (813) 885-7481
electronic training systems, simulators

Regency Cruises, Inc. SHIP
260 Madison Avenue
New York, NY 10016 (212) 972-4774
operates cruise ships

Regency Electronics, Inc. RGCY
7707 Records Street
Indianapolis, IN 46226 (317) 545-4281
radio communications

Regency Equities Corporation RGEQ
131 S. Rodeo Drive
Beverly Hills, CA 90212 (213) 276-6224
financial services

Relational Technology, Inc. RELY
1080 Marina Village Parkway
Alameda, CA 94501 (415) 769-1400
database management and application
software

Reliability, Inc. REAL
16400 Park Row, P.O. Box 218370
Houston, TX 77218 (713) 492-0550
integrated circuit testing equipment

Repco, Inc. RPCO
2421 North Orange Blossom
Orlando, FL 32804 (305) 843-8484
radio communications, mobile telephones

Repligen Corporation RGEN
1 Kendall Square
Cambridge, MA 02139 (617) 225-6000
health care products using recombinant DNA

Republic Automotive Parts, Inc. RAUT
500 Wilson Pike Circle
Brentwood, TN 37027 (615) 373-2050
auto replacement parts

Republic Pictures Corporation RPICA
12636 Beatrice Street
Los Angeles, CA 90066 (213) 306-4040
motion pictures, TV series, videocassettes

Resdel Industries RSDL
Suite 550, 4000 MacArthur Boulevard
Newport Beach, CA 92660 (714) 955-0515
high-technology electronic communications
equipment

Research Frontiers, Inc. REFR
240 Crossways Park Drive
Woodbury, NY 11797 (516) 364-1902
light-control technology development

Research, Inc. RESR
P.O. Box 24064
Minneapolis, MN 55424 (612) 941-3300
process control instruments, heating devices

Research Industries Corporation
1847 West 2300 South
Salt Lake City, UT 84119 (801) 972-5500
cardiovacular devices, nerve repair implants,
drugs

Reserve Industries ROIL
Suite 308, 20 First Plaza
Albuquerque, NM 87102 (505) 247-2384
recycles magnesium waste streams, silica
mining

Respironics, Inc. RESP
530 Seco Road
Monroeville, PA 15146 (412) 373-8114
respiratory medical products

Retailing Corporation of America RCOA
111 East Wisconsin Avenue
Milwaukee, WI 53202 (414) 272-5373
health and beauty aid retailing

Reuter, Inc. REUT
410 - 11th Avenue South
Hopkins, MN 55343 (612) 935-6921
disc-pack spindles for computer
manufacturers

Reuters Holdings PLC RTRSY
85 Fleet Street
London EC4P 4AJ UK (01) 250-1122
financial information and news services

Revere Fund, Inc. PREV
575 Fifth Avenue
New York, NY 10017 (212) 808-9090
closed-end corporate bond investment
company

Rexon, Inc. REXN
5800 Uplander Way
Culver City, CA 90230 (213) 641-7110
word processing computers, data storage

Rheometrics, Inc. RHEM
1 Possumtown Road
Piscataway, NJ 08854 (201) 560-8550
rheological instruments measure material
flow

Ribi Immunochem Research, Inc. RIBI
N.E. 581 Old Corvallis Road, P.O. Box 1409
Hamilton, MT 59840 (406) 363-6214
immune system biomedical agents

Richardson Electronics, Ltd. RELL
40W267 Keslinger Road
LaFox, IL 60147 (312) 232-6400
semiconductors to control electric power

Richfood Holdings RCHFA
2000 Richfood Road
Richmond, VA 23261 (804) 746-6000
wholesale food distribution

Richton International Corporation RIHL
1345 Avenue of the Americas
New York, NY 10105 (212) 765-6480
makes and markets fashion jewelry

Riggs National Corporation RIGS
1503 Pennsylvania Avenue, N.W.
Washington, DC 20005 (202) 835-6000
banking

Ripley Company, Inc. RIPY
46 Nooks Hill Road
Cromwell, CT 06416 (203) 635-2200
outdoor lighting controls for highway fixtures

Ritzy's, Inc. (G.D.) RITZ
1496 Old Henderson Road
Columbus, OH 43220 (614) 459-3250
restaurants

River Forest Bancorp RFBC
7727 Lake Street
River Forest, IL 60305 (312) 771-2500
banking

Riverside Group, Inc. RSGI
10 West Adams Street
Jacksonville, FL 32202 (904) 350-1150
collateral protection, mobile home, credit
insurance

Roadmaster Industries, Inc. WHEL
7315 East Peakview Avenue
Englewood, CO 80111 (303) 796-8940
makes bicycles, tricycles, children's toys

Roadway Services, Inc. ROAD
1077 Gorge Boulevard, P.O. Box 88
Akron, OH 44309 (216) 384-8184
trucking DRP 0

Roanoke Electric Steel Corporation RESC
102 Miller Street, N.W.
Roanoke, VA 24017 (703) 342-1831
steel mills

Robbins & Myers, Inc. ROBN
1400 Kettering Tower
Dayton, OH 45423 (513) 222-2610
industrial pumps, electric motors, controls

Robert Half International, Inc. RHII
111 Pine Street
San Francisco, CA 94111 (415) 362-4253
temporary and permanent personnel services

Robeson Industries Corporation RBSN
49 Windsor Avenue
Mineola, NY 11501 (516) 741-0420
household electric appliances, fans, heaters

Robinson Nugent, Inc. RNIC
800 East Eighth Street, P.O. Box 1208
New Albany, IN 47150 (812) 945-0211
electronic connectors, integrated circuit
sockets

Robotic Vision Systems, Inc. ROBV
425 Rabro Drive East
Hauppauge, NY 11788 (516) 273-9700
3-D machine vision for manufacturing

Rochester Community Savings Bank RCSB
40 Franklin Street
Rochester, NY 14604 (716) 262-5800
savings banking

Rockwood Holding Company RKWD
118 West Main Street
Somerset, PA 15501 (814) 443-1471
insurance

Rockwood National Corporation RNC
300 1 Jackson Place, 188 East Capitol Street
Jackson, MS 39201 (601) 948-4091
real estate development

Rocky Mount Undergarment Company, Inc.
RMUC
1536 Boone Street
Rocky Mount, NC 27801 (919) 446-5188
fashion and basic underwear

Rodime PLC RODMY
Rothesay House, Rothesay Place
Glenrothes, Scotland KY& 6PW
makes magnetic rigid disk drives

Rogers Communications, Inc. RCI.A
Suite 2600, Commercial Union Tower
Toronto, Ontario, CDA M5K 1J5
(416) 864-2373
radio and television stations, cellular
telephone

Ronson Corporation RONC
Campus Drive, P.O. Box 6707
Somerset, NJ 08875 (201) 469-8300
lighter flints, aerospace valves, flight controls

Roosevelt Financial Group RFED
900 Roosevelt Parkway
Chesterfield, MO 63017 (314) 532-6200
savings banking

Ropak Corporation ROPK
660 South State College Boulevard
Fullerton, CA 92631 (714) 870-9757
plastic shipping containers

Rose's Stores, Inc. RSTO
218 South Garnett Street
Henderson, NC 27536 (919) 492-8111
discount and variety stores

Rospatch Corporation RPCH
3101 Walkent Drive, N.W.
Walker, MI 49504 (616) 956-8000
ready-to-assemble furniture, avionics

Ross Cosmetics Distribution Centers, Inc.
RCDC
111 Commerce Court
Duncan, SC 29334 (803) 439-7854
cosmetics, fragrances, health and beauty
aids

Ross Stores, Inc. ROST
P.O. Box 728
Newark, CA 94560 (415) 790-4400
off-price retail apparel stores

RoTech Medical Corporation ROTC
4506 L.B. McLeod Road
Orlando, FL 32811 (305) 841-2115
outpatient medical products and services

Roto-Rooter, Inc. ROTO
Suite 1400, DuBois Tower, 511 Walnut Street
Cincinnati, OH 45202 (513) 762-6690
sewer and drain cleaning services

Rouse Company (The) ROUS
10275 Little Patuxent Parkway
Columbia, MD 21044 (301) 992-6000
real estate development

Rowe Furniture Corporation ROWE
239 Rowan Street
Salem, VA 24153 (703) 389-8671
contemporary upholstered furniture

Royal Gold, Inc. RGLD
Suite 1000, 1660 Wynkoop
Denver, CO 80202 (303) 573-1660
gold mining

Royal Palm Savings Association RPAL
100 Australian Avenue
West Palm Beach, FL 33406 (305) 478-0500
savings banking

Royal Par Industries ROYL
40 South Street
Hartford, CT 06110 (203) 249-6315
temporary personnel for aerospace industry

RPM, Inc. RPOW
2628 Pearl Road, P.O. Box 777
Medina, OH 44258 (216) 225-3192
specialty chemicals, building products DRP

RSI Corporation RSIC
1 Shelter Centre
Greenville, SC 29601 (803) 271-7171
outdoor power equipment, furniture, doors

RTI, Inc. RTII
51 Gibraltar Road
Morris Plains, NJ 07950 (201) 898-0042
irradiation treatment for food and chemicals

Rule Industries, Inc. RULE
Cape Ann Industrial Park
Gloucester, MA 01930 (508) 281-0440
fasteners, marine and hardware products

Ryan's Family Steak Houses, Inc. RYAN
405 Lancaster Avenue
Greer, SC 29651 (803) 879-1000
restaurants

SafeCard Services, Inc. SFCD
6400 N.W. 6th Way
Fort Lauderdale, FL 33309 (305) 776-2500
credit card protection services

Safeco Corporation SAFC
Safeco Plaza T-14
Seattle, WA 98185 (206) 545-5000
property-casualty, life insurance, investments
O

Safeguard Health Enterprises SFGD
505 North Euclid Street
Anaheim, CA 92803 (714) 778-1284
operates dental care plan

Sage Software, Inc. SGSI
3200 Monroe Street
Rockville, MD 20852 (301) 230-3200
computer-aided software engineering

Sahara Resorts SHRE
2535 Las Vegas Boulevard South
Las Vegas, NV 89109 (702) 737-2111
casinos and hotels

Sahlen & Associates, Inc. SALN
600 Hillsboro Boulevard
Deerfield Beach, FL 33441 (305) 429-3301
private investigation services, security guards

St. Helena Gold Mines, Ltd. SGOLY
General Mining Building, 6 Hollard Street
Johannesburg 2001, South Africa
gold mining

St. Ives Laboratories Corporation SWIS
8944 Mason Avenue
Chatsworth, CA 91311 (818) 709-5500
shampoos, skin care lotions, hair sprays

St. Jude Medical, Inc. STJM
1 Lillehei Plaza
St. Paul, MN 55117 (612) 483-2000
makes mechanical heart valves O

St. Paul Bancorp SPBC
6700 West North Avenue
Chicago, IL 60635 (312) 622-5000
savings banking

St. Paul Companies, Inc. STPL
385 Washington Street
St. Paul, MN 55102 (612) 221-7911
property-casualty insurance, investments DRP
O

Salem Carpet Mills, Inc. SLCR
Suite 1100, NCNB Plaza
Winston-Salem, NC 27101 (919) 727-1200
carpeting

Salick Health Care, Inc. SHCI
407 North Maple Drive
Beverly Hills, CA 90210 (213) 276-0732
diagnostic and cancer treatment, kidney
dialysis

Samna Corporation SMNA
5600 Glenridge Drive
Atlanta, GA 30342 (404) 851-0007
word processing software

Sanderson Farms, Inc. SAFM
225 North 13th Avenue
Laurel, MS 39440 (601) 649-4030
produces fresh and frozen chicken

Sands Regent SNDS
345 North Arlington Avenue
Reno, NV 89501 (702) 348-2200
casino, hotel

Sandwich Chef, Inc. SHEF
3514 Lornaridge Drive
Birmingham, AL 35216 (205) 822-3960
sandwich shops, convenience stores

Sanford Corporation SANF
2740 Washington Boulevard
Bellwood, IL 60104 (312) 547-6650
disposable writing and marking instruments

Santa Monica Bank SANT
1251 Fourth Street
Santa Monica, CA 90401 (213) 394-9611
banking

Satellite Music Network SMNI
12655 North Central Expressway
Dallas, TX 75243 (214) 991-9200
live radio programming network

Savannah Foods & Industries, Inc. SVAN
P.O. Box 339
Savannah, GA 31402 (912) 234-1261
sugar refining DRP

Saxon Oil Company SAXO
717 North Harwood
Dallas, TX 75201 (214) 745-1300
oil and gas

Scanforms, Inc. SCFM
181 Rittenhouse Circle Keystone Park
Bristol, PA 19007 (215) 785-0101
direct mail specialty continuous forms

Scan-Optics, Inc. SOCR
22 Prestige Park Circle
East Hartford, CT 06108 (203) 289-6001
optical data capture systems

Scherer (R. P.) Corporation SCHC
2075 West Big Beaver Road
Troy, MI 48007 (313) 649-0900
soft gelatin capsules for nutrition, drugs

Schulman (A)., Inc. SHLM
3550 West Market Street
Akron, OH 44313 (216) 666-3751
engineered plastic compounds

Scicom Data Services, Ltd. SCIE
10101 Bren Road East
Minnetonka, MN 55343 (612) 933-4200
computerized direct mail services

Schultz Sav-O Stores, Inc. SAVO
2215 Union Avenue
Sheboygan, WI 53801 (414) 457-4433
wholesale food distribution, supermarkets

Science Accessories Corporation SEAS
200 Watson Boulevard
Stratford, CT 06497 (203) 386-9978
sonic digitizers to measure distances

Science Dynamics Corporation SIDY
1919 Springdale Road
Cherry Hill, NJ 08003 (609) 424-0068
electronics

Scientific Measurement Systems, Inc. SCMS
2201 Donley Drive
Austin, TX 78758 (512) 837-4712
tomographic and digital radiographic systems

Scientific Software-Intercomp, Inc. SSFT
1801 California Street
Denver, CO 80202 (303) 292-1111
software for petroleum industry

SciMed Life Systems, Inc. SMLS
13000 County Road 6
Minneapolis, MN 55441 (612) 559-9504
oxygenator systems, angioplasty catheters

SCI Systems, Inc. SCIS
5000 Technology Drive
Huntsville, AL 35805 (302) 998-0592
computer products, electronic subsystems O

Scitex Corporation, Ltd. SCIXF
Hamada Street
Herzlia B 46 103, Israel (052) 549-2222
computer imaging systems

Scott's Liquid Gold, Inc. SLIQ
4880 Havana Street
Denver, CO 80239 (303) 373-4860
wood preservatives, air fresheners, cigarette
filters

Scott & Stringfellow Financial, Inc. SCOT
909 East Main Street
Richmond, VA 23219 (804) 643-1811
securities brokerage, investment banking

Scribe Systems, Inc. SSIX
163 Pioneer Drive
Leominster, MA 01453 (508) 537-4001
electronic publishing systems

Scripps, E.W. Company EWSCA
1409 Foulk Road
Wilmington, DE 19803 (302) 478-4141
newspapers, radio and TV stations, cable TV

Scripps-Howard Broadcasting Co. SCRP
1100 Central Trust Tower
Cincinnati, OH 45202 (513) 977-3000
television and radio stations, cable TV
systems

SCS/Compute, Inc. SCOM
1714 Deer Tracks Trail
St. Louis, MO 63131 (314) 966-1040
income tax return processing

Sea Galley Stores, Inc. SEAG
6920-220th S.W.
Mountlake Terrace, WA 98043
(206) 775-0411
seafood restaurants

Seacoast Banking Corporation of Florida
SBCFA
815 Colorado Avenue
Stuart, FL 34994 (407) 287-4000
banking

Seagate Technology, Inc. SGAT
920 Disc Drive
Scotts Valley, CA 95066 (408) 438-6550
computer disk drives O

Sealright Company, Inc. SRCO
Suite 500, 8330 Ward Parkway
Kansas City, MO 64114 (816) 926-2000
ice cream packaging, plastic food packaging

Seattle FilmWorks, Inc. FOTO
1260 16th Avenue West
Seattle, WA 98119 (206) 281-1390
direct mail marketer of film and
photofinishing

Seaway Food Town, Inc. SEWY
1020 Ford Street
Maumee, OH 43537 (419) 893-9401
supermarkets and drugstores

Second National Federal Savings SNFS
2045 West Street
Annapolis, MD 21401 (301) 749-8415
savings banking

Security American Financial Enterprises, Inc.
SAFE
6681 Country Club Drive
Minneapolis, MN 55427 (612) 544-2121
life and health insurance

Security Bancorp, Inc. SECB
16333 Trenton Road
Southgate, MI 48195 (313) 281-5000
banking DRP

Security Federal Savings Bank SFBM
219 North 26th Street
Billings, MT 59103 (406) 259-4571
savings banking

Security Tag Systems, Inc. STAG
1615 118th Avenue North
St. Petersburg, FL 33716 (813) 576-6399
electronic article surveillance systems

SEEQ Technology, Inc. SEEQ
1849 Fortune Drive
San Jose, CA 95131 (408) 432-7400
semiconductor memory devices

Seibels Bruce Group, Inc. (The) SBIG
1501 Lady Street
Columbia, SC 29201 (803) 748-2000
property-casualty insurance DRP 5%

SEI Corporation SEIC
680 East Swedesford Road
Wayne, PA 19087 (215) 254-1000
information for banks, investment
management

Selecterm, Inc. SLTM
153 Andover Street
Danvers, MA 01923 (617) 246-1300
computer systems management, rental

Selective Insurance Group, Inc. SIGI
Wantage Avenue
Branchville, NJ 07890 (201) 948-3000
property-casualty insurance

Selvac Corporation SLVC
1752 Limkiln Pike
Dresher, PA 19025 (215) 628-2020
hair removal appliance, non-aerosol
dispensing system

Senior Service Corporation SENR
354 Nod Hill Road
Wilton, CT 06897 (203) 834-1644
large print publishing, adult day care

Sensormatic Electronics Corporation SNSR
500 N.W. 12th Avenue
Deerfield Beach, FL 33441 (305) 427-9700
electronic and video surveillance for retailers

Sequent Computer Systems, Inc. SQNT
15450 S.W. Koll Parkway
Beaverton, OR 97006 (503) 626-5700
parallel computer systems for databases

Service Fracturing Company SERF
Highway 152W, P.O. Box 1741
Pampa, TX 79066 (806) 665-7221
oil and gas services

Seven Oaks International, Inc. QPON
Suite 100, 700 Colonial Road
Memphis, TN 38117 (901) 683-7055
coupon processing

SFE Technologies SFEM
1501 First Street
San Fernando, CA 91340 (818) 361-1176
capacitors, crystal control devices

SFFed Corporation SFFD
88 Kearny Street
San Francisco, CA 94108 (415) 955-5800
savings and loan

Shared Medical Systems Corporation SMED
51 Valley Stream Parkway
Malvern, PA 19355 (215) 296-6300
hospital computer information services O

Sharper Image Corporation SHRP
650 Davis Street
San Francisco, CA 94111 (415) 445-6000
catalog and retail merchandising of unique
items

Shelby Furniture, Inc. SWIX
1348 Merchandise Mart
Chicago, IL 60654 (312) 527-3593
furniture

Sheldahl, Inc. SHEL
P.O. Box 170
Northfield, MN 55057 (507) 663-8000
electronic circuitry, adhesives, plastic devices

SHL Systemhouse, Inc. SHKI
99 Bank Street
Ottawa, Ont. CDA K1P 6B9 (613) 236-9734
systems integration services

Shopsmith, Inc. SHOP
3931 Image Drive
Dayton, OH 45414 (513) 898-6070
woodworking tools for do-it-yourselfers

Shorewood Packaging Corporation SHOR
55 Engineers Lane
Farmingdale, NY 11735 (516) 694-2900
packaging for music and other industries

Showscan Film Corporation SHOW
1801 Century Park East
Los Angeles, CA 90067 (213) 553-2364
specialized motion picture film process

Sierra On-Line, Inc. SIER
40033 Sierra Way
Oakhurst, CA 93644 (209) 683-4468
interactive entertainment software products

Sierra Real Estate Equity Trust '83 SETB
Suite 1600, One Market Plaza
San Francisco, CA 94105 (415) 543-4141
real estate equity trust

Sierra Real Estate Equity Trust '84 SETC
Suite 1600, One Market Plaza
San Francisco, CA 94105 (415) 543-4141
real estate equity trust

Sigma-Aldrich Corporation SIAL
3050 Spruce Street
St. Louis, MO 63103 (314) 771-5765
biochemical and organic products for
research

Sigma Designs, Inc. SIGM
46501 Landing Parkway
Fremont, CA 94538 (415) 770-0100
color graphics adapters, high-resolution
monitors

SI Handling Systems, Inc. SIHS
Kesslersville Road
Easton, PA 18042 (215) 252-7321
automated manufacturing and warehousing

Silicon General, Inc. SILN
85 West Tasman Drive
San Jose, CA 95134 (408) 943-9403
telephone equipment, data conversion
products

Silicon Graphics, Inc. SGIC
2011 North Shoreline Boulevard
Mountain View, CA 94039 (415) 960-1980
3-D engineering workstations

Silicon Valley Group, Inc. SVGI
541 East Trimble Road
San Jose, CA 95131 (408) 432-9300
semiconductor processing equipment

Siliconix, Inc. SILI
2201 Laurelwood Road
Santa Clara, CA 95054 (408) 988-8000
specialty semiconductors and integrated
circuits

Silk Greenhouse, Inc. SGHI
1401 Tampa East Boulevard
Tampa, FL 33619 (813) 622-7886
artificial flower stores

Silvar-Lisco SVRL
1080 Marsh Road
Menlo Park, CA 94025 (415) 324-0700
computer-aided engineering software

Silver King Mines, Inc. SILV
2319 Foothill Drive
Salt Lake City, UT 84109 (801) 483-1116
gold and silver mining

Silverado Mines, Ltd. SLVRF
Suite 2580, 1066 West Hastings Street
Vancouver, BC, CDA V6E 3X2 (604) 689-1535
gold mining

Simpson Industries, Inc. SMPS
32100 Telegraph Road
Birmingham, MI 48010 (313) 540-6200
automotive components and assemblies DRP

Sizzler Restaurants International, Inc. SIZZ
12655 West Jefferson Boulevard
Los Angeles, CA 90066 (213) 827-2300
restaurants

S&K Famous Brands, Inc. SKFB
11100 West Broad Street
Richmond, VA 23294 (804) 346-2500
specialty retailer of men's clothing

S-K-I Ltd. SKII
c/o Killington Ltd.
Killington, VT 05751 (802) 422-3333
lodging and skiing

Skipper's, Inc. SKIP
14450 N.E. 29th Place
Bellevue, WA 98007 (206) 885-2116
seafood restaurants

Smith Laboratories, Inc. SMLB
3940 Ruffin Road
San Diego, CA 92123 (619) 569-4941
medical surgical products

Smithfield Foods, Inc. SFDS
501 North Church Street
Smithfield, VA 23430 (804) 357-4321
pork and other meat products

Society Corporation SOCI
800 Superior Avenue
Cleveland, OH 44114 (216) 622-9000
banking DRP

Society For Savings Bancorp SOCS
31 Pratt Street, P.O. Box 2200
Hartford, CT 06145 (203) 727-5000
savings banking

SofTech, Inc. SOFT
460 Totten Pond Road
Waltham, MA 02254 (617) 890-6900
custom defense software

Software Publishing Corporation SPCO
1901 Landings Drive
Mountain View, CA 94043 (415) 962-8910
productivity applications software

Solitec, Inc. SOLI
1715 Wyatt Drive
Santa Clara, CA 95054 (408) 980-1355
semiconductor test equipment

Somerset Bancorp, Inc. SOMB
P. O. Box 711
Somerville, NJ 08876 (201) 685-8852
banking

Sonoco Products Company SONO
North Second Street
Hartsville, SC 29550 (803) 383-7000
paper and plastic packaging DRP O

Sonora Gold Corporation SONNF
595 Howe Street
Vancouver, BC, CDA V6C 2T5 (604) 669-1814
gold mining

Sooner Federal S&L Association SFOK
5100 East Skelly Drive
Tulsa, OK 74135 (918) 665-6600
savings and loan

Sound Advice, Inc. SUND
1401 Tigertail Boulevard
Dania, FL 33004 (305) 922-4434
consumer electronics retailing

South Carolina National Corporation SCNC
1426 Main Street
Columbia, SC 29226 (803) 765-3000
banking

Southeastern Michigan Gas Enterprises, Inc.
SMGS
405 Water Street
Port Huron, MI 48061 (313) 987-2200
gas utility DRP

Southeastern Savings and Loan Company
SESL
112 South Tryon Street
Charlotte, NC 28284 (704) 379-1200
savings and loan

Southern California Water Company SWTR
3625 West Sixth Street
Los Angeles, CA 90020 (213) 251-3600
water utility DRP

Southern National Corporation SNAT
500 North Chestnut Street
Lumberton, NC 28358 (919) 671-2000
banking

Southland Financial Corporation SFIN
5215 North O'Connor Boulevard
Irving, TX 75039 (214) 556-0500
real estate development

SouthTrust Corporation SOTR
420 North 20th Street
Birmingham, AL 35203 (205) 254-5509
banking

Southwest National Corporation SWPA
111 South Main Street
Greensburg, PA 15601 (412) 834-2310
banking

Southwest Water Company SWWC
16340 East Maplegrove Street
La Puente, CA 91744 (818) 918-1231
water utility DRP

Sovran Financial Corporation SOVN
One Commercial Place
Norfolk, VA 23510 (804) 441-4000
banking DRP 5%

Span-America Medical Systems, Inc. SPAN
70 Commerce Drive
Greenville, SC 29615 (803) 288-8877
foam patient positioners, packaging

Spartan Motors, Inc. SPAR
1000 Reynolds Road
Charlotte, MI 48813 (517) 543-6400
custom heavy truck chassis

Spearhead Industries, Inc. SPRH
9971 Valley View Road
Minneapolis, MN 55344 (612) 941-9171
markets seasonal items, toys

Spec's Music SPEK
1666 N.W. 82nd Avenue
Miami, FL 33126 (305) 592-7288
music and video retailing

SpecTran Corporation SPTR
SpecTran Industrial Park, 50 Hall Road
Sturbridge, MA 01566 (617) 347-2261
fiberoptic cables

Spectra Pharmaceutical Services, Inc. SPCT
155 Webster Street
Hanover, MA 02339 (617) 871-3991
eyecare products

Spectrum Control, Inc. SPEC
2185 West Eighth Street
Erie, PA 16505 (814) 455-0966
electronic pollution control devices

Sphinx Mining SPNXF
101 North Second Street
Fort Smith, AR 72902 (501) 783-1145
gold mining

Spiegel, Inc. SPGLA
1515 West 22nd Street
Oak Brook, IL 60522 (312) 986-7500
catalog retailing of apparel, home furnishings

S.P.I.-Suspension and Parts Inds. Ltd. SPILF
Ha-Yotzrim Street
Carmiel 20100, Israel (972) 4988301
suspension systems for military vehicles

Spire Corporation SPIR
Patriots Park
Bedford, MA 01730 (617) 275-6000
semiconductor structures and surfaces

Square Industries, Inc. SQAI
921 Bergen Avenue
Jersey City, NJ 07306 (201) 798-0090
parking lots, gasoline stations

STAAR Surgical Company STAA
1911 Walker Avenue
Monrovia, CA 91016 (818) 303-7902
cataract surgery products, lenses

Staff Builders, Inc. SBLI
1981 Marcus Avenue
Lake Success, NY 11042 (516) 358-1000
temporary and permanent personnel

Standard Microsystems Corporation SMSC
35 Marcus Boulevard
Hauppauge, NY 11788 (516) 273-3100
standard and custom semiconductors

Standard Register Company (The) SREG
600 Albany Street
Dayton, OH 45401 (513) 443-1000
business forms

Stanford Telecommunications, Inc. STII
2421 Mission College Boulevard
Santa Clara, CA 95054 (408) 748-1010
satellite earth stations

Stanley Interiors Corporation STHF
Route 57
Stanleytown, VA 24168 (703) 629-7561
furniture and fabric products

Stansbury Mining Corporation STBY
1831 North Fort Canyon Road
Alpine, UT 84003 (801) 756-5464
mining

Stan West Mining Corporation SWMC
6045 Scottsdale Road
Scottsdale, AZ 85253 (602) 483-8000
precious metals mining

Staodynamics, Inc. SDYN
1225 Florida Avenue
Longmont, CO 80501 (303) 772-3631
medical electronic products

Star Banc Corporation STRZ
425 Walnut Street
Cincinnati, OH 45202 (513) 632-4000
banking DRP

Starstream Communications Group, Inc.
SCGI
Suite 300, 9800 Richmond Avenue
Houston, TX 77042 (713) 781-0781
radio promotions and programs

Star Technologies, Inc. STRR
515 Shaw Road
Sterling, VA 22170 (703) 689-4400
array processors

State Street Boston Corporation STBK
225 Franklin Street
Boston, MA 02110 (617) 786-3000
banking, mutual fund custodian

Statesman Group, Inc. (The) STTG
1400 Des Moines Building
Des Moines, IA 50309 (215) 284-7500
life insurance, investment banking

Steel of West Virginia SWVA
17th Street and 2nd Avenue
Huntington, WV 25726 (304) 529-7171
steel mini-mill

Steel Technologies, Inc. STTX
15415 Shelbyville Road
Louisville, KY 40223 (502) 245-2110
steel processing

Sterner Lighting Systems, Inc. SLTG
351 Lewis Avenue West
Winsted, MN 55395 (612) 473-1251
lighting equipment, energy management

Steve's Homemade Ice Cream, Inc. STVEA
5 Lawrence Street
Bloomfield, NJ 07003 (201) 429-7661
ice cream manufacturer and retailer

Stewart & Stevenson Services, Inc. SSSS
2707 North Loop West
Houston, TX 77251 (713) 868-7700
makes, distributes diesel engines, parts

Stewart Information Services Corporation
SISC
2200 West Loop South
Houston, TX 77027 (713) 871-1100
title insurance

Stewart Sandwiches, Inc. STEW
5732 Curlew Drive
Norfolk, VA 23502 (804) 466-9200
prepackaged sandwiches

Stockholder Systems, Inc. SSIAA
4411 East Jones Bridge Road
Norcross, GA 30092 (404) 441-3387
financial software

Stokely U.S.A, Inc. STKY
626 East Wisconsin Avenue
Oconomowoc, WI 53066 (414) 567-1731
processes, packages food products

Stolt Tankers and Terminals STLTF
8 Sound Shore Drive
Greenwich, CT 06836 (203) 625-9400
ocean shipping of specialty liquids

Strategic Planning Associates, Inc. SPAIB
600 New Hampshire Avenue N.W.
Washington, DC 20037 (202) 298-3300
corporate strategy and management
consulting

Stratus Computer, Inc. STRA
55 Fairbanks Blvd.
Marlborough, MA 01752 (508) 460-2000
fault-tolerant computer systems [O]

Strawbridge & Clothier STRWA
801 Market Street
Philadelphia, PA 19107 (215) 629-6779
department, self-service stores

Strober Organization (The) STRB
550 Hamilton Avenue
Brooklyn, NY 11232 (718) 875-9700
building materials supplier

Structural Dynamics Research Corporation
SDRC
2000 Eastman Drive
Milford, OH 45150 (513) 576-2400
engineering software, services supplier

Stryker Corporation STRY
420 East Alcott Street
Kalamazoo, MI 49001 (616) 385-2600
specialty surgical, medical supplies

Stuart Hall Company, Inc. STUH
117 West 20th St.
Kansas City, MO 64108 (816) 221-8480
office and school supplies, stationery

Stuarts Department Stores, Inc. STUH
45 South Street
Hopkinton, MA 01748 (508) 435-9711
discount department stores

Sturm, Ruger & Company, Inc. STRM
Lacey Place
Southport, CT 06490 (203) 259-7843
manufactures rifles, handguns

STV Engineers, Inc. STVI
11 Robinson Street
Pottstown, PA 19464 (215) 326-4600
engineering and architectural services

Subaru of America, Inc. SBRU
2235 Route 70 West
Cherry Hill, NJ 08002 (609) 488-8500
imports, distributes automobiles [O]

Suburban Bancorp SUBBA
50 North Brockway
Palatine, IL 60067 (312) 359-1077
banking

Sudbury, Inc. SUDS
25800 Science Park Drive, Suite 250
Cleveland, OH 44122 (216) 464-7026
manufactures industrial products

Suffield Savings Bank SSBK
66 North Main Street
Suffield, CT 06078 (203) 668-1261
banking

Sumitomo Bank Of California SUMI
365 California Street
San Francisco, CA 94104 (415) 445-8000
banking

Summagraphics Corporation SUGR
777 Commerce Drive
Fairfield, CT 06430 (203) 384-1344
digitizing tablets for computer graphics
systems

Summa Medical Corporation SUMA
4255 Balloon Park Road, N.E.
Albuquerque, NM 87109 (505) 345-8891
develops, produces drugs

Summcorp SMCR
One Summit Square
Fort Wayne, IN 46801 (219) 427-8333
banking

Summit Bancorporation (The) SUBN
367 Springfield Avenue
Summit, NJ 07901 (201) 522-8400
banking DRP

Summit Health Ltd. SUMH
1800 Avenue of the Stars
Los Angeles, CA 90067 (213) 201-4000
operates hospitals, nursing homes

Sun Coast Plastics, Inc. SUNI
8214 Westchester, Suite 900
Dallas, TX 75225 (214) 363-5615
designs, manufactures plastic caps

Sunair Electronics, Inc. SNRU
3101 S.W. Third Avenue
Fort Lauderdale, FL 33315 (305) 525-1505
radio communications equipment

SunGard Data Systems, Inc. SNDT
2 Glenhardie Corporate Center
1285 Drummers Lane
Wayne, PA 19087 (215) 341-8700
specialized computer services

SunGroup, Inc. SUNNC
226 Third Avenue North
Nashville, TN 37201 (615) 254-1070
radio broadcasting stations

Sunlite, Inc. SNLT
6045 Barfield Road
Atlanta, GA 30328 (404) 256-4766
oil and gas production

Sun Microsystems, Inc. SUNW
2550 Garcia Avenue
Mountain View, CA 94043 (415) 960-1300
high-performance computer workstations

Sunrise Medical, Inc. SNMD
2355 Crenshaw Boulevard, Suite 150
Torrance, CA 90501 (213) 328-8018
home health care products

Sunstar Foods, Inc. SUNF
7575 Golden Valley Road
Minneapolis, MN 55427 (612) 546-2506
consumer foods and ingredients

Sunstates Corporation SUST
1325 San Marco Blvd.
Jacksonville, FL 32207 (904) 396-1600
real estate

Sun State Savings and Loan Association
SSSL
4222 East Camelback Road
Phoenix, AZ 85018 (602) 224-1000
real estate lending and investment

Sunwest Financial Services, Inc. SFSI
303 Roma Avenue N.W.
Albuquerque, NM 87102 (505) 765-2403
banking

Super Rite Foods, Inc. SRFI
3900 Industrial Road
Harrisburg, PA 17110 (717) 232-6821
wholsesale grocery operations

Superior Electric Company (The) SUPE
383 Middle Street
Bristol, CT 06010 (203) 582-9561
manufactures electronic equipment

Supertex, Inc. SUPX
1225 Bordeaux Drive
Sunnyvale, CA 94088 (408) 744-0100
integrated circuits, semiconductor
components

Supradur Companies SUPD
411 Theodore Fremd Avenue
Rye, NY 10580 (914) 967-8230
roofing and siding products

Supreme Equipment & Systems Corporation
SEQP
170 53rd Street
Brooklyn, NY 11232 (718) 439-3800
office filing equipment

Surgical Care Affiliates, Inc. SCAF
4515 Harding Road
Nashville, TN 37205 (615) 385-3541
outpatient surgical care facilities

Survival Technology, Inc. SURV
8101 Glenbrook Road
Bethesda, MD 20814 (301) 656-5600
emergency health care products

Susquehanna Bancshares, Inc. SUSQ
9 East Main Street
Lititz, PA 17543 (717) 626-4721
banking

Swank, Inc. SNKI
6 Hazel Street
Attleboro, MA 02703 (508) 222-3400
men's, women's leather goods, jewelry

Switcho, Inc. SXCO
329 Alfred Avenue
Teaneck, NJ 07666 (201) 837-5100
telecommunications products, radio paging

Symbion, Inc. SYMB
350 West 800 North
Salt Lake City, UT 84103 (801) 531-7022
designs, produces artificial organs

Symbolics, Inc. SMBX
8 New England Executive Park
Burlington, MA 01803 (617) 221-1000
artificial intelligence computer systems

Sym-Tek Systems, Inc. SYMK
3912 Calle Fortunada
San Diego, CA 92123 (619) 569-6800
computers testing equipment

Synbiotics Corporation SBIO
11011 Via Frontera
San Diego, CA 92127 (619) 451-3770
biomedical products and services

Syncor International Corporation SCOR
20001 Prairie Street
Chatsworth, CA 91311 (818) 886-7400
radiopharmaceutical distributor

Synercom Technology, Inc. SYNR
2500 City West Boulevard Suite 1100
Houston, TX 77042 (713) 954-7000
mapping information management systems

Synergen, Inc. SYGN
1885 33rd Street
Boulder, CO 80301 (303) 938-6200
develops human, animal pharmaceuticals

Syntech International, Inc. SYNE
4955 Energy Way
Reno, NV 89502 (702) 329-6969
on-line player-activated lottery systems

Syntrex Inc. STRX
246 Industrial Way West
Eatontown, NJ 07724 (201) 542-1500
office automation equipment

Syntro Corporation SYNT
10655 Sorrento Valley Road
San Diego, CA 92121 (619) 453-4000

Systematics, Inc. SYST
4001 Rodney Perham Road
Little Rock, AK 72212 (501) 223-5100
data processing services, software

Systems & Computer Technology Corporation
SCTC
4 Country View Road
Malvern, PA 19355 (215) 647-5930
applications software for education and
government

System Software Associates SSAX
500 West Madison
Chicago, IL 60606 (312) 641-2900
manufacturing and financial software

Taco Villa, Inc. TVLA
1801 Royal Lane, Suite 902
Dallas, TX 75229 (214) 556-0955
Mexican fast-food restaurants

Taco Viva, Inc. TVIV
1500 N.W. 62 Street
Ft. Lauderdale, FL 33309 (305) 772-4224
Mexican fast-food restaurants

Talman Home Federal Savings and Loan
TLMN
30 West Monroe Street
Chicago, IL 60603 (312) 726-8915
savings and loan

Tandon Corporation TCOR
301 Science Drive
Moorpark, CA 93021 (805) 523-0340
microcomputer systems and subsystems

Taro Vit Industries, Ltd. TAROF
333 Halstead Avenue
Mamaroneck, NY 10543 (914) 381-4810
manufactures generic pharmaceuticals

Taylor Devices, Inc. TAYD
90 Taylor Drive
North Tonawanda, NY 14120 (716) 694-0800
tension control devices for machinery

TBC Corporation TBCC
4770 Hickory Hill Road
Memphis, TN 38115 (901) 363-8030
produces, distributes auto parts

TCA Cable TV, Inc. TCAT
3015 S.E. Loop 323
Tyler, TX 75701 (214) 595-3701
operates cable TV systems

TCF Financial Corporation TCFC
801 Marquette Avenue, Suite 302
Minneapolis, MN 55402 (612) 370-7000
savings and loan

TCI International, Inc. TCII
34175 Ardenwood Boulevard
Fremont, CA 94536 (415) 795-7800
specialty communications equipment

Tech Data Corporation TECD
5777 Myerlake Circle
Clearwater, FL 33520 (813) 539-7429
computer products and printers

Techdyne, Inc. TCDN
2230 West 77th Street
Hialeah, FL 33016 (305) 556-9210
manufactures electronic assemblies

Technalysis Corporation TECN
6700 France Avenue South
Minneapolis, MN 55435 (612) 925-5900
computer system design, programming

Technical Communications Corporation TCCO
100 Domino Drive
Concord, MA 01742 (617) 862-6035
electrical equipment

Techniclone International Corporation TCLN
14282 Franklin Avenue
Tustin, CA 92680 (714) 838-0500
biotechnology

Technology for Communications International
TCII
1625 Stierlin Drive
Mountain View, CA 94043 (415) 962-5200
communications equipment

Tecogen, Inc. TCGN
45 First Avenue
Waltham, MA 02254 (617) 622-1400
makes cogeneration systems

Tecumseh Products Company TECU
100 East Patterson Street
Tecumseh, MI 49286 (517) 423-8411
refrigeration compressors and products

Tekelec TKLC
26540 Agoura Road
Calabasas, CA 91302 (818) 880-5656
telecommunications test equipment

Telco Systems, Inc. TELC
63 Nahaten Street
Norwood, MA 02062 (617) 551-0300
fiber optic telecommunications equipment

Tele-Communications, Inc. TCOMA
Terminal Annex, P.O. Box 5630
Denver, CO 80217 (303) 721-5500
cable television systems [O]

Telecommunications Network, Inc. TNII
146 Midland Avenue
Kearny, NJ 07032 (201) 997-8400
radio paging, telephone answering systems

Telecom Plus International, Inc. TELE
48-40 34th Street
Long Island City, NY 11101 (718) 392-7700
communications equipment

Telecrafter Corporation TLCR
11350 Technology Circle
Duluth, MN 30136 (404) 623-0096
satellite communications equipment

Telecredit, Inc. TCRD
6171 West Century Boulevard
Los Angeles, CA 90045 (213) 410-4600
check and credit card payment systems

Telefonos de Mexico SA de CV TFONY
Parque Via 198
Mexico City, DF, Mexico (905) 518-8220
telephone service for Mexico

Telematics International, Inc. TMAX
1201 Cypress Creek Road
Ft. Lauderdale, FL 33309 (305) 772-3070
computer products for communications
networks

Telenetics Corporation TNET
895 Yorba Linda Boulevard
Placentia, CA 92670 (714) 779-2766
manufactures modems for data transmission

Teleprobe Systems, Inc. PROB
1385 Akron Street
Copiague, NY 11726 (516) 789-5000
telecommunications equipment

TeleQuest, Inc. TELQ
7740 Kenmar Court
San Diego, CA 92121 (619) 549-6200
manufactures residential telephones

Teletimer International, Inc. TLTMC
1801 Clint Moore Road
Boca Raton, FL 33487 (407) 994-9044
computerized energy management systems

Televideo Systems, Inc. TELV
550 East Brokaw Road
San Jose, CA 95161 (408) 954-8333
manufactures computer terminals

Tellabs, Inc. TLAB
4951 Indiana Avenue
Lisle, IL 60532 (312) 969-8800
telecommunications equipment

TEL Offshore Trust TELOZ
712 Main Street
Houston, TX 77002 (713) 236-6369
oil and gas royalties

Telos Corporation TLOS
3420 Ocean Park Boulevard
Santa Monica, CA 90405 (213) 450-2424
computer software for military use

Telxon Corporation TLXN
3330 West Market Street
Akron, OH 44313 (216) 867-3700
hand-held microcomputers

TEMPEST Technologies, Inc. TTOI
460 Herndon Parkway
Herndon, VA 22070 (703) 471-0157
modifies computer, peripheral equipment

Temtex Industries, Inc. TMTX
1601 LBJ Freeway, Suite 605
Dallas, TX 75234 (214) 484-1845
fabricated metal products for consumers

Tennant Company TANT
701 North Lilac Drive
Minneapolis, MN 55440 (612) 540-1200
commercial floor care equipment

Teradata Corporation TDAT
12945 Jefferson Boulevard
Los Angeles, CA 90066 (213) 827-8777
database management computer systems

Terex Corporation TERX
201 West Walnut Street
Green Bay, WI 54303 (414) 435-5322
construction, industrial equipment

Terminal Data Corporation TERM
5898 Condor Drive
Moorpark, CA 93021 (805) 529-1500
document microfilming

Terra Mines, Ltd. TMEXF
7606 103rd Street, Suite 202
Edmonton, Canada T6E 4Z8 (403) 432-1212

Teva Pharmaceutical Industries Ltd. TEVIY
5 Basel Street
Petach Tikva, Israel (3) 926-7267
generic pharmacueticals

TGX Corporation XTGX
400 Templeton Energy Center
Houston, TX 77060 (713) 820-0333
oil and gas acquisition and production

Thermal Profiles, Inc. THPR
59 Mall Drive
Commack, NY 11725 (516) 543-3030
window units, patio doors

Thermodynetics, Inc. TDYN
651 Day Hill Road
Windsor, CT 06095 (203) 683-2005
metal tubing for heating and A/C equipment

Thomas Nelson, Inc. TNEL
Nelson Place at Elm Hill Pike
Nashville, TN 37214 (615) 889-9000
bible publishing

Thomson Newspapers, Ltd. THM.A
65 Queen Street West
Toronto, Ontario, CDA M5H 2M8
(416) 864-1710
newspaper publishing

Thorn Apple Valley, Inc. TAVI
18700 West Ten Mile Road
Southfield, MI 48075 (313) 552-0700
food products

Thousand Trails, Inc. TRLS
12301 Northeast 10th Place
Bellvue, WA 98005 (206) 455-3155
campground resort systems

3Com Corporation COMS
3165 Kifer Road
Santa Clara, CA 95052 (408) 562-6400
local and area computer network systems

Thrifty Rent-A-Car System, Inc. TFTY
4608 South Garnett Road
Tulsa, OK 74146 (918) 665-3930
car rental network

TIC International Corporation TICI
3901 North Meridian Street
Indianapolis, IN 46208 (317) 924-5311
consultant service for employee benefit plans

Tierco Group, Inc. (The) TIER
1140 N.W. 63rd Street, Suite G-120
Oklahoma City, OK 73116 (405) 843-9906
development, management of real estate

Tigera Group, Inc. TYGR
300 Harbor Boulevard
Belmont, CA 94002 (415) 598-9597
computer software

Timberjack Corporation TJCK
925 Devonshire Avenue
Woodstock, Ontario N4S 7X1 (519) 537-6271
lumber harvesting machinery

Timberline Software Corporation
9405 S.W. Gemini
Beaverton, OR 97005 (503) 626-6775
construction, engineering software

Tinsley Laboratories, Inc. TNSL
3900 Lakeside Drive
Richmond, CA 94806 (415) 222-8110
precision optical components for aerospace

TJ International, Inc. TJCO
9777 West Chinden Boulevard
Boise, ID 83714 (208) 375-4450
construction products

TM Communications, Inc. TMCI
1349 Regal Row
Dallas, TX 75247 (214) 634-8511
broadcast services for advertisers

Tokio Marine & Fire Insurance Co. TKIOY
55 Water Street
New York, NY 10041 (212) 530-0700
auto, fire, cargo and personal insurance

Tom Brown, Inc. TMBR
500 Empire Plaza Building
Midland, TX 79701 (915) 682-9715
oil and gas exploration and development

Tony Lama Company, Inc. TLAM
1137 Tony Lama Street
El Paso, TX 79915 (915) 778-8311
western boots and leather products

Topps Company, Inc. (The) TOPPC
254 36th Street
Brooklyn, NY 11232 (718) 768-8900
bubble gum picture cards and novelties

Toronto-Dominion Bank TD
P.O. Box 1, Toronto-Dominion Centre
Toronto, Ontario, Canada M5K 1A2
(416) 866-8222
banking [O]

Total System Services, Inc. TSYS
1000 Fifth Avenue
Columbus, GA 31902 (404) 649-2387
bank card data processing services

TPI Enterprises, Inc. TPIE
885 Third Avenue
New York, NY 10022 (212) 230-2233
restaurants

Trace Products TRCE
2190 Bering Drive
San Jose, CA 95131 (408) 435-7800
computer disk and tape duplication

Traditional Industries, Inc. TRAD
5155 North Clareton Drive
Agoura Hills, CA 91301 (818) 991-2773

Trak Auto Corporation TRKA
3300 75th Avenue
Landover, MD 20785 (301) 731-1200
auto parts retailer

Transact International Inc. TACT
6 Thorndal Circle
Darien, CT 06820 (203) 656-0777
air cargo handling systems

TransAlta Utilities Corporation TAU
110-12 Avenue S.W.
Calgary, Alberta T2P 2M1 (403) 267-7110
electric utility

Trans-Industries, Inc. TRNI
2637 North Adams Road
Auburn Heights, MI 48057 (313) 852-1990
mass transit component manufacturing

Trans Lousiana Gas Company, Inc. TRLA
201 Rue Iberville
Lafayette, LA 70508 (318) 234-4782
gas utility

Transmation, Inc. TRNS
977 Mount Read Boulevard
Rochester, NY 14606 (716) 254-9000
electronic monitoring instrumentation

Trans Mountain Pipe Line Co., Ltd. TMP
601 West Broadway
Vancouver, British Columbia V5Z 4C5
(608) 876-6711
crude oil pipeline

Transnational Industries, Inc. TRSL
8 Sound Shore Drive, Suite 250
Greenwich, CT 06830 (203) 661-3188
jet engine and airframe components

TransNet Corporation TRNT
1945 Route 22
Union, NJ 07083 (201) 688-7800
sale, lease and rental of computers

Transtech Industries, Inc. TRTI
25 Chambers Brook Road
Branchburg, NJ 08876 (201) 218-9500
waste management facilities

Trans World Music TWMC
38 Corporate Circle
Albany, NY 12203 (518) 452-1242
music and video retailing

Trenwick Group, Inc. TREN
Metro Center, 1 Station Plaza
Stamford, CT 06902 (203) 226-8116
reinsurance

Triad Systems Corporation TRSC
3055 Triad Drive
Livermore, CA 94550 (415) 449-0606
computer systems

Trico Products Corporation TRCO
817 Washington Street
Buffalo, NY 14203 (716) 852-5700
auto windshield wiping and washing systems

Trimedyne, Inc. TMED
2501 Pullman Street
Santa Ana, CA 92705 (714) 852-9963
fiberoptic laser catheters

Trion, Inc. TRON
101 McNeill Road
Sanford, NC 27331 (919) 775-2201
electronic air cleaners

Trio-Tech International TRTC
355 Parkside Drive
San Fernando, CA 91340 (818) 365-9200
semiconductor testing equipment

Trustco Bank Corp NY TRST
320 State Street
Schenectady, NY 12305 (518) 377-3311
banking

Trustcompany Bancorp TCBC
35 Journal Square
Jersey City, NJ 07306 (201) 420-2500
banking

T.R.V. Minerals Corporation TRVMF
1800-1500 West Georgia Street
Vancouver, BC, CDA V6G 2Z6 (604) 689-5300
minerals, oil and gas exploration

Trustcorp, Inc. TTCO
Three SeaGate
Toledo, OH 43603 (419) 259-8264
banking

TS Industries, Inc. TNDS
1865 South 3480 West
Salt Lake City, UT 84104 (801) 973-7500
fire and security door systems

TSI, Inc. TSII
500 Cardigan Road
St. Paul, MN 55164 (612) 483-0900
instruments to measure fluid flows

TSR, Inc. TSRI
400 Oser Avenue
Hauppauge, NY 11788 (516) 231-0333
software, toys and games

Tucker Drilling Company, Inc. TUCK
P.O. Box 1876
San Angelo, TX 76902 (915) 655-6773
oil and gas drilling services

Tuesday Morning, Inc. TUES
14621 Inwood Road
Dallas, TX 75244 (214) 387-3562
close-out merchandise retailing

Turf Paradise, Inc. TURF
1501 West Bell Road
Phoenix, AZ 85023 (602) 942-1101
thoroughbred horse race track

Tuscarora Plastics, Inc. TUSC
737 Fifth Avenue
New Brighton, PA 15066 (412) 843-8200
molded foam plastic packaging products

TVI Corporation TVIE
10700 Hanna Street
Beltsville, MD 20705 (301) 595-5252
military thermal signature targets

TVX Broadcast Group, Inc. TVXGC
Suite 300, 5501 Greenwich Road
Virginia Beach, VA 23462 (804) 499-9800
television stations

202 Data Systems, Inc. TOOT
1275 Drummer Lane
Wayne, PA 19087 (215) 964-1170
software to monitor power plant equipment

20th Century Industries TWEN
6301 Owensmouth Avenue, Suite 700
Woodland Hills, CA 91367 (818) 704-3700
auto, homeowners insurance

Twistee Treat Corporation TWST
3434 Hancock Bridge Parkway
North Fort Myers, FL 33093 (813) 997-8800
soft-serve ice cream stores

Tyco Toys, Inc. TTOY
540 Glen Avenue
Moorestown, NJ 08057 (609) 234-7400
electric and radio-controlled toys

Tylan Corporation TYLN
359 Van Ness Way
Torrance, CA 90501 (213) 212-5533
semiconductor equipment

Tyrex Oil Co. TYRX
777 North Overland Trail
Casper, WY 86201 (307) 234-4260
buys and sell undeveloped land

Tyson Foods, Inc. TYSNA
2210 Oaklawn Drive
Springdale, AK 72764 (501) 756-4000
poultry producer

Ultra Bancorporation ULTB
1125 Route 22 West
Bridgewater, NJ 08807 (201) 685-8486
banking

Ungermann-Bass, Inc. UNGR
2560 Mission College Blvd.
Santa Clara, CA 95052 (408) 496-0111
computer network systems

Unifi, Inc. UNFI
7201 West Friendly Road
Greensboro, NC 27419 (919) 294-4410
manufactures polyester yarns

Uniforce Temporary Personnel, Inc. UNFR
1335 Jericho Turnpike
New Hyde Park, NY 11040 (516) 437-3300
temporary personnel

Uni-Marts, Inc. UNMAA
477 East Beaver Avenue
State College, PA 16801 (814) 234-6000
operates convenience stores

Unimed, Inc. UMED
35 Columbia Road
Somerville, NJ 08876 (201) 526-6894
pharmaceutical products

Union Bank UNBK
350 California Street
San Francisco, CA 94194 (415) 445-0200
banking

Union Enterprises UEL
21 St. Clair Avenue E
Toronto, Ontario M4T 2T7 (416) 964-6300
natural gas distributor

Union National Corporation UNBC
620 Washington Road
Mt. Lebanon, PA 15228 (412) 644-6200
banking

United Artists Communications, Inc. UNCI
5655 South Yosemite, Suite 450
Englewood, CO 80111 (303) 220-8800
movie theaters, cable TV systems

United Bankers, Inc. UBKR
510 North Valley Mills Drive
Waco, TX 76710 (817) 776-7600
banking

United Banks Of Colorado, Inc. UBKS
One United Bank Center, 1700 Lincoln Street
Denver, CO 80274 (303) 861-4700
banking

United Carolina Bancshares Corporation
UCAR
306 South Madison Street
Whiteville, NC 28472 (919) 642-5131
banking

United Cities Gas Company UCIT
5300 Maryland Way
Brentwood, TN 37027 (615) 373-0104
gas utility DRP

United Coasts Corporation UCOA
One Corporate Center
Hartford, CT 06103 (203) 560-1670
asbestos abatement insurance

United Companies Financial Corporation
UNCF
One United Plaza, 4041 Essen Lane
Baton Rouge, LA 70821 (504) 924-6007
life, accident, health insurance

United Dominion Realty Trust, Inc. UDRT
5 East Franklin Street
Richmond, VA 23219 (804) 780-2691
real estate investment trust

United Education & Software, Inc. UESS
15720 Ventura Boulevard
Encino, CA 91436 (818) 907-6649
vocational education

United Fire & Casualty Company UFCS
118 Second Avenue S.E.
Cedar Rapids, IA 52407 (319) 399-5700
property-casualty, life insurance

United Gaming, Inc. UGAM
3101 West Spring Mountain Road
Las Vegas, NV 89102 (702) 732-2672
gaming machine operations, equipment

United-Guardian, Inc. UNIR
230 Marcus Boulevard
Hauppauge, NY 11788 (516) 273-0900
pharmaceuticals, fine chemicals

United HealthCare Corporation UNIH
300 Opus Center, 9900 Bren Road East
Minnetonka, MN 55343 (612) 936-1300
health maintenance organizations

United Home Life Insurance Company UHLI
1000 North Madison Avenue
Greenwood, IN 46142 (317) 888-4421
insurance

United Insurance Company UICI
5215 North O'Connor
Irvine, TX 75039 (214) 869-4800
life, accident, health insurance

United Investors Management Company
UTDMK
2001 Third Avenue South
Birmingham, AL 35233 (205) 325-4200
financial services, mutual funds, brokerage

United Missouri Bancshares, Inc. UMSB
1010 Grand Avenue
Kansas City, MO 64141 (816) 556-7000
banking

United New Mexico Financial Corporation
BNKS
P.O. Box 1081
Albuquerque, NM 87103 (505) 765-5086
banking

United Newspapers PLC UNEWY
23-27 Tudor Street
London, UK EC4Y OHR 01-583-9199
international publishing, information services

United Presidential Corporation UPCO
217 Southway Blvd. East
Kokomo, IN 46902 (317) 453-0602
insurance

United Savings Bank, FA UBMT
601 First Avenue North
Great Falls, MT 59401 (406) 761-2200
savings banking

United Services Advisors, Inc. USVSP
11330 I.H. 10 West
San Antonio, TX 78249 (512) 696-1234
mutual funds marketing

United States Antimony Corporation USAC
P.O. Box 643
Thompson Falls, MT 59873 (406) 827-3523
antimony mining

United Stationers Inc. USTR
2200 East Golf Road
Des Plaines, IL 60016 (312) 699-5000
office supplies and products

United Television, Inc. UTVI
8501 Wilshire Boulevard
Beverly Hills, CA 90211 (213) 854-0426
broadcast television stations

United Tote, Inc. TOTE
10115 Cabin Creek Road
Shepherd, MT 59079 (406) 373-5507
pari-mutuel wagering systems

United Vermont Bancorporation UVTB
80 West Street
Rutland, VT 05701 (802) 775-2525
banking

United Virginia Bankshares, Inc. UVBK
919 East Main Street
Richmond, VA 23261 (804) 782-5000
banking

Universal Furniture, Ltd. UFURF
2622 Uwharrie Road
High Point, NC 27263 (919) 884-4322
furniture

Universal Health Services, Inc UHSI
367 South Gulph Road
King of Prussia, PA 19406 (215) 768-3300
hospital management

Universal Holding Corporation UHCO
100 Jericho Quadrangle
Jericho, NY 11753 (516) 935-8940
life insurance

Universal Security Instruments, Inc. USEC
10324 South Dolfield Road
Owings Mills, MD 21117 (301) 363-3000
video products, security devices

Universal Voltronics Corporation UVOL
27 Radio Circle Drive
Mt. Kisco, NY 10549 (914) 241-1300
power conversion systems, modulators

UNR Industries, Inc. UNRIQ
332 South Michigan Avenue
Chicago, IL 60604 (312) 341-1234

Upper Peninsula Energy Corporation UPEN
616 Shelden Avenue
Houghton, MI 49931 (906) 482-0220
electric utility DRP

U.S. Bancorp USBC
111 S.W. Fifth Avenue
Portland, OR 97208 (503) 275-6111
banking, financial services

U.S. Capital Corporation USCC
1400 Main Street
Columbia, SC 29201 (803) 779-2170
residential construction

U.S. Energy Corporation USEG
Glen L. Larson Bldg.
Riverton, WY 82501 (307) 856-9271
metal mining

US Facilities Corporation USRE
650 Town Center Drive
Costa Mesa, CA 92626 (714) 549-1600
property, casualty reinsurance

U.S. Gold Corporation USGL
1600 Hudson's Bay Centre, 1600 Stout Street
Denver, CO 80202 (303) 629-1515
gold mining

U.S. Healthcare, Inc. USHC
980 Jolly Road
Blue Bell, PA 19422 (215) 628-4800
health maintenance organizations

U.S. Intec INTK
1212 Brai Drive
Port Arthur, TX 77643 (409) 724-7024
single-ply roofing products

USMX, Inc. USMX
141 Union Boulevard
Lakewood, CO 80228 (303) 985-4665
gold mining

U.S. Precious Metals, Inc. USPM
535 Howe Street, 6th Floor
Vancouver, BC V6C 2C2 (604) 669-6115
metal mining

UST Corporation USTB
40 Court Street
Boston, MA 02108 (617) 726-7000
banking

U.S. Trust Corporation USTC
45 Wall Street
New York, NY 10005 (212) 806-4500
banking, financial services DRP

US West NewVector Group, Inc. USWNA
3350 161 Avenue S.E.
Bellevue, WA 98008 (206) 747-4900
cellular telephone and mobile
communications

Utah Medical Products, Inc. UTMD
7043 South 300 West
Midvale, UT 84047 (801) 566-1200
health care products

Utah Shale Land & Minerals UTAH
111 West Monroe Street
Chicago, IL 60603 (312) 346-9126
land development

UTL Corporation UTLC
1508 West Mockingbird Lane
Dallas, TX 75235 (214) 638-6688
military electronic systems

Vaal Reefs Exploration & Mining Co. VAALY
44 Main Street
Johannesburg 2001 South Africa
South African metals mining

Vacation Spa Resorts VSPA
4310 Paradise Road
Las Vegas, NV 89109 (702) 737-3700
markets time-share vacation plans

Valid Logic Systems Inc. VLID
2820 Orchard Pkwy.
San Jose, CA 95134 (408) 432-9400
computer engineering workstations

Vallen Corporation VALN
13333 Northwest Freeway
Houston, TX 77040 (713) 462-8700
industrial health and safety products

Valley Bancorporation VYBN
100 West Lawrence Street
Appleton, WI 54912 (414) 738-3830
banking DRP

Valley Federal S & L Association VFED
6842 Van Nuys Boulevard
Van Nuys, CA 91405 (818) 904-3000
savings and loan

Valley National Bancorp VNBP
615 Main Avenue
Passaic, NJ 07055 (201) 777-1800
banking

Valley National Corporation VNCP
241 North Central Avenue
Phoenix, AZ 85001 (602) 261-2900
banking

Valmont Industries, Inc. VALM
West Highway 275
Valley, NE 68064 (402) 359-2201
steel tubing

Value Line, Inc. VALU
711 Third Avenue
New York, NY 10017 (212) 687-3965
investment advisory services

Vanderbilt Gold Corporation VAGO
3311 South Jones Boulevard
Las Vegas, NV 89102 (702) 362-3152
gold and silver mining

Vari-Care, Inc. VCRE
814 Medical Arts Building
Rochester, NY 14607 (716) 325-6940
long-term health care services

Varitronic Systems, Inc. VRSY
300 Interchange Tower, 600 South County
Road 18
Minneapolis, MN 55426 (612) 542-1500
electronic lettering systems

Varlen Corporation VRLN
305 East Shulman Boulevard, Suite 500
Naperville, IL 60566 (312) 420-0400
industrial metal products

V Band Corporation VBAN
5 Odell Plaza
Yonkers, NY 10701 (914) 964-0900
electronic key telephone systems

Velcro Industries N.V. VELCF
15 Pietermaai, Willemstad
Curacao, Netherlands Antilles
fabric fasteners

VeloBind, Inc. VBND
47212 Mission Falls Court
Fremont, CA 94539 (415) 657-8200
book and document binding supplies

Ventrex Laboratories, Inc. VTRX
217 Read Street
Portland, ME 04103 (207) 773-7231
medical supplies

Venturian Corporation VENT
1600 Second Street South
Hopkins, MN 55343 (612) 931-2500
markets military equipment

Verdix Corporation VRDX
14130-A Sullyfield Circle
Chantilly, VA 22021 (703) 378-7600
computer systems and software

Vermont Financial Services Corporation VFSC
100 Main Street
Brattleboro, VT 05301 (802) 257-7151
banking

Veronex Resources Ltd. VEOXF
1200-625 Howe Street
Vancouver, British Columbia V6C 2T6
(604) 669-5650
natural resources exploration, development

Versa Technologies, Inc. VRSA
1300 South Green Bay Road
Racine, WI 53405 (414) 632-6622
industrial rubber, silicone products

Vertex Communications Corporation VTEX
2600 North Longview Street
Kilgore, TX 75662 (214) 984-0555
satellite communications equipment

Vestar, Inc. VSTR
939 East Walnut Street
Pasadena, CA 91106 (818) 792-6101
cancer diagnostics and therapeutics

Vicorp Restaurants, Inc. VRES
400 West 48th Avenue
Denver, CO 80216 (303) 296-2121
family-style restaurants

Victoria Bankshares, Inc. VICT
One O'Conner Plaza
Victoria, TX 77902 (512) 573-5151
banking

Victoria Creations, Inc. VITC
30 Jefferson Park Road
Warwick, RI 02888 (401) 467-7150
costume jewelry manufacturer

Video Display Corporation VIDE
5530 East Ponce de Leon Avenue
Stone Mountain, GA 30086 (404) 938-2080
cathode ray tubes for display screens

Video Jukebox Network JUKE
2550 Biscayne Boulevard
Miami, FL 33137 (305) 573-6122
music video cable TV channels

Vie De France Corporation VDEF
8201 Greensboro Drive
McLean, VA 22102 (703) 442-9205
French breads, pastries, cafes

View-Master Ideal Group, Inc. VMIG
8585 Southwest Hall Boulevard
Beaverton, OR 97005 (503) 644-1181
slide viewers, classic toys

Vipont Pharmaceutical VLAB
1625 Sharp Point Drive
Fort Collins, CO 80524 (303) 482-3126
plaque-control toothpaste, periodontal
products

Viragen, Inc. VRGN
2343 West 76th Street
Hialeah, FL 33016 (305) 557-6000
immunological product research,
development

Viral Response Systems, Inc. VRSI
34 East Putnam Avenue
Greenwich, CT 06830 (203) 661-1550
nose, mouth and nasal medical treatments

Viratek, Inc. VIRA
ICN Plaza, 3300 Hyland Avenue
Costa Mesa, CA 92626 (714) 545-0100
anti-respiratory virus drugs

Virginia Beach Federal S & L Association
VABF
210 25th Street
Virginia Beach, VA 23451 (804) 428-9331
savings & loan

Virginia First Savings, FSB VFSB
P.O. Box 2009
Petersburg, VA 23804 (804) 733-0333
banking

Visual Electronics Corporation VISC
285 Emmet Street
Newark, NJ 07114 (201) 242-6600
Electronics

Vita Plus Industries, Inc.
953 East Sahara Avenue, #21-B
Las Vegas, NV 89104 (702) 733-8805
health, personal care products

Vitalink Communications Corporation VITA
6607 Kaiser Drive
Fremont, CA 94555 (415) 794-1100
data communications products

Vivigen, Inc. VIVI
435 St. Michael's Drive
Santa Fe, NM 87501 (505) 988-9744
cell analysis

VLSI Technology Inc. VLSI
1109 McKay Drive
San Jose, CA 95131 (408) 434-3000
specialized semiconductors

VMS Mortgage Investors L.P. VMLP
8700 West Bryn Mawr Avenue
Chicago, IL 60631 (312) 399-8700
real estate partnership

VMX, Inc. VMXI
110 Rose Orchard Way
San Jose, CA 95134 (408) 943-0878
voice mail systems

Volt Information Sciences, Inc. VOLT
101 Park Avenue
New York, NY 10178 (212) 309-0200
services to telecommunications companies

Volvo AB VOLVY
S-405 08
Goteborg, Sweden (011) 46-31-59-00-00
vehicle, industrial manufacturing

Votrax, Inc. VOTX
38455 Hills Tech Drive
Farmington Hills, MI 48331 (313) 553-0580
audio automation systems

VSE Corporation VSEC
2550 Huntington Avenue
Alexandria, VA 22303 (703) 960-4600
engineering services

VWR Corporation VWRX
1900 Koll Center 500 108th Avenue N.E.
Bellevue, WA 98004 (206) 646-6550
distributes photography, printing supplies

Walbro Corporation WALB
6242 Garfield Avenue
Cass City, MI 48726 (517) 872-2131
carburetors for small engines, fuel pumps

Walker Telecommunications Corporation
WTEL
200 Oser Avenue
Hauppauge, NY 11788 (516) 435-1100
electronic key telephone systems

Wall to Wall Sound & Video, Inc. WTWS
200 South Route 130
Cinnaminson, NJ 08077 (609) 786-8300
consumer electronics stores

Warehouse Club, Inc. WCLB
7235 North Linder Avenue
Skokie, IL 60077 (312) 679-6800
member-only warehouse stores

Warwick Insurance Managers, Inc. WIMI
4 Gatehall Drive, Routes 10 & 202
Parsippany, NJ 07950 (201) 993-9200
property, casualty insurance

Washington Energy Company WECO
815 Mercer Street
Seattle, WA 98109 (206) 622-6767
gas utilities DRP

Washington Federal Savings & Loan WFSL
425 Pike Street
Seattle, WA 98101 (206) 624-7930
savings and loan

Washington Mutual Savings Bank WAMU
1101 Second Avenue
Seattle, WA 98101 (206) 464-4400
savings banking

Washington Scientific Industries,Inc. WSCI
2605 West Wayzata Blvd.
Long Lake, MN 55356 (612) 473-1271
precision-machined equipment

Waste Recovery, Inc. WRII
2606 Gaston Avenue
Dallas, TX 75226 (214) 741-3865
processes tires into fuel supplement

Waterhouse Investor Services, Inc. WHOO
44 Wall Street
New York, NY 10005 (212) 344-7500
discount securities brokerage services

Waters Instruments, Inc. WTRS
2411 Seventh Streeet, N.W.
Rochester, MN 55903 (507) 288-7777
computer cable harnesses, electromedical
equipment

Watts Industries, Inc. WATTA
Route 114 & Chestnut Street
North Andover, MA 01845 (617) 688-1811
water safety and quality valves

Wausau Paper Mills Co. WSAU
1 Clark's Island
Wausau, WI 54402 (715) 845-5266
writing, printing and specialty papers

Waverly, Inc. WAVR
428 E. Preston Street
Baltimore, MD 21202 (301) 528-4000
publishing of medical journals, books

Wavetek Corporation WVTK
9145 Balboa Avenue
San Diego, CA 92123 (619) 450-9971
electronic test and measurement instruments

Waxman Industries, Inc. WAXM
24460 Aurora Road
Bedford Heights, OH 44146 (216) 439-1830
home plumbing, electrical and hardware
products

WD - 40 Company WDFC
1061 Cudahy Place
San Diego, CA 92110 (619) 275-1400
petroleum-based lubricants

Webster Clothes, Inc. WEBS
8901 Yellow Brick Road
Baltimore, MD 21237 (301) 391-8811
men's retail clothing stores

Weigh-Tronix, Inc. WGHT
1000 Armstrong Drive
Fairmont, MN 56031 (507) 238-4461
electronic industrial scales

Weisfield's, Inc. WEIS
800 South Michigan Street
Seattle, WA 98108 (206) 767-5011
jewelry retailing

Weitek Corporation WWTK
1060 East Arques Avenue
Sunnyvale, CA 94086 (408) 738-8400
numeric processing circuits, software

Welkom Gold Holdings WLKMY
44 Main Street
Johannesburg 2001, South Africa
investment holding company

Werner Enterprises, Inc. WERN
I-80 & Highway 50
Omaha, NE 68137 (402) 895-6640
trucking

Western Capital Investment Corporation
WECA
1675 Broadway
Denver, CO 80202 (303) 623-5577
savings and loan

Western Commercial WCCC
4995 East Clinton Avenue
Fresno, CA 93727 (209) 252-8711
banking

Western Deep Levels Ltd. WDEPY
44 Main Street
Johannesburg 2001, South Africa
gold mining

Western Federal Savings Bank WFPR
P.O. Box WFS
Mayaguez, PR 00709 (809) 834-8000
banking

Western Financial Corporation WSTF
715 Merchant
Emporia, KN 66801 (316) 342-5425
savings and loan

Western Micro Technology, Inc. WSTM
12900 Saratoga Avenue
Saratoga, CA 95070 (408) 725-1660
semiconductor component distributor

Western Publishing Group WPGI
444 Madison Avenue
New York, NY 10022 (212) 688-4500
children's book publisher

Western Waste Industries WWIN
1125 West 190th Street
Gardena, CA 90248 (213) 329-1425
solid waste collection services

WestMarc Communications WSMCA
4643 South Ulster Street
Denver, CO 80237 (303) 796-9100
operates cable TV systems

Westmark International Inc. WMRK
Columbia Center, 701 Fifth Avenue,
Suite 6800
Seattle, WA 98104 (206) 682-6800
high-technology medical equipment

Westmin Resources Ltd. WMI
255-5th Avenue, SW
Calgary, Alberta T2P 3G6 (403) 298-2000
oil and gas exploration, development

Westmoreland Coal Company WMOR
2500 Fidelity Building
Philadelphia, PA 19109 (215) 545-2500
coal mining

Weston (Roy F.), Inc. WSTNA
Weston Way
West Chester, PA 19380 (215) 692-3030
environmental engineering and consulting

Weston (George) Ltd.
22 St. Clair Avenue East
Toronto, Ontario M4T 2S7 (414) 922-2500
food distribution and processing

Westwood One, Inc. WONE
9540 Washington Blvd.
Culver City, CA 90232 (213) 204-5000
radio network, program production

Wetterau Inc. WETT
8920 Pershall Road
Hazelwood, MO 63042 (314) 524-5000
grocery wholesaling DRP

Weyenberg Shoe Manufacturing Company
WEYS
234 East Reservoir Avenue
Milwaukee, WI 53201 (414) 374-8900
footwear

Wheelabrator Group (The), Inc. WHGP
Liberty Lane
Hampton, NH 03842 (603) 926-5611
holding company

Wheelabrator Technologies, Inc. WHTI
55 Ferncroft Road
Danvers, MA 01923 (617) 777-2207
refuse-to-energy facilities, services

Wholesale Club (The), Inc. WHLS
7260 Shadeland Station
Indianapolis, IN 46250 (317) 842-0351
member-only warehouse stores

WICAT Systems, Inc. WCAT
1875 South State Street
Orem, UT 84057 (801) 224-6400
educational computers

Wiland Services, Inc. WSVS
1426 Pearl Street
Boulder, CO 80302 (303) 449-5347
business data processing

Wiley (John) & Sons, Inc. WILLB
605 Third Avenue
New York, NY 10158 (212) 850-6000
educational, professional book publishing

Willamette Industries, Inc. WMTT
3800 First Interstate Tower
Portland, OR 97201 (503) 227-5581
forest, paper products

Williams Industries, Inc. WMSI
2849 Meadow View Road
Falls Church, VA 22042 (703) 560-1505
industrial construction, manufacturing

W. W. Williams Company (The) WWWM
835 West Goodale Boulevard
Columbus, OH 43212 (614) 228-5000
construction machinery rentals and sales

Williams-Sonoma, Inc. WSGC
100 North Point Street
San Francisco, CA 94133 (415) 421-7900
mail order cookware and gardening
equipment

Wilmington Trust Company WILM
Rodney Square North
Wilmington, DE 19890 (302) 651-1000
banking

Windmere Corporation WDMR
4920 N.W. 165th Street
Hialeah, FL 33014 (305) 621-2611
personal care products

Wisconsin Southern Gas WISC
120 East Sheridan Springs Road
Lake Geneva, WI 53147 (414) 248-8861
gas utility

Wisconsin Toy Company, Inc. WTOY
710 North Plankinton Avenue
Milwaukee, WI 53203 (414) 274-2575
wholesale, retail toys

Wiser Oil Company (The) WISE
P.O. Box 192
Sisterville, WV 26175 (304) 652-3861
oil and gas production, distribution

WNS, Inc. WNSI
P.O. Box 4586
Houston, TX 77210 (713) 874-0800
decorative accessories, art stores

Wolohan Lumber Company WLHN
1740 Midland Road
Saginaw, MI 48603 (517) 793-4532
retail building materials

Wolverine Technologies, Inc. WOLA
1650 Howard Street
Lincoln Park, MI 48146 (313) 386-0800
finished metal products

Woodhead Industries, Inc. WDHD
3411 Woodhead Drive
Northbrook, IL 60062 (312) 272-7990
electrical industrial products

Woodward's Ltd. WDSA
101 West Hastings Street
Vancouver, British Columbia V6B 1H4
(604) 684-5231
retail department stores

Worlco, Inc. WORLA
215 West Church Road
King of Prussia, PA 19406 (215) 265-2200
life, accident and health insurance

Worldwide Computer Services Inc. WCSI
7 Doig Road
Wayne, NJ 07470 (201) 694-8876
temporary computer, communications
personnel

Worthington Industries, Inc. WTHG
1205 Dearborn Drive
Columbus, OH 43085 (614) 438-3210
steel processing, production DRP

Writer Corporation (The) WRTC
27 Inverness Drive East
Englewood, CO 80112 (303) 790-2870
homebuilder

WSMP, Inc. WSMP
Ham House Drive, P.O. Box 399
Claremont, NC 28610 (704) 459-7626
restaurants, pork products

WTD Industries, Inc. WTDI
2 Lincoln Center,
10260 S.W. Greenburg Road, Suite 1200
Portland, OR 97223 (503) 246-3440
woods products, pulp and paper

Wyman-Gordon Company WYMN
105 Madison Street
Worcester, MA 01613 (617) 756-5111
forged metal components

Wyoming National Bancorporation WYNB
152 North Durbin Street
Casper, WY 82601 (307) 235-7797
banking

Xicor, Inc. XICO
1511 Buckeye Drive
Milpitas, CA 95035 (408) 946-6920
semiconductor memory products

XL/Datacomp, Inc. XLDC
908 North Elm Street
Hinsdale, IL 60521 (312) 323-1200
mid-range computer equipment and services

XOMA Corporation XOMA
2910 Seventh Street
Berkeley, CA 94710 (415) 644-1170
monoclonal antibody products

X-Rite, Inc. XRIT
3100 44th Street. S.W.
Grandville, MI 49418 (616) 534-7663
advanced electronics and optics products

Xscribe Corproation XSCR
6160 Cornerstone Court East
San Diego, CA 92121 (619) 457-5091
stenographic transcription software

Xylogics, Inc. XLGX
53 Third Avenue
Burlington, MA 01803 (617) 272-8140
high performance computer controllers

Xyvision, Inc. XYVI
101 Edgewater Drive
Wakefield, MA 01880 (617) 245-4100
computer-integrated publishing systems

Yellow Freight System, Inc. of Delaware YELL
10990 Roe Avenue
Overland Park, KS 66207 (913) 345-1020
trucking

York Federal S & L Association YFED
101 South George Street
York, PA 17405 (717) 846-8777
savings & loan

Zentec Corporation ZENT
2400 Walsh Avenue
Santa Clara, CA 95051 (408) 727-7662
customized intelligent terminal systems

Zeus Components, Inc. ZEUS
100 Midland Avenue
Port Chester, NY 10573 (914) 937-7400
distributes semiconductors to aerospace
contractors

Ziegler Company, Inc. (The) ZEGL
215 North Main Street
West Bend, WI 53095 (414) 334-5521
financial services

Zions Bancorporation ZION
1380 Kennecott Building
Salt Lake City, UT 84133 (801) 524-4787
banking

Zitel Corporation ZITL
630 Adler Drive
Milpitas, CA 95035 (408) 946-9600
semiconductor memory systems

Z-Seven Fund, Inc. ZSEV
2302 Monterey Circle
Mesa, AZ 85202 (602) 897-6214
closed-end stock mutual fund

Zycad Corporation ZCAD
1380 Willow Road
Menlo Park, CA 94025 (415) 321-8574
electronic systems computers, software

Zygo Corporation ZIGO
Laurel Brook Road
Middlefield, CT 06455 (203) 347-8506
laser electro-optical instruments

ZyMOS Corporation ZMOS
477 North Mathilda Avenue
Sunnyvale, CA 94086 (408) 730-8800
semiconductor equipment

Zytec Systems, Inc. ZSLIF
2474 Manana, Suite 121
Dallas, TX 75220 (214) 358-1350
communication terminal leasing

TORONTO STOCK EXCHANGE

Abitibi-Price Inc. A
2 First Canadian Place, Suite 1300, Box 39
Toronto, ON M5X 1A9 (416) 369-6700
forest products, newsprint, building supplies
[O]

Acklands Ltd. ACK
945 Wilson Avenue
Downsview, ON M3K 1E8 (416) 635-1200
replacement auto parts, industrial products

Agnico-Eagle Mines Ltd. AGE
Suite 2302, 401 Bay Street, P.O. Box 102
Toronto, ON M5H 2Y4 (416) 947-1212
gold, silver mining

Air Canada AC
Place Air Canada,
500 Rene Levesque Boulevard West
Montreal, PQ H2Z 1X5 (514) 879-7000
airline   [O]

Alberta Energy Company Ltd. AEC
Suite 2400, 639 5th Avenue S.W.
Calgary, AB T2P 0M9 (403) 266-8111
oil and gas exploration, distribution

Alberta Natural Gas Company Ltd. ANG
East Tower, ESSO Plaza, Suite 2400,
425 1st Street S.W.
Calgary, AB T2P 3L8 (403) 260-9000
natural gas, specialty chemicals, magnesium

Alcan Aluminium Ltd. AL
1188 Sherbrooke Street West
Montreal, PQ H3A 3G2 (514) 848-8000
aluminum products   [O]

Algoma Central Railway ALC
289 Bay Street, P.O. Box 7000
Sault Ste. Marie, ON P6A 5P6 (705) 949-2113
rail, water transportation

Amca International Ltd. AIL
200 Ronson Drive
Toronto, ON M9W 5Z9 (416) 243-9343
industrial and building products, services

American Barrick Resources Co. ABX
24 Hazelton Avenue
Toronto, ON M5R 2E2 (416) 923-9400
gold mining   [O]

ATCO Ltd. ACO.X
1600 Canadian Western Centre,
909 11th Avenue S.W.
Calgary, AB T2R 1N6 (403) 292-7500
utilities, oil and gas, building products

AUR Resources Inc. AUR
Suite 3202, 130 Adelaide Street West
Toronto, ON M5H 3P5 (416) 362-2614
exploration, development of mineral resources

Bank of Montreal BMO
1 First Canadian Place
Toronto, ON M5X 1A1 (416) 867-5000
banking

Bank of Nova Scotia (The) BNS
Scotia Plaza, 44 King Street West
Toronto, ON M5H 1H1 (416) 866-6161
banking   [O]

Baton Broadcasting Inc. BNB
P.O. Box 9, Postal Station O
Toronto, ON M4A 2M9 (416) 299-2000
TV, radio and film broadcasting, production

BC Gas Inc. BCG
1066 West Hastings Street
Vancouver, BC V6E 3G3 (604) 684-0484
oil and natural gas distribution

BC Sugar Refinery, Ltd. BCS.A
P.O. Box 2150
Vancouver, BC V6B 3V2 (604) 253-1131
sugar, specialty chemical products

BCE Development Corp. BD
P.O. Box 3, Suite 3850, TD Bank Tower,
Toronto-Dominion Centre
Toronto, ON M5K 1A1 (416) 369-2300
real estate development

BCE Inc. B
2000 McGill College Avenue, Suite 2100
Montreal, PQ H3A 3H7 (514) 499-7000
telecommunications, publishing, real estate
[O]

BCE Mobile Communications Inc. BCX
Suite 200, 6505 Trans Canada Highway
St.-Laurent, PQ H4T 1S3 (514) 748-3200
mobile, cellular communications

Belmoral Mines Ltd. BME
Suite 1215, 111 Richmond Street West
Toronto, ON M5H 2G4 (416) 364-0444
mining exploration, development, gold

BGR Precious Metals Inc. BPT.A
The Dynamic Building, 6 Adelaide St. East
Toronto, ON M5C 1H6 (416) 365-5100
precious metals closed-end mutual fund

Bombardier Inc. BBD.A
Suite 1700,
800 Rene-Levesque Boulevard West
Montreal, PQ H3B 1Y8 (514) 861-9481
rail, recreational, marine, aerospace
products

Bow Valley Industries Ltd. BVI
1800, 321 6th Avenue S.W.,
P.O. Box 6610, Station D
Calgary, AB T2P 3R2 (403) 261-6100
oil and gas exploration, development   [0]

BP Canada Inc. BPC
333 Fifth Avenue S.W.
Calgary, AB T2P 3B6 (403) 237-1234
oil, gas and metals exploration, production

Bramalea Ltd. BCD
1867 Yonge Street
Toronto, ON M4S 1Y5 (416) 487-3861
real estate development, housing

Brascan Ltd. BL.A
Suite 4800, Commerce Court West
Toronto, ON M5L 1B7 (416) 363-9491
natural resources, consumer products,
finance

Breakwater Resources Ltd. BWR
Suite 900, 999 West Hastings Street
Vancouver, BC V6C 2W2 (604) 669-1918
precious metals mining, development

Brenda Mines Ltd. BND
P.O. Box 45, Commerce Court West
Toronto, ON M5L 1B6 (416) 867-7111
metals mining, oil and gas exploration

British Columbia Telephone Co. BCT
3777 Kingsway
Burnaby, BC V5H 3Z7 (800) 663-9455
telecommunications services, equipment

Bruncor Inc. BRR
One Brunswick Square, P.O. Box 5030
Saint John, NB E2L 4L4 (800) 561-9030
telecommunications services

Brunswick Mining and Smelting Co. Ltd. BMS
Suite 900, 4 King Street West
Toronto, ON M5H 3X2 (416) 982-7111
metals mining, operations

CAE Industries Ltd. CAE
Suite 3060, P.O. Box 30, Royal Bank Plaza
Toronto, ON M5J 2J1 (416) 865-0070
aerospace, electronics, industrial products

Cambior Inc. CBJ
Suite 1075, 3rd Avenue East, C.P. 9999
Val d'Or, PQ J9P 6M1 (819) 825-0211
gold mining, production

Cambridge Shopping Centres Ltd. CBG
Suite 300, 95 Wellington Street West
Toronto, ON M5J 2R2 (416) 369-1200
real estate investment, shopping centres

Campbell Resources Inc. CCH
Suite 2701, P.O Box 498,
1 First Canadian Place
Toronto, ON M5X 1E5 (416) 366-5201
gold mining, natural resource production

Campbell Soup Co. Ltd. CSC
60 Birmingham Street
Toronto, ON M8V 2B8 (416) 251-1131
convenience food processing, distribution

Campeau Co. CMP
Suite 5800, 40 King Street West
Toronto, ON M5H 3Y8 (416) 868-6460
real estate development, retailing   [0]

Canada Malting Co. Ltd. CMG
21 Four Seasons Place, Suite 325
Etobicoke, ON M9B 6J8 (416) 620-7575
malt, mushroom production

Canada Northwest Energy Ltd. CNW
Suite 2700, 300 5th Avenue S.W.
Calgary, AB T2P 3C4 (403) 260-2900
hydrocarbon, oil and gas exploration

Canada Packers Inc. CK
30 St. Clair Avenue West
Toronto, ON M4V 3A2 (416) 766-4311
consumer, industrial food product
processing

Canada Southern Petroleum Ltd. CSW
Suite 1410, One Palliser Square,
125 Ninth Avenue, S.E.
Calgary, AB T2G 0P6 (403) 269-7741
petroleum exploration, development

Canadian Express Ltd. XE
P.O. Box 129, Suite 4400,
Commerce Court West
Toronto, ON M5L 1K5 (416) 865-0430
investment company

Canadian General Investments Ltd. CGI
Suite 1702, 110 Yonge Street
Toronto, ON M5C 1T4 (416) 366-2931
closed-end investment company

Canadian Imperial Bank of Commerce CM
Commerce Court
Toronto, ON M5L 1A2 (416) 980-2211
banking, financial services

Canadian Marconi Co. CMW
2442 Trenton Avenue
Montreal, PQ H3P 1Y9 (514) 341-7630
aerospace, communications technology

Canadian Occidental Petroleum Ltd. CXY
Suite 1500, 635 8th Avenue Southwest
Calgary, AB T2P 3Z1 (403) 234-6700
energy and chemicals production

Canadian Pacific Forest Products Ltd. PFP
1155 Metcalfe Street
Montreal, PQ H3B 2X1 (514) 878-4811
forest products, newsprint

Canadian Pacific Ltd. CP
P.O. Box 6042, Postal Station A
Montreal, PQ H3C 3E4 (514) 395-5151
transportation, energy, real estate,
communications [O]

Canadian Roxy Petroleum Ltd. CNR
Suite 2200, Pacific Plaza,
700 6th Avenue Southwest
Calgary, AB T2P 0T8 (403) 260-9400
oil and gas exploration

Canadian Tire Co., Ltd. CTR.A
2180 Yonge Street, P.O. Box 770, Station K
Toronto, ON M4P 2V8 (416) 480-3000
auto products, sporting goods, housewares

Canadian Utilities Ltd. CU
10035 105 Street
Edmonton, AB T5J 2V6 (403) 420-7310
natural gas, electricity distribution

Canam Manac Group Inc. (The) CAM.A
Suite 700, 11535 1st Avenue
Ville St-Georges, PQ G5Y 2C7 (418) 228-8031
metal products, services, steel

Canamax Resources Inc. CMX
Suite 1100, 181 University Avenue
Toronto, ON M5H 3M7 (416) 364-6188
gold mining, and natural resource
development

Canfor Corp. CFP
2800-1055 Dunsmuir Street, P.O. Box 49420,
Bentall Postal Station
Vancouver, BC V7X 1B5 (604) 661-5241
wood, paper, building products

Cara Operations Ltd. CAO
230 Bloor Street West
Toronto, ON M5S 1T8 (416) 962-4571
food services, restaurants

Carena Developments CDN
P.O. Box 129, Suite 4400,
Commerce Court West
Toronto, ON M5L 1K5 (416) 865-0430
real estate development

Cascades Inc. CAS
404 Marie-Victorin Street, P.O. Box 30
Kingsey-Falls, PQ J0A 1B0 (819) 363-2245
paper and building products

Cassiar Mining Corp. CSQ
Suite 2000, 1055 West Hastings Street
Vancouver, BC V6E 3V3 (604) 688-2511
metals mining, copper

CB Pak Inc. CBK
2070 Hadwen Road
Mississauga, ON L5K 2C9 (416) 823-3860
packaging, glass tableware products

CCL Industries Inc. CCQ.B
105 Gordon Baker Road
Willowdale, ON M2H 3P8 (416) 756-8500
consumer products, containers

Celanese Canada Inc. CCL
800 Rene-Levesque Boulevard West
Montreal, PQ H3B 1Z1 (514) 871-5511
fiber, chemical and industrial goods
production

Central Capital Corp. CEH
1801 Hollis Street
Halifax, NS B3J 3C8 (902) 420-2000
financial services, brokerage, insurance

Central Fund of Canada Ltd. CEF.A
P.O. Box 7319
Ancaster, ON L9G 3N6 (416) 648-7878
gold and silver bullion investment company

Central Guaranty Trustco Ltd. CGA
366 Bay Street
Toronto, ON M5H 2W5 (416) 975-4500
real estate, lending

Centurion Gold Ltd. CEU
6th Floor, 535 Howe St.
Vancouver, BC V6C 2C2 (604) 681-8466
gold mining, production

CFCF Inc. CF
405 Ogilvy Avenue
Montreal, PQ H3N 1M4 (514) 273-6311
broadcast TV stations

CGC Inc. GYP
777 Bay Street, Suite 1800
Toronto, ON M5W 1K8 (416) 595-8853
building products, gypsum,
bathroom fixtures

Charan Industries Inc. CHN
9850 Parkway Boulevard
Montreal, PQ H1J 1P6 (514) 353-2950
sporting goods, children's products

Chum Ltd. CHM.B
1331 Yonge Street
Toronto, ON M4T 1Y1 (416) 925-6666
broadcast TV, radio stations

Cineplex Odeon Co. CPX
1303 Yonge St.
Toronto, ON M4T 2Y9 (416) 323-6600
movie theaters, production, distribution
                                                    [O]

Coho Resources Ltd. COH.A
Suite 3700, 700 2nd Street S.W.
Calgary, AB T2P 2W2 (403) 261-9800
oil and gas exploration, production

Cominco Ltd. CLT
2600-200 Granville Street
Vancouver, BC V6C 2R2 (604) 682-0611
mining, production of metals and fertilizer
                                                    [O]

Computalog L CGH
Suite 800, 600 6th Avenue Southwest
Calgary, AB T2P 0S5 (403) 265-6060
oil and gas drilling services

Connaught Biosciences Inc. CSE
Suite 1500, P.O. Box 23, 55 University Avenue
Toronto, ON M5J 2H7 (416) 941-8770
health care products, drugs

Consolidated HCI Holdings Corp. CXA.A
Suite 2200, Commercial Union Tower,
P.O. Box 8, TD Centre
Toronto, ON M5K1A1 (416) 862-1734
real estate development, securities

Consolidated TVX Mining Corp. CVX
Suite 2010, 145 King Street West
Toronto, ON M5H 1J8 (416) 366-8160
gold mining

Consumers' Gas Company Ltd. (The) CGT
100 Simcoe Street
Toronto, ON M5H 3G2 (416) 591-6611
natural gas distribution, production, storage

Consumers Packaging Inc. CGC
401 The West Mall, Suite 900
Etobicoke (Toronto), ON M9C 5J7
(416) 232-3283
glass and plastic packaging products

Conwest Exploration Co. Ltd. CEX.A
Suite 2000, 95 Wellington Street West
Toronto ON, BM5J 2N7 (416) 362-6721
oil and gas exploration, production

Corby Distilleries Ltd. CDL.A
1201 Ouest Rue Sherbrooke
Montreal, PQ H3A 1J1 (514) 288-4181
distilled spirits and wine production,
distribution

Cornucopia Resources Ltd. CNP
Suite 520, Marine Building, 355 Burrard Street
Vancouver, BC V6C 2G8 (604) 687-0619
exploration, development of precious metals
properties

Corona Co. ICR.A
Suite 1900, 120 Adelaide Street West
Toronto, ON M5H 1T1 (416) 862-2000
precious metals production

Coscan Development Corp. COT
2 First Canadian Place, Suite 2200, Box 428
Toronto, ON M5X 1H9 (416) 369-8200
residential, commercial real estate
development

Co-Steel Inc. CEI
P.O. Box 130, 40 King Street West
Toronto, ON M5H 3Y2 (416) 366-4500
steel building products

Crownx Inc. CRX
120 Bloor Street East
Toronto, ON M4W 1B8 (416) 928-7722
financial, health care services

Denison Mines Ltd. DEN.A
P.O. Box 40, Royal Bank Plaza,
Suite 3900, South Tower
Toronto, ON M5J 2K2 (416) 865-1991
natural resource mining, oil and gas
production

Derlan Industries Ltd. DRL
Suite 200, 95 King Street East
Toronto, ON M5C 1G4 (416) 364-5852
aerospace, automotive, industrial
manufacturing

Dickenson Mines Ltd. DML.A
Suite 2600, 130 Adelaide Street West
Toronto, ON M5H 3P5 (416) 361-0402
gold, silver, limestone mining and production
[O]

Dofasco Inc. DFS
P.O. Box 2460
Hamilton, ON L8N 3J5 (416) 544-3761
steel products

Dominion Textile Inc. DTX
1950 Sherbrooke Street West
Montreal, PQ H3H 1E7 (514) 989-6000
textile manufacturing, distribution

Domtar Inc. DTC
395 De Maisonneuve-Boulevard West
Montreal, PQ H3A 1L6 (514) 848-5400
paper, packaging, building and chemical
products

Donohue Inc. DHC
1150 Claire-Fontaine
Quebec, PQ G1R 5G4 (418) 522-6471
forest products, newsprint, pulp, lumber

Dumagami Mines Ltd. (NPL) DMI
Suite 2302, 401 Bay Street
Toronto, ON M5H 2Y4 (416) 947-1212
precious metals property development

Du Pont Canada Inc. DUP.A
Box 2200, Streetsville
Mississauga, ON L5M 2H3 (416) 821-3300
chemical products, fibers, plastics and films

Dylex Ltd. DLX.A
637 Lake Shore Boulevard West
Toronto, ON M5V 1A8 (416) 586-7000
retail fashion clothing stores

Echo Bay Mines Ltd. ECO
3300 Manulife Place, 10180 101 Street
Edmonton, AB T5J 3S4 (403) 429-5811
gold mining

E-L Financial Corp. Ltd. ELF
10th Floor, 165 University Avenue
Toronto, ON M5H 3B8 (416) 868-1880
insurance underwriting, investment services

Emco Ltd. EML
Box 5252, 620 Richmond Street
London, ON N6A 4L6 (519) 645-3900
plumbing and heating product distribution

Empire Co. Ltd. EMP.A
115 King Street
Stellarton, NS B0K 1S0 (902) 755-4440
food distribution, real estate development

Enfield Corp. Ltd. (The) ENF
Suite 2300, 1100 Eglinton Avenue East
Toronto, ON M3C 1H8 (416) 445-7438
investment and management company

Equity Silver Mines Ltd. EST.A
P.O. Box 49330, Bentall Postal Station
Vancouver, BC V7X 1P1 (604) 682-7082
gold, silver and copper mining

Fairfax Financial Holdings Ltd. FFH
95 Wellington Street West, Suite 800
Toronto, ON M5J 2N7 (416) 367-4941
insurance and financial services

Falconbridge Ltd. FL
40th Floor, Commerce Court West
Toronto, ON M5L 1B4 (416) 863-7000
metals and minerals mining, production, nickel
[O]

FCA International Ltd. FC
3rd Floor, 160 Vanderhoof Avenue
Toronto, ON M4G 4B8 (416) 467-8300
collection agency

Federal Industries Ltd. FIL.A
Suite 2400, 1 Lombard Place
Winnipeg, MB R3B 0X3 (204) 942-8161
consumer, industrial, transportation services

Federal Pioneer Ltd. FPE
19 Waterman Avenue
Toronto, ON M4B 1Y2 (416) 752-8020
electrical power distribution equipment

Finning Ltd. FTT
555 Great Northern Way
Vancouver, BC V5T 1E2 (604) 872-4444
heavy equipment leasing, selling, servicing

First City Financial Corp. Ltd. FCY
First City Building, 777 Hornby Street
Vancouver, BC V6Z 1S4 (604) 685-2489
financial, real estate, investment services

First Marathon Inc. FMS.A
The Exchange Tower, 2 First Canadian Place,
Suite 3100, P.O. Box 21
Toronto, ON M5X 1J9 (416) 869-3707
financial services, brokerage

Fletcher Challenge Canada Ltd. FCC.A
P.O. Box 10058, Pacific Centre, 9th Floor,
700 West Georgia Street
Vancouver, BC V7Y IJ7 (604) 654-4000
forest products, newsprint, paper, lumber

Ford Motor Company of Canada, Ltd. FMC
The Canadian Road
Oakville, ON L6J 5E4 (416) 845-2511
auto manufacturing, distribution

Fortis Inc. FTS
55 Kenmount Road, P.O. Box 8837
St. John's, NF A1B 3T2 (709) 737-5600
investment company, electric utility

Four Seasons Hotels Inc. FSH
1165 Leslie Street
Toronto, ON M3C 2K8 (416) 449-1750
luxury hotels

FPI Ltd. FPL
70 O'Leary Avenue, P.O. Box 550
St. John's, NF A1C 5L1 (709) 570-0000
seafood harvesting, processing, marketing

Franco-Nevada Mining Corp. Ltd. FN
20 Eglinton Avenue West, #2000
Toronto, ON M4R 1K8 (416) 485-1010
development of precious metals properties

Galactic Resources Ltd. GLC
Suite 935, 355 Burrard Street
Vancouver, BC V6C 2G8 (604) 687-7169
development of gold mining properties

[O]

Gandalf Technologies Inc. GAN
130 Colonnade Road South
Nepean, ON K2E 7M5 (613) 723-6500
communications software, hardware

Gendis Inc. GDS.A
1370 Sony Place
Winnipeg, MB R3T 1N5 (204) 474-5200
oil and gas exploration, real estate
development

General Trustco of Canada, Inc. TTG
1100 University Street
Montreal, PQ H3B 2G7 (514) 871-7100
trust and financial services, real estate
brokerage

Giant Yellowknife Mines Ltd. GYK
Suite 1601, P.O. Box 13, 95 Wellington Street
Toronto, ON M5J 2N7 (416) 363-5470
gold mining

Glamis Gold Ltd. GLG
3324 Four Bentall Centre,
1055 Dunsmuir Street, P.O. Box 49287
Vancouver, BC V7X 1L3 (604) 681-3541
gold mining

Goldcorp Investments Ltd. G
Suite 2804, IBM Tower, P.O. Box 68
Toronto-Dominion Centre
Toronto, ON M5K 1E7 (416) 865-0326
gold bullion and gold mining shares
investment company

Golden Knight Resources Inc. GKR
1199 West Hastings Street
Vancouver, BC V6E 2K5 (604) 687-1117
natural resource production

Grafton Group Ltd. GFG.A
9 Sunlight Park Road
Toronto, ON M4M 3G1 (416) 461-9411
apparel, footwear and home furnishings
retailer

Granges Inc. GXL
Suite 2300, 885 West Georgia Street
Vancouver, BC V6C 3E8 (604) 687-2831
natural resource property development,
minerals

Great Lakes Group Inc. GLZ
Suite 4800, Commerce Court West
Toronto, ON M5L 1B7 (416) 367-4056
investment banking, securities company

Great-West Lifeco Inc. GWO
100 Osborne Street North
Winnipeg, MB R3C 3A5 (204) 946-1190
investment company, insurance

Greyhound Lines of Canada Ltd. GHL
877 Greyhound Way Southwest
Calgary, AB T3C 3V8 (403) 260-0877
bus transportation and manufacturing

Groupe Videotron LTEE (Le) VDO
2000 Berri Street
Montreal, PQ H2L 4V7 (514) 281-1232
cable and broadcast TV stations

Gulf Canada Resources Ltd. GOU
401 9th Avenue S.W., P.O. Box 130
Calgary, AB T2P 2H7 (403) 233-4000
oil and gas exploration

GW Utilities Ltd. GWT
Suite 2700, 2 First Canadian Place, P.O. Box 20
Toronto, ON M5X 1B5 (416) 862-5300
investment company in gas utilities

Haley Industries Ltd. HLY
Haley, ON K0J 1Y0 (613) 432-8841
high-technology aerospace products, castings

Harris Steel Group, Inc. HSG.A
20 Queen Street West, Box 67, Suite 2210
Toronto, ON M5H 3R3 (416) 585-9425
steel building products

Hawker Siddeley Canada Inc. HSC
3 Robert Speck Parkway
Mississauga, ON L4Z 2G5 (416) 897-7161
transportation, industrial, mining and logging
products

Hayes-Dana Inc. HAY
One St. Paul, P.O. Box 3029
St. Catharines, ON L2R 7K9 (416) 687-4200
heavy vehicle parts and products

Hees International Bancorp Inc. HIL
P.O. Box 129, Suite 4400,
Commerce Court West
Toronto, ON M5L 1K5 (416) 865-0430
merchant banking   [O]

Hemlo Gold Mines Inc. HEM
Suite 1300, 4 King Street West
Toronto, ON M5H 3X2 (416) 982-7116
gold mining   [O]

Hollinger Inc. HLG
10 Toronto Street
Toronto, ON M5C 2B7 (416) 363-8721
newspaper publishing, printing, distributing

Horsham Corp. (The) HSM
5 Hazelton Avenue
Toronto, ON M5R 2E1 (416) 924-6665
investment company, mining

Hudson Bay Mining and Smelting Co., Ltd.
HBM.S
Suite 200, 3 Lombard Place,
Bank of Canada Building
Winnipeg, MB R3T 0E1 (204) 942-8148
metals mining and production, oil and gas

Hudson's Bay Company HBC
401 Bay Street
Toronto, ON M5H 2Y4 (416) 861-6112
retail stores, real estate development

Imasco Ltd. IMS
600 de Maisonneuve Boulevard West,
20th Floor
Montreal, PQ H3A 3K7 (514) 982-9111
consumer products and services, drugstores,
mortgages

Imperial Oil Ltd. IMO.A
111 St. Clair Avenue West
Toronto, ON M5W 1K3 (416) 968-4111
oil and chemical production   [O]

Inco Ltd. N
Royal Trust Tower, P.O. Box 44,
Toronto-Dominion Centre,
Toronto, ON M5K 1N4 (416) 361-7511
metal and alloy products, nickel, copper
                                              [O]

Innopac Inc. INA
Suite 900, Sussex Centre,
50 Burnhamthorpe Road West
Mississauga, ON L5B 3C2 (416) 566-7500
packaging products and services

Inter-City Gas Corp. ICG
Box 32, 20 Queen Street West
Toronto, ON M5H 3R3 (416) 598-0101
natural gas distribution   [O]

Interhome Energy Inc. IHE
3200 Home Oil Tower,
324 8th Avenue Southwest
Calgary, AB T2P 2Z5 (403) 232-5500
oil and hydrocarbon distribution, pipeline

International Forest Products Ltd. IFP.A
P.O. Box 49114, Suite 3500, Bentall Tower,
1055 Dunsmuir Street
Vancouver, BC V7X 1H7 (604) 681-3221
forest products, logging operations

International Semi-Tech Microelectronics Inc.
ISE
131 McNabb Street
Markham, ON L3R 5V7 (416) 475-2670
microelectronics research and development

Investors Group Inc. IGI
One Canada Centre, 447 Portage Avenue
Winnipeg, MB R3C 3B6 (204) 943-0361
individual and group financial services

IPSCO Inc. ISP
P.O. Box 1670
Regina, SK S4P 3C7 (306) 949-3530
steel and steel products

Jannock Ltd. JN
Suite 5203, 52nd Floor,
Toronto Dominion Bank Tower
Toronto, ON M5K 1B7 (416) 364-8586
brick products, electrical components

Kerr Addison Mines Ltd. KER
P.O. Box 91, Suite 3970,
Commerce Court West
Toronto, ON M5L 1C7 (416) 982-7270
metals mining, smelting, oil and gas
operations

Jean Coutu Group (PCJ) Inc. (The) PJC.A
530 Rue Beriault
Longueuil, PQ J4G 1S8 (514) 646-9760
health and beauty products, retailing

John Labatt Ltd. LBT
451 Ridout North
London, ON N6A 5L3 (519) 667-7500
brewing, dairy, grain, grocery products   [O]

Lac Minerals Ltd. LAC
P.O. Box 156, Suite 2105, North Tower,
Royal Bank Plaza
Toronto, ON M5J 2J4 (416) 865-0722
gold and metals mining, tin

Lafarge Canada Inc. LCI.PR.E
Suite 800, 606 Cathcart Street
Montreal, PQ H3B 1L7 (514) 861-1411
cement products, concrete, aggregates

Laidlaw Transportation Ltd. LDM.B
3221 North Service Road
Burlington, ON L7N 3G2 (416) 336-1800
transportation, waste services

Laurentian Bank of Canada LB
Tour Banque Laurentienne,
1981 Avenue McGill College, 17th Floor
Montreal, PQ H3A 3K3 (514) 284-3911
banking, financial services

Laurentian Group Corp. (The) LGC.B
The Laurentian Building,
1100 Rene-Levesque Boulevard West
Montreal, PQ H3B 4N4 (514) 392-6392
financial services, banking, insurance,
investment management

Lawson Mardon Group Ltd. LMP.A
Suite 401, 6711 Mississauga Road
Mississauga, ON L5N 2W3 (416) 821-9711
packaging products, printing

Loblaw Companies Ltd. L
22 St. Clair Avenue East, Suite 1500
Toronto, ON M4T 2S8 (416) 922-8500
food distribution

Lonvest Corp. LNV
Suite 3800, Royal Trust Tower,
Toronto-Dominion Centre
Toronto, ON M5K 1G8 (416) 981-6677
insurance services

MacKenzie Financial Corp. MKF
150 Bloor Street West, 4th Floor
Toronto, ON M5S 2X9 (416) 922-5322
investment portfolio management, mutual
funds

MacLean Hunter Ltd. MHP.X
MacLean Hunter Building, 777 Bay Street
Toronto, ON M5W 1A7 (416) 596-5000
publishing, printing, broadcasting

MacMillan Bloedel Ltd. MB
1075 West Georgia Street
Vancouver, BC V6E 3R9 (604) 661-8000
forest products, newsprint, packaging

Magna International Inc. MG.A
36 Apple Creek Boulevard
Markham, ON L3R 4Y4 (416) 477-7766
automotive components and systems   [O]

Maritime Telegraph and Telephone Company,
   Ltd. MTT
Maritime Centre, 1505 Barrington Street,
P.O. Box 880
Halifax, NS B3J 2W3 (902) 421-4311
telecommunications services

Mark Resources Inc. MKC
Suite 1300, 800 5th Avenue S.W.
Calgary, AB T2P 4A4 (403) 267-1500
oil and gas exploration, development

MDS Health Group Ltd. MHG.B
100 International Boulevard
Etobicoke, ON M9W 6J6 (416) 675-7661
health care services, clinical laboratories

Memotec Data Inc. MDI
600 McCaffrey Street
Laurent, PQ H4T 1N1 (514) 738-4781
networking, telecommunications services

Metall Mining Corp. MLM
Suite 2812, P.O. Box 19, TD Bank Tower,
Toronto-Dominion Centre
Toronto, ON M5K 1A1 (416) 361-6400
gold, silver and metal mining

Midland Doherty Financial Corp. MDG
121 King Street West
Toronto, ON M5H 3W6 (416) 369-7400
investment company, mutual funds,
securities

Minnova Inc. MVA
Suite 3970, P.O. Box 91,
Commerce Court West
Toronto, ON M5L 1C7 (416) 982-7270
exploration, development of mineral
properties

Minven Gold Corp. MVG
Suite 303, 7596 West Jewel Avenue
Lakewood, CO 80226 (303) 980-5615
mining production financing

Mitel Corp. MLT
350 Legget Drive, P.O. Box 13089
Kanata, ON K2K 1X3 (613) 592-2122
telecommunications products

Molson Companies Ltd. (The) MOL.A
2 International Boulevard
Toronto, ON M9W 1A2 (416) 675-1786
brewing, chemical products, lumber retail
outlets

Moore Corp. Ltd. MCL
P.O. Box 78, 1 First Canadian Place
Toronto, ON M5X 1G5 (416) 364-2600
business forms, software products and
services

Muscocho Explorations Ltd. MUS
Suite 950, 36 Toronto Street
Toronto, ON M5C 2C5 (416) 363-1124
gold and silver metals mining

National Bank of Canada NA
National Bank Tower,
600 de la Gauchetiere West
Montreal, PQ H3B 4L2 (514) 394-4000
banking

National Trustco Inc. NT
21 King Street East
Toronto, ON M5C 1B3 (416) 361-3611
trust and fiduciary services

Newtel Enterprises Ltd. NEL
Fort William Building, P.O. Box 12110
St. John's, NF A1C 6J7 (709) 739-2108
telecommunications services

Noma Industries Ltd. NMA.A
4211 Yonge Street, Suite 315
Willowdale, ON M2P 2A9 (416) 222-6662
mechanical and electrical products

Noranda Forest Inc. NF
P.O. Box 7, Toronto Dominion Bank Tower,
Toronto Dominion Centre
Toronto, ON M5K 1A1 (416) 982-7444
forest products, paper, building materials,
packaging

Noranda Inc. NOR
P.O. Box 45, Commerce Court West
Toronto, ON M5L 1B6 (416) 982-7111
mineral, oil and gas production, forest
products

Norcen Energy Resources Ltd. NCN
715 5th Avenue Southwest
Calgary, AB T2P 2X7 (403) 231-0111
hydrocarbon production, oil, gas and propane
distribution

North Canadian Oils Ltd. NCO
Suite 700, 112 4th Avenue Southwest
Calgary, AB T2P 4B2 (403) 261-3100
oil and gas production, lead and zinc mining

Northern Telecom Ltd. NTL
3 Robert Speck Parkway
Mississauga, ON L4Z 3C8 (416) 897-9000
telecommunications products, services
[O]

Northgate Exploration Ltd. NGX
Suite 2701, P.O. Box 143,
1 First Canadian Place
Toronto, ON M5X 1C7 (416) 362-6683
gold, mineral exploration and production

Nova Corp. of Alberta NVA
801 7th Avenue Southwest, P.O. Box 2535,
Postal Station M
Calgary, AB T2P 2N6 (403) 290-6000
gas transportation, oil production,
petrochemicals   [O]

Noverco Inc. NVC
1170 Peel Street, Suite 410
Montreal, PQ H3B 4P2 (514) 393-2650
energy investment company

Nowsco Well Service Ltd. NWS
Suite 1300, 801 6th Avenue Southwest
Calgary, AB T2P 4E1 (403) 261-2990
oil and gas drilling products, services

Numac Oil & Gas Ltd. NMC
Petroleum Plaza, South Tower,
1400, 9915 108th Street
Edmonton, AB T5K 2G8 (403) 423-1718
oil and gas exploration, production,
uranium

Ocelot Industries Ltd. OIL.B
Suite 2400, 400 3rd Avenue Southwest
Calgary, AB T2P 4H2 (403) 261-2100
oil and gas products and services,
petrochemicals

Onex Corp. OCX
29th Floor, Commerce Court West,
P.O. Box 153
Toronto, ON M5L 1E7 (416) 362-7711
acquires companies in leveraged buyouts,
investments

Oshawa Group Ltd. (The) OSH.A
302 The East Mall
Etobicoke, ON M9B 6B8 (416) 236-1971
food, health, drug, beauty product marketing

Pagurian Corp. Ltd. (The) PGC.A
13 Hazelton Avenue
Toronto, ON M5R 2E1 (416) 968-0255
investment company   [O]

Pamour Inc. PAM
Suite 1601, Box 13, 95 Wellington Street West
Toronto, ON M5J 2N7 (416) 363-5470
holding company for gold and minerals
mining firms

Pancanadian Petroleum Ltd. PCP
P.O. Box 2850
Calgary, AB T2P 2S5 (403) 290-2000
oil and gas exploration, production

Placer Dome Inc. PDG
P.O. Box 49330, Bentall Postal Station
Vancouver, BC V7X 1P1 (604) 682-7082
gold, silver, copper, molybdenum mining,
oil and gas   [O]

Pegasus Gold Inc. PGU
Suite 400, North 9 Post Street
Spokane, WA 99201 (509) 624-4653
gold, silver, zinc and lead mining

Peoples Jewellers Ltd. PCJ.A
1440 Don Mills Road
Don Mills, ON M3B 3M1 (416) 441-1515
retail jewelry stores

Pioneer Metals Corp. PSM
Suite 1770, 885 West Georgia
Vancouver, BC V6C 3E8 (604) 669-3383
metal exploration, production, oil and gas

Poco Petroleums Ltd. POC
Suite 2600, 250 6th Avenue Southwest
Calgary, AB T2P 3H7 (403) 260-8000
oil and gas exploration, production

Power Corporation of Canada POW
800 Place Victoria, 44th Floor
Montreal, PQ H4Z 1E3 (514) 286-7400
financial services, paper products, publishing

Power Financial Corporation PWF
800 Place Victoria, 44th Floor, C.P. 206
Montreal, PQ H4Z 1E3 (514) 286-7430
financial, fiduciary services, insurance

Provigo Inc. PGI
800 Boulevarde Rene-Levesque Ouest
Montreal, PQ H3B 1Y2 (514) 878-8300
food and health care products, retail stores

PWA Corp. PWA
Suite 2800, 700 2nd Street West
Calgary, AB T2P 2W2 (403) 294-2000
airline

Quebecor Inc. QBR.A
612 St.-Jacques West
Montreal, PQ H3C 4M8 (514) 282-9600
publishing, printing, forest products

Quebec-Telephone QT
6 Rue Jules-a-Brillant
Rimouski, PQ G5L 7E4 (418) 723-2271
telecommunications services

Ranger Oil Ltd. RGO
2700 Esso Plaza East,
25 First Street Southwest
Calgary, AB T2P 3L8 (403) 263-1500
oil and gas exploration, development   [O]

Rayrock Yellowknife Resources Inc. RAY
65 Granby Street
Toronto, ON M5B 1H8 (416) 977-6644
gold, oil and mineral products, fertilizer

Reed Stenhouse Companies Ltd. RSS.S
20 Bay Street, 24th Floor
Toronto, ON M5J 2N9 (416) 868-5500
risk management consulting, insurance

Reitmans (Canada) Ltd. RET
250 Suave Street West
Montreal, PQ H3L 1Z2 (514) 384-1140
women's retail clothing stores

Renaissance Energy Ltd. RES
Suite 3300, 400 3rd Avenue Southwest
Calgary, AB T2P 4H2 (403) 267-1400
oil and gas exploration, development   [O]

Repap Enterprises Inc. RPP
Suite 3200, 1150 Peel Street
Montreal, PQ H3B 3V2 (514) 879-1316
pulp and paper products

Rio Algom Ltd. ROM
120 Adelaide Street West, Suite 2600
Toronto, ON M5H 1W5 (416) 367-4000
uranium, copper ore mining, steel milling

Rogers Communications Inc. RCI.B
Suite 2600, Commercial Union Tower,
Toronto-Dominion Centre
Toronto, ON M5K 1J5 (416) 864-2373
radio, TV stations, cable systems, cellular
telephone systems

Roman Corp. Ltd. RMN
Suite 3900, South Tower, Royal Bank Plaza,
P.O. Box 40
Toronto, ON M5J 2K2 (416) 865-1991
packaging, printing services

Rothmans Inc. ROC
1500 Don Mills Road
North York, ON M3B 3L1 (416) 449-5525
tobacco products

Royal Bank of Canada (The) RY
P.O. Box 6001, 1 Place Ville Marie
Montreal, PQ H3C 3A9 (514) 874-2110
banking   [0]

Royal Lepage Ltd. RLG
Suite 1000, 33 Yonge Street
Toronto, ON M5E 1S9 (416) 862-0611
real estate management and investment
services

Royal Trustco Ltd. RYL
Royal Trust Tower, Suite 3900
Toronto, ON M5W 1P9 (416) 864-7000
trust company, financial services

St. Lawrence Cement Inc. ST.A
1945 Graham Boulevard
Mont-Royal, PQ H3R 1H1 (514) 340-1881
cement, concrete and aggregates manufacturing, distribution

Samuel Manu-Tech Inc. SMT
191 The West Mall, Suite 418
Etobicoke, ON M9C 5K8 (416) 626-2190
steel and aluminum products, air
compressors

Saskatchewan Oil and Gas Corp. SKO
1500 Saskoil Tower, 1945 Hamilton Street,
P.O. Box 1550
Regina, SK S4P 3C4 (306) 781-8200
oil and gas exploration, production

Sceptre Resources Ltd. SRL
Suite 2000, 400 3rd Avenue Southwest
Calgary, AB T2P 4H2 (403) 298-9800
oil and gas exploration, production

Schneider Corp. SCD.A
321 Courtland Avenue East, P.O. Box 130
Kitchener, ON N2G 3X8 (519) 864-6500
fresh and processed meat, dairy and grocery
products

Scott Paper Ltd. SPL
P.O. Box 3600, 1111 Melville Street, 12th Floor
Vancouver, BC V6E 3V6 (604) 688-8131
household paper products

Scott's Hospitality Inc. SRC.C
89 Chestnut Street
Toronto, ON M5G 1R1 (416) 977-6001
food, restaurant, hotel, transportation
services, photofinishing

Seagram Company Ltd. (The) VO
1430 Peel Street
Montreal, PQ H3A 1S9 (514) 849-5271
distilled spirits and wine producer, distributor
                                                     [0]

Sears Canada Inc. SCC
222 Jarvis Street
Toronto, ON M5B 2B8 (416) 362-1711
retail, catalog, insurance services, real estate
                                                     [0]

Shaw Cablesystems Ltd. SCL.B
7605 50 Street
Edmonton, AB T6B 2W9 (403) 468-1230
cable TV systems, radio stations, newspapers

Shell Canada Ltd. SHC
Shell Centre, 400 4th Avenue Southwest
Calgary, AB T2P 0J4 (403) 232-3111
oil, gas, chemical production, distribution
                                                     [0]

Sherritt Gordon Ltd. SE
P.O. Box 28, Commerce Court West
Toronto, ON M5L 1B1 (416) 363-9241
fertilizer, nickel, cobalt, specialty metals,
chemicals   [0]

SHL Systemhouse Inc. SHK
50 O'Connor Street, 5th Floor
Ottawa, ON K1P 6L2 (613) 236-9734
information systems integration

Sico Inc. SIC
3280 Ste.-Anne Boulevard
Beauport, PQ G1E 3K9 (418) 663-3551
paint, varnish and stain products

SNC Group Inc. (The) SNU.A
2 Place Felix-Martin
Montreal, PQ H2Z 1Z3 (514) 866-1000
engineering, construction project management

Southam Inc. STM
Suite 900, 150 Bloor Street West
Toronto, ON M5S 2Y8 (416) 927-1877
newspaper and magazine publishing, retail
bookstores

Spar Aerospace Ltd. SPZ
Suite 900, 5090 Explorer Drive
Mississauga, ON L4W 4X6 (416) 629-7727
aerospace, defense, communications systems

Stelco Inc. STE.A
IBM Tower, Toronto-Dominion Centre
Toronto, ON M5K 1J4 (416) 362-2161
steel, steel products   [O]

Steinberg Inc. SBG.A
2 Place Alexis Nihon,
3500 de Maisonneuve West
Westmount, PQ H3Z 1Y3 (514) 931-9131
supermarkets, convenience stores,
restaurants, real estate

Sonora Gold Corp. SON
Suite 2701, P.O. Box 143,
1 First Canadian Place
Toronto, ON M5X 1C7 (416) 362-6683
gold mining

T.C.C. Beverages Ltd. KOC
42 Overlea Boulevard
Toronto, ON M4H 1B8 (416) 424-6000
soft drink bottling, distribution

Teck Corp. TEK.B
1199 West Hastings Street
Vancouver, BC V6E 2K5 (604) 687-1117
gold, silver, copper, zinc, coal, oil and gas
production

Tele-Metropole Inc. TM.B
Case Postale 170, Station C
Montreal, PQ H2L 4P6 (514) 526-9251
TV broadcast, film and video production

Tembec Inc. TBC.A
800 Rene-Levesque Boulevard West
Montreal, PQ H3B 1X9 (514) 871-0137
sulphite chemical wood-cellulose products

Terra Mines ltd. TER
Suite 202, 7608 103rd Street
Edmonton, AB T6E 4Z8 (403) 432-1212
exploration, development of precious metal
properties

Thomson Corp. (The) TOC
Suite 2706, Box 24, TD Bank Tower,
Toronto-Dominion Centre
Toronto, ON M5K 1A1 (416) 360-8700
publishing, travel services

Toronto-Dominion Bank (The) TD
P.O. Box 1, Toronto-Dominion Centre,
King Street and Bay Street
Toronto, ON M5K 1A2 (416) 982-8222
banking   [O]

Toronto Sun Publishing Corp. TSP
333 King Street East
Toronto, ON M5A 3X5 (416) 947-2222
newspaper publishing

Torstar Corp. TS.B
1 Yonge Street
Toronto, ON M5E 1P9 (416) 367-4595
newspaper and book publishing, printing

Total Petroleum (North America) Ltd. TPN
639 Fifth Avenue, Southwest, Suite 700
Calgary, AB T2P 0M9 (403) 267-3000
petroleum production, refining

Transalta Utilities Corp. TAU
P.O. Box 1900
Calgary, AB T2P 2M1 (403) 267-7253
electric utility

Trans Canada Glass ltd. TCG
2000-4330 Kingsway
Burnaby, BC V5H 4G7 (604) 438-1000
replacement auto parts

Transcanada Pipelines Ltd. TRP
P.O. Box 54, Commerce Court West
Toronto, ON M5L 1C2 (416) 869-2111
natural gas distribution

Trilon Financial Corp. TFC.A
Suite 3800, Royal Trust Tower,
Toronto-Dominion Centre
Toronto, ON M5K 1G8 (416) 363-0061
financial services, property-casualty insurance
                                                               [O]

Trimac Ltd. TMA
P.O. Box 3500, 2100 Trimac House
Calgary, AB T2P 2P9 (403) 298-5100
trucking and drilling services, waste
management

Trizec Corp. Ltd. TZC.A
Suite 3000, 700 2nd Street Southwest
Calgary, AB T2P 2W2 (403) 269-8241
real estate development, homebuilder,
retirement homes

Turbo Resources Ltd. TBR
815 8th Avenue Southwest
Calgary, AB T2P 3P2 (403) 294-6400
refinery operations

UAP Inc. UAP.A
7025 Ontario Street East
Montreal, PQ H1N 2B3 (514) 256-5031
auto parts distributor

Ulster Petroleums Ltd. ULP
Suite 1400, 144 4th Avenue Southwest,
Sun Life Plaza 1
Calgary, AB T2P 3N4 (403) 269-6911
oil and gas exploration, development

Unicorp Canada Corp. UNI.A
21 St. Clair Avenue East
Toronto, ON M4T 2T7 (416) 961-1200
merchant banking, energy, real estate and
financial services

Union Carbide Canada Ltd. UCC
123 Eglinton Avenue East
Toronto, ON M4P 1J3 (416) 488-1444
chemical and plastic products, industrial gases

United Corporations Ltd. UNC
26th Floor, South Tower, Royal Bank Plaza
Toronto, ON M5J 2J5 (416) 974-0616
investment company, finance, mining, real
estate, industrial goods

Unigesco Inc. UGO.B
1 Place Ville Marie, Suite 3315
Montreal, PQ H3B 3N2 (514) 871-1212
investment and management company

Union Enterprises Ltd. UEL
Unicorp Building, 21 St. Clair Avenue East
Toronto, ON M4T 2T7 (416) 964-6300
oil and gas distribution, financial services

Varity Corp. VAT
595 Bay Street
Toronto, ON M5G 2C3 (416) 593-3811
auto parts, farm and heavy machinery
products

Viceroy Resource Corp. VOY
Suite 880, 999 West Hastings Street
Vancouver, BC V6C 2W2 (604) 688-9780
mineral property exploration, development,
gold mining

Wajax Ltd. WJX.A
Place Mercantile, Suite 1750,
770 Sherbrooke Street West
Montreal, PQ H3A 1G1 (514) 849-0583
mechanical equipment distribution

West Fraser Timber Co., Ltd. WFT
Suite 1000, 1100 Melville Street
Vancouver, BC V6E 4A6 (604) 681-8282
forest products, paper, building supply
stores

Weldwood of Canada Ltd. WLW
P.O. Box 2179
Vancouver, BC V6B 3V8 (604) 687-7366
forest, building products

Westar Group Ltd. WGL
Suite 1900, 1176 West Georgia Street
Vancouver, BC V6E 4B9 (604) 687-2600
lumber, coal, oil and gas production,
distribution

Westcoast Energy Inc. W
1333 West Georgia Street
Vancouver, BC V6E 3K9 (604) 664-5500
natural gas exploration, production,
distribution

Westmin Resources Ltd. WMI
Suite 1800, 255 5th Avenue Southwest
Calgary, AB T2P 3G6 (403) 298-2000
oil and gas, metals, coal exploration,
development

George Weston Ltd. WN
22 St. Clair Avenue East, Suite 1901
Toronto, ON M4T 2S7 (416) 922-2500
food processing, distribution services, fish,
forest products

Wharf Resources Ltd. WFR
Suite 2600, 130 Adelaide Street West
Toronto, ON M5H 3P5 (416) 592-5080
gold, silver mining

WIC Western International Communications
Ltd. WIC.B
Suite 1960, One Bentall Centre,
505 Burrard Street
Vancouver, BC V7X 1M6 (604) 687-2844
broadcast TV, radio stations

Woodward's Ltd. WDS.A
101 West Hastings Street
Vancouver, BC V6B 1H4 (604) 684-5231
retail merchandising

Xerox Canada Inc. XXC
5650 Yonge Street
North York (Toronto), ON M2M 4G7
(416) 229-3769
office technology, equipment, services,
copiers

AMERICAN DEPOSITARY RECEIPTS (ADRs)

Investors wishing to buy shares in some companies headquartered outside the United States can avoid dealing directly with foreign exchanges by purchasing American Depositary Receipts in U.S. markets. ADRs are traded on the New York Stock Exchange, the American Stock Exchange and the Over-the-Counter market. ADRs are receipts for foreign-based corporation's shares, which are held in American bank vaults. A buyer of an ADR in America is entitled to the same dividends and capital gains accruing to a shareholder purchasing shares on an exchange in the home country of the company. ADRs are denominated in dollars, so quoted prices reflect the latest currency exchange rates. ADR prices are listed in the Wall Street Journal and other newspapers, as well as in electronic databases.

The companies with ADRs generally are well-established, financially stable corporations with worldwide operations. In many cases, Americans would be familiar with their products and services because they are offered in the United States. A total of about 700 ADRs are traded. Most of the trading activity, however, is limited to some 100 issues. It is these actively traded issues that are presented here in alphabetical order, courtesy of Wilshire Associates [1299 Ocean Avenue, Santa Monica, California 90401 (213) 451-3051.] The entry for each company includes (1) the firm's name, (2) it's stock symbol, (3) the exchange where it trades (NYSE for New York Stock Exchange, AMEX for American Stock Exchange and OTC for Over-The-Counter market), (4) its main line of business, and (5) the country where it is headquartered.

ADT Limited [ADTL] OTC, Construction, United Kingdom

Aegon Insurance Group [AEGNY] OTC, Insurance, Netherlands

Airship Industries [AIRSY] OTC, Aerospace, United Kingdom

American Israeli Paper Mills [AIP] AMEX, Paper Manufacturing, Israel

Anglo American Corporation [ANGLY] OTC, Gold, South Africa

Anglo American Gold Investors [AAGIY] OTC, Gold Mining, South Africa

ASEA AB [ASEA] OTC, Power Engineering, Sweden

Attwoods PLC [ATTWY] OTC, Waste Management, United Kingdom

BAT Industries Limited [BTI] AMEX, Tobacco and Retailing, United Kingdom

BET Pub Limited [BEP] NYSE, Industrial Services, United Kingdom

Banco Balboa Vizcaya [BBV] NYSE, Banking, Spain

Banco Central S.A. [BCM] NYSE, Banking, Spain

Banco De Santander [STD] NYSE, Banking, Spain

Bank Leumi Le Israel [BKLMY] OTC, Banking, Israel

Barclays PLC [BCS] NYSE, Banking, United Kingdom

Beazer, C.H. Holdings PLC [BEZRY] NYSE, Building Materials, United Kingdom

Beecham Group Limited [BECHY] OTC, Health and Personal Care, United Kingdom

Blue Arrow PLC [BAW] NYSE, Employment Services, United Kingdom

Blyvoorjitzicht Gold Mining [BLYVY] OTC, Gold Mining, South Africa

Bowater Industries PLC [BWTRY] OTC, Packaging & Associated Products, United Kingdom

British Airways PLC [BAB] NYSE, Airlines, United Kingdom

British Gas PLC [BRG] NYSE, Purchase/Sale/Transport of Natural Gas, United Kingdom

British Petroleum Limited [BP] NYSE, Oil/Natural Gas Exploration, United Kingdom

British Petroleum PLC [BPPP] NYSE, Oil, United Kingdom

British Steel PLC [BST] NYSE, Iron & Steel Making, United Kingdom

British Telecommunications PLC [BTT] NYSE, Telecommunications, United Kingdom

Broken Hill Proprietary Company [BHP] NYSE, Petroleum, Minerals & Steel, Australia

Buffelsfontein Gold Mines [BFELY] OTC, Gold Mining, South Africa

Burmah Oil, Limited [BURMY] OTC, Oil Refining and Marketing, United Kingdom

Cadbury-Schweppes PLC [CADBY] OTC, Confectioners & Beverages, United Kingdom

Cambridge Instrument Company [CAMBY] OTC, Electronics, United Kingdom

Canon Inc. [CANNY] OTC, Business Equipment, Japan

Carlton Communications [CCTVY] OTC, Broadcasting, United Kingdom

Central Pacific Minerals, N.L. [CPMNY] OTC, Metals Mining, Australia

Coles Myer Limited [CM] NYSE, Retail Department Stores, Australia

Compania De Alumbrad [ELSA] OTC, Utility, El Salvador

Courtaulds Limited [COU] AMEX, Textiles and Fibers, United Kingdom

CSK Corporation [CSKKY] OTC, Computer Services, Japan

Daiei Inc. [DAIEY] OTC, Retail Food Stores, Japan

De Beers Consolidated Mines [DBRSY] OTC, Diamonds Mining, South Africa

Deltec International [DLTC] NYSE, Finance, British Columbia

Dixons Group PLC [DXN] NYSE, Consumer Electronics Appliances, United Kingdom

Dresdner Bank A.G. [DRSDY] OTC, Banking, Germany

Driefontein Consolidated Limited [DRFNY] OTC, Gold Mining, South Africa

Dunlop Holdings ADR [DUNQ] AMEX, Tires , United Kingdom

Eagle Limited [EGCLY] OTC, Chemicals, Australia

Elan PLC [ELANY] OTC, Drugs Research & Development, Ireland

Electrolux, A B [ELXSN] OTC, Electrical Equipment, Sweden

EMI Limited [EMIL] NYSE, Records, United Kingdom

Empresa Nacional de Celulosas [ELE] NYSE, Paper Pulp Products, Spain

English China Clays PLC [ECLAY] OTC, Building Materials, United Kingdom

Ericsson, LM [ERICY] OTC, Communications Equipment, Sweden

Fairhaven International Limited [NIMSY] OTC, Photographic Equipment, Germany

Fisons PLC [FISNY] OTC, Drugs/Scientific Equipment, United Kingdom

Free State Consolidated Gold Mines [FSCNY] OTC, Gold Mining, South Africa

Fuji Photo Film Ltd. [FUJIY] OTC, Photographic Equipment, Japan

Gambro A.B. [GAMBY] OTC, Health Services/ Supplies, Sweden

Gateway Corporation PLC [GAT] NYSE, Retail/ Food Stores, United Kingdom

Glaxo Holdings PLC [GLX] NYSE, Drugs, United Kingdom

Gold Fields of South Africa Limited [GLDF] OTC, Gold Mining, South Africa

Great Eastern Mines Limited [GOLDY] OTC, Mining, Australia

Hard Rock Cafe PLC [HRK] AMEX, Restaurants, United Kingdom

Harvard Group PLC [HARVY] OTC, Finance, United Kingdom

Highveld Steel and Vanadium [HSVLY] OTC, Steel, South Africa

Hitachi Limited [HIT] NYSE, Electronic Equipment, Japan

Honda Motor Limited [HMC] NYSE, Auto and Motorcycle Manufacturer, Japan.

Hong Kong Telecommunications Limited [HKT] NYSE, Communications, Japan

Huntington International Holding [HRCLY] OTC, Drugs, United Kingdom

IDB Bankholding Company [IDBBY] OTC, Banking, Israel

Imperial Chemical Industries [ICI] NYSE, Pharmaceuticals, United Kingdom

Imperial Group PLC [IMT] AMEX, Tobacco and Food, United Kingdom

Instrumentarium Corporation [INMRY] OTC, Health Services and Supplies, Finland

Ito Yokado Limited [IYCOY] OTC, Retailing, Japan

Japan Air Lines Limited [JAPNY] OTC, Airline, Japan

Kirin Brewery Limited [KNBWY] OTC, Brewers and Wineries, Japan

Kloof Gold Mining [KLOFY] OTC, Gold Mining, South Africa

Kubota Limited [KUB] NYSE, Farm, Construction and Mining Machinery, Japan

Kyocera Limited [KYO] NYSE, Electronics and Ceramics, Japan

LVMH Moet Hennessy Louis Vuitton [LVMHY] OTC, Champagne, Perfumes and Luggage, France

LEP Group PLC [LEPY] OTC, Shipping and Distribution, United Kingdom

Lydenburg Platinum [LYDPY] OTC, Platinum Mining, South Africa

Makita Electric Works Limited [MKTAY] OTC, Electrical Equipment, Japan

Matsushita Electric Industrial [MC] NYSE, Electronic Equipment, Japan

Melcorp Securities Limited [AGLY] OTC, Gold, Australia

Meridian Oil, N.L. [MEOLY] OTC, Oil Drilling and Refining, Netherlands

Michigan Consolidated Gas Company [MIC] NYSE, Energy and Utilities, Germany

Minorco [MNRCY] OTC, Mining/Rare Metals, Luxembourg

Mitsui & Company Limited [MITSY] OTC, Conglomerate, Japan

Montedison SpA [MNT.P] NYSE, Chemicals, Italy

NEC Corporation [NIPNY] OTC, Electronics Equipment, Japan

National Australia Bank Limited [NAB] NYSE, Banking, Australia

National Westminster Bank PLC [NW] NYSE, Banking, United States

New Zealand Petroleum Ltd. [NZPCY] OTC, Oil, New Zealand

News Corporation Limited [NWS] NYSE, Media, Australia

Nissan Motors [NSANY] OTC, Auto Manufacturer, Japan

Norsk-Data, A.S. [NORKZ] OTC, Computers and Data Processing, Norway

Norsk Hydro A S [NHY] NYSE, Oil, Norway

Novo Industri A/S [NVO] NYSE, Drugs, Denmark

Oce-Van Der Grinten [OCENY] OTC, Copying Machines, Netherlands

O'Okiep Copper Company Limited [OKP] AMEX, Copper Mining, South Africa

Orange Free State Investment Limited [OESLY] OTC, Gold, South Africa

Pacific Dunlop Limited [PDLPY] OTC, Consumer Products, Australia

Pelsart Resources, N.L. [PELR] OTC, Energy, Netherlands

Pharmacia,A.B. [PHABY] OTC, Drugs, Sweden

Philips, N.V. [PHG] NYSE, Electrical Equipmenmt, Netherlands

Pioneer Electronic Corporation [PIO] NYSE, Radio and TV Equipment, Japan

Plessey Company PLC [PLY] NYSE, Communications Equipment, United Kingdom

PNC Financial Corporation [PNCFN] NYSE, Banking, United Kingdom

Racal Telecommunications Group [RTG] NYSE, Cellular Networks, United Kingdom

Ramtron Australia Limited [MEMR] OTC, Business Machines, Australia

Rank Organization PLC [RANKD] OTC, Movies, United Kingdom

Ratners Group, PLC [RATNY] OTC, Retail/Department Stores, United Kingdom

Reuters Holding PLC [RTRSY] OTC, Electronic Publishing, United Kingdom

Rhone-Poulenc S.A. [RHPOY] OTC, Chemicals, France

Rodime PLC [RODMY] OTC, Electronics, United Kingdom

Royal Dutch Petroleum Company [RPETY] OTC, Oil Refining and Marketing, Netherlands

Saatchi and Saatchi Company PLC [SAA] NYSE, Advertising and Financial Services, United Kingdom

Santos Limited [STOSY] OTC, Oil and Gas Production, Australia

Sanyo Electric Limited [SANYY] OTC, Electronics, Japan

Sasol Limited [SASOY] OTC, Oil Refining and Marketing, South Africa

Senetek PLC [SNTKY] OTC, Business Services, United Kingdom

Shell Transport & Trading Company PLC [SC] NYSE, Oil Refining and Marketing, United Kingdom

Sir Speedy Printing Centers [SPEDY] OTC, Printing Services, United Kingdom

SKF A.G. [SKFRY] OTC, Precision Engineering Equipment, Sweden

Sony Corp [SNE] NYSE, Consumer and Commercial Electronics, Japan

Southern Pacific Petroleum, N.L. [SPPTY] OTC, Oil Refining and Food, Australia

St Helena Gold Mines [SGOLY] OTC, Gold Mining, South Africa

Svenska Cellulosa Aktiebolaget [SCAPY] OTC, Forest Industry, Sweden

Swan Resources Limited [SWANY] OTC, Natural Resources, Austrailia

TDK Electronics, Limited [TDK] NYSE, Electronic Equipment, Japan

Telefonica de Espana S.A. [TEF] NYSE, Telephone Service, Spain

Telephonos de Mexico S.A. [TFONY] OTC, Telephone Utility, Mexico

Teva Pharaceutical [TEVIY] OTC, Drugs, Israel

Thomson - CSF [TCSFY] OTC, Defense Electronics, France

Tokio Marine & Fire [TKIOY] OTC, Fire, Marine, Casualty and Title Insurance, Japan

Tomkins PLC [TOMK] OTC, Industrial Management, United Kingdom

Toyota Motor Company [TOYOY] OTC, Auto Manufacturer, Japan

Tubos de Acero de me [TAM] AMEX, Steel, Mexico

Unilever Limited PLC [UL] NYSE, Food, United Kingdom

Unilever N.V. [UN] NYSE, Soaps and Cleansers, Netherlands

United Newspapers PLC [UNEWY] OTC, Publishing, United Kingdom

Vaal Reefs Exploration & Mining [VAAL] OTC, Gold Mining, South Africa

Volvo A.B., VOLVY [OTC] Auto Manufacturer, Sweden

WCRS Group PLC [WCRSY] OTC, Advertising Agency, United Kingdom

Ward White Group [WWGPY] OTC, Retail/Apparel, United Kingdom

Waterford Glass Group PLC [WATFZ] OTC, Glassware, Ireland

Welkom Gold Mining Limited [WLKMY] OTC, Gold Mining, South Africa

Western Deep Levels [WDEPY] OTC, Gold Mining, South Africa

FREE AND DISCOUNTED GOODS FOR SHAREHOLDERS

The following is a list of American corporations that give free or discounted merchandise or services to their shareholders. In order to make a claim, shareholders usually must write or call the company, since most companies do not know the names of their shareholders (shares often are held in street name by a brokerage firm). These freebies usually are not taxed as income to shareholders—if they are, the company will so inform their shareholders.

This list is provided courtesy of Gene Walden, who has written a book, The 100 Best Stocks To Own In America (Longman Financial Services Publishing, 520 North Dearborn Street, Chicago, Illinois, 60610). The book describes some of these shareholder perks in more detail.

Albertson's Inc.: Product pack of private-label groceries for shareholders attending the annual meeting.

American Brands, Inc.: Product pack including cigarettes, office products, locks and food for shareholders who attend the annual meeting.

American Home Products Corporation: Coupons for food and health-care products.

Anheuser-Busch Companies, Inc.: Free beer samples to shareholders attending the annual meeting. Also, discounts on admission to all the company's theme parks.

Borden, Inc.: Product pack including glue, popcorn and potato chips for shareholders who attend the annual meeting.

Bristol-Myers: Product pack including over-the-counter drugs, shampoos and toiletries for new shareholders.

Brown-Forman Corporation: Discount of 50% on Lenox china, crystal dinnerware and Christmas tree ornaments during the holiday season.

Campbell Soup Company: Shareholders attending the annual meeting receive free foods, a product pack to take home and coupons. Also, coupons are included in quarterly and annual reports.

ConAgra, Inc.: Coupons and discounts for meat and other foods products.

Dean Foods Company: Product pack including groceries and coupons for shareholders attending the annual meeting.

Flowers Industries, Inc.: Small gift to shareholders attending the annual meeting.

General Mills, Inc.: Shareholders attending the annual meeting receive product pack of cereals, cake mixes and coupons.

Gillette Company: Pack of new toiletry products for shareholders attending the annual meeting.

Gulf + Western, Inc.: Small gifts to shareholders attending the annual meeting.

H.J. Heinz Company: New stockholders with at least 30 shares receive a welcome gift such as a crock pot or clock. Shareholders who attend the annual meeting are offered a product pack.

Hershey Foods Corporation: Product pack of chocolates and coupons to Friendly's restaurants for shareholders who attend the annual meeting. Also, a Christmas gift catalog exclusively for shareholders who want gifts wrapped and mailed directly from the chocolate factory.

James River Corporation: Product pack of tissues, Dixie Cups and industrial wipes for shareholders attending the annual meeting. Also, product coupons.

Johnson & Johnson: Gift pack of hygiene products to shareholders attending the annual meeting.

Kellogg Company: New shareholders receive a welcome gift of coupons for free grocery products. Shareholders attending the annual meeting recieve a product pack of cereals, waffles and other goods, along with coupons and special gifts.

Kimberly-Clark Corporation: Christmas pack filled with the company's paper products such as tissues, napkins and stationery that shareholders can order for themselves or others.

Marriott Corporation: Special resort packages and discounts of up to 50% on stays at the company's hotels.

McDonald's Corporation: Shareholders attending the annual meeting at Hamburger University in Oak Brook, Illinois, receive a free tour and complimentary meal.

Minnesota Mining and Manufacturing Company: Product pack of scotch tape, office products and brushes for new shareholders. Also, special holiday packages can be ordered as gifts. For shareholders attending the annual meeting, a product pack and discounts at the company store are available.

Noxell Corporation: Shareholders attending the annual meeting receive a product pack of cosmetics, chili and liquid cleaner.

PepsiCo Inc.: Shareholders attending the annual meeting receive gift packs of soft drinks, food products and coupons for Kentucky Fried Chicken and Pizza Hut. They also are given special collector's item gifts.

Prime Motor Inns, Inc.: Discounts of 50% on weekends and 25% on weekdays for lodging at hotels and motels.

Quaker Oats: Discount coupons mailed to shareholders with quarterly dividend checks. Product pack given to shareholders attending the annual meeting.

Ralston Purina Company: Shareholders attending the annual meeting recieve bakery, cereal and other food products, along with batteries and pet food coupons. Also, discount coupons for Keystone ski resort are sent out with dividend checks each September.

Ramada, Inc.: Discounts on hotel accomodations.

Rubbermaid, Inc.: Shareholders attending the annual meeting receive a free Rubbermaid product. Also, shareholders may shop in the company store and receive discounts on products.

Sara Lee Corporation: Shareholders attending the annual meeting recieve a product pack of shoe polish, hosiery and coupons for meat and bakery products.

Scott Paper Company: Product pack of tissues, paper towels, napkins and other paper goods for shareholders attending the annual meeting. Also, shareholders can have Scott mail a gift pack of paper products to themselves or to friends at Christmas.

Sonoco Products Company: Gift box of products for which Sonoco makes packaging, such as Crisco shortening, masking tape or Pringles potato chips, to shareholders attending the annual meeting.

Super Valu Stores, Inc.: Product pack of private-label groceries for shareholders attending the annual meeting.

UST, Inc.: Product pack of cigars, smokeless tobacco and company keychains to shareholders attending the annual meeting.

The Walgreen Company: Shareholders at the annual meeting receive one or two private-label products.

The Walt Disney Company: Admission to the Magic Kingdom Club, discounts of 10% on theme park admission, 5% to 20% on accomodations, 10% on purchases and access to special cruise and travel packages. Also, discounts on Delta Airlines flights to Disney areas.

William Wrigley Jr. Company: Christmas gift boxes of gum and 20 packs of gum to shareholders attending the annual meeting.

7. STOCK SYMBOLS

This section of the Handbook lists over 6000 stock symbols of companies listed on the New York Stock Exchange, the American Stock Exchange and on the NASDAQ over-the-counter market. The symbols are listed in alphabetical order, with the accompanying company name.

This list will be useful to investors who see stock symbols on the broad tape in a broker's office, on a computer screen with stock quotations, or on cable television, but do not know which companies are represented by each symbol.

This list was provided courtesy of Quotron Systems, Inc., a leading provider of real-time, online financial information services for more than 30 years. If you would like to receive Quotron's North American Symbol Directory, International Symbol Directory or QUOTIPS —Quotron's monthly updates of U.S. stock symbols—please call Betty Frazier at (213) 302-4138 or write to her at: Quotron Systems, Inc. 12731 West Jefferson Boulevard, Mail Stop G1-00, Los Angeles, California 90066.

A	A	American Medical Buildings Inc	ACPI	Q	American Consumer Products Inc
AA	N	Aluminum Co of America	ACPT	Q	Acceptance Insurance Holdings Inc
AA*	A	Aluminum Co of America $3.75 Cum Pfd	ACR	N	Angell Real Estate Co
AAC	N	Anacomp Inc	ACS	N	American Capital Convertible Securities Inc
AAE	N	Amerace Corp	ACT	N	American Century Corp
AAF	N	American Government Income Portfolio Inc	ACU	A	Acme United Corp
AAGC	Q	All American Gourmet Co	ACV	N	Alberto Culver Co
AAHS	Q	Alco Health Services Corp	ACVA	N	Alberto Culver Co Cl A
AAL	N	Alexander & Alexander Services Inc	ACWWS	A	Associates Corp of North America Currency
AAME	Q	Atlantic American Corp			Wts
AAPL	Q	Apple Computer	ACX	A	Action Industries Inc
AAST	Q	Action Auto Stores Inc	ACXM	Q	Acxion Corp
AATI	Q	Analysis & Technology Inc	ACY	N	American Cyanamid Co
ABBK	Q	Abington Bancorp Inc	ADAC	Q	A D A C Laboratories
ABC	N	Ambase Corp	ADB	N	Adobe Resources Corp
ABCV	Q	Affiliated Banc Corp	ADB*A	N	Adobe Resources Corp 9.2% Cv Pfd
ABD	A	Abiomed Inc	ADB*B	N	Adobe Resources Corp 12% Pfd
ABF	N	Airborne Freight Corp	ADBE	Q	Adobe Systems Inc
ABG	N	American Ship Building Co	ADCT	Q	A D C Telecommunications Inc
ABGA	Q	Allied Bancshares Inc Georgia	ADD	N	Ames Department Stores Inc
ABI	A	Ambrit Inc	ADDR	Q	Addington Resources Inc
ABIG	Q	American Bankers Insurance Group Inc	ADGE	Q	Adage Inc
ABIO	Q	Applied Biosystems Inc	ADI	N	Analog Devices Inc
ABKR	Q	Anchor Savings Bank F S B	ADIA	Q	A D I A Services Inc
ABL	A	American Biltrite Inc	ADIE	Q	Autodie Corp
ABM	N	American Building Maintenance Industries	ADL	A	Andal Corp
ABP	N	American Business Products Inc	ADM	N	Archer Daniels Midland Co
ABQC	Q	A B Q Corp	ADMG	Q	Advanced Magnetics Inc
ABRI	Q	Abrams Industries Inc	ADMS	Q	Advanced Marketing Services Inc
ABS	N	Albertsons Inc	ADO	A	Audiotronics Corp
ABSB	Q	Alex Brown Inc	ADP	N	Allied Products Corp
ABSI	Q	A B S Industries Inc	ADPT	Q	Adaptec Inc
ABT	N	Abbott Laboratories	ADTLY	Q	A D T Ltd ADR
ABW	N	Armada Corp	ADU	N	Amdura Corp
ABX	N	American Barrick Resources Corp	ADU*D	N	Amdura Corp 9 3 4% Cv Pfd Ser D
ABY	N	Abitibi Price Inc	ADV	N	Advest Group Inc
AC	N	Alliance Capital Management L P	ADVC	Q	Advanced Circuits Inc
ACA	N	American Capital Management & Research	ADVN	Q	Advanta Corp
		Inc	ADVO	Q	A D V O System Inc
ACAD	Q	Autodesk Inc	ADX	N	Adams Express Co
ACB	N	American Capital Bond Fund Inc	AE	A	Adams Resources & Energy Inc
ACC	A	American Capital Corp	AEAGF	Q	Agnico Eagle Mines Ltd
ACC*	A	American Capital Corp Ser A Pfd	AEE	N	Aileen Inc
ACCC	Q	A C Teleconnect Corp	AEGNY	Q	Aegon N V
ACCMA	Q	Associated Communications Corp Cl A	AELNA	Q	A E L Industries Inc Cl A
ACCMB	Q	Associated Communications Corp Cl B	AEN	A	A M C Entertainment Inc
ACCOB	Q	Coors Adolph Brewing Co Cl B	AEP	N	American Electric Power Co Inc
ACD	N	American Capital Income Trust S B I	AEPI	Q	A E P Industrial Inc
ACE	N	Acme Electric Corp	AESM	Q	Aero Systems Inc
ACET	Q	Aceto Corp	AET	N	Aetna Life & Casualty Co
ACG	N	A C M Government Income Fund Inc	AEW*B	N	Appalachian Power Co 8.12% Cum Pfd
ACHV	Q	Archive Corp	AEW*C	N	Appalachian Power Co 7.40% Cum Pfd
ACI	N	Ashland Coal Inc	AEW*D	N	Appalachian Power Co $2.65 Cum Pfd
ACIG	Q	Academy Insurance Group Inc	AEX	A	Air Express Intl Corp
ACK	N	Armstrong World Industries Inc	AEZNS	Q	Asiamerica Equities Ltd S B I
ACLE	Q	Accel Intl Corp	AFBK	Q	Affiliated Bankshares of Colorado Inc
ACLV	Q	Autoclave Engineers Inc	AFCA	A	American Fructose Corp Cl A
ACMB	A	Atlas Consolidated Mining & Development	AFCB	A	American Fructose Corp Cl B
		Corp Cl B	AFED	Q	Atlanfed Bancorp Inc
ACME	Q	Acme Steel Co	AFFFZ	Q	America First Financial Fund 1987 A Ltd
ACMS	Q	C M S Enhancements Inc			Partner
ACMT	Q	Acmat Corp	AFGI	Q	Ambassador Financial Group Inc
ACMTA	Q	Acmat Corp Cl A	AFIL	Q	American Filtrona Corp
ACN	Q	Acuson Corp	AFL	N	American Family Corp
ACOL	Q	American Colloid Co	AFMBZ	Q	America First Federally Grntd Mtge Fund
ACOM	Q	Astrocom Corp			Two
ACP	N	American Real Estate Partners L P	AFN	A	Alfin Inc

AFP	N	Affiliated Publications Inc
AFPFZ	Q	First Part Pfd Eqty Mtg Fund L P Ex Units
AFTXZ	Q	America First Tax Exempt Mtg Fund LP Units
AFWY	Q	Arkansas Freightways Corp
AG	N	Allegheny Intl Inc
AG*B	N	Allegheny Intl Inc $2.19 Cum Pfd
AG*C	N	Allegheny Intl Inc $11.25 Cv Pfd
AGC	N	American General Corp
AGCWS	N	American General Corp Wts
AGE	N	Edwards A G Inc
AGF	N	American Government Income Fund Inc
AGH	A	Atlantis Group Inc Cl A
AGI	A	Alpine Group Inc
AGII	Q	Argonaut Group Inc
AGL	Q	Angelica Corp
AGN	N	Allergan Inc
AGNC	Q	Agency Rent A Car
AGO	A	A B M Gold Corp
AGPH	Q	Agouron Pharmaceuticals Inc
AGREA	Q	American Greetings Corp Cl A
AGT	N	American Government Term Trust Inc
AHA	A	Alpha Industries Inc
AHC	N	Amerada Hess Corp
AHE	N	American Health Properties Inc
AHH	A	Amerihealth Inc
AHI	A	American Healthcare Management Inc
AHL	N	American Heritage Life Investment Corp
AHM	N	Ahmanson H F Co
AHP	N	American Home Products Corp
AHP*	N	American Home Products Corp $2.00 Cv Pfd
AHR	N	Americana Hotels & Realty Corp
AHS	A	A M I Holdings Inc
AHSC	Q	American Home Shield Corp
AHT	A	Aircoa Hotel Partners L P
AHTS	Q	American Health Services Corp
AI	A	Arrow Automotive Industries Inc
AIB*	N	Allied Irish Banks Plc Pfd
AIC	N	Asset Investors Corp
AIF	A	A I F S Inc
AIFC	Q	American Indemnity Financial Corp
AIG	N	American Intl Group Inc
AII	A	Altex Industries Inc
AIIC	Q	American Integrity Corp
AIL	N	A M C A Intl Ltd
AILP	Q	Automated Language Processing Systems Inc
AIMAZ	Q	American Insured Mtge Investors Dep Units
AIMBZ	Q	Integrated Resour Amer Insured Mtg Inv Cal L P
AIMT	Q	Aim Telephone Inc
AIN	N	Albany Intl Corp Cl A
AIND	Q	Arnold Industry Inc
AINVS	Q	Ameribanc Investors Group S B I
AIP	A	American Israeli Paper Mills Ltd
AIR	N	A A R Corp
AIRC	Q	Associated Inns & Restaurants Co of America
AIRSY	Q	Airship Industries Ltd ADR
AISA	Q	Ampal American Israel Corp Cl A
AIT	N	Ameritech
AIX	A	Astrotech Intl
AIX*	A	Astrotech Intl Pfd
AIXWS	A	Astrotech Intl Wts
AIXWW	A	Astrotech Intl Wts W I
AIZ	N	Amcast Industrial Corp

AJG	N	Gallagher Arthur J & Co
AK	A	Ackerley Communications Inc
AKLM	Q	Acclaim Entertainment Inc
AKLMZ	Q	Acclaim Entertainment Inc Ser A Wts 1 30 90
AKRN	Q	Akorn Inc
AKZOY	N	Akso N V ADR
AL	N	Alcan Aluminum Ltd
ALBC	Q	Alameda Bancorp Inc
ALCCC	Q	A L C Communications Corp
ALCI	Q	Allcity Insurance Co
ALCO	Q	Alico Inc
ALD	N	Allied Signal Corp Inc
ALD*F	N	Allied Signal Corp Inc Adj Rate Cum Pfd F
ALDC	Q	Aldus Corp
ALET	Q	Aloette Cosmetics Inc
ALEX	Q	Alexander & Baldwin Inc
ALFA	Q	Alfa Corp
ALFB	Q	Abraham Lincoln F S B
ALFL	Q	Alliance Financial Corp
ALG	N	Arkla Inc
ALG*A	N	Arkla Inc $3.00 Cv Ex Pfd Ser A
ALGH	Q	Allegheny & Western Energy Corp
ALGI	Q	American Locker Group Inc
ALGO	Q	Algorex Corp
ALGR	Q	Allied Group Inc
ALI	N	Allstate Municipal Premium Income Trust
ALK	N	Alaska Air Group Inc
ALL	N	Allstate Municipal Income Trust III
ALLC	Q	Allied Capital Corp
ALLP	Q	Alliance Pharmaceutical Corp
ALLPW	Q	Alliance Pharmaceutical Corp Wts 5 28 90
ALM	N	Allstate Municipal Income Trust
ALMI	Q	Alpha Microsystems Inc
ALN	N	Allen Group Inc
ALN*A	N	Allen Group Inc $1.75 Cv Exch Pfd Ser A
ALNT	Q	Alliant Computer Systems Corp
ALOG	Q	Analogic Corp New
ALOT	Q	Astromed Inc New
ALOY	Q	Alloy Computer Products Inc
ALP*B	N	Alabama Power 8.28% Cum Pfd
ALP*C	N	Alabama Power 8.16% Cum Pfd
ALP*D	N	Alabama Power 9.44% Pfd
ALP*E	N	Alabama Power 11% Cum Pfd
ALP*F	N	Alabama Power 9% Cum Pfd
ALP*G	N	Alabama Power Adj Rate Cl A Pfd
ALP*S	N	Alabama Power Dep Pfd Shares
ALRN	Q	Altron Inc
ALS	N	Allegheny Ludlum Corp
ALT	N	Allstate Municipal Income Trust II
ALTI	Q	Altai Inc
ALTO	Q	Altos Computer Systems
ALTR	Q	Altera Corp
ALTS	Q	Altus Bank F S B
ALU	A	Allou Health & Beauty Care Inc Cl A
ALUWS	A	Allou Health & Beauty Care Inc Cl A Wts
ALW	N	Williams A L Corp
ALWS	Q	Allwaste Inc
ALX	N	Alexanders Inc
AM	N	A M Intl
AM*	N	A M Intl Inc $2.00 Cv Exch Pfd
AMA	N	Advanced Medical Technology Inc
AMA*	N	Advanced Medical Technology Inc 10% Pfd
AMAT	Q	Applied Materials Inc
AMB	N	American Brands Inc
AMB*A	N	American Brands Inc $2.67 Cv Pfd A
AMB*B	N	American Brands Inc $2.75 Pfd B

AMBJ	Q	American City Business Journals Inc	AOF	N	A C M Government Opportunity Fund Inc
AMCO	Q	American Midland Corp	AOG	A	American Oil & Gas
AMD	N	Advanced Micro Devices Inc	AOI	A	A O I Coal Co
AMD*	N	Advanced Micro Devices Inc Dep Cv Ex Pfd	AOP	A	Americus Trust for Amoco Shares Prime
AME	N	Ametek Inc	AORGB	Q	Allen Organ Co Cl B
AMEI	Q	American Medical Electronics Inc	AOS	A	Americus Trust for Amoco Shares Score
AMF	N	A C M Managed Income Fund Inc	AOT	N	Allstate Municipal Income Opp Trust II S B I
AMFI	Q	Amcor Financial Inc	AOU	A	Americus Trust for Amoco Shares Units
AMFLP	Q	American S & L Assn of Florida Ser A Pfd	AP	N	Ampco Pittsburgh Corp
AMGD	Q	American Vanguard Corp	APA	N	Apache Corp
AMGN	Q	Amgen	APB	N	Asia Pacific Fund Inc
AMH	A	Amdahl Corp	APBI	Q	Applied Bioscience Intl Inc
AMI	N	American Medical Intl Inc	APC	N	Anadarko Petroleum Corp
AMIWD	N	American Medical Intl Inc W D	APCC	Q	American Power Conversion Corp
AMJX	Q	American Fed S & L Assn of Duval County	APD	N	Air Products & Chemicals Inc
AMK	A	American Technical Ceramics Corp	APFC	Q	American Pacific Corp
AMKG	Q	Amoskeag Bank Shares Inc	APGI	Q	A P Green Industries Inc
AMLWS	A	A M Intl Inc Wts	APIA	A	American Petrofina Inc Cl A
AMM	N	A M R E Inc	APIO	Q	American Pioneer Inc
AMMG	Q	American Magnetics Corp	APK	N	Apple Bancorp Inc Holding Co
AMN	N	Ameron Inc	APM	N	Applied Magnetics Corp
AMO	N	Allstate Municipal Income Opportunities Trust	APOG	Q	Apogee Enterprises Inc
			APOS	Q	Advanced Polymer Systems Inc
AMOS	Q	Amoskeag Co	APPB	Q	Applebees Intl Inc
AMP	N	A M P Inc	APR	A	American Precision Industries Inc
AMPH	Q	American Physicians Service Group Inc	APS	N	American President Co Ltd
AMPI	Q	Amplicon Inc	APSWD	N	American President Co Ltd W D
AMR	N	A M R Corp	APT	A	Angeles Participating Mortgage Trust
AMRI	Q	Amerifirst F S B	APU	A	N R M Energy Co L P
AMS	A	American Shared Hospital Services	APWRA	Q	Applied Power Inc Cl A
AMSB	Q	American Savings Financial Corp	APX	N	Apex Municipal Fund Inc
AMSR	Q	Amserv Inc	AQM	N	Q M S Inc
AMSWA	Q	American Software Inc Cl A	AQTN	N	Aequitron Medical Inc
AMSY	Q	American Management System	AR	N	A S A R C O Inc
AMT	N	Acme Cleveland Corp	AR*	N	A S A R C O Inc $2.25 Dep Cv Exch Pfd
AMTA	Q	Amistar Corp	ARAI	Q	Allied Research Corp
AMTR	Q	Ameritrust Corp	ARB	N	American Realty Trust Inc
AMTY	Q	Amity Bancorp Inc	ARBC	Q	American Republic Bancorp
AMV	N	A M E V Securities Inc	ARBR	Q	Arbor Drugs Inc
AMW	A	Amwest Insurance Group	ARC	N	Atlantic Richfield Co
AMWD	Q	American Woodmark Corp	ARC*A	N	Atlantic Richfield Co $3.00 Cum Cv Pfd A
AMWI	Q	Air Midwest Inc	ARC*B	N	Atlantic Richfield Co $3.75% Cum Pfd B
AMX	N	Amax Inc	ARC*C	N	Atlantic Richfield Co $2.80 Cum Cv Pfd C
AMX*B	N	Amax Inc Cv Pfd B	ARDNA	Q	Arden Group Inc Cl A
AMZ	N	American List Corp	AREL	Q	Alpharel Inc
AN	N	Amoco Corp	ARG	N	Airgas Inc
ANAT	Q	American National Insurance Co	ARIB	Q	Aspen Ribbon Inc
ANC	N	Anchor Glass Container Corp	ARIG	Q	American Reliance Group Inc
AND	A	Andrea Radio Corp	ARIT	Q	Aritech Corp
ANDB	Q	Andover Savings Bank	ARIX	Q	A R I X Corp
ANDR	Q	Andersen Group Inc	ARMR	Q	Armor All Products Corp
ANDW	Q	Andrew Corp	ARON	Q	Aaron Rents
ANDY	Q	Andros Analyzers Inc	AROS	Q	Advance Ross Corp
ANEN	Q	Anaren Microwave Inc	AROW	Q	Arrow Bank Corp
ANF	A	Angeles Financial Partners	ARP*Q	N	Arizona Public Service Co Adj Cum Pfd Q
ANG	A	Angeles Corp	ARS	N	Aristech Chemical Corp
ANGWS	A	Angeles Corp Wts	ARSD	Q	Arabian Shield Development Co
ANLY	Q	Analysts Intl Corp	ART	A	Armatron Intl Inc
ANM	A	Angeles Mortgage Partners Ltd	ARTW	Q	Arts Way Manufacturing Co Inc
ANP*	N	A N R Pipeline Co $2.675 Cum Pfd	ARV	N	Arvin Industries Inc
ANP*B	N	A N R Pipeline Co $2.12 Cum Pfd	ARV*	N	Arvin Industries Inc $3.75 Cv Exch Pfd
ANPID	Q	Alaska Northwest Properties Inc	ARW	N	Arrow Electronics Inc
ANSL	Q	Action Savings Bank S & L Assn	ARW*	N	Arrow Electronics Inc $19.375 Cv Exch Pfd
ANSY	Q	American Nursery Products Inc	ARWS	Q	Air Wis Services Inc
ANT	N	Anthony Industries Inc	ARX	N	A R X Inc
ANUC	Q	American Nuclear Corp	AS	N	Armco Inc
AOC	N	Aon Corp	AS*	N	Armco Inc $2.10 Cum Cv Pfd

AS*A	N	Armco Inc $4.50 Cum Cv Pfd
ASA	N	A S A Ltd
ASAI	Q	Atlantic Southeast Airlines
ASAL	Q	Atlantic Federal S & L Assn of Ft Lauderdale
ASB	N	American Savings Bank F S B
ASB*A	N	American Savings Bank F S B $1.8125 Cum Cv Ex Pfd A
ASBC	Q	Associated Banc Corp
ASBI	Q	Ameriana Savings Bank F S B
ASC	N	American Stores Co
ASC*A	N	American Stores Co $4.375 Cum Cv Exch Pfd
ASE	A	American Science & Engineering Inc
ASEWS	A	American Science & Engineering Inc Wts
ASFN	Q	Allstate Financial Corp
ASH	N	Ashland Oil Inc
ASI	A	Astrex Inc
ASII	Q	Automated Systems Inc
ASIPY	Q	American Shipholdings Ltd Cl A ADR
ASIX	Q	Assix Intl Inc
ASIXW	Q	Assix Intl Inc Wts 7 18 91
ASKI	Q	Ask Computer Systems Inc
ASMIF	Q	Advanced Semiconductor Materials Intl
ASN	N	Alco Standard Corp
ASNWD	N	Alco Standard Corp W D
ASO	N	Amsouth Bancorp
ASR	A	American Southwest Mortgage Investment Corp
AST	A	Aim Strategic Income Fund Inc
ASTA	Q	A S T Research Inc
ASTE	Q	Astec Industries Inc
ASTR	Q	Astrosystems Inc
AT	N	Alltel Corp
AT*	N	Alltel Corp $2.06 Cum Cv Pfd C
ATA	N	Artra Group Inc
ATAXZ	Q	American First Tax Exempt Mtg Fund 2 L P
ATC	A	Atari Corp
ATCC	Q	Airtran Corp
ATCMA	Q	American Television & Communications Corp A
ATE	N	Atlantic Energy Inc
ATEKF	Q	Amertek Inc
ATEL	Q	Advanced Telecommunications Corp
ATF	A	Equity Income Fund of A T & T U U I
ATFC	Q	Atico Financial Corp
ATG	N	Atlanta Gas & Light Co
ATH	N	Athlone Industries Inc
ATI	A	A T I Medical Inc
ATKM	Q	Atek Metals Center Inc
ATKN	Q	Guy F Atkinson Co of Cal
ATL	N	Atalanta Sosnoff Capital Corp
ATLF	Q	Atlantic Financial Federal
ATLFP	Q	Atlantic Financial Federal Cum Cv Pfd A
ATM	N	Anthem Electronics Inc
ATN	A	Acton Corp
ATN*	A	Acton Corp $3.75 Pfd
ATNG	Q	Alatenn Resources Inc
ATO	N	Atmos Energy Corp
ATOG	N	Andover Togs Inc
ATP	A	Americus Trust for A T & T 2 Prime
ATPC	Q	Athey Products Corp
ATRO	Q	Astronics Corp
ATS	A	Americus Trust for A T & T 2 Score
ATTC	Q	Auto Trol Technology Corp
ATTWY	Q	Attwoods Plc ADR
ATU	A	Americus Trust for A T & T 2 Units
ATV	A	A R C Intl Inc
ATVC	Q	American Travelers Corp
ATW	A	A T & E Corp
ATWD	Q	Atwood Oceanics Inc
ATXA	A	Cross A T Co
AU	N	Amax Gold Inc
AUD	N	Automatic Data Processing Inc
AUG	N	Augat Inc
AUS	N	Ausimont N V
AUTO	Q	Auto Info Inc
AUTR	Q	Autotrol Corp
AVA	N	Audio Video Affiliates Inc
AVAK	Q	Avantek Inc
AVDL	Q	Avondale Industries Inc
AVE	N	A V E M C O Corp
AVFC	Q	Amvestors Financial Corp
AVL	N	Avalon Corp
AVP	N	Avon Products Inc
AVP*	N	Avon Products Inc $2.00 Pfd
AVT	N	Avnet Inc
AVTR	Q	Avatar Holding
AVWS	N	Avco Corp Wts
AVX	N	A V X Corp
AVY	N	Avery Intl Corp
AWAL	Q	America West Airlines
AWK	N	American Water Works
AWK*A	N	American Water Works 5% Cum Pfd A
AWK*B	N	American Water Works 5% Cum Pfd B
AWS	A	Alba Waldensian Inc
AWST	Q	American Western Corp New
AWT	A	Air & Water Technologies Corp Cl A
AX	A	American Exploration Co
AXO	A	Alamco Inc
AXP	N	American Express Co
AXR	N	A M R E P Corp
AXWS	A	American Exploration Co Wts
AXXN	Q	Action Auto Rental Inc
AXXX	Q	Artel Communications Corp
AYD	N	Aydin Corp
AYP	N	Allegheny Power System Inc
AZ	N	Atlas Corp
AZA	N	Alza Corp
AZAU	A	Alza Corp Units
AZB	A	Arizona Commerce Bank
AZEA	A	American Maize Products Co Cl A
AZEB	A	American Maize Products Co Cl B
AZIC	Q	Arizona Instrument Corp
AZL	N	Arizona Land Income Corp
AZTC	Q	Aztec Manufacturing Co
AZWS	A	Atlas Corp Wts
B	N	Barnes Group Inc
BA	N	Boeing Co
BAB	N	British Airways Plc
BAC	N	Bankamerica Corp
BAC*A	N	Bankamerica Corp Cum Adj Pfd A
BAC*B	N	Bankamerica Corp Cum Adj Pfd B
BAC*C	N	Bankamerica Corp Cum Pfd
BAIB	Q	Bailey Corp
BAL	A	Baldwin Securities Corp
BAMI	Q	Basic American Medical Inc
BAN	A	Banister Continental Ltd
BANG	A	Bangor Hydro Electric Co Com
BANQ	Q	Burritt Interfinancial Bancorp
BARC	Q	Barrett Resources Corp
BARD	N	Barden Corp
BARY	Q	Barrys Jewelers Inc
BAS	N	Basix Corp
BASEA	Q	Base Ten Systems Inc Cl A

BAT	N	Blackstone Star Trust Inc
BAW	N	Blue Arrow Plc ADR
BAX	N	Baxter Intl Inc
BAX*A	N	Baxter Intl Inc Adj Rate Pfd
BAX*B	N	Baxter Intl Inc Pfd
BAY	N	Bay Financial Corp
BB	A	Bank Building & Equipment Corp of America
BBB	N	Baltimore Bancorp
BBC	A	Bergen Brunswig Corp Cl A
BBE	A	Belden & Blake Energy Co
BBGS	Q	Babbages Inc
BBI	N	Barnett Banks Inc
BBN	N	Bolt Beranek & Newman Inc
BBNK	Q	Baybanks Inc
BBRC	Q	Burr Brown Corp
BBTF	Q	B B & T Financial Corp
BBV	N	Banco Bilbao Vizcaya S A
BBY	N	Best Buy Co Inc
BC	N	Brunswick Corp
BCB*A	N	Barclays Bank Plc ADS Cum Pfd A
BCB*B	N	Barclays Bank Plc ADS Cum Pfd B
BCC	N	Boise Cascade Corp
BCE	N	Bell Canada Enterprises Inc
BCF	N	Burlington Coat Factory Warehouse Corp
BCKY	Q	Buckeye Financial Corp
BCL	N	Biocraft Laboratories Inc
BCM	N	Banco S A ADS
BCNJ	Q	Bancorp New Jersey
BCO	A	Blessings Corp
BCP	N	Borden Chemicals & Plastics Ltd Units
BCR	N	Bard C R Inc
BCS	N	Barclays Plc ADS
BCU	N	Borden Chemicals & Plastics Ltd
BCV	A	Bancroft Convertible Fund Inc
BDEP	Q	Banco De Ponce Corp
BDF	N	Bond Debenture Trading Fund 1838
BDG	N	Bandag Inc
BDK	N	Black & Decker Corp
BDL	A	Flanigans Enterprises Inc
BDX	N	Becton Dickinson & Co
BE	N	Benguet Corp Cl B
BEBA	Q	Beebas Creations Inc
BEC	N	Beckman Instruments Inc
BEIH	Q	B E I Holdings Ltd
BEII	Q	B E I Electronics Inc
BEL	N	Bell Atlantic Corp
BELF	Q	Bel Fuse Inc
BEM	A	Bergstrom Capital Corp
BEN	N	Franklin Resources Inc
BENH	Q	Bankeast Corp
BENJ	Q	Ben Franklin S & L Assn
BEP	N	Bet Public Ltd Co
BER	N	Bearings Inc
BET	A	Bethlehem Corp
BETZ	Q	Betz Laboratories Inc
BEV	N	Beverly Enterprises
BEZ	N	Baldor Electric Co
BF*	A	Brown Foreman Pfd
BFA	A	Brown Foreman Cl A
BFB	A	Brown Foreman Cl B
BFBS	Q	Brookfield Bancshares Corp
BFC	A	Bank Atlantic Financial Corp
BFCP	Q	Broadway Financial Corp
BFCS	Q	Boston Five Bancorp Inc
BFEN	Q	B F Enterprises Inc
BFI	N	Browning Ferris Industries Inc
BFL	N	Bancflorida Financial Corp

BFO	A	Baruch Foster Corp
BFSI	Q	B F S Bank Corp Inc
BFX	A	Buffton Corp
BG	N	Brown Group Inc
BGAS	Q	Berkshire Gas Co
BGC	N	Bay State Gas Co
BGE	N	Baltimore Gas & Electric
BGE*B	N	Baltimore Gas & Electric 4 1 2% Cum Pfd B
BGEN	Q	Biogen Inc
BGENP	Q	Biogen Inc Cv Ex Pfd
BGENW	Q	Biogen Inc 6 30 94 Wts
BGG	N	Briggs & Stratton Corp
BGO	N	Butes Gas & Oil Co
BGSS	Q	B G S Systems Inc
BH	N	Benequity Holdings Ltd
BHA	A	Biscayne Holding Inc
BHAGA	Q	B H A Group Inc Cl A
BHAGB	Q	B H A Group Inc Cl B
BHC	A	B H C Communications Inc
BHI	N	Baker Hughes Inc
BHI*	N	Baker Hughes Inc $3.50 Cv Exch Pfd
BHK	A	B & H Crude Carriers Ltd
BHL	N	Bunker Hill Income Securities Inc
BHM	A	B & H Maritime Ltd
BHO	A	B & H Ocean Carriers Ltd
BHP	N	Broken Hill Proprietary Co Ltd
BHT	N	Ballys Health & Tennis Corp
BHWD	N	Benequity Holdings Ltd W D
BHY	N	Belding Hemingway Co
BI	N	Bell Industries
BIC	A	B I C Corp
BID	A	Sothebys Holdings Inc Cl A
BIG	N	Bond Intl Gold Inc
BIGB	Q	Big B Inc
BIGO	Q	Big O Tires Inc
BIGWS	N	Bond Intl Gold Inc Wts
BILT	Q	Microbilt Corp
BIM	A	I C N Biomedical
BIN	A	Binks Manufacturing Co
BINC	Q	Biospherics Inc
BIND	N	Bindley Western Industries Inc
BIOA	A	Bio Rad Laboratories Inc Cl A
BIOB	A	Bio Rad Laboratories Inc Cl B
BIOT	Q	Biotechnica Intl Inc
BIOW	Q	Banks of Iowa Inc
BIR	N	Birmingham Steel Corp
BIRD	Q	Bird Inc
BIRT	Q	Birtcher Corp
BIS	A	Barister Information Corp
BJICA	Q	Ben & Jerrys Homemade Inc Cl A
BK	N	Bank of New York Co
BK*	N	Bank of New York Co Adj Rate Non Cum Pfd
BK*A	N	Bank of New York Co Adj Rate Non Cum Pfd
BKB	N	Bank of Boston
BKB*A	N	Bank of Boston Pfd A
BKB*B	N	Bank of Boston Adj Rate Cum Pfd B
BKB*C	N	Bank of Boston Adj Rate Cum Pfd C
BKC	A	American Bank of Connecticut
BKF	N	Baker Fentress & Co
BKH	N	Black Hills Corp
BKLY	Q	Berkley W R Corp
BKNG	Q	Banknorth Group Inc New
BKNT	Q	Bankers Note Inc
BKP	N	Burger King Investors Masters L P Units
BKQ	N	Burger King Investors Masters L P I I
BKR	A	Baker Michael Corp
BKSO	Q	Bank South Corp

BKT	N	Blackstone Income Trust
BKY	N	Berkey Inc
BL	A	Blair Corp
BLAK	Q	Black Industries Inc
BLAU	Q	Barry Blau & Partners Inc
BLC	N	Belo A H Corp
BLCC	Q	Balchem Corp
BLD	A	Baldwin Technology Co
BLI	N	Businessland Inc
BLIS	Q	Bliss & Laughlin Industries Inc
BLL	N	Ball Corp
BLLW	Q	Bell W Co Inc
BLOCA	Q	Block Drug Co Cl A
BLR	A	Bolar Pharmaceutical Co
BLRGZ	Q	Blue Ridge Real Estate Units
BLS	N	Bellsouth Corp
BLSC	Q	Bio Logic Systems Corp
BLTA	A	Blount Inc Cl A
BLTB	A	Blount Inc Cl B
BLU	N	Blue Chip Value Fund
BLUD	Q	Immucor Inc
BLV	A	Belvedere Corp
BLVD	Q	Boulevard Bancorp Inc
BLY	N	Bally Manufacturing Corp
BMAC	Q	B M A Corp
BMC	N	B M C Industries Inc
BMCC	Q	Bando Mc Glocklin Capital Corp
BMCS	Q	B M C Software Inc
BMD	N	A L Laboratories Inc Cl A
BMDS	Q	Bio Medicus Inc
BMED	Q	Ballard Medical Products
BMEEF	Q	Belmoral Mines Ltd
BMET	Q	Biomet Inc
BMG	N	Battle Mountain Gold Co Cl A
BMI	A	Badger Meter Inc
BMJF	Q	B M J Financial Corp
BML	A	Balfour Maclaine Corp
BMRG	Q	B M R Financial Group Inc
BMS	N	Bemis Co
BMT	A	Biomagnetic Technologies Inc
BMTC	Q	Bryn Mawr Bank Corp
BMY	N	Bristol Myers Squibb Co
BMY*	N	Bristol Myers Squibb Co $2.00 Cum Cv Pfd
BN	N	Borden Inc
BNBC	Q	Broad National Bancorp
BNBGA	Q	Bull & Bear Group Inc Cl A
BNC	N	Regional Financial Shares Investment Fund Inc
BNE	A	Bowne & Co Inc
BNG	N	Benetton Group S P A ADR
BNGO	Q	Bingo King Co Inc
BNHB	Q	B N H Bancshares Inc
BNHC	Q	Bank of New Hampshire Corp
BNHI	Q	Bancorp Hawaii Inc
BNHN	Q	Benihana National Corp
BNI	N	Burlington Northern Inc
BNI*	N	Burlington Northern 5 1 2% Cum Pfd
BNK	N	Bangor Punta Corp
BNKF	Q	Bankers First Corp
BNKS	Q	United New Mexico Financial Corp
BNKW	Q	Bank Worcester Corp
BNL	N	Beneficial Corp
BNL*A	N	Beneficial Corp $4.50 Cum Pfd
BNL*B	N	Beneficial Corp $4.30 Cum Pfd
BNL*C	N	Beneficial Corp $5.50 Cum Cv Pfd
BNL*V	N	Beneficial Corp 5% Cum Pfd
BNP	A	Boddie Noell Restaurant Properties Inc

BNR	N	Banner Industries Inc
BNS	N	Brown Sharp Manufacturing Co Cl A
BNTA	Q	Banta Corp
BOAT	Q	Boatmens Bancshares Inc
BOBE	Q	Bob Evans Farms Inc
BOC	A	Beard Oil Co
BOCB	Q	Buffets Inc
BOF	A	Bank of San Francisco Co Cl A
BOF*	A	Bank of San Francisco Co 8% Ser B Cv Pfd
BOGO	Q	Bogert Oil Co
BOHM	Q	Bohemia Inc
BOL	N	Bausch & Lomb Inc
BOM	A	Bowmar Instruments Corp
BOMA	Q	Banks of Mid America Inc
BOMS	Q	Bank of Mississippi Inc
BOOL	Q	Boole & Babbage Inc
BOON	Q	Boonton Electronics Corp
BOS	N	Boston Celtics L P
BOSA	Q	Boston Acoustics Inc
BOST	Q	Boston Digital Corp
BOW	N	Bowater Inc
BP	N	British Petroleum Co Ltd
BPAO	Q	Baldwin Piano & Organ Co
BPCO	Q	Bonneville Pacific Corp
BPH	A	Biopharmaceutics Inc
BPI	A	Bamberger Polymers
BPILF	Q	Basic Petroleum Intl Ltd
BPL	N	Buckeye Partners L P
BPMI	Q	Badger Paper Mills Inc
BPOP	Q	Banco Popular De Puerto Rico
BPP	A	Burnham Pacific
BPT	N	B P Prudhoe Bay Royalty Trust
BPWS	N	British Petroleum Co Ltd Plc Wts
BQC	N	Quantel Corp
BQR	N	Quick & Reilly Group Inc
BR	N	Burlington Resources Inc
BRAE	N	B R A E Corp
BRAN	Q	Brand Cos Inc
BRC	N	Baroid Corp
BRCOA	Q	W H Brady Co Cl A
BRD	N	Brad Ragan Inc
BRDL	Q	Brendles Inc
BRDN	Q	Brandon Systems Corp
BRE	N	Bankamerica Realty Investors S B I
BREN	Q	Brenco Inc
BRG	N	British Gas Public Ltd Co ADS
BRID	Q	Bridgfords Foods Corp
BRJS	Q	Brajdas Corp
BRK	N	Berkshire Hathaway & Co
BRL	A	Barr Laboratories Inc
BRLN	Q	Brooklyn Savings Bank
BRN	N	Barnwell Industries Inc
BRNO	Q	Brunos Inc
BRO	N	Broad Inc
BRSA	A	Brascan Ltd Cl A
BRT	N	B R T Realty Trust
BRX	A	Bio Therapeutics Inc
BRY	N	Berry Petroleum Co Cl A
BS	N	Bethlehem Steel Corp
BS*	N	Bethlehem Steel Corp $5.00 Cum Cv Pfd
BS*B	N	Bethlehem Steel Corp $2.50 Cum Cv Pfd
BSBC	Q	Branford Savings Bank
BSBN	Q	B S B Bancorp
BSBX	Q	Bell Savings Holdings Inc
BSC	N	Bear Sterns Co
BSC*A	N	Bear Sterns Co Inc Adj Cum Pfd Ser A
BSCWD	N	Bear Sterns Co W D

BSD	A	B S D Bancorp Inc
BSE	N	Boston Edison Co
BSE*	N	Boston Edison Co 8.88% Cum Pfd
BSE*C	N	Boston Edison Co $1.46 Cum Pfd
BSET	Q	Bassett Furniture Industries Inc
BSH	A	Bush Industries Inc
BSIM	Q	Burnup & Sims Inc
BSN	A	B S N Corp
BST	N	British Steel Plc
BSY	N	Bear Stearns Options
BT	N	Bankers Trust New York Corp
BTEC	Q	Banctec Inc
BTEK	Q	Baltek Corp
BTFC	Q	B T Financial Corp
BTHL	Q	Bethel Bancorp
BTI	A	B A T Industries Ord Shares
BTLR	Q	Butler Manufacturing Co Com
BTR	A	Bradley Real Estate Trust
BTRI	Q	B T R Realty Inc
BTRL	Q	Biotech Research Labs Inc
BTSB	Q	Braintree Savings Bank
BTT	N	Blackstone Target Term Trust Inc
BTUI	Q	B T U Intl Inc
BTX	N	Banctexas Group Inc
BTY	N	British Telecommunications Plc ADR
BU	N	Brooklyn Union Gas Co
BU*	N	Brooklyn Union Gas Co $2.47 Pfd I
BUD	N	Anheuser Busch Co Inc
BUDWD	N	Anheuser Busch Co Inc W D
BUE	A	Buell Industries Inc
BULKF	Q	B & H Bulk Carriers Ltd
BULL	Q	Bull Run Gold Mines Ltd
BUTI	Q	Beautycontrol Cosmetics Inc
BV	N	Blockbuster Entertainment Corp
BVFS	Q	Bay View Capital Corp
BVI	A	Bow Valley Industries Ltd
BVSI	Q	Brite Voice Systems Inc
BW	N	Brush Wellman Inc
BWINA	Q	Baldwin & Lyons Inc Cl A
BWINB	Q	Baldwin & Lyons Inc Cl B
BWLA	A	Bowl America Inc Cl A
BWRLF	Q	Breakwater Resources Inc Capital Stock
BYP	A	Americus Trust for Bristol Myers Prime
BYS	A	Americus Trust for Bristol Myers Score
BYTE	Q	Compucom Systems Inc
BYTX	Q	Bytex Corp
BYU	A	Americus Trust for Bristol Myers Units
BYX	A	Bayou Steel Corp
BZ	N	Bairnco Corp
BZF	N	Brazil Fund Inc
BZMT	Q	Bizmart Inc
BZP	A	Americus Trust for I B M Shares Prime
BZR	N	Beazer Plc ADS
BZS	A	Americus Trust for I B M Shares Score
BZU	A	Americus Trust for I B M Shares Units
C	N	Chrysler Corp
CA	N	Computer Associates Intl Inc
CABL	Q	Communication Cable Inc
CACCB	Q	Colonial Life & Accident Ins Cl B
CACH	Q	Cache Inc
CACIA	Q	C A C I Inc Cl A
CACOA	Q	Cato Corp Cl A
CADBY	Q	Cadbury Schweppes Plc ADR
CADE	Q	Cade Industries Inc
CAF	N	Furrs Bishop Cafeterias L P
CAFS	Q	Cardinal Financial Group Inc
CAG	N	Conagra Inc

CAII	Q	Capital Associates Inc
CAL	N	Calfed Inc
CALI	Q	Calumet Industries Inc
CAMBY	Q	Cambridge Instrument Co Plc ADR
CAMD	Q	California Micro Devices Corp
CAME	Q	Carme Inc
CAMP	Q	California Amplifier Inc
CANLZ	Q	Canal Randolph L P Units
CANNY	Q	Canon Inc ADR
CANO	Q	Canonie Enviromental Services Corp
CANX	Q	Cannon Express Inc
CAO	N	Carolina Freight Corp
CAP	A	Capital Housing & Mortgage Partners
CAPB	Q	Capitol Bancorp
CAR	N	Carter Wallace Inc
CARL	Q	Carl Karcher Enterprises Inc
CARN	Q	Carrington Laboratories Inc
CAS	A	Castle A M & Co
CASC	Q	Cascade Corp
CASY	Q	Caseys General Stores Inc
CAT	N	Caterpillar Tractor Co
CATA	Q	Capitol Transamerica Corp
CATLB	Q	Cantel Industries Inc Cl B
CAUT	Q	Computer Automation Inc
CAVN	Q	C V N Cos Inc
CAVR	Q	Carver Corp
CAW	N	Caesars World Inc
CAYB	Q	Cayuga Savings Bank
CB	N	Chubb Corp
CBAM	Q	Cambrex Corp
CBCF	Q	Citizens Banking Corp
CBCT	Q	Cenvest Inc
CBCX	Q	Cambridge Bioscience Corp
CBE	N	Cooper Industries Inc
CBH	N	C B I Industries Inc
CBI	A	Curtice Burns Inc Cl A
CBIO	Q	California Biotechnology Inc
CBK	N	Continental Bank Corp
CBK*	N	Continental Bank Corp Adj Rate Pfd
CBK*A	N	Continental Bank Corp Adj Rate Cum Pfd Ser 2
CBKI	Q	Community Banks Inc
CBKS	Q	Commonwealth Bancshares Corp
CBL	N	Corroon & Black Corp
CBNB	Q	Commerce Bancorp
CBNE	Q	Constitution Bancorp of New England Inc
CBNH	Q	Community Bancshares Inc
CBOCA	Q	Commercial Bancorp of Colorado
CBOT	Q	Cabot Medical Corp
CBPA	Q	Community Bancorp Inc
CBR	N	Crystal Brands Inc
CBRL	Q	Cracker Barrel Old Country Stores Inc
CBRYA	Q	Northland Cranberries Inc Cl A
CBS	N	C B S Inc
CBS*	N	C B S Inc $1.00 Cum Cv Pfd
CBSH	Q	Commerce Bancshares Inc
CBSI	Q	Community Bank Systems Inc
CBSS	Q	Central Bancshares of the South Inc
CBT	N	Cabot Corp
CBTF	Q	C B T Financial Corp
CBU	Q	Commodore Intl Ltd
CBWA	Q	Central Bancorp
CC	N	Circuit City Stores Inc
CCAM	Q	C C A Industries Inc
CCAR	Q	C C Air Inc
CCAX	Q	Corrections Corp of America
CCB	N	Capital Cities A B C Inc

CCBF	Q	C C B Financial Corp
CCBL	Q	C C O R Electronics
CCBT	Q	Cape Cod Bank & Trust Co
CCCI	Q	Three C I Inc
CCE	N	Coca Cola Enterprises Inc
CCEM	Q	Compuchem Corp
CCH	N	Campbell Resources Inc
CCI	N	Citicorp
CCI*	N	Citicorp Adj Rate Ser 2 Pfd
CCI*A	N	Citicorp Adj Rate Ser 3 Pfd
CCI*B	N	Citicorp Adj Rate Ser 4 Pfd
CCK	N	Crown Cork & Seal Co Inc
CCL	A	Carnival Cruise Lines Inc Cl A
CCLPZ	Q	Callon Consolidated Partners L P Units
CCLR	Q	Commerce Clearing House Inc
CCN	N	Chris Craft Industries Inc
CCN*A	N	Chris Craft Industries Inc $1.00 Pfd
CCN*B	N	Chris Craft Industries Inc $1.40 Cv Pfd
CCNC	Q	C C N B Corp
CCOA	Q	Comcoa Inc
CCON	Q	Circon Corp
CCP	A	Corcap Inc
CCPT	Q	Concept Inc
CCR	N	Countrywide Credit Industries Inc
CCRS	Q	Corporate Capital Resources Inc
CCTC	Q	Computer & Communications Technology Corp
CCTVY	Q	Carlton Communications Plc ADR
CCU	A	Clear Channel Inc
CCUR	Q	Concurrent Computer Corp
CCX	N	C C X Inc
CCX*	N	C C X Inc 5% Cum Pfd
CCXLA	Q	Contel Cellular Inc Cl A
CDA	N	Control Data Corp
CDA*	N	Control Data Corp 4 1 2% Cum Pfd
CDC	A	Compudyne Corp
CDCC	Q	Chemdesign Corp
CDCRA	Q	Childrens Discovery Centers of America Inc Cl A
CDE	A	Coeur D'alene Mines Corp
CDGA	A	Canandaigua Wine Co Inc Cl A
CDGB	A	Canandaigua Wine Co Inc Cl B
CDGI	Q	Courier Dispatch Group
CDI	N	C D I Corp
CDIC	Q	Cardinal Distribution Inc
CDL	A	Citadel Holding Corp
CDMS	Q	Cadmus Communications Corp
CDNC	Q	Cadence Design Systems Inc
CDO	N	Comdisco Inc
CDVA	A	Chambers Development Co Inc Cl A
CDVB	A	Chambers Development Co Inc Cl B
CE	A	California Energy Co
CEA	N	Cessna Aircraft Co
CEBK	Q	Central Cooperative Bank
CECX	Q	Castle Energy Corp
CEE	N	C Three Inc
CEF	A	Central Fund of Canada Cl A
CEFT	Q	Concord Computing Corp
CELG	Q	Celegne Corp
CELL	Q	Cell Technology Inc
CELLW	Q	Cell Technology Inc Wts
CEMX	Q	C E M Corp
CENT	Q	Centuri Inc
CEP	A	Convest Energy Partners Ltd
CEQ	A	Centennial Group
CER	N	Cilcorp Inc Holding Co
CER*	N	Central Illinois Light Co 4 1 2% Cum Pfd
CER*B	N	Central Illinois Light Co $2.625 Cum Pfd A
CERB	Q	Cerbco Inc
CERN	Q	Cerner Corp
CES	N	Commonwealth Energy Systems S B I
CET	A	Central Securities Corp
CET*D	A	Central Securities Corp $1.25 Pfd D
CETH	Q	Catalyst Thermal Energy Corp
CEUMF	Q	Centurion Gold Ltd
CF	N	Collins Foods Intl Inc
CFA	N	Computer Factory Inc
CFB	A	Citizens First Bancorp Inc
CFB*A	A	Citizens First Bancorp Inc Cum Cv Pfd A
CFBI	Q	Cullen Frost Bankers Inc
CFBS	Q	Central Fidelity Banks Inc
CFCN	Q	Commercial Federal Corp
CFED	Q	Charter Federal Savings Bank
CFER	Q	Confertech Intl Inc
CFFS	Q	Columbia First Federal S & L Assn
CFHC	Q	California Financial Holding Co
CFI	N	Calfed Income Partners L P
CFIB	Q	Consolidated Fibres Inc
CFIN	Q	Consumers Financial Corp
CFINP	Q	Consumers Financial Corp Pfd
CFIP	Q	C F & I Steel Corp
CFIX	Q	Chemfix Technologies Inc
CFIXW	Q	Chemfix Technologies Inc Wts 12 15 89
CFK	A	Comfed Bancorp Inc
CFNE	Q	Circle Fine Art Corp
CFNH	Q	Cheshire Financial Corp
CFQ	A	Quaker Fabric Corp
CFSC	Q	C F S Financial Corp
CFSF	Q	Coast Federal S & L Assn
CG	N	Columbia Gas System Inc
CG*D	N	Columbia Gas System Inc Adj Cum Pfd D
CGAS	Q	Clinton Gas Systems Inc
CGC	N	Cascade Natural Gas Corp
CGE	N	Carriage Industries Inc
CGEN	Q	Collagen Corp
CGES	Q	Colonial Gas Co
CGIC	Q	Continental General Corp
CGLA	A	Cagles Inc Cl A
CGN	N	Cognitronics Corp
CGNE	Q	Calgene Inc
CGNEP	Q	Calgene Inc Cv Exch Pfd
CGNX	Q	Cognex Corp
CGP	N	Coastal Corp
CGP*A	N	Coastal Corp $1.19 Cum Cv Pfd A
CGP*B	N	Coastal Corp $1.83 Cum Cv Pfd B
CGPS	Q	Stamford Capital Group Inc
CGR	A	Chariot Group Inc
CGT	N	Colonial Government Income Trust
CH	N	Chile Fund
CHA	N	Champion Intl Corp
CHANF	Q	Chandler Insurance Co Ltd
CHB	A	Champion Enterprises Inc
CHCO	Q	City Holding Co
CHCR	Q	Chancellor Corp
CHD	N	Chelsa Industries Inc
CHE	N	Chemed Corp
CHEK	Q	Checkpoint System Inc
CHEM	Q	Chempower Inc
CHER	Q	Cherry Corp
CHEY	Q	Cheyenne Software Inc
CHF	N	Chock Full O' Nuts Corp
CHFC	Q	Chemical Financial Corp
CHFD	Q	Charter Federal Savings Bank (Virginia)
CHG	N	Chicago Milwaukee Corp

CHG*	N	Chicago Milwaukee Corp $5.00 Prior Pfd
CHH	N	Carter Hawley Hale Stores Inc
CHHC	Q	C H Heist Corp
CHIK	Q	Golden Poultry Co Inc
CHIR	Q	Chiron Corp
CHL	N	Chemical Banking Corp
CHL*A	N	Chemical Banking Corp Adj Cv Pfd A
CHL*B	N	Chemical Banking Corp Adj Cum Pfd B
CHL*C	N	Chemical Banking Corp Adj Cum Pfd C
CHL*D	N	Chemical Banking Corp Dep Cum Pfd
CHLB	N	Chemical Banking Corp Cl B
CHLN	Q	Chalone Inc
CHMX	Q	Chemex Pharmaceuticals Inc
CHMXL	Q	Chemex Pharmaceuticals Inc 89 1 Wts 3 31 94
CHN	A	Chilton Corp
CHOL	Q	Central Holding Co
CHP	A	Charter Power Systems Inc
CHPK	Q	Chesapeake Utilities Corp
CHPN	Q	Chapman Energy Inc
CHPS	Q	Chips & Technologies Inc
CHR	N	Charter Co
CHR*	N	Charter Co Cv Dep Pfd Shares
CHRS	Q	Charming Shoppes Inc
CHRZ	Q	Computer Horizons
CHS	N	Bernard Chaus Inc
CHT	N	Chart House Enterprises Inc
CHTB	Q	Cohasset Savings Bank
CHTT	N	Chattem Inc
CHV	N	Chevron Corp
CHW	N	Chemical Waste Management Inc
CHX	N	Pilgrims Pride Corp
CHY	N	Chyron Corp
CI	N	Cigna Corp
CIBA	Q	Citizens Bank
CIBC	Q	Citizens Bancorp
CIC	N	Continental Corp
CID	A	Chieftain Intl Inc
CIDN	Q	Computer Identics Corp
CIF	N	Colonial Intermediate High Income Fund
CIFR	Q	Cipher Data Products Inc
CIH	N	Continental Illinois Holding Corp
CII	N	C R I Insured Mortgage Investments II Inc
CIM	A	C I M High Yield Securities
CIMC	Q	Cimco Inc
CIN	N	Cincinnati Gas & Electric Co
CIN*A	N	Cincinnati Gas & Electric Co 4% Cum Pfd
CIN*B	N	Cincinnati Gas & Electric Co 4 3 4% Cum Pfd
CIN*C	N	Cincinnati Gas & Electric Co 9.30% Cum Pfd
CIN*D	N	Cincinnati Gas & Electric Co 7.44% Cum Pfd
CIN*E	N	Cincinnati Gas & Electric Co 9.28% Cum Pfd
CIN*F	N	Cincinnati Gas & Electric Co 9.52% Cum Pfd
CIN*G	N	Cincinnati Gas & Electric Co 10.20% Cum Pfd
CINF	Q	Cincinnati Financial Corp
CINNA	Q	Citizens Insurance Co of America Cl A
CINS	Q	Circle Income Shares
CIP	N	Central Illinois Public Service Co
CIR	N	Circus Circus Enterprises Inc
CIS	A	Concord Fabrics Inc
CISA	Q	Citizens Savings Bank F S B N Y
CISB	A	Concord Fabrics Inc Cl B

CISI	Q	C I S Technologies Inc
CITGS	Q	Citizens Growth Properties S B I
CITUA	Q	Citizens Utilities A
CITUB	Q	Citizens Utilities B
CITY	Q	First City Bancorp Inc
CIV	A	Columbia Real Estate Investment Inc
CIW	N	Cameron Iron Works Inc Holding Co
CIX	A	Cardinal Investment Properties
CIZCF	Q	City Resources Canada Ltd
CJ	A	California Jockey Co
CJER	Q	Central Jersey Bancorp
CJN	A	Caesars New Jersey Inc
CJSB	Q	Central Jersey Savings Bank S & L Assn
CKCP	Q	Cybertek Corp
CKDN	Q	Circadian Inc
CKE	N	Castle Cooke Inc
CKL	N	Clark Equipment Co
CKN*	N	Crocker National Corp $3.00 Cum Cv Pfd
CKP	N	Circle K Corp
CKSB	Q	C K Federal Savings Bank
CKT	A	Continental Circuits Corp
CL	N	Colgate Palmolive Co
CL*	N	Colgate Palmolive Co $4.25 Pfd
CLBGA	Q	Colonial Bancgroup Cl A
CLCM	Q	Cellcom Corp
CLD	N	Computerland Corp
CLDA	Q	Clinical Data Inc
CLDR	Q	Cliffs Drilling Co
CLDRP	Q	Cliffs Drilling Co Cv Exch Pfd
CLE	N	Claires Stores Inc
CLEA	Q	Chemical Leaman Corp
CLF	N	Cleveland Cliffs Inc
CLFI	Q	Country Lake Foods Inc
CLG	N	Clabir Corp
CLG*	A	Clabir Corp $3.3125 Cum Pfd
CLGWS	A	Clabir Corp Wts
CLHB	Q	Clean Harbors Inc
CLICC	Q	Clairson Intl Corp
CLIX	Q	Compression Lab Inc
CLM	N	Clemente Global Growth Fund Inc
CLO	N	Coleco Industries Inc
CLR	A	Color System Technology Inc
CLRI	Q	Computer Language Research Inc
CLRK	Q	Clarcor Inc
CLRX	Q	Colorocs Corp
CLSC	Q	Clinical Sciences Inc
CLT	A	Cominco Ltd
CLX	N	Clorox Co
CM	N	Coles Myer Ltd ADR
CMA	N	Commonwealth Mortgage Co of America L P
CMAFC	Q	Campau Corp
CMB	N	Chase Manhattan Corp
CMB*B	N	Chase Manhattan Corp 6 3 4% Pfd B
CMB*C	N	Chase Manhattan Corp 7.60% Pfd C
CMB*D	N	Chase Manhattan Corp 10 1 2% Pfd D
CMB*E	N	Chase Manhattan Corp Floating Rate Pfd E
CMB*F	N	Chase Manhattan Corp Floating Rate Pfd F
CMB*G	N	Chase Manhattan Corp 10 1 2 Ser G Pfd
CMB*H	N	Chase Manhattan Corp 9.76% Cum Pfd H
CMBK	Q	Cumberland Federal Bancorporation Inc
CMC	N	Commercial Metals Co
CMCA	Q	Comerica Inc
CMCAP	Q	Comerica Inc $4.32 Ser B Pfd
CMCSA	Q	Comcast Corp Cl A
CMCSK	Q	Comcast Corp Spl Cl A
CMDL	Q	Comdial Corp

CMDT	Q	Comdata Holdings Corp
CMETS	Q	Continental Mortgage & Equity Trust S B I
CMFB	Q	Chemical Fabrics Corp
CMH	N	Clayton Homes Inc
CMI	N	Club Med Inc
CMIC	Q	California Microwave Inc
CMIKA	Q	Carmike Cinemas Inc Cl A
CMIN	Q	Computer Memories Inc
CMK	N	Colonial Intermarket Income Trust
CML	N	C M L Group Inc
CMLE	Q	Casual Male Corp
CMN	N	Callahan Mining Corp
CMP	N	Comprehensive Care Corp
CMPX	Q	Comptronix Corp
CMR	A	Commtron Corp Cl A
CMRE	Q	Comstock Resources Inc
CMRO	Q	Comarco
CMS	N	C M S Energy Corp Holding Co
CMS*A	N	Consumers Power Co $4.16 Cum Pfd A
CMS*B	N	Consumers Power Co $4.50 Cum Pfd B
CMS*C	N	Consumers Power Co $4.52 Cum Pfd C
CMS*D	N	Consumers Power Co $7.45 Cum Pfd D
CMS*E	N	Consumers Power Co $7.72 Cum Pfd E
CMS*G	N	Consumers Power Co $7.76 Cum Pfd G
CMS*H	N	Consumers Power Co $7.68 Cum Pfd H
CMS*N	N	Consumers Power Co $3.85 Cum Pfd
CMS*P	N	Consumers Power Co $3.98 Cum Pfd
CMS*U	N	Consumers Power Co $3.60 Cum Pfd
CMS*V	N	Consumers Power Co $4.50 Cum Pfd B
CMS*W	N	Consumers Power Co $7.45 Cum Pfd D
CMS*X	N	Consumers Power Co $7.72 Cum Pfd E
CMS*Y	N	Consumers Power Co $7.76 Cum Pfd G
CMS*Z	N	Consumers Power Co $7.68 Cum Pfd H
CMTK	Q	Cimflex Teknowledge Corp
CMU	N	Colonial Municipal Income Trust
CMW	A	Canadian Marconi Co
CMX	A	C M I Corp
CMY	N	Community Psychiatric Centers
CMZ	N	Cincinnati Milacron Inc
CN	N	Calton Inc
CNA	N	C N A Financial Corp
CNBA	Q	County Bank F S B
CNBE	Q	C N B Bancshares Inc
CNBKA	Q	Century Bancorp Inc Cl A
CNBT	Q	Community National Bancorp Inc
CNC	N	Conseco Inc
CNC*	N	Conseco Inc Ser A Cv Exch Pfd
CNCD	Q	Concorde Career Colleges Inc
CNCL	Q	Commercial National Corp
CNCR	Q	Cencor Inc New
CNDN	Q	Chittenden Corp
CNE	N	Connecticut Energy Corp
CNET	Q	Comnet Corp
CNF	N	Consolidated Freightways Inc
CNG	N	Consolidated Natural Gas Co
CNG*A	N	Consolidated Natural Gas Co 10.96% Pfd A
CNH	N	Central Hudson Gas & Electric Corp
CNH*	N	Central Hudson Gas & Electric Corp Dep Pfd
CNK	N	Crompton Knowles Corp
CNL	N	Central Louisiana Electric Co Inc
CNL*	N	Central Louisiana Electric Co Inc $4.18 Pfd
CNLF	Q	C N L Financial Corp
CNMD	Q	Conmed Corp
CNMW	Q	Cincinnati Microwave Inc
CNN	N	C N A Income Shares Inc
CNNR	Q	Conner Peripherals Inc
CNO	A	Casten Oil Inc
CNO*	A	Casten Oil Inc $1.80 Cv Pfd
CNPA	A	Crown Central Petroleum Corp Cl A
CNPB	A	Crown Central Petroleum Corp Cl B
CNPGF	Q	Cornucopia Resources Ltd
CNS	N	Consolidated Stores Corp
CNSB	Q	Centennial Savings Bank F S B
CNSL	Q	Consul Restaurant Corp
CNSP	Q	Central Sprinkler Corp
CNT	N	Centel Corp
CNTO	Q	Centocor Inc
CNTX	Q	Centex Telemanagement Inc
CNU	A	Continuum Co
CNV	N	Convertible Holdings Inc Capital Shares
CNV*	N	Convertible Holdings Inc Income Shares
CNVLZ	Q	City Investing Liquidating Trust U B I
CNVX	Q	Convex Computers Corp
CNW	N	C N W Holdings Co
CNW*	N	C N W Holdings Co $2.125 Cv Exch Pfd
CNY	N	Continental Information Systems
COA	N	Coachmen Industries Inc
COB	A	Columbia Laboratories Inc
COBA	N	Commerce Bancorp Inc NJ
COBAP	Q	Commerce Bancorp Inc Cum Cv Pfd B
COBB	Q	Cobb Resources Corp
COBE	Q	Cobe Laboratories Inc
COBK	Q	Co Operative Bank of Concord
COC*B	N	Columbus Southern Power Co $2.42 Cum Pfd B
COC*C	N	Columbus Southern Power Co $15.25 Cum Pfd
COC*D	N	Columbus Southern Power Co $3.45 Cum Pfd
COC*S	N	Columbus Southern Power Co $15.25 Cum Pfd S D
COCA	Q	Coca Mines Inc
COCAW	Q	Coca Mines Inc Wts 5 5 94
CODL	Q	Code Alarm Inc
CODN	Q	Codenoll Technology Corp
CODNW	Q	Codenoll Technology Corp Wts 9 10 90
CODS	Q	Corporate Data Sciences Inc
COES	Q	Commodore Environmental Services Inc
COFD	Q	Collective Bancorp Inc
COFI	Q	Charter One Financial Inc
COGNF	Q	Cognos Inc
COGRA	Q	Colonial Group Inc Cl A
COH	A	Cohu Inc
COHR	Q	Coherent Inc
COILP	Q	Crystal Oil Co Ser A Cv Vtg Pfd
COKE	Q	Coca Cola Bottling Co Consolidated
COKR	Q	Cooker Restaurant Corp
COLC	Q	Colorado National Bankshares Inc
COM	A	Crowley Milner Co
COMM	Q	Cellular Communications Inc
COMR	Q	Comair Holdings Inc
COMS	Q	Three Com Corp
CON	A	Connelly Containers Inc
COND	N	Condor Services Inc
CONH	Q	Continental Homes Holding Corp
CONT	Q	Continental Medical Systems Inc
CONW	N	Consumers Water Co
COO	N	Cooper Cos Inc
COOL	Q	Cooper Development Co
COP	A	Copley Property Inc
COPI	Q	Consolidated Products Inc
COPY	Q	Copytele Inc
COR	A	Crystal Oil Co
CORC	Q	Corcom Inc

CORD	Q	Cordis Corp
COS	N	Copperweld Corp
COSF	Q	Cosmetic & Fragrance Concept Inc
COST	Q	Costco Wholesale Corp
COTG	Q	Cottage Savings Assn
COU	A	Courtaulds Ltd ADR Ord Reg
COUS	Q	Cousins Properties Inc
COVT	Q	Covington Technologies Inc
COW	N	Canal Capital Corp
COW*	N	Canal Capital Corp $1.30 Exch Pfd
CP	N	Canadian Pacific Ltd
CPAK	Q	Cpac Inc
CPB	N	Campbell Soup Co
CPBI	Q	C P B Inc
CPC	N	C P C Intl Inc
CPCI	Q	Ciprico Inc
CPE	A	Colorado Prime Corp
CPER	Q	Consolidated Papers Inc
CPF	N	Comstock Partners Strategy Fund Inc
CPH	N	Capital Holding Corp
CPH*F	N	Capital Holding Corp Adj Rate Cum Pfd
CPL	N	Carolina Power & Light
CPL*	A	Carolina Power & Light $5.00 Cum Pfd
CPLS	Q	Care Plus Inc
CPLSZ	Q	Care Plus Inc Cl A Wts
CPP	A	Calprop Corp
CPQ	N	Compaq Computer Corp
CPRD	Q	Computer Products Inc
CPSA	N	Central Pennsylvania Financial Corp
CPSL	Q	C S C Industries Inc
CPST	Q	C P C Rexcel Inc
CPT	A	Compumat Inc
CPTC	Q	C P T Corp
CPTD	Q	Computer Data Systems Inc
CPX	N	Cineplex Odeon Corp
CPY	N	C P I Corp
CQ	N	Communications Satellite Corp
CQX	A	Conquest Exploration Co
CR	N	Crane Co
CRA	N	Craig Corp
CRAB	Q	Captain Crab Inc
CRAN	Q	Crown Anderson Inc
CRAW	Q	Crawford & Company
CRBI	Q	Cal Rep Bancorp Inc
CRBN	N	Calgon Carbon Corp
CRC	N	Carolco Pictures Inc
CRCC	Q	Craftmatic Contour Industries
CRCH	Q	Church & Dwight Co Inc
CRCWS	N	Carolco Pictures Inc Wts
CRDN	Q	Ceradyne Inc
CREB	Q	Champion Parts Inc
CRES	N	Crestmont Federal S & L Assn
CRFC	Q	Crestar Financial Corp
CRHCY	Q	C R H Plc ADR
CRI	N	Core Industries Inc
CRIC	N	Collaborative Research Inc
CRIX	Q	Control Resource Industries Inc
CRL	N	Crossland Savings F S B
CRL*A	N	Crossland Savings F S B $1.8125 Cum Pfd A
CRL*B	N	Crossland Savings F S B $12.75 Cum Pfd B
CRLC	Q	Central Reserve Life Corp
CRM	N	C R I Insured Mtge Inv L P
CRNR	Q	Chronar Corp
CRNS	Q	Cronus Industries Inc
CRO	N	Chromalloy American Corp
CROP	Q	Crop Genetics Intl N V
CRR	N	Consolidated Rail Corp
CRRC	Q	Courier Corp
CRRS	Q	Crown Resources Corp
CRS	N	Carpenter Technology Corp
CRUS	Q	Cirrus Logic Inc
CRV	A	Coast R V Inc
CRW	A	Crown Crafts Inc
CRWN	Q	Crown Books Corp
CRX	N	C R S Sirrine Inc
CS	N	Cabletron Systems Inc
CSA	N	Coast Savings Financial Inc
CSAR	Q	Calstar Inc
CSAV	Q	Continental Savings of America
CSBC	Q	Central & Southern Holding Co
CSC	N	Computer Sciences Corp
CSESF	Q	Connaught Biosciences Inc
CSFCB	Q	Citizens Savings Financial Corp Cl B
CSFN	Q	Corestates Financial Corp
CSII	Q	Communications Systems Inc
CSIM	Q	Consilium Inc
CSK	N	Chesapeake Corp
CSL	N	Carlisle Co Inc
CSLH	Q	Cotton States Life & Health Insurance
CSM	N	Chaparral Steel Co
CSMO	Q	Cosmo Communications Corp
CSN	N	Cincinnati Bell Inc
CSOF	Q	Corporate Software Inc
CSOL	Q	Convergent Solutions Inc
CSP	N	Combustion Engineering Inc
CSPI	Q	C S P Inc
CSR	N	Central South West Corp
CSRE	Q	Comshare Inc
CSS	A	C S S Industries Co
CST	N	Christiana Cos Inc
CSTB	Q	California State Bank
CSTL	Q	Constellation Bancorp
CSTN	Q	Cornerstone Financial Corp
CSTP	Q	Congress Street Properties Inc
CSTR	Q	Costar Corp
CSV	N	Columbia S & L Assn
CSV*A	N	Columbia S & L Assn Cum Cv Pfd A
CSWC	Q	Capital Southwest Corp
CSX	N	C S X Corp
CSX*A	N	C S X Corp $7.00 Cum Cv Pfd A
CSXWD	N	C S X Corp W D
CSY	N	Central Soya Co Inc
CSYS	Q	Central Banking System Inc
CT	N	California Real Estate Investment Trust S B I
CTA	A	Central Pacific Corp
CTAS	Q	Cintas Corp
CTB	N	Cooper Tire & Rubber Co
CTBX	Q	Centerbank
CTC	N	Contel Corp
CTCO	Q	Cross & Trecker Corp
CTCQ	Q	Check Technology Corp
CTEK	Q	Commercial Intertech Corp
CTEX	Q	C T E C Corp
CTF	N	Counsellors Tandem Securities Fund Inc
CTF*	N	Counsellors Tandem Securities Fund Inc Pfd
CTG	N	Connecticut Natural Gas Corp
CTH	N	C R I Insured Mtge Inv I I I Ltd
CTHL	Q	Continental Health Affiliates
CTIA	Q	Communications Transmission Inc
CTK	A	Comptek Research Inc
CTL	N	Century Telephone Enterprises Inc
CTLC	Q	Consolidated Tomoka Land Co
CTM	A	Com Systems Inc

CTME	Q	Clothes Time Inc
CTO	A	Commerce Total Return Fund Inc
CTP	N	Central Maine Power
CTP*	A	Central Maine Power 3.50% Pfd
CTR	N	Constar Intl Inc
CTRIS	Q	Clevetrust Realty Investors S B I
CTS	N	C T S Corp
CTUS	Q	Cetus
CTWL	Q	Chartwell Group Ltd
CTWS	Q	Connecticut Water Services Inc
CTWSA	N	California Real Estate Investment Trust S B I Wts A
CTX	N	Centex Corp
CTY	A	Century Communications Corp Cl A
CTYF	Q	City Fed Financial Corp
CTYFN	Q	Cityfed Financial Corp Jr Pfd C
CTYFO	Q	City Fed Financial Corp Pfd B
CTYN	Q	City National Corp
CTZ	N	Citizens & Southern Corp
CU	N	C U C Intl Inc
CUB	A	Cubic Corp
CUC	N	Culbro Corp
CUE	N	Quantum Chemical Corp
CULP	Q	Culp Inc
CUM	N	Cummins Engine Co Inc
CUM*	N	Cummins Engine Co Inc $3.50 Dep Cv Pfd Ser A
CUO	A	Continental Materials Corp
CUR	A	Current Income Shares Inc
CUS	A	Customedix Corp
CV	N	Central Vermont Public Service Corp
CVBF	Q	C V B Financial Corp
CVC	A	Cablevision Systems Corp Cl A
CVD	A	Conversion Industries Inc
CVF	A	Castle Convertible Fund Inc
CVI	A	Cenvill Investors Inc
CVL	A	Cenvill Development Corp
CVN	N	Computervision Corp
CVP	A	Americus Trust for Chevron Shares Prime
CVR	A	Chicago Rivet & Machine Co
CVS	A	Americus Trust for Chevron Shares Score
CVT	N	T C W Convertible Securities Fund Inc
CVU	A	Americus Trust for Chevron Shares Units
CVX*	N	Cleveland Electric Illuminating Co $7.40 Pfd A
CVX*B	N	Cleveland Electric Illuminating Co $7.56 Pfd B
CVX*L	N	Cleveland Electric Illuminating Co Adj Rate Pfd L
CW	N	Curtiss Wright Corp
CWE	N	Commonwealth Edison
CWE*A	N	Commonwealth Edison $1.425 Cum Cv Pfd A
CWE*C	N	Commonwealth Edison $1.90 Cum Pfd C
CWE*D	N	Commonwealth Edison $2.00 Cum Pfd D
CWE*E	N	Commonwealth Edison $7.24 Cum Pfd E
CWE*F	N	Commonwealth Edison $8.40 Cum Pfd F
CWE*G	N	Commonwealth Edison $2.875 Cum Pfd G
CWE*H	N	Commonwealth Edison $2.375 Cum Pfd
CWE*I	N	Commonwealth Edison $8.38 Cum Pfd
CWE*J	N	Commonwealth Edison $8.40 Pfd B
CWE*K	N	Commonwealth Edison $11.70 Cum Pfd
CWE*L	N	Commonwealth Edison $12.75 Cum Pfd
CWET	N	Commonwealth Edison Wts B
CWEW	N	Commonwealth Edison Wts A
CWLD	Q	Childworld Inc
CWM	N	Countrywide Mortgage Investment Inc
CWP	N	Cable & Wireless Plc
CWTR	Q	California Water Service Co
CWTS	Q	Country Wide Transport Services Inc
CX	N	Centerior Energy Corp
CXE	N	Colonial High Income Municipal Trust
CXH	N	Colonial Investment Grade Municipal Trust
CXI	A	Cuplex Inc
CXIM	Q	Criticare Systems Inc
CXR	A	C X R Telecom Corp
CXV	A	Cavalier Homes
CXY	A	Canadian Occidental Petroleum Ltd
CY	N	Cypress Semiconductor Corp
CYC	N	Cyclops Industries Inc
CYM	N	Cyprus Minerals Co
CYM*	N	Cyprus Minerals Co $3.75 Cv Exch Pfd
CYR	N	Cray Research Inc
CYS	N	Cycare System Inc
CYT	N	Citytrust Bancorp Inc
CYTO	Q	Cytogen Corp
CZ	N	Celanese Corp
CZM	N	Calmat Co
D	N	Dominion Resources Inc of Va
DAHL	Q	Dahlberg Inc
DAIO	Q	Data I O
DAL	N	Delta Air Lines Inc
DAN	N	Daniel Industries Inc
DAPN	Q	Dauphin Deposit Corp
DARTA	Q	Dark Group Corp Cl A
DASW	Q	Data Switch Corp
DATM	Q	Datum Inc
DATX	Q	Data Translation Inc
DAVX	Q	Davox Corp
DAY	N	Dayco Corp
DAZX	Q	Daisy Systems Corp
DBAS	Q	D B A Systems Inc
DBD	N	Diebold Inc
DBHI	Q	Dow B Hickam Inc
DBIO	Q	Damon Biotech
DBRL	Q	Dibrell Brothers Inc
DBRN	Q	Dress Barn
DC	A	Datametrics Corp
DCA	N	Digital Communications Associates Inc
DCI	N	Donaldson Co Inc
DCM	N	Dreyfus California Municipal Income Inc
DCN	N	Dana Corp
DCO	A	Ducommun Inc
DCOR	Q	Decor Corp
DCPI	Q	Dick Clark Productions Inc
DCY	N	D C N Y Corp
DD	N	Du Pont E I De Nemours & Co
DD*A	N	Du Pont E I De Nemours & Co $3.50 Pfd
DD*B	N	Du Pont E I De Nemours & Co $4.50 Pfd
DDIX	Q	D D I Pharmaceutical Inc
DDL	N	Data Design Laboratories
DDS	N	Dillard Department Stores Inc Cl A
DE	N	Deere & Co
DEAL	Q	Dial REIT Inc
DEBS	Q	Deb Shops Inc
DEC	N	Digital Equipment Corp
DEER	Q	Deerfield Fed S & L Assn
DEFI	Q	Defiance Inc
DEI	N	Diversified Energies Inc
DELE	Q	Del Electronics Corp
DELL	Q	Dell Computer Corpration
DEMP	Q	Drug Emporium Inc
DEPA	A	Damson Energy Co L P Cl A
DEPB	A	Damson Energy Co L P Cl B

DEPC	Q	D E P Corp
DEPS	Q	Deposit Guaranty Corp
DESI	Q	Designs Inc
DETA	Q	Del Taco Restaurants Inc
DETC	Q	Detection Systems Inc
DEVC	Q	Devcon Intl Corp
DEVN	Q	Devon Group Inc
DEW	N	Delmarva Power & Light Co
DEX	N	Dexter Corp
DF	N	Dean Foods Co
DFI	A	Duty Free Intl Inc
DFII	Q	Duty Free Intl Inc
DFLX	Q	Dataflex Corp
DFSE	Q	D F Southeastern Inc
DGAS	Q	Delta Natural Gas Co Inc
DGIC	Q	Donegal Group Inc
DGII	Q	Digi Intl Inc
DGN	N	Data General Corp
DGWD	N	Associated Dry Goods Corp W D
DH	N	Dayton Hudson Corp
DHR	N	Danaher Corp
DHTK	Q	D H Technology Inc
DHULZ	Q	Dorchester Hugoton Ltd D D R
DI	N	Dresser Industries Inc
DIA	A	Diasonics Inc
DIBK	Q	Dime Financial Corp
DICN	Q	Diceon Electronics Inc
DIG	N	Di Giorgio Corp
DIGI	Q	D S C Communications Corp
DIGWD	N	Di Giorgio Corp W D
DII	A	Decorator Industries Inc
DILO	Q	Digilog Systems Inc
DING	Q	Diversified Investment Group Inc
DIO	A	Diodes Inc
DIS	N	Disney Walt Co
DIV	A	P C L Diversifund Inc
DIX	A	Dixieline Products Inc Cl A
DJ	N	Dow Jones & Co Inc
DJCO	Q	Daily Journal Corp (Sc)
DJI	A	Designcraft Industries Inc
DKAI	Q	D A K A Intl Inc
DKEY	Q	Datakey Inc
DLCH	Q	Delchamps Inc
DLI	A	Del Laboratories Inc
DLOG	Q	Distributed Logic Corp
DLP	A	Centrust Bank
DLP*	A	Centrust Bank Ser 1 Part Pfd
DLPH	Q	Delphi Information Systems Inc
DLS	N	Dallas Corp
DLT	N	Deltona Corp
DLTK	Q	Deltak Corp
DLW	N	Delta Woodside Industries Inc
DLX	N	Deluxe Corp
DMAR	Q	Datamarine Intl Inc
DMBK	Q	Dominion Bankshares Corp
DMC	N	Diversified Industries Inc
DMCB	Q	Data Measurement Corp
DMCVA	Q	Dairy Mart Convenience Stores Inc Cl A
DMCVB	Q	Dairy Mart Convenience Stores Inc Cl B
DMD	A	Delmed Inc
DME	N	Dime Savings Bank of New York
DMF	A	Dreyfus Municipal Income Inc
DMGIF	Q	Dumagami Mines Ltd
DMIC	Q	Digital Microwave Corp
DMK	A	Direct Action Marketing Inc
DMLA	A	Dickenson Mines Ltd Cl A
DMLB	A	Dickenson Mines Ltd Cl B
DNA	N	Diana Corp
DNAP	Q	D N A Plant Technology Corp
DNB	N	Dun & Bradstreet Corp
DNEX	Q	Dionex Corp
DNFC	Q	D & N Financial Corp
DNM	A	Dreyfus New York Municipal Income Inc
DNNY	Q	Frances Denney Co Inc
DNP	N	Duff & Phelps Selected Utilities Inc
DNY	N	Donnelley R R & Sons Co
DOCKS	Q	Chicago Dock & Canal Trust S B I
DOCO	Q	D O C Optics Corp
DOCP	Q	Delaware Ostego Corp
DOLR	Q	Dollar General Corp
DOMNQ	Q	Domain Technology Inc
DOMZ	Q	Dominquez Water Corp
DON	A	Donnely Corp
DOP	A	Americus Trust for Dow Shares Prime
DOS	A	Americus Trust for Dow Shares Score
DOSK	Q	Doskocil Cos Inc
DOTX	Q	Dotronix Inc
DOU	A	Americus Trust for Dow Shares Units
DOUG	Q	Douglas & Lomason Co
DOV	N	Dover Corp
DOW	N	Dow Chemical Co
DP	N	Diagnostic Products Corp
DPC	A	Dataproducts Corp
DPHZ	Q	Dataphaz Inc
DPL	N	D P L Inc Holding Co
DPL*D	N	Dayton Power & Light 7.48% Cum Pfd D
DPL*E	N	Dayton Power & Light 7.70% Cum Pfd E
DPL*F	N	Dayton Power & Light 7.375% Cum Pfd F
DPL*J	N	Dayton Power & Light 11.60% Cum Pfd J
DPP	A	Americus Trust for Dupont Prime
DPS	A	Americus Trust for Dupont Score
DPT	N	Datapoint Corp
DPT*	N	Datapoint Corp $4.94 Ex Pfd
DPU	A	Americus Trust for Dupont Units
DPX	A	Duplex Products Inc
DQE	N	D Q E Inc Holding Co
DQU*A	N	Duquesne Light Co $2.10 Cum Pfd A
DQU*B	N	Duquesne Light Co 3.75% Cum Pfd B
DQU*C	N	Duquesne Light Co 4% Cum Pfd C
DQU*D	N	Duquesne Light Co 4.10% Cum Pfd D
DQU*E	N	Duquesne Light Co 4.15% Cum Pfd E
DQU*G	N	Duquesne Light Co 4.20% Cum Pfd G
DQU*H	N	Duquesne Light Co $7.20 Cum Pfd H
DQU*J	N	Duquesne Light Co $2.315 Pfd
DQU*K	N	Duquesne Light Co $2.10 Pfd K
DR*B	N	National Distillers & Chem Corp 4 1 2% Cum Pfd B
DRCO	Q	Dynamics Research Corp
DRE	N	Duke Realty Investments Inc
DRE*U	N	Duke Realty Investments Inc Units
DREW	Q	Drew Industries Inc
DRH	Q	Driver Harris Co
DRI	A	De Rose Industries Inc
DRKN	Q	Durakon Industries Inc
DRL	A	D I Industries Inc
DRM	N	Diamond Shamrock R & M Inc
DRM*	N	Diamond Shamrock R & M Inc $2.00 Cv Exch Pfd
DRMD	Q	Duramed Pharmaceuticals
DRSA	A	Diagnostic Retrieval Systems Inc Cl A
DRSB	A	Diagnostic Retrieval Systems Inc Cl B
DRTK	Q	Duratek Corp
DRV	N	Dravo Corp
DRXR	Q	Drexler Technology Corp

DRY	N	Dreyfus Corp
DRYR	Q	Dreyers Grand Ice Cream Inc
DSBC	Q	Derby Savings Bank
DSCC	Q	Datasouth Computer Corp
DSCP	Q	Datascope Corp
DSG	A	Designatronics Inc
DSI	N	Dreyfus Strategic Government Income Inc
DSII	Q	Decom System Inc
DSL	N	Downey S & L Assn
DSMI	Q	Dallas Semiconductor Corp
DSN	N	Dennison Manufacturing Co
DSO	N	De Soto Inc
DSP	N	Diamond Shamrock Offshore Partners L P Dep Units
DSR	N	Dresher Inc
DSTS	Q	D S T Systems Inc
DTC	N	Domtar Inc
DTE	N	Detroit Edison Co
DTE*	N	Detroit Edison Co 5 1 2% Cum Cv Pfd
DTE*A	N	Detroit Edison Co 9.32% Cum Pfd
DTE*B	N	Detroit Edison Co $2.75 Ser B Pfd
DTE*C	N	Detroit Edison Co 7.68% Pfd C
DTE*D	N	Detroit Edison Co 7.45% Pfd D
DTE*E	N	Detroit Edison Co 7.36% Pfd E
DTE*F	N	Detroit Edison Co $2.75 Cum Pfd F
DTE*G	N	Detroit Edison Co $2.28 Pfd G
DTE*H	N	Detroit Edison Co 9.72% Cum Pfd H
DTM	A	Dataram Corp
DTMD	Q	Dento Med Industries Inc
DTRX	Q	Detrex Corp
DTSI	Q	Datron Systems Inc
DUCO	Q	Durham Corp
DUFM	Q	Durr Fillauer Medical Inc
DUK	N	Duke Power
DUK*	N	Duke Power 6 3 4% Cum Cv Pfd A A
DUK*F	N	Duke Power 8.70% Cum Pfd F
DUK*G	N	Duke Power 8.20% Cum Pfd G
DUK*H	N	Duke Power 7.80% Cum Pfd H
DUK*K	N	Duke Power 8.28% Cum Pfd K
DUK*M	N	Duke Power 8.84% Cum Pfd M
DUK*N	N	Duke Power 8.84% Cum Pfd
DUNK	Q	Dunkin Donuts Inc
DURI	Q	Duriron Co Inc
DVH	A	Divi Hotels
DVL	N	Del Val Financial Corp
DVN	N	Devon Energy Corp
DVN*	A	Devon Energy Corp Pfd
DVRS	Q	Diversco Inc
DWG	A	D W G Corp
DWPWS	A	Del E Webb Investment Properties Wts
DWSN	Q	Dawson Geophysical Co
DWW	N	Davis Water & Waste Industries Inc
DWWS	A	Citicorp Currency Exchange Wts Germany
DXN	N	Dixons Group Plc
DXR	Q	Daxor Corp
DXT	A	Dixon Ticonderoga Co
DXTK	Q	Diagnostek Inc
DXYN	Q	Dixie Yarns Inc
DYA	N	Dynamics Corp of America
DYAN	Q	Dyansen Corp
DYCO	Q	Dycom Industries Inc
DYN	N	Dyncorp
DYNA	Q	Dynascan Corp
DYR	A	Dyneer Corp
DYTC	Q	Dynatech Corp
DYTR	Q	Dyatron Corp
E	N	Transco Energy Co

E*A	N	Transco Energy Co Cum Cv 4.75 Pfd
EA	N	Electronic Associates Inc
EAC	A	E A C Industries Inc
EACO	Q	E A Engineering Science & Technology Inc
EAFC	Q	Eastland Financial Corp
EAG	A	Eagle Financial Corp
EAL*D	A	Eastern Airlines 11.36% Pfd
EAL*E	A	Eastern Airlines $2.27 Pfd
EAL*F	A	Eastern Airlines $3.24 Pfd
EAL*G	A	Eastern Airlines $3.12 Pfd
EASI	Q	Engineers Support Systems Inc
EASTS	Q	Eastover Corp S B I
EAT	N	Chilis Inc
EAVN	Q	Eaton Vance Corp
EB	A	Ehrlich Bober Financial Corp
EBCI	Q	Eagle Bancorp Inc
EBF	N	Ennis Business Forms Inc
EBKC	Q	Eliot Savings Bank
EBMI	Q	E & B Marine Inc
EBNC	Q	Equitable Bancorp
EBS	N	Edison Brothers Stores Inc
EBSI	Q	Eagle Bancshares Inc
EC	N	Engelhard Corp
ECC	N	E C C Intl Corp
ECF	A	Elsworth Cv Growth & Income Fund
ECFC	Q	Eastchester Financial Corp
ECGC	Q	Essex County Gas Co
ECGI	Q	Environmental Control Group Inc
ECH	N	Echlin Inc
ECILF	Q	E C I Telecom Ltd
ECL	N	Ecolab Inc
ECLAY	Q	English China Clays Public Ltd Co ADR
ECO	A	Echo Bay Mines Ltd
ECOL	Q	American Ecology Corp
ECP	N	Central Newspapers Inc Cl A
ECRC	Q	Employers Casualty Co
ECTL	Q	Elcotel Inc
ED	N	Consolidated Edison Co N Y
ED*A	N	Consolidated Edison Co N Y $5.00 Cum Pfd
ED*B	N	Consolidated Edison Co N Y 6% Cum Cv Pfd B
ED*C	N	Consolidated Edison Co N Y 4.65% Cum Pfd C
EDAT	Q	Electronic Data Technologies
EDCO	Q	Edison Control Corp
EDE	N	Empire District Electric
EDE*A	N	Empire District Electric 4 3 4% Cum Pfd A
EDE*B	N	Empire District Electric 5% Cum Pfd B
EDO	N	E D O Corp
EDP	N	Energy Development Partners Units
EDSE	Q	E S E L C O Inc
EE	A	Esquire Radio & Electronics Inc
EEC	A	E E C O Inc
EECN	Q	Ecogen Inc
EED	N	Entex Energy Development Ltd
EEI	A	Ecology & Environment Inc
EEMWS	A	Emerson Electric Co Wts
EESI	Q	Eastern Environmental Services Inc
EFG	N	Equitec Financial Group Inc
EFIC	Q	E F I Corp
EFSB	Q	Elmwood Federal Savings Bank
EFU	N	Eastern Enterprises
EFX	N	Equifax Inc
EGA	N	E Q K Green Acres L P
EGG	N	E G G Inc
EGGS	Q	Egghead Inc
EGL	A	Eagle Clothes Inc

EGLE	Q	Eagle Food Centers Inc
EGN	N	Energen Corp
EGP	A	Eastgroup Properties S B I
EGX	A	Engex Inc
EHP	N	Emerald Homes L P
EI	A	Endevco Inc
EIC	N	Emerald Mortgage Investment Corp
EILI	Q	E I L Instruments Inc
EIPM	Q	E I P Microwave Inc
EIS	N	Excelsior Income Shares Inc
EJA	A	Everest & Jennings Intl Cl A
EJB	A	Everest & Jennings Intl Cl B
EK	N	Eastman Kodak Co
EKO	N	Ekco Group Inc
EKR	N	E Q K Realty Investors Ser 1 S B I
ELANY	Q	Elan Corp Plc ADR
ELB	A	Eldorado Bancorp
ELBTF	Q	Elbit Computers Ltd
ELCH	Q	El Chico Corp
ELCN	Q	Elco Industries Inc
ELD	N	Eldon Industries Inc
ELDC	Q	Eldec Corp
ELE	N	Empresa Nacional De Electricidad S A
ELJ	N	Eljer Industries Inc
ELK	N	Elcor Corp
ELMG	Q	Electromagnetic Sciences Inc
ELPA	Q	El Paso Electric Co Com
ELRC	N	Electro Rent Corp
ELRNF	Q	Elron Electronics Industries Inc
ELS	A	Elsinore Corp
ELSE	Q	Electro Sensors Inc
ELT	N	Elscint Ltd
ELUXY	Q	A B Electrolux ADR
ELXS	Q .	E L X S I Corp
EM	A	Entertainment Marketing Inc
EMC	N	E M C Corp
EMCI	Q	E M C Insurance Group Inc
EMCO	Q	Engineering Measurements Co
EME	N	Emerson Radio Corp
EMF	A	Templeton Emerging Markets Fund Inc
EMI	A	Encore Marketing Intl Inc
EML	A	Eastern Co
EMLX	Q	Emulex Corp
EMP	A	Empire of Carolina Inc
EMPI	Q	Empi Inc
EMPR	Q	Empire Financial Corp
EMR	N	Emerson Electric Co
EN	N	Enterra Corp
ENCC	Q	Encore Computer Corp
ENCL	Q	Enclean Inc
ENE	N	Enron Corp
ENE*J	N	Enron Corp $10.50 Cum Cv 2nd Pfd J
ENEX	Q	E N E X Resources Corp
ENG	N	Enron Oil & Gas Co
ENGH	Q	Engraph Inc
ENNI	Q	Energy North Inc
ENRGB	Q	Dekalb Energy Co Cl B
ENS	N	Enserch Corp
ENS*D	N	Enserch Corp Adj Rate Cum Pfd D
ENS*E	N	Enserch Corp Adj Rate Cum Pfd E
ENT	A	Entertainment Publications Inc
ENTC	Q	Entronics Corp
ENV	N	Enviropact Inc
ENVI	Q	Envirosafe Services Inc
ENVT	Q	Environmental Tectonics Corp
ENX	A	E N S R
ENZ	A	Enzo Biochem Inc

ENZN	Q	Enzon Inc
EOA	A	Empire of America Federal Savings Bank
EOG	N	Enron Oil & Gas Co
EORR	Q	Empire Orr Inc
EP	N	Enserch Exploration Partners Ltd Dep Receipts
EPI	N	Eagle Picher Industries
EPSI	Q	Epsilon Data Management Inc
EQICB	Q	Equitable of Iowa Cos Cl B
EQK	N	Equimark Corp
EQK*	N	Equimark Corp $2.31 Cum Cv Pfd
EQK*C	N	Equimark Corp Cum Cv Pfd C
EQM	N	Equitable Real Estate Shopping Centers L P
EQT	N	Equitable Resources Inc
EQT*	N	Equitable Resources Inc $2.00 Pfd
EQTX	Q	Equitex Inc
EQTY	Q	Equity Oil Co
ERB	N	Erbamont N V
ERC	N	E R C Intl Inc
ERCE	Q	E R C Environmental & Energy Services Co Inc
ERICY	Q	Ericsson Telephone Co ADR
ERIE	Q	Erie Lackawanna Inc
ERLYE	Q	E R L Y Industries Inc
ERTS	Q	Electronic Arts
ESB	N	Esselte Business Systems Inc
ESC	N	Environmental Systems Co
ESC*A	N	Environmental Systems Co $1.75 Cum Cv Exch Pfd A
ESCA	Q	Escalade Inc
ESCC	Q	Evans & Sutherland Computer Corp
ESEX	Q	Essex Corp
ESG	A	Electrosound Group Inc
ESH	A	Earl Scheib Inc
ESI	A	E S I Industries Inc
ESIO	Q	Electro Scientific Industries Inc
ESIWS	A	E S I Industries Inc Wts
ESL	N	Esterline Corp
ESN	A	Escagenetics Corp
ESP	A	Espey Manufacturing & Electronics Corp
ESR*	A	Enstar Indonesia Inc Pfd
ESSF	Q	E S S E F Corp
ESTO	Q	Eastco Industrial Safety Corp
ESV	N	Energy Service Co Inc
ESV*	A	Energy Service Co $1.50 Cum Cv Exch Pfd
ESX	A	Essex Financial Partners L P Units
ESY	N	E Systems Inc
ET	N	El Torito Restaurants Inc
ETCIA	Q	Electronic Tele Communication Inc Cl A
ETCO	Q	Earth Technology Corp
ETEX	Q	Eastex Energy Inc
ETN	N	Eaton Corp
ETR	N	Entergy Corp
ETRC	Q	Entree Corp
ETZ	A	Etz Lavud Ltd
EUA	N	Eastern Utilities Associates
EVAN	Q	Evans Inc Com
EVGN	Q	Evergreen Bancorp
EVRX	Q	Everex Systems Inc
EVSB	Q	Evansville Federal Savings Bank
EWAT	Q	E Town Corp
EWSCA	Q	E W Scripps Co Cl A
EXAR	Q	Exar Corp
EXC	A	Excell Industries Inc
EXCG	Q	Exchange Bancorp Inc
EXCWD	A	Excell Industries Inc W D
EXP	N	Transco Exploration Partners Ltd Dep Units

EXPD	Q	Expeditors Intl of Washington Inc
EY	N	Ethyl Corp
EY*	N	Ethyl Corp $2.40 Cum Cv Pfd A
EZEM	Q	E Z Em Inc
F	N	Ford Motor Co
FABC	Q	First Alabama Bancshares Inc
FABK	Q	First of America Bank Corp
FABKM	Q	First of America Bank Corp 9% Ser G Pfd
FABKN	Q	First of America Bank Corp 10% Ser E Pfd
FABKO	Q	First of America Bank Corp Pfd
FACT	Q	First Albany Cos Inc
FAHS	Q	Farm & Home Financial Corp
FAHSP	Q	Farm & Home Financial Corp 13% Ser A Cum Ex Pfd
FAI	N	F A I Insurances Ltd ADR
FAL	A	Falcon Cable Systems Co Units
FAMA	Q	First Amarillo Bancorp Inc
FAMB	Q	First American Bank for Savings
FAME	Q	Flamemaster Corp
FAMF	Q	First Amfed Corp
FAMRA	Q	First American Financial Corp Cl A
FAMS	Q	Famous Restaurants Inc
FARA	Q	Faradyne Electronics Corp
FARC	Q	Farr Co
FARF	Q	Fairfield Noble Corp
FARM	Q	Farmer Brothers Co Com
FASB	Q	First American Savings Bank
FAST	Q	Fastenal Co
FATN	Q	First American Corp
FAU	N	Freeport Mc Moran Gold Corp
FAX	A	First Australia Prime Income Fund
FAXM	Q	Hotelecopy Inc
FAY	N	Fays Inc
FBAC	Q	First National Bancorp of Gainesville
FBD	A	Fireboard Corp
FBF	N	First Boston Income Fund Inc
FBH	N	Hall Frank B & Co
FBH*B	N	Hall Frank B & Co Ser B Cv Pfd
FBI	N	First Boston Strategic Income Fund Inc
FBIC	Q	Firstbank of Illinois Co
FBNC	Q	First Bancorp
FBO	N	Federal Paperboard Co Inc
FBO*A	N	Federal Paperboard Co Inc $2.875 Cum Cv Pfd
FBO*B	N	Federal Paperboard Co Inc $1.20 Cum Cv Pfd
FBOH	Q	First Bancorp of Ohio
FBRC	Q	Fabric Wholesalers Inc
FBRX	Q	Fibronics Intl Inc
FBS	N	First Bank System Inc
FBS*A	N	First Bank System Inc 10.50% Pfd
FBSI	Q	First Banc Securities Inc
FBT	N	First City Bancorp of Texas
FBT*B	N	First City Bancorp of Texas $5.50 Cum Cv Pfd
FBXC	Q	F B X Corp
FC	A	Ford Motor Co of Canada Ltd
FCA	N	Fabri Centers of America Inc
FCAP	Q	First Capital Corp
FCB	N	Foote Cone & Belding Communications Inc
FCBK	Q	Fairfield County Bancorp Inc
FCBN	Q	Fluorocarbon Co
FCC	A	First Central Financial Corp
FCEA	A	Forest City Enterprises Inc Cl A
FCEB	A	Forest City Enterprises Inc Cl B
FCH	N	First Capital Holding Corp
FCH*	N	First Capital Holding Corp $2.0625 Cum Cv Pfd
FCHT	Q	First Chattanooga Financial Corp
FCI	N	Fairfield Communities Inc
FCIT	Q	First Citizens Financial Corp
FCLR	Q	First Commercial Corp
FCNCA	Q	First Citizens Bancshares Inc Cl A
FCNCB	Q	First Citizens Bancshares Inc Cl B
FCO	A	First Connecticut Small Business Inv
FCOA	Q	Foremost Corp of America
FCOB	Q	First Commercial Bancorp
FCOLA	Q	First Colonial Bancshares Corp Cl A
FCOM	Q	First Commerce Corp
FCON	Q	First Constitution Financial Corp
FCP	A	Americus Trust for Ford Prime
FCR	A	First Corp Inc Cl A
FCRES	Q	First Continental Real Estate Investment Trust S B I
FCS	A	Americus Trust for Ford Score
FCTR	Q	First Charter Corp
FCU	A	Americus Trust for Ford Units
FCX	N	Freeport Mc Moran Copper Co Inc
FDLNA	Q	Food Lion Inc Cl A
FDLNB	Q	Food Lion Inc Cl B
FDO	N	Family Dollar Stores Inc
FDOS	Q	Franklin Computer Corp
FDPC	Q	F D P Corp
FDX	N	Federal Express Corp
FE	A	Fries Entertainment Inc
FEBC	Q	First Eastern Corp
FED	N	Firstfed Financial Corp
FEDF	Q	Federated Financial S & L Assn
FEI	A	Frequency Electronics Inc
FELE	Q	Franklin Electric Co Inc
FEN*A	N	Fairchild Industries Inc Cv Pfd A
FERO	Q	Ferrofluidics Corp
FERT	Q	Nu West Industries Inc
FERTP	Q	Nu West Industries Inc Pfd A
FES	A	First Empire State Corp
FESX	Q	First Essex Bancorp Inc
FEXC	Q	First Executive Corp
FEXCM	Q	First Executive Corp Ser G Cum Pfd
FEXCO	Q	First Executive Corp Dep Cum Pfd F
FEXCP	Q	First Executive Corp Dep Pfd Shares
FEXCR	Q	First Executive Corp Rts 10 11 89
FEXCW	Q	First Executive Corp Wts
FEXNV	Q	First Executive Corp Dep Preference Shares
FEXZV	Q	First Executive Corp Wts 10 9 92 W I
FF	N	First Financial Fund Inc
FFA	A	Firstfed America Inc
FFAL	Q	First Federal of Alabama F S B
FFAM	Q	First Family Group Inc
FFB	N	First Fidelity Bancorp
FFB*B	N	First Fidelity Bancorp $2.15 Cum Cv Pfd B
FFB*D	N	First Fidelity Bancorp Ser D Adj Rate Pfd
FFBC	Q	First Financial Bancorp
FFBK	Q	First Florida Banks Inc
FFC	N	Firemans Fund Corp
FFCA	Q	Carolina Bancorp Inc
FFCH	Q	First Financial Holdings
FFES	Q	First Federal S & L Assn of East Hartford
FFFC	Q	Franklin First Financial Corp
FFFG	Q	F F O Financial Group Inc
FFH	A	Fairfield Homes L P
FFHC	Q	First Financial Corp
FFHP	Q	First Harrisburg Bancor Inc
FFHS	Q	First Franklin Corp
FFKY	Q	First Federal Savings Bank Elizabethtown

FFMA	Q	Fidelity Federal Savings Bank	FLFC	Q	First Liberty Financial Corp
FFMC	Q	First Financial Management Corp	FLFE	Q	Florida Federal Savings Bank
FFMY	Q	First Federal S & L Assn of Ft Myers	FLGF	Q	Flagship Financial Corp
FFNS	Q	First Savings Bancorp	FLGLA	Q	Flagler Bancorp Cl A
FFOM	Q	Firstfed Michigan Corp	FLM	N	Fleming Cos
FFP	A	Food N Fuel Partners L P	FLO	N	Flowers Industries Inc
FFPC	Q	Florida First Federal Savings Bank	FLOG	Q	Falcon Oil & Gas
FFPR	Q	First Federal Savings Bank Puerto Rico	FLOW	Q	Flow Intl Corp
FFRV	Q	Fidelity Federal Savings Bank	FLP	N	Floating Point Systems Inc
FFS	A	First Federal Bank Corp	FLR	N	Fluor Corp
FFSB	Q	Fulton Federal Savings Bank	FLSHP	Q	F L S Holdings Ser A Pfd
FFSD	Q	First Federal Savings Bank Alabama	FLTI	Q	Flight Intl Group Inc
FFSM	Q	First Federal Savings Bank of Montana	FLX	A	Flexible Bond Trust Inc
FFSW	Q	First Federal Financial Services Corp	FLXS	Q	Flexsteel Industries Inc
FFTN	Q	Fidelity Federal S & L Assn of Tennessee	FLY	N	Airlease Ltd
FFUT	Q	First Fed S & L of Salt Lake City	FMBC	Q	First Michigan Bankcorp
FFWP	Q	First Federal of Western Pennsylvania	FMBI	Q	First Midwest Bancorp Inc
FFWV	Q	First Fidelity Bancorp	FMC	N	F M C Corp
FG	N	U S F & G Corp	FMCO	Q	F M S Financial Corp
FG*A	N	U S F & G Corp $4.10 Ser A Cv Ex Pfd	FMFS	Q	F & M Financial Service Inc
FGBC	Q	First Golden Bancorp	FMLY	Q	Danielson Federal S & L Assn
FGC	N	F G I C Corp	FMNT	Q	F & M National Corp
FGE	A	Fitchburg Gas & Electric Light Co	FMO	N	Federal Mogul Corp
FGHC	Q	First Georgia Holdings Inc	FMP	N	Freeport Mc Moran Energy Partners Ltd Dep
FGI	N	Foothill Group Inc Cl A			Receipts
FGL	N	F M C Gold Co	FMR	N	Freeport Mc Moran Oil & Gas Royalty Trust
FGN	N	Flow General Inc			U B I
FHC	N	F H C Compcare Inc	FMSB	Q	First Mutual Savings Bank
FHI	N	Fine Homes Intl L P Dep Units	FN	A	First National Corp
FHO	A	Fredericks of Hollywood Inc	FNB	N	First Chicago Corp
FHPC	Q	F H P Corp	FNB*	N	First Chicago Corp Adj Div Cum Pfd
FHWN	Q	First Hawaiian Inc	FNB*A	N	First Chicago Corp $3.75 Cum Cv Pfd
FIA	N	Fiat S P A Ordinary ADS	FNB*B	N	First Chicago Corp Adj Cum Pfd B
FIA*	N	Fiat S P A Preference ADS	FNB*C	N	First Chicago Corp Adj Div Cum Pfd C
FIA*A	N	Fiat S P A Savings ADS	FNBF	Q	Florida National Banks of Florida
FIAMA	Q	First American Bank & Trust of Palm Beach	FNBR	Q	F N B Rochester Corp
		Cl A	FNF	A	Fidelity National Financial Inc
FICI	Q	Fair Isaac & Company Inc	FNG	N	Fleet Norstar Financial Group Inc
FIF	N	Financial News Composite Fund Inc	FNG*	N	Fleet Norstar Financial Group Inc Cum Adj
FIGI	Q	Figgie Intl Holding Cl B			Pfd
FIGIA	Q	Figgie Intl Holding Cl A	FNG*A	N	Fleet Norstar Financial Group Inc Pfd
FIIA	Q	First Interstate of Iowa Inc	FNGB	Q	First Northern Savings Bank S A
FILE	Q	Filenet Corp	FNL	N	Fansteel Inc
FIN	N	Financial Corp of America	FNM	N	Federal National Mortgage Assn
FIN*	N	Financial Corp of America 6% Pfd	FNMWS	N	Federal National Mortgage Assn Wts
FIN*A	N	Financial Corp of America Flt Rate Pfd A	FNMWW	N	Federal National Mortgage Assn Wts W I
FINX	Q	Fingermatrix Inc	FNNG	Q	Finnigan Corp
FIRF	Q	First Financial Savings Assn	FNNI	Q	Financial News Network Inc
FIRO	Q	First Ohio Bancshares	FNPC	Q	First National Pennsylvania Corp
FIS	N	Fischbach Corp	FNWB	Q	F N W Bancorp Inc
FISB	Q	First Indiana Savings Bank	FNYB	Q	First New York Business Bank Corp
FISV	Q	Fiserv Inc	FOBBA	Q	First Oak Brook Bancshares Inc Cl A
FIT	A	Fab Industries	FOE	N	Ferro Corp
FITB	Q	Fifth Third Bancorp	FOFF	Q	Fifty Off Stores Inc
FITC	Q	Financial Trust Corp	FOIL	N	Forest Oil Corp
FIWI	Q	First Interstate Corp of Wisconsin	FONR	N	Fonar Corp
FJQ	N	Fedders Corp	FOOT	Q	Foothill Independent Bancorp
FKFD	Q	Frankford Corp	FORF	Q	Fortune Financial Group Inc
FKL	A	Franklin Corp	FOTO	Q	Seattle Film Works Inc
FKM	A	Fluke John Manufacturing Co	FOUR	Q	Forum Group Inc
FLA	N	Florida East Coast Industries Inc	FOX	N	Foxboro Co
FLAEF	Q	Florida Employers Insurance Co	FP	A	Fischer & Porter Co
FLAG	Q	First Federal Savings Bank of La Grange	FPA	N	First Pennsylvania Corp
FLAI	Q	Fleet Aerospace Inc	FPC	N	Florida Progress Corp
FLD	N	Fieldcrest Cannon Inc	FPI	A	Fountain Powerboat Industries Inc
FLE	N	Fleetwood Enterprises Inc	FPL	N	F P L Group Inc
FLEX	Q	Flextronics Inc	FPNJ	Q	First Peoples Financial Corp

FPO	A	F P A Corp
FPRY	Q	First Federal Savings Bank of Perry
FPT	N	Franklin Principal Maturity Trust
FPUT	Q	Florida Public Utilities Co
FQA	N	Fuqua Industries Inc
FRA	N	Farah Inc
FRBK	Q	Fairfield First Bank & Trust Co
FRC	A	First Republic Bancorp Inc
FRCC	Q	First Financial Caribbean Corp
FRD	A	Friedman Industries
FRE	N	Federal Home Loan Mortgage Corp
FRFD	Q	First Community Bancorp Inc
FRK	A	Florida Rock Industries Inc
FRL	A	Forum Retirement Partners L P
FRM	N	First Mississippi Corp
FRMBF	Q	Forum Re Group (Bermuda) Ltd
FRME	Q	First Merchants Corp
FRMG	Q	First Miss Gold Inc
FRML	Q	Freymiller Trucking Inc
FRMT	Q	Freemont General Corp
FRN	N	France Fund Inc
FRP	N	Freeport Mc Moran Resources Partners L P
FRPP	Q	F R P Properties Inc
FRS	A	Frischs Restaurants Inc
FRST	Q	Firstier Financial Inc
FRT	N	Federal Realty Investment Trust S B I
FRTH	Q	Fourth Financial Corp
FRTR	Q	Frontier Insurance Group
FRV	A	Fur Vault Inc
FRX	A	Forest Laboratories Inc Cl A
FSAK	Q	Franklin Savings Association
FSB	N	Financial Corp of Santa Barbara
FSBC	Q	First Savings Bank F S B
FSBG	Q	First Federal Savings Bank Georgia
FSBX	Q	Framington Savings Bank
FSCB	Q	First Commercial Bancshares Inc
FSCC	Q	First Federal Savings Bank of Charlotte County
FSCO	Q	First Security Corp
FSCR	Q	Federal Screw Works
FSEB	Q	First Home Federal S & L Assn
FSFC	Q	First Security Financial Corp
FSFI	Q	First State Financial Services Inc
FSI	N	Flight Safety Intl Inc
FSII	Q	F S I Intl Inc
FSKY	Q	First Security Corp of Kentucky
FSM	A	Foodarama Supermarkets
FSNR	Q	Forschner Group Inc
FSPG	Q	First Home Saving Bank S & L Assn
FSR	N	Firstar Corp
FSR*B	N	Firstar Corp Cum Adj Pfd
FSS	N	Federal Signal Corp
FSTRA	Q	L B Foster Co Cl A
FSVA	Q	Fidelity Savings Association
FSVB	Q	Franklin Savings Bank F S B
FT	N	Franklin Universal Trust
FTD	N	Fort Dearborn Income Securities Inc
FTEN	Q	First Tennessee National Corp
FTIL	Q	First Illinois
FTK	N	Filtertek Inc
FTL	A	Fruit of the Loom
FTSC	Q	First Federal S & L Assn of South Carolina
FTTR	Q	Fretter Inc
FTU	N	First Union Corp
FTX	N	Freeport Mc Moran Inc
FTX*	N	Freeport Mc Moran Inc $1.875 Cv Exch Pfd
FTXWD	N	Freeport Mc Moran Inc W D
FULL	Q	Fuller H B Co Minnesota
FULT	Q	Fulton Financial Corp
FUN	N	Cedar Fair L P
FUR	N	First Union Real Estate Equity Mtg Inv S B I
FVB	N	First Virginia Banks Inc
FVF	N	Finevest Foods Inc
FW	N	First Wachovia Corp
FWBI	Q	First Western Bancorp Inc
FWC	N	Foster Wheeler Corp
FWCH	Q	First World Cheese Inc
FWCHW	Q	First World Cheese Inc Wts
FWES	Q	First Western Financial Corp
FWF	N	Far West Financial Corp
FWFWD	N	Far West Financial Corp W D
FWNC	Q	Fort Wayne National Corp
FXM	N	Foxmeyer Corp
FYBR	Q	Critical Industries Inc
FYCWS	A	Ford Motor Credit Co Yen Wts
FYWS	A	Ford Motor Credit Co Wts
FYYWS	A	Ford Motor Credit Co Wts Yen
G	N	Greyhound Corp
G*	N	Greyhound Corp $4.75 Pfd
GA	A	General Automation Inc
GAB	N	Gabelli Equity Trust Inc
GACC	Q	Great American Communications Co
GAEO	Q	Galileo Electro Optics Corp
GAL	N	Galoob Lewis Toys Inc
GAL*	N	Galoob Lewis Toys Inc Dep Cv Exch Pfd
GAM	N	General American Investors Co Inc
GAMA	Q	Gamma Biologicals
GAN	A	Garan Inc
GANDF	Q	Gandalf Technologies Inc
GAP	N	Great Atlantic & Pacific Tea Co
GARN	Q	Garnett Resources Corp
GAS	N	N I C O R Inc
GAS*	N	N I C O R Inc $1.90 Cum Cv Pfd
GAT	N	Gateway Corp Plc
GATS	Q	Gulf Applied Technologies Inc
GATW	Q	Gateway Federal S & L Assn
GB	Q	Guardian Bancorp
GBAN	Q	Gateway Bancorp Inc
GBBS	Q	Great Bay Bankshares Inc
GBCB	Q	G B C Bancorp
GBE	N	Grubb & Ellis Co
GBFH	Q	Georgia Bonded Fibers Inc
GBI	A	Granada Biosciences Inc
GBLD	Q	General Building Products Corp
GBND	Q	General Binding Corp
GBP	A	Global Asset Portfolio Inc
GBW	A	Great Lakes Recreation Co
GBYLF	Q	Giant Bay Resources Ltd
GCBK	Q	Great Country Bank
GCCC	Q	General Computer Corp
GCGI	Q	Geneve Capital Group Inc
GCGWS	A	General Electric Capital Corp Currency Exch Wts
GCI	N	Gannett Co Inc
GCN	N	General Cinema Corp
GCN*A	N	General Cinema Corp Cum Cv Pfd A
GCO	N	Genesco Inc
GCOR	Q	Gencor Industries Inc
GCP	A	Americus Trust for G M Shares Prime
GCR	A	Gaylord Container Corp
GCRA	Q	Golden Corral Realty Corp
GCS	A	Americus Trust for G M Shares Score
GCU	A	Americus Trust for G M Shares Units
GD	N	General Dynamics Corp

GDC	N	General Datacomm Industries Inc
GDM	N	Goldome
GDMK	Q	Goodmark Foods Inc
GDSB	A	Glenmore Distilleries Co Cl B
GDV	N	General Development Corp
GDW	N	Golden West Financial Corp
GDXA	A	Genovese Drug Stores Inc Cl A
GDYN	Q	Geodynamics Corp
GE	N	General Electric Co
GEB	N	Gerber Products Co
GEC	N	Geico Corp
GECM	Q	Genicom Corp
GECWD	N	Geico Corp W D
GEF	N	Nicholas Applegate Growth Equity Fund
GEG	N	Grace Energy Corp
GEL*	N	Gelco Corp Dep Rcpts Cum Pfd
GEM*	N	Gemini Fund Inc Income Shares
GEMC	Q	Geriatric & Medical Centers Inc
GEN	N	Genrad Inc
GENA	Q	General Automation Inc
GENI	Q	Genetics Institute Inc
GENIP	Q	Genetics Institute Inc Cv Ex Pfd
GENZ	Q	Genzyme Corp
GEO	A	Geothermal Resources Intl Inc
GEO*A	A	Geothermal Resources Intl Inc Pfd A
GEOD	Q	Geodyne Resources Inc
GEOWS	A	Geothermal Resources Intl Inc Wts
GEOX	Q	Geonex Corp
GER	N	Germany Fund Inc
GES	A	Genisco Technology Corp
GEST	Q	Guest Supply Inc
GEYWS	A	General Electric Capital Corp Yen Wts
GF	A	American First Guaranteed Income Fund L P
GFB	N	G F Corp Holding Co
GFC	N	Gilbraltar Financial Corp
GFCT	Q	Greenwich Financial Corp
GFD	N	Guilford Mills Inc
GFGC	Q	Great Falls Gas Co
GFH	N	Gifford Hill & Co
GFI	A	Graham Sealed Health Products Inc
GFSA	A	Giant Food Inc Cl A
GFX	A	P L M Equipment Growth Fund Dep Units
GGC	N	Georgia Gulf Corp
GGCWD	N	Georgia Gulf Corp W D
GGG	N	Graco Inc
GGGWD	N	Graco Inc W D
GGNS	Q	Genus Inc
GGP*	N	General Growth Properties $1.90 Cum Cv Pfd A
GGUY	Q	Good Guys Inc
GH	N	General Host Corp
GHM	A	Graham Corp
GHO	N	General Homes Corp
GHW	N	General Housewares Corp
GHX	N	Galveston Houston Co
GIB	A	C R Gibson Co
GIBG	Q	Gibson Greetings Inc
GIDL	Q	Giddings & Lewis Inc
GIGA	Q	Giga Tronics Inc
GII	A	Greiner Engineering Inc
GIL	A	Gilbarco Inc
GILBA	Q	Gilbert Associates Inc Cl A
GIM	N	Templeton Global Income Fund Inc
GIS	N	General Mills Inc
GISH	Q	Gish Biomedical Inc
GIT	N	Gitano Group Inc
GIYWS	A	General Mills Inc Currency Exch Wts

GKSRA	Q	G & K Services Inc Cl A
GLBC	Q	Great Lakes Bancorp
GLC	A	Galactic Resources Ltd
GLDC	Q	Golden Enterprises Inc
GLE	N	Gleason Works
GLF*A	N	General Telephone Co Florida $1.25 Cum Pfd A
GLF*B	N	General Telephone Co Florida $1.30 Cum Pfd B
GLF*C	N	General Telephone Co Florida $8.16 Cum Pfd C
GLGVF	Q	Glamis Gold Ltd
GLI	N	Global Income Plus Fund Inc
GLK	N	Great Lakes Chemical Corp
GLM	N	Global Marine Inc
GLMWS	N	Global Marine Inc Wts W I
GLN	N	Glenfed Inc
GLO	A	Global Ocean Carriers Ltd
GLP	A	Gould Investors L P Units
GLT	A	Glatfelter P H Co
GLTX	Q	Goldtex Inc
GLW	N	Corning Inc
GLX	N	Glaxo Holdings Plc
GLXIF	Q	Glenex Industries Inc
GLYT	Q	Genlyte Group Inc
GM	N	General Motors Corp
GM*A	N	General Motors Corp $3.75 Pfd A
GM*B	N	General Motors Corp $5.00 Pfd B
GMCC	Q	General Magnaplate Corp
GME	N	General Motors Corp Cl E
GMFD	Q	Germania Bank F S B
GMGW	Q	Geraghty & Miller Inc
GMH	N	General Motors Corp Cl H
GMI	N	Gemini II Inc Capital Shares
GMI*	N	Gemini II Inc Income Shares
GMN	A	Greenman Bros
GMP	N	Green Mountain Power Corp
GMT	N	G A T X Corp
GMT*	N	G A T X Corp $2.50 Cum Cv Pfd
GMT*A	N	G A T X Corp Cv Adj Rate Pfd
GMW	A	General Microwave Corp
GNA	A	Gainsco Inc
GNBC	Q	Glendale Bancorp
GNC	N	General Nutrition Corp
GNDR	Q	Gander Mountain Inc
GNE	N	Genentech Inc
GNEX	Q	Genex Corp
GNEXP	Q	Genex Corp Ser B Pfd
GNF	A	Granada Foods Corp
GNG	N	Golden Nugget Inc
GNI	N	Great Northern Iron Ore Prop Tr Ctfs
GNL	A	Gemco National Corp
GNN	A	Great Northern Nekoosa Corp
GNO	N	Ginos Inc
GNP	A	Americus Trust for G E Prime
GNR	A	Global Natural Resources Inc
GNS	A	Americus Trust for G E Score
GNT	N	Greentree Acceptance Inc
GNTE	Q	Granite Corporative Bank
GNTX	Q	Gentex Corp
GNU	A	Americus Trust for G E Units
GNUC	Q	G N I Inc
GNWF	Q	G N W Financial Corp
GO	A	Collins Industries Inc
GOAL	Q	Goal Systems Intl
GOOD	Q	Goody Products
GOSHA	Q	Oshkosh B Gosh Inc Cl A

GOSHB	Q	Oshkosh B Gosh Inc Cl B
GOT	N	Gottschalks Inc
GOU	A	Gulf Canada Resources
GOU*	A	Gulf Canada Corp Ser 1 Pfd Shares
GOV	N	Global Government Plus Fund Inc
GP	N	Georgia Pacific Corp
GPAR	Q	General Parametrics Corp
GPC	N	Genuine Parts Co
GPE*	N	Georgia Power Co $7.72 Cum Pfd
GPE*A	N	Georgia Power Co $2.75 Cl A Pfd
GPE*B	N	Georgia Power Co $7.80 Pfd
GPE*C	N	Georgia Power Co $2.52 Pfd A
GPE*D	N	Georgia Power Co $2.56 Cl A Pfd
GPE*G	N	Georgia Power Co Adj Cl A Pfd
GPE*H	N	Georgia Power Co $3.00 Cl A Pfd
GPE*I	N	Georgia Power Co Adj Cl A 1985 Ser Pfd
GPE*J	N	Georgia Power Co Adj Rate Cl A 2nd Ser Pfd
GPE*K	N	Georgia Power Co $2.30 Pfd A
GPE*L	N	Georgia Power Co $2.47 Pfd L
GPE*M	N	Georgia Power Co $2.50 Cl A Pfd
GPE*N	N	Georgia Power Co $2.43 Cl A Pfd
GPEC	Q	Guber Peters Entertainment Co
GPI	N	Guardsman Products Inc
GPO	N	Giant Portland Masonry Cement Co
GPRO	Q	Gen Probe Inc
GPS	N	Gap Inc
GPU	N	General Public Utilities Corp
GQ	N	Grumman Corp
GQ*	N	Grumman Corp $2.80 Cum Pfd
GR	N	Goodrich B F Co
GR*	N	Goodrich B F Co $7.85 Cum Pfd A
GR*D	N	Goodrich B F Co Ser D $3.50 Cum Cv Pfd
GRA	N	Grace W R Co
GRAN	Q	Bank of Granite Corp
GRARE	Q	Great American Recreation Inc
GRB	N	Gerber Scientific Inc
GRC	A	Gorman Rupp Co
GRCO	Q	Gradco System Inc
GRD	N	Guardian Industries Corp
GRE	N	Gulf Resources & Chemical Corp
GRE*B	N	Gulf Resources & Chemical $1.30 Cum Cv Pfd B
GREY	Q	Grey Advertising Inc
GRGI	Q	Greenery Rehabilitation Group Inc
GRH	N	M G M Grand Hotels Inc
GRIF	Q	Griffin Technology Inc
GRIT	Q	Grubb & Ellis Realty Income Trust
GRL	N	General Instrument Corp
GRLWD	N	General Instrument Corp W D
GRN	N	General Re Corp
GRO	N	Grow Group Inc
GROS	Q	Grossmans Inc
GROV	Q	Grovebank for Savings
GRPH	Q	Graphic Industries Inc
GRPI	Q	Greenwich Pharmaceuticals Inc
GRR	A	G R I Corp
GRST	Q	Grist Mill Co
GRT	A	Graphic Technology Inc
GRTR	Q	Greater New York Savings Bank
GS	N	Gillette Co
GSBI	Q	Granite State Bancshares Inc
GSBK	Q	Germantown Savings Bank
GSC	A	Gelman Sciences Inc
GSCC	Q	Graphic Scanning Corp
GSF	N	A C M Government Securities Fund Inc
GSK*A	N	Gamble Skogmo Inc $1.75 Cum Cv Pfd A
GSO	N	Growth Stock Outlook Trust Inc
GSOF	Q	Group I Software Inc
GSSC	Q	Grunta Sunburst Systems Corp
GSU	N	Gulf States Utilities Co
GSU*B	N	Gulf States Utilities Co $4.40 Cum Pfd
GSU*D	N	Gulf States Utilities Co Adj Rate Cum Pfd
GSU*E	N	Gulf States Utilities Co $5.08 Cum Pfd
GSU*G	N	Gulf States Utilities Co $4.52 Cum Pfd
GSU*K	N	Gulf States Utilities Co $8.80 Cum Pfd
GSU*M	N	Gulf States Utilities Co $4.40 Pfd
GSU*N	N	Gulf States Utilities Co $3.85 Div Pfd
GSV	N	Gas Service Co
GSX	N	General Signal Corp
GT	N	Goodyear Tire & Rubber Co
GTA	N	Great American Bank S S B
GTCH	Q	G Tech Corp
GTE	N	G T E Corp
GTE*	N	G T E Corp 5% Cum Cv Pfd
GTE*B	N	G T E Corp $2.475 Pfd
GTE*C	N	G T E Corp $2.00 Cv Pfd
GTI	A	G T I Corp
GTOS	Q	Gantos Inc
GTR	A	Gould Investors Trust S B I
GTV	A	Galaxy Cable Vision L P
GTWY	Q	Gateway Financial Corp
GTY	N	Getty Petroleum Corp
GUL	N	Gulton Industries Inc
GULD	Q	Goulds Pumps Inc Com
GULL	Q	Gull Laboratories Inc
GUN	A	Gundle Environment Systems Inc
GV	A	Goldfield Corp
GVF	N	Golden Valley Microwave Foods Inc
GVMI	Q	G V Medical Inc
GVT	N	Dean Witter Government Income Trust
GWA	A	Greater Washington Investors Inc
GWAY	Q	Gateway Communications Inc
GWCC	Q	G W C Corp
GWF	N	Great Western Financial Corp
GWOX	Q	Goodheart Willcox Co Inc
GWT	A	G W Utilities Ltd
GWTI	Q	Groundwater Technology Inc
GWW	N	Grainger W W Inc
GX	N	Geo Intl Corp
GXL	A	Granges Inc
GXLWS	A	Granges Inc Wts
GY	N	Gencorp Inc
GYK	A	Giant Yellowknife Mines Ltd
GZEA	Q	G Z A Geo Environmental Technologies Inc
H	A	Helm Resources Inc
HA	A	H A L Inc
HACH	Q	Hach Co
HAD	N	Hadson Corp
HAI	A	Hampton Industries
HAKO	Q	Hako Minuteman Inc
HAL	N	Halliburton Co
HALL	Q	Hall Financial Group Inc
HAML	Q	Hamilton Oil Corp
HAMS	Q	Smithfield Cos
HAN	N	Hanson Trust Plc ADS
HANA	Q	Hana Biologics Inc
HAND	Q	Handex Environmental Recovery Inc
HANWS	N	Hanson Trust Inc Wts
HAO	A	Harrow Industries Inc
HAR	N	Harman Intl Industries Inc
HARG	Q	Harper Group Inc
HARL	Q	Harleysville Savings Association
HAS	A	Hasbro Corp
HASR	Q	Hauserman Inc

HAT	N	Hatteras Income Securities Inc
HATH	Q	Hathaway Corp
HAVT	Q	Haverty Furniture Co Inc
HAVTA	Q	Harverty Furniture Co Inc Cl A
HB	N	Hillenbrand Industries Inc
HBAN	Q	Huntington Bancshares Inc
HBENB	Q	Home Beneficial Corp
HBJ	N	Harcourt Brace Jovanovich
HBJ*	N	Harcourt Brace Jovanovich 12% Pfd
HBOC	Q	H B O & Co
HBOL	Q	Hartford Steam Boiler Inspection & Ins Co
HBSI	Q	Hampton Bancshares Inc
HBUF	Q	Homestyle Buffet Inc
HBW	A	Wolf Howard B Inc
HC	N	Helene Curtis Industries Inc
HCCC	Q	Healthcare Compare Corp
HCCI	Q	H C C Industries
HCH	A	Health Chem Corp
HCI*B	N	Heritage Communications Inc Cv Pfd B
HCN	A	Healthcare R E I T Inc
HCO	A	Hubco Inc
HCP	N	Healthcare Property Investors Inc
HCS	A	Healthcare Services Inc
HCSB	Q	Home & City Savings Bank
HCSG	Q	Health Care Services Group Inc
HD	N	Home Depot Inc
HDCO	Q	Hadco Corp
HDG	A	Halsey Drug Co Inc
HDGH	Q	Hodgson Houses Inc
HDGWS	A	Halsey Drug Co Inc Wts
HDI	N	Harley Davidson Inc
HDL	N	Handleman Co
HDR	A	Heldor Industries Inc
HDRP	Q	H D R Power Systems Inc
HDS	N	Hills Department Stores Inc
HDYN	Q	Healthdyne Inc
HE	N	Hawaiian Electric Industries Inc
HEAL	Q	Healthwatch Inc
HEBC	Q	Heritage Bancorp Inc
HEC	N	Harken Energy Corp
HECHA	Q	Hechinger Co Cl A
HECHB	Q	Hechinger Co Cl B
HEI	A	Heico Corp
HEIC	Q	H E I Corp
HEII	Q	H E I Inc
HEKN	Q	Heekin Can Inc
HELE	Q	Helen of Troy Corp
HELX	Q	Helix Technology Inc
HEM*	N	Hemisphere Fund Income Shares
HENG	Q	Henley Group Inc Cl A
HEP	A	Hallwood Energy Partners L P
HERS	Q	Heritage Financial Services Inc
HESI	Q	Hunter Environmental Services Inc
HF	N	House of Fabrics Inc
HFD	N	Homefed Corp Holding Co
HFED	Q	Heart Federal S & L Assn
HFET	Q	Home Federal S & L Assn of Upper East Tenn
HFGA	Q	Home Federal Savings Bank of Georgia
HFI	A	Hudson Foods Cl A
HFIN	Q	Horizon Financial Services Inc
HFL	N	Homestead Financial Corp
HFLB	Q	Homestead Financial Corp Cl B
HFMD	Q	Home Federal Savings Bank Maryland
HFOX	Q	Home Federal S & L Assn
HFS	N	Home Owners Savings Bank F S B
HFSF	Q	Home Federal S & L Assn of San Francisco
HFSLP	Q	Home Owners Savings Bank F S B Ser A Pfd
HGC	A	Hudson General Corp
HGIC	Q	Harleysville Group Inc
HH	A	Hooper Holmes Inc
HHC	N	Horizon Healthcare Corp
HHH	A	Heritage Entertainment Inc
HHHWS	A	Heritage Entertainment Inc Wts
HHOT	Q	H & H Oil Tool Co Inc
HI	N	Household Intl Inc
HI*D	N	Household Intl Inc $6.25 Cum Cv Vtg Pfd D
HIA	N	Holiday Inns
HIBCA	Q	Hibernia Corp Cl A
HIFS	Q	Hingham Institution for Savings
HIG*A	N	Hartford Fire Insurance Co Cl A Pfd
HIGH	Q	Highland Super Stores Inc
HII	A	Healthcare Intl Cl A
HIMG	Q	Health Images Inc
HIN*A	N	Home Insurance Co Pfd
HINS	Q	Hanover Insurance Co New York
HIP	A	Hipotronics Inc
HIPC	Q	High Plains Corp
HIS	N	Cigna High Income Shares S B I
HIT	N	Hitachi Ltd ADR
HIVT	Q	Health Insurance of Vermont Inc
HIWDF	Q	Highwood Resources Ltd
HKF	N	Hancock Fabrics Inc
HKT	N	Hong Kong Telecommunications Ltd
HL	N	Hecla Mining Co
HLCO	Q	Healthco Intl Inc
HLP	A	Americus Trust for Hewlett Packard Shares Prime
HLS	A	Americus Trust for Hewlett Packard Shares Score
HLT	N	Hilton Hotels Corp
HLU	A	Americus Trust for Hewlett Packard Shares Units
HM	N	Homestake Mining Co
HMC	N	Honda Motor Co Ltd ADR
HMDY	Q	Hemodynamics Inc
HMF	A	Hastings Manufacturing Co
HMG	A	H M G Courtland Property Inc
HMI	A	Health Mor Inc
HMOA	Q	H M O America Inc
HMP	A	Americus Trust for Phillip Morris Shares Prime
HMS	A	Americus Trust for Phillip Morris Shares Score
HMSB	Q	Home Savings Bank
HMSD	Q	Homestead Holding Corp
HMSS	Q	H M S S Inc
HMT	N	Himont Inc
HMU	A	Americus Trust for Phillip Morris Shares Units
HMW	N	H M W Industries Inc
HMX	N	Hartmarx Corp
HMY	N	Heilig Meyers Co
HNBC	Q	Harleysville National Corp
HND	A	Hinderliter Industries Inc
HNH	N	Handy & Harman
HNIS	Q	Heritage Bancorp Inc
HNW	A	Hein Werner Corp
HNZ	N	Heinz H J Co
HNZ*	N	Heinz H J Co Third Cum $1.70 Cv Pfd
HO	A	Houston Oil Trust U B I
HOBC	Q	Howard Bancorp
HOC	A	Holly Corp
HOF	A	Hofmann Industries Inc

HOGN	Q	Hogan Systems Inc
HOLA	A	Holco Mortgage Acceptance Corp
HOME	Q	International American Homes Inc
HOMF	Q	Home Federal Savings Bank
HOMG	Q	Homeowners Group Inc
HON	N	Honeywell Inc
HONI	Q	H O N Industries Inc
HOR	A	Horn & Hardart Co
HORL	Q	Home Office Reference Laboratory Inc
HOSP	Q	Hosposable Products Inc
HOT	N	Hotel Investors Trust S B I
HOTWB	A	Hotel Investors Trust Wts B
HOU	N	Houston Industries Inc
HOV	N	Hovnanian Enterprises Inc
HOW	A	Howell Industries Inc
HP	N	Helmerich & Payne Inc
HPBC	Q	Home Port Bancorp Inc
HPC	N	Hercules Inc
HPH	N	Harnischfeger Corp
HPH*B	N	Harnischfeger Corp $3.402 Pfd
HPP	A	Americus Trust for Home Products Shares Prime
HPS	A	Americus Trust for Home Products Shares Score
HPSC	Q	H P S C Inc
HPU	A	Americus Trust for Home Products Shares Units
HQH	N	H & Q Healthcare Fund
HRA	A	Harvey Group Inc
HRB	N	Block H & R Inc
HRC	N	Healthsouth Rehabilitation Corp
HRD	N	Hannaford Brothers Inc
HRDG	Q	Harding Associates
HRE	N	H R E Properties
HRHC	Q	Hilb Rogal & Hamilton Co
HRI	A	Howe Richardson Corp
HRIZ	Q	Horizon Gold Shares Inc
HRL	A	Hormel George A & Co
HRLD	Q	Harolds Stores Inc
HRLY	Q	Herley Microwave Systems Inc
HRMN	Q	Harmon Industries Inc
HRN	A	Harlyn Products Inc
HROK	Q	Home Federal S & L Assn of the Rockies
HRP	N	Health & Rehabilitation Prop Trust
HRS	N	Harris Corp
HRZB	Q	Horizon Bank
HRZN	Q	Horizon Industries Inc
HS	N	Hopper Soliday Corp
HSBK	Q	Hibernia Savings Bank
HSC	N	Harsco Corp
HSI	N	Hi Shear Industries Inc
HSLD	Q	Home S & L Assn
HSN	A	Home Shopping Network Inc
HSO	A	Hershey Oil Corp
HSSI	Q	Hospital Staffing Services Inc
HSY	N	Hershey Foods Corp
HTCH	Q	Hutchinson Technology Inc
HTD	N	Huntingdon Intl Holdings Plc ADR
HTEK	Q	Hytek Microsystems Inc
HTG	A	Heritage Media Corp Cl A
HTHR	Q	Hawthorne Financial Corp
HTK	A	Howtek Inc
HTLD	Q	Hartland Express Inc
HTN	N	Houghton Mifflin Co
HTR	N	Hyperion Total Return & Income Fund Inc
HTWN	Q	Hometown Bancorp Inc
HTXA	Q	Hitox Corp of America
HU	A	Hampton Utilities Trust
HU*	A	Hampton Utilities Trust Pfd
HUBA	A	Hubbel Inc Cl A
HUBB	A	Hubbel Inc Cl B
HUF	N	Huffy Corp
HUFK	Q	Huffman Koos Inc
HUG	N	Hughes Supply Inc
HUHO	Q	Hughes Homes Inc
HUHOW	Q	Hughes Homes Inc Wts 1993
HUM	N	Humana Inc
HUN	N	Hunt Manufacturing Co
HURC	Q	Hurco Cos Inc
HUSB	Q	Home Unity S & L Assn
HVDK	Q	Harvard Knitwear Inc
HVFD	Q	Haverfield Corp
HVT	A	Healthvest
HWEC	Q	Hallwood Energy Corp
HWG	N	Hallwood Group Inc
HWKB	Q	Hawkeye Bancorp
HWKN	Q	Hawkins Chemical Inc
HWL	N	Howell Corp
HWP	N	Hewlett Packard Co
HWR	N	Walker Hiram Resources Ltd
HWRD	Q	Howard Bank New Jersey
HWY	N	Huntway Partners L P
HX	A	Halifax Engineering Inc
HXL	N	Hexcel Corp
HYB	N	New America High Income Fund Inc
HYDE	Q	Hyde Athletic Industries Inc
HYF	N	T C W High Yield Fund Inc
HYI	N	High Yield Income Fund
HYP	N	High Yield Plus Fund Inc
HYU	A	Lilly Eli & Co Cont Payment Oblig Unit
HZN	N	Horizon Corp
I	N	First Interstate Bancorp
I*A	N	First Interstate Bancorp Ser A Cv Pfd
I*B	N	Interstate Bancorp Adj Cum Pfd
IA	N	First Interstate Bancorp Cl A
IACI	Q	Industrial Acoustics Co Inc
IAD	N	Inland Steel Industries
IAF	A	First Australia Fund Inc
IAL	N	International Aluminum Corp
IBAN	Q	Imperial Bancorp
IBCA	Q	International Broadcasting Corp
IBCP	Q	Independent Bank Corp Michigan
IBF	A	First Iberian Fund Inc
IBK	A	International Banknote Co
IBL	N	Iroquois Brands Ltd
IBM	N	International Business Machines Corp
IBP	N	I B P Inc
ICA	N	Imperial Corp of America
ICAR	Q	Intercargo Corp
ICB	N	Intercapital Income Securities Inc
ICE	A	Arctic Alaska Fisheries Corp
ICEYF	Q	International Capital Equipment Ltd
ICG	A	Inter City Gas Corp The Amalgamated Co
ICH	A	I C H Corp
ICH*A	A	I C H Corp $1.75 Cum Cv Exch Pfd
ICI	N	Imperial Chemical Industries Ltd Plc ADR
ICM	A	I C M Property Investors Inc
ICN	N	I C N Pharmaceuticals Inc
ICOC	Q	I C O Inc
ICOT	Q	Icot Corp
ICPYY	Q	Institute of Clinical Pharmacology Plc ADR
ICRA	A	Corona Corp Cl A Vtg Shares
ICSI	Q	International Container Systems Inc
ICU	A	United Capital Corp

IDA	N	Idaho Power Co
IDBX	Q	I D B Communications Group Inc
IDL	N	Ideal Basic Industries
IDTI	Q	Integrated Device Technology Inc
IEC	A	P E C Israel Economic Corp
IEHC	Q	I E H Corp
IEI	N	Indiana Energy Inc
IEL	N	I E Industries Inc Holding Co
IEX	N	Idex Corp
IF	A	I R E Financial Corp
IFC	N	I F R B Corp
IFED	Q	Inter Federal Savings Bank
IFEI	Q	Imagine Films Entertainment Inc
IFEIW	Q	Imagine Films Entertainment Inc Wts
IFF	N	International Flavors & Fragrances Inc
IFG	N	Inter Regional Financial Group Inc
IFII	Q	Indiana Financial Investors Inc
IFL	N	I M C Fertilizer Group Inc
IFMX	Q	Informix Corp
IFRS	Q	I F R Systems Inc
IFSB	Q	Independent Federal Savings Bank
IFSIA	Q	Interface Inc Cl A
IFSL	Q	Indiana Federal S & L Assn
IG	A	I G I Inc
IGAM	Q	International Game Technology
IGC	A	Interstate General Co L P
IGEI	Q	International Genetic Engineering Inc
IGF	N	India Growth Fund Inc
IGL	N	International Minerals & Chemicals
IGL*	N	International Minerals & Chemicals 4% Cum Pfd
IGL*B	N	International Minerals & Chemicals $3.25 Cv Pfd B
IGLSF	Q	Insituform Group Ltd
IGLWF	Q	Insituform Group Ltd Wts
IGSI	Q	Insituform Gulf South Inc
IHEIF	Q	Interhome Energy Inc
IHK	A	Imperial Holly Corp
IHS	N	Ipco Corp
III	A	Insteel Industries Inc
IINT	Q	Information Intl Inc
IIP	A	International Income Property Inc
IIS	N	I N A Investment Securities Inc
IISLF	Q	I I S Intelligent Information Systems Ltd
IIVI	Q	Two V I Inc
IK	N	Interlake Corp Holding Co
ILCT	Q	I L C Technology Inc
ILFC	N	International Lease Financial
ILFCW	Q	International Lease Finance Corp Wts 1994
IMAT	Q	Imatron Inc
IMATW	Q	Imatron Inc Wts 11 90
IMC	N	International Multifoods Corp
IMD	N	Imo Delaval Inc
IME*	N	Indiana Michigan Power Co 7.08% Cum Pfd
IME*B	N	Indiana Michigan Power Co 7.76% Cum Pfd B
IME*C	N	Indiana Michigan Power Co 8.68% Cum Pfd C
IME*D	N	Indiana Michigan Power Co 12% Cum Pfd D
IME*E	N	Indiana Michigan Power Co $2.15 Cum Pfd E
IME*F	N	Indiana Michigan Power Co $2.25 Cum Pfd F
IME*G	N	Indiana Michigan Power Co $2.75 Cum Pfd G
IMET	Q	Intermetrics
IMGE	Q	Imnet Inc

IMI	A	Intermark Inc
IMI*	A	Intermark Inc Partic Pfd
IMKTA	Q	Ingles Markets Inc Cl A
IMMC	Q	International Mobile Machines
IMMCO	Q	International Mobile Machines Cum Cv Pfd
IMMU	Q	Immunomedics Inc
IMNX	Q	Immunex Corp
IMOA	A	Imperial Oil Ltd Cl A
IMPX	Q	International Microelectronic Products Inc
IMRGA	Q	Imreg Inc Cl A
IMRI	Q	I M C O Recycling Inc
INAC	Q	Inacomp Computer Centers Inc
INAI	Q	Intellicorp
INBC	Q	Independence Bancorp Inc
INBF	Q	I N B Financial Corp
INBS	Q	Iowa National Bankshares Corp
INCL	Q	Intellicall Inc
INCRF	Q	I N C O Resources Ltd
INDB	Q	Independent Bank Corp
INDHK	Q	Independent Insurance Group Inc Non Vtg
INDQA	Q	International Dairyqueen Cl A
INDQB	Q	International Dairyqueen Cl B
INDR	Q	Industrial Resources Inc
INDX	Q	Index Technology Corp
INEI	Q	Insituform East Inc
INEL	Q	Intelligent Electronics Inc
INFD	Q	Infodata Systems Inc
INFN	Q	Infotron Systems Corp
INGR	Q	Intergraph Corp
INMA	Q	Intermagnetics General Corp
INMC	Q	Inmac Corp
INMT	Q	Intermet Corp
INP	A	Intelligent Systems Corp
INPH	Q	Interphase Corp
INRD	Q	Inrad Inc
INS	A	International Seaway Trading Corp
INSH	Q	International Shipholding Corp
INSI	Q	Information Science Inc
INSMA	Q	Insituform Mid America Inc Cl A
INSP	Q	Inspeech Inc
INSUA	Q	Insituform of North America Inc Cl A
INSY	Q	Interim Systems Corp
INT	A	International Recovery Corp
INTC	Q	Intel Corp
INTCW	Q	Intel Corp 95 Wts
INTCZ	Q	Intel Corp Wts 92
INTE	Q	Intech Inc
INTF	Q	Interface Systems Inc
INTGC	Q	Intergroup Corp
INTK	Q	U S Intec Inc
INTLA	Q	Intertel Inc Cl A
INTO	Q	Initio Inc
INTP	Q	Interpoint Corp
INTR	Q	Intermec Corp
INTV	Q	Intervoice Inc
INVF	Q	Investors Financial Corp
INVG	Q	I N V G Mortgage Securities Corp
INVN	Q	Invitron Corp
INVS	Q	Investors Savings Corp
INVX	Q	Innovex Inc
IOMG	Q	Iomega Corp
ION	A	Ionics Inc
IOR	N	Iowa Resources Inc
IOT	N	Income Opportunity Realty Trust S B I
IOTWS	A	Income Opportunity Realty Trust Wts
IP	N	International Paper Co
IPC	N	Illinois Power Co

IPC*A	N	Illinois Power Co 4.08% Cum Pfd A		ITT*K	N	I T T Corp $4.00 Cum Cv Pfd K
IPC*B	N	Illinois Power Co 4.20% Cum Pfd B		ITT*N	N	I T T Corp $2.25 Cum Cv Pfd N
IPC*C	N	Illinois Power Co 4.26% Cum Pfd C		ITT*O	N	I T T Corp $5.00 Cum Cv Pfd O
IPC*D	N	Illinois Power Co 4.42% Cum Pfd D		ITW	N	Illinois Tool Works Inc
IPC*E	N	Illinois Power Co 4.70% Cum Pfd E		ITX	N	International Technology Corp
IPC*G	N	Illinois Power Co 8.24% Cum Pfd G		IUTL	Q	Iowa Southern Inc
IPC*H	N	Illinois Power Co 7.56% Cum Pfd H		IV	N	Mark I V Industries Inc
IPC*I	N	Illinois Power Co 8.94% Cum Pfd I		IVCR	Q	Invacare Corp
IPC*J	N	Illinois Power Co 8% Cum Pfd J		IVT	A	Iverson Technology Corp
IPC*L	N	Illinois Power Co Adj Rate Cum Pfd A		IVX	A	Ivax Corp
IPC*M	N	Illinois Power Co 11.75% Cum Pfd		IWCR	Q	I W C Resources Corp
IPC*N	N	Illinois Power Co Adj Rate Cum Pfd B		IWG	N	Iowa Illinois Gas & Electric
IPC*O	N	Illinois Power Co 8.52 Cum Pfd		IX	A	I R T Corp
IPC*P	N	Illinois Power Co 8% Cum Pfd		IYCOY	Q	I T O Yokado Co Ltd ADR
IPG	N	Interpublic Group of Cos Inc		J	N	Jackpot Enterprises Inc
IPL	N	Ipalco Enterprises Inc		JACO	Q	Jaco Electronics
IPLSA	Q	I P L Systems Inc Cl A		JAGRY	Q	Jaguar Plc ADR
IPM	A	I P M Technology Inc		JAIL	Q	Adtec Inc
IPT	N	I P Timberland Cl A Dep Units		JALC	Q	John Adams Life Corp
IPW	N	Interstate Power Co		JASN	Q	Jason Inc
IPW*	N	Interstate Power Co $2.28 Pfd		JAYJ	Q	Jay Jacobs Inc
IR	N	Ingersoll Rand Co		JBAK	Q	J Baker Inc
IRC	N	Inspiration Resources Corp		JBBB	Q	J B S Restaurants Inc
IRDV	Q	International Research Development Corp		JBHT	Q	J B Hunt Transport Services Inc
IRE	N	Integrated Resources Inc		JBM	A	Jan Bell Marketing Inc
IRE*C	N	Integrated Resources Inc Adj Rate Cum Pfd		JBNK	Q	Jefferson Bankshares Inc
IRE*D	N	Integrated Resources Inc $4.25 Cum Cv Pfd		JC	N	Jewelcor Inc
IRE*E	N	Integrated Resources $1.8125 Cum Cv Ex Pfd		JCBS	Q	Jacobson Stores Inc
				JCI	N	Johnson Controls Inc
IRF	N	International Rectifier Corp		JCOR	Q	Jacor Communications
IRIC	Q	Information Resources Inc		JCP	N	Penney J C Co Inc
IRIS	Q	International Remote		JEC	A	Jacobs Engineering Group Inc
IRON	Q	Ironstone Group Inc		JEFG	Q	Jefferies Group Inc
IRT	N	I R T Property Co		JEM	A	Jewelmasters Inc Cl A
IS	N	Interstate Johnson Lane Inc		JEP	N	Jepson Corp
ISBJ	Q	Interchange State Bank		JERR	Q	Jerrico Inc
ISEC	Q	Insituform Southeast Inc		JET	A	Jetronic Industries Inc
ISI	A	I S S Intl Service System Inc		JETS	Q	Jetborne Intl Inc
ISKO	Q	Isco Inc		JFFN	Q	Jefferson Bank
ISLH	Q	International Holding Capital Corp		JGIN	Q	J G Industries Inc
ISMX	Q	Isomedix Inc		JGRP	Q	Jesup Group Inc
ISN	A	Instron Corp		JH	N	Harland John H Co
ISPC	Q	Interspec Inc		JHI	N	John Hancock Investors Trust
ISR	A	Incstar Corp		JHM	N	J H M Mortgage Securities L P Pfd Units
ISS	N	Interco Inc		JHS	N	John Hancock Income Securities Trust
ISY	A	Instrument Systems Corp		JHSL	Q	John Hanson Savings Bank F S B
ISY*I	A	Instrument Systems Corp Cv 2nd Pfd I		JHSN	Q	Johnson Electronics Inc
IT	N	Intelogic Trace Inc		JII	N	Johnston Industries Inc
ITA	N	Italy Fund Inc		JIT	A	Frozen Food Express Industries Inc
ITB	N	International Thoroughbred Breeders Inc		JJS	A	Jumping Jacks Shoes Inc
ITB*A	A	International Thoroughbred Breeders Inc Cv Pfd A		JJSC	Q	Jefferson Smurfit Corp
				JJSF	Q	J & J Snack Food Corp
ITCC	Q	Industrial Training Corp		JKHY	Q	Jack Henry & Assoc Inc
ITCH	Q	Infotechnology Inc		JLGI	Q	J L G Industries Inc
ITG	N	Integra A Hotel & Restaurant Co		JLN	A	Jaclyn Inc
ITG*	N	Integra A Hotel & Restaurant Co Cum Div Cv Pfd		JLUBC	Q	Jiffy Lube Intl Inc
				JMBRS	Q	J M B Realty Trust S B I
ITGN	Q	Integon Corp		JMED	Q	Jones Medical Industries
ITGR	Q	Integra Financial Corp		JML	A	James Madison Ltd Cl A
ITI	A	International Telecharge Inc		JMLC	Q	James Madison Ltd
ITIC	Q	Investors Title Co		JMP	A	J M Peters Co Inc
ITL	N	Itel Corp		JMY	N	Jamesway Corp
ITL*C	N	Itel Corp $3.375 Cl B Ser C Cv Pfd		JNBK	Q	Jefferson National Bank
ITN	N	Intertan Inc		JNJ	N	Johnson & Johnson
ITRN	Q	Intertrans Corp		JNP	A	Americus Trust for J & J Shares Prime
ITSI	Q	International Totalizator Systems Inc		JNS	A	Americus Trust for J & J Shares Score
ITT	N	I T T Corp		JNU	A	Americus Trust for J & J Shares Units

JOB	A	General Employment Enterprises Inc
JOIN	Q	Jones Intercable Inc
JOINA	Q	Jones Intercable Inc Cl A
JOL	A	Joule Inc
JOR	N	Jorgenson Earle M Co
JOS	N	Jostens Inc
JOSL	Q	Joslyn Corp
JOSWD	N	Jostens Inc W D
JP	N	Jefferson Pilot Corp
JPC	A	Johnson Products Co Inc
JPI	N	J P Industries Inc
JPM	N	Morgan J P & Co Inc
JPM*A	N	Morgan J P & Co Inc Adj Cum Pfd A
JPS	A	Jones Plumbing Systems Inc
JR	N	James River Corp of Virginia
JR*K	N	James River Corp of Virginia Ser K $3.375 Cum Pfd
JR*L	N	James River Corp of Virginia Ser L $14.00 Cum Pfd
JRMX	Q	J R M Holdings Inc
JSBK	Q	Johnstown Savings Bank F S B
JSTN	Q	Justin Industries Inc
JTC	A	Jet Capital Corp
JTV	A	Jones Intercable Investors L P
JUNO	Q	Juno Lighting Inc
JWAIA	Q	Johnson Worldwide Associates Inc Cl A
JWC*	N	Jim Walter Corp 5% Cum Pfd
JWL	N	Jewel Co Inc
JWP	N	J W P Inc
JYP*	N	Jersey Central Power & Light 4% Cum Pfd
JYP*C	N	Jersey Central Power & Light 8.12% Cum Pfd
JYP*D	N	Jersey Central Power & Light 8% Cum Pfd
JYP*E	N	Jersey Central Power & Light 7.88% Cum Pfd
JYP*H	N	Jersey Central Power & Light 8.75% Pfd H
K	N	Kellogg Co
KAB	N	Kaneb Services Inc
KAB*A	N	Kaneb Services Inc Adj Rate Cum Pfd A
KAB*W	N	Kaneb Services Inc Adj Rate Cum Pfd A W D
KAMNA	Q	Kaman Corp Cl A Non Vtg
KAN	N	Kansas Power & Light Co
KAN*	N	Kansas Power & Light Co $2.32 Pfd
KASL	Q	Kasler Corp
KAY	A	Kay Corp
KBA	N	Kleinwort Benson Australian Income Fund Inc
KBALB	Q	Kimball Intl Inc Cl B
KBH	N	Kaufman & Broad Home Corp
KCH	A	Ketchum & Co Inc
KCS	A	Conston Corp Cl A
KCSG	Q	K C S Group Inc
KDNY	Q	Home Intensive Care Inc
KDON	Q	Kaydon Corp
KDP	A	Americus Trust for Kodak Shares Prime
KDS	A	Americus Trust for Kodak Shares Score
KDU	A	Americus Trust for Kodak Shares Units
KE	A	Koger Equity Inc
KEA	A	Keane Inc
KEC	A	Kent Electronics Corp
KEI	A	Kiethley Instruments Inc
KELYA	Q	Kelly Services Inc Cl A
KELYB	Q	Kelly Services Inc Cl B
KEM	N	Kemper Corp
KENCA	Q	Kentucky Central Life Ins Co Cl A Non Vtg
KEP	N	Kaneb Energy Partners Ltd

KEQU	Q	Kewaunee Scientific Equipment Corp
KES	N	Keystone Consolidated Industries
KEVN	Q	Kimmins Environmental Service Corp
KEX	A	Kirby Exploration Co Inc
KEY	N	Keycorp
KEYC	Q	Key Centurian Bankshares Inc
KF	N	Korea Fund Inc
KFV	N	Quest for Value Dual Purpose Fund Inc Capital Shares
KFV*	N	Quest for Value Dual Purpose Fund Inc Shares
KGE	N	Kansas Gas & Electric Co
KGE*	A	Kansas Gas & Electric Co 4 1 2% Pfd
KGM	N	Kerr Glass Manufacturing Corp
KGM*D	N	Kerr Glass Manufacturing Corp $1.70 Cum Cv Pfd D
KGT	N	Kemper Intermediate Government Trust
KH	N	K H Corp
KH*A	N	K H Corp $3.68 Cum Ex Pfd A
KHGI	Q	Keystone Heritage Group Inc
KHI	N	Kemper High Income Trust
KHLR	Q	Kahler Corp
KII	N	Keystone Intl Inc
KIN	A	Kin Ark Corp
KIND	Q	Kinder Care Learning Centers Inc
KIT	N	Kit Manufacturing Co
KITS	Q	Meridian Diagnostics Inc
KIX	A	Kerkhoff Industries Inc
KJI	N	Kay Jewelers Inc
KKP	A	Americus Trust for Coca Cola Shares Prime
KKS	A	Americus Trust for Coca Cola Shares Score
KKU	A	Americus Trust for Coca Cola Shares Units
KLAC	Q	K L A Instruments Corp
KLIC	Q	Kulicke & Soffa Industries Inc
KLLM	Q	K L L M Transport Services Inc
KLM	N	K L M Royal Dutch Airlines
KLT	N	Kansas City Power & Light Co
KLT*A	N	Kansas City Power & Light Co $3.80 Cum Pfd A
KLT*D	N	Kansas City Power & Light Co 4.35% Cum Pfd D
KLT*E	N	Kansas City Power & Light Co 4.50% Cum Pfd E
KLT*F	N	Kansas City Power & Light Co $2.33 Cum Pfd F
KLT*G	N	Kansas City Power & Light Co $2.20 Cum Pfd G
KLY	A	Kelly Oil & Gas Partners Ltd
KM	N	K Mart Corp
KMAG	Q	Komag Inc
KMB	N	Kimberly Clark Corp
KMDC	Q	Kirschner Medical Corp
KMG	N	Kerr Mc Gee Corp
KML	A	Carmel Container Systems Ltd Ord
KMM	N	Kemper Multimarket Income Trust
KMSI	Q	K M S Industries Inc
KMT	N	Kennametal Inc
KMW	A	K M W Systems Corp
KNAP	Q	Knape & Vogt Manufacturing Co
KNCI	Q	Kinetic Concepts Inc
KNDR	Q	Kinder Care Inc
KNE	N	K N Energy Inc
KNO	N	Knogo Corp
KNOWD	N	Knogo Corp W D
KO	N	Coca Cola Co
KOA	A	Koala Technologies Corp
KOE	N	Koehring Co

KOG	N	Koger Properties Inc	LCIC	Q	Leisure Concepts Inc
KOL	N	Kollmorgen Corp	LCLD	Q	Laclede Steel Co
KOSM	Q	Cascade Intl Inc	LCNB	Q	Lincoln Bancorp
KOSS	Q	Koss Corp	LCSI	Q	L C S Industries Inc
KPA	A	Kappa Network Inc	LDBC	Q	L D B Corp
KPCI	Q	Key Production Co	LDDSA	Q	L D D S Communications Inc Cl A
KPE	N	Columbia Pictures Entertainment Inc	LDDSW	Q	L D D S Communications Inc Wts 10 20 89
KPI	A	Killearn Properties Inc	LDG	N	Longs Drug Stores
KPP	N	Kaneb Pipeline Partners L P	LDGX	Q	Logistix Inc
KPTL	Q	Keptel Inc	LDIC	Q	L D I Corp
KR	N	Kroger Co	LDL	A	Lydall Inc
KRI	N	Knight Ridder Inc	LDMFA	Q	Laidlaw Transportation Ltd Cl A
KRSL	Q	Kreisler Manufacturing Co	LDMFB	Q	Laidlaw Transportation Ltd Cl B
KRUG	Q	Krug Intl Corp	LDMK	Q	Landmark Bank for Savings
KSF	N	Quaker State Corp	LDP	A	Americus Trust for G T E Shares Prime
KSM	N	Kemper Strategic Municipal Income Trust	LDS	A	Americus Trust for G T E Shares Score
KSS	A	Kessler Products Ltd	LDU	A	Americus Trust for G T E Shares Units
KSTN	Q	Keystone Financial Inc	LE	N	Lands End Inc
KSU	N	Kansas City Southern Industries	LEAF	Q	Interleaf Inc
KSU*	N	Kansas City Southern Industries 4% Pfd	LECH	Q	Lechters Inc
KT	N	Katy Industries	LECT	Q	Lectec Corp
KT*B	N	Katy Industries $1.46 Cum Cv Pfd B	LEDA	Q	Lee Data Corp
KTCC	Q	Key Tronic Corp	LEE	N	Lee Enterprises Inc
KTCO	Q	Kenan Transport Co	LEG	N	Leggett & Platt Inc
KTF	N	Kemper Municipal Income Trust	LEIX	Q	Lowrance Electronics Inc
KTII	Q	K Tron Intl Inc	LEM	N	Lehman Corp
KTM	A	Ketema Inc	LEN	N	Lennar Corp
KU	N	Kentucky Utilities Co	LENS	Q	Concord Camera Corp
KUB	N	Kubota Ltd ADR	LEO	N	Dreyfus Strategic Municipals Inc
KUH	N	Kuhlman Corp	LEPGY	Q	L E P Group Plc ADR
KUST	Q	Kustom Electronics Inc	LES	N	Leslie Fay
KV	A	K V Pharmaceuticals Co	LEXB	Q	Lexington Savings Bank
KVLM	Q	Kevlin Microwave Corp	LEXI	Q	Lexicon Corp
KVU	A	Kleer Vu Industries Inc	LEXP	Q	Lexington Precision Corp
KWD	N	Kellwood Co	LFA	A	Littlefield Adams & Co
KWIKF	Q	Kwik Products Intl Corp	LFB	N	Longview Fibre Co
KWN	A	Kenwin Shops Inc	LFC	N	Lomas Financial Corp
KWP	N	King World Productions Inc	LFE	N	L F E Corp
KWPWD	N	King World Productions Inc W D	LFIN	Q	Lincoln Financial Corp
KYC	A	Keystone Camera Products	LFSA	Q	First Federal S & L Assn of Lenawee County
KYCWB	A	Keystone Camera Products Wts 1991	LFT	N	Lifetime Corp
KYCWS	A	Keystone Camera Products Wts	LG	N	Laclede Gas Co
KYMDA	Q	Kentucky Medical Insurance Co Cl A	LGL	A	Lynch Corp
KYO	N	Kyocera Corp ADR	LGN	N	Logicon Inc
KZ	N	Kysor Industrial Corp	LGNT	Q	Legent Corp
LA	N	L A Gear Inc	LGS	N	Louisiana General Services Inc
LAB	A	Nichols Institute	LGSWD	N	Louisiana General Services Inc W D
LABB	A	Beauty Labs Inc	LHC	N	L & N Housing Corp
LABL	Q	Multi Color Corp	LIBHA	Q	Liberty Homes Inc Cl A
LAC	N	Lac Minerals Ltd	LIBHB	Q	Liberty Homes Inc Cl B
LADF	Q	Ladd Furniture Inc	LICF	Q	Long Island City Financial Corp
LAF	N	Lafarge Corp	LICIA	Q	Lilly Industrial Coatings Inc Cl A
LAFCB	Q	Loan America Financial Corp Cl B	LIFE	Q	Lifeline Systems Inc
LAKE	Q	Lakeland Industries Inc	LIG	N	Liggett Group Inc
LAN	A	Lancer Corp	LII	A	Larizza Industries
LANC	Q	Lancaster Colony Corp	LIL	N	Long Island Lighting
LAS	A	Laser Industries Ltd	LIL*B	N	Long Island Lighting 5% Cum Pfd B
LASR	Q	Laser Precision Corp	LIL*E	N	Long Island Lighting 4.35% Cum Pfd E
LAT	A	Latshaw Enterprises Inc	LIL*I	N	Long Island Lighting 5 3 4% Cum Cv Pfd I
LAW	N	Lawter Intl Inc	LIL*J	N	Long Island Lighting 8.12% Cum Pfd J
LAWS	Q	Lawson Products Inc	LIL*K	N	Long Island Lighting 8.30% Cum Pfd K
LB	A	La Barge Inc	LIL*O	N	Long Island Lighting $2.47 Cum Pfd O
LBC	N	Landmark Bancshares Corp	LIL*P	N	Long Island Lighting $2.43 Cum Pfd P
LC	N	Liberty Corp	LIL*S	N	Long Island Lighting 9.80% Pfd S
LCBI	Q	Landmark Community Bancorp Inc	LIL*T	N	Long Island Lighting $3.31 Pfd T
LCBM	Q	Lifecore Biomedical Inc	LIL*U	N	Long Island Lighting $4.25 Cum Pfd U
LCE	N	Lone Star Industries Inc	LIL*V	N	Long Island Lighting $3.50 Cum Pfd V

LIL*W	N	Long Island Lighting $3.52 Cum Pfd W
LIL*X	N	Long Island Lighting $3.50 Pfd X
LINB	Q	Lin Broadcasting Corp
LIND	Q	Lindberg Corp
LINN	Q	Lincoln Food Services Product Inc
LINZ	Q	Lindsay Manufacturing Co
LIO	A	Lionel Corp
LIPO	Q	Liposome Co Inc
LIQB	Q	Liqui Box Corp
LIT	N	Litton Industries
LIT*B	N	Litton Industries $2.00 Cum Cv Pfd B
LIVE	Q	Live Entertainment Inc
LIZC	Q	Liz Claiborne Inc
LJC	A	La Jolla Bancorp
LK	N	Lockheed Corp
LKI	A	Lazare Kaplan Inc
LLB	A	Computrac Computer Inc
LLEC	N	Long Lake Energy Corp
LLOG	Q	Lincoln Logs Ltd
LLSL	Q	Lakeland First Financial Group Inc
LLTC	Q	Linear Technology Inc
LLX	N	Louisiana Land & Exploration Co
LLY	N	Lilly Eli & Co
LLYWS	N	Lilly Eli & Co Wts
LM	N	Legg Mason Inc
LMC	N	Lomas Mortgage Corp
LMED	Q	Lyphomed Inc
LMG	A	Lawson Mardon Group Ltd
LMK	N	Lifemark Corp
LML	A	Landmark Land Co Inc
LMR	N	Lamaur Inc
LMRK	Q	Landmark Graphics Corp
LMS	N	Lamson & Sessions Co
LNBC	Q	Liberty National Bancorp Inc
LNC	N	Lincoln National Corp
LNC*	N	Lincoln National Corp $3.00 Cum Cv Pfd A
LNCE	Q	Lance Inc North Carolina
LND	N	Lincoln National Income Fund Inc
LNDL	Q	Lindal Cedar Homes Inc
LNSB	Q	Lincoln Savings Bank
LNV	N	Lincoln National Cv Securities Fund Inc
LOC	N	Loctite Corp
LOG	N	Rayonier Timberlands L P Cl A Dep Units
LOGC	Q	Logic Devices Inc
LOM	N	Lomas Nettleton Mortgage Investors S B I
LOMWS	N	Lomas Nettleton Mortgage Investors Wts
LOR	N	Loral Corp
LOTS	Q	Lotus Development Corp
LOU	N	Louisville Gas & Electric Co
LOW	N	Lowes Cos Inc
LOYC	Q	Loyola Capital Corp
LPAI	Q	La Petite Academy Inc
LPF	A	Landsing Pacific Fund
LPH	A	Lee Pharmaceuticals
LPL*	N	Louisiana Power & Light Co 12.64% Cum Pfd
LPLI	Q	L P L Technologies Inc Cl A
LPO	A	Linpro Specified Properties S B I
LPT	N	Lear Petroleum Corp
LPX	N	Louisiana Pacific Corp
LQ	A	Laurentain Capital Corp
LQM	N	La Quinta Motor Inns
LQP	N	La Quinta Motor Inns Partnership
LRC	A	Lori Corp
LRCX	Q	Lam Research Corp
LRF	A	Lincoln N C Realty Fund Inc
LRFWS	A	Lincoln N C Realty Fund Inc Wts W I

LRI	N	Lea Ronal Inc
LRT	N	L L & E Royalty Trust U B I
LSA	A	Landmark Savings Assn
LSB	A	L S B Industries Inc
LSB*C	A	L S B Industries Inc Ser 1 Cv Exch Cl C Pfd
LSC	A	Shopco Laurel Center L P
LSCO	Q	Lesco Inc
LSER	Q	Laser Corp
LSF	N	Lomas Mortgage Securities Fund Inc
LSI	N	L S I Logic Corp
LSNB	Q	Lake Shore Bancorp
LSST	Q	Lone Technologies Inc
LTD	N	Limited The Inc
LTEC	Q	Lincoln Telecommunications Co
LTEK	Q	Life Technology Inc
LTG	A	Catalina Lighting Co
LTIZ	Q	Liposome Technology Inc
LTR	N	Loews Corp
LTV	N	L T V Corp
LTV*	N	L T V Corp $5.00 Cum Pfd A
LTV*B	N	L T V Corp $3.06 Cum Cv Pfd B
LTV*C	N	L T V Corp $5.25 Cum Cv Pfd
LTV*D	N	L T V Corp $1.25 Cum Cv Pfd
LTXX	Q	L T X Corp
LUB	N	Lubys Cafeterias Inc
LUC	N	Lukens Inc
LUK	N	Leucadia National Corp
LUK*G	N	Leucadia National Corp Adj Rate Cum Pfd G
LUM	A	Lumex Inc
LUND	Q	Lund Enterprises Inc
LUR	A	Lauria L & Sons Inc
LUSK	Q	Luskins Inc
LUV	N	Southwest Airlines Co
LVC	N	Lillian Vernon Corp
LVI	N	L V I Group Inc
LVI*	N	L V I Group Inc 2.0625 Cum Cv Pfd
LVMHY	Q	L V M H Moet Hennessy Louis Vuitton ADR
LVX	N	Leisure Technology Inc
LVX*	N	Leisure Technology Inc $2.25 Cum Cv Exch Pfd
LWR	A	Lawrence Insurance Group Inc
LXBK	Q	L S B Bancshares Inc
LYO	N	Lyondell Petrochemical Co
LYTS	Q	L S I Lighting Systems Inc
LZ	N	Lubrizol Corp
LZB	N	La Z Boy Chair Co
M	N	M Corp
M*A	N	M Corp $3.50 Cum Cv Pfd
MA	N	May Department Stores
MAAR	Q	Marcor Resorts Inc
MAB	A	Mangood Corp
MABC	Q	Mid America Bancorp
MACD	Q	Mac Dermid Inc
MACK	Q	Mack Trucks Inc
MAG	N	Magnetek Inc
MAGAF	Q	Magna Intl Inc Cl A Sub Vtg
MAGI	Q	Magna Group Inc
MAH	N	M A Hanna Co
MAHI	Q	Monarch Avalon Inc
MAI	N	M A Com Inc
MAIL	Q	Mail Boxes Etc
MAIR	Q	Metro Airlines
MAJL	Q	Michael Anthony Jewelers Inc
MAJR	Q	Major Realty Corp
MAKL	Q	Markel Corp
MALC	Q	Mallard Coach Co Inc
MALTZ	Q	Management Assistant Inc Liquidating Trust

U B I
MANA	Q	Manatron Inc
MANT	Q	Manitowoc Co Inc
MAP	A	Maine Public Service Co
MAR	N	Marcade Group Inc
MARC	Q	M A R C Inc
MARS	Q	Marsh Supermarkets Inc
MAS	N	Masco Corp
MASB	Q	Massbank for Savings
MASX	Q	Masco Industries
MAT	N	Mattel Inc
MATWS	N	Mattel Inc Wts
MAXC	Q	Maxco Inc
MAXE	Q	Max & Ermas Restaurant Inc
MAXEW	Q	Max & Ermas Restaurants Inc 10 7 89 Wts
MAYS	Q	J W Mays Inc
MBC	N	Mickelberry Corp
MBF	N	M A I Basic Four Inc
MBI	N	M B I A Inc
MBK	N	Mitsubishi Bank Ltd ADR
MBLA	Q	National Mercantile Bancorp
MBLE	Q	Mobile Gas Service
MBN	A	Metrobank N A
MBNY	Q	Merchants Bank of New York
MBP	A	Americus Trust for Mobil Shares Prime
MBS	A	Americus Trust for Mobil Shares Score
MBU	A	Americus Trust for Mobil Shares Units
MBVT	Q	Merchants Bancshares Inc
MBY	A	Middleby Corp
MC	N	Matsushita Electric Industrial Co Ltd ADR
MCA	N	M C A Inc
MCAWA	Q	Mc Caw Cellular Communications Cl A
MCBKA	Q	Merchants Capital Corp Cl A
MCBKB	Q	Merchants Capital Corp Cl B
MCC	N	Mestek Inc
MCCL	Q	Mc Clain Industries Inc
MCCRK	Q	Mc Cormick Co Non Vtg
MCCS	Q	Medco Containment Services Inc
MCD	N	Mc Donalds Corp
MCDY	Q	Microdyne Corp
MCFE	Q	Mc Farland Energy Inc
MCH	A	Medchem Products Inc
MCHN	Q	Merchants National Corp
MCI	A	Massmutual Corporate Investors Inc
MCIC	Q	M C I Communications Corp
MCK	N	Mc Kesson Corp
MCK*	N	Mc Kesson Corp $1.80 Cum Cv Pfd A
MCL	N	Moore Corp Ltd
MCN	N	M C N Corp Holding Co
MCN*	N	Michigan Consolidated Gas Co $2.50 Cum Pfd
MCOM	Q	Midwest Communications Corp
MCON	Q	E M C O N Associates
MCOR	Q	Marine Corp
MCR	N	M F S Charter Income Trust
MCRN	Q	Micron Technology
MCRS	Q	Micros Systems Inc
MCU	A	Magma Copper Co Cl B
MCUWS	A	Magma Copper Co Wts
MCX	A	M C Shipping Inc
MD	N	Mc Donnell Douglas Corp
MDA	N	Mapco Inc
MDC	N	M D C Holdings Inc
MDCI	Q	Medical Action Industries Inc
MDCO	Q	Marine Drilling Co
MDD	N	Mc Donald & Co Investments Inc
MDE*A	N	Mc Dermott Intl Inc $2.20 Cum Cv Pfd A
MDE*B	N	Mc Dermott Intl Inc $2.60 Cum Cv Pfd B
MDEV	Q	Medical Devices
MDEX	Q	Medex Inc
MDIN	Q	Medalist Industries Inc
MDK	A	Medicore Inc
MDMWS	A	Morgan J P & Co Wts
MDP	N	Meredith Corp
MDR	N	Mc Dermott Intl Inc
MDRWS	N	Mc Dermott Intl Inc Wts
MDSN	Q	Madison Gas & Electric Co
MDST	Q	Medstat Systems Inc
MDT	N	Medtronic Inc
MDTA	Q	Megadata Corp
MDTC	Q	M D T Corp
MDU	N	M D U Resources Group Inc
MDW	N	Midway Airlines Inc
MDXR	Q	Medar Inc
MDY	A	Morgan Drive Away Inc
MEA	N	Mead Corp
MED	A	Mediq Inc
MED*	A	Mediq Inc Dep Pfd
MEDC	Q	Medical Care Intl Inc
MEGA	A	Media General Inc Cl A
MEI	N	M E I Diversified Inc
MEL	N	Mellon Bank Corp
MEL*A	N	Mellon Bank Corp $2.80 Pfd A
MEL*B	N	Mellon Bank Corp Pfd B
MEM	A	M E M Co Inc
MEN	N	Munienhanced Fund Inc
MENT	Q	Mentor Graphics Corp
MER	N	Merrill Lynch Co Inc
MERY	Q	Merry Land & Investment Co Inc
MES	N	Melville Corp
MESA	Q	Mesa Airlines Inc
MET	A	Metropolitan Realty Corp
METB	Q	Metropolitan Bancorp Inc
METC	Q	Metcalf & Eddy Co Inc
METHA	Q	Methode Electronics Inc Cl A
METHB	Q	Methode Electronics Inc Cl B
METS	Q	Met Coil Systems Corp
MEYR	Q	Meyer Fred Inc
MF	N	Malaysia Fund Inc
MFAC	Q	Market Facts Inc
MFBZ	Q	Mutual Federal Savings Bank A Stock Corp
MFC	N	Metropolitan Financial Corp
MFC*A	N	Metropolitan Financial Corp $2.00 Cum Cv Pfd
MFCO	Q	Microwave Filter Co Inc
MFD	N	Munford Inc
MFED	Q	Maury Federal Savings Bank
MFFC	Q	Mayflower Financial Corp
MFGC	Q	Midwest Financial Group
MFGR	Q	Metrobank Financial Group Inc
MFLR	Q	Mayflower Co Operative Bank
MFM	N	M F S Municipal Income Trust
MFN	N	Mercury Finance Co
MFO	N	M F S Income Opportunity Trust
MFSB	Q	Pinnacle Bancorp Inc
MFSL	Q	Maryland Federal S & L Assn
MFT	N	M F S Multimarket Total Return Trust
MFTN	Q	Metropolitan Federal S & L Assn
MGC	N	Morgan Grenfell Smallcap Fund
MGCC	Q	Medical Graphics Corp
MGF	N	M F S Government Market Income Trust
MGI	N	M G I Properties
MGLL	Q	Mc Gill Manufacturing Co Inc
MGM	N	M G M U A Communications Co

MGMA	Q	Magma Power Co
MGN	N	Morgan Products Ltd
MGNC	Q	Mediagenic
MGP	A	Merchants Group Inc
MGR	N	Mc Graw Edison Co
MGRC	Q	Mc Grath Rent Corp
MGRE	Q	Merry Go Round Enterprises Inc
MGT	A	Mac Gregor Team Sports
MH	N	M H I Group Inc
MHBK	Q	Mid Hudson Savings Bank F S B
MHC	N	Manufacturers Hanover Corp
MHC*	N	Manufacturers Hanover Corp Cum Adj Pfd
MHC*B	N	Manufacturers Hanover Corp Cum Adj Pfd B
MHCO	Q	Moore Handsen Andley Inc
MHF	N	Municipal High Income Fund Inc
MHG	A	Malartic Hygrade Mines Canada Ltd
MHP	N	Mc Graw Hill Inc
MHS	N	Marriott Corp
MI	N	Marshall Industries
MIAM	Q	Mid American National Bank & Trust
MICA	Q	Microage Inc
MIDC	Q	Mid Conn Bank
MIDL	Q	Midlantic Corp
MIDS	Q	Mid South Insurance Co
MIF	A	Muni Insured Fund Inc
MIGI	Q	Meridian Insurance Group Inc
MIHO	Q	M I Schottenstein Home Inc
MII	N	Morton Intl Inc
MIKA	Q	Medical Imaging Centers of America Inc
MIKL	Q	Michael Foods Inc
MIL	N	Millipore Corp
MILL	Q	Millicom Inc
MILT	Q	Miltope Group Inc
MILW	Q	Milwaukee Insurance Group Inc
MIN	N	M F S Intermediate Income Trust
MIND	Q	Mindscape Inc
MINYE	Q	Miniscribe Corp
MIP	A	Mortgage Investment Plus Inc
MITSY	Q	Mitsui & Co Ltd ADR
MK	N	Mark Controls Corp
MKC	N	Marion Laboratories
MKCO	Q	M Kamenstein Inc
MKE	A	Michaels Stores Inc
MKP	A	Americus Trust for Merck Shares Prime
MKS	A	Americus Trust for Merck Shares Score
MKTAY	Q	Makita Electric Works Ltd ADR
MKU	A	Americus Trust for Merck Shares Units
ML	N	Martin Marietta Corp
MLA	A	Midland Co
MLC	N	Manhattan National Corp
MLHR	Q	Miller Herman Inc
MLIS	Q	Micropolis Corp
MLK	A	Matlack Systems Inc
MLLE	Q	Martin Lawrence Ltd Editions Inc
MLP	N	Mesa L P
MLP*A	N	Mesa L P Pfd A
MLRC	N	Mallon Resources Corp
MLT	N	Mitel Corp
MLTF	Q	Multibank Financial Corp
MLW	N	Miller Wohl Co Inc
MLXX	Q	M L X Corp
MM*A	N	Marine Midland Banks Inc Adj Cum Pfd A
MMA	A	Medical Management of America Inc
MMBLF	Q	Mac Millan Bloedell Ltd
MMC	N	Marsh & Mc Lennan Cos Inc
MMD	A	Moore Medical Corp
MMEDC	Q	Multimedia Inc New

MMIM	Q	M M I Medical Inc
MMM	N	Minnesota Mining & Manufacturing Co
MMO	N	Monarch Machine Tool Co
MMP	A	Americus Trust for 3 M Shares Prime
MMPI	Q	Marquest Medical Products Inc
MMRH	Q	M M R Holding Corp
MMS	A	Americus Trust for 3 M Shares Score
MMSB	Q	Mid Maine Savings Bank F S B
MMT	N	M F S Multimarket Income Trust
MMU	A	Americus Trust for 3 M Shares Units
MMZA	A	Metro Mobile C T S Inc Cl A
MMZB	A	Metro Mobile C T S Inc Cl B
MNBC	Q	Mimers National Bancorp Inc
MNC	N	M N C Financial Inc
MNCO	Q	Michigan National Corp
MND	A	Mitchell Energy Development Corp
MNE	A	Monumental Energy Services Inc
MNES	Q	Mine Safety Appliances Co
MNH	A	Manufactured Home Inc Cl A
MNI	N	Mc Clatchy Newspapers Inc Cl A
MNPI	Q	Microcom Inc
MNR	N	Manor Care Inc
MNRTS	Q	Monmouth Real Estate Investment Trust S B I
MNS	A	Mac Neal Schwendler
MNT	N	Montedison S P A ADS
MNT*	N	Montedison S P A Ordinary ADS
MNTL	Q	Manufacturers National Corp
MNTR	Q	Mentor Corp
MNTX	Q	Minntech Corp
MNXI	Q	M N X Inc
MO	N	Philip Morris Cos Inc Holding Co
MOB	N	Mobil Corp
MOBI	Q	Molecular Biosystems Inc
MOCO	Q	Modern Controls Inc
MODI	Q	Modine Manufacturing Co
MOGA	A	Moog Inc Cl A
MOGB	A	Moog Inc Cl B
MOGN	Q	Molecular Genetics Inc
MOIL	Q	Maynard Oil Co
MOLE	Q	Flow Mole Corp
MOLX	Q	Molex Inc
MON	N	Monarch Capital Corp
MON*A	N	Monarch Capital Corp $5.00 Ser Pfd
MOR	N	Morgan Keegan Inc
MORF	Q	Mor Flow Industries Inc
MORP	Q	Moore Products Co
MORR	Q	Morrison Inc
MOS	N	Mesa Offshore Trust U B I
MOSI	Q	Mosinee Paper Corp
MOT	N	Motorola Inc
MOTO	Q	Moto Photo Inc
MOTOP	Q	Moto Photo Inc Cum Cv Pfd
MOTOZ	Q	Moto Photo Inc 11 25 90 Wts
MOTR	Q	Motor Club of America
MPAC	Q	Impact Systems Inc
MPB	A	Metropolitan Circuits Inc
MPH	N	Murphy G C Co
MPL	N	Minnesota Power & Light Co
MPL*A	N	Minnesota Power & Light Co 5% Pfd A
MPL*B	N	Minnesota Power & Light Co $7.36 Pfd B
MPMTS	Q	Mellon Partic Mtge Trust Comm Prop S B I
MPN*A	A	Monongahela Power Co 4.40% Pfd A
MPN*C	A	Monongahela Power Co 4.50% Pfd C
MPP	A	Medical Properties Inc
MPP*	A	Medical Properties Inc Pfd
MPR	A	Met Pro Corp

MPSG	Q	M P S I Systems Inc
MPV	N	Massmutual Participation Investors
MR	A	Morgan Foods Inc
MRAC	Q	Microamerica Inc
MRBK	Q	Mercantile Bankshares Corp
MRBL	Q	Marble Financial Corp
MRC	N	Milton Roy Co
MRCC	Q	Mark Controls Corp
MRCS	Q	Marcus Corp
MRCY	Q	Mercury General Corp
MRDN	Q	Meridian Bankcorp Inc
MRET	Q	Meret Inc
MRGC	Q	M R Gasket Co
MRGO	Q	Margo Nursery Farms Inc
MRIA	A	Mc Rae Industries Inc Cl A
MRIB	A	Mc Rae Industries Inc Cl B
MRIS	Q	Marshall & Ilsley Corp
MRK	N	Merck & Co Inc
MRLL	Q	Merrill Corp
MRM	A	Merrimac Industries Inc
MRMK	Q	Merrimack Bancorp Inc
MRN	N	Morrison Knudsen Corp Holding Co
MRP	A	Mission Resource Partners L P Units
MRT	N	Mortgage & Realty Trust S B I
MRTA	Q	Marietta Corp
MRTN	Q	Marten Transport Ltd
MRTWS	A	Mortgage & Realty Trust S B I Wts
MS	N	Morgan Stanley Group Inc
MSA	N	Medusa Corp
MSAI	Q	Management Science America Inc
MSAM	Q	Marsam Pharmaceuticals Inc
MSB	N	Mesabi Trust Ctfs of Beneficial Interest
MSBI	Q	Monyclair Bancorp Inc
MSBK	Q	Medford Savings Bank
MSC	A	Material Sciences Corp
MSCA	Q	M S Carriers Inc
MSCC	Q	Micro Semi Corp
MSCM	Q	M O S C O M Corp
MSCO	Q	Masstor Systems Corp
MSEX	Q	Middlesex Water Co
MSFT	Q	Microsoft Corp
MSHK	Q	Medstone Intl Inc
MSII	Q	Medicine Shoppe Intl Inc
MSL	N	Mercury S & L Assn
MSM	A	Motts Super Markets Inc
MSR	A	M S R Exploration Ltd
MSRR	Q	Midsouth Corp
MSSB	Q	Mid State Federal Savings Bank
MST	N	Mercantile Stores Co Inc
MSTI	Q	Medical Sterilization Inc
MSW	A	Missionwest Properties Inc
MT	N	Meditrust S B I
MTBS	Q	Metro Bancshares
MTC	N	Monsanto Co
MTCL	Q	First National Bank Corp
MTE	A	M I T E Corp
MTIK	Q	Miller Building Systems Inc
MTIX	Q	Mechanical Technology Inc
MTL	Q	Materials Research Corp
MTLI	Q	Marine Transport Lines Inc
MTN	A	Mountain Medical Equipment Inc
MTNR	Q	Mountaineer Bancshares of West Virginia
MTOR	Q	Meritor Savings Bank
MTP	N	Montana Power Co
MTR	N	Mesa Royalty Trust U B I
MTRC	Q	Mercantile Bancorp
MTRM	Q	Moniterm Corp

MTRO	Q	Metro Tel Corp
MTS	N	Montgomery Street Income Securities Inc
MTSC	Q	M T S Systems Corp
MTT*C	N	Metropolitan Edison 3.90% Cum Pfd C
MTT*F	N	Metropolitan Edison 8.12% Cum Pfd F
MTT*G	N	Metropolitan Edison 7.68% Cum Pfd G
MTT*H	N	Metropolitan Edison 8.32% Cum Pfd H
MTT*I	N	Metropolitan Edison 8.12% Cum Pfd I
MTT*J	N	Metropolitan Edison 8.32% Cum Pfd J
MTTL	Q	Mobile Telecommunications Technologies Corp
MTWN	Q	Mark Twain Bancshares Inc
MTWO	Q	Melamine Chemicals Inc
MTY	A	Marlton Technologies Inc
MUEL	Q	Mueller Paul Co
MUN	N	Munsingwear Inc
MUO	N	Mutual of Omaha Interest Shares Inc
MUR	N	Murphy Oil Corp
MUTU	Q	Mutual Federal S & L Assn
MVBC	Q	Mission Valley Bancorp
MVF	A	Munivest Fund Inc
MVL	N	Manville Corp
MVL*	N	Manville Corp $1.00 Cum Pfd
MVLWS	N	Manville Corp Wts
MW	N	Matthews & Wright Group Inc
MWAV	Q	Microwave Labs Inc
MWE	N	Midwest Energy Co
MWGP	Q	Midwest Grain Products Inc
MWSB	Q	Mountain West Savings Bank F S B
MX	N	Measurex Corp
MXC	A	Matec Corp
MXF	N	Mexico Fund Inc
MXFWD	N	Mexico Fund Inc W D
MXIM	Q	Maxim Integrated Products Inc
MXM	A	Maxxam Inc
MXS	N	Maxus Energy Corp
MXS*	N	Maxus Energy Corp $4.00 Cum Cv Pfd
MXTR	Q	Max Tor Corp
MXWL	Q	Maxwell Labs Inc
MYCO	Q	Mycogen Corp
MYE	A	Myers Industries Inc
MYFRA	Q	Mayfair Supermarkets Inc Cl A
MYG	N	Maytag Corp
MYL	N	Mylan Laboratories Inc
MYM	N	M O N Y Real Estate Investors
MYR	N	Myers L E Co Group
MZ	N	Macy Acquiring Corp
N	N	I N C O Co Ltd
NAB	N	National Australia Bank Ltd ADS
NAC*A	N	National Can Corp $1.50 Cum Cv Pfd A
NAFC	Q	Nash Finch Co
NAIG	Q	National Insurance Group
NAMC	Q	North American National Corp
NAN	A	Nantucket Industries Inc
NANO	Q	Nanometrics Inc
NAPE	Q	National Properties Corp
NAS	A	Nasta Intl
NATL	Q	North Atlantic Industries
NATR	Q	Natures Sunshine Products Inc
NAV	N	Navistar Intl Corp Hldg Co
NAV*D	N	Navistar Intl Corp Hldg Co Cv Jr Pfd D
NAV*G	N	Navistar Intl Corp Hldg Co $6.00 Cum Cv Pfd Ser G
NAVG	Q	Navigator Group Inc
NAVI	Q	North American Ventures Inc
NAVWA	N	Navistar Intl Corp Hldg Co Wts A
NAVWB	N	Navistar Intl Corp Hldg Co Wts B

NAVWC	N	Navistar Intl Corp Hldg Co Wts C
NBAK	Q	National Bancorp of Alaska Inc
NBB	N	N B B Bancorp Inc
NBCC	Q	National Banc of Commerce Co
NBCTC	Q	National Bancshares Corp of Texas
NBD	N	N B D Bancorp Inc
NBF	A	Northbay Financial Corp
NBI	N	N B I Inc
NBIC	Q	Northeast Bancorp Inc
NBIO	Q	North American Biologicals Inc
NBL	A	Noble Affiliates Inc
NBR	A	Nabors Industries Inc
NBRWS	A	Nabors Industries Inc Wts
NBSC	Q	New Brunswick Scientific Co
NBTY	Q	Natures Bounty Inc
NC	N	Nacco Corp Cl A
NCA	N	Nuveen California Municipal Value Fund Inc
NCB	N	N C N B Corp
NCBC	Q	National Commerce Bancorp
NCBM	Q	National City Bancorp
NCBR	Q	National Community Bank Inc
NCC	N	National City Corp
NCD	A	North Canadian Oils Ltd
NCEL	Q	Nationwide Cellular Service Inc
NCELW	Q	Nationwide Cellular Service Inc Wts 5 4 92
NCH	N	N C H Corp
NCL	A	Nichols S E Inc
NCM	N	Nuveen California Municipal Income Fund
NCMC	Q	National Capital Management Corp
NCN	A	Norcen Energy Resources Ltd
NCNA	A	Norcen Energy Resources Ltd Sub Flt Ordinary Shares
NCNG	Q	North Carolina Natural Gas Corp
NCR	N	N C R Corp
NCS	N	National Convenience Stores Inc
NDCO	Q	Noble Drilling Corp
NDSN	Q	Nordson Corp
NDTA	Q	National Data Corp
NEB	N	Bank of New England
NEBS	Q	New England Business Inc
NEC	N	National Education Corp
NECC	Q	New England Critical Care Inc
NEEC	Q	N E E C O Inc
NEG	A	National Environment Inc
NEI	N	National Enterprises Inc
NELL	Q	Nellcor Inc
NEM	N	Newmont Mining Corp
NEMWD	N	Newmont Mining Corp W D
NER	N	N E R C O Inc
NERX	Q	Neorx Corp
NES	N	New England Electric System
NESB	Q	N E S B Corp
NET	N	North European Oil Royalty Trust U B I
NETG	Q	Network General Corp
NEW	A	Newcor Inc
NEWE	Q	Newport Electronics Inc
NEWP	Q	Newport Corp
NFBC	Q	North Fork Bancorp Inc
NFC	A	N C F Financial Corp
NFG	N	National Fuel Gas Co
NFSF	Q	N F S Financial Corp
NFSL	Q	Newnan Federal S & L Assn
NGAS	Q	Associated Natural Gas Corp
NGC	N	Newmont Gold Co
NGE	N	New York State Electric & Gas
NGE*	N	New York State Electric & Gas 3.75% Cum Pfd

NGE*A	N	New York State Electric & Gas Adj Cum Pfd A
NGE*B	N	New York State Electric & Gas 8.80% Cum Pfd
NGE*C	N	New York State Electric & Gas 8.48% Cum Pfd
NGFCF	Q	Nevada Goldfields Corp
NGNA	Q	Neutrogena Corp
NGS	N	Niagara Share Corp
NGX	N	Northgate Exploration Ltd
NHC	A	National Health Corp
NHDI	Q	N H D Stores Inc
NHI	A	Nelson Holding Intl
NHL	N	Newhall Land & Farming Co
NHLI	Q	National Health Laboratories Inc
NHMO	Q	National H M O Corp
NHP	N	National Health Properties Inc
NHR	N	National Heritage Inc
NHSB	Q	New Hampshire Savings Bank Corp
NHTB	Q	New Hampshire Thrift Bancshares Inc
NHY	N	Norsk Hydro A S ADS
NI	N	Nipsco Industries Inc
NI*	A	Northern Indiana Public Service 4 1 4% Pfd
NI*A	N	Northern Indiana Public Service Adjust Cum Pfd A
NIC	N	Nicolet Instrument Corp
NICL	Q	Nickel Resources Development Corp
NIEX	Q	Niagara Exchange Corp
NII	N	National Intergroup Inc
NII*	N	National Intergroup Inc $5.00 Cum Cv Pfd
NIIS	Q	New Image Industries Inc
NIKE	Q	Nike Inc Cl B
NIPNY	Q	N E C Corp ADR
NIRTS	Q	National Income Realty Trust S B I
NJR	N	New Jersey Resources Corp
NJST	Q	New Jersey Steel Corp
NL	N	N L Industries Inc
NLBK	Q	National Loan Bank
NLC	N	Nalco Chemical Co
NLCS	Q	National Computer Systems Inc
NLG	A	National Gas & Oil Co
NLI	A	Newmark & Lewis Inc
NLN	A	New Line Cinema Corp
NLON	Q	New London Inc
NLP	A	National Realty L P
NLT	N	N L T Corp
NLWD	N	N L Industries Inc W D
NMBC	Q	Merchants Bancorp Inc
NMC	A	Numac Oil & Gas Ltd
NMCO	Q	National Media Corp
NMD	N	National Medical Care Inc
NMDY	Q	Normandy Oil & Gas Co
NME	N	National Medical Enterprises Inc
NMG	N	Neiman Marcus Group Inc
NMI	N	Nuveen Municipal Income Fund Inc
NMIC	Q	National Micronetics
NMK	N	Niagara Mohawk Power
NMK*	N	Niagara Mohawk Power Adj Pfd A
NMK*A	N	Niagara Mohawk Power 3.40% Cum Pfd A
NMK*B	N	Niagara Mohawk Power 3.60% Cum Pfd B
NMK*C	N	Niagara Mohawk Power 3.90% Cum Pfd C
NMK*D	N	Niagara Mohawk Power 4.10% Cum Pfd D
NMK*E	N	Niagara Mohawk Power 4.85% Cum Pfd E
NMK*G	N	Niagara Mohawk Power 5.25% Cum Pfd G
NMK*H	N	Niagara Mohawk Power 6.10% Cum Pfd H
NMK*I	N	Niagara Mohawk Power 7.72% Cum Pfd I
NMK*J	N	Niagara Mohawk Power 10.60% Cum Pfd J

NMK*K	N	Niagara Mohawk Power Adj Rate Pfd C
NMK*L	N	Niagara Mohawk Power 8.75% Pfd L
NMS	N	National Mine Service Co
NMSB	Q	New Milford Savings Bank
NMTX	Q	Novametrix Medical Systems Inc
NNCXF	Q	Newbridge Networks Corp
NNM	N	Nuveen N Y Municipal Income Fund
NNSL	Q	Newport News S & L Assn
NNY	N	Nuveen N Y Municipal Value Fund Inc
NOAX	Q	N E O A X Inc
NOB	N	Norwest Corp
NOBE	Q	Nordstrom Inc
NOBLF	Q	Nobel Insurance Ltd
NOC	N	Northrop Corp
NOHL	Q	North Hills Electronics Inc
NOLD	Q	Noland Co
NOR*	N	Norstar Bancorp Cum Adj Pfd
NORKZ	Q	Norsk Data As Cl B ADR
NOVL	Q	Novell Inc
NOVR	Q	Novar Electronics Corp
NOVX	Q	Nova Pharmaceutical Corp
NOVXL	Q	Nova Pharmaceutical Corp Cl D Wts 6 30 98
NOVXM	Q	Nova Pharmaceutical Corp Cl C Wts 6 30 93
NOWT	Q	Northwest Telecommunications
NOXLB	Q	Noxell Corp Cl B Non Vtg
NPBC	Q	National Penn Bancshares Inc
NPD	A	National Patent Development Corp
NPI	N	Nuveen Premium Income Municipal Fund Inc
NPK	N	National Presto Industries Inc
NPL*	N	Northwest Pipeline Corp $2.50 Cum Pfd
NPL*A	N	Northwest Pipeline Corp $2.36 Cum Pfd
NPP	N	Nuveen Performance Plus Municipal Fund Inc
NPR	N	New Plan Realty Trust S B I
NPT	A	N E C O Enterprises Inc
NRD	N	Nord Resources Corp
NREC	Q	N A C R E Corp
NRES	Q	Nichols Research Corp
NRM	A	N R M Energy Co L P Dep Units
NRM*	A	N R M Energy Co L P Dep Units $2.60 Cum Cv Pfd
NRMC	A	N R M Energy Co L P Bond
NRRD	Q	Norstan Inc
NRT	N	Norton Co
NRTI	Q	Nooney Realty Trust
NSB	N	Northeast Savings F A
NSB*A	N	Northeast Savings F A $2.25 Cum Cv Pfd
NSBA	Q	National Savings Bank of the City of Albany
NSBK	Q	North Side Savings Bank
NSC	N	Norfolk Southern Corp
NSCB	Q	N B S C Corp
NSCO	Q	Network Systems Corp
NSD	N	National Standard Co
NSH	N	Nashua Corp
NSI	N	National Service Industries
NSIC	Q	National Security Insurance Co
NSM	N	National Semiconductor Corp
NSM*	N	National Semiconductor Corp $4.00 Cum Cv Exch Pfd
NSM*U	N	National Semiconductor Corp Units
NSMWS	N	National Semiconductor Corp Wts
NSO	N	New American Shoe Co
NSP	N	Northern States Power
NSP*A	N	Northern States Power $3.60 Cum Pfd A
NSP*B	N	Northern States Power $4.08 Cum Pfd B
NSP*C	N	Northern States Power $4.10 Cum Pfd C
NSP*D	N	Northern States Power $4.11 Cum Pfd D
NSP*E	N	Northern States Power $4.16 Cum Pfd E
NSP*G	N	Northern States Power $4.56 Cum Pfd G
NSP*H	N	Northern States Power $6.80 Cum Pfd H
NSP*I	N	Northern States Power $7.00 Cum Pfd I
NSP*J	N	Northern States Power $8.80 Cum Pfd J
NSP*K	N	Northern States Power $7.84 Cum Pfd K
NSRU	Q	North Star Universal Inc
NSS	A	N S Group Inc
NSSB	Q	Norwich Financial Corp
NSSC	Q	Napco Security Systems Inc
NSSI	Q	Nuclear Support Services Inc
NSSX	Q	National Sanitary Supply Co
NSTS	Q	Northwestern States Portland Cement Co
NT	N	Northern Telecom Ltd
NTK	N	Nortek Inc
NTLB	Q	National Lumber & Supply Inc
NTRS	Q	Northern Trust Corp
NTSC	Q	National Technical Systems Inc
NU	N	Northeast Utilities
NUCM	Q	Nuclear Metals Inc
NUCO	Q	Nucorp Inc Delaware
NUCOL	Q	Nucorp Inc Wts Bc 10 31 90
NUE	N	Nucor Corp
NUH	A	Nu Horizons Electronics Corp
NUHWS	A	Nu Horizons Electronics Corp Wts
NUI	N	N U I Corp
NUME	Q	Numerica Financial Corp
NUMR	Q	Numerex Corp
NUMS	Q	Nu Med Inc
NUT	N	Mauna Loa Macadamia Partners L P
NUTM	Q	Nutmeg Industries Inc
NUV	N	Nuveen Municipal Value Fund
NUVI	Q	Nuvision Inc
NVA	N	Nova Corp of Alberta
NVBC	Q	Napa Valley Bancorp
NVLS	Q	Norvellus Systems Inc
NVO	N	Novo Nordisk A S
NVP	N	Nevada Power Co
NVR	A	N V R L P
NW	N	National Westminister Bank Plc ADR
NWGI	Q	N W Group Inc
NWIB	Q	Northwest Illinois Bancorp Inc
NWK	N	Network Equipment Technologies Inc
NWL	N	Newell Co Holding Inc
NWLIA	Q	National Western Life Insurance Co Cl A
NWNG	Q	Northwest Natural Gas Co
NWNL	Q	N W N L Cos Inc
NWOR	Q	Neworld Bancorp Inc
NWPH	Q	Newport Pharmaceuticals Intl Inc
NWPS	Q	Northwestern Public Service Co
NWRK	Q	Networks Electronics Corp
NWS	N	News Corp Ltd ADR
NWS*	N	News Corp Cayman Island Ltd Pfd
NWTL	Q	Northwest Teleproductions Inc
NX	N	Quanex Corp
NX*	N	Quantex Corp Dep Cum Cv Exch Pfd
NXA	A	Norex America Inc
NYBC	Q	New York Bancorp Inc
NYCO	Q	Nycor Inc
NYCOP	Q	Nycor Inc Cv Ex Pfd
NYMG	Q	N Y Magic Inc
NYN	N	N Y N E X Corp
NYTA	A	New York Times Cl A
NZ	N	New Mexico & Arizona Land Co
OA	A	Odetics Inc Cl A
OAK	N	Oak Industries Inc

OAR	A	Ohio Art Co
OAT	N	Quaker Oats Co
OB	A	Odetics Inc Cl B
OBS	A	O'Brein Energy Systems Inc Cl A
OC	N	Orion Capital Corp
OC*	N	Orion Capital Corp $2.125 Cv Exch Pfd
OC*A	N	Orion Capital Corp Adj Rate Pfd
OC*B	N	Orion Capital Corp $1.90 Cum Cv Exch Pfd
OCAS	Q	Ohio Casualty Corp
OCC	N	Oppenheimer Capital L P
OCER	Q	Oceaneering Intl Inc
OCF	N	Owens Corning Fiberglas Corp
OCGI	Q	Omni Capital Group Inc
OCLB	Q	Office Club Inc
OCLI	Q	Optical Coating Labs
OCOMA	Q	Outlet Communications Inc Cl A
OCQ	N	Oneida Ltd
OCR	N	Omnicare Inc
OCTL	Q	Octel Communications Corp
ODEP	Q	Office Depot Inc
ODR	N	Ocean Drilling & Exploration Co
ODSI	Q	Old Dominion Systems Inc
OEA	A	O E A Inc
OEC	N	Ohio Edison Co
OEC*A	N	Ohio Edison Co 3.90% Cum Pfd A
OEC*B	N	Ohio Edison Co 4.40% Cum Pfd B
OEC*C	N	Ohio Edison Co 4.44% Cum Pfd C
OEC*D	N	Ohio Edison Co 4.56% Cum Pfd D
OEC*E	N	Ohio Edison Co 7.24% Cum Pfd E
OEC*G	N	Ohio Edison Co 7.36% Cum Pfd G
OEC*H	N	Ohio Edison Co 8.20% Cum Pfd H
OEC*K	N	Ohio Edison Co 8.64% Cum Pfd K
OEC*L	N	Ohio Edison Co 9.12% Cum Pfd L
OEC*P	N	Ohio Edison Co Adj Cv Pfd A
OEC*Q	N	Ohio Edison Co Adj Cl B Cum Pfd
OEH	N	Orient Express Hotels Inc
OEN	A	Oxford Energy Co
OFFI	Q	Old Fashioned Foods Inc
OFSB	Q	Oriental Federal Savings Bank
OG	N	Ogden Corp
OG*	N	Ogden Corp $1.875 Cum Cv Pfd
OGE	N	Oklahoma Gas & Electric Co
OGE*A	N	Oklahoma Gas & Electric Co 4% Cum Pfd A
OGLE	Q	Oglebay Norton Co
OGP	A	Americus Trust for Proctor & Gamble Prime
OGS	A	Americus Trust for Proctor & Gamble Score
OGT	N	Oppenheimer Multi Government Trust
OGU	A	Americus Trust for Proctor & Gamble Units
OH	N	Oakwood Homes Corp
OHBC	Q	Ohio Bancorp
OHCA	A	Oriole Homes Corp Cl A
OHCB	A	Oriole Homes Corp Cl B
OHM	N	O H M Corp
OHSC	Q	Oak Hill Sportswear Corp
OICO	Q	O I Corp
OIF	N	American Opportunity Income Fund Inc
OIL	N	Triton Energy Corp
OIL*	N	Triton Energy Corp $2.00 Cv Exch Pfd
OILC	Q	Oildri Corp of America
OJ	N	Orange Co Inc
OKE	N	Oneok Inc
OKEN	Q	Old Kent Financial Corp
OKP	A	O'Okiep Copper Co Ltd ADR
OLCC	Q	Olympus Capital Corp
OLDB	Q	Old National Bancorp
OLDR	Q	Old Republic Intl Corp
OLGR	Q	Oilgear Co

OLN	N	Olin Corp
OLOG	Q	Offshore Logistics Inc
OLP	A	One Liberty Properties Inc
OLP*	A	One Liberty Properties Inc $15.50 Cum Cv Pfd
OLS	A	Olsten Corp
OM	N	Outboard Marine Corp
OMCM	Q	Omnicom Group Inc
OMD	A	Ormand Industries Inc
OMET	Q	Orthomet Inc
OMI	N	Owens & Minor Inc
OMM	A	O M I Corp
OMS	N	Oppenheimer Multi Sector Income Trust
ONA	A	Oneida Industries Inc
ONBK	Q	Onbancorp
ONCS	Q	Oncogene Science Inc
ONE	N	Banc One Corp
ONPR	Q	One Price Clothing Stores Inc
OPC	N	Orion Pictures Corp
OPI	N	Ogden Projects Inc
OPP	A	Oppenheimer Industries Inc
OPTKF	Q	Optrotech Ltd
OPTO	Q	O P T O Mechanik Inc
OPTX	Q	Optek Technology Inc
OPW*	N	Ohio Power Co 8.04% Cum Pfd
OPW*B	N	Ohio Power Co 7.60% Cum Pfd B
OPW*C	N	Ohio Power Co 7.60% Cum Pfd C
OPW*D	N	Ohio Power Co 7.76% Cum Pfd D
OPW*E	N	Ohio Power Co 8.48% Cum Pfd E
OPW*G	N	Ohio Power Co $2.27 Cum Pfd G
ORBT	Q	Orbit Instrument
ORCL	Q	Oracle Systems Corp
ORCO	Q	Optical Radiation Corp
OREM	Q	Oregon Metallurgical Corp
ORFA	Q	O R F A Corp of Amer
ORG	A	Organogensis Inc
ORU	N	Orange & Rockland Utilities Inc
ORX	N	Oryx Energy Co
OS	A	Oregon Steel Mills Inc
OSBN	Q	Osborn Communications Corp
OSBW	Q	Olympic Savings Bank
OSG	N	Overseas Shipholding Group Inc
OSHM	Q	Oshmans Sporting Goods Inc
OSI	N	On Line Software Intl Inc
OSIC	Q	Osicom Technologies Inc
OSL	A	O'Sullivan Corp
OSMO	Q	Osmonics Inc
OST	N	Austria Fund Inc
OSTN	Q	Old Stone Corp
OSTNO	Q	Old Stone Corp Pfd B
OSW	A	Old Spaghetti Warehouse Inc
OTRKB	Q	Osh Kosh Truck Corp Cl B
OTTR	Q	Otter Tail Power Co
OTU	N	Outlet Co
OUCH	Q	Occupational Urgent Health Care
OVWV	Q	One Valley Bancorp of West Virginia
OXID	Q	Oxidyne Group Inc
OXM	N	Oxford Industries Inc
OXY	N	Occidental Petroleum Corp
OXY*H	N	Occidental Petroleum Corp $14.00 Cum Pfd
P	N	Phillips Petroleum Co
PA	N	Primerica Corp
PAB	N	Pan American Banks Inc
PABC	Q	Pacific Bancorp
PAC	N	Pacific Telesis Group
PACCA	Q	Provident Life & Accident Insr Co of America Cl A

PACCB   Q   Provident Life & Accident Ins Co of Amer Cl B
PACE   Q   Pacesetter Homes Inc
PACN   Q   Pacific Nuclear Systems Inc
PAE   A   Pioneer Systems Inc
PAG   N   Pargas Inc
PAGH   Q   Pacific Agricultural Holdings Inc
PAHC   Q   Pioneer American Holding Co Corp
PAI   N   Pacific American Income Shares Inc
PALM   Q   Palmetto Fed Savings Sc
PAMX   Q   Ponchos Mexican Buffet
PANTQ   Q   Panteras Corp
PAR   A   Precision Aerotech
PARC   Q   Park Communications Inc
PASI   Q   Pacific Silver Corp
PAT   N   Patten Corp
PATK   Q   Patrick Industries Inc
PATL   Q   Pan Atlantic Inc
PAXTA   Q   Paxton Frank Co Cl A
PAY   N   Pay Less Drug Stores Northwest Inc
PAYC   Q   Payco American Corp
PAYX   Q   Paychex Inc
PBCT   Q   Peoples Bank Bridgeport Conn
PBEN   Q   Puritan Bennett Corp
PBFI   Q   Paris Business Forms Inc
PBGI   Q   Piedmont Bankgroup Inc
PBI   N   Pitney Bowes Inc
PBI*   N   Pitney Bowes Inc $2.12 Cv Pfd
PBK   A   Peoples Bank Corp
PBKB   Q   Peoples Savings Bank of Brockton
PBKC   Q   Premier Bankshares Corp
PBKS   Q   Provident Bankshares Corp
PBNB   Q   Peoples Savings Financial Corp
PBS   N   Pilgrim Regional Inc
PBT   N   Permian Basin Royalty Trust U B I
PBY   N   Pep Boys Manny Moe & Jack
PC   N   Penn Central Corp
PCAI   Q   P C A Intl Inc
PCAR   Q   Paccar Inc
PCC   N   Pathe Communications Corp
PCE   A   Professional Care Inc
PCEP   Q   Perception Technology Corp
PCF   N   Putnam High Income Cv & Bond Fund
PCG   N   Pacific Gas & Electric
PCG*A   A   Pacific Gas & Electric 6% Pfd A
PCG*B   A   Pacific Gas & Electric 5 1 2% Pfd B
PCG*C   A   Pacific Gas & Electric 5% Pfd C
PCG*D   A   Pacific Gas & Electric 5% Pfd D
PCG*E   A   Pacific Gas & Electric 5% Ser A Pfd E
PCG*G   A   Pacific Gas & Electric 4.80% Pfd G
PCG*H   A   Pacific Gas & Electric 4.50% Pfd H
PCG*I   A   Pacific Gas & Electric 4.36% Pfd I
PCG*J   A   Pacific Gas & Electric 9.28% Pfd J
PCG*K   A   Pacific Gas & Electric 8.16% Pfd K
PCG*L   A   Pacific Gas & Electric 9% Pfd L
PCG*M   A   Pacific Gas & Electric 7.84% Pfd M
PCG*O   A   Pacific Gas & Electric 8% Pfd O
PCG*P   A   Pacific Gas & Electric 8.20% Pfd P
PCG*R   A   Pacific Gas & Electric 9.48% Pfd R
PCG*S   A   Pacific Gas & Electric 10.46% Pfd S
PCG*T   A   Pacific Gas & Electric 10.18% Pfd T
PCG*V   A   Pacific Gas & Electric 9.30% Pfd V
PCG*W   A   Pacific Gas & Electric 10.28% Pfd W
PCH   N   Potlatch Corp
PCI   N   Paramount Communications Inc
PCI*S   N   Paramount Communications Inc $5.75 Pfd
PCL   N   Plum Creek Timber Co L P

PCLB   Q   Price Co
PCO   N   Pittston Co
PCOR   Q   Psicor Inc
PCR   A   Perini Corp
PCR*   A   Perini Corp Pfd
PCSI   Q   P C S Inc
PCSNC   Q   Precision Standard Inc
PCST   Q   Precision Castparts Corp
PCT   A   Property Capital Trust
PD   N   Phelps Dodge Corp
PDA   A   Princeton Diagnostic Laboratories of America
PDAE   A   Princeton Diagnostic Laboratories of America Units
PDAS   Q   P D A Engineering
PDAWS   A   Princeton Diagnostic Laboratories of America Wts
PDF   N   Patriot Premium Dividend Fund Inc
PDG   N   Placer Dome Inc
PDI   N   Putnam Dividend Income Fund
PDLA   A   Presidential Realty Corp Cl A
PDLB   A   Presidential Realty Corp Cl B
PDLPY   Q   Pacific Dunlop Ltd ADR
PDM   A   Pitt Des Moines Inc
PDN   N   Paradyne Corp
PDP   N   Parker & Parsley Development L P
PDQ   N   Prime Motor Inns Inc
PDS   N   Perry Drug Stores Inc
PE   N   Philadelphia Electric Co
PE*A   N   Philadelphia Electric Co 3.80% Cum Pfd A
PE*B   N   Philadelphia Electric Co 4.30% Cum Pfd B
PE*C   N   Philadelphia Electric Co 4.40% Cum Pfd C
PE*D   N   Philadelphia Electric Co 4.68% Cum Pfd D
PE*E   N   Philadelphia Electric Co 7.00% Cum Pfd E
PE*G   N   Philadelphia Electric Co 8.75% Cum Pfd G
PE*H   N   Philadelphia Electric Co 7.85% Cum Pfd H
PE*I   N   Philadelphia Electric Co 7.75% Cum Pfd I
PE*J   N   Philadelphia Electric Co 7.80% Cum Pfd J
PE*K   N   Philadelphia Electric Co 9.50% Cum Pfd K
PE*L   N   Philadelphia Electric Co 9.52% Cum Pfd L
PE*M   N   Philadelphia Electric Co 15.25% Pfd M
PE*O   N   Philadelphia Electric Co Dep Pfd Shares
PE*P   N   Philadelphia Electric Co 13.35 Dep Pfd Shares
PE*Q   N   Philadelphia Electric Co 14.625% Pfd
PE*R   N   Philadelphia Electric Co 14.15% Dep Pfd
PE*S   N   Philadelphia Electric Co 9.50% Pfd S
PE*T   N   Philadelphia Electric Co 9.875% Pfd
PEBK   Q   Peoples Bank
PEBW   Q   Peoples Bancorp of Worcester Inc
PECN   Q   Publishers Equipment Corp
PEG   N   Public Service Entpr Group
PEG*   N   Public Service Entpr Group 1.40 Cum Pfd
PEG*A   N   Public Service Entpr Group 4.08% Cum Pfd A
PEG*B   N   Public Service Entpr Group 4.18% Cum Pfd B
PEG*C   N   Public Service Entpr Group 4.30% Cum Pfd C
PEG*D   N   Public Service Entpr Group 5.05% Cum Pfd D
PEG*E   N   Public Service Entpr Group 5.28% Cum Pfd E
PEG*G   N   Public Service Entpr Group 6.80% Cum Pfd G
PEG*H   N   Public Service Entpr Group 9.26% Cum Pfd H

PEG*I	N	Public Service Entpr Group 7.40% Cum Pfd I
PEG*J	N	Public Service Entpr Group 7.52% Cum Pfd J
PEG*K	N	Public Service Entpr Group 8.08% Cum Pfd K
PEG*L	N	Public Service Entpr Group 7.80% Cum Pfd L
PEG*M	N	Public Service Entpr Group 7.70% Cum Pfd M
PEG*N	N	Public Service Entpr Group 12.25% Cum Pfd N
PEG*O	N	Public Service Entpr Group 9.75% Cum Pfd O
PEG*P	N	Public Service Entpr Group 8.70% Cum Pfd P
PEG*R	N	Public Service Entpr Group 13.44% Pfd R
PEG*S	N	Public Service Entpr Group 12.80% Cum Pfd
PEG*T	N	Public Service Entpr Group 11.62% Cum Pfd
PEG*U	N	Public Service Entpr Group 8.16% Cum Pfd
PEI	A	Pennsylvania Real Estate Inv Trust
PEL	N	Panhandle Eastern Corp
PENG	Q	Prima Energy Corp
PENT	Q	Pennsylvania Enterprises Inc
PENW	Q	Penwest Ltd
PEO	N	Petroleum Resources Corp
PEO*A	N	Petroleum Resources Corp $1.57 1 2 Cv Pfd
PEP	N	Pepsico Inc
PER	A	Pope Evans & Robbins Inc
PERC	Q	Perceptronics Inc
PERLF	Q	Pearle Systems Ltd
PET	N	Pacific Enterprises
PET*A	A	Pacific Enterprises 4.36 Cum Pfd A
PET*B	A	Pacific Enterprises 4.40 Cum Pfd B
PET*C	A	Pacific Enterprises 4.50 Cum Pfd C
PET*D	A	Pacific Enterprises 4.75 Cum Pfd D
PET*E	A	Pacific Enterprises 7.64 Cum Pfd E
PETD	Q	Petroleum Development Corp
PETTV	Q	Pettibone Corp New W I
PF	A	America First Prep Fund L P
PFBK	Q	Pioneer Federal Savings Bank
PFBS	Q	Ponce Federal Bank F S B
PFCP	Q	Perpetual Financial Corp
PFCPP	Q	Perpetual Financial Corp Cv Ser A Pfd
PFDC	Q	Peoples Federal Savings Bank of Dekalb Cty
PFE	N	Pfizer Inc
PFFS	Q	Pacific First Financial Corp
PFINA	Q	P & F Industries Inc Cl A
PFLY	Q	Polifly Financial Corp
PFNC	Q	Progress Financial Corp
PFP	A	Prime Partners Cl A Units
PFP*	A	Prime Partners Pfd
PFR	N	Perkins Family Restaurant L P
PFSB	Q	Piedmont Federal Corp
PFSI	Q	Pioneer Financial Services Inc
PFSIP	Q	Pioneer Financial Services Inc $2.12 Cum Cv Ex Pfd
PFTS	Q	Profit Systems Inc
PG	N	Proctor & Gamble Co
PGA	A	Punta Gorda Isles Inc
PGI	A	Ply Gem Industries
PGL	N	Peoples Energy Corp
PGN	N	Portland General Corp
PGN*B	N	Portland General Electric Co $2.60 Pfd B
PGR	N	Progressive Corp
PGRWD	N	Progressive Corp W D
PGT	N	Putnam Intermediate Government Income Trust
PGU	A	Pegasus Gold Ltd
PGY	N	Global Yield Fund Inc
PH	N	Parker Hannifin Corp
PHABY	Q	Pharmacia A B ADR New
PHAR	Q	Pharmacontrol Corp
PHBK	Q	Peoples Heritage Financial Group Inc
PHC	A	Pratt Hotels Inc
PHF	A	U S F & G Pacholder Fund Inc
PHG	N	Philips N V
PHH	N	P H H Corp
PHI	A	Philippine Long Distance Telephone Co
PHL	N	Philips Industries Inc
PHL*	N	Philips Industries Inc $1.00 Cum Cv Special Pfd
PHM	N	P H M Corp Holding Co
PHNX	Q	Phoenix Medical Technology Inc
PHOC	Q	Photo Control Corp
PHP	A	Petroleum Heat & Power Co Inc Cl B
PHPH	Q	P H P Healthcare Corp
PHR	A	Phoenix Realty Investors Inc
PHRS	Q	Paul Harris Stores Inc
PHSY	Q	Pacificare Health Systems Inc
PHX	N	P H L Corp Inc
PHXA	Q	Phoenix American Inc
PHXWD	N	P H L Corp Inc W D
PHY	N	Prospect Street High Income Portfolio Inc
PHYB	N	Pioneer Hi Bred Intl Inc
PICC	Q	Piccadilly Cafeterias
PICN	Q	Pic N Save Corp
PICOA	Q	Physicians Insurance Co Ohio Cl A
PIF	N	Prudential Intermediate Income Fund Inc
PIL	N	Petroleum Investment Ltd Units
PIM	N	Putnam Master Intermediate Income Trust S B I
PIN	N	P S I Holdings Inc
PIN*B	N	Public Service Co of Indiana 4.16% Cum Pfd B
PIN*C	N	Public Service Co of Indiana 4.32% Cum Pfd C
PIN*D	N	Public Service Co of Indiana 7.15% Cum Pfd D
PIN*F	N	Public Service Co of Indiana 8.52% Cum Pfd
PIN*G	N	Public Service Co of Indiana 8.38% Cum Pfd G
PIN*H	N	Public Service Co of Indiana 8.96% Cum Pfd
PIN*I	N	Public Service Co of Indiana 9.60% Cum Pfd
PIO	N	Pioneer Electronic Co ADR
PIOG	Q	Pioneer Group Inc
PION	Q	Pioneer Financial Corp
PIOS	Q	Pioneer Standard Electronics Inc
PIPR	Q	Piper Jaffray Inc
PIR	N	Pier 1 Imports Inc
PISC	Q	Pacific Intl Services Corp
PIZA	Q	National Pizza Co
PKD	N	Parker Drilling Co
PKE	N	Park Electrochemical Corp
PKLB	Q	Pharma Kinetics Laboratories
PKN	N	Perkin Elmer Corp
PKOH	Q	Park Ohio Industries Inc
PKPS	Q	Poughkeepsie Savings Bank F S B
PKWY	Q	Parkway Co

PLA	N	Playboy Enterprises Inc
PLAB	Q	Photronic Labs Inc
PLEN	Q	Plenum Publishing Corp
PLFC	Q	Pulaski Furniture Corp
PLFE	Q	Presidential Life Corp
PLI	A	P Leiner Nutritional Products Corp
PLIT	Q	Petrolite Corp
PLL	A	Pall Corp
PLM	A	P L M Intl Inc
PLN	N	Planning Research Corp
PLNS	Q	Plains Resources Inc
PLNSP	Q	Plains Resources Inc Cum Cv Pfd
PLP	N	Plains Petroleum Co
PLRA	A	Plymouth Rubber Co Inc Cl A
PLRB	A	Plymouth Rubber Co Inc Cl B
PLS	A	Peerless Tube Co
PLT*A	A	Pacific Lighting Corp $4.36 Cum Pfd A
PLT*B	A	Pacific Lighting Corp $4.40 Cum Pfd B
PLT*C	A	Pacific Lighting Corp $4.50 Cum Pfd C
PLT*D	A	Pacific Lighting Corp $4.75 Cum Pfd D
PLT*E	A	Pacific Lighting Corp $7.64 Cum Pfd E
PLTZ	Q	Pulitzer Publishing Co
PLXS	Q	Plexus Corp
PLY	N	Plessey Co Ltd ADR
PLZA	Q	Plaza Commerce Bancorp
PM	A	Pratt Lambert Inc
PMAN	Q	Piedmont Management Co Inc
PMBK	Q	Primebank Federal Savings Bank
PMBS	Q	Prime Bancshares Inc
PMC	A	Promed Capital Corp
PMFG	Q	Peerless Manufacturing Co
PMI	N	Premark Intl Inc
PMK	N	Primark Corp
PMM	N	Putnam Managed Municipal Income Trust
PMP	N	Prime Motor Inns L P
PMR	A	Micron Products Inc
PMSC	Q	Policy Management Systems Corp
PMSI	Q	Prime Medical System Inc
PMT	N	Putnam Master Income Trust
PMWD	A	Pratt & Lambert Inc W I
PMWI	Q	Pace Membership Warehouse Inc
PN	N	Pan American World Airways Inc
PNA	N	Pioneer Corp
PNBT	Q	Planters Corp
PNC	N	P N C Financial Corp
PNC*C	N	P N C Financial Corp $1.60 Cum Cv Pfd
PNC*D	N	P N C Financial Corp $1.80 Cum Cv Pfd
PNC*E	N	P N C Financial Corp $2.60 Cum Non Vtg Pfd
PNET	Q	Pronet Inc
PNF	A	Penn Trafic Co
PNH	N	Public Service Co of New Hampshire
PNH*	N	Public Service Co of New Hampshire 11% Cum
PNH*B	N	Public Service Co of New Hampshire 11.24% Pfd
PNH*C	N	Public Service Co of New Hampshire 17% Cum Pfd
PNH*D	N	Public Service Co of New Hampshire 15% Cum Pfd
PNH*E	N	Public Service Co of New Hampshire 15.44% S F Pfd
PNH*F	N	Public Service Co of New Hampshire 13% S F
PNH*G	N	Public Service Co of New Hampshire 13.80% Cum S F Pfd
PNL	A	Penril Corp
PNM	N	Public Service Co of New Mexico
PNN	A	Penn Engineering Mfg Corp
PNS	N	Pansophic Systems Inc
PNTA	Q	Pentair Inc
PNTAP	Q	Pentair Inc Cum Cv Pfd
PNTC	Q	Panatech Research & Develop Corp
PNTK	Q	Pentech Intl Inc
PNU	A	Pneumatic Scale Corp
PNV	A	Perini Investment Properties Inc
PNW	N	Pinnacle West Capital Corp
PNWS	N	Pan American World Airways Inc Wts
PNY	N	Piedmont Natural Gas Co
POAI	Q	Properties of America Inc
POBS	Q	Portsmouth Bank Shares Inc
POCI	Q	Ports of Call Inc
POLK	Q	Polk Audio Inc
POM	N	Potomac Electric Power Co
POM*	N	Potomac Electric Power Co $2.44 Cum Cv Pfd
POM*H	N	Potomac Electric Power Co $3.37 Pfd Ser P
POOL	Q	Poseidon Pools of America
POP	N	Pope Talbot Inc
POPX	N	Pop Radio Corp
POR	N	Portec Inc
POS	A	Pool Energy Services Co
POSS	Q	Possis Corp
POW	A	P S E Inc
POWL	Q	Powell Industries Inc
POWR	Q	Environmental Power Corp
POY	A	Prairie Oil Royalties Co Ltd
PP	A	Pauley Petroleum Corp
PPA*	N	Permian Partners L P Cum Cv Pfd
PPC	N	Patrick Petroleum Co
PPD	A	Prepaid Legal Services Inc
PPG	N	P P G Industries Inc
PPI	A	Pico Products Inc
PPL	N	Pennsylvania Power & Light
PPL*A	N	Pennsylvania Power & Light 4.40% Cum Pfd A
PPL*B	N	Pennsylvania Power & Light 4.50% Cum Pfd B
PPL*G	N	Pennsylvania Power & Light 8.60% Cum Pfd G
PPL*H	N	Pennsylvania Power & Light 8.40% Cum Pfd H
PPL*I	N	Pennsylvania Power & Light 8.70% Cum Pfd I
PPL*J	N	Pennsylvania Power & Light 8.00% Cum Pfd J
PPL*M	N	Pennsylvania Power & Light 9.24% Cum Pfd M
PPL*P	N	Pennsylvania Power & Light Dep Pfd Shares P
PPL*R	N	Pennsylvania Power & Light Dep Pfd Shares R
PPP	N	Pogo Producing Co
PPS	N	Paco Pharmaceutical Services Inc
PPSA	Q	Prospect Park Financial Corp
PPT	N	Putnam Premier Income Trust
PPW	N	Pacificorp
PPW*	A	Pacificorp 5% Pfd
PQB	A	Quebecor Inc
PQBB	A	Quebecor Inc Cl B
PQBWS	A	Quebecor Inc Cl B Wts
PR	A	Price Communications Corp
PRBC	Q	Premier Bancorp Inc
PRBK	Q	Provident Bancorp Inc

PRCO	Q	Pricor Inc
PRCWD	N	Products Research & Chemical Corp W D
PRD	N	Polaroid Corp
PRDE	Q	Pride Petroleum Services Inc
PRE	N	Premier Industrial Corp
PREM	Q	Premier Financial Services Inc
PREV	Q	Revere Inc Fund
PRFT	Q	Proffitts Inc
PRGR	Q	Progroup Inc
PRIA	Q	Priam Corp
PRLX	Q	Parlex Corp
PRM	N	Prime Computer Inc
PRN	N	Puerto Rican Cement Co Inc
PRO	A	International Proteins Corp
PROF	Q	Professional Investors Insurance Group
PROP	Q	Production Operators Corp
PROS	Q	Prospect Group Inc
PROT	Q	Protective Life Corp
PRR	A	Perrigo Corp
PRS*	A	Presidio Oil Co 9.5% Cum Cv Pfd
PRSA	A	Presidio Oil Co Cl A
PRSB	A	Presidio Oil Co Cl B
PRT	N	Prudential Realty Trust Capital Shares
PRT*	N	Prudential Realty Trust Income Shares
PRX	N	Par Pharmaceutical Inc
PRXS	Q	Praxis Biologics Inc
PRY	A	Pittway Corp
PRZ	A	Prism Entertainment Corp
PS	N	Proler Intl Corp
PSA	A	Storage Properties Inc
PSAB	Q	Prime Bancorp Inc
PSB	A	Psychiatric Bio Science Inc
PSBE	A	Psychiatric Bio Science Inc Units
PSBF	Q	Pioneer Savings Bank F S B
PSBK	Q	Pawling Savings Bank
PSBN	Q	Pioneer Bancorp Inc
PSBWS	A	Psychiatric Bio Science Inc Wts
PSBX	Q	Peoples Savings Bank F S B
PSC	N	Philadelphia Suburban Corp
PSD	N	Puget Sound Power & Light Co
PSD*D	A	Puget Sound Power & Light Co 9.36% Cum Pfd D
PSF	N	Prudential Strategic Income Fund Inc
PSG	N	P S Group Inc
PSI	A	Porta Systems Inc
PSLA	Q	Preferred Savings Bank
PSNB	Q	Puget Sound Bancorp
PSNC	Q	Public Service Co of North Carolina
PSO	A	Penobscot Shoe Co
PSPA	Q	Pennview Savings Association
PSR	N	Public Service Co of Colorado
PSR*	A	Public Service Co of Colorado 4 1 4% Pfd
PSR*A	N	Public Service Co of Colorado 7.15% Cum Pfd
PSR*B	N	Public Service Co of Colorado 8.40% Cum Pfd
PSSP	Q	Price Stern Sloan Inc
PST	N	Petrie Stores Corp
PSX	N	Pacific Scientific Co
PSYS	Q	Programming & Systems Inc
PTA	N	Careercom Corp
PTAC	Q	Penn Treaty American Corp
PTC	N	Par Technology Corp
PTCM	Q	Pacific Telecom Inc
PTCO	Q	Petroleum Equipment Tools
PTEC	Q	Phoenix Technologies Ltd
PTG	A	Portage Industries Corp
PTI	A	Patient Technology Inc
PTLX	Q	Patlex Corp
PTNM	Q	Putnam Trust Co
PTNX	Q	Printronix Inc
PTR	N	Property Trust of America S B I
PTRK	Q	Preston Corp
PTRL	Q	Petrol Industries Inc
PTRO	Q	Petrominerals Corp
PTRWD	N	Property Trust of America W D
PTSI	Q	P A M Transportation Services Inc
PUBO	Q	Pubco Corp
PUL	N	Publicker Industries Inc
PULS	Q	Pulawski S & L Assn
PVH	N	Phillips Van Heusen Corp
PVIR	Q	Penn Virginia Corp
PVNA	Q	Provena Foods Inc
PVSA	Q	Parkvale Financial Corp
PVY	A	Providence Energy Corp
PW	A	Pittsburgh West Virginia Railroad S B I
PWB	A	Pacific Western Bancshares
PWJ	A	Paine Webber Group
PWJ*	N	Paine Webber Group $1.375 Cum Cv Exch Pfd
PWN	A	Cash America Investments Inc
PWR	A	International Power Machine Corp
PWRR	Q	Providence & Worcester Railroad Inc
PWSB	Q	Peoples Westchester Savings Bank
PXR	A	Paxer Corp
PXRE	Q	Phoenix Re Corp
PY	A	Preferred Health Care Ltd
PYF	A	Pay Fone Systems Inc
PYM	N	Putnam High Yield Municipal Trust
PYRD	Q	Pyramid Technology Corp
PZL	N	Pennzoil Co
QCHM	Q	Quaker Chemical
QEDX	Q	Q E D Exploration Inc
QFCI	Q	Quality Food Centers Inc
QLTIF	Q	Quadra Logic Technologies Inc
QMED	Q	Quest Medical Inc
QNTM	Q	Quantum Corp
QNTX	Q	Qintex Entertainment Inc
QPON	Q	Seven Oaks Intl Inc
QRXI	Q	Quarex Industries Inc
QTEC	Q	Questech Inc
QUAD	Q	Quadrex Corp
QUAN	Q	Quantronix Corp
QUIK	Q	Quiksilver Inc
QUIP	Q	Quipp Inc
QUIX	Q	Quixote Corp
QUME	Q	Qume Corp
QVCN	Q	Q V C Network Inc
QZMGF	Q	Quartz Mountain Gold Corp
R	N	Ryder Systems Inc
RABT	Q	Rabbit Software Corp
RAD	N	Rite Aid Corp
RADS	Q	Radiation Systems Inc
RAH	N	Robins A H Co Inc
RAL	N	Ralston Purina Co
RAM	N	Ramada Inc
RANG	Q	Rangaire Corp
RARB	Q	Raritan Bancorp Inc
RATNY	Q	Ratners Group Plc ADR
RAUT	Q	Republic Automotive Parts Inc
RAV	A	Raven Industries Inc
RAXR	Q	Rax Restaurants Inc
RAY	N	Raytech Corp
RAYM	Q	Raymond Corp

RB	N	Reading & Bates Corp
RB*	N	Reading & Bates Corp $2.125 Cum Cv Pfd
RB*A	N	Reading & Bates Corp Adj Rate Cum Pfd Ser 5
RBC	A	Regal Beloit Corp
RBCO	Q	Ryanbeck & Co
RBD	N	Rubbermaid Inc
RBK	N	Reebok Intl Ltd
RBNC	Q	Republic Bancorp Inc
RBPAA	Q	Royal Bank of Pennsylvania Cl A
RBSN	Q	Robeson Industries Corp
RBW	A	R B & W Corp
RCBI	Q	Robert C Brown & Co Inc
RCC	A	Re Capital Corp
RCDC	Q	Ross Cosmetics Distribution Centers Inc
RCE	N	Reece Corp
RCHFA	Q	Richfood Holdings Inc Cl A
RCHI	Q	Rauch Industries
RCM	N	Arco Chemical Co
RCOA	Q	Retailing Corp of America
RCOT	Q	Recoton Corp
RCP	N	Rockefeller Center Properties Inc
RCSB	Q	Rochester Community Savings Bank
RCT	N	Real Estate Investment Trust of California
RD	N	Royal Dutch Petroleum Co
RDC	N	Rowan Cos Inc
RDGC	Q	Reading Co
RDK	A	Ruddick Corp
RDK*	A	Ruddick Corp $0.56 Cv Pfd
RDL	A	Redlaw Industries Inc
RDLWA	A	Redlaw Industries Inc Wts A
RDWI	Q	Roadway Motor Plazas Inc
REAL	Q	Reliability Inc
REC	N	Recognition Equipment Inc
RECWD	N	Recognition Equipment Inc W D
RED	A	Red Lions Inns L P Units
REDI	Q	Readi Care Inc
REDX	Q	Red Eagle Resources Corp
REED	Q	Reeds Jewelers Inc
REFC	Q	Refac Technology Development Co
REGB	Q	Regional Bancorp Inc
REIC	Q	Research Industries
REL	N	Reliance Group Holding
RELL	Q	Richardson Electronics Ltd
RELY	Q	Relational Technology Inc
REN	N	Rollins Environmental Services Inc
RENT	Q	Rentrak Corp
REP	N	Repsol S A
RES	N	R P C Energy Services Inc
RESC	Q	Roanoke Electric Steel Corp
RESP	Q	Respironics Inc
RESR	Q	Research Inc
REUT	Q	Reuter Inc
REXI	Q	Resource America Inc
REXL	Q	Rexhall Industries Inc
REXN	Q	Rexon Inc
REXW	Q	Rexworks Inc
REY	N	Reynolds & Reynolds Co Cl A
RFBC	Q	River Forest Bancorp
RFBK	Q	R S Financial Corp
RFED	Q	Roosevelt Bank F S B
RFIN	Q	Rock Financial Corp
RFP	A	Americus Trust for Arco Shares Prime
RFS	A	Americus Trust for Arco Shares Score
RFSB	Q	Reisterstown Fed Savings Bank
RFTN	Q	Reflectone Inc
RFU	A	Americus Trust for Arco Shares Units

RGB	A	Barry R G Corp
RGC	N	Republic Gypsum Co
RGCY	Q	Regency Electronics Inc
RGEN	Q	Repligen Corp
RGEQ	Q	Regency Equities Corp
RGL	N	Regal Intl Inc
RGLD	Q	Royal Gold Inc
RGO	N	Ranger Oil Ltd
RGS	N	Rochester Gas & Electric Corp
RHCC	Q	Rocking Horse Child Care Centers of America
RHCI	Q	Ramsay Health Care Inc
RHEM	Q	Rheometrics Inc
RHH	N	Robertson H H Corp
RHII	Q	Robert Half Intl Inc
RHPOY	Q	Rhone Poulenc S A ADR
RHR	N	Rohr Industries Inc
RI	N	Radice Corp
RIBI	Q	Ribi Immunochem Research Inc
RICE	Q	American Rice Inc
RIE	A	Riedel Environment Technologies Inc
RIF	A	Real Estate Securities Income Fund
RIGS	Q	Riggs National Corp
RIHL	Q	Richton Intl Corp
RII	A	Resort Income Investors Inc
RIO	N	Royal Intl Optical Corp
RIV	A	Riverbend Intl Corp
RJF	N	Raymond James Financial Inc
RJR*A	N	R J R Nabisco Inc Cum Pfd A
RK	N	Ark Restaurant Corp
RLC	N	R L C Corp
RLI	N	R L I Corp
RLM	N	Reynolds Metals Co
RM	A	Rymac Mortgage Investment Corp
RMC	A	American Restaurant Partners L P
RMCI	Q	Right Management Consultants Inc
RMF	N	R A C Income Fund Inc
RMI	A	Residential Mortgage Investment Inc
RMKA	A	Robert Mark Inc Cl A
RMKE	A	Robert Mark Inc Units
RMKWS	A	Robert Mark Inc Wts
RML	N	Russell Corp
RMPO	Q	Ramapo Financial Corp
RMR	N	R A C Mortgage Investment Corp
RMS	A	R M S Intl Inc
RMUC	Q	Rocky Mount Undergarment Co Inc
RNB	N	Republic New York Corp
RNB*B	N	Republic New York Corp Floating Rate Cum Pfd B
RNBO	Q	Rainbow Technologies Inc
RNIC	Q	Robinson Nugent
RNRC	Q	Riverside National Bank
ROAD	Q	Roadway Services Inc
ROBN	Q	Robbins & Meyers Inc
ROBV	Q	Robotic Vision Systems Inc
ROC	N	R O C Taiwan Fund
RODS	Q	American Steel & Wire Corp
ROE	N	Roebling Property Investors Inc
ROG	A	Rogers Corp
ROH	N	Rohm & Haas Co
ROI	N	River Oaks Industries Inc
ROIL	Q	Reserve Industries Corp
ROK	N	Rockwell Intl Corp
ROK*	N	Rockwell Intl Corp $4.75 Cum Cv Pfd A
ROK*B	N	Rockwell Intl Corp $1.35 Cum Cv Pfd B
ROL	N	Rollins Inc
ROM	A	Rio Algom Ltd

RONC	Q	Ronson Corp
ROPK	Q	Ropak Corp
ROR	N	Rorer Group Inc
ROST	Q	Ross Stores Inc
ROTC	Q	Rotech Medical Corp
ROTO	Q	Roto Rooter Inc
ROUS	Q	Rouse Co
ROW	A	Rowe Furniture Corp
ROYL	Q	Royalpar Industries Inc
ROYLW	Q	Royalpar Industries Inc Wts
RPAPF	Q	Repap Enterprises Corp Inc
RPB	A	Royal Palm Beach Colony L P
RPCH	Q	Rospatch Corp
RPICA	Q	Republic Pictures Corp Cl A
RPOW	Q	R P M Inc
RPS	N	R P S Realty Trust
RR	N	Rodman & Renshaw Capital Group Inc
RRF	N	Realty Refund Trust S B I
RRMN	Q	Railroadmens Fed S & L Assn of Indianapolis
RRT	A	Resource Recycling Co Inc
RS	N	Republic Steel Corp
RS*	N	Republic Steel Corp $5.25 Cum Cv Pfd
RSDL	Q	Resdel Industries Inc
RSFC	Q	Republic Savings Financial Corp
RSGI	Q	Riverside Group Inc
RSI	A	Realty South Investors Inc
RSIC	Q	R S I Corp
RSIWS	A	Realty South Investors Inc Wts
RSLA	Q	Republic S & L Assn of Wisconsin
RSP	A	Americus Trust for Sears Shares Prime
RSR	A	Riser Foods Inc Cl A
RSS	A	Americus Trust for Sears Shares Score
RSTO	Q	Roses Stores Inc
RSTOB	Q	Roses Stores Inc Cl B Non Vtg
RSU	A	Americus Trust for Sears Shares Units
RTC	N	Rochester Telephone Corp
RTCH	Q	Radiation Technology Inc
RTG	N	Racal Telecom Plc
RTH	N	Houston Oil Royalty Trust U B I
RTI	N	R M I Titanium Co
RTN	N	Raytheon Co
RTP	N	Reich & Tang L P
RTRSY	Q	Reuters Holding Plc ADR
RTS	N	Russ Togs Inc
RULE	Q	Rule Industries Inc
RUS	N	Russ Berrie & Co
RVCC	Q	Reeves Communications Corp
RVEE	Q	Holiday R V Superstores Inc
RVR	A	Cruise America Inc
RVT	N	Royce Value Trust Inc
RXN	N	Rexeen Corp
RYAN	Q	Ryans Family Steak Houses
RYC	N	Raychem Corp
RYFL	Q	Family Steak Houses of Florida Inc
RYK	N	Rykoff Sexton Inc
RYL	N	Ryland Group Inc
RYR	N	Rymer Co
RYR*	N	Rymer Co $1.175 Cum Cv Exchangeable Pfd
RYRWS	A	Rymer Co Wts
S	N	Sears Roebuck & Co
SA	A	Stage I I Apparel Corp
SAA	N	Saatchi & Saatchi Co Plc
SAC*	N	South Carolina Electric & Gas Co 5% Cum Pfd
SAF	N	Scudder New Asia Fund Inc

SAFC	Q	Safeco Corp Com
SAFE	Q	Security American Financial Enterprises Inc
SAFM	Q	Sanderson Farms Inc
SAH	N	Sahara Casino Partners L P
SAI	A	Allstar Inns L P Dep Units
SAJ	N	Saint Joseph Light & Power Co
SAM	A	Samson Energy Co L P
SAN	A	San Carlos Milling Co Inc
SANF	Q	Sanford Corp
SAR	N	Santa Anita Realty Enterprises Inc
SAT	N	Schafer Value Trust Inc
SATI	Q	Satellite Information Systems Co
SAV*A	N	Savannah Electric & Power Co $9.50 Pfd
SAVO	Q	Schultz Sav O Stores Inc
SAX	A	Saxon Oil Development Partners L P Dep Units
SAY	A	Southbay Corp
SB	N	Salomon Inc
SBA	A	Sbarro Inc
SBC	N	Southwestern Bell Corp
SBCFA	Q	Seacoast Banking Corp Florida Cl A
SBE	N	Smithkline Beecham ADR Units
SBH	N	Smithkline Beecham Plc ADR
SBIG	Q	Seibels Bruce Group Inc
SBIO	Q	Synbiotics Corp
SBK	N	Signet Banking Corp
SBL	N	Symbol Technologies Inc
SBLI	Q	Staff Builders Inc Del
SBM	A	Speed O Print Business Machine Corp
SBN	A	Sunbelt Nursery Group Inc
SBO	N	Showboat Inc
SBOS	Q	Boston Bancorp
SBP	N	Standard Brands Paint Co
SBR	N	Sabine Royalty Trust U B I
SBRU	Q	Subaru of America Inc
SBS	A	Salem Corp
SBTC	Q	S B T Corp
SC	N	Shell Transport & Trading Plc Ltd
SCAF	Q	Surgical Care Affiliates Inc
SCAPY	Q	Svenska Cellulosa Aktiebolaget S C A Spons ADR
SCE	N	S C E Corp Holding Co
SCE*B	A	Southern California Edison 4.08% Cum Pfd B
SCE*C	A	Southern California Edison 4.24% Cum Pfd C
SCE*D	A	Southern California Edison 4.32% Cum Pfd D
SCE*E	A	Southern California Edison 4.78% Cum Pfd E
SCE*G	A	Southern California Edison 5.80% Cum Pfd G
SCE*I	A	Southern California Edison 8.96% Cum Pfd I
SCE*J	A	Southern California Edison 8.70% Cum Pfd J
SCE*K	A	Southern California Edison 7.58% Cum Pfd K
SCE*O	A	Southern California Edison 8.54% Cum Pfd O
SCE*P	A	Southern California Edison 12% Cum Pfd P
SCF	A	Scandanavia Fund Inc
SCFB	Q	South Carolina Federal Corp
SCFM	Q	Scanforms Inc
SCG	N	Scana Corp
SCH	N	Charles Schwab & Co
SCIS	Q	S C I Systems Inc
SCIXF	Q	Scitex Corp Ltd

SCL	A	Stephan Co
SCNC	Q	South Carolina National Corp
SCO	N	Smith Corona Corp
SCOM	Q	S C S Compute Inc
SCOR	Q	Syncor Intl Corp
SCOT	Q	Scott & Stringfellow Financial Inc
SCP	A	Scope Industries
SCR	N	Sea Containers Ltd
SCR*	N	Sea Containers Ltd $1.4625 Cum Pfd
SCR*B	N	Sea Containers Ltd $2.10 Cum Pfd
SCR*C	N	Sea Containers Ltd $2.10 1982 Cum Pfd
SCR*D	N	Sea Containers Ltd $4.125 Cum Cv Pfd
SCRP	Q	Scripps Howard Broadcasting Co
SCSL	Q	Suncoast S & L Assn
SCT	N	Scotsman Industries Inc
SCTC	Q	Systems & Computer Technology Corp
SCX	N	Starrett L S Co
SCZ	N	Schwitzer Inc
SDNB	Q	S D N B Financial Corp
SDO	N	San Diego Gas & Electric
SDO*A	A	San Diego Gas & Electric 5% Pfd A
SDO*B	A	San Diego Gas & Electric 4.50% Cum Pfd B
SDO*C	A	San Diego Gas & Electric 4.40% Cum Pfd C
SDO*E	A	San Diego Gas & Electric 7.80% Cum Pfd E
SDO*G	A	San Diego Gas & Electric 7.20% Cum Pfd G
SDO*I	A	San Diego Gas & Electric $2.475 Cum Pfd I
SDP	N	Sun Distributors L P
SDRC	Q	Structural Dynamics Research Corp
SDW	N	Southdown Inc
SDY	A	Sandy Corp
SDYN	Q	Stadynamics Inc
SE	N	Sun Electric Corp
SEAB	Q	Seaboard S & L Assn
SEAG	Q	Sea Galley Stores Inc
SEB	A	Seaboard Corp
SEC	A	Sterling Electronic Corp
SECB	Q	Security Bancorp Inc
SECR	Q	Secor Bank F S B
SED	N	S E D C O Inc
SEE	N	Sealed Air Corp
SEEDB	Q	Dekalb Genetics Corp Cl B
SEEQ	Q	S E E Q Technology Inc
SEH	A	Spartech Corp
SEI	A	Seitel Inc
SEIC	Q	S E I Corp
SEMI	Q	All American Semiconductor Inc
SENE	Q	Seneca Foods Corp
SEO	A	Seaport Corp
SEO*A	A	Seaport Corp $0.56 Cum Cv Pfd A
SEQ	N	Storage Equities Inc
SEQP	Q	Supreme Equipment & Systems Corp
SER	A	Sierracin Corp
SERF	Q	Service Fracturing Co
SESL	Q	Southeastern Savings Bank Inc
SETBS	Q	Sierra Real Estate Equity Trust 83 S B I
SETC	Q	Sierra Real Estate Equity Trust 84
SEVN	Q	Sevenson Environmental Services Inc
SEWY	Q	Seaway Food Town Inc
SF	N	Stifel Financial Corp
SFA	N	Scientific Atlanta Inc
SFB	N	Standard Federal Bank
SFBM	Q	Security Federal Savings Bank
SFCD	Q	Safecard Services Inc
SFCP	Q	Suffield Financial Corp
SFD	N	Smiths Food & Drug Center Inc Cl B
SFDS	Q	Smithfield Foods Inc
SFE	N	Safeguard Scientifics Inc

SFEM	Q	S F E Technologies
SFF	N	Santa Fe Industries Inc
SFFD	Q	S F Fed Corp
SFGD	Q	Safeguard Health Enterprises Inc
SFGI	Q	Security Financial Group Inc
SFI	A	Spendthrift Farm Inc
SFIWS	A	Spendthrift Farm Inc Wts
SFL	N	Sante Fe Pacific Pipeline Partner L P
SFM	A	S F M Corp
SFNS	Q	Spear Financial Services Inc
SFP	N	Santa Fe Energy Partners L P
SFS	A	Super Food Services Inc
SFSI	A	Sunwest Financial Services Inc
SFX	N	Sante Fe Pacific Corp
SFXWD	N	Santa Fe Southern Pacific W D
SFY	A	Swift Energy Co
SG	N	Stotler Group Inc
SGAT	Q	Seagate Technology
SGC	A	Superior Surgical Mfg Co
SGCWD	A	Superior Surgical Manufacturing Co W D
SGHB	Q	Sag Habor Savings Bank
SGHI	Q	Silk Greenhouse Inc
SGI	N	Slattery Group Inc
SGIC	Q	Silicone Graphics Inc
SGO	N	Seagull Energy Corp
SGOPP	Q	Seagull Energy Corp Cv Exch Pfd A
SGP	N	Schering Plough Corp
SGSI	Q	Sage Software Inc
SGWS	A	Stotler Group Inc Wts
SHB	N	Scottys Inc
SHBS	Q	Sharebase Corp
SHBZ	Q	Showbiz Pizza Time Inc
SHCI	Q	Salick Health Care Inc
SHCO	Q	Schult Homes Corp
SHD	A	Sherwood Group Inc
SHEF	Q	Sandwich Chef Inc
SHEL	Q	Sheldahl Co
SHIP	Q	Regency Cruises Inc
SHKIF	Q	S H L Systemhouse Inc
SHLB	Q	Shelby Federal Savings Bank
SHLM	Q	Schulman A Inc
SHN	N	Shoneys Inc
SHO	A	Starrett Housing Corp
SHOP	N	Shopsmith Inc
SHOR	Q	Shorewood Packaging Corp
SHOW	Q	Showscan Film Corp
SHP	A	Bay Ocean Carriers Ltd
SHRE	Q	Sahara Resorts
SHRP	Q	Sharper Image Corp
SHS	A	Shaer Shoe Corp
SHW	N	Sherwin Williams Co
SHX	N	Shaw Industries Inc
SI	N	A C M Government Spectrum Fund Inc
SIA	N	Signal Apparel Co
SIA*	N	Signal Apparel Co $1.60 Cum Cv Pfd
SIAL	Q	Sigma Aldrich Corp
SIDY	Q	Science Dynamics Corp
SIE	A	Sierra Health Services Inc
SIER	Q	Sierra On Line Inc
SIF	A	Sifco Industries Inc
SIG	N	Southern Indiana Gas & Electric Co
SIGI	Q	Selective Insurance Group Inc
SIGM	Q	Sigma Designs Inc
SIGN	Q	Plasti Line Inc
SII	N	Smith Intl Inc
SILI	Q	Siliconix Inc
SILN	Q	Silicone General Inc

SILV	Q	Silver King Mines Inc Nevada
SISC	Q	Stewart Information Services Corp
SIVB	Q	Silicon Valley Bancshares
SIX	N	Motel Six L P Dep Units
SIZ	N	Sizelers Property Investors Inc
SIZZ	Q	Sizzler Restaurants
SJI	N	South Jersey Industries Inc
SJM	N	Smucker J M Co
SJNB	Q	S J N B Financial Corp
SJR	N	San Juan Racing Assoc Inc
SJS	A	Sunshine Jr Stores Inc
SJT	N	San Juan Basin Royalty Trust U B I
SJW	A	S J W Corp
SK	N	Safety Kleen Corp
SKA	A	Sikes Corp Cl A
SKAN	Q	Skaneateles Savings Bank
SKFB	Q	S & K Famous Brands Inc
SKFRY	Q	Ab Skf ADR
SKII	Q	S K I Ltd
SKIP	Q	Skippers Inc
SKN	A	Skolniks Inc
SKNWS	A	Skolniks Inc Wts
SKY	N	Skyline Corp
SKYW	Q	Skywest Inc
SL	N	S L Industries Inc
SLB	N	Schlumberger Ltd
SLCR	Q	Salem Carpet Mills Inc
SLE	N	Sara Lee Corp
SLE*	N	Sara Lee Corp Adj Cv Pfd
SLFX	Q	Selfix Inc
SLG	A	Seligman Associates Inc
SLH	N	Shearson Lehman Hutton Holding Inc
SLM	N	Student Loan Marketing Assn
SLM*A	N	Student Loan Marketing Assn Adj Rate Cum Pfd A
SLMAJ	Q	Student Loan Marketing Assn Vtg
SLN	N	Sea Land Corp
SLP	N	Sun Energy Partners L P
SLRV	Q	Sellersville S & L Assn
SLS	A	Selas Corp of America
SLT	N	Salant Corp
SLTI	Q	Surgical Laser Technologies Inc
SLTM	Q	Selecterm Inc
SLV	A	Silvercrest Industries Inc
SM	N	Southmark Corp
SM*D	N	Southmark Corp Adj Cum Pfd D
SM*H	N	Southmark Corp Ser H 9 1 4% Cum Cv Pfd
SMBX	Q	Symbolics Inc
SMC*C	A	Smith A O Corp $2.125 Cv Exch Pfd
SMCA	A	Smith A O Corp Cl A
SMCB	A	Smith A O Corp Cl B
SMCR	Q	Summcorp
SME	N	Service Merchandise Co
SMED	Q	Shared Medical Systems Corp
SMET	Q	S I M E T C O Inc
SMG	A	Science Management Corp
SMGS	Q	Southeastern Michigan Gas Enterprises Inc
SMH	A	Semtech Corp
SMI	N	Spring Industries Inc
SMIN	Q	Southern Mineral Corp
SMK	A	Sandmark Stardust Inc
SMLB	Q	Smith Laboratories Inc
SMLS	Q	Scimed Life Systems Inc
SMMT	Q	Summit Savings Association
SMMWS	A	Student Loan Marketing Assn Ger Currency Wts
SMN	A	Seamans Corp
SMNA	Q	Samna Corp
SMP	N	Standard Motor Products Inc
SMPS	Q	Simpson Industries Inc
SMS	N	State Mutual Securities Trust
SMSC	Q	Standard Microsystems Corp
SMX	N	Systems Center Inc
SMYWS	A	Student Loan Marketing Assn Japan Wts
SNA	N	Snap On Tools Corp
SNAT	Q	Southern National Corp
SNC	N	Shawnut National Corp
SNCO	Q	Sensor Control Corp
SNDS	Q	Sands Regent
SNDT	Q	Sunguard Data Systems Inc
SNE	N	Sony Corp ADR
SNEL	Q	Snelling & Snelling Co
SNF	N	Spain Fund Inc
SNFS	Q	Second National Federal Savings Bank
SNG	N	Southern New England Telecom
SNI	A	Sun City Industries Inc
SNLFA	Q	S N L Financial Corp Cl A
SNLT	Q	Sunlite Inc
SNMD	A	Sunrise Medical Inc
SNO	A	Polaris Equity Income Partnership L P
SNPX	Q	Synoptics Communications Inc
SNRU	Q	Sunair Electronics Inc
SNS	N	Sundstrand Corp
SNSR	Q	Sensormatic Electronics Corp
SNSTA	Q	Sonesta Intl Hotels Corp Cl A New
SNT	N	Sonat Inc
SNTC	Q	Synetic Inc
SNV	N	Synovus Financial Corp
SO	N	Southern Co
SOBK	N	Southern Bankshares Inc
SOCI	Q	Society Corp
SOCR	Q	Scan Optics Inc
SOCS	Q	Society for Savings Bancorp Inc
SOD	N	Solitron Devices Inc
SODA	Q	A & W Brands Inc
SOFS	Q	Softsel Computer Products Inc
SOFT	Q	Softech Inc
SOI	N	Snyder Oil Partners
SOI*A	N	Snyder Oil Partners L P Pfd A
SOLR	Q	Applied Solar Energy Corp
SOME	Q	State O Maine Inc
SOMR	Q	Somerset Group Inc
SONNF	Q	Sonora Gold Corp
SONO	Q	Sonoco Products Co
SOO	N	Soo Line Corp
SOR	N	Source Capital Inc
SOR*	N	Source Capital Inc $2.40 Cum Pfd
SOSA	Q	Somerset Bankshares Inc
SOTR	Q	Southtrust Corp
SOV	N	Sovran Financial Corp
SP	A	Aaron Spelling Production Inc Cl A
SPA	N	Sparton Corp
SPAIB	Q	Strategic Planning Associates Inc Cl B
SPAN	Q	Span America Medical Systems Inc
SPAR	Q	Spartan Motor Inc
SPBC	Q	St Paul Bancorp Inc
SPC	N	Security Pacific Corp
SPCO	Q	Software Publishing Corp
SPD	N	Standard Products Co
SPEC	Q	Spectrum Control Inc
SPEK	Q	Specs Music Inc
SPF	N	Standard Pacific Corp
SPG	N	Sprague Technologies Inc
SPGLA	Q	Spiegel Inc Cl A Non Vtg

SPGWD	N	Sprague Technologies Inc W D
SPH*	A	S P I Holdings 16% Pfd
SPI	A	S P I Pharmaceuticals Inc
SPILF	Q	S P I Suspension & Parts Industries Ltd
SPIR	Q	Spire Corp
SPKR	Q	Spinnaker Software Corp
SPLKA	Q	Jones Spacelink Ltd Cl A
SPLS	Q	Staples Inc
SPP	N	Scott Paper Co
SPR	A	Sterling Capital Corp
SPRH	Q	Spearhead Industries Inc
SPS	N	Southwestern Public Service Co
SPTR	Q	Spectran Corp
SPW	N	S P X Corp
SQA*	N	Sequa Corp $5.00 Cv Pfd
SQAA	N	Sequa Corp Cl A
SQAB	N	Sequa Corp Cl B
SQAI	Q	Square Industries Inc
SQD	N	Square D Co
SQNT	Q	Sequent Computer Systems Inc
SR*	N	Southern Railway $2.60 Cum Pfd A
SRB	A	Scurry Rainbow Oil Ltd
SRBC	Q	Sunrise Bancorp
SRC	N	Service Resources Corp
SRCE	Q	First Source Corp
SRCO	Q	Sealright Co Inc
SRE	N	Stoneridge Resources Inc
SREG	Q	Standard Register Co
SRG	A	Sorg Co
SRL	A	Sceptre Resources Ltd
SRP	N	Sierra Pacific Resources
SRR	N	Stride Rite Corp
SRSL	Q	Sunrise Bancorp Inc
SRV	N	Service Corp Intl
SSAX	Q	System Software Associates Inc
SSBA	Q	Seacoast Savings Bank
SSBB	Q	Southington Savings Bank
SSBC	Q	Shelton Bancorp Inc
SSC	N	Sunshine Mining Co Hldg Co
SSC*	N	Sunshine Mining Co Hldg Co $11.94 Cum Red Pfd
SSFT	Q	Scientific Software Intercomp Inc
SSIAA	Q	Stockholders Systems Inc Cl A
SSIF	Q	Southeastern Savings Institutions Fund Inc
SSLN	Q	Security Investments Group Inc
SSM	N	S S M C Inc
SSOA	Q	Software Services of America
SSS	A	M S A Realty Corp
SSSS	Q	Stewart & Stevenson Services Inc
SST	A	Shelter Components Corp
SSW	A	Sterling Software Inc
SSW*	A	Sterling Software Inc Pfd
SSWWD	A	Sterling Software Inc W D
ST	N	S P S Technologies Inc
STAG	Q	Security Tag System Inc
STB	N	Southeast Banking Corp
STBK	Q	State Street Boston Corp
STBY	Q	Stansbury Mining
STD	N	Banco De Santander Sociedad Anonima De Credito
STEC	Q	Serv Tech Inc
STF	N	Stauffer Chemical Co
STG	N	Steego Corp
STH	N	Stanhome Inc
STI	N	Suntrust Banks Inc
STII	Q	Stanford Telecommunications Inc
STIZ	Q	Scientific Technology Inc

STJM	Q	St Jude Medical Inc
STK	N	Storage Technology Corp
STK*	N	Storage Technology Corp Cv Exch Pfd
STKLF	Q	Stake Technology Ltd
STKY	Q	Stokely U S A Inc
STL	N	Sterling Bancorp
STLTF	Q	Stolt Tankers & Terminals Hlds S A
STM	N	Strategic Mortgage Investment Inc
STNWD	N	Stevens J P Co Inc W D
STO	N	Stone Container Corp
STPL	N	Saint Paul Cos Inc
STPT	Q	Starpointe Savings Bank
STR	N	Questar Corp Holding Co
STRA	Q	Stratus Computer Inc
STRB	Q	Strober Organization Inc
STRC	Q	Stratford American Corp
STRM	Q	Sturm Ruger & Co Inc
STRR	Q	Star Resources Inc
STRS	Q	Sprouse Reitz Stores
STRU	Q	Structofab Inc
STRWA	Q	Strawbridge & Clothier Cl A
STRX	N	Syntrex Inc
STRY	Q	Stryker Corp
STRZ	Q	Star Banc Corp
STSS	Q	Star States Corp
STT	A	Superior Teletec Inc
STTG	Q	Statesman Group Inc
STTX	Q	Steel Technologies Inc
STUH	Q	Stuart Hall Co Inc
STUS	Q	Stuart Department Stores Inc
STVI	Q	S T V Engineering Inc
STW	N	Standard Commercial Corp
STWB	Q	Statewide Bancorp
STX	N	Sterling Chemicals Inc
SUA	A	Summit Tax Exempt Bond Fund
SUBBA	Q	Suburban Bancorp Inc Cl A
SUBK	Q	Suffolk Bancorp
SUBN	Q	Summit Bancorp
SUDS	Q	Sudbury Inc
SUG	N	Southern Union Co
SUGR	Q	Summagraphics Corp
SUHC	Q	Summit Holding Corp
SUMA	Q	Summa Medical Corp
SUMH	Q	Summit Health Ltd
SUMI	Q	Sumitomo Bank of California
SUN	N	Sun Co Inc
SUND	Q	Sound Advice Inc
SUNF	Q	Sunstar Foods Inc
SUNI	Q	Suncoast Plastics Inc
SUNW	Q	Sun Micro Systems Inc
SUP	A	Superior Industries Intl
SUPX	Q	Supertex Inc
SUR	N	Scor U S Corp
SURV	Q	Survival Technology Inc
SUSQ	Q	Susquehanna Bancshares Inc
SUW	A	Struthers Wells Corp
SVAN	Q	Savannah Foods & Industries Inc
SVB	N	Savin Corp
SVB*A	N	Savin Corp $1.50 Cum Cv Pfd A
SVB*B	N	Savin Corp $0.80 Cum Cv Pfd B
SVB*D	N	Savin Corp $0.10 Cum Cv Pfd D
SVC*	N	Stokely Van Camp Inc 5% Cum Pr Pfd
SVGA	A	Stevens Graphics Cl A
SVGB	A	Stevens Graphics Cl B
SVGI	Q	Silicon Valley Group Inc
SVM	N	Service Master Ltd
SVMHF	Q	Silver Hart Mines Ltd

SVRL	Q	Silvar Lisco
SVRN	Q	Sovereign Bancorp Inc
SVT	A	Servotronics Inc
SVU	N	Super Valu Stores Inc
SW	N	Stone Webster Inc
SWARA	Q	Schwartz Brothers Inc Cl A
SWB	A	Southwest Bancorp
SWCB	Q	Sandwich Cooperative Bank
SWD	A	Standard Shares Inc
SWEL	Q	Southwestern Electric Service Co
SWIS	Q	St Ives Laboratories Corp
SWIX	Q	Shelby Williams Industries Inc
SWK	N	Stanley Works
SWL	A	Southwest Realty Ltd
SWN	N	Southwestern Energy Co
SWPA	Q	Southwest National Corp
SWTR	Q	Southern California Water Co
SWTX	Q	Southwall Technology Inc
SWV	N	Suave Shoe Corp
SWVA	Q	Steel of West Virginia Inc
SWVWD	N	Suave Shoe Corp W D
SWWC	Q	Southwest Water Co
SWX	N	Southwest Gas Corp
SWZ	N	Helvetia Fund Inc
SXI	N	Standex Intl Corp
SY	N	Shelby Williams Industries Inc
SYB	N	Sybron Corp
SYB*	N	Sybron Corp $2.40 Cv Pfd
SYDWS	A	Student Loan Marketing Assn Yen Wts 3 1 93
SYGN	Q	Synergen Inc
SYI	A	System Industries Inc
SYM	N	Syms Corp
SYMB	Q	Symbion Inc
SYMC	Q	Symantec Corp
SYMK	Q	Sym Tek Systems Inc
SYN	N	Syntex Corp
SYNE	Q	Syntech Intl Inc
SYNR	Q	Synercom Technology
SYNT	Q	Syntro Corp
SYO	A	Synalloy Corp
SYRA	Q	Syracuse Supply Co
SYRWS	A	Student Loan Marketing Assn Yen Wts
SYS	A	I S I Systems Inc
SYST	Q	Systematics Inc
SYY	N	Sysco Corp
SZD	A	Sierra Capital Realty Trust IV
SZF	A	Sierra Capital Realty Trust VI
SZF*	A	Sierra Capital Realty Trust VI Pfd
SZG	A	Sierra Capital Realty Trust
SZG*	A	Sierra Capital Realty Trust Pfd
SZH	A	Sierra Capital Realty Trust VIII
SZH*	A	Sierra Capital Realty Trust VIII Pfd
T	N	American Telephone & Telegraph
TA	N	Transamerica Corp
TAB	N	Tandy Brands Inc
TAC	N	Tandycraft Inc
TAI	N	Transamerica Income Shares
TAL	N	Talley Industries Inc
TAL*B	N	Talley Industries Inc $1.00 Cum Cv Pfd B
TAM	A	Tubos De Acero De Mexico ADR S Com
TAN	N	Tandy Corp
TANT	A	Tennant Co
TATE	Q	Ashton Tate
TAVI	Q	Thorn Apple Valley Inc
TBC	A	Tasty Baking Co
TBCC	Q	T B C Corp

TBL	A	Timberland Co
TBO	N	Tacoma Boatbuilding Co
TBP	A	Tab Products Co
TBS*A	A	Turner Broadcasting Systems Inc Cum Pfd A
TBSA	A	Turner Broadcasting Systems Inc Cl A
TBSB	A	Turner Broadcasting Systems Inc Cl B
TBY	N	T C B Y Enterprises Inc
TCA	A	Thermocardio Systems
TCAT	Q	T C A Cable T V Inc
TCB	N	T C F Financial Corp
TCBC	Q	Trust Co Bancorp
TCC	A	Teleconcepts Corp
TCCO	Q	Technical Communications Corp
TCEL	A	T Cell Sciences Inc
TCGN	Q	Tecogen Inc
TCI	N	Transcontinental Realty Investors
TCII	Q	T C I Intl Inc
TCIWS	N	Transcontinental Realty Investors Wts
TCL	N	Transcon Inc
TCM	A	T S F Communications Corp
TCOMA	Q	Tele Communications Inc Cl A
TCOMB	Q	Tele Communications Inc Cl B
TCOMR	Q	Tele Communications Inc Rts 1 31 95
TCOR	Q	Tandon Corp
TCR	Q	Trammell Crow Real Estate Investors S B I
TCRD	Q	Telecredit Inc
TCS	A	T C S Enterprises Inc
TCSFY	Q	Thomson C S F ADR
TCTC	Q	Tompkins County Trust Co
TCYWS	A	A T & T Credit Corp Currency Exch Wts
TDAT	Q	Teradata Corp
TDCX	Q	Technology Development Corp
TDDA	A	Three D Department Stores Cl A
TDDB	A	Three D Departments Inc Cl B
TDI	N	Twin Disc Inc
TDK	N	T D K Corp ADR
TDM	N	Tandem Computers
TDRLF	Q	Tudor Corp Ltd
TDS	A	Telephone & Data Systems Inc
TDW	N	Tidewater Inc
TDW*	N	Tidewater Inc Cv Adj Pfd
TDX	A	Tridex Corp
TDY	N	Teledyne Inc
TE	N	Teco Energy Inc
TECD	Q	Tech Data Corp
TECN	Q	Technalysis Corp
TECU	Q	Tecumseh Products Co
TED*A	A	Toledo Edison Co 8.32% Cum Pfd A
TED*B	A	Toledo Edison Co 4.25% Cum Pfd B
TED*C	A	Toledo Edison Co 7.76% Cum Pfd C
TED*D	A	Toledo Edison Co 10% Cum Pfd D
TED*E	A	Toledo Edison Co 8.84% Cum Pfd E
TED*F	N	Toledo Edison Co $2.365 Cum Pfd F
TED*K	N	Toledo Edison Co Adj Rate Pfd Sr A
TED*L	N	Toledo Edison Co Adj Rate Pfd B
TED*M	N	Toledo Edison Co $2.81 Cum Pfd
TEF	N	Telefonica De Espana S A ADR
TEJS	Q	Tejas Gas Corp
TEK	N	Tektronix Inc
TEL	N	Telecom Corp
TELC	Q	Telco Systems Inc
TELV	Q	Televideo Systems Inc
TEM	A	Temco National Corp
TEMWS	A	Temco National Corp Wts
TEP	N	Tucson Electric Power Co
TER	N	Teradyne Inc
TERM	Q	Terminal Data Corp

TERX	Q	Terex Corp
TEV	A	Thermo Enviromental Corp
TEVIY	Q	Teva Pharmaceuticals Inc
TEX	A	Texas Air Corp
TFC	N	Transcapital Financial Corp
TFLX	Q	Termiflex Corp
TFSB	Q	Federal Savings Bank
TFX	A	Teleflex Inc
TG	N	Tredegar Industries Inc
TGDGF	Q	Total Energold Corp
TGG	N	Templeton Global Trust Inc
TGI	N	T G I Fridays Inc
TGL	N	Triton Group Ltd
TGP*	N	Transcontinental Gas Pipe Line Corp $2.50
TGP*B	N	Transcontinental Gas Pipe Line Corp $6.65 Cum Pfd
TGP*C	N	Transcontinental Gas Pipe Line Corp $8.64 Cum Pfd
TGT	N	Tenneco Inc
TGT*B	N	Tenneco Inc $7.40 Cum Pfd
TGTWD	N	Tenneco Inc W D
THC	N	Hydraulic Co
THCO	Q	Hammond Co
THFI	Q	Plymouth Five Cents Savings Bank
THI	A	Thermo Instrument Systems Inc
THK	N	Thackeray Corp
THO	N	Thor Industries Inc
THP	A	Triangle Home Products Inc
THPR	Q	Thermal Profiles Inc
THR	A	Thor Energy Resources Inc
THT	N	Thoratec Intl Inc
TI	A	T I I Industries Inc
TIBI	N	Image Bank Inc
TIC	N	Travelers Corp
TIE	A	T I E Communications Inc
TIERC	Q	Tierco Group Inc
TIF	N	Tiffany & Co
TII	N	Thomas Industries Inc
TIN	N	Temple Inland Inc
TIS	N	T I S Mortgage Investment Co
TJCO	Q	T J Intl
TJX	N	T J X Cos Inc
TKA	N	Tonka Corp
TKC	N	Thiokol Corp
TKIOY	Q	Tokio Marine & Fire Insurance Co ADR
TKLC	Q	Tekelec
TKR	N	Timken Co
TL	N	Time Warner Inc
TLAB	Q	Tellabs Inc
TLAM	Q	Tony Lama
TLII	Q	Trans Leasing Intl Inc
TLMD	Q	Telemundo Group Inc
TLMN	Q	Talman Home Fed S & L Assn of Ill
TLMT	Q	T L M Corp
TLOS	Q	Telos Corp
TLP	A	Tenera L P Dep Units
TLR	N	Telerate Inc
TLX	A	Trans Lux Corp
TLXN	Q	Telxon Corp
TLY	A	Technology Applications Inc Cl A
TMA	N	Thomson Mc Kinnon Asset Management L P
TMAS	Q	Trimas Corp
TMAX	Q	Telmatics Intl Inc
TMB	N	Tambrands Inc
TMBR	Q	Tom Brown Inc
TMBS	Q	Timberline Software Corp

TMC	N	Times Mirror Co
TMCI	Q	T M Communications Inc
TMD	A	Thermedics Inc
TMED	Q	Trimedyne Inc
TMI	A	Team Inc
TMK	N	Torchmark Corp
TMK*A	N	Torchmark Corp Adj Rate Cum Pfd A
TMKWD	N	Torchmark Corp W D
TMO	N	Thermo Electron Corp
TMR	A	Texas Meridan Resources Ltd
TMSTA	Q	Thomaston Mills Inc Cl A
TMSTB	Q	Thomaston Mills Inc Cl B
TMTX	Q	Temtex Industries Inc
TNB	N	Thomas Betts Corp
TNC	A	Town & Country Corp
TND	A	Technodyne Inc
TNEL	Q	Thomas Nelson Inc
TNIA	A	Transcisco Cl A
TNIB	A	Transcisco Cl B
TNII	Q	Telecommunications Network Inc
TNL	A	Technitrol Inc
TNP	N	T N P Enterprises Inc
TNV	N	Trinova Corp
TNY	A	Tenney Engineering Inc
TNZ	A	Tranzonic Cos
TNZB	A	Tranzonic Cos Cl B
TO	A	Tech Ops Landauer Inc
TOBK	Q	Tolland Bank
TOC	A	Tech Ops Sevcon Inc
TOCRZ	Q	Tocor Inc Units 12 31 94
TOD	N	Todd Shipyards Corp
TOD*A	N	Todd Shipyards Corp $3.08 Cv Ex Pfd Ser A
TODDA	Q	Todd A O Corp Cl A
TOF	A	Tofutti Brands Inc
TOK	N	Tokheim Corp
TOL	N	Toll Brothers Inc
TOMKY	Q	Tomkins Plc ADR
TONE	Q	One Bancorp
TOOL	Q	Easco Hand Tools Inc
TOOT	Q	Two Zero Two Data Systems Inc
TOPPC	Q	Topps Co Inc
TOPT	Q	Tele Optics Inc
TOS	Q	Tosco Corp
TOS*E	N	Tosco Corp $2.375 Ser C Cv Pfd
TOTE	Q	Unite Tote Inc
TOY	N	Toys R Us Inc
TPI	A	Thermo Process Systems Inc
TPIE	Q	T P I Enterprises Inc
TPL	N	Texas Pacific Land Trust Sub Shares Ctfs
TPN	A	Total Petroleum North America
TPN*	A	Total Petroleum North America $2.88 Cv Pfd
TR	N	Tootsie Roll Industries Inc
TRAD	Q	Traditional Industries Inc
TRB	N	Tribune Co
TRBK	Q	Trustbank Savings F S B
TRC	A	Tejon Ranch Co
TRCO	Q	Trico Products Corp
TREN	Q	Trenwick Group Inc
TREX	Q	Intrex Financial Services Inc
TRFI	Q	Trans Financial Bancorp
TRG	A	Triangle Corp
TRGL	Q	Toreador Royalty Corp
TRKA	Q	Trak Auto Corp
TRLS	Q	Thousand Trails Inc
TRN	N	Trinity Industries Inc
TRNI	Q	Trans Industries Inc
TRNS	Q	Transmation Inc

TRNT	Q	Transnet Corp
TRON	Q	Trion Inc
TROW	Q	T Rowe Price Associates Inc
TRP	N	Transcanada Pipelines Ltd
TRR	A	T R C Cos Inc
TRROO	Q	Triton Group Ltd Ser C Pfd
TRS	A	Trust America
TRSC	Q	Traid Systems Corp
TRSL	Q	Trans National Industries Inc
TRST	Q	Trustco Bank Corp NY
TRTI	Q	Transtech Industries Inc
TRUK	Q	Builders Transport Inc
TRW	N	T R W Inc
TRW*B	N	T R W Inc $4.40 Cum Cv II Pfd B
TRW*D	N	T R W Inc $4.50 Cum Cv II Pfd 3 D
TSII	Q	T S I Inc
TSK	N	Computer Task Group Inc
TSM	A	Tri State Motor Transit Co
TSNG	Q	Tseng Labs Inc
TSO	N	Tesoro Petroleum Corp
TSO*	N	Tesoro Petroleum Corp $2.16 Cum Cv Pfd
TSP	A	Telesphere Communications Inc
TSQ	A	T Square Medical Inc Cl A
TSRI	Q	T S R Inc
TSS	AN	T S S Seedmans Inc
TSY	N	Tech Sym Corp
TT	N	Transtechnology Corp
TTC	N	Toro Co
TTCO	Q	Trustcorp Inc
TTF	N	Thai Fund Inc
TTL	A	Torotel Inc
TTN	N	Titan Corp
TTN*	N	Titan Corp $1.00 Cum Cv Pfd
TTNWD	N	Titan Corp W D
TTOI	Q	Tempest Technologies Inc
TTOR	Q	Transtector Systems Inc
TTOY	Q	Tyco Toys Inc
TTOYW	Q	Tyco Toys Inc Wts 6 7 93
TTT	N	Telecom U S A Inc
TTX	N	Tultex Corp
TUCK	Q	Tucker Drilling Co Inc
TUES	Q	Tuesday Morning Inc
TUG	N	Maritrans Partners L P
TUR	A	Turner Corp
TUSC	Q	Tuscarora Plastics Inc
TVF	N	Templeton Value Fund Inc
TVOPZ	Q	Vista Organization Partnership
TVXGC	Q	T V X Broadcast Group Inc
TW	N	T W Services Inc
TW*B	N	Transworld Corp $1.90 Cum Pfd B
TWA*	N	Trans World Airlines Inc $2.25 Cum Pfd
TWBC	Q	Transworld Bancorp
TWEN	Q	Twentieth Century Industries
TWI	A	Tidwell Industries
TWMC	Q	Trans World Music Corp
TWN	N	Taiwan Fund Inc
TWP	A	Two Pesos Inc
TWRX	Q	Software Toolworks Inc
TWSTQ	Q	Twistee Treat Corp
TX	N	Texaco Inc
TX*C	N	Texaco Inc Ser C Var Rate Cum Pfd
TXF	N	Texfi Industries Inc
TXF*	N	Texfi Industries Inc Cum Pfd
TXF*B	N	Texfi Industries Inc Cum Pfd B
TXI	N	Texas Industries Inc
TXN	N	Texas Instruments Inc
TXT	N	Textron Inc

TXT*A	N	Textron Inc $2.08 Cum Cv Pfd A
TXT*B	N	Textron Inc $1.40 Cum Cv Pfd B
TXU	N	Texas Utilities Co
TY	N	Tri Continental Corp
TY*	N	Tri Continental Corp $2.50 Cum Pfd
TYC	N	Tyco Laboratories Inc
TYGR	Q	Tigera Group Inc
TYL	N	Tyler Corp
TYSNA	Q	Tyson Foods Inc Cl A
U	N	U S Air Group Inc
UAC	A	Unicorp American Corp
UAECA	Q	United Artists Entertainment Co Cl A
UAECB	Q	United Artists Entertainment Co Cl B
UAL	N	U A L Corp
UAM	N	United Asset Management Corp
UB	N	United Brands Co
UBKR	Q	United Bankers Inc Texas
UBKS	Q	United Banks of Colorado
UBMT	Q	United Savings Bank F A
UBN	A	University Bank National Assn
UBNK	Q	Union Bank
UBSI	Q	United Bankshares Inc
UCAR	Q	United Carolina Bancshares
UCC	N	Union Camp Corp
UCIT	Q	United Cities Gas Co
UCL	N	Unocal Corp Delaware
UCO	N	Union Corp
UCOA	Q	United Coasts Corp
UCS	A	Universal Communication Systems Inc
UCU	N	Utilicorp United Inc
UCU*	N	Utilicorp United Inc $2.4375 Cum Pfd
UCU*B	N	Utilicorp United Inc $2.1625 Cum Pfd
UCU*C	N	Utilicorp United Inc $1.775 Cum Cv Pfd
UDC	N	U D C Universal Development L P Dep Receipts
UDC*	N	U D C Universal Development L P $15.00 Pfd
UDC*B	N	U D C Universal Development L P Ser B Pfd
UDCWD	N	U D C Universal Development L P Dep Receipts W D
UDRT	Q	United Dominion Realty Trust
UDS	A	Ultrasystems Defense & Space Inc
UEP	N	Union Electric Co
UEP*A	N	Union Electric Co $3.50 Cum Pfd A
UEP*C	N	Union Electric Co $4.00 Cum Pfd C
UEP*D	N	Union Electric Co $4.50 Cum Pfd D
UEP*E	N	Union Electric Co $4.56 Cum Pfd E
UEP*G	N	Union Electric Co $6.40 Cum Pfd G
UEP*H	N	Union Electric Co $8.00 Cum Pfd H
UEP*I	N	Union Electric Co $7.44 Cum Pfd I
UEP*L	N	Union Electric Co $8.00 Cum Pfd L
UESS	Q	United Education & Software
UFBK	Q	United Federal Bancorp Inc
UFC	N	Universal Foods Corp
UFCS	Q	United Fire & Casualty Co
UFDA	A	United Foods Inc Cl A
UFDB	A	United Foods Inc Cl B
UFF	N	Unionfed Financial Corp
UFN	A	Unicare Financial Corp
UFST	Q	Unifast Industries Inc
UGAM	Q	United Gaming Inc
UGI	N	U G I Corp
UGNE	Q	Unigene Laboratories Inc
UGNEW	Q	Unigene Laboratories Inc Wts
UH	N	United States Home Corp
UHCO	Q	Universal Holding Corp
UHLI	Q	United Home Life Insurance Co

UHSIB	Q	Universal Health Services Inc Cl B
UHT	N	Universal Health Realty Inc Tr Shares
UI	N	United Inns Inc
UIC	N	United Industrial Corp
UICI	Q	United Insurance Cos
UIF	N	U S L I F E Income Fund Inc
UIL	N	United Illuminating Co
UIL*	N	United Illuminating Co 8.80% Pfd
UIL*D	N	United Illuminating Co 19% Pfd
UIS	N	Unisys Corp
UIS*A	N	Unisys Corp Ser A Cum Cv Pfd
UJB	N	U J B Financial Corp
UJB*B	N	U J B Financial Corp Adj Rate Cum Pfd
UK	N	Union Carbide Corp
UKM	N	United Kingdom Fund Inc
UL	N	Unilever Plc American Shares
ULT	N	Ultimate Corp
UM	A	United Medical Corp
UMB	N	Universal Medical Buildings L P
UMB*A	N	Universal Medical Buildings L P Cv Pfd A
UMED	N	Unimed Inc
UMG	N	Universal Matchbox Group Ltd
UMM	N	United Merchants & Manufacturers Inc
UMR	N	Unimar Co Indonesia Partic Units
UMSB	Q	United Missouri Bancshares
UN	N	Unilever N V New York Shares
UNAM	Q	Unico American Corp
UNBJ	Q	United National Bancorp
UNC	N	U N C Inc
UNCF	Q	United Cos Financial Corp
UNEWY	Q	United Newspapers Public Ltd Co ADR
UNF	N	Unifirst Corp
UNFI	Q	Unifi Inc
UNFR	Q	Uniforce Temporary Personnel Inc
UNIH	Q	United Healthcare Corp
UNIR	Q	United Guardian Inc
UNM	N	U N U M Corp
UNMAA	Q	Uni Marts Inc Cl A
UNMWD	N	U N U M Corp W D
UNNB	Q	University National Bank & Trust Co
UNO	A	Uno Restaurants Corp
UNP	N	Union Pacific Corp
UNR*	N	Uniroyal Inc 8% Pfd
UNRI	Q	U N R Industries Inc
UNRIW	Q	U N R Industries Inc Wts 6 14 95
UNSA	Q	United Financial Corp of South Carolina Inc
UNSL	Q	U N S L Financial Corp
UNSVA	Q	United Savings Assn Cl A
UNT	N	Unit Corp
UNTD	Q	First United Bancshares Inc
UNV	A	Unitel Video Inc
UPC	N	Union Partners Corp
UPEN	Q	Upper Peninsula Energy Corp
UPJ	N	Upjohn Co
UPK	N	United Park City Mines Co
UPP	A	Americus Trust for Union Pacific Shares Prime
UPS	A	Americus Trust for Union Pacific Shares Score
UPT	A	University Patents Inc
UPU	A	Americus Trust for Union Pacific Shares Units
URT	A	U S P Real Estate Investment Trust
USA	N	Liberty All Star Equity Fund
USAB	Q	U S A Bancorp Inc
USBA	Q	United Savings Bank Mutual
USBC	Q	U S Bancorp Oregon

USBI	Q	United Savers Bancorp Inc
USBK	Q	United Savings Bank
USBP	Q	U S Bancorp Inc Pa
USBPP	Q	U S Bancorp Inc Cum Cv Pfd A
USC	N	U S L I C O Corp
USEG	Q	United States Energy Corp
USF	N	U S A Cafes L P
USG	N	U S G Corp
USGL	Q	U S Gold Corp
USGWD	N	U S G Corp W D
USH	N	U S L I F E Corp
USH*C	N	U S L I F E Corp $3.33 Cum Pfd C
USHC	Q	U S Health Care Inc
USM	A	United States Cellular Corp
USMX	Q	U S M X Inc
USPMF	Q	U S Precious Metals Inc
USR	N	United States Shoe Corp
USRE	Q	U S Facilities Corp
USS	N	United States Surgical Corp
UST	N	U S T Inc
USTB	Q	U S T Corp
USTC	Q	U S Trust Corp
USTR	Q	United Stationers Inc
USVC	Q	U S L I C O Corp
USW	N	U S West Inc
USWNA	Q	U S West New Vector Group Inc Cl A
UT	N	United Telecommunications Inc
UT*	N	United Telecommunications Inc 1st Cv Pfd
UT*A	N	United Telecommunications Inc 2nd Cv Pfd
UTDMK	Q	United Investors Management Co Non Vtg
UTH	N	Union Texas Petroleum Holdings Inc
UTL	A	U N I T I L Corp
UTLC	Q	U T L Corp
UTMD	Q	Utah Medical Inc
UTOG	Q	Unitog Co
UTR	N	Unitrode Corp
UTRX	Q	Unitronix Corp
UTVI	Q	United Television Inc
UTX	N	United Technologies Corp
UVC	A	Union Valley Corp
UVCWS	A	Union Valley Corp Wts
UVOL	Q	Universal Voltronics Corp
UVTB	Q	United Vermont Bancorp
UVV	N	Universal Leaf Tobacco Co Inc
UVX	N	Univar Corp
UWR	N	United Water Resources Inc
UXP	N	Union Explorations Partnership Ltd Dep Units
V	N	Vivra Inc
VABF	Q	Virginia Beach F S B
VACA	Q	Vermont American Corp Cl A
VAGO	Q	Vanderbilt Gold Corp
VAL	A	Valspar Corp
VALM	Q	Valmont Industries Inc
VALN	Q	Vallen Corp
VALU	Q	Value Line Inc
VANF	Q	Vanfed Bancorp
VAR	N	Varian Associates
VAT	N	Varity Corp
VAT*A	N	Varity Corp $1.30 Cum Cv Pfd A
VBAN	Q	V Bank Corp
VBND	Q	Velo Bind Inc
VC	N	Vista Chemical Co
VCC	N	Volunteer Capital Corp
VCCN	Q	Valley Capital Corp
VCELA	Q	Vanguard Cellular Systems Inc Cl A
VCOR	Q	Vencor Inc

VCRE	Q	Vari Care Inc
VDC	N	Van Dorn Co
VDEF	Q	Vie De France Corp
VDR	A	Vader Group Inc
VEL*E	N	Virginia Electric & Power Co $5.00 Cum Pfd E
VEL*F	N	Virginia Electric & Power Co $7.72 Cum Pfd F
VEL*G	N	Virginia Electric & Power Co $8.84 Cum Pfd G
VEL*H	N	Virginia Electric & Power Co $7.45 Cum Pfd H
VEL*I	N	Virginia Electric & Power Co $7.20 Cum Pfd I
VEL*J	N	Virginia Electric & Power Co $7.72 Cum Pfd J
VEL*L	N	Virginia Electric & Power Co $9.75 Cum Pfd L
VEL*M	N	Virginia Electric & Power Co $8.60 Cum Pfd
VEL*S	N	Virginia Electric & Power Co $8.60 Cum Pfd M S D
VENT	Q	Venturian Corp
VEOXF	Q	Veronex Resources Ltd
VER	A	Verit Industries Inc
VES	N	Vestaur Securities Inc
VF	A	Valley Forge Corp
VFBK	Q	Eastern Bancorp Inc
VFC	N	V F Corp
VFCWD	N	V F Corp W D
VFED	Q	Valley Federal S & L Assn
VFSB	Q	Virginia First Savings F S B
VFSC	Q	Vermont Financial Services Corp
VHI	N	Valhi Inc
VHT	A	V M S Hotels Investment Trust S B I
VHTWS	A	V M S Hotels Investment Trust S B I Wts
VI	N	Valley Industries
VIA	A	Viacom Intl Inc
VICT	Q	Victoria Bankshares Inc
VIDE	Q	Video Display Corp
VII	N	Vicon Industries Inc
VIN	A	Vintage Enterprises Inc
VIPTS	Q	Vinland Property Trust S B I
VIR	A	Virco Manufacturing Corp
VIRA	Q	Viratek Inc
VISA	Q	Vista Organization Ltd
VIT	N	Van Kampen Merritt Intermediate High Income Trust
VITA	Q	Vitalink Communications Corp
VITC	Q	Victoria Creations Inc
VIVI	Q	Vivigen Inc
VKC	A	Van Kampen Merritt Cal Municipal Trust
VKSI	Q	Vikonics Inc
VLAB	Q	Vipont Pharmaceutical Inc
VLANS	Q	V M S Strategic Land Trust S B I
VLC	A	Northtankers Inc
VLCM	Q	Valcom Inc
VLGEA	Q	Village Super Market Inc Cl A
VLID	Q	Valid Logic Systems Inc
VLO	N	Valero Energy Corp
VLO*	N	Valero Energy Corp Depository Pfd Shares
VLP	N	Valero Natural Gas Partners L P
VLSI	Q	V L S I Technology Inc
VLT	N	Van Kampen Merritt Term High Inco Tr
VLT*	N	Van Kampen Merritt Term High Inco Tr 9.50% Cum Pfd
VLU	N	Worldwide Value Fund Inc
VMC	N	Vulcan Materials Co
VMG	N	V M S Mortgage Investment Fund
VMLPZ	Q	V M S Mortgage Investors L P Dep Units
VMORZ	Q	V M S Mortgage Investors L P I I I Units Lpi
VMT	N	Van Kampen Municipal Income Trust
VMTGZ	Q	V M S Mortgage Investors L P I I Dep Units
VMXI	Q	V M X Inc
VNBP	Q	Valley National Bancorp
VNCP	Q	Valley National Corp
VNO	N	Vornado Inc
VO	N	Seagram Co Ltd
VOLT	Q	Volt Information Sciences Inc
VOLVY	Q	Volvo A B ADR
VON	N	Vons Cos Inc
VOT	A	Voplex Corp
VOX	A	Audiovox Corp Cl A
VR	A	Valley Resources Inc
VRC	N	Varco Intl Inc
VRE	A	Vermont Research Corp
VREOS	Q	Vanguard R E Fund I A Sales Comm Fr Income Prop SBI
VRES	Q	Vicorp Restaurant Inc
VRLN	Q	Varlen Corp
VRO	N	Varo Inc
VRSA	N	Versa Technologies Inc
VRSY	Q	Varitronic Systems Inc
VSBC	Q	V S B Bancorp
VSEC	Q	V S E Corp
VSH	N	Vishay Intertechnology Inc
VSLF	Q	V M S Strategic Land Fund II
VSR	A	Versar Inc
VST	A	V M S Short Term Income Trust S B I
VSTR	Q	Vestar Inc
VTC	N	Vitronics Corp
VTEX	Q	Vertex Communications Corp
VTK	N	Viatech Inc
VTRX	Q	Ventrex Laboratories Inc
VTX	A	V T X Electronics Corp
VUL	A	Vulcan Corp
VV	N	Vestron Inc
VWRX	Q	V W R Corp
VY	A	Vyquest Inc
VYBN	Q	Valley Bancorp
W	N	Westvaco Corp
WA*	N	Wabash Railroad Co 4 1 2% Non Cum Pfd
WAB	A	Westamerica Bancorp
WAC	A	Wells American Corp
WAE	N	Wilfred American Educational Corp
WAG	N	Walgreen Co
WAH	A	Westarr Holding Inc
WAIN	Q	Wainwright Bank & Trust Co
WAK	N	Wackenhut Corp
WALB	Q	Walbro Corp
WALS	Q	Walshire Assurance Co
WAMU	Q	Washington Mutual Savings Bank
WAMUP	Q	Washington Mutual Savings Bank Pfd
WANB	A	Wang Laboratories Cl B
WANC	A	Wang Laboratories Cl C Cv
WATFZ	Q	Waterford Wedgwood Plc ADR Units
WATTA	Q	Watts Industries Inc Cl A
WAVR	Q	Waverly Inc
WAX	N	Waxman Industries Inc
WBAT	Q	Westport Bancorp Inc
WBB	N	Webb Del Corp
WBC	A	Westbridge Capital Corp
WBK	N	Westpac Banking Corp ADS
WBN	N	Waban Inc
WBNC	Q	Washington Bancorp Inc

WBST	Q	Webster Financial Corp
WC	A	Weiman Co Inc
WCAT	Q	Wicat Systems Inc
WCBC	Q	West Coast Bancorp
WCBK	Q	Workingmens Corp
WCCC	Q	Western Commercial
WCE	A	Western Centers Equity Trust
WCH*	A	W C I Holdings Corp 15 1 2% Cum Ex Red Pfd
WCI	N	Warner Communications
WCLB	Q	Warehouse Club Inc
WCP	N	Warner Computer Systems Inc
WCRSY	Q	V C R S Group Plc ADR
WCS	N	Wallace Computer Services Inc
WDC	A	Western Digital Corp
WDFC	Q	W D Forty Co
WDG	N	Wedgestone Financial Inc S B I
WDH	N	Winchells Donut Houses L P
WDHD	Q	Woodhead Industrials Inc
WDST	Q	Wordstar Intl Inc
WE	N	Westcoast Energy Inc
WEBS	Q	Webster Clothes Inc
WEC	N	Wisconsin Energy Corp Holding Co
WECA	Q	Western Capital Investment Corp
WECO	Q	Washington Energy Co
WED	A	Wedco Technology Inc
WEIS	Q	Weisfields Inc
WEN	N	Wendys Intl Inc
WERN	Q	Werner Enterprises Inc
WES	A	Wescorp Inc
WEST	Q	West One Bancorp
WETT	Q	Wetterau Inc
WEXCC	Q	Wolverine Exploration Co
WEXWC	Q	Wolverine Exploration Co Cl A Wts
WEYS	Q	Weyenberg Shoe Mfg Co
WFC	N	Wells Fargo Co
WFC*A	N	Wells Fargo Co Adj Rate Cum Pfd A
WFC*B	N	Wells Fargo Co Adj Rate Cum Pfd Ser B
WFM	N	Wells Fargo Mortgage & Equity Trust
WFOR	N	Washington Federal Savings Bank Oregon
WFPR	Q	Western Federal Savings Bank Puerto Rico
WFRAF	Q	Wharf Resources Ltd
WFSB	Q	Washington Federal Savings Bank Jersey
WFSL	Q	Washington Federal S & L Assn of Seattle
WG	N	Wilcox & Gibbs Inc
WGA	A	Wells Gardner Electronics Corp
WGHT	Q	Weightronix Inc
WGL	N	Washington D C Gas Light Co
WGNR	Q	Wegener Corp
WGO	N	Winnebago Industries Inc
WGP*	N	Western Gas Processing Ltd Pfd
WH	N	Whitman Corp
WHIT	Q	Whitman Medical
WHLS	Q	Wholesale Club Inc
WHOO	Q	Waterhouse Investor Services Inc
WHR	N	Whirlpool Corp
WHT	N	Whitehall Corp
WHX	N	Wheeling Pittsburgh Steel Corp
WHX*	N	Wheeling Pittsburgh Steel Corp $5.oo Cum Pfd
WHX*B	N	Wheeling Pittsburgh Steel Corp 6% Cum Pfd
WIC	N	W I C O R Inc
WID	N	Wean Inc
WID*A	N	Wean Inc 5 1 4% Cum Cv Pfd A
WII	A	Weatherford Intl Inc
WII*	A	Weatherford Intl Inc $2.625 Cum Cv Pfd

WIL	A	Wilsons Sporting Goods
WILLA	Q	Wiley John & Sons Cl A
WILM	Q	Wilmington Trust Co Delaware
WIMI	Q	Warwick Insurance Managers Inc
WIN	N	Winn Dixie Stores Inc
WINB	N	Winn Dixie Stores Inc Cl B Cum Cv Vtg
WIR	A	Western Investment Real Estate Trust S B I
WIS*	A	Wisconsin Power & Light 4 1 2% Pfd
WISC	Q	Wisconsin Southern Gas Co
WISE	Q	Wiser Oil Co
WIT	N	Witco Corp
WIX*A	A	Wickes Cos Inc $2.50 Cv Pfd A
WIXWS	A	Wickes Cos Inc Wts
WJ	N	Watkins Johnson Co
WJR	A	Cypress Fund Inc
WJRWD	A	Cypress Fund Inc W D
WKR	N	Whittaker Corp
WKRWD	N	Whittaker Corp W D
WLA	N	Warner Lambert Co
WLBK	Q	Waltham Corp
WLC	A	Wellco Enterprises Inc
WLD	N	Weldotron Corp
WLE	N	Wheeling Lake Erie Railway
WLHN	Q	Wolohan Lumber Co
WLM	N	Wellman Inc
WLPI	Q	Wellington Leisure Products Inc
WLRF	Q	W L R Foods Inc
WMB	N	Williams Cos
WMB*	N	Williams Cos $3.875 Cv Exch Pfd
WMBS	Q	West Mass Bancshares Inc
WMD	A	Mars Graphic Services Inc
WMI	A	Winthrop Insured Mortgage Investors
WMIC	Q	Western Microwave Inc
WMK	N	Weis Markets Inc
WMOR	Q	Westmoreland Coal Co Delaware
WMRK	Q	Westmark Intl Inc
WMS	N	W M S Industries Inc
WMSI	Q	Williams Industry Inc
WMT	N	Wal Mart Stores Inc
WMTT	Q	Willamette Industries Inc
WMX	N	Waste Management Inc
WN	N	Wynns Intl Inc
WND	N	Windmere Corp
WNG*	N	Williams Natural Gas Co Adj Rate Cum Pfd
WNSB	Q	West Newton Savings Bank
WNSI	Q	W N S Inc
WNT	N	Washington National Corp
WNT*	N	Washington National Corp $2.50 Cv Pfd
WOA	N	Worldcorp Inc
WOBS	Q	First Woburn Bancorp Inc
WOC	N	Wilshire Oil Co of Texas
WOI	A	World Income Fund Inc
WOL	N	Wainoco Oil Corp
WONE	Q	Westwood One Inc
WOR	N	Worthen Banking Corp
WOTK	Q	World Wide Technology Inc
WPB	A	Wiener Enterprises Inc
WPGI	Q	Western Publishing Group Inc
WPH	N	W P L Holdings Inc
WPM	N	West Point Pepperell Inc
WPOB	A	Washington Post Co Cl B
WPPGY	Q	W P P Group Plc ADR
WPS	N	Wisconsin Public Service Corp
WRE	A	Washington Real Estate Investment Trust S B I
WRI	N	Weingarten Realty Investors S B I
WRNB	Q	Warren Bancorp Inc

WRO	A	Wichita River Oil
WRS	A	Winston Resources Inc
WRTC	Q	Writer Corp
WS	N	Weirton Steel Corp
WSAU	Q	Wausau Paper Mills Co
WSBC	Q	Wesbanco Inc
WSBK	Q	Western Bank
WSBX	Q	Washington Savings Bank
WSC	A	Wesco Financial Corp
WSCI	Q	Washington Scientific Industries Inc
WSGC	Q	Williams Sonoma Inc
WSMCA	Q	Westmarc Communications Inc Cl A
WSMP	Q	W S M P Inc
WSN	N	Western Co of North America
WSOA	A	Watsco Inc Cl A
WSOB	A	Watsco Inc Cl B
WSP*	N	West Penn Power Co 4 1 2% Pfd Vtg
WST	N	West Co Inc
WSTF	Q	Western Financial Corp
WSTM	Q	Western Micro Technology Inc
WSTNA	Q	Roy Western Inc Cl A
WSVS	Q	Wiland Services Inc
WT	A	Woolworth F W Co Ltd ADR S
WTBK	Q	Westerbeke Corp
WTDI	Q	W T D Industries Inc
WTEL	N	Walker Telecommunication Corp
WTHG	Q	Worthington Industries Inc
WTI	N	Wheelabrator Technologies Inc
WTOY	Q	Wisconsin Toy Co Inc
WTPR	Q	Wetterau Properties Inc
WTRS	Q	Waters Instrument Inc
WTWS	Q	Wall To Wall Sound & Video Inc
WTX*	A	West Texas Utilities $4.40 Pfd
WU	N	Western Union Corp
WU*A	N	Western Union Corp 4.60% Cum Cv Pfd A
WU*AW	N	Western Union Corp $4.60% Cum Cv Pfd A W D
WU*B	N	Western Union Corp Cl B Cum Cv Pfd
WU*C	N	Western Union Corp 4.90% Cum Cv 2nd Pfd C
WU*E	N	Western Union Corp Dep Pfd E
WU*S	N	Western Union Corp Dep Pfd Shares
WUR	N	Wurltech Industries Inc
WUT*	N	Western Union Telegraph 6% Cum Pfd
WUT*A	N	Western Union Telegraph 10.25% Cum Pfd A
WVTK	Q	Wavetek Corp
WWBC	Q	Washington Bancorp
WWIN	Q	Western Waste Industries
WWP	N	Washington Water Power Co
WWTK	Q	Weitek Corp
WWW	N	Wolverine World Wide Inc
WWWM	Q	Williams W W Co
WWY	N	Wrigley Wm Jr Co
WX	N	Westinghouse Electric
WY	N	Weyerhaeuser Co
WY*	N	Weyerhaeuser Co 2.625 Cv Exch Pfd
WYL	N	Wyle Laboratories
WYMN	Q	Wyman Gordon Co
WYNB	Q	Wyoming National Bancorp
WYS	N	Wyse Technology
X	N	U S X Corp
X*	N	U S X Corp Adj Rate Cum Pfd
X$D	N	U S X Corp $10.75 Cum Red Pfd
X*E	N	U S X Corp $3.50 Cv Exch Pfd
XCEL	Q	Excel Bancorp Inc
XCOL	Q	Exploration Co of Louisiana Inc

XCWWS	A	Xerox Currency Wts
XFF	N	French Franc
XICO	Q	Xicor Inc
XLDC	Q	X L Datacomp Inc
XLGX	Q	Xylogics Inc
XNP	A	Americus Trust for Exxon Shares Prime
XNS	A	Americus Trust for Exxon Shares Score
XNU	A	Americus Trust for Exxon Shares Units
XOL	A	Xoil Energy Resources Inc
XOMA	Q	Xoma Corp
XON	N	Exxon Corp
XPLR	Q	Xplor Corp
XPP	A	Americus Trust for American Express Shares Prime
XPS	A	Americus Trust for American Express Shares Score
XPU	A	Americus Trust for American Express Shares Units
XRAY	Q	Gendix Corp
XRIT	Q	X Rite Inc
XRX	N	Xerox Corp
XRX*A	N	Xerox Corp $3.6875 Pfd
XRX*B	N	Xerox Corp $4.125 Pfd
XRXWD	N	Xerox Corp W D
XSCR	Q	Xscribe Corp
XSY	N	Swiss Franc Option
XTGX	Q	T G X Corp
XTON	Q	Executone Information Systems Inc
XTR	N	X T R A Inc
XTR*B	N	X T R A Inc 1.9375 Ser B Cum Cv Pfd
XTX	A	New York Tax Exempt Income Fund
XXP	A	Americus Trust for Xerox Shares Prime
XXS	A	Americus Trust for Xerox Shares Score
XXU	A	Americus Trust for Xerox Shares Units
XYVI	Q	Xyvision Inc
Y	N	Alleghany Corp
YCO	N	Yardney Corp
YCSL	Q	Yorkridge Calvert S & L Assn
YELL	Q	Yellow Freight Systems Inc of Delaware
YESS	Q	Yankee Energy Systems Inc
YFED	Q	York Financial Corp
YLD	N	High Income Advantage Trust
YLH	N	High Income Advantage Trust III
YLT	N	High Income Advantage Trust II
YNK	A	Yankee Cos
YNK*	A	Yankee Cos $1.15 Cum Pfd
YORK	Q	York Research
YWWS	A	Citicorp Currency Exchange Wts Japan
YYWWS	A	Citicorp Currency Exchange Yen 1993 Wts
Z	N	Woolworth Corp Holding Co
Z*A	N	Woolworth Corp Holding Co $2.20 Cum Cv Pfd A
ZAL	N	Zale Corp
ZAPS	Q	Cooper Life Sciences Inc
ZCAD	Q	Zycad Corp
ZE	N	Zenith Electronics Corp
ZEGL	Q	Zeigler Co Inc
ZEN	N	Zenith Laboratories Inc
ZENT	Q	Zentec Corp
ZEUS	Q	Zeus Components Inc
ZF	N	Zweig Fund Inc
ZIF	N	Zenith Income Fund Inc
ZIGO	Q	Zygo Corp
ZION	Q	Zions Bancorp
ZITL	Q	Zitel Corp
ZMOS	Q	Zymos Corp
ZMX	N	Zemex Corp

ZNT	N	Zenith National Insurance Corp
ZOS	N	Zapata Corp
ZRN	N	Zurn Industries Inc
ZRO	N	Zero Corp
ZTR	N	Zweig Total Return Fund Inc

Appendix

SELECTED FURTHER READING

Overall Bibliography

Daniells, Lorna M. *Business Information Sources*. rev. ed. Berkeley: University of California Press, 1985.

Economics

Friedman, Milton. *Capitalism and Freedom*. Chicago: University of Chicago Press, 1981.

A leading exponent of the monetarist ("Chicago") school of economics sets forth his views in this basic work, first published in 1962.

Heilbroner, Robert L. and Lester C. Thurow. *The Economic Problem*. 7th ed. Englewood Cliffs: Prentice-Hall, 1984.

An established introductory text by two noted economists; covers the background, economic tools, market systems, and major challenges in both macroeconomics and microeconomics.

Keynes, John Maynard. *The General Theory of Employment, Interest and Money*. London: Macmillan, 1936.

The definitive work of the British economist and government advisor, whose influential theories advocating government intervention (fiscal policy) as a solution to economic problems have become known as Keynesian economics.

McConnell, Campbell R. *Economics: Principles, Problems, and Policies*. 9th ed. New York: McGraw-Hill, 1984.

A highly regarded introduction to the fundamental problems and principles of economics and the policy alternatives available to countries, both from a national and international perspective.

Samuelson, Paul A. and W. Nordhaus: *Economics*. 12th ed. New York: McGraw-Hill, 1985.

This famous and widely used introductory economics text has been thoroughly revised and updated. It takes students from fundamental to sophisticated levels of understanding of income and production factors including international trade and finance and current economic problems.

Smith, Adam. *An Inquiry into the Nature and Causes of the Wealth of Nations*. New York: Random House (Modern Library), 1937.

The definitive work, first published in 1776, of the most famous of the classical economists, who held that economies function best when under a laissez-faire system in which market forces are free to operate without government interference.

International Economics, Finance, and Investment

George, Abraham M. and Ian H. Giddy, eds. *International Finance Handbook*. 2 vol. New York: John Wiley & Sons, 1983.

A massive reference written by 56 authorities for the nonspecialist practitioner in international financing, banking, and investment.

Lindert, Peter H. and Charles P. Kindleberger. *International Economics*. 7th ed. Homewood, Illinois: Dow Jones-Irwin, 1982.

A classic text covering aspects of international economics and finance on theoretical and practical levels, plus an examination of larger problems concerning international mobility of people and factors of production.

Pring, Martin J. *International Investing Made Easy*. New York: McGraw-Hill, 1980.

A wide-ranging discussion for the investor new to foreign securities, clearly written by a well-known authority.

Root, Franklin R. *International Trade and Investment*. 5th ed. Cincinnati: South-Western, 1984.

Covers theory, policy, and the marketplace of international trade, including international payments, development financing, and international investments and multinational enterprises.

Roussakis, Emmanuel N., ed. *International Banking: Principles and Practices*. New York: Praeger, 1983.

Twenty-three experts discuss international banking, focusing on lending policies and procedures and on risk and credit analysis.

Walker, Townsend. *A Guide for Using the Foreign Exchange Market*. New York: John Wiley and Sons, 1981.

This beginner's explanatory guide, with case studies and exercises, emphasizes techniques, analysis, and calculations used in foreign exchange.

Money and Banking

Cochran, John A. *Money, Banking and the Economy*. 5th ed. New York: Macmillan, 1983.

An introductory text covering money; the money and capital markets; commercial banks and their competitors; commercial banking practices; central banking; monetary and income theory; and public policy.

DeRosa, Paul and Gary H. Stern. *In the Name of Money: A Professional's Guide to the Federal Reserve, Interest Rates & Money*. New York: McGraw-Hill, 1981.

A practical (rather than theoretical) discussion of Federal Reserve policy and operations and their effects on interest rates, money supply, and the financial markets. Not for the beginner.

Kaufman, George G. *The U.S. Financial System: Money, Markets and Institutions*. 2d ed. Englewood Cliffs: Prentice-Hall, 1983.

Assuming a basic knowledge of economics, this text covers in terms of theory and practice the evolution and operations of the national and international financial markets as well as instruments, institutions, and regulation. The Federal Reserve System and other aspects of the economic macrostructure are also examined.

Ritter, Lawrence S. and William L. Silber. *Principles of Money, Banking and Financial Markets*. 4th ed. New York: Basic Books, 1983.

A comprehensive introductory text that covers money and banking fundamentals; banks and other intermediaries; central banking; monetary theory; financial markets and interest rates; and international finance.

Bond and Money Markets

Darst, David M. *The Handbook of the Bond and Money Markets*. New York: McGraw-Hill, 1981.

For professionals and nonprofessionals, this volume analyzes long- and short-term fixed-income securities, the marketplace, and investment strategies. Comprehensively covers such related subjects as Federal Reserve operations and the makeup and meaning of economic and debt statistics.

Donoghue, William E. with Thomas Tilling. *William E. Donoghue's Complete Money Market Guide*. New York: Harper & Row, 1981.

A readable guide to the money market and investing through money market funds, by a prominent specialist in the field.

Fabozzi, Frank J. and Irving M. Pollock, eds. *The Handbook of Fixed Income Securities*. Homewood, Illinois: Dow Jones-Irwin, 1983.

Includes 47 chapters, each by an expert, covering general investment information; securities and instruments; bond investment management; interest rates and rate forecasting. More extensive than the volume by David M. Darst, but similarly designed for the layperson and professional.

Holt, Robert L. *The Complete Book of Bonds*. rev. ed. San Diego: Harcourt Brace Jovanovich, 1985.

An in-depth examination of bonds and the markets in which they are traded; for both the beginner and the professional.

Stigum, Marcia. *The Money Market*. rev. ed. Homewood, Illinois: Dow Jones-Irwin, 1983.

A comprehensive guide, by a working professional, to the U.S. money market. It covers (1) the various instruments traded, how yields are calculated, and the role of the Federal Reserve; (2) the major participants, including Eurobanks; and (3) particular markets, such as those for commercial paper, Treasury bills, and CDs. Includes financial futures.

Corporate Finance

Altman, Edward I., ed. *Financial Handbook*. 5th ed. New York: John Wiley and Sons, 1981.

With 38 chapters written by 45 authorities, this exhaustive reference divides the world of finance into four sections: U.S. Financial Markets and Institutions; International Financial Markets and Institutions; Securities and Portfolio Management; and Corporate Financial Management. The last category includes 15 chapters on such subjects as planning and control techniques, financial forecasting, capital budgeting, and mergers and acquisitions.

Brigham, Eugene F. *Financial Management: Theory and Practice.* 4th ed. Hinsdale, Illinois: Dryden Press, 1985.

A well-written discussion of basic concepts in financial management and their use in maximizing the value of a firm. Using real-life examples, the text covers financial forecasting, working capital management, capital budgeting, and other relevant subjects, including international financial management and mergers and acquisitions.

Van Horne, James C. *Fundamentals of Financial Management.* 6th ed. Englewood Cliffs: Prentice-Hall, 1986.

An excellent introductory text with sections on principles of financial returns, tools of financial analysis and planning, working capital management, investing in capital assets, capital structure and dividend policies, long-term financing and markets, and special areas including cash-management models and option pricing.

Weston, J. Fred and Eugene F. Brigham. *Essentials of Managerial Finance.* 7th ed. Hinsdale, Illinois: Dryden Press. 1985.

A fine introductory text emphasizing decision rather than theory, with sections on fundamental concepts; financial analysis, planning and control; working capital management; investment decisions; cost of capital and valuation; long-term financing decisions; and integrated topics in managerial finance.

Securities Markets, Securities Analysis, and Portfolio Management

Amling, Frederick. *Investments, An Introduction to Analysis and Management.* 5th ed. Englewood Cliffs: Prentice-Hall, 1984.

A text for the beginning investor or aspiring investment professional. Using practical cases to demonstrate principles, the book deals with various aspects of fundamental analysis, modern portfolio theory, and technical analysis.

Arbel, Avner. *How to Beat the Market with High-Performance Generic Stocks.* New York: William Morrow, 1985.

In an original contribution to the literature of investing, Professor Arbel sets forth an investment strategy based on generic stocks, which lack name recognition but represent potential appreciation because their values have been ignored by the brokerage community.

Cohen, Jerome B., Edward D. Zinbarg, and Arthur Zeikel. *Investment Analysis and Portfolio Management.* 4th ed. Homewood, Illinois: Dow Jones-Irwin, 1982.

An introductory text, notable because it is comprehensive and discusses modern portfolio theory and security valuation techniques in a nonmathematical, readable fashion. It also covers the current investment scene and industry and company analysis.

Dreman, David. *The New Contrarian Investment Strategy: The Psychology of Stock Market Success.* New York: Random House, 1983.

An updated version of an established title, this book discusses a contrarian's approach to successful investing in a 1980s environment marked by widely fluctuating interest rates and market prices.

Engel, Louis and Brendan Boyd. *How to Buy Stocks.* 7th ed. Boston: Atlantic-Little Brown, 1983.

A highly readable, clear, and informative introduction to investing in the stock market, this book has been a deserved fixture in the literature on investing for over three decades.

Fischer, Donald E. and Ronald J. Jordan. *Security Analysis and Portfolio Management.* 3d ed. Englewood Cliffs: Prentice-Hall, 1983.

By using the fast-food industry and McDonald's Corporation as an example to illustrate the practical applications of security analysis and portfolio management theory, the authors of this introductory text manage to keep an essentially mathematical subject relatively nonmathematical and understandable.

Graham, Benjamin, David L. Dodd, and Sidney Cottle. *Security Analysis: Principles and Techniques.* 4th ed. New York: McGraw-Hill, 1962.

This classic work, originally published in 1934, remains the bible for students of the fundamentalist approach to securities analysis. It consists of six parts: survey and approach; analysis of financial statements; fixed-income securities; the valuation of common stocks; senior securities with speculative features; and other aspects of security analysis.

Loll, Leo M. and Julian G. Buckley. *The Over-The-Counter Securities Markets.* 4th ed. Englewood Cliffs: Prentice-Hall, 1981.

A training manual for would-be stockbrokers preparing for the NASD examination and a generally valuable book for any investor wishing to learn more about the over-the-counter markets, securities underwriting, stock and bond trading, regulation, and the securities business in general.

Pring, Martin J. *Technical Analysis Explained: The Successful Investor's Guide to Spotting Investment Trends and Turning Points.* 2d ed. New York: McGraw-Hill, 1985.

An excellent and comprehensive introduction to technical analysis, made especially useful by its many illustrative charts.

Rolo, Charles J. *Gaining on the Market: Your Complete Guide to Investment Strategy.* Boston: Atlantic-Little Brown, 1982.

A superb guide to investing in stocks. It discusses stock picking and market timing as well as forces influencing stock prices and includes practical advice on dealing with brokers and using information sources.

Teweles, Richard J. and Edward S. Bradley. *The Stock Market.* 4th ed. New York: John Wiley and Sons, 1982.

This is a revision of a work originally authored by George L. Leffler in 1951. It examines the stock market in five sections dealing with fundamental information, the exchanges, securities houses, regulations, investing practices, and special instruments.

Train, John. *The Money Masters.* New York: Harper & Row, 1980.

Interesting stories, by an investment counselor, about the investment strategies of nine distinguished portfolio managers, such as T. Rowe Price, Benjamin Graham, and John Templeton, with commentary on their methods and personalities.

Commodity and Financial Futures Markets

Huff, Charles and Barbara Marinacci. *Commodity Speculation for Beginners: A Guide to the Futures Market.* New York: Macmillan, 1980.

Using an informal, chatty narrative style, this book takes the beginner to a considerable depth of understanding of commodities trading and its marketplace, including personal trading programs.

Kaufman, Perry J. *Handbook of Futures Markets: Commodity, Financial, Stock Index, Options.* New York: John Wiley and Sons, 1984.

An extensive manual and reference guide comprising 49 chapters written by over 50 experts. Twenty-five chapters deal with individual commodities, including financial futures. Others deal with markets, forecasting, hedging, risk and money management, and other technical aspects.

Powers, Mark J. *Getting Started in Commodity Futures Trading.* 4th ed. Cedar Falls, Iowa: Investor Publications, 1983.

A combination of theory and practical information for the beginner; includes history, exchanges, choosing a broker, trading programs, hedging, and forecasting. Deals with financial futures.

Rothstein, Nancy H. and James M. Little, eds. *The Handbook of Financial Futures: A Guide for Investors and Professional Financial Managers.* New York: McGraw-Hill, 1984.

A comprehensive reference focusing on concepts and methods for using and analyzing financial futures for hedging and trading purposes, including regulatory, accounting, and tax implications. For the professional as well as the novice.

Schwager, Jack D. *A Complete Guide to the Futures Markets: Fundamental Analysis, Technical Analysis, Trading, Spreads, and Options.* New York: John Wiley and Sons, 1984.

Assumes a basic familiarity with futures trading, but otherwise provides a nontechnical discussion of various analytical techniques, including regression analysis and chart analysis. Has sample charts and a section on trading guidelines.

Options Markets

Ansbacher, Max G. *The New Options Market.* rev. ed. New York: Walker & Co., 1979.

An easy-to-read, yet comprehensive rundown, by a professional trader, of options and option strategies. For the speculator as well as the conservative investor.

——. *The New Stock-Index Market, Strategies for Profit in Stock Index Futures and Options.* New York: Walker & Co., 1983.

This veteran trader and clearheaded writer discusses the relatively new and growing area of index futures and options; for beginner as well as seasoned investors and speculators.

Gastineau, Gary L. *The Stock Options Manual.* 2d ed. New York: McGraw-Hill, 1979.

Assuming a basic knowledge of options and how they are used, Gastineau discusses option valuation methods and their applications in portfolio analysis and management. The book also covers option investment and trading strategies and tax implications.

McMillan, Lawrence G. *Options as a Strategic Investment.* Englewood Cliffs: Prentice-Hall, 1980.

An advanced discussion of option strategies, focusing on which ones work where and why. Includes chapters on arbitrage, mathematical applications, and tax ramifications.

Tso, Lin. *Complete Investor's Guide to Listed Options: Calls & Puts.* Englewood Cliffs: Prentice-Hall, 1981.

A leading expert discusses the fundamentals of puts and calls and the uses, risks, and rewards of listed options for investors of all types.

CURRENCIES OF THE WORLD

This is a list of the currencies of most of the countries on earth. The countries are listed alphabetically, with the name of the currency, followed by the denomination that currency is broken down into. For example, one dollar is made up of 100 cents. This listing should be useful to anyone traveling or doing business in any of these countries.

Of course, the value of these currencies is constantly changing in relation to the amount of dollars necessary to buy them. For current exchange rates of the currencies of most major countries, one must consult the financial tables of newspapers such as the *Wall Street Journal* or *London's Financial Times*.

Abu Dhabi 1 Dinar = 1,000 fils
Aden 1 Dinar = 1,000 fils
Afghanistan 1 Afghani = 100 puls
Albania 1 Lek = 100 qintar
Algeria 1 Dinar = 100 centimes
Andorra 1 Peseta = 100 centimos
Angola 1 Kwanza = 100 centavos
Antigua 1 Dollar= 100 cents
Argentina 1 Austral = 100 cents
Australia 1 Dollar = 100 cents
Austria 1 Schilling= 100 groschen
Azores 1 Escudo = 100 cents
Bahamas 1 Dollar = 100 cents
Bahrain 1 Dinar = 100 fils
Bangladesh 1 Taka = 100 paise
Barbados 1 Dollar = 100 cents
Belgium 1 Franc = 100 centimes
Bermuda 1 Pound = 100 pence
Bhutan 1 Ngultrum = 100 chetzrum
Bolivia 1 Peso = 100 centavos
Botswana 1 Pula = 100 cents
Brazil 1 Cruzado = 100 new centavos
Brunei 1 Dollar = 100 cents
Bulgaria 1 Lev = 100 stotinki
Burkina Fasso 1 Franc = 100 centimes
Burma 1 Kyat = 100 pyas
Burundi 1 Franc = 100 centimes
Cambodia 1 Riel = 100 sen
Cameroon 1 Franc = 100 centimes
Canada 1 Dollar = 100 cents
Canary Islands 1 Peseta = 100 centimos
Cape Verde Islands 1 Escudo = 100 centavos

Central African Republic 1 Franc = 100 centimes
Chad 1 Franc = 100 centimes
Chile 1 Peso = 100 centavos
China (Communist) 1 Yuan = 10,000 jen min piao
Colombia 1 Peso = 100 centavos
Congo 1 Franc = 100 centimos
Costa Rica 1 Colon = 100 centimos
Cuba 1 Peso = 100 centavos
Cyprus 1 Pound = 1,000 mils
Czechoslovakia 1 Koruna = 100 hellers
Denmark 1 Krone = 100 øre
Djibouti 1 Franc = 100 centimes
Dominica 1 Dollar = 100 cents
Dominican Republic 1 Peso = 100 centavos
Dubai 1 Gulf Riyal = 100 dirhams
Ecuador 1 Sucre = 100 centavos
Egypt 1 Pound = 100 piasters
El Salvador 1 Colon = 100 centavos
Equatorial Guinea 1 Franc = 100 centimes
Ethiopia 1 Birr = 100 cents
Fiji Islands 1 Dollar = 100 cents
Finland 1 Markka = 100 pennis
France 1 Franc = 100 centimes
Gabon 1 Franc = 100 centimes
Gambia 1 Dalasi = 100 bututs
Germany (West) 1 Deutsche mark = 100 pfennig
Ghana 1 Cedi = 100 pesewas
Gibraltar 1 Pound = 100 pence
Grand Cayman Island 1 Pound = 100 pence
Greece 1 Drachma = 100 lepta

Grenada 1 Dollar = 100 cents
Guadeloupe 1 Franc = 100 centimes
Guam 1 U.S. Dollar = 100 cents
Guatemala 1 Quetzal= 100 centavos
Guiana (French) 1 Franc = 100 centimes
Guinea-Bissau 1 Peso = 100 centavos
Guinea 1 Syli = 100 centimes
Guyana 1 Dollar = 100 cents
Haiti 1 Gourde = 100 centimes
Honduras 1 Lempira = 100 centavos
Hong Kong 1 Dollar = 100 cents
Hungary 1 Forint = 100 fils
Iceland 1 Krona = 100 aurar
India 1 Rupee = 100 paise
Indonesia 1 Rupiah = 100 sen
Iran 1 Rial = 100 dinars
Iraq 1 Dinar = 1,000 fils
Ireland 1 Pound = 100 pence
Israel 1 Shekel = 100 new agorot
Italy 1 Lira = 100 centesimi
Ivory Coast 1 Franc = 100 centimes
Jamaica 1 Dollar = 100 cents
Japan 1 Yen = 100 sen
Jordan 1 Dinar = 1,000 fils
Kampuchea 1 Riel = 100 sen
Kenya 1 Shilling = 100 cents
Korea (North and South) 1 Won = 100 chon
Kuwait 1 Dinar = 1,000 fils
Laos 1 Kip = 100 at
Lebanon 1 Pound = 100 piasters
Lesotho 1 Loti = 100 cents
Liberia 1 U.S. Dollar = 100 cents
Libya 1 Dinar = 1,000 fils
Liechtenstein 1 Franc = 100 centimes
Luxembourg 1 Franc = 100 centimes
Macao 1 Pataca = 100 avos
Madagascar 1 Franc = 100 centimes
Madeira 1 Escudo = 100 centavos
Malawi 1 Kwacha = 100 tambala
Malaysia 1 Ringgit = 100 sen
Maldive Islands 1 Rufiya = 100 cents
Mali 1 Franc = 100 centimes
Malta 1 Lire = 100 centesimi
Marshall Islands 1 U.S. Dollar = 100 cents
Martinique 1 Franc = 100 centimes
Mauritania 1 Ouguiya = 5 khoums
Mauritius 1 Rupee = 100 cents
Mexico 1 Peso = 100 centavos
Monaco 1 Franc = 100 centimes
Mongolia 1 Tughrik = 100 mongos
Montserrat 1 Dollar = 100 cents
Morocco 1 Dirham = 100 Moroccan francs
Mozambique 1 Metical= 100 cents

Nauru 1 Dollar = 100 cents
Nepal 1 Rupee = 100 pice
Netherlands 1 Guilder = 100 cents
Netherlands Antilles 1 Guilder = 100 cents
New Caledonia 1 Franc = 100 centimes
New Guinea 1 Dollar = 100 cents
New Hebrides Islands 1 Franc = 100 centimes
New Zealand 1 Dollar = 100 cents
Nicaragua 1 Cordoba = 100 centavos
Niger 1 Franc = 100 centimes
Nigeria 1 Naira = 100 kobo
Norway 1 Krone = 100 øre
Oman 1 Rial = 100 dinars
Pakistan 1 Rupee = 100 paisa
Panama 1 Balboa = 100 centesimos
Papua New Guinea 1 Kina = 100 cents
Paraguay 1 Guarani = 100 centimos
Peru 1 Sol = 100 centavos
Philippines 1 Peso = 100 centavos
Poland 1 Zloty = 100 grosze
Portugal 1 Escudo = 100 centavos
Puerto Rico 1 U.S. Dollar = 100 cents
Qatar 1 Gulf Riyal = 100 dirhams
Romania 1 Leu = 100 bani
Rwanda 1 Franc = 100 centimes
St. Kitts Island 1 Dollar = 100 cents
St. Lucia Island 1 Dollar = 100 cents
St. Vincent Island 1 Dollar = 100 cents
Samoa 1 Tala = 100 sene
San Marino 1 Lira = 100 centesimi
Saudi Arabia 1 Riyal = 20 gurshes
Senegal 1 Franc = 100 centimes
Seychelles Islands 1 Rupee = 100 cents
Sierra Leone 1 Leone = 100 cents
Singapore 1 Dollar = 100 cents
Solomon Islands 1 Dollar = 100 cents
Somalia Somalian Shilling = 100 centesimi
South Africa 1 Rand = 100 cents
South West Africa (Namibia) 1 Rand = 100 cents
South Yemen 1 Dinar = 1,000 fils
Spain 1 Peseta = 100 centimos
Sri Lanka 1 Rupee = 100 paise
Sudan 1 Pound = 100 piasters
Suriname 1 Guilder = 100 cents
Swaziland 1 Lilangeni = 100 cents
Sweden 1 Krona = 100 öre
Switzerland 1 Franc = 100 centimes
Syria 1 Pound = 100 piasters
Tahiti 1 Franc = 100 centimes
Taiwan 1 Dollar = 100 cents
Tanzania 1 Shilling = 100 cents
Thailand 1 Baht = 100 satang

Timor 1 Escudo = 100 centavos
Togo 1 Franc = 100 centimes
Tonga islands 1 Pa'anga = 100 cents
Trinidad and Tobago 1 Dollar = 100 cents
Tunisia 1 Dinar = 1,000 milliemes
Turkey 1 Lira 100 centensimi
Uganda 1 Shilling = 100 cents
United Arab Emirates 1 Dirham = 100 francs
United Kingdom 1 Pound = 100 pence
United States 1 Dollar = 100 cents

Uruguay 1 New Peso = 100 centesimos
USSR 1 Ruble = 100 kopeks
Vatican City 1 Lira = 100 centesimi
Venezuela 1 Bolivar = 100 centimos
Vietnam 1 Dong = 100 cents
Virgin Islands (U.S.) 1 Dollar = 100 cents
Yugoslavia 1 Dinar = 100 paras
Zaire 1 Zaire = 100 makutu
Zambia 1 Kwacha = 100 newee
Zimbabwe 1 Dollar = 100 cents

ABBREVIATIONS AND ACRONYMS

A

A Includes Extra (or Extras) (in stock listings of newspapers)

AAII American Association of Individual Investors

AB Aktiebolag (Swedish stock company)

ABA American Bankers Association

ABA American Bar Association

ABLA American Business Law Association

ABWA American Business Women's Association

ACE AMEX Commodities Exchange

ACRS Accelerated Cost Recovery System

A-D Advance-Decline Line

ADB Adjusted Debit Balance

ADR Automatic Dividend Reinvestment

ADR Asset Depreciation Range System

ADRS Asset Depreciation Range System

AE Account Executive

AFL-CIO American Federation of Labor-Congress of Industrial Organizations

AG Aktiengesellschaft (West German stock company)

AICPA American Institute of Certified Public Accountants

AID Agency for International Development

AIM American Institute for Management

AMA American Management Association

AMA Asset Management Account

AMEX American Stock Exchange

AON All or None

APB Accounting Principles Board

APR Annual Percentage Rate

Arb Arbitrageur

ARF American Retail Federation

ARM Adjustable Rate Mortgage

ARPS Adjustable Rate Preferred Stock

ASAP As Soon as Possible

ASE American Stock Exchange

ATM Automatic Teller Machine

B

B Annual Rate Plus Stock Dividend (in stock listings of newspapers)

BAC Business Advisory Council

BAN Bond Anticipation Note

BBB Better Business Bureau

BD Bank Draft

BD Bills Discontinued

B/D Broker-Dealer

BE Bill of Exchange

BF Brought Forward

BL Bill of Lading

BLS Bureau of Labor Statistics

BO Branch Office

BO Buyer's Option

BOM Beginning of the Month

BOP Balance of Payments

BOT Balance of Trade

BOT Bought

BOT Board of Trustees

BPW Business and Professional Women's Foundation

BR Bills Receivable

BS Balance Sheet

BS Bill of Sale

BS Bureau of Standards

BW Bid Wanted

C

C Liquidating Dividend (in stock listings of newspapers)

CA Capital Account

CA Chartered Accountant

CA Commercial Agent

CA Credit Account

CA Current Account

CACM Central American Common Market

CAD Cash against Documents

CAF Cost Assurance and Freight

C&F Cost and Freight

CAPM Capital Asset Pricing Model

CATS Certificate of Accrual on Treasury Securities

CATV Community Antenna Television

CBA Cost Benefit Analysis

CBD Cash Before Delivery

CBOE Chicago Board Options Exchange

CBT Chicago Board of Trade

CC Chamber of Commerce

CCH Commerce Clearing House

CD Certificate of Deposit

CD Commercial Dock

CEA Council of Economic Advisors

CEO Chief Executive Officer

CF Certificates (in bond listings of newspapers)

CF Carried Forward

CFC Chartered Financial Counselor

CFC Consolidated Freight Classification

CFI Cost, Freight, and Insurance

CFO Chief Financial Officer

CFP Certified Financial Planner

CFTC Commodities Futures Trading Commission

CH Clearing House

CH Custom House

Cía Compañía (Spanish company)

Cie Compagnie (French company)

CIF Corporate Income Fund

CIF Cost, Insurance, and Freight

CLD Called (in stock listings of newspapers)

CLU Chartered Life Underwriter

CME Chicago Mercantile Exchange

CMO Collateralized Mortgage Obligation

CMV Current Market Value

CN Consignment Note

CN Credit Note

CNS Continuous Net Settlement

CO Cash Order

CO Certificate of Origin

Co. Company

COB Close of Business (with date)

COD Cash on Delivery

COD Collect on Delivery

CODA Cash or Deferred Arrangement

COLA Cost-of-Living Adjustment

COMEX Commodity Exchange (New York)

COMSAT Communications Satellite Corporation

CPA Certified Public Accountant

CPD Commissioner of Public Debt

CPFF Cost Plus Fixed Fee

CPI Consumer Price Index

CPM Cost per Thousand

CPPC Cost plus a Percentage of Cost
CR Carrier's Risk
CR Class Rate
CR Company's Risk
CR Current Rate
CRCE Chicago Rice and Cotton Exchange
CSCE Coffee, Sugar and Cocoa Exchange
CSE Cincinnati Stock Exchange
CSVLI Cash Surrender Value of Life Insurance
CUNA Credit Union National Association
CUSIP Committee on Uniform Securities Identification Procedures
CV Convertible Security
CWO Cash with Order

D

DA Deposit Account
DA Documents against Acceptance
DAC Delivery against Cost
D&B Dun and Bradstreet
DC Deep Discount Issue (in bond listings of newspapers)
DCFM Discounted Cash Flow Method
DDB Double-Declining-Balance Depreciation Method
DF Damage Free
DIDC Depository Institutions Deregulatory Committee
DISC Domestic International Sales Corporation
DJIA Dow Jones Industrial Average
DJTA Dow Jones Transportation Average
DJUA Dow Jones Utility Average
DK Don't Know
DN Debit Note
DNR Do Not Reduce
D/O Delivery Order

DP Documents against Payment
DPI Disposable Personal Income
DS Days After Sight
DTC Depository Trust Company
DUNS Data Universal Numbering System (Dun's Number)
DVP Delivery Versus Payment

E

E Declared or Paid in the Preceding 12 Months (in stock listings of newspapers)
E&OE Errors and Omissions Excepted
EBIT Earnings Before Interest and Taxes
ECM European Common Market
ECT Estimated Completion Time
EDD Estimated Delivery Date
EEC European Economic Community
EEOC Equal Employment Opportunity Commission
EMP End-of-Month Payment
EOA Effective On or About
EOM End of Month
EPR Earnings Price Ratio
EPS Earnings Per Share
ERISA Employee Retirement Income Security Act of 1974
ERTA Economic Recovery Tax Act of 1981
ESOP Employee Stock Ownership Plan
ETA Estimated Time of Arrival
ETD Estimated Time of Departure
ETLT Equal To or Less Than
EUA European Unit of Account
EXIMBANK Export-Import Bank

F

F Dealt in Flat (in bond listings in newspapers)

FA Free Alongside

FACT Factor Analysis Chart Technique

FAS Free Alongside

FASB Financial Accounting Standards Board

FAT Fixed Asset Transfer

FAX Facsimile

FB Freight Bill

FCA Fellow of the Institute of Chartered Accountants

FCC Federal Communications Commission

FCUA Federal Credit Union Administration

FDIC Federal Deposit Insurance Corporation

Fed Federal Reserve System

FET Federal Excise Tax

F&F Furniture and Fixtures

FFCS Federal Farm Credit System

FGIC Financial Guaranty Insurance Corporation

FHA Farmers Home Administration

FHA Federal Housing Administration

FHLBB Federal Home Loan Bank Board

FHLMC Federal Home Loan Mortgage Corporation (Freddie Mac)

FICA Federal Insurance Contributions Act

FICB Federal Intermediate Credit Bank

FIFO First In, First Out

FIGS Future Income and Growth Securities

FIT Federal Income Tax

FITW Federal Income Tax Withholding

FLB Federal Land Bank

FMC Federal Maritime Commission

FNMA Federal National Mortgage Association (Fannie Mae)

FOB Free on Board

FOC Free of Charge

FOCUS Financial and Operations Combined Uniform Single Report

FOI Freedom of Information Act

FOK Fill or Kill

FOMC Federal Open Market Committee

FOR Free on Rail (or Road)

FOT Free on Truck

FP Floating Policy

FP Fully Paid

FRA Federal Reserve Act

FRB Federal Reserve Bank

FRB Federal Reserve Board

FRD Federal Reserve District

FREIT Finite Life REIT

FRS Federal Reserve System

FS Final Settlement

FSC Foreign Sales Corporation

FSLIC Federal Savings and Loan Insurance Corporation

FTC Federal Trade Commission

FTI Federal Tax Included

FVO For Valuation Only

FX Foreign Exchange

FY Fiscal Year

FYA For Your Attention

FYI For Your Information

G

G Dividends and Earnings In Canadian Dollars (in stock listings of newspapers)

GAAP Generally Accepted Accounting Principles

GAAS Generally Accepted Auditing Standards

GAI Guaranteed Annual Income

GAINS Growth and Income Securities

GAO General Accounting Office

GATT General Agreement on Tariffs and Trade

GDR German Democratic Republic (East Germany)

GE Federal Republic of Germany (West Germany)

GINNIE MAE Government National Mortgage Association

GM General Manager

GmbH Gesellschaft mit beschränkter Haftung (West German limited liability company)

GNMA Government National Mortgage Association

GNP Gross National Product

GO General Obligation Bond

GPM Graduated Payment Mortgage

GTC Good Till Canceled

GTM Good This Month

GTW Good This Week

H

H Declared or Paid After Stock Dividend or Split-Up (in stock listings of newspapers)

H/F Held For

HFR Hold For Release

HQ Headquarters

HR U.S. House of Representatives

HR U.S. House of Representatives Bill (with number)

HUD Department of Housing and Urban Development

I

I Paid This Year, Dividend Omitted, Deferred, or No Action Taken at Last Dividend Meeting (in stock listings of newspapers)

IBES Institutional Broker's Estimate System

IBRD International Bank for Reconstruction and Development (World Bank)

ICC Interstate Commerce Commission

ICFTU International Confederation of Free Trade Unions

ICMA Institute of Cost and Management Accountants

IDB Industrial Development Bond

IET Interest Equalization Tax

IFC International Finance Corporation

ILA International Longshoremen's Association

ILGWU International Ladies' Garment Workers' Union

ILO International Labor Organization

IMF International Monetary Fund

IMM International Monetary Market of the Chicago Mercantile Exchange

Inc. Incorporated

INSTINET Institutional Networks Corporation

IOC Immediate-Or-Cancel Order

IOU I Owe You

IPO Initial Public Offering

IR Investor Relations

IRA Individual Retirement Account

IRB Industrial Revenue Bond

IRC Internal Revenue Code

IRR Internal Rate of Return

IRS Internal Revenue Service

ISBN International Standard Book Number

ISSN International Standard Serial Number

ITC Investment Tax Credit

ITS Intermarket Trading System

J

JA Joint Account

Jeep Graduated Payment Mortgage

K

K Declared or Paid This Year on a Cumulative Issue with Dividends in Arrears (in stock listings of newspapers)

K Kilo- (prefix meaning multiplied by one thousand)

KCBT   Kansas City Board of Trade

KD   Knocked Down (disassembled)

KK   Kabushiki-Kaisha (Japanese stock company)

KW   Kilowatt

KWH   Kilowatt-hour

KYC   Know Your Customer Rule

L

L   Listed (securities)

LBO   Leveraged Buyout

L/C   Letter Of Credit

LCL   Less-Than-Carload Lot

LCM   Least Common Multiple (mathematics)

LDC   Less Developed Country

L/I   Letter of Intent

LIBOR   London Interbank Offered Rate

LIFO   Last In, First Out

LMRA   Labor-Management Relations Act

LP   Limited Partnership

Ltd   Limited (British Corporation)

LYONS   Liquid Yield Option Notes

M

M   Matured Bonds (in bond listings in newspapers)

M   Mill- (prefix meaning divided by one thousand)

M   Mega- (prefix meaning multiplied by one million)

M   One Thousand (Roman Numeral)

MACE   MidAmerica Commodity Exchange

Max   Maximum

MBA   Master of Business Administration

MBIA   Municipal Bond Insurance Association

MBO   Management By Objective

MBS   Mortgage-backed Security

MC   Marginal Credit

MC   Member of Congress

M-CATS   Municipal Certificates of Accrual on Tax-exempt Securities

MD   Months After Date

ME   Montreal Exchange

MFN   Most Favored Nation (tariff regulations)

MGE   Minneapolis Grain Exchange

MGM   Milligram

MHR   Member of the U.S. House of Representatives

MIG-1   Moody's Investment Grade

MIMC   Member of the Institute of Management Consultants

Min   Minimum

MIS   Management Information System

Misc   Miscellaneous

MIT   Market if Touched

MIT   Municipal Investment Trust

M&L   Matched And Lost

MLR   Minimum Lending Rate

MM   Millimeter (metric unit)

MMDA   Money Market Deposit Account

MO   Money Order

MSB   Mutual Savings Bank

MSE   Midwest Stock Exchange

MSRB   Municipal Securities Rulemaking Board

MTU   Metric Units

N

N   New Issue (in stock listings of newspapers)

NA   National Association (National Bank)

NAIC   National Association of Investment Clubs

NAM   National Association of Manufacturers

NAPA   National Association of Purchasing Agents

NASA   National Aeronautics and Space Administration

NASD   National Association of Securities Dealers

NASDAQ   National Association of Securities Dealers Automated Quotations system

NAV   Net Asset Value

NBS   National Bureau of Standards

NC   No Charge

NCUA   National Credit Union Administration

NCV   No Commercial Value

ND   Next Day Delivery (in stock listings of newspapers)

NEMS   National Exchange Market System

NH   Not Held

NIP   Normal Investment Practice

NIT   Negative Income Tax

NL   No Load

NLRA   National Labor Relations Act

NLRB   National Labor Relations Board

NMAB   National Market Advisory Board

NMB   National Mediation Board

NMS   National Market System

NNP   Net National Product

NOW   National Organization for Women

NOW   Negotiable Order Of Withdrawal

NP   No Protest (banking)

NP   Notary Public

N/P   Notes Payable

NPV   Net Present Value

NPV   No Par Value

NQB   National Quotation Bureau

NQB   No Qualified Bidders

NR   Not Rated

NSBA   National Small Business Association

NSCC   National Securities Clearing Corporation

NSF   Not Sufficient Funds

NSTS   National Securities Trading System

NTU   Normal Trading Unit

NV   Naamloze Vennootschap (Dutch corporation)

NYCE   New York Cotton Exchange

NYCSCE   New York Coffee, Sugar and Cocoa Exchange

NYCTN,CA   New York Cotton Exchange, Citrus Associates

NYFE   New York Futures Exchange

NYME   New York Mercantile Exchange

NYSE   New York Stock Exchange

O

O   Old (in options listing of newspapers)

OAPEC   Organization of Arab Petroleum Exporting Countries

OB   Or Better

OBV   On-Balance Volume

OCC   Options Clearing Corporation

OD   Overdraft, overdrawn

OECD   Organization for Economic Cooperation and Development

OMB   Office of Management and Budget

OPD   Delayed Opening

OPEC   Organization of Petroleum Exporting Countries

OPM   Options Pricing Model

OPM   Other People's Money

O/T   Overtime

1224

Abbreviations and Acronyms

OTC Over The Counter

OW Offer Wanted

P

P Paid this Year (in stock listings of newspapers)

P Put (in options listings of newspapers)

PA Power of Attorney

PA Public Accountant

PA Purchasing Agent

PAC Put and Call (options market)

P&L Profit and Loss Statement

PAYE Pay as You Earn

PBGC Pension Benefit Guaranty Corporation

PC Participation Certificate

PE Price Earnings Ratio (in stock listings of newspapers)

PER Price Earnings Ratio

PF Preferred Stock (stock tables)

PFD Preferred Stock

PHLX Philadelphia Stock Exchange

PL Price List

PLC (British) Public Limited Company

PN Project Note

PN Promissory Note

POA Power of Attorney

POD Pay on Delivery

POE Port of Embarkation

POE Port of Entry

POR Pay on Return

PPS Prior Preferred Stock

PR Preferred Stock (ticker tape)

PR Public Relations

PRIME Prescribed Right to Income and Maximum Equity

Prop Proprietor

PSA Public Securities Association

PSE Pacific Stock Exchange

PUC Public Utilities Commission

PUHCA Public Utility Holding Company Act of 1935

PVR Profit/Volume Ratio

Q

QB Qualified Buyers

QC Quality Control

QI Quarterly Index

QT Questioned Trade

QTIP Qualified Terminable Interest Property Trust

R

R Declared or Paid in the Preceding 12 Months plus Stock Dividend (in stock listings of newspapers)

R Option Not Traded (in option listings in newspapers)

RAM Reverse Annuity Mortgage

RAN Revenue Anticipation Note

R&D Research and Development

RCIA Retail Credit Institute of America

RCMM Registered Competitive Market Maker

REIT Real Estate Investment Trust

REMIC Real Estate Mortgage Investment Conduit

Repo Repurchase Agreement

ROC Return on Capital

ROE Return on Equity

ROI Return on Investment (Return on Invested Capital)

ROP Registered Options Principal

ROS Return on Sales

RP Repurchase Agreement

RRP Reverse Repurchase Agreement

RT Royalty Trust

RTW Right to Work

S

S   No Option Offered (in option listings of newspapers)

S   Signed (before signature on typed copy of a document, original of which was signed)

S   Split or Stock Dividend (in stock listings of newspapers)

SA   Sociedad Anónima (Spanish corporation)

SA   Société Anonyme (French corporation)

SAA   Special Arbitrage Account

SAB   Special Assessment Bond

S&L   Savings and Loan

S&L   Sale and Leaseback

S&P   Standard and Poor's

SB   Savings Bond

SB   Short Bill

SBA   Small Business Administration

SBIC   Small Business Investment Corporation

SBLI   Savings Bank Life Insurance

SCORE   Special Claim on Residual Equity

SD   Standard Deduction

SDB   Special District Bond

SDBL   Sight Draft, Bill of Lading Attached

SDRs   Special Drawing Rights

SE   Shareholders' Equity

SEAQ   Stock Exchange Automated Quotations

SEC   Securities and Exchange Commission

SEP   Simplified Employee Pension Plan

SF   Sinking Fund

SG&A   Selling, General and Administrative Expenses

SIA   Securities Industry Association

SIAC   Securities Industry Automation Corporation

SIC   Standard Industrial Classification

SIPC   Securities Investor Protection Corporation

SL   Sold

SLMA   Student Loan Marketing Association (Sallie Mae)

SLO   Stop-Limit Order, Stop-Loss Order

SMA   Society of Management Accountants

SMA   Special Miscellaneous Account

SML   Security Market Line

SN   Stock Number

Snafu   Situation Normal, All Fouled Up

SOP   Standard Operating Procedure

SOYD   Sum of the Years' Digits Method

SpA   Società per Azioni (Italian corporation)

SPDA   Single Premium Deferred Annuity

SPQR   Small Profits, Quick Returns

SPRI   Société de Personnes à Responsabilité Limitée (Belgian corporation)

Sr   Senior

SRO   Self-Regulatory Organization

SRP   Salary Reduction Plan

SRT   Spousal Remainder Trust

SS   Social Security

SSA   Social Security Administration

STAGS   Sterling Transferable Accruing Government Securities

STB   Special Tax Bond

STRIPS   Seperate Trading of Registered Interest and Principal of Securities

SU   Set Up (freight)

T

T-   Treasury (as in T-bill, T-bond, T-note)

TA   Trade Acceptance

TA   Transfer Agent

TAB   Tax Anticipation Bill

TAN   Tax Anticipation Note

TC   Tax Court of the United States

TD   Time Deposit

TEFRA   Tax Equity and Fiscal Responsibility Act of 1982

TFE   Toronto Futures Exchange

TIGER   Treasury Investors Growth Receipt

TIP   To Insure Promptness

TL   Trade-Last

TM   Trademark

TSE   Toronto Stock Exchange

TT   Testamentary Trust

TVA   Tennessee Valley Authority

U

UAW   United Automobile Workers

UCC   Uniform Commercial Code

UGMA   Uniform Gifts To Minors Act

UIT   Unit Investment Trust

UL   Underwriters' Laboratories

ULC   Underwriter's Laboratories of Canada

ULI   Underwriter's Laboratories, Inc

UMW   United Mine Workers

UN   United Nations

UPC   Uniform Practice Code

US   United States (of America)

USA   United States of America

USBS   United States Bureau of Standards

USC   United States Code

USCC   United States Chamber of Commerce

USIT   Unit Share Investment Trust

USJCC   United States Junior Chamber of Commerce (JAYCEES)

USS   United States Senate

USS   United States Ship

UW   Underwriter

V

VA   Veterans Administration

VAT   Value Added Tax

VD   Volume Deleted

Veep   Vice President

VI   In bankruptcy or receivership; being reorganized under the Bankruptcy Act; securities assumed by such companies (in bond and stock listings of newspapers)

VIP   Very Important Person

VL   Value Line Investment Survey

VOL   Volume

VP   Vice President

VRM   Variable Rate Mortgage

VSE   Vancouver Stock Exchange

VTC   Voting Trust Certificate

W

WB   Waybill

WCA   Workmen's Compensation Act

WCE   Winnipeg Commodity Exchange

WD   When Distributed (in stock listings of newspapers)

WHOOPS   Washington Public Power Supply System

WI   When Issued (in stock listings of newspapers)

WR   Warehouse Receipt

WSJ   Wall Street Journal

WT   Warrant (in stock listings of newspapers)

W/Tax   Withholding Tax

WW   With Warrants (in bond and stock listings of newspapers)

X

X   Ex-Interest (in bond listings of newspapers)

XD   Ex-Dividend (in stock listings of newspapers)

X-Dis   Ex-Distribution (in stock listings of newspapers)

XR Ex-Rights (in stock listings of newspapers)

XW Ex-Warrants (in bond and stock listings of newspapers)

Y

Y Ex-Dividend and Sales in Full (in stock listings of newspapers)

YLD Yield (in stock listings of newspapers)

YTB Yield to Broker

YTC Yield to Call

YTM Yield to Maturity

Z

Z Zero

ZBA Zero Bracket Amount

ZBB Zero-Based Budgeting

ZR Zero Coupon Issue (Security) (in bond listings of newspapers)

INDEX

This index is coordinated with the Dictionary of Finance and Investment on pages 157 to 566. Entries found there usually are not duplicated in the Index. It is advisable for the user of the *Handbook* to do a double lookup: once in this Index and once in the Dictionary.

Accounting firms
  eight largest, 193
  list of, 694
ADB (adjusted debit
  balance), 171
Adjustable rate preferred
  stock, 68
ADR. *See* American
  Depositary Receipts;
  Asset Depreciation
  Range System
Advertisements
  advice on, 125
  for securities
    offerings 127–29
Agencies. *See* Government
  agency securities
American Depositary
  Receipts, 24, 65
  list of companies with,
    1150–53
American Stock Exchange
  financial pages'
    reports on, 134–40
  list of publicly
    traded companies on,
    977–1018
  meaning of trading on,
    124
  options traded on, 143
  options traded on, list
    of, 774–75
  stock indexes of, 354,
    498
  ticker-tape identifier for,
    159
Americus Shareowner
  Service Corporation,
  420, 463
Amex. *See* American
  Stock Exchange
Amex Commodities
  Corporation, 774–75
Amex Market Value Index,
  data of, 847
Analysis. *See* Securities
  analysis
Annual reports, how to
  read, 89–120
Annuities, 9–11
  deferred payment,
    241–42
  fixed, 280
  hybrid, 312
  immediate payment,
    313
  joint and survivor, 341
  nonqualifying, 381
  qualifying, 430
  single-premium
    deferred, 483
  variable, 547
  wraparound, 559
Arbitrage
  risk, 455
  special account in, 486
ARM (adjustable rate
  mortgage), 171

Asset Depreciation Range
  System, 182
Assets of firm in annual
  report, 98–100
  turnover ratios, 114–15
Associated Press, special
  abbreviations of, 138,
  140, 144
Australian exchanges,
  810–13
Average collection period,
  91, 114, 221

Baby bonds, 12, 150
Balance sheets, 89–92,
  97–102
  ratios applied to, 113–16
Bankruptcy
  discharge of, 248
  trustee in, 526
  voluntary, 552
Banks
  Certificates of Deposit
    of, 76
  commercial, list of,
    638–642
  dealing in securities by,
    297
  deposit accounts in, 76
  deregulation of, 245,
    250
  financial pages'
    listing of highest
    interest rates of, 131
  float of, 283, 528
  foreign, 259
  investment, 326
  list of Federal
    Reserve, 631–34
  list of primary
    government securities
    dealers, 643–37
  merchant, 357
  money center vs.
    regional, 360, 438
  mortgage, 354
  mutual savings, 369
  national, 371
  prime rate of, 1968-
    1989 data on, 888
  regulators, list of,
    577–80
  revolving credit of, 452
  savings, 462, 526
  savings, list of 644–49
  state, 495
  state regulators of,
    577–80
  See also Federal
    Reserve
BANs. *See* Bond
  Anticipation Notes
Barron's Group Stock
  Averages, 499
*Barron's National Business
  and Financial Weekly,*
  121, 131, 140, 141,
  146, 189

Boilerplate, 128
Bond Anticipation Notes,
  48
Bond Buyer Index (11
  bonds), data of, 848–50
Bond Buyer Index (20
  bonds), data of 850–52
Bonds
  adjustment, 171
  agency. *See*
    Government agency
    securities
  authority, 184
  bellwether, 191
  blocks of, 195
  bond power in transfer
    of, 197
  collateral trust, 220
  commodity-backed, 223
  common stock
    equivalent for, 223
  convertible. *See*
    Convertible securities
  corporate. *See*
    Corporate bonds
  coupon, 233, 236, 292,
    480
  current yield of, 237
  cushion, 237
  deferred interest, 241
  discount, 240, 248
  dollar, 251
  double-barrelled, 48,
    252
  Dow Jones 40 Bond
    Average, 499
  equipment trust
    certificate, 261
  Eurodollar, 264
  financial pages'
    coverage of, 122–23
  first call dates of, 278
  flat trading in, 282
  flower, 285
  foreign, 24–27, 561
  going away, 298
  gold, 299
  guaranteed, 303
  high-grade, 307
  inactive, 312
  income, 313
  industrial
    development, 48
  Japanese, 551
  joint, 331
  junk, 12, 705
  letter security, 339
  long, 346
  moral obligation, 364
  mortgage. *See*
    Mortgage bonds
  municipal. *See*
    Municipal securities
  optional payment, 393
  par, 400
  passive, 402
  performance, 405
  perpetual, 406

pickup, 407
  point changes in, 409
  positive and negative
    yield curves for, 249,
    412
  prior-lien 421
  put, 429
  with put options, 48
  rate of return for, 433
  ratings of, 150, 197,
    434, 555
  registered, 438
  reorganization, 445
  revenue. *See* Revenue
    obligations
  savings, 77, 462, 477
  secured, 465
  serial, 477
  short, 480
  short and long coupons
    of, 346, 480
  special assessment, 486
  special tax, 489
  super sinker, 508
  telephone, financial
    pages' reports on, 131
  terms of, 322, 346, 357,
    482
  toll revenue, 528
  Treasury. *See* Treasury
    securities
  unamortized bond
    discounts, 538
  zero-coupon. *See*
    Zero-coupon securities
Bonds premium, 415
Boston Stock Exchange,
  160
Brokers
  ABC agreement for
    employees of, 165
  aged-fail contracts
    between, 174
  arbitration between, 196
  back offices, of, 196,
    390
  board, 195
  bond, 197
  boutique, 200
  commissions to, 222
  contra, 228
  as dealers, 239
  discount, 3, 248, 479
  discount, list of, 663–64
  floor, 284
  full-service, 3, 292
  full-service, list of,
    659–63
  golden handcuffs of,
    299
  haircuts in calculation
    of net capital of, 304
  independent, 316
  institutional, 320
  list of primary
    government securities
    dealers, 634–37
  loan rate for, 202

capital requirement
)r, 375
clearing, 380
stered representatives
f, 439
cial bids by, 486
sting by, 538
e houses, 557
an futures
hanges, 812–15
future exchanges,
–27
ility of bonds, 153
ate, first, 278
otions, 53–56, 483
p in/out of the
money of, 240
a
mpanies traded on
oronto Stock
xchange, 1137–50
a of Toronto stock
ndex, 875
of futures and
ptions traded in,
04–807
of life insurance
ompanies, 652–58
of stock and
ommodity exchanges
n, 697
ntreal Exchange,
utures, 804–805
vincial and
erritorial agencies
f, 588–89
ulatory
rganizations in,
47–50
onto Futures
xchange, 804–807
t and loan
ssociations in,
49–52
l
t of, 232
remental cost of, 315
rginal efficiency of,
60
ative working, 372
l-in, 399
rn of, 450
rn on invested, 450
ture, 495, 549
king, 558
lization. See
erage
l stock, overissue
res of, 397
value life insurance,
38
(Certificate of
crual on Treasury
urities), 84
See Certificates of
posit
cates of Deposit
77
odollar, 264
bo (negotiable),
32, 373
. See Commodities
ures Trading

Commission
Chart patterns for stocks,
215
accumulation area, 169
advance-decline line,
172
ascending tops, 181
back up, 186
breakout, 201
correction, 231, 232
descending tops, 246
dip, 247
double bottom, 253
double top, 254
flag, 282
gap, 294
head and shoulders, 305
horizontal price
movement, 309
moving average, 366
pennant, 404
point and figure chart,
409
resistance level, 427,
428
reversal, 451
rising bottoms, 453,
454
saucer, 460
selling climax, 473
trading pattern, 531
trendline, 534
triangle, 534
vertical line charting,
549
V formation, 550
wedge, 554
W formation, 554
Checks
kiting of, 334
registered, 438
third-party, 524
Chicago Board of Trade,
467
list of futures and
futures options traded
on, 776–81
See also MidAmerica
Commodity Exchange
Chicago Board Options
Exchange, 143, 195,
467
list of options traded
on, 780–81
Chicago Mercantile
Exchange, 147
list of futures and
futures options traded
on, 780–85
See also International
Monetary Market
Chicago Rice and Cotton
Exchange, 467
list of futures traded on,
786–87
Cincinnati Stock
Exchange, 160
Closed-end funds, 14–16
dual purpose, 225
in financial pages, 157
for securities of
precious-metals
companies, 65
Closed-end mutual

funds. See Mutual
funds—closed-end
CME. See Chicago
Mercantile Exchange
CMOs. See
Collaterized mortgage
obligations
Coffee, Sugar & Cocoa
Exchange, 467
list of futures and
futures options traded
on, 786–87
Coins
as collectibles, 17
gold, 65, 335
COLAs, 232
Collateralized mortgage
obligations, 45
Collectibles, 19
stock and bond
certificates, 463
COMEX. See
Commodity Exchange
Commercial banks, list of,
638–43
Commodities
actuals, 170
cash, 212
controlled, 229
daily trading limits for,
238
financial pages'
coverage of, 155
index of, 133
intercommodity spread
in, 321
list of worldwide
exchanges for,
696–704
moving average of, 366
physical, 407
position limit in, 411
regulated, 442
spot, 490
See also Futures
contracts
Commodities Futures
Trading Commission,
28, 570
Commodity Exchange
(COMEX), 132
list of futures and
futures options traded
on, 788–89
Commodity Research
Bureau Index, 133
Common stock, 19–21
blue chip, 195
classified, 217
conversion parties for,
229
fully diluted earnings
per share of, 292
net income per share of,
376
rate of return for, 434
underlying securities
for, 539
Computerized databases
for investors, list of,
621–26
Computer software for
investing and financial
planning, list of, 627–30

Computer Technology
Index, 774
Condominiums, 73
Condominium time-shares,
73
Conduit theory, 503
Consumer Price Index,
data of, 880
Contrarian investors, odd-
lot trading and, 138,
384
Convertible preferred
stock, 21–22
Convertible securities,
21–24
investment value of, 329
zero-coupon, 84
Cooperatives, 73
Corporate bonds, 11–14
in financial pages,
150–53
Corporate zero-income
securities, 84
Cost of goods sold, in
annual report, 105
Credit unions, 526
Certificate of Deposits
of, 76
Cumulative preferred
stock, 68
Curb. See American Stock
Exchange
Currencies
futures contracts on
62–64
hard, 305
newspaper tables of
exchange rates for,
133–34
par value of, 502
soft, 485
units of, 1215–18
Current ratio, 91, 113
Cushion rule, 20%, 538
CVs. See Convertible
securities
Cycles
business, 203
cash conversion
(earnings), 212
Kondratieff wave
theory of, 334
presidential election
theory of, 418

Databases for investors,
computerized, list of,
627–30
DDB (double-declining-
balance depreciation),
253
Debentures, 11, 22
high-premium
convertible, 307
Debt options, 58–60
Debt to equity ratio (debt
ratio), 92, 116
Debt to total assets ratio,
115–17
Delphi forecast, 332
Deposit accounts, 75
Depreciation
accelerated, 166
ACRS, 166

in annual reports, 103
double-declining-
balance, 253
in GNP, 199
recapture of, 436
straight-line, 502
sum-of-the-years'-
digits method of, 507
written-down value
after, 550
Directors and officers in
annual report, 113
Discount rate
data of, 881–83
in financial pages, 130
risk-adjusted, 454
Dividend payout ratio, 117
Dividend reports in
financial pages, 127,
139
Dividends
cash, 212
extra, 267
illegal, 312
liquidating, 343
optional, 393
stock, 497
trading, 531
unpaid, 545
DJIA. See Dow Jones
Industrial Averages
Dollars
constant, 227
hard, 305
index of value of, 133
newspaper tables of
exchange rates for,
133–34
purchasing power of,
435
soft, 485
Donoghue's money fund
average, 157
Double-barrelled bonds, 48
Dow Jones 15 Utility
Stock Average, 498
data of, 859–61
Dow Jones 40 Bond
Average, 499
Dow Jones Industrial
Average, 124, 125–26,
136, 189, 254, 341, 499
data of, 852–55
Dow Jones Municipal Bond
Yield Average, 499
Dow Jones 65
Composite Stock
Average, 499
data of, 861–62
Dow Jones 30 Industrials
Stock Average. See Dow
Jones Industrial Average
Dow Jones 20
Transportation Stock
Average, 499
data of, 856–58
Drilling. See Limited
partnerships—oil and gas
Dual-purpose funds, 14–15
income shares of, 314

Earnings reports in
financial pages, 126–27
Economic and financial

indicators in financial
pages, 125–34
Economic Recovery and
Tax Act of 1981, 176,
314, 355, 431, 459
ACRS in, 166
ADR under, 182
Economics, financial
pages' coverage of, 122
Enhanced securities, 48
Equity real estate
investment trusts, 70
ERISA (Employment
Retirement Income
Security Act of 1974),
404
ERTA. See Economic
Recovery and Tax Act
of 1981
EUAs. See European Units
of Account
Eurobonds, 25
Eurodollars, 25, 131
European Units of
Account, 25
Exchange rates, floating,
284, 403
Exchanges, securities and
commodities, list of,
696–704

Face value of bonds, 12
Federal funds
financial pages' report
on, 130–31
rate of, data on, 884–85
Federal Home Loan Bank
Board, 461
Federal Home Loan
Mortgage Corporation,
securities of, 33, 44
Federal National Mortgage
Association, securities
of, 33, 44
Federal Open Market
Committee, matched
sale purchase transaction
of, 356
Federal regulatory
organizations, list of,
569–572
Federal Reserve, 547–49
Board of Governors of,
632
borrowed reserves from,
199
discount rate, data of,
881–83
discount rate of, 249
dollar index of, 133
draining reserves by,
255
federal funds of, 270
Fed wire of, 273
as fiscal agent for
agencies, 34
general accounts in, 295
"go around" of, 297
list of banks and
branch banks of,
632–34
member banks of, 357
open-market
operations of, 390

Regulation T of, 396,
442, 471
FHLMC. See Federal
Home Loan Mortgage
Corporation
FIFO method, 97, 103
Finance and investment
organizations list of,
589–95
Finance and investment
publications, list of,
596–620
Financial pages, how to
read, 121–59
Financial statement in
annual report, 95–111
combined vs.
consolidated 221, 226
comparative, 224
source and application of
funds statement in, 485
spreadsheets for, 492
Financial supermarkets, 3
Financial Times, 121
FINEX, list of futures
traded on, 796–97
Finite life real estate
investment trusts, 70
First in, first out. See FIFO
Fitch Investor's Service,
150, 195, 434
Fixed annuities, 9
Fixed charge coverage, 116
Floating-rate municipal
securities, 48
Floating-rate notes, 12
Floating-rate preferred
stock, 68
FNMA. See Federal
National Mortgage
Association
Forecasting, jury of
executive opinion
(Delphi), 332
Foreign banks, 259
Foreign governments'
defaults, 486
Foreign stock and
commodity exchanges,
list of, 696–704
Foreign stocks and bonds,
24–27
financial pages'
information on,
142–43
Foreign trade, U.S. bank
for, 267
Form 10-K, 112
Form FR-1, 369
Fraud
blue-sky laws vs., 195
fidelity bonds vs., 194
manipulating as, 349,
453
pyramiding, 430
Free and discounted
goods and services for
shareholders, list of
companies offering,
1153–54
FREITs. See Finite life real
estate investment trusts
French futures exchanges,
828–31

Funds
closed-end. See
Closed-end funds
money market, 42–45
Futures contracts
on commodities, 27–30
on currencies, 62–65
dates of expiration of,
535
by exchange, list of,
767–845
financial, 275
in financial pages,
149–51
on interest rates, 30–31
intracommodity spread
in, 323
list of, by contract,
767–845
option contracts on,
56–58
random-walk theory of,
443
on stock indexes, 32–33
underlying, 539

General obligation notes
and bonds, 47–48
GNMA. See
Government National
Mortgage Association
Gold, 64–65
bonds backed by, 299
demonetization of, 245,
299
London Morning
Fixed Price data on,
863
prices of, financial
pages' reports on, 132
Gold coins, 65
Gold mining shares,
South African, 333
Government agency
securities, 33–35
in financial pages, 155
Government National
Mortgage Association
mobile home
certificate of, 360
securities of, 33, 45,
51, 155, 175
Government securities, list
of primary dealers in,
634–36
GPMs (graduated-payment
mortgages), 301
Growth stocks, 19

Highlights of annual
reports, 92–93
Historical data, 846–91
Hong Kong Futures
Exchange, 830–31
Hospital revenue bonds, 48
Housing bonds, 48

IBRD (International Bank
for Reconstruction and
Development), 322
ICC (Interstate Commerce
Commission), 323
IDBS. See Industrial
development bonds

x, 321
international
netary Fund), 322
International
netary Market), 323
e statements in
ual report, 90,
–105
e stocks, 19
e taxes
nnual reports, 105
me averaging for,
14
riage penalty on,
55
ative, 372
of Leading
nomic Indicators,
t of, 884–85
options, 60–62
tracts for 768–70
hanges for, 467
inancial pages,
45–46
rial development
ds, 48
n
t-push, 233
nand-pull, 244
estments that
utperformed, 16
flation, 493
also Dollars
t, 290
er-tape identifier for,
60
nce
nsurance, 220
dit, 234
surance, 444
e regulators of,
80–83
also Life insurance
nce companies,
ngs of, 192, 434
st
rued, 168
npound, 225
n corporate bonds,
1–14
n, 390
nary, 395
rt, in financial
ages, 129
ple, 483
arned, 542
st rates
ancial pages'
overage of 122–23,
30–31
res contracts on,
0–31
ion contracts on,
8–60
l, 435
e of 72 for, 458
ational Monetary
rket, 467
ational Networks
poration. *See* Instinet
ories
nnual report, 91–92,
8, 114
petual, 406

See also FIFO; LIFO
Investment companies
closed-end
management, 14–16,
757–61
diversified, 251
income, 314
leveraged, 340
open-end
management, 705–56
registered, 439
regulated, 442
See also Mutual funds;
Unit investment trusts
Investment
organizations, list of,
589–95
Investment, personal, 3–86
alternative, chart on,
6–7
list of computerized
databases for, 621–26
personal computer
software for, 627–30
Investor's Daily, 121
Investor's information in
annual report, 112
IRR (internal rate of
return), 322
ITS (International Trading
System), 321, 438

Japanese bonds, 551
Japanese futures
exchanges, 832–37
Junk bonds, 12, 332

Kansas City Board of
Trade, 467
list of futures and
futures options traded
on, 790–91
Know your customer rules,
457
Kuala Lumpur Commodity
Exchange, 836–37

Last in, first out. *See* LIFO
Leading Economic
Indicators, data of,
885–86
Letter to shareholders in
annual report, 94
Leverage, ratios for
measurement of, 115–16
Leveraged programs in
limited partnerships, 39
Liabilities of firm, in
annual report, 100–101
LIBOR. *See* London
Interbank Offered Rate
Life insurance
cash value, 36–38
single premium, 36, 483
term, 36
universal, 36, 544
universal variable, 36
variable, 36, 547
whole, 556
Life insurance
companies, list of,
652–57
regulators, list of,
580–83

LIFO method, 97 103
Limited partnerships,
38–41, 664–94
blind pool, 195
equipment leasing, 261
general partners of, 296,
490
income, 314
leveraged programs, 39
Liquidity Fund
buy-outs of, 343
list of sponsors of,
664–94
master, 39
mini-warehouse, 360
prospectuses for, 425
public, 426
reachback ability of,
435
research and
development, 445
resyndication, 447
silent partners in, 482
unleveraged programs,
39
venture capital, 549
See *also* Private
limited partnerships
London futures exchanges,
814–27
London Interbank
Offered Rate, 25, 131
London Morning Fix
Price, data on, 863
Long-term debt to total
capitalization ratio, 116
Lottery, oil and gas, 386
LPs. *See* Limited
partnerships

Malaysian futures
exchanges, 836–37
Margins, 170
fictitious credit and, 274
$500 rule for, 280
in futures markets, 28
Hunt brothers' failure to
meet call for, 483
initial, 319
remargining, 444
special arbitrage account
for, 486
special bond account
for, 486
Market diary, 135, 136
Market-to-book ratio, 117
M-CATS, 84
Mergers
financial pages'
coverage of, 123
purchase acquisition in,
428
MidAmerica Commodity
Exchange, 467
list of futures and
futures options traded
on, 790–93
Midwest Stock Exchange,
160
Minneapolis Grain
Exchange, 467
list of futures and
futures options
traded on, 794–95

MIT's (mutual investment
trusts), 367
MMDAs. *See* Money
Market Deposit
Accounts
Money
supply of, financial
pages' reports on, 132
supply of, data on,
886–87
velocity of, 548
Money Market Deposit
Accounts, 76
Money market funds,
42–44
in financial pages,
157–58
historical yields of, 307
Moody's Investors Service,
150, 197, 434
Morgan Guaranty Trust
Co., dollar index of,
133
Mortgage-backed (pass-
through) securities,
44–47, 296, 402
Mortgage bonds, 11, 349
consolidated, 226
obligation, 382
Mortgages
after acquired clauses
in, 173
adjustable rate, 171
closed-end, 218
conventional, 229
first, 279
foreclosures on, 286
general, 295
graduated-payment, 301
junior, 332
open-end, 388
reverse annuity, 451
second, 308, 465
secondary market for,
465
variable-rate (VRM),
548
Veterans
Administration, 550
wraparound, 559
See also Collateralized
mortgage obligations
Municipal securities,
47–50, 367
advance refunding of,
172
Blue List of, 195
Bond Buyer's index of,
197
certificateless, 214, 217
Dow Jones Municipal
Bond Yield Average,
499
financial pages' reports
on, 131, 155
general obligation,
47–48, 155, 296
private purpose, 47
public purpose, 47
rate covenants in, 433
revenue obligations, 48
special tax, 489
as triple tax exempt,
535

25% rules for, 537, 538
utility revenue, 545
zero-coupon, 89
Mutual funds, 14–16, 50,
53, 705–66
aggressive growth, 705
allocation of sales
charges in, 228
balanced, 705
breakpoint sale in, 201
capital gains
distribution of, 209
closed-end, 14–16
closed-end, list of,
757–66
common stock, 223
contractual plans of, 228
corporate bond, 705
discretionary trust, 249
diversified, 251
energy, 261
exchange privilege in,
265
family of, 269
in financial pages,
156–58
flexible portfolio, 706
global bond, 706
GNMA, 706
go-go, 298
gold, 299
growth, 706
growth and income, 706
high-yield, 706
income, 707
index, 316
international, 707
Lipper industry average
for, 342
load, 344
long-term municipal
bond, 707
maximum capital gains,
356
money market, 707
net asset value in, 374
no-load, 379, 510, 522
open end, 50–53
open-end, list of,
705–56
option income, 707
performance, 405
precious metals and
gold, 707
prospectuses for, 425
for securities of
precious-metals
companies, 65
selling dividends in, 474
short-term municipal
bond, 707
single-state municipal
bond, 707
social consciousness,
485
specialized, 488
sponsors of, 490
state municipal bond—
long-term, 707
state municipal bond—
short-term, 707
tax-managed utility, 517
12b–1, 537
U.S. government

income, 707
See also Money market
funds

Naked writers, 53, 353,
537
NASD, *See* National
Association of
Securities Dealers
NASDAQ, 355, 447
financial pages'
reports on, 140–42
list of most actively
traded companies
on, 1018–1136
meaning of trading on,
124
ticker-tape identifier
for, 160
NASDAQ 100 Index, as
index option, 795
NASDAQ National Market
System Composite
Index, data of, 864
NASDAQ-OTC Price
Index, 499
National Association of
Securities Dealers,
140, 157
Rules of Fair Practice,
220, 280, 291, 298,
334, 458
Uniform Practice Code,
543
National Credit Union
Administration, 267
*National OTC Stock
Journal*, 140
National Quotation Bureau,
407, 561
National Securities
Clearing Corporation,
228
NAV (net asset value),
156, 375
Negotiated Order of
Withdrawal Accounts,
75
Netherlands futures
exchanges, 838–39
Net profit margin, 115
Newsletters, Hulbert rating
of, 312
Newspapers, financial,
121–59
New York Cotton
Exchange, 467
list of futures and
futures options
traded on, 794–97
New York Futures
Exchange, 467, 490
list of futures and
futures options
traded on, 796–99
New York Mercantile
Exchange, 407
list of futures traded
on, 798–99
New York Stock Exchange,
467
ABC agreement and, 165
basket trading, 800–801
as Big Board, 193

bond crowds in, 170,
197, 206, 288, 345
broad tape not allowed
on floor of, 201
financial pages'
coverage of, 125–26,
134–43
garage annex floor of,
295
list of companies traded
on, 895
meaning of trading on,
124,
Nine Bond Rule of,
151, 379
registered competitive
traders of, 439
Rule 405 of, 457
stock watch
department of, 501
ticker-tape identifier for,
160
New York Stock Exchange
Composite Index, 32
128, 499
New York Stock Exchange
Telephone Index, 499
New York Times, The, 123,
128, 129–35, 146,
154–55
New Zealand futures
exchanges, 840–41
NH (not held), 393
Noncumulative preferred
stock, 68
Notes
floating-rate, 12
general obligation,
47–48
promissory, 425
Treasury, 79, 154–55
variable-rate demand,
548
NOW Accounts. *See*
Negotiated Order of
Withdrawal Accounts
NPV method, 376

OCC. *See* Options
Clearing Corporation
Odd-lot trading, financial
pages' reports on,
35–39
OMB (Office of
Management and
Budget), 396
Open-end mutual funds.
See under Mutual
funds—open-end
Operating profit margin,
92, 115
Option contracts, 53–56
Black-Scholes model of,
194
conventional, 229
covered, 234
on currencies, 62–64
daily trading limits for,
238
dates of expiration of,
535
delta measurement of,
243
European, 264

"farther out" and
"farther in" of, 269
on futures contracts,
56–58
on interest rates, 58–60
intrinsic value in, 324
mini-manipulation of,
360
position limit in, 412
spreads in, 176, 192,
203, 207, 247, 309,
344, 417, 491–92,
527, 549
on stock indexes. *See*
Index options
uncovered, 539
underlying securities
for, 539
Options, stock. *See* Stock
options
Options Clearing
Corporation, 53, 146
Over the counter market,
524
financial pages' reports
on, 140–42
meaning of trading on,
124
pink and yellow sheets
for prices in, 407
regulation of, 348
stock index of, 499
unlisted securities of,
544
OW (offer wanted), 386

Pacific Stock Exchange,
160, 468
specifications on index
option of, 800–801
Palladium, 64, 65
Participating preferred
stock, 68
Partnerships, limited.
See Limited
partnerships
Par value of bonds, 12
Pass-through securities.
See Mortgage-backed
securities
PBGC (Pension Benefit
Guaranty Corporation),
394
Penny stocks, 65
information about, 140
PE ratio, 139
Periodicals, finance and
investment, list of,
596–620
Philadelphia Stock
Exchange, 143, 160
list of futures and
options traded on,
800–803
Platinum, 64–65
Port Authority of New
York and New Jersey,
184
Portfolio management
programs, computer
software for, 627–30
Precious metals, 64–67
Preference shares, 68
Preferred stock, 67–69

nual reports, 101
non stock
  uivalent for, 223
  ertible, 21–24, 67
  lative, 68
  279
  money, 376
  allable, 380
  onvertible, 67–69
  umulative, 68, 380
  -, 421
  of return for, 433
  nd-, 465
  rnings ratio,
  17, 139
  ate in financial
  s, 130
  on, 888
  eferred stock, 68
limited
  erships, 38
mortgage
  cipation
  ficates, 45
  er Price Index, data
  89
  ility ratios, 92, 115
  ions, finance and
  stment, list of,
  620
imited
  erships, 39
  traded
  panies
merican Stock
  xchange, 977–1017
  ew York Stock
  xchange, 895–976
  ASDAQ National
  arket System,
  18–1136
  oronto Stock
  xchange, 1137–49
  ions, 53–56
  quire stock, 550
  s with, 48
  -secured, 550
  in/out of the
  oney of, 240
  ied, 355
  d, financial, 276
ly reports, how to
  118
  atio, 91, 113–14
See Revenue
  cipation Notes
  sts for annual
  rt, 90–93, 113–17
  tate investment
  s, 70–72
  gage, 365
  otion notices in
  cial pages, 129
  al stock exchanges,
  cial pages'
  ports on, 136, 142
  f, 696–704
  ors, list of, 569–88
See Real estate
  tment trusts
  ', 45

Report of independent
  accountants in annual
  report, 95–96
Return on equity, 92, 115
Revenue Anticipation
  Notes, 48
Revenue obligations, 48,
  184, 309, 317, 368,
  451, 528, 545
Review of operations in
  annual report, 94–95
Rules of Fair Practice, 220,
  280, 291, 299, 334, 458

Savings alternatives, 75–77
Savings and loan
  associations,
  Certificates of Deposit
  of, 75
  list of, 644–48
  mutual, 368
Savings Bonds, U.S., 76
SBA (Small Business
  Administration), 484
SDRs. *See* Special
  Drawing Rights
Securities
  borrowing power of,
  199
  convertible, 21–24
  CUSIP identification
  for, 223
  exempt, 266
  government agency,
  33–36
  historic trading range
  of, 307
  junior, 332
  lending, 338
  listed, 344
  marketable, 352
  mutilated, 368
  of precious-metals
  companies, 65
  prospectuses for, 425
  registered, 440
  residual, 447
  secondary distribution
  of, 464
  segregation of, 472
  shelf registration of,
  480
  state regulators of,
  584–87
  undigested, 532
  See also Bonds; Stocks
Securities analysis, 466,
  521
  contrarian, 138
  Dow theory in, 254
  fundamental, 303
  Graham and Dodd
  method of, 301
  hemline theory of,
  307
  mean return in, 356
  on-balance volume
  method of, 387
  personal computer
  software for, 627–30
  portfolio theory, 511
  projection in, 424
  qualitative analysis in,
  431

regression analysis in,
  440
  research department
  for, 446
  short interest theory
  in, 481
  technical, 521
  testing concept in, 523
  top-down approach in,
  527
  See also Chart patterns
  for stocks
Securities and Exchange
  Commission
  foreign bonds not
  subject to, 25
  list of rules of, 471
  National Market
  Advisory Board of,
  361
  net capital requirement
  of, 365
  registered companies
  with, 439
  20-day period of, 537
Securities firms. *See*
  Securities Brokers
Securities Investor
  Protection Corporation,
  42
Securities offerings in
  financial pages, 127–29
Securities regulators, list
  of, 584–87
Segment reporting in
  annual report, 111
Separate Trading of
  Interest and Principal of
  Securities. *See* STRIPS
SEP (simplified employee
  pension) plan, 483
Shareholders' equity in
  annual report, 101–102
Shareholders, free and
  discounted goods and
  services for, list of
  companies offering,
  1153–54
Short interest data in
  financial pages, 129
Silver, 64–65
Singapore International
  Monetary Exchange,
  840–43
SIPC. *See* Securities
  Investor Protection
  Corporation
65 Stock Average, 499
SMA (special
  miscellaneous account),
  488
Small business
  corporations, 505
SPDA (single-premium
  deferred annuity), 483
Special Drawing Rights, 25
Specialists, trading posts
  of, 532
Standard & Poor's bond
  ratings by, 162, 196, 434
  20 Transportation
  Stock Index, data of,
  867–68
  40 Stock Financial

Index, data of,
  871
  40 Utilities Stock,
  Index, data of,
  869–70
  100 Stock Index, 499
  400 Industrial Stock
  Index, data of,
  866–67
  500 Stock Index, 32,
  125, 136, 189, 499,
  500
  500 Stock Index, data
  of, 867–68
Statement of changes in
  financial condition in
  annual report, 108–11
States, U.S. attorney
  generals' offices of,
  573–76
  banking regulators of,
  577–79
  insurance regulators
  of, 580–83
  securities regulators
  of, 584–87
Stock exchanges
  companies traded on,
  lists of, 895–1017,
  1137–49
  financial pages'
  coverage of,
  123–24, 125–26,
  134–43
  Intermarket Trading
  System of, 321, 438
  list of, 696–704
  member firms of, 342
  open outcry method at,
  390
  regional, 438
  surveillance
  departments of, 501,
  509, 553
  suspended trading on,
  509
  ticker-tape identifiers
  for, 160
Stock indexes, 353
  futures contracts on,
  30–31, 500
  listed by exchange,
  468
  listed by name, 499
  market value-
  weighted, 354
  option contracts on,
  60–62, 145–46
  price-weighted, 419
Stock markets. *See* Stock
  exchanges
Stock options
  financial pages'
  reports on, 143–47
  incentive, 314
  nonqualifying, 382
  qualifying, 421
Stocks
  abbreviated names of,
  138, 141, 1155
  active market for, 170
  air pocket, 175
  in annual reports,
  101–103

bear raids on, 191
bellwether, 192
charting of. See Chart
    patterns for stocks
common. See
    Common stock
cyclical, 238
debenture, 239
distribution, 250
financial pages' daily
    summaries on,
    134–43
foreign, 24–27
fractional shares of,
    290
general considerations
    on, 3–5
glamor, 297
high tech, 307
inactive, 312
interest-sensitive, 321
letter security, 339
leveraged, 340
most active list of, 365
nonvoting and voting,
    382, 552
no-par value, 382
OTC margin, 396
out-of-favor, 396
penny, 65
point changes in, 409
preferred. See
    Preferred stock
publicly traded lists
    of, 895–1149
ratios to measure value
    of, 116–17
splits of, 489
stopped, 502
tape symbols for,
    1155–1204
treasury, 533
unissued, 543
watered, 553
widow-and-orphan,
    536
See also Common
    stock; Preferred stock
Strike price in options
    tables, 143–46
Strips, 84
STRIPS, 84
Super NOW Accounts, 76
Swedish futures
    exchanges, 842–45
Syndicates. See
    Underwriters

TAB (Tax Anticipation
    Bill), 514
Takeovers
    crown jewels in, 235
    financial pages'
        coverage of, 123
    firms specializing in
        early detection of, 480
    killer bees in, 334
    leveraged buyout, 340
    Pac-Man strategy vs.,
        399

poison-pill defense
    vs., 410
proxy fights in, 426
radar alert for, 433
raiders, 433
safe harbor defense
    vs., 459
scorched-earth policy
    vs., 463
shark repellent vs.,
    479
"sleeping beauty"
    terminology in, 484
tender offers for,
    460, 522
target companies for,
    513
Williams Act and, 547
TANs. See Tax
    Anticipation Notes
Tapes. See Ticker tapes
Tax Anticipation Notes, 48
Taxes
    accumulated profits,
        169
    alternative minimum,
        176
    capital gains, 209
    deferral of, 241
    estate, 263
    estate, flower bonds
        for, 285
    estimated, 263
    excess profits, 265
    excise, 265
    flat vs. progressive,
        283, 424
    franchise, 290
    gift, 296
    interest equalization,
        321
    Laffer curve theory of,
        335
    luxury, 347
    marginal rate of, 351
    real rate of return
        after, 173
    regressive, 441
    transfer, 532
    unified credit vs., 542
    value-added (VAT), 546
    See also Income taxes
Tax Exempt Authority
    Bonds. See Municipal
    securities
Tax Exempt commercial
    paper, 48
Tax-option corporations,
    505
Tax shelters, abusive, 166
Tender offer
    announcements in
        financial pages, 129
Term life insurance, 36
Ticker tapes, 513
    broad, 201
    consolidated, 226
    delayed, 247
    flashes on, 282
    how to read, 159

OPD symbol on, 388
"painting" of, 399
reading of, 253
TIGRs (Treasury
    Investment Growth
    Receipts), 84
Times interest earned, 116
Tokyo Commodity
    Exchange, 832–33
Tokyo Grain Exchange,
    834–35
Tokyo Stock Exchange,
    834–35
Tokyo Sugar Exchange,
    834–35
Tombstone ads, 127–29
Toronto 300 Composite
    Stock Index, data of,
    875
Treasury bills, 79
    in financial pages,
        131, 132, 153–54
    noncompetitive bid
        for, 380
    3-month, yields of,
        data on, 876
Treasury securities, 79–81
    agencies compared to, 33
    bills, 79–81
    bond 20-year yields,
        data on, 877
    bonds, 79–81
    financial pages'
        reports on, 131, 132,
        153
    notes, 79–81
    strips and STRIPS, 84
    See also Treasury bills
Trusts
    bypass, 205
    diamond investment,
        247
    discretionary, 249
    inter vivos, 323
    irrevocable, 330
    Q-tip, 430
    qualified, 430
    revocable, 452
    royalty, 457
    spousal remainder, 491
    testamentary, 523
    unit investment, 81–83
    See also Unit
        investment trusts

UITs. See Unit investment
    trusts
Underwriters (syndicate)
    agreement between,
        175, 201, 428
    circles by, 216
    distributing, 250
    green shoe clause of, 302
    managing, 348
    mezzanine bracket of,
        348
    negotiated
        underwriting by, 374
    piggyback registration
        by, 407

"pipeline" phrase of,
    408
spreads of, 491
standby, 494
sticky deals of, 496
Unemployment rate, data
    on, 891–92
United press International,
    special abbreviations of,
    138, 140, 141
Unit investment trusts,
    81–83
    discretionary, 249
    diversified, 251
    fixed, 282
    municipal, 367
    PRIME and SCORE,
        463
Universal life insurance,
    244
Universal variable life
    insurance, 36
Unleveraged programs in
    limited partnerships, 40
USA Today, 121
Utilities, rate bases for,
    433
Utility revenue bonds, 48

Value Line Composite
    Index, 32, 136, 139,
    499, 500
    data of, 758
Vancouver Stock
    Exchange, 806–807
Variable annuities, 9
Variable life insurance, 36
Variable rate preferred
    stock, 68
VAT (value-added tax),
    546
VRM (Variable-rate
    mortgages), 548

Wall Street Journal, The,
    121, 126, 127, 129,
    131, 134, 135, 155
Washington Public Power
    Supply System, 556
Wash rule, 30-day, 524
Wholesale drug industry,
    EOM dating in, 261
Wilshire 5000 Equity
    Index, 134, 137
    data of, 879
Winnipeg Commodity
    Exchange, 808–809

Yield to maturity, 153

Zero-coupon securities,
    83–86
    CATS, M-CATS, 84
    convertible, 84
    corporate, 84
    municipal, 84
    reinvestment rate on,
        444
    STRIPS, 84
    TIGRs, 84